VISUAL BASIC® .NET FOR EXPERIENCED PROGRAMMERS

DEITEL™ DEVELOPER SERIES

Deitel™ Books, Cyber Classrooms, Complete Tra
published by

DEITEL™ *Developer* Series

C#: A Programmer's Introduction

C# for Experienced Programmers

Java™ Web Services for Experienced Programmers

Visual Basic® .NET for Experienced Programmers

*Visual C++® .NET: A Managed Code Approach
For Experienced Programmers*

Web Services: A Technical Introduction

Java 2 Micro Edition for Experienced Programmers (Spring 2003)

Java 2 Enterprise Edition for Experienced Programmers (Spring 2003)

*ASP .NET and Web Services with Visual Basic® .NET for Experienced
Programmers (Fall 2002)*

*ASP .NET and Web Services with C# for Experienced Programmers
(Spring 2003)*

How to Program Series

*Advanced Java™ 2 Platform How to
Program*

C How to Program, 3/E

C++ How to Program, 3/E

C# How to Program

*e-Business and e-Commerce How to
Program*

*Internet and World Wide Web How to
Program, 2/E*

Java™ How to Program, 4/E

Perl How to Program

Python How to Program

Visual Basic® 6 How to Program

*Visual Basic® .NET How to
Program, 2/E*

*Wireless Internet & Mobile Business
How to Program*

XML How to Program

.NET How to Program Series

C# How to Program

Visual Basic® .NET How to Program, 2/E

Visual Studio® Series

C# How to Program

Visual Basic® .NET How to Program, 2/E

*Getting Started with Microsoft® Visual
C++™ 6 with an Introduction to
MFC*

Visual Basic® 6 How to Program

For Managers Series

*e-Business and e-Commerce for
Managers*

Coming Soon

e-books and e-whitepapers

*Premium CourseCompass, WebCT and
Blackboard Multimedia Cyber
Classroom versions*

ining Courses and Web-Based Training Courses
Prentice Hall

Multimedia Cyber Classroom and *Web-Based Training* Series

(For information regarding Deitel™ Web-based training visit **www.ptgtraining.com**)

C++ Multimedia Cyber Classroom, 3/E

C# Multimedia Cyber Classroom

e-Business and e-Commerce Multimedia Cyber Classroom

Internet and World Wide Web Multimedia Cyber Classroom, 2/E

Java™ 2 Multimedia Cyber Classroom, 4/E

Perl Multimedia Cyber Classroom

Python Multimedia Cyber Classroom

Visual Basic® 6 Multimedia Cyber Classroom

Visual Basic® .NET Multimedia Cyber Classroom, 2/E

Wireless Internet & Mobile Business Programming Multimedia Cyber Classroom

XML Multimedia Cyber Classroom

The Complete Training Course Series

The Complete C++ Training Course, 3/E

The Complete C# Training Course

The Complete e-Business and e-Commerce Programming Training Course

The Complete Internet and World Wide Web Programming Training Course, 2/E

The Complete Java™ 2 Training Course, 4/E

The Complete Perl Training Course

The Complete Python Training Course

The Complete Visual Basic® 6 Training Course

The Complete Visual Basic® .NET Training Course, 2/E

The Complete Wireless Internet & Mobile Business Programming Training Course

The Complete XML Programming Training Course

To communicate with the authors, send e-mail to:

deitel@deitel.com

For information on corporate on-site seminars and public seminars offered by Deitel & Associates, Inc. worldwide, visit:

www.deitel.com

For continuing updates on Prentice Hall and Deitel publications visit:

www.deitel.com,
www.prenhall.com/deitel or
www.InformIT.com/deitel

To follow the Deitel publishing program, please register at

www.deitel.com/newsletter/subscribe.html

for the *DEITEL™ BUZZ ONLINE* e-mail newsletter.

Library of Congress Cataloging-in-Publication Data

On file

Acquisitions Editor: *Karen McLean*
Project Manager: *Mike Ruel*
Executive Managing Editor: *Vince O'Brien*
Formatters: *Chirag Thakkar, John Lovell*
Director of Creative Services: *Paul Belfanti*
Art Editor: *Xiaohong Zhu*
Creative Director: *Carole Anson*
Design Technical Support: *John Christiana*
Chapter Opener and Cover Designers: *Dr. Harvey M. Deitel, Laura Treibick and Tamara L. Newnam*
Manufacturing Manager: *Trudy Pisciotti*
Manufacturing Buyer: *Lisa McDowell*
Marketing Manager: *Kate Hargett*
Marketing Assistant: *Corrine Mitchell*

© 2003 Pearson Education, Inc.
Upper Saddle River, New Jersey 07458

Cover photo: *Colin Samuels/Amana America/Photonica*

10 9 8 7 6 5 4 3

ISBN 0-13-046131-8

Pearson Education Ltd., *London*
Pearson Education Australia Pty. Ltd., *Sydney*
Pearson Education Singapore, Pte. Ltd.
Pearson Education North Asia Ltd., *Hong Kong*
Pearson Education Canada, Inc., *Toronto*
Pearson Educacion de Mexico, S.A. de C.V.
Pearson Education–Japan, *Tokyo*
Pearson Education Malaysia, Pte. Ltd.
Pearson Education, Inc., *Upper Saddle River, New Jersey*

VISUAL BASIC® .NET FOR EXPERIENCED PROGRAMMERS

DEITEL™ DEVELOPER SERIES

H. M. Deitel
Deitel & Associates, Inc.

P. J. Deitel
Deitel & Associates, Inc.

T. R. Nieto
Deitel & Associates, Inc.

C. H. Yaeger
Deitel & Associates, Inc.

PRENTICE HALL, Upper Saddle River, New Jersey 07458

To the members of the Microsoft Visual Basic .NET team:

For your efforts in evolving Visual Basic into a world-class, enterprise-development programming language.

Harvey and Paul Deitel

To Erin Flanagan:

For being the loving, compassionate person that you are and for inspiring me to be a better person.

Tem R. Nieto

In memory of Charles Yaeger and Oscar Kesten. I wish I could have gotten to know both of you.

Cheryl H. Yaeger

Trademarks

Contents

Illustrations

6   Object-Oriented Programming: Inheritance   191

7   Object-Oriented Programming: Polymorphism   227

17 ASP .NET, Web Forms and Web Controls   742

21 Mobile Internet Toolkit   **985**

A Operator Precedence Chart   **1036**

B Visual Studio .NET Debugger   **1038**

Preface

Live in fragments no longer. Only connect.
Edward Morgan Forster

We wove a web in childhood,
A web of sunny air.
Charlotte Brontë

Welcome to Visual Basic .NET and the world of Windows, Internet and World-Wide-Web programming with Visual Studio .NET and the .NET platform! This book is the third in the new *Deitel™ Developer Series*, which presents leading-edge computing technologies to software developers and IT professionals.

Visual Basic .NET was created from Visual Basic 6.0 by Microsoft expressly for its .NET platform. Visual Basic .NET provides the features that are most important to programmers, such as object-oriented programming, graphics, graphical-user-interface (GUI) components, exception handling, multithreading, multimedia (audio, images, animation and video), file processing, prepackaged data structures, database processing, Internet and World-Wide-Web-based multi-tier application development, networking, Web services and distributed computing. The language is appropriate for implementing Internet- and World-Wide-Web-based applications that integrate seamlessly with Windows-based applications.

The .NET platform offers powerful capabilities for software development and deployment, including language and platform independence. For example, developers writing code in any (or several) of the .NET languages (such as Visual Basic .NET, C# and Visual C++ .NET) can contribute components to the same software product. In addition to providing language independence, .NET extends program portability by enabling .NET applications to reside on, and communicate across, multiple platforms. This facilitates the creation and use of *Web services*, which are applications that expose functionality to clients over the Internet.

The .NET platform enables Web-based applications to be distributed to consumer-electronic devices, such as wireless phones and personal digital assistants (PDAs), as well as to desktop computers. The capabilities that Microsoft has incorporated into the .NET platform increase programmer productivity and decrease development time.

Who Should Read This Book

Deitel & Associates, Inc. currently has two Visual Basic .NET publications, intended for different audiences. We provide information on **www.deitel.com**, here and inside this book's back cover to help you determine which publication is best for you.

Our first Visual Basic .NET book, *Visual Basic .NET How to Program, Second Edition*, was published as part of our *How to Program Series*, for college and university students. It provides a comprehensive treatment of Visual Basic .NET and includes learning aids and extensive ancillary support. *Visual Basic .NET How to Program, Second Edition* assumes that the reader has little or no programming experience. Early chapters focus on fundamental programming principles. The book builds on this to create increasingly complex and sophisticated programs that demonstrate how to use Visual Basic .NET to create graphical user interfaces, networking applications, multithreaded applications, Web-based applications and more. We encourage professors and professionals to consider the *The Complete Visual Basic .NET Training Course*. This package includes *Visual Basic .NET How to Program, Second Edition*, as well as the *Visual Basic .NET Multimedia Cyber Classroom, Second Edition*, an interactive multimedia CD-ROM that provides extensive e-Learning features. *The Complete Visual Basic .NET Training Course, Second Edition* and *Visual Basic .NET Multimedia Cyber Classroom, Second Edition* are discussed in detail later in this Preface.

This book, *Visual Basic .NET for Experienced Programmers*, is part of the new *Deitel™ Developer Series*, intended for professional software developers—from novices through experienced programmers. This publication is a part of the *For Experienced Programmers* subseries, designed for the experienced software developer who wants a deep treatment of a new technology with minimal, if any, introductory material. *Visual Basic .NET for Experienced Programmers* provides a brief introduction to programming principles in general and to Visual Basic .NET fundamentals, then delves deeply into more sophisticated topics, such as Web development and distributed computing. There is considerable overlap between this book and *Visual Basic .NET How to Program, Second Edition*.

A third publication, *ASP .NET with Visual Basic .NET for Experienced Programmers*, is forthcoming. This book was originally titled *Advanced Visual Basic .NET for Experienced Programmers*.

Each of our Visual Basic .NET books presents many complete, working Visual Basic .NET programs and depicts their inputs and outputs in actual screen shots of running programs. This is our signature *LIVE-CODE™ approach*—we present concepts in the context of complete working programs. Each book's source code is available free for download at **www.deitel.com**.

Please examine both the *Deitel™ Developer Series* professional books and the *How to Program Series* textbooks to determine which best suits your needs. *Visual Basic .NET for Experienced Programmers* is derived from *Visual Basic .NET How to Program, Second Edition*. Depending on your particular needs, you should purchase either this book or *Visual Basic .NET How to Program, Second Edition*.

This book was written after *Visual Basic .NET How to Program, Second Edition*. We added to this *Deitel™ Developer Series* book a chapter on the new Microsoft Mobile Internet Toolkit for our readers who wish to develop wireless Internet applications for wireless phones, pagers and PDAs. This material will be added to the third edition of *Visual Basic .NET How to Program*.

For a detailed listing of Deitel™ products and services, please see the "advertorial" pages at the back of this book and visit **www.deitel.com**. Readers may also want to register for our new *Deitel™ Buzz Online* e-mail newsletter (**www.deitel.net/newsletter/subscribe.html**), which provides information about our publications, company announcements, links to informative technical articles, programming tips, teaching tips, challenges and anecdotes.

As you proceed, if you would like to communicate with us, please send an e-mail to **deitel@deitel.com**—we always respond promptly. Please check our Web sites, **www.deitel.com**, **www.prenhall.com/deitel** and **www.InformIT.com/ deitel** for frequent updates, errata, FAQs, etc. When sending an e-mail, please include the book's title and edition number. We sincerely hope that you enjoy learning Visual Basic .NET with our publications.

Features of *Visual Basic .NET for Experienced Programmers*

This edition contains many features, including:

- *Syntax Highlighting* . This book uses five-way syntax highlighting to emphasize Visual Basic .NET programming elements in a manner similar to that of Visual Studio .NET. Our syntax-highlighting conventions are as follows:

```
comments
keywords
literal values
errors and ASP .NET directives
text, class, method and variable names
```

- *"Code Washing."* This is our term for the process we use to format the book's programs so that they have a carefully commented, open layout. The code is grouped into small, well-documented pieces. This greatly improves code readability—an especially important goal for us, considering that this book contains approximately 20,300 lines of code in 192 complete LIVE-CODE™ programs.

- *Web Forms, Web Controls and ASP .NET* . The .NET platform enables developers to create robust, scalable Web-based applications. Microsoft's .NET server-side technology, Active Server Pages (ASP) .NET, allows programmers to build Web documents that respond to client requests. To enable interactive Web pages, server-side programs process information users input into HTML forms. ASP .NET is a significant departure from ASP 3.0, allowing developers to program Web-based applications using .NET's powerful object-oriented languages such as Visual Basic .NET and C#, rather than using only scripting languages. ASP .NET also provides enhanced visual programming capabilities, similar to those used in building Windows forms for desktop programs. Programmers can create Web pages visually, by dragging and dropping Web controls onto Web forms. Chapter 17, ASP .NET, Web Forms and Web Controls, introduces these powerful technologies.

- *Web Services and ASP .NET* . Microsoft's .NET strategy embraces the Internet and Web as integral to software development and deployment. Web services technology enables information sharing, e-commerce and other interactions using standard Internet protocols and technologies, such as Hypertext Transfer Protocol (HTTP), Extensible Markup Language (XML) and Simple Object Access Protocol (SOAP). Web services enable programmers to package application functionality in a manner that turns the Web into a library of reusable software components. In Chapter 18, ASP .NET and Web Services, we present a Web service that allows users to manipulate "huge integers"—integers too large to be contained in Visual Basic .NET's built-in data types. In this example, a user enters two huge integers and presses buttons to invoke Web services that add, subtract and compare the two integers.

- *Object-Oriented Programming.* Object-oriented programming is the most widely employed technique for developing robust, reusable software. This text offers a rich treatment of Visual Basic .NET's object-oriented programming features. Chapter 5, Object-Based Programming, introduces how to create classes and objects. These concepts are extended in Chapter 6, Object-Oriented Programming: Inheritance, which discusses how programmers can create powerful new classes quickly by "absorbing" the capabilities of existing classes. Chapter 7, Object-Oriented Programming: Polymorphism, familiarizes the reader with the crucial concepts of polymorphism, abstract classes, concrete classes and interfaces, which facilitate powerful manipulations among objects belonging to an inheritance hierarchy.

- *XML.* Use of Extensible Markup Language (XML) is exploding in the software-development industry, in the e-business and e-commerce communities, and is pervasive throughout the .NET platform. Because XML is a platform-independent technology for describing data and for creating markup languages, XML's data portability integrates well with Visual Basic .NET-based portable applications and services. Chapter 15, Extensible Markup Language (XML), introduces XML. In this chapter, we introduce basic XML markup and discuss the technologies such as DTDs and Schema, which are used to validate XML documents' contents. We also explain how to manipulate XML documents programmatically using the Document Object Model (DOM™) and how to transform XML documents into other types of documents via Extensible Stylesheet Language Transformations (XSLT).

- *Multithreading* . Computers enable programmers to perform many tasks in parallel (i.e., concurrently), such as printing documents, downloading files from a network and surfing the Web. Multithreading is the technology through which programmers can develop applications that perform concurrent tasks. Historically, a computer has contained a single, expensive processor, which its operating system would share among all applications. Today, processors are becoming increasingly inexpensive, making it possible to build affordable computers with many processors working in parallel—such computers are called multiprocessors. Multithreading is effective on both single-processor and multiprocessor systems. .NET's multithreading capabilities make the platform and its related technologies better prepared to handle today's sophisticated multimedia-intensive, database-intensive, network-based, multiprocessor-based, distributed applications. Chapter 11, Multithreading, introduces this powerful capability.

- *ADO .NET.* Databases store vast amounts of information that individuals and organizations must access to conduct business. As an evolution of Microsoft's ActiveX Data Objects (ADO) technology, ADO .NET represents a new approach for building applications that interact with databases. ADO .NET uses XML and an enhanced object model to provide developers with the tools they need to access and manipulate databases for large-scale, extensible, mission-critical multi-tier applications. Chapter 16, Database, SQL and ADO .NET, introduces the capabilities of ADO .NET and the Structured Query Language (SQL) to manipulate databases.

- *Wireless Development.* By some estimates, about a billion people worldwide are using mobile devices, such as wireless phones and PDAs, and this number is increasing rapidly. To simplify the creation of Web content for mobile devices, Microsoft provides the Mobile Internet Toolkit (MIT). The MIT, which is built on ASP .NET, allows wireless content to be created using Visual Studio .NET's object-oriented languages. One program can be created that will be compatible with a variety of devices and able to display different content based on the type of device (e.g., a wireless phone versus a PDA). Chapter 21, Mobile Internet Toolkit, introduces wireless Web application development.

- *Visual Studio .NET Debugger* . Debuggers help programmers find and correct logic errors in program code. In Appendix B, Visual Studio .NET Debugger, we explain how to use key debugger features, such as setting "breakpoints" and "watches," stepping into and out of methods, and examining the method call stack.

- *Unicode*®. As computer systems evolved worldwide, computer vendors developed numeric representations of character sets and special symbols for the local languages spoken in different countries. In some cases, different representations were developed for the same languages. Such disparate character sets hindered communication among computer systems. Visual Basic .NET supports the *Unicode Standard* (maintained by a non-profit organization called the *Unicode Consortium*), which maintains a single character set that specifies unique numeric values for characters and special symbols in most of the world's languages. Appendix D, Unicode®, discusses the standard, overviews the Unicode Consortium Web site, **www.unicode.org** and presents a Visual Basic .NET application that displays "Welcome to Unicode!" in several languages.

Pedagogic Approach

Visual Basic .NET for Experienced Programmers contains a rich collection of examples that have been tested on Windows 2000 and Windows XP. The book concentrates on the principles of good software engineering and stresses program clarity. We are educators who teach edge-of-the-practice topics in industry classrooms worldwide. We avoid arcane terminology and syntax specifications in favor of teaching by example. The text emphasizes good pedagogy.

We use fonts to distinguish between Visual Studio .NET's Integrated Development Environment (IDE) features (such as menu names and menu items) and other elements that appear in the IDE. Our convention is to emphasize IDE features in a sans-serif bold Helvetica font (e.g., **Project** menu) and to emphasize program text in a serif bold Courier font (e.g., **Dim x As Integer**).

LIVE-CODE™ Teaching Approach

Visual Basic .NET for Experienced Programmers is loaded with numerous LIVE-CODE™ examples. This style exemplifies the way we teach and write about programming and is the focus of our multimedia *Cyber Classrooms* and Web-based training courses as well. Each new concept is presented in the context of a complete, working example that is followed by one or more windows showing the program's input/output dialog. We call this method of teaching and writing the **LIVE-CODE™ Approach**. *We use programming languages to teach programming languages.* Reading the examples in the text is much like entering and running them on a computer. Readers have the option of downloading all of the book's code examples from **www.deitel.com**, under the **Downloads/Resources** link. Other links provide errata and answers to frequently asked questions.

World Wide Web Access

All of the source code for the examples in *Visual Basic .NET for Experienced Programmers* (and our other publications) is available on the Internet as downloads from the following Web sites:

> **www.deitel.com**
> **www.prenhall.com/deitel**

Registration is quick and easy and these downloads are free. We suggest downloading all the examples, then running each program as you read the corresponding portion of the book. Make changes to the examples and immediately see the effects of those changes—this is a great way to improve your programming skills. Any instructions for running the examples assumes that the user is running Windows 2000 or Windows XP and is using Microsoft's Internet Information Services (IIS). Additional setup instructions for IIS and other software can be found at our Web sites along with the examples. [*Note:* This is copyrighted material. Feel free to use it as you study, but you may not republish any portion of it in any form without explicit permission from Prentice Hall and the authors.]

Visual Studio .NET belongs to a family of products that are available for purchase and download from Microsoft. Visual Studio .NET, which includes Visual Basic .NET, comes in four different editions—Academic, Professional, Enterprise Developer and Enterprise Architect. Visual Studio .NET Academic contains Visual Studio .NET Professional's features in addition to features designed for students and professors (e.g., an Assignment Manager that documents assignment submission, Application Publishing Tools that aid in the notification of assignments, code samples and more).

Microsoft also offers stand-alone products (Visual C# .NET Standard, Visual C++ .NET Standard and Visual Basic .NET Standard) for various .NET-languages. Each product provides an integrated development environment (similar to Visual Studio .NET) and a compiler. Visit **msdn.microsoft.com/vstudio/howtobuy** for descriptions and ordering information.

Objectives

Each chapter begins with objectives that inform readers of what to expect and gives them an opportunity, after reading the chapter, to determine whether they have met the intended goals.

Quotations

The chapter objectives are followed by sets of quotations. Some are humorous, some are philosophical and some offer interesting insights. We have found that readers enjoy relating the quotations to the chapter material. Many of the quotations are worth a "second look" *after* you read each chapter.

Outline

The chapter outline enables readers to approach the material in top-down fashion. Along with the chapter objectives, the outline helps users anticipate topics and set a comfortable and effective learning pace.

Approximately 20,300 Lines of Code in 192 Example Programs (with Program Outputs)

We present Visual Basic .NET features in the context of complete, working Visual Basic .NET programs. The programs range in size from just a few lines of code to substantial examples containing hundreds of lines of code. All examples are available as downloads from our Web site, **www.deitel.com**.

559 Illustrations/Figures

An abundance of charts, line drawings and program outputs is included.

319 Programming Tips

We have included programming tips to help readers focus on important aspects of program development. We highlight hundreds of these tips in the form of *Good Programming Practices*, *Common Programming Errors*, *Testing and Debugging Tips*, *Performance Tips*, *Portability Tips*, *Software Engineering Observations* and *Look-and-Feel Observations*. These tips and practices represent the best the authors have gleaned from many decades of programming and teaching experience. One of our customers—a mathematics major—told us that she feels this approach is like the highlighting of axioms, theorems and corollaries in mathematics books; it provides a foundation on which to build good software.

32 Good Programming Practices

Good Programming Practices are tips that call attention to techniques that will help developers produce programs that are clearer, more understandable and more maintainable.

100 Common Programming Errors

Developers learning a language tend to make certain kinds of errors frequently. Pointing out these Common Programming Errors *reduces the likelihood that readers will make the same mistakes.*

34 Testing and Debugging Tips

When we first designed this "tip type," we thought the tips would contain suggestions strictly for exposing bugs and removing them from programs. In fact, many of the tips describe aspects of Visual Basic .NET that prevent "bugs" from getting into programs in the first place, thus simplifying the testing and debugging processes.

39 Performance Tips

Developers like to "turbo charge" their programs. We have included 39 Performance Tips *that highlight opportunities for improving program performance—making programs run faster or minimizing the amount of memory that they occupy.*

11 Portability Tips

We include Portability Tips *to help developers write portable code and to provide insights on how Visual Basic .NET achieves its high degree of portability.*

86 Software Engineering Observations

The object-oriented programming paradigm necessitates a complete rethinking of the way we build software systems. Visual Basic .NET is an effective language for achieving good software engineering. The Software Engineering Observations *highlight architectural and design issues that affect the construction of software systems, especially large-scale systems.*

17 Look-and-Feel Observations

We provide Look-and-Feel Observations *to highlight graphical-user-interface conventions. These observations help developers design attractive, user-friendly graphical user interfaces that conform to industry norms.*

Summary

Each chapter ends with a summary that helps readers review and reinforce key concepts.

Approximately 3,683 Index Entries (with approximately 4,490 Page References)

We have included an extensive Index. This resource enables readers to search for any term or concept by keyword. The Index is especially useful to practicing programmers who use the book as a reference.

"Double Indexing" of All Visual Basic .NET L   IVE-CODE™ Examples

Visual Basic .NET for Experienced Programmers has 192 LIVE-CODE™ examples, which we have "double indexed." For every Visual Basic .NET source-code program in the book, we took the file name with the **.vb** extension, such as **ShowColors.vb**, and indexed it both alphabetically (in this case, under "S") and as a subindex item under "Examples." This makes it easier to find examples using particular features.

Visual Basic .NET Multimedia Cyber Classroom, Second Edition and The Complete Visual Basic .NET Training Course, Second Edition

We have prepared an interactive, CD-ROM-based, software version of *Visual Basic .NET How to Program, Second Edition,* called the *Visual Basic .NET Multimedia Cyber Classroom, Second Edition.* This resource, ideal for corporate training and college courses, is loaded with interactive e-learning features. The *Cyber Classroom* is packaged with the *Visual Basic .NET How to Program, Second Edition* textbook at a discount in *The Complete Visual Basic .NET Training Course, Second Edition.* If you already have that book and would like to purchase the *Visual Basic .NET Multimedia Cyber Classroom, Second Edition* separately, please visit **www.InformIT.com/cyberclassrooms**. The ISBN number for the *Visual Basic .NET Multimedia Cyber Classroom, Second Edition* is 0-13-

065193-1. Many Deitel™ *Cyber Classrooms* are available in CD-ROM and Web-based training formats.

The CD-ROM provides an introduction in which the authors overview the *Cyber Classroom*'s features. The textbook's 249 LIVE-CODE™ example Visual Basic .NET programs truly "come alive" in the *Cyber Classroom*. If you are viewing a program and want to execute it, you simply click the lightning-bolt icon, and the program will run. You immediately will see—and hear, when working with audio-based multimedia programs—the program's output. Click the audio icon, and one of the authors will discuss the program and "walk you through" the code.

The *Cyber Classroom* also provides navigational aids, including extensive hyperlinking. The *Cyber Classroom* is browser based, so it remembers sections that you have visited recently and allows you to move forward or backward among those sections. The thousands of index entries are hyperlinked to their text occurrences. Furthermore, when you key in a term using the "find" feature, the *Cyber Classroom* will locate occurrences of that term throughout the text. The Table of Contents entries are "hot," so clicking a chapter name takes you immediately to that chapter.

Readers like the fact that solutions to approximately half the exercises in *Visual Basic .NET How to Program, Second Edition* are included with the *Cyber Classroom*. Studying and running these extra programs is a great way for readers to enhance their learning experience.

Professionals and student users of our *Cyber Classrooms* tell us that they like the interactivity and that the *Cyber Classroom* is an effective reference due to its extensive hyperlinking and other navigational features. We received an e-mail from a reader who said he lives "in the boonies" and cannot attend a live course at a university, so the *Cyber Classroom* provided an ideal solution to his educational needs.

Professors tell us that their students enjoy using the *Cyber Classroom* and spend more time on the courses and master more of the material than in textbook-only courses. For a complete list of the available and forthcoming *Cyber Classrooms* and *Complete Training Courses*, see the *Deitel™ Series* page at the beginning of this book, the product listing and ordering information at the end of this book or visit **www.deitel.com**, **www.prenhall.com/deitel** or **www.InformIT.com/deitel**.

Deitel e-Learning Initiatives

e-Books and Support for Wireless Devices

Wireless devices will play an enormous role in the future of the Internet. Given recent bandwidth enhancements and the emergence of 2.5 and 3G wireless technologies, it is projected that, within two years, more people will access the Internet through wireless devices than through desktop computers. Deitel & Associates, Inc., is committed to wireless accessibility and has recently published *Wireless Internet & Mobile Business How to Program*. To fulfill the needs of a wide range of customers, we are developing our content in traditional print formats and in new electronic formats, such as e-books, so that readers can access content virtually anytime, anywhere. Visit **www.deitel.com** for periodic updates on all Deitel technology initiatives.

e-Matter

Deitel & Associates, Inc., is partnering with Prentice Hall's parent company, Pearson PLC, and its information technology Web site, **InformIT.com**, to launch the Deitel e-Matter series at **www.InformIT.com/deitel** in Fall 2002. The Deitel e-Matter series will provide professionals with an additional source of information on specific programming topics at modest prices. e-Matter consists of stand-alone sections taken from published texts, forthcoming texts or pieces written during the Deitel research-and-development process. Developing e-Matter based on pre-publication manuscripts allows us to offer significant amounts of the material well before our books are published.

Course Management Systems: WebCT, Blackboard, CourseCompass and Premium CourseCompass

We are working with Prentice Hall to integrate our *How to Program Series* courseware into four series of Course Management Systems-based products: WebCT, Blackboard™, CourseCompass and Premium CourseCompass. These enable instructors to create, manage and use sophisticated Web-based educational programs. Course Management Systems feature course customization (such as posting contact information, policies, syllabi, announcements, assignments, grades, performance evaluations and progress tracking), class and student management tools, a grade book, reporting tools, communication tools (such as chat rooms), a whiteboard, document sharing, bulletin boards and more. Instructors can use these products to communicate with their students, create online quizzes and exams from questions directly linked to the text and efficiently grade and track test results. For more information about these upcoming products, visit **www.prenhall.com/cms**. For demonstrations of WebCT, Blackboard and CourseCompass course materials, visit **cms.prenhall.com/webct**, **cms.prenhall.com/blackboard** and **cms.prenhall.com/coursecompass**, respectively.

Deitel and InformIT Newsletters

Deitel Column in the InformIT Newsletters

Deitel & Associates, Inc., contributes articles to the free *InformIT* weekly e-mail newsletter, subscribed to by more than 750,000 IT professionals worldwide. For registration information, visit **www.InformIT.com** and click the **MyInformIT** tab.

Deitel™ Buzz Online Newsletter

Our own free newsletter, the *Deitel™ Buzz Online*, includes commentary on industry trends and developments, links to articles and resources from our published books and upcoming publications, product-release schedules, challenges, anecdotes and more. For registration information, visit **www.deitel.com/newsletter/subscribe.html**.

The Deitel™ Developer Series

Deitel & Associates, Inc., is making a major commitment to .NET programming through our *Deitel™ Developer Series. C# A Programmer's Introduction, C# for Experienced Programmers, Visual Basic .NET for Experienced Programmers* and *Visual C++ .NET for Experienced Programmers* are the first .NET books in this new series. These will be followed by several advanced books, beginning with *ASP .NET with Visual Basic .NET for Experienced Programmers* and *ASP .NET with C# for Experienced Programmers.*

The *Deitel™ Developer Series* is divided into three subseries. The *A Technical Introduction* subseries provides IT managers and developers with detailed overviews of emerging technologies. The *A Programmer's Introduction* subseries is designed to teach the fundamentals of new languages and software technologies to developers from the ground up. These books discuss programming fundamentals, followed by brief introductions to more sophisticated topics. Finally, the *For Experienced Programmers* subseries is designed for seasoned developers seeking to learn new programming languages and technologies without the encumbrance of introductory material. The books in this subseries move quickly to in-depth coverage of the intermediate features of the programming languages and software technologies being covered.

ASP .NET with Visual Basic .NET for Experienced Programmers

Our forthcoming publication *ASP .NET with Visual Basic .NET for Experienced Programmers* (available in 2003) is geared toward experienced .NET developers. This new book will cover enterprise-level Web-programming topics, including: Creating multi-tier, database intensive ASP .NET applications using ADO .NET and XML; constructing custom Web controls and developing Web services. This book also will include configuration and security topics. Updates on the status of this publication are posted at **www.deitel.com**. Before reading this book you should be familiar with Visual Basic .NET at the level of either *Visual Basic .NET How to Program, Second Edition* or *Visual Basic .NET for Experienced Programmers*.

Acknowledgments

One of the great pleasures of writing a book is acknowledging the efforts of many people whose names may not appear on the cover, but whose hard work, cooperation, friendship and understanding were crucial to the production of the book. Because this publication has been derived from *Visual Basic .NET How to Program, Second Edition*, we would like to acknowledge those who have helped us with both publications.

Many other people at Deitel & Associates, Inc., devoted long hours to this project. Below is a list of our full-time employees who contributed to this publication:

> Matthew R. Kowalewski
> Jonathan Gadzik
> Kyle Lomelí
> Lauren Trees
> Rashmi Jayaprakash
> Laura Treibick
> Betsy DuWaldt
> Barbara Deitel

We would also like to thank the participants in the Deitel & Associates, Inc., College Internship Program who contributed to this publication.[1]

---

1. The *Deitel & Associates, Inc. College Internship Program* offers a limited number of salaried positions to Boston-area college students majoring in Computer Science, Information Technology, Marketing, Management and English. Students work at our corporate headquarters in Maynard, Massachusetts full-time in the summers and (for those attending college in the Boston area) part-time during the academic year. We also offer full-time internship positions for students interested in taking a semester off from school to gain industry experience. Regular full-time positions are available to college graduates. For more information about this competitive program, please contact Abbey Deitel at **deitel@deitel.com** and visit **www.deitel.com**.

Andrew Jones (Harvard)
Jeffrey Hamm (Northeastern)
Su Kim (Carnegie Mellon)
Jeng Lee (Carnegie Mellon)
Thiago Lucas da Silva (Northeastern)
Wilson Wu (Carnegie Mellon)
Brian Foster (Northeastern)

We are fortunate to have been able to work with the talented and dedicated team of publishing professionals at Prentice Hall. We especially appreciate the extraordinary efforts of our editors, Petra Recter and Karen McLean of Prentice Hall and PH/PTR, respectively and Michael Ruel, who managed the extraordinary review processes for our *Deitel™ Developer Series* Visual Basic .NET publication. We would also like to thank Mark L. Taub, Editor-in-Chief for computer publications at PH/PTR, for conceptualizing the *Deitel™ Developer Series*. He provided the necessary environment and resources to help us generate the many books in this series. A special note of appreciation goes to Marcia Horton, Editor-in-Chief of Engineering and Computer Science at Prentice Hall. Marcia has been our mentor and our friend for 18 years at Prentice Hall. She is responsible for all aspects of Deitel publications at all Pearson divisions including Prentice Hall, PH/PTR and Pearson International.

Laura Treibick, the Director of Multimedia at Deitel & Associates, Inc., designed the cover. Tamara Newnam (**smart_art@earthlink.net**) carried the cover through to completion, and produced the art work for our programming-tip icons.

We wish to acknowledge the efforts of our first- and second-round reviewers. Adhering to a tight time schedule, these reviewers scrutinized the text and the programs, providing countless suggestions for improving the accuracy and completeness of the presentation. We sincerely appreciate the time these people took from their busy professional schedules to help us ensure the quality, accuracy and timeliness of this book.

Merged reviewer list from *Visual Basic .NET How to Program, Second Edition* and *Visual Basic .NET for Experienced Programmers*:
Lars Bergstrom (Microsoft)
Christopher Brumme (Microsoft)
Alan Carter (Microsoft)
Greg Lowney (Microsoft)
Cameron McColl (Microsoft)
Tania Means (Microsoft)
Dale Michalk (Microsoft)
Shanku Niyogi (Microsoft)
Eric Olson (Microsoft)
Paul Vick (Microsoft)
Jeff Welton (Microsoft)
Joan Aliprand (Unicode Consortium)
Douglas Bass (University of St. Thomas)
Paul Bohman (Technology Coordinator, WebAIM)
Harlan Brewer (Utah State University)
Carl Burnham (Southpoint)

Clinton Chadwick (Valtech)
Mario Chavez-Rivas (Trane Corp.)
Ram Choppa (Baker Hughes)
Ken Cox (Sympatico)
Christopher Crane (University of New Foundland)
Anthony Fadale (State of Kansas, Accessibility Committee)
Corrine Gregory (Hart Gregory Group)
James Huddleston (IBM)
J. Mel Harris (OnLineLiveTraining.com)
Terry Hull (CEO, Enterprise Component Technologies, Inc.)
Balaji Janamanchi (Texas Tech)
Amit Kalani (MobiCast, co-author of *Inside ASP.NET* and *.NET Mobile Web Developer's Guide*)
Stan Kurkovsky (Columbus State University)
Stephen Longo (LaSalle University)
Rick McGowan (Unicode Consortium)
John Mueller
Michael Paciello (Founder, WebABLE)
Chris Panell (Heald College)
Kevin Parker (Idaho State College)
Bryan Plaster (Valtech)
Andre Pool (Florida Community College-Jacksonville)
T. J. Racoosin (rSolutions)
Teri Radichel (Radical Software)
Nancy Reyes (Heald College)
Chris Ridpath (A-Prompt Project, University of Toronto)
Wally Roth (Taylor University)
Craig Shofding (CAS Training)
Bill Stutzman (Consultant)
Jutta Treviranus (A-Prompt Project, University of Toronto)
Tim Thomas (Xtreme Computing)
Mark Thomas (University of Cincinnati)
Bill Tinker (Aries Software)
Joel Weinstein (Northeastern University)

We would sincerely appreciate your comments, criticisms, corrections and suggestions for improving the book. Please address all correspondence to:

deitel@deitel.com

We will respond promptly.

Well, that's it for now. Welcome to the exciting world of Visual Basic .NET programming. We hope you enjoy this look at Microsoft's premier .NET language. Good luck!

Dr. Harvey M. Deitel
Tem R. Nieto
Cheryl H. Yaeger

About the Authors

Dr. Harvey M. Deitel, Chairman and Chief Strategy Officer of Deitel & Associates, Inc., has 41 years experience in the computing field, including extensive industry and academic experience. Dr. Deitel earned B.S. and M.S. degrees from the Massachusetts Institute of Technology and a Ph.D. from Boston University. He worked on the pioneering virtual-memory operating-systems projects at IBM and MIT that developed techniques now widely implemented in systems such as Unix, Linux™ and Windows XP. He has 20 years of college teaching experience, including earning tenure and serving as the Chairman of the Computer Science Department at Boston College before founding Deitel & Associates, Inc., with his son, Paul J. Deitel. He is the author or co-author of several dozen books and multimedia packages and is writing many more. With translations published in Japanese, Russian, Spanish, Traditional Chinese, Simplified Chinese, Korean, French, Polish, Italian, Portuguese and Greek, Dr. Deitel's texts have earned international recognition. Dr. Deitel has delivered professional seminars to major corporations, and to government organizations and various branches of the military.

Paul J. Deitel, CEO and Chief Technical Officer of Deitel & Associates, Inc., is a graduate of the Massachusetts Institute of Technology's Sloan School of Management, where he studied Information Technology. Through Deitel & Associates, Inc., he has delivered Java, C, C++ and Internet and World Wide Web programming courses to industry clients including Compaq, Sun Microsystems, White Sands Missile Range, Rogue Wave Software, Boeing, Dell, Stratus, Fidelity, Cambridge Technology Partners, Open Environment Corporation, One Wave, Hyperion Software, Lucent Technologies, Adra Systems, Entergy, CableData Systems, NASA at the Kennedy Space Center, the National Severe Storms Laboratory, IBM and many other organizations. He has lectured on C++ and Java for the Boston Chapter of the Association for Computing Machinery and has taught satellite-based Java courses through a cooperative venture of Deitel & Associates, Inc., Prentice Hall and the Technology Education Network. He and his father, Dr. Harvey M. Deitel, are the world's best-selling programming language textbook authors.

Tem R. Nieto, Director of Product Development of Deitel & Associates, Inc., is a graduate of the Massachusetts Institute of Technology, where he studied engineering and computing. Through Deitel & Associates, Inc., he has delivered courses for industry clients including Sun Microsystems, Compaq, EMC, Stratus, Fidelity, NASDAQ, Art Technology, Progress Software, Toys "R" Us, Operational Support Facility of the National Oceanographic and Atmospheric Administration, Jet Propulsion Laboratory, Nynex, Motorola, Federal Reserve Bank of Chicago, Banyan, Schlumberger, University of Notre Dame, NASA, Hewlett-Packard, various military installations and many others. He has co-authored numerous books and multimedia packages with the Deitels and has contributed to virtually every Deitel & Associates, Inc., publication.

Cheryl H. Yaeger, Director of Microsoft Software Publications with Deitel & Associates, Inc., graduated from Boston University in three years with a bachelor's degree in Computer Science. Cheryl has co-authored various Deitel & Associates publications, including *C# How to Program*, *C# A Programmer's Introduction*, *C# for Experienced Programmers* and *Visual Basic .NET for Experienced Programmers* as well as contributed to other Deitel publications including *Perl How to Program*, *Wireless Internet & Mobile Business How to Program*, *Internet and World Wide Web How to Program, Second Edition* and *Visual Basic .NET How to Program, Second Edition*.

About Deitel & Associates, Inc.

Deitel & Associates, Inc., is an internationally recognized corporate instructor-led training and content-creation organization specializing in Internet/World Wide Web software technology, e-business/e-commerce software technology, object technology and computer programming languages education. The company provides courses in Internet and World Wide Web programming, wireless Internet programming, Web services (in both Java and .NET languages), object technology, and major programming languages and platforms, such as Visual Basic .NET, C#, Visual C++ .NET, Java, Advanced Java, C, C++, XML, Perl, Python, ASP .NET, ADO .NET and more. Deitel & Associates, Inc., was founded by Dr. Harvey M. Deitel and Paul J. Deitel, the world's leading programming-language textbook authors. The company's clients include many of the largest computer companies, government agencies, branches of the military and business organizations. Through its 25-year publishing partnership with Prentice Hall, Deitel & Associates, Inc., publishes leading-edge programming textbooks, professional books, interactive CD-ROM-based multimedia *Cyber Classrooms*, *Complete Training Courses*, e-books, e-matter, Web-based training courses and course management systems e-content. Deitel & Associates, Inc., and the authors can be reached via e-mail at:

> `deitel@deitel.com`

To learn more about Deitel & Associates, Inc., its publications and its worldwide corporate on-site curriculum, see the last few pages of this book or visit:

> `www.deitel.com`

Individuals wishing to purchase Deitel books, *Cyber Classrooms*, *Complete Training Courses* and Web-based training courses can do so through bookstores, online booksellers and:

> `www.deitel.com`
> `www.prenhall.com/deitel`
> `www.InformIT.com/deitel`
> `www.InformIT.com/cyberclassrooms`

Bulk orders by corporations and academic institutions should be placed directly with Prentice Hall. See the last few pages of this book for worldwide ordering details. To follow the Deitel publishing program, please register at

> `www.deitel.com/newsletter/subscribe.html`.

The World Wide Web Consortium (W3C)

 Deitel & Associates, Inc., is a member of the *World Wide Web Consortium (W3C)*. The W3C was founded in 1994 "to develop common protocols for the evolution of the World Wide Web." As a W3C member, Deitel & Associates, Inc., holds a seat on the W3C Advisory Committee (the company's representative is our CEO and Chief Technology Officer, Paul Deitel). Advisory Committee members help provide "strategic direction" to the W3C through meetings held around the world. Member organizations also help develop standards recommendations for Web technologies (such as XHTML, XML and many others) through participation in W3C activities and groups. Membership in the W3C is intended for companies and large organizations. To obtain information on becoming a member of the W3C visit **www.w3.org/Consortium/Prospectus/Joining**.

1

Introduction to .NET and Visual Basic .NET

Objectives

- To learn the history of the Internet and the World Wide Web.
- To become familiar with the World Wide Web Consortium (W3C).
- To learn what the Extensible Markup Language (XML) is and why it is an important technology.
- To understand the impact of object technology on software development.
- To understand the Microsoft® .NET initiative.
- To preview the remaining chapters of the book.

Things are always at their best in their beginning.
Blaise Pascal

High thoughts must have high language.
Aristophanes

Our life is frittered away by detail…Simplify, simplify.
Henry David Thoreau

Before beginning, plan carefully….
Marcus Tullius Cicero

Look with favor upon a bold beginning.
Virgil

I think I'm beginning to learn something about it.
Auguste Renoir

Outline

1.1 Introduction

Welcome to Visual Basic .NET! We have worked hard to provide programmers with the most accurate and complete information regarding the Visual Basic .NET language and the .NET platform. We hope that this book will provide an informative, entertaining and challenging learning experience for you. In this chapter, we present the history of the Internet and World Wide Web, and introduce Microsoft's .NET initiative. The chapter concludes with a tour of the remainder of the book.

1.2 History of the Internet and World Wide Web

In the late 1960s, at a conference at the University of Illinois Urbana-Champaign, ARPA—the Advanced Research Projects Agency of the Department of Defense—rolled out the blueprints for networking the main computer systems of approximately a dozen ARPA-funded universities and research institutions. The computers were to be connected with communications lines operating at a then-stunning 56 Kbps (1 Kbps is equal to 1,024 bits per second), at a time when most people (of the few who had access to networking technologies) were connecting over telephone lines to computers at a rate of 110 bits per second. Researchers at Harvard talked about communicating with the Univac 1108 "supercomputer," which was located across the country at the University of Utah, to handle calculations related to their computer graphics research. Many other intriguing possibilities were discussed. Academic research was about to take a giant leap forward. Shortly after this conference, ARPA proceeded to implement what quickly became called the *ARPAnet*, the grandparent of today's *Internet*.

Things worked out differently from the original plan. Although the ARPAnet did enable researchers to network their computers, its chief benefit proved to be the capability for quick and easy communication via what came to be known as *electronic mail (e-mail)*. This is true even on today's Internet, with e-mail, instant messaging and file transfer facilitating communications among hundreds of millions of people worldwide.

The network was designed to operate without centralized control. This meant that if a portion of the network should fail, the remaining working portions would still be able to route data packets from senders to receivers over alternative paths.

The protocol (i.e., set of rules) for communicating over the ARPAnet became known as the *Transmission Control Protocol (TCP)*. TCP ensured that messages were routed properly from sender to receiver and that those messages arrived intact.

In parallel with the early evolution of the Internet, organizations worldwide were implementing their own networks to facilitate both intra-organization (i.e., within the organization) and inter-organization (i.e., between organizations) communication. A huge variety of networking hardware and software appeared. One challenge was to enable these diverse products to communicate with each other. ARPA accomplished this by developing the *Internet Protocol (IP),* which created a true "network of networks," the current architecture of the Internet. The combined set of protocols is now commonly called *TCP/IP.*

Initially, use of the Internet was limited to universities and research institutions; later, the military adopted the technology. Eventually, the government decided to allow access to the Internet for commercial purposes. When this decision was made, there was resentment among the research and military communities—it was felt that response times would become poor as "the Net" became saturated with so many users.

In fact, the opposite has occurred. Businesses rapidly realized that, by making effective use of the Internet, they could refine their operations and offer new and better services to their clients. Companies started spending vast amounts of money to develop and enhance their Internet presence. This generated fierce competition among communications carriers and hardware and software suppliers to meet the increased infrastructure demand. The result is that *bandwidth* (i.e., the information-carrying capacity of communications lines) on the Internet has increased tremendously, while hardware costs have plummeted. The Internet has played a significant role in the economic growth that many industrialized nations experienced over the last decade.

The *World Wide Web* allows computer users to locate and view multimedia-based documents (i.e., documents with text, graphics, animations, audios or videos) on almost any subject. Even though the Internet was developed more than three decades ago, the introduction of the World Wide Web (WWW) was a relatively recent event. In 1989, Tim Berners-Lee of CERN (the European Organization for Nuclear Research) began to develop a technology for sharing information via hyperlinked text documents. Basing the new language on the well-established *Standard Generalized Markup Language (SGML)*—a standard for business data interchange—Berners-Lee called his invention the *HyperText Markup Language (HTML)*. He also wrote communication protocols to form the backbone of his new hypertext information system, which he referred to as the World Wide Web.

Surely, historians will list the Internet and the World Wide Web among the most important and profound creations of humankind. In the past, most computer applications ran on "stand-alone" computers (computers that were not connected to one another). Today's applications can be written to communicate among the world's hundreds of millions of computers. The Internet and World Wide Web merge computing and communications technologies, expediting and simplifying our work. They make information instantly and conveniently accessible to large numbers of people. They enable individuals and small businesses to achieve worldwide exposure. They are changing the way we do business and conduct our personal lives.

1.3 World Wide Web Consortium (W3C)

In October 1994, Tim Berners-Lee founded an organization, called the *World Wide Web Consortium (W3C)*, that is devoted to developing nonproprietary, interoperable technologies for the World Wide Web. One of the W3C's primary goals is to make the Web universally accessible—regardless of its users' disabilities, languages or cultures.

The W3C is also a standardization organization and is composed of three *hosts*—the Massachusetts Institute of Technology (MIT), France's INRIA (Institut National de Recherche en Informatique et Automatique) and Keio University of Japan—and over 400 members, including Deitel & Associates, Inc. Members provide the primary financing for the W3C and help provide the strategic direction of the Consortium. To learn more about the W3C, visit **www.w3.org**.

Web technologies standardized by the W3C are called *Recommendations*. Current W3C Recommendations include *Extensible HyperText Markup Language (XHTML™)* for marking up content for the Web, *Cascading Style Sheets (CSS™)* for describing how content is formatted and the *Extensible Markup Language (XML)* for creating markup languages. Recommendations are not actual software products, but documents that specify the role, syntax and rules of a technology. Before becoming a W3C Recommendation, a document passes through three major phases: *Working Draft*, which, as its name implies, specifies an evolving draft; *Candidate Recommendation,* a stable version of the document that industry can begin to implement; and *Proposed Recommendation*, a Candidate Recommendation that is considered mature (i.e., has been implemented and tested over a period of time) and is ready to be considered for W3C Recommendation status. For detailed information about the W3C Recommendation track, see "6.2 The W3C Recommendation track" at

```
www.w3.org/Consortium/Process/Process-19991111/
process.html#RecsCR
```

1.4 Extensible Markup Language (XML)

As the popularity of the Web exploded, HTML's limitations became apparent. HTML's lack of *extensibility* (the ability to change or add features) frustrated developers, and its ambiguous definition allowed erroneous HTML to proliferate. In response to these problems, the W3C added limited extensibility to HTML. This was, however, only a temporary solution—the need for a standardized, fully extensible and structurally strict language was apparent. As a result, XML was developed by the W3C. XML combines the power and extensibility of its parent language, Standard Generalized Markup Language (SGML), with the simplicity that the Web community demands.

Data independence, the separation of content from its presentation, is an essential characteristic of XML. Because an XML document describes data, any application conceivably can process such a document. Recognizing this, software developers are integrating XML into their applications to improve Web functionality and interoperability. XML's flexibility and power make it perfect for the middle tier of client/server systems, which must interact with a wide variety of clients. Much of the processing that was once limited to server computers now can be performed by client computers, because XML's semantic and structural information enables it to be manipulated by any application that can process text. This reduces server loads and network traffic, resulting in a faster, more efficient Web.

XML is not limited to Web applications. Increasingly, XML is being employed in databases—the structure of an XML document enables it to be integrated easily with database applications. As applications become more Web enabled, it seems likely that XML will become the universal technology for data representation. All applications employing XML will be able to communicate, provided that they can understand each other's XML markup, or *vocabulary*.

Simple Object Access Protocol (SOAP) is a technology for the distribution of data (marked up as XML) over the Internet. Developed initially by Microsoft and Develop-Mentor, SOAP is a W3C Working Draft that provides a framework for expressing application semantics, encoding data and packaging data. Microsoft .NET (discussed in Sections 1.6 and 1.7) uses XML and SOAP to mark up and transfer data over the Internet. XML and SOAP are at the core of .NET—they allow software components to interoperate (i.e., communicate easily with one another). SOAP is supported by many platforms, because of its foundations in XML and HTTP. We discuss XML in Chapter 15, Extensible Markup Language (XML), and SOAP in Chapter 18, ASP .NET and Web Services.

1.5 Key Software Trend: Object Technology

Object technology is a packaging scheme that facilitates the creation of meaningful software units. These units are large and focused on particular application areas. There are date objects, time objects, paycheck objects, invoice objects, audio objects, video objects, file objects, record objects and so on. In fact, almost any noun can be represented as a software object. Objects have *properties* (i.e., *attributes*, such as color, size and weight) and perform *actions* (i.e., *behaviors*, such as moving, sleeping or drawing). Classes represent groups of related objects. For example, all cars belong to the "car" class, even though individual cars vary in make, model, color and options packages. A class specifies the general format of its objects; the properties and actions available to an object depend on its class.

We live in a world of objects. Just look around you—there are cars, planes, people, animals, buildings, traffic lights, elevators and so on. Before object-oriented languages appeared, *procedural programming languages* (such as Fortran, Pascal, BASIC and C) focused on actions (verbs) rather than things or objects (nouns). We live in a world of objects, but earlier programming languages forced individuals to program primarily with verbs. This paradigm shift made program writing a bit awkward. However, with the advent of popular object-oriented languages, such as C++, Java, C# and Visual Basic .NET, programmers can program in an object-oriented manner that reflects the way in which they perceive the world. This process, which seems more natural than procedural programming, has resulted in significant productivity gains.

One of the key problems with procedural programming is that the program units created do not mirror real-world entities effectively and therefore are difficult to reuse. Programmers often write and rewrite similar software for various projects. This wastes precious time and money as programmers repeatedly "reinvent the wheel." With object technology, properly designed software entities (called objects) can be reused on future projects. Using libraries of reusable componentry can reduce the amount of effort required to implement certain kinds of systems (as compared to the effort that would be required to reinvent these capabilities in new projects). Visual Basic .NET programmers use the .NET Framework Class Library (known commonly as the FCL), which is introduced in Section 1.9.

Some organizations report that software reusability is not, in fact, the key benefit of object-oriented programming. Rather, they indicate that object-oriented programming tends to produce software that is more understandable because it is better organized and has fewer maintenance requirements. As much as 80 percent of software costs are not associated with the original efforts to develop the software, but instead are related to the continued evolution and maintenance of that software throughout its lifetime. Object orientation allows programmers to abstract the details of software and focus on the "big picture." Rather than worrying about minute details, the programmer can focus on the behaviors and interactions of objects. A roadmap that showed every tree, house and driveway would be difficult, if not impossible, to read. When such details are removed and only the essential information (roads) remains, the map becomes easier to understand. In the same way, a program that is divided into objects is easy to understand, modify and update because it hides much of the detail. It is clear that object-oriented programming will be the key programming methodology for at least the next decade.

Software Engineering Observation 1.1

Use a building-block approach to create programs. By using existing pieces in new projects, programmers avoid reinventing the wheel. This is called software reuse, *and it is central to object-oriented programming.*

[*Note*: We will include many of these *Software Engineering Observations* throughout the book to explain concepts that affect and improve the overall architecture and quality of a software system and, particularly, of large software systems. We also will highlight *Good Programming Practices* (practices that can help programmers write programs that are clearer, more understandable, more maintainable and easier to test and debug), *Common Programming Errors* (problems we highlight to ensure that programmers avoid the most common errors), *Performance Tips* (techniques that will help programmers write programs that run faster and use less memory), *Portability Tips* (techniques that will help programmers write programs that can run, with little or no modification, on a variety of computers), *Testing and Debugging Tips* (techniques that will help programmers remove bugs from their programs and, more importantly, write bug-free programs in the first place) and *Look-and-Feel Observations* (techniques that will help programmers design the "look and feel" of their graphical user interfaces for appearance and ease of use). Many of these techniques and practices are only guidelines; you will, no doubt, develop your own preferred programming style.]

The advantage of writing your own code is that you will know exactly how it works. The code will be yours to examine, modify and improve. The disadvantage is the time and effort that goes into designing, developing and testing new code.

Performance Tip 1.1

Reusing proven code components instead of writing your own versions can improve program performance, because these components normally are written to perform efficiently.

Software Engineering Observation 1.2

Extensive class libraries of reusable software components are available over the Internet and the World Wide Web; many are offered free of charge.

1.6 Introduction to Microsoft .NET

In June 2000, Microsoft announced its *.NET* (pronounced "dot-net") *initiative*. The *.NET platform* is one that provides significant enhancements to earlier developer platforms. .NET offers a new software-development model that allows applications created in disparate programming languages to communicate with each other. The platform also allows developers to create Web-based applications that can be distributed to a great variety of devices (even wireless phones) and to desktop computers.

Microsoft's .NET initiative is a broad new vision for embracing the Internet and the Web in the development, engineering and use of software. One key aspect of the .NET strategy is its independence from a specific language or platform. Rather than requiring programmers to use a single programming language, developers can create a .NET application by using any combination of .NET-compatible languages (Fig. 1.1). Programmers can contribute to the same software project, writing code in the .NET languages (such as Visual Basic .NET, C#, Visual C++ .NET and many others) in which they are most proficient. Part of the initiative includes Microsoft's *Active Server Pages (ASP) .NET* technology, which allows programmers to create applications for the Web. With ASP .NET, developers can create Web-based, database-intensive applications quickly by harnessing the power of .NET's object-oriented languages. Developers can use ASP .NET to develop powerful and robust Web applications, taking advantage of ASP .NET's optimizations for performance, testing and security.

A key component of the .NET architecture is *Web services*, which are applications that expose (i.e., make available) functionality to clients via the Internet. Clients and other applications can use these Web services as reusable building blocks. One example of a Web service is Dollar Rent A Car's reservation system, known as Quick Keys.[1] Dollar wanted to expose the functionality of its mainframe-based system, so that other companies could provide customers with the ability to make rental-car reservations. Dollar could have created individual, proprietary solutions for its business partners. To expose its functionality in a reusable way, Dollar implemented its solution using Web services. The results have been phenomenal. Through this Web service, airlines and hotels can use Dollar's reservation system to reserve cars for their clients. Dollar's business partners do not need to use the same platform as Dollar uses, nor do they need to understand how the reservation system is implemented. Reimplementing its application as a Web service has provided Dollar with millions of dollars of additional revenue, as well as thousands of new customers.

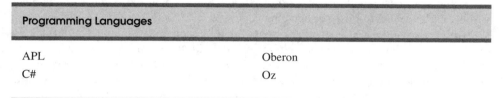

Programming Languages	
APL	Oberon
C#	Oz

Fig. 1.1   .NET Languages (table information from Microsoft Web site, `www.microsoft.com`.). (Part 1 of 2.)

1. Microsoft Corporation, "Dollar Rent A Car Breathes New Life Into Legacy Systems Using .NET Connected Software," 15 March 2002, `<www.microsoft.com/business/casestudies/b2c/dollarrentacar.asp>`.

Programming Languages (Cont.)	
COBOL	Pascal
Component Pascal	Perl
Curriculum	Python
Eiffel	RPG
Fortran	Scheme
Haskell	Smalltalk
J#	Standard ML
JScript .NET	Visual Basic .NET
Mercury	Visual C++ .NET

Fig. 1.1   .NET Languages (table information from Microsoft Web site, **www.microsoft.com**). (Part 2 of 2.)

Web services extend tncept of software reuse by allowing programmers to concentrate on their specialties without having to implement every component of every application. Instead, companies can buy Web services and devote their time and energy to developing their products. Visual programming (discussed in Chapter 2) has become popular, because it enables programmers to create applications easily, using such prepackaged components as buttons, textboxes and labels. Similarly, programmers may create an application using Web services for databases, security, authentication, data storage and language translation without having to know the internal details of those components.

When companies link their products via Web services, a new user experience emerges. For example, a single application could manage bill payments, tax refunds, loans and investments, using Web services from various companies. An online merchant could buy Web services for online credit-card payments, user authentication, network security and inventory databases to create an e-commerce Web site.

The keys to this interaction are XML and SOAP, which enable Web services to communicate. XML gives meaning to data, and SOAP is the protocol that allows Web services to communicate easily with one another. XML and SOAP act as the "glue" that combines various Web services to form applications.

Universal data access is another essential .NET concept. If two copies of a file exist (e.g., on a personal and a company computer), the oldest version must be updated constantly—this is called file *synchronization*. If the files are different, they are *unsynchronized*, a situation that could lead to errors. With .NET, data can reside in one central location rather than on separate systems. Any Internet-connected device can access the data (under tight control, of course), which would then be formatted appropriately for use or display on the accessing device. Thus, the same document could be seen and edited on a desktop PC, a PDA, a wireless phone or other device. Users would not need to synchronize the information, because it would be fully up-to-date in a central location.

.NET is an immense undertaking. We discuss various aspects of .NET throughout this book. Additional information is available at **www.microsoft.com/net**.

1.7 Visual Basic .NET

Visual Basic .NET evolved from BASIC (Beginner's All-purpose Symbolic Instruction Code), developed in the mid-1960s by Professors John Kemeny and Thomas Kurtz of Dartmouth College as a language for writing simple programs. BASIC's primary purpose was to familiarize novices with programming concepts.

The widespread use of BASIC on various types of computers (sometimes called *hardware platforms*) led to many enhancements to the language. When Bill Gates founded Microsoft Corporation, he implemented BASIC on several early personal computers. With the development of the Microsoft Windows graphical user interface (GUI) in the late 1980s and the early 1990s, the natural evolution of BASIC was Visual Basic, introduced by Microsoft in 1991.

Until Visual Basic appeared in 1991, developing Microsoft Windows-based applications was a difficult and cumbersome process. Although Visual Basic is derived from the BASIC programming language, it is a distinctly different language that offers powerful features such as graphical user interfaces, event handling, access to the *Windows 32-bit Application Programming Interface (Win32 API)*, object-based programming and error handling. Like Visual Basic, Visual Basic .NET is an event-driven, visual programming language in which programs are created using an *Integrated Development Environment (IDE)*. With the IDE, a programmer can write, run, test and debug Visual Basic programs quickly and efficiently, thereby reducing the time it takes to produce a working program to a fraction of the time it would have taken without using the IDE. The process of creating an application rapidly is typically referred to as *Rapid Application Development (RAD)*. Visual Basic is the world's most widely used RAD language.

The advancement of programming tools and consumer-electronic devices created many challenges. Integrating software components from diverse languages proved difficult, and installation problems were common because new versions of shared components were incompatible with old software. Developers also discovered that they needed Web-based applications that could be accessed and used via the Internet. As programmable devices, such as *personal digital assistants* (*PDAs*) and cell phones, grew in popularity in the late 1990s, the need for these components to interact with others via the Internet rose dramatically. As a result of the popularity of mobile electronic devices, software developers realized that their clients were no longer restricted to desktop users. Developers recognized the need for software accessible to anyone from almost any type of device.

Microsoft's .NET strategy addresses these needs. The .NET platform is one over which Web-based applications can be distributed to a variety of devices (such as cell phones) and to desktop computers. The .NET platform offers a new programming model that allows programs created in disparate programming languages to communicate with each other.

Microsoft has designed a version of Visual Basic for .NET. Earlier versions of Visual Basic did offer object-oriented capabilities, but Visual Basic .NET offers enhanced object orientation, including a powerful library of components, allowing programmers to develop applications even more quickly. Visual Basic .NET also enables enhanced language interoperability: Software components from different languages can interact as never before. Developers can package old software to work with new Visual Basic .NET programs. Also, Visual Basic .NET applications can interact via the Internet, using industry standards such as the Simple Object Access Protocol (SOAP) and XML, which we discuss in Chapter 15, Extensible Markup Language (XML). Visual Basic .NET is crucial to

Microsoft's .NET strategy, enabling existing Visual Basic developers to migrate to .NET easily. The advances embodied in .NET and Visual Basic .NET will lead to a new programming style, in which applications are created from components called Web Services, which are accessed over the Internet.

1.8 C, C++, Java™ and C#

As high-level languages develop, new offerings build on aspects of their predecessors. C++ evolved from C, which in turn evolved from two previous languages, BCPL and B. Martin Richards developed BCPL in 1967 as a language for writing operating systems, software and compilers. Ken Thompson modeled his language, B, after BCPL. In 1970, Thompson used B to create early versions of the UNIX operating system. Both BCPL and B were "typeless" languages, meaning that every data item occupied one "word" in memory. Using these languages, programmers assumed responsibility for treating each data item as a whole number or real number.

The C language, which Dennis Ritchie evolved from B at Bell Laboratories, was originally implemented in 1973. Although C employs many of BCPL and B's important concepts, it also offers data typing and other features. C first gained widespread recognition as a development language of the UNIX operating system. However, C is now available for most computers, and many of today's major operating systems are written in C or C++. C is a hardware-independent language, and, with careful design, it is possible to write C programs that are portable to most computers.

C++, an extension of C using elements from Simula 67 (a simulation programming language), was developed by Bjarne Stroustrup in the early 1980s at Bell Laboratories. C++ provides a number of features that "spruce up" the C language, but, more importantly, it provides capabilities for *object-oriented programming (OOP)*.

At a time when demand for new and more powerful software is soaring, the ability to build software quickly, correctly and economically remains an elusive goal. However, this problem can be addressed in part through the use of objects, or reusable software components that model items in the real world (see Section 1.5). Software developers are discovering that a modular, object-oriented approach to design and implementation can make software development groups much more productive than is possible using only previously popular programming techniques, such as structured programming. Furthermore, object-oriented programs are often easier to understand, correct and modify.

In addition to C++, many other object-oriented languages have been developed. These include Smalltalk, which was created at Xerox's Palo Alto Research Center (PARC). Smalltalk is a pure object-oriented language, which means that literally everything is an object. C++ is a hybrid language—it is possible to program in a C-like style, an object-oriented style or both. Although some perceive this range of options as a benefit, most programmers today believe that it is best to program in a purely object-oriented manner.

In the early 1990s, many individuals projected that intelligent consumer-electronic devices would be the next major market in which microprocessors would have a profound impact. Recognizing this, Sun Microsystems in 1991 funded an internal corporate research project code-named Green. The project resulted in the development of a language based on C and C++. Although the language's creator, James Gosling, called it Oak (after an oak tree outside his window at Sun), it was later discovered that a computer language called Oak already existed. When a group of Sun employees visited a local coffee place, the name Java was suggested, and it stuck.

But the Green project ran into some difficulties. The marketplace for intelligent consumer-electronic devices was not developing as quickly as Sun had anticipated. Worse yet, a major contract for which Sun competed was awarded to another company. The project was, at this point, in danger of being canceled. By sheer good fortune, the World Wide Web exploded in popularity in 1993, and Sun saw immediate potential for using Java to create *dynamic content* (i.e., animated and interactive content) for Web pages.

Sun formally announced Java at a conference in May 1995. Ordinarily, an event like this would not generate much publicity. However, Java grabbed the immediate attention of the business community because of the new, widespread interest in the World Wide Web. Developers now use Java to create Web pages with dynamic content, to build large-scale enterprise applications, to enhance the functionality of World Wide Web servers (the computers that provide the content distributed to our Web browsers when we browse Web sites), to provide applications for consumer devices (e.g., cell phones, pagers and PDAs) and for many other purposes.

The C# programming language, developed at Microsoft by Anders Hejlsberg and Scott Wiltamuth, was designed specifically for the .NET platform. It has roots in C, C++ and Java, adapting the best features of each. Like Visual Basic .NET, C#[2] is object-oriented and contains a powerful class library of prebuilt components, enabling programmers to develop applications quickly.

1.9 .NET Framework and the Common Language Runtime

The *.NET Framework* is at the heart of .NET. This framework manages and executes applications, contains a class library (called the *Framework Class Library* or *FCL*), enforces security and provides many other programming capabilities. The details of the .NET Framework are found in the *Common Language Specification* (*CLS*), which contains information about the storage of objects and so on. The CLS has been submitted for standardization to ECMA (the European Computer Manufacturers Association). This allows independent software vendors to create the .NET Framework for other platforms. The .NET Framework exists only for the Windows platform, but is being developed for other platforms, as well, such as Microsoft's *Shared Source CLI* (*Common Language Infrastructure*). The Shared Source CLI is an archive of source code that provides a subset of the Microsoft .NET Framework for both Windows XP and the FreeBSD[3] operating systems.[4] For more information on the Shared Source CLI, visit **msdn.microsoft.com/library/en-us/Dndotnet/html/mssharsourcecli.asp**.

The *Common Language Runtime (CLR)* is another central part of the .NET Framework—it executes Visual Basic .NET programs. Programs are compiled into machine-spe-

---

2. Readers interested in learning C# may want to consider one of our C# publications. Information about these publications can be found at **www.deitel.com**.
3. The FreeBSD project provides a freely available and open-source UNIX-like operating system that is based on UC Berkeley's *Berkeley System Distribution* (*BSD*). For more information on BSD, visit **www.freebsd.org**.
4. Microsoft Corporation, "The Microsoft Shared Source CLI Implementation," March 2002, <**msdn.microsoft.com/library/en-us/Dndotnet/html/mssharsource-cli.asp**>.

cific instructions in two steps. First, the program is compiled into *Microsoft Intermediate Language (MSIL)*, which defines instructions for the CLR. Code converted into MSIL from other languages and sources is woven together by the CLR. Then, another compiler in the CLR compiles the MSIL into machine code (for a particular platform), creating a single application.

Why bother having the extra step of converting from Visual Basic .NET to MSIL, instead of compiling directly into machine language? The key reasons are portability between operating systems, interoperability between languages and execution-management features such as memory management and security.

If the .NET Framework exists (and is installed) for a platform, that platform can run any .NET program. The ability of a program to run (without modification) across multiple platforms is known as *platform independence*. Code written once can be used on another machine without modification, saving both time and money. In addition, software can target a wider audience—previously, companies had to decide whether converting (or *porting*) their programs to other platforms was worth the cost. With .NET, porting is simplified.

The .NET Framework also provides a high level of *language interoperability*. Programs written in different languages are all compiled into MSIL—the different parts can be combined to create a single, unified program. MSIL allows the .NET Framework to be *language independent*, because MSIL is not tied to a particular programming language. Any language that can be compiled into MSIL is called a *.NET-compliant language*.

Language interoperability offers many benefits to software companies. Visual Basic .NET, C# and Visual C++ .NET developers, for example, can work side-by-side on the same project without having to learn another programming language—all their code is compiled into MSIL and linked together to form one program. In addition, the .NET Framework can package preexisting components (i.e., components created using tools that predate .NET) and .NET components to work together. This allows companies to reuse the code that they have spent years developing and integrate it with the .NET code that they write. Integration is crucial, because companies cannot migrate easily to .NET unless they can stay productive, using their existing developers and software.

Another benefit of the .NET Framework is the CLR's execution-management features. The CLR manages memory, security and other features, relieving the programmer of these responsibilities. With languages like C++, programmers must manage their own memory. This leads to problems if programmers request memory and never release it—programs could consume all available memory, which would prevent applications from running. By managing the program's memory, the .NET Framework allows programmers to concentrate on program logic.

The .NET Framework also provides programmers with a huge library of reusable classes. This library, called the Framework Class Library (FCL), can be used by any .NET language.

This book explains how to develop .NET software with Visual Basic .NET and the FCL. Steve Ballmer, Microsoft's CEO, stated in May 2001 that Microsoft was "betting the company" on .NET. Such a dramatic commitment surely indicates a bright future for Visual Basic .NET and its community of developers.

1.10 Tour of the Book

In this section, we tour the chapters and appendices of *Visual Basic .NET for Experienced Programmers*. In addition to the topics presented in each chapter, several of the chapters contain an Internet and Web Resources section that lists additional sources from which readers can enhance their knowledge of Visual Basic .NET programming.

Chapter 1—Introduction to .NET and Visual Basic .NET

The first chapter presents the history of the Internet, World Wide Web and various technologies (such as XML and SOAP) that have led to advances in computing. We introduce the Microsoft .NET initiative and the Visual Basic .NET programming language, including Web services. We explore the impact of .NET on software development and software reusability. The chapter concludes with a tour of the book.

Chapter 2—Introduction to the Visual Studio® IDE and Visual Basic .NET Programming

Chapter 2 introduces Visual Studio .NET, an integrated development environment (IDE) that allows programmers to create Visual Basic .NET programs. Visual Studio .NET enables *visual programming*, in which *controls* (such as buttons and textboxes) are "dragged" and "dropped" into place, rather than added by typing code. Visual programming increases software-development productivity by eliminating many tedious programming tasks. For example, a graphical user interface's (GUI's) properties (information such as size and color) can be modified through the Visual Studio .NET IDE, allowing changes to be made quickly and causing the results to appear immediately on the screen. Rather than having to guess how the GUI will appear while writing a program, programmers view the GUI exactly as it will appear when the finished program runs. Visual Studio .NET also contains tools for debugging, documenting and writing code. The chapter presents features of Visual Studio .NET, including its key windows, and shows how to compile and run programs. We use the capabilities of Visual Studio .NET to create a simple Windows application without typing a single line of code. The chapter also introduces readers to non-visual programming in Visual Basic .NET. Every concept is presented in the context of a complete working Visual Basic .NET program and is followed by one or more screen shots showing actual inputs and outputs as the program executes. This is our LIVE-CODE™ approach. We discuss fundamental tasks, such as how a program inputs data from its users and how to write arithmetic expressions. This chapter also demonstrates displaying text in a window called a **MessageBox**.

Chapter 3—Control Structures

This chapter introduces the principles of structured programming, a set of techniques that will help the reader develop clear, understandable and maintainable programs. The chapter then introduces the use of control structures that affect the sequence in which statements are executed. Control structures produce programs that are easily understood, debugged and maintained. We discuss the three forms of program control—sequence, selection and repetition—focusing on the **If/Then/Else**, **While**, **For/Next**, **Do While/Loop**, **Do Until/Loop**, **Do/Loop While**, **Do/Loop Until** and **Select Case** structures. We explain the **Exit** keyword and the logical operators. We build on information presented in the previous chapter to create programs that are interactive (i.e., they change their behavior to suit user-supplied inputs). We present an example that combines visual and non-visual programming techniques. This example builds upon the first example presented in Chapter 2.

Chapter 4—Procedures and Arrays

A *procedure* allows the programmer to create a block of code that can be called upon from various points in a program. Larger programs can be divided into interacting classes, each consisting of procedures—this is sometimes called the "divide and conquer" strategy. Programs are divided into simple components that interact in straightforward ways. We discuss how to create our own procedures that can take inputs, perform calculations and return outputs. *Recursive* procedures (procedures that call themselves) and procedure overloading, which allows multiple procedures to have the same name, are introduced. We demonstrate overloading by creating two **Square** procedures that each take an integer (i.e., a whole number) and a floating-point number (i.e., a number with a decimal point), respectively. This chapter also introduces arrays, our first data structure. Data structures are crucial to storing, sorting, searching and manipulating large amounts of information. *Arrays* are groups of related data items that allow the programmer to access any element directly. Rather than creating 100 separate variables that are all related in some way, the programmer instead can create an array of 100 elements and access these elements by their location in the array. We discuss how to declare and allocate arrays, and we build on the techniques of the previous chapter by passing arrays to procedures. Chapter 3 provides essential background for the discussion of arrays, because repetition structures are used to iterate through elements in the array. The combination of these concepts helps programmers create highly structured and well-organized programs. We discuss multidimensional arrays, which can be used to store tables of data. We introduce the **For Each/Next** structure, which iterates through arrays.

Chapter 5—Object-Based Programming

Chapter 5 introduces objects and classes. Object technology has led to considerable improvements in software development, allowing programmers to create reusable software components. Objects allow programs to be organized in natural and intuitive ways. This chapter presents the fundamentals of object-based programming, such as encapsulation, data abstraction and abstract data types (ADTs). These techniques hide the details of components so that the programmer can concentrate on the "big picture." We create a **CTime** class, which displays the time in standard and universal formats. We show how to create reusable software components with assemblies, namespaces and dynamic link library (DLL) files. We create classes and namespaces, and discuss properties and the **ReadOnly** and **Const** keywords. This chapter lays the groundwork for the next two chapters, which introduce object-oriented programming.

Chapter 6—Object-Oriented Programming: Inheritance

In this chapter, we discuss inheritance—a form of software reusability in which classes (called *derived classes*) are created by absorbing attributes and methods of existing classes (called *base classes*). The inheriting class (i.e., the derived class) can contain additional attributes and methods. We show how finding the commonality between classes of objects can reduce the amount of work it takes to build large software systems. A detailed case study demonstrates software reuse and good programming techniques by finding the commonality among a three-level inheritance hierarchy: the **CPoint**, **CCircle** and **CCylinder** classes. We discuss the software engineering benefits of object-oriented programming. Crucial object-oriented programming concepts, such as creating and extending classes, are presented in this chapter.

Chapter 7—Object-Oriented Programming: Polymorphism

Chapter 7 continues our presentation of object-oriented programming. We discuss polymorphic programming and its advantages. *Polymorphism* permits classes to be treated in a general manner, allowing the same method call to act differently depending on context (e.g., "move" messages sent to a bird and a fish result in dramatically different types of action—a bird flies and a fish swims). In addition to treating existing classes in a general manner, polymorphism allows new classes to be added to a system easily. We identify situations in which polymorphism is useful. A payroll system case study demonstrates polymorphism—the system determines the wages for each employee differently to suit the type of employee (bosses who are paid fixed salaries, hourly workers who are paid by the hour, commission workers who receive a base salary plus commission and piece workers who are paid per item produced). These programming techniques and those of the previous chapter allow the programmer to create extensible and reusable software components.

Chapter 8—Exception Handling
Exception handling is one of the most important topics in Visual Basic .NET from the standpoint of building mission-critical and business-critical applications. Users can enter incorrect data, data can be corrupted and clients can try to access records that do not exist or are restricted. A simple division-by-zero error may cause a calculator program to crash, but what if such an error occurs in the navigation system of an airplane while it is in flight? In some cases, the results of program failure could be disastrous. Programmers need to know how to recognize the errors (*exceptions*) that could occur in software components and handle those exceptions effectively, allowing programs to deal with problems and continue executing instead of "crashing." Programmers who construct software systems from reusable components built by other programmers must deal with the exceptions that those components may "throw." This chapter covers the details of Visual Basic .NET exception handling, the termination model of exception handling, throwing and catching exceptions, and FCL class **Exception**.

Chapter 9—Graphical User Interface Concepts: Part 1
Chapter 9 explains how to add sophisticated GUIs to programs. By using the techniques of rapid application development (RAD), programmers can create GUIs from reusable components, rather than explicitly programming every detail. The Visual Studio .NET IDE makes developing GUIs even easier by allowing the programmer to position components in a window through so-called visual programming. We discuss how to construct user interfaces with *Windows Forms controls* such as labels, buttons, textboxes and picture boxes. We also introduce *events*, which are messages sent by a program to signal to an object or a set of objects that an action has occurred. Events most commonly signal user interactions with GUI controls, but also can signal internal actions in a program. We overview event handling and discuss how to handle events specific to controls, the mouse and the keyboard.

Chapter 10—Graphical User Interface Concepts: Part 2
Chapter 10 introduces more complex GUI components, including menus, link labels, panels, list boxes, combo boxes and tab controls. *Multiple Document Interface (MDI)* programming is presented, which allows multiple documents (i.e., forms) to be open simultaneously in a single GUI. We conclude with an introduction to visual inheritance, which enables programmers to combine the GUI concepts presented in this chapter with the object-oriented concepts presented in Chapter 6 to create user interfaces that can be used and extended by other programmers. Tips are included throughout the chapter to help the programmer create visually appealing, well-organized and consistent GUIs.

Chapter 11—Multithreading

Users have come to expect much from applications. Users want to download files from the Internet, listen to music, print documents and browse the Web—all at the same time! To do this, programmers need a feature called *multithreading*, which allows applications to perform multiple activities concurrently. The .NET Framework includes built-in capabilities to enable multithreaded applications, while shielding programmers from complex details. The .NET languages are better equipped to deal with more sophisticated multimedia, network-based and multiprocessor-based applications than those languages that do not have multithreading features. This chapter introduces the FCL's threading classes and covers threads, thread life-cycles, time-slicing, scheduling and priorities. We analyze the producer-consumer relationship, thread synchronization and circular buffers. This chapter lays the foundation for creating the multithreaded programs that clients demand.

Chapter 12—Strings, Characters and Regular Expressions

In this chapter, we discuss the processing of words, sentences, characters and groups of characters. In Visual Basic .NET, **String**s (groups of characters) are objects. This is yet another benefit of Visual Basic .NET's emphasis on object-oriented programming. Objects of type **String** contain methods that can copy, search, extract substrings and concatenate strings with one another. We introduce class **StringBuilder**, which defines string-like objects that can be modified after initialization. As an interesting example of strings, we create a card shuffling-and-dealing simulation. We discuss regular expressions, a powerful tool for searching and manipulating text.

Chapter 13—Graphics and Multimedia

In this chapter, we discuss *GDI+* (an extension of the *Graphics Device Interface—GDI*), the Windows service that provides the graphical features used by .NET applications. The extensive graphical capabilities of GDI+ can make programs more visual and fun to create and use. We discuss Visual Basic .NET's treatment of graphics objects and color control. We also discuss how to draw arcs, polygons and other shapes. This chapter also demonstrates how to use various pens and brushes to create color effects and includes an example that demonstrates gradient fills and textures. We also introduce techniques for turning text-only applications into exciting, aesthetically pleasing programs that even novice programmers can write with ease. The second half of the chapter focuses on audio, video and speech technology. We discuss adding sound, video and animated characters to programs (primarily using existing audio and video clips). You will see how easy it is to incorporate multimedia into Visual Basic .NET applications. This chapter introduces an exciting technology called *Microsoft Agent* for adding *interactive animated characters* to a program. Each character allows users to interact with the application, using more natural human communication techniques, such as speech. The agent characters respond to mouse and keyboard events, speak and hear (i.e., they support speech synthesis and speech recognition). With these capabilities, your applications can speak to users and actually respond to their voice commands!

Chapter 14—Files and Streams

Imagine a program that could not save data to a file. Once the program is closed, all the work performed by the program is lost forever. For this reason, this chapter is one of the most important for programmers who will be developing commercial applications. We introduce FCL classes for inputting and outputting data. A detailed example demonstrates these concepts by allowing users to read and write bank account information to and from files. We introduce the FCL classes and methods that help perform input and output conveniently—they demonstrate the power of object-oriented programming and reusable classes. We discuss benefits of sequential files, random-access files and buffering. This chapter lays the groundwork for the material presented in Chapter 19, Networking: Streams-Based Sockets and Datagrams.

Chapter 15—Extensible Markup Language (XML)

The Extensible Markup Language (XML) derives from SGML (Standard Generalized Markup Language), which became an industry standard in 1986. Although SGML is employed in publishing applications worldwide, it has not been incorporated into the mainstream programming community because of its sheer size and complexity. XML is an effort to make SGML-like technology available to a much broader community. XML, created by the World Wide Web Consortium (W3C), describes data in a portable format. XML differs in concept from markup languages such as HTML, which only describes how information is rendered in a browser. XML is a technology for creating markup languages for virtually any type of information. Document authors use XML to create entirely new markup languages to describe specific types of data, including mathematical formulas, chemical molecular structures, music, recipes and much more. Markup languages created with XML include XHTML (Extensible HyperText Markup Language, for Web content), MathML (for mathematics), VoiceXML™ (for speech), SMIL™ (Synchronized Multimedia Integration Language, for multimedia presentations), CML (Chemical Markup Language, for chemistry) and XBRL (Extensible Business Reporting Language, for financial data exchange). The extensibility of XML has made it one of the most important technologies in industry today and it is being integrated into almost every field. Companies and individuals constantly are finding new and innovative uses for XML. In this chapter, we present examples that illustrate the basics of marking up data as XML. We demonstrate XML-derived markup languages, such as *XML Schema* (for checking an XML document's grammar), *XSLT (Extensible Stylesheet Language Transformations*, for transforming an XML document's data into another text-based format such as XHTML) and Microsoft's *BizTalk*™ (for marking up business transactions).

Chapter 16—Database, SQL and ADO .NET

Data storage and access are integral to creating powerful software applications. This chapter discusses .NET support for database manipulation. Today's most popular database systems are relational databases. In this chapter, we introduce the Structured Query Language (SQL) for performing queries on relational databases. We introduce *ActiveX Data Objects* ADO .NET—an extension of ADO that enables .NET applications to access and manipulate databases. ADO .NET allows data to be exported as XML, which enables applications that use ADO .NET to communicate with a variety of programs that understand XML. We show the reader how to create database connections, using tools provided in Visual Studio .NET and how to use ADO .NET classes to query a database.

Chapter 17—ASP .NET, Web Forms and Web Controls

Previous chapters demonstrated how to create applications that execute locally on the user's computer. In this chapter and Chapters 18 and 21, we discuss how to create Web-based applications using *Active Server Pages (ASP) .NET*. This is a crucial aspect of .NET and of Microsoft's vision of how software should be developed and deployed on the Internet. ASP .NET is an integral technology for creating dynamic Web content marked up as HTML. *Web Forms* provide GUIs for ASP .NET pages and can contain *Web controls*, such as labels, buttons and textboxes with which users interact. Like Windows Forms, Web Forms are designed using visual programming. This chapter presents many interesting examples, which include an online guest book application and a multi-tier, database-intensive application that allows users to query a database for a list of publications by a specific author. Debugging Web Forms using the **Trace** property also is discussed.

Chapter 18—ASP .NET and Web Services

Chapter 18 continues our discussion of ASP .NET. In this chapter, we introduce *Web services*, which are programs that "expose" services (i.e., methods) to clients over the Internet, intranets and extranets. Web services offer increased software reusability by allowing services on disparate platforms to interact with each other seamlessly. This chapter presents several interesting examples that include Web services for manipulating huge numbers (up to 100 digits), simulating the card game of blackjack and implementing an airline reservation system. One particularly interesting example is our temperature server, a Web service that gathers weather information for dozens of cities in the United States.

Chapter 19—Networking: Streams-Based Sockets and Datagrams

Chapter 19 introduces the fundamental techniques of streams-based networking. We demonstrate how streams-based *sockets* allow programmers to hide many networking details. With sockets, networking is as simple as if the programmer were reading from and writing to a file. We also introduce *datagrams* in which packets of information are sent between programs. Each packet is addressed to its recipient and sent out to the network, which routes the packet to its destination. The examples in this chapter focus on communication between applications. One example demonstrates using streams-based sockets to communicate between two Visual Basic .NET programs. Another similar example sends datagrams between applications. We also show how to create a multithreaded-server application that can communicate with multiple clients in parallel. In this client/server tic-tac-toe game, the server maintains the status of the game and two clients communicate with the server to play the game.

Chapter 20—Data Structures and Collections

This chapter discusses arranging data into aggregations such as linked lists, stacks, queues and trees. Each data structure has properties that are useful in a wide variety of applications, from sorting elements to keeping track of procedure calls. We discuss how to build each of these data structures. This is also a valuable experience in crafting useful classes. In addition, we cover pre-built collection classes in the FCL. These collections classes store sets, or collections, of data and provide functionality that allows the developer to sort, insert, delete and retrieve data items. Different collection classes store data in different ways. This chapter focuses on classes **Array**, **ArrayList**, **Stack** and **Hashtable**, discussing the details of each. When possible, Visual Basic .NET programmers should use the FCL to find appropriate data structures, rather than implementing these data structures themselves. This chapter reinforces much of the object technology discussed in Chapters 5–7, including classes, inheritance and composition.

Chapter 21—Mobile Internet Toolkit

The demand for wireless applications is growing rapidly. Within the next two years, the number of people browsing the Web from wireless devices will exceed the number browsing from desktop computers. The *Mobile Internet Toolkit* (*MIT*) extends Visual Studio .NET by providing a set of FCL classes for creating Web applications for mobile devices. We introduce mobile Web controls and mobile Web Forms that can be used to create ASP .NET applications that target a wide range of mobile devices. Furthermore, mobile Web applications created using the MIT can be designed to determine the type of device making the request and generate markup appropriate for that specific device. For example, a personal digital assistant and mobile phone can both request the same page, but receive different markup. This is known as device-specific rendering, a process demonstrated in this chapter. Finally, we demonstrate how to consume a Web service from a mobile Web application. In this example, we show how similar it is to access a Web service from a mobile application, as it is to access a Web service from a Windows application.

Appendix A—Operator Precedence Chart

This appendix lists Visual Basic .NET operators and their precedence.

Appendix B—Visual Studio .NET Debugger

This appendix introduces the Visual Studio .NET debugger for locating logic errors in programs. Key features include setting "breakpoints," stepping through programs line-by-line and "watching" variables.

Appendix C—ASCII Character Set

This appendix contains a table of the 128 ASCII (American Standard Code for Information Interchange) alphanumeric symbols and their corresponding integer values.

Appendix D—Unicode®

This appendix introduces the Unicode Standard, an encoding scheme that assigns unique numeric values to the characters of most of the world's languages. We include a Windows application that uses Unicode encoding to print welcome messages in several languages.

1.11 Summary

In the late 1960s, at a conference at the University of Illinois Urbana-Champaign, ARPA—the Advanced Research Projects Agency of the Department of Defense—rolled out the blueprints for networking the main computer systems of approximately a dozen ARPA-funded universities and research institutions. Shortly after this conference, ARPA proceeded to implement the ARPAnet, the grandparent of today's Internet.

Although the ARPAnet did enable researchers to network their computers, its chief benefit proved to be the capability for quick and easy communication via what came to be known as electronic mail (e-mail). This is true even on today's Internet, with e-mail, instant messaging and file transfer facilitating communications among hundreds of millions of people worldwide.

The protocol (i.e., set of rules) for communicating over the ARPAnet became known as the Transmission Control Protocol (TCP). TCP ensured that messages were routed properly from sender to receiver and that those messages arrived intact. ARPA developed the

Internet Protocol (IP), which created a true "network of networks," the current architecture of the Internet. The combined set of protocols is now commonly called TCP/IP.

The World Wide Web allows computer users to locate and view multimedia-based documents (i.e., documents with text, graphics, animations, audios or videos) on almost any subject. In 1989, Tim Berners-Lee of CERN (the European Organization for Nuclear Research) began to develop a technology for sharing information via hyperlinked text documents. Berners-Lee called his invention the HyperText Markup Language (HTML). He also wrote communication protocols to form the backbone of his new hypertext information system, which he referred to as the World Wide Web.

In October 1994, Berners-Lee founded an organization, called the World Wide Web Consortium (W3C), that is devoted to developing nonproprietary, interoperable technologies for the World Wide Web. One of the W3C's primary goals is to make the Web universally accessible—regardless of disabilities, language or culture.

The Extensible Markup Language (XML) combines the power and extensibility of its parent language, Standard Generalized Markup Language, with the simplicity that the Web community demands. Data independence, the separation of content from its presentation, is an essential characteristic of XML. Because an XML document describes data, any application conceivably can process such a document. XML's flexibility and power make it perfect for client/server systems, which must interact with a wide variety of clients.

Simple Object Access Protocol (SOAP) is a technology for the distribution of data (marked up as XML) over the Internet. Developed initially by Microsoft and Develop-Mentor, SOAP is a W3C Working Draft that provides a framework for expressing application semantics, encoding data and packaging data. Microsoft .NET uses XML and SOAP to mark up and transfer data over the Internet. XML and SOAP are at the core of .NET—they allow software components to communicate easily with one another.

Object technology is a packaging scheme that facilitates the creation of meaningful software units. Objects have properties (i.e., attributes, such as color, size and weight) and perform actions (i.e., behaviors, such as moving, sleeping and drawing). Classes represent groups of related objects.

With the advent of popular object-oriented languages, such as C++, Java, C# and Visual Basic .NET, programmers can program in an object-oriented manner that reflects the way in which they perceive the world. This process, which seems more natural than procedural programming, has resulted in significant productivity gains.

With object technology, properly designed software entities (called classes) can be reused on future projects. Using libraries of reusable componentry can reduce the amount of effort required to implement certain kinds of systems (as compared to the effort that would be required to reinvent these capabilities in new projects). Visual Basic .NET programmers use the .NET Framework Class Library (known commonly as the FCL).

In June 2000, Microsoft announced its .NET initiative. The .NET platform is one that provides significant enhancements to earlier developer platforms. .NET offers a new software-development model that allows applications created in disparate programming languages to communicate with each other. The platform also allows developers to create Web-based applications that can be distributed to a great variety of devices (even wireless phones) and to desktop computers.

One key aspect of the .NET strategy is its independence from a specific language or platform. Rather than requiring programmers to use a single programming language, developers can create a .NET application by using any combination of .NET-compatible languages. Programmers can contribute to the same software project, writing code in the .NET languages in which they are most proficient. Part of the initiative includes Microsoft's Active Server Pages (ASP) .NET technology, which allows programmers to create applications for the Web.

A key component of the .NET architecture is Web services, which are applications that expose functionality to clients via the Internet. Clients and other applications can use these Web services as reusable building blocks.

Universal data access is another essential .NET concept. With .NET, data can reside in one central location rather than on separate systems. Any Internet-connected device can access the data (under tight control, of course), which would then be formatted appropriately for use or display on the accessing device.

Visual Basic .NET is an event-driven, fully object-oriented, visual programming language in which programs are created using an Integrated Development Environment (IDE). With the IDE, a programmer can create, run, test and debug Visual Basic .NET programs quickly and efficiently, thereby reducing the time it takes to produce a working program to a fraction of the time it would have taken without using the IDE.

Visual Basic .NET evolved from BASIC (Beginner's All-purpose Symbolic Instruction Code), developed in the mid-1960s by Professors John Kemeny and Thomas Kurtz of Dartmouth College as a language for writing simple programs. BASIC's primary purpose was to familiarize novices with programming techniques. When Bill Gates founded Microsoft Corporation, he implemented BASIC on several early personal computers. With the development of the Microsoft Windows graphical user interface (GUI) in the late 1980s and the early 1990s, the natural evolution of BASIC was Visual Basic, introduced by Microsoft in 1991.

The .NET Framework manages and executes applications, contains the FCL, enforces security, and provides many other programming capabilities. The details of the .NET Framework are found in the Common Language Specification (CLS), which contains information about the storage of data types, objects and so on.

The Common Language Runtime (CLR) executes Visual Basic .NET programs. Programs are compiled into machine-specific instructions in two steps. First, the program is compiled into Microsoft Intermediate Language (MSIL), which defines instructions for the CLR. Code converted into MSIL from other languages and sources is woven together by the CLR. Then, another compiler in the CLR compiles the MSIL into machine code (for a particular platform), creating a single application.

1.12 Internet and World Wide Web Resources

www.deitel.com
This is the official Deitel & Associates, Inc. Web site. Here you will find updates, corrections, downloads and additional resources for all Deitel publications. In addition, this site provides information about Deitel & Associates, Inc., downloads and resources related to our publications, information on international translations, and much more.

www.deitel.com/newsletter/subscribe.html
You can register here to receive the *DEITEL™ BUZZ ONLINE* e-mail newsletter. This free newsletter updates readers on our publishing program, instructor-led corporate training courses, hottest industry trends and topics, and much more. The newsletter is available in full-color HTML and plain-text formats.

www.prenhall.com/deitel
This is Prentice Hall's Web site for Deitel publications, which contains information about our products and publications, downloads, Deitel curriculum, and author information.

www.InformIT.com/deitel
This is the Deitel & Associates, Inc. page on Pearson's InformIT Web site. (Pearson owns our publisher Prentice Hall.) InformIT is a comprehensive resource for IT professionals providing articles, electronic publications and other resources for today's hottest information technologies. The Deitel kiosk at **InformIT.com** provides two or three free articles per week and for-purchase electronic publications. All Deitel publications can be purchased at this site.

www.microsoft.com
The Microsoft Corporation Web site provides information and technical resources for all Microsoft products, including .NET, enterprise software and the Windows operating system.

www.microsoft.com/net
The .NET home page provides downloads, news and events, certification information, and subscription information.

www.w3.org
The World Wide Web Consortium (W3C) is an organization that develops and recommends technologies for the Internet and World Wide Web. This site includes links to W3C technologies, news, mission statements and frequently asked questions (FAQs). Deitel and Associates, Inc. is a member of the W3C.

www.netvalley.com/intval.html
This site presents the history of the Internet and the World Wide Web.

Introduction to the Visual Studio IDE and VB .NET Programming

Objectives

- To become familiar with the Visual Studio .NET integrated development environment (IDE).
- To use the commands contained in the IDE's menus and toolbars.
- To understand the various kinds of windows in Visual Studio .NET.
- To use the features provided by the IDE's toolbar.
- To understand Visual Studio .NET's help features.
- To create, compile and execute a simple Visual Basic .NET program.
- To use input and output statements.
- To become familiar with primitive data types.
- To use arithmetic operators.
- To write decision-making statements.
- To use relational and equality operators.

Seeing is believing.
Proverb

Form ever follows function.
Louis Henri Sullivan

Intelligence… is the faculty of making artificial objects, especially tools to make tools.
Henri-Louis Bergson

Outline

2.1 Introduction

Visual Studio .NET is Microsoft's integrated development environment (IDE) for creating, documenting, running and debugging programs written in a variety of .NET programming languages. Visual Studio .NET also offers editing tools for manipulating several types of files. It is a powerful and sophisticated tool for creating business-critical and mission-critical applications. In this chapter, we provide an overview of the Visual Studio .NET features needed to create simple Visual Basic .NET programs. We introduce additional IDE features throughout the book.

This chapter also introduces Visual Basic .NET programming and presents examples that illustrate several important features of the language. Examples are analyzed one line at a time. Later in this chapter, we present *console applications*—applications that contain predominantly textual output. There are several types of projects that programmers can create in Visual Basic .NET; the console application is one of the basic types. Text output in a console application is displayed in a *console window* (also called a *command window*). On Microsoft Windows 95/98, the console window is the **MS-DOS prompt**. On Microsoft Windows NT/2000/XP, the console window is called the **Command Prompt**. With Visual Basic .NET, a program can be created with multiple types of output (windows, dialogs and so on). Such programs are called *Windows applications* and provide graphical user interfaces. This chapter provides a brief overview of the creation of both Windows and console applications in Visual Basic .NET. In the next chapter, we provide a detailed treatment of *program development* and *program control* in Visual Basic .NET.

2.2 Visual Studio .NET Integrated Development Environment (IDE) Overview

When Visual Studio .NET is executed for the first time, the **Start Page** is displayed (Fig. 2.1). This page contains helpful links, which appear on the left side of the **Start Page**. Users can click the name of a section (such as **Get Started**) to browse its contents. We refer to clicking once with the left mouse button as *selecting* or *clicking* and to clicking twice with the left mouse button as *double-clicking*. [*Note*: The user should be aware that there are slight differences in the way that Visual Studio .NET appears, based on the version being used.]

Figure 2.1 displays the **Start Page** when the **Get Started** link is selected. The **Get Started** section contains links to recently opened *projects* (i.e., a group of related files that form a program), such as **WindowsApplication1** in Fig. 2.1, along with their modification dates. Alternatively, the user can select **Recent Projects** from the **File** menu to display the links. The first time that Visual Studio .NET is loaded, the project list will be empty. Notice the two *buttons* on the page: **Open Project** and **New Project**.

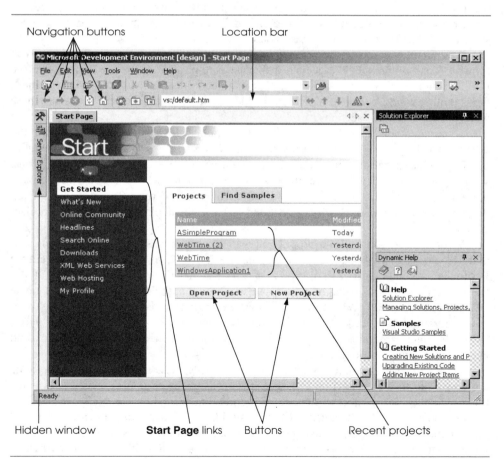

Fig. 2.1   Start Page in Visual Studio .NET.

We now provide a brief overview of the other **Start Page** links, shown in Fig. 2.1. The ***What's New*** section displays new features and updates for Visual Studio .NET, including downloads for code samples and new programming tools. The ***Online Community*** section includes ways to contact other software developers, using newsgroups, Web pages and other online resources. The ***Headlines*** section provides a way to browse news, articles and how-to guides. Use the ***Search Online*** section to browse through the *Microsoft Developer Network (MSDN)* online library. The MSDN site includes numerous articles, downloads and tutorials for a variety of technologies. The ***Downloads*** section allows the user to obtain updates and code samples. The ***XML Web Services*** page provides programmers with information about *Web services*, which are reusable pieces of software that are accessed via the Internet. We discuss this technology in Chapter 18, ASP .NET and Web Services. The ***Web Hosting*** section provides information for developers who wish to post their software (such as Web services) online for public use. Finally, the ***My Profile*** page allows users to customize Visual Studio .NET, such as by setting keyboard and window layout preferences. Users also can customize Visual Studio .NET by selecting **Options...** or **Customize...** from the **Tools** menu. [*Note*: From this point forward, we use the **>** character to indicate the selection of a menu command. For example, we use the notation **Tools > Options...** and **Tools > Customize...** to indicate the selection of the **Options...** and **Customize...** commands, respectively.]

Programmers can even browse the Web from the IDE—the Internet Explorer Web browser is part of the IDE. To access a Web page, type its address into the location bar (see Fig. 2.1), and press the *Enter* key. [*Note*: The computer must be connected to the Internet.] Several other windows appear in the IDE in addition to the **Start Page**. We discuss these windows in subsequent sections.

To create a new Visual Basic .NET program, click the **New Project** button in the **Get Started** section. This action displays the *dialog* shown in Fig. 2.2. Visual Studio .NET organizes programs into *projects* and *solutions*. A project is a group of related files, such as Visual Basic .NET code, images and documentation. A solution is a group of projects that represent a complete application or a set of related applications. Each project in a solution may perform a different task. In this book, we create single-project solutions.

Visual Studio .NET allows programmers to create projects in a variety of programming languages. This book focuses on Visual Basic .NET, so select the **Visual Basic Projects** folder in the **New Project** dialog (Fig. 2.2). There are a variety of project types from which to choose, several of which are used throughout this book. In this case, create a *Windows application*. Windows applications are programs that execute inside the Windows operating system, like Microsoft Word, Internet Explorer and Visual Studio .NET. Typically, such programs contain *controls*—graphical elements, such as buttons and labels—with which the user interacts.

By default, Visual Studio .NET assigns the name `WindowsApplication1` to the project and to the solution (Fig. 2.2). The default location for storing related files is the folder where the last project was created. The first time Visual Studio .NET executes, the default folder is the **Visual Studio Projects** folder in the **My Documents** folder. The programmer can change both the name and the location of the folder in which to save the project. After selecting a name and location for the project, click **OK** in the **New Project** dialog. The IDE will then change its appearance, as shown in Fig. 2.3.

Visual Basic Projects folder

Visual Basic **Windows application** (selected)

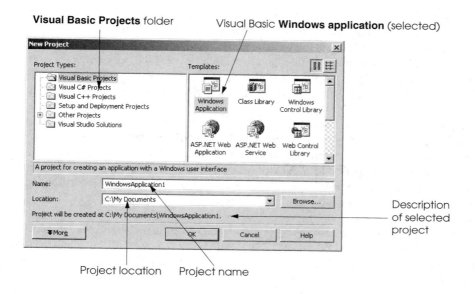

Project location   Project name

Description of selected project

Fig. 2.2   New Project dialog.

Tabs   Menu   Title bar   Menu bar   **Solution Explorer**

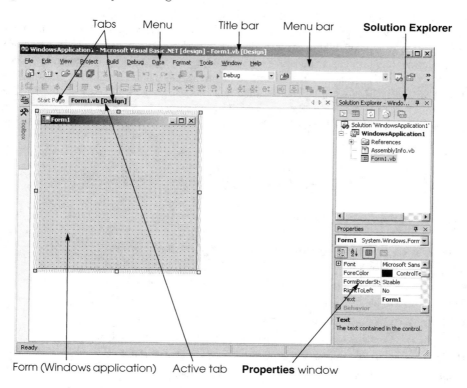

Form (Windows application)   Active tab   **Properties** window

Fig. 2.3   Visual Studio .NET environment after a new project has been created.

In this figure, the large gray box to the left represents the window for our application. This rectangle is called the *form*. We discuss how to add controls to the form later in this chapter. The form and controls are the *graphical user interface (GUI)* of the program; they are the graphical components through which users interact with the program. Users enter data (*inputs*) into the program by entering information from the keyboard and by clicking the mouse buttons. The program displays instructions and other information (*outputs*) for users to read in the GUI.

The top of the IDE window (the *title bar* in Fig. 2.3) displays the text **Windows-Application1 - Microsoft Visual Basic .NET [design] - Form1.vb [Design]**. This title provides the name of the project (**WindowsApplication1**), the programming language (**Microsoft Visual Basic .NET**), the *mode of the IDE* (**design** mode), the name of the file being viewed (**Form1.vb**) and the mode of the file being viewed (**Design** mode). The file name **Form1.vb** is the default for Windows applications. We discuss the various modes in Section 2.6.

Notice how a tab appears for each open document (Fig. 2.3). In our case, the documents are the **Start Page** and **Form1.vb [Design]**. To view a tab's content, click the tab with the name of the document you wish to view. Tabs save space and allow easy access to multiple documents.

2.3 Menu Bar and Toolbar

Commands for managing the IDE and for developing, maintaining and executing programs are contained in the menus. Figure 2.4 shows the menus that are displayed on the menu bar. Menus contain groups of related commands that, when selected, cause the IDE to perform various actions (e.g., open a window). For example, new projects can be created by selecting **File > New > Project...**. The contents of the menus shown in Fig. 2.4 are summarized in Fig. 2.5. Visual Studio .NET provides different modes in which the user can work. One of these modes is the design mode, which will be discussed in Section 2.6. Certain menu items appear only in particular IDE modes.

File   Edit   View   Project   Build   Debug   Data   Format   Tools   Window   Help

Fig. 2.4   Visual Studio .NET menu bar.

Menu	Description
File	Contains commands for opening projects, closing projects, printing projects, etc.
Edit	Contains commands such as cut, paste, find and undo.
View	Contains commands for displaying IDE windows and toolbars.
Project	Contains commands for adding features, such as forms, to a project.
Build	Contains commands for compiling a program.

Fig. 2.5   Visual Studio .NET menus summary. (Part 1 of 2.)

Menu	Description
Debug	Contains commands for debugging and executing a program.
Data	Contains commands for interacting with databases.
Format	Contains commands for arranging a form's controls.
Tools	Contains commands for additional IDE tools and options for customizing the environment.
Window	Contains commands for arranging and displaying windows.
Help	Contains commands for getting help.

Fig. 2.5   Visual Studio .NET menus summary. (Part 2 of 2.)

Rather than having to navigate the menus for certain commonly used commands, the programmer can access the commands from the *toolbar* (Fig. 2.6). The toolbar contains pictures, called *icons*, that represent commands. To execute a command, click its icon. Some icons provide the option of executing multiple commands. Click the *down arrow* beside such an icon to display related commands. Figure 2.6 shows the standard (default) toolbar and an icon that uses the down arrow.

Holding the mouse pointer over an icon on the toolbar highlights that icon and displays a description called a *tooltip* (Fig. 2.7). Tooltips help users understand the purposes of unfamiliar icons.

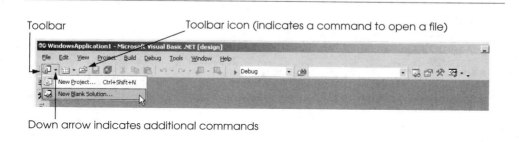

Fig. 2.6   Visual Studio .NET toolbar.

Fig. 2.7   Tooltip demonstration.

2.4 Visual Studio .NET Windows

Visual Studio .NET provides users with windows for exploring files and customizing controls. In this section, we discuss the windows that are essential for developing Visual Basic .NET applications. These windows can be accessed via the toolbar icons below the menu bar and on the right edge of the toolbar (Fig. 2.8) or by selecting the name of the desired window from the **View** menu.

2.4.1 Solution Explorer

The **Solution Explorer** window (Fig. 2.9) lists all the files in the open solution. When Visual Studio .NET is first loaded (the left window in Fig. 2.9), the **Solution Explorer** is empty—there are no files to display. After a new project has been created or an existing project has been loaded, the **Solution Explorer** displays that project's contents (the right window in Fig. 2.9).

The solution's *start-up project* is the project that runs when the solution is executed. It appears in bold text in the **Solution Explorer**. For our single-project solution, the startup project, **WindowsApplication1**, is the only project. The Visual Basic .NET file is **Form1.vb**; it contains the program's code. We discuss the other files and folders later in the book.

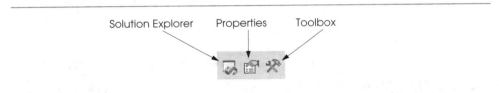

Fig. 2.8   Toolbar icons for various Visual Studio .NET windows.

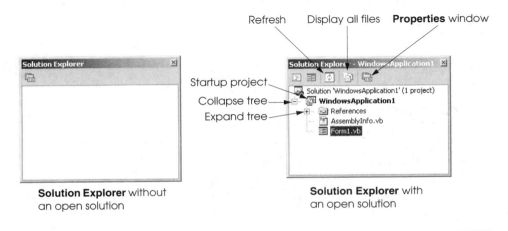

Fig. 2.9   **Solution Explorer** window.

The plus and minus boxes to the left of the **Solution Explorer** elements expand and collapse the tree, respectively (similar to plus and minus boxes in Windows Explorer). Click a plus box to display more options; click a minus box to collapse a tree that already is expanded. Users also can expand or collapse a tree by double-clicking the name of the folder. Many other Visual Studio .NET windows also use the plus–minus convention.

The **Solution Explorer** contains a toolbar. One icon on the toolbar reloads the files in the solution (refreshes), and another icon displays all files in the solution (including hidden files, or files that are located in the project's directory, but are not generally viewed as part of the project). The number of icons in the toolbar changes, depending on the type of file selected. We discuss these icons later in the book.

2.4.2 Toolbox

The **Toolbox** window (Fig. 2.10) contains reusable software components (or controls) that can be used to customize applications. Using *visual programming*, programmers can "drag and drop" controls onto a form instead of writing code themselves. Just as people do not need to know how to build an engine to drive a car, programmers do not need to build a control to use it. This capability of visual programming allows programmers to concentrate on the big picture, rather than the complex details of every control. The wide variety of tools available to programmers is a powerful feature of Visual Basic .NET. We demonstrate the power of the controls in the **Toolbox** when we create our own Visual Basic .NET program visually later in the chapter.

The **Toolbox** contains groups of related components (e.g., **Data**, **Components** and **Windows Forms**) located toward the top (Fig. 2.10). Expand the members of a group by clicking the name of the group. Scroll through the individual items by using the black scroll arrows on the right side of the **Toolbox**.

To add that item to their application the programmer can either double-click the item or select the item (by clicking it once) and use the mouse pointer to drag the item onto the form. The first item in each group is not a control—it is the mouse pointer (the selected item in Fig. 2.10). Clicking this icon allows the user to deselect the current control in the **Toolbox**, thus restoring the normal uses of the mouse pointer. Note that there are no tooltips, because the **Toolbox** icons already are labeled with the names of the controls. In later chapters, we discuss many of these controls.

Initially, the **Toolbox** may be hidden, with a **Toolbox** icon showing on the side of the IDE (Fig. 2.11). Moving the mouse pointer over the name **Toolbox** opens this window. Moving the mouse pointer outside the window causes the window to disappear. This feature is known as *auto-hide*. To "pin down" the **Toolbox** (i.e., to disable auto-hide), click the *pin icon* in the upper right corner of the window (see Fig. 2.11). If the window is not hidden (i.e., auto-hide is disabled), the pin icon has a vertical orientation. To enable auto-hide (if it has been disabled), click the pin icon again. Notice that when auto-hide is enabled, the pin icon has a horizontal orientation, as is shown in Fig. 2.11.

2.4.3 Properties Window

The **Properties** window (Fig. 2.12) allows manipulation of the *properties* of a form or control. Properties specify information about a control, such as its size, color and position.

Each control has its own set of properties. The bottom of the **Properties** window contains a description of the selected property.

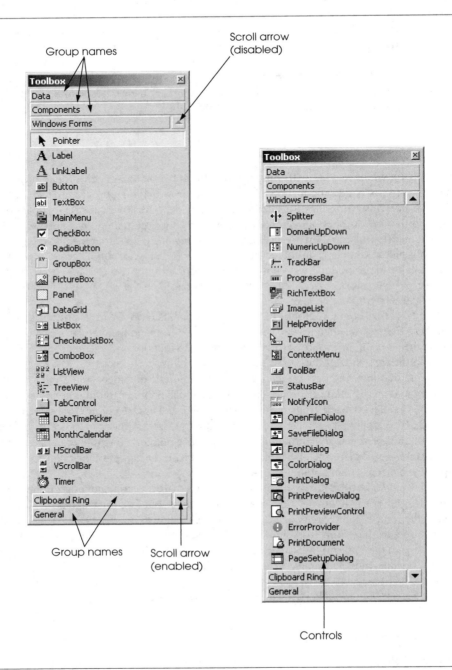

Fig. 2.10 Toolbox window.

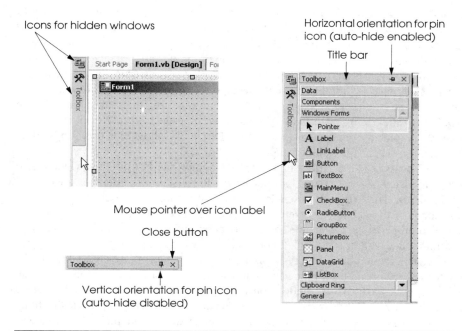

Fig. 2.11   Demonstrating window auto-hide.

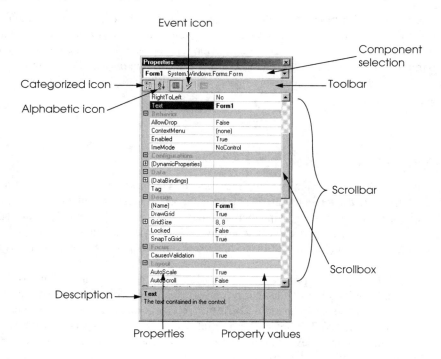

Fig. 2.12   Properties window.

The left column of the **Properties** window shows the properties of the control (a form in Fig. 2.12). The right column displays their current values. Icons on the toolbar sort the properties either alphabetically (by clicking the *alphabetic icon*) or categorically (by clicking the *categorized icon*), meaning that the properties are organized into groups based on their purpose. Users can scroll through the list of properties by *dragging* the scrollbox up or down (i.e., holding down the left mouse button while the mouse cursor is over the scrollbox, moving the mouse up or down and releasing the mouse button). The *event icon* allows the control or form to respond to certain user actions. We discuss events in Chapter 9, Graphical User Interface Concepts: Part 1. We show how to set individual properties later in this chapter and throughout the book.

Like the **Toolbox** and **Solution Explorer** windows, the **Properties** window also is important to visual programming. Controls usually are customized after they are created from the **Toolbox**. The **Properties** window allows programmers to modify controls visually (i.e, without writing code). This setup has a number of benefits. First, the programmer can see which properties are available for modification and what the possible values are; the programmer does not have to look up or remember what settings a particular property can have. Second, the window displays a brief description of each property, allowing the programmer to understand each property's purpose. Third, a property's value can be set quickly by using the **Properties** window; only a single click is required, and no code need be written. Fourth, the **Properties** window displays modified property values in bold, enabling developers to see which properties have been changed from their default values. All these features are designed to help software developers program without performing many repetitive tasks.

At the top of the **Properties** window is a drop-down list, which is a control containing a down arrow that, when clicked, displays a list of options. This drop-down list is called the *component selection box*. It indicates which component's properties are being displayed. The programmer can use the list to select any component in the project. For example, if a GUI contains several buttons, the programmer can select the name of a specific button to configure.

2.5 Using Help

Visual Studio .NET has an extensive help mechanism. The **Help** *menu* contains a variety of options. The **Contents** menu item displays a categorized table of contents of help topics. Menu item **Index** displays an alphabetical index that users can browse. The **Search** feature allows users to find particular help articles, based on a few search words. In each case, a subset of available topics, or filter, can narrow the search to articles related only to Visual Basic .NET.

Dynamic help (Fig. 2.13) provides a list of articles, based on the current context (i.e., the items around the location of the mouse cursor). To open dynamic help (if it is not already open), select the **Help** menu's **Dynamic Help** command. Once you click an object in Visual Studio .NET, relevant help articles will appear in the **Dynamic Help** window. The window lists relevant help entries, samples and "Getting Started" information, in addition to providing a toolbar for the regular help features. Dynamic help is an excellent way to get information about the features of Visual Studio .NET.

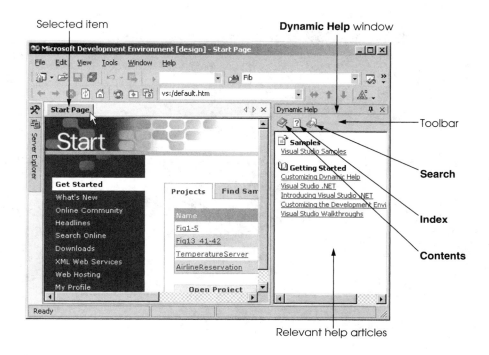

Fig. 2.13   **Dynamic Help** window.

Performance Tip 2.1

If you experience slow response time from Visual Studio .NET, you can disable (i.e., close) **Dynamic Help** *by clicking the* **x** *in the upper right corner of the* **Dynamic Help** *window.*

In addition to dynamic help, Visual Studio .NET provides *context-sensitive help.* Context-sensitive help is similar to dynamic help, except that the former immediately brings up a relevant help article rather than presenting a list. To use context-sensitive help, select an item and press the *F1* key. Help can appear either *internally* or *externally.* With external help, a relevant article immediately pops up in a separate window, outside the IDE. With internal help, a help article appears as a tabbed window inside Visual Studio .NET. The help options can be set from the **My Profile** section of the **Start Page**.

2.6 Simple Program: Displaying Text and an Image

In this section, we create a program that displays "**Welcome to Visual Basic!**" and an image of the Deitel & Associates mascot. The program consists of a single form that uses a label to display text and a picture box to display an image. Figure 2.14 shows the program as it executes. The example here (as well as the image file used in the example) is available on our Web Site (**www.deitel.com**) under the **Downloads/Resources** link.

Fig. 2.14 Simple program as it executes.

We do not write a single line of program code in this example. Instead, we use the techniques of visual programming. Various programmer *gestures* (such as using the mouse for pointing, clicking, dragging and dropping) provide Visual Studio .NET with sufficient information for it to generate all or a major portion of the program code. Later in this chapter, we begin our discussion of writing program code. Throughout the book, we produce increasingly substantial and powerful programs. Visual Basic .NET programming usually involves a combination of writing a portion of the program code and having Visual Studio .NET generate the remaining code.

To create, run and terminate this first program, perform the following steps:

1. *Create the new project.* If a project is already open, close it by selecting **File > Close Solution** in the IDE. A dialog asking whether to save the current solution may appear. To keep any unsaved changes, save the solution. Then create a new Windows application for the program. To do so, open Visual Studio .NET and select **File > New > Project... > Visual Basic .NET Projects > Windows Application** (Fig. 2.15). Name the project **ASimpleProject**, and select a directory in which to save the project. To select the directory, click the **Browse...** button, which opens a **Project Location** dialog (Fig. 2.16). Navigate through the directories, find one in which to place the project and select **OK**. This selection returns you to the **New Project** dialog; the selected folder appears in the **Location** text field. When you are satisfied with the location of the project, click **OK**. Visual Studio .NET will load the new solution, and a form labeled **Form1** will appear. We already have seen an example of this form in Fig. 2.3.

Project types

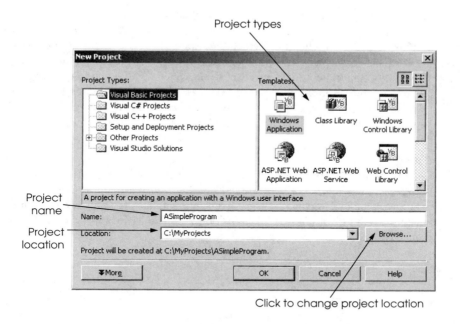

Project name

Project location

Click to change project location

Fig. 2.15 Creating a new Windows application.

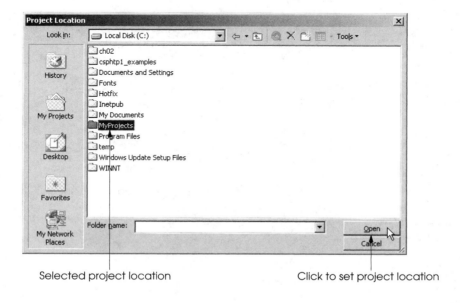

Selected project location

Click to set project location

Fig. 2.16 Setting the project location.

2. *Set the form's title bar.* First, set the text that appears in the title bar. This text is determined by the form's **Text** property (Fig. 2.17). If the form's **Properties** window is not open, click the **Properties** icon in the toolbar or select **View > Properties Window**. Use the mouse to select the form; the **Properties** window shows information about the currently selected item. In the window, click in the box to the right of the **Text** property's box. To set a value for the **Text** property, type the value in the box. In this case, type **A Simple Program**, as in Fig. 2.17. When you have finished, press the *Enter* key to update the form's title bar in the design area.

3. *Resize the form.* Click and drag one of the form's enabled *sizing handles* (the small squares around the form shown in Fig. 2.18) to change the size of the form. Enabled sizing handles are white. The mouse cursor changes appearance when it is over an enabled sizing handle. Disabled sizing handles are gray. The grid on the background of the form is used to align controls and does not appear when the program executes.

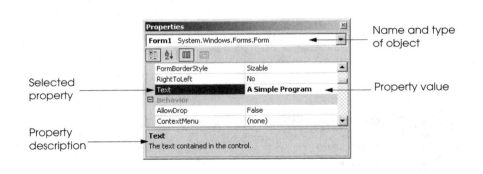

Fig. 2.17   Setting the form's **Text** property.

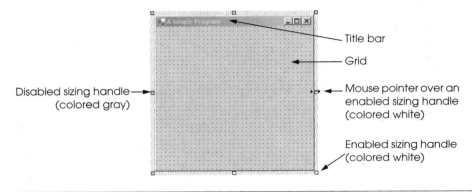

Fig. 2.18   Form with sizing handles.

4. *Change the form's background color.* The **BackColor** property specifies a form's or control's background color. Clicking **BackColor** in the **Properties** window causes a down-arrow button to appear next to the property value (Fig. 2.19). When clicked, the down arrow drops down to display other options. (The options vary, depending on the property.) In this case, it displays the tabs **System** (the default), **Web** and **Custom**. Click the **Custom** tab to display the *palette* (a selection box of colors). Select the box that represents light blue. The palette will disappear, and the form's background color will change to light blue.

5. *Add a label control to the form.* Double-click the label control in the **Toolbox**. This action creates a label with sizing handles in the upper left corner of the form (Fig. 2.20). Double-clicking any **Toolbox** control places it on the form. Alternatively, programmers can drag controls from the **Toolbox** to the form. Labels display text; our label displays **Label1** by default. Notice that our label is the same color as the form's background color. The form's background color is also the default background color of controls added to the form.

6. *Set the label's text.* Select the label so that its properties appear in the **Properties** window. The label's **Text** property determines the text (if any) that the label displays. The form and label each have their own **Text** property. Forms and controls can have the same types of properties without conflict. We will see that many controls have property names in common. Set the **Text** property of the label to **Welcome to Visual Basic!** (Fig. 2.21). Resize the label (using the sizing handles) if the text does not fit. Move the label to the top center of the form by dragging it or by using the arrow keys. Alternatively, you can move the label by selecting **Format > Center in Form > Horizontally**.

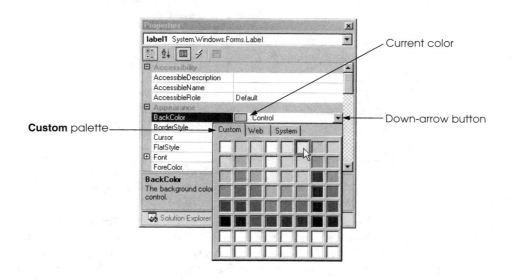

Fig. 2.19   Changing property **BackColor**.

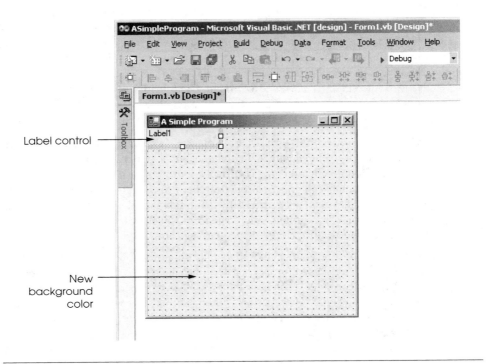

Fig. 2.20   Adding a new label to the form.

Fig. 2.21   Label in position, with its **Text** property set.

7. *Set the label's font size, and align the label's text.* Clicking the **Font** property value causes an *ellipsis* button (...) to appear next to the value, as in Fig. 2.22. The ellipsis button indicates that a dialog will appear when the programmer clicks the button. When the button is clicked, the **Font** *window* shown in Fig. 2.23 is displayed. Users can select the font name (**Microsoft Sans Serif**, **Arial**, etc.), font style (**Regular**, **Bold**, etc.) and font size (**8**, **10**, etc.) in this window. The text in

the **Sample** *area* displays the selected font. Under the **Size** category, select **24**, and click **OK**. If the text does not fit on a single line, it will wrap to the next line. Resize the label if it is not large enough to hold the text. Next, select the label's **TextAlign** property, which determines how the text is aligned within the label. A three-by-three grid of alignment choices is displayed, corresponding to where the text appears in the label (Fig. 2.24). Select the top center grid item, so that the text will appear at the top center of the label.

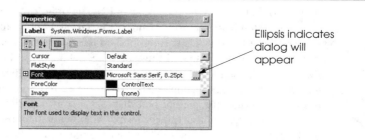

Fig. 2.22   Properties window displaying the label's properties.

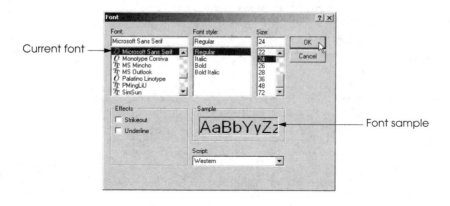

Fig. 2.23   Font window for selecting fonts, styles and sizes.

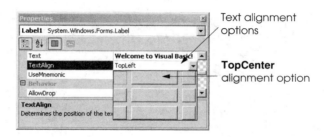

**Fig. 2.24   Centering the text in the label.

8. *Add a picture box to the form.* The picture-box control displays images. This step is similar to Step 5. Find the picture box in the toolbox, and add it to the form. Move it underneath the label, by either dragging it or using the arrow keys (Fig. 2.25).

9. *Insert an image.* Click the picture box to load its properties in the **Properties** window, and find the ***Image*** *property.* The **Image** property shows a preview of the current picture. No picture has been assigned, so the **Image** property displays **(none)** (Fig. 2.26). Click the ellipsis button to display an **Open** dialog (Fig. 2.27). Browse for and select a picture to insert; then press the *Enter* key. The proper formats of an image include PNG (Portable Networks Graphic), GIF (Graphic Interchange Format) and JPEG (Joint Photographic Experts Group). Each of these file formats is supported on the Internet. To create a new picture, it is necessary to use image-editing software, such as Jasc Paint Shop Pro, Adobe Photoshop Elements or Microsoft Paint. We use the picture **bug.png**, which is located with this example on our Web site (**www.deitel.com**). After the image has been inserted, the picture box displays as much of the picture as it can (depending on size), and the **Image** property shows a small preview. To display the entire image, resize the picture box by dragging its handles (Fig. 2.28).

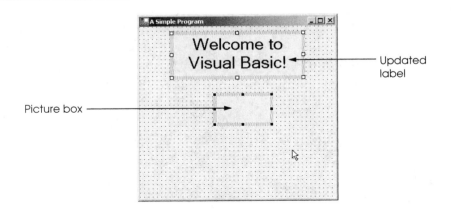

Picture box

Updated label

Fig. 2.25   Inserting and aligning the picture box.

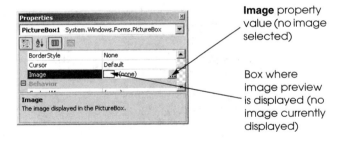

Image property value (no image selected)

Box where image preview is displayed (no image currently displayed)

Fig. 2.26   **Image** property of the picture box.

Fig. 2.27 Selecting an image for the picture box.

Fig. 2.28 Picture box after the image has been inserted.

10. *Save the project.* Select **File > Save All** to save the entire solution. To save an individual file, select it in the **Solution Explorer**, and select **File > Save**. The created program stores the source code in the Visual Basic .NET file **Form1.vb**. The project file (**.vbproj** extension) contains the names and locations of all the files in the project. The solution file (**.sln** extension) contains the names and locations of all projects in the solution. Choosing **Save All** saves all the files in the current solution.

11. *Run the project.* Prior to this step, we have been working in the IDE *design mode* (i.e., the program being created is not executing). This mode is indicated by the text **Microsoft Visual Basic .NET [design]** in the title bar. While in design mode, programmers have access to all the environment windows (i.e., **Toolbox**

and **Properties**), menus, toolbars and so forth. While in *run mode*, however, the program is executing, and users can interact with only a few IDE features. Features that are not available are disabled or grayed out. The text **Form1.vb [Design]** in the title bar indicates that we are designing the form visually, rather than programming it by using code. If we had been writing code, the title bar would have contained only the text **Form1.vb**. To execute or run our program, we first need to compile it, which is accomplished by selecting **Build > Build Solution** (or by pressing *Ctrl + Shift + B*). The program then can be executed by clicking the **Start** button (the blue triangle), selecting **Debug > Start** command (or pressing the *F5* key). Figure 2.29 shows the IDE in run mode. Note that the IDE title bar displays **[run]** and that many toolbar icons are disabled.

12. *Terminate execution.* To terminate the program, click the running application's close button (the **x** in the top right corner). Alternatively, click the **End** button (the blue square) in the toolbar. Either action stops program execution and puts the IDE into design mode.

Fig. 2.29   IDE in run mode, with the running application in the foreground.

Software Engineering Observation 2.1

Visual programming can be simpler and faster than writing code.

Software Engineering Observation 2.2

Most programs require more than visual programming. In such programs, some code must be written by the programmer. Examples of such programs include applications that use event handlers (used to respond to the user's actions), databases, security, networking, text editing, graphics and multimedia.

2.7 Simple Program: Printing a Line of Text

We now turn our discussion towards nonvisual, or conventional, programming; we will demonstrate how to create programs by using only code. As we will see throughout the text, Visual Basic .NET programming is a mixture of two styles: Visual programming allows us to develop a GUI and avoid tedious tasks, while conventional programming specifies the behavior of our program.

We begin by considering a simple program that displays a line of text. Figure 2.30 shows the program, followed by an output window that displays the program's results. When you execute this program, the output will appear in a console window.

This program illustrates several important features of Visual Basic .NET. Line 7 in Fig. 2.30 does the "real work" of the program, displaying the phrase **Welcome to Visual Basic!** on the screen.

Line 1 begins with a *single-quote character* (**'**), indicating that the remainder of the line is a *comment*. A comment that begins with **'** is called a *single-line comment*, because the comment terminates at the end of the line. Comments are ignored by the compiler. In the Visual Studio .NET IDE, all comment text appears in green.

Lines 4–10 define our first *module*. (These lines collectively are called a *module definition*.) Visual Basic console applications consist of modules, which are logical groupings of *procedures* that simplify program organization. Procedures perform tasks and can return information when the tasks are completed. Every console application in Visual Basic consists of at least one module definition and one procedure. In Chapter 4, Procedures and Arrays, we discuss modules and procedures in detail.

```
1   ' Fig. 2.30: Welcome1.vb
2   ' Simple Visual Basic program.
3
4   Module modFirstWelcome
5
6      Sub Main()
7         Console.WriteLine("Welcome to Visual Basic!")
8      End Sub ' Main
9
10  End Module ' modFirstWelcome
```

```
Welcome to Visual Basic!
```

Fig. 2.30 Simple Visual Basic program.

The word **Module** is an example of a *keyword* (or *reserved word*). Keywords are reserved for use by Visual Basic. (A complete list of Visual Basic keywords is presented in the next chapter.) The name of the **Module** (**modFirstWelcome** in this example) is known as an *identifier*, which is a series of characters consisting of letters, digits, and underscores (_). Identifiers cannot begin with a digit and cannot contain spaces. Examples of valid identifiers are **value1**, **xy_coordinate**, **__total** and **cmdExit**. The name **7Welcome** is not a valid identifier, because it begins with a digit, and the name **input field** is not a valid identifier, because it contains a space.

Good Programming Practice 2.1

Begin each module identifier with **mod** *to make modules easier to identify.*

Visual Basic keywords and identifiers are not *case sensitive*. This means that uppercase and lowercase letters are considered to be identical, which causes **modfirstwelcome** and **modFirstWelcome** to be interpreted as the same identifier. Although keywords appear to be case sensitive, they are not: Visual Studio .NET applies the "proper" case to each letter of a keyword. For example, although **module** may have been typed in, it is changed to **Module** when the *Enter* key is pressed.

Line 6 is present in all Visual Basic .NET console applications. These applications begin executing at **Main**, which is known as the *entry point* of the program. The parentheses after **Main** indicate that **Main** is a program building block, called a *procedure*. Visual Basic .NET modules normally contain one or more procedures. For Visual Basic .NET console applications, exactly one of those procedures must be named **Main**, and it must be defined as shown on line 6; otherwise, the program is not executable.

Line 7 instructs the computer to perform an *action*, namely, to print the series of characters contained between the double quotation marks. Characters delimited in this manner are called *strings*, *character strings* or *string literals*. We refer to characters between double quotation marks generically as *strings*. Whitespace characters (e.g., spaces and tabs) in strings are significant; the compiler does not ignore these characters when they appear in strings.

As discussed in Chapter 1, classes represent groups of related objects. The **Console** *class* enables programs to output information to the computer's *standard output*, normally the screen. Class **Console** provides *methods* (a type of procedure we discuss further in Chapter 4) that allow Visual Basic .NET programs to display strings and other types of information in the console window.

Method **Console.WriteLine** *displays* (or *prints*) a line of text in the console window. When **Console.WriteLine** completes its task, it positions the *output cursor* (the location where the next character will be displayed) at the beginning of the next line in the console window.

The entire line, including **Console.WriteLine** and its *argument* in parentheses (**"Welcome to Visual Basic!"**), is called a *statement*. When this statement executes, it displays the message **Welcome to Visual Basic!** in the console window (Fig. 2.31).

Now that we have presented our first console application, we provide a step-by-step explanation of how to create and run it, using the features of the Visual Studio .NET IDE:

Fig. 2.31 Executing the program shown in Fig. 2.30.

1. *Create the console application.* Select **File > New > Project...** to display the **New Project** dialog (Fig. 2.32). In the left pane, select ***Visual Basic Projects***, and in the right pane, select ***Console Application***. In the dialog's **Name** field, type **Welcome1**. The location in which project files will be created is specified in the **Location** field. By default, projects are saved in the folder **Visual Studio Projects** inside the **My Documents** folder (on the Windows desktop). Click **OK** to create the project. The IDE now contains the open console application, as shown in Fig. 2.33. Notice that the editor window contains four lines of code provided by the IDE. The color scheme used by the IDE is called *syntax-color highlighting*, and it helps programmers visually differentiate programming elements. Keywords appear in blue, whereas text is black. When present, comments are colored green. In Step 4, we discuss how to use the editor window to write code.

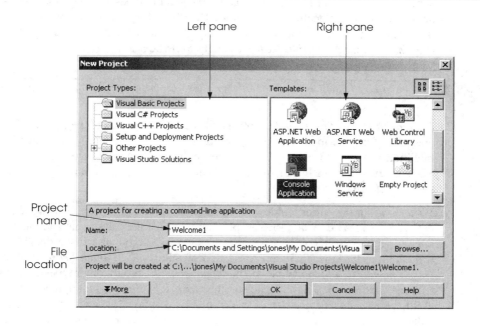

Fig. 2.32 Creating a **Console Application** with the **New Project** dialog.

Editor window
(containing program code)

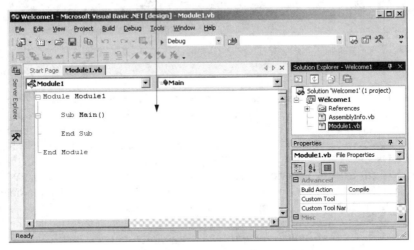

Fig. 2.33   IDE with an open console application.

2. *Change the name of the program file.* For programs in this book, we change the name of the program file (i.e., **Module1.vb**) to a more descriptive name. To rename the file, click **Module1.vb** in the **Solution Explorer** window; this action will display the program file's properties in the **Properties** window (Fig. 2.34). Change the *File Name* property to **Welcome1.vb**.

Testing and Debugging Tip 2.1

Syntax-color highlighting helps programmers avoid the accidental misuse of keywords.

3. *Change the name of the module.* Notice that changing the name of the program file does not affect the module name in the program code. Module names must be modified in the editor window. To do so, replace the identifier **Module1** with **modFirstWelcome** by deleting the old name and typing the new name after the keyword **Module**.

4. *Write code.* In the editor window, type the code contained in line 7 of Fig. 2.30 between **Sub Main()** and **End Sub**. After you type the class name and the dot operator (i.e., **Console.**), a window containing a scrollbar will be displayed (Fig. 2.35). This Visual Studio .NET IDE feature, called *IntelliSense*, lists a class's *members*, which include method names. As the programmer types characters, the first member that matches all the characters typed is highlighted, and a tooltip containing a description of that member is displayed. The programmer can either type the complete member name (e.g., **WriteLine**), double-click the member name in the list or press the *Tab* key to complete the name. Once the complete name is provided, the IntelliSense window closes. When the programmer

types the open parenthesis character, **(**, after **Console.WriteLine**, two additional windows are displayed (Fig. 2.36)—the *Parameter Info* and *Parameter List* windows. The Parameter Info window displays information about a method's arguments. This window indicates how many versions of the selected method are available and provides *up and down arrows* for scrolling through the different versions. For example, there are 18 versions of the **WriteLine** method one of which is used in our example. The Parameter List window lists possible arguments for the method shown in the Parameter Info window. These windows are part of the many features provided by the IDE to aid program development. You will learn more about the information displayed in these windows in the next chapter. In this case, because we know that we want to use the version of **WriteLine** that takes a string argument, we can close these windows by pressing the *Escape* key twice (i.e., once for each of the windows).

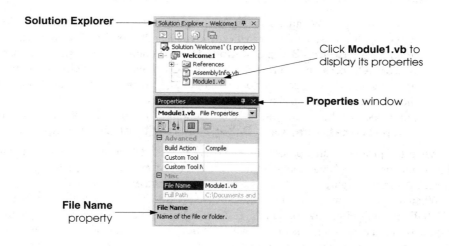

Fig. 2.34   Renaming the program file in the **Properties** window.

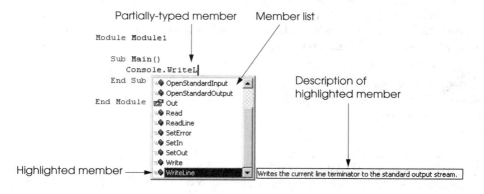

Fig. 2.35   IntelliSense feature of the Visual Studio .NET IDE.

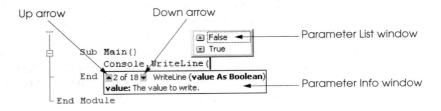

Fig. 2.36   Parameter Info and Parameter List windows.

 Testing and Debugging Tip 2.2

Visual Basic provides a large number of classes and methods. The Parameter Info and Parameter List windows help ensure that a method is being used correctly.

5. *Run the program.* We are now ready to compile and execute our program. To do so, we simply follow steps similar to those provided in Section 2.6. To compile the program, select **Build > Build Solution**. This selection creates a new file, named **Welcome1.exe**, in the project's directory that contains the Microsoft Intermediate Language (MSIL) code for our program. The **.exe** file extension denotes that the file is executable (i.e., contains instructions that can be executed by another program, such as the Common Language Runtime). To run this console application (i.e., **Welcome1.exe**), select **Debug > Start Without Debugging**.[1]

When the program runs, procedure **Main** is invoked, which is considered the entry point to the program. Next, the statement on line 7 of **Main** displays **Welcome to Visual Basic!**. Figure 2.31 shows the result of program execution.

When the programmer types a line of code and presses the *Enter* key, the Visual Studio .NET IDE responds either by applying syntax-color highlighting or by generating a *syntax error* (also called a *compile-time error*), which indicates a violation of the language syntax (i.e., one or more statements are not written correctly). Syntax errors occur for various reasons, such as when keywords are misspelled. When a syntax error occurs, the Visual Studio .NET IDE underlines the error in blue and provides a description of the error in the ***Task List*** *window* (Fig. 2.37). If the **Task List** window is not visible in the IDE, select **View > Other Windows > Task List** to display it. [*Note*: One syntax error can lead to multiple entries in the **Task List** window.]

 Software Engineering Observation 2.3

Visual Studio .NET often will catch syntax errors as you are creating the program, even before the program is compiled. Look out for jagged blue lines that appear directly below a syntax error.

---

1. Selecting **Debug > Start Without Debugging** causes the console window to prompt the user to press a key after the program terminates, allowing the user to observe the program's output. In contrast, if we run this program by selecting **Debug > Start**, as we did for the Windows application in Section 2.6, a console window opens, the program displays the message **Welcome to Visual Basic!** and the console window closes immediately thereafter.

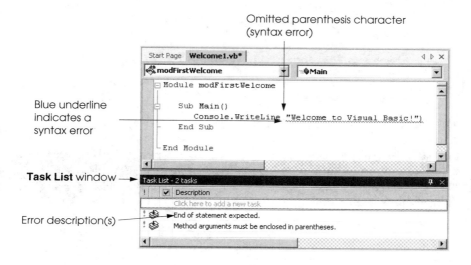

Omitted parenthesis character
(syntax error)

Blue underline
indicates a
syntax error

Task List window

Error description(s)

Fig. 2.37   IDE indicating a syntax error.

Testing and Debugging Tip 2.3

*When the compiler reports a syntax error, the error might not be on the line indicated by the
error message. First, check the line where the error was reported. If that line does not contain syntax errors, check the lines that precede the one reported.*

Although the programs discussed thus far display output in the console window, most
Visual Basic programs use *dialogs* to display output. Dialogs are windows that typically
display messages to the user. Visual Basic provides class **MessageBox** for creating dialogs. The program in Fig. 2.38 uses a dialog to display the square root of two.

In our next example, we present a program that contains a simple GUI (i.e., the dialog).
The .NET Framework Class Library (FCL) contains a rich collection of classes that can be
used to construct GUIs. FCL classes are grouped by functionality into *namespaces*. Line 4
is an **Imports** statement which indicates that we are using the features provided by the
System.Windows.Forms namespace. **System.Windows.Forms** contains win-
dows-related classes (i.e., forms and dialogs). We discuss this namespace in detail after we
discuss the code in this example.

```
1   ' Fig. 2.38: SquareRoot.vb
2   ' Displaying the square root of 2 in dialog.
3
4   Imports System.Windows.Forms ' namespace containing MessageBox
5
6   Module modSquareRoot
7
8      Sub Main()
9
```

Fig. 2.38   Displaying text in a dialog. (Part 1 of 2.)

```
10          ' calculate square root of 2
11          Dim root As Double = Math.Sqrt(2)
12
13          ' display results in dialog
14          MessageBox.Show("The square root of 2 is " & root, _
15             "The Square Root of 2")
16
17      End Sub ' Main
18
19  End Module ' modSquareRoot
```

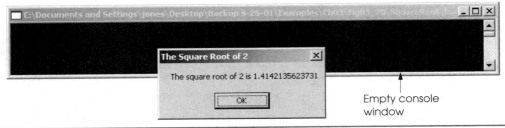

Empty console window

Fig. 2.38 Displaying text in a dialog. (Part 2 of 2.)

Line 11 calls the **Sqrt** method of the **Math** class to compute the square root of two. The value returned is a floating-point number, so we declare the variable **root** as type **Double**. The **Double** data type stores floating-point numbers (i.e., numbers such as 2.3456 and –845.7840). We declare and initialize **root** on a single line.

Notice the use of spacing in lines 14–15 of Fig. 2.38. To improve readability, long statements may be split over several lines, using the *line-continuation character*, _ . Line 14 uses the line-continuation character to indicate that line 15 is a continuation of the previous line. A single statement can contain as many line-continuation characters as necessary. However, at least one whitespace character must precede each line-continuation character.

 Common Programming Error 2.1

Splitting a statement over several lines without including the line-continuation character is a syntax error.

 Common Programming Error 2.2

Failure to precede the line-continuation character with at least one whitespace character is a syntax error.

 Common Programming Error 2.3

Placing anything, including comments, after a line-continuation character is a syntax error.

 Common Programming Error 2.4

Splitting a statement in the middle of an identifier or string is a syntax error.

 Good Programming Practice 2.2

A lengthy statement may be spread over several lines. If a single statement must be split across lines, choose breaking points that make sense, such as after a comma in a comma-separated list or after an operator in a lengthy expression. If a statement is split across two or more lines, indent all subsequent lines with one level of indentation.

Lines 14–15 (Fig. 2.38) call method *Show* of class *MessageBox*. This method takes two arguments. The first argument is the **String** that is displayed in the dialog. The second argument is the **String** that is displayed in the dialog's title bar.

In this case, the first argument to method **Show** is the expression

```
"The square root of 2 is " & root
```

which uses the *string concatenation operator*, **&**, to combine a **String** (the literal **"The square root of 2 is "**) and the value of the variable **root** (the **Double** variable containing the square root of **2**). The string concatenation operator combines two **String**s. This operation results in a new, longer **String**. If an argument given to the string concatenation operator is not of type **String**, the program creates a **String** representation of the argument.

When executed, lines 14–15 display the dialog shown in Fig. 2.39. The dialog includes an **OK** button that allows the user to *dismiss* (or *close*) the dialog by positioning the *mouse pointer* (also called the *mouse cursor*) over the **OK** button and clicking the mouse. Once the dialog has been dismissed, the program terminates.

Many classes provided by Visual Basic .NET (such as **MessageBox**) must be added to the project before they can be used in a program. These *compiled classes* are located in a file, called an assembly, that has a *.dll* (or *dynamic link library*) extension.

Information about the assembly that we need can be found in the Visual Studio .NET documentation (also called the *MSDN Documentation*). The easiest way to locate this information is by selecting **Help > Index...** to display the **Index** dialog (Fig. 2.40).

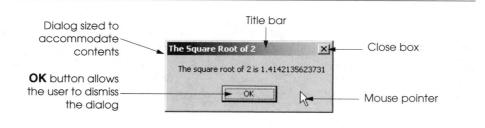

Fig. 2.39   Dialog displayed by calling **MessageBox.Show**.

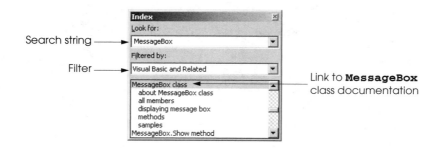

Fig. 2.40   Obtaining documentation for a class by using the **Index** dialog.

Type the class name in the **Look for:** box, and select the appropriate *filter*, which narrows the search to a subset of the documentation. Visual Basic programmers should select **Visual Basic and Related**. Next, click the **about MessageBox class** link to display documentation for the **MessageBox** class (Fig. 2.41). The **Requirements** section of the documentation lists the assembly that contains the class. Class **MessageBox** is located in assembly *System.Windows.Forms.dll*.

It is necessary to *add a reference* to this assembly (i.e., to place an assembly in the **Solution Explorer**'s **References** folder) if we wish to use class **MessageBox** in our program. Visual Studio .NET provides a simple process by which to add a reference. Let us discuss the process of adding a reference to **System.Windows.Forms**.

To add a reference to an existing project, select **Project > Add Reference...** to display the **Add Reference** *dialog* (Fig. 2.42). Find and double-click **System.Windows.Forms.dll** to add this file to the **References** folder, and click **OK**. Notice that **System.Windows.Forms** is now listed in the **References** folder of the **Solution Explorer** (Fig. 2.42).

Now that the assembly **System.Windows.Forms.dll** is referenced, we can use the classes that are a part of the assembly. The namespace that includes class **MessageBox**, **System.Windows.Forms**, also is specified with the **Imports** statement in line 4 of the program (Fig. 2.38). [*Note*: The **Imports** statement is not added to the program by Visual Studio .NET; programmers must add this line to their code.]

Common Programming Error 2.5

*Forgetting to add an **Imports** statement for a referenced assembly is a syntax error. Likewise, forgetting to reference an assembly that is specified with an **Imports** statement is a syntax error.*

We did not have to add references to any of our previous programs, because Visual Studio .NET adds some references to assemblies when the project is created. The references added depend on the project type that is selected in the **New Project** dialog. Some assemblies do not need to be referenced. Class **Console**, for instance, is located in the assembly *mscorlib.dll*, but we do not need to reference this assembly explicitly to use it.

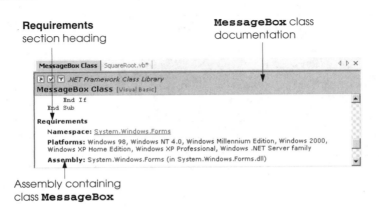

Fig. 2.41   Documentation for the **MessageBox** class.

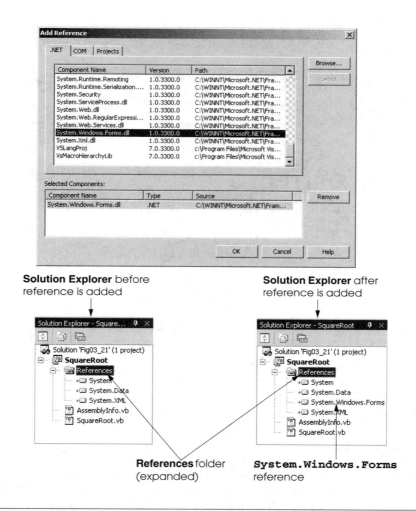

Fig. 2.42 Adding a reference to an assembly in the Visual Studio .NET IDE.

The **System.Windows.Forms** namespace contains many classes that help Visual Basic programmers define GUIs for their applications. *GUI components* (such as buttons) facilitate both data entry by the user and the formatting or presentation of data outputs to the user. For example, Fig. 2.43 shows an Internet Explorer window with a menu bar containing various menus, such as **File**, **Edit** and **View**. Below the menu bar is a toolbar that consists of buttons. Each button, when clicked, executes a task. Beneath the toolbar is a *combo box* in which the user can type the location of a World Wide Web site to visit. To the left of the combo box is a *label* that indicates the purpose of the combo box. The menus, buttons, labels, etc. are part of Internet Explorer's GUI; they enable users to interact with the Internet Explorer program. Visual Basic provides classes for creating the GUI components shown here. Other classes that create GUI components will be described in Chapters 9 and 10, Graphical User Interface Concepts: Part 1 and Graphical User Interface Concepts: Part 2, respectively.

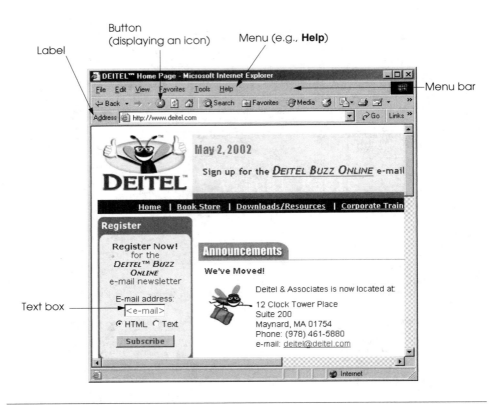

Fig. 2.43   Internet Explorer window with GUI components.

2.8 Arithmetic

Most programs perform arithmetic calculations. The *arithmetic operators* are summarized in Fig. 2.44. Note the use of various special symbols not used in algebra. For example, the *asterisk* (*****) indicates multiplication, and the keyword **Mod** represents the *modulus operator*, which is discussed shortly. The majority of the arithmetic operators listed in Fig. 2.44 are binary operators, because each operates on two operands. For example, the expression **sum + value** contains the binary operator **+** and the two operands **sum** and **value**. Visual Basic also provides *unary operators*, i.e., operators that take only one operand. For example, unary versions of plus (**+**) and minus (**−**) are provided, so that programmers can write expressions such as **+9** and **−19**.

Visual Basic applies the operators in arithmetic expressions in a precise sequence, determined by the following *rules of operator precedence*, which are generally the same as those followed in algebra:

1. Operators in expressions contained within a pair of parentheses are evaluated first. Thus, *parentheses can be used to force the order of evaluation to occur in any sequence desired by the programmer.* Parentheses are at the highest level of precedence. With *nested* (or *embedded*) parentheses, the operators contained in the innermost pair of parentheses are applied first.

Visual Basic operation	Arithmetic operator	Algebraic expression	Visual Basic expression
Addition	+	$f + 7$	f + 7
Subtraction	–	$p - c$	p - c
Multiplication	*	bm	b * m
Division (float)	/	x/y or $\dfrac{x}{y}$ or $x \div y$	x / y
Division (integer)	\	none	v \ u
Modulus	*Mod*	r modulo s	r *Mod* s
Exponentiation	^	q^p	q ^ p
Unary negative	–	$-e$	-e
Unary positive	+	$+g$	+g

Fig. 2.44 Arithmetic operators.

2. Exponentiation is applied next. If an expression contains several exponentiation operations, operators are applied from left to right.

3. Unary positive and negative operators, **+** and **–**, respectively, are applied next. If an expression contains several sign operations, operators are applied from left to right. Sign operations **+** and **–** have the same level of precedence.

4. Multiplication and floating-point division operations are applied next. If an expression contains several multiplication and floating-point division operations, operators are applied from left to right. Multiplication and floating-point division have the same level of precedence.

5. **Integer** division is applied next. If an expression contains several **Integer** division operations, operators are applied from left to right.

6. Modulus operations are applied next. If an expression contains several modulus operations, operators are applied from left to right.

7. Addition and subtraction operations are applied last. If an expression contains several addition and subtraction operations, operators are applied from left to right. Addition and subtraction have the same level of precedence.

The rules of operator precedence enable Visual Basic to apply operators in the correct order. When we say that operators are applied from left to right, we are referring to the *associativity* of the operators. If there are multiple operators, each with the same precedence, the order in which the operators are applied is determined by the operators' associativity. Figure 2.45 summarizes the rules of operator precedence. This table will be expanded as we introduce additional Visual Basic operators in subsequent chapters. A complete operator-precedence chart is available in Appendix A.

Operator(s)	Operation	Order of evaluation (precedence)
( )	Parentheses	Evaluated first. If the parentheses are nested, the expression in the innermost pair is evaluated first. If there are several pairs of parentheses "on the same level" (i.e., not nested), they are evaluated from left to right.
^	Exponentiation	Evaluated second. If there are several such operators, they are evaluated from left to right.
+, −	Sign operations	Evaluated third. If there are several such operators, they are evaluated from left to right.
*, /	Multiplication and division	Evaluated fourth. If there are several such operators, they are evaluated from left to right.
\	*Integer* division	Evaluated fifth. If there are several such operators, they are evaluated from left to right.
Mod	Modulus	Evaluated sixth. If there are several such operators, they are evaluated from left to right.
+, −	Addition and subtraction	Evaluated last. If there are several such operators, they are evaluated from left to right.

Fig. 2.45   Precedence of arithmetic operators.

2.9 Decision Making: Equality and Relational Operators

This section introduces Visual Basic's **If/Then** structure, which allows a program to make a decision based on the truth or falsity of some expression. The expression in an **If/Then** structure is called the *condition*. If the condition is met (i.e., the condition is *true*), then the statement in the body of the **If/Then** structure executes. If the condition is not met (i.e., the condition is *false*), then the body statement is not executed. Conditions in **If/Then** structures can be formed by using the *equality operators* and *relational operators* (also called *comparison operators*), which are summarized in Fig. 2.46. The relational and equality operators all have the same level of precedence and associate from left to right.

The next example uses six **If/Then** statements to compare two numbers entered into a program by the user. If the condition in any of these **If/Then** statements is true, the output statement associated with that **If/Then** statement executes. The user inputs the values, which are converted to **Integer**s and stored in variables **number1** and **number2**, respectively. The comparisons are performed, and the results of the comparison are displayed in the console window. The program and some sample outputs are shown in Fig. 2.47.

Line 9 declares the variables that are used in procedure **Main**. In this line, two variables of type **Integer** are declared. Remember that variables of the same type may be declared either in one declaration or in multiple declarations. Also recall that, when more than one variable is placed in a declaration, the variables must be separated by commas (**,**). The comment that precedes the declaration indicates the purpose of the variables in the program.

Standard algebraic equality operator or relational operator	Visual Basic equality or relational operator	Example of Visual Basic condition	Meaning of Visual Basic condition
Equality operators			
=	=	x = y	**x** is equal to **y**
≠	<>	x <> y	**x** is not equal to **y**
Relational operators			
>	>	x > y	**x** is greater than **y**
<	<	x < y	**x** is less than **y**
≥	>=	x >= y	**x** is greater than or equal to **y**
≤	<=	x <= y	**x** is less than or equal to **y**

Fig. 2.46   Equality and relational operators.

```
1    ' Fig. 2.47: Comparison.vb
2    ' Using equality and relational operators.
3
4    Module modComparison
5
6       Sub Main()
7
8          ' declare Integer variables for user input
9          Dim number1, number2 As Integer
10
11         ' read first number from user
12         Console.Write("Please enter first integer: ")
13         number1 = Console.ReadLine()
14
15         ' read second number from user
16         Console.Write("Please enter second integer: ")
17         number2 = Console.ReadLine()
18
19         If number1 = number2 Then
20            Console.WriteLine("{0} = {1}", number1, number2)
21         End If
22
23         If number1 <> number2 Then
24            Console.WriteLine("{0} <> {1}", number1, number2)
25         End If
26
27         If number1 < number2 Then
28            Console.WriteLine("{0} < {1}", number1, number2)
29         End If
30
```

Fig. 2.47   Performing comparisons with equality and relational operators. (Part 1 of 2.)

```
31            If number1 > number2 Then
32                Console.WriteLine("{0} > {1}", number1, number2)
33            End If
34
35            If number1 <= number2 Then
36                Console.WriteLine("{0} <= {1}", number1, number2)
37            End If
38
39            If number1 >= number2 Then
40                Console.WriteLine("{0} >= {1}", number1, number2)
41            End If
42
43        End Sub ' Main
44
45    End Module ' modComparison
```

```
Please enter first integer: 1000
Please enter second integer: 2000
1000 <> 2000
1000 < 2000
1000 <= 2000
```

```
Please enter first integer: 515
Please enter second integer: 49
515 <> 49
515 > 49
515 >= 49
```

```
Please enter first integer: 333
Please enter second integer: 333
333 = 333
333 <= 333
333 >= 333
```

Fig. 2.47 *Performing comparisons with equality and relational operators. (Part 2 of 2.)*

Lines 13 and 17 both retrieve inputs from the user, convert the inputs to type **Integer** and assign the values to the appropriate variables (i.e., **number1** or **number2**) in one step.

The **If/Then** structure on lines 19–21 compares the values of the variables **number1** and **number2** for equality. If the values are equal, the program outputs the **String** generated by the arguments that are given to **WriteLine** in line 20.

For example, if **number1** contains the value **1000** and **number2** contains the value **1000**, the expression evaluates as follows: **number1** and **number2** are converted to **String**s and put in the string **"{0} = {1}"** in place of the **{0}** and **{1}** formats, respectively. At this point, the **String**, namely **"1000 = 1000"**, is sent to **WriteLine** to be printed. As the program proceeds through the **If/Then** structures, additional **String**s are output by the **Console.WriteLine** statements. For example, when given the value **1000** for **number1** and **number2**, the **If/Then** conditions in lines 35 (**<=**) and 39 (**>=**) are true. Thus, the output displayed is

```
1000 = 1000
1000 <= 1000
1000 >= 1000
```

Good Programming Practice 2.3

Indent the statements in the body of an **If/Then** *structure to emphasize the body of the structure and to enhance program readability.*

Common Programming Error 2.6

Omission of the **Then** *keyword in an* **If/Then** *structure is a syntax error.*

The table in Fig. 2.48 shows the precedence of the operators introduced in this chapter. The operators are displayed from top to bottom in decreasing order of precedence. All operators in Visual Basic associate from left to right.

Testing and Debugging Tip 2.4

When uncertain about the order of evaluation in a complex expression, use parentheses to force the order, as you would do in an algebraic expression. Doing so can help avoid the introduction of subtle bugs.

2.10 Summary

The Visual Studio .NET integrated development environment (IDE) is the environment used for creating, documenting, running and debugging programs. There are various windows used in Visual Studio .NET, including the **Solution Explorer**, which lists all the files in a solution; the **Toolbox**, which contains controls that customize forms; and the **Properties** window, which displays a control's characteristics (e.g., colors and fonts). Visual Studio .NET provides several help features, including context-sensitive and dynamic help.

Most Visual Basic .NET programs are constructed by using a combination of visual and nonvisual programming. One form of nonvisual programming is to create console applications, i.e., applications that predominantly write text to the console window.

Operators	Type
( )	parentheses
^	exponentiation
* /	multiplicative
\	*Integer* division
Mod	modulus
+ -	additive
= <> < <= > >=	equality and relational

Fig. 2.48   Precedence of operators introduced in this chapter.

There are various pieces that make up Visual Basic .NET programs, such as modules, procedures and namespaces. All Visual Basic .NET console applications contain procedure **Main**, known as the entry point of the program. Procedures can perform tasks and return information when their tasks are completed. Data can be passed to a method, if such data are necessary for the procedure to complete its task. The .NET Framework Class Library (FCL) provides many namespaces, one of which includes the class that contains the method which displays a message dialog.

Visual Basic .NET provides arithmetic, equality and relational operators for manipulating values in a program. Often, values will need to be input by the user. Data can be read from the user via method **ReadLine**.

Control Structures

Objectives

- To use the **If/Then** and **If/Then/Else** selection structures to choose among alternative actions.
- To use the **While**, **Do While/Loop** and **Do Until/Loop** repetition structures to execute statements in a program repeatedly.
- To use the assignment operators.
- To use the **For/Next**, **Do/Loop While** and **Do/Loop Until** repetition structures to execute statements in a program repeatedly.
- To understand multiple selection as implemented by the **Select Case** selection structure.
- To use the **Exit Do** and **Exit For** program control statements.
- To use logical operators.

Who can control his fate?
William Shakespeare

Man is a tool-making animal.
Benjamin Franklin

Intelligence... is the faculty of making artificial objects, especially tools to make tools.
Henri Bergson

Let's all move one place on.
Lewis Carroll

Outline

3.1 Introduction

In this chapter, we present control structures that enable programmers to control the order of events in their programs. Visual Basic's sequence, selection and repetition structures are used to select and repeat various statements and thereby execute complex algorithms. In the process, we introduce commonly used shorthand operators that allow the programmer quickly to calculate and assign new values to variables. When we study object-based programming in more depth in Chapter 5, we will see that control structures are helpful in building and manipulating objects.

3.2 Control Structures

Normally, statements in a program are executed one after another in the order in which they are written. This process is called *sequential execution*. However, various Visual Basic statements enable the programmer to specify that the next statement to be executed might not be the next one in sequence. A *transfer of control* occurs when a statement other than the next one in the program executes.

Visual Basic provides seven types of repetition structures: **While**, **Do While/Loop**, **Do/Loop While**, **Do Until/Loop**, **Do/Loop Until**, **For/Next** and **For Each/Next**. (**For Each/Next** is covered in Chapter 4, Procedures and Arrays.) The words **If**, **Then**,

Else, **End**, **Select**, **Case**, **While**, **Do**, **Until**, **Loop**, **For**, **Next** and **Each** are all Visual Basic keywords. (See Fig. 3.1 for a list of all the Visual Basic keywords.) We discuss many of Visual Basic's keywords and their respective purposes throughout this book.

Visual Basic Keywords			
AddHandler	AddressOf	Alias	And
AndAlso	Ansi	As	Assembly
Auto	Boolean	ByRef	Byte
ByVal	Call	Case	Catch
CBool	CByte	CChar	CDate
CDec	CDbl	Char	CInt
Class	CLng	CObj	Const
CShort	CSng	CStr	CType
Date	Decimal	Declare	Default
Delegate	Dim	DirectCast	Do
Double	Each	Else	ElseIf
End	Enum	Erase	Error
Event	Exit	False	Finally
For	Friend	Function	Get
GetType	GoTo	Handles	If
Implements	Imports	In	Inherits
Integer	Interface	Is	Lib
Like	Long	Loop	Me
Mod	Module	MustInherit	MustOverride
MyBase	MyClass	Namespace	New
Next	Not	Nothing	NotInheritable
NotOverridable	Object	On	Option
Optional	Or	OrElse	Overloads
Overridable	Overrides	ParamArray	Preserve
Private	Property	Protected	Public
RaiseEvent	ReadOnly	ReDim	REM
RemoveHandler	Resume	Return	Select
Set	Shadows	Shared	Short
Single	Static	Step	Stop
String	Structure	Sub	SyncLock
Then	Throw	To	True

Fig. 3.1   Keywords in Visual Basic. (Part 1 of 2.)

Visual Basic Keywords			
Try	*TypeOf*	*Unicode*	*Until*
When	*While*	*With*	*WithEvents*
WriteOnly	*Xor*		

The following are retained as keywords, although they are no longer supported in Visual Basic .NET:

Let	*Variant*

Fig. 3.1   Keywords in Visual Basic. (Part 2 of 2.)

3.3 If/Then Selection Structure

In a program, a selection structure chooses among alternative courses of action. For example, suppose that the passing grade on an examination is 60 (out of 100). Then the Visual Basic .NET code

```
If studentGrade >= 60 Then
    Console.WriteLine("Passed")
End If
```

determines whether the condition **studentGrade >= 60** is true or false. If the condition is true, then "**Passed**" is printed, and the next statement in order is "performed." If the condition is false, the **Console.WriteLine** statement is ignored, and the next statement in order is performed. A decision can be made on any expression that evaluates to a value of Visual Basic's *Boolean* type (i.e., any expression that evaluates to **True** or **False**).

3.4 If/Then/Else Selection Structure

The **If/Then** selection structure performs an indicated action only when the condition evaluates to true; otherwise, the action is skipped. The **If/Then/Else** selection structure allows the programmer to specify that a different action be performed when the condition is true than that performed when the condition is false. For example, the statement

```
If studentGrade >= 60 Then
    Console.WriteLine("Passed")
Else
    Console.WriteLine("Failed")
End If
```

prints "**Passed**" if the student's grade is greater than or equal to **60** and prints "**Failed**" if the student's grade is less than **60**. In either case, after printing occurs, the next statement in sequence is "performed."

3.5 `While` Repetition Structure

A *repetition structure* allows the programmer to specify that an action be repeated a number of times, depending on the value of a condition. Visual Basic .NET provides seven repetition structures—one of which is the *While* repetition structure.

As an example of a **While** structure, consider a program segment designed to find the first power of two larger than **1000**. Suppose **Integer** variable **product** contains the value **2**. When the following **While** structure finishes executing, **product** contains the result:

```
Dim product As Integer = 2

While product <= 1000
   product = product * 2
End While
```

When the **While** structure begins executing, **product** is **2**. Variable **product** is multiplied by **2** repeatedly, taking on the values **4**, **8**, **16**, **32**, **64**, **128**, **256**, **512** and **1024**, successively. When **product** becomes **1024**, the condition **product <= 1000** in the **While** structure becomes false. This condition causes the repetition to terminate, with **1024** as **product**'s final value. Execution continues with the next statement after the **While** structure. [*Note*: If a **While** structure's condition is initially false, the body statement(s) will never be executed.]

3.6 Do `While`/`Loop` Repetition Structure

The *Do While/Loop* repetition structure behaves like the **While** repetition structure. As an example of a **Do While/Loop** structure, consider another version of the segment designed to find the first power of two larger than **1000**:

```
Dim product As Integer = 2

Do While product <= 1000
   product = product * 2
Loop
```

When the **Do While/Loop** structure is entered, the value of **product** is **2**. The variable **product** is multiplied by **2** repeatedly, taking on the values **4**, **8**, **16**, **32**, **64**, **128**, **256**, **512** and **1024** successively. When **product** becomes **1024**, the condition in the **Do While/Loop** structure, **product <= 1000**, becomes false. This condition causes the repetition to terminate, with **1024** as **product**'s final value. Program execution continues with the next statement after the **Do While/Loop** structure.

3.7 Do `Until`/`Loop` Repetition Structure

Unlike the **While** and **Do While/Loop** repetition structures, the *Do Until/Loop* repetition structure tests a condition for falsity for repetition to continue. Statements in the body of a **Do Until/Loop** are executed repeatedly as long as the loop-continuation test evaluates to false. As an example of a **Do Until/Loop** repetition structure, once again consider the segment designed to find the first power of two larger than **1000**:

```
Dim product As Integer = 2

Do Until product >= 1000
    product = product * 2
Loop
```

3.8 Do/Loop While Repetition Structure

The *Do/Loop While* repetition structure is similar to the **While** and **Do While/Loop** structures. In the **While** and **Do While/Loop** structures, the loop-continuation condition is tested at the beginning of the loop, before the body of the loop always is performed. The **Do/Loop While** structure tests the loop-continuation condition *after* the body of the loop is performed. Therefore, in a **Do/Loop While** structure, the body of the loop is always executed at least once. When a **Do/Loop While** structure terminates, execution continues with the statement after the **Loop While** clause. As an example of a **Do/Loop While** repetition structure, once again consider the segment designed to find the first power of two larger than **1000**:

```
Dim product As Integer = 1

Do
    product = product * 2
Loop While produce <= 1000
```

3.9 Do/Loop Until Repetition Structure

The **Do/Loop Until** structure is similar to the **Do Until/Loop** structure, except that the loop-continuation condition is tested after the body of the loop is performed; therefore, the body of the loop executes at least once. When a **Do/Loop Until** terminates, execution continues with the statement after the **Loop Until** clause. As an example of a **Do/Loop Until** repetition structure, once again consider the segment designed to find the first power of two larger than **1000**:

```
Dim product As Integer = 1

Do
    product = product * 2
Loop Until product >= 1000
```

3.10 Assignment Operators

Visual Basic .NET provides several assignment operators for abbreviating assignment statements. For example, the statement

```
value = value + 3
```

can be abbreviated with the *addition assignment operator* (**+=**) as

```
value += 3
```

The **+=** operator adds the value of the right operand to the value of the left operand and stores the result in the left operand's variable. Any statement of the form

>   *variable* **=** *variable   operator   expression*

where *operator* is one of the binary operators **+, −, *, ^, &, /** or ****, can be written in the form

>   *variable   operator***=** *expression*

Figure 3.2 lists the arithmetic assignment operators and provides sample expressions using these operators and corresponding explanations.

Although the symbols **=, +=, −=, *=, /=, \=, ^=** and **&=** are operators, we do not include them in operator-precedence tables. When an assignment statement is evaluated, the expression to the right of the operator always is evaluated first and subsequently assigned to the variable on the left. Unlike Visual Basic's other operators, the assignment operators can occur only once in a statement.

3.11 **For/Next** Repetition Structure

The **For/Next** repetition structure handles the details of counter-controlled repetition. The example in Fig. 3.3 uses the **For/Next** structure to display the even digits from 2–10.

Assignment operator	Sample expression	Explanation	Assigns
Assume: **c = 4, d = "He"**			
+=	**c += 7**	**c = c + 7**	11 to **c**
−=	**c −= 3**	**c = c − 3**	1 to **c**
*=	**c *= 4**	**c = c * 4**	16 to **c**
/=	**c /= 2**	**c = c / 2**	2 to **c**
\=	**c \= 3**	**c = c \ 3**	1 to **c**
^=	**c ^= 2**	**c = c ^ 2**	16 to **c**
&=	**d &= "llo"**	**d = d & "llo"**	"Hello" to **d**

Fig. 3.2   Assignment operators.

```
1    ' Fig. 3.3: ForCounter.vb
2    ' Using the For/Next structure to demonstrate counter-controlled
3    ' repetition.
4
5    Module modForCounter
6
7       Sub Main()
8          Dim counter As Integer
9
```

Fig. 3.3   Counter-controlled repetition with the **For/Next** structure. (Part 1 of 2.)

```
10          ' initialization, repetition condition and
11          ' incrementing are all included in For structure
12          For counter = 2 To 10 Step 2
13             Console.Write(counter & " ")
14          Next
15
16       End Sub ' Main
17
18    End Module ' modForCounter
```

```
2 4 6 8 10
```

Fig. 3.3   Counter-controlled repetition with the **For/Next** structure. (Part 2 of 2.)

The **Main** procedure of the program operates as follows: When the **For/Next** structure (lines 12–14) begins its execution, the control variable **counter** is initialized to **2**, thus addressing the first two elements of counter-controlled repetition—control variable *name* and *initial value*. Next, the implied loop-continuation condition **counter <= 10** is tested. The **To** *keyword* is required in the **For/Next** structure. The optional **Step** *keyword* specifies the increment (i.e., the amount that is added to **counter** each time the body of the **For/Next** structure is executed). The increment of a **For/Next** structure could be negative, in which case it is a decrement, and the loop actually counts downwards. If **Step** and the value following it are omitted, the increment defaults to **1**. Thus, programmers typically omit the **Step** portion for increments of **1**.

Because, the initial value of **counter** is **2**, the implied condition is satisfied (i.e., **True**), and the **counter**'s value (**2**) is output in line 13. The required **Next** *keyword* marks the end of the **For/Next** repetition structure. When the **Next** keyword is reached, variable **counter** is incremented by the specified value of **2**, and the loop begins again with the loop-continuation test.

At this point, the control variable is equal to **4**. This value does not exceed the final value, so the program performs the body statement again. This process continues until the **counter** value of **10** has been printed and the control variable **counter** is incremented to **12**, causing the loop-continuation test to fail and repetition to terminate. The program continues by performing the first statement after the **For/Next** structure. (In this case, procedure **Main** terminates, because the program reaches the **End Sub** statement on line 16.)

3.12 Example: Using the For/Next Structure to Compute Compound Interest

The next example computes compound interest, using the **For/Next** structure. Consider the following problem:

A person invests $1000.00 in a savings account that yields 5% interest. Assuming that all interest is left on deposit, calculate and print the amount of money in the account at the end of each year, over a period of 10 years. To determine these amounts, use the following formula:

$$a = p (1 + r)^n$$

where

> *p* is the original amount invested (i.e., the principal)
> *r* is the annual interest rate (e.g., .05 stands for 5%)
> *n* is the number of years
> *a* is the amount on deposit at the end of the *n*th year.

This problem involves a loop that performs the indicated calculation for each of the 10 years that the money remains on deposit. The solution is shown in Fig. 3.4.

Line 9 declares two **Decimal** variables. Type **Decimal** is used for monetary calculations. Line 10 declares **rate** as type **Double**, and lines 14–15 initialize **principal** to **1000.00** and **rate** to **0.05** (i.e., 5%).

The body of the **For/Next** structure is executed 10 times, varying control variable **year** from **1** to **10** in increments of **1**. Line 21 performs the calculation from statement of the problem, that is,

$$a = p\,(1 + r)^{\,n}$$

where *a* is **amount**, *p* is **principal**, *r* is **rate** and *n* is **year**.

```
1   ' Fig. 3.4: Interest.vb
2   ' Calculating compound interest.
3
4   Imports System.Windows.Forms
5
6   Module modInterest
7
8      Sub Main()
9         Dim amount, principal As Decimal  ' dollar amounts
10        Dim rate As Double                ' interest rate
11        Dim year As Integer               ' year counter
12        Dim output As String              ' amount after each year
13
14        principal = 1000.00
15        rate = 0.05
16
17        output = "Year" & vbTab & "Amount on deposit" & vbCrLf
18
19        ' calculate amount after each year
20        For year = 1 To 10
21           amount = principal * (1 + rate) ^ year
22           output &= year & vbTab & _
23              String.Format("{0:C}", amount) & vbCrLf
24        Next
25
26        ' display output
27        MessageBox.Show(output, "Compound Interest", _
28           MessageBoxButtons.OK, MessageBoxIcon.Information)
29
30     End Sub ' Main
31
32  End Module ' modInterest
```

Fig. 3.4   **For/Next** structure used to calculate compound interest. (Part 1 of 2.)

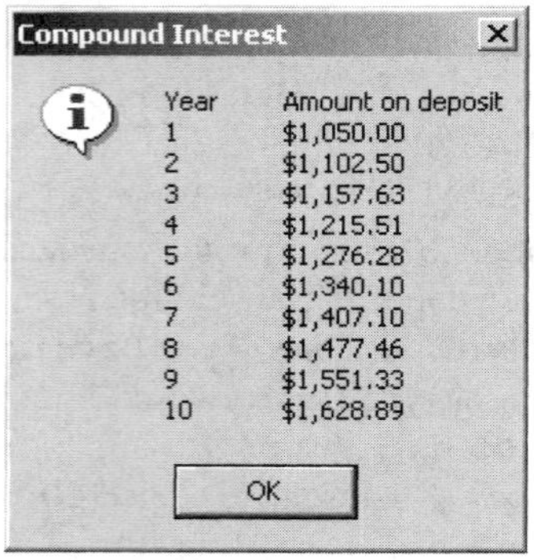

Fig. 3.4   For/Next structure used to calculate compound interest. (Part 2 of 2.)

Lines 22–23 append additional text to the end of **String output**. The text includes the current value of **year**, a tab character (**vbTab**) to position the cursor to the second column, the result of the method call **String.Format("{0:C}", amount)** and, finally, a newline character (**vbCrLf**) to start the next output on the next line. The first argument passed to **Format** is the format string. Previously in the text, we have seen **String**s containing **{0}**, **{1}** and so on, where the digit within the braces indicates the argument being displayed. In more complicated format strings, such as **"{0:C}"**, the first digit (**0**) serves the same purpose. The information specified after the colon (**:**) is called the *formatting code*. The **C** (for "currency") *formatting code* indicates that its corresponding argument (**amount**) should be displayed in monetary format. Figure 3.5 explains several formatting codes; a complete list can be found in the MSDN documentation "Standard Numeric Format Strings." All formatting codes are case insensitive. Note that format codes **D** and **X** can be used only with integer values. [*Note*: Method **Format** uses .NET's string formatting codes to represent numeric and monetary values according to the user's *localization settings*.[1] For example, in the United States, an amount would be expressed in dollars (e.g., **$634,307.08**), while in Malaysia, the amount would be expressed in ringgits (e.g., **R634.307,08**).]

Format Code	Description
c	Currency. Precedes the number with **$**, separates every three digits with commas and sets the number of decimal places to two.

Fig. 3.5   Formatting codes for **String**s. (Part 1 of 2.)

---

1. Localization is the customization of software (e.g., an operating system) to display information by means of the customs and languages of a geographical region. Localization settings can be customized through the **Start Menu** by selecting **Control Panel > Regional and Language Options > Regional Options** in Windows XP and by selecting **Control Panel > Regional Options** in Windows 2000.

Format Code	Description
E	Scientific notation. Displays one digit to the left of the decimal point and six digits to the right of the decimal point, followed by the character **E** and a three-digit integer representing the exponent of a power of 10. For example, **956.2** is formatted as **9.562000E+002**.
F	Fixed point. Sets the number of decimal places to two.
G	General. Visual Basic chooses either **E** or **F** for you, depending on which representation generates a shorter string.
D	Decimal integer. Displays an integer as a whole number in standard base-10 format.
N	Number. Separates every three digits with a comma and sets the number of decimal places to two.
X	Hexadecimal integer. Displays the integer in hexadecimal (base-16) notation.

Fig. 3.5   Formatting codes for **String**s. (Part 2 of 2.)

Variables **amount** and **principal** are of type **Decimal**. We use this type because we are dealing with fractional parts of dollars and need a type that allows precise calculations with monetary amounts; **Single** and **Double** do not.

Good Programming Practice 3.1

*Do not use variables of type **Single** or **Double** to perform precise monetary calculations. The imprecision of floating-point numbers can cause errors that result in incorrect monetary values. Use the data type **Decimal** for monetary calculations.*

Variable **rate** is also of type **Double**, because it is used in the calculation **1.0 + rate**, which appears as the right operand of the exponentiation operator. In fact, this calculation produces the same result each time through the loop, so performing the calculation in the body of the **For/Next** loop is wasteful.

Performance Tip 3.1

Avoid placing inside a loop the calculation of an expression whose value does not change each time through the loop. Such an expression should be evaluated only once, prior to the loop.

The FCL and Visual Basic .NET allow multiple procedures with the same name to be defined. Programmers often use this technique, known as *procedure overloading*, to define several procedures that perform similar actions, but take a different set of arguments. One example of the use of procedure overloading is method **MessageBox.Show**. In a previous example, we have provided only one argument to this method—a **String** to be displayed in a message dialog. Figure 3.4 uses a version of method **MessageBox.Show** (lines 27–28) that takes four arguments. The dialog in the output of Fig. 3.4 illustrates the four arguments. The first argument is the message to display. The second argument is the string to display in the dialog's title bar. The third argument is a value indicating which button(s) to display. The fourth argument indicates which icon to display to the left of the message. Figures 3.6 and 3.7

provide a listing of the **MessageBoxButtons** and **MessageBoxIcon** choices. Information about other versions of method **MessageBox.Show** can be found in the MSDN documentation provided with Visual Studio .NET. We discuss procedure overloading in more detail in Chapter 4, Procedures and Arrays.

MessageBoxIcon Constants	Icon	Description
MessageBoxIcon.Exclamation		Icon containing an exclamation point. Typically used to warn the user of potential problems.
MessageBoxIcon.Information		Icon containing the letter "i." Typically used to display information about the state of the application.
MessageBoxIcon.Question		Icon containing a question mark. Typically used to ask the user a question.
MessageBoxIcon.Error		Icon containing an ∞ in a red circle. Typically used to alert the user of errors or critical situations.

Fig. 3.6   Message-dialog icon constants.

MessageBoxButtons constants	Description
MessageBoxButtons.OK	**OK** button. Allows the user to acknowledge a message. Included by default.
MessageBoxButtons.OKCancel	**OK** and **Cancel** buttons. Allows the user to either continue or cancel an operation.
MessageBoxButtons.YesNo	**Yes** and **No** buttons. Allows the user to respond to a question.
MessageBoxButtons.YesNoCancel	**Yes**, **No** and **Cancel** buttons. Allows the user to respond to a question or cancel an operation.
MessageBoxButtons.RetryCancel	**Retry** and **Cancel** buttons. Typically used to allow the user either to retry or to cancel an operation that has failed.
MessageBoxButtons.AbortRetryIgnore	**Abort**, **Retry** and **Ignore** buttons. When one of a series of operations has failed, these buttons allow the user to abort the entire sequence, retry the failed operation, or ignore the failed operation and continue.

Fig. 3.7   Message-dialog button constants.

3.13 Select Case Multiple-Selection Structure

Occasionally, an algorithm contains a series of decisions in which the algorithm tests a variable or expression separately for each value that the variable or expression might assume. The algorithm then takes different actions based on those values. Visual Basic provides the **Select Case** *multiple-selection structure* to handle such decision making. The program in Fig. 3.8 uses a **Select Case** structure to count the number of different letter grades on an exam. Assume that the exam is graded as follows: 90 and above is an "A," 80–89 is a "B," 70–79 is a "C," 60–69 is a "D" and 0–59 is an "F." The instructor generously gives a minimum grade of 10 for students who were present for the exam. Students not present for the exam receive a 0.

Line 7 in Fig. 3.8 declares variable **grade** as type **Integer**. This variable stores each grade that is input. Lines 8–12 declare variables that store the total number grades of each type. Lines 18–57 use a **While** loop to control repetition.

Line 20,

> **Select Case grade**

begins the **Select Case** structure. The expression following the keywords **Select Case** is called the *controlling expression*. The controlling expression (i.e., the value of **grade**) is compared sequentially with each **Case**. If a matching **Case** is found, the code in the **Case** executes, and program control proceeds to the first statement after the **Select Case** structure (line 55).

Common Programming Error 3.1

*Duplicate **Case** statements are logic errors. At execution time, the first matching **Case** statement is executed.*

The first **Case** statement (line 22) determines whether the value of **grade** is exactly equal to **100**. The next **Case** statement (line 27) determines whether **grade** is between **90** and **99**, inclusive. Keyword **To** specifies the range. Lines 31–44 use this keyword to present a series of similar **Case**s.

Common Programming Error 3.2

*If the value on the left side of the **To** keyword in a **Case** statement is larger than the value on the right side, the **Case** statement is ignored during program execution, potentially causing a logic error.*

```
1   ' Fig. 3.8: SelectTest.vb
2   ' Using the Select Case structure.
3
4   Module modEnterGrades
5
6      Sub Main()
7         Dim grade As Integer = 0 ' one grade
8         Dim aCount As Integer = 0 ' number of As
9         Dim bCount As Integer = 0 ' number of Bs
10        Dim cCount As Integer = 0 ' number of Cs
11        Dim dCount As Integer = 0 ' number of Ds
```

Fig. 3.8   **Select Case** structure used to count grades. (Part 1 of 3.)

```
12          Dim fCount As Integer = 0 ' number of Fs
13
14          Console.Write("Enter a grade, -1 to quit: ")
15          grade = Console.ReadLine()
16
17          ' input and process grades
18          While grade <> -1
19
20              Select Case grade      ' determine which grade was input
21
22                  Case 100           ' student scored 100
23                      Console.WriteLine("Perfect Score!" & vbCrLf & _
24                          "Letter grade: A" & vbCrLf)
25                      aCount += 1
26
27                  Case 90 To 99      ' student scored 90-99
28                      Console.WriteLine("Letter Grade: A" & vbCrLf)
29                      aCount += 1
30
31                  Case 80 To 89      ' student scored 80-89
32                      Console.WriteLine("Letter Grade: B" & vbCrLf)
33                      bCount += 1
34
35                  Case 70 To 79      ' student scored 70-79
36                      Console.WriteLine("Letter Grade: C" & vbCrLf)
37                      cCount += 1
38
39                  Case 60 To 69      ' student scored 60-69
40                      Console.WriteLine("Letter Grade: D" & vbCrLf)
41                      dCount += 1
42
43                  ' student scored 0 or 10-59 (10 points for attendance)
44                  Case 0, 10 To 59
45                      Console.WriteLine("Letter Grade: F" & vbCrLf)
46                      fCount += 1
47
48                  Case Else
49
50                      ' alert user that invalid grade was entered
51                      Console.WriteLine("Invalid Input. " & _
52                          "Please enter a valid grade." & vbCrLf)
53              End Select
54
55              Console.Write("Enter a grade, -1 to quit: ")
56              grade = Console.ReadLine()
57          End While
58
59          ' display count of each letter grade
60          Console.WriteLine(vbCrLf & _
61              "Totals for each letter grade are: " & vbCrLf & _
62              "A: " & aCount & vbCrLf & "B: " & bCount _
63              & vbCrLf & "C: " & cCount & vbCrLf & "D: " & _
64              dCount & vbCrLf & "F: " & fCount)
```

Fig. 3.8   **Select Case** structure used to count grades. (Part 2 of 3.)

```
65
66      End Sub ' Main
67
68  End Module ' modEnterGrades
```

```
Enter a grade, -1 to quit: 84
Letter Grade: B

Enter a grade, -1 to quit: 100
Perfect Score!
Letter grade: A

Enter a grade, -1 to quit: 3000
Invalid Input. Please enter a valid grade.

Enter a grade, -1 to quit: 95
Letter Grade: A

Enter a grade, -1 to quit: 78
Letter Grade: C

Enter a grade, -1 to quit: 64
Letter Grade: D

Enter a grade, -1 to quit: 10
Letter Grade: F

Enter a grade, -1 to quit: -1

Totals for each letter grade are:
A: 2
B: 1
C: 1
D: 1
F: 1
```

Fig. 3.8   Select Case structure used to count grades. (Part 3 of 3.)

When multiple values are tested in a **Case** statement, they are separated by commas. On line 44, either **0** or any value in the range **10** to **59**, inclusive, matches to this **Case**. Line 48 contains the optional **Case Else**, which is executed when the input does not match the controlling expression in any of the previous **Case**s. **Case Else** commonly is used to check for invalid input. When employed, the **Case Else** must be the last **Case**. The required **End Select** keywords terminate the **Select Case** structure.

Common Programming Error 3.3

*When using the optional **Case Else** statement in a **Select Case** structure, failure to place the **Case Else** as the last **Case** is a syntax error.*

Case statements also can use relational operators to determine whether the controlling expression satisfies a condition. For example,

```
Case Is < 0
```

uses keyword *Is* along with the relational operator **<** to test for values less than **0**.

Testing and Debugging Tip 3.1

*Provide a **Case Else** in **Select Case** structures. **Case**s not handled in a **Select Case** structure are ignored unless a **Case Else** is provided. The inclusion of a **Case Else** statement facilitates the processing of exceptional conditions. In some situations, no **Case Else** processing is needed.*

3.14 Using the **Exit** Keyword in a Repetition Structure

The **Exit Do**, **Exit While** and **Exit For** statements alter the flow of control by causing immediate exit from a repetition structure. The **Exit Do** statement can be executed in a **Do While/Loop, Do/Loop While, Do Until/Loop** or **Do/Loop Until** structure and causes the program to exit immediately from that repetition structure. Similarly, the **Exit For** and **Exit While** statements cause immediate exit from **For/Next** and **While** loops, respectively. Execution continues with the first statement that follows the repetition structure. Figure 3.9 demonstrates the **Exit For**, **Exit Do** and **Exit While** statements in various repetition structures.

```
1    ' Fig. 3.9: ExitTest.vb
2    ' Using the Exit keyword in repetition structures.
3
4    Imports System.Windows.Forms
5
6    Module modExitTest
7
8       Sub Main()
9          Dim output As String
10         Dim counter As Integer
11
12         For counter = 1 To 10
13
14            ' skip remaining code in loop only if counter = 3
15            If counter = 3 Then
16               Exit For
17            End If
18
19         Next
20
21         output = "counter = " & counter & _
22            " after exiting For/Next structure" & vbCrLf
23
24         Do Until counter > 10
25
26            ' skip remaining code in loop only if counter = 5
27            If counter = 5 Then
28               Exit Do
29            End If
```

Fig. 3.9   Exit keyword in repetition structures. (Part 1 of 2.)

```
30
31              counter += 1
32          Loop
33
34          output &= "counter = " & counter & _
35              " after exiting Do Until/Loop structure" & vbCrLf
36
37          While counter <= 10
38
39              ' skip remaining code in loop only if counter = 7
40              If counter = 7 Then
41                 Exit While
42              End If
43
44              counter += 1
45          End While
46
47          output &= "counter = " & counter & _
48              " after exiting While structure"
49
50          MessageBox.Show(output, "Exit Test", _
51              MessageBoxButtons.OK, MessageBoxIcon.Information)
52      End Sub ' Main
53
54  End Module ' modExitTest
```

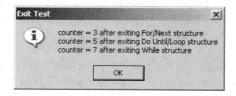

Fig. 3.9   Exit keyword in repetition structures. (Part 2 of 2.)

The header of the **For/Next** structure (line 12) indicates that the body of the loop should execute 10 times. During each execution, the **If/Then** structure (lines 15–17) determines if the control variable, **counter**, is equal to **3**. If so, the **Exit For** statement (line 16) executes. Thus, as the body of the **For/Next** structure executes for the third time (i.e, **counter** is **3**), the **Exit For** statement terminates execution of the loop. Program control then proceeds to the assignment statement (lines 21–22), which appends the current value of **counter** to **String** variable **output**.

The header of the **Do Until/Loop** structure (line 24) indicates that the loop should continue executing until **counter** is greater than **10**. (Note that **counter** is **3** when the **Do Until/Loop** structure begins executing.) When **counter** has the values **3** and **4**, the body of the **If/Then** structure (lines 27–29) does not execute, and **counter** is incremented (line 31). However, when **counter** is **5**, the **Exit Do** statement (line 28) executes, terminating the loop. The assignment statement (lines 34–35) appends the value of **counter** to **String** variable **output**. Note that the program does not increment **counter** (line 31) after the **Exit Do** statement executes.

The **While** structure (lines 37–45) behaves similarly to the **Do While/Loop**. In this case, the value of **counter** is **5** when the loop begins executing. When **counter** is **7**, the **Exit While** statement (line 41) executes, terminating execution of the **While** structure. Lines 47–48 append the final value of **counter** to **String** variable **output**, which is displayed in a message dialog (lines 50–51).

Software Engineering Observation 3.1

*Some programmers feel that **Exit Do**, **Exit While** and **Exit For** violate the principles of structured programming.*

Software Engineering Observation 3.2

Debates abound regarding the relative importance of quality software engineering and program performance. Often, one of these goals is accomplished at the expense of the other. For all but the most performance-intensive situations, apply the following guidelines: First, make your code simple and correct; then make it fast and small, but only if necessary.

3.15 Logical Operators

So far, we have studied only *simple conditions*, such as **count <= 10**, **total > 1000** and **number <> sentinelValue**. Each selection and repetition structure evaluated only one condition with one of the operators **>**, **<**, **>=**, **<=**, **=** and **<>**. To make a decision that relied on the evaluation of multiple conditions, we performed these tests in separate statements or in nested **If/Then** or **If/Then/Else** structures.

To handle multiple conditions more efficiently, Visual Basic provides *logical operators* that can be used to form complex conditions by combining simple ones. The logical operators are **AndAlso**, **And**, **OrElse**, **Or**, **Xor** and **Not**. We consider examples that use each of these operators.

Suppose we wish to ensure that two conditions are *both* true in a program before a certain path of execution is chosen. In such a case, we can use the logical **AndAlso** operator as follows:

```
If gender = "F" AndAlso age >= 65 Then
   seniorFemales += 1
End If
```

This **If/Then** statement contains two simple conditions. The condition **gender = "F"** determines whether a person is female, and the condition **age >= 65** determines whether a person is a senior citizen. The two simple conditions are evaluated first, because the precedences of **=** and **>=** are both higher than the precedence of **AndAlso**. The **If/Then** statement then considers the combined condition

```
gender = "F" AndAlso age >= 65
```

This condition evaluates to true *if and only if* both of the simple conditions are true. When this combined condition is true, the count of **seniorFemales** is incremented by **1**. However, if either or both of the simple conditions are false, the program skips the incrementation step and proceeds to the statement following the **If/Then** structure. The readability of the preceding combined condition can be improved by adding redundant (i.e., unnecessary) parentheses:

```
(gender = "F") AndAlso (age >= 65)
```

Figure 3.10 illustrates the effect of using the **AndAlso** operator with two expressions. The table lists all four possible combinations of true and false values for *expression1* and *expression2*. Such tables often are called *truth tables*. Visual Basic evaluates to true or false expressions that include relational operators, equality operators and logical operators.

Now let us consider the **OrElse** operator. Suppose we wish to ensure that either *or* both of two conditions are true before we choose a certain path of execution. We use the **OrElse** operator in the following program segment:

```
If (semesterAverage >= 90 OrElse finalExam >= 90) Then
   Console.WriteLine("Student grade is A")
End If
```

This statement also contains two simple conditions. The condition **semesterAverage >= 90** is evaluated to determine whether the student deserves an "A" in the course because of an outstanding performance throughout the semester. The condition **finalExam >= 90** is evaluated to determine whether the student deserves an "A" in the course because of an outstanding performance on the final exam. The **If/Then** statement then considers the combined condition

```
(semesterAverage >= 90 OrElse finalExam >= 90)
```

and awards the student an "A" if either or both of the conditions are true. Note that the text "**Student grade is A**" is *always* printed, unless both of the conditions are false. Figure 3.11 provides a truth table for the **OrElse** operator.

expression1	expression2	expression1 AndAlso expression2
False	*False*	*False*
False	*True*	*False*
True	*False*	*False*
True	*True*	*True*

Fig. 3.10 Truth table for the **AndAlso** operator.

expression1	expression2	expression1 OrElse expression2
False	*False*	*False*
False	*True*	*True*
True	*False*	*True*
True	*True*	*True*

Fig. 3.11 Truth table for the **OrElse** operator.

The **AndAlso** operator has a higher precedence than the **OrElse** operator. An expression containing **AndAlso** or **OrElse** operators is evaluated only until truth or falsity is known. For example, evaluation of the expression

```
(gender = "F" AndAlso age >= 65)
```

stops immediately if **gender** is not equal to **"F"** (i.e., the entire expression is false); the evaluation of the second expression is irrelevant because the first condition is false. Evaluation of the second condition occurs if and only if **gender** is equal to **"F"** (i.e., the entire expression could still be true if the condition **age >= 65** is true). This performance feature for the evaluation of **AndAlso** and **OrElse** expressions is called *short-circuit evaluation*.

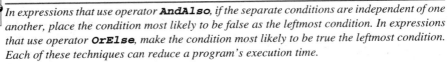

Performance Tip 3.2

*In expressions that use operator **AndAlso**, if the separate conditions are independent of one another, place the condition most likely to be false as the leftmost condition. In expressions that use operator **OrElse**, make the condition most likely to be true the leftmost condition. Each of these techniques can reduce a program's execution time.*

The *logical AND operator without short-circuit evaluation* (**And**) and the *logical inclusive OR operator without short-circuit evaluation* (**Or**) are similar to the **AndAlso** and **OrElse** operators, respectively, with one exception: The **And** and **Or** logical operators always evaluate both of their operands. No short-circuit evaluation occurs when **And** and **Or** are employed. For example, the expression

```
(gender = "F" And age >= 65)
```

evaluates **age >= 65**, even if **gender** is not equal to **"F"**.

Normally, there is no compelling reason to use the **And** and **Or** operators instead of **AndAlso** and **OrElse**. However, some programmers make use of them when the right operand of a condition produces a *side effect* (such as a modification of a variable's value) or when the right operand includes a required method call, as in the following program segment:

```
Console.WriteLine("How old are you?")
If (gender = "F" And Console.ReadLine() >= 65) Then
    Console.WriteLine("You are a female senior citizen.")
End If
```

Here, the **And** operator guarantees that the condition **Console.ReadLine() >= 65** is evaluated, so **ReadLine** is called regardless of whether the overall expression is true. It would be better to write this code as two separate statements; the first would store the result of **Console.ReadLine()** in a variable, and the second would use that variable with the **AndAlso** operator in the condition.

Testing and Debugging Tip 3.2

Avoid expressions with side effects in conditions, as side effects often cause subtle errors.

A condition containing the *logical exclusive OR* (**Xor**) operator is true *if and only if one of its operands results in a true value and the other results in a false value.* If both operands are true or both are false, the entire condition is false. Figure 3.12 presents a truth table for the logical exclusive OR operator (**Xor**). This operator always evaluates both of its operands (i.e., there is no short-circuit evaluation).

expression1	expression2	expression1 Xor expression2
False	False	False
False	True	True
True	False	True
True	True	False

Fig. 3.12 Truth table for the logical exclusive OR (**Xor**) operator.

Visual Basic's **Not** (logical negation) operator enables a programmer to "reverse" the meaning of a condition. Unlike the logical operators **AndAlso**, **And**, **OrElse**, **Or** and **Xor**, which each combine two conditions (i.e., they are all binary operators), the logical negation operator is a unary operator, requiring only one operand. The logical negation operator is placed before a condition to choose a path of execution if the original condition (without the logical negation operator) is false. The following program segment demonstrates the logical negation operator:

```
If Not (grade = sentinelValue) Then
    Console.WriteLine("The next grade is " & grade)
End If
```

The parentheses around the condition **grade = sentinelValue** are necessary, because the logical negation operator (**Not**) has a higher precedence than the equality operator. Figure 3.13 provides a truth table for the logical negation operator.

In most cases, the programmer can avoid the use of logical negation by expressing the condition differently with relational or equality operators. For example, the preceding statement can be written as follows:

```
If grade <> sentinelValue Then
    Console.WriteLine("The next grade is " & grade)
End If
```

This flexibility aids programmers in expressing conditions more naturally. The console application in Fig. 3.14 demonstrates the use of the logical operators by displaying their truth tables.

expression	Not expression
False	True
True	False

Fig. 3.13 Truth table for the **Not** operator (logical NOT).

```
1   ' Fig. 3.14: LogicalOperator.vb
2   ' Using logical operators.
3
4   Module modLogicalOperator
5
6      Sub Main()
7
8         ' create truth table for AndAlso
9         Console.Write("AndAlso" & vbCrLf & _
10           "False AndAlso False: " & (False AndAlso False) & _
11           vbCrLf & "False AndAlso True: " & _
12           (False AndAlso True) & vbCrLf & _
13           "True AndAlso False: " & (True AndAlso False) & _
14           vbCrLf & "True AndAlso True: " & _
15           (True AndAlso True) & vbCrLf & vbCrLf)
16
17         ' create truth table for OrElse
18         Console.Write("OrElse" & vbCrLf & "False OrElse False: " & _
19           (False OrElse False) & vbCrLf & "False OrElse True: " & _
20           (False OrElse True) & vbCrLf & "True OrElse False: " & _
21           (True OrElse False) & vbCrLf & "True OrElse True: " & _
22           (True OrElse True) & vbCrLf & vbCrLf)
23
24         ' create truth table for And
25         Console.Write("And" & vbCrLf & "False And False: " & _
26           (False And False) & vbCrLf & "False And True: " & _
27           (False And True) & vbCrLf & "True And False: " & _
28           (True And False) & vbCrLf & "True And True: " & _
29           (True And True) & vbCrLf & vbCrLf)
30
31         ' create truth table for Or
32         Console.Write("Or" & vbCrLf & "False Or False: " & _
33           (False Or False) & vbCrLf & "False Or True: " & _
34           (False Or True) & vbCrLf & "True Or False: " & _
35           (True Or False) & vbCrLf & "True Or True: " & _
36           (True Or True) & vbCrLf & vbCrLf)
37
38         ' create truth table for Xor
39         Console.Write("Xor" & vbCrLf & "False Xor False: " & _
40           (False Xor False) & vbCrLf & "False Xor True: " & _
41           (False Xor True) & vbCrLf & "True Xor False: " & _
42           (True Xor False) & vbCrLf & "True Xor True: " & _
43           (True Xor True) & vbCrLf & vbCrLf)
44
45         ' create truth table for Not
46         Console.Write("Not" & vbCrLf & "Not False: " & _
47           (Not False) & vbCrLf & "Not True: " & (Not True) & _
48           vbCrLf & vbCrLf)
49
50      End Sub ' Main
51
52   End Module ' modLogicalOperator
```

Fig. 3.14 Logical-operator truth tables. (Part 1 of 2.)

```
AndAlso
False AndAlso False: False
False AndAlso True: False
True AndAlso False: False
True AndAlso True: True

OrElse
False OrElse False: False
False OrElse True: True
True OrElse False: True
True OrElse True: True

And
False And False: False
False And True: False
True And False: False
True and True: True

Or
False Or False: False
False Or True: True
True Or False: True
True Or True: True

Xor
False Xor False: False
False Xor True: True
True Xor False: True
True Xor True: False

Not
Not False: True
Not True: False
```

Fig. 3.14   Logical-operator truth tables. (Part 2 of 2.)

Lines 9–15 demonstrate operator **AndAlso**; lines 18–22 demonstrate operator **OrElse**. The remainder of procedure **Main** demonstrates the **And**, **Or**, **Xor** and **Not** operators. We use keywords **True** and **False** in the program to specify values of the **Boolean** data type. Notice that when a **Boolean** value is concatenated to a **String**, Visual Basic concatenates the string **"False"** or **"True"** on the basis of the **Boolean**'s value.

The chart in Fig. 3.15 displays the precedence of the Visual Basic operators introduced thus far. The operators are shown from top to bottom in decreasing order of precedence.

Operators	Type
( )	parentheses
^	exponentiation

Fig. 3.15   Precedence of the operators discussed so far. (Part 1 of 2.)

Operators	Type
+ -	unary plus and minus
* /	multiplicative
\	integer division
Mod	modulus
+ -	additive
&	concatenation
< <= > >= = <>	relational and equality
Not	logical NOT
And AndAlso	logical AND
Or OrElse	logical inclusive OR
Xor	logical exclusive OR

Fig. 3.15   Precedence of the operators discussed so far. (Part 2 of 2.)

3.16 Introduction to Windows Application Programming

Today, users demand software with rich graphical user interfaces (GUIs) that allow them to click buttons, select items from menus and much more. In this chapter and the previous one, we have created console applications. However, the vast majority of Visual Basic programs used in industry are Windows applications with GUIs. For this reason, we have chosen to introduce Windows applications early in the book, although doing so exposes some concepts that cannot be explained fully until later chapters.

In Chapter 2, we introduced the concept of visual programming, which allows programmers to create GUIs without writing any program code. In this section, we combine visual programming with the conventional programming techniques introduced in this chapter and the previous chapter. Through this combination, we can enhance considerably the Windows application introduced in Chapter 2.

Before proceeding, load the project **ASimpleProgram** from Chapter 2 into the IDE, and change the **(Name)** properties of the form, label and picture box to **FrmASimpleProgram**, **lblWelcome** and **picBug**, respectively. The modification of these names enables us easily to identify the form and its controls in the program code. [*Note*: In this section, we change the file name from **Form1.vb** to **ASimpleProgram.vb**, to enhance clarity.]

 Good Programming Practice 3.2

The prefixes **Frm**, **lbl** *and* **pic** *allow forms, labels and picture boxes; respectively, easily to be identified easily in program code.*

With visual programming, the IDE generates the program code that creates the GUI. This code contains instructions for creating the form and every control on it. Unlike with a console application, a Windows application's program code is not displayed initially in the editor window. Once the program's project (e.g., **ASimpleProgram**) is opened in the IDE, the program code can be viewed by selecting **View > Code**. Figure 3.16 shows the code editor displaying the program code.

Notice that no module is present. Instead, Windows applications use classes. We already have seen examples of classes, such as **Console** and **MessageBox**, which are defined within the .NET Framework Class Library (FCL). Like modules, classes are logical groupings of procedures and data that simplify program organization. Modules are discussed in detail in Chapter 4, Procedures. In-depth coverage of classes is provided in Chapter 5, Object-Based Programming.

Every Windows application consists of at least one class that *Inherits* from class *Form* (which represents a form) in the FCL's **System.Windows.Forms** namespace. The keyword **Class** begins a class definition and is followed immediately by the class name (**FrmASimpleProgram**). Recall that the form's name is set by means of the **(Name)** property. Keyword **Inherits** indicates that the class **FrmASimpleProgram** inherits existing pieces from another class.

The class from which **FrmASimpleProgram** inherits—here, **System.Windows.Forms.Form**—appears to the right of the **Inherits** keyword. In this inheritance relationship, **Form** is called the *superclass*, or *base class*, and **FrmASimpleProgram** is called the *subclass*, or *derived class*. The use of inheritance results in a **FrmASimpleProgram** class definition that has the *attributes* (data) and *behaviors* (methods) of class **Form**. We discuss the significance of the keyword **Public** in Chapter 5.

A key benefit of inheriting from class **Form** is that someone else previously has defined "what it means to be a form." The Windows operating system expects every window (e.g., a form) to have certain capabilities (attributes and behaviors). However, because class **Form** already provides those capabilities, programmers do not need to "reinvent the wheel" by defining all those capabilities themselves. In fact, class **Form** has over 400 methods! In our programs up to this point, we have used only one method (i.e., **Main**), so you can imagine how much work went into creating class **Form**. The use of **Inherits** to extend from class **Form** enables programmers to create forms quickly and easily.

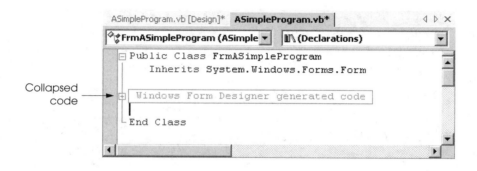

Fig. 3.16   IDE showing code for the program in Fig. 2.14.

In the editor window (Fig. 3.16), notice the text **Windows Form Designer generated code**, which is colored gray and has a plus box next to it. The plus box indicates that this section of code is *collapsed*. Although collapsed code is not visible, it is still part of the program. Code collapsing allows programmers to hide code in the editor, so that they can focus on key code segments. Notice that the entire class definition also can be collapsed, by clicking the minus box to the left of **Public**. In Fig. 3.16, the description to the right of the plus box indicates that the collapsed code was created by the *Windows Form Designer* (i.e., the part of the IDE that creates the code for the GUI). This collapsed code contains the code created by the IDE for the form and its controls, as well as code that enables the program to run. Click the plus box to view the code.

Upon initial inspection, the *expanded code* (Fig. 3.17) appears complex. This code is created by the IDE and normally is not edited by the programmer. However, we feel that it is important for readers to see the code that is generated by the IDE, even though much of the code is not explained until later in the book. This type of code is present in every Windows application. Allowing the IDE to create this code saves the programmer considerable development time. If the IDE did not provide the code, the programmer would have to write it, which would require a considerable amount of time. The vast majority of the code shown has not been introduced yet, so you are not expected to understand how it works. However, certain programming constructs, such as comments and control structures, should be familiar. Our explanation of this code will enable us to discuss visual programming in greater detail. As you continue to study Visual Basic, especially in Chapters 5–10, the purpose of this code will become clearer.

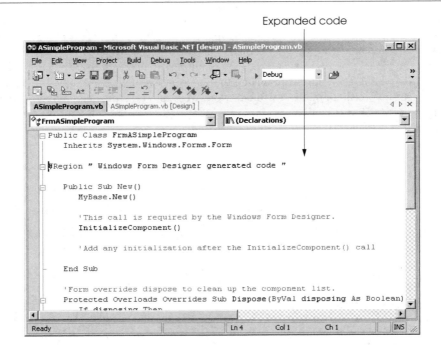

Fig. 3.17 Windows Form Designer-generated code when expanded.

When we created this application in Chapter 2, we used the **Properties** window to set properties for the form, label and picture box. Once a property was set, the form or control was updated immediately. Forms and controls contain a set of *default properties*, which are displayed initially in the **Properties** window when a form or control is created. These default properties provide the initial characteristics of a form or control when it is created. When a control, such as a label, is placed on the form, the IDE adds code to the class (e.g., `FrmASimpleProgram`) that creates the control and that sets some of the control's property values, such as the name of the control and its location on the form. Figure 3.18 shows a portion of the code generated by the IDE for setting the label's (i.e., `lblWelcome`'s) properties, including the label's **Font**, **Location**, **Name**, **Text** and **TextAlign** properties. Recall from Chapter 2 that we explicitly set values for the label's **Text** and **TextAlign** properties. Other properties, such as **Location**, are set only when the label is placed on the form.

The values assigned to the properties are based on the values in the **Properties** window. We now demonstrate how the IDE updates the Windows Form Designer–generated code created when a property value in the **Properties** window changes. During this process, we must switch between code view and design view. To switch views, select the corresponding tabs: **ASimpleProgram.vb** for code view and **ASimpleProgram.vb [Design]** for design view. Alternatively, you can select **View > Code** or **View > Designer**. Perform the following steps:

1. *Modify the file name.* First, change the name of the file from **Form1.vb** to **ASimpleProgram.vb** by clicking the file name in the **Solution Explorer** and changing the **File Name** property.

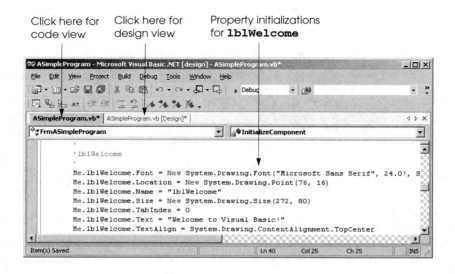

Fig. 3.18   Code generated by the IDE for `lblWelcome`.

2. *Modify the label control's* **Text** *property, using the* **Properties** *window.* Recall that properties can be changed in design view by clicking a form or control to select it and modifying the appropriate property in the **Properties** window. Change the **Text** property of the label to "**Deitel and Associates**" (Fig. 3.19).

3. *Examine the changes in code view.* Switch to code view, and examine the code. Notice that the label's **Text** property is now assigned the text that we entered in the **Properties** window (Fig. 3.20). When a property is changed in design mode, the Windows Form Designer updates the appropriate line of code in the class to reflect the new value.

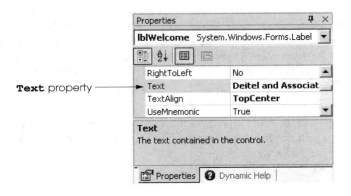

Text property ——

Fig. 3.19   **Properties** window as used to set a property value.

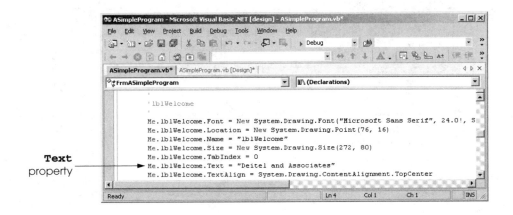

Text property ——

Fig. 3.20   Windows Form Designer-generated code reflecting new property values.

4. *Modify a property value in code view.* In the code-view editor, locate the three lines of comments indicating the initialization for **lblWelcome**, and change the **String** assigned to **Me.lblWelcome.Text** from "**Deitel and Associates**" to "**Visual Basic .NET**" (Fig. 3.21).Then switch to design mode. The label now displays the updated text, and the **Properties** window for **lblWelcome** displays the new **Text** value (Fig. 3.22). [*Note*: Property values should not be set using the techniques presented in this step. Here, we modify the property value in the IDE-generated code only as a demonstration of the relationship between program code and the Windows Form Designer.]

5. *Change the label's* **Text** *property at runtime.* In the previous steps, we set properties at design time. Often, however, it is necessary to modify a property while a program is running. For example, to display the result of a calculation, a label's text can be assigned a **String** containing the result. In console applications, such code is located in **Main**. In Windows applications, we must create a method that executes when the form is loaded into memory during program execution. Like **Main**, this method is invoked when the program is run. Double-clicking the form in design view adds a method named **FrmASimpleProgram_Load** to the class (Fig. 3.23). Notice that **FrmASimpleProgram_Load** is not part of the Windows Form Designer-generated code. Add the statement **lblWelcome.Text = "Visual Basic"** into the body of the method definition (Fig. 3.24). In Visual Basic, properties are accessed by placing the property name (i.e., **Text** in this case) after the class name (i.e., **lblWelcome** in this case), separated by the dot operator. This syntax is similar to that used when accessing class methods. Notice that the IntelliSense feature displays the **Text** property in the member list after the class name and dot operator have been typed (Fig. 3.23). In Chapter 5, Object-Based Programming, we discuss how programmers can create their own properties.

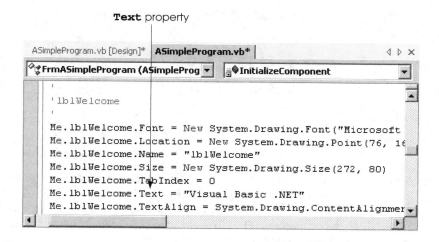

Text property

Fig. 3.21 Changing a property in the code-view editor.

Text property value

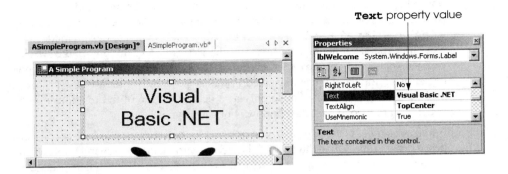

Fig. 3.22 New **Text** property value as reflected in design mode.

FrmASimpleProgram_Load method

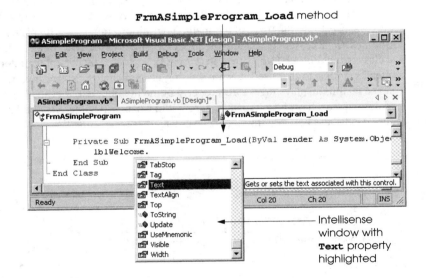

Intellisense window with **Text** property highlighted

Fig. 3.23 Adding program code to **FrmASimpleProgram_Load**.

6. *Examine the results of the* **FrmASimpleProgram_Load** *method.* Notice that the text in the label looks the same in **Design** mode as it did in Fig. 3.22. Note also that the **Property** window still displays the value "**Visual Basic .NET**" as the label's **Text** property. The IDE-generated code has not changed either. Select **Build > Build Solution** and **Debug > Start** to run the program. Once the form is displayed, the text in the label reflects the property assignment in **FrmASimpleProgram_Load** (Fig. 3.25).

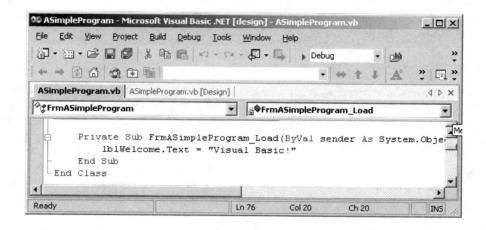

Fig. 3.24   Method `FrmASimpleProgram_Load` containing program code.

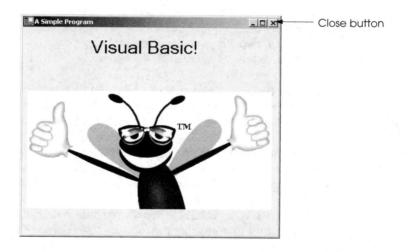

Fig. 3.25   Changing a property value at runtime.

7. *Terminate program execution.* Click the close button to terminate program execution. Once again, notice that both the label and the label's **Text** property contain the text **Visual Basic .NET**. The IDE-generated code also contains the text **Visual Basic .NET**, which is assigned to the label's **Text** property.

This chapter discussed how to compose programs from control structures that contain actions and decisions. In Chapter 4, Procedures and Arrays, we introduce another program-structuring unit, called the *procedure*. We will discuss how to compose programs by combining procedures that are composed of control structures. We also discuss how procedures promote software reusability. In Chapter 5, Object-Based Programming, we discuss in more detail another Visual Basic program-structuring unit, called the *class*. We then create objects from classes and proceed with our treatment of object-oriented programming—a key focus of this book.

3.17 Summary

The **If/Then** single-selection structure selects or ignores a single action (or a single group of actions), based on the truth or falsity of a condition. The **If/Then/Else** double-selection structure selects between two different actions (or groups of actions), based on the truth or falsity of a condition.

The **While** and **Do While/Loop** repetition structures allow the programmer to specify that an action is to be repeated while a specific condition remains true. Eventually, the condition in a **While**, **Do While/Loop** or **Do/Loop While** structure becomes false. At this point, the repetition terminates, and the first statement after the repetition structure executes.

The **Do Until/Loop** and **Do/Loop Until** repetition structures allow the programmer to specify that an action is to be repeated while a specific condition remains false. Eventually, the condition in a **Do Until/Loop** or **Do/Loop Until** structure becomes true. At this point, the repetition terminates, and the first statement after the repetition structure executes. The **For/Next** repetition structure handles the details of counter-controlled repetition. The required **To** keyword specifies the initial value and the final value of the control variable. The optional **Step** keyword specifies the increment. The **Exit Do**, **Exit While** and **Exit For** statements alter the flow of control by causing immediate exit from a repetition structure.

Visual Basic provides the **Select Case** multiple-selection structure so that a variable or expression may be tested separately for each value that the variable or expression might assume. The **Select Case** structure consists of a series of **Case** labels and an optional **Case Else**.

The logical operators are **AndAlso** (logical AND with short-circuit evaluation), **And** (logical AND without short-circuit evaluation), **OrElse** (logical inclusive OR with short-circuit evaluation), **Or** (logical inclusive OR without short-circuit evaluation), **Xor** (logical exclusive OR) and **Not** (logical NOT, also called logical negation).

With visual programming, the IDE actually generates program code that creates the GUI. This code contains instructions for creating the form and every control on it. Windows application code is contained in a class. Like modules, classes are logical groupings of procedures and data that simplify program organization.

Forms and controls contain a set of default properties, which are displayed initially in the **Properties** window when a form or control is selected. These default properties provide the initial characteristics that a form or control has when it is created. When a change is made in design mode, such as when a property value is changed, the Windows Form Designer creates code that implements the change. Often, it is necessary to modify a property while a program is running. In Windows applications, the code that implements the change is placed in a procedure that executes when the form is loaded, which can be created by double-clicking the form in design view.

Procedures and Arrays

Objectives

- To construct programs modularly from procedures.
- To understand the mechanisms used to pass information between procedures.
- To understand how the visibility of identifiers is limited to specific regions of programs.
- To understand how to write and use recursive procedures (procedures that call themselves).
- To introduce the array data structure.
- To declare and manipulate multidimensional arrays.

Form ever follows function.
Louis Henri Sullivan

E pluribus unum.
(One composed of many.)
Virgil

O! call back yesterday, bid time return.
William Shakespeare

Call me Ishmael.
Herman Melville

When you call me that, smile.
Owen Wister

Outline

4.1 Introduction

Most computer programs that solve real-world problems are much larger than the programs presented in the first few chapters of this text. Experience has shown that the best way to develop and maintain a large program is to construct it from small, manageable pieces. This technique is known as *divide and conquer*. In this chapter, we describe many key features of the Visual Basic language that facilitate the design, implementation, operation and maintenance of large programs.

This chapter also introduces data structures. *Arrays* are data structures consisting of data items of the same type. Arrays are "static" entities, in that they remain the same size once they are created. In this chapter we show how to create and access arrays. We then demonstrate how to create more sophisticated arrays that have multiple dimensions. Chapter 20, Data Structures and Collections, introduces dynamic data structures such as lists, queues, stacks and trees, which can grow and shrink as programs execute. We also introduce Visual Basic .NET's predefined data structures, that enable the programmer to use existing data structures for lists, queues, stacks and trees, rather than having to "reinvent the wheel."

4.2 Modules, Classes and Procedures

Visual Basic programs consist of many pieces, including modules and classes. The programmer combines new modules and classes with "prepackaged" classes available in the .NET Framework Class Library (FCL). These modules and classes are composed of smaller pieces called *procedures*. When procedures are contained in a class, we refer to them as *methods*.

The FCL provides a rich collection of classes and methods for performing common mathematical calculations, string manipulations, character manipulations, input/output operations, error checking and many other useful operations. This framework makes the programmer's job easier, because the methods provide many of the capabilities that programmers need. In earlier chapters, we introduced some FCL classes, such as **Console**, which provides methods for inputting and outputting data.

 Software Engineering Observation 4.1

> *When possible, use .NET Framework classes and methods instead of writing new classes and methods. This practice reduces program development time and helps prevent the introduction of new errors.*

Programmers write their own *programmer-defined procedures* to meet the unique requirements of a particular problem. Three types of procedures exist: **Sub** *procedures*, **Function** *procedures* and *event procedures*. Throughout this chapter, the term "procedure" refers to both **Sub** procedures and **Function** procedures, unless otherwise noted.

A procedure is *invoked* (i.e., made to perform its designated task) by a *procedure call*. The procedure call specifies the procedure name and provides information (as *arguments*) that the *callee* (i.e, the procedure being called) requires to do its job. When the procedure completes its task, it returns control to the *caller* (i.e., the *calling procedure*). In some cases, the procedure also returns a result to the caller. We will see momentarily how this *hiding of implementation details* promotes good software engineering.

4.3 Sub Procedures

The programs presented earlier in the book each contained at least one procedure definition (e.g., **Main**) that called FCL methods (such as **Console.WriteLine**) to accomplish the program's tasks. We now consider how to write customized procedures.

Consider the console application in Fig. 4.1, which uses a **Sub** procedure (invoked from the application's **Main** procedure) to print a worker's payment information.

```
1    ' Fig. 4.1: Payment.vb
2    ' Sub procedure that prints payment information.
3
4    Module modPayment
5
6       Sub Main()
7
8          ' call Sub procedure PrintPay four times
9          PrintPay(40, 10.5)
10         PrintPay(38, 21.75)
```

Fig. 4.1   **Sub** procedure for printing payment information. (Part 1 of 2.)

```
11            PrintPay(20, 13)
12            PrintPay(50, 14)
13
14      End Sub ' Main
15
16      ' print dollar amount earned in command window
17      Sub PrintPay(ByVal hours As Double, ByVal wage As Decimal)
18
19         ' pay = hours * wage
20         Console.WriteLine("The payment is {0:C}", hours * wage)
21      End Sub ' PrintPay
22
23   End Module ' modPayment
```

```
The payment is $420.00
The payment is $826.50
The payment is $260.00
The payment is $700.00
```

Fig. 4.1   **Sub** procedure for printing payment information. (Part 2 of 2.)

The program contains two *procedure definitions*. Lines 6–14 define **Sub** procedure **Main**, which executes when the console application is loaded. Lines 17–21 define **Sub** procedure **PrintPay**, which executes when it is *invoked*, or *called*, from another procedure—in this case, **Main**.

Main makes four calls (lines 9–12) to **Sub** procedure **PrintPay**, causing **PrintPay** to execute four times. Although the procedure arguments in this case are constants, arguments also can be variables or expressions. For example, the statement

```
PrintPay(employeeOneExtraHours, employeeOneWage * 1.5)
```

could be used to display payment information for an employee who is being paid time-and-a-half for working overtime.

When **Main** calls **PrintPay**, the program makes a copy of the value of each argument (e.g., **40** and **10.5** on line 9), and program control transfers to the first line of procedure **PrintPay**. Procedure **PrintPay** receives the copied values and stores them in the *parameter variables* **hours** and **wage**. Then **PrintPay** calculates **hours * wage** and displays the result, using the currency format (line 20). When the **End Sub** statement on line 21 is encountered, control is returned to the calling procedure, **Main**.

The first line of procedure **PrintPay** (line 17) shows (inside the parentheses) that **PrintPay** declares a **Double** variable **hours** and a **Decimal** variable **wage**. These parameters hold the values passed to **PrintPay** within the definition of this procedure. Notice that the entire procedure definition of **PrintPay** appears within the body of module **modPayment**. All procedures must be defined inside a module or a class.

The format of a **Sub** procedure definition is

```
Sub procedure-name(parameter-list)
   declarations and statements
End Sub
```

Common Programming Error 4.1

Defining a procedure outside of a module or class definition is a syntax error.

The first line of a procedure is sometimes known as the *procedure header*. The *procedure-name*, which directly follows the **Sub** keyword in the procedure header, can be any valid identifier.

The *parameter-list* is a comma-separated list in which the **Sub** procedure declares each parameter variable's type and name. There must be one argument in the procedure call for each parameter in the procedure header. The arguments also must be compatible with the parameter's type (i.e., Visual Basic must be able to assign the value of the argument to the parameter). For example, a parameter of type **Double** could receive a value of 7.35, 22 or –.03546, but not **"hello"**, because a **Double** value cannot contain a **String**. In Section 4.6, we discuss this issue in detail. If a procedure does not receive any values, the parameter list is empty (i.e., the procedure name is followed by an empty set of parentheses).

Notice that the parameter declarations in the procedure header for **PrintPay** (line 17) look similar to variable declarations, but use keyword **ByVal** instead of **Dim**. **ByVal** specifies that the calling procedure should pass a copy of the value of the argument in the procedure call to the parameter, which can be used in the **Sub** procedure body. Section 4.9 discusses argument passing in detail.

Common Programming Error 4.2

Declaring a variable in a procedure's body with the same name as a parameter variable in the procedure header is a syntax error.

Testing and Debugging Tip 4.1

Although it is not prohibited, an argument passed to a procedure should not have the same name as the corresponding parameter in the procedure definition. This distinction prevents ambiguity that could lead to logic errors.

The declarations and statements in the procedure definition form the *procedure body*. The procedure body contains Visual Basic code that performs actions, generally by manipulating or interacting with the parameters. The procedure body must be terminated with keywords **End Sub**, which define the end of the procedure. The procedure body also is referred to as a *block*. A block is a sequence of statements grouped together as the body of some structure and terminated with an **End**, **Next**, **Else** or **Loop** statement, depending on the type of structure. Variables can be declared in any block, and blocks can be nested.

Common Programming Error 4.3

Defining a procedure inside another procedure is a syntax error; procedures cannot be nested.

Control returns to the caller when execution reaches the **End Sub** statement (i.e., the end of the procedure body). Alternatively, keywords **Return** and **Exit Sub** can be used anywhere in a procedure to return control to the point at which a **Sub** procedure was invoked. We discuss **Return** and **Exit Sub** in detail momentarily.

Software Engineering Observation 4.2

The procedure header and procedure calls all must agree in terms of the number, type and order of parameters.

4.4 Function Procedures

Function procedures are similar to **Sub** procedures, with one important difference: **Function** procedures *return a value* (i.e., send a value) to the caller, whereas **Sub** procedures do not. The console application in Fig. 4.2 uses **Function** procedure **Square** to calculate the squares of the **Integer**s from 1–10.

The **For** structure (lines 12–14) displays the results of squaring the **Integer**s from **1**–**10**. Each iteration of the loop calculates the square of control variable **i** and displays it in the console window.

Function procedure **Square** is invoked (line 13) with the expression **Square(i)**. When program control reaches this expression, the program calls **Function Square** (lines 20–22). At this point, the program makes a copy of the value of **i** (the argument), and program control transfers to the first line of **Function Square**. **Square** receives the copy of **i**'s value and stores it in the parameter **y**. Line 21 is a **Return** *statement*, which terminates execution of the procedure and returns the result of **y ^ 2** to the calling program. The result is returned to the point on line 13 where **Square** was invoked. Line 13 displays the value of **i** and the value returned by **Square** in the console window. This process is repeated 10 times.

The format of a **Function** procedure definition is

> **Function** *procedure-name*(*parameter-list*) **As** *return-type*
>   *declarations and statements*
> **End Function**

The *procedure-name*, *parameter-list* and the *declarations and statements* in a **Function** procedure definition behave like the corresponding elements in a **Sub** procedure definition. In the **Function** header, the *return-type* indicates the data type of the result returned from the **Function** to its caller. The statement

> **Return** *expression*

can occur anywhere in a **Function** procedure body and returns the value of *expression* to the caller. If necessary, Visual Basic attempts to convert the *expression* to the **Function** procedure's *return-type*. **Function**s **Return** exactly one value. When a **Return** statement is executed, control returns immediately to the point at which the procedure was invoked.

```
1   ' Fig. 4.2: SquareInteger.vb
2   ' Function procedure to square a number.
3
4   Module modSquareInteger
5
6      Sub Main()
7         Dim i As Integer ' counter
8
9         Console.WriteLine("Number" & vbTab & "Square" & vbCrLf)
10
```

Fig. 4.2   **Function** procedure for squaring an integer. (Part 1 of 2.)

```
11          ' square numbers from 1 to 10
12          For i = 1 To 10
13              Console.WriteLine(i & vbTab & Square(i))
14          Next
15
16      End Sub ' Main
17
18      ' function Square is executed
19      ' only when function is explicitly called
20      Function Square(ByVal y As Integer) As Integer
21          Return y ^ 2
22      End Function ' Square
23
24  End Module ' modSquareInteger
```

```
Number   Square

1        1
2        4
3        9
4        16
5        25
6        36
7        49
8        64
9        81
10       100
```

Fig. 4.2   **Function** procedure for squaring an integer. (Part 2 of 2.)

Common Programming Error 4.4

*If the expression in a **Return** statement cannot be converted to the **Function** procedure's return-type, a runtime error is generated.*

Common Programming Error 4.5

*Failure to return a value from a **Function** procedure (e.g., by forgetting to provide a **Return** statement) causes the procedure to return the default value for the return-type, often producing incorrect output.*

Software Engineering Observation 4.3

*Write **Function**s which have only one return statement instead of a separate return statement for each path of execution.*

4.5 Methods

A method is any procedure that is contained within a class. We already have presented several FCL methods (i.e., methods contained in classes that are part of the FCL). Programmers also can define custom methods in programmer-defined classes, such as a class used to define a Windows application. The Windows application in Fig. 4.3 uses two methods to calculate the largest of three **Double**s.

Until now, many of our applications have facilitated user interaction via either the console window (in which the user can type an input value into the program) or a message dialog (which displays a message to the user and allows the user to click the **OK** button to dismiss the dialog). In the last chapter, we introduced Windows applications by creating a program that displays information in a label on a form.

```vb
1   ' Fig. 4.3: Maximum.vb
2   ' Program finds the maximum of three numbers input.
3
4   Public Class FrmMaximum
5       Inherits System.Windows.Forms.Form
6
7       ' prompts for three inputs
8       Friend WithEvents lblOne As System.Windows.Forms.Label
9       Friend WithEvents lblTwo As System.Windows.Forms.Label
10      Friend WithEvents lblThree As System.Windows.Forms.Label
11
12      ' displays result
13      Friend WithEvents lblMaximum As System.Windows.Forms.Label
14
15      ' read three numbers
16      Friend WithEvents txtFirst As System.Windows.Forms.TextBox
17      Friend WithEvents txtSecond As System.Windows.Forms.TextBox
18      Friend WithEvents txtThird As System.Windows.Forms.TextBox
19
20      ' reads inputs and calculate results
21      Friend WithEvents cmdMaximum As System.Windows.Forms.Button
22
23      ' Visual Studio .NET generated code
24
25      ' obtain values in each text box, call procedure Maximum
26      Private Sub cmdMaximum_Click(ByVal sender As System.Object, _
27          ByVal e As System.EventArgs) Handles cmdMaximum.Click
28
29          Dim value1, value2, value3 As Double
30
31          value1 = txtFirst.Text
32          value2 = txtSecond.Text
33          value3 = txtThird.Text
34
35          lblMaximum.Text = Maximum(value1, value2, value3)
36      End Sub ' cmdMaximum_Click
37
38      ' find maximum of three parameter values
39      Function Maximum(ByVal valueOne As Double, _
40          ByVal valueTwo As Double, ByVal valueThree As Double) _
41          As Double
42
43          Return Math.Max(Math.Max(valueOne, valueTwo), valueThree)
44      End Function ' Maximum
45
46  End Class ' FrmMaximum
```

Fig. 4.3   Method that determines the largest of three numbers. (Part 1 of 2.)

Fig. 4.3   Method that determines the largest of three numbers. (Part 2 of 2.)

Although console windows and message dialogs are valid ways to receive input from a user and display output, they are limited in their capabilities: The console window can obtain only one line of input at a time from the user, and a message dialog can display only one message. Often it is required that multiple inputs be received at the same time (such as the three values in this example) or that many pieces of data be displayed at once. To introduce more sophisticated user-interface programming, the program in Fig. 4.3 uses GUI *event handling* (i.e., the ability to respond to a state change in the GUI, such as when the user clicks a button).

Class **FrmMaximum** uses a GUI consisting of three **TextBox**es (**txtFirst, txtSecond** and **txtThird**) for user input, a **Button** (**cmdMaximum**) to invoke the calculation and four **Label**s, including **lblMaximum**, which displays the results. We create these controls visually, using the **Toolbox**, and change their properties in the **Properties** window. Lines 8–21 are declarations indicating the name of each control. Although these lines of code are actually part of the Visual Studio .NET-generated code, we display them to indicate the objects that are part of the form. (As always, the complete code for this program is downloadable from **www.deitel.com**.)

Line 5 indicates that class **FrmMaximum Inherits** from **System.Windows.Forms.Form**. All forms inherit from class **System.Windows.Forms.Form**. A class can inherit attributes and behaviors (data and methods) from another class if the latter class is specified to the right of the **Inherits** keyword. We discuss inheritance in detail in Chapter 6, Object-Oriented Programming: Inheritance.

FrmMaximum contains two programmer-defined methods. Method **Maximum** (lines 39–44) takes three **Double** parameters and returns the value of the largest parameter. Note that this method definition looks just like the definition of a **Function** procedure in a module. The program also includes method **cmdMaximum_Click** (lines 26–36). When the user double-clicks a control, such as a **Button**, in **Design** mode, the IDE generates a method that **Handles** an event (i.e., an *event handler*). An event represents an action taken by the user, such as clicking a **Button** or altering a value. An event handler is a method that is executed (called) when a certain event is *raised* (occurs). In this case, method **cmdMaximum_Click** handles the event in which **Button cmdMaximum** is clicked. Programmers write code to perform certain tasks when such events occur. By employing both events and objects, programmers can create applications that enable more sophisticated user interactions than those we have seen previously. Event-handler names created by the IDE begin with the object's name, followed by an underscore and the name of the event. We explain how to create our own event handlers, which can be given any name, in Chapter 9, Graphical User Interface Concepts: Part 1.

When the user clicks **Maximum**, procedure **cmdMaximum_Click** (lines 26–36) executes. Lines 31–33 retrieve the values in the three **TextBox**es, using the **Text** properties. The values are converted implicitly to type **Double** and stored in variables **value1**, **value2** and **value3**.

Line 35 calls method **Maximum** (lines 39–44) with the arguments **value1**, **value2** and **value3**. The values of these arguments are stored in parameters **valueOne**, **valueTwo** and **valueThree**, respectively, in method **Maximum**. **Maximum** returns the result of the expression on line 43, which makes two calls to *method Max* of the **Math** class. Method **Max** returns the largest of its two **Double** arguments, meaning that the computation on line 43 first compares **valueOne** and **valueTwo** and thereafter compares the value returned by the first method call with **valueThree**. Calls to *Shared methods*,[1] such as **Math.Max**, that are defined in a class in the FCL must include the class name and the dot (**.**) operator (also called the *member access operator*). However, calls to methods defined in the class that contains the method call need specify only the method name.

When control returns to method **cmdMaximum_Click**, line 35 assigns the value returned by method **Maximum** to **lblMaximum**'s **Text** property, causing it to be displayed for the user.

4.6 Argument Promotion

An important feature of procedure definitions is the *coercion of arguments* (i.e., the forcing of arguments to the appropriate data type so that they can be passed to a procedure). Visual Basic supports both widening and narrowing conversions. *Widening conversion* occurs when a type is converted to another type (usually one that can hold more data) without losing data, whereas a *narrowing conversion* occurs when there is potential for data loss during the conversion (usually to a type that holds a smaller amount of data). Figure 4.4 provides size information for the various built-in types of Visual Basic .NET and Fig. 4.5 lists the widening conversions supported by Visual Basic.

Type	Size in bits	Values	Standard
Boolean	16	**True** or **False**	
Char	16	One Unicode character	(Unicode character set)
Byte	8	0 to **255**	
Date	64	1 January 0001 to 31 December 9999 0:00:00 to 23:59:59	

Fig. 4.4   Visual Basic primitive data types. (Part 1 of 2.)

---

1. We discuss Shared methods in more detail in Chapter 5, Object-Based Programming.

Type	Size in bits	Values	Standard
Decimal	128	1.0E-28 to 7.9E+28	
Short	16	-32,768 to 32,767	
Integer	32	-2,147,483,648 to 2,147,483,647	
Long	64	-9,223,372,036,854,775,808 to 9,223,372,036,854,775,807	
Single	32	±1.5E-45 to ±3.4E+38	(IEEE 754 floating point)
Double	64	±5.0E-324 to ±1.7E+308	(IEEE 754 floating point)
Object	32	Data of any type	
String		0 to ~2,000,000,000 Unicode characters	(Unicode character set)

Fig. 4.4   Visual Basic primitive data types. (Part 2 of 2.)

Type	Conversion Types
Boolean	*Object*
Byte	*Short*, *Integer*, *Long*, *Decimal*, *Single*, *Double* or *Object*
Char	*String* or *Object*
Date	*Object*
Decimal	*Single*, *Double* or *Object*
Double	*Object*
Integer	*Long*, *Decimal*, *Single*, *Double* or *Object*
Long	*Decimal*, *Single*, *Double* or *Object*
Object	none
Short	*Integer*, *Long*, *Decimal*, *Single*, *Double* or *Object*
Single	*Double* or *Object*
String	*Object*

Fig. 4.5   Widening conversions.

For example, the **Math** class method **Sqrt** can be called with an **Integer** argument, even though the method is defined in the **Math** class to receive a **Double** argument. The statement

```
Console.Write(Math.Sqrt(4))
```

correctly evaluates **Math.Sqrt(4)** and prints the value **2**. Visual Basic promotes (i.e., converts) the **Integer** value **4** to the **Double** value **4.0** before the value is passed to **Math.Sqrt**. In this case, the argument value does not correspond precisely to the parameter type in the method definition, so an implicit widening conversion changes the value to the proper type before the method is called. Visual Basic also performs narrowing conversions on arguments passed to procedures. For example, if **String** variable **number** contains the value **"4"**, the method call **Math.Sqrt(number)** correctly evaluates to **2**. However, some implicit narrowing conversions can fail, resulting in runtime errors and logic errors. For example, if **number** contains the value **"hello"**, passing it as an argument to method **Math.Sqrt** causes a runtime error. In the next section, we discuss some measures the programmer can take to help avoid such issues.

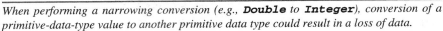

Common Programming Error 4.6

*When performing a narrowing conversion (e.g., **Double** to **Integer**), conversion of a primitive-data-type value to another primitive data type could result in a loss of data.*

Argument promotion applies not only to primitive-data-type values passed as arguments to methods, but also to expressions containing values of two or more data types. Such expressions are referred to as *mixed-type expressions*. In a mixed-type expression, each value is promoted to the "highest" data type in the expression (i.e., widening conversions are made until the values are of the same type). For example, if **singleNumber** is of type **Single** and **integerNumber** is of type **Integer**, then when Visual Basic evaluates the expression

```
singleNumber + integerNumber
```

the value of **integerNumber** is converted to type **Single** and added to **singleNumber**, producing a **Single** result. Although the values' original data types are maintained, a temporary version of each value is created for use in the expression, and the data types of the temporary versions are modified appropriately.

4.7 Option Strict and Data-Type Conversions

Visual Basic provides several options for controlling the way in which the compiler handles data types. These options can help programmers eliminate such errors as those caused by narrowing conversions, thereby making code more reliable and secure. The first option is *Option Explicit*, which is set to **On** by default, meaning that it was enabled in the Visual Basic programs created in Chapters 2 and 3. **Option Explicit** forces the programmer to declare explicitly all variables before they are used in a program. Forcing explicit declarations eliminates subtle errors that may occur if **Option Explicit** is turned off. For example, when **Option Explicit** is set to **Off**, the compiler interprets misspelled variable names as new variable declarations, which creates subtle errors that can be difficult to debug.

A second option, which is set to **Off** by default, is *Option Strict*. Visual Basic provides **Option Strict** as a means by which to increase program clarity and reduce debugging time. When set to **On**, **Option Strict** causes the compiler to check all conversions and requires the programmer to perform an *explicit conversion* for all narrowing conversions that could cause data loss (e.g., conversion from **Double** to **Integer**) or program termination (e.g., conversion of a **String**, such as **"hello"**, to type **Integer**).

The methods in class *Convert* can be used to change data types explicitly. The name of each conversion method is the word **To**, followed by the name of the data type to which the method converts its argument. For instance, to store a **String** input by the user in variable **number** of type **Integer** (represented in Visual Basic .NET as type *Int32*, a 32-bit integer), with **Option Strict** set to **On**, we use the statement

```
number = Convert.ToInt32(Console.ReadLine())
```

When **Option Strict** is set to **Off**, Visual Basic performs such type conversions implicitly, meaning that the programmer might not realize that a narrowing conversion is being performed. If the data being converted are incompatible with the new data type, a runtime error occurs. **Option Strict** draws the programmer's attention to narrowing conversions so that they can be eliminated or handled properly. In Chapter 8, Exception Handling, we discuss how to handle the errors caused by failed narrowing conversions.

Software Engineering Observation 4.4

Performing explicit conversions allows programs to execute more efficiently by eliminating the need to determine the data type of the value being changed before the conversion executes.

From this point forward, all code examples have **Option Strict** set to **On**. **Option Strict** can be activated through the IDE by right-clicking the project name in the **Solution Explorer**. From the resulting menu, select **Properties** to open the **Property Pages** dialog (Fig. 4.6). From the directory tree on the left side of the dialog, select **Build** from the **Common Properties** list. In the middle of the dialog is a drop-down box labeled **Option Strict:**. By default, the option is set to **Off**. Choose **On** from the drop-down box, and click the **Apply** button.

Setting **Option Strict** to **On** in the **Property Pages** dialog applies the change globally, that is, to the entire project. The programmer also can enable **Option Strict** within an individual code file by typing **Option Strict On** at the start of the file, above any declarations or **Imports** statements.

WindowsApplication1 Property Pages ⊠

| Configuration: N/A ▼ | Platform: N/A ▼ | Configuration Manager... |

- 📁 Common Properties
  - General
  - ⇨ Build
  - Imports
  - Reference Path
  - Strong Name
  - Designer Defaults
- 📁 Configuration Properties

Application icon:

(Default Icon) ▼ ...

Compiler Defaults

Option Explicit: On ▼

Option Strict: On ▼

Option Compare: Binary ▼

| OK | Cancel | Apply | Help |

Fig. 4.6   Property Pages dialog with **Option Strict** set to **On**.

4.8 Value Types and Reference Types

In the next section, we discuss passing arguments to procedures by value and by reference. To understand these concepts, we first need to make a distinction between data types in Visual Basic. All Visual Basic data types can be categorized as either *value types* or *reference types*. A variable of a value type contains data of that type. Normally, value types are used for a single piece of data, such as an **Integer** or a **Double** value. By contrast, a variable of a reference type (sometimes called a *reference*) contains a location in memory where data are stored. The location in memory can contain many individual pieces of data. Collectively, reference types are known as objects and are discussed in detail in Chapters 5, 6 and 7, Object-Based Programming, Object-Oriented Programming: Inheritance and Object-Oriented Programming: Polymorphism, respectively.

Both value types and reference types include built-in types and types that the programmer can create. The built-in value types include the *integral types* (**Byte**, **Short**, **Integer** and **Long**), the *floating-point types* (**Single** and **Double**) and types **Boolean**, **Date**, **Decimal** and **Char**. The built-in reference types include **Object** and **String** (although type **String** often behaves more like a value type, as we discuss in the next section). The value types that can be constructed by the programmer include **Structure**s and **Enum**erations. The reference types that can be created by the programmer include classes, interfaces and delegates. Programmer-defined types are discussed in greater detail in Chapters 5, 6 and 7.

The table in Fig. 4.4 lists the primitive data types, which form the building blocks for more complicated types, such as classes. If **Option Explicit** is set to **On**, all variables must have a type before they can be used in a program. This requirement is referred to as *strong typing*.

Each value type in the table is accompanied by its size in bits (there are eight bits to a byte) and its range of values. To promote portability, Microsoft chose to use internationally recognized standards for both character formats (Unicode®) and floating-point numbers (IEEE 754). We discuss the Unicode® character formats in Appendix D, Unicode®.

Values typed directly in program code are called *literals*. Each literal corresponds to one of the primitive data types. We already have seen literals for commonly used types, such as **String**, **Integer** and **Double**. However, some of Visual Basic's data types use special notations for creating literals. For instance, to create a literal of type **Char**, follow a single-character **String** with the *type character c*. The statement

```
Dim character As Char = "Z"c
```

declares **Char** variable **character** and initializes it to the **"Z"** character. Figure 4.7 displays Visual Basic's type characters and examples of literals for each data type. All literals must be within the range for the literal's type, as specified in Fig. 4.4.

Type	Type character	Example
Char	c	"u"c
Single	F	9.802E+31F

Fig. 4.7   Literals with type characters. (Part 1 of 2.)

Type	Type character	Example
Double	R	6.04E-187R
Decimal	D	128309.76D
Short	S	3420S
Integer	I	-867I
Long	L	19235827493259374L

Fig. 4.7   Literals with type characters. (Part 2 of 2.)

4.9 Passing Arguments: Pass-by-Value vs. Pass-by-Reference

Arguments are passed in one of two ways: *Pass-by-value* and *pass-by-reference* (also called *call-by-value* and *call-by-reference*, respectively). When an argument is passed by value, the program makes a *copy* of the argument's value and passes that copy to the called procedure. With pass-by-value, changes to the called procedure's copy do not affect the original variable's value. In contrast, when an argument is passed by reference, the caller gives the called procedure the ability to access and modify the caller's original data directly. Figure 4.8 demonstrates the passing of value-type arguments by value and by reference.

The program passes three value-type variables, **number1**, **number2** and **number3**, in different ways to procedures **SquareByValue** (lines 40–46) and **SquareByReference** (lines 49–55). Keyword **ByVal** in the procedure header of **SquareByValue** (line 40) indicates that value-type arguments should be passed by value. When **number1** is passed to **SquareByValue** (line 13), a copy of the value stored in **number1** (i.e., **2**) is passed to the procedure. Therefore, the value of **number1** in the calling procedure, **Main**, is not modified when parameter **number** is squared in procedure **SquareByValue** (line 43).

Procedure **SquareByReference** uses *keyword **ByRef*** (line 49) to receive its value-type parameter by reference. When **Main** calls **SquareByReference** (line 23), a reference to the value stored in **number2** is passed, which gives **SquareByReference** direct access to the value stored in the original variable. Thus, the value stored in **number2** after **SquareByReference** finishes executing is the same as the final value of parameter **number**.

When arguments are enclosed in parentheses, **( )**, a copy of the value of the argument is passed to the procedure, even if the procedure header includes keyword **ByRef**. Thus, the value of **number3** does not change after it is passed to **SquareByReference** (line 33) via parentheses.

```
1   ' Fig. 4.8: ByRefTest.vb
2   ' Demonstrates passing by reference.
3
4   Module modByRefTest
5
```

Fig. 4.8   **ByVal** and **ByRef** used to pass value-type arguments. (Part 1 of 3.)

```vb
6      ' squares three values ByVal and ByRef, displays results
7      Sub Main()
8         Dim number1 As Integer = 2
9
10        Console.WriteLine("Passing a value-type argument by value:")
11        Console.WriteLine("Before calling SquareByValue, " & _
12           "number1 is {0}", number1)
13        SquareByValue(number1)   ' passes number1 by value
14        Console.WriteLine("After returning from SquareByValue, " & _
15           "number1 is {0}" & vbCrLf, number1)
16
17        Dim number2 As Integer = 2
18
19        Console.WriteLine("Passing a value-type argument" & _
20           " by reference:")
21        Console.WriteLine("Before calling SquareByReference, " & _
22           "number2 is {0}", number2)
23        SquareByReference(number2) ' passes number2 by reference
24        Console.WriteLine("After returning from " & _
25           "SquareByReference, number2 is {0}" & vbCrLf, number2)
26
27        Dim number3 As Integer = 2
28
29        Console.WriteLine("Passing a value-type argument" & _
30           " by reference, but in parentheses:")
31        Console.WriteLine("Before calling SquareByReference " & _
32           "using parentheses, number3 is {0}", number3)
33        SquareByReference((number3)) ' passes number3 by value
34        Console.WriteLine("After returning from " & _
35           "SquareByReference, number3 is {0}", number3)
36
37     End Sub ' Main
38
39     ' squares number by value (note ByVal keyword)
40     Sub SquareByValue(ByVal number As Integer)
41        Console.WriteLine("After entering SquareByValue, " & _
42           "number is {0}", number)
43        number *= number
44        Console.WriteLine("Before exiting SquareByValue, " & _
45           "number is {0}", number)
46     End Sub ' SquareByValue
47
48     ' squares number by reference (note ByRef keyword)
49     Sub SquareByReference(ByRef number As Integer)
50        Console.WriteLine("After entering SquareByReference" & _
51           ", number is {0}", number)
52        number *= number
53        Console.WriteLine("Before exiting SquareByReference" & _
54           ", number is {0}", number)
55     End Sub ' SquareByReference
56
57  End Module ' modByRefTest
```

Fig. 4.8   **ByVal** and **ByRef** used to pass value-type arguments. (Part 2 of 3.)

```
Passing a value-type argument by value:
Before calling SquareByValue, number1 is 2
After entering SquareByValue, number is 2
Before exiting SquareByValue, number is 4
After returning from SquareByValue, number1 is 2

Passing a value-type argument by reference:
Before calling SquareByReference, number2 is 2
After entering SquareByReference, number is 2
Before exiting SquareByReference, number is 4
After returning from SquareByReference, number2 is 4

Passing a value-type argument by reference, but in parentheses:
Before calling SquareByReference using parentheses, number3 is 2
After entering SquareByReference, number is 2
Before exiting SquareByReference, number is 4
After returning from SquareByReference, number3 is 2
```

Fig. 4.8   **ByVal** and **ByRef** used to pass value-type arguments. (Part 3 of 3.)

Passing value-type arguments with keyword **ByRef** is useful when procedures need to alter argument values directly. However, passing by reference can weaken security, because the called procedure can modify the caller's data. Reference-type variables passed with keyword **ByVal** are passed by reference, as the value that is copied is the reference for the object.

Testing and Debugging Tip 4.2

When passing arguments by value, changes to the called procedure's copy do not affect the original variable's value. This condition prevents possible side effects that could hinder the development of correct and reliable software systems. Always pass value-type arguments by value, unless you explicitly intend for the called procedure to modify the caller's data.

Software Engineering Observation 4.5

*Although keywords **ByVal** and **ByRef** may be used to pass reference-type variables by value or by reference, the called procedure can manipulate the caller's reference-type variable directly in both cases. Therefore, it is rarely appropriate to use **ByRef** with reference-type variables. We discuss this subtle issue in detail in Section 4.17.*

Software Engineering Observation 4.6

*When returning information from a **Function** procedure via a **Return** statement, value-type variables always are returned by value (i.e., a copy is returned), whereas reference-type variables always are returned by reference (i.e., a reference to an object is returned).*

4.10 Duration of Identifiers

In earlier chapters of this book, we have used identifiers for various purposes, including as variable names and as the names of modules and programmer-defined procedures. Every identifier has certain attributes, including *duration* and *scope*.

An identifier's *duration* (also called its *lifetime*) is the period during which the identifier exists in memory. Some identifiers exist briefly, others are created and destroyed repeatedly, and yet others are maintained through the entire execution of a program.

The *scope* of an identifier is the portion of a program in which the variable's identifier can be referenced. Some identifiers can be referenced throughout an entire program; others can be referenced only from limited portions of a program (such as within a single procedure). This section discusses the duration of identifiers. Section 4.11 discusses the scope of identifiers.

Identifiers that represent local variables in a procedure (i.e., parameters and variables declared in the procedure body) have *automatic duration*. Automatic-duration variables are created when program control enters the procedure in which they are declared, exist while the procedure is active and are destroyed when the procedure is exited.[2] For the remainder of the text, we refer to variables of automatic duration simply as *automatic variables*, or *local variables*.

Variables declared inside a module or class, but outside any procedure definition, exist as long as their containing class or module is loaded in memory. Variables declared in a module exist throughout a program's execution. By default, a variable declared in a class, such as a **Form** class for a Windows application, is an *instance variable*. In the case of a **Form**, this means that the variable is created when the **Form** loads and exists until the **Form** is unloaded from memory. We discuss instance variables in detail in Chapter 5.

4.11 Scope Rules

The *scope* (sometimes called the *declaration space*) of a variable, reference or procedure identifier is the portion of the program in which the identifier can be accessed. The possible scopes for an identifier are *class scope*, *module scope*, *namespace scope* and *block scope*.

Members of a class have class scope, which means that they are visible in what is known as the *declaration space of a class*. Class scope begins at the class identifier after keyword **Class** and terminates at the **End Class** statement. This scope enables a method of that class to invoke directly all members defined in that class and to access members inherited by that class.[3] In a sense, members of a class are global to the methods of the class in which they are defined. This means that the methods can modify instance variables of the class (i.e., variables declared in the class definition, but outside any method definition) directly and invoke other methods of the class.

In Visual Basic, identifiers declared inside a block, such as the body of a procedure definition or the body of an **If/Then** selection structure, have block scope (*local-variable declaration space*). Block scope begins at the identifier's declaration and ends at the block's **End** statement (or equivalent, e.g., **Next**). Local variables of a procedure have block scope. Procedure parameters also have block scope, because they are considered local variables of the procedure. Any block can contain variable declarations. When blocks are nested in a body of a procedure, an error is generated if an identifier declared in an outer block has the same name as an identifier declared in an inner block. However, if a local variable in a called procedure shares its name with a variable with class scope, such as an instance variable, the class-scope variable is "hidden" until the called procedure terminates execution.

---

2. Variables in a procedure also can be declared by using keyword **Static**, in which case the variable is created and initialized during the first execution of the procedure and maintains its value between subsequent calls to the procedure.
3. In Chapter 5, we see that **Shared** members are an exception to this rule.

Variables declared in a module have module scope, which is similar to class scope. Variables declared in a module are accessible to all procedures defined in the module. Module scope and class scope are sometimes referred to collectively as module scope. Like class-scope variables, module-scope variables are hidden when they have the same identifier as that of a local variable.

By default, procedures defined in a module have namespace scope, which generally means that they may be accessed throughout a project. Namespace scope is useful in projects that contain multiple pieces (i.e., modules and classes). If a project contains a module and a class, methods in the class can access the procedures of the module. Although variables declared in a module have module scope, they can be given namespace scope by replacing keyword **Dim** with keyword **Public** in the declaration. We discuss how to add modules to projects in Section 4.14.

 Good Programming Practice 4.1

Avoid local-variable names that hide class-variable or module-variable names.

The program in Fig. 4.9 demonstrates scoping issues with instance variables and local variables. Instance variable **value** is declared and initialized to **1** in line 12. As explained previously, this variable is hidden in any procedure that declares a variable named **value**. The **FrmScoping_Load** method declares a local variable **value** (line 19) and initializes it to **5**. This variable is displayed in **lblOutput** (note the declaration on line 7, which is actually part of the Visual Studio .NET-generated code) to illustrate that the instance variable **value** is hidden in **FrmScoping_Load**.

```
1   ' Fig. 4.9: Scoping.vb
2   ' Demonstrates scope rules and instance variables.
3
4   Public Class FrmScoping
5       Inherits System.Windows.Forms.Form
6
7       Friend WithEvents lblOutput As System.Windows.Forms.Label
8
9       ' Visual Studio .NET generated code
10
11      ' instance variable can be used anywhere in class
12      Dim value As Integer = 1
13
14      ' demonstrates class scope and block scope
15      Private Sub FrmScoping_Load(ByVal sender As System.Object, _
16          ByVal e As System.EventArgs) Handles MyBase.Load
17
18          ' variable local to FrmScoping_Load hides instance variable
19          Dim value As Integer = 5
20
21          lblOutput.Text = "local variable value in" & _
22              " FrmScoping_Load is " & value
23
24          MethodA() ' MethodA has automatic local value
25          MethodB() ' MethodB uses instance variable value
```

Fig. 4.9   Scoping rules in a class. (Part 1 of 2.)

```
26          MethodA() ' MethodA creates new automatic local value
27          MethodB() ' instance variable value retains its value
28
29          lblOutput.Text &= vbCrLf & vbCrLf & "local variable " & _
30             "value in FrmScoping_Load is " & value
31       End Sub ' FrmScoping_Load
32
33       ' automatic local variable value hides instance variable
34       Sub MethodA()
35          Dim value As Integer = 25 ' initialized after each call
36
37          lblOutput.Text &= vbCrLf & vbCrLf & "local variable " & _
38             "value in MethodA is " & value & " after entering MethodA"
39          value += 1
40          lblOutput.Text &= vbCrLf & "local variable " & _
41             "value in MethodA is " & value & " before exiting MethodA"
42       End Sub ' MethodA
43
44       ' uses instance variable value
45       Sub MethodB()
46          lblOutput.Text &= vbCrLf & vbCrLf & "instance variable" & _
47             " value is " & value & " after entering MethodB"
48          value *= 10
49          lblOutput.Text &= vbCrLf & "instance variable " & _
50             "value is " & value & " before exiting MethodB"
51       End Sub ' MethodB
52
53    End Class ' FrmScoping
```

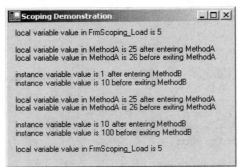

Fig. 4.9   Scoping rules in a class. (Part 2 of 2.)

The program defines two other methods—**MethodA** and **MethodB**, which take no arguments and return nothing. Each method is called twice from **FrmScoping_Load**. **MethodA** defines local variable **value** (line 35) and initializes it to **25**. When **MethodA** is called, the variable is displayed in the label **lblOutput**, incremented and displayed again before exiting the method. Automatic variable **value** is destroyed when **MethodA** terminates. Thus, each time this method is called, **value** must be re-created and reinitialized to **25**.

MethodB does not declare any variables. Therefore, when this procedure refers to variable **value**, the instance variable **value** (line 12) is used. When **MethodB** is called, the instance variable is displayed, multiplied by **10** and displayed again before exiting the method. The next time method **MethodB** is called, the instance variable retains its modified value, **10**, and line 48 causes **value** (line 12) to become **100**. Finally, the program again displays the local variable **value** in method **FrmScoping_Load**, to show that none of the method calls modified this variable **value**—both methods refer to variables in other scopes.

4.12 Recursion

In most of the programs we have discussed so far, procedures have called one another in a disciplined, hierarchical manner. However, in some instances, it is useful to enable procedures to call themselves. A *recursive procedure* is a procedure that calls itself, either directly or indirectly (i.e., through another procedure). In this section, we present a simple example of recursion.

Prior to examining actual programs containing recursive procedures, we first consider recursion conceptually. Recursive problem-solving approaches have a number of elements in common. A recursive procedure is called to solve a problem. The procedure actually is able to solve only the simplest case(s), or *base case(s)*. If the procedure is called with a base case, the procedure returns a result. If the procedure is called with a more complex problem, the procedure divides the problem into two conceptual pieces—a piece that the procedure knows how to perform (base case) and a piece that the procedure does not know how to perform. To make recursion feasible, the latter piece must resemble the original problem, but be a slightly simpler or smaller version of it. The procedure then invokes (calls) a fresh copy of itself to work on the smaller problem; this action is referred to as a *recursive call*, or a *recursion step*. The recursion step also normally includes the keyword **Return**, because its result will be combined with the portion of the problem that the procedure was able to solve. Such a combination will form a result that will be passed back to the original caller.

The recursion step executes while the original call to the procedure is still "open" (i.e., has not finished executing). The recursion step can result in many more recursive calls as the procedure divides each new subproblem into two conceptual pieces. As the procedure continues to call itself with slightly simpler versions of the original problem, the sequence of smaller and smaller problems must converge on the base case, so that the recursion can eventually terminate. At that point, the procedure operates on the base case and returns a result to the previous copy of the procedure. A sequence of returns ensues up the line until the original procedure call returns the final result to the caller. As an example of these concepts, let us write a recursive program that performs a common mathematical calculation.

The factorial of a nonnegative integer *n,* written *n*! (and read "*n* factorial"), is the product

$$n \cdot (n-1) \cdot (n-2) \cdot \ldots \cdot 1$$

with 1! equal to 1 and 0! defined as 1. For example, 5! is the product $5 \cdot 4 \cdot 3 \cdot 2 \cdot 1$, which is equal to 120.

The factorial of an integer **number** greater than or equal to **0** can be calculated *iteratively* (nonrecursively), using a **For** repetition structure, as follows:

```
Dim counter, factorial As Integer = 1

For counter = number To 1 Step -1
   factorial *= counter
Next
```

We arrive at a recursive definition of the factorial procedure by using the following relationship:

$$n! = n \cdot (n - 1)!$$

For example, 5! is clearly equal to 5 · 4!, as is shown by the following equations:

$$5! = 5 \cdot 4 \cdot 3 \cdot 2 \cdot 1$$
$$5! = 5 \cdot (4 \cdot 3 \cdot 2 \cdot 1)$$
$$5! = 5 \cdot (4!)$$

The program in Fig. 4.10 recursively calculates and prints factorials. (The choice of the data type **Long** will be explained soon). The recursive method **Factorial** (lines 33–41) first tests (line 35) to determine whether its terminating condition is true (i.e., whether **number** is less than or equal to **1**). If **number** is less than or equal to **1**, **Factorial** returns **1**, no further recursion is necessary and the method returns. If **number** is greater than **1**, line 38 expresses the problem as the product of **number** and a recursive call to **Factorial**, evaluating the factorial of **number - 1**. Note that **Factorial(number - 1)** is a slightly simpler problem than the original calculation, **Factorial(number)**.

Function Factorial (line 33) receives a parameter of type **Long** and returns a result of type **Long**. As is seen in the output window of Fig. 4.10, factorial values escalate quickly. We choose data type **Long** to enable the program to calculate factorials greater than 12!. Unfortunately, the values produced by the **Factorial** method increase at such a rate that the range of even the **Long** type is exceeded quickly.

```
1    ' Fig. 4.10: Factorial.vb
2    ' Calculating factorials using recursion.
3
4    Public Class FrmFactorial
5       Inherits System.Windows.Forms.Form
6
7       Friend WithEvents lblEnter As Label        ' prompts for Integer
8       Friend WithEvents lblFactorial As Label ' indicates output
9
10      Friend WithEvents txtInput As TextBox      ' reads an Integer
11      Friend WithEvents txtDisplay As TextBox ' displays output
12
13      Friend WithEvents cmdCalculate As Button ' generates output
14
15      ' Visual Studio .NET generated code
16
17      Private Sub cmdCalculate_Click(ByVal sender As System.Object, _
18         ByVal e As System.EventArgs) Handles cmdCalculate.Click
19
20         Dim value As Integer = Convert.ToInt32(txtInput.Text)
21         Dim i As Integer
```

Fig. 4.10   Recursive factorial program. (Part 1 of 2.)

```
22            Dim output As String
23
24            txtDisplay.Text = ""
25
26            For i = 0 To value
27               txtDisplay.Text &= i & "! = " & Factorial(i) & vbCrLf
28            Next
29
30         End Sub ' cmdCalculate_Click
31
32         ' recursively generates factorial of number
33         Function Factorial(ByVal number As Long) As Long
34
35            If number <= 1 Then ' base case
36               Return 1
37            Else
38               Return number * Factorial(number - 1)
39            End If
40
41         End Function ' Factorial
42
43      End Class ' FrmFactorial
```

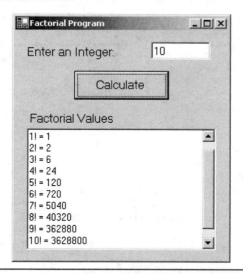

Fig. 4.10 Recursive factorial program. (Part 2 of 2.)

Common Programming Error 4.7

Forgetting to return a value from a recursive procedure when a return value is required can result in logic errors.

Common Programming Error 4.8

Omitting the base case or writing the recursive step so that it does not converge on the base case will cause infinite recursion, *eventually exhausting memory. This situation is analogous to the problem of an infinite loop in an iterative (nonrecursive) solution.*

4.13 Procedure Overloading and Optional Arguments

Visual Basic provides several ways of allowing procedures to have variable sets of parameters. *Overloading* allows the programmer to create multiple procedures with the same name, but differing numbers and types of arguments. This feature allows the programmer to reduce the complexity of the program and create a more flexible application. Procedures also can receive *optional arguments*. Defining an argument as optional allows the calling procedure to determine which arguments to pass. Optional arguments normally specify a default value that is assigned to the parameter if the optional argument is not passed. Overloaded procedures are generally more flexible than procedures with optional arguments. For instance, the programmer can specify varying return types for overloaded procedures. However, optional arguments present a simple way of specifying default values.

4.13.1 Procedure Overloading

By overloading, a programmer can define several procedures with the same name, as long as the procedures have different sets of parameters (in terms of the number of parameters, the types of parameters or the order of the parameters). When an overloaded procedure is called, the compiler selects the proper procedure by examining the number, types and order of the call's arguments. Often, procedure overloading is used to create several procedures with the same name that perform similar tasks on different data types.

Good Programming Practice 4.2

The overloading of procedures that perform closely related tasks can make programs more readable and understandable.

The program in Fig. 4.11 uses overloaded method **Square** to calculate the square of both an **Integer** and a **Double**.

```
1    ' Fig. 4.11: Overload.vb
2    ' Using overloaded methods.
3
4    Public Class FrmOverload
5        Inherits System.Windows.Forms.Form
6
7        Friend WithEvents outputLabel As Label
8
9        ' Visual Studio .NET generated code
10
11       Private Sub FrmOverload_Load(ByVal sender As System.Object, _
12           ByVal e As System.EventArgs) Handles MyBase.Load
13
14           outputLabel.Text = "The square of Integer 7 is " & _
15               Square(7) & vbCrLf & "The square of Double " & _
16               "7.5 is " & Square(7.5)
17       End Sub ' FrmOverload_Load
18
19       Function Square(ByVal value As Integer) As Integer
20           Return Convert.ToInt32(value ^ 2)
21       End Function ' Square
```

Fig. 4.11 Overloaded methods. (Part 1 of 2.)

```
22
23      Function Square(ByVal value As Double) As Double
24          Return value ^ 2
25      End Function ' Square
26
27   End Class ' FrmOverload
```

Fig. 4.11   Overloaded methods. (Part 2 of 2.)

Overloaded procedures are distinguished by their *signatures*, which are a combination of the procedure's name and parameter types. If the compiler were to examine only procedure names during compilation, the code in Fig. 4.11 would be ambiguous—the compiler would not know how to differentiate between the two **Square** methods. The compiler uses a logical process known as *overload resolution* to determine which procedure should be called. This process first searches for all procedures that *could* be used, on the basis of the number and type of arguments that are present. Although it might seem that only one procedure would match, it is important to remember that Visual Basic promotes variables with implicit conversions when they are passed as arguments. Once all matching procedures are found, the compiler then selects the closest match. This match is based on a "best-fit" algorithm, which analyzes the implicit conversions that will take place.

Let us look at an example. In Fig. 4.11, the compiler might use the logical name "**Square** of **Integer**" for the **Square** method that specifies an **Integer** parameter (line 19) and "**Square** of **Double**" for the **Square** method that specifies a **Double** parameter (line 23). If a procedure **ExampleSub**'s definition begins as

```
Function ExampleSub(ByVal a As Integer, ByVal b As Double) _
    As Integer
```

the compiler might use the logical name "**ExampleSub** of **Integer** and **Double**." Similarly, if the parameters are specified as

```
Function ExampleSub(ByVal a As Double, ByVal b As Integer) _
    As Integer
```

the compiler might use the logical name "**ExampleSub** of **Double** and **Integer**." The order of the parameters is important to the compiler; it considers the preceding two **ExampleSub** procedures to be distinct.

So far, the logical procedure names used by the compiler have not mentioned the procedures' return types. This is because procedure calls cannot be distinguished by return type. The program in Fig. 4.12 illustrates the syntax error that is generated when two methods have the same signature and different return types. Overloaded procedures with different parameter lists can have different return types. Overloaded procedures need not have the same number of parameters.

```
1   ' Fig. 4.12: Overload2.vb
2   ' Using overloaded procedures with identical signatures and
3   ' different return types.
4
5   Public Class FrmOverload2
6      Inherits System.Windows.Forms.Form
7
8      Friend WithEvents outputLabel As Label
9
10     ' Visual Studio .NET generated code
11
12     Private Sub FrmOverload2_Load(ByVal sender As System.Object, _
13        ByVal e As System.EventArgs) Handles MyBase.Load
14
15        outputLabel.Text = "The square of Integer 7 is " & _
16           Square(7) & vbCrLf & "The square of Double " & _
17           "7.5 is " & Square(7.5)
18     End Sub ' FrmOverload2_Load
19
20     Function Square(ByVal value As Double) As Integer
21        Return Convert.ToInt32(value ^ 2)
22     End Function ' Square
23
24     Function Square(ByVal value As Double) As Double
25        Return value ^ 2
26     End Function ' Square
27
28  End Class ' FrmOverload2
```

Fig. 4.12   Syntax error generated from overloaded procedures with identical parameter lists and different return types.

 Common Programming Error 4.9

Creating overloaded procedures with identical parameter lists and different return types produces a syntax error.

The output window displayed in Fig. 4.12 is the **Task List** of Visual Studio .NET. By default, the **Task List** is displayed at the bottom of the IDE when a compiler error is generated.

4.13.2 Optional Arguments

Visual Basic allows programmers to create procedures that take one or more optional arguments. When a parameter is declared as optional, the caller has the *option* of passing that particular argument. Optional arguments are specified in the procedure header with keyword **Optional**. For example, the procedure header

```
Sub ExampleProcedure(ByVal value1 As Boolean, Optional _
    ByVal value2 As Long = 0)
```

specifies the last parameter as **Optional**. Any call to **ExampleProcedure** must pass at least one argument, or else a syntax error is generated. If the caller so chooses, a second argument can be passed to **ExampleProcedure** as well. This condition is demonstrated by the following calls to **ExampleProcedure**:

```
ExampleProcedure()
ExampleProcedure(True)
ExampleProcedure(False, 10)
```

The first call to **ExampleProcedure** generates a syntax error, because a minimum of one argument is required. The second call to **ExampleProcedure** is valid, because one argument is being passed. The **Optional** argument, **value2**, is not specified in the procedure call. The last call to **ExampleProcedure** also is valid: **False** is passed as the one required argument, and **10** is passed as the **Optional** argument.

In the call that passes only one argument (**True**) to **ExampleProcedure**, **value2** defaults to **0**, which is the value specified in the procedure header. **Optional** arguments must specify a *default value*, using the equals sign followed by the value. For example, the header for **ExampleProcedure** sets **0** as the default value for **value2**. Default values can be used only with parameters declared as **Optional**.

Common Programming Error 4.10

*Not specifying a default value for an **Optional** parameter is a syntax error.*

Common Programming Error 4.11

*Declaring a non-**Optional** parameter to the right of an **Optional** parameter is a syntax error.*

The example in Fig. 4.13 demonstrates the use of optional arguments. The program calculates the result of raising a base to an exponent, both of which are specified by the user. If the user does not specify an exponent, however, the **Optional** argument is omitted, and the default value, **2**, is used.

```
1   ' Fig. 4.13 Power.vb
2   ' Calculates the power of a value, defaults to square.
3
4   Public Class FrmPower
5       Inherits System.Windows.Forms.Form
6
7       Friend WithEvents txtBase As TextBox    ' reads base
8       Friend WithEvents txtPower As TextBox  ' reads power
9
10      Friend WithEvents inputGroup As GroupBox
11
12      Friend WithEvents lblBase As Label      ' prompts for base
13      Friend WithEvents lblPower As Label     ' prompts for power
14      Friend WithEvents lblOutput As Label    ' displays output
15
```

Fig. 4.13 **Optional**-argument demonstration with method **Power**. (Part 1 of 2.)

```
16       Friend WithEvents cmdCalculate As Button ' generates output
17
18       ' Visual Studio .NET generated code
19
20       ' reads input and displays result
21       Private Sub cmdCalculate_Click(ByVal sender As System.Object, _
22          ByVal e As System.EventArgs) Handles cmdCalculate.Click
23
24          Dim value As Integer
25
26          ' call version of Power depending on power input
27          If Not txtPower.Text = "" Then
28             value = Power(Convert.ToInt32(txtBase.Text), _
29                Convert.ToInt32(txtPower.Text))
30          Else
31             value = Power(Convert.ToInt32(txtBase.Text))
32          End If
33
34          lblOutput.Text = Convert.ToString(value)
35       End Sub ' cmdCalculate_Click
36
37       ' use iteration to calculate power
38       Function Power(ByVal base As Integer, _
39          Optional ByVal exponent As Integer = 2) As Integer
40
41          Dim total As Integer = 1
42          Dim i As Integer
43
44          For i = 1 To exponent
45             total *= base
46          Next
47
48          Return total
49       End Function ' Power
50
51    End Class ' FrmPower
```

Fig. 4.13 **Optional**-argument demonstration with method **Power**. (Part 2 of 2.)

Line 27 determines whether **txtPower** contains a value. If the condition evaluates to **True**, the values in the **TextBox**es are converted to **Integer**s and passed to **Power**. Otherwise, **txtBase**'s value is converted to an **Integer** and passed as the first of two arguments to **Power** in line 31. The second argument, which has a value of **2**, is provided by the Visual Basic compiler and is not visible to the programmer in the call.

Method **Power** (lines 38–49) specifies that its second argument is **Optional**. When omitted, the second argument defaults to the value **2**.

4.14 Modules

Programmers use modules to group related procedures so that they can be reused in other projects. Modules are similar in many ways to classes; they allow programmers to build reusable components without a full knowledge of object-oriented programming. Using modules in a project requires knowledge of scoping rules, because some procedures and variables in a module are accessible from other parts of a project. In general, modules should be self-contained, meaning that the procedures in the module should not require access to variables and procedures outside the module, except when such values are passed as arguments.

Figure 4.14 presents **modDice**, which groups several dice-related procedures into a module for reuse in other programs that use dice. Function **RollDie** (lines 11–13) simulates a single die roll and returns the result. We use FCL class *Random* (line 8) to generate random numbers. Line 12 calls method *Next* to generate a number in the range **1** to **6**, inclusive. Function **RollAndSum** (lines 16–27) uses a **For** structure (lines 22–24) to call **RollDie** for the number of times indicated by **diceNumber** and totals the results. Function **Get-DieImage** (lines 30–37) returns a die **Image** that corresponds to parameter **dieValue**. **Optional** parameter **baseImageName** represents the prefix of the image name to be used. If the argument is omitted, the default prefix **"die"** is used. [*Note*: New modules are added to a project by selecting **Project > Add Module**.]

```
1    ' Fig. 4.14: DiceModule.vb
2    ' A collection of common dice procedures.
3
4    Imports System.IO
5
6    Module modDice
7
8       Dim randomObject As Random = New Random()
9
10      ' rolls single die
11      Function RollDie() As Integer
12         Return randomObject.Next(1, 7)
13      End Function ' RollDie
14
15      ' die summation procedure
16      Function RollAndSum(ByVal diceNumber As Integer) _
17         As Integer
18
19         Dim i As Integer
20         Dim sum As Integer = 0
21
22         For i = 1 To diceNumber
23            sum += RollDie()
24         Next
25
26         Return sum
27      End Function ' RollAndSum
28
```

Fig. 4.14   Module used to define a group of related procedures. (Part 1 of 2.)

```
29      ' returns die image
30      Function GetDieImage(ByVal dieValue As Integer, _
31         Optional ByVal baseImageName As String = "die") _
32         As System.Drawing.Image
33
34         Return Image.FromFile( _
35            Directory.GetCurrentDirectory & _
36            "\Images\" & baseImageName & dieValue & ".png")
37      End Function ' GetDieImage
38
39   End Module ' modDice
```

Fig. 4.14   Module used to define a group of related procedures. (Part 2 of 2.)

FrmDiceModuleTest (Fig. 4.15) demonstrates the use of the **modDice** procedures to respond to button clicks. Procedure **cmdRollDie1_Click** (lines 23–27) rolls a
die and obtains the default image. We call procedures contained in **modDice** by following
the module name with the dot (.) operator and the procedure name. Due to the functionality
provided by **modDice**, the body of this procedure requires only one statement (line 26).
Thus, we easily can create a similar **Button, cmdRollDie2**. In this case, procedure
cmdRollDie2_Click (lines 29–34) uses the **Optional** argument to prefix the image
name and select a different image. Procedure **cmdRollTen_Click** (lines 36–40) sets the
Text property of **lblSum** to the result of 10 rolls.

```
1    ' Fig. 4.15: DiceModuleTest.vb
2    ' Demonstrates modDiceModule procedures
3
4    Imports System.Drawing
5
6    Public Class FrmDiceModuleTest
7       Inherits System.Windows.Forms.Form
8
9       Friend WithEvents lblSum As Label ' displays 10-roll sum
10
11      Friend WithEvents diceGroup As GroupBox
12
13      ' dice images
14      Friend WithEvents picDie1 As PictureBox
15      Friend WithEvents picDie2 As PictureBox
16
17      Friend WithEvents cmdRollDie1 As Button ' rolls blue die
18      Friend WithEvents cmdRollTen As Button  ' simulates 10 rolls
19      Friend WithEvents cmdRollDie2 As Button ' rolls red die
20
21      ' Visual Studio .NET generated code
22
23      Private Sub cmdRollDie1_Click(ByVal sender As System.Object, _
24         ByVal e As System.EventArgs) Handles cmdRollDie1.Click
25
```

Fig. 4.15   Testing the **modDice** procedures. (Part 1 of 2.)

```
26          picDie1.Image = modDice.GetDieImage(modDice.RollDie())
27      End Sub ' cmdRollDie1_Click
28
29      Private Sub cmdRollDie2_Click(ByVal sender As System.Object, _
30          ByVal e As System.EventArgs) Handles cmdRollDie2.Click
31
32          picDie2.Image = modDice.GetDieImage(modDice.RollDie(), _
33              "redDie")
34      End Sub ' cmdRollDie2_Click
35
36      Private Sub cmdRollTen_Click(ByVal sender As System.Object, _
37          ByVal e As System.EventArgs) Handles cmdRollTen.Click
38
39          lblSum.Text = Convert.ToString(modDice.RollAndSum(10))
40      End Sub ' cmdRollTen_Click
41
42  End Class ' FrmDiceModuleTest
```

Fig. 4.15   Testing the **modDice** procedures. (Part 2 of 2.)

For the program in Fig. 4.15, we add **DiceModule.vb** to the project to give it access to the procedures defined in **modDice**. To include a module in a project, select **File > Add Existing Item…**. In the dialog that is displayed, select the module's file name, and click the **Open** button. Once a module has been added to a project, the procedures contained in the module have namespace scope. By default, procedures with namespace scope are accessible to all other parts of a project, such as methods in classes and procedures in other modules. Although it is not necessary, the programmer may place the file containing the module's code in the same directory as the other files for the project.

4.15 Arrays

An array is a group of memory locations that have the same name and the same type. Array names follow the same conventions that apply to other variable names, as was discussed in Chapter 2. To refer to a particular location or element in an array, we specify the name of the array and the *position number* of the element to which we refer. Position numbers are values that indicate specific locations within arrays. The position number in parentheses more formally is called an *index* (or a *subscript*). An index must be an integer or an integer expression.

Arrays occupy space in memory. The amount of memory required by an array depends on the length of the array and the size of the data type of the elements in the array. The declaration of an array creates a variable that can store a reference to an array, but does not create the array in memory. To declare an array reference, the programmer provides the array's name and data type. For example, the declaration

```
Dim numberArray As Integer()
```

declares **numberArray** to be a reference to an **Integer** array. The parentheses that follow the data type indicate that an array is being referenced. Arrays can be declared to contain any data type. In an array of primitive data types, every element of the array contains one value of the declared data type. For example, every element of an **Integer** array contains an **Integer** value.

Before the array can be used, the programmer must specify the size of the array and allocate memory for the array, using keyword **New**. Keyword **New** creates an object. Arrays are represented as objects in Visual Basic, so they, too, must be allocated by using keyword **New**. The value stored in the array variable is actually a *reference* to the location in the computer's memory where the array object is created. All non-primitive-type variables are reference variables. For example, to allocate memory for the array **numberArray** after it has been declared, we use the statement

```
numberArray = New Integer(11) {}
```

In our example, the number **11** defines the upper bound for the array. *Array bounds* determine what indices can be used to access an element in the array. Here, the array bounds are **0** (which is implicit in the preceding statement) and **11**, meaning that an index outside these bounds cannot be used to access elements in the array. Notice that the actual size of the array is one larger than the upper bound specified in the allocation.

The zero or more items contained within required braces (**{** and **}**) are called an *initializer list* and specify the initial values of the elements in the array. When the initializer list is empty, the elements in the array are initialized to the default value for the data type of the elements of the array. The default value is **0** for numeric primitive-data-type variables, **False** for **Boolean** variables and **Nothing** for references. Keyword **Nothing** denotes an empty reference (i.e., a value indicating that a reference variable has not been assigned an address in the computer's memory). The initializer list also can contain a comma-separated list specifying the initial values of the elements in the array. For instance,

```
Dim numbers As Integer()
numbers = New Integer() {1, 2, 3, 6}
```

declares and allocates an array containing four **Integer** values. Visual Basic can determine the array bounds from the number of elements in the initializer list. Thus, it is not necessary to specify the size of the array when a nonempty initializer list is present.

The allocation of an array can be combined into the declaration, as in the statement

```
Dim numberArray As Integer() = New Integer(11) {}
```

Separating the declaration and allocation statements is useful, however, when the size of an array depends on user input or on values calculated at runtime.

Programmers can declare arrays via several alternative methods, which we discuss throughout this chapter. For example, several arrays can be declared with a single statement; the following statement declares two array references of type **Double()**:

```
Dim array1, array2 As Double()
```

The program in Fig. 4.16 creates three **Integer** arrays of 10 elements each and sets the values of the elements, using default initialization, an initializer list and a **For** structure. The arrays are displayed in tabular format in a message dialog.

```
1   ' Fig. 4.16: CreateArray.vb
2   ' Declaring, allocating and initializing arrays.
3
4   Imports System.Windows.Forms
5
6   Module modCreateArray
7
8      Sub Main()
9         Dim output As String
10        Dim i As Integer
11
12        Dim array As Integer()          ' declare array variable
13        Dim array1, array2 As Integer() ' declare two arrays
14
15        array = New Integer(9) {} ' allocate memory for array
16
17        ' initializer list specifies number of elements
18        ' and value of each element
19        array1 = New Integer() {32, 27, 64, 18, 95, _
20           14, 90, 70, 60, 37}
21
22        ' allocate array2 based on length of array1
23        array2 = New Integer(array1.GetUpperBound(0)) {}
24
25        ' set values in array2 by a calculation
26        For i = 0 To array2.GetUpperBound(0)
27           array2(i) = 2 + 2 * i
28        Next
29
30        output &= "Subscript " & vbTab & "Array" & vbTab & _
31           "Array1" & vbTab & "Array2" & vbCrLf
32
33        ' display values in array
34        For i = 0 To array.GetUpperBound(0)
35           output &= i & vbTab & array(i) & vbTab & _
36              array1(i) & vbTab & array2(i) & vbCrLf
37        Next
38
39        output &= vbCrLf & "The array contains " & _
40           array.Length & " elements."
41
```

Fig. 4.16 Creating arrays. (Part 1 of 2.)

```
42              MessageBox.Show(output, "Array of Integer Values", _
43                  MessageBoxButtons.OK, MessageBoxIcon.Information)
44        End Sub ' Main
45
46   End Module ' modCreateArray
```

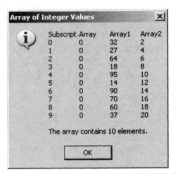

Fig. 4.16   Creating arrays. (Part 2 of 2.)

Line 12 declares **array**—a variable capable of storing a reference to an array of **Integer** elements. Line 15 allocates an array of 10 elements, using **New**, and assigns it to **array**. Line 13 uses one statement to declare **array1** and **array2** as variables that are capable of referring to arrays of **Integer**s. Lines 19–20 allocate the 10 elements of **array1** with **New** and initialize the values in the array, using an initializer list. Line 23 allocates **array2**, whose size is determined by the expression **array1.GetUpper-Bound(0)**, meaning that **array1** and **array2**, in this particular program, have the same upper bound.

The **For** structure in lines 26–28 initializes each element in **array2**. The elements in **array2** are initialized (line 27) to the even integers **2, 4, 6, ..., 20**. The **For** structure in lines 34–37 uses the values in the arrays to build **String output**, which is displayed in a **MessageBox** (lines 42–43).

Every array in Visual Basic "knows" its own length. The ***Length*** property (line 40) returns the number of elements in the array referenced by **array**.

4.16 Passing Arrays to Procedures

To pass an array argument to a procedure, specify the name of the array without using parentheses. For example, if array **hourlyTemperatures** has been declared as

    Dim hourlyTemperatures As Integer() = New Integer(24) {}

then the procedure call

        DayData(hourlyTemperatures)

passes array **hourlyTemperatures** to procedure **DayData**.

For a procedure to receive an array through a procedure call, the procedure's parameter list must specify that an array will be received. For example, the procedure header for **Day-Data** might be written as

```
Sub DayData(ByVal temperatureData As Integer())
```

indicating that **DayData** expects to receive an **Integer** array in parameter **temperatureData**. In Visual Basic, arrays always are passed by reference; however, it normally is inappropriate to use keyword **ByRef** in the procedure definition header. We discuss this subtle (and somewhat complex) issue in more detail in Section 4.17.

Although entire arrays are always passed by reference, individual array elements can be passed in the same manner as simple variables of that type. For instance, array element values of primitive data types, such as **Integer**, can be passed by value or by reference, depending on the procedure definition. To pass an array element to a procedure, use the indexed name of the array element as an argument in the call to the procedure. The program in Fig. 4.17 demonstrates the difference between passing an entire array and passing an array element.

```
1   ' Fig. 4.17: PassArray.vb
2   ' Passing arrays and individual array elements to procedures.
3
4   Imports System.Windows.Forms
5
6   Module modPassArray
7      Dim output As String
8
9      Sub Main()
10        Dim array1 As Integer() = New Integer() {1, 2, 3, 4, 5}
11        Dim i As Integer
12
13        output = "EFFECTS OF PASSING ENTIRE ARRAY " & _
14           "BY REFERENCE:" & vbCrLf & vbCrLf & _
15           "The values of the original array are:" & vbCrLf
16
17        ' display original elements of array1
18        For i = 0 To array1.GetUpperBound(0)
19           output &= "   " & array1(i)
20        Next
21
22        ModifyArray(array1) ' array is passed by reference
23
24        output &= vbCrLf & _
25           "The values of the modified array are:" & vbCrLf
26
27        ' display modified elements of array1
28        For i = 0 To array1.GetUpperBound(0)
29           output &= "   " & array1(i)
30        Next
31
32        output &= vbCrLf & vbCrLf & _
33           "EFFECTS OF PASSING ARRAY ELEMENT " & _
34           "BY VALUE:" & vbCrLf & vbCrLf & "array1(3) " & _
35           "before ModifyElementByVal: " & array1(3)
36
37        ' array element passed by value
38        ModifyElementByVal(array1(3))
```

Fig. 4.17 Passing arrays and individual array elements to procedures. (Part 1 of 3.)

```
39
40        output &= vbCrLf & "array1(3) after " & _
41           "ModifyElementByVal: " & array1(3)
42
43        output &= vbCrLf & vbCrLf & "EFFECTS OF PASSING " & _
44           "ARRAY ELEMENT BY REFERENCE: " & vbCrLf & vbCrLf & _
45           "array1(3) before ModifyElementByRef: " & array1(3)
46
47        ' array element passed by reference
48        ModifyElementByRef(array1(3))
49
50        output &= vbCrLf & "array1(3) after " & _
51           "ModifyElementByRef: " & array1(3)
52
53        MessageBox.Show(output, "Passing Arrays", _
54           MessageBoxButtons.OK, MessageBoxIcon.Information)
55     End Sub ' Main
56
57     ' procedure modifies array it receives (note ByVal)
58     Sub ModifyArray(ByVal arrayParameter As Integer())
59        Dim j As Integer
60
61        For j = 0 To arrayParameter.GetUpperBound(0)
62           arrayParameter(j) *= 2
63        Next
64
65     End Sub ' ModifyArray
66
67     ' procedure modifies integer passed to it
68     ' original is not to be modified (note ByVal)
69     Sub ModifyElementByVal(ByVal element As Integer)
70
71        output &= vbCrLf & "Value received in " & _
72           "ModifyElementByVal: " & element
73        element *= 2
74        output &= vbCrLf & "Value calculated in " & _
75           "ModifyElementByVal: " & element
76     End Sub ' ModifyElementByVal
77
78     ' procedure modifies integer passed to it
79     ' original is to be modified (note ByRef)
80     Sub ModifyElementByRef(ByRef element As Integer)
81
82        output &= vbCrLf & "Value received in " & _
83           "ModifyElementByRef: " & element
84        element *= 2
85        output &= vbCrLf & "Value calculated in " & _
86           "ModifyElementByRef: " & element
87     End Sub ' ModifyElementByRef
88
89  End Module ' modPassArray
```

Fig. 4.17   Passing arrays and individual array elements to procedures. (Part 2 of 3.)

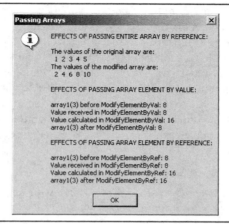

Fig. 4.17   Passing arrays and individual array elements to procedures. (Part 3 of 3.)

The **For/Next** structure on lines 18–20 appends the five elements of integer array **array1** (line 10) to **String output**. Line 22 passes **array1** to procedure **Modify-Array** (line 58), which then multiplies each element by **2** (line 62). To illustrate that **array1**'s elements were modified in the called procedure (i.e., as enabled by passing by reference), the **For/Next** structure on lines 28–30 appends the five elements of **array1** to **output**. As the screen capture indicates, the elements of **array1** are indeed modified by **ModifyArray**.

To show the value of **array1(3)** before the call to **ModifyElementByVal**, lines 32–35 append the value of **array1(3)** to **String output**. Line 38 invokes procedure **ModifyElementByVal** and passes it **array1(3)**. When **array1(3)** is passed by value, the **Integer** value in the fourth position of array **array1** (now **8**) is copied and is passed to procedure **ModifyElementByVal**, where it becomes the value of argument **element**. Procedure **ModifyElementByVal** then multiplies **element** by **2** (line 73). The parameter of **ModifyElementByVal** is a local variable that is destroyed when the procedure terminates. Thus, when control is returned to **Main**, the unmodified value of **array1(3)** is appended to the string variable **output** (lines 40–41).

Lines 43–51 demonstrate the effects of procedure **ModifyElementByRef** (lines 80–87). This procedure performs the same calculation as that in **ModifyElementByVal** i.e., multiplying **element** by **2**. In this case, **array1(3)** is passed by reference, meaning that the value of **array1(3)** appended to **output** (lines 50–51) is the same as the value calculated in the procedure.

Common Programming Error 4.12

In passing an array to a procedure, including an empty pair of parentheses after the array name is a syntax error.

4.17 Passing Arrays: `ByVal` vs. `ByRef`

In Visual Basic .NET, a variable that "stores" an object, such as an array, does not actually store the object itself. Instead, such a variable stores a reference to the object (i.e., the location in the computer's memory where the object is already stored). The distinction between reference variables and primitive data type variables raises some subtle issues that programmers must understand to create secure, stable programs.

When used to declare a value-type parameter, keyword **ByVal** causes the value of the argument to be copied to a local variable in the procedure. Changes to the local variable are reflected in the local copy of that variable, but not in the original variable in the calling program. However, if the argument passed using keyword **ByVal** is of a reference type, the value copied is also a reference to the original object in the computer's memory. Thus, reference types (like arrays and other objects) passed via keyword **ByVal** actually are passed by reference, meaning that changes to the objects in called procedures affect the original objects in the callers.

Performance Tip 4.1

Passing arrays and other objects by reference makes sense for performance reasons. If arrays were passed by value, a copy of each element would be passed. For large, frequently passed arrays, this procedure would waste time and consume considerable storage with the copies of the arrays. Both of these problems cause poor performance.

Visual Basic also allows procedures to pass references by means of keyword **ByRef**. This capability is subtle and, if misused, can lead to problems. For instance, when a reference-type object like an array is passed via **ByRef**, the called procedure actually gains control over the passed reference itself, allowing the called procedure to replace the original reference in the caller with a different object, or even with **Nothing**. Such behavior can lead to unpredictable effects, which can be disastrous in mission-critical applications. The program in Fig. 4.18 demonstrates the subtle difference between passing a reference **ByVal** and passing a reference **ByRef**.

Lines 11–12 declare two integer array variables, **firstArray** and **firstArray-Copy**. (We make the copy so that we can determine whether reference **firstArray** gets overwritten.) Line 15 allocates an array containing **Integer** values **1**, **2** and **3** and stores the array reference in variable **firstArray**. The assignment statement on line 16 copies reference **firstArray** to variable **firstArrayCopy**, causing these variables to reference the same array object. The **For/Next** structure on lines 24–26 prints the contents of **firstArray** before it is passed to procedure **FirstDouble** on line 29, so we can verify that this array is passed by reference (i.e., that the called method indeed changes the array's contents).

```
1    ' Fig. 4.18: ArrayReferenceTest.vb
2    ' Testing the effects of passing array references using
3    ' ByVal and ByRef.
4
5    Module modArrayReferenceTest
6
7       Sub Main()
8          Dim i As Integer
9
10         ' declare array references
11         Dim firstArray As Integer()
12         Dim firstArrayCopy As Integer()
```

Fig. 4.18 Passing an array reference with **ByVal** and **ByRef**. (Part 1 of 4.)

```
13
14        ' allocate firstArray and copy its reference
15        firstArray = New Integer() {1, 2, 3}
16        firstArrayCopy = firstArray
17
18        Console.WriteLine("Test passing array reference " & _
19           "using ByVal.")
20        Console.Write("Contents of firstArray before " & _
21           "calling FirstDouble: ")
22
23        ' print contents of firstArray
24        For i = 0 To firstArray.GetUpperBound(0)
25           Console.Write(firstArray(i) & " ")
26        Next
27
28        ' pass firstArray using ByVal
29        FirstDouble(firstArray)
30
31        Console.Write(vbCrLf & "Contents of firstArray after " & _
32           "calling FirstDouble: ")
33
34        ' print contents of firstArray
35        For i = 0 To firstArray.GetUpperBound(0)
36           Console.Write(firstArray(i) & " ")
37        Next
38
39        ' test whether reference was changed by FirstDouble
40        If firstArray Is firstArrayCopy Then
41           Console.WriteLine(vbCrLf & "The references are " & _
42              "equal.")
43        Else
44           Console.WriteLine(vbCrLf & "The references are " & _
45              "not equal.")
46        End If
47
48        ' declare array references
49        Dim secondArray As Integer()
50        Dim secondArrayCopy As Integer()
51
52        ' allocate secondArray and copy its reference
53        secondArray = New Integer() {1, 2, 3}
54        secondArrayCopy = secondArray
55
56        Console.WriteLine(vbCrLf & "Test passing array " & _
57           "reference using ByRef.")
58        Console.Write("Contents of secondArray before " & _
59           "calling SecondDouble: ")
60
61        ' print contents of secondArray before procedure call
62        For i = 0 To secondArray.GetUpperBound(0)
63           Console.Write(secondArray(i) & " ")
64        Next
65
```

Fig. 4.18 Passing an array reference with **ByVal** and **ByRef**. (Part 2 of 4.)

```
66              ' pass secondArray using ByRef
67              SecondDouble(secondArray)
68
69              Console.Write(vbCrLf & "Contents of secondArray " & _
70                 "after calling SecondDouble: ")
71
72              ' print contents of secondArray after procedure call
73              For i = 0 To secondArray.GetUpperBound(0)
74                 Console.Write(secondArray(i) & " ")
75              Next
76
77              ' test whether reference was changed by SecondDouble
78              If secondArray Is secondArrayCopy Then
79                 Console.WriteLine(vbCrLf & "The references are " & _
80                    "equal.")
81              Else
82                 Console.WriteLine(vbCrLf & "The references are " & _
83                    "not equal.")
84              End If
85
86           End Sub ' Main
87
88        ' procedure modifies elements of array and assigns
89        ' new reference (note ByVal)
90        Sub FirstDouble(ByVal array As Integer())
91           Dim i As Integer
92
93              ' double each element value
94              For i = 0 To array.GetUpperBound(0)
95                 array(i) *= 2
96              Next
97
98              ' create new reference, assign it to array
99              array = New Integer() {11, 12, 13}
100        End Sub ' FirstDouble
101
102       ' procedure modifies elements of array and assigns
103       ' new reference (note ByRef)
104       Sub SecondDouble(ByRef array As Integer())
105          Dim i As Integer
106
107             ' double contents of array
108             For i = 0 To array.GetUpperBound(0)
109                array(i) *= 2
110             Next
111
112             ' create new reference, assign it to array
113             array = New Integer() {11, 12, 13}
114       End Sub ' SecondDouble
115
116    End Module ' modArrayReferenceTest
```

Fig. 4.18   Passing an array reference with **ByVal** and **ByRef**. (Part 3 of 4.)

```
Test passing array reference using ByVal.
Contents of firstArray before calling FirstDouble: 1 2 3
Contents of firstArray after calling FirstDouble: 2 4 6
The references are equal.

Test passing array reference using ByRef.
Contents of secondArray before calling SecondDouble: 1 2 3
Contents of secondArray after calling SecondDouble: 11 12 13
The references are not equal.
```

Fig. 4.18 Passing an array reference with **ByVal** and **ByRef**. (Part 4 of 4.)

The **For/Next** structure in procedure **FirstDouble** (lines 94–96) multiplies the values of all the elements in the array by **2**. Line 99 allocates a new array containing the values **11**, **12** and **13**; the reference for this array then is assigned to parameter **array** (in an attempt to overwrite reference **firstArray** in **Main**—this, of course, will not happen, because the reference was passed **ByVal**). After procedure **FirstDouble** executes, the **For/Next** structure on lines 35–37 prints the contents of **firstArray**, demonstrating that the values of the elements have been changed by the procedure (and confirming that in Visual Basic, arrays always are passed by reference). The **If** structure on lines 40–46 uses the **Is** operator to compare references **firstArray** (which we just attempted to overwrite) and **firstArrayCopy**. Visual Basic provides operator **Is** for comparing references to determine whether they are referencing the same object. The expression on line 40 is true if the operands to binary operator **Is** indeed reference the same object. In this case, the object represented is the array allocated in line 15—not the array allocated in procedure **FirstDouble** (line 99).

Lines 48–84 in procedure **Main** perform similar tests, using array variables **secondArray** and **secondArrayCopy** and procedure **SecondDouble** (lines 104–114). Procedure **SecondDouble** performs the same operations as **FirstDouble**, but receives its array argument via keyword **ByRef**. In this case, the reference stored in **secondArray** after the procedure call is a reference to the array allocated on line 113 of **SecondDouble**, demonstrating that a reference passed via keyword **ByRef** can be modified by the called procedure so that the reference actually points to a different object—in this case, an array allocated in procedure **SecondDouble**. The **If** structure on lines 78–84 demonstrates that **secondArray** and **secondArrayCopy** no longer represent the same array.

Software Engineering Observation 4.7

*Using **ByVal** to receive a reference-type object parameter does not cause the object to be passed by value—the object is still passed by reference. Rather, **ByVal** causes the object's reference to be passed by value. This condition prevents a called procedure from overwriting a reference in the caller. In the vast majority of cases, protecting the caller's reference from modification is the desired behavior. If you encounter a situation where you truly want the called procedure to modify the caller's reference, pass the reference-type object **ByRef**— but, again, such situations are rare.*

Software Engineering Observation 4.8

In Visual Basic, reference-type objects (including arrays) are always passed by reference. So, a called procedure receiving a reference to an object in a caller can change the caller's object.

4.18 Multidimensional Rectangular and Jagged Arrays

So far, we have studied *one-dimensional* (or *single-subscripted*) arrays—i.e., arrays that contain one row of values. In this section, we introduce *multidimensional* (often called *multiple-subscripted*) arrays, which require two or more indices to identify particular elements. We concentrate on *two-dimensional* (often called *double-subscripted*) arrays, or arrays that contain multiple rows of values. There are two types of multidimensional arrays—*rectangular* and *jagged*. Rectangular arrays with two indices often represent *tables* of values consisting of information arranged in *rows* and *columns*. Each row is the same size, and each column is the same size (hence the term "rectangular"). To identify a particular table element, we must specify the two indices; by convention, the first identifies the element's row, and the second identifies the element's column. Figure 4.19 illustrates a two-dimensional rectangular array, **a**, containing three rows and four columns. A rectangular two-dimensional array with *m* rows and *n* columns is called an *m-by-n array*; the array in Fig. 4.19 is referred to as a three-by-four array.

Every element in array **a** is identified in Fig. 4.19 by an element name of the form **a(i, j)**, where **a** is the name of the array and **i** and **j** are the indices that uniquely identify the row and column of each element in array **a**. Notice that, because array indices are determined through zero-based counting, the names of the elements in the first row have a first index of **0**; likewise, the names of the elements in the fourth column have a second index of **3**.

Multidimensional arrays are initialized in declarations by means of the same process and notations employed for one-dimensional arrays. For example, a two-dimensional rectangular array **numbers** with two rows and two columns could be declared and initialized as follows:

```
Dim numbers As Integer(,) = New Integer(1,1) {}

numbers(0, 0) = 1
numbers(0, 1) = 2
numbers(1, 0) = 3
numbers(1, 1) = 4
```

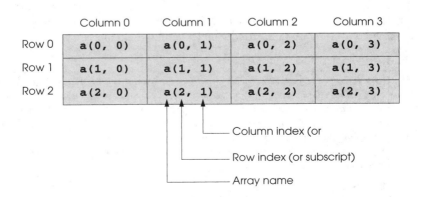

Fig. 4.19   Two-dimensional array with three rows and four columns.

Alternatively, the initialization can be written on one line as follows:

```
Dim numbers As Integer(,) = New Integer(,) {{1, 2}, {3, 4}}
```

The values are grouped by row in braces, with **1** and **2** initializing **numbers(0,0)** and **numbers(0,1)**, respectively, and **3** and **4** initializing **numbers(1,0)** and **numbers(1,1)**, respectively. The compiler determines the number of rows by counting the number of subinitializer lists (represented by sets of braces) in the main initializer list. Then, the compiler determines the number of columns in each row by counting the number of initializer values in the subinitializer list for that row. In rectangular arrays, each row has the same number of values.

Jagged arrays are maintained as arrays of arrays. Unlike rectangular arrays, rows in jagged arrays can be of different lengths. The statements

```
Dim array2 As Integer()()      ' declare jagged array

array2 = New Integer(1)() {} ' allocate two rows

' allocate columns for row 0
array2(0) = New Integer() {1, 2}

' allocate columns for row 1
array2(1) = New Integer() {3, 4, 5}
```

create **Integer** array **array2** with row **0** (which is an array itself) containing two elements (**1** and **2**) and row **1** containing three elements (**3**, **4** and **5**). Notice that the array name, followed by a single index (e.g., **array2(0)**), behaves exactly like a normal one-dimensional array variable. A one-dimensional array can be created and assigned to that value.

The program in Fig. 4.20 demonstrates the initialization of a rectangular array (**array1**) and a jagged array (**array2**) in declarations and the use of nested **For/Next** loops to traverse the arrays (i.e., to manipulate every array element).

```
1    ' Fig. 4.20: MultidimensionalArrays.vb
2    ' Initializing multidimensional arrays.
3
4    Imports System.Windows.Forms
5
6    Module modMultidimensionalArrays
7
8       Sub Main()
9          Dim output As String
10         Dim i, j As Integer
11
12            ' create rectangular two-dimensional array
13            Dim array1 As Integer(,)
14            array1 = New Integer(,) {{1, 2, 3}, {4, 5, 6}}
15
16            ' create jagged two-dimensional array
17            Dim array2 As Integer()() = New Integer(2)() {}
```

Fig. 4.20   Initializing multidimensional arrays. (Part 1 of 2.)

```
18
19        array2(0) = New Integer() {1, 2}
20        array2(1) = New Integer() {3}
21        array2(2) = New Integer() {4, 5, 6}
22
23        output = "Values in array1 by row are " & vbCrLf
24
25        For i = 0 To array1.GetUpperBound(0)
26
27           For j = 0 To array1.GetUpperBound(1)
28              output &= array1(i, j) & "   "
29           Next
30
31           output &= vbCrLf
32        Next
33
34        output &= vbCrLf & "Values in array2 by row are " & _
35           vbCrLf
36
37        For i = 0 To array2.GetUpperBound(0)
38
39           For j = 0 To array2(i).GetUpperBound(0)
40              output &= array2(i)(j) & "   "
41           Next
42
43           output &= vbCrLf
44        Next
45
46        MessageBox.Show(output, _
47           "Initializing Multi-Dimensional Arrays", _
48           MessageBoxButtons.OK, MessageBoxIcon.Information)
49     End Sub ' Main
50
51  End Module ' modMultidimensionalArrays
```

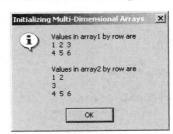

Fig. 4.20   Initializing multidimensional arrays. (Part 2 of 2.)

The program declares two arrays in method **Main**. The allocation of **array1** (line 14) provides six initializers in two sublists. The first sublist initializes the first row (row **0**) of the array to the values **1**, **2** and **3**; the second sublist initializes the second row (row **1**) of the array to the values **4**, **5** and **6**. The declaration and allocation of **array2** (line 17) create a jagged array of three arrays (specified by the **2** in the first set of parentheses after keyword **Integer**). Lines 19–21 initialize each subarray so that the first subarray contains the values **1** and **2**, the second contains the value **3**, and the last contains the values **4**, **5** and **6**.

The nested **For/Next** structures in lines 24–31 append the elements of **array1** to string **output**. The nested **For/Next** structures traverse the arrays in two dimensions. The outer **For/Next** structure traverses the rows; the inner **For/Next** structure traverses the columns within a row. Each **For/Next** structure calls method **GetUpperBound** to obtain the upper bound of the dimension it traverses. Notice that the dimensions are zero based, meaning the rows are dimension **0** and the columns are dimension **1**.

The nested **For/Next** structures in lines 37–44 behave similarly for **array2**. However, in a jagged two-dimensional array, the second dimension is actually the first dimension of a separate array. In the example, the inner **For/Next** structure determines the number of columns in each row of the array by passing argument **0** to method **GetUpper-Bound**, called on the array returned by accessing a single row of the jagged array. Arrays of dimensions higher than two can be traversed by using one nested **For/Next** structure for each dimension.

Many common array manipulations use **For/Next** repetition structures. Imagine a jagged array **jaggedArray** that contains three rows, or arrays. The following **For/Next** repetition structure sets all the elements in the third row of array **jaggedArray** to zero:

```
For column = 0 To jaggedArray(2).GetUpperBound(0)
   jaggedArray(2)(column) = 0
Next
```

We specified the *third* row; therefore, we know that the first index is always **2** (because **0** is the first row and **1** is the second row). The **For/Next** loop varies only the second index (i.e., the column index). Notice the use of **jaggedArray(2).GetUpperBound(0)** as the end value of the loop counter. In this expression, we call the **GetUpperBound** method on the array contained in the third row of **jaggedArray**. This statement demonstrates that each row of **jaggedArray** is itself an array, and therefore, methods called on this value behave as they would for a typical array. The preceding **For/Next** structure is equivalent to the assignment statements

```
jaggedArray(2)(0) = 0
jaggedArray(2)(1) = 0
jaggedArray(2)(2) = 0
jaggedArray(2)(3) = 0
```

The following nested **For/Next** structure determines the total of all the elements in array **jaggedArray**:

```
Dim total, row, column As Integer

For row = 0 To jaggedArray.GetUpperBound(0)

   For column = 0 To jaggedArray(row).GetUpperBound(0)
      total += jaggedArray(row)(column)
   Next

Next
```

We use method **GetUpperBound** in the headers of the **For/Next** structures to determine the number of rows in **jaggedArray** and the number of columns in each row. The nested **For/Next** structure totals the elements of the array, one row at a time. The outer

For/Next structure begins by setting the **row** index to **0**, so that the elements of the first row can be totaled by the inner **For/Next** structure. The outer **For/Next** structure then increments **row** to **1**, so that the elements of the second row can be totaled. Finally, the outer **For/Next** structure increments **row** to **2**, so that the elements of the third row can be totaled. The result can be displayed when the outer **For/Next** structure terminates.

4.19 For Each/Next Repetition Structure

Visual Basic provides the **For Each/Next** repetition structure for iterating through the values in a data structure, such as an array. When used with one-dimensional arrays, **For Each/Next** behaves like a **For/Next** structure that iterates through the range of indices from **0** to the value returned by **GetUpperBound(0)**. Instead of a counter, **For Each/Next** uses a variable to represent the value of each element. The program in Fig. 4.21 uses the **For Each/Next** repetition structure to determine the minimum value in a two-dimensional array of grades.

The header of the **For Each** repetition structure (line 13) specifies a variable, **grade**, and an array, **gradeArray**. The **For Each/Next** structure iterates through all the elements in **gradeArray**, sequentially assigning each value to variable **grade**. The values are compared with variable **lowGrade** (line 15), which stores the lowest grade in the array.

```
1   ' Fig. 4.21: ForEach.vb
2   ' Program uses For Each/Next to find a minimum grade.
3
4   Module modForEach
5
6      Sub Main()
7         Dim gradeArray As Integer(,) = New Integer(,) _
8            {{77, 68, 86, 73}, {98, 87, 89, 81}, {70, 90, 86, 81}}
9
10        Dim grade As Integer
11        Dim lowGrade As Integer = 100
12
13        For Each grade In gradeArray
14
15           If grade < lowGrade Then
16              lowGrade = grade
17           End If
18
19        Next
20
21        Console.WriteLine("The minimum grade is: {0}", lowGrade)
22     End Sub ' Main
23
24  End Module ' modForEach
```

```
The minimum grade is: 68
```

Fig. 4.21 Using **For Each/Next** with an array.

For rectangular arrays, the repetition of the **For Each/Next** structure begins with the element whose indices are all zero and subsequently iterates through all possible combinations of indices, incrementing the rightmost index first. When the rightmost index reaches its upper bound, it is reset to zero, and the index to the left of it is incremented by one. In this case, **grade** takes the values as they are ordered in the initializer list in line 8. When all the grades have been processed, **lowGrade** is displayed.

Although many array calculations are handled best with a counter, **For Each/Next** is useful when the indices of the elements are not important. **For Each/Next** particularly is useful for looping through arrays of objects, as we discuss in Chapter 7.

In this chapter, we have introduced procedures and arrays. We have also mentioned that Visual Basic .NET arrays are objects. In Chapter 5, we show how to create classes, which are essentially the "blueprints" from which objects are instantiated (i.e., created).

4.20 Summary

Experience has shown that the best way to develop and maintain a large program is to construct it from small, manageable pieces. This technique is known as divide and conquer. Visual Basic programs consist of many pieces, including modules and classes. Modules and classes are composed of smaller pieces called procedures. Procedures promote software reusability—the ability to use existing procedures as building blocks for new programs.

Three types of procedures exist: **Sub** procedures (which do not return a value), **Function** procedures (which return a value) and event procedures (which respond to user actions called events).

All data types can be categorized as either value types or reference types. A variable of a value type contains data of that type. A variable of a reference type contains the location in memory where the data are stored. Both value and reference types include built-in types and types that programmers can create.

Arguments are passed in one of two ways—pass-by-value and pass-by-reference (also called call-by-value and call-by-reference, respectively). When an argument is passed by value, the program makes a copy of the argument's value and passes that copy to the called procedure. Changes to the called procedure's copy do not affect the original variable's value. When an argument is passed by reference, the caller gives the procedure the ability to access and modify the caller's original data directly.

An identifier's duration (also called its lifetime) is the period during which the identifier exists in memory. Identifiers that represent local variables in a procedure (i.e., parameters and variables declared in the procedure body) have automatic duration. Automatic-duration variables are created when program control enters the procedure in which they are declared, exist while the procedure is active and are destroyed when the procedure is exited.

The scope (sometimes called declaration space) of a variable, reference or procedure identifier is the portion of the program in which the identifier can be accessed. The possible scopes for an identifier are class scope, module scope, namespace scope and block scope.

A widening conversion occurs when a type is converted to another type (usually one that can hold more data) without losing data. A narrowing conversion occurs when there is potential for data loss during a conversion (usually to a type that holds a smaller amount of data). When set to **On**, **Option Strict** requires the programmer to perform all narrowing conversions explicitly.

Overloading allows the programmer to define several procedures with the same name, as long as the procedures have different sets of parameters (in terms of the number of parameters, the types of the parameters and the order of the parameters). This feature allows the programmer to reduce the complexity of the program and create a more flexible application. Overloaded procedures are distinguished by their signatures, which are a combination of the procedure's name and parameter types. The compiler uses a logical process known as overload resolution to determine which procedure should be called.

Programmers use modules to group related procedures so that they can be reused in other projects. Modules are similar in many ways to classes; they allow programmers to build reusable components without a full knowledge of object-oriented programming.

Visual Basic allows programmers to create procedures that take one or more optional arguments. When a parameter is declared as optional, the caller has the option of passing that particular argument. Optional arguments are specified in the procedure header by using keyword **Optional**.

A recursive procedure is a procedure that calls itself, either indirectly (i.e., through another procedure) or directly. Both **Sub** and **Function** procedures may be recursive.

An array is a group of memory locations that have the same name and are of the same type. The first element in every array is the zeroth element (i.e., element **0**).

The declaration of an array creates a variable that can store a reference to an array, but does not create the array in memory. Arrays can be declared to contain elements of any data type. Arrays are represented as objects in Visual Basic, so they must also be allocated via keyword **New**.

To pass an array argument to a procedure, specify the name of the array, and do not include parentheses. Although entire arrays are passed by reference, individual array elements of primitive data types can be passed by value.

There are two types of multidimensional arrays—rectangular and jagged. Rectangular arrays with two indices often are used to represent tables of values consisting of information arranged in rows and columns. Each row is the same size, and each column is the same size (hence to the term "rectangular"). Jagged arrays are maintained as arrays of arrays. Unlike with rectangular arrays, rows in jagged arrays can be of different lengths. Visual Basic provides the **For Each/Next** repetition structure for iterating through the values in a data structure, such as an array.

Object-Based Programming

Objectives

- To understand encapsulation and data hiding.
- To understand the concepts of data abstraction and abstract data types (ADTs).
- To create, use and destroy objects.
- To control access to object instance variables and methods.
- To use properties to keep objects in consistent states.
- To understand the use of the **Me** reference.
- To understand namespaces and assemblies.
- To use the **Class View** and **Object Browser**.

My object all sublime
I shall achieve in time.
W. S. Gilbert

Is it a world to hide virtues in?
William Shakespeare

Your public servants serve you right.
Adlai Stevenson

Classes struggle, some classes triumph, others are
eliminated.
Mao Zedong

This above all: to thine own self be true.
William Shakespeare

Outline

5.1 Introduction

In this chapter, we investigate object orientation in Visual Basic. Some readers might ask, why did we defer this topic until now? There are several reasons. First, the objects we build in this chapter are composed partially of structured program pieces; to explain the organization of objects, we needed to establish a basis in structured programming with control structures. We also wanted to study methods in detail before introducing object orientation. Finally, we wanted to familiarize readers with arrays, which are Visual Basic objects.

In our discussions of object-oriented programs in Chapters 1–4, we introduced many basic concepts (i.e., "object think") and terminology (i.e., "object speak") that relate to Visual Basic object-oriented programming. We also discussed our program-development methodology: We analyzed many typical problems that required a program to be built and determined what classes from the .NET Framework Library were needed to implement each program. We then selected appropriate instance variables and methods for each program, as well as specifying the manner in which an object of our class collaborated with objects from the .NET Framework classes to accomplish the program's overall goals.

Let us briefly review some key concepts and terminology of object orientation. Object orientation uses classes to *encapsulate* instance variables (*data*) and methods (*behaviors*). Objects have the ability to hide their implementation from other objects (this principle is called *information hiding*). Although some objects can communicate with one another across well-defined *interfaces,* objects are unaware of how other objects are implemented.

Normally, implementation details are hidden within the objects themselves. Surely, it is possible to drive a car effectively without knowing the details of how engines, transmissions and exhaust systems operate. Later, we will see why information hiding is so crucial to good software engineering.

In C and other *procedural programming languages,* programming tends to be *action oriented.* Visual Basic programming, however, is *object oriented.* In C, the unit of programming is the *function* (called *procedures* in Visual Basic). In Visual Basic, the unit of programming is the *class* (although programs often are written with modules as well). Objects eventually are *instantiated* (i.e., created) from these classes, whereas procedures are encapsulated within the "boundaries" of classes as methods.

C programmers concentrate on writing functions. They group actions that perform some task into a function and then group functions to form a program. Data is certainly important in C, but it exists primarily to support the actions that functions perform. The *verbs* in a system-requirements document help a C programmer determine the set of functions that will work together to implement the system.

Visual Basic programmers concentrate on creating their own *user-defined types* called *classes.* We also refer to classes as *programmer-defined types.* Each class contains both data and a set of methods that manipulate the data. The data components, or *data members*, of a class are called *instance variables*, or *member variables.* Just as we call an instance of a built-in type—such as **Integer**—a *variable,* we call an *instance* of a user-defined type (i.e., a class) an *object.* In Visual Basic, attention is focused on classes, rather than methods. The *nouns* in a system-requirements document help the Visual Basic programmer determine an initial set of classes with which to begin the design process. These classes then are used to instantiate objects that work together to implement the system.

This chapter explains how to create and use classes and objects, a subject known as *object-based programming (OBP).* Chapters 6 and 7 introduce *inheritance* and *polymorphism*—two key technologies that enable *object-oriented programming (OOP).* Although we do not discuss inheritance in detail until Chapter 6, it is part of several Visual Basic class definitions. An example of inheritance was demonstrated when we derived a class from **System.Windows.Forms.Form** in Chapter 3.

Software Engineering Observation 5.1

All Visual Basic objects are passed by reference. Visual Basic classes are reference types.

5.2 Implementing a Time Abstract Data Type with a Class

Classes in Visual Basic facilitate the creation of special data types, called *abstract data types (ADT)*, which hide their implementation from clients. A problem in procedural programming languages is that client code often is implementation-dependent; client code has to be written so that it uses specific data members and must be rewritten if the code with which it interfaces changes. ADTs eliminate this problem by providing implementation-independent interfaces to their clients. The creator of a class can change the implementation of that class without having to change the clients of that class.

Software Engineering Observation 5.2

It is important to write programs that are understandable and easy to maintain. Change is the rule rather than the exception. Programmers should anticipate that their code will be modified. As we will see, classes facilitate program modifiability.

Before discussing classes in detail, we review how to add classes to a project in Visual Studio. By now, you are familiar with adding a module to a project. The process of adding a class to a project is almost identical to that of adding a module to a project. To add a class to a project, select **Project > Add Class**. Enter the class name in the **Name** text field and click the **Open** button. Note that the class name (ending with the **.vb** file extension) appears in the **Solution Explorer** below the project name.

The following application consists of class **CTime** (Fig. 5.1) and module **modTimeTest** (Fig. 5.2). Class **CTime** contains the information needed to represent a specific time; module **modTimeTest** contains method **Main**, which uses an instance of class **CTime** to run the application.

In Fig. 5.1, lines 4–5 begin the **CTime** class definition, indicating that class **CTime** inherits from class *Object* (of namespace **System**). Visual Basic programmers use *inheritance* to create classes from existing classes. The **Inherits** keyword (line 5) followed by class name **Object** indicates that class **CTime** inherits existing pieces of class **Object**. If the programmer does not include line 5, the Visual Basic compiler includes it implicitly. Because this is the first chapter that exposes classes, we include these declarations for the classes in this chapter; however, we remove them in Chapter 6. A complete understanding of inheritance is not necessary to the understanding of the concepts and programs in this chapter. We explore inheritance in detail in Chapter 6.

```
1   ' Fig. 5.1: CTime.vb
2   ' Represents time in 24-hour format.
3
4   Class CTime
5      Inherits Object
6
7      ' declare Integer instance values for hour, minute and second
8      Private mHour As Integer ' 0 - 23
9      Private mMinute As Integer ' 0 - 59
10     Private mSecond As Integer ' 0 - 59
11
12     ' Method New is the CTime constructor method, which initializes
13     ' instance variables to zero
14     Public Sub New()
15        SetTime(0, 0, 0)
16     End Sub ' New
17
18     ' set new time value using universal time;
19     ' perform validity checks on data;
20     ' set invalid values to zero
21     Public Sub SetTime(ByVal hourValue As Integer, _
22        ByVal minuteValue As Integer, ByVal secondValue As Integer)
23
24        ' check if hour is between 0 and 23, then set hour
25        If (hourValue >= 0 AndAlso hourValue < 24) Then
26           mHour = hourValue
27        Else
28           mHour = 0
29        End If
```

Fig. 5.1   Abstract data type representing time in 24-hour format. (Part 1 of 2.)

```
30
31          ' check if minute is between 0 and 59, then set minute
32          If (minuteValue >= 0 AndAlso minuteValue < 60) Then
33              mMinute = minuteValue
34          Else
35              mMinute = 0
36          End If
37
38          ' check if second is between 0 and 59, then set second
39          If (secondValue >= 0 AndAlso secondValue < 60) Then
40              mSecond = secondValue
41          Else
42              mSecond = 0
43          End If
44
45      End Sub ' SetTime
46
47      ' convert String to universal-time format
48      Public Function ToUniversalString() As String
49          Return String.Format("{0}:{1:D2}:{2:D2}", _
50              mHour, mMinute, mSecond)
51      End Function ' ToUniversalString
52
53      ' convert to String in standard-time format
54      Public Function ToStandardString() As String
55          Dim suffix As String = " PM"
56          Dim format As String = "{0}:{1:D2}:{2:D2}"
57          Dim standardHour As Integer
58
59          ' determine whether time is AM or PM
60          If mHour < 12 Then
61              suffix = " AM"
62          End If
63
64          ' convert from universal-time format to standard-time format
65          If (mHour = 12 OrElse mHour = 0) Then
66              standardHour = 12
67          Else
68              standardHour = mHour Mod 12
69          End If
70
71          Return String.Format(format, standardHour, mMinute, _
72              mSecond) & suffix
73      End Function ' ToStandardString
74
75  End Class ' CTime
```

Fig. 5.1   Abstract data type representing time in 24-hour format. (Part 2 of 2.)

Lines 4 and 75 delineate the *body* of the **CTime** class definition with keywords **Class** and **End Class**. Any information that we place in this body is contained within the class. For example, class **CTime** contains three **Integer** instance variables—**mHour, mMinute** and **mSecond** (lines 8–10)—that represent the time in *universal-time* format (*24-*

hour clock format). Note that our member-naming preference is to prefix an 'm' to each instance variable.[1]

Good Programming Practice 5.1

Begin class names using a capital "C" to distinguish those names as class names.

Keywords **Public** and **Private** are *member access modifiers*. Instance variables or methods with member access modifier **Public** are accessible wherever the program has a reference to a **CTime** object. The declaration of instance variables or methods with member access modifier **Private** makes them accessible only to methods of that class. Member access modifiers can appear in any order in a class definition.

Good Programming Practice 5.2

For clarity, every instance variable or method definition should be preceded by a member access modifier.

Good Programming Practice 5.3

Group members in a class definition according to their member access modifiers to enhance clarity and readability.

Lines 8–10 declare each of the three **Integer** instance variables—**mHour, mMinute** and **mSecond**—with member access modifier **Private**, indicating that these instance variables of the class are accessible only to members of the class. When an object of the class encapsulates such instance variables, only methods of that object's class can access the variables. Normally, instance variables are declared **Private**, whereas methods are declared **Public**. However, it is possible to have **Private** methods and **Public** instance variables, as we will see later. Often, **Private** methods are called *utility methods*, or *helper methods*, because they can be called only by other methods of that class, and their purpose is to support the operation of those methods. The creation of **Public** data members in a class is an uncommon and dangerous programming practice. The provision of such access to a class's data members is unsafe; foreign code could set these members to invalid values, producing potentially disastrous results.

Software Engineering Observation 5.3

*Make a class member **Private** if there is no reason for it to be accessed outside of the class definition.*

Access methods can read or display data. Another common use for access methods is to test the truth of conditions—such methods often are called *predicate methods*. For example, we could design predicate method **IsEmpty** for a *container class*—a class capable of holding many objects, such as a linked list, a stack or a queue (these data structures are discussed in detail in Chapter 20, Data Structures and Collections). This method would return **True** if the container is empty and **False** otherwise. A program might test **IsEmpty** before attempting to read another item from the container object. Similarly, a program might call another predicate method (e.g., **IsFull**) before attempting to insert another item into a container object.

---

1. For a list of Microsoft recommended naming conventions visit **msdn.microsoft.com/library/default.asp?url=/library/en-us/vbcon98/html/vbconobject-namingconventions.asp**.

Class **CTime** contains the following **Public** methods—**New** (lines 14–16), **Set-Time** (lines 21–45), **ToUniversalString** (lines 48–51) and **ToStandardString** (lines 54–73). These are the *Public methods* (also called the *Public services*, or *Public interfaces*) of the class. *Clients*, such as module **modTimeTest** (discussed momentarily), use these methods to manipulate the data stored in the class objects or to cause the class to perform some service.

New is a *constructor* method. (As we will see, a class can have many constructors— all share the same name (**New**), but each must have unique parameters.) A constructor is a special method that initializes an object's instance variables. The instantiation of an object of a class calls that class's constructor method. This constructor method (lines 14–16) then calls method **SetTime** (discussed shortly) with **mHour**, **mMinute** and **mSecond** values specified as **0**. Constructors can take arguments but cannot return values. An important difference between constructors and other methods is that constructors cannot specify a return data type—for this reason, Visual Basic constructors are implemented as **Sub** procedures (because **Sub** procedures cannot return values). Generally, constructors are **Public** methods of a class.

Common Programming Error 5.1

*Attempting to declare a constructor as a **Function** and/or attempting to **Return** a value from a constructor is a syntax error.*

Method **SetTime** (lines 21–45) is a **Public** method that uses three **Integer** arguments to set the time. A conditional expression tests each argument to determine whether the value is in a specified range. For example, the **mHour** value must be greater than or equal to 0 and less than 24, because universal-time format represents hours as integers from **0** to **23**. Similarly, both minute and second values must fall between **0** and **59**. Any values outside these ranges are invalid values and default to zero, at least ensuring that a **CTime** object always contains valid data. This is also known as *keeping the object in a consistent state*. When users supply invalid data to **SetTime**, the program might want to indicate that the entered time setting was invalid.

Good Programming Practice 5.4

Always define a class so that its instance variables maintain a consistent state.

Method **ToUniversalString** (lines 48–51) takes no arguments and returns a **String** in universal-time format, consisting of six digits—two for the hour, two for the minute and two for the second. For example, if the time were 1:30:07 PM, method **ToUniversalString** would return the **String "13:30:07"**. **String** method **Format** helps to configure the universal time. Line 49 passes to the method the *format control string* **"{0}:{1:D2}:{2:D2}"**, which indicates that argument **0** (the first argument after the format **String** argument) should take the default format; and that arguments **1** and **2** (the last two arguments after the **String** argument) should take the format **D2** (base 10 decimal number format using two digits) for display purposes—thus, **8** would be converted to **08**. The two colons that separate the curly braces **}** and **{** represent the colons that separate the hour from the minute and the minute from the second, respectively.

Method **ToStandardString** (lines 54–73) takes no arguments and returns a **String** in standard-time format, consisting of the **mHour**, **mMinute** and **mSecond** values separated by colons and followed by an AM or PM indicator (e.g., **1:27:06 PM**).

Like method **ToUniversalString**, method **ToStandardString** calls method **Format** of class **String** to guarantee that the **mMinute** and **mSecond** values each appear as two digits. Lines 60–69 determine the proper formatting for the hour.

After defining the class, we can use it as a type in declarations such as

    Dim **sunset** *As* **CTime**   *' reference to object of type CTime*

The class name (**CTime**) is a type. A class can yield many objects, just as a primitive data type (e.g., **Integer**) can yield many variables. Programmers can create class types as needed; this is one reason why Visual Basic is known as an *extensible language*.

Module **modTimeTest** (Fig. 5.2) uses an instance of class **CTime**. Method **Main** (lines 8–33) declares and initializes instance **time** of class **CTime** (line 9). When the object is instantiated, *keyword* **New** allocates the memory in which the **CTime** object will be stored, then calls the **CTime** constructor (method **New** in lines 14–16 of Fig. 5.1) to initialize the instance variables of the **CTime** object. As mentioned before, this constructor invokes method **SetTime** of class **CTime** to initialize each **Private** instance variable explicitly to **0**. Method **New** then returns a reference to the newly created object; this reference is assigned to **time**.

Note that the **TimeTest.vb** file does not use keyword **Imports** to import the namespace that contains class **CTime**. If a class is in the same namespace and **.vb** file as the class that uses it, the **Imports** statement is not required. Every class in Visual Basic is part of a namespace. If a programmer does not specify a namespace for a class, the class is placed in the *default namespace*, which includes the compiled classes in the current directory (in Visual Studio, this is a project's directory). We must import classes from the .NET Framework, because their namespaces and source files are located in a different directory than those compiled with each program we write.

Line 10 declares a **String** reference **output** that will store the **String** containing the results, which later will be displayed in a **MessageBox**. Lines 12–15 assign the time to **output** in universal-time format (by invoking method **ToUniversalString** of **CTime**) and standard-time format (by invoking method **ToStandardString** of **CTime**).

```
1    ' Fig. 5.2: TimeTest.vb
2    ' Demonstrating class CTime.
3
4    Imports System.Windows.Forms
5
6    Module modTimeTest
7
8       Sub Main()
9          Dim time As New CTime() ' call CTime constructor
10         Dim output As String
11
12         output = "The initial universal times is: " & _
13            time.ToUniversalString() & vbCrLf & _
14            "The initial standard time is: " & _
15            time.ToStandardString()
16
```

Fig. 5.2   Using an abstract data type. (Part 1 of 2.)

```
17        time.SetTime(13, 27, 6) ' set time with valid settings
18
19        output &= vbCrLf & vbCrLf & _
20          "Universal time after setTime is: " & _
21          time.ToUniversalString() & vbCrLf & _
22          "Standard time after setTime is: " & _
23          time.ToStandardString()
24
25        time.SetTime(99, 99, 99) ' set time with invalid settings
26
27        output &= vbCrLf & vbCrLf & _
28          "After attempting invalid settings: " & vbCrLf & _
29          "Universal time: " & time.ToUniversalString() & _
30          vbCrLf & "Standard time: " & time.ToStandardString()
31
32        MessageBox.Show(output, "Testing Class CTime")
33      End Sub ' Main
34
35    End Module ' modTimeTest
```

Fig. 5.2   Using an abstract data type. (Part 2 of 2.)

 Software Engineering Observation 5.4

*When keyword **New** creates an object of a class, that class's method **New** (constructor method) is called to initialize the instance variables of that object.*

Line 17 sets the time of the **CTime** object by passing valid time arguments to **CTime**'s method **SetTime**. Lines 19–23 concatenate the time to **output** in both universal and standard formats to confirm that the time was set correctly.

To illustrate that method **SetTime** validates the values passed to it, line 25 passes invalid time arguments to method **SetTime**. Lines 27–30 concatenates the time to **output** in both formats, and line 32 displays a **MessageBox** with the results of our program. Notice in the last two lines of the output window that the time is set to midnight, which is the default value of a **CTime** object.

CTime is our first example of a *nonapplication class*, which is a class that does not define a **Main** method and therefore not executable. A module (**modTimeTest**), though technically not a class, acts like an *application class* in the sense that it defines a **Main** method, which is the starting point (referred to as the entry point) for an executable program in Visual Basic. Class **CTime** does not define **Main** and thus cannot be used as a starting point in this program.

Note that the program declares instance variables **mHour**, **mMinute** and **mSecond** as **Private**. Instance variables declared **Private** are not accessible outside the class in which they are defined. The class's clients are not concerned with the actual data representation of that class. For example, the class could represent the time internally as the number of seconds that have elapsed since the previous midnight. Suppose this representation changes. Clients still are able to use the same **Public** methods and obtain the same results (**Return** values) without becoming aware of the change in internal representation. In this sense, the implementation of a class is said to be *hidden* from its clients.

Software Engineering Observation 5.5

Information hiding promotes program modifiability and simplifies the client's perception of a class.

Software Engineering Observation 5.6

Clients of a class can (and should) use the class without knowing the internal details of how the class is implemented. If the class implementation is changed (to improve performance, for example), provided that the class's interface remains constant, the class clients' source code need not change. This makes it much easier to modify systems.

In this program, the **CTime** constructor initializes the instance variables to **0** (i.e., the universal time equivalent of 12 AM) to ensure that the object is created in a *consistent state* (i.e., all instance variable values are valid). The instance variables of a **CTime** object cannot store invalid values, because the constructor (which calls **SetTime**) is called when the **CTime** object is created. Method **SetTime** scrutinizes subsequent attempts by a client to modify the instance variables.

Normally, instance variables are initialized in a class's constructor, but they also can be initialized when they are declared in the class body. If a programmer does not initialize instance variables explicitly, the compiler initializes them. When this occurs, the compiler sets primitive numeric variables to **0**, **Boolean**s to **False** and references to **Nothing**).

Methods **ToUniversalString** and **ToStandardString** take no arguments because these methods manipulate the instance variables of the particular **CTime** object for which they are invoked. This makes method calls more concise than conventional function calls in procedural programming. It also reduces the likelihood of passing the wrong arguments, the wrong types of arguments or the wrong number of arguments.

Software Engineering Observation 5.7

The use of an object-oriented programming approach often simplifies method calls by reducing the number of parameters that must be passed. This benefit of object-oriented programming derives from the fact that encapsulation of instance variables and methods within an object gives the object's methods the right to access its instance variables.

Classes simplify programming, because the client (or user of the class object) need be concerned only with the **Public** operations encapsulated in the object. Usually, such operations are designed to be client-oriented, rather than implementation-oriented. Clients are neither aware of, nor involved in, a class's implementation. Interfaces change less frequently than do implementations. When an implementation changes, implementation-dependent code must change accordingly. By hiding the implementation, we eliminate the possibility that other program parts will become dependent on the class-implementation details.

Often, programmers do not have to create classes "from scratch." Rather, they can derive classes from other classes that provide behaviors required by the new classes. Classes also can include references to objects of other classes as members. Such *software reuse* can greatly enhance programmer productivity. Chapter 6 discusses *inheritance*—the process by which new classes are derived from existing classes. Section 5.8 discusses *composition* (*aggregation*), in which classes include as members references to objects of other classes.

5.3 Class Scope

In Section 4.11, we discussed method scope; now, we discuss class *scope*. A class's instance variables and methods belong to that class's scope. Within a class's scope, class members are accessible to all of that class's methods and can be referenced by name. Outside a class's scope, class members cannot be referenced directly by name. Those class members that are visible (such as **Public** members) can be accessed only through a "handle" (i.e., members can be referenced via the format *objectReferenceName* **.** *memberName*).

If a variable is defined in a method, only that method can access the variable (i.e., the variable is a local variable of that method). Such variables are said to have *block scope*. If a method defines a variable that has the same name as a variable with class scope (i.e., an instance variable), the method-scope variable hides the class-scope variable in that method's scope. A hidden instance variable can be accessed in a method by preceding its name with the keyword **Me** and the dot operator, as in **Me.mHour**. We discuss keyword **Me** later in this chapter.

5.4 Controlling Access to Members

The member access modifiers **Public** and **Private** control access to a class's instance variables and methods. (In Chapter 6, we introduce the additional access modifiers **Protected** and **Friend**.)

As we stated previously, **Public** methods serve primarily to present to the class's clients a view of the *services* that the class provides (i.e., the **Public** interface of the class). We have mentioned the merits of writing methods that perform only one task. If a method must execute other tasks to calculate its final result, these tasks should be performed by a utility method. A client does not need to call these utility methods, nor does it need to be concerned with how the class uses its utility methods. For these reasons, utility methods are declared as **Private** members of a class.

Common Programming Error 5.2

*Attempting to access a **Private** class member from outside that class is a syntax error.*

The application of Fig. 5.3 demonstrates that **Private** class members are not accessible outside the class. Line 9 attempts to access **Private** instance variable **mHour** of **CTime** object **time**. The compiler generates an error stating that the **Private** member **mHour** is not accessible. [*Note*: This program assumes that the **CTime** class from Fig. 5.1 is used.]

Good Programming Practice 5.5

We prefer to list instance variables of a class first, so that, when reading the code, programmers see the name and type of each instance variable before it is used in the methods of the class.

```
1   ' Fig. 5.3: RestrictedAccess.vb
2   ' Demonstrate error from attempt to access Private class member.
3
4   Module modRestrictedAccess
5
6      Sub Main()
7         Dim time As New CTime()
8
9         time.mHour = 7 ' error
10     End Sub ' Main
11
12  End Module ' modRestrictedAccess
```

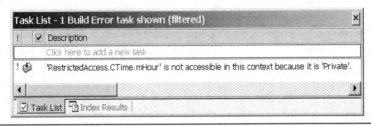

Fig. 5.3   Attempting to access restricted class members results in a syntax error.

Good Programming Practice 5.6

*Even though **Private** and **Public** members can be repeated and intermixed, list all the **Private** members of a class first in one group, then list all the **Public** members in another group.*

Software Engineering Observation 5.8

*Declare all instance variables of a class as **Private**. When necessary, provide **Public** methods to set and get the values of **Private** instance variables. This architecture hides the class's implementation from its clients, reduces bugs and improves program modifiability.*

Access to **Private** data should be controlled carefully by a class's methods. To allow clients to read the values of **Private** data, the class can provide a *property definition*, which enables users to access this **Private** data safely. Properties, which we discuss in detail in Section 5.7, contain *accessors*, or portions of code that handle the details of modifying and returning data. A property definition can contain a ***Get*** *accessor*, a ***Set*** *accessor* or both. A **Get** accessor enables a client to read a **Private** data value, whereas a **Set** accessor enables the client to modify that value. Such modification would seem to violate the notion of **Private** data. However, a **Set** accessor can provide data-validation capabilities (such as range checking) to ensure that the value is set properly. A **Set** accessor also can translate between the format of the data used in the interface and the format used in the implementation. A **Get** accessor need not expose the data in "raw" format; rather, the **Get** accessor can edit the data and limit the client's view of that data.

Testing and Debugging Tip 5.1

*Declaring the instance variables of a class as **Private** and the methods of the class as **Public** facilitates debugging, because problems with data manipulations are localized to the class's methods.*

5.5 Initializing Class Objects: Constructors

A constructor method initializes its class's members. The programmer writes code for the constructor, which is invoked each time an object of that class is instantiated. Instance variables can be initialized implicitly to their default values (**0** for primitive numeric types, **False** for **Boolean**s and **Nothing** for references). Visual Basic initializes variables to their default values when they are declared at runtime. Variables can be initialized when declared in either the class body or constructor. Regardless of whether an instance variable is initialized in a constructor, that variable is initialized (either to its default value or to the value assigned in its declaration) by the runtime before any constructors are called. Classes can contain overloaded constructors to provide multiple ways to initialize objects of that class.

Performance Tip 5.1

Because instance variables are always initialized to default values by the runtime, avoid initializing instance variables to their default values in the constructor.

It is important to note that, although references do not need to be initialized immediately by invoking a constructor, an uninitialized reference cannot be used until it refers to an actual object. If a class does not define any constructors, the compiler provides a default constructor.

Software Engineering Observation 5.9

When appropriate, provide a constructor to ensure that every object is initialized with meaningful values.

When creating an object of a class, the programmer can provide *initializers* in parentheses to the right of the class name. These initializers are the arguments to the class's constructor. In general, declarations take the form

　　　　Dim *objectReference* **As New** *ClassName*(*arguments*)

where *objectReference* is a reference of the appropriate data type, **New** indicates that an object is being created, *ClassName* indicates the type of the new object and *arguments* specifies the values used by the class's constructor to initialize the object. A constructor that takes arguments often is called a *parameterized constructor*. The next example (Fig. 5.4) demonstrates the use of initializers.

If a class does not have any defined constructors, the compiler provides a default constructor. This constructor contains no code (i.e., the constructor is empty) and takes no arguments. Programmers also can provide a default constructor, as we demonstrated in class **CTime** (Fig. 5.1), and as we will see in the next example.

Common Programming Error 5.3

*If constructors are provided for a class, but none of the **Public** constructors is a default constructor, and an attempt is made to call a default constructor to initialize an object of the class, a syntax error occurs. A constructor can be called with no arguments only if there are no constructors for the class (the default constructor is called) or if the class includes a default constructor.*

5.6 Using Overloaded Constructors

Like methods, constructors of a class can be *overloaded*. This means that several constructors in a class can have the exact same method name (i.e., **New**). To overload a constructor of a class, provide a separate method definition with the same name for each version of the method. Remember that overloaded constructors must have different numbers and/or types and/or orders of parameters.

Common Programming Error 5.4

Attempting to overload a constructor of a class with another method that has the exact same signature (method name and number, types and order of parameters) is a syntax error.

The **CTime** constructor in Fig. 5.1 initialized **mHour**, **mMinute** and **mSecond** to **0** (i.e., 12 midnight in universal time) with a call to the class's **SetTime** method. Class **CTime2** (Fig. 5.4) overloads the constructor method to provide a variety of ways to initialize **CTime2** objects. Each constructor calls method **SetTime** of the **CTime2** object, which ensures that the object begins in a consistent state by setting out-of-range values to zero. The Visual Basic runtime invokes the appropriate constructor by matching the number, types and order of the arguments specified in the constructor call with the number, types and order of the parameters specified in each constructor method definition.

Because most of the code in class **CTime2** is identical to that in class **CTime**, this section concentrates only on the overloaded constructors. Line 14 defines the default constructor. Line 20 defines a **CTime2** constructor that receives a single **Integer** argument, representing the **mHour**. Line 26 defines a **CTime2** constructor that receives two **Integer** arguments, representing the **mHour** and **mMinute**. Line 33 defines a **CTime2** constructor that receives three **Integer** arguments representing the **mHour**, **mMinute** and **mSecond**. Line 40 defines a **CTime2** constructor that receives a reference to another **CTime2** object. When this last constructor is employed, the values from the **CTime2** argument are used to initialize the **mHour**, **mMinute** and **mSecond** values. Even though class **CTime2** declares these values as **Private** (lines 8–10), the **CTime2** object can access these values directly using the expressions **timeValue.mHour**, **timeValue.mMinute** and **timeValue.mSecond**.

No constructor specifies a return type; doing so is a syntax error. Also, notice that each constructor receives a different number or different types of arguments. Even though only two of the constructors receive values for the **mHour**, **mMinute** and **mSecond**, each constructor calls **SetTime** with values for **mHour**, **mMinute** and **mSecond** and substitutes zeros for the missing values to satisfy **SetTime**'s requirement of three arguments.

Software Engineering Observation 5.10

*When one object of a class has a reference to another object of the same class, the first object can access all the second object's data and methods (including those that are **Private**).*

```
1    ' Fig. 5.4: CTime2.vb
2    ' Represents time and contains overloaded constructors.
3
4    Class CTime2
5       Inherits Object
6
7       ' declare Integers for hour, minute and second
8       Private mHour As Integer    ' 0 - 23
9       Private mMinute As Integer  ' 0 - 59
10      Private mSecond As Integer  ' 0 - 59
11
```

Fig. 5.4   Overloading constructors. (Part 1 of 3.)

```
12      ' constructor initializes each variable to zero and
13      ' ensures that each CTime2 object starts in consistent state
14      Public Sub New()
15         SetTime()
16      End Sub ' New
17
18      ' CTime2 constructor: hour supplied;
19      ' minute and second default to 0
20      Public Sub New(ByVal hourValue As Integer)
21         SetTime(hourValue)
22      End Sub ' New
23
24      ' CTime2 constructor: hour and minute supplied;
25      ' second defaulted to 0
26      Public Sub New(ByVal hourValue As Integer, _
27         ByVal minuteValue As Integer)
28
29         SetTime(hourValue, minuteValue)
30      End Sub ' New
31
32      ' CTime2 constructor: hour, minute and second supplied
33      Public Sub New(ByVal hourValue As Integer, _
34         ByVal minuteValue As Integer, ByVal secondValue As Integer)
35
36         SetTime(hourValue, minuteValue, secondValue)
37      End Sub ' New
38
39      ' CTime2 constructor: another CTime2 object supplied
40      Public Sub New(ByVal timeValue As CTime2)
41         SetTime(timeValue.mHour, timeValue.mMinute, timeValue.mSecond)
42      End Sub ' New
43
44      ' set new time value using universal time;
45      ' perform validity checks on data;
46      ' set invalid values to zero
47      Public Sub SetTime(Optional ByVal hourValue As Integer = 0, _
48         Optional ByVal minuteValue As Integer = 0, _
49         Optional ByVal secondValue As Integer = 0)
50
51         ' perform validity checks on hour, then set hour
52         If (hourValue >= 0 AndAlso hourValue < 24) Then
53            mHour = hourValue
54         Else
55            mHour = 0
56         End If
57
58         ' perform validity checks on minute, then set minute
59         If (minuteValue >= 0 AndAlso minuteValue < 60) Then
60            mMinute = minuteValue
61         Else
62            mMinute = 0
63         End If
64
```

Fig. 5.4   Overloading constructors. (Part 2 of 3.)

```
65          ' perform validity checks on second, then set second
66          If (secondValue >= 0 AndAlso secondValue < 60) Then
67              mSecond = secondValue
68          Else
69              mSecond = 0
70          End If
71
72      End Sub ' SetTime
73
74      ' convert String to universal-time format
75      Public Function ToUniversalString() As String
76          Return String.Format("{0}:{1:D2}:{2:D2}", _
77              mHour, mMinute, mSecond)
78      End Function ' ToUniversalString
79
80      ' convert to String in standard-time format
81      Public Function ToStandardString() As String
82          Dim suffix As String = " PM"
83          Dim format As String = "{0}:{1:D2}:{2:D2}"
84          Dim standardHour As Integer
85
86          ' determine whether time is AM or PM
87          If mHour < 12 Then
88              suffix = " AM"
89          End If
90
91          ' convert from universal-time format to standard-time format
92          If (mHour = 12 OrElse mHour = 0) Then
93              standardHour = 12
94          Else
95              standardHour = mHour Mod 12
96          End If
97
98          Return String.Format(format, standardHour, mMinute, _
99              mSecond) & suffix
100     End Function ' ToStandardString
101
102 End Class ' CTime2
```

Fig. 5.4   Overloading constructors. (Part 3 of 3.)

Common Programming Error 5.5

A constructor can call other class methods that use instance variables not yet initialized. Using instance variables before they have been initialized can lead to logic errors.

Figure 5.5 (**modTimeTest2**) demonstrates the use of overloaded constructors (Fig. 5.4). Lines 11–16 create six **CTime2** objects that invoke various constructors of the class. Line 11 specifies that it invokes the default constructor by placing an empty set of parentheses after the class name. Lines 12–16 of the program demonstrate the passing of arguments to the **CTime2** constructors. To invoke the appropriate constructor, pass the proper number, types and order of arguments (specified by the constructor's definition) to that constructor. For example, line 13 invokes the constructor that is defined in lines 26–30 of

Fig. 5.4. Lines 21–55 invoke methods **ToUniversalString** and **ToStandardString** for each **CTime2** object to demonstrate how the constructors initialize the objects.

```vb
1    ' Fig. 5.5: TimeTest2.vb
2    ' Demonstrates overloading constructors.
3
4    Imports System.Windows.Forms
5
6    Module modTimeTest2
7
8       Sub Main()
9
10         ' use overloaded constructors
11         Dim time1 As New CTime2()
12         Dim time2 As New CTime2(2)
13         Dim time3 As New CTime2(21, 34)
14         Dim time4 As New CTime2(12, 25, 42)
15         Dim time5 As New CTime2(27, 74, 99)
16         Dim time6 As New CTime2(time4) ' use time4 as initial value
17
18         Const SPACING As Integer = 13 ' spacing between output text
19
20         ' invoke time1 methods
21         Dim output As String = "Constructed with: " & vbCrLf & _
22            " time1: all arguments defaulted" & vbCrLf & _
23            Space(SPACING) & time1.ToUniversalString() & _
24            vbCrLf & Space(SPACING) & time1.ToStandardString()
25
26         ' invoke time2 methods
27         output &= vbCrLf & _
28            " time2: hour specified; minute and second defaulted" & _
29            vbCrLf & Space(SPACING) & _
30            time2.ToUniversalString() & vbCrLf & Space(SPACING) & _
31            time2.ToStandardString()
32
33         ' invoke time3 methods
34         output &= vbCrLf & _
35            " time3: hour and minute specified; second defaulted" & _
36            vbCrLf & Space(SPACING) & time3.ToUniversalString() & _
37            vbCrLf & Space(SPACING) & time3.ToStandardString()
38
39         ' invoke time4 methods
40         output &= vbCrLf & _
41            " time4: hour, minute and second specified" & _
42            vbCrLf & Space(SPACING) & time4.ToUniversalString() & _
43            vbCrLf & Space(SPACING) & time4.ToStandardString()
44
45         ' invoke time5 methods
46         output &= vbCrLf & _
47            " time5: hour, minute and second specified" & _
48            vbCrLf & Space(SPACING) & time5.ToUniversalString() & _
49            vbCrLf & Space(SPACING) & time5.ToStandardString()
50
```

Fig. 5.5   Overloaded-constructor demonstration. (Part 1 of 2.)

```
51            ' invoke time6 methods
52            output &= vbCrLf & _
53                " time6: Time2 object time4 specified" & vbCrLf & _
54                Space(SPACING) & time6.ToUniversalString() & _
55                vbCrLf & Space(SPACING) & time6.ToStandardString()
56
57            MessageBox.Show(output, _
58                "Demonstrating Overloaded Constructor")
59        End Sub ' Main
60
61    End Module ' modTimeTest2
```

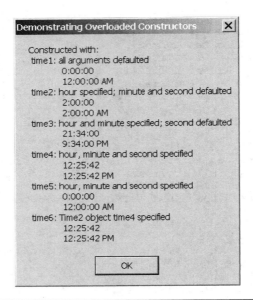

Fig. 5.5   Overloaded-constructor demonstration. (Part 2 of 2.)

Each **CTime2** constructor can be written to include a copy of the appropriate statements from method **SetTime**. This might be slightly more efficient, because it eliminates the extra call to **SetTime**. However, consider what would happen if the programmer changes the representation of the time from three **Integer** values (requiring 12 bytes of memory) to a single **Integer** value representing the total number of seconds that have elapsed in the day (requiring 4 bytes of memory). Placing identical code in the **CTime2** constructors and method **SetTime** makes such a change in the class definition more difficult. If the implementation of method **SetTime** changes, the implementation of the **CTime2** constructors would need to change accordingly. If the **CTime2** constructors call **SetTime** directly, any changes to the implementation of **SetTime** must be made only once, thus reducing the likelihood of a programming error when altering the implementation.

Software Engineering Observation 5.11

If a method of a class provides functionality required by a constructor (or other method) of the class, call that method from the constructor (or other method). This simplifies the maintenance of the code and reduces the likelihood of introducing an error in the code.

5.7 Properties

Methods of a class can manipulate that class's **Private** instance variables. A typical manipulation might be the adjustment of a customer's bank balance—a **Private** instance variable of a class **CBankAccount**—a **ComputeInterest** method.

Classes often provide **Public** *properties* to allow clients to *set* (i.e., assign values to) or *get* (i.e., obtain the values of) **Private** instance variables. In Fig. 5.6, we show how to create three properties—**Hour**, **Minute** and **Second**. **Hour** accesses variable **mHour**, **Minute** accesses variable **mMinute** and **Second** accesses variable **mSecond**. Each property contains a *Get accessor* (to retrieve the variable value) and a *Set accessor* (to modify the variable value).

Although providing **Set** and **Get** accessors appears to be the same as making the instance variables **Public**, this is not the case. This is another one of Visual Basic's subtleties that makes the language so attractive from a software-engineering standpoint. If an instance variable is **Public**, the instance variable can be read or written by any method in the program. If an instance variable is **Private**, a **Public** get method seems to allow other methods to read the data at will. However, the get method can control the formatting and display of the data. A **Public** set method can scrutinize attempts to modify the instance variable's value, thus ensuring that the new value is appropriate for that data member. For example, an attempt to set the day of the month to 37 would be rejected, and an attempt to set a person's weight to a negative value would be rejected. Therefore, although set and get methods provide access to **Private** data, the implementation of these methods can restrict access to that data.

The declaration of instance variables as **Private** does not guarantee data integrity. Programmers must provide validity checking—Visual Basic provides only the framework with which programmers can design better programs.

Testing and Debugging Tip 5.2

*Methods that set the values of **Private** data should verify that the intended new values are proper; if they are not, the **Set** methods should place the **Private** instance variables into an appropriate consistent state.*

A class's **Set** accessors cannot return values indicating a failed attempt to assign invalid data to objects of the class. Such return values could be useful to a class's clients for handling errors. In this case, clients could take appropriate actions if the objects occupy invalid states. Chapter 8 presents exception handling—a mechanism that can be used to notify a class's clients of failed attempts to set objects of that class to consistent states.

Figure 5.6 enhances our **CTime** class (now called **CTime3**) to include properties for the **mHour**, **mMinute** and **mSecond Private** instance variables. The **Set** accessors of these properties strictly control the setting of the instance variables to valid values. An attempt to set any instance variable to an incorrect value causes the instance variable to be set to zero (thus leaving the instance variable in a consistent state). Each **Get** accessor returns the appropriate instance variable's value.

```
1    ' Fig. 5.6: CTime3.vb
2    ' Represents time in 24-hour format and contains properties.
3
```

Fig. 5.6   Properties in a class. (Part 1 of 4.)

```
4    Class CTime3
5       Inherits Object
6
7       ' declare Integers for hour, minute and second
8       Private mHour As Integer
9       Private mMinute As Integer
10      Private mSecond As Integer
11
12      ' CTime3 constructor: initialize each instance variable to zero
13      ' and ensure that each CTime3 object starts in consistent state
14      Public Sub New()
15         SetTime(0, 0, 0)
16      End Sub ' New
17
18      ' CTime3 constructor:
19      ' hour supplied, minute and second defaulted to 0
20      Public Sub New(ByVal hourValue As Integer)
21         SetTime(hourValue, 0, 0)
22      End Sub ' New
23
24      ' CTime3 constructor:
25      ' hour and minute supplied; second defaulted to 0
26      Public Sub New(ByVal hourValue As Integer, _
27         ByVal minuteValue As Integer)
28
29         SetTime(hourValue, minuteValue, 0)
30      End Sub ' New
31
32      ' CTime3 constructor: hour, minute and second supplied
33      Public Sub New(ByVal hourValue As Integer, _
34         ByVal minuteValue As Integer, ByVal secondValue As Integer)
35
36         SetTime(hourValue, minuteValue, secondValue)
37            ' New
38
39      ' CTime3 constructor: another CTime3 object supplied
40      Public Sub New(ByVal timeValue As CTime3)
41         SetTime(timeValue.mHour, timeValue.mMinute, _
42            timeValue.mSecond)
43      End Sub ' New
44
45      ' set new time value using universal time;
46      ' uses properties to perform validity checks on data
47      Public Sub SetTime(ByVal hourValue As Integer, _
48         ByVal minuteValue As Integer, ByVal secondValue As Integer)
49
50         Hour = hourValue       ' looks
51         Minute = minuteValue   ' dangerous
52         Second = secondValue   ' but it is correct
53      End Sub ' SetTime
54
```

Fig. 5.6   Properties in a class. (Part 2 of 4.)

```
55      ' property Hour
56      Public Property Hour() As Integer
57
58          ' return mHour value
59          Get
60              Return mHour
61          End Get
62
63          ' set mHour value
64          Set(ByVal value As Integer)
65
66              If (value >= 0 AndAlso value < 24) Then
67                  mHour = value
68              Else
69                  mHour = 0
70              End If
71
72          End Set
73
74      End Property ' Hour
75
76      ' property Minute
77      Public Property Minute() As Integer
78
79          ' return mMinute value
80          Get
81              Return mMinute
82          End Get
83
84          ' set mMinute value
85          Set(ByVal value As Integer)
86
87              If (value >= 0 AndAlso value < 60) Then
88                  mMinute = value
89              Else
90                  mMinute = 0
91              End If
92
93          End Set
94
95      End Property ' Minute
96
97      ' property Second
98      Public Property Second() As Integer
99
100         ' return mSecond value
101         Get
102             Return mSecond
103         End Get
104
```

Fig. 5.6   Properties in a class. (Part 3 of 4.)

```
105                ' set mSecond value
106                Set(ByVal value As Integer)
107
108                    If (value >= 0 AndAlso value < 60) Then
109                        mSecond = value
110                    Else
111                        mSecond = 0
112                    End If
113
114                End Set
115
116          End Property ' Second
117
118          ' convert String to universal-time format
119          Public Function ToUniversalString() As String
120                Return String.Format("{0}:{1:D2}:{2:D2}", _
121                    mHour, mMinute, mSecond)
122          End Function ' ToUniversalString
123
124          ' convert to String in standard-time format
125          Public Function ToStandardString() As String
126                Dim suffix As String = " PM"
127                Dim format As String = "{0}:{1:D2}:{2:D2}"
128                Dim standardHour As Integer
129
130                ' determine whether time is AM or PM
131                If mHour < 12 Then
132                    suffix = " AM"
133                End If
134
135                ' convert from universal-time format to standard-time format
136                If (mHour = 12 OrElse mHour = 0) Then
137                    standardHour = 12
138                Else
139                    standardHour = mHour Mod 12
140                End If
141
142                Return String.Format(format, standardHour, mMinute, _
143                    mSecond) & suffix
144          End Function ' ToStandardString
145
146    End Class    ' CTime3
```

Fig. 5.6   Properties in a class. (Part 4 of 4.)

Lines 56–74, 77–95 and 98–116 define the properties **Hour**, **Minute** and **Second** of class **CTime3**, respectively. Each property begins with a declaration line, which includes an access modifier (**Public**), the property's name (**Hour**, **Minute** or **Second**) and the property's type (**Integer**).

The body of the property contains **Get** and **Set** accessors, which are declared using the keywords **Get** and **Set**. The **Get** accessor method declarations are on lines 59–61, 80–82 and 101–103. These **Get** methods return the **mHour**, **mMinute** and **mSecond** instance variable values that objects request. The **Set** accessors are declared on lines 64–72, 85–93 and 106–114. The body of each **Set** accessor performs the same conditional statement that was previously in method **SetTime** for setting the **mHour**, **mMinute** or **mSecond**.

Method **SetTime** (lines 47–53) now uses properties **Hour**, **Minute** and **Second** to ensure that instance variables **mHour**, **mMinute** and **mSecond** have valid values. After we define a property, we can use it in the same way that we use a variable. We assign values to properties using the **=** (assignment) operator. When this assignment occurs, the code in the definition of the **Set** accessor for that property is executed. Referencing the property (for instance, using it in a mathematical calculation) executes the code within the definition of the **Get** accessor for that property.

When we employ **Set** and **Get** accessor methods in class **CTime3**, we minimize the changes that we must make to the class definition, in the event that we alter the data representation from **mHour**, **mMinute** and **mSecond** to another representation (such as total elapsed seconds in the day). We must provide only new **Set** and **Get** accessor bodies. Using this technique, programmers can change the implementation of a class without affecting the clients of that class (as long as all the **Public** methods of the class are called in the same way).

Software Engineering Observation 5.12

*Accessing **Private** data through **Set** and **Get** accessors not only protects the instance variables from receiving invalid values, but also hides the internal representation of the instance variables from that class's clients. Thus, if representation of the data changes (typically, to reduce the amount of required storage or to improve performance), only the properties implementations need to change—the clients' implementations need not change as long as the service provided by the properties is preserved.*

Figure 5.7 (class **FrmTimeTest3**), which represents the GUI for class **CTime3** (line 30 represents the condensed region of code generated by the Visual Studio's *Windows Form Designer*), declares and instantiates an object of class **CTime3** (line 28). The GUI contains three text fields in which the user can input values for the **CTime3** object's **mHour**, **mMinute** and **mSecond** variables, respectively. Lines 68–92 declare three methods that use the **Hour**, **Minute** and **Second** properties of the **CTime3** object to alter their corresponding values. The GUI also contains a button that enables the user to increment the **mSecond** value by **1** without having to use the text box. Using properties, method **cmdAddSecond_Click** (lines 43–65) determines and sets the new time. For example, **23:59:59** becomes **00:00:00** when the user presses the button.

```
1   ' Fig. 5.7: TimeTest3.vb
2   ' Demonstrates Properties.
3
4   Imports System.Windows.Forms
5
6   Class FrmTimeTest3
7      Inherits Form
8
9      ' Label and TextBox for hour
10     Friend WithEvents lblSetHour As Label
11     Friend WithEvents txtSetHour As TextBox
12
```

Fig. 5.7   Graphical user interface for class **CTime3**. (Part 1 of 3.)

```
13        ' Label and TextBox for minute
14        Friend WithEvents lblSetMinute As Label
15        Friend WithEvents txtSetMinute As TextBox
16
17        ' Label and TextBox for second
18        Friend WithEvents lblSetSecond As Label
19        Friend WithEvents txtSetSecond As TextBox
20
21        ' Labels for outputing time
22        Friend WithEvents lblOutput1 As Label
23        Friend WithEvents lblOutput2 As Label
24
25        ' Button for adding one second to time
26        Friend WithEvents cmdAddSecond As Button
27
28        Dim time As New CTime3()
29
30        ' Visual Studio .NET generated code
31
32        ' update time display
33        Private Sub UpdateDisplay()
34           lblOutput1.Text = "Hour: " & time.Hour & "; Minute: " & _
35              time.Minute & "; Second: " & time.Second
36
37           lblOutput2.Text = "Standard time is: " & _
38              time.ToStandardString & "; Universal Time is: " _
39              & time.ToUniversalString()
40        End Sub ' UpdateDisplay
41
42        ' invoked when user presses Add Second button
43        Protected Sub cmdAddSecond_Click( _
44           ByVal sender As System.Object, _
45           ByVal e As System.EventArgs) Handles cmdAddSecond.Click
46
47           ' add one second
48           time.Second = (time.Second + 1) Mod 60
49           txtSetSecond.Text = time.Second
50
51           ' add one minute if 60 seconds have passed
52           If time.Second = 0 Then
53              time.Minute = (time.Minute + 1) Mod 60
54              txtSetMinute.Text = time.Minute
55
56              ' add one hour if 60 minutes have passed
57              If time.Minute = 0 Then
58                 time.Hour = (time.Hour + 1) Mod 24
59                 txtSetHour.Text = time.Hour
60              End If
61
62           End If
63
64           UpdateDisplay()
65        End Sub ' cmdAddSecond_Click
```

Fig. 5.7   Graphical user interface for class **CTime3**. (Part 2 of 3.)

```
66
67        ' handle event when txtSetHour's text changes
68        Protected Sub txtSetHour_TextChanged(ByVal sender As _
69           System.Object, ByVal e As System.EventArgs) _
70           Handles txtSetHour.TextChanged
71
72           time.Hour = Convert.ToInt32(txtSetHour.Text)
73           UpdateDisplay()
74        End Sub ' txtSetHour_TextChanged
75
76        ' handle event when txtSetMinute's text changes
77        Protected Sub txtSetMinute_TextChanged(ByVal sender As _
78           System.Object, ByVal e As System.EventArgs) _
79           Handles txtSetMinute.TextChanged
80
81           time.Minute = Convert.ToInt32(txtSetMinute.Text)
82           UpdateDisplay()
83        End Sub ' txtSetMinute_TextChanged
84
85        ' handle event when txtSetSecond's text changes
86        Protected Sub txtSetSecond_TextChanged(ByVal sender _
87           As System.Object, ByVal e As System.EventArgs) _
88           Handles txtSetSecond.TextChanged
89
90           time.Second = Convert.ToInt32(txtSetSecond.Text)
91           UpdateDisplay()
92        End Sub ' txtSetSecond_TextChanged
93
94     End Class ' FrmTimeTest3
```

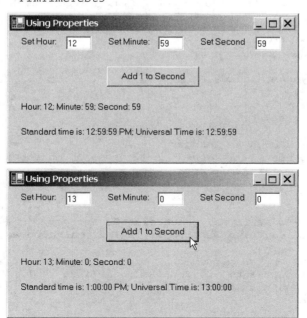

Fig. 5.7   Graphical user interface for class **CTime3**. (Part 3 of 3.)

Not all properties need to have **Get** and **Set** accessors. A property with only a **Get** accessor is called a read-only property and must be declared using keyword **ReadOnly**. By contrast, a property with only a **Set** accessor is called a write-only property and must be declared using keyword **WriteOnly**. Generally, **WriteOnly** properties are seldom used. In Section 5.11, we use **ReadOnly** properties to prevent our programs from changing the values of instance variables.

5.8 Composition: Objects as Instance Variables of Other Classes

In many situations, referencing existing objects is more convenient than rewriting the objects' code for new classes in new projects. Suppose we were to implement a **CAlarm-Clock** class object that needs to know when to sound its alarm. It would be easier to reference an existing **CTime** object (like those from the previous examples in this chapter) than it would be to write a new **CTime** object. The use of references to objects of preexisting classes as members of new objects is called *composition*.

Software Engineering Observation 5.13

One form of software reuse is composition, in which a class has as members references to objects of other classes.

The application of Fig. 5.8, Fig. 5.9 and Fig. 5.10 demonstrates composition. Class **CDay** (Fig. 5.8) encapsulates information relating to a specific date. Lines 9–11 declare **Integer**s **mMonth**, **mDay** and **mYear**. Lines 15–35 define the constructor, which receives values for **mMonth**, **mDay** and **mYear** as arguments, then assigns these values to the class variables after ensuring that the variables are in a consistent state.

```
1    ' Fig. 5.8: CDay.vb
2    ' Encapsulates month, day and year.
3
4    Imports System.Windows.Forms
5
6    Class CDay
7       Inherits Object
8
9       Private mMonth As Integer ' 1-12
10      Private mDay As Integer ' 1-31 based on month
11      Private mYear As Integer ' any year
12
13      ' constructor confirms proper value for month, then calls
14      ' method CheckDay to confirm proper value for day
15      Public Sub New(ByVal monthValue As Integer, _
16         ByVal dayValue As Integer, ByVal yearValue As Integer)
17
18         ' ensure month value is valid
19         If (monthValue > 0 AndAlso monthValue <= 12) Then
20            mMonth = monthValue
21         Else
22            mMonth = 1
```

Fig. 5.8   **CDay** class encapsulates day, month and year information. (Part 1 of 2.)

```vbnet
23
24              ' inform user of error
25              Dim errorMessage As String = _
26                 "Month invalid. Set to month 1."
27
28              MessageBox.Show(errorMessage, "", _
29                 MessageBoxButtons.OK, MessageBoxIcon.Error)
30           End If
31
32           mYear = yearValue
33           mDay = CheckDay(dayValue) ' validate day
34
35       End Sub ' New
36
37       ' confirm proper day value based on month and year
38       Private Function CheckDay(ByVal testDayValue As Integer) _
39          As Integer
40
41          Dim daysPerMonth() As Integer = _
42             {0, 31, 28, 31, 30, 31, 30, 31, 31, 30, 31, 30, 31}
43
44          If (testDayValue > 0 AndAlso _
45             testDayValue <= daysPerMonth(mMonth)) Then
46
47             Return testDayValue
48          End If
49
50          ' check for leap year in February
51          If (mMonth = 2 AndAlso testDayValue = 29 AndAlso _
52             mYear Mod 400 = 0 OrElse mYear Mod 4 = 0 AndAlso _
53             mYear Mod 100 <> 0) Then
54
55             Return testDayValue
56          Else
57
58             ' inform user of error
59             Dim errorMessage As String = _
60                "day " & testDayValue & "invalid. Set to day 1. "
61
62             MessageBox.Show(errorMessage, "", _
63                MessageBoxButtons.OK, MessageBoxIcon.Error)
64
65             Return 1 ' leave object in consistent state
66          End If
67
68       End Function ' CheckDay
69
70       ' create string containing month/day/year format
71       Public Function ToStandardString() As String
72          Return mMonth & "/" & mDay & "/" & mYear
73       End Function ' ToStandardString
74
75    End Class ' CDay
```

Fig. 5.8   **CDay** class encapsulates day, month and year information. (Part 2 of 2.)

Class **CEmployee** (Fig. 5.9) holds information relating to an employee's birthday and hire date (lines 7–10) using instance variables **mFirstName**, **mLastName**, **mBirthDate** and **mHireDate**. Members **mBirthDate** and **mHireDate** are references to **CDay** objects, each of which contains instance variables **mMonth**, **mDay** and **mYear**. In this example, class **CEmployee** is *composed of* two references of class **CDay**. The **CEmployee** constructor (lines 13–32) takes eight arguments (**firstNameValue**, **lastNameValue**, **birthMonthValue**, **birthDayValue**, **birthYearValue**, **hireMonthValue**, **hireDayValue** and **hireYearValue**). Lines 26–27 pass arguments **birthMonthValue**, **birthDayValue** and **birthYearValue** to the **CDay** constructor to create the **mBirthDate** object. Similarly, lines 30–31 pass arguments **hireMonthValue**, **hireDayValue** and **hireYearValue** to the **CDay** constructor to create the **mHireDate** object.

Module **modCompositionTest** (Fig. 5.10) runs the application with method **Main**. Lines 9–10 instantiate a **CEmployee** object (**"Bob Jones"** with birthday **7/24/1949** and hire date **3/12/1988**), and lines 12–13 display the information to the user in a **MessageBox**.

```
1    ' Fig. 5.9: CEmployee.vb
2    ' Represent employee name, birthday and hire date.
3
4    Class CEmployee
5       Inherits Object
6
7       Private mFirstName As String
8       Private mLastName As String
9       Private mBirthDate As CDay ' member object reference
10      Private mHireDate As CDay ' member object reference
11
12      ' CEmployee constructor
13      Public Sub New(ByVal firstNameValue As String, _
14         ByVal lastNameValue As String, _
15         ByVal birthMonthValue As Integer, _
16         ByVal birthDayValue As Integer, _
17         ByVal birthYearValue As Integer, _
18         ByVal hireMonthValue As Integer, _
19         ByVal hireDayValue As Integer, _
20         ByVal hireYearValue As Integer)
21
22         mFirstName = firstNameValue
23         mLastName = lastNameValue
24
25         ' create CDay instance for employee birthday
26         mBirthDate = New CDay(birthMonthValue, birthDayValue, _
27            birthYearValue)
28
29         ' create CDay instance for employee hire date
30         mHireDate = New CDay(hireMonthValue, hireDayValue, _
31            hireYearValue)
32      End Sub ' New
```

Fig. 5.9   CEmployee class encapsulates employee name, birthday and hire date. (Part 1 of 2.)

```
33
34       ' return employee information as standard-format String
35       Public Function ToStandardString() As String
36          Return mLastName & ", " & mFirstName & " Hired: " _
37             & mHireDate.ToStandardString() & " Birthday: " & _
38             mBirthDate.ToStandardString()
39       End Function ' ToStandardString
40
41    End Class ' CEmployee
```

Fig. 5.9   **CEmployee** class encapsulates employee name, birthday and hire date. (Part 2 of 2.)

```
1     ' Fig. 5.10: CompositionTest.vb
2     ' Demonstrate an object with member object reference.
3
4     Imports System.Windows.Forms
5
6     Module modCompositionTest
7
8        Sub Main()
9           Dim employee As New CEmployee( _
10             "Bob", "Jones", 7, 24, 1949, 3, 12, 1988)
11
12          MessageBox.Show(employee.ToStandardString(), _
13             "Testing Class Employee")
14       End Sub ' Main
15
16    End Module ' modCompositionTest
```

Fig. 5.10   Composition demonstration.

5.9 Using the Me Reference

Every object can access a reference to itself via the *Me reference*. The **Me** reference is used implicitly refer to instance variables, properties and methods of an object. We begin with an example of using reference **Me** explicitly and implicitly to display the **Private** data of an object.

Class **CTime4** (Fig. 5.11) defines three **Private** instance variables—**mHour**, **mMinute** and **mSecond** (line 5). The constructor (lines 8–14) receives three **Integer** arguments to initialize a **CTime4** object. Note that for this example, we have made the constructor's parameter names (lines 8–9) identical to the class's instance variable names (line 5). A method's local variable that has the same name as a class's instance variable hides the instance variable in that method's scope. However, the method can use reference **Me** to refer to these instance variables explicitly. Lines 11–13 of Fig. 5.11 demonstrate this feature.

```
1    ' Fig. 5.11: CTime4.vb
2    ' Encapsulate time using Me reference.
3
4    Class CTime4
5       Private mHour, mMinute, mSecond As Integer
6
7       ' CTime4 constructor
8       Public Sub New(ByVal mHour As Integer, _
9          ByVal mMinute As Integer, ByVal mSecond As Integer)
10
11          Me.mHour = mHour
12          Me.mMinute = mMinute
13          Me.mSecond = mSecond
14       End Sub ' New
15
16       ' create String using Me and implicit references
17       Public Function BuildString() As String
18          Return "Me.ToUniversalString(): " & Me.ToUniversalString() _
19             & vbCrLf & "ToUniversalString(): " & ToUniversalString()
20       End Function ' BuildString
21
22       ' convert to String in standard-time format
23       Public Function ToUniversalString() As String
24          Return String.Format("{0:D2}:{1:D2}:{2:D2}", _
25             mHour, mMinute, mSecond)
26       End Function ' ToUniversalString
27
28    End Class ' CTime4
```

Fig. 5.11 Class using **Me** reference.

Method **BuildString** (lines 17–20) returns a **String** created by a statement that uses the **Me** reference explicitly and implicitly. Line 18 uses the **Me** reference explicitly to call method **ToUniversalString**, whereas line 19 uses the **Me** reference implicitly to call method **ToUniversalString**. Note that both lines perform the same task (i.e., generate identical output). Because of this, programmers usually do not use the **Me** reference explicitly to reference methods.

Common Programming Error 5.6

For a method in which a parameter has the same name as an instance variable, use reference **Me** *to access the instance variable explicitly; otherwise, the method parameter is referenced.*

Testing and Debugging Tip 5.3

Avoidance of method-parameter names that conflict with instance variable names helps prevent certain subtle, hard-to-trace bugs.

Good Programming Practice 5.7

The explicit use of the **Me** *reference can increase program clarity where* **Me** *is optional.*

Module **modMeTest** (Fig. 5.12) runs the application that demonstrates the use of the **Me** reference. Line 9 instantiates an instance of class **CTime4**. Lines 11–12 invoke method **BuildString**, then display the results to the user in a **MessageBox**.

```
1   ' Fig. 5.12: MeTest.vb
2   ' Demonstrates Me reference.
3
4   Imports System.Windows.Forms
5
6   Module modMeTest
7
8      Sub Main()
9         Dim time As New CTime4(12, 30, 19)
10
11        MessageBox.Show(time.BuildString(), _
12           "Demonstrating the 'Me' Reference")
13     End Sub ' Main
14
15  End Module ' modMeTest
```

Fig. 5.12 **Me** reference demonstration.

5.10 Garbage Collection

In previous examples, we have seen how a constructor method initializes data in an object of a class after the object is created. Keyword **New** allocates memory for the object, then calls that object's constructor. The constructor might acquire other system resources, such as network connections and database connections. Objects must have a disciplined way to return memory and release resources when the program no longer uses those objects. Failure to release such resources causes *resource leaks.*

Unlike C and C++, in which programmers must manage memory explicitly, Visual Basic performs memory management internally. The .NET Framework performs *garbage collection* of memory to return memory that is no longer needed back to the system. When the *garbage collector* executes, it locates objects for which the application has no references. Such objects can be collected at that time or in a subsequent execution of the garbage collector. Therefore, the *memory leaks* that are common in such languages as C and C++, where memory is not reclaimed automatically, are rare in Visual Basic.

Dependence on Visual Basic's automatic garbage collection, however, might not be the best way to manage resources. Certain resources, such as network connections, database connections and file streams, are better handled explicitly by the programmer. One technique employed to handle these resources (in conjunction with the garbage collector) is to define a *finalizer* method that returns resources to the system. The garbage collector calls an object's finalizer method to perform *termination housekeeping* on that object just before the garbage collector reclaims the object's memory (this process is called *finalization*).

Class **Object** defines method **Finalize**, which is the finalizer method for all Visual Basic objects. Because all Visual Basic classes inherit from class **Object**, they inherit method **Finalize** and can *override* it to free resources specific to those classes. The overridden method is called before garbage collection occurs—however, we cannot determine exactly when this method is called, because we cannot determine exactly when garbage collection occurs. We discuss method **Finalize** in greater detail in Chapter 6, when we discuss inheritance.

5.11 **Shared** Class Members

Each object of a class has its own copy of all the instance variables of the class. However, in certain cases, all class objects should share only one copy of a particular variable. A *Shared class variable* is such a variable; a program contains only one copy of this variable in memory, no matter how many objects of the variable's class have been instantiated. A **Shared** class variable represents *class-wide information*—all class objects share the same piece of data. The declaration of a **Shared** member begins with the keyword **Shared**.

In Visual Basic, programmers can define what is known as a *shared constructor*, which is used only to initialize **Shared** class members. **Shared** constructors are optional and must be declared with the **Shared** keyword. Normally, **Shared** constructors are used when it is necessary to initialize a **Shared** class variable before any objects of that class are instantiated. **Shared** constructors are called before any **Shared** class members are used and before any class objects are instantiated.

We now employ a video-game example to explain the need for **Shared** class-wide data. Suppose we have a video game in which **CMartian**s attack with other space creatures. Each **CMartian** tends to be brave and willing to attack other space creatures when the **CMartian** is aware that there are at least four other **CMartian**s present. If there are fewer than a total of five **CMartian**s present, each **CMartian** becomes cowardly. For this reason, each **CMartian** must know the **martianCount**. We could endow class **CMartian** with **martianCount** as instance data. If we were to do this, then every **CMartian** would have a separate copy of the instance data, and, every time we create a **CMartian**, we would have to update the instance variable **martianCount** in every **CMartian**. The redundant copies waste space, and the updating of those copies is time-consuming. Instead, we declare **martianCount** to be **Shared** so that **martianCount** is class-wide data. Each **CMartian** can see the **martianCount** as if it were instance data of that **CMartian**, but Visual Basic maintains only one copy of the **Shared martianCount** to save space. We also save time, in that the **CMartian** constructor increments only the **Shared martianCount**. Because there is only one copy, we do not have to increment separate copies of **martianCount** for each **CMartian** object.

Performance Tip 5.2

*When a single copy of the data will suffice, use **Shared** class variables to save storage.*

Although **Shared** class variables might seem like *global variables* in C and C++ (variables that can be referenced directly by name in any C function or C++ class or method in a program), they are not the same thing. **Shared** class variables have class scope. A class's **Public Shared** members can be accessed through the class name using the dot operator (e.g., *className*.*sharedMemberName*). A class's **Private Shared** class members can be accessed only through methods of the class. **Shared** class members are available as soon as the class is loaded into memory at execution time; like other variables with class scope, they exist for the duration of program execution, even when no objects of that class exist. To access a **Private Shared** class member when no objects of the class exist, programmers must provide a **Public Shared** method or property.

A **Shared** method cannot access non-**Shared** class members. Unlike non-**Shared** methods, a **Shared** method has no **Me** reference, because **Shared** class variables and **Shared** class methods exist independently of any class objects and even when there are no objects of that class.

Common Programming Error 5.7

*Using the **Me** reference in a **Shared** method or **Shared** property is a syntax error.*

Class **CEmployee2** (Fig. 5.13) demonstrates the use of a **Private Shared** class variable and a **Public Shared Property**. The **Shared** class variable **mCount** is initialized to zero by default (line 11). Class variable **mCount** maintains a count of the number of objects of class **CEmployee2** that have been instantiated and currently reside in memory, including those objects that have already been marked for garbage collection but have not yet been reclaimed by the garbage collector.

When objects of class **CEmployee2** exist, **Shared** member **mCount** can be used in any method of a **CEmployee2** object—in this example, the constructor (lines 14–24) increments **mCount** (line 20) and method **Finalize** (lines 27–32) decrements **mCount** (line 28). (Note that method **Finalize** is declared using keywords **Protected** and **Overrides**—method **Finalize**'s header must contain these keywords, and we will explain them in detail in Chapter 6.) If no objects of class **CEmployee2** exist, member **mCount** can be referenced through a call to **Property Count** (lines 53–59). Because this **Property** is **Shared**, we do not have to instantiate a **CEmployee2** object to call the **Get** method inside the **Property**. Also, by declaring property **Count** as **ReadOnly**, we prevent clients from changing **mCount**'s value directly, thus ensuring that clients can change **mCount**'s value only via the class **CEmployee2** constructors and finalizer.

Module **modSharedTest** (Fig. 5.14) runs the application that demonstrates the use of **Shared** members (Fig. 5.13). Lines 11–12 use the **ReadOnly Shared Property Count** of class **CEmployee2** to obtain the current **mCount** value. Lines 14–18 then instantiate two **CEmployee2** objects, which increment the **mCount** value by two. Lines 26–29 display the names of the employees. Lines 32–33 set these objects' references to **Nothing**, so that references **employee1** and **employee2** no longer refer to the **CEmployee2** objects. This "marks" the objects for garbage collection, because there are no more references to these objects in the program.

```
1   ' Fig. 5.13: CEmployee2.vb
2   ' Class CEmployee2 uses Shared variable.
3
4   Class CEmployee2
5      Inherits Object
6
7      Private mFirstName As String
8      Private mLastName As String
9
```

Fig. 5.13 **CEmployee2** class objects share **Shared** variable. (Part 1 of 2.)

```
10        ' number of objects in memory
11        Private Shared mCount As Integer
12
13        ' CEmployee2 constructor
14        Public Sub New(ByVal firstNameValue As String, _
15           ByVal lastNameValue As String)
16
17           mFirstName = firstNameValue
18           mLastName = lastNameValue
19
20           mCount += 1 ' increment shared count of employees
21           Console.WriteLine _
22              ("Employee object constructor: " & mFirstName & _
23              " " & mLastName)
24        End Sub ' New
25
26        ' finalizer method decrements Shared count of employees
27        Protected Overrides Sub Finalize()
28           mCount -= 1 ' decrement mCount, resulting in one fewer object
29           Console.WriteLine _
30              ("Employee object finalizer: " & mFirstName & _
31              " " & mLastName & "; count = " & mCount)
32        End Sub ' Finalize
33
34        ' return first name
35        Public ReadOnly Property FirstName() As String
36
37           Get
38              Return mFirstName
39           End Get
40
41        End Property ' FirstName
42
43        ' return last name
44        Public ReadOnly Property LastName() As String
45
46           Get
47              Return mLastName
48           End Get
49
50        End Property ' LastName
51
52        ' property Count
53        Public ReadOnly Shared Property Count() As Integer
54
55           Get
56              Return mCount
57           End Get
58
59        End Property ' Count
60
61     End Class ' CEmployee2
```

Fig. 5.13 **CEmployee2** class objects share **Shared** variable. (Part 2 of 2.)

Performance Tip 5.3

Invocation of the garbage collector incurs a performance penalty because of such factors as the complex algorithm that determines which objects should be collected.

Common Programming Error 5.8

*A call to an instance method or an attempt to access an instance variable from a **Shared** method is a syntax error.*

Normally, the garbage collector is not invoked directly by the user. Either the garbage collector reclaims the memory for objects when it deems garbage collection is appropriate, or the operating system recovers the unneeded memory when the program terminates. Line 35 uses **Public Shared** method **Collect** from class **GC** of namespace **System** to request that the garbage collector execute. Before the garbage collector releases the memory occupied by the two **CEmployee2** objects, it invokes method **Finalize** for each **CEmployee2** object, which decrements the **mCount** value by two.

The last two lines of the console output (green window) show that the **CEmployee2** object for **Bob Jones** was finalized before the **CEmployee2** object for **Susan Baker**. However, the output of this program on your system could differ. The garbage collector is not guaranteed to collect objects in a specific order.

```
1    ' Fig. 5.14: SharedTest.vb
2    ' Demonstrates Shared members.
3
4    Imports System.Windows.Forms
5
6    Module modSharedTest
7
8       Sub Main()
9          Dim output As String
10
11         Console.WriteLine("Employees before instantiation: " & _
12            CEmployee2.Count)
13
14         Dim employee1 As CEmployee2 = _
15            New CEmployee2("Susan", "Baker")
16
17         Dim employee2 As CEmployee2 = _
18            New CEmployee2("Bob", "Jones")
19
20         ' output of employee2 after instantiation
21         Console.WriteLine(vbCrLf & _
22            "Employees after instantiation: " & vbCrLf & _
23            "via Employee.Count: " & CEmployee2.Count)
24
25         ' display name of first and second employee
26         Console.WriteLine(vbCrLf & "Employees 1: " & _
27            employee1.FirstName & " " & employee1.LastName & _
28            vbCrLf & "Employee 2: " & employee2.FirstName & " " & _
29            employee2.LastName)
30
```

Fig. 5.14 Shared class member demonstration. (Part 1 of 2.)

```
31              ' mark employee1 and employee2 for garbage collection
32              employee1 = Nothing
33              employee2 = Nothing
34
35              System.GC.Collect() ' request garbage collection
36      End Sub ' Main
37
38   End Module ' modSharedTest
```

```
Employees before instantiation: 0
Employee object constructor: Susan Baker
Employee object constructor: Bob Jones

Employees after instantiation:
via Employee.Count: 2

Employees 1: Susan Baker
Employee 2: Bob Jones
Employee object finalizer: Bob Jones; count = 1
Employee object finalizer: Susan Baker; count = 0
```

Fig. 5.14   Shared class member demonstration. (Part 2 of 2.)

Good Programming Practice 5.8

Although **.vb** *files import namespace* **System***, we prefer to invoke method* **GC.Collect** *by preceding* **GC** *with namespace* **System** *and a dot (* **.** *) operator to indicate explicitly that class* **GC** *belongs to namespace* **System***. This helps make programs more readable.*

5.12 Const and ReadOnly Members

Visual Basic allows programmers to create *constants*, or members whose values cannot change during program execution. To create a constant data member of a class, declare that member using either the **Const** or **ReadOnly** keyword. A data member declared as **Const** must be initialized in its declaration; a data member declared as **ReadOnly** can be initialized either in its declaration or in the class constructor. Neither a **Const** nor a **ReadOnly** value can be modified once initialized.

Testing and Debugging Tip 5.4

If a variable's value should never change, making it a constant prevents it from changing. This helps eliminate errors that might occur if the value of the variable were to change.

Common Programming Error 5.9

Declaring a class data member as **Const** *but failing to initialize it in that declaration is a syntax error.*

Common Programming Error 5.10

Assigning a value to a **Const** *data member during runtime is a syntax error.*

Members that are declared as **Const** must be assigned values at compile time. Therefore, **Const** members can be initialized only to other constant values, such as integers, string literals, characters and other **Const** members. Constant members with values that cannot be determined at compile time must be declared with the keyword **ReadOnly**. We mentioned previously that a **ReadOnly** member can be assigned a value only once, either when it is declared or within that class's constructor. When we choose to define such a member within a constructor, a **Shared** constructor must be used to initialize **Shared ReadOnly** members, and a separate non-**Shared** (instance) constructor is used to initialize non-**Shared ReadOnly** members.

Common Programming Error 5.11

*Declaring a class data member as **ReadOnly** and attempting to use it before it is initialized is a logic error.*

Common Programming Error 5.12

*A **Shared ReadOnly** data member cannot be defined in a non-**Shared** constructor for that class, and an instance **ReadOnly** data member cannot be defined in a **Shared** constructor for that class. Attempting to define a **ReadOnly** data member in an inappropriate constructor is a syntax error.*

Common Programming Error 5.13

*The declaration of a **Const** member as **Shared** is a syntax error, because a **Const** member is **Shared** implicitly.*

Class **CCircleConstants** (Fig. 5.15) demonstrates the use of constants. Line 7 creates constant **PI** using keyword **Const** and assigns the **Double** value **3.14159**, an approximation of π. We could have used pre-defined **Const PI** of class **Math** (**Math.PI**) as the value, but we wanted to demonstrate how to create a **Const** data member explicitly. The compiler must be able to determine a **Const**'s value for that value to be assigned to the **Const** data member. The value **3.14159** is acceptable (line 7), but the expression:

```
Convert.ToDouble( "3.14159" )
```

would generate a syntax error if used in place of that value. Although this expression uses a constant value (**String** literal **"3.14159"**) as an argument, a syntax error occurs, because the compiler cannot evaluate the executable statement **Convert.ToDouble**. This restriction is lifted with **ReadOnly** members, which are assigned values at runtime. Note that line 14 (at runtime) assigns the value of constructor parameter **radiusValue** to **ReadOnly** member **mRadius**. Also, we could have used an executable statement, such as **Convert.ToDouble**, to assign a value to this **ReadOnly** member.

```
1   ' Fig. 5.15: CCircleConstants.vb
2   ' Encapsulate constants PI and radius.
3
4   Class CCircleConstants
5
6      ' PI is constant data member
7      Public Const PI As Double = 3.14159
8
9      ' radius is uninitialized constant
10     Public ReadOnly RADIUS As Integer
```

Fig. 5.15   Constants used in class **CCircleConstants**. (Part 1 of 2.)

```
11
12        ' constructor of class CCircleConstants
13        Public Sub New(ByVal radiusValue As Integer)
14           RADIUS = radiusValue
15        End Sub ' New
16
17    End Class ' CCircleConstants
```

Fig. 5.15 Constants used in class **CCircleConstants**. (Part 2 of 2.)

Module **modConstAndReadOnly** (Fig. 5.16) illustrates the use of **Const** and **ReadOnly** values. Lines 9–11 use class **Random** to generate a random **Integer** between **1–20** that corresponds to a circle's radius. Line 11 passes this value to the **CCircleConstant** constructor to instantiate a **CCircleConstant** object. Line 13 then accesses the **ReadOnly** variable **mRadius** through a reference to its class instance. Lines 15–17 compute the circle's circumference and assign the value to **String output**. This calculation employs the **Const** member **PI**, which we access in line 17 through its **Shared** class reference. Lines 19–20 output the radius and circumference values to a **MessageBox**.

```
1    ' Fig. 5.16: ConstAndReadOnly.vb
2    ' Demonstrates Const and ReadOnly members.
3
4    Imports System.Windows.Forms
5
6    Module modConstAndReadOnly
7
8       Sub Main()
9          Dim random As Random = New Random()
10         Dim circle As CCircleConstants = _
11            New CCircleConstants(random.Next(1, 20))
12
13         Dim radius As String = Convert.ToString(circle.RADIUS)
14
15         Dim output As String = "Radius = " & radius & vbCrLf _
16            & "Circumference = " + String.Format("{0:N3}", _
17            circle.RADIUS * 2 * CCircleConstants.PI)
18
19         MessageBox.Show(output, "Circumference", _
20            MessageBoxButtons.OK, MessageBoxIcon.Information)
21      End Sub ' Main
22
23   End Module ' modConstAndReadOnly
```

Fig. 5.16 **Const** and **ReadOnly** class member demonstration.

5.13 Data Abstraction and Information Hiding

As we pointed out at the beginning of this chapter, classes normally hide the details of their implementation from their clients. This is called *information hiding*. As an example of information hiding, let us consider a data structure called a *stack*.

Readers can think of a stack as analogous to a pile of dishes. When a dish is placed on the pile, it is always placed at the top (referred to as *pushing* the dish onto the stack). Similarly, when a dish is removed from the pile, it is always removed from the top (referred to as *popping* the dish off the stack). Stacks are known as *last-in, first-out (LIFO) data structures*—the last item pushed (inserted) on the stack is the first item popped (removed) from the stack.

Stacks can be implemented with arrays and with other methods, such as linked lists (we discuss linked lists in Chapter 20, Data Structures and Collections). A client of a stack class need not be concerned with the stack's implementation. The client knows only that when data items are placed in the stack, these items will be retrieved in last-in, first-out order. The client cares about *what* functionality a stack offers, but not about *how* that functionality is implemented. This concept is referred to as *data abstraction*. Although programmers might know the details of a class's implementation, they should not write code that depends on these details. This enables a particular class (such as one that implements a stack and its operations, *push* and *pop*) to be replaced with another version without affecting the rest of the system. As long as the **Public** services of the class do not change (i.e., every method or property still has the same name, return type and parameter list in the new class definition), the rest of the system is not affected.

Most programming languages emphasize actions. In these languages, data exists to support the actions that programs must take. Data is "less interesting" than actions. Data is "crude." Only a few built-in data types exist, and it is difficult for programmers to create their own data types. Visual Basic and the object-oriented style of programming elevates the importance of data. The primary activities of object-oriented programming in Visual Basic is the creation of data types (i.e., classes) and the expression of the interactions among objects of those data types. To create languages that emphasize data, the programming-languages community needed to formalize some notions about data. The formalization we consider here is the notion of *abstract data types (ADTs)*. ADTs receive as much attention today as structured programming did decades earlier. ADTs, however, do not replace structured programming. Rather, they provide an additional formalization to improve the program-development process.

Consider built-in type **Integer**, which people would associate an **Integer** with an integer in mathematics. Unlike mathematical integers, computer **Integer**s are fixed in size. For example, **Integer** on a 32-bit machine is limited approximately to the range ±2 billion. If the result of a calculation falls outside this range, an error occurs, and the computer responds in some machine-dependent manner. It might for example, "quietly" produce an incorrect result. Mathematical integers do not have this problem. Therefore, the notion of a computer **Integer** is only an approximation of the notion of a real-world integer. The same is true of **Double** and other built-in types.

We have taken the notion of **Integer** for granted until this point, but we now consider a new perspective. Types like **Integer**, **Double**, **Char** and others are all examples of abstract data types, representations of real-world notions to some satisfactory level of precision within a computer system.

An ADT actually captures two notions: A *data representation* and the *operations* that can be performed on that data. For example, in Visual Basic, an **Integer** contains an integer value (data) and provides addition, subtraction, multiplication, division and modulus operations; however, division by zero is undefined. In Visual Basic, programmers use classes to implement abstract data types.

Software Engineering Observation 5.14

Programmers can create types through the use of the class mechanism. These new types can be designed so that they are as convenient to use as the built-in types. This marks Visual Basic as an extensible language. Although the language is easy to extend via new types, the programmer cannot alter the base language itself.

Another abstract data type we discuss is a *queue*, which is similar to a "waiting line." Computer systems use many queues internally. We write programs that simulate queues and their behavior. A queue offers well-understood behavior to its clients: Clients place items in a queue one at a time via an *enqueue* operation, then get those items back one at a time via a *dequeue* operation. A queue returns items in *first-in, first-out (FIFO)* order, which means that the first item inserted in a queue is the first item removed. Conceptually, a queue can become infinitely long, whereas real queues are finite.

The queue hides an internal data representation that keeps track of the items currently waiting in line, and it offers a set of operations to its clients (*enqueue* and *dequeue*). The clients are not concerned about the implementation of the queue—clients depend on the queue to operate "as advertised." When a client enqueues an item, the queue should accept that item and place it in some kind of internal FIFO data structure. Similarly, when the client wants the next item from the front of the queue, the queue should remove the item from its internal representation and deliver the item in FIFO order (i.e., the item that has been in the queue the longest should be the next one returned by the next dequeue operation).

The queue ADT guarantees the integrity of its internal data structure. Clients cannot manipulate this data structure directly—only the queue ADT has access to its internal data. Clients are able to perform only allowable operations on the data representation; the ADT rejects operations that its public service does not provide.

5.14 Software Reusability

Visual Basic programmers concentrate on both crafting new classes and reusing existing classes. Many *class libraries* exist, and developers worldwide are creating others. Software is constructed from existing, well-defined, carefully tested, well-documented, portable, widely available components. Software reusability speeds the development of powerful, high-quality software. *Rapid application development (RAD)* is of great interest today in the software industry.

To realize the full potential of software reusability, we need to improve cataloging and licensing schemes, protection mechanisms that ensure master copies of classes are not corrupted, description schemes that system designers use to determine whether existing classes meet their needs and browsing mechanisms that determine whether classes are available and how closely these classes meet software developer requirements. These efforts will be worthwhile, because the value of convenient and effective software reuse is enormous.

Consider the earlier application examples of this chapter. Many of them contained a definition for some variation of a **CTime** class and a **modTimeTest** module. These definitions often contained repeated code. Programmers should not have to rewrite code. With the **CTime/modTimeTest** case, each application could have been engineered to import the functionality, thus decreasing programming overhead. We show in Section 5.15 how to import functionality.

5.15 Namespaces and Assemblies

As we have seen in almost every example in the text, classes from preexisting libraries, such as the .NET Framework, must be imported into a Visual Basic program by including a reference to those libraries (a process we demonstrated in Chapter 2). Remember that each class in the Framework Class Library belongs to a specific namespace. This preexisting code provides a mechanism that facilitates software reuse.

As we discussed in Section 5.14, when appropriate, programmers should concentrate on making the software components they create reusable. However, doing so often results in *naming collisions*, which occur when the same name is used for two classes in the same namespace, for two methods in the same class, etc.

 Common Programming Error 5.14

Attempting to compile code that contains naming collisions generates a syntax error.

Namespaces help minimize this problem by providing a convention for *unique class names*. No two classes in a given namespace can have the same name, but different namespaces can contain classes with the same name. With millions of people writing Visual Basic programs, the names that one programmer chooses for classes will likely conflict with the names that other programmers choose for their classes.

Figure 5.17, which provides the code for class **CEmployee3**, demonstrates the creation of a reusable class library. Notice that this class is identical to class **CEmployee2** (Fig. 5.13), except we have declared class **CEmployee3** as a **Public** class. When other projects make use of a class library, only **Public** classes are accessible—thus, if we did not declare **CEmployee3** as **Public**, other projects could not use it. We demonstrate momentarily how to package class **CEmployee3** into **EmployeeLibrary.dll**—the *dynamic link library* that we create for reuse with other systems. As we mentioned in Chapter 2, a dynamic link library contains related classes that projects can use.

```
1    ' Fig. 5.17: CEmployee3.vb
2    ' Class CEmployee3 uses Shared variable.
3
4    Public Class CEmployee3
5       Inherits Object
6
7       Private mFirstName As String
8       Private mLastName As String
9
10      ' number of objects in memory
11      Private Shared mCount As Integer
```

Fig. 5.17 **CEmployee3** class to store in class library. (Part 1 of 2.)

```
12
13        ' CEmployee3 constructor
14        Public Sub New(ByVal firstNameValue As String, _
15           ByVal lastNameValue As String)
16
17           mFirstName = firstNameValue
18           mLastName = lastNameValue
19
20           mCount += 1 ' increment shared count of employees
21           Console.WriteLine _
22              ("Employee object constructor: " & mFirstName & _
23              " " & mLastName)
24        End Sub ' New
25
26        ' finalizer method decrements Shared count of employees
27        Protected Overrides Sub Finalize()
28           mCount -= 1 ' decrement mCount, resulting in one fewer object
29           Console.WriteLine _
30              ("Employee object finalizer: " & mFirstName & _
31              " " & mLastName & "; count = " & mCount)
32        End Sub ' Finalize
33
34        ' return first name
35        Public ReadOnly Property FirstName() As String
36
37           Get
38              Return mFirstName
39           End Get
40
41        End Property ' FirstName
42
43        ' return last name
44        Public ReadOnly Property LastName() As String
45
46           Get
47              Return mLastName
48           End Get
49
50        End Property ' LastName
51
52        ' property Count
53        Public ReadOnly Shared Property Count() As Integer
54
55           Get
56              Return mCount
57           End Get
58
59        End Property ' Count
60
61     End Class ' CEmployee3
```

Fig. 5.17   **CEmployee3** class to store in class library. (Part 2 of 2.)

We now describe how to create a class library that includes class **CEmployee3**:

1. *Create a class library project.* Select **File > New > Project...** to display the **New Project** dialog. Select **Visual Basic Projects** from the **Project Types:** pane, then select **Class Library** from the **Templates:** pane. Name the project **EmployeeLibrary,** and choose a directory in which you would like the project to be located (you many choose any directory you wish). A class library is created, as shown in Fig. 5.18. There are two important points to note about the class library's code. The first is that there is no **Main** method. This indicates that a class library is not an executable program. Class libraries are software components that are loaded and used (and reused) by executable programs. It is not designed as a standalone application—rather, it is designed to be used by running programs. The second key point is that **Class1** is a **Public** class, so that it is accessible to other projects (Fig. 5.18).

2. In the **Solution Explorer**, rename **Class1.vb** to **CEmployee3.vb** (right-click **Class1.vb** and select **Rename**). Replace the following code generated by the development environment:

    ```
    Public Class Class1

    End Class
    ```

    with the entire code listing from class **CEmployee3** *(Fig. 5.17).*

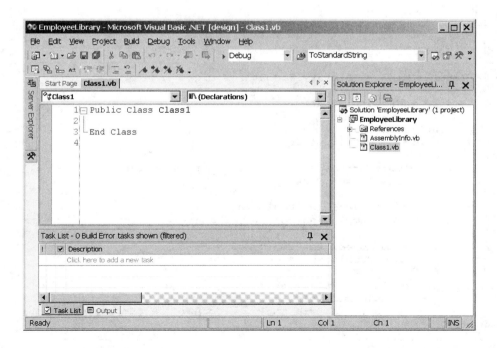

Fig. 5.18 Simple class library project.

3. Select **Build > Build Solution** to compile the code. Remember that this code is not executable. If the programmer attempts to execute the class library by selecting **Debug > Start Without Debugging**, Visual Studio displays an error message.

When the class library is compiled successfully, an assembly is created. This assembly is located in the project's **bin** directory, and by default is named **EmployeeLibrary.dll**. The assembly file contains class **CEmployee3**, which other modules, classes and systems can use. Assembly files, which have file extensions **.dll** and **.exe**, are at the core of Visual Basic application development. The Windows operating system uses executable files (**.exe**) to run applications and library files (**.dll**, or *dynamic link library*) to create code libraries.

 Portability Tip 5.1

Focus on creating unique namespace names to avoid naming collisions. This is especially helpful when using someone else's code (or when someone else uses your code).

Module **modAssemblyTest** (Fig. 5.19) demonstrates the use of the assembly file in a running application. The module employs class **CEmployee3** in **EmployeeLibrary.dll** to create and mark two **CEmployee3** for garbage collection. A reference to the assembly is created by selecting **Project > Add Reference**. Using the **Browse** button, select **EmployeeLibrary.dll** (located in the **bin** directory of our **EmployeeLibrary** project), then click **OK** to add the resource to the project. Once the reference has been added, we use keyword **Imports** followed by the namespace's name (**EmployeeLibrary**) to inform the compiler that we are using classes from this namespace (line 4).

```
1   ' Fig. 5.19: AssemblyTest.vb
2   ' Demonstrates assembly files and namespaces.
3
4   Imports EmployeeLibrary ' contains class CEmployee3
5
6   Module modAssemblyTest
7
8      Public Sub Main()
9         Dim output As String
10
11        Console.WriteLine("Employees before instantiation: " & _
12           CEmployee3.Count)
13
14        Dim employee1 As CEmployee3 = _
15           New CEmployee3("Susan", "Baker")
16
17        Dim employee2 As CEmployee3 = _
18           New CEmployee3("Bob", "Jones")
19
20        ' output of employee after instantiation
21        Console.WriteLine(vbCrLf & "Employees after instantiation:" _
22           & vbCrLf & "via Employee.Count: " & CEmployee3.Count)
23
```

Fig. 5.19 Module **modAssemblyTest** references **EmployeeLibrary.dll**. (Part 1 of 2.)

```
24        ' display name of first and second employee
25        Console.WriteLine(vbCrLf & "Employees 1: " & _
26          employee1.FirstName & " " & employee1.LastName & _
27          vbCrLf & "Employee 2: " & employee2.FirstName & " " & _
28          employee2.LastName)
29
30        ' mark employee1 and employee2 for garbage collection
31        employee1 = Nothing
32        employee2 = Nothing
33
34        System.GC.Collect() ' request garbage collection
35     End Sub ' Main
36
37  End Module ' modAssemblyTest
```

```
Employees before instantiation: 0
Employee object constructor: Susan Baker
Employee object constructor: Bob Jones

Employees after instantiation:
via Employee.Count: 2

Employees 1: Susan Baker
Employee 2: Bob Jones
Employee object finalizer: Bob Jones; count = 1
Employee object finalizer: Susan Baker; count = 0
```

Fig. 5.19 Module **modAssemblyTest** references **EmployeeLibrary.dll**.
(Part 2 of 2.)

5.16 Class View and Object Browser

Now that we have introduced key concepts of object-based programming, we present two features that Visual Studio provides to facilitate the design of object-oriented applications—**Class View** and **Object Browser**.

The **Class View** displays a project's class members. To access this feature, select **View > Class View**. Figure 5.20 depicts the **Class View** for the **TimeTest** project of Fig. 5.1 and Fig. 5.2 (class **CTime** and module **modTimeTest**). **Class View** follows a hierarchical structure, with the project name (**TimeTest**) as the root. Beneath the root is a series of nodes (e.g., classes, variables, methods, etc.). If a node contains a plus box (**+**) next to it, that node is collapsed. By contrast, if a node contains a minus box (**-**) next to it, that node has been expanded (and can be collapsed). In Fig. 5.20, project **TimeTest** contains class **CTime** and module **modTimeTest** as *children*. Class **CTime** contains a constructor, methods **SetTime**, **ToStandardString** and **ToUniversalString** (indicated by purple boxes) and variables **mHour**, **mMinute** and **mSecond** (indicated by blue boxes). The lock icons, placed to the left of the blue-box icons, indicate that the variables are **Private**. Module **modTimeTest** contains method **Main**. Note that class **CTime** contains the **Bases and Interfaces** node, which contains class **Object**. This is because class **CTime** inherits from class **System.Object** (which we discuss in Chapter 6).

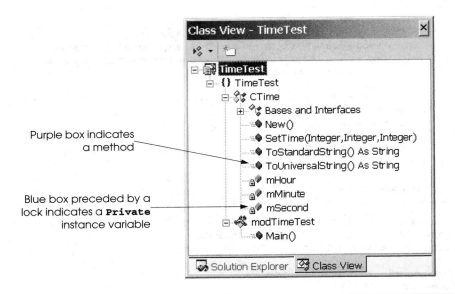

Purple box indicates
a method

Blue box preceded by a
lock indicates a **Private**
instance variable

Fig. 5.20   **Class View** of Fig. 5.1 and Fig. 5.2.

The second feature that Visual Studio provides is the **Object Browser**, which lists the Framework Class Library (FCL) classes available in Visual Basic. Developers use the **Object Browser** to learn about the functionality provided by a specific object. To open the **Object Browser**, right click any Visual Basic class or method in the code editor and select **Go To Definition** (Fig. 5.21). Figure 5.22 shows the **Object Browser** when the user selects keyword **Object** in the code editor. Note that the **Object Browser** lists all non-**Private** members provided by class **Object** in the *Members of 'Object'* window—this window offers developers "instant access" to information regarding the services of various objects. Note also that the **Object Browser** lists in the **Objects** window all objects that Visual Basic provides.

5.17 Summary

Instance variables and methods that are declared with member access modifier **Public** are accessible wherever the program has a reference to an object of the class in which the **Public** members are defined. Instance variables and methods that are declared with member access modifier **Private** are accessible only to methods of the class in which the **Private** members are defined.

A class's constructor is called when an object of the class is instantiated. Constructors initialize an object's instance variables and can be overloaded. If no constructors are defined for a class, a default constructor is provided by the compiler. The default constructor takes no parameters and has an empty body.

To allow clients to manipulate the value of **Private** data, the class can provide a property definition. Property definitions contain accessor methods that handle the details of modifying and returning data. A property definition can contain a **Set** accessor, a **Get** accessor or both. A **Get** accessor enables the client to read the variable's value, and the **Set** accessor enables the client to modify the variable's value.

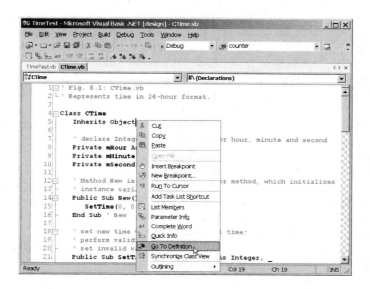

Fig. 5.21 Invoking the **Object Browser** from the development environment.

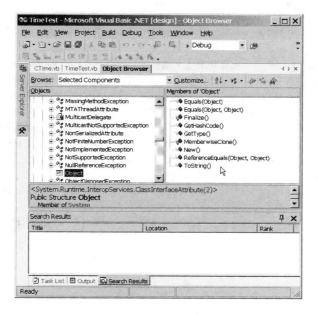

Fig. 5.22 **Object Browser** when user selects **Object** from development environment.

A class's instance variables, properties and methods belong to that class's scope. Within a class's scope, class members are accessible to all of that class's methods and can be referenced simply by name. Outside a class's scope, class members cannot be referenced directly by name. If a method defines a variable that has the same name as a variable with class scope (i.e., an instance variable), the class-scope variable is hidden by the method-scope variable in that method's scope.

The .NET Framework performs automatic garbage collection. When an object is no longer used in the program (i.e., there are no references to the object), the object is marked for garbage collection. The memory for such an object then is reclaimed when the garbage collector executes. Every class contains a finalizer that typically returns resources to the system. The finalizer for an object is guaranteed to be called to perform termination house-keeping on the object just before the garbage collector reclaims the memory for the object (a process called finalization).

In certain cases, all objects of a class should share only one copy of a particular variable. Programmers use **Shared** class variables for this and other reasons. A **Shared** class variable represents class-wide information; all objects of the class share the same piece of data. The declaration of a **Shared** member begins with the keyword **Shared**. Although **Shared** class variables might seem like global variables, **Shared** class variables have class scope. **Public Shared** class members can be accessed by specifying the class name and the dot operator (e.g., *className.sharedMemberName*). **Private Shared** class members can be accessed only through methods of the class. A **Shared** method cannot access non-**Shared** class members.

Visual Basic allows programmers to create members whose values cannot change during program execution. Such members are called constants. To create a constant member of a class, the programmer must declare that member with either the **Const** or the **ReadOnly** keyword. Members declared with **Const** must be initialized in the declaration; those declared with **ReadOnly** can be initialized in the constructor, but must be initialized before they are used.

Each class in the .NET Framework belongs to a specific namespace (or library) that contains a group of related classes. Namespaces provide a mechanism for software reuse. It is likely that the names programmers create for classes will conflict with names that other programmers create. Namespaces help resolve this problem.

Assembly files are either **.dll** (library code) or **.exe** (executables) files. The **Imports** statement informs the compiler what assembly files a **.vb** file references. Classes, by default, are placed in the **.exe** assembly file of an application, unless they are compiled as **.dll** assembly files and imported into a program.

Class View displays the variables, properties and methods for all classes in a project. The **Object Browser** lists all classes in the Visual Basic library. Developers use the **Object Browser** to learn about the functionality provided by a specific object.

Object-Oriented Programming: Inheritance

Objectives

- To understand inheritance and software reusability.
- To understand the concepts of base classes and derived classes.
- To understand member access modifiers **Protected** and **Friend**.
- To use the **MyBase** reference to access base-class members.
- To understand the use of constructors and finalizers in base classes and derived classes.
- To present a case study that demonstrates the mechanics of inheritance.

Say not you know another entirely, till you have divided an inheritance with him.
Johann Kasper Lavater

This method is to define as the number of a class the class of all classes similar to the given class.
Bertrand Russell

Good as it is to inherit a library, it is better to collect one.
Augustine Birrell

6.1 Introduction

In this chapter, we begin our discussion of object-oriented programming (OOP) by introducing one of its main features—*inheritance*. Inheritance is a form of software reusability in which classes are created by absorbing an existing class's data and behaviors and embellishing them with new capabilities. Software reusability saves time during program development. It also encourages the reuse of proven and debugged high-quality software, which increases the likelihood that a system will be implemented effectively.

When creating a class, instead of writing completely new instance variables and methods, the programmer can designate that the new class should *inherit* the class variables, properties and methods of another class. The previously defined class is called the *base class*, and the new class is referred to as the *derived class.* (Other programming languages, such as Java, refer to the base class as the *superclass*, and the derived class as the *subclass*.) Once created, each derived class can become the base class for future derived classes. A derived class, to which unique class variables, properties and methods normally are added, is often larger than its base class. Therefore, a derived class is more specific than its base class and represents a more specialized group of objects. Typically, the derived class contains the behaviors of its base class and additional behaviors. The *direct base class* is the base class from which the derived class explicitly inherits. An *indirect base class* is inherited from two or more levels up the *class hierarchy*. In the case of *single inheritance,* a class is derived from one base class. Visual Basic does not support *multiple inheritance* (which occurs when a class is derived from more than one direct base class), as does C++. (We explain in Chapter 7 how Visual Basic can use interfaces to realize many of the benefits of multiple inheritance while avoiding the associated problems.)

Every object of a derived class is also an object of that derived class's base class. However, base-class objects are not objects of their derived classes. For example, all cars are vehicles, but not all vehicles are cars. As we continue our study of object-oriented programming in Chapters 6 and 7, we take advantage of this relationship to perform some interesting manipulations.

Experience in building software systems indicates that significant amounts of code deal with closely related special cases. When programmers are preoccupied with special cases, the details can obscure the "big picture." With object-oriented programming, programmers focus on the commonalities among objects in the system, rather than on the special cases. This process is called *abstraction*.

We distinguish between the *"is-a" relationship* and the *"has-a" relationship*. "Is-a" represents inheritance. In an "is-a" relationship, an object of a derived class also can be treated as an object of its base class. For example, a car *is a* vehicle. By contrast, "has-a" stands for composition (composition is discussed in Chapter 5). In a "has-a" relationship, a class contains one or more object references as members. For example, a car *has a* steering wheel.

Derived class methods might require access to their base-class instance variables, properties and methods. A derived class can access the non-**Private** members of its base class. Base-class members that should not be accessible to properties or methods of a class derived from that base class via inheritance are declared **Private** in the base class. A derived class can effect state changes in **Private** base-class members, but only through non-**Private** methods and properties provided in the base class and inherited by the derived class.

Software Engineering Observation 6.1

*Properties and methods of a derived class cannot directly access **Private** members of their base class.*

Software Engineering Observation 6.2

*Hiding **Private** members helps test, debug and correctly modify systems. If a derived class could access its base class's **Private** members, classes that inherit from that derived class could access that data as well. This would propagate access to what should be **Private** data, and the benefits of information hiding would be lost.*

One problem with inheritance is that a derived class can inherit properties and methods it does not need or should not have. It is the class designer's responsibility to ensure that the capabilities provided by a class are appropriate for future derived classes. Even when a base-class property or method is appropriate for a derived class, that derived class often requires the property or method to perform its task in a manner specific to the derived class. In such cases, the base-class property or method can be *overridden* (redefined) in the derived class with an appropriate implementation.

New classes can inherit from abundant *class libraries*. Although organizations often develop their own class libraries, they also can take advantage of other libraries available worldwide. Someday, the vast majority of new software likely will be constructed from *standardized reusable components*, as most hardware is constructed today. This will facilitate the development of more powerful and abundant software.

6.2 Base Classes and Derived Classes

Often, an object of one class "is an" object of another class, as well. For example, a rectangle *is a* quadrilateral (as are squares, parallelograms and trapezoids). Thus, class **CRectangle** can be said to *inherit* from class **CQuadrilateral**. In this context, class **CQuadrilateral** is a base class, and class **CRectangle** is a derived class. A rectangle *is a* specific type of quadrilateral, but it is incorrect to claim that a quadrilateral *is a* rectangle—the quadrilateral could be a parallelogram or some other type of **CQuadrilateral**. Figure 6.1 lists several simple examples of base classes and derived classes.

Base class	Derived classes
CStudent	CGraduateStudent CUndergraduateStudent
CShape	CCircle CTriangle CRectangle
CLoan	CCarLoan CHomeImprovementLoan CMortgageLoan
CEmployee	CFacultyMember CStaffMember
CAccount	CCheckingAccount CSavingsAccount

Fig. 6.1   Inheritance examples.

Every derived-class object "is an" object of its base class, and one base class can have many derived classes; therefore, the set of objects represented by a base class typically is larger than the set of objects represented by any of its derived classes. For example, the base class **CVehicle** represents all vehicles, including cars, trucks, boats, bicycles and so on. By contrast, derived-class **CCar** represents only a small subset of all **CVehicle**s.

Inheritance relationships form tree-like hierarchical structures. A class exists in a hierarchical relationship with its derived classes. Although classes can exist independently, once they are employed in inheritance arrangements, they become affiliated with other classes. A class becomes either a base class, supplying data and behaviors to other classes, or a derived class, inheriting its data and behaviors from other classes.

Let us develop a simple inheritance hierarchy. A university community has thousands of members. These members consist of employees, students and alumni. Employees are either faculty members or staff members. Faculty members are either administrators (such as deans and department chairpersons) or teachers. This organizational structure yields the inheritance hierarchy, depicted in Fig. 6.2. Note that the inheritance hierarchy could contain many other classes. For example, students can be graduate or undergraduate students. Undergraduate students can be freshmen, sophomores, juniors and seniors. Each arrow in the hierarchy represents an "is-a" relationship. For example, as we follow the arrows in this class hierarchy, we can state, "a **CEmployee** *is a* **CCommunityMember**" or "a **CTeacher** *is a* **CFaculty** member." **CCommunityMember** is the *direct base class* of **CEmployee**, **CStudent** and **CAlumnus**. In addition, **CCommunityMember** is an *indirect base class* of all the other classes in the hierarchy diagram.

Starting from the bottom of the diagram, the reader can follow the arrows and apply the *is-a* relationship to the topmost base class. For example, a **CAdministrator** *is a* **CFaculty** member, *is a* **CEmployee** and *is a* **CCommunityMember**. In Visual Basic, a **CAdministrator** also *is an* **Object**, because all classes in Visual Basic have **Object** as either a direct or indirect base class. Thus, all classes in Visual Basic are connected via a hierarchical relationship in which they share the eight methods defined by class **Object**. We discuss some of these methods inherited from **Object** throughout the text.

Another inheritance hierarchy is the **CShape** hierarchy of Fig. 6.3. To specify that class **CTwoDimensionalShape** is derived from (or inherits from) class **CShape**, class **CTwoDimensionalShape** could be defined in Visual Basic as follows:

> *Class* **CTwoDimensionalShape**
>   *Inherits* **CShape**

In Chapter 5, we briefly discussed *has-a* relationships, in which classes have as members references to objects of other classes. Such relationships create classes by *composition* of existing classes. For example, given the classes **CEmployee**, **CBirthDate** and **CTelephoneNumber**, it is improper to say that a **CEmployee** *is a* **CBirthDate** or that a **CEmployee** *is a* **CTelephoneNumber**. However, it is appropriate to say that a **CEmployee** *has a* **CBirthDate** and that a **CEmployee** *has a* **CTelephoneNumber**.

With inheritance, **Private** members of a base class are not accessible directly from that class's derived classes, but these **Private** base-class members are still inherited. All other base-class members retain their original member access when they become members of the derived class (e.g., **Public** members of the base class become **Public** members of the derived class, and, as we will soon see, **Protected** members of the base class become **Protected** members of the derived class). Through these inherited base-class members, the derived class can manipulate **Private** members of the base class (if these inherited members provide such functionality in the base class).

It is possible to treat base-class objects and derived-class objects similarly; their commonalities are expressed in the member variables, properties and methods of the base class. Objects of all classes derived from a common base class can be treated as objects of that base class. In Chapter 7, we consider many examples that take advantage of this relationship.

Software Engineering Observation 6.3

Constructors never are inherited—they are specific to the class in which they are defined.

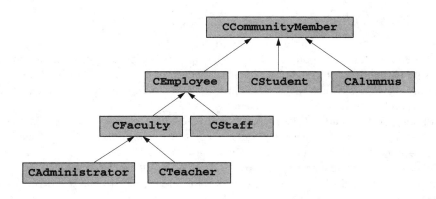

Fig. 6.2   Inheritance hierarchy for university **CCommunityMember**s.

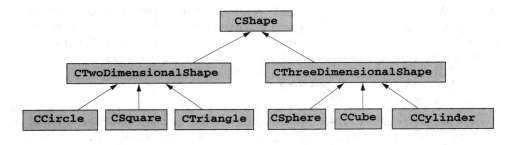

Fig. 6.3   Portion of a **CShape** class hierarchy.

6.3 **Protected** and **Friend** Members

Chapter 5 discussed **Public** and **Private** member access modifiers. A base class's **Public** members are accessible anywhere that the program has a reference to an object of that base class or one of its derived classes. A base class's **Private** members are accessible only within the body of that base class. In this section, we introduce two additional member access modifiers, *Protected* and *Friend*.

Protected access offers an intermediate level of protection between **Public** and **Private** access. A base class's **Protected** members can be accessed only in that base class or in any classes derived from that class.

Another intermediate level of access is known as **Friend** access. A base class's **Friend** members can be accessed only by objects declared in the same assembly. Note that a **Friend** member is accessible in any part of the assembly in which that **Friend** member is declared—not only in classes derived from the base class that defines the member.

Derived-class methods normally can refer to **Public**, **Protected** and **Friend** members of the base class simply by using the member names. When a derived-class method overrides a base-class member, the base-class member can be accessed from the derived class by preceding the base-class member name with keyword *MyBase*, followed by the dot operator (**.**). We discuss keyword **MyBase** in Section 6.4.

6.4 Relationship Between Base Classes and Derived Classes

In this section, we use a point-circle hierarchy to discuss the relationship between a base class and a derived class. The point-circle relationship may seem slightly unnatural when we discuss it in the context of a circle "is a" point; however, this mechanical example teaches *structural inheritance*, which focuses primarily on how a base class and a derived class relate to one another. In Chapter 7, we present more "natural" inheritance examples.

We divide our discussion of the point-circle relationship into several parts. First, we create class **CPoint**, which directly inherits from class **System.Object** and contains as **Private** data an *x-y* coordinate pair. Then, we create class **CCircle**, which also directly inherits from class **System.Object** and contains as **Private** data an *x-y* coordinate pair (representing the location of the center of the circle) and a radius. We do not use inheritance to create class **CCircle**; rather, we construct the class by writing every line of code the class requires. Next, we create a separate **CCircle2** class, which directly inherits from class **CPoint** (i.e., class **CCircle2** "is a" **CPoint** but also contains a radius) and attempts to use the **CPoint Private** members—this results in compilation errors, because the derived class does not have access to the base-class's **Private** data. We then show how by declaring **CPoint**'s data as **Protected**, a separate **CCircle3** class that also inherits from class **CPoint** can access that data. Both the inherited and non-inherited **CCircle** classes contain identical functionality, but we show how the inherited **CCircle3** class is easier to create and manage. After discussing the merits of using **Protected** data, we set the **CPoint** data back to **Private**, then show how a separate **CCircle4** class (which also inherits from class **CPoint**) can use **CPoint** methods to manipulate **CPoint**'s **Private** data.

Let us first examine the **CPoint** (Fig. 6.4) class definition. The **Public** services of class **CPoint** include two **CPoint** constructors (lines 11–25), properties **X** and **Y** (lines 28–51) and method **ToString** (lines 54–56). The instance variables **mX** and **mY** of **CPoint** are specified as **Private** (line 8), so objects of other classes cannot access **mX** and **mY** directly. Technically, even if **CPoint**'s variables **mX** and **mY** were made **Public**, **CPoint** can never maintain an inconsistent state, because the *x-y* coordinate plane is infinite in both directions, so **mX** and **mY** can hold any **Integer** value. However, declaring this data as **Private**, while providing non-**Private** properties to manipulate and perform validation checking on this data, enforces good software engineering.

We mentioned in Section 6.2 that class constructors are never inherited. Therefore, class **CPoint** does not inherit class **Object**'s constructor. However, class **CPoint**'s constructors (lines 11–25) call class **Object**'s constructor implicitly. In fact, the first task undertaken by any derived-class constructor is to call its direct base class's constructor, either implicitly or explicitly. (The syntax for calling a base-class constructor is discussed later in this section.) If the code does not include an explicit call to the base-class constructor, an implicit call is made to the base class's default (no-argument) constructor. The comments in lines 13 and 22 indicate where the calls to the base-class **Object**'s default constructor occur.

 Common Programming Error 6.1

If a constructor makes an implicit call to a default base-class constructor that does not exist, a compilation error occurs.

```
1   ' Fig. 6.4: Point.vb
2   ' CPoint class represents an x-y coordinate pair.
3
4   Public Class CPoint
5      ' implicitly Inherits Object
6
7      ' point coordinate
8      Private mX, mY As Integer
9
10     ' default constructor
11     Public Sub New()
12
13        ' implicit call to Object constructor occurs here
14        X = 0
15        Y = 0
16     End Sub ' New
17
```

Fig. 6.4   **CPoint** class represents an *x-y* coordinate pair. (Part 1 of 2.)

```
18          ' constructor
19          Public Sub New(ByVal xValue As Integer, _
20             ByVal yValue As Integer)
21
22             ' implicit call to Object constructor occurs here
23             X = xValue
24             Y = yValue
25          End Sub ' New
26
27          ' property X
28          Public Property X() As Integer
29
30             Get
31                Return mX
32             End Get
33
34             Set(ByVal xValue As Integer)
35                mX = xValue ' no need for validation
36             End Set
37
38          End Property ' X
39
40          ' property Y
41          Public Property Y() As Integer
42
43             Get
44                Return mY
45             End Get
46
47             Set(ByVal yValue As Integer)
48                mY = yValue ' no need for validation
49             End Set
50
51          End Property ' Y
52
53          ' return String representation of CPoint
54          Public Overrides Function ToString() As String
55             Return "[" & mX & ", " & mY & "]"
56          End Function ' ToString
57
58       End Class ' CPoint
```

Fig. 6.4   **CPoint** class represents an *x-y* coordinate pair. (Part 2 of 2.)

Note that method **ToString** (lines 54–56) contains the keyword ***Overrides*** in its declaration. Every class in Visual Basic (such as class **CPoint**) inherits either directly or indirectly from class **System.Object**, which is the root of the class hierarchy. As we mentioned previously, this means that every class inherits the eight methods defined by class **Object**. One of these methods is ***ToString***, which returns a **String** containing the object's type preceded by its namespace—this method obtains an object's **String** representation and sometimes is called implicitly by the program (such as when an object is concatenated to a **String**). Method **ToString** of class **CPoint** *overrides* the original **ToString** from class **Object**—when invoked, method **ToString** of class **CPoint** returns a **String** containing an ordered pair of the values **mX** and **mY** (line 55), instead of returning a **String** containing the object's class and namespace.

Software Engineering Observation 6.4

*The Visual Basic compiler sets the base class of a derived class to **Object** when the program does not specify a base class explicitly.*

In Visual Basic, a base-class method must be declared **Overridable** if that method is to be overridden in a derived class. Method **ToString** of class **Object** is declared **Overridable**, which enables derived class **CPoint** to override this method. To view the method header for **ToString**, select **Help > Index...**, and enter **Object.ToString method** in the search textbox. The page displayed contains a description of method **ToString**, which includes the following header:

Overridable Public Function ToString() As String

Keyword **Overridable** allows programmers to specify those methods that a derived class can override—a method that has not been declared **Overridable** cannot be overridden. We use this later in this section to enable certain methods in our base classes to be overridden.

Common Programming Error 6.2

*A derived class attempting to override (using keyword **Overrides**) a method that has not been declared **Overridable** is a syntax error.*

Module **modPointTest** (Fig. 6.5) tests class **CPoint**. Line 12 instantiates an object of class **CPoint** and assigns **72** as the x-coordinate value and **115** as the y-coordinate value. Lines 15–16 use properties **X** and **Y** to retrieve these values, then append the values to **String output**. Lines 18–19 change the values of properties **X** and **Y**, and lines 22–23 call **CPoint**'s **ToString** method to obtain the **CPoint**'s **String** representation.

```
1   ' Fig. 6.5: PointTest.vb
2   ' Testing class CPoint.
3
4   Imports System.Windows.Forms
5
6   Module modPointTest
7
8      Sub Main()
9         Dim point As CPoint
10        Dim output As String
11
12        point = New CPoint(72, 115) ' instantiate CPoint object
13
14        ' display point coordinates via X and Y properties
15        output = "X coordinate is " & point.X & _
16           vbCrLf & "Y coordinate is " & point.Y
17
18        point.X = 10 ' set x-coordinate via X property
19        point.Y = 10 ' set y-coordinate via Y property
20
```

Fig. 6.5   modPointTest demonstrates class **CPoint** functionality. (Part 1 of 2.)

```
21            ' display new point value
22            output &= vbCrLf & vbCrLf & _
23               "The new location of point is " & point.ToString()
24
25            MessageBox.Show(output, "Demonstrating Class Point")
26       End Sub ' Main
27
28    End Module ' modPointTest
```

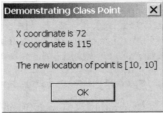

Fig. 6.5   modPointTest demonstrates class **CPoint** functionality. (Part 2 of 2.)

We now discuss the second part of our introduction to inheritance by creating and testing class **CCircle** (Fig. 6.6), which directly inherits from class **System.Object** and represents an *x-y* coordinate pair (representing the center of the circle) and a radius. Lines 7–8 declare the instance variables **mX**, **mY** and **mRadius** as **Private** data. The **Public** services of class **CCircle** include two **CCircle** constructors (lines 11–27), properties **X**, **Y** and **Radius** (lines 30–70), methods **Diameter** (lines 73–75), **Circumference** (lines 78–80), **Area** (lines 83–85) and **ToString** (lines 88–91). These properties and methods encapsulate all necessary features (i.e., the "analytic geometry") of a circle; in the next section, we show how this encapsulation enables us to reuse and extend this class.

```
1     ' Fig. 6.6: Circle.vb
2     ' CCircle class contains x-y coordinate pair and radius.
3
4     Public Class CCircle
5
6        ' coordinate of center of CCircle
7        Private mX, mY As Integer
8        Private mRadius As Double ' CCircle's radius
9
10       ' default constructor
11       Public Sub New()
12
13          ' implicit call to Object constructor occurs here
14          X = 0
15          Y = 0
16          Radius = 0
17       End Sub ' New
18
```

Fig. 6.6   CCircle class contains an *x-y* coordinate and a radius. (Part 1 of 3.)

```
19      ' constructor
20      Public Sub New(ByVal xValue As Integer, _
21         ByVal yValue As Integer, ByVal radiusValue As Double)
22
23         ' implicit call to Object constructor occurs here
24         X = xValue
25         Y = yValue
26         Radius = radiusValue
27      End Sub ' New
28
29      ' property X
30      Public Property X() As Integer
31
32         Get
33            Return mX
34         End Get
35
36         Set(ByVal xValue As Integer)
37            mX = xValue ' no need for validation
38         End Set
39
40      End Property ' X
41
42      ' property Y
43      Public Property Y() As Integer
44
45         Get
46            Return mY
47         End Get
48
49         Set(ByVal yValue As Integer)
50            mY = yValue ' no need for validation
51         End Set
52
53      End Property ' Y
54
55      ' property Radius
56      Public Property Radius() As Double
57
58         Get
59            Return mRadius
60         End Get
61
62         Set(ByVal radiusValue As Double)
63
64            If radiusValue > 0
65               mRadius = radiusValue
66            End If
67
68         End Set
69
70      End Property ' Radius
71
```

Fig. 6.6   CCircle class contains an *x-y* coordinate and a radius. (Part 2 of 3.)

```
72      ' calculate CCircle diameter
73      Public Function Diameter() As Double
74          Return mRadius * 2
75      End Function ' Diameter
76
77      ' calculate CCircle circumference
78      Public Function Circumference() As Double
79          Return Math.PI * Diameter()
80      End Function ' Circumference
81
82      ' calculate CCircle area
83      Public Function Area() As Double
84          Return Math.PI * mRadius ^ 2
85      End Function ' Area
86
87      ' return String representation of CCircle
88      Public Overrides Function ToString() As String
89          Return "Center = " & "[" & mX & ", " & mY & "]" & _
90              "; Radius = " & mRadius
91      End Function ' ToString
92
93  End Class ' CCircle
```

Fig. 6.6   `CCircle` class contains an *x-y* coordinate and a radius. (Part 3 of 3.)

Module **modCircleTest** (Fig. 6.7) tests class **CCircle**. Line 12 instantiates an object of class **CCircle**, assigning **37** as the *x*-coordinate value, **43** as the *y*-coordinate value and **2.5** as the radius value. Lines 15–17 use properties **X**, **Y** and **Radius** to retrieve these values, then concatenate the values to **String output**. Lines 20–22 use **CCircle**'s **X**, **Y** and **Radius** properties to change the *x-y* coordinate pair value and radius value, respectively. Property **Radius** ensures that member variable **mRadius** cannot be assigned a negative value. Line 27 calls **CCircle**'s **ToString** method to obtain the **CCircle**'s **String** representation, and lines 31–38 call **CCircle**'s **Diameter**, **Circumference** and **Area** methods.

After writing all the code for class **CCircle** (Fig. 6.6), note that a major portion of the code in this class is similar, if not identical, to much of the code in class **CPoint**. For example, the declaration in **CCircle** of **Private** variables **mX** and **mY** and properties **X** and **Y** are identical to those of class **CPoint**. In addition, the class **CCircle** constructors and method **ToString** are almost identical to those of class **CPoint**, except that they also supply **mRadius** information. In fact, the only other additions to class **CCircle** are **Private** member variable **mRadius**, property **Radius** and methods **Diameter**, **Circumference** and **Area**.

```
1   ' Fig. 6.7: CircleTest.vb
2   ' Testing class CCircle.
3
4   Imports System.Windows.Forms
5
```

Fig. 6.7   `modCircleTest` demonstrates class `CCircle` functionality. (Part 1 of 2.)

```
6   Module modCircleTest
7
8      Sub Main()
9         Dim circle As CCircle
10        Dim output As String
11
12        circle = New CCircle(37, 43, 2.5) ' instantiate CCircle
13
14        ' get CCircle's initial x-y coordinates and radius
15        output = "X coordinate is " & circle.X & vbCrLf & _
16           "Y coordinate is " & circle.Y & vbCrLf & "Radius is " & _
17           circle.Radius
18
19        ' set CCircle's x-y coordinates and radius to new values
20        circle.X = 2
21        circle.Y = 2
22        circle.Radius = 4.25
23
24        ' display CCircle's String representation
25        output &= vbCrLf & vbCrLf & _
26           "The new location and radius of circle are " & _
27           vbCrLf & circle.ToString() & vbCrLf
28
29        ' display CCircle's diameter
30        output &= "Diameter is " & _
31           String.Format("{0:F}", circle.Diameter()) & vbCrLf
32
33        ' display CCircle's circumference
34        output &= "Circumference is " & _
35           String.Format("{0:F}", circle.Circumference()) & vbCrLf
36
37        ' display CCircle's area
38        output &= "Area is " & String.Format("{0:F}", circle.Area())
39
40        MessageBox.Show(output, "Demonstrating Class CCircle")
41     End Sub ' Main
42
43  End Module ' modCircleTest
```

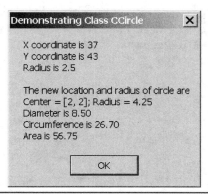

Fig. 6.7   **modCircleTest** demonstrates class **CCircle** functionality.
(Part 2 of 2.)

It appears that we literally copied code from class **CPoint**, pasted this code in the code from class **CCircle**, then modified class **CCircle** to include a radius. This "copy-and-paste" approach is often error-prone and time-consuming. Worse yet, it can result in many physical copies of the code existing throughout a system, creating a code-maintenance "nightmare."

In the next examples, we use a more elegant approach emphasizing the benefits of using inheritance. Now, we create and test a class **CCircle2** (Fig. 6.8) that inherits variables **mX** and **mY** and properties **X** and **Y** from class **CPoint** (Fig. 6.4). This class **CCircle2** "is a" **CPoint**, but also contains **mRadius** (line 7). The *Inherits* keyword in the class declaration (line 5) indicates inheritance. As a derived class, **CCircle2** inherits all the members of class **CPoint**, except for the constructors. Thus, the **Public** services of **CCircle2** include the two **CCircle2** constructors; the **Public** methods inherited from class **CPoint**; property **Radius**; and the **CCircle2** methods **Diameter**, **Circumference**, **Area** and **ToString**.

```
1   ' Fig. 6.8: Circle2.vb
2   ' CCircle2 class that inherits from class CPoint.
3
4   Public Class CCircle2
5      Inherits CPoint ' CCircle2 Inherits from class CPoint
6
7      Private mRadius As Double ' CCircle2's radius
8
9      ' default constructor
10     Public Sub New()
11
12        ' implicit call to CPoint constructor occurs here
13        Radius = 0
14     End Sub ' New
15
16     ' constructor
17     Public Sub New(ByVal xValue As Integer, _
18        ByVal yValue As Integer, ByVal radiusValue As Double)
19
20        ' implicit call to CPoint constructor occurs here
21        mX = xValue
22        mY = yValue
23        Radius = radiusValue
24     End Sub ' New
25
26     ' property Radius
27     Public Property Radius() As Double
28
29        Get
30           Return mRadius
31        End Get
32
33        Set(ByVal radiusValue As Double)
34
```

Fig. 6.8   **CCircle2** class that inherits from class **CPoint**. (Part 1 of 2.)

```
35                If radiusValue > 0
36                    mRadius = radiusValue
37                End If
38
39            End Set
40
41        End Property ' Radius
42
43        ' calculate CCircle2 diameter
44        Public Function Diameter() As Double
45            Return mRadius * 2
46        End Function ' Diameter
47
48        ' calculate CCircle2 circumference
49        Public Function Circumference() As Double
50            Return Math.PI * Diameter()
51        End Function ' Circumference
52
53        ' calculate CCircle2 area
54        Public Function Area() As Double
55            Return Math.PI * mRadius ^ 2
56        End Function ' Area
57
58        ' return String representation of CCircle2
59        Public Overrides Function ToString() As String
60            Return "Center = " & "[" & mX & ", " & mY & "]" & _
61                "; Radius = " & mRadius
62        End Function ' ToString
63
64    End Class ' CCircle2
```

!	✔	Description	File	Line
		Task List – 4 Build Error tasks shown (filtered)		
		Click here to add a new task		
!	🖋	'CircleTest.CPoint.mX' is not accessible in this context because it is 'Private'.	C:\...\Circle2.vb	21
!	🖋	'CircleTest.CPoint.mY' is not accessible in this context because it is 'Private'.	C:\...\Circle2.vb	22
!	🖋	'CircleTest.CPoint.mX' is not accessible in this context because it is 'Private'.	C:\...\Circle2.vb	60
!	🖋	'CircleTest.CPoint.mY' is not accessible in this context because it is 'Private'.	C:\...\Circle2.vb	60

Fig. 6.8 **CCircle2** class that inherits from class **CPoint**. (Part 2 of 2.)

Lines 12 and 20 in the **CCircle2** constructors (lines 10–24) invoke the default **CPoint2** constructor implicitly to initialize the base-class portion (variables **mX** and **mY**, inherited from class **CPoint**) of a **CCircle2** object to **0**. However, because the parameterized constructor (lines 17–24) should set the x-y coordinate to a specific value, lines 21–22 attempt to assign argument values to **mX** and **mY** directly. Even though lines 21–22 attempt to set **mX** and **mY** values explicitly, line 20 first calls the **CPoint** default constructor to initialize these variables to their default values. The compiler generates a syntax error for lines 21–22 (and line 60, where **CCircle2**'s method **ToString** attempts to use the values of **mX** and **mY** directly), because the derived class **CCircle2** is not allowed to access the base class **CPoint**'s **Private** members **mX** and **mY**. Visual Basic rigidly enforces restriction on accessing **Private** data members, so that even derived classes (i.e,. which are closely related to their base class) cannot access base-class **Private** data.

To enable class **CCircle2** to access **CPoint** member variables **mX** and **mY** directly, we declare those variables as **Protected**. As we discussed in Section 6.3, a base class's **Protected** members can be accessed only in that base class or in any classes derived from that class. Class **CPoint2** (Fig. 6.9) modifies class **CPoint** (Fig. 6.4) to declare variables **mX** and **mY** as **Protected** (line 8) instead of **Private**.

```
1    ' Fig. 6.9: Point2.vb
2    ' CPoint2 class contains an x-y coordinate pair as Protected data.
3
4    Public Class CPoint2
5       ' implicitly Inherits Object
6
7       ' point coordinate
8       Protected mX, mY As Integer
9
10      ' default constructor
11      Public Sub New()
12
13         ' implicit call to Object constructor occurs here
14         X = 0
15         Y = 0
16      End Sub ' New
17
18      ' constructor
19      Public Sub New(ByVal xValue As Integer, _
20         ByVal yValue As Integer)
21
22         ' implicit call to Object constructor occurs here
23         X = xValue
24         Y = yValue
25      End Sub ' New
26
27      ' property X
28      Public Property X() As Integer
29
30         Get
31            Return mX
32         End Get
33
34         Set(ByVal xValue As Integer)
35            mX = xValue ' no need for validation
36         End Set
37
38      End Property ' X
39
40      ' property Y
41      Public Property Y() As Integer
42
```

Fig. 6.9   **CPoint2** class represents an x-y coordinate pair as **Protected** data. (Part 1 of 2.)

```
43              Get
44                  Return mY
45              End Get
46
47              Set(ByVal yValue As Integer)
48                  mY = yValue ' no need for validation
49              End Set
50
51          End Property ' Y
52
53          ' return String representation of CPoint2
54          Public Overrides Function ToString() As String
55              Return "[" & mX & ", " & mY & "]"
56          End Function ' ToString
57
58      End Class ' CPoint2
```

Fig. 6.9   `CPoint2` class represents an *x-y* coordinate pair as **Protected** data. (Part 2 of 2.)

Class **CCircle3** (Fig. 6.10) modifies class **CCircle2** (Fig. 6.4) to inherit from class **CPoint2** rather than inherit from class **CPoint**. Because class **CCircle3** is a class derived from class **CPoint2**, class **CCircle3** can access class **CPoint2**'s **Protected** member variables **mX** and **mY** directly, and the compiler does not generate errors when compiling Fig. 6.10. Note that we declare method **Area** as **Overridable** (line 54), so that derived classes (such as class **CCylinder**, as we will see in Section 6.5) can override this method to provide a specific implementation.

Module **modCircleTest3** (Fig. 6.11) performs identical tests on class **CCircle3** as module **modCircleTest** (Fig. 6.7) performed on class **CCircle** (Fig. 6.6). Note that the outputs of the two programs are identical. We created class **CCircle** without using inheritance and created class **CCircle3** using inheritance; however, both classes provide the same functionality. However, observe that the code listing for class **CCircle3**, which is 64 lines, is considerably shorter than the code listing for class **CCircle**, which is 93 lines, because class **CCircle3** absorbs part of its functionality from **CPoint2**, whereas class **CCircle** does not.

In the previous example, we declared the base class instance variables as **Protected**, so that a derived class could modify their values directly. The use of **Protected** variables allows for a slight increase in performance, because we avoid incurring the overhead of a method call to a property's **Set** or **Get** accessor. However, in most Visual Basic application, in which user interaction comprises a large part of the execution time, the optimization offered through the use of **Protected** variables is negligible.

```
1   ' Fig. 6.10: Circle3.vb
2   ' CCircle3 class that inherits from class CPoint2.
3
4   Public Class CCircle3
5       Inherits CPoint2 ' CCircle3 Inherits from class CPoint2
```

Fig. 6.10   `CCircle3` class that inherits from class **CPoint2**. (Part 1 of 3.)

```
6
7        Private mRadius As Double ' CCircle3's radius
8
9        ' default constructor
10       Public Sub New()
11
12          ' implicit call to CPoint2 constructor occurs here
13          Radius = 0
14       End Sub ' New
15
16       ' constructor
17       Public Sub New(ByVal xValue As Integer, _
18          ByVal yValue As Integer, ByVal radiusValue As Double)
19
20          ' implicit call to CPoint2 constructor occurs here
21          mX = xValue
22          mY = yValue
23          Radius = radiusValue
24       End Sub ' New
25
26       ' property Radius
27       Public Property Radius() As Double
28
29          Get
30             Return mRadius
31          End Get
32
33          Set(ByVal radiusValue As Double)
34
35             If radiusValue > 0
36                mRadius = radiusValue
37             End If
38
39          End Set
40
41       End Property ' Radius
42
43       ' calculate CCircle3 diameter
44       Public Function Diameter() As Double
45          Return mRadius * 2
46       End Function ' Diameter
47
48       ' calculate CCircle3 circumference
49       Public Function Circumference() As Double
50          Return Math.PI * Diameter()
51       End Function ' Circumference
52
53       ' calculate CCircle3 area
54       Public Overridable Function Area() As Double
55          Return Math.PI * mRadius ^ 2
56       End Function ' Area
57
```

Fig. 6.10 **CCircle3** class that inherits from class **CPoint2**. (Part 2 of 3.)

```
58        ' return String representation of CCircle3
59        Public Overrides Function ToString() As String
60           Return "Center = " & "[" & mX & ", " & mY & "]" & _
61              "; Radius = " & mRadius
62        End Function ' ToString
63
64     End Class ' CCircle3
```

Fig. 6.10 `CCircle3` class that inherits from class **CPoint2**. (Part 3 of 3.)

Unfortunately, the inclusion of **Protected** instance variables often yields two major problems. First, the derived-class object does not have to use a property to set the value of the base-class's **Protected** data. Therefore, a derived-class object can assign an illegal value to the **Protected** data, thus leaving that object in an inconsistent state. For example, if we declare **CCircle3**'s variable **mRadius** as **Protected**, a derived-class object (e.g., **CCylinder**), can assign a negative value to **mRadius**. The second problem in using **Protected** data is that derived class methods are more likely to be written to depend on base-class implementation. In practice, derived classes should depend only on the base-class services (i.e., non-**Private** methods and properties) and not depend on base-class implementation. With **Protected** data in the base class, if the base-class implementation changes, we may need to modify all derived classes of that base class. For example, if we change the names of variables **mX** and **mY** to **mXCoordinate** and **mYCo-ordinate**, we must do so for all occurrences in which a derived class references these variables directly. If this happens, the base class is considered *fragile*, or *brittle*. The base class should be able to change its implementation freely, while providing the same services to derived classes. (Of course, if the base class changes its services, we must reimplement our derived classes, but good object-oriented design attempts to prevent this.)

Software Engineering Observation 6.5

The most appropriate time to use the **Protected** *access modifier is when a base class should provide a service only to its derived classes (i.e., should not provide the service to other clients). In this case, declare the base-class property or method as* **Protected***.*

```
1     ' Fig. 6.11: CircleTest3.vb
2     ' Testing class CCircle3.
3
4     Imports System.Windows.Forms
5
6     Module modCircleTest3
7
8        Sub Main()
9           Dim circle As CCircle3
10          Dim output As String
11
12          circle = New CCircle3(37, 43, 2.5) ' instantiate CCircle3
13
```

Fig. 6.11 `modCircleTest3` demonstrates class **CCircle3** functionality. (Part 1 of 2.)

```
14              ' get CCircle3's initial x-y coordinates and radius
15              output = "X coordinate is " & circle.X & vbCrLf & _
16                 "Y coordinate is " & circle.Y & vbCrLf & "Radius is " & _
17                 circle.Radius
18
19              ' set CCircle3's x-y coordinates and radius to new values
20              circle.X = 2
21              circle.Y = 2
22              circle.Radius = 4.25
23
24              ' display CCircle3's String representation
25              output &= vbCrLf & vbCrLf & _
26                 "The new location and radius of circle are " & _
27                 vbCrLf & circle.ToString() & vbCrLf
28
29              ' display CCircle3's diameter
30              output &= "Diameter is " & _
31                 String.Format("{0:F}", circle.Diameter()) & vbCrLf
32
33              ' display CCircle3's circumference
34              output &= "Circumference is " & _
35                 String.Format("{0:F}", circle.Circumference()) & vbCrLf
36
37              ' display CCircle3's area
38              output &= "Area is " & String.Format("{0:F}", circle.Area())
39
40              MessageBox.Show(output, "Demonstrating Class CCircle3")
41           End Sub ' Main
42
43        End Module ' modCircleTest3
```

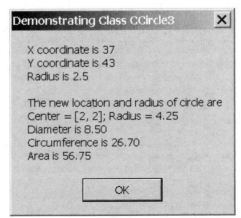

Fig. 6.11 `modCircleTest3` demonstrates class `CCircle3` functionality. (Part 2 of 2.)

Software Engineering Observation 6.6

Declaring base-class instance variables ***Private*** *(as opposed to declaring them* ***Protected****) helps programmers change base-class implementation without having to change derived-class implementation.*

Testing and Debugging Tip 6.1

*When possible, avoid including **Protected** data in a base class. Rather, include non-**Private** properties and methods that access **Private** data, ensuring that the object maintains a consistent state.*

We reexamine our point-circle hierarchy example once more; this time, attempting to use the best software engineering technique. We use **CPoint** (Fig. 6.4), which declares variables **mX** and **mY** as **Private**, and we show how derived class **CCircle4** (Fig. 6.12) can invoke base-class methods and properties to manipulate these variables.

```
1   ' Fig. 6.12: Circle4.vb
2   ' CCircle4 class that inherits from class CPoint.
3
4   Public Class CCircle4
5       Inherits CPoint ' CCircle4 Inherits from class CPoint
6
7       Private mRadius As Double
8
9       ' default constructor
10      Public Sub New()
11
12          ' implicit call to CPoint constructor occurs here
13          Radius = 0
14      End Sub ' New
15
16      ' constructor
17      Public Sub New(ByVal xValue As Integer, _
18          ByVal yValue As Integer, ByVal radiusValue As Double)
19
20          ' use MyBase reference to CPoint constructor explicitly
21          MyBase.New(xValue, yValue)
22          Radius = radiusValue
23      End Sub ' New
24
25      ' property Radius
26      Public Property Radius() As Double
27
28          Get
29              Return mRadius
30          End Get
31
32          Set(ByVal radiusValue As Double)
33
34              If radiusValue > 0
35                  mRadius = radiusValue
36              End If
37
38          End Set
39
40      End Property ' Radius
```

Fig. 6.12 **CCircle4** class that inherits from class **CPoint**, which does not provide **Protected** data. (Part 1 of 2.)

```
41
42        ' calculate CCircle4 diameter
43        Public Function Diameter() As Double
44            Return mRadius * 2
45        End Function ' Diameter
46
47        ' calculate CCircle4 circumference
48        Public Function Circumference() As Double
49            Return Math.PI * Diameter()
50        End Function ' Circumference
51
52        ' calculate CCircle4 area
53        Public Overridable Function Area() As Double
54            Return Math.PI * mRadius ^ 2
55        End Function ' Area
56
57        ' return String representation of CCircle4
58        Public Overrides Function ToString() As String
59
60            ' use MyBase reference to return CPoint String representation
61            Return "Center= " & MyBase.ToString() & _
62                "; Radius = " & mRadius
63        End Function ' ToString
64
65   End Class ' CCircle4
```

Fig. 6.12 **CCircle4** class that inherits from class **CPoint**, which does not provide **Protected** data. (Part 2 of 2.)

For the purpose of this example, to demonstrate both explicit and implicit calls to base-class constructors, we include a second constructor that calls the base-class constructor explicitly. Lines 17–23 declare the **CCircle4** constructor that invokes the second **CPoint** constructor explicitly using the *base-class constructor-call syntax* (i.e., reference **MyBase** followed by a set of parentheses containing the arguments to the base-class constructor). In this case, **xValue** and **yValue** are passed to initialize the base-class members **mX** and **mY**. The insertion of the **MyBase** reference followed by the dot operator accesses the base-class version of that method—in this constructor, **MyBase.New** invokes the **CPoint** constructor explicitly (line 21). By making this explicit call, we can initialize **mX** and **mY** to specific values, rather than to **0**. When calling the base-class constructor explicitly, the call to the base-class constructor must be the first statement in the derived-class-constructor definition.

 Common Programming Error 6.3

It is a syntax error if a derived class uses MyBase to call its base-class constructor, and the arguments do not match exactly the parameters specified in one of the base-class constructor definitions.

Class **CCircle4**'s **ToString** method (line 58–63) overrides class **CPoint**'s **ToString** method (lines 54–56 of Fig. 6.4). As we discussed earlier, overriding this method is possible, because method **ToString** of class **System.Object** (class **CPoint**'s base class) is declared **Overridable**. Method **ToString** of class **CCircle4** displays the **Private** instance variables **mX** and **mY** of class **CPoint** by calling the base class's **ToString** method (in this case, **CPoint**'s **ToString** method). The call is made in line 61 via the expression **MyBase.ToString** and causes the values of **mX** and **mY** to become part of the **CCircle4**'s **String** representation. Using this approach is a good software engineering practice: If an object's method performs the actions needed by another object, call that method rather than duplicating its code body. Duplicate code creates code-maintenance problems. By having **CCircle4**'s **ToString** method use the formatting provided by **CPoint**'s **ToString** method, we prevent the need to duplicate code. Also, **CPoint**'s **ToString** method performs part of the task of **CCircle4**'s **ToString** method, so we call **CPoint**'s **ToString** method from class **CCircle4** with the expression **MyBase.ToString**.

Software Engineering Observation 6.7

A redefinition in a derived class of a base-class method that uses a different signature than that of the base-class method is method overloading rather than method overriding.

Software Engineering Observation 6.8

*Although method **ToString** could be overridden to perform several actions that do not pertain to returning a **String**, the general understanding in the Visual Basic .NET community is that method **ToString** should be overridden to obtain an object's **String** representation.*

Good Programming Practice 6.1

*Each class should override method **ToString**, so that it returns useful information about objects of that class.*

Module **modCircleTest4** (Fig. 6.13) performs identical manipulations on class **CCircle4** as did modules **modCircleTest** (Fig. 6.7) and **modCircleTest3** (Fig. 6.11). Note that the outputs of all three modules are identical. Therefore, although each "circle" class appears to behave identically, class **CCircle4** is the most properly engineered. Using inheritance, we have constructed a class that has a strong commitment to **Private** data, in which a change in **CPoint**'s implementation does not affect class **CCircle4**.

```
1   ' Fig. 6.13: CircleTest4.vb
2   ' Testing class CCircle4.
3
4   Imports System.Windows.Forms
5
6   Module modCircleTest4
7
8      Sub Main()
9         Dim circle As CCircle4
10        Dim output As String
11
12        circle = New CCircle4(37, 43, 2.5) ' instantiate CCircle4
13
```

Fig. 6.13 **modCircleTest4** demonstrates class **CCircle4** functionality. (Part 1 of 2.)

```
14          ' get CCircle4's initial x-y coordinates and radius
15          output = "X coordinate is " & circle.X & vbCrLf & _
16             "Y coordinate is " & circle.Y & vbCrLf & "Radius is " & _
17             circle.Radius
18
19          ' set CCircle4's x-y coordinates and radius to new values
20          circle.X = 2
21          circle.Y = 2
22          circle.Radius = 4.25
23
24          ' display CCircle4's String representation
25          output &= vbCrLf & vbCrLf & _
26             "The new location and radius of circle are " & _
27             vbCrLf & circle.ToString() & vbCrLf
28
29          ' display CCircle4's diameter
30          output &= "Diameter is " & _
31             String.Format("{0:F}", circle.Diameter()) & vbCrLf
32
33          ' display CCircle4's circumference
34          output &= "Circumference is " & _
35             String.Format("{0:F}", circle.Circumference()) & vbCrLf
36
37          ' display CCircle4's area
38          output &= "Area is " & String.Format("{0:F}", circle.Area())
39
40          MessageBox.Show(output, "Demonstrating Class CCircle4")
41       End Sub ' Main
42
43    End Module ' modCircleTest4
```

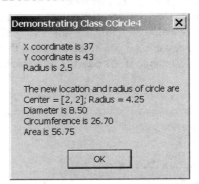

Fig. 6.13 `modCircleTest4` demonstrates class `CCircle4` functionality. (Part 2 of 2.)

6.5 Case Study: Three-Level Inheritance Hierarchy

Let us consider a substantial inheritance example, in which we study a point-circle-cylinder hierarchy. In Section 6.4, we developed classes **CPoint** (Fig. 6.4) and **CCircle4** (Fig. 6.12). Now, we present an example in which we derive class **CCylinder** from class **CCircle4**.

The first class that we use in our case study is class **CPoint** (Fig. 6.4). We declared **CPoint**'s instance variables as **Private**. Class **CPoint** also contains properties **X** and **Y** for accessing **mX** and **mY** and method **ToString** (which **CPoint** overrides from class **Object**) for obtaining a **String** representation of the *x-y* coordinate pair.

We also created class **CCircle4** (Fig. 6.12), which inherits from class **CPoint**. Class **CCircle4** contains the **CPoint** functionality, in addition to providing property **Radius**, which ensures that the **mRadius** member variable cannot hold a negative value, and methods **Diameter**, **Circumference**, **Area** and **ToString**. Recall that method **Area** was declared **Overridable** (line 53). As we discussed in Section 6.4, this key-word enables derived classes to override a base-class method. Derived classes of class **CCircle4** (such as class **CCylinder**, which we introduce momentarily) can override these methods and provide specific implementations. A circle has an area that is calculated by the equation

$$\pi r^2$$

in which *r* represents the circle's radius. However, a cylinder has a surface area that is cal-culated by a different equation:

$$(2\pi r^2) + (2\pi rh)$$

in which *r* represents the cylinder's radius and *h* represents the cylinder's height. Therefore, class **CCylinder** must override method **Area** to include this calculation, so we declared class **CCircle4**'s method **Area** as **Overridable**.

Figure 6.14 presents class **CCylinder**, which inherits from class **CCircle4** (line 5). Class **CCylinder**'s **Public** services include the inherited **CCircle4** methods **Diameter**, **Circumference**, **Area** and **ToString**; the inherited **CCircle4** prop-erty **Radius**; the indirectly inherited **CPoint** properties **X** and **Y**; the **CCylinder** con-structor, property **Height** and method **Volume**. Method **Area** (lines 43–45) overrides method **Area** of class **CCircle4**. Note that, if class **CCylinder** were to attempt to override **CCircle4**'s methods **Diameter** and **Circumference**, syntax errors would occur, because class **CCircle4** did not declare these methods **Overridable**. Method **ToString** (lines 53–55) overrides method **ToString** of class **CCircle4** to obtain a **String** representation for the cylinder. Class **CCylinder** also includes method **Volume** (lines 48–50) to calculate the cylinder's volume. Because we do not declare method **Volume** as **Overridable**, no derived class of class **CCylinder** can override this method.

```
1   ' Fig. 6.14: Cylinder.vb
2   ' CCylinder class inherits from class CCircle4.
3
4   Public Class CCylinder
5       Inherits CCircle4
6
7       Private mHeight As Double
```

Fig. 6.14 **CCylinder** class inherits from class **CCircle4** and **Overrides** method **Area**. (Part 1 of 2.)

```
8
9       ' default constructor
10      Public Sub New()
11         Height = 0
12      End Sub ' New
13
14      ' four-argument constructor
15      Public Sub New(ByVal xValue As Integer, _
16         ByVal yValue As Integer, ByVal radiusValue As Double, _
17         ByVal heightValue As Double)
18
19         ' explicit call to CCircle4 constructor
20         MyBase.New(xValue, yValue, radiusValue)
21         Height = heightValue ' set CCylinder height
22      End Sub ' New
23
24      ' property Height
25      Public Property Height() As Double
26
27         Get
28            Return mHeight
29         End Get
30
31         ' set CCylinder height if argument value is positive
32         Set(ByVal heightValue As Double)
33
34            If heightValue >= 0 Then
35               mHeight = heightValue
36            End If
37
38         End Set
39
40      End Property ' Height
41
42      ' override method Area to calculate CCylinder area
43      Public Overrides Function Area() As Double
44         Return 2 * MyBase.Area + MyBase.Circumference * mHeight
45      End Function ' Area
46
47      ' calculate CCylinder volume
48      Public Function Volume() As Double
49         Return MyBase.Area * mHeight
50      End Function ' Volume
51
52      ' convert CCylinder to String
53      Public Overrides Function ToString() As String
54         Return MyBase.ToString() & "; Height = " & mHeight
55      End Function ' ToString
56
57   End Class ' CCylinder
```

Fig. 6.14 **CCylinder** class inherits from class **CCircle4** and **Overrides** method **Area**. (Part 2 of 2.)

Figure 6.15 is a **modCylinderTest** application that tests the **CCylinder** class. Line 11 instantiates an object of class **CCylinder**. Lines 15–17 use properties **X**, **Y**, **Radius** and **Height** to obtain information about the **CCylinder** object, because **modCylinderTest** cannot reference the **Private** data of class **CCylinder** directly. Lines 20–23 use properties **X**, **Y**, **Height** and **Radius** to reset the **CCylinder**'s *x-y* coordinates (we assume the cylinder's *x-y* coordinates specify its position on the *x-y* plane), height and radius. Class **CCylinder** can use class **CPoint**'s **X** and **Y** properties, because class **CCylinder** inherits them indirectly from class **CPoint**—Class **CCylinder** inherits properties **X** and **Y** directly from class **CCircle4**, which inherited them directly from class **CPoint**. Line 28 invokes method **ToString** to obtain the **String** representation of the **CCylinder** object. Lines 32–36 invoke methods **Diameter** and **Circumference** of the **CCylinder** object—because class **CCylinder** inherits these methods from class **CCircle4** but cannot override them, these methods, as listed in **CCircle4**, are invoked. Lines 40–44 invoke methods **Area** and **Volume**.

Using the point-circle-cylinder example, we have shown the use and benefits of inheritance. We were able to develop classes **CCircle4** and **CCylinder** using inheritance much faster than if we had developed these classes by duplicating code. Inheritance avoids duplicating code and therefore helps avoid code-maintenance problems.

```
1   ' Fig. 6.15: CylinderTest.vb
2   ' Tests class CCylinder.
3
4   Imports System.Windows.Forms
5
6   Module modCylinderTest
7
8      Sub Main()
9
10        ' instantiate object of class CCylinder
11        Dim cylinder As New CCylinder(12, 23, 2.5, 5.7)
12        Dim output As String
13
14        ' properties get initial x-y coordinate, radius and height
15        output = "X coordinate is " & cylinder.X & vbCrLf & _
16           "Y coordinate is " & cylinder.Y & vbCrLf & "Radius is " & _
17           cylinder.Radius & vbCrLf & "Height is " & cylinder.Height
18
19        ' properties set new x-y coordinate, radius and height
20        cylinder.X = 2
21        cylinder.Y = 2
22        cylinder.Height = 10
23        cylinder.Radius = 4.25
24
25        ' get new x-y coordinate and radius
26        output &= vbCrLf & vbCrLf & "The new location, radius " & _
27           "and height of cylinder are" & vbCrLf & "Center = [" & _
28           cylinder.ToString() & vbCrLf & vbCrLf
29
```

Fig. 6.15 Testing class **CCylinder**. (Part 1 of 2.)

```
30          ' display CCylinder's diameter
31          output &= "Diameter is " & _
32              String.Format("{0:F}", cylinder.Diameter()) & vbCrLf
33
34          ' display CCylinder's circumference
35          output &= "Circumference is " & _
36              String.Format("{0:F}", cylinder.Circumference()) & vbCrLf
37
38          ' display CCylinder's area
39          output &= "Area is " & _
40              String.Format("{0:F}", cylinder.Area()) & vbCrLf
41
42          ' display CCylinder's volume
43          output &= "Volume is " & _
44              String.Format("{0:F}", cylinder.Volume())
45
46          MessageBox.Show(output, "Demonstrating Class CCylinder")
47      End Sub ' Main
48
49  End Module ' modCylinderTest
```

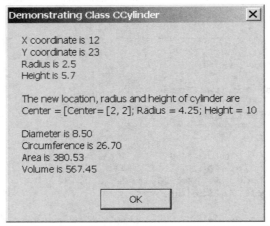

Fig. 6.15 Testing class **CCylinder**. (Part 2 of 2.)

6.6 Constructors and Finalizers in Derived Classes

As we explained in the previous section, instantiating a derived-class object begins a chain of constructor calls in which the derived-class constructor, before performing its own tasks, invokes the base-class constructor either explicitly or implicitly. Similarly, if the base-class was derived from another class, the base-class constructor must invoke the constructor of the next class up in the hierarchy, and so on. The last constructor called in the chain is class **Object**'s constructor whose body actually finishes executing first— the original derived class's body finishes executing last. Each base-class constructor initializes the base-class instance variables that the derived-class object inherits. For example, consider the **CPoint/CCircle4** hierarchy from Fig. 6.4 and Fig. 6.12. When a program creates a **CCircle4** object, one of the **CCircle4** constructors is called. That constructor calls class **CPoint**'s constructor, which in turn calls class **Object**'s constructor. When class **Object**'s constructor completes execution, it returns control to class **CPoint**'s constructor, which initializes the *x-y* coordinates of **CCircle4**. When class **CPoint**'s constructor completes execution, it returns control to class **CCircle4**'s constructor, which initializes the **CCircle4**'s radius.

Software Engineering Observation 6.9

When a program creates a derived-class object, the derived-class constructor calls the base-class constructor, the base-class constructor executes, then the remainder of the derived-class constructor's body executes.

When the garbage collector removes an object from memory, the garbage collector calls that object's finalizer method. This begins a chain of finalizer calls in which the derived-class finalizer and the finalizers of the direct and indirect base classes execute in the reverse order of the constructors. Executing the finalizer method should free all resources acquired by the object before the garbage collector reclaims the memory for that object. When the garbage collector calls an object's finalizer, the finalizer performs its task. Then, the programmer can use keyword **MyBase** to invoke the finalizer of the base class.

We discussed in Chapter 5 that class **Object** defines **Protected Overridable** method **Finalize**, which is the finalizer for a Visual Basic object. Because all Visual Basic classes inherit from class **Object** (either directly or indirectly), these classes inherit method **Finalize** and can *override* it to free resources specific to those objects. Although we cannot determine exactly when a **Finalize** call occurs (because we cannot determine exactly when garbage collection occurs), we still are able to specify code to execute before the garbage collector removes an object from memory.

Our next example revisits the point-circle hierarchy by defining versions of class **CPoint3** (Fig. 6.16) and class **CCircle5** (Fig. 6.17) that contain constructors *and* finalizers, each of which prints a message when it runs.

Class **CPoint3** (Fig. 6.16) contains the features as shown in Fig. 6.4, and we modified the two constructors (lines 10–16 and 19–26) to output a line of text when they are called and added method **Finalize** (lines 29–32) that also outputs a line of text when it is called. Each output statement (lines 15, 25 and 30) adds reference **Me** to the output string. This implicitly invokes the class's **ToString** method to obtain the **String** representation of **CPoint3**'s coordinates.

Because constructors are not inherited, lines 12 and 22 make implicit calls to the **Object** constructor. However, method **Finalize** is inherited and overridden from class **Object**, so line 31 uses reference **MyBase** to call the **Object** base-class method **Finalize** explicitly. If we omitted line 31, the **Object**'s **Finalize** method would not get called.

Class **CCircle5** (Fig. 6.17) contains the features in Fig. 6.8, and we modified the two constructors (lines 10–15 and 18–25) to output a line of text when they are called. We also added method **Finalize** (lines 28–31) that also outputs a line of text when it is called. Note again that line 30 uses **MyBase** to invoke **CPoint3**'s **Finalize** method explicitly—this method is not called if we omit this line. Each output statement (lines 14, 24 and 29) adds reference **Me** to the output string. This implicitly invokes the **CCircle5**'s **ToString** method to obtain the **String** representation of **CCircle5**'s coordinates and radius.

```vb
1    ' Fig. 6.16: Point3.vb
2    ' CPoint3 class represents an x-y coordinate pair.
3
4    Public Class CPoint3
5
6       ' point coordinate
7       Private mX, mY As Integer
8
9       ' default constructor
10      Public Sub New()
11
12         ' implicit call to Object constructor occurs here
13         X = 0
14         Y = 0
15         Console.Writeline("CPoint3 constructor: {0}", Me)
16      End Sub ' New
17
18      ' constructor
19      Public Sub New(ByVal xValue As Integer, _
20         ByVal yValue As Integer)
21
22         ' implicit call to Object constructor occurs here
23         X = xValue
24         Y = yValue
25         Console.Writeline("CPoint3 constructor: {0}", Me)
26      End Sub ' New
27
28      ' finalizer overrides version in class Object
29      Protected Overrides Sub Finalize()
30         Console.Writeline("CPoint3 Finalizer: {0}", Me)
31         MyBase.Finalize() ' call Object finalizer
32      End Sub ' Finalize
33
34      ' property X
35      Public Property X() As Integer
36
37         Get
38            Return mX
39         End Get
40
41         Set(ByVal xValue As Integer)
42            mX = xValue ' no need for validation
43         End Set
44
45      End Property ' X
46
47      ' property Y
48      Public Property Y() As Integer
49
50         Get
51            Return mY
52         End Get
53
```

Fig. 6.16 CPoint3 base class contains constructors and finalizer. (Part 1 of 2.)

```
54              Set(ByVal yValue As Integer)
55                 mY = yValue ' no need for validation
56              End Set
57
58          End Property ' Y
59
60          ' return String representation of CPoint3
61          Public Overrides Function ToString() As String
62             Return "[" & mX & ", " & mY & "]"
63          End Function ' ToString
64
65      End Class ' CPoint3
```

Fig. 6.16 `CPoint3` base class contains constructors and finalizer. (Part 2 of 2.)

Module **modConstructorAndFinalizer** (Fig. 6.18) demonstrates the order in which constructors and finalizers are called for objects of classes that are part of an inheritance class hierarchy. Method **Main** (lines 7–17) begins by instantiating an object of class **CCircle5**, then assigns it to reference **circle1** (line 10). This invokes the **CCircle5** constructor, which invokes the **CPoint3** constructor immediately. Then, the **CPoint3** constructor invokes the **Object** constructor. When the **Object** constructor (which does not print anything) returns control to the **CPoint3** constructor, the **CPoint3** constructor initializes the x-y coordinates, then outputs a **String** indicating that the **CPoint3** constructor was called. The output statement also calls method **ToString** implicitly (using reference **Me**) to obtain the **String** representation of the object being constructed. Then, control returns to the **CCircle5** constructor, which initializes the radius and outputs the **CCircle5**'s x-y coordinates and radius by calling method **ToString** implicitly.

Notice that the first two lines of the output from this program contain values for the x-y coordinate and the radius of **CCircle5**. When constructing a **CCircle5** object, the **Me** reference used in the body of both the **CCircle5** and **CPoint3** constructors refers to the **CCircle5** object being constructed. When a program invokes method **ToString** on an object, the version of **ToString** that executes is always the version defined in that object's class. Because reference **Me** refers to the current **CCircle5** object being constructed, **CCircle5**'s **ToString** method executes even when **ToString** is invoked from the body of class **CPoint3**'s constructor. [*Note:* This would not be the case if the **CPoint3** constructor were called to initialize a new **CPoint3** object.] When the **CPoint3** constructor invokes method **ToString** for the **CCircle5** being constructed, the program displays **0** for the **mRadius** value, because the **CCircle5** constructor's body has not yet initialized the **mRadius**. Remember that **0** is the default value of a **Double** variable. The second line of output shows the proper **mRadius** value (**4.5**), because that line is output after the **mRadius** is initialized.

```
1    ' Fig. 6.17: Circle5.vb
2    ' CCircle5 class that inherits from class CPoint3.
3
```

Fig. 6.17 `CCircle5` class inherits from class `CPoint3` and overrides a finalizer method. (Part 1 of 3.)

```vbnet
4   Public Class CCircle5
5       Inherits CPoint3 ' CCircle5 Inherits from class CPoint3
6
7       Private mRadius As Double
8
9       ' default constructor
10      Public Sub New()
11
12          ' implicit call to CPoint3 constructor occurs here
13          Radius = 0
14          Console.WriteLine("CCircle5 constructor: {0}", Me)
15      End Sub ' New
16
17      ' constructor
18      Public Sub New(ByVal xValue As Integer, _
19          ByVal yValue As Integer, ByVal radiusValue As Double)
20
21          ' use MyBase reference to CPoint3 constructor explicitly
22          MyBase.New(xValue, yValue)
23          Radius = radiusValue
24          Console.WriteLine("CCircle5 constructor: {0}", Me)
25      End Sub ' New
26
27      ' finalizer overrides version in class CPoint3
28      Protected Overrides Sub Finalize()
29          Console.Writeline("CCircle5 Finalizer: {0}", Me)
30          MyBase.Finalize() ' call CPoint3 finalizer
31      End Sub ' Finalize
32
33      ' property Radius
34      Public Property Radius() As Double
35
36          Get
37              Return mRadius
38          End Get
39
40          Set(ByVal radiusValue As Double)
41
42              If radiusValue > 0
43                  mRadius = radiusValue
44              End If
45
46          End Set
47
48      End Property ' Radius
49
50      ' calculate CCircle5 diameter
51      Public Function Diameter() As Double
52          Return mRadius * 2
53      End Function ' Diameter
54
```

Fig. 6.17 CCircle5 class inherits from class CPoint3 and overrides a finalizer method. (Part 2 of 3.)

```
55        ' calculate CCircle5 circumference
56        Public Function Circumference() As Double
57            Return Math.PI * Diameter()
58        End Function ' Circumference
59
60        ' calculate CCircle5 area
61        Public Overridable Function Area() As Double
62            Return Math.PI * mRadius ^ 2
63        End Function ' Area
64
65        ' return String representation of CCircle5
66        Public Overrides Function ToString() As String
67
68            ' use MyBase reference to return CPoint3 String
69            Return "Center = " & MyBase.ToString() & _
70                "; Radius = " & mRadius
71        End Function ' ToString
72
73    End Class ' CCircle5
```

Fig. 6.17 `CCircle5` class inherits from class `CPoint3` and overrides a finalizer method. (Part 3 of 3.)

Line 11 instantiates an object of class **CCircle5**, then assigns it to reference **circle2**. Again, this begins the chain of constructor calls in which the **CCircle5** constructor, the **CCircle5** constructor and the **Object** constructor are called. In the output, notice that the body of the **CPoint3** constructor executes before the body of the **CCircle5** constructor. This demonstrates that objects are constructed "inside out" (i.e., the base-class constructor is called first).

Lines 13–14 set references **circle1** and **circle2** to **Nothing**. This removes the only references to the two **CCircle5** objects in the program. Thus, the garbage collector can release the memory that these objects occupy. Remember that we cannot guarantee when the garbage collector executes, nor can we guarantee that it collects all available objects when it does execute. To demonstrate the finalizer calls for the two **CCircle5** objects, line 16 invokes class **GC**'s method **Collect** to request the garbage collector to run. Notice that each **CCircle5** object's finalizer outputs information before calling class **CPoint3**'s **Finalize** method. Objects are finalized "outside in" (i.e., the derived-class finalizer completes its tasks before calling the base-class finalizer).

```
1    ' Fig. 6.18: ConstructorAndFinalizer.vb
2    ' Display order in which base-class and derived-class constructors
3    ' and finalizers are called.
4
5    Module modConstructorAndFinalizer
6
7        Sub Main()
8            Dim circle1, circle2 As CCircle5
9
```

Fig. 6.18 Demonstrating order in which constructors and finalizers are called. (Part 1 of 2.)

```
10        circle1 = New CCircle5(72, 29, 4.5) ' instantiate objects
11        circle2 = New CCircle5(5, 5, 10)
12
13        circle1 = Nothing ' mark objects for garbage collection
14        circle2 = Nothing
15
16        System.GC.Collect() ' request garbage collector to execute
17     End Sub ' Main
18
19  End Module ' modConstructorAndFinalizer
```

```
CPoint3 constructor: Center = [72, 29]; Radius = 0
CCircle5 constructor: Center = [72, 29]; Radius = 4.5
CPoint3 constructor: Center = [5, 5]; Radius = 0
CCircle5 constructor: Center = [5, 5]; Radius = 10
CCircle5 Finalizer: Center = [5, 5]; Radius = 10
CPoint3 Finalizer: Center = [5, 5]; Radius = 10
CCircle5 Finalizer: Center = [72, 29]; Radius = 4.5
CPoint3 Finalizer: Center = [72, 29]; Radius = 4.5
```

Fig. 6.18   Demonstrating order in which constructors and finalizers are called.
(Part 2 of 2.)

Software Engineering Observation 6.10

*The last statement in a **Finalize** method of a derived class should invoke the base class's **Finalize** method (via keyword **MyBase**) to free any base-class resources.*

Common Programming Error 6.4

*When a base-class method is overridden in a derived class, the derived-class version often calls the base-class version to do additional work. Failure to use the **MyBase** reference when referencing the base class's method causes infinite recursion, because the derived-class method would then call itself.*

Common Programming Error 6.5

*The use of "chained" **MyBase** references to refer to a member (a method, property or variable) several levels up the hierarchy (as in **MyBase.MyBase.mX**) is a syntax error.*

6.7 Software Engineering with Inheritance

In this section, we discuss the use of inheritance to customize existing software. When we use inheritance to create a class from an existing one, the new class inherits the member variables, properties and methods of the existing class. Once the class is created, we can customize it to meet our needs both by including additional member variables, properties and methods, and by overriding base-class members.

Sometimes, it is difficult for developers to appreciate the scope of problems faced by designers who work on large-scale software projects in industry. People experienced with such projects invariably say that practicing software reuse improves the software-development process. Object-oriented programming facilitates the reuse of software, thus shortening development times.

Visual Basic encourages software reuse by providing substantial class libraries, which deliver the maximum benefits of software reuse through inheritance. As interest in Visual Basic grows (it is already the world's most widely used programming language), interest in Visual Basic .NET class libraries also increases. There is a worldwide commitment to the continued evolution of Visual Basic .NET class libraries for a wide variety of applications.

Software Engineering Observation 6.11

At the design stage in an object-oriented system, the designer often determines that certain classes are closely related. The designer should "factor out" common attributes and behaviors and place them in a base class. Then the designer should use inheritance to form derived classes, endowing them with capabilities beyond those inherited from the base class.

Software Engineering Observation 6.12

The creation of a derived class does not affect the base class's source code. Inheritance preserves the integrity of a base class.

Software Engineering Observation 6.13

Just as designers of non-object-oriented systems should avoid proliferation of functions, designers of object-oriented systems should avoid proliferation of classes. Proliferation of classes creates management problems and can hinder software reusability, because it becomes difficult for a client to find the most appropriate class of a huge class library. The alternative is to create fewer classes, where each class provides more substantial functionality, but such classes might provide too much functionality.

Performance Tip 6.1

If classes produced through inheritance are larger than they need to be (i.e., they contain too much functionality), memory and processing resources might be wasted. Inherit from the class whose functionality is "closest" to what is needed.

Reading derived-class definitions can be confusing, because inherited members are not shown physically in the derived class, but nevertheless are present in the derived class. A similar problem exists when documenting derived-class members.

In this chapter, we have introduced inheritance—the ability to create classes by absorbing an existing class's data members and behaviors and embellishing them with new capabilities. In Chapter 7, we build upon our discussion of inheritance by introducing *polymorphism*—an object-oriented technique that enables us to write programs that handle, in a more general manner, a wide variety of classes related by inheritance. After studying Chapter 7, you will be familiar with encapsulation, inheritance and polymorphism—the most crucial aspects of object-oriented programming.

6.8 Summary

Software reusability reduces program-development time. Inheritance is the process by which one class "absorbs" the capabilities of an existing class (via keyword **Inherits**). When a new class is created by inheriting from an existing class, the new class is called a derived class. The class from which the derived class inherited is called the base class.

Because derived classes can include their own instance variables, properties and methods, derived classes are often larger than their base classes. A derived class is more specific than its base class and represents a smaller group of objects.

Inheritance is an "is-a" relationship; an object of a derived class also can be treated as an object of the derived class' base class. However, base-class objects are not objects of that class's derived classes. Composition is a "has-a" relationship; an object has references to one or more objects of other classes as members.

A base class's **Public** members are accessible anywhere that the program has a reference to an object of the base class or to an object of one of that base class's derived classes. A base class's **Private** members are accessible only within the definition of that base class. A base class's **Protected** members have an intermediate level of protection between **Public** and **Private** access; they can be accessed only in the base class or in any classes derived from that base class. A base class's **Friend** members can be accessed only by objects in the same assembly.

When a base-class method is inappropriate for a derived class, that method can be overridden (redefined) in the derived class by using an appropriate implementation. When a method is overridden in a derived class and that method is called on a derived-class object, the derived-class version (not the base-class version) is called.

When an object of a derived class is instantiated, the base class's constructor is called immediately (either explicitly or implicitly) to do any necessary initialization of the base-class instance variables in the derived-class object (before the derived-class instance variable are initialized). Base-class constructors are not inherited by derived classes.

7

Object-Oriented Programming: Polymorphism

Objectives

- To understand the concept of polymorphism.
- To understand how polymorphism makes systems extensible and maintainable.
- To understand the distinction between abstract classes and concrete classes.
- To learn how to create abstract classes, interfaces and delegates.

One Ring to rule them all, One Ring to find them,
One Ring to bring them all and in the darkness bind them.
John Ronald Reuel Tolkien

General propositions do not decide concrete cases.
Oliver Wendell Holmes

A philosopher of imposing stature doesn't think in a vacuum.
Even his most abstract ideas are, to some extent, conditioned
by what is or is not known in the time when he lives.
Alfred North Whitehead

Outline

7.1 Introduction

The previous chapter's object-oriented programming (OOP) discussion focussed on one of its key component technologies, inheritance. In this chapter, we continue our study of OOP *polymorphism*. Both inheritance and polymorphism are crucial technologies in the development of complex software. Polymorphism enables us to write programs that handle a wide variety of related classes and facilitates adding new classes and capabilities to a system.

Using polymorphism, it is possible to design and implement systems that are easily extensible. Programs can process objects of all classes in a class hierarchy generically as objects of a common base class. Furthermore, a new class can be added with little or no modification to the generic part of the program, as long as those new classes are part of the inheritance hierarchy that the program generically processes. The only parts of a program that must be altered to accommodate new classes are those program components that require direct knowledge of the new classes that the programmer adds to the hierarchy. In this chapter, we demonstrate two substantial class hierarchies and manipulate objects from those hierarchies polymorphically.

7.2 Derived-Class-Object to Base-Class-Object Conversion

Section 6.4 created a point-circle class hierarchy, in which class **CCircle** inherited from class **CPoint**. The programs that manipulated objects of these classes always used **CPoint** references to refer to **CPoint** objects and **CCircle** references to refer to **CCircle** objects. In this section, we discuss the relationship between classes in a hierarchy that enables a program to assign derived-class objects to base-class references—a fundamental part of programs that process objects polymorphically. This section also discusses explicit casting between types in a class hierarchy.

An object of a derived class can be treated as an object of its base class. This enables various interesting manipulations. For example, a program can create an array of base-class references that refer to objects of many derived-class types. This is allowed despite the fact that the derived-class objects are of different data types. However, the reverse is not true—

a base-class object is not an object of any of its derived classes. For example, a **CPoint** is not a **CCircle** based on the hierarchy defined in Chapter 6. If a base-class reference refers to a derived-class object, it is possible to convert the base-class reference to the object's actual data type and manipulate the object as that type.

Common Programming Error 7.1

Treating a base-class object as a derived-class object can cause errors.

The example in Fig. 7.1–Fig. 7.3 demonstrates assigning derived-class objects to base-class references and casting base-class references to derived-class references. Class **CPoint** (Fig. 7.1), which we discussed in Chapter 6, represents an *x-y* coordinate pair. Class **CCircle** (Fig. 7.2), which we also discussed in Chapter 6, represents a circle and inherits from class **CPoint**. Each **CCircle** object "is a" **CPoint** and also has a radius (represented via variable **mRadius**). We declare method **Area** as **Overridable**, so that a derived class (such as class **CCylinder**) can calculate its area. Class **CTest** (Fig. 7.3) demonstrates the assignment and cast operations.

```
1    ' Fig. 7.1: Point.vb
2    ' CPoint class represents an x-y coordinate pair.
3
4    Public Class CPoint
5
6       ' point coordinate
7       Private mX, mY As Integer
8
9       ' default constructor
10      Public Sub New()
11
12         ' implicit call to Object constructor occurs here
13         X = 0
14         Y = 0
15      End Sub ' New
16
17      ' constructor
18      Public Sub New(ByVal xValue As Integer, _
19         ByVal yValue As Integer)
20
21         ' implicit call to Object constructor occurs here
22         X = xValue
23         Y = yValue
24      End Sub ' New
25
26      ' property X
27      Public Property X() As Integer
28
29         Get
30            Return mX
31         End Get
32
```

Fig. 7.1   **CPoint** class represents an *x-y* coordinate pair. (Part 1 of 2.)

```
33          Set(ByVal xValue As Integer)
34             mX = xValue  ' no need for validation
35          End Set
36
37       End Property  ' X
38
39       ' property Y
40       Public Property Y() As Integer
41
42          Get
43             Return mY
44          End Get
45
46          Set(ByVal yValue As Integer)
47             mY = yValue  ' no need for validation
48          End Set
49
50       End Property  ' Y
51
52       ' return String representation of CPoint
53       Public Overrides Function ToString() As String
54          Return "[" & mX & ", " & mY & "]"
55       End Function  ' ToString
56
57    End Class  ' CPoint
```

Fig. 7.1 `CPoint` class represents an *x-y* coordinate pair. (Part 2 of 2.)

```
1    ' Fig. 7.2: Circle.vb
2    ' CCircle class that inherits from class CPoint.
3
4    Public Class CCircle
5       Inherits CPoint  ' CCircle Inherits from class CPoint
6
7       Private mRadius As Double
8
9       ' default constructor
10      Public Sub New()
11
12         ' implicit call to CPoint constructor occurs here
13         Radius = 0
14      End Sub  ' New
15
16      ' constructor
17      Public Sub New(ByVal xValue As Integer, _
18         ByVal yValue As Integer, ByVal radiusValue As Double)
19
20         ' use MyBase reference to CPoint constructor explicitly
21         MyBase.New(xValue, yValue)
22         Radius = radiusValue
23      End Sub  ' New
24
```

Fig. 7.2 `CCircle` class that inherits from class `CPoint`. (Part 1 of 2.)

```
25      ' property Radius
26      Public Property Radius() As Double
27
28         Get
29             Return mRadius
30         End Get
31
32         Set(ByVal radiusValue As Double)
33
34             If radiusValue >= 0 ' mRadius must be nonnegative
35                 mRadius = radiusValue
36             End If
37
38         End Set
39
40      End Property ' Radius
41
42      ' calculate CCircle diameter
43      Public Function Diameter() As Double
44          Return mRadius * 2
45      End Function ' Diameter
46
47      ' calculate CCircle circumference
48      Public Function Circumference() As Double
49          Return Math.PI * Diameter()
50      End Function ' Circumference
51
52      ' calculate CCircle area
53      Public Overridable Function Area() As Double
54          Return Math.PI * mRadius ^ 2
55      End Function ' Area
56
57      ' return String representation of CCircle
58      Public Overrides Function ToString() As String
59
60         ' use MyBase reference to return CCircle String representation
61         Return "Center= " & MyBase.ToString() & _
62             "; Radius = " & mRadius
63      End Function ' ToString
64
65   End Class ' CCircle
```

Fig. 7.2   `CCircle` class that inherits from class `CPoint`. (Part 2 of 2.)

Class **CTest** (Fig. 7.3) demonstrates assigning derived-class references to base-class references and casting base-class references to derived-class references. Lines 11–12 declare two **CPoint** references (**point1** and **point2**) and two **CCircle** references (**circle1** and **circle2**). Lines 14–15 assign to **point1** a new **CPoint** object and assign to **circle1** a new **CCircle** object. Lines 17–18 invoke each object's **ToString** method, then append the **String** representations to **String output** to show the values used to initialize each object. Because **point1** is a **CPoint** object, method **ToString** of **point1** prints the object as a **CPoint**. Similarly, because **circle1** is a **CCircle** object, method **ToString** of **circle1** prints the object as a **CCircle**.

```
1    ' Fig. 7.3: Test.vb
2    ' Demonstrating inheritance and polymorphism.
3
4    Imports System.Windows.Forms
5
6    Class CTest
7
8       ' demonstrate "is a" relationship
9       Shared Sub Main()
10         Dim output As String
11         Dim point1, point2 As CPoint
12         Dim circle1, circle2 As CCircle
13
14         point1 = New CPoint(30, 50)
15         circle1 = New CCircle(120, 89, 2.7)
16
17         output = "CPoint point1: " & point1.ToString() & _
18            vbCrLf & "CCircle circle1: " & circle1.ToString()
19
20         ' use is-a relationship to assign CCircle to CPoint reference
21         point2 = circle1
22
23         output &= vbCrLf & vbCrLf & _
24            "CCircle circle1 (via point2): " & point2.ToString()
25
26         ' downcast (cast base-class reference to derived-class
27         ' data type) point2 to circle2
28         circle2 = CType(point2, CCircle) ' allowed only via cast
29
30         output &= vbCrLf & vbCrLf & _
31            "CCircle circle1 (via circle2): " & circle2.ToString()
32
33         output &= vbCrLf & "Area of circle1 (via circle2): " & _
34            String.Format("{0:F}", circle2.Area())
35
36         ' assign CPoint object to CCircle reference
37         If (TypeOf point1 Is CCircle) Then
38            circle2 = CType(point1, CCircle)
39            output &= vbCrLf & vbCrLf & "cast successful"
40         Else
41            output &= vbCrLf & vbCrLf & _
42               "point1 does not refer to a CCircle"
43         End If
44
45         MessageBox.Show(output, _
46            "Demonstrating the 'is a' relationship")
47      End Sub ' Main
48
49   End Class ' CTest
```

Fig. 7.3   Assigning derived-class references to base-class references. (Part 1 of 2.)

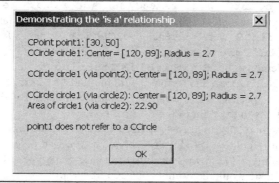

Fig. 7.3   Assigning derived-class references to base-class references. (Part 2 of 2.)

Line 21 assigns **circle1** (a reference to a derived-class object) to **point2** (a base-class reference). In Visual Basic, it is acceptable to assign a derived-class reference to a base-class reference, because of the inheritance "is-a" relationship. A **CCircle** *is a* **CPoint** (in a structural sense, at least), because class **CCircle** inherits from class **CPoint**. However, assigning a base-class reference to a derived-class reference is potentially dangerous, as we will discuss.

Lines 23–24 invoke **point2.ToString** and append the result to **output**. When Visual Basic encounters an **Overridable** method invocation (such as method **ToString**), Visual Basic determines which version of the method to call based on the type of the object on which the method is called, not based on the type of the reference that refers to the object. In this case, **point2** refers to a **CCircle** object, so Visual Basic calls **CCircle** method **ToString** (line 24), rather than calling **CPoint** method **ToString** (as one might expect off the **point2** reference, which was declared as a **CPoint**). The decision of which method to call is an example of *polymorphism*, a concept that we discuss in detail throughout this chapter. Note that, if **point2** referenced a **CPoint** object rather than a **CCircle** object, Visual Basic would invoke **CPoint**'s **ToString** method.

Previous chapters used methods such as **Convert.ToInt32** and **Convert.ToDouble** to convert between various built-in Visual Basic types. Now, we convert between object references of user-defined types. We use method **CType** to perform this conversion, which is known as a *cast*. If the cast is valid, our program can treat a base-class reference as a derived-class reference. If the cast is invalid, Visual Basic throws an **InvalidCastException**, which indicates that the cast operation is not allowed. Exceptions are discussed in detail in Chapter 8, Exception Handling.

Common Programming Error 7.2

Assigning a base-class object (or a base-class reference) to a derived-class reference (without a cast) is a syntax error.

Software Engineering Observation 7.1

If a derived-class object has been assigned to a reference of one of its direct or indirect base classes, it is acceptable to cast that base-class reference back to a reference of the derived-class type. In fact, this must be done to send that object messages that do not appear in the base class. [Note: We sometimes use the term "messages" to represent invoking methods and properties on an object.]

Line 28 casts **point2**, which currently refers to a **CCircle** (**circle1**), to a **CCircle** and assigns the result to **circle2**. As we discuss momentarily, this cast would be dangerous if **point2** were referencing a **CPoint**. Lines 30–31 invoke method **ToString** of the **CCircle** object to which **circle2** now refers (note that the fourth line of the output demonstrates that **CCircle**'s **ToString** method is called). Lines 33–34 calculate **circle2**'s **Area** and format it with method **String.Format**. The format **"{0:F}"** (line 34) specifies the formatting for this number. By default, the number appears with two digits to the right of the decimal point.

Line 38 uses method **CType** to cast **point1** to a **CCircle**. This is a dangerous operation, because point refers to a **CPoint** object and a **CPoint** object is not a **CCircle**. Objects can be cast only to their own type or to their base-class types. If this statement were to execute, Visual Basic would determine that **point1** references a **CPoint** object, recognize the cast to **CCircle** as dangerous and indicate an improper cast with an **InvalidCastException** message. However, we prevent this statement from executing by including the **If/Else** structure (lines 37–43). The condition at line 37 uses operator **TypeOf** to determine whether the object to which **point1** refers "is a" **CCircle**. Operator **TypeOf** determines the type of the object to which **TypeOf**'s operand refers. We then compare that type to **CCircle**. In our example, **point1** does not refer to a **CCircle**, so the condition fails, and lines 41–42 append to **output** a **String** indicating the result. Note that the **Is** comparison will be **True** if the two operands are the same type or if the left operand is a derived-class of the right operand.

 Common Programming Error 7.3

*Attempting to cast a base-class reference to a derived-class type causes an **Invalid-CastException** if the reference refers to a base-class object rather than a derived-class object.*

If we were to execute line 38 without the **If/Else** structure, Visual Basic displays a **MessageBox** containing the message:

```
An unhandled exception of type 'System.InvalidCastException'
occurred in
```

followed by the name and path of the executing program. We discuss how to deal with this situation in Chapter 8.

Despite the fact that a derived-class object also "is a" base-class object, the derived-class and base-class objects are different. As we have discussed previously, derived-class objects can be treated as if they were base-class objects. This is a logical relationship, because the derived class contains members that correspond to all members in the base class. The derived class can have additional members as well. For this reason, assigning base-class objects to derived-class references is not allowed without an explicit cast (when **Option Strict** is **On**). Such an assignment would leave the additional derived-class members undefined.

There are four ways to mix base-class references and derived-class references with base-class objects and derived-class objects:

1. Referring to a base-class object with a base-class reference is straightforward.

2. Referring to a derived-class object with a derived-class reference is straightforward.

3. Referring to a derived-class object with a base-class reference is safe, because the derived-class object *is an* object of its base class. However, this reference can refer only to base-class members. If this code refers to derived-class-only members through the base-class reference, the compiler reports an error.

4. Referring to a base-class object with a derived-class reference generates a compiler error (when **Option Strict** is **On**). To avoid this error, the derived-class reference first must be cast to a base-class reference. In this cast, the derived-class reference must reference a derived-class object, or Visual Basic generates an **InvalidCastException**.

Common Programming Error 7.4

After assigning a derived-class object to a base-class reference, attempting to reference derived-class-only members with the base-class reference is a syntax error.

Common Programming Error 7.5

Treating a base-class object as a derived-class object can cause errors.

Though it is convenient to treat derived-class objects as base-class objects by manipulating derived-class objects with base-class references, doing so can cause significant problems. For example, in a payroll system we need to be able to walk through an array of employees and calculate the weekly pay for each person. Intuition suggests that using base-class references would enable the program to call only the base-class payroll calculation routine (if there is such a routine in the base class). We need a way to invoke the proper payroll calculation routine for each object, whether it is a base-class object or a derived-class object, and to do this simply by using the base-class reference. We learn how to create classes that include this behavior as we introduce polymorphism throughout this chapter.

7.3 Type Fields and Select Case Statements

One way to determine the type of an object that is incorporated in a larger program is to use a **Select Case** statement. This allows us to distinguish among object types, then invoke an appropriate action for a particular object. For example, in a hierarchy of shapes in which each shape object has an **mShapeType** instance variable, a **Select Case** structure could employ the object's **mShapeType** to determine which **Print** method to call.

However, using **Select-Case** logic exposes programs to a variety of potential problems. For example, the programmer might forget to include a type test when one is warranted or the programmer might forget to test all possible cases in a **Select Case**. When modifying a **Select-Case**-based system by adding new types, the programmer might forget to insert the new cases in all relevant **Select-Case** statements. Every addition or deletion of a class requires the modification of every **Select-Case** statement in the system; tracking these statements down can be time-consuming and error-prone.

Software Engineering Observation 7.2

*Polymorphic programming can eliminate the need for unnecessary **Select-Case** logic. By using Visual Basic's polymorphism mechanism to perform the equivalent logic, programmers can avoid the kinds of errors typically associated with **Select-Case** logic.*

Testing and Debugging Tip 7.1

An interesting consequence of using polymorphism is that programs take on a simplified appearance. They contain less branching logic and more simple, sequential code. This simplification facilitates testing, debugging and program maintenance.

7.4 Polymorphism Examples

In this section, we discuss several examples of polymorphism. If class **CRectangle** is derived from class **CQuadrilateral**, then a **CRectangle** object is a more specific version of a **CQuadrilateral** object. Any operation (such as calculating the perimeter or the area) that can be performed on an object of class **CQuadrilateral** also can be performed on an object of class **CRectangle**. Such operations also can be performed on other kinds of **CQuadrilateral**s, such as **CSquare**s, **CParallelogram**s and **CTrapezoid**s. When a program invokes a derived-class method through a base-class (i.e., **CQuadrilateral**) reference, Visual Basic polymorphically chooses the correct overridden method in the derived class from which the object was instantiated. We will soon investigate this behavior in LIVE-CODE™ examples.

Suppose that we design a video game that manipulates objects of many different types, including objects of classes **CMartian**, **CVenutian**, **CPlutonian**, **CSpace-Ship** and **CLaserBeam**. Also imagine that each of these classes inherits from the common base class called **CSpaceObject**, which contains a method called **DrawYourself**. Each derived class implements this method. A Visual Basic screen-manager program would maintain a container (such as a **CSpaceObject** array) of references to objects of the various classes. To refresh the screen, the screen manager periodically sends each object the same message—namely, **DrawYourself**. However, each object responds in a unique way. For example, a **CMartian** object draws itself in red with the appropriate number of antennae. A **CSpaceShip** object draws itself as a bright, silver flying saucer. A **CLaserBeam** object draws itself as a bright red beam across the screen. Thus the same message sent to a variety of objects would have "many forms" of results—hence the term *polymorphism*.

A polymorphic screen manager makes it especially easy to add new types of objects to a system with minimal modifications to the system's code. Suppose we want to add class **CMercurian**s to our video game. To do so, we must build a class **CMercurian** that inherits from **CSpaceObject**, but provides its own definition of the **DrawYourself** method. Then, when objects of class **CMercurian** appear in the container, the programmer does not need to alter the screen manager. The screen manager invokes method **DrawYourself** on every object in the container, regardless of the object's type, so the new **CMercurian** objects simply "plug right in." Thus, without modifying the system (other than to build and include the classes themselves), programmers can use polymorphism to include additional types of classes that were not envisioned when the system was created.

With polymorphism, one method call can cause different actions to occur, depending on the type of the object receiving the call. This gives the programmer tremendous expressive capability. In the next several sections, we provide LIVE-CODE™ examples that demonstrate polymorphism.

Software Engineering Observation 7.3

With polymorphism, the programmer can deal in generalities and let the execution-time environment concern itself with the specifics. The programmer can command a wide variety of objects to behave in manners appropriate to those objects, even if the programmer does not know the objects' types.

Software Engineering Observation 7.4

Polymorphism promotes extensibility. Software used to invoke polymorphic behavior is written to be independent of the types of the objects to which messages (i.e., method calls) are sent. Thus, programmers can include into a system additional types of objects that respond to existing messages and can do this without modifying the base system.

7.5 Abstract Classes and Methods

When we think of a class as a type, we assume that programs will create objects of that type. However, there are cases in which it is useful to define classes for which the programmer never intends to instantiate any objects. Such classes are called *abstract classes*. Because such classes are normally used as base classes in inheritance situations, we normally refer to them as *abstract base classes*. These classes cannot be used to instantiate objects. Abstract classes are incomplete. Derived classes must define the "missing pieces." Abstract classes normally contain one or more *abstract methods* or *abstract properties*, which are methods and properties that do not provide an implementation. Derived classes must override inherited abstract methods and properties to enable objects of those derived classes to be instantiated.

The purpose of an abstract class is to provide an appropriate base class from which other classes may inherit (we will see examples shortly). Classes from which objects can be instantiated are called *concrete classes*. Such classes provide implementations of every method and property they define. We could have an abstract base class **CTwoDimensionalObject** and derive concrete classes, such as **CSquare**, **CCircle**, **CTriangle**. We could also have an abstract base class **CThreeDimensionalObject** and derive such concrete classes as **CCube**, **CSphere** and **CCylinder**. Abstract base classes are too generic to define real objects; we need to be more specific before we can think of instantiating objects. For example, if someone tells you to "draw the shape," what shape would you draw? Concrete classes provide the specifics that make it reasonable to instantiate objects.

A class is made abstract by declaring it with keyword *MustInherit*. A hierarchy does not need to contain any **MustInherit** classes, but as we will see, many good object-oriented systems have class hierarchies headed by **MustInherit** base classes. In some cases, **MustInherit** classes constitute the top few levels of the hierarchy. A good example of this is the shape hierarchy in Fig. 6.3. The hierarchy begins with **MustInherit** (abstract) base-class **CShape**. On the next level of the hierarchy, we have two more **MustInherit** base classes, namely **CTwoDimensionalShape** and **CThreeDimensionalShape**. The next level of the hierarchy would start defining concrete classes for two-dimensional shapes such as **CCircle** and **CSquare** and such three-dimensional shapes such as **CSphere** and **CCube**.

Software Engineering Observation 7.5

A MustInherit class defines a common set of Public methods for the various members of a class hierarchy. A MustInherit class typically contains one or more abstract methods or properties that derived classes will override. All classes in the hierarchy can use this common set of Public methods.

MustInherit classes must specify their abstract methods or properties. Visual Basic provides keyword **MustOverride** to declare a method or property as abstract. **MustOverride** methods and properties do not provide implementations—attempting to do so is a syntax error. Every derived class must override all base-class **MustOverride** methods and properties (using keyword **Overrides**) and provide concrete implementations of those methods or properties. Any class with a **MustOverride** method in it must be declared **MustInherit**. The difference between a **MustOverride** method and an **Overridable** method is that an **Overridable** method has an implementation and provides the derived class with the option of overriding the method; by contrast, a **MustOverride** method does not provide an implementation and forces the derived class to override the method (for that derived class to be concrete).

Common Programming Error 7.6

It is a syntax error to define a **MustOverride** *method in a class that has not been declared as* **MustInherit**.

Common Programming Error 7.7

Attempting to instantiate an object of a **MustInherit** *class is an error.*

Common Programming Error 7.8

Failure to override a **MustOverride** *method in a derived class is a syntax error, unless the derived class also is a* **MustInherit** *class.*

Software Engineering Observation 7.6

An abstract class can have instance data and nonabstract methods (including constructors), which are subject to the normal rules of inheritance by derived classes.

Although we cannot instantiate objects of **MustInherit** base classes, we *can* use **MustInherit** base classes to declare references; these references can refer to instances of any concrete classes derived from the **MustInherit** class. Programs can use such references to manipulate instances of the derived classes polymorphically.

Let us consider another application of polymorphism. A screen manager needs to display a variety of objects, including new types of objects that the programmer will add to the system after writing the screen manager. The system might need to display various shapes, such as **CCircle**, **CTriangle** or **CRectangle**, which are derived from **MustInherit** class **CShape**. The screen manager uses base-class references of type **CShape** to manage the objects that are displayed. To draw any object (regardless of the level at which that object's class appears in the inheritance hierarchy), the screen manager uses a base-class reference to the object to invoke the object's **Draw** method. Method **Draw** is a **MustOverride** method in base-class **CShape**; therefore each derived class must override method **Draw**. Each **CShape** object in the inheritance hierarchy knows how to draw itself. The screen manager does not have to worry about the type of each object or whether the screen manager has ever encountered objects of that type.

Polymorphism is particularly effective for implementing layered software systems. In operating systems, for example, each type of physical device could operate quite differently from the others. Even so, commands to *read* or *write* data from and to devices can have a certain uniformity. The write message sent to a device-driver object needs to be interpreted specifically in the context of that device driver and how that device driver manipulates devices of a specific type. However, the write call itself is really no different from the write to any other device in the system—simply place some number of bytes from memory onto that device. An object-oriented operating system might use a **MustInherit** base class to provide an interface appropriate for all device drivers. Then, through inheritance from that **MustInherit** base class, derived classes are formed that all operate similarly. The capabilities (i.e., the **Public** interface) offered by the device drivers are provided as **MustOverride** methods in the **MustInherit** base class. The implementations of these **MustOverride** methods are provided in the derived classes that correspond to the specific types of device drivers.

It is common in object-oriented programming to define an *iterator class* that can walk through all the objects in a container (such as an array). For example, a program can print a list of objects in a linked list by creating an iterator object, then using the iterator to obtain the next element of the list each time the iterator is called. Iterators often are used in polymorphic programming to traverse an array or a linked list of objects from various levels of a hierarchy. The references in such a list are all base-class references. (See Chapter 20, Data Structures and Collections, to learn more about linked lists.) A list of objects of base class **CTwoDimensionalShape** could contain objects from classes **CSquare**, **CCircle**, **CTriangle** and so on. Using polymorphism to send a **Draw** message to each object in the list would draw each object correctly on the screen.

7.6 Case Study: Inheriting Interface and Implementation

Our next example (Fig. 7.4–Fig. 7.8) reexamines the **CPoint**, **CCircle**, **CCylinder** hierarchy that we explored in Chapter 6. In this example, the hierarchy begins with **MustInherit** base class **CShape** (Fig. 7.4). This hierarchy mechanically demonstrates the power of polymorphism.

```vb
1   ' Fig. 7.4: Shape.vb
2   ' Demonstrate a shape hierarchy using MustInherit class.
3
4   Imports System.Windows.Forms
5
6   Public MustInherit Class CShape
7
8      ' return shape area
9      Public Overridable Function Area() As Double
10        Return 0
11     End Function ' Area
12
13     ' return shape volume
14     Public Overridable Function Volume() As Double
15        Return 0
16     End Function ' Volume
17
18     ' overridable method that should return shape name
19     Public MustOverride ReadOnly Property Name() As String
20
21   End Class ' CShape
```

Fig. 7.4   Abstract **CShape** base class.

Class **CShape** defines two concrete methods and one abstract property. Because all shapes have an area and a volume, we include methods **Area** (lines 9–11) and **Volume** (lines 14–16), which return the shape's area and volume, respectively. The volume of two-dimensional shapes is always zero, whereas three-dimensional shapes have a positive, non-zero volume. In class **CShape**, methods **Area** and **Volume** return zero, by default. Programmers can override these methods in derived classes when those classes should have a different area calculation [e.g., classes **CCircle2** (Fig. 7.6) and **CCylinder2** (Fig. 7.7)] and/or a different volume calculation (e.g., **CCylinder2**). Property **Name** (line 19) is declared as **MustOverride**, so derived classes must override this property to become concrete classes.

Class **CPoint2** (Fig. 7.5) inherits from **MustInherit** class **CShape** and overrides the **MustOverride** property **Name**, which makes **CPoint2** a concrete class. A point's area and volume are zero, so class **CPoint2** does not override base-class methods **Area** and **Volume**. Lines 59–65 implement property **Name**. If we did not provide this implementation, class **CPoint2** would be an abstract class that would require **MustInherit** in the first line of the class definition.

```
1    ' Fig. 7.5: Point2.vb
2    ' CPoint2 class represents an x-y coordinate pair.
3
4    Public Class CPoint2
5       Inherits CShape ' CPoint2 inherits from MustInherit class CShape
6
7       ' point coordinate
8       Private mX, mY As Integer
9
10      ' default constructor
11      Public Sub New()
12
13         ' implicit call to Object constructor occurs here
14         X = 0
15         Y = 0
16      End Sub ' New
17
18      ' constructor
19      Public Sub New(ByVal xValue As Integer, _
20         ByVal yValue As Integer)
21
22         ' implicit call to Object constructor occurs here
23         X = xValue
24         Y = yValue
25      End Sub ' New
26
27      ' property X
28      Public Property X() As Integer
29
30         Get
31            Return mX
32         End Get
```

Fig. 7.5   **CPoint2** class inherits from **MustInherit** class **CShape**. (Part 1 of 2.)

```
33
34              Set(ByVal xValue As Integer)
35                 mX = xValue ' no need for validation
36              End Set
37
38          End Property ' X
39
40          ' property Y
41          Public Property Y() As Integer
42
43             Get
44                Return mY
45             End Get
46
47             Set(ByVal yValue As Integer)
48                mY = yValue ' no need for validation
49             End Set
50
51          End Property ' Y
52
53          ' return String representation of CPoint2
54          Public Overrides Function ToString() As String
55             Return "[" & mX & ", " & mY & "]"
56          End Function ' ToString
57
58          ' implement MustOverride property of class CShape
59          Public Overrides ReadOnly Property Name() As String
60
61             Get
62                Return "CPoint2"
63             End Get
64
65          End Property ' Name
66
67       End Class ' CPoint2
```

Fig. 7.5   **CPoint2** class inherits from **MustInherit** class **CShape**. (Part 2 of 2.)

Fig. 7.6 defines class **CCircle2** that inherits from class **CPoint2**. Class **CCircle2** contains member variable **mRadius** and provides property **Radius** (lines 26–40) to access the **mRadius**. Note that we do not declare property **Radius** as **Overridable**, so classes derived from this class cannot override this property. A circle has a volume of zero, so we do not override base-class method **Volume**. Rather, **CCircle2** inherits this method from class **CPoint2**, which inherited the method from **CShape**. However, a circle does have an area, so **CCircle2** overrides **CShape**'s method **Area** (lines 53–55). Property **Name** (lines 66–72) of class **CCircle2** overrides property **Name** of class **CPoint2**. If this class did not override property **Name**, the class would inherit the **CPoint2** version of property **Name**. In that case, **CCircle2**'s **Name** property would erroneously return "**CPoint2**."

```vb
1    ' Fig. 7.6: Circle2.vb
2    ' CCircle2 class inherits from CPoint2 and overrides key members.
3
4    Public Class CCircle2
5       Inherits CPoint2  ' CCircle2 Inherits from class CPoint2
6
7       Private mRadius As Double
8
9       ' default constructor
10      Public Sub New()
11
12         ' implicit call to CPoint2 constructor occurs here
13         Radius = 0
14      End Sub ' New
15
16      ' constructor
17      Public Sub New(ByVal xValue As Integer, _
18         ByVal yValue As Integer, ByVal radiusValue As Double)
19
20         ' use MyBase reference to CPoint2 constructor explicitly
21         MyBase.New(xValue, yValue)
22         Radius = radiusValue
23      End Sub ' New
24
25      ' property Radius
26      Public Property Radius() As Double
27
28         Get
29            Return mRadius
30         End Get
31
32         Set(ByVal radiusValue As Double)
33
34            If radiusValue >= 0 ' mRadius must be nonnegative
35               mRadius = radiusValue
36            End If
37
38         End Set
39
40      End Property ' Radius
41
42      ' calculate CCircle2 diameter
43      Public Function Diameter() As Double
44         Return mRadius * 2
45      End Function ' Diameter
46
47      ' calculate CCircle2 circumference
48      Public Function Circumference() As Double
49         Return Math.PI * Diameter()
50      End Function ' Circumference
51
```

Fig. 7.6   **CCircle2** class that inherits from class **CPoint2**. (Part 1 of 2.)

```
52        ' calculate CCircle2 area
53        Public Overrides Function Area() As Double
54            Return Math.PI * mRadius ^ 2
55        End Function ' Area
56
57        ' return String representation of CCircle2
58        Public Overrides Function ToString() As String
59
60            ' use MyBase to return CCircle2 String representation
61            Return "Center = " & MyBase.ToString() & _
62                "; Radius = " & mRadius
63        End Function ' ToString
64
65        ' override property Name from class CPoint2
66        Public Overrides ReadOnly Property Name() As String
67
68            Get
69                Return "CCircle2"
70            End Get
71
72        End Property ' Name
73
74    End Class ' CCircle2
```

Fig. 7.6   `CCircle2` class that inherits from class `CPoint2`. (Part 2 of 2.)

Figure 7.7 defines class **CCylinder2** that inherits from class **CCircle2**. Class **CCylinder2** contains member variable **mHeight** and property **Height** (lines 27–42) to access the **mHeight**. Note that we do not declare property **Height** as **Overridable**, so classes derived from class **CCylinder2** cannot override this property. A cylinder has different area and volume calculations than a circle, so this class overrides method **Area** (lines 45–47) to calculate the cylinder's surface area (i.e., $2\pi r^2 + 2\pi rh$) and defines method **Volume** (lines 50–52). Property **Name** (lines 60–66) overrides property **Name** of class **CCircle2**. If this class did not override property **Name**, the class would inherit property **Name** of class **CCircle2**, and this property would erroneously return "**CCircle2**."

```
1     ' Fig. 7.7: Cylinder2.vb
2     ' CCylinder2 inherits from CCircle2 and overrides key members.
3
4     Public Class CCylinder2
5         Inherits CCircle2 ' CCylinder2 inherits from class CCircle2
6
7         Private mHeight As Double
8
9         ' default constructor
10        Public Sub New()
11
12            ' implicit call to CCircle2 constructor occurs here
13            Height = 0
14        End Sub ' New
15
```

Fig. 7.7   `CCylinder2` class inherits from class `CCircle2`. (Part 1 of 2.)

```
16         ' four-argument constructor
17         Public Sub New(ByVal xValue As Integer, _
18            ByVal yValue As Integer, ByVal radiusValue As Double, _
19            ByVal heightValue As Double)
20
21            ' explicit call to CCircle2 constructor
22            MyBase.New(xValue, yValue, radiusValue)
23            Height = heightValue ' set CCylinder2 height
24         End Sub ' New
25
26         ' property Height
27         Public Property Height() As Double
28
29            Get
30               Return mHeight
31            End Get
32
33            ' set CCylinder2 height if argument value is positive
34            Set(ByVal heightValue As Double)
35
36               If heightValue >= 0 Then ' mHeight must be nonnegative
37                  mHeight = heightValue
38               End If
39
40            End Set
41
42         End Property ' Height
43
44         ' override method Area to calculate CCylinder2 surface area
45         Public Overrides Function Area() As Double
46            Return 2 * MyBase.Area + MyBase.Circumference * mHeight
47         End Function ' Area
48
49         ' calculate CCylinder2 volume
50         Public Overrides Function Volume() As Double
51            Return MyBase.Area * mHeight
52         End Function ' Volume
53
54         ' convert CCylinder2 to String
55         Public Overrides Function ToString() As String
56            Return MyBase.ToString() & "; Height = " & mHeight
57         End Function ' ToString
58
59         ' override property Name from class CCircle2
60         Public Overrides ReadOnly Property Name() As String
61
62            Get
63               Return "CCylinder2"
64            End Get
65
66         End Property ' Name
67
68      End Class ' CCylinder2
```

Fig. 7.7   CCylinder2 class inherits from class CCircle2. (Part 2 of 2.)

Figure 7.8 defines class **CTest2** whose method **Main** creates an object of each of the three concrete classes and manipulates the objects polymorphically using an array of **CShape** references. Lines 11–13 instantiate **CPoint2** object **point**, **CCircle2** object **circle**, and **CCylinder2** object **cylinder**, respectively. Next, line 16 instantiates array **arrayOfShapes**, which contains three **CShape** references. Line 19 assigns reference **point** to array element **arrayOfShapes(0)**, line 22 assigns reference **circle** to array element **arrayOfShapes(1)** and line 25 assigns reference **cylinder** to array element **arrayOfShapes(2)**. These assignments are possible, because a **CPoint2** is a **CShape**, a **CCircle2** is a **CShape** and a **CCylinder2** is a **CShape**. Therefore, we can assign instances of derived-classes **CPoint2**, **CCircle2** and **CCylinder2** to base-class **CShape** references.

```
1    ' Fig. 7.8: Test2.vb
2    ' Demonstrate polymorphism in Point-Circle-Cylinder hierarchy.
3
4    Imports System.Windows.Forms
5
6    Class CTest2
7
8       Shared Sub Main()
9
10         ' instantiate CPoint2, CCircle2 and CCylinder2 objects
11         Dim point As New CPoint2(7, 11)
12         Dim circle As New CCircle2(22, 8, 3.5)
13         Dim cylinder As New CCylinder2(10, 10, 3.3, 10)
14
15         ' instantiate array of base-class references
16         Dim arrayOfShapes As CShape() = New CShape(2){}
17
18         ' arrayOfShapes(0) refers to CPoint2 object
19         arrayOfShapes(0) = point
20
21         ' arrayOfShapes(1) refers to CCircle2 object
22         arrayOfShapes(1) = circle
23
24         ' arrayOfShapes(2) refers to CCylinder2 object
25         arrayOfShapes(2) = cylinder
26
27         Dim output As String = point.Name & ": " & _
28            point.ToString() & vbCrLf & circle.Name & ": " & _
29            circle.ToString() & vbCrLf & cylinder.Name & _
30            ": " & cylinder.ToString()
31
32         Dim shape As CShape
33
34         ' display name, area and volume for each object in
35         ' arrayOfShapes polymorphically
36         For Each shape In arrayOfShapes
37            output &= vbCrLf & vbCrLf & shape.Name & ": " & _
38               shape.ToString() & vbCrLf & "Area = " & _
```

Fig. 7.8   **CTest2** demonstrates polymorphism in Point-Circle-Cylinder hierarchy. (Part 1 of 2.)

```
39                  String.Format("{0:F}", shape.Area) & vbCrLf & _
40                  "Volume = " & String.Format("{0:F}", shape.Volume)
41          Next
42
43          MessageBox.Show(output, "Demonstrating Polymorphism")
44       End Sub ' Main
45
46    End Class ' CTest2
```

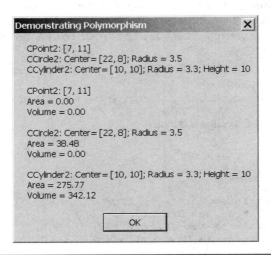

Fig. 7.8   **CTest2** demonstrates polymorphism in Point-Circle-Cylinder hierarchy.
(Part 2 of 2.)

Lines 27–30 invoke property **Name** and method **ToString** for objects **point**, **circle** and **cylinder**. Property **Name** returns the object's class name and method **ToString** returns the object's **String** representation (i.e., *x-y* coordinate pair, radius and height, depending on each object's type). Note that lines 27–30 use derived-class references to invoke each derived-class object's methods and properties.

By contrast, the **For Each** structure (lines 36–41) uses base-class **CShape** references to invoke each derived-class object's methods and properties. The **For Each** structure calls property **Name** and methods **ToString**, **Area** and **Volume** for each **CShape** reference in **arrayOfShapes**. The property and methods are invoked on each object in **arrayOfShapes**. When the compiler looks at each method/property call, the compiler determines whether each **CShape** reference (in **arrayOfShapes**) can make these calls. This is the case for property **Name** and methods **Area** and **Volume**, because they are defined in class **CShape**. However, class **CShape** does not define method **ToString**. For this method, the compiler proceeds to **CShape**'s base class (class **Object**), and determines that **CShape** inherited a no-argument **ToString** method from class **Object**.

The screen capture of Fig. 7.8 illustrates that the "appropriate" property **Name** and methods **ToString**, **Area** and **Volume** were invoked for each type of object in **arrayOfShapes**. By "appropriate," we mean that Visual Basic maps each property and method call to the proper object. For example, in the **For Each** structure's first iteration, reference **arrayOfShapes(0)** (which is of type **CShape**) refers to the same object as **point** (which is of type **CPoint2**). Class **CPoint2** overrides property **Name** and method **ToString**, and inherits method **Area** and **Volume** from class **CShape**. At runtime, **arrayOfShapes(0)** invokes property **Name** and methods **ToString**, **Area** and **Volume** of the **CPoint** object. Visual Basic determines the correct object type, then uses that type to determine the appropriate methods to invoke. Through polymorphism, the call to property **Name** returns the string **"CPoint2:"**; the call to method **ToString** returns the **String** representation of **point**'s *x-y* coordinate pair; and methods **Area** and **Volume** each return **0** (as shown in the second group of outputs in Fig. 7.8).

Polymorphism occurs in the next two iterations of the **For Each** structure as well. Reference **arrayOfShapes(1)** refers to the same object as **circle** (which is of type **CCircle2**). Class **CCircle2** provides implementations for property **Name**, method **ToString** and method **Area**, and inherits method **Volume** from class **CPoint2** (which, in turn, inherited method **Volume** from class **CShape**). Visual Basic associates property **Name** and methods **ToString**, **Area** and **Volume** of the **CCircle2** object to reference **arrayOfShapes(1)**. As a result, property **Name** returns the string **"CCircle2:"**; method **ToString** returns the **String** representation of **circle**'s *x-y* coordinate pair and radius; method **Area** returns the area (**38.48**); and method **Volume** returns **0**.

For the final iteration of the **For Each** structure, reference **arrayOfShapes(2)** refers to the same object as **cylinder** (which is of type **CCylinder2**). Class **CCylinder2** provides its own implementations for property **Name** and methods **ToString**, **Area** and **Volume**. Visual Basic associates property **Name** and methods **ToString**, **Area** and **Volume** of the **CCylinder2** object to reference **arrayOf-Shapes(2)**. Property **Name** returns the string **"CCylinder2:"**; method **ToString** returns the **String** representation of **cylinder**'s *x-y* coordinate pair, radius and height; method **Area** returns the cylinder's surface area (**275.77**); and method **Volume** returns the cylinder's volume (**342.12**).

7.7 **NotInheritable** Classes and **NotOverridable** Methods

A class that is declared **NotInheritable** cannot be a base class. Programmers use this feature to prevent inheritance beyond the **NotInheritable** class in the hierarchy. A **NotInheritable** class is the "opposite" of a **MustInherit** class. A **NotInherit-able** class is a concrete class that cannot act as a base class, whereas a **MustInherit** class is an abstract class that can only act as a base class.

A method that was declared **Overridable** in a base class can be declared **NotOverridable** in a derived class. This prevents overriding the method in classes that inherit from the derived class. All classes derived from the class that contains the **Not-Overridable** method use that class's method implementation. Methods that are declared **Shared** and methods that are declared **Private** implicitly are **Not-Overridable**.

Software Engineering Observation 7.7

*If a method is declared **NotOverridable**, it cannot be overridden in derived classes. Calls to **NotOverridable** methods cannot be sent polymorphically to objects of those derived classes.*

Software Engineering Observation 7.8

*A class that is declared **NotInheritable** cannot be a base class (i.e., a class cannot inherit from a **NotInheritable** class). All methods in a **NotInheritable** class implicitly are **NotOverridable**.*

7.8 Case Study: Payroll System Using Polymorphism

Let us use abstract classes (declared as **MustInherit**), abstract methods (declared as **MustOverride**) and polymorphism to perform different payroll calculations for various types of employees. We begin by creating an abstract base class **CEmployee**. The derived classes of **CEmployee** are **CBoss** (paid a fixed weekly salary, regardless of the number of hours worked), **CCommissionWorker** (paid a flat base salary plus a percentage of the worker's sales), **CPieceWorker** (paid a flat fee per item produced) and **CHourlyWorker** (paid by the hour with "time-and-a-half" for overtime). In this example, we declare all classes that inherit from class **CEmployee** as **NotInheritable**, because we do not intend to derive classes from them.

The application must determine the weekly earnings for all types of employees, so each class derived from **CEmployee** requires method **Earnings**. However, each derived class uses a different calculation to determine earnings for a specific type of employee. Therefore, we declare method **Earnings** as **MustOverride** in **CEmployee** and declare **CEmployee** to be a **MustInherit** class. Each derived class overrides this method to calculate earnings for that employee type.

To calculate any employee's earnings, the program can use a base-class reference to a derived-class object and invoke method **Earnings**. In a real payroll system, the various **CEmployee** objects might be referenced by individual elements in an array of **CEmployee** references. The program would traverse the array one element at a time, using the **CEmployee** references to invoke the appropriate **Earnings** method of each object.

Software Engineering Observation 7.9

*The ability to declare an abstract (**MustOverride**) method gives the class designer considerable control over how derived classes are defined in a class hierarchy. Any class that inherits directly from a base class containing an abstract method must override the abstract method. Otherwise, the new class also would be abstract, and attempts to instantiate objects of that class would fail.*

Let us consider class **CEmployee** (Fig. 7.9). The **Public** members include a constructor (lines 10–15) that takes as arguments an employee's first and last names; properties **FirstName** (lines 18–28) and **LastName** (lines 31–41); method **ToString** (lines 44–46) that returns the first name and last name separated by a space; and **MustOverride** method **Earnings** (line 50). The **MustInherit** keyword (line 4) indicates that class **CEmployee** is abstract; thus, it cannot be used to instantiate **CEmployee**. Method **Earnings** is declared as **MustOverride**, so the class does not provide a method implementation. All classes derived directly from class **CEmployee**—except for abstract derived classes—must define this method. Method **Earnings** is abstract in **CEmployee**, because we cannot calculate the earnings for a generic employee. To determine earnings, we first must know of what *kind* of employee it is. By declaring this method **MustOverride**, we indicate that we will provide an implementation in each concrete derived class, but not in the base class itself.

```
1    ' Fig. 7.9: Employee.vb
2    ' Abstract base class for employee derived classes.
3
4    Public MustInherit Class CEmployee
5
6       Private mFirstName As String
7       Private mLastName As String
8
9       ' constructor
10      Public Sub New(ByVal firstNameValue As String, _
11         ByVal lastNameValue As String)
12
13         FirstName = firstNameValue
14         LastName = lastNameValue
15      End Sub ' New
16
17      ' property FirstName
18      Public Property FirstName() As String
19
20         Get
21            Return mFirstName
22         End Get
23
24         Set(ByVal firstNameValue As String)
25            mFirstName = firstNameValue
26         End Set
27
28      End Property ' FirstName
29
30      ' property LastName
31      Public Property LastName() As String
32
33         Get
34            Return mLastName
35         End Get
36
37         Set(ByVal lastNameValue As String)
38            mLastName = lastNameValue
39         End Set
40
41      End Property ' LastName
42
43      ' obtain String representation of employee
44      Public Overrides Function ToString() As String
45         Return mFirstName & " " & mLastName
46      End Function ' ToString
47
48      ' abstract method that must be implemented for each derived
49      ' class of CEmployee to calculate specific earnings
50      Public MustOverride Function Earnings() As Decimal
51
52   End Class ' CEmployee
```

Fig. 7.9   MustInherit class CEmployee definition.

Class **CBoss** (Fig. 7.10) inherits from **CEmployee**. Class **CBoss**'s constructor (lines 10–15) receives as arguments a first name, a last name and a salary. The constructor passes the first name and last name to the **CEmployee** constructor (line 13), which initializes the **FirstName** and **LastName** members of the base-class part of the derived-class object. Other **Public** methods contained in **CBoss** include method **Earnings** (lines 36–38), which defines the calculation of a boss' earnings, and method **ToString** (lines 41–43), which returns a **String** indicating the type of employee (i.e., **"CBoss: "**) and the boss's name. Class **CBoss** also includes property **WeeklySalary** (lines 18–33), which sets and gets the value for member variable **mSalary**. Note that this property ensures only that **mSalary** cannot hold a negative value—in a real payroll system, this validation would be more extensive and carefully controlled.

```
1   ' Fig. 7.10: Boss.vb
2   ' Boss class derived from CEmployee.
3
4   Public NotInheritable Class CBoss
5      Inherits CEmployee
6
7      Private mSalary As Decimal
8
9      ' constructor for class CBoss
10     Public Sub New(ByVal firstNameValue As String, _
11        ByVal lastNameValue As String, ByVal salaryValue As Decimal)
12
13        MyBase.New(firstNameValue, lastNameValue)
14        WeeklySalary = salaryValue
15     End Sub ' New
16
17     ' property WeeklySalary
18     Public Property WeeklySalary() As Decimal
19
20        Get
21           Return mSalary
22        End Get
23
24        Set(ByVal bossSalaryValue As Decimal)
25
26           ' validate mSalary
27           If bossSalaryValue > 0
28              mSalary = bossSalaryValue
29           End If
30
31        End Set
32
33     End Property ' WeeklySalary
34
35     ' override base-class method to calculate Boss earnings
36     Public Overrides Function Earnings() As Decimal
37        Return WeeklySalary
38     End Function ' Earnings
39
```

Fig. 7.10 **CBoss** class inherits from class **CEmployee**. (Part 1 of 2.)

```
40          ' return Boss' name
41          Public Overrides Function ToString() As String
42              Return "CBoss: " & MyBase.ToString()
43          End Function ' ToString
44
45      End Class ' CBoss
```

Fig. 7.10 **CBoss** class inherits from class **CEmployee**. (Part 2 of 2.)

Class **CCommissionWorker** (Fig. 7.11) also inherits from class **CEmployee**. The constructor for this class (lines 12–21) receives as arguments a first name, a last name, a salary, a commission and a quantity of items sold. Line 17 passes the first name and last name to the base-class **CEmployee** constructor. Class **CCommissionWorker** also provides properties **Salary** (lines 24–39), **Commission** (lines 42–57) and **Quantity** (lines 60–75); method **Earnings** (lines 78–80), which calculates the worker's wages; and method **ToString** (lines 83–85), which returns a **String** indicating the employee type (i.e., **"CCommissionWorker: "**) and the worker's name.

```
1       ' Fig. 7.11: CommissionWorker.vb
2       ' CEmployee implementation for a commission worker.
3
4       Public NotInheritable Class CCommissionWorker
5           Inherits CEmployee
6
7           Private mSalary As Decimal ' base salary per week
8           Private mCommission As Decimal ' amount per item sold
9           Private mQuantity As Integer ' total items sold
10
11          ' constructor for class CCommissionWorker
12          Public Sub New(ByVal firstNameValue As String, _
13              ByVal lastNameValue As String, ByVal salaryValue As Decimal, _
14              ByVal commissionValue As Decimal, _
15              ByVal quantityValue As Integer)
16
17              MyBase.New(firstNameValue, lastNameValue)
18              Salary = salaryValue
19              Commission = commissionValue
20              Quantity = quantityValue
21          End Sub ' New
22
23          ' property Salary
24          Public Property Salary() As Decimal
25
26              Get
27                  Return mSalary
28              End Get
29
```

Fig. 7.11 **CCommissionWorker** class inherits from class **CEmployee**. (Part 1 of 3.)

```
30             Set(ByVal salaryValue As Decimal)
31
32                ' validate mSalary
33                If salaryValue > 0 Then
34                   mSalary = salaryValue
35                End If
36
37             End Set
38
39          End Property ' Salary
40
41          ' property Commission
42          Public Property Commission() As Decimal
43
44             Get
45                Return mCommission
46             End Get
47
48             Set(ByVal commissionValue As Decimal)
49
50                ' validate mCommission
51                If commissionValue > 0 Then
52                   mCommission = commissionValue
53                End If
54
55             End Set
56
57          End Property ' Commission
58
59          ' property Quantity
60          Public Property Quantity() As Integer
61
62             Get
63                Return mQuantity
64             End Get
65
66             Set(ByVal QuantityValue As Integer)
67
68                ' validate mQuantity
69                If QuantityValue > 0 Then
70                   mQuantity = QuantityValue
71                End If
72
73             End Set
74
75          End Property ' Quantity
76
77          ' override method to calculate CommissionWorker earnings
78          Public Overrides Function Earnings() As Decimal
79             Return Salary + Commission * Quantity
80          End Function ' Earnings
81
```

Fig. 7.11 CCommissionWorker class inherits from class CEmployee. (Part 2 of 3.)

```
82      ' return commission worker's name
83      Public Overrides Function ToString() As String
84          Return "CCommissionWorker: " & MyBase.ToString()
85      End Function ' ToString
86
87  End Class ' CCommissionWorker
```

Fig. 7.11 `CCommissionWorker` class inherits from class **CEmployee**. (Part 3 of 3.)

Class **CPieceWorker** (Fig. 7.12) inherits from class **CEmployee**. The constructor for this class (lines 11–19) receives as arguments a first name, a last name, a wage per piece and a quantity of items produced. Line 16 then passes the first name and last name to the base-class **CEmployee** constructor. Class **CPieceWorker** also provides properties **WagePerPiece** (lines 22–37) and **Quantity** (lines 40–55); method **Earnings** (lines 58–60), which calculates a piece worker's earnings; and method **ToString** (lines 63–65), which returns a **String** indicating the type of the employee (i.e., **"CPieceWorker: "**) and the piece worker's name.

Class **CHourlyWorker** (Fig. 7.13) inherits from class **CEmployee**. The constructor for this class (lines 11–18) receives as arguments a first name, a last name, a wage and the number of hours worked. Line 15 passes the first name and last name to the base-class **CEmployee** constructor. Class **CHourlyWorker** also provides properties **HourlyWage** (lines 21–36) and **Hours** (lines 39–54); method **Earnings** (lines 57–67), which calculates an hourly worker's earnings; and method **ToString** (lines 70–72), which returns a **String** indicating the type of the employee (i.e., **"CHourlyWorker:"**) and the hourly worker's name. Note that hourly workers are paid "time-and-a-half" for "overtime" (i.e., hours worked in excess of 40 hours).

```
1   ' Fig. 7.12: PieceWorker.vb
2   ' CPieceWorker class derived from CEmployee.
3
4   Public NotInheritable Class CPieceWorker
5      Inherits CEmployee
6
7      Private mAmountPerPiece As Decimal ' wage per piece output
8      Private mQuantity As Integer ' output per week
9
10     ' constructor for CPieceWorker
11     Public Sub New(ByVal firstNameValue As String, _
12        ByVal lastNameValue As String, _
13        ByVal wagePerPieceValue As Decimal, _
14        ByVal quantityValue As Integer)
15
16        MyBase.New(firstNameValue, lastNameValue)
17        WagePerPiece = wagePerPieceValue
18        Quantity = quantityValue
19     End Sub ' New
20
```

Fig. 7.12 `CPieceWorker` class inherits from class **CEmployee**. (Part 1 of 2.)

```
21        ' property WagePerPiece
22        Public Property WagePerPiece() As Decimal
23
24           Get
25               Return mAmountPerPiece
26           End Get
27
28           Set(ByVal wagePerPieceValue As Decimal)
29
30               ' validate mAmountPerPiece
31               If wagePerPieceValue > 0 Then
32                   mAmountPerPiece = wagePerPieceValue
33               End If
34
35           End Set
36
37        End Property ' WagePerPiece
38
39        ' property Quantity
40        Public Property Quantity() As Integer
41
42           Get
43               Return mQuantity
44           End Get
45
46           Set(ByVal quantityValue As Integer)
47
48               ' validate mQuantity
49               If quantityValue > 0 Then
50                   mQuantity = quantityValue
51               End If
52
53           End Set
54
55        End Property ' Quantity
56
57        ' override base-class method to calculate PieceWorker's earnings
58        Public Overrides Function Earnings() As Decimal
59           Return Quantity * WagePerPiece
60        End Function ' Earnings
61
62        ' return piece worker's name
63        Public Overrides Function ToString() As String
64           Return "CPieceWorker: " & MyBase.ToString()
65        End Function ' ToString
66
67     End Class ' CPieceWorker
```

Fig. 7.12 CPieceWorker class inherits from class **CEmployee**. (Part 2 of 2.)

Method **Main** (lines 8–50) of class **CTest** (Fig. 7.14) declares **CEmployee** reference **employee** (line 9). Each employee type is handled similarly in **Main**, so we discuss only the manipulations of the **CBoss** object.

```
1   ' Fig. 7.13: HourlyWorker.vb
2   ' CEmployee implementation for an hourly worker.
3
4   Public NotInheritable Class CHourlyWorker
5      Inherits CEmployee
6
7      Private mWage As Decimal ' wage per hour
8      Private mHoursWorked As Double ' hours worked for week
9
10      ' constructor for class CHourlyWorker
11      Public Sub New(ByVal firstNameValue As String, _
12         ByVal lastNameValue As String, _
13         ByVal wageValue As Decimal, ByVal hourValue As Double)
14
15         MyBase.New(firstNameValue, lastNameValue)
16         HourlyWage = wageValue
17         Hours = hourValue
18      End Sub ' New
19
20      ' property HourlyWage
21      Public Property HourlyWage() As Decimal
22
23         Get
24            Return mWage
25         End Get
26
27         Set(ByVal hourlyWageValue As Decimal)
28
29            ' validate mWage
30            If hourlyWageValue > 0 Then
31               mWage = hourlyWageValue
32            End If
33
34         End Set
35
36      End Property ' HourlyWage
37
38      ' property Hours
39      Public Property Hours() As Double
40
41         Get
42            Return mHoursWorked
43         End Get
44
45         Set(ByVal hourValue As Double)
46
47            ' validate mHoursWorked
48            If hourValue > 0 Then
49               mHoursWorked = hourValue
50            End If
51
52         End Set
53
```

Fig. 7.13 **CHourlyWorker** class inherits from class **CEmployee**. (Part 1 of 2.)

```vb
54          End Property ' Hours
55
56          ' override base-class method to calculate HourlyWorker earnings
57          Public Overrides Function Earnings() As Decimal
58
59              ' calculate for "time-and-a-half"
60              If mHoursWorked <= 40
61                  Return Convert.ToDecimal(mWage * mHoursWorked)
62              Else
63                  Return Convert.ToDecimal((mWage * mHoursWorked) + _
64                      (mHoursWorked - 40) * 0.5 * mWage)
65              End If
66
67          End Function ' Earnings
68
69          ' return hourly worker's name
70          Public Overrides Function ToString() As String
71              Return "CHourlyWorker: " & MyBase.ToString()
72          End Function ' ToString
73
74      End Class ' CHourlyWorker
```

Fig. 7.13   `CHourlyWorker` class inherits from class **CEmployee**. (Part 2 of 2.)

```vb
1   ' Fig. 7.14: Test.vb
2   ' Displays the earnings for each CEmployee.
3
4   Imports System.Windows.Forms
5
6   Class CTest
7
8       Shared Sub Main()
9           Dim employee As CEmployee ' base-class reference
10          Dim output As String
11
12          Dim boss As CBoss = New CBoss("John", "Smith", 800)
13
14          Dim commissionWorker As CCommissionWorker = _
15              New CCommissionWorker("Sue", "Jones", 400, 3, 150)
16
17          Dim pieceWorker As CPieceWorker = _
18              New CPieceWorker("Bob", "Lewis", _
19                  Convert.ToDecimal(2.5), 200)
20
21          Dim hourlyWorker As CHourlyWorker = _
22              New CHourlyWorker("Karen", "Price", _
23                  Convert.ToDecimal(13.75), 40)
24
25          ' employee reference to a CBoss
26          employee = boss
27          output &= GetString(employee) & boss.ToString() & _
28              " earned " & boss.Earnings().ToString("C") & vbCrLf & vbCrLf
```

Fig. 7.14   **CTest** class tests the **CEmployee** class hierarchy. (Part 1 of 2.)

```
29
30          ' employee reference to a CCommissionWorker
31          employee = commissionWorker
32          output &= GetString(employee) & _
33             commissionWorker.ToString() & " earned " & _
34             commissionWorker.Earnings().ToString("C") & vbCrLf & vbCrLf
35
36          ' employee reference to a CPieceWorker
37          employee = pieceWorker
38          output &= GetString(employee) & pieceWorker.ToString() & _
39             " earned " & pieceWorker.Earnings().ToString("C") _
40             & vbCrLf & vbCrLf
41
42          ' employee reference to a CHourlyWorker
43          employee = hourlyWorker
44          output &= GetString(employee) & _
45             hourlyWorker.ToString() & " earned " & _
46             hourlyWorker.Earnings().ToString("C") & vbCrLf & vbCrLf
47
48          MessageBox.Show(output, "Demonstrating Polymorphism", _
49             MessageBoxButtons.OK, MessageBoxIcon.Information)
50       End Sub ' Main
51
52       ' return String containing employee information
53       Shared Function GetString(ByVal worker As CEmployee) As String
54          Return worker.ToString() & " earned " & _
55             worker.Earnings().ToString("C") & vbCrLf
56       End Function ' GetString
57
58    End Class ' CTest
```

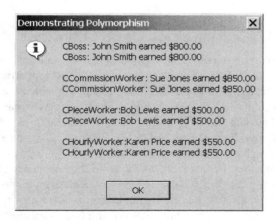

Fig. 7.14 **CTest** class tests the **CEmployee** class hierarchy. (Part 2 of 2.)

Line 12 assigns to **CBoss** reference **boss** a **CBoss** object and passes to its constructor the boss's first name ("**John**"), last name ("**Smith**") and fixed weekly salary (**800**). Line 26 assigns the derived-class reference **boss** to the base-class **CEmployee** reference **employee**, so that we can demonstrate the polymorphic determination of **boss**'s earnings. Line 27 passes reference **employee** as an argument to **Private** method **GetString** (lines 53–56), which polymorphically invokes methods **ToString** and **Earnings** on the **CEmployee** object the method receives as an argument. At this point, Visual Basic determines that the object passed to **GetString** is of type **CBoss**, so lines 54–55 invoke **CBoss** methods **ToString** and **Earnings**. These are classic examples of polymorphic behavior.

Method **Earnings** returns a **Decimal** object on which line 55 then calls method **ToString**. In this case, the string **"C"**, which is passed to an overloaded version of **Decimal** method **ToString**, stands for **Currency** and **ToString** formats the string as a currency amount.

When method **GetString** returns to **Main**, lines 27–28 explicitly invoke methods **ToString** and **Earnings** through derived-class **CBoss** reference **boss** to show the method invocations that do not use polymorphic processing. The output generated in lines 27–28 is identical to that generated by methods **ToString** and **Earnings** through base-class reference **employee** (i.e., the methods that use polymorphism), verifying that the polymorphic methods invoke the appropriate methods in derived class **CBoss**.

To prove that the base-class reference **employee** can invoke the proper derived-class versions of methods **ToString** and **Earnings** for the other types of employees, lines 31, 37 and 43 assign to base-class reference **employee** a different type of **CEmployee** object (**CCommissionWorker**, **CPieceWorker** and **CHourlyWorker**, respectively). After each assignment, the application calls method **GetString** to return the results via the base-class reference. Then, the application calls methods **ToString** and **Earnings** of each derived-class reference to show that Visual Basic correctly associates each method call to its corresponding derived-class object.

7.9 Case Study: Creating and Using Interfaces

We now present two more examples of polymorphism through the use of an *interface*, which specifies a set of **Public** services (i.e., methods and properties) that classes must implement. An interface is used when there is no default implementation to inherit (i.e., no instance variables and no default-method implementations). Whereas an abstract class is best used for providing data and services for objects in a hierarchical relationship, an interface can be used for providing services that "bring together" disparate objects that relate to one another only through that interface's services.

An interface definition begins with the keyword **Interface** and contains a list of **Public** methods and properties. To use an interface, a class must specify that it **Implements** the interface and must provide implementations for every method and property specified in the interface definition. Having a class implement an interface is like signing a contract with the compiler that states, "this class will define all the methods and properties specified by the interface."

 Common Programming Error 7.9

When a class **Implements** *an* **Interface**, *leaving even a single* **Interface** *method or property undefined is an error. The class must define every method and property in the* **Interface**.

Common Programming Error 7.10

*In Visual Basic, an **Interface** can be declared only as **Public** or **Friend**; the declaration of an **Interface** as **Private** or **Protected** is an error.*

Common Programming Error 7.11

*When implementing an **Interface** method, failure to include keyword **Implements** followed by that **Interface** method's name is a syntax error.*

Interfaces provide a uniform set of methods and properties to objects of disparate classes. These methods and properties enable programs to process the objects of those disparate classes polymorphically. For example, consider disparate objects that represent a person, a tree, a car and a file. These objects have "nothing to do" with each other—a person has a first name and last name; a tree has a trunk, a set of branches and a bunch of leaves; a car has wheels, gears and several other mechanisms enabling the car to move; and a file contains data. Because of the lack in commonality among these classes, modeling them via an inheritance hierarchy with an abstract class seems illogical. However, these objects certainly have at least one common characteristic—an age. A person's age is represented by the number of years since that person was born; a tree's age is represented by the number of rings in its trunk; a car's age is represented by its manufacture date; and a file's age is represented by its creation date. We can use an interface that provides a method or property that objects of these disparate classes can implement to return each object's age.

In this example, we use interface **IAge** (Fig. 7.15) to return the age information for classes **CPerson** (Fig. 7.16) and **CTree** (Fig. 7.17). The definition of interface **IAge** begins at line 4 with **Public Interface** and ends at line 10 with **End Interface**. Lines 7–8 specify properties **Age** and **Name**, for which every class that implements interface **IAge** must provide implementations. Interface **IAge** declares these properties as **ReadOnly**, but doing so is not required—an interface can also provide methods (**Sub**s and **Function**s), **WriteOnly** properties and properties with both get and set accessors. By containing these property declarations, interface **IAge** provides an opportunity for an object that implements **IAge** to return its age and name, respectively. However, the classes that implement these methods are not "required" by either interface **IAge** or Visual Basic to return an age and a name. The compiler requires only that classes implementing interface **IAge** provide implementations for the interface's properties. (Technically, interface **IAge** should not provide the opportunity for an object to return its name. However, as we will see later, clients that process interface objects polymorphically can interact with those objects only through the interface; therefore, property **Name** gives an object a chance to "identify" itself in our example.)

Line 5 of Fig. 7.16 uses keyword **Implements** to indicate that class **CPerson** implements interface **IAge**. In this example, class **CPerson** implements only one interface. A class can implement any number of interfaces in addition to inheriting from one class. To implement more than one interface, the class definition must provide a comma-separated list of interface names after keyword **Implements**. Class **CPerson** has member variables **mYearBorn**, **mFirstName** and **mLastName** (lines 7–9), for which the constructor (lines 12–29) set the values. Because class **CPerson** implements interface **IAge**, class **CPerson** must implement properties **Age** and **Name**—defined on lines 32–39 and lines 42–49, respectively. Property **Age** allows the client to obtain the person's age, and property **Name** returns a **String** containing **mFirstName** and **mLastName**. Note that property **Age** calculates the person's age by subtracting **mYearBorn** from the current year (via property **Year** of property **Date.Now**, which returns the current date). These properties satisfy the implementation requirements defined in interface **IAge**, so class **CPerson** has fulfilled its "contract" with the compiler.

```
1    ' Fig. 7.15: IAge.vb
2    ' Interface IAge declares property for setting and getting age.
3
4    Public Interface IAge
5
6       ' classes that implement IAge must define these properties
7       ReadOnly Property Age() As Integer
8       ReadOnly Property Name() As String
9
10   End Interface ' IAge
```

Fig. 7.15 **Interface** for returning age of objects of disparate classes.

```
1    ' Fig. 7.16: Person.vb
2    ' Class CPerson has a birthday.
3
4    Public Class CPerson
5       Implements IAge
6
7       Private mYearBorn As Integer
8       Private mFirstName As String
9       Private mLastName As String
10
11      ' constructor receives first name, last name and birth date
12      Public Sub New(ByVal firstNameValue As String, _
13         ByVal lastNameValue As String, _
14         ByVal yearBornValue As Integer)
15
16         ' implicit call to Object constructor
17         mFirstName = firstNameValue
18         mLastName = lastNameValue
19
20         ' validate year
21         If (yearBornValue > 0 AndAlso _
22            yearBornValue <= Date.Now.Year)
23
24            mYearBorn = yearBornValue
25         Else
26            mYearBorn = Date.Now.Year
27         End If
28
29      End Sub ' New
30
31      ' property Age implementation of interface IAge
32      ReadOnly Property Age() As Integer _
33         Implements IAge.Age
34
```

Fig. 7.16 **CPerson** class implements **IAge** interface. (Part 1 of 2.)

```
35          Get
36              Return Date.Now.Year - mYearBorn
37          End Get
38
39      End Property ' Age
40
41      ' property Name implementation of interface IAge
42      ReadOnly Property Name() As String _
43          Implements IAge.Name
44
45          Get
46              Return mFirstName & " " & mLastName
47          End Get
48
49      End Property ' Name
50
51  End Class ' CPerson
```

Fig. 7.16 **CPerson** class implements **IAge** interface. (Part 2 of 2.)

Class **CTree** (Fig. 7.17) also implements interface **IAge**. Class **CTree** has member variables **mRings** (line 7), which represents the number of rings inside the tree's trunk—this variable corresponds directly with the tree's age. The **CTree** constructor (lines 10–14) receives as an argument an **Integer** that specifies when the tree was planted. Class **CTree** includes method **AddRing** (lines 17–19), which enables a user to increment the number of rings in the tree. Because class **CTree** implements interface **IAge**, class **CTree** must implement properties **Age** and **Name**—defined on lines 22–29 and lines 32–39, respectively. Property **Age** returns the value of **mRings**, and property **Name** returns **String** "Tree."

```
1   ' Fig. 7.17: Tree.vb
2   ' Class CTree contains number of rings corresponding to age.
3
4   Public Class CTree
5       Implements IAge
6
7       Private mRings As Integer
8
9       ' constructor receives planting date
10      Public Sub New(ByVal yearPlanted As Integer)
11
12          ' implicit call to Object constructor
13          mRings = Date.Now.Year - yearPlanted
14      End Sub ' New
15
16      ' increment mRings
17      Public Sub AddRing()
18          mRings += 1
19      End Sub ' AddRing
20
```

Fig. 7.17 **CTree** class implements **IAge** interface. (Part 1 of 2.)

```
21      ' property Age
22      ReadOnly Property Age() As Integer _
23         Implements IAge.Age
24
25         Get
26            Return mRings
27         End Get
28
29      End Property ' Age
30
31      ' property Name implementation of interface IAge
32      ReadOnly Property Name() As String _
33         Implements IAge.Name
34
35         Get
36            Return "Tree"
37         End Get
38
39      End Property ' Name
40
41   End Class ' CTree
```

Fig. 7.17 **CTree** class implements **IAge** interface. (Part 2 of 2.)

Class **CTest** (Fig. 7.18) demonstrates polymorphism on the objects of disparate classes **CPerson** and **CTree**. Line 11 instantiates object tree of class **CTree**, and line 12 instantiates object **person** of class **CPerson**. Line 15 declares **iAgeArray**—an array of two references to **IAge** objects. Line 18 and 21 assign **tree** and **person** to the first and second reference in **iAgeArray**, respectively. Lines 24–26 invoke method **ToString** on tree, then invoke its properties **Age** and **Name** to return age and name information for object **tree**. Lines 29–31 invoke method **ToString** on **person**, then invoke its properties **Age** and **Name** to return age and name information for object **person**. Next, we manipulate these objects polymorphically through the **iAgeArray** of references to **IAge** objects. Lines 36–39 define a **For-Each** structure that uses properties **Age** and **Name** to obtain age and name information for each **IAge** object in **iAgeArray**. Note that we use **Name** so that each object in **iAgeArray** can "identify" itself in our program's output. Objects **tree** and **person** can use method **ToString** to do this, because classes **CTree** and **CPerson** both inherit from class **Object**. However, when **CTest** interacts with these objects polymorphically, **CTest** can use only properties **Age** and **Name** for each interface object. Because interface **IAge** does not provide method **ToString**, clients cannot invoke method **ToString** through interface **IAge** references.

```
1   ' Fig. 7.18: Test.vb
2   ' Demonstrate polymorphism.
3
4   Imports System.Windows.Forms
5
6   Class CTest
7
```

Fig. 7.18 Demonstrate polymorphism on objects of disparate classes. (Part 1 of 2.)

```
8        Shared Sub Main()
9
10          ' instantiate CTree and CPerson objects
11          Dim tree As New CTree(1976)
12          Dim person As New CPerson("Bob", "Jones", 1983)
13
14          ' instantiate array of interface references
15          Dim iAgeArray As IAge() = New IAge(1){}
16
17          ' iAgeArray(0) references CTree object
18          iAgeArray(0) = tree
19
20          ' iAgeArray(1) references CPerson object
21          iAgeArray(1) = person
22
23          ' display tree information
24          Dim output As String = tree.ToString() & ": " & _
25             tree.Name & vbCrLf & "Age is " & tree.Age & vbCrLf & _
26             vbCrLf
27
28          ' display person information
29          output &= person.ToString() & ": " & _
30             person.Name & vbCrLf & "Age is " & person.Age & _
31             vbCrLf
32
33          Dim ageReference As IAge
34
35          ' display name and age for each IAge object in iAgeArray
36          For Each ageReference In iAgeArray
37             output &= vbCrLf & ageReference.Name & ": " & _
38                "Age is " & ageReference.Age
39          Next
40
41          MessageBox.Show(output, "Demonstrating Polymorphism")
42       End Sub ' Main
43
44    End Class ' CTest
```

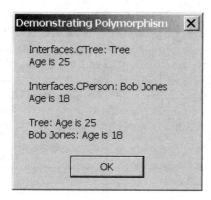

Fig. 7.18 Demonstrate polymorphism on objects of disparate classes. (Part 2 of 2.)

Our next example reexamines the **CPoint–CCircle–CCylinder** hierarchy using an interface, rather than using an abstract class, to describe the common methods and properties of the classes in the hierarchy. We now show how a class can implement an interface, then act as a base class for derived classes to inherit the implementation. We create interface **IShape** (Fig. 7.19), which specifies methods **Area** and **Volume** and property **Name** (lines 7–9). Every class that implements interface **IShape** must provide implementations for these two methods and this property. Note that, even though the methods in this interface do not receive arguments, interface methods can receive arguments (just as regular methods can).

Good Programming Practice 7.1

*By convention, begin the name of each interface with "**I**."*

Because class **CPoint3** (Fig. 7.20) implements interface **IShape**, class **CPoint3** must implement all three **IShape** members. Lines 55–59 implement method **Area**, which returns **0**, because points have an area of zero. Lines 62–66 implement method **Volume**, which also returns **0**, because points have a volume of zero. Lines 69–76 implement **ReadOnly** property **Name**, which returns the class name as a **String** (**"CPoint3"**). Note the inclusion of keyword **Implements** followed by the interface method/property name in these method/property implementations—this keyword informs the compiler that each method/property is an implementation of its corresponding interface method/property. Also note that class **CPoint3** specifies these methods/properties as **Overridable**, enabling derived classes to override them.

When a class implements an interface, the class enters the same kind of *is-a* relationship that inheritance establishes. In our example, class **CPoint3** implements interface **IShape**. Therefore, a **CPoint3** object *is an* **IShape**, and objects of any class that inherits from **CPoint3** are also **IShape**s. For example, class **CCircle3** (Fig. 7.21) inherits from class **CPoint3**; thus, a **CCircle3** *is an* **IShape**. Class **CCircle3** implements interface **IShape** implicitly, because class **CCircle3** inherits the **IShape** methods that class **CPoint** implemented. Because circles do not have volume, class **CCircle3** inherits class **CPoint3**'s **Volume** method, which returns zero. However, we do not want to use the class **CPoint3** method **Area** or property **Name** for class **CCircle3**. Class **CCircle3** should provide its own implementation for these, because the area and name of a circle differ from those of a point. Lines 51–53 override method **Area** to return the circle's area, and lines 56–62 override property **Name** to return **String "CCircle3"**.

Class **CCylinder3** (Fig. 7.22) inherits from class **CCircle3**. Class **CCylinder3** implements interface **IShape** implicitly, because class **CCylinder3** inherits method **Area** and property **Name** from class **CCircle3** and method **Volume** from class **CPoint3**. However, class **CCylinder3** overrides property **Name** and methods **Area** and **Volume** to perform **CCylinder3**-specific operations. Lines 43–45 override method **Area** to return the cylinder's surface area, lines 48–50 override method **Volume** to return the cylinder's volume and lines 58–64 override property **Name** to return **String "CCylinder3"**.

```
1    ' Fig. 7.19: Shape.vb
2    ' Interface IShape for Point, Circle, Cylinder hierarchy.
```

Fig. 7.19 **IShape** interface provides **Area**, **Volume** and **Name**. (Part 1 of 2.)

```
3
4   Public Interface IShape
5
6       ' classes that implement IShape must define these methods
7       Function Area() As Double
8       Function Volume() As Double
9       ReadOnly Property Name() As String
10
11   End Interface ' IShape
```

Fig. 7.19 **IShape** interface provides **Area**, **Volume** and **Name**. (Part 2 of 2.)

```
1   ' Fig. 7.20: Point3.vb
2   ' Class CPoint3 implements IShape.
3
4   Public Class CPoint3
5      Implements IShape
6
7      ' point coordinate
8      Private mX, mY As Integer
9
10     ' default constructor
11     Public Sub New()
12        X = 0
13        Y = 0
14     End Sub ' New
15
16     ' constructor
17     Public Sub New(ByVal xValue As Integer, _
18        ByVal yValue As Integer)
19        X = xValue
20        Y = yValue
21     End Sub ' New
22
23     ' property X
24     Public Property X() As Integer
25
26        Get
27           Return mX
28        End Get
29
30        Set(ByVal xValue As Integer)
31           mX = xValue ' no need for validation
32        End Set
33
34     End Property ' X
35
```

Fig. 7.20 **CPoint3** class implements interface **IShape**. (Part 1 of 2.)

```vb
36          ' property Y
37          Public Property Y() As Integer
38
39             Get
40                Return mY
41             End Get
42
43             Set(ByVal yValue As Integer)
44                mY = yValue ' no need for validation
45             End Set
46
47          End Property ' Y
48
49          ' return String representation of CPoint3
50          Public Overrides Function ToString() As String
51             Return "[" & mX & ", " & mY & "]"
52          End Function ' ToString
53
54          ' implement interface IShape method Area
55          Public Overridable Function Area() As Double _
56             Implements IShape.Area
57
58             Return 0
59          End Function ' Area
60
61          ' implement interface IShape method Volume
62          Public Overridable Function Volume() As Double _
63             Implements IShape.Volume
64
65             Return 0
66          End Function ' Volume
67
68          ' implement interface IShape property Name
69          Public Overridable ReadOnly Property Name() As String _
70             Implements IShape.Name
71
72             Get
73                Return "CPoint3"
74             End Get
75
76          End Property ' Name
77
78       End Class ' CPoint3
```

Fig. 7.20 **CPoint3** class implements interface **IShape**. (Part 2 of 2.)

```vb
1        ' Fig. 7.21: Circle3.vb
2        ' CCircle3 inherits CPoint3 and overrides some of its methods.
3
4        Public Class CCircle3
5           Inherits CPoint3 ' CCircle3 Inherits from class CPoint3
6
```

Fig. 7.21 **CCircle3** class inherits from class **CPoint3**. (Part 1 of 3.)

```
7        Private mRadius As Double
8
9        ' default constructor
10       Public Sub New()
11          Radius = 0
12       End Sub ' New
13
14       ' constructor
15       Public Sub New(ByVal xValue As Integer, _
16          ByVal yValue As Integer, ByVal radiusValue As Double)
17
18          ' use MyBase reference to CPoint constructor explicitly
19          MyBase.New(xValue, yValue)
20          Radius = radiusValue
21       End Sub ' New
22
23       ' property Radius
24       Public Property Radius() As Double
25
26          Get
27             Return mRadius
28          End Get
29
30          Set(ByVal radiusValue As Double)
31
32             If radiusValue >= 0
33                mRadius = radiusValue ' mRadius cannot be negative
34             End If
35
36          End Set
37
38       End Property ' Radius
39
40       ' calculate CCircle3 diameter
41       Public Function Diameter() As Double
42          Return mRadius * 2
43       End Function ' Diameter
44
45       ' calculate CCircle3 circumference
46       Public Function Circumference() As Double
47          Return Math.PI * Diameter()
48       End Function ' Circumference
49
50       ' calculate CCircle3 area
51       Public Overrides Function Area() As Double
52          Return Math.PI * mRadius ^ 2
53       End Function ' Area
54
55       ' override interface IShape property Name from class CPoint3
56       Public ReadOnly Overrides Property Name() As String
57
```

Fig. 7.21   CCircle3 class inherits from class CPoint3. (Part 2 of 3.)

```
58            Get
59                Return "CCircle3"
60            End Get
61
62       End Property ' Name
63
64       ' return String representation of CCircle3
65       Public Overrides Function ToString() As String
66
67          ' use MyBase to return CCircle3 String representation
68          Return "Center = " & MyBase.ToString() & _
69             "; Radius = " & mRadius
70       End Function ' ToString
71
72   End Class ' CCircle3
```

Fig. 7.21 **CCircle3** class inherits from class **CPoint3**. (Part 3 of 3.)

```
1    ' Fig. 7.22: Cylinder3.vb
2    ' CCylinder3 inherits from CCircle3 and overrides key members.
3
4    Public Class CCylinder3
5       Inherits CCircle3 ' CCylinder3 inherits from class CCircle3
6
7       Private mHeight As Double
8
9       ' default constructor
10      Public Sub New()
11         Height = 0
12      End Sub ' New
13
14      ' four-argument constructor
15      Public Sub New(ByVal xValue As Integer, _
16         ByVal yValue As Integer, ByVal radiusValue As Double, _
17         ByVal heightValue As Double)
18
19         ' explicit call to CCircle2 constructor
20         MyBase.New(xValue, yValue, radiusValue)
21         Height = heightValue ' set CCylinder2 height
22      End Sub ' New
23
24      ' property Height
25      Public Property Height() As Double
26
27         Get
28            Return mHeight
29         End Get
30
31         ' set CCylinder3 height if argument value is positive
32         Set(ByVal heightValue As Double)
33
```

Fig. 7.22 **CCylinder3** class inherits from class **CCircle3**. (Part 1 of 2.)

```
34                If heightValue >= 0 Then
35                    mHeight = heightValue
36                End If
37
38          End Set
39
40       End Property ' Height
41
42       ' override method Area to calculate CCylinder2 area
43       Public Overrides Function Area() As Double
44          Return 2 * MyBase.Area + MyBase.Circumference * mHeight
45       End Function ' Area
46
47       ' calculate CCylinder3 volume
48       Public Overrides Function Volume() As Double
49          Return MyBase.Area * mHeight
50       End Function ' Volume
51
52       ' convert CCylinder3 to String
53       Public Overrides Function ToString() As String
54          Return MyBase.ToString() & "; Height = " & mHeight
55       End Function ' ToString
56
57       ' override property Name from class CCircle3
58       Public Overrides ReadOnly Property Name() As String
59
60          Get
61             Return "CCylinder3"
62          End Get
63
64       End Property ' Name
65
66   End Class ' CCylinder3
```

Fig. 7.22 **CCylinder3** class inherits from class **CCircle3**. (Part 2 of 2.)

Class **CTest3** (Fig. 7.23) demonstrates our point-circle-cylinder hierarchy that uses interfaces. Class **CTest3** has only two differences from the version in Fig. 7.8, which tested the class hierarchy created from the **MustInherit** base class **CShape**. In Fig. 7.23, line 16 declares **arrayOfShapes** as an array of **IShape** interface references, rather than **CShape** base-class references. In Fig. 7.8, calls to method **ToString** were made through **CShape** base-class references—however, because interface **IShape** does not provide method **ToString**, clients cannot invoke method **ToString** on each **IShape** object.

Software Engineering Observation 7.10

In Visual Basic, an interface reference may invoke only those methods and/or properties that the interface declares.

In this example, interface **IShape** declares methods **Area** and **Volume** and property **Name**, but does not declare method **ToString**. Even though every reference refers to some type of **Object**, and every **Object** has method **ToString**, if we attempt to use

IShape interface references to invoke **ToString**, the compiler will generate the following syntax error:

> "ToString is not a member of InterfaceTest.IShape"

(where **InterfaceTest** is the assembly/namespace that contains interface **IShape**). Figure 7.8 was able to invoke method **ToString** through a **CShape** base-class reference, because class **CShape** inherited method **ToString** from base class **Object**. Note that the output of the program demonstrates that interface references can be used to perform polymorphic processing of objects that implement the interface.

Software Engineering Observation 7.11

*In Visual Basic, an interface provides only those **Public** services declared in the interface, whereas a **MustInherit** (abstract) class provides the **Public** services defined in the MustInherit class and those members inherited from the **MustInherit** class's base class.*

```
1   ' Fig. 7.23: Test3.vb
2   ' Demonstrate polymorphism in Point-Circle-Cylinder hierarchy.
3
4   Imports System.Windows.Forms
5
6   Class CTest3
7
8      Shared Sub Main()
9
10        ' instantiate CPoint3, CCircle3 and CCylinder3 objects
11        Dim point As New CPoint3(7, 11)
12        Dim circle As New CCircle3(22, 8, 3.5)
13        Dim cylinder As New CCylinder3(10, 10, 3.3, 10)
14
15        ' instantiate array of interface references
16        Dim arrayOfShapes As IShape() = New IShape(2){}
17
18        ' arrayOfShapes(0) references CPoint3 object
19        arrayOfShapes(0) = point
20
21        ' arrayOfShapes(1) references CCircle3 object
22        arrayOfShapes(1) = circle
23
24        ' arrayOfShapes(2) references CCylinder3 object
25        arrayOfShapes(2) = cylinder
26
27        Dim output As String = point.Name & ": " & _
28           point.ToString() & vbCrLf & circle.Name & ": " & _
29           circle.ToString() & vbCrLf & cylinder.Name & _
30           ": " & cylinder.ToString()
31
32        Dim shape As IShape
33
```

Fig. 7.23 **CTest3** uses interfaces to demonstrate polymorphism in Point-Circle-Cylinder hierarchy. (Part 1 of 2.)

```
34        ' display name, area and volume for each object in
35        ' arrayOfShapes
36        For Each shape In arrayOfShapes
37           output &= vbCrLf & vbCrLf & shape.Name & ": " & _
38              vbCrLf & "Area = " & _
39              String.Format("{0:F}", shape.Area()) & vbCrLf & _
40              "Volume = " & String.Format("{0:F}", shape.Volume())
41        Next
42
43        MessageBox.Show(output, "Demonstrating Polymorphism")
44     End Sub ' Main
45
46  End Class ' CTest3
```

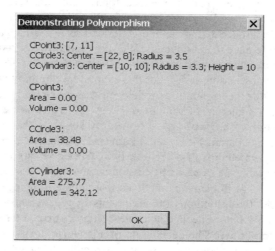

Fig. 7.23   **CTest3** uses interfaces to demonstrate polymorphism in Point-Circle-Cylinder hierarchy. (Part 2 of 2.)

7.10 Delegates

In Chapter 4, we discussed how objects can pass member variables as arguments to methods. However, sometimes it is beneficial for objects to pass methods as arguments to other methods. For example, suppose that you wish to sort a series of values in ascending and descending order. Rather than providing separate ascending and descending sorting methods (one for each type of comparison), we could use a single method that receives as an argument a reference to the comparison method to use. To perform an ascending sort, we could pass to the sorting method the reference to the ascending-sort-comparison method; to perform an descending sort, we could pass to the sorting method the reference to the descending-sort-comparison method. The sorting method then would use this reference to sort the list—the sorting method would not need to know whether it is performing an ascending or descending sort.

Visual Basic does not allow passing method references directly as arguments to other methods, but does provide *delegates*, which are classes that encapsulate a set of references to methods. A delegate object that contains method references can be passed to another method. Rather than send a method reference directly, an object can send the delegate instance, which contains the reference of the method that we would like to send. The method that receives the reference to the delegate then can invoke the methods the delegate contains.

Delegates containing a single method are known as *singlecast delegates* and are created or derived from class **Delegate**. Delegates containing multiple methods are *multicast delegates* and are created or derived from class **MulticastDelegate**. Both delegate classes belong to namespace **System**.

To use a delegate, we first must declare one. The delegate's declaration specifies a method signature (parameters and return value). Methods whose references will be contained within a delegate object, must have the same method signature as that defined in the delegate declaration. We then create methods that have this signature. The third step is to create a delegate instance via keyword **AddressOf**, which implicitly creates a delegate instance enclosing a reference to that method. After we create the delegate instance, we can invoke the method reference that it contains. We show this process in our next example.

Class **CDelegateBubbleSort** (Fig. 7.24) uses delegates to sort an **Integer** array in ascending or descending order. For this example we employ the bubble sort technique. Lines 7–9 provide the declaration for delegate **Comparator**. To declare a delegate (line 7), we declare a signature of a method—keyword **Delegate** after the member-access modifier (in this case, **Public**), followed by keyword **Function** (or keyword **Sub**), the delegate name, parameter list and return type. Delegate **Comparator** defines a method signature for methods that receive two **Integer** arguments and return a **Boolean**. Note that delegate **Comparator** contains no body. As we soon demonstrate, our application (Fig. 7.25) implements methods that adhere to delegate **Comparator**'s signature, then passes these methods (as arguments of type **Comparator**) to method **SortArray**. Note also that we declare delegate **Comparator** as a **Function**, because it returns a value (**Boolean**). The declaration of a delegate does not define its intended role or implementation; our application uses this particular delegate when *comparing* two **Integer**s, but other applications might use it for different purposes.

```
1    ' Fig. 7.24: DelegateBubbleSort.vb
2    ' Uses delegates to sort random numbers (ascending or descending).
3
4    Public Class CDelegateBubbleSort
5
6       ' delegate definition
7       Public Delegate Function Comparator( _
8          ByVal element1 As Integer, _
9          ByVal element2 As Integer) As Boolean
10
11      ' sort array depending on comparator
12      Public Sub SortArray(ByVal array As Integer(), _
13         ByVal Compare As Comparator)
14
15         Dim i, pass As Integer
16
```

Fig. 7.24 Bubble sort using delegates. (Part 1 of 2.)

```
17          For pass = 0 To array.GetUpperBound(0)
18
19              ' comparison inner loop
20              For i = 0 To array.GetUpperBound(0) - 1
21
22                  If Compare(array(i), array(i + 1)) Then
23                      Swap(array(i), array(i + 1))
24                  End If
25
26              Next ' inner loop
27
28          Next ' outer loop
29
30      End Sub ' SortArray
31
32      ' swap two elements
33      Private Sub Swap(ByRef firstElement As Integer, _
34          ByRef secondElement As Integer)
35
36          Dim hold As Integer
37
38          hold = firstElement
39          firstElement = secondElement
40          secondElement = hold
41      End Sub ' Swap
42
43  End Class ' CDelegateBubbleSort
```

Fig. 7.24 Bubble sort using delegates. (Part 2 of 2.)

Lines 12–30 define method **SortArray**, which takes an array and a reference to a **Comparator** delegate object as arguments. Method **SortArray** modifies the array by sorting its contents. Line 22 uses the delegate method to determine how to sort the array. Line 22 invokes the method enclosed within the delegate object by treating the delegate reference as the method that the delegate object contains. Visual Basic invokes the enclosed method reference directly, passing it parameters **array(i)** and **array(i+1)**. The **Comparator** determines the sorting order for its two arguments. If the **Comparator** returns **True**, the two elements are out of order, so line 23 invokes method **Swap** (lines 33–41) to swap the elements. If the **Comparator** returns **False**, the two elements are in the correct order. To sort in ascending order, the **Comparator** returns **True** when the first element being compared is greater than the second element being compared. Similarly, to sort in descending order, the **Comparator** returns **True** when the first element being compared is less than the second element being compared.

Class **CFrmBubbleSort** (Fig. 7.25) displays a **Form** with two text boxes and three buttons. The first text box displays a list of unsorted numbers, and the second box displays the same list of numbers after they are sorted. The **Create Data** button creates the list of unsorted values. The **Sort Ascending** and **Sort Descending** buttons sort the array in ascending and descending order, respectively. Methods **SortAscending** (lines 31–35) and **SortDescending** (lines 38–42) each have a signature that corresponds with the signature defined by the **Comparator** delegate declaration (i.e., each receives two **Integer**s and returns a *Boolean*). As we will see, the program passes to **CDelegateBubbleSort** method **SortArray** delegates containing references to methods **SortAscending** and **SortDescending**, which will specify class **CDelegateBubbleSort**'s sorting behavior.

```
1   ' Fig. 7.25: FrmBubbleSort.vb
2   ' Create GUI that enables user to sort array.
3
4   Imports System.Windows.Forms
5
6   Public Class CFrmBubbleSort
7      Inherits Form
8
9      ' TextBox that contains original list
10     Friend WithEvents txtOriginal As TextBox
11     Friend WithEvents lblOriginal As Label
12
13     ' TextBox that contains sorted list
14     Friend WithEvents txtSorted As TextBox
15     Friend WithEvents lblSorted As Label
16
17     ' Buttons for creating and sorting lists
18     Friend WithEvents cmdCreate As Button
19     Friend WithEvents cmdSortAscending As Button
20     Friend WithEvents cmdSortDescending As Button
21
22     ' Windows Form Designer generate code
23
24     ' reference to object containing delegate
25     Dim mBubbleSort As New CDelegateBubbleSort()
26
27     ' original array with unsorted elements
28     Dim mElementArray As Integer() = New Integer(9){}
29
30     ' delegate implementation sorts in asending order
31     Private Function SortAscending(ByVal element1 As Integer, _
32        ByVal element2 As Integer) As Boolean
33
34        Return element1 > element2
35     End Function ' SortAscending
36
37     ' delegate implementation sorts in descending order
38     Private Function SortDescending(ByVal element1 As Integer, _
39        ByVal element2 As Integer) As Boolean
40
41        Return element1 < element2
42     End Function ' SortDescending
43
44     ' creates random generated numbers
45     Private Sub cmdCreate_Click(ByVal sender As System.Object, _
46        ByVal e As System.EventArgs) Handles cmdCreate.Click
47
48        txtSorted.Clear()
```

Fig. 7.25 Bubble-sort **Form** application. (Part 1 of 3.)

```
49
50          Dim output As String
51          Dim randomNumber As Random = New Random()
52          Dim i As Integer
53
54          ' create String with 10 random numbers
55          For i = 0 To mElementArray.GetUpperBound(0)
56             mElementArray(i) = randomNumber.Next(100)
57             output &= mElementArray(i) & vbCrLf
58          Next
59
60          txtOriginal.Text = output ' display numbers
61
62          ' enable sort buttons
63          cmdSortAscending.Enabled = True
64          cmdSortDescending.Enabled = True
65       End Sub ' cmdCreate_Click
66
67    ' display array contents in specified TextBox
68    Private Sub DisplayResults()
69
70          Dim output As String
71          Dim i As Integer
72
73          ' create string with sorted numbers
74          For i = 0 To mElementArray.GetUpperBound(0)
75             output &= mElementArray(i) & vbCrLf
76          Next
77
78          txtSorted.Text = output ' display numbers
79           Sub ' DisplayResults
80
81    ' sorts randomly generated numbers in ascending manner
82    Private Sub cmdSortAscending_Click(ByVal sender As _
83          System.Object, ByVal e As System.EventArgs) _
84          Handles cmdSortAscending.Click
85
86          ' sort array
87          mBubbleSort.SortArray(mElementArray, AddressOf SortAscending)
88
89          DisplayResults() ' display results
90
91          cmdSortAscending.Enabled = False
92          cmdSortDescending.Enabled = True
93              ' cmdSortAscending_Click
94
95    ' sorts randomly generated numbers in descending manner
96              cmdSortDescending_Click(ByVal sender As _
97          System.Object, ByVal e As System.EventArgs) _
98          Handles cmdSortDescending.Click
99
100         ' create sort object and sort array
101         mBubbleSort.SortArray(mElementArray, AddressOf SortDescending)
```

Fig. 7.25 Bubble-sort **Form** application. (Part 2 of 3.)

```
102
103          DisplayResults()  ' display results
104
105          cmdSortDescending.Enabled = False
106          cmdSortAscending.Enabled = True
107       End Sub ' cmdSortDescending_Click
108
109    End Class ' CFrmBubbleSort
```

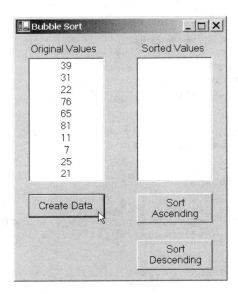

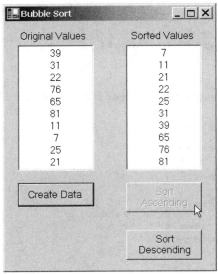

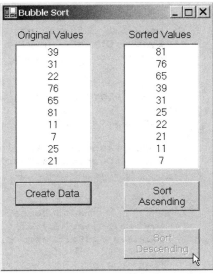

Fig. 7.25   Bubble-sort **Form** application. (Part 3 of 3.)

Methods **cmdSortAscending_Click** (lines 82–93) and **cmdSort-Descending_Click** (lines 96–107) are invoked when the user clicks the **Sort Ascending** and **Sort Descending** buttons, respectively. In method **cmdSortAscending_Click**, line 87 passes to **CDelegateBubbleSort** method **SortArray** the unsorted **mElementArray** and a reference to method **SortAscending**. Keyword **AddressOf** returns a reference to method **SortAscending**. Visual Basic implicitly converts the method reference into a delegate object that contains the method reference. The second argument of line 87 is equivalent to

New **CDelegateBubbleSort.Comparator(***AddressOf* **SortAscending)**

which explicitly creates a **CDelegateBubbleSort Comparator** delegate object. In method **cmdSortDescending_Click**, line 101 passes the unsorted **mElementArray** and a reference to method **SortDescending** to method **SortArray**. We continue to use delegates in Chapters 9–11, when we discuss event handling and multithreading.

In Chapter 8, Exception Handling, we discuss how to handle problems that might occur during a program's execution. The features presented in Chapter 8 enable programmers to write more robust and fault-tolerant programs.

7.11 Summary

Polymorphism enables programmers to write programs in a general fashion to handle a wide variety of existing and future related classes. One means of processing objects of many different types is to use a **Select Case** statement to perform an appropriate action on each object, based on the object's type. Polymorphic programming can eliminate the need for such **Select Case** logic.

Polymorphism allows one method call to perform different actions, depending on the type of the object receiving the call. The same message assumes "many forms"—hence the term polymorphism. With polymorphism, the programmer can deal in generalities and let the executing program manage the specifics.

Abstract classes, which are declared with keyword **MustInherit**, define common behavior for an inheritance hierarchy. When we apply the **MustInherit** keyword to a class, we cannot create instances of that class. Instead, we create classes that inherit from the **MustInherit** class and create instances of those derived classes. Although we cannot instantiate objects of **MustInherit** base classes, we can declare references to **MustInherit** base classes. Such references can manipulate instances of the derived classes polymorphically.

A class declared **NotInheritable** cannot be a base class and therefore represents the end of the inheritance hierarchy.

Delegates are classes that encapsulate a set of references to methods. Delegates facilitate polymorphism by enabling the programmer to specify calls to methods that will not be defined until later.

Exception Handling

Objectives

- To understand exceptions and error handling.
- To use **Try** blocks to delimit code in which
  exceptions might occur.
- To **Throw** exceptions.
- To use **Catch** blocks to specify exception handlers.
- To use the **Finally** block to release resources.
- To understand the Visual Basic exception class
  hierarchy.
- To create programmer-defined exceptions.

*It is common sense to take a method and try it. If it fails,
admit it frankly and try another. But above all, try something.*
Franklin Delano Roosevelt

*O! throw away the worser part of it,
And live the purer with the other half.*
William Shakespeare

*If they're running and they don't look where they're going
I have to come out from somewhere and catch them.*
Jerome David Salinger

*And oftentimes excusing of a fault
Doth make the fault the worse by the excuse.*
William Shakespeare

I never forget a face, but in your case I'll make an exception.
Groucho (Julius Henry) Marx

Outline

8.1 Introduction

In this chapter, we introduce *exception handling*. An *exception* is an indication of a problem that occurs during a program's execution. The name "exception" comes from the fact that, although the problem can occur, it occurs infrequently. If the "rule" is that a statement normally executes correctly, then the occurrence of the problem represents the "exception to the rule." Exception handling enables programmers to create applications that can resolve (or handle) exceptions. In many cases, the handling of an exception allows a program to continue executing as if no problems were encountered. However, more severe problems might prevent a program from continuing normal execution, instead requiring the program to notify the user of the problem and then terminate in a controlled manner. The features presented in this chapter enable programmers to write clear, robust and more *fault-tolerant programs*.

The style and details of exception handling in Visual Basic .NET are based in part on the work of Andrew Koenig and Bjarne Stroustrup, as presented in their paper, "Exception Handling for C++ (revised)."[1] Visual Basic's designers implemented an exception-handling mechanism similar to that used in C++, using Koenig's and Stroustrup's work as a model.

This chapter begins with an overview of exception-handling concepts and demonstrations of basic exception-handling techniques. The chapter also offers an overview of the exception-handling class hierarchy. Programs typically request and release resources (such as files on disk) during program execution. Often, the supply of these resources is limited, or the resources can be used by only one program at a time. We demonstrate a part of the exception-handling mechanism that enables a program to use a resource and then guarantees that the program releases the resource for use by other programs. The chapter continues with an example that demonstrates several properties of class `System.Exception` (the base class of all exception classes); this is followed by an example that shows programmers how to create and use their own exception classes. The chapter concludes with a practical application of exception handling, in which a program handles exceptions generated by arithmetic calculations that result in out-of-range values for a particular data type—a condition known as *arithmetic overflow*.

---

1. Koenig, A. and B. Stroustrup, "Exception Handling for C++ (revised)", *Proceedings of the Usenix C++ Conference*, 149–176, San Francisco, April 1990.

8.2 Exception Handling Overview

The logic of a program frequently tests conditions that determine how program execution proceeds. Consider the following pseudocode:

Perform a task

If the preceding task did not execute correctly
     Perform error processing

Perform next task

If the preceding task did not execute correctly
     Perform error processing

...

In this pseudocode, we begin by performing a task. We then test whether that task executed correctly. If not, we perform error processing. Otherwise, we continue on to the next task and start the entire process again. Although this form of error handling works, the intermixing of program logic with error-handling logic can make the program difficult to read, modify, maintain and debug. This is especially true in large applications. In fact, if many of the potential problems occur infrequently, the intermixing of program logic and error handling can degrade the performance of the program, because the program must test extra conditions to determine whether the next task can be performed.

Exception handling enables the programmer to remove error-handling code from the "main line" of the program's execution. This improves program clarity and enhances modifiability. Programmers can decide to handle whatever exceptions arise—all types of exceptions, all exceptions of a certain type or all exceptions of a group of related types. Such flexibility reduces the likelihood that errors will be overlooked, thereby increasing a program's robustness.

Testing and Debugging Tip 8.1

Exception handling helps improve a program's fault tolerance. If it is easy to write error-processing code, programmers are more likely to use it.

Software Engineering Observation 8.1

Although it is possible to do so, do not use exceptions for conventional flow of control. It is difficult to keep track of a large number of exception cases, and programs with a large number of exception cases are hard to read and maintain.

Good Programming Practice 8.1

Avoid using exception handling for purposes other than error handling, because such usage can reduce program clarity.

When using programming languages that do not support exception handling, programmers often postpone the writing of error-processing code and sometimes forget to include it. This results in less robust software products. Visual Basic enables the programmer to deal with exception handling in a convenient manner from the inception of a project. However, the programmer still must put considerable effort into incorporating an exception-handling strategy into software projects.

Software Engineering Observation 8.2

Try to incorporate an exception-handling strategy into a system from the inception of the design process. It can be difficult to add effective exception handling to a system after it has been implemented.

Software Engineering Observation 8.3

In the past, programmers used many techniques to implement error-processing code. Exception handling provides a single, uniform technique for processing errors. This helps programmers working on large projects to understand each other's error-processing code.

The exception-handling mechanism also is useful for processing problems that occur when a program interacts with software elements, such as methods, properties, assemblies and classes. Rather than handling all problems internally, such software elements often use exceptions to notify programs when problems occur. This enables programmers to implement error handling customized for each application.

Common Programming Error 8.1

Aborting a program could leave a resource—such as file stream or I/O device—in a state that causes the resource to be unavailable to other programs. This is known as a "resource leak."

Performance Tip 8.1

When no exceptions occur, exception-handling code does not hinder the program's performance. Thus, programs that implement exception handling operate more efficiently than do programs that perform error handling throughout the program logic.

Performance Tip 8.2

Exception-handling should be used only for problems that occur infrequently. As a "rule of thumb," if a problem occurs at least 30 percent of the time when a particular statement executes, the program should test for the error inline, because the overhead of exception handling will cause the program to execute more slowly.[2]

Software Engineering Observation 8.4

*Methods with common error conditions should return **Nothing** (or another appropriate value), rather than throwing exceptions. A program calling such a method can check the return value to determine the success or failure of the method call.[3]*

A complex application normally consists of predefined software components (such as those defined in the .NET Framework) and components specific to the application that uses the predefined components. When a predefined component encounters a problem, that component must have a mechanism by which it can communicate the problem to the application-specific component. This is because the predefined component cannot know in advance how a specific application will process a problem that occurs. Exception handling facilitates efficient collaboration between software components by enabling predefined components to communicate the occurrence of problems to application-specific components, which then can process the problems in an application-specific manner.

---

2. "Best Practices for Handling Exceptions [Visual Basic]," *.NET Framework Developer's Guide*, Visual Studio .NET Online Help.
3. "Best Practices for Handling Exceptions [Visual Basic]."

Exception handling is designed to process *synchronous errors*—errors that occur during the normal flow of program control. Common examples of these errors are out-of-range array subscripts, arithmetic overflow (i.e., the occurrence of a value that is outside the representable range of values), division by zero for integral types, invalid method parameters and running out of available memory. Exception handling is not designed to process *asynchronous* events, such as disk-I/O completions, network-message arrivals, mouse clicks and keystrokes.

Exception handling is geared toward situations in which the method that detects an error is unable to handle it. Such a method *throws an exception*. There is no guarantee that the program contains an *exception handler*—code that executes when the program detects an exception—to process that kind of exception. If an appropriate exception handler exists, the exception will be *caught* and *handled*. The result of an *uncaught exception* is dependant on whether the program is executing in debug mode or standard execution mode. In debug mode, when the runtime environment detects an uncaught exception, a dialog appears that enables the programmer to view the problem in the debugger or to continue program execution by ignoring the problem. In standard execution mode, a Windows application presents a dialog that allows the user to continue or terminate program execution. A console application presents a dialog that enables the user to open the program in the debugger or terminate program execution.

Visual Basic .NET uses **Try** *blocks* to enable exception handling. A **Try** block consists of keyword **Try**, followed by a block of code in which exceptions might occur. The **Try** block encloses statements that could cause exceptions and statements that should not execute if an exception occurs. Immediately following the **Try** block are zero or more **Catch** *blocks* (also called **Catch** *handlers*). Each **Catch** block specifies an exception parameter representing the type of exception that the **Catch** block can handle. If an exception parameter includes an optional parameter name, the **Catch** handler can use that parameter name to interact with a caught exception object. Optionally, programmers can include a *parameterless* **Catch** *block* that catches all exception types. After the last **Catch** block, an optional **Finally** *block* contains code that always executes, regardless of whether an exception occurs.

When a method called in a program detects an exception, or when the Common Language Runtime (CLR) detects a problem, the method or CLR *throws an exception*. The point in the program at which an exception occurs is called the *throw point*—an important location for debugging purposes (as we demonstrate in Section 8.6). Exceptions are objects of classes that extend class **Exception** of namespace **System**. If an exception occurs in a **Try** block, the **Try** block *expires* (i.e., terminates immediately), and program control transfers to the first **Catch** handler (if there is one) following the **Try** block. Visual Basic is said to use the *termination model of exception handling*, because the **Try** block enclosing a thrown exception expires immediately when that exception occurs.[4] As with any other block of code, when a **Try** block terminates, local variables defined in the block go out of scope. Next, the CLR searches for the first **Catch** handler that can process the type of exception that occurred. The CLR locates the matching **Catch** by comparing the thrown exception's type to each **Catch**'s exception-parameter type. A match occurs if the types

---

4. Some languages use the *resumption model of exception handling* in which, after handling the exception, control returns to the point at which the exception was thrown and execution resumes from that point.

are identical or if the thrown exception's type is a derived class of the exception-parameter type. Once an exception is matched to a **Catch** handler, the other **Catch** handlers are ignored.

Testing and Debugging Tip 8.2

If several handlers match the type of an exception, and if each of these handles the exception differently, then the order of the handlers will affect the manner in which the exception is handled.

Common Programming Error 8.2

It is a logic error if a catch that catches a base-class object is placed before a catch for that class's derived-class types.

If no exceptions occur in a **Try** block, the CLR ignores the exception handlers for that block. Program execution continues with the next statement after the **Try/Catch** sequence, regardless of whether an exception occurs. If an exception that occurs in a **Try** block has no matching **Catch** handler, or if an exception occurs in a statement that is not in a **Try** block, the method containing that statement terminates immediately, and the CLR attempts to locate an enclosing **Try** block in a calling method. This process is called *stack unwinding* and is discussed in Section 8.6.

8.3 Example: `DivideByZeroException`

Let us consider a simple example of exception handling. The application in Fig. 8.1 uses **Try** and **Catch** to specify a block of code that might throw exceptions and to handle those exceptions if they occur. The application displays two **TextBox**es in which the user can type integers. When the user presses the **Click to Divide** button, the program invokes **cmdDivide_Click** (lines 25–61), which obtains the user's input, converts the input values to type **Integer** and divides the first number (**numerator**) by the second number (**denominator**). Assuming that the user provides integers as input and does not specify **0** as the denominator for the division, **cmdDivide_Click** displays the division result in **lblOutput**. However, if the user inputs a non-integer value or supplies **0** as the denominator, exceptions occur. This program demonstrates how to catch such exceptions.

Before we discuss the details of this program, let us consider the sample output windows in Fig. 8.1. The first window shows a successful calculation, in which the user inputs the numerator **100** and the denominator **7**. Note that the result (**14**) is an **Integer**, because **Integer** division always yields an **Integer** result. The next two windows depict the result of inputting a non-**Integer** value—in this case, the user entered **"hello"** in the second **TextBox**. When the user presses **Click to Divide**, the program attempts to convert the input **String**s into **Integer** values using method **Convert.ToInt32**. If an argument passed to **Convert.ToInt32** does not represent an integer value, the method generates a *FormatException* (namespace **System**). The program detects the exception and displays an error message dialog, indicating that the user must enter two **Integers**. The last two output windows demonstrate the result after an attempt to divide by zero. In integer arithmetic, the CLR tests for division by zero and generates a *DivideByZeroException* (namespace **System**) if the denominator is zero.

The program detects the exception and displays an error message dialog, indicating that an attempt has been made to divide by zero.[5]

```vb
1    ' Fig. 8.1: DivideByZeroTest.vb
2    ' Basics of Visual Basic exception handling.
3
4    Imports System.Windows.Forms.Form
5
6    Public Class FrmDivideByZero
7       Inherits Form
8
9       ' Label and TextBox for specifying numerator
10      Friend WithEvents lblNumerator As Label
11      Friend WithEvents txtNumerator As TextBox
12
13      ' Label and TextBox for specifying denominator
14      Friend WithEvents lblDenominator As Label
15      Friend WithEvents txtDenominator As TextBox
16
17      ' Button for dividing numerator by denominator
18      Friend WithEvents cmdDivide As Button
19
20      Friend WithEvents lblOutput As Label ' output for division
21
22      ' Visual Studio .NET generated code
23
24      ' obtain integers from user and divide numerator by denominator
25      Private Sub cmdDivide_Click(ByVal sender As System.Object, _
26         ByVal e As System.EventArgs) Handles cmdDivide.Click
27
28         lblOutput.Text = ""
29
30         ' retrieve user input and call Quotient
31         Try
32
33            ' Convert.ToInt32 generates FormatException if argument
34            ' is not an integer
35            Dim numerator As Integer = _
36               Convert.ToInt32(txtNumerator.Text)
37
38            Dim denominator As Integer = _
39               Convert.ToInt32(txtDenominator.Text)
```

Fig. 8.1   Exception handlers for **FormatException** and **DivideByZeroException**. (Part 1 of 2.)

---

5. The CLR allows floating-point division by zero, which produces a positive or negative infinity result, depending on whether the numerator is positive or negative. Dividing zero by zero is a special case that results in a value called "not a number." Programs can test for these results using constants for positive infinity (**PositiveInfinity**), negative infinity (**NegativeInfinity**) and not a number (**NaN**) that are defined in type **Double** (for **Double** calculations) and **Single** (for floating-point calculations).

```
40
41              ' division generates DivideByZeroException if
42              ' denominator is 0
43              Dim result As Integer = numerator \ denominator
44
45              lblOutput.Text = result.ToString()
46
47          ' process invalid number format
48          Catch formatExceptionParameter As FormatException
49              MessageBox.Show("You must enter two integers", _
50                  "Invalid Number Format", MessageBoxButtons.OK, _
51                  MessageBoxIcon.Error)
52
53          ' user attempted to divide by zero
54          Catch divideByZeroExceptionParameter As DivideByZeroException
55              MessageBox.Show(divideByZeroExceptionParameter.Message, _
56                  "Attempted to Divide by Zero", _
57                  MessageBoxButtons.OK, MessageBoxIcon.Error)
58
59          End Try
60
61      End Sub ' cmdDivide_Click
62
63  End Class ' FrmDivideByZero
```

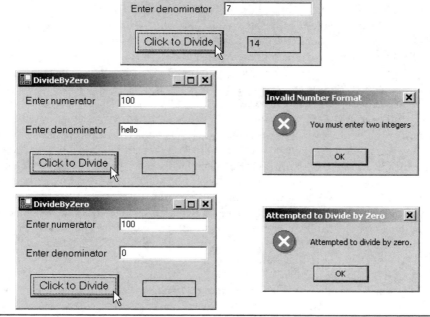

Fig. 8.1   Exception handlers for **FormatException** and
DivideByZeroException. (Part 2 of 2.)

Now, we consider the user interactions and flow of control that yield the results shown in the sample output windows. The user inputs values into the **TextBox**es that represent the numerator and denominator and then presses **Click to Divide**. At this point, the program invokes method **cmdDivide_Click**. Line 28 assigns the empty **String** to **lblOutput** to clear any prior result, because the program is about to attempt a new calculation. Lines 31–59 define a **Try** block enclosing the code that might throw exceptions, as well as the code that should not execute if an exception occurs. For example, the program should not display a new result in **lblOutput** (line 45) unless the calculation (line 43) completes successfully. Remember that the **Try** block terminates immediately if an exception occurs, so the remaining code in the **Try** block will not execute.

Software Engineering Observation 8.5

*Enclose in a **Try** block a significant logical section of the program in which several statements can throw exceptions, rather than using a separate **Try** block for every statement that might throw an exception. However, each **Try** block should enclose a small enough section of code such that when an exception occurs, the specific context is known, and the **Catch** handlers can process the exception properly.*

The two statements that read the **Integer**s from the **TextBox**es (lines 35–39) call method **Convert.ToInt32** to convert **String**s to **Integer** values. This method throws a **FormatException** if it cannot convert its **String** argument to an **Integer**. If lines 35–39 convert the values properly (i.e., no exceptions occur), then line 43 divides the **numerator** by the **denominator** and assigns the result to variable **result**. If the denominator is zero, line 43 causes the CLR to throw a **DivideByZeroException**. If line 43 does not cause an exception to be thrown, then line 45 displays the result of the division. If no exceptions occur in the **Try** block, the program successfully completes the **Try** block by ignoring the **Catch** handlers at lines 48–51 and 54–57 and reaching line 59. Then, the program executes the first statement following the **Try/Catch** sequence. In this example, the program reaches the end of event handler **cmdDivide_Click** (line 61), so the method terminates, and the program awaits the next user interaction.

Immediately following the **Try** block are two **Catch** handlers. Lines 48–51 define the **Catch** handler for a **FormatException**, and lines 54–57 define the **Catch** handler for the **DivideByZeroException**. Each **Catch** handler begins with keyword **Catch**, followed by an exception parameter that specifies the type of exception handled by the **Catch** block. The exception-handling code appears in the **Catch**-handler body. In general, when an exception occurs in a **Try** block, a **Catch** block catches the exception and handles it. In Fig. 8.1, the first **Catch** handler specifies that it catches **FormatException**s (thrown by method **Convert.ToInt32**), and the second **Catch** block specifies that it catches **DivideByZeroException**s (thrown by the CLR). If an exception occurs, the program executes only the matching **Catch** handler. Both the exception handlers in this example display an error message dialog. When program control reaches the end of a **Catch** handler, the program considers the exception to be handled, and program control continues with the first statement after the **Try/Catch** sequence (the end of the method, in this example).

In the second sample output, the user input **hello** as the denominator. When lines 38–39 execute, **Convert.ToInt32** cannot convert this **String** to an **Integer**, so **Convert.ToInt32** creates a **FormatException** object and throws it to indicate that the method was unable to convert the **String** to an **Integer**. When the exception occurs, the **Try** block expires (terminates). Any local variables defined in the **Try** block go out of scope; therefore, those variables are not available to the exception handlers. Next, the CLR attempts to locate a matching **Catch** handler. Starting with the **Catch** in line 48, the program compares the type of the thrown exception (**FormatException**) with the exception type in the **Catch**-block declaration (also **FormatException**). A match occurs, so the exception handler executes, and the program ignores all other exception handlers following the **Try** block. If a match did not occur, the program would compare the type of the thrown exception with the next **Catch** handler in sequence, repeating this process until a match is found.

Common Programming Error 8.3

*An attempt to access a **Try** block's local variables in one of that **Try** block's associated **Catch** handlers is a syntax error. Before a corresponding **Catch** handler can execute, the **Try** block expires, and its local variables go out of scope.*

Common Programming Error 8.4

*Specifying a comma-separated list of exception parameters in a **Catch** handler is a syntax error. Each **Catch** handler can have at most one exception parameter.*

In the third sample output, the user inputs **0** as the denominator. When line 43 executes, the CLR throws a **DivideByZeroException** object to indicate the occurrence of an attempt to divide by zero. Once again, the **Try** block terminates immediately upon encountering the exception, and the program attempts to locate a matching **Catch** handler. Starting from the **Catch** handler in line 48, the program compares the type of the thrown exception (**DivideByZeroException**) with the exception type in the **Catch**-handler declaration (**FormatException**). In this case, the first **Catch** handler does not produce a match. This is because the exception type in the **Catch**-handler declaration is not the same as the type of the thrown exception, and **FormatException** is not a base class of **DivideByZeroException**. Therefore, the program proceeds to line 54 and compares the type of the thrown exception (**DivideByZeroException**) with the exception type in the **Catch**-handler declaration (**DivideByZeroException**). A match occurs, which causes that exception handler to execute, using property *Message* of class **Exception** to display the error message. If there were additional **Catch** handlers, the program would ignore them.

8.4 .NET **Exception** Hierarchy

The exception-handling mechanism allows only objects of class **Exception** and its derived classes to be thrown and caught. This section overviews several of the .NET Framework's exception classes. In addition, we discuss how to determine whether a particular method throws exceptions.

Class **Exception** of namespace **System** is the base class of the .NET Framework exception hierarchy. Two of the most important classes derived from **Exception** are *ApplicationException* and *SystemException*. ApplicationException is a base class that programmers can extend to create exception data types that are specific to their applications. We discuss the creation of programmer-defined exception classes in Section 8.7. Programs can recover from most **ApplicationException**s and continue execution.

The CLR generates **SystemException**s, which can occur at any point during the execution of the program. Many of these exceptions can be avoided if applications are coded properly. These are called *runtime exceptions*. Runtime exceptions are are derived from class *SystemException*. For example, if a program attempts to access an out-of-range array subscript, the CLR throws an exception of type **IndexOutOfRangeException** (a derived class of **SystemException**). Similarly, a runtime exception occurs when a program uses an object reference to manipulate an object that does not yet exist (i.e., the reference has a **Nothing** value). Attempting to use a **Nothing** reference causes a *NullReferenceException* (another derived class of **SystemException**). According to Microsoft's "Best Practices for Handling Exceptions [Visual Basic],"[6] programs typically cannot recover from most exceptions that the CLR throws. Therefore, programs generally should not throw or catch **SystemException**s. [*Note:* For a complete list of the derived classes of **Exception**, search for "**Exception** class" in the **Index** of the Visual Studio .NET online documentation.]

A benefit of using the exception class hierarchy is that a **Catch** handler can catch exceptions of a particular type or can use a base-class type to catch exceptions in a hierarchy of related exception types. For example, Section 8.2 discussed the parameterless **Catch** handler, which catches exceptions of all types. A **Catch** handler that specifies an exception parameter of type **Exception** also can catch all exceptions, because **Exception** is the base class of all exception classes. The advantage of using this approach is that the exception handler can use the exception parameter to access the information of the caught exception.

The use of inheritance with exceptions enables an exception handler to catch related exceptions using a concise notation. An exception handler certainly could catch each derived-class exception type individually, but catching the base-class exception type is more concise. However, this makes sense only if the handling behavior is the same for a base class and all derived classes. Otherwise, catch each derived-class exception individually.

We know that many different exception types exist and we also know that methods, properties and the CLR can throw exceptions. But, how do we determine that an exception might occur in a program? For methods contained in the .NET Framework classes, programmers can investigate the detailed description of the methods in the online documentation. If a method throws an exception, its description contains a section called **Exceptions** that specifies the types of exceptions thrown by the method and briefly describes potential causes for the exceptions. For example, search for "**Convert.ToInt32** method" in the **Index** of the Visual Studio .NET online documentation. In the document that describes the method, click the link **Overloads Public Shared Function ToInt32(String) As Integer**. In the document that appears, the **Exceptions** section indicates that method **Convert.ToInt32** throws three exception types—**ArgumentException**, **FormatException** and **OverflowException**—and describes the reason why each exception type might occur.

Software Engineering Observation 8.6

*If a method throws exceptions, statements that invoke the method should be placed in **Try** blocks, and those exceptions should be caught and handled.*

---

6. "Best Practices for Handling Exceptions [Visual Basic]," *.NET Framework Developer's Guide*, Visual Studio .NET Online Help.

It is more difficult to determine when the CLR throws exceptions. Typically, such information appears in the *Visual Basic Language Specification*, which is located in the online documentation. To access the language specification, select **Help > Contents...** in Visual Studio. In the **Contents** dialogue, expand **Visual Studio .NET**, **Visual Basic and Visual C#**, **Reference**, **Visual Basic Language** and **Visual Basic .NET Language Specification**.

The language specification defines the syntax of the language and specifies cases in which exceptions are thrown. For example, in Fig. 8.1, we demonstrated that the CLR throws a **DivideByZeroException** when a program attempts to divide by zero in integer arithmetic. Section 10.5.4 of the language specification discusses the division operator. In this section, programmers find a detailed analysis of when a **DivideByZeroException** occurs.

8.5 **Finally** Block

Programs frequently request and release resources dynamically (i.e., at execution time). For example, a program that reads a file from disk first requests to open that file. If that request succeeds, the program reads the contents of the file. Operating systems typically prevent more than one program from manipulating a file at once. Therefore, when a program finishes processing a file, the program normally closes the file (i.e., releases the resource). This enables other programs to use the file. Closing the file helps prevent a *resource leak*; this occurs when the file resource is not available to other programs, because a program using the file never closed it. Programs that obtain certain types of resources (such as files) must return those resources explicitly to the system to avoid resource leaks.

In programming languages such as C and C++, in which the programmer is responsible for dynamic memory management, the most common type of resource leak is a *memory leak*. A memory leak occurs when a program allocates memory (as Visual Basic programmers do via keyword **New**), but does not deallocate the memory when the memory is no longer needed in the program. Normally, this is not an issue in Visual Basic, because the CLR performs "garbage collection" of memory that is no longer needed by an executing program. However, other kinds of resource leaks (such as the unclosed files that we mentioned previously) can occur in Visual Basic.

Testing and Debugging Tip 8.3

The CLR does not eliminate memory leaks completely. The CLR will not garbage collect an object until the program contains no more references to that object. Thus, memory leaks can occur if programmers erroneously keep references to unwanted objects.

Potential exceptions are associated with the processing of most resources that require explicit release. For example, a program that processes a file might receive **IOException**s during the processing. For this reason, file-processing code normally appears in a **Try** block. Regardless of whether a program successfully processes a file, the program should close the file when the file is no longer needed. Suppose a program places all resource-request and resource-release code in a **Try** block. If no exceptions occur, the **Try** block executes normally and releases the resources after using them. However, if an exception occurs, the **Try** block may expire before the resource-release code can execute. We could duplicate all resource-release code in the **Catch** handlers, but this would make the code more difficult to modify and maintain.

To address this problem, Visual Basic's exception handling mechanism provides the **Finally** block, which is guaranteed to execute if program control enters the corresponding **Try** block. The **Finally** block executes regardless of whether that **Try** block executes successfully or an exception occurs. This guarantee makes the **Finally** block an ideal location in which to place resource deallocation code for resources that are acquired and manipulated in the corresponding **Try** block. If the **Try** block executes successfully, the **Finally** block executes immediately after the **Try** block terminates. If an exception occurs in the **Try** block, the **Finally** block executes immediately after a **Catch** handler completes. If the exception is not caught by a **Catch** handler associated with that **Try** block, or if a **Catch** handler associated with that **Try** block throws an exception, the **Finally** block executes before the exception is processed by the next enclosing **Try** block (if there is one).

Testing and Debugging Tip 8.4

*A **Finally** block typically contains code to release resources acquired in the corresponding **Try** block; this makes the **Finally** block an effective way to eliminate resource leaks.*

Testing and Debugging Tip 8.5

*The only reason that a **Finally** block will not execute if program control enters the corresponding **Try** block is if the application terminates before **Finally** can execute.*

Performance Tip 8.3

As a rule, resources should be released as soon as it is apparent that they are no longer needed in a program. This makes the resources available for reuse, thus enhancing resource utilization in the program.

If one or more **Catch** handlers follow a **Try** block, the **Finally** block is optional. However, if no **Catch** handlers follow a **Try** block, a **Finally** block must appear immediately after the **Try** block. If any **Catch** handlers follow a **Try** block, the **Finally** block appears after the last **Catch** handler. Only whitespace and comments can separate the blocks in a **Try/Catch/Finally** sequence.

Common Programming Error 8.5

*Placing the **Finally** block before a **Catch** handler is a syntax error.*

The Visual Basic application in Fig. 8.2 demonstrates that the **Finally** block always executes, regardless of whether an exception occurs in the corresponding **Try** block. The program consists of method **Main** (lines 8–52) and four other **Shared** methods that **Main** invokes to demonstrate **Finally**. These methods are **DoesNotThrowException** (lines 55–73), **ThrowExceptionWithCatch** (lines 76–97), **ThrowException-WithoutCatch** (lines 100–118) and **ThrowExceptionCatchRethrow** (lines 121–149). [*Note:* We use **Shared** methods in this example so that **Main** can invoke these methods directly, without creating **CUsingExceptions** objects. This enables us to focus on the mechanics of the **Try/Catch/Finally** sequence.]

Line 12 of **Main** invokes method **DoesNotThrowException** (lines 55–73). The **Try** block (lines 58–70) for this method begins by outputting a message (line 59). Because the **Try** block does not throw any exceptions, program control ignores the **Catch** handler (lines 62–63) and executes the **Finally** block (lines 66–68), which outputs a message. At this point, program control continues with the first statement after the **End Try** statement (line 72), which outputs a message indicating that the end of the method has been reached. Then, program control returns to **Main**.

Line 18 of **Main** invokes method **ThrowExceptionWithCatch** (lines 76–97); which begins in its **Try** block (lines 79–94) by outputting a message. Next, the **Try** block creates an **Exception** object and uses a ***Throw*** *statement* to throw the exception object (lines 82–83). The **String** passed to the constructor becomes the exception object's error message. When a **Throw** statement in a **Try** block executes, the **Try** block expires immediately, and program control continues at the first **Catch** (lines 86–87) following the **Try** block. In this example, the type thrown (**Exception**) matches the type specified in the **Catch**, so line 87 outputs a message indicating the type of exception that occurred. Then, the **Finally** block (lines 90–92) executes and outputs a message. At this point, program control continues with the first statement after the **End Try** statement (line 96), which outputs a message indicating that the end of the method has been reached. Program control then returns to **Main**. In line 87, note that we use the exception object's ***Message*** *property* to retrieve the error message associated with the exception (i.e., the message passed to the **Exception** constructor). Section 8.6 discusses several properties of class **Exception**.

Lines 26–34 of **Main** define a **Try** block in which **Main** invokes method **ThrowExceptionWithoutCatch** (lines 100–118). The **Try** block enables **Main** to catch any exceptions thrown by **ThrowExceptionWithoutCatch**. The **Try** block in lines 103–114 of **ThrowExceptionWithoutCatch** begins by outputting a message. Next, the **Try** block throws an **Exception** (lines 106–107), and the **Try** block expires immediately.

```vb
1    ' Fig. 8.2: UsingExceptions.vb
2    ' Using Finally blocks.
3
4    ' demonstrating that Finally always executes
5    Class CUsingExceptions
6
7       ' entry point for application
8       Shared Sub Main()
9
10         ' Case 1: No exceptions occur in called method
11         Console.WriteLine("Calling DoesNotThrowException")
12         DoesNotThrowException()
13
14         ' Case 2: Exception occurs and is caught in called method
15         Console.WriteLine(vbCrLf & _
16            "Calling ThrowExceptionWithCatch")
17
18         ThrowExceptionWithCatch()
19
20         ' Case 3: Exception occurs, but not caught in called method
21         ' because no Catch handler.
22         Console.WriteLine(vbCrLf & _
23            "Calling ThrowExceptionWithoutCatch")
24
```

Fig. 8.2   **Finally** statements always execute, regardless of whether an exception occurs. (Part 1 of 4.)

```
25          ' call ThrowExceptionWithoutCatch
26          Try
27             ThrowExceptionWithoutCatch()
28
29          ' process exception returned from ThrowExceptionWithoutCatch
30          Catch
31             Console.WriteLine("Caught exception from " & _
32                "ThrowExceptionWithoutCatch in Main")
33
34          End Try
35
36          ' Case 4: Exception occurs and is caught in called method,
37          ' then rethrown to caller.
38          Console.WriteLine(vbCrLf & _
39             "Calling ThrowExceptionCatchRethrow")
40
41          ' call ThrowExceptionCatchRethrow
42          Try
43             ThrowExceptionCatchRethrow()
44
45          ' process exception returned from ThrowExceptionCatchRethrow
46          Catch
47             Console.WriteLine("Caught exception from " & _
48                "ThrowExceptionCatchRethrow in Main")
49
50          End Try
51
52       End Sub ' Main
53
54       ' no exceptions thrown
55       Public Shared Sub DoesNotThrowException()
56
57          ' Try block does not throw any exceptions
58          Try
59             Console.WriteLine("In DoesNotThrowException")
60
61          ' this Catch never executes
62          Catch
63             Console.WriteLine("This Catch never executes")
64
65          ' Finally executes because corresponding Try executed
66          Finally
67             Console.WriteLine( _
68                "Finally executed in DoesNotThrowException")
69
70          End Try
71
72          Console.WriteLine("End of DoesNotThrowException")
73       End Sub ' DoesNotThrowException
74
```

Fig. 8.2   **Finally** statements always execute, regardless of whether an exception occurs. (Part 2 of 4.)

```vb
75          ' throws exception and catches it locally
76      Public Shared Sub ThrowExceptionWithCatch()
77
78            ' Try block throws exception
79          Try
80              Console.WriteLine("In ThrowExceptionWithCatch")
81
82              Throw New Exception( _
83                  "Exception in ThrowExceptionWithCatch")
84
85          ' catch exception thrown in Try block
86          Catch exceptionParameter As Exception
87              Console.WriteLine("Message: " & exceptionParameter.Message)
88
89          ' Finally executes because corresponding Try executed
90          Finally
91              Console.WriteLine( _
92                  "Finally executed in ThrowExceptionWithCatch")
93
94          End Try
95
96          Console.WriteLine("End of ThrowExceptionWithCatch")
97      End Sub ' ThrowExceptionWithCatch
98
99      ' throws exception and does not catch it locally
100     Public Shared Sub ThrowExceptionWithoutCatch()
101
102           ' throw exception, but do not catch it
103         Try
104             Console.WriteLine("In ThrowExceptionWithoutCatch")
105
106             Throw New Exception( _
107                 "Exception in ThrowExceptionWithoutCatch")
108
109         ' Finally executes because corresponding Try executed
110         Finally
111             Console.WriteLine("Finally executed in " & _
112                 "ThrowExceptionWithoutCatch")
113
114         End Try
115
116           ' unreachable code; logic error
117         Console.WriteLine("End of ThrowExceptionWithoutCatch")
118     End Sub ' ThrowExceptionWithoutCatch
119
120     ' throws exception, catches it and rethrows it
121     Public Shared Sub ThrowExceptionCatchRethrow()
122
123           ' Try block throws exception
124         Try
125             Console.WriteLine("In ThrowExceptionCatchRethrow")
126
```

Fig. 8.2 **Finally** statements always execute, regardless of whether an exception occurs. (Part 3 of 4.)

```
127              Throw New Exception( _
128                 "Exception in ThrowExceptionCatchRethrow")
129
130           ' catch any exception and rethrow
131           Catch exceptionParameter As Exception
132              Console.WriteLine("Message: " & _
133                 exceptionParameter.Message)
134
135              ' rethrow exception for further processing
136              Throw exceptionParameter
137
138              ' unreachable code; logic error
139
140           ' Finally executes because corresponding Try executed
141           Finally
142              Console.WriteLine("Finally executed in " & _
143                 "ThrowExceptionCatchRethrow")
144
145        End Try
146
147           ' any code placed here is never reached
148           Console.WriteLine("End of ThrowExceptionCatchRethrow")
149     End Sub ' ThrowExceptionCatchRethrow
150
151  End Class ' UsingExceptions
```

```
Calling DoesNotThrowException
In DoesNotThrowException
Finally executed in DoesNotThrowException
End of DoesNotThrowException

Calling ThrowExceptionWithCatch
In ThrowExceptionWithCatch
Message: Exception in ThrowExceptionWithCatch
Finally executed in ThrowExceptionWithCatch
End of ThrowExceptionWithCatch

Calling ThrowExceptionWithoutCatch
In ThrowExceptionWithoutCatch
Finally executed in ThrowExceptionWithoutCatch
Caught exception from ThrowExceptionWithoutCatch in Main

Calling ThrowExceptionCatchRethrow
In ThrowExceptionCatchRethrow
Message: Exception in ThrowExceptionCatchRethrow
Finally executed in ThrowExceptionCatchRethrow
Caught exception from ThrowExceptionCatchRethrow in Main
```

Fig. 8.2   **Finally** statements always execute, regardless of whether an exception occurs. (Part 4 of 4.)

Normally, program control would continue at the first **Catch** following this **Try** block. However, this **Try** block does not have any corresponding **Catch** handlers. Therefore, the exception is not caught in method **ThrowExceptionWithoutCatch**. Normal program control cannot continue until the exception is caught and processed. Thus, the CLR terminates **ThrowExceptionWithoutCatch**, and program control returns to **Main**. Before control returns to **Main**, the **Finally** block (lines 110–112) executes and outputs a message. At this point, program control returns to **Main**—any statements appearing after the **Finally** block (e.g., line 117) do not execute. In this example, such statements could cause logic errors, because the exception thrown in lines 106–107 is not caught. In **Main**, the **Catch** handler in lines 30–32 catches the exception and displays a message indicating that the exception was caught in **Main**.

Common Programming Error 8.6

*The argument of a **Throw**—an exception object—must be of class **Exception** or one of its derived classes.*

Lines 42–50 of **Main** define a **Try** block in which **Main** invokes method **Throw-ExceptionCatchRethrow** (lines 121–149). The **Try** block enables **Main** to catch any exceptions thrown by **ThrowExceptionCatchRethrow**. The **Try** block in lines 124–145 of **ThrowExceptionCatchRethrow** begins by outputting a message. Next, the **Try** block throws an **Exception** (lines 127–128). The **Try** block expires immediately, and program control continues at the first **Catch** (lines 131–136) following the **Try** block. In this example, the type thrown (**Exception**) matches the type specified in the **Catch**, so lines 132–133 outputs a message indicating where the exception occurred. Line 136 uses the **Throw** statement to *rethrow* the exception. This indicates that the **Catch** handler performed partial processing of the exception and now is passing the exception back to the calling method (in this case, **Main**) for further processing. Note that the argument to the **Throw** statement is the reference to the exception that was caught. When rethrowing the original exception, you also can use the statement

> *Throw*

with no argument. Section 8.6 demonstrates using a **Throw** statement with an argument from a **Catch** handler. After an exception is caught, such a **Throw** statement enables programmers to create an exception object then throw a different type of exception from the **Catch** handler. Class-library designers often do this to customize the exception types thrown from methods in their class libraries or to provide additional debugging information.

Software Engineering Observation 8.7

Before rethrowing an exception to a calling method, the method that rethrows the exception should release any resources it acquired before the exception occurred.[7]

Software Engineering Observation 8.8

Whenever possible, a method should handle exceptions that are thrown in that method, rather than passing the exceptions to another region of the program.

The exception handling in method **ThrowExceptionCatchRethrow** does not complete, because the program cannot run code in the **Catch** handler placed after the invocation of the **Throw** statement (line 136). Therefore, method **Throw-ExceptionCatchRethrow** terminates and returns control to **Main**. Once again, the

---

7. "Best Practices for Handling Exceptions [Visual Basic]."

Finally block (lines 141–143) executes and outputs a message before control returns to **Main**. When control returns to Main, the **Catch** handler in lines 46–48 catches the exception and displays a message indicating that the exception was caught. Then, the program terminates.

Note that the location to which program control returns after the **Finally** block executes depends on the exception-handling state. If the **Try** block successfully completes, or if a **Catch** handler catches and handles an exception, control continues with the next statement after the **End Try** statement. However, if an exception is not caught, or if a **Catch** handler rethrows an exception, program control continues in the next enclosing **Try** block. The enclosing **Try** could be in the calling method or in one of its callers. It also is possible to nest a **Try/Catch** sequence in a **Try** block; in such a case, the outer **Try** block's **Catch** handlers would process any exceptions that were not caught in the inner **Try/Catch** sequence. If a **Try** block executes and has a corresponding **Finally** block, the **Finally** block always executes—even if the **Try** block terminates due to a **Return** statement. The **Return** occurs after the execution of the **Finally** block.

Common Programming Error 8.7

*Throwing an exception from a **Finally** block can be dangerous. If an uncaught exception is awaiting processing when the **Finally** block executes, and the **Finally** block throws a new exception that is not caught in the **Finally** block, the first exception is lost, and the new exception is passed to the next enclosing **Try** block.*

Testing and Debugging Tip 8.6

*When placing code that can throw an exception in a **Finally** block, always enclose that code in a **Try/Catch** sequence that catches the appropriate exception types. This prevents the loss of any uncaught and rethrown exceptions that occur before the **Finally** block executes.*

Software Engineering Observation 8.9

*Visual Basic's exception-handling mechanism removes error-processing code from the main line of a program to improve program clarity. Do not place **Try/Catch/Finally** around every statement that might throw an exception, because this can make programs difficult to read. Rather, place one **Try** block around a significant portion of code, and follow this **Try** block with **Catch** handlers that handle each of the possible exceptions. Then, follow the **Catch** handlers with a single **Finally** block.*

8.6 Exception Properties

As we discussed in Section 8.4, exception data types derive from class **Exception**, which has several properties. These properties frequently are used to formulate error messages indicating a caught exception. Two important properties are *Message* and *StackTrace*. Property **Message** stores the error message associated with an **Exception** object. This message can be a default message associated with the exception type or a customized message passed to an **Exception** object's constructor when the **Exception** object is thrown. Property **StackTrace** contains a **String** that represents the *method-call stack*. The runtime environment keeps a list of method calls that have been made up to a given moment. The **StackTrace String** represents this sequential list of methods that had not finished processing at the time the exception occurred. The exact location at which the exception occurs in the program is called the exception's *throw point*.

Testing and Debugging Tip 8.7

A stack trace shows the complete method-call stack at the time an exception occurred. This enables the programmer to view the series of method calls that led to the exception. Information in the stack trace includes the names of the methods on the call stack at the time of the exception, names of the classes in which those methods are defined and names of the namespaces in which those classes are defined. The stack trace also includes line numbers; the first line number indicates the throw point, and subsequent line numbers indicate the locations from which the methods in the stack trace were called.

Another property used frequently by class-library programmers is **InnerException**. Typically, programmers use this property to "wrap" exception objects caught in their code so that they then can throw new exception types that are specific to their libraries. For example, a programmer implementing an accounting system might have some account-number processing code in which account numbers are input as **String**s, but represented as **Integer**s in the code. Recall, a program can convert **String**s to **Integer** values with **Convert.ToInt32**, which throws a **FormatException** when it encounters an invalid number format. When an invalid account-number format occurs, the accounting-system programmer might wish employ a different error message than the default message supplied by **FormatException** or might wish to indicate a new exception type, such as **InvalidAccountNumberFormatException**. In these cases, the programmer would provide code to catch the **FormatException** and then would create an **Exception** object in the **Catch** handler, passing the original exception as one of the constructor arguments. The original exception object becomes the **InnerException** of the new exception object. When an **InvalidAccountNumberFormatException** occurs in code that uses the accounting-system library, the **Catch** block that catches the exception can obtain a reference to the original exception via property **InnerException**. Thus, the exception indicates both that the user specified an invalid account number and that the particular problem was an invalid number format.

Class **Exception** provides other properties, including *HelpLink*, *Source* and *TargetSite*. Property **HelpLink** specifies the location of the help file that describes the problem that occurred. This property is **Nothing** if no such file exists. Property **Source** specifies the name of the application where the exception occurred. Property **TargetSite** specifies the method where the exception originated.

Our next example (Fig. 8.3) demonstrates properties **Message**, **StackTrace** and **InnerException** and method **ToString** of class **Exception**. In addition, this example introduces *stack unwinding*, which is the process of attempting to locate an appropriate **Catch** handler for an uncaught exception. As we discuss this example, we keep track of the methods on the call stack so that we can discuss property **StackTrace** and the stack-unwinding mechanism.

Program execution begins with the invocation of **Main**, which becomes the first method on the method call stack. Line 13 of the **Try** block in **Main** invokes **Method1** (defined in lines 37–39), which becomes the second method on the stack. If **Method1** throws an exception, the **Catch** handler in lines 17–30 handles the exception and outputs information about the exception that occurred. Line 38 of **Method1** invokes **Method2** (lines 42–44), which becomes the third method on the stack. Then, line 43 of **Method2** invokes **Method3** (lines 47–61) which becomes the fourth method on the stack.

At this point, the method call stack for the program is:

```
Method3
Method2
Method1
Main
```

Notice the most recent method to be called (**Method3**) appears at the top of the list, whereas the first method called (**Main**) appears at the bottom. The **Try** block (lines 50–59) in **Method3** invokes method **Convert.ToInt32** (line 51), which attempts to convert a **String** to an **Integer**. At this point, **Convert.ToInt32** becomes the fifth and final method on the call stack.

Because the argument to **Convert.ToInt32** is not in **Integer** format, line 51 throws a **FormatException** that is caught in line 54 of **Method3**. The exception terminates the call to **Convert.ToInt32**, so the method is removed from the method-call stack. The **Catch** handler in **Method3** then creates and throws an **Exception** object. The first argument to the **Exception** constructor is the custom error message for our example, "**Exception occurred in Method3.**" The second argument is the **InnerException**—the **FormatException** that was caught. The **StackTrace** for this new exception object reflects the point at which the exception was thrown (line 56). Now, **Method3** terminates, because the exception thrown in the **Catch** handler is not caught in the method body. Thus, control returns to the statement that invoked **Method3** in the prior method in the call stack (**Method2**). This removes, or *unwinds,* **Method3** from the method-call stack.

When control returns to line 42 in **Method2**, the CLR determines that line 42 is not in a **Try** block. Therefore, the exception cannot be caught in **Method2**, and **Method2** terminates. This unwinds **Method2** from the call stack and returns control to line 37 in **Method1**.

Here again, line 37 is not in a **Try** block, so the exception cannot be caught in **Method1**. The method terminates and unwinds from the call stack, returning control to line 13 in **Main**, which is located in a **Try** block. The **Try** block in **Main** expires and the **Catch** handler (lines 17–30) catches the exception. The **Catch** handler uses method **ToString** and properties **Message**, **StackTrace** and **InnerException** to create the output. Stack unwinding continues until a **Catch** handler catches the exception or the program terminates.

The first block of output (reformatted for readability) in Fig. 8.3 contains the exception's **String** representation, which is returned from method **ToString**. The **String** begins with the name of the exception class followed by the **Message** property value. The next ten lines present the **String** representation of the **InnerException** object. The remainder of the block of output shows the **StackTrace** for the exception thrown in **Method3**. Note that the **StackTrace** represents the state of the method-call stack at the throw point of the exception, rather than at the point where the exception eventually is caught. Each **StackTrace** line that begins with "**at**" represents a method on the call stack. These lines indicate the method in which the exception occurred, the file in which that method resides and the line number in the file where the exception is thrown (throw point). Also, note that the stack trace includes the inner exception stack trace.

Testing and Debugging Tip 8.8

When reading a stack trace, start from the top of the stack trace and read the error message first. Then, read the remainder of the stack trace, searching for the first line that references code from your program. Normally, this is the location that caused the exception.

```vb
1   ' Fig. 8.3: Properties.vb
2   ' Stack unwinding and Exception class properties.
3
4   ' demonstrates using properties Message, StackTrace and
5   ' InnerException
6   Class CProperties
7
8      Shared Sub Main()
9
10         ' call Method1; any Exception generated is caught
11         ' in Catch handler that follows
12         Try
13            Method1()
14
15         ' output String representation of Exception, then output
16         ' properties InnerException, Message and StackTrace
17         Catch exceptionParameter As Exception
18            Console.WriteLine("exceptionParameter.ToString: " & _
19               vbCrLf & "{0}" & vbCrLf, exceptionParameter.ToString())
20
21            Console.WriteLine("exceptionParameter.Message: " & _
22               vbCrLf & "{0}" & vbCrLf, exceptionParameter.Message)
23
24            Console.WriteLine("exceptionParameter.StackTrace: " & _
25               vbCrLf & "{0}" & vbCrLf, exceptionParameter.StackTrace)
26
27            Console.WriteLine( _
28               "exceptionParameter.InnerException: " & _
29               vbCrLf & "{0}" & vbCrLf, _
30               exceptionParameter.InnerException.ToString())
31
32         End Try
33
34      End Sub ' Main
35
36      ' calls Method2
37      Public Shared Sub Method1()
38         Method2()
39      End Sub
40
41      ' calls Method3
42      Public Shared Sub Method2()
43         Method3()
44      End Sub
45
46      ' throws an Exception containing InnerException
47      Public Shared Sub Method3()
48
49         ' attempt to convert String to Integer
50         Try
51            Convert.ToInt32("Not an integer")
52
```

Fig. 8.3   **Exception** properties and stack unwinding. (Part 1 of 3.)

```
53              ' wrap FormatException in new Exception
54              Catch formatExceptionParameter As FormatException
55
56                  Throw New Exception("Exception occurred in Method3", _
57                      formatExceptionParameter)
58
59              End Try
60
61          End Sub ' Method3
62
63      End Class ' CProperties
```

```
exceptionParameter.ToString:
System.Exception: Exception occurred in Method3 --->
   System.FormatException: Input string was not in a correct format.
   at System.Number.ParseInt32(String s, NumberStyles style,
      NumberFormatInfo info)
   at System.Int32.Parse(String s, NumberStyles style,
      IFormatProvider provider)
   at System.Int32.Parse(String s)
   at System.Convert.ToInt32(String value)
   at Properties.CProperties.Method3() in
 C:\Fig08_03\Properties\Properties.vb:line 51
   --- End of inner exception stack trace ---
   at Properties.CProperties.Method3() in
 C:\Fig08_03\Properties\Properties.vb:line 56
   at Properties.CProperties.Method2() in
 C:\Fig08_03\Properties\Properties.vb:line 43
   at Properties.CProperties.Method1() in
 C:\Fig08_03\Properties\Properties.vb:line 38
   at Properties.CProperties.Main() in
 C:\Fig08_03\Properties\Properties.vb:line 13

exceptionParameter.Message:
Exception occurred in Method3

exceptionParameter.StackTrace:
   at Properties.CProperties.Method3() in
 C:\Fig08_03\Properties\Properties.vb:line 56
   at Properties.CProperties.Method2() in
 C:\Fig08_03\Properties\Properties.vb:line 43
   at Properties.CProperties.Method1() in
 C:\Fig08_03\Properties\Properties.vb:line 38
   at Properties.CProperties.Main() in
 C:\Fig08_03\Properties\Properties.vb:line 13

exceptionParameter.InnerException:
System.FormatException: Input string was not in a correct format.
   at System.Number.ParseInt32(String s, NumberStyles style,
      NumberFormatInfo info)
```

(continued on next page)

Fig. 8.3   **Exception** properties and stack unwinding. (Part 2 of 3.)

```
                                            (continued from previous page)
   at System.Int32.Parse(String s, NumberStyles style,
      IFormatProvider provider)
   at System.Int32.Parse(String s)
   at System.Convert.ToInt32(String value)
   at Properties.CProperties.Method3() in
C:\Fig08_03\Properties\Properties.vb:line 51
```

Fig. 8.3   **Exception** properties and stack unwinding. (Part 3 of 3.)

Testing and Debugging Tip 8.9

When catching and rethrowing an exception, provide additional debugging information in the rethrown exception. To do so, create an **Exception** *object containing more specific debugging information and then pass the original caught exception to the new exception object's constructor to initialize the* **InnerException** *property.*[8]

The next block of output (two lines) simply displays the **Message** property's value (**Exception occurred in Method3**) of the exception thrown in **Method3**.

The third block of output displays the **StackTrace** property of the exception thrown in **Method3**. Note that this **StackTrace** property contains the stack trace starting from line 56 in **Method3**, because that is the point at which the **Exception** object was created and thrown. The stack trace always begins from the exception's throw point.

Finally, the last block of output displays the **ToString** representation of the **InnerException** property, which includes the namespace and class name of that exception object, as well as its **Message** property and **StackTrace** property.

8.7 Programmer-Defined Exception Classes

In many cases, programmers can use existing exception classes from the .NET Framework to indicate exceptions that occur in their programs. However, in some cases, programmers might wish to create new exception types that are specific to the problems that occur in their programs. *Programmer-defined exception classes* should derive directly or indirectly from class **ApplicationException** of namespace **System**.

Good Programming Practice 8.2

The association of each type of malfunction with an appropriately named exception class improves program clarity.

Software Engineering Observation 8.10

Before creating programmer-defined exception classes, investigate the existing exception classes in the .NET Framework to determine whether an appropriate exception type already exists.

Software Engineering Observation 8.11

Programmers should create exception classes only if they need to catch and handle the new exceptions in a different manner than other existing exception types.

---

8. "Best Practices for Handling Exceptions [Visual Basic]," *.NET Framework Developer's Guide*, Visual Studio .NET Online Help.

Figure 8.4 and Fig. 8.5 demonstrate a programmer-defined exception class. Class **NegativeNumberException** (Fig. 8.4) is a programmer-defined exception class representing exceptions that occur when a program performs an illegal operation on a negative number, such as attempting to calculate the square root of a negative number.

According to Microsoft,[9] programmer-defined exceptions should extend class **ApplicationException**, should have a class name that ends with "Exception" and should define three constructors—a default constructor, a constructor that receives a **String** argument (the error message) and a constructor that receives a **String** argument and an **Exception** argument (the error message and the inner exception object).

NegativeNumberExceptions most likely occur during arithmetic operations, so it seems logical to derive class **NegativeNumberException** from class **ArithmeticException**. However, class **ArithmeticException** derives from class **SystemException**—the category of exceptions thrown by the CLR. The base class for programmer-defined exception classes should inherit from **ApplicationException**, rather than **SystemException**.

Class **FrmSquareRoot** (Fig. 8.5) demonstrates our programmer-defined exception class. The application enables the user to input a numeric value and then invokes method **SquareRoot** (lines 23–34) to calculate the square root of that value. To perform this calculation, **SquareRoot** invokes class **Math**'s *Sqrt* method, which receives a **Double** value as its argument. Normally, if the argument is negative, method **Sqrt** returns constant **NaN** from class **Double**. In this program, we would like to prevent the user from calculating the square root of a negative number. If the numeric value that the user enters is negative, **SquareRoot** throws a **NegativeNumberException** (lines 27–28). Otherwise, **SquareRoot** invokes class **Math**'s method *Sqrt* to compute the square root (line 33).

When the user inputs a value and clicks the **Square Root** button, the program invokes event handler **cmdSquareRoot_Click** (lines 37–67). The **Try** block (lines 44–65) attempts to invoke **SquareRoot** using the value input by the user. If the user input is not a valid number, a **FormatException** occurs, and the **Catch** handler in lines 51–54 processes the exception. If the user inputs a negative number, method **SquareRoot** throws a **NegativeNumberException** (lines 27–28). The **Catch** handler in lines 57–63 catches and handles this type of exception.

```
1    ' Fig. 8.4: NegativeNumberExceptionDefinition.vb
2    ' NegativeNumberException represents exceptions caused by
3    ' illegal operations performed on negative numbers.
4
5    Public Class NegativeNumberException
6       Inherits ApplicationException
7
8       ' default constructor
9       Public Sub New()
10          MyBase.New("Illegal operation for a negative number")
11       End Sub ' New
```

Fig. 8.4   **ApplicationException** derived class thrown when a program performs an illegal operation on a negative number. (Part 1 of 2.)

9. "Best Practices for Handling Exceptions [Visual Basic]," *.NET Framework Developer's Guide*, Visual Studio .NET Online Help.

```
12
13        ' constructor for customizing error message
14        Public Sub New(ByVal messageValue As String)
15           MyBase.New(messageValue)
16        End Sub ' New
17
18        ' constructor for customizing error message and specifying
19        ' InnerException object
20        Public Sub New(ByVal messageValue As String, _
21           ByVal inner As Exception)
22
23           MyBase.New(messageValue, inner)
24        End Sub ' New
25
26     End Class ' NegativeNumberException
```

Fig. 8.4   `ApplicationException` derived class thrown when a program performs an illegal operation on a negative number. (Part 2 of 2.)

```
1      ' Fig. 8.5: SquareRootTest.vb
2      ' Demonstrating a programmer-defined exception class.
3
4      Imports System.Windows.Forms
5
6      Public Class FrmSquareRoot
7         Inherits Form
8
9         ' Label for showing square root
10        Friend WithEvents lblOutput As Label
11        Friend WithEvents lblInput As Label
12
13        ' Button invokes square-root calculation
14        Friend WithEvents cmdSquareRoot As Button
15
16        ' TextBox receives user's Integer input
17        Friend WithEvents txtInput As TextBox
18
19        ' Visual Studio .NET generated code
20
21        ' computes square root of parameter; throws
22        ' NegativeNumberException if parameter is negative
23        Public Function SquareRoot(ByVal value As Double) As Double
24
25           ' if negative operand, throw NegativeNumberException
26           If value < 0 Then
27              Throw New NegativeNumberException( _
28                 "Square root of negative number not permitted")
29
30           End If
31
```

Fig. 8.5   `FrmSquareRoot` class throws an exception if an error occurs when calculating the square root. (Part 1 of 2.)

```
32              ' compute square root
33              Return Math.Sqrt(value)
34          End Function ' SquareRoot
35
36          ' obtain user input, convert to Double, calculate square root
37          Private Sub cmdSquareRoot_Click( _
38              ByVal sender As System.Object, _
39              ByVal e As System.EventArgs) Handles cmdSquareRoot.Click
40
41              lblOutput.Text = ""
42
43              ' catch any NegativeNumberException thrown
44              Try
45                  Dim result As Double = _
46                      SquareRoot(Convert.ToDouble(txtInput.Text))
47
48                  lblOutput.Text = result.ToString()
49
50              ' process invalid number format
51              Catch formatExceptionParameter As FormatException
52                  MessageBox.Show(formatExceptionParameter.Message, _
53                      "Invalid Number Format", MessageBoxButtons.OK, _
54                      MessageBoxIcon.Error)
55
56              ' display MessageBox if negative number input
57              Catch negativeNumberExceptionParameter As _
58                  NegativeNumberException
59
60                  MessageBox.Show( _
61                      negativeNumberExceptionParameter.Message, _
62                      "Invalid Operation", MessageBoxButtons.OK, _
63                      MessageBoxIcon.Error)
64
65              End Try
66
67          End Sub ' cmdSquareRoot_Click
68
69      End Class ' FrmSquareRoot
```

Fig. 8.5   **FrmSquareRoot** class throws an exception if an error occurs when calculating the square root. (Part 2 of 2.)

8.8 Handling Overflows

In Visual Basic, primitive data types can represent values only within a fixed range. For instance, the maximum value of an **Integer** is 2,147,483,647. In **Integer** arithmetic, a value larger than 2,147,483,647 causes *overflow*—type **Integer** cannot represent such a number. Overflow also can occur with other Visual Basic primitive types. Overflows often cause programs to produce incorrect results.

Visual Basic enables the user to specify whether arithmetic occurs in a *checked context* or *unchecked context*. In a checked context, the CLR throws an **OverflowException** (namespace **System**) if overflow occurs during the evaluation of an arithmetic expression. In an unchecked context, overflow produces a truncated result.

By default, calculations occur in a checked context. However, the programmer can modify a project's properties to disable checking for arithmetic overflow—a dangerous practice. To do so, first select the project in the **Solution Explorer**. Next, select **View > Property Pages**. In the **Property Pages** dialog, select the **Configuration Properties** folder. Under **Optimizations**, select the checkbox named **Remove integer overflow checks** to disable checking for arithmetic overflow.

> **Performance Tip 8.4**
>
> *The removal of integer-overflow checking improves runtime performance, but can yield faulty program results if an overflow occurs. Programmers should disable integer-overflow checking only if they have tested a program thoroughly and are certain that no overflows can occur.*

The operators *****, **/**, **+** and **–** can cause overflow when used with integral data types (such as **Integer** and **Long**). In addition, conversions between integral data types can cause overflow. For example, the conversion of 1,000,000 from an **Integer** to a **Short** results in overflow because a **Short** can store a maximum value of 32,767. Figure 8.6 demonstrates overflows occurring in both checked and unchecked contexts. The first output depicts the program execution when integer-overflow checking is enabled, whereas the second output illustrates program execution without checking.

```
1   ' Fig. 8.6: Overflow.vb
2   ' Demonstrating overflows with and without checking.
3
4   ' demonstrates overflows with and without checking
5   Class COverflow
6
7      Shared Sub Main()
8
9         ' calculate sum of number1 and number 2
10        Try
11
12           Dim number1 As Integer = Int32.MaxValue ' 2,147,483,647
13           Dim number2 As Integer = Int32.MaxValue ' 2,147,483,647
14           Dim sum As Integer = 0
15
```

Fig. 8.6   **OverflowException** cannot occur if user disables integer-overflow checking. (Part 1 of 2.)

```
16                   ' output numbers
17                   Console.WriteLine("number1: {0}" & vbCrLf & _
18                      "number2: {1}", number1, number2)
19
20                   Console.WriteLine(vbCrLf & _
21                      "Sum integers in checked context:")
22
23                   sum = number1 + number2 ' compute sum
24
25                   ' this statement will not throw OverflowException if user
26                   ' removes integer-overflow checks
27                   Console.WriteLine(vbCrLf & _
28                      "Sum after operation: {0}", sum)
29
30                ' catch overflow exception
31                Catch overflowExceptionParameter As OverflowException
32                   Console.WriteLine(overflowExceptionParameter.ToString())
33
34                End Try
35
36          End Sub ' Main
37
38    End Class ' COverflow
```

```
number1: 2147483647
number2: 2147483647

Sum integers in checked context:
System.OverflowException: Arithmetic operation resulted in an overflow.
   at Overflow.COverflow.Main() in
C:\books\2001\vbhtp2\ch11\Overflow\Overflow.vb:line 23
```

```
number1: 2147483647
number2: 2147483647

Sum integers in checked context:

Sum after operation: -2
```

Fig. 8.6   **OverflowException** cannot occur if user disables integer-overflow checking. (Part 2 of 2.)

The **Try** block in lines 10–34 begins by defining **Integer** variables **number1** and **number2** (lines 12–13), and assigning to each variable the maximum value for an **Integer**, which is 2,147,483,647. (This maximum is defined by *Int32.MaxValue*.) Next, line 23 calculates the total of **number1** and **number2** and stores the result in variable **sum**. Because variables **number1** and **number2** already contain the maximum value for an **Integer**, adding these values when integer-overflow checking is enabled causes an **OverflowException**. The **Catch** handler in lines 31–32 catches the exception and outputs its **String** representation. Note that, if integer-overflow checking is disabled (as represented by the second output window), line 23 does not generate an **OverflowException**. Lines 27–28 output the **sum** of **number1** and **number2**. The result of the calculation should be 4,294,967,294. However, this value is too large to be represented as an **Integer**, so Visual Basic truncates part of the value, resulting in a sum of **-2** in the output. The result of the unchecked calculation does not resemble the actual sum of the variables.

In this chapter, we demonstrated the exception-handling mechanism and discussed how to make applications more robust by writing exception handlers to process potential problems. As programmers develop applications, it is important that they investigate potential exceptions thrown by the methods that their program invokes or by the CLR. They then should implement appropriate exception-handling code to make their applications more robust. In the next chapter, we begin a more in-depth treatment of graphical user interfaces.

Testing and Debugging Tip 8.10

Use a checked context when performing calculations that can result in overflows. The programmer-defined exception handlers to deal with the overflow situations.

8.9 Summary

An exception is an indication of a problem that occurs during a program's execution. Exception handling enables programmers to create applications that can resolve exceptions, often allowing a program to continue execution as if no problems were encountered. Exception handling enables programmers to write clear, robust and more fault-tolerant programs. Exception handling enables the programmer to remove error-handling code from the "main line" of the program's execution.

When a method detects an error and is unable to handle it, the method throws an exception. There is no guarantee that there will be an exception handler to process that kind of exception. If there is, the exception will be caught and handled. Exception-handling code uses **Try/Catch/Finally** sequences.

A **Try** block encloses the code that could throw exceptions and the code that should not execute if an exception occurs. A **Try** block consists of keyword **Try** followed by a block of code in which exceptions could occur. If an exception occurs in a **Try** block, the block expires and program control transfers to the first **Catch** handler following the **Try** block. Each **Catch** handler begins with keyword **Catch** followed by an optional exception parameter that specifies the type of exception handled by the **Catch** handler. The exception-handling code appears in the body of the **Catch** handler. The CLR searches for the first **Catch** handler that can process the type of exception that occurred. The appropriate handler is the first one in which the thrown exception's type matches, or is derived from, the exception type specified by the **Catch** handler's exception parameter.

After the last **Catch** handler, an optional **Finally** block contains code that always executes, regardless of whether an exception occurs. The **Finally** block is an ideal location to place resource-deallocation code for resources acquired and manipulated in the corresponding **Try** block. If no exceptions occur or if an exception is caught and handled, the program resumes execution with the next statement after the **Try/Catch/Finally** sequence.

Class **Exception** (namespace **System**) is the base class of the .NET Framework exception hierarchy. **ApplicationException** is a base class programmers can extend to create new exception data types that are specific to their applications. Programs can recover from most **ApplicationException**s and continue execution. The CLR generates **SystemException**s. Programs typically cannot recover from most exceptions thrown by the CLR. Therefore, programs generally should not throw **SystemExceptions** nor attempt to **Catch** such exceptions.

A **Throw** statement throws an exception object. A **Throw** statement can be used in a **Catch** handler to rethrow an exception. This indicates that the **Catch** handler performed partial processing of the exception and is now passing the exception back to a calling method for further processing.

Exception property **Message** stores the error message associated with an **Exception** object. This message may be a default message associated with the exception type or a customized message passed to an exception object's constructor at the time a program creates the exception. **Exception** property **StackTrace** contains a **String** that represents the method-call stack at the throw point of the exception. **Exception** property **InnerException** typically is used to "wrap" a caught exception object in a new exception object, then throw the object of that new exception type.

Overflow occurs in integer arithmetic when the value of an expression is greater than the maximum value that can be stored in a particular data type. Visual Basic enables the user to specify whether arithmetic occurs in a *checked context* or *unchecked context*. In a checked context, the CLR throws an **OverflowException** if overflow occurs during the evaluation of an arithmetic expression. In an unchecked context, overflow produces a truncated result (normally, a dangerous thing to allow).

Graphical User Interface Concepts: Part 1

Objectives

- To understand the design principles of graphical user interfaces.
- To use events.
- To understand namespaces that contain graphical user interface components and event-handling classes.
- To create graphical user interfaces.
- To create and manipulate buttons, labels, lists, textboxes and panels.
- To use mouse and keyboard events.

...the wisest prophets make sure of the event first.
Horace Walpole

...The user should feel in control of the computer; not the other way around. This is achieved in applications that embody three qualities: responsiveness, permissiveness, and consistency.
Inside Macintosh, Volume 1
Apple Computer, Inc. 1985

All the better to see you with, my dear.
The Big Bad Wolf to Little Red Riding Hood

Outline

9.1 Introduction

A *graphical user interface* (*GUI*) allows a user to interact visually with a program. A GUI gives a program a distinctive "look" and "feel." By providing different applications with a consistent set of intuitive user-interface components, GUIs enable users to spend less time trying to remember which keystroke sequences perform what functions, freeing up time that can be spent using the program in a productive manner.

Look-and-Feel Observation 9.1

Consistent user interfaces enable a user to learn new applications more quickly.

As an example of a GUI, Fig. 9.1 depicts an Internet Explorer window in which various *GUI components* have been labeled. Near the top of the window, there is a *menu bar* containing *menus*, including **File**, **Edit**, **View**, **Favorites**, **Tools** and **Help**. Below the menu bar is a set of *buttons*, each of which has a defined task in Internet Explorer. Below these buttons lies a *textbox,* in which users can type the locations of World Wide Web sites that they wish to visit. To the left of the textbox is a *label* that indicates the textbox's purpose. Scrollbars are situated on the far right and bottom of the window. Usually, scrollbars are employed when a window contains more information than can be displayed in the window's viewable area. By clicking the scrollbars, the user can view different portions of the window. These components form a user-friendly interface through which the user interacts with the Internet Explorer Web browser.

GUIs are built from GUI components (which are sometimes called *controls* or *widgets*—short for *window gadgets*). A GUI component is an object with which the user interacts via the mouse or keyboard. Several common GUI components are listed in Fig. 9.2. In the sections that follow, we discuss each of these GUI components in detail. The next chapter explores the features and properties of more advanced GUI components.

Fig. 9.1   GUI components in a sample Internet Explorer window.

Component	Description
Label	An area in which icons or uneditable text is displayed.
TextBox	An area in which the user inputs data from the keyboard. This area also can display information.
Button	An area that triggers an event when clicked.
CheckBox	A component that is either selected or unselected.
ComboBox	A drop-down list of items from which the user can make a selection either by clicking an item in the list or by typing into a box.
ListBox	An area in which a list of items is displayed. The user can make a selection from the list by clicking on any item. Multiple elements can be selected.
Panel	A container in which components can be placed.
Scrollbar	A component that allows the user to access a range of elements that normally cannot fit in the control's container.

Fig. 9.2   Some basic GUI components.

9.2 Windows Forms

Windows Forms (also called *WinForms*) are used to create the GUIs for programs. A *form* is a graphical element that appears on the desktop; it can be a dialog, a window or an *MDI window* (*multiple document interface window*, discussed in Chapter 10, Graphical User Interface Concepts: Part 2). A *component* is an instance of a class that implements the **ICom-ponent** *interface*, which defines the behaviors that components must implement. A *control*, such as a button or label, is a component that has a graphical representation at runtime. Controls are visible, whereas components that lack a graphical representation (e.g., class **Timer** of namespace **System.Windows.Forms**, see Chapter 10) are not.

Figure 9.3 displays the Windows Forms controls and components that are contained in the **Toolbox**. The first two screenshots show the controls, and the last screenshot shows the components. To add a component or control to a Windows Form, a user selects that component or control from the **Toolbox** and drags it onto the Windows Form. Note that the **Pointer** (the icon at the top of the list) is not a component; rather, it allows the programmer to use the mouse pointer and does not add an item to the form. In this chapter and the next, we discuss many of these controls.

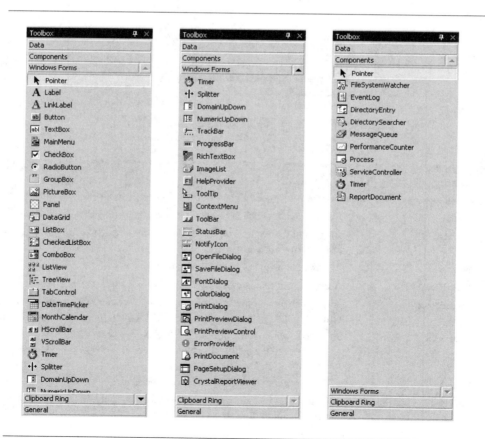

Fig. 9.3   Components and controls for Windows Forms.

In a series of windows, the *active window* is the frontmost window and has a highlighted title bar. A window becomes the active window when the user clicks somewhere inside it. During interaction with windows, the active window is said to have the *focus*.

The form acts as a *container* for components and controls. As we saw in Chapter 3, Control Structures, when we drag a control from the **Toolbox** onto the form, Visual Studio .NET generates this code for us, instantiating the component and setting its basic properties. Although we could write the code ourselves, it is much easier to create and modify controls using the **Toolbox** and **Properties** windows and allow Visual Studio .NET to handle the details. We introduced basic concepts relating to this kind of *visual programming* earlier in the book. In this chapter and the next, we use visual programming to build much richer and more complex GUIs.

When the user interacts with a control via the mouse or keyboard, events (discussed in Section 9.3) are generated. Typically, events are messages sent by a program to signal to an object or a set of objects that an action has occurred. Events are used most commonly used to signal user interactions with GUI components, but also can signal internal actions in a program. For example, clicking the **OK** button in a **MessageBox** generates an event. The **MessageBox** *handles* this event. The **MessageBox** component is designed to close when the event is handled, which occurs when the **OK** button is clicked. Section 9.3 describes how to design components so that they react differently to various types of events.

Each class we present in this chapter (i.e., form, component and control) is in the **System.Windows.Forms** namespace. Class **Form**, the basic window used by Windows applications, is fully qualified as **System.Windows.Forms.Form**. Likewise, class **Button** actually is **System.Windows.Forms.Button**.

The general design process for creating Windows applications requires generating a Windows Form, setting its properties, adding controls, setting their properties and implementing the *event handlers* (methods that are called in response to an event). Figure 9.4 lists common **Form** properties, methods and events.

Form Properties and Events	Description / Delegate and Event Arguments
Common Properties	
AcceptButton	Button that is clicked when *Enter* is pressed.
AutoScroll	**Boolean** value that allows or disallows scrollbars to appear when needed.
CancelButton	Button that is clicked when the *Escape* key is pressed.
FormBorderStyle	Border style for the form (e.g., **none**, **single**, **3D**, **sizable**).
Font	Font of text displayed on the form, and the default font of controls added to the form.
Text	Text in the form's title bar.
Common Methods	
Close	Closes a form and releases all resources. A closed form cannot be reopened.

Fig. 9.4   Common **Form** properties, methods and events. (Part 1 of 2.)

Form Properties and Events	Description / Delegate and Event Arguments
Hide	Hides form (does not destroy the form or release its resources).
Show	Displays a hidden form.
Common Events	*(Delegate EventHandler, event arguments EventArgs)*
Load	Occurs before a form is displayed to the user. The handler for this event is displayed in the editor when the form is double-clicked in the Visual Studio .NET designer.

Fig. 9.4   Common **Form** properties, methods and events. (Part 2 of 2.)

When we create controls and event handlers, Visual Studio .NET generates a large amount of the GUI–related code. Constructing GUIs can be performed graphically, by dragging and dropping components onto the form and setting properties via the **Properties** window. In visual programming, the IDE generally maintains GUI-related code and the programmer writes the necessary event handlers.

9.3 Event-Handling Model

GUIs are *event driven*—they *generate events* when a program's user interacts with the GUI. Typical interactions include moving the mouse, clicking the mouse, clicking a button, typing in a textbox, selecting an item from a menu and closing a window. Event information is passed to *event handlers*, which are methods that are called as a result of specific events. For example, consider a form that changes color when a button is clicked. Clicking the button generates an event and passes it to the button's event handler, causing the event-handler code to change the form's color.

Events are based on the notion of *delegates*, which are objects that reference methods (see Section 7.10). Event delegates are *multicast* (class **MulticastDelegate**), which means that they represent a set of delegates with the same signature. Multicast delegates enable event calls to be sent sequentially to all delegates contained within the multicast delegate. To learn more about delegates, see Chapter 7, Object-Oriented Programming: Polymorphism. In the event-handling model, delegates act as intermediaries between the objects creating (raising) events and the methods handling the events (Fig. 9.5).

Fig. 9.5   Event-handling model using delegates.

Delegates enable classes to specify methods that will not be named or implemented until the class is instantiated. This is extremely helpful in creating event handlers. For example, the creator of the **Form** class does not need to name or define the method that will handle the **Click** event. Using delegates, the class can specify when such an event handler would be called. Programmers who create their own forms can then name and define this event handler. As long as the event handler has been registered with the proper delegate, the method will be called at the proper time.

Once an event is generated, the system calls every method (event handler) referenced by the delegate. Every method in the delegate must have the same signature, because all the methods are being passed the same information.

Many situations require handling events generated by .NET controls, such as buttons and scrollbars. These controls already have predefined delegates corresponding to every event they can generate. The programmer creates the event handler and registers it with the delegate; Visual Studio .NET helps automate this task. In the following example, we create a form that displays a message box when clicked. Afterwards, we analyze the event code generated by Visual Studio .NET.

Following the steps we outlined in Chapter 3, Control Structures, create a **Form** containing a **Label**. First, create a new Windows application. Then, select the **Label** element from the **Windows Forms** list in the **Toolbox** window. Drag the **Label** element over the form to create a label. In the **Properties** window, set the **(Name)** property to **lblOutput** and the **Text** property to **"Click Me!"**.

We have been working in **Design** mode, which provides a graphical representation of our program. However, Visual Studio .NET has been creating code in the background, and that code can be accessed using the tab for the code or by right-clicking anywhere in the **Design** window and selecting **View Code**. To define and register an event handler for **lblOutput**, the IDE must be displaying the code listing for the Window application.

While viewing the code, notice the two drop-down menus above the editor window. (Fig. 9.6). The drop-down menu on the left-hand side, called the *Class Name* menu, contains a list of all components contained in our **Form** other than those elements that correspond to the **Form** base class. The Class Name drop-down menu for our **Form** should list one **Label**, named **lblOutput**. Select this element from the menu. On the right-hand side, the *Method Name* drop-down menu allows the programmer to access, modify and create event handlers for a component. This drop-down menu lists the events that the object can generate.

For the purposes of this exercise, we want the label to respond when clicked. Select the **Click** event in the Method Name drop-down menu. This creates an empty event handler inside the program code.

```
Private Sub lblOutput_Click(ByVal sender As Object, _
    ByVal e As System.EventArgs) Handles lblOutput.Click

End Sub
```

This is the method that is called when the form is clicked. We program the form to respond to the event by displaying a message box. To do this, insert the statement

```
MessageBox.Show("Label was clicked.")
```

into the event handler. The event handler now should appear as follows:

```
Private Sub lblOutput_Click(ByVal sender As Object, _
    ByVal e As System.EventArgs) Handles lblOutput.Click

    MessageBox.Show("Label was clicked.")
End Sub
```

Now we can compile and execute the program, which appears in Fig. 9.7. Whenever the label is clicked, a message box appears displaying the text **"Label was clicked"**. In previous examples, we commented out the code generated by the Visual Studio IDE. In this example, we present the complete code listing which we discuss in detail.

The Visual Studio .NET IDE generated the code pertaining to the creation and initialization of the application that we built through the GUI design window. The code generated by Visual Studio is contained within **#Region** and **#End Region** *preprocessor directives* (lines 7–69). In Visual Studio, these preprocessor directives allow code to be collapsed into a single line, enabling the programmer to focus on only certain portions of a program at a time. The only code that this example required us to write is the event-handling code (line 75).

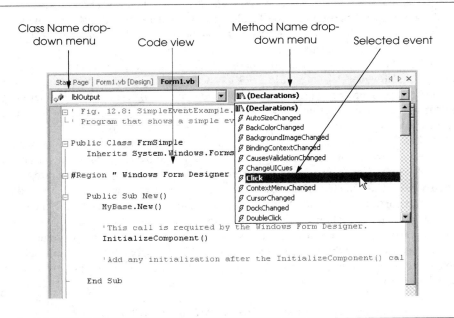

Fig. 9.6   Events section in the Method Name drop-down menu.

```
1    ' Fig. 9.7: SimpleEventExample.vb
2    ' Program demonstrating simple event handler.
3
4    Public Class FrmSimple
5        Inherits System.Windows.Forms.Form
```

Fig. 9.7   Simple event-handling example using visual programming. (Part 1 of 3.)

```
 6
 7   #Region " Windows Form Designer generated code "
 8
 9      Public Sub New()
10         MyBase.New()
11
12            ' This call is required by the Windows Form Designer.
13            InitializeComponent()
14
15
16            ' Add any initialization after the
17            ' InitializeComponent() call
18      End Sub
19
20      ' Form overrides dispose to clean up the component list.
21      Protected Overloads Overrides Sub Dispose( _
22         ByVal disposing As Boolean)
23
24         If disposing Then
25
26            If Not (components Is Nothing) Then
27               components.Dispose()
28            End If
29
30         End If
31
32         MyBase.Dispose(disposing)
33      End Sub
34
35      Friend WithEvents lblOutput As System.Windows.Forms.Label
36
37      ' Required by the Windows Form Designer
38      Private components As System.ComponentModel.Container
39
40      ' NOTE: The following procedure is required by
41      ' the Windows Form Designer.
42      ' It can be modified using the Windows Form Designer.
43      ' Do not modify it using the code editor.
44      <System.Diagnostics.DebuggerStepThrough()> _
45      Private Sub InitializeComponent()
46         Me.lblOutput = New System.Windows.Forms.Label()
47         Me.SuspendLayout()
48         '
49         'lblOutput
50         '
51         Me.lblOutput.Location = New System.Drawing.Point(32, 48)
52         Me.lblOutput.Name = "lblOutput"
53         Me.lblOutput.Size = New System.Drawing.Size(168, 40)
54         Me.lblOutput.TabIndex = 0
55         Me.lblOutput.Text = "Click Me!"
56         '
57         'FrmSimple
58         '
```

Fig. 9.7   Simple event-handling example using visual programming. (Part 2 of 3.)

```
59            Me.AutoScaleBaseSize = New System.Drawing.Size(5, 13)
60            Me.ClientSize = New System.Drawing.Size(272, 237)
61            Me.Controls.AddRange( _
62                New System.Windows.Forms.Control() {Me.lblOutput})
63
64            Me.Name = "FrmSimple"
65            Me.Text = "SimpleEventExample"
66            Me.ResumeLayout(False)
67        End Sub
68
69   #End Region
70
71        ' handler for click event on lblOutput
72        Private Sub lblOutput_Click(ByVal sender As Object, _
73            ByVal e As System.EventArgs) Handles lblOutput.Click
74
75            MessageBox.Show("Label was clicked")
76        End Sub ' lblOutput_Click
77
78   End Class ' FrmSimple
```

Fig. 9.7   Simple event-handling example using visual programming. (Part 3 of 3.)

The Visual Studio-generated code contains all references to the controls that we created through the GUI design window (in this case, **lblOutput**), the non-parameterized constructor (lines 9–18), the destructor (lines 21–33) and the initialization code for each of the controls (lines 44–67). The initialization code corresponds to the changes made to the **Properties** window for each control. Note that as we have learned in previous chapters, Visual Studio .NET adds comments to the code that it generates. The comments appear throughout the code, such as in lines 40–43. To make programs more concise and readable, we remove some of these generated comments in future examples, leaving only those comments that pertain to new concepts.

Lines 9–18 define the constructor. Because class **FrmSimple** inherits from **System.Windows.Forms.Form**, line 10 of the default constructor calls the base-class constructor. This allows the base-class constructor to perform initialization before class **FrmSimpleExample** instantiates. Line 13 calls the Visual Studio-generated method **InitializeComponent** (lines 44–67), which regulates the property settings for all the controls that we created in the **Design** window. The property settings method **InitializeComponent** establishes such properties as the **Form** title, the **Form** size, component sizes and text within components. Visual Studio .NET examines this method to create the design view of the code. If we change this method, Visual Studio .NET might not recognize our modifications, in which case it would display the design improperly. It is important to note that the design view is based on the code, and not vice versa. A program can run even if its design view displays incorrectly.

Software Engineering Observation 9.1

*The complexity of the Visual Studio generated code favors a recommendation that programmers modify individual control's properties through the **Properties** window.*

Visual Studio also places within the **#Region** and **#End Region** preprocessor directives a declaration for each control that is created via the design window. Line 35 declares the **lblOutput** control. There are three things to note about the declaration of reference **lblOutput**. First, the declaration has a **Friend** access modifier. By default, all variable declarations for controls created through the design window have a **Friend** access modifier. Second, line 35 declares a member variable (**lblOutput**) to class **Frm-Simple**. Although **lblOutput** is declared within the **#Region** and **#End Region** preprocessor directives, it is still a class member of **FrmSimple**. This is because the compiler does not consider the block of code encapsulated by the **#Region** and **#End Region** preprocessor directives to be a separate block of code. This means that the scope of variables declared within the **#Region** and **#End Region** preprocessor directives is not affected—the variables are included in the scope of the main class. Finally, the member variable **lblOutput** is declared with the keyword **WithEvents**.

The **WithEvents** keyword tells the compiler that methods handling events triggered by this component are identified by the inclusion of the suffix **Handles** *componentName.eventName* in their method declaration. When we selected event **Click** from the Method Name drop-down menu, the Visual Studio .NET IDE created a method signature that matched the **Click** event-handler delegate, placing the suffix **Handles lblOutput.Click** at the end of the method signature. This tells the Visual Basic compiler that the method will handle **Click** events triggered by **lblOutput**. However, it is possible to define additional methods that also handle **lblOutput Click** events. To register additional event handlers, we simply create a new method that has the same signature as the **Click** delegate and is accompanied by the method declaration suffix **Handles lblOutput.Click**.

The inclusion of multiple handlers for one event is called *event multicasting*. Although all event handlers are called when the event occurs, the order in which the event handlers are called is indeterminate.

Common Programming Error 9.1

The assumption that multiple event handlers registered for the same event are called in a particular order can lead to logic errors. If the order is important, register the first event handler and have it call the others in order, passing the event arguments to each handler.

As previously mentioned, every event handler must have a unique signature, which is specified by the event delegate. Two objects are passed to event handlers: A reference to the object that generated the event (**sender**) and an event arguments object (**e**). Argument **e** is of type **EventArgs**. Class **EventArgs** is the base class for objects that contain event information. We discuss the information contained in **EventArgs** objects later in the chapter.

To create the event handler, we first must find the delegate's signature. When we click an event name in the Method Name drop-down menu, Visual Studio .NET creates a method with the proper signature. The naming convention is *ControlName_EventName*; in our previous examples, the event handler is **lblOutput_Click**. Instead of using the Method Name drop-down menu, we also can look up the event-arguments class. Consult the documentation under each control's class (i.e., **Form class**), and click the **events** section (Fig. 9.8). This displays a list of all the events that the class can generate. Click the name of an event to bring up its delegate, its event argument type and a description (Fig. 9.9).

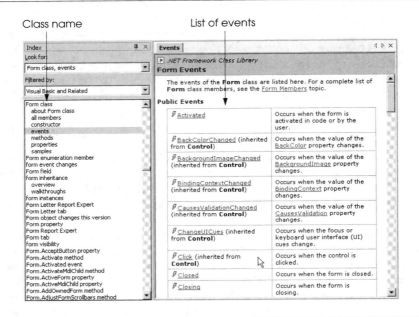

Fig. 9.8   List of **Form** events.

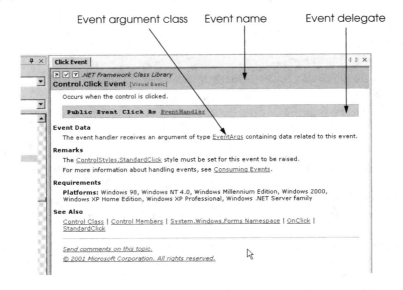

Fig. 9.9   **Click** event details.

In general, the format of the event-handling method is,

```
Private Sub ControlName_EventName(ByVal sender As Object, _
    ByVal e As System.EventArgs) Handles ControlName.EventName

        event-handling code
End Sub
```

where the name of the event handler is, by default, the name of the control, followed by an underscore (_) and the name of the event. Event handlers are methods that take two arguments: An **Object** (usually **sender**), and an instance of an **EventArgs** class. The differences between the various **EventArgs** classes are discussed later in this chapter.

Software Engineering Observation 9.2

*The handlers for predefined events (such as **Click**) are procedures. The programmer should not expect return values from event handlers; rather, event handlers are designed to execute code based on an action and then return control to the main program.*

Good Programming Practice 9.1

Use the event-handler naming convention ControlName_EventName, *so that method names are meaningful. Such names tell users what event a method handles, and for what control. Visual Studio .NET uses this naming convention when creating event handlers from the Method Name drop-down menu.*

In the upcoming sections, we indicate the *EventArgs* class and the *EventHandler* delegate that correspond to each event we present. To locate additional information about a particular type of event, review the help documentation under **ClassName class, events**.

9.4 Control Properties and Layout

This section overviews properties that are common to many controls. Controls derive from class **Control** (namespace **System.Windows.Forms**). Figure 9.10 lists some of class **Control**'s properties and methods; these properties can be set for many controls. The **Text** property determines the text that appears on a control. The appearance of this text can vary depending on the context. For example, the text of a Windows Form is its title bar, but the text of a button appears on its face.

Class **Control** Properties and Methods	Description
Common Properties	
BackColor	Sets the control's background color.
BackgroundImage	Sets the control's background image.
Enabled	Indicates whether the control is enabled (i.e., if the user can interact with it). A disabled control is displayed, but portions of the control appear in gray.

Fig. 9.10 Class **Control** properties and methods. (Part 1 of 2.)

Class `Control` Properties and Methods	Description
`Focused`	Indicates whether a control has the focus.
`Font`	Sets the `Font` used to display the control's text.
`ForeColor`	Sets the control's foreground color. This usually determines the color of the `Text` property.
`TabIndex`	Sets the tab order of the control. When the *Tab* key is pressed, the focus transfers to various controls according to the tab order. This order can be set by the programmer.
`TabStop`	Indicates whether users can employ the *Tab* key to select the control. If `True`, then a user can select this control through the *Tab* key.
`Text`	Sets the text associated with the control. The location and appearance varies depending on the type of control.
`TextAlign`	Establishes the alignment of the text on the control—possibilities are one of three horizontal positions (left, center or right) and one of three vertical positions (top, middle or bottom).
`Visible`	Indicates whether the control is visible.
Common Methods	
`Focus`	Acquires the focus.
`Hide`	Hides the control (sets `Visible` to `False`).
`Show`	Shows the control (sets `Visible` to `True`).

Fig. 9.10 Class `Control` properties and methods. (Part 2 of 2.)

The **Focus** method transfers the focus to a control. A control that has the focus is referred to as the *active control*. When the *Tab* key is pressed, controls are given the focus in the order specified by their **TabIndex** property. The **TabIndex** property is set by Visual Studio .NET, but can be changed by the programmer. **TabIndex** is helpful for users who enter information in many different locations—the user can enter information and quickly select the next control by pressing the *Tab* key. The **Enabled** property indicates whether a control can be used; often, if a control is disabled, it is because an option is unavailable to the user. In most cases, a disabled control's text appears in gray (rather than in black) when a control is disabled. However, a programmer can hide a control's text from the user without disabling the control by setting the **Visible** property to **False** or by calling method **Hide**. When a control's **Visible** property is set to **False**, the control still exists, but it is not shown on the form.

Visual Studio .NET enables control *anchoring* and *docking*, which allow the programmer to specify the layout of controls inside a container (such as a form). Anchoring causes controls to remain at a fixed distance from the sides of the container even when the control is resized. Docking sets the dimensions of a control to the dimensions of the parent container at all times.

For example, a programmer might want a control to appear in a certain position (top, bottom, left or right) in a form even if that form is resized. The programmer can specify this by *anchoring* the control to a side (top, bottom, left or right). The control then maintains a fixed distance between itself and the side to its parent container. Although most parent containers are forms, other controls also can act as parent containers.

When parent containers are resized, all controls move. Unanchored controls move relative to their original position on the form, whereas anchored controls move so that their distance from the sides to which they are anchored does not vary. For example, in Fig. 9.11, the top-most button is anchored to the top and left sides of the parent form. When the form is resized, the anchored button moves so that it remains a constant distance from the top and left sides of the form (its parent). By contrast, the unanchored button changes position as the form is resized.

To see the effects of anchoring a control, create a simple Windows application that contains two buttons (Fig. 9.12). Anchor one control to the right side by setting the **Anchor** property as shown in Fig. 9.12. Leave the other control unanchored. Now, enlarge the form by dragging its right side. Notice that both controls move. The anchored control moves so that it is always at the same distance from the top-right corner of the form, whereas the unanchored control adjusts its location relative to each side of the form.

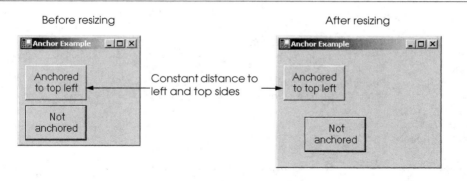

Fig. 9.11   Anchoring demonstration.

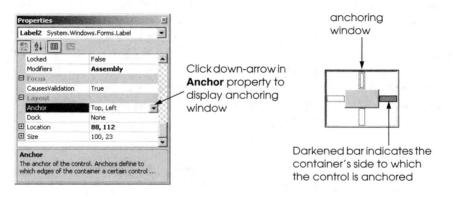

Fig. 9.12   Manipulating the **Anchor** property of a control.

Sometimes, it is desirable that a control span an entire side of the form, even when the form is resized. This is useful when we want one control, such as a status bar, to remain prevalent on the form. *Docking* allows a control to span an entire side (left, right, top or bottom) of its parent container. When the parent is resized, the docked control resizes as well. In Fig. 9.13, a button is docked at the top of the form (it spans the top portion). When the form is resized horizontally, the button is resized to the form's new width. Windows Forms provide property **DockPadding**, which specifies the distance between the docked controls and the form edges. The default value is zero, which results in docked controls that are attached to the edge of the form. The control layout properties are summarized in the table in Fig. 9.14.

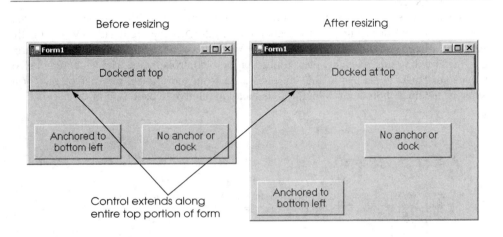

Fig. 9.13   Docking demonstration.

Common Layout Properties	Description
Anchor	Attaches control to the side of parent container. Used during resizing. Possible values include top, bottom, left and right.
Dock	Allows controls to span along the sides of their containers—values cannot be combined.
DockPadding (for containers)	Sets the space between a container's edges and docked controls. Default is zero, causing controls to appear flush with the sides of the container.
Location	Specifies the location of the upper-left corner of the control, in relation to its container.
Size	Specifies the size of the control. Takes a **Size** type, which has properties **Height** and **Width**.

Fig. 9.14   Control layout properties. (Part 1 of 2.)

Common Layout Properties	Description
MinimumSize, **MaximumSize** (for Windows Forms)	Indicates the minimum and maximum size of the form.

Fig. 9.14 **Control** layout properties. (Part 2 of 2.)

The docking and anchoring options refer to the parent container, which includes the form as well as other parent containers we discuss later in the chapter. The minimum and maximum form sizes can be set via properties ***MinimumSize*** and ***MaximumSize***, respectively. Both properties use the ***Size*** *type*, which has properties ***Height*** and ***Width***, to specify the size of the form. Properties **MinimumSize** and **MaximumSize** allow the programmer to design the GUI layout for a given size range. To set a form to a fixed size, set its minimum and maximum size to the same value.

Look-and-Feel Observation 9.2

Allow Windows Forms to be resized whenever possible—this enables users with limited screen space or multiple applications running at once to use the application more easily. Make sure that the GUI layout appears consistent across different permissible form sizes.

9.5 Labels, TextBoxes and Buttons

Labels provide text instructions or information and are defined with class ***Label***, which is derived from class **Control**. A **Label** displays *read-only text* (i.e., text that the user cannot modify). At runtime, a **Label**'s text can be changed by setting **Label**'s **Text** property. Figure 9.15 lists common **Label** properties.

A *textbox* (class ***TextBox***) is an area in which text can either be displayed by the program or be input by the user via the keyboard. A *password textbox* is a **TextBox** that hides the information entered by the user. As the user types in characters, the password textbox masks the user input by displaying characters (usually *****). If a value is provided for the ***PasswordChar*** property, the textbox becomes a password textbox. Otherwise it is a textbox.

Common **Label** Properties	Description / Delegate and Event Arguments
Font	The font used by the text on the **Label**.
Text	The text that appears on the **Label**.
TextAlign	The alignment of the **Label**'s text on the control. Possibilities are one of three horizontal positions (left, center or right) and one of three vertical positions (top, middle or bottom).

Fig. 9.15 Common **Label** properties.

Users often encounter both types of textboxes, when logging into a computer or Web site. The username textbox allows users to input their usernames; the password textbox allows users to enter their passwords. Figure 9.16 lists the common properties and events of **TextBox**es.

A *button* is a control that the user clicks to trigger a specific action. A program can employ several specific types of buttons, such as *checkboxes* and *radio buttons*. All the button types are derived from **ButtonBase** (namespace **System.Windows.Forms**), which defines common button features. In this section, we concentrate on the class **Button**, which initiates a command. The other button types are covered in subsequent sections. The text on the face of a **Button** is called a *button label*. Figure 9.17 lists the common properties and events of **Button**s.

Look-and-Feel Observation 9.3

*Although **Label**s, **TextBox**es and other controls can respond to mouse clicks, **Button**s more naturally convey this meaning. Use a **Button** (such as **OK**), rather than another type of control, to initiate a user action.*

The program in Fig. 9.18 uses a **TextBox**, a **Button** and a **Label**. The user enters text into a password box and clicks the **Button**, causing the text input to be displayed in the **Label**. Normally, we would not display this text—the purpose of password textboxes is to hide the text being entered by the user from anyone who might be looking over the user's shoulder. Figure 9.18 demonstrates that the text input into the password textbox is unaffected by property **PasswordChar**'s value.

First, we create the GUI by dragging the controls (a **Button**, a **Label** and a **TextBox**) onto the form. Once the controls are positioned, we change their names in the **Properties** window (by setting the **(Name)** property) from the default values—**TextBox1**, **Label1** and **Button1**—to the more descriptive **lblOutput**, **txtInput** and **cmdShow**. Visual Studio .NET creates the necessary code and places it inside method **InitializeComponent**. The **(Name)** property in the **Properties** window enables us to change the variable name of the object reference.

TextBox Properties and Events	Description / Delegate and Event Arguments
Common Properties	
AcceptsReturn	If **True**, pressing *Enter* creates a new line (if textbox is configured to contain multiple lines.) If **False**, pressing *Enter* clicks the default button of the form.
Multiline	If **True**, **Textbox** can span multiple lines. The default value is **False**.
PasswordChar	If a character is provided for this property, the **TextBox** becomes a password box, and the specified character masks each character typed by the user. If no character is specified, **Textbox** displays the typed text.

Fig. 9.16   **TextBox** properties and events. (Part 1 of 2.)

TextBox Properties and Events	Description / Delegate and Event Arguments
ReadOnly	If **True**, **TextBox** has a gray background, and its text cannot be edited. The default value is **False**.
ScrollBars	For multiline textboxes, indicates which scrollbars appear (**none**, **horizontal**, **vertical** or **both**).
Text	The textbox's text content.
Common Events	*(Delegate **EventHandler**, event arguments **EventArgs**)*
TextChanged	Generated when text changes in **TextBox** (i.e., when the user adds or deletes characters). When a programmer double-clicks the **Text-Box** control in **Design** view, an empty event handler for this event is generated.

Fig. 9.16　**TextBox** properties and events. (Part 2 of 2.)

Button properties and events	Description / Delegate and Event Arguments
Common Properties	
Text	Specifies text displayed on the **Button** face.
Common Events	*(Delegate **EventHandler**, event arguments **EventArgs**)*
Click	Generated when user clicks the control. When a programmer double-clicks the **Button** control in design view, an empty event handler for this event is created.

Fig. 9.17　**Button** properties and events.

```vb
1    ' Fig. 9.18: LabelTextBoxButtonTest.vb
2    ' Using a textbox, label and button to display the hidden
3    ' text in a password box.
4
5    Imports System.Windows.Forms
6
7    Public Class FrmButtonTest
8       Inherits Form
9
10      Friend WithEvents txtInput As TextBox  ' input field
11      Friend WithEvents lblOutput As Label   ' display label
12      Friend WithEvents cmdShow As Button    ' activation button
13
14      ' Visual Studio .NET generated code
15
```

Fig. 9.18　Program to display hidden text in a password box. (Part 1 of 2.)

```
16        ' handles cmdShow_Click events
17        Private Sub cmdShow_Click(ByVal sender As System.Object, _
18           ByVal e As System.EventArgs) Handles cmdShow.Click
19
20           lblOutput.Text = txtInput.Text
21        End Sub ' cmdShow_Click
22
23     End Class ' FrmButtonTest
```

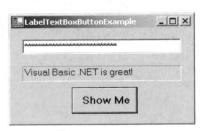

Fig. 9.18   Program to display hidden text in a password box. (Part 2 of 2.)

We then set **cmdShow**'s **Text** property to "**Show Me**" and clear the **Text** of **lblOutput** and **txtInput** so that they are blank when the program begins its execution. The **BorderStyle** property of **lblOutput** is set to **Fixed3D**, giving our **Label** a three-dimensional appearance. Notice that the **BorderStyle** property of all **TextBox**es is set to **Fixed3D** by default. The password character is set by assigning the asterisk character (*****) to the **PasswordChar** property. This property accepts only one character.

We create an event handler for **cmdShow** by selecting **cmdShow** from the Class Name drop-down menu and by selecting **Click** from the Method Name drop-down menu. This generates an empty event handler. We add line 20 to the event-handler code. When the user clicks **Button Show Me**, line 20 obtains user-input text in **txtInput** and displays it in **lblOutput**.

9.6 GroupBoxes and Panels

GroupBoxes and **Panel**s arrange controls on a GUI. For example, buttons with similar functionality can be placed inside a **GroupBox** or **Panel** within the Visual Studio .NET Form Designer. All these buttons move together when the **GroupBox** or **Panel** is moved.

The main difference between the two classes is that **GroupBox**es can display a caption (i.e., text) and do not include scrollbars, whereas **Panel**s can include scrollbars and do not include a caption. **GroupBox**es have thin borders by default; **Panel**s can be set so that they also have borders, by changing their **BorderStyle** property.

Look-and-Feel Observation 9.4
Panels and GroupBoxes can contain other Panels and GroupBoxes.

Look-and-Feel Observation 9.5
Organize the GUI by anchoring and docking controls (of similar functionality) inside a GroupBox or Panel. The GroupBox or Panel then can be anchored or docked inside a form. This divides controls into functional "groups" that can be arranged easily.

To create a **GroupBox**, drag it from the toolbar and place it on a form. Then, create new controls and place them inside the **GroupBox**. These controls are added to the **GroupBox**'s *Controls property* and become part of the **GroupBox** class. The **GroupBox**'s **Text** property determines its caption. The following tables list the common properties of **GroupBox**es (Fig. 9.19) and **Panel**s (Fig. 9.20).

To create a **Panel**, drag it onto the form, and add controls to it. To enable the scroll-bars, set the **Panel**'s **AutoScroll** property to **True**. If the **Panel** is resized and cannot display all of its controls, scrollbars appear (Fig. 9.21). The scrollbars then can be used to view all the controls in the **Panel** (both when running and designing the form). This allows the programmer to see the GUI exactly as it appears to the client.

GroupBox Properties	Description
Controls	Lists the controls that the **GroupBox** contains.
Text	Specifies text displayed at the top of the **GroupBox** (its caption).

Fig. 9.19 GroupBox properties.

Panel Properties	Description
AutoScroll	Indicates whether scrollbars appear when the **Panel** is too small to display all of its controls. Default is **False**.
BorderStyle	Sets the border of the **Panel** (default **None**; other options are **Fixed3D** and **FixedSingle**).
Controls	Lists the controls that the **Panel** contains.

Fig. 9.20 Panel properties.

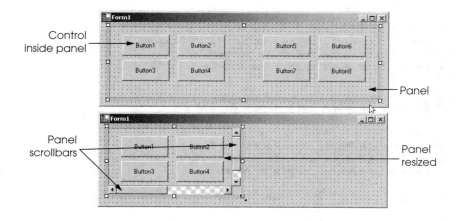

Fig. 9.21 Creating a **Panel** with scrollbars.

Look-and-Feel Observation 9.6

*Use **Panel**s with scrollbars to avoid cluttering a GUI and to reduce the GUI's size.*

The program in Fig. 9.22 uses a **GroupBox** and a **Panel** to arrange buttons. These buttons change the text on a **Label**.

The **GroupBox** (named **mainGroupBox**, line 10) has two buttons, **cmdHi** (labeled **Hi**, line 11) and **cmdBye** (labeled **Bye**, line 12). The **Panel** (named **mainPanel**, line 18) also has two buttons, **cmdLeft** (labeled **Far Left**, line19) and **cmdRight** (labeled **Far Right**, line 20). The **mainPanel** control has its **AutoScroll** property set to **True**, allowing scrollbars to appear when the contents of the **Panel** require more space than the **Panel**'s visible area. The **Label** (named **lblMessage**) is initially blank.

To add controls to **mainGroupBox**, Visual Studio .NET creates a **Windows.Forms.Control** array containing the controls. It then passes the array to method **AddRange** of the **Controls** collection in the **GroupBox**. Similarly, to add controls to **mainPanel**, Visual Studio .NET creates a **Windows.Forms.Control** array and passes it to the **mainPanel**'s **Controls.AddRange** method. Method **Controls.Add** adds a single control to a **Panel** or **GroupBox**.

The event handlers for the four buttons are located in lines 25–50. To create an empty **Click** event handler, double click the button in design mode (instead of using the Method Name drop-down menu). We then add a line in each handler to change the text of **lblMessage**.

```vb
1   ' Fig. 9.22: GroupBoxPanelExample.vb
2   ' Using GroupBoxes and Panels to hold buttons.
3
4   Imports System.Windows.Forms
5
6   Public Class FrmGroupBox
7      Inherits Form
8
9      ' top group box and controls
10     Friend WithEvents mainGroupBox As GroupBox
11     Friend WithEvents cmdHi As Button
12     Friend WithEvents cmdBye As Button
13
14     ' middle display
15     Friend WithEvents lblMessage As Label
16
17     ' bottom panel and controls
18     Private WithEvents mainPanel As Panel
19     Friend WithEvents cmdLeft As Button
20     Friend WithEvents cmdRight As Button
21
22     ' Visual Studio .NET generated code
23
```

Fig. 9.22 Using **GroupBox**es and **Panel**s to arrange **Button**s. (Part 1 of 2.)

```
24      ' event handlers to change lblMessage
25      Private Sub cmdHi_Click(ByVal sender As System.Object, _
26         ByVal e As System.EventArgs) Handles cmdHi.Click
27
28         lblMessage.Text = "Hi pressed"
29      End Sub ' cmdHi_Click
30
31      ' bye button handler
32      Private Sub cmdBye_Click(ByVal sender As System.Object, _
33         ByVal e As System.EventArgs) Handles cmdBye.Click
34
35         lblMessage.Text = "Bye pressed"
36      End Sub ' cmdBye_Click
37
38      ' far left button handler
39      Private Sub cmdLeft_Click(ByVal sender As System.Object, _
40         ByVal e As System.EventArgs) Handles cmdLeft.Click
41
42         lblMessage.Text = "Far left pressed"
43      End Sub ' cmdLeft_Click
44
45      ' far right button handler
46      Private Sub cmdRight_Click(ByVal sender As System.Object, _
47         ByVal e As System.EventArgs) Handles cmdRight.Click
48
49         lblMessage.Text = "Far right pressed"
50      End Sub ' cmdRight_Click
51
52   End Class ' FrmGroupBox
```

 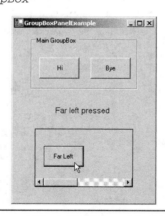 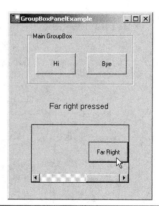

Fig. 9.22   Using **GroupBox**es and **Panel**s to arrange **Button**s. (Part 2 of 2.)

9.7 CheckBoxes and RadioButtons

Visual Basic .NET has two types of *state buttons*—***CheckBox*** and ***RadioButton***—that can be in the on/off or true/false state. Classes **CheckBox** and **RadioButton** are derived from class **ButtonBase**. A **RadioButton** is different from a **CheckBox** in that **RadioButton**s are usually organized into groups and that only one of the **RadioButton**s in the group can be selected (**True**) at any time.

A checkbox is a small white square that either is blank or contains a checkmark. When a checkbox is selected, a black checkmark appears in the box. There are no restrictions on how checkboxes are used—any number of boxes can be selected at a time. The text that appears alongside a checkbox is referred to as the *checkbox label*. A list of common properties and events of class **Checkbox** appears in Fig. 9.23.

The program in Fig. 9.24 allows the user to select a **CheckBox** to change the font style of a **Label**. One **CheckBox** applies a bold style, whereas the other applies an italic style. If both **CheckBox**es are selected, the style of the font is both bold and italic. When the program initially executes, neither **CheckBox** is checked.

CheckBox events and properties	Description / Delegate and Event Arguments
Common Properties	
Checked	Indicates whether the **CheckBox** is checked (contains a black checkmark) or unchecked (blank).
CheckState	Indicates whether the **Checkbox** is checked or unchecked. An enumeration with values **Checked**, **Unchecked** or **Indeterminate** (checks and shades checkbox).
Text	Specifies the text displayed to the right of the **CheckBox** (called the label).
Common Events	*(Delegate **EventHandler**, event arguments **EventArgs**)*
CheckedChanged	Generated every time the **Checkbox** is either checked or unchecked. When a user double-clicks the **CheckBox** control in design view, an empty event handler for this event is generated.
CheckStateChanged	Generated when the **CheckState** property changes.

Fig. 9.23 **CheckBox** properties and events.

```
1    ' Fig. 9.24: CheckBoxTest.vb
2    ' Using CheckBoxes to toggle italic and bold styles.
3
4    Imports System.Windows.Forms
5
6    Public Class FrmCheckBox
7       Inherits Form
8
9       ' display label
10      Friend WithEvents lblOutput As Label
11
12      ' font checkboxes
13      Friend WithEvents chkBold As CheckBox
14      Friend WithEvents chkItalic As CheckBox
15
16      ' Visual Studio .NET generated code
17
```

Fig. 9.24 Using **CheckBox**es to change font styles. (Part 1 of 2.)

```
18          ' use Xor to toggle italic, keep other styles same
19          Private Sub chkItalic_CheckedChanged _
20             (ByVal sender As System.Object, ByVal e As System.EventArgs) _
21             Handles chkItalic.CheckedChanged
22
23             lblOutput.Font = New Font(lblOutput.Font.Name, _
24                lblOutput.Font.Size, lblOutput.Font.Style _
25                Xor FontStyle.Italic)
26          End Sub ' chkItalic_CheckedChanged
27
28          ' use Xor to toggle bold, keep other styles same
29          Private Sub chkBold_CheckedChanged _
30             (ByVal sender As System.Object, ByVal e As System.EventArgs) _
31             Handles chkBold.CheckedChanged
32
33             lblOutput.Font = New Font(lblOutput.Font.Name, _
34                lblOutput.Font.Size, lblOutput.Font.Style _
35                Xor FontStyle.Bold)
36          End Sub ' chkBold_CheckedChanged
37
38       End Class ' FrmCheckBox
```

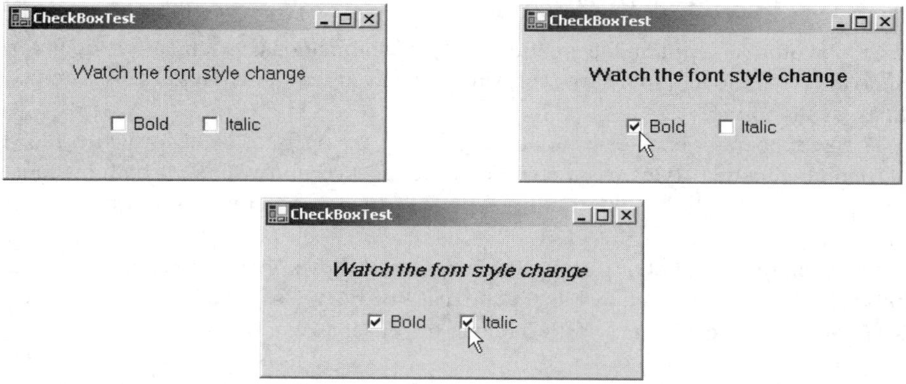

Fig. 9.24   Using **CheckBox**es to change font styles. (Part 2 of 2.)

The first **CheckBox**, named **chkBold** (line 13), has its **Text** property set to **Bold**. The other **CheckBox** is named **chkItalic** (line 14) and labeled **Italic**. The **Text** property of the **Label**, named **lblOutput**, is set to **Watch the font style change**.

After creating the controls, we define their event handlers. Double clicking the **CheckBox** named **chkBold** at design time creates an empty **CheckedChanged** event handler (line 29). To understand the code added to the event handler, we first discuss the **Font** property of **lblOutput**.

To enable the font to be changed, the programmer must set the **Font** property to a **Font** object. The **Font** constructor (lines 23–25 and 33–35) that we use takes the font name, size and style. The first two arguments namely **lblOutput.Font.Name** and **lblOutput.Font.Size** (lines 24 and 34), make use of **lblOutput**'s **Font** object. The style is a member of the **FontStyle** enumeration, which contains the font styles **Regular**, **Bold**, **Italic**, **Strikeout** and **Underline**. (The **Strikeout** style displays text with a line through it; the **Underline** style displays text with a line below it.) A **Font** object's **Style** property, which is read-only, is set when the **Font** object is created.

Styles can be combined via *bitwise operators*—operators that perform manipulation on bits. Recall from Chapter 1 that all data is represented on the computer as a series of 0s and 1s. Each 0 or 1 represents a bit. The FCL documentation indicates that **FontStyle** is a **System.FlagAttribute**, meaning that the **FontStyle** bit-values are selected in a way that allows us to combine different **FontStyle** elements to create compound styles, using bitwise operators. These styles are not mutually exclusive, so we can combine different styles and remove them without affecting the combination of previous **Font-Style** elements. We can combine these various font styles, using either the **Or** operator or the **Xor** operator. As a result of applying the **Or** operator to two bits, if at least one bit out of the two bits is 1, then the result is 1. The combination of styles using the **Or** operator works as follows. Assume that **FontStyle.Bold** is represented by bits **01** and that **FontStyle.Italic** is represented by bits **10**. When we **Or** both styles, we obtain the bitset **11**.

```
        01      = Bold
 Or     10      = Italic
        --
        11      = Bold and Italic
```

The **Or** operator is helpful in the creation of style combinations, as long as we do not need to undo the bitwise operation. However, what happens if we want to undo a style combination, as we did in Fig. 9.24?

The **Xor** operator enables us to accomplish the **Or** operator behavior while allowing us to undo compound styles. As a result of applying **Xor** to two bits, if both bits are the same ([1, 1] or [0, 0]), then the result is 0. If both bits are different ([1, 0] or [0, 1]), then the result is 1.

The combination of styles using **Xor** works as follows. Assume, again, that **Font-Style.Bold** is represented by bits **01** and that **FontStyle.Italic** is represented by bits **10**. When we **Xor** both styles, we obtain the bitset **11**.

```
        01      = Bold
 Xor    10      = Italic
        --
        11      = Bold and Italic
```

Now, suppose that we would like to remove the **FontStyle.Bold** style from the previous combination of **FontStyle.Bold** and **FontStyle.Italic**. The easiest way to do so is to reapply the **Xor** operator to the compound style and **Font-Style.Bold**.

```
        11      = Bold and Italic
 Xor    01      = Bold
        ----
        10      = Italic
```

This is a simple example. The advantages of using bitwise operators to combine **Font-Style** elements become more evident when we consider that there are five different **FontStyle** elements (**Bold**, **Italic**, **Regular**, **Strikeout** and **Underline**), resulting in 16 different **FontStyle** combinations. Using bitwise operators to combine font styles greatly reduces the amount of code required to check all possible font combinations.

In Fig. 9.24, we need to set the **FontStyle** so that the text appears bold if it was not bold originally, and vice versa. Notice that, in line 35, we use the bitwise **Xor** operator to do this. If **lblOutput.Font.Style** (line 34) is bold, then the resulting style is not bold. If the text is originally italicized, the resulting style is italicized and bold, rather than just bold. The same applies for **FontStyle.Italic** in line 25.

If we did not use bitwise operators to compound **FontStyle** elements, we would have to test for the current style and change it accordingly. For example, in the method **chkBold_CheckChanged**, we could test for the regular style and make it bold; test for the bold style and make it regular; test for the italic style and make it bold italic; and test for the italic bold style and make it italic. However, this method is cumbersome because, for every new style we add, we double the number of combinations. If we added a checkbox for underline, we would have to test for eight possible styles. To add a checkbox for strikeout then would require an additional 16 tests in each event handler. By using the bitwise **Xor** operator, we save ourselves from this trouble.

Radio buttons (defined with class *RadioButton*) are similar to checkboxes in that they also have two states—*selected* and *not selected* (also called *deselected*). However, radio buttons normally appear as a *group*, in which only one radio button can be selected at a time. The selection of one radio button in the group forces all other radio buttons in the group to be deselected. Therefore, radio buttons are used to represent a set of *mutually exclusive* options (i.e., a set in which multiple options cannot be selected at the same time).

Look-and-Feel Observation 9.7
Use RadioButtons when the user should choose only one option in a group.

Look-and-Feel Observation 9.8
Use CheckBoxes when the user should be able to choose multiple options in a group.

All radio buttons added to a form become part of the same group. To separate radio buttons into several groups, the radio buttons must be added to **GroupBox**es or **Panel**s. The common properties and events of class **RadioButton** are listed in Fig. 9.25.

RadioButton properties and events	Description / Delegate and Event Arguments
Common Properties	
Checked	Indicates whether the **RadioButton** is checked.
Text	Specifies the text displayed to the right of the **RadioButton** (called the label).
Common Events	*(Delegate **EventHandler**, event arguments **EventArgs**)*
Click	Generated when user clicks the control.

Fig. 9.25   RadioButton properties and events. (Part 1 of 2.)

RadioButton properties and events	Description / Delegate and Event Arguments
CheckedChanged	Generated every time the **RadioButton** is checked or unchecked. When a user double-clicks the **RadioButton** control in design view, an empty event handler for this event is generated.

Fig. 9.25 **RadioButton** properties and events. (Part 2 of 2.)

 Software Engineering Observation 9.3

Forms, GroupBoxes, and Panels can act as logical groups for radio buttons. The radio buttons within each group are mutually exclusive with each other, but not with radio buttons in different groups.

The program in Fig. 9.26 uses radio buttons to enable the selection of options for a **MessageBox**. After selecting the desired attributes, the user presses **Button Display**, causing the **MessageBox** to appear. A **Label** in the lower-left corner shows the result of the **MessageBox** (**Yes**, **No**, **Cancel** etc.). The different **MessageBox** icons and button types are illustrated and explained in Chapter 3, Control Structures.

To store the user's choice of options, the objects **iconType** and **buttonType** are created and initialized (lines 9–10). Object **iconType** is a **MessageBoxIcon** enumeration that can have values **Asterisk**, **Error**, **Exclamation**, **Hand**, **Information**, **Question**, **Stop** and **Warning**. In this example, we use only **Error**, **Exclamation**, **Information** and **Question**.

```
1   ' Fig. 9.26: RadioButtonTest.vb
2   ' Using RadioButtons to set message window options.
3
4   Imports System.Windows.Forms
5
6   Public Class FrmRadioButton
7      Inherits Form
8
9      Private iconType As MessageBoxIcon
10     Private buttonType As MessageBoxButtons
11
12     ' button type group box and controls
13     Friend WithEvents buttonTypeGroupBox As GroupBox
14     Friend WithEvents radOk As RadioButton
15     Friend WithEvents radOkCancel As RadioButton
16     Friend WithEvents radAbortRetryIgnore As RadioButton
17     Friend WithEvents radYesNoCancel As RadioButton
18     Friend WithEvents radYesNo As RadioButton
19     Friend WithEvents radRetryCancel As RadioButton
20
21     ' icon group box and controls
22     Friend WithEvents iconGroupBox As GroupBox
23     Friend WithEvents radAsterisk As RadioButton
```

Fig. 9.26 Using **RadioButton**s to set message-window options. (Part 1 of 6.)

```
24      Friend WithEvents radError As RadioButton
25      Friend WithEvents radExclamation As RadioButton
26      Friend WithEvents radHand As RadioButton
27      Friend WithEvents radInformation As RadioButton
28      Friend WithEvents radQuestion As RadioButton
29      Friend WithEvents radStop As RadioButton
30      Friend WithEvents radWarning As RadioButton
31
32      ' display button
33      Friend WithEvents cmdDisplay As Button
34
35      ' output label
36      Friend WithEvents lblDisplay As Label
37
38      ' Visual Studio .NET generated code
39
40      ' display message box and obtain dialogue button clicked
41      Private Sub cmdDisplay_Click(ByVal sender _
42         As System.Object, ByVal e As System.EventArgs) _
43         Handles cmdDisplay.Click
44
45         Dim dialog As DialogResult = MessageBox.Show( _
46            "This is Your Custom MessageBox", "Custom MessageBox", _
47            buttonType, iconType)
48
49         ' check for dialog result and display on label
50         Select Case dialog
51
52            Case DialogResult.OK
53               lblDisplay.Text = "OK was pressed"
54
55            Case DialogResult.Cancel
56               lblDisplay.Text = "Cancel was pressed"
57
58            Case DialogResult.Abort
59               lblDisplay.Text = "Abort was pressed"
60
61            Case DialogResult.Retry
62               lblDisplay.Text = "Retry was pressed"
63
64            Case DialogResult.Ignore
65               lblDisplay.Text = "Ignore was pressed"
66
67            Case DialogResult.Yes
68               lblDisplay.Text = "Yes was pressed"
69
70            Case DialogResult.No
71               lblDisplay.Text = "No was pressed"
72         End Select
73
74      End Sub ' cmdDisplay_Click
75
```

Fig. 9.26   Using **RadioButton**s to set message-window options. (Part 2 of 6.)

```
76      ' set button type to OK
77      Private Sub radOk_CheckedChanged(ByVal sender _
78         As System.Object, ByVal e As System.EventArgs) _
79         Handles radOk.CheckedChanged
80
81         buttonType = MessageBoxButtons.OK
82      End Sub ' radOk_CheckedChanged
83
84      ' set button type to OkCancel
85      Private Sub radOkCancel_CheckedChanged(ByVal sender _
86         As System.Object, ByVal e As System.EventArgs) _
87         Handles radOkCancel.CheckedChanged
88
89         buttonType = MessageBoxButtons.OKCancel
90      End Sub ' radOkCancel_CheckedChanged
91
92      ' set button type to AbortRetryIgnore
93      Private Sub radAbortRetryIgnore_CheckedChanged(ByVal sender _
94         As System.Object, ByVal e As System.EventArgs) _
95         Handles radAbortRetryIgnore.CheckedChanged
96
97         buttonType = MessageBoxButtons.AbortRetryIgnore
98      End Sub ' radAbortRetryIgnore_CheckedChanged
99
100     ' set button type to YesNoCancel
101     Private Sub radYesNoCancel_CheckedChanged(ByVal sender _
102        As System.Object, ByVal e As System.EventArgs) _
103        Handles radYesNoCancel.CheckedChanged
104
105        buttonType = MessageBoxButtons.YesNoCancel
106     End Sub ' radYesNoCancel_CheckedChanged
107
108     ' set button type to YesNo
109     Private Sub radYesNo_CheckedChanged(ByVal sender _
110        As System.Object, ByVal e As System.EventArgs) _
111        Handles radYesNo.CheckedChanged
112
113        buttonType = MessageBoxButtons.YesNo
114     End Sub ' radYesNo_CheckedChanged
115
116     ' set button type to RetryCancel
117     Private Sub radRetryCancel_CheckedChanged(ByVal sender _
118        As System.Object, ByVal e As System.EventArgs) _
119        Handles radRetryCancel.CheckedChanged
120
121        buttonType = MessageBoxButtons.RetryCancel
122     End Sub ' radRetryCancel_CheckedChanged
123
124     ' set icon type to Asterisk when Asterisk checked
125     Private Sub radAsterisk_CheckedChanged(ByVal sender _
126        As System.Object, ByVal e As System.EventArgs) _
127        Handles radAsterisk.CheckedChanged
128
```

Fig. 9.26 Using **RadioButton**s to set message-window options. (Part 3 of 6.)

```
129        iconType = MessageBoxIcon.Asterisk
130    End Sub ' radAsterisk_CheckedChanged
131
132    ' set icon type to Error when Error checked
133    Private Sub radError_CheckedChanged(ByVal sender _
134        As System.Object, ByVal e As System.EventArgs) _
135        Handles radError.CheckedChanged
136
137        iconType = MessageBoxIcon.Error
138    End Sub ' radError_CheckedChanged
139
140    ' set icon type to Exclamation when Exclamation checked
141    Private Sub radExclamation_CheckedChanged(ByVal sender _
142        As System.Object, ByVal e As System.EventArgs) _
143        Handles radExclamation.CheckedChanged
144
145        iconType = MessageBoxIcon.Exclamation
146    End Sub ' radExclamation_CheckedChanged
147
148    ' set icon type to Hand when Hand checked
149    Private Sub radHand_CheckedChanged(ByVal sender _
150        As System.Object, ByVal e As System.EventArgs) _
151        Handles radHand.CheckedChanged
152
153        iconType = MessageBoxIcon.Hand
154    End Sub ' radHand_CheckedChanged
155
156    ' set icon type to Information when Information checked
157    Private Sub radInformation_CheckedChanged(ByVal sender _
158        As System.Object, ByVal e As System.EventArgs) _
159        Handles radInformation.CheckedChanged
160
161        iconType = MessageBoxIcon.Information
162    End Sub ' radInformation_CheckedChanged
163
164    ' set icon type to Question when Question checked
165    Private Sub radQuestion_CheckedChanged(ByVal sender _
166        As System.Object, ByVal e As System.EventArgs) _
167        Handles radQuestion.CheckedChanged
168
169        iconType = MessageBoxIcon.Question
170    End Sub ' radQuestion_CheckedChanged
171
172    ' set icon type to Stop when Stop checked
173    Private Sub radStop_CheckedChanged(ByVal sender _
174        As System.Object, ByVal e As System.EventArgs) _
175        Handles radStop.CheckedChanged
176
177        iconType = MessageBoxIcon.Stop
178    End Sub ' radStop_CheckedChanged
179
```

Fig. 9.26   Using **RadioButton**s to set message-window options. (Part 4 of 6.)

```
180        ' set icon type to Warning when Warning checked
181        Private Sub radWarning_CheckedChanged(ByVal sender _
182           As System.Object, ByVal e As System.EventArgs) _
183           Handles radWarning.CheckedChanged
184
185           iconType = MessageBoxIcon.Warning
186        End Sub ' radWarning_CheckedChanged
187
188     End Class ' FrmRadioButton
```

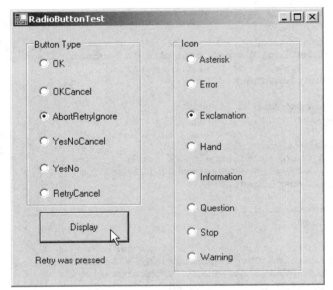

Exclamation icon type

(**OKCancel** button type)

Error icon type

(**OK** button type)

Information icon type

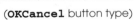

(**AbortRetryIgnore** button type)

Question icon type

(**YesNoCancel** button type)

Fig. 9.26   Using **RadioButton**s to set message-window options. (Part 5 of 6.)

(**YesNo** button type)   (**RetryCancel** button type)

Fig. 9.26   Using **RadioButton**s to set message-window options. (Part 6 of 6.)

Object **buttonType** is a **MessageBoxButton** enumeration with values **Abort-RetryIgnore, OK, OKCancel, RetryCancel, YesNo** and **YesNoCancel**. The name indicates the options that are presented to the user. This example employs all **MessageBoxButton** enumeration values.

Two **GroupBox**es are created, one for each enumeration. Their captions are **Button Type** and **Icon**. There is also a button (**cmdDisplay**, line 33) labeled **Display**; when a user clicks it, a customized message box is displayed. A **Label** (**lblDisplay**, line 36) displays which button within the message box was pressed. **RadioButton**s are created for the enumeration options, and their labels are set appropriately. Because the radio buttons are grouped, only one **RadioButton** can be selected from each **GroupBox**.

Each radio button has an event handler that handles the radio button's **Checked-Changed** event. When a radio button contained in the **Button Type GroupBox** is checked, the checked radio button's corresponding event-handler sets **buttonType** to the appropriate value. Lines 77–122 contain the event handling for these radio buttons. Similarly, when the user checks the radio buttons belonging to the **Icon GroupBox**, the event handlers associated to these events (lines 125–186) sets **iconType** to its corresponding value.

To create the event handler for an event, it is necessary to use the functionality provided by Visual Studio. Note that each check box has its own event handler. This design has several advantages. First, it allows developers to modify the functionality of their code (i.e., by adding or removing check boxes) with minimal structural changes. The design structure also partitions the event-handling code to each respective event handler, reducing the potential for the accidental introduction of bugs into the code when an event handler for a particular check box must change. One common alternative design employs one event handler to handle all **CheckedChanged** events from a set of radio buttons. A "monolithic control structure" typically determines which code to execute on the basis of the control that triggered the event. This design offers the benefit that all event-handling code is localized to one event handler. However, the design complicates the process of extending the code for each event handler. Whenever the programmer modifies the event-handling code for a given **CheckBox**, a bug could be introduced into the monolithic control structure and could affect the code for the other, unmodified event handlers. This event-handling scheme is not recommended. It is always a good idea to separate unrelated sections of code from one another. This reduces the potential for bugs, thus decreasing development time.

The **Click** handler for **cmdDisplay** (lines 41–74) creates a **MessageBox** (lines 45–47). The **MessageBox** options are set by **iconType** and **buttonType**. The result of the message box is a **DialogResult** enumeration that has possible values **Abort, Cancel, Ignore, No, None, OK, Retry** or **Yes**. The **Select Case** statement on lines 50–72 tests for the result and sets **lblDisplay.Text** appropriately.

9.8 PictureBoxes

A picture box (class **PictureBox**) displays an image. The image, set by an object of class **Image**, can include a bitmap, a *GIF (Graphics Interchange Format)*, a *JPEG (Joint Photographic Expert Group)*, icon or metafile format. (Images and multimedia are discussed in Chapter 13, Graphics and Multimedia.)

The **Image** property specifies the image that is displayed, and the **SizeMode** property indicates how the image is displayed (**Normal, StretchImage, Autosize** or **CenterImage**). Figure 9.27 describes important properties and events of class **PictureBox**.

The program in Fig. 9.28 uses **PictureBox picImage** to display one of three bitmap images—**image0, image1** or **image2**. These images are located in the directory **images** (in the **bin/images** directory of our project), where the executable file is located. Whenever a user clicks **picImage**, the image changes. The **Label** (named **lblPrompt**) at the top of the form displays the text **Click On Picture Box to View Images**.

PictureBox properties and events	Description / Delegate and Event Arguments
Common Properties	
Image	Sets the image to display in the **PictureBox**.
SizeMode	Enumeration that controls image sizing and positioning. Values are **Normal** (default), **StretchImage, AutoSize** and **CenterImage**. **Normal** places the image in top-left corner of **PictureBox**, and **CenterImage** puts the image in middle (both truncate the image if it is too large). **StretchImage** resizes the image to fit in **PictureBox**. **AutoSize** resizes **PictureBox** to hold the image.
Common Events	*(Delegate **EventHandler**, event arguments **EventArgs**)*
Click	Generated when a user clicks the control. Default event when this control is double clicked in the designer.

Fig. 9.27 **PictureBox** properties and events.

```
1   ' Fig. 9.28: PictureBoxTest.vb
2   ' Using a PictureBox to display images.
3
4   Imports System.IO
5   Imports System.Windows.Forms
6
7   Public Class FrmPictureBox
8      Inherits Form
9
10     Private imageNumber As Integer = -1
11
12     ' instructions display label
13     Friend WithEvents lblPrompt As Label
```

Fig. 9.28 Using a **PictureBox** to display images. (Part 1 of 2.)

```
14
15       ' image display area
16       Friend WithEvents picImage As PictureBox
17
18       ' Visual Studio .NET generated code
19
20       ' replace image in picImage
21       Private Sub picImage_Click(ByVal sender As System.Object, _
22          ByVal e As System.EventArgs) Handles picImage.Click
23
24          ' imageNumber from 0 to 2
25          imageNumber = (imageNumber + 1) Mod 3
26
27          ' create Image object from file, display in PictureBox
28          picImage.Image = Image.FromFile _
29             (Directory.GetCurrentDirectory & "\images\image" & _
30             imageNumber & ".bmp")
31       End Sub ' picImage_Click
32
33    End Class ' FrmPictureBox
```

Fig. 9.28   Using a **PictureBox** to display images. (Part 2 of 2.)

To respond to the user's clicks, the program must handle the **Click** event. Inside the event handler, **picImage_Click** (lines 21–31), we use an **Integer** (**imageNumber**) to store the image we want to display. We then set the **Image** property of **picImage** to an **Image** (lines 28–30). Although class **Image** is discussed in Chapter 13, Graphics and Multimedia, we now overview method **FromFile**, which takes a **String** (the image file) and creates an **Image** object.

To find the images, we use class **Directory** (namespace **System.IO**, specified on line 4) method **GetCurrentDirectory** (line 29). This returns the current directory of the executable file as a **String**. To access the **images** subdirectory, we append "**\images**" and the file name to the name of the current directory. We use **image-Number** to append the proper number, enabling us to load either **image0**, **image1** or **image2**. The value of **Integer imageNumber** stays between **0** and **2** because of the modulus calculation in line 25. Finally, we append **".bmp"** to the filename. Thus, if we want to load **image0**, the **String** becomes "*CurrentDir***\images\image0.bmp**", where *CurrentDir* is the directory of the executable.

9.9 Mouse-Event Handling

This section explains the handling of *mouse events,* such as *clicks, presses* and *moves,* which are generated when the mouse interacts with a control. Mouse events can be handled for any control that derives from class **System.Windows.Forms.Control**. Mouse-event information is passed through class *MouseEventArgs,* and the delegate used to create mouse-event handlers is *MouseEventHandler.* Each mouse-event-handling method requires an **Object** and a **MouseEventArgs** object as arguments. For example, the **Click** event, which we covered earlier, uses delegate **EventHandler** and event arguments **EventArgs**.

Class **MouseEventArgs** contains information related to the mouse event, such as the *x*- and *y*-coordinates of the mouse pointer, the mouse button pressed (**Right**, **Left** or **Middle**), the number of times the mouse was clicked and the number of notches through which the mouse wheel turned. Note that the *x*- and *y*-coordinates of the **MouseEventArgs** object are relative to the control that generated the event. Point *(0,0)* represents the upper-left corner of the control. Several mouse events are described in Fig. 9.29.

Mouse Events, Delegates and Event Arguments	
Mouse Events (Delegate **EventHandler**, *event arguments* **EventArgs**)	
MouseEnter	Generated if the mouse cursor enters the area of the control.
MouseLeave	Generated if the mouse cursor leaves the area of the control.
Mouse Events (Delegate **MouseEventHandler**, *event arguments* **MouseEventArgs**)	
MouseDown	Generated if the mouse button is pressed while its cursor is over the area of the control.
MouseHover	Generated if the mouse cursor hovers over the area of the control.

Fig. 9.29   Mouse events, delegates and event arguments. (Part 1 of 2.)

Mouse Events, Delegates and Event Arguments	
MouseMove	Generated if the mouse cursor is moved while in the area of the control.
MouseUp	Generated if the mouse button is released when the cursor is over the area of the control.
Class **MouseEventArgs** *Properties*	
Button	Specifies the mouse button that was pressed (**left**, **right**, **middle** or **none**).
Clicks	Indicates the number of times that the mouse button was clicked.
X	The *x*-coordinate of the event, within the control.
Y	The *y*-coordinate of the event, within the control.

Fig. 9.29   Mouse events, delegates and event arguments. (Part 2 of 2.)

The program in Fig. 9.30 uses mouse events to draw on a form. Whenever the user drags the mouse (i.e., moves the mouse while holding down a button), a line is drawn on the form.

In line 7, the program declares variable **shouldPaint**, which determines whether to draw on the form. We want the program to draw only while the mouse button is pressed (i.e., held down). Thus, in the event handler for event **MouseDown** (lines 28–33), **shouldPaint** is set to **True**. As soon as the mouse button is released, the program stops drawing: **shouldPaint** is set to **False** in the **FrmPainter_MouseUp** event handler (lines 36–41).

Whenever the mouse moves, the system generates a **MouseMove** event at a rate predefined by the operating system. Inside the **FrmPainter_MouseMove** event handler (lines 18–23), the program draws only if **shouldPaint** is **True** (indicating that the mouse button is pressed). Line 19 creates the form's **Graphics** object, which offers methods that draw various shapes. For example, method **FillEllipse** (lines 21–22) draws a circle at every point over which the mouse cursor moves (while the mouse button is pressed). The first parameter to method **FillEllipse** is a *SolidBrush* object, which specifies the color of the shape drawn. We create a new **SolidBrush** object by passing a **Color** value to the constructor. Type *Color* contains numerous predefined color constants—we selected **Color.BlueViolet** (line 22). The **SolidBrush** fills an elliptical region that lies inside a bounding rectangle. The bounding rectangle is specified by the *x*- and *y*-coordinates of its upper-left corner, its height and its width. These are the final four arguments to method **FillEllipse**. The *x*- and *y*-coordinates represent the location of the mouse event and can be taken from the mouse-event arguments (**e.X** and **e.Y**). To draw a circle, we set the height and width of the bounding rectangle so that they are equal—in this example, both are 4 pixels.

```
1    ' Fig. 9.30: Painter.vb
2    ' Using the mouse to draw on a form.
3
```

Fig. 9.30   Using the mouse to draw on a form. (Part 1 of 2.)

```
4    Public Class FrmPainter
5       Inherits System.Windows.Forms.Form
6
7       Dim shouldPaint As Boolean = False
8
9       ' Visual Studio .NET generated code
10
11      ' draw circle if shouldPaint is True
12      Private Sub FrmPainter_MouseMove( _
13         ByVal sender As System.Object, _
14         ByVal e As System.Windows.Forms.MouseEventArgs) _
15         Handles MyBase.MouseMove
16
17         ' paint circle if mouse pressed
18         If shouldPaint Then
19            Dim graphic As Graphics = CreateGraphics()
20
21            graphic.FillEllipse _
22               (New SolidBrush(Color.BlueViolet), e.X, e.Y, 4, 4)
23         End If
24
25      End Sub ' FrmPainter_MouseMove
26
27      ' set shouldPaint to True
28      Private Sub FrmPainter_MouseDown(ByVal sender As Object, _
29         ByVal e As System.Windows.Forms.MouseEventArgs) _
30         Handles MyBase.MouseDown
31
32         shouldPaint = True
33      End Sub ' FrmPainter_MouseDown
34
35      ' set shouldPaint to False
36      Private Sub FrmPainter_MouseUp(ByVal sender As Object, _
37         ByVal e As System.Windows.Forms.MouseEventArgs) _
38         Handles MyBase.MouseUp
39
40         shouldPaint = False
41      End Sub ' FrmPainter_MouseUp
42
43   End Class ' FrmPainter
```

Fig. 9.30   Using the mouse to draw on a form. (Part 2 of 2.)

Whenever the user clicks or holds down a mouse button, the system generates a **MouseDown** event. **FrmPainter_MouseDown** (lines 28–33) handles the **MouseDown** event. Line 32 sets **shouldPaint** to **True**. Unlike **MouseMove** events, the system generates a **MouseDown** event only once while the mouse button is down.

When the user releases the mouse button (to complete a "click" operation), the system generates a single **MouseUp** event. **FrmPainter_MouseUp** handles the **MouseUp** event (lines 36–41). Line 40 sets **shouldPaint** to **False**.

9.10 Keyboard-Event Handling

This section explains the handling of *key events*, which are generated when keys on the keyboard are pressed and released. Such events can be handled by any control that inherits from **System.Windows.Forms.Control**. There are two types of key events. The first is event **KeyPress**, which fires when a key representing an ASCII character is pressed (determined by **KeyPressEventArgs** property **KeyChar**). ASCII is a 128-character set of alphanumeric symbols, a full listing of which can be found in Appendix C, ASCII Character Set.

However the **KeyPress** event does not enable us to determine whether *modifier keys* (e.g., *Shift*, *Alt* and *Control*) were pressed. It is necessary to handle the second type of key events, the **KeyUp** or **KeyDown** events, to determine such actions. Class **KeyEventArgs** contains information about special modifier keys. The key's **Key** *enumeration* value can be returned, providing information about a wide range of non-ASCII keys. Often, modifier keys are used in conjunction with the mouse to select or highlight information. **KeyEventHandler** (event argument class **KeyEventArgs**) and **KeyPressEventHandler** (event argument class **KeyPressEventArgs**) are the delegates for the two classes. Figure 9.31 lists important information about key events.

Keyboard Events, Delegates and Event Arguments	
*Key Events (Delegate **KeyEventHandler**, event arguments **KeyEventArgs**)*	
KeyDown	Generated when the key is initially pressed.
KeyUp	Generated when the key is released.
*Key Events (Delegate **KeyPressEventHandler**, event arguments **KeyPressEventArgs**)*	
KeyPress	Generated when the key is pressed. Occurs repeatedly while key is held down, at a rate specified by the operating system.
Class **KeyPressEventArgs** *Properties*	
KeyChar	Returns the ASCII character for the key pressed.
Handled	Indicates whether the **KeyPress** event was handled.
Class **KeyEventArgs** *Properties*	
Alt	Indicates whether the *Alt* key was pressed.
Control	Indicates whether the *Control* key was pressed.
Shift	Indicates whether the *Shift* key was pressed.

Fig. 9.31   Keyboard events, delegates and event arguments. (Part 1 of 2.)

Keyboard Events, Delegates and Event Arguments	
Handled	Indicates whether the event was handled.
KeyCode	Returns the key code for the key as a **Keys** enumeration. This does not include modifier-key information. Used to test for a specific key.
KeyData	Returns the key code for a key as a **Keys** enumeration, combined with modifier information. Contains all information about the pressed key.
KeyValue	Returns the key code as an **Integer**, rather than as a **Keys** enumeration. Used to obtain a numeric representation of the pressed key.
Modifiers	Returns a **Keys** enumeration for any modifier keys pressed (*Alt*, *Control* and *Shift*). Used to determine modifier-key information only.

Fig. 9.31   Keyboard events, delegates and event arguments. (Part 2 of 2.)

Figure 9.32 demonstrates the use of the key-event handlers to display a key pressed by a user. The program is a form with two **Label**s. It displays the pressed key on one **Label** and modifier information on the other.

Initially, the two **Label**s (**lblCharacter** and **lblInformation**) are empty. The **lblCharacter** label displays the character value of the key pressed, whereas **lblInformation** displays information relating to the pressed key. Because the **KeyDown** and **KeyPress** events convey different information, the form (**FrmKeyDemo**) handles both.

The **KeyPress** event handler (lines 18–23) accesses the **KeyChar** property of the **KeyPressEventArgs** object. This returns the pressed key as a **Char** and displays the result in **lblCharacter** (line 22). If the pressed key is not an ASCII character, then the **KeyPress** event will not fire, and **lblCharacter** remains empty. ASCII is a common encoding format for letters, numbers, punctuation marks and other characters. It does not support keys such as the *function keys* (like *F1*) or the modifier keys (*Alt*, *Control* and *Shift*).

```
1   ' Fig. 9.32: KeyDemo.vb
2   ' Displaying information about a user-pressed key.
3
4   Imports System.Windows.Forms
5
6   Public Class FrmKeyDemo
7      Inherits Form
8
9      ' KeyPressEventArgs display label
10     Friend WithEvents lblCharacter As Label
11
12     ' KeyEventArgs display label
13     Friend WithEvents lblInformation As Label
14
```

Fig. 9.32   Demonstrating keyboard events. (Part 1 of 3.)

```
15      ' Visual Studio .NET generated code
16
17      ' event handler for key press
18      Private Sub FrmKeyDemo_KeyPress(ByVal sender As System.Object, _
19         ByVal e As System.windows.Forms.KeyPressEventArgs) _
20         Handles MyBase.KeyPress
21
22         lblCharacter.Text = "Key pressed: " & e.KeyChar
23      End Sub
24
25      ' display modifier keys, key code, key data and key value
26      Private Sub FrmKeyDemo_KeyDown(ByVal sender As System.Object, _
27         ByVal e As System.Windows.Forms.KeyEventArgs) _
28         Handles MyBase.KeyDown
29
30         lblInformation.Text = ""
31
32         ' if key is Alt
33         If e.Alt Then
34            lblInformation.Text &= "Alt: Yes" & vbCrLf
35         Else
36            lblInformation.Text &= "Alt: No" & vbCrLf
37         End If
38
39         ' if key is Shift
40         If e.Shift Then
41            lblInformation.Text &= "Shift: Yes" & vbCrLf
42         Else
43            lblInformation.Text &= "Shift: No" & vbCrLf
44         End If
45
46         ' if key is Ctrl
47         If e.Control Then
48            lblInformation.Text &= "Ctrl: Yes" & vbCrLf
49         Else
50            lblInformation.Text &= "Ctrl: No" & vbCrLf
51         End If
52
53         lblInformation.Text &= "KeyCode: " & e.KeyCode.ToString & _
54            vbCrLf & "KeyData: " & e.KeyData.ToString & _
55            vbCrLf & "KeyValue: " & e.KeyValue
56      End Sub ' FrmKeyDemo_KeyDown
57
58      ' clear labels when key is released
59      Private Sub FrmKeyDemo_KeyUp(ByVal sender As System.Object, _
60         ByVal e As System.windows.Forms.KeyEventArgs) _
61         Handles MyBase.KeyUp
62
63         lblInformation.Text = ""
64         lblCharacter.Text = ""
65      End Sub ' FrmKeyDemo_KeyUp
66
67   End Class ' FrmKeyDemo
```

Fig. 9.32   Demonstrating keyboard events. (Part 2 of 3.)

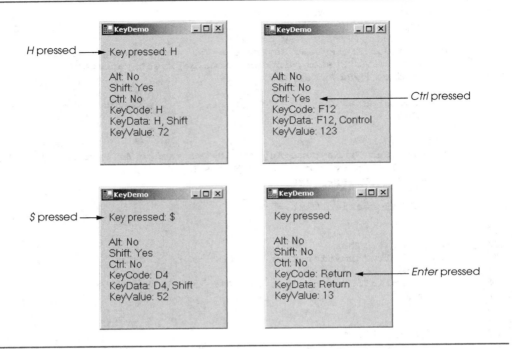

Fig. 9.32   Demonstrating keyboard events. (Part 3 of 3.)

The **KeyDown** event handler (lines 26–56) displays information from its **KeyEventArgs** object. It tests for the *Alt*, *Shift* and *Control* keys by using the **Alt**, **Shift** and **Control** properties, each of which returns **Boolean**—**True** if their respective keys are pressed, **False** otherwise. It then displays the **KeyCode**, **KeyData** and **KeyValue** properties.

The **KeyCode** property returns a **Keys** enumeration, which is converted to a **String** via method **ToString** (line 53). The **KeyCode** property returns the pressed key, but does not provide any information about modifier keys. Thus, both a capital and a lowercase "a" are represented as the *A* key.

The **KeyData** property (line 54) also returns a **Keys** enumeration, but this property includes data about modifier keys. Thus, if "A" is input, the **KeyData** shows that the *A* key and the *Shift* key were pressed. Lastly, **KeyValue** (line 55) returns the key code of the pressed key as an **Integer**. This **Integer** is the *Windows virtual key code*, which provides an **Integer** value for a wide range of keys and for mouse buttons. The Windows virtual key code is useful when one is testing for non-ASCII keys (such as *F12*).

The **KeyUp** event handler (lines 59–65) clears both labels when the key is released. As we can see from the output, non-ASCII keys are not displayed in **lblCharacter**, because the **KeyPress** event is not generated. However, the **KeyDown** event still is generated, and **lblInformation** displays information about the key. The **Keys** enumeration can be used to test for specific keys by comparing the key pressed to a specific **KeyCode**. The Visual Studio. NET documentation contains a complete list of the **Keys** enumeration constants, under the topic **Keys enumeration**.

Software Engineering Observation 9.4

*To cause a control to react when a certain key is pressed (such as Enter), handle a key event and test for the pressed key. To cause a button to be clicked when the Enter key is pressed on a form, set the form's **AcceptButton** property.*

Throughout the chapter we introduced various GUI controls. We named the variables that referenced these controls according to their use in each program. We added a prefix that describes each control's type. This prefix enhances program readability by identifying a control's type. We include a table (Fig. 9.33) that contains the prefixes we use in this book.

In this chapter, we explored several GUI components in greater detail. In the next chapter, we continue our discussion of GUI components and GUI development by introducing additional controls.

9.11 Summary

A graphical user interface (GUI) presents a pictorial interface to a program. A GUI gives a program a distinctive "look" and "feel." By providing different applications with a consistent set of intuitive user interface components, GUIs allow the user to concentrate on using programs productively.

GUIs are built from GUI components (sometimes called controls or widgets). A GUI control is a visual object with which the user interacts via the mouse or keyboard. When the user interacts with a control, an event is generated. This event can trigger methods that respond to the user's actions. Events are based on the notion of delegates. Delegates act as an intermediate step between the object creating (raising) the event and the method handling it.

The general design process for creating Windows applications involves creating a Windows Form, setting its properties, adding controls, setting their properties and configuring event handlers. All forms, components and controls are classes.

GUIs are event driven. When a user interaction occurs, an event is generated. The event information then is passed to event handlers. Events are based on the notion of delegates. Delegates act as an intermediate step between the object creating (raising) the event and the method(s) handling it. The Class Name and Method Name drop-down menus are used to create and register event handlers. The information the programmer needs to register an event is the **EventArgs** class (to define the event handler) and the **EventHandler** delegate (to register the event handler). Visual Studio .NET usually can register the event handler on behalf of the programmer.

Prefix	Control
Frm	Form
lbl	Label
txt	TextBox
cmd	Button

Fig. 9.33 Abbreviations for controls introduced in chapter. (Part 1 of 2.)

Prefix	Control
chk	CheckBox
rad	RadioButton
pic	PictureBox

Fig. 9.33   Abbreviations for controls introduced in chapter. (Part 2 of 2.)

Labels (class **Label**) display read-only text to the user. A **TextBox** is a single-line area in which text can be entered. A password textbox masks each character input with a special character (e.g., *****). A **Button** is a control that the user clicks to trigger a specific action. **Button**s typically respond to the **Click** event.

GroupBoxes and **Panel**s help arrange components on a GUI. The main difference between these classes is that **GroupBox**es can display text, and **Panel**s can have scrollbars.

Visual Basic .NET has two types of state buttons—**CheckBox**es and **RadioButton**s—that have on/off or true/false values. A checkbox is a small white square that is either empty or contains a checkmark. Radio buttons appear as a group in which only one radio button can be selected at a time. To create new groups, radio buttons must be added to a container (e.g., **GroupBox**es or **Panel**s). Radio buttons and checkboxes raise the **CheckChanged** event.

Mouse events (clicks, presses and moves) can be handled for any GUI control that derives from **System.Windows.Forms.Control**. Mouse events use class **MouseEventArgs** (whose corresponding delegate is **MouseEventHandler**) and **EventArgs** (whose corresponding delegate is **EventHandler**).

Class **MouseEventArgs** contains information about the x- and y-coordinates, the button used, the number of clicks and the number of notches through which the mouse wheel turned.

Key events are generated when the keyboard's keys are pressed and released. These events can be handled by any control that inherits from **System.Windows.Forms.Control**.

Event **KeyPress** can return a **Char** for any ASCII character pressed. Events **KeyUp** and **KeyDown** test for special modifier keys (using **KeyEventArgs**). The delegates are **KeyPressEventHandler** (class **KeyPressEventArgs**) and **KeyEventHandler** (class **KeyEventArgs**).

Graphical User Interface
Concepts: Part 2

Objectives

- To be able to create menus, tabbed windows and multiple-document-interface (MDI) programs.
- To understand the use of the **ListView** and **TreeView** controls for displaying information.
- To create hyperlinks using the **LinkLabel** control.
- To display lists of information in **ListBox**es and **ComboBox**es.
- To create custom controls.

I claim not to have controlled events, but confess plainly that events have controlled me.
Abraham Lincoln

A good symbol is the best argument, and is a missionary to persuade thousands.
Ralph Waldo Emerson

Capture its reality in paint!
Paul Cézanne

But, soft! what light through yonder window breaks?
It is the east, and Juliet is the sun!
William Shakespeare

An actor entering through the door, you've got nothing. But if he enters through the window, you've got a situation.
Billy Wilder

Outline

10.1 Introduction

This chapter continues our study of GUIs. We begin our discussion of more advanced topics with a frequently used GUI component, the *menu*, which presents a user with several logically organized commands (or options). We discuss how to develop menus with the tools provided by Visual Studio .NET. We introduce **LinkLabel**s, powerful GUI components that enable the user to click the mouse to be taken to one of several destinations.

We consider GUI components that encapsulate smaller GUI components. We demonstrate how to manipulate a list of values via a **ListBox** and how to combine several checkboxes in a **CheckedListBox**. We also create drop-down lists using **ComboBox**es and display data hierarchically with a **TreeView** control. We present two important GUI components—tab controls and multiple-document-interface windows. These components enable developers to create real-world programs with sophisticated GUIs.

Visual Studio .NET provides a large set of GUI components, many of which are discussed in this chapter. Visual Studio .NET enables programmers to design custom controls and add those controls to the **ToolBox**. The techniques presented in this chapter form the groundwork for creating complex GUIs and custom controls.

10.2 Menus

Menus provide groups of related commands for Windows applications. Although these commands depend on the program, some—such as **Open** and **Save**—are common to many applications. Menus are an integral part of GUIs, because they organize commands without "cluttering" the GUI.

In Fig. 10.1, an expanded menu lists various commands (called *menu items*), plus *submenus* (menus within a menu). Notice that the top-level menus appear in the left portion of the figure, whereas any submenus or menu items are displayed to the right. The menu that contains a menu item is called that menu item's *parent menu*. A menu item that contains a submenu is considered to be the parent of that submenu.

All menu items can have *Alt* key shortcuts (also called *access shortcuts* or *hot keys*), which are accessed by pressing *Alt* and the underlined letter (for example, *Alt + F* expands the **File** menu). Menus that are not top-level menus can have shortcut keys as well (combinations of *Ctrl*, *Shift*, *Alt*, *F1*, *F2*, letter keys, etc.). Some menu items display checkmarks, usually indicating that multiple options on the menu can be selected at once.

To create a menu, open the **Toolbox** and drag a **MainMenu** control onto the form. This creates a menu bar on the top of the form and places a **MainMenu** icon at the bottom of the IDE. To select the **MainMenu**, click this icon. This configuration is known as the Visual Studio .NET Menu Designer, which allows the user to create and edit menus. Menus, like other controls, have properties, which can be accessed through the **Properties** window or the Menu Designer (Fig. 10.2), and events, which can be accessed through the **Class Name** and **Method Name** drop-down menus.

To add command names to the menu, click the **Type Here** textbox (Fig. 10.2) and type the menu command's name. Each entry in the menu is of type **MenuItem** from the **System.Windows.Forms** namespace. The menu itself is of type **MainMenu**. After the programmer presses the *Enter* key, the menu item name is added to the menu. Then, more **Type Here** textboxes appear, allowing the programmer to add items underneath or to the side of the original menu item (Fig. 10.3).

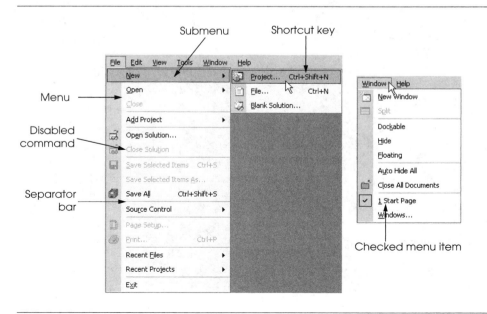

Fig. 10.1   Expanded and checked menus.

To create an *access shortcut* (or *keyboard shortcut*), type an ampersand (**&**) in front of the character to be underlined. For example, to create the **F̲ile** menu item, type **&File**. The ampersand character is displayed by typing **&&**. To add other shortcut keys (e.g., *Ctrl + F9*), set the **Shortcut** property of the **MenuItem**.

Look-and-Feel Observation 10.1

Button̲s also can have access shortcuts. Place the & symbol immediately before the desired character. To click the button, the user then presses Alt *and the underlined character.*

Programmers can remove a menu item by selecting it with the mouse and pressing the *Delete* key. Menu items can be grouped logically by creating *separator bars*. Separator bars are inserted by right-clicking the menu and selecting **Insert Separator** or by typing "**-**" for the menu text.

Menu items generate a **Click** event when selected. To create an empty event handler, enter code-view mode and select the **MenuItem** instance from the Class Name drop-down menu. Then, select the desired event from the Method Name drop-down menu. Common menu actions include displaying dialogs an d setting properties. Menus also can display the names of open windows in multiple-document-interface (MDI) forms (see Section 10.9). Menu properties and events are summarized in Fig. 10.4.

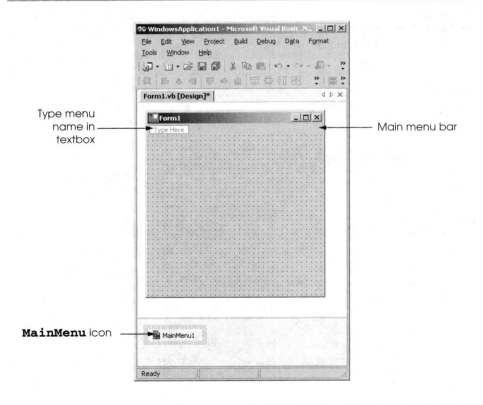

Fig. 10.2   Visual Studio .NET Menu Designer.

Place & character
before letter to
underline in the
menu

Text boxes for
adding items to
the menu

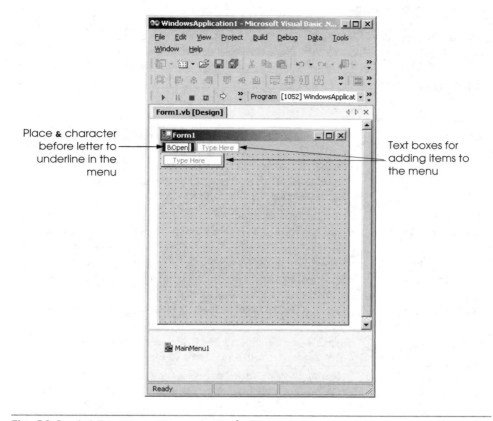

Fig. 10.3   Adding **MenuItem**s to **MainMenu**.

Look-and-Feel Observation 10.2

*It is convention to place an ellipsis (...) after a menu item that displays a dialog (such as **Save As...**). Menu items that produce an immediate action without prompting the user (such as **Save**) should not have an ellipsis following their name.*

Look-and-Feel Observation 10.3

Using common Windows shortcuts (such as Ctrl+F for Find operations and Ctrl+S for Save operations) decreases an application's learning curve.

MainMenu and MenuItem events and properties	Description / Delegate and Event Arguments
MainMenu Properties	
MenuItems	Lists the **MenuItem**s that are contained in the **MainMenu**.

Fig. 10.4   **MainMenu** and **MenuItem** properties and events. (Part 1 of 2.)

MainMenu and MenuItem events and properties	Description / Delegate and Event Arguments
RightToLeft	Causes text to display from right to left. Useful for languages, such as Arabic, that are read from right to left.
MenuItem Properties	
Checked	Indicates whether a menu item is checked (according to property **RadioCheck**). Default value is **False**, meaning that the menu item is unchecked.
Index	Specifies an item's position in its parent menu. A value of **0** places the **MenuItem** at the beginning of the menu.
MenuItems	Lists the submenu items for a particular menu item.
RadioCheck	Specifies whether a selected menu item appears as a radio button (black circle) or as a checkmark. **True** displays a radio button, and **False** displays a checkmark; default **False**.
Shortcut	Specifies the shortcut key for the menu item (e.g., *Ctrl + F9* is equivalent to clicking a specific item).
ShowShortcut	Indicates whether a shortcut key is shown beside menu item text. Default is **True**, which displays the shortcut key.
Text	Specifies the menu item's text. To create an *Alt* access shortcut, precede a character with **&** (e.g., **&File** for **File**).
Common Event	*(Delegate EventHandler, event arguments EventArgs)*
Click	Generated when item is clicked or shortcut key is used. This is the default event when the menu is double-clicked in the designer.

Fig. 10.4 MainMenu and **MenuItem** properties and events. (Part 2 of 2.)

Class **FrmMenu** (Fig. 10.5) creates a simple menu on a form. The form has a top-level **File** menu with menu items **About** (displays a message box) and **Exit** (terminates the program).The menu also includes a **Format** menu, which changes the text on a label. The **Format** menu has submenus **Color** and **Font**, which change the color and font of the text on a label.

```
1   ' Fig. 10.5: MenuTest.vb
2   ' Using menus to change font colors and styles.
3
4   Imports System.Windows.Forms
5
6   Public Class FrmMenu
7      Inherits Form
8
9      ' display label
10     Friend WithEvents lblDisplay As Label
11
```

Fig. 10.5 Menus for changing text font and color. (Part 1 of 5.)

```
12      ' main menu (contains file and format menus)
13      Friend WithEvents mnuMainMenu As MainMenu
14
15      ' file menu
16      Friend WithEvents mnuFile As MenuItem
17      Friend WithEvents mnuitmAbout As MenuItem
18      Friend WithEvents mnuitmExit As MenuItem
19
20      ' format menu (contains format and font submenus)
21      Friend WithEvents mnuFormat As MenuItem
22
23      ' color submenu
24      Friend WithEvents mnuitmColor As MenuItem
25      Friend WithEvents mnuitmBlack As MenuItem
26      Friend WithEvents mnuitmBlue As MenuItem
27      Friend WithEvents mnuitmRed As MenuItem
28      Friend WithEvents mnuitmGreen As MenuItem
29
30      ' font submenu
31      Friend WithEvents mnuitmFont As MenuItem
32      Friend WithEvents mnuitmTimes As MenuItem
33      Friend WithEvents mnuitmCourier As MenuItem
34      Friend WithEvents mnuitmComic As MenuItem
35      Friend WithEvents mnuitmDash As MenuItem
36      Friend WithEvents mnuitmBold As MenuItem
37      Friend WithEvents mnuitmItalic As MenuItem
38
39      ' Visual Studio .NET generated code
40
41      ' display MessageBox
42      Private Sub mnuitmAbout_Click( _
43         ByVal sender As System.Object, _
44         ByVal e As System.EventArgs) Handles mnuitmAbout.Click
45
46         MessageBox.Show("This is an example" & vbCrLf & _
47            "of using menus.", "About", MessageBoxButtons.OK, _
48            MessageBoxIcon.Information)
49      End Sub ' mnuitmAbout_Click
50
51      ' exit program
52      Private Sub mnuitmExit_Click( _
53         ByVal sender As System.Object, _
54         ByVal e As System.EventArgs) Handles mnuitmExit.Click
55
56         Application.Exit()
57      End Sub ' mnuitmExit_Click
58
59      ' reset font color
60      Private Sub ClearColor()
61
62         ' clear all checkmarks
63         mnuitmBlack.Checked = False
64         mnuitmBlue.Checked = False
```

Fig. 10.5   Menus for changing text font and color. (Part 2 of 5.)

```vbnet
65          mnuitmRed.Checked = False
66          mnuitmGreen.Checked = False
67      End Sub ' ClearColor
68
69      ' update menu state and color display black
70      Private Sub mnuitmBlack_Click(ByVal sender As System.Object, _
71          ByVal e As System.EventArgs) Handles mnuitmBlack.Click
72
73          ' reset checkmarks for color menu items
74          ClearColor()
75
76          ' set color to black
77          lblDisplay.ForeColor = Color.Black
78          mnuitmBlack.Checked = True
79      End Sub ' mnuitmBlack_Click
80
81      ' update menu state and color display blue
82      Private Sub mnuitmBlue_Click(ByVal sender As System.Object, _
83          ByVal e As System.EventArgs) Handles mnuitmBlue.Click
84
85          ' reset checkmarks for color menu items
86          ClearColor()
87
88          ' set color to blue
89          lblDisplay.ForeColor = Color.Blue
90          mnuitmBlue.Checked = True
91      End Sub ' mnuitmBlue_Click
92
93      ' update menu state and color display red
94      Private Sub mnuitmRed_Click(ByVal sender As System.Object, _
95          ByVal e As System.EventArgs) Handles mnuitmRed.Click
96
97          ' reset checkmarks for color menu items
98          ClearColor()
99
100         ' set color to red
101         lblDisplay.ForeColor = Color.Red
102         mnuitmRed.Checked = True
103     End Sub ' mnuitmRed_Click
104
105     ' update menu state and color display green
106     Private Sub mnuitmGreen_Click(ByVal sender As System.Object, _
107         ByVal e As System.EventArgs) Handles mnuitmGreen.Click
108
109         ' reset checkmarks for color menu items
110         ClearColor()
111
112         ' set color to green
113         lblDisplay.ForeColor = Color.Green
114         mnuitmGreen.Checked = True
115     End Sub ' mnuitmGreen_Click
116
```

Fig. 10.5 Menus for changing text font and color. (Part 3 of 5.)

```
117     ' reset font type
118     Private Sub ClearFont()
119
120         ' clear all checkmarks
121         mnuitmTimes.Checked = False
122         mnuitmCourier.Checked = False
123         mnuitmComic.Checked = False
124     End Sub ' ClearFont
125
126     ' update menu state and set font to Times
127     Private Sub mnuitmTimes_Click(ByVal sender As System.Object, _
128         ByVal e As System.EventArgs) Handles mnuitmTimes.Click
129
130         ' reset checkmarks for font menu items
131         ClearFont()
132
133         ' set Times New Roman font
134         mnuitmTimes.Checked = True
135         lblDisplay.Font = New Font("Times New Roman", 30, _
136             lblDisplay.Font.Style)
137     End Sub ' mnuitmTimes_Click
138
139     ' update menu state and set font to Courier
140     Private Sub mnuitmCourier_Click(ByVal sender As System.Object, _
141         ByVal e As System.EventArgs) Handles mnuitmCourier.Click
142
143         ' reset checkmarks for font menu items
144         ClearFont()
145
146         ' set Courier font
147         mnuitmCourier.Checked = True
148         lblDisplay.Font = New Font("Courier New", 30, _
149             lblDisplay.Font.Style)
150     End Sub ' mnuitmCourier_Click
151
152     ' update menu state and set font to Comic Sans MS
153     Private Sub mnuitmComic_Click(ByVal sender As System.Object, _
154         ByVal e As System.EventArgs) Handles mnuitmComic.Click
155
156         ' reset check marks for font menu items
157         ClearFont()
158
159         ' set Comic Sans font
160         mnuitmComic.Checked = True
161         lblDisplay.Font = New Font("Comic Sans MS", 30, _
162             lblDisplay.Font.Style)
163     End Sub ' mnuitmComic_Click
164
165     ' toggle checkmark and toggle bold style
166     Private Sub mnuitmBold_Click( _
167         ByVal sender As System.Object, _
168         ByVal e As System.EventArgs) Handles mnuitmBold.Click
169
```

Fig. 10.5   Menus for changing text font and color. (Part 4 of 5.)

```
170            ' toggle checkmark
171            mnuitmBold.Checked = Not mnuitmBold.Checked
172
173            ' use Xor to toggle bold, keep all other styles
174            lblDisplay.Font = New Font( _
175               lblDisplay.Font.FontFamily, 30, _
176               lblDisplay.Font.Style Xor FontStyle.Bold)
177      End Sub ' mnuitmBold_Click
178
179         ' toggle checkmark and toggle italic style
180      Private Sub mnuitmItalic_Click( _
181         ByVal sender As System.Object, _
182         ByVal e As System.EventArgs) Handles mnuitmItalic.Click
183
184            ' toggle checkmark
185            mnuitmItalic.Checked = Not mnuitmItalic.Checked
186
187            ' use Xor to toggle italic, keep all other styles
188            lblDisplay.Font = New Font( _
189               lblDisplay.Font.FontFamily, 30, _
190               lblDisplay.Font.Style Xor FontStyle.Italic)
191         End Sub ' mnuitmItalic_Click
192
193   End Class ' FrmMenu
```

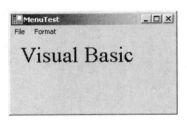

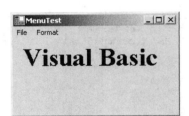
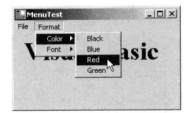

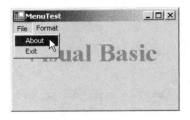

Fig. 10.5   Menus for changing text font and color. (Part 5 of 5.)

We begin by dragging the **MainMenu** from the **ToolBox** onto the form. We then create our entire menu structure, using the Menu Designer. The **File** menu (**mnuFile**, line 16) has menu items **About** (**mnuitmAbout**, line 17) and **Exit** (**mnuitmExit**, line 18); the **Format** menu (**mnuFormat**, line 21) has two submenus. The first submenu, **Color** (**mnuitmColor**, line 24), contains menu items **Black** (**mnuitmBlack**, line 25), **Blue** (**mnuitmBlue**, line 26), **Red** (**mnuitmRed**, line 27) and **Green** (**mnuitmGreen**, line 28). The second submenu, **Font** (**mnuitmFont**, line 31), contains menu items **Times New Roman** (**mnuitmTimes**, line 32), **Courier** (**mnuitmCourier**, line 33), **Comic Sans** (**mnuitmComic**, line 34), a separator bar (**mnuitmDash**, line 35), **Bold** (**mnuitmBold**, line 36) and **Italic** (**mnuitmItalic**, line 37).

The **About** menu item in the **File** menu displays a **MessageBox** when clicked (lines 46–48). The **Exit** menu item closes the application through **Shared** method *Exit* of class *Application* (line 56). Class **Application**'s **Shared** methods control program execution. Method **Exit** causes our application to terminate.

We made the items in the **Color** submenu (**Black**, **Blue**, **Red** and **Green**) mutually exclusive—the user can select only one at a time (we explain how we did this shortly). To indicate this fact to the user, we set each **Color** menu item's *RadioCheck* properties to **True**. This causes a radio button to appear (instead of a checkmark) when a user selects a **Color**-menu item.

Each **Color** menu item has its own event handler. The method handler for color **Black** is **mnuitmBlack_Click** (lines 70–79). Similarly, the event handlers for colors **Blue**, **Red** and **Green** are **mnuitmBlue_Click** (lines 82–91), **mnuitmRed_Click** (lines 94–103) and **mnuitmGreen_Click** (lines 106–115), respectively. Each **Color** menu item must be mutually exclusive, so each event handler calls method **ClearColor** (lines 60–67) before setting its corresponding **Checked** property to **True**. Method **ClearColor** sets the **Checked** property of each color **MenuItem** to **False**, effectively preventing more than one menu item from being selected at a time.

 Software Engineering Observation 10.1

*The mutual exclusion of menu items is not enforced by the **MainMenu**, even when the **RadioCheck** property is **True**. This behavior must be programmed.*

 **Look-and-Feel Observation 10.4**

*Set the **RadioCheck** property to reflect the desired behavior of menu items. Use radio buttons (**RadioCheck** property set to **True**) to indicate mutually exclusive menu items. Use check marks (**RadioCheck** property set to **False**) for menu items that have no logical restriction.*

The **Font** menu contains three menu items for font types (**Courier**, **Times New Roman** and **Comic Sans**) and two menu items for font styles (**Bold** and **Italic**). We added a separator bar between the font-type and font-style menu items to indicate the distinction: Font types are mutually exclusive; styles are not. This means that a **Font** object can specify only one font type at a time but can set multiple styles at once (e.g., a font can be both bold and italic). We set the font-type menu items to display checks. As with the **Color** menu, we also must enforce mutual exclusion in our event handlers.

Event handlers for font-type menu items **TimesRoman**, **Courier** and **ComicSans** are **mnuitmTimes_Click** (lines 127–137), **mnuitmCourier_Click** (lines 140–150) and **mnuitmComic_Click** (lines 153–163), respectively. These event handlers behave in a manner similar to that of the event handlers for the **Color** menu items. Each event handler clears the **Checked** properties for all font-type menu items by calling method **ClearFont** (lines 118–124), then sets the **Checked** property of the menu item that raised the event to **True**. This enforces the mutual exclusion of the font-type menu items.

The event handlers for the **Bold** and **Italic** menu items (lines 166–191) use the bitwise **Xor** operator. For each font style, the **Xor** operator changes the text to include the style or, if that style is already applied, to remove it. The toggling behavior provided by the **Xor** operator is explained in Chapter 9, Graphical User Interface Concepts: Part 1. As explained in Chapter 9, this program's event-handling structure allows the programmer to add and remove menu entries while making minimal structural changes to the code.

10.3 **LinkLabels**

The *LinkLabel* control displays links to other resources, such as files or Web pages (Fig. 10.6). A **LinkLabel** appears as underlined text (colored blue by default). When the mouse moves over the link, the pointer changes to a hand; this is similar to the behavior of a hyperlink in a Web page. The link can change color to indicate whether the link is new, previously visited or active. When clicked, the **LinkLabel** generates a *LinkClicked* event (see Fig. 10.7). Class **LinkLabel** is derived from class **Label** and therefore inherits all of class **Label**'s functionality.

> **Look-and-Feel Observation 10.5**
>
> *Although other controls can perform actions similar to those of a **LinkLabel** (such as the opening of a Web page), **LinkLabel**s indicate that a link can be followed—a regular label or button does not necessarily convey that idea.*

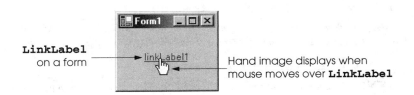

Fig. 10.6   LinkLabel control in running program.

LinkLabel properties and events	Description / Delegate and Event Arguments
Common Properties	
ActiveLinkColor	Specifies the color of the active link when clicked. Red is the default.
LinkArea	Specifies which portion of text in the **LinkLabel** is part of the link.

Fig. 10.7   LinkLabel properties and events. (Part 1 of 2.)

LinkLabel properties and events	Description / Delegate and Event Arguments
LinkBehavior	Specifies the link's behavior, such as how the link appears when the mouse is placed over it.
LinkColor	Specifies the original color of all links before they have been visited. Blue is the default.
Links	Lists the **LinkLabel.Link** objects, which are the links contained in the **LinkLabel**.
LinkVisited	If **True**, link appears as though it were visited (its color is changed to that specified by property **VisitedLinkColor**). Default value is **False**.
Text	Specifies the control's text.
UseMnemonic	If **True**, **&** character in **Text** property acts as a shortcut (similar to the *Alt* shortcut in menus).
VisitedLinkColor	Specifies the color of visited links. Purple is the default.
Common Event	*(Delegate **LinkLabelLinkClickedEventHandler**, event arguments **LinkLabelLinkClickedEventArgs**)*
LinkClicked	Generated when the link is clicked. This is the default event when the control is double-clicked in designer.

Fig. 10.7 **LinkLabel** properties and events. (Part 2 of 2.)

Class **FrmLinkLabel** (Fig. 10.8) uses three **LinkLabel**s, to link to the **C:** drive, the Deitel Web site (**www.deitel.com**) and the Notepad application, respectively. The **Text** properties of the **LinkLabel**'s **lnklblCDrive** (line 10), **lnklblDeitel** (line 11) and **lnklblNotepad** (line 12) describe each link's purpose.

The event handlers for the **LinkLabel** instances call method **Start** of class **Process** (namespace **System.Diagnostics**). This method allows us to execute other programs from our application. Method **Start** can take as arguments either the file to open (a **String**) or the application to run and its command-line arguments (two **String**s). Method **Start**'s arguments can be in the same form as if they were provided for input to the Windows **Run** command. For applications, full path names are not needed, and the **.exe** extension often can be omitted. To open a file that has a file type that Windows recognizes, simply insert the file's full path name. The Windows operating system must be able to use the application associated with the given file's extension to open the file.

The event handler for **lnklblCDrive**'s **LinkClicked** events browses the **C:** drive (lines 17–24). Line 22 sets the **LinkVisited** property to **True**, which changes the link's color from blue to purple (the **LinkVisited** colors are configured through the **Properties** window in Visual Studio). The event handler then passes **"C:\"** to method **Start** (line 23), which opens a **Windows Explorer** window.

The event handler for **lnklblDeitel**'s **LinkClicked** event (lines 27–35) opens the Web page **www.deitel.com** in Internet Explorer. We achieve this by passing the Web-page address as a **String** (lines 33–34), which opens Internet Explorer. Line 32 sets the **LinkVisited** property to **True**.

```vb
1    ' Fig. 10.8: LinkLabelTest.vb
2    ' Using LinkLabels to create hyperlinks.
3
4    Imports System.Windows.Forms
5
6    Public Class FrmLinkLabel
7       Inherits Form
8
9       ' linklabels to C:\ drive, www.deitel.com and Notepad
10      Friend WithEvents lnklblCDrive As LinkLabel
11      Friend WithEvents lnklblDeitel As LinkLabel
12      Friend WithEvents lnklblNotepad As LinkLabel
13
14      ' Visual Studio .NET generated code
15
16      ' browse C:\ drive
17      Private Sub lnklblCDrive_LinkClicked( _
18         ByVal sender As System.Object, ByVal e As _
19         System.Windows.Forms.LinkLabelLinkClickedEventArgs) _
20         Handles lnklblCDrive.LinkClicked
21
22         lnklblCDrive.LinkVisited = True
23         System.Diagnostics.Process.Start("C:\")
24      End Sub ' lnklblCDrive
25
26      ' load www.deitel.com in Web browser
27      Private Sub lnklblDeitel_LinkClicked( _
28         ByVal sender As System.Object, ByVal e As _
29         System.Windows.Forms.LinkLabelLinkClickedEventArgs) _
30         Handles lnklblDeitel.LinkClicked
31
32         lnklblDeitel.LinkVisited = True
33         System.Diagnostics.Process.Start( _
34            "IExplore", "http://www.deitel.com")
35      End Sub ' lnklblDeitel
36
37      ' run application Notepad
38      Private Sub lnklblNotepad_LinkClicked( _
39         ByVal sender As System.Object, ByVal e As _
40         System.Windows.Forms.LinkLabelLinkClickedEventArgs) _
41         Handles lnklblNotepad.LinkClicked
42
43         lnklblNotepad.LinkVisited = True
44
45         ' run notepad application
46         ' full path not needed
47         System.Diagnostics.Process.Start("notepad")
48      End Sub ' lnklblNotepad_LinkClicked
49
50   End Class ' FrmLinkLabelList
```

Fig. 10.8 **LinkLabel**s used to link to a drive, a Web page and an application. (Part 1 of 2.)

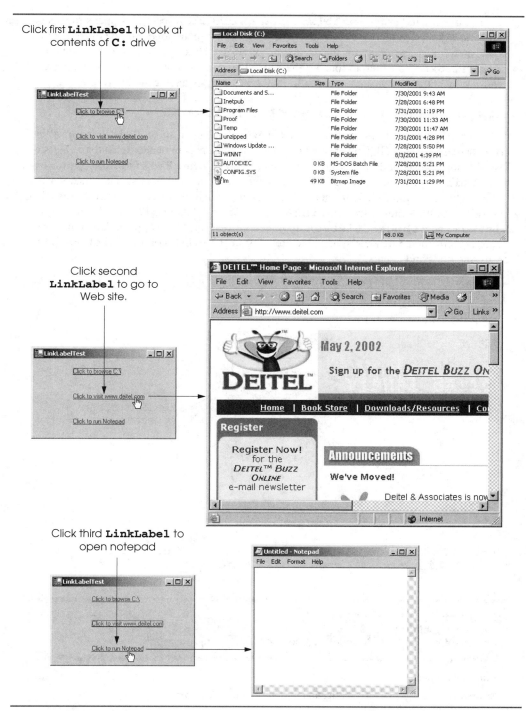

The event handler for **lnklblNotepad**'s **LinkClicked** events opens the specified Notepad application (lines 38–48). Line 43 sets the link to appear in the event handler as a visited link. Line 47 passes the argument **"notepad"** to method **Start**, which runs **notepad.exe**. Note that, in line 47, the **.exe** extension is not required—Windows can determine whether the argument given to method **Start** is an executable file.

10.4 **ListBoxes** and **CheckedListBoxes**

The **ListBox** control allows the user to view and select from multiple items in a list. **ListBox**es are static GUI entities, which means that users cannot add items to the list, unless the application adds items programmatically. The **CheckedListBox** control extends a **ListBox** by including check boxes next to each item in the list. This allows users to place checks on multiple items at once, as is possible in a **CheckBox** control (users also can select multiple items from a **ListBox**, but not by default). Figure 10.9 displays a **ListBox** and a **CheckedListBox**. In both controls, scrollbars appear if the number of items exceeds the **ListBox**'s viewable area. Figure 10.10 lists common **ListBox** properties, methods and events.

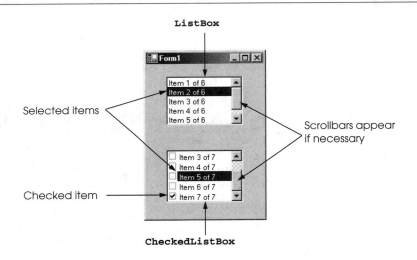

Fig. 10.9 **ListBox** and **CheckedListBox** on a form.

ListBox properties, methods and events	Description / Delegate and Event Arguments
Common Properties	
Items	The collection of items in the **ListBox**.

Fig. 10.10 **ListBox** properties, methods and events. (Part 1 of 2.)

ListBox properties, methods and events	Description / Delegate and Event Arguments
MultiColumn	Indicates whether the **ListBox** can break a list into multiple columns. Multiple columns eliminate vertical scrollbars from the display.
SelectedIndex	Returns the index of the selected item. If the user selects multiple items, this property arbitrarily returns one of the selected indices; if no items have been selected, the property returns **-1**.
SelectedIndices	Returns a collection containing the indices for all selected items.
SelectedItem	Returns a reference to the selected item (if multiple items are selected, it returns the item with the lowest index number).
SelectedItems	Returns a collection of the selected item(s).
SelectionMode	Determines the number of items that can be selected, and the means through which multiple items can be selected. Values **None**, **One**, **MultiSimple** (multiple selection allowed) or **MultiExtended** (multiple selection allowed using a combination of arrow keys or mouse clicks and *Shift* and *Control* keys).
Sorted	Indicates whether items are sorted alphabetically. Setting this property's value to **True** sorts the items. The default value is **False**.
Common Method	
GetSelected	Takes an index as an argument, and returns **True** if the corresponding item is selected.
Common Event	*(Delegate **EventHandler**, event arguments **EventArgs**)*
SelectedIndex-Changed	Generated when selected index changes. This is the default event when the control is double-clicked in the designer.

Fig. 10.10 ListBox properties, methods and events. (Part 2 of 2.)

The **SelectionMode** property determines the number of items that can be selected. This property has the possible values **None**, **One**, **MultiSimple** and **MultiExtended** (from the **SelectionMode** *enumeration*)—the differences among these settings are explained in Fig. 10.10. The **SelectedIndexChanged** event occurs when the user selects a new item.

Both the **ListBox** and **CheckedListBox** have properties **Items**, **SelectedItem** and **SelectedIndex**. Property **Items** returns all the list items as a collection. Collections are a common way of exposing lists of **Object**s in the .NET framework. Many .NET GUI components (e.g., **ListBox**es) use collections to expose lists of internal objects (e.g., items contained within a **ListBox**). We discuss collections further in Chapter 20, Data Structures and Collections. Property **SelectedItem** returns the **ListBox**'s currently selected item. If the user can select multiple items, use collection **SelectedItems** to return all the selected items as a collection. Property **SelectedIndex** returns the index of the selected item—if there could be more than one, use property **SelectedIndices**. If no items are selected, property **SelectedIndex** returns **-1**. Method **GetSelected** takes an index and returns **True** if the corresponding item is selected.

To add items to a **ListBox** or to a **CheckedListBox** we must add objects to its **Items** collection. This can be accomplished by calling method **Add** to add a **String** to the **ListBox**'s or **CheckedListBox**'s **Items** collection. For example, we could write

> *myListBox*.**Items.Add(** *myListItem* **)**

to add **String** *myListItem* to **ListBox** *myListBox*. To add multiple objects, programmers can either call method **Add** multiple times or call method **AddRange** to add an array of objects. Classes **ListBox** and **CheckedListBox** each call the submitted object's **ToString** method to determine the label for the corresponding object's entry in the list. This allows programmers to add different objects to a **ListBox** or a **CheckedListBox** that later can be returned through properties **SelectedItem** and **SelectedItems**.

Alternatively, we can add items to **ListBox**es and **CheckedListBox**es visually by examining the **Items** property in the **Properties** window. Clicking the ellipsis button opens the **String Collection Editor**, a text area in which programmers add items; each item appears on a separate line (Fig. 10.11). Visual Studio .NET then adds these **String**s to the **Items** collection inside method **InitializeComponent**.

10.4.1 ListBoxes

Figure 10.12 uses class **FrmListBox** to add, remove and clear items from **ListBox** **lstDisplay** (line 10). Class **FrmListBox** uses **TextBox txtInput** (line 13) to allow the user to type in a new item. When the user clicks the **Add** button (**cmdAdd** in line 16), the new item appears in **lstDisplay**. Similarly, if the user selects an item and clicks **Remove** (**cmdRemove** in line 17), the item is deleted. When clicked, **Clear** (**cmdClear** in line 18) deletes all entries in **lstDisplay**. The user terminates the application by clicking **Exit** (**cmdExit** in line 19).

Fig. 10.11 String Collection Editor.

```
1   ' Fig. 10.12: ListBoxTest.vb
2   ' Program to add, remove and clear list box items.
3
4   Imports System.Windows.Forms
```

Fig. 10.12 Program that adds, removes and clears **ListBox** items. (Part 1 of 3.)

```vb
 5
 6    Public Class FrmListBox
 7       Inherits Form
 8
 9       ' contains user-input list of elements
10       Friend WithEvents lstDisplay As ListBox
11
12       ' user-input textbox
13       Friend WithEvents txtInput As TextBox
14
15       ' add, remove, clear and exit command buttons
16       Friend WithEvents cmdAdd As Button
17       Friend WithEvents cmdRemove As Button
18       Friend WithEvents cmdClear As Button
19       Friend WithEvents cmdExit As Button
20
21       ' Visual Studio .NET generated code
22
23       ' add new item (text from input box) and clear input box
24       Private Sub cmdAdd_Click(ByVal sender As System.Object, _
25          ByVal e As System.EventArgs) Handles cmdAdd.Click
26
27          lstDisplay.Items.Add(txtInput.Text)
28          txtInput.Text = ""
29       End Sub ' cmdAdd_Click
30
31       ' remove item if one is selected
32       Private Sub cmdRemove_Click (ByVal sender As System.Object, _
33          ByVal e As System.EventArgs) Handles cmdRemove.Click
34
35          ' remove only if item is selected
36          If lstDisplay.SelectedIndex <> -1 Then
37             lstDisplay.Items.RemoveAt(lstDisplay.SelectedIndex)
38          End If
39
40       End Sub ' cmdRemove_Click
41
42       ' clear all items
43       Private Sub cmdClear_Click (ByVal sender As System.Object, _
44          ByVal e As System.EventArgs) Handles cmdClear.Click
45
46          lstDisplay.Items.Clear()
47       End Sub ' cmdClear_Click
48
49       ' exit application
50       Private Sub cmdExit_Click (ByVal sender As System.Object, _
51          ByVal e As System.EventArgs) Handles cmdExit.Click
52
53          Application.Exit()
54       End Sub ' cmdExit_Click
55
56    End Class ' FrmListBox
```

Fig. 10.12 Program that adds, removes and clears **ListBox** items. (Part 2 of 3.)

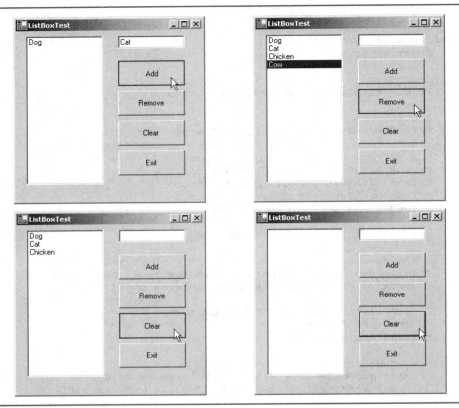

Fig. 10.12 Program that adds, removes and clears **ListBox** items. (Part 3 of 3.)

The **cmdAdd_Click** event handler (lines 24–29) calls method **Add** of the **Items** collection in the **ListBox**. This method takes a **String** as the item to add to **lstDisplay**. In this case, the **String** used is the user-input text, or **txtInput.Text** (line 27). After the item is added, **txtInput.Text** is cleared (line 28).

The **cmdRemove_Click** event handler (lines 32–40) calls method **Remove** of the **Items** collection. Event handler **cmdRemove_Click** first uses property **Selected-Index** to determine which index is selected. Unless **SelectedIndex** is empty (**-1**) (line 36), the handler removes the item that corresponds to the selected index.

The event handler for **cmdClear_Click** (lines 43–47) calls method **Clear** of the **Items** collection (line 46). This removes all the entries in **lstDisplay**. Finally, event handler **cmdExit_Click** (lines 50–54) terminates the application, by calling method **Application.Exit** (line 53).

10.4.2 CheckedListBoxes

The **CheckedListBox** control derives from class **ListBox** and includes a checkbox next to each item. As in **ListBox**es, items can be added via methods **Add** and **AddRange** or through the **String Collection Editor**. **CheckedListBox**es imply that multiple items can be selected, and the only possible values for the **SelectionMode** property are

None and **One**. **One** allows multiple selection, because checkboxes imply that there are no logical restrictions on the items—the user can select as many items as required. Thus, the only choice is whether to give the user multiple selection or no selection at all. This keeps the **CheckedListBox**'s behavior consistent with that of **CheckBox**es. The programmer is unable to set the last two **SelectionMode** values, **MultiSimple** and **MultiExtended**, because the only logical two selection modes are handled by **None** and **One**. Common properties and events of **CheckedListBox**es appear in Fig. 10.13.

Common Programming Error 10.1

*The IDE displays an error message if the programmer attempts to set the **SelectionMode** property to **MultiSimple** or **MultiExtended** in the **Properties** window of a **CheckedListBox**; If this value is set programmatically, a runtime error occurs.*

Event **ItemCheck** is generated whenever a user checks or unchecks a **CheckedListBox** item. Event argument properties **CurrentValue** and **NewValue** return **CheckState** values for the current and new state of the item, respectively. A comparison of these values allows the programmer to determine whether the **CheckedListBox** item was checked or unchecked. The **CheckedListBox** control retains the **SelectedItems** and **SelectedIndices** properties (it inherits them from class **ListBox**). However, it also includes properties **CheckedItems** and **CheckedIndices**, which return information about the checked items and indices.

CheckedListBox properties, methods and events	Description / Delegate and Event Arguments
Common Properties	*(All the **ListBox** properties and events are inherited by **CheckedListBox**.)*
CheckedItems	Contains the collection of items that are checked. This is distinct from the selected item, which is highlighted (but not necessarily checked). [*Note:* There can be at most one selected item at any given time.]
CheckedIndices	Returns indices for all checked items. This is not the same as the selected index.
SelectionMode	Determines how many items can be checked. Only possible values are **One** (allows multiple checks to be placed) or **None** (does not allow any checks to be placed).
Common Method	
GetItemChecked	Takes an index and returns **True** if the corresponding item is checked.
Common Event	*(Delegate **ItemCheckEventHandler**, event arguments **ItemCheckEventArgs**)*
ItemCheck	Generated when an item is checked or unchecked.
***ItemCheckEventArgs** Properties*	
CurrentValue	Indicates whether the current item is checked or unchecked. Possible values are **Checked**, **Unchecked** and **Indeterminate**.

Fig. 10.13 **CheckedListBox** properties, methods and events. (Part 1 of 2.)

CheckedListBox properties, methods and events	Description / Delegate and Event Arguments
Index	Returns index of the item that changed.
NewValue	Specifies the new state of the item.

Fig. 10.13 CheckedListBox properties, methods and events. (Part 2 of 2.)

In Fig. 10.14, class **FrmCheckedListBox** uses a **CheckedListBox** and a **ListBox** to display a user's selection of books. The **CheckedListBox** named **chklstInput** (line 10), allows the user to select multiple titles. In the **String Collection Editor**, items were added for some Deitel™ books: C++, Java™, Visual Basic, Internet & WWW, Perl, Python, Wireless Internet and Advanced Java (the acronym HTP stands for "How to Program"). The **ListBox**, named **lstDisplay** (line 13), displays the user's selection. In the screenshots accompanying this example, the **CheckedListBox** appears to the left, the **ListBox** on the right.

When the user checks or unchecks an item in **CheckedListBox chklstInput**, an **ItemCheck** event is generated. Event handler **chklstInput_ItemCheck** (lines 18–34) handles the event. An **If/Else** control structure (lines 28–32) determines whether the user checked or unchecked an item in the **CheckedListBox**. Line 28 uses the **NewValue** property to determine whether the item is being checked (**CheckState.Checked**). If the user checks an item, line 29 adds the checked entry to the **ListBox lstDisplay**. If the user unchecks an item, line 31 removes the corresponding item from **lstDisplay**.

```
1    ' Fig. 10.14: CheckedListBoxTest.vb
2    ' Using the checked list boxes to add items to a list box.
3
4    Imports System.Windows.Forms
5
6    Public Class FrmCheckedListBox
7       Inherits Form
8
9       ' list of available book titles
10      Friend WithEvents chklstInput As CheckedListBox
11
12      ' user selection list
13      Friend WithEvents lstDisplay As ListBox
14
15      ' Visual Studio .NET generated code
16
17      ' item about to change, add or remove from lstDisplay
18      Private Sub chklstInput_ItemCheck( _
19         ByVal sender As System.Object, _
20         ByVal e As System.Windows.Forms.ItemCheckEventArgs) _
21         Handles chklstInput.ItemCheck
```

Fig. 10.14 CheckedListBox and ListBox used in a program to display a user selection. (Part 1 of 2.)

```
22
23          ' obtain reference of selected item
24          Dim item As String = chklstInput.SelectedItem
25
26          ' if item checked add to listbox
27          ' otherwise remove from listbox
28          If e.NewValue = CheckState.Checked Then
29              lstDisplay.Items.Add(item)
30          Else
31              lstDisplay.Items.Remove(item)
32          End If
33
34       End Sub ' chklstInput_ItemCheck
35
36   End Class ' FrmCheckedListBox
```

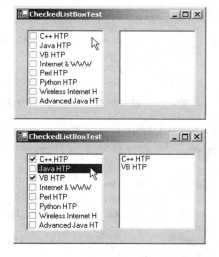
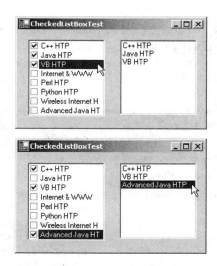

Fig. 10.14 **CheckedListBox** and **ListBox** used in a program to display a user selection. (Part 2 of 2.)

10.5 ComboBoxes

The ***ComboBox*** control combines **TextBox** features with a *drop-down list*. A drop-down list is a GUI component that contains a list from which a value can be selected. It usually appears as a text box with a down arrow to its right. By default, the user can enter text into the text box or click the down arrow to display a list of predefined items. If a user chooses an element from this list, that element is displayed in the text box. If the list contains more elements than can be displayed in the drop-down list, a scrollbar appears. The maximum number of items that a drop-down list can display at one time is set by property ***MaxDrop-DownItems***. Figure 10.15 shows a sample **ComboBox** in three different states.

As with the **ListBox** control, the programmer can add objects to collection **Items** programmatically, using methods **Add** and **AddRange**, or visually, with the **String Collection Editor**. Figure 10.16 lists common properties and events of class **ComboBox**.

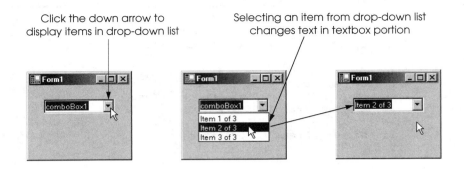

Fig. 10.15 **ComboBox** demonstration.

Look-and-Feel Observation 10.6

*Use a **ComboBox** to save space on a GUI. The disadvantage is that, unlike with a **ListBox**, the user cannot see available items without expanding the drop-down list.*

ComboBox events and properties	Description / Delegate and Event Arguments
Common Properties	
DropDownStyle	Determines the type of combo box. Value **Simple** means that the text portion is editable and the list portion is always visible. Value **DropDown** (the default) means that the text portion is editable, but the user must click an arrow button to see the list portion. Value **DropDownList** means that the text portion is not editable and the user must click the arrow button to see the list portion.
Items	The collection of items in the **ComboBox** control.
MaxDropDownItems	Specifies the maximum number of items (between **1** and **100**) that the drop-down list can display. If the number of items exceeds the maximum number of items to display, a scrollbar appears.
SelectedIndex	Returns the index of the selected item. If there is no selected item, **-1** is returned.
SelectedItem	Returns a reference to the selected item.
Sorted	Indicates whether items are sorted alphabetically. Setting this property's value to **True** sorts the items. Default is **False**.
Common Event	*(Delegate **EventHandler**, event arguments **EventArgs**)*
SelectedIndex-Changed	Generated when the selected index changes (such as when a different item is selected). This is the default event when the control is double-clicked in the designer.

Fig. 10.16 **ComboBox** properties and events.

Property ***DropDownStyle*** determines the type of **ComboBox**. Style ***Simple*** does not display a drop-down arrow. Instead, a scrollbar appears next to the control, allowing the user to select a choice from the list. The user also can type in a selection. Style ***DropDown*** (the default) displays a drop-down list when the down arrow is clicked (or the down-arrow key is pressed). The user can type a new item into the **ComboBox**. The last style is ***Drop-DownList***, which displays a drop-down list but does not allow the user to enter a new item.

The **ComboBox** control has properties **Items** (a collection), **SelectedItem** and **SelectedIndex**, which are similar to the corresponding properties in **ListBox**. There can be at most one selected item in a **ComboBox** (if zero, then **SelectedIndex** is **-1**). When the selected item changes, event **SelectedIndexChanged** is generated.

Class **FrmComboBox** (Fig. 10.17) allows users to select a shape to draw—an empty or filled circle, ellipse, square or pie—by using a **ComboBox**. The combo box in this example is uneditable, so the user cannot input a custom item.

Look-and-Feel Observation 10.7

*Make lists (such as **ComboBox**es) editable only if the program is designed to accept user-submitted elements. Otherwise, the user might try to enter a custom item and be unable to use it.*

```
1   ' Fig. 10.17: ComboBoxTest.vb
2   ' Using ComboBox to select shape to draw.
3
4   Imports System.Windows.Forms
5   Imports System.Drawing
6
7   Public Class FrmComboBox
8      Inherits Form
9
10      ' contains shape list (circle, square, ellipse, pie)
11      Friend WithEvents cboImage As ComboBox
12
13      ' Visual Studio .NET generated code
14
15      ' get selected index, draw shape
16      Private Sub cboImage_SelectedIndexChanged( _
17         ByVal sender As System.Object, _
18         ByVal e As System.EventArgs) _
19         Handles cboImage.SelectedIndexChanged
20
21         ' create graphics object, pen and brush
22         Dim myGraphics As Graphics = MyBase.CreateGraphics()
23
24         ' create Pen using color DarkRed
25         Dim myPen As New Pen(Color.DarkRed)
26
27         ' create SolidBrush using color DarkRed
28         Dim mySolidBrush As New SolidBrush(Color.DarkRed)
29
30         ' clear drawing area by setting it to color White
31         myGraphics.Clear(Color.White)
```

Fig. 10.17 ComboBox used to draw a selected shape. (Part 1 of 3.)

```
32
33              ' find index, draw proper shape
34          Select Case cboImage.SelectedIndex
35
36              Case 0 ' case circle is selected
37                  myGraphics.DrawEllipse(myPen, 50, 50, 150, 150)
38
39              Case 1 ' case rectangle is selected
40                  myGraphics.DrawRectangle(myPen, 50, 50, 150, 150)
41
42              Case 2 ' case ellipse is selected
43                  myGraphics.DrawEllipse(myPen, 50, 85, 150, 115)
44
45              Case 3 ' case pie is selected
46                  myGraphics.DrawPie(myPen, 50, 50, 150, 150, 0, 45)
47
48              Case 4 ' case filled circle is selected
49                  myGraphics.FillEllipse( _
50                      mySolidBrush, 50, 50, 150, 150)
51
52              Case 5 ' case filled rectangle is selected
53                  myGraphics.FillRectangle( _
54                      mySolidBrush, 50, 50, 150, 150)
55
56              Case 6 ' case filled ellipse is selected
57                  myGraphics.FillEllipse( _
58                      mySolidBrush, 50, 85, 150, 115)
59
60              Case 7 ' case filled pie is selected
61                  myGraphics.FillPie( _
62                      mySolidBrush, 50, 50, 150, 150, 0, 45)
63
64          End Select
65
66      End Sub ' cboImage_SelectedIndexChanged
67
68  End Class ' FrmComboBox
```

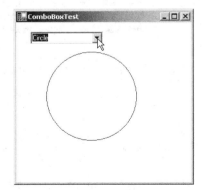

Fig. 10.17 ComboBox used to draw a selected shape. (Part 2 of 3.)

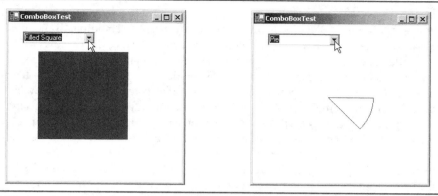

Fig. 10.17 **ComboBox** used to draw a selected shape. (Part 3 of 3.)

After creating **ComboBox cboImage** (line 11), we make it uneditable by setting its **DropDownStyle** to **DropDownList** in the **Properties** window. Next, we add items **Circle**, **Square**, **Ellipse**, **Pie**, **Filled Circle**, **Filled Square**, **Filled Ellipse** and **Filled Pie** to the **Items** collection using the **String Collection Editor**. Whenever the user selects an item from **cboImage**, a **SelectedIndexChanged** event is generated. Event handler **cboImage_SelectedIndexChanged** (lines 16–66) handles these events. Lines 22–28 create a **Graphics** object, a **Pen** and a **SolidBrush**, which are used to draw on the form. The **Graphics** object (line 22) allows a pen or brush to draw on a component using one of several **Graphics** methods. The **Pen** object is used by methods **drawEllipse**, **drawRectangle** and **drawPie** (lines 37, 40, 43 and 46) to draw the outlines of their corresponding shapes. The **Solid-Brush** object is used by methods **fillEllipse**, **fillRectangle** and **fillPie** (lines 49–50, 53–54, 57–58 and 61–62) to draw their corresponding solid shapes. Line 31 colors the entire form **White**, using **Graphics** method **Clear**. These methods are discussed in greater detail in Chapter 13, Graphics and Multimedia.

The application draws a particular shape on the basis of the selected item's index. The **Select Case** statement (lines 34–64) uses **cboImage.SelectedIndex** to determine which item the user selected. Class **Graphics** method *DrawEllipse* (line 37) takes a **Pen**, the *x*- and *y*- coordinates of the center and the width and height of the ellipse to draw. The origin of the coordinate system is in the upper-left corner of the form; the *x*-coordinate increases to the right, and the *y*-coordinate increases downward. A circle is a special case of an ellipse (the height and width are equal). Line 37 draws a circle. Line 43 draws an ellipse that has different values for height and width.

Class **Graphics** method *DrawRectangle* (line 40) takes a **Pen**, the *x*- and *y*-coordinates of the upper-left corner and the width and height of the rectangle to draw. Method *DrawPie* (line 46) draws a pie as a portion of an ellipse. The ellipse is bounded by a rectangle. Method **DrawPie** takes a **Pen**, the *x*- and *y*- coordinates of the upper-left corner of the rectangle, its width and height, the start angle (in degrees) and the sweep angle (in degrees) of the pie. Angles increase clockwise. The *FillEllipse* (lines 49–50 and 57–58), *FillRectange* (lines 53–54) and *FillPie* (lines 61–62) methods are similar to their unfilled counterparts, except that they take a **SolidBrush** instead of a **Pen**. Some of the drawn shapes are illustrated in the screen shots at the bottom of Fig. 10.17.

10.6 TreeViews

The **TreeView** control displays *nodes* hierarchically in a *tree*. Traditionally, nodes are objects that contain values and can refer to other nodes. A *parent node* contains *child nodes*, and the child nodes can be parents of other nodes. Two child nodes that have the same parent node are considered *sibling nodes*. A tree is a collection of nodes, usually organized in hierarchical manner. The first parent node of a tree is the *root* node (a **TreeView** can have multiple roots). For example, the file system of a computer can be represented as a tree. The top-level directory (perhaps **C:**) would be the root, each subfolder of **C:** would be a child node and each child folder could have its own children. **TreeView** controls are useful for displaying hierarchal information, such as the file structure that we just mentioned. We cover nodes and trees in greater detail in Chapter 20, Data Structures and Collections. Figure 10.18 displays a sample **TreeView** control on a form.

A parent node can be expanded or collapsed by clicking the plus box or minus box to its left. Nodes without children do not have these boxes.

The nodes displayed in a **TreeView** are instances of class **TreeNode**. Each **TreeNode** has a **Nodes** *collection* (type **TreeNodeCollection**), which contains a list of other **TreeNode**s—its children. The **Parent** property returns a reference to the parent node (or **Nothing** if the node is a root node). Figure 10.19 and Fig. 10.20 list the common properties of **TreeView**s and **TreeNode**s, and a **TreeView** event.

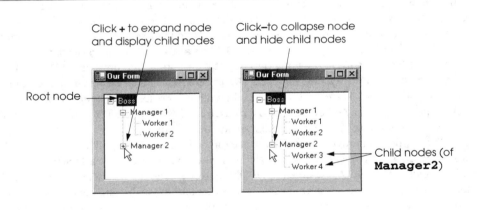

Fig. 10.18 TreeView displaying a sample tree.

TreeView properties and events	Description / Delegate and Event Arguments
Common Properties	
CheckBoxes	Indicates whether checkboxes appear next to nodes. A value of **True** displays checkboxes. The default value is **False**.

Fig. 10.19 TreeView properties and events. (Part 1 of 2.)

TreeView properties and events	Description / Delegate and Event Arguments
ImageList	Specifies the **ImageList** containing the node icons. An *Image-List* is a collection that contains **Image** objects.
Nodes	Lists the collection of **TreeNode**s in the control. Contains methods **Add** (adds a **TreeNode** object), **Clear** (deletes the entire collection) and **Remove** (deletes a specific node). Removing a parent node deletes all its children.
SelectedNode	The selected node.
Common Event	*(Delegate **TreeViewEventHandler**, event arguments **TreeViewEventArgs**)*
AfterSelect	Generated after selected node changes. This is the default event when the control is double-clicked in the designer.

Fig. 10.19 TreeView properties and events. (Part 2 of 2.)

TreeNode properties and methods	Description / Delegate and Event Arguments
Common Properties	
Checked	Indicates whether the **TreeNode** is checked (**CheckBoxes** property must be set to **True** in parent **TreeView**).
FirstNode	Specifies the first node in the **Nodes** collection (i.e., first child in tree).
FullPath	Indicates the path of the node, starting at the root of the tree.
ImageIndex	Specifies the index of the image shown when the node is deselected.
LastNode	Specifies the last node in the **Nodes** collection (i.e., last child in tree).
NextNode	Next sibling node.
Nodes	The collection of **TreeNode**s contained in the current node (i.e., all the children of the current node). Contains methods **Add** (adds a **TreeNode** object), **Clear** (deletes the entire collection) and **Remove** (deletes a specific node). Removing a parent node deletes all its children.
PrevNode	Indicates the previous sibling node.
SelectedImageIndex	Specifies the index of the image to use when the node is selected.
Text	Specifies the **TreeView**'s text.

Fig. 10.20 TreeNode properties and methods. (Part 1 of 2.)

TreeNode properties and methods	Description / Delegate and Event Arguments
Common Methods	
`Collapse`	Collapses a node.
`Expand`	Expands a node.
`ExpandAll`	Expands all the children of a node.
`GetNodeCount`	Returns the number of child nodes.

Fig. 10.20 `TreeNode` properties and methods. (Part 2 of 2.)

To add nodes to the **TreeView** visually, click the ellipsis by the **Nodes** property in the **Properties** window. This opens the *TreeNode Editor*, which displays an empty tree representing the **TreeView** (Fig. 10.21). There are buttons to create a root, to add or delete a node, and to rename a node.

To add nodes programmatically, we first must create a root node. Create a new **TreeNode** object and pass it a **String** to display. Then, call method **Add** to add this new **TreeNode** to the **TreeView**'s **Nodes** collection. Thus, to add a root node to **TreeView** *myTreeView*, write

$$myTreeView.\texttt{Nodes.Add(}\textit{New }\texttt{TreeNode(}RootLabel\texttt{))}$$

where *myTreeView* is the **TreeView** to which we are adding nodes, and *RootLabel* is the text to display in *myTreeView*. To add children to a root node, add new **TreeNode**s to its **Nodes** collection. We select the appropriate root node from the **TreeView** by writing

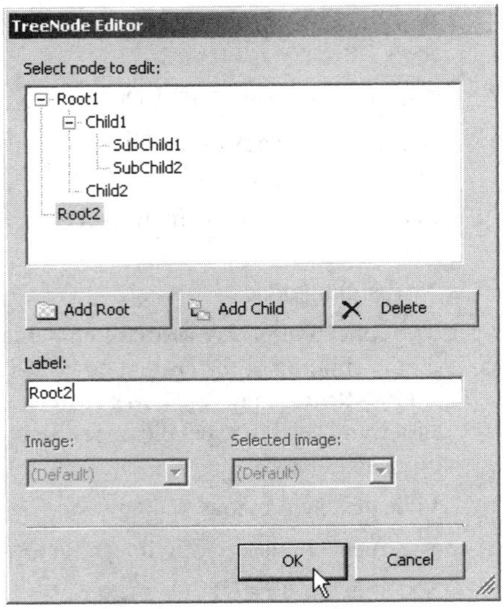

Fig. 10.21 TreeNode Editor.

myTreeView.**Nodes**(*myIndex*)

where *myIndex* is the root node's index in *myTreeView*'s **Nodes** collection. We add nodes to child nodes through the same process by which we added root nodes to *myTreeView*. To add a child to the root node at index *myIndex*, write

myTreeView.**Nodes**(*myIndex*).**Nodes**.**Add**(**New TreeNode**(*ChildLabel*))

Class **FrmTreeViewDirectory** (Fig. 10.22) uses a **TreeView** to display the directory file structure on a computer. The root node is the **C:** drive, and each subfolder of **C:** becomes a child. This layout is similar to that used in **Windows Explorer**. Folders can be expanded or collapsed by clicking the plus or minus boxes that appear to their left.

When **FrmTreeViewDirectory** loads, a **Load** event is generated, that is handled by event handler **FrmTreeViewDirectory_Load** (lines 56–62). Line 60 adds a root node (**C:**) to our **TreeView**, named **treDirectory**. **C:** is the root folder for the entire directory structure. Line 61 calls method **PopulateTreeView** (lines 16–53), which takes a directory (a **String**) and a parent node. Method **PopulateTreeView** then creates child nodes corresponding to the subdirectories of the directory that was passed to it.

Method **PopulateTreeView** (lines 16–53) obtains a list of subdirectories, using method **GetDirectories** of class **Directory** (namespace **System.IO**) on lines 23–24. Method **GetDirectories** takes a **String** (the current directory) and returns an array of **String**s (the subdirectories). If a directory is not accessible for security reasons, an **UnauthorizedAccessException** is thrown. Line 49 catches this exception and adds a node containing "**Access Denied**" instead of displaying the subdirectories.

```
1    ' Fig. 10.22: TreeViewDirectoryStructureTest.vb
2    ' Using TreeView to display directory structure.
3
4    Imports System.Windows.Forms
5    Imports System.IO
6
7    Public Class FrmTreeViewDirectory
8       Inherits Form
9
10      ' contains view of c:\ drive directory structure
11      Friend WithEvents treDirectory As TreeView
12
13      ' Visual Studio .NET generated code
14
15      ' add all subfolders of 'directoryValue' to 'parentNode'
16      Private Sub PopulateTreeView(ByVal directoryValue As String, _
17         ByVal parentNode As TreeNode)
18
19         ' populate current node with subdirectories
20         Try
21
22            ' get all subfolders
23            Dim directoryArray As String() = _
24               Directory.GetDirectories(directoryValue)
```

Fig. 10.22 TreeView used to display directories. (Part 1 of 3.)

```
25
26             If directoryArray.Length <> 0 Then  ' if at least one
27
28          Dim currentDirectory As String
29
30          ' for every subdirectory, create new TreeNode,
31          ' add as child of current node and
32          ' recursively populate child nodes with subdirectories
33          For Each currentDirectory In directoryArray
34
35             ' create TreeNode for current directory
36             Dim myNode As TreeNode = _
37                New TreeNode(currentDirectory)
38
39             ' add current directory node to parent node
40             parentNode.Nodes.Add(myNode)
41
42             ' recursively populate every subdirectory
43             PopulateTreeView(currentDirectory, myNode)
44          Next
45
46          End If
47
48       ' catch exception
49       Catch unauthorized As UnauthorizedAccessException
50          parentNode.Nodes.Add("Access Denied")
51       End Try
52
53    End Sub ' PopulateTreeView
54
55    ' called by system when form loads
56    Private Sub FrmTreeViewDirectory_Load(ByVal sender As Object, _
57       ByVal e As System.EventArgs) Handles MyBase.Load
58
59       ' add c:\ drive to treDirectory and insert its subfolders
60       treDirectory.Nodes.Add("C:")
61       PopulateTreeView("C:\", treDirectory.Nodes(0))
62    End Sub ' FrmTreeViewDirectory_Load
63
64 End Class ' FrmTreeViewDirectory
```

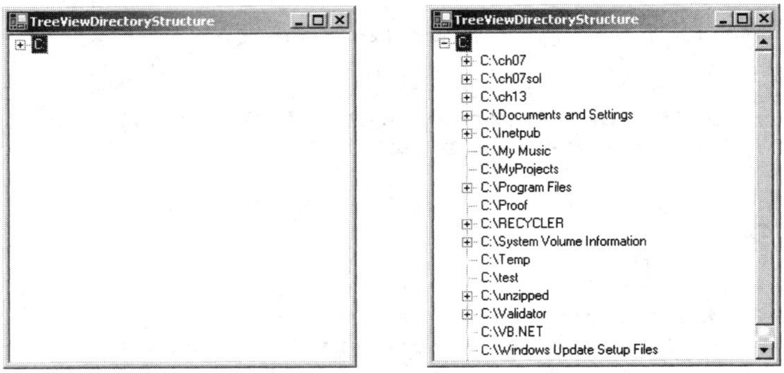

Fig. 10.22 TreeView used to display directories. (Part 2 of 3.)

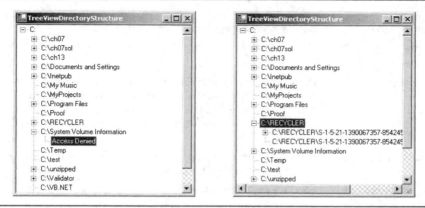

Fig. 10.22 `TreeView` used to display directories. (Part 3 of 3.)

If there are accessible subdirectories, each **String** in the **directoryArray** is used to create a new child node (lines 36–37). We use method **Add** (line 40) to add each child node to the parent. Then, method **PopulateTreeView** is called recursively on every subdirectory (line 43) and eventually populates the entire directory structure. Our recursive algorithm causes our program to have an initial delay when it loads—it must create a tree for the entire **C:** drive. However, once the drive folder names are added to the appropriate **Nodes** collection, they can be expanded and collapsed without delay. In the next section, we present an alternate algorithm to solve this problem.

10.7 ListViews

The **_ListView_** control is similar to a **ListBox** in that both display lists from which the user can select one or more items (to see an example of a **ListView**, look ahead to the output of Fig. 10.25). The important difference between the two classes is that a **ListView** can display icons alongside the list items in a variety of ways (controlled by its **ImageList** property). Property **_MultiSelect_** (a boolean) determines whether multiple items can be selected. Checkboxes can be included by setting property **CheckBoxes** (a **Boolean**) to **True**, making the **ListView**'s appearance similar to that of a **CheckedListBox**. The **View** property specifies the layout of the **ListView**. Property **_Activation_** determines the method by which the user selects a list item. The details of these properties are explained in Fig. 10.23.

ListView allows the programmer to define the images used as icons for **ListView** items. To display images, an **ImageList** component is required. Create one by dragging it onto a form from the **ToolBox**. Then, click the **Images** collection in the **Properties** window to display the **Image Collection Editor** (Fig. 10.24). Here, developers can browse for images that they wish to add to the **ImageList**, which contains an array of **Image**s. Once the images have been defined, set property **SmallImageList** of the **ListView** to the new **ImageList** object. Property **SmallImageList** specifies the image list for the small icons. Property **LargeImageList** sets the **ImageList** for large icons. Icons for the **ListView** items are selected by setting the item's **ImageIndex** property to the appropriate index.

ListView events and properties	Description / Delegate and Event Arguments
Common Properties	
Activation	Determines how the user activates an item. This property takes a value in the **ItemActivation** enumeration. Possible values are **OneClick** (single-click activation), **TwoClick** (double-click activation, item changes color when selected) and **Standard** (double-click activation).
CheckBoxes	Indicates whether items appear with checkboxes. **True** displays checkboxes. **False** is the default.
LargeImageList	Specifies the **ImageList** containing large icons for display.
Items	Returns the collection of **ListViewItem**s in the control.
MultiSelect	Determines whether multiple selection is allowed. Default is **True**, which enables multiple selection.
SelectedItems	Lists the collection of selected items.
SmallImageList	Specifies the **ImageList** containing small icons for display.
View	Determines appearance of **ListViewItem**s. Values **LargeIcon** (large icon displayed, items can be in multiple columns), **SmallIcon** (small icon displayed), **List** (small icons displayed, items appear in a single column) and **Details** (like **List**, but multiple columns of information can be displayed per item).
Common Event	*(Delegate* **EventHandler**, *event arguments* **EventArgs***)*
ItemActivate	Raised when an item in the **ListView** is activated. Does not contain the specifics of which item is activated.

Fig. 10.23 **ListView** properties and events.

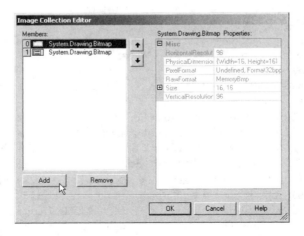

Fig. 10.24 Image Collection Editor window for an **ImageList** component.

Class **FrmListView** (Fig. 10.25) displays files and folders in a **ListView**, along with small icons representing each file or folder. If a file or folder is inaccessible because of permission settings, a message box appears. The program scans the contents of the directory as it browses, rather than indexing the entire drive at once.

To display icons beside list items, we must create an **ImageList** for the **ListView** **lvwBrowser** (line 15). First, drag and drop an **ImageList** onto the form and open the **Image Collection Editor**. Create two simple bitmap images—one for a folder (array index 0) and another for a file (array index 1). Then, set the object **lvwBrowser** property **SmallImageList** to the new **ImageList** in the **Properties** window. Developers can create such icons with any image software, such as Adobe® Photoshop™, Jasc® Paint Shop Pro™ or Microsoft® Paint.

```
1    ' Fig. 10.25: ListViewTest.vb
2    ' Displaying directories and their contents in ListView.
3
4    Imports System.Windows.Forms
5    Imports System.IO
6
7    Public Class FrmListView
8       Inherits Form
9
10      ' display labels for current location in directory tree
11      Friend WithEvents lblCurrent As Label
12      Friend WithEvents lblDisplay As Label
13
14      ' displays contents of current directory
15      Friend WithEvents lvwBrowser As ListView
16
17      ' specifies images for file icons and folder icons
18      Friend WithEvents ilsFileFolder As ImageList
19
20      ' Visual Studio .NET generated code
21
22      ' get current directory
23      Dim currentDirectory As String = _
24         Directory.GetCurrentDirectory()
25
26      ' browse directory user clicked or go up one level
27      Private Sub lvwBrowser_Click(ByVal sender As System.Object, _
28         ByVal e As System.EventArgs) Handles lvwBrowser.Click
29
30         ' ensure item selected
31         If lvwBrowser.SelectedItems.Count <> 0 Then
32
33            ' if first item selected, go up one level
34            If lvwBrowser.Items(0).Selected Then
35
36               ' create DirectoryInfo object for directory
37               Dim directoryObject As DirectoryInfo = _
38                  New DirectoryInfo(currentDirectory)
```

Fig. 10.25 **ListView** displaying files and folders. (Part 1 of 4.)

```
39
40              ' if directory has parent, load it
41              If Not (directoryObject.Parent Is Nothing) Then
42                  LoadFilesInDirectory( _
43                      directoryObject.Parent.FullName)
44              End If
45
46          ' selected directory or file
47          Else
48
49              ' directory or file chosen
50              Dim chosen As String = _
51                  lvwBrowser.SelectedItems(0).Text
52
53              ' if item selected is directory
54              If Directory.Exists(currentDirectory & _
55                  "\" & chosen) Then
56
57                  ' load subdirectory
58                  ' if in c:\, do not need "\", otherwise we do
59                  If currentDirectory = "C:\" Then
60                      LoadFilesInDirectory(currentDirectory & chosen)
61                  Else
62                      LoadFilesInDirectory(currentDirectory & _
63                          "\" & chosen)
64                  End If
65
66              End If
67
68          End If
69
70          ' update lblDisplay
71          lblDisplay.Text = currentDirectory
72      End If
73
74  End Sub ' lvwBrowser_Click
75
76  ' display files/subdirectories of current directory
77  Public Sub LoadFilesInDirectory( _
78      ByVal currentDirectoryValue As String)
79
80      ' load directory information and display
81      Try
82
83          ' clear ListView and set first item
84          lvwBrowser.Items.Clear()
85          lvwBrowser.Items.Add("Go Up One Level")
86
87          ' update current directory
88          currentDirectory = currentDirectoryValue
89          Dim newCurrentDirectory As DirectoryInfo = _
90              New DirectoryInfo(currentDirectory)
91
```

Fig. 10.25 **ListView** displaying files and folders. (Part 2 of 4.)

```
92                  ' put files and directories into arrays
93                  Dim directoryArray As DirectoryInfo() = _
94                     newCurrentDirectory.GetDirectories()
95
96                  Dim fileArray As FileInfo() = _
97                     newCurrentDirectory.GetFiles()
98
99                  ' add directory names to ListView
100                 Dim dir As DirectoryInfo
101
102                 For Each dir In directoryArray
103
104                    ' add directory to listview
105                    Dim newDirectoryItem As ListViewItem = _
106                       lvwBrowser.Items.Add(dir.Name)
107
108                    ' set directory image
109                    newDirectoryItem.ImageIndex = 0
110                 Next
111
112                 ' add file names to ListView
113                 Dim file As FileInfo
114
115                 For Each file In fileArray
116
117                    ' add file to ListView
118                    Dim newFileItem As ListViewItem = _
119                       lvwBrowser.Items.Add(file.Name)
120
121                    newFileItem.ImageIndex = 1      ' set file image
122                 Next
123
124              ' access denied
125              Catch exception As UnauthorizedAccessException
126                 MessageBox.Show("Warning: Some files may " & _
127                    "not be visible due to permission settings", _
128                    "Attention", 0, MessageBoxIcon.Warning)
129              End Try
130
131           End Sub ' LoadFilesInDirectory
132
133           ' handle load event when Form displayed for first time
134           Private Sub FrmListView_Load(ByVal sender As System.Object, _
135              ByVal e As System.EventArgs) Handles MyBase.Load
136
137              ' set image list
138              Dim folderImage As Image = Image.FromFile _
139                 (currentDirectory & "\images\folder.bmp")
140
141              Dim fileImage As Image = Image.FromFile _
142                 (currentDirectory & "\images\file.bmp")
143
144              ilsFileFolder.Images.Add(folderImage)
```

Fig. 10.25 ListView displaying files and folders. (Part 3 of 4.)

```
145          ilsFileFolder.Images.Add(fileImage)
146
147          ' load current directory into browserListView
148          LoadFilesInDirectory(currentDirectory)
149          lblDisplay.Text = currentDirectory
150      End Sub ' FrmListView_Load
151
152  End Class ' FrmListView
```

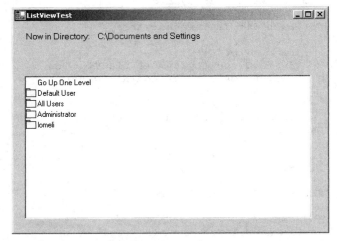

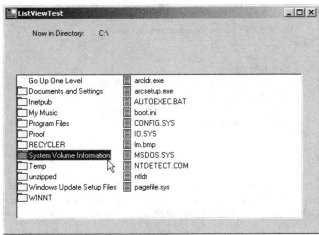

Fig. 10.25 ListView displaying files and folders. (Part 4 of 4.)

Method **LoadFilesInDirectory** (lines 77–131) populates **lvwBrowser** with the directory passed to it (**currentDirectoryValue**). It clears **lvwBrowser** and adds the element **"Go Up One Level"**. When the user clicks this element, the program attempts to move up one level (we see how shortly). The method then creates a **DirectoryInfo** object initialized with the **String currentDirectory** (lines 89–90). If permission is not given to browse the directory, an exception is thrown (caught on line 125). Method **LoadFilesInDirectory** works differently from method **PopulateTreeView** in the previous program (Fig. 10.22). Instead of loading all the folders in the entire hard drive, method **LoadFilesInDirectory** loads only the folders in the current directory.

Class *DirectoryInfo* (namespace **System.IO**) enables us to browse or manipulate the directory structure easily. Method **GetDirectories** (lines 93–94) returns an array of **DirectoryInfo** objects containing the subdirectories of the current directory. Similarly, method **GetFiles** (lines 96–97) returns an array of class **FileInfo** objects containing the files in the current directory. Property *Name* (of both class **Directory-Info** and class **FileInfo**) contains only the directory or file name, such as **temp** instead of **C:\myfolder\temp**. To access the full name, use property *FullName*.

Lines 102–110 and lines 115–122 iterate through the subdirectories and files of the current directory and add them to **lvwBrowser**. Lines 109 and 121 set the **ImageIndex** properties of the newly created items. If an item is a directory, we set its icon to a directory icon (index 0); if an item is a file, we set its icon to a file icon (index 1).

Method **lvwBrowser_Click** (lines 27–74) responds when the user clicks control **lvwBrowser**. Line 31 checks whether anything is selected. If a selection has been made, line 34 determines whether the user chose the first item in **lvwBrowser**. The first item in **lvwBrowser** is always **Go up one level**; if it is selected, the program attempts to go up a level. Lines 37–38 create a **DirectoryInfo** object for the current directory. Line 41 tests property **Parent** to ensure that the user is not at the root of the directory tree. Property **Parent** indicates the parent directory as a **DirectoryInfo** object; if it does not exist, **Parent** returns the value **Nothing**. If a parent directory exists, then lines 42–43 pass the full name of the parent directory to method **LoadFilesInDirectory**.

If the user did not select the first item in **lvwBrowser**, lines 47–68 allow the user to continue navigating through the directory structure. Lines 50–51 create **String chosen**, which receives the text of the selected item (the first item in collection **SelectedItems**). Lines 54–55 determine whether the user has selected a valid directory (rather than a file). The program combines variables **currentDirectory** and **chosen** (the new directory), separated by a slash (****), and passes this value to class **Directory**'s method *Exists*. Method **Exists** returns **True** if its **String** parameter is a directory. If this occurs, the program passes the **String** to method **LoadFilesInDirectory**. Because the **C:** directory already includes a slash, a slash is not needed when combining **currentDirectory** and **chosen** (line 60). However, other directories must include the slash (lines 62–63). Finally, **lblDisplay** is updated with the new directory (line 71).

This program loads quickly, because it indexes only the files in the current directory. This means that, rather than having a large delay in the beginning, a small delay occurs whenever a new directory is loaded. In addition, changes in the directory structure can be shown by reloading a directory. The previous program (Fig. 10.22) needs to be restarted to reflect any changes in the directory structure. This type of trade-off is typical in the software world. When designing applications that run for long periods of time, developers might choose a large initial delay to improve performance throughout the rest of the program. However, when creating applications that run for only short periods of time, developers often prefer fast initial loading times and a small delay after each action.

10.8 Tab Control

The *TabControl* control creates tabbed windows, such as the ones we have seen in the Visual Studio .NET IDE (Fig. 10.26). This allows the programmer to specify more information in the same space on a form, such as in the items of the Windows **Control Panel**.

TabControls contain *TabPage* objects, which are similar to **Panel**s and **GroupBox**es in that **TabPage**s also can contain controls. The programmer first adds controls to the **TabPage** objects, then adds the **TabPage**s to the **TabControl**. Only one **TabPage** is displayed at a time. To add objects to the **TabPage** and the **TabControl**, write

> *myTabPage*.**Controls.Add(***myControl***)**
> *myTabControl*.**Controls.Add(***myTabPage***)**

These statements call method **Add** of the **Controls** collection. The example adds **TabControl** *myControl* to **TabPage** *myTabPage*, then adds *myTabPage* to *myTabControl*. Alternatively, we can use method **AddRange** to add an array of **TabPage**s and an array of controls to **TabControl** and **TabPage** instances, respectively. Figure 10.27 depicts a sample **TabControl**.

Tab Windows

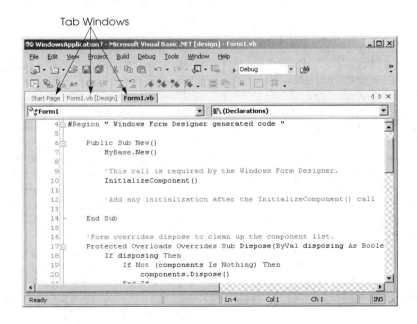

Fig. 10.26 Tabbed windows in Visual Studio .NET.

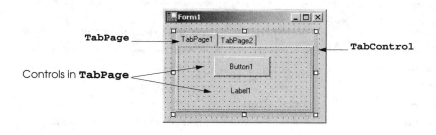

Fig. 10.27 `TabControl` with `TabPage`s example.

Programmers can add **TabControl**s visually by dragging and dropping them onto a form in design mode. To add **TabPage**s in the Visual Studio .NET designer, right-click the **TabControl**, and select **Add Tab** (Fig. 10.28). Alternatively, click the **TabPages** collection in the **Properties** window, and add tabs in the dialog that appears. To change a tab label, set the **Text** property of the **TabPage**. Note that clicking the tabs selects the **TabControl**—to select the **TabPage**, click the control area underneath the tabs. The programmer can add controls to the **TabPage** by dragging and dropping items from the **ToolBox**. To view different **TabPage**s, click the appropriate tab (in either design or run mode). Common properties and events of **TabControl**s are described in Fig. 10.29.

Each **TabPage** raises its own **Click** event when its tab is clicked. Remember, events for controls can be handled by any event handler that is registered with the control's event delegate. This also applies to controls contained in a **TabPage**. For convenience, Visual Studio .NET generates the empty event handlers for these controls.

Class **FrmTabs** (Fig. 10.30) uses a **TabControl** to display various options relating to the text on a label (**Color**, **Size** and **Message**). The last **TabPage** displays an **About** message, which describes the use of **TabControl**s.

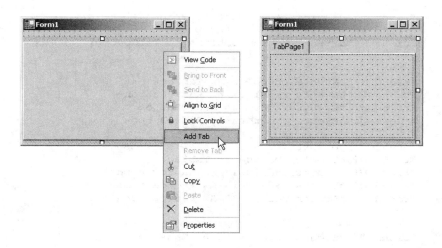

Fig. 10.28 `TabPage`s added to a `TabControl`.

TabControl properties and events	Description / Delegate and Event Arguments
Common Properties	
ImageList	Specifies images to be displayed on tabs.
ItemSize	Specifies tab size.
MultiLine	Indicates whether multiple rows of tabs can be displayed.
SelectedIndex	Index of selected TabPage.
SelectedTab	The selected TabPage.
TabCount	Returns the number of tab pages.
TabPages	Collection of TabPages within the TabControl.
Common Event	*(Delegate* EventHandler, *event arguments* EventArgs*)*
SelectedIndexChanged	Generated when SelectedIndex changes (i.e., another TabPage is selected).

Fig. 10.29 TabControl properties and events.

```
1   ' Fig. 10.30: UsingTabs.vb
2   ' Using TabControl to display various font settings.
3
4   Imports System.Windows.Forms
5
6   Public Class FrmTabs
7      Inherits Form
8
9      ' output label reflects text changes
10     Friend WithEvents lblDisplay As Label
11
12     ' table control containing table pages tbpColor,
13     ' tbpSize, tbpMessage and tbpAbout
14     Friend WithEvents tbcTextOptions As TabControl
15
16     ' table page containing color options
17     Friend WithEvents tbpColor As TabPage
18     Friend WithEvents radBlack As RadioButton
19     Friend WithEvents radRed As RadioButton
20     Friend WithEvents radGreen As RadioButton
21
22     ' table page containing font size options
23     Friend WithEvents tbpSize As TabPage
24     Friend WithEvents radSize12 As RadioButton
25     Friend WithEvents radSize16 As RadioButton
26     Friend WithEvents radSize20 As RadioButton
27
28     ' table page containing text display options
29     Friend WithEvents tbpMessage As TabPage
```

Fig. 10.30 TabControl used to display various font settings. (Part 1 of 3.)

```
30          Friend WithEvents radHello As RadioButton
31          Friend WithEvents radGoodbye As RadioButton
32
33          ' table page containing about message
34          Friend WithEvents tbpAbout As TabPage
35          Friend WithEvents lblMessage As Label
36
37          ' Visual Studio .NET generated code
38
39          ' event handler for black radio button
40          Private Sub radBlack_CheckedChanged( _
41             ByVal sender As System.Object, ByVal e As System.EventArgs) _
42             Handles radBlack.CheckedChanged
43
44             lblDisplay.ForeColor = Color.Black
45          End Sub ' radBlack_CheckedChanged
46
47          ' event handler for red radio button
48          Private Sub radRed_CheckedChanged( _
49             ByVal sender As System.Object, ByVal e As System.EventArgs) _
50             Handles radRed.CheckedChanged
51
52             lblDisplay.ForeColor = Color.Red
53          End Sub ' radRed_CheckedChanged
54
55          ' event handler for green radio button
56          Private Sub radGreen_CheckedChanged( _
57             ByVal sender As System.Object, ByVal e As System.EventArgs) _
58             Handles radGreen.CheckedChanged
59
60             lblDisplay.ForeColor = Color.Green
61          End Sub ' radGreen_CheckedChanged
62
63          ' event handler for size 12 radio button
64          Private Sub radSize12_CheckedChanged( _
65             ByVal sender As System.Object, ByVal e As System.EventArgs) _
66             Handles radSize12.CheckedChanged
67
68             lblDisplay.Font = New Font(lblDisplay.Font.Name, 12)
69          End Sub ' radSize12_CheckedChanged
70
71          ' event handler for size 16 radio button
72          Private Sub radSize16_CheckedChanged( _
73             ByVal sender As System.Object, ByVal e As System.EventArgs) _
74             Handles radSize16.CheckedChanged
75
76             lblDisplay.Font = New Font(lblDisplay.Font.Name, 16)
77          End Sub ' radSize16_CheckedChanged
78
79          ' event handler for size 20 radio button
80          Private Sub radSize20_CheckedChanged( _
81             ByVal sender As System.Object, ByVal e As System.EventArgs) _
82             Handles radSize20.CheckedChanged
```

Fig. 10.30 TabControl used to display various font settings. (Part 2 of 3.)

```
83
84          lblDisplay.Font = New Font(lblDisplay.Font.Name, 20)
85     End Sub ' radSize20_CheckedChanged
86
87     ' event handler for message "Hello!" radio button
88     Private Sub radHello_CheckedChanged( _
89        ByVal sender As System.Object, ByVal e As System.EventArgs) _
90        Handles radHello.CheckedChanged
91
92          lblDisplay.Text = "Hello!"
93     End Sub ' radHello_CheckedChanged
94
95     ' event handler for message "Goodbye!" radio button
96     Private Sub radGoodbye_CheckedChanged( _
97        ByVal sender As System.Object, ByVal e As System.EventArgs) _
98        Handles radGoodbye.CheckedChanged
99
100         lblDisplay.Text = "Goodbye!"
101    End Sub ' radGoodbye_CheckedChanged
102
103 End Class ' FrmTabs
```

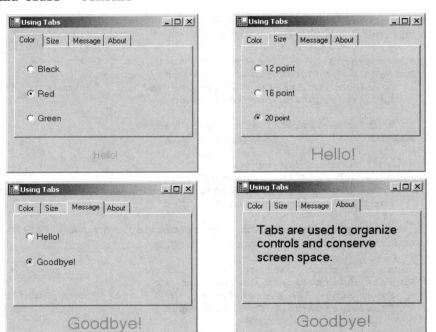

Fig. 10.30 TabControl used to display various font settings. (Part 3 of 3.)

The **TabControl tbcTextOptions** (line 14) and **TabPage**s **tbpColor** (line 17), **tbpSize** (line 23), **tbpMessage** (line 29) and **tbpAbout** (line 34) are created in the designer (as described previously). **TabPage tbpColor** contains three radio buttons for the colors black (**radBlack**, line 18), red (**radRed**, line 19) and green (**radGreen**, line 20). The **CheckChanged** event handler for each button updates the color of the text in **lblDisplay** (lines 44, 52 and 60). **TabPage tbpSize** has three radio buttons, corresponding to font sizes **12** (**radSize12**, line 24), **16** (**radSize16**, line 25) and **20** (**radSize20**, line 26), which change the font size of **lblDisplay**—lines 68, 76 and 84, respectively. **TabPage tbpMessage** contains two radio buttons for the messages **Hello!** (**radHello**, line 30) and **Goodbye!** (**radGoodbye**, line 31). The two radio buttons determine the text on **lblDisplay** (lines 92 and 100, respectively). The last **TabPage** (**tbpAbout**, line 34) contains a **Label** (**lblMessage**, line 35) describing the purpose of **TabControl**s.

Software Engineering Observation 10.2

*A **TabPage** can act as a container for a single logical group of radio buttons and enforce their mutual exclusivity. To place multiple radio-button groups inside a single **TabPage**, programmers should group radio buttons within **Panel**s or **GroupBox**es contained within the **TabPage**.*

10.9 Multiple-Document-Interface (MDI) Windows

In previous chapters, we have built only *single-document-interface (SDI)* applications. Such programs (including Notepad or Paint) can support only one open window or document at a time. SDI applications usually have contracted abilities—Paint and Notepad, for example, have limited image- and text-editing features. To edit multiple documents, the user must create another instance of the SDI application.

Multiple document interface (MDI) programs (such as PaintShop Pro or Adobe Photoshop) enable users to edit multiple documents at once. MDI programs also tend to be more complex—PaintShop Pro and Photoshop have a greater number of image-editing features than does Paint. Until now, we had not mentioned that the applications we created were SDI applications. We define this here to emphasize the distinction between the two types of programs.

The application window of an MDI program is called the *parent window*, and each window inside the application is referred to as a *child window*. Although an MDI application can have many child windows, each has only one parent window. Furthermore, a maximum of one child window can be active at once. Child windows cannot be parents themselves and cannot be moved outside their parent. Otherwise, a child window behaves like any other window (with regard to closing, minimizing, resizing etc.). A child window's functionality can be different from the functionality of other child windows of the parent. For example, one child window might edit images, another might edit text and a third might display network traffic graphically, but all could belong to the same MDI parent. Figure 10.31 depicts a sample MDI application.

To create an MDI form, create a new **Form** and set its *IsMDIContainer* property to **True**. The form changes appearance, as in Fig. 10.32.

Next, create a child form class to be added to the form. To do this, right-click the project in the **Solution Explorer**, select **Add Windows Form...** and name the file. To add the child form to the parent, we must create a new child form object, set its **MdiParent** property to the parent form and call method **Show**. In general, to add a child form to a parent, write

```
Dim frmChild As New ChildFormClass()
frmChild.MdiParent = frmParent
frmChild.Show()
```

In most cases, the parent form creates the child so that the *frmParent* reference is **Me**. The code to create a child usually lies inside an event handler, which creates a new window in response to a user action. Menu selections (such as **File** followed by a submenu option of **New** followed by a submenu option of **Window**) are common methods of creating new child windows.

Class **Form** property **MdiChildren** returns an array of child **Form** references. This is useful if the parent window wants to check the status of all its children (such as to ensure that all are saved before the parent closes). Property **ActiveMdiChild** returns a reference to the active child window; it returns **Nothing** if there are no active child windows. Other features of MDI windows are described in Fig. 10.33.

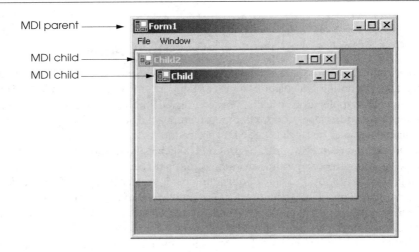

Fig. 10.31 MDI parent window and MDI child windows.

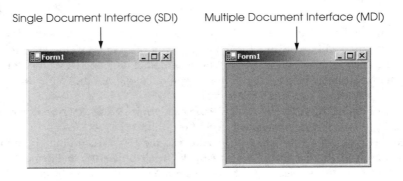

Fig. 10.32 SDI and MDI forms.

MDI Form events and properties	Description / Delegate and Event Arguments
Common MDI Child Properties	
IsMdiChild	Indicates whether the **Form** is an MDI child. If **True**, **Form** is an MDI child (read-only property).
MdiParent	Specifies the MDI parent **Form** of the child.
Common MDI Parent Properties	
ActiveMdiChild	Returns the **Form** that is the currently active MDI child (returns **Nothing** if no children are active).
IsMdiContainer	Indicates whether a **Form** can be an MDI parent. If **True**, the **Form** can be an MDI parent. The default value is **False**.
MdiChildren	Returns the MDI children as an array of **Form**s.
Common Method	
LayoutMdi	Determines the display of child forms on an MDI parent. Takes as a parameter an **MdiLayout** enumeration with possible values **ArrangeIcons**, **Cascade**, **TileHorizontal** and **TileVertical**. Figure 10.36 depicts the effects of these values.
Common Event	*(Delegate **EventHandler**, event arguments **EventArgs**)*
MdiChildActivate	Generated when an MDI child is closed or activated.

Fig. 10.33 MDI parent and MDI child events and properties.

Child windows can be minimized, maximized and closed independently of each other and of the parent window. Figure 10.34 shows two images, one containing two minimized child windows and a second containing a maximized child window. When the parent is minimized or closed, the child windows are minimized or closed as well. Notice that the title bar in the second image of Fig. 10.34 is **Parent Window - [Child]**. When a child window is maximized, its title bar is inserted into the parent window's title bar. When a child window is minimized or maximized, its title bar displays a restore icon, which can be used to return the child window to its previous size (its size before it was minimized or maximized).

The parent and child forms can have different menus, which are merged whenever a child window is selected. To specify how the menus merge, programmers can set the *MergeOrder* and the *MergeType* properties for each **MenuItem**. **MergeOrder** determines the order in which **MenuItem**s appear when two menus are merged. **MenuItem**s with a lower **MergeOrder** value appear first. For example, if **Menu1** has items **File**, **Edit** and **Window** (and their orders are 0, 10 and 20) and **Menu2** has items **Format** and **View** (and their orders are 7 and 15), then the merged menu contains menu items **File**, **Format**, **Edit**, **View** and **Window**, in that order.

Each **MenuItem** instance has its own **MergeOrder** property. It it likely that, at some point in an application, two **MenuItem**s with the same **MergeOrder** value will merge. Property **MergeType** resolves this conflict by determining the order in which the two menus are displayed.

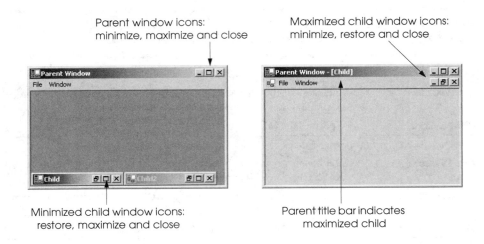

Parent window icons:
minimize, maximize and close

Maximized child window icons:
minimize, restore and close

Minimized child window icons:
restore, maximize and close

Parent title bar indicates
maximized child

Fig. 10.34 Minimized and maximized child windows.

The **MergeType** property takes a *MenuMerge* enumeration value and determines which menu items are displayed when two menus are merged. A menu item with value *Add* is added to its parent's menu as a new menu on the menu bar (the parent's menu items come first). If a child form's menu item has value *Replace*, it attempts to take the place of its parent form's corresponding menu item during merging. A menu with value *MergeItems* combines its items with that of its parent's corresponding menu (if parent and child menus originally occupy the same space, their submenus are combined as one menu). A child's menu item with value *Remove* disappears when the menu is merged with that of its parent.

Value **MergeItems** acts passively—if the parent's menu has a **MergeType** that is different from the child menu's **MergeType**, the child's menu setting determines the outcome of the merge. When the child window is closed, the parent's original menu is restored.

Software Engineering Observation 10.3

*Set the parent's menu items' **MergeType** property to value **MergeItems**. This allows the child window to add most menu items according to its own settings. Parent menu items that must remain should have value **Add**, and those that must be removed should have value **Remove**.*

Visual Basic .NET provides a property that facilitates the tracking of which child windows are opened in an MDI container. Property *MdiList* (a **Boolean**) of class **MenuItem** determines whether a **MenuItem** displays a list of open child windows. The list appears at the bottom of the menu following a separator bar (first screen in Figure 10.35). When a new child window is opened, an entry is added to the list. If nine or more child windows are open, the list includes the option **More Windows...**, which allows the user to select a window from a list, using a scrollbar. Multiple **MenuItem**s can have their **MdiList** property set; each displays a list of open child windows.

Good Programming Practice 10.1

*When creating MDI applications, include a menu item with its **MdiList** property set to **True**. This helps the user select a child window quickly, rather than having to search for it in the parent window.*

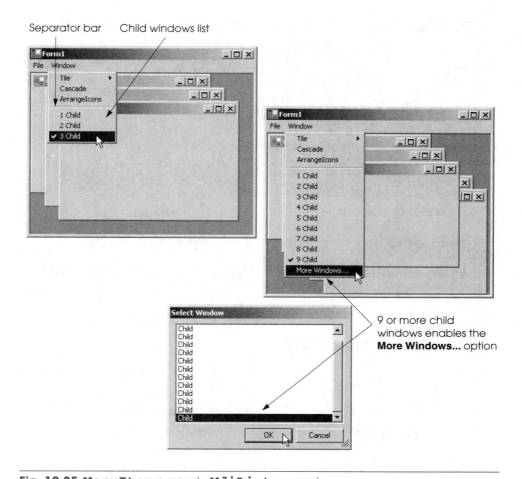

Fig. 10.35 MenuItem property **MdiList** example.

MDI containers allow developers to organize the placement of child windows. The child windows in an MDI application can be arranged by calling method **LayoutMdi** of the parent form. Method **LayoutMdi** takes a **MdiLayout** *enumeration*, which can have values **ArrangeIcons**, **Cascade**, **TileHorizontal** and **TileVertical**. *Tiled windows* completely fill the parent and do not overlap; such windows can be arranged horizontally (value **TileHorizontal**) or vertically (value **TileVertical**). *Cascaded windows* (value **Cascade**) overlap—each is the same size and displays a visible title bar, if possible. Value **ArrangeIcons** arranges the icons for any minimized child windows. If minimized windows are scattered around the parent window, value **ArrangeIcons** orders them neatly at the bottom-left corner of the parent window. Figure 10.36 illustrates the values of the **MdiLayout** enumeration.

Class **FrmUsingMDI** (Fig. 10.37) demonstrates the use of MDI windows. Class **FrmUsingMDI** uses three instances of child form **FrmChild** (Fig. 10.38), each containing a **PictureBox** that displays an image. The parent MDI form contains a menu enabling users to create and arrange child forms.

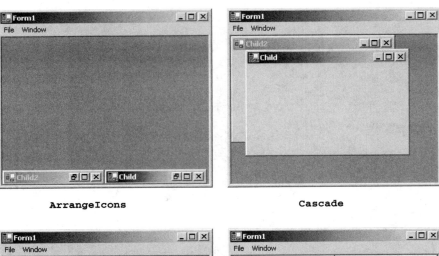

ArrangeIcons   Cascade

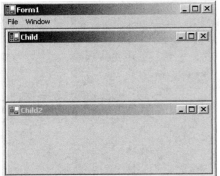   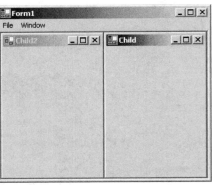

TileHorizontal   TileVertical

Fig. 10.36 **LayoutMdi** enumeration values.

```
1   ' Fig. 10.37: UsingMDI.vb
2   ' Demonstrating use of MDI parent and child windows.
3
4   Imports System.Windows.Forms
5
6   Public Class FrmUsingMDI
7      Inherits Form
8
9      ' main menu containing menu items File and Window
10     Friend WithEvents mnuMain As MainMenu
11
12     ' menu containing submenu New and menu item Exit
13     Friend WithEvents mnuitmFile As MenuItem
14     Friend WithEvents mnuitmExit As MenuItem
15
```

Fig. 10.37 MDI parent-window class. (Part 1 of 4.)

```
16      ' submenu New
17      Friend WithEvents mnuitmNew As MenuItem
18      Friend WithEvents mnuitmChild1 As MenuItem
19      Friend WithEvents mnuitmChild2 As MenuItem
20      Friend WithEvents mnuitmChild3 As MenuItem
21
22      ' menu containing menu items Cascade, TileHorizontal and
23      ' TileVertical
24      Friend WithEvents mnuitmWindow As MenuItem
25      Friend WithEvents mnuitmCascade As MenuItem
26      Friend WithEvents mnuitmTileHorizontal As MenuItem
27      Friend WithEvents mnuitmTileVertical As MenuItem
28
29      ' Visual Studio .NET generated code
30
31      ' create Child1 when menu clicked
32      Private Sub mnuitmChild1_Click( _
33         ByVal sender As System.Object, _
34         ByVal e As System.EventArgs) Handles mnuitmChild1.Click
35
36         ' create image path
37         Dim imagePath As String = _
38            Directory.GetCurrentDirectory() & "\images\image0.jpg"
39
40         ' create new child
41         childWindow = New FrmChild(imagePath, "Child1")
42         childWindow.MdiParent = Me   ' set parent
43         childWindow.Show()           ' display child
44      End Sub ' mnuitmChild1_Click
45
46      ' create Child2 when menu clicked
47      Private Sub mnuitmChild2_Click( _
48         ByVal sender As System.Object, _
49         ByVal e As System.EventArgs) Handles mnuitmChild2.Click
50
51         ' create image path
52         Dim imagePath As String = _
53            Directory.GetCurrentDirectory() & "\images\image1.jpg"
54
55         ' create new child
56         childWindow = New FrmChild(imagePath, "Child2")
57         childWindow.MdiParent = Me   ' set parent
58         childWindow.Show()           ' display child
59      End Sub ' mnuitmChild2_Click
60
61      ' create Child3 when menu clicked
62      Private Sub mnuitmChild3_Click( _
63         ByVal sender As System.Object, _
64         ByVal e As System.EventArgs) Handles mnuitmChild3.Click
65
66         ' create image path
67         Dim imagePath As String = _
68            Directory.GetCurrentDirectory() & "\images\image2.jpg"
```

Fig. 10.37 MDI parent-window class. (Part 2 of 4.)

```vbnet
69
70          ' create new child
71          childWindow = New FrmChild(imagePath, "Child3")
72          childWindow.MdiParent = Me   ' set parent
73          childWindow.Show()           ' display child
74      End Sub ' mnuitmChild3_Click
75
76      ' exit application
77      Private Sub mnuitmExit_Click(ByVal sender As System.Object, _
78         ByVal e As System.EventArgs) Handles mnuitmExit.Click
79
80         Application.Exit()
81      End Sub ' mnuitmExit_Click
82
83      ' set cascade layout
84      Private Sub mnuitmCascade_Click(ByVal sender As System.Object, _
85         ByVal e As System.EventArgs) Handles mnuitmCascade.Click
86
87         Me.LayoutMdi(MdiLayout.Cascade)
88      End Sub ' mnuitmCascade_Click
89
90      ' set TileHorizontal layout
91      Private Sub mnuitmTileHorizontal_Click( _
92         ByVal sender As System.Object, ByVal e As System.EventArgs) _
93         Handles mnuitmTileHorizontal.Click
94
95         Me.LayoutMdi(MdiLayout.TileHorizontal)
96      End Sub ' mnuitmTileHorizontal_Click
97
98      ' set TileVertical layout
99      Private Sub mnuitmTileVertical_Click( _
100        ByVal sender As System.Object, _
101        ByVal e As System.EventArgs) Handles mnuitmTileVertical.Click
102
103        Me.LayoutMdi(MdiLayout.TileVertical)
104     End Sub ' mnuitmTileVertical_Click
105
106  End Class ' FrmUsingMDI
```

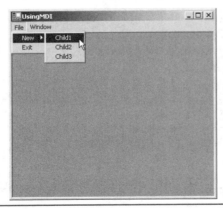 

Fig. 10.37 MDI parent-window class. (Part 3 of 4.)

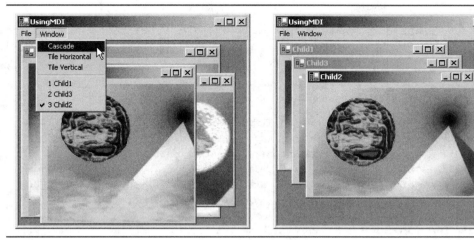

Fig. 10.37 MDI parent-window class. (Part 4 of 4.)

The program in Fig. 10.37 is the application. The MDI parent form, which is created first, contains two top-level menus. The first of these menus, **File** (**mnuitmFile**, line 13), contains both an **Exit** item (**mnuitmExit**, line 14) and a **New** submenu (**mnuitmNew**, line 17) consisting of items for each child window. The second menu, **Window** (**mnuit-mWindow**, line 24), provides options for laying out the MDI children, plus a list of the active MDI children.

```
1   ' Fig. 10.38: Child.vb
2   ' A child window of the MDI parent.
3
4   Imports System.Windows.Forms
5
6   Public Class FrmChild
7      Inherits Form
8
9      ' contains image loaded from disk
10     Friend WithEvents picDisplay As PictureBox
11
12     ' Visual Studio .NET generated code
13
14     ' constructor
15     Public Sub New(ByVal picture As String, _
16        ByVal name As String)
17
18        ' call Visual Studio generated default constructor
19        Me.New()
20
21        ' set title
22        Me.Text = name
23
```

Fig. 10.38 MDI child **FrmChild**. (Part 1 of 2.)

```
24          ' set image for picture box
25          picDisplay.Image = Image.FromFile(picture)
26      End Sub   ' New
27
28  End Class  ' FrmChild
```

Fig. 10.38 MDI child **FrmChild**. (Part 2 of 2.)

In the **Properties** window, we set the **Form**'s **IsMdiContainer** property to **True**, making the **Form** an MDI parent. In addition, we set the **mnuitmWindow MdiList** property to **True**. This enables **mnuitmWindow** to contain the list of child MDI windows.

The **Cascade** menu item (**mnuitmCascade**, line 25) has an event handler (**mnuitmCascade_Click**, lines 84–88) that arranges the child windows in a cascading manner. The event handler calls method **LayoutMdi** with the argument **Cascade** from the **MdiLayout** enumeration (line 87).

The **Tile Horizontal** menu item (**mnuitmTileHorizontal**, line 26) has an event handler (**mnuitmTileHorizontal_Click**, lines 91–96) that arranges the child windows in a horizontal manner. The event handler calls method **LayoutMdi** with the argument **TileHorizontal** from the **MdiLayout** enumeration (line 95).

Finally, the **Tile Vertical** menu item (**mnuitmTileVertical**, line 27) has an event handler (**mnuitmTileVertical_Click**, lines 99–104) that arranges the child windows in a vertical manner. The event handler calls method **LayoutMdi** with the argument **TileVertical** from the **MdiLayout** enumeration (line 103).

At this point the application is still incomplete—we must define the MDI child class. To do this, right-click the project in the **Solution Explorer** and select **Add**, then **Add Windows Form...** Then, name the new class in the dialog as **FrmChild** (Fig. 10.38). Next, we add a **PictureBox** (**picDisplay**, line 10) to form **FrmChild**. We override the constructor generated by Visual Studio. Line 19 calls the default Visual Studio generated constructor to allow the form and all of its components to initialize. Line 22 sets the title bar text. Line 25 sets **picDisplay**'s **Image** property to an **Image**, using method **FromFile**. Method **FromFile** takes as a **String** argument the path of the image to load.

After the MDI child class is defined, the parent MDI form (Fig. 10.37) can create new instances of them. The event handlers in lines 32–74 create a new child form corresponding to the menu item clicked. Each event handler creates a **String** representing the image file path each **FrmChild** displays (lines 37–38, 52–53 and 67–68). Lines 41, 56 and 71 create new instances of **FrmChild**. Lines 42, 57 and 72 sets each **FrmChild**'s **MdiParent** property to the parent form. Lines 43, 58 and 73 call method **Show** to display each child form.

10.10 Visual Inheritance

In Chapter 6, Object-Oriented Programming: Inheritance, we discussed how to create classes by inheriting from other classes. In Visual Basic, we also can use inheritance to create **Form**s that display a GUI, because **Form**s are classes that derive from class **System.Windows.Forms.Form**. Visual inheritance allows us to create a new **Form** by inheriting from another **Form**. The derived **Form** class contains the functionality of its **Form** base class, including any base-class properties, methods, variables and controls. The derived class also inherits all visual aspects—such as sizing, component layout, spacing between GUI components, colors and fonts—from its base class.

Visual inheritance enables developers to achieve visual consistency across applications by reusing code. For example, a company could define a base form that contains a product's logo, a static background color, a predefined menu bar and other elements. Programmers then could use the base form throughout an application for purposes of uniformity and branding.

Class **FrmInheritance** (Fig. 10.39) is a derived class of class **Form**. The output depicts the workings of the program. The GUI contains two labels with text **Bugs, Bugs, Bugs** and **Copyright 2002, by Bug2Bug.com.**, as well as one button displaying the text **Learn More**. When a user presses the **Learn More** button, method **cmdLearn_Click** (lines 16–22) is invoked. This method displays a message box that provides some informative text.

To allow other forms to inherit from **FrmInheritance**, we must package **Frm-Inheritance** as a **.dll**. Right click the project's name in the **Solution Explorer** and choose **Properties**. Under **Common Properties > General**, change **Output Type** to **Class Library**. Building the project produces the **.dll**.

To visually inherit from **FrmInheritance**, we create an empty project. From the **Project** menu, select **Add Inherited Form...** to display the **Add New Item** dialog. Select **Inherited Form** from the **Templates** pane. Clicking **Open** displays the **Inheritance Picker** tool. The **Inheritance Picker** tool enables programmers to create a form which inherits from a specified form. Click button **Browse** and select the **.dll** file corresponding to **FrmInheritance**. This **.dll** file normally is located within the project's **bin** directory. Click **OK**. The Form Designer should now display the inherited form (Fig. 10.40). We can add components to the form.

```
1   ' Fig. 10.39: FrmInheritance.vb
2   ' Form template for use with visual inheritance.
3
4   Imports System.Windows.Forms
5
6   Public Class FrmInheritance
7      Inherits Form
8
9      Friend WithEvents lblBug As Label          ' top label
10     Friend WithEvents lblCopyright As Label    ' bottom label
11     Friend WithEvents cmdLearn As Button       ' left button
12
13     ' Visual Studio .NET generated code
14
15     ' invoked when user clicks Learn More button
16     Private Sub cmdLearn_Click(ByVal sender As System.Object, _
17        ByVal e As System.EventArgs) Handles cmdLearn.Click
18
19        MessageBox.Show("Bugs, Bugs, Bugs is a product of " & _
20           " Bug2Bug.com.", "Learn More", MessageBoxButtons.OK, _
21           MessageBoxIcon.Information)
22     End Sub ' cmdLearn_Click
23
24  End Class ' FrmInheritance
```

Fig. 10.39 Class **FrmInheritance**, which inherits from class **Form**, contains a button (**Learn More**). (Part 1 of 2.)

Fig. 10.39 Class **FrmInheritance**, which inherits from class **Form**, contains a button (**Learn More**). (Part 2 of 2.)

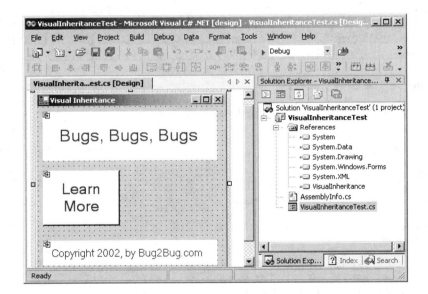

Fig. 10.40 Visual Inheritance through the Form Designer.

Class **FrmVisualTest** (Fig. 10.41) is a derived class of class **Visual-Form.FrmInheritance**. The output illustrates the functionality of the program. The GUI contains those components derived from class **FrmInheritance**, as well as an additional button with text **Learn The Program**. When a user presses this button, method **cmdProgram_Click** (lines 13–20) is invoked. This method displays another message box providing different informative text.

Figure 10.41 demonstrates that the components, their layouts and the functionality of base-class **FrmInheritance** (Fig. 10.39) are inherited by **FrmVisualTest**. If a user clicks button **Learn More**, the base-class event handler **cmdLearn_Click** displays a **MessageBox**. **FrmInheritance** uses a **Friend** access modifier to declare its controls, so class **FrmVisualTest** cannot modify the controls inherited from class **Frm-**

Inheritance. As we discussed in Chapter 6, **Friend** access modifiers allow access only to other classes or modules belonging to the same assembly. In this example, **FrmVisualTest** does not belong to the assembly of **FrmInheritance** (**VisualForm**), so **FrmVisualTest** cannot modify the controls that it inherits from **FrmInheritance**.

```vb
1   ' Fig. 10.41: VisualTest.vb
2   ' A form that uses visual inheritance.
3
4   Public Class FrmVisualTest
5      Inherits VisualForm.FrmInheritance
6
7      ' new button added to form
8      Friend WithEvents cmdProgram As Button
9
10     ' Visual Studio .NET generated code
11
12     ' invoke when user clicks Learn the Program button
13     Private Sub cmdProgram_Click(ByVal sender As System.Object, _
14        ByVal e As System.EventArgs) Handles cmdProgram.Click
15
16        MessageBox.Show( _
17           "This program was created by Deitel & Associates", _
18           "Learn the Program", MessageBoxButtons.OK, _
19           MessageBoxIcon.Information)
20     End Sub ' cmdProgram_Click
21
22  End Class ' FrmVisualTest
```

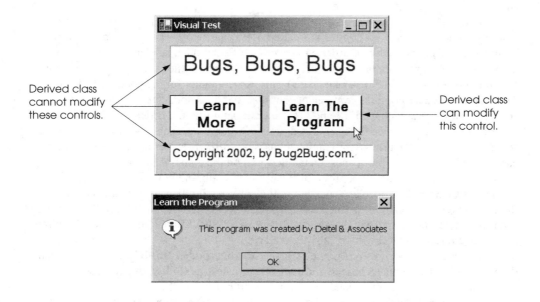

Fig. 10.41 Class **FrmVisualTest**, which inherits from class **VisualForm.FrmInheritance**, contains an additional button.

10.11 User-Defined Controls

The .NET Framework allows programmers to create *customized controls* or *custom controls* that inherit from a variety of classes. These customized controls appear in the user's **Toolbox** and can be added to **Form**s, **Panel**s or **GroupBox**es in the same way that we add **Button**s, **Label**s, and other predefined controls. The simplest way to create a customized control is to derive a class from an existing Windows Forms control, such as a **Label**. This is useful if the programmer wants to add functionality to an existing control, rather than having to reimplement the existing control in addition to including the desired functionality. For example, we can create a new type of label that behaves like a normal **Label** but has a different appearance. We accomplish this by inheriting from class **Label** and overriding method **OnPaint**.

Look-and-Feel Observation 10.8

*To change the appearance of any control, override method **OnPaint**.*

All controls contain method **OnPaint**, which the system calls when a component must be redrawn (such as when the component is resized). Method **OnPaint** is passed a ***PaintEventArgs*** object, which contains graphics information—property ***Graphics*** is the graphics object used to draw, and property ***ClipRectangle*** defines the rectangular boundary of the control. Whenever the system raises the **Paint** event, our control's base class catches the event. Through polymorphism, our control's **OnPaint** method is called. Our base class's **OnPaint** implementation is not called, so we must call it explicitly from our **OnPaint** implementation before we execute our custom-paint code. Alternately, if we do not wish to let our base class paint itself, we should not call our base class's **OnPaint** method implementation.

To create a new control composed of existing controls, use class ***UserControl***. Controls added to a custom control are called *constituent controls*. For example, a programmer could create a **UserControl** composed of a button, a label and a text box, each associated with some functionality (such as if the button sets the label's text to that contained in the text box). The **UserControl** acts as a container for the controls added to it. The **UserControl** contains constituent controls, so it does not determine how these constituent controls are displayed. Method **OnPaint** cannot be overridden in these custom controls—their appearance can be added only by handling each constituent control's **Paint** event. The **Paint** event handler is passed a **PaintEventArgs** object, which can be used to draw graphics (lines, rectangles etc.) on the constituent controls.

Using another technique, a programmer can create a brand new control by inheriting from class **Control**. This class does not define any specific behavior; that task is left to the programmer. Instead, class **Control** handles the items associated with all controls, such as events and sizing handles. Method **OnPaint** should contain a call to the base class's **OnPaint** method, which calls the **Paint** event handlers. The programmer must then add code that adds custom graphics inside the overridden **OnPaint** method when drawing the control. This technique allows for the greatest flexibility, but also requires the most planning. All three approaches are summarized in Fig. 10.42.

We create a "clock" control in Fig. 10.43. This is a **UserControl** composed of a label and a timer—whenever the timer raises an event, the label is updated to reflect the current time.

Custom Control Techniques and `PaintEventArgs` Properties	Description
Inherit from Windows Forms control	Add functionality to a preexisting control. If overriding method **OnPaint**, call base class **OnPaint**. Can add only to the original control appearance, not redesign it.
Create a `UserControl`	Create a **UserControl** composed of multiple preexisting controls (and combine their functionality). Cannot override **OnPaint** methods of custom controls. Instead, add drawing code to a **Paint** event handler. Can add only to the original control appearance, not redesign it.
Inherit from class `Control`	Define a brand-new control. Override **OnPaint** method, call base class method **OnPaint** and include methods to draw the control. Can customize control appearance and functionality.
`PaintEventArgs` *Properties*	*Use this object inside method* **OnPaint** *or* **Paint** *to draw on the control.*
`Graphics`	The graphics object of the control. Used to draw on the control.
`ClipRectangle`	Specifies the rectangle indicating the boundary of the control.

Fig. 10.42 Custom control creation.

Timers (**System.Windows.Forms** namespace) are non-visible components that reside on a form, generating *Tick* events at a set interval. This interval is set by the **Timer**'s *Interval* property, which defines the number of milliseconds (thousandths of a second) between events. By default, timers are disabled.

```
1   ' Fig. 10.43: CClockUserControl.vb
2   ' User-defined control with timer and label.
3
4   Imports System.Windows.Forms
5
6   ' create clock control that inherits from UserControl
7   Public Class CClockUserControl
8      Inherits UserControl
9
10     ' displays time
11     Friend WithEvents lblDisplay As Label
12
13     ' non-visible event-triggering timer object
14     Friend WithEvents tmrClock As Timer
15
16     ' Visual Studio .NET generated code
17
```

Fig. 10.43 `UserControl`-defined clock. (Part 1 of 2.)

```
18        ' update label at every tick
19        Private Sub tmrClock_Tick(ByVal sender As System.Object, _
20           ByVal e As System.EventArgs) Handles tmrClock.Tick
21
22           ' get current time (Now), convert to string
23           lblDisplay.Text = DateTime.Now.ToLongTimeString
24        End Sub ' tmrClock_Tick
25
26     End Class ' CClockUserControl
```

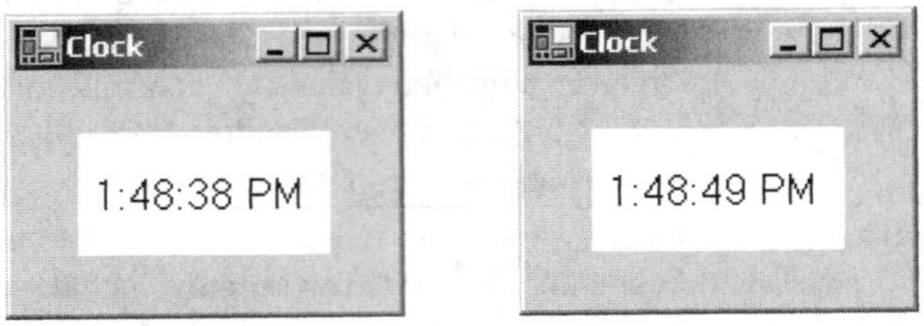

Fig. 10.43 UserControl-defined clock. (Part 2 of 2.)

We create a **Form** that displays our custom control, **CClockUserControl** (Fig. 10.43). Next, we create a **UserControl** class for the project by selecting **Project > Add User Control....** This displays a dialog from which we can select the type of control to add—user controls are already selected. We then name the file (and the class) **CClock-UserControl**. This brings up our empty **CClockUserControl** as a grey rectangle.

We can treat this control like a Windows **Form**, meaning that we can add controls using the **ToolBox** and set properties, using the **Properties** window. However, instead of creating an application (notice there is no **Main** method in the **Control** class), we are simply creating a new control composed of other controls. We add a **Label** (**lblDis-play**, line 11) and a **Timer** (**tmrClock**, line 14) to the **UserControl**. We set the **Timer** interval to 100 milliseconds and set **lblDisplay**'s text with each event (lines 19–24). Note that **tmrClock** must be enabled by setting property **Enabled** to **True** in the **Properties** window.

Structure **DateTime** (namespace **System**) contains member **Now**, which is the current time. Method **ToLongTimeString** converts **Now** to a **String** containing the current hour, minute and second (along with AM or PM). We use this to set **lblDisplay** on line 23.

Once created, our clock control appears as an item on the **ToolBox**. To use the control, we can simply drag it onto a form and run the Windows application. The **CClockUser-Control** object has a white background to make it stand out in the form. Figure 10.43 shows the output of **FrmClock**, which contains our **CClockUserControl**.

The above steps are useful when we need to define a custom control for the project on which we are working. Visual Studio .NET allows developers to share their custom controls with other developers. To create a **UserControl** that can be exported to other solutions, do the following:

1. Create a new **Windows Control Library** project.

2. Inside the project, add controls and functionality to the **UserControl** (Fig. 10.44).

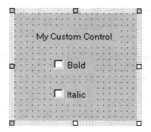

Fig. 10.44 Custom-control creation.

3. Build the project. Visual Studio .NET creates a **.dll** file for the **UserControl** in the output directory. The file is not executable: **Control** classes do not have a **Main** method. Select **Project > Properties** to find the output directory and output file (Fig. 10.45).

4. Create a new Windows application.

5. Import the **UserControl**. In the new Windows application, right click the **ToolBox**, and select **Customize Toolbox...**. In the dialog that appears, select the **.NET Framework Components** tab. Browse for the **.dll** file, which is in the output directory for the Windows control library project. Click the checkbox next to the control, and click **OK** (Fig. 10.46).

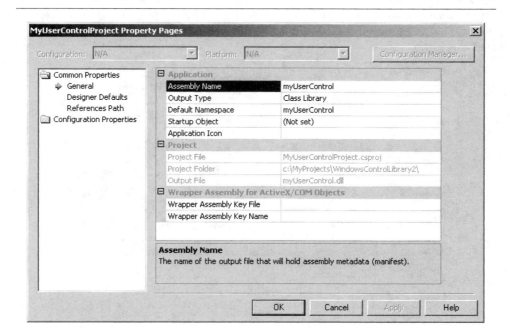

Fig. 10.45 Project properties dialog.

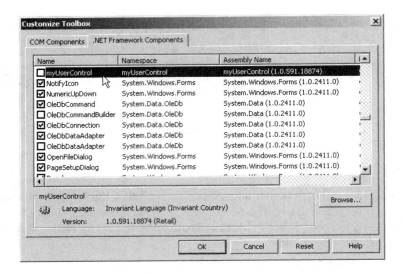

Fig. 10.46 Custom control added to the **ToolBox**.

      6. The **UserControl** appears on the **ToolBox** and can be added to the form as if it were any other control (Fig. 10.47).

Testing and Debugging Tip 10.1

*Control classes do not have a **Main** method—they cannot be run by themselves. To test their functionality, add them to a sample Windows application and run them there.*

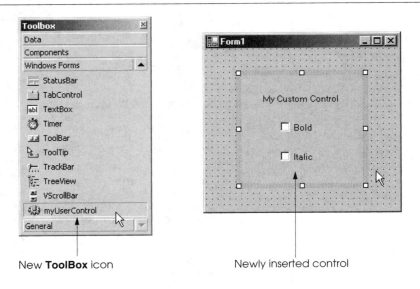

New **ToolBox** icon   Newly inserted control

Fig. 10.47 Custom control added to a **Form**.

As mentioned in Chapter 9, prefixing a variable name with an abbreviation of its type improves code readability. Figure 10.48 lists the abbreviations for the controls introduced in this chapter's code examples.

Many of today's most successful commercial programs provide GUIs that are easy to use and manipulate. Because of this demand for user-friendly GUIs, the ability to design sophisticated GUIs is an essential programming skill. Fortunately, Visual Studio .NET provides an IDE that makes GUI development quick and easy. In the last two chapters, we have presented the basic techniques required to add various GUI components to a program. The next chapter explores a more behind-the-scenes topic, *multithreading*. In many programming languages, the programmer can create multiple *threads*, enabling several processes to occur at once. By learning to create and manage multithreading in Visual Basic .NET, readers begin their study of a more mission-critical type of software.

10.12 Summary

Menus provide groups of related commands for Windows applications and enable user-application interaction without unnecessarily "cluttering" the GUI.

The **LinkLabel** control is used to display links to other objects, such as files or Web pages. When clicked, a **LinkLabel** generates a **LinkClicked** event.

The **ListBox** control allows the user to view and select multiple items from a list. The **CheckedListBox** control extends a **ListBox** by preceding each item in the list with a checkbox. This allows multiple items to be selected with no logical restriction. The **SelectedIndexChanged** event occurs when the user selects a new item in a **CheckedListBox**. Property **SelectedItem** returns the currently selected item. **SelectedIndex** returns the index of the selected item.

The **ComboBox** control combines **TextBox** features with a drop-down list. The user can either select an option from the list or type one in (if allowed by the program). Property **DropDownStyle** determines the type of **ComboBox**. The **ComboBox** control has properties **Items** (a collection), **SelectedItem** and **SelectedIndex**, which are similar to the corresponding properties in **ListBox**.

Prefix	Control
mnu	Menu
mnuitm	MenuItem
lnklbl	LinkLabel
lst	ListBox
chklst	CheckedListBox
cbo	ComboBox
tre	TreeView
lvw	ListView
ils	ImageList

Fig. 10.48 Prefixes for controls used in chapter. (Part 1 of 2.)

Prefix	Control
tbc	TabControl
tbp	TabPage
tmr	Timer

Fig. 10.48 Prefixes for controls used in chapter. (Part 2 of 2.)

The **TreeView** control can display nodes hierarchically in a tree. A node is one element in the tree. Nodes contain data as well as references to other nodes. A parent node contains child nodes, and the child nodes can be parents themselves. Each node has a **Nodes** collection, which contains a list of the **Node**'s children.

The **ListView** control is similar to a **ListBox** except that it can display icons alongside the list items in a variety of ways. To specify the images that will be used for the various icons, the programmer must use an **ImageList** component.

The **TabControl** control creates tabbed windows. This allows the programmer to logically organize information and save screen space. **TabControl**s contain **TabPage** objects, which can contain controls. Each **TabPage** generates its own **Click** event when its tab is clicked.

Multiple-document-interface (MDI) programs allow users to open multiple documents (i.e. windows) within the applications main window. Each window inside an MDI application is called a child window, and the application window is called the parent window. The parent and child windows of an application can have different menus, which are merged (combined) whenever a child window is selected.

The .NET Framework allows the programmer to create customized controls. To create a new control composed of existing controls, use class **UserControl**. To create a new control from the ground up, inherit from class **Control**. We create a **UserControl** class for the project by selecting **Project > Add User Control....** This control can be treated like a Windows Form.

11

Multithreading

Objectives

- To understand the concept of multithreading.
- To appreciate how multithreading can improve program performance.
- To understand how to create, manage and destroy threads.
- To understand the life cycle of a thread.
- To understand thread synchronization.
- To understand thread priorities and scheduling.

The spider's touch, how exquisitely fine!
Feels at each thread, and lives along the line.
Alexander Pope

A person with one watch knows what time it is; a person with two watches is never sure.
Proverb

Learn to labor and to wait.
Henry Wadsworth Longfellow

The most general definition of beauty...Multeity in Unity.
Samuel Taylor Coleridge

Outline

11.1 Introduction

The human body performs a great variety of operations *in parallel*—or, as we will say throughout this chapter, *concurrently*. Respiration, blood circulation and digestion, for example, can occur concurrently. Similarly, all the senses—sight, touch, smell, taste and hearing—can occur at once. Computers, too, perform operations concurrently. It is common for a desktop personal computer to compile a program, send a file to a printer and receive electronic mail messages over a network concurrently.

Ironically, some programming languages do not enable programmers to specify concurrent activities. Rather, these programming languages provide only a simple set of control structures that allow programmers to organize successive actions; a program proceeds to the next action after the previous action is completed. Historically, the type of concurrency that computers perform today generally has been implemented as operating-system "primitives" available only to highly experienced "systems programmers."

The Ada programming language, developed by the United States Department of Defense, made concurrency primitives widely available to defense contractors building military command-and-control systems. However, Ada has not been widely adopted by universities or commercial industry.

The .NET Framework Class Library makes concurrency primitives available to applications programmers. A programmer can specify that an application contains "threads of execution," where each thread designates a portion of a program that might execute concurrently with other threads. This capability is called *multithreading*. Multithreading is available in all .NET programming languages, including Visual Basic, C# and Visual C++.

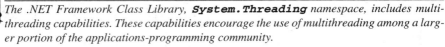

Software Engineering Observation 11.1

The .NET Framework Class Library, **System.Threading** *namespace, includes multi-threading capabilities. These capabilities encourage the use of multithreading among a larger portion of the applications-programming community.*

In this chapter, we discuss various applications of concurrent programming. For example, when programs download large files, such as audio clips or video clips from the World Wide Web, users do not want to wait until an entire clip downloads before starting the playback. To solve this problem, we can put multiple threads to work—one thread downloads a clip, and another plays the clip. This enables these activities, or *tasks*, to proceed concurrently. To avoid choppy playback, we *synchronize* the threads so that the player thread does not begin until the amount of the clip contained in memory is sufficient to keep the player thread busy while the downloading thread completes its execution.

Another example of multithreading is Visual Basic's automatic *garbage collection*. In C and C++, the programmer must assume responsibility for reclaiming dynamically allocated memory. By contrast, Visual Basic provides a *garbage-collector thread* that reclaims dynamically allocated memory when it is no longer needed.

Testing and Debugging Tip 11.1

In C and C++, programmers must provide statements explicitly for reclaiming dynamically allocated memory. When memory is not reclaimed (because a programmer forgets to do so, because of a logic error or because an exception diverts program control), an error called a memory leak *occurs. Over time, memory leaks can exhaust the supply of free memory and even cause program termination. Visual Basic's automatic garbage collection eliminates the vast majority of memory leaks.*

Performance Tip 11.1

One reason that C and C++ have remained popular over the years is that these languages memory management techniques were more efficient than those of languages that used garbage collectors. However, memory management in Visual Basic often is faster than in C or C++.[1]

Good Programming Practice 11.1

Set an object reference to **Nothing** *when the program no longer needs that object. This enables the garbage collector to determine at the earliest possible moment that the object can be garbage collected. If the program retains other references to the object, that object cannot be collected.*

The writing of multithreaded programs can be tricky. Although the human mind can perform functions concurrently, people often find it difficult to jump between parallel "trains of thought." To perceive why multithreading can be difficult to program and understand, try the following experiment: Open three books to page one and try reading the books concurrently. Read a few words from the first book, then read a few words from the second book, then read a few words from the third book, then loop back and read the next few words from the first book, etc. After conducting this experiment, readers will appreciate the challenges presented by multithreading. It is exceedingly difficult to switch between books, read each book briefly, remember your place in each book, move the book you are reading closer so you can see it and push books you are not reading aside. Moreover, it is nearly impossible to comprehend the content of the books amidst all this chaos!

Performance Tip 11.2

A problem with single-threaded applications is that lengthy activities must complete before other activities can begin. In a multithreaded application, threads can share a processor (or set of processors), enabling multiple tasks to be performed in parallel.

---

1. E. Schanzer, "Performance Considerations for Run-Time Technologies in the .NET Framework," August 2001 **<http://msdn.microsoft.com/library/default.asp?url= /library/en-us/dndotnet/html/dotnetperftechs.asp>**.

11.2 Thread States: Life Cycle of a Thread

At any time, a thread is said to be in one of several *thread states* (illustrated in Fig. 11.1). This section discusses the various states, as well as the transitions between states. Two classes that are essential to multithreaded applications are **Thread** and **Monitor** (**System.Threading** namespace). This section also discusses several methods of classes **Thread** and **Monitor** that cause state transitions.

When a program creates a new thread, the new thread begins its life cycle in the *Unstarted* state. The thread remains in the *Unstarted* state until the program calls **Thread** method **Start**, which places the thread in the *Started* state (sometimes called the *Ready* or *Runnable* state) and then immediately returns control to the calling thread. At this point, the thread that invoked **Start**, the newly *Started* thread and any other threads in the program can execute concurrently.

The highest priority *Started* thread enters the *Running* state (i.e., begins executing) when the operating system assigns a processor to the thread (Section 11.3 discusses thread priorities). When a *Started* thread receives a processor for the first time and becomes a *Running* thread, the thread executes its **ThreadStart** delegate, which specifies the actions that the thread will perform during its life cycle. When a program creates a new **Thread**, the program specifies the **Thread**'s **ThreadStart** delegate as an argument to the **Thread** constructor. The **ThreadStart** delegate must be a procedure that takes no arguments.

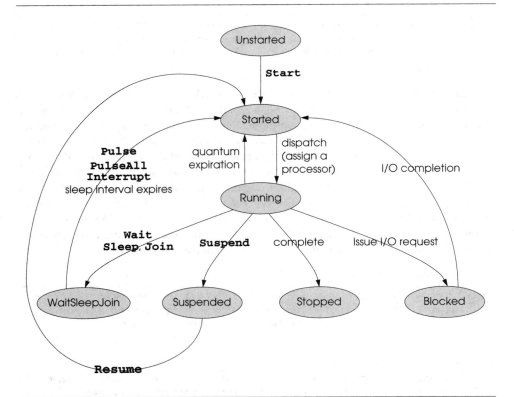

Fig. 11.1   Thread life cycle.

A *Running* thread enters the *Stopped* (or *Dead*) state when its **ThreadStart** delegate terminates. Note that a program can force a thread into the *Stopped* state by calling **Thread** method **Abort** on the appropriate **Thread** object. Method **Abort** throws a ***ThreadAbortException*** in the thread, normally causing the thread to terminate. When a thread is in the *Stopped* state and no references to the thread object remain in the program, the garbage collector can remove the thread object from memory.

A thread enters the *Blocked* state when the thread issues an input/output request. The operating system blocks the thread from executing until the operating system can complete the I/O for which the thread is waiting. Once the request is complete, the thread returns to the *Started* state and can resume execution. A *Blocked* thread cannot use a processor, even if one is available.

There are three ways in which a *Running* thread enters the *WaitSleepJoin* state. If a thread encounters code that it cannot execute yet (normally because a condition is not satisfied), the thread can call **Monitor** method **Wait** to enter the *WaitSleepJoin* state. Once in this state, a thread returns to the *Started* state when another thread invokes **Monitor** method **Pulse** or **PulseAll**. Method **Pulse** moves the next waiting thread back to the *Started* state. Method **PulseAll** moves all waiting threads back to the *Started* state.

Alternatively, a *Running* thread can call **Thread** method **Sleep** to enter the *WaitSleepJoin* state for a number of milliseconds specified as the argument to **Sleep**. A sleeping thread returns to the *Started* state when its designated sleep time expires. Like *Blocked* threads, sleeping threads cannot use a processor, even if one is available.

Any thread that enters the *WaitSleepJoin* state by calling **Monitor** method **Wait** or by calling **Thread** method **Sleep** leaves the *WaitSleepJoin* state and returns to the *Started* state if the sleeping or waiting **Thread**'s **Interrupt** method is called by another thread in the program.

If a thread (which we will call the dependent thread) cannot continue executing unless another thread terminates, the dependent thread calls the other thread's **Join** method to "join" the two threads. When two threads are "joined," the dependent thread leaves the *WaitSleepJoin* state when the other thread finishes execution (enters the *Stopped* state).

If a *Running* **Thread**'s **Suspend** method is called, the *Running* thread enters the *Suspended* state. A *Suspended* thread returns to the *Started* state when another thread in the program invokes the Suspended thread's **Resume** method.

11.3 Thread Priorities and Thread Scheduling

Every thread has a priority in the range from **ThreadPriority.Lowest** to **ThreadPriority.Highest**. These two values come from the **ThreadPriority** enumeration (namespace **System.Threading**), which consists of the values **Lowest**, **BelowNormal**, **Normal**, **AboveNormal** and **Highest**. By default, each thread has priority **Normal**. The *thread scheduler* determines when each thread executes based on the thread's priority.

The Windows platform supports a concept called *timeslicing*, which enables threads of equal priority to share a processor. Without timeslicing, each thread in a set of equal-priority threads runs to completion (unless the thread leaves the *Running* state and enters the *WaitSleepJoin*, *Suspended* or *Blocked* state) before the thread's peers get a chance to execute. With timeslicing, each thread receives a brief burst of processor time, called a *quantum*, during which the thread can execute. At the completion of the quantum, even if the thread has not finished executing, the processor is taken away from that thread and given to the next thread of equal priority, if one is available.

The job of the thread scheduler is to keep the highest-priority thread running at all times and, if there is more than one highest-priority thread, to ensure that all such threads execute for a quantum in round-robin fashion. Figure 11.2 illustrates the multilevel priority queue for threads. In Fig. 11.2, assuming that we are using a single-processor computer, threads A and B each execute for a quantum in round-robin fashion until both threads complete execution. This means that A gets a quantum of time to run, then B gets a quantum, then A gets another quantum and B gets another quantum. This continues until one thread completes. The processor then devotes all its power to the thread that remains (unless another thread of that priority is *Started*). Once A and B have finished executing, thread C runs to completion. Next threads D, E and F each execute for a quantum in round-robin fashion until they all complete execution. This process continues until all threads run to completion. Note that, depending on the operating system, new higher-priority threads could postpone—possibly indefinitely—the execution of lower-priority threads. Such *indefinite postponement* often is referred to more colorfully as *starvation*.

A thread's priority can be adjusted via the **Priority** property, which accepts values from the **ThreadPriority** enumeration. If the argument is not one of the valid thread-priority constants, an **ArgumentException** occurs.

A thread executes until it dies, becomes *Blocked* for input/output (or for some other reason), calls **Sleep**, calls **Monitor** methods **Wait** or **Join**, is preempted by a thread of higher priority or has its quantum expire. A thread with a higher priority than the *Running* thread can become *Started* (and hence preempt the *Running* thread) if a sleeping thread wakes up, if I/O completes for a thread that *Blocked* for that I/O, if either **Pulse** or **PulseAll** is called for an object on which a thread is waiting, or if a thread to which the high-priority thread was **Join**ed completes.

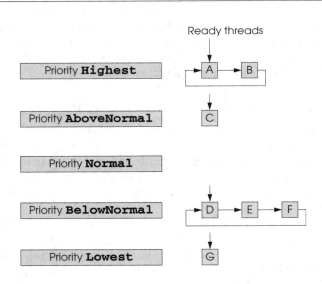

Fig. 11.2   Thread-priority scheduling.

Figure 11.3 and Figure 11.4 demonstrate basic threading techniques, including the construction of a **Thread** object and the use of the **Thread** class's **Shared** method **Sleep**. Module **modThreadTester** (Fig. 11.4) creates three threads that each have default priority **Normal**. Each thread displays a message indicating that it is going to sleep for a random interval between 0 and 5000 milliseconds and then goes to sleep. When each threads awakens, the thread displays a message indicating its name and that it is done sleeping and enters the *Stopped* state. Readers will see that method **Main** (i.e., the *Main thread of execution*) terminates before the application terminates. The program consists of one module—**modThreadTester** (Fig. 11.4), which creates the three threads—and one class—**CMessagePrinter** (Fig. 11.3), which defines a **Print** method containing the actions that each thread will perform.

```vb
1   ' Fig. 11.3: MessagePrinter.vb
2   ' Thread control method prints verbose message,
3   ' sleeps and prints waking up verbose message.
4
5   Imports System.Threading
6
7   Public Class CMessagePrinter
8
9      Private sleepTime As Integer
10     Private Shared randomObject As New Random()
11
12        ' constructor to initialize a CMessagePrinter object
13     Public Sub New()
14
15        ' pick random sleep time between 0 and 5 seconds
16        sleepTime = randomObject.Next(5001)
17     End Sub ' New
18
19     ' method Print controls thread that prints messages
20     Public Sub Print()
21
22        ' obtain reference to currently executing thread
23        Dim current As Thread = Thread.CurrentThread
24
25        ' put thread to sleep for sleepTime amount of time
26        Console.WriteLine(current.Name & " going to sleep for " & _
27           sleepTime)
28
29        Thread.Sleep(sleepTime)
30
31        ' print thread name
32        Console.WriteLine(current.Name & " done sleeping")
33     End Sub ' Print
34
35   End Class ' CMessagePrinter
```

Fig. 11.3 **ThreadStart** delegate **Print** displays message and sleeps for arbitrary duration of time.

Objects of class **CMessagePrinter** (Fig. 11.3) control the life cycle of each of the three threads that module **modThreadTester**'s **Main** method creates. Class **CMessagePrinter** consists of instance variable **sleepTime** (line 9), **Shared** variable **randomObject** (line 10), a constructor (lines 13–17) and a **Print** method (lines 20–33). Variable **sleepTime** stores a random **Integer** value chosen when a new **CMessage-Printer** object's constructor is called. Each thread controlled by a **CMessagePrinter** object sleeps for the amount of time specified by the corresponding **CMessagePrinter** object's **sleepTime**.

The **CMessagePrinter** constructor (lines 13–17) initializes **sleepTime** to a random **Integer** from 0 up to, but not including, 5001 (i.e., from 0 to 5000).

Method **Print** (lines 20–33) begins by obtaining a reference to the currently executing thread (line 23) via class **Thread**'s **Shared** property *CurrentThread*. The currently executing thread is the one that invokes method **Print**. Next, lines 26–27 display a message containing the name of the currently executing thread and an indication that the thread is going to sleep for a certain number of milliseconds. Note that line 26 uses the currently executing thread via the thread's **Name** property, which is set in method **Main** (Fig. 11.4, lines 8–35) when each thread is created. Line 29 invokes **Shared Thread** method **Sleep** to place the thread into the *WaitSleepJoin* state. At this point, the thread loses the processor, and the system allows another thread to execute. When the thread awakens, it reenters the *Started* state until the system assigns a processor to the thread. When the **CMessage-Printer** object enters the *Running* state again, line 32 outputs the thread's name in a message that indicates the thread is done sleeping, and method **Print** terminates.

Module **modThreadTester**'s **Main** method (Fig. 11.4, lines 8–35) creates three objects of class **CMessagePrinter**, in lines 11–13. Lines 17–19 create and initialize the three **Thread** objects that correspond to the **CMessagePrinter** objects created. Lines 22–24 set each **Thread**'s **Name** property, which we use for output purposes. Note that each **Thread**'s constructor receives a **ThreadStart** delegate as an argument. Remember that a **ThreadStart** delegate specifies the actions that a thread performs during its life cycle. Line 17 specifies that the delegate for **thread1** will be method **Print** of the object to which **printer1** refers. When **thread1** enters the *Running* state for the first time, **thread1** invokes **printer1**'s **Print** method to perform the tasks specified in method **Print**'s body. Thus, **thread1** prints its name, displays the amount of time for which it will go to sleep, sleeps for that amount of time, wakes up and displays a message indicating that the thread is done sleeping. At that point, method **Print** terminates. A thread completes its task when the method specified by a **Thread**'s **ThreadStart** delegate terminates, placing the thread in the *Stopped* state. When **thread2** and **thread3** enter the *Running* state for the first time, they invoke the **Print** methods of **printer2** and **printer3**, respectively. Threads **thread2** and **thread3** perform the same tasks that **thread1** performs by executing the **Print** methods of the objects to which **printer2** and **printer3** refer (each of which has its own randomly chosen sleep time).

Testing and Debugging Tip 11.2

*The naming of threads assists in the debugging of a multithreaded program. Visual Studio .NET's debugger provides a **Threads** window that displays the name of each thread and enables programmers to view the execution of any thread in the program.*

Lines 30–32 invoke each **Thread**'s **Start** method to place the threads in the *Started* state (this process sometimes is called *launching a thread*). Method **Start** returns immediately from each invocation; line 34 then outputs a message indicating that the threads were started, and the **Main** thread of execution terminates. The program itself does not terminate, however, because it still contains threads that are alive (i.e., threads that were *Started* and have not reached the *Stopped* state yet). The program will not terminate until its last thread dies. When the system assigns a processor to a thread, the thread enters the *Running* state and calls the method specified by the thread's **ThreadStart** delegate. In this program, each thread invokes method **Print** of the appropriate **CMessage-Printer** object to perform the tasks discussed previously.

Note that the sample outputs for this program display the name and sleep time of each thread as the thread goes to sleep. The thread with the shortest sleep time normally awakens first, then indicates that it is done sleeping and terminates. Section 11.7 discusses multithreading issues that may prevent the thread with the shortest sleep time from awakening first.

```vb
1   ' Fig. 11.4: ThreadTester.vb
2   ' Shows multiple threads that print at different intervals.
3
4   Imports System.Threading
5
6   Module modThreadTester
7
8      Sub Main()
9
10        ' create CMessagePrinter instances
11        Dim printer1 As New CMessagePrinter()
12        Dim printer2 As New CMessagePrinter()
13        Dim printer3 As New CMessagePrinter()
14
15        ' create each thread. Use CMessagePrinter's
16        ' Print method as argument to ThreadStart delegate
17        Dim thread1 As New Thread(AddressOf printer1.Print)
18        Dim thread2 As New Thread(AddressOf printer2.Print)
19        Dim thread3 As New Thread(AddressOf printer3.Print)
20
21        ' name each thread
22        thread1.Name = "thread1"
23        thread2.Name = "thread2"
24        thread3.Name = "thread3"
25
26        Console.WriteLine("Starting threads")
27
28        ' call each thread's Start method to place each
29        ' thread in Started state
30        thread1.Start()
31        thread2.Start()
32        thread3.Start()
33
34        Console.WriteLine("Threads started" & vbCrLf)
35     End Sub ' Main
36
37  End Module ' modThreadTester
```

Fig. 11.4   Threads sleeping and printing. (Part 1 of 2.)

```
Starting threads
Threads started

thread1 going to sleep for 1977
thread2 going to sleep for 4513
thread3 going to sleep for 1261
thread3 done sleeping
thread1 done sleeping
thread2 done sleeping
```

```
Starting threads
Threads started

thread1 going to sleep for 1466
thread2 going to sleep for 4245
thread3 going to sleep for 1929
thread1 done sleeping
thread3 done sleeping
thread2 done sleeping
```

Fig. 11.4   Threads sleeping and printing. (Part 2 of 2.)

11.4 Thread Synchronization and Class `Monitor`

Often, multiple threads of execution manipulate shared data. If threads that have access to shared data simply read that data, there is no need to prevent the data from being accessed by more than one thread at a time. However, when multiple threads share data and that data is modified by one or more of those threads, then indeterminate results might occur. If one thread is in the process of updating the data and another thread tries to update it too, the data will reflect the most recent update. If the data is an array or other data structure in which the threads could update separate parts of the data concurrently, it is possible that part of the data would reflect the information from one thread, whereas another part of the data would reflect information from a different thread. When this happens, it is difficult for the program to determine whether the data has been updated properly.

Programmers can solve this problem by giving any thread that is manipulating shared data exclusive access to that data during the manipulating. While one thread is manipulating the data, other threads desiring to access the data should be kept waiting. When the thread with exclusive access to the data completes its manipulation of the data, one of the waiting threads should be allowed to proceed. In this fashion, each thread accessing the shared data excludes all other threads from doing so simultaneously. This is called *mutual exclusion,* or *thread synchronization.*

Visual Basic uses the .NET Framework's monitors[2] to perform synchronization. Class **Monitor** provides methods for *locking objects,* which enables the implementation of synchronized access to shared data. The locking of an object means that only one thread can

---

2. Hoare, C. A. R. "Monitors: An Operating System Structuring Concept," *Communications of the ACM.* Vol. 17, No. 10, October 1974: 549–557. *Corrigendum, Communications of the ACM.* Vol. 18, No. 2, February 1975: 95.

access that object at a time. When a thread wishes to acquire exclusive control over an object, the thread invokes **Monitor** method **Enter** to acquire the lock on that data object. Each object has a *SyncBlock* that maintains the state of that object's lock. Methods of class **Monitor** use the data in an object's *SyncBlock* to determine the state of the lock for that object. After acquiring the lock for an object, a thread can manipulate that object's data. While the object is locked, all other threads attempting to acquire the lock on that object are blocked (i.e., they enter the *Blocked* state) from acquiring the lock. When the thread that locked the shared object no longer requires the lock, that thread invokes **Monitor** method **Exit** to release the lock. This updates the *SyncBlock* of the shared object to indicate that the lock for the object is available again. At this point, if there is a thread that was previously blocked from acquiring the lock on the shared object, that thread acquires the lock and can begin its processing of the object. If all threads with access to an object must acquire the object's lock before manipulating the object, only one thread at a time will be allowed to manipulate the object. This helps ensure the integrity of the data.

Common Programming Error 11.1

Make sure that all code that updates a shared object locks the object before doing so. Otherwise, a thread calling a method that does not lock the object can make the object unstable, even when another thread has acquired the lock for the object.

Common Programming Error 11.2

Deadlock occurs when a waiting thread (let us call this thread1*) cannot proceed, because it is waiting for another thread (let us call this* thread2*) to proceed. Similarly,* thread2 *cannot proceed, because it is waiting for* thread1 *to proceed. Because the two threads are waiting for each other, the actions that would enable each thread to continue execution never occur.*

Visual Basic also provides another means of manipulating an object's lock—keyword **SyncLock**. The placement of **SyncLock** before a block of code, as in:

```
SyncLock ( objectReference )
    ' code that requires synchronization goes here
End SyncLock
```

obtains the lock on the object to which the *objectReference* in parentheses refers. The *objectReference* is the same reference that normally would be passed to **Monitor** methods **Enter**, **Exit**, **Pulse** and **PulseAll**. When a **SyncLock** block terminates for any reason, Visual Basic releases the lock on the object to which the *objectReference* refers. We explain **SyncLock** further in Section 11.7.

If a thread determines that it cannot perform its task on a locked object, the thread can call **Monitor** method **Wait**, passing as an argument the object on which the thread will wait until the thread can perform its task. Calling method **Wait** from a thread releases the lock the thread has on the object that method **Wait** receives as an argument. Method **Wait** then places the calling thread into the *WaitSleepJoin* state for that object. A thread in the *WaitSleepJoin* state for an object leaves the *WaitSleepJoin* state when a separate thread invokes **Monitor** method **Pulse** or **PulseAll** with the object as an argument. Method **Pulse** transitions the object's first waiting thread from the *WaitSleepJoin* state to the *Started* state. Method **PulseAll** transitions all threads in the object's *WaitSleepJoin* state to the *Started* state. The transition to the *Started* state enables the thread (or threads) to prepare to continue executing.

There is a difference between threads waiting to acquire the lock for an object and threads waiting in an object's *WaitSleepJoin* state. Threads waiting in an object's *WaitSleepJoin* state call **Monitor** method **Wait** with the object as an argument. By contrast, threads that are waiting to acquire the lock enter the *Blocked* state and wait there until the object's lock becomes available. Then, one of the blocked threads can acquire the object's lock.

Common Programming Error 11.3

A thread in the WaitSleepJoin *state cannot reenter the* Started *state to continue execution until a separate thread invokes* **Monitor** *method* **Pulse** *or* **PulseAll** *with the appropriate object as an argument. If this does not occur, the waiting thread will wait forever and so can cause deadlock.*

Testing and Debugging Tip 11.3

When multiple threads manipulate a shared object using monitors, the programmer should ensure that, if one thread calls **Monitor** *method* **Wait** *to enter the* WaitSleepJoin *state for the shared object, a separate thread eventually will call* **Monitor** *method* **Pulse** *to transition the thread waiting on the shared object back to the* Started *state. If multiple threads might be waiting for the shared object, a separate thread can call* **Monitor** *method* **PulseAll** *as a safeguard to ensure that all waiting threads have another opportunity to perform their tasks.*

Performance Tip 11.3

Synchronization of threads in multithreaded programs can make programs runs more slowly, due to monitor overhead and the frequent transitioning of threads among the Running, WaitSleepJoin *and* Started *states. There is not much to say, however, for highly efficient, incorrect multithreaded programs!*

Monitor methods **Enter**, **Exit**, **Wait**, **Pulse** and **PulseAll** all take a reference to an object—usually the keyword **Me**—as their argument.

11.5 Producer/Consumer Relationship without Thread Synchronization

In a *producer/consumer relationship*, the *producer* portion of an application generates data, and the *consumer* portion of the application uses that data. In a multithreaded producer/consumer relationship, a *producer thread* calls a *produce method* to generate data and place it into a shared region of memory, called a *buffer*. A *consumer thread* then calls a *consume method* to read that data. If the producer waiting to put the next data into the buffer determines that the consumer has not yet read the previous data from the buffer, the producer thread should call **Wait**; otherwise, the consumer never sees the previous data, and that data is lost to the application. When the consumer thread reads the data, it should call **Pulse** to allow a waiting producer to proceed. If a consumer thread finds the buffer empty or determines that it has already read the data in the buffer, the consumer should call **Wait**; otherwise, the consumer might read "garbage" from the buffer, or the consumer might process a previous data item more than once. Any of these possibilities results in a logic error in the application. When the producer places the next data into the buffer, the producer should call **Pulse** to allow the consumer thread to proceed.

Now, let us consider how logic errors can arise if we do not synchronize access among multiple threads manipulating shared data. Imagine a producer/consumer relationship in which a producer thread writes a sequence of numbers (we use 1–4) into a *shared buffer*—a memory location shared among multiple threads. The consumer thread reads this data from the shared buffer and then displays the data. We display in the program's output the values that the producer writes (produces) and that the consumer reads (consumes). Figure 11.8 demonstrates a producer and a consumer accessing a single shared cell (**Integer** variable **mBuffer**, Fig. 11.5 line 9) of memory without any synchronization. Both the consumer and the producer threads access this single cell: The producer thread writes to the cell, whereas the consumer thread reads from it. We would like each value that the producer thread writes to the shared cell to be consumed exactly once by the consumer thread. However, the threads in this example are not synchronized. Therefore, data can be lost if the producer places new data into the slot before the consumer consumes the previous data. In addition, data can be incorrectly repeated if the consumer consumes data again before the producer produces the next item. To illustrate these possibilities, the consumer thread in the following example keeps a total of all the values it reads. The producer thread produces values from 1 to 4. If the consumer reads each value once and only once, the total would be 10. However, if readers execute this program several times, they will see that the total is rarely, if ever, 10. To emphasize our point, the producer and consumer threads in the example each sleep for random intervals of up to three seconds between performing their tasks. Thus, we do not know exactly when the producer thread will attempt to write a new value, nor do we know when the consumer thread will attempt to read a value.

The program consists of module **modSharedCell** (Fig. 11.8) and three classes—**CHoldIntegerUnsynchronized** (Fig. 11.5), **CProducer** (Fig. 11.6) and **CConsumer** (Fig. 11.7).

Class **CHoldIntegerUnsynchronized** (Fig. 11.5) consists of instance variable **mBuffer** (line 9) and property **Buffer** (lines 12–28), which provides **Get** and **Set** accessors. Property **Buffer**'s accessors do not synchronize access to instance variable **mBuffer**. Note that each accessor uses class **Thread**'s **Shared** property **CurrentThread** to obtain a reference to the currently executing thread and then uses that thread's property **Name** to obtain the thread's name.

```
1   ' Fig. 11.5: HoldIntegerUnsynchronized.vb
2   ' Definition of a shared integer without synchronization mechanisms.
3
4   Imports System.Threading
5
6   Public Class CHoldIntegerUnsynchronized
7
8       ' buffer shared by producer and consumer threads
9       Private mBuffer As Integer = -1
10
11      ' property Buffer
12      Property Buffer() As Integer
13
14         Get
15            Console.WriteLine(Thread.CurrentThread.Name & _
16               " reads " & mBuffer)
17
18            Return mBuffer
19         End Get
```

Fig. 11.5 Unsynchronized shared **Integer** buffer. (Part 1 of 2.)

```
20
21          Set(ByVal Value As Integer)
22             Console.WriteLine(Thread.CurrentThread.Name & _
23                " writes " & Value)
24
25             mBuffer = Value
26          End Set
27
28       End Property ' Buffer
29
30   End Class ' CHoldIntegerUnsynchronized
```

Fig. 11.5   Unsynchronized shared **Integer** buffer. (Part 2 of 2.)

Class **CProducer** (Fig. 11.6) consists of instance variable **sharedLocation** (line 8), instance variable **randomSleepTime** (line 9), a constructor (lines 12–17) to initialize the instance variables and a **Produce** method (lines 20–33). The constructor initializes instance variable **sharedLocation** so that it refers to the **CHoldIntegerUnsynchronized** object received from method **Main**. The producer thread in this program executes the tasks specified in method **Produce** of class **CProducer**. Method **Produce** contains a **For** structure (lines 25–28) that loops four times. Each iteration of the loop first invokes **Thread** method **Sleep** to place the producer thread into the *WaitSleep-Join* state for a random time interval of between 0 and 3 seconds (line 26). When the thread awakens, line 27 assigns the value of control variable **count** to the **CHoldIntegerUnsynchronized** object's **Buffer** property, which causes the **Set** accessor of **CHoldIntegerUnsynchronized** to modify the **mBuffer** instance variable of the **CHoldIntegerUnsynchronized** object. When the loop completes, lines 30–32 display a line of text in the command window to indicate that the thread finished producing data and is terminating. Then, the **Produce** method terminates, placing the producer thread in the *Stopped* state.

```
1    ' Fig. 11.6: Producer.vb
2    ' Produces integers from 1 to 4 and places them in
3    ' unsynchronized buffer.
4
5    Imports System.Threading
6
7    Public Class CProducer
8       Private sharedLocation As CHoldIntegerUnsynchronized
9       Private randomSleepTime As Random
10
11      ' constructor
12      Public Sub New(ByVal sharedObject As _
13         CHoldIntegerUnsynchronized, ByVal randomObject As Random)
14
15         sharedLocation = sharedObject
16         randomSleepTime = randomObject
17      End Sub ' New
18
```

Fig. 11.6   Producer places **Integer**s in unsynchronized shared buffer. (Part 1 of 2.)

```
19         ' store values 1-4 in object sharedLocation
20         Public Sub Produce()
21            Dim count As Integer
22
23               ' sleep for random interval up to 3000 milliseconds
24               ' set sharedLocation's Buffer property
25               For count = 1 To 4
26                  Thread.Sleep(randomSleepTime.Next(3000))
27                  sharedLocation.Buffer = count
28               Next
29
30               Console.WriteLine(Thread.CurrentThread.Name & _
31                  " done producing." & vbCrLf & "Terminating " & _
32                  Thread.CurrentThread.Name & ".")
33         End Sub ' Produce
34
35      End Class ' CProducer
```

Fig. 11.6   Producer places **Integer**s in unsynchronized shared buffer. (Part 2 of 2.)

Class **CConsumer** (Fig. 11.7) consists of instance variable **sharedLocation** (line 7), instance variable **randomSleepTime** (line 8), a constructor (lines 11–16) to initialize the instance variables and a **Consume** method (lines 19–32). The constructor initializes **sharedLocation** so that it refers to the **CHoldIntegerUnsynchronized** received from **Main** as the argument **sharedObject**. The consumer thread in this program performs the tasks specified in class **CConsumer**'s **Consume** method. The method contains a **For** structure (lines 24–27) that loops four times. Each iteration of the loop invokes **Thread** method **Sleep** to put the consumer thread into the *WaitSleepJoin* state for a random time interval of between 0 and 3 seconds (line 25). Next, line 26 gets the value of the **CHoldIntegerUnsynchronized** object's **Buffer** property and adds the value to the variable **sum**. When the loop completes, lines 29–31 display a line in the command window indicating the sum of all values that were read. Then the **Consume** method terminates, placing the consumer thread in the *Stopped* state.

```
1      ' Fig. 11.7: Consumer.vb
2      ' Consumes 4 integers from unsynchronized buffer.
3
4      Imports System.Threading
5
6      Public Class CConsumer
7         Private sharedLocation As CHoldIntegerUnsynchronized
8         Private randomSleepTime As Random
9
10        ' constructor
11        Public Sub New(ByVal sharedObject As _
12           CHoldIntegerUnsynchronized, ByVal randomObject As Random)
13
14           sharedLocation = sharedObject
15           randomSleepTime = randomObject
16        End Sub ' New
```

Fig. 11.7   Consumer reads **Integer**s from unsynchronized shared buffer. (Part 1 of 2.)

```
17
18          ' store values 1-4 in object sharedLocation
19      Public Sub Consume()
20         Dim count, sum As Integer
21
22            ' sleep for random interval up to 3000 milliseconds
23            ' then add sharedLocation's Buffer property value to sum
24            For count = 1 To 4
25               Thread.Sleep(randomSleepTime.Next(3000))
26               sum += sharedLocation.Buffer
27            Next
28
29            Console.WriteLine(Thread.CurrentThread.Name & _
30               " read values totaling: " & sum & "." & vbCrLf & _
31               "Terminating " & Thread.CurrentThread.Name & ".")
32         End Sub ' Consume
33
34      End Class ' CConsumer
```

Fig. 11.7   Consumer reads **Integer**s from unsynchronized shared buffer. (Part 2 of 2.)

Note: We use method **Sleep** in this example to emphasize the fact that, in multi-threaded applications, it is unclear when each thread will perform its task and how long it will take to perform that task when it has the processor. Normally, dealing with these thread-scheduling issues is the job of the computer's operating system. In this program, our thread's tasks are quite simple—the producer must loop four times and perform an assignment statement; the consumer must loop four times and add a value to variable **sum**. If we omit the **Sleep** method call, and if the producer executes first, the producer would complete its task before the consumer ever gets a chance to execute. In the same situation, if the consumer executes first, it would consume **-1** four times and then terminate before the producer can produce the first real value.

Module **modSharedCell**'s **Main** method (Fig. 11.8) instantiates a shared **CHold-IntegerUnsynchronized** object (line 14) and a **Random** object (line 17) for generating random sleep times; it then passes these objects as arguments to the constructors for the objects of classes **CProducer** (**producer**, line 20) and **CConsumer** (**consumer**, line 21). The **CHoldIntegerUnsynchronized** object contains the data that will be shared between the producer and consumer threads. Line 25 creates **producerThread**. The **ThreadStart** delegate for **producerThread** specifies that the thread will execute method **Produce** of object **producer**. Line 26 creates the **consumerThread**. The **ThreadStart** delegate for the **consumerThread** specifies that the thread will execute method **Consume** of object **consumer**. Lines 29–30 name threads **producer-Thread** and **consumerThread**. Finally, lines 33–34 place the two threads in the *Started* state by invoking each thread's **Start** method. Then, the **Main** thread terminates.

Ideally, we would like every value produced by the **CProducer** object to be consumed exactly once by the **CConsumer** object. However, when we study the first output of Fig. 11.8, we see that the consumer retrieved a value (**-1**) before the producer ever placed a value in the shared buffer, and that the value **1** was consumed three times. The consumer finished executing before the producer had an opportunity to produce the values **2**, **3** and **4**. Therefore, those three values were lost. In the second output, we see that the

```vb
1    ' Fig. 11.8: SharedCell.vb
2    ' Creates producer and consumer threads which interact
3    ' with each other through common CHoldIntegerUnsynchronized
4    ' object.
5
6    Imports System.Threading
7
8    Module modSharedCell
9
10      ' create producer and consumer threads and start
11      Sub Main()
12
13         ' create shared object used by threads
14         Dim holdInteger As New CHoldIntegerUnsynchronized()
15
16         ' Random object used by each thread
17         Dim randomObject As New Random()
18
19         ' create Producer and Consumer objects
20         Dim producer As New CProducer(holdInteger, randomObject)
21         Dim consumer As New CConsumer(holdInteger, randomObject)
22
23         ' create threads for producer and consumer
24         ' set delegates for each thread
25         Dim producerThread As New Thread(AddressOf producer.Produce)
26         Dim consumerThread As New Thread(AddressOf consumer.Consume)
27
28         ' name each thread
29         producerThread.Name = "Producer"
30         consumerThread.Name = "Consumer"
31
32         ' start each thread
33         producerThread.Start()
34         consumerThread.Start()
35      End Sub ' Main
36
37   End Module ' modSharedCell
```

```
Consumer reads -1
Producer writes 1
Consumer reads 1
Consumer reads 1
Consumer reads 1
Consumer read values totaling: 2.
Terminating Consumer.
Producer writes 2
Producer writes 3
Producer writes 4
Producer done producing.
Terminating Producer.
```

Fig. 11.8   Producer and consumer threads accessing a shared object without synchronization. (Part 1 of 2.)

```
Producer writes 1
Producer writes 2
Consumer reads 2
Producer writes 3
Consumer reads 3
Producer writes 4
Producer done producing.
Terminating Producer.
Consumer reads 4
Consumer reads 4
Consumer read values totaling: 13.
Terminating Consumer.
```

```
Producer writes 1
Consumer reads 1
Producer writes 2
Consumer reads 2
Producer writes 3
Consumer reads 3
Producer writes 4
Producer done producing.
Terminating Producer.
Consumer reads 4
Consumer read values totaling: 10.
Terminating Consumer.
```

Fig. 11.8   Producer and consumer threads accessing a shared object without
synchronization. (Part 2 of 2.)

value **1** was lost, because the values **1** and **2** were produced before the consumer thread
could read the value **1**. In addition, the value **4** was consumed twice. The last sample output
demonstrates that it is possible, with some luck, to achieve a proper output, in which each
value that the producer produces is consumed once and only once by the consumer. This
example clearly demonstrates that access to shared data by concurrent threads must be controlled carefully; otherwise, a program might produce incorrect results.

To solve the problems that occur in the previous example regarding lost and repeatedly
consumed data, we will (in Fig. 11.9) synchronize the concurrent producer and consumer
threads access to the shared data by using **Monitor** class methods **Enter**, **Wait**, **Pulse**
and **Exit**. When a thread uses synchronization to access a shared object, the object is
locked, and no other thread can acquire the lock for that shared object until the thread
holding the lock releases it.

11.6 Producer/Consumer Relationship with Thread Synchronization

Figure 11.12 demonstrates a producer and a consumer accessing a shared cell of memory
with synchronization. The consumer consumes only after the producer produces a value,
and the producer produces a new value only after the consumer consumes the previously
produced value. Classes **CProducer** (Fig. 11.10), **CConsumer** (Fig. 11.11) and module

modSharedCell (Fig. 11.12) are identical to those in Fig. 11.6, Fig. 11.7 and Fig. 11.8, respectively, except that they use the new class **CHoldIntegerSynchronized** (Fig. 11.9). [Note: In this example, we demonstrate synchronization with class **Monitor**'s **Enter** and **Exit** methods. In the next example, we demonstrate the same concepts using a **SyncLock** block.]

```vb
1    ' Fig. 11.9: HoldIntegerSynchronized.vb
2    ' Synchronizes access to an Integer.
3
4    Imports System.Threading
5
6    Public Class CHoldIntegerSynchronized
7
8       ' buffer shared by producer and consumer threads
9       Private mBuffer As Integer = -1
10
11      ' occupiedBufferCount maintains count of occupied buffers
12      Private occupiedBufferCount As Integer
13
14      Public Property Buffer() As Integer
15
16         Get
17
18            ' obtain lock on this object
19            Monitor.Enter(Me)
20
21            ' if there is no data to read, place invoking
22            ' thread in WaitSleepJoin state
23            If occupiedBufferCount = 0 Then
24               Console.WriteLine(Thread.CurrentThread.Name & _
25                  " tries to read.")
26
27               DisplayState("Buffer empty. " & _
28                  Thread.CurrentThread.Name & " waits.")
29
30               Monitor.Wait(Me)
31            End If
32
33            ' indicate that producer can store another value
34            ' because consumer just retrieved buffer value
35            occupiedBufferCount -= 1
36
37            DisplayState(Thread.CurrentThread.Name & " reads " & _
38               mBuffer)
39
40            ' tell waiting thread (if there is one) to
41            ' become ready to execute (Started state)
42            Monitor.Pulse(Me)
43
44            ' Get copy of buffer before releasing lock.
45            ' It is possible that the producer could be
46            ' assigned the processor immediately after the
```

Fig. 11.9 Synchronized shared **Integer** buffer. (Part 1 of 3.)

```
47              ' monitor is released and before the return
48              ' statement executes. In this case, the producer
49              ' would assign a new value to buffer before the
50              ' return statement returns the value to the
51              ' consumer. Thus, the consumer would receive the
52              ' new value. Making a copy of buffer and
53              ' returning the copy helps ensure that the
54              ' consumer receives the proper value.
55              Dim bufferCopy As Integer = mBuffer
56
57              ' release lock on this object
58              Monitor.Exit(Me)
59
60           Return bufferCopy
61        End Get
62
63        Set(ByVal Value As Integer)
64
65              ' acquire lock for this object
66              Monitor.Enter(Me)
67
68              ' if there are no empty locations, place invoking
69              ' thread in WaitSleepJoin state
70              If occupiedBufferCount = 1 Then
71                 Console.WriteLine(Thread.CurrentThread.Name & _
72                    " tries to write.")
73
74                 DisplayState("Buffer full. " & _
75                    Thread.CurrentThread.Name & " waits.")
76
77                 Monitor.Wait(Me)
78              End If
79
80              ' set new buffer value
81              mBuffer = Value
82
83              ' indicate producer cannot store another value
84              ' until consumer retrieves current buffer value
85              occupiedBufferCount += 1
86
87              DisplayState(Thread.CurrentThread.Name & " writes " & _
88                 mBuffer)
89
90              ' tell waiting thread (if there is one) to
91              ' become ready to execute (Started state)
92              Monitor.Pulse(Me)
93
94              ' release lock on this object
95              Monitor.Exit(Me)
96        End Set
97
98     End Property ' Buffer
99
```

Fig. 11.9 Synchronized shared **Integer** buffer. (Part 2 of 3.)

```
100        Public Sub DisplayState(ByVal operation As String)
101           Console.WriteLine("{0,-35}{1,-9}{2}" & vbCrLf, _
102              operation, mBuffer, occupiedBufferCount)
103        End Sub ' DisplayState
104
105     End Class ' CHoldIntegerSynchronized
```

Fig. 11.9 Synchronized shared **Integer** buffer. (Part 3 of 3.)

```
1    ' Fig. 11.10: Producer.vb
2    ' Produce 4 integers and place them in synchronized buffer.
3
4    Imports System.Threading
5
6    Public Class CProducer
7       Private sharedLocation As CHoldIntegerSynchronized
8       Private randomSleepTime As Random
9
10      ' constructor
11      Public Sub New(ByVal sharedObject As _
12         CHoldIntegerSynchronized, ByVal randomObject As Random)
13
14         sharedLocation = sharedObject
15         randomSleepTime = randomObject
16      End Sub ' New
17
18      ' store values 1-4 in object sharedLocation
19      Public Sub Produce()
20         Dim count As Integer
21
22         ' sleep for random interval up to 3000 milliseconds
23         ' set sharedLocation's Buffer property
24         For count = 1 To 4
25            Thread.Sleep(randomSleepTime.Next(3000))
26            sharedLocation.Buffer = count
27         Next
28
29         Console.WriteLine(Thread.CurrentThread.Name & _
30            " done producing. " & vbCrLf & "Terminating " & _
31            Thread.CurrentThread.Name & "." & vbCrLf)
32      End Sub ' Produce
33
34   End Class ' CProducer
```

Fig. 11.10 Producer places **Integer**s in synchronized shared buffer.

```
1    ' Fig. 11.11: Consumer.vb
2    ' Consumes 4 Integers from synchronized buffer.
3
4    Imports System.Threading
5
```

Fig. 11.11 Consumer reads **Integer**s from synchronized shared buffer. (Part 1 of 2.)

```
 6    Public Class CConsumer
 7       Private sharedLocation As CHoldIntegerSynchronized
 8       Private randomSleepTime As Random
 9
10       ' constructor
11       Public Sub New(ByVal sharedObject As _
12          CHoldIntegerSynchronized, ByVal randomObject As Random)
13
14          sharedLocation = sharedObject
15          randomSleepTime = randomObject
16       End Sub ' New
17
18       ' read sharedLocation's value four times
19       Public Sub Consume()
20          Dim count, sum As Integer
21
22          ' sleep for random interval up to 3000 milliseconds
23          ' add sharedLocation's Buffer property value to sum
24          For count = 1 To 4
25             Thread.Sleep(randomSleepTime.Next(3000))
26             sum += sharedLocation.Buffer
27          Next
28
29          Console.WriteLine(Thread.CurrentThread.Name & _
30             " read values totaling: " & sum & "." & vbCrLf & _
31             "Terminating " & Thread.CurrentThread.Name & "." & _
32             vbCrLf)
33       End Sub ' Consume
34
35    End Class ' CConsumer
```

Fig. 11.11 Consumer reads **Integer**s from synchronized shared buffer. (Part 2 of 2.)

```
 1    ' Fig. 11.12: SharedCell.vb
 2    ' Create producer and consumer threads.
 3
 4    Imports System.Threading
 5
 6    Module modSharedCell
 7
 8       Sub Main()
 9
10          ' create shared object used by threads
11          Dim holdInteger As New CHoldIntegerSynchronized()
12
13          ' Random object used by each thread
14          Dim randomObject As New Random()
15
16          ' create CProducer and CConsumer objects
17          Dim producer As New CProducer(holdInteger, randomObject)
18          Dim consumer As New CConsumer(holdInteger, randomObject)
```

Fig. 11.12 Producer and consumer threads accessing a shared object with synchronization. (Part 1 of 3.)

```
19
20          Console.WriteLine("{0,-35}{1,-9}{2}" & vbCrLf, _
21              "Operation", "Buffer", "Occupied Count")
22
23          holdInteger.DisplayState("Initial State")
24
25          ' create threads for producer and consumer
26          ' set delegates for each thread
27          Dim producerThread As _
28              New Thread(AddressOf producer.Produce)
29
30          Dim consumerThread As _
31              New Thread(AddressOf consumer.Consume)
32
33          ' name each thread
34          producerThread.Name = "Producer"
35          consumerThread.Name = "Consumer"
36
37          ' start each thread
38          producerThread.Start()
39          consumerThread.Start()
40      End Sub ' Main
41
42  End Module ' modSharedCell
```

Operation	Buffer	Occupied Count
Initial state	-1	0
Producer writes 1	1	1
Consumer reads 1	1	0
Consumer tries to read. Buffer empty. Consumer waits.	1	0
Producer writes 2	2	1
Consumer reads 2	2	0
Producer writes 3	3	1
Producer tries to write. Buffer full. Producer waits.	3	1
Consumer reads 3	3	0
Producer writes 4	4	1
Producer done producing. Terminating Producer.		
Consumer reads 4	4	0
Consumer read values totaling: 10. Terminating Consumer.		

Fig. 11.12 Producer and consumer threads accessing a shared object with synchronization. (Part 2 of 3.)

Operation	Buffer	Occupied Count
Initial state	-1	0
Consumer tries to read. Buffer empty. Consumer waits.	-1	0
Producer writes 1	1	1
Consumer reads 1	1	0
Producer writes 2	2	1
Consumer reads 2	2	0
Producer writes 3	3	1
Producer tries to write. Buffer full. Producer waits.	3	1
Consumer reads 3	3	0
Producer writes 4	4	1
Producer done producing. Terminating Producer.		
Consumer reads 4	4	0
Consumer read values totaling: 10. Terminating Consumer.		

Operation	Buffer	Occupied Count
Initial state	-1	0
Producer writes 1	1	1
Consumer reads 1	1	0
Producer writes 2	2	1
Consumer reads 2	2	0
Producer writes 3	3	1
Consumer reads 3	3	0
Producer writes 4	4	1
Producer done producing. Terminating Producer.		
Consumer reads 4	4	0
Consumer read values totaling: 10. Terminating Consumer.		

Fig. 11.12 Producer and consumer threads accessing a shared object with synchronization. (Part 3 of 3.)

Class **CHoldIntegerSynchronized** (Fig. 11.9) contains two instance variables—**mBuffer** (line 9) and **occupiedBufferCount** (line 12). Property **Buffer**'s **Get** (lines 16–61) and **Set** (lines 63–96) accessors now use methods of class **Monitor** to synchronize access to property **Buffer**. Thus, each object of class **CHoldIntegerSynchronized** has a *SyncBlock* to maintain synchronization. Instance variable **occupiedBufferCount** is known as a *condition variable*—property **Buffer**'s accessors use this **Integer** in conditions to determine whether it is the producer's turn to perform a task or the consumer's turn to perform a task. If **occupiedBufferCount** is **0**, property **Buffer**'s **Set** accessor can place a value into variable **mBuffer**, because the variable currently does not contain information. However, this means that property **Buffer**'s **Get** accessor currently cannot read the value of **mBuffer**. If **occupiedBufferCount** is **1**, the **Buffer** property's **Get** accessor can read a value from variable **mBuffer**, because the variable currently contains information. In this case, property **Buffer**'s **Set** accessor currently cannot place a value into **mBuffer**.

As in Fig. 11.6, the producer thread (Fig. 11.10) performs the tasks specified in the **producer** object's **Produce** method. When line 26 sets the value of **CHoldIntegerSynchronized** property **Buffer**, the producer thread invokes the **Set** accessor in lines 63–96 (Fig. 11.9). Line 66 invokes **Monitor** method **Enter** to acquire the lock on the **CHoldIntegerSynchronized** object. The **If** structure in lines 70–78 then determines whether **occupiedBufferCount** is **1**. If this condition is **True**, lines 71–72 output a message indicating that the producer thread tried to write a value, and lines 74–75 invoke method **DisplayState** (lines 100–103) to output another message indicating that the buffer is full and that the producer thread waits. Line 77 invokes **Monitor** method **Wait** to place the calling thread (i.e., the producer) in the *WaitSleepJoin* state for the **CHoldIntegerSynchronized** object and releases the lock on the object. The *WaitSleepJoin* state for an object is maintained by that object's *SyncBlock*. Now, another thread can invoke an accessor method of the **CHoldIntegerSynchronized** object's **Buffer** property.

The producer thread remains in state *WaitSleepJoin* until the thread is notified that it can proceed—at which point the thread returns to the *Started* state and waits to be assigned a processor. When the thread returns to the *Running* state, the thread implicitly reacquires the lock on the **CHoldIntegerSynchronized** object, and the **Set** accessor continues executing with the next statement after **Wait**. Line 81 assigns **Value** to **mBuffer**. Line 85 increments the **occupiedBufferCount** to indicate that the shared buffer now contains a value (i.e., a consumer can read the value, and a producer cannot yet put another value there). Lines 87–88 invoke method **DisplayState** to output a line to the command window indicating that the producer is writing a new value into the **mBuffer**. Line 92 invokes **Monitor** method **Pulse** with the **CHoldIntegerSynchronized** object as an argument. If there are any waiting threads in that object's *SyncBlock*, the first waiting thread enters the *Started* state; this thread can attempt its task again as soon as the thread is assigned a processor. The **Pulse** method returns immediately. Line 95 invokes **Monitor** method **Exit** to release the lock on the **CHoldIntegerSynchronized** object, and the **Set** accessor returns to its caller.

Common Programming Error 11.4

Failure to release the lock on an object when that lock is no longer needed is a logic error. This will prevent other threads that require the lock from acquiring the lock and proceeding with their tasks. These threads will be forced to wait (unnecessarily, because the lock is no longer needed). Such waiting can lead to deadlock and indefinite postponement.

The **Get** and **Set** accessors are implemented similarly. As in Fig. 11.7, the consumer thread (Fig. 11.11) performs the tasks specified in the **consumer** object's **Consume** method. The consumer thread gets the value of the **CHoldIntegerSynchronized** object's **Buffer** property (Fig. 11.11, line 26) by invoking the **Get** accessor at Fig. 11.9, lines 16–61. In Fig. 11.9, line 19 invokes **Monitor** method **Enter** to acquire the lock on the **CHoldIntegerSynchronized** object.

The **If** structure in lines 23–31 determines whether **occupiedBufferCount** is **0**. If this condition is **True**, lines 24–25 output a message indicating that the consumer thread tried to read a value, and lines 27–28 invoke method **DisplayState** to output another message indicating that the buffer is empty and that the consumer thread waits. Line 30 invokes **Monitor** method **Wait** to place the calling thread (i.e., the consumer) in the *WaitSleepJoin* state for the **CHoldIntegerSynchronized** object and releases the lock on the object. Now, another thread can invoke an accessor method of the **CHoldIntegerSynchronized** object's **Buffer** property.

The consumer thread object remains in the *WaitSleepJoin* state until the thread is notified that it can proceed—at which point the thread returns to the *Started* state and waits for the system to assign a processor to the thread. When the thread reenters the *Running* state, the thread implicitly reacquires the lock on the **CHoldIntegerSynchronized** object, and the **Get** accessor continues executing with the next statement after **Wait**. Line 35 decrements **occupiedBufferCount** to indicate that the shared buffer now is empty (i.e., a consumer cannot read the value, but a producer can place another value into the shared buffer). Lines 37–38 output a line to the command window specifying the value that the consumer is reading, and line 42 invokes **Monitor** method **Pulse** with the **CHoldIntegerSynchronized** object as an argument. If there are any waiting threads in that object's *SyncBlock*, the first waiting thread enters the *Started* state, indicating that the thread can attempt its task again as soon as the thread is assigned a processor. The **Pulse** method returns immediately. Line 55 creates a copy of **mBuffer** before releasing lock. It is possible that the producer could be assigned the processor immediately after the lock is released (line 58) and before the **Return** statement executes (line 60). In this case, the producer would assign a new value to **mBuffer** before the **Return** statement returns the value to the consumer. Thus, the consumer would receive the new value. By making a copy of **mBuffer** and returning the copy, we ensure that the consumer receives the proper value. Line 58 invokes **Monitor** method **Exit** to release the lock on the **CHoldIntegerSynchronized** object, and the **Get** accessor returns **bufferCopy** to its caller.

Study the outputs depicted in Fig. 11.12. Observe that every **Integer** produced is consumed exactly once—no values are lost, and no values are consumed more than once. This occurs because the producer and consumer cannot perform tasks unless it is "their turn." The producer must go first; the consumer must wait if the producer has not produced a value since the consumer last consumed; and the producer must wait if the consumer has not yet consumed the value that the producer most recently produced. Execute this program several times to confirm that every **Integer** produced is consumed exactly once.

In the first and second sample outputs, notice the lines indicating when the producer and consumer must wait to perform their respective tasks. In the third sample output, notice that the producer and consumer were able to perform their tasks without waiting.

11.7 Producer/Consumer Relationship: Circular Buffer

Figure 11.9 uses thread synchronization to guarantee that two threads correctly manipulate data in a shared buffer. However, the application might not perform optimally. If the two threads operate at different speeds, one of the threads will spend more (or most) of its time waiting. For example, in Fig. 11.12, we shared a single **Integer** between the two threads. If the producer thread produces values faster than the consumer can consume those values, then the producer thread waits for the consumer, because there are no other memory locations in which to place the next value. Similarly, if the consumer consumes faster than the producer can produce values, the consumer waits until the producer places the next value into the shared location in memory. Even when we have threads that operate at the same relative speeds, over a period of time, those threads could become "out of sync," causing one of the threads to wait for the other. We cannot make assumptions about the relative speeds of asynchronous concurrent threads. Too many interactions occur among the operating system, the network, the user and other components, and these interactions can cause the threads to operate a different speeds. When this happens, threads wait. When threads wait, programs become less productive, user-interactive programs become less responsive and network applications suffer longer delays.

To minimize waiting by threads that share resources and operate at the same relative speeds, we can implement a *circular buffer*, which provides extra buffers into which the producer can place values and from which the consumer can retrieve those values. Let us assume the buffer is implemented as an array. The producer and consumer work from the beginning of the array. When either thread reaches the end of the array, it simply returns to the first element of the array to perform its next task. If the producer temporarily produces values faster than the consumer can consume them, the producer can write additional values into the extra buffers (if cells are available). This enables the producer to perform its task, even though the consumer is not ready to receive the value currently being produced. Similarly, if the consumer consumes faster than the producer produces new values, the consumer can read additional values from the buffer (if there are any). This enables the consumer to perform its task, even though the producer is not ready to produce additional values.

Readers should note that the circular buffer would be inappropriate if the producer and consumer operate at different speeds. If the consumer always executes faster than the producer, then a buffer with one location would suffice. Additional locations would waste memory. If the producer always executes faster, a buffer with an infinite number of locations would be required to absorb the extra production.

The key to using a circular buffer is to define it with enough extra cells so that it can handle the expected "extra" production. If, over a period of time, we determine that the producer often produces as many as three more values than the consumer can consume, we can define a buffer of at least three cells to handle the extra production. We do not want the buffer to be too small, because that would result in waiting threads. On the other hand, we do not want the buffer to be too large, because that would waste memory.

Performance Tip 11.4

Even when using a circular buffer, it is possible that a producer thread could fill the buffer, which would force the producer thread to wait until a consumer consumes a value to free an element in the buffer. Similarly, if the buffer is empty at any given time, the consumer thread must wait until the producer produces another value. The key to using a circular buffer is to optimize the buffer size, thus minimizing the amount of thread-wait time.

Figure 11.16 demonstrates a producer and a consumer accessing a circular buffer (in this case, a shared array of three cells) with synchronization. In this version of the producer/consumer relationship, the consumer consumes a value only when the array is not empty, and the producer produces a value only when the array is not full. This program is implemented as a Windows application that sends its output to a **TextBox**. Classes **CProducer** (Fig. 11.14) and **CConsumer** (Fig. 11.15) perform the same tasks as in Fig. 11.10 and Fig. 11.11, respectively, except that they output messages to the **TextBox** in the application window. The statements that created and started the thread objects in the **Main** methods of module **mod-SharedCell** (Fig. 11.8 and Fig. 11.12) now appear in class **FrmCircularBuffer** (Fig. 11.16), where the **Load** event handler (lines 15–50) performs the statements.

The most significant differences between this and the previous synchronized example occur in class **CHoldIntegerSynchronized** (Fig. 11.13), which now contains five instance variables. Array **mBuffer** is a three-element **Integer** array that represents the circular buffer. Variable **occupiedBufferCount** is the condition variable used to determine whether a producer can write into the circular buffer (i.e., **occupiedBufferCount** is less than the number of elements in array **mBuffer**) and whether a consumer can read from the circular buffer (i.e., **occupiedBufferCount** is greater than **0**). Variable **readLocation** indicates the position from which the next value can be read by a consumer. Variable **writeLocation** indicates the next location in which a value can be placed by a producer. The program displays output in **txtOutput** (a **TextBox** control).

The **Set** accessor (lines 73–115) of property **Buffer** performs the same tasks that it did in Fig. 11.9, but with a few modifications. Rather than using **Monitor** methods **Enter** and **Exit** to acquire and release the lock on the **CHoldIntegerSynchronized** object, we use a block of code preceded by keyword **SyncLock** (line 77) to lock the **CHoldIntegerSynchronized** object. As program control enters the **SyncLock** block, the currently executing thread acquires the lock (assuming the lock currently is available) on the **CHoldIntegerSynchronized** object (i.e., **Me**). When the **SyncLock** block terminates, the thread releases the lock automatically.

Common Programming Error 11.5

*When using class **Monitor**'s **Enter** and **Exit** methods to manage an object's lock, **Exit** must be called explicitly to release the lock. If an exception occurs in a method before **Exit** can be called and that exception is not caught, the method could terminate without calling **Exit**. If so, the lock is not released. To avoid this error, place code that might throw exceptions in a **Try** block, and then place the call to **Exit** in the corresponding **Finally** block. This ensures that the lock is released.*

Software Engineering Observation 11.2

*Using a **SyncLock** block to manage the lock on a synchronized object eliminates the possibility of forgetting to release the lock via a call to **Monitor** method **Exit**. When a **SyncLock** block terminates for any reason, Visual Basic implicitly calls **Monitor** method **Exit**. Thus, even if an exception occurs in the block, the lock will be released.*

The **If** structure in lines 81–88 of the **Set** accessor determines whether the producer must wait (i.e., all buffers are full). If the producer thread must wait, lines 82–83 append text to the **txtOutput** indicating that the producer is waiting to perform its task, and line 87 invokes **Monitor** method **Wait** to place the producer thread in the *WaitSleepJoin* state of the **CHoldIntegerSynchronized** object. When execution continues at line 92 after the **If** structure, the value written by the producer is placed in the circular buffer at location **writeLocation**. Next, lines 94–96 append to the **TextBox** a message containing the produced value. Line 100 increments **occupiedBufferCount**, because the buffer now contains at least one value that the consumer can read. Then, lines 104–105 update **writeLocation** for the next call to the **Set** accessor of property **Buffer**. In line 107 method **CreateStateOutput** (lines 120–165) creates output indicating the number of occupied buffers, the contents of the buffers and the current **writeLocation** and **readLocation**. Finally, line 112 invokes **Monitor** method **Pulse** to indicate that a thread waiting on the **CHoldIntegerSynchronized** object (if there is a waiting thread) should transition to the *Started* state. Note that reaching the closing **SyncLock** statement (**End SyncLock**) in line 113 causes the thread to release the lock on the **CHoldIntegerSynchronized** object.

The **Get** accessor (lines 29–71) of property **Buffer** also performs the same tasks in this example that it did in Fig. 11.9, but with a few minor modifications. The **If** structure in lines 37–43 of the **Get** accessor determines whether the consumer must wait (i.e., all buffers are empty). If the consumer thread must wait, lines 38–39 append text to the **txtOutput** indicating that the consumer is waiting to perform its task, and line 42 invokes **Monitor** method **Wait** to place the consumer thread in the *WaitSleepJoin* state of the **CHoldIntegerSynchronized** object. Once again, we use a **SyncLock** block to acquire and release the lock on the **CHoldIntegerSynchronized** object, rather than using **Monitor** methods **Enter** and **Exit**. When execution continues at line 47 after the **If** structure, **readValue** is assigned the value at location **readLocation** in the circular buffer. Lines 49–51 appends the consumed value to the **TextBox**. Line 55 decrements the **occupiedBufferCount**, because the buffer contains at least one open position in which the producer thread can place a value. Then, line 59 updates **readLocation** for the next call to the **Get** accessor of **Buffer**. Line 61 invokes method **CreateStateOutput** to output the number of occupied buffers, the contents of the buffers and the current **writeLocation** and **readLocation**. Finally, line 66 invokes method **Pulse** to transition the next thread waiting for the **CHoldIntegerSynchronized** object into the *Started* state, and line 68 returns the consumed value to the calling method.

```
1   ' Fig. 11.13: HoldIntegerSynchronized.vb
2   ' Synchronize access to circular Integer buffer.
3
4   Imports System.Threading
5   Imports System.Windows.Forms
6
7   Public Class CHoldIntegerSynchronized
8
9      ' each array element is a buffer
10     Private mBuffer As Integer() = {-1, -1, -1}
11
12     ' occupiedBufferCount maintains count of occupied buffers
13     Private occupiedBufferCount As Integer
14
15     ' maintains read and write buffer locations
16     Private readlocation, writeLocation As Integer
```

Fig. 11.13 Synchronized shared circular buffer. (Part 1 of 4.)

```
17
18          ' GUI component to display output
19          Private txtOutput As TextBox
20
21          ' constructor
22          Public Sub New(ByVal output As TextBox)
23             txtOutput = output
24          End Sub ' New
25
26          ' property Buffer
27          Property Buffer() As Integer
28
29             Get
30
31                ' lock this object while getting value
32                ' from mBuffer array
33                SyncLock (Me)
34
35                   ' if there is no data to read, place invoking
36                   ' thread in WaitSleepJoin state
37                   If occupiedBufferCount = 0 Then
38                      txtOutput.Text &= vbCrLf & "All buffers empty. " & _
39                         Thread.CurrentThread.Name & " waits."
40
41                      txtOutput.ScrollToCaret()
42                      Monitor.Wait(Me)
43                   End If
44
45                   ' obtain value at current readLocation
46                   ' add string indicating consumed value to output
47                   Dim readValue As Integer = mBuffer(readlocation)
48
49                   txtOutput.Text &= vbCrLf & _
50                      Thread.CurrentThread.Name & " reads " & _
51                      mBuffer(readlocation) & " "
52
53                   ' just consumed value, so decrement number of
54                   ' occupied buffers
55                   occupiedBufferCount -= 1
56
57                   ' update readLocation for future read operation
58                   ' add current state to output
59                   readlocation = (readlocation + 1) Mod mBuffer.Length
60
61                   txtOutput.Text &= CreateStateOutput()
62                   txtOutput.ScrollToCaret()
63
64                   ' return waiting thread (if there is one)
65                   ' to Started state
66                   Monitor.Pulse(Me)
67
68                   Return readValue
69                End SyncLock
```

Fig. 11.13 Synchronized shared circular buffer. (Part 2 of 4.)

```
70
71          End Get
72
73          Set(ByVal Value As Integer)
74
75              ' lock this object while setting value
76              ' in mBuffer array
77              SyncLock (Me)
78
79                  ' if there are no empty locations, place invoking
80                  ' thread in WaitSleepJoin state
81                  If occupiedBufferCount = mBuffer.Length Then
82                      txtOutput.Text &= vbCrLf & "All buffers full. " & _
83                          Thread.CurrentThread.Name & " waits."
84
85                      txtOutput.ScrollToCaret()
86
87                      Monitor.Wait(Me)
88                  End If
89
90                  ' place value in writeLocation of mBuffer, then
91                  ' add string indicating produced value to output
92                  mBuffer(writeLocation) = Value
93
94                  txtOutput.Text &= vbCrLf & _
95                      Thread.CurrentThread.Name & " writes " & _
96                      mBuffer(writeLocation) & " "
97
98                  ' just produced value, so increment number of
99                  ' occupied mBuffer elements
100                 occupiedBufferCount += 1
101
102                 ' update writeLocation for future write operation,
103                 ' then add current state to output
104                 writeLocation = (writeLocation + 1) Mod _
105                     mBuffer.Length
106
107                 txtOutput.Text &= CreateStateOutput()
108                 txtOutput.ScrollToCaret()
109
110                 ' return waiting thread (if there is one)
111                 ' to Started state
112                 Monitor.Pulse(Me)
113             End SyncLock
114
115         End Set
116
117     End Property ' Buffer
118
119     ' create state output
120     Public Function CreateStateOutput() As String
121
122         Dim i As Integer
```

Fig. 11.13 Synchronized shared circular buffer. (Part 3 of 4.)

```
123
124            ' display first line of state information
125            Dim output As String = "(buffers occupied: " & _
126               occupiedBufferCount & ")" & vbCrLf & "buffers: "
127
128            For i = 0 To mBuffer.GetUpperBound(0)
129               output &= " " & mBuffer(i) & "   "
130            Next
131
132            output &= vbCrLf
133
134            ' display second line of state information
135            output &= "             "
136
137            For i = 0 To mBuffer.GetUpperBound(0)
138               output &= "---- "
139            Next
140
141            output &= vbCrLf
142
143            ' display third line of state information
144            output &= "            "
145
146            For i = 0 To mBuffer.GetUpperBound(0)
147
148               If (i = writeLocation AndAlso _
149                  writeLocation = readlocation) Then
150
151                  output &= " WR  "
152               ElseIf i = writeLocation Then
153                  output &= " W   "
154               ElseIf i = readlocation Then
155                  output &= "  R  "
156               Else
157                  output &= "     "
158               End If
159
160            Next
161
162            output &= vbCrLf
163
164            Return output
165         End Function ' CreateStateOutput
166
167   End Class ' CHoldIntegerSynchronized
```

Fig. 11.13 Synchronized shared circular buffer. (Part 4 of 4.)

```
1    ' Fig. 11.14: Producer.vb
2    ' Produce 10 Integers into synchronized Integer buffer.
3
4    Imports System.Threading
```

Fig. 11.14 Producer places **Integer**s in synchronized circular buffer. (Part 1 of 2.)

```
 5    Imports System.Windows.Forms
 6
 7    Public Class CProducer
 8       Private sharedLocation As CHoldIntegerSynchronized
 9       Private randomSleepTime As Random
10       Private txtOutput As TextBox
11
12       ' constructor
13       Public Sub New(ByVal sharedObject As CHoldIntegerSynchronized, _
14          ByVal randomObject As Random, ByVal output As TextBox)
15
16          sharedLocation = sharedObject
17          randomSleepTime = randomObject
18          txtOutput = output
19       End Sub ' New
20
21       ' store values 11-20 and place them
22       ' in sharedLocation's buffer
23       Public Sub Produce()
24          Dim count As Integer
25
26          ' sleep for random interval up to 3000 milliseconds
27          ' set sharedLocation's Buffer property
28          For count = 11 To 20
29             Thread.Sleep(randomSleepTime.Next(1, 3000))
30             sharedLocation.Buffer = count
31          Next
32
33          txtOutput.Text &= vbCrLf & Thread.CurrentThread.Name & _
34             " done producing. " & vbCrLf & _
35             Thread.CurrentThread.Name & " terminated." & vbCrLf
36       End Sub ' Produce
37
38    End Class ' CProducer
```

Fig. 11.14 Producer places **Integer**s in synchronized circular buffer. (Part 2 of 2.)

```
 1    ' Fig. 11.15: Consumer.vb
 2    ' Consume 10 Integers from synchronized circular buffer.
 3
 4    Imports System.Threading
 5    Imports System.Windows.Forms
 6
 7    Public Class CConsumer
 8       Private sharedLocation As CHoldIntegerSynchronized
 9       Private randomSleepTime As Random
10       Private txtOutput As TextBox
11
12       ' constructor
13       Public Sub New(ByVal sharedObject As CHoldIntegerSynchronized, _
14          ByVal randomObject As Random, ByVal output As TextBox)
15
```

Fig. 11.15 Consumer reads **Integer**s from synchronized circular buffer. (Part 1 of 2.)

```vbnet
16            sharedLocation = sharedObject
17            randomSleepTime = randomObject
18            txtOutput = output
19         End Sub ' New
20
21         ' consume 10 Integers from buffer
22         Public Sub Consume()
23            Dim count, sum As Integer
24
25            ' loop 10 times and sleep for random interval up to
26            ' 3000 milliseconds
27            ' add sharedLocation's Buffer property value to sum
28            For count = 1 To 10
29               Thread.Sleep(randomSleepTime.Next(1, 3000))
30               sum += sharedLocation.Buffer
31            Next
32
33            txtOutput.Text &= vbCrLf & "Total " & _
34               Thread.CurrentThread.Name & " consumed: " & sum & vbCrLf & _
35               Thread.CurrentThread.Name & " terminated." & vbCrLf
36
37            txtOutput.ScrollToCaret()
38         End Sub ' Consume
39
40      End Class ' CConsumer
```

Fig. 11.15 Consumer reads **Integer**s from synchronized circular buffer. (Part 2 of 2.)

```vbnet
1  ' Fig. 11.16: FrmCircularBuffer.vb
2  ' Create display form and start threads.
3
4  Imports System.Threading
5  Imports System.Windows.Forms
6
7  Public Class FrmCircularBuffer
8     Inherits Form
9
10    Friend WithEvents txtOutput As TextBox
11
12    ' Visual Studio .NET generated code
13
14    ' initialize threads upon loading
15    Private Sub FrmCircularBuffer_Load(ByVal sender As Object, _
16       ByVal e As System.EventArgs) Handles MyBase.Load
17
18       ' create shared object
19       Dim sharedLocation As _
20          New CHoldIntegerSynchronized(txtOutput)
21
22       ' display sharedLocation state before producer
23       ' and consumer threads begin execution
24       txtOutput.Text = sharedLocation.CreateStateOutput()
```

Fig. 11.16 Producer and consumer threads accessing a circular buffer. (Part 1 of 4.)

```
25
26          ' Random object used by each thread
27          Dim randomObject As New Random()
28
29          ' create CProducer and CConsumer objects
30          Dim producer As New CProducer(sharedLocation, _
31              randomObject, txtOutput)
32
33          Dim consumer As New CConsumer(sharedLocation, _
34              randomObject, txtOutput)
35
36          ' create threads
37          Dim producerThread As _
38              New Thread(AddressOf producer.Produce)
39
40          Dim consumerThread As _
41              New Thread(AddressOf consumer.Consume)
42
43          ' name threads
44          producerThread.Name = "Producer"
45          consumerThread.Name = "Consumer"
46
47          ' start threads
48          producerThread.Start()
49          consumerThread.Start()
50      End Sub ' FrmCircularBuffer_Load
51
52   End Class ' FrmCircularBuffer
```

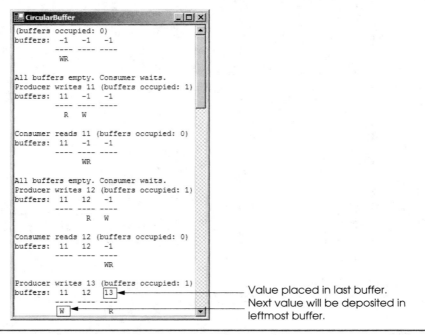

Value placed in last buffer.
Next value will be deposited in
leftmost buffer.

Fig. 11.16 Producer and consumer threads accessing a circular buffer. (Part 2 of 4.)

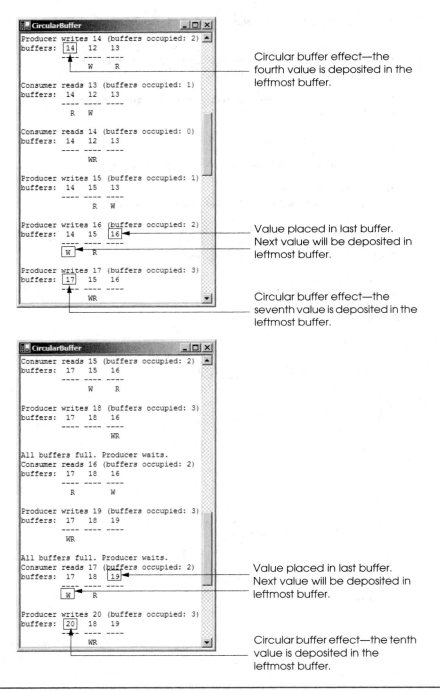

```
CircularBuffer                    _ □ ×
Producer writes 14 (buffers occupied: 2)
buffers:  14    12    13
          ---- ---- ----
                W     R


Consumer reads 13 (buffers occupied: 1)
buffers:  14    12    13
          ---- ---- ----
           R    W

Consumer reads 14 (buffers occupied: 0)
buffers:  14    12    13
          ---- ---- ----
                WR

Producer writes 15 (buffers occupied: 1)
buffers:  14    15    13
          ---- ---- ----
           R    W

Producer writes 16 (buffers occupied: 2)
buffers:  14    15    16
          ---- ---- ----
           W         R

Producer writes 17 (buffers occupied: 3)
buffers:  17    15    16
          ---- ---- ----
                WR
```

Circular buffer effect—the fourth value is deposited in the leftmost buffer.

Value placed in last buffer. Next value will be deposited in leftmost buffer.

Circular buffer effect—the seventh value is deposited in the leftmost buffer.

```
CircularBuffer                    _ □ ×
Consumer reads 15 (buffers occupied: 2)
buffers:  17    15    16
          ---- ---- ----
                W     R

Producer writes 18 (buffers occupied: 3)
buffers:  17    18    16
          ---- ---- ----
                     WR

All buffers full. Producer waits.
Consumer reads 16 (buffers occupied: 2)
buffers:  17    18    16
          ---- ---- ----
           R          W

Producer writes 19 (buffers occupied: 3)
buffers:  17    18    19
          ---- ---- ----
           WR

All buffers full. Producer waits.
Consumer reads 17 (buffers occupied: 2)
buffers:  17    18    19
          ---- ---- ----
           W          R

Producer writes 20 (buffers occupied: 3)
buffers:  20    18    19
          ---- ---- ----
                WR
```

Value placed in last buffer. Next value will be deposited in leftmost buffer.

Circular buffer effect—the tenth value is deposited in the leftmost buffer.

Fig. 11.16 Producer and consumer threads accessing a circular buffer. (Part 3 of 4.)

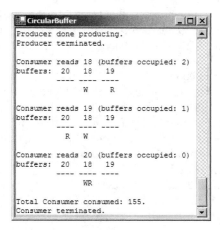

Fig. 11.16 Producer and consumer threads accessing a circular buffer. (Part 4 of 4.)

In Fig. 11.16, the outputs include the current **occupiedBufferCount**, the contents of the buffers and the current **writeLocation** and **readLocation**. In the output, the letters **W** and **R** represent the current **writeLocation** and **readLocation**, respectively. Notice that, after the third value is placed in the third element of the buffer, the fourth value is inserted at the beginning of the array. This produces the circular buffer effect.

11.8 Summary

Computers perform operations concurrently. Programming languages generally provide only a simple set of control structures that enable programmers to perform one action at a time and proceed to the next action after the previous one finishes. The FCL provides the Visual Basic .NET programmer with the ability to specify that applications contain threads of execution, each thread designating a portion of a program that may execute concurrently with other threads—this capability is called multithreading.

A thread is initialized using the **Thread** class's constructor, which receives a **ThreadStart** delegate. This delegate specifies the method that contains the tasks a thread will perform. A thread remains in the *Unstarted* state until the thread's **Start** method is called; this causes the thread to enter the *Started* state. A thread in the *Started* state enters the *Running* state when the system assigns a processor to the thread. The system assigns the processor to the highest-priority *Started* thread. A thread enters the *Stopped* state when its **ThreadStart** delegate completes or terminates. A thread is forced into the *Stopped* state when its **Abort** method is called (by itself or by another thread). A *Running* thread enters the *Blocked* state when the thread issues an input/output request. A *Blocked* thread becomes *Started* when the I/O it is waiting for completes. A *Blocked* thread cannot use a processor, even if one is available.

If a thread needs to sleep, it calls method **Sleep**. A thread wakes up when the designated sleep interval expires. If a thread (the dependent thread) cannot continue executing unless another thread terminates, the dependent thread calls the other thread's **Join** method to "join" the two threads. When two threads are "joined," the dependent thread leaves the *WaitSleepJoin* state when the other thread finishes execution.

When a thread encounters code that it cannot yet run, the thread can call **Monitor** method **Wait** until certain actions occur that enable the thread to continue executing. This puts the thread into the *WaitSleepJoin* state. Any thread in the *WaitSleepJoin* state can leave that state if another thread invokes **Thread** method **Interrupt** on the thread in the *WaitSleepJoin* state. If a thread called **Monitor** method **Wait**, a corresponding call to the **Monitor** method **Pulse** or **PulseAll** by another thread in the program will transition the original thread from the *WaitSleepJoin* state to the *Started* state.

If **Thread** method **Suspend** is called on a thread, the thread enters the *Suspended* state. A thread leaves the *Suspended* state when a separate thread invokes **Thread** method **Resume** on the suspended thread.

Every Visual Basic thread has a priority. The job of the thread scheduler is to keep the highest-priority thread running at all times and, if there is more than one highest-priority thread, to ensure that all equally high-priority threads execute for a quantum at a time in round-robin fashion. A thread's priority can be adjusted with the **Priority** property, which is assigned an argument from the **ThreadPriority** enumeration.

A thread that updates shared data calls **Monitor** method **Enter** to acquire the lock on that data. It updates the data and calls **Monitor** method **Exit** upon completion of the update. While those data are locked, all other threads attempting to acquire the lock on that data must wait. If you place the **SyncLock** keyword before a block of code, the lock is acquired on the specified object as program control enters the block; the lock is released when the block terminates.

12

Strings, Characters and Regular Expressions

Objectives

- To create and manipulate nonmodifiable character string objects of class **String**.
- To create and manipulate modifiable character string objects of class **StringBuilder**.
- To use regular expressions in conjunction with classes **Regex** and **Match**.

The chief defect of Henry King
Was chewing little bits of string.
Hilaire Belloc

Vigorous writing is concise. A sentence should contain no
unnecessary words, a paragraph no unnecessary sentences.
William Strunk, Jr.

I have made this letter longer than usual, because I lack the
time to make it short.
Blaise Pascal

The difference between the almost-right word and the right
word is really a large matter—it's the difference between the
lightning bug and the lightning.
Mark Twain

Mum's the word.
Miguel de Cervantes

12.1 Introduction

This chapter introduces Visual Basic string and character processing capabilities and demonstrate using regular expressions to search for patterns in text. The techniques presented in this chapter can be employed to develop text editors, word processors, page-layout software, computerized typesetting systems and other kinds of text-processing software. Previous chapters have already presented several string-processing capabilities. In this chapter, we expand on this information by detailing the capabilities of class *String* and type *Char* from the *System* namespace, class *StringBuilder* from the *System.Text* namespace and classes *Regex* and *Match* from the *System.Text.RegularExpressions* namespace.

12.2 Fundamentals of Characters and Strings

Characters are the fundamental building blocks of Visual Basic source code. Every program is composed of characters that, when grouped together meaningfully, create a sequence that the compiler interprets as a series of instructions that describe how to accomplish a task. In addition to normal characters, a program also can contain *character constants*. A character constant is a character that is represented as an integer value, called a *character code*. For example, the integer value of **122** corresponds to the character constant **"z"c**. Character constants are established according to the *Unicode character set*, an international character set that contains many more symbols and letters than does the ASCII character set (see Appendix C, ASCII Character Set). To learn the integer equivalents of many common Unicode characters, see Appendix D, Unicode®.

A string is a series of characters treated as a single unit. These characters can be uppercase letters, lowercase letters, digits and various *special characters,* such as **+, -, *, /, $** and others. A string is an object of class **String** in the **System** namespace. We write *string literals,* or *string constants* (often called *literal **String** objects*), as sequences of characters in double quotation marks, as follows:

```
"John Q. Doe"
"9999 Main Street"
"Waltham, Massachusetts"
"(201) 555-1212"
```

A declaration can assign a **String** literal to a **String** reference. The declaration

```
Dim color As String = "blue"
```

initializes **String** reference **color** to refer to the **String** literal object **"blue"**.

Performance Tip 12.1

*If there are multiple occurrences of the same **String** literal object in an application, a single copy of the **String** literal object will be referenced from each location in the program that uses that **String** literal. It is possible to share the object in this manner, because **String** literal objects are implicitly constant. Such sharing conserves memory.*

12.3 **String** Constructors

Class **String** provides three constructors for initializing **String** objects in various ways. Figure 12.1 demonstrates the use of three of the constructors.

```
1    ' Fig. 12.1: StringConstructor.vb
2    ' Demonstrating String class constructors.
3
4    Imports System.Windows.Forms
5
6    Module modStringConstructor
7
8       Sub Main()
9          Dim characterArray As Char()
10         Dim output As String
11         Dim quotes As Char = ChrW(34)
12         Dim originalString, string1, string2, string3, _
13                 string4 As String
14
15         characterArray = New Char() {"b"c, "i"c, "r"c, _
16            "t"c, "h"c, " "c, "d"c, "a"c, "y"c}
17
18         ' string initialization
19         originalString = "Welcome to VB.NET Programming!"
20         string1 = originalString
21         string2 = New String(characterArray)
```

Fig. 12.1   String constructors. (Part 1 of 2.)

```
22          string3 = New String(characterArray, 6, 3)
23          string4 = New String("C"c, 5)
24
25          output = "string1 = " & quotes & string1 & quotes & _
26             vbCrLf & "string2 = " & quotes & string2 & quotes & _
27             vbCrLf & "string3 = " & quotes & string3 & quotes & _
28             vbCrLf & "string4 = " & quotes & string4 & quotes
29
30          MessageBox.Show(output, "String Class Constructors", _
31             MessageBoxButtons.OK, MessageBoxIcon.Information)
32       End Sub ' Main
33
34    End Module ' modStringConstructor
```

Fig. 12.1   String constructors. (Part 2 of 2.)

In line 11, we declare variable **quotes** and give it the value returned by function **ChrW** when **ChrW** is passed a value of **34**. The value passed to function **ChrW** is a Unicode character code. Function **ChrW** returns as a **Char** data type the character that corresponds to the specified Unicode character code. In this case, function **ChrW** returns a double quote character (**"**). (To learn more about character codes, see Appendix D, Unicode®.)

Lines 15–16 allocate **Char** array **characterArray**, which contains nine characters. The **c** suffix that follows each **String** converts it to a character literal. We do this because **Option Strict** prohibits the implicit conversion from type **String** to type **Char**.

Line 19 assigns literal string **"Welcome to VB.NET Programming!"** to **String** reference **originalString**. Line 20 sets **string1** to reference **String** literal **originalString**.

Software Engineering Observation 12.1

*In most cases, it is not necessary to make a copy of an existing **String** object. All **String** objects are immutable—their character contents cannot be changed after they are created. Also, if there are one or more references to a **String** object (or any object for that matter), the object cannot be reclaimed by the garbage collector.*

Line 21 assigns to **string2** a new **String** object, using the **String** constructor that takes a character array as an argument. The new **String** object contains a copy of the characters in array **characterArray**.

Line 22 assigns to **string3** a new **String** object, using the **String** constructor that takes a **Char** array and two **Integer** arguments. The second argument specifies the starting index position (the *offset*) from which characters in the array are copied. The third argument specifies the number of characters (the *count*) to be copied from the specified starting position in the array. The new **String** object contains a copy of the specified characters in the array. If the specified offset or count indicates that the program should access an element outside the bounds of the character array, an **ArgumentOutOfRangeException** is thrown.

Line 23 assigns to **string4** a new **String** object, using the **String** constructor that takes as arguments a character and an **Integer** specifying the number of times to repeat that character in the **String**.

Each instance of variable **quotes** (lines 25–28) represents a double quote character (**"**). Visual Studio .NET treats double quotes as delimiters for **String**s and does not treat them as part of a **String**. We can represent a quotation mark within a **String** by using the numerical code of the character (e.g., line 11) or by placing consecutive double quote characters (**""**) in the **String**.

12.4 `String` `Length` and `Chars` Properties, and `CopyTo` Method

The application in Fig. 12.2 presents the **String** property *Chars*, which facilitates the retrieval of any character in the **String**, and the **String** property *Length*, which returns the length of the **String**. The **String** method *CopyTo* copies a specified number of characters from a **String** into a **Char** array.

```
1    ' Fig. 12.2: StringMiscellaneous.vb
2    ' Using properties Length and Chars, and method CopyTo
3    ' of class string.
4
5    Imports System.Windows.Forms
6
7    Module modMiscellaneous
8
9       Sub Main()
10          Dim string1, output As String
11          Dim characterArray As Char()
12          Dim i As Integer
13          Dim quotes As Char = ChrW(34)
14
15          string1 = "hello there"
16          characterArray = New Char(5) {}
17
18          ' output string
19          output = "string1: " & quotes & string1 & quotes
20
21          ' test Length property
22          output &= vbCrLf & "Length of string1: " & string1.Length
23
24          ' loop through characters in string1 and display
25          ' reversed
26          output &= vbCrLf & "The string reversed is: "
27
28          For i = string1.Length - 1 To 0 Step -1
29             output &= string1.Chars(i)
30          Next
```

Fig. 12.2 `String Length` and `Chars` properties, and `CopyTo` method. (Part 1 of 2.)

```
31
32          ' copy characters from string1 into characterArray
33          string1.CopyTo(0, characterArray, 0, 5)
34          output &= vbCrLf & "The character array is: "
35
36          For i = 0 To characterArray.GetUpperBound(0)
37             output &= characterArray(i)
38          Next
39
40          MessageBox.Show(output, "Demonstrating String" & _
41             " properties Length and Chars", _
42             MessageBoxButtons.OK, MessageBoxIcon.Information)
43       End Sub ' Main
44
45    End Module ' modMiscellaneous
```

Fig. 12.2 String Length and **Chars** properties, and **CopyTo** method. (Part 2 of 2.)

In this example, we create an application that determines the length of a **String**, reverses the order of the characters in the **String** and copies a series of characters from the **String** into a character array.

Line 22 uses **String** property **Length** to determine the number of characters in **String string1**. Like arrays, **String**s always know their own size.

Lines 28–30 append to **output** the characters of the **String string1** in reverse order. The **String** property **Chars** returns the character located in a specific index in the **String**. Property **Chars** takes an **Integer** argument specifying the index and returns the character at that index. As in arrays, the first element of a **String** is at index **0**.

 Common Programming Error 12.1

*Attempting to access a character that is outside the bounds of a **String** (i.e., an index less than 0 or an index greater than or equal to the **String**'s length) results in an **Index-OutOfRangeException.***

Line 33 uses **String** method **CopyTo** to copy the characters of a **String** (**string1**) into a character array (**characterArray**). The first argument given to method **CopyTo** is the index from which the method begins copying characters in the **String**. The second argument is the character array into which the characters are copied. The third argument is the index specifying the location at which the method places the copied characters in the character array. The last argument is the number of characters that the method will copy from the **String**. Lines 36–38 append the **Char** array contents to **String output** one character at a time.

12.5 Comparing Strings

The next two examples demonstrate the various methods that Visual Basic provides for comparing **String** objects. To understand how one **String** can be "greater than" or "less than" another **String**, consider the process of alphabetizing a series of last names. The reader would, no doubt, place **"Jones"** before **"Smith"**, because the first letter of **"Jones"** comes before the first letter of **"Smith"** in the alphabet. The alphabet is more than just a set of 26 letters—it is an ordered list of characters in which each letter occurs in a specific position. For example, **Z** is more than just a letter of the alphabet; **Z** is specifically the twenty-sixth letter of the alphabet.

Computers can order characters alphabetically because the characters are represented internally as Unicode numeric codes. When comparing two **String**s, computers simply compare the numeric codes of the characters in the **String**s.

Class **String** provides several ways to compare **String**s. The application in Fig. 12.3 demonstrates the use of method **Equals**, method **CompareTo** and the equality operator (**=**).

```
1    ' Fig. 12.3: StringCompare.vb
2    ' Comparing strings.
3
4    Imports System.Windows.Forms
5
6    Module modCompare
7
8       Sub Main()
9          Dim string1 As String = "hello"
10         Dim string2 As String = "good bye"
11         Dim string3 As String = "Happy Birthday"
12         Dim string4 As String = "happy birthday"
13         Dim output As String
14         Dim quotes As Char = ChrW(34)
15
16         ' output values of four Strings
17         output = "string1 = " & quotes & string1 & quotes & _
18            vbCrLf & "string2 = " & quotes & string2 & quotes & _
19            vbCrLf & "string3 = " & quotes & string3 & quotes & _
20            vbCrLf & "string4 = " & quotes & string4 & quotes & _
21            vbCrLf & vbCrLf
22
23         ' test for equality using Equals method
24         If (string1.Equals("hello")) Then
25            output &= "string1 equals " & quotes & "hello" & _
26               quotes & vbCrLf
27
28         Else
29            output &= "string1 does not equal " & quotes & _
30               "hello" & quotes & vbCrLf
31         End If
32
```

Fig. 12.3 **String** test to determine equality. (Part 1 of 2.)

```
33              ' test for equality with =
34         If string1 = "hello" Then
35            output &= "string1 equals " & quotes & "hello" & _
36               quotes & vbCrLf
37
38         Else
39            output &= "string1 does not equal " & quotes & _
40               "hello" & quotes & vbCrLf
41         End If
42
43              ' test for equality comparing case
44         If (String.Equals(string3, string4)) Then
45            output &= "string3 equals string4" & vbCrLf
46         Else
47            output &= "string3 does not equal string4" & vbCrLf
48         End If
49
50              ' test CompareTo
51         output &= vbCrLf & "string1.CompareTo(string2) is " & _
52            string1.CompareTo(string2) & vbCrLf & _
53            "string2.CompareTo(string1) is " & _
54            string2.CompareTo(string1) & vbCrLf & _
55            "string1.CompareTo(string1) is " & _
56            string1.CompareTo(string1) & vbCrLf & _
57            "string3.CompareTo(string4) is " & _
58            string3.CompareTo(string4) & vbCrLf & _
59            "string4.CompareTo(string3) is " & _
60            string4.CompareTo(string3) & vbCrLf & vbCrLf
61
62         MessageBox.Show(output, "Demonstrating string" & _
63            " comparisons", MessageBoxButtons.OK, _
64            MessageBoxIcon.Information)
65      End Sub ' Main
66
67   End Module ' modCompare
```

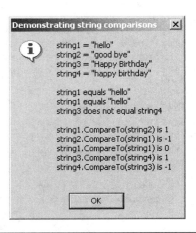

Fig. 12.3 **String** test to determine equality. (Part 2 of 2.)

The **If** structure condition (line 24) uses method **Equals** to compare **string1** and literal **String "hello"** to determine whether they are equal. Method **Equals** (inherited by **String** from class **Object**) tests any two objects for equality (i.e., checks whether the objects contain identical contents). The method returns **True** if the objects are equal and **False** otherwise. In this instance, the preceding condition returns **True**, because **string1** references **String** literal object **"hello"**. Method **Equals** uses a *lexicographical comparison*—the integer Unicode values that represent each character in each **String** are compared. Method **Equals** compares the **Integer** Unicode values that represent the characters in each **String**. A comparison of the **String "hello"** with the **String "HELLO"** would return **False**, because the **Integer** representations of lowercase letters are different from the **Integer** representations of corresponding uppercase letters.

The condition in the second **If** structure (line 34) uses the equality operator (=) to compare **String string1** with the literal **String "hello"** for equality. In Visual Basic, the equality operator also uses a lexicographical comparison to compare two **String**s. Thus, the condition in the **If** structure evaluates to **True**, because the values of **string1** and **"hello"** are equal. As with any reference type, the **Is** operator may be used to determine whether two **String**s reference the same object.

We present the test for **String** equality between **string3** and **string4** (line 44) to illustrate that comparisons are indeed case sensitive. Here, **Shared** method **Equals** (as opposed to the instance method in line 24) is used to compare the values of two **String**s. **"Happy Birthday"** does not equal **"happy birthday"**, so the condition of the **If** structure fails, and the message **"string3 does not equal string4"** is added to the output message (line 47).

Lines 52–60 use the **String** method **CompareTo** to compare **String** objects. Method **CompareTo** returns **0** if the **String**s are equal, a **-1** if the **String** that invokes **CompareTo** is less than the **String** that is passed as an argument and a **1** if the **String** that invokes **CompareTo** is greater than the **String** that is passed as an argument. Method **CompareTo** uses a lexicographical comparison.

Notice that **CompareTo** considers **string3** to be larger than **string4**. The only difference between these two strings is that **string3** contains two uppercase letters. This example illustrates that an uppercase letter has a higher value in the Unicode character set than its corresponding lowercase letter.

The application in Fig. 12.4 shows how to test whether a **String** instance begins or ends with a given **String**. Method *StartsWith* determines if a **String** instance starts with the **String** text passed to it as an argument. Method *EndsWith* determines if a **String** instance ends with the **String** text passed to it as an argument. Application **modStartEnd**'s **Main** method defines an array of **String**s (called **strings**), which contains **"started"**, **"starting"**, **"ended"** and **"ending"**. The remainder of method **Main** tests the elements of the array to determine whether they start or end with a particular set of characters.

Line 20 uses method **StartsWith**, which takes a **String** argument. The condition in the **If** structure determines whether the **String** at index **i** of the array starts with the characters **"st"**. If so, the method returns **True** and appends **strings(i)** to **String output** for display purposes.

Line 32 uses method **EndsWith**, which also takes a **String** argument. The condition in the **If** structure determines whether the **String** at index **i** of the array ends with

```
1    ' Fig. 12.4: StringStartEnd.vb
2    ' Demonstrating StartsWith and EndsWith methods.
3
4    Imports System.Windows.Forms
5
6    Module modStartEnd
7
8       Sub Main()
9          Dim strings As String()
10         Dim output As String = ""
11         Dim i As Integer
12         Dim quotes As Char = ChrW(34)
13
14         strings = New String() {"started", "starting", _
15            "ended", "ending"}
16
17         ' test every string to see if it starts with "st"
18         For i = 0 To strings.GetUpperBound(0)
19
20            If strings(i).StartsWith("st") Then
21               output &= quotes & strings(i) & quotes & _
22                  " starts with " & quotes & "st" & quotes & vbCrLf
23            End If
24
25         Next
26
27         output &= vbCrLf
28
29         ' test every string to see if it ends with "ed"
30         For i = 0 To strings.GetUpperBound(0)
31
32            If strings(i).EndsWith("ed") Then
33               output &= quotes & strings(i) & quotes & _
34                  " ends with " & quotes & "ed" & quotes & vbCrLf
35            End If
36
37         Next
38
39         MessageBox.Show(output, "Demonstrating StartsWith and" & _
40            " EndsWith methods", MessageBoxButtons.OK, _
41            MessageBoxIcon.Information)
42      End Sub ' Main
43
44   End Module ' modStartEnd
```

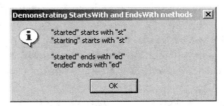

Fig. 12.4   StartsWith and EndsWith methods.

the characters **"ed"**. If so, the method returns **True**, and **strings(i)** is appended to **String output** for display purposes.

12.6 String Method GetHashCode

Often, it is necessary to store **String**s and other data types in a manner that enables the information to be found quickly. One of the best ways to make information easily accessible is to store it in a hash table. A *hash table* stores an object by performing a special calculation on that object, which produces a *hash code*. The object then is stored at a location in the hash table determined by the calculated hash code. When a program needs to retrieve the information, the same calculation is performed, generating the same hash code. Any object can be stored in a hash table. Class **Object** defines method **GetHashCode** to perform the hash-code calculation. Although all classes inherit this method from class **Object**, it is recommended that they override **Object**'s default implementation. **String Overrides** method **GetHashCode** to provide a good hash-code distribution based on the contents of the **String**. We will discuss hashing in detail in Chapter 20, Data Structures and Collections.

The example in Fig. 12.5 demonstrates the application of the **GetHashCode** method to two **String**s (**"hello"** and **"Hello"**). Here, the hash-code value for each **String** is different. However, **String**s that are not identical can have the same hash-code value.

```
1    ' Fig. 12.5: StringHashCode.vb
2    ' Demonstrating method GetHashCode of class String.
3
4    Imports System.Windows.Forms
5
6    Module modHashCode
7
8       Sub Main()
9          Dim string1 As String = "hello"
10         Dim string2 As String = "Hello"
11         Dim output As String
12         Dim quotes As Char = ChrW(34)
13
14         output = "The hash code for " & quotes & string1 & _
15            quotes & " is " & string1.GetHashCode() & vbCrLf
16
17         output &= "The hash code for " & quotes & string2 & _
18            quotes & " is " & string2.GetHashCode()
19
20         MessageBox.Show(output, _
21            "Demonstrating String Method GetHashCode")
22      End Sub ' Main
23
24   End Module ' modHashCode
```

Fig. 12.5 **GetHashCode** method demonstration. (Part 1 of 2.)

Fig. 12.5 GetHashCode method demonstration. (Part 2 of 2.)

12.7 Locating Characters and Substrings in `Strings`

In many applications, it is necessary to search for a character or set of characters in a
String. For example, a programmer creating a word processor would want to provide capabilities for searching through documents. The application in Fig. 12.6 demonstrates some
of the many versions of **String** methods *IndexOf*, *IndexOfAny*, *LastIndexOf*
and *LastIndexOfAny*, which search for a specified character or substring in a **String**.
We perform all searches in this example on the **String letters** (initialized with **"ab-
cdefghijklmabcdefghijklm"**) located in method **Main** of module **modIn-
dexMethods**. Notice that this program makes use of adjacent quotation marks instead of
creating a **quotes** variable with the value **ChrW(34)**.

Lines 14–21 use method **IndexOf** to locate the first occurrence of a character or substring in a **String**. If **IndexOf** finds a character, **IndexOf** returns the index of the specified character in the **String**; otherwise, **IndexOf** returns **–1**. The expression on line 18
uses a version of method **IndexOf** that takes two arguments—the character to search for
and the starting index at which the search of the **String** should begin. The method does
not examine any characters that occur prior to the starting index (in this case **1**). The expression in line 21 uses another version of method **IndexOf** which takes three arguments—
the character to search for, the index at which to start searching and the number of characters to search.

```
1   ' Fig. 12.6: StringIndexMethods
2   ' Using String searching methods.
3
4   Imports System.Windows.Forms
5
6   Module modIndexMethods
7
8      Sub Main()
9         Dim letters As String = "abcdefghijklmabcdefghijklm"
10        Dim output As String
11        Dim searchLetters As Char() = New Char() {"c"c, "a"c, "$"c}
12
13        ' test IndexOf to locate a character in a string
14        output &= """c"" is located at index " & _
15           letters.IndexOf("c"c)
16
17        output &= vbCrLf & """a"" is located at index " & _
18           letters.IndexOf("a"c, 1)
```

Fig. 12.6   Searching for characters and substrings in **String**s. (Part 1 of 3.)

```
19
20          output &= vbCrLf & """$"" is located at index " & _
21             letters.IndexOf("$"c, 3, 5)
22
23          ' test LastIndexOf to find a character in a string
24          output &= vbCrLf & vbCrLf & "Last ""c"" is located at " & _
25             "index " & letters.LastIndexOf("c"c)
26
27          output &= vbCrLf & "Last ""a"" is located at index " & _
28             letters.LastIndexOf("a"c, 25)
29
30          output &= vbCrLf & "Last ""$"" is located at index " & _
31             letters.LastIndexOf("$"c, 15, 5)
32
33          ' test IndexOf to locate a substring in a string
34          output &= vbCrLf & vbCrLf & """def"" is located at" & _
35             " index " & letters.IndexOf("def")
36
37          output &= vbCrLf & """def"" is located at index " & _
38             letters.IndexOf("def", 7)
39
40          output &= vbCrLf & """hello"" is located at index " & _
41             letters.IndexOf("hello", 5, 15)
42
43          ' test LastIndexOf to find a substring in a string
44          output &= vbCrLf & vbCrLf & "Last ""def"" is located " & _
45             "at index " & letters.LastIndexOf("def")
46
47          output &= vbCrLf & "Last ""def"" is located at " & _
48             letters.LastIndexOf("def", 25)
49
50          output &= vbCrLf & "Last ""hello"" is located at " & _
51             "index " & letters.LastIndexOf("hello", 20, 15)
52
53          ' test IndexOfAny to find first occurrence of character
54          ' in array
55          output &= vbCrLf & vbCrLf & "First occurrence of ""c""," & _
56             " ""a"" or ""$"" is located at " & _
57             letters.IndexOfAny(searchLetters)
58
59          output &= vbCrLf & "First occurrence of ""c"", ""a"" or " & _
60             """$"" is located at " & _
61             letters.IndexOfAny(searchLetters, 7)
62
63          output &= vbCrLf & "First occurrence of ""c"", ""a"" or " & _
64             """$"" is located at " & _
65             letters.IndexOfAny(searchLetters, 20, 5)
66
67          ' test LastIndexOfAny to find first occurrence of character
68          ' in array
69          output &= vbCrLf & vbCrLf & "Last occurrence of ""c""," & _
70             " ""a"" or ""$"" is located at " & _
71             letters.LastIndexOfAny(searchLetters)
```

Fig. 12.6　Searching for characters and substrings in **String**s. (Part 2 of 3.)

```
72
73          output &= vbCrLf & "Last occurrence of ""c"", ""a"" or " & _
74              """$"" is located at " & _
75              letters.LastIndexOfAny(searchLetters, 1)
76
77          output &= vbCrLf & "Last occurrence of ""c"", ""a"" or " & _
78              """$"" is located at " & _
79              letters.LastIndexOfAny(searchLetters, 25, 5)
80
81          MessageBox.Show(output, _
82              "Demonstrating String class index methods")
83      End Sub ' Main
84
85  End Module ' modIndexMethods
```

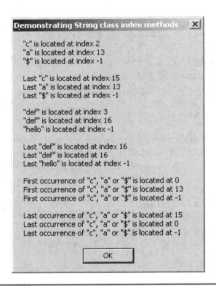

Fig. 12.6   Searching for characters and substrings in **String**s. (Part 3 of 3.)

Lines 24–31 use method **LastIndexOf** to locate the last occurrence of a character in a **String**. Method **LastIndexOf** performs the search from the end of the **String** toward the beginning of the **String**. If method **LastIndexOf** finds the character, **LastIndexOf** returns the index of the specified character in the **String**; otherwise, **LastIndexOf** returns **-1**. There are three versions of **LastIndexOf** that search for characters in a **String**. The expression in line 25 uses the version of method **LastIn-dexOf** that takes as an argument the character for which to search. The expression in line 28 uses the version of method **LastIndexOf** that takes two arguments—the character for which to search and the highest index from which to begin searching backward for the character. The expression in line 31 uses a third version of method **LastIndexOf** that takes three arguments—the character for which to search, the starting index from which to start searching backward and the number of characters (the portion of the **String**) to search.

Lines 34–51 use versions of **IndexOf** and **LastIndexOf** that take a **String** instead of a character as the first argument. These versions of the methods perform identically to those described above except that they search for sequences of characters (or substrings) that are specified by their **String** arguments.

Lines 55–79 use methods **IndexOfAny** and **LastIndexOfAny**, which take an array of characters as the first argument. These versions of the methods also perform identically to those described above except that they return the index of the first occurrence of any of the characters in the character array argument.

Common Programming Error 12.2

*In the overloaded methods **LastIndexOf** and **LastIndexOfAny** that take three parameters, the second argument must always be greater than or equal to the third argument. This might seem counterintuitive, but remember that the search moves from the end of the string toward the start of the string.*

12.8 Extracting Substrings from Strings

Class **String** provides two **Substring** methods, which are used to create a new **String** object by copying part of an existing **String** object. Each method returns a new **String** object. The application in Fig. 12.7 demonstrates the use of both methods.

```
1   ' Fig. 12.7: SubString.vb
2   ' Demonstrating the String Substring method.
3
4   Imports System.Windows.Forms
5
6   Module modSubString
7
8      Sub Main()
9         Dim letters As String = "abcdefghijklmabcdefghijklm"
10        Dim output As String
11        Dim quotes As Char = ChrW(34)
12
13        ' invoke SubString method and pass it one parameter
14        output = "Substring from index 20 to end is " & _
15           quotes & letters.Substring(20) & quotes & vbCrLf
16
17        ' invoke SubString method and pass it two parameters
18        output &= "Substring from index 0 to 6 is " & _
19           quotes & letters.Substring(0, 6) & quotes
20
21        MessageBox.Show(output, _
22           "Demonstrating String method Substring")
23     End Sub ' Main
24
25  End Module ' modSubString
```

Fig. 12.7   Substrings generated from **String**s.

The statement in lines 14–15 uses the **Substring** method that takes one **Integer** argument. The argument specifies the starting index from which the method copies characters in the original **String**. The substring returned contains a copy of the characters from the starting index to the end of the **String**. If the index specified in the argument is outside the bounds of the **String**, the program throws an **ArgumentOutOfRangeException**.

The second version of method **Substring** (line 19) takes two **Integer** arguments. The first argument specifies the starting index from which the method copies characters from the original **String**. The second argument specifies the length of the substring to be copied. The substring returned contains a copy of the specified characters from the original **String**.

12.9 Concatenating **Strings**

The **&** operator (discussed in Chapter 2, Introduction to the Visual Studio IDE and VB .NET Programming) is not the only way to perform **String** concatenation. The **Shared** method **Concat** of class **String** (Fig. 12.8) concatenates two **String** objects and returns a new **String** object containing the combined characters from both original **String**s. Line 18 appends the characters from **string2** to the end of **string1** using method **Concat**. The statement on line 18 does not modify the original **String**s.

 Common Programming Error 12.3

*In Visual Basic, the **+** operator also can be used to concatenate **String**s. However, using the **+** operator in this way can lead to subtle errors and ambiguous program code.*

```
1    ' Fig. 12.8: StringConcatenation.vb
2    ' Demonstrating String class Concat method.
3
4    Imports System.Windows.Forms
5
6    Module modStringConcatenation
7
8       Sub Main()
9          Dim string1 As String = "Happy "
10         Dim string2 As String = "Birthday"
11         Dim output As String
12
13         output = "string1 = """ & string1 & """" & _
14            vbCrLf & "string2 = """ & string2 & """"
15
16         output &= vbCrLf & vbCrLf & _
17            "Result of String.Concat(string1, string2) = " & _
18            String.Concat(string1, string2)
19
20         MessageBox.Show(output, _
21            "Demonstrating String method Concat")
22      End Sub ' Main
23
24   End Module ' modStringConcatenation
```

Fig. 12.8   **Concat Shared** method. (Part 1 of 2.)

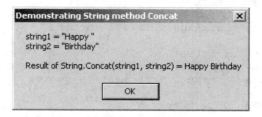

Fig. 12.8   **Concat Shared** method. (Part 2 of 2.)

12.10 Miscellaneous **String** Methods

Class **String** provides several methods that return modified copies of **String**s. The application in Fig. 12.9 demonstrates the use of these methods, which include **String** methods *Replace*, *ToLower*, *ToUpper*, *Trim* and *ToString*.

```
1    ' Fig. 12.9: StringMiscellaneous.vb
2    ' Demonstrating String methods Replace, ToLower, ToUpper, Trim,
3    ' and ToString.
4
5    Imports System.Windows.Forms
6
7    Module modStringMiscellaneous
8
9       Sub Main()
10         Dim string1 As String = "cheers!"
11         Dim string2 As String = "GOOD BYE "
12         Dim string3 As String = "   spaces   "
13         Dim output As String
14         Dim quotes As Char = ChrW(34)
15         Dim i As Integer
16
17         output = "string1 = " & quotes & string1 & quotes & _
18            vbCrLf & "string2 = " & quotes & string2 & quotes & _
19            vbCrLf & "string3 = " & quotes & string3 & quotes
20
21         ' call method Replace
22         output &= vbCrLf & vbCrLf & "Replacing " & quotes & "e" & _
23            quotes & " with " & quotes & "E" & quotes & _
24            " in string1: " & quotes & string1.Replace("e"c, "E"c) & _
25            quotes
26
27         ' call ToLower and ToUpper
28         output &= vbCrLf & vbCrLf & "string1.ToUpper() = " & _
29            quotes & string1.ToUpper() & quotes & vbCrLf & _
30            "string2.ToLower() = " & quotes & string2.ToLower() & _
31            quotes
32
```

Fig. 12.9   **String** methods **Replace**, **ToLower**, **ToUpper**, **Trim** and **ToString**. (Part 1 of 2.)

```
33          ' call Trim method
34          output &= vbCrLf & vbCrLf & "string3 after trim = " & _
35             quotes & string3.Trim() & quotes
36
37          ' call ToString method
38          output &= vbCrLf & vbCrLf & "string1 = " & _
39             quotes & string1.ToString() & quotes
40
41          MessageBox.Show(output, _
42             "Demonstrating miscellaneous String methods")
43    End Sub ' Main
44
45  End Module ' modStringMiscellaneous
```

Fig. 12.9 `String` methods `Replace`, `ToLower`, `ToUpper`, `Trim` and `ToString`. (Part 2 of 2.)

Line 24 uses **String** method **Replace** to return a new **String** object, replacing every occurrence in **string1** of character **"e"**c with character **"E"**c. Method **Replace** takes two arguments—a **String** for which to search and another **String** with which to replace all matching occurrences of the first argument. The original **String** remains unchanged. If there are no occurrences of the first argument in the **String**, the method returns the original **String**.

String method **ToUpper** generates a new **String** object (line 29) that replaces any lowercase letters in **string1** with their uppercase equivalent. The method returns a new **String** object containing the converted **String**; the original **String** remains unchanged. If there are no characters to convert to uppercase, the method returns the original **String**. Line 30 uses **String** method **ToLower** to return a new **String** in which any uppercase letters in **string2** are replaced by their lowercase equivalents. The original **String** is unchanged. As with **ToUpper**, if there are no characters to convert to lowercase, method **ToLower** returns the original **String**.

Line 35 uses **String** method **Trim** to remove all whitespace characters that appear at the beginning and end of a **String**. Without altering the original **String**, the method returns a new **String** object that contains the **String**, but omits leading or trailing whitespace characters. Another version of method **Trim** takes a character array, removes all whitespace characters from the beginning and end of the array and returns the result in a **String**.

Line 39 uses class **String**'s method **ToString** to show that the various other methods employed in this application have not modified **string1**. Why is the **ToString** method provided for class **String**? In Visual Basic .NET, all objects are derived from class **Object**, which defines **Overridable** method **ToString**. Thus, method **ToString** can be called to obtain a **String** representation any object. If a class that inherits from **Object** (such as **String**) does not override method **ToString**, the class uses the default version from class **Object**, which returns a **String** consisting of the object's class name. Classes usually override method **ToString** to express the contents of an object as text. Class **String** overrides method **ToString** so that, instead of returning the class name, it simply returns the **String**.

12.11   Class StringBuilder

The **String** class provides many capabilities for processing **String**s. However a **String**'s contents can never change. Operations which seem to concatenate **String**s are in fact assigning **String** references to newly created **String**s (e.g., the **&=** operator creates a new **String** and assigns the initial **String** reference to the newly created **String**).

The next several sections discuss the features of class **StringBuilder** (namespace **System.Text**), which is used to create and manipulate dynamic string information—i.e., modifiable strings. Every **StringBuilder** can store a certain number of characters that is specified by its capacity. Exceeding the capacity of a **StringBuilder** causes the capacity to expand to accommodate the additional characters. As we will see, members of class **StringBuilder**, such as methods **Append** and **AppendFormat**, can be used for concatenation like the operators **&** and **&=** for class **String**.

Software Engineering Observation 12.2

String objects are constant strings, whereas StringBuilder objects are modifiable strings. Visual Basic can perform certain optimizations involving String objects (such as the sharing of one String object among multiple references), because it knows these objects will not change.

Performance Tip 12.2

When given the choice between using a String object to represent a string and using a StringBuilder object to represent that string, always use a String object if the contents of the object will not change. When appropriate, using String objects instead of StringBuilder objects improves performance.

Class **StringBuilder** provides six overloaded constructors. Module **modBuilderConstructor** (Fig. 12.10) demonstrates the use of three of these overloaded constructors.

```
1   ' Fig. 12.10: StringBuilderConstructor.vb
2   ' Demonstrating StringBuilder class constructors.
3
4   Imports System.Text
5   Imports System.Windows.Forms
6
```

Fig. 12.10 StringBuilder class constructors. (Part 1 of 2.)

```
7   Module modBuilderConstructor
8
9      Sub Main()
10         Dim buffer1, buffer2, buffer3 As StringBuilder
11         Dim quotes As Char = ChrW(34)
12         Dim output As String
13
14         buffer1 = New StringBuilder()
15         buffer2 = New StringBuilder(10)
16         buffer3 = New StringBuilder("hello")
17
18         output = "buffer1 = " & quotes & buffer1.ToString() & _
19            quotes & vbCrLf
20
21         output &= "buffer2 = " & quotes & _
22            buffer2.ToString() & quotes & vbCrLf
23
24         output &= "buffer3 = " & quotes & _
25            buffer3.ToString() & quotes
26
27         MessageBox.Show(output, _
28            "Demonstrating StringBuilder class constructors")
29      End Sub ' Main
30
31   End Module ' modBuilderConstructor
```

Fig. 12.10 `StringBuilder` class constructors. (Part 2 of 2.)

Line 14 employs the no-argument **StringBuilder** constructor to create a **StringBuilder** that contains no characters and has a default initial capacity of 16 characters. Line 15 uses the **StringBuilder** constructor that takes an **Integer** argument to create a **StringBuilder** that contains no characters and has the initial capacity specified in the **Integer** argument (i.e., **10**). Line 16 uses the **StringBuilder** constructor that takes a **String** argument to create a **StringBuilder** containing the characters of the **String** argument. The initial capacity is the smallest power of two greater than the number of characters in the **String** passed as an argument.

Lines 18–25 use **StringBuilder** method **ToString** to obtain a **String** representation of the **StringBuilder**'s contents. This method returns the **StringBuilder**'s underlying string.

12.12 StringBuilder Indexer, Length and Capacity Properties, and EnsureCapacity Method

Class **StringBuilder** provides the *Length* and *Capacity* properties to return the number of characters currently in a **StringBuilder** and the number of characters that a **StringBuilder** can store without allocating more memory, respectively. These properties also can increase or decrease the length or the capacity of the **StringBuilder**.

Method ***EnsureCapacity*** allows programmers to guarantee that a **String-Builder** has a capacity that reduces the number of times the capacity must be increased. Method **EnsureCapacity** doubles the **StringBuilder** instance's current capacity. If this doubled value is greater than the value that the programmer wishes to ensure, it becomes the new capacity. Otherwise, **EnsureCapacity** alters the capacity to make it one more than the requested number. For example, if the current capacity is 17 and we wish to make it 40, 17 multiplied by 2 is not greater than 40, so the call will result in a new capacity of 41. If the current capacity is 23 and we wish to make it 40, 23 will be multiplied by 2 to result in a new capacity of 46. Both 41 and 46 are greater than 40, and so a capacity of 40 is indeed ensured by method **EnsureCapacity**. The program in Fig. 12.11 demonstrates the use of these methods and properties.

The program contains one **StringBuilder**, called **buffer**. Lines 11–12 of the program use the **StringBuilder** constructor that takes a **String** argument to instantiate the **StringBuilder** and initialize its value to **"Hello, how are you?"**. Lines 15–17 append to **output** the content, length and capacity of the **StringBuilder**. In the output window, notice that the capacity of the **StringBuilder** is initially 32. Remember, the **StringBuilder** constructor that takes a **String** argument creates a **StringBuilder** object with an initial capacity that is the smallest power of two greater than the number of characters in the **String** passed as an argument.

```
1    ' Fig. 12.11: StringBuilderFeatures.vb
2    ' Demonstrating some features of class StringBuilder.
3
4    Imports System.Text
5    Imports System.Windows.Forms
6
7    Module modBuilderFeatures
8
9       Sub Main()
10         Dim i As Integer
11         Dim buffer As StringBuilder = _
12            New StringBuilder("Hello, how are you?")
13
14         ' use Length and Capacity properties
15         Dim output As String = "buffer = " & buffer.ToString & _
16            vbCrLf & "Length = " & buffer.Length & vbCrLf & _
17            "Capacity = " & buffer.Capacity
18
19         ' use EnsureCapacity method
20         buffer.EnsureCapacity(75)
21
22         output &= vbCrLf & vbCrLf & "New capacity = " & _
23            buffer.Capacity
24
25         ' truncate StringBuilder by setting Length property
26         buffer.Length = 10
27
```

Fig. 12.11 **StringBuilder** size manipulation. (Part 1 of 2.)

```
28          output &= vbCrLf & vbCrLf & "New Length = " & _
29             buffer.Length & vbCrLf & "buffer = "
30
31          ' use StringBuilder Indexer
32          For i = 0 To buffer.Length - 1
33             output &= buffer(i)
34          Next
35
36          MessageBox.Show(output, "StringBuilder features")
37       End Sub ' Main
38
39    End Module ' modBuilderFeatures
```

Fig. 12.11 `StringBuilder` size manipulation. (Part 2 of 2.)

Line 20 expands the capacity of the **StringBuilder** to a minimum of 75 characters. The current capacity (**32**) multiplied by two is less than 75, so method **EnsureCapacity** increases the capacity to one greater than 75 (i.e., 76). If new characters are added to a **String-Builder** so that its length exceeds its capacity, the capacity grows to accommodate the additional characters in the same manner as if method **EnsureCapacity** had been called.

Line 26 uses **Length**'s **Set** accessor to set the length of the **StringBuilder** to **10**. If the specified length is less than the current number of characters in the **String-Builder**, the contents of **StringBuilder** are truncated to the specified length (i.e., the program discards all characters in the **StringBuilder** that occur after the specified length). If the specified length is greater than the number of characters currently in the **StringBuilder**, null characters (characters with the numeric representation **0** that signal the end of a **String**) are appended to the **StringBuilder** until the total number of characters in the **StringBuilder** is equal to the specified length.

 Common Programming Error 12.4

*Assigning **Nothing** to a **String** reference can lead to logic errors. The keyword **Nothing** is a null reference, not a **String**. Do not confuse **Nothing** with the empty string, **" "** (the **String** that is of length 0 and contains no characters).*

12.13 `StringBuilder` Append and AppendFormat Methods

Class **StringBuilder** provides 19 overloaded **Append** methods that allow various data-type values to be added to the end of a **StringBuilder**. Visual Basic provides versions for each of the primitive data types and for character arrays, **String**s and **Object**s. (Remember that method **ToString** produces a **String** representation of any **Object**.) Each of the methods takes an argument, converts it to a **String** and appends it to the **StringBuilder**. Figure 12.12 demonstrates the use of several **Append** methods.

```vb
1    ' Fig. 12.12: StringBuilderAppend.vb
2    ' Demonstrating StringBuilder Append methods.
3
4    Imports System.Text
5    Imports System.Windows.Forms
6
7    Module modBuilderAppend
8
9       Sub Main()
10         Dim objectValue As Object = "hello"
11         Dim stringValue As String = "good bye"
12         Dim characterArray As Char() = {"a"c, "b"c, "c"c, _
13            "d"c, "e"c, "f"c}
14
15         Dim booleanValue As Boolean = True
16         Dim characterValue As Char = "Z"c
17         Dim integerValue As Integer = 7
18         Dim longValue As Long = 1000000
19         Dim singleValue As Single = 2.5
20         Dim doubleValue As Double = 33.333
21         Dim buffer As StringBuilder = New StringBuilder()
22
23         ' use method Append to append values to buffer
24         buffer.Append(objectValue)
25         buffer.Append("   ")
26         buffer.Append(stringValue)
27         buffer.Append("   ")
28         buffer.Append(characterArray)
29         buffer.Append("   ")
30         buffer.Append(characterArray, 0, 3)
31         buffer.Append("   ")
32         buffer.Append(booleanValue)
33         buffer.Append("   ")
34         buffer.Append(characterValue)
35         buffer.Append("   ")
36         buffer.Append(integerValue)
37         buffer.Append("   ")
38         buffer.Append(longValue)
39         buffer.Append("   ")
40         buffer.Append(singleValue)
41         buffer.Append("   ")
42         buffer.Append(doubleValue)
43
44         MessageBox.Show("buffer = " & buffer.ToString(), _
45            "Demonstrating StringBuilder Append methods", _
46            MessageBoxButtons.OK, MessageBoxIcon.Information)
47      End Sub ' Main
```

Fig. 12.12 Append methods of **StringBuilder**. (Part 1 of 2.)

```
48
49    End Module ' modBuilderAppend
```

Fig. 12.12 Append methods of **StringBuilder**. (Part 2 of 2.)

Lines 24–42 use 10 different overloaded **Append** methods to attach the objects created in lines 10–21 to the end of the **StringBuilder**. **Append** behaves similarly to the **&** operator which is used with **String**s. Just as **&** seems to append objects to a **String**, method **Append** can append data types to a **StringBuilder**'s underlying string.

Class **StringBuilder** also provides method **AppendFormat**, which converts a **String** to a specified format and then appends it to the **StringBuilder**. The example in Fig. 12.13 demonstrates the use of this method.

```
1    ' Fig. 12.13: StringBuilderAppendFormat.vb
2    ' Demonstrating method AppendFormat.
3
4    Imports System.Text
5    Imports System.Windows.Forms
6
7    Module modBuilderAppendFormat
8
9       Sub Main()
10          Dim buffer As StringBuilder = New StringBuilder()
11          Dim string1, string2 As String
12
13          ' formatted string
14          string1 = "This {0} costs: {1:C}." & vbCrLf
15
16          ' string1 argument array
17          Dim objectArray As Object() = New Object(1) {}
18
19          objectArray(0) = "car"
20          objectArray(1) = 1234.56
21
22          ' append to buffer formatted string with argument
23          buffer.AppendFormat(string1, objectArray)
24
25          ' formatted string
26          string2 = "Number:{0:D3}. " & vbCrLf & _
27             "Number right aligned with spaces:{0, 4}." & vbCrLf & _
28             "Number left aligned with spaces:{0, -4}."
29
30          ' append to buffer formatted string with argument
31          buffer.AppendFormat(string2, 5)
```

Fig. 12.13 **StringBuilder**'s **AppendFormat** method. (Part 1 of 2.)

```
32
33              ' display formatted strings
34          MessageBox.Show(buffer.ToString(), "Using AppendFormat", _
35              MessageBoxButtons.OK, MessageBoxIcon.Information)
36      End Sub ' Main
37
38  End Module ' modBuilderAppendFormat
```

Fig. 12.13 StringBuilder's AppendFormat method. (Part 2 of 2.)

Line 14 creates a **String** that contains formatting information. The information enclosed within the braces determines how to format a specific piece of information. Formats have the form **{X[,Y][:FormatString]}**, where **X** is the number of the argument to be formatted, counting from zero. **Y** is an optional argument, which can be positive or negative, indicating how many characters should be in the result of formatting. If the resulting **String** is less than the number **Y**, the **String** will be padded with spaces to make up for the difference. A positive integer aligns the string to the right; a negative integer aligns it to the left. The optional **FormatString** applies a particular format to the argument: Currency, decimal, scientific, as well as others. In this case, "**{0}**" means the first argument will be printed out. "**{1:C}**" specifies that the second argument will be formatted as a currency value.

Line 23 shows a version of **AppendFormat**, which takes two parameters—a **String** specifying the format and an array of objects to serve as the arguments to the format **String**. The argument referred to by "**{0}**" is in the object array at index **0**, and so on.

Lines 26–28 define another **String** used for formatting. The first format "**{0:D3}**" specifies that the first argument will be formatted as a three-digit decimal, meaning any number that has fewer than three digits will have leading zeros placed in front to make up the difference. The next format, "**{0, 4}**" specifies that the formatted **String** should have four characters and should be right aligned. The third format, "**{0, -4}**" specifies that the **String**s should be aligned to the left. For more formatting options, please refer to the documentation.

Line 31 uses a version of **AppendFormat**, which takes two parameters: a **String** containing a format and an object to which the format is applied. In this case, the object is the number **5**. The output of Fig. 12.13 displays the result of applying these two version of **AppendFormat** with their respective arguments.

12.14 StringBuilder Insert, Remove and Replace Methods

Class **StringBuilder** provides 18 overloaded *Insert* methods to allow various data-type values to be inserted at any position in a **StringBuilder**. The class provides versions for each of the primitive data types and for character arrays, **String**s and **Object**s.

(Remember that method **ToString** produces a **String** representation of any **Object**.)
Each method takes its second argument, converts it to a **String** and inserts the **String**
in the **StringBuilder** in front of the index specified by the first argument. The index
specified by the first argument must be greater than or equal to **0** and less than the length
of the **StringBuilder**; otherwise, the program throws an **ArgumentOutOfRange-
Exception**.

Class **StringBuilder** also provides method **Remove** for deleting any portion of a
StringBuilder. Method **Remove** takes two arguments—the index at which to begin
deletion and the number of characters to delete. The sum of the starting subscript and the
number of characters to be deleted must always be less than the length of the **String-
Builder**; otherwise, the program throws an **ArgumentOutOfRangeException**.
The **Insert** and **Remove** methods are demonstrated in Fig. 12.14.

```
1    ' Fig. 12.14: StringBuilderInsertRemove.vb
2    ' Demonstrating methods Insert and Remove of the
3    ' StringBuilder class.
4
5    Imports System.Text
6    Imports System.Windows.Forms
7
8    Module modBuilderInsertRemove
9
10      Sub Main()
11         Dim objectValue As Object = "hello"
12         Dim stringValue As String = "good bye"
13         Dim characterArray As Char() = {"a"c, "b"c, "c"c, _
14            "d"c, "e"c, "f"c}
15
16         Dim booleanValue As Boolean = True
17         Dim characterValue As Char = "K"c
18         Dim integerValue As Integer = 7
19         Dim longValue As Long = 10000000
20         Dim singleValue As Single = 2.5
21         Dim doubleValue As Double = 33.333
22         Dim buffer As StringBuilder = New StringBuilder()
23         Dim output As String
24
25         ' insert values into buffer
26         buffer.Insert(0, objectValue)
27         buffer.Insert(0, "  ")
28         buffer.Insert(0, stringValue)
29         buffer.Insert(0, "  ")
30         buffer.Insert(0, characterArray)
31         buffer.Insert(0, "  ")
32         buffer.Insert(0, booleanValue)
33         buffer.Insert(0, "  ")
34         buffer.Insert(0, characterValue)
35         buffer.Insert(0, "  ")
36         buffer.Insert(0, integerValue)
37         buffer.Insert(0, "  ")
```

Fig. 12.14 StringBuilder text insertion and removal. (Part 1 of 2.)

```
38            buffer.Insert(0, longValue)
39            buffer.Insert(0, "   ")
40            buffer.Insert(0, singleValue)
41            buffer.Insert(0, "   ")
42            buffer.Insert(0, doubleValue)
43            buffer.Insert(0, "   ")
44
45            output = "buffer after inserts:" & vbCrLf & _
46                buffer.ToString() & vbCrLf & vbCrLf
47
48            buffer.Remove(12, 1) ' delete 5 in 2.5
49            buffer.Remove(2, 4) ' delete 33.3 in 33.333
50
51            output &= "buffer after Removes:" & vbCrLf & _
52                buffer.ToString()
53
54            MessageBox.Show(output, "Demonstrating StringBuilder " & _
55                "Insert and Remove Methods", MessageBoxButtons.OK, _
56                MessageBoxIcon.Information)
57        End Sub ' Main
58
59    End Module ' modBuilderInsertRemove
```

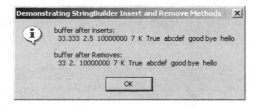

Fig. 12.14 **StringBuilder** text insertion and removal. (Part 2 of 2.)

Another useful method included with **StringBuilder** is **Replace**. **Replace** searches for a specified **String** or character and substitutes another **String** or character in its place. Figure 12.15 demonstrates this method.

```
1    ' Fig. 12.15: StringBuilderReplace.vb
2    ' Demonstrating method Replace.
3
4    Imports System.Text
5    Imports System.Windows.Forms
6
7    Module modBuilderReplace
8
9        Sub Main()
10           Dim builder1 As StringBuilder = _
11               New StringBuilder("Happy Birthday Jane")
12
13           Dim builder2 As StringBuilder = _
14               New StringBuilder("good bye greg")
```

Fig. 12.15 **StringBuilder** text replacement. (Part 1 of 2.)

```
15
16          Dim output As String = "Before Replacements:" & vbCrLf & _
17              builder1.ToString() & vbCrLf & builder2.ToString()
18
19          builder1.Replace("Jane", "Greg")
20          builder2.Replace("g"c, "G"c, 0, 5)
21
22          output &= vbCrLf & vbCrLf & "After Replacements:" & _
23              vbCrLf & builder1.ToString() & vbCrLf & _
24              builder2.ToString()
25
26          MessageBox.Show(output, _
27              "Using StringBuilder method Replace", _
28              MessageBoxButtons.OK, MessageBoxIcon.Information)
29      End Sub ' Main
30
31  End Module ' modBuilderReplace
```

Fig. 12.15 **StringBuilder** text replacement. (Part 2 of 2.)

Line 19 uses method **Replace** to replace all instances of the **String "Jane"** with the **String "Greg"** in **builder1**. Another overload of this method takes two characters as parameters and replaces all occurrences of the first with the second. Line 20 uses an overload of **Replace** that takes four parameters, the first two of which are characters and the second two of which are **Integer**s. The method replaces all instances of the first character with the second, beginning at the index specified by the first **Integer** and continuing for a count specified by the second. Thus, in this case, **Replace** looks through only five characters starting with the character at index **0**. As the outputs illustrates, this version of **Replace** replaces **g** with **G** in the word **"good"**, but not in **"greg"**. This is because the **g**s in **"greg"** do not fall in the range indicated by the **Integer** arguments (i.e., between indexes **0** and **4**).

12.15 Char Methods

Visual Basic provides a program building block, called a *structure*, which is similar to a class. Although structures and classes are comparable in many ways, structures encapsulate value types. Like classes, structures include methods and properties. Both use the same modifiers (such as **Public**, **Private** and **Protected**) and access members via the member access operator (**.**). However, classes are created by using the keyword **Class**, and structures are created using the keyword **Structure**.

Many of the primitive data types that we have used in this book are actually aliases for different structures. For instance, an **Integer** is defined by structure **System.Int32**, a **Long** by **System.Int64**, and so on. These structures are derived from class **Value-Type**, which in turn is derived from class **Object**. In this section, we present structure **Char**, which is the structure for characters.

Most **Char** methods are **Shared**, take at least one character argument and perform either a test or a manipulation on the character. We present several of these methods in the next example. Figure 12.16 demonstrates **Shared** methods that test characters to determine whether they are a specific character type and **Shared** methods that perform case conversions on characters.

```
1    ' Fig. 12.16: CharMethods.vb
2    ' Demonstrates Shared character testing methods
3    ' from Char structure
4
5    Public Class FrmCharacter
6       Inherits Form
7
8       Friend WithEvents lblEnter As Label ' prompts for input
9
10      Friend WithEvents txtInput As TextBox   ' reads a Char
11      Friend WithEvents txtOutput As TextBox ' displays results
12
13      ' reads and displays information about input
14      Friend WithEvents cmdAnalyze As Button
15
16      ' Visual Studio .NET generated code
17
18      ' handle cmdAnalyze Click
19      Private Sub cmdAnalyze_Click(ByVal sender As System.Object, _
20         ByVal e As System.EventArgs) Handles cmdAnalyze.Click
21
22         Dim character As Char = Convert.ToChar(txtInput.Text)
23
24         BuildOutput(character)
25      End Sub ' cmdAnalyze_Click
26
27      ' display character information in txtOutput
28      Public Sub BuildOutput(ByVal inputCharacter As Char)
29         Dim output As String
30
31         output = "is digit: " & _
32            Char.IsDigit(inputCharacter) & vbCrLf
33
34         output &= "is letter: " & _
35            Char.IsLetter(inputCharacter) & vbCrLf
36
37         output &= "is letter or digit: " & _
38            Char.IsLetterOrDigit(inputCharacter) & vbCrLf
39
```

Fig. 12.16 Char's Shared character-testing methods and case-conversion methods. (Part 1 of 2.)

```
40          output &= "is lower case: " & _
41              Char.IsLower(inputCharacter) & vbCrLf
42
43          output &= "is upper case: " & _
44              Char.IsUpper(inputCharacter) & vbCrLf
45
46          output &= "to upper case: " & _
47              Char.ToUpper(inputCharacter) & vbCrLf
48
49          output &= "to lower case: " & _
50              Char.ToLower(inputCharacter) & vbCrLf
51
52          output &= "is punctuation: " & _
53              Char.IsPunctuation(inputCharacter) & vbCrLf
54
55          output &= "is symbol: " & Char.IsSymbol(inputCharacter)
56
57          txtOutput.Text = output
58      End Sub ' BuildOutput
59
60  End Class ' FrmCharacter
```

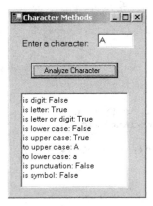 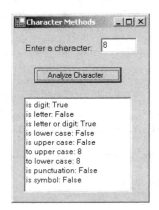 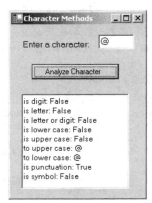

Fig. 12.16 Char's **Shared** character-testing methods and case-conversion methods. (Part 2 of 2.)

This Windows application contains a prompt, a **TextBox** into which the user can input a character, a button that the user can press after entering a character and a second **TextBox** that displays the output of our analysis. When the user clicks the **Analyze Character** button, event handler **cmdAnalyze_Click** (lines 19–25) is invoked. This method converts the entered data from a **String** to a **Char** using method **Convert.ToChar** (line 22). On line 24, we call method **BuildOutput**, which is defined in lines 28–58.

Line 32 uses **Char** method *IsDigit* to determine whether character **inputCharacter** is defined as a digit. If so, the method returns **True**; otherwise, it returns **False**.

Line 35 uses **Char** method *IsLetter* to determine whether character **inputCharacter** is a letter. If so, the method returns **True**; otherwise, it returns **False**. Line 38 uses **Char** method *IsLetterOrDigit* to determine whether character **inputCharacter** is a letter or a digit. If so, the method returns **True**; otherwise, it returns **False**.

Line 41 uses **Char** method *IsLower* to determine whether character **inputCharacter** is a lowercase letter. If so, the method returns **True**; otherwise, it returns **False**. Line 44 uses **Char** method *IsUpper* to determine whether character **inputCharacter** is an uppercase letter. If so, the method returns **True**; otherwise, it returns **False**. Line 47 uses **Char** method *ToUpper* to convert the character **inputCharacter** to its uppercase equivalent. The method returns the converted character if the character has an uppercase equivalent; otherwise, the method returns its original argument. Line 50 uses **Char** method *ToLower* to convert the character **inputCharacter** to its lowercase equivalent. The method returns the converted character if the character has a lowercase equivalent; otherwise, the method returns its original argument.

Line 53 uses **Char** method *IsPunctuation* to determine whether character **inputCharacter** is a punctuation mark. If so, the method returns **True**; otherwise, it returns **False**. Line 55 uses **Char** method *IsSymbol* to determine whether character **inputCharacter** is a symbol. If so, the method returns **True**; otherwise it returns **False**.

Structure type **Char** also contains other methods not shown in this example. Many of the **Shared** methods are similar; for instance, *IsWhiteSpace* is used to determine whether a certain character is a whitespace character (e.g., newline, tab or space). The structure also contains several **Public** instance methods; many of these, such as methods **ToString** and **Equals**, are methods that we have seen before in other classes. This group includes method *CompareTo*, which is used to compare two character values with one another.

12.16 Card Shuffling and Dealing Simulation

In this section, we use random-number generation to develop a program that simulates the shuffling and dealing of cards. Once created, this program can be implemented in programs that imitate specific card games.

We develop application **DeckOfCards** (Fig. 12.18), which creates a deck of 52 playing cards using **CCard** objects. Users can deal each card by clicking the **Deal Card** button. Each dealt card is displayed in a **Label**. Users also can shuffle the deck at any time by clicking the **Shuffle Cards** button.

```
1   ' Fig. 12.17: Card.vb
2   ' Stores suit and face information on each card.
3
4   Public Class CCard
5      Private face As String
6      Private suit As String
7
```

Fig. 12.17 CCard class. (Part 1 of 2.)

```
8         Public Sub New(ByVal faceValue As String, _
9            ByVal suitValue As String)
10
11            face = faceValue
12            suit = suitValue
13         End Sub ' New
14
15         Public Overrides Function ToString() As String
16            Return face & " of " & suit
17         End Function ' ToString
18
19      End Class ' CCard
```

Fig. 12.17 CCard class. (Part 2 of 2.)

```
1       ' Fig. 12.18: DeckOfCards.vb
2       ' Simulating card dealing and shuffling.
3
4       Public Class FrmDeck
5          Inherits Form
6
7          Friend WithEvents lblDisplay As Label ' displays dealt card
8          Friend WithEvents lblStatus As Label  ' number of cards dealt
9
10         Friend WithEvents cmdDeal As Button     ' deal one card
11         Friend WithEvents cmdShuffle As Button ' shuffle cards
12
13         ' Visual Studio .NET generated code
14
15         Private currentCard As Integer
16         Private randomObject As Random = New Random()
17         Private deck As CCard() = New CCard(51) {}
18
19         ' handles form at load time
20         Public Sub FrmDeck_Load(ByVal sender As System.Object, _
21            ByVal e As System.EventArgs) Handles MyBase.Load
22
23            Dim faces As String() = {"Ace", "Deuce", "Three", _
24               "Four", "Five", "Six", "Seven", "Eight", "Nine", _
25               "Ten", "Jack", "Queen", "King"}
26
27            Dim suits As String() = {"Hearts", "Diamonds", "Clubs", _
28               "Spades"}
29
30            Dim i As Integer
31
32            ' no cards have been drawn
33            currentCard = -1
34
```

Fig. 12.18 Card dealing and shuffling simulation. (Part 1 of 4.)

```vb
35              ' initialize deck
36              For i = 0 To deck.GetUpperBound(0)
37                  deck(i) = New CCard(faces(i Mod 13), suits(i Mod 4))
38              Next
39
40          End Sub ' FrmDeck_Load
41
42          ' handles cmdDeal Click
43          Private Sub cmdDeal_Click(ByVal sender As System.Object, _
44              ByVal e As System.EventArgs) Handles cmdDeal.Click
45
46              Dim dealt As CCard = DealCard()
47
48              ' if dealt card is Null, then no cards left
49              ' player must shuffle cards
50              If Not (dealt Is Nothing) Then
51                  lblDisplay.Text = dealt.ToString()
52                  lblStatus.Text = "Card #: " & currentCard
53              Else
54                  lblDisplay.Text = "NO MORE CARDS TO DEAL"
55                  lblStatus.Text = "Shuffle cards to continue"
56              End If
57
58          End Sub ' cmdDeal_Click
59
60          ' shuffle cards
61          Public Sub Shuffle()
62              Dim i As Integer
63              Dim j As Integer
64              Dim temporaryValue As CCard
65
66              currentCard = -1
67
68              ' swap each card with random card
69              For i = 0 To deck.GetUpperBound(0)
70                  j = randomObject.Next(52)
71
72                  ' swap cards
73                  temporaryValue = deck(i)
74                  deck(i) = deck(j)
75                  deck(j) = temporaryValue
76              Next
77
78              cmdDeal.Enabled = True
79          End Sub ' Shuffle
80
81          Public Function DealCard() As CCard
82
83              ' if there is a card to deal then deal it
84              ' otherwise signal that cards need to be shuffled by
85              ' disabling cmdDeal and returning Nothing
86              If (currentCard + 1) < deck.GetUpperBound(0) Then
87                  currentCard += 1
```

Fig. 12.18 Card dealing and shuffling simulation. (Part 2 of 4.)

```
88
89              Return deck(currentCard)
90          Else
91              cmdDeal.Enabled = False
92
93              Return Nothing
94          End If
95
96      End Function ' DealCard
97
98      ' cmdShuffle_Click
99      Private Sub cmdShuffle_Click(ByVal sender As System.Object, _
100         ByVal e As System.EventArgs) Handles cmdShuffle.Click
101
102         lblDisplay.Text = "SHUFFLING..."
103
104         Shuffle()
105
106         lblDisplay.Text = "DECK IS SHUFFLED"
107     End Sub ' cmdShuffle_Click
108
109  End Class ' FrmDeck
```

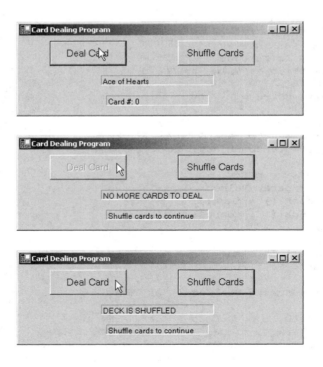

Fig. 12.18 Card dealing and shuffling simulation. (Part 3 of 4.)

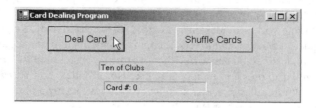

Fig. 12.18 Card dealing and shuffling simulation. (Part 4 of 4.)

Class **CCard** (Fig. 12.17) contains two **String** instance variables—**face** and **suit**—that store references to the face name and suit name of a specific card. The constructor for the class receives two **String**s that it uses to initialize **face** and **suit**. Method **ToString** creates a **String** consisting of the **face** of the card and the **suit** of the card.

Method **FrmDeck_Load** (lines 20–40 of Fig. 12.18) uses the **For** structure (lines 36–38) to fill the **deck** array with **CCard**s. Note that each **CCard** is instantiated and initialized with two **String**s—one from the **faces** array (**String**s **"Ace"** through **"King"**) and one from the **suits** array (**"Hearts"**, **"Diamonds"**, **"Clubs"** or **"Spades"**). The calculation **i Mod 13** always results in a value from **0** to **12** (the thirteen subscripts of the **faces** array), and the calculation **i Mod 4** always results in a value from **0** to **3** (the four subscripts in the **suits** array). The initialized **deck** array contains the cards with faces ace through king for each suit.

When users click the **Deal Card** button, event handler **cmdDeal_Click** (line 43) invokes method **DealCard** (defined in lines 81–96) to get the next card in the **deck** array. If the **deck** is not empty, the method returns a **CCard** object reference; otherwise, it returns **Nothing**. If the reference is not **Nothing**, lines 51–52 display the **CCard** in **lblDisplay** and display the card number in the **lblStatus**.

If **dealCard** returns a **Nothing** reference, the **String "NO MORE CARDS TO DEAL"** is displayed in **lblDisplay**, and the **String "Shuffle cards to continue"** is displayed in **lblStatus**.

When users click the **Shuffle Cards** button, its event-handling method **cmdShuffle_Click** (lines 99–107) invokes method **Shuffle** (defined in line 61) to shuffle the cards. The method loops through all 52 cards (array subscripts **0–51**). For each card, the method randomly picks a number between **0** and **51**. Then the current **CCard** object and the randomly selected **CCard** object are swapped in the array. To shuffle the cards, method **Shuffle** makes a total of only 52 swaps during a single pass of the entire array. When the shuffling is complete, **lblDisplay** displays the **String "DECK IS SHUFFLED"**.

12.17 Regular Expressions and Class Regex

Regular expressions are specially formatted **String**s used to find patterns in text and can be useful during information validation, to ensure that data is in a particular format. For example, a ZIP code must consist of five digits, and a last name must start with a capital letter. One application of regular expressions is to facilitate the construction of a compiler. Often, a large and complex regular expression is used to validate the syntax of a program. If the program code does not match the regular expression, the compiler knows that there is a syntax error within the code.

The .NET Framework provides class **Regex** (**System.Text.RegularExpressions** namespace) to help developers recognize and manipulate regular expressions. Class **Regex** provides method **Match**, which returns an object of class **Match** that represents a single regular expression match. **RegEx** also provides method **Matches**, which finds all matches of a regular expression in an arbitrary **String** and returns a *MatchCollection* object—i.e., a set of **Match**es.

Common Programming Error 12.5

*When using regular expressions, do not confuse class **Match** with the method **Match**, which belongs to class **Regex**.*

Common Programming Error 12.6

*Visual Studio does not add **System.Text.RegularExpressions** to the list of namespaces imported in the project properties, so a programmer must import it manually with the statement **Imports System.Text.RegularExpressions**.*

The table in Fig. 12.19 specifies some *character classes* that can be used with regular expressions. A character class is an escape sequence that represents a group of characters.

A *word character* is any alphanumeric character or underscore. A *whitespace* character is a space, a tab, a carriage return, a newline or a form feed. A *digit* is any numeric character. Regular expressions are not limited to these character classes, however. The expressions employ various operators and other forms of notation to search for complex patterns. We discuss several of these techniques in the context of the next example.

Figure 12.20 presents a simple example that employs regular expressions. This program takes birthdays and tries to match them to a regular expression. The expression only matches birthdays that do not occur in April and that belong to people whose names begin with **"J"**.

Character	Matches	Character	Matches
\d	any digit	\D	any non-digit
\w	any word character	\W	any non-word character
\s	any whitespace	\S	any non-whitespace

Fig. 12.19 Character classes.

```
1   ' Fig. 12.20: RegexMatches.vb
2   ' Demonstrating Class Regex.
3
4   Imports System.Text.RegularExpressions
5   Imports System.Windows.Forms
6
7   Module modRegexMatches
8
```

Fig. 12.20 Regular expressions checking birthdays. (Part 1 of 2.)

```
9     Sub Main()
10       Dim output As String = ""
11       Dim myMatch As Match
12
13       ' create regular expression
14       Dim expression As Regex = _
15          New Regex("J.*\d[0-35-9]-\d\d-\d\d")
16
17       Dim string1 As String = "Jane's Birthday is 05-12-75" & _
18          vbCrLf & "Dave's Birthday is 11-04-68" & vbCrLf & _
19          "John's Birthday is 04-28-73" & vbCrLf & _
20          "Joe's Birthday is 12-17-77"
21
22       ' match regular expression to string and
23       ' print out all matches
24       For Each myMatch In expression.Matches(string1)
25          output &= myMatch.ToString() & vbCrLf
26       Next
27
28       MessageBox.Show(output, "Using Class Regex", _
29          MessageBoxButtons.OK, MessageBoxIcon.Information)
30    End Sub ' Main
31
32   End Module ' modRegexMatches
```

Fig. 12.20 Regular expressions checking birthdays. (Part 2 of 2.)

Line 15 creates an instance of class **Regex** and defines the regular expression pattern for which **Regex** will search. The first character in the regular expression, **"J"**, is treated as a literal character. This means that any **String** matching this regular expression is required to start with **"J"**.

In a regular expression, the dot character **"."** matches any single character except a newline character. However, when the dot character is followed by an asterisk, as in the expression **".*"**, it matches any number of unspecified characters. In general, when the operator **"*"** is applied to any expression, the expression will match zero or more occurrences of the expression. By contrast, the application of the operator **"+"** to an expression causes the expression to match one or more occurrences of that expression. For example, both **"A*"** and **"A+"** will match **"A"**, but only **"A*"** will match an empty **String**.

As indicated in Fig. 12.19, **"\d"** matches any numeric digit. To specify sets of characters other than those that have a character class, characters can be listed in square brackets, **[]**. For example, the pattern **"[aeiou]"** can be used to match any vowel. Ranges of characters can be represented by placing a dash (**-**) between two characters. In the example, **"[0-35-9]"** matches only digits in the ranges specified by the pattern. In this case, the pattern matches any digit between **0** and **3** or between **5** and **9**; therefore, it matches any digit except **4**. If the first character in the brackets is the **"^"**, the expression accepts any character other than those indicated. However, it is important to note that **"[^4]"** is not the same as **"[0-35-9]"**, as the former matches any non-digit in addition to the digits other than **4**.

Although the **"-"** character indicates a range when it is enclosed in square brackets, instances of the **"-"** character outside grouping expressions are treated as literal characters. Thus, the regular expression in line 15 searches for a **String** that starts with the letter **"J"**, followed by any number of characters, followed by a two-digit number (of which the second digit cannot be **4**), followed by a dash, another two-digit number, a dash and another two-digit number.

Lines 24-26 use a **For Each** loop to iterate through each **Match** obtained from **expression.Matches**, which used **string1** as an argument. The output in Fig. 12.20 indicates the two matches that were found in **string1**. Notice that both matches conform to the patter specified by the regular expression.

The asterisk (*****) and plus (**+**) in the previous example are called *quantifiers*. Figure 12.21 lists various quantifiers and their uses.

We have already discussed how the asterisk (*****) and plus (**+**) work. The question mark (**?**) matches zero or one occurrences of the expression that it quantifies. A set of braces containing one number (**{n}**), matches exactly **n** occurrences of the expression it quantifies. We demonstrate this quantifier in the next example. Including a comma after the number enclosed in braces matches at least **n** occurrences of the quantified expression. The set of braces containing two numbers (**{n,m}**), matches between **n** and **m** occurrences of the expression that it qualifies. All of the quantifiers are *greedy*. This means that they will match as many occurrences as they can as long as the match is successful. However, if any of these quantifiers is followed by a question mark (**?**), the quantifier becomes *lazy*. It then will match as few occurrences as possible as long as the match is successful.

The Windows application in Fig. 12.22 presents a more involved example that validates user input via regular expressions.

Quantifier	Matches
*	Matches zero or more occurrences of the pattern.
+	Matches one or more occurrences of the pattern.
?	Matches zero or one occurrences of the pattern.
{n}	Matches exactly **n** occurrences.
{n,}	Matches at least **n** occurrences.
{n,m}	Matches between **n** and **m** (inclusive) occurrences.

Fig. 12.21 Quantifiers used in regular expressions.

```
1    ' Fig. 12.22: Validate.vb
2    ' Validate user information using regular expressions.
3
```

Fig. 12.22 Validating user information using regular expressions. (Part 1 of 5.)

```
4   Imports System.Text.RegularExpressions
5
6   Public Class FrmValid
7      Inherits Form
8
9      ' field labels
10     Friend WithEvents lblLast As Label
11     Friend WithEvents lblFirst As Label
12     Friend WithEvents lblAddress As Label
13     Friend WithEvents lblCity As Label
14     Friend WithEvents lblState As Label
15     Friend WithEvents lblZip As Label
16     Friend WithEvents lblPhone As Label
17
18     ' field inputs
19     Friend WithEvents txtLast As TextBox
20     Friend WithEvents txtFirst As TextBox
21     Friend WithEvents txtAddress As TextBox
22     Friend WithEvents txtCity As TextBox
23     Friend WithEvents txtState As TextBox
24     Friend WithEvents txtZip As TextBox
25     Friend WithEvents txtPhone As TextBox
26
27     Friend WithEvents cmdOK As Button ' validate all fields
28
29     ' Visual Studio .NET generated code
30
31     ' handles cmdOK Click event
32     Private Sub cmdOK_Click(ByVal sender As System.Object, _
33        ByVal e As System.EventArgs) Handles cmdOK.Click
34
35        ' ensures no textboxes are empty
36        If (txtPhone.Text = "" OrElse txtZip.Text = "" OrElse _
37           txtState.Text = "" OrElse txtCity.Text = "" OrElse _
38           txtAddress.Text = "" OrElse txtFirst.Text = "" OrElse _
39           txtLast.Text = "") Then
40
41           ' display popup box
42           MessageBox.Show("Please fill in all fields", "Error", _
43              MessageBoxButtons.OK, MessageBoxIcon.Error)
44
45           ' set focus to txtLast
46           txtLast.Focus()
47
48           Return
49        End If
50
51        ' if last name format invalid show message
52        If Not Regex.Match(txtLast.Text, _
53           "^[A-Z][a-zA-Z]*$").Success Then
54
55           ' last name was incorrect
56           MessageBox.Show("Invalid Last Name", "Message")
```

Fig. 12.22 Validating user information using regular expressions. (Part 2 of 5.)

```
57                  txtLast.Focus()
58
59                  Return
60              End If
61
62              ' if first name format invalid show message
63              If Not Regex.Match(txtFirst.Text, _
64                  "^[A-Z][a-zA-Z]*$").Success Then
65
66                  ' first name was incorrect
67                  MessageBox.Show("Invalid First Name", "Message")
68                  txtFirst.Focus()
69
70                  Return
71              End If
72
73              ' if address format invalid show message
74              If Not Regex.Match(txtAddress.Text, "^[0-9]+\s+([a-zA-Z]" & _
75                  "+|[a-zA-Z]+\s[a-zA-Z]+)$").Success Then
76
77                  ' address was incorrect
78                  MessageBox.Show("Invalid Address", "Message")
79                  txtAddress.Focus()
80
81                  Return
82              End If
83
84              ' if city format invalid show message
85              If Not Regex.Match(txtCity.Text, "^([a-zA-Z]+|[a-zA-Z]" & _
86                  "+\s[a-zA-Z]+)$").Success Then
87
88                  ' city was incorrect
89                  MessageBox.Show("Invalid City", "Message")
90                  txtCity.Focus()
91
92                  Return
93              End If
94
95              ' if state format invalid show message
96              If Not Regex.Match(txtState.Text, _
97                  "^([a-zA-Z]+|[a-zA-Z]+\s[a-zA-Z]+)$").Success Then
98
99                  ' state was incorrect
100                 MessageBox.Show("Invalid State", "Message")
101                 txtState.Focus()
102
103                 Return
104             End If
105
106             ' if zip code format invalid show message
107             If Not Regex.Match(txtZip.Text, "^\d{5}$").Success Then
108
```

Fig. 12.22 Validating user information using regular expressions. (Part 3 of 5.)

```
109              ' zip code was incorrect
110              MessageBox.Show("Invalid zip code", "Message")
111              txtZip.Focus()
112
113              Return
114          End If
115
116          ' if phone number format invalid show message
117          If Not Regex.Match(txtPhone.Text, "^[1-9]" & _
118              "\d{2}-[1-9]\d{2}-\d{4}$").Success Then
119
120              ' phone was incorrect
121              MessageBox.Show("Invalid Phone Number", "Message")
122              txtPhone.Focus()
123
124              Return
125          End If
126
127          ' information is valid, signal user and exit application
128          Me.Hide()
129          MessageBox.Show("Thank you!", "Information Correct", _
130              MessageBoxButtons.OK, MessageBoxIcon.Information)
131
132          Application.Exit()
133      End Sub ' cmdOK_Click
134
135  End Class ' FrmValid
```

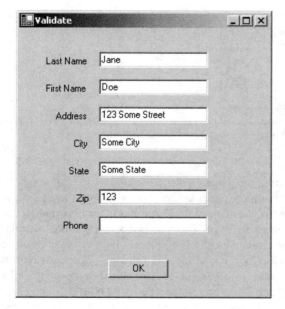

Fig. 12.22 Validating user information using regular expressions. (Part 4 of 5.)

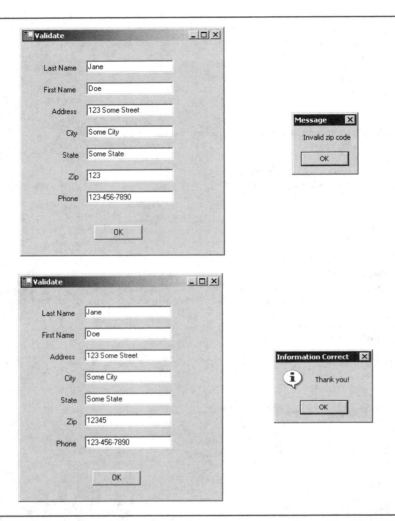

Fig. 12.22 Validating user information using regular expressions. (Part 5 of 5.)

When a user clicks the **OK** button, the program checks to make sure that none of the fields are empty (lines 36–39). If one or more fields are empty, the program signals the user that all fields must be filled before the program can validate the input information (lines 42–43). Line 46 calls instance method **Focus** of class **TextBox**. Method **Focus** places the cursor within the **TextBox** that made the call. The program then exits the event handler (line 48). If there are no empty fields, the user input is validated. The **Last Name** is validated first (lines 52–60). If it passes the test (i.e., if the **Success** property of the **Match** instance is **True**), control moves on to validate the **First Name** (lines 63–71). This process continues until all **TextBox**es are validated, or until a test fails (**Success** is **False**) and the program sends an appropriate error message. If all fields contain valid information, success is signaled, and the program quits.

In the previous example, we searched for substrings that matched a regular expression. In this example, we want to check whether an entire **String** conforms to a regular expression. For example, we want to accept **"Smith"** as a last name, but not **"9@Smith#"**. We achieve this effect by beginning each regular expression with a **"^"** character and ending it with a **"$"** character. The **"^"** and **"$"** characters match the positions at the beginning and end of a **String**, respectively. This forces the regular expression to evaluate the entire **String** and not return a match if a substring matches successfully.

In this program, we use the **Shared** version of **Regex** method *Match*, which takes an additional parameter specifying the regular expression that we are trying to match. The expression in line 53 uses the square bracket and range notation to match an uppercase first letter, followed by letters of any case—**a-z** matches any lowercase letter, and **A-Z** matches any uppercase letter. The ***** quantifier signifies that the second range of characters may occur zero or more times in the **String**. Thus, this expression matches any **String** consisting of one uppercase letter, followed by zero or more additional letters.

The notation **\s** matches a single whitespace character (lines 74–75 and 86). The expression **\d{5}**, used in the **Zip** (zip code) field, matches any five digits (line 107). In general, an expression with a positive integer **x** in the curly braces will match any **x** digits. (Notice the importance of the **"^"** and **"$"** characters to prevent zip codes with extra digits from being validated.)

The character "**|**" matches the expression to its left or to its right. For example, **Hi (John|Jane)** matches both **Hi John** and **Hi Jane**. Note the use of parentheses to group parts of the regular expression. Quantifiers may be applied to patterns enclosed in parentheses to create more complex regular expressions.

The **Last Name** and **First Name** fields both accept **String**s of any length, which begin with an uppercase letter. The **Address** field matches a number of at least one digit, followed by a space and either one or more letters or one or more letters followed by a space and another series of one or more letters (lines 74–75). Therefore, **"10 Broadway"** and **"10 Main Street"** are both valid addresses. The **City** (lines 85–86) and **State** (lines 96–97) fields match any word of at least one character or, alternatively, any two words of at least one character if the words are separated by a single space. This means both **Waltham** and **West Newton** would match. As previously stated, the **Zip** code must be a five-digit number (line 107). The **Phone** number must be of the form **xxx-yyy-yyyy**, where the **x**s represent the area code and **y**s the number (lines 117–118). The first **x** and the first **y** may not be zero.

Sometimes it is useful to replace parts of a **String** with another, or split a **String** according to a regular expression. For this purpose, the **Regex** class provides **Shared** and instance versions of methods *Replace* and *Split*, which are demonstrated in Fig. 12.23.

```
1    ' Fig. 12.23: RegexSubstitution.vb
2    ' Using Regex method Replace.
3
4    Imports System.Text.RegularExpressions
5    Imports System.Windows.Forms
6
7    Module modRegexSubstitution
```

Fig. 12.23 Regex methods **Replace** and **Split**. (Part 1 of 3.)

```
8
9       Sub Main()
10          Dim testString1 As String = _
11              "This sentence ends in 5 stars *****"
12
13          Dim testString2 As String = "1, 2, 3, 4, 5, 6, 7, 8"
14          Dim testRegex1 As Regex = New Regex("stars")
15          Dim testRegex2 As Regex = New Regex("\d")
16          Dim results As String()
17          Dim resultString As String
18          Dim output As String = "Original String 1" & vbTab & _
19              vbTab & vbTab & testString1
20
21          testString1 = Regex.Replace(testString1, "\*", "^")
22
23          output &= vbCrLf & "^ substituted for *" & vbTab & _
24              vbTab & vbTab & testString1
25
26          testString1 = testRegex1.Replace(testString1, "carets")
27
28          output &= vbCrLf & """carets"" substituted for " & _
29              """stars""" & vbTab & testString1
30
31          output &= vbCrLf & "Every word replaced by " & _
32              """word""" & vbTab & _
33              Regex.Replace(testString1, "\w+", "word")
34
35          output &= vbCrLf & vbCrLf & "Original String 2" & _
36              vbTab & vbTab & vbTab & testString2
37
38          output &= vbCrLf & "First 3 digits replaced by " & _
39              """digit""" & vbTab & _
40              testRegex2.Replace(testString2, "digit", 3)
41
42          output &= vbCrLf & "String split at commas" & vbTab & _
43              vbTab & "["
44
45          results = Regex.Split(testString2, ",\s*")
46
47          For Each resultString In results
48              output &= """" & resultString & """, "
49          Next
50
51          output = output.Substring(0, output.Length - 2) & "]"
52
53          MessageBox.Show(output, _
54              "Substitution using regular expressions")
55      End Sub ' Main
56
57  End Module ' modRegexSubstitution
```

Fig. 12.23 Regex methods **Replace** and **Split**. (Part 2 of 3.)

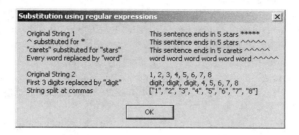

Fig. 12.23 Regex methods **Replace** and **Split**. (Part 3 of 3.)

Method **Replace** replaces text in a **String** with new text wherever the original **String** matches a regular expression. We present two versions of this method in Fig. 12.23. The first version (line 21) is **Shared** and takes three parameters—the **String** to modify, the **String** containing the regular expression to match and the replacement **String**. Here, **Replace** replaces every instance of **"*"** in **testString1** with **"^"**. Notice that the regular expression (**"*"**) precedes character * with a backslash, \. Normally, * is a quantifier indicating that a regular expression should match any number of occurrences of a preceding pattern. However, in line 21, we want to find all occurrences of the literal character *; to do this, we must escape character * with character \. By escaping a special regular expression character with a \, we inform the regular-expression matching engine to find the actual character, as opposed to what it represents in a regular expression. The second version of method **Replace** (line 26) is an instance method that uses the regular expression passed to the constructor for **testRegex1** (line 14) to perform the replacement operation. In this case, every match for the regular expression **"stars"** in **testString1** is replaced with **"carets"**.

Line 15 instantiates **testRegex2** with argument **"\d"**. The call to instance method **Replace** in line 40 takes three arguments—a **String** to modify, a **String** containing the replacement text and an **Integer** specifying the number of replacements to make. In other words, this version of **Replace** replaces the first three instances of a digit (**"\d"**) in **testString2** with the text **"digit"** (line 40).

Method **Split** divides a **String** into several substrings. The original **String** is broken in any location that matches a specified regular expression. Method **Split** returns an array containing the substrings between matches for the regular expression. In line 45, we use the **Shared** version of method **Split** to separate a **String** of comma-separated integers. The first argument is the **String** to split, and the second argument is the regular expression. In this case, we use the regular expression **", \s*"** to separate the substrings wherever a comma occurs. By matching any whitespace characters, we eliminate extra spaces from the resulting substrings.

12.18 Summary

Characters are the fundamental building blocks of Visual Basic program code. Every program is composed of a sequence of characters that is interpreted by the compiler as a series of instructions used to accomplish a task.

A **String** is a series of characters treated as a single unit. A **String** may include letters, digits and various special characters, such as +, -, *, /, $ and others. All characters correspond to numeric codes. When the computer compares two **String**s, it actually compares the numeric codes of the characters in the **String**s. Once a **String** is created, its contents can never change. Class **StringBuilder** provides a modifiable **String**-like entity that can grow and shrink in size.

A hash table stores information, using a special calculation on the object to be stored that produces a hash code. The hash code is used to choose the location in the table at which to store the object. Class **Object** defines method **GetHashCode** to perform the hash-code calculation.

The braces in a format **String** specify how to format a specific piece of information. Formats have the form **{X[,Y][:FormatString]}**, where **X** is the number of the argument to be formatted, counting from zero. **Y** is an optional argument, which can be positive or negative. **Y** indicates how many characters should be in the result of formatting; if the resulting **String** is less than this number, it will be padded with spaces to make up for the difference. A positive integer means the **String** will be right aligned; a negative one means it will be left aligned. The optional **FormatString** indicates what kind of formatting should be applied to the argument: currency, decimal, or scientific, among others.

Structures are in many ways similar to classes, the primary difference between them being that structures encapsulate value types, whereas classes encapsulate reference types. Many of the primitive data types that we have been using are actually aliases for different structures. These structures are derived from class **ValueType**, which in turn is derived from class **Object**. **Char** is a structure that represents characters.

Regular expressions match patterns in text. The .NET Framework provides class **Regex** to aid developers in recognizing and manipulating regular expressions. **Regex** provides method **Match**, which returns an object of class **Match**. This object represents a single match in a regular expression. **Regex** also provides the method **Matches**, which finds all matches of a regular expression in an arbitrary **String** and returns a **Match-Collection**—a set of **Match**es.

Graphics and Multimedia

Objectives

- To understand graphics contexts and graphics objects.
- To manipulate colors and fonts.
- To understand and be able to use GDI+ **Graphics** methods to draw lines, rectangles, **String**s and images.
- To use class **Image** to manipulate and display images.
- To draw complex shapes from simple shapes with class **GraphicsPath**.
- To use Windows Media Player and Microsoft Agent in a Visual Basic .NET application.

One picture is worth ten thousand words.
Chinese proverb

Treat nature in terms of the cylinder, the sphere, the cone, all in perspective.
Paul Cezanne

Nothing ever becomes real till it is experienced—even a proverb is no proverb to you till your life has illustrated it.
John Keats

A picture shows me at a glance what it takes dozens of pages of a book to expound.
Ivan Sergeyevich

Outline

13.1 Introduction

In this chapter, we overview Visual Basic's tools for drawing two-dimensional shapes and for controlling colors and fonts. Visual Basic supports graphics that enable programmers to enhance their Windows applications visually. The language contains many sophisticated drawing capabilities as part of namespace **System.Drawing** and the other namespaces that make up the .NET resource *GDI+*. GDI+, an extension of the Graphical Device Interface, is an application programming interface (API) that provides classes for creating two-dimensional vector graphics (a high-performance technique for creating graphics), manipulating fonts and inserting images. GDI+ expands GDI by simplifying the programming model and introducing several new features, such as graphics paths, extended image file format support and alpha blending. Using the GDI+ API, programmers can create images without worrying about the platform-specific details of their graphics hardware.

We begin with an introduction to Visual Basic's drawing capabilities. We then present more powerful drawing capabilities, such as changing the styles of lines used to draw shapes and controlling the colors and patterns of filled shapes.

Figure 13.1 depicts a portion of the **System.Drawing** class hierarchy, which includes several of the basic graphics classes and structures covered in this chapter. The most commonly used components of GDI+ reside in the **System.Drawing** and **System.Drawing.Drawing2D** namespaces.

Class **Graphics** contains methods used for drawing **String**s, lines, rectangles and other shapes on a **Control**. The drawing methods of class **Graphics** usually require a **Pen** or **Brush** object to render a specified shape. The **Pen** draws shape outlines; the **Brush** draws solid objects.

Structure **Color** contains numerous **Shared** properties, which set the colors of various graphical components, as well as methods that allow users to create new colors. Class

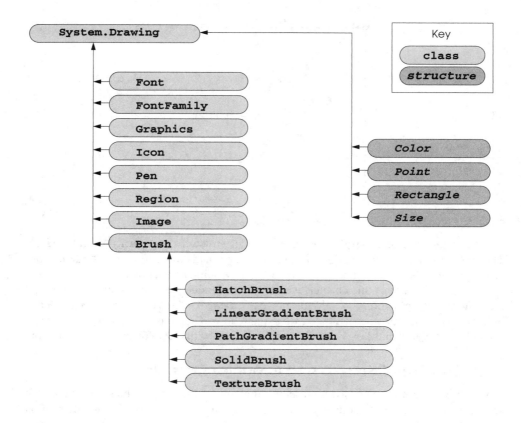

Fig. 13.1　**System.Drawing** namespace's Classes and Structures.

Font contains properties that define unique fonts. Class *FontFamily* contains methods for obtaining font information.

To begin drawing in Visual Basic, we first must understand GDI+'s *coordinate system* (Fig. 13.2), a scheme for identifying every point on the screen. By default, the upper-left corner of a GUI component (such as a **Panel** or a **Form**) has the coordinates (0, 0). A coordinate pair has both an *x-coordinate* (the *horizontal coordinate*) and a *y-coordinate* (the *vertical coordinate*). The *x*-coordinate is the horizontal distance (to the right) from the upper-left corner. The *y*-coordinate is the vertical distance (downward) from the upper-left corner. The *x-axis* defines every horizontal coordinate, and the *y-axis* defines every vertical coordinate. Programmers position text and shapes on the screen by specifying their (*x*,*y*) coordinates. Coordinate units are measured in *pixels* ("picture elements"), which are the smallest units of resolution on a display monitor.

 Portability Tip 13.1

Different display monitors have different resolutions, so the density of pixels on such monitors will vary. This might cause the sizes of graphics to appear different on different monitors.

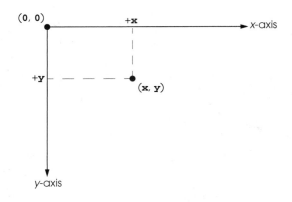

Fig. 13.2   GDI+ coordinate system. Units are measured in pixels.

The **System.Drawing** namespace provides structures **Rectangle** and **Point**. The *Rectangle* *structure* defines rectangular shapes and dimensions. The *Point* *structure* represents the *x-y* coordinates of a point on a two-dimensional plane.

In the remainder of this chapter, we explore techniques of manipulating images and creating smooth animations. We also discuss class *Image*, which can store and manipulate images from many file formats. Later, we explain how to combine the graphical rendering capabilities covered in the early sections of the chapter with those for image manipulation.

13.2 Graphics Contexts and Graphics Objects

A Visual Basic *graphics context* represents a drawing surface and enables drawing on the screen. A **Graphics** object manages a graphics context by controlling how information is drawn. **Graphics** objects contain methods for drawing, font manipulation, color manipulation and other graphics-related actions. Every Windows application that derives from class **System.Windows.Forms.Form** inherits an **Overridable** *OnPaint* method where most graphics operations are performed. The arguments to the **OnPaint** method include a **PaintEventArgs** object from which we can obtain a **Graphics** object for the control. We must obtain the **Graphics** object on each call to the method, because the properties of the graphics context that the graphics object represents could change. The **OnPaint** method triggers the **Control**'s *Paint* event.

When displaying graphical information on a **Form**'s client area, programmers can override the **OnPaint** method to retrieve a **Graphics** object from argument **Paint-EventArgs** or to create a new **Graphics** object associated with the appropriate surface. We demonstrate these techniques of drawing in applications later in the chapter.

To override the inherited **OnPaint** method, use the following method definition:

```
Protected Overrides Sub OnPaint(ByVal e As PaintEventArgs)
```

Next, extract the incoming **Graphics** object from the **PaintEventArgs** argument:

```
Dim graphicsObject As Graphics = e.Graphics
```

Variable **graphicsObject** now is available to draw shapes and **String**s on the form.

Calling the **OnPaint** method raises the **Paint** event. Instead of overriding the **OnPaint** method, programmers can add an event handler for the **Paint** event. First, write the code for the **Paint** event handler in this form:

```
Public Sub MyEventHandler_Paint( _
    ByVal sender As Object, ByVal e As PaintEventArgs) _
    Handles MyBase.Paint
```

Programmers seldom call the **OnPaint** method directly, because the drawing of graphics is an *event-driven process*. An event—such as the covering, uncovering or resizing of a window—calls the **OnPaint** method of that form. Similarly, when any control (such as a **TextBox** or **Label**) is displayed, the program calls that control's **Paint** method.

If programmers need to invoke method **OnPaint** explicitly, they can call the **Invalidate** method (inherited from **Control**). This method refreshes a control's client area and repaints all graphical components. Visual Basic contains several overloaded **Invalidate** methods that allow programmers to update portions of the client area.

Performance Tip 13.1

*Calling the **Invalidate** method to refresh the **Control** often is inefficient. Instead, call **Invalidate** with a **Rectangle** parameter to refresh only the area designated by the rectangle. This improves program performance.*

Controls, such as **Label**s and **Button**s, also have their own graphics contexts. To draw on a control, first obtain its graphics object by invoking the **CreateGraphics** method:

```
Dim graphicsObject As Graphics = label1.CreateGraphics()
```

Then, you can use the methods provided in class **Graphics** to draw on the control.

13.3 Color Control

Colors can enhance a program's appearance and help convey meaning. For example, a red traffic light indicates stop, yellow indicates caution and green indicates go.

Structure **Color** defines methods and constants used to manipulate colors. Because it is a lightweight object that performs only a handful of operations and stores **Shared** fields, **Color** is implemented as a structure, rather than as a class.

Every color can be created from a combination of alpha, red, green and blue components. Together, these components are called *ARGB values*. All four ARGB components are **Byte**s that represent integer values in the range from 0 to 255. The alpha value determines the intensity of the color. For example, the alpha value 0 results in a transparent color, whereas the value 255 results in an opaque color. Alpha values between 0 and 255 result in a weighted blending effect of the color's RGB value with that of any background color, causing a semi-transparent effect. The first number in the RGB value defines the amount of red in the color, the second defines the amount of green and the third defines the amount of blue. The larger the value, the greater the amount of that particular color. Visual Basic enables programmers to choose from almost 17 million colors. If a particular computer cannot display all these colors, it will display the color closest to the one specified. Figure 13.3 summarizes some predefined color constants, and Fig. 13.4 describes several **Color** methods and properties.

Constants in structure Color (all are Public Shared)	RGB value	Constants in structure Color (all are Public Shared)	RGB value
Orange	255, 200, 0	White	255, 255, 255
Pink	255, 175, 175	Gray	28, 128, 128
Cyan	0, 255, 255	DarkGray	64, 64, 64
Magenta	255, 0, 255	Red	255, 0, 0
Yellow	255, 255, 0	Green	0, 255, 0
Black	0, 0, 0	Blue	0, 0, 255

Fig. 13.3   **Color** structure **Shared** constants and their RGB values.

Structure Color methods and properties	Description
Common Methods	
Shared **FromArgb**	Creates a color based on red, green and blue values expressed as **Integers** from 0 to 255. Overloaded version allows specification of alpha, red, green and blue values.
Shared **FromName**	Creates a color from a name, passed as a **String**.
Common Properties	
A	**Integer** between 0 and 255, representing the alpha component.
R	**Integer** between 0 and 255, representing the red component.
G	**Integer** between 0 and 255, representing the green component.
B	**Integer** between 0 and 255, representing the blue component.

Fig. 13.4   **Color** structure members.

The table in Fig. 13.4 describes two **FromArgb** method calls. One takes three **Integer** arguments, and one takes four **Integer** arguments (all argument values must be between 0 and 255). Both take **Integer** arguments specifying the amount of red, green and blue. The overloaded version takes four arguments and allows the user to specify alpha; the three-argument version defaults the alpha to 255. Both methods return a **Color** object representing the specified values. **Color** properties **A**, **R**, **G** and **B** return **Byte**s that represent **Integer** values from 0 to 255, corresponding to the amounts of alpha, red, green and blue, respectively.

Programmers draw shapes and **String**s using **Brush**es and **Pen**s. A **Pen**, which functions similarly to an ordinary pen, is used to draw lines. Most drawing methods require a **Pen** object. The overloaded **Pen** constructors allow programmers to specify the colors and widths of the lines that they wish to draw. The **System.Drawing** namespace also provides a **Pens** collection containing predefined **Pen**s.

All classes derived from abstract class **Brush** define objects that color the interiors of graphical shapes (for example, the **SolidBrush** constructor takes a **Color** object—the color to draw). In most **Fill** methods, **Brush**es fill a space with a color, pattern or image. Figure 13.5 summarizes various **Brush**es and their functions.

The application in Fig. 13.6 demonstrates several of the methods described in Fig. 13.4. It displays two overlapping rectangles, allowing the user to experiment with color values and color names.

Class	Description
HatchBrush	Uses a rectangular brush to fill a region with a pattern. The pattern is defined by a member of the **HatchStyle** enumeration, a foreground color (with which the pattern is drawn) and a background color.
LinearGradient-Brush	Fills a region with a gradual blend of one color into another. Linear gradients are defined along a line. They can be specified by the two colors, the angle of the gradient and either the width of a rectangle or two points.
SolidBrush	Fills a region with one color. Defined by a **Color** object.
TextureBrush	Fills a region by repeating a specified **Image** across the surface.

Fig. 13.5   Classes that derive from class **Brush**.

```
1    ' Fig. 13.6: ShowColors.vb
2    ' Using different colors in Visual Basic.
3
4    Public Class FrmColorForm
5       Inherits System.Windows.Forms.Form
6
7       ' input text boxes
8       Friend WithEvents txtColorName As TextBox
9       Friend WithEvents txtGreenBox As TextBox
10      Friend WithEvents txtRedBox As TextBox
11      Friend WithEvents txtAlphaBox As TextBox
12      Friend WithEvents txtBlueBox As TextBox
13
14      ' set color command buttons
15      Friend WithEvents cmdColorName As Button
16      Friend WithEvents cmdColorValue As Button
17
18      ' color labels
19      Friend WithEvents lblBlue As Label
20      Friend WithEvents lblGreen As Label
21      Friend WithEvents lblRed As Label
22      Friend WithEvents lblAlpha As Label
23
24      ' group boxes
25      Friend WithEvents nameBox As GroupBox
26      Friend WithEvents colorValueGroup As GroupBox
```

Fig. 13.6   Color value and alpha demonstration. (Part 1 of 3.)

```
27
28        ' Visual Studio .NET generated code
29
30        ' color for back rectangle
31        Private mBehindColor As Color = Color.Wheat
32
33        ' color for front rectangle
34        Private mFrontColor As Color = Color.FromArgb(100, 0, 0, 255)
35
36        ' overrides Form OnPaint method
37        Protected Overrides Sub OnPaint(ByVal e As PaintEventArgs)
38           Dim graphicsObject As Graphics = e.Graphics ' get graphics
39
40           Dim textBrush As SolidBrush = _
41              New SolidBrush(Color.Black) ' create text brush
42
43           Dim brush As SolidBrush = _
44              New SolidBrush(Color.White) ' create solid brush
45
46           ' draw white background
47           graphicsObject.FillRectangle(brush, 4, 4, 275, 180)
48
49           ' display name of behindColor
50           graphicsObject.DrawString(mBehindColor.Name, Me.Font, _
51              textBrush, 40, 5)
52
53           ' set brush color and display back rectangle
54           brush.Color = mBehindColor
55
56           graphicsObject.FillRectangle(brush, 45, 20, 150, 120)
57
58           ' display Argb values of front color
59           graphicsObject.DrawString("Alpha: " & mFrontColor.A & _
60              " Red: " & mFrontColor.R & " Green: " & mFrontColor.G _
61              & " Blue: " & mFrontColor.B, Me.Font, textBrush, _
62              55, 165)
63
64           ' set brush color and display front rectangle
65           brush.Color = mFrontColor
66
67           graphicsObject.FillRectangle(brush, 65, 35, 170, 130)
68        End Sub ' OnPaint
69
70        ' handle cmdColorValue click event
71        Private Sub cmdColorValue_Click(ByVal sender As _
72           System.Object, ByVal e As System.EventArgs) _
73           Handles cmdColorValue.Click
74
75           ' obtain new front color from text boxes
76           mFrontColor = Color.FromArgb(txtAlphaBox.Text, _
77              txtRedBox.Text, txtGreenBox.Text, txtBlueBox.Text)
78
```

Fig. 13.6 Color value and alpha demonstration. (Part 2 of 3.)

```
79          Invalidate() ' refresh Form
80       End Sub ' cmdColorValue_Click
81
82       Private Sub cmdColorName_Click(ByVal sender As _
83          System.Object, ByVal e As System.EventArgs) _
84          Handles cmdColorName.Click
85
86          ' set behindColor to color specified in text box
87          mBehindColor = Color.FromName(txtColorName.Text)
88
89          Invalidate() ' refresh Form
90       End Sub ' cmdColorName_Click
91
92    End Class ' FrmColorForm
```

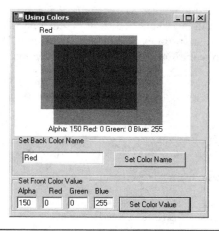

Fig. 13.6 Color value and alpha demonstration. (Part 3 of 3.)

When the application begins its execution, it calls class **ShowColors' OnPaint** method to paint the window. Line 38 gets a reference to **PaintEventArgs e**'s **Graphics** object and assigns it to **Graphics** object **graphicsObject**. Lines 40–44 create a black and a white **SolidBrush** for drawing on the form. Class **SolidBrush** derives from abstract base class **Brush**; programmers can draw solid shapes with the **SolidBrush**.

Graphics method *FillRectangle* draws a solid white rectangle with the **Brush** supplied as a parameter (line 47). It takes as parameters a brush, the *x*- and *y*-coordinates of a point and the width and height of the rectangle to draw. The point represents the upper-left corner of the rectangle. Lines 50–51 display the **String Name** property of the **Brush**'s **Color** property with the **Graphics DrawString** method. The programmer has access to several overloaded **DrawString** methods; the version demonstrated in lines 50–51 takes a **String** to display, the display **Font**, a **Brush** and the x- and y-coordinates of the location for the **String**'s first character.

Lines 54–56 assign the **Color mBehindColor** value to the **Brush**'s **Color** property and display a rectangle. Lines 59–62 extract and display the ARGB values of **Color mFrontColor** and then display a filled rectangle that overlaps the first.

Button event-handler method **cmdColorValue_Click** (lines 71–80) uses **Color** method **FromARGB** to construct a new **Color** object from the ARGB values that a user specifies via text boxes. It then assigns the newly created **Color** to **mFrontColor**. **Button** event-handler method **cmdColorName_Click** (lines 82–90) uses the **Color** method **FromName** to create a new **Color** object from the **colorName** that a user enters in a text box. This **Color** is assigned to **mBehindColor**.

If the user assigns an alpha value between 0 and 255 for the **mFrontColor**, the effects of alpha blending are apparent. In the screenshot output, the red back rectangle blends with the blue front rectangle to create purple where the two overlap.

Software Engineering Observation 13.1

No methods in class **Color** *enable programmers to change the characteristics of the current color. To use a different color, create a new* **Color** *object.*

The predefined GUI component *ColorDialog* is a dialog box that allows users to select from a palette of available colors. It also offers the option of creating custom colors. The program in Fig. 13.7 demonstrates the use of such a dialog. When a user selects a color and presses **OK**, the application retrieves the user's selection via the **ColorDialog**'s *Color* property.

```
1   ' Fig. 13.7: ShowColorsComplex.vb
2   ' Change the background and text colors of a form.
3
4   Imports System.Windows.Forms
5
6   Public Class FrmColorDialogTest
7      Inherits System.Windows.Forms.Form
8
9      Friend WithEvents cmdBackgroundButton As Button
10     Friend WithEvents cmdTextButton As Button
11
12     ' Visual Studio .NET generated code
13
14     ' change text color
15     Private Sub cmdTextButton_Click (ByVal sender As System.Object, _
16        ByVal e As System.EventArgs) Handles cmdTextButton.Click
17
18        ' create ColorDialog object
19        Dim colorBox As ColorDialog = New ColorDialog()
20        Dim result As DialogResult
21
22        ' get chosen color
23        result = colorBox.ShowDialog()
24
25        If result = DialogResult.Cancel Then
26           Return
27        End If
28
```

Fig. 13.7 **ColorDialog** used to change background and text color. (Part 1 of 2.)

```
29        ' assign forecolor to result of dialog
30        cmdBackgroundButton.ForeColor = colorBox.Color
31        cmdTextButton.ForeColor = colorBox.Color
32     End Sub ' cmdTextButton_Click
33
34     ' change background color
35     Private Sub cmdBackgroundButton_Click( _
36        ByVal sender As System.Object, _
37        ByVal e As System.EventArgs) _
38        Handles cmdBackgroundButton.Click
39
40        ' create ColorDialog object
41        Dim colorBox As ColorDialog = New ColorDialog()
42        Dim result As DialogResult
43
44        ' show ColorDialog and get result
45        colorBox.FullOpen = True
46        result = colorBox.ShowDialog()
47
48        If result = DialogResult.Cancel Then
49           Return
50        End If
51
52        ' set background color
53        Me.BackColor = colorBox.Color
54     End Sub  ' cmdBackgroundButton_Click
55
56  End Class ' FrmColorDialogTest
```

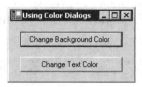

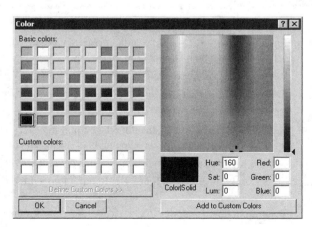

Fig. 13.7 ColorDialog used to change background and text color. (Part 2 of 2.)

The GUI for this application contains two **Button**s. The top one, **cmdBackground**, allows the user to change the form and button background colors. The bottom one, **cmd-TextButton**, allows the user to change the button text colors.

Lines 15–32 define **Button cmdTextButton**'s event handler, which creates a new **ColorDialog** named **colorBox** and invokes its **ShowDialog** method to display the window. Property **Color** of **colorBox** stores users' selections. Lines 30–31 set the text color of both buttons to the selected color.

Lines 35–54 define the event handler for button **cmdBackgroundButton**. The method modifies the background color of the form by setting **BackColor** equal to the dialog's **Color** property. The method creates a new **ColorDialog** and sets the dialog's ***FullOpen*** property to **True**. The dialog now displays all available colors, as shown in the screen capture in Fig. 13.7. The regular color display does not show the right-hand portion of the screen.

Users are not restricted to the **ColorDialog**'s 48 colors. To create a custom color, users can click anywhere in the **ColorDialog**'s large rectangle—this displays the various color shades. Adjust the slider, hue and other features to refine the color. When finished, click the **Add to Custom Colors** button, which adds the custom color to a square in the custom colors section of the dialog. Clicking **OK** sets the **Color** property of the **ColorDialog** to that color. Selecting a color and pressing the dialog's **OK** button causes the application's background color to change.

13.4 Font Control

This section introduces methods and constants that are related to font control. Once a **Font** has been created, its properties cannot be modified. If programmers require a different **Font**, they must create a new **Font** object—there are many overloaded versions of the **Font** constructor for creating custom **Font**s. Some properties of class **Font** are summarized in Fig. 13.8.

Property	Description
Bold	Tests a font for a bold font style. Returns **True** if the font is bold.
FontFamily	Represents the **FontFamily** of the **Font** (a grouping structure to organize fonts and define their similar properties).
Height	Represents the height of the font.
Italic	Tests a font for an italic font style. Returns **True** if the font is italic.
Name	Represents the font's name as a **String**.
Size	Returns a **Single** value indicating the current font size measured in design units (design units are any specified units of measurement for the font).
SizeInPoints	Returns a **Single** value indicating the current font size measured in points.
Strikeout	Tests a font for a strikeout font style. Returns **True** if the font is in strikeout format.
Underline	Tests a font for an underline font style. Returns **True** if the font is underlined.

Fig. 13.8 **Font** class read-only properties.

Note that property **Size** returns the font size as measured in design units, whereas **SizeInPoints** returns the font size as measured in points (the more common measurement). When we say that the **Size** property measures the size of the font in *design units*, we mean that the font size can be specified in a variety of ways, such as inches or millimeters. Some versions of the **Font** constructor accept a **GraphicsUnit** argument—an enumeration that allows users to specify the unit of measurement employed to describe the font size. Members of the **GraphicsUnit** enumeration include **Point** (1/72 inch), **Display** (1/75 inch), **Document** (1/300 inch), **Millimeter**, **Inch** and **Pixel**. If this argument is provided the **Size** property contains the size of the font as measured in the specified design unit, and the **SizeInPoints** property converts the size of the font into points. For example, if we create a **Font** with a size of **1** and specify that **Graphics-Unit.Inch** be used to measure the font, the **Size** property will be **1**, and the **SizeIn-Points** property will be **72**. If we employ a constructor that does not accept a member of the **GraphicsUnit**, the default measurement for the font size is **Graphics-Unit.Point** (thus, the **Size** and **SizeInPoints** properties will be equal).

Class **Font** has a number of constructors. Most require a *font name*, which is a **String** representing the default font currently supported by the system. Common fonts include Microsoft *SansSerif* and *Serif*. Constructors also usually require the *font size* as an argument. Lastly, **Font** constructors usually require the *font style*, which is a member of the *FontStyle* enumeration: *Bold*, *Italic*, *Regular*, *Strikeout*, *Underline*. Font styles can be combined via the **Or** operator (for example, **FontStyle.Italic Or FontStyle.Bold**, makes a font both italic and bold).

Graphics method *DrawString* sets the current drawing font—the font in which the text displays—to its **Font** argument.

Common Programming Error 13.1

Specifying a font that is not available on a system is a logic error. If this occurs, Visual Basic will substitute that system's default font.

The program in Fig. 13.9 displays text in four different fonts, each of a different size. The program uses the **Font** constructor to initialize **Font** objects (lines 17–29). Each call to the **Font** constructor passes a font name (e.g., Arial, Times New Roman, Courier New or Tahoma) as a **String**, a font size (a **Single**) and a **FontStyle** object (**style**). **Graphics** method **DrawString** sets the font and draws the text at the specified location. Note that line 14 creates a **DarkBlue SolidBrush** object (**brush**), causing all **String**s drawn with that brush to appear in **DarkBlue**.

Software Engineering Observation 13.2

*There is no way to change the properties of a **Font** object—to use a different font, programmers must create a new **Font** object.*

```
1   ' Fig. 13.9: UsingFonts.vb
2   ' Demonstrating various font settings.
3
4   Public Class FrmFonts
5      Inherits System.Windows.Forms.Form
6
```

Fig. 13.9 **Font**s and **FontStyle**s. (Part 1 of 2.)

```
7      ' Visual Studio .NET generated code
8
9      ' demonstrate various font and style settings
10     Protected Overrides Sub OnPaint( _
11        ByVal paintEvent As PaintEventArgs)
12
13        Dim graphicsObject As Graphics = paintEvent.Graphics
14        Dim brush As SolidBrush = New SolidBrush(Color.DarkBlue)
15
16        ' arial, 12 pt bold
17        Dim style As FontStyle = FontStyle.Bold
18        Dim arial As Font = New Font( _
19           New FontFamily("Arial"), 12, style)
20
21        ' times new roman, 12 pt regular
22        style = FontStyle.Regular
23        Dim timesNewRoman As Font = New Font( _
24           "Times New Roman", 12, style)
25
26        ' courier new, 16 pt bold and italic
27        style = FontStyle.Bold Or FontStyle.Italic
28        Dim courierNew As Font = New Font("Courier New", _
29           16, style)
30
31        ' tahoma, 18 pt strikeout
32        style = FontStyle.Strikeout
33        Dim tahoma As Font = New Font("Tahoma", 18, style)
34
35        graphicsObject.DrawString(arial.Name & " 12 point bold.", _
36           arial, brush, 10, 10)
37
38        graphicsObject.DrawString(timesNewRoman.Name & _
39           " 12 point plain.", timesNewRoman, brush, 10, 30)
40
41        graphicsObject.DrawString(courierNew.Name & _
42           " 16 point bold and italic.", courierNew, brush, 10, 54 )
43
44        graphicsObject.DrawString(tahoma.Name & _
45           " 18 point strikeout.", tahoma, brush, 10, 75)
46     End Sub ' OnPaint
47
48  End Class ' FrmFonts
```

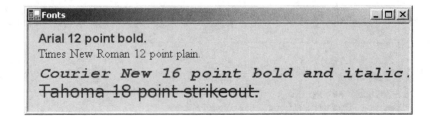

Fig. 13.9 **Font**s and **FontStyle**s. (Part 2 of 2.)

Programmers can define precise information about a font's *metrics* (or properties), such as *height*, *descent* (the amount that characters dip below the baseline), *ascent* (the amount that characters rise above the baseline) and *leading* (the difference between the ascent of one line and the descent of the previous line). Figure 13.10 illustrates these properties.

Class **FontFamily** defines characteristics common to a group of related fonts. Class **FontFamily** provides several methods used to determine the font metrics that are shared by members of a particular family. These methods are summarized in Fig. 13.11.

The program shown in Fig. 13.12 calls method **ToString** to display the metrics of two fonts. Line 21 creates **Font arial** and sets it to 12-point Arial font. Line 22 uses class **Font** property **FontFamily** to obtain object **arial**'s **FontFamily** object. Lines 30–31 call **ToString** to output the **String** representation of the font. Lines 33–47 then use methods of class **FontFamily** to return integers specifying the ascent, descent, height and leading of the font. Lines 50–68 repeat this process for font **sansSerif**, a **Font** object derived from the MS Sans Serif **FontFamily**.

Fig. 13.10 An illustration of font metrics.

Method	Description
GetCellAscent	Returns an **Integer** representing the ascent of a font as measured in design units.
GetCellDescent	Returns an **Integer** representing the descent of a font as measured in design units.
GetEmHeight	Returns an **Integer** representing the height of a font as measured in design units.
GetLineSpacing	Returns an **Integer** representing the distance between two consecutive lines of text as measured in design units.

Fig. 13.11 FontFamily methods that return font-metric information.

```
1   ' Fig. 13.12: UsingFontMetrics.vb
2   ' Displaying font metric information.
3
4   Imports System
5   Imports System.Drawing
6   Imports System.Drawing.Text
```

Fig. 13.12 FontFamily class used to obtain font-metric information. (Part 1 of 3.)

```vbnet
7
8   Public Class FrmFontMetrics
9      Inherits System.Windows.Forms.Form
10
11     ' Visual Studio .NET generated code
12
13     Protected Overrides Sub OnPaint( _
14        ByVal paintEvent As PaintEventArgs)
15
16        Dim graphicsObject As Graphics = paintEvent.Graphics
17        Dim brush As SolidBrush = New SolidBrush(Color.Red)
18        Dim pen As Pen = New Pen(brush, Convert.ToSingle(2.5))
19
20        ' Arial font metrics
21        Dim arial As Font = New Font("Arial", 12)
22        Dim family As FontFamily = arial.FontFamily
23        Dim sanSerif As Font = New Font("Microsoft Sans Serif", _
24           14, FontStyle.Italic)
25
26        pen.Color = brush.Color
27        brush.Color = Color.DarkBlue
28
29        ' display Arial font metrics
30        graphicsObject.DrawString("Current Font: " & arial.ToString, _
31           arial, brush, 10, 10)
32
33        graphicsObject.DrawString("Ascent: " & _
34           family.GetCellAscent(FontStyle.Regular), arial, brush, _
35           10, 30)
36
37        graphicsObject.DrawString("Descent: " & _
38           family.GetCellDescent(FontStyle.Regular), arial, brush, _
39           10, 50)
40
41        graphicsObject.DrawString("Height: " & _
42           family.GetEmHeight(FontStyle.Regular), _
43           arial, brush, 10, 70)
44
45        graphicsObject.DrawString("Leading: " & _
46           family.GetLineSpacing(FontStyle.Regular), arial, brush, _
47           10, 90)
48
49        ' display Sans Serif font metrics
50        family = sanSerif.FontFamily
51
52        graphicsObject.DrawString("Current Font: " & _
53           sanSerif.ToString(), sanSerif, brush, 10, 130)
54
55        graphicsObject.DrawString("Ascent: " & _
56           family.GetCellAscent(FontStyle.Italic), _
57           sanSerif, brush, 10, 150)
58
```

Fig. 13.12 FontFamily class used to obtain font-metric information. (Part 2 of 3.)

```
59            graphicsObject.DrawString("Descent: " & _
60              family.GetCellDescent(FontStyle.Italic), sanSerif, _
61              brush, 10, 170)
62
63            graphicsObject.DrawString("Height: " & family.GetEmHeight _
64              (FontStyle.Italic), sanSerif, brush, 10, 190)
65
66            graphicsObject.DrawString("Leading: " & _
67              family.GetLineSpacing(FontStyle.Italic), sanSerif, _
68              brush, 10, 210)
69      End Sub   ' OnPaint
70
71   End Class ' FrmFontMetrics
```

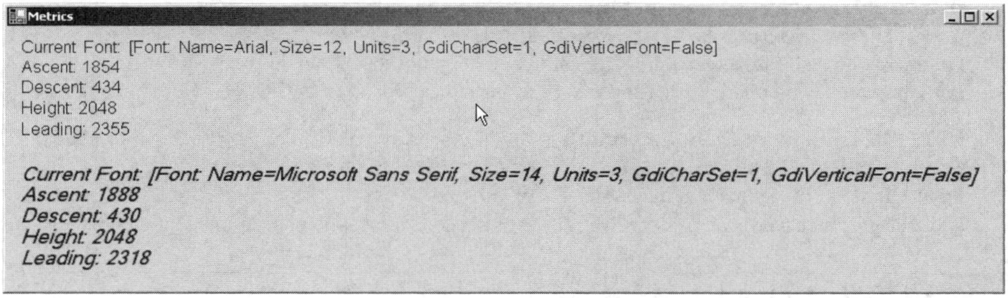

Fig. 13.12 FontFamily class used to obtain font-metric information. (Part 3 of 3.)

13.5 Drawing Lines, Rectangles and Ovals

This section presents a variety of **Graphics** methods for drawing lines, rectangles and ovals. Each of the drawing methods has several overloaded versions. When employing methods that draw shape outlines, we use versions that take a **Pen** and four **Integer**s; when employing methods that draw solid shapes, we use versions that take a **Brush** and four **Integer**s. In both instances, the first two **Integer** arguments represent the coordinates of the upper-left corner of the shape or its enclosing area, and the last two **Integer**s indicate the shape's width and height. Figure 13.13 summarizes the **Graphics** methods and their parameters.

Graphics Drawing Methods and Descriptions.

Note: Many of these methods are overloaded—consult the documentation for a full listing.

DrawLine(ByVal p As Pen, ByVal x1 As Integer, ByVal y1 As Integer, ByVal x2 As Integer, ByVal y2 As Integer)
Draws a line from (**x1**, **y1**) to (**x2**, **y2**). The **Pen** determines the color, style and width of the line.

Fig. 13.13 Graphics methods that draw lines, rectangles and ovals. (Part 1 of 2.)

Graphics Drawing Methods and Descriptions.

DrawRectangle(*ByVal* p *As* Pen, *ByVal* x *As* Integer, *ByVal* y *As* Integer, *ByVal* width *As* Integer, *ByVal* height *As* Integer)
Draws a rectangle of the specified width and height. The top-left corner of the rectangle is at point (**x**, **y**). The **Pen** determines the color, style, and border width of the rectangle.

FillRectangle(*ByVal* b *As* Brush, *ByVal* x *As* Integer, *ByVal* y *As* Integer, *ByVal* width *As* Integer, *ByVal* height *As* Integer)
Draws a solid rectangle of the specified width and height. The top-left corner of the rectangle is at point (**x**, **y**). The **Brush** determines the fill pattern inside the rectangle.

DrawEllipse(*ByVal* p *As* Pen, *ByVal* x *As* Integer, *ByVal* y *As* Integer, *ByVal* width *As* Integer, *ByVal* height *As* Integer)
Draws an ellipse inside a rectangle. The width and height of the rectangle are as specified, and its top-left corner is at point (**x**, **y**). The **Pen** determines the color, style and border width of the ellipse.

FillEllipse(*ByVal* b *As* Brush, *ByVal* x *As* Integer, *ByVal* y *As* Integer, *ByVal* width *As* Integer, *ByVal* height *As* Integer)
Draws a filled ellipse inside a rectangle. The width and height of the rectangle are as specified, and its top-left corner is at point (**x**, **y**). The **Brush** determines the pattern inside the ellipse.

Fig. 13.13 Graphics methods that draw lines, rectangles and ovals. (Part 2 of 2.)

The application in Fig. 13.14 draws lines, rectangles and ellipses. In this application, we also demonstrate methods that draw filled and unfilled shapes.

```
1   ' Fig. 13.14: LinesRectanglesOvals.vb
2   ' Demonstrating lines, rectangles, and ovals.
3
4   Public Class FrmDrawing
5      Inherits System.Windows.Forms.Form
6
7      ' Visual Studio .NET generated code
8
9      ' display ovals lines, and rectangles
10     Protected Overrides Sub OnPaint( _
11        ByVal paintEvent As PaintEventArgs)
12
13        ' get graphics object
14        Dim g As Graphics = paintEvent.Graphics
15        Dim brush As SolidBrush = New SolidBrush(Color.Blue)
16        Dim pen As Pen = New Pen(Color.AliceBlue)
17
18        ' create filled rectangle
19        g.FillRectangle(brush, 90, 30, 150, 90)
20
21        ' draw lines to connect rectangles
22        g.DrawLine(pen, 90, 30, 110, 40)
```

Fig. 13.14 Drawing lines, rectangles and ellipses. (Part 1 of 2.)

```
23            g.DrawLine(pen, 90, 120, 110, 130)
24            g.DrawLine(pen, 240, 30, 260, 40)
25            g.DrawLine(pen, 240, 120, 260, 130)
26
27            ' draw top rectangle
28            g.DrawRectangle(pen, 110, 40, 150, 90)
29
30            ' set brush to red
31            brush.Color = Color.Red
32
33            ' draw base Ellipse
34            g.FillEllipse(brush, 280, 75, 100, 50)
35
36            ' draw connecting lines
37            g.DrawLine(pen, 380, 55, 380, 100)
38            g.DrawLine(pen, 280, 55, 280, 100)
39
40            ' draw Ellipse outline
41            g.DrawEllipse(pen, 280, 30, 100, 50)
42      End Sub ' OnPaint
43
44   End Class ' FrmDrawing
```

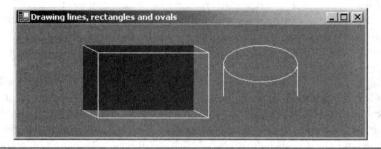

Fig. 13.14 Drawing lines, rectangles and ellipses. (Part 2 of 2.)

Methods *FillRectangle* and *DrawRectangle* (lines 19 and 28) draw rectangles on the screen. For each method, the first argument specifies the drawing object to use. The **DrawRectangle** method uses a **Pen** object, whereas the **FillRectangle** method uses a **Brush** object (in this case, an instance of **SolidBrush**—a class that derives from **Brush**). The next two arguments specify the coordinates of the upper-left corner of the *bounding rectangle*, which represents the area in which the rectangle will be drawn. The fourth and fifth arguments specify the rectangle's width and height. Method *DrawLine* (lines 22–25) takes a **Pen** and two pairs of **Integer**s, specifying the start and endpoint of the line. The method then draws a line, using the **Pen** object passed to it.

Methods *DrawEllipse* and *FillEllipse* each provide overloaded versions that take five arguments. In both methods, the first argument specifies the drawing object to use. The next two arguments specify the upper-left coordinates of the bounding rectangle representing the area in which the ellipse will be drawn. The last two arguments specify the bounding rectangle's width and height, respectively. Figure 13.15 depicts an ellipse bounded by a rectangle. The ellipse touches the midpoint of each of the four sides of the bounding rectangle. The bounding rectangle is not displayed on the screen.

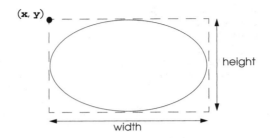

Fig. 13.15 Ellipse bounded by a rectangle.

13.6 Drawing Arcs

*Arc*s are portions of ellipses and are measured in degrees, beginning at a *starting angle* and continuing for a specified number of degrees (called the *arc angle*). An arc is said to *sweep* (traverse) its arc angle, beginning from its starting angle. Arcs that sweep in a clockwise direction are measured in positive degrees, whereas arcs that sweep in a counterclockwise direction are measured in negative degrees. Figure 13.16 depicts two arcs. Note that the left portion of the figure sweeps downward from zero degrees to approximately 110 degrees. Similarly, the arc in the right portion of the figure sweeps upward from zero degrees to approximately –110 degrees.

Notice the dashed boxes around the arcs in Fig. 13.16. We draw each arc as part of an oval (the rest of which is not visible). When drawing an oval, we specify the oval's dimensions in the form of a bounding rectangle that encloses the oval. The boxes in Fig. 13.16 correspond to these bounding rectangles. The **Graphics** methods used to draw arcs—**DrawArc**, **DrawPie** and **FillPie**—are summarized in Fig. 13.17.

The program in Fig. 13.18 draws six images (three arcs and three filled pie slices) to demonstrate the arc methods listed in Fig. 13.17. To illustrate the bounding rectangles that determine the sizes and locations of the arcs, the arcs are displayed inside red rectangles that have the same *x*-coordinates, *y*-coordinates, width and height arguments as those that define the bounding rectangles for the arcs.

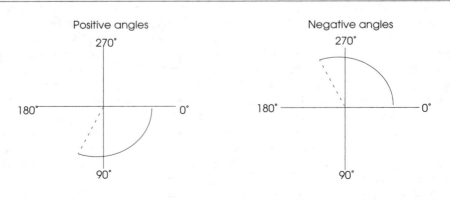

Fig. 13.16 Positive and negative arc angles.

Graphics Methods And Descriptions

Note: Many of these methods are overloaded—consult the documentation for a full listing.

DrawArc(*ByVal* **p** *As* **Pen,** *ByVal* **x** *As* **Integer,** *ByVal* **y** *As* **Integer,**
    ByVal **width** *As* **Integer,** *ByVal* **height** *As* **Integer,**
    ByVal **startAngle** *As* **Integer,** *ByVal* **sweepAngle** *As* **Integer)**
Draws an arc of an ellipse, beginning from angle **startAngle** (in degrees) and sweeping
sweepAngle degrees. The ellipse is defined by a bounding rectangle of width **w**, height **h** and
upper-left corner (**x,y**). The **Pen** determines the color, border width and style of the arc.

DrawPie(*ByVal* **p** *As* **Pen,** *ByVal* **x** *As* **Integer,** *ByVal* **y** *As* **Integer,**
    ByVal **width** *As* **Integer,** *ByVal* **height** *As* **Integer,**
    ByVal **startAngle** *As* **Integer,** *ByVal* **sweepAngle** *As* **Integer)**
Draws a pie section of an ellipse, beginning from angle **startAngle** (in degrees) and sweeping
sweepAngle degrees. The ellipse is defined by a bounding rectangle of width **w**, height **h** and
upper-left corner (**x,y**). The **Pen** determines the color, border width and style of the arc.

FillPie(*ByVal* **b** *As* **Brush,** *ByVal* **x** *As* **Integer,** *ByVal* **y** *As* **Integer,**
    ByVal **width** *As* **Integer,** *ByVal* **height** *As* **Integer,**
    ByVal **startAngle** *As* **Integer,** *ByVal* **sweepAngle** *As* **Integer)**
Functions similarly to **DrawPie**, except draws a solid arc (i.e., a sector). The **Brush** determines
the fill pattern for the solid arc.

Fig. 13.17 Graphics methods for drawing arcs.

```
1   ' Fig. 13.18: DrawArcs.vb
2   ' Drawing various arcs on a form.
3
4   Public Class FrmArcTest
5      Inherits System.Windows.Forms.Form
6
7      ' Visual Studio .NET generated code
8
9      Protected Overrides Sub OnPaint( _
10        ByVal paintEvent As PaintEventArgs)
11
12        ' get graphics object
13        Dim graphicsObject As Graphics = paintEvent.Graphics
14        Dim rectangle1 As Rectangle = New Rectangle(15, 35, 80, 80)
15        Dim brush1 As SolidBrush = New SolidBrush(Color.FireBrick)
16        Dim pen1 As Pen = New Pen(brush1, 1)
17        Dim brush2 As SolidBrush = New SolidBrush(Color.DarkBlue)
18        Dim pen2 As Pen = New Pen(brush2, 1)
19
20        ' start at 0 and sweep 360 degrees
21        graphicsObject.DrawRectangle(pen1, rectangle1)
22        graphicsObject.DrawArc(pen2, rectangle1, 0, 360)
23
```

Fig. 13.18 Arc method demonstration. (Part 1 of 2.)

```
24              ' start at 0 and sweep 110 degrees
25              rectangle1.Location = New Point(100, 35)
26              graphicsObject.DrawRectangle(pen1, rectangle1)
27              graphicsObject.DrawArc(pen2, rectangle1, 0, 110)
28
29              ' start at 0 and sweep -270 degrees
30              rectangle1.Location = New Point(185, 35)
31              graphicsObject.DrawRectangle(pen1, rectangle1)
32              graphicsObject.DrawArc(pen2, rectangle1, 0, -270)
33
34              ' start at 0 and sweep 360 degrees
35              rectangle1.Location = New Point(15, 120)
36              rectangle1.Size = New Size(80, 40)
37              graphicsObject.DrawRectangle(pen1, rectangle1)
38              graphicsObject.FillPie(brush2, rectangle1, 0, 360)
39
40              ' start at 270 and sweep -90 degrees
41              rectangle1.Location = New Point(100, 120)
42              graphicsObject.DrawRectangle(pen1, rectangle1)
43              graphicsObject.FillPie(brush2, rectangle1, 270, -90)
44
45              ' start at 0 and sweep -270 degrees
46              rectangle1.Location = New Point(185, 120)
47              graphicsObject.DrawRectangle(pen1, rectangle1)
48              graphicsObject.FillPie(brush2, rectangle1, 0, -270)
49          End Sub ' OnPaint
50
51      End Class ' FrmArcTest
```

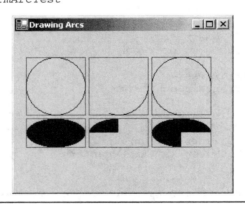

Fig. 13.18 Arc method demonstration. (Part 2 of 2.)

Lines 13–18 create the objects that we need to draw various arcs: **Graphics** objects, **Rectangle**s, **SolidBrush**es and **Pen**s. Lines 21–22 then draw a rectangle and an arc inside the rectangle. The arc sweeps 360 degrees, becoming a circle. Line 25 changes the location of the **Rectangle** by setting its **Location** property to a new **Point**. The **Point** constructor takes the *x*- and *y*-coordinates of the new point. The **Location** property determines the upper-left corner of the **Rectangle**. After drawing the rectangle, the program draws an arc that starts at 0 degrees and sweeps 110 degrees. Because angles in Visual Basic increase in a clockwise direction, the arc sweeps downward.

Lines 30–32 perform similar functions, except that the specified arc sweeps -270 degrees. The **Size** property of a **Rectangle** determines the arc's height and width. Line 36 sets the **Size** property to a new **Size** object, which changes the size of the rectangle.

The remainder of the program is similar to the portions described above, except that a **SolidBrush** is used with method **FillPie**. The resulting arcs, which are filled, can be seen in the bottom half of the screenshot Fig. 13.18.

13.7 Drawing Polygons and Polylines

Polygons are multisided shapes. There are several **Graphics** methods used to draw polygons: **DrawLines** draws a series of connected points, **DrawPolygon** draws a closed polygon and **FillPolygon** draws a solid polygon. These methods are described in Fig. 13.19. The program in Fig. 13.20 allows users to draw polygons and connected lines via the methods listed in Fig. 13.19.

Method	Description
DrawLines	Draws a series of connected lines. The coordinates of each point are specified in an array of **Point**s. If the last point is different from the first point, the figure is not closed.
DrawPolygon	Draws a polygon. The coordinates of each point are specified in an array of **Point** objects. This method draws a closed polygon, even if the last point is different from the first point.
FillPolygon	Draws a solid polygon. The coordinates of each point are specified in an array of **Points**. This method draws a closed polygon, even if the last point is different from the first point.

Fig. 13.19 Graphics methods for drawing polygons.

```
1    ' Fig. 13.20: DrawPolygons.vb
2    ' Demonstrating polygons.
3
4    Public Class FrmPolygon
5       Inherits System.Windows.Forms.Form
6
7       ' polygon type options
8       Friend WithEvents filledPolygonRadio As RadioButton
9       Friend WithEvents lineRadio As RadioButton
10      Friend WithEvents polygonRadio As RadioButton
11
12      ' command buttons
13      Friend WithEvents cmdClear As Button
14      Friend WithEvents cmdNewColor As Button
15
16      Friend WithEvents drawWindow As Panel
17      Friend WithEvents typeGroup As GroupBox
```

Fig. 13.20 Polygon drawing demonstration. (Part 1 of 4.)

```
18
19      ' Visual Studio .NET generated code
20
21      ' contains list of polygon points
22      Private mPoints As ArrayList = New ArrayList()
23
24      ' initialize default pen and brush
25      Dim mPen As Pen = New Pen(Color.DarkBlue)
26      Dim mBrush As SolidBrush = New SolidBrush(Color.DarkBlue)
27
28      ' draw panel mouse down event handler
29      Private Sub drawWindow_MouseDown(ByVal sender _
30         As Object, ByVal e As _
31         System.Windows.Forms.MouseEventArgs) _
32         Handles drawWindow.MouseDown
33
34         ' Add mouse position to vertex list
35         mPoints.Add(New Point(e.X, e.Y))
36         drawWindow.Invalidate() ' refresh panel
37      End Sub ' drawWindow_MouseDown
38
39      ' draw panel paint event handler
40      Private Sub drawWindow_Paint(ByVal sender As Object, _
41         ByVal e As System.Windows.Forms.PaintEventArgs) _
42         Handles drawWindow.Paint
43
44         ' get graphics object for panel
45         Dim graphicsObject As Graphics = e.Graphics
46
47         ' if arraylist has 2 or more points, display shape
48         If mPoints.Count > 1 Then
49
50            ' get array for use in drawing functions
51            Dim pointArray() As Point = _
52               mPoints.ToArray(mPoints(0).GetType())
53
54            If polygonRadio.Checked Then ' draw polygon
55               graphicsObject.DrawPolygon(mPen, pointArray)
56
57            ElseIf lineRadio.Checked Then ' draw lines
58               graphicsObject.DrawLines(mPen, pointArray)
59
60            ElseIf filledPolygonRadio.Checked Then ' draw filled
61               graphicsObject.FillPolygon(mBrush, pointArray)
62            End If
63
64         End If
65
66      End Sub ' drawWindow_Paint
67
68      ' handle cmdClear click event
69      Private Sub cmdClear_Click(ByVal sender As System.Object, _
70         ByVal e As System.EventArgs) Handles cmdClear.Click
```

Fig. 13.20 Polygon drawing demonstration. (Part 2 of 4.)

```
71
72          mPoints = New ArrayList() ' remove points
73
74          drawWindow.Invalidate() ' refresh panel
75       End Sub ' cmdClear_Click
76
77       ' handle polygon radio button CheckedChange event
78       Private Sub polygonRadio_CheckedChanged(ByVal sender As _
79          System.Object, ByVal e As System.EventArgs) _
80          Handles polygonRadio.CheckedChanged
81
82          drawWindow.Invalidate() ' refresh panel
83       End Sub ' polygonRadio_CheckedChanged
84
85       ' handle line radio button CheckChanged event
86       Private Sub lineRadio_CheckedChanged(ByVal sender As _
87          System.Object, ByVal e As System.EventArgs) _
88          Handles lineRadio.CheckedChanged
89
90          drawWindow.Invalidate() ' refresh panel
91       End Sub ' lineRadio_CheckedChanged
92
93       ' handle filled polygon radio button CheckChanged event
94       Private Sub filledPolygonRadio_CheckedChanged(ByVal sender _
95          As System.Object, ByVal e As System.EventArgs) _
96          Handles filledPolygonRadio.CheckedChanged
97
98          drawWindow.Invalidate() ' refresh panel
99       End Sub ' filledPolygonRadio_CheckedChanged
100
101      ' handle cmdNewColor click event
102      Private Sub cmdNewColor_Click(ByVal sender As _
103         System.Object, ByVal e As System.EventArgs) _
104         Handles cmdNewColor.Click
105
106         ' create new color dialog
107         Dim colorBox As ColorDialog = New ColorDialog()
108
109         ' show dialog and obtain result
110         Dim result As DialogResult = colorBox.ShowDialog()
111
112         ' return if user cancels
113         If result = DialogResult.Cancel Then
114            Return
115         End If
116
117         mPen.Color = colorBox.Color ' set pen to new color
118         mBrush.Color = colorBox.Color ' set brush
119         drawWindow.Invalidate() ' refresh panel
120      End Sub ' cmdNewColor_Click
121
122   End Class ' FrmPolygon
```

Fig. 13.20 Polygon drawing demonstration. (Part 3 of 4.)

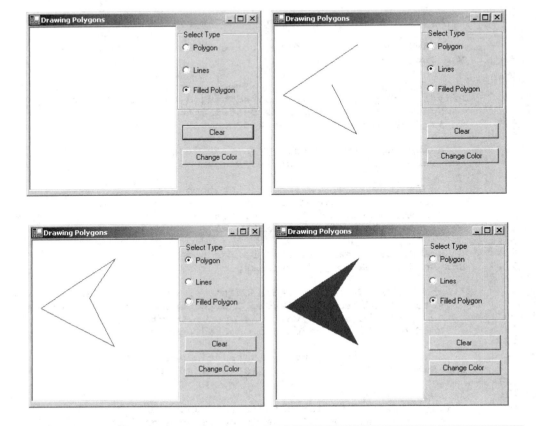

Fig. 13.20 Polygon drawing demonstration. (Part 4 of 4.)

To allow the user to specify a variable number of points, line 22 declares **ArrayList mPoints** as a container for our **Point** objects. Lines 25–26 declare the **Pen** and **Brush** used to color our shapes. The **MouseDown** event handler (lines 29–37) for **Panel draw-Window** stores mouse-click locations in the **mPoints ArrayList**. It then calls method **Invalidate** of **drawWindow** to ensure that the panel refreshes to accommodate the new point. Method **drawWindow_Paint** (lines 40–66) handles the **Panel's Paint** event. It obtains the panel's **Graphics** object (line 45) and, if the **ArrayList mPoints** contains two or more **Point**s, displays the polygon using the method that the user selected via the GUI radio buttons (lines 54–62). In lines 51–52, we extract an **Array** from the **ArrayList** via method **ToArray**. Method **ToArray** can take a single argument to determine the type of the returned array; we obtain the type from the first element in the **ArrayList**.

Method **cmdClear_Click** (lines 69–75) handles the **Clear** button's click event, creates an empty **ArrayList** (causing the old list to be erased) and refreshes the display. Lines 78–99 define the event handlers for the radio buttons' **CheckedChanged** event. Each method refreshes **Panel drawWindow** to ensure that the panel display reflects the selected drawing type. Event method **cmlNewColor_Click** (102–120) allows the user to select a new drawing color with a **ColorDialog**, using the same technique demonstrated in Fig. 13.7.

13.8 Advanced Graphics Capabilities

Visual Basic offers many additional graphics capabilities. The **Brush** hierarchy, for example, also includes *HatchBrush*, *LinearGradientBrush*, *PathGradientBrush* and *TextureBrush*.

The program in Fig. 13.21 demonstrates several graphics features, such as dashed lines, thick lines and the ability to fill shapes with patterns. These represent just a few of the additional capabilities of the **System.Drawing** namespace.

Lines 12–82 define the overridden **OnPaint** method for our form. Lines 19–21 create **LinearGradientBrush** (namespace **System.Drawing.Drawing2D**) object **brush**. A **LinearGradientBrush** enables users to draw with a color gradient. The **LinearGradientBrush** used in this example takes four arguments: A **Rectangle**, two **Color**s and a member of enumeration **LinearGradientMode**. In Visual Basic, all linear gradients are defined along a line that determines the gradient endpoint. This line can be specified either by starting and ending points or by the diagonal of a rectangle. The first argument, **Rectangle boundingRectangle**, specifies the defining line for **LinearGradientBrush brush**. This **Rectangle** argument represents the endpoints of the linear gradient—the upper-left corner is the starting point, and the bottom-right corner is the ending point. The second and third arguments specify the colors that the gradient will use. In this case, the color of the ellipse will gradually change from **Color.Blue** to **Color.Yellow**. The last argument, a type from the enumeration *LinearGradientMode*, specifies the linear gradient's direction. In our case, we use *LinearGradientMode.ForwardDiagonal*, which creates a gradient from the upper-left to the lower-right corner. We then use **Graphics** method **FillEllipse** in line 38 to draw an ellipse with **brush**; the color gradually changes from blue to yellow, as described above.

```
1    ' Fig. 13.21: DrawShapes.vb
2    ' Drawing various shapes on a form.
3
4    Imports System.Drawing.Drawing2D
5
6    Public Class FrmDrawShapes
7       Inherits System.Windows.Forms.Form
8
9       ' Visual Studio .NET generated code
10
11      ' draw various shapes on form
12      Protected Overrides Sub OnPaint(ByVal e As PaintEventArgs)
13
14         ' references to object we will use
15         Dim graphicsObject As Graphics = e.Graphics
16
17         ' ellipse rectangle and gradient brush
18         Dim drawArea1 As Rectangle = New Rectangle(5, 35, 30, 100)
```

Fig. 13.21 Shapes drawn on a form. (Part 1 of 3.)

```
19        Dim linearBrush As LinearGradientBrush = _
20           New LinearGradientBrush(drawArea1, Color.Blue, _
21           Color.Yellow, LinearGradientMode.ForwardDiagonal)
22
23        ' pen and location for red outline rectangle
24        Dim thickRedPen As Pen = New Pen(Color.Red, 10)
25        Dim drawArea2 As Rectangle = New Rectangle(80, 30, 65, 100)
26
27        ' bitmap texture
28        Dim textureBitmap As Bitmap = New Bitmap(10, 10)
29        Dim graphicsObject2 As Graphics = _
30           Graphics.FromImage(textureBitmap) ' get bitmap graphics
31
32        ' brush and pen used throughout program
33        Dim solidColorBrush As SolidBrush = _
34           New SolidBrush(Color.Red)
35        Dim coloredPen As Pen = New Pen(solidColorBrush)
36
37        ' draw ellipse filled with a blue-yellow gradient
38        graphicsObject.FillEllipse(linearBrush, 5, 30, 65, 100)
39
40        ' draw thick rectangle outline in red
41        graphicsObject.DrawRectangle(thickRedPen, drawArea2)
42
43        ' fill textureBitmap with yellow
44        solidColorBrush.Color = Color.Yellow
45        graphicsObject2.FillRectangle(solidColorBrush, 0, 0, 10, 10)
46
47        ' draw small black rectangle in textureBitmap
48        coloredPen.Color = Color.Black
49        graphicsObject2.DrawRectangle(coloredPen, 1, 1, 6, 6)
50
51        ' draw small blue rectangle in textureBitmap
52        solidColorBrush.Color = Color.Blue
53        graphicsObject2.FillRectangle(solidColorBrush, 1, 1, 3, 3)
54
55        ' draw small red square in textureBitmap
56        solidColorBrush.Color = Color.Red
57        graphicsObject2.FillRectangle(solidColorBrush, 4, 4, 3, 3)
58
59        ' create textured brush and display textured rectangle
60        Dim texturedBrush As TextureBrush = _
61           New TextureBrush(textureBitmap)
62
63        graphicsObject.FillRectangle( _
64           texturedBrush, 155, 30, 75, 100)
65
66        ' draw pie-shaped arc in white
67        coloredPen.Color = Color.White
68        coloredPen.Width = 6
69        graphicsObject.DrawPie( _
70           coloredPen, 240, 30, 75, 100, 0, 270)
71
```

Fig. 13.21 Shapes drawn on a form. (Part 2 of 3.)

```
72          ' draw lines in green and yellow
73          coloredPen.Color = Color.Green
74          coloredPen.Width = 5
75          graphicsObject.DrawLine(coloredPen, 395, 30, 320, 150)
76
77          ' draw a rounded, dashed yellow line
78          coloredPen.Color = Color.Yellow
79          coloredPen.DashCap = LineCap.Round
80          coloredPen.DashStyle = DashStyle.Dash
81          graphicsObject.DrawLine(coloredPen, 320, 30, 395, 150)
82      End Sub ' OnPaint
83
84  End Class ' FrmDrawShapes
```

Fig. 13.21 Shapes drawn on a form. (Part 3 of 3.)

In line 24, we create a **Pen** object **pen**. We pass to **pen**'s constructor **Color.Red** and **Integer** argument **10**, indicating that we want **pen** to draw red lines that are 10 pixels wide.

Line 28 creates a new *Bitmap* image, which initially is empty. Class **Bitmap** can produce images in color and gray scale; this particular **Bitmap** is 10 pixels wide and 10 pixels tall. Method *FromImage* (line 29–30) is a **Shared** member of class **Graphics** and retrieves the **Graphics** object associated with an **Image**, which may be used to draw on an image. Lines 44–53 draw on the **Bitmap** a pattern consisting of black, blue, red and yellow rectangles and lines. A **TextureBrush** is a brush that fills the interior of a shape with an image, rather than a solid color. In line 60–64, **TextureBrush** object **textureBrush** fills a rectangle with our **Bitmap**. The **TextureBrush** constructor version that we use takes as an argument an image that defines its texture.

Next, we draw a pie-shaped arc with a thick white line. Lines 67–70 set **pen**'s color to **White** and modify its width to be six pixels. We then draw the pie on the form by specifying the **Pen**, *x*-coordinate, *y*-coordinate, length and width of the bounding rectangle, start angle and sweep angle.

Finally, lines 79–80 make use of **System.Drawing.Drawing2D** enumerations *DashCap* and *DashStyle* to draw a diagonal dashed line. Line 79 sets the *DashCap* property of **pen** (not to be confused with the **DashCap** enumeration) to a member of the **DashCap** enumeration. The **DashCap** enumeration specifies the styles for the start and end of a dashed line. In this case, we want both ends of the dashed line to be rounded, so we use *DashCap.Round*. Line 80 sets the *DashStyle* property of **pen** (not to be confused with the **DashStyle** enumeration) to **DashStyle.Dash**, indicating that we want our line to consist entirely of dashes.

Our next example demonstrates the use of a *general path*. A general path is a shape constructed from straight lines and complex curves. An object of class **GraphicsPath** (**System.Drawing.Drawing2D** namespace) represents a general path. The **GraphicsPath** class provides functionality that enables the creation of complex shapes from vector-based primitive graphics objects. A **GraphicsPath** object consists of figures defined by simple shapes. The start point of each vector-graphics object (such as a line or arc) that is added to the path is connected by a straight line to the end point of the previous object. When called, the **CloseFigure** method attaches the final graphic object endpoint to the initial starting point for the current figure by a straight line then starts a new figure. Method **StartFigure** begins a new figure within the path without closing the previous figure.

The program of Fig. 13.22 draws general paths in the shape of five-pointed stars. Line 29 sets the origin of the **Graphics** object. The arguments to method **TranslateTransform** indicate that the origin should be translated to the coordinates (150, 150). Lines 20–23 define two **Integer** arrays, representing the *x*- and *y*-coordinates of the points in the star, and line 26 defines **GraphicsPath** object **star**. A **For** loop then creates lines to connect the points of the star and adds these lines to **star**. We use **GraphicsPath** method **AddLine** to append a line to the shape. The arguments of **AddLine** specify the coordinates for the line's endpoints; each new call to **AddLine** adds a line from the previous point to the current point. Line 38 uses **GraphicsPath** method *CloseFigure* to complete the shape.

```
1    ' Fig. 13.22: DrawStars.vb
2    ' Using paths to draw stars on a form.
3
4    Imports System.Drawing.Drawing2D
5
6    Public Class FrmDrawStars
7       Inherits System.Windows.Forms.Form
8
9       ' Visual Studio .NET generated code
10
11      ' create path and draw stars along it
12      Protected Overrides Sub OnPaint(ByVal e As PaintEventArgs)
13         Dim graphicsObject As Graphics = e.Graphics
14         Dim i As Integer
15         Dim random As Random = New Random()
16         Dim brush As SolidBrush = _
17            New SolidBrush(Color.DarkMagenta)
18
19         ' x and y points of path
20         Dim xPoints As Integer() = _
21            {55, 67, 109, 73, 83, 55, 27, 37, 1, 43}
22         Dim yPoints As Integer() = _
23            {0, 36, 36, 54, 96, 72, 96, 54, 36, 36}
24
25         ' create graphics path for star
26         Dim star As GraphicsPath = New GraphicsPath()
27
```

Fig. 13.22 Paths used to draw stars on a form. (Part 1 of 2.)

```
28              ' translate origin to (150, 150)
29              graphicsObject.TranslateTransform(150, 150)
30
31              ' create star from series of points
32              For i = 0 To 8 Step 2
33                 star.AddLine(xPoints(i), yPoints(i), _
34                    xPoints(i + 1), yPoints(i + 1))
35              Next
36
37              ' close shape
38              star.CloseFigure()
39
40              ' rotate origin and draw stars in random colors
41              For i = 1 To 18
42                 graphicsObject.RotateTransform(20)
43
44                 brush.Color = Color.FromArgb(random.Next(200, 255), _
45                    random.Next(255), random.Next(255), random.Next(255))
46
47                 graphicsObject.FillPath(brush, star)
48              Next
49
50           End Sub ' OnPaint
51
52        End Class ' FrmDrawStars
```

Fig. 13.22 Paths used to draw stars on a form. (Part 2 of 2.)

The **For** structure in lines 41–48 draws the **star** 18 times, rotating it around the origin. Line 42 uses **Graphics** method *RotateTransform* to move to the next position on the form; the argument specifies the rotation angle in degrees. **Graphics** method **FillPath** (line 47) then draws a filled version of the **star** with the **Brush** created on lines 44–45. The application determines the **SolidBrush**'s color randomly, using **Random** variable **random**'s method **Next**.

13.9 Introduction to Multimedia

Visual Basic offers many convenient ways to include images and animations in programs. People who entered the computing field decades ago used computers primarily to perform arithmetic calculations. As the discipline evolves, we are beginning to realize the importance of computers' data-manipulation capabilities. We are seeing a wide variety of exciting new three-dimensional applications. Multimedia programming is an entertaining and innovative field, but one that presents many challenges

Multimedia applications demand extraordinary computing power. Until recently, affordable computers with this amount of power were not available. However, today's ultrafast processors are making multimedia-based applications commonplace. As the market for multimedia explodes, users are purchasing faster processors, larger memories and wider communications bandwidths needed to support multimedia applications. This benefits the computer and communications industries, which provide the hardware, software and services fueling the multimedia revolution.

In the remaining sections of this chapter, we introduce the use and manipulation of images, as well as other multimedia features and capabilities. Section 13.10 discusses how to load, display and scale images; Section 13.11 demonstrates image animation; Section 13.12 presents the video capabilities of the Windows Media Player control; and Section 13.13 explores Microsoft Agent technology.

13.10 Loading, Displaying and Scaling Images

Visual Basic's multimedia capabilities include graphics, images, animations and video. Previous sections demonstrated Visual Basic's vector-graphics capabilities; this section concentrates on image manipulation. The Windows form that we create in Fig. 13.23 demonstrates the loading of an **Image** (**System.Drawing** namespace). The application allows users to enter a desired height and width for the **Image**, which then is displayed in the specified size.

```
1    ' Fig. 13.23: DisplayLogo.vb
2    ' Displaying and resizing an image.
3
4    Public Class FrmDisplayLogo
5       Inherits System.Windows.Forms.Form
6
7       ' width controls
8       Friend WithEvents txtWidth As TextBox
9       Friend WithEvents lblWidth As Label
10
11      ' height controls
12      Friend WithEvents lblHeight As Label
13      Friend WithEvents txtHeight As TextBox
14
15      Private mGraphicsObject As Graphics
16      Private mImage As Image
17
```

Fig. 13.23 Image resizing. (Part 1 of 3.)

```vbnet
18      ' sets member variables on form load
19      Private Sub FrmDisplayLogo_Load(ByVal sender As _
20         System.Object, ByVal e As System.EventArgs) _
21         Handles MyBase.Load
22
23         ' get Form's graphics object
24         mGraphicsObject = Me.CreateGraphics
25
26         ' load image
27         mImage = Image.FromFile("images/pyramid.png")
28
29      End Sub ' FrmDisplayLogo_Load
30
31      ' Visual Studio .NET generated code
32
33      Private Sub cmdSetButton_Click (ByVal sender As System.Object, _
34         ByVal e As System.EventArgs) Handles cmdSetButton.Click
35
36         ' get user input
37         Dim width As Integer = Convert.ToInt32(txtWidth.Text)
38         Dim height As Integer = Convert.ToInt32(txtHeight.Text)
39
40         ' if specified dimensions are too large display problem
41         If (width > 375 OrElse height > 225) Then
42            MessageBox.Show("Height or Width too large")
43
44            Return
45         End If
46         mGraphicsObject.Clear(Me.BackColor) ' clear Windows Form
47
48         ' draw image
49         mGraphicsObject.DrawImage(mImage, 5, 5, width, height)
50      End Sub ' cmdSetButton_Click
51
52   End Class ' FrmDisplayLogo
```

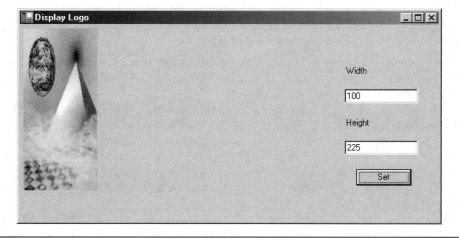

Fig. 13.23 Image resizing. (Part 2 of 3.)

Fig. 13.23 Image resizing. (Part 3 of 3.)

Line 16 declares **Image** reference **mImage**. The **Shared Image** method *From-File* then retrieves an image stored on disk and assigns it to **mImage** (line 27). Line 24 uses **Form** method *CreateGraphics* to create a **Graphics** object associated with the **Form**; we use this object to draw on the **Form**. Method **CreateGraphics** is inherited from class **Control**; all Windows controls, such as **Button**s and **Panel**s, also provide this method. When users click **Set**, the width and height parameters are validated to ensure that they are not too large. If the parameters are valid, line 46 calls **Graphics** method *Clear* to paint the entire **Form** in the current background color. Line 49 calls **Graphics** method *DrawImage* with the following parameters: the image to draw, the *x*-coordinate of the upper-left corner, the *y*-coordinate of the upper-left corner, the width of the image and the height of the image. If the width and height do not correspond to the image's original dimensions, the image is scaled to fit the new specifications.

13.11 Animating a Series of Images

The next example animates a series of images stored in an array. The application uses the same techniques to load and display **Image**s as those illustrated in Fig. 13.23. The images were created with Adobe Photoshop.

The animation in Fig. 13.24 uses a **PictureBox**, which contains the images that we animate. We use a **Timer** to cycle through the images, causing a new image to display every 50 milliseconds. Variable **count** keeps track of the current image number and increases by one every time we display a new image. The array includes 30 images (numbered 0–29); when the application reaches image 29, it returns to image 0. The 30 images were prepared in advance with a graphics software package and placed in the **images** folder inside the **bin/Debug** directory of the project.

Lines 19–22 load each of 30 images and place them in an *ArrayList*. *ArrayList* method *Add* allows us to add objects to the **ArrayList**; we use this method in lines 20–21 to add each **Image**. Line 25 places the first image in the **PictureBox**, using the

ArrayList indexer. Line 28 modifies the size of the **PictureBox** so that it is equal to the size of the **Image** it is displaying. The event handler for **timer**'s **Tick** event (line 38–46) then displays the next image from the **ArrayList**.

```
1   ' Fig. 13.24: LogoAnimator.vb
2   ' Program that animates a series of images.
3
4   Public Class FrmLogoAnimator
5      Inherits System.Windows.Forms.Form
6
7      Private mImages As ArrayList = New ArrayList()
8      Private mCount As Integer = 1
9
10     Public Sub New()
11        MyBase.New()
12
13        ' This call is required by Windows Form Designer.
14        InitializeComponent()
15
16        ' load all images
17        Dim i As Integer
18
19        For i = 0 To 29
20           mImages.Add(Image.FromFile("images/deitel" & i _
21              & ".gif"))
22        Next
23
24        ' load first image
25        logoPictureBox.Image = CType(mImages(0), Image)
26
27        ' set PictureBox to be same size as Image
28        logoPictureBox.Size = logoPictureBox.Image.Size
29     End Sub ' New
30
31     Friend WithEvents timer As System.Windows.Forms.Timer
32
33     Friend WithEvents logoPictureBox As _
34        System.Windows.Forms.PictureBox
35
36     ' Visual Studio .NET generated code
37
38     Private Sub timer_Tick(ByVal sender As System.Object, _
39        ByVal e As System.EventArgs) Handles timer.tick
40
41        ' increment counter
42        mCount = (mCount + 1) Mod 30
43
44        ' load next image
45        logoPictureBox.Image = CType(mImages(mCount), Image)
46     End Sub ' Timer_Tick
47
48  End Class ' FrmLogoAnimator
```

Fig. 13.24 Animation of a series of images. (Part 1 of 2.)

Fig. 13.24 Animation of a series of images. (Part 2 of 2.)

Performance Tip 13.2

It is more efficient to load an animation's frames as one image than to load each image separately. (A painting program, such as Adobe Photoshop®, Jasc® or Paint Shop Pro™, can be used to combine the animation's frames into one image.) If the images are being loaded separately from the Web, each loaded image requires a separate connection to the site on which the images are stored; this process can result in poor performance.

Performance Tip 13.3

Loading animation frames can cause program delays, because the program waits for all frames to load before displaying them.

The following chess example demonstrates the capabilities of GDI+ as they pertain to a chess-game application. These include techniques for two-dimensional *collision detection*, the selection of single frames from a multi-frame image and *regional invalidation* (refreshing only the required parts of the screen) to increase performance. Two-dimensional collision detection is the detection of an overlap between two shapes. In the next example, we demonstrate the simplest form of collision detection, which determines whether a point (the mouse-click location) is contained within a rectangle (a chess-piece image).

Class **CChessPiece** (Fig. 13.25) is a container class for the individual chess pieces. Lines 7–14 define a public enumeration of constants that identify each chess-piece type. The constants also serve to identify the location of each piece in the chess-piece image file. **Rectangle** object **mLocationRectangle** (lines 20–21) identifies the image location on the chess board. The **x** and **y** properties of the rectangle are assigned in the **CChessPiece** constructor, and all chess-piece images have heights and widths of **75**.

```
1    ' Fig. 13.25 : Chesspiece.vb
2    ' Storage class for chess piece attributes.
3
4    Public Class CChessPiece
5
6        ' define chess-piece type constants
7        Public Enum Types
8            KING
9            QUEEN
10           BISHOP
11           KNIGHT
12           ROOK
```

Fig. 13.25 Container class for chess pieces. (Part 1 of 2.)

```
13          PAWN
14      End Enum
15
16      Private mCurrentType As Integer ' this object's type
17      Private mPieceImage As Bitmap ' this object's image
18
19      ' default display location
20      Private mLocationRectangle As Rectangle = _
21         New Rectangle(0, 0, 75, 75)
22
23      ' construct piece
24      Public Sub New(ByVal type As Integer, _
25         ByVal xLocation As Integer, ByVal yLocation As Integer, _
26         ByVal sourceImage As Bitmap)
27
28         mCurrentType = type ' set current type
29         mLocationRectangle.X = xLocation ' set current x location
30         mLocationRectangle.Y = yLocation ' set current y location
31
32          ' obtain pieceImage from section of sourceImage
33          mPieceImage = sourceImage.Clone(New Rectangle(type * 75, _
34             0, 75, 75), Drawing.Imaging.PixelFormat.DontCare)
35      End Sub ' constructor
36
37      ' draw this piece
38      Public Sub Draw(ByVal graphicsObect As Graphics)
39         graphicsObect.DrawImage(mPieceImage, mLocationRectangle)
40      End Sub ' Draw
41
42      ' obtain this piece's location rectangle
43      Public Readonly Property LocationRectangle As Rectangle
44         Get
45             Return mLocationRectangle
46         End Get
47      End Property ' LocationRectangle
48
49      ' set this piece's location
50      Public Sub SetLocation(ByVal xLocation As Integer, _
51         ByVal yLocation As Integer)
52
53         mLocationRectangle.X = xLocation
54         mLocationRectangle.Y = yLocation
55      End Sub ' SetLocation
56
57   End Class ' CChesspiece
```

Fig. 13.25 Container class for chess pieces. (Part 2 of 2.)

The **CChessPiece** constructor (lines 24–35) requires that the calling class define a chess-piece type, its **x** and **y** location and the **Bitmap** containing all chess-piece images. Rather than loading the chess-piece image within the class, we allow the calling class to pass the image. This avoids the image-loading overhead for each piece. It also increases the flexibility of the class by allowing the user to change images; for example, in this case, we use the class for both black and white chess-piece images. Lines 33–34 extract a subimage that contains only the current piece's bitmap data. Our chess-piece images are defined in a specific manner: One image contains six chess-piece images, each defined within a 75-pixel block, resulting in a total image size of 450-by-75. We obtain a single image via **Bitmap**'s **Clone** method, which allows us to specify a rectangle image location and the desired pixel format. The location is a 75-by-75 pixel block with its upper-left corner **x** equal to **75 * type** and the corresponding **y** equal to **0**. For the pixel format, we specify constant **DontCare**, causing the format to remain unchanged.

Method **Draw** (lines 38–40) causes the **CChessPiece** to draw **mPieceImage** in **mLocationRectangle** on the passed **Graphics** object. **Readonly Property LocationRectangle** returns the object **mLocationRectangle** for use in collision detection, and **SetLocation** allows the calling class to specify a new piece location.

Class **FrmChessSurface** (Fig. 13.26) defines the game and graphics code for our chess game. Lines 20–30 define class-scope variables that are required by the program. **ArrayList mChessTile** (line 20) stores the board tile images; it contains four images: Two light tiles and two dark tiles (to increase board variety). **ArrayList mChessPieces** (line 23) stores all active **CChessPiece** objects, and **Integer mSelectedIndex** (line 26) identifies the index in **mChessPieces** of the currently selected piece. The **mBoard** (line 27) is an 8-by-8, two-dimensional **Integer** array corresponding to the squares of a Chess board. Each board element is an integer from 0 to 3 that corresponds to an index in **mChessTile** and is used to specify the Chess-board square image. **Integer TILESIZE** (line 30) is a constant defining the size of each tile in pixels.

```
1    ' Fig. 13.26: ChessGame.vb
2    ' Chess Game graphics code.
3
4    Imports System.Drawing.Drawing2D
5
6    Public Class FrmChessSurface
7        Inherits System.Windows.Forms.Form
8
9        ' display box
10       Friend WithEvents pieceBox As PictureBox
11
12       ' game menu
13       Friend WithEvents gameMenu As MainMenu
14       Friend WithEvents gameItem As MenuItem
15       Friend WithEvents newGame As MenuItem
16
17       ' Visual Studio .NET generated code
18
19       ' ArrayList for board tile images
20       Dim mChessTile As ArrayList = New ArrayList()
21
22       ' ArrayList for chess pieces
23       Dim mChessPieces As ArrayList = New ArrayList()
24
25       ' define index for selected piece
26       Dim mSelectedIndex As Integer = -1
27       Dim mBoard As Integer(,) = New Integer(7,7) {} ' board array
```

Fig. 13.26 Chess-game code. (Part 1 of 9.)

```
28
29       ' define chess tile size in pixels
30       Private Const TILESIZE As Integer = 75
31
32       ' load tile bitmaps and reset game
33       Private Sub FrmChessSurface_Load(ByVal sender _
34          As System.Object, ByVal e As System.EventArgs) _
35          Handles MyBase.Load
36
37          ' load chess board tiles
38          mChessTile.Add(Bitmap.FromFile("lightTile1.png"))
39          mChessTile.Add(Bitmap.FromFile("lightTile2.png"))
40          mChessTile.Add(Bitmap.FromFile("darkTile1.png"))
41          mChessTile.Add(Bitmap.FromFile("darkTile2.png"))
42
43          ResetBoard() ' initialize board
44          Invalidate() ' refresh form
45       End Sub ' FrmChessSurface_Load
46
47       ' initialize pieces to start positions and rebuild board
48       Private Sub ResetBoard()
49          Dim column As Integer = 0
50          Dim row As Integer = 0
51          Dim current As Integer
52          Dim piece As CChessPiece
53          Dim random As Random = New Random()
54          Dim light As Boolean = False
55          Dim type As Integer
56
57          ' ensure empty arraylist
58          mChessPieces = New ArrayList()
59
60          ' load whitepieces image
61          Dim whitePieces As Bitmap = _
62             Bitmap.FromFile("whitePieces.png")
63
64          ' load blackpieces image
65          Dim blackPieces As Bitmap = _
66             Bitmap.FromFile("blackPieces.png")
67
68          ' set whitepieces drawn first
69          Dim selected As Bitmap = whitePieces
70
71          ' traverse board rows in outer loop
72          For row = 0 To mBoard.GetUpperBound(0)
73
74             ' if at bottom rows, set to black piece images
75             If row > 5 Then
76                selected = blackPieces
77             End If
78
```

Fig. 13.26 Chess-game code. (Part 2 of 9.)

```
79              ' traverse board columns in inner loop
80              For column = 0 To mBoard.GetUpperBound(1)
81
82                  ' if first or last row, organize pieces
83                  If (row = 0 OrElse row = 7) Then
84
85                      Select Case column
86
87                          Case 0, 7 ' set current piece to rook
88                              current = CChessPiece.Types.ROOK
89
90                          Case 1, 6 ' set current piece to knight
91                              current = CChessPiece.Types.KNIGHT
92
93                          Case 2, 5 ' set current piece to bishop
94                              current = CChessPiece.Types.BISHOP
95
96                          Case 3 ' set current piece to king
97                              current = CChessPiece.Types.KING
98
99                          Case 4 ' set current piece to queen
100                             current = CChessPiece.Types.QUEEN
101                     End Select
102
103                     ' create current piece at start position
104                     piece = New CChessPiece(current, _
105                         column * TILESIZE, row * TILESIZE, selected)
106
107                     ' add piece to ArrayList
108                     mChessPieces.Add(piece)
109                 End If
110
111                 ' if second or seventh row, organize pawns
112                 If (row = 1 OrElse row = 6) Then
113                     piece = New CChessPiece(CChessPiece.Types.PAWN, _
114                         column * TILESIZE, row * TILESIZE, selected)
115
116                     mChessPieces.Add(piece)
117                 End If
118
119                 ' determine board piece type
120                 type = random.Next(0, 2)
121
122                 If light Then ' set light tile
123                     mBoard(row, column) = type
124                     light = False
125                 Else ' set dark tile
126                     mBoard(row, column) = type + 2
127                     light = True
128                 End If
129
130             Next ' next column
131
```

Fig. 13.26 Chess-game code. (Part 3 of 9.)

```
132                ' account for new row tile color switch
133                light = Not light
134           Next ' next row
135
136    End Sub ' ResetBoard
137
138    ' display board in form OnPaint event
139    Protected Overrides Sub OnPaint(ByVal paintEvent _
140       As PaintEventArgs)
141
142       ' obtain graphics object
143       Dim graphicsObject As Graphics = paintEvent.Graphics
144       Dim row, column As Integer
145
146       For row = 0 To mBoard.GetUpperBound(0)
147
148          For column = 0 To mBoard.GetUpperBound(1)
149
150             ' draw image specified in board array
151             graphicsObject.DrawImage( _
152                CType(mChessTile(mBoard(row, column)), _
153                Image), New Point(TILESIZE * column, _
154                TILESIZE * row))
155          Next
156
157       Next
158
159    End Sub ' OnPaint
160
161    ' return index of piece that intersects point
162    ' optionally exclude a value
163    Private Function CheckBounds(ByVal point As Point, _
164       Optional ByVal exclude As Integer = -1) As Integer
165
166       Dim rectangle As Rectangle ' current bounding rectangle
167       Dim i As Integer
168
169       For i = 0 To mChessPieces.Count - 1
170
171          ' get piece rectangle
172          rectangle = Getpiece(i).LocationRectangle()
173
174          ' check if rectangle contains point
175          If (rectangle.Contains(point) AndAlso i <> exclude) Then
176             Return i
177          End If
178
179       Next
180
181       Return -1
182    End Function ' CheckBounds
183
```

Fig. 13.26 Chess-game code. (Part 4 of 9.)

```
184      ' handle pieceBox paint event
185      Private Sub pieceBox_Paint(ByVal sender As System.Object, _
186         ByVal e As System.Windows.Forms.PaintEventArgs) _
187         Handles pieceBox.Paint
188
189         Dim i As Integer
190
191         ' draw all pieces
192         For i = 0 To mChessPieces.Count - 1
193            Getpiece(i).Draw(e.Graphics)
194         Next
195
196      End Sub ' pieceBox_Paint
197
198      ' on MouseDown event, select chess piece
199      Private Sub pieceBox_MouseDown(ByVal sender As System.Object, _
200         ByVal e As System.Windows.Forms.MouseEventArgs) _
201         Handles pieceBox.MouseDown
202
203         ' determine selected piece
204         mSelectedIndex = CheckBounds(New Point(e.X, e.Y))
205      End Sub ' pieceBox_MouseDown
206
207      ' if piece is selected, move it
208      Private Sub pieceBox_MouseMove(ByVal sender As System.Object, _
209         ByVal e As System.Windows.Forms.MouseEventArgs) _
210         Handles pieceBox.MouseMove
211
212         If mSelectedIndex > -1 Then
213
214            Dim region As Rectangle = New Rectangle(e.X - _
215               TILESIZE * 2, e.Y - TILESIZE * 2, TILESIZE * 4, _
216               TILESIZE * 4)
217
218            ' set piece center to mouse
219            Getpiece(mSelectedIndex).SetLocation(e.X - _
220               TILESIZE / 2, e.Y - TILESIZE / 2)
221
222            ' refresh immediate area
223            pieceBox.Invalidate(region)
224         End If
225
226      End Sub ' pieceBox_MouseMove
227
228      ' on mouse up, deselect chess piece and remove taken piece
229      Private Sub pieceBox_MouseUp(ByVal sender As _
230         System.Object, ByVal e As _
231         System.Windows.Forms.MouseEventArgs) _
232         Handles pieceBox.MouseUp
233
234         Dim remove As Integer = -1
235
```

Fig. 13.26 Chess-game code. (Part 5 of 9.)

```
236         If mSelectedIndex > -1 Then ' if chess piece was selected
237
238             Dim current As Point = New Point(e.X, e.Y)
239             Dim newPoint As Point = New Point(current.X - _
240                 current.X Mod TILESIZE, current.Y - _
241                 current.Y Mod TILESIZE)
242
243             ' check bounds with point, exclude selected piece
244             remove = CheckBounds(current, mSelectedIndex)
245
246             ' snap piece into center of closest square
247             Getpiece(mSelectedIndex).SetLocation(newPoint.X, _
248                 newPoint.Y)
249
250             mSelectedIndex = -1 ' deselect piece
251
252             ' remove taken piece
253             If remove > -1 Then
254                 mChessPieces.RemoveAt(remove)
255             End If
256
257         End If
258
259         ' refresh pieceBox to ensure artifact removal
260         pieceBox.Invalidate()
261     End Sub ' pieceBox_MouseUp
262
263     ' helper function to convert ArrayList object as CChesspiece
264     Private Function Getpiece(ByVal i As Integer) _
265         As CChessPiece
266
267         Return CType(mChessPieces(i), CChessPiece)
268     End Function ' Getpiece
269
270     ' handle NewGame menu option click
271     Private Sub NewGame_Click(ByVal sender As Object, _
272         ByVal e As System.EventArgs) Handles NewGame.Click
273
274         ResetBoard() ' re-initialize board
275         Invalidate() ' refresh form
276     End Sub ' NewGame_Click
277
278 End Class ' FrmChessSurface
```

Fig. 13.26 Chess-game code. (Part 6 of 9.)

The chess game GUI consists of **Form FrmChessSurface**, the area in which we draw the tiles; **PictureBox pieceBox**, the window in which we draw the pieces (note that **pieceBox** background color is set to **"transparent"**); and a **Menu** that allows the user to begin a new game. Although the pieces and tiles could have been drawn on the same form, doing so would decrease performance. We would be forced to refresh the board as well as the pieces every time we refreshed the control.

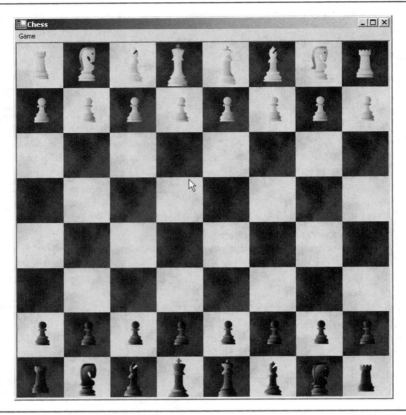

Fig. 13.26 Chess-game code. (Part 7 of 9.)

The **FrmChessSurface Load** event (lines 33–45) loads each tile image into **mChessTile**. It then calls method **ResetBoard** to refresh the **Form** and begin the game. Method **ResetBoard** (lines 48–136) assigns **mChessPieces** to a new **Array-List**, loading images for both the black and white chess-piece sets, and creates **Bitmap selected** to define the currently selected **Bitmap** set. Lines 72–134 loop through 64 positions on the chess board, setting the tile color and piece for each tile. Lines 75–77 cause the currently selected image to switch to the **blackPieces** after the fifth row. If the row counter is on the first or last row, lines 83–109 add a new piece to **mChessPieces**. The type of the piece is based on the current column we are initializing. Pieces in chess are positioned in the following order, from left to right: Rook, knight, bishop, queen, king, bishop, knight and rook. Lines 112–117 add a new pawn at the current location if the current **row** is second or seventh.

A chess board is defined by alternating light and dark tiles across a row in a pattern where the color that starts each row is equal to the color of the last tile of the previous row. Lines 122–128 assign the current board-tile color as an index in the **mBoard** array. Based on the alternating value of **Boolean** variable **light** and the results of the random operation on line 120, **0** and **1** are light tiles, whereas **2** and **3** are dark tiles. Line 133 inverts the value of **light** at the end of each row to maintain the staggered effect of a chess board.

Fig. 13.26 Chess-game code. (Part 8 of 9.)

Method **OnPaint** (lines 139–159) overrides class **Form**'s **OnPaint** method and draws the tiles according to their values in the board array. Method **pieceBox_Paint**, which handles the **pieceBox PictureBox paint** event, iterates through each element of the **mChessPiece ArrayList** and calls its **Draw** method.

The **MouseDown** event handler (lines 199–205) calls method **CheckBounds** with the location of the user's click to determine whether the user selected a piece. **Check-Bounds** returns an integer locating a collision from a given point.

The **MouseMove** event handler (lines 208–226) moves the currently selected piece with the mouse. Lines 219–220 set the selected piece location to the mouse cursor position, adjusting the location by half a tile to center the image on the mouse. Lines 214–216 define and refresh a region of the **PictureBox** that spans two tiles in every direction from the mouse. As mentioned earlier in the chapter, the **Invalidate** method is slow. This means that the **MouseMove** event handler might be called again several times before the **Inval-idate** method completes. If a user working on a slow computer moves the mouse quickly, the application could leave behind *artifacts*. An artifact is any unintended visual abnormality in a graphical program. By causing the program to refresh a two-square rectangle, which should suffice in most cases, we achieve a significant performance enhancement over an entire component refresh during each **MouseMove** event.

Fig. 13.26 Chess-game code. (Part 9 of 9.)

Lines 229–261 define the **MouseUp** event handler. If a piece has been selected, lines 236–257 determine the index in **mChessPieces** of any piece collision, remove the collided piece, snap (align) the current piece into a valid location and deselect the piece. We check for piece collisions to allow the chess piece to "take" other chess pieces. Line 244 checks whether any piece (excluding the currently selected piece) is beneath the current mouse location. If a collision is detected, the returned piece index is assigned to **Integer remove**. Lines 247–248 determine the closest valid chess tile and "snap" the selected piece to that location. If **remove** contains a positive value **mChessPieces**, line 254 removes it from the **mChessPieces ArrayList**. Finally, the entire **PictureBox** is **Invalidate**d in line 260 to display the new piece location and remove any artifacts created during the move.

Method **CheckBounds** (lines 163–182) is a collision-detection helper method; it iterates through the **mChessPieces ArrayList** and returns the index of any piece rectangle containing the point value passed to the method (the mouse location, in this example). Method **CheckBounds** optionally can exclude a single piece index (to ignore the selected index in the **MouseUp** event handler, in this example).

Lines 264–268 define helper function **GetPiece**, which simplifies the conversion from **Object**s in the **ArrayList mChessPieces** to **CChessPiece** types. Method

NewGame_Click handles the **NewGame** menu item click event, calls **RefreshBoard** to reset the game and **Invalidate**s the entire form.

13.12 Windows Media Player

The Windows Media Player control enables an application to play video and sound in many multimedia formats. These include MPEG (Motion Pictures Experts Group) audio and video, AVI (audio–video interleave) video, WAV (Windows wave-file format) audio and MIDI (Musical Instrument Digital Interface) audio. Users can find preexisting audio and video on the Internet, or they can create their own files using available sound and graphics packages.

The application in Fig. 13.27 demonstrates the Windows Media Player control, which enables users to play multimedia files. To use the Windows Media Player control, programmers must add the control to the **Toolbox**. This is accomplished by first selecting **Customize Toolbox** from the **Tool** menu to display the **Customize Toolbox** dialog box. In the dialog box, scroll down and select the option **Windows Media Player**. Then, click the **OK** button to dismiss the dialog box. The icon for the Windows Media Player control now should appear at the bottom of the **Toolbox**.

```vb
1    ' Fig. 13.27: MediaPlayerTest.vb
2    ' Demonstrates the Windows Media Player control
3
4    Public Class FrmMediaPlayer
5       Inherits System.Windows.Forms.Form
6
7       ' action menus
8       Friend WithEvents applicationMenu As MainMenu
9       Friend WithEvents fileItem As MenuItem
10      Friend WithEvents openItem As MenuItem
11      Friend WithEvents exitItem As MenuItem
12      Friend WithEvents aboutItem As MenuItem
13      Friend WithEvents aboutMessageItem As MenuItem
14
15      ' media player control
16      Friend WithEvents player As AxMediaPlayer.AxMediaPlayer
17      Friend WithEvents openMediaFileDialog As OpenFileDialog
18
19      ' Visual Studio .NET generated code
20
21      ' open new media file in Windows Media Player
22      Private Sub openItem_Click(ByVal sender As System.Object, _
23         ByVal e As System.EventArgs) Handles openItem.Click
24
25         openMediaFileDialog.ShowDialog()
26
27         player.FileName = openMediaFileDialog.FileName
28
29         ' adjust the size of the Media Player control and the
30         ' Form according to the size of the image
31         player.Size = New Size( _
32            player.ImageSourceWidth, player.ImageSourceHeight)
```

Fig. 13.27 Windows Media Player demonstration. (Part 1 of 2.)

```
33
34          Me.Size = New Size(player.Size.Width + 20, _
35              player.Size.Height + 60)
36      End Sub ' openItem_Click
37
38      ' exit application
39      Private Sub exitItem_Click(ByVal sender As System.Object, _
40          ByVal e As System.EventArgs) Handles exitItem.Click
41
42          Application.Exit()
43      End Sub ' exitItem_Click
44
45      ' show the About box for Windows Media Player
46      Private Sub aboutMessageItem_Click(ByVal sender As _
47          System.Object, ByVal e As System.EventArgs) _
48          Handles aboutMessageItem.Click
49
50          player.AboutBox()
51      End Sub ' aboutMessageItem_Click
52
53  End Class ' FrmMediaPlayer
```

Fig. 13.27 Windows Media Player demonstration. (Part 2 of 2.)

The Windows Media Player control provides several buttons that allow the user to play the current file, pause, stop, play the previous file, rewind, forward and play the next file. The control also includes a volume control and trackbars to select a specific position in the media file.

The application provides a **MainMenu**, which includes **File** and **About** menus. The **File** menu contains the **Open** and **Exit** menu items; the **About** menu contains the **About Windows Media Player** menu item.

When a user chooses **Open** from the **File** menu, the **openMenuItem_Click** event handler (lines 22–36) executes. An **OpenFileDialog** box displays (line 25), allowing the user to select a file. The program then sets the **FileName** property of the player (the Windows Media Player control object of type **AxMediaPlayer**) to the name of the file chosen by the user. The **FileName** property specifies the file that Windows Media Player currently is using. Lines 31–35 adjust the size of **player** and the application to reflect the size of the media contained in the file.

The event handler that executes when the user selects **Exit** from the **File** menu (lines 39–43) simply calls **Application.Exit** to terminate the application. The event handler that executes when the user chooses **About Windows Media Player** from the **About** menu (lines 46–51) calls the **AboutBox** method of the player. **AboutBox** simply displays a preset message box containing information about Windows Media Player.

13.13 Microsoft Agent

Microsoft Agent is a technology used to add *interactive animated characters* to Windows applications or Web pages. Interactivity is the key function of Microsoft Agent technology: Microsoft Agent characters can speak and respond to user input via speech recognition and synthesis. Microsoft employs its Agent technology in applications such as Word, Excel and PowerPoint. Agents in these programs aid users in finding answers to questions and in understanding how the applications function.

The Microsoft Agent control provides programmers with access to four predefined characters—*Genie* (a genie), *Merlin* (a wizard), *Peedy* (a parrot) and *Robby* (a robot). Each character has a unique set of animations that programmers can use in their applications to illustrate different points and functions. For instance, the Peedy character-animation set includes different flying animations, which the programmer might use to move Peedy on the screen. Microsoft provides basic information on Agent technology at its Web site:

> **www.microsoft.com/msagent**

Microsoft Agent technology enables users to interact with applications and Web pages through speech, the most natural form of human communication. When the user speaks into a microphone, the control uses a *speech recognition engine,* an application that translates vocal sound input from a microphone into language that the computer understands. The Microsoft Agent control also uses a *text-to-speech engine*, which generates characters' spoken responses. A text-to-speech engine is an application that translates typed words into audio sound that users hear through headphones or speakers connected to a computer. Microsoft provides speech recognition and text-to-speech engines for several languages at its Web site:

> **www.microsoft.com/products/msagent/downloads.htm**

Programmers can even create their own animated characters with the help of the *Microsoft Agent Character Editor* and the *Microsoft Linguistic Sound Editing Tool*. These products are available free for download from:

www.microsoft.com/products/msagent/devdownloads.htm

This section introduces the basic capabilities of the Microsoft Agent control. For complete details on downloading this control, visit:

www.microsoft.com/products/msagent/downloads.htm

The following example, Peedy's Pizza Palace, was developed by Microsoft to illustrate the capabilities of the Microsoft Agent control. Peedy's Pizza Palace is an online pizza shop where users can place their orders via voice input. The Peedy character interacts with users by helping them choose toppings and then calculating the totals for their orders.

Readers can view this example at:

agent.microsoft.com/agent2/sdk/samples/html/peedypza.htm

To run this example, readers must download the Peedy character file, a text-to-speech engine and a speech-recognition engine. When the page loads, the browser prompts for these downloads. Follow the directions provided by Microsoft to complete installation.

When the window opens, Peedy introduces himself (Fig. 13.28), and the words he speaks appear in a cartoon bubble above his head. Notice that Peedy's animations correspond to the words he speaks.

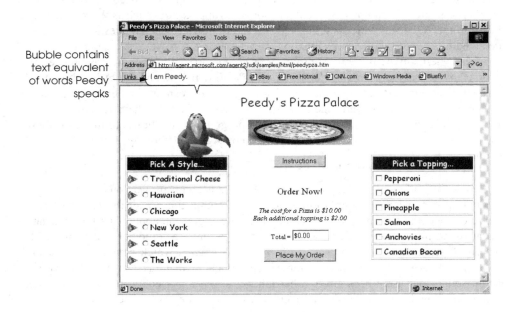

Fig. 13.28 Peedy introducing himself when the window opens.

Programmers can synchronize character animations with speech output to illustrate a point or to convey a character's mood. For instance, Fig. 13.29 depicts Peedy's *Pleased* animation. The Peedy character-animation set includes eighty-five different animations, each of which is unique to the Peedy character.

Look-and-Feel Observation 13.1

Agent characters remain on top of all active windows while a Microsoft Agent application is running. Their motions are not limited to within the boundaries of the browser or application window.

Peedy also responds to input from the keyboard and mouse. Figure 13.30 shows what happens when a user clicks Peedy with the mouse pointer. Peedy jumps up, ruffles his feathers and exclaims, "Hey that tickles!" or, "Be careful with that pointer!" Users can relocate Peedy on the screen by clicking and dragging him with the mouse. However, even when the user moves Peedy to a different part of the screen, he continues to perform his pre-set animations and location changes.

Many location changes involve animations. For instance, Peedy can hop from one screen location to another, or he can fly (Fig. 13.31).

Once Peedy completes the ordering instructions, a text box appears beneath him indicating that he is listening for a voice command (Fig. 13.32). Users can enter the type of pizza they wish to order either by speaking the style name into a microphone or by clicking the radio button corresponding to their choice.

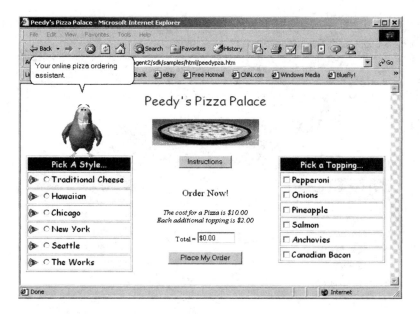

Fig. 13.29 Peedy's *Pleased* animation.

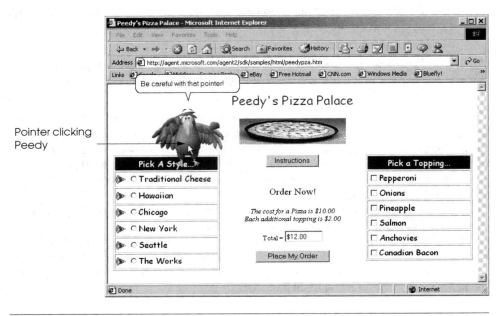

Pointer clicking
Peedy

Fig. 13.30 Peedy's reaction when he is clicked.

Fig. 13.31 Peedy flying animation.

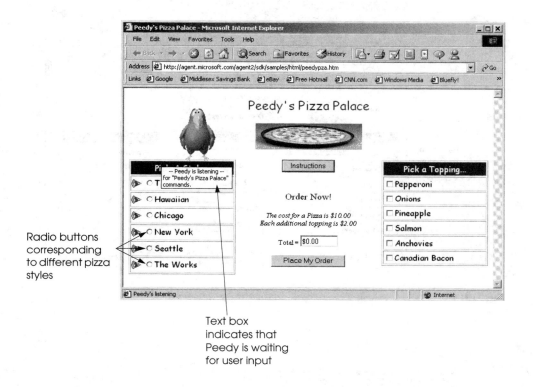

Radio buttons
corresponding
to different pizza
styles

Text box
indicates that
Peedy is waiting
for user input

Fig. 13.32 Peedy waiting for speech input.

If a user chooses speech input, a box appears below Peedy displaying the words that Peedy "heard" (i.e., the words translated to the program by the speech-recognition engine). Once he recognizes the user input, Peedy gives the user a description of the selected pizza. Figure 13.33 shows what happens when the user chooses **Seattle** as the pizza style.

Peedy then asks the user to choose additional toppings. Again, the user can either speak or use the mouse to make a selection. Check boxes corresponding to toppings that come with the selected pizza style are checked for the user. Figure 13.34 shows what happens when a user chooses anchovies as an additional topping. Peedy makes a wisecrack about the user's choice.

The user can submit the order either by pressing the **Place My Order** button or by speaking, "Place order" into the microphone. Peedy recounts the order while writing down the order items on his notepad (Fig. 13.35). He then calculates the figures on his calculator and reports the total to the user (Fig. 13.36).

Text box
indicates
recognized
speech

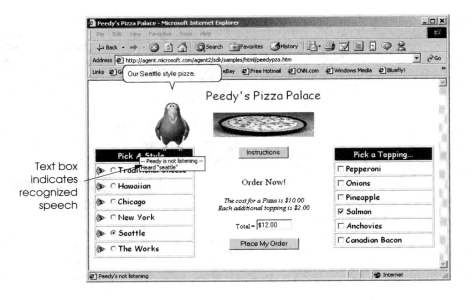

Fig. 13.33 Peedy repeating the user's request for Seattle style pizza.

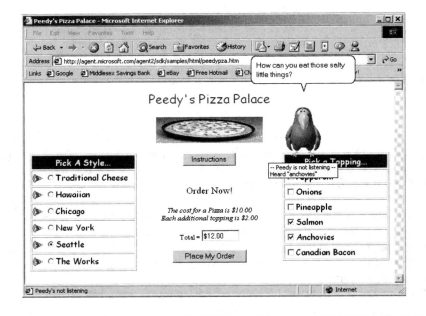

Fig. 13.34 Peedy repeating the user's request for anchovies as an additional
topping.

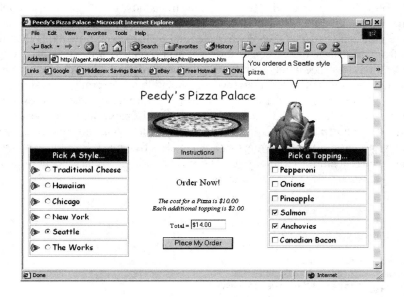

Fig. 13.35 Peedy recounting the order.

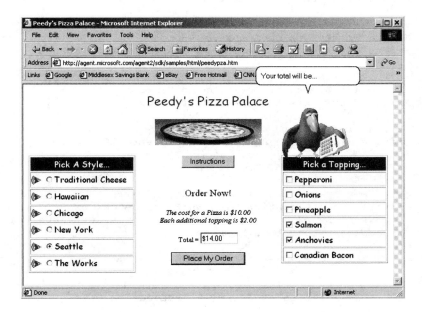

Fig. 13.36 Peedy calculating the total.

The following example (Fig. 13.37) demonstrates how to build a simple application using the Microsoft Agent control. This application contains two drop-down lists from which the user can choose an Agent character and a character animation. When the user chooses from these lists, the chosen character appears and performs the chosen animation. The application uses speech recognition and synthesis to control the character animations and speech: Users can tell the character which animation to perform by pressing the *Scroll Lock* key and then speaking the animation name into a microphone. The example also allows the user to switch to a new character by speaking its name, and also creates a custom command, **MoveToMouse**. In addition, the characters also speak any text that a user enters into the text box. Before running this example, readers first must download and install the control, speech recognition engine, text to speech engine and the character definitions from the Microsoft Agent Web site listed previously.

```vb
1   ' Fig. 13.37:   Agent.vb
2   ' Demonstrating Microsoft Agent.
3
4   Imports System.IO
5   Imports System.Collections
6   Imports System.Windows.Forms
7
8   Public Class FrmAgent
9       Inherits System.Windows.Forms.Form
10
11      ' options
12      Friend WithEvents characterCombo As ComboBox
13      Friend WithEvents actionsCombo As ComboBox
14
15      Friend WithEvents GroupBox1 As GroupBox
16      Friend WithEvents cmdSpeak As Button
17      Friend WithEvents mainAgent As AxAgentObjects.AxAgent
18
19      ' input boxes
20      Friend WithEvents txtLocation As TextBox
21      Friend WithEvents txtSpeech As TextBox
22
23      ' current agent object
24      Private mSpeaker As AgentObjects.IAgentCtlCharacter
25
26      ' Visual Studio .NET generated code
27
28      ' keyDown event handler for locationTextBox
29      Private Sub txtLocation_KeyDown(ByVal sender As _
30          Object, ByVal e As System.Windows.Forms.KeyEventArgs)_
31          Handles txtLocation.KeyDown
32
33          If e.KeyCode = Keys.Enter Then
34
35              ' set character location to text box value
36              Dim location As String = txtLocation.Text
37
```

Fig. 13.37 Microsoft Agent demonstration. (Part 1 of 6.)

```
38              ' initialize characters
39          Try
40
41              ' load characters into agent object
42              mainAgent.Characters.Load( _
43                  "Genie", location & "Genie.acs")
44
45              mainAgent.Characters.Load( _
46                  "Merlin", location & "Merlin.acs")
47
48              mainAgent.Characters.Load( _
49                  "Peedy", location & "Peedy.acs")
50
51              mainAgent.Characters.Load( _
52                  "Robby", location & "Robby.acs")
53
54              ' disable TextBox location and enable other controls
55              txtLocation.Enabled = False
56              txtSpeech.Enabled = True
57              cmdSpeak.Enabled = True
58              characterCombo.Enabled = True
59              actionsCombo.Enabled = True
60
61              ' set current character to Genie and show
62              mSpeaker = mainAgent.Characters("Genie")
63              GetAnimationNames() ' obtain animation name list
64              mSpeaker.Show(0)
65
66          Catch fileNotFound As FileNotFoundException
67              MessageBox.Show("Invalid character location", _
68                  "Error", MessageBoxButtons.OK, _
69                  MessageBoxIcon.Error)
70          End Try
71
72      End If
73
74   End Sub ' txtLocation_KeyDown
75
76   ' speak button event handler
77   Private Sub cmdSpeak_Click(ByVal sender As System.Object, _
78      ByVal e As System.EventArgs) Handles cmdSpeak.Click
79
80      ' if TextBox is empty, have character ask
81      ' user to type words into TextBox, otherwise
82      ' have character say words in TextBox
83      If txtSpeech.Text = "" Then
84          mSpeaker.Speak( _
85              "Please type the words you want me to speak", "")
86      Else
87          mSpeaker.Speak(txtSpeech.Text, "")
88      End If
89
90   End Sub ' cmdSpeak_Click
```

Fig. 13.37 Microsoft Agent demonstration. (Part 2 of 6.)

```
91
92        ' click event for agent
93        Private Sub mainAgent_ClickEvent(ByVal sender As Object _
94           Object, ByVal e As AxAgentObjects._AgentEvents_ClickEvent)_
95           Handles mainAgent.ClickEvent
96
97           mSpeaker.Play("Confused")
98           mSpeaker.Speak("Why are you poking me?", "")
99           mSpeaker.Play("RestPose")
100       End Sub ' mainAgent_ClickEvent
101
102       ' comboBox changed event, switch active agent
103       Private Sub characterCombo_SelectedIndexChanged(ByVal _
104          sender As System.Object, ByVal e As System.EventArgs) _
105          Handles characterCombo.SelectedIndexChanged
106
107          ChangeCharacter(characterCombo.Text)
108       End Sub ' characterCombo_SelectedIndexChanged
109
110       ' hide current character and show new
111       Private Sub ChangeCharacter(ByVal name As String)
112          mSpeaker.Hide(0)
113          mSpeaker = mainAgent.Characters(name)
114          GetAnimationNames() ' regenerate animation name list
115          mSpeaker.Show(0)
116       End Sub ' ChangeCharacter
117
118       ' get animation names and store in arraylist
119       Private Sub GetAnimationNames()
120
121          ' ensure thread safety
122          SyncLock (Me)
123
124             ' get animation names
125             Dim enumerator As IEnumerator = _
126                mainAgent.Characters.Character( _
127                mSpeaker.Name).AnimationNames.GetEnumerator()
128
129             Dim voiceString As String
130
131             ' clear cboActions combo box
132             actionsCombo.Items.Clear()
133             mSpeaker.Commands.RemoveAll()
134
135             ' copy enumeration to ArrayList
136             While enumerator.MoveNext()
137
138                ' remove underscores in speech string
139                voiceString = Convert.ToString(enumerator.Current)
140                voiceString = voiceString.Replace("_", "underscore")
141
142                actionsCombo.Items.Add(enumerator.Current)
143
```

Fig. 13.37 Microsoft Agent demonstration. (Part 3 of 6.)

```
144                     ' add all animations as voice enabled commands
145                     mSpeaker.Commands.Add(Convert.ToString( _
146                         enumerator.Current, , voiceString, True, False)
147                 End While
148
149                 ' add custom command
150                 mSpeaker.Commands.Add("MoveToMouse", "MoveToMouse", _
151                     "MoveToMouse", True, True)
152             End SyncLock
153
154     End Sub ' GetAnimationNames
155
156     ' user selects new action
157     Private Sub actionsCombo_SelectedIndexChanged(ByVal sender _
158         As System.Object, ByVal e As System.EventArgs) _
159         Handles actionsCombo.SelectedIndexChanged
160
161         mSpeaker.Stop()
162         mSpeaker.Play(actionsCombo.Text)
163         mSpeaker.Play("RestPose")
164     End Sub ' actionsCombo_SelectedIndexChanged
165
166     ' handles agent commands
167     Private Sub mainAgent_Command(ByVal sender As System.Object, _
168         ByVal e As AxAgentObjects._AgentEvents_CommandEvent) _
169         Handles mainAgent.Command
170
171         ' get UserInput object
172         Dim command As AgentObjects.IAgentCtlUserInput = _
173             CType(e.userInput, AgentObjects.IAgentCtlUserInput)
174
175         ' change character if user speaks character name
176         If (command.Voice = "Peedy" OrElse _
177             command.Voice = "Robby" OrElse _
178             command.Voice = "Merlin" OrElse _
179             command.Voice = "Genie") Then
180             ChangeCharacter(command.Voice)
181
182             Return
183         End If
184
185         ' send agent to mouse
186         If command.Name = "MoveToMouse" Then
187             mSpeaker.MoveTo(Convert.ToInt16( _
188                 Cursor.Position.X - 60), Convert.ToInt16( _
189                 Cursor.Position.Y - 60))
190
191             Return
192         End If
193
194         ' play new animation
195         mSpeaker.Stop()
196         mSpeaker.Play(command.Name)
```

Fig. 13.37 Microsoft Agent demonstration. (Part 4 of 6.)

```
197
198    End Sub  ' mainAgent_Command
199
200  End Class  ' FrmAgent
```

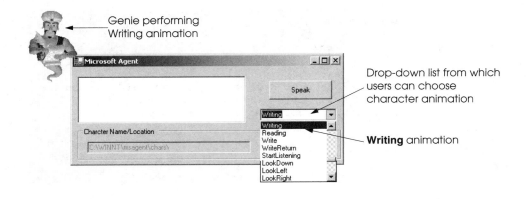

Genie performing
Writing animation

Drop-down list from which
users can choose
character animation

Writing animation

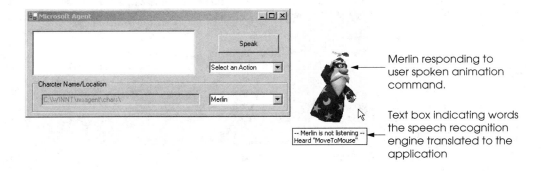

Merlin responding to
user spoken animation
command.

Text box indicating words
the speech recognition
engine translated to the
application

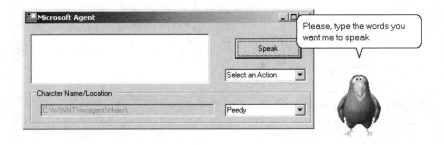

Fig. 13.37 Microsoft Agent demonstration. (Part 5 of 6.)

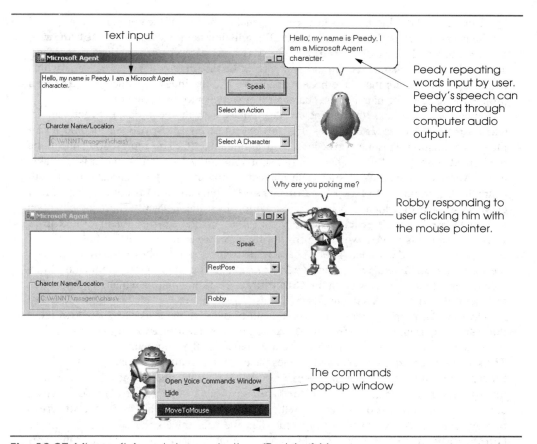

Fig. 13.37 Microsoft Agent demonstration. (Part 6 of 6.)

To use the Microsoft Agent control, the programmer first must add it to the **Toolbox**. Begin by selecting **Customize Toolbox** from the **Tools** menu to display the **Customize Toolbox** dialog. In the dialog, scroll down and select the option **Microsoft Agent Control 2.0**. When this option is selected properly, a small check mark appears in the box to the left of the option. Then, click **OK** to dismiss the dialog. The icon for the Microsoft Agent control now should appear at the bottom of the **Toolbox**.

In addition to the Microsoft Agent object **mainAgent** (of type **AxAgent**) that manages all the characters, we also need an object (of type **IAgentCtlCharacter**) to represent the current character. We create this object, named **mSpeaker**, in line 24.

When the program begins, the only enabled control is the **txtLocation**. This text box contains the default location for the character files, but the user can change this location if the files are located elsewhere on the user's computer. Once the user presses *Enter* in the **TextBox**, event handler **txtLocation_KeyDown** (lines 29–74) executes. Lines 42–52 load the character descriptions for the predefined animated characters. If the specified location of the characters is incorrect, or if any character is missing, a **FileNotFoundException** is thrown.

Lines 55–59 disable **txtLocation** and enable the rest of the controls. Lines 62–64 set Genie as the default character, obtain all animation names via method **GetAnimationNames** and then call **IAgentCtlCharacter** method *Show* to display the character. We access characters through property *Characters* of **mainAgent**, which contains all characters that have been loaded. We use the indexer of the **Characters** property to specify the name of the character that we wish to load (Genie).

When a user clicks the character (i.e., pokes it with the mouse), event handler **mainAgent_ClickEvent** (lines 93–100) executes. First, **mSpeaker** method **Play** plays an animation. This method accepts as an argument a **String** representing one of the predefined animations for the character (a list of animations for each character is available at the Microsoft Agent Web site; each character provides over 70 animations). In our example, the argument to **Play** is **"Confused"**—this animation is defined for all four characters, each of which expresses this emotion in a unique way. The character then speaks, **"Why are you poking me?"** via a call to method *Speak*. Finally, the *Rest-Pose* animation is played, which returns the character to its neutral, resting pose.

The list of valid commands for a character is contained in the **Commands** property of the **IAgentCtlCharacter** object (**mSpeaker**, in this example). The commands for an Agent character can be viewed in the **Commands** pop-up window, which displays when the user right-clicks an Agent character (the last screenshot in Fig. 13.37). Method **Add** of the **Commands** property adds a new command to the command list. Method **Add** takes three **String** arguments and two **Boolean** arguments. The first **String** argument identifies the name of the command, which we use to identify the command programmatically. The second **String** is optional and defines the command name as it appears in the **Commands** pop-up window. The third **String** also is optional and defines the voice input that triggers the command. The first **Boolean** specifies whether the command is active, and the second **Boolean** indicates whether the command is visible in the **Commands** pop-up window. A command is triggered when the user selects the command from the **Commands** pop-up window or speaks the voice input into a microphone. Command logic is handled in the **Command** event of the **AxAgent** control (**mainAgent**, in this example). In addition, Agent defines several global commands that have predefined functions (for example, speaking a character name causes that character to appear).

Method **GetAnimationNames** (lines 119–154) fills the **actionsCombo** **ComboBox** with the current character's animation listing and defines the valid commands that can be used with the character. The method contains a **SyncLock** block to prevent errors resulting from rapid character changes. The method obtains the current character's animations as an enumerator (125–127), then clears the existing items in the **ComboBox** and character's **Commands** property. Lines 136–147 iterate through all items in the animation name enumerator. For each animation, in line 139, we assign the animation name to **String voiceString**. Line 140 removes any underscore characters (_) and replaces them with the **String "underscore"**; this changes the **String** so that a user can pronounce and employ it as a command activator. The **Add** method (lines 145–146) of the **Commands** property adds a new command to the current character. The **Add** method adds all animations as commands by providing the following arguments: the animation name as the new command's **name** and **voiceString** for the voice activation **String**. The method's **Boolean** arguments enable the command, but make it unavailable in the **Commands** pop-up window. Thus, the command can be activated only by voice input. Lines

150–151 create a new command, named **MoveToMouse**, which is visible in the **Commands** pop-up window.

After the **GetAnimationNames** method has been called, the user can select a value from the **actionsCombo ComboBox**. Event-handler method **actionsCombo.SelectedIndexChanged** stops any current animation and then displays the animation that the user selected from the **ComboBox**.

The user also can type text into the **TextBox** and click **Speak**. This causes event handler **cmdSpeak_Click** (line 77–90) to call **mSpeaker**'s method **Speak**, supplying as an argument the text in **txtSpeech**. If the user clicks **Speak** without providing text, the character speaks, **"Please, type the words you want me to speak"**.

At any point in the program, the user can choose to display a different character from the **ComboBox**. When this happens, the **SelectedIndexChanged** event handler for **characterCombo** (lines 103–108) executes. The event handler calls method **ChangeCharacter** (lines 111–116) with the text in the **characterCombo ComboBox** as an argument. Method **ChangeCharacter** calls the **Hide** method of **mSpeaker** (line 112) to remove the current character from view. Line 113 assigns the newly selected character to **mSpeaker**, line 114 generates the character's animation names and commands, and line 115 displays the character via a call to method **Show**.

Each time a user presses the *Scroll Lock* key and speaks into a microphone or selects a command from the **Commands** pop-up window, event handler **mainAgent_Command** is called. This method is passed an argument of type **AxAgentObjects._AgentEvents_CommandEvent**, which contains a single method, **userInput**. The **userInput** method returns an **Object** that can be converted to type **AgentObjects.IAgentCtlUserInput**. The **userInput** object is assigned to a **IAgentCtlUserInput** object **command**, which is used to identify the command and then take appropriate action. Lines 176–180 use method **ChangeCharacter** to change the current Agent character if the user speaks a character name. Microsoft Agent always will show a character when a user speaks its name; however, by controlling the character change, we can ensure that only one Agent character is displayed at a time. Lines 186–192 move the character to the current mouse location if the user invokes the **MoveToMouse** command. The Agent method *MoveTo* takes x- and y-coordinate arguments and moves the character to the specified screen position, applying appropriate movement animations. For all other commands, we **Play** the command name as an animation on line 196.

In this chapter, we explored various graphics capabilities of GDI+, including pens, brushes and images, as well as some multimedia capabilities of the .NET Famework Class Library. In the next chapter, we cover the reading, writing and accessing of sequential- and random-access files. We also explore several types of streams included in Visual Studio .NET.

13.14 Summary

A coordinate system identifies every possible point on the screen. The upper left corner of a GUI component has coordinates *(0, 0)*. A coordinate pair is composed of an *x*-coordinate (the horizontal coordinate) and a *y*-coordinate (the vertical coordinate). Coordinate units are measured in pixels. A pixel is the smallest unit of resolution on a display monitor.

A graphics context represents a drawing surface on the screen. A **Graphics** object provides access to the graphics context of a control. **Graphics** objects contain methods for drawing, font manipulation, color manipulation and other graphics-related actions.

Class **Graphics** provides methods **DrawLine**, **DrawRectangle**, **DrawEllipse**, **DrawArc**, **DrawLines**, **DrawPolygon** and **DrawPie**, which draw lines and shape outlines. Methods **FillRectangle**, **FillEllipse**, **FillPolygon** and **FillPie** draw solid shapes. Classes **HatchBrush**, **LinearGradientBrush**, **PathGradientBrush** and **TextureBrush** all derive from class **Brush** and represent shape-filling styles.

Method **OnPaint** normally is called in response to an event, such as the uncovering of a window. This method, in turn, triggers a **Paint** event.

Structure **Color** defines constants for manipulating colors in a Visual Basic program. **Color** properties **R**, **G** and **B** return **int** values from 0 to 255, representing the amounts of red, green and blue, respectively, that exist in a **Color**. The larger the value, the greater the amount of that particular color.

Class **Font**'s constructors all take at least three arguments—the font name, the font size and the font style. The font name is any font currently supported by the system. The font style is a member of the **FontStyle** enumeration. Class **FontMetrics** defines several methods for obtaining font metrics (e.g., ascent, descent, etc.). The **FontFamily** class provides information about such font metrics as the family's spacing and height.

Class **GraphicsPath** represents a shape constructed from straight lines and curves. **GraphicsPath** method **AddLine** appends a line to the shape that is encapsulated by the object. **GraphicsPath** method **CloseFigure** completes the shape that is represented by the **GraphicsPath** object.

Class **Image** is used to manipulate images. Class **Image** provides method **FromFile** to retrieve an image stored on disk and load it into an instance of class **Image**. **Graphics** method **FromImage** retrieves the **Graphics** object associated with the image file that is its argument. **Graphics** method **DrawImage** draws the specified **Image** on the **Control**.

Using Visual Studio .NET and Visual Basic, programmers can create applications that use components such as Windows Media Player and Microsoft Agent. The Windows Media Player allows programmers to create applications that can play multimedia files. Microsoft Agent is a technology that allows programmers to include interactive animated characters in their applications.

14

Files and Streams

Objectives

- To create, read, write and update files.
- To understand the Visual Basic streams class hierarchy.
- To use classes **File** and **Directory**.
- To use the **FileStream** and **BinaryFormatter** classes to read objects from, and write objects to, files.
- To become familiar with sequential-access and random-access file processing.

I can only assume that a "Do Not File" document is filed in a "Do Not File" file.
Senator Frank Church

Consciousness ... does not appear to itself chopped up in bits. ... A "river" or a "stream" are the metaphors by which it is most naturally described.
William James

I read part of it all the way through.
Samuel Goldwyn

Outline

14.1 Introduction

Variables and arrays offer only temporary storage of data—the data are lost when a local variable "goes out of scope" or when the program terminates. By contrast, *files* are used for long-term retention of data, even after the program that created the data terminates. Data maintained in files often are called *persistent data*. Computers store files on *secondary storage devices*, such as magnetic disks, optical disks and magnetic tapes. In this chapter, we explain how to create, update and process data files in Visual Basic programs. We consider both "sequential-access" files and "random-access" files, indicating the kinds of applications for which each is best suited. We have two goals in this chapter: To introduce the sequential-access and random-access file-processing paradigms and to provide the reader with sufficient stream-processing capabilities to support the networking features that we introduce in Chapter 19, Networking: Streams-Based Sockets and Datagrams.

File processing is one of a programming language's most important capabilities, because it enables a language to support commercial applications that typically process massive amounts of persistent data. This chapter discusses Visual Basic's powerful and abundant file-processing and stream-input/output features.

14.2 Data Hierarchy

Ultimately, all data items processed by a computer are reduced to combinations of zeros and ones. This occurs because it is simple and economical to build electronic devices that can assume two stable states—**0** represents one state, and **1** represents the other. It is remarkable that the impressive functions performed by computers involve only the most fundamental manipulations of **0**s and **1**s.

The smallest data items that computers support are called *bits* (short for "*binary digit*"—a digit that can assume one of two values). Each data item, or bit, can assume either the value **0** or the value **1**. Computer circuitry performs various simple bit manipulations, such as examining the value of a bit, setting the value of a bit and reversing a bit (from **1** to **0** or from **0** to **1**).

Programming with data in the low-level form of bits is cumbersome. It is preferable to program with data in forms such as *decimal digits* (i.e., 0, 1, 2, 3, 4, 5, 6, 7, 8 and 9), *letters* (i.e., A through Z and a through z) and *special symbols* (i.e., $, @, %, &, *, (,), -, +, ", :, ?, / and many others). Digits, letters and special symbols are referred to as *characters*. The set of all characters used to write programs and represent data items on a particular computer is called that computer's *character set*. Because computers can process only **1**s and **0**s, every character in a computer's character set is represented as a pattern of **1**s and **0**s. *Bytes* are composed of eight bits (characters in Visual Basic are *Unicode* characters, which are composed of 2 bytes). Programmers create programs and data items with characters; computers manipulate and process these characters as patterns of bits.

Just as characters are composed of bits, *fields* are composed of characters. A field is a group of characters that conveys some meaning. For example, a field consisting of uppercase and lowercase letters can represent a person's name.

Data items processed by computers form a *data hierarchy* (Fig. 14.1) in which data items become larger and more complex in structure as we progress from bits, to characters, to fields and up to larger data structures.

Typically, a *record* (e.g., a **Class** in Visual Basic) is composed of several fields (called member variables in Visual Basic). In a payroll system, for example, a record for a particular employee might include the following fields:

1.   Employee identification number

2.   Name

3.   Address

4.   Hourly pay rate

5.   Number of exemptions claimed

6.   Year-to-date earnings

7.   Amount of taxes withheld

Thus, a record is a group of related fields. In the preceding example, each field is associated with the same employee. A *file* is a group of related records.[1] A company's payroll file normally contains one record for each employee. Thus, a payroll file for a small company might contain only 22 records, whereas a payroll file for a large company might contain 100,000 records. It is not unusual for a company to have many files, some containing millions, billions, or even trillions of characters of information.

To facilitate the retrieval of specific records from a file, at least one field in each record is chosen as a *record key*. A record key identifies a record as belonging to a particular person or entity and distinguishes that record from all other records. In the payroll record described previously, the employee identification number normally would be chosen as the record key.

---

1.   Generally, a file can contain arbitrary data in arbitrary formats. In some operating systems, a file is viewed as nothing more than a collection of bytes. In such an operating system, any organization of the bytes in a file (such as organizing the data into records) is a view created by the applications programmer.

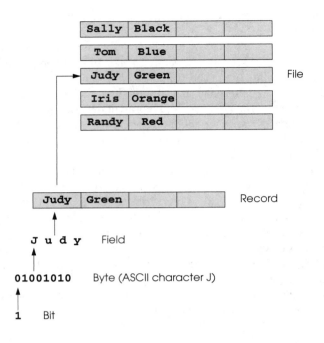

Fig. 14.1   Data hierarchy.

There are many ways of organizing records in a file. The most common type of organization is called a *sequential file*, in which records typically are stored in order by the record-key field. In a payroll file, records usually are placed in order by employee identification number. The first employee record in the file contains the lowest employee identification number, and subsequent records contain increasingly higher employee identification numbers.

Most businesses use many different files to store data. For example, a company might have payroll files, accounts receivable files (listing money due from clients), accounts payable files (listing money due to suppliers), inventory files (listing facts about all the items handled by the business) and many other types of files. Sometimes, a group of related files is called a *database*. A collection of programs designed to create and manage databases is called a *database management system* (DBMS). We discuss databases in detail in Chapter 16, Database, SQL and ADO .NET.

14.3 Files and Streams

Visual Basic views each file as a sequential *stream* of bytes (Fig. 14.2). Each file ends either with an *end-of-file marker* or at a specific byte number that is recorded in a system-maintained administrative data structure. When a file is *opened*, Visual Basic creates an object and then associates a stream with that object. The runtime environment creates three stream objects upon program execution, each accessible via properties **Console.Out**, **Console.In** and **Console.Error**, respectively. These objects facilitate communication between a program and a particular file or device. Property **Console.In** returns the *standard input stream object*, which enables a program to input data from the keyboard. Property **Console.Out** returns the *standard output stream object*, which enables a program to output data to the screen. Property **Console.Error** returns the *standard error stream object*, which enables a program to output error messages to the screen. We have been using **Console.Out** and **Console.In** in our console applications—**Console** methods **Write** and **WriteLine** use **Console.Out** to perform output, and methods **Read** and **ReadLine** use **Console.In** to perform input.

To perform file processing in Visual Basic, namespace **System.IO** must be referenced. This namespace includes definitions for stream classes such as **StreamReader** (for text input from a file), **StreamWriter** (for text output to a file) and **FileStream** (for both input and output to a file). Files are opened by creating objects of these stream classes, which inherit from **MustInherit** classes **TextReader**, **TextWriter** and **Stream**, respectively. Actually, **Console.In** and **Console.Out** are properties of class **TextReader** and **TextWriter**, respectively. These classes are **MustInherit**; **StreamReader** and **StreamWriter** are classes that derive from classes **TextReader** and **TextWriter**.

Visual Basic provides class *BinaryFormatter*, which is used in conjunction with a **Stream** object to perform input and output of objects. *Serialization* involves converting an object into a format that can be written to a file without losing any of that object's data. *Deserialization* consists of reading this format from a file and reconstructing the original object from it. A **BinaryFormatter** can serialize objects to, and deserialize objects from, a specified **Stream**.

Class *System.IO.Stream* provides functionality for representing streams as bytes. This class is **MustInherit**, so objects of this class cannot be instantiated. Classes *FileStream*, *MemoryStream* and *BufferedStream* (all from namespace **System.IO**) inherit from class **Stream**. Later in the chapter, we use **FileStream** to read data to, and write data from, sequential-access and random-access files. Class **MemoryStream** enables the transferal of data directly to and from memory—this type of transfer is much faster than other types of data transfer (e.g., to and from disk). Class **BufferedStream** uses *buffering* to transfer data to or from a stream. Buffering is an I/O-performance-enhancement technique, in which each output operation is directed to a region in memory called a *buffer* that is large enough to hold the data from many output operations. Then, actual transfer to the output device is performed in one large *physical output operation* each time the buffer fills. The output operations directed to the output buffer in memory often are called *logical output operations*.

Visual Basic offers many classes for performing input and output. In this chapter, we use several key stream classes to implement a variety of file-processing programs that create, manipulate and destroy sequential-access files and random-access files. In Chapter 19, Networking: Streams-Based Sockets and Datagrams, we use stream classes extensively to implement networking applications.

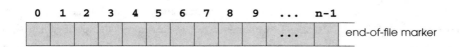

Fig. 14.2   Visual Basic's view of an *n-byte* file.

14.4 Classes `File` and `Directory`

Information on computers is stored in files, which are organized in directories. Class **`File`** is provided for manipulating files, and class **`Directory`** is provided for manipulating directories. Class **`File`** cannot write to or read from files directly; we discuss methods for reading and writing files in the following sections.

Note that the **** *separator character* separates directories and files in a path. On UNIX systems, the separator character is **/**. Visual Basic actually processes both characters as identical in a path name. This means that, if we specified the path **c:\VisualBasic/ README**, which uses one of each separator character, Visual Basic still processes the file properly.

Figure 14.3 lists some methods in class **`File`** for manipulating and determining information about particular files. Class **`File`** contains only **`Shared`** methods—you cannot instantiate objects of type **`File`**. We use several of these methods in the example of Fig. 14.5.

Class **`Directory`** provides the capabilities for manipulating directories with the .NET framework. Figure 14.4 lists some methods that can be used for directory manipulation. We use several of these methods in the example of Fig. 14.5.

The **`DirectoryInfo`** object returned by method **`CreateDirectory`** contains information about a directory. Much of the information contained in this class also can be accessed via the **`Directory`** methods.

Shared Method	Description
`AppendText`	Returns a **`StreamWriter`** that appends to an existing file or creates a file if one does not exist.
`Copy`	Copies a file to a new file.
`Create`	Returns a **`FileStream`** associated with the file just created.
`CreateText`	Returns a **`StreamWriter`** associated with the new text file.
`Delete`	Deletes the specified file.
`GetCreationTime`	Returns a **`DateTime`** object representing the time that the file was created.
`GetLastAccessTime`	Returns a **`DateTime`** object representing the time that the file was last accessed.
`GetLastWriteTime`	Returns a **`DateTime`** object representing the time that the file was last modified.
`Move`	Moves the specified file to a specified location.
`Open`	Returns a **`FileStream`** associated with the specified file and equipped with the specified read/write permissions.
`OpenRead`	Returns a read-only **`FileStream`** associated with the specified file.
`OpenText`	Returns a **`StreamReader`** associated with the specified file.
`OpenWrite`	Returns a read/write **`FileStream`** associated with the specified file.

Fig. 14.3 `File` class methods (partial list).

Shared Method	Description
CreateDirectory	Returns the **DirectoryInfo** object associated with the newly created directory.
Delete	Deletes the specified directory.
Exists	Returns **True** if the specified directory exists; otherwise, it returns **False**.
GetLastWriteTime	Returns a **DateTime** object representing the time that the directory was last modified.
GetDirectories	Returns a **String** array representing the names of the directories in the specified directory.
GetFiles	Returns a **String** array representing the names of the files in the specified directory.
GetCreationTime	Returns a **DateTime** object representing the time that the directory was created.
GetLastAccessTime	Returns a **DateTime** object representing the time that the directory was last accessed.
GetLastWriteTime	Returns a **DateTime** object representing the time that items were last written to the directory.
Move	Moves the specified directory to specified location.

Fig. 14.4 Directory class methods (partial list).

Class **FrmFileTest** (Fig. 14.5) uses various the methods described in Fig. 14.3 and Fig. 14.4 to access file and directory information. This class contains **TextBox txtInput** (line 15), which enables the user to input a file or directory name. For each key that the user presses in the text box, the program calls method **txtInput_KeyDown** (lines 20–84). If the user presses the *Enter* key (line 25), this method displays either file or directory contents, depending on the text the user input in the **TextBox**. (Note that, if the user does not press the *Enter* key, this method returns without displaying any content.) Line 33 uses method **Exists** of class **File** to determine whether the user-specified text is a file. If the user specifies an existing file, line 36 invokes **Private** method **GetInformation** (lines 87–108), which calls methods **GetCreationTime** (line 97), **GetLast-WriteTime** (line 101) and **GetLastAccessTime** (line 105) of class **File** to access information on the file. When method **GetInformation** returns, lines 42–43 instantiate a **StreamReader** for reading text from the file. The **StreamReader** constructor takes as an argument a **String** containing the name of the file to open. Line 44 calls method **ReadToEnd** of the **StreamReader** to read the file content from the file and then displays the content.

If line 33 determines that the user-specified text is not a file, line 56 determines whether it is a directory using method **Exists** of class **Directory**. If the user specified an existing directory, line 62 invokes method **GetInformation** to access the directory information. Line 65 calls method **GetDirectories** of class **Directory** to obtain a

String array containing the names of subdirectories in the specified directory. Lines 71–73 display each element in the **String** array. Note that, if line 56 determines that the user-specified text is neither a file nor a directory, lines 77–79 notify the user (via a **MessageBox**) that the file or directory does not exist.

```
1    ' Fig. 14.5: FileTest.vb
2    ' Using classes File and Directory.
3
4    Imports System.IO
5    Imports System.Windows.Forms
6
7    Public Class FrmFileTest
8       Inherits Form
9
10      ' label that gives directions to user
11      Friend WithEvents lblDirections As Label
12
13      ' text boxes for inputting and outputting data
14      Friend WithEvents txtOutput As TextBox
15      Friend WithEvents txtInput As TextBox
16
17      ' Visual Studio .NET generated code
18
19      ' invoked when user presses key
20      Protected Sub txtInput_KeyDown(ByVal sender As Object, _
21         ByVal e As System.Windows.Forms.KeyEventArgs) Handles _
22         txtInput.KeyDown
23
24         ' determine whether user pressed Enter key
25         If e.KeyCode = Keys.Enter Then
26
27            Dim fileName As String ' name of file or directory
28
29            ' get user-specified file or directory
30            fileName = txtInput.Text
31
32            ' determine whether fileName is a file
33            If File.Exists(fileName) Then
34
35               ' get file's creation date, modification date, etc.
36               txtOutput.Text = GetInformation(fileName)
37
38               ' display file contents through StreamReader
39               Try
40
41                  ' obtain reader and file contents
42                  Dim stream As StreamReader
43                  stream = New StreamReader(fileName)
44                  txtOutput.Text &= stream.ReadToEnd()
45
```

Fig. 14.5 **FrmFileTest** class tests classes **File** and **Directory**. (Part 1 of 3.)

```
46                     ' handle exception if StreamReader is unavailable
47                     Catch exceptionCatch As IOException
48
49                        ' display error
50                        MessageBox.Show("FILE ERROR", "FILE ERROR", _
51                           MessageBoxButtons.OK, MessageBoxIcon.Error)
52
53                     End Try
54
55                  ' determine whether fileName is a directory
56                  ElseIf Directory.Exists(fileName) Then
57
58                     Dim directoryList As String() ' array for directories
59                     Dim i As Integer
60
61                     ' get directory's creation date, modification date, etc
62                     txtOutput.Text = GetInformation(fileName)
63
64                     ' obtain directory list of specified directory
65                     directoryList = Directory.GetDirectories(fileName)
66
67                     txtOutput.Text &= vbCrLf & vbCrLf & _
68                        "Directory contents:" & vbCrLf
69
70                     ' output directoryList contents
71                     For i = 0 To directoryList.Length - 1
72                        txtOutput.Text &= directoryList(i) & vbCrLf
73                     Next
74
75                  ' notify user that neither file nor directory exists
76                  Else
77                     MessageBox.Show(txtInput.Text & " does not exist", _
78                        "FILE ERROR", MessageBoxButtons.OK, _
79                        MessageBoxIcon.Error)
80                  End If
81
82               End If ' determine whether user pressed Enter key
83
84         End Sub ' txtInput_KeyDown
85
86         ' get information on file or directory
87         Private Function GetInformation(ByRef fileName As String) _
88            As String
89
90            Dim information As String
91
92            ' output that file or directory exists
93            information = fileName & " exists" & vbCrLf & vbCrLf
94
95            ' output when file or directory was created
96            information &= "Created : " & _
97               File.GetCreationTime(fileName) & vbCrLf
98
```

Fig. 14.5 **FrmFileTest** class tests classes **File** and **Directory**. (Part 2 of 3.)

```
99          ' output when file or directory was last modified
100         information &= "Last modified: " & _
101             File.GetLastWriteTime(fileName) & vbCrLf
102
103         ' output when file or directory was last accessed
104         information &= "Last accessed: " & _
105             File.GetLastAccessTime(fileName) & vbCrLf & vbCrLf
106
107         Return information
108      End Function ' GetInformation
109
110  End Class ' FrmFileTest
```

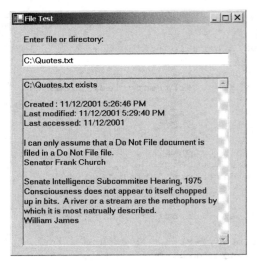
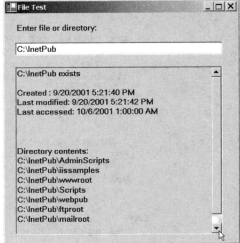
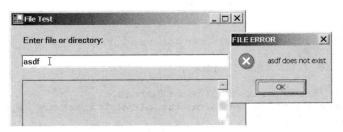

Fig. 14.5 **FrmFileTest** class tests classes **File** and **Directory**. (Part 3 of 3.)

We now consider another example that uses Visual Basic's file and directory-manipulation capabilities. Class **FrmFileSearch** (Fig. 14.6) uses classes **File** and **Directory** in conjunction with classes for performing regular expressions to report the number of files of each file type in the specified directory path. The program also serves as a "cleanup" utility—when the program encounters a file that has the **.bak** extension (i.e., a backup file), the program displays a **MessageBox** asking if that file should be removed and then responds appropriately to the user's input.

When the user presses the *Enter* key or clicks the **Search Directory** button, the program invokes method **cmdSearch_Click** (lines 47–88), which searches recursively through the directory path that the user provides. If the user inputs text in the **TextBox**, line 56 calls method **Exists** of class **Directory** to determine whether that text indicates a valid directory. If the user specifies an invalid directory, lines 65–66 notify the user of the error.

If the user specifies a valid directory, line 78 passes the directory name as an argument to **Private** method **SearchDirectory** (lines 91–181). This method locates files on the basis of the regular expression defined in lines 100–101 by the **Regex** object, which matches any sequence of numbers or letters followed by a period and one or more letters. Notice an unfamiliar substring of format **(?<extension>***regular-expression***)** contained in the argument to the **Regex** constructor (line 101). All **String**s with the substring *regular-expression* are tagged with the name **extension**. In this program, we assign to the variable **extension** any **String** matching one or more characters.

```
1    ' Fig. 14.6: FileSearch.vb
2    ' Using regular expressions to determine file types.
3
4    Imports System.IO
5    Imports System.Text.RegularExpressions
6    Imports System.Collections.Specialized
7    Imports System.Windows.Forms
8
9    Public Class FrmFileSearch
10       Inherits Form
11
12       ' label that displays current directory
13       Friend WithEvents lblDirectory As Label
14
15       ' label that displays directions to user
16       Friend WithEvents lblDirections As Label
17
18       ' button that activates search
19       Friend WithEvents cmdSearch As Button
20
21       ' text boxes for inputting and outputting data
22       Friend WithEvents txtInput As TextBox
23       Friend WithEvents txtOutput As TextBox
24
25       ' Visual Studio .NET generated code
26
27       Dim currentDirectory As String = Directory.GetCurrentDirectory
28       Dim directoryList As String() ' subdirectories
29       Dim fileArray As String() ' files in current directory
30
31       ' store extensions found and number found
32       Dim found As NameValueCollection = New NameValueCollection()
```

Fig. 14.6 FrmFileSearch class uses regular expressions to determine file types. (Part 1 of 5.)

```
33
34      ' invoked when user types in text box
35      Private Sub txtInput_KeyDown(ByVal sender As System.Object, _
36         ByVal e As System.Windows.Forms.KeyEventArgs) _
37         Handles txtInput.KeyDown
38
39         ' determine whether user pressed Enter
40         If (e.KeyCode = Keys.Enter) Then
41            cmdSearch_Click(sender, e)
42         End If
43
44      End Sub ' txtInput_KeyDown
45
46      ' invoked when user clicks "Search Directory" button
47      Private Sub cmdSearch_Click(ByVal sender As System.Object, _
48         ByVal e As System.EventArgs) Handles cmdSearch.Click
49
50         Dim current As String
51
52         ' check for user input; default is current directory
53         If txtInput.Text <> "" Then
54
55            ' verify that user input is a valid directory name
56            If Directory.Exists(txtInput.Text) Then
57               currentDirectory = txtInput.Text
58
59               ' reset input text box and update display
60               lblDirectory.Text = "Current Directory:" & vbCrLf & _
61                  currentDirectory
62
63               ' show error if user does not specify valid directory
64            Else
65               MessageBox.Show("Invalid Directory", "Error", _
66                  MessageBoxButtons.OK, MessageBoxIcon.Error)
67
68               Return
69            End If
70
71         End If
72
73         ' clear text boxes
74         txtInput.Text = ""
75         txtOutput.Text = ""
76
77         ' search directory
78         SearchDirectory(currentDirectory)
79
80         ' summarize and print results
81         For Each current In found
82            txtOutput.Text &= "* Found " & found(current) & " " _
83               & current & " files." & vbCrLf
84         Next
```

Fig. 14.6 **FrmFileSearch** class uses regular expressions to determine file types.
(Part 2 of 5.)

```vbnet
85
86          ' clear output for new search
87        found.Clear()
88    End Sub ' cmdSearch_Click
89
90    ' search directory using regular expression
91    Private Sub SearchDirectory(ByVal currentDirectory As String)
92
93       ' for file name without directory path
94       Try
95          Dim fileName As String = ""
96          Dim myFile As String
97          Dim myDirectory As String
98
99          ' regular expression for extensions matching pattern
100         Dim regularExpression As Regex = _
101            New Regex("([a-zA-Z0-9]+\.(?<extension>\w+))")
102
103         ' stores regular-expression-match result
104         Dim matchResult As Match
105
106         Dim fileExtension As String ' holds file extensions
107
108         ' number of files with given extension in directory
109         Dim extensionCount As Integer
110
111         ' get directories
112         directoryList = _
113            Directory.GetDirectories(currentDirectory)
114
115         ' get list of files in current directory
116         fileArray = Directory.GetFiles(currentDirectory)
117
118         ' iterate through list of files
119         For Each myFile In fileArray
120
121            ' remove directory path from file name
122            fileName = myFile.Substring( _
123               myFile.LastIndexOf("\") + 1)
124
125            ' obtain result for regular-expression search
126            matchResult = regularExpression.Match(fileName)
127
128            ' check for match
129            If (matchResult.Success) Then
130               fileExtension = matchResult.Result("${extension}")
131            Else
132               fileExtension = "[no extension]"
133            End If
```

Fig. 14.6 **FrmFileSearch** class uses regular expressions to determine file types. (Part 3 of 5.)

```
134
135                    ' store value from container
136                    If (found(fileExtension) = Nothing) Then
137                        found.Add(fileExtension, "1")
138                    Else
139                        extensionCount = _
140                            Convert.ToInt32(found(fileExtension)) + 1
141
142                        found(fileExtension) = extensionCount.ToString()
143                    End If
144
145                    ' search for backup(.bak) files
146                    If fileExtension = "bak" Then
147
148                        ' prompt user to delete (.bak) file
149                        Dim result As DialogResult = _
150                            MessageBox.Show("Found backup file " & _
151                            fileName & ". Delete?", "Delete Backup", _
152                            MessageBoxButtons.YesNo, _
153                            MessageBoxIcon.Question)
154
155                        ' delete file if user clicked 'yes'
156                        If (result = DialogResult.Yes) Then
157                            File.Delete(myFile)
158                            extensionCount = _
159                                Convert.ToInt32(found("bak")) - 1
160
161                            found("bak") = extensionCount.ToString()
162                        End If
163
164                    End If
165
166                Next
167
168                ' recursive call to search files in subdirectory
169                For Each myDirectory In directoryList
170                    SearchDirectory(myDirectory)
171                Next
172
173            ' handle exception if files have unauthorized access
174            Catch unauthorizedAccess As UnauthorizedAccessException
175                MessageBox.Show("Some files may not be visible due to" _
176                    & " permission settings", "Warning", _
177                    MessageBoxButtons.OK, MessageBoxIcon.Information)
178
179            End Try
180
181        End Sub ' SearchDirectory
182
183    End Class ' FrmFileSearch
```

Fig. 14.6 **FrmFileSearch** class uses regular expressions to determine file types. (Part 4 of 5.)

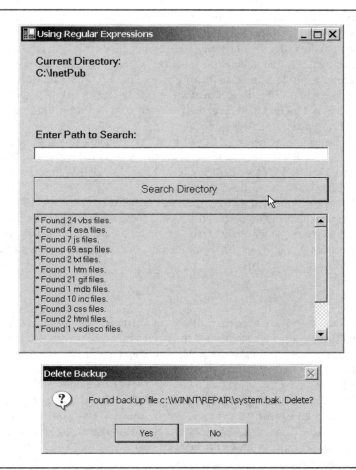

Fig. 14.6 **FrmFileSearch** class uses regular expressions to determine file types. (Part 5 of 5.)

Lines 112–113 call method **GetDirectories** of class **Directory** to retrieve the names of all directories that belong to the current directory. Line 116 calls method **Get-Files** of class **Directory** to store the names of all current-directory files in **String** array **fileArray**. The **For Each** loop in line 119 searches for files with extension **bak**; it then calls **SearchDirectory** recursively for each subdirectory in the current directory. Lines 122–123 eliminate the directory path, so the program can test only the file name when using the regular expression. Lines 126 uses method **Match** of the **Regex** object to match the regular expression with the file name and then returns the result to object **matchResult** of type **Match**. If the match is successful, line 130 uses method **Result** of object **matchResult** to store the extension **String** from object **matchResult** in **fileExtension** (the **String** that will contain the current file's extension). If the match is unsuccessful, line 132 sets **fileExtension** to hold a value of **"[no extension]"**.

Class **FrmFileSearch** uses an instance of class *NameValueCollection* (declared in line 32) to store each file-extension type and the number of files for each type.

A **NameValueCollection** contains a collection of key/value pairs, each of which is a **String**, and provides method **Add** to add a key/value pair. The indexer for this pair can index according to the order that the items were added or according to the entry key—both means of indexing return the value corresponding to that key. Line 136 uses **NameValueCollection** variable **found** to determine whether this is the first occurrence of the file extension. If so, line 137 adds to **found** that extension as a key with the value **1**. Otherwise, lines 139–142 increment the value associated with the extension in **found** to indicate another occurrence of that file extension.

Line 146 determines whether **fileExtension** equals "bak"—i.e., the file is a backup file. Lines 149–153 prompt the user to indicate whether the file should be removed—if the user clicks **Yes** (line 156), lines 157–159 delete the file and decrement the value for the "**bak**" file type in **found**.

Lines 169–171 call method **SearchDirectory** for each subdirectory. Using recursion, we ensure that the program performs the same logic for finding **bak** files on each subdirectory. After each subdirectory has been checked for **bak** files, method **SearchDirectory** returns to the event handler (i.e., method **cmdSearch_Click**), and lines 81–84 display the results.

14.5 Creating a Sequential-Access File

Visual Basic imposes no structure on a file. Thus, concepts like that of a "record" do not exist in Visual Basic files. This means that the programmer must structure files to meet the requirements of applications. In this example, we use text and special characters to organize our own concept of a "record."

As we will see, the GUIs for most of the programs in this chapter are similar; therefore, we created class **FrmBankUI** (Fig. 14.7) to encapsulate this GUI (see the screen capture in Fig. 14.7). Class **FrmBankUI** contains four **Label**s (lines 10–13) and four **Text-Box**es (lines 16–19). Methods **ClearTextBoxes** (lines 35–52), **SetTextBoxValues** (lines 55–72) and **GetTextBoxValues** (lines 75–86) clear, set the values of, and get the values of the text in the **TextBox**es, respectively.

```
1    ' Fig. 14.7: BankUI.vb
2    ' A reusable windows form for the examples in this chapter.
3
4    Imports System.Windows.Forms
5
6    Public Class FrmBankUI
7       Inherits Form
8
9       ' labels for TextBoxes
10      Public WithEvents lblAccount As Label
11      Public WithEvents lblFirstName As Label
12      Public WithEvents lblLastName As Label
13      Public WithEvents lblBalance As Label
14
```

Fig. 14.7 **FrmBankUI** class is the base class for GUIs in our file-processing applications. (Part 1 of 3.)

```vb
15        ' text boxes that receive user input
16        Public WithEvents txtAccount As TextBox
17        Public WithEvents txtFirstName As TextBox
18        Public WithEvents txtLastName As TextBox
19        Public WithEvents txtBalance As TextBox
20
21        ' Visual Studio .NET generated code
22
23        ' number of TextBoxes on Form
24        Protected TextBoxCount As Integer = 4
25
26        ' enumeration constants specify TextBox indices
27        Public Enum TextBoxIndices
28           ACCOUNT
29           FIRST
30           LAST
31           BALANCE
32        End Enum
33
34        ' clear all TextBoxes
35        Public Sub ClearTextBoxes()
36           Dim myControl As Control ' current GUI component
37           Dim i As Integer
38
39           ' iterate through every Control on form
40           For i = 0 To Controls.Count - 1
41              myControl = Controls(i) ' get Control
42
43              ' determine whether Control is TextBox
44              If (TypeOf myControl Is TextBox) Then
45
46                 ' clear Text property (set to empty String)
47                 myControl.Text = ""
48              End If
49
50           Next
51
52        End Sub ' ClearTextBoxes
53
54        ' set TextBox values to String-array values
55        Public Sub SetTextBoxValues(ByVal values As String())
56
57           ' determine whether String array has correct length
58           If (values.Length <> TextBoxCount) Then
59
60              ' throw exception if not correct length
61              Throw New ArgumentException("There must be " & _
62                 TextBoxCount + 1 & " strings in the array")
63
64           ' else set array values to TextBox values
65           Else
66              txtAccount.Text = values(TextBoxIndices.ACCOUNT)
```

Fig. 14.7 **FrmBankUI** class is the base class for GUIs in our file-processing applications. (Part 2 of 3.)

```
67              txtFirstName.Text = values(TextBoxIndices.FIRST)
68              txtLastName.Text = values(TextBoxIndices.LAST)
69              txtBalance.Text = values(TextBoxIndices.BALANCE)
70           End If
71
72        End Sub ' SetTextBoxValues
73
74        ' return TextBox values as String array
75        Public Function GetTextBoxValues() As String()
76
77           Dim values(TextBoxCount) As String
78
79           ' copy TextBox fields to String array
80           values(TextBoxIndices.ACCOUNT) = txtAccount.Text
81           values(TextBoxIndices.FIRST) = txtFirstName.Text
82           values(TextBoxIndices.LAST) = txtLastName.Text
83           values(TextBoxIndices.BALANCE) = txtBalance.Text
84
85           Return values
86        End Function ' GetTextBoxValues
87
88     End Class ' FrmBankUI
```

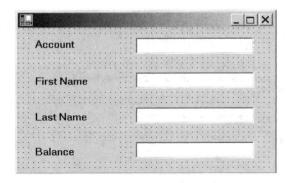

Fig. 14.7 **FrmBankUI** class is the base class for GUIs in our file-processing
          applications. (Part 3 of 3.)

To reuse class **FrmBankUI**, we compile the GUI into a DLL library by creating a
project of type **Windows Control Library** (the DLL we create is called **BankLibrary**). This library, as well as all the code in this book, can be found at our Web site,
www.deitel.com, under the **Downloads/Resources** link. However, readers might
need to change the reference to this library, as it most likely resides in a different location
on their systems.

Figure 14.8 contains the **CRecord** class that the programs of Fig. 14.9, Fig. 14.11 and
Fig. 14.12 use for reading records from, and writing records to, a file sequentially. This
class also belongs to the **BankLibrary** DLL, which means that it is located in the same
project as is class **FrmBankUI**. (When readers add class **CRecord** to the project containing **FrmBankUI**, they must remember to rebuild the project.)

```
1    ' Fig. 14.8: CRecord.vb
2    ' Serializable class that represents a data record.
3
4    <Serializable()> Public Class CRecord
5
6       Private mAccount As Integer
7       Private mFirstName As String
8       Private mLastName As String
9       Private mBalance As Double
10
11      ' default constructor sets members to default values
12      Public Sub New()
13         Me.New(0, "", "", 0.0)
14      End Sub ' New
15
16      ' overloaded constructor sets members to parameter values
17      Public Sub New(ByVal accountValue As Integer, _
18         ByVal firstNameValue As String, _
19         ByVal lastNameValue As String, _
20         ByVal balanceValue As Double)
21
22         Account = accountValue
23         FirstName = firstNameValue
24         LastName = lastNameValue
25         Balance = balanceValue
26      End Sub ' New
27
28      ' property Account
29      Public Property Account() As Integer
30
31         Get
32            Return mAccount
33         End Get
34
35         Set(ByVal accountValue As Integer)
36            mAccount = accountValue
37         End Set
38
39      End Property ' Account
40
41      ' property FirstName
42      Public Property FirstName() As String
43
44         Get
45            Return mFirstName
46         End Get
47
48         Set(ByVal firstNameValue As String)
49            mFirstName = firstNameValue
50         End Set
51
52      End Property ' FirstName
```

Fig. 14.8 **CRecord** class represents a record for sequential-access file-processing applications. (Part 1 of 2.)

```
53
54        ' property LastName
55        Public Property LastName() As String
56
57           Get
58              Return mLastName
59           End Get
60
61           Set(ByVal lastNameValue As String)
62              mLastName = lastNameValue
63           End Set
64
65        End Property ' LastName
66
67        ' property Balance
68        Public Property Balance() As Double
69
70           Get
71              Return mBalance
72           End Get
73
74           Set(ByVal balanceValue As Double)
75              mBalance = balanceValue
76           End Set
77
78        End Property ' Balance
79
80     End Class ' CRecord
```

Fig. 14.8   **CRecord** class represents a record for sequential-access file-processing applications. (Part 2 of 2.)

The ***Serializable*** attribute (line 4) indicates to the compiler that objects of class **CRecord** can be *serialized*, or represented as sets of bytes—we then either can write these bytes to streams or store stream data into these sets. Objects that we wish to write to or read from a stream must include this attribute tag before their class definitions.

Class **CRecord** contains **Private** data members **mAccount**, **mFirstName**, **mLastName** and **mBalance** (lines 6–9), which collectively represent all information necessary to store record data. The default constructor (lines 12–14) sets these members to their default (i.e., empty) values, and the overloaded constructor (lines 17–26) sets these members to specified parameter values. Class **CRecord** also provides properties **Account** (lines 29–39), **FirstName** (lines 42–52), **LastName** (lines 55–65) and **Balance** (lines 68–78) for accessing the account number, first name, last name and balance of each customer, respectively.

Class **FrmCreateSequentialAccessFile** (Fig. 14.9) uses instances of class **CRecord** to create a sequential-access file that might be used in an accounts-receivable system—i.e., a program that organizes data regarding money owed by a company's credit clients. For each client, the program obtains an account number and the client's first name, last name and balance (i.e., the amount of money that the client owes to the company for previously received goods or services). The data obtained for each client constitutes a record for that client. In this application, the account number represents the record key—

files are created and maintained in account-number order. This program assumes that the user enters records in account-number order. However, in comprehensive accounts-receivable system would provide a sorting capability. The user could enter the records in any order, and the records then could be sorted and written to the file in order. (Note that all outputs in this chapter should be read row by row, from left to right in each row.)

Figure 14.9 contains the code for class **FrmCreateSequentialAccessFile**, which either creates or opens a file (depending on whether one exists) and then allows the user to write bank information to that file. Line 11 imports the **BankLibrary** namespace; this namespace contains class **FrmBankUI**, from which class **FrmCreateSequentialAccessFile** inherits (line 14). Because of this inheritance relationship, the **FrmCreateSequentialAccessFile** GUI is similar to that of class **FrmBankUI** (shown in the Fig. 14.9 output), except that the inherited class contains buttons **Save As**, **Enter** and **Exit**.

```vb
1   ' Fig. 14.9: CreateSequentialAccessFile.vb
2   ' Creating a sequential-access file.
3
4   ' Visual Basic namespaces
5   Imports System.IO
6   Imports System.Runtime.Serialization.Formatters.Binary
7   Imports System.Runtime.Serialization
8   Imports System.Windows.Forms
9
10  ' Deitel namespaces
11  Imports BankLibrary
12
13  Public Class FrmCreateSequentialAccessFile
14      Inherits FrmBankUI
15
16      ' GUI buttons to save file, enter data and exit program
17      Friend WithEvents cmdSave As Button
18      Friend WithEvents cmdEnter As Button
19      Friend WithEvents cmdExit As Button
20
21      ' Visual Studio .NET generated code
22
23      ' serializes CRecord in binary format
24      Private formatter As BinaryFormatter = New BinaryFormatter()
25
26      ' stream through which serializable data is written to file
27      Private output As FileStream
28
29      ' invoked when user clicks Save button
30      Protected Sub cmdSave_Click(ByVal sender As Object, _
31          ByVal e As System.EventArgs) Handles cmdSave.Click
32
33          ' create dialog box enabling user to save file
34          Dim fileChooser As SaveFileDialog = New SaveFileDialog()
35          Dim result As DialogResult = fileChooser.ShowDialog()
36          Dim fileName As String ' name of file to save data
```

Fig. 14.9 **FrmCreateSequentialAccessFile** class creates and writes to sequential-access files. (Part 1 of 5.)

```
37
38            ' allow user to create file
39            fileChooser.CheckFileExists = False
40
41            ' exit event handler if user clicked "Cancel"
42            If result = DialogResult.Cancel Then
43               Return
44            End If
45
46            fileName = fileChooser.FileName ' get specified file name
47
48            ' show error if user specified invalid file
49            If (fileName = "" OrElse fileName = Nothing) Then
50               MessageBox.Show("Invalid File Name", "Error", _
51                  MessageBoxButtons.OK, MessageBoxIcon.Error)
52            Else
53
54               ' save file via FileStream if user specified valid file
55               Try
56
57                  ' open file with write access
58                  output = New FileStream(fileName, _
59                     FileMode.OpenOrCreate, FileAccess.Write)
60
61                  cmdSave.Enabled = False ' disable Save button
62                  cmdEnter.Enabled = True ' enable Enter button
63
64               ' notify user if file does not exist
65               Catch fileException As FileNotFoundException
66                  MessageBox.Show("File Does Not Exist", "Error", _
67                     MessageBoxButtons.OK, MessageBoxIcon.Error)
68
69               End Try
70
71            End If
72
73      End Sub ' cmdSave_Click
74
75      ' invoked when user clicks Enter button
76      Protected Sub cmdEnter_Click(ByVal sender As Object, _
77         ByVal Be As System.EventArgs) Handles cmdEnter.Click
78
79            ' account-number value from TextBox
80            Dim accountNumber As Integer
81
82            ' store TextBox-values String array
83            Dim values As String() = GetTextBoxValues()
84
85            ' CRecord containing TextBox values to serialize
86            Dim record As New CRecord()
87
```

Fig. 14.9 **FrmCreateSequentialAccessFile** class creates and writes to sequential-access files. (Part 2 of 5.)

```
 88              ' determine whether TextBox account field is empty
 89          If values(TextBoxIndices.ACCOUNT) <> "" Then
 90
 91                  ' store TextBox values in CRecord and serialize CRecord
 92              Try
 93
 94                      ' get account-number value from TextBox
 95                  accountNumber = _
 96                      Convert.ToInt32(values(TextBoxIndices.ACCOUNT))
 97
 98                      ' determine whether accountNumber is valid
 99                  If accountNumber > 0 Then
100
101                          ' store TextBox fields in CRecord
102                      record.Account = accountNumber
103                      record.FirstName = values(TextBoxIndices.FIRST)
104                      record.LastName = values(TextBoxIndices.LAST)
105                      record.Balance = Convert.ToDouble( _
106                          values(TextBoxIndices.BALANCE))
107
108                          ' write CRecord to FileStream (Serialize object)
109                      formatter.Serialize(output, record)
110
111                      ' notify user if invalid account number
112                  Else
113                      MessageBox.Show("Invalid Account Number", _
114                          "Error", MessageBoxButtons.OK, _
115                          MessageBoxIcon.Error)
116                  End If
117
118              ' notify user if error occurs in serialization
119              Catch serializableException As SerializationException
120                  MessageBox.Show("Error Writing to File", "Error", _
121                      MessageBoxButtons.OK, MessageBoxIcon.Error)
122
123              ' notify user if error occurs regarding parameter format
124              Catch formattingException As FormatException
125                  MessageBox.Show("Invalid Format", "Error", _
126                      MessageBoxButtons.OK, MessageBoxIcon.Error)
127
128              End Try
129
130          End If
131
132          ClearTextBoxes() ' clear TextBox values
133      End Sub ' cmdEnter_Click
134
135      ' invoked when user clicks Exit button
136      Protected Sub cmdExit_Click(ByVal sender As Object, _
137          ByVal e As System.EventArgs) Handles cmdExit.Click
138
```

Fig. 14.9 **FrmCreateSequentialAccessFile** class creates and writes to
sequential-access files. (Part 3 of 5.)

```
139           ' determine whether file exists
140        If (output Is Nothing) = False Then
141
142             ' close file
143           Try
144              output.Close()
145
146             ' notify user of error closing file
147           Catch fileException As IOException
148              MessageBox.Show("Cannot close file", "Error", _
149                 MessageBoxButtons.OK, MessageBoxIcon.Error)
150
151           End Try
152
153        End If
154
155        Application.Exit()
156     End Sub ' cmdExit_Click
157
158  End Class ' FrmCreateSequentialAccessFile
```

BankUI graphical
user interface

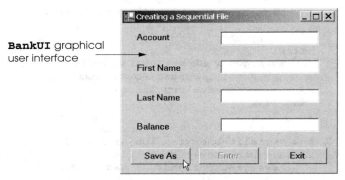

SaveFileDialog

Files and directories

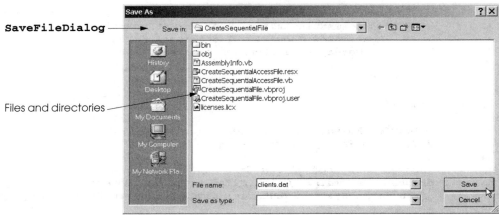

Fig. 14.9   FrmCreateSequentialAccessFile class creates and writes to
sequential-access files. (Part 4 of 5.)

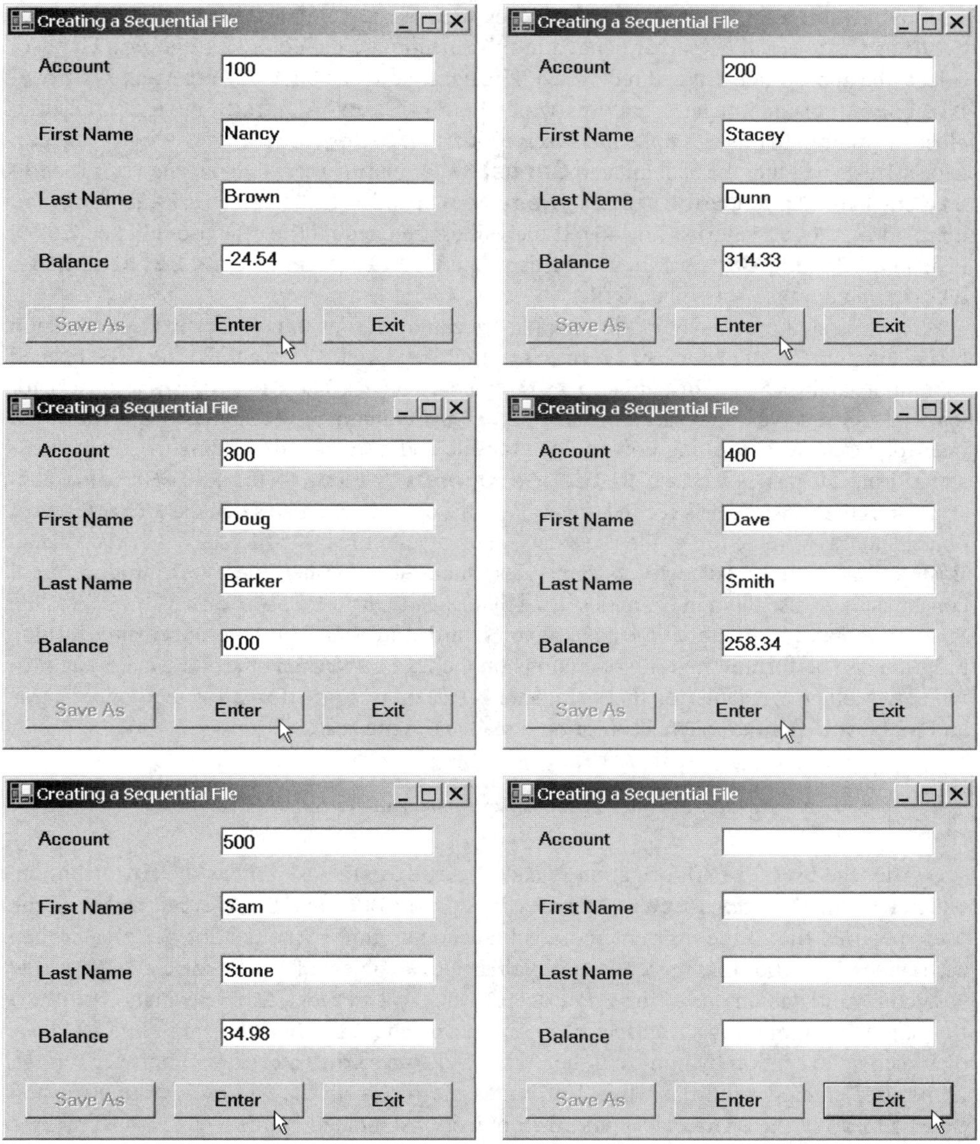

Fig. 14.9 FrmCreateSequentialAccessFile class creates and writes to sequential-access files. (Part 5 of 5.)

When the user clicks the **Save As** button, the program invokes method **cmdSave_Click** (lines 30–73). Line 34 instantiates an object of class **SaveFileDialog**, which belongs to the **System.Windows.Forms** namespace. Objects of this class are used for selecting files (see the second screen in Fig. 14.9). Line 36 calls method **ShowDialog** of the **SaveFileDialog** object to display the **SaveFileDialog**.

When displayed, a **SaveFileDialog** prevents the user from interacting with any other window in the program until the user closes the **SaveFileDialog** by clicking either **Save** or **Cancel**. Dialogs that behave in this fashion are called *modal dialogs*. The user selects the appropriate drive, directory and file name and then clicks **Save**. Method **Show-Dialog** returns an integer specifying which button (**Save** or **Cancel**) the user clicked to close the dialog. In this example, the **Form** property **DialogResult** receives the integer. Line 42 tests whether the user clicked **Cancel** by comparing the value returned by property **DialogResult** to **Const** *DialogResult.Cancel*. If the values are equal, method **cmdSave_Click** returns (line 43). If the values are unequal (i.e., the user clicked **Save**, instead of clicking **Cancel**), line 46 uses property *FileName* of class **SaveFileDialog** to obtain the user-selected file.

As we stated previously in this chapter, we can open files to perform text manipulation by creating objects of classes **FileStream**. In this example, we want the file to be opened for output, so lines 58–59 instantiate a **FileStream** object. The **FileStream** constructor that we use receives three arguments—a **String** containing the name of the file to be opened, a **Const** describing how to open the file and a **Const** describing the file permissions. Line 59 passes **Const FileMode.OpenOrCreate** to the **FileStream** constructor as the constructor's second argument. This constant indicates that the **FileStream** object should open the file, if the file exists, or create the file if the file does not exist. Visual Basic offers other **FileMode** constants describing how to open files; we introduce these constants as we use them in examples. Line 59 passes **Const FileAccess.Write** to the **FileStream** constructor as the constructor's third argument. This constant ensures that the program can perform write-only operations on the **FileStream** object. Visual Basic provides two other constants for this parameter—**FileAccess.Read** for read-only access and **FileAccess.ReadWrite** for both read and write access.

 Good Programming Practice 14.1

When opening files, use the **FileAccess** *enumeration to control user access.*

After the user types information in each **TextBox**, the user clicks the **Enter** button, which calls method **cmdEnter_Click** (lines 76–133) to save the **TextBox** data in the user-specified file. If the user entered a valid account number (i.e., an integer greater than zero), lines 102–106 store the **TextBox** values into an object of type **CRecord**. If the user entered invalid data in one of the **TextBox**es (such as entering a **String** in the **Balance** field), the program throws a **FormatException**. The **Catch** statement in line 124 handles such an exception by notifying the user (via a **MessageBox**) of the improper format. If the user entered valid data, line 109 writes the record to the file by invoking method **Serialize** of the **BinaryFormatter** object (instantiated in line 24). Class **Binary-Formatter** uses methods *Serialize* and *Deserialize* to write and read objects into streams, respectively. Method **Serialize** writes the object's representation to a file. Method **Deserialize** reads this representation from a file and reconstructs the original object. Both methods throw **SerializationException**s if an error occurs during serialization or deserialization (errors results when the methods attempt to access streams or records that do not exist). Both methods **Serialize** and **Deserialize** require a **Stream** object (e.g., the **FileStream**) as a parameter so that the **BinaryFormatter** can access the correct file; the **BinaryFormatter** must receive an instance of a class that derives from class **Stream**, because **Stream** is **MustInherit**. Class **BinaryFor-**

matter belongs the *System.Runtime.Serialization.Formatters.Binary* namespace.

Common Programming Error 14.1

Failure to open a file before attempting to reference it in a program is a logic error.

When the user clicks the **Exit** button, the program invokes method **cmdExit_Click** (lines 136–156) to exit the application. Line 144 closes the **FileStream** if one has been opened, and line 155 exits the program.

Performance Tip 14.1

Close each file explicitly when the program no longer needs to reference the file. This can reduce resource usage in programs that continues executing long after they finish using a specific file. The practice of explicitly closing files also improves program clarity.

Performance Tip 14.2

Releasing resources explicitly when they are no longer needed makes them immediately available for reuse by the program, thus improving resource utilization.

In the sample execution for the program of Fig. 14.9, we entered information for five accounts (Fig. 14.10). The program does not depict how the data records are rendered in the file. To verify that the file has been created successfully, in the next section we create a program to read and display the file.

14.6 Reading Data from a Sequential-Access File

Data are stored in files so that they can be retrieved for processing when they are needed. The previous section demonstrated how to create a file for sequential access. In this section, we discuss how to read (or retrieve) data sequentially from a file.

Class **FrmReadSequentialAccessFile** (Fig. 14.11) reads records from the file created by the program in Fig. 14.9 and then displays the contents of each record. Much of the code in this example is similar to that of Fig. 14.9, so we discuss only the unique aspects of the application.

When the user clicks the **Open File** button, the program calls method **cmdOpen_Click** (lines 29–58). Line 33 instantiates an object of class *OpenFileDialog*, and line 34 calls the object's *ShowDialog* method to display the **Open** dialog (see the second screenshot in Fig. 14.11). The behavior and GUI between the two dialog types are the same (except that **Save** is replaced by **Open**). If the user inputs a valid file name, lines 52–53 create a **FileStream** object and assign it to reference **input**. We pass **Const FileMode.Open** as the second argument to the **FileStream** constructor. This constant indicates that the **FileStream** should open the file if one exists and throw a **FileNotFoundException** if the file does not exist. (In this example, the **FileStream** constructor will not throw a **FileNotFoundException**, because the **OpenFileDialog** requires the user to enter a file that exists.) In the last example (Fig. 14.9), we wrote text to the file using a **FileStream** object with write-only access. In this example, (Fig. 14.11), we specify read-only access to the file by passing **Const FileAccess.Read** as the third argument to the **FileStream** constructor.

Account Number	First Name	Last Name	Balance
100	Nancy	Brown	-25.54
200	Stacey	Dunn	314.33
300	Doug	Barker	0.00
400	Dave	Smith	258.34
500	Sam	Stone	34.98

Fig. 14.10 Sample data for the program of Fig. 14.9.

```
1   ' Fig. 14.11: ReadSequentialAccessFile.vb
2   ' Reading a sequential-access file.
3
4   ' Visual Basic namespaces
5   Imports System.IO
6   Imports System.Runtime.Serialization.Formatters.Binary
7   Imports System.Runtime.Serialization
8   Imports System.Windows.Forms
9
10  ' Deitel namespaces
11  Imports BankLibrary
12
13  Public Class FrmReadSequentialAccessFile
14      Inherits FrmBankUI
15
16      ' GUI buttons for opening file and reading records
17      Friend WithEvents cmdOpen As Button
18      Friend WithEvents cmdNext As Button
19
20      ' Visual Studio .NET generated code
21
22      ' stream through which serializable data is read from file
23      Private input As FileStream
24
25      ' object for deserializing CRecord in binary format
26      Private reader As BinaryFormatter = New BinaryFormatter()
27
28      ' invoked when user clicks Open button
29      Protected Sub cmdOpen_Click(ByVal sender As Object, _
30          ByVal e As EventArgs) Handles cmdOpen.Click
31
32          ' create dialog box enabling user to open file
33          Dim fileChooser As OpenFileDialog = New OpenFileDialog()
34          Dim result As DialogResult = fileChooser.ShowDialog()
35          Dim fileName As String ' name of file containing data
36
```

Fig. 14.11 `FrmReadSequentialAccessFile` class reads sequential-access files. (Part 1 of 4.)

```
37                ' exit event handler if user clicked Cancel
38           If result = DialogResult.Cancel Then
39                Return
40           End If
41
42           fileName = fileChooser.FileName ' get specified file name
43           ClearTextBoxes()
44
45           ' show error if user specified invalid file
46           If (fileName = "" OrElse fileName = Nothing) Then
47                MessageBox.Show("Invalid File Name", "Error", _
48                   MessageBoxButtons.OK, MessageBoxIcon.Error)
49           Else ' open file if user specified valid file
50
51                ' create FileStream to obtain read access to file
52                input = New FileStream(fileName, FileMode.Open, _
53                   FileAccess.Read)
54
55                cmdNext.Enabled = True ' enable Next Record button
56
57           End If
58      End Sub ' cmdOpen_Click
59
60      ' invoked when user clicks Next button
61      Protected Sub cmdNext_Click(ByVal sender As Object, _
62          ByVal e As EventArgs) Handles cmdNext.Click
63
64           ' deserialize CRecord and store data in TextBoxes
65           Try
66
67                ' get next CRecord available in file
68                Dim record As CRecord = _
69                   CType(reader.Deserialize(input), CRecord)
70
71                ' store CRecord values in temporary String array
72                Dim values As String() = New String() { _
73                   record.Account.ToString(), _
74                   record.FirstName.ToString(), _
75                   record.LastName.ToString(), _
76                   record.Balance.ToString()}
77
78                ' copy String-array values to TextBox values
79                SetTextBoxValues(values)
80
81           ' handle exception when no CRecords in file
82           Catch serializableException As SerializationException
83
84                input.Close() ' close FileStream if no CRecords in file
85
86                cmdOpen.Enabled = True ' enable Open Record button
87                cmdNext.Enabled = False ' disable Next Record button
88
```

Fig. 14.11 `FrmReadSequentialAccessFile` class reads sequential-access files. (Part 2 of 4.)

```
89              ClearTextBoxes()
90
91          ' notify user if no CRecords in file
92          MessageBox.Show("No more records in file", "", _
93              MessageBoxButtons.OK, MessageBoxIcon.Information)
94      End Try
95
96   End Sub ' cmdNext_Click
97
98 End Class ' FrmReadSequentialAccessFile
```

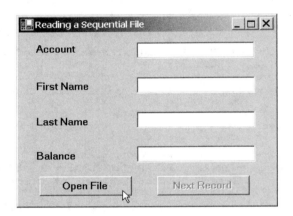

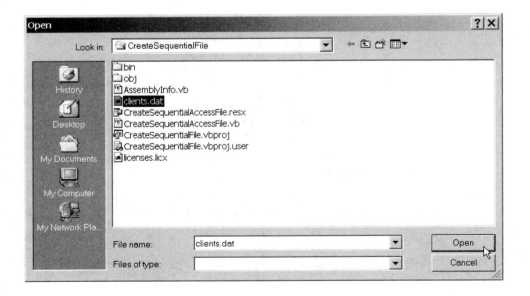

Fig. 14.11 **FrmReadSequentialAccessFile** class reads sequential-access files. (Part 3 of 4.)

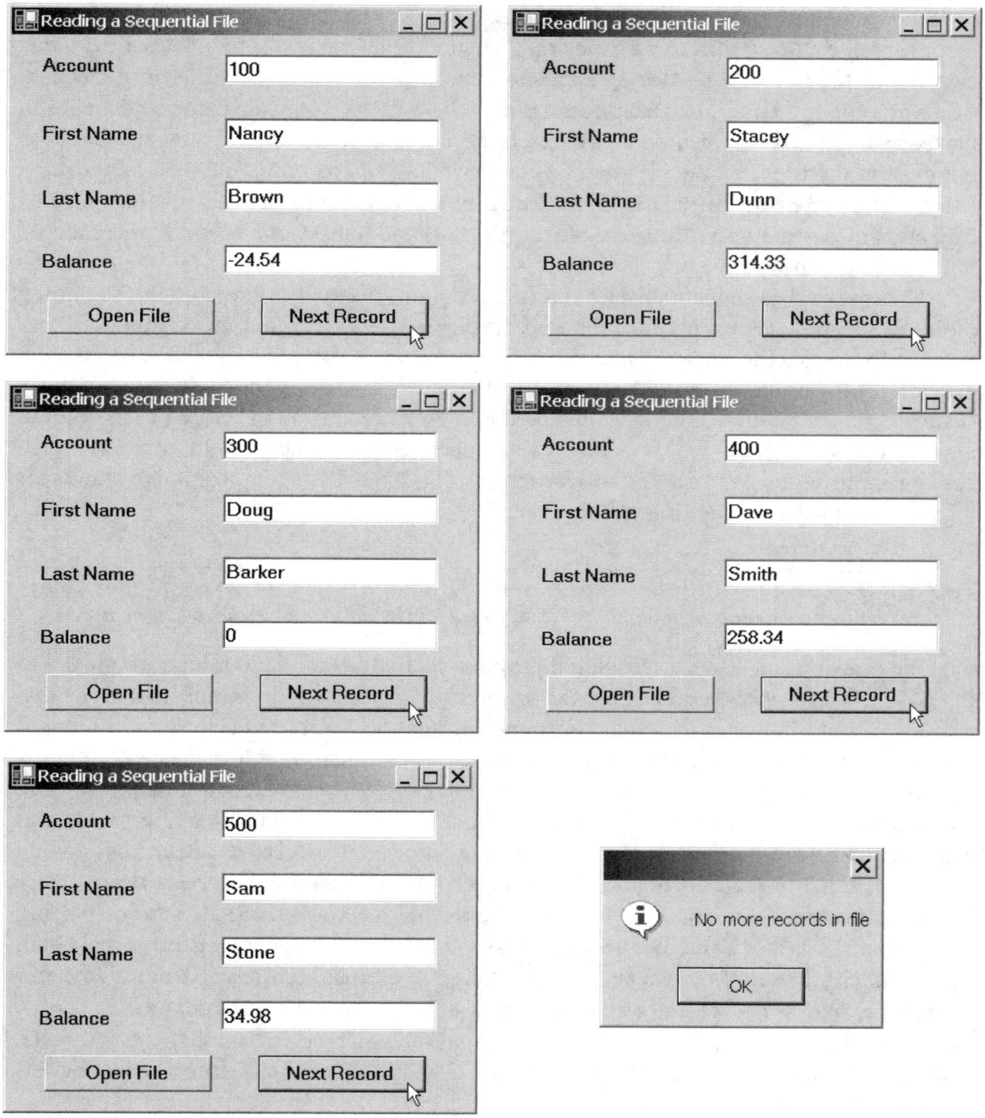

Fig. 14.11 FrmReadSequentialAccessFile class reads sequential-access files. (Part 4 of 4.)

Testing and Debugging Tip 14.1

*Open a file with the **FileAccess.Read** file-open mode if the contents of the file should not be modified. This prevents unintentional modification of the file's contents.*

When the user clicks the **Next Record** button, the program calls method **cmdNext_Click** (lines 61–96), which reads the next record from the user-specified file.

(The user must click **Next Record** to view the first record after opening the file.) Lines 68–69 call method **Deserialize** of the **BinaryFormatter** object to read the next record. Method **Deserialize** reads the data and casts the result to a **CRecord**—this cast is necessary, because **Deserialize** returns a reference to an instance of class **Object** (not of **BinaryFormatter**). Lines 72–79 then display the **CRecord** values in the **TextBox**es. When method **Deserialize** attempts to deserialize a record that does not exist in the file (i.e., the program has displayed all file records), the method throws a **SerializationException**. The **Catch** block (defined in line 82) that handles this exception closes the **FileStream** object (line 84) and notifies the user that there are no more records (lines 92–93).

To retrieve data sequentially from a file, programs normally start from the beginning of the file, reading data consecutively until the desired data are found. It sometimes is necessary to process a file sequentially several times (from the beginning of the file) during the execution of a program. A **FileStream** object can reposition its *file-position pointer* (which contains the byte number of the next byte to be read from or written to the file) to any position in the file—we show this feature when we introduce random-access file-processing applications. When a **FileStream** object is opened, its file-position pointer is set to zero (i.e., the beginning of the file)

Performance Tip 14.3

It is time-consuming to close and reopen a file for the purpose of moving the file-position pointer to the file's beginning. Doing so frequently could slow program performance.

We now present a more substantial program that builds on the concepts employed in Fig. 14.11. Class **FrmCreditInquiry** (Fig. 14.12) is a credit-inquiry program that enables a credit manager to display account information for those customers with credit balances (i.e., customers to whom the company owes money), zero balances (i.e., customers who do not owe the company money) and debit balances (i.e., customers who owe the company money for previously received goods and services). Note that line 18 declares a **RichTextBox** that will display the account information. **RichTextBox**es provide more functionality than do regular **TextBox**es—for example, **RichTextBox**es offer method **Find** for searching individual **String**s and method **LoadFile** for displaying file contents. Class **RichTextBox** does not inherit from class **TextBox**; rather, both classes inherit directly from **MustInherit** class **System.Windows.Forms.Text-BoxBase**. We use a **RichTextBox** in this example, because, by default, a **RichTextBox** displays multiple lines of text, whereas a regular **TextBox** displays only one. Alternatively, we could have specified multiple lines of text for a **TextBox** object by setting its **Multiline** property to **True**.

```
1    ' Fig. 14.12: CreditInquiry.vb
2    ' Read a file sequentially and display contents based on account
3    ' type specified by user (credit, debit or zero balances).
4
5    ' Visual Basic namespaces
6    Imports System.IO
```

Fig. 14.12 FrmCreditInquiry class is a program that displays credit inquiries. (Part 1 of 7.)

```
 7   Imports System.Runtime.Serialization.Formatters.Binary
 8   Imports System.Runtime.Serialization
 9   Imports System.Windows.Forms
10
11   ' Deitel namespaces
12   Imports BankLibrary
13
14   Public Class FrmCreditInquiry
15      Inherits Form
16
17      ' displays several lines of output
18      Friend WithEvents txtDisplay As RichTextBox
19
20      ' buttons to open file, read records and exit program
21      Friend WithEvents cmdOpen As Button
22      Friend WithEvents cmdCredit As Button
23      Friend WithEvents cmdDebit As Button
24      Friend WithEvents cmdZero As Button
25      Friend WithEvents cmdDone As Button
26
27      ' Visual Studio .NET generated code
28
29      ' stream through which serializable data is read from file
30      Private input As FileStream
31
32      ' object for deserializing CRecord in binary format
33      Dim reader As BinaryFormatter = New BinaryFormatter()
34
35      ' name of file that stores credit, debit and zero balances
36      Private fileName As String
37
38      ' invoked when user clicks Open File button
39      Protected Sub cmdOpen_Click(ByVal sender As Object, _
40         ByVal e As System.EventArgs) Handles cmdOpen.Click
41
42         ' create dialog box enabling user to open file
43         Dim fileChooser As OpenFileDialog = New OpenFileDialog()
44         Dim result As DialogResult = fileChooser.ShowDialog()
45
46         ' exit event handler if user clicked Cancel
47         If result = DialogResult.Cancel Then
48            Return
49         End If
50
51         fileName = fileChooser.FileName ' get file name from user
52
53         ' enable buttons allowing user to display balances
54         cmdCredit.Enabled = True
55         cmdDebit.Enabled = True
56         cmdZero.Enabled = True
57
```

Fig. 14.12 FrmCreditInquiry class is a program that displays credit inquiries.
(Part 2 of 7.)

```
58              ' show error if user specified invalid file
59              If (fileName = "" OrElse fileName = Nothing) Then
60                 MessageBox.Show("Invalid File Name", "Error", _
61                    MessageBoxButtons.OK, MessageBoxIcon.Error)
62
63              ' else enable all GUI buttons, except for Open File button
64              Else
65                 cmdOpen.Enabled = False
66                 cmdCredit.Enabled = True
67                 cmdDebit.Enabled = True
68                 cmdZero.Enabled = True
69              End If
70
71          End Sub ' cmdOpen_Click
72
73          ' invoked when user clicks Credit Balances, Debit Balances
74          ' or Zero Balances button
75          Protected Sub cmdGet_Click(ByVal senderObject As Object, _
76             ByVal e As System.EventArgs) Handles cmdCredit.Click, _
77             cmdZero.Click, cmdDebit.Click
78
79              ' convert senderObject explicitly to object of type Button
80              Dim senderButton As Button = CType(senderObject, Button)
81
82              ' get text from clicked Button, which stores account type
83              Dim accountType As String = senderButton.Text
84
85              ' used to store each record read from file
86              Dim record As CRecord
87
88              ' read and display file information
89              Try
90
91                 ' close file from previous operation
92                 If (input Is Nothing) = False Then
93                    input.Close()
94                 End If
95
96                 ' create FileStream to obtain read access to file
97                 input = New FileStream(fileName, FileMode.Open, _
98                    FileAccess.Read)
99
100                txtDisplay.Text = "The accounts are:" & vbCrLf
101
102                ' traverse file until end of file
103                While True
104
105                   ' get next CRecord available in file
106                   record = CType(reader.Deserialize(input), CRecord)
107
108                   ' store record's last field in balance
109                   Dim balance As Double = record.Balance
```

Fig. 14.12 FrmCreditInquiry class is a program that displays credit inquiries. (Part 3 of 7.)

```
110
111                    ' determine whether to display balance
112                    If ShouldDisplay(balance, accountType) = True Then
113
114                        ' display record
115                        Dim output As String = record.Account & vbTab & _
116                            record.FirstName & vbTab & record.LastName & _
117                            Space(6) & vbTab
118
119                        ' display balance with correct monetary format
120                        output &= _
121                            String.Format("{0:F}", balance) & vbCrLf
122
123                        txtDisplay.Text &= output ' copy output to screen
124                    End If
125
126                End While
127
128           ' handle exception when file cannot be closed
129           Catch fileException As IOException
130              MessageBox.Show("Cannot Close File", "Error", _
131                 MessageBoxButtons.OK, MessageBoxIcon.Error)
132
133           ' handle exception when no more records
134           Catch serializableException As SerializationException
135              input.Close() ' close FileStream if no CRecords in file
136
137         End Try
138
139      End Sub ' cmdGet_Click
140
141      ' determine whether to display given record
142      Private Function ShouldDisplay(ByVal balance As Double, _
143         ByVal accountType As String) As Boolean
144
145         If balance > 0 Then
146
147             ' display Credit Balances
148             If accountType = "Credit Balances" Then
149                Return True
150             End If
151
152         ElseIf balance < 0 Then
153
154             ' display Debit Balances
155             If accountType = "Debit Balances" Then
156                Return True
157             End If
158
```

Fig. 14.12 **FrmCreditInquiry** class is a program that displays credit inquiries. (Part 4 of 7.)

```vbnet
159            Else ' balance = 0
160
161                ' display Zero Balances
162                If accountType = "Zero Balances" Then
163                    Return True
164                End If
165
166            End If
167
168            Return False
169        End Function ' ShouldDisplay
170
171        ' invoked when user clicks Done button
172        Protected Sub cmdDone_Click(ByVal sender As Object, _
173            ByVal e As System.EventArgs) Handles cmdDone.Click
174
175            ' determine whether file exists
176            If input Is Nothing = False Then
177
178                ' close file
179                Try
180                    input.Close()
181
182                ' notify user of error closing file
183                Catch fileException As IOException
184                    MessageBox.Show("Cannot close file", "Error", _
185                        MessageBoxButtons.OK, MessageBoxIcon.Error)
186
187                End Try
188
189            End If
190
191            Application.Exit()
192        End Sub ' cmdDone_Click
193
194  End Class ' FrmCreditInquiry
```

Fig. 14.12 FrmCreditInquiry class is a program that displays credit inquiries. (Part 5 of 7.)

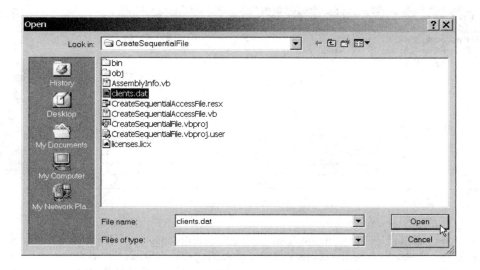

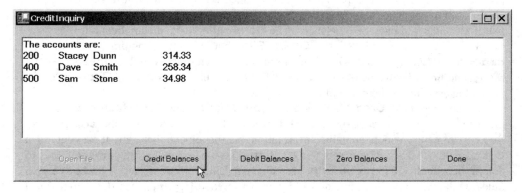

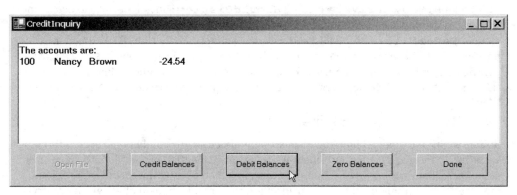

Fig. 14.12 FrmCreditInquiry class is a program that displays credit inquiries. (Part 6 of 7.)

Fig. 14.12 FrmCreditInquiry class is a program that displays credit inquiries. (Part 7 of 7.)

The program displays buttons that enable a credit manager to obtain credit information. The **Open File** button opens a file for gathering data. The **Credit Balances** button produces a list of accounts that have credit balances. The **Debit Balances** button produces a list of accounts that have debit balances. The **Zero Balances** button produces a list of accounts that have zero balances. The **Done** button exits the application.

When the user clicks the **Open File** button, the program calls method **cmdOpen_Click** (lines 39–71). Line 43 instantiates an object of class *OpenFileDialog*, and line 44 calls the object's *ShowDialog* method to display the **Open** dialog, in which the user inputs the name of the file to open.

When user clicks **Credit Balances**, **Debit Balances** or **Zero Balances**, the program invokes method **cmdGet_Click** (lines 75–139). Line 80 casts the **senderObject** parameter, which contains information on the object that sent the event, to a **Button** object. Line 83 extracts the **Button** object's text, which the program uses to determine which GUI **Button** the user clicked. Lines 97–98 create a **FileStream** object with read-only file access and assign it to reference **input**. Lines 103–126 define a **While** loop that uses **Private** method **ShouldDisplay** (lines 142–169) to determine whether to display each record in the file. The **While** loop obtains each record by calling method **Deserialize** of the **FileStream** object repeatedly (line 106). When the file-position pointer reaches the end of file, method **Deserialize** throws a **SerializationException**, which the **Catch** statement in line 134 handles—line 135 calls the **Close** method of **FileStream** to close the file, and method **cmdGet_Click** returns.

14.7 Random-Access Files

So far, we have explained how to create sequential-access files and how to search through such files to locate particular information. However, sequential-access files are inappropriate for so-called *"instant-access" applications*, in which a particular record of information must be located immediately. Popular instant-access applications include airline-reservation systems, banking systems, point-of-sale systems, automated-teller machines and other kinds of *transaction-processing systems* that require rapid access to specific data. The bank at which an individual has an account might have hundreds of thousands or even millions of other customers, however, when that individual uses an automated teller machine, the appropriate account is checked for sufficient funds in seconds. This type of instant access is made possible by *random-access files*. Individual records of a random-access file can be accessed directly (and quickly) without searching through potentially large numbers of other records, as is necessary with sequential-access files. Random-access files sometimes are called *direct-access files*.

As we discussed earlier in this chapter, Visual Basic does not impose structure on files, so applications that use random-access files must create the random-access capability. There are a variety of techniques for creating random-access files. Perhaps the simplest involves requiring that all records in a file be of uniform fixed length. The use of fixed-length records enables a program to calculate (as a function of the record size and the record key) the exact location of any record in relation to the beginning of the file. We soon demonstrate how this facilitates immediate access to specific records, even in large files.

Figure 14.13 illustrates the view we will create of a random-access file composed of fixed-length records (each record in this figure is 100 bytes long). Readers can consider a random-access file as analogous to a railroad train with many cars, some of which are empty and some of which contain contents.

Data can be inserted into a random-access file without destroying other data in the file. In addition, previously stored data can be updated or deleted without rewriting the entire file. In the following sections, we explain how to create a random-access file, write data to that file, read the data both sequentially and randomly, update the data and delete data that is no longer needed.

Figure 14.14 contains class **CRandomAccessRecord**, which is used in the random-access file-processing applications in this chapter. This class also belongs to the **Bank-Library** DLL—i.e., it is part of the project that contains classes **FrmBankUI** and **CRecord**. (When adding class **CRandomAccessRecord** to the project containing **FrmBankUI** and **CRecord**, remember to rebuild the project.)

Like class **CRecord** (Fig. 14.8), class **CRandomAccessRecord** contains **Private** data members (lines 18–21) for storing record information, two constructors for setting these members to default and parameter-specified values, and properties for accessing these members. However, class **CRandomAccessRecord** does not contain attribute **<Serializable>** before its class definition. We do not serialize this class, because Visual Basic does not provide a means to obtain an object's size at runtime. This means that we cannot guarantee a fixed-length record size.

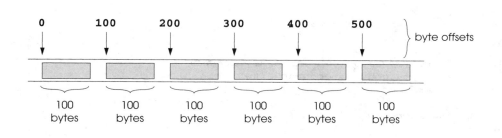

Fig. 14.13 Random-access file with fixed-length records.

```vb
1    ' Fig. 14.14: CRandomAccessRecord.vb
2    ' Data-record class for random-access applications.
3
4    Public Class CRandomAccessRecord
5
6       ' length of mFirstName and mLastName
7       Private Const CHAR_ARRAY_LENGTH As Integer = 15
8
9       Private Const SIZE_OF_CHAR As Integer = 2
10      Private Const SIZE_OF_INT32 As Integer = 4
11      Private Const SIZE_OF_DOUBLE As Integer = 8
12
13      ' length of record
14      Public Const SIZE As Integer = SIZE_OF_INT32 + _
15         2 * (SIZE_OF_CHAR * CHAR_ARRAY_LENGTH) + SIZE_OF_DOUBLE
16
17      ' record data
18      Private mAccount As Integer
19      Private mFirstName(CHAR_ARRAY_LENGTH) As Char
20      Private mLastName(CHAR_ARRAY_LENGTH) As Char
21      Private mBalance As Double
22
23      ' default constructor sets members to default values
24      Public Sub New()
25         Me.New(0, "", "", 0.0)
26      End Sub ' New
27
28      ' overloaded constructor sets members to parameter values
29      Public Sub New(ByVal accountValue As Integer, _
30         ByVal firstNameValue As String, _
31         ByVal lastNameValue As String, _
32         ByVal balanceValue As Double)
33
34         Account = accountValue
35         FirstName = firstNameValue
36         LastName = lastNameValue
37         Balance = balanceValue
38      End Sub ' New
39
40      ' property Account
41      Public Property Account() As Integer
42
43         Get
44            Return mAccount
45         End Get
46
47         Set(ByVal accountValue As Integer)
48            mAccount = accountValue
49         End Set
50
51      End Property ' Account
52
```

Fig. 14.14 CRandomAccessRecord class represents a record for random-access file-processing applications. (Part 1 of 3.)

```
53          ' property FirstName
54          Public Property FirstName() As String
55
56             Get
57                Return mFirstName
58             End Get
59
60             Set(ByVal firstNameValue As String)
61
62                ' determine length of String parameter
63                Dim stringSize As Integer = firstNameValue.Length()
64
65                ' recordFirstName String representation
66                Dim recordFirstNameString As String = firstNameValue
67
68                ' append spaces to String parameter if too short
69                If CHAR_ARRAY_LENGTH >= stringSize Then
70                   recordFirstNameString = firstNameValue & _
71                      Space(CHAR_ARRAY_LENGTH - stringSize)
72
73                ' remove characters from String parameter if too long
74                Else
75                   recordFirstNameString = _
76                      firstNameValue.Substring(0, CHAR_ARRAY_LENGTH)
77                End If
78
79                ' convert String parameter to Char array
80                mFirstName = recordFirstNameString.ToCharArray()
81
82             End Set
83
84          End Property ' FirstName
85
86          ' property LastName
87          Public Property LastName() As String
88
89             Get
90                Return mLastName
91             End Get
92
93             Set(ByVal lastNameValue As String)
94
95                ' determine length of String parameter
96                Dim stringSize As Integer = lastNameValue.Length()
97
98                ' recordLastName String representation
99                Dim recordLastNameString As String = lastNameValue
100
101               ' append spaces to String parameter if too short
102               If CHAR_ARRAY_LENGTH >= stringSize Then
103                  recordLastNameString = lastNameValue & _
104                     Space(CHAR_ARRAY_LENGTH - stringSize)
```

Fig. 14.14 CRandomAccessRecord class represents a record for random-access file-processing applications. (Part 2 of 3.)

```
105
106                ' remove characters from String parameter if too long
107                Else
108                   recordLastNameString = _
109                      lastNameValue.Substring(0, CHAR_ARRAY_LENGTH)
110                End If
111
112                ' convert String parameter to Char array
113                mLastName = recordLastNameString.ToCharArray()
114
115          End Set
116
117       End Property ' LastName
118
119       ' property Balance
120       Public Property Balance() As Double
121
122          Get
123             Return mBalance
124          End Get
125
126          Set(ByVal balanceValue As Double)
127             mBalance = balanceValue
128          End Set
129
130       End Property ' Balance
131
132    End Class ' CRandomAccessRecord
```

Fig. 14.14 **CRandomAccessRecord** class represents a record for random-access
file-processing applications. (Part 3 of 3.)

Instead of serializing the class, we fix the length of the **Private** data members and
then write those data as a byte stream to the file. To fix this length, the **Set** accessors of
properties **FirstName** (lines 60–82) and **LastName** (lines 93–115) ensure that members
mFirstName and **mLastName** are **Char** arrays of exactly 15 elements. Each **Set**
accessor receives as an argument a **String** representing the first name and last name,
respectively. If the **String** parameter contains fewer than 15 **Char**s, the property's **Set**
accessor copies the **String**'s values to the **Char** array and then populates the remainder
with spaces. If the **String** parameter contains more than 15 **Char**s, the **Set** accessor
stores only the first 15 **Char**s of the **String** parameter into the **Char** array.

Lines 14–15 declare **Const SIZE**, which specifies the record's length. Each record
contains **mAccount** (4-byte **Integer**), **mFirstName** and **mLastName** (two 15-ele-
ment **Char** arrays, where each **Char** occupies two bytes, resulting in a total of 60 bytes)
and **mBalance** (8-byte **Double**). In this example, each record (i.e., the four **Private**
data members that our programs will read to and write from files) occupies 72 bytes (4
bytes + 60 bytes + 8 bytes).

14.8 Creating a Random-Access File

Consider the following problem statement for a credit-processing application:

> *Create a transaction-processing program capable of storing a maximum of 100 fixed-length records for a company that can have a maximum of 100 customers. Each record consists of an account number (that acts as the record key), a last name, a first name and a balance. The program can update an account, create an account and delete an account.*

The next several sections introduce the techniques necessary to create this credit-processing program. We now discuss the program used to create the random-access file that the programs of Fig. 14.16 and Fig. 14.17 and the transaction-processing application use to manipulate data. Class **CCreateRandomAccessFile** (Fig. 14.15) creates a random-access file.

```vb
1    ' Fig. 14.15: CreateRandomAccessFile.vb
2    ' Creating a random file.
3
4    ' Visual Basic namespaces
5    Imports System.IO
6    Imports System.Windows.Forms
7
8    ' Deitel namespaces
9    Imports BankLibrary
10
11   Public Class CCreateRandomAccessFile
12
13      ' number of records to write to disk
14      Private Const NUMBER_OF_RECORDS As Integer = 100
15
16      ' start application
17      Shared Sub Main()
18
19         ' create random file, then save to disk
20         Dim file As CCreateRandomAccessFile = _
21            CCreateRandomAccessFile()
22
23         file.SaveFile()
24      End Sub ' Main
25
26      ' write records to disk
27      Private Sub SaveFile()
28
29         ' record for writing to disk
30         Dim blankRecord As CRandomAccessRecord = _
31            New CRandomAccessRecord()
32
33         ' stream through which serializable data is written to file
34         Dim fileOutput As FileStream
35
36         ' stream for writing bytes to file
37         Dim binaryOutput As BinaryWriter
```

Fig. 14.15 CCreateRandomAccessFile class creates files for random-access file-processing applications. (Part 1 of 3.)

```
38
39            ' create dialog box enabling user to save file
40            Dim fileChooser As SaveFileDialog = New SaveFileDialog()
41            Dim result As DialogResult = fileChooser.ShowDialog
42
43            ' get file name from user
44            Dim fileName As String = fileChooser.FileName
45            Dim i As Integer
46
47            ' exit event handler if user clicked Cancel
48            If result = DialogResult.Cancel Then
49               Return
50            End If
51
52            ' show error if user specified invalid file
53            If (fileName = "" OrElse fileName = Nothing) Then
54               MessageBox.Show("Invalid File Name", "Error", _
55                  MessageBoxButtons.OK, MessageBoxIcon.Error)
56            Else
57
58               ' write records to file
59               Try
60
61                  ' create FileStream to hold records
62                  fileOutput = New FileStream(fileName, _
63                     FileMode.Create, FileAccess.Write)
64
65                  ' set length of file
66                  fileOutput.SetLength( _
67                     CRandomAccessRecord.SIZE * NUMBER_OF_RECORDS)
68
69                  ' create object for writing bytes to file
70                  binaryOutput = New BinaryWriter(fileOutput)
71
72                  ' write empty records to file
73                  For i = 0 To NUMBER_OF_RECORDS - 1
74
75                     ' set file-position pointer in file
76                     fileOutput.Position = i * CRandomAccessRecord.SIZE
77
78                     ' write blank record to file
79                     binaryOutput.Write(blankRecord.Account)
80                     binaryOutput.Write(blankRecord.FirstName)
81                     binaryOutput.Write(blankRecord.LastName)
82                     binaryOutput.Write(blankRecord.Balance)
83                  Next
84
85                  ' notify user of success
86                  MessageBox.Show("File Created", "Success", _
87                     MessageBoxButtons.OK, MessageBoxIcon.Information)
88
```

Fig. 14.15 CCreateRandomAccessFile class creates files for random-access file-processing applications. (Part 2 of 3.)

```
89                  ' show error if error occurs during writing
90              Catch fileException As IOException
91                  MessageBox.Show("Cannot write to file", "Error", _
92                     MessageBoxButtons.OK, MessageBoxIcon.Error)
93
94              End Try
95
96          End If
97
98          ' close FileStream
99              (fileOutput             ) <>
100             fileOutput.Close()
101
102
103         ' close BinaryWriter
104             (binaryOutput           ) <>
105             binaryOutput.Close()
106
107
108     End Sub ' SaveFile
109
110  End Class ' CCreateRandomAccessFile
```

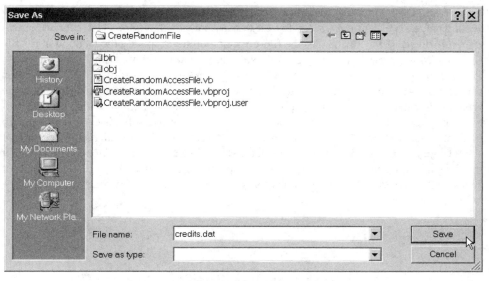

Fig. 14.15 `CCreateRandomAccessFile` class creates files for random-access file-processing applications. (Part 3 of 3.)

Method **Main** (lines 17–24) starts the application, which creates a random-access file by calling user-defined method **SaveFile** (lines 27–108). Method **SaveFile** populates a file with 100 copies of the default (i.e., empty) values for **Private** data members **mAccount**, **mFirstName**, **mLastName** and **mBalance** of class **CRandomAccess-Record**. Lines 40–41 create and display the **SaveFileDialog**, which enables a user to specify the file to which the program writes data. Using this file, lines 62–63 instantiate the **FileStream**—note that lines 63 passes **Const FileMode.Create**, which either creates the specified file, if the file does not exist, or overwrites the specified file if it does exist. Lines 66–67 sets the **FileStream**'s length, which is equal to the size of an individual **CRandomAccessRecord** (obtained through constant **CRandomAccess-Record.SIZE**) multiplied by the number of records we want to copy (obtained through constant **NUMBER_OF_RECORDS** in line 14, which we set to value **100**).

We now require a means to write bytes to a file. Class *BinaryWriter* of namespace **System.IO** provides methods for writing bytes to streams, rather than files. The **BinaryWriter** constructor receives as an argument a reference to an instance of class **System.IO.Stream** through which the **BinaryWriter** can write bytes. Because class **FileStream** provides methods for writing streams to files and inherits from class **Stream**, we can pass the **FileStream** object as an argument to the **BinaryWriter** constructor (line 70). Now, we can use the **BinaryWriter** to write bytes directly to the file.

Lines 73–83 define the **For** loop that populates the file with 100 copies of the empty record values (i.e., default values for **Private** data members of class **CRandomAccessRecord**). Line 76 changes the file-position pointer to specify the location in the file in which to write the next empty record. Now that we are working with a random-access file, we must set the file-pointer explicitly using the **Set** accessor of the **FileStream** object's **Position** property. This method receives as an argument a **Long** value describing where to position the pointer relative to the beginning of the file—in this example, we set the pointer so that it advances a number of bytes that is equal to the record size (obtained by **CRandomAccessRecord.SIZE**). Lines 79–82 call method **Write** of the **BinaryWriter** object to write the data. Method **Write** is an overloaded method that receives as an argument any primitive data type and then writes that type to a stream of bytes. After the **For** loop exits, lines 99–106 close the **FileStream** and **BinaryWriter** objects.

14.9 Writing Data Randomly to a Random-Access File

Now that we have created a random-access file, we use class **FrmWriteRandomAccessFile** (Fig. 14.16) to write data to that file. When a user clicks the **Open File** button, the program invokes method **cmdOpen_Click** (lines 30–75), which displays the **OpenFileDialog** for specifying the file to serialize data (lines 34–35), and then uses the specified file to create **FileStream** object with write-only access (lines 57–58). Line 61 uses the **FileStream** reference to instantiate an object of class **BinaryWriter**, enabling the program to write bytes to files. We used the same approach with class **CCreateRandomAccessFile** (Fig. 14.15).

The user enters values in the **TextBox**es for the account number, first name, last name and balance. When the user clicks the **Enter** button, the program invokes method **cmdEnter_Click** (lines 78–131), which writes the data in the **TextBox**es to the file. Line 85 calls method **GetTextBoxValues** (provided by base class **FrmBankUI**) to retrieve the data. Lines 98–99 determine whether the **Account Number TextBox** holds valid information (i.e., the account number is in the **1–100** range).

```vb
1    ' Fig. 14.16: WriteRandomAccessFile.vb
2    ' Write data to a random-access file.
3
4    ' Visual Basic namespaces
5    Imports System.IO
6    Imports System.Windows.Forms
7
8    ' Deitel namespaces
9    Imports BankLibrary
10
11   Public Class FrmWriteRandomAccessFile
12      Inherits FrmBankUI
13
14      ' buttons for opening file and entering data
15                       cmdOpen      Button
16                       cmdEnter     Button
17
18      ' Visual Studio .NET generated code
19
20      ' number of CRandomAccessRecords to write to disk
21      Private Const NUMBER_OF_RECORDS As Integer = 100
22
23      ' stream through which data is written to file
24      Private fileOutput As FileStream
25
26      ' stream for writing bytes to file
27      Private binaryOutput As BinaryWriter
28
29      ' invoked when user clicks Open button
30      Public Sub cmdOpen_Click(ByVal sender As System.Object, _
31         ByVal e As System.EventArgs) Handles cmdOpen.Click
32
33         ' create dialog box enabling user to open file
34         Dim fileChooser As OpenFileDialog = New OpenFileDialog()
35         Dim result As DialogResult = fileChooser.ShowDialog()
36
37         ' get file name from user
38         Dim fileName As String = fileChooser.FileName
39
40         ' exit event handler if user clicked Cancel
41         If result = DialogResult.Cancel Then
42            Return
43         End If
44
```

Fig. 14.16 **FrmWriteRandomAccessFile** class writes records to random-access files. (Part 1 of 5.)

```
45            ' show error if user specified invalid file
46            If (fileName = "" OrElse fileName = Nothing) Then
47               MessageBox.Show("Invalid File Name", "Error", _
48                  MessageBoxButtons.OK, MessageBoxIcon.Error)
49
50            ' open file if user specified valid file
51            Else
52
53               ' open file if file already exists
54               Try
55
56                  ' create FileStream to hold records
57                  fileOutput = New FileStream(fileName, FileMode.Open, _
58                     FileAccess.Write)
59
60                  ' create object for writing bytes to file
61                  binaryOutput = New BinaryWriter(fileOutput)
62
63                  cmdOpen.Enabled = False ' disable Open button
64                  cmdEnter.Enabled = True ' enable Enter button
65
66               ' notify user if file does not exist
67               Catch fileException As IOException
68                  MessageBox.Show("File Does Not Exist", "Error", _
69                     MessageBoxButtons.OK, MessageBoxIcon.Error)
70
71               End Try
72
73         End If
74
75      End Sub ' cmdOpen_Click
76
77      ' invoked when user clicks Enter button
78      Private Sub cmdEnter_Click(ByVal sender As System.Object, _
79         ByVal e As System.EventArgs) Handles cmdEnter.Click
80
81         ' account-number value from TextBox
82         Dim accountNumber As Integer
83
84         ' TextBox-values String array
85         Dim values As String() = GetTextBoxValues()
86
87         ' determine whether TextBox account field is empty
88         If (values(TextBoxIndices.ACCOUNT) <> "") Then
89
90            ' write record to file at appropriate position
91            Try
92
93               ' get account-number value from TextBox
94               accountNumber = _
95                  Convert.ToInt32(values(TextBoxIndices.ACCOUNT))
96
```

Fig. 14.16 FrmWriteRandomAccessFile class writes records to random-access files. (Part 2 of 5.)

```
97                        ' determine whether accountNumber is valid
98                        If (accountNumber > 0 AndAlso _
99                           accountNumber <= NUMBER_OF_RECORDS) Then
100
101                           ' move file-position pointer
102                           fileOutput.Seek((accountNumber - 1) * _
103                              CRandomAccessRecord.SIZE, SeekOrigin.Begin)
104
105                           ' write data to file
106                           binaryOutput.Write(accountNumber)
107                           binaryOutput.Write(values(TextBoxIndices.FIRST))
108                           binaryOutput.Write(values(TextBoxIndices.LAST))
109                           binaryOutput.Write( Convert.ToDouble( _
110                              values(TextBoxIndices.BALANCE)))
111
112                        ' notify user if invalid account number
113                        Else
114                           MessageBox.Show("Invalid Account Number", _
115                              "Error", MessageBoxButtons.OK, _
116                              MessageBoxIcon.Error)
117                        End If
118
119                        ClearTextBoxes()
120
121                     ' notify user if error occurs when formatting numbers
122                     Catch formattingException As FormatException
123                        MessageBox.Show("Invalid Balance", "Error", _
124                           MessageBoxButtons.OK, MessageBoxIcon.Error)
125
126                     End Try
127
128               End If
129
130         ClearTextBoxes() ' clear TextBox values
131      End Sub ' cmdEnter_Click
132
133   End Class ' FrmWriteRandomAccessFile
```

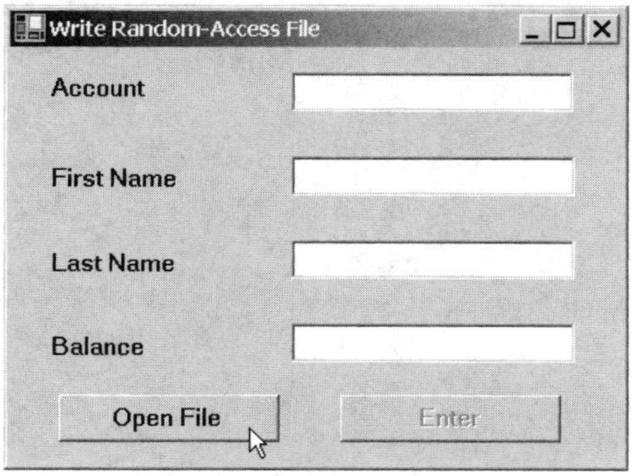

Fig. 14.16 FrmWriteRandomAccessFile class writes records to random-access files. (Part 3 of 5.)

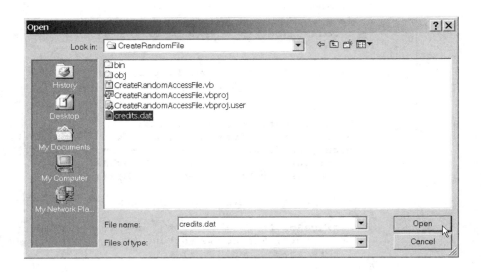

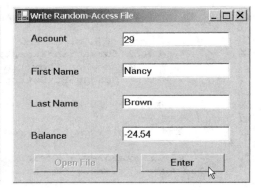

Fig. 14.16 FrmWriteRandomAccessFile class writes records to random-access files. (Part 4 of 5.)

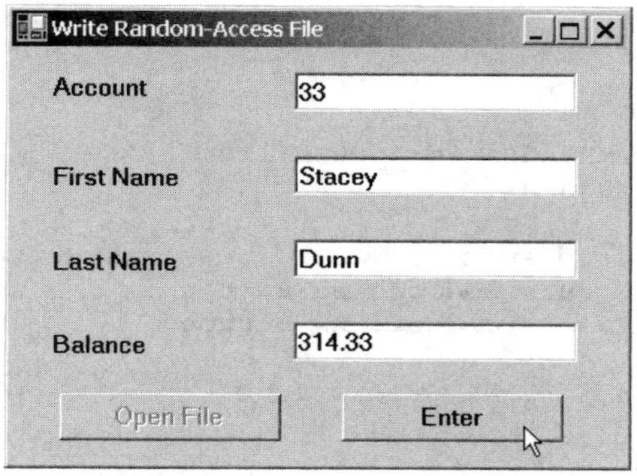

Fig. 14.16 `FrmWriteRandomAccessFile` class writes records to random-access files. (Part 5 of 5.)

Class **FrmWriteRandomAccessFile** must determine the position in the **FileStream** in which to insert the data from the **TextBox**es. Lines 102–103 use method **Seek** of the **FileStream** object to locate an exact location in the file. In this case, method **Seek** sets the position of the file-position pointer for the **FileStream** object to the byte location calculated by **(accountNumber - 1) * CRandomAccess-Record.SIZE**. Because the account numbers range from **1** to **100**, we subtract **1** from the account number when calculating the byte location of the record. For example, our use of method **Seek** sets the first record's file-position pointer to byte 0 of the file (the file's beginning). The second argument to method **Seek** is a member of the enumeration *Seek-Origin* and specifies the location in which the method should begin seeking. We use **Const *SeekOrigin.Begin***, because we want the method to seek in relation to the beginning of the file. After the program determines the file location at which to place the record, lines 106–110 write the record to the file using the **BinaryWriter** (discussed in the previous section).

14.10 Reading Data Sequentially from a Random-Access File

In the previous sections, we created a random-access file and wrote data to that file. Here, we develop a program (Fig. 14.17) that opens the file, reads records from it and displays only those records containing data (i.e., those records in which the account number is not zero). This program also provides an additional benefit. Readers should see if they can determine what it is—we will reveal it at the end of this section.

```
1    ' Fig. 14.17: ReadRandomAccessFile.vb
2    ' Reads and displays random-access file contents.
3
4    ' Visual Basic namespaces
5    Imports System.IO
6    Imports System.Windows.Forms
```

Fig. 14.17 `FrmReadRandomAccessFile` class reads records from random-access files sequentially. (Part 1 of 5.)

```
7
8    ' Deitel namespaces
9    Imports BankLibrary
10
11   Public Class FrmReadRandomAccessFile
12      Inherits FrmBankUI
13
14      ' buttons for opening file and reading records
15      Friend WithEvents cmdOpen As Button
16      Friend WithEvents cmdNext As Button
17
18      ' Visual Studio .NET generated code
19
20      ' stream through which data is read from file
21      Private fileInput As FileStream
22
23      ' stream for reading bytes from file
24      Private binaryInput As BinaryReader
25
26      ' index of current record to be displayed
27      Private currentRecordIndex As Integer
28
29      ' invoked when user clicks Open button
30      Protected Sub cmdOpen_Click(ByVal sender As System.Object, _
31         ByVal e As System.EventArgs) Handles cmdOpen.Click
32
33         ' create dialog box enabling user to open file
34         Dim fileChooser As OpenFileDialog = New OpenFileDialog()
35         Dim result As DialogResult = fileChooser.ShowDialog()
36
37         ' get file name from user
38         Dim fileName As String = fileChooser.FileName
39
40         ' exit event handler if user clicked Cancel
41         If result = DialogResult.Cancel Then
42            Return
43         End If
44
45         ' show error if user specified invalid file
46         If (fileName = "" OrElse fileName = Nothing) Then
47            MessageBox.Show("Invalid File Name", "Error", _
48               MessageBoxButtons.OK, MessageBoxIcon.Error)
49
50         ' open file if user specified valid file
51         Else
52
53            ' create FileStream to obtain read access to file
54            fileInput = New FileStream(fileName, FileMode.Open, _
55               FileAccess.Read)
56
57            ' use FileStream for BinaryWriter to read bytes from file
58            binaryInput = New BinaryReader(fileInput)
```

Fig. 14.17 FrmReadRandomAccessFile class reads records from random-access files sequentially. (Part 2 of 5.)

```
59
60            cmdOpen.Enabled = False ' disable Open button
61            cmdNext.Enabled = True ' enable Next button
62
63            currentRecordIndex = 0
64            ClearTextBoxes()
65        End If
66
67     End Sub ' cmdOpen_Click
68
69     ' invoked when user clicks Next button
70     Protected Sub cmdNext_Click(ByVal sender As System.Object, _
71        ByVal e As System.EventArgs) Handles cmdNext.Click
72
73        ' record to store file data
74        Dim record As CRandomAccessRecord = _
75           New CRandomAccessRecord()
76
77        ' read record and store data in TextBoxes
78        Try
79           Dim values As String() ' for storing TextBox values
80
81           ' get next record available in file
82           While (record.Account = 0)
83
84              ' set file-position pointer to next record in file
85              fileInput.Seek( _
86                 currentRecordIndex * CRandomAccessRecord.SIZE, 0)
87
88              currentRecordIndex += 1
89
90              ' read data from record
91              record.Account = binaryInput.ReadInt32()
92              record.FirstName = binaryInput.ReadString()
93              record.LastName = binaryInput.ReadString()
94              record.Balance = binaryInput.ReadDouble()
95           End While
96
97           ' store record values in temporary String array
98           values = New String() { _
99              record.Account.ToString(), _
100             record.FirstName.ToString(), _
101             record.LastName.ToString(), _
102             record.Balance.ToString()}
103
104          ' copy String-array values to TextBox values
105          SetTextBoxValues(values)
106
107          ' handle exception when no records in file
108       Catch fileException As IOException
109
```

Fig. 14.17 FrmReadRandomAccessFile class reads records from random-access files sequentially. (Part 3 of 5.)

```vb
110            ' close streams if no records in file
111            fileInput.Close()
112            binaryInput.Close()
113
114            cmdOpen.Enabled = True   ' enable Open button
115            cmdNext.Enabled = False ' disable Next button
116            ClearTextBoxes()
117
118            ' notify user if no records in file
119            MessageBox.Show("No more records in file", "", _
120               MessageBoxButtons.OK, MessageBoxIcon.Information)
121
122         End Try
123
124      End Sub ' cmdNext_Click
125
126   End Class ' FrmReadRandomAccessFile
```

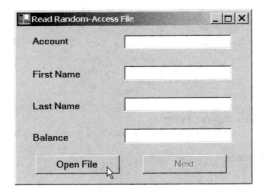

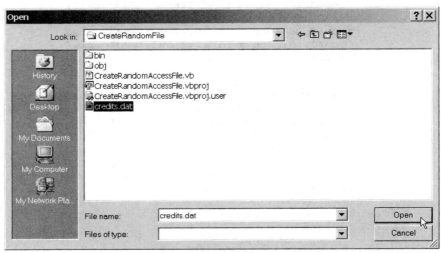

Fig. 14.17 FrmReadRandomAccessFile class reads records from random-access files sequentially. (Part 4 of 5.)

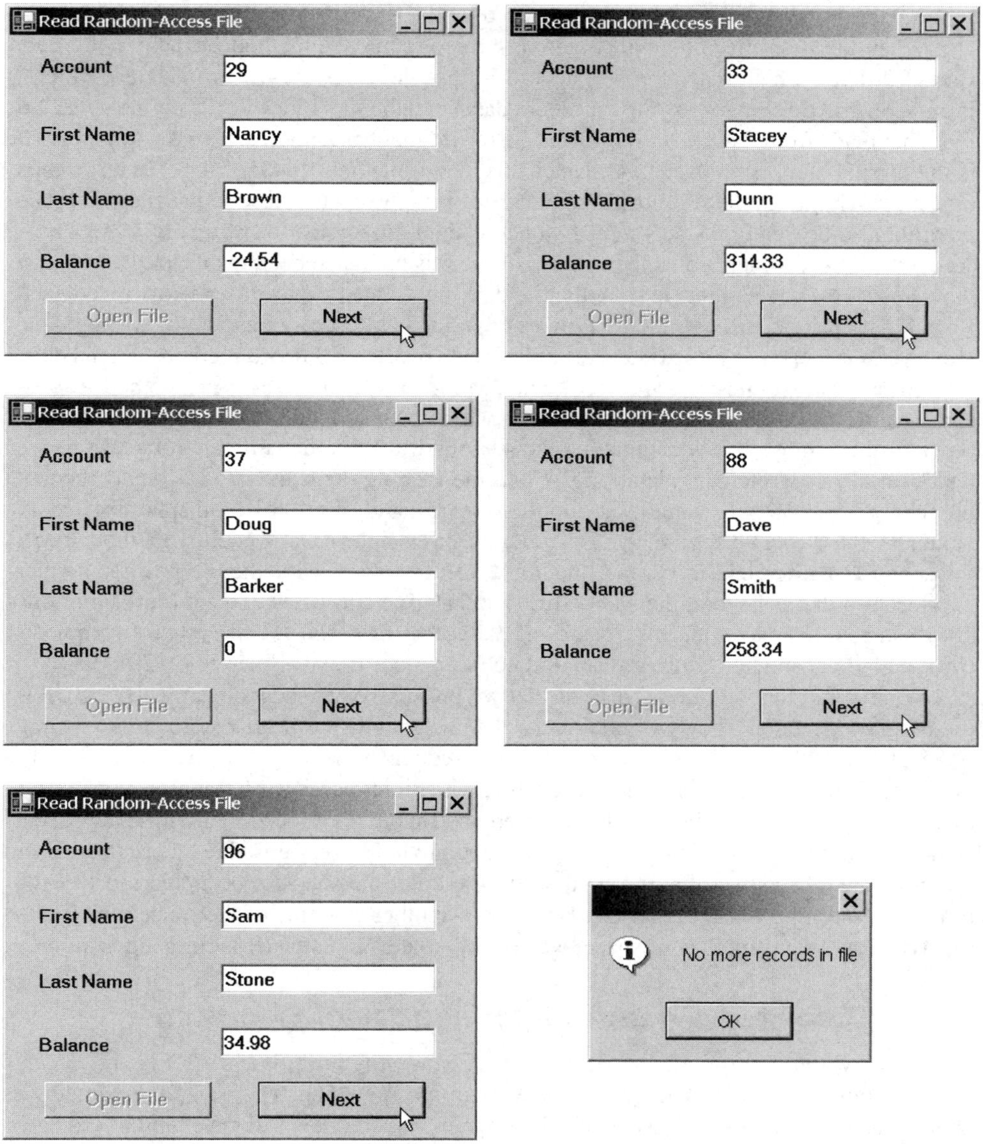

Fig. 14.17 FrmReadRandomAccessFile class reads records from random-access files sequentially. (Part 5 of 5.)

When the user clicks the **Open File** button, class **FrmReadRandomAccessFile** invokes method **cmdOpen_Click** (lines 30–67), which displays the **OpenFileDialog** for specifying the file from which to read data. Lines 54–55 instantiate a **FileStream** object that opens a file with read-only access. Line 58 creates an instance of class **BinaryReader**, which reads bytes from a stream. We pass the **FileStream** object as an argument to the **BinaryReader** constructor, thus enabling the **BinaryReader** to read bytes from the file created by the **BinaryWriter** in Fig. 14.9.

When the user clicks the **Next** button, the program calls method **cmdNext_Click** (lines 70–124), which reads the next record in the file. Lines 74–75 instantiate a **CRandomAccessRecord** for storing the record data from the file. Lines 82–95 define a **While** loop that reads from the file until it reaches a record that has a non-zero account number (**0** is the initial value for the account). Lines 85–86 call method **Seek** of the **FileStream** object, which moves the file-position pointer to the appropriate place in the file where the record must be read. To accomplish this, method **Seek** uses **Integer currentRecordIndex**, which stores the number of records that have been read. Lines 91–94 use the **BinaryReader** object to store the file data in the **CRandomAccessRecord** object. Recall that class **BinaryWriter** provides overloaded **Write** methods for writing data. However, class **BinaryReader** does not provide overloaded **Read** methods to read data. This means that we must use method **ReadInt32** to read an **Integer**, method **ReadString** to read a **String** and method **ReadDouble** to read a **Double**. Note that the order of these method invocations must correspond to the order in which the **BinaryWriter** object wrote each data type. When the **BinaryReader** reads a valid account number (i.e., a non-zero value), the loop terminates, and lines 98–105 display the record values in the **TextBox**es. When the program has displayed all records, method **Seek** throws an **IOException** (because method **Seek** tries to position the file-position pointer to a location that is beyond the end-of-file marker). The **Catch** statement (defined in line 108) handles this exception by closing the **FileStream** and **BinaryReader** objects (lines 111–112) and notifying the user that no more records exist (lines 119–120).

What about that additional benefit that we promised? If readers examine the GUI as the program executes, they will notice that the program displays the records in ascending order by account number! This is a simple consequence of using our direct-access techniques to store these records in the file. Sorting with direct-access techniques is much faster than sorting with the bubble sort presented in Chapter 4, Procedures and Arrays. We achieve this speed by making the file large enough to hold every possible record that a user might create. Of course, this means that the file could be sparsely occupied most of the time, resulting in a waste of storage. Here is yet another example of the space/time trade-off: By using large amounts of space, we are able to develop a faster sorting algorithm.

14.11 Case Study: A Transaction-Processing Program

We now develop a substantial transaction-processing program (Fig. 14.18–Fig. 14.23) using a random-access file to achieve "instant-access" processing. The program maintains a bank's account information. Users of this program can add new accounts, update existing accounts and delete accounts that are no longer needed. First, we discuss the transaction-processing behavior (i.e., the class enables the addition, updating and removal of accounts). We then discuss the GUI, which contains windows that display the account information and enable the user to invoke the application's transaction-processing behavior.

Transaction-Processing Behavior

In this case study, we create class **CTransaction** (Fig. 14.18), which acts as a *proxy* to handle all transaction processing. The objects in this application do not provide the transaction-processing behavior—rather, these objects use an instance of **CTransaction** to provide this functionality. The use of a proxy enables us to encapsulate transaction-processing behavior in only one class, enabling various classes in our application to reuse it. Furthermore, if we decide to modify this behavior, we modify only the proxy (i.e., class **CTransaction**), rather than having to modify the behavior of each class that uses the proxy.

```vb
1    ' Fig. 14.18: CTransaction.vb
2    ' Handles record transactions.
3
4    ' Visual Basic namespaces
5    Imports System.IO
6    Imports System.Windows.Forms
7
8    ' Deitel namespaces
9    Imports BankLibrary
10
11   Public Class CTransaction
12
13       ' number of records to write to disk
14       Private Const NUMBER_OF_RECORDS As Integer = 100
15
16       ' stream through which data moves to and from file
17       Private file As FileStream
18
19       ' stream for reading bytes from file
20       Private binaryInput As BinaryReader
21
22       ' stream for writing bytes to file
23       Private binaryOutput As BinaryWriter
24
25       ' create/open file containing empty records
26       Public Sub OpenFile(ByVal fileName As String)
27
28           ' write empty records to file
29           Try
30
31               ' create FileStream from new file or existing file
32               file = New FileStream(fileName, FileMode.OpenOrCreate)
33
34               ' use FileStream for BinaryWriter to read bytes from file
35               binaryInput = New BinaryReader(file)
36
37               ' use FileStream for BinaryWriter to write bytes to file
38               binaryOutput = New BinaryWriter(file)
39
40               ' determine whether file has just been created
41               If file.Length = 0 Then
42
43                   ' record to be written to file
44                   Dim blankRecord As CRandomAccessRecord = _
45                       New CRandomAccessRecord()
46
```

Fig. 14.18 CTransaction class handles record transactions for the transaction-processor case study. (Part 1 of 4.)

```
47                     Dim i As Integer ' counter
48
49                     ' new record can hold NUMBER_OF_RECORDS records
50                     file.SetLength( _
51                        CRandomAccessRecord.SIZE * NUMBER_OF_RECORDS)
52
53                     ' write blank records to file
54                     For i = 0 To NUMBER_OF_RECORDS - 1
55
56                        ' move file-position pointer to next position
57                        file.Position = i * CRandomAccessRecord.SIZE
58
59                        ' write blank record to file
60                        binaryOutput.Write(blankRecord.Account)
61                        binaryOutput.Write(blankRecord.FirstName)
62                        binaryOutput.Write(blankRecord.LastName)
63                        binaryOutput.Write(blankRecord.Balance)
64                     Next
65
66                  End If
67
68               ' notify user of error during writing of blank records
69               Catch fileException As IOException
70                  MessageBox.Show("Cannot create file", "Error", _
71                     MessageBoxButtons.OK, MessageBoxIcon.Error)
72
73               End Try
74
75            End Sub ' OpenFile
76
77            ' retrieve record depending on whether account is valid
78            Public Function GetRecord(ByVal accountValue As String) _
79               As CRandomAccessRecord
80
81               ' store file data associated with account in record
82               Try
83
84                  ' record to store file data
85                  Dim record As CRandomAccessRecord = _
86                     New CRandomAccessRecord()
87
88                  ' get value from TextBox's account field
89                  Dim accountNumber As Integer = _
90                     Convert.ToInt32(accountValue)
91
92                  ' if account is invalid, do not read data
93                  If (accountNumber < 1 OrElse _
94                     accountNumber > NUMBER_OF_RECORDS) Then
95
96                     ' set record's account field with account number
97                     record.Account = accountNumber
98
```

Fig. 14.18 CTransaction class handles record transactions for the transaction-processor case study. (Part 2 of 4.)

```
99                 ' get data from file if account is valid
100              Else
101
102                  ' locate position in file where record exists
103                  file.Seek( _
104                     (accountNumber - 1) * CRandomAccessRecord.SIZE, 0)
105
106                  ' read data from record
107                  record.Account = binaryInput.ReadInt32()
108                  record.FirstName = binaryInput.ReadString()
109                  record.LastName = binaryInput.ReadString()
110                  record.Balance = binaryInput.ReadDouble()
111              End If
112
113              Return record
114
115          ' notify user of error during reading
116          Catch fileException As IOException
117             MessageBox.Show("Cannot read file", "Error", _
118                MessageBoxButtons.OK, MessageBoxIcon.Error)
119
120          ' notify user of error in parameter mismatch
121          Catch formattingException As FormatException
122             MessageBox.Show("Invalid Account", "Error", _
123                MessageBoxButtons.OK, MessageBoxIcon.Error)
124
125          End Try
126
127          Return Nothing
128      End Function ' GetRecord
129
130      ' add record to file at position determined by accountNumber
131      Public Function AddRecord(ByVal record As CRandomAccessRecord, _
132          ByVal accountNumber As Integer) As Boolean
133
134          ' write record to file
135          Try
136
137              ' move file-position pointer to appropriate position
138              file.Seek( _
139                 (accountNumber - 1) * CRandomAccessRecord.SIZE, 0)
140
141              ' write data to file
142              binaryOutput.Write(record.Account)
143              binaryOutput.Write(record.FirstName)
144              binaryOutput.Write(record.LastName)
145              binaryOutput.Write(record.Balance)
146
147          ' notify user if error occurs during writing
148          Catch fileException As IOException
149             MessageBox.Show("Error Writing To File", "Error", _
150                MessageBoxButtons.OK, MessageBoxIcon.Error)
```

Fig. 14.18 CTransaction class handles record transactions for the transaction-processor case study. (Part 3 of 4.)

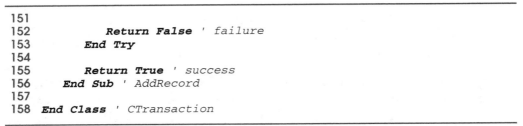

```
151
152            Return False ' failure
153         End Try
154
155         Return True ' success
156      End Sub ' AddRecord
157
158   End Class ' CTransaction
```

Fig. 14.18 CTransaction class handles record transactions for the transaction-processor case study. (Part 4 of 4.)

Class **CTransaction** contains methods **OpenFile, GetRecord** and **AddRecord**. Method **OpenFile** (lines 26–75) uses **Const FileMode.OpenOrCreate** (line 32) to create a **FileStream** object from either an existing file or one not yet created. Lines 35–38 use this **FileStream** to create **BinaryReader** and **BinaryWriter** objects for reading and writing bytes to the file. If the file is new, lines 54–64 populate the **FileStream** object with empty records. Readers might recall that we used these techniques in Section 14.8.

Method **GetRecord** (lines 78–128) returns the record associated with the account-number parameter. Lines 85–86 instantiate a **CRandomAccessRecord** object that will store the file data. If the account parameter is valid, lines 103–104 call method **Seek** of the **FileStream** object, which uses the parameter to determine the position of the specified record in the file. Lines 107–110 then call methods **ReadInt32, ReadString** and **ReadDouble** of the **BinaryReader** object to store the file data in the **CRandomAccessRecord** object. Line 113 returns the **CRandomAccessRecord** object. We used these techniques in Section 14.10.

Method **AddRecord** (lines 131–156) inserts a record into the file. Lines 138–139 call method **Seek** of the **FileStream** object, which uses the account-number parameter to locate the position which to insert the record in the file. Lines 142–145 call the overloaded **Write** methods of the **BinaryWriter** object to write the **CRandomAccessRecord** object's data to the file. We used these techniques in Section 14.9. Note that, if an error occurs when adding the record (i.e., either the **FileStream** or the **BinaryWriter** throws an **IOException**), lines 149–152 notify the user of the error and return **False** (failure).

Transaction-Processor GUI
The GUI for this program consists of a window containing internal frames (an MDI). Class **FrmTransactionProcessor** (Fig. 14.19) is the parent window, which acts as the driver for the application and displays one of its children windows—an object of type **FrmStartDialog** (Fig. 14.20), **FrmNewDialog** (Fig. 14.21), **FrmUpdateDialog** (Fig. 14.22) or **FrmDeleteDialog** (Fig. 14.23). **FrmStartDialog** allows the user to open a file containing account information and provides access to the **FrmNewDialog**, **FrmUpdateDialog** and **FrmDeleteDialog** internal frames. These frames allow us-

ers to update, create and delete records, respectively (using a reference to the **CTransaction** object).

Initially, **FrmTransactionProcessor** displays the **FrmStartDialog** object, this window provides the user with various options. It contains four buttons that enable the user to create or open a file, create a record, update an existing record or delete an existing record.

Before the user can modify records, the user must either create or open a file. When the user clicks the **New/Open File** button, the program calls method **cmdOpen_Click** (lines 36–94 of Fig. 14.20), which opens a file that the application uses for modifying records. Lines 40–48 display the **OpenFileDialog** for specifying the file from which to read data and then uses this file to create the **FileStream** object. Note that line 46 sets property **CheckFileExists** of the **OpenFileDialog** object to **False**—this enables the user to create a file if the specified file does not exist. If this property were **True** (its default value), the dialog would notify the user that the specified file does not exist, thus preventing the user from creating a file.

If the user specifies a file name, line 67 instantiates an object of class **CTransaction** (Fig. 14.18), which acts as the proxy for creating, reading records from and writing records to random-access files. Line 68 calls its method **OpenFile**, which either creates or opens the specified file, depending on whether the file exists.

Class **FrmStartDialog** also creates internal windows that enable the user to create, update and delete records. We do not use the default constructor created by Visual Studio .NET for these classes; instead, we use an overloaded constructor that takes as arguments the **CTransaction** object and a delegate object that references method **ShowStartDialog** (lines 121–123). Each child window uses the second delegate parameter to display the **FrmStartDialog** GUI when the user closes a child window. Lines 77–86 instantiate objects of classes **FrmUpdateDialog**, **FrmNewDialog** and **FrmDeleteDialog**, which serve as the child windows.

```
1   ' Fig. 14.19: TransactionProcessor.vb
2   ' MDI parent for transaction-processor application.
3
4   Imports System.Windows.Forms
5
6   Public Class FrmTransactionProcessor
7      Inherits Form
8
9      ' Visual Studio .NET generated code
10
11     ' reference to Multiple-Document-Interface client
12     Private childForm As MdiClient
13
14     ' reference to StartDialog
15     Private startDialog As FrmStartDialog
16
17  End Class ' FrmTransactionProcessor
```

Fig. 14.19 **FrmTransactionProcessor** class runs the transaction-processor application.

```vb
1   ' Fig. 14.20: StartDialog.vb
2   ' Initial dialog box displayed to user. Provides buttons for
3   ' creating/opening file and for adding, updating and removing
4   ' records from file.
5
6   ' Visual Basic namespaces
7   Imports System.Windows.Forms
8
9   ' Deitel namespaces
10  Imports BankLibrary
11
12  Public Class FrmStartDialog
13     Inherits Form
14
15     ' buttons for displaying other dialogs
16     Friend WithEvents cmdOpen As Button
17     Friend WithEvents cmdNew As Button
18     Friend WithEvents cmdUpdate As Button
19     Friend WithEvents cmdDelete As Button
20
21     ' Visual Studio .NET generated code
22
23     ' reference to dialog box for adding record
24     Private newDialog As FrmNewDialog
25
26     ' reference to dialog box for updating record
27     Private updateDialog As FrmUpdateDialog
28
29     ' reference to dialog box for removing record
30     Private deleteDialog As FrmDeleteDialog
31
32     ' reference to object that handles transactions
33     Private transactionProxy As CTransaction
34
35     ' invoked when user clicks New/Open File button
36     Protected Sub cmdOpen_Click(ByVal sender As System.Object, _
37        ByVal e As System.EventArgs) Handles cmdOpen.Click
38
39        ' create dialog box enabling user to create or open file
40        Dim fileChooser As OpenFileDialog = New OpenFileDialog()
41        Dim result As DialogResult
42        Dim fileName As String
43
44        ' enable user to create file if file does not exist
45        fileChooser.Title = "Create File / Open File"
46        fileChooser.CheckFileExists = False
47
48        result = fileChooser.ShowDialog() ' show dialog box to user
49
50        ' exit event handler if user clicked Cancel
51        If result = DialogResult.Cancel Then
52           Return
```

Fig. 14.20 FrmStartDialog class enables users to access dialog boxes
associated with various transactions. (Part 1 of 4.)

```
53              End If
54
55          ' get file name from user
56          fileName = fileChooser.FileName
57
58          ' show error if user specified invalid file
59          If (fileName = "" OrElse fileName = Nothing) Then
60             MessageBox.Show("Invalid File Name", "Error", _
61                MessageBoxButtons.OK, MessageBoxIcon.Error)
62
63          ' open or create file if user specified valid file
64          Else
65
66              ' create CTransaction with specified file
67              transactionProxy = New CTransaction()
68              transactionProxy.OpenFile(fileName)
69
70              ' enable GUI buttons except for New/Open File button
71              cmdNew.Enabled = True
72              cmdUpdate.Enabled = True
73              cmdDelete.Enabled = True
74              cmdOpen.Enabled = False
75
76              ' instantiate dialog box for creating records
77              newDialog = New FrmNewDialog(transactionProxy, _
78                 AddressOf ShowStartDialog)
79
80              ' instantiate dialog box for updating records
81              updateDialog = New FrmUpdateDialog(transactionProxy, _
82                 AddressOf ShowStartDialog)
83
84              ' instantiate dialog box for removing records
85              deleteDialog = New FrmDeleteDialog(transactionProxy, _
86                 AddressOf ShowStartDialog)
87
88              ' set StartDialog as MdiParent for dialog boxes
89              newDialog.MdiParent = Me.MdiParent
90              updateDialog.MdiParent = Me.MdiParent
91              deleteDialog.MdiParent = Me.MdiParent
92          End If
93
94      End Sub ' cmdOpen_Click
95
96      ' invoked when user clicks New Record button
97      Protected Sub cmdNew_Click(ByVal sender As System.Object, _
98         ByVal e As System.EventArgs) Handles cmdNew.Click
99
100         Hide() ' hide StartDialog
101         newDialog.Show() ' show NewDialog
102     End Sub ' cmdNew_Click
103
```

Fig. 14.20 FrmStartDialog class enables users to access dialog boxes associated with various transactions. (Part 2 of 4.)

```
104        ' invoked when user clicks Update Record button
105        Protected Sub cmdUpdate_Click(ByVal sender As System.Object, _
106           ByVal e As System.EventArgs) Handles cmdUpdate.Click
107
108           Hide() ' hide StartDialog
109           updateDialog.Show() ' show UpdateDialog
110        End Sub ' cmdUpdate_Click
111
112        ' invoked when user clicks Delete Record button
113        Protected Sub cmdDelete_Click(ByVal sender As System.Object, _
114           ByVal e As System.EventArgs) Handles cmdDelete.Click
115
116           Hide() ' hide StartDialog
117           deleteDialog.Show() ' show DeleteDialog
118        End Sub ' cmdDelete_Click
119
120        ' displays StartDialog
121        Protected Sub ShowStartDialog()
122           Show()
123        End Sub ' ShowStartDialog
124
125     End Class ' FrmStartDialog
```

Fig. 14.20 FrmStartDialog class enables users to access dialog boxes associated with various transactions. (Part 3 of 4.)

Fig. 14.20 `FrmStartDialog` class enables users to access dialog boxes associated with various transactions. (Part 4 of 4.)

When the user clicks the **New Record** button in the **Start Dialog**, the program invokes method `cmdNew_Click` of class `FrmStartDialog` (Fig. 14.20, lines 97–102), which displays the `FrmNewDialog` internal frame. Class `FrmNewDialog` (Fig. 14.21) enables the user to create records in the file that `FrmStartDialog` opened (or created). Line 23 defines `MyDelegate` as a delegate to a method that does not return a value and has no parameters—method `ShowStartDialog` of class `FrmStartDialog` (Fig. 14.20, lines 121–123) conforms to these requirements. Class `FrmNewDialog` receives a `MyDelegate` object, which references this method as a parameter—therefore, `FrmNewDialog` can invoke this method to display the start window when the user exits the `FrmNewDialog`. Classes `FrmUpdateDialog` and `FrmDeleteDialog` also receive `MyDelegate` references as arguments, enabling them to display `FrmStartDialog` after completing their tasks.

After the user enters data in the `TextBox`es and clicks the **Save Record** button, the program invokes method `cmdSave_Click` (lines 47–62) to write the record to disk. Lines 50–52 call method `GetRecord` of the `CTransaction` object, which should return an empty `CRandomAccessRecord`. If method `GetRecord` returns a `CRandomAccessRecord` that contains content, the user is attempting to overwrite that `CRandomAccessRecord` with a new one. Line 56 calls `Private` method `InsertRecord` (lines 65–108). If the `CRandomAccessRecord` is empty, method `InsertRecord` calls method `AddRecord` of the `CTransaction` object (lines 93–94), which inserts the newly created `CRandomAccessRecord` into the file. If the user is attempting to overwrite an existing file, lines 76–80 notify the user that the file already exists and return from the method.

```
1   ' Fig. 14.21: NewDialog.vb
2   ' Enables user to insert new record into file.
3
4   ' Visual Basic namespaces
5   Imports System.Windows.Forms
6
```

Fig. 14.21 `FrmNewDialog` class enables users to create records in transaction-processor case study. (Part 1 of 4.)

```vbnet
 7   ' Deitel namespaces
 8   Imports BankLibrary
 9
10   Public Class FrmNewDialog
11      Inherits FrmBankUI
12
13      ' buttons for creating record and canceling action
14      Friend WithEvents cmdSave As Button
15      Friend WithEvents cmdCancel As Button
16
17      ' Windows Form Designer generated code
18
19      ' reference to object that handles transactions
20      Private transactionProxy As CTransaction
21
22      ' delegate for method that displays previous window
23      Delegate Sub MyDelegate()
24      Public showPreviousWindow As MyDelegate
25
26      ' initialize components and set members to parameter values
27      Public Sub New(ByVal transactionProxyValue As CTransaction, _
28         ByVal delegateValue As MyDelegate)
29
30         InitializeComponent()
31         showPreviousWindow = delegateValue
32
33         ' instantiate object that handles transactions
34         transactionProxy = transactionProxyValue
35      End Sub ' New
36
37      ' invoked when user clicks Cancel button
38      Protected Sub cmdCancel_Click(ByVal sender As System.Object, _
39         ByVal e As System.EventArgs) Handles cmdCancel.Click
40
41         Hide()
42         ClearTextBoxes()
43         showPreviousWindow()
44      End Sub ' cmdCancel_Click
45
46      ' invoked when user clicks Save As button
47      Protected Sub cmdSave_Click(ByVal sender As System.Object, _
48         ByVal e As System.EventArgs) Handles cmdSave.Click
49
50         Dim record As CRandomAccessRecord = _
51            transactionProxy.GetRecord( _
52               GetTextBoxValues(TextBoxIndices.ACCOUNT))
53
54         ' if record exists, add it to file
55         If (record Is Nothing) = False Then
56            InsertRecord(record)
57         End If
58
```

Fig. 14.21 **FrmNewDialog** class enables users to create records in transaction-processor case study. (Part 2 of 4.)

```
59          Hide()
60          ClearTextBoxes()
61          showPreviousWindow()
62       End Sub ' cmdSave_Click
63
64       ' insert record in file at position specified by accountNumber
65       Private Sub InsertRecord(ByVal record As CRandomAccessRecord)
66
67          ' store TextBox values in String array
68          Dim textBoxValues As String() = GetTextBoxValues()
69
70          ' store TextBox account field
71          Dim accountNumber As Integer = _
72             Convert.ToInt32(textBoxValues(TextBoxIndices.ACCOUNT))
73
74          ' notify user and return if record account is not empty
75          If record.Account <> 0 Then
76             MessageBox.Show( _
77                "Record Already Exists or Invalid Number", "Error", _
78                MessageBoxButtons.OK, MessageBoxIcon.Error)
79
80             Return
81          End If
82
83          ' store values in record
84          record.Account = accountNumber
85          record.FirstName = textBoxValues(TextBoxIndices.FIRST)
86          record.LastName = textBoxValues(TextBoxIndices.LAST)
87          record.Balance = Convert.ToDouble( _
88             textBoxValues(TextBoxIndices.BALANCE))
89
90          ' add record to file
91          Try
92
93             If (transactionProxy.AddRecord( _
94                record, accountNumber) = False ) Then
95
96                Return ' if error
97             End If
98
99          ' notify user if error occurs in parameter mismatch
100         Catch formattingException As FormatException
101            MessageBox.Show("Invalid Balance", "Error", _
102               MessageBoxButtons.OK, MessageBoxIcon.Error)
103
104         End Try
105
106         MessageBox.Show("Record Created", "Success", _
107            MessageBoxButtons.OK, MessageBoxIcon.Information)
108      End Sub ' InsertRecord
109
110   End Class ' FrmNewDialog
```

Fig. 14.21 **FrmNewDialog** class enables users to create records in transaction-processor case study. (Part 3 of 4.)

Fig. 14.21 FrmNewDialog class enables users to create records in transaction-processor case study. (Part 4 of 4.)

When the user clicks the **Update Record** button in the **Start Dialog**, the program invokes method **cmdUpdate_Click** of class **FrmStartDialog** (Fig. 14.20, lines 105–110), which displays the **FrmUpdateDialog** internal frame (Fig. 14.22). Class **FrmUpdateDialog** enables the user to update existing records in the file. To update a record, users must enter the account number associated with the record they wish to update. When the user presses *Enter*, **FrmUpdateDialog** calls method **txtAccount-Number_KeyDown** (lines 42–82) to display the record contents. This method calls method **GetRecord** of the **CTransaction** object (lines 51–53) to retrieve the specified **CRandomAccessRecord**. If the record is not empty, lines 64–67 populate the **Text-Box**es with the **CRandomAccessRecord** values.

```
1   ' Fig. 14.22: UpdateDialog.vb
2   ' Enables user to update records in file.
3
4   ' Visual Basic namespaces
5   Imports System.Windows.Forms
6
7   ' Deitel namespaces
8   Imports BankLibrary
9
10  Public Class FrmUpdateDialog
11      Inherits FrmBankUI
```

Fig. 14.22 FrmUpdateDialog class enables users to update records in transaction-processor case study. (Part 1 of 6.)

```vb
12
13       ' label and textbox for user to enter transaction data
14       Friend WithEvents lblTransaction As Label
15       Friend WithEvents txtTransaction As TextBox
16
17       ' buttons for saving data to file and canceling save
18       Friend WithEvents cmdSave As Button
19       Friend WithEvents cmdCancel As Button
20
21       ' Visual Studio .NET generated code
22
23       ' reference to object that handles transactions
24       Private transactionProxy As CTransaction
25
26       ' delegate for method that displays previous window
27       Delegate Sub MyDelegate()
28       Public showPreviousWindow As MyDelegate
29
30       ' initialize components and set members to parameter values
31       Public Sub New(ByVal transactionProxyValue As CTransaction, _
32          ByVal delegateValue As MyDelegate)
33
34          InitializeComponent()
35          showPreviousWindow = delegateValue
36
37          ' instantiate object that handles transactions
38          transactionProxy = transactionProxyValue
39       End Sub ' New
40
41       ' invoked when user enters text in Account TextBox
42       Protected Sub txtAccountNumber_KeyDown( _
43          ByVal sender As System.Object, _
44          ByVal e As System.Windows.Forms.KeyEventArgs) _
45          Handles txtAccount.KeyDown
46
47          ' determine whether user pressed Enter Key
48          If e.KeyCode = Keys.Enter Then
49
50             ' retrieve record associated with account from file
51             Dim record As CRandomAccessRecord = _
52                transactionProxy.GetRecord( _
53                   GetTextBoxValues(TextBoxIndices.ACCOUNT))
54
55             ' return if record does not exist
56             If (record Is Nothing) = True Then
57                Return
58             End If
59
60             ' determine whether record is empty
61             If record.Account <> 0 Then
62
```

Fig. 14.22 **FrmUpdateDialog** class enables users to update records in transaction-processor case study. (Part 2 of 6.)

```
63                  ' store record values in String array
64                  Dim values As String() = {record.Account.ToString(), _
65                     record.FirstName.ToString(), _
66                     record.LastName.ToString(), _
67                     record.Balance.ToString()}
68
69                  ' copy String-array value to TextBox values
70                  SetTextBoxValues(values)
71                  txtTransaction.Text = "[Charge or Payment]"
72
73               ' notify user if record does not exist
74               Else
75                  MessageBox.Show("Record Does Not Exist", "Error", _
76                     MessageBoxButtons.OK, MessageBoxIcon.Error)
77
78            End If
79
80         End If
81
82      End Sub ' txtAccountNumber_KeyDown
83
84      ' invoked when user enters text in Transaction TextBox
85      Protected Sub txtTransactionNumber_KeyDown( _
86         ByVal sender As System.Object, _
87         ByVal e As System.Windows.Forms.KeyEventArgs) _
88         Handles txtTransaction.KeyDown
89
90         ' determine whether user pressed Enter key
91         If e.KeyCode = Keys.Enter Then
92
93            ' calculate balance using Transaction TextBox value
94            Try
95
96               ' retrieve record associated with account from file
97               Dim record As CRandomAccessRecord = _
98                  transactionProxy.GetRecord( _
99                     GetTextBoxValues(TextBoxIndices.ACCOUNT))
100
101              ' get Transaction TextBox value
102              Dim transactionValue As Double = _
103                 Convert.ToDouble(txtTransaction.Text)
104
105              ' calculate new balance (old balance + transaction)
106              Dim newBalance As Double = _
107                 record.Balance + transactionValue
108
109              ' store record values in String array
110              Dim values As String() = {record.Account.ToString(), _
111                 record.FirstName.ToString(), _
112                 record.LastName.ToString(), newBalance.ToString()}
113
```

Fig. 14.22 FrmUpdateDialog class enables users to update records in transaction-processor case study. (Part 3 of 6.)

```vb
114                   ' copy String-array value to TextBox values
115                   SetTextBoxValues(values)
116
117                   ' clear txtTransactionNumber
118                   txtTransaction.Text = ""
119
120               ' notify user if error occurs in parameter mismatch
121               Catch formattingException As FormatException
122                  MessageBox.Show("Invalid Transaction", "Error", _
123                     MessageBoxButtons.OK, MessageBoxIcon.Error)
124
125            End Try
126
127         End If
128
129      End Sub ' txtTransactionNumber_KeyDown
130
131      ' invoked when user clicks Save button
132      Protected Sub cmdSave_Click(ByVal sender As System.Object, _
133         ByVal e As System.EventArgs) Handles cmdSave.Click
134
135         Dim record As CRandomAccessRecord = _
136            transactionProxy.GetRecord( _
137               GetTextBoxValues(TextBoxIndices.ACCOUNT))
138
139         ' if record exists, update in file
140         If (record Is Nothing) = False Then
141            UpdateRecord(record)
142         End If
143
144         Hide()
145         ClearTextBoxes()
146         showPreviousWindow()
147      End Sub ' cmdSave_Click
148
149      ' invoked when user clicks Cancel button
150      Protected Sub cmdCancel_Click(ByVal sender As System.Object, _
151         ByVal e As System.EventArgs) Handles cmdCancel.Click
152
153         Hide()
154         ClearTextBoxes()
155         showPreviousWindow()
156      End Sub ' cmdCancel_Click
157
158      ' update record in file at position specified by accountNumber
159      Public Sub UpdateRecord(ByVal record As CRandomAccessRecord)
160
161         ' store TextBox values in record and write record to file
162         Try
163            Dim accountNumber As Integer = record.Account
164            Dim values As String() = GetTextBoxValues()
165
```

Fig. 14.22 FrmUpdateDialog class enables users to update records in transaction-processor case study. (Part 4 of 6.)

```
166            ' store values in record
167            record.Account = accountNumber
168            record.FirstName = values(TextBoxIndices.FIRST)
169            record.LastName = values(TextBoxIndices.LAST)
170            record.Balance = _
171               Double.Parse(values(TextBoxIndices.BALANCE))
172
173            ' add record to file
174            If (transactionProxy.AddRecord( _
175               record, accountNumber) = False ) Then
176
177               Return ' if error
178            End If
179
180         ' notify user if error occurs in parameter mismatch
181         Catch formattingException As FormatException
182            MessageBox.Show("Invalid Balance", "Error", _
183               MessageBoxButtons.OK, MessageBoxIcon.Error)
184
185            Return
186         End Try
187
188         MessageBox.Show("Record Updated", "Success", _
189            MessageBoxButtons.OK, MessageBoxIcon.Information)
190      End Sub ' UpdateRecord
191
192 End Class ' FrmUpdateDialog
```

Fig. 14.22 FrmUpdateDialog class enables users to update records in transaction-processor case study. (Part 5 of 6.)

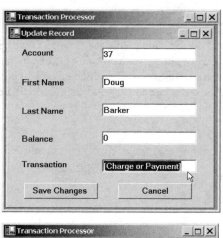

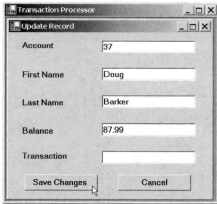

Fig. 14.22 FrmUpdateDialog class enables users to update records in transaction-processor case study. (Part 6 of 6.)

The **Transaction TextBox** initially contains the string **Charge or Payment**. The user should select this text, type the transaction amount (a positive value for a charge or a negative value for a payment) and then press *Enter*. The program calls method **txtTransactionNumber_KeyDown** (lines 85–129) to add the user-specified transaction amount to the current balance.

The user clicks the **Save Changes** button to write the altered contents of the **Text-Box**es to the file. (Note that pressing **Save Changes** does not update the **Balance** field—the user must press *Enter* to update this field before pressing **Save Changes**.) When the user clicks **Save Changes**, the program invokes method **cmdSave_Click** (lines 132–147), which calls **Private** method **UpdateRecord** (lines 159–190). This method calls method **AddRecord** of the **CTransaction** object (lines 174–175) to store the **TextBox** values in a **CRandomAccessRecord** and overwrite the existing file record with the **CRandomAccessRecord** containing the new data.

When the user clicks the **Delete Record** button of the **Start Dialog**, the program invokes method **cmdDelete_Click** of class **FrmStartDialog** (Fig. 14.20, lines

113–118), which displays the **FrmDeleteDialog** internal frame (Fig. 14.23). Class **FrmDeleteDialog** enables the user to remove existing records from the file. To remove a record, users must enter the account number associated with the record they wish to delete. When the user clicks the **Delete Record** button (now, from the **FrmDeleteDialog** internal frame), **FrmDeleteDialog** calls method **cmdDelete_Click** (lines 42–55). This method calls method **DeleteRecord** (lines 66–97), which ensures that the record to be deleted exists and then calls method **AddRecord** of the **CTransaction** object (lines 83–84) to overwrite the file record with an empty one.

```vb
1    ' Fig. 14.23: DeleteDialog.vb
2    ' Enables user to delete records in file.
3
4    ' Visual Basic namespaces
5    Imports System.Windows.Forms
6
7    ' Deitel namespaces
8    Imports BankLibrary
9
10   Public Class FrmDeleteDialog
11      Inherits Form
12
13      ' label and TextBox enabling user to input account number
14      Friend WithEvents lblAccount As Label
15      Friend WithEvents txtAccount As TextBox
16
17      ' buttons for deleting record and canceling action
18      Friend WithEvents cmdDelete As Button
19      Friend WithEvents cmdCancel As Button
20
21      ' Visual Studio .NET generated code
22
23      ' reference to object that handles transactions
24      Private transactionProxy As CTransaction
25
26      ' delegate for method that displays previous window
27      Delegate Sub MyDelegate()
28      Public showPreviousWindow As MyDelegate
29
30      ' initialize components and set members to parameter values
31      Public Sub New(ByVal transactionProxyValue As CTransaction, _
32         ByVal delegateValue As MyDelegate)
33
34         InitializeComponent()
35         showPreviousWindow = delegateValue
36
37         ' instantiate object that handles transactions
38         transactionProxy = transactionProxyValue
39      End Sub ' New
40
```

Fig. 14.23 FrmDeleteDialog class enables users to remove records from files in transaction-processor case study. (Part 1 of 3.)

```
41      ' invoked when user clicks Delete Record button
42      Protected Sub cmdDelete_Click(ByVal sender As System.Object, _
43         ByVal e As System.EventArgs) Handles cmdDelete.Click
44
45         Dim record As CRandomAccessRecord = _
46            transactionProxy.GetRecord(txtAccount.Text)
47
48         ' if record exists, delete it in file
49         If (record Is Nothing) = False Then
50            DeleteRecord(record)
51         End If
52
53         Me.Hide()
54         showPreviousWindow()
55      End Sub ' cmdDelete_Click
56
57      ' invoked when user clicks Cancel button
58      Protected Sub cmdCancel_Click(ByVal sender As System.Object, _
59         ByVal e As System.EventArgs) Handles cmdCancel.Click
60
61         Me.Hide()
62         showPreviousWindow()
63      End Sub ' cmdCancel_Click
64
65      ' delete record in file at position specified by accountNumber
66      Public Sub DeleteRecord(ByVal record As CRandomAccessRecord)
67
68         Dim accountNumber As Integer = record.Account
69
70         ' display error message if record does not exist
71         If record.Account = 0 Then
72            MessageBox.Show("Record Does Not Exist", "Error", _
73               MessageBoxButtons.OK, MessageBoxIcon.Error)
74            txtAccount.Clear()
75
76            Return
77         End If
78
79         ' create blank record
80         record = New CRandomAccessRecord()
81
82         ' write over file record with empty record
83         If (transactionProxy.AddRecord( _
84            record, accountNumber) = True) Then
85
86            ' notify user of successful deletion
87            MessageBox.Show("Record Deleted", "Success", _
88               MessageBoxButtons.OK, MessageBoxIcon.Information)
89         Else
90
91            ' notify user of failure
92            MessageBox.Show("Record could not be deleted", "Error", _
```

Fig. 14.23 `FrmDeleteDialog` class enables users to remove records from files in transaction-processor case study. (Part 2 of 3.)

```
93                    MessageBoxButtons.OK, MessageBoxIcon.Error)
94          End If
95
96          txtAccount.Clear() ' clear text box
97       End Sub ' DeleteRecord
98
99    End Class ' FrmDeleteDialog
```

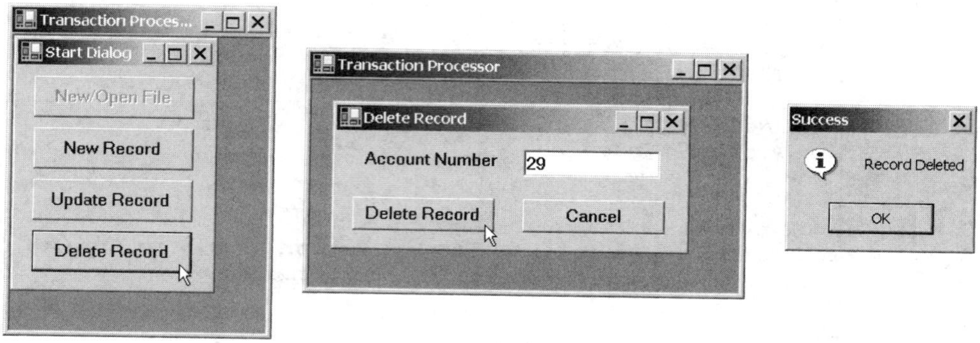

Fig. 14.23 FrmDeleteDialog class enables users to remove records from files in transaction-processor case study. (Part 3 of 3.)

14.12 Summary

All data items processed by a computer ultimately are reduced to combinations of zeros and ones. The smallest data items that computers support are called bits and can assume either the value **0** or the value **1**. Digits, letters and special symbols are referred to as characters. The set of all characters used to write programs and represent data items on a particular computer is called that computer's character set. Every character in a computer's character set is represented as a pattern of **1**s and **0**s.

A field is a group of characters that conveys some meaning. A record is a group of related fields. At least one field in a record is chosen as a record key, which identifies that record as belonging to a particular person or entity and distinguishes that record from all other records in the file. A file is a group of related records. Files are used for long-term retention of large amounts of data and can store those data even after the program that created the data terminates. Data maintained in files often are called persistent data.

Visual Basic imposes no structure on files. This means that concepts like that of a "record" do not exist in Visual Basic. The programmer must structure each file appropriately to meet the requirements of an application. Visual Basic views each file as a sequential stream of bytes. Each file ends in some machine-dependent form of end-of-file marker.

To perform file processing in Visual Basic, the namespace **System.IO** must be referenced. This namespace includes definitions for stream classes such as **StreamReader**, **StreamWriter** and **FileStream**. Files are opened by instantiating objects of these classes. When a file is opened, an object is created, and a stream is associated with the object. Streams provide communication channels between files and programs.

The most common type of file organization is the sequential file, in which records typically are stored in order by the record-key field. To retrieve data sequentially from a file, programs normally start from the beginning of the file, reading all data consecutively until the desired data are found. With a sequential-access file, each successive input/output request reads or writes the next consecutive set of data in the file.

BinaryFormatter provides methods **Serialize** and **Deserialize** to write and to read objects. Only classes with the **Serializable** attribute can be serialized to and deserialized from files. Method **Serialize** writes the object's representation to a stream. Method **Deserialize** reads this representation from a stream and reconstructs the original object. Methods **Serialize** and **Deserialize** each require a **Stream** object as a parameter, enabling the **BinaryFormatter** to access the correct file.

Instant data access is possible with random-access files. A program can access individual records of a random-access file directly (and quickly) without searching through other records. Random-access files sometimes are called direct-access files. With a random-access file, each successive input/output request can be directed to any part of the file, which can be any distance from the part of the file referenced in the previous request.

There are a variety of techniques for creating random-access files. Perhaps the simplest involves requiring that all records in a file be of the same fixed length. The use of fixed-length records makes it easy for a program to calculate (as a function of the record size and the record key) the exact location of any record in relation to the beginning of the file.

Classes **BinaryReader** and **BinaryWriter** provide methods for reading and writing bytes to streams, respectively. The **BinaryReader** and **BinaryWriter** constructors receive as arguments references to instances of class **System.IO.Stream**. Class **FileStream** inherits from class **Stream**, so we can pass the **FileStream** object as an argument to either the **BinaryReader** or the **BinaryWriter** constructor to create an object that can transfer bytes directly to or from a file.

15

Extensible Markup Language (XML)

Objectives

- To mark up data using XML.
- To understand the concept of an XML namespace.
- To understand the relationship between DTDs, Schemas and XML.
- To create Schemas.
- To create and use simple XSLT documents.
- To transform XML documents into XHTML using class `XslTransform`.
- To become familiar with BizTalk™.

Knowing trees, I understand the meaning of patience.
Knowing grass, I can appreciate persistence.
Hal Borland

Like everything metaphysical, the harmony between thought and reality is to be found in the grammar of the language.
Ludwig Wittgenstein

I played with an idea, and grew willful; tossed it into the air; transformed it; let it escape and recaptured it; made it iridescent with fancy, and winged it with paradox.
Oscar Wilde

15.1 Introduction

The *Extensible Markup Language* (XML) was developed in 1996 by the *World Wide Web Consortium's (W3C's) XML Working Group*. XML is a portable, widely supported, *open technology* (i.e., non-proprietary technology) for describing data. XML is becoming the standard for storing data that is exchanged between applications. Using XML, document authors can describe any type of data, including mathematical formulas, software-configuration instructions, music, recipes and financial reports. XML documents are readable by both humans and machines.

The .NET Framework uses XML extensively. The Framework Class Library provides an extensive set of XML-related classes. Much of Visual Studio's internal implementation also employs XML. In this chapter, we introduce XML, XML-related technologies and key classes for creating and manipulating XML documents.

15.2 XML Documents

In this section, we present our first XML document, which describes an article (Fig. 15.1). The line numbers shown are not part of the XML document.

```
1    <?xml version = "1.0"?>
2
3    <!-- Fig. 15.1: article.xml        -->
4    <!-- Article structured with XML -->
5
6    <article>
7
8        <title>Simple XML</title>
9
```

Fig. 15.1 XML used to mark up an article. (Part 1 of 2.)

```
10      <date>December 6, 2001</date>
11
12      <author>
13         <firstName>John</firstName>
14         <lastName>Doe</lastName>
15      </author>
16
17      <summary>XML is pretty easy.</summary>
18
19      <content>In this chapter, we present a wide variety of examples
20         that use XML.
21      </content>
22
23   </article>
```

Fig. 15.1   XML used to mark up an article. (Part 2 of 2.)

This document begins with an optional *XML declaration* (line 1), which identifies the document as an XML document. The **version** *information parameter* specifies the version of XML that is used in the document. XML comments (lines 3–4), which begin with **<!--** and end with **-->**, can be placed almost anywhere in an XML document. As in a Visual Basic program, comments are used in XML for documentation purposes.

Common Programming Error 15.1

The placement of any characters, including whitespace, before the XML declaration is a syntax error.

Portability Tip 15.1

Although the XML declaration is optional, documents should include the declaration to identify the version of XML used. Otherwise, in the future, a document that lacks an XML declaration might be assumed to conform to the latest version of XML, and errors could result.

In XML, data are marked up using *tags*, which are names enclosed in *angle brackets* (**<>**). Tags are used in pairs to delimit character data (e.g., **Simple XML**). A tag that begins *markup* (i.e., XML data) is called a *start tag*, whereas a tag that terminates markup is called an *end tag*. Examples of start tags are **<article>** and **<title>** (lines 6 and 8, respectively). End tags differ from start tags in that they contain a *forward slash* (*/*) character immediately after the **<** character. Examples of end tags are **</title>** and **</article>** (lines 8 and 23, respectively). XML documents can contain any number of tags.

Common Programming Error 15.2

Failure to provide a corresponding end tag for a start tag is a syntax error.

Individual units of markup (i.e., everything included between a start tag and its corresponding end tag) are called *elements*. An XML document includes one element (called a *root element*) that contains every other element. The root element must be the first element after the XML declaration. In Fig. 15.1, **article** (line 6) is the root element. Elements are *nested* within each other to form hierarchies—with the root element at the top of the hierarchy. This allows document authors to create explicit relationships between data. For example, elements **title**, **date**, **author**, **summary** and **content** are nested within **article**. Elements **firstName** and **lastName** are nested within **author**.

Common Programming Error 15.3

Attempting to create more than one root element in an XML document is a syntax error.

Element **title** (line 8) contains the title of the article, **Simple XML**, as character data. Similarly, **date** (line 10), **summary** (line 17) and **content** (lines 19–21) contain as character data the date, summary and content, respectively. XML element names can be of any length and may contain letters, digits, underscores, hyphens and periods—they must begin with a letter or an underscore.

Common Programming Error 15.4

XML is case sensitive. The use of the wrong case for an XML element name is a syntax error.

By itself, this document is simply a text file named **article.xml**. Although it is not required, most XML documents end in the file extension **.xml**. The processing of XML documents requires a program called an *XML parser*. Parsers are responsible for checking an XML document's syntax and making the XML document's data available to applications. Often, XML parsers are built into applications such as Visual Studio or available for download over the Internet. Popular parsers include Microsoft's *msxml*, the Apache Software Foundation's *Xerces* and IBM's *XML4J*. In this chapter, we use msxml.

When the user loads **article.xml** into Internet Explorer (IE),[1] msxml parses the document and passes the parsed data to IE. IE then uses a built-in *style sheet* to format the data. Notice that the resulting format of the data (Fig. 15.2) is similar to the format of the XML document shown in Fig. 15.1. As we soon demonstrate, style sheets play an important and powerful role in the transformation of XML data into formats suitable for display.

Notice the minus (−) and plus (+) signs in Fig. 15.2. Although these are not part of the XML document, IE places them next to all *container elements* (i.e., elements that contain other elements). Container elements also are called *parent elements*. A minus sign indicates that the parent element's *child elements* (i.e., nested elements) are being displayed. When clicked, a minus sign becomes a plus sign (which collapses the container element and hides all children). Conversely, clicking a plus sign expands the container element and changes the plus sign to a minus sign. This behavior is similar to the viewing of the directory structure on a Windows system using Windows Explorer. In fact, a directory structure often is modeled as a series of tree structures, in which each drive letter (e.g., **C:**, etc.) represents the *root* of a tree. Each folder is a *node* in the tree. Parsers often place XML data into trees to facilitate efficient manipulation, as discussed in Section 15.4.

Common Programming Error 15.5

Nesting XML tags improperly is a syntax error. For example, `<x><y>hello</x></y>` is an error, because the `</y>` tag must precede the `</x>` tag.

We now present a second XML document (Fig. 15.3), which marks up a business letter. This document contains significantly more data than did the previous XML document.

---

1. IE 5 and higher.

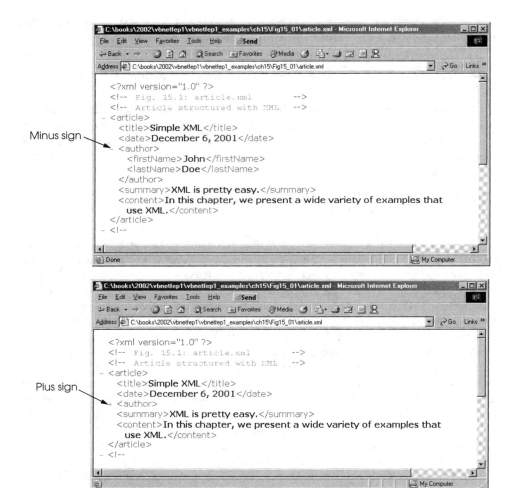

Fig. 15.2   article.xml displayed by Internet Explorer.

```
1   <?xml version = "1.0"?>
2
3   <!-- Fig. 15.3: letter.xml               -->
4   <!-- Business letter formatted with XML -->
5
6   <letter>
7      <contact type = "from">
8         <name>Jane Doe</name>
9         <address1>Box 12345</address1>
10        <address2>15 Any Ave.</address2>
11        <city>Othertown</city>
12        <state>Otherstate</state>
```

Fig. 15.3   XML to mark up a business letter. (Part 1 of 2.)

```
13              <zip>67890</zip>
14              <phone>555-4321</phone>
15              <flag gender = "F" />
16          </contact>
17
18          <contact type = "to">
19              <name>John Doe</name>
20              <address1>123 Main St.</address1>
21              <address2></address2>
22              <city>Anytown</city>
23              <state>Anystate</state>
24              <zip>12345</zip>
25              <phone>555-1234</phone>
26              <flag gender = "M" />
27          </contact>
28
29          <salutation>Dear Sir:</salutation>
30
31              <paragraph>It is our privilege to inform you about our new
32              database managed with <technology>XML</technology>. This
33              new system allows you to reduce the load on
34              your inventory list server by having the client machine
35              perform the work of sorting and filtering the data.
36              </paragraph>
37
38              <paragraph>Please visit our Web site for availability
39              and pricing.
40              </paragraph>
41
42          <closing>Sincerely</closing>
43
44          <signature>Ms. Doe</signature>
45      </letter>
```

Fig. 15.3 XML to mark up a business letter. (Part 2 of 2.)

Root element **letter** (lines 6–45) contains the child elements **contact** (lines 7–16 and 18–27), **salutation**, **paragraph**, **closing** and **signature**. In addition to being placed between tags, data also can be placed in *attributes*, which are name-value pairs in start tags. Elements can have any number of attributes in their start tags. The first **contact** element (lines 7–16) has attribute **type** with attribute *value* **"from"**, which indicates that this contact element marks up information about the letter's sender. The second **contact** element (lines 18–27) has attribute **type** with value **"to"**, which indicates that this contact element marks up information about the letter's recipient. Like element names, attribute names are case sensitive, can be any length; may contain letters, digits, underscores, hyphens and periods; and must begin with either a letter or underscore character. A **contact** element stores a contact's name, address, phone number and gender. Element **salutation** (line 29) marks up the letter's salutation. Lines 31–40 mark up the letter's body with **paragraph** elements. Elements **closing** (line 42) and **signature** (line 44) mark up the closing sentence and the signature of the letter's author, respectively.

Common Programming Error 15.6

*Failure to enclose attribute values in double (**" "**) or single (**' '**) quotes is a syntax error.*

In line 15, we introduce *empty element* **flag**, which is used to indicate the gender of the contact. Empty elements do not contain character data (i.e., they do not contain text between the start and end tags). Such elements are closed either by placing a slash at the end of the element (as shown in line 15) or by explicitly writing a closing tag, as in

```
<flag gender = "F"></flag>
```

15.3 XML Namespaces

Object-oriented programming languages, such as C++ and Visual Basic, provide massive class libraries that group their features into namespaces. These namespaces prevent *naming collisions* between programmer-defined identifiers and identifiers in class libraries. For example, we might use class **CBook** to represent information on one of our publications; however, a stamp collector might use class **CBook** to represent a book of stamps. A naming collision would occur if we use these two classes in the same assembly, without using namespaces to differentiate them.

Like Visual Basic, XML also provides *namespaces*, which provide a means of uniquely identifying XML elements. In addition, XML-based languages—called *vocabularies*, such as XML Schema (Section 15.5), Extensible Stylesheet Language (Section 15.6) and BizTalk (Section 15.7)—often use namespaces to identify their elements.

Elements are differentiated via *namespace prefixes*, which identify the namespace to which an element belongs. For example,

```
<deitel:book>Visual Basic How to Program</deitel:book>
```

qualifies element **book** with namespace prefix **deitel**. This indicates that element **book** is part of namespace **deitel**. Document authors can use any name for a namespace prefix except the reserved namespace prefix **xml**.

 Common Programming Error 15.7

*Attempting to create a namespace prefix named **xml** in any mixture of case is a syntax error.*

The mark up in Fig. 15.4 demonstrates the use of namespaces. This XML document contains two **file** elements that are differentiated using namespaces.

```
1   <?xml version = "1.0"?>
2
3   <!-- Fig. 15.4: namespace.xml -->
4   <!-- Demonstrating namespaces -->
5
6   <text:directory xmlns:text = "urn:deitel:textInfo"
7      xmlns:image = "urn:deitel:imageInfo">
8
```

Fig. 15.4 XML namespaces demonstration. (Part 1 of 2.)

```
9    <text:file filename = "book.xml">
10       <text:description>A book list</text:description>
11   </text:file>
12
13   <image:file filename = "funny.jpg">
14       <image:description>A funny picture</image:description>
15       <image:size width = "200" height = "100" />
16   </image:file>
17
18   </text:directory>
```

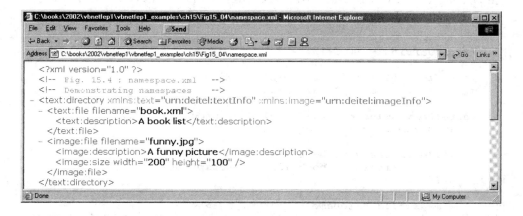

Fig. 15.4   XML namespaces demonstration. (Part 2 of 2.)

 ### Software Engineering Observation 15.1

Attributes need not be qualified with namespace prefixes, because they always are associated with elements.

Lines 6–7 use attribute **xmlns** to create two namespace prefixes: **text** and **image**. Each namespace prefix is bound to a series of characters called a *uniform resource identifier (URI)* that uniquely identifies the namespace. Document authors create their own namespace prefixes and URIs.

To ensure that namespaces are unique, document authors must provide unique URIs. Here, we use the text **urn:deitel:textInfo** and **urn:deitel:imageInfo** as URIs. A common practice is to use *Universal Resource Locators (URLs)* for URIs, because the domain names (such as, **www.deitel.com**) used in URLs are guaranteed to be unique. For example, lines 6–7 could have been written as

```
<text:directory xmlns:text =
    "http://www.deitel.com/xmlns-text"
    xmlns:image = "http://www.deitel.com/xmlns-image">
```

In this example, we use URLs related to the Deitel & Associates, Inc, domain name to identify namespaces. The parser never visits these URLs—they simply represent a series of characters used to differentiate names. The URLs need not refer to actual Web pages or be formed properly.

Lines 9–11 use the namespace prefix **text** to describe elements **file** and **descrip-tion**. Notice that the namespace prefix **text** is applied to the end tags as well. Lines 13–16 apply namespace prefix **image** to elements **file**, **description** and **size**.

To eliminate the need to precede each element with a namespace prefix, document authors can specify a *default namespace*. Figure 15.5 demonstrates the creation and use of default namespaces.

Line 6 declares a default namespace using attribute **xmlns** with a URI as its value. Once we define this default namespace, child elements belonging to the namespace need not be qualified by a namespace prefix. Element **file** (line 9–11) is in the namespace corresponding to the URI **urn:deitel:textInfo**. Compare this to Fig. 15.4, where we prefixed **file** and **description** with **text** (lines 9–11).

```
1    <?xml version = "1.0"?>
2
3    <!-- Fig. 15.5: defaultnamespace.xml -->
4    <!-- Using a default namespace         -->
5
6    <directory xmlns = "urn:deitel:textInfo"
7       xmlns:image = "urn:deitel:imageInfo">
8
9       <file filename = "book.xml">
10         <description>A book list</description>
11      </file>
12
13      <image:file filename = "funny.jpg">
14         <image:description>A funny picture</image:description>
15         <image:size width = "200" height = "100" />
16      </image:file>
17
18   </directory>
```

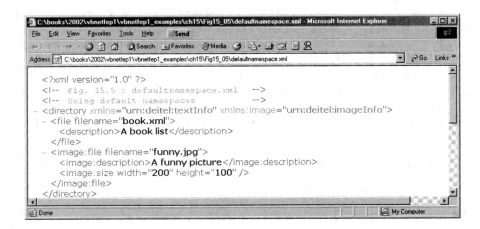

Fig. 15.5 Default namespace demonstration.

The default namespace applies to the **directory** element and all elements that are not qualified with a namespace prefix. However, we can use a namespace prefix to specify a different namespace for particular elements. For example, the **file** element in line 13 is prefixed with **image** to indicate that it is in the namespace corresponding to the URI **urn:deitel:imageInfo**, rather than the default namespace.

15.4 Document Object Model (DOM)

Although XML documents are text files, retrieving data from them via sequential-file access techniques is neither practical nor efficient, especially in situations where data must be added or deleted dynamically.

Upon successful parsing of documents, some XML parsers store document data as tree structures in memory. Figure 15.6 illustrates the tree structure for the document **article.xml** discussed in Fig. 15.1. This hierarchical tree structure is called a *Document Object Model (DOM)* tree, and an XML parser that creates this type of structure is known as a *DOM parser*. The DOM tree represents each component of the XML document (e.g., **article**, **date**, **firstName**, etc.) as a node in the tree. Nodes (such as **author**) that contain other nodes (called *child nodes*) are called *parent nodes*. Nodes that have the same parent (such as, **firstName** and **lastName**) are called *sibling nodes*. A node's *descendant nodes* include that node's children, its children's children and so on. Similarly, a node's *ancestor nodes* include that node's parent, its parent's parent and so on. Every DOM tree has a single *root node* that contains all other nodes in the document.

Classes for creating, reading and manipulating XML documents are located in the Visual Basic namespace *System.Xml*. This namespace also contains additional namespaces that contain other XML-related operations.

In this section, we present several examples that use DOM trees. Our first example, the program in Fig. 15.7, loads the XML document presented in Fig. 15.1 and displays its data in a text box. This example uses an *XmlReader* derived class named *XmlNodeReader*, which iterates through each node in the XML document. Class **XmlReader** is a **MustInherit** class that defines the interface for reading XML documents.

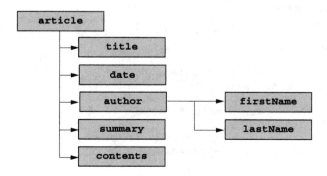

Fig. 15.6 Tree structure for Fig. 15.1.

Line 4 includes the **System.Xml** namespace, which contains the XML classes used in this example. Line 23 creates a reference to an ***XmlDocument*** object that conceptually represents an empty XML document. The XML document **article.xml** is parsed and loaded into this **XmlDocument** object when method ***Load*** is invoked in line 24. Once an XML document is loaded into an **XmlDocument**, its data can be read and manipulated programmatically. In this example, we read each node in the **XmlDocument**, which is the DOM tree. In successive examples, we demonstrate how to manipulate node values.

```
1    ' Fig. 15.7: XmlReaderTest.vb
2    ' Reading an XML document.
3
4    Imports System.Xml
5    Imports System.Windows.Forms
6
7    Public Class FrmXMLReaderTest
8       Inherits Form
9
10      ' TextBox displays XML output
11      Friend WithEvents txtOutput As TextBox
12
13      Public Sub New()
14         MyBase.New()
15
16         ' This call is required by the Windows Form Designer.
17         InitializeComponent()
18
19         ' add any initialization after
20         ' InitializeComponent() call
21
22         ' reference to "XML document"
23         Dim document As XmlDocument = New XmlDocument()
24         document.Load("article.xml")
25
26         ' create XmlNodeReader for document
27         Dim reader As XmlNodeReader = New XmlNodeReader(document)
28
29         ' show form before txtOutput is populated
30         Me.Show()
31
32         ' tree depth is -1, no indentation
33         Dim depth As Integer = -1
34
35         ' display each node's content
36         While reader.Read
37
38            Select Case reader.NodeType
39
40               ' if Element, display its name
41               Case XmlNodeType.Element
42
43                  ' increase tab depth
44                  depth += 1
```

Fig. 15.7 **XmlNodeReader** iterates through an XML document. (Part 1 of 3.)

```vbnet
45                      TabOutput(depth)
46                      txtOutput.Text &= "<" & reader.Name & ">" & _
47                          vbCrLf
48
49                      ' if empty element, decrease depth
50                      If reader.IsEmptyElement Then
51                          depth -= 1
52                      End If
53
54                  Case XmlNodeType.Comment ' if Comment, display it
55                      TabOutput(depth)
56                      txtOutput.Text &= "<!--" & reader.Value & _
57                          "-->" & vbCrLf
58
59                  Case XmlNodeType.Text ' if Text, display it
60                      TabOutput(depth)
61                      txtOutput.Text &= vbTab & reader.Value & vbCrLf
62
63                      ' if XML declaration, display it
64                  Case XmlNodeType.XmlDeclaration
65                      TabOutput(depth)
66                      txtOutput.Text &= "<?" & reader.Name & " " & _
67                          reader.Value & "?>" & vbCrLf
68
69                      ' if EndElement, display it and decrement depth
70                  Case XmlNodeType.EndElement
71                      TabOutput(depth)
72                      txtOutput.Text &= "</" & reader.Name & ">/" & _
73                          vbCrLf
74
75                      depth -= 1
76
77              End Select
78
79          End While
80
81      End Sub ' New
82
83      ' Visual Studio .NET generated code
84
85      ' insert tabs
86      Private Sub TabOutput(ByVal number As Integer)
87          Dim i As Integer
88
89          For i = 0 To number - 1
90              txtOutput.Text &= vbTab
91          Next
92
93      End Sub ' TabOutput
94
95  End Class ' FrmXmlReaderTest
```

Fig. 15.7 **XmlNodeReader** iterates through an XML document. (Part 2 of 3.)

Fig. 15.7 XmlNodeReader iterates through an XML document. (Part 3 of 3.)

In line 27, we create an **XmlNodeReader** and assign it to reference **reader**, which enables us to read each node sequentially from the **XmlDocument**. Method *Read* of **XmlReader** reads one node from the DOM tree. By placing this statement in the **While** loop (lines 36–79), **reader Read**s all the document nodes. The **Select Case** statement (lines 38–77) processes each node. Either the *Name* property (line 46), which contains the node's name, or the *Value* property (line 56), which contains the node's data, is formatted and concatenated to the **String** assigned to the text box **Text** property. The **NodeType** property contains the node type (specifying whether the node is an element, comment, text etc.). Notice that each **Case** specifies a node type using *XmlNodeType* enumeration constants. Note that our line breaks use the Visual Basic constant **vbCrLf**, which denotes a carriage return followed by a line feed. This is the standard line break for Windows-based applications and controls.

The displayed output emphasizes the structure of the XML document. Variable **depth** (line 33) sets the number of tab characters for indenting each element. The depth is incremented each time an **Element** type is encountered and is decremented each time an **EndElement** or empty element is encountered. We use a similar technique in the next example to emphasize the tree structure of the XML document in the display.

The Visual Basic program in Fig. 15.8 demonstrates how to manipulate DOM trees programmatically. This program loads **letter.xml** (Fig. 15.3) into the DOM tree and then creates a second DOM tree that duplicates the DOM tree containing **letter.xml**'s contents. The GUI for this application contains a text box, a **TreeView** control and three buttons—**Build**, **Print** and **Reset**. When clicked, **Build** copies **letter.xml** and displays the document's tree structure in the **TreeView** control, **Print** displays the XML element values and names in a text box and **Reset** clears the **TreeView** control and text-box content.

```
1    ' Fig. 15.8: XmlDom.vb
2    ' Demonstrates DOM tree manipulation.
3
4    Imports System.Xml
5    Imports System.Windows.Forms
6    Imports System.CodeDom.Compiler ' contains TempFileCollection
7
8    Public Class FrmXmlDom
9       Inherits Form
10
11      ' TextBox and TreeView for displaying data
12      Friend WithEvents txtConsole As TextBox
13      Friend WithEvents treXml As TreeView
14
15      ' Buttons for building, printing and reseting DOM tree
16      Friend WithEvents cmdBuild As Button
17      Friend WithEvents cmdPrint As Button
18      Friend WithEvents cmdReset As Button
19
20      Private source As XmlDocument ' reference to "XML document"
21
22      ' reference copy of source's "XML document"
23      Private copy As XmlDocument
24
25      Private tree As TreeNode ' TreeNode reference
26
27      Public Sub New()
28         MyBase.New()
29
30         ' This call is required by the Windows Form Designer.
31         InitializeComponent()
32
33         ' add any initialization after
34         ' InitializeComponent() call
35
36         ' create XmlDocument and load letter.xml
37         source = New XmlDocument()
38         source.Load("letter.xml")
39
40         ' initialize references to Nothing
41         copy = Nothing
42         tree = Nothing
43
44      End Sub ' New
45
46      ' Visual Studio .NET generated code
47
48      ' event handler for cmdBuild click event
49      Private Sub cmdBuild_Click(ByVal sender As System.Object, _
50         ByVal e As System.EventArgs) Handles cmdBuild.Click
51
52         ' determine if copy has been built already
53         If Not copy Is Nothing Then
```

Fig. 15.8 DOM structure of an XML document. (Part 1 of 5.)

```
54                Return ' document already exists
55          End If
56
57          ' instantiate XmlDocument and TreeNode
58          copy = New XmlDocument()
59          tree = New TreeNode()
60
61          ' add root node name to TreeNode and add
62          ' TreeNode to TreeView control
63          tree.Text = source.Name ' assigns #root
64          treXml.Nodes.Add(tree)
65
66          ' build node and tree hierarchy
67          BuildTree(source, copy, tree)
68       End Sub ' cmdBuild_Click
69
70       ' event handler for cmdPrint click event
71       Private Sub cmdPrint_Click(ByVal sender As System.Object, _
72          ByVal e As System.EventArgs) Handles cmdPrint.Click
73
74          ' exit if copy does not reference an XmlDocument
75          If copy Is Nothing Then
76             Return
77          End If
78
79          ' create temporary XML file
80          Dim file As TempFileCollection = New TempFileCollection()
81
82          ' create file that is deleted at program termination
83          file.AddExtension("xml", False)
84          Dim filename As String() = New String(0) {}
85          file.CopyTo(filename, 0)
86
87          ' write XML data to disk
88          Dim writer As XmlTextWriter = _
89             New XmlTextWriter(filename(0), _
90             System.Text.Encoding.UTF8)
91
92          copy.WriteTo(writer)
93          writer.Close()
94
95          ' parse and load temporary XML document
96          Dim reader As XmlTextReader = _
97             New XmlTextReader(filename(0))
98
99          ' read, format and display data
100         While reader.Read
101
102            If reader.NodeType = XmlNodeType.EndElement Then
103               txtConsole.Text &= "/"
104            End If
105
```

Fig. 15.8   DOM structure of an XML document. (Part 2 of 5.)

```
106                    If reader.Name <> String.Empty Then
107                        txtConsole.Text &= reader.Name & vbCrLf
108                    End If
109
110                    If reader.Value <> String.Empty Then
111                        txtConsole.Text &= vbTab & reader.Value & vbCrLf
112                    End If
113
114                End While
115
116                reader.Close()
117            End Sub ' cmdPrint_Click
118
119            ' handle cmdReset click event
120            Private Sub cmdReset_Click(ByVal sender As System.Object, _
121                ByVal e As System.EventArgs) Handles cmdReset.Click
122
123                ' remove TreeView nodes
124                If Not tree Is Nothing Then
125                    treXml.Nodes.Remove(tree)
126                End If
127
128                treXml.Refresh() ' force TreeView update
129
130                ' delete XmlDocument and tree
131                copy = Nothing
132                tree = Nothing
133
134                txtConsole.Clear() ' clear text box
135            End Sub ' cmdReset_Click
136
137            ' construct DOM tree
138            Private Sub BuildTree(ByVal xmlSourceNode As XmlNode, _
139                ByVal documentValue As XmlNode, _
140                ByVal treeNode As TreeNode)
141
142                ' create XmlNodeReader to access XML document
143                Dim nodeReader As XmlNodeReader = _
144                    New XmlNodeReader(xmlSourceNode)
145
146                ' represents current node in DOM tree
147                Dim currentNode As XmlNode = Nothing
148
149                ' treeNode to add to existing tree
150                Dim newNode As TreeNode = New TreeNode()
151
152                ' references modified node type for CreateNode
153                Dim modifiedNodeType As XmlNodeType
154
155                While nodeReader.Read
156
157                    ' get current node type
158                    modifiedNodeType = nodeReader.NodeType
```

Fig. 15.8 DOM structure of an XML document. (Part 3 of 5.)

```vbnet
159
160            ' check for EndElement, store as Element
161            If modifiedNodeType = XmlNodeType.EndElement Then
162               modifiedNodeType = XmlNodeType.Element
163            End If
164
165            ' create node copy
166            currentNode = copy.CreateNode(modifiedNodeType, _
167               nodeReader.Name, nodeReader.NamespaceURI)
168
169            ' build tree based on node type
170            Select Case nodeReader.NodeType
171
172               ' if Text node, add its value to tree
173               Case XmlNodeType.Text
174                  newNode.Text = nodeReader.Value
175                  treeNode.Nodes.Add(newNode)
176
177                  ' append Text node value to currentNode data
178                  CType(currentNode, XmlText).AppendData _
179                     (nodeReader.Value)
180
181                  documentValue.AppendChild(currentNode)
182
183               ' if EndElement, move up tree
184               Case XmlNodeType.EndElement
185                  documentValue = documentValue.ParentNode
186                  treeNode = treeNode.Parent
187
188               ' if new element, add name and traverse tree
189               Case XmlNodeType.Element
190
191                  ' determine if element contains content
192                  If Not nodeReader.IsEmptyElement Then
193
194                     ' assign node text, add newNode as child
195                     newNode.Text = nodeReader.Name
196                     treeNode.Nodes.Add(newNode)
197
198                     ' set treeNode to last child
199                     treeNode = newNode
200
201                     documentValue.AppendChild(currentNode)
202                     documentValue = documentValue.LastChild
203
204                  Else ' do not traverse empty elements
205
206                     ' assign NodeType string to newNode
207                     newNode.Text = nodeReader.NodeType.ToString
208
209                     treeNode.Nodes.Add(newNode)
210                     documentValue.AppendChild(currentNode)
211                  End If
```

Fig. 15.8   DOM structure of an XML document. (Part 4 of 5.)

```
212
213                    Case Else ' all other types, display node type
214                        newNode.Text = nodeReader.NodeType.ToString
215                        treeNode.Nodes.Add(newNode)
216                        documentValue.AppendChild(currentNode)
217
218                End Select
219
220                newNode = New TreeNode()
221            End While
222
223            ' update TreeView control
224            treXml.ExpandAll()
225            treXml.Refresh()
226        End Sub ' BuildTree
227
228    End Class ' FrmXmlDom
```

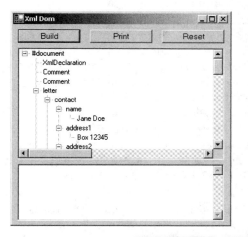

Fig. 15.8 DOM structure of an XML document. (Part 5 of 5.)

Lines 20 and 23 create references to **XmlDocument**s **source** and **copy**. Line 37 assigns a new **XmlDocument** object to reference **source**. Line 38 then invokes method **Load** to parse and load **letter.xml**. We discuss reference **copy** shortly.

Unfortunately, **XmlDocument**s do not provide any features for displaying their content graphically. In this example, we display the document's contents using a *TreeView* control. We use class *TreeNode* to represent each node in the tree. Class **TreeView** and class **TreeNode** are part of the **System.Windows.Forms.Form** namespace. **TreeNode**s are added to the **TreeView** to emphasize the structure of the XML document.

When clicked, the **Build** button triggers the event handler **cmdBuild_Click** (lines 49–68), which creates a copy of **letter.xml** dynamically. Lines 58–59 create the **Xml-Document** and **TreeNode**s (i.e., the nodes for graphical representation in the **Tree-View**). Line 63 retrieves the **Name** of the node referenced by **source** (i.e., **#root**, which represents the document root) and assigns it to **tree**'s **Text** property. This **TreeNode** then is inserted into the **TreeView** control's node list. Method **Add** is called to add each new **TreeNode** to the **TreeView**'s **Nodes** collection. Line 67 calls method **Build-Tree** to copy the **XMLDocument** referenced by **source** and to update the **TreeView**.

Method **BuildTree** (line 138–226) receives an **XmlNode** representing the source node, an empty **XmlNode** and a **treeNode** to place in the DOM tree. Parameter **treeNode** references the current location in the tree (i.e., the **TreeNode** most recently added to the **TreeView** control). Lines 143–144 instantiate an **XmlNodeReader** for iterating through the DOM tree. Lines 147–150 declare **XmlNode** and **TreeNode** references that indicate the next nodes added to **document** (i.e., the DOM tree referenced by **copy**) and **treeNode**. Lines 155–221 iterate through each node in the tree.

Lines 158–167 create a node containing a copy of the current **nodeReader** node. Method *CreateNode* of **XmlDocument** takes a **NodeType**, a **Name** and a *NamespaceURI* as arguments. The **NodeType** cannot be an **EndElement**. If the **NodeType** is an **EndElement** type, lines 161–162 assign **modifiedNodeType** type **Element**.

The **Select Case** statement in lines 170–218 determines the node type, creates and adds nodes to the **TreeView** and updates the DOM tree. When a text node is encountered, the new **TreeNode**'s **newNode**'s **Text** property is assigned the current node's value. This **TreeNode** is added to the **TreeView** control. In lines 178–179, we downcast **currentNode** to **XmlText** and append the node's value. The **currentNode** then is appended to the **document**. Lines 184–186 match an **EndElement** node type. This **Case** moves up the tree, because the end of an element has been encountered. The *ParentNode* and *Parent* properties retrieve the **documentValue**'s and **treeNode**'s parents, respectively.

Line 189 matches **Element** node types. Each non-empty **Element NodeType** (line 192) increases the depth of the tree; thus, we assign the current **nodeReader Name** to the **newNode**'s **Text** property and add the **newNode** to the **treeNode** node list. Lines 199–202 reorder the nodes in the node list to ensure that **newNode** is the last **TreeNode** in the node list. **XmlNode currentNode** is appended to **documentValue** as the last child, and **document** is set to its *LastChild*, which is the child we just added. If it is an empty element (line 204), we assign to the **newNode**'s **Text** property the **String** representation of the **NodeType**. Next, the **newNode** is added to the **treeNode** node list. Line 216 appends the **currentNode** to the **documentValue**. The **Case Else** case assigns the

String representation of the node type to the **NewNode Text** property, adds the **newNode** to the **TreeNode** node list and appends the **currentNode** to the **document**.

After the DOM trees are built, the **TreeNode** node list is displayed in the **TreeView** control. The clicking of the nodes (i.e., the **+** or **–** boxes) in the **TreeView** either expands or collapses them. When **Print** is clicked, the event handler method **cmdPrint_Click** (lines 71–117) is invoked. Lines 80–85 create a temporary file for storing the XML. Lines 88–90 create an **XmlTextWriter** for streaming the XML data to disk. Method **WriteTo** is called to write the XML representation to the **XmlTextWriter** stream (line 92). Lines 96–97 create an **XmlTextReader** to read from the file. The **While** loop (line 100–114) reads each node in the DOM tree and writes tag names and character data to the text box. If it is an end element, a slash is concatenated. If the node has a **Name** or **Value**, that name or value is concatenated to the text box text.

The **Reset** button's event handler, **cmdReset_Click**, deletes both dynamically generated trees and updates the **TreeView** control's display. Reference **copy** is assigned **Nothing** (to allow its tree to be garbage collected in line 131), and the **TreeNode** node list reference **tree** is assigned **Nothing**.

Although **XmlReader** includes methods for reading and modifying node values, it is not the most efficient means of locating data in a DOM tree. Microsoft .NET provides class **XPathNavigator** in the **System.Xml.XPath** namespace for iterating through node lists that match search criteria, which are written as an *XPath expression*. XPath (XML Path Language) provides a syntax for locating specific nodes in XML documents effectively and efficiently. XPath is a string-based language of expressions used by XML and many of its related technologies (such as XSLT, discussed in Section 15.6).

Figure 15.9 demonstrates how to navigate through an XML document using an **XPathNavigator**. Like Fig. 15.8, this program uses a **TreeView** control and **TreeNode** objects to display the XML document's structure. However, instead of displaying the entire DOM tree, the **TreeNode** node list is updated each time the **XPath-Navigator** is positioned to a new node. Nodes are added to and deleted from the **TreeView** to reflect the **XPathNavigator**'s location in the DOM tree. The XML document **games.xml** that we use in this example is presented in Fig. 15.10.

```
1    ' Fig. 15.9: PathNavigator.vb
2    ' Demonstrates Class XPathNavigator
3
4    Imports System.Windows.Forms
5    Imports System.Xml.XPath ' contains XPathNavigator
6
7    Public Class FrmPathNavigator
8       Inherits Form
9
10      ' GroupBox contains Controls for locating XML file
11      Friend WithEvents locateGroupBox As GroupBox
12      Friend WithEvents cmdSelect As Button
13      Friend WithEvents cboSelect As ComboBox
14      Friend WithEvents txtSelect As TextBox
15
```

Fig. 15.9 **XPathNavigator** class navigates selected nodes. (Part 1 of 7.)

```
16         ' GroupBox contains Controls for navigating DOM tree
17         Friend WithEvents navigateGroupBox As GroupBox
18         Friend WithEvents cmdNext As Button
19         Friend WithEvents cmdPrevious As Button
20         Friend WithEvents cmdParent As Button
21         Friend WithEvents cmdFirstChild As Button
22
23         ' TreeView displays DOM-tree results
24         Friend WithEvents trePath As TreeView
25
26         ' navigator to traverse document
27         Private xPath As XPathNavigator
28
29         ' references document for use by XPathNavigator
30         Private document As XPathDocument
31
32         ' references TreeNode list used by TreeView control
33         Private tree As TreeNode
34
35         Public Sub New()
36            MyBase.New()
37
38            ' This call is required by the Windows Form Designer.
39            InitializeComponent()
40
41            ' add any initialization after
42            ' InitializeComponent() call
43
44            ' load in XML document
45            document = New XPathDocument("sports.xml")
46
47            ' create nagivator
48            xPath = document.CreateNavigator
49
50            ' create root node for TreeNodes
51            tree = New TreeNode()
52
53            tree.Text = xPath.NodeType.ToString ' #root
54            trePath.Nodes.Add(tree)                ' add tree
55
56            ' update TreeView control
57            trePath.ExpandAll()
58            trePath.Refresh()
59            trePath.SelectedNode = tree            ' highlight root
60         End Sub ' New
61
62         ' Visual Studio .NET generated code
63
64         ' traverse to first child
65         Private Sub cmdFirstChild_Click( _
66            ByVal sender As System.Object, _
67            ByVal e As System.EventArgs) Handles cmdFirstChild.Click
```

Fig. 15.9 **XPathNavigator** class navigates selected nodes. (Part 2 of 7.)

```vbnet
68
69          Dim newTreeNode As TreeNode
70
71          ' move to first child
72          If xPath.MoveToFirstChild Then
73            newTreeNode = New TreeNode() ' create new node
74
75              ' set node's Text property to either
76              ' navigator's name or value
77            DetermineType(newTreeNode, xPath)
78
79              ' add node to TreeNode node list
80            tree.Nodes.Add(newTreeNode)
81            tree = newTreeNode ' assign tree newTreeNode
82
83              ' update TreeView control
84            trePath.ExpandAll()
85            trePath.Refresh()
86            trePath.SelectedNode = tree
87
88          Else ' node has no children
89            MessageBox.Show("Current Node has no children.", _
90                "", MessageBoxButtons.OK, MessageBoxIcon.Information)
91          End If
92
93       End Sub ' cmdFirstChild_Click
94
95       ' traverse to node's parent on cmdParent_Click event
96       Private Sub cmdParent_Click(ByVal sender As System.Object, _
97          ByVal e As System.EventArgs) Handles cmdParent.Click
98
99          ' move to parent
100         If xPath.MoveToParent Then
101
102            tree = tree.Parent
103
104              ' get number of child nodes, not including sub trees
105            Dim count As Integer = tree.GetNodeCount(False)
106
107              ' remove all children
108            Dim i As Integer
109            For i = 0 To count - 1
110               tree.Nodes.Remove(tree.FirstNode)
111            Next
112
113              ' update TreeView control
114            trePath.ExpandAll()
115            trePath.Refresh()
116            trePath.SelectedNode = tree
117
```

Fig. 15.9   XPathNavigator class navigates selected nodes. (Part 3 of 7.)

```
118              Else ' if node has no parent (root node)
119                 MessageBox.Show("Current node has no parent.", "", _
120                    MessageBoxButtons.OK, MessageBoxIcon.Information)
121
122           End If
123
124        End Sub ' cmdParent_Click
125
126        ' find next sibling on cmdNext_Click event
127        Private Sub cmdNext_Click(ByVal sender As System.Object, _
128           ByVal e As System.EventArgs) Handles cmdNext.Click
129
130           Dim newTreeNode As TreeNode = Nothing
131           Dim newNode As TreeNode = Nothing
132
133           ' move to next sibling
134           If xPath.MoveToNext Then
135
136              newTreeNode = tree.Parent ' get parent node
137
138              newNode = New TreeNode() ' create new node
139              DetermineType(newNode, xPath)
140              newTreeNode.Nodes.Add(newNode)
141
142              ' set current position for display
143              tree = newNode
144
145              ' update TreeView control
146              trePath.ExpandAll()
147              trePath.Refresh()
148              trePath.SelectedNode = tree
149
150           Else ' node has no additional siblings
151              MessageBox.Show("Current node is last sibling.", "", _
152                 MessageBoxButtons.OK, MessageBoxIcon.Information)
153
154           End If
155
156        End Sub ' cmdNext_Click
157
158        ' get previous sibling on cmdPrevious_Click
159        Private Sub cmdPrevious_Click( _
160           ByVal sender As System.Object, _
161           ByVal e As System.EventArgs) Handles cmdPrevious.Click
162
163           Dim parentTreeNode As TreeNode = Nothing
164
165           ' move to previous sibling
166           If xPath.MoveToPrevious Then
167
168              parentTreeNode = tree.Parent ' get parent node
169
```

Fig. 15.9 **XPathNavigator** class navigates selected nodes. (Part 4 of 7.)

```
170                ' delete current node
171                parentTreeNode.Nodes.Remove(tree)
172
173                ' move to previous node
174                tree = parentTreeNode.LastNode
175
176                ' update TreeView control
177                trePath.ExpandAll()
178                trePath.Refresh()
179                trePath.SelectedNode = tree
180
181          Else ' if current node has no previous siblings
182             MessageBox.Show("Current node is first sibling.", "", _
183                MessageBoxButtons.OK, MessageBoxIcon.Information)
184
185          End If
186
187       End Sub ' cmdPrevious_Click
188
189       ' process cmdSelect_Click event
190       Private Sub cmdSelect_Click(ByVal sender As System.Object, _
191          ByVal e As System.EventArgs) Handles cmdSelect.Click
192
193          Dim iterator As XPathNodeIterator ' enables node iteration
194
195          ' get specified node from ComboBox
196          Try
197             iterator = xPath.Select(cboSelect.Text)
198             DisplayIterator(iterator) ' print selection
199
200          ' catch invalid expressions
201          Catch argumentException As System.ArgumentException
202             MessageBox.Show(argumentException.Message, "Error", _
203                MessageBoxButtons.OK, MessageBoxIcon.Error)
204
205          End Try
206
207       End Sub ' cmdSelect_Click
208
209       ' print values for XPathNodeIterator
210       Private Sub DisplayIterator( _
211          ByVal iterator As XPathNodeIterator)
212
213          txtSelect.Clear()
214
215          ' prints selected node's values
216          While iterator.MoveNext
217             txtSelect.Text &= iterator.Current.Value.Trim & vbCrLf
218          End While
219
220       End Sub ' DisplayIterator
221
```

Fig. 15.9 **XPathNavigator** class navigates selected nodes. (Part 5 of 7.)

```
222        ' determine if TreeNode should display current node
223        ' name or value
224        Private Sub DetermineType(ByVal node As TreeNode, _
225           ByVal xPath As XPathNavigator)
226
227           ' determine NodeType
228           Select Case xPath.NodeType
229
230              Case XPathNodeType.Element ' if Element, get its name
231
232                 ' get current node name, and remove whitespaces
233                 node.Text = xPath.Name.Trim
234
235              Case Else   ' obtain node values
236
237                 ' get current node value and remove whitespaces
238                 node.Text = xPath.Value.Trim
239
240           End Select
241
242        End Sub ' DetermineType
243
244     End Class ' FrmPathNavigator
```

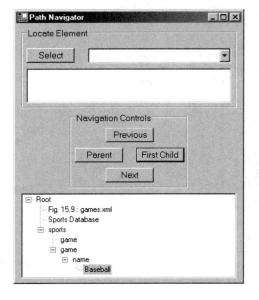

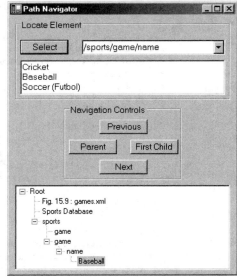

Fig. 15.9 XPathNavigator class navigates selected nodes. (Part 6 of 7.)

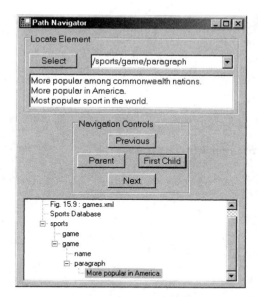

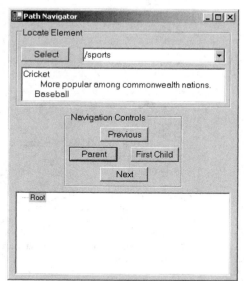

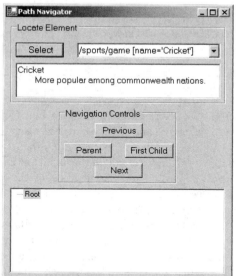

Fig. 15.9 **XPathNavigator** class navigates selected nodes. (Part 7 of 7.)

This program loads XML document **sports.xml** into an **XPathDocument** object by passing the document's file name to the **XPathDocument** constructor (line 45). Method **CreateNavigator** (line 48) creates and returns an **XPathNavigator** reference to the **XPathDocument**'s tree structure.

```
1    <?xml version = "1.0"?>
2
3    <!-- Fig. 15.10: games.xml -->
4    <!-- Sports Database        -->
5
6    <sports>
7
8      <game id = "783">
9          <name>Cricket</name>
10
11          <paragraph>
12              More popular among commonwealth nations.
13          </paragraph>
14      </game>
15
16      <game id = "239">
17          <name>Baseball</name>
18
19          <paragraph>
20              More popular in America.
21          </paragraph>
22      </game>
23
24      <game id = "418">
25          <name>Soccer(Futbol)</name>
26          <paragraph>Most popular sport in the world</paragraph>
27      </game>
28    </sports>
```

Fig. 15.10 XML document that describes various sports.

The navigation methods of **XPathNavigator** in Fig. 15.9 are *MoveToFirst-Child* (line 72), *MoveToParent* (line 100), *MoveToNext* (line 134) and *MoveToPrevious* (line 166). Each method performs the action that its name implies. Method **MoveToFirstChild** moves to the first child of the node referenced by the **XPathNavigator**, **MoveToParent** moves to the parent node of the node referenced by the **XPathNavigator**, **MoveToNext** moves to the next sibling of the node referenced by the **XPathNavigator** and **MoveToPrevious** moves to the previous sibling of the node referenced by the **XPathNavigator**. Each method returns a **Boolean** indicating whether the move was successful. In this example, we display a warning in a **MessageBox**, whenever a move operation fails. Furthermore, each method is called in the event handler of the button that matches its name (e.g., button **First Child** triggers **cmdFirstChild_Click**, which calls **MoveToFirstChild**).

Whenever we move forward using the **XPathNavigator**, as with **MoveToFirstChild** and **MoveToNext**, nodes are added to the **TreeNode** node list. **Private** Method **DetermineType** (lines 224–242) determines whether to assign the **Node**'s *Name* property or *Value* property to the **TreeNode** (lines 233 and 238). Whenever **MoveToParent** is called, all children of the parent node are removed from the display. Similarly, a call to **MoveToPrevious** removes the current sibling node. Note that the nodes are removed only from the **TreeView**, not from the tree representation of the document.

The other event handler corresponds to button **Select** (line 190–207). Method **Select** (line 197) takes search criteria in the form of either an *XPathExpression* or a **String** that represents an XPath expression and returns as an **XPathNodeIterator** object any nodes that match the search criteria. Figure 15.11 summarizes the XPath expressions provided by this program's combo box.

Method **DisplayIterator** (defined in lines 210–220) appends the node values from the given **XPathNodeIterator** to the **txtSelect** text box. Note that we call the **String** method **Trim** to remove unnecessary whitespace. Method *MoveNext* (line 216) advances to the next node, which property *Current* (line 217) can access.

15.5 Document Type Definitions (DTDs), Schemas and Validation

XML documents can reference optional documents that specify how the XML documents should be structured. These optional documents are called *Document Type Definitions* (*DTDs*) and *Schemas*. When a DTD or Schema document is provided, some parsers (called *validating parsers*) can read the DTD or Schema and check the XML document's structure against it. If the XML document conforms to the DTD or Schema, then the XML document is *valid*. Parsers that cannot check for document conformity against the DTD or Schema and are called *non-validating parsers*. If an XML parser (validating or non-validating) is able to process an XML document (that does not reference a DTD or Schema), the XML document is considered to be *well formed* (i.e., it is syntactically correct). By definition, a valid XML document is also a well-formed XML document. If a document is not well formed, parsing halts, and the parser issues an error.

 Software Engineering Observation 15.2

DTD and Schema documents are essential components for XML documents used in business-to-business (B2B) transactions and mission-critical systems. These documents help ensure that XML documents are valid.

Expression	Description
/sports	Matches all **sports** nodes that are child nodes of the document root node.
/sports/game/name	Matches all **name** nodes that are child nodes of **game**. The **game** is a child of **sports**, which is a child of the document root.
/sports/game/paragraph	Matches all **paragraph** nodes that are child nodes of **game**. The **game** is a child of **sports**, which is a child of the document root.
/sports/game[name='Cricket']	Matches all **game** nodes that contain element **name** whose name is **Cricket**. The **game** is a child of **sports**, which is a child of the document root.

Fig. 15.11 XPath expressions and descriptions.

Software Engineering Observation 15.3

Because XML document content can be structured in many different ways, an application cannot determine whether the document data it receives is complete, missing data or ordered properly. DTDs and Schemas solve this problem by providing an extensible means of describing a document's contents. An application can use a DTD or Schema document to perform a validity check on the document's contents.

15.5.1 Document Type Definitions

Document type definitions (DTDs) provide a means for type checking XML documents and thus verifying their *validity* (confirming that elements contain the proper attributes, elements are in the proper sequence, etc.). DTDs use *EBNF* (*Extended Backus-Naur Form*) *grammar* to describe an XML document's content. XML parsers need additional functionality to read EBNF grammar, because it is not XML syntax. Although DTDs are optional, they are recommended to ensure document conformity. The DTD in Fig. 15.12 defines the set of rules (i.e., the grammar) for structuring the business letter document contained in Fig. 15.13.

Portability Tip 15.2

DTDs can ensure consistency among XML documents generated by different programs.

Line 4 uses the **ELEMENT** *element type declaration* to define rules for element **letter**. In this case, **letter** contains one or more **contact** elements, one **salutation** element, one or more **paragraph** elements, one **closing** element and one **signature** element, in that sequence. The *plus sign* (**+**) *occurrence indicator* specifies that an element must occur one or more times. Other indicators include the *asterisk* (*****), which indicates an optional element that can occur any number of times, and the *question mark* (**?**), which indicates an optional element that can occur at most once. If an occurrence indicator is omitted, exactly one occurrence is expected.

```
1    <!-- Fig. 15.12: letter.dtd      -->
2    <!-- DTD document for letter.xml -->
3
4    <!ELEMENT letter ( contact+, salutation, paragraph+,
5       closing, signature )>
6
7    <!ELEMENT contact ( name, address1, address2, city, state,
8       zip, phone, flag )>
9    <!ATTLIST contact type CDATA #IMPLIED>
10
11   <!ELEMENT name ( #PCDATA )>
12   <!ELEMENT address1 ( #PCDATA )>
13   <!ELEMENT address2 ( #PCDATA )>
14   <!ELEMENT city ( #PCDATA )>
15   <!ELEMENT state ( #PCDATA )>
16   <!ELEMENT zip ( #PCDATA )>
17   <!ELEMENT phone ( #PCDATA )>
18   <!ELEMENT flag EMPTY>
```

Fig. 15.12 Document Type Definition (DTD) for a business letter. (Part 1 of 2.)

```
19    <!ATTLIST flag gender (M | F) "M">
20
21    <!ELEMENT salutation ( #PCDATA )>
22    <!ELEMENT closing ( #PCDATA )>
23    <!ELEMENT paragraph ( #PCDATA )>
24    <!ELEMENT signature ( #PCDATA )>
```

Fig. 15.12 Document Type Definition (DTD) for a business letter. (Part 2 of 2.)

The **contact** element definition (line 7) specifies that it contains the **name**, **address1**, **address2**, **city**, **state**, **zip**, **phone** and **flag** elements—in that order. Exactly one occurrence of each is expected.

Line 9 uses the ***ATTLIST*** *element type declaration* to define an attribute (i.e., **type**) for the **contact** element. Keyword ***#IMPLIED*** specifies that, if the parser finds a **contact** element without a **type** attribute, the application can provide a value or ignore the missing attribute. The absence of a **type** attribute cannot invalidate the document. Other types of default values include ***#REQUIRED*** and ***#FIXED***. Keyword ***#REQUIRED*** specifies that the attribute must be present in the document and the keyword ***#FIXED*** specifies that the attribute (if present) must always be assigned a specific value. For example,

> **<!ATTLIST address zip #FIXED "01757">**

indicates that the value **01757** must be used for attribute **zip**; otherwise, the document is invalid. If the attribute is not present, then the parser, by default, uses the fixed value that is specified in the **ATTLIST** declaration. Flag ***CDATA*** specifies that attribute **type** contains a **String** that is not processed by the parser, but instead is passed to the application as is.

Software Engineering Observation 15.4

DTD syntax does not provide any mechanism for describing an element's (or attribute's) data type.

Flag ***#PCDATA*** (line 11) specifies that the element can store *parsed character data* (i.e., text). Parsed character data cannot contain markup. The characters less than (**<**) and ampersand (**&**) must be replaced by their *entities* (i.e., **<** and **&**). However, the ampersand character can be inserted when used with entities.

Line 18 defines an empty element named **flag**. Keyword ***EMPTY*** specifies that the element cannot contain child elements or character data. Empty elements commonly are used for their attributes.

Common Programming Error 15.8

Any element, attribute or relationship not explicitly defined by a DTD results in an invalid document.

XML documents must explicitly reference a DTD. Figure 15.13 is an XML document that conforms to **letter.dtd** (Fig. 15.12).

This XML document is similar to that in Fig. 15.3. Line 6 references a DTD file. This markup contains three pieces: The name of the root element (**letter** in line 8) to which the DTD is applied, the keyword ***SYSTEM*** (which in this case denotes an *external DTD*—a DTD defined in a separate file) and the DTD's name and location (i.e., **letter.dtd** in the current directory). Though almost any file extension can be used, DTD documents typically end with the **.dtd** extension.

```
1   <?xml version = "1.0"?>
2
3   <!-- Fig. 15.13: letter2.xml          -->
4   <!-- Business letter formatted with XML -->
5
6   <!DOCTYPE letter SYSTEM "letter.dtd">
7
8   <letter>
9      <contact type = "from">
10        <name>Jane Doe</name>
11        <address1>Box 12345</address1>
12        <address2>15 Any Ave.</address2>
13        <city>Othertown</city>
14        <state>Otherstate</state>
15        <zip>67890</zip>
16        <phone>555-4321</phone>
17        <flag gender = "F" />
18     </contact>
19
20     <contact type = "to">
21        <name>John Doe</name>
22        <address1>123 Main St.</address1>
23        <address2></address2>
24        <city>Anytown</city>
25        <state>Anystate</state>
26        <zip>12345</zip>
27        <phone>555-1234</phone>
28        <flag gender = "M" />
29     </contact>
30
31     <salutation>Dear Sir:</salutation>
32
33     <paragraph>It is our privilege to inform you about our new
34        database managed with XML. This new system
35        allows you to reduce the load on your inventory list
36        server by having the client machine perform the work of
37        sorting and filtering the data.
38     </paragraph>
39
40     <paragraph>Please visit our Web site for availability
41        and pricing.
42     </paragraph>
43     <closing>Sincerely</closing>
44     <signature>Ms. Doe</signature>
45   </letter>
```

Fig. 15.13 XML document referencing its associated DTD.

Various tools (many of which are free) check document conformity against DTDs and Schemas (discussed momentarily). The output in Fig. 15.14 shows the results of the validation of **letter2.xml** using Microsoft's *XML Validator*. Visit **www.w3.org/XML/Schema.html** for a list of validating tools. Microsoft XML Validator is available free for download from **msdn.microsoft.com/downloads/samples/Internet/xml/xml_validator/sample.asp**.

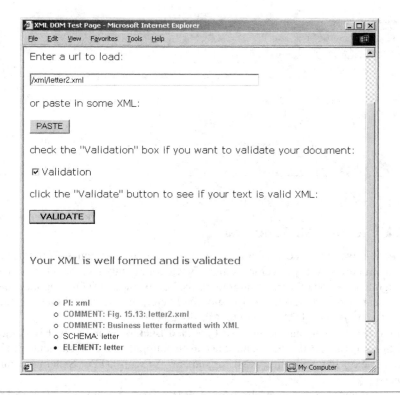

Fig. 15.14 XML Validator validates an XML document against a DTD.

Microsoft XML Validator can validate XML documents against DTDs locally or by uploading the documents to the XML Validator Web site. Here, **letter2.xml** and **letter.dtd** are placed in folder **C:\XML**. This XML document (**letter2.xml**) is well formed and conforms to **letter.dtd**.

XML documents that fail validation are still well-formed documents. When a document fails to conform to a DTD or Schema, Microsoft XML Validator displays an error message. For example, the DTD in Fig. 15.12 indicates that the **contact** element must contain child element **name**. If the document omits this child element, the document is well formed, but not valid. In such a scenario, Microsoft XML Validator displays the error message shown in Fig. 15.15.

Visual Basic programs can use msxml to validate XML documents against DTDs. For information on how to accomplish this, visit:

```
msdn.microsoft.com/library/default.asp?
url=/library/en-us/cpguidnf/html/
cpconvalidationagainstdtdwithxmlvalidatingreader.asp
```

As mentioned earlier, Schemas are the preferred means of defining structures for XML documents in .NET. Although several types of Schemas exist, the two most popular are Microsoft Schema and W3C Schema. We begin our discussion of Schemas in the next section.

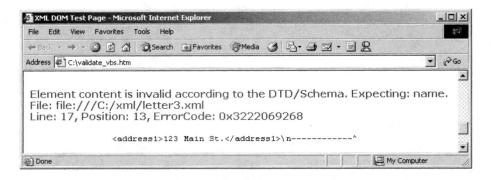

Fig. 15.15 XML Validator displaying an error message.

15.5.2 Microsoft XML Schemas

In this section, we introduce an alternative to DTDs—called Schemas—for defining XML document structures. Many developers in the XML community feel that DTDs are not flexible enough to meet today's programming needs. For example, DTDs cannot be manipulated (e.g., searched, programmatically modified, etc.) in the same manner that XML documents can, because DTDs are not XML documents.

Unlike DTDs, Schemas do not use Extended Backus-Naur Form (EBNF) grammar. Instead, Schemas are XML documents that can be manipulated (e.g., elements can be added or removed, etc.) like any other XML document. As with DTDs, Schemas require validating parsers.

In this section, we focus on Microsoft's *XML Schema* vocabulary.[2] Figure 15.16 presents an XML document that conforms to the Microsoft Schema document shown in Figure 15.17. By convention, Microsoft XML Schema documents use the file extension **.xdr**. Line 6 (Fig. 15.16) references the Schema document **book.xdr**.

```
1    <?xml version = "1.0"?>
2
3    <!-- Fig. 15.16: book.xml              -->
4    <!-- XML file that marks up book data -->
5
6    <books xmlns = "x-schema:book.xdr">
7       <book>
8          <title>C# How to Program</title>
9       </book>
10
11      <book>
12         <title>Java How to Program, 4/e</title>
13      </book>
```

Fig. 15.16 XML document that conforms to a Microsoft Schema document. (Part 1 of 2.)

---

2. For those readers who are interested in W3C Schema, we provide such examples on our Web site, **www.deitel.com**. We also provide a detailed treatment of W3C Schema in *XML for Experienced Programmers* (available 2003).

```
14
15      <book>
16         <title>Visual Basic .NET How to Program</title>
17      </book>
18
19      <book>
20         <title>Advanced Java 2 Platform How to Program</title>
21      </book>
22
23      <book>
24         <title>Python How to Program</title>
25      </book>
26   </books>
```

Fig. 15.16 XML document that conforms to a Microsoft Schema document. (Part 2 of 2.)

```
1    <?xml version = "1.0"?>
2
3    <!-- Fig. 15.17: book.xdr                    -->
4    <!-- Schema document to which book.xml conforms -->
5
6    <Schema xmlns = "urn:schemas-microsoft-com:xml-data">
7       <ElementType name = "title" content = "textOnly"
8          model = "closed" />
9
10      <ElementType name = "book" content = "eltOnly" model = "closed">
11         <element type = "title" minOccurs = "1" maxOccurs = "1" />
12      </ElementType>
13
14      <ElementType name = "books" content = "eltOnly" model = "closed">
15         <element type = "book" minOccurs = "0" maxOccurs = "*" />
16      </ElementType>
17   </Schema>
```

Fig. 15.17 Schema file that contains structure to which **book.xml** conforms.

Software Engineering Observation 15.5

Schemas are XML documents that conform to DTDs, which define the structure of a Schema. These DTDs, which are bundled with the parser, are used to validate the Schemas that authors create.

Software Engineering Observation 15.6

Many organizations and individuals are creating DTDs and Schemas for a broad range of categories (e.g., financial transactions, medical prescriptions, etc.). Often, these collections—called repositories*—are available free for download from the Web.[3]*

In line 6, root element **Schema** begins the Schema markup. Microsoft Schemas use the namespace URI **"urn:schemas-microsoft-com:data"**. Line 7 uses the **ElementType** element to define element **title**. Attribute **content** specifies that this element contains parsed character data (i.e., text only). Element **title** is not permitted to

---

3. See, for example, **opengis.net/schema.htm**

contain child elements. Setting the *model* *attribute* to *"closed"* specifies that a con-
forming XML document can contain only elements defined in this Schema. Line 10 defines
element **book**; this element's **content** is "elements only" (i.e., *eltOnly*). This means
that the element cannot contain mixed content (i.e., text and other elements). Within the **ElementType** element named **book**, the *element* element indicates that **title** is a **child**
element of **book**. Attributes *minOccurs* and *maxOccurs* are set to **"1"**, indicating that
a **book** element must contain exactly one **title** element. The asterisk (*****) in line 15 indicates that the Schema permits any number of **book** elements in element **books**.

Class *XmlValidatingReader* validates an XML document against a Schema. The
program in Fig. 15.18 validates an XML document that the user provides (such as,
Fig. 15.16 or Fig. 15.19) against a Microsoft Schema document (Fig. 15.17).

Line 17 creates an *XmlSchemaCollection* reference named **schemas**. Line 33
calls its *Add* method to add an *XmlSchema* object to the Schema collection. Method **Add**
receives as arguments a name that identifies the Schema (e.g., **"book"**) and the name of
the Schema file (e.g., **"book.xdr"**).

The XML document to be validated against the Schema(s) contained in the
XmlSchemaCollection must be passed to the **XmlValidatingReader** constructor (line 48–49). Lines 44–45 create an **XmlReader** for the file that the user selected
from **filesComboBox**. The **XmlReader** passed to this constructor is created using the
file name selected from **cboFiles** (lines 44–45).

Line 52 **Add**s the Schema collection referenced by **Schemas** to the *Schemas* property. This property sets the Schema(s) used to validate the document. The *Validation-
Type* property (line 55) is set to the *ValidationType* *enumeration* constant for
Microsoft Schema. Lines 58–59 register method **ValidationError** with *ValidationEventHandler*. Method **ValidationError** (lines 79–84) is called if the document is invalid or an error occurs, such as if the document cannot be found. Failure to
register a method with **ValidationEventHandler** causes an exception to be thrown
when the document is missing or invalid.

```
1    ' Fig. 15.18: ValidationTest.vb
2    ' Validating XML documents against Schemas.
3
4    Imports System.Windows.Forms
5    Imports System.Xml
6    Imports System.Xml.Schema ' contains Schema classes
7
8    ' determines XML document Schema validity
9    Public Class FrmValidationTest
10       Inherits Form
11
12       ' Controls for validating XML document
13       Friend WithEvents cboFiles As ComboBox
14       Friend WithEvents cmdValidate As Button
15       Friend WithEvents lblConsole As Label
16
17       Private schemas As XmlSchemaCollection ' Schemas
18       Private valid As Boolean ' validation result
```

Fig. 15.18 Schema-validation example. (Part 1 of 3.)

```
19
20      Public Sub New()
21         MyBase.New()
22
23         ' This call is required by the Windows Form Designer.
24         InitializeComponent()
25
26         ' add any initialization after
27         ' InitializeComponent() call
28
29         valid = True ' assume document is valid
30
31         ' get Schema(s) for validation
32         schemas = New XmlSchemaCollection()
33         schemas.Add("book", "book.xdr")
34      End Sub ' New
35
36   ' Visual Studio .NET generated code
37
38   ' handle cmdValidate click event
39   Private Sub cmdValidate_Click( _
40      ByVal sender As System.Object, _
41      ByVal e As System.EventArgs) Handles cmdValidate.Click
42
43         ' get XML document
44         Dim reader As XmlTextReader = _
45            New XmlTextReader(cboFiles.Text)
46
47         ' get validator
48         Dim validator As XmlValidatingReader = _
49            New XmlValidatingReader(reader)
50
51         ' assign Schema(s)
52         validator.Schemas.Add(schemas)
53
54         ' Microsoft XDR validation
55         validator.ValidationType = ValidationType.XDR
56
57         ' register event handler for validation error(s)
58         AddHandler validator.ValidationEventHandler, _
59            AddressOf ValidationError
60
61         ' validate document node-by-node
62         While validator.Read
63
64            ' empty body
65         End While
66
67         ' check validation result
68         If valid Then
69            lblConsole.Text = "Document is valid"
70         End If
71
```

Fig. 15.18 Schema-validation example. (Part 2 of 3.)

```
72            valid = True ' reset variable
73
74            ' close reader stream
75            validator.Close()
76        End Sub ' cmdValidate_Click
77
78        ' event handler for validation error
79        Private Sub ValidationError(ByVal sender As Object, _
80            ByVal arguments As ValidationEventArgs)
81
82            lblConsole.Text = arguments.Message
83            valid = False ' validation failed
84        End Sub ' ValidationError
85
86    End Class ' FrmValidationTest
```

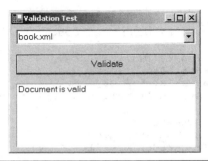

Fig. 15.18 Schema-validation example. (Part 3 of 3.)

Validation is performed node-by-node by calling method **Read** of the **ValidatingReader** object (line 62). Each call to **Read** validates the next node in the document. The loop terminates either when all nodes have been validated successfully or if a node fails validation.

When validated against the Schema, the XML document in Fig. 15.16 validates successfully. However, when the XML document of Fig. 15.19 is provided, validation fails, because the **book** element defined by lines 19–22 contains more than one **title** element.

```
1    <?xml version = "1.0"?>
2
3    <!-- Fig. 15.19: fail.xml                              -->
4    <!-- XML file that does not conform to Schema book.xdr -->
5
6    <books xmlns = "x-schema:book.xdr">
7       <book>
8          <title>XML How to Program</title>
9       </book>
10
11      <book>
12         <title>Java How to Program, 4/e</title>
13      </book>
```

Fig. 15.19 XML file that does not conform to the Schema in Fig. 15.17. (Part 1 of 2.)

```
14
15      <book>
16          <title>Visual Basic .NET How to Program</title>
17      </book>
18
19      <book>
20          <title>C++ How to Program, 3/e</title>
21          <title>Python How to Program</title>
22      </book>
23
24      <book>
25          <title>C# How to Program</title>
26      </book>
27  </books>
```

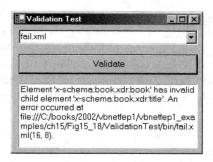

Fig. 15.19 XML file that does not conform to the Schema in Fig. 15.17. (Part 2 of 2.)

15.6 Extensible Stylesheet Language and `XslTransform`

Extensible Stylesheet Language (XSL) is an XML vocabulary for formatting XML data. In this section, we discuss the portion of XSL—called *XSL Transformations (XSLT)*—that creates formatted text-based documents from XML documents. This process is called a *transformation* and involves two tree structures: the *source tree*, which is the XML document being transformed, and the *result tree*, which is the result (e.g., *Extensible Hypertext Markup Language or XHTML*) of the transformation.[4] The source tree is not modified when a transformation occurs.

To perform transformations, an XSLT processor is required. Popular XSLT processors include Microsoft's msxml and the Apache Software Foundation's *Xalan 2*. The XML document, shown in Fig. 15.20, is transformed by msxml into an XHTML document (Fig. 15.21).

Line 6 is a *processing instruction (PI)*, which contains application-specific information that is embedded into the XML document. In this particular case, the processing instruction is specific to IE and specifies the location of an XSLT document with which to transform the XML document. The characters **<?** and **?>** delimit a processing instruction,

---

4. XHTML is the W3C technical recommendation that replaces HTML for marking up content for the Web. For more information on XHTML, see the XHTML Appendices J and K and visit **www.w3.org**.

which consists of a *PI target* (e.g., **xml:stylesheet**) and *PI value* (e.g., **type = "text/xsl" href = "sorting.xsl"**). The portion of this particular PI value that follows **href** specifies the name and location of the style sheet to apply—in this case, **sorting.xsl**, which is located in the same directory as this XML document.

Fig. 15.21 presents the XSLT document (**sorting.xsl**) that transforms **sorting.xml** (Fig. 15.20) to XHTML.

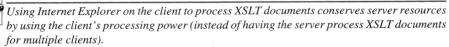

Performance Tip 15.1

Using Internet Explorer on the client to process XSLT documents conserves server resources by using the client's processing power (instead of having the server process XSLT documents for multiple clients).

Line 1 of Fig. 15.21 contains the XML declaration. Recall that an XSL document is an XML document. Line 6 is the **xsl:stylesheet** root element. Attribute **version** specifies the version of XSLT to which this document conforms. Namespace prefix **xsl** is defined and bound to the XSLT URI defined by the W3C. When processed, lines 11–13 write the document type declaration to the result tree. Attribute **method** is assigned **"xml"**, which indicates that XML is being output to the result tree. Attribute **omit-xml-declaration** is assigned **"no"**, which outputs an XML declaration to the result tree. Attribute **doctype-system** and **doctype-public** write the **Doctype** DTD information to the result tree.

```
1    <?xml version = "1.0"?>
2
3    <!-- Fig. 15.20: sorting.xml                  -->
4    <!-- XML document containing book information -->
5
6    <?xml:stylesheet type = "text/xsl" href = "sorting.xsl"?>
7
8    <book isbn = "999-99999-9-X">
9        <title>Deitel&apos;s XML Primer</title>
10
11       <author>
12           <firstName>Paul</firstName>
13           <lastName>Deitel</lastName>
14       </author>
15
16       <chapters>
17           <frontMatter>
18               <preface pages = "2" />
19               <contents pages = "5" />
20               <illustrations pages = "4" />
21           </frontMatter>
22
23           <chapter number = "3" pages = "44">
24               Advanced XML</chapter>
25           <chapter number = "2" pages = "35">
26               Intermediate XML</chapter>
27           <appendix number = "B" pages = "26">
28               Parsers and Tools</appendix>
```

Fig. 15.20 XML document containing book information. (Part 1 of 2.)

```
29          <appendix number = "A" pages = "7">
30             Entities</appendix>
31          <chapter number = "1" pages = "28">
32             XML Fundamentals</chapter>
33       </chapters>
34
35       <media type = "CD" />
36    </book>
```

Fig. 15.20 XML document containing book information. (Part 2 of 2.)

```
1    <?xml version = "1.0"?>
2
3    <!-- Fig. 15.21 : sorting.xsl                    -->
4    <!-- Transformation of book information into XHTML -->
5
6    <xsl:stylesheet version = "1.0"
7       xmlns:xsl = "http://www.w3.org/1999/XSL/Transform">
8
9       <!-- write XML declaration and DOCTYPE DTD information -->
10      <xsl:output method = "xml" omit-xml-declaration = "no"
11         doctype-system =
12            "http://www.w3.org/TR/xhtml1/DTD/xhtml1-strict.dtd"
13         doctype-public = "-//W3C//DTD XHTML 1.0 Strict//EN"/>
14
15      <!-- match document root -->
16      <xsl:template match = "/">
17         <html xmlns = "http://www.w3.org/1999/xhtml">
18            <xsl:apply-templates/>
19         </html>
20      </xsl:template>
21
22      <!-- match book -->
23      <xsl:template match = "book">
24         <head>
25            <title>ISBN <xsl:value-of select = "@isbn" /> -
26               <xsl:value-of select = "title" /></title>
27         </head>
28
29         <body>
30            <h1 style = "color: blue">
31               <xsl:value-of select = "title"/></h1>
32
33            <h2 style = "color: blue">by <xsl:value-of
34               select = "author/lastName" />,
35               <xsl:value-of select = "author/firstName" /></h2>
36
37            <table style =
38               "border-style: groove; background-color: wheat">
39
```

Fig. 15.21 XSL document that transforms **sorting.xml** into XHTML. (Part 1 of 3.)

```
40                    <xsl:for-each select = "chapters/frontMatter/*">
41                       <tr>
42                          <td style = "text-align: right">
43                             <xsl:value-of select = "name()" />
44                          </td>
45
46                          <td>
47                             ( <xsl:value-of select = "@pages" /> pages )
48                          </td>
49                       </tr>
50                    </xsl:for-each>
51
52                    <xsl:for-each select = "chapters/chapter">
53                       <xsl:sort select = "@number" data-type = "number"
54                          order = "ascending" />
55                       <tr>
56                          <td style = "text-align: right">
57                             Chapter <xsl:value-of select = "@number" />
58                          </td>
59
60                          <td>
61                             ( <xsl:value-of select = "@pages" /> pages )
62                          </td>
63                       </tr>
64                    </xsl:for-each>
65
66                    <xsl:for-each select = "chapters/appendix">
67                       <xsl:sort select = "@number" data-type = "text"
68                          order = "ascending" />
69                       <tr>
70                          <td style = "text-align: right">
71                             Appendix <xsl:value-of select = "@number" />
72                          </td>
73
74                          <td>
75                             ( <xsl:value-of select = "@pages" /> pages )
76                          </td>
77                       </tr>
78                    </xsl:for-each>
79                 </table>
80
81                 <br /><p style = "color: blue">Pages:
82                    <xsl:variable name = "pagecount"
83                       select = "sum(chapters//*/@pages)" />
84                    <xsl:value-of select = "$pagecount" />
85                 <br />Media Type:
86                    <xsl:value-of select = "media/@type" /></p>
87              </body>
88           </xsl:template>
89
90     </xsl:stylesheet>
```

Fig. 15.21 XSL document that transforms **sorting.xml** into XHTML. (Part 2 of 3.)

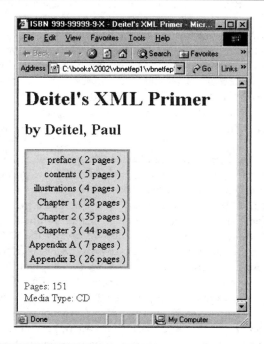

Fig. 15.21 XSL document that transforms **sorting.xml** into XHTML. (Part 3 of 3.)

XSLT documents contain one or more **xsl:template** elements that specify which information is outputted to the result tree. The template on line 16 **match**es the source tree's document root. When the document root is encountered in the transformation, this template is applied, and any text marked up by this element that is not in the namespace referenced by **xsl** is outputted to the result tree. Line 18 calls for all the **template**s that match children of the document root to be applied. Line 23 specifies a **template** that **match**es element **book**.

Lines 25–26 create the title for the XHTML document. We use the ISBN of the book from attribute **isbn** and the contents of element **title** to create the title **String ISBN 999-99999-9-X - Deitel's XML Primer**. Element **xsl:value-of** selects the **book** element's **isbn** attribute.

Lines 33–35 create a header element that contains the book's author. Because the *context node* (i.e., the current node being processed) is **book**, the XPath expression **author/ lastName** selects the author's last name, and the expression **author/firstName** selects the author's first name.

Line 40 selects each element (indicated by an asterisk) that is a child of element **frontMatter**. Line 43 calls *node-set function* **name** to retrieve the current node's element name (e.g., **preface**). The current node is the context node specified in the **xsl:for-each** (line 40).

Lines 53–54 sort **chapter**s by number in ascending order. Attribute **select** selects the value of context node **chapter**'s attribute **number**. Attribute *data-type* with value **"number"**, specifies a numeric sort and attribute *order* specifies **"ascending"** order. Attribute **data-type** also can be assigned the value *"text"* (line 67) and attribute **order** also may be assigned the value *"descending"*.

Lines 82–83 use an *XSL variable* to store the value of the book's page count and output it to the result tree. Attribute **name** specifies the variable's name, and attribute **select** assigns it a value. Function *sum* totals the values for all **page** attribute values. The two slashes between **chapters** and * indicate that all descendent nodes of **chapters** are searched for elements that contain an attribute named **pages**.

Figure 15.22 applies a style sheet (**games.xsl**) to **games.xml** (Fig. 15.10). The transformation result is written to a text box and to a file. We also show the transformation results rendered in IE.

Line 7 imports the *System.Xml.Xsl* namespace, which contains classes for applying XSLT style sheets to XML documents. Specifically, an object of class *Xsl-Transform* performs the transformation.

Line 19 declares **XslTransform** reference **transformer**. An object of this type is necessary to transform the XML data to another format. In line 33, the XML document is parsed and loaded into memory by calling method **Load** of the **XMLDocument** object. Method **CreateNavigator** of the **XMLDocument** object is called in line 36 to create an **XPathNavigator** object for navigating the XML document during the transformation. A call to method *Load* of the **XslTransform** object (line 40) parses and loads the style sheet that this application uses. The argument that is passed contains the name and location of the style sheet.

Event handler **cmdTransform_Click** (lines 46–66) calls method *Transform* of class **XslTransform** to apply the style sheet (**games.xsl**) to **games.xml** (line 51). This method takes three arguments: an **XPathNavigator** (created from **games.xml**'s **XmlDocument**); an instance of class *XsltArgumentList*, which is a list of **String** parameters that can be applied to a style sheet (**Nothing** in this case); and an instance of a derived class of **TextWriter** (in this example, an instance of class **StringWriter**). The results of the transformation are stored in the **StringWriter** object referenced by **output**. Lines 57–61 write the transformation results to disk. The third screen shot depicts the created XHTML document rendered in IE.

```
1    ' Fig. 15.22: TransformTest.vb
2    ' Applying a style to an XML document.
3
4    Imports System.Windows.Forms
5    Imports System.Xml
6    Imports System.Xml.XPath
7    Imports System.Xml.Xsl
8    Imports System.IO
9
10   Public Class FrmTransformTest
11      Inherits Form
12
13      ' Controls for starting and displaying transformation
14      Friend WithEvents cmdTransform As Button
15      Friend WithEvents txtConsole As TextBox
16
```

Fig. 15.22 XSL style sheet applied to an XML document. (Part 1 of 3.)

```vb
17      Private document As XmlDocument        ' Xml document root
18      Private navigator As XPathNavigator    ' navigate document
19      Private transformer As XslTransform    ' transform document
20      Private output As StringWriter         ' display document
21
22      Public Sub New()
23         MyBase.New()
24
25         ' This call is required by the Windows Form Designer.
26         InitializeComponent()
27
28         ' add any initialization after
29         ' InitializeComponent() call
30
31         ' load XML data
32         document = New XmlDocument()
33         document.Load("games.xml")
34
35         ' create navigator
36         navigator = document.CreateNavigator
37
38         ' load style sheet
39         transformer = New XslTransform()
40         transformer.Load("games.xsl")
41      End Sub ' New
42
43      ' Visual Studio .NET generated code
44
45      ' cmdTransform click event
46      Private Sub cmdTransform_Click( ByVal sender As System.Object, _
47         ByVal e As System.EventArgs) Handles cmdTransform.Click
48
49         ' transform XML data
50         output = New StringWriter()
51         transformer.Transform(navigator, Nothing, output)
52
53         ' display transformation in text box
54         txtConsole.Text = output.ToString
55
56         ' write transformation result to disk
57         Dim stream As FileStream = _
58            New FileStream("games.html", FileMode.Create)
59
60         Dim writer As StreamWriter = New StreamWriter(stream)
61         writer.Write(output.ToString)
62
63         ' close streams
64         writer.Close()
65         output.Close()
66      End Sub ' cmdTransform_Click
67
68   End Class ' FrmTransformTest
```

Fig. 15.22 XSL style sheet applied to an XML document. (Part 2 of 3.)

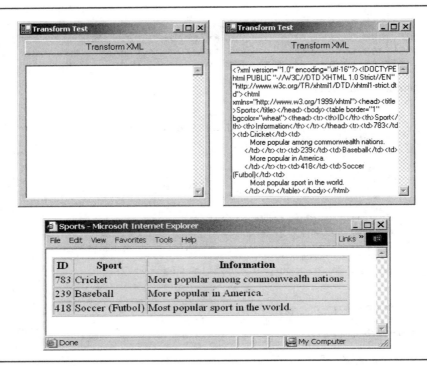

Fig. 15.22 XSL style sheet applied to an XML document. (Part 3 of 3.)

15.7 Microsoft BizTalk™

Increasingly, organizations are using the Internet to exchange critical data. However, transferring data between these organizations can become difficult, because organizations often use different platforms, applications and data specifications that complicate data transfer. To help resolve this complication, Microsoft developed *BizTalk* ("business talk"), an XML-based technology that helps to manage and facilitate business transactions.

BizTalk consists of three parts: The BizTalk Server, the BizTalk Framework and the BizTalk Schema Library. The *BizTalk Server* (*BTS*) parses and translates all inbound and outbound messages (or documents) that are sent to and from a business. The *BizTalk Framework* is a Schema for structuring those messages. The *BizTalk Schema Library* is a collection of Framework Schemas. Businesses can design their own Schemas or choose existing Schemas from the BizTalk Schema Library. Figure 15.23 summarizes BizTalk terminology.

BizTalk	Description
Framework	A specification that defines a format for messages.
Schema library	A repository of Framework XML Schemas.

Fig. 15.23 BizTalk terminology. (Part 1 of 2.)

BizTalk	Description
Server	An application that assists vendors in converting their messages to BizTalk format. For more information, visit **www.microsoft.com/biztalkserver**
JumpStart Kit	A set of tools for developing BizTalk applications.

Fig. 15.23 BizTalk terminology. (Part 2 of 2.)

Fig. 15.24 is an example BizTalk message for a product offer from a retail company. The message Schema for this example was developed by Microsoft to facilitate online shopping. We use this Schema for a fictitious company, named ExComp.

```
1   <?xml version = "1.0"?>
2   <BizTalk xmlns =
3      "urn:schemas-biztalk-org:BizTalk/biztalk-0.81.xml">
4
5   <!-- Fig. 15.24: biztalkmarkup.xml        -->
6   <!-- Example of standard BizTalk markup -->
7
8      <Route>
9         <From locationID = "8888888" locationType = "DUNS"
10           handle = "23" />
11
12        <To locationID = "454545445" locationType = "DUNS"
13           handle = "45" />
14     </Route>
15
16     <Body>
17        <Offers xmlns =
18           "x-schema:http://schemas.biztalk.org/eshop_msn_com/
t7ntoqnq.xml">
19           <Offer>
20              <Model>12-a-3411d</Model>
21              <Manufacturer>ExComp, Inc.</Manufacturer>
22              <ManufacturerModel>DCS-48403</ManufacturerModel>
23
24              <MerchantCategory>
25                 Clothes | Sports wear
26              </MerchantCategory>
27
28              <MSNClassId></MSNClassId>
29
30              <StartDate>2001-06-05 T13:12:00</StartDate>
31              <EndDate>2001-12-05T13:12:00</EndDate>
32
33              <RegularPrice>89.99</RegularPrice>
34              <CurrentPrice>25.99</CurrentPrice>
35              <DisplayPrice value = "3" />
36              <InStock value = "15" />
```

Fig. 15.24 BizTalk markup using an offer Schema. (Part 1 of 2.)

```
37
38              <ReferenceImageURL>
39                 http://www.Example.com/clothes/index.jpg
40              </ReferenceImageURL>
41
42              <OfferName>Clearance sale</OfferName>
43
44              <OfferDescription>
45                 This is a clearance sale
46              </OfferDescription>
47
48              <PromotionalText>Free Shipping</PromotionalText>
49
50              <Comments>
51                 Clothes that you would love to wear.
52              </Comments>
53
54              <IconType value = "BuyNow" />
55
56              <ActionURL>
57                 http://www.example.com/action.htm
58              </ActionURL>
59
60              <AgeGroup1 value = "Infant" />
61              <AgeGroup2 value = "Adult" />
62
63              <Occasion1 value = "Birthday" />
64              <Occasion2 value = "Anniversary" />
65              <Occasion3 value = "Christmas" />
66
67           </Offer>
68        </Offers>
69     </Body>
70  </BizTalk>
```

Fig. 15.24 BizTalk markup using an offer Schema. (Part 2 of 2.)

All Biztalk documents have the root element **BizTalk** (line 2). Line 3 defines a default namespace for the **BizTalk** framework elements. Element **Route** (lines 8–14) contains the routing information, which is mandatory for all BizTalk documents. Element **Route** also contains elements **To** and **From** (lines 9–12), which specify the document's destination and source, respectively. This makes it easier for the receiving application to communicate with the sender. Attribute **locationType** specifies the type of business that sends or receives the information, and attribute **locationID** specifies a business identity (the unique identifier for a business). These attributes facilitate source and destination organization. Attribute **handle** provides information to routing applications that handle the document.

Element **Body** (lines 16–69) contains the actual message, whose Schema is defined by the businesses themselves. Lines 17–18 specify the default namespace for element **Offers** (lines 17–68), which is contained in element **Body** (note that line 18 wraps—if we split this line, Internet Explorer cannot locate the namespace). Each offer is marked up using an **Offer** element (lines 19–67) that contains elements describing the offer. For additional information on BizTalk, visit **www.biztalk.com**.

In this chapter, we studied the Extensible Markup Language and several of its related technologies. In Chapter 16, we begin our discussion of databases, which are crucial to the development of multi-tier Web-based applications.

15.8 Summary

XML is a widely supported, open technology (i.e., nonproprietary technology) for data exchange. XML is quickly becoming the standard by which applications maintain data. XML is highly portable. Any text editor that supports ASCII or Unicode characters can render or display XML documents. Because XML elements describe the data they contain, they are both human and machine readable.

XML permits document authors to create custom markup for virtually any type of information. This extensibility enables document authors to create entirely new markup languages that describe specific types of data, including mathematical formulas, chemical molecular structures, music, recipes, etc.

The processing of XML documents—which programs typically store in files whose names end with the **.xml** extension—requires a program called an XML parser. A parser is responsible for identifying components of XML documents and for storing those components in a data structure for manipulation.

An XML document can reference another optional document that defines the XML document's structure. Two types of optional structure-defining documents are Document Type Definitions (DTDs) and Schemas.

Data are marked up with tags whose names are enclosed in angle brackets (**<>**). Tags are used in pairs to delimit markup. A tag that begins markup is called a start tag, and a tag that terminates markup is called an end tag. End tags differ from start tags in that they contain a forward slash (**/**) character.

Individual units of markup are called elements, which are the most fundamental XML building blocks. XML documents contain one element, called a root element, that contains every other element in the document. Elements are embedded or nested within each other to form hierarchies, with the root element at the top of the hierarchy.

In addition to being placed between tags, data also can be placed in attributes, which are name-value pairs in start tags. Elements can have any number of attributes.

Since XML allows document authors to create their own tags, naming collisions (i.e., two different elements that have the same name) can occur. As in Visual Basic, XML namespaces provide a means for document authors to prevent collisions. Elements are qualified with namespace prefixes to specify the namespace to which they belong.

Each namespace prefix is bound to a uniform resource identifier (URI) that uniquely identifies the namespace. A URI is a series of characters that differentiate names. Document authors create their own namespace prefixes. Virtually any name can be used as a namespace prefix except the reserved namespace prefix **xml**. To eliminate the need to place a namespace prefix in each element, document authors can specify a default namespace for an element and its children.

When an XML parser successfully parses a document, the parser stores a tree structure containing the document's data in memory. This hierarchical tree structure is called a Document Object Model (DOM) tree. The DOM tree represents each component of the XML document as a node in the tree. Nodes that contain other nodes (called child nodes) are called parent nodes. Nodes that have the same parent are called sibling nodes. A node's descendant nodes include that node's children, its children's children and so on. A node's ancestor nodes include that node's parent, its parent's parent and so on. The DOM tree has a single root node that contains all other nodes in the document.

Namespace **System.Xml** contains classes for creating, reading and manipulating XML documents. **XmlReader**-derived class **XmlNodeReader** iterates through each node in the XML document. An **XmlDocument** object conceptually represents an empty XML document. The XML documents are parsed and loaded into an **XmlDocument** object when method **Load** is invoked. Once an XML document is loaded into an **Xml-Document**, its data can be read and manipulated programmatically. An **XmlNode-Reader** allows programmers to read one node at a time from an **XmlDocument**. An **XmlTextWriter** streams XML data to disk. An **XmlTextReader** reads XML data from a file.

XPath (XML Path Language) provides a syntax for locating specific nodes in XML documents effectively and efficiently. XPath is a string-based language of expressions used by XML and many of its related technologies. Class **XPathNavigator** in the **System.Xml.XPath** namespace can iterate through node lists that match search criteria, written as an XPath expression.

Whereas XML contains only data, XSLT is capable of transforming XML into any text-based format. XSLT documents typically have the extension **.xsl**. When transforming an XML document via XSLT, two tree structures are involved: the source tree, which is the XML document being transformed, and the result tree, which is the result (e.g., XHTML) of the transformation. XML documents can be transformed programmatically through Visual Basic. The **System.Xml.Xsl** namespace facilitates the application of XSLT style sheets to XML documents.

15.9 Internet and World Wide Web Resources

www.w3.org/xml
The W3C (World Wide Web Consortium) facilitates the development of common protocols to ensure interoperability on the Web. Their XML page includes information about upcoming events, publications, software and discussion groups. Visit this site to read about the latest developments in XML.

www.xml.org
xml.org is a reference for XML, DTDs, schemas and namespaces.

www.w3.org/style/XSL
This W3C page provides information on XSL, including the topics such as XSL development, learning XSL, XSL-enabled tools, the XSL specification, FAQs and XSL history.

www.w3.org/TR
This is the W3C technical reports and publications page. It contains links to working drafts, proposed recommendations and other resources.

www.xmlbooks.com
This site provides a list of XML books recommended by Charles Goldfarb, one of the original designers of GML (General Markup Language), from which SGML was derived.

www.xml-zone.com
The Development Exchange XML Zone is a complete resource for XML information. This site includes a FAQ, news, articles and links to other XML sites and newsgroups.

wdvl.internet.com/Authoring/Languages/XML
Web Developer's Virtual Library XML site includes tutorials, a FAQ, the latest news and extensive links to XML sites and software downloads.

www.xml.com
This site provides the latest news and information about XML, conference listings, links to XML Web resources organized by topic, tools and other resources.

msdn.microsoft.com/xml/default.asp
The MSDN Online XML Development Center features articles on XML, Ask-the-Experts chat sessions, samples, demos, newsgroups and other helpful information.

msdn.microsoft.com/downloads/samples/Internet/xml/xml_validator/ sample.asp
The Microsoft XML validator, which can be downloaded from this site, can validate both online and offline documents.

www.oasis-open.org/cover/xml.html
The SGML/XML Web Page is an extensive resource that includes links to several FAQs, online resources, industry initiatives, demos, conferences and tutorials.

www.gca.org/whats_xml/default.htm
The GCA site offers an XML glossary, list of books, brief descriptions of the draft standards for XML and links to online drafts.

www-106.ibm.com/developerworks/xml
The IBM XML Zone site is a great resource for developers. It provides news, tools, a library, case studies and information about events and standards.

developer.netscape.com/tech/xml/index.html
The XML and Metadata Developer Central site has demos, technical notes and news articles related to XML.

www.projectcool.com/developer/xmlz
The Project Cool Developer Zone site includes several tutorials covering introductory through advanced XML topics.

www.ucc.ie/xml
This site is a detailed XML FAQ. Developers can check out responses to some popular questions or submit their own questions through the site.

16

Database, SQL and ADO .NET

Objectives

- To understand the relational database model.
- To understand basic database queries written in Structured Query Language (SQL).
- To use the classes and interfaces of namespace **System.Data** to manipulate databases.
- To understand and use ADO .NET's disconnected model.
- To use the classes and interfaces of namespace **System.Data.OleDb**.

It is a capital mistake to theorize before one has data.
Arthur Conan Doyle

Now go, write it before them in a table, and note it in a book, that it may be for the time to come for ever and ever.
The Holy Bible: The Old Testament

Let's look at the record.
Alfred Emanuel Smith

Get your facts first, and then you can distort them as much as you please.
Mark Twain

I like two kinds of men: domestic and foreign.
Mae West

Outline

16.1 Introduction

A *database* is an integrated collection of data. Many different strategies exist for organizing data in databases to facilitate easy access to and manipulation of the data. A *database management system* (*DBMS*) provides mechanisms for storing and organizing data in a manner that is consistent with the database's format. Database management systems enable programmers to access and store data without worrying about the internal representation of databases.

Today's most popular database systems are *relational databases*. Almost universally, relational databases use a language called *Structured Query Language* (*SQL*—pronounced as its individual letters or as "sequel") to perform *queries* (i.e., to request information that satisfies given criteria) and to manipulate data. [*Note*: The writing in this chapter assumes that SQL is pronounced as its individual letters. For this reason, we often precede SQL with the article "an" as in "an SQL database" or "an SQL statement."]

Some popular, enterprise-level relational database systems include Microsoft SQL Server, Oracle™, Sybase™, DB2™, Informix™ and MySQL™. This chapter presents examples using *Microsoft Access*—a relational database system that comes with *Microsoft Office*.

A programming language connects to, and interacts with, a relational database via an *interface*—software that facilitates communication between a database management system and a program. Visual Basic .NET programmers communicate with databases and manipulate their data through *Microsoft ActiveX Data Objects™* (ADO), *ADO .NET*.

16.2 Relational Database Model

The *relational database model* is a logical representation of data that allows relationships among data to be considered without concern for the physical structure of the data. A relational database is composed of *tables*. Figure 16.1 illustrates an example table that might be used in a personnel system. The table name is **Employee**, and its primary purpose is to illustrate the specific attributes of various employees. A particular row of the table is called a *record* (or *row*). This table consists of six records. The **number** *field* (or *column*) of each record in the table is the *primary key* for referencing data in the table. A primary key is a field (or fields) in a table that contain(s) unique data, or data that is not duplicated in other records of that table. This guarantees that each record can be identified by at least one unique value. Examples of primary-key fields are columns that contain social security numbers, employee IDs and part numbers in an inventory system. The records of Fig. 16.1 are *ordered* by primary key. In this case, the records are listed in increasing order (they also could be in decreasing order).

Each column of the table represents a different field. Records normally are unique (by primary key) within a table, but particular field values might be duplicated in multiple records. For example, three different records in the **Employee** table's **Department** field contain the number 413.

Often, different users of a database are interested in different data and different relationships among those data. Some users require only subsets of the table columns. To obtain table subsets, we use SQL statements to specify certain data to *select* from a table. SQL provides a complete set of commands (including **SELECT**) that enable programmers to define complex *queries* to select data from a table. The results of a query commonly are called *result sets* (or *record sets*). For example, we might select data from the table in Fig. 16.1 to create a new result set containing only the location of each department. This result set appears in Fig. 16.2. SQL queries are discussed in Section 16.4.

number	name	department	salary	location
23603	Jones	413	1100	New Jersey
24568	Kerwin	413	2000	New Jersey
34589	Larson	642	1800	Los Angeles
35761	Myers	611	1400	Orlando
47132	Neumann	413	9000	New Jersey
78321	Stephens	611	8500	Orlando

Record/Row — Primary key — Field/Column

Fig. 16.1 Relational-database structure of an **Employee** table.

department	location
413	New Jersey
611	Orlando
642	Los Angeles

Fig. 16.2 Result set formed by selecting **Department** and **Location** data from the **Employee** table.

16.3 Relational Database Overview: Books Database

This section provides an overview of SQL in the context of a sample **Books** database we created for this chapter. Before we discuss SQL, we explain the various tables of the **Books** database. We use this database to introduce various database concepts, including the use of SQL to manipulate and obtain useful information from the database.

The database consists of four tables: **Authors**, **Publishers**, **AuthorISBN** and **Titles**. The **Authors** table (described in Fig. 16.3) consists of three fields (or columns) that maintain each author's unique ID number, first name and last name. Figure 16.4 contains the data from the **Authors** table of the **Books** database.

Field	Description
authorID	Author's ID number in the database. In the **Books** database, this **Integer** field is defined as an *auto-incremented field*. For each new record inserted in this table, the database increments the **authorID** value, ensuring that each record has a unique **authorID**. This field represents the table's primary key.
firstName	Author's first name (a **String**).
lastName	Author's last name (a **String**).

Fig. 16.3 **Authors** table from **Books**.

authorID	firstName	lastName
1	Harvey	Deitel
2	Paul	Deitel
3	Tem	Nieto
4	Kate	Steinbuhler
5	Sean	Santry

Fig. 16.4 Data from the **Authors** table of **Books**. (Part 1 of 2.)

authorID	firstName	lastName
6	Ted	Lin
7	Praveen	Sadhu
8	David	McPhie
9	Cheryl	Yaeger
10	Marina	Zlatkina
11	Ben	Wiedermann
12	Jonathan	Liperi

Fig. 16.4 Data from the **Authors** table of **Books**. (Part 2 of 2.)

The **Publishers** table (Fig. 16.5) consists of two fields, representing each publisher's unique ID and name. Figure 16.6 contains the data from the **Publishers** table of the **Books** database.

The **AuthorISBN** table (Fig. 16.7) consists of two fields, which maintain ISBN numbers for each book and their corresponding authors' ID numbers. This table helps associate the names of the authors with the titles of their books. Figure 16.8 contains the data from the **AuthorISBN** table of the **Books** database. ISBN is an abbreviation for "International Standard Book Number"—a numbering scheme by which publishers worldwide give every book a unique identification number. [*Note*: To save space, we have split the contents of this figure into two columns, each containing the **authorID** and **isbn** fields.]

Field	Description
publisherID	The publisher's ID number in the database. This auto-incremented **Integer** field is the table's primary-key field.
publisherName	The name of the publisher (a **String**).

Fig. 16.5 **Publishers** table from **Books**.

publisherID	publisherName
1	Prentice Hall
2	Prentice Hall PTG

Fig. 16.6 Data from the **Publishers** table of **Books**.

Field	Description
`authorID`	The author's ID number, which allows the database to associate each book with a specific author. The integer ID value in this field must correspond to an ID value in the **Authors** table.
`isbn`	The ISBN number for a book (a **String**).

Fig. 16.7 `AuthorISBN` table from **Books**.

The **Titles** table (Fig. 16.9) consists of seven fields, which maintain general information about the books in the database. This information includes each book's ISBN number, title, edition number, copyright year and publisher's ID number, as well as the name of a file containing an image of the book cover, and finally, each book's price. Figure 16.10 contains the data from the **Titles** table.

authorID	isbn	authorID	isbn
1	0130895725	2	0139163050
1	0132261197	2	013028419x
1	0130895717	2	0130161438
1	0135289106	2	0130856118
1	0139163050	2	0130125075
1	013028419x	2	0138993947
1	0130161438	2	0130852473
1	0130856118	2	0130829277
1	0130125075	2	0134569555
1	0138993947	2	0130829293
1	0130852473	2	0130284173
1	0130829277	2	0130284181
1	0134569555	2	0130895601
1	0130829293	3	013028419x
1	0130284173	3	0130161438
1	0130284181	3	0130856118
1	0130895601	3	0134569555
2	0130895725	3	0130829293
2	0132261197	3	0130284173
2	0130895717	3	0130284181
2	0135289106	4	0130895601

Fig. 16.8 Data from `AuthorISBN` table in **Books**.

Field	Description
isbn	ISBN number of the book (a **String**).
title	Title of the book (a **String**).
editionNumber	Edition number of the book (a **String**).
publisherID	Publisher's ID number (an **Integer**). This value must correspond to an ID number in the **Publishers** table.
copyright	Copyright year of the book (an **Integer**).
imageFile	Name of the file containing the book's cover image (a **String**).
price	Suggested retail price of the book (a real number). [*Note*: The prices shown in this database are for example purposes only.]

Fig. 16.9 **Titles** table from **Books**.

isbn	title	edition-Number	publish-erID	copy-right	imageFile	price
0130923613	Python How to Program	1	1	2002	**python.jpg**	$69.95
0130622214	C# How to Program	1	1	2002	**cshtp.jpg**	$69.95
0130341517	Java How to Program	4	1	2002	**jhtp4.jpg**	$69.95
0130649341	The Complete Java Training Course	4	2	2002	**javactc4.jpg**	$109.95
0130895601	Advanced Java 2 Platform How to Program	1	1	2002	**advjhtp1.jpg**	$69.95
0130308978	Internet and World Wide Web How to Program	2	1	2002	**iw3htp2.jpg**	$69.95
0130293636	Visual Basic .NET How to Program	2	1	2002	**vbnet.jpg**	$69.95
0130895636	The Complete C++ Training Course	3	2	2001	**cppctc3.jpg**	$109.95
0130895512	The Complete e-Business & e-Commerce Programming Training Course	1	2	2001	**ebecctc.jpg**	$109.95
013089561X	The Complete Internet & World Wide Web Programming Training Course	2	2	2001	**iw3ctc2.jpg**	$109.95

Fig. 16.10 Data from the **Titles** table of **Books**. (Part 1 of 3.)

isbn	title	edition-Number	publish-erID	copy-right	imageFile	price
0130895547	The Complete Perl Training Course	1	2	2001	**perl.jpg**	$109.95
0130895563	The Complete XML Program-ming Training Course	1	2	2001	**xmlctc.jpg**	$109.95
0130895725	C How to Program	3	1	2001	**chtp3.jpg**	$69.95
0130895717	C++ How to Pro-gram	3	1	2001	**cpphtp3.jpg**	$69.95
013028419X	e-Business and e-Commerce How to Program	1	1	2001	**ebechtp1.jpg**	$69.95
0130622265	Wireless Internet and Mobile Busi-ness How to Pro-gram	1	1	2001	**wireless.jpg**	$69.95
0130284181	Perl How to Pro-gram	1	1	2001	**perlhtp1.jpg**	$69.95
0130284173	XML How to Pro-gram	1	1	2001	**xmlhtp1.jpg**	$69.95
0130856118	The Complete Internet and World Wide Web Pro-gramming Training Course	1	2	2000	**iw3ctc1.jpg**	$109.95
0130125075	Java How to Pro-gram (Java 2)	3	1	2000	**jhtp3.jpg**	$69.95
0130852481	The Complete Java 2 Training Course	3	2	2000	**javactc3.jpg**	$109.95
0130323640	e-Business and e-Commerce for Managers	1	1	2000	**ebecm.jpg**	$69.95
0130161438	Internet and World Wide Web How to Program	1	1	2000	**iw3htp1.jpg**	$69.95
0130132497	Getting Started with Visual C++ 6 with an Introduc-tion to MFC	1	1	1999	**gsvc.jpg**	$49.95
0130829293	The Complete Visual Basic 6 Training Course	1	2	1999	**vbctc1.jpg**	$109.95
0134569555	Visual Basic 6 How to Program	1	1	1999	**vbhtp1.jpg**	$69.95

Fig. 16.10 Data from the **Titles** table of **Books**. (Part 2 of 3.)

isbn	title	edition-Number	publish-erID	copy-right	imageFile	price
0132719746	Java Multimedia Cyber Classroom	1	2	1998	`javactc.jpg`	$109.95
0136325890	Java How to Program	1	1	1998	`jhtp1.jpg`	$69.95
0139163050	The Complete C++ Training Course	2	2	1998	`cppctc2.jpg`	$109.95
0135289106	C++ How to Program	2	1	1998	`cpphtp2.jpg`	$49.95
0137905696	The Complete Java Training Course	2	2	1998	`javactc2.jpg`	$109.95
0130829277	The Complete Java Training Course (Java 1.1)	2	2	1998	`javactc2.jpg`	$99.95
0138993947	Java How to Program (Java 1.1)	2	1	1998	`jhtp2.jpg`	$49.95
0131173340	C++ How to Program	1	1	1994	`cpphtp1.jpg`	$69.95
0132261197	C How to Program	2	1	1994	`chtp2.jpg`	$49.95
0131180436	C How to Program	1	1	1992	`chtp.jpg`	$69.95

Fig. 16.10 Data from the **Titles** table of **Books**. (Part 3 of 3.)

Figure 16.11 illustrates the relationships among the tables in the **Books** database. The first line in each table is the table's name. The field whose names appearing in italics identify that table's primary keys. A table's primary key uniquely identifies each record in the table. Every record must have a value in the primary-key field, and the value must be unique. This is known as the *Rule of Entity Integrity*. Note that the **AuthorISBN** table contains two fields whose names are italicized. This indicates that these two fields form a *composite primary key*—each record in the table must have a unique **authorID–isbn** combination. For example, several records might have an **authorID** of **2**, and several records might have an **isbn** of **0130895601**, but only one record can have both an **authorID** of **2** and an **isbn** of **0130895601**.

Common Programming Error 16.1

Failure to provide a value for a primary-key field in every record breaks the Rule of Entity Integrity and causes the DBMS to report an error.

Common Programming Error 16.2

Providing duplicate values for the primary-key field in multiple records causes the DBMS to report an error.

The lines connecting the tables in Fig. 16.11 represent the *relationships* among the tables. Consider the line between the **Publishers** and **Titles** tables. On the **Publishers** end of the line, there is a **1**, and on the **Titles** end, there is an infinity (∞) symbol. This line indicates a *one-to-many relationship*, in which every publisher in the

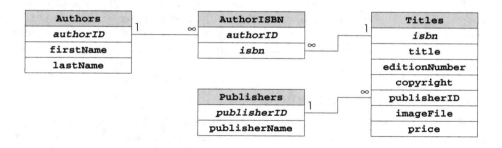

Fig. 16.11 Table relationships in **Books**.

Publishers table can have an arbitrarily large number of books in the **Titles** table. Note that the relationship line links the **publisherID** field in the **Publishers** table to the **publisherID** field in **Titles** table. In the **Titles** table, the **publisherID** field is a *foreign key*—a field for which every entry has a unique value in another table and where the field in the other table is the primary key for that table (e.g., **publisherID** in the **Publishers** table). Programmers specify foreign keys when creating a table. The foreign key helps maintain the *Rule of Referential Integrity*: Every foreign-key field value must appear in another table's primary-key field. Foreign keys enable information from multiple tables to be *joined* together for analysis purposes. There is a one-to-many relationship between a primary key and its corresponding foreign key. This means that a foreign-key field value can appear many times in its own table, but must appear exactly once as the primary key of another table. The line between the tables represents the link between the foreign key in one table and the primary key in another table.

 Common Programming Error 16.3

Providing a foreign-key value that does not appear as a primary-key value in another table breaks the Rule of Referential Integrity and causes the DBMS to report an error.

The line between the **AuthorISBN** and **Authors** tables indicates that, for each author in the **Authors** table, there can be an arbitrary number of ISBNs for books written by that author in the **AuthorISBN** table. The **authorID** field in the **AuthorISBN** table is a foreign key of the **authorID** field (the primary key) of the **Authors** table. Note, again, that the line between the tables links the foreign key in table **AuthorISBN** to the corresponding primary key in table **Authors**. The **AuthorISBN** table links information in the **Titles** and **Authors** tables.

Finally, the line between the **Titles** and **AuthorISBN** tables illustrates a one-to-many relationship; a title can be written by any number of authors. In fact, the sole purpose of the **AuthorISBN** table is to represent a many-to-many relationship between the **Authors** and **Titles** tables; an author can write any number of books, and a book can have any number of authors.

16.4 Structured Query Language (SQL)

In this section, we provide an overview of Structured Query Language (SQL) in the context of our **Books** sample database. The SQL queries discussed here form the foundation for the SQL used in the chapter examples.

Figure 16.12 lists SQL keywords programmers use in the context of complete SQL queries. In the next several subsections, we discuss these SQL keywords in the context of complete SQL queries. Other SQL keywords exist, but are beyond the scope of this text. [*Note*: To locate additional information on SQL, please refer to the bibliography at the end of this chapter.]

16.4.1 Basic **SELECT** Statement

Let us consider several SQL queries that extract information from database **Books**. A typical SQL query "selects" information from one or more tables in a database. Such selections are performed by ***SELECT*** *queries*. The simplest format for a **SELECT** statement is:

> ***SELECT * FROM*** *tableName*

In this query, the asterisk (*****) indicates that all columns from the *tableName* table of the database should be selected. For example, to select the entire contents of the **Authors** table (i.e., all the data in Fig. 16.13), use the query:

> ***SELECT * FROM*** **Authors**

To select specific fields from a table, replace the asterisk (*****) with a comma-separated list of the field names to select. For example, to select only the fields **authorID** and **lastName** for all rows in the **Authors** table, use the query

> ***SELECT*** **authorID, lastName** ***FROM*** **Authors**

This query only returns the data presented in Fig. 16.13. [*Note*: If a field name contains spaces, the entire field name must be enclosed in square brackets (**[ ]**) in the query. For example, if the field name is **first name**, it must appear in the query as **[first name]**.]

SQL keyword	Description
SELECT	Selects (retrieves) fields from one or more tables.
FROM	Specifies tables from which to get fields or delete records. Required in every *SELECT* and *DELETE* statement.
WHERE	Specifies criteria that determines the rows to be retrieved.
INNER JOIN	Joins records from multiple tables to produce a single set of records.
GROUP BY	Specifies criteria for grouping records.
ORDER BY	Specifies criteria for ordering records.
INSERT	Inserts data into a specified table.
UPDATE	Updates data in a specified table.
DELETE	Deletes data from a specified table.

Fig. 16.12 SQL query keywords.

authorID	lastName	authorID	lastName
1	Deitel	7	Sadhu
2	Deitel	8	McPhie
3	Nieto	9	Yaeger
4	Steinbuhler	10	Zlatkina
5	Santry	11	Wiedermann
6	Lin	12	Liperi

Fig. 16.13 `authorID` and `lastName` from the **Authors** table.

Common Programming Error 16.4

*If a program assumes that an SQL statement using the asterisk (*) to select fields always returns those fields in the same order, the program could process the result set incorrectly. If the field order in the database table(s) changes, the order of the fields in the result set would change accordingly.*

Performance Tip 16.1

If a program does not know the order of fields in a result set, the program must process the fields by name. This could require a linear search of the field names in the result set. If users specify the field names that they wish to select from a table (or several tables), the application receiving the result set can know the order of the fields in advance. When this occurs, the program can process the data more efficiently, because fields can be accessed directly by column number.

16.4.2 WHERE Clause

In most cases, users search a database for records that satisfy certain *selection criteria*. Only records that match the selection criteria are selected. SQL uses the optional **WHERE** *clause* in a **SELECT** statement to specify the selection criteria for the query. The simplest format of a **SELECT** statement that includes selection criteria is:

> **SELECT** *fieldName1,* *fieldName2,* ... **FROM** *tableName* **WHERE** *criteria*

For example, to select the **title**, **editionNumber** and **copyright** fields from those rows of table **Titles** in which the **copyright** date is greater than **1999**, use the query

```
SELECT title, editionNumber, copyright
FROM Titles
WHERE copyright > 1999
```

Figure 16.14 shows the result set of the preceding query. [*Note*: When we construct a query for use in Visual Basic .NET, we simply create a **String** containing the entire query. However, when we display queries in the text, we often use multiple lines and indentation to enhance readability.]

Title	editionNumber	copyright
Internet and World Wide Web How to Program	2	2002
Java How to Program	4	2002
The Complete Java Training Course	4	2002
The Complete e-Business & e-Commerce Programming Training Course	1	2001
The Complete Internet & World Wide Web Programming Training Course	2	2001
The Complete Perl Training Course	1	2001
The Complete XML Programming Training Course	1	2001
C How to Program	3	2001
C++ How to Program	3	2001
The Complete C++ Training Course	3	2001
e-Business and e-Commerce How to Program	1	2001
Internet and World Wide Web How to Program	1	2000
The Complete Internet and World Wide Web Programming Training Course	1	2000
Java How to Program (Java 2)	3	2000
The Complete Java 2 Training Course	3	2000
XML How to Program	1	2001
Perl How to Program	1	2001
Advanced Java 2 Platform How to Program	1	2002
e-Business and e-Commerce for Managers	1	2000
Wireless Internet and Mobile Business How to Program	1	2001
C# How To Program	1	2002
Python How to Program	1	2002
Visual Basic .NET How to Program	2	2002

Fig. 16.14 Titles with copyrights after 1999 from table **Titles**.

Performance Tip 16.2

Using selection criteria improves performance, because queries that involve such criteria normally select a portion of the database that is smaller than the entire database. Working with a smaller portion of the data is more efficient than working with the entire set of data stored in the database.

The **WHERE** clause condition can contain operators **<**, **>**, **<=**, **>=**, **=**, **<>** and **LIKE**. Operator **LIKE** is used for *pattern matching* with wildcard characters *asterisk* (*****) and *question mark* (**?**). Pattern matching allows SQL to search for similar strings that "match a pattern."

A pattern that contains an asterisk (*****) searches for strings in which zero or more characters take the asterisk character's place in the pattern. For example, the following query
locates the records of all authors whose last names start with the letter **D**:

```
SELECT authorID, firstName, lastName
FROM Authors
WHERE lastName LIKE 'D*'
```

The preceding query selects the two records shown in Fig. 16.15, because two of the authors in our database have last names that begin with the letter **D** (followed by zero or more
characters). The ***** in the **WHERE** clause's **LIKE** pattern indicates that any number of characters can appear after the letter **D** in the **lastName** field. Notice that the pattern string is
surrounded by single-quote characters.

Portability Tip 16.1

*Not all database systems support the **LIKE** operator, so be sure to read the database system's documentation carefully before employing this operator.*

Portability Tip 16.2

*Most databases use the **%** character in place of the ***** character in **LIKE** expressions.*

Portability Tip 16.3

In some databases, string data is case sensitive.

Portability Tip 16.4

In some databases, table names and field names are case sensitive.

Good Programming Practice 16.1

*By convention, SQL keywords should be written entirely in uppercase letters on systems that
are not case sensitive. This emphasizes the SQL keywords in an SQL statement.*

A pattern string including a question mark (**?**) character searches for strings in which
exactly one character takes the question mark's place in the pattern. For example, the following query locates the records of all authors whose last names start with any character
(specified with **?**), followed by the letter **i**, followed by any number of additional characters (specified with *****):

```
SELECT authorID, firstName, lastName
FROM Authors
WHERE lastName LIKE '?i*'
```

authorID	firstName	lastName
1	Harvey	Deitel
2	Paul	Deitel

Fig. 16.15 Authors from the **Authors** table whose last names start with **D**.

The preceding query produces the records listed in Fig. 16.16; four authors in our database have last names that contain the letter **i** as the second letter.

 Portability Tip 16.5

Most databases use the _ character in place of the ? character in **LIKE** *expressions.*

16.4.3 ORDER BY Clause

The results of a query can be arranged in ascending or descending order using the optional *ORDER BY clause*. The simplest form of an **ORDER BY** clause is:

> *SELECT fieldName1, fieldName2, ... FROM tableName ORDER BY field ASC*
> *SELECT fieldName1, fieldName2, ... FROM tableName ORDER BY field DESC*

where **ASC** specifies ascending order (lowest to highest), **DESC** specifies descending order (highest to lowest) and *field* specifies the field that determines the sorting order.

For example, to obtain the list of authors that is arranged in ascending order by last name (Fig. 16.17), use the query:

> *SELECT* authorID, firstName, lastName
> *FROM* Authors
> *ORDER BY* lastName ASC

Note that the default sorting order is ascending; therefore **ASC** is optional.

authorID	firstName	lastName
3	Tem	Nieto
6	Ted	Lin
11	Ben	Wiedermann
12	Jonathan	Liperi

Fig. 16.16 Authors from table **Authors** whose last names contain **i** as their second letter.

authorID	firstName	lastName
2	Paul	Deitel
1	Harvey	Deitel
6	Ted	Lin
12	Jonathan	Liperi
8	David	McPhie

Fig. 16.17 Authors from table **Authors** in ascending order by **lastName**. (Part 1 of 2.)

authorID	firstName	lastName
3	Tem	Nieto
7	Praveen	Sadhu
5	Sean	Santry
4	Kate	Steinbuhler
11	Ben	Wiedermann
9	Cheryl	Yaeger
10	Marina	Zlatkina

Fig. 16.17 Authors from table **Authors** in ascending order by **lastName**. (Part 2 of 2.)

To obtain the same list of authors arranged in descending order by last name (Fig. 16.18), use the query:

```
SELECT authorID, firstName, lastName
FROM Authors
ORDER BY lastName DESC
```

The **ORDER BY** clause also can be used to order records by multiple fields. Such queries are written in the form:

```
ORDER BY field1 sortingOrder, field2 sortingOrder, ...
```

where *sortingOrder* is either **ASC** or **DESC**. Note that the *sortingOrder* does not have to be identical for each field.

authorID	firstName	lastName
10	Marina	Zlatkina
9	Cheryl	Yaeger
11	Ben	Wiedermann
4	Kate	Steinbuhler
5	Sean	Santry
7	Praveen	Sadhu
3	Tem	Nieto
8	David	McPhie
12	Jonathan	Liperi
6	Ted	Lin
2	Paul	Deitel
1	Harvey	Deitel

Fig. 16.18 Authors from table **Authors** in descending order by **lastName**.

For example, the query:

```
SELECT authorID, firstName, lastName
FROM Authors
ORDER BY lastName, firstName
```

sorts all authors in ascending order by last name, then by first name. This means that, if any authors have the same last name, their records are returned sorted by first name (Fig. 16.19).

The **WHERE** and **ORDER BY** clauses can be combined in one query. For example, the query

```
SELECT isbn, title, editionNumber, copyright, price
FROM Titles
WHERE title
LIKE '*How to Program' ORDER BY title ASC
```

returns the ISBN, title, edition number, copyright and price of each book in the **Titles** table that has a **title** ending with "**How to Program**"; it lists these records in ascending order by **title**. The results of the query are depicted in Fig. 16.20.

16.4.4 Merging Data from Multiple Tables: **INNER JOIN**

Database designers often split related data into separate tables to ensure that a database does not store data redundantly. For example, the **Books** database has tables **Authors** and **Titles**. We use an **AuthorISBN** table to provide "links" between authors and titles. If we did not separate this information into individual tables, we would need to include author information with each entry in the **Titles** table. This would result in the database storing duplicate author information for authors who wrote multiple books.

authorID	firstName	lastName
1	Harvey	Deitel
2	Paul	Deitel
6	Ted	Lin
12	Jonathan	Liperi
8	David	McPhie
3	Tem	Nieto
7	Praveen	Sadhu
5	Sean	Santry
4	Kate	Steinbuhler
11	Ben	Wiedermann
9	Cheryl	Yaeger
10	Marina	Zlatkina

Fig. 16.19 Authors from table **Authors** in ascending order by **lastName** and by **firstName**.

isbn	title	edition-Number	copy-right	price
0130895601	Advanced Java 2 Platform How to Program	1	2002	$69.95
0131180436	C How to Program	1	1992	$69.95
0130895725	C How to Program	3	2001	$69.95
0132261197	C How to Program	2	1994	$49.95
0130622214	C# How To Program	1	2002	$69.95
0135289106	C++ How to Program	2	1998	$49.95
0131173340	C++ How to Program	1	1994	$69.95
0130895717	C++ How to Program	3	2001	$69.95
013028419X	e-Business and e-Commerce How to Program	1	2001	$69.95
0130308978	Internet and World Wide Web How to Program	2	2002	$69.95
0130161438	Internet and World Wide Web How to Program	1	2000	$69.95
0130341517	Java How to Program	4	2002	$69.95
0136325890	Java How to Program	1	1998	$0.00
0130284181	Perl How to Program	1	2001	$69.95
0130923613	Python How to Program	1	2002	$69.95
0130293636	Visual Basic .NET How to Program	2	2002	$69.95
0134569555	Visual Basic 6 How to Program	1	1999	$69.95
0130622265	Wireless Internet and Mobile Business How to Program	1	2001	$69.95
0130284173	XML How to Program	1	2001	$69.95

Fig. 16.20 Books from table **Titles** whose titles end with **How to Program** in ascending order by **title**.

Often, it is necessary for analysis purposes to merge data from multiple tables into a single set of data. Referred to as *joining* the tables, this is accomplished via an **INNER JOIN** operation in the **SELECT** statement. An **INNER JOIN** merges records from two tables by testing for matching values in fields that are common to the tables. The simplest format of an **INNER JOIN** operation is:

```
SELECT fieldName1, fieldName2, …
FROM table1
INNER JOIN table2
    ON table1.fieldName = table2.fieldName
```

The **ON** clause of the **INNER JOIN** operation specifies the fields from each table that are compared to determine which records are joined. For example, the following query produces a list of authors accompanied by the ISBN numbers for books written by each author:

```
SELECT firstName, lastName, isbn
FROM Authors
INNER JOIN AuthorISBN
    ON Authors.authorID = AuthorISBN.authorID
ORDER BY lastName, firstName
```

The query merges the **firstName** and **lastName** fields from table **Authors** and the **isbn** field from table **AuthorISBN**, sorting the results in ascending order by **lastName** and **firstName**. Notice the use of the syntax *tableName.fieldName* in the **ON** clause of the **INNER JOIN**. This syntax (called a *qualified name*) specifies the fields from each table that should be compared to join the tables. The "*tableName.*" syntax is required if the fields have the same name in both tables. The same syntax can be used in any query to distinguish among fields in different tables that have the same name. Qualified names that start with the database name can be used to perform cross-database queries.

Software Engineering Observation 16.1

*If an SQL statement includes fields from multiple tables that have the same name, the statement must precede those field names with their table names and the dot operator (e.g., **Authors.authorID**).*

Common Programming Error 16.5

In a query, failure to provide qualified names for fields that have the same name in two or more tables is an error.

As always, the query can contain an **ORDER BY** clause. Figure 16.21 depicts the results of the preceding query, ordered by **lastName** and **firstName**. [*Note:* To save space, we split the results of the query into two columns, each containing the **firstName**, **lastName** and **isbn** fields.]

firstName	lastName	isbn	firstName	lastName	isbn
Harvey	Deitel	0130895601	Harvey	Deitel	0130856118
Harvey	Deitel	0130284181	Harvey	Deitel	0130161438
Harvey	Deitel	0130284173	Harvey	Deitel	013028419x
Harvey	Deitel	0130829293	Harvey	Deitel	0139163050
Harvey	Deitel	0134569555	Harvey	Deitel	0135289106
Harvey	Deitel	0130829277	Harvey	Deitel	0130895717
Harvey	Deitel	0130852473	Harvey	Deitel	0132261197
Harvey	Deitel	0138993947	Harvey	Deitel	0130895725
Harvey	Deitel	0130125075	Paul	Deitel	0130895601

Fig. 16.21 Authors from table **Authors** and ISBN numbers of the authors' books, sorted in ascending order by **lastName** and **firstName**. (Part 1 of 2.)

firstName	lastName	isbn	firstName	lastName	isbn
Paul	Deitel	0130284181	Paul	Deitel	0135289106
Paul	Deitel	0130284173	Paul	Deitel	0130895717
Paul	Deitel	0130829293	Paul	Deitel	0132261197
Paul	Deitel	0134569555	Paul	Deitel	0130895725
Paul	Deitel	0130829277	Tem	Nieto	0130284181
Paul	Deitel	0130852473	Tem	Nieto	0130284173
Paul	Deitel	0138993947	Tem	Nieto	0130829293
Paul	Deitel	0130125075	Tem	Nieto	0134569555
Paul	Deitel	0130856118	Tem	Nieto	0130856118
Paul	Deitel	0130161438	Tem	Nieto	0130161438
Paul	Deitel	013028419x	Tem	Nieto	013028419x
Paul	Deitel	0139163050	Sean	Santry	0130895601

Fig. 16.21 Authors from table **Authors** and ISBN numbers of the authors' books, sorted in ascending order by **lastName** and **firstName**. (Part 2 of 2.)

16.4.5 Joining Data from Tables Authors, AuthorISBN, Titles and Publishers

The **Books** database contains one predefined query (**TitleAuthor**), which selects as its results the title, ISBN number, author's first name, author's last name, copyright year and publisher's name for each book in the database. For books that have multiple authors, the query produces a separate composite record for each author. The **TitleAuthor** query is shown in Fig. 16.22. Figure 16.23 contains a portion of the query results.

```
1   SELECT Titles.title, Titles.isbn, Authors.firstName,
2          Authors.lastName, Titles.copyright,
3          Publishers.publisherName
4   FROM
5      ( Publishers INNER JOIN Titles
6        ON Publishers.publisherID = Titles.publisherID )
7      INNER JOIN
8      ( Authors INNER JOIN AuthorISBN
9        ON Authors.authorID = AuthorISBN.authorID )
10     ON Titles.isbn = AuthorISBN.isbn
11   ORDER BY Titles.title
```

Fig. 16.22 Joining tables to produce a result set in which each record contains an author, title, ISBN number, copyright and publisher name.

title	isbn	first-Name	last-Name	copy-right	publisher-Name
Advanced Java 2 Platform How to Program	0130895601	Paul	Deitel	2002	Prentice Hall
Advanced Java 2 Platform How to Program	0130895601	Harvey	Deitel	2002	Prentice Hall
Advanced Java 2 Platform How to Program	0130895601	Sean	Santry	2002	Prentice Hall
C How to Program	0131180436	Harvey	Deitel	1992	Prentice Hall
C How to Program	0131180436	Paul	Deitel	1992	Prentice Hall
C How to Program	0132261197	Harvey	Deitel	1994	Prentice Hall
C How to Program	0132261197	Paul	Deitel	1994	Prentice Hall
C How to Program	0130895725	Harvey	Deitel	2001	Prentice Hall
C How to Program	0130895725	Paul	Deitel	2001	Prentice Hall
C# How To Program	0130622214	Tem	Nieto	2002	Prentice Hall
C# How To Program	0130622214	Paul	Deitel	2002	Prentice Hall
C# How To Program	0130622214	Cheryl	Yaeger	2002	Prentice Hall
C# How To Program	0130622214	Marina	Zlatkina	2002	Prentice Hall
C# How To Program	0130622214	Harvey	Deitel	2002	Prentice Hall
C++ How to Program	0130895717	Paul	Deitel	2001	Prentice Hall
C++ How to Program	0130895717	Harvey	Deitel	2001	Prentice Hall
C++ How to Program	0131173340	Paul	Deitel	1994	Prentice Hall
C++ How to Program	0131173340	Harvey	Deitel	1994	Prentice Hall
C++ How to Program	0135289106	Harvey	Deitel	1998	Prentice Hall
C++ How to Program	0135289106	Paul	Deitel	1998	Prentice Hall
e-Business and e-Commerce for Managers	0130323640	Harvey	Deitel	2000	Prentice Hall
e-Business and e-Commerce for Managers	0130323640	Kate	Stein-buhler	2000	Prentice Hall
e-Business and e-Commerce for Managers	0130323640	Paul	Deitel	2000	Prentice Hall
e-Business and e-Commerce How to Program	013028419X	Harvey	Deitel	2001	Prentice Hall
e-Business and e-Commerce How to Program	013028419X	Paul	Deitel	2001	Prentice Hall
e-Business and e-Commerce How to Program	013028419X	Tem	Nieto	2001	Prentice Hall

Fig. 16.23 Portion of the result set produced by the query in Fig. 16.22.

We added indentation to the query of Fig. 16.22 to make the query more readable. Let us now break down the query into its various parts. Lines 1–3 contain a comma-separated list of the fields that the query returns; the order of the fields from left to right specifies the fields' order in the returned table. This query selects fields **title** and **isbn** from table **Titles**, fields **firstName** and **lastName** from table **Authors**, field **copyright** from table **Titles** and field **publisherName** from table **Publishers**. For the purpose of clarity, we qualified each field name with its table name (e.g., **Titles.isbn**).

Lines 5–10 specify the **INNER JOIN** operations used to combine information from the various tables. There are three **INNER JOIN** operations. It is important to note that, although an **INNER JOIN** is performed on two tables, either of those two tables can be the result of another query or another **INNER JOIN**. We use parentheses to nest the **INNER JOIN** operations; The most straightforward way to evaluate an SQL statement is to begin with the innermost set of parentheses and then move outward. We begin with the **INNER JOIN**:

```
( Publishers INNER JOIN Titles
    ON Publishers.publisherID = Titles.publisherID )
```

which joins the **Publishers** table and the **Titles** table **ON** the condition that the **publisherID** number in each table matches. The resulting temporary table contains information about each book and its publisher.

The other nested set of parentheses contains the **INNER JOIN**:

```
( Authors INNER JOIN AuthorISBN ON
    Authors.AuthorID = AuthorISBN.AuthorID )
```

which joins the **Authors** table and the **AuthorISBN** table **ON** the condition that the **authorID** field in each table matches. Remember that the **AuthorISBN** table has multiple entries for **ISBN** numbers of books that have more than one author.

The third **INNER JOIN**:

```
( Publishers INNER JOIN Titles
    ON Publishers.publisherID = Titles.publisherID )
INNER JOIN
( Authors INNER JOIN AuthorISBN
    ON Authors.authorID = AuthorISBN.authorID )
ON Titles.isbn = AuthorISBN.isbn
```

joins the two temporary tables produced by the prior inner joins **ON** the condition that the **Titles.isbn** field for each record in the first temporary table matches the corresponding **AuthorISBN.isbn** field for each record in the second temporary table. The result of all these **INNER JOIN** operations is a temporary table from which the appropriate fields are selected to produce the results of the query.

Finally, line 11 of the query:

```
ORDER BY Titles.title
```

indicates that all the titles should be sorted in ascending order (the default).

16.4.6 INSERT Statement

The *INSERT* statement inserts a new record in a table. The simplest form for this statement is:

> *INSERT INTO* tableName (*fieldName1, fieldName2, ..., fieldNameN*)
> *VALUES* (*value1, value2, ..., valueN*)

where *tableName* is the table in which to insert the record. The *tableName* is followed by a comma-separated list of field names in parentheses. The list of field names is followed by the SQL keyword **VALUES** and a comma-separated list of values in parentheses. The specified values in this list must match the field names listed after the table name in both order and type (for example, if *fieldName1* is specified as the **firstName** field, then *value1* should be a string in single quotes representing the first name). The **INSERT** statement:

> *INSERT INTO* Authors (firstName, lastName)
> *VALUES* ('Sue', 'Smith')

inserts a record into the **Authors** table. The first comma-separated list indicates that the statement provides data for the **firstName** and **lastName** fields. The corresponding values to insert, which are contained in the second comma-separated list, are **'Sue'** and **'Smith'**. We do not specify an **authorID** in this example, because **authorID** is an auto-increment field in the database. Every new record that we add to this table is assigned a unique **authorID** value that is the next value in the auto-increment sequence (i.e., 1, 2, 3, etc.). In this case, **Sue Smith** would be assigned **authorID** number 13. Figure 16.24 shows the **Authors** table after we perform the **INSERT** operation.

authorID	firstName	lastName
1	Harvey	Deitel
2	Paul	Deitel
3	Tem	Nieto
4	Kate	Steinbuhler
5	Sean	Santry
6	Ted	Lin
7	Praveen	Sadhu
8	David	McPhie
9	Cheryl	Yaeger
10	Marina	Zlatkina
11	Ben	Wiedermann
12	Jonathan	Liperi
13	Sue	Smith

Fig. 16.24 Table **Authors** after an **INSERT** operation to add a record.

Common Programming Error 16.6

*SQL statements use the single-quote (') character as a delimiter for strings. To specify a string containing a single quote (such as O'Malley) in an SQL statement, the string must include two single quotes in the position where the single-quote character should appear in the string (e.g., **'O''Malley'**). The first of the two single-quote characters acts as an escape character for the second. Failure to escape single-quote characters in a string that is part of an SQL statement is an SQL syntax error.*

16.4.7 UPDATE Statement

An **UPDATE** statement modifies data in a table. The simplest form for an **UPDATE** statement is:

```
UPDATE tableName
    SET fieldName1 = value1, fieldName2 = value2, ..., fieldNameN = valueN
    WHERE criteria
```

where *tableName* is the table in which to update a record (or records). The *tableName* is followed by keyword **SET** and a comma-separated list of field name/value pairs written in the format, *fieldName = value*. The **WHERE** clause specifies the criteria used to determine which record(s) to update. For example, the **UPDATE** statement:

```
UPDATE Authors
    SET lastName = 'Jones'
    WHERE lastName = 'Smith' AND firstName = 'Sue'
```

updates a record in the **Authors** table. The statement indicates that the **lastName** will be assigned the new value **Jones** for the record in which **lastName** currently is equal to **Smith** and **firstName** is equal to **Sue**. If we know the **authorID** in advance of the **UPDATE** operation (possibly because we searched for the record previously), the **WHERE** clause could be simplified as follows:

```
WHERE AuthorID = 13
```

Figure 16.25 depicts the **Authors** table after we perform the **UPDATE** operation.

authorID	firstName	lastName
1	Harvey	Deitel
2	Paul	Deitel
3	Tem	Nieto
4	Kate	Steinbuhler
5	Sean	Santry
6	Ted	Lin

Fig. 16.25 Table **Authors** after an **UPDATE** operation to change a record. (Part 1 of 2.)

authorID	firstName	lastName
7	Praveen	Sadhu
8	David	McPhie
9	Cheryl	Yaeger
10	Marina	Zlatkina
11	Ben	Wiedermann
12	Jonathan	Liperi
13	Sue	Jones

Fig. 16.25 Table **Authors** after an **UPDATE** operation to change a record. (Part 2 of 2.)

Common Programming Error 16.7

*Failure to use a **WHERE** clause with an **UPDATE** statement could lead to logic errors.*

16.4.8 DELETE Statement

An SQL **DELETE** statement removes data from a table. The simplest form for a **DELETE** statement is:

> *DELETE FROM* tableName *WHERE* criteria

where *tableName* is the table from which to delete a record (or records). The **WHERE** clause specifies the criteria used to determine which record(s) to delete. For example, the **DELETE** statement:

```
DELETE FROM Authors
    WHERE lastName = 'Jones' AND firstName = 'Sue'
```

deletes the record for **Sue Jones** from the **Authors** table.

Common Programming Error 16.8

***WHERE** clauses can match multiple records. When deleting records from a database, be sure to define a **WHERE** clause that matches only the records to be deleted.*

Figure 16.26 shows the **Authors** table after we perform the **DELETE** operation.

authorID	firstName	lastName
1	Harvey	Deitel
2	Paul	Deitel

Fig. 16.26 Table **Authors** after a **DELETE** operation to remove a record. (Part 1 of 2.)

authorID	firstName	lastName
3	Tem	Nieto
4	Kate	Steinbuhler
5	Sean	Santry
6	Ted	Lin
7	Praveen	Sadhu
8	David	McPhie
9	Cheryl	Yaeger
10	Marina	Zlatkina
11	Ben	Wiedermann
12	Jonathan	Liperi

Fig. 16.26 Table **Authors** after a **DELETE** operation to remove a record. (Part 2 of 2.)

16.5 ADO .NET Object Model

The ADO .NET object model provides an API for accessing database systems programmatically. ADO .NET was created for the .NET framework and is the next generation of *ActiveX Data Objects*™ (ADO), which was designed to interact with Microsoft's *Component Object Model*™ (COM) framework.

The primary namespaces for ADO .NET are *System.Data*, *System.Data.OleDb* and *System.Data.SqlClient*. These namespaces contain classes for working with databases and other types of data sources (such as, XML files). Namespace **System.Data** is the root namespace for the ADO .NET API. Namespaces **System.Data.OleDb** and **System.Data.SqlClient** contain classes that enable programs to connect with and modify data sources. Namespace **System.Data.OleDb** contains classes that are designed to work with any data source, whereas the **System.Data.SqlClient** namespace contains classes that are optimized to work with Microsoft SQL Server 2000 databases.

Instances of class *System.Data.DataSet*, which consist of a set of **DataTable**s and relationships among those **DataTable**s, represent a *cache* of data—data that a program stores temporarily in local memory. The structure of a **DataSet** mimics the structure of a relational database. An advantage of using class **DataSet** is that it is *disconnected*—the program does not need a persistent connection to the data source to work with data in a **DataSet**. The program connects to the data source only during the initial population of the **DataSet** and then to store any changes made in the **DataSet**. Hence, the program does not require any active, permanent connection to the data source.

Instances of class *OleDbConnection* of namespace **System.Data.OleDb** represent a connection to a data source. Instances of class *OleDbDataAdapter* connect to a data source through an instance of class **OleDbConnection** and can populate **DataSet**s with data from a data source. We discuss the details of creating and populating **DataSet**s later in this chapter.

Instances of class **OleDbCommand** of namespace **System.Data.OleDb** represent an arbitrary SQL command to be executed on a data source. A program can use instances of class **OleDbCommand** to manipulate a data source through an **OleDbConnection**. The programmer must close the active connection to the data source explicitly once no further changes are to be made. Unlike **DataSet**s, **OleDbCommand** objects do not cache data in local memory.

16.6 Programming with ADO .NET: Extracting Information from a Database

In this section, we present two examples that introduce how to connect to a database, query the database and display the results of the query. The database used in these examples is the Microsoft Access **Books** database that we have discussed throughout this chapter. It can be found in the project directory for the application of Fig. 16.27. Every program employing this database must specify the database's location on the computer's hard drive. When executing these examples, this location must be updated for each program. For example, before readers can run the application in Fig. 16.27 on their computers, they must change lines 230–246 so that the code specifies the correct location for the database file.

16.6.1 Connecting to and Querying an Access Data Source

The first example (Fig. 16.27) performs a simple query on the **Books** database that retrieves the entire **Authors** table and displays the data in a *DataGrid* (a component from namespace **System.Windows.Forms** that can display a data source in a GUI). The program illustrates the process of connecting to the database, querying the database and displaying the results in a **DataGrid**. The discussion following the example presents the key aspects of the program. [*Note*: We present all of Visual Studio's auto-generated code in Fig. 16.27 so that readers are aware of what Visual Studio generates for the example.]

```
1   ' Fig. 16.27: DisplayTable.vb
2   ' Displaying data from a database table.
3
4   Public Class FrmTableDisplay
5      Inherits System.Windows.Forms.Form
6
7   #Region " Windows Form Designer generated code "
8
9      Public Sub New()
10        MyBase.New()
11
12        ' This call is required by the Windows Form Designer.
13        InitializeComponent()
14
15        ' Add any initialization after the
16        ' InitializeComponent call
17
18        ' fill DataSet1 with data
19        OleDbDataAdapter1.Fill(DataSet1, "Authors")
20
```

Fig. 16.27 Database access and information display. (Part 1 of 7.)

```
21              ' bind data in Users table in DataSet1 to dgdAuthors
22              dgdAuthors.SetDataBinding(DataSet1, "Authors")
23       End Sub ' New
24
25       ' Form overrides Dispose to clean up the component list.
26       Protected Overloads Overrides Sub Dispose( _
27          ByVal disposing As Boolean)
28
29          If disposing Then
30             If Not (components Is Nothing) Then
31                components.Dispose()
32             End If
33          End If
34          MyBase.Dispose(disposing)
35       End Sub ' Dispose
36
37       Friend WithEvents dgdAuthors As System.Windows.Forms.DataGrid
38       Friend WithEvents OleDbSelectCommand1 As _
39          System.Data.OleDb.OleDbCommand
40
41       Friend WithEvents OleDbInsertCommand1 As _
42             System.Data.OleDb.OleDbCommand
43
44       Friend WithEvents OleDbUpdateCommand1 As _
45          System.Data.OleDb.OleDbCommand
46
47       Friend WithEvents OleDbDeleteCommand1 As _
48          System.Data.OleDb.OleDbCommand
49
50       Friend WithEvents OleDbConnection1 As _
51          System.Data.OleDb.OleDbConnection
52
53       Friend WithEvents OleDbDataAdapter1 As _
54          System.Data.OleDb.OleDbDataAdapter
55
56       Friend WithEvents DataSet1 As System.Data.DataSet
57
58       ' Required by the Windows Form Designer
59       Private components As System.ComponentModel.Container
60
61       ' NOTE: The following procedure is required by the
62       ' Windows Form Designer
63       ' It can be modified using the Windows Form Designer.
64       ' Do not modify it using the code editor.
65       <System.Diagnostics.DebuggerStepThrough()> _
66       Private Sub InitializeComponent()
67
68          Me.dgdAuthors = New System.Windows.Forms.DataGrid()
69          Me.OleDbSelectCommand1 = _
70             New System.Data.OleDb.OleDbCommand()
71
72          Me.OleDbInsertCommand1 = _
73             New System.Data.OleDb.OleDbCommand()
```

Fig. 16.27 Database access and information display. (Part 2 of 7.)

```
74
75          Me.OleDbUpdateCommand1 = _
76             New System.Data.OleDb.OleDbCommand()
77
78          Me.OleDbDeleteCommand1 = _
79             New System.Data.OleDb.OleDbCommand()
80
81          Me.OleDbConnection1 = _
82             New System.Data.OleDb.OleDbConnection()
83
84          Me.OleDbDataAdapter1 = _
85             New System.Data.OleDb.OleDbDataAdapter()
86
87          Me.DataSet1 = New System.Data.DataSet()
88          CType(Me.dgdAuthors, _
89             System.ComponentModel.ISupportInitialize).BeginInit()
90
91          CType(Me.DataSet1, _
92             System.ComponentModel.ISupportInitialize).BeginInit()
93
94          Me.SuspendLayout()
95
96          '
97          ' dgdAuthors
98          '
99          Me.dgdAuthors.DataMember = ""
100         Me.dgdAuthors.Location = New System.Drawing.Point(8, 8)
101         Me.dgdAuthors.Name = "dgdAuthors"
102         Me.dgdAuthors.Size = New System.Drawing.Size(304, 256)
103         Me.dgdAuthors.TabIndex = 0
104
105         '
106         ' OleDbSelectCommand1
107         '
108         Me.OleDbSelectCommand1.CommandText = _
109            "SELECT authorID, firstName, lastName FROM Authors"
110
111         Me.OleDbSelectCommand1.Connection = Me.OleDbConnection1
112
113         '
114         ' OleDbInsertCommand1
115         '
116         Me.OleDbInsertCommand1.CommandText = _
117            "INSERT INTO Authors(authorID, firstName, lastName)" & _
118            "VALUES (?, ?, ?)"
119
120         Me.OleDbInsertCommand1.Connection = _
121            Me.OleDbConnection1
122
123         Me.OleDbInsertCommand1.Parameters.Add _
124            (New System.Data.OleDb.OleDbParameter("authorID", _
125            System.Data.OleDb.OleDbType.Numeric, 0, _
126            System.Data.ParameterDirection.Input, False, _
```

Fig. 16.27 Database access and information display. (Part 3 of 7.)

```
127            CType(10, Byte), CType(0, Byte), "authorID", _
128            System.Data.DataRowVersion.Current, Nothing))
129
130        Me.OleDbInsertCommand1.Parameters.Add _
131            (New System.Data.OleDb.OleDbParameter("firstName", _
132            System.Data.OleDb.OleDbType.Char, 50, _
133            System.Data.ParameterDirection.Input, False, _
134            CType(0, Byte), CType(0, Byte), "firstName", _
135            System.Data.DataRowVersion.Current, Nothing))
136
137        Me.OleDbInsertCommand1.Parameters.Add _
138            (New System.Data.OleDb.OleDbParameter("lastName", _
139            System.Data.OleDb.OleDbType.Char, 50, _
140            System.Data.ParameterDirection.Input, False, _
141            CType(0, Byte), CType(0, Byte), "lastName", _
142            System.Data.DataRowVersion.Current, Nothing))
143
144        '
145        ' OleDbUpdateCommand1
146        '
147        Me.OleDbUpdateCommand1.CommandText = _
148            "UPDATE Authors SET authorID = ?, firstName = ?, " & _
149            "lastName = ? WHERE (authorID = ?)" & _
150            " AND (firstName = ?) AND (lastName = ?)"
151
152        Me.OleDbUpdateCommand1.Connection = Me.OleDbConnection1
153        Me.OleDbUpdateCommand1.Parameters.Add ( _
154            New System.Data.OleDb.OleDbParameter("authorID", _
155            System.Data.OleDb.OleDbType.Numeric, 0, _
156            System.Data.ParameterDirection.Input, False, _
157            CType(10, Byte), CType(0, Byte), "authorID", _
158            System.Data.DataRowVersion.Current, Nothing))
159
160        Me.OleDbUpdateCommand1.Parameters.Add _
161            (New System.Data.OleDb.OleDbParameter("firstName", _
162            System.Data.OleDb.OleDbType.Char, 50, _
163            System.Data.ParameterDirection.Input, False, _
164            CType(0, Byte), CType(0, Byte), "firstName", _
165            System.Data.DataRowVersion.Current, Nothing))
166
167        Me.OleDbUpdateCommand1.Parameters.Add _
168            (New System.Data.OleDb.OleDbParameter("lastName", _
169            System.Data.OleDb.OleDbType.Char, 50, _
170            System.Data.ParameterDirection.Input, False, _
171            CType(0, Byte), CType(0, Byte), "lastName", _
172            System.Data.DataRowVersion.Current, Nothing))
173
174        Me.OleDbUpdateCommand1.Parameters.Add _
175            (New System.Data.OleDb.OleDbParameter _
176            ("Original_authorID", _
177            System.Data.OleDb.OleDbType.Numeric, 0, _
178            System.Data.ParameterDirection.Input, False, _
```

Fig. 16.27 Database access and information display. (Part 4 of 7.)

```
179        CType(10, Byte), CType(0, Byte), "authorID", _
180        System.Data.DataRowVersion.Original, Nothing))
181
182     Me.OleDbUpdateCommand1.Parameters.Add _
183        (New System.Data.OleDb.OleDbParameter _
184        ("Original_firstName", _
185        System.Data.OleDb.OleDbType.Char, 50, _
186        System.Data.ParameterDirection.Input, False, _
187        CType(0, Byte), CType(0, Byte), "firstName", _
188        System.Data.DataRowVersion.Original, Nothing))
189
190     Me.OleDbUpdateCommand1.Parameters.Add _
191        (New System.Data.OleDb.OleDbParameter _
192        ("Original_lastName", _
193        System.Data.OleDb.OleDbType.Char, 50, _
194        System.Data.ParameterDirection.Input, False, _
195        CType(0, Byte), CType(0, Byte), "lastName", _
196        System.Data.DataRowVersion.Original, Nothing))
197
198        '
199        ' OleDbDeleteCommand1
200        '
201     Me.OleDbDeleteCommand1.CommandText = _
202        "DELETE FROM Authors WHERE (authorID = ?) AND " & _
203        "(firstName = ?) AND (lastName = ?)"
204
205     Me.OleDbDeleteCommand1.Connection = Me.OleDbConnection1
206     Me.OleDbDeleteCommand1.Parameters.Add _
207        (New System.Data.OleDb.OleDbParameter("authorID", _
208        System.Data.OleDb.OleDbType.Numeric, 0, _
209        System.Data.ParameterDirection.Input, False, _
210        CType(10, Byte), CType(0, Byte), "authorID", _
211        System.Data.DataRowVersion.Original, Nothing))
212
213     Me.OleDbDeleteCommand1.Parameters.Add _
214        (New System.Data.OleDb.OleDbParameter("firstName", _
215        System.Data.OleDb.OleDbType.Char, 50, _
216        System.Data.ParameterDirection.Input, False, _
217        CType(0, Byte), CType(0, Byte), "firstName", _
218        System.Data.DataRowVersion.Original, Nothing))
219
220     Me.OleDbDeleteCommand1.Parameters.Add _
221        (New System.Data.OleDb.OleDbParameter("lastName", _
222        System.Data.OleDb.OleDbType.Char, 50, _
223        System.Data.ParameterDirection.Input, False, _
224        CType(0, Byte), CType(0, Byte), "lastName", _
225        System.Data.DataRowVersion.Original, Nothing))
226
227        '
228        'OleDbConnection1
229        '
230     Me.OleDbConnection1.ConnectionString = _
231        "Provider=Microsoft.Jet.OLEDB.4.0;Password="""";" & _
```

Fig. 16.27 Database access and information display. (Part 5 of 7.)

```
232             "User ID=Admin;Data Source=C:\Documen" & _
233             "ts and Settings\thiago\Desktop\vbhtp2e\examples\" & _
234             "Ch19\Fig16_27\Books.mdb;Mode=Sha" & _
235             "re Deny None;Extended Properties="""";" & _
236             "Jet OLEDB:System database="""";Jet OLEDB:Regis" & _
237             "try Path="""";Jet OLEDB:Database Password="""";" & _
238             "Jet OLEDB:Engine Type=5;Jet OLEDB:Dat" & _
239             "abase Locking Mode=1;Jet OLEDB:Global Partial " & _
240             "Bulk Ops=2;Jet OLEDB:Global Bulk T" & _
241             "ransactions=1;Jet OLEDB:New Database " & _
242             "Password="""";Jet OLEDB:Create System Databas" & _
243             "e=False;Jet OLEDB:Encrypt Database=False;" & _
244             "Jet OLEDB:Don't Copy Locale on Compact=" & _
245             "False;Jet OLEDB:Compact Without Replica " & _
246             "Repair=False;Jet OLEDB:SFP=False"
247
248         '
249         ' OleDbDataAdapter1
250         '
251         Me.OleDbDataAdapter1.DeleteCommand = _
252             Me.OleDbDeleteCommand1
253
254         Me.OleDbDataAdapter1.InsertCommand = _
255             Me.OleDbInsertCommand1
256
257         Me.OleDbDataAdapter1.SelectCommand = _
258             Me.OleDbSelectCommand1
259
260         Me.OleDbDataAdapter1.TableMappings.AddRange _
261             (New System.Data.Common.DataTableMapping() _
262             {New System.Data.Common.DataTableMapping("Table", _
263             "Authors", New System.Data.Common.DataColumnMapping() _
264             {New System.Data.Common.DataColumnMapping("authorID", _
265             "authorID"), New System.Data.Common.DataColumnMapping _
266             ("firstName", "firstName"), _
267             New System.Data.Common.DataColumnMapping("lastName", _
268             "lastName")})})
269
270         Me.OleDbDataAdapter1.UpdateCommand = _
271             Me.OleDbUpdateCommand1
272
273         '
274         ' DataSet1
275         '
276         Me.DataSet1.DataSetName = "NewDataSet"
277         Me.DataSet1.Locale = _
278             New System.Globalization.CultureInfo("en-US")
279
280         '
281         ' FrmTableDisplay
282         '
283         Me.AutoScaleBaseSize = New System.Drawing.Size(5, 13)
284         Me.ClientSize = New System.Drawing.Size(320, 273)
```

Fig. 16.27 Database access and information display. (Part 6 of 7.)

```
285          Me.Controls.AddRange(New System.Windows.Forms.Control() _
286            {Me.dgdAuthors})
287
288          Me.Name = "FrmTableDisplay"
289          Me.Text = "Table Display"
290          CType(Me.dgdAuthors, System.ComponentModel. _
291            ISupportInitialize).EndInit()
292
293          CType(Me.DataSet1, System.ComponentModel. _
294            ISupportInitialize).EndInit()
295
296          Me.ResumeLayout(False)
297
298      End Sub ' InitializeComponent
299
300  #End Region
301
302  End Class ' FrmTableDisplay
```

Fig. 16.27 Database access and information display. (Part 7 of 7.)

This example uses an Access database. To register the **Books** database as a data source, right click the **Data Connections** node in the **Server Explorer** and then click **Add Connection**. In the **Provider** tab of the window that appears, choose "**Microsoft Jet 4.0 OLE DB Provider**", which is the driver for Access databases. In the **Connection** tab, click the ellipsis button (**...**) to the right of the textbox for the database name; this opens the **Select Access Database** window. Go to the appropriate folder, select the **Books** database and click **OK**. Then, click the **Add Connection** window's **OK** button. Now, the database is listed as a connection in the **Server Explorer**. Drag the database node onto the Windows Form. This creates an **OleDbConnection** to the source, which the Windows Form designer shows as **OleDbConnection1**.

Next, drag an **OleDbDataAdapter** from the **Toolbox**'s **Data** subheading onto the Windows Form designer. This displays the **Data Adapter Configuration Wizard**, which configures the **OleDbDataAdapter** instance with a custom query for populating a **DataSet**. Click **Next** to display a drop-down list of possible connections. Select the connection created in the previous step from the drop-down list and click **Next**. The resulting screen allows us to choose how the **OleDbDataAdapter** should access the database. Keep the default **Use SQL Statement** option and click **Next**. Click the "**Query Builder**" button, then select the **Authors** table from the "**Add**" menu and then **Close** that menu. Place a check mark in the "***All Columns**" box from the small "**Authors**" window. Note how that particular window lists all columns of the **Authors** table. Click **OK** and then **Finish**.

Next, we create a **DataSet** to store the query results. To do so, drag **DataSet** from the **Data** tab in the **Toolbox** onto the form. This displays the **Add DataSet** window. Choose the "**Untyped DataSet (no schema)**"—the query with which we populate the **DataSet** dictates the **DataSet**'s *schema*, or structure (i.e., the tables that make up the **DataSet** and the relationships among those tables). Finally, add **DataGrid dgdAuthors** to the **Form**.

Figure 16.27 includes all of the auto-generated code. Normally, we omit this code from examples, because this code consists solely of GUI components. In this case, however, we must discuss database functionality that is contained in the auto-generated code. Furthermore, we have left Visual Studio's default naming conventions in this example to show exactly the code Visual Studio creates. Normally, we would change these names to conform to our programming conventions and style.

 Good Programming Practice 16.2

Use clear, descriptive variable names in code. This makes programs easier to understand.

Lines 230–246 initialize the **OleDbConnection** for this program. Property **ConnectionString** specifies the path to the database file on the computer's hard drive.

An instance of class **OleDbDataAdapter** populates the **DataSet** in this example with data from the **Books** database. The instance properties *DeleteCommand* (lines 251–252), *InsertCommand* (lines 254–255), *SelectCommand* (lines 257–258) and *UpdateCommand* (lines 270–271) are **OleDbCommand** objects that specify how the **OleDbDataAdapter** deletes, inserts, selects and updates data in the database.

Each **OleDbCommand** object must have an **OleDbConnection** through which the **OleDbCommand** can communicate with the database. Property **Connection** is set to the **OleDbConnection** to the **Books** database. For **OleDbUpdateCommand1**, line 152 sets the **Connection** property, and lines 147–150 set the **CommandText**.

Although Visual Studio .NET generates most of this program's code, we manually enter code in the **FrmTableDisplay** constructor (lines 9–23); this code populates **dataSet1** using an **OleDbDataAdapter**. Line 19 calls **OleDbDataAdapter** method *Fill* to retrieve information from the database associated with the **OleDbConnection**, placing this information in the **DataSet** provided as an argument. The second argument to method **Fill** is a **String** specifying the name of the table in the database from which to **Fill** the **DataSet**.

Line 22 invokes **DataGrid** method **SetDataBinding** to bind the **DataGrid** to a data source. The first argument is the **DataSet**—in this case, **DataSet1**—whose data the **DataGrid** should display. The second argument is a **String** representing the name of the table within the data source that we want to bind to the **DataGrid**. Once this line executes, the **DataGrid** is filled with the information in the **DataSet**. The information in **DataSet1** is used to set the correct number of rows and columns in the **DataGrid** and to provide the columns with default names.

16.6.2 Querying the Books Database

The code example in Fig. 16.28 demonstrates how to execute SQL **SELECT** statements on a database and display the results. Although Fig. 16.28 uses only **SELECT** statements to query the data, the application could be used to execute many different SQL statements with a few minor modifications.

```
1    ' Fig. 16.28: DisplayQueryResults.vb
2    ' Displays the contents of the authors database.
3
4    Imports System.Windows.Forms
5
6    Public Class FrmDisplayQueryResult
7       Inherits Form
8
9       ' SQL query input textbox and submit button
10      Friend WithEvents txtQuery As TextBox
11      Friend WithEvents cmdSubmit As Button
12
13      ' dataset display grid
14      Friend WithEvents dgdResults As DataGrid
15
16      ' database connection
17      Friend WithEvents BooksConnection As _
18         System.Data.OleDb.OleDbConnection
19
20      ' database adapter
21      Friend WithEvents BooksDataAdapter As _
22         System.Data.OleDb.OleDbDataAdapter
23
24      ' query dataset
25      Friend WithEvents BooksDataSet As System.Data.DataSet
26
27      ' Visual Studio .NET generated code
28
29      ' perform SQL query on data
30      Private Sub cmdSubmit_Click(ByVal sender As System.Object, _
31         ByVal e As System.EventArgs) Handles cmdSubmit.Click
32
33         Try
34
35            ' set text of SQL query to what user typed
36            BooksDataAdapter.SelectCommand.CommandText = _
37               txtQuery.Text
38
39            ' clear dataSet from previous operation
40            BooksDataSet.Clear()
41
42            ' fill dataset with information that results
43            ' from SQL query
44            BooksDataAdapter.Fill(BooksDataSet, "Authors")
45
```

Fig. 16.28 SQL statements executed on a database. (Part 1 of 2.)

```
46                    ' bind DataGrid to contents of DataSet
47                    dgdResults.SetDataBinding(BooksDataSet, "Authors")
48
49             ' display database connection message
50          Catch oleDbExceptionParameter As _
51             System.Data.OleDb.OleDbException
52
53             MessageBox.Show("Invalid Query")
54          End Try
55
56       End Sub ' cmdSubmit_Click
57
58    End Class ' FrmDisplayQueryResult
```

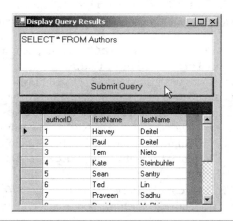
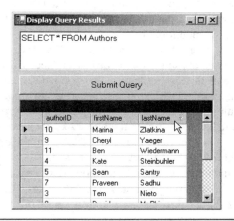

Fig. 16.28 SQL statements executed on a database. (Part 2 of 2.)

Form FrmDisplayQueryResult (Fig. 16.28) contains **TextBox txtQuery** (line 10), in which users input **SELECT** statements. After entering a query, the user clicks **Button cmdSubmit** (line 11), labeled **Submit Query**, to view the results of the query. The results then are displayed in **DataGrid dgdResults** (line 14).

Event handler **cmdSubmit_Click** (lines 30–56) is the key part of this program. When the program invokes this event handler in response to a button click, lines 36–37 assign the **SELECT** statement that the user typed in **txtQuery** as the value of the **Ole-DbDataAdapter**'s **SelectCommand** property. This **String** is parsed into an SQL query and executed on the database via the **OleDbDataAdapter**'s method **Fill** (line 44). This method, as discussed in the previous section, places the data from the database into **BooksDataSet**. Line 40 calls method **Clear** of class **DataSet**. Method **Clear** removes all previous information contained within a **DataSet**.

Common Programming Error 16.9

*If a **DataSet** already has been **Fill**ed at least once, failure to call the **DataSet**'s **Clear** method before calling the **Fill** method will lead to logic errors.*

To display or redisplay contents in the **DataGrid**, use method **SetDataBinding**. Again, the first argument to this method is the data source to be displayed in the table—a **DataSet**, in this case. The second argument is the **String** name of the data source member to be displayed (line 47)—a table name, in this case. Readers can try entering their own queries in the text box and then pressing the **Submit Query** button to execute the query.

Fig. 16.28 displays the output for **FrmDisplayQueryResult**. The first screenshot demonstrates the query results of retrieving all records from the **Authors** table. As the second screen capture demonstrates, clicking any column sorts the rows according to the contents of that column in either ascending or descending order.

16.7 Programming with ADO .NET: Modifying a Database

Our next example implements a simple address-book application that enables users to insert, retrieve and update records in the Microsoft Access database **Addressbook**.

The **Addressbook** application (Fig. 16.29) provides a GUI through which users can execute SQL statements on the database. Earlier in the chapter, we presented examples explaining the use of **SELECT** statements to query a database. This example provides that same functionality.

Event handler **cmdFind_Click** (lines 72–119) performs the **SELECT** statement on the database for the record associated with the **String** entered in **txtLast**. This represents the last name of the person whose record the user wishes to retrieve. Line 81 invokes method **Clear** of class **DataSet** to empty the **DataSet** of any prior data. Lines 85–87 modify the text of the SQL query to perform the appropriate **SELECT** operation. The **OleDbDataAdapter** method **Fill** then executes this statement (line 91). Notice how a different overload of method **Fill** from the previous example has been used in this situation. Only the **DataSet** to be filled is passed as an argument. Finally, the **TextBox**es are updated with a call to method **Display** (line 94).

Methods **cmdAdd_Click** (lines 122–173) and **cmdUpdate_Click** (lines 176–232) perform **INSERT** and **UPDATE** operations, respectively. Each method uses members of class **OleDbCommand** to perform operations on a database. The instance properties **InsertCommand** and **UpdateCommand** of class **OleDbDataAdapter** are instances of class **OleDbCommand**.

```
1   ' Fig. 16.29: AddressBook.vb
2   ' Using SQL statements to manipulate a database.
3
4   Imports System.Windows.Forms
5
6   Public Class FrmAddressBook
7      Inherits Form
8
9      ' top set of command buttons
10     Friend WithEvents cmdFind As Button
11     Friend WithEvents cmdAdd As Button
12     Friend WithEvents cmdUpdate As Button
13     Friend WithEvents cmdClear As Button
14     Friend WithEvents cmdHelp As Button
15
16     ' textbox identifier labels
17     Friend WithEvents lblId As Label
```

Fig. 16.29 Database modification demonstration. (Part 1 of 9.)

```
18      Friend WithEvents lblFirst As Label
19      Friend WithEvents lblLast As Label
20      Friend WithEvents lblAddress As Label
21      Friend WithEvents lblCity As Label
22      Friend WithEvents lblState As Label
23      Friend WithEvents lblZip As Label
24      Friend WithEvents lblCountry As Label
25      Friend WithEvents lblEmail As Label
26      Friend WithEvents lblPhone As Label
27      Friend WithEvents lblFax As Label
28
29      ' input textboxes
30      Friend WithEvents txtId As TextBox
31      Friend WithEvents txtFirst As TextBox
32      Friend WithEvents txtLast As TextBox
33      Friend WithEvents txtAddress As TextBox
34      Friend WithEvents txtCity As TextBox
35      Friend WithEvents txtState As TextBox
36      Friend WithEvents txtZip As TextBox
37      Friend WithEvents txtCountry As TextBox
38      Friend WithEvents txtEmail As TextBox
39      Friend WithEvents txtPhone As TextBox
40      Friend WithEvents txtFax As TextBox
41
42      ' query status display textbox
43      Friend WithEvents txtStatus As TextBox
44
45      ' database connection
46      Friend WithEvents AddressBookConnection As _
47         System.Data.OleDb.OleDbConnection
48
49      ' database adapter
50      Friend WithEvents AddressBookDataAdapter As _
51         System.Data.OleDb.OleDbDataAdapter
52
53      ' query dataset
54      Friend WithEvents AddressBookDataSet As System.Data.DataSet
55
56      ' constructor
57      Public Sub New()
58         MyBase.New()
59
60         ' This call is required by the Windows Form Designer.
61         InitializeComponent()
62
63         ' Add any initialization after the InitializeComponent call
64
65         ' open connection
66         AddressBookConnection.Open()
67      End Sub ' New
68
69      ' Visual Studio .NET generated code
70
```

Fig. 16.29 Database modification demonstration. (Part 2 of 9.)

```
71         ' find record in database
72         Private Sub cmdFind_Click(ByVal sender As System.Object, _
73            ByVal e As System.EventArgs) Handles cmdFind.Click
74
75            Try
76
77               ' ensure user input last name
78               If txtLast.Text <> "" Then
79
80                  ' clear DataSet from last operation
81                  AddressBookDataSet.Clear()
82
83                  ' create SQL query to find contact
84                  ' with specified last name
85                  AddressBookDataAdapter.SelectCommand.CommandText = _
86                     "SELECT * FROM addresses WHERE " & _
87                     "lastname = '" & txtLast.Text & "' "
88
89                  ' fill AddressBookDataSet with the rows resulting
90                  ' from the query
91                  AddressBookDataAdapter.Fill(AddressBookDataSet)
92
93                  ' display information
94                  Display(AddressBookDataSet)
95                  txtStatus.Text &= vbCrLf & "Query Successful " & _
96                     vbCrLf
97
98               ' prompt user for last name
99               Else
100                  txtLast.Text = _
101                     "Enter last name here then press Find"
102              End If
103
104           ' display verbose information with database exception
105           Catch oleDbExceptionParameter As _
106              System.Data.OleDb.OleDbException
107
108              Console.WriteLine(oleDbExceptionParameter.StackTrace)
109              txtStatus.Text &= oleDbExceptionParameter.ToString
110
111           ' display message box when invalid operation
112           Catch invalidOperationExceptionParameter As _
113              InvalidOperationException
114
115              MessageBox.Show( _
116                 invalidOperationExceptionParameter.Message)
117           End Try
118
119        End Sub ' cmdFind_Click
120
```

Fig. 16.29 Database modification demonstration. (Part 3 of 9.)

```
121        ' adds record to database
122        Private Sub cmdAdd_Click(ByVal sender As System.Object, _
123           ByVal e As System.EventArgs) Handles cmdAdd.Click
124
125           Try
126
127              ' ensure first and last name input
128              If (txtLast.Text <> "" AndAlso txtFirst.Text <> "") Then
129
130                 ' create the SQL query to insert a row
131                 AddressBookDataAdapter.InsertCommand.CommandText = _
132                    "INSERT INTO addresses(firstname, " & _
133                    "lastname, address, city, " & _
134                    "stateorprovince, postalcode, country, " & _
135                    "emailaddress, homephone, faxnumber) " & _
136                    "VALUES('" & txtFirst.Text & "' , " & _
137                    "'" & txtLast.Text & "' , " & _
138                    "'" & txtAddress.Text & "' , " & _
139                    "'" & txtCity.Text & "' , " & _
140                    "'" & txtState.Text & "' , " & _
141                    "'" & txtZip.Text & "' , " & _
142                    "'" & txtCountry.Text & "' , " & _
143                    "'" & txtEmail.Text & "' , " & _
144                    "'" & txtPhone.Text & "' , " & _
145                    "'" & txtFax.Text & "')"
146
147                 ' notify the user the query is being sent
148                 txtStatus.Text &= vbCrLf & "Sending query: " & _
149                    AddressBookDataAdapter.InsertCommand. _
150                       CommandText & vbCrLf
151
152                 ' send query
153                 AddressBookDataAdapter.InsertCommand. _
154                    ExecuteNonQuery()
155
156                 txtStatus.Text &= vbCrLf & "Query successful"
157
158              ' prompt user to input first and last name
159              Else
160                 txtStatus.Text &= vbCrLf & _
161                    "Enter at least first and last name then " & _
162                    "press Add" & vbCrLf
163              End If
164
165           ' display verbose information when database exception
166           Catch oleDbExceptionParameter As _
167              System.Data.OleDb.OleDbException
168
169              Console.WriteLine(oleDbExceptionParameter.StackTrace)
170              txtStatus.Text &= oleDbExceptionParameter.ToString
171           End Try
172
173        End Sub ' cmdAdd_Click
```

Fig. 16.29 Database modification demonstration. (Part 4 of 9.)

```
174
175          ' updates entry in database
176          Private Sub cmdUpdate_Click(ByVal sender As System.Object, _
177             ByVal e As System.EventArgs) Handles cmdUpdate.Click
178
179             Try
180
181                ' make sure user has already found
182                ' record to update
183                If txtId.Text <> "" Then
184
185                   ' set SQL query to update all fields in
186                   ' table where id number matches id in
187                   ' idTextBox
188                   AddressBookDataAdapter.UpdateCommand.CommandText = _
189                      "UPDATE addresses SET firstname=" & _
190                      "'" & txtFirst.Text & "' , " & _
191                      "lastname = '" & txtLast.Text & "' , " & _
192                      "address='" & txtAddress.Text & "' , " & _
193                      "city='" & txtCity.Text & "' , " & _
194                      "stateorprovince= " & _
195                      "'" & txtState.Text & "', " & _
196                      "postalcode='" & txtZip.Text & "', " & _
197                      "country='" & txtCountry.Text & "' , " & _
198                      "emailaddress='" & txtEmail.Text & "' , " & _
199                      "homephone='" & txtPhone.Text & "' , " & _
200                      "faxnumber='" & txtFax.Text & "' " & _
201                      "WHERE id=" & txtId.Text & " ;  "
202
203                   ' notify user that query is being sent
204                   txtStatus.Text &= vbCrLf & "Sending query: " & _
205                      AddressBookDataAdapter.UpdateCommand. _
206                         CommandText & vbCrLf
207
208                   ' execute query
209                   AddressBookDataAdapter.UpdateCommand. _
210                      ExecuteNonQuery()
211
212                   txtStatus.Text &= vbCrLf & "Query Successful" & _
213                      vbCrLf
214
215                ' prompt user to input existing record
216                Else
217                   txtStatus.Text &= vbCrLf & _
218                      "You may only update an existing record. " & _
219                      "Use Find to locate the record, then " & _
220                      "modify the information and press Update." & _
221                      vbCrLf
222                End If
223
224             ' display verbose information when database exception
225             Catch oleDbExceptionParameter As _
226                System.Data.OleDb.OleDbException
```

Fig. 16.29 Database modification demonstration. (Part 5 of 9.)

```
227
228              Console.WriteLine(oleDbExceptionParameter.StackTrace)
229              txtStatus.Text &= oleDbExceptionParameter.ToString
230         End Try
231
232      End Sub ' cmdUpdate_Click
233
234      ' clears all information in textboxes
235      Private Sub cmdClear_Click(ByVal sender As System.Object, _
236         ByVal e As System.EventArgs) Handles cmdClear.Click
237
238         txtId.Clear()
239         ClearTextBoxes()
240      End Sub ' cmdClear_Click
241
242      ' displays information on application use
243      Private Sub cmdHelp_Click(ByVal sender As System.Object, _
244         ByVal e As System.EventArgs) Handles cmdHelp.Click
245
246         txtStatus.AppendText(vbCrLf & _
247            "Click Find to locate a record" & vbCrLf & _
248            "Click Add to insert a new record." & vbCrLf & _
249            "Click Update to update the information in a " & _
250            "record " & vbCrLf & "Click Clear to empty the " & _
251            "textboxes")
252      End Sub ' cmdHelp_Click
253
254      ' displays data in dataset
255      Private Sub Display(ByVal dataset As DataSet)
256
257         Try
258
259            ' get first DataTable - there will be one
260            Dim dataTable As DataTable = dataset.Tables(0)
261
262            ' ensure dataTable not empty
263            If dataTable.Rows.Count <> 0 Then
264               Dim recordNumber As Integer = _
265                  Convert.ToInt32(dataTable.Rows(0)(0))
266
267               txtId.Text = recordNumber.ToString
268               txtFirst.Text = _
269                  Convert.ToString(dataTable.Rows(0)(1))
270
271               txtLast.Text = _
272                  Convert.ToString(dataTable.Rows(0)(2))
273
274               txtAddress.Text = _
275                  Convert.ToString(dataTable.Rows(0)(3))
276
277               txtCity.Text = _
278                  Convert.ToString(dataTable.Rows(0)(4))
279
```

Fig. 16.29 Database modification demonstration. (Part 6 of 9.)

```vb
280                    txtState.Text = _
281                       Convert.ToString(dataTable.Rows(0)(5))
282
283                    txtZip.Text = _
284                       Convert.ToString(dataTable.Rows(0)(6))
285
286                    txtCountry.Text = _
287                       Convert.ToString(dataTable.Rows(0)(7))
288
289                    txtEmail.Text = _
290                       Convert.ToString(dataTable.Rows(0)(8))
291
292                    txtPhone.Text = _
293                       Convert.ToString(dataTable.Rows(0)(9))
294
295                    txtFax.Text = _
296                       Convert.ToString(dataTable.Rows(0)(10))
297
298                 ' display not-found message
299                 Else
300                    txtStatus.Text &= vbCrLf & "No record found" & vbCrLf
301                 End If
302
303              ' display verbose information when database exception
304              Catch oleDbExceptionParameter As _
305                 System.Data.OleDb.OleDbException
306
307                 Console.WriteLine(oleDbExceptionParameter.StackTrace)
308                 txtStatus.Text &= oleDbExceptionParameter.ToString
309              End Try
310
311        End Sub ' Display
312
313        ' clears text boxes
314        Private Sub ClearTextBoxes()
315           txtFirst.Clear()
316           txtLast.Clear()
317           txtAddress.Clear()
318           txtCity.Clear()
319           txtState.Clear()
320           txtZip.Clear()
321           txtCountry.Clear()
322           txtEmail.Clear()
323           txtPhone.Clear()
324           txtFax.Clear()
325        End Sub    ' ClearTextBoxes
326
327  End Class ' FrmAddressBook
```

Fig. 16.29 Database modification demonstration. (Part 7 of 9.)

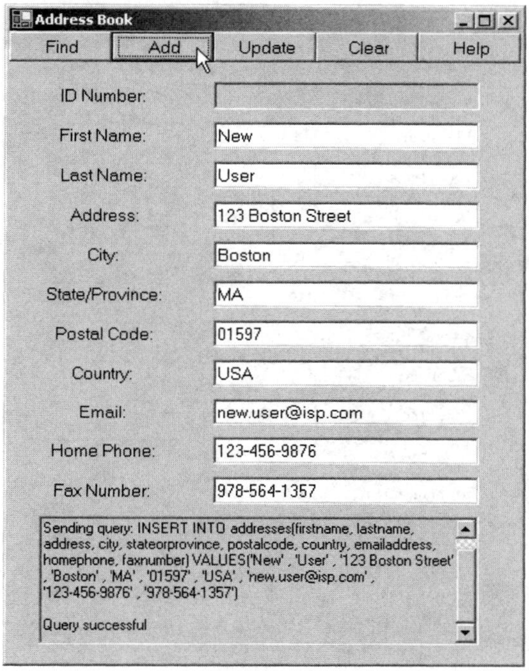

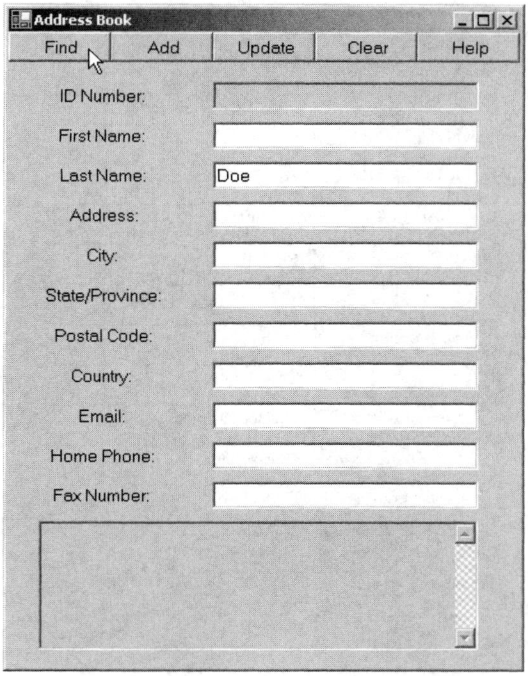

Fig. 16.29 Database modification demonstration. (Part 8 of 9.)

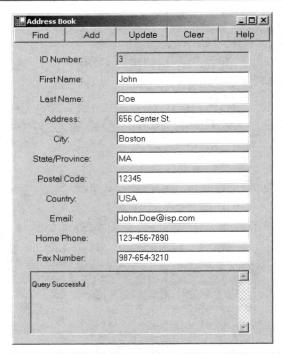

Fig. 16.29 Database modification demonstration. (Part 9 of 9.)

Property **CommandText** of class **OleDbCommand** is a **String** representing the SQL statement that the **OleDbCommand** object executes. Event handler **cmdAdd_Click** sets property **CommandText** of the **OleDbCommand** object (accessed through **AddressBookDataAdapter**'s property **InsertCommand**) to execute the appropriate **INSERT** statement on the database (lines 131–145). Method **cmdUpdate_Click** sets this property of **UpdateCommand** to execute the appropriate **UPDATE** statement on the database (lines 188–201).

The *ExecuteNonQuery* method of class **OleDbCommand** performs the action specified by **CommandText**. Hence, the **INSERT** statement defined by **Address-BookDataAdapter.InsertCommand.CommandText** in the **cmdAdd_Click** event handler is executed when lines 153–154 invoke method **AddressBookData-Adapter.InsertCommand.ExecuteNonQuery**. Similarly, the **UPDATE** statement defined by **AddressBookDataAdapter.UpdateCommand.CommandText** in the event handler **cmdUpdate_Click** is executed by invoking method **AddressBook-DataAdapter.UpdateCommand.ExecuteNonQuery** (lines 209–210).

Method **Display** (lines 255-311) updates the user interface with data from the newly retrieved address book record. Line 260 obtains a **DataTable** from the **DataSet**'s **Tables** collection. This **DataTable** contains the results of our SQL query. Line 263 checks whether the query returned any rows. The **Rows** property in class **DataTable** provides access to all records retrieved by the query. The **Rows** property is much like a two-dimensional rectangular array. Lines 264–265 retrieve the field with index *0, 0* (i.e., the first record's first column of data) and store the value in variable **recordNumber**. Lines 267–296 then retrieve the remaining fields of data from the **DataTable** to populate the user interface.

The application's **Help** button prints instructions in the console at the bottom of the application window (lines 246–251). The event handler for this button is **cmdHelp_Click** (lines 243–252). The **Clear** button clears the text from the **TextBox**es using method **ClearTextBoxes** (line 314).

16.8 Reading and Writing XML Files

A powerful feature of ADO .NET is its ability to convert data stored in a data source to XML. Class **DataSet** of namespace **System.Data** provides methods *WriteXml*, *ReadXml* and *GetXml*, which enable developers to create XML documents from data sources and to convert data from XML into data sources. The application of Fig. 16.30 populates a **DataSet** with statistics about baseball players and then writes the data to files as XML. The application also displays the XML in a **TextBox**.

```
1  ' Fig. 16.30: XMLWriter.vb
2  ' Demonstrates generating XML from an ADO .NET DataSet.
3
4  Imports System.Windows.Forms
5
6  Public Class FrmXMLWriter
7     Inherits Form
8
```

Fig. 16.30 XML representation of a **DataSet** written to a file. (Part 1 of 3.)

```
 9        ' constructor
10        Public Sub New()
11           MyBase.New()
12
13           ' This call is required by the Windows Form Designer.
14           InitializeComponent()
15
16           ' Add any initialization after the
17           ' InitializeComponent() call
18
19           ' open database connection
20           BaseballConnection.Open()
21
22           ' fill DataSet with data from OleDbDataAdapter
23           BaseballDataAdapter.Fill(BaseballDataSet, "Players")
24
25           ' bind DataGrid to DataSet
26           dgdPlayers.SetDataBinding(BaseballDataSet, "Players")
27        End Sub
28
29        ' form controls
30        Friend WithEvents cmdWrite As Button
31        Friend WithEvents dgdPlayers As DataGrid
32        Friend WithEvents txtOutput As TextBox
33
34        ' database connection
35        Friend WithEvents BaseballConnection As _
36           System.Data.OleDb.OleDbConnection
37
38        ' database adapter
39        Friend WithEvents BaseballDataAdapter As _
40           System.Data.OleDb.OleDbDataAdapter
41
42        ' results dataset
43        Friend WithEvents BaseballDataSet As System.Data.DataSet
44
45        ' Visual Studio .NET generated code
46
47        ' write XML representation of DataSet when button clicked
48        Private Sub cmdWrite_Click(ByVal sender As System.Object, _
49           ByVal e As System.EventArgs) Handles cmdWrite.Click
50
51           ' write XML representation of DataSet to file
52           BaseballDataSet.WriteXml("Players.xml")
53
54           ' display XML in TextBox
55           txtOutput.Text &= "Writing the following XML:" & _
56              vbCrLf & BaseballDataSet.GetXml() & vbCrLf
57        End Sub ' cmdWrite_Click
58
59     End Class ' FrmXMLWriter
```

Fig. 16.30 XML representation of a **DataSet** written to a file. (Part 2 of 3.)

Fig. 16.30 XML representation of a **DataSet** written to a file. (Part 3 of 3.)

The **FrmXMLWriter** constructor (lines 10–27) establishes a connection to the **Baseball** database in line 20. Line 23 calls method **Fill** of class **OleDbDataAdapter** to populate **BaseballDataSet** with data from the **Players** table in the **Baseball** database. Line 26 binds the **dgdPlayers** to **BaseballDataSet** to display the information to the user.

Event handler **cmdWrite_Click** (lines 48–57) defines the event handler for the **Write to XML** button. When the user clicks this button, line 52 invokes **DataSet** method **WriteXml**, which generates an XML representation of the data contained in the **DataSet** and then writes the XML to the specified file. Figure 16.31 depicts this XML representation. Each **Players** element represents a record in the **Players** table. The **firstName**, **lastName**, **battingAverage** and **playerID** elements correspond to the fields that have these names in the **Players** database table.

```
1    <?xml version="1.0" standalone="yes"?>
2    <NewDataSet>
3       <Players>
4          <firstName>John</firstName>
5          <lastName>Doe</lastName>
6          <battingAverage>0.375</battingAverage>
7          <playerID>1</playerID>
8       </Players>
9
10      <Players>
11         <firstName>Jack</firstName>
12         <lastName>Smith</lastName>
13         <battingAverage>0.223</battingAverage>
14         <playerID>2</playerID>
15      </Players>
16
17      <Players>
18         <firstName>George</firstName>
19         <lastName>O'Malley</lastName>
```

Fig. 16.31 XML document generated from **WriteXML**. (Part 1 of 2.)

```
20                    <battingAverage>0.444</battingAverage>
21                    <playerID>3</playerID>
22              </Players>
23      </NewDataSet>
```

Fig. 16.31 XML document generated from **WriteXML**. (Part 2 of 2.)

16.9 Summary

A database is an integrated collection of data. A database management system (DBMS) provides mechanisms for storing and organizing data. Today's most popular database systems are relational databases.

A relational database is composed of tables. A row of a table is called a record. A primary key is a field that contains unique data, or data that are not duplicated in other records of that table. Each column in a table represents a different field. A primary key can be composed of more than one column (or field) in the database. A one-to-many relationship between tables indicates that a record in one table can have many corresponding records in a separate table. A foreign key is a field for which every entry in one table has a unique value in another table and where the field in the other table is the primary key for that table.

A language called Structured Query Language (SQL) is used almost universally with relational-database systems to perform queries and manipulate data. SQL provides a complete set of commands, enabling programmers to define complex queries to select data from tables. The results of a query commonly are called result sets (or record sets).

The **SELECT** statement is used to extract data from a database. The optional **WHERE** clause specifies the selection criteria for the query. The **WHERE** clause condition can contain operators **<, >, <=, >=, =, <>** and **LIKE**. Operator **LIKE** is used for pattern matching with wildcard characters asterisk (*****) and question mark (**?**). The results of a query can be arranged in ascending or descending order via the optional **ORDER BY** clause. A join query merges records from two tables by testing for matching values in fields that are common to both tables. An **INSERT** statement inserts a new record in a table. An **UPDATE** statement modifies data in a table. A **DELETE** statement removes data from a table.

A programming language connects to, and interacts with, relational databases via an interface. Visual Basic programmers communicate with databases and manipulate their data via ADO .NET. **System.Data**, **System.Data.OleDb** and **System.Data.SqlClient** are the three main namespaces in ADO .NET. Class **DataSet** is from the **System.Data** namespace. Instances of this class represent in-memory caches of data. The advantage of using class **DataSet** is that it allows the contents of a data source to be modified without having to maintain an active connection. Class **OleDbCommand** of the **System.Data.OleDb** namespace enables the programmer to execute SQL statements directly on the data source.

Use the **Add Connection** option to create a database connection. Use the **Data Adapter Configuration Wizard** to set up an **OleDbDataAdapter** and generate queries. **OleDbCommand** commands are what the **OleDbDataAdapter** executes on the database in the form of SQL queries. **OleDbCommand** instance property **Connection** is set to the **OleDbConnection** that the command will be executed on, and the instance property **CommandText** is set to the SQL query that will be executed on the database.

OleDbDataAdapter method **Fill** retrieves information from the database associated with the **OleDbConnection** and places this information in the **DataSet** provided as an argument. **DataGrid** method **SetDataBinding** binds a **DataGrid** to a data source. Method **ExecuteNonQuery** of class **OleDbCommand** performs the action specified by **CommandText** on the database.

A powerful feature of ADO .NET is its ability to convert data stored in a data source to XML, and vice versa. Method **WriteXml** of class **DataSet** writes the XML representation of the **DataSet** instance to the first argument passed to it. Method **ReadXml** of class **DataSet** reads the XML representation of the first argument passed to it into its own **DataSet**.

17

ASP .NET, Web Forms and Web Controls

Objectives

- To become familiar with Web Forms in ASP .NET.
- To create Web Forms.
- To create an ASP .NET application consisting of multiple Web Forms.
- To control user access to Web applications through forms authentication.
- To use files and databases in an ASP .NET application.
- To learn how to use tracing with Web Forms.

If any man will draw up his case, and put his name at the foot of the first page, I will give him an immediate reply. Where he compels me to turn over the sheet, he must wait my leisure.
Lord Sandwich

Rule One: Our client is always right
Rule Two: If you think our client is wrong, see Rule One.
Anonymous

A fair question should be followed by a deed in silence.
Dante Alighieri

You will come here and get books that will open your eyes, and your ears, and your curiosity, and turn you inside out or outside in.
Ralph Waldo Emerson

Outline

17.1 Introduction

In previous chapters, we used Windows Forms and Windows controls to develop Windows applications. In this chapter, we introduce *Web-based application development*, which employs Microsoft's ASP .NET technology. Web-based applications create Web content for Web browser clients. This Web content includes Hypertext Markup Language (HTML),[1] client-side scripting, images and binary data.

We present several examples that demonstrate Web-based applications development using *Web Forms* (also known as *Web Form pages*), *Web controls* (also known as *ASP .NET server controls*) and Visual Basic programming. Web Forms files have the file extension **.aspx** and contain the Web page's GUI. Programmers customize Web Forms by adding Web controls, which include labels, textboxes, images, buttons and other GUI components. The Web Form file represents the Web page that is sent to the client browser. [*Note*: From this point onward, we refer to Web Forms files as *ASPX files*.]

Every ASPX file created in Visual Studio has a corresponding class written in a .NET language, such as Visual Basic; this class includes event handlers, initialization code, utility methods and other supporting code. The Visual Basic file that contains this class is called the *code-behind file* and provides the ASPX file's programmatic implementation.

---

1. This chapter assumes readers are familiar with HTML.

17.2 Simple HTTP Transaction

Before exploring Web-based applications development further, a basic understanding of networking and the World Wide Web is necessary. In this section, we examine the inner workings of the *Hypertext Transfer Protocol (HTTP)* and discuss what occurs behind the scenes when a browser displays a Web page. HTTP specifies a set of *methods* and *headers* that allow clients and servers to interact and exchange information in a uniform and predictable way.

In its simplest form, a Web page is nothing more than an HTML document. This document is a plain text file containing markings (*markup* or *tags*) that describe to a Web browser how to display and format the document's information. For example, the HTML markup

```
<title>My Web Page</title>
```

indicates to the browser that the text contained between the `<title>` *start tag* and the `</title>` *end tag* is the Web page's title. HTML documents also can contain *hypertext* data (usually called *hyperlinks*), which create links to different pages or to other parts of the same page. When the user activates a hyperlink (usually by clicking it with the mouse), the requested Web page (or different part of the same Web page) is loaded into the user's browser window.

Any HTML document available for viewing over the Web has a corresponding *Uniform Resource Locator (URL)*, which is an address indicating the location of a resource. The URL contains information that directs a browser to the resource document that the user wishes to access. Computers that run *Web server* software provide such resources. When developing ASP .NET Web applications, Microsoft *Internet Information Services (IIS)* is the Web server.

Let us examine the components of the URL

```
http://www.deitel.com/books/downloads.htm
```

The `http://` indicates that the resource is to be obtained using HTTP. The middle portion, **www.deitel.com**, is the fully qualified *hostname* of the server. The hostname is the name of the computer on which the resource resides. This computer usually is referred to as the *host*, because it houses and maintains resources. The hostname **www.deitel.com** is translated into an *IP address* (**207.60.134.230**), which identifies the server in a manner similar to that in which a telephone number uniquely defines a particular phone line. The translation of the hostname into an IP address normally is performed by a *domain name server (DNS)*, a computer that maintains a database of hostnames and their corresponding IP addresses. This translation operation is called a *DNS lookup*.

The remainder of the URL provides the name of the requested resource, **/books/downloads.htm** (an HTML document). This portion of the URL specifies both the name of the resource (**downloads.htm**) and its path, or location (**/books**), on the Web server. The path could specify the location of an actual directory on the Web server's file system. However, for security reasons, the path often specifies the location of a *virtual directory*. In such systems, the server translates the virtual directory into a real location on the server (or on another computer on the server's network), thus hiding the true location of the resource. Furthermore, some resources are created dynamically and do not reside anywhere on the server computer. The hostname in the URL for such a resource specifies the correct server, and the path and resource information identify the location of the resource with which to respond to the client's request.

When given a URL, a browser performs a simple HTTP transaction to retrieve and display a Web page. Figure 17.1 illustrates the transaction in detail. This transaction consists of interaction between the Web browser (the client side) and the Web-server application (the server side).

In Fig. 17.1, the Web browser sends an HTTP request to the server. The request (in its simplest form) is

```
GET /books/downloads.htm HTTP/1.1
```

The word **GET** is an HTTP method indicating that the client wishes to obtain a resource from the server. The remainder of the request provides the path name of the resource (an HTML document) and the protocol's name and version number (**HTTP/1.1**).

Any server that understands HTTP (version 1.1) can translate this request and respond appropriately. Figure 17.2 depicts the results of a successful request. The server first responds by sending a line of text that indicates the HTTP version, followed by a numeric code and phrase describing the status of the transaction. For example,

```
HTTP/1.1 200 OK
```

indicates success, whereas

```
HTTP/1.1 404 Not found
```

informs the client that the Web server could not locate the requested resource.

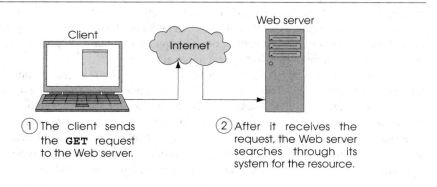

① The client sends the **GET** request to the Web server.

② After it receives the request, the Web server searches through its system for the resource.

Fig. 17.1 Client interacting with Web server. Step 1: The **GET** request, `GET /books/downloads.htm HTTP/1.1`.

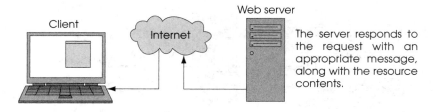

The server responds to the request with an appropriate message, along with the resource contents.

Fig. 17.2 Client interacting with Web server. Step 2: The HTTP response, `HTTP/1.1 200 OK`.

The server then sends one or more *HTTP headers,* which provide additional information about the data that will be sent. In this case, the server is sending an HTML text document, so the HTTP header for this example reads:

```
Content-type: text/html
```

The information provided in this header specifies the *Multipurpose Internet Mail Extensions (MIME)* type of the content that the server is transmitting to the browser. MIME is an Internet standard that specifies the way in which certain data must be formatted so that programs can interpret the data correctly. For example, the MIME type **text/plain** indicates that the sent information is text that can be displayed directly, without any interpretation of the content as HTML markup. Similarly, the MIME type **image/gif** indicates that the content is a GIF image. When the browser receives this MIME type, it attempts to display the image.

The header or set of headers is followed by a blank line, which indicates to the client that the server is finished sending HTTP headers. The server then sends the contents of the requested HTML document (**downloads.htm**). The server terminates the connection when the transfer of the resource is complete. At this point, the client-side browser parses the HTML it has received and *renders* (or displays) the results.

17.3 System Architecture

Web-based applications are *multi-tier applications*, which sometimes are referred to as *n*-tier applications. Multi-tier applications divide functionality into separate *tiers* (i.e., logical groupings of functionality). Although tiers can be located on the same computer, the tiers of Web-based applications typically reside on separate computers. Figure 17.3 presents the basic structure of a three-tier Web-based application.

The *information tier* (also called the *data tier* or the *bottom tier*) maintains data pertaining to the application. This tier typically stores data in a *relational database management system (RDBMS)*. We discussed RDBMSs in Chapter 16. For example, a retail store might have a database for storing product information, such as descriptions, prices and quantities in stock. The same database also might contain customer information, such as user names, billing addresses and credit-card numbers. This tier can be composed of multiple databases, which together contain the data needed for our application.

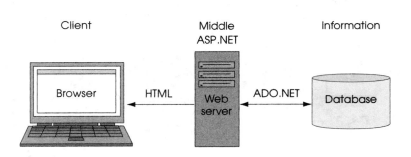

Fig. 17.3   Three-tier architecture.

The *middle tier* implements *business logic*, *controller logic* and *presentation logic* to control interactions between application clients and application data. The middle tier acts as an intermediary between data in the information tier and the application's clients. The middle-tier controller logic processes client requests (such as requests to view a product catalog) and retrieves data from the database. The middle-tier presentation logic then processes data from the information tier and presents the content to the client. Web applications typically present data to clients in the form of HTML documents.

Business logic in the middle tier enforces *business rules* and ensures that data are reliable before the server application updates the database or presents data to users. Business rules dictate how clients can and cannot access application data and how applications process data.

The *client tier*, or *top tier*, is the application's user interface, which is typically a Web browser. Users interact directly with the application through the user interface. The client tier interacts with the middle tier to make requests and to retrieve data from the information tier. The client tier then displays to the user the data retrieved from the middle tier.

17.4 Creating and Running a Simple Web-Form Example

In this section, we present our first example, which displays the time of day as maintained on the Web server in a browser window. When run, this program displays the text **A Simple Web Form Example**, followed by the Web server's time. As mentioned previously, the program consists of two related files—an ASPX file (Fig. 17.4) and a Visual Basic code-behind file (Fig. 17.5). We display the markup, code and output first; then, we carefully guide the reader through the step-by-step process of creating this program. [*Note*: The markup in Fig. 17.4 and other ASPX file listings in this chapter have been reformatted for presentation purposes.]

```
1    <%-- Fig. 17.4: WebTime.aspx          --%>
2    <%-- A page that contains two labels. --%>
3
4    <%@ Page Language="vb" AutoEventWireup="false"
5       Codebehind="WebTime.aspx.vb" Inherits="WebTime.WebTimer"
6       enableViewState="False" EnableSessionState="False" %>
7
8    <!DOCTYPE HTML PUBLIC "-//W3C//DTD HTML 4.0 Transitional//EN">
9    <HTML>
10      <HEAD>
11         <title>WebTime</title>
12         <meta name="GENERATOR"
13            content="Microsoft Visual Studio.NET 7.0">
14         <meta name="CODE_LANGUAGE" content="Visual Basic 7.0">
15         <meta name="vs_defaultClientScript" content="JavaScript">
16         <meta name="vs_targetSchema"
17            content="http://schemas.microsoft.com/intellisense/ie5">
18      </HEAD>
19      <body MS_POSITIONING="GridLayout">
20         <form id="Form1" method="post" runat="server">
21
```

Fig. 17.4 ASPX page that displays the Web server's time. (Part 1 of 2.)

```
22              <asp:Label id="displayLabel" style="Z-INDEX: 101;
23                 LEFT: 42px; POSITION: absolute; TOP: 36px"
24                 runat="server" Width="186px">
25                 A Simple Web Form Example
26              </asp:Label>
27
28              <asp:Label id="timeLabel" style="Z-INDEX: 102;
29                 LEFT: 33px; POSITION: absolute; TOP: 84px"
30                 runat="server" Width="225px" Height="55px"
31                 ForeColor="#C0FFC0" BackColor="Black"
32                 Font-Size="XX-Large">
33              </asp:Label>
34
35          </form>
36        </body>
37    </HTML>
```

Fig. 17.4   ASPX page that displays the Web server's time. (Part 2 of 2.)

Visual Studio generates the markup shown in Fig. 17.4 when the programmer drags two **Label**s onto the Web Form and sets their properties. Notice that the ASPX file contains other information in addition to HTML.

Lines 1–2 of Fig. 17.4 are *ASP .NET comments* that indicate the figure number, the file name and the purpose of the file. ASP.NET comments begin with **<%--** and terminate with **--%>**. We added these comments to the file. Lines 4–6 use a **<%@ Page...%>** *directive* to specify information needed by the Common Language Runtime (CLR) to process this file. The *language* of the code-behind file is specified as *vb*; the code-behind file is named **WebTime.aspx.vb**.

The **AutoEventWireup** attribute determines how Web Form events are handled. When the **AutoEventWireup** is set to **true**, ASP .NET determines which methods in the class are called in response to an event generated by the **Page**. For example, ASP .NET will call methods **Page_Load** and **Page_Init** in the code-behind file to handle the **Page**'s **Load** and **Init** events respectively, without the use of the **Handles** keyword. When Visual Studio .NET generates an **aspx** file it sets **AutoEventWireup** to **false**. This is because Visual Studio .NET generates the **Page_Load** and **Page_Init** event handlers using the **Handles** keyword when the project is created. For this reason, always set **AutoEventWireup false** when using Visual Studio.

The **Inherits** attribute specifies the class in the code-behind file from which this ASP .NET class inherits—in this case, **WebTimer**. We say more about **Inherits** momentarily. [*Note*: We explicitly set the **EnableViewState** attribute and the **EnableSessionState** attribute to **False**. We explain the significance of these attributes later in the chapter.]

For this first ASPX file, we provide a brief discussion of the HTML markup. We do not discuss the **HTML** contained in subsequent ASPX files. Line 8 is called the *document type declaration*, which specifies the document element name (**HTML**) and the **PUBLIC** Uniform Resource Identifier (URI) for the DTD.

Lines 9–10 contain the **<HTML>** and **<HEAD>** start tags, respectively. **HTML** documents have root element HTML and mark up information about the document in the **HEAD** element. Line 11 sets the title for this Web page. Lines 12–17 are a series of *meta elements*, which contain information about the document. Two important **meta**-element attributes are *name*, which identifies the **meta** element, and *content*, which stores the **meta** element's data. Visual Studio generates these **meta** elements when an ASPX file is created.

Line 19 contains the **<body>** start tag, which begins the HTML body; the body contains the main content that the browser displays. The **Form** that contains our controls is defined in lines 20–35. Notice the *runat* attribute in line 20, which is set to *"server"*. This attribute indicates that the **form** executes on the server. The corresponding HTML will be generated and sent to the client.

Lines 22–26 and 28–33 mark up two label Web controls. The properties that we set in the **Properties** window, such as **Font-Size** and **Text**, are attributes here. The *asp: tag prefix* in the declaration of the *Label* tag indicates that the label is an ASP .NET Web control. Each Web control maps to a corresponding HTML element.

 Portability Tip 17.1

The same Web control can map to different HTML elements, depending on the client browser and the Web control's property settings.

In this example, the **asp:Label** control maps to the HTML *span* element. A **span** element contains text that is displayed in a Web page. This particular element is used because **span** elements facilitate the application of styles to text. Several of the property values that were applied to our labels are represented as part of the **style** of the **span** element. Soon we will see the **span** elements that are created.

Each of the Web controls in our example contains the **runat="server"** attribute-value pair, because these controls must be processed on the server. If this attribute pair is not present, the **asp:Label** element is written as text to the client (i.e., the control would not be converted into a **span** element and would not be rendered properly).

Figure 17.5 presents the code-behind file. Recall that the ASPX file in Fig. 17.4 references this file in line 5. To explain the code, we present the entire code-behind file for this example.

```
1   ' Fig. 17.5: WebTime.aspx.vb
2   ' The code-behind file for a page
3   ' that displays the current time.
4
5   Imports System
6   Imports System.Web
7   Imports System.Web.UI
8   Imports System.Web.UI.WebControls
9
10  Public Class WebTimer
11     Inherits System.Web.UI.Page
12
13     Protected WithEvents displayLabel As _
14        System.Web.UI.WebControls.Label
15
16     Protected WithEvents timeLabel As _
17        System.Web.UI.WebControls.Label
18
```

Fig. 17.5 Code-behind file for a page that displays the Web server's time. (Part 1 of 2.)

```
19          ' This call is required by the Web Form Designer
20                      InitializeComponent()
21
22
23       Private Sub Page_Init(ByVal sender As System.Object, _
24          ByVal e As System.EventArgs) Handles MyBase.Init
25
26          InitializeComponent()
27
28          timeLabel.Text = _
29             String.Format("{0:D2}:{1:D2}:{2:D2}", _
30             DateTime.Now.Hour, DateTime.Now.Minute, _
31             DateTime.Now.Second)
32       End Sub ' Page_Init
33
34                   Page_Load(        sender      System.Object, _
35                e     System.EventArgs)                .Load
36          ' Put user code to initialize the page here
37                   ' Page_Load
38    End Class ' WebTimer
```

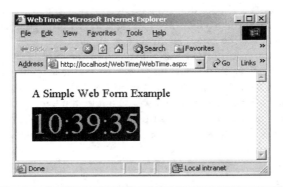

Fig. 17.5   Code-behind file for a page that displays the Web server's time.
(Part 2 of 2.)

Notice the **Imports** statements in lines 5–8. These statements specify namespaces that contain classes for developing Web-based applications. The key namespace on which we initially focus is *System.Web*, which contains classes that manage client requests and server responses. The other namespaces define the controls available and how they can be manipulated; these are discussed throughout the chapter as they become more relevant.

Line 10 begins the class definition for **WebTimer**, which inherits from class *Page*. This class defines the requested Web page and is located in the *System.Web.UI* namespace (line 7), which contains classes pertinent to the creation of Web-based applications and controls. Class **Page** also provides event handlers and objects necessary for creating Web-based applications. In addition to the **Page** class (from which all Web applications directly or indirectly inherit), **System.Web.UI** also includes the *Control* class. This class is the base class that provides common functionality for all Web controls.

Lines 13–17 declare references to two **Label**s. These **Label**s are Web controls, defined in namespace **System.Web.UI.WebControls** (line 8). This namespace contains Web controls employed in the design of the page's user interface. Web controls in this namespace derive from class **WebControl**.

Lines 23–32 define method **Page_Init**, which handles the page's **Init** event. This event, which is the first event raised, indicates that the page is ready to be initialized. Method **Page_Init** calls method **InitializeComponent** (lines 20–21). Like Windows Forms, this method is used to programmatically set some initial properties of the application's components. After this call, **timeLabel**'s **Text** property is set to the Web server's time (lines 28–31).

How are the ASPX file and the code-behind file used to create the Web page that is sent to the client? First, recall that class **WebTimer** is the base class specified in line 5 of the ASPX file (Fig. 17.4). This class inherits from **Page**, which defines the general functionality of a Web page. Class **WebTimer** inherits this functionality and defines some of its own (i.e., displaying the current time). The code-behind file is the file that defines this functionality, whereas the ASPX file defines the GUI. When a client requests an ASPX file, a class is created behind the scenes that contains both the visual aspect of our page (defined in the ASPX file) and the logic of our page (defined in the code-behind file). This new class inherits from **Page**. The first time that our Web page is requested, this class is compiled, and an instance is created. This instance represents our page—it creates the HTML that is sent to the client. The assembly created from our compiled class is placed in the project's **bin** directory.

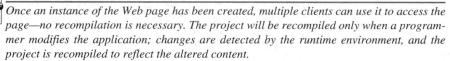

Performance Tip 17.1

Once an instance of the Web page has been created, multiple clients can use it to access the page—no recompilation is necessary. The project will be recompiled only when a programmer modifies the application; changes are detected by the runtime environment, and the project is recompiled to reflect the altered content.

Let us look briefly at how the code in our Web page executes. When an instance of our page is created, the **Init** event occurs first, invoking method **Page_Init**. This method calls **InitializeComponent**. In addition to this call, method **Page_Init** might contain code needed to initialize objects. After this occurs, the **Load** event is generated and the **Page_Load** event handler executes any processing that is necessary to restore data from previous requests. After this event handler has finished executing, the page processes any events raised by the page's controls. This includes the handling of any events generated by the user, such as button clicks. When the Web-Form object is ready for garbage collection, an **Unload** event is generated. Although not present, event handler **Page_Unload** is inherited from class **Page**. This event handler contains any code that releases resources, especially any *unmanaged resources* (i.e., resources not managed by the CLR).

Figure 17.6 shows the HTML generated by the ASP .NET application. To view this HTML, select **View > Source** in Internet Explorer.

The contents of this page are similar to those of the ASPX file. Lines 7–15 define a document header comparable to that in Fig. 17.4. Lines 17–35 define the body of the document. Line 18 begins the form, which is a mechanism for collecting user information and sending it to the Web server. In this particular program, the user does not submit data to the Web server for processing; however, this is a crucial part of many applications and is facilitated by the form.

```
1    <!-- Fig. 17.6: WebTime.html                          -->
2    <!-- The HTML generated when WebTime is loaded. -->
3
4    <!DOCTYPE HTML PUBLIC "-//W3C//DTD HTML 4.0 Transitional//EN" >
5
6    <HTML>
7       <HEAD>
8          <title>WebTime</title>
9          <meta name="GENERATOR"
10            Content="Microsoft Visual Studio 7.0">
11         <meta name="CODE_LANGUAGE" Content="Visual Basic 7.0">
12         <meta name="vs_defaultClientScript" content="JavaScript">
13         <meta name="vs_targetSchema"
14            content="http://schemas.microsoft.com/intellisense/ie5">
15      </HEAD>
16
17      <body MS_POSITIONING="GridLayout">
18         <form name="Form1" method="post"
19            action="WebTime.aspx" id="Form1">
20            <input type="hidden" name="__VIEWSTATE"
21               value="dDw1OTc3ODM2Mzk7Oz4=" />
22
23            <span id="displayLabel"
24               style="width:186px;Z-INDEX: 101;
25               LEFT: 42px; POSITION: absolute; TOP: 36px">
26               A Simple Web Form Example
27            </span>
28            <span id="timeLabel" style="color:#C0FFC0;
29               background-color:Black;font-size:XX-Large;
30               height:55px;width:225px;Z-INDEX: 102;
31               LEFT: 33px; POSITION: absolute; TOP: 84px">
32               10:39:35
33            </span>
34         </form>
35      </body>
36   </HTML>
```

Fig. 17.6   HTML response when the browser requests **WebTime.aspx**.

HTML forms can contain visual and nonvisual components. Visual components include clickable buttons and other GUI components with which users interact. Nonvisual components, called *hidden inputs*, store any data that the document author specifies, such as e-mail addresses. One of these hidden inputs is defined in lines 20–21. We discuss the precise meaning of this hidden input later in the chapter. Attribute **method** specifies the method by which the Web browser submits the form to the server. The **action** attribute in the **<form>** tag identifies the name and location of the resource that will be requested when this form is submitted; in this case, **WebTime.aspx**. Recall that the ASPX file's **form** elements contained the **runat="server"** attribute-value pair. When the **form** is processed on the server, the **name="Form1"** and **action="WebTime.aspx"** attribute-value pairs are added to the HTML **form** sent to the client browser.

In the ASPX file, the form's labels were Web controls. Here, we are viewing the HTML created by our application, so the **form** contains **span** elements to represent the text in our labels. In this particular case, ASP .NET maps the label Web controls to HTML **span** elements. Each **span** element contains formatting information, such as size and placement, for the text being displayed. Most of the information specified as properties for **timeLabel** and **displayLabel** are specified by the **style** attribute of each **span**.

Now that we have presented the ASPX file and the code-behind file,[2] we outline the process by which we created this application. To create the application, perform the following steps:

1. *Create the project.* Select **File > New > Project...** to display the **New Project** dialog (Fig. 17.7). In this dialog, select **Visual Basic Projects** in the left pane and then *ASP .NET Web Application* in the right pane. Notice that the field for the project name is grayed out. Rather than using this field, we specify the name and location of the project in the **Location** field. We want our project to be located in **http://localhost**, which is the URL for IIS' root directory (typically **C:\InetPub\wwwroot**). The name *localhost* indicates that the client and server reside on the same machine. If the Web server were located on a different machine, localhost would be replaced with the appropriate IP address or hostname. By default, Visual Studio assigns the project name **WebApplication1**, which we change to **WebTime**. IIS must be running for this project to be created successfully. IIS can be started by executing **inetmgr.exe**, right-clicking **Default Web Site** and selecting **Start**. [*Note:* You might need to expand the node representing your computer to display the **Default Web Site**.] Below the **Location** textbox, the text "**Project will be created at http://localhost/VB/WebTime**" appears. This indicates that the project's folder is located in the root directory on the Web server. When the developer clicks **OK**, the project is created; this action also produces a virtual directory, which is linked to the project folder. The *Create New Web* dialog is displayed next, while Visual Studio is creating the Web site on the server (Fig. 17.8).

2. *Examine the newly created project.* The next several figures describe the new project's content; we begin with the **Solution Explorer** shown in Fig. 17.9. As occurs with Windows applications, Visual Studio creates several files when a new project is created. **WebForm1.aspx** is the Web Form (**WebForm1** is the default name for this file). As mentioned previously, a code-behind file is included as part of the project. To view the ASPX file's code-behind file, right click the ASPX file, and select **View Code**. Alternatively, the programmer can click an icon to display all files, then expand the node for our ASPX page (see Fig. 17.9.)

   Figure 17.10, shows the **Web Forms** controls listed in the **Toolbox**. The left figure displays the beginning of the Web controls list, and the right figure displays the remaining Web controls. Notice that some controls are similar to the Windows controls presented earlier in the book.

   Figure 17.11 shows the Web Form designer for **WebForm1.aspx**. It consists of a grid on which users drag and drop components, such as buttons and labels, from the **Toolbox**.

---

2. To run the examples included in this chapter, you must create a virtual directory in Microsoft Internet Information Services. For instructions visit the **FAQs** link at **www.deitel.com**.

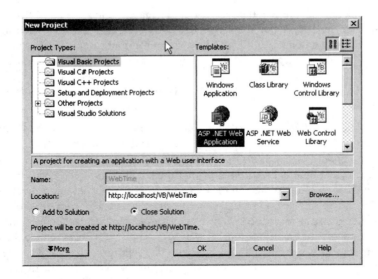

Fig. 17.7   Creating an **ASP .NET Web Application** in Visual Studio.

Fig. 17.8   Visual Studio creating and linking a virtual directory for the **WebTime** project folder.

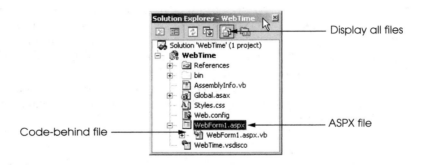

Fig. 17.9   **Solution Explorer** window for project **WebTime**.

Fig. 17.10 **Web Forms** menu in the **Toolbox**.

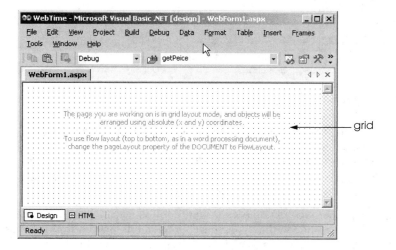

Fig. 17.11 **Design** mode of Web Form designer.

Figure 17.12 portrays the Web Form designer in **HTML** mode, which allows the programmer to view the markup that represents the user interface shown in design mode. When a developer clicks the **HTML** button in the lower-left corner of the Web Form designer, the Web Form designer switches to HTML mode. Similarly, the clicking of the **Design** button (to the left of the **HTML** button) returns the Web Form designer to design mode.

The next figure (Fig. 17.13) displays **WebForm1.aspx.vb**—the code-behind file for **WebForm1.aspx**. Recall that Visual Studio .NET generates this code-behind file when the project is created; it has been reformatted for presentation.

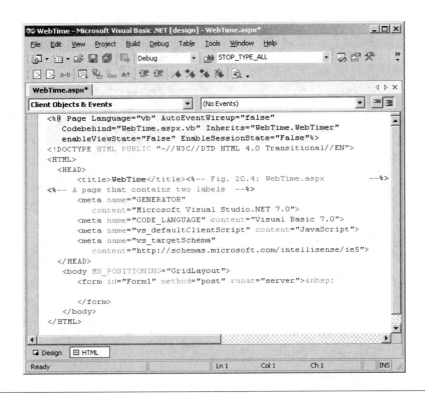

Fig. 17.12 HTML mode of Web-Form designer.

3. *Rename the ASPX file.* We have displayed the contents of the default ASPX and code-behind files. We now rename these files. Right click the ASPX file in the **Solution Explorer** and select **Rename**. Enter the new file name and hit *Enter*. This updates the name of both the ASPX file and the code-behind file. In this example, we use the name **WebTime.aspx**.

4. *Design the page.* Designing a Web Form is as simple as designing a Windows Form. To add controls to the page, drag and drop them from the **Toolbox** onto the Web Form. Like the Web Form itself, each control is an object that has properties, methods and events. Developers can set these properties and events, using the **Properties** window.

The ***PageLayout*** property determines how controls are arranged on the form (Fig. 17.15). By default, property **PageLayout** is set to *GridLayout*, which specifies that all controls are located exactly where they are dropped on the Web Form. This is called *absolute positioning*. Alternatively, the developer can set the Web Form's **PageLayout** property to *FlowLayout*, which causes controls to be placed sequentially on the Web Form. To view the Web Form's properties, select ***Document*** from the drop-down list in the **Properties** window; **Document** is the name used to represent the Web Form in the **Properties** window. This is called *relative positioning*, because the controls' positions are relative to the Web Form's upper-left corner. We use **GridLayout** for many of our examples.

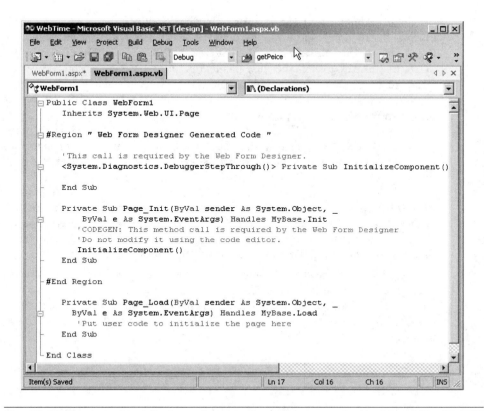

Fig. 17.13 Code-behind file for **WebForm1.aspx** generated by Visual Studio .NET.

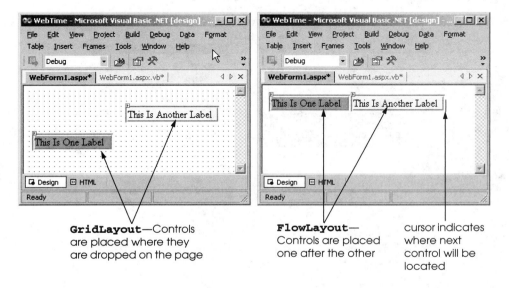

GridLayout—Controls are placed where they are dropped on the page

FlowLayout— Controls are placed one after the other

cursor indicates where next control will be located

Fig. 17.14 **FlowLayout** and **GridLayout** illustration.

In this example, we use two **Label**s, which developers can place on the Web Form either by drag-and-drop or by double-clicking the **Toolbox**'s **Label** control. Name the first **Label displayLabel** and the second **timeLabel**. We delete **timeLabel**'s text, because this text is set in the code-behind file. When a **Label** does not contain text, the name is displayed in square brackets in the Web Form designer, but is not displayed at run time (Fig. 17.15). We set the text for **promptLabel** to **A Simple Web Form Example**.

We set **timeLabel**'s **BackColor**, **ForeColor** and **Font-Size** properties to **Black**, **LimeGreen** and **XX-Large**, respectively. To change font properties, the programmer must expand the **Font** node in the **Properties** window, then change each relevant property individually. We also set the labels' locations and sizes by dragging the controls. Finally, we set the Web Form's **EnableSessionState** and **EnableViewState** properties to **False** (we discuss these properties later in the chapter). Once the **Label**s' properties are set in the **Properties** window, Visual Studio updates the ASPX file's contents. Figure 17.15 shows the IDE after these properties are set.

5. *Add page logic.* Once the user interface has been designed, Visual Basic code must be added to the code-behind file. In this example, lines 28–31 of Fig. 17.5 are added to the code-behind file. The statement retrieves the current time and formats it so that the time is in the format *HH*:*MM*:*SS*. For example, 9 a.m. is formatted as **09:00:00**.

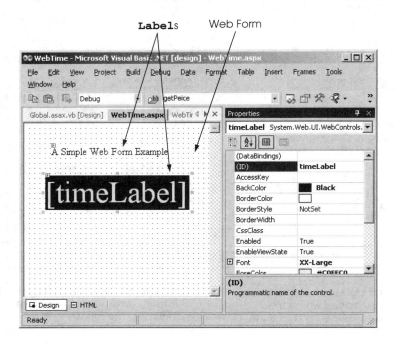

Fig. 17.15 **WebForm.aspx** after adding two **Label**s and setting their properties.

6. *Run the program.* Select **Debug > Start**. An Internet Explorer window opens and loads the Web page (the ASPX file). Notice that the URL is `http://local-host/VB/WebTime/WebTime.aspx` (Fig. 17.4), indicating that our ASPX file is located within the directory **WebTime**, which is located in the Web server's **VB** directory.

After the Web Form is created, the programmer can view it four different ways. First, the programmer can select **Debug > Start** (as described previously), which runs the application by opening a browser window. The IDE exits **Run** or **Debug** mode when the browser is closed.

The programmer also can right-click either the Web Form designer or the ASPX file name (in the **Solution Explorer**) and select *Build and Browse* or *View In Browser*. These each open a browser window within Visual Studio and displays preview of the page. This preview shows the user what the page would look like when requested by a client. The third way to run an ASP .NET application is to open a browser window and type in the Web page's URL. When testing an ASP .NET application on the same computer, type `http://localhost/`*ProjectFolder/PageName*`.aspx`, where *ProjectFolder* is the folder in which the page resides (usually the name of the project), and *PageName* is the name of the ASP .NET page. The first two methods of running the application compile the project for the programmer. The third and fourth methods require that the programmer compile the project by selecting **Build > Build Solution** in Visual Studio.

17.5 Web Controls

This section introduces some of the Web controls located on the **Web Form** tab in the **Toolbox** (Fig. 17.10). Figure 17.16 summarizes some of the Web controls used in the chapter examples.

17.5.1 Text and Graphics Controls

Figure 17.17 depicts a simple form for gathering user input. This example uses all the controls listed in Fig. 17.16. [*Note:* This example does not contain any functionality (i.e., no action occurs when the user clicks **Register**). In successive examples, we demonstrate how to add functionality to many of these Web controls.]

Web Control	Description
Label	Displays text that the user cannot edit.
Button	Triggers an event when clicked.
TextBox	Gathers user input and displays text.
Image	Displays images (e.g., GIF and JPG).

Fig. 17.16 Commonly used Web controls. (Part 1 of 2.)

Web Control	Description
RadioButtonList	Groups radio buttons.
DropDownList	Displays a drop-down list of choices from which a user can select one item.

Fig. 17.16 Commonly used Web controls. (Part 2 of 2.)

Lines 50–54 define an **Image** control, which inserts an image into a Web page. The image can be downloaded from our Web site, **www.deitel.com**, under the **Downloads/Resources** link. The **ImageUrl** property (line 53) specifies the file location of the image to display. To specify an image, click the ellipsis next to the **ImageUrl** property and use the resulting dialog to browse for the desired image. The top of this dialog displays the contents of this application. If the image is not explicitly part of the project, the programmer will need to use the **Browse** button. When the programmer right-clicks the image in the **Solution Explorer** and selects **Include in Project**, this image will be displayed in the top portion of the dialog.

```
1   <%-- Fig. 17.17: Controls.aspx  --%>
2   <%-- Demonstrates web controls. --%>
3
4   <%@ Page Language="vb" AutoEventWireup="false"
5      Codebehind="Controls.aspx.vb"
6      Inherits="Controls.WebForm1"
7      enableViewState="False" EnableSessionState="False" %>
8
9   <!DOCTYPE HTML PUBLIC "-//W3C//DTD HTML 4.0 Transitional//EN">
10  <HTML>
11     <HEAD>
12        <title>WebForm1</title>
13        <meta name="GENERATOR"
14           content="Microsoft Visual Studio.NET 7.0">
15        <meta name="CODE_LANGUAGE" content="Visual Basic 7.0">
16        <meta name="vs_defaultClientScript" content="JavaScript">
17        <meta name="vs_targetSchema"
18           content="http://schemas.microsoft.com/intellisense/ie5">
19     </HEAD>
20     <body MS_POSITIONING="GridLayout">
21        <form id="Form1" method="post" runat="server">
22
23           <asp:Label id="WelcomeLabel" style="Z-INDEX: 101;
24              LEFT: 44px; POSITION: absolute; TOP: 27px"
25              runat="server" Width="451px" Height="28px"
26              Font-Size="X-Large">
27              This is a simple registration form.
28           </asp:Label>
29
```

Fig. 17.17 Web-controls demonstration. (Part 1 of 5.)

```
30      <asp:Label id="RegisterLabel" style="Z-INDEX: 102;
31         LEFT: 48px; POSITION: absolute; TOP: 71px"
32         runat="server" Width="376px" Height="26px"
33         Font-Italic="True" Font-Size="Medium">
34         Please fill in all fields and click Register.
35      </asp:Label>
36
37      <asp:Image id="UserLabel" style="Z-INDEX: 103;
38         LEFT: 42px; POSITION: absolute; TOP: 135px"
39         runat="server" Width="439px" Height="28px"
40         ImageUrl="images/user.png">
41      </asp:Image>
42
43      <asp:Label id="FillLabel" style="Z-INDEX: 104;
44         LEFT: 50px; POSITION: absolute; TOP: 189px"
45         runat="server" Width="225px" ForeColor="Lime"
46         Font-Size="Medium">
47         Please fill out the fields below.
48      </asp:Label>
49
50      <asp:Image id="FirstImage" style="Z-INDEX: 105;
51         LEFT: 49px; POSITION: absolute; TOP: 224px"
52         runat="server" Width="84px" Height="36px"
53         ImageUrl="images/fname.png">
54      </asp:Image>
55
56      <asp:Image id="EmailImage" style="Z-INDEX: 106;
57         LEFT: 49px; POSITION: absolute; TOP: 280px"
58         runat="server" Width="86px" Height="29px"
59         ImageUrl="images/email.png">
60      </asp:Image>
61
62      <asp:TextBox id="FirstTextBox" style="Z-INDEX: 107;
63         LEFT: 145px; POSITION: absolute; TOP: 231px"
64         runat="server" Width="115px" Height="20px">
65      </asp:TextBox>
66
67      <asp:TextBox id="EmailTextBox" style="Z-INDEX: 108;
68         LEFT: 147px; POSITION: absolute; TOP: 284px"
69         runat="server" Width="112px" Height="18px">
70      </asp:TextBox>
71
72      <asp:Image id="LastImage" style="Z-INDEX: 109;
73         LEFT: 292px; POSITION: absolute; TOP: 227px"
74         runat="server" Width="77px" Height="33px"
75         ImageUrl="images/lname.png">
76      </asp:Image>
77
78      <asp:Image id="PhoneImage" style="Z-INDEX: 110;
79         LEFT: 292px; POSITION: absolute; TOP: 273px"
80         runat="server" Width="80px" Height="30px"
81         ImageUrl="images/phone.png">
82      </asp:Image>
```

Fig. 17.17 Web-controls demonstration. (Part 2 of 5.)

```
83
84        <asp:TextBox id="LastTextBox" style="Z-INDEX: 111;
85            LEFT: 400px; POSITION: absolute; TOP: 232px"
86            runat="server" Width="109px" Height="20px">
87        </asp:TextBox>
88
89        <asp:TextBox id="PhoneTextBox" style="Z-INDEX: 112;
90            LEFT: 399px; POSITION: absolute; TOP: 277px"
91            runat="server" Width="108px" Height="18px">
92        </asp:TextBox>
93
94        <asp:Label id="PhoneLabel" style="Z-INDEX: 113;
95            LEFT: 309px; POSITION: absolute; TOP: 318px"
96            runat="server" Width="223px" Height="18px">
97            Must be in the form (555)555-5555.
98        </asp:Label>
99
100       <asp:Image id="PublicationImage" style="Z-INDEX: 114;
101           LEFT: 50px; POSITION: absolute; TOP: 356px"
102           runat="server" Width="435px" Height="27px"
103           ImageUrl="images/downloads.png">
104       </asp:Image>
105
106       <asp:Label id="Booklabel" style="Z-INDEX: 115;
107           LEFT: 54px; POSITION: absolute; TOP: 411px"
108           runat="server" Width="348px" Height="23px"
109           ForeColor="Lime" Font-Size="Medium">
110           Which book would you like information about?
111       </asp:Label>
112
113       <asp:DropDownList id="BookDropDownList"
114           style="Z-INDEX: 116; LEFT: 60px; POSITION:
115           absolute; TOP: 448px" runat="server"
116           Width="326px" Height="29px">
117
118       <asp:ListItem Value="XML How to Program 1e">
119           XML How to Program 1e
120       </asp:ListItem>
121       <asp:ListItem Value="C# How to Program 1e">
122           C# How to Program 1e
123       </asp:ListItem>
124       <asp:ListItem Value="Java How to Program 4e">
125           Java How to Program 4e
126       </asp:ListItem>
127       <asp:ListItem Value=
128           "Advanced Java How to Program 1e">
129           Advanced Java How to Program 1e
130       </asp:ListItem>
131       <asp:ListItem Value=
132           "Visual Basic .NET How to Program 2e">
133           Visual Basic .NET How to Program 2e
134       </asp:ListItem>
```

Fig. 17.17 Web-controls demonstration. (Part 3 of 5.)

```
135        <asp:ListItem Value="C++ How to Program 3e">
136           C++ How to Program 3e
137        </asp:ListItem>
138     </asp:DropDownList>
139
140     <asp:HyperLink id="BooksHyperLink"
141        style="Z-INDEX: 117; LEFT: 64px; POSITION:
142        absolute; TOP: 486px" runat="server"
143        Width="385px" Height="22px"
144        NavigateUrl="http://www.deitel.com">
145        Click here to view more information about our books.
146     </asp:HyperLink>
147
148     <asp:Image id="OperatingImage" style="Z-INDEX: 118;
149        LEFT: 53px; POSITION: absolute; TOP: 543px"
150        runat="server" Width="431px" Height="32px"
151        ImageUrl="images/os.png">
152     </asp:Image>
153
154     <asp:Label id="OperatingLabel" style="Z-INDEX: 119;
155        LEFT: 63px; POSITION: absolute; TOP: 591px"
156        runat="server" Width="328px" Height="29px"
157        ForeColor="Lime" Font-Size="Medium">
158        Which operating system are you using?
159     </asp:Label>
160
161     <asp:Button id="RegisterButton" style="Z-INDEX: 124;
162        LEFT: 69px; POSITION: absolute; TOP: 760px"
163        runat="server" Width="120px" Height="33px"
164        Text="Register">
165     </asp:Button>
166
167     <asp:RadioButtonList id="OperatingRadioButtonList"
168        style="Z-INDEX: 125; LEFT: 65px; POSITION:
169        absolute; TOP: 624px" runat="server"
170        Height="122px" Width="155px">
171
172        <asp:ListItem Value="Windows NT">
173           Windows NT
174        </asp:ListItem>
175        <asp:ListItem Value="Windows 2000">
176           Windows 2000
177        </asp:ListItem>
178        <asp:ListItem Value="Windows XP">
179           Windows XP
180        </asp:ListItem>
181        <asp:ListItem Value="Linux">
182           Linux
183        </asp:ListItem>
184        <asp:ListItem Value="Other">
185           Other
186        </asp:ListItem>
187     </asp:RadioButtonList>
```

Fig. 17.17 Web-controls demonstration. (Part 4 of 5.)

```
188
189         </form>
190     </body>
191 </HTML>
```

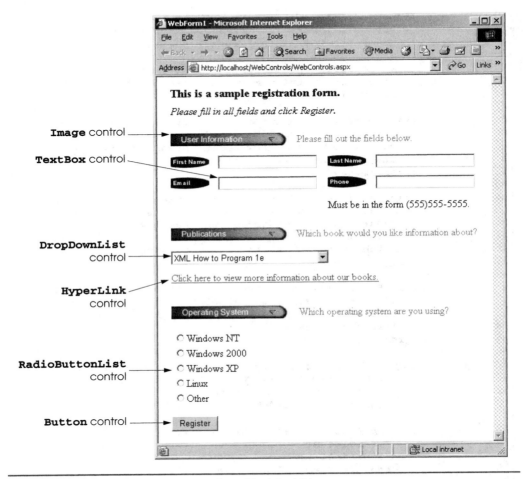

Image control

TextBox control

DropDownList control

HyperLink control

RadioButtonList control

Button control

Fig. 17.17 Web-controls demonstration. (Part 5 of 5.)

Lines 62–65 define a **TextBox** control, which allows the programmer to read and display text. Lines 167–187 define a **RadioButtonList** control, which provides a series of radio buttons from which the user can select only one. Each radio button is defined by a **ListItem** element (lines 172–186). The **HyperLink** control (lines 140–146) adds a hyperlink to a Web page. The **NavigateUrl** property (line 144) of this control specifies the resource that is requested (i.e., **http://www.deitel.com**) when a user clicks the hyperlink. Lines 113–138 define a **DropDownList**. This control is similar to a **RadioButtonList**, in that it allows the user to select exactly one option. When a user clicks the drop-down list, it expands and displays a list from which the user can make a selection. Lines 118–137 define the **ListItem**s that display when the drop-down list is expanded. Like the **Button** Windows control, the ***Button*** Web control (lines 161–165) represents a button; a button Web control typically maps to an **input** HTML element that has attribute **type** and value **"button"**.

17.5.2 AdRotator Control

Web pages often contain product or service advertisements, and these advertisements usually consist of images. Although Web site authors want to include as many sponsors as possible, Web pages can display only a limited number of advertisements. To address this problem, ASP .NET provides the ***AdRotator*** Web control for displaying advertisements. Using advertisement data located in an XML file, the **AdRotator** control randomly selects an image to display and then generates a hyperlink to the Web page associated with that image. Browsers that do not support images instead display alternate text that is specified in the XML document. If a user clicks the image or substituted text, the browser loads the Web page associated with that image.

Figure 17.18 demonstrates the **AdRotator** Web control. In this example, our advertisements that we rotate are the flags of eleven countries. When a user clicks the displayed flag image, the browser is redirected to a Web page containing information about the country that the flag represents. If a user clicks refresh or re-requests the page, one of the eleven flags is again chosen at random and displayed.

```
1    <%-- Fig. 17.18: CountryRotator.aspx             --%>
2    <%-- A Web Form that demonstrates class AdRotator. --%>
3
4    <%@ Page Language="vb" AutoEventWireup="false"
5       Codebehind="CountryRotator.aspx.vb"
6       Inherits="AdRotator.AdRotator"
7       enableViewState="False" EnableSessionState="False" %>
8
9    <!DOCTYPE HTML PUBLIC "-//W3C//DTD HTML 4.0 Transitional//EN">
10   <HTML>
11      <HEAD>
12         <title>WebForm1</title>
13         <meta content="Microsoft Visual Studio.NET 7.0"
14            name="GENERATOR">
15         <meta content="Visual Basic 7.0" name="CODE_LANGUAGE">
16         <meta content="JavaScript" name="vs_defaultClientScript">
17         <meta name="vs_targetSchema"
18            content="http://schemas.microsoft.com/intellisense/ie5">
19      </HEAD>
20      <body background=
21         "images/background.png"
22         MS_POSITIONING="GridLayout">
23         <form id="Form1" method="post" runat="server">
24
25            <asp:label id="displayLabel" style="Z-INDEX: 101;
26               LEFT: 36px; POSITION: absolute; TOP: 22px"
27               runat="server" Font-Size="Medium" Height="28px"
28               Width="268px">AdRotator Example
29            </asp:label>
```

Fig. 17.18 AdRotator class demonstrated on a Web form. (Part 1 of 2.)

```
30
31                    <asp:adrotator id="countryRotator" style="Z-INDEX: 102;
32                        LEFT: 36px; POSITION: absolute; TOP: 47px"
33                        runat="server" Height="72px" Width="108px"
34                        AdvertisementFile="AdRotatorInformation.xml">
35                    </asp:adrotator>
36
37                </form>
38            </body>
39        </HTML>
```

Fig. 17.18 `AdRotator` class demonstrated on a Web form. (Part 2 of 2.)

The ASPX file in Fig. 17.18 is similar to that in Fig. 17.4. However, instead of two **Label**s, this page contains one **Label** and one **AdRotator** control named **country-Rotator**. The **background** property for our page is set to display the image **background.png**. To specify this file, click the ellipsis provided next to the **Background** property and use the resulting dialog to browse for **background.png**.

In the **Properties** window, we set the **AdRotator** control's *Advertisement-File* property to **AdRotatorInformation.xml** (line 33). The Web control determines which advertisement to display from this file. We present the contents of this XML file momentarily. As illustrated in Fig. 17.19, the programmer does not need to add any additional code to the code-behind file, because the **adRotator** control does "all the work." The output depicts two different requests—the first time the page is requested, the American flag is shown, and, in the second request, the Latvian flag is displayed. The last image depicts the Web page that loads when the Latvian flag is clicked.

```
1    ' Fig. 17.19: CountryRotator.aspx.vb
2    ' The code-behind file for a page that
3    ' demonstrates the AdRotator class.
4
5    Public Class AdRotator
6        Inherits System.Web.UI.Page
7
8        Protected WithEvents displayLabel As _
9            System.Web.UI.WebControls.Label
10
11       Protected WithEvents countryRotator As _
12           System.Web.UI.WebControls.AdRotator
13
14       ' This call is required by the Web Form Designer.
15       Private Sub InitializeComponent()
16       End Sub
17
18       Private Sub Page_Init(ByVal sender As System.Object, _
19           ByVal e As System.EventArgs) Handles MyBase.Init
20
```

Fig. 17.19 Code-behind file for page demonstrating the **AdRotator** class. (Part 1 of 2.)

```
21          ' CODEGEN: This method call is required by the Web Form Designer
22          ' Do not modify it using the code editor.
23              InitializeComponent()
24      End Sub ' Page_Init
25
26      Private Sub Page_Load(ByVal sender As System.Object, _
27          ByVal e As System.EventArgs) Handles MyBase.Load
28              ' Put user code to initialize the page here
29          End Sub
30      End Class ' AdRotator
```

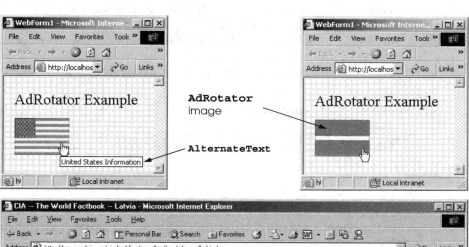

Fig. 17.19 Code-behind file for page demonstrating the **AdRotator** class. (Part 2 of 2.)

XML document **AdRotatorInformation.xml** (Fig. 17.20) contains several *Ad* elements, each of which provides information about a different advertisement. Element *ImageUrl* specifies the path (location) of the advertisement's image, and element *NavigateUrl* specifies the URL for the web page that loads when a user clicks the advertisement. The **AlternateText** element contains text that displays in place of the image when the browser cannot locate or render the image for some reason (i.e., because the file is missing, or the browser is not capable of displaying it). The **AlternateText** element's text is also a *tooltip* that Internet Explorer displays when a user places the mouse pointer over the image (Fig. 17.19). A tooltip is a caption that appears when the mouse hovers over a control and provides the user with information about that control. The *Impressions* element specifies how often a particular image appears, relative to the other images. An advertisement that has a higher **Impressions** value displays more frequently than an advertisement with a lower value. In our example, the advertisements display with equal probability, because each **Impressions**'s value is set to **1**.

```xml
1    <?xml version="1.0" encoding="utf-8"?>
2
3    <!-- Fig. 17.20: AdRotatorInformation.xml              -->
4    <!-- XML file containing advertisement information. -->
5
6    <Advertisements>
7       <Ad>
8          <ImageUrl>images/us.png</ImageUrl>
9          <NavigateUrl>
10            http://www.odci.gov/cia/publications/factbook/geos/us.html
11         </NavigateUrl>
12         <AlternateText>United States Information</AlternateText>
13         <Impressions>1</Impressions>
14      </Ad>
15
16      <Ad>
17         <ImageUrl>images/france.png</ImageUrl>
18         <NavigateUrl>
19            http://www.odci.gov/cia/publications/factbook/geos/fr.html
20         </NavigateUrl>
21         <AlternateText>France Information</AlternateText>
22         <Impressions>1</Impressions>
23      </Ad>
24
25      <Ad>
26         <ImageUrl>images/germany.png</ImageUrl>
27         <NavigateUrl>
28            http://www.odci.gov/cia/publications/factbook/geos/gm.html
29         </NavigateUrl>
30         <AlternateText>Germany Information</AlternateText>
31         <Impressions>1</Impressions>
32      </Ad>
33
34      <Ad>
35         <ImageUrl>images/italy.png</ImageUrl>
```

Fig. 17.20 AdvertisementFile used in **AdRotator** example. (Part 1 of 3.)

```
36              <NavigateUrl>
37                  http://www.odci.gov/cia/publications/factbook/geos/it.html
38              </NavigateUrl>
39              <AlternateText>Italy Information</AlternateText>
40              <Impressions>1</Impressions>
41          </Ad>
42
43          <Ad>
44              <ImageUrl>images/spain.png</ImageUrl>
45              <NavigateUrl>
46                http://www.odci.gov/cia/publications/factbook/geos/sp.html
47              </NavigateUrl>
48              <AlternateText>Spain Information</AlternateText>
49              <Impressions>1</Impressions>
50          </Ad>
51
52          <Ad>
53              <ImageUrl>images/latvia.png</ImageUrl>
54              <NavigateUrl>
55                  http://www.odci.gov/cia/publications/factbook/geos/lg.html
56              </NavigateUrl>
57              <AlternateText>Latvia Information</AlternateText>
58              <Impressions>1</Impressions>
59          </Ad>
60
61          <Ad>
62              <ImageUrl>images/peru.png</ImageUrl>
63              <NavigateUrl>
64                  http://www.odci.gov/cia/publications/factbook/geos/pe.html
65              </NavigateUrl>
66              <AlternateText>Peru Information</AlternateText>
67              <Impressions>1</Impressions>
68          </Ad>
69
70          <Ad>
71              <ImageUrl>images/senegal.png</ImageUrl>
72              <NavigateUrl>
73                  http://www.odci.gov/cia/publications/factbook/geos/sg.html
74              </NavigateUrl>
75              <AlternateText>Senegal Information</AlternateText>
76              <Impressions>1</Impressions>
77          </Ad>
78
79          <Ad>
80              <ImageUrl>images/sweden.png</ImageUrl>
81              <NavigateUrl>
82                  http://www.odci.gov/cia/publications/factbook/geos/sw.html
83              </NavigateUrl>
84              <AlternateText>Sweden Information</AlternateText>
85              <Impressions>1</Impressions>
86          </Ad>
87
```

Fig. 17.20 **AdvertisementFile** used in **AdRotator** example. (Part 2 of 3.)

```
88      <Ad>
89          <ImageUrl>images/thailand.png</ImageUrl>
90          <NavigateUrl>
91              http://www.odci.gov/cia/publications/factbook/geos/th.html
92          </NavigateUrl>
93          <AlternateText>Thailand Information</AlternateText>
94          <Impressions>1</Impressions>
95      </Ad>
96
97      <Ad>
98          <ImageUrl>images/unitedstates.png</ImageUrl>
99          <NavigateUrl>
100             http://www.odci.gov/cia/publications/factbook/geos/us.html
101         </NavigateUrl>
102         <AlternateText>United States Information</AlternateText>
103         <Impressions>1</Impressions>
104     </Ad>
105 </Advertisements>
```

Fig. 17.20 **AdvertisementFile** used in **AdRotator** example. (Part 3 of 3.)

17.5.3 Validation Controls

This section introduces a different type of Web control, called a *validation control* (or *validator*), which determines whether the data in another Web control are in the proper format. For example, validators could determine whether a user has provided information in a required field or whether a ZIP-code field contains exactly five digits. Validators provide a mechanism for validating user input on the client. When the HTML for our page is created, the validator is converted into *ECMAScript*[3] that performs the validation. ECMAScript is a scripting language that enhances the functionality and appearance of Web pages. ECMAScript is typically executed on the client. However, if the client does not support scripting or scripting is disabled, validation is performed on the server.

The example in this section prompts the user to input a phone number, in the form 555–4567. After the user enters a number, validators ensure that the phone-number field is filled and that the number is in the correct format before the program sends the number to the Web server. Once the phone number is submitted, the Web Server responds by sending an HTML page containing all possible letter combinations that represent the phone number. The letters used for each digit are the letters found on a phone's key pad. For instance, the 5-button displays the letters J, K and L. For the position in the phone number where there is a 5, we can substitute one of these three letters. Businesses often use this technique to make their phone numbers easy to remember. Figure 17.21 presents the ASPX file.

The HTML page sent to the client browser accepts a phone number in the form **555–4567** and then lists all the possible words that can be generated from both the first three digits and the last four digits. This example uses a ***RegularExpressionValidator***

---

3. ECMAScript (commonly known as JavaScript) is a scripting standard created by the ECMA (European Computer Manufacturer's Association). Both Netscape's JavaScript and Microsoft's JScript implement the ECMAScript standard, but each provides additional features beyond the specification. For information on the current ECMAScript standard, visit **www.ecma.ch** and click the **Publications** link. From here the reader can access a list of ECMA standards documents. The ECMAScript standard will be listed as **ECMA-262**.

```
1   <%-- Fig. 17.21: Generator.aspx                  --%>
2   <%-- A Web Form demonstrating the use of validators. --%>
3
4   <%@ Page Language="vb" AutoEventWireup="false"
5       Codebehind="Generator.aspx.vb"
6       Inherits="WordGenerator.Generator"
7       enableViewState="False" EnableSessionState="False" %>
8
9   <!DOCTYPE HTML PUBLIC "-//W3C//DTD HTML 4.0 Transitional//EN">
10  <HTML>
11      <HEAD>
12          <title>WebForm1</title>
13          <meta name="GENERATOR"
14              content="Microsoft Visual Studio.NET 7.0">
15          <meta name="CODE_LANGUAGE" content="Visual Basic 7.0">
16          <meta name="vs_defaultClientScript" content="JavaScript">
17          <meta name="vs_targetSchema"
18              content="http://schemas.microsoft.com/intellisense/ie5">
19      </HEAD>
20      <body MS_POSITIONING="GridLayout">
21          <form id="Form1" method="post" runat="server">
22
23              <asp:Label id="promptLabel" style="Z-INDEX: 101;
24                  LEFT: 22px; POSITION: absolute; TOP: 17px"
25                  runat="server" EnableViewState="False">
26                  Please enter a phone number in the form 555-4567.
27              </asp:Label>
28
29              <asp:TextBox id="outputTextBox" style="Z-INDEX: 106;
30                  LEFT: 22px; POSITION: absolute; TOP: 118px"
31                  runat="server" TextMode="MultiLine" Visible="False"
32                  EnableViewState="False" Height="198px" Width="227px"
33                  Font-Bold="True" Font-Names="Courier New">
34              </asp:TextBox>
35
36              <asp:RegularExpressionValidator id="phoneNumberValidator"
37                  style="Z-INDEX: 105; LEFT: 196px; POSITION: absolute;
38                  TOP: 70px" runat="server" ErrorMessage=
39                  "The phone number must be in the form 555-4567."
40                  ControlToValidate="phoneTextBox"
41                  ValidationExpression="^\d{3}-\d{4}$">
42              </asp:RegularExpressionValidator>
43
44              <asp:RequiredFieldValidator id="phoneInputValidator"
45                  style="Z-INDEX: 104; LEFT: 196px; POSITION:
46                  absolute; TOP: 45px" runat="server"
47                  ControlToValidate="phoneTextBox"
48                  ErrorMessage=
49                      "Please enter a phone number.">
50              </asp:RequiredFieldValidator>
51
```

Fig. 17.21 Validators used in a Web Form that generates possible letter combinations from a phone number. (Part 1 of 2.)

```
52                  <asp:Button id="submitButton" style="Z-INDEX: 103;
53                     LEFT: 22px; POSITION: absolute; TOP: 77px"
54                     runat="server" Text="Submit">
55                  </asp:Button>
56
57                  <asp:TextBox id="phoneTextBox" style="Z-INDEX: 102;
58                     LEFT: 22px; POSITION: absolute; TOP: 42px"
59                     runat="server">
60                  </asp:TextBox>
61
62         </form>
63      </body>
64   </HTML>
```

Fig. 17.21 Validators used in a Web Form that generates possible letter combinations from a phone number. (Part 2 of 2.)

to match another Web control's content against a regular expression. (The use of regular expressions is introduced in Chapter 12, Strings, Characters and Regular Expressions.) Lines 36–42 create a **RegularExpressionValidator** named **phoneNumber-Validator**. Property **ErrorMessage**'s text (lines 38–39) is displayed on the Web Form if the validation fails. The regular expression that validates the input is assigned to property **ValidationExpression** in line 41. The input is valid if it matches the regular expression **^\d{3}-\d{4}$** (i.e., if exactly 3 digits are followed by a hyphen and exactly 4 digits, where the 3 digits are at the beginning of the string and the 4 digits are at the end of the string).

The clicking of property **ValidationExpression** in the **Properties** window displays a dialog that contains a list of common regular expressions for phone numbers, ZIP codes and other formatted information. However, we write our own regular expression in this example, because the phone number input should not contain an area code. Line 40 associates **phoneTextBox** with **phoneNumberValidator** by setting property **ControlToValidate** to **phoneTextBox**. This indicates that **phoneNumber-Validator** verifies the **phoneTextBox**'s contents. If the user inputs text that does not have the correct format and attempts to submit the form, the **ErrorMessage** text is displayed in red.

This example also uses a **RequiredFieldValidator** to ensure that the text box is not empty when the HTML form is submitted. Lines 44–50 define **RequiredField-Validator phoneInputValidator**, which confirms that **phoneTextBox**'s content is not empty. If the user does not input any data in **phoneTextBox** and attempts to submit the form, validation fails, and the **ErrorMessage** for this validator is displayed in red. If the validator is successful, a multiline **TextBox** named **outputTextBox** (lines 29–34) displays the words generated from the phone number. Notice that the **Visible** property initially is set to **False** when the server returns its HTML response.

Figure 17.22 depicts the code-behind file for the ASPX file in Fig. 17.21. Notice that this code-behind file does not contain any implementation related to the validators. We say more about this soon.

```
1    ' Fig. 17.22: Generator.aspx.vb
2    ' The code-behind file for a page that
3    ' generates words when given a phone number.
4
5    Imports System.Web.UI.WebControls
6
7    Public Class Generator
8       Inherits System.Web.UI.Page
9
10      Protected WithEvents phoneInputValidator As _
11         RequiredFieldValidator
12
13      Protected WithEvents phoneNumberValidator As _
14         RegularExpressionValidator
15
16      Protected WithEvents promptLabel As Label
17      Protected WithEvents outputTextBox As TextBox
18      Protected WithEvents submitButton As Button
19      Protected WithEvents phoneTextBox As TextBox
20
21      ' Web Form Designer generated code
22
23      Private Sub Page_Load(ByVal sender As System.Object, _
24         ByVal e As System.EventArgs) Handles MyBase.Load
25
26         ' if not first time page loads
27         If IsPostBack Then
28            Dim number As String
29
30            outputTextBox.Text() = ""
31
32            ' retrieve number and remove "-"
33            number = Request.Form("phoneTextBox")
34            number = number.Remove(3, 1)
35
36            ' generate words for first 3 digits
37            outputTextBox.Text &= "Here are the words for the " & _
38               "first three digits" & vbCrLf
39
40            ComputeWords(number.Substring(0, 3), "")
41            outputTextBox.Text &= vbCrLf
42
43            ' generate words for last 4 digits
44            outputTextBox.Text &= "Here are the words for the " & _
45               "last 4 digits" & vbCrLf
46
47            ComputeWords(number.Substring(3), "")
48
49            outputTextBox.Visible = True
50         End If
51
52      End Sub ' Page_Load
53
```

Fig. 17.22 Code-behind file for the word-generator page. (Part 1 of 4.)

```
54    Private Sub ComputeWords(ByVal number As String, _
55       ByVal temporaryWord As String)
56
57       Dim current As Integer
58
59       ' if number is empty, print word
60       If number = "" Then
61          outputTextBox.Text &= temporaryWord & vbCrLf
62          Return
63       End If
64
65       ' retrieve first number and convert to Integer
66       current = Convert.ToInt32(number.Substring(0, 1))
67
68       ' delete first number
69       number = number.Remove(0, 1)
70
71       ' determine number, call ComputeWord recursively
72       Select Case current
73
74          ' 0 can be q or z
75          Case 0
76             ComputeWords(number, temporaryWord & "Q")
77             ComputeWords(number, temporaryWord & "Z")
78
79             ' 1 has no letter associated with it
80          Case 1
81             ComputeWords(number, temporaryWord & "")
82
83             ' 2 can be a, b or c
84          Case 2
85             ComputeWords(number, temporaryWord & "A")
86             ComputeWords(number, temporaryWord & "B")
87             ComputeWords(number, temporaryWord & "C")
88
89             ' 3 can be d, e or f
90          Case 3
91             ComputeWords(number, temporaryWord & "D")
92             ComputeWords(number, temporaryWord & "E")
93             ComputeWords(number, temporaryWord & "F")
94
95             ' 4 can be g, h or i
96          Case 4
97             ComputeWords(number, temporaryWord & "G")
98             ComputeWords(number, temporaryWord & "H")
99             ComputeWords(number, temporaryWord & "I")
100
101            ' 5 can be j, k or l
102         Case 5
103            ComputeWords(number, temporaryWord & "J")
104            ComputeWords(number, temporaryWord & "K")
105            ComputeWords(number, temporaryWord & "L")
106
```

Fig. 17.22 Code-behind file for the word-generator page. (Part 2 of 4.)

```
107                  ' 6 can be m, n or o
108            Case 6
109               ComputeWords(number, temporaryWord & "M")
110               ComputeWords(number, temporaryWord & "N")
111               ComputeWords(number, temporaryWord & "O")
112
113                  ' 7 can be p, r or s
114            Case 7
115               ComputeWords(number, temporaryWord & "P")
116               ComputeWords(number, temporaryWord & "R")
117               ComputeWords(number, temporaryWord & "S")
118
119                  ' 8 can be t, u or v
120            Case 8
121               ComputeWords(number, temporaryWord & "T")
122               ComputeWords(number, temporaryWord & "U")
123               ComputeWords(number, temporaryWord & "V")
124
125                  ' 9 can be w, x or y
126            Case 9
127               ComputeWords(number, temporaryWord & "W")
128               ComputeWords(number, temporaryWord & "X")
129               ComputeWords(number, temporaryWord & "Y")
130         End Select
131
132      End Sub ' ComputeWords
133   End Class ' Generator
```

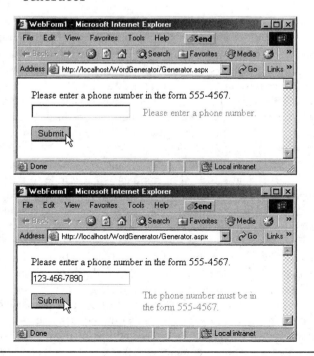

Fig. 17.22 Code-behind file for the word-generator page. (Part 3 of 4.)

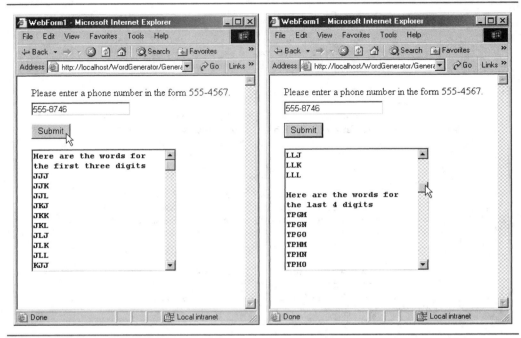

Fig. 17.22 Code-behind file for the word-generator page. (Part 4 of 4.)

Web programmers using ASP .NET often design their Web pages so that the current page reloads when the user submits the form; this enables the program to receive input, process it as necessary and display the results in the same page when it is reloaded. These pages usually contain a form that, when submitted, causes the current page to be requested again. This event is known as a *postback*. Line 27 uses the ***IsPostBack*** property of class **Page** to determine whether the page is being loaded due to a postback. The first time that the Web page is requested, **IsPostBack** is **False**. When the postback occurs (from the users clicking of **Submit**), **IsPostBack** is **True**. To prepare the **outputTextBox** for display, its **Text** property is set to an empty string (**""**) in line 30. Line 33 then uses the ***Request*** object to retrieve **phoneTextBox**'s value from the ***Form*** array. When data is posted to the Web server, the HTML **form**'s data is accessible to the Web application through the **Request** object's **Form** array. The hyphen is **Remove**d from the phone number string in line 34. Method **ComputeWords** is passed a substring containing the first three numbers and an empty **String** (line 40). Line 49 sets the **outputTextBox**'s **Visible** property to **True**.

Method **ComputeWords**, defined in lines 54–132, is a recursive method that generates the list of words from the **String** containing the digits of the phone number, minus the hyphen. The first argument, **number**, contains the digits that are being converted to letters. The first call to this method (line 40) passes in the first three digits, and the second call (line 47) passes in the last four digits. The second argument, **temporaryWord**, builds up the list that is displayed by the program. Each time this method is called, as we will see shortly, **number** contains one less character than the previous call and **temporaryWord** contains one more character more than the previous call. Lines 60–63 define the base case, which occurs when **number** equals the empty string. When this occurs, the **temporary-Word** that has been built up from the previous calls is added to **outputTextBox**, and the method returns.

Let us discuss how **ComputeWords** works when we do not have the base case. On line 57, we declare variable **current** and initialize its value to the first character in **number**. We then remove this character from **number**. The remainder of the method uses a **Select Case** structure (lines 72–130) to make the correct recursive calls based on the number in **current**. For each digit, we wish to add the appropriate letter to **temporaryWord**. For most of the digits, there are two or three letters that can be represented by the number in **current**. The keypad button for the number 3, for instance, also represents the letters d, e or f. In this example we want to exhaust all possible letter combinations, so we make a recursive call to **ComputeWords** for each option (lines 91–93). Each call passes **number** as the first argument (which contains one digit fewer, as a result of the call to method **Remove** on line 69). The second argument contains **temporary-Word**, concatenated with the new letter. Each call continues to add a letter for the current number, until all the numbers have been processed. At this point we reach the base case, and **temporaryWord** is appended to **outputTextBox**.

Figure 17.23 shows the HTML sent to the client browser. Notice that lines 25–28 and lines 71–113 contain ECMAScript, which provides the implementation for the validation controls. Visual Studio generates this ECMAScript. The programmer does not need to be able to create or even understand ECMAScript—the functionality defined for the controls in our application is converted to working ECMAScript for us.

```
1   <!-- Fig. 17.23: Generator.html                        -->
2   <!-- The HTML page that is sent to the client browser. -->
3
4   <!DOCTYPE HTML PUBLIC "-//W3C//DTD HTML 4.0 Transitional//EN" >
5   <HTML>
6      <HEAD>
7         <title>WebForm1</title>
8         <meta name="GENERATOR"
9            content="Microsoft Visual Studio 7.0">
10        <meta name="CODE_LANGUAGE" content="Visual Basic 7.0" >
11        <meta name="vs_defaultClientScript"
12           content="JavaScript">
13        <meta name="vs_targetSchema"
14           content="http://schemas.microsoft.com/intellisense/ie5">
15     </HEAD>
16
17     <body MS_POSITIONING="GridLayout">
18
19        <form name="Form1" method="post"
20           action="Generator.aspx" language="javascript"
21           onsubmit="ValidatorOnSubmit();" id="FORM1">
22           <input type="hidden" name="__VIEWSTATE"
23              value="dDwxMjgyMzM3ozs+" />
24
25           <script language="javascript"
```

Fig. 17.23 HTML and JavaScript sent to the client browser. (Part 1 of 3.)

```
26              src=
27          "/aspnet_client/system_web/1_0_3215_11/WebUIValidation.js">
28          </script>
29
30          <span id="phoneNumberValidator"
31             controltovalidate="phoneTextBox"
32             errormessage=
33                "The phone number must be in the form 555-4567."
34             evaluationfunction=
35                "RegularExpressionValidatorEvaluateIsValid"
36             validationexpression="^\d{3}-\d{4}$"
37             style="color:Red;Z-INDEX:106;LEFT:217px;
38                POSITION:absolute;TOP:73px;visibility:hidden;">
39                The phone number must be in the form 555-4567.
40          </span>
41
42          <input name="phoneTextBox" type="text"
43             id="phoneTextBox"
44             style="Z-INDEX: 102; LEFT: 16px;
45             POSITION: absolute; TOP: 52px" />
46
47          <input type="submit" name="submitButton"
48             value="Submit"
49             onclick= "if ( " +
50                "typeof(Page_ClientValidate) == 'function') " +
51                "Page_ClientValidate(); " language="javascript"
52                id="submitButton" style="Z-INDEX: 103;
53             LEFT: 16px;
54             POSITION: absolute;
55             TOP: 86px" />
56
57          <span id="phoneInputValidator"
58             controltovalidate="phoneTextBox"
59             errormessage="Please enter a phone number."
60             evaluationfunction=
61                "RequiredFieldValidatorEvaluateIsValid"
62             initialvalue="" style="color:Red;Z-INDEX:105;
63                LEFT:217px;POSITION:absolute;TOP:47px;
64                visibility:hidden;">Please enter a phone number.
65          </span>
66
67          <span id="promptLabel" style="Z-INDEX: 101;
68             LEFT: 16px; POSITION: absolute; TOP: 23px">
69             Please enter a phone number in the form 555-4567:
70          </span>
71
72          <script language="javascript">
73          <!--
74             var Page_Validators = new Array(
75                document.all["phoneNumberValidator"],
76                document.all["phoneInputValidator"] );
77          // -->
78          </script>
```

Fig. 17.23 HTML and JavaScript sent to the client browser. (Part 2 of 3.)

```
79
80          <script language="javascript">
81          <!--
82              var Page_ValidationActive = false;
83
84              if (
85                  typeof(clientInformation) != "undefined" &&
86                  clientInformation.appName.indexOf("Explorer")
87                  != -1 ) {
88
89                  if ( typeof(Page_ValidationVer) == "undefined" )
90                      alert(
91                          "Unable to find script library " +
92                          "'/aspnet_client/system_web/'"+
93                          "'1_0_3215_11/WebUIValidation.js'. " +
94                          "Try placing this file manually, or " +
95                          "reinstall by running 'aspnet_regiis -c'.");
96                  else if ( Page_ValidationVer != "125" )
97                      alert(
98                          "This page uses an incorrect version " +
99                          "of WebUIValidation.js. The page " +
100                         "expects version 125. " +
101                         "The script library is " +
102                         Page_ValidationVer + ".");
103                 else
104                     ValidatorOnLoad();
105             }
106
107             function ValidatorOnSubmit() {
108                 if (Page_ValidationActive) {
109                     ValidatorCommonOnSubmit();
110                 }
111             }
112         // -->
113         </script>
114      </form>
115   </body>
116 </HTML>
```

Fig. 17.23 HTML and JavaScript sent to the client browser. (Part 3 of 3.)

In earlier ASPX files, we explicitly set the **EnableViewState** attribute to **False**. This attribute determines whether a Web control's value persists (i.e., is retained) when a postback occurs. By default, this attribute is **true**, which indicates that control values persist. In the screen shots (Fig. 17.22), notice that the phone number input still appears in the text box after the postback occurs. A **hidden** input in the HTML document (line 22–23) contains the data of the controls on this page. This element is always named __**VIEWSTATE** and stores the controls' data as an encoded string.

Performance Tip 17.2

*The setting of **EnableViewState** to **false** reduces the amount of data passed to the Web server.*

17.6 Session Tracking

Originally, critics accused the Internet and e-business of failing to provide the kind of customized service typically experienced in bricks-and-mortar stores. To address this problem, e-businesses began to establish mechanisms by which they could personalize users' browsing experiences, tailoring content to individual users while enabling them to bypass irrelevant information. Businesses achieve this level of service by tracking each customer's movement through the Internet and combining the collected data with information provided by the consumer, including billing information, personal preferences, interests and hobbies.

Personalization makes it possible for e-businesses to communicate effectively with their customers and also improves users' ability to locate desired products and services. Companies that provide content of particular interest to users can establish relationships with customers and build on those relationships over time. Furthermore, by targeting consumers with personal offers, advertisements, promotions and services, e-businesses create customer loyalty. At such Web sites as **MSN.com** and **CNN.com**, sophisticated technology allows visitors to customize home pages to suit their individual needs and preferences. Similarly, online shopping sites often store personal information for customers and target them with notifications and special offers tailored to their interests. Such services can create customer bases that visit sites more frequently and make purchases from those sites more regularly.

A trade-off exists, however, between personalized e-business service and protection of *privacy*. Whereas some consumers embrace the idea of tailored content, others fear that the release of information that they provide to e-businesses or that is collected about them by tracking technologies will have adverse consequences on their lives. Consumers and privacy advocates ask: What if the e-business to which we give personal data sells or gives that information to another organization without our knowledge? What if we do not want our actions on the Internet—a supposedly anonymous medium—to be tracked and recorded by unknown parties? What if unauthorized parties gain access to sensitive private data, such as credit-card numbers or medical history? All of these are questions that must be debated and addressed by consumers, e-businesses and lawmakers alike.

To provide personalized services to consumers, e-businesses must be able to recognize clients when they request information from a site. As we have discussed, the request/response system on which the Web operates is facilitated by HTTP. Unfortunately, HTTP is a stateless protocol—it does not support persistent connections that would enable Web servers to maintain state information regarding particular clients. This means that Web servers have no capacity to determine whether a request comes from a particular client or whether the same or different clients generate a series of requests. To circumvent this problem, sites such as **MSN.com** and **CNN.com** provide mechanisms by which they identify individual clients. A session represents a unique client on the Internet. If the client leaves a site and then returns later, the client will still be recognized as the same user. To help the server distinguish among clients, each client must identify itself to the server. The tracking of individual clients, known as *session tracking*, can be achieved in a number of ways. One popular technique involves the use of cookies (Section 17.6.1); another employs .NET's **HttpSessionState** object (Section 17.6.2). Additional session-tracking techniques include the use of input form elements of type **"hidden"** and URL rewriting. Using **"hidden"** form elements, a Web Form can write session-tracking data into a **form** in the Web page that it returns to the client in response to a prior request. When the user submits the form in the new Web page, all the form data, including the **"hidden"** fields, are sent to the form handler on the Web server. When a Web site employs URL rewriting, the Web Form embeds session-tracking information directly in the URLs of hyperlinks that the user clicks to send subsequent requests to the Web server.

The reader should note that, in previous examples, we usually set the Web Form's **EnableSessionState** property to **false**. However, because we wish to use session tracking in the following examples, we leave this property in its default mode, which is **true**.

17.6.1 Cookies

A popular way to customize interactions with Web pages is via *cookies*. A cookie is a text file stored by a Web site on an individual's computer that allows the site to track the actions of the visitor. The first time that a user visits the Web site, the user's computer might receive a cookie; this cookie is then reactivated each time the user revisits that site. The collected information is intended to be an anonymous record containing data that are used to personalize the user's future visits to the site. For example, cookies in a shopping application might store unique identifiers for users. When a user adds items to an online shopping cart or performs another task resulting in a request to the Web server, the server receives a cookie containing the user's unique identifier. The server then uses the unique identifier to locate the shopping cart and perform any necessary processing.

In addition to identifying users, cookies also can indicate clients' shopping preferences. When a Web Form receives a request from a client, the Web Form could examine the cookie(s) it sent to the client during previous communications, identify the client's preferences and immediately display products that are of interest to the client.

Every HTTP-based interaction between a client and a server includes a header containing information either about the request (when the communication is from the client to the server) or about the response (when the communication is from the server to the client). When a Web Form receives a request, the header includes information such as the request type (e.g., **GET**) and any cookies that have been sent previously from the server to be stored on the client machine. When the server formulates its response, the header information includes any cookies the server wants to store on the client computer and other information, such as the MIME type of the response.

If the programmer of a cookie does not set an *expiration date*, the Web browser maintains the cookie for the duration of the browsing session. Otherwise, the Web browser maintains the cookie until the expiration date occurs. When the browser requests a resource from a Web server, cookies previously sent to the client by that Web server are returned to the Web server as part of the request formulated by the browser. Cookies are deleted when they *expire*. The expiration date of a cookie can be set in that cookie's **Expires** property.

The next Web application demonstrates the use of cookies. The example contains two pages. In the first page (Fig. 17.24 and Fig. 17.25), users select a favorite programming language from a group of radio buttons and then submit the HTML **form** to the Web server for processing. The Web server responds by creating a cookie that stores a record of the chosen language, as well as the ISBN number for a book on that topic. The server then returns an HTML document to the browser, allowing the user either to select another favorite programming language or to view the second page in our application (Fig. 17.26 and Fig. 17.27), which lists recommended books pertaining to the programming language that the user selected previously. When the user clicks the hyperlink, the cookies previously stored on the client are read and used to form the list of book recommendations.

```
1    <%-- Fig. 17.24: OptionsPage.aspx                    --%>
2    <%-- allows clients to select a programming language --%>
3    <%-- to get recommendations.                         --%>
4
5    <%@ Page Language="vb" AutoEventWireup="false"
6       Codebehind="OptionsPage.aspx.vb"
7       Inherits="Cookies.Cookie"%>
8
9    <!DOCTYPE HTML PUBLIC "-//W3C//DTD HTML 4.0 Transitional//EN">
10   <HTML>
11      <HEAD>
12         <title>Cookies</title>
13         <meta content="Microsoft Visual Studio.NET 7.0"
14            name="GENERATOR">
15         <meta content="Visual Basic 7.0" name="CODE_LANGUAGE">
16         <meta content="JavaScript" name="vs_defaultClientScript">
17         <meta name="vs_targetSchema"
18            content="http://schemas.microsoft.com/intellisense/ie5">
19      </HEAD>
20      <body MS_POSITIONING="GridLayout">
21         <form id="Form1" method="post" runat="server">
22
23            <asp:label id="promptLabel" style="Z-INDEX: 101;
24               LEFT: 42px; POSITION: absolute; TOP: 22px"
25               runat="server" Font-Bold="True" Font-Size="Large">
26               Select a programming language.
27            </asp:label>
28
29            <asp:radiobuttonlist id="LanguageList"
30               style="Z-INDEX: 111; LEFT: 42px; POSITION:
31               absolute; TOP: 52px" runat="server">
32
33               <asp:ListItem Value="Visual Basic .NET"
34                  >Visual Basic .NET</asp:ListItem>
35
36               <asp:ListItem Value="C#">C#</asp:ListItem>
37               <asp:ListItem Value="C">C</asp:ListItem>
38               <asp:ListItem Value="C++">C++</asp:ListItem>
39               <asp:ListItem Value="Python">Python</asp:ListItem>
40            </asp:radiobuttonlist>
41
42            <asp:hyperlink id="recommendationsLink"
43               style="Z-INDEX: 110; LEFT: 42px; POSITION:
44               absolute; TOP: 90px" runat="server"
45               Visible="False" NavigateUrl=
46               "RecommendationPage.aspx">
47               Click here to get book recommendations
48            </asp:hyperlink>
49
50            <asp:hyperlink id="languageLink" style="Z-INDEX:
51               109; LEFT: 42px; POSITION: absolute;
52               TOP: 55px" runat="server" Visible="False"
53               NavigateUrl="OptionsPage.aspx">
```

Fig. 17.24 ASPX file that presents a list of programming languages. (Part 1 of 2.)

```
54                     Click here to choose another language
55              </asp:hyperlink>
56
57              <asp:label id="welcomeLabel" style="Z-INDEX: 108;
58                 LEFT: 42px; POSITION: absolute; TOP: 23px"
59                 runat="server" Visible="False" Font-Bold="True"
60                 Font-Size="Large">Welcome to cookies! You selected
61              </asp:label>
62
63              <asp:button id="submitButton" style="Z-INDEX: 107;
64                 LEFT: 42px; POSITION: absolute; TOP: 196px"
65                 runat="server" Text="Submit">
66              </asp:button>
67
68          </form>
69       </body>
70    </HTML>
```

Fig. 17.24 ASPX file that presents a list of programming languages. (Part 2 of 2.)

The ASPX file in Fig. 17.24 contains five radio buttons (lines 29–40), having the values **Visual Basic .NET**, **C#**, **C**, **C++**, and **Python**. A programmer sets these values by clicking the **Items** property in the **Properties** window and then adding items via the **List Item Collection Editor**. This process is similar to the customizing of a **ListBox** in a Windows application. The user selects a programming language by clicking one of the radio buttons. The page contains a **Submit** button, which, when clicked, creates a cookie containing a record of the selected language. Once created, this cookie is added to the HTTP response header, and a postback occurs. Each time the user chooses a language and clicks **Submit**, a cookie is written to the client.

When the postback occurs, certain components are hidden and others are displayed. Towards the bottom of the page, two hyperlinks are displayed: One that requests this page (lines 50–55), and one that requests **Recommendations.aspx** (lines 42–48). Notice that clicking the first hyperlink (the one that requests the current page) does not cause a postback to occur. The file **OptionsPage.aspx** is specified in the **NavigateUrl** property of the hyperlink. When the hyperlink is clicked, this page is requested as a completely new request.

Figure 17.25 presents the code-behind file. Line 14 defines **books** as a **Hashtable** (namespace **System.Collections**), which is a data structure that stores *key–value pairs* (we introduced hash tables briefly in Chapter 12, Strings, Characters and Regular Expressions). The program uses the key to store and retrieve the associated value in the **Hashtable**. In this example, the keys are **String**s containing the programming language name's and the values are **String**s containing the ISBN numbers for the recommended books. Class **Hashtable** provides method *Add*, which takes as arguments a key and a value. A value that is added via method **Add** is placed in the **Hashtable** at a location determined by the key. The value for a specific **Hashtable** entry can be determined by indexing the hash table with that value's key. For instance,

> *HashtableName* (*keyName*)

returns the value in the key-value pair in which *keyName* is the key. An example of this is shown in line 65; **books(language)** returns the value that corresponds to the key contained in **language**. Class **Hashtable** is discussed in detail in Chapter 20, Data Structures and Collections.

```
1    ' Fig. 17.25: OptionsPage.aspx.vb
2    ' Page that allows the user to choose a different language.
3
4    Imports System.Web.UI.WebControls
5
6    Public Class Cookie
7        Inherits System.Web.UI.Page
8        Protected WithEvents languageLink As HyperLink
9        Protected WithEvents recommendationsLink As HyperLink
10       Protected WithEvents promptLabel As Label
11       Protected WithEvents LanguageList As RadioButtonList
12       Protected WithEvents welcomeLabel As Label
13       Protected WithEvents submitButton As Button
14       Private books = New Hashtable()
15
16       ' Visual Studio .NET generated code
17
18       Private Sub Page_Init(ByVal sender As System.Object, _
19          ByVal e As System.EventArgs) Handles MyBase.Init
20
21          InitializeComponent()
22
23          ' add values to Hastable
24          books.Add("Visual Basic .NET", "0-13-456955-5")
25          books.Add("C#", "0-13-062221-4")
26          books.Add("C", "0-13-089572-5")
27          books.Add("C++", "0-13-089571-7")
28          books.Add("Python", "0-13-092361-3")
29       End Sub ' Page_Init
30
31       Private Sub Page_Load(ByVal sender As System.Object, _
32          ByVal e As System.EventArgs) Handles MyBase.Load
33
34          If IsPostBack Then
35
36             ' if postback is True, user has submitted information
37             ' display welcome message and appropriate hyperlinks
38             welcomeLabel.Visible = True
39             languageLink.Visible = True
40             recommendationsLink.Visible = True
41
42             ' hide option information
43             submitButton.Visible = False
44             promptLabel.Visible = False
45             LanguageList.Visible = False
46
47             If (LanguageList.SelectedItem Is Nothing) = False Then
48                welcomeLabel.Text &= " " & _
49                   LanguageList.SelectedItem.Text.ToString & "."
```

Fig. 17.25 Code-behind file that writes cookies to the client. (Part 1 of 3.)

```
50              Else
51                  welcomeLabel.Text &= "no language."
52              End If
53          End If
54      End Sub ' Page_Load
55
56      Private Sub submitButton_Click(ByVal sender As System.Object, _
57          ByVal e As System.EventArgs) Handles submitButton.Click
58
59          Dim language, ISBN As String
60          Dim cookie As HttpCookie
61
62          ' if choice was made by user
63          If (LanguageList.SelectedItem Is Nothing) = False Then
64              language = LanguageList.SelectedItem.ToString()
65              ISBN = books(language).ToString()
66
67              ' create cookie, name/value pair is
68              ' language chosen and ISBN number from Hashtable
69              cookie = New HttpCookie(language, ISBN)
70
71              ' add cookie to response,
72              ' thus placing it on user's machine
73              Response.Cookies.Add(cookie)
74          End If
75
76      End Sub ' submitButton_Click
77  End Class ' Cookie
```

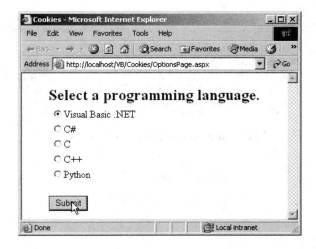

Fig. 17.25 Code-behind file that writes cookies to the client. (Part 2 of 3.)

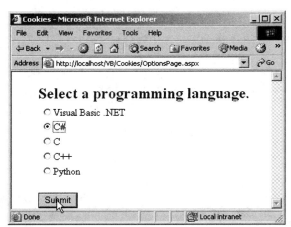

Fig. 17.25 Code-behind file that writes cookies to the client. (Part 3 of 3.)

Clicking the **Submit** button creates a cookie if a language is selected and causes a postback to occur. A new cookie object (of type ***HttpCookie***) is created to store the **language** and its corresponding **ISBN** number (line 69). This cookie is then **Add**ed to the ***Cookies*** collection sent as part of the HTTP response header (line 73). The postback causes the condition in the **If** structure of **Page_Load** (line 34) to evaluate to **True**, and lines 38–53 execute. Line 47 determines whether the user selected a language. If so, that language is displayed in **welcomeLabel** (lines 48–49). Otherwise, text indicating that a language was not selected is displayed in **welcomeLabel** (line 51). The two hyperlinks are made visible on lines 38–39.

After the postback request, the user may request a book recommendation. The book recommendation hyperlink forwards the user to **RecomendationPage.aspx** (Fig. 17.26) to display a recommendation.

```
1   <%-- Fig. 17.26: RecommendationPage.aspx        --%>
2   <%-- Displays book recommendations using cookies. --%>
3
4   <%@ Page Language="vb" AutoEventWireup="false"
5      Codebehind="RecommendationPage.aspx.vb"
6      Inherits="Cookies.Recommendations"%>
7
8   <!DOCTYPE HTML PUBLIC "-//W3C//DTD HTML 4.0 Transitional//EN">
9   <HTML>
10     <HEAD>
11        <title>Book recommendations</title>
12        <meta content="Microsoft Visual Studio.NET 7.0"
13          name="GENERATOR">
14        <meta content="Visual Basic 7.0" name="CODE_LANGUAGE">
15        <meta content="JavaScript" name="vs_defaultClientScript">
16        <meta name="vs_targetSchema"
17          content="http://schemas.microsoft.com/intellisense/ie5">
18     </HEAD>
19     <body MS_POSITIONING="GridLayout">
20        <form id="Form1" method="post" runat="server">
21
22           <asp:label id="recommendationsLabel"
23              style="Z-INDEX: 101; LEFT: 55px; POSITION:
24              absolute; TOP: 38px" runat="server"
25              Font-Size="X-Large">Recommendations
26           </asp:label>
27
28           <asp:listbox id="booksListBox" style="Z-INDEX: 102;
29              LEFT: 50px; POSITION: absolute; TOP: 80px"
30              runat="server" Width="442px" Height="125px">
31           </asp:listbox>
32
33        </form>
34     </body>
35   </HTML>
```

Fig. 17.26 ASPX page that displays book information.

RecommendationsPage.aspx contains a label (lines 22–26) and a list box (lines 28–31). The label displays the text **Recommendations** if the user has selected one or more languages; otherwise, it displays **No Recommendations**. The list box displays the recommendations created by the code-behind file, which is shown in Fig. 17.27.

Method **Page_Init** (lines 13–43) retrieves the cookies from the client, using the **Request** object's **Cookies** property (line 22). This returns a collection of type *Http-CookieCollection*, containing cookies that have previously been written to the client. Cookies can be read by an application only if they were created in the domain in which our application is running—a Web server can never access cookies created outside the domain associated with that server. For example, a cookie created by a Web server in the **deitel.com** domain cannot be downloaded by a Web server in the **bug2bug.com** domain.

```vb
1    ' Fig. 17.27: RecommendationsPage.aspx.vb
2    ' Reading cookie data from the client.
3
4    Imports System.Web.UI.WebControls
5
6    Public Class Recommendations
7       Inherits Page
8       Protected WithEvents recommendationsLabel As Label
9       Protected WithEvents booksListBox As ListBox
10
11      ' Visual Studio .NET generated code
12
13      Private Sub Page_Init(ByVal sender As System.Object, _
14         ByVal e As System.EventArgs) Handles MyBase.Init
15
16         InitializeComponent()
17
18         ' retrieve client's cookies
19         Dim cookies As HttpCookieCollection
20         Dim i As Integer
21
22         cookies = Request.Cookies
23
24         ' if there are cookies besides the ID cookie,
25         ' list appropriate books and ISBN numbers
26         If (((cookies Is Nothing) = False) _
27            AndAlso cookies.Count <> 1) Then
28
29            For i = 1 To cookies.Count - 1
30               booksListBox.Items.Add(cookies(i).Name & _
31                  " How to Program. ISBN#: " & _
32                  cookies(i).Value)
33            Next
34
35            ' if no cookies besides ID, no options were
36            ' chosen. no recommendations made
```

Fig. 17.27 Cookies being read from a client in an ASP .NET application. (Part 1 of 2.)

```
37              Else
38                  recommendationsLabel.Text = "No Recommendations"
39                  booksListBox.Items.Clear()
40                  booksListBox.Visible = False
41              End If
42
43          End Sub ' Page_Init
44
45          Private Sub Page_Load(ByVal sender As System.Object, _
46              ByVal e As System.EventArgs) Handles MyBase.Load
47
48              ' Put user code to initialize the page here
49          End Sub ' Page_Load
50      End Class ' Recommendations
```

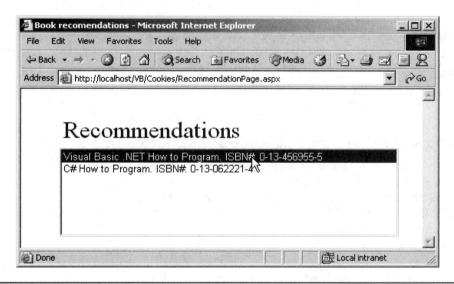

Fig. 17.27 Cookies being read from a client in an ASP .NET application. (Part 2 of 2.)

Lines 26–27 determine whether at least two cookies exist. ASP .NET always adds a cookie named **ASP.NET_SessionId** to the response, so lines 26–27 ensure that there is at least one cookie besides the **ASP.NET_SessionId** cookie. Lines 29–33 add the information in the other cookie(s) to our list box. The **For** structure iterates through all the cookies except for the first one, the **ASP.NET_SessionID** cookie. The application retrieves the name and value of each cookie by using **i**, the control variable in our **For** structure, to determine the current value in our cookie collection. The **Name** and **Value** properties of class **HttpCookie** containing the language and corresponding ISBN, respectively, are concatenated with **" How to Program. ISBN# "** and added to the **ListBox**. The list box displays a maximum of five books. Lines 38–40 execute if no language was selected. We summarize some commonly used **HttpCookie** properties in Fig. 17.28.

Properties	Description
Domain	Returns a **String** containing the cookie's domain (i.e., the domain of the Web server from which the cookie was downloaded). This determines which Web servers can receive the cookie. By default, cookies are sent to the Web server that originally sent the cookie to the client.
Expires	Returns a **DateTime** object indicating when the browser can delete the cookie.
Name	Returns a **String** containing the cookie's name.
Path	Returns a **String** containing the URL prefix for the cookie. Cookies can be "targeted" to specific URLs that include directories on the Web server, enabling the programmer to specify the location of the cookie. By default, a cookie is returned to services operating in the same directory as the service that sent the cookie or a subdirectory of that directory.
Secure	Returns a **Boolean** value indicating whether the cookie should be transmitted through a secure protocol. The value **True** causes a secure protocol to be used.
Value	Returns a **String** containing the cookie's value.

Fig. 17.28 **HttpCookie** properties.

17.6.2 Session Tracking with **HttpSessionState**

Visual Basic provides session-tracking capabilities in the Framework Class Library's **HttpSessionState** class. To demonstrate basic session-tracking techniques, we modified Fig. 17.27 so that it employs **HttpSessionState** objects. Figure 17.29 presents the ASPX file, and Fig. 17.30 presents the code-behind file. The ASPX file is similar to that presented in Fig. 17.24.

```
1   <%-- Fig. 17.29: OptionsPage.aspx     --%>
2   <%-- displays a list of book options --%>
3
4   <%@ Page Language="vb" AutoEventWireup="false"
5      Codebehind="OptionsPage.aspx.vb"
6      Inherits="Sessions.Options2"%>
7
8   <!DOCTYPE HTML PUBLIC "-//W3C//DTD HTML 4.0 Transitional//EN">
9   <HTML>
10    <HEAD>
11       <title>Session Tracking</title>
12       <meta name="GENERATOR"
13          content="Microsoft Visual Studio.NET 7.0">
14       <meta name="CODE_LANGUAGE" content="Visual Basic 7.0">
15       <meta name="vs_defaultClientScript" content="JavaScript">
16       <meta name="vs_targetSchema"
17          content="http://schemas.microsoft.com/intellisense/ie5">
18    </HEAD>
```

Fig. 17.29 Options supplied on an ASPX page. (Part 1 of 3.)

```
19      <body MS_POSITIONING="GridLayout">
20         <form id="Form1" method="post" runat="server">
21
22            <asp:label id="promptLabel" style="Z-INDEX: 106;
23               LEFT: 43px; POSITION: absolute; TOP: 32px"
24               runat="server" Font-Bold="True" Font-Size="Large">
25               Select a programming language.
26            </asp:label>
27
28            <asp:Label id="timeOutLabel" style="Z-INDEX: 108;
29               LEFT: 42px; POSITION: absolute; TOP: 100px"
30               runat="server">
31            </asp:Label>
32
33            <asp:Label id="idLabel" style="Z-INDEX: 107;
34               LEFT: 42px; POSITION: absolute; TOP: 66px"
35               runat="server">
36            </asp:Label>
37
38            <asp:radiobuttonlist id="LanguageList" style="Z-INDEX: 105;
39               LEFT: 43px; POSITION: absolute; TOP: 69px" runat="server">
40
41               <asp:ListItem Value="Visual Basic .NET"
42                  Selected="True">Visual Basic .NET</asp:ListItem>
43
44               <asp:ListItem Value="C#">C#</asp:ListItem>
45               <asp:ListItem Value="C">C</asp:ListItem>
46               <asp:ListItem Value="C++">C++</asp:ListItem>
47               <asp:ListItem Value="Python">Python</asp:ListItem>
48            </asp:radiobuttonlist>
49
50            <asp:hyperlink id="recommendationsLink" style="Z-INDEX: 104;
51               LEFT: 42px; POSITION: absolute; TOP: 172px"
52               runat="server" NavigateUrl="RecommendationPage.aspx"
53               Visible="False">
54               Click here to get book recommendations
55            </asp:hyperlink>
56
57            <asp:hyperlink id="languageLink" style="Z-INDEX: 103;
58               LEFT: 42px; POSITION: absolute; TOP: 137px"
59               runat="server" NavigateUrl="OptionsPage.aspx"
60               Visible="False">
61               Click here to choose another language
62            </asp:hyperlink>
63
64            <asp:label id="welcomeLabel" style="Z-INDEX: 102;
65               LEFT: 42px; POSITION: absolute; TOP: 32px"
66               runat="server" Visible="False" Font-Bold="True"
67               Font-Size="Large">Welcome to sessions! You selected
68            </asp:label>
69
```

Fig. 17.29 Options supplied on an ASPX page. (Part 2 of 3.)

```
70                <asp:button id="submitButton" style="Z-INDEX: 101;
71                    LEFT: 42px; POSITION: absolute; TOP: 207px"
72                    runat="server" Text="Submit">
73                </asp:button>
74
75            </form>
76        </body>
77    </HTML>
```

Fig. 17.29 Options supplied on an ASPX page. (Part 3 of 3.)

Every Web Form includes an **HttpSessionState** object, which is accessible through property **Session** of class **Page**. Throughout this section, we use property **Session** to manipulate our page's **HttpSessionState** object. When the Web page is requested, an **HttpSessionState** object is created and assigned to the **Page**'s **Session** property. As a result, we often refer to property **Session** as the **Session** object. When the user presses **Submit**, **submitButton_Click** is invoked in the code-behind file (Fig. 17.30). Method **submitButton_Click** responds by adding a key-value pair to our **Session** object, specifying the language chosen and the ISBN number for a book on that language. These key-value pairs are often referred to as *session items*. Next, a postback occurs. Each time the user clicks **Submit**, **submitButton_Click** adds a new session item to the **HttpSessionState** object. Because much of this example is identical to the last example, we concentrate on the new features.

```
1    ' Fig. 17.30: OptionsPage.aspx.vb
2    ' A listing of programming languages,
3    ' cookie is created based on choice made.
4
5    Imports System.Web.UI.WebControls
6
7    Public Class Options2
8        Inherits System.Web.UI.Page
9        Protected WithEvents languageLink As HyperLink
10       Protected WithEvents recommendationsLink As HyperLink
11       Protected WithEvents LanguageList As RadioButtonList
12       Protected WithEvents idLabel As Label
13       Protected WithEvents timeOutLabel As Label
14       Protected WithEvents promptLabel As Label
15       Protected WithEvents welcomeLabel As Label
16       Protected WithEvents submitButton As Button
17       Private books = New Hashtable()
18
19       ' Visual Studio .NET generated code
20
21       Private Sub Page_Init(ByVal sender As System.Object, _
22           ByVal e As System.EventArgs) Handles MyBase.Init
23
24           InitializeComponent()
25
```

Fig. 17.30 Sessions are created for each user in an ASP .NET Web application. (Part 1 of 4.)

```
26              ' add values to Hastable
27              books.Add("Visual Basic .NET", "0-13-456955-5")
28              books.Add("C#", "0-13-062221-4")
29              books.Add("C", "0-13-089572-5")
30              books.Add("C++", "0-13-089571-7")
31              books.Add("Python", "0-13-092361-3")
32           End Sub ' Page_Init
33
34           Private Sub Page_Load(ByVal sender As System.Object, _
35                 ByVal e As System.EventArgs) Handles MyBase.Load
36
37              If IsPostBack Then
38
39                 ' if postback is True, user has submitted information
40                 ' display welcome message and appropriate hyperlinks
41                 welcomeLabel.Visible = True
42                 languageLink.Visible = True
43                 recommendationsLink.Visible = True
44
45                 ' hide option information
46                 submitButton.Visible = False
47                 promptLabel.Visible = False
48                 LanguageList.Visible = False
49
50                 If (LanguageList.SelectedItem Is Nothing) = False Then
51                    welcomeLabel.Text &= " " & _
52                       LanguageList.SelectedItem.Text.ToString & "."
53                 Else
54                    welcomeLabel.Text &= "no language."
55                 End If
56
57                 idLabel.Text = "Your unique session ID is: " & _
58                    Session.SessionID
59
60                 timeOutLabel.Text = "Timeout: " & Session.Timeout & _
61                    " minutes."
62
63              End If
64
65           End Sub ' Page_Load
66
67           Private Sub submitButton_Click(ByVal sender As System.Object, _
68              ByVal e As System.EventArgs) Handles submitButton.Click
69
70              Dim language, ISBN As String
71
72              ' if choice was made by user
73              If (LanguageList.SelectedItem Is Nothing) = False Then
74                 language = LanguageList.SelectedItem.ToString()
75                 ISBN = books(language).ToString()
76
```

Fig. 17.30 Sessions are created for each user in an ASP .NET Web application. (Part 2 of 4.)

```
77                  ' add name/value pair to Session
78              Session.Add(language, ISBN)
79          End If
80
81      End Sub ' submitButton_Click
82  End Class ' Options2
```

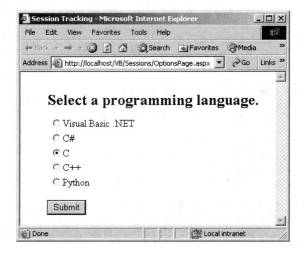

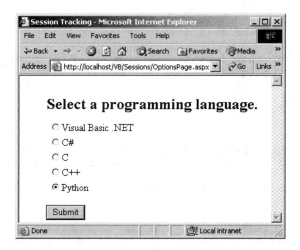

Fig. 17.30 Sessions are created for each user in an ASP .NET Web application. (Part 3 of 4.)

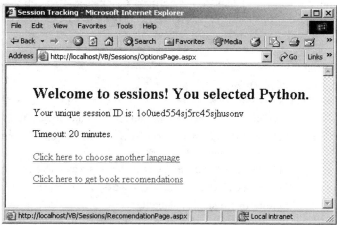

Fig. 17.30 Sessions are created for each user in an ASP .NET Web application. (Part 4 of 4.)

Software Engineering Observation 17.1

*A Web Form should not use instance variables to maintain client state information, because clients accessing that Web Form in parallel might overwrite the shared instance variables. Web Forms should maintain client state information in **HttpSessionState** objects, because such objects are specific to each client.*

Like a cookie, an **HttpSessionState** object can store name-value pairs. These session items are placed into an **HttpSessionState** object by calling method **Add**. Line 78 calls **Add** to place the language and its corresponding recommended book's ISBN number into the **HttpSessionState** object. One of the primary benefits of using **HttpSessionState** objects (rather than cookies) is that **HttpSessionState** objects can store any type of object (not just **String**s) as attribute values. This provides Visual Basic programmers with increased flexibility in determining the type of state information they wish to maintain for their clients. If the application calls method **Add** to add an attribute that has the same name as an attribute previously stored in a session, the object associated with that attribute is replaced.

After the values are added to the **HttpSessionState** object, the application handles the postback event (lines 37–63) in method **Page_Load**. Here, we retrieve information about the current client's session from the **Session** object's properties and display this information in the Web page. The ASP .NET application contains information about the **HttpSessionState** object for the current client. Property *SessionID* (lines 57–58) contains the *session's unique ID*. The first time a client connects to the Web server, a unique session ID is created for that client. When the client makes additional requests, the client's session ID is compared with the session IDs stored in the Web server's memory. Property *Timeout* (line 60) specifies the maximum amount of time that an **Http-SessionState** object can be inactive before it is discarded. Figure 17.31 lists some common **HttpSessionState** properties.

As in the cookies example, this application provides a link to **Recommendations-Page.aspx** (Fig. 17.32), which displays a list of book recommendations that is based on the user's language selections. Lines 28–31 define a **ListBox** Web control that is used to present the recommendations to the user. Figure 17.33 presents the code-behind file for this ASPX file.

Properties	Description
Count	Specifies the number of key-value pairs in the **Session** object.
IsNewSession	Indicates whether this is a new session (i.e., whether the session was created during loading of this page).
IsReadOnly	Indicates whether the **Session** object is read only.
Keys	Returns a collection containing the **Session** object's keys.
SessionID	Returns the session's unique ID.
Timeout	Specifies the maximum number of minutes during which a session can be inactive (i.e., no requests are made) before the session expires. By default, this property is set to 20 minutes.

Fig. 17.31 HttpSessionState properties.

```
1   <%-- Fig. 17.32: RecommendationPage.aspx          --%>
2   <%-- Displays book recommendations based on session --%>
3   <%-- information       .                          --%>
4
5   <%@ Page Language="vb" AutoEventWireup="false"
6      Codebehind="RecommendationPage.aspx.vb"
7      Inherits="Sessions.Recommendations" %>
8
9   <!DOCTYPE HTML PUBLIC "-//W3C//DTD HTML 4.0 Transitional//EN">
```

Fig. 17.32 Session information displayed in a **ListBox**. (Part 1 of 2.)

```
10  <HTML>
11     <HEAD>
12        <meta content="Microsoft Visual Studio.NET 7.0"
13           name="GENERATOR">
14        <meta content="Visual Basic 7.0" name="CODE_LANGUAGE">
15        <meta content="JavaScript" name="vs_defaultClientScript">
16        <meta name="vs_targetSchema"
17           content="http://schemas.microsoft.com/intellisense/ie5">
18     </HEAD>
19     <body MS_POSITIONING="GridLayout">
20        <form id="Form1" method="post" runat="server">
21
22           <asp:label id="recommendationLabel"
23              style="Z-INDEX: 101; LEFT: 55px;
24              POSITION: absolute; TOP: 38px" runat="server"
25              Font-Size="X-Large">Recommendations
26           </asp:label>
27
28           <asp:listbox id="booksListBox" style="Z-INDEX: 102;
29              LEFT: 50px; POSITION: absolute; TOP: 80px"
30              runat="server" Width="442px" Height="125px">
31           </asp:listbox>
32
33        </form>
34     </body>
35  </HTML>
```

Fig. 17.32 Session information displayed in a **ListBox**. (Part 2 of 2.)

```
 1  ' Fig. 17.33: RecommendationPage.aspx.vb
 2  ' Reading cookie data from the client
 3
 4  Imports System.Web.UI.WebControls
 5
 6  Public Class Recommendations
 7     Inherits Page
 8     Protected WithEvents recommendationLabel As Label
 9     Protected WithEvents booksListBox As ListBox
10
11     ' Visual Studio .NET generated code
12
13     Private Sub Page_Init(ByVal sender As System.Object, _
14        ByVal e As System.EventArgs) Handles MyBase.Init
15
16        InitializeComponent()
17
18        Dim i As Integer
19        Dim keyName As String
20
```

Fig. 17.33 Session data read by an ASP .NET Web application to provide recommendations for the user. (Part 1 of 2.)

```
21              ' determine if Session contains information
22          If Session.Count <> 0 Then
23
24              ' iterate through Session values,
25              ' display in ListBox
26              For i = 0 To Session.Count - 1
27
28                  ' store current key in sessionName
29                  keyName = Session.Keys(i)
30
31                  ' use current key to display
32                  ' Session's name/value pairs
33                  booksListBox.Items.Add(keyName & _
34                      " How to Program. ISBN#: " & _
35                      Session(keyName))
36              Next
37          Else
38              recommendationLabel.Text = "No Recommendations"
39              booksListBox.Visible = False
40          End If
41      End Sub ' Page_Init
42
43      Private Sub Page_Load(ByVal sender As System.Object, _
44          ByVal e As System.EventArgs) Handles MyBase.Load
45
46          ' Put user code to initialize the page here
47      End Sub ' Page_Load
48  End Class ' Recommendations
```

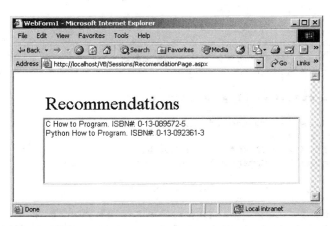

Fig. 17.33 Session data read by an ASP .NET Web application to provide recommendations for the user. (Part 2 of 2.)

Event handler **Page_Init** (lines 13–41) retrieves the session information. If a user has not selected any language during any visit to this site, our **Session** object's *Count* property will be zero. This property provides the number of session items contained in a **Session** object. If **Session** object's **Count** property is zero (i.e., no language was ever selected) then we display the text **No Recommendations**.

If the user has chosen a language, the **For** structure (lines 26–36) iterates through our **Session** object's session items (line 29). The value in a key-value pair is retrieved from the **Session** object by indexing the **Session** object with the key name, using the same process by which we retrieved a value from our hash table in the last section.

We then access the *Keys* property of class **HttpSessionState** (line 29), which returns a collection containing all the keys in the session. Line 29 indexes our collection to retrieve the current key. Lines 33–35 concatenate **keyName**'s value to the **String " How to Program. ISBN#: "** and to the value from the session object for which **keyName** is the key. This **String** is the recommendation that appears in the **ListBox**.

17.7 Case Study: Online Guest book

Many Web sites allow users to provide feedback about the Web site in a *guest book*. Typically, users click a link on the Web site's home page to request the guest-book page. This page usually consists of an HTML **form** that contains fields for the user's name, e-mail address, message/feedback and so on. Data submitted on the guest-book **form** often are stored in a database located on the Web server's machine. In this section, we create a guest-book Web Form application. The GUI is slightly more complex, containing a **DataGrid**, as shown in Fig. 17.34.

The HTML **form** presented to the user consists of a user-name field, an e-mail address field and a message field. Figure 17.35 presents the ASPX file and Fig. 17.36 presents the code–behind file for the guest-book application. For the sake of simplicity, we write the guest-book information to a text file.

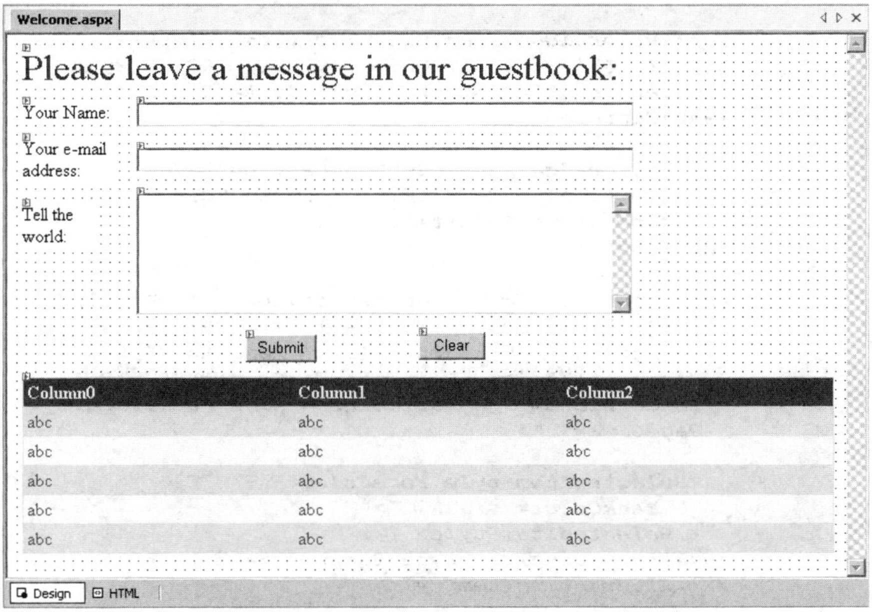

Fig. 17.34 Guest-book application GUI.

```
1   <%-- Fig. 17.35: GuestbookPage.aspx              --%>
2   <%-- Controls and layout for guestbook application. --%>
3
4   <%@ Page Language="vb" AutoEventWireup="false"
5      Codebehind="GuestbookPage.aspx.vb"
6      Inherits="Guestbook.Guestbook"%>
7
8   <!DOCTYPE HTML PUBLIC "-//W3C//DTD HTML 4.0 Transitional//EN">
9   <HTML>
10     <HEAD>
11       <title>GuestBook</title>
12       <meta content="Microsoft Visual Studio.NET 7.0"
13          name="GENERATOR">
14       <meta content="Visual Basic 7.0" name="CODE_LANGUAGE">
15       <meta content="JavaScript" name="vs_defaultClientScript">
16       <meta content=
17          "http://schemas.microsoft.com/intellisense/ie5"
18          name="vs_targetSchema">
19     </HEAD>
20     <body MS_POSITIONING="GridLayout">
21       <form id="Form1" method="post" runat="server">
22
23          <asp:Label id="promptLabel" style="Z-INDEX: 101;
24             LEFT: 39px; POSITION: absolute; TOP: 20px"
25             runat="server" Font-Size="X-Large"
26             ForeColor="Blue">
27             Please leave a message in our guestbook:
28          </asp:Label>
29
30          <asp:Button id="clearButton" style="Z-INDEX: 110;
31             LEFT: 383px; POSITION: absolute; TOP: 318px"
32             runat="server" Width="56px" Text="Clear">
33          </asp:Button>
34
35          <asp:Button id="submitButton" style="Z-INDEX: 109;
36             LEFT: 187px; POSITION: absolute; TOP: 319px"
37             runat="server" Text="Submit">
38          </asp:Button>
39
40          <asp:DataGrid id="DataGrid1" style="Z-INDEX: 108;
41             LEFT: 39px; POSITION: absolute; TOP: 372px"
42             runat="server" Width="541px" Height="95px"
43             HorizontalAlign="Left" BorderColor="#E7E7FF"
44             BorderWidth="1px" GridLines="None" CellPadding="3"
45             PageSize="5">
46
47             <SelectedItemStyle ForeColor="#F7F7F7"
48                BackColor="#738A9C">
49             </SelectedItemStyle>
50             <AlternatingItemStyle BackColor="#F7F7F7">
51             </AlternatingItemStyle>
```

Fig. 17.35 ASPX file for the guest-book application. (Part 1 of 2.)

```
52              <ItemStyle HorizontalAlign="Left" Width="100px"
53                 ForeColor="#4A3C8C" BackColor="#E7E7FF">
54              </ItemStyle>
55              <HeaderStyle ForeColor="#F7F7F7"
56                 BackColor="#4A3C8C">
57              </HeaderStyle>
58              <FooterStyle ForeColor="#4A3C8C"
59                 BorderColor="#B5C7DE">
60              </FooterStyle>
61              <PagerStyle HorizontalAlign="Right"
62                 ForeColor="#4A3C8C" BackColor="#E7E7FF"
63                 Mode="NumericPages">
64              </PagerStyle>
65           </asp:DataGrid>
66
67           <asp:TextBox id="messageTextBox" style="Z-INDEX: 107;
68              LEFT: 135px; POSITION: absolute; TOP: 181px"
69              runat="server" Width="449px" Height="113px"
70              TextMode="MultiLine">
71           </asp:TextBox>
72
73           <asp:TextBox id="emailTextBox" style="Z-INDEX: 106;
74              LEFT: 135px; POSITION: absolute; TOP: 132px"
75              runat="server" Width="449px">
76           </asp:TextBox>
77
78           <asp:TextBox id="nameTextBox" style="Z-INDEX: 105;
79              LEFT: 135px; POSITION: absolute; TOP: 85px"
80              runat="server" Width="449px">
81           </asp:TextBox>
82
83           <asp:Label id="messageLabel" style="Z-INDEX: 104;
84              LEFT: 39px; POSITION: absolute; TOP: 167px"
85              runat="server" Width="51px">Tell the world:
86           </asp:Label>
87
88           <asp:Label id="emailLabel" style="Z-INDEX: 103;
89              LEFT: 39px; POSITION: absolute; TOP: 118px"
90              runat="server" Width="69px">Your email address:
91           </asp:Label>
92
93           <asp:Label id="nameLabel" style="Z-INDEX: 102;
94              LEFT: 39px; POSITION: absolute; TOP: 90px"
95              runat="server">Your name:
96           </asp:Label>
97
98        </form>
99     </body>
100 </HTML>
```

Fig. 17.35 ASPX file for the guest-book application. (Part 2 of 2.)

The ASPX file generated by the GUI is shown in Fig. 17.35. After dragging the two buttons onto the form, double-click each button to create its corresponding event handler.

Visual Studio adds the event handlers to the code-behind file (Fig. 17.36). A **DataGrid** named **dataGrid** displays all guest-book entries. This control can be added from the **Toolbox**, just as could a button or label. The colors for the **DataGrid** are specified through the **Auto Format...** link that is located near the bottom of the **Properties** window when we are looking at the properties of our **DataGrid**. A dialog will open with several choices. In this example, we chose **Colorful 4**. We discuss adding information to this **DataGrid** shortly.

The event handler for **clearButton** (lines 35–41) clears each **TextBox** by setting its **Text** property to an empty string. Lines 84–107 contain the event-handling code for **submitButton**, which will add the user's information to **guestbook.txt**, a text file stored in our project. The various entries in this file will be displayed in the **DataGrid**, including the newest entry. Let us look at how this is done in the code.

Lines 90–92 create a **StreamWriter** that references the file containing the guest-book entries. We use the **Request** object's **PhysicalApplicationPath** property to retrieve the path of the application's root directory (this will be the path of the project folder for the current application) and then concatenate to it the file name (i.e., **guest-book.txt**). The second argument (**True**) specifies that new information will be appended to the file (i.e., added at the end). Lines 95–98 append the appropriate message to the guest-book file. Before the event handler exits, it calls method **FillMessage-Table** (line 106).

```
1    ' Fig. 17.36: GuestbookPage.aspx.vb
2    ' The code-behind file for the guest book page.
3
4    Imports System.Web.UI.WebControls
5    Imports System.Data
6    Imports System.IO
7
8    ' allows users to leave message
9    Public Class Guestbook
10       Inherits System.Web.UI.Page
11
12       Protected WithEvents promptLabel As Label
13       Protected WithEvents nameLabel As Label
14       Protected WithEvents emailLabel As Label
15       Protected WithEvents messageLabel As Label
16       Protected WithEvents dataGrid As DataGrid
17       Protected WithEvents submitButton As Button
18       Protected WithEvents messageTextBox As TextBox
19       Protected WithEvents emailTextBox As TextBox
20       Protected WithEvents nameTextBox As TextBox
21       Protected WithEvents clearButton As Button
22       Protected WithEvents dataView As System.Data.DataView
23
24       ' Visual Studio .NET generated code
25
26       Private Sub Page_Load(ByVal sender As System.Object, _
27          ByVal e As System.EventArgs) Handles MyBase.Load
28
```

Fig. 17.36 Code-behind file for the guest-book application. (Part 1 of 4.)

```
29              'Put user code to initialize the page here
30              dataView = New DataView(New DataTable())
31
32          End Sub
33
34          ' clear text boxes; user can enter new input
35          Private Sub clearButton_Click(ByVal sender As System.Object, _
36              ByVal e As System.EventArgs) Handles clearButton.Click
37
38              nameTextBox.Text = ""
39              emailTextBox.Text = ""
40              messageTextBox.Text = ""
41          End Sub ' clearButton_Click
42
43          Public Sub FillMessageTable()
44              Dim table As New DataTable()
45              Dim reader As StreamReader
46              Dim separator As Char()
47              Dim message As String
48              Dim parts As String()
49
50              table = dataView.Table
51
52              table.Columns.Add("Date")
53              table.Columns.Add("FirstName")
54              table.Columns.Add("email")
55              table.Columns.Add("Message")
56
57              ' open guestbook file for reading
58              reader = New StreamReader( _
59                  Request.PhysicalApplicationPath & "guestbook.txt")
60
61              separator = New Char() {vbTab}
62
63              ' read one line from file
64              message = reader.ReadLine()
65
66              While message <> ""
67
68                  ' split String into four parts
69                  parts = message.Split(separator)
70
71                  ' load data into table
72                  table.LoadDataRow(parts, True)
73
74                  ' read one line from file
75                  message = reader.ReadLine()
76              End While
77
78              dataGrid.DataBind() ' update grid
79
80              reader.Close()
81          End Sub ' FillMessageTable
```

Fig. 17.36 Code-behind file for the guest-book application. (Part 2 of 4.)

```
82
83         ' add user's entry to guestbook
84      Private Sub submitButton_Click(ByVal sender As System.Object, _
85         ByVal e As System.EventArgs) Handles submitButton.Click
86
87         Dim guestbook As StreamWriter
88
89          ' open stream for appending to file
90         guestbook = New StreamWriter( _
91            Request.PhysicalApplicationPath & _
92            "guestbook.txt", True)
93
94          ' write new message to file
95         guestbook.WriteLine( _
96            DateTime.Now.Date.ToString().Substring(0, 10) & _
97            vbTab & nameTextBox.Text & vbTab & emailTextBox.Text & _
98            vbTab & messageTextBox.Text)
99
100         ' clear textboxes and close stream
101        nameTextBox.Text = ""
102        emailTextBox.Text = ""
103        messageTextBox.Text = ""
104        guestbook.Close()
105
106        FillMessageTable()
107     End Sub ' submitButton_Click
108  End Class ' Guestbook
```

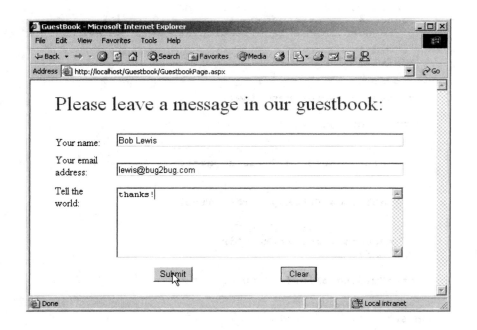

Fig. 17.36 Code-behind file for the guest-book application. (Part 3 of 4.)

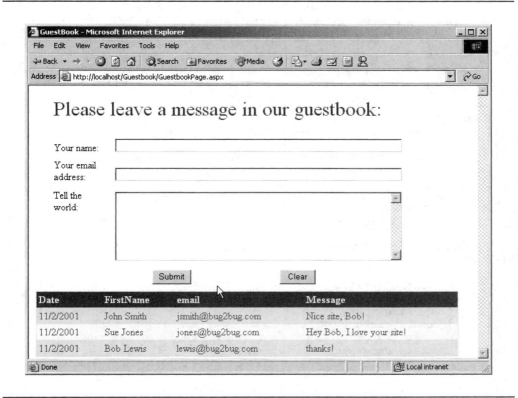

Fig. 17.36 Code-behind file for the guest-book application. (Part 4 of 4.)

Method **FillMessageTable** (lines 43–81) places the guest-book entries in **DataTable table**. Lines 50–55 create a **DataTable** object from our **DataView**'s **Table** property and then form the necessary columns, using the **Columns** collection's **Add** method. Lines 66–76 read each line in the text file. Method **Split** breaks each line read from the file into four tokens, which are added to the **table** by calling method **LoadDataRow** (line 72). The second argument to method **LoadDataRow** is **True**, indicating that any changes resulting from the addition will be accepted. The **DataTable** places one piece of data in each column. After the **DataTable** is populated, the data are bound to the **DataGrid**. Method **DataBind** is called to refresh the **DataView**. [*Note*: **DataView dataView** was assigned to the **DataSource** property of the **DataGrid** in the Web Form designer, after it was declared in the code.]

17.8 Case Study: Connecting to a Database in ASP .NET

This case study presents a Web-based application in which a user can view a list of publications by an author. This program consists of two Web Forms. The first page that a user requests is **Login.aspx** (Fig. 17.37). After accessing this page, users select their names from the drop-down list and then enter their passwords. If their passwords are valid, they are redirected to **Authors.aspx** (Fig. 17.40), which provides a list of authors. When the user chooses an author and clicks the **Select** button, a postback occurs, and the updated page displays a table containing the titles, ISBNs and publishers of books by the selected author.

Much of the information provided by this Web page is accessed through databases stored in our project. **Login.aspx** retrieves valid user names for this site through **Login.mdb**, and all the author information is retrieved from the **Books.mdb** database. The reader can view these databases by opening the **Database** project for this chapter.

```
1   <%-- Fig. 17.37: login.aspx                    --%>
2   <%-- Controls and formatting for login page. --%>
3
4   <%@ Register TagPrefix="Header" TagName="ImageHeader"
5       Src="ImageHeader.ascx" %>
6
7   <%@ Page Language="vb" AutoEventWireup="false"
8       Codebehind="login.aspx.vb"
9       Inherits="Database.Login"%>
10
11  <!DOCTYPE HTML PUBLIC "-//W3C//DTD HTML 4.0 Transitional//EN">
12  <HTML>
13     <HEAD>
14        <title></title>
15        <meta content="Microsoft Visual Studio.NET 7.0"
16           name="GENERATOR">
17        <meta content="Visual Basic 7.0" name="CODE_LANGUAGE">
18        <meta content="JavaScript" name="vs_defaultClientScript">
19        <meta name="vs_targetSchema"
20           content="http://schemas.microsoft.com/intellisense/ie5">
21     </HEAD>
22     <body bgColor="#ffebff" MS_POSITIONING="GridLayout">
23        <form id="Form1" method="post" runat="server">
24
25           <asp:label id="promptLabel" style="Z-INDEX: 108;
26              LEFT: 20px; POSITION: absolute; TOP: 144px"
27              runat="server">Please select your name and enter
28                 your password to log in:
29           </asp:label>
30
31           <asp:label id="nameLabel" style="Z-INDEX: 101;
32              LEFT: 15px; POSITION: absolute; TOP: 188px"
33              runat="server">Name
34           </asp:label>
35
36           <asp:dropdownlist id="nameList" style="Z-INDEX: 105;
37              LEFT: 92px; POSITION: absolute; TOP: 185px"
38              runat="server" Width="154px">
39           </asp:dropdownlist>
40
41           <asp:label id="passwordLabel" style="Z-INDEX: 102;
42              LEFT: 15px; POSITION: absolute; TOP: 220px"
43              runat="server">Password
44           </asp:label>
45
```

Fig. 17.37 Login Web Form. (Part 1 of 2.)

```
46        <asp:textbox id="passwordTextBox" style="Z-INDEX: 103;
47           LEFT: 92px; POSITION: absolute; TOP: 221px"
48           runat="server" TextMode="Password">
49        </asp:textbox>
50
51        <asp:customvalidator id="invalidPasswordValidator"
52           style="Z-INDEX: 107; LEFT: 262px; POSITION:
53           absolute; TOP: 221px" runat="server"
54           ControlToValidate="passwordTextBox" Font-Bold="True"
55           ForeColor="DarkCyan" ErrorMessage="Invalid password!">
56        </asp:customvalidator>
57
58        <asp:requiredfieldvalidator id=
59           "requiredPasswordValidator" style="Z-INDEX: 106;
60           LEFT: 262px; POSITION: absolute; TOP: 221px"
61           runat="server" ControlToValidate="passwordTextBox"
62           Font-Bold="True" ForeColor="DarkCyan"
63           ErrorMessage="Please enter a password!">
64        </asp:requiredfieldvalidator>
65
66        <asp:button id="submitButton" style="Z-INDEX: 104;
67           LEFT: 92px; POSITION: absolute; TOP: 263px"
68           runat="server" Text="Submit">
69        </asp:button>
70
71        <Header:ImageHeader id="ImageHeader1" runat="server">
72        </Header:ImageHeader>
73
74      </form>
75    </body>
76 </HTML>
```

Fig. 17.37 Login Web Form. (Part 2 of 2.)

Lines 4–5 add one *Web user control* to the ASPX file. Readers might recall that we covered the definition of user controls for Windows applications in Chapter 10, Graphical User Interface Concepts: Part 2; we can define user controls for Web Forms by a similar technique. Because the ASPX files that users request do not define user controls for Web Forms, such controls do not have **HTML** or **BODY** elements. Rather, programmers specify these controls via the **<%@ Register...%>** directive. For example, a programmer might want to include a *navigation bar* (i.e., a series of buttons for navigating a Web site) on every page of a site. If the site encompasses a large number of pages, the addition of markup to create the navigation bar for each page can be time consuming. Moreover, if the programmer subsequently modifies the navigation bar, every page on the site that uses it must be updated. By creating a user control, the programmer can specify where on each page the navigation bar is placed with only a few lines of markup. If the navigation bar changes, the pages that use it are updated the next time the page is requested.

Like Web Forms, most Web user controls consist of two pages: An *ASCX file* and a code-behind file. Lines 4–5 define the user control's *tag name* (the name of this instance of the control) and tag prefix, which are **ImageHeader** and **Header**, respectively. The **ImageHeader** element is added to the file in lines 71–72. The tag definition is located in the *Src* file **HeaderImage.ascx** (Fig. 17.38). The programmer can create this file by right clicking the project name in the **Solution Explorer** and selecting **Add > Add New Item...**. From the dialog that opens, select **Web User Control**, and a new ASCX file will be added to the solution. At this point, the programmer can add items to this file as if it were an ASPX document, defining any functionality in the Web user control's code-behind file. After creating the user control, the programmer can drag it from the **Solution Explorer** directly onto an open ASPX file. An instance of the control then will be created and added to the Web Form.

The form (Fig. 17.37) includes several **Label**s, a **TextBox** (**passwordTextbox**) and a **DropDownList** (**nameList**), which is populated in the code-behind file, **Login.aspx.vb** (Fig. 17.39), with user names retrieved from a database. We also include two validators: A **RequiredFieldValidator**, and a *CustomValidator*. A **CustomValidator** allows us to specify the circumstances under which a field is valid. We define these circumstances in the event handler for the *ServerValidate* event of the **CustomValidator**. The event-handling code is placed in the code-behind file for **Login.aspx.vb** and is discussed shortly. Both validators' **ControlToValidate** properties are set to **passwordTextbox**.

```
1    <%-- Fig. 17.38: ImageHeader.ascx          --%>
2    <%-- Listing for the header user control. --%>
3
4    <%@ Control Language="vb" AutoEventWireup="false"
5       Codebehind="ImageHeader.ascx.vb"
6       Inherits="Database.ImageHeader"
7       TargetSchema="http://schemas.microsoft.com/intellisense/ie5" %>
8
9    <asp:Image id="Image1" runat="server"
10      ImageUrl="http://localhost/VB/Database/bug2bug.png">
11   </asp:Image>
```

Fig. 17.38 ASCX code for the header.

```
1    ' Fig. 17.39: Login.aspx.vb
2    ' The code-behind file for the page that logs the user in.
3
4    Imports System
5    Imports System.Collections
6    Imports System.ComponentModel
7    Imports System.Data
8    Imports System.Data.OleDb
9    Imports System.Drawing
10   Imports System.Web
11   Imports System.Web.SessionState
12   Imports System.Web.UI
13   Imports System.Web.UI.WebControls
14   Imports System.Web.UI.HtmlControls
15   Imports System.Web.Security
16
```

Fig. 17.39 Code-behind file for the login page for authors application. (Part 1 of 5.)

```
17   Public Class Login
18       Inherits System.Web.UI.Page
19
20       Protected WithEvents requiredPasswordValidator As _
21       RequiredFieldValidator
22
23       Protected WithEvents invalidPasswordValidator As _
24           CustomValidator
25
26       Protected WithEvents submitButton As Button
27       Protected WithEvents passwordTextBox As TextBox
28       Protected WithEvents passwordLabel As Label
29       Protected WithEvents nameList As DropDownList
30       Protected WithEvents nameLabel As Label
31       Protected WithEvents OleDbDataAdapter1 As OleDbDataAdapter
32       Protected WithEvents OleDbSelectCommand1 As OleDbCommand
33       Protected WithEvents OleDbInsertCommand1 As OleDbCommand
34       Protected WithEvents OleDbUpdateCommand1 As OleDbCommand
35       Protected WithEvents OleDbDeleteCommand1 As OleDbCommand
36       Protected WithEvents OleDbConnection1 As OleDbConnection
37       Protected WithEvents promptLabel As Label
38       Protected dataReader As OleDbDataReader
39
40       ' Visual Studio .NET generated code
41
42       Private Sub Page_Init(ByVal sender As System.Object, _
43           ByVal e As System.EventArgs) Handles MyBase.Init
44
45           InitializeComponent()
46
47           ' if page loads due to postback, process information
48           ' otherwise, page is loading for first time, so
49           ' do nothing
50           If Not IsPostBack Then
51
52               ' open database and read data
53               Try
54                   ' open database connection
55                   OleDbConnection1.Open()
56
57                   ' execute query
58                   dataReader = _
59                       OleDbDataAdapter1.SelectCommand.ExecuteReader()
60
61                   ' while we can read row from query result,
62                   ' add first item to drop-down list
63                   While (dataReader.Read())
64                       nameList.Items.Add(dataReader.GetString(0))
65                   End While
66
67                   ' catch error if database cannot be opened
68               Catch exception As OleDbException
69                   Response.Write("Unable to open database!")
```

Fig. 17.39 Code-behind file for the login page for authors application. (Part 2 of 5.)

```
70
71                     ' close database
72                 Finally
73                     ' close database connection
74                     OleDbConnection1.Close()
75                 End Try
76         End If
77     End Sub ' Page_Init
78
79     ' validate user name and password
80     Private Sub invalidPasswordValidator_ServerValidate( _
81         ByVal source As Object, _
82         ByVal args As ServerValidateEventArgs) _
83         Handles invalidPasswordValidator.ServerValidate
84
85         ' open database and check password
86         Try
87             ' open database connection
88             OleDbConnection1.Open()
89
90             ' set select command to find password of username
91             ' from drop-down list
92             OleDbDataAdapter1.SelectCommand.CommandText = _
93                 "SELECT * FROM Users WHERE loginID = '" & _
94                 Request.Form("nameList").ToString() & "'"
95
96             dataReader = _
97                 OleDbDataAdapter1.SelectCommand.ExecuteReader()
98
99             dataReader.Read()
100
101            ' if password user provided is correct create
102            ' authentication ticket for user and redirect
103            ' user to Authors.aspx; otherwise set IsValid to false
104            If args.Value = dataReader.GetString(1) Then
105                FormsAuthentication.SetAuthCookie( _
106                    Request.Form("namelist"), False)
107                Session.Add("name", _
108                        Request.Form("nameList").ToString())
109                Response.Redirect("Authors.aspx")
110            Else
111                args.IsValid = False
112
113            End If
114
115            ' display error if unable to open database
116         Catch exception As OleDbException
117             Response.Write("Unable to open database!")
118
119             ' close database
120         Finally
121             ' close database connection
122             OleDbConnection1.Close()
```

Fig. 17.39 Code-behind file for the login page for authors application. (Part 3 of 5.)

```
123          End Try
124      End Sub ' InvalidPasswordValidator_ServerValidate
125  End Class ' Login
```

Fig. 17.39 Code-behind file for the login page for authors application. (Part 4 of 5.)

Fig. 17.39 Code-behind file for the login page for authors application. (Part 5 of 5.)

In Fig. 17.39, the **Page_Init** event handler is defined in lines 42–77. If the page is being loaded for the first time, lines 50–76 execute. The database code is contained within a **Try/Catch/Finally** block (lines 53–75) to handle any database connectivity exceptions and to ensure that the database is closed. Lines 58–59 execute the SQL query that Visual Studio generates at design time—this query simply retrieves all the rows from the **Users** table of the **Login** database. Lines 63–65 iterate through the rows, placing the item in the first column of each row (the user name) into **nameList**.

The reader might notice that we use an *OleDbDataReader*, an object that reads data from a database. We did not use an object of this type before, because the **OleDbData-Reader** is not as flexible as other readers we discussed in Chapter 16. The object can read data, but cannot update it. However, we use **OleDbDataReader** in this example because we need only read the users' names; this object provides a fast and simple way to do so.

In this example, we use a **CustomValidator** to validate the user's password. We define a handler (lines 80–124) for the *ServerValidate* event of the **CustomValidator**, which executes every time the user clicks **Submit**. This event handler contains a *ServerValidateEventArgs* parameter called **args**. The object referenced by **args** has two important properties: *Value*, which contains the value of the control that the **CustomValidator** is validating, and *IsValid*, which contains a **Boolean** representing the validation result. Once the event handler completes, if **IsValid** is **True**, the HTML form is submitted to the Web server; if **IsValid** is **False**, the **Custom-Validator**'s **ErrorMessage** is displayed, and the HTML **form** is not submitted to the Web server.

To create and attach an event handler for the **ServerValidate** event, double-click **CustomValidator**. The definition for this event handler (lines 80–124) tests the selected user name against the password provided by the user. If they match, the user is *authenticated* (i.e., the user's identity is confirmed), and the browser is redirected to **Authors.aspx** (Fig. 17.40). Lines 104–110 authenticate the user and provide access to **Authors.aspx** by calling method *SetAuthCookie* of class *FormsAuthentication*. This class is in the **System.Web.Security** namespace (line 15). Method **SetAuthCookie** writes to the client an *encrypted* cookie containing information necessary to authenticate the user. Encrypted data is data translated into a code that only the sender and receiver can understand thereby keeping it private. Method **SetAuthCookie** takes two arguments: A **String** containing the user name, and a **Boolean** value that specifies whether this cookie should persist (i.e., remain on the client's computer) beyond the current session. Because we want the application to authenticate the user only for the current session, we set this value to **False**. After the user is authenticated, the user's Web browser is redirected to **Authors.aspx**. If the database query did not verify the user's identity, property *IsValid* of the **CustomValidator** is set to **False**; the *ErrorMessage* is displayed, and the user can attempt to log in again.

This example uses a technique known as *forms authentication*, which protects a page so that only authenticated users can access it. Authentication is a crucial tool for sites that allow only members to enter the site or a portion of the site. Authentication and denial of access to unauthorized users involves the placement of several lines in *Web.config* (a file used for application configuration). This XML file is a part of every ASP .NET application created in Visual Studio. If readers open this file, they will see the default authentication element, which is only one line and appears as follows:

```
<authentication mode="None" />
```

To deny access to unauthorized users, replace this line with

```
<authentication mode="Forms">
   <forms name="DatabaseCookie"
      loginUrl="Login.aspx" protection="Encryption" />
</authentication>

<authorization>
   <deny users="?" />
</authorization>
```

This replacement alters the value of the *mode* attribute in the **authentication** element from **"None"** to **"Forms"**, specifying that we want to use forms authentication. The *forms* element defines the way in which users are validated. Inside the forms element, **name** attribute sets the name of the cookie that is created on the user's machine—in this case, we named it **DatabaseCookie**. Attribute *loginUrl* specifies the login page for our application; users who attempt to access any page in our application without logging in are redirected to this page. Attribute *protection* specifies whether the value of the cookie is encrypted. In this case, we set the value of **protection** to **"Encryption"** to encrypt the cookie's data.

Element *authorization* indicates the type of access that specific users can have. In this application, we want to allow authenticated users access to all pages on the site. We place the *deny* element inside the **authorization** element to specify to what users we wish to deny access. When we set this attribute's value to **"?"**, all anonymous (i.e., unauthenticated) users are denied access to the site.

A user who has been authenticated will be redirected to **Authors.aspx** (Fig. 17.40). This page provides a list of authors, from which the user can choose one. After a choice has been made, a table is displayed with information about books that author has written.

```
1    <%-- Fig. 17.40: Authors.aspx                    --%>
2    <%-- Displays book titles based on author name --%>
3    <%-- from database.                             --%>
4
5    <%@ Page Language="vb" AutoEventWireup="false"
6        Codebehind="Authors.aspx.vb"
7        Inherits="Database.Authors"%>
8
9    <%@ Register TagPrefix="Header" TagName="ImageHeader"
10       Src="ImageHeader.ascx" %>
11
12   <!DOCTYPE HTML PUBLIC "-//W3C//DTD HTML 4.0 Transitional//EN">
13   <HTML>
14       <HEAD>
15           <title>Authors</title>
16           <meta name="GENERATOR"
17               content="Microsoft Visual Studio.NET 7.0">
18           <meta name="CODE_LANGUAGE" content="Visual Basic 7.0">
19           <meta name="vs_defaultClientScript" content="JavaScript">
20           <meta name="vs_targetSchema"
21               content="http://schemas.microsoft.com/intellisense/ie5">
22       </HEAD>
23       <body MS_POSITIONING="GridLayout" bgColor="#ffebff">
24           <form id="Form1" method="post" runat="server">
25
26               <asp:DataGrid id="dataGrid" style="Z-INDEX: 106;
27                   LEFT: 15px; POSITION: absolute; TOP: 131px"
28                   runat="server" ForeColor="Black" AllowPaging="True"
29                   DataSource="<%# dataView %>" AllowSorting="True"
30                   Visible="False" Width="700px" Height="23px">
31
32                   <EditItemStyle BackColor="White"></EditItemStyle>
33                   <AlternatingItemStyle ForeColor="Black"
34                       BackColor="LightGoldenrodYellow">
35                   </AlternatingItemStyle>
36                   <ItemStyle BackColor="White"></ItemStyle>
37                   <HeaderStyle BackColor="LightGreen"></HeaderStyle>
38                   <PagerStyle NextPageText="Next &amp;gt;"
39                       PrevPageText="&amp;lt; Previous">
40                   </PagerStyle>
41               </asp:DataGrid>
42
43               <asp:Button id="Button1" style="Z-INDEX: 104;
44                   LEFT: 29px; POSITION: absolute; TOP: 188px"
45                   runat="server" Width="78px" Text="Select">
46               </asp:Button>
```

Fig. 17.40 ASPX file that allows a user to select an author from a drop-down list. (Part 1 of 2.)

```
47
48              <asp:DropDownList id="nameList" style="Z-INDEX: 103;
49                  LEFT: 90px; POSITION: absolute; TOP: 157px"
50                  runat="server" Width="158px" Height="22px">
51              </asp:DropDownList>
52
53              <asp:Label id="Label2" style="Z-INDEX: 102;
54                  LEFT: 28px; POSITION: absolute; TOP: 157px"
55                  runat="server" Width="48px" Height="22px">
56                  Authors:
57              </asp:Label>
58
59              <asp:Label id="Label3" style="Z-INDEX: 105;
60                  LEFT: 19px; POSITION: absolute; TOP: 127px"
61                  runat="server" Visible="False" Width="210px">
62                  You chose
63              </asp:Label>
64
65              <Header:ImageHeader id="ImageHeader1" runat="server">
66              </Header:ImageHeader>
67
68          </form>
69      </body>
70  </HTML>
```

Fig. 17.40 ASPX file that allows a user to select an author from a drop-down list. (Part 2 of 2.)

The ASPX file for this page creates a number of controls: A **DropDownList**, three **Label**s, a **Button** and a **DataGrid**. Notice that some of the controls—one of the **Label**s and the **DataGrid**—have their **Visible** properties set to **false** (line 30 and line 61). This means that the controls are not visible when the page first loads, because there is no author information to display because the user has not yet chosen an author. Users select an author from the **DropDownList** and click **Select**, causing a postback to occur. When the postback is handled, the **DataGrid** is filled and displayed. Figure 17.41 lists the code-behind file for this ASPX file.

Method **Page_Load** (lines 34–106) contains most of the code for this example. The condition (line 38) determines whether the page was loaded as a result of a postback event. If it is not a postback, line 41 adds a session item to the **Session** object to help us sort the data. Line 45 then opens the database connection, and lines 48–49 execute the database command, which retrieves all the authors' first and last names from the database. Lines 53–56 iterate through the result set and add the authors' first and last names to **nameList**.

```
1   ' Fig. 17.41: Authors.aspx.vb
2   ' The code-behind file for a page that allows a user to choose
3   ' an author and then view that author's books.
4
5   Imports System
6   Imports System.Data.OleDb
```

Fig. 17.41 Database information being inputted into a **DataGrid**. (Part 1 of 5.)

```
7    Imports System.Collections
8    Imports System.ComponentModel
9    Imports System.Data
10   Imports System.Drawing
11   Imports System.Web
12   Imports System.Web.SessionState
13   Imports System.Web.UI
14   Imports System.Web.UI.WebControls
15   Imports System.Web.UI.HtmlControls
16
17   Public Class Authors
18      Inherits System.Web.UI.Page
19
20      Protected WithEvents Label3 As Label
21      Protected WithEvents Label2 As Label
22      Protected WithEvents nameList As DropDownList
23      Protected WithEvents Button1 As Button
24      Protected WithEvents dataGrid As dataGrid
25      Protected WithEvents OleDbDataAdapter1 As OleDbDataAdapter
26      Protected WithEvents OleDbSelectCommand1 As OleDbCommand
27      Protected WithEvents OleDbConnection1 As OleDbConnection
28      Protected WithEvents dataView As DataView
29      Protected dataTable As New DataTable()
30      Protected dataReader As OleDbDataReader
31
32      ' Visual Studio .NET generated code
33
34      Private Sub Page_Load(ByVal sender As System.Object, _
35         ByVal e As System.EventArgs) Handles MyBase.Load
36
37         ' test if the page was loaded due to a post back
38         If Not IsPostBack Then
39
40            ' add data sort string
41            Session.Add("sortString", "Title")
42
43            ' open database connection
44            Try
45               OleDbConnection1.Open()
46
47               ' execute query
48               dataReader = _
49                  OleDbDataAdapter1.SelectCommand.ExecuteReader()
50
51               ' while we can read a row from the result of the
52               ' query, add the first item to the dropdown list
53               While (dataReader.Read())
54                  nameList.Items.Add(dataReader.GetString(0) & _
55                     " " & dataReader.GetString(1))
56               End While
57
```

Fig. 17.41 Database information being inputted into a **DataGrid**. (Part 2 of 5.)

```vbnet
58            ' if database cannot be found
59            Catch exception As System.Data.OleDb.OleDbException
60               Label3.Text = "Server Error: Unable to load database!"
61
62         Finally ' close database connection
63               OleDbConnection1.Close()
64         End Try
65      Else
66         ' set some controls to be invisible
67         nameList.Visible = False
68         Button1.Visible = False
69         Label2.Visible = False
70
71         ' set other controls to be visible
72         Label3.Visible = True
73         dataGrid.Visible = True
74
75         ' add author name to label
76         Label3.Text = "You Chose " & nameList.SelectedItem.Text _
77            & "."
78         Dim authorID As Integer = nameList.SelectedIndex + 1
79
80         Try
81            ' open database connection
82            OleDbConnection1.Open()
83
84            ' grab the title, ISBN and publisher name for each book
85            OleDbDataAdapter1.SelectCommand.CommandText = _
86               "SELECT Titles.Title, Titles.ISBN, " & _
87               "Publishers.PublisherName FROM AuthorISBN " & _
88               "INNER JOIN Titles ON AuthorISBN.ISBN = " & _
89               "Titles.ISBN, Publishers WHERE " & _
90               "(AuthorISBN.AuthorID = " & authorID & ")"
91
92            ' fill dataset with results
93            OleDbDataAdapter1.Fill(dataTable)
94            dataView = New DataView(dataTable)
95            dataView.Sort = Session("sortString")
96            dataGrid.DataBind() ' bind grid to data source
97
98         ' if database cannot be found
99         Catch exception As System.Data.OleDb.OleDbException
100
101            Label3.Text = "Server Error: Unable to load database!"
102         Finally ' close database connection
103            OleDbConnection1.Close()
104         End Try
105      End If
106   End Sub ' Page_Load
107
```

Fig. 17.41 Database information being inputted into a **DataGrid**. (Part 3 of 5.)

```
108      ' handles DataGrid page changed event
109      Private Sub OnNewPage(ByVal sender As Object, _
110         ByVal e As DataGridPageChangedEventArgs) _
111         Handles dataGrid.PageIndexChanged
112
113         ' set current page to next page
114         dataGrid.CurrentPageIndex = e.NewPageIndex
115
116         dataView.Sort = Session("sortString")
117         dataGrid.DataBind() ' rebind data
118
119      End Sub ' OnNewPage
120
121      ' handles Sort event
122      Private Sub dataGrid_SortCommand(ByVal source As Object, _
123         ByVal e As DataGridSortCommandEventArgs) _
124         Handles dataGrid.SortCommand
125
126         ' get table to sort
127         Session.Add("sortString", e.SortExpression.ToString())
128         dataView.Sort = Session("sortString") ' sort
129         dataGrid.DataBind() ' rebind data
130
131      End Sub ' dataGrid_SortCommand
132   End Class ' Authors
```

Fig. 17.41 Database information being inputted into a **DataGrid**. (Part 4 of 5.)

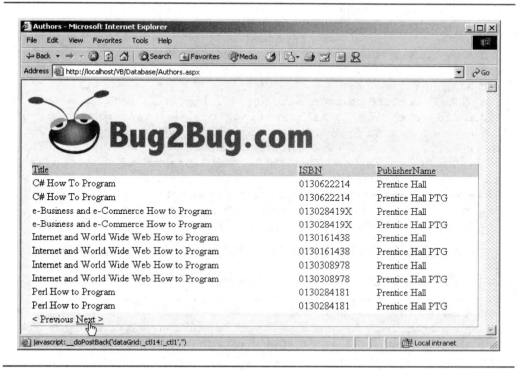

Fig. 17.41 Database information being inputted into a **DataGrid**. (Part 5 of 5.)

Once the user has selected an author and submitted the form, the condition (line 38) is **False**, which causes lines 65–105 to execute. The initial set of controls displayed to the user (i.e., the label, drop-down list and button) are hidden in the postback. However, the label and the data grid that previously were invisible are made visible. Line 76 adds the selected author's name to the label control.

Lines 85–90 create a database query to retrieve the title, ISBN and publisher name for each of the author's books and assign them to the command's **CommandText** property. Method **Fill** (line 93) populates its **DataTable** argument with the rows returned by our query on 85–90. The **DataView** class's **Sort** property sorts its data by the **String** assigned to it (this value is stored in the **Session** object with key value **sortString**). This value is set initially to **"Title"** on line 41, indicating that rows in our table are to be sorted by title, in ascending order. Ascending order is the default. If the session value were **"TitleDESC"**, the rows in our table would also be sorted by title, but in descending order.

Method **OnNewPage** (lines 109–119) handles the **DataGrid**'s **PageIndex-Changed** event, which is fired when the user clicks the **Next** link at the bottom of the **DataGrid** control to display the next page of data. To enable paging, the **AllowPaging** property of the **DataGrid** is set to **True** in the Web-Form designer. **DataGrid**'s **PageSize** property determines the number of entries per page, and its **PagerStyle** property customizes the display of our **DataGrid** during paging. This **DataGrid** control displays ten books per page. After the **DataGrid**'s **CurrentPageIndex** property is assigned the event argument **NewPageIndex** (line 114), we sort the data and rebind it, so that the next page of data can be displayed (lines 116–117). This technique for displaying data makes the site more readable and enables pages to load more quickly (because less data is displayed at one time).

Method **dataGrid_SortCommand** (lines 122–131) handles the **Sort** event of the **DataGrid** control. When the **AllowSorting** property in the Web-Form designer is enabled, the **DataGrid** displays all table headings as *LinkButton* controls (i.e., buttons that act as hyperlinks). The **SortCommand** event is raised when the user clicks a column header name. On line 127, we use the *SortExpression* property of **e**. This property indicates the column by which the data is sorted. This value is added to the current **Session** object's **sortString** key, which is then assigned to our **DataView**'s **Sort** property on line 128. On line 129, we rebind the sorted data to our **DataGrid**.

17.9 Tracing

ASP .NET provides a *tracing* feature for the debugging of Web-based applications. Tracing is the process of placing statements throughout the code-behind file that output information during execution about the program's status.

In Windows applications, message boxes can be used as an aid in debugging; in Web Forms, a programmer might use **Response.Write** for this purpose. However, the employment of **Response.Write** for tracing in ASP .NET has several drawbacks.

One of these drawbacks is that, once an application is executing correctly, the programmer must remove all **Response.Write** statements from the program. This is time-consuming and can introduce errors, because the programmer must differentiate between statements that are part of the program's logic and statements that are used for testing purposes. ASP .NET provides the programmer with two forms of built-in tracing: *page tracing* and *application tracing*.

Page tracing involves the tracing of the actions of an individual page. Setting the *Trace* property of the page to **True** in the **Properties** window enables tracing for that page. Instead of calling the **Response** object's **Write** method, we call the *Trace* object's *Write* method. Object **Trace** is an instance of the *TraceContext* class and provides tracing capabilities. In addition to method **Write**, the **Trace** object includes method *Warn*, which prints warning statements in red. When tracing is disabled by setting the **Trace** property to **False**, **Trace** statements are not executed.

Figure 17.42 depicts a simple page that displays a sentence (we do not show the code for this page, as it is quite simplistic). The **Page_Load** event for this page includes the statement **Trace.Warn("Using warnings")**. Notice that **"Using warnings"** is not displayed on the page; we will see shortly when and where trace statements are displayed.

Figure 17.43 displays the same page when the **Trace** property is set to **True**. The top of the figure depicts the original page, and the tracing information generated by ASP .NET appears below. The *Request Details* section provides information about the request. The *Trace Information* section contains the information output by calling the **Write** and **Warn** methods. The second row contains the message, which displays in red.

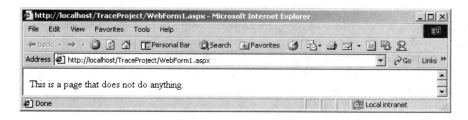

Fig. 17.42 ASPX page with tracing turned off.

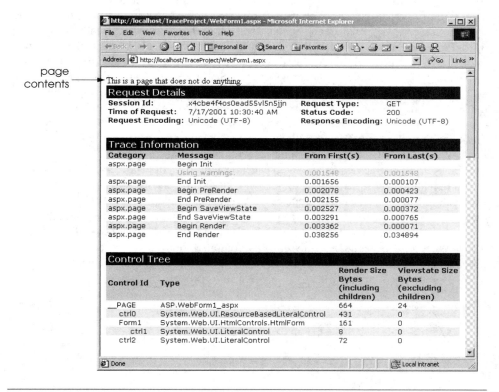

Fig. 17.43 Tracing enabled on a page.

The **Control Tree** section lists all the controls contained on the page. Several additional tables also appear in this page. The **Cookies Collection** section contains information about the program's cookies, the **Headers Collection** section catalogs the HTTP headers for the page and the **Server Variables** section provides a list of server variables (i.e., information sent by the browser with each request) and their values.

Tracing for the entire project is also available. To turn on application-level tracing, open the **Web.config** file for the project. Set the **Enabled** property to **True** in the **trace** element. To view the project's tracing information, navigate the browser to the

trace.axd file in the project folder. This file does not actually exist on the hard drive; it is generated when the user requests **trace.axd**. Figure 17.44 shows the Web page that is generated when the programmer views the **trace.axd** file.

This page lists all the requests made to this application and the times when the pages were accessed. The clicking of one of the **View Details** links directs the browser to a page similar to the one portrayed in Fig. 17.43.

17.10 Summary

Microsoft's ASP .NET technology is used for Web-based application development. Web-based applications create Web content for Web browser clients using Web-Form files. The Web-Form file represents the Web page that is sent to the client browser. Web-Form files have the file extension **.aspx** and contain the GUI of the Web page currently being developed. Programmers customize Web Forms by adding Web controls, which include text boxes, images and buttons. Every ASPX file created in Visual Studio has a corresponding class located in the code-behind file that provides the ASPX file's programmatic implementation.

Visual Studio generates the markup in the ASPX page when controls are dragged onto the Web Form. When a control's **runat** attribute is set to **"server"**, this control is executed on a server, generating HTML equivalent markup for the control. The **asp:** tag prefix in the declaration of a control indicates that the control is an ASP .NET Web control. Each Web control maps to a corresponding HTML element.

Class **Page** defines a standard Web page, providing event handlers and objects necessary for creating Web-based applications. All code-behind classes for ASPX forms inherit from class **Page**. When a client requests an ASPX file, a class is created behind the scenes that contains both the visual aspect of the page (defined in the ASPX file) and the page's logic (defined in the code-behind file). This new class inherits from **Page**. The first time that a Web page is requested, this class is compiled, and an instance is created. This instance represents the page—it will create the HTML that is sent to the client.

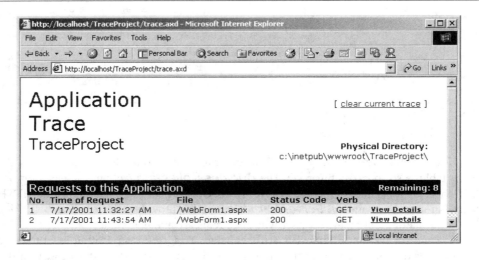

Fig. 17.44 Tracing information for a project.

Method **Page_Init** is called when the **Init** event is raised. This event indicates that the page is ready to be initialized. The **Load** event is raised every time a page is requested/reloaded. The **Page_Load** event handler typically is used to execute any processing that is necessary to restore data from previous requests. After **Page_Load** has finished executing, the page processes any events raised by the page's controls. When a Web Form object is ready for garbage collection, an **Unload** event is raised. Event handler **Page_Unload** is inherited from class **Page** and contains any code that releases resources.

The **PageLayout** property determines how controls are arranged on the form. By default, property **PageLayout** is set to **GridLayout**, meaning that all controls remain exactly where they are dropped on the Web Form.

Image controls insert an image into a Web page. A **TextBox** control allows the programmer to read and display text. A **RadioButtonList** control provides a series of radio buttons for the user. A **DropDownList** control provides a list of options to the user. The **HyperLink** control adds a hyperlink to a Web page. The **AdRotator** Web control is used for displaying advertisements.

A validation control (or validator) checks whether the data in another Web control is in the proper format. A **RegularExpressionValidator** matches a Web control's content against a regular expression. The regular expression that validates the input is assigned to property **ValidationExpressison**. A validator's **ControlToValidate** property indicates which control will be validated. A **RequiredFieldValidator** is used to ensure that a control receives input from the user when the form is submitted. A **CustomValidator** allows programmers to specify the circumstances under which a field is valid. We define these circumstances in the event handler for the **ServerValidate** event of the **CustomValidator**.

Web programmers using ASP .NET often design their Web pages so that, when submitted, the current page is requested again. This event is known as a postback. The **Page**'s **IsPostBack** property can be used to determine whether the page is being loaded as a result of a postback. The **EnableViewState** attribute determines whether a Web control's state persists (i.e., is retained) when a postback occurs.

A session represents a unique client. If the client leaves a site and returns later, the client should still be recognized as the same user. To help the server distinguish among clients, each client must identify itself to the server. The tracking of individual clients is known as session tracking.

A cookie is a text file stored by a Web site on an individual's computer that allows the site to track the actions of the visitor. When a Web Form receives a request, the header includes such information as the request type and any cookies that have been sent previously from the server to be stored on the client machine. When the server formulates its response, the header information includes any cookies the server wants to store on the client computer and other information, such as the MIME type of the response.

A cookie object is of type **HttpCookie**. Cookies are sent and received in the form of a collection of cookies, of type **HttpCookieCollection**. The **Name** and **Value** properties of class **HttpCookie** can be used to retrieve the key and value of the key-value pair in a cookie.

Visual Basic provides session-tracking capabilities in the FCL's **HttpSessionState** class. Every Web Form includes an **HttpSessionState** object, which is accessible through property **Session** of class **Page**. When the Web page is requested, an **HttpSessionState** object is created and is assigned to the **Page**'s **Session** property.

Web Forms should maintain client state information in **HttpSessionState** objects, because such objects are specific to each client. Like a cookie, an **HttpSessionState** object can store name-value pairs. **HttpSessionState** objects can store any type of object (not just **String**s) as attribute values. A value in a key-value pair is retrieved from the **Session** object by indexing the **Session** object with the key name, using the same process by which a value can be retrieved from a hash table. The **Keys** property of class **HttpSessionState** returns a collection containing all the keys in the session.

When a user's identity is confirmed, the user has been authenticated. Method **SetAuthCookie** writes to the client an encrypted cookie containing information necessary to authenticate the user. Encrypted data are data translated into a code that only the sender and receiver can understand thereby keeping it private.

A technique known as forms authentication protects a page so that only authenticated users can access it. Authentication and denial of access to unauthorized users involves the placement of several lines in **Web.config** (a file used for application configuration).

ASP .NET provides a tracing feature for the debugging of Web-based applications. Tracing is the process of placing statements throughout the code-behind file that output information during execution about the program's status. ASP .NET provides the programmer with two forms of built-in tracing—page tracing and application tracing. Page tracing involves the tracing of the actions of an individual page. Application-level tracing enables the programmer to trace the entire project, rather than simply one ASPX page.

17.11 Internet and Web Resources

www.asp.net

The Microsoft site overviews ASP .NET and provides a link for downloading ASP .NET. This site includes the IBuy Spy e-commerce storefront example that uses ASP .NET. Links to the Amazon and Barnes & Noble Web sites where the user can purchase books also are included.

www.asp101.com/aspplus

This site overviews ASP .NET, and includes articles, code examples and links to ASP .NET resources. The code samples demonstrate the use of cookies in an ASP .NET application and show how to establish a connection to a database—two key capabilities of multi-tier applications.

www.411asp.net

This resource site provides programmers with ASP .NET tutorials and code samples. The community pages allows programmers to ask questions, answer questions and post messages.

www.aspfree.com

This site provides free ASP .NET demos and source code. The site also provides a list of articles for various topics and a frequently asked questions (FAQs) page.

www.aspng.com

This site offers tutorials, links and recommendations for books on ASP .NET. Links to different mailing lists are also provides. These links are organized by topic. This site also contains articles related to many ASP .NET topics, such as "Performance Tips and Tricks."

www.aspnetfaq.com

This site provides answers to frequently asked questions (FAQs) about ASP .NET.

www.123aspx.com

This site offers a directory of links to ASP .NET resources. The site also includes daily and weekly newsletters.

18

ASP .NET and Web Services

Objectives

- To understand what a Web service is.
- To create Web services.
- To understand the elements that compose a Web service, such as service descriptions and discovery files.
- To create a client that uses a Web service.
- To use Web services with Windows and Web applications.
- To understand session tracking in Web services.
- To pass user-defined data types to a Web service.

A client is to me a mere unit, a factor in a problem.
Sir Arthur Conan Doyle

...if the simplest things of nature have a message that you understand, rejoice, for your soul is alive.
Eleonora Duse

Protocol is everything.
Francoise Giuliani

They also serve who only stand and wait.
John Milton

18.1 Introduction[1]

Throughout this book, we have created dynamic link libraries (DLLs) to facilitate software reusability and modularity—the cornerstones of good object-oriented programming. However, the use of DLLs is limited, because a DLL must reside on the same machine as the program that uses it. This chapter introduces the use of Web services (sometimes called *XML Web services*) to promote software reusability over distributed systems. Distributed-systems technologies allow applications to execute across multiple computers on a network. A Web service is a class that enables distributed computing by allowing one machine to call methods on other machines via common data formats and protocols, such as XML and HTTP. In .NET, the method calls are implemented through the Simple Object Access Protocol (SOAP), an XML-based protocol describing how to mark up requests and responses so that they can be transferred via protocols such as HTTP. Using SOAP, applications represent and transmit data in a standardized format—XML. The underlying implementation of the Web service is usually not relevant to the client using the Web service.

Microsoft is encouraging software vendors and e-businesses toward the deployment of Web services. As larger numbers of people worldwide connect to the Internet, the concept of applications that call methods across a network becomes more practical. Earlier in this text, we delineated the merits of object-oriented programming. Web services represent the next step in object-oriented programming: Instead of developing software from a small number of class libraries provided at one location, programmers can access countless libraries in multiple locations. This technology also makes it easier for businesses to collaborate and grow together. By purchasing Web services that are relevant to their businesses, companies that create applications can spend less time coding and more time developing new products. In addition, e-businesses can employ Web services to provide their customers with an enhanced shopping experience. Let us look at an online music store as a simple example. The store's Web site provides links to various CDs, enabling users to purchase the CDs or to obtain information about the artists. Another company that sells concert tickets provides a Web service that displays the dates of upcoming concerts by various artists then allows users to buy concert tickets. By deploying the concert-ticket Web

1. IIS must be running to create a Web service in Visual Studio.

service on its site, the online music store can provide an additional service to its customers that will likely result in increased traffic to its site. The company that sells concert tickets also benefits from the business relationship. In addition to selling more tickets, it receives revenue from the online music store for the use of its Web service.

Visual Studio and the .NET framework provide a simple, user-friendly way to create Web services like the one discussed in this example. In this chapter, we explore the steps involved in both the creation and the use of Web services. For each example, we provide the code for the Web service, then give an example of an application that might use the Web service. Our first examples are designed to offer an in-depth analysis of Web services and how they work in Visual Studio. Then, we move on to demonstrate more sophisticated Web services that use session tracking and complex data types.

18.2 Web Services

A Web service is a class stored on one machine that can be accessed on another machine over a network. Because of this relationship, the machine on which the Web service resides commonly is referred to as a *remote machine*. The application that desires access to the Web service sends a method call and its arguments to the remote machine, which processes the call and sends a response to the caller. This kind of distributed computing can benefit various systems, including slow systems, those with limited amounts of memory or resources, those without access to certain data and those lacking the code necessary to perform specific computations. Another advantage of Web services is that code and data can be stored on another computer. For instance, a Web service can be defined at one location to execute several common queries to a database. Not only does the Web service define the necessary code for the client, but the database is stored on the same machine as is the Web service. The client does not need to access or store the database on its machine.

A Web service is, in its simplest form, a class. In previous chapters, when we wanted to include a class in a project, we would have to either define the class in our project or add a reference to the compiled DLL. This compiled DLL is placed in the **bin** directory of our application by default. As a result, all pieces of our application reside on one machine. When we are using Web services, the class we wish to include in our project is instead stored on a remote machine—a compiled version of this class will not be placed in the current application. What actually does happen is discussed shortly.

Methods in a Web service are executed through a *Remote Procedure Call (RPC)*. These methods, which are marked with the **WebMethod** attribute, are often referred to as *Web-service methods*. Declaring a method with this attribute makes the method accessible to other classes through an RPC. The declaration of a Web-service method with attribute **WebMethod** is known as *exposing* a Web-service method.

 Common Programming Error 18.1

Trying to call a remote method in a Web service where the method is not declared with the **WebMethod** *attribute is a compile-time error.*

Method calls to and responses from Web services are transmitted via SOAP. This means that any client capable of generating and processing SOAP messages can use a Web service, regardless of the language in which the Web service is written.

Web services have important implications for *business-to-business (B2B) transactions*—ones that occur between two or more businesses. Now, businesses are able to conduct their transactions via Web services, rather than via custom-created applications—a much simpler and more efficient means of conducting business. Because Web services and SOAP are platform independent, companies can collaborate and use each others' Web services without worrying about the compatibility of technologies or programming languages. In this way, Web services are an inexpensive, readily-available solution to facilitate B2B transactions.

A Web service in .NET has two parts: An *ASMX* file, and a code-behind file. The ASMX file can be viewed in any Web browser and contains valuable information about the Web service, such as descriptions of Web-service methods and ways to test these methods. The code-behind file provides the implementation for the methods that the Web service encompasses. Figure 18.1 depicts Internet Explorer rendering an ASMX file.

The top of the page provides a link to the Web service's **Service Description**. A service description is an XML document that conforms to the *Web Service Description Language (WSDL)*, an XML vocabulary that describes how a Web service behaves. A WSDL document defines the methods that the Web service makes available and the ways in which clients can interact with those methods. The document also specifies lower-level information that clients might need, such as the required format in which to send requests to the Web service and the format of the Web service's response. Visual Studio .NET generates the WSDL service description. Client programs can use the service description to confirm the correctness of method calls when those client programs are compiled.

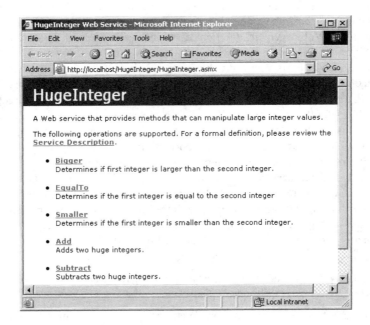

Fig. 18.1   ASMX file rendered in Internet Explorer.

The programmer should not alter this document, for it defines how a Web service works. When a user clicks the **Service Description** link at the top of the ASMX page, WSDL is displayed that defines the service description for this Web service (Fig. 18.2).

Below the **Service Description** link, the Web page shown in Fig. 18.1 lists the methods that the Web service provides (i.e., all methods in the application that are declared with **WebMethod** attributes). Clicking any method name requests a test page that describes the method (Fig. 18.3). After explaining the method's arguments, the page allows users to execute a test run of the method by entering the proper parameters and clicking **Invoke**. (We discuss the process of testing a Web-service method shortly.) Below the **Invoke** button, the page displays sample request and response messages, using SOAP, HTTP GET and HTTP POST. These protocols are the three options for sending and receiving messages in Web services. The protocol used for request and response messages is sometimes known as the Web service's *wire protocol* or *wire format*, because the wire format specifies how information is sent "along the wire." Notice that Fig. 18.3 uses the HTTP GET protocol to test a method. Later in this chapter, when we use Web services in our Visual Basic programs, we instead employ SOAP, because SOAP is the default protocol for Web services in Visual Studio. As we will demonstrate, the use of SOAP to execute calls to Web-service methods can be quite advantageous.

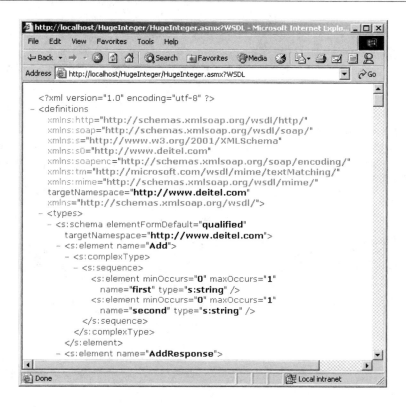

Fig. 18.2   Service description for a Web service.

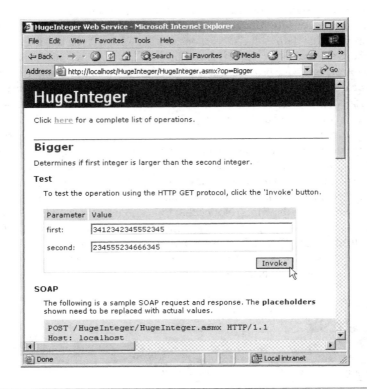

Fig. 18.3 Invoking a method of a Web service from a Web browser.

Users can test the method above by entering **Value**s in the **first:** and **second:** fields and then clicking **Invoke**. The method executes, and a new Web-browser window opens to display an XML document containing the result (Fig. 18.4). Now that we have introduced a simple example using a Web service, the next several sections explore the role of XML in Web services, as well as other aspects of Web services' functionality.

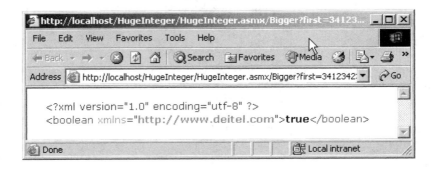

Fig. 18.4 Results of invoking a Web-service method from a Web browser.

Testing and Debugging Tip 18.1

Using the ASMX page of a Web service to test and debug methods makes that Web service more reliable and robust; it also reduces the likelihood that others who use the Web service will encounter errors.

18.3 Simple Object Access Protocol (SOAP) and Web Services

Simple Object Access Protocol (SOAP) is a platform-independent protocol that uses XML to make remote procedure calls over HTTP. Each call and response is packaged in a *SOAP message*—an XML message containing all the information necessary to process its contents. SOAP messages are quite popular, because they are written in the easy-to-understand and platform-independent XML. Similarly, HTTP was chosen to transmit SOAP messages because HTTP is a standard protocol for sending information across the Internet. The use of XML and HTTP enables different operating systems to send and receive SOAP messages. Another benefit of HTTP is that it can be used with networks that contain *firewalls*—security barriers that restrict communication among networks.

Another reason that programmers creating Web services use SOAP is its extensive set of supported data types. Readers should note that the wire format used to transmit requests and responses must support all data types passed between the applications. Web services that use SOAP support a wider variety of data types than do Web services that employ other wire formats. The data types supported by SOAP include the basic data types, **DataSet**, **DateTime**, **XmlNode** and several others. SOAP also permits transmission of arrays of all these types. In addition, user-defined types can be used; we demonstrate how to do this in Section 18.8.

ASP .NET Web services send requests and responses to and from Web services via SOAP. When a program invokes a Web-service method, the request and all relevant information is packaged in a SOAP request message and sent to the appropriate destination. When the Web service receives this SOAP message, it begins to process the contents called the *SOAP envelope*, which specifies the method that the client wishes to execute and the arguments the client is passing to that method. After the Web service receives this request and parses it, the proper method is called with the specified arguments (if there are any), and the response is sent back to the client in a SOAP response message. The client parses the response to retrieve the result of the method call.

The SOAP request message portrayed in Fig. 18.5 was taken directly from the **Bigger** method of the **HugeInteger** Web service (Fig. 18.3). This Web service provides programmers with several methods that manipulate integers larger than those that can be stored as a **Long** variable. Most programmers do not manipulate SOAP messages, allowing the Web service to handle the details of transmission.

```
1   POST /HugeInteger/HugeInteger.asmx HTTP/1.1
2   Host: localhost
3   Content-Type: text/xml; charset=utf-8
4   Content-Length: length
5   SOAPAction: "http://www.deitel.com/Bigger"
6
```

Fig. 18.5 SOAP request message for the **HugeInteger** Web service. (Part 1 of 2.)

```
 7   <?xml version="1.0" encoding="utf-8"?>
 8
 9   <soap:Envelope
10     xmlns:xsi="http://www.w3.org/2001/XMLSchema-instance"
11     xmlns:xsd="http://www.w3.org/2001/XMLSchema"
12     xmlns:soap="http://schemas.xmlsoap.org/soap/envelope/">
13
14     <soap:Body>
15       <Bigger xmlns="http://www.deitel.com">
16         <first>string</first>
17         <second>string</second>
18       </Bigger>
19     </soap:Body>
20   </soap:Envelope>
```

Fig. 18.5 SOAP request message for the **HugeInteger** Web service. (Part 2 of 2.)

Figure 18.5 displays a standard SOAP request message, which is created when a client wishes to execute the **HugeInteger** Web service's method **Bigger**. When a request to a Web service causes such a SOAP request message to be created, the MIME **content-length**'s value (**length**) and elements **first** and **second**'s character data (**String**s) would contain the actual values entered by the user (line 4 and lines 16–17, respectively). If this envelope were transmitting the request from Fig. 18.3, element **first** and element **second** instead would be the numbers represented in the figure. Placeholder "**length**" would contain the length of this SOAP request message.

18.4 Publishing and Consuming Web Services

This section presents several examples of creating (also known as *publishing*) and using (also known as *consuming*) a Web service. An application that consumes a Web service actually consists of two parts: A *proxy* class representing the Web service and a client application that accesses the Web service via an instance of the proxy class. A proxy class handles the transfer of the arguments for a Web-service method from the client application to the Web service and the transfer of the result from the Web-service method back to the client application. Visual Studio can generate a proxy class—we demonstrate how to do this momentarily.

Figure 18.6 presents the code-behind file for the **HugeInteger** Web service (Fig. 18.1). This Web service is designed to perform calculations with integers that contain a maximum of 100 digits. As we mentioned earlier, **Long** variables cannot handle integers of this size (i.e., an overflow occurs). The Web service provides a client with methods that take two "huge integers" and immediately determines which one is larger or smaller, whether the two numbers are equal, their sum and their difference. The reader can think of these methods as services that one application provides for the programmers of other applications (hence the term, Web services). Any programmer can access this Web service, use the methods and thus avoid writing over 200 lines of code. We hide portions of the Visual Studio generated code in the code-behind files. We do this for both brevity and presentation purposes.

Line 14 assigns the Web service namespace to **www.deitel.com** to uniquely identify this Web service. This namespace is specified in the **Namespace** property of a **Web-Service** attribute. In lines 15–16, we use property **Description** to provide information about our Web service that appears in the ASMX file. In line 18, notice that our class derives from **System.Web.Services.WebService**—by default, Visual Studio defines our Web service so that it inherits from the **WebService** class. Although a Web service is not required to derive from **WebService**, this class provides members that are useful in determining information about the client and the Web service itself. Several methods in class **HugeInteger** are tagged with the *WebMethod* attribute, which exposes a method so that it can be called remotely. When this attribute is absent, the method is not accessible through the Web service. Notice that this attribute, like the **WebService** attribute, contains a **Description** property, which provides information about the method to our ASMX page. Readers can see these descriptions in the output of Fig. 18.6.

```vb
1    ' Fig. 18.6: HugeInteger.asmx.vb
2    ' HugeInteger WebService.
3
4    Imports System
5    Imports System.Collections
6    Imports System.ComponentModel
7    Imports System.Data
8    Imports System.Diagnostics
9    Imports System.Web
10   Imports System.Web.Services ' contains Web service classes
11
12   ' performs operation on large integers
13
14   <WebService(Namespace:="http://www.deitel.com", _
15      Description := "A Web service that provides methods that" _
16      & " can manipulate large integer values." ) > _
17   Public Class HugeInteger
18      Inherits System.Web.Services.WebService
19
20      Private Const MAXIMUM As Integer = 100
21      Public number() As Integer
22
23      ' default constructor
24      Public Sub New()
25
26         ' CODEGEN: This call is required by the ASP.NET Web
27         ' Services Designer
28         InitializeComponent()
29
30         number = New Integer(MAXIMUM) {}
31      End Sub ' New
32
33      ' Visual Studio .NET generated code
34
35      ' property that accepts an integer parameter
36      Public Property Digits(ByVal index As Integer) As Integer
37         Get
38            Return number(index)
39         End Get
40
```

Fig. 18.6   HugeInteger Web service. (Part 1 of 5.)

```
41              Set(ByVal Value As Integer)
42                 number(index) = Value
43              End Set
44
45           End Property ' Property
46
47           ' returns String representation of HugeInteger
48           Public Overrides Function ToString() As String
49              Dim returnString As String = ""
50
51              Dim digit As Integer
52              For Each digit In number
53                 returnString = digit & returnString
54              Next
55
56              Return returnString
57           End Function
58
59
60           ' creates HugeInteger based on argument
61           Public Shared Function FromString(ByVal value As String) _
62              As HugeInteger
63
64              Dim parsedInteger As New HugeInteger()
65              Dim i As Integer
66
67              For i = 0 To value.Length - 1
68                 parsedInteger.Digits(i) = Int32.Parse( _
69                    value.Chars(value.Length - i - 1).ToString())
70              Next
71
72
73              Return parsedInteger
74           End Function
75
76           ' WebMethod that performs the addition of integers
77           'represented by the string arguments
78           <WebMethod( Description := "Adds two huge integers." )> _
79           Public Function Add(ByVal first As String, _
80              ByVal second As String) As String
81
82              Dim carry As Integer = 0
83              Dim i As Integer
84
85              Dim operand1 As HugeInteger = _
86                 HugeInteger.FromString(first)
87
88              Dim operand2 As HugeInteger = _
89                 HugeInteger.FromString(second)
90
91              ' store result of addition
92              Dim result As New HugeInteger()
93
```

Fig. 18.6   HugeInteger Web service. (Part 2 of 5.)

```vbnet
94          ' perform addition algorithm for each digit
95          For i = 0 To MAXIMUM
96
97              ' add two digits in same column
98              ' result is their sum, plus carry from
99              ' previous operation modulo 10
100             result.Digits(i) = _
101                (operand1.Digits(i) + operand2.Digits(i)) _
102                   Mod 10 + carry
103
104             ' set carry to remainder of dividing
105             ' sums of two digits by 10
106             carry = (operand1.Digits(i) + operand2.Digits(i)) \ 10
107         Next
108
109         Return result.ToString()
110
111     End Function ' Add
112
113     ' WebMethod that performs the subtraction of integers
114     ' represented by the String arguments
115     <WebMethod( Description := "Subtracts two huge integers." )> _
116     Public Function Subtract(ByVal first As String, _
117        ByVal second As String) As String
118
119        Dim i As Integer
120        Dim operand1 As HugeInteger = _
121           HugeInteger.FromString(first)
122
123        Dim operand2 As HugeInteger = _
124           HugeInteger.FromString(second)
125
126        Dim result As New HugeInteger()
127
128        ' subtract top digit from bottom digit
129        For i = 0 To MAXIMUM
130           ' if top digit is smaller than bottom
131           ' digit we need to borrow
132           If operand1.Digits(i) < operand2.Digits(i) Then
133              Borrow(operand1, i)
134           End If
135
136           ' subtract bottom from top
137           result.Digits(i) = operand1.Digits(i) - _
138              operand2.Digits(i)
139        Next
140
141        Return result.ToString()
142     End Function ' Subtract
143
```

Fig. 18.6   HugeInteger Web service. (Part 3 of 5.)

```
144        ' borrows 1 from next digit
145        Private Sub Borrow(ByVal hugeInteger As HugeInteger, _
146           ByVal place As Integer)
147
148           ' if no place to borrow from, signal problem
149           If place >= MAXIMUM - 1 Then
150              Throw New ArgumentException()
151
152           ' otherwise if next digit is zero,
153           ' borrow from digit to left
154           ElseIf hugeInteger.Digits(place + 1) = 0 Then
155              Borrow(hugeInteger, place + 1)
156           End If
157
158           ' add ten to current place because we borrowed
159           ' and subtract one from previous digit -
160           ' this is digit borrowed from
161           hugeInteger.Digits(place) += 10
162           hugeInteger.Digits(place + 1) -= 1
163
164        End Sub ' Borrow
165
166        ' WebMethod that returns true if first integer is
167        ' bigger than second
168        <WebMethod( Description := "Determines if first integer is " & _
169           "larger than the second integer." )> _
170        Public Function Bigger(ByVal first As String, _
171           ByVal second As String) As Boolean
172
173           Dim zeroes As Char() = {"0"}
174
175           Try
176              ' if elimination of all zeroes from result
177              ' of subtraction is an empty string,
178              ' numbers are equal, so return false,
179              ' otherwise return true
180              If Subtract(first, second).Trim(zeroes) = "" Then
181                 Return False
182              Else
183                 Return True
184              End If
185
186              ' if ArgumentException occurs, first number
187              ' was smaller, so return False
188           Catch exception As ArgumentException
189              Return False
190           End Try
191        End Function ' Bigger
192
```

Fig. 18.6   HugeInteger Web service. (Part 4 of 5.)

```
193     ' WebMethod returns True if first integer is
194     ' smaller than second
195     <WebMethod( Description := "Determines if the first integer " & _
196         "is smaller than the second integer.")> _
197     Public Function Smaller(ByVal first As String, _
198         ByVal second As String) As Boolean
199
200         ' if second is bigger than first, then first is
201         ' smaller than second
202         Return Bigger(second, first)
203     End Function
204
205     ' WebMethod that returns true if two integers are equal
206     <WebMethod( Description := "Determines if the first integer " & _
207         "is equal to the second integer" )> _
208     Public Function EqualTo(ByVal first As String, _
209         ByVal second As String) As Boolean
210
211         ' if either first is bigger than second, or first is
212         ' smaller than second, they are not equal
213         If (Bigger(first, second) OrElse _
214             Smaller(first, second)) Then
215             Return False
216         Else
217             Return True
218         End If
219     End Function ' EqualTo
220 End Class ' HugeInteger
```

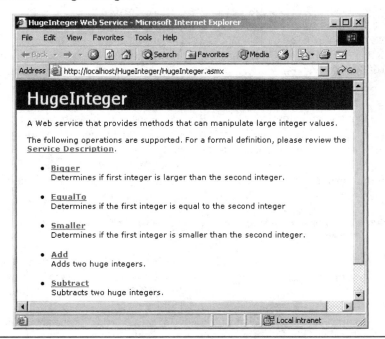

Fig. 18.6 HugeInteger Web service. (Part 5 of 5.)

Good Programming Practice 18.1

Specify a namespace for each Web service so that it can be uniquely identified.

Good Programming Practice 18.2

Specify descriptions for all Web services and Web-service methods so that clients can obtain additional information about the Web service and its contents.

Common Programming Error 18.2

*No method with the **WebMethod** attribute can be declared **Shared**—for a client to access a Web-service method, an instance of that Web service must exist.*

Lines 36–45 define a **Property** that enables us to access any digit in a **HugeInteger** through property **Digits**. Lines 78 and 115 define **WebMethod**s **Add** and **Subtract**, which perform addition and subtraction, respectively. Method **Borrow** (defined in lines 145–164) handles the case in which the digit that we are currently looking at in the left operand is smaller than the corresponding digit in the right operand. For instance, when we subtract 19 from 32, we usually go digit by digit, starting from the right. The number 2 is smaller than 9, so we add 10 to 2 (resulting in 12), which subtracts 9, resulting in 3 for the right most digit in the solution. We then subtract 1 from the next digit over (3), making it 2. The corresponding digit in the right operand is now the "1" in 19. The subtraction of 1 from 2 is 1, making the corresponding digit in the result 1. The final result, when the resulting digits are put together, is 13. Method **Borrow** is the method that adds ten to the appropriate digits and subtracts 1 from the digits to the left. Because this is a utility method that is not intended to be called remotely, it is not qualified with attribute **WebMethod**.

The screen capture in Fig. 18.6 is identical to the one in Fig. 18.1. A client application can invoke only the five methods listed in the screen shot (i.e., the methods qualified with the **WebMethod** attribute).

Let us demonstrate how to create this.[2] To begin, we must create a project of type **ASP .NET Web Service**. Like Web Forms, Web services are stored in the Web server's **wwwroot** directory on the server (e.g., **localhost**). By default, Visual Studio places the solution file (**.sln**) in the **Visual Studio Projects** folder.

Notice that, when the project is created, the code-behind file is displayed by default in design view (Fig. 18.7). If this file is not open, it can be opened by double-clicking **Service1.asmx**. The file that will be opened, however, is **Service1.asmx.vb** (the code-behind file for our Web service). This is because, when creating Web services in Visual Studio, programmers work almost exclusively in the code-behind file. In fact, if a programmer were to open the ASMX file, it would contain only the lines

```
<%@ WebService Language="vb" Codebehind="Service1.asmx.vb"
    Class="WebService1.Service1" %>
```

indicating the name of the code-behind file, the programming language in which the code-behind file is written and the class that defines our Web service. This is the extent of the information that this file must contain. [*Note:* By default, the code-behind file is not listed

---

2. Visit the **Downloads/Resources** link at **www.deitel.com** to download the code examples for this book, and visit the FAQs link for step-by-step configuration instructions for the Web Services examples.

in the **Solution Explorer**. It is displayed when the ASMX file is double clicked. It can be listed in the **Solution Explorer** if the icon to show all files is clicked.]

It may seem strange that there is a design view for a Web service, when a Web service does not have a graphical user interface. The answer is that more sophisticated Web services contain methods that manipulate more than just strings or numbers. For example, a Web-service method could manipulate a database. Instead of typing all the code necessary to create a database connection, we simply drop the proper ADO .NET components into the design view and manipulate them as we would in a Windows or Web application. We will see an example of this in Section 18.6.

Now that we have defined our Web service, we demonstrate how to use it. First, a client application must be created. In this first example, we create a Windows application as our client. Once this application has been created, the client must add a proxy class that can be used to access the Web service. A proxy class (or *proxy*) is a class created from the Web service's WSDL file that enables the client to call Web-service methods over the Internet. The proxy class handles all the "plumbing" required for method calls to Web-service methods. Whenever a call is made in the client application to a Web-service method, the application actually calls a corresponding method in the proxy class. This method takes the method name and arguments and then formats them so that they can be sent as a request in a SOAP envelope. The Web service receives this request and executes the method call, sending back the result in another SOAP envelope. When the client application receives the SOAP envelope containing the response, the proxy class decodes it and formats the results so that they are understandable to the client. This information then is returned to the client. It is important to note that the proxy class essentially is hidden from the program. We cannot, in fact, view it in the **Solution Explorer** unless we choose to show all the files. The purpose of the proxy class is to make it seem to clients as if they are calling the Web-service methods directly— the client should have no need to view or manipulate the proxy class.

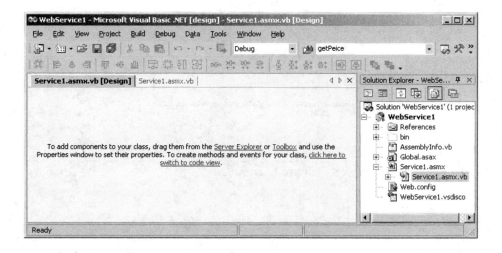

Fig. 18.7   Design view of a Web service.

The next example demonstrates how to create a Web-service client and its corresponding proxy class. We must begin by creating a project and then adding a *Web reference* to the project. When we add a Web reference to a client application, the proxy class is created. The client then creates an instance of the proxy class, which is in turn used to call methods included in the Web service.

To create a proxy in Visual Studio, right click the **References** folder in **Solution Explorer**, and select **Add Web Reference** (Fig. 18.8). In the **Add Web Reference** dialog that appears (Fig. 18.9), enter the Web address[3] of the Web service, and press *Enter*. When the description of the Web service appears, click **Add Reference** (Fig. 18.9). This adds to the **Solution Explorer** (Fig. 18.10) a **Web References** folder with a node named after the domain name where the Web service is located. In this case, the name is **localhost**, because we are using the local Web server. This means that, when we reference class **HugeInteger**, we will be doing so through class **HugeInteger** in namespace **localhost** (the Web service class and proxy class have the same name). Visual Studio generates a proxy for the Web service and adds it as a reference (Fig. 18.10).

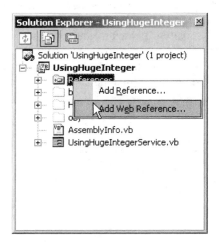

Fig. 18.8   Adding a Web reference to a project.

---

3. In this chapter, we store the Web service in the root directory of our local Web server (**http://localhost**, whose physical location is **C:\Inetpub\wwwroot**). We do not store the services in the **VB** directory used in the previous chapter.

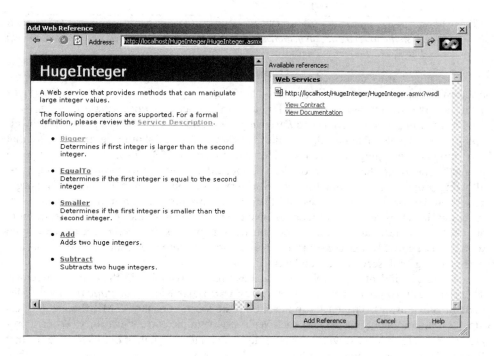

Fig. 18.9 Web reference selection and description.

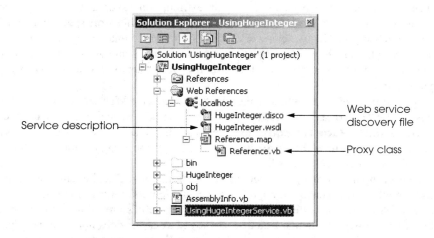

Fig. 18.10 Solution Explorer after adding a Web reference to a project.

Good Programming Practice 18.3

When creating a program that uses Web services, add the Web reference first. This enables Visual Studio to recognize an instance of the Web-service class, allowing Intellisense to help developers use the Web service.

The steps that we described previously work well if the programmer knows the appropriate Web-service reference. However, what if we are trying to locate a new Web service? There are two technologies that can facilitate this process: *Universal Description, Discovery and Integration (UDDI)* and *Discovery files (DISCO)*. UDDI is a project for developing a set of specifications that define how Web services should be exposed, so that programmers searching for Web services can find them. Microsoft began an ongoing project to facilitate the locating of Web services that conform to certain specifications, allowing programmers to find different Web services through search engines. UDDI organizes and describes Web services and then places this information in a central location. Although UDDI is beyond the scope of what we are teaching, the reader can learn more about this project and view a demonstration by visiting **www.uddi.org** and **uddi.microsoft.com/default.aspx**. Both of these sites contain search tools that make finding Web services fast and easy.

A DISCO file catalogs any Web services that are available in the current directory. There are both *dynamic discovery* files (**.vsdisco** extension) and *static discovery* files (**.disco** extension). These files indicate both the location of the ASMX file and the service description (a WSDL file) for each Web service in the current directory. When a programmer creates a Web service, Visual Studio generates a dynamic discovery file for that Web service. When a client is adding a Web reference, the dynamic discovery file is then used to point out the Web service. Once the Web reference is created, a static discovery file is placed in the client's project. The static discovery file hard-codes the location for the ASMX and WSDL files (by "hard code," we mean that the location is entered directly into the file). Dynamic discovery files, on the other hand, are created such that the list of Web services are created dynamically on the server when a client is searching for Web services. The use of dynamic discovery enables certain extra options, such as the hiding of certain Web services in subdirectories. Discovery files are a Microsoft-specific technology, whereas UDDI is not. The two can work together, though, to enable a client to find a Web service. Using both technologies, the client can use a search engine to find a location with various Web services on a topic, and then use discovery files to view all the Web services in that location.

Once the Web reference is added, the client can access the Web service through a proxy. Because **HugeInteger** is located as a proxy class in namespace **localhost**, we must use **localhost.HugeInteger** to reference this class. The Windows Form in Fig. 18.11 uses the **HugeInteger** Web service to perform computations with positive integers that are up to **100** digits long.

The user inputs two integers, each up to 100 digits long. Clicking any button invokes a remote method to perform the appropriate calculation and return the result. The return value of each operation is displayed, and all leading zeroes are eliminated by **String** method **TrimStart**. Note that **FrmUsingHugeInteger** does not have the capability to perform operations with 100-digit numbers. It instead creates **String** representations of these numbers and passes them as arguments to Web-service methods that handle such tasks for us.

```vb
1    ' Fig. 18.11: UsingHugeIntegerService.vb
2    ' Using the HugeInteger Web Service.
3
4    Imports System
5    Imports System.Drawing
6    Imports System.Collections
7    Imports System.ComponentModel
8    Imports System.Windows.Forms
9    Imports System.Web.Services.Protocols
10
11   ' allows user to perform operations on large integers
12   Public Class FrmUsingHugeInteger
13      Inherits Windows.Forms.Form
14
15      ' declare a reference Web service
16      Private remoteInteger As localhost.HugeInteger
17
18      ' HugeInteger operation buttons
19      Friend WithEvents cmdAdd As Button
20      Friend WithEvents cmdEqual As Button
21      Friend WithEvents cmdSmaller As Button
22      Friend WithEvents cmdLarger As Button
23      Friend WithEvents cmdSubtract As Button
24
25      ' input text boxes
26      Friend WithEvents txtSecond As TextBox
27      Friend WithEvents txtFirst As TextBox
28
29      ' question and answer labels
30      Friend WithEvents lblPrompt As Label
31      Friend WithEvents lblResult As Label
32
33      Private zeroes() As Char = {"0"}
34
35      ' default constructor
36      Public Sub New()
37         MyBase.New()
38
39         InitializeComponent()
40
41         ' instantiate remoteInteger
42         remoteInteger = New localhost.HugeInteger()
43      End Sub
44
45      ' Visual Studio .NET generated code
46
47      Public Shared Sub Main()
48         Application.Run(New FrmUsingHugeInteger())
49      End Sub ' Main
50
```

Fig. 18.11 Using the **HugeInteger** Web service. (Part 1 of 5.)

```vbnet
51     ' checks if two numbers user input are equal
52     Private Sub cmdEqual_Click(ByVal sender As System.Object, _
53        ByVal e As System.EventArgs) Handles cmdEqual.Click
54
55        ' make sure HugeIntegers do not exceed 100 digits
56        If SizeCheck(txtFirst, txtSecond) Then
57           Return
58        End If
59
60        ' call Web-service method to determine if integers are equal
61        If remoteInteger.EqualTo( _
62           txtFirst.Text, txtSecond.Text) Then
63
64           lblResult.Text = _
65              txtFirst.Text.TrimStart(zeroes) & _
66              " is equal to " & _
67              txtSecond.Text.TrimStart(zeroes)
68        Else
69           lblResult.Text = _
70              txtFirst.Text.TrimStart(zeroes) & _
71              " is NOT equal to " & _
72              txtSecond.Text.TrimStart(zeroes)
73        End If
74
75     End Sub ' cmdEqual_Click
76
77     ' checks if first integer input
78     ' by user is smaller than second
79     Private Sub cmdSmaller_Click(ByVal sender As System.Object, _
80        ByVal e As System.EventArgs) Handles cmdSmaller.Click
81
82        ' make sure HugeIntegers do not exceed 100 digits
83        If SizeCheck(txtFirst, txtSecond) Then
84           Return
85        End If
86
87        ' call Web-service method to determine if first
88        ' integer is smaller than second
89        If remoteInteger.Smaller( _
90           txtFirst.Text, txtSecond.Text) Then
91
92           lblResult.Text = _
93              txtFirst.Text.TrimStart(zeroes) & _
94              " is smaller than " & _
95              txtSecond.Text.TrimStart(zeroes)
96        Else
97           lblResult.Text = _
98              txtFirst.Text.TrimStart(zeroes) & _
99              " is NOT smaller than " & _
100             txtSecond.Text.TrimStart(zeroes)
101       End If
102
103    End Sub ' cmdSmaller_Click
```

Fig. 18.11 Using the **HugeInteger** Web service. (Part 2 of 5.)

```
104
105      ' checks if first integer input
106      ' by user is bigger than second
107      Private Sub cmdLarger_Click(ByVal sender As System.Object, _
108         ByVal e As System.EventArgs) Handles cmdLarger.Click
109
110         ' make sure HugeIntegers do not exceed 100 digits
111         If SizeCheck(txtFirst, txtSecond) Then
112            Return
113         End If
114
115         ' call Web-service method to determine if first
116         ' integer is larger than the second
117         If remoteInteger.Bigger(txtFirst.Text, _
118            txtSecond.Text) Then
119
120            lblResult.Text = _
121               txtFirst.Text.TrimStart(zeroes) & _
122               " is larger than " & _
123               txtSecond.Text.TrimStart(zeroes)
124         Else
125            lblResult.Text = _
126               txtFirst.Text.TrimStart(zeroes) & _
127               " is NOT larger than " & _
128               txtSecond.Text.TrimStart(zeroes)
129         End If
130
131      End Sub ' cmdLarger_Click
132
133      ' subtract second integer from first
134      Private Sub cmdSubtract_Click(ByVal sender As System.Object, _
135         ByVal e As System.EventArgs) Handles cmdSubtract.Click
136
137         ' make sure HugeIntegers do not exceed 100 digits
138         If SizeCheck(txtFirst, txtSecond) Then
139            Return
140         End If
141
142         ' perform subtraction
143         Try
144            Dim result As String = remoteInteger.Subtract( _
145               txtFirst.Text, txtSecond.Text).TrimStart(zeroes)
146
147            If result = "" Then
148               lblResult.Text = "0"
149            Else
150               lblResult.Text = result
151            End If
152
153         ' if WebMethod throws an exception, then first
154         ' argument was smaller than second
```

Fig. 18.11 Using the **HugeInteger** Web service. (Part 3 of 5.)

```
155            Catch exception As SoapException
156               MessageBox.Show( _
157                  "First argument was smaller than the second")
158            End Try
159
160         End Sub ' cmdSubtract_Click
161
162         ' adds two integers input by user
163         Private Sub cmdAdd_Click(ByVal sender As System.Object, _
164            ByVal e As System.EventArgs) Handles cmdAdd.Click
165
166            ' make sure HugeInteger does not exceed 100 digits
167            ' and be sure both are not 100 digits long
168            ' which would result in overflow
169
170            If txtFirst.Text.Length > 100 OrElse _
171               txtSecond.Text.Length > 100 OrElse _
172               (txtFirst.Text.Length = 100 AndAlso _
173               txtSecond.Text.Length = 100) Then
174
175               MessageBox.Show("HugeIntegers must not be more " _
176                  & "than 100 digits" & vbCrLf & "Both integers " _
177                  & "cannot be of length 100: this causes an overflow", _
178                  "Error", MessageBoxButtons.OK, _
179                  MessageBoxIcon.Information)
180               Return
181            End If
182
183            ' perform addition
184            lblResult.Text = _
185               remoteInteger.Add(txtFirst.Text, _
186               txtSecond.Text).TrimStart(zeroes)
187
188         End Sub ' cmdAdd_Click
189
190         ' determine if size of integers is too big
191         Private Function SizeCheck(ByVal first As TextBox, _
192            ByVal second As TextBox) As Boolean
193
194            If first.Text.Length > 100 OrElse _
195               second.Text.Length > 100 Then
196
197               MessageBox.Show("HugeIntegers must be less than 100" _
198                  & " digits", "Error", MessageBoxButtons.OK, _
199                  MessageBoxIcon.Information)
200
201               Return True
202            End If
203
204            Return False
205         End Function ' SizeCheck
206      End Class ' FrmUsingHugeInteger
```

Fig. 18.11 Using the **HugeInteger** Web service. (Part 4 of 5.)

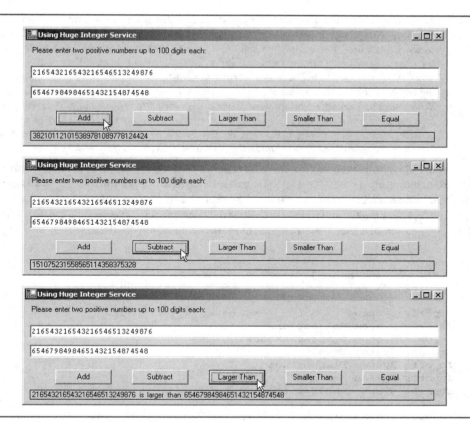

Fig. 18.11 Using the **HugeInteger** Web service. (Part 5 of 5.)

18.5 Session Tracking in Web Services

In Chapter 17, we described the importance of maintaining information about users to personalize their experiences. In the context of that discussion, we explored session tracking using cookies and sessions. In this section, we incorporate session tracking into a Web service. Sometimes, it makes sense that a client application would call several methods from the same Web service, and it might call some methods possibly several times. It would be beneficial for such a Web service to maintain state information for the client. Using session tracking can be beneficial because information that is stored as part of the session will not need to be passed back and forth between the Web service and the client. This will not only cause the client application to run faster, but also require less effort on the part of the programmer (who likely will have to pass less information to a method).

Storing session information also can provide for a more intuitive Web service. In the following example, we create a Web service designed to assist with the computations involved in playing a game of Blackjack (Fig. 18.12). We will then use this Web service to create a dealer for a game of Blackjack. This dealer handles the details for our deck of cards. The information is stored as part of the session, so that one deck of cards does not get mixed up with another deck being used by another client application. Our example uses casino Blackjack rules:

Two cards each are dealt to the dealer and the player. The player's cards are dealt face up. Only one of the dealer's cards is dealt face up. Then, the player can begin taking additional cards one at a time. These cards are dealt face up, and the player decides when to stop taking cards. If the sum of the player's cards exceeds 21, the game is over, and the player loses. When the player is satisfied with the current set of cards, the player "stays" (i.e., stops taking cards) and the dealer's hidden card is revealed. If the dealer's total is less than 17, the dealer must take another card; otherwise, the dealer must stay. The dealer must continue to take cards until the sum of the dealer's cards is greater than or equal to 17. If the dealer exceeds 21, the player wins. Otherwise, the hand with the higher point total wins. If both sets of cards have the same point total, the game is a push (i.e., a tie) and no one wins.

The Web service that we create provides methods to deal a card and to count cards in a hand, determining a value for a specific hand. Each card is represented by a **String** in the form "**face suit**" where **face** is a digit representing the face of the card, and **suit** is a digit representing the suit of the card. After the Web service is created, we create a Windows application that uses these methods to implement a game of Blackjack.

```
1   ' Fig. 18.12: BlackjackService.asmx.vb
2   ' Blackjack Web Service which deals and counts cards.
3
4   Imports System
5   Imports System.Collections
6   Imports System.ComponentModel
7   Imports System.Data
8   Imports System.Diagnostics
9   Imports System.Web
10  Imports System.Web.Services
11
12  <WebService(Namespace:="http://www.deitel.com", Description := _
13     "A Web service that provides methods to manipulate a deck " _
14     & "of cards" )> _
15  Public Class BlackjackService
16     Inherits System.Web.Services.WebService
17
18     ' Visual Studio .NET generated code
19
20     ' deals card that has not yet been dealt
21     <WebMethod(EnableSession:=True, Description := "Deal a new " _
22        & "card from the deck." )> _
23     Public Function DealCard() As String
24
25        Dim card As String = "2 2"
26
27        ' get client's deck
28        Dim deck As ArrayList = CType(Session("deck"), ArrayList)
29        card = Convert.ToString(deck(0))
30        deck.RemoveAt(0)
31        Return card
32
33     End Function ' DealCard
34
```

Fig. 18.12 Blackjack Web service. (Part 1 of 3.)

```vb
35    <WebMethod(EnableSession:=True, Description := "Create and " _
36      & "shuffle a deck of cards." )> _
37    Public Sub Shuffle()
38
39       Dim temporary As Object
40       Dim randomObject As New Random()
41       Dim newIndex As Integer
42       Dim i, j As Integer
43
44       Dim deck As New ArrayList()
45
46       ' generate all possible cards
47       For i = 1 To 13
48          For j = 0 To 3
49             deck.Add(i & " " & j)
50          Next
51       Next
52
53       ' swap each card with another card randomly
54       For i = 0 To deck.Count - 1
55
56          newIndex = randomObject.Next(deck.Count - 1)
57          temporary = deck(i)
58          deck(i) = deck(newIndex)
59          deck(newIndex) = temporary
60       Next
61
62       ' add this deck to user's session state
63       Session.Add("deck", deck)
64    End Sub ' Shuffle
65
66    ' computes value of hand
67    <WebMethod( Description := "Compute a numerical value" _
68      & " for the current hand." )> _
69    Public Function CountCards(ByVal dealt As String) As Integer
70
71       ' split string containing all cards
72       Dim tab As Char() = {vbTab}
73       Dim cards As String() = dealt.Split(tab)
74       Dim drawn As String
75       Dim total As Integer = 0
76       Dim face, numAces As Integer
77       numAces = 0
78
79       For Each drawn In cards
80
81          ' get face of card
82          face = Int32.Parse( _
83             drawn.Substring(0, drawn.IndexOf(" ")))
84
85          Select Case face
86             Case 1 ' if ace, increment numAces
87                numAces += 1
```

Fig. 18.12 Blackjack Web service. (Part 2 of 3.)

```
88                    Case 11 To 13 ' if jack, queen or king, add 10
89                        total += 10
90                    Case Else ' otherwise, add value of face
91                        total += face
92                End Select
93            Next
94
95            ' if there are any aces, calculate optimum total
96            If numAces > 0 Then
97
98                ' if it is possible to count one Ace as 11, and rest
99                ' 1 each, do so; otherwise, count all Aces as 1 each
100               If (total + 11 + numAces - 1 <= 21) Then
101                   total += 11 + numAces - 1
102               Else
103                   total += numAces
104               End If
105           End If
106
107           Return total
108
109   End Function ' CountCards
110
111 End Class ' BlackjackService
```

Fig. 18.12 Blackjack Web service. (Part 3 of 3.)

Lines 21–23 define method **DealCard** as a **WebMethod**, with property **EnableSession** set to **True**. This property needs to be set to **True** for session information to be maintained. This simple step provides an important advantage to our Web service. The Web service can now use an **HttpSessionState** object (called **Session**) to maintain the deck of cards for each client application that wishes to use this Web service (line 28). We can use **Session** to store objects for a specific client between method calls. We discussed session state in detail in Chapter 17, ASP .NET, Web Forms and Web Controls.

As we discuss shortly, method **DealCard** removes a card from the deck and returns it to the client. Without using a session variable, the deck of cards would need to be passed back and forth with each method call. Not only does the use of session state make the method easy to call (it requires no arguments), but we avoid the overhead that would occur from sending this information back and forth. This makes our Web service faster.

Right now, we simply have methods that use session variables. The Web service, however, still cannot determine which session variables belong to which user. This is an important point—if the Web service cannot uniquely identify a user, it has failed to perform session tracking properly. If two clients successfully call the **DealCard** method, the same deck would be manipulated. In order to identify various users, the Web service creates a cookie for each user. A client application that wishes to use this Web service will need to accept this cookie in a **CookieContainer** object. We discuss this in more detail shortly, when we look into the client application that uses the Blackjack Web service.

Method **DealCard** (lines 21–33) obtains the current user's deck as an **ArrayList** from the Web service's **Session** object (line 28). You can think of an **ArrayList** as a dynamic array (i.e., its size can change at runtime). Class **ArrayList** is discussed in greater detail in Chapter 20, Data Structures and Collections. The class's method **Add** places an **Object** in the **ArrayList**. Method **DealCard** then removes the top card from the deck (line 30) and returns the card's value as a **String** (line 31).

Method **Shuffle** (lines 35–64) generates an **ArrayList** representing a card deck, shuffles it and stores the shuffled cards in the client's **Session** object. Lines 47–51 include **For** loops to generate **String**s in the form "**face suit**" to represent each possible card in a deck. Lines 54–60 shuffle the recreated deck by swapping each card with another random card in the deck. Line 63 adds the **ArrayList** to the **Session** object to maintain the deck between method calls.

Method **CountCards** (lines 67–109) counts the values of the cards in a hand by trying to attain the highest score possible without going over 21. Precautions need to be taken when calculating the value of the cards, because an ace can be counted as either 1 or 11, and all face cards count as 10.

The **String dealt** is tokenized into its individual cards by calling **String** method **Split** and passing it an array containing the tab character. The **For Each** loop (line 79) counts the value of each card. Lines 82–83 retrieve the first integer—the face—and use that value as input to the **Select Case** statement in line 85. If the card is 1 (an ace), the program increments variable **aceCount**. Because an ace can have two values, additional logic is required to process aces. If the card is a 13, 12 or 11 (King, Queen or Jack), the program adds 10 to the total. If the card is anything else, the program increases the total by that value.

In lines 96–105, the aces are counted after all the other cards. If several aces are included in a hand, only one can be counted as 11 (e.g., if two were counted as 11 we would already have a hand value of 22, which is a losing hand). We then determine whether counting one ace as 11 and the rest as 1will result in a total that does not exceed 21. If this is possible, line 101 adjusts the total accordingly. Otherwise, line 103 adjusts the total, counting each ace as 1 point.

CountCards attempts to maximize the value of the current cards without exceeding 21. Imagine, for example, that the dealer has a 7 and then receives an ace. The new total could be either 8 or 18. However, **CountCards** always tries to maximize the value of the cards without going over 21, so the new total is 18.

Now, we use the Blackjack Web service in a Windows application called **Game** (Fig. 18.13). This program uses an instance of **BlackjackService** to represent the dealer, calling its **DealCard** and **CountCards** methods. The Web service keeps track of both the player's and the dealer's cards (i.e., all the cards that have been dealt).

Each player has eleven **PictureBox**es—the maximum number of cards that can be dealt without automatically exceeding 21. These **PictureBox**es are placed in an **ArrayList**, allowing us to index the **ArrayList** to determine which **PictureBox** will display the card image.

```
1   ' Fig. 18.13: Blackjack.vb
2   ' Blackjack game that uses the Blackjack Web service.
3
```

Fig. 18.13 Blackjack game that uses the **Blackjack** Web service. (Part 1 of 9.)

```vb
4    Imports System
5    Imports System.Drawing
6    Imports System.Collections
7    Imports System.ComponentModel
8    Imports System.Windows.Forms
9    Imports System.Data
10   Imports System.Net ' for cookieContainer
11
12   ' game that uses Blackjack Web Service
13   Public Class FrmBlackJack
14      Inherits System.Windows.Forms.Form
15
16      Private dealer As localhost.BlackjackService
17      Private dealersCards, playersCards As String
18      Private cardBoxes As ArrayList
19      Private playerCard, dealerCard As Integer
20      Friend WithEvents pbStatus As System.Windows.Forms.PictureBox
21
22      Friend WithEvents cmdStay As System.Windows.Forms.Button
23      Friend WithEvents cmdHit As System.Windows.Forms.Button
24      Friend WithEvents cmdDeal As System.Windows.Forms.Button
25
26      Friend WithEvents lblDealer As System.Windows.Forms.Label
27      Friend WithEvents lblPlayer As System.Windows.Forms.Label
28
29      Public Enum GameStatus
30         PUSH
31         LOSE
32         WIN
33         BLACKJACK
34      End Enum
35
36
37      Public Sub New()
38
39         InitializeComponent()
40
41         dealer = New localhost.BlackjackService()
42
43         ' allow session state
44         dealer.CookieContainer = New CookieContainer()
45
46         cardBoxes = New ArrayList()
47
48         ' put PictureBoxes into ArrayList
49         cardBoxes.Add(pictureBox1)
50         cardBoxes.Add(pictureBox2)
51         cardBoxes.Add(pictureBox3)
52         cardBoxes.Add(pictureBox4)
53         cardBoxes.Add(pictureBox5)
54         cardBoxes.Add(pictureBox6)
55         cardBoxes.Add(pictureBox7)
56         cardBoxes.Add(pictureBox8)
```

Fig. 18.13 Blackjack game that uses the **Blackjack** Web service. (Part 2 of 9.)

```
57        cardBoxes.Add(pictureBox9)
58        cardBoxes.Add(pictureBox10)
59        cardBoxes.Add(pictureBox11)
60        cardBoxes.Add(pictureBox12)
61        cardBoxes.Add(pictureBox13)
62        cardBoxes.Add(pictureBox14)
63        cardBoxes.Add(pictureBox15)
64        cardBoxes.Add(pictureBox16)
65        cardBoxes.Add(pictureBox17)
66        cardBoxes.Add(pictureBox18)
67        cardBoxes.Add(pictureBox19)
68        cardBoxes.Add(pictureBox20)
69        cardBoxes.Add(pictureBox21)
70        cardBoxes.Add(pictureBox22)
71     End Sub ' New
72
73     ' Visual Studio .NET generated code
74
75     ' deals cards to dealer while dealer's total is
76     ' less than 17, then computes value of each hand
77     ' and determines winner
78     Private Sub cmdStay_Click(ByVal sender As System.Object, _
79        ByVal e As System.EventArgs) Handles cmdStay.Click
80        cmdStay.Enabled = False
81        cmdHit.Enabled = False
82        cmdDeal.Enabled = True
83        DealerPlay()
84     End Sub ' cmdStay_Click
85
86     ' process dealers turn
87     Private Sub DealerPlay()
88
89        ' while value of dealer's hand is below 17,
90        ' dealer must take cards
91        While dealer.CountCards(dealersCards) < 17
92           dealersCards &= vbTab & dealer.DealCard()
93           DisplayCard(dealerCard, "")
94           dealerCard += 1
95           MessageBox.Show("Dealer takes a card")
96        End While
97
98
99        Dim dealersTotal As Integer = _
100          dealer.CountCards(dealersCards)
101       Dim playersTotal As Integer = _
102          dealer.CountCards(playersCards)
103
104       ' if dealer busted, player wins
105       If dealersTotal > 21 Then
106          GameOver(GameStatus.WIN)
107          Return
108       End If
109
```

Fig. 18.13 Blackjack game that uses the **Blackjack** Web service. (Part 3 of 9.)

```vbnet
110            ' if dealer and player have not exceeded 21,
111            ' higher score wins; equal scores is a push
112            If dealersTotal > playersTotal Then
113               GameOver(GameStatus.LOSE)
114            ElseIf playersTotal > dealersTotal Then
115               GameOver(GameStatus.WIN)
116            Else
117               GameOver(GameStatus.PUSH)
118            End If
119
120      End Sub 'DealerPlay
121
122      ' deal another card to player
123      Private Sub cmdHit_Click(ByVal sender As System.Object, _
124         ByVal e As System.EventArgs) Handles cmdHit.Click
125
126            ' get player another card
127            Dim card As String = dealer.DealCard()
128            playersCards &= vbTab & card
129            DisplayCard(playerCard, card)
130            playerCard += 1
131
132            Dim total As Integer = _
133               dealer.CountCards(playersCards)
134
135            ' if player exceeds 21, house wins
136            If total > 21 Then
137               GameOver(GameStatus.LOSE)
138            End If
139            ' if player has 21, they cannot take more cards
140            ' the dealer plays
141            If total = 21 Then
142               cmdHit.Enabled = False
143               DealerPlay()
144            End If
145
146
147      End Sub ' cmdHit_Click
148
149      ' deal two cards each to dealer and player
150      Private Sub cmdDeal_Click(ByVal sender As System.Object, _
151         ByVal e As System.EventArgs) Handles cmdDeal.Click
152
153            Dim card As String
154            Dim cardImage As PictureBox
155
156            ' clear card images
157            For Each cardImage In cardBoxes
158               cardImage.Image = Nothing
159            Next
160
161            pbStatus.Image = Nothing
162
```

Fig. 18.13 Blackjack game that uses the **Blackjack** Web service. (Part 4 of 9.)

```
163          dealer.Shuffle()
164
165          ' deal two cards to player
166          playersCards = dealer.DealCard()
167          DisplayCard(0, playersCards)
168          card = dealer.DealCard()
169          DisplayCard(1, card)
170          playersCards &= vbTab & card
171
172          ' deal two cards to dealer, only display face
173          ' of first card
174          dealersCards = dealer.DealCard()
175          DisplayCard(11, dealersCards)
176          card = dealer.DealCard()
177          DisplayCard(12, "")
178          dealersCards &= vbTab & card
179
180          cmdStay.Enabled = True
181          cmdHit.Enabled = True
182          cmdDeal.Enabled = False
183
184          Dim dealersTotal As Integer = _
185             dealer.CountCards(dealersCards)
186
187          Dim playersTotal As Integer = _
188             dealer.CountCards(playersCards)
189
190          ' if hands equal 21, it is a push
191          If dealersTotal = playersTotal AndAlso _
192             dealersTotal = 21 Then
193             GameOver(GameStatus.PUSH)
194
195          ' if dealer has 21, dealer wins
196          ElseIf dealersTotal = 21 Then
197             GameOver(GameStatus.LOSE)
198
199          ' if player has 21, the player has blackjack
200          ElseIf playersTotal = 21 Then
201             GameOver(GameStatus.BLACKJACK)
202          End If
203
204          playerCard = 2
205          dealerCard = 13
206
207       End Sub ' cmdDeal_Click
208
209       ' displays card represented by card value in
210       ' PictureBox with number card
211       Public Sub DisplayCard(ByVal card As Integer, _
212          ByVal cardValue As String)
213
```

Fig. 18.13 Blackjack game that uses the **Blackjack** Web service. (Part 5 of 9.)

```
214          ' retrieve appropriate PictureBox from ArrayList
215          Dim displayBox As PictureBox = _
216             CType(cardBoxes(card), PictureBox)
217
218          ' if String representing card is empty,
219          ' set displayBox to display back of card
220          If cardValue = "" Then
221             displayBox.Image = _
222                Image.FromFile("blackjack_images\\cardback.png")
223             Return
224          End If
225
226          ' retrieve face value of card from cardValue
227          Dim faceNumber As Integer = Int32.Parse( _
228             cardValue.Substring(0, cardValue.IndexOf(" ")))
229
230          Dim face As String = faceNumber.ToString()
231
232          ' retrieve the suit of the card from cardValue
233          Dim suit As String = cardValue.Substring( _
234             cardValue.IndexOf(" ") + 1)
235
236          Dim suitLetter As Char
237
238          ' determine if suit is other then clubs
239          Select Case (Convert.ToInt32(suit))
240             Case 0 ' suit is clubs
241                suitLetter = "c"
242             Case 1 ' suit is diamonds
243                suitLetter = "d"
244             Case 2 ' suit is hearts
245                suitLetter = "h"
246             Case Else 'suit is spades
247                suitLetter = "s"
248          End Select
249
250          ' set displayBox to display appropriate image
251          displayBox.Image = Image.FromFile( _
252             "blackjack_images\\" & face & suitLetter & ".png")
253
254       End Sub ' DisplayCard
255
256       ' displays all player cards and shows
257       ' appropriate game status message
258       Public Sub GameOver(ByVal winner As GameStatus)
259
260          Dim tab As Char() = {vbTab}
261          Dim cards As String() = dealersCards.Split(tab)
262          Dim i As Integer
263
264          For i = 0 To cards.Length - 1
265             DisplayCard(i + 11, cards(i))
266          Next
```

Fig. 18.13 Blackjack game that uses the **Blackjack** Web service. (Part 6 of 9.)

```
267
268          ' push
269          If winner = GameStatus.PUSH Then
270             pbStatus.Image = _
271                Image.FromFile("blackjack_images\\tie.png")
272
273          ' player loses
274          ElseIf winner = GameStatus.LOSE Then
275             pbStatus.Image = _
276                Image.FromFile("blackjack_images\\lose.png")
277
278          ' player has blackjack
279          ElseIf winner = GameStatus.BLACKJACK Then
280             pbStatus.Image = _
281                Image.FromFile("blackjack_images\\blackjack.png")
282
283          ' player wins
284          Else
285             pbStatus.Image = _
286                Image.FromFile("blackjack_images\\win.png")
287          End If
288
289          cmdStay.Enabled = False
290          cmdHit.Enabled = False
291          cmdDeal.Enabled = True
292
293       End Sub ' GameOver
294
295    End Class ' Blackjack
```

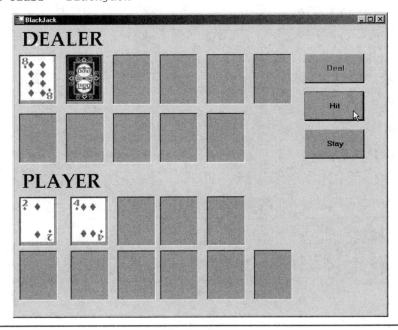

Fig. 18.13 Blackjack game that uses the **Blackjack** Web service. (Part 7 of 9.)

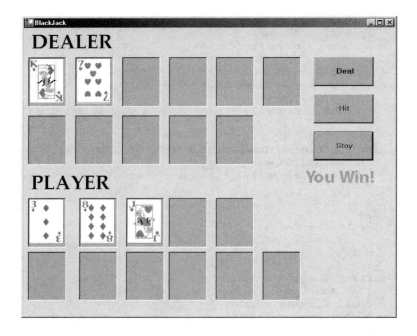

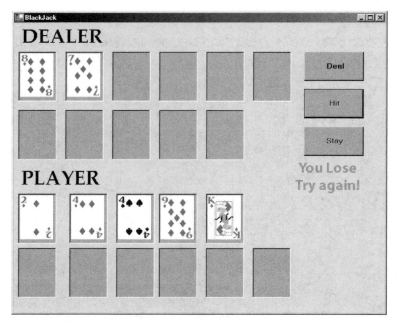

Fig. 18.13 Blackjack game that uses the **Blackjack** Web service. (Part 8 of 9.)

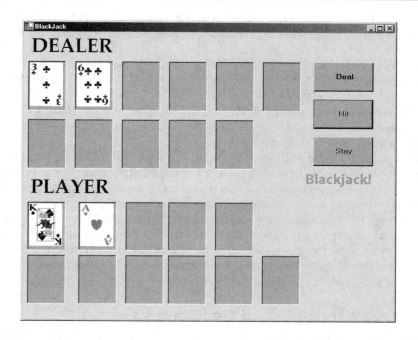

Fig. 18.13 Blackjack game that uses the **Blackjack** Web service. (Part 9 of 9.)

Previously we mentioned that the client must provide a way to accept any cookies created by the Web service to identify users. Line 44 in the constructor creates a new **CookieContainer** object for the **CookieContainer** property of **dealer**. Class **CookieContainer** (defined in namespace **System.Net**) acts as a storage space for an object of the **HttpCookie** class. Creating the **CookieContainer** allows the Web service to maintain a session state for this client. This **CookieContainer** contains a **Cookie** with a unique identifier that the server can use to recognize the client when the client makes future requests. By default, the **CookieContainer** is **Nothing**, and a new **Session** object is created by the Web Service for each request.

Method **GameOver** (line 258–293) displays all the dealer's cards (many of which are face-down during the game) and shows the appropriate message in the status **PictureBox**. Method **GameOver** receives as an argument a member of the **GameStatus** enumeration (defined in lines 29–34). The enumeration represents whether the player tied, lost or won the game; its four members are: **PUSH**, **LOSE**, **WIN** and **BLACKJACK**.

When the player clicks the **Deal** button (event handler on lines 150–207), all the **PictureBox**es are cleared, the deck is shuffled and the player and dealer receive two cards each. If both obtain scores of 21, method **GameOver** is called and is passed **GameStatus.PUSH**. If only the player has 21 after the first two cards are dealt, **GameOver** is called and is passed **GameStatus.BLACKJACK**. If only the dealer has 21, method **GameOver** is called and is passed **GameStatus.LOSE**.

If **GameOver** is not called, the player can take additional cards by clicking the **Hit** button (event handler on line 123–147). Each time a player clicks **Hit**, the player is dealt one card, which is displayed in the GUI. If the player exceeds 21, the game is over, and the player loses. If the player has exactly 21, the player is not allowed to take any more cards.

Players can click the **Stay** button to indicate that they do not want to risk being dealt another card. In the event handler for this event (lines 78–84), all the **Hit** and **Stay** buttons are disabled, and method **DealerPlay** is called. This method (lines 87–120) causes the dealer to keep taking cards until the dealer's hand is worth 17 or more. If the dealer exceeds 21, the player wins; otherwise, the values of the hands are compared, and **GameOver** is called with the appropriate argument.

Method **DisplayCard** (lines 211–254) retrieves the appropriate card image. It takes as arguments an integer representing the index of the **PictureBox** in the **ArrayList** that must have its image set and a **String** representing the card. An empty **String** indicates that we wish to display the back of a card; otherwise, the program extracts the face and suit from the **String** and uses this information to find the correct image. The **Select Case** statement (lines 239–248) converts the number representing the suit into an integer and assigns the appropriate character to **suitLetter** (**c** for Clubs, **d** for Diamonds, **h** for Hearts and **s** for Spades). The character **suitLetter** is used to complete the image's file name.

18.6 Using Web Forms and Web Services

In the previous examples, we have accessed Web services from Windows applications. However, we can just as easily use them in Web applications. Because Web-based businesses are becoming more and more prevalent, it often is more practical for programmers to design Web services as part of Web applications. Figure 18.14 presents an airline reservation Web service that receives information regarding the type of seat the customer wishes to reserve and then makes a reservation if such a seat is available.

```
1    ' Fig. 18.14: Reservation.asmx.vb
2    ' Airline reservation Web Service.
3
4    Imports System
5    Imports System.Data
6    Imports System.Diagnostics
7    Imports System.Web
8    Imports System.Web.Services
9    Imports System.Data.OleDb
10
11   ' performs reservation of a seat
12   <WebService(Namespace:="http://www.deitel.com/", Description := _
13      "Service that enables a user to reserve a seat on a plane.")> _
14   Public Class Reservation
15      Inherits System.Web.Services.WebService
16
17      Friend WithEvents oleDbDataAdapter1 As _
18         System.Data.OleDb.OleDbDataAdapter
```

Fig. 18.14 Airline reservation Web service. (Part 1 of 3.)

```
19
20      Friend WithEvents oleDbDeleteCommand1 As _
21         System.Data.OleDb.OleDbCommand
22
23      Friend WithEvents oleDbConnection1 As _
24         System.Data.OleDb.OleDbConnection
25
26      Friend WithEvents oleDbInsertCommand1 As _
27         System.Data.OleDb.OleDbCommand
28
29      Friend WithEvents oleDbSelectCommand1 As _
30         System.Data.OleDb.OleDbCommand
31
32      Friend WithEvents oleDbUpdateCommand1 As _
33         System.Data.OleDb.OleDbCommand
34
35      ' Visual Studio .NET generated code
36
37      ' checks database to determine if matching seat is available
38      <WebMethod(Description := "Method to reserve a seat.")> _
39      Public Function Reserve(ByVal seatType As String, _
40         ByVal classType As String) As Boolean
41
42         ' try database connection
43         Try
44            Dim dataReader As OleDbDataReader
45
46            ' open database connection
47            oleDbConnection1.Open()
48
49            ' set and execute SQL query
50            oleDbDataAdapter1.SelectCommand.CommandText = _
51               "SELECT Number FROM Seats WHERE Type = '" & _
52               seatType & "' AND Class = '" & classType & _
53               "' AND Taken = '0'"
54            dataReader = _
55               oleDbDataAdapter1.SelectCommand.ExecuteReader()
56
57            ' if there were results, seat is available
58            If dataReader.Read() Then
59
60               Dim seatNumber As String = dataReader.GetString(0)
61               dataReader.Close()
62
63               ' update the first available seat to be taken
64               oleDbDataAdapter1.UpdateCommand.CommandText = _
65                  "Update Seats Set Taken = '1' WHERE Number = '" _
66                  & seatNumber & "'"
67
68               oleDbDataAdapter1.UpdateCommand.ExecuteNonQuery()
69
70               Return True
71            End If
```

Fig. 18.14 Airline reservation Web service. (Part 2 of 3.)

```
72
73              dataReader.Close()
74
75      Catch exception As OleDbException  ' if connection problem
76          Return False
77
78      Finally
79          oleDbConnection1.Close()
80      End Try
81
82      ' no seat was reserved
83      Return False
84
85   End Function  ' Reserve
86
87 End Class  ' Reservation
```

Fig. 18.14 Airline reservation Web service. (Part 3 of 3.)

The airline reservation Web service has a single **WebMethod**—**Reserve** (line 38–85)—which searches its seat database to locate a seat matching a user's request. If it finds an appropriate seat, **Reserve** updates the database, makes the reservation, and returns **True**; otherwise, no reservation is made, and the method returns **False**.

Reserve takes two arguments—a **String** representing the desired seat type (the choices are window, middle and aisle) and a **String** representing the desired class type (the choices are economy and first class). Our database contains four columns: The seat number, the seat type, the class type and a column containing either 0 or 1 to indicate whether the seat is taken. Lines 50–53 define an SQL query that retrieves the number of available seats matching the requested seat and class type. The statement in lines 54–55 executes the query. If the result of the query is not empty, the application reserves the first seat number that the query returns. The database is updated with an **UPDATE** statement, and **Reserve** returns **True**, indicating that the reservation was successful. If the result of the **SELECT** query is not successful, **Reserve** returns **False**, indicating that no seats available matched the request.

Earlier in the chapter, we displayed a Web service in design view (Fig. 18.7), and we explained that design view allows the programmer to add components to a Web service in a visual manner. In our airline reservation Web service (Fig. 18.14), we used various data components. Figure 18.15 shows these components in design view. Notice that it is easier to drop these components into our Web service using the **Toolbox** rather than typing the equivalent code.

Figure 18.16 presents the ASPX listing for the Web Form through which users can select seat types. This page allows users to reserve a seat on the basis of its class and location in a row of seats. The page then uses the airline-reservation Web service to carry out users' requests. If the database request is not successful, the user is instructed to modify the request and try again.

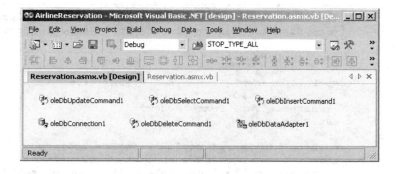

Fig. 18.15 Airline Web Service in design view.

```
1   <%-- Fig. 18.16: TicketReservation.aspx              --%>
2   <%-- A Web Form to allow users to select the kind of seat --%>
3   <%-- they wish to reserve.                            --%>
4
5   <%@ Page Language="vb" AutoEventWireup="false"
6      Codebehind="TicketReservation.aspx.vb"
7      Inherits="MakeReservation.TicketReservation"%>
8
9   <!DOCTYPE HTML PUBLIC "-//W3C//DTD HTML 4.0 Transitional//EN">
10  <HTML>
11     <HEAD>
12       <title>Ticket Reservation</title>
13       <meta content="Microsoft Visual Studio.NET 7.0" name=GENERATOR>
14       <meta content="Visual Basic 7.0" name=CODE_LANGUAGE>
15       <meta content=JavaScript name=vs_defaultClientScript>
16       <meta name=vs_targetSchema content=
17          http://schemas.microsoft.com/intellisense/ie5>
18     </HEAD>
19     <body MS_POSITIONING="GridLayout">
20
21       <form id=Form1 method=post runat="server">
22
23          <asp:DropDownList id=seatList style="Z-INDEX: 105;
24             LEFT: 23px; POSITION: absolute; TOP: 43px"
25             runat="server" Width="105px" Height="22px">
26
27             <asp:ListItem Value="Aisle">Aisle</asp:ListItem>
28             <asp:ListItem Value="Middle">Middle</asp:ListItem>
29             <asp:ListItem Value="Window">Window</asp:ListItem>
30
31          </asp:DropDownList>
32
33          <asp:DropDownList id=classList style="Z-INDEX: 102;
34             LEFT: 145px; POSITION: absolute; TOP: 43px"
35             runat="server" Width="98px" Height="22px">
36
```

Fig. 18.16 ASPX file that takes reservation information. (Part 1 of 2.)

```
37                <asp:ListItem Value="Economy">Economy</asp:ListItem>
38                <asp:ListItem Value="First">First</asp:ListItem>
39
40          </asp:DropDownList>
41
42          <asp:Button id=reserveButton style="Z-INDEX: 103;
43             LEFT: 21px; POSITION: absolute; TOP: 83px"
44             runat="server" Text="Reserve">
45          </asp:Button>
46
47          <asp:Label id=Label1 style="Z-INDEX: 104;
48             LEFT: 17px; POSITION: absolute; TOP: 13px"
49             runat="server">Please select the type of seat and
50             class you wish to reserve:
51          </asp:Label>
52
53       </form>
54    </body>
55 </HTML>
```

Fig. 18.16 ASPX file that takes reservation information. (Part 2 of 2.)

This page defines two **DropDownList** objects and a **Button**. One **DropDown-List** displays all the seat types from which users can select. The second lists choices for the class type. Users click the **Button**, named **reserveButton**, to submit requests after making selections from the **DropDownList**s. The code-behind file (Fig. 18.17) attaches an event handler for this button.

```
1  ' Fig. 18.17: TicketReservation.aspx.vb
2  ' Making a reservation using a Web Service.
3
4  Imports System
5  Imports System.Collections
6  Imports System.ComponentModel
7  Imports System.Data
8  Imports System.Drawing
9  Imports System.Web
10 Imports System.Web.SessionState
11 Imports System.Web.UI
12 Imports System.Web.UI.WebControls
13 Imports System.Web.UI.HtmlControls
14
15 ' allows visitors to select seat type to reserve, and
16 ' then make the reservation
17 Public Class TicketReservation
18    Inherits System.Web.UI.Page
19
20    Protected WithEvents Label1 As Label
21    Protected WithEvents reserveButton As Button
22    Protected WithEvents classList As DropDownList
23    Protected WithEvents seatList As DropDownList
```

Fig. 18.17 Code-behind file for the reservation page. (Part 1 of 3.)

```
24      Private Agent As New localhost.Reservation()
25
26      ' Visual Studio .NET generated code
27
28      Private Sub Page_Load(ByVal sender As System.Object, _
29         ByVal e As System.EventArgs) Handles MyBase.Load
30
31         If IsPostBack
32            classList.Visible = False
33            seatList.Visible = False
34            reserveButton.Visible = False
35            Label1.Visible = False
36         End If
37      End Sub
38
39      ' calls Web Service to try to reserve the specified seat
40      Private Sub reserveButton_Click(ByVal sender As _
41         System.Object, ByVal e As System.EventArgs) _
42         Handles reserveButton.Click
43
44         ' if WebMethod returned true, signal success
45         If Agent.Reserve(seatList.SelectedItem.Text, _
46            classList.SelectedItem.Text.ToString) Then
47
48            Response.Write("Your reservation has been made." _
49               & "   Thank you.")
50
51            ' WebMethod returned False, so signal failure
52         Else
53            Response.Write("This seat is not available, " & _
54               "please hit the back button on your browser " & _
55               "and try again.")
56         End If
57
58      End Sub ' reserveButton_Click
59
60   End Class ' TicketReservation
```

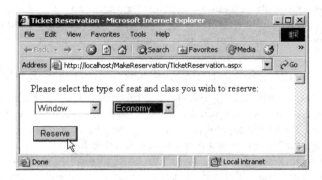

Fig. 18.17 Code-behind file for the reservation page. (Part 2 of 3.)

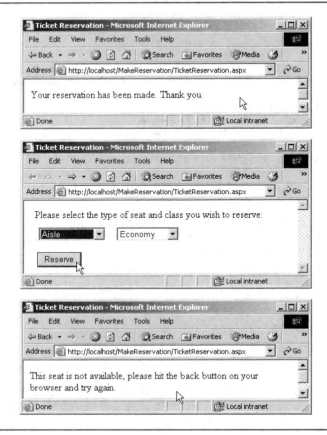

Fig. 18.17 Code-behind file for the reservation page. (Part 3 of 3.)

Line 24 creates a **Reservation** object. When the user clicks **Reserve**, the **reserveButton_Click** event handler executes, and the page reloads. The event handler (lines 40–58) calls the Web service's **Reserve** method and passes it the selected seat and class type as arguments. If **Reserve** returns **True**, the application displays a message thanking the user for making a reservation; otherwise, the user is notified that the type of seat requested is not available, and the user is instructed to try again.

18.7 Case Study: Temperature Information Application

This case study discusses both a Web service that presents weather forecasts for various cities around the United States and a Windows application that employs the Web service. The Web service uses networking capabilities to display the forecasts; it parses a Web page containing the required information and then extracts weather forecast information.

First, we present Web service **TemperatureServer**, in Fig. 18.18. This Web service reads a Web page and collects information about the temperature and weather conditions in an assortment of American cities. [*Note*: At the time of publication, this program runs in the manner that we depict. However, if changes are made to the Web page from which the program retrieves data, the program might work differently or not at all. Please check our Web site at **www.deitel.com** for updates.]

```vb
1   ' Fig. 18.18: TemperatureServer.asmx.vb
2   ' TemperatureServer Web Service that extract weather
3   ' information from a Web page.
4
5   Imports System
6   Imports System.Collections
7   Imports System.ComponentModel
8   Imports System.Data
9   Imports System.Diagnostics
10  Imports System.Web
11  Imports System.Web.Services
12  Imports System.IO
13  Imports System.Net
14
15  <WebService(Namespace:="http://www.deitel.com", Description := _
16     "A Web service that provides information from the " _
17     & "National Weather Service.")> _
18  Public Class TemperatureServer
19     Inherits System.Web.Services.WebService
20
21     Dim cityList As ArrayList
22
23     Public Sub New()
24        MyBase.New()
25
26        'This call is required by the Web Services Designer.
27        InitializeComponent()
28     End Sub
29
30     ' Visual Studio .Net generated code
31
32     <WebMethod(EnableSession := true, Description := "Method to " _
33        & "read information from the National Weather Service.")> _
34     Public Sub UpdateWeatherConditions()
35        ' create a WebClient to get access to the web
36        ' page
37        Dim myClient As New WebClient()
38        Dim cityList As New ArrayList()
39
40        ' get a StreamReader for response so we can read
41        ' the page
42        Dim input As New StreamReader( _
43           myClient.OpenRead( _
44           "http://iwin.nws.noaa.gov/iwin/us/" & _
45           "traveler.html"))
46
47        Dim separator As String = "TAV12"
48
49        'locate first horizontal line on Web page
```

Fig. 18.18 TemperatureServer Web service. (Part 1 of 3.)

```
50        While Not input.ReadLine().StartsWith( _
51           separator)
52           ' do nothing
53        End While
54
55        ' s1 is the day format and s2 is the night format
56        Dim dayFormat As String = _
57           "CITY              WEA     HI/LO   WEA      HI/LO"
58        Dim nightFormat As String = _
59           "CITY              WEA     LO/HI   WEA      LO/HI"
60
61        Dim inputLine As String = ""
62
63        ' locate header that begins weather information
64        Do
65           inputLine = input.ReadLine()
66        Loop While (Not inputLine.Equals(dayFormat)) AndAlso _
67           (Not inputLine.Equals(nightFormat))
68
69        ' get first city's info
70        inputLine = input.ReadLine()
71
72        While inputLine.Length > 28
73
74           ' create WeatherInfo object for city
75           Dim cityWeather As New CityWeather( _
76              inputLine.Substring(0, 16), _
77              inputLine.Substring(16, 7), _
78              inputLine.Substring(23, 7))
79
80           ' add to List
81           cityList.Add(cityWeather)
82
83           ' get next city's info
84           inputLine = input.ReadLine()
85        End While
86
87        ' close connection to NWS server
88        input.Close()
89
90        ' add city list to user session
91        Session.Add("cityList", cityList)
92
93     End Sub 'UpdateWeatherConditions
94
95     <WebMethod(EnableSession := true, Description := "Method to " _
96        & "retrieve a list of cities.")> _
97     Public Function Cities() As String()
98
99        Dim cityList As ArrayList = _
100          Ctype(Session("cityList"), ArrayList)
101
102       Dim currentCities(cityList.Count-1) As String
```

Fig. 18.18 TemperatureServer Web service. (Part 2 of 3.)

```
103          Dim i As Integer
104
105          ' retrieve the names of all cities
106          For i = 0 To cityList.Count - 1
107            Dim weather As CityWeather = _
108               CType(cityList(i), CityWeather)
109            currentCities(i) = weather.CityName
110          Next
111
112          Return currentCities
113       End Function ' Cities
114
115       <WebMethod(EnableSession := true, Description := "Method to " _
116          & "retrieve a list of weather descriptions for cities.")> _
117       Public Function Descriptions() As String()
118
119          Dim cityList As ArrayList = _
120             Ctype(Session("cityList"), ArrayList)
121
122          Dim cityDescriptions(cityList.Count-1) As String
123          Dim i As Integer
124          ' retrieve weather descriptions of all cities
125          For i = 0 To cityList.Count - 1
126
127             Dim weather As CityWeather = _
128                CType(cityList(i), CityWeather)
129             cityDescriptions(i) = weather.Description
130          Next
131
132          Return cityDescriptions
133       End Function ' Descriptions
134
135       <WebMethod(EnableSession := true, Description := "Method to " _
136          & "retrieve a list of temperatures for a list of cities.")> _
137       Public Function Temperatures() As String()
138
139          Dim cityList As ArrayList = _
140             Ctype(Session("cityList"), ArrayList)
141
142          Dim cityTemperatures(cityList.Count-1) As String
143          Dim i As Integer
144
145          ' retrieve temperatures for all cities
146          For i = 0 To cityList.Count - 1
147
148             Dim weather As CityWeather = _
149                CType(cityList(i), CityWeather)
150             cityTemperatures(i) = weather.Temperature
151          Next
152
153          Return cityTemperatures
154       End Function ' Temperatures
155    End Class ' TemperatureServer
```

Fig. 18.18 TemperatureServer Web service. (Part 3 of 3.)

Method **UpdateWeatherConditions**, which gathers weather data from a Web page, is the first **WebMethod** that a client must call from the Web service. The service also provides the **WebMethod**s **Cities**, **Descriptions** and **Temperatures**, which return different kinds of forecast-related information.

When **UpdateWeatherConditions** (line 32–93) is invoked, the method connects to a Web site containing the traveler's forecasts from the National Weather Service (NWS). Line 37 creates a *WebClient* object, which we use because the **WebClient** class is designed for interaction with a source specified by a URL. In this case, the URL for the NWS page is **http://iwin.nws.noaa.gov/iwin/us/traveler.html**. Lines 43–45 call **WebClient** method *OpenRead*; the method retrieves a **Stream** from the URL containing the weather information and then uses this **Stream** to create a **StreamReader** object. Using a **StreamReader** object, the program can read the Web page's HTML markup line-by-line.

The section of the Web page in which we are interested starts with the **String** "**TAV12**." Therefore, lines 50–53 read the HTML markup one line at a time until this **String** is encountered. Once the string "**TAV12**" is reached, the **Do/Loop While** structure (lines 64–67) continues to read the page one line at a time until it finds the header line (i.e., the line at the beginning of the forecast table). This line starts with either **dayFormat**, indicating day format, or **nightFormat**, indicating night format. Because the line could be in either format, the structure checks for both. Line 70 reads the next line from the page, which is the first line containing temperature information.

The **While** structure (lines 72–85) creates a new **CityWeather** object to represent the current city. It parses the **String** containing the current weather data, separating the city name, the weather condition and the temperature. The **CityWeather** object is added to **cityList** (an **ArrayList** that contains a list of the cities, their descriptions and their current temperatures); then, the next line from the page is read and is stored in **inputLine** for the next iteration. This process continues until the length of the **String** read from the Web page is less than or equal to **28**. This signals the end of the temperature section. Line 91 adds the **ArrayList cityList** to the **Session** object so that the values are maintained between method calls.

Method **Cities** (line 95–113) creates an array of **String**s that can contain as many **String**s as there are elements in **cityList**. Lines 99–100 obtain the list of cities from the **Session** object. Lines 106–110 iterate through each **CityWeather** object in **cityList** and insert the city name into the array that is returned in line 109. Methods **Descriptions** (lines 115–133) and **Temperatures** (lines 135–154) behave similarly, except that they return weather descriptions and temperatures, respectively.

Figure 18.19 contains the code listing for the **CityWeather** class. The constructor takes three arguments: The city's name, the weather description and the current temperature. The class provides the properties **CityName**, **Temperature** and **Description**, so that these values can be retrieved by the Web service.

```
1   ' Fig. 18.19: CityWeather.vb
2   ' Class representing the weather information for one city.
3
4   Imports System
```

Fig. 18.19 Class that stores weather information about a city. (Part 1 of 2.)

```
5
6    Public Class CityWeather
7
8       Private mCityName, mTemperature, mDescription As String
9
10      Public Sub New(ByVal city As String, ByVal description _
11         As String, ByVal temperature As String)
12         mCityName = city
13         mDescription = description
14         mTemperature = temperature
15      End Sub
16
17      ' name of city
18      Public ReadOnly Property CityName() As String
19         Get
20            Return mCityName
21         End Get
22      End Property
23
24      ' temperature of city
25      Public ReadOnly Property Temperature() As String
26         Get
27            Return mTemperature
28         End Get
29      End Property
30
31      ' description of forecast
32      Public ReadOnly Property Description() As String
33         Get
34            Return mDescription
35         End Get
36      End Property
37   End Class ' CityWeather
```

Fig. 18.19 Class that stores weather information about a city. (Part 2 of 2.)

The Windows application in Fig. 18.20 uses the **TemperatureServer** Web service to display weather information in a user-friendly format.

```
1    ' Fig. 18.20: Client.vb
2    ' Class that displays weather information which it receives
3    ' from a Web Service.
4
5    Imports System
6    Imports System.Drawing
7    Imports System.Collections
8    Imports System.ComponentModel
9    Imports System.Windows.Forms
10   Imports System.Net
11
12   Public Class FrmClient
13      Inherits System.Windows.Forms.Form
```

Fig. 18.20 Receiving temperature and weather data from a Web service. (Part 1 of 4.)

```
14
15        Public Sub New()
16           MyBase.New()
17
18           ' This call is required by the Windows Form Designer.
19           InitializeComponent()
20
21           Dim client As New localhost.TemperatureServer()
22           client.CookieContainer = New CookieContainer()
23           client.UpdateWeatherConditions()
24
25           Dim cities As String() = client.Cities()
26           Dim descriptions As String() = client.Descriptions()
27           Dim temperatures As String() = client.Temperatures()
28
29           label35.BackgroundImage = New Bitmap( _
30              "images/header.jpg")
31           label36.BackgroundImage = New Bitmap( _
32              "images/header.jpg")
33
34           ' create Hashtable and populate with every label
35           Dim cityLabels As New Hashtable()
36           cityLabels.Add(1, label1)
37           cityLabels.Add(2, label2)
38           cityLabels.Add(3, label3)
39           cityLabels.Add(4, label4)
40           cityLabels.Add(5, label5)
41           cityLabels.Add(6, label6)
42           cityLabels.Add(7, label7)
43           cityLabels.Add(8, label8)
44           cityLabels.Add(9, label9)
45           cityLabels.Add(10, label10)
46           cityLabels.Add(11, label11)
47           cityLabels.Add(12, label12)
48           cityLabels.Add(13, label13)
49           cityLabels.Add(14, label14)
50           cityLabels.Add(15, label15)
51           cityLabels.Add(16, label16)
52           cityLabels.Add(17, label17)
53           cityLabels.Add(18, label18)
54           cityLabels.Add(19, label19)
55           cityLabels.Add(20, label20)
56           cityLabels.Add(21, label21)
57           cityLabels.Add(22, label22)
58           cityLabels.Add(23, label23)
59           cityLabels.Add(24, label24)
60           cityLabels.Add(25, label25)
61           cityLabels.Add(26, label26)
62           cityLabels.Add(27, label27)
63           cityLabels.Add(28, label28)
64           cityLabels.Add(29, label29)
65           cityLabels.Add(30, label30)
66           cityLabels.Add(31, label31)
```

Fig. 18.20 Receiving temperature and weather data from a Web service. (Part 2 of 4.)

```
67          cityLabels.Add(32, label32)
68          cityLabels.Add(33, label33)
69          cityLabels.Add(34, label34)
70
71          ' create Hashtable and populate with all weather
72          ' conditions
73          Dim weather As New Hashtable()
74          weather.Add("SUNNY", "sunny")
75          weather.Add("PTCLDY", "pcloudy")
76          weather.Add("CLOUDY", "mcloudy")
77          weather.Add("MOCLDY", "mcloudy")
78          weather.Add("TSTRMS", "rain")
79          weather.Add("RAIN", "rain")
80          weather.Add("SNOW", "snow")
81          weather.Add("VRYHOT", "vryhot")
82          weather.Add("FAIR", "fair")
83          weather.Add("RNSNOW", "rnsnow")
84          weather.Add("SHWRS", "showers")
85          weather.Add("WINDY", "windy")
86          weather.Add("NOINFO", "noinfo")
87          weather.Add("MISG", "noinfo")
88          weather.Add("DRZL", "rain")
89          weather.Add("HAZE", "noinfo")
90          weather.Add("SMOKE", "mcloudy")
91          weather.Add("FOG", "mcloudy")
92
93          Dim i As Integer
94          Dim background As New Bitmap("images/back.jpg")
95          Dim font As New Font("Courier New", 8, _
96             FontStyle.Bold)
97
98          ' for every city
99          For i = 0 To cities.Length - 1
100
101             ' use Hashtable to find the next Label
102             Dim currentCity As Label = _
103                CType(cityLabels(i + 1), Label)
104
105             ' set current Label's image to the image
106             ' corresponding to its weather condition -
107             ' find correct image name in Hashtable weather
108             currentCity.Image = New Bitmap("images/" & _
109                weather(descriptions(i).Trim()).ToString & ".jpg")
110
111             ' set background image, font and forecolor
112             ' of Label
113             currentCity.BackgroundImage = background
114             currentCity.Font = font
115             currentCity.ForeColor = Color.White
116
```

Fig. 18.20 Receiving temperature and weather data from a Web service. (Part 3 of 4.)

```
117                    ' set label's text to city name
118                    currentCity.Text = vbCrLf & cities(i) & " " & _
119                       temperatures(i)
120             Next
121
122        End Sub ' New
123
124        ' Visual Studio .NET generated code
125    End Class ' FrmClient
```

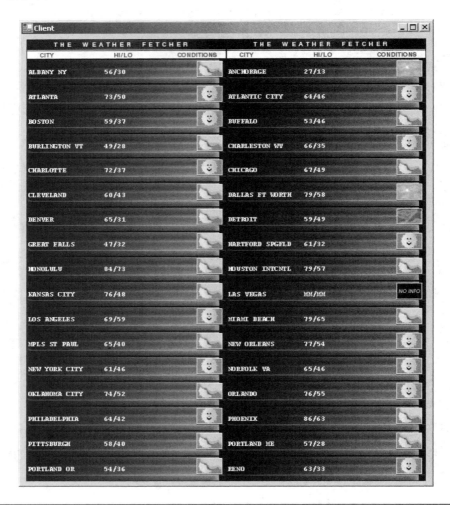

Fig. 18.20 Receiving temperature and weather data from a Web service. (Part 4 of 4.)

FrmClient (Fig. 18.20) is a Windows application that uses the **Temperature-Server** Web service to display weather information in a graphical and easy-to-read manner. This application consists of 36 **Label**s, placed in two columns. Each **Label** displays the weather information for a different city.

Lines 21–23 of the constructor instantiate a **TemperatureServer** object, create a new **CookieContainer** object and update the weather data by calling method **UpdateWeatherConditions**. Lines 25–27 call **TemperatureServer** methods **Cities**, **Descriptions** and **Temperatures** to retrieve the city's weather and description information. Because the application presents weather data for so many cities, we must establish a way to organize the information in the **Label**s and to ensure that each weather description is accompanied by an appropriate image. To address these concerns, the program uses class **Hashtable** (discussed further in Chapter 20, Data Structures and Collections) to store all the **Label**s, the weather descriptions and the names of their corresponding images. A **Hashtable** stores key–value pairs, in which both the key and the value can be any type of object. Method **Add** adds key-value pairs to a **Hashtable**. The class also provides an indexer to return the key value on which the **Hashtable** is indexed. Line 35 creates a **Hashtable** object, and lines 36–69 add the **Label**s to the **Hashtable**, using the numbers **1** through **36** as keys. Then, line 73 creates a second **Hashtable** object (**weather**) to contain pairs of weather conditions and the images associated with those conditions. Note that a given weather description does not necessarily correspond to the name of the PNG file containing the correct image. For example, both "**TSTRMS**" and "**RAIN**" weather conditions use the **rain.png** file.

Lines 74–91 set each **Label** so that it contains a city name, the current temperature in the city and an image corresponding to the weather condition for that city. Line 103 uses the **Hashtable** indexer to retrieve the next **Label** by passing as an argument the current value of **i** plus **1**. We do this because the **Hashtable** indexer begins at 0, despite the fact that both the labels and the **Hashtable** keys are numbered from 1–36.

Lines 108–109 set the **Label**'s image to the PNG image that corresponds to the city's weather condition. The application does this by retrieving the name of the PNG image from the **weather Hashtable**. The program eliminates any spaces in the description **String** by calling **String** method **Trim**. Lines 113–119 set several **Label**s' properties to achieve the visual effect seen in the output. For each label, we specify a blue-and-black background image (line 113). Lines 118–119 set each label's text so that it displays the correct information for each city (i.e., the city name and temperature information).

18.8 User-Defined Types in Web Services

Notice that the Web service discussed in the previous section returns arrays of **String**s. It would be much more convenient if **TemperatureServer** could return an array of **CityWeather** objects, instead of an array of **String**s. Fortunately, it is possible to define and use user-defined types in a Web service. These types can be passed into or returned from Web-service methods. Web-service clients also can use user-defined types, because the proxy class created for the client contains these type definitions. There are, however, some subtleties to keep in mind when using user-defined types in Web services; we point these out as we encounter them in the next example.

The case study in this section presents a math tutoring program. The Web service generates random equations of type **Equation**. The client inputs information about the kind of mathematical example that the user wants (addition, subtraction or multiplication) and the skill level of the user (1 creates equations using 1-digit numbers; 2, more difficult equations, involving 2 digits; 3, the most difficult equations, containing 3-digit numbers); it then generates an equation consisting of random numbers that have the proper number of digits.

The client receives the **Equation** and uses a Windows form to display the sample questions to the user.

We mentioned earlier that data types passed to and from Web services must be supported by SOAP. How, then, can SOAP support a type that is not even created yet? In Chapter 14, Files and Streams, we discussed the serializing of data types, which enables them to be written to files. Similarly, custom types that are sent to or from a Web service are serialized, so that they can be passed in XML format. This process is referred to as *XML serialization*.

In this example, we define class **Equation** (Fig. 18.21). This class is included in the Web-service project and contains fields, properties and methods. Before explaining class **Equation**, we briefly discuss the process of returning objects from Web-service methods. Any object returned by a Web-service method must have a default constructor. Although all objects can be instantiated by a default **Public** constructor (even if this constructor is not defined explicitly), a class returned from a Web service must have an explicitly defined constructor, even if its body is empty.

```vb
1    ' Fig. 18.21: Equation.vb
2    ' Class Equation that contains
3    ' information about an equation.
4
5    Imports System
6
7    Public Class Equation
8
9        Private mLeft, mRight, mResult As Integer
10       Private mOperation As String
11
12       ' required default constructor
13       Public Sub New()
14           Me.New(0, 0, "+")
15       End Sub ' New
16
17       ' constructor for class Equation
18       Public Sub New(ByVal leftValue As Integer, _
19           ByVal rightValue As Integer, _
20           ByVal operationType As String)
21
22           mLeft = leftValue
23           mRight = rightValue
24           mOperation = operationType
25
26           Select Case operationType
27
28               Case "+" ' addition operator
29                   mResult = mLeft + mRight
30               Case "-" ' subtraction operator
31                   mResult = mLeft - mRight
32               Case "*" ' multiplication operator
33                   mResult = mLeft * mRight
34           End Select
35       End Sub ' New
```

Fig. 18.21 Class that stores equation information. (Part 1 of 3.)

```vb
36
37     Public Overrides Function ToString() As String
38
39        Return Left.ToString() & " " & mOperation & " " & _
40           mRight.ToString() & " = " & mResult.ToString()
41     End Function ' ToString
42
43     ' readonly property returning a string representing
44     ' left-hand side
45     Public Property LeftHandSide() As String
46        Get
47           Return mLeft.ToString() & " " & mOperation & " " & _
48              mRight.ToString()
49        End Get
50        Set(ByVal Value As String)
51        End Set
52     End Property
53
54     ' readonly property returning a string representing
55     ' the right hand side
56     Public Property RightHandSide() As String
57        Get
58           Return mResult.ToString()
59        End Get
60        Set(ByVal Value As String)
61        End Set
62     End Property
63
64     ' left operand get and set property
65     Public Property Left() As Integer
66        Get
67           Return mLeft
68        End Get
69        Set(ByVal value As Integer)
70
71           mLeft = value
72        End Set
73     End Property
74
75     ' right operand get and set property
76     Public Property Right() As Integer
77        Get
78           Return mRight
79        End Get
80
81        Set(ByVal Value As Integer)
82           mRight = Value
83        End Set
84     End Property
85
```

Fig. 18.21 Class that stores equation information. (Part 2 of 3.)

```
86        ' get and set property of result of applying
87        ' operation to left and right operands
88        Public Property Result() As Integer
89           Get
90              Return mResult
91           End Get
92           Set(ByVal Value As Integer)
93              mResult = Value
94           End Set
95        End Property
96
97        ' get and set property for the operation
98        Public Property Operation() As String
99           Get
100             Return mOperation
101          End Get
102          Set(ByVal Value As String)
103             Operation = Value
104          End Set
105       End Property
106 End Class 'Equation
```

Fig. 18.21 Class that stores equation information. (Part 3 of 3.)

Common Programming Error 18.3

*Failure to define explicitly a **Public** constructor for a type being used in a Web service results in a runtime error.*

A few additional requirements apply to custom types in Web services. Any variables of our custom type that we wish to access during runtime must be declared **Public**. We also must define both the **Get** and **Set** accessors of any properties that we wish to access at run time. The Web service needs to have a way both to retrieve and to manipulate such properties, because objects of the custom type will be converted into XML (when the objects are serialized) then converted back to objects (when they are deserialized). During serialization, the property value must be read (through the **Get** accessor); during deserialization, the property value of the new object must be set (through the **Set** accessor). If only one of the accessors is present, the client application will not have access to the property.

Common Programming Error 18.4

*Defining only the **Get** or **Set** accessor of a property for a custom type being used in a Web service results in a property that is inaccessible to the client.*

Common Programming Error 18.5

*Clients of a Web service can access only that service's **Public** members. To allow access to **Private** data, the programmer should provide **Public** properties.*

Now, let us discuss class **Equation** (Fig. 18.21). Lines 18–35 define a constructor that takes three arguments—two **Integers** representing the left and right operands and a **String** that represents the algebraic operation to carry out. The constructor sets the **mLeft**, **mRight** and **mOperation** fields, then calculates the appropriate result. The default constructor (line 13–15) calls the other constructor and passes some default values. We do not use the default constructor, but it must be defined in the program.

Class **Equation** defines properties **LeftHandSide**, **RightHandSide**, **Left**, **Right**, **Operation** and **Result**. The program does not need to modify the values of these properties, but an implementation for the **Set** accessor must be provided. **LeftHandSide** returns a **String** representing everything to the left of the "**=**" sign, and **RightHandSide** returns a **String** representing everything to the right of the "**=**" sign. **Left** returns the **Integer** to the left of the operator (known as the left operand), and **Right** returns the **Integer** to the right of the operator (known as the right operand). **Result** returns the answer to the equation, and **Operation** returns the operator. The program does not actually need the **RightHandSide** property, but we have chosen to include it in case other clients choose to use it. Figure 18.22 presents the **Generator** Web service that creates random, customized **Equation**s.

```
1   ' Fig. 18.22: Generator.asmx.vb
2   ' Web Service to generate random equations based on the
3   ' operation and difficulty level.
4
5   Imports System
6   Imports System.Collections
7   Imports System.ComponentModel
8   Imports System.Data
9   Imports System.Diagnostics
10  Imports System.Web
11  Imports System.Web.Services
12
13  <WebService(Namespace:="http://www.deitel.com/", Description:= _
14     "Web service that generates a math equation.")> _
15  Public Class Generator
16     Inherits System.Web.Services.WebService
17
18     ' Visual Studio .NET generated code
19
20     <WebMethod(Description:="Method to generate a " _
21        & "math equation.")> _
22     Public Function GenerateEquation(ByVal operation As String, _
23        ByVal level As Integer) As Equation
24
25        ' find maximum and minimum number to be used
26        Dim maximum As Integer = Convert.ToInt32( _
27           Math.Pow(10, level))
28
29        Dim minimum As Integer = Convert.ToInt32( _
30           Math.Pow(10, level - 1))
31
32        Dim randomObject As New Random()
33
34        ' create equation consisting of two random numbers
35        ' between minimum and maximum parameters
36        Dim equation As New Equation( _
37           randomObject.Next(minimum, maximum), _
38           randomObject.Next(minimum, maximum), operation)
39
```

Fig. 18.22 Web service that generates random equations. (Part 1 of 2.)

```
40          Return equation
41      End Function ' Generate Equation
42  End Class ' Generator
```

Fig. 18.22 Web service that generates random equations. (Part 2 of 2.)

Web service **Generator** contains only one method, **GenerateEquation**. This method takes as arguments a **String** representing the operation we wish to perform and an **Integer** representing the difficulty level. Figure 18.23 demonstrates the result of executing a test call of this Web service. Notice that the return value from our Web service method is XML. However, this example differs from previous ones in that the XML specifies the values for all **Public** properties and fields of the object that is being returned. The return object has been serialized into XML. Our proxy class takes this return value and deserializes it into an object that then is passed back to the client.

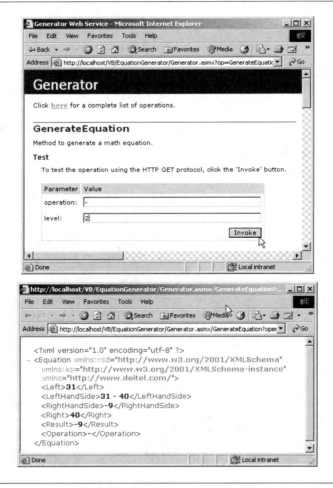

Fig. 18.23 Returning an object from a Web-service method.

Lines 26–30 define the lower and upper bounds for the random numbers that the method generates. To set these limits, the program first calls **Shared** method **Pow** of class **Math**—this method raises its first argument to the power of its second argument. **Integer maximum** represents the upper bound for a randomly generated number. The program raises **10** to the power of the specified **level** argument and then passes this value as the upper bound. For instance, if **level** is **1**, **maximum** is **10**; if **level** is **2**, **minimum** is **100**; and so on. Variable **minimum**'s value is determined by raising **10** to a power one less than **level**. This calculates the smallest number with **level** digits. If **level** is **2**, **min** is **10**; if **level** is **3**, **minimum** is **100**; and so on.

Lines 36–38 create a new **Equation** object. The program calls **Random** method **Next**, which returns an **Integer** that is greater than or equal to a specified lower bound, but less than a specified upper bound. This method generates a left operand value that is greater than or equal to **minimum** but less than **maximum** (i.e., a number with **level** digits). The right operand is another random number with the same characteristics. The operation passed to the **Equation** constructor is the **String operation** that was received by **GenerateEquation**. The new **Equation** object is returned.

Figure 18.24 lists the math-tutoring application that uses the **Generator** Web service. The application calls **Generator**'s **GenerateEquation** method to create an **Equation** object. The tutor then displays the left-hand side of the **Equation** and waits for user input. In this example, the program accesses both class **Generator** and class **Equation** from within the **localhost** namespace—both are placed in this namespace when the proxy is generated.

The math-tutor application displays a question and waits for input. The default setting for the difficulty level is **1**, but the user can change this at any time by choosing a level from among the bottom row of **RadioButton**s. Clicking any of the levels invokes its click event handler (lines 78–94), which sets integer **level** to the level selected by the user. Although the default setting for the question type is **Addition**, the user also can change this at any time by selecting one of the top-row **RadioButton**s. Doing so invokes the radio-button event handlers on lines 97–121, which set **String operation** so that it contains the symbol corresponding to the user's selection.

```
1   ' Fig. 18.24: Tutor.vb
2   ' Math Tutor program.
3
4   Public Class FrmTutor
5      Inherits System.Windows.Forms.Form
6
7      Friend WithEvents cmdGenerate As Button
8      Friend WithEvents cmdOk As Button
9
10     Friend WithEvents txtAnswer As TextBox
11     Friend WithEvents lblQuestion As Label
12
13     Friend WithEvents pnlOperations As Panel
14     Friend WithEvents pnlLevel As Panel
```

Fig. 18.24 Math-tutor application. (Part 1 of 4.)

```
15
16        ' select math operation
17        Friend WithEvents subtractRadio As RadioButton
18        Friend WithEvents addRadio As RadioButton
19        Friend WithEvents multiplyRadio As RadioButton
20
21        ' select question level radio buttons
22        Friend WithEvents levelOne As RadioButton
23        Friend WithEvents levelTwo As RadioButton
24        Friend WithEvents levelThree As RadioButton
25
26        Private operation As String = "+"
27        Private level As Integer = 1
28        Private equation As localhost.Equation
29        Private generator As New localhost.Generator()
30
31        ' Visual Studio .NET generated code
32
33        ' generates new equation on click event
34        Private Sub cmdGenerate_Click(ByVal sender As _
35           System.Object, ByVal e As System.EventArgs) _
36           Handles cmdGenerate.Click
37
38           ' generate equation using current operation
39           ' and level
40           equation = generator.GenerateEquation(operation, _
41              level)
42
43           ' display left-hand side of equation
44           lblQuestion.Text = equation.LeftHandSide
45
46           cmdOk.Enabled = True
47           txtAnswer.Enabled = True
48        End Sub ' cmdGenerate_Click
49
50        ' check user's answer
51        Private Sub cmdOk_Click(ByVal sender As _
52           System.Object, ByVal e As System.EventArgs) _
53           Handles cmdOk.Click
54
55           ' determine correct result from Equation object
56           Dim answer As Integer = equation.Result
57
58           If txtAnswer.Text = "" Then
59              Return
60           End If
61
62           ' get user's answer
63           Dim myAnswer As Integer = Int32.Parse( _
64              txtAnswer.Text)
65
```

Fig. 18.24 Math-tutor application. (Part 2 of 4.)

```
66              ' test if user's answer is correct
67          If answer = myAnswer Then
68
69              lblQuestion.Text = ""
70              txtAnswer.Text = ""
71              cmdOk.Enabled = False
72              MessageBox.Show("Correct! Good job!")
73          Else
74              MessageBox.Show("Incorrect. Try again.")
75          End If
76      End Sub ' cmdOk_Click
77
78      Private Sub levelOne_Click(ByVal sender As Object, _
79          ByVal e As System.EventArgs) Handles levelOne.Click
80
81          level = 1
82      End Sub ' levelOne_Click
83
84      Private Sub levelTwo_Click(ByVal sender As Object, _
85          ByVal e As System.EventArgs) Handles levelTwo.Click
86
87          level = 2
88      End Sub ' levelTwo_Click
89
90      Private Sub levelThree_Click(ByVal sender As Object, _
91          ByVal e As System.EventArgs) Handles levelThree.Click
92
93          level = 3
94      End Sub ' levelThree_Click
95
96      ' set the add operation
97      Private Sub addRadio_Click(ByVal sender As Object, _
98          ByVal e As System.EventArgs) Handles addRadio.Click
99
100         operation = "+"
101         cmdGenerate.Text = "Generate " & addRadio.Text & _
102             " Example"
103     End Sub ' addRadio_Click
104
105     ' set the subtract operation
106     Private Sub subtractRadio_Click(ByVal sender As Object, _
107         ByVal e As System.EventArgs) Handles subtractRadio.Click
108
109         operation = "-"
110         cmdGenerate.Text = "Generate " & subtractRadio.Text & _
111             " Example"
112     End Sub ' subtractRadio_Click
113
114     ' set the multiply operation
115     Private Sub multiplyRadio_Click(ByVal sender As Object, _
116         ByVal e As System.EventArgs) Handles multiplyRadio.Click
117
118         operation = "*"
```

Fig. 18.24 Math-tutor application. (Part 3 of 4.)

```
119         cmdGenerate.Text = "Generate " & multiplyRadio.Text & _
120             " Example"
121     End Sub ' multiplyRadio_Click
122 End Class ' FrmTutor
```

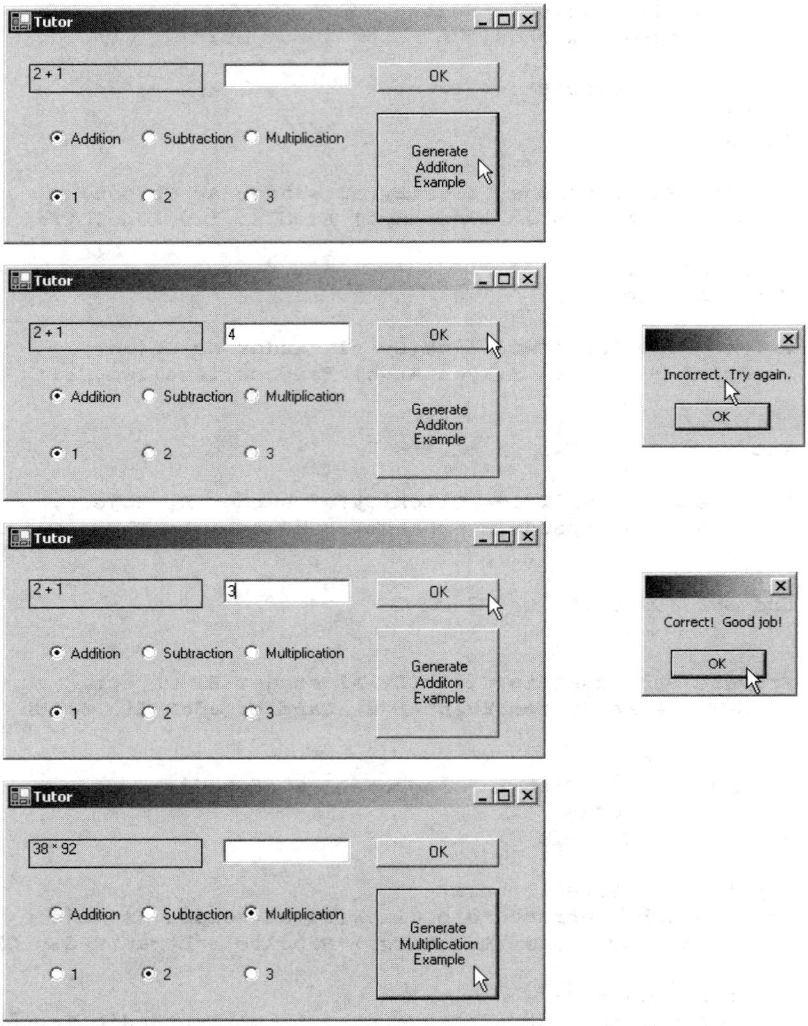

Fig. 18.24 Math-tutor application. (Part 4 of 4.)

Event handler **cmdGenerate_Click** (line 34–48) invokes **Generator** method **GenerateEquation**. The left-hand side of the equation is displayed in **lblQuestion** (line 44), and **cmdOk** is enabled (line 46) so that the user can enter an answer. When the user clicks **OK**, **cmdOk_Click** (line 51–76) checks whether the user provided the correct answer.

The last two chapters familiarized the user with the creation of Web applications and Web services, both of which enable users to request and receive data via the Internet. In the next chapter, we discuss the low-level details of how data is sent from one location to another (networking). Topics discussed in the next chapter include the implementation of servers and clients and the sending of data via sockets.

18.9 Summary

A Web service is an application stored on a remote machine and accessed through a remote procedure call. Web-service method calls are implemented using Simple Object Access Protocol (SOAP), an XML-based protocol describing how requests and responses are marked up so that they can be transferred via protocols such as HTTP. These methods are marked with the **WebMethod** attribute and are often referred to as Web-service methods. By default, requests to and responses from Web services are sent as SOAP messages. As long as a client can create and understand SOAP messages, the client can use Web services, regardless of the programming languages in which the Web services are written.

A Web service in .NET has two parts: an ASMX file and a code-behind file. The ASMX file can be viewed in any Web browser and displays information about the Web service. The code-behind file contains the definition for the methods in the Web service.

A service description is an XML document that conforms to the Web Service Description Language (WSDL). WSDL is an XML vocabulary that describes how Web services behave. The service description can be used by a client program to confirm the correctness of method calls at compile time.

The Simple Object Access Protocol (SOAP) is a platform-independent protocol that uses XML to describe remote-procedure calls over HTTP. Requests to and responses from a Web-service method are packaged in a SOAP message—an XML message containing all the information necessary to process its contents. SOAP allows Web services to employ a variety of data types, including user-defined data types. When a program invokes a Web-service method, the request and all relevant information are packaged in a SOAP message and sent to the appropriate destination. When the Web service receives the SOAP message, it processes the message's contents, which specifies the method that the client wishes to execute and the arguments the client is passing to that method. The method is executed and the response is sent back to the client as another SOAP message.

An application that uses a Web service consists of two parts: a proxy class for the Web service and a client application that accesses the Web service via the proxy. A proxy class handles the task of transferring the arguments passed from the client into a SOAP message that is sent to the Web service. The proxy likewise handles the transfer of information in the SOAP response to the client. A proxy class is created from the Web service's WSDL file that enables the client to call Web-service methods over the Internet. Whenever a call is made in a client application to a Web-service method, a method in the proxy class is called. This method takes the method name and arguments passed by the client and formats them so that they can be sent as a request in a SOAP message.

Class **WebService** provides members that determine information about the user, the application and other topics relevant to the Web service. A Web service is not required to inherit from class **WebService**. A programmer specifies a class as a Web service by tagging it with the **WebService** attribute. A programmer specifies a method as a Web-service method by tagging it with a **WebMethod** attribute.

UDDI (Universal Description, Discovery and Integration) is a project for developing a set of specifications that define how Web services should be discovered so that clients searching for Web services can find them. A DISCO (discovery) file specifies any Web services that are available in the current directory. There are both dynamic discovery files (**.vsdisco** extension) and static discovery files (**.disco** extension). Once a Web reference is created, a static discovery file is placed in the client's project. The static discovery file contains the locations of the ASMX and WSDL files. Dynamic discovery files are created so that a list of Web services is created when a client is searching for Web services.

To store session information, the **EnableSession** property of the **WebMethod** attribute must be set to **True**. When storing session information, a Web service must have a way of identifying users between method calls. The approach is implemented using cookies, which are stored in a **CookieContainer**.

Types can be defined by a programmer and used in a Web service. These types can be passed into or returned from Web-service methods. User-defined types can be sent to or returned from Web-service methods, because the types are defined in the proxy class created for the client. Custom types that are sent to or from a Web service are serialized as XML. When an object is returned from a Web service, all its **Public** properties and fields are marked up in XML. This information can then be transferred back into an object on the client side.

18.10 Internet and Web Resources

msdn.microsoft.com/webservices
This Microsoft site includes .NET Web service technology specifications and white papers with XML/SOAP articles, columns and links.

www.webservices.org
This site provides industry related news, articles, resources and links.

www.w3.org/TR/wsdl
This site provides extensive documentation on WSDL. It provides a thorough discussion of Web Service related technologies such as XML, SOAP, HTTP and MIME types in the context of WSDL.

www-106.ibm.com/developerworks/library/w-wsdl.html
This IBM site discusses WSDL. The page demonstrates the current WSDL XML Web Service specification with XML examples.

www.devxpert.com/tutors/wsdl/wsdl.asp
This site presents a high-level introduction to Web Services. The discussion includes several diagrams and examples.

msdn.microsoft.com/soap
This Microsoft site includes documentation, headlines and overviews SOAP. ASP .NET examples that use SOAP are available at this site.

www.w3.org/TR/SOAP
This site provides extensive SOAP documentation. The site describes SOAP messages, using SOAP with HTTP and SOAP security issues.

www.uddi.com
The Universal Description, Discovery and Integration site provides discussions, specifications, white pages and general information on UDDI.

19

Networking: Streams-Based Sockets and Datagrams

Objectives

- To implement Visual Basic networking applications using sockets and datagrams.
- To understand how to create clients and servers that communicate with one another.
- To understand the implementation of network-based applications.
- To construct a multithreaded server.

If the presence of electricity can be made visible in any part of a circuit, I see no reason why intelligence may not be transmitted instantaneously by electricity.
Samuel F. B. Morse

Mr. Watson, come here, I want you.
Alexander Graham Bell

What networks of railroads, highways and canals were in another age, the networks of telecommunications, information and computerization … are today.
Bruno Kreisky

Science may never come up with a better office-communication system than the coffee break.
Earl Wilson

19.1 Introduction

The Internet and the World Wide Web have generated a great deal of excitement in the business and computing communities. The Internet ties the "information world" together; the Web makes the Internet easy to use while providing the flair of multimedia. Organizations see both the Internet and the Web as crucial to their information-systems strategies. Visual Basic and the .NET Framework offer a number of built-in networking capabilities that facilitate Internet-based and Web-based applications development. Visual Basic not only can specify parallelism through multithreading, but also can enable programs to search the Web for information and collaborate with programs running on other computers internationally.

In Chapters 17 and 18, we began our presentation of Visual Basic's networking and distributed-computing capabilities. We discussed Web Forms and Web Services, two high-level networking technologies that enable programmers to develop distributed applications in Visual Basic. In this chapter, we focus on the networking technologies that support Visual Basic's ASP .NET capabilities and can be used to build distributed applications.

Our discussion of networking focuses on both sides of a *client–server relationship*. The *client* requests that some action be performed; the *server* performs the action and responds to the client. A common implementation of this request–response model is between Web browsers and Web servers. When users select Web sites that they wish to view through a browser (the client application), the browser makes a request to the appropriate Web server (the server application). The server normally responds to the client by sending the appropriate HTML Web pages.

Visual Basic's networking capabilities are grouped into several namespaces. The fundamental networking capabilities are defined by classes and interfaces of namespace **System.Net.Sockets**. Through this namespace, Visual Basic offers *socket-based communications*, which enable developers to view networking as if it were file I/O. This means that a program can read from a *socket* (network connection) or write to a socket as easily as it can read from or write to a file. Sockets are the fundamental way to perform network communications in the .NET Framework. The term "socket" refers to the Berkeley Sockets Interface, which was developed in 1978 for network programming with UNIX and was popularized by C and C++ programmers.

The classes and interfaces of namespace **System.Net.Sockets** also offer *packet-based communications*, through which individual *packets* of information are transmitted— this is a common method of transmitting audio and video over the Internet. In this chapter, we show how to create and manipulate sockets and how to communicate via packets of data.

Socket-based communications in Visual Basic employ *stream sockets*. With stream sockets, a *process* (running program) establishes a *connection* to another process. While the connection is in place, data flows between the processes in continuous *streams*. For this reason, stream sockets are said to provide a *connection-oriented service*. The popular *TCP (Transmission Control Protocol)* facilitates stream-socket transmission.

By contrast, packet-based communications in Visual Basic employ *datagram sockets*, through which individual *packets* of information are transmitted. Unlike TCP, the protocol used to enable datagram sockets—*UDP, the User Datagram Protocol*—is a *connectionless service* and does not guarantee that packets will arrive in any particular order. In fact, packets can be lost or duplicated and can arrive out of sequence. Applications that use UDP often require significant extra programming to deal with these problems. UDP is most appropriate for network applications that do not require the error checking and reliability of TCP. Stream sockets and the TCP protocol will be the most desirable method of communication for the vast majority of Visual Basic programmers.

Performance Tip 19.1

Connectionless services generally offer better performance but less reliability than do connection-oriented services.

Portability Tip 19.1

The TCP protocol and its related set of protocols enable intercommunication among a wide variety of heterogeneous computer systems (i.e., computer systems with different processors and different operating systems).

19.2 Establishing a Simple Server (Using Stream Sockets)

Typically, with TCP and stream sockets, a server "waits" for a connection request from a client. Often, the server program contains a control structure or block of code that executes continuously until the server receives a request. On receiving a request, the server establishes a connection with the client. The server then uses this connection to handle future requests from that client and to send data to the client.

The establishment of a simple server with TCP and stream sockets in Visual Basic requires five steps. The first step is to create an object of class **TcpListener**, which belongs to namespace **System.Net.Sockets**. This class represents a TCP stream socket through which a server can listen for requests. A call to the **TcpListener** constructor, such as

```
Dim server As TcpListener = New TcpListener( port )
```

binds (assigns) the server to the specified *port number*. A port number is a numeric identifier that a process uses to identify itself at a given *network address*, also known as an *Internet Protocol Address* (*IP Address*). IP addresses identify computers on the Internet. In fact, Web-site names, such as **www.deitel.com**, are aliases for IP addresses. Any process that performs networking identifies itself via an *IP address/port number pair*. Hence, no two processes can have the same port number at a given IP address. The explicit binding of a socket to a port (using method **Bind** of class **Socket**) is usually unnecessary, because class **TcpListener** and other classes discussed in this chapter hide this binding (i.e., bind sockets to ports implicitly), plus they perform other socket-initialization operations.

Software Engineering Observation 19.1

Port numbers can have values between 0 and 65535. Many operating systems reserve port numbers below 1024 for system services (such as e-mail and Web servers). Applications must be granted special privileges to use these reserved port numbers. Usually, a server-side application should not specify port numbers below 1024 as connection ports, because some operating systems might reserve these numbers.

Common Programming Error 19.1

Attempting to bind an already assigned port at a given IP address is a logic error.

To receive requests, the **TcpListener** first must listen for them. The second step in our connection process is to call **TcpListener**'s **Start** method, which causes the **TcpListener** object to begin listening for connection requests. The third step establishes the connection between the server and client. The server listens indefinitely for a request—i.e., the execution of the server-side application waits until some client attempts to connect with it. The server creates a connection to the client upon receipt of a connection request. An object of class **System.Net.Sockets.Socket** manages each connection to the client. Method **AcceptSocket** of class **TcpListener** waits for a connection request, then creates a connection when a request is received. This method returns a **Socket** object upon connection, as in the statement

Dim connection *As* Socket = server.AcceptSocket()

When the server receives a request, method **AcceptSocket** calls method **Accept** of the **TcpListener**'s underlying **Socket** to make the connection. This is an example of Visual Basic's hiding networking complexity from the programmer. The programmer can write the preceding statement into a server-side program, then allow the classes of namespace **System.Net.Sockets** to handle the details of accepting requests and establishing connections.

Step four is the processing phase, in which the server and the client communicate via methods **Receive** and **Send** of class **Socket**. These methods return references to **Socket** objects for reading from, and writing to, respectively. Note that these methods, as well as TCP and stream sockets, can be used only when the server and client are connected. In contrast, through **Socket** methods **SendTo** and **ReceiveFrom**, UDP and datagram sockets can be used when no connection exists.

The fifth step is the connection-termination phase. When the client and server have finished communicating, the server uses method **Close** of the **Socket** object to close the connection. Most servers then return to step two (i.e., wait for another client's connection request).

One problem associated with the server scheme described in this section is that step four *blocks* other requests while processing a client's request, so that no other client can connect with the server while the code that defines the processing phase is executing. The most common technique for addressing this problem is to use multithreaded servers, which place the processing-phase code in a separate thread. When the server receives a connection request, the server *spawns*, or creates, a **Thread** to process the connection, leaving its **TcpListener** (or **Socket**) free to receive other connections.

Software Engineering Observation 19.2

Using Visual Basic's multithreading capabilities, we can create servers that can manage simultaneous connections with multiple clients. This multithreaded-server architecture is precisely what popular UNIX and Windows network servers use.

Software Engineering Observation 19.3

*A multithreaded server can be implemented to create a thread that manages network I/O across a reference to a **Socket** object returned by method **AcceptSocket**. A multithreaded server also can be implemented to maintain a pool of threads that manage network I/O across newly created **Socket**s.*

Performance Tip 19.2

*In high-performance systems with abundant memory, a multithreaded server can be implemented to create a pool of threads. These threads can be assigned quickly to handle network I/O across each newly created **Socket**. Thus, when a connection is received, the server does not incur the overhead of thread creation.*

19.3 Establishing a Simple Client (Using Stream Sockets)

We create TCP-stream-socket clients via a process that requires four steps. In the first step, we create an object of class ***TcpClient*** (which belongs to namespace **System.Net.Sockets**) to connect to the server. This connection is established through method ***Connect*** of class **TcpClient**. One overloaded version of this method receives two arguments—the server's IP address and the port number—as in the following:

```
Dim client As TcpClient = New TcpClient()
client.Connect( serverAddress, serverPort )
```

Here, **serverPort** is an **Integer** that represents the server's port number; **serverAddress** can be either an ***IPAddress*** instance (that encapsulates the server's IP address) or a **String** that specifies the server's hostname. Alternatively, the programmer could pass an object reference of class ***IPEndPoint***, which represents an IP address/port number pair, to a different overload of method **Connect**. Method **Connect** of class **TcpClient** calls method ***Connect*** of class **Socket** to establish the connection. If the connection is successful, method **TcpClient.Connect** returns a positive integer; otherwise, it returns **0**.

In step two, the **TcpClient** uses its method ***GetStream*** to get a ***NetworkStream*** so that it can write to and read from the server. **NetworkStream** methods ***WriteByte*** and ***Write*** can be used to output individual bytes or sets of bytes to the server, respectively; similarly, **NetworkStream** methods ***ReadByte*** and ***Read*** can be used to input individual bytes or sets of bytes from the server, respectively.

The third step is the processing phase, in which the client and the server communicate. In this phase, the client uses methods **Read**, **ReadByte**, **Write** and **WriteByte** of class **NetworkStream** to perform the appropriate communications. Using a process similar to that used by servers, a client can employ threads to prevent blocking of communications with other servers while processing data from one connection.

After the transmission is complete, step four requires the client to close the connection by calling method ***Close*** of the **NetworkStream** object. This closes the underlying **Socket** (if the **NetworkStream** has a reference to that **Socket**). Then, the client calls method **Close** of class **TcpClient** to terminate the TCP connection. At this point, a new connection can be established through method **Connect**, as we have described.

19.4 Client/Server Interaction via Stream-Socket Connections

The applications in Fig. 19.1 and Fig. 19.2 use the classes and techniques discussed in the previous two sections to construct a simple *client/server chat application*. The server waits for a client's request to make a connection. When a client application connects to the server, the server application sends an array of bytes to the client, indicating that the connection was successful. The client then displays a message notifying the user that a connection has been established.

Both the client and the server applications contain **TextBox**es that enable users to type messages and send them to the other application. When either the client or the server sends message "**TERMINATE**," the connection between the client and the server terminates. The server then waits for another client to request a connection. Figure 19.1 and Fig. 19.2 provide the code for classes **FrmServer** and **FrmClient**, respectively. Figure 19.2 also contains screen captures displaying the execution between the client and the server.

```vb
1    ' Fig. 19.1: Server.vb
2    ' Set up a Server that receives connections from clients and sends
3    ' String data to clients.
4
5    Imports System.Windows.Forms
6    Imports System.Threading
7    Imports System.Net.Sockets
8    Imports System.IO
9
10   Public Class FrmServer
11      Inherits Form
12
13      ' TextBoxes for receiving user input and displaying information
14      Friend WithEvents txtInput As TextBox
15      Friend WithEvents txtDisplay As TextBox
16
17      Private connection As Socket  ' Socket object handles connection
18      Private readThread As Thread  ' server thread
19
20      ' Stream through which to transfer data
21      Private socketStream As NetworkStream
22
23      ' objects for writing and reading data
24      Private writer As BinaryWriter
25      Private reader As BinaryReader
26
27      Public Sub New()
28         MyBase.New()
29
30         ' required by the Windows Form Designer.
31         InitializeComponent()
```

Fig. 19.1   Server portion of a client/server stream-socket connection. (Part 1 of 4.)

```
32
33                ' add any initialization after the
34                ' InitializeComponent call
35
36                ' create thread from server
37                readThread = New Thread(AddressOf RunServer)
38                readThread.Start()
39            End Sub ' New
40
41        ' Visual Studio .NET generated code
42
43        ' invoked when user closes server
44        Private Sub FrmServer_Closing( _
45            ByVal sender As System.Object, _
46            ByVal e As system.ComponentModel.CancelEventArgs) _
47            Handles MyBase.Closing
48
49            System.Environment.Exit(System.Environment.ExitCode)
50        End Sub ' FrmServer_Closing
51
52        ' send server text to client
53        Private Sub txtInput_KeyDown( ByVal sender As System.Object, _
54            ByVal e As system.Windows.Forms.KeyEventArgs) _
55            Handles txtInput.KeyDown
56
57            ' send text to client
58            Try
59
60                ' send text if user pressed Enter and connection exists
61                If (e.KeyCode = Keys.Enter AndAlso _
62                    Not connection Is Nothing) Then
63
64                    writer.Write("SERVER>>> " & txtInput.Text) ' send data
65
66                    txtDisplay.Text &= vbCrLf & "SERVER>>> " & _
67                        txtInput.Text
68
69                    ' close connection if server's user signals termination
70                    If txtInput.Text = "TERMINATE" Then
71                        connection.Close()
72                    End If
73
74                    txtInput.Clear()
75                End If
76
77            ' handle exception if error occurs when server sends data
78            Catch exception As SocketException
79                txtDisplay.Text &= vbCrLf & "Error writing object"
80
81            End Try
82
83        End Sub ' txtInput_KeyDown
84
```

Fig. 19.1 Server portion of a client/server stream-socket connection. (Part 2 of 4.)

```
85          ' allow client to connect and display text sent by user
86          Public Sub RunServer()
87             Dim listener As TcpListener
88             Dim counter As Integer = 1
89
90             ' wait for request, then establish connection
91             Try
92
93                ' Step 1: create TcpListener
94                listener = New TcpListener(5000)
95
96                ' Step 2: TcpListener waits for connection request
97                listener.Start()
98
99                ' Step 3: establish connection upon client request
100               While True
101                  txtDisplay.Text = "Waiting for connection" & vbCrLf
102
103                  ' accept an incoming connection
104                  connection = listener.AcceptSocket()
105
106                  ' create NetworkStream object associated with socket
107                  socketStream = New NetworkStream(connection)
108
109                  ' create objects for transferring data across stream
110                  writer = New BinaryWriter(socketStream)
111                  reader = New BinaryReader(socketStream)
112
113                  txtDisplay.Text &= "Connection " & counter & _
114                     " received." & vbCrLf
115
116                  ' inform client that connection was successfull
117                  writer.Write("SERVER>>> Connection successful")
118
119                  txtInput.ReadOnly = False
120                  Dim theReply As String = ""
121
122                  ' Step 4: read String data sent from client
123                  Try
124
125                     ' loop until client signals termination
126                     Do
127                        theReply = reader.ReadString() ' read data
128
129                        ' display message
130                        txtDisplay.Text &= vbCrLf & theReply
131
132                     Loop While (theReply <> "CLIENT>>> TERMINATE" _
133                        AndAlso connection.Connected)
134
135                  ' handle exception if error reading data
136                  Catch inputOutputException As IOException
137                     MessageBox.Show("Client application closing")
```

Fig. 19.1   Server portion of a client/server stream-socket connection. (Part 3 of 4.)

```vbnet
138
139                    ' close connections
140                Finally
141
142                    txtDisplay.Text &= vbCrLf & _
143                        "User terminated connection"
144
145                    txtInput.ReadOnly = True
146
147                    ' Step 5: close connection
148                    writer.Close()
149                    reader.Close()
150                    socketStream.Close()
151                    connection.Close()
152
153                    counter += 1
154                End Try
155
156            End While
157
158        ' handle exception if error occurs in establishing connection
159        Catch inputOutputException As IOException
160            MessageBox.Show("Server application closing")
161
162        End Try
163
164    End Sub ' RunServer
165
166 End Class ' FrmServer
```

Fig. 19.1   Server portion of a client/server stream-socket connection. (Part 4 of 4.)

```vbnet
1  ' Fig. 19.2: Client.vb
2  ' Set up a client that reads and displays data sent from server.
3
4  Imports System.Windows.Forms
5  Imports System.Threading
6  Imports System.Net.Sockets
7  Imports System.IO
8
9  Public Class FrmClient
10     Inherits Form
11
12     ' TextBoxes for inputting and displaying information
13     Friend WithEvents txtInput As TextBox
14     Friend WithEvents txtDisplay As TextBox
15
16     ' stream for sending data to server
17     Private output As NetworkStream
18
19     ' objects for writing and reading bytes to streams
20     Private writer As BinaryWriter
```

Fig. 19.2   Client portion of a client/server stream-socket connection. (Part 1 of 5.)

```vbnet
21         Private reader As BinaryReader
22
23         Private message As String = ""  ' message sent to server
24
25         ' thread prevents client from blocking data transfer
26         Private readThread As Thread
27
28         Public Sub New()
29            MyBase.New()
30
31            ' required by the Windows Form Designer.
32            InitializeComponent()
33
34            ' add any initialization after the
35            ' InitializeComponent call
36
37            readThread = New Thread(AddressOf RunClient)
38            readThread.Start()
39         End Sub ' New
40
41      ' Visual Studio .NET generated code
42
43      ' invoked when user closes application
44      Private Sub FrmClient_Closing(ByVal sender As System.Object, _
45         ByVal e As System.ComponentModel.CancelEventArgs) _
46         Handles MyBase.Closing
47
48         System.Environment.Exit(System.Environment.ExitCode)
49      End Sub
50
51      ' send user input to server
52      Private Sub txtInput_KeyDown(ByVal sender As System.Object, _
53         ByVal e As System.windows.Forms.KeyEventArgs) _
54         Handles txtInput.KeyDown
55
56         ' send user input if user pressed Enter
57         Try
58
59            ' determine whether user pressed Enter
60            If e.KeyCode = Keys.Enter Then
61
62               ' send data to server
63               writer.Write("CLIENT>>> " & txtInput.Text)
64
65               txtDisplay.Text &= vbCrLf & "CLIENT>>> " & _
66                  txtInput.Text
67
68               txtInput.Clear()
69            End If
70
```

Fig. 19.2   Client portion of a client/server stream-socket connection. (Part 2 of 5.)

```
71              ' handle exception if error occurs in sending data to server
72          Catch exception As SocketException
73              txtDisplay.Text &= vbCrLf & "Error writing object"
74          End Try
75
76      End Sub ' txtInput_KeyDown
77
78      ' connect to server and display server-generated text
79      Public Sub RunClient()
80          Dim client As TcpClient
81
82              ' instantiate TcpClient for sending data to server
83          Try
84
85              txtDisplay.Text &= "Attempting connection" & vbCrLf
86
87              ' Step 1: create TcpClient and connect to server
88              client = New TcpClient()
89              client.Connect("localhost", 5000)
90
91              ' Step 2: get NetworkStream associated with TcpClient
92              output = client.GetStream()
93
94              ' create objects for writing and reading across stream
95              writer = New BinaryWriter(output)
96              reader = New BinaryReader(output)
97
98              txtDisplay.Text &= vbCrLf & "Got I/O streams" & vbCrLf
99
100             txtInput.ReadOnly = False
101
102             ' Step 3: processing phase
103             Try
104
105                 ' loop until server signals termination
106                 Do
107
108                     ' read message from server
109                     message = reader.ReadString
110                     txtDisplay.Text &= vbCrLf & message
111
112                 Loop While message <> "SERVER>>> TERMINATE"
113
114             ' handle exception if error in reading server data
115             Catch inputOutputException As IOException
116                 MessageBox.Show("Client application closing")
117
118             ' Step 4: close connection
119             Finally
120
121                 txtDisplay.Text &= vbCrLf & "Closing connection." & _
122                     vbCrLf
123
```

Fig. 19.2 Client portion of a client/server stream-socket connection. (Part 3 of 5.)

```
124                    writer.Close()
125                    reader.Close()
126                    output.Close()
127                    client.Close()
128
129               End Try
130
131               Application.Exit()
132
133           ' handle exception if error in establishing connection
134           Catch inputOutputException As Exception
135              MessageBox.Show("Client application closing")
136
137           End Try
138
139     End Sub ' RunClient
140
141  End Class ' FrmClient
```

Fig. 19.2   Client portion of a client/server stream-socket connection. (Part 4 of 5.)

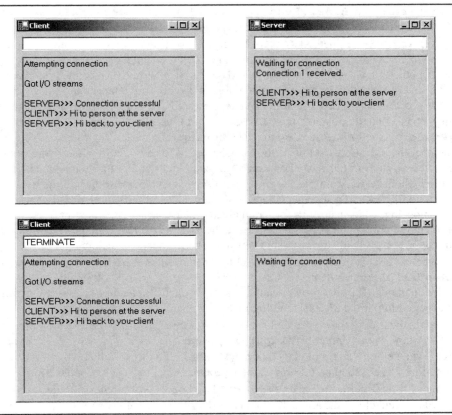

Fig. 19.2   Client portion of a client/server stream-socket connection. (Part 5 of 5.)

As we analyze this example, we begin by discussing class **FrmServer** (Fig. 19.1). In the constructor, line 37 creates a **Thread** that will accept connections from clients. Line 38 starts the **Thread**, which invokes method **RunServer** (lines 86–164). Method **Run-Server** initializes the server to receive connection requests and process connections. Line 94 instantiates the **TcpListener** to listen for a connection request from a client at port **5000** (Step 1). Line 97 then calls method **Start** of the **TcpListener** object, which requires the **TcpListener** to wait for requests (Step 2).

Lines 100–156 declare an infinite **While** loop that establishes connections requested by clients (Step 3). Line 104 calls method **AcceptSocket** of the **TcpListener** object, which returns a **Socket** upon successful connection. Method **AcceptSocket** blocks other services until a client request is made (i.e., the thread in which method **Accept-Socket** is called stops executing until a connection is established). The **Socket** object will manage the connection. Line 107 passes this **Socket** object as an argument to the constructor of a **NetworkStream** object. Class **NetworkStream** provides access to streams across a network—in this example, the **NetworkStream** object provides access to the **Socket** connection. Lines 110–111 create instances of the *BinaryWriter* and *BinaryReader* classes for writing and reading data. We pass the **NetworkStream** object as an argument to each constructor; **BinaryWriter** can write bytes to the **Net-**

workStream, and **BinaryReader** can read bytes from **NetworkStream**. Lines 113–114 append text to the **TextBox**, indicating that a connection was received.

BinaryWriter method *Write* has many overloaded versions, which enable the method to write various types to a stream. (You might remember that we used these overloaded methods in Chapter 14 to write record data to files.) Line 117 uses method **Write** to send to the client a **String** notifying the user of a successful connection. Lines 126–133 declare a **Do/Loop While** structure that executes until the server receives a message indicating connection termination (i.e., **CLIENT>>> TERMINATE**). Line 127 uses **BinaryReader** method *ReadString* to read a **String** from the stream (Step 4). (You might remember that we also used this method in Chapter 14 to read records' first-name and last-name **String**s from files.) Method **ReadString** blocks until a **String** is read. To prevent the whole server from blocking, we use a separate **Thread** to handle the transfer of information. The **While** statement loops until there is more information to read—this results in I/O blocking, which causes the program always to appear frozen. However, if we run this portion of the program in a separate **Thread**, the user can interact with the Windows **Form** and send messages while the program waits in the background for incoming messages.

When the chat is complete, lines 148–151 close the **BinaryWriter**, **BinaryReader**, **NetworkStream** and **Socket** (Step 5) by invoking their respective **Close** methods. The server then waits for another client connection request by returning to the beginning of the **While** loop (line 100).

When the user of the server application enters a **String** in the **TextBox** and presses the *Enter* key, event handler **txtInput_KeyDown** (lines 53–83) reads the **String** and sends it via method **Write** of class **BinaryWriter**. If a user terminates the server application, line 71 calls method **Close** of the **Socket** object to close the connection.

Lines 44–50 define the **frmServer_Closing** event handler for the **Closing** event. The event closes the application and uses **System.Environment.Exit** method with parameter **System.Environment.ExitCode** to terminate all threads. Method **Exit** of class **Environment** closes all threads associated with the application.

Figure 19.2 depicts the code for the **Client** object. Like the **Server** object, the **Client** object creates a **Thread** (lines 37–38) in its constructor to handle all incoming messages. **Client** method **RunClient** (lines 79–139) connects to the **Server**, receives data from the **Server** and sends data to the **Server** (when the user presses *Enter*). Lines 88–89 instantiate a **TcpClient** object, then call its method **Connect** to establish a connection (Step 1). The first argument to method **Connect** is the name of the server—in our case, the server's name is *"localhost"*, meaning that the server is located on the same machine as the client. The **localhost** is also known as the *loopback IP address* and is equivalent to the IP address *127.0.0.1*. This value sends the data transmission back to the sender's IP address. [*Note:* We chose to demonstrate the client/server relationship by connecting between programs that are executing on the same computer (**localhost**). Normally, this argument would contain the Internet address of another computer.] The second argument to method **Connect** is the server port number. This number must match the port number at which the server waits for connections.

The **Client** uses a **NetworkStream** to send data to and receive data from the server. The client obtains the **NetworkStream** in line 92 through a call to **TcpClient** method **GetStream** (Step 2). The **Do/Loop While** structure in lines 106–112 loops until the client receives the connection-termination message (**SERVER>>> TERMINATE**). Line 109 uses

BinaryReader method **ReadString** to obtain the next message from the server (Step 3). Lines 121–122 display the message and lines 124–127 close the **BinaryWriter**, **BinaryReader**, **NetworkStream** and **TcpClient** objects (Step 4).

When the user of the client application enters a **String** in the **TextBox** and presses the *Enter* key, the event handler **txtInput_KeyDown** (lines 52–76) reads the **String** from the **TextBox** and sends it via **BinaryWriter** method **Write**. Notice that, here, the **Server** receives a connection, processes it, closes it and waits for the next one. In a real-world application, a server would likely receive a connection, set up the connection to be processed as a separate thread of execution and wait for new connections. The separate threads that process existing connections can continue to execute while the **Server** concentrates on new connection requests.

19.5 Connectionless Client/Server Interaction via Datagrams

Up to this point, we have discussed connection-oriented, streams-based transmission. Now, we consider connectionless transmission using datagrams.

Connection-oriented transmission is similar to interaction over a telephone system, in which a user dials a number and is *connected* to the telephone of the party they wish to connect. The system maintains the connection for the duration of the phone call, regardless of whether the users are speaking.

By contrast, connectionless transmission via *datagrams* more closely resembles the method by which the postal service carries and delivers mail. Connectionless transmission bundles and sends information in *packets* called datagrams, which can be thought of as similar to posted letters. If a large message will not fit in one envelope, that message is broken into separate message pieces and placed in separate, sequentially numbered envelopes. All the letters are mailed at once. The letters might arrive in order, out of order or not at all. The person at the receiving end reassembles the message pieces into sequential order before attempting to interpret the message. If the message is small enough to fit in one envelope, the sequencing problem is eliminated, but it is still possible that the message will never arrive. (Unlike with posted mail, duplicates of datagrams could reach a receiving computer.) Visual Basic provides the **UdpClient** class for connectionless transmission. Like **TcpListener** and **TcpClient**, **UdpClient** uses methods from class **Socket**. The **UdpClient** methods **Send** and **Receive** are used to transmit data with **Socket**'s **SendTo** method and to read data with **Socket**'s **ReceiveFrom** method, respectively.

The programs in Fig. 19.3 and Fig. 19.4 use datagrams to send *packets* of information between a client and server application. In the **Client** application, the user types a message into a **TextBox** and presses *Enter*. The client converts the message to a **Byte** array and sends it to the server. The server receives the packet and displays the packet's information, then *echoes*, or returns, the packet back to the client. When the client receives the packet, the client displays the packet's information. In this example, the implementations of the **Client** and **Server** classes are similar.

```
1   ' Fig. 19.3: Server.vb
2   ' Server receives packets from a client, then echoes packets back
3   ' to clients.
```

Fig. 19.3   Server portion of connectionless client/server computing. (Part 1 of 3.)

```
 4
 5   Imports System.Windows.Forms
 6   Imports System.Net
 7   Imports System.Net.Sockets
 8   Imports System.Threading
 9
10   Public Class FrmDatagramServer
11      Inherits Form
12
13      ' TextBox displays packet information
14      Friend WithEvents txtDisplay As TextBox
15
16      ' reference to client that will send packet information
17      Private client As UdpClient
18
19      ' client IP address/port number pair
20      Private receivePoint As IPEndPoint
21
22      Public Sub New()
23         MyBase.New()
24
25         ' required by the Windows Form Designer.
26         InitializeComponent()
27
28         ' add any initialization after the
29         ' InitializeComponent call
30
31         ' instantiate UdpClient listening for requests at port 5000
32         client = New UdpClient(5000)
33
34         ' hold IP address and port number of client
35         receivePoint = New IPEndPoint(New IPAddress(0), 0)
36
37         Dim readThread As Thread = New Thread _
38            (New ThreadStart(AddressOf WaitForPackets))
39
40         readThread.Start() ' wait for packets
41      End Sub ' New
42
43   ' Visual Studio .NET generated code
44
45   ' invoked when user closes server
46   Protected Sub Server_Closing(ByVal sender As system.Object, _
47      ByVal e As System.ComponentModel.CancelEventArgs) _
48      Handles MyBase.Closing
49
50      System.Environment.Exit(System.Environment.ExitCode)
51   End Sub ' Server_Closing
52
53   ' wait for packets to arrive from client
54   Public Sub WaitForPackets()
55
```

Fig. 19.3 Server portion of connectionless client/server computing. (Part 2 of 3.)

```
56          ' use infinite loop to wait for data to arrive
57          While True
58
59              ' receive byte array from client
60              Dim data As Byte() = client.Receive(receivePoint)
61
62              ' output packet data to TextBox
63              txtDisplay.Text &= vbCrLf & "Packet received:" & _
64                  vbCrLf & "Length: " & data.Length & vbCrLf & _
65                  "Containing: " & _
66                  System.Text.Encoding.ASCII.GetString(data)
67
68              txtDisplay.Text &= vbCrLf & vbCrLf & _
69                  "Echo data back to client..."
70
71              ' echo information from packet back to client
72              client.Send(data, data.Length, receivePoint)
73              txtDisplay.Text &= vbCrLf & "Packet sent" & _
74                  vbCrLf
75
76          End While
77
78      End Sub ' WaitForPackets
79
80  End Class ' FrmDatragramServer
```

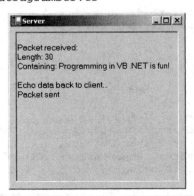

Fig. 19.3 Server portion of connectionless client/server computing. (Part 3 of 3.)

```
1   ' Fig. 19.4: Client.vb
2   ' Client sends packets to, and receives packets from, a server.
3
4   Imports System.Windows.Forms
5   Imports System.Net
6   Imports System.Net.Sockets
7   Imports System.Threading
8
9   Public Class FrmDatagramClient
10      Inherits Form
```

Fig. 19.4 Client portion of connectionless client/server computing. (Part 1 of 3.)

```vbnet
11
12      ' TextBoxes for inputting and displaying packet information
13      Friend WithEvents txtInput As TextBox
14      Friend WithEvents txtDisplay As TextBox
15
16      ' UdpClient that sends packets to server
17      Private client As UdpClient
18
19      ' hold IP address and port number of clients
20      Private receivePoint As IPEndPoint
21
22      Public Sub New()
23         MyBase.New()
24
25         ' required by the Windows Form Designer.
26         InitializeComponent()
27
28         ' add any initialization after the
29         ' InitializeComponent() call
30
31         receivePoint = New IPEndPoint(New IPAddress(0), 0)
32
33         ' instantiate UdpClient to listen on port 5001
34         client = New UdpClient(5001)
35
36         Dim thread As Thread = New Thread _
37            (New ThreadStart(AddressOf WaitForPackets))
38
39         thread.Start() ' wait for packets
40      End Sub ' New
41
42      ' Visual Studio .NET generated code
43
44      ' invoked when user closes client
45      Private Sub FrmDatagramClient_Closing( _
46         ByVal sender As System.Object, _
47         ByVal e As System.ComponentModel.CancelEventArgs) _
48         Handles MyBase.Closing
49
50         System.Environment.Exit(System.Environment.ExitCode)
51      End Sub ' FrmDatagramClient_Closing
52
53      ' invoked when user presses key
54      Private Sub txtInput_KeyDown( ByVal sender As System.Object, _
55         ByVal e As System.Windows.Forms.KeyEventArgs) _
56         Handles txtInput.KeyDown
57
58         ' determine whether user pressed Enter
59         If e.KeyCode = Keys.Enter Then
60
61            ' create packet (datagram) as String
62            Dim packet As String = txtInput.Text
63
```

Fig. 19.4   Client portion of connectionless client/server computing. (Part 2 of 3.)

```
64                txtDisplay.Text &= vbCrLf & _
65                   "Sending packet containing: " & packet
66
67                ' convert packet to byte array
68                Dim data As Byte() = _
69                   System.Text.Encoding.ASCII.GetBytes(packet)
70
71                ' send packet to server on port 5000
72                client.Send(data, data.Length, "localhost", 5000)
73
74                txtDisplay.Text &= vbCrLf & "Packet sent" & vbCrLf
75                txtInput.Clear()
76             End If
77
78          End Sub ' txtInput_KeyDown
79
80          ' wait for packets to arrive
81          Public Sub WaitForPackets()
82
83             While True
84
85                ' receive byte array from client
86                Dim data As Byte() = client.Receive(receivePoint)
87
88                ' output packet data to TextBox
89                txtDisplay.Text &= vbCrLf & "Packet received:" & _
90                   vbCrLf & "Length: " & data.Length & vbCrLf & _
91                   System.Text.Encoding.ASCII.GetString(data)
92
93             End While
94
95          End Sub ' WaitForPackets
96
97       End Class ' FrmDatagramClient
```

Client window before sending   **Client** window after sending a packet to
a packet to the server   the server and receiving it back

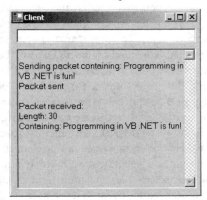

Fig. 19.4   Client portion of connectionless client/server computing. (Part 3 of 3.)

The code in Fig. 19.3 defines the **Server** for this application. Line 32 in the constructor for class **Server** creates an instance of the **UdpClient** class that receives data at port **5000**. This initializes the underlying **Socket** for communications. Line 35 creates an instance of class **IPEndPoint** to hold the IP address and port number of the client(s) that transmit to **Server**. The first argument to the constructor of **IPEndPoint** is an **IPAddress** object; the second argument to the constructor for **IPEndPoint** is the port number of the endpoint. These values are both **0**, because we need only instantiate an empty **IPEndPoint** object. The IP addresses and port numbers of clients are copied into the **IPEndPoint** when datagrams are received from clients.

Server method **WaitForPackets** (lines 54–78) executes an infinite loop while waiting for data to arrive at the **Server**. When information arrives, the **UdpClient** method **Receive** (line 60) receives a byte array from the client. We include **Receive** in the **IPEndPoint** object created in the constructor; this provides the method with a reference to an **IPEndPoint** into which the program copies the client's IP address and port number. This program will compile and run without an exception even if the reference to the **IPEndPoint** object is **Nothing**, because method **Receive** (or some method that method **Receive** subsequently calls) initializes the **IPEndPoint** if it is **Nothing**.

Good Programming Practice 19.1

*Initialize all references to objects (to a value other than **Nothing**). This protects code from methods that do not check their parameters for **Nothing** references.*

Lines 63–66 update the **Server**'s display to include the packet's information and content. Line 72 echoes the data back to the client, using **UdpClient** method **Send**. This version of **Send** takes three arguments: the byte array to send, an **Integer** representing the array's length and the **IPEndPoint** to which to send the data. We use array **Byte()** returned by method **Receive** as the data, the length of array **Byte()** as the length and the **IPEndPoint** passed to method **Receive** as the data's destination. The IP address and port number of the client that sent the data to **Server** are stored in **receivePoint**, so merely passing **receivePoint** to **Send** allows **Server** to respond to the client.

Class **Client** (Fig. 19.4) works similarly to class **Server**, except that the **Client** object sends packets only when the user types a message in a **TextBox** and presses the *Enter* key. When this occurs, the program calls event handler **txtInput_KeyDown** (lines 54–78). Lines 68–69 convert the **String** that the user entered in the **TextBox** to a **Byte** array. Line 72 calls **UdpClient** method **Send** to send the **Byte** array to the **Server** that is located on **localhost** (i.e., the same machine). We specify the port as **5000**, which we know to be **Server**'s port.

Line 34 instantiates a **UdpClient** object to receive packets at port **5001**—we choose port **5001**, because the **Server** already occupies port **5000**. Method **WaitForPackets** of class **FrmDatagramClient** (lines 81–95) uses an infinite loop to wait for these packets. The **UdpClient** method **Receive** blocks until a packet of data is received (line 86). However, this does not prevent the user from sending a packet, because Visual Basic provides a separate thread for handling GUI events. The blocking performed by method **Receive** does not prevent class **Client** from performing other services (e.g., handling user input), because a separate thread runs method **WaitForPackets**.

When a packet arrives, lines 89–91 display its contents in the **TextBox**. The user can type information into the **Client** window's **TextBox** and press the *Enter* key at any

time, even while a packet is being received. The event handler for the **TextBox** processes
the event and sends the data to the server.

19.6 Client/Server Tic-Tac-Toe Using a Multithreaded Server

In this section, we present our capstone networking example—the popular game Tic-Tac-
Toe, implemented with stream sockets and client/server techniques. The program consists
of a **FrmServer** application (Fig. 19.5) and two **FrmClient** applications (Fig. 19.7);
FrmServer allows the **FrmClient**s to connect to the server and play Tic-Tac-Toe. We
depict the output in Fig. 19.7. When the server receives a client connection, lines 67–78 of
Fig. 19.5 create an instance of class **CPlayer** (Fig. 19.6) to process the client in a separate
thread of execution. This enables the server to handle requests from both clients. The server
assigns value **"X"** to the first client that connects (player **X** makes the first move), then assigns value **"O"** to the second client. Throughout the game, the server maintains information regarding the status of the board so that the server can validate players' requested
moves. However, neither the server nor the client can establish whether a player has won
the game—in this application, method **GameOver** (lines 166–170) always returns **False**.
As an added challenge, the reader may wish to implement this functionality on their own.
Each **FrmClient** maintains its own GUI version of the Tic-Tac-Toe board to display the
game. The clients can place marks only in empty squares on the board. Class **CSquare**
(Fig. 19.8) is used to define squares on the Tic-Tac-Toe board.

```
1    ' Fig. 19.5: Server.vb
2    ' Server maintains a Tic-Tac-Toe game for two client applications.
3
4    Imports System.Windows.Forms
5    Imports System.Net.Sockets
6    Imports System.Threading
7
8    Public Class FrmServer
9       Inherits Form
10
11      ' TextBox for displaying results
12      Friend WithEvents txtDisplay As TextBox
13
14      Private board As Char() ' Tic-Tac-Toe game board
15
16      Private players As CPlayer() ' player-client applications
17      Private playerThreads As Thread() ' Threads that run clients
18
19      ' indicates current player ("X" or "O")
20      Private currentPlayer As Integer
21
22      ' indicates whether server has disconnected
23      Private disconnect As Boolean = False
24
25      Public Sub New()
26         MyBase.New()
27
```

Fig. 19.5 Client/server Tic-Tac-Toe program server. (Part 1 of 4.)

```vbnet
28              ' required by the Windows Form Designer
29              InitializeComponent()
30
31              ' add any initialization after the
32              ' InitializeComponent call
33
34              board = New Char(8) {} ' create board with nine squares
35
36              players = New CPlayer(1) {} ' create two players
37
38              ' create one thread for each player
39              playerThreads = New Thread(1) {}
40              currentPlayer = 0
41
42              ' use separate thread to accept connections
43              Dim getPlayers As Thread = New Thread(New ThreadStart( _
44                 AddressOf SetUp))
45
46              getPlayers.Start()
47           End Sub ' New
48
49        ' Visual Studio .NET generated code
50
51        ' invoked when user closes server window
52        Private Sub FrmServer_Closing(ByVal sender As System.Object, _
53           ByVal e As System.ComponentModel.CancelEventArgs) _
54           Handles MyBase.Closing
55
56           disconnect = True
57        End Sub ' FrmServer_Closing
58
59        ' accept connections from two client applications
60        Public Sub SetUp()
61
62           ' server listens for requests on port 5000
63           Dim listener As TcpListener = New TcpListener(5000)
64           listener.Start()
65
66           ' accept first client (player) and start its thread
67           players(0) = New CPlayer(listener.AcceptSocket(), Me, "X"c)
68           playerThreads(0) = _
69              New Thread(New ThreadStart(AddressOf players(0).Run))
70
71           playerThreads(0).Start()
72
73           ' accept second client (player) and start its thread
74           players(1) = New CPlayer(listener.AcceptSocket, Me, "O"c)
75           playerThreads(1) = _
76              New Thread(New ThreadStart(AddressOf players(1).Run))
77
78           playerThreads(1).Start()
79
```

Fig. 19.5 Client/server Tic-Tac-Toe program server. (Part 2 of 4.)

```
80              ' inform first player of other player's connection to server
81              SyncLock (players(0))
82
83                 players(0).threadSuspended = False
84                 Monitor.Pulse(players(0))
85              End SyncLock
86
87          End Sub ' SetUp
88
89          ' display message argument in txtDisplay
90          Public Sub Display(ByVal message As String)
91             txtDisplay.Text &= message & vbCrLf
92          End Sub ' Display
93
94          ' determine whether move is valid
95          Public Function ValidMove(ByVal location As Integer, _
96             ByVal player As Char) As Boolean
97
98             ' prevent other threads from making moves
99             SyncLock(Me)
100
101                Dim playerNumber As Integer = 0
102
103                ' playerNumber = 0 if player = "X", else playerNumber = 1
104                If player = "O"c
105                   playerNumber = 1
106                End If
107
108                ' wait while not current player's turn
109                While playerNumber <> currentPlayer
110                   Monitor.Wait(Me)
111                End While
112
113                ' determine whether desired square is occupied
114                If Not IsOccupied(location) Then
115
116                   ' place either an "X" or an "O" on board
117                   If currentPlayer = 0 Then
118                      board(location) = "X"c
119                   Else
120                      board(location) = "O"c
121                   End If
122
123                   ' set currentPlayer as other player (change turns)
124                   currentPlayer = (currentPlayer + 1) Mod 2
125
126                   ' notify other player of move
127                   players(currentPlayer).OtherPlayerMoved(location)
128
129                   ' alert other player to move
130                   Monitor.Pulse(Me)
131
132                   Return True
```

Fig. 19.5   Client/server Tic-Tac-Toe program server. (Part 3 of 4.)

```
133                 Else
134                     Return False
135                 End If
136
137             End SyncLock
138
139         End Function ' ValidMove
140
141         ' determine whether specified square is occupied
142         Public Function IsOccupied(ByVal location As Integer) _
143             As Boolean
144
145             ' return True if board location contains "X" or "O"
146             If (board(location) = "X"c OrElse _
147                 board(location) = "O"c) Then
148
149                 Return True
150             Else
151                 Return False
152             End If
153
154         End Function ' IsOccupied
155
156         ' allow clients to see if server has disconnected
157         Public ReadOnly Property Disconnected() As Boolean
158
159             Get
160                 Return disconnect
161             End Get
162
163         End Property ' Disconnected
164
165         ' determine whether game is over
166         Public Function GameOver() As Boolean
167
168             ' place code here to test for winner of game
169             Return False
170         End Function ' GameOver
171
172     End Class ' FrmServer
```

Fig. 19.5   Client/server Tic-Tac-Toe program server. (Part 4 of 4.)

```
1   ' Fig. 19.6: Player.vb
2   ' Represents a Tic-Tac-Toe player.
3
4   Imports System.Threading
5   Imports System.Net.Sockets
6   Imports System.IO
7
8   Public Class CPlayer
9
```

Fig. 19.6   **CPlayer** class represents a Tic-Tac-Toe player. (Part 1 of 4.)

```
10      Private connection As Socket ' connection to server
11      Private server As FrmServer ' reference to Tic-Tac-Toe server
12
13      ' object for sending data to server
14      Private socketStream As NetworkStream
15
16      ' objects for writing and reading bytes to streams
17      Private writer As BinaryWriter
18      Private reader As BinaryReader
19
20      Private mark As Char ' "X" or "O"
21      Friend threadSuspended As Boolean = True
22
23      Sub New(ByVal socketValue As Socket, _
24         ByVal serverValue As FrmServer, ByVal markValue As Char)
25
26         ' assign argument values to class-member values
27         connection = socketValue
28         server = serverValue
29         mark = markValue
30
31         ' use Socket to create NetworkStream object
32         socketStream = New NetworkStream(connection)
33
34         ' create objects for writing and reading bytes across streams
35         writer = New BinaryWriter(socketStream)
36         reader = New BinaryReader(socketStream)
37      End Sub ' New
38
39      ' inform other player that move was made
40      Public Sub OtherPlayerMoved(ByVal location As Integer)
41
42         ' notify opponent
43         writer.Write("Opponent moved")
44         writer.Write(location)
45      End Sub ' OtherPlayerMoved
46
47      ' inform server of move and receive move from other player
48      Public Sub Run()
49
50         Dim done As Boolean = False   ' indicates whether game is over
51
52         ' indicate successful connection and send mark to server
53         If mark = "X"c Then
54            server.Display("Player X connected")
55            writer.Write(mark)
56            writer.Write("Player X connected" & vbCrLf)
57         Else
58            server.Display("Player O connected")
59            writer.Write(mark)
60            writer.Write("Player O connected, please wait" & vbCrLf)
61         End If
62
```

Fig. 19.6   CPlayer class represents a Tic-Tac-Toe player. (Part 2 of 4.)

```
63              ' wait for other player to connect
64          If mark = "X"c Then
65              writer.Write("Waiting for another player")
66
67                  ' wait for notification that other player has connected
68              SyncLock (Me)
69
70                  While ThreadSuspended
71                      Monitor.Wait(Me)
72                  End While
73
74              End SyncLock
75
76              writer.Write("Other player connected. Your move")
77          End If
78
79          ' play game
80          While Not done
81
82              ' wait for data to become available
83              While connection.Available = 0
84                  Thread.Sleep(1000)
85
86                  ' end loop if server disconnects
87                  If server.Disconnected Then
88                      Return
89                  End If
90
91              End While
92
93              ' receive other player's move
94              Dim location As Integer = reader.ReadInt32()
95
96              ' determine whether move is valid
97              If server.ValidMove(location, mark) Then
98
99                  ' display move on server
100                 server.Display("loc: " & location)
101
102                 ' notify server of valid move
103                 writer.Write("Valid move.")
104
105             Else   ' notify server of invalid move
106                 writer.Write("Invalid move, try again")
107             End If
108
109             ' exit loop if game over
110             If server.GameOver Then
111                 done = True
112             End If
113
114         End While
115
```

Fig. 19.6 CPlayer class represents a Tic-Tac-Toe player. (Part 3 of 4.)

```
116         ' close all connections
117         writer.Close()
118         reader.Close()
119         socketStream.Close()
120         connection.Close()
121     End Sub ' Run
122
123 End Class ' CPlayer
```

Fig. 19.6 **CPlayer** class represents a Tic-Tac-Toe player. (Part 4 of 4.)

```
1  ' Fig. 19.7: Client.vb
2  ' Client for the Tic-Tac-Toe program.
3
4  Imports System.Windows.Forms
5  Imports System.Net.Sockets
6  Imports System.Threading
7  Imports System.IO
8
9  Public Class FrmClient
10     Inherits Form
11
12     ' board contains nine panels where user can place "X" or "O"
13     Friend WithEvents Panel1 As Panel
14     Friend WithEvents Panel2 As Panel
15     Friend WithEvents Panel3 As Panel
16     Friend WithEvents Panel4 As Panel
17     Friend WithEvents Panel5 As Panel
18     Friend WithEvents Panel6 As Panel
19     Friend WithEvents Panel7 As Panel
20     Friend WithEvents Panel8 As Panel
21     Friend WithEvents Panel9 As Panel
22
23     ' TextBox displays game status and other player's moves
24     Friend WithEvents txtDisplay As TextBox
25     Friend WithEvents lblId As Label ' Label displays player
26
27     Private board As CSquare(,) ' Tic-Tac-Toe board
28
29     ' square that user previously clicked
30     Private mCurrentSquare As CSquare
31
32     Private connection As TcpClient ' connection to server
33     Private stream As NetworkStream ' stream to tranfser data
34
35     ' objects for writing and reader bytes to streams
36     Private writer As BinaryWriter
37     Private reader As BinaryReader
38
39     Private mark As Char ' "X" or "O"
40     Private turn As Boolean ' indicates which player should move
41
```

Fig. 19.7 Client/server Tic-Tac-Toe program Client. (Part 1 of 7.)

```
42        Private brush As SolidBrush ' brush for painting board
43
44        Private done As Boolean = False ' indicates whether game is over
45
46        Public Sub New()
47           MyBase.New()
48
49           ' required by the Windows Form Designer
50           InitializeComponent()
51
52           ' add any initialization after the
53           ' InitializeComponent call
54
55           board = New CSquare(2, 2) {} ' create 3 x 3 board
56
57           ' create nine CSquare's and place their Panels on board
58           board(0, 0) = New CSquare(Panel1, " "c, 0)
59           board(0, 1) = New CSquare(Panel2, " "c, 1)
60           board(0, 2) = New CSquare(Panel3, " "c, 2)
61           board(1, 0) = New CSquare(Panel4, " "c, 3)
62           board(1, 1) = New CSquare(Panel5, " "c, 4)
63           board(1, 2) = New CSquare(Panel6, " "c, 5)
64           board(2, 0) = New CSquare(Panel7, " "c, 6)
65           board(2, 1) = New CSquare(Panel8, " "c, 7)
66           board(2, 2) = New CSquare(Panel9, " "c, 8)
67
68           ' create SolidBrush for writing on Squares
69           brush = New SolidBrush(Color.Black)
70
71           ' make connection request to server at port 5000
72           connection = New TcpClient("localhost", 5000)
73           stream = connection.GetStream()
74
75           ' create objects for writing and reading bytes to streams
76           writer = New BinaryWriter(stream)
77           reader = New BinaryReader(stream)
78
79           ' create thread for sending and receiving messages
80           Dim outputThread As Thread = New Thread(AddressOf Run)
81           outputThread.Start()
82        End Sub ' New
83
84     ' Visual Studio .NET generated code
85
86     ' invoked on screen redraw
87     Private Sub FrmClient_Paint(ByVal sender As System.Object, _
88        ByVal e As System.Windows.Forms.PaintEventArgs) _
89        Handles MyBase.Paint
90
91        PaintSquares()
92     End Sub
93
```

Fig. 19.7   Client/server Tic-Tac-Toe program Client. (Part 2 of 7.)

```
94        ' invoked when user closes client application
95        Private Sub FrmClient_Closing(ByVal sender As System.Object, _
96           ByVal e As System.ComponentModel.CancelEventArgs) _
97           Handles MyBase.Closing
98
99           done = True
100       End Sub
101
102       ' redraw Tic-Tac-Toe board
103       Public Sub PaintSquares()
104          Dim graphics As Graphics
105
106          ' counters for traversing Tic-Tac-Toe board
107          Dim row As Integer
108          Dim column As Integer
109
110          ' draw appropriate mark on each panel
111          For row = 0 To 2
112
113             For column = 0 To 2
114
115                ' get Graphics for each Panel
116                graphics = board(row, column).Panel.CreateGraphics()
117
118                ' draw appropriate letter on panel
119                graphics.DrawString(board(row, _
120                   column).Mark.ToString(), Me.Font, brush, 8, 8)
121             Next
122          Next
123
124       End Sub ' PaintSquares
125
126       ' invoked when user clicks Panels
127       Private Sub square_MouseUp(ByVal sender As System.Object, _
128          ByVal e As System.Windows.Forms.MouseEventArgs) Handles _
129          Panel1.MouseUp, Panel2.MouseUp, Panel3.MouseUp, _
130          Panel4.MouseUp, Panel5.MouseUp, Panel6.MouseUp, _
131          Panel7.MouseUp, Panel8.MouseUp, Panel9.MouseUp
132
133          ' counters for traversing Tic-Tac-Toe board
134          Dim row As Integer
135          Dim column As Integer
136
137          For row = 0 To 2
138
139             For column = 0 To 2
140
141                ' determine which Panel was clicked
142                If board(row, column).Panel Is sender Then
143                   mCurrentSquare = board(row, column)
144
```

Fig. 19.7   Client/server Tic-Tac-Toe program Client. (Part 3 of 7.)

```
145                        ' send move to server
146                        SendClickedSquare(board(row, column).Location)
147                     End If
148
149           Next
150       Next
151
152    End Sub ' square_MouseUp
153
154    ' continuously update TextBox display
155    Public Sub Run()
156
157       Dim quote As Char = ChrW(34) ' single quote
158
159       ' get player's mark ("X" or "O")
160       mark = Convert.ToChar(stream.ReadByte())
161       lblId.Text = "You are player " & quote & mark & quote
162
163       ' determine which player should move
164       If mark = "X" Then
165          turn = True
166       Else
167          turn = False
168       End If
169
170       ' process incoming messages
171       Try
172
173          ' receive messages sent to client
174          While True
175             ProcessMessage(reader.ReadString())
176          End While
177
178          ' notify user if server closes connection
179       Catch exception As EndOfStreamException
180          txtDisplay.Text = "Server closed connection.  Game over."
181
182       End Try
183
184    End Sub ' Run
185
186    ' process messages sent to client
187    Public Sub ProcessMessage(ByVal messageValue As String)
188
189       ' if valid move, set mark to clicked square
190       If messageValue = "Valid move." Then
191          txtDisplay.Text &= "Valid move, please wait." & vbCrLf
192          mCurrentSquare.Mark = mark
193          PaintSquares()
194
```

Fig. 19.7   Client/server Tic-Tac-Toe program Client. (Part 4 of 7.)

```
195              ' if invalid move, inform user to try again
196              ElseIf messageValue = "Invalid move, try again" Then
197                 txtDisplay.Text &= messageValue & vbCrLf
198                 turn = True
199
200                 ' if opponent moved, mark opposite mark on square
201              ElseIf messageValue = "Opponent moved" Then
202
203                 ' find location of opponent's move
204                 Dim location As Integer = reader.ReadInt32()
205
206                 ' mark that square with opponent's mark
207                 If mark = "X" Then
208                    board(location \ 3, location Mod 3).Mark = "O"c
209                 Else
210                    board(location \ 3, location Mod 3).Mark = "X"c
211                 End If
212
213                 PaintSquares()
214
215                 txtDisplay.Text &= "Opponent moved. Your turn." & vbCrLf
216
217                 turn = True ' change turns
218
219                 ' display message as default case
220              Else
221                 txtDisplay.Text &= messageValue & vbCrLf
222              End If
223
224           End Sub ' ProcessMessage
225
226           ' send square position to server
227           Public Sub SendClickedSquare(ByVal location As Integer)
228
229              ' send location to the server if current turn
230              If turn Then
231                 writer.Write(location)
232                 turn = False ' change turns
233              End If
234
235           End Sub ' SendClickedSquare
236
237           ' Property CurrentSquare
238           Public WriteOnly Property CurrentSquare() As CSquare
239
240              Set(ByVal Value As CSquare)
241                 mCurrentSquare = Value
242              End Set
243
244           End Property ' CurrentSquare
245
246        End Class ' FrmClient
```

Fig. 19.7   Client/server Tic-Tac-Toe program Client. (Part 5 of 7.)

1.
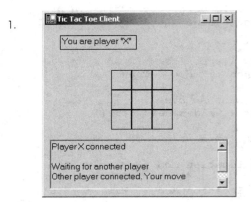

2.
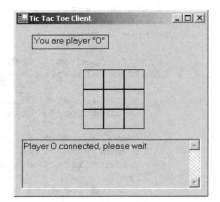

3.
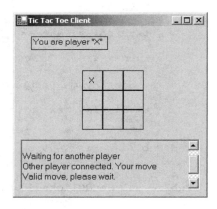

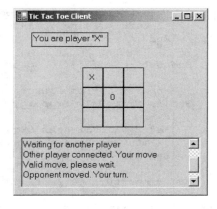

Fig. 19.7   Client/server Tic-Tac-Toe program Client. (Part 6 of 7.)

4.

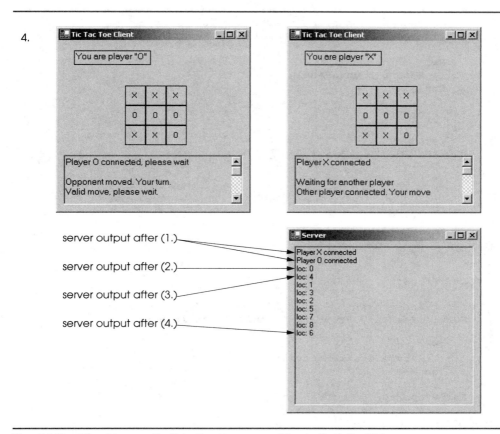

Fig. 19.7   Client/server Tic-Tac-Toe program Client. (Part 7 of 7.)

```
1    ' Fig. 19.8: Square.vb
2    ' Represents a square on the Tic-Tac-Toe board.
3
4    Public Class CSquare
5
6       Private squarePanel As Panel ' panel on which user clicks
7       Private squareMark As Char ' "X" or "O"
8       Private squareLocation As Integer ' position on board
9
10      ' constructor assigns argument values to class-member values
11      Public Sub New(ByVal panelValue As Panel, _
12         ByVal markValue As Char, ByVal locationValue As Integer)
13
14         squarePanel = panelValue
15         squareMark = markValue
16         squareLocation = locationValue
17      End Sub ' New
18
```

Fig. 19.8   **CSquare** class represents a square on the Tic-Tac-Toe board (Part 1 of 2.).

```
19        ' return panel on which user can click
20        Public ReadOnly Property Panel() As Panel
21
22           Get
23              Return squarePanel
24           End Get
25
26        End Property ' Panel
27
28        ' set and get squareMark ("X" or "O")
29        Public Property Mark() As Char
30
31           Get
32              Return squareMark
33           End Get
34
35           Set(ByVal Value As Char)
36              squareMark = Value
37           End Set
38
39        End Property ' Mark
40
41        ' return squarePanel position on Tic-Tac-Toe board
42        Public ReadOnly Property Location() As Integer
43
44           Get
45              Return squareLocation
46           End Get
47
48        End Property ' Location
49
50     End Class ' CSquare
```

Fig. 19.8 **CSquare** class represents a square on the Tic-Tac-Toe board (Part 2 of 2.).

FrmServer (Fig. 19.5) uses its constructor (lines 25–47) to create a **Char** array to store the moves the players have made (line 34). The program creates an array of two references to **CPlayer** objects (line 36) and an array of two references to **Thread** objects (line 39). Each element in both arrays corresponds to a Tic-Tac-Toe player. Variable **currentPlayer** is set to **0** (line 40), which corresponds to player **"X."** In our program, player **"X"** makes the first move. Lines 43–46 create and start **Thread getPlayers**, which the **FrmServer** uses to accept connections so that the current **Thread** does not block while awaiting players.

Thread **getPlayers** executes method **SetUp** (lines 60–87), which creates a **TcpListener** object to listen for requests on port **5000** (lines 63–64). This object then listens for connection requests from the first and second players. Lines 67 and 74 instantiate **CPlayer** objects representing the players, and lines 68–69 and 75–76 create two **Thread**s that execute the **Run** methods of each **CPlayer** object.

The **CPlayer** constructor (Fig. 19.6, lines 23–37) receives as arguments a reference to the **Socket** object (i.e., the connection to the client), a reference to the **FrmServer** object and a **Char** indicating the mark (**"X"** or **"O"**) used by that player. In this case study, **FrmServer** calls method **Run** (lines 48–121) after instantiating a **CPlayer** object. Lines 53–

61 notify the server of a successful connection and send to the client the **Char** that the client will place on the board when making a move. If **Run** is executing for **CPlayer "X"**, lines 65–76 execute, causing **CPlayer "X"** to wait for a second player to connect. Lines 70–72 define a **While** loop that suspends the **CPlayer "X" Thread** until the server signals that **CPlayer "O"** has connected. The server notifies the **CPlayer** of the connection by setting the **CPlayer**'s **threadSuspended** variable to **False** (Fig. 19.5, lines 81–85). When **threadSuspended** becomes **False**, **CPlayer** exits the **While** loop of lines 70–72.

Method **Run** executes the **While** structure (lines 80–114), enabling the user to play the game. Each iteration of this structure waits for the client to send an **Integer** specifying where on the board to place the **"X"** or **"O"**—the **CPlayer** then places the mark on the board, if the specified mark location is valid (e.g., that location does not already contain a mark). Note that the **While** structure continues execution only if **Boolean** variable **done** is **False**. This variable is set to **True** by event handler **FrmServer_Closing** of class **FrmServer**, which is invoked when the server closes the connection.

Line 83 of Fig. 19.6 begins a **While** that loops until **Socket** property **Available** indicates that there is information to receive from the **Socket** (or until the server disconnects from the client). If there is no information, the thread goes to sleep for one second. Upon awakening, the thread uses property **Disconnected** to check for whether server variable **disconnect** is **True** (lines 87–89). If the value is **True**, the **Thread** exits the method (thus terminating the **Thread**); otherwise, the **Thread** loops again. However, if property **Available** indicates that there is data to receive, the **While** loop of lines 83–91 terminates, enabling the information to be processed.

This information contains an **Integer** representing the location in which the client wants to place a mark. Line 94 calls method **ReadInt32** of the **BinaryReader** object (which reads from the **NetworkStream** created with the **Socket**) to read this **Integer**. Line 97 then passes the **Integer** to **Server** method **ValidMove**. If this method validates the move, the **CPlayer** places the mark in the desired location.

Method **ValidMove** (Fig. 19.5, lines 95–139) sends to the client a message indicating whether the move was valid. Locations on the board correspond to numbers from **0**–**8** (**0**–**2** for the first row, **3**–**5** for the second and **6**–**8** for the third). All statements in method **ValidMove** are enclosed in a **SyncLock** statement that allows only one move to be attempted at a time. This prevents two players from modifying the game's state information simultaneously. If the **CPlayer** attempting to validate a move is not the current player (i.e., the one allowed to make a move), that **CPlayer** is placed in a *wait* state until it is that **CPlayer**'s turn to move. If the user attempts to place a mark on a location that already contains a mark, method **ValidMove** returns **False**. However, if the user has selected an unoccupied location (line 114), lines 117–121 place the mark on the local representation of the board. Line 127 notifies the other **CPlayer** that a move has been made, and line 130 invokes the **Pulse** method so that the waiting **CPlayer** can validate a move. The method then returns **True** to indicate that the move is valid.

When a **FrmClient** application (Fig. 19.7) executes, it creates a **TextBox** to display messages from the server and the Tic-Tac-Toe board representation. The board is created out of nine **CSquare** objects (Fig. 19.8) that contain **Panel**s on which the user can click, indicating the position on the board in which to place a mark. The **FrmClient**'s constructor (line 46–82) opens a connection to the server (line 72) and obtains a reference to the connection's associated **NetworkStream** object from **TcpClient** (line 73). Lines 80–81 start a thread to read messages sent from the server to the client. The server passes messages (for example, whether each move is valid) to method **ProcessMessage** (lines 187–224). If the message indicates that a move is valid (line 190), the client sets its mark to the current square (the square that the user clicked) and repaints the board. If the message indicates that a move is invalid (line 196), the client notifies the user to click a different square. If the message indicates that the opponent made a move (line 201), line 204 reads from the server an **Integer** specifying where on the board the client should place the opponent's mark.

In this chapter, we discussed how to use Visual Basic's networking technologies by providing both connection-oriented (i.e., streams-based) transmission and connectionless (i.e., packet-based) transmission. We showed how to create a simple server and client via stream sockets, then showed how to create a multithreaded server. In Chapter 20, Data Structures and Collections, we discuss how to store data dynamically and discuss several of the key classes that belong to the Visual Basic **System.Collections** namespace.

19.7 Summary

The two most popular types of sockets are stream sockets and datagram sockets. Stream sockets provide a connection-oriented service, meaning that one process establishes a connection to another process, and data can flow between the processes in continuous streams. Datagram sockets provide a connectionless service that uses messages to transmit data. Connectionless services generally offer greater performance, but less reliability than connection-oriented services.

Transmission Control Protocol (TCP) is the preferred protocol for stream sockets. It is a reliable and relatively fast way to send data through a network. The User Datagram Protocol (UDP) is the preferred protocol for datagram sockets. UDP is unreliable. There is no guarantee that packets sent with UDP will arrive in the order in which they were sent or that they will arrive at all.

The establishment of a simple server with TCP and stream sockets in Visual Basic requires five steps. Step 1 is to create a **TcpListener** object. This class represents a TCP stream socket that a server can use to receive connections. To receive connections, the **TcpListener** must be listening for them. For the **TcpListener** to listen for client connections, its **Start** method must be called (Step 2). **TcpListener** method **AcceptSocket** blocks indefinitely until a connection is established, at which point it returns a **Socket** (Step 3). Step 4 is the processing phase, in which the server and the client communicate via methods **Read** and **Write** via a **NetworkStream** object. When the client and server have finished communicating, the server closes the connection with the **Close** method on the **Socket** (Step 5). Most servers will then, by means of a control loop, return to the **AcceptSocket** call step to wait for another client's connection.

A port number is a numeric ID number that a process uses to identify itself at a given network address, also known as an Internet Protocol address (IP address). An individual process running on a computer is identified by an IP address/port number pair. Hence, no two processes can have the same port number at a given IP address. Class **IPAddress** represents an Internet Protocol address. Class **IPEndPoint** represents an endpoint on a network, including an IP address/port number pair.

The establishment of a simple client requires four steps. In Step 1, we create a **Tcp-Client** to connect to the server. This connection is established through a call to the **Tcp-Client** method **Connect** containing two arguments—the server's IP address and the port number. In Step 2, the **TcpClient** uses method **GetStream** to get a **Stream** to write to and read from the server. Step 3 is the processing phase, in which the client and the server communicate. Step 4 has the client close the connection by calling the **Close** method on the **NetworkStream**. **NetworkStream** methods **WriteByte** and **Write** can be used to output individual bytes or sets of bytes to a stream, respectively. **Network-Stream** methods **ReadByte** and **Read** can be used to read individual bytes or sets of bytes from a stream, respectively.

Class **UdpClient** is provided for connectionless transmission of data. Class **Udp-Client** methods **Send** and **Receive** are used to transmit data.

Multithreaded servers can manage many simultaneous connections with multiple clients. Using multithreaded servers, the programmer can place processing-phase code into a separate thread. This leaves the **TCPListener** free to listen for other connections.

20

Data Structures and Collections

Objectives

- To form linked data structures using references, self-referential classes and recursion.
- To create and manipulate dynamic data structures, such as linked lists, queues, stacks and binary trees.
- To understand various applications of linked data structures.
- To understand how to create reusable data structures with classes, inheritance and composition.

Much that I bound, I could not free;
Much that I freed returned to me.
Lee Wilson Dodd

'Will you walk a little faster?' said a whiting to a snail,
'There's a porpoise close behind us, and he's treading on my
tail.'
Lewis Carroll

There is always room at the top.
Daniel Webster

Push on—keep moving.
Thomas Morton

I think that I shall never see
A poem lovely as a tree.
Joyce Kilmer

20.1　Introduction

The *data structures* that we have studied thus far, such as single-subscripted and double-subscripted arrays, have been of fixed sizes. This chapter introduces *dynamic data structures*, which can grow and shrink at execution time. *Linked lists* are collections of data items "lined up in a row"—users can make insertions and deletions anywhere in a linked list. *Stacks* are important in compilers and operating systems; insertions and deletions are made only at the stack's *top*. *Queues* represent waiting lines; insertions are made only at the back (also referred to as the *tail*) of a queue, and deletions are made only from the front (also referred to as the *head*) of a queue. *Binary trees* facilitate high-speed searching and sorting of data, efficient elimination of duplicate data items, representation of file-system hierarchies and compilation of expressions into machine language. The various data structures we just mentioned have many other interesting applications, as well.

In this chapter, we discuss each of the major types of data structures and then implement programs that create and manipulate these data structures. We use classes, inheritance and composition to create and package the data structures in ways that enhance reusability and maintainability.

The chapter examples are practical programs that readers will find useful in advanced courses and in industrial applications. The programs devote special attention to reference manipulation.

20.2　Self-Referential Classes

A *self-referential class* contains a reference member referring to an object of the same class type. For example, the class definition in Fig. 20.1 defines type **CNode**. This type has two

Private instance variables (lines 5–6)—**Integer mData** and **CNode** reference **mNextNode**. Member **mNextNode** references an object of type **CNode**, the same type as the current class—hence the term, "self-referential class." Member **mNextNode** is referred to as a *link* (this means that **mNextNode** can be used to "tie" an object of type **CNode** to another object of the same type). Class **CNode** also has two properties: One for variable **mData**, named **Data** (lines 13–23), and another for variable **mNextNode**, named **NextNode** (lines 26–36).

Self-referential objects can be linked together to form useful data structures, such as lists, queues, stacks and trees. Figure 20.2 illustrates the linking of two self-referential objects to form a list. A backslash (representing a **Nothing** reference) is placed in the link member of the second self-referential object to indicate that the link does not refer to another object. A **Nothing** reference usually defines the end(s) of a data structure.

```
1    ' Fig. 20.1: Node.vb
2    ' Self-referential Node class.
3
4    Class CNode
5       Private mData As Integer
6       Private mNextNode As CNode
7
8       Public Sub New(ByVal dataValue As Integer)
9          ' constructor body
10      End Sub ' New
11
12      ' Property Data
13      Public Property Data() As Integer
14
15         Get
16            ' get body
17         End Get
18
19         Set(ByVal dataValue As Integer)
20            ' set body
21         End Set
22
23      End Property ' Data
24
25      ' Property NextNode
26      Public Property NextNode As CNode
27
28         Get
29            ' get next node
30         End Get
31
32         Set(ByVal nodeValue As CNode)
33            ' set next node
34         End Set
35
36      End Property ' NextNode
37
38   End Class 'CNode
```

Fig. 20.1 Self-referential **CNode** class definition.

Fig. 20.2 Self-referential class objects linked together.

 Common Programming Error 20.1

Failure to set the link in the last node of a list (or other linear data structure) to **Nothing** *is a common logic error.*

Creating and maintaining dynamic data structures requires *dynamic memory allocation*—a program's ability to obtain additional memory (to hold new variables) and to release unneeded memory at execution time. Recall that, instead of releasing dynamically allocated memory explicitly, Visual Basic programs perform automatic garbage collection.

Dynamic memory allocation is limited by the amount of available physical memory in the computer (and the amount of available disk space in a virtual-memory system). In most cases, the limits for an individual program are much smaller—the computer's available memory must be shared among many applications.

Keyword **New** is essential to dynamic memory allocation. Keyword **New** takes the class name of an object as an operand. It then dynamically allocates the memory for a new object, calls the class constructor and returns a reference to the newly created object. For example, the statement:

> *Dim* nodeToAdd *As* CNode = *New* CNode(10)

allocates the appropriate amount of memory to store a **CNode**, calls the **CNode** constructor with an argument of **10** (for the **CNode**'s **mData** member) and stores a reference to this object in **nodeToAdd**. If no memory is available, **New** throws an **OutOfMemoryException**.

The following sections discuss lists, stacks, queues and trees. These data structures are created and maintained with dynamic memory allocation and self-referential classes.

 Good Programming Practice 20.1

When creating an object, it is a good idea to test for an **OutOfMemoryException.** *Perform appropriate error processing if the requested memory is not allocated.*

20.3 Linked Lists

A *linked list* is a linear collection (i.e., a sequence) of self-referential class objects, called *nodes,* that are connected by reference links—hence the term, "linked" list. A program accesses a linked list via a reference to the first node of the list. Each subsequent node is accessed via the current node's link-reference member. By convention, the link reference in the last node of a list is set to **Nothing**, marking the end of the list. Data is stored in a linked list dynamically—each node is created as necessary. A node can contain data of any type.

Although arrays also can store lists of data, linked lists provide several advantages over arrays. It is appropriate to use a linked list when the number of data elements to be represented in the data structure is unpredictable. Unlike a linked list, the size of a "conventional" Visual Basic array cannot be altered, because the array size is fixed when the array is created. Conventional arrays can become full, but linked lists become full only when the system has insufficient memory to satisfy dynamic storage allocation requests.

Performance Tip 20.1

An array can be declared to contain more elements than the expected number of items, but this would waste memory. Linked lists can provide better memory utilization in these situations. In general, the use of dynamic memory allocation (instead of arrays) for data structures that grow and shrink at execution time can save memory.

Programmers can maintain linked lists in sorted order simply by inserting each new element at the proper point in the list. Although locating the proper insertion point does take time, it is not necessary to move existing list elements.

Performance Tip 20.2

Insertion and deletion in a sorted array can consume time, because all elements following the inserted or deleted element must be shifted appropriately.

Performance Tip 20.3

The elements of an array are stored contiguously in memory to allow immediate access to any array element—the address of any element can be calculated directly as its offset from the beginning of the array. Linked lists do not afford such immediate access to their elements—an element can be accessed only by traversing the list from the front.

Normally, memory does not store linked-list nodes contiguously. Rather, the nodes are logically contiguous. Figure 20.3 illustrates a linked list containing several nodes.

The program of Fig. 20.4–Fig. 20.6 uses an object of class **CList** to manipulate a list of objects of type **Object**. Method **Main** of module **modListTest** (Fig. 20.7) creates a list of objects, inserts objects at the beginning of the list (using **CList** method **InsertAtFront**), inserts objects at the end of the list (using **CList** method **InsertAtBack**), deletes objects from the front of the list (using **CList** method **RemoveFromFront**) and deletes objects from the end of the list (using **CList** method **RemoveFromBack**). Each insertion or deletion operation invokes **CList** method **Print** to display the current list contents. A detailed discussion of the program follows. An **EmptyListException** occurs if an attempt is made to remove an item from an empty list.

The program consists of four classes—**CListNode** (Fig. 20.4), **CList** (Fig. 20.5), **EmptyListException** (Fig. 20.6) and module **modListTest** (Fig. 20.7). The classes in Fig. 20.4–Fig. 20.6 create a linked-list library. These classes belong to namespace **LinkedListLibrary** (i.e., we store them in the **LinkedListLibrary** class library), enabling us to reuse the classes throughout this chapter.

Encapsulated in each **CList** object is a linked list of **CListNode** objects. Class **CListNode** (Fig. 20.4) consists of two member variables—**mData** and **mNextNode**. Member **mData** can refer to any **Object**. Member **mNextNode** stores a reference to the next **CListNode** object in the linked list. A **CList** accesses the **CListNode** member variables via properties **Data** (lines 22–28) and **NextNode** (lines 31–41), respectively.

Class **CList** (Fig. 20.5) contains **Private** members **firstNode** (a reference to the first **CListNode** in a **CList**) and **lastNode** (a reference to the last **CListNode** in a **CList**). The constructors (lines 10–14 and 17–19) initialize both references to **Nothing**. Methods **InsertAtFront** (lines 22–36), **InsertAtBack** (lines 39–54),

RemoveFromFront (lines 57–81) and **RemoveFromBack** (lines 84–117) are the primary methods of class **CList**. Each method uses a **SyncLock** block to ensure that **CList** objects are *thread safe* when used in a multithreaded program. This means that, if one thread is modifying the contents of a **CList** object, no other thread can modify the same **CList** object at the same time. Method **IsEmpty** (lines 120–132) is a *predicate method* that determines whether the list is empty (i.e., whether the reference to the first node of the list is **Nothing**). Predicate methods typically test a condition and do not modify the object on which they are called. If the list is empty, method **IsEmpty** returns **True**; otherwise, it returns **False**. Method **Print** (lines 135–159) displays the list's contents. Both method **IsEmpty** and method **Print** use **SyncLock** blocks, ensuring that the state of the list does not change while the methods are performing their tasks.

Class **EmptyListException** (Fig. 20.6) defines an exception class to handle illegal operations on an empty **CList**. For example, an **EmptyListException** occurs if the program attempts to remove a node from an empty **CList**.

Module **modListTest** (Fig. 20.7) uses the linked-list library to create and manipulate a linked list. Line 10 creates an instance of type **CList** named **list**. Then, lines 13–16 create data to add to the list. Lines 19–29 use **CList** insertion methods to insert these objects and use **CList** method **Print** to output the contents of **list** after each insertion. The code inside the **Try** block (lines 35–70) removes objects (using **CList** deletion methods), outputs the removed object and outputs **list** after every deletion. If there is an attempt to remove an object from an empty list, the **Catch** block (lines 66–68) catches the **EmptyListException**. Note that module **modListTest** uses namespace **LinkedListLibrary** (Fig. 20.4); thus, the project containing module **modListTest** must contain a reference to the **LinkedListLibrary** class library.

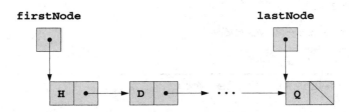

Fig. 20.3 Linked-list graphical representation.

```
1   ' Fig. 20.4: ListNodes.vb
2   ' Class to represent one node in a CList.
3
4   Public Class CListNode
5       Private mData As Object
6       Private mNextNode As CListNode
7
```

Fig. 20.4 Self-referential class **CListNode**. (Part 1 of 2.)

```
8            ' create CListNode with dataValue in list
9            Public Sub New(ByVal dataValue As Object)
10              MyClass.New(dataValue, Nothing)
11           End Sub ' New
12
13           ' create CListNode with dataValue and nextNodeValue in list
14           Public Sub New(ByVal dataValue As Object, _
15              ByVal nextNodeValue As Object)
16
17              mData = dataValue
18              mNextNode = nextNodeValue
19           End Sub ' New
20
21           ' property Data
22           Public ReadOnly Property Data() As Object
23
24              Get
25                 Return mData
26              End Get
27
28           End Property ' Data
29
30           ' property mNext
31           Public Property NextNode() As CListNode
32
33              Get
34                 Return mNextNode
35              End Get
36
37              Set(ByVal value As CListNode)
38                 mNextNode = value
39              End Set
40
41           End Property ' NextNode
42
43       End Class ' CListNode
```

Fig. 20.4   Self-referential class **CListNode**. (Part 2 of 2.)

```
1     ' Fig. 20.5: List.vb
2     ' Class CList definition.
3
4     Public Class CList
5        Private firstNode As CListNode
6        Private lastNode As CListNode
7        Private name As String
8
9        ' construct empty List with specified name
10       Public Sub New(ByVal listName As String)
11          name = listName
12          firstNode = Nothing
```

Fig. 20.5   Linked-list **CList** class. (Part 1 of 4.)

```vbnet
13          lastNode = Nothing
14      End Sub ' New
15
16      ' construct empty List with "list" as its name
17      Public Sub New()
18          MyClass.New("list")
19      End Sub ' New
20
21      ' insert object at front of List
22      Public Sub InsertAtFront(ByVal insertItem As Object)
23
24          SyncLock (Me) ' ensure thread safe
25
26              ' if this list is empty, create node
27              If IsEmpty() Then
28                  lastNode = New CListNode(insertItem)
29                  firstNode = lastNode
30              Else ' create node and insert before first node
31                  firstNode = New CListNode(insertItem, firstNode)
32              End If
33
34          End SyncLock
35
36      End Sub ' InsertAtFront
37
38      ' insert object at end of List
39      Public Sub InsertAtBack(ByVal insertItem As Object)
40
41          SyncLock (Me) ' ensure thread safety
42
43              ' if list is empty create node and set firstNode
44              If IsEmpty() Then
45                  lastNode = New CListNode(insertItem)
46                  firstNode = lastNode
47              Else ' create node and insert after last node
48                  lastNode.NextNode = New CListNode(insertItem)
49                  lastNode = lastNode.NextNode
50              End If
51
52          End SyncLock
53
54      End Sub ' InsertAtBack
55
56      ' remove first node from list
57      Public Function RemoveFromFront() As Object
58
59          SyncLock (Me) ' ensure thread safety
60              Dim removeItem As Object = Nothing
61
62              ' throw exception if removing node from empty list
63              If IsEmpty() Then
64                  Throw New EmptyListException(name)
65              End If
```

Fig. 20.5 Linked-list **CList** class. (Part 2 of 4.)

```
66
67              removeItem = firstNode.Data ' retrieve data
68
69              ' reset firstNode and lastNode references
70              If firstNode Is lastNode Then
71                 firstNode = Nothing
72                 lastNode = Nothing
73              Else
74                 firstNode = firstNode.NextNode
75              End If
76
77              Return removeItem ' return removed item
78
79           End SyncLock
80
81      End Function ' RemoveFromFront
82
83      ' remove last node from CList
84      Public Function RemoveFromBack() As Object
85
86           SyncLock (Me) ' ensure thread safe
87              Dim removeItem As Object = Nothing
88
89              ' throw exception if removing node from empty list
90              If IsEmpty() Then
91                 Throw New EmptyListException(name)
92              End If
93
94              removeItem = lastNode.Data ' retrieve data
95
96              ' reset firstNode and last node references
97              If firstNode Is lastNode Then
98                 lastNode = Nothing
99                 firstNode = lastNode
100             Else
101                Dim current As CListNode = firstNode
102
103                ' loop while current node is not lastNode
104                While (Not (current.NextNode Is lastNode))
105                   current = current.NextNode ' move to next node
106                End While
107
108                ' current is new lastNode
109                lastNode = current
110                current.NextNode = Nothing
111             End If
112
113             Return removeItem ' return removed data
114
115          End SyncLock
116
117     End Function ' RemoveFromBack
118
```

Fig. 20.5 Linked-list **CList** class. (Part 3 of 4.)

```vb
119       ' return true if list is empty
120       Public Function IsEmpty() As Boolean
121
122          SyncLock (Me)
123
124             If firstNode Is Nothing Then
125                Return True
126             Else
127                Return False
128             End If
129
130          End SyncLock
131
132       End Function ' IsEmpty
133
134       ' output List contents
135       Public Overridable Sub Print()
136
137          SyncLock (Me)
138
139             If IsEmpty() Then
140                Console.WriteLine("Empty " & name)
141
142                Return
143             End If
144
145             Console.Write("The " & name & " is: ")
146
147             Dim current As CListNode = firstNode
148
149             ' output current node data while not at end of list
150             While Not current Is Nothing
151                Console.Write(current.Data & " ")
152                current = current.NextNode
153             End While
154
155             Console.WriteLine(vbCrLf)
156
157          End SyncLock
158
159       End Sub ' Print
160
161    End Class ' CList
```

Fig. 20.5   Linked-list **CList** class. (Part 4 of 4.)

```vb
1     ' Fig. 20.6: EmptyListException.vb
2     ' Class EmptyListException definition.
3
4     Public Class EmptyListException
5        Inherits ApplicationException
6
```

Fig. 20.6   Exception thrown when removing node from empty linked list. (Part 1 of 2.)

```
7        Public Sub New(ByVal name As String)
8            MyBase.New("The " & name & " is empty")
9        End Sub ' New
10
11    End Class ' EmptyListException
```

Fig. 20.6 Exception thrown when removing node from empty linked list. (Part 2 of 2.)

```
1    ' Fig. 20.7: ListTest.vb
2    ' Testing class CList.
3
4    ' Deitel namespaces
5    Imports LinkedListLibrary
6
7    Module modListTest
8
9        Sub Main()
10            Dim list As CList = New CList() ' create CList container
11
12            ' create data to store in CList
13            Dim aBoolean As Boolean = True
14            Dim aCharacter As Char = "$"c
15            Dim anInteger As Integer = 34567
16            Dim aString As String = "hello"
17
18            ' use CList insert methods
19            list.InsertAtFront(aBoolean) ' insert Boolean at front
20            list.Print()
21
22            list.InsertAtFront(aCharacter) ' insert Char at front
23            list.Print()
24
25            list.InsertAtBack(anInteger) ' insert Integer at back
26            list.Print()
27
28            list.InsertAtBack(aString) ' insert String at back
29            list.Print()
30
31            ' use CList remove methods
32            Dim removedObject As Object
33
34            ' remove data from list and print after each removal
35            Try
36
37                ' remove object from front of list
38                removedObject = list.RemoveFromFront()
39                Console.WriteLine(Convert.ToString(removedObject) & _
40                    " removed")
41
42                list.Print()
```

Fig. 20.7 Linked-list demonstration. (Part 1 of 2.)

```
43
44              ' remove object from front of list
45              removedObject = list.RemoveFromFront()
46              Console.WriteLine(Convert.ToString(removedObject) & _
47                  " removed")
48
49              list.Print()
50
51              ' remove object from back of list
52              removedObject = list.RemoveFromBack()
53              Console.WriteLine(Convert.ToString(removedObject) & _
54                  " removed")
55
56              list.Print()
57
58              ' remove object from back of list
59              removedObject = list.RemoveFromBack()
60              Console.WriteLine(Convert.ToString(removedObject) & _
61                  " removed")
62
63              list.Print()
64
65          ' Catch exception if list is empty
66          Catch emptyListException As EmptyListException
67              Console.Error.WriteLine(vbCrLf & _
68                  Convert.ToString(emptyListException))
69
70          End Try
71
72      End Sub ' Main
73
74  End Module ' modListTest
```

```
The list is: True

The list is: $ True

The list is: $ True 34567

The list is: $ True 34567 hello

$ removed
The list is: True 34567 hello

True removed
The list is: 34567 hello

hello removed
The list is: 34567

34567 removed
Empty list
```

Fig. 20.7   Linked-list demonstration. (Part 2 of 2.)

Over the next several pages, we discuss each of the methods of class **CList** in detail. Method **InsertAtFront** (Fig. 20.5, lines 22–36) places a new node at the front of the list. This method consists of three steps, which are outlined below:

1. Call **IsEmpty** to determine whether the list is empty (Fig. 20.5, line 27).

2. If the list is empty, set both **firstNode** and **lastNode** to refer to a new **CListNode** initialized with object **insertItem** (lines 28–29). The **CList-Node** constructor in lines 9–11 (Fig. 20.4) calls the **CListNode** constructor in lines 14–19 (Fig. 20.4) to set instance variable **mData** to refer to the **Object** passed as the first argument and then sets the **mNextNode** reference to **Nothing**.

3. If the list is not empty, the new node is "threaded" (not to be confused with mul-tithreading) into the list by setting **firstNode** to refer to a new **CListNode** object initialized with object **insertItem** and **firstNode** (line 31). When the **CListNode** constructor (lines 14–19 of Fig. 20.4) executes, it sets instance variable **mData** to refer to the **Object** passed as the first argument and performs the insertion by setting the **mNextNode** reference to the **CListNode** passed as the second argument.

Figure 20.8 illustrates method **InsertAtFront**. Part (a) of the figure depicts the list and the new node during the **InsertAtFront** operation and before the threading of the new **ListNode** (containing value **12**) into the list. The dotted arrows in part (b) illustrate step 3 of the **InsertAtFront** operation, which enables the **ListNode** to become the new list front.

Method **InsertAtBack** (Fig. 20.5, lines 39–54) places a new node at the back of the list. This method consists of three steps:

1. Call **IsEmpty** to determine whether the list is empty (Fig. 20.5, line 44).

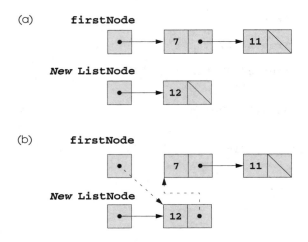

Fig. 20.8 InsertAtFront graphical representation.

2. If the list is empty, set both **firstNode** and **lastNode** to refer to a new **CListNode** initialized with object **insertItem** (lines 45–46). The **CList-Node** constructor in lines 9–11 (Fig. 20.4) calls the **CListNode** constructor in lines 14–19 (Fig. 20.4) to set instance variable **mData** to refer to the **Object** passed as the first argument and then sets the **mNextNode** reference to **Nothing**.

3. If the list is not empty, thread the new node into the list by setting **lastNode** and **lastNode.NextNode** to refer to a new **CListNode** object initialized with object **insertItem** (Fig. 20.5, lines 48–49). When the **CListNode** constructor (lines 9–11 of Fig. 20.4) executes, it sets instance variable **mData** to refer to the **Object** passed as an argument and sets the **mNextNode** reference to **Nothing**.

Figure 20.9 illustrates method **InsertAtBack**. Part (a) of the figure depicts the list and the new **ListNode** (containing value **5**) during the **InsertAtBack** operation and before the new node has been threaded into the list. The dotted arrows in part (b) illustrate the steps of method **InsertAtBack** that enable a new **ListNode** to be added to the end of a list that is not empty.

Method **RemoveFromFront** (Fig. 20.5, lines 57–81) removes the front node of the list and returns a reference to the removed data. The method throws a **EmptyList-Exception** (line 64) if the program tries to remove a node from an empty list. This method consists of four steps:

1. Assign **firstNode.Data** (the data being removed from the list) to reference **removeItem** (line 67).

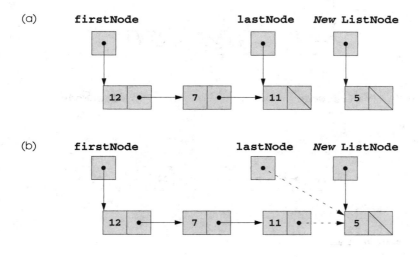

Fig. 20.9 InsertAtBack graphical representation.

2. If the objects to which **firstNode** and **lastNode** refer are the same object, this indicates that the list contains only one element prior to the removal attempt. In this case, the method sets **firstNode** and **lastNode** to **Nothing** (lines 71–72) to "dethread" (remove) the node from the list (leaving the list empty).

3. If the list contains more than one node prior to removal, then the method leaves reference **lastNode** as is and simply assigns **firstNode.NextNode** to reference **firstNode** (line 74). Thus, **firstNode** references the node that was the second node prior to the **RemoveFromFront** call.

4. Return the **removeItem** reference (line 77).

Figure 20.10 illustrates method **RemoveFromFront**. Part (a) illustrates the list before the removal operation. Part (b) portrays the actual reference manipulations.

Method **RemoveFromBack** (Fig. 20.5, lines 84–117) removes the last node of a list and returns a reference to the removed data. The method throws a **EmptyListException** (line 91) if the program attempts to remove a node from an empty list. This method consists of seven steps:

1. Assign **lastNode.Data** (the data being removed from the list) to reference **removeItem** (line 94).

2. If the objects to which **firstNode** and **lastNode** refer are the same object (line 97), this indicates that the list contains only one element prior to the removal attempt. In this case, the method sets **firstNode** and **lastNode** to **Nothing** (lines 98–99) to dethread (remove) that node from the list (leaving the list empty).

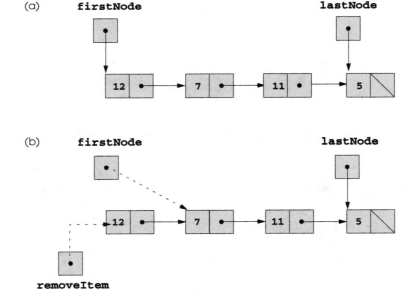

Fig. 20.10 RemoveFromFront graphical representation.

3. If the list contains more than one node prior to removal, create the **CListNode** reference **current** and assign it **firstNode** (line 101).

4. Use **current** to traverse the list until **current** references the node directly preceding the last node. The **While** loop (lines 104–106) assigns **current.NextNode** to reference **current** as long as **current.NextNode** is not equal to **lastNode**.

5. After locating the second-to-last node, assign **current** to **lastNode** (line 109) to dethread the last node from the list.

6. Set **current.NextNode** to **Nothing** (line 110) in the new last node of the list to ensure proper list termination.

7. Return the **removeItem** reference (line 113).

Figure 20.11 illustrates method **RemoveFromBack**. Part (a) illustrates the list before the removal operation. Part (b) portrays the actual reference manipulations.

Method **Print** (Fig. 20.5, lines 135–159) first determines whether the list is empty (line 139). If so, **Print** displays a **String** consisting of **"Empty "** and the list's **name** and then returns control to the calling method. Otherwise, **Print** outputs the data in the list. The method prints a **String** consisting of the string **"The "**, the **name** of the list and the string **" is: "**. Then, line 147 creates **CListNode** reference **current** and initializes it with **firstNode**. While **current** is not **Nothing**, there are more items in the list. Therefore, the method prints **current.Data** (line 151) then assigns **current.NextNode** to **current** (line 152) thus moving to the next node in the list. Note that, if the link in the last node of the list is not **Nothing**, the printing algorithm will erroneously attempt to print past the end of the list. The printing algorithm is identical for linked lists, stacks and queues.

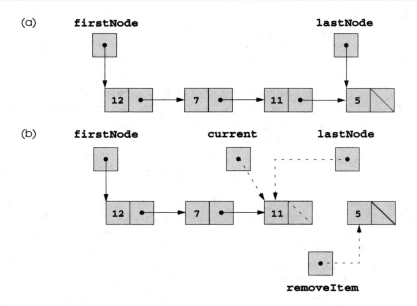

Fig. 20.11 RemoveFromBack graphical representation.

20.4 Stacks

A *stack* is a constrained version of a linked list—new nodes can be added to a stack and removed from a stack only at its top. For this reason, a stack is referred to as a *last-in, first-out (LIFO)* data structure. The link member in the bottom (i.e., last) node of the stack is set to **Nothing** to indicate the bottom of the stack.

The primary operations used to manipulate a stack are *push* and *pop*. Operation *push* adds a new node to the top of the stack. Operation *pop* removes a node from the top of the stack and returns the data from the popped node.

Stacks have many interesting applications. For example, when a program calls a method, the called method must know how to return to its caller, so the return address is pushed onto the *program execution stack*. If a series of method calls occurs, the successive return values are pushed onto the stack in last-in, first-out order so that each method can return to its caller. Stacks support recursive method calls in the same manner that they support conventional nonrecursive method calls.

The program execution stack contains the space created for local variables on each invocation of a method during a program's execution. When the method returns to its caller, the space for that method's local variables is popped off the stack, and those variables are no longer known to the program.

Compilers use stacks to evaluate arithmetic expressions and to generate machine-language code required to process the expressions. The **System.Collections** namespace contains class **Stack** for implementing and manipulating stacks that can grow and shrink during program execution. Section 20.7 discusses class **Stack**.

We take advantage of the close relationship between lists and stacks to implement our own stack class by reusing a list class. We demonstrate two different forms of reusability. First, we implement the stack class by inheriting from class **CList** of Fig. 20.5. Then, we implement an identically performing stack class through composition by including a **CList** object as a **Private** member of a stack class. This chapter implements list, stack and queue data structures to store **Object** references, which encourages further reusability—objects of any type can be stored in such a list, stack or queue.

The program of Fig. 20.12 and Fig. 20.13 creates a stack class by inheriting from class **CList** of Fig. 20.5. We want the stack to provide methods **Push**, **Pop**, **IsEmpty** and **Print**. Essentially, these are the methods **InsertAtFront**, **RemoveFromFront**, **IsEmpty** and **Print** of class **CList**. Class **CList** contains other methods, such as **InsertAtBack** and **RemoveFromBack**, which we would rather not make accessible through the **Public** interface of the stack. It is important to remember that all methods in the **Public** interface of class **CList** are also **Public** methods of the derived class **CStackInheritance** (Fig. 20.12).

When we implement the stack's methods, we have each **CStackInheritance** method call the appropriate **CList** method—method **Push** calls **InsertAtFront**, and method **Pop** calls **RemoveFromFront**. Class **CStackInheritance** does not define methods **IsEmpty** and **Print**, because **CStackInheritance** inherits these methods from class **CList** into **CStackInheritance**'s **Public** interface. The methods in class **CStackInheritance** do not use **SyncLock** statements. Each of the methods in this class calls a method from class **CList** that uses **SyncLock**. If two threads call **Push** on the same stack object, only one thread at a time will be able to call **CList** method **InsertAtFront**. Note that class **CStackInheritance** uses namespace **LinkedListLibrary** (Fig. 20.4); thus, the project that contains class **CStackInheritance** must contain a reference to the **LinkedListLibrary** class library.

Module **modStackInheritanceTest**'s **Main** method (Fig. 20.13) uses class **CStackInheritance** to instantiate a stack of **Object**s, called **stack**. Lines 15–18 define four objects that will be pushed onto the stack and popped off the stack. The program pushes onto the stack (lines 21, 24, 27 and 30) a **Boolean** with value **True**, a **Char** with value **$**, an **Integer** with value **34567** and a **String** with value **"hello"**. An infinite **While** loop (lines 40–44) pops the elements from the stack. When there are no objects left to pop, method **Pop** throws an **EmptyListException**, and the program displays the exception's stack trace, which depicts the program execution stack at the time the exception occurred. The program uses method **Print** (inherited from class **CList**) to output the contents of the stack after each operation. Note that module **modStackInheritanceTest** uses namespaces **LinkedListLibrary** (Fig. 20.4) and **CStackInheritanceLibrary** (Fig. 20.12); thus, the project containing module **modStackInheritanceTest** must contain references to both class libraries.

```vb
1    ' Fig. 20.12: StackInheritance.vb
2    ' Implementing a stack by inheriting from class CList.
3
4    ' Deitel namespaces
5    Imports LinkedListLibrary
6
7    ' class CStackInheritance inherits class CList
8    Public Class CStackInheritance
9       Inherits CList
10
11      ' pass name "stack" to CList constructor
12      Public Sub New()
13         MyBase.New("stack")
14      End Sub ' New
15
16      ' place dataValue at top of stack by inserting dataValue at
17      ' front of linked list
18      Public Sub Push(ByVal dataValue As Object)
19         MyBase.InsertAtFront(dataValue)
20      End Sub ' Push
21
22      ' remove item from top of stack by removing item at front of
23      ' linked list
24      Public Function Pop() As Object
25         Return MyBase.RemoveFromFront()
26      End Function ' Pop
27
28   End Class ' CStackInheritance
```

Fig. 20.12 Stack implementation by inheritance from class **CList**.

```vb
1    ' Fig. 20.13: StackTest.vb
2    ' Testing stack implementations.
3
4    ' Deitel namespaces
5    Imports LinkedListLibrary
6    Imports StackInheritanceLibrary
7
8    ' demonstrates functionality of stack implementations
9    Module modStackInheritanceTest
10
11      Sub Main()
12         Dim stack As CStackInheritance = New CStackInheritance()
13
14         ' create objects to store in stack
15         Dim aBoolean As Boolean = True
16         Dim aCharacter As Char = Convert.ToChar("$")
17         Dim anInteger As Integer = 34567
18         Dim aString As String = "hello"
19
20         ' use method Push to add items to stack
21         stack.Push(aBoolean) ' add Boolean
22         stack.Print()
23
24         stack.Push(aCharacter) ' add Char
25         stack.Print()
26
27         stack.Push(anInteger) ' add Integer
28         stack.Print()
29
30         stack.Push(aString) ' add String
31         stack.Print()
32
33         ' use method Pop to remove items from stack
34         Dim removedObject As Object = Nothing
35
36         ' remove items from stack
37         Try
38
39            ' pop item and output removed item
40            While True
41               removedObject = stack.Pop()
42               Console.WriteLine(removedObject & " popped")
43               stack.Print()
44            End While
45
46         ' catch exception if Pop was called while stack empty
47         Catch emptyListException As EmptyListException
48            Console.Error.WriteLine(emptyListException.StackTrace)
49         End Try
50
51      End Sub ' Main
52
53   End Module ' modStackInheritanceTest
```

Fig. 20.13 Stack-by-inheritance test. (Part 1 of 2.)

```
The stack is: True

The stack is: $ True

The stack is: 34567 $ True

The stack is: hello 34567 $ True

hello popped
The stack is: 34567 $ True

34567 popped
The stack is: $ True

$ popped
The stack is: True

True popped
Empty stack
   at LinkedListLibrary.CList.RemoveFromFront() in
C:\books\2001\vbhtp2\ch20\Examples\Fig20_04\LinkedListLi-
brary\List.vb:line 64
   at StackInheritanceLibrary.CStackInheritance.Pop() in
C:\books\2001\vbhtp2\ch20\Examples\Fig20_12\StackInheritanceLi-
brary\StackInheritance.vb:line 25
   at StackInheritanceTest.modStackInheritance.Main() in
C:\books\2001\vbhtp2\ch20\Examples\Fig20_13\StackTest\Stack-
Test.vb:line 41
```

Fig. 20.13 Stack-by-inheritance test. (Part 2 of 2.)

Another way to implement a stack class is by reusing a list class through composition. The class in Fig. 20.14 uses a **Private** object of class **CList** (line 9) in the definition of class **CStackComposition**. Composition enables us to hide the methods of class **CList** that should not appear in our stack's **Public** interface by providing **Public** interface methods only to the required **CList** methods. Class **CStackComposition** implements each stack method by delegating its work to an appropriate **CList** method. In particular, **CStackComposition** calls **CList** methods **InsertAtFront**, **Remove-FromFront**, **IsEmpty** and **Print**. We do not show module **modStackComposi-tionTest** for this example, because this class differs from that in Fig. 20.13 only in that we change the type of the stack from **CStackInheritance** to **CStackComposi-tion** in line 12 (Fig. 20.13). If readers execute the application (downloadable from **www.deitel.com**), they will see that the output for the two applications are identical.

```
1   ' Fig. 20.14: StackComposition.vb
2   ' StackComposition definition with composed CList object.
3
4   ' Deitel namespaces
5   Imports LinkedListLibrary
```

Fig. 20.14 Stack-by-composition test. (Part 1 of 2.)

```
6
7    ' class CStackComposition encapsulates CList's capabilities
8    Public Class CStackComposition
9       Private stack As CList
10
11      ' construct empty stack
12      Public Sub New()
13         stack = New CList("stack")
14      End Sub ' New
15
16      ' add object to stack
17      Public Sub Push(ByVal dataValue As Object)
18         stack.InsertAtFront(dataValue)
19      End Sub ' Push
20
21      ' remove object from stack
22      Public Function Pop() As Object
23         Return stack.RemoveFromFront()
24      End Function ' Pop
25
26      ' determine whether stack is empty
27      Public Function IsEmpty() As Boolean
28         Return stack.IsEmpty()
29      End Function ' IsEmpty
30
31      ' output stack content
32      Public Sub Print()
33         stack.Print()
34      End Sub ' Print
35
36   End Class ' CStackComposition
```

Fig. 20.14 Stack-by-composition test. (Part 2 of 2.)

20.5 Queues

Another common data structure is the *queue.* A queue is similar to a checkout line in a super-market—the first person in line is served first, and other customers enter the line at the end and wait to be served. Queue nodes are removed only from the *head* of the queue and are inserted only at the *tail* of the queue. For this reason, a queue is a *first-in, first-out (FIFO)* data structure. The insert and remove operations are known as *enqueue* and *dequeue.*

Queues have many applications in computer systems. Most computers contain only a single processor, enabling them to provide service for at most one user at a time. Thus, entries for other users are placed in a queue. The entry at the front of the queue receives the first available service. Each entry gradually advances to the front of the queue as users receive service.

Information packets in computer networks wait in queues. Each time a packet arrives at a network node, the routing node must route it to the next node on the network, following the path to the packet's final destination. The routing node routes one packet at a time, so additional packets are enqueued until the router can route them.

Another example of queries is presented by the file server in a computer network, which handles file-access requests from many clients throughout the network. Servers have a limited capacity to service requests from clients. When client requests exceed that capacity, the requests wait in queues.

The program of Fig. 20.15 and Fig. 20.16 creates a queue class through inheritance from a list class. We want the **CQueueInheritance** class (Fig. 20.15) to include methods **Enqueue**, **Dequeue**, **IsEmpty** and **Print**. Note that these methods essentially are the **InsertAtBack**, **RemoveFromFront**, **IsEmpty** and **Print** methods of class **CList**. This class contains other methods, such as methods **InsertAtFront** and **RemoveFromBack**, which we would rather not make accessible through the **Public** interface to the queue class. Remember that all methods in the **Public** interface of the **CList** class are also **Public** methods of the derived class **CQueueInheritance**.

When we implement the queue's methods, we have each **CQueueInheritance** method call the appropriate **CList** method—method **Enqueue** calls **InsertAtBack**, and method **Dequeue** calls **RemoveFromFront**, whereas **IsEmpty** and **Print** calls invoke their base-class versions. Class **CQueueInheritance** does not define methods **IsEmpty** and **Print**, because **CQueueInheritance** inherits these methods from class **CList** into **CQueueInheritance**'s **Public** interface. The methods in class **CQueueInheritance** do not use **SyncLock** statements. Each method in this class calls a corresponding method from class **CList** that uses **Synclock**. Note that class **CQueueInheritance** uses namespace **LinkedListLibrary** (Fig. 20.4); thus, the project that contains class **CQueueInheritance** must include a reference to the **LinkedListLibrary** class library.

Module **modQueueInheritanceTest**'s **Main** method (Fig. 20.16) uses class **CQueueInheritance** to instantiate a queue of **Object**s, called **queue**. Lines 15–18 define four objects that will be pushed onto the stack and popped off the stack. The program enqueues (lines 21, 24, 27 and 30) a **Boolean** with value **True**, a **Char** with value **'$'**, an **Integer** with value **34567** and a **String** with value **"hello"**.

```
1    ' Fig. 20.15: QueueInheritance.vb
2    ' Implementing a queue by inheriting from class CList.
3
4    ' Deitel namespaces
5    Imports LinkedListLibrary
6
7    ' class CQueueInheritance inherits from class CList
8    Public Class CQueueInheritance
9       Inherits CList
10
11      ' pass name "queue" to CList constructor
12      Public Sub New()
13         MyBase.New("queue")
14      End Sub
15
16      ' place dataValue at end of queue by inserting dataValue at end
17      ' of linked list
18      Public Sub Enqueue(ByVal dataValue As Object)
19         MyBase.InsertAtBack(dataValue)
20      End Sub ' Enqueue
21
```

Fig. 20.15 Queue implemented by inheritance from class **CList**. (Part 1 of 2.)

```
22        ' remove item from front of queue by removing item at front of
23        ' linked list
24        Public Function Dequeue() As Object
25           Return MyBase.RemoveFromFront()
26        End Function ' Dequeue
27
28     End Class ' CQueueInheritance
```

Fig. 20.15 Queue implemented by inheritance from class **CList**. (Part 2 of 2.)

An infinite **While** loop (lines 40–44) dequeues the elements from the queue. When no objects are left to dequeue, method **Dequeue** throws an **EmptyListException**. At this point, the program displays the exception's stack trace, which shows the program execution stack at the time the exception occurred. The program uses method **Print** (inherited from class **CList**) to output the contents of the queue after each operation. Note that class **CQueueInheritance** uses namespaces **LinkedListLibrary** and **QueueInheritanceLibrary** (Fig. 20.15); thus, the project containing module **modQueueInheritanceTest** must include references to both class libraries.

```
1     ' Fig. 20.16: QueueTest.vb
2     ' Testing queue implementation.
3
4     ' Deitel namespaces
5     Imports LinkedListLibrary
6     Imports QueueInheritanceLibrary
7
8     ' demonstrate queue functionality
9     Module modQueueTest
10
11       Sub Main()
12          Dim queue As CQueueInheritance = New CQueueInheritance()
13
14          ' create data to store in queue
15          Dim aBoolean As Boolean = True
16          Dim aCharacter As Char = Convert.ToChar("$")
17          Dim anInteger As Integer = 34567
18          Dim aString As String = "hello"
19
20          ' use method Enqueue to add items to queue
21          queue.Enqueue(aBoolean) ' add Boolean
22          queue.Print()
23
24          queue.Enqueue(aCharacter) ' add Char
25          queue.Print()
26
27          queue.Enqueue(anInteger) ' add Integer
28          queue.Print()
29
30          queue.Enqueue(aString) ' add String
31          queue.Print()
```

Fig. 20.16 Queue-by-inheritance test. (Part 1 of 2.)

```
32
33        ' use method Dequeue to remove items from queue
34        Dim removedObject As Object = Nothing
35
36        ' remove items from queue
37        Try
38
39            ' dequeue item and output removed item
40            While True
41                removedObject = queue.Dequeue()
42                Console.WriteLine(removedObject & " dequeue")
43                queue.Print()
44            End While
45
46            ' if exception occurs, print stack trace
47        Catch emptyListException As EmptyListException
48            Console.Error.WriteLine(emptyListException.StackTrace)
49        End Try
50
51    End Sub ' Main
52
53  End Module ' modQueueTest
```

```
The queue is: True

The queue is: True $

The queue is: True $ 34567

The queue is: True $ 34567 hello

True dequeue
The queue is: $ 34567 hello

$ dequeue
The queue is: 34567 hello

34567 dequeue
The queue is: hello

hello dequeue
Empty queue
   at LinkedListLibrary.CList.RemoveFromFront() in
C:\books\2001\vbhtp2\ch20\Examples\Fig20_04\LinkedListLi-
brary\List.vb:line 64
   at QueueInheritanceLibrary.CQueueInheritance.Dequeue() in
C:\books\2001\vbhtp2\ch20\Examples\Fig20_15\QueueInheritanceLi-
brary\QueueInheritance.vb:line 25
   at QueueTest.modQueueInheritanceTest.Main() in
C:\books\2001\vbhtp2\ch20\Examples\Fig20_16\QueueTest\QueueTest.vb:
line 41
```

Fig. 20.16 Queue-by-inheritance test. (Part 2 of 2.)

20.6 Trees

Linked lists, stacks and queues are *linear data structures* (i.e., *sequences*). By contrast, a *tree* is a nonlinear, two-dimensional data structure with special properties. Tree nodes contain two or more links. This section discusses *binary trees* (Fig. 20.17), or trees whose nodes each contain two links (none, one or both of which can be **Nothing**). The *root node* is the first node in a tree. Each link in the root node refers to a *child*. The *left child* is the first node in the *left subtree,* and the *right child* is the first node in the *right subtree.* The children of a specific node are called *siblings*. A node with no children is called a *leaf node.* Computer scientists normally draw trees as cascading down from the root node—exactly opposite to the way most trees grow in nature.

Common Programming Error 20.2

*Failure to set to **Nothing** the links in leaf nodes of a tree is a common logic error.*

Our binary-tree example creates a special binary tree called a *binary search tree*. A binary search tree (with no duplicate node values) has the characteristic that the values in any left subtree are less than the value in the subtree's parent node, and the values in any right subtree are greater than the value in the subtree's parent node. Figure 20.18 depicts a binary search tree containing 12 integers. Note that the shape of a binary search tree that corresponds to a set of data can vary depending on the order in which the values are inserted into the tree.

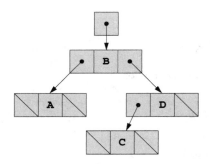

Fig. 20.17 Binary tree graphical representation.

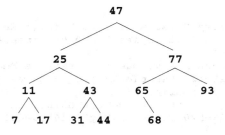

Fig. 20.18 Binary search tree containing 12 values.

20.6.1 Binary Search Tree of **Integer** Values

The application of Fig. 20.19, Fig. 20.20 and Fig. 20.21 creates a binary search tree of integers and then traverses it (i.e., walks through all its nodes) in three ways—using recursive *inorder, preorder* and *postorder traversals*. The program generates 10 random numbers and inserts each into the tree. Figure 20.20 defines class **CTree** in namespace **BinaryTreeLibrary** (for reuse purposes). Figure 20.21 defines module **modTreeTest**, which demonstrates class **CTree**'s functionality. Method **Main** of module **modTreeTest** instantiates an empty **CTree** object, randomly generates 10 integers and inserts each value in the binary tree using **CTree** method **InsertNode**. The program then performs preorder, inorder and postorder traversals of the tree. We will discuss these traversals shortly.

Class **CTreeNode** (Fig. 20.19) is a self-referential class containing three **Private** data members—**mLeftNode** and **mRightNode** of type **CTreeNode** and **mData** of type **Integer** (lines 5–7). Initially, every **CTreeNode** is a leaf node, so the constructor (lines 10–14) initializes references **mLeftNode** and **mRightNode** to **Nothing**. Properties **LeftNode** (lines 17–27), **Data** (lines 30–40) and **RightNode** (lines 43–53) provide access to a **CTreeNode**'s **Private** data members. We discuss **CTreeNode** method **Insert** (lines 56–84) shortly.

Class **CTree** (Fig. 20.20) manipulates objects of class **CTreeNode**. Class **CTree** contains a **Private** root node (line 5)—a reference to the root node of the tree. The class also contains **Public** method **InsertNode** (lines 13–26), which inserts a node in the tree, and **Public** methods **PreorderTraversal** (lines 29–35), **InorderTraversal** (lines 56–62) and **PostorderTraversal** (lines 83–89), which begin traversals of the tree. Each traversal method calls a separate recursive utility method to perform the traversal operations on the internal representation of the tree. The **CTree** constructor (lines 8–10) initializes **root** to **Nothing** to indicate that the tree initially is empty.

The **CTree** class's method **InsertNode** first locks the **CTree** object (to ensure thread safety) and then determines whether the tree is empty. If so, line 19 instantiates a **CTreeNode** object, initializes the node with the integer being inserted in the tree and assigns the new node to **root**. If the tree is not empty, method **InsertNode** calls **CTreeNode** (Fig. 20.19) method **Insert** (lines 56–84), which recursively determines the location for the new node in the tree and inserts the node at that location. In a binary search tree, nodes can be inserted only as leaf nodes.

The **CTreeNode** method **Insert** compares the value to insert with the **mData** value in the root node. If the insert value is less than the root-node data, the program determines whether the left subtree is empty (line 62). If so, line 63 instantiates a **CTreeNode** object, initializes it with the integer being inserted and assigns the new node to reference **mLeftNode**. Otherwise, line 67 recursively calls method **Insert** on the left subtree to insert the value into the left subtree. If the insert value is greater than the root node data, the program determines whether the right subtree is empty (line 74). If so, line 75 instantiates a **CTreeNode** object, initializes it with the integer being inserted and assigns the new node to reference **mRightNode**. Otherwise, line 79 recursively calls method **Insert** on the right subtree to insert the value in the right subtree.

Methods **InorderTraversal**, **PreorderTraversal** and **PostorderTraversal** call helper methods **InorderHelper** (lines 65–80), **PreorderHelper** (lines 38–53) and **PostorderHelper** (lines 92–107), respectively, to traverse the tree and print the node values. The helper methods in class **CTree** allow the programmer to

```vb
1    ' Fig. 20.19: TreeNode.vb
2    ' Class CTreeNode represents a node in a CTree.
3
4    Public Class CTreeNode
5       Private mLeftNode As CTreeNode
6       Private mData As Integer
7       Private mRightNode As CTreeNode
8
9       ' initialize data and make that a leaf node
10      Public Sub New(ByVal nodeData As Integer)
11         mData = nodeData
12         mRightNode = Nothing ' node has no children
13         LeftNode = Nothing ' node has no children
14      End Sub ' New
15
16      ' property LeftNode
17      Public Property LeftNode() As CTreeNode
18
19         Get
20            Return mLeftNode
21         End Get
22
23         Set(ByVal value As CTreeNode)
24            mLeftNode = value
25         End Set
26
27      End Property ' LeftNode
28
29      ' property Data
30      Public Property Data() As Integer
31
32         Get
33            Return mData
34         End Get
35
36         Set(ByVal value As Integer)
37            mData = value
38         End Set
39
40      End Property ' Data
41
42      ' property RightNode
43      Public Property RightNode() As CTreeNode
44
45         Get
46            Return mRightNode
47         End Get
48
49         Set(ByVal value As CTreeNode)
50            mRightNode = value
51         End Set
52
53      End Property ' RightNode
```

Fig. 20.19 Tree-node data structure. (Part 1 of 2.)

```
54
55      ' insert node into tree
56      Public Sub Insert(ByVal insertValue As Integer)
57
58         ' insert in left subtree
59         If insertValue < mData Then
60
61            ' insert new CTreeNode
62            If mLeftNode Is Nothing Then
63               LeftNode = New CTreeNode(insertValue)
64
65            ' continue traversing left subtree
66            Else
67               LeftNode.Insert(insertValue)
68            End If
69
70         ' insert in right subtree
71         ElseIf insertValue > mData Then
72
73            ' insert new CTreeNode
74            If RightNode Is Nothing Then
75               RightNode = New CTreeNode(insertValue)
76
77            ' continue traversing right subtree
78            Else
79               RightNode.Insert(insertValue)
80            End If
81
82         End If
83
84      End Sub ' Insert
85
86   End Class ' CTreeNode
```

Fig. 20.19 Tree-node data structure. (Part 2 of 2.)

start a traversal without first obtaining a reference to the **root** node and then calling the recursive method with that reference. Methods **InorderTraversal**, **PreorderTraversal** and **PostorderTraversal** simply take the **Private** reference **root** and pass it to the appropriate helper method to initiate a traversal of the tree. For the following discussion, we use the binary search tree shown in Fig. 20.22.

```
1    ' Fig. 20.20: Tree.vb
2    ' Class CTree is a tree containing CTreeNodes.
3
4    Public Class CTree
5       Private root As CTreeNode
6
```

Fig. 20.20 Tree data structure. (Part 1 of 3.)

```
7        ' construct an empty CTree of integers
8        Public Sub New()
9           root = Nothing
10       End Sub ' New
11
12       ' insert new node in binary search tree
13       Public Sub InsertNode(ByVal insertValue As Integer)
14
15          SyncLock (Me)
16
17             ' if node does not exist, create node
18             If root Is Nothing Then
19                root = New CTreeNode(insertValue)
20             Else ' otherwise insert node into tree
21                root.Insert(insertValue)
22             End If
23
24          End SyncLock
25
26       End Sub ' InsertNode
27
28       ' begin preorder traversal
29       Public Sub PreorderTraversal()
30
31          SyncLock (Me)
32             PreorderHelper(root)
33          End SyncLock
34
35       End Sub ' PreorderTraversal
36
37       ' recursive method to perform preorder traversal
38       Private Sub PreorderHelper(ByVal node As CTreeNode)
39
40          If node Is Nothing Then
41             Return
42          End If
43
44          ' output node data
45          Console.Write(node.Data & " ")
46
47          ' traverse left subtree
48          PreorderHelper(node.LeftNode)
49
50          ' traverse right subtree
51          PreorderHelper(node.RightNode)
52
53       End Sub ' PreorderHelper
54
55       ' begin inorder traversal
56       Public Sub InorderTraversal()
57
58          SyncLock (Me)
59             InorderHelper(root)
```

Fig. 20.20 Tree data structure. (Part 2 of 3.)

```vbnet
60                End SyncLock
61
62          End Sub ' InorderTraversal
63
64          ' recursive method to perform inorder traversal
65          Private Sub InorderHelper(ByVal node As CTreeNode)
66
67             If node Is Nothing Then
68                Return
69             End If
70
71             ' traverse left subtree
72             InorderHelper(node.LeftNode)
73
74             ' output node data
75             Console.Write(node.Data & " ")
76
77             ' traverse right subtree
78             InorderHelper(node.RightNode)
79
80          End Sub ' InorderHelper
81
82          ' begin postorder traversal
83          Public Sub PostorderTraversal()
84
85             SyncLock (Me)
86                PostorderHelper(root)
87             End SyncLock
88
89          End Sub ' PostorderTraversal
90
91          ' recursive method to perform postorder traversal
92          Private Sub PostorderHelper(ByVal node As CTreeNode)
93
94             If node Is Nothing Then
95                Return
96             End If
97
98             ' traverse left subtree
99             PostorderHelper(node.LeftNode)
100
101            ' traverse right subtree
102            PostorderHelper(node.RightNode)
103
104            ' output node data
105            Console.Write(node.Data & " ")
106
107         End Sub ' PostorderHelper
108
109      End Class ' CTree
```

Fig. 20.20 Tree data structure. (Part 3 of 3.)

```vb
1    ' Fig. 20.21: TreeTest.vb
2    ' This program tests class CTree.
3
4    ' Deitel namespaces
5    Imports BinaryTreeLibrary
6
7    Module modTreeTest
8
9       ' test class CTree
10      Sub Main()
11         Dim tree As CTree = New CTree()
12         Dim insertValue As Integer
13         Dim i As Integer
14
15         Console.WriteLine("Inserting Values: ")
16         Dim randomNumber As Random = New Random()
17
18         ' insert 10 random integers from 0-99 in tree
19         For i = 1 To 10
20            insertValue = randomNumber.Next(100)
21            Console.Write(insertValue & " ")
22            tree.InsertNode(insertValue)
23         Next
24
25         ' perform preorder traversal of tree
26         Console.WriteLine(vbCrLf & vbCrLf & "Preorder Traversal")
27         tree.PreOrderTraversal()
28
29         ' perform inorder traversal of tree
30         Console.WriteLine(vbCrLf & vbCrLf & "Inorder Traversal")
31         tree.InOrderTraversal()
32
33         ' perform postorder traversal of tree
34         Console.WriteLine(vbCrLf & vbCrLf & "Postorder Traversal")
35         tree.PostOrderTraversal()
36
37         Console.WriteLine()
38      End Sub ' Main
39
40   End Module ' modTreeTest
```

```
Inserting Values:
83 13 83 96 81 26 25 13 10 89

Preorder Traversal
83 13 10 81 26 25 96 89

Inorder Traversal
10 13 25 26 81 83 89 96

Postorder Traversal
10 25 26 81 13 89 96 83
```

Fig. 20.21 Tree-traversal demonstration.

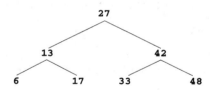

Fig. 20.22 A binary search tree.

Method **InorderHelper** (lines 65–80) defines the steps for an inorder traversal. Those steps are as follows:

1. If the argument is **Nothing**, return immediately.

2. Traverse the left subtree with a call to **InorderHelper** (line 72).

3. Process the value in the node (line 75).

4. Traverse the right subtree with a call to **InorderHelper** (line 78).

The inorder traversal does not process the value in a node until the values in that node's left subtree are processed. The inorder traversal of the tree in Fig. 20.22 is:

    6 13 17 27 33 42 48

Note that the inorder traversal of a binary search tree prints the node values in ascending order. The process of creating a binary search tree actually sorts the data; thus, this process is called the *binary tree sort.*

Method **PreorderHelper** (lines 38–53) defines the steps for a preorder traversal. Those steps are as follows:

1. If the argument is **Nothing**, return immediately.

2. Process the value in the node (line 45).

3. Traverse the left subtree with a call to **PreorderHelper** (line 48).

4. Traverse the right subtree with a call to **PreorderHelper** (line 51).

The preorder traversal processes the value in each node as the node is visited. After processing the value in a given node, the preorder traversal processes the values in the left subtree, then the values in the right subtree. The preorder traversal of the tree in Fig. 20.22 is:

    27 13 6 17 42 33 48

Method **PostorderHelper** (lines 92–107) defines the steps for a postorder traversal. Those steps are as follows:

1. If the argument is **Nothing**, return immediately.

2. Traverse the left subtree with a call to **PostorderHelper** (line 99).

3. Traverse the right subtree with a call to **PostorderHelper** (line 102).

4. Process the value in the node (line 105).

The postorder traversal processes the value in each node after the values of all that node's children are processed. The postorder traversal of the tree in Fig. 20.22 is:

6 17 13 33 48 42 27

The binary search tree facilitates *duplicate elimination*. During the construction of a binary search tree, the insertion operation recognizes attempts to insert a duplicate value, because a duplicate follows the same "go left" or "go right" decisions on each comparison as does the original value. Thus, the insertion operation eventually compares the duplicate with a node containing the same value. At this point, the insertion operation might discard the duplicate value.

Searching a binary tree for a value that matches a key value can be fast, especially in *tightly packed* binary trees. In a tightly packed binary tree, each level contains approximately twice as many elements as does the previous level. Figure 20.22 is a tightly packed binary tree. A binary search tree with n elements has a minimum of $\log_2 n$ levels. Thus, at least $\log_2 n$ comparisons could be required either to find a match or to determine that no match exists. For example, searching a (tightly packed) 1000-element binary search tree requires at most 10 comparisons, because $2^{10} > 1000$. Similarly, searching a (tightly packed) 1,000,000-element binary search tree requires at most 20 comparisons, because $2^{20} > 1,000,000$.

Although not discussed in this book, other binary-tree operations, such as a *level-order traversal of a binary tree* exist. Such a traversal visits the nodes of the binary tree row by row, starting at the root-node level. On each level of the tree, a level-order traversal visits the nodes from left to right.

20.6.2 Binary Search Tree of **IComparable** Objects

The binary-tree example in Section 20.6.1 works nicely when all data is of type **Integer**. However, suppose that a programmer wants to manipulate a binary tree consisting of double values. The programmer could rewrite the **CTreeNode** and **CTree** classes with different names and customize the classes so that they manipulate double values. In fact, programmers could create similar customized versions of classes **CTreeNode** and **CTree** for each data type. This would result in a proliferation of code, which can become difficult to manage and maintain.

Ideally, we would like to define the binary-tree functionality once and reuse that functionality for many data types. Visual Basic provides polymorphic capabilities that enable all objects to be manipulated in a uniform manner. The use of these capabilities enables us to design a more flexible data structure.

In our next example, we take advantage of Visual Basic's polymorphic capabilities. We implement classes **CTreeNode** and **CTree**, which manipulate objects that implement interface **IComparable** (of namespace **System**). It is imperative that we be able to compare objects stored in a binary search tree so that we can determine the path to the insertion point of a new node. Classes that implement interface **IComparable** define method **CompareTo**, which compares the object that invokes the method with the object that the method receives as an argument. The method returns an **Integer** value less than zero if the calling object is less than the argument object, zero if the objects are equal or an **Integer** greater than zero if the calling object is greater than the argument object. Also, both the calling and argument objects must be of the same data type; otherwise, the method throws an **ArgumentException**.

The program of Fig. 20.23 and Fig. 20.24 enhances the program from Section 20.6.1 to manipulate **IComparable** objects. One restriction on the new versions of classes **CTreeNode** and **CTree** (Fig. 20.23 and Fig. 20.24) is that each **CTree** object can contain objects of only one data type (e.g., all **String**s or all **Double**s). If a program attempts to insert multiple data types in the same **CTree** object, **ArgumentException**s will occur. We modified only seven lines of code in class **CTreeNode** (lines 6, 10, 30, 36, 56, 59 and 71) and one line of code in class **CTree** (line 13) to enable the processing of **IComparable** objects. With the exception of lines 59 and 71, all other changes simply replaced the type **Integer** with the type **IComparable**. Lines 59 and 71 previously used the < and > operators to compare the value being inserted with the value in a given node. These lines now compare **IComparable** objects using the interface's method **CompareTo**; the method's return value then is tested to determine whether it is less than zero (the calling object is less than the argument object), zero (the calling and argument objects are equal) or greater than zero (the calling object is greater than the argument object).

```
1    ' Fig. 20.23: TreeNode2.vb
2    ' Class CTreeNode uses IComparable objects for objects
3
4    Public Class CTreeNode
5       Private mLeftNode As CTreeNode
6       Private mData As IComparable
7       Private mRightNode As CTreeNode
8
9       ' initialize data and make this a leaf node
10      Public Sub New(ByVal nodeData As IComparable)
11         mData = nodeData
12         mRightNode = Nothing ' node has no children
13         LeftNode = Nothing ' node has no children
14      End Sub ' New
15
16      ' property LeftNode
17      Public Property LeftNode() As CTreeNode
18
19         Get
20            Return mLeftNode
21         End Get
22
23         Set(ByVal value As CTreeNode)
24            mLeftNode = value
25         End Set
26
27      End Property ' LeftNode
28
29      ' property Data
30      Public Property Data() As IComparable
31
32         Get
33            Return mData
34         End Get
```

Fig. 20.23 Tree node contains **IComparable**s as data. (Part 1 of 2.)

```vb
35
36          Set(ByVal value As IComparable)
37             mData = value
38          End Set
39
40       End Property ' Data
41
42       ' property RightNode
43       Public Property RightNode() As CTreeNode
44
45          Get
46             Return mRightNode
47          End Get
48
49          Set(ByVal value As CTreeNode)
50             mRightNode = value
51          End Set
52
53       End Property ' RightNode
54
55       ' insert node into tree
56       Public Sub Insert(ByVal insertValue As IComparable)
57
58          'insert in left subtree
59          If insertValue.CompareTo(mData) < 0 Then
60
61             ' insert new TreeNode
62             If mLeftNode Is Nothing Then
63                LeftNode = New CTreeNode(insertValue)
64
65             ' continue traversing left subtree
66             Else
67                LeftNode.Insert(insertValue)
68             End If
69
70          ' insert in right subtree
71          ElseIf insertValue.CompareTo(mData) Then
72
73             ' insert new TreeNode
74             If RightNode Is Nothing Then
75                RightNode = New CTreeNode(insertValue)
76
77             ' continue traversing right subtree
78             Else
79                RightNode.Insert(insertValue)
80             End If
81
82          End If
83
84       End Sub ' Insert
85
86    End Class ' CTreeNode
```

Fig. 20.23 Tree node contains **IComparable**s as data. (Part 2 of 2.)

```vb
1    ' Fig. 20.24: Tree2.vb
2    ' Class CTree contains nodes with IComparable data
3
4    Public Class CTree
5       Private root As CTreeNode
6
7       ' construct an empty CTree of integers
8       Public Sub New()
9          root = Nothing
10      End Sub ' New
11
12      ' insert new node in binary search tree
13      Public Sub InsertNode(ByVal insertValue As IComparable)
14
15         SyncLock (Me)
16
17            ' if node does not exist, create one
18            If root Is Nothing Then
19               root = New CTreeNode(insertValue)
20            Else ' otherwise insert node in tree
21               root.Insert(insertValue)
22            End If
23
24         End SyncLock
25
26      End Sub ' InsertNode
27
28      ' begin preorder traversal
29      Public Sub PreorderTraversal()
30
31         SyncLock (Me)
32            PreorderHelper(root)
33         End SyncLock
34
35      End Sub ' PreorderTraversal
36
37      ' recursive method to perform preorder traversal
38      Private Sub PreorderHelper(ByVal node As CTreeNode)
39
40         If node Is Nothing Then
41            Return
42         End If
43
44         ' output node data
45         Console.Write(Convert.ToString(node.Data) & " ")
46
47         ' traverse left subtree
48         PreOrderHelper(node.LeftNode)
49
50         ' traverse right subtree
51         PreOrderHelper(node.RightNode)
52
53      End Sub ' PreorderHelper
```

Fig. 20.24 Binary tree stores nodes with **IComparable** data. (Part 1 of 3.)

```
54
55          ' begin inorder traversal
56          Public Sub InorderTraversal()
57
58             SyncLock (Me)
59                InorderHelper(root)
60             End SyncLock
61
62          End Sub ' InorderTraversal
63
64          ' recursive method to perform inorder traversal
65          Private Sub InorderHelper(ByVal node As CTreeNode)
66
67             If node Is Nothing Then
68                Return
69             End If
70
71             ' traverse left subtree
72             InorderHelper(node.LeftNode)
73
74             ' output node data
75             Console.Write(Convert.ToString(node.Data) & " ")
76
77             ' traverse right subtree
78             InorderHelper(node.RightNode)
79
80          End Sub ' InorderHelper
81
82          ' begin postorder traversal
83          Public Sub PostorderTraversal()
84
85             SyncLock (Me)
86                PostOrderHelper(root)
87             End SyncLock
88
89          End Sub ' PostorderTraversal
90
91          ' recursive method to perform postorder traversal
92          Private Sub PostorderHelper(ByVal node As CTreeNode)
93
94             If node Is Nothing Then
95                Return
96             End If
97
98             ' traverse left subtree
99             PostorderHelper(node.LeftNode)
100
101            ' traverse right subtree
102            PostorderHelper(node.RightNode)
103
```

Fig. 20.24 Binary tree stores nodes with **IComparable** data. (Part 2 of 3.)

```
104              ' output node data
105              Console.Write(Convert.ToString(node.Data) & " ")
106
107          End Sub ' PostorderHelper
108
109    End Class ' CTree
```

Fig. 20.24 Binary tree stores nodes with **IComparable** data. (Part 3 of 3.)

Module **modTreeTest2** (Fig. 20.25) creates three **CTree** objects to store **Integer**, **Double** and **String** values, all of which the .NET Framework defines as **IComparable** types. The program populates the trees from the values in arrays **integerArray** (line 11), **doubleArray** (lines 12–13) and **stringArray** (lines 15–16), respectively, and then calls method **TraverseTree** to output the preorder, inorder and postorder traversals of the three **CTree**s. Method **PopulateTree** (lines 36–47) receives as arguments an **Array** containing the initializer values for the **CTree**, a **CTree** into which the array elements will be placed and a **String** representing the **CTree** name. Method **PopulateType** then inserts each **Array** element in the **CTree**.

Note that the inorder traversal of each **CTree** outputs the data in sorted order, regardless of the data type stored in the **CTree**. Our polymorphic implementation of class **CTree** invokes the appropriate data type's **CompareTo** method, which uses standard binary search tree insertion rules to determine the path to each value's insertion point. In addition, notice that the **CTree** of **String**s is output in alphabetical order.

```
1    ' Fig. 20.25: TreeTest2.vb
2    ' This program tests class CTree.
3
4    ' Deitel namespaces
5    Imports BinaryTreeLibrary2
6
7    Module modTreeTest2
8
9        ' test class CTree.
10       Sub Main()
11           Dim integerArray As Integer() = {8, 2, 4, 3, 1, 7, 5, 6}
12           Dim doubleArray As Double() = _
13               {8.8, 2.2, 4.4, 3.3, 1.1, 7.7, 5.5, 6.6}
14
15           Dim stringArray As String() = {"eight", "two", "four", _
16               "three", "one", "seven", "five", "six"}
17
18           ' create Integer tree
19           Dim integerTree As CTree = New CTree()
20           PopulateTree(integerArray, integerTree, "integerTree")
21           TraverseTree(integerTree, "integerTree")
22
```

Fig. 20.25 **IComparable** binary-tree demonstration. (Part 1 of 3.)

```
23              ' create Double tree
24              Dim doubleTree As CTree = New CTree()
25              populateTree(doubleArray, doubleTree, "doubleTree")
26              TraverseTree(doubleTree, "doubleTree")
27
28              ' create String tree
29              Dim stringTree As CTree = New CTree()
30              populateTree(stringArray, stringTree, "stringTree")
31              TraverseTree(stringTree, "stringTree")
32
33      End Sub ' Main
34
35      ' populate tree with array elements
36      Public Sub PopulateTree(ByVal array As Array, _
37         ByVal tree As CTree, ByVal name As String)
38
39         Dim data As IComparable
40         Console.WriteLine(vbCrLf & "Inserting into " & name & ":")
41
42         For Each data In array
43            Console.Write(Convert.ToString(data) & " ")
44            tree.InsertNode(data)
45         Next
46
47      End Sub ' PopulateTree
48
49      ' perform traversals
50      Public Sub TraverseTree(ByVal tree As CTree, _
51         ByVal treeType As String)
52
53         ' perform preorder traversal of tree
54         Console.WriteLine(vbCrLf & vbCrLf & _
55            "Preorder Traversal of " & treeType)
56
57         tree.PreorderTraversal()
58
59         ' perform inorder traversal of tree
60         Console.WriteLine(vbCrLf & vbCrLf & _
61            "Inorder Traversal of " & treeType)
62
63         tree.InorderTraversal()
64
65         ' perform postorder traversal of tree
66         Console.WriteLine(vbCrLf & vbCrLf & _
67            "Postorder Traversal of " & treeType)
68
69         tree.PostorderTraversal()
70
71         Console.WriteLine(vbCrLf)
72      End Sub ' TraverseTree
73
74   End Module ' CTreeTest2
```

Fig. 20.25 IComparable binary-tree demonstration. (Part 2 of 3.)

```
Inserting into integerTree:
8  2  4  3  1  7  5  6

Preorder Traversal of integerTree
8  2  1  4  3  7  5  6

Inorder Traversal of integerTree
1  2  3  4  5  6  7  8

Postorder Traversal of integerTree
1  3  6  5  7  4  2  8


Inserting into doubleTree:
8.8  2.2  4.4  3.3  1.1  7.7  5.5  6.6

Preorder Traversal of doubleTree
8.8  2.2  1.1  4.4  3.3  7.7  5.5  6.6

Inorder Traversal of doubleTree
1.1  2.2  3.3  4.4  5.5  6.6  7.7  8.8

Postorder Traversal of doubleTree
1.1  3.3  6.6  5.5  7.7  4.4  2.2  8.8


Inserting into stringTree:
eight  two  four  three  one  seven  five  six

Preorder Traversal of stringTree
eight  two  four  five  three  one  seven  six

Inorder Traversal of stringTree
eight  five  four  one  seven  six  three  two

Postorder Traversal of stringTree
five  six  seven  one  three  four  two  eight
```

Fig. 20.25 `IComparable` binary-tree demonstration. (Part 3 of 3.)

 Common Programming Error 20.3

*When comparing **IComparable** objects, the argument to method **CompareTo** must be of the same type as the object on which **CompareTo** is invoked; otherwise, an **Argument-Exception** occurs.*

20.7 Collection Classes

In the previous sections of this chapter, we discussed how to create and manipulate data structures. The discussion was "low level," in the sense that we painstakingly created each element of each data structure dynamically using keyword **New** and then modified the data structures by directly manipulating their elements and references to those elements. In this section, we consider the prepackaged data-structure classes provided by the .NET Framework. These classes are known as *collection classes*—they store collections of data. Each instance of one of these classes is known as a *collection*, which is a set of items.

With collection classes, instead of creating data structures, the programmer uses existing data structures without worrying about how the data structures are implemented. This methodology represents a marvelous example of code reuse. Programmers can code more quickly and can expect excellent performance, maximizing execution speed and minimizing memory consumption.

Examples of collections include the cards that players hold in a card game, a group of favorite songs stored in a computer and the real-estate records in the local registry of deeds (which map book numbers and page numbers to properties). The .NET Framework provides several collections. We demonstrate four collection classes—**Array**, **ArrayList**, **Stack** and **Hashtable**—and built-in array capabilities. Namespace **System.Collections** also provides several other data structures, including **BitArray** (a collection of **True/False** values), **Queue** and **SortedList** (a collection of key/value pairs that are sorted by key and can be accessed either by key or by index).

The .NET Framework provides ready-to-go, reusable components; programmers do not need to write their own collection classes. The collections are standardized so that applications can use them easily, without requiring knowledge of the implementation details. These collections are written for broad reuse. They are tuned for rapid execution, as well as for efficient use of memory. The .NET collections encourage further reusability—as new data structures and algorithms that fit this framework are developed, a large base of programmers already will be familiar with the interfaces and algorithms implemented by those data structures.

20.7.1 Class **Array**

Chapter 4 presented basic array-processing capabilities, and many subsequent chapters used the techniques that were demonstrated in that chapter. We mentioned that all arrays inherit from class **Array** (of namespace **System**), which defines property **Length** specifying the number of elements in an array. In addition, class **Array** provides **Shared** methods that define algorithms for processing arrays. These class **Array** methods are overloaded to provide multiple options for performing algorithms. For example, **Array** method **Reverse** can reverse the order of the elements in an entire array or can reverse the elements in a specified range of elements in an array. For a complete list of class **Array**'s **Shared** methods and their overloaded versions, see the online documentation for the class. Figure 20.26 demonstrates several **Shared** methods of class **Array**.

```
1   ' Fig. 20.26: UsingArray.vb
2   ' Using class Array to perform common array manipulations.
3
4   Imports System.Windows.Forms
5   Imports System.Collections
6
7   ' demonstrate algorithms of class Array
8   Public Class CUsingArray
9       Private integerValues As Integer() = {1, 2, 3, 4, 5, 6}
```

Fig. 20.26 Array class demonstration. (Part 1 of 3.)

```vb
10      Private doubleValues As Double() = _
11         {8.4, 9.3, 0.2, 7.9, 3.4}
12
13      Private integerValuesCopy(6) As Integer
14      Private output As String
15
16      ' build and display program output
17      Public Sub Start()
18         Dim result As Integer
19
20         output = "Initial Array Values:" & vbCrLf
21         PrintArray() ' output initial array contents
22
23         ' sort doubleValues
24         Array.Sort(doubleValues)
25
26         ' copy integerValues into integerValuesCopy
27         Array.Copy(integerValues, integerValuesCopy, _
28            integerValues.Length)
29
30         output &= vbCrLf & vbCrLf & _
31            "Array values after Sort and Copy:" & vbCrLf
32
33         PrintArray() ' output array contents
34         output &= vbCrLf & vbCrLf
35
36         ' search for value 5 in integerValues
37         result = Array.BinarySearch(integerValues, 5)
38
39         If result >= 0 Then
40            output &= "5 found at element " & result & _
41               " in integerValues"
42         Else
43            output &= "5 not found" & " in integerValues"
44         End If
45
46         output &= vbCrLf
47
48         ' search for value 8763 in integerValues
49         result = Array.BinarySearch(integerValues, 8763)
50
51         If result >= 0 Then
52            output &= "8763 found at element " & _
53               result & " in integerValues"
54         Else
55            output &= "8763 was not found" & " in integerValues"
56         End If
57
58         MessageBox.Show(output, "Using Class Array", _
59            MessageBoxButtons.OK, MessageBoxIcon.Information)
60
61      End Sub ' Start
62
```

Fig. 20.26 Array class demonstration. (Part 2 of 3.)

```
63          ' append array output to output string
64          Private Sub PrintArray()
65             Dim doubleElement As Double
66             Dim integerElement As Integer
67
68             output &= "doubleValues: "
69
70             ' output each element in array doubleValues
71             For Each doubleElement In doubleValues
72                output &= doubleElement & " "
73             Next
74
75             output &= vbCrLf & " integerValues: "
76
77             ' output each element in array integerValues
78             For Each integerElement In integerValues
79                output &= integerElement & " "
80             Next
81
82             output &= vbCrLf & " integerValuesCopy: "
83
84             ' output each element in array integerValuesCopy
85             For Each integerElement In integerValuesCopy
86                output &= integerElement & " "
87             Next
88
89          End Sub ' PrintArray
90
91          ' main entry point for application
92          Shared Sub Main()
93             Dim application As CUsingArray = New CUsingArray()
94             application.Start()
95          End Sub ' Main
96
97       End Class ' CUsingArray
```

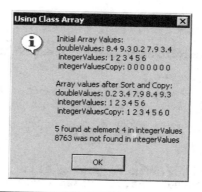

Fig. 20.26 Array class demonstration. (Part 3 of 3.)

Line 24 uses **Shared Array** method **Sort** to sort an array of **Double** values. When this method returns, the array contains its original elements sorted in ascending order.

Lines 27–28 uses **Shared Array** method *Copy* to copy elements from array **integerValues** into array **integerValuesCopy**. The first argument is the array to copy (**integerValues**), the second argument is the destination array (**integerValuesCopy**) and the third argument is an integer representing the number of elements to copy (in this case, property **integerValues.Length** specifies "all elements").

Lines 37 and 49 invoke **Shared Array** method *BinarySearch* to perform binary searches on array **integerValues**. Method **BinarySearch** receives the *sorted* array in which to search and the key for which to search. The method returns the index in the array at which it finds the key, or if the key is not found, the method returns a negative number.

Other **Shared Array** methods include *Clear* (to set a range of elements to **0** or **Nothing**), *CreateInstance* (to create an array of a specified data type), *IndexOf* (to locate the first occurrence of a specific object in an array or portion of an array), *LastIndexOf* (to locate the last occurrence of a specific object in an array or portion of an array) and *Reverse* (to reverse the contents of an array or portion of an array).

20.7.2 Class **ArrayList**

In most programming languages, conventional arrays have a fixed size—they cannot be changed dynamically to an application's execution-time memory requirements. In some applications, this fixed-size limitation presents a problem for programmers. Such programmers must choose whether to use fixed-size arrays that are large enough to store the maximum number of elements the program might require, or to use dynamic data structures, which can grow or shrink at execution time to accommodate a program's memory needs.

Visual Basic's *ArrayList* collection (namespace **System.Collections**) mimics the functionality of conventional arrays and provides dynamic resizing capabilities. At any time, an **ArrayList** contains a certain number of elements, which is either less than or equal to its *capacity*—the number of elements currently reserved for the **ArrayList**. A program can manipulate the capacity with **ArrayList** property **Capacity**. If an **ArrayList** needs to grow, it by default doubles its current **Capacity**.

Performance Tip 20.4

*As with linked lists, the insertion of additional elements into an **ArrayList** whose current size is less than its capacity is a fast operation.*

Performance Tip 20.5

*Inserting an element into an **ArrayList** that must grow larger to accommodate a new element is a slow operation.*

Performance Tip 20.6

*If storage is at a premium, use method **TrimToSize** of class **ArrayList** to trim an **ArrayList** to its exact size. This optimizes an **ArrayList**'s memory use. However be careful—if the program later needs to insert additional elements, the process will be slower, because the **ArrayList** must grow dynamically (trimming leaves no room for growth).*

Performance Tip 20.7

*The default capacity increment, which is a doubling of the **ArrayList**'s size might seem to waste storage, but doubling is an efficient way for an **ArrayList** to grow quickly to "about the right size." This is a much more efficient use of time than growing the **ArrayList** by one element at a time in response to insert operations.*

ArrayLists store references to **Object**s. All classes derive from class **Object**, so an **ArrayList** can contain objects of any type. Figure 20.27 lists some useful methods of class **ArrayList**.

Figure 20.28 demonstrates class **ArrayList** and several of its methods. Users can type a **String** into the user interface's **TextBox** and then press a button representing an **ArrayList** method to see that method's functionality. A **TextBox** displays messages indicating each operation's results.

The **ArrayList** in this example stores **String**s that users input in the **TextBox**. Line 32 creates an **ArrayList** with an initial capacity of one element. This **ArrayList** will double in size each time the user fills the array and then attempts to add another element.

ArrayList method *Add* appends an element to the end of an **ArrayList**. When the user clicks **Add**, event handler **cmdAdd_Click** (lines 35–41) invokes method **Add** (line 38) to append the **String** in the **inputTextBox** to the **ArrayList**.

Method	Description
Add	Adds an **Object** to the **ArrayList**. Returns an **Integer** specifying the index at which the **Object** was added.
Clear	Removes all elements from the **ArrayList**.
Contains	Returns **True** if the specified **Object** is in the **ArrayList**; otherwise, returns **False**.
IndexOf	Returns the index of the first occurrence of the specified **Object** in the **ArrayList**.
Insert	Inserts an **Object** at the specified index.
Remove	Removes the first occurrence of the specified **Object**.
RemoveAt	Removes an object at the specified index.
RemoveRange	Removes a specified number of elements starting at a specified index in the **ArrayList**.
Sort	Sorts the **ArrayList**.
TrimToSize	Sets the **Capacity** of the **ArrayList** to the number of elements that the **ArrayList** currently contains.

Fig. 20.27 **ArrayList** methods (partial list).

```
1    ' Fig. 20.28: ArrayListTest.vb
2    ' Demonstrating class ArrayList functionality.
3
4    Imports System.Collections
5    Imports System.Text
6    Imports System.Windows.Forms
7
8    Public Class FrmArrayList
9       Inherits Form
10
```

Fig. 20.28 **ArrayList** class demonstration. (Part 1 of 5.)

```
11        ' Buttons for invoking ArrayList functionality
12        Friend WithEvents cmdAdd As Button
13        Friend WithEvents cmdRemove As Button
14        Friend WithEvents cmdFirst As Button
15        Friend WithEvents cmdLast As Button
16        Friend WithEvents cmdIsEmpty As Button
17        Friend WithEvents cmdContains As Button
18        Friend WithEvents cmdLocation As Button
19        Friend WithEvents cmdTrim As Button
20        Friend WithEvents cmdStatistics As Button
21        Friend WithEvents cmdDisplay As Button
22
23        ' TextBox for user input
24        Friend WithEvents txtInput As TextBox
25        Friend WithEvents lblEnter As Label
26
27        Friend WithEvents txtConsole As TextBox ' TextBox for output
28
29        ' Visual Studio .NET generated code
30
31        ' ArrayList for manipulating Strings
32        Private arrayList As ArrayList = New ArrayList(1)
33
34        ' add item to end of arrayList
35        Private Sub cmdAdd_Click(ByVal sender As System.Object, _
36           ByVal e As System.EventArgs) Handles cmdAdd.Click
37
38           arrayList.Add(txtInput.Text)
39           txtConsole.Text = "Added to end: " & txtInput.Text
40           txtInput.Clear()
41        End Sub ' cmdAdd_Click
42
43        'remove specified item from arrayList
44        Private Sub cmdRemove_Click(ByVal sender As System.Object, _
45           ByVal e As System.EventArgs) Handles cmdRemove.Click
46
47           arrayList.Remove(txtInput.Text)
48           txtConsole.Text = "Removed: " & txtInput.Text
49           txtInput.Clear()
50        End Sub ' cmdRemove_Click
51
52        ' display first element
53        Private Sub cmdFirst_Click(ByVal sender As System.Object, _
54           ByVal e As System.EventArgs) Handles cmdFirst.Click
55
56           ' get first element
57           Try
58              txtConsole.Text = "First element: " & arrayList(0)
59
60              ' show exception if no elements in arrayList
61           Catch outOfRange As ArgumentOutOfRangeException
62              txtConsole.Text = outOfRange.ToString()
63           End Try
```

Fig. 20.28 ArrayList class demonstration. (Part 2 of 5.)

```
64
65          End Sub ' cmdFirst_Click
66
67          ' display last element
68          Private Sub cmdLast_Click(ByVal sender As System.Object, _
69             ByVal e As System.EventArgs) Handles cmdLast.Click
70
71             ' get last element
72             Try
73                txtConsole.Text = "Last element: " & _
74                   arrayList(arrayList.Count - 1)
75
76             ' show exception if no elements in arrayList
77             Catch outOfRange As ArgumentOutOfRangeException
78                txtConsole.Text = outOfRange.ToString()
79             End Try
80
81          End Sub ' cmdLast_Click
82
83          ' determine whether arrayList is empty
84          Private Sub cmdIsEmpty_Click(ByVal sender As System.Object, _
85             ByVal e As System.EventArgs) Handles cmdIsEmpty.Click
86
87             If arrayList.Count = 0 Then
88                txtConsole.Text = "arrayList is empty"
89             Else
90                txtConsole.Text = "arrayList is not empty"
91             End If
92
93          End Sub ' cmdIsEmpty_Click
94
95          ' determine whether arrayList contains specified object
96          Private Sub cmdContains_Click(ByVal sender As System.Object, _
97             ByVal e As System.EventArgs) Handles cmdContains.Click
98
99             If arrayList.Contains(txtInput.Text) Then
100               txtConsole.Text = "arrayList contains " & _
101                  txtInput.Text()
102            Else
103               txtConsole.Text = txtInput.Text & " not found"
104            End If
105
106         End Sub ' cmdContains_Click
107
108         ' determine location of specified object
109         Private Sub cmdLocation_Click(ByVal sender As System.Object, _
110            ByVal e As System.EventArgs) Handles cmdLocation.Click
111
112            txtConsole.Text = "Element is at location " & _
113               arrayList.IndexOf(txtInput.Text)
114         End Sub ' cmdLocation_Click
115
```

Fig. 20.28 ArrayList class demonstration. (Part 3 of 5.)

```
116      ' trim arrayList to current size
117      Private Sub cmdTrim_Click(ByVal sender As System.Object, _
118          ByVal e As System.EventArgs) Handles cmdTrim.Click
119
120          arrayList.TrimToSize()
121          txtConsole.Text = "Vector trimmed to size"
122      End Sub ' cmdTrim_Click
123
124      ' show arrayList current size and capacity
125      Private Sub cmdStatistics_Click(ByVal sender As System.Object, _
126          ByVal e As System.EventArgs) Handles cmdStatistics.Click
127
128          txtConsole.Text = "Size = " & arrayList.Count & _
129          "; capacity = " & arrayList.Capacity
130      End Sub ' cmdStatistics_Click
131
132      ' display contents of arrayList
133      Private Sub cmdDisplay_Click(ByVal sender As System.Object, _
134          ByVal e As System.EventArgs) Handles cmdDisplay.Click
135
136          Dim enumerator As IEnumerator = arrayList.GetEnumerator()
137          Dim buffer As StringBuilder = New StringBuilder()
138
139          While enumerator.MoveNext()
140              buffer.Append(enumerator.Current & " ")
141          End While
142
143          txtConsole.Text = buffer.ToString()
144      End Sub ' cmdDisplay_Click
145
146  End Class ' FrmArrayList
```

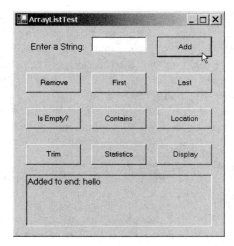

Fig. 20.28 ArrayList class demonstration. (Part 4 of 5.)

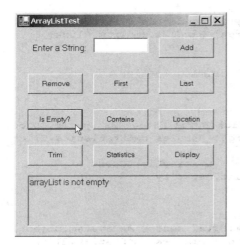 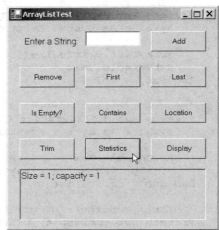

Fig. 20.28 **ArrayList** class demonstration. (Part 5 of 5.)

ArrayList method *Remove* deletes a specified item from an **ArrayList**. When the user clicks **Remove**, event handler **cmdRemove_Click** (line 44–50) invokes **Remove** (line 47) to remove the **String** specified in the **inputTextBox** from the **ArrayList**. If the object passed to **Remove** is in the **ArrayList**, the first occurrence of that object is removed, and all subsequent elements shift toward the beginning of the **ArrayList** to fill the empty position.

A program can access **ArrayList** elements in the same way that conventional array elements are accessed: By following the **ArrayList** reference name with the array subscript operator (**()**) and the desired index of the element. Event handlers **cmdFirst_Click** (lines 53–65) and **cmdLast_Click** (lines 68–81) use the **Array-List** subscript operator to retrieve the first element (line 58) and last element (line 74), respectively. An **ArgumentOutOfRangeException** occurs if the specified index is less than zero or greater than the number of elements currently stored in the **ArrayList**.

Event handler **cmdIsEmpty_Click** (lines 84–93) uses **ArrayList** property *Count* (line 87) to determine whether the **ArrayList** is empty. Event handler **cmdContains_Click** (lines 96–106) uses **ArrayList** method **Contains** (line 99) to determine whether the object that **Contains** receives as an argument currently is in the **ArrayList**. If so, the method returns **True**; otherwise, it returns **False**.

Performance Tip 20.8

*ArrayList method **Contains** performs a linear search, which is a costly operation for large **ArrayList**s. If the **ArrayList** is sorted, use **ArrayList** method **Binary-Search** to perform a more efficient search.*

When the user clicks **Location**, event handler **cmdLocation_Click** (lines 109–114) invokes **ArrayList** method *IndexOf* (line 113) to determine the index of a particular object in the **ArrayList**. **IndexOf** returns **-1** if the element is not found.

When the user clicks **Trim**, event handler **cmdTrim_Click** (lines 117–122) invokes method *TrimToSize* (line 120) to set the *Capacity* property so that it is equal to the

Count property. This reduces the storage capacity of the **ArrayList** to the exact number of elements currently in the **ArrayList**.

When users click **Statistics**, **cmdStatistics_Click** (lines 125–130) uses the **Count** and **Capacity** properties to display the current number of elements in the **ArrayList** and the maximum number of elements that can be stored without the allocation of more memory to the **ArrayList**.

When users click **Display**, **cmdDisplay_Click** (lines 133–144) outputs the contents of the **ArrayList**. This event handler uses an *IEnumerator* (sometimes called an *enumerator*, or an *iterator*) to traverse the elements of an **ArrayList** one element at a time. Interface **IEnumerator** defines methods *MoveNext* and *Reset* and property *Current*. **MoveNext** moves the enumerator to the next element in the **ArrayList**. The first call to **MoveNext** positions the enumerator at the first element of the **ArrayList**. **MoveNext** returns **True** if there is at least one more element in the **ArrayList**; otherwise, the method returns **False**. Method **Reset** positions the enumerator before the first element of the **ArrayList**. Methods **MoveNext** and **Reset** throw an **InvalidOperationException** if the contents of the collection are modified after the enumerator's creation. Property **Current** returns the object at the current location in the **ArrayList**.

Line 136 creates an **IEnumerator**, called **enumerator**, and assigns it the result of a call to **ArrayList** method *GetEnumerator*. Lines 139–141 use **enumerator** to iterate the **ArrayList** (as long as **MoveNext** returns **True**), retrieve the current item via property **Count** and append it to **StringBuilder buffer**. When the loop terminates, line 143 displays the contents of **buffer**.

20.7.3 Class **Stack**

The **Stack** class (namespace **System.Collections**) implements a stack data structure. This class provides much of the functionality that we defined in our implementation in Section 20.4. The application in Fig. 20.29 provides a GUI that enables the user to test many **Stack** methods. Line 31 of the **FrmStackTest** constructor creates a **Stack** with the default initial capacity (10 elements).

Class **Stack** provides methods **Push** and **Pop** to perform the basic stack operations. Method **Push** takes an **Object** as an argument and adds it to the top of the **Stack**. If the number of items on the **Stack** (the **Count** property) is equal to the capacity at the time of the **Push** operation, the **Stack** grows to accommodate more **Object**s. Event handler **cmdPush_Click** (lines 37–42) uses method **Push** to add a user-specified string to the stack (line 40).

```
1   ' Fig. 20.29: StackTest.vb
2   ' Demonstrates class Stack functionality.
3
4   Imports System.Collections
5   Imports System.Text
6   Imports System.Windows.Forms
7
8   Public Class FrmStackTest
9      Inherits Form
```

Fig. 20.29 **Stack** class demonstration. (Part 1 of 4.)

```vbnet
10
11       ' Buttons invoking Stack functionality
12       Friend WithEvents cmdPush As Button
13       Friend WithEvents cmdPop As Button
14       Friend WithEvents cmdPeek As Button
15       Friend WithEvents cmdIsEmpty As Button
16       Friend WithEvents cmdSearch As Button
17       Friend WithEvents cmdDisplay As Button
18
19       ' TextBox receives input from user
20       Friend WithEvents txtInput As TextBox
21       Friend WithEvents lblStatus As Label
22       Friend WithEvents lblEnter As Label
23
24       Private stack As Stack
25
26       Public Sub New()
27          MyBase.New()
28
29          InitializeComponent()
30
31          stack = New Stack() ' create stack
32       End Sub ' New
33
34       ' Visual Studio .NET generated code
35
36       ' push element onto stack
37       Private Sub cmdPush_Click(ByVal sender As System.Object, _
38          ByVal e As System.EventArgs) Handles cmdPush.Click
39
40          Stack.Push(txtInput.Text)
41          lblStatus.Text = "Pushed: " & txtInput.Text
42       End Sub ' cmdPush_Click
43
44       ' pop element from stack
45       Private Sub cmdPop_Click(ByVal sender As System.Object, _
46          ByVal e As System.EventArgs) Handles cmdPop.Click
47
48          ' pop element
49          Try
50             lblStatus.Text = "Popped: " & stack.Pop()
51
52          ' print message if stack is empty
53          Catch invalidOperation As InvalidOperationException
54             lblStatus.Text = invalidOperation.ToString()
55          End Try
56
57       End Sub ' cmdPop_Click
58
59       ' peek at top element of stack
60       Private Sub cmdPeek_Click(ByVal sender As System.Object, _
61          ByVal e As System.EventArgs) Handles cmdPeek.Click
62
```

Fig. 20.29 Stack class demonstration. (Part 2 of 4.)

```vbnet
63                ' view top element
64            Try
65               lblStatus.Text = "Top: " & stack.Peek()
66
67                  ' print message if stack is empty
68            Catch invalidOperation As InvalidOperationException
69               lblStatus.Text = invalidOperation.ToString()
70            End Try
71
72         End Sub ' cmdPeek_Click
73
74         ' determine whether stack is empty
75         Private Sub cmdIsEmpty_Click(ByVal sender As System.Object, _
76            ByVal e As System.EventArgs) Handles cmdIsEmpty.Click
77
78            If stack.Count = 0 Then
79               lblStatus.Text = "Stack is empty"
80            Else
81               lblStatus.Text = "Stack is not empty"
82            End If
83
84         End Sub ' cmdIsEmpty_Click
85
86         ' determine whether specified element is on stack
87         Private Sub cmdSearch_Click(ByVal sender As System.Object, _
88            ByVal e As System.EventArgs) Handles cmdSearch.Click
89
90            If stack.Contains(txtInput.Text) Then
91               lblStatus.Text = txtInput.Text & " found"
92            Else
93               lblStatus.Text = txtInput.Text & " not found"
94            End If
95
96         End Sub ' cmdSearch_Click
97
98         ' display stack contents
99         Private Sub cmdDisplay_Click(ByVal sender As System.Object, _
100           ByVal e As System.EventArgs) Handles cmdDisplay.Click
101
102           Dim enumerator As IEnumerator = stack.GetEnumerator()
103           Dim buffer As StringBuilder = New StringBuilder()
104
105           While enumerator.MoveNext()
106              buffer.Append(enumerator.Current & " ")
107           End While
108
109           lblStatus.Text = buffer.ToString()
110        End Sub ' cmdDisplay_Click
111
112  End Class ' FrmStackTest
```

Fig. 20.29 Stack class demonstration. (Part 3 of 4.)

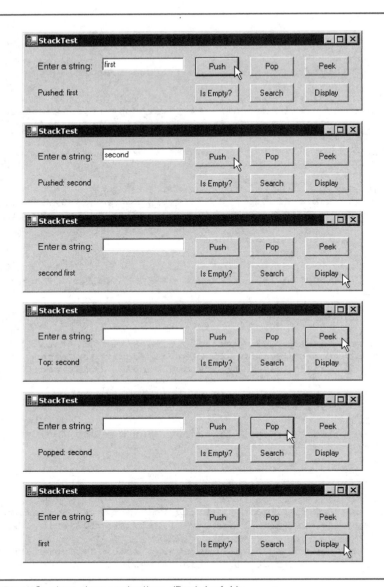

Fig. 20.29 **Stack** class demonstration. (Part 4 of 4.)

Method **Pop** takes no arguments. This method removes and returns the object currently on top of the **Stack**. Event handler **cmdPop_Click** (lines 45–57) calls method **Pop** (line 50) to remove an object from the **Stack**. An **InvalidOperationException** occurs if the **Stack** is empty when the program calls **Pop**.

Method **Peek** returns the value of the top stack element, but does not remove the element from the **Stack**. We demonstrate **Peek** in line 65 of event handler **cmdPeek_Click** (lines 60–72) to view the object on top of the **Stack**. As with **Pop**, an **InvalidOperationException** occurs if the **Stack** is empty when the program calls **Peek**.

Common Programming Error 20.4

*Attempting to **Peek** or **Pop** an empty **Stack** (a **Stack** whose **Count** property equals zero) causes an **InvalidOperationException**.*

Event handler **cmdIsEmpty_Click** (lines 75–84) determines whether the **Stack** is empty by comparing the **Stack**'s **Count** property to zero. If it is zero, the **Stack** is empty; otherwise, it is not. Event handler **cmdSearch_Click** (lines 87–96) uses **Stack** method **Contains** (lines 90) to determine whether the **Stack** contains the object specified as its argument. **Contains** returns **True** if the **Stack** contains the specified object and **False** otherwise.

Event handler **cmdDisplay_Click** (lines 99–110) uses an **IEnumerator** to traverse the **Stack** and display its contents.

20.7.4 Class `Hashtable`

Object-oriented programming languages facilitate creating types. When a program creates objects of new or existing types, it then must manage those objects efficiently. This includes storing and retrieving objects. It is efficient to store and retrieve information in arrays if some aspect of the data directly matches the key values and if those keys are unique and tightly packed. If a company has 100 employees with nine-digit Social Security numbers and wants to store and retrieve employee data using Social Security numbers as keys, nominally this would require an array with 999,999,999 elements, because there are 999,999,999 unique nine-digit numbers. This is impractical for virtually all applications that key on Social Security numbers. If it were possible to have an array that large, programmers could achieve very high performance storing and retrieving employee records by simply using the Social Security number as the array index.

Many applications have this problem—namely, either that the keys are of the wrong type (i.e., negative integers) or that they are of the right type, but they are spread sparsely over a large range.

The solution to this problem must involve a high-speed scheme for converting keys, such as Social Security numbers and inventory part numbers, to unique array subscripts. Then, when an application needs to store some value, the scheme could convert the application key rapidly to a subscript, and the record of information could be stored at that location in the array. Retrieval occurs the same way. Once the application has a key for retrieving the data record, the application applies the same conversion to the key, producing the appropriate array subscript, and retrieves the data.

The scheme we describe here provides the basis for a technique called *hashing*. When we convert a key to an array subscript, we literally scramble the bits, forming a kind of "mishmash" number. The number has no real significance beyond its usefulness in storing and retrieving the particular data record.

Problems in the scheme arise when *collisions* occur (i.e., two different keys "hash into" the same cell (or element) in the array). Because we cannot store two different data records into the same space, we need to find alternative homes for all records beyond the first that hash to a particular array subscript. Many schemes exist for doing this. One is to "hash again" (i.e., to reapply the hashing operation to the key to produce a next candidate cell in the array). Because the hashing process is designed to be random, we can assume that, with just a few hashes, an available cell will be found.

Another scheme uses one hash to locate the first candidate cell. If the cell is occupied, successive cells are searched linearly until an available cell is found. Retrieval works the same way—the key is hashed once, the resulting cell is checked to determine whether it contains the desired data. If it does, the search is complete. If it does not, successive cells are searched linearly until the desired data is found.

The most popular solution to hash-table collisions is to have each cell of the table be a hash "bucket," which typically is a linked list of all the key/value pairs that hash to that cell. This is the solution that Visual Basic's **Hashtable** class (namespace **System.Collections**) implements.

The *load factor* affects the performance of hashing schemes. The load factor is the ratio of the number of occupied cells in the hash table to the size of the hash table. The closer the ratio gets to 1.0, the greater the chance of collisions.

Performance Tip 20.9

The load factor in a hash table is a classic example of a space/time trade-off: By increasing the load factor, we achieve better memory utilization, but cause the program to be slowed by increased hashing collisions. By decreasing the load factor, we achieve better program speed due to a reduction in hashing collisions, but we get poorer memory utilization, because a larger portion of the hash table remains empty.

The proper programming of hash tables is too complex for most casual programmers. Recognizing the value of hashing, Visual Basic provides class **Hashtable** and some related features to enable programmers to take advantage of hashing without studying the complex details of the technique.

The preceding sentence is profoundly important in our study of object-oriented programming. Classes encapsulate and hide complexity (i.e., implementation details) while offering user-friendly interfaces. Crafting classes to do this properly is one of the most valued skills in the field of object-oriented programming.

A *hash function* performs a calculation that determines where to place data in the hashtable. The hash function is applied to the key in a key/value pair of objects. Class **Hashtable** can accept any object as a key. For this reason, class **Object** defines method **GetHashCode**, which is inherited by all Visual Basic objects. Most classes that can be used as keys in hash tables override this method to provide one that performs efficient hashcode calculations for the specific data type. For example, a **String** has a hashcode calculation that is based on the contents of the **String**. Figure 20.30 demonstrates several methods of class **Hashtable**.

```
1   ' Fig. 20.30: FrmHashTableTest.vb
2   ' Demonstrate class Hashtable functionality.
3
4   Imports System.Collections
5   Imports System.Text
6   Imports System.Windows.Forms
7
8   Public Class FrmHashTableTest
9       Inherits Form
```

Fig. 20.30 Hashtable class demonstration. (Part 1 of 5.)

```
10
11       ' Buttons invoke Hashtable functionality
12       Friend WithEvents cmdAdd As Button
13       Friend WithEvents cmdGet As Button
14       Friend WithEvents cmdRemove As Button
15       Friend WithEvents cmdEmpty As Button
16       Friend WithEvents cmdContains As Button
17       Friend WithEvents cmdClear As Button
18       Friend WithEvents cmdListObjects As Button
19       Friend WithEvents cmdListKeys As Button
20
21       ' TextBoxes enable user to input hashtable data
22       Friend WithEvents txtFirst As TextBox
23       Friend WithEvents txtLast As TextBox
24       Friend WithEvents txtConsole As TextBox
25
26       Friend WithEvents lblFirst As Label
27       Friend WithEvents lblLast As Label
28       Friend WithEvents lblStatus As Label
29
30       Private table As Hashtable
31
32       Public Sub New()
33          MyBase.New()
34
35          'This call is required by the Windows Form Designer.
36          InitializeComponent()
37
38          table = New Hashtable() ' create Hashtable object
39       End Sub ' New
40
41       ' Visual Studio .NET generated code
42
43       ' add last name and CEmployee object to table
44       Private Sub cmdAdd_Click(ByVal sender As System.Object, _
45          ByVal e As System.EventArgs) Handles cmdAdd.Click
46
47          Dim employee As New CEmployee(txtFirst.Text, txtLast.Text)
48
49          ' add new key/value pair
50          Try
51             table.Add(txtLast.Text, employee)
52             lblStatus.Text = "Put: " & employee.ToString()
53
54          ' if key does not exist or is in table, throw exception
55          Catch argumentException As ArgumentException
56             lblStatus.Text = argumentException.ToString()
57          End Try
58
59       End Sub ' cmdAdd_Click
60
```

Fig. 20.30 Hashtable class demonstration. (Part 2 of 5.)

```
61      ' get object for given key
62      Private Sub cmdGet_Click(ByVal sender As System.Object, _
63         ByVal e As System.EventArgs) Handles cmdGet.Click
64
65         Dim result As Object = table(txtLast.Text)
66
67         If Not result Is Nothing Then
68            lblStatus.Text = "Get: " & result.ToString()
69         Else
70            lblStatus.Text = "Get: " & txtLast.Text & " not in table"
71         End If
72
73      End Sub ' cmdGet_Click
74
75      ' remove key/value pair from table
76      Private Sub cmdRemove_Click(ByVal sender As System.Object, _
77         ByVal e As System.EventArgs) Handles cmdRemove.Click
78
79         table.Remove(txtLast.Text)
80         lblStatus.Text = "Object Removed"
81      End Sub ' cmdRemove_Click
82
83      ' determine whether table is empty
84      Private Sub cmdEmpty_Click(ByVal sender As System.Object, _
85         ByVal e As System.EventArgs) Handles cmdEmpty.Click
86
87         lblStatus.Text = "Table is "
88
89         If table.Count = 0 Then
90            lblStatus.Text &= "empty"
91         Else
92            lblStatus.Text &= "not empty"
93         End If
94
95      End Sub ' cmdEmpty_Click
96
97      ' determine whether table contains specified key
98      Private Sub cmdContains_Click(ByVal sender As System.Object, _
99         ByVal e As System.EventArgs) Handles cmdContains.Click
100
101        lblStatus.Text = "Contains key: " & _
102           table.ContainsKey(txtLast.Text)
103     End Sub ' cmdContains_Click
104
105     ' discard all table contents
106     Private Sub cmdClear_Click(ByVal sender As System.Object, _
107        ByVal e As System.EventArgs) Handles cmdClear.Click
108
109        table.Clear()
110        lblStatus.Text = "Clear: Table is now empty"
111     End Sub ' cmdClear_Click
112
```

Fig. 20.30 Hashtable class demonstration. (Part 3 of 5.)

```vb
113      ' display list of all objects in table
114      Private Sub cmdListObjects_Click( _
115         ByVal sender As System.Object, ByVal e As System.EventArgs) _
116         Handles cmdListObjects.Click
117
118         Dim enumerator As IDictionaryEnumerator = _
119         table.GetEnumerator()
120
121         Dim buffer As StringBuilder = New StringBuilder()
122
123         While enumerator.MoveNext()
124            buffer.Append(Convert.ToString(enumerator.Value) & _
125               vbCrLf)
126         End While
127
128         txtConsole.Text = buffer.ToString()
129      End Sub ' cmdListObjects_Click
130
131      ' display list of keys in table
132      Private Sub cmdListKeys_Click(ByVal sender As System.Object, _
133         ByVal e As System.EventArgs) Handles cmdListKeys.Click
134
135         Dim enumerator As IDictionaryEnumerator = _
136               table.GetEnumerator()
137
138         Dim buffer As StringBuilder = New StringBuilder()
139
140         While enumerator.MoveNext()
141            buffer.Append(enumerator.Key & vbCrLf)
142         End While
143
144         txtConsole.Text = buffer.ToString()
145      End Sub ' cmdListKeys_Click
146
147  End Class ' FrmHashTableTest
```

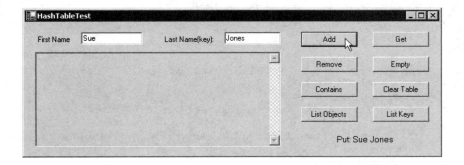

Fig. 20.30 Hashtable class demonstration. (Part 4 of 5.)

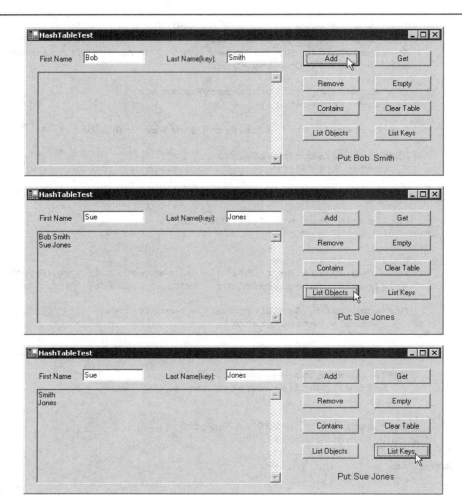

Fig. 20.30 Hashtable class demonstration. (Part 5 of 5.)

```
1    ' Fig. 20.31: Employee.vb
2    ' Class CEmployee for use with HashTable.
3
4    Public Class CEmployee
5       Private firstName, lastName As String
6
7       Public Sub New(ByVal first As String, ByVal last As String)
8          firstName = first
9          lastName = last
10      End Sub ' New
11
```

Fig. 20.31 CEmployee class. (Part 1 of 2.)

```
12        ' return Employee first and last names as String
13        Public Overrides Function ToString() As String
14           Return firstName & " " & lastName
15        End Function ' ToString
16
17   End Class ' CEmployee
```

Fig. 20.31 `CEmployee` class. (Part 2 of 2.)

Event handler **cmdAdd_Click** (lines 44–59) reads the first name and last name of an employee from the user interface, creates an object of class **CEmployee** (Fig. 20.31) and adds that **CEmployee** to the **Hashtable** with method **Add** (line 51). This method receives two arguments——a key object and a value object. In this example, the key is the last name of the **CEmployee** (a **String**), and the value is the corresponding **CEmployee** object. An **ArgumentException** occurs if the **Hashtable** already contains the key or if the key is **Nothing**.

Event handler **cmdGet_Click** (lines 62–73) retrieves the object associated with a specific key using the **Hashtable**'s subscript operator (as shown on line 65). The expression in parentheses is the key for which the **Hashtable** should return the corresponding object. If the key is not found, the result is **Nothing**.

Event handler **cmdRemove_Click** (lines 76–81) invokes **Hashtable** method **Remove** to delete a key and its associated object from the **Hashtable**. If the key does not exist in the table, nothing happens.

Event handler **cmdEmpty_Click** (lines 84–95) uses **Hashtable** property **Count** to determine whether the **Hashtable** is empty (i.e., **Count** is **0**).

Event handler **cmdContainsKey_Click** (lines 98–103) invokes **Hashtable** method **ContainsKey** to determine whether the **Hashtable** contains the specified key. If so, the method returns **True**; otherwise, it returns **False**.

Event handler **cmdClear_Click** (lines 106–111) invokes **Hashtable** method **Clear** to delete all **Hashtable** entries.

Class **Hashtable** provides method **GetEnumerator**, which returns an enumerator of type **IDictionaryEnumerator**, which is derived from **IEnumerator**. Such enumerators provide properties **Key** and **Value** to access the information for a key/value pair. The event handler in lines 114–129 (**cmdListObjects_click**) uses property **Value** of the enumerator to output the objects in the **Hashtable**. The event handler in lines 132–145 (**cmdListKeys_click**) uses the **Key** property of the enumerator to output the keys in the **Hashtable**.

20.8 Summary

Dynamic data structures can grow and shrink at execution time. Creating and maintaining dynamic data structures requires dynamic memory allocation—the ability for a program to obtain more memory at execution time (to hold new nodes) and to release memory no longer needed. The limit for dynamic memory allocation can be as large as the available physical memory in the computer or the amount of available disk space in a virtual-memory system.

A self-referential class contains a data member that refers to an object of the same class type. Self-referential objects can be linked to form useful data structures such as lists, queues, stacks and trees.

A linked list is a linear collection (i.e., a sequence) of self-referential class objects called nodes, connected by reference links. A node can contain data of any type, including objects of other classes. A linked list is accessed via a reference to the first node of the list. Each subsequent node is accessed via the link-reference member stored in the previous node. By convention, the link reference in the last node of a list is set to **Nothing** to mark the end of the list.

Stacks are important in compilers and operating systems. A stack is a constrained version of a linked list—new nodes can be added to a stack and removed from a stack only at the top. A stack is referred to as a last-in, first-out (LIFO) data structure. The primary stack operations are push and pop. Operation push adds a new node to the top of the stack. Operation pop removes a node from the top of the stack and returns the data object from the popped node.

Queues represent waiting lines. Insertions occur at the back (also referred to as the tail) of a queue, and deletions occur from the front (also referred to as the head) of a queue. A queue is similar to a checkout line in a supermarket: The first person in line is served first; other customers enter the line only at the end and wait to be served. Queue nodes are removed only from the head of the queue and are inserted only at the tail of the queue. For this reason, a queue is referred to as a first-in, first-out (FIFO) data structure. The insert and remove operations for a queue are known as enqueue and dequeue.

Binary trees facilitate high-speed searching and sorting of data. Tree nodes contain two or more links. A binary tree is a tree whose nodes all contain two links. The root node is the first node in a tree. Each link in the root node refers to a child. The left child is the first node in the left subtree, and the right child is the first node in the right subtree. The children of a node are called siblings. A node with no children is called a leaf node.

A binary search tree (with no duplicate node values) has the characteristic that the values in any left subtree are less than the values that subtree's parent node and the values in any right subtree are greater than the values in that subtree's parent node. A node can be inserted only as a leaf node in a binary search tree.

An inorder traversal of a binary search tree processes the node values in ascending order. The process of creating a binary search tree actually sorts the data—hence, the term "binary tree sort." In a preorder traversal, the value in each node is processed as the node is visited. After the value in a given node is processed, the values in the left subtree are processed. Then the values in the right subtree are processed. In a postorder traversal, the value in each node is processed after the node's left and right subtrees are processed.

The binary search tree facilitates duplicate elimination. As the tree is created, attempts to insert a duplicate value are recognized because a duplicate follows the same "go left" or "go right" decisions on each comparison as the original value did. Thus, the duplicate eventually is compared with a node containing the same value. The duplicate value may simply be discarded at this point.

The prepackaged data-structure classes provided by the .NET Framework are known as collection classes—they store collections of data. Each instance of one of these classes is known as a collection, which is a set of items.

21

Mobile Internet Toolkit

Objectives

- To become familiar with the Mobile Internet Toolkit (MIT).
- To use ASP .NET and Visual Basic .NET to create mobile Web content.
- To use Mobile Web controls.
- To create code-behind files.
- To create scripts for Mobile Web Forms.
- To use style sheets and templates with a Web Form.
- To access Web services from mobile applications.

It was ordained at the beginning of the world that certain signs should prefigure certain events.
Marcus Tullius Cicero

Oh, never mind the fashion. When one has a style of one's own, it is always twenty times better.
Margaret Oliphant

Outline

21.1 Introduction

Wireless technologies bring the power of communications and the Internet to users worldwide. Wireless communications affect many aspects of society, including business management and operations, employee productivity, consumer purchasing behavior, marketing strategies and personal communications. In addition to Web applications and Windows applications, programmers must develop applications for wireless platforms.

In this chapter, we introduce the Microsoft® *Mobile Internet Toolkit (MIT)*,[1] which allows programmers to create mobile Web applications. The MIT extends Visual Studio .NET's functionality and uses the .NET Framework to create Web content for mobile devices, using languages such as Visual Basic .NET and C#. In this chapter, we explore the MIT in depth as we create wireless applications, using ASP .NET, XML and Visual Basic.NET. We discuss handling user input, displaying images, accessing Web services, mobile Web design and how to make Web pages accessible to multiple devices with the MIT.

21.2 Mobile Internet Toolkit Client Devices

In 1997, the *Wireless Application Protocol (WAP)* was developed by dominant cell-phone manufacturers Nokia, Ericsson, Motorola and others to facilitate the introduction and standardization of wireless Internet access.[2] WAP is a set of communications protocols that are designed to enable wireless devices to access the Internet.

The *Wireless Markup Language (WML)*, which is an XML vocabulary, is the markup language used to describe content for WAP devices. *Microbrowsers*, browsers designed with limited bandwidth and memory requirements, can access the Web via the wireless Internet. WAP supports WML to deliver the content to microbrowsers.

---

1. Setup instructions for the Mobile Internet Toolkit, 1.0, Microsoft Mobile Explorer (MME) 3.0 and Pocket PC 2002 can be downloaded from the **Downloads/Resources** page at **www.deitel.com**.
2. T. Hughes, "The Web Unwired," *Global Technology Business* December 1999: 33.

Although WAP and WML have many proponents, they also have many opponents. Many view WAP technology as a short-term solution for the delivery of wireless Internet access. WAP opponents cite various disadvantages that are associated with the protocol, including possible security breaches, limited bandwidth and unreliability.[3] Another disadvantage cited is that the WAP standard has been implemented only loosely for the various WAP microbrowsers on the market. This means that some microbrowsers support only a subset of WML tags and thus have limited functionality.

Portability Tip 21.1

Different WAP microbrowsers can have inconsistent WML implementations. This makes it difficult to use WML uniformly across a variety of WAP microbrowsers.

The fast pace at which the wireless community is growing has led to the development of other standards, some of which will be discussed shortly. Multiple standards have created a significant challenge for wireless developers. In a world of clients attempting to communicate over disparate technologies, it is a difficult task to build one application that will run correctly on a variety of wireless devices. This chapter introduces the MIT, which helps developers handle disparate mobile devices uniformly. Before we begin our discussion of the MIT's features, let us briefly overview the types of devices that can be targeted by the MIT.

The MIT supports three main clients—*HTML devices*, *WAP devices* and *iMode devices*. HTML devices are those that display HTML markup, such as Internet Explorer (IE), Pocket PC and Palm-based browsers. WAP devices are those that support WAP microbrowsers, which render WML markup. WAP devices can include mobile phones equipped with Nokia or Openwave WAP microbrowsers.

The relationship between WAP browsers and WML is similar to that between IE and HTML. WML's design fits the needs of small devices with low memory capabilities and limited display screens.

Finally, iMode devices are those that support *cHTML (compact HyperText Markup Language) content*. cHTML conforms to a subset of the HTML 2.0 specification. Unlike HTML, cHTML does not support image maps, tables, frames or JPEG images. cHTML pages cannot have a background color or image. Style sheets (e.g., CSS) and scripts (e.g., JavaScript) cannot be used with cHTML.

When learning about mobile communications, it is vital to understand that the process by which mobile devices connect to and interact with the Internet is different for each application type. For example, WAP applications communicate with a WAP gateway—a link between mobile devices and the Internet— using WAP and the WAP gateway communicates with a Web server via HTTP, whereas iMode applications communicate with a Web server directly via HTTP. The MIT eliminates the burden of understanding the various protocols and languages. Rather than creating WML markup for WAP devices, cHTML markup for iMode devices and HTML markup for HTML devices, the developer can now create one application that produces the proper markup needed for disparate devices. For a list of mobile devices supported by the MIT, visit **msdn.microsoft.com/vstudio/device/mitdevices.asp**.

---

3. Further information about WAP can be found at the WAP Forum Web site, **www.wapforum.org**.

21.3 Introduction to the Microsoft Mobile Internet Toolkit and Microsoft Mobile Web Forms

The MIT extends ASP .NET (Chapter 17) functionality to include mobile clients. When an ASPX page is requested by the *incoming device* (i.e., the mobile device), the MIT generates HTML for IE 6.0 and Pocket IE, cHTML for iMode clients and WML for WAP clients.

Creating a mobile Web application in Visual Studio .NET generates an ASPX page (with the **.aspx** file extension), which contains the markup for the page's user interface. The business logic (e.g., event handlers for buttons) for the application can be embedded in the ASPX file as a script or in a code-behind file. The business logic is executed on the Web server. In this chapter, we use both methods of code containment.

Software Engineering Observation 21.1

Most developers use a code-behind file, especially when an application contains significant amounts of code. Using a code-behind file makes programs easier to maintain, debug and modify, because the interface is separated from the implementation.

In this section, we present two mobile Web applications and guide the reader through the steps necessary to create the applications. Figure 21.1 displays the **Welcome.aspx** Web page. The markup in this example is generated by Visual Studio .NET when the user interface is created in design view. Later, we manipulate this markup to include Visual Basic .NET code and device specific functionality. Lines 10–11 use the ***Page*** directive to set the language (via the ***Language*** attribute) in which the code-behind file is written to Visual Basic .NET and set the code-behind file (**CodeBehind** attribute) to **Welcome.aspx.vb**. We discuss this code-behind file (Fig. 21.2) momentarily. Attribute ***Inherits*** indicates the class from which this page inherits. In this example, we are inheriting from the class **Welcome.WelcomePage**, defined in the code-behind file.

```
1   <%-- Fig. 21.1: Welcome.aspx --%>
2   <%-- A simple Web Form.        --%>
3
4   <%-- directive specifies file where code is stored and --%>
5   <%-- programming language in which the code is written --%>
6   <%@ Register TagPrefix="mobile"
7       Namespace="System.Web.UI.MobileControls"
8       Assembly="System.Web.Mobile, Version=1.0.3300.0,
Culture=neutral, PublicKeyToken=b03f5f7f11d50a3a" %>
9
10  <%@ Page Language="vb" AutoEventWireup="false"
11      Codebehind="Welcome.aspx.vb" Inherits="Welcome.CWelcome" %>
12
13  <meta name="GENERATOR" content="Microsoft Visual Studio.NET 7.0">
14  <meta name="CODE_LANGUAGE" content="Visual Basic 7.0">
15  <meta name="vs_targetSchema"
16     content="http://schemas.microsoft.com/Mobile/Page">
17
18  <body Xmlns:mobile="http://schemas.microsoft.com/Mobile/WebForm">
19
20      <mobile:Form id="frmStart" runat="server">
```

Fig. 21.1   Multiple forms in a mobile Web form page. (Part 1 of 2.)

```
21
22          <mobile:Label id="lblStart" runat="server">
23             Click Start!
24          </mobile:Label>
25
26          <%-- command object that will execute method --%>
27          <%-- cmdStart_Click when it is clicked        --%>
28          <mobile:Command id="cmdStart" runat="server">
29             Start
30          </mobile:Command>
31       </mobile:Form>
32
33       <%-- form frmResult --%>
34       <%-- when activated, the method frmResult_Activate --%>
35       <%-- is called --%>
36       <mobile:Form id="frmResult" runat="server">
37          <mobile:Label id="lblResult" runat="server"></mobile:Label>
38       </mobile:Form>
39
40    </body>
```

Fig. 21.1 Multiple forms in a mobile Web form page. (Part 2 of 2.)

The **Register** directive (lines 6–8) specifies the namespace and assembly to which this mobile Web Form's controls belong and the *tag prefix*, which qualifies the Mobile control tag names. The tag prefix is assigned to the **TagPrefix** attribute. The default value for this attribute is **mobile**. The **Namespace** attribute's value (**System.Web.UI.Mobile-Controls**) indicates that any control with the prefix **mobile** is defined in the namespace **System.Web.UI.MobileControls**. The **Assembly** attribute's value (**System.Web.Mobile**) specifies the library file where the mobile FCL classes are located.

Mobile Web Form controls (or *mobile controls*) are the objects used to create mobile applications. Some basic mobile controls include labels and buttons. Every mobile control's start tag has its **runat** attribute set to **"server"** to indicate that the control must be executed on the server. Lines 20–31 define the first mobile control, a **Form**. The **id** attribute's value (line 20) provides a programmatic identifier for the control. In this case, we chose the identifier **frmStart**, because this is the initial form that is displayed to mobile clients. Programmers can assign almost any value to the **id** attribute via the **(ID)** property, provided that it is a valid Visual Basic .NET identifier. Programmers can access and manipulate this control in their code-behind files, using the identifier **frmStart**.

This form contains a **Label** control and a **Command** control. Like Web Form **Label** controls, Mobile **Label** controls display textual information. Setting the **Label**'s **Text** property to **Click Start!** and its **(ID)** property to **lblStart** in design view creates a **Label** control in the markup, such as

```
<mobile:Label id="lblStart" runat="server">
   Click Start!
</mobile:Label>
```

Look-and-Feel Observation 21.1

In design view, **Command** *controls look like buttons. However, some microbrowsers, such as the Openwave™ 5.0 browser, render* **Command** *controls as hyperlinks.*

When the **Command** control is clicked by the user, method **cmdStart_Click** is called to handle the **Click** event. This method is defined in the code-behind file (discussed in Fig. 21.2). Notice that, in the output of Fig. 21.2, the **Command** control is rendered below the **Label** control. By default, controls are placed one below the other on the form in design view. We discuss how to change the layout of the form's controls later in the chapter. Because screen size is limited on most mobile devices, content usually is divided into multiple forms, to reduce the user's need to scroll through the page. On lines 36–38 of Fig. 21.1, the second form is provided, which is the equivalent of another Web page. When this form becomes *active* (i.e., is being displayed), its code-behind file's **frmResult_Activate** method is called to handle the ***Activate*** event. [*Note*: The form being displayed is called the *active form*. Only one form can be active at a time.]

Common Programming Error 21.1

Web Form pages must contain a minimum of one form. A page with no forms results in a compilation error.

In Fig. 21.2, we present the code-behind file **Welcome.aspx.vb** for the ASPX file presented in Fig. 21.1. Class **CWelcome** begins on line 4 and is the base class specified on line 11 in Fig. 21.1. On lines 26–31, we define method **cmdStart_Click**, which handles the **Click** event raised when the user presses the **Start** button. Line 30 sets **frmResult** as the active form by assigning it to property **ActiveForm**. Forms must be activated in this manner because ASPX files can contain multiple forms. Only one form can be active at a time. Method **frmResult_Activate** (lines 34–42) sets **lblResult**'s **Text** property to a welcome message (lines 39–40). In this example, the text displayed by **lblResult** is **Welcome to the Microsoft Mobile Internet Toolkit!**.

The *Microsoft Mobile Explorer* (MME) is a phone emulator that includes two *soft keys* (labeled in Fig. 21.2). These keys allow users interact with the application. For example, the left MME output window in Fig. 21.2 shows the **Start** button highlighted and the left soft key displaying **OK**. Pressing the left soft key selects (i.e., presses) the **Start** button. The *scroll keys* allow users to scroll through Web pages.

```
1    ' Fig. 21.2: Welcome.aspx.vb
2    ' A simple code-behind file.
3
4    Public Class CWelcome
5       Inherits System.Web.UI.MobileControls.MobilePage
6
7       ' forms
8       Protected WithEvents frmStart As _
9          System.Web.UI.MobileControls.Form
10      Protected WithEvents frmResult As _
11         System.Web.UI.MobileControls.Form
12
```

Fig. 21.2   Code-behind file for a mobile application that displays a welcome message. (Part 1 of 3.)

```
13        ' labels
14        Protected WithEvents lblStart As _
15           System.Web.UI.MobileControls.Label
16        Protected WithEvents lblResult As _
17           System.Web.UI.MobileControls.Label
18
19        ' button
20        Protected WithEvents cmdStart As _
21           System.Web.UI.MobileControls.Command
22
23        ' Visual Studio .NET generated code
24
25        ' changes current form when cmdStart is clicked
26        Private Sub cmdStart_Click(ByVal sender As System.Object, _
27           ByVal e As System.EventArgs) Handles cmdStart.Click
28
29           ' change the current form to frmResult
30           ActiveForm = frmResult
31        End Sub ' cmdStart_Click
32
33        ' displays text when frmResult is activated
34        Private Sub frmResult_Activate( _
35           ByVal sender As System.Object, _
36           ByVal e As System.EventArgs) Handles frmResult.Activate
37
38           ' change value to be displayed
39           lblResult.Text = _
40              "Welcome to the Microsoft Mobile Internet Toolkit!"
41
42        End Sub ' frmResult
43
44     End Class ' CWelcome
```

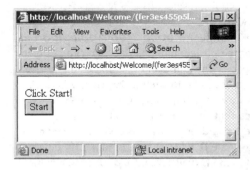

Fig. 21.2   Code-behind file for a mobile application that displays a welcome message. (Part 2 of 3.)

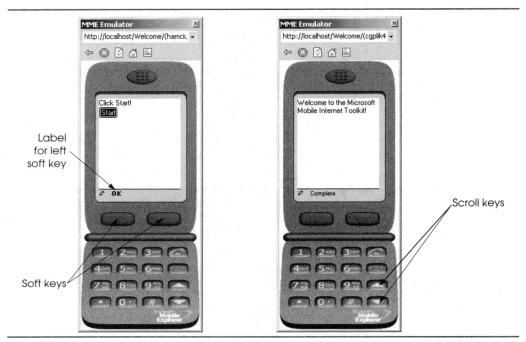

Fig. 21.2   Code-behind file for a mobile application that displays a welcome
            message. (Part 3 of 3.)

Now that we have presented the ASPX file and the code-behind file,[4] we outline the
process by which we created this application. To create the application, perform the following steps:[5]

1. *Create the project.* Open Visual Studio .NET and select **File > New > Project...**
to display the **New Project** dialog (Fig. 21.3). In this dialog, select **Visual
Basic .NET Projects** in the left pane and then *Mobile Web Application* in
the right pane.[6] Notice that the field for the project name is disabled (i.e., grayed
out). Rather than using this field, we specify the name and location of the project
in the **Location** field. We want our project to be located in **http://local-
host**, which is the URL for IIS's root directory (typically, **C:\InetPub\ww-
wroot**). The name *localhost* indicates that the client and server reside on the
same machine. If the Web server were located on a different machine, **localhost** would be replaced with the appropriate IP address or hostname. By default,
Visual Studio .NET assigns the project name **MobileWebApplication1**, which

---

4. To run the chapter examples provided at **www.deitel.com**, you must create a virtual directory
in IIS. For instructions on how to create a virtual directory, visit the **Downloads/Resources**
link at **www.deitel.com**.

5. IIS must be running for this project to be created successfully. IIS can be started by executing **in-
etmgr.exe**, right clicking **Default Web Site** and selecting **Start**. You might need to expand
the node representing your computer to display the **Default Web Site**.

6. The **Mobile Web Application** project will not appear in the **New Project** dialog until after the
MIT has been installed.

we changed to **Welcome**. Below the **Location** textbox, the text **Project will be created at http://localhost/Welcome.** appears. This indicates that the project's folder is located in the root directory on the Web server. Clicking **OK** creates the project and creates a virtual directory, which is linked to the project folder. The **Create New Web** dialog is displayed next, while Visual Studio .NET is creating the Web site on the server (Fig. 21.4).

2. *Examine the newly created project.* The next several figures describe the new project's content; we begin with the **Solution Explorer** shown in Fig. 21.5. Visual Studio .NET generates several files when a new **Mobile Web Application** project is created. **MobileWebForm1.aspx** is the mobile Web Form, which includes a code-behind file. To view the ASPX file's code-behind file, right click the ASPX file and select **View Code**. Alternatively, the programmer can click the icon to display all files, then expand the node for the ASPX page, as shown in Fig. 21.5.

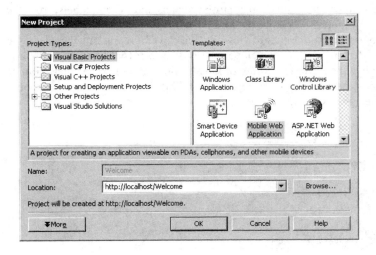

Fig. 21.3   Creating a **Mobile Web Application** in Visual Studio .NET.

Fig. 21.4   Visual Studio .NET creating and linking a virtual directory for the **Welcome** project folder.

Display all files

Code-behind file

ASPX file

Fig. 21.5   **Solution Explorer** window for project **WebTime**.

Figure 21.6 shows the *Mobile Web Form Designer* for **MobileWebForm1.aspx** in *design mode*. It consists of a form on which programmers drag and drop controls, such as buttons and labels, from the **Toolbox**.

Figure 21.7 shows the Mobile Web Form Designer in *HTML mode*, which allows the programmer to view the markup that represents the user interface shown in design mode. A developer can switch to HTML mode by clicking the *HTML tab* in the lower left corner of the Mobile Web Form Designer. Similarly, clicking the *Design* tab (to the left of the **HTML** button) returns the Mobile Web Form Designer to design mode.

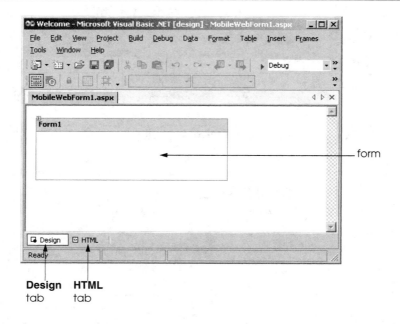

form

Design   **HTML**
tab   tab

Fig. 21.6   Design mode of the Mobile Web Form Designer.

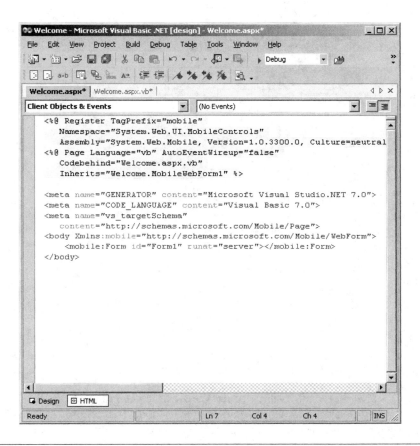

Fig. 21.7 HTML mode of Mobile Web Form Designer.

The next figure (Fig. 21.8) displays **MobileWebForm1.aspx.vb**—the code-behind file for **MobileWebForm1.aspx**. Recall that Visual Studio .NET generates this code-behind file when the project is created; we have reformatted the file's contents for presentation purposes.

3. *Rename the ASPX file.* We have displayed the contents of the default ASPX and code-behind files. We now rename these files. Right click the ASPX file in the **Solution Explorer**, and select **Rename**. Enter the new file name, and press *Enter*. This updates the name of both the ASPX file and the code-behind file. In this example, we use the name **Welcome.aspx**.

4. *Design the page.* The process of designing a mobile Web Form is the same as that for designing a Web Form. To add mobile controls to the page, drag and drop them from the **Toolbox** onto the mobile Web Form. Like the mobile Web Form itself, each control is an object that has properties, methods and events. Programmers can set these properties and events, using the **Properties** window. To view the properties of the mobile Web Form, select ***Document*** from the drop-down list in the **Properties** window.

Fig. 21.8   Code-behind file for `WebForm1.aspx` generated by Visual Studio .NET.

Figure 21.9 shows the **Mobile Web Forms** controls listed in the **Toolbox**. The left figure displays the beginning of the Mobile Web controls list, and the right figure displays the remaining Mobile Web controls. Many of these controls are similar to the Windows controls and Web controls presented earlier in the book.

Fig. 21.9   **Mobile Web Forms** group in the **Toolbox**.

We set the form's **(ID)** property to **frmStart**. We then add a **Label** control and a **Command** control to the form. We set the **Label**'s **(ID)** property to **lblStart** and its **Text** property to **Click Start!**. Notice that the **Command** control appears below the **Label** control. In the Mobile Web Form Designer, the controls are placed one after another, vertically. Changing how the form is rendered by a client requires using such properties as **BreakAfter** (discussed momentarily). Changing the value of a property in the designer changes that control's corresponding markup in the ASPX document.

We now add the second form. We set its **(ID)** property to **frmResult** and add a **Label** to it. The **Label**'s **(ID)** property is set to **lblResult**. We delete the default value (**Label**) for **lblResult**'s **Text** property in design view, because the **Text** property's value is set programmatically in the code-behind file. When a **Label**'s **Text** property does not contain text, the **Label**'s name is displayed in square brackets in the Mobile Web Form Designer. This text is not displayed at run time. The resulting ASPX page is shown in Fig. 21.10.

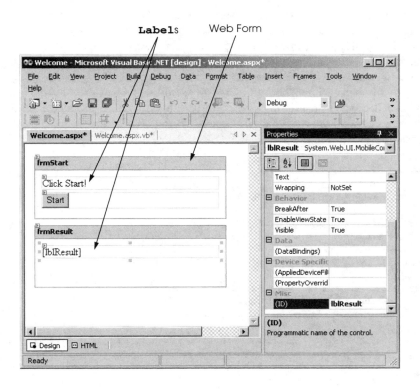

Fig. 21.10 **WebForm.aspx** after adding two **Label**s and setting their properties.

5. *Add page logic.* Once the user interface has been designed, Visual Basic .NET code can be added to the code-behind file. In this example, lines 25–42 of Fig. 21.2 are added to the code-behind file. When the command button in **frm-Start** is clicked, method **cmdStart_Click** (lines 26–31) is called to handle the **Click** event. The statement within this method sets **frmResult** as the active form so method **frmResult_Activate** (lines 34–42) is called. This method sets and displays the contents of **lblResult**.

6. *Run the program.*[7] Select **Build > Build Solution** to build the solution. Next, select **File > Browse With....** From the list of browsers on the left side of the dialog, select ***Microsoft Mobile Explorer Emulator***, and click **Browse**. The MME window opens and loads the Web page (the ASPX file). Notice that the URL is **http://localhost/Welcome/Welcome.aspx** (Fig. 21.2), indicating that our ASPX file is located within the directory **Welcome**.

  After the mobile Web Form is created, the programmer can view it by opening the MME. (Click **BrowseWith...** in the **File** menu, select the MME from the list of browsers and click **Browse**.) When testing an ASP .NET application on the same computer, type **http://localhost/***ProjectFolder***/***Page-Name***.aspx**, where *ProjectFolder* is the folder in which the page resides (usually the name of the project) and *PageName* is the name of the ASP .NET page.

In the next example (Fig. 21.11), we create a tip calculator, which calculates a tip amount based on a dollar amount and a tip percentage. We also demonstrate how to embed a Visual Basic .NET script in an ASPX file. The script begins with a ***<script>*** tag on line 18, wherein we specify the language (via the **Language** attribute) that is used in the script. On lines 21–38, we define method **cmdCalculate_Click**, which calculates the tip amount from the amount and tip-percentage information entered by the user. This method is called when the user clicks the **Calculate Tip** button. Users enter information into two **TextBox** controls (lines 61–62 and 75–76). [*Note:* For simplicity, we do not check the user input for numeric values.]

```
1   <%-- Fig. 21.11: TipCalculator.aspx    --%>
2   <%-- A Web Form that calculates tips. --%>
3
4   <%@ Register TagPrefix="mobile"
5       Namespace="System.Web.UI.MobileControls"
6       Assembly="System.Web.Mobile, Version=1.0.3300.0,
Culture=neutral, PublicKeyToken=b03f5f7f11d50a3a" %>
7
8   <%@ Page Language="vb" AutoEventWireup="false"
9       Codebehind="TipCalculator.aspx.vb"
10      Inherits="TipCalculator.CTipCalculator" %>
11
```

Fig. 21.11 Web Form with embedded Visual Basic .NET code. (Part 1 of 4.) (Image courtesy Openwave Systems, Inc.)

---

7. Before this step, the MME must be installed. This software can be downloaded at **msdn.microsoft.com/downloads/default.asp?url=/downloads/sample.asp?url=/msdn-files/027/001/706/msdncompositedoc.xml**.

```
12   <meta content="Microsoft Visual Studio.NET 7.0" name="GENERATOR">
13   <meta content="Visual Basic 7.0" name="CODE_LANGUAGE">
14   <meta content="http://schemas.microsoft.com/Mobile/Page"
15      name="vs_targetSchema">
16
17   <%-- embedded script containing Visual Basic .NET code --%>
18   <script language="vb" runat="server">
19
20      ' calculate tip
21      Private Sub cmdCalculate_Click(ByVal sender As System.Object, _
22         ByVal e As System.EventArgs) Handles cmdCalculate.Click
23
24         If Page.IsValid Then
25
26            Dim tip As Decimal
27            Dim dollarAmount As String
28
29            tip = Convert.ToDecimal(txtTotal.Text) * _
30               (Convert.ToDecimal(txtTip.Text) / 100)
31
32            ' change tip to dollar value
33            dollarAmount = String.Format( "{0:C}", tip)
34            lblResult.Text = "Tip Amount:" & dollarAmount
35
36         End If
37
38      End Sub ' cmdCalculate_Click
39
40      ' clear form
41      Private Sub cmdClear_Click(ByVal sender As System.Object, _
42         ByVal e As System.EventArgs) Handles cmdClear.Click
43
44            txtTip.Text = ""
45            txtTotal.Text = ""
46            lblResult.Text = ""
47
48      End Sub ' cmdClear_Click
49
50   </script>
51
52   <body Xmlns:mobile="http://schemas.microsoft.com/Mobile/WebForm">
53
54      <mobile:Form id="frmTipCalculator" runat="server">
55
56         <mobile:Label id="lblInstruction1" runat="server"
57            BreakAfter="False">
58            Enter Tip Percentage:
59         </mobile:Label>
60
61         <mobile:TextBox id="txtTip" runat="server">
62         </mobile:TextBox>
63
```

Fig. 21.11 Web Form with embedded Visual Basic .NET code. (Part 2 of 4.) (Image courtesy Openwave Systems, Inc.)

```
64          <mobile:RequiredFieldValidator id="tipValidator"
65             runat="server" ControlToValidate="txtTip"
66             ErrorMessage="RequiredFieldValidator">
67             Please enter the tip percentage
68          </mobile:RequiredFieldValidator>
69
70          <mobile:Label id="lblInstruction2" runat="server"
71             BreakAfter="False">
72             Enter Total Amount:
73          </mobile:Label>
74
75          <mobile:TextBox id="txtTotal" runat="server">
76          </mobile:TextBox>
77
78          <mobile:RequiredFieldValidator id="totalAmountValidator"
79             runat="server" ControlToValidate="txtTotal"
80             ErrorMessage="RequiredFieldValidator">
81             Please enter the total amount
82          </mobile:RequiredFieldValidator>
83
84          <mobile:Label id="lblResult" runat="server">
85          </mobile:Label>
86
87          <mobile:Command id="cmdCalculate" runat="server"
88             BreakAfter="False">
89             Calculate Tip
90          </mobile:Command>
91
92          <mobile:Command id="cmdClear" runat="server">
93             Clear
94          </mobile:Command>
95
96      </mobile:Form> <%-- end form Calculator --%>
97
98   </body>
```

Fig. 21.11 Web Form with embedded Visual Basic .NET code. (Part 3 of 4.) (Image courtesy Openwave Systems, Inc.)

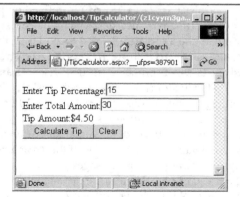

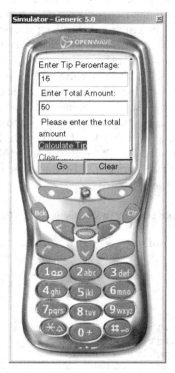

Fig. 21.11 Web Form with embedded Visual Basic .NET code. (Part 4 of 4.) (Image courtesy Openwave Systems, Inc.)

Below each **TextBox** control we included a *validation control*. Validation controls examine user input. For example, if users enter incorrect information or omit required information, most applications cannot proceed, because the information submitted is not in the proper format or is missing. In this example, we use the ***RequiredFieldValidator*** control, which ensures that another control contains data when users attempt to submit the page. In this example, the two **TextBox**es are required to have data, because both the tip percentage and the total amount are required to perform the calculation. The first of these validation controls (**tipValidator**) is defined on lines 64–68. The **Con-trolToValidate** attribute (line 65) specifies which control is validated. In this case, our validator is set to validate the **TextBox** named **txtTip**. If this **TextBox** is empty when the user clicks **Calculate Tip**, the **RequiredFieldValidator** displays the error message specified in its **Text** property (in this case, **Please enter the tip percentage**). The second validator (lines 78–82) behaves in a similar manner, but validates **txtTotal**. Calling method **cmdCalculate_Click** tests the condition **Page.IsValid** on line 24. This condition tests for whether the page is *valid*, i.e., no errors were raised by the validators. If valid, the remainder of **cmdCalculate_Click** will execute. If the page is not valid (i.e., at least one of the **TextBox**es is empty), then the page reloads and displays one or more error messages.

Once **cmdCalculate_Click** calculates the tip amount and displays it, the user has the ability to enter new values. Notice, however, that there are some differences between the ways this program renders in the IE browser and on the Openwave™ browser. In later examples, we demonstrate how to write programs that perform different actions, depending on the browser. For example, the **TextBox**es are displayed next to their respective labels in IE, but the Openwave™ browser displays them on separate lines. Controls can be placed on the same line by setting the control's **BreakAfter** *property* to **False**. The MIT checks on whether the control can fit on the same line or the control must be placed on the next line, by checking the device's screen size. Each device's screen size and other device-specific information, such as support for color graphics and the ability to initiate a phone call, are stored in the **machine.config** file. For example, Fig. 21.12 shows a section of the **machine.config** file that lists the features the MME supports. The markup in Fig. 21.12 indicates that the MME supports HTML markup (line 6) and GIF images (line 7). The **machine.config** file is located in the

C:\WINDOWS\Microsoft.NET\Framework\v1.0.3705\CONFIG

directory. [*Note*: The version number (i.e., **v1.0.3705**) is subject to change.]

```
1   <!-- HTML-oriented capabilities of the HTML MME browsers -->
2   <filter
3       match=".+"
4       with="${httpRequest}">
5       preferredRenderingType = "html32"
6       preferredRenderingMime = "text/html"
7       preferredImageMime = "image/gif"
8       supportsImageSubmit = "true"
9       supportsBold = "true"
10      supportsItalic = "true"
11      supportsFontSize = "true"
12      supportsFontName = "true"
13      supportsFontColor = "true"
14      supportsBodyColor = "true"
15      supportsDivAlign = "true"
16      supportsDivNoWrap = "false"
17  </filter>
```

Fig. 21.12 Section of **machine.config** file.

21.4 Advanced Mobile Web Forms Controls

In this section, we introduce a more sophisticated example that plays the popular game of chance called Craps. The basic rules of the game are provided as part of the example. Figures 21.13 and 21.14 display the ASPX page and code-behind file, respectively. The ASPX page (Fig. 21.13) contains two forms—one that displays the rules to the user (**frm-Rules**) and one provides the game's user interface (**frmGame**). The instructions in **frm-Rules** are displayed in a **Label** control.

```
 1   <%-- Fig. 21.13: Craps.aspx           --%>
 2   <%-- An interactive mobile craps game. --%>
 3
 4   <%@ Page Language="vb" AutoEventWireup="false"
 5       Codebehind="Craps.aspx.vb" Inherits="Craps.CCrapsGame" %>
 6
 7   <%@ Register TagPrefix="mobile"
 8       Namespace="System.Web.UI.MobileControls"
 9       Assembly="System.Web.Mobile, Version=1.0.3300.0,
Culture=neutral, PublicKeyToken=b03f5f7f11d50a3a"%>
10
11   <meta content="Microsoft Visual Studio.NET 7.0" name="GENERATOR">
12   <meta content="Visual Basic 7.0" name="CODE_LANGUAGE">
13   <meta content="http://schemas.microsoft.com/Mobile/Page"
14       name="vs_targetSchema">
15
16   <body Xmlns:mobile="http://schemas.microsoft.com/Mobile/WebForm">
17
18       <mobile:form id="frmRules" runat="server">
19
20          <%-- centered Label --%>
21          <mobile:Label id="lblTitle" runat="server"
22            Alignment="Center">
23            --Craps Rules--
24          </mobile:Label>
25
26          <%-- game rules for user --%>
27          <mobile:Label id="lblRules" runat="server">A player
28            rolls two dice. Each die has six faces. These faces
29            contain 1, 2, 3, 4, 5 and 6 spots. After the dice have
30            come to rest,the sum of the spots on the two upward
31            faces is calculated. If the sum is 7 or 11 on the
32            first throw, the player wins. If the sum is 2
33            (snake eyes), 3 (trey) or 12 (boxcars) on the first
34            throw (called craps), the player loses
35            (i.e., the house wins). If the sum is 4, 5, 6, 8, 9 or 10
36            on the first throw, then that sum becomes the player's
37            'point.' To win, you must continue rolling the dice until
38            you make your point. The player loses by rolling a 7
39            before making the point.
40          </mobile:Label>
41
```

Fig. 21.13 ASPX page for mobile Craps program. (Part 1 of 2.)

```
42              <mobile:Command id="cmdNewGame" runat="server">
43                 New Game
44              </mobile:Command>
45
46         </mobile:form> <%-- end frmRules --%>
47
48         <mobile:form id="frmGame" runat="server">
49
50              <%-- lblStatus displays 'point' or      --%>
51              <%-- message if user won or lost         --%>
52              <mobile:Label id="lblStatus" runat="server">
53              </mobile:Label>
54
55              <%-- Panel object groups a Label and two Images --%>
56              <mobile:Panel id="dicePanel" runat="server">
57                 <mobile:Label id="lblRollValue" runat="server">
58                 </mobile:Label>
59
60                 <mobile:Image id="imgFirst" runat="server"
61                    BreakAfter="False">
62                 </mobile:Image>
63
64                 <mobile:Image id="imgSecond" runat="server">
65                 </mobile:Image>
66              </mobile:Panel>
67
68              <mobile:Command id="cmdPlay" runat="server"
69                 BreakAfter="False">
70                 Play
71              </mobile:Command>
72
73              <mobile:Command id="cmdRoll" runat="server"
74                 BreakAfter="False">
75                 Roll Again
76              </mobile:Command>
77
78              <mobile:Command id="cmdQuit" runat="server">
79                 Quit
80              </mobile:Command>
81
82         </mobile:form> <%-- end frmGame --%>
83
84     </body>
```

Fig. 21.13 ASPX page for mobile Craps program. (Part 2 of 2.)

The second form (**frmGame**) is activated when the user begins a new game. Form **frmGame**'s **lblStatus** (lines 52–53) displays information about the current game's status. On lines 56–66, two new controls—***Panel*** and ***Image***—are introduced. The **Panel** control groups related controls. Setting the **Panel**'s **Visible** property to **false** causes each control on the **Panel** to be hidden. In this example, the **Panel** (**dice-Panel**) contains a **Label** (**rollValueLabel**) and two **Image** controls (**imgFirst** and **imgSecond**). **Label lblRollValue** displays the result of the user's roll, and the two **Image** controls display the dice that correspond to the user's roll. Buttons are provided that allow the user to play, roll again or quit (lines 68–80).

Figure 21.14 shows the code-behind file (**Craps.aspx.vb**). This file defines several methods, including **cmdNewGame_Click**, **frmGame_Activate**, **cmdPlay_Click**, **cmdRoll_Click**, **cmdQuit_Click** and **RollDice**. Clicking the **New Game** button on the rules page calls method **cmdNewGame_Click** (lines 51–58), which sets form **frm-Game** (line 54) as the active form and sets **dicePanel**'s **Visible** property (line 57) to **False**.

```
1    ' Fig. 21.14: Craps.aspx.vb
2    ' The code-behind file for a game of craps.
3
4    Public Class CCrapsGame
5       Inherits System.Web.UI.MobileControls.MobilePage
6
7       ' first form
8       Protected WithEvents frmRules As _
9          System.Web.UI.MobileControls.Form
10
11      ' frmRules form controls
12      Protected WithEvents lblTitle As _
13         System.Web.UI.MobileControls.Label
14      Protected WithEvents lblRules As _
15         System.Web.UI.MobileControls.Label
16      Protected WithEvents cmdNewGame As _
17         System.Web.UI.MobileControls.Command
18
19      ' second form
20      Protected WithEvents frmGame As _
21         System.Web.UI.MobileControls.Form
22
23      ' frmGame form controls
24      Protected WithEvents lblStatus As _
25         System.Web.UI.MobileControls.Label
26      Protected WithEvents lblRollValue As _
27         System.Web.UI.MobileControls.Label
28      Protected WithEvents imgFirst As _
29         System.Web.UI.MobileControls.Image
30      Protected WithEvents imgSecond As _
31         System.Web.UI.MobileControls.Image
32      Protected WithEvents cmdPlay As _
33         System.Web.UI.MobileControls.Command
34      Protected WithEvents cmdRoll As _
35         System.Web.UI.MobileControls.Command
36      Protected WithEvents dicePanel As _
37         System.Web.UI.MobileControls.Panel
38      Protected WithEvents cmdQuit As _
39         System.Web.UI.MobileControls.Command
40
41      ' Visual Studio .NET generated code
```

Fig. 21.14 Code-behind file for craps application. (Part 1 of 6.) (Image courtesy Openwave System, Inc.)

```
42
43          ' special values
44          Enum Names
45              SNAKE_EYES = 2
46              TREY = 3
47              YO_LEVEN = 11
48              BOX_CARS = 12
49          End Enum
50
51          Private Sub cmdNewGame_Click(ByVal sender As System.Object, _
52              ByVal e As System.EventArgs) Handles cmdNewGame.Click
53
54              ActiveForm = frmGame
55
56              ' game has not begun, dice not shown
57              dicePanel.Visible = False
58          End Sub ' cmdNewGame_Click
59
60          Private Sub frmGame_Activate(ByVal sender As System.Object, _
61              ByVal e As System.EventArgs) Handles frmGame.Activate
62
63              ' user is given option to start game
64              cmdPlay.Visible = True
65              cmdPlay.Text = "Play"
66              cmdRoll.Visible = False
67              lblStatus.Text = "Press Play to start!"
68          End Sub ' frmGame_Activate
69
70          ' begins game and analyzes first roll
71          Private Sub cmdPlay_Click(ByVal sender As System.Object, _
72              ByVal e As System.EventArgs) Handles cmdPlay.Click
73
74              Dim sum As Integer
75
76              lblStatus.Text = ""
77              sum = RollDice()
78
79              ' display dice for this roll, store point
80              dicePanel.Visible = True
81              Session.Add( "myPoint", sum.ToString() )
82
83              ' analyze first roll
84              Select Case sum
85
86                  ' user has won
87                  Case 7, Convert.ToInt32(Names.YO_LEVEN)
88
89                      ' game is over; user cannot roll again
90                      cmdRoll.Visible = False
91                      lblStatus.Text = "*YOU WIN!!!*"
92                      cmdPlay.Text = "Play Again"
93
```

Fig. 21.14 Code-behind file for craps application. (Part 2 of 6.) (Image courtesy Openwave System, Inc.)

```
94              ' user has lost
95              Case Convert.ToInt32(Names.SNAKE_EYES), _
96                 Convert.ToInt32(Names.TREY), _
97                 Convert.ToInt32(Names.BOX_CARS)
98                 cmdRoll.Visible = False
99                 lblStatus.Text = "*SORRY. YOU LOSE.*"
100                cmdPlay.Text = "Play Again"
101
102             ' users continue to play if they
103             ' have neither won nor lost
104             Case Else
105                Session("myPoint") = sum.ToString()
106                lblStatus.Text = "Point is " & _
107                   Session("myPoint") & "."
108                cmdPlay.Visible = False
109
110                ' user is given option to roll
111                cmdRoll.Visible = True
112
113          End Select
114
115     End Sub ' cmdPlay_Click
116
117     Private Sub cmdRoll_Click(ByVal sender As System.Object, _
118        ByVal e As System.EventArgs) Handles cmdRoll.Click
119
120        Dim roll As Integer
121        Dim point As Integer = _
122           Convert.ToInt32(Session("myPoint").ToString())
123
124        roll = RollDice()
125
126        ' analyze current roll
127        ' if both cases are False, users roll again
128        If roll = point Then
129           lblStatus.Text = "*YOU WIN!!!*"
130           cmdPlay.Text = "Play Again"
131           cmdRoll.Visible = False
132           cmdPlay.Visible = True
133
134        Else
135
136           If roll = 7 Then
137              lblStatus.Text = "*SORRY. YOU LOSE.*"
138              cmdPlay.Text = "Play Again"
139              cmdRoll.Visible = False
140              cmdPlay.Visible = True
141           End If
142
143        End If
144
145     End Sub ' cmdRoll_Click
```

Fig. 21.14 Code-behind file for craps application. (Part 3 of 6.) (Image courtesy Openwave System, Inc.)

```
146
147     ' creates random values for a roll
148     Private Function RollDice() As Integer
149        Dim die1, die2, dieSum As Integer
150        Dim randomNumber As Random = New Random()
151
152        die1 = 1 + randomNumber.Next(6)
153        die2 = 1 + randomNumber.Next(6)
154
155        ' display the proper dice images
156        imgFirst.ImageUrl = "redDie" & die1.ToString & ".png"
157        imgSecond.ImageUrl = "redDie" & die2.ToString & ".png"
158
159        ' calculate sum of roll
160        dieSum = die1 + die2
161        lblRollValue.Text = "Your roll was " & dieSum.ToString & ":"
162
163        Return dieSum
164
165     End Function ' RollDice
166
167     Private Sub cmdQuit_Click(ByVal sender As System.Object, _
168        ByVal e As System.EventArgs) Handles cmdQuit.Click
169
170        ActiveForm = frmRules
171     End Sub ' cmdQuit_Click
172
173 End Class ' CrapsGame
```

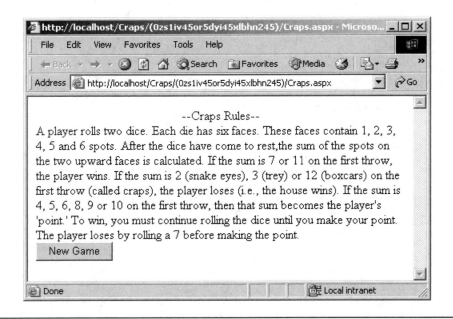

Fig. 21.14 Code-behind file for craps application. (Part 4 of 6.) (Image courtesy Openwave System, Inc.)

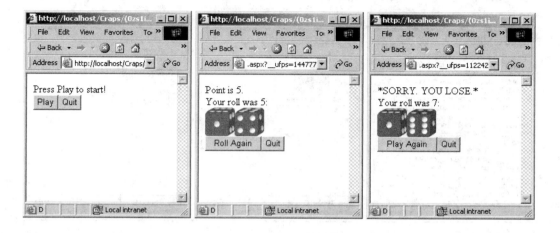

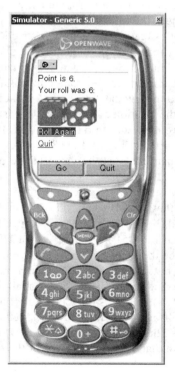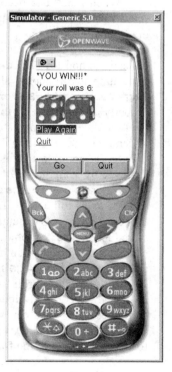

Fig. 21.14 Code-behind file for craps application. (Part 5 of 6.) (Image courtesy Openwave System, Inc.)

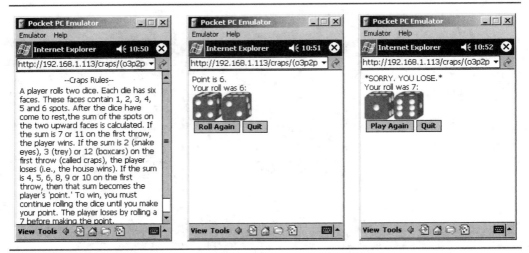

Fig. 21.14 Code-behind file for craps application. (Part 6 of 6.) (Image courtesy Openwave System, Inc.)

When **frmGame** becomes the active form, the **Play** button's **Visible** property is set to **True** and the **Roll Again** button's **Visible** property is set to **False** (i.e., this is the first roll and not a "point" situation). When the user clicks the **Play** button, method **cmdPlay_Click** is called (lines 71–115) to handle the player's initial roll. On line 77, we call method **RollDice** (lines 148–165), which simulates the rolling of two dice by generating two random values in the range from 1 to 6. On lines 156–157, the images **imgFirst** and **imgSecond** display the dice images. Notice that we use the **ImageUrl** property and set its value to the location of the image we wish to display. On line 160, we total the dice values and store their sum in **dieSum**. Line 163 returns **dieSum**'s value, which is assigned to variable **sum** on line 77. Line 81 creates the key–value pair to store in our **Session** object. This pair contains the value of the player's point, which can be retrieved by using the key **"myPoint"**.

We use a **Select Case** statement to determine the value of the first roll (lines 84–113). If users roll a 7 or 11, they win. If users roll a 2, 3 or 12, they lose. Otherwise, the **Case Else** case is executed (lines 104–111). In the **Case Else** case, the user's roll is stored in a **Session** object (line 105) and displayed via **lblStatus**'s **Text** property (lines 106–107). We then hide the **Play** button and show the **Roll Again** button. When users click the **Roll Again** button, method **rollCommand_Click** (defined on lines 117–145) is called to roll the dice again (line 124) and analyze their sum. The player wins if the "point" is rolled (line 128), but loses if a 7 is rolled (line 136). Otherwise, the game continues, and users can roll again or quit playing. Method **quitCommand_Click** (lines 167–171) is called when the **Quit** button is clicked. This method changes the active form to **frmRules**, the form that displays the rules of the game.

21.5 Example: Deitel Wireless Portal

In this example (Fig. 21.15), we create the Deitel Wireless Portal Web site. This site contains links to many WAP-accessible sites. The links are organized into four categories (news, travel and food, financial and contact information), each of which is displayed on separate form controls. The ASPX page consists of five forms and one Visual Basic .NET script. The first form welcomes users and displays the category headings; the other forms contain the links for each category.

The Visual Basic .NET script in this file contains method **frmContact_Activate** (lines 19–29), which adds items to **contactList**, a *List* control. The **List** control renders a list of items in a mobile Web page. Each list item is of type *MobileListItem*. The **List** class contains property *Items*, which can be used to **Get** and **Set MobileListItem**s. The **Get** accessor returns the items as a *MobileListItemCollection* object. The **MobileListItemCollection** class, unlike the **List** class, provides functionality for manipulating a list of items programmatically. Lines 24–27 call **MobileListItemCollection** methods *Clear* and *Add* to update **contactList**. Method **Clear** (line 24) removes all items in the list; method **Add** (lines 25–27) inserts items into the list.

Lines 35–66 define form **frmWelcome**, which is the Web site's main menu. This form consists of a **Label** control and four *Link* controls, which create hyperlinks that redirect users to other forms and sites, depending on the value of the *NavigateUrl* property. For example, on line 56, the *NavigateUrl* property is set to **#frmTravelFood**. The **Text** property is set to **Travel/Food**. The Web site displays the value of the **Link** control's **Text** property (**Travel/Food**) as a hyperlink when the example is run. When users click this **Link**, they are redirected to the value specified in the **NavigateUrl** property. In this case, users are redirected to the form **frmTravelFood** (defined in lines 103–118). The pound (**#**) sign in each **NavigateUrl** value denotes that the resource is located in the ASPX file. **NavigateUrl** values preceded by a **#** are called *internal links* (sometimes referred to as *page anchors*). Later, we will see that **NavigateUrl** values also can be set to *external links* (i.e., locations outside the ASPX file). External links do not contain the **#** symbol.

Lines 66–118 define the forms that contain different categories of Web links. Each form contains multiple external links. Lines 120–129 define the form **frmContact** that displays the items in the **List** control (defined on lines 127–128).

Many of the links connect to WAP sites when clicked at runtime and thus cannot be displayed in IE. In the next section, we examine how the MIT provide ways to handle device-specific functionality.

```
1   <%-- Fig. 21.15: DeitelWirelessPortal1.aspx --%>
2   <%-- A simple mobile Web portal.            --%>
3
4   <%@ Page Language="vb" AutoEventWireup="false"
5       Codebehind="DeitelWirelessPortal1.aspx.vb"
6       Inherits="DeitelWirelessPortal1.MobileWebForm1" %>
7   <%@ Register TagPrefix="mobile"
8       Namespace="System.Web.UI.MobileControls"
9       Assembly="System.Web.Mobile, Version=1.0.3300.0,
Culture=neutral, PublicKeyToken=b03f5f7f11d50a3a" %>
10
```

Fig. 21.15 Demonstrating **List**s and **Link**s. (Part 1 of 5.) (Image courtesy Openwave System, Inc.) (Courtesy of Screaming Media, Inc.)

```vb
11   <meta content="Microsoft Visual Studio.NET 7.0" name="GENERATOR">
12   <meta content="Visual Basic 7.0" name="CODE_LANGUAGE">
13   <meta content="http://schemas.microsoft.com/Mobile/Page"
14      name="vs_targetSchema">
15
16   <script runat="server" language="vb">
17
18      ' add items to list
19      Private Sub frmContact_Activate(ByVal sender As System.Object, _
20         ByVal e As System.EventArgs) Handles frmContact.Activate
21
22         ' clear list (from previous executions)
23         ' add three phone numbers
24         contactList.Items.Clear()
25         contactList.Items.Add("DWP Sales (555)555-1234")
26         contactList.Items.Add("DWP Tech Support (555)555-2468")
27         contactList.Items.Add("DWP Main (555)555-3696")
28
29      End Sub ' frmContact_Activate
30
31   </script>
32
33   <body Xmlns:mobile="http://schemas.microsoft.com/Mobile/WebForm">
34
35      <mobile:form id="frmWelcome" runat="server">
36
37         <mobile:Label id="lblWelcome" runat="server">
38            Welcome to the Deitel Wireless Portal!
39         </mobile:Label>
40
41         <%-- when link is clicked users are sent --%>
42         <%-- to URL specified by NavigateUrl    --%>
43
44         <%-- # indicates internal link --%>
45         <mobile:Link id="newsLink" runat="server"
46            NavigateUrl="#frmNews">
47            News
48         </mobile:Link>
49
50         <mobile:Link id="financialLink" runat="server"
51            NavigateUrl="#frmFinancial">
52            Financial
53         </mobile:Link>
54
55         <mobile:Link id="travelFoodLink" runat="server"
56            NavigateUrl="#frmTravelFood">
57            Travel/Food
58         </mobile:Link>
59
60         <mobile:Link id="contactLink" runat="server"
61            NavigateUrl="#frmContact">
62            Contact
```

Fig. 21.15 Demonstrating **List**s and **Link**s. (Part 2 of 5.) (Image courtesy Openwave System, Inc.) (Courtesy of Screaming Media, Inc.)

```
63          </mobile:Link>
64       </mobile:form>
65
66       <mobile:form id="frmNews" runat="server">
67
68          <%-- NavigateUrl contains external link --%>
69          <%-- users are sent to another site    --%>
70          <mobile:Link id="bloombergLink" runat="server"
71             NavigateUrl=
72             "http://www.bloomberg.com/delivery/hdml/home.hdml">
73             Bloomberg
74          </mobile:Link>
75
76          <mobile:Link id="cnetLink" runat="server"
77             NavigateUrl="http://wap.cnet.com/">
78             CNET News
79          </mobile:Link>
80
81          <mobile:Link id="nytLink" runat="server"
82             NavigateUrl="http://www.nytimes.com/wap">
83             New York Times
84          </mobile:Link>
85       </mobile:form>
86
87       <mobile:form id="frmFinancial" runat="server">
88          <mobile:Link id="wallStreetLink" runat="server"
89             NavigateUrl="http://wap.wsj.com/">
90             Wall Street Journal
91          </mobile:Link>
92          <mobile:Link id="finWinLink" runat="server"
93             NavigateUrl="http://finwin.com">
94             FinWin
95          </mobile:Link>
96          <mobile:Link id="stockPointLink" runat="server"
97             NavigateUrl=
98             "http://wml.stockpoint.com/index.wml">
99             StockPoint
100         </mobile:Link>
101      </mobile:form>
102
103      <mobile:form id="frmTravelFood" runat="server">
104         <mobile:Link id="citiWizLink" runat="server"
105            NavigateUrl="http://wap.citiwiz.com/index.wml">
106            CitiWiz
107         </mobile:Link>
108
109         <mobile:Link id="tenBestLink" runat="server"
110            NavigateUrl="http://wap.10best.com/ ">
111            10Best
112         </mobile:Link>
113
```

Fig. 21.15 Demonstrating **List**s and **Link**s. (Part 3 of 5.) (Image courtesy Openwave System, Inc.) (Courtesy of Screaming Media, Inc.)

```
114          <mobile:Link id="expediaLink" runat="server"
115             NavigateUrl="http://mobile.msn.com/hdml/travel.asp">
116             Expedia
117          </mobile:Link>
118       </mobile:form>
119
120       <mobile:form id="frmContact" runat="server">
121
122          <mobile:Label id="lblContact" runat="server">
123             Contact Information
124          </mobile:Label>
125
126          <%-- list object contains phone numbers --%>
127          <mobile:List id="contactList" runat="server">
128          </mobile:List>
129       </mobile:form>
130    </body>
```

Fig. 21.15 Demonstrating **List**s and **Link**s. (Part 4 of 5.) (Image courtesy Openwave System, Inc.) (Courtesy of Screaming Media, Inc.)

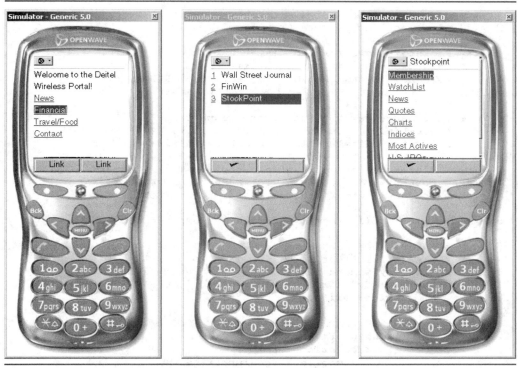

Fig. 21.15 Demonstrating **List**s and **Link**s. (Part 5 of 5.) (Image courtesy Openwave System, Inc.) (Courtesy of Screaming Media, Inc.)

21.6 Device-Independent Web Design Using Stylesheets and Templates

In this section, we enhance the Deitel Wireless Portal Web site's look and feel by using additional controls, such as the **AdRotator** control that randomly selects and displays advertisements. We also discuss how to use "templates" and "style sheets" to maximize the capabilities of the incoming device. In this section, we present an important aspect of mobile Web applications development—programming sites to handle requests from disparate devices. We begin by examining the ASPX file (Fig. 21.16) and the files accessed by our application (Figures 21.17 and 21.18), before we move on to discuss the code-behind file (Fig. 21.19).

A **Stylesheet** control is a collection of **Style** elements. Most MIT controls have a **StyleReference** property, which sets the control's font, color, alignment and so on. This property's value is set to the **Name** attribute of the **Style** element it references. **Stylesheet** controls allow the developer to specify the style of the page elements (headers, fonts, colors, etc.) separately from the structure of the document (i.e., mobile tags) and allow developers to target a specific device (called *Device-Specific Rendering*). For example, developers can write code to enrich the display for HTML-based browsers without compromising mobile accessibility. In this chapter, IE and the Openwave™ Mobile browser are used to test the examples. However, IE browsers are capable of displaying higher-resolution graphics and more sophisticated Web pages.

```
1   <%-- Fig. 21.16: DeitelWirelessPortal2.aspx --%>
2   <%-- A device-independent Web portal.      --%>
3
4   <%@ Register TagPrefix="mobile"
5       Namespace="System.Web.UI.MobileControls"
6       Assembly="System.Web.Mobile, Version=1.0.3300.0,
Culture=neutral, PublicKeyToken=b03f5f7f11d50a3a" %>
7
8   <%@ Page Language="vb" AutoEventWireup="false"
9       Codebehind="DeitelWirelessPortal2.aspx.vb"
10      Inherits="DeitelWirelessPortal2.DeitelWirelessPortal2" %>
11
12  <meta content="Microsoft Visual Studio.NET 7.0" name="GENERATOR">
13  <meta content="Visual Basic 7.0" name="CODE_LANGUAGE">
14  <meta content="http://schemas.microsoft.com/Mobile/Page"
15     name="vs_targetSchema">
16  <body Xmlns:mobile="http://schemas.microsoft.com/Mobile/WebForm">
17
18     <%-- Stylesheet rendered for     --%>
19     <%-- each form that specifies it --%>
20     <mobile:stylesheet id="Stylesheet1" runat="server">
21        <mobile:Style Name="DWPStyles">
22           <DeviceSpecific>
23
24              <%-- templates created for HTML browsers --%>
25              <Choice Filter="isHTML32">
26                 <HeaderTemplate>
27                    <mobile:Image runat="server"
28                       ImageUrl="top.jpg">
29                    </mobile:Image>
30                 </HeaderTemplate>
31              </Choice>
32
33              <%-- templates created for other browsers --%>
34              <Choice>
35                 <HeaderTemplate>
36                    <Mobile:Label runat="server"
37                       StyleReference="Title"
38                       Text="Deitel Wireless Portal" ID="Label1" />
39                 </HeaderTemplate>
40              </Choice>
41           </DeviceSpecific>
42        </mobile:Style>
43     </mobile:stylesheet> <%-- end style sheet --%>
44
45     <%-- opening page showing dwp image --%>
46     <mobile:form id="frmWelcome" runat="server">
47
48        <mobile:Image id="imgWelcome" runat="server"
49           AlternateText="DeitelWireless" ImageUrl="logo.wbmp">
50           <DeviceSpecific>
51              <Choice Filter="isHTML32" ImageUrl="logocolor.jpg">
52              </Choice>
```

Fig. 21.16 Stylesheets and templates in a Mobile Web Form. (Part 1 of 4.)

```
53              </DeviceSpecific>
54          </mobile:Image>
55
56          <mobile:Link id="enterLink" runat="server"
57              Alignment="Center" NavigateUrl="#frmMain">
58              Enter
59          </mobile:Link>
60      </mobile:form> <%-- end form frmWelcome --%>
61
62      <%-- Stylesheet 'DWPStyles' specified --%>
63      <mobile:form id="frmMain" runat="server"
64          StyleReference="DWPStyles">
65
66          <mobile:Link id="newsLink" runat="server"
67              NavigateUrl="#frmNews">
68              News
69          </mobile:Link>
70
71          <mobile:Link id="financialLink" runat="server"
72              NavigateUrl="#frmFinancial">
73              Financial
74          </mobile:Link>
75
76          <mobile:Link id="travelFoodLink" runat="server"
77              NavigateUrl="#frmTravelFood">
78              Travel/Food
79          </mobile:Link>
80
81          <mobile:Link id="contactLink" runat="server"
82              NavigateUrl="#frmContact">
83              Contact
84          </mobile:Link>
85
86          <mobile:Label id="lblSpecials" runat="server"
87              Font-Bold="True">
88              Specials:
89          </mobile:Label>
90
91          <mobile:Label id="lblBookTitle" runat="server"
92              Font-Italic="True">
93          </mobile:Label>
94
95          <mobile:Label id="lblDescription" runat="server">
96          </mobile:Label>
97
98          <mobile:AdRotator id="AdRotator1" runat="server"
99              ImageKey="WirelessImageUrl"
100                 AdvertisementFile="adBanners.xml">
101             <DeviceSpecific>
102                 <Choice Filter="isMME" ImageKey="JpgImageUrl">
103                 </Choice>
104                 <Choice Filter="isHTML32" ImageKey="ImageUrl"
105                     NavigateUrlKey="IENavigateUrl">
```

Fig. 21.16 Stylesheets and templates in a Mobile Web Form. (Part 2 of 4.)

```
106                    </Choice>
107                 </DeviceSpecific>
108              </mobile:AdRotator>
109       </mobile:form> <%-- end form frmMain --%>
110
111       <mobile:form id="frmNews" runat="server"
112          StyleReference="DWPStyles">
113
114          <mobile:Link id="bloombergLink" runat="server"
115             NavigateUrl=
116             "http://www.bloomberg.com/delivery/hdml/home.hdml">
117             Bloomberg
118          </mobile:Link>
119
120          <mobile:Link id="cnetLink" runat="server"
121             NavigateUrl="http://wap.cnet.com/ ">
122             CNET News
123          </mobile:Link>
124
125          <mobile:Link id="newYorkTimesLink" runat="server"
126             NavigateUrl="http://www.nytimes.com/wap">
127             New York Times
128          </mobile:Link>
129
130          <mobile:Link id="mainLink1" runat="server"
131             NavigateUrl="#frmMain">
132             Main
133          </mobile:Link>
134       </mobile:form> <%-- end form frmNews --%>
135
136       <mobile:form id="frmFinancial" runat="server"
137          StyleReference="DWPStyles">
138
139          <mobile:Link id="wallStreetLink" runat="server"
140             NavigateUrl="http://wap.wsj.com/">
141             Wall Street Journal
142          </mobile:Link>
143
144          <mobile:Link id="finWinLink" runat="server"
145             NavigateUrl="http://finwin.com">
146             FinWin
147          </mobile:Link>
148
149          <mobile:Link id="stockPointLink" runat="server"
150             NavigateUrl=
151             "http://wml.stockpoint.com/index.wml">
152             StockPoint
153          </mobile:Link>
154
155          <mobile:Link id="MainLink2" runat="server"
156             NavigateUrl="#frmMain">
157             Main
158          </mobile:Link>
```

Fig. 21.16 Stylesheets and templates in a Mobile Web Form. (Part 3 of 4.)

```
159     </mobile:form> <%-- end form frmFinancial --%>
160
161     <mobile:form id="frmTravelFood" runat="server"
162        StyleReference="DWPStyles">
163
164        <mobile:Link id="citiWizLink" runat="server"
165           NavigateUrl="http://wap.citiwiz.com/index.wml">
166           CitiWiz
167        </mobile:Link>
168
169        <mobile:Link id="tenBestLink" runat="server"
170           NavigateUrl="http://wap.10best.com/ ">
171           10Best
172        </mobile:Link>
173
174        <mobile:Link id="expediaLink" runat="server"
175           NavigateUrl="http://mobile.msn.com/hdml/travel.asp">
176           Expedia
177        </mobile:Link>
178
179        <mobile:Link id="mainLink3" runat="server"
180           NavigateUrl="#frmMain">
181           Main
182        </mobile:Link>
183     </mobile:form> <%-- end form frmTravelFood --%>
184
185     <mobile:form id="frmContact" runat="server"
186        StyleReference="DWPStyles">
187
188        <mobile:Label id="lblContact" runat="server">
189           Contact Information
190        </mobile:Label>
191
192        <mobile:List id="contactList" runat="server">
193           <Item Value="DWP Sales (555)555-1234"
194              Text="DWP Sales (555)555-1234">
195           </Item>
196           <Item Value="DWP Tech Support (555)555-2468"
197              Text="DWP Tech Support (555)555-2468">
198           </Item>
199           <Item Value="DWP Main (555)555-3696"
200              Text="DWP Main (555)555-3696">
201           </Item>
202        </mobile:List>
203        <mobile:Link id="mainLink4" runat="server"
204           NavigateUrl="#frmMain">
205           Main
206        </mobile:Link>
207     </mobile:form> <%-- end form frmContact --%>
208
209  </body>
```

Fig. 21.16 Stylesheets and templates in a Mobile Web Form. (Part 4 of 4.)

Software Engineering Observation 21.2

Separating structure from content allows greater manageability of a site and makes changing the site's style easier.

We begin with the ASPX file, shown in Fig. 21.16. Lines 20–43 define a style sheet. Although **Stylesheet** controls can contain multiple **Style** objects, ours contains only one. The **Style** element (lines 21–42) has its *Name* attribute's value set to **DWPStyles**. Forms use the **Name** attribute's value to reference (via the *StyleReference* attribute) the style sheet.

Style DWPStyles contains a *DeviceSpecific* element when multiple devices are being targeted. A **DeviceSpecific** element contains one or more *Choice* elements, which provide the display information for a particular device (or set of devices). The **Choice** element contains a *Filter* attribute that is evaluated and compared to the **Filter**s specified within the *DeviceFilters* element of our **Web.config** file (Fig. 21.17) to discover whether the microbrowser running the application supports the specified property. Each **filter** element in **Web.config** contains three attributes: *name*, *compare* and *argument*. The **name** attribute's value is selected by the programmer from a predefined list in the **Web.config** file. The **compare** attribute's value must be one of several predefined browser properties specified in the **machine.config** file (discussed earlier in Fig. 21.12). The **argument** attribute is the expected value (e.g., **True**) of the browser property.

```
1    <?xml version="1.0" encoding="utf-8" ?>
2
3    <configuration>
4       <system.web>
5          <deviceFilters>
6
7             <!-- Markup Languages -->
8             <filter name="isHTML32"
9                compare="PreferredRenderingType"
10               argument="html32" />
11            <filter name="isWML11"
12               compare="PreferredRenderingType"
13               argument="wml11" />
14            <filter name="isCHTML10"
15               compare="PreferredRenderingType"
16               argument="chtml10" />
17
18            <!-- Device Browsers -->
19            <filter name="isGoAmerica"
20               compare="Browser" argument="Go.Web" />
21            <filter name="isMME" compare="Browser"
22               argument="Microsoft Mobile Explorer" />
23            <filter name="isMyPalm" compare="Browser"
24               argument="MyPalm" />
25            <filter name="isPocketIE" compare="Browser"
26               argument="Pocket IE" />
```

Fig. 21.17 **Web.config** file used for **DeitelWirelessPortal2.aspx**. (Part 1 of 2.)

```
27          <filter name="isUP3x" compare="Type"
28             argument="Phone.com 3.x Browser" />
29          <filter name="isUP4x" compare="Type"
30            argument="Phone.com 4.x Browser" />
31
32          <!-- Specific Devices -->
33          <filter name="isEricssonR380" compare="Type"
34             argument="Ericsson R380" />
35          <filter name="isNokia7110" compare="Type"
36             argument="Nokia 7110" />
37
38          <!-- Device Capabilities -->
39          <filter name="prefersGIF"
40             compare="PreferredImageMIME"
41             argument="image/gif" />
42          <filter name="prefersWBMP"
43             compare="PreferredImageMIME"
44             argument="image/vnd.wap.wbmp" />
45          <filter name="supportsColor" compare="IsColor"
46             argument="true" />
47          <filter name="supportsCookies" compare="Cookies"
48             argument="true" />
49          <filter name="supportsJavaScript"
50             compare="Javascript" argument="true" />
51          <filter name="supportsVoiceCalls"
52             compare="CanInitiateVoiceCall"
53             argument="true" />
54
55       </deviceFilters>
56     </system.web>
57   </configuration>
```

Fig. 21.17 Web.config file used for **DeitelWirelessPortal2.aspx**.
   (Part 2 of 2.)

Filter elements describe the microbrowser's properties. These properties allow
developers to evaluate the incoming device programmatically. To do this, the developer
can call method **HasCapability** (class **MobileCapabilities**), which takes information about a specific **Filter** as an argument and returns **True** if the incoming device
supports those capabilities. On lines 25–31, the first **Choice** element is specified. The
filter **"isHTML32"** indicates that this element is for HTML browsers and is defined in
Fig. 21.17 on lines 7–9. The **name** of this filter (line 7) is used for identification purposes.
The **compare** attribute is set to **preferredRenderingType** (line 8), which differen-
tiates between the possible devices. The **argument** attribute sets the value for the device.
This value can be anything from a **Boolean** value to a MIME type. In this example, the
Choice element is based on the **preferredRenderingType**. This property repre-
sents the image's MIME type that the incoming device supports. The rendering type is set
by the **argument** attribute, in this case **html32**. This indicates that the **Choice** with this
Filter is selected if the incoming device is **html32**. The code that follows (lines 27–29
of Fig. 21.16) displays **top.jpg**, an image format supported by HTML browsers. The
Openwave™ Mobile browser cannot display JPEGs, so the contents of the **HeaderTemplate** element (discussed momentarily) located within the default **Choice** element

(lines 34–40) are displayed. This **Choice** element is the default choice because it does not contain a **Filter** attribute. For HTML browsers, lines 25–31 execute; for other browsers, lines 39–40 execute.

Notice that, within each **Choice** element, there is a *templated control*, which contains a set of template elements (e.g., **HeaderTemplate** elements). Templates mark up content for display on incoming devices. We use a set of templates, rather than just one template, to support the variety of devices targeted by this application. However, only one template is applied for per targeted device. In this example, we use templates to create a header that is displayed on all devices. For HTML devices (e.g., IE and MME), the header is a full-color image; non-HTML clients display the header as text. Where the content is rendered is determined by the template element type. On lines 26–30, we use the **HeaderTemplate**, which is rendered at the top of a **Form** control or a **List** control in Web pages. In this template, the image **top.jpg** is displayed. For the default **HeaderTemplate** (lines 35–39), we display the text **Deitel Wireless Portal**. To create content that is displayed at the bottom of a **Form** control or a **List** control, the **FooterTemplate** is used.

Lines 46–60 define form **frmWelcome**, which greets users entering the Web site. This form does not reference style sheet **DWPStyles**. Instead, we use the **DeviceSpecific** and **Choice** elements to show that Device-Specific Rendering can be accomplished without a style sheet. If the incoming device is capable of displaying colors, a large, full-color **.jpg** image will be displayed. Otherwise, the default device displays a bitmap version of the company logo. Lines 56–59 provide a **Link** object that redirects the user to form **frmMain**.

Lines 63–109 define form **frmMain**. This form and the remainder of the forms in the document use the **StyleReference** attribute to reference the **DWPStyles** style sheet. Form **frmMain** contains several **Link**s (lines 66–84) and three **Label**s, two of which are used in the **AdRotator1_AdCreated** method to provide a text description of the item being advertised. The **AdRotator** itself is defined on lines 98–108.

The advertisements are stored in the programmer-defined XML file specified in the **AdvertisementFile** property. This file (**AdBanners.xml**) is shown in Fig. 21.18. Information for three different advertisements is marked up. Each advertisement's information is specified within an **Ad** element. Each advertisement has five elements—**ImageUrl**, **WirelessImageUrl**, **NavigateUrl**, **AlternateText** and **Impressions**.

```
1    <?xml version="1.0" ?>
2
3    <Advertisements>
4       <Ad>
5          <ImageUrl>banner1.gif</ImageUrl>
6          <WirelessImageUrl>buyMe.wbmp</WirelessImageUrl>
7          <JpgImageUrl>buyMe.jpg</JpgImageUrl>
8          <NavigateUrl></NavigateUrl>
9          <IENavigateUrl>http://www.amazon.com/exec/obidos/ASIN/
013028419X/deitelassociatin/107-7206886-3349351</IENavigateUrl>
10         <AlternateText>banner1Text</AlternateText>
11         <Impressions>80</Impressions>
12      </Ad>
```

Fig. 21.18 AdBanners.xml file used for **DeitelWirelessPortal2.aspx**.
   (Part 1 of 2.)

```
13       <Ad>
14          <ImageUrl>banner2.gif</ImageUrl>
15          <WirelessImageUrl>buyMe.wbmp</WirelessImageUrl>
16          <JpgImageUrl>buyMe.jpg</JpgImageUrl>
17          <NavigateUrl></NavigateUrl>
18          <IENavigateUrl>http://www.amazon.com/exec/obidos/ASIN/
0130284173/deitelassociatin/107-7206886-3349351</IENavigateUrl>
19          <AlternateText>banner2Text</AlternateText>
20          <Impressions>80</Impressions>
21       </Ad>
22       <Ad>
23          <ImageUrl>banner3.gif</ImageUrl>
24          <WirelessImageUrl>buyMe.wbmp</WirelessImageUrl>
25          <JpgImageUrl>buyMe.jpg</JpgImageUrl>
26          <NavigateUrl></NavigateUrl>
27          <IENavigateUrl>http://www.amazon.com/exec/obidos/ASIN/
0130323640/deitelassociatin/107-7206886-3349351</IENavigateUrl>
28          <AlternateText>banner3Text</AlternateText>
29          <Impressions>80</Impressions>
30       </Ad>
31    </Advertisements>
```

Fig. 21.18 `AdBanners.xml` file used for `DeitelWirelessPortal2.aspx`. (Part 2 of 2.)

Each advertisement in our file can have multiple images associated with it. One of these images is selected to match the capabilities of the incoming device. To specify these capabilities, we again use a **DeviceSpecific** element (lines 101–107) that contains one or more **Choice** elements. We assign the **Choice** element's **Filter** attribute to specify one of the filters (e.g., **isHTML32**) in our **Web.config** file. In this example, we introduce another attribute—*ImageKey*. We use element *WirelessImageUrl* to reference the image specified by the **ImageKey** attribute. For instance, if the value of **ImageKey** is **JPEGImageUrl**, the image displayed is the one specified in element **JPEGImageUrl**. In this example, the **Filter** we use is **"isMME"** (defined in our **Web.config** file), which is specified on line 102 of Fig. 21.16 and defined on lines 19–20 of Fig. 21.17. If the incoming device is the MME (version 3.0), the image displayed is selected from one of the **WirelessImageUrl** elements in **AdBanners.xml** (lines 6, 15 and 24 of Fig. 21.18). If the incoming device is not the MME, the program examines the next **Choice** element. The default image is used for other microbrowsers, because additional **Choice** elements have not been provided. The default image is specified in the *ImageUrl* element. If the image cannot be displayed for some reason (either we specified an image that is not supported by the microbrowser or the image cannot be located), text marked up in the **AlternateText** element is displayed in place of the image.

Each advertisement also contains *NavigateUrl* and *Impressions* elements. **NavigateUrl** marks up the location where users are redirected when the advertisement is clicked. In this example, we leave this element empty (i.e., nothing happens if the image is clicked). The **Impressions** element marks up the advertisement's weight. Advertisements with larger weights are displayed more frequently.

Forms **frmNews**, **frmFinancial** and **frmTravelFood** (lines 111–184 of Fig. 21.16) are similar to those used in the previous example, with one important difference—

these forms call the **ResolveLinks** method, which determines whether the user is redirected to an HTML site or a WAP site. We discuss method **ResolveLinks** shortly.

Lines 185–207 of Fig. 21.16 define the **frmContact** form, which contains a **List** object populated with phone numbers. In this case, the **List** items are added directly in the form instead of in the **<script>** section, as in the last example. All forms contain a **Link** back to the main menu, except for **frmMain** itself.

Portability Tip 21.2

*When using the **NavigateUrl** element, it is the programmer's responsibility to ensure that the Web site specified by the URL can be rendered on the incoming device.*

Let us now discuss the code-behind file (Fig. 21.19), which contains two methods: **AdRotator1_AdCreated** (lines 88–115) and **ResolveLinks** (lines 117–137). Method **AdRotator1_AdCreated** is an event handler for our **AdRotator**'s *AdCreated* event, which is raised when an advertisement of our **AdRotator** is displayed. This event contains an **AlternateText** property which provides access to the value of the **AlternateText** in the XML file. Lines 92, 99 and 106 of **AdRotator1_AdCreated** use this property to determine the advertisement and to set appropriate values to the **Text** properties of **lblBookTitle** and **lblDescription**. For instance, if the image chosen is that of our *XML How to Program* publication, method **AdRotator1_AdCreated** would display the title of our XML book in **lblBookTitle**, and information about this specific publication in **lblDescription**.

Method **ResolveLinks**, defined on lines 117–137, is an event handler for the **Activate** events of forms **frmNews**, **frmFinancial** and **frmTravelFood**. This method is used to determine the destination of a form's links based on the capabilities of an incoming device. Some Web sites, such as **www.finwin.com**, detect the incoming device and return the appropriate markup. Other sites, such as the *Wall Street Journal*, have separate URLs for their wireless sites. To access the *Wall Street Journal* wireless site, users visit **wap.wsj.com** instead of **www.wsj.com**. **ResolveLinks** determines the capabilities of the incoming device programmatically by using the **MobileCapabilities** class. This class inherits from class *HttpBrowserCapabilities*, which encapsulates information about the current browser. Notice the *Request.Browser* property (line 123), which is part of the *HttpRequest* class and returns an **HttpBrowserCapabilities** object. On lines 46–48, we cast this object to type **MobileCapabilities** and assign it to our **MobileCapabilities** instance, referenced by **capability**. By accessing the *Browser* property of **capabilities**, we can discover whether the incoming device is IE. If it is, the user is redirected to the appropriate HTML sites.

```
1    ' Fig. 21.19: DeitelWirelessPortal2.aspx.vb
2    ' Code-behind file for the Deitel Wireless Portal 2.
3
4    Public Class DeitelWirelessPortal2
5        Inherits System.Web.UI.MobileControls.MobilePage
6
7        ' style sheet
8        Protected WithEvents Stylesheet1 As _
9            System.Web.UI.MobileControls.StyleSheet
```

Fig. 21.19 Code-behind file for the Deitel Wireless Portal. (Part 1 of 6.)

```
10
11    ' welcome form and its controls
12    Protected WithEvents frmWelcome As _
13        System.Web.UI.MobileControls.Form
14    Protected WithEvents imgWelcome As _
15        System.Web.UI.MobileControls.Image
16    Protected WithEvents enterLink As _
17        System.Web.UI.MobileControls.Link
18
19    ' main form and its controls
20    Protected WithEvents frmMain As _
21        System.Web.UI.MobileControls.Form
22    Protected WithEvents newsLink As _
23        System.Web.UI.MobileControls.Link
24    Protected WithEvents financialLink As _
25        System.Web.UI.MobileControls.Link
26    Protected WithEvents travelFoodLink As _
27        System.Web.UI.MobileControls.Link
28    Protected WithEvents contactLink As _
29        System.Web.UI.MobileControls.Link
30    Protected WithEvents lblSpecials As _
31        System.Web.UI.MobileControls.Label
32    Protected WithEvents lblBookTitle As _
33        System.Web.UI.MobileControls.Label
34    Protected WithEvents lblDescription As _
35        System.Web.UI.MobileControls.Label
36    Protected WithEvents AdRotator1 As _
37        System.Web.UI.MobileControls.AdRotator
38
39    ' news form and its controls
40    Protected WithEvents frmNews As _
41        System.Web.UI.MobileControls.Form
42    Protected WithEvents bloombergLink As _
43        System.Web.UI.MobileControls.Link
44    Protected WithEvents cnetLink As _
45        System.Web.UI.MobileControls.Link
46    Protected WithEvents newYorkTimesLink As _
47        System.Web.UI.MobileControls.Link
48    Protected WithEvents mainLink1 As _
49        System.Web.UI.MobileControls.Link
50
51    ' financial form and its controls
52    Protected WithEvents frmFinancial As _
53        System.Web.UI.MobileControls.Form
54    Protected WithEvents wallStreetLink As _
55        System.Web.UI.MobileControls.Link
56    Protected WithEvents finWinLink As _
57        System.Web.UI.MobileControls.Link
58    Protected WithEvents stockPointLink As _
59        System.Web.UI.MobileControls.Link
60    Protected WithEvents MainLink2 As _
61        System.Web.UI.MobileControls.Link
62
```

Fig. 21.19 Code-behind file for the Deitel Wireless Portal. (Part 2 of 6.)

```
63      ' travel/food form and its controls
64      Protected WithEvents frmTravelFood As _
65          System.Web.UI.MobileControls.Form
66      Protected WithEvents citiWizLink As _
67          System.Web.UI.MobileControls.Link
68      Protected WithEvents tenBestLink As _
69          System.Web.UI.MobileControls.Link
70      Protected WithEvents expediaLink As _
71          System.Web.UI.MobileControls.Link
72      Protected WithEvents mainLink3 As _
73          System.Web.UI.MobileControls.Link
74
75      ' contacts form and its controls
76      Protected WithEvents frmContact As _
77          System.Web.UI.MobileControls.Form
78      Protected WithEvents lblContact As _
79          System.Web.UI.MobileControls.Label
80      Protected WithEvents contactList As _
81          System.Web.UI.MobileControls.List
82      Protected WithEvents mainLink4 As _
83          System.Web.UI.MobileControls.Link
84
85      ' Visual Studio .NET generated code
86
87      ' displays the proper text for the current ad
88      Private Sub AdRotator1_AdCreated(ByVal sender As System.Object, _
89          ByVal e As System.Web.UI.WebControls.AdCreatedEventArgs) _
90          Handles AdRotator1.AdCreated
91
92          If e.AlternateText = "banner1Text" Then
93              lblBookTitle.Text = "e-Business and e-Commerce " & _
94                  "How To Program:"
95              lblDescription.Text = "This book carefully " & _
96                  "explains how to program multi-tiered, " & _
97                  "client/server, database-intensive, Web-based," & _
98                  " e-Business and e-Commerce applications."
99          ElseIf e.AlternateText = "banner2Text" Then
100             lblBookTitle.Text = "XML How to Program:"
101             lblDescription.Text = "Offers a careful explanation " & _
102                 "of XML-based systems development, for faculty " & _
103                 "students and professionals. Includes " & _
104                 "extensive pedagogic features, including " & _
105                 "Internet resources."
106         ElseIf e.AlternateText = "banner3Text" Then
107             lblBookTitle.Text = "e-Business and e-Commerce " & _
108                 "For Managers:"
109             lblDescription.Text = "For all managers, business " & _
110                 "owners and others who need a comprehensive " & _
111                 "overview of how to build and manage " & _
112                 "and e-Business."
113         End If
114
115     End Sub ' AdRotator1_AdCreated
```

Fig. 21.19 Code-behind file for the Deitel Wireless Portal. (Part 3 of 6.)

```
116
117    Private Sub ResolveLinks(ByVal sender As System.Object, _
118       ByVal e As EventArgs) _
119       Handles frmNews.Activate, frmFinancial.Activate, _
120       frmContact.Activate, frmTravelFood.Activate
121
122       Dim capability As System.Web.Mobile.MobileCapabilities = _
123          CType(Request.Browser, _
124          System.Web.Mobile.MobileCapabilities)
125
126       If capability.Browser.IndexOf("IE") <> -1 Then
127          bloombergLink.NavigateUrl = "http://www.bloomberg.com"
128          cnetLink.NavigateUrl = "http://www.cnet.com"
129          newYorkTimesLink.NavigateUrl = "http://www.nyt.com"
130          wallStreetLink.NavigateUrl = "http://www.wsj.com"
131          stockPointLink.NavigateUrl = "http://stockpoint.com/"
132          citiWizLink.NavigateUrl = "http://www.citiwiz.com"
133          tenBestLink.NavigateUrl = "http://www.10best.com"
134          expediaLink.NavigateUrl = "http://www.expedia.com"
135       End If
136
137    End Sub ' ResolveLinks
138
139 End Class ' DeitelWirelessPortal2
```

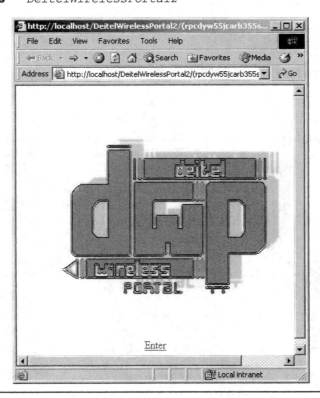

Fig. 21.19 Code-behind file for the Deitel Wireless Portal. (Part 4 of 6.)

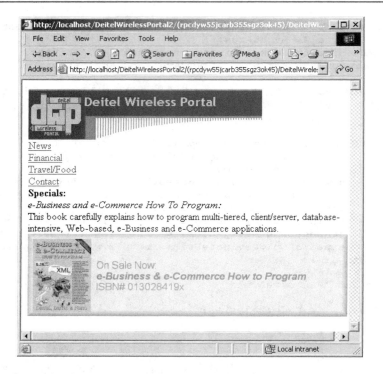

Fig. 21.19 Code-behind file for the Deitel Wireless Portal. (Part 5 of 6.)

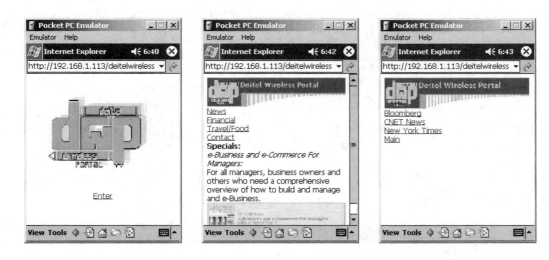

Fig. 21.19 Code-behind file for the Deitel Wireless Portal. (Part 6 of 6.)

21.7 Consuming a Web Service from a Mobile Application

In Chapter 18, ASP .NET and Web Services, we created an Airline Reservation example where users can reserve a seat on a flight. In this example, we show how to access the same Web service from a mobile device. The only difference between this example and the example presented in Chapter 18 is the client, which we built by using the MIT.

The airline reservation Web service receives information regarding the type of seat the customer wishes to reserve and then makes a reservation if the seat is available. The logic for the airline reservation Web service has a single **WebMethod**—**Reserve**—which searches its seat database to locate a seat matching a user's request. If it finds an appropriate seat, **Reserve** updates the database, makes the reservation and returns **True**; otherwise, no reservation is made, and the method returns **False**. [*Note*: We do not show the code listing for the Web service here, because it is listed in Chapter 18, ASP .NET and Web Services.]

Reserve takes two arguments—a **String** representing the desired seat type (i.e., window, middle or aisle) and a **String** representing the desired class type (i.e., economy or first class). If the result of the query is not empty, the application reserves the first seat number that the query returns and **Reserve** returns **True**, indicating that the reservation was successful. If the result of the query is not successful, **Reserve** returns **False**, indicating that no available seats matched the request.

Figure 21.20 presents the ASPX listing for the mobile Web Form through which users can select seat types. This page allows users to reserve a seat on the basis of its class and location in a row of seats. The page then uses the airline-reservation Web service to carry out users' requests. If the database request is not successful, the user is instructed to modify the request and try again.

This page defines two ***DropDownList*** objects, each of which displays a short list of choices, and a **Button**. One **DropDownList** displays all the seat types from which users can select. The second lists the class types. Users click the **Button**, named **cmdReserve**, to submit requests after making selections from the **DropDownList**s. The code-behind file (Fig. 21.21) contains the event handler for this button.

```
1    <%-- Fig. 21.20: AirlineReservation.aspx --%>
2    <%-- Airline Reservation client.          --%>
3
4    <%@ Register TagPrefix="mobile"
5        Namespace="System.Web.UI.MobileControls"
6        Assembly="System.Web.Mobile, Version=1.0.3300.0,
Culture=neutral, PublicKeyToken=b03f5f7f11d50a3a" %>
7
8    <%@ Page Language="vb" AutoEventWireup="false"
9        Codebehind="AirlineReservation.aspx.vb"
10       Inherits="MobileAirlineReservation.CAirlineReservation" %>
11
12   <meta content="Microsoft Visual Studio.NET 7.0" name="GENERATOR">
13   <meta content="Visual Basic 7.0" name="CODE_LANGUAGE">
14   <meta content="http://schemas.microsoft.com/Mobile/Page"
15      name="vs_targetSchema">
16
17   <body Xmlns:mobile="http://schemas.microsoft.com/Mobile/WebForm">
18
19       <mobile:form id="frmReservation" runat="server">
20
21          <mobile:Label id="lblInstruction" runat="server">
22             Please select the type of seat and class
23             you wish to reserve:
24          </mobile:Label>
25
26          <mobile:Label id="lblSeat" runat="server"
27             Font-Size="Large">
28             Seat:
29          </mobile:Label>
30
31          <mobile:SelectionList id="seatList" runat="server">
32             <Item Value="Aisle" Text="Aisle"></Item>
33             <Item Value="Middle" Text="Middle"></Item>
34             <Item Value="Window" Text="Window"></Item>
35          </mobile:SelectionList>
36
37          <mobile:Label id="lblClass" runat="server"
38             Font-Size="Large">
39             Class:
40          </mobile:Label>
41
42          <mobile:SelectionList id="classList" runat="server">
43             <Item Value="Economy" Text="Economy"></Item>
44             <Item Value="First" Text="First"></Item>
45          </mobile:SelectionList>
46
```

Fig. 21.20 ASPX page that allows a mobile device to access a Web service. (Part 1 of 2.)

```
47        <mobile:Command id="cmdReserve" runat="server">
48           Reserve!
49        </mobile:Command>
50     </mobile:form>
51
52     <mobile:form id="frmConfirmation" runat="server">
53
54        <mobile:Label id="lblConfirmation" runat="server">
55        </mobile:Label>
56
57        <mobile:Label id="lblconfirmSeat" runat="server">
58        </mobile:Label>
59
60        <mobile:Label id="lblconfirmClass" runat="server">
61        </mobile:Label>
62     </mobile:form>
63
64  </body>
```

Fig. 21.20 ASPX page that allows a mobile device to access a Web service.
(Part 2 of 2.)

Line 41 creates a **Reservation** object (i.e., an instance of the Web service). When the
user clicks **Reserve**, the **cmdReserve_Click** event handler executes, and the page
reloads. The event handler (lines 50–73) calls the Web service's **Reserve** method and
passes it the selected seat and class type as arguments. If **Reserve** returns **True**, the application displays a message thanking the user for making a reservation; otherwise, the user is
notified that the type of seat requested is not available, and the user is instructed to try again.

```
1   ' Fig. 21.21: AirlineReservation.aspx.vb
2   ' Making a reservation using a Web Service
3
4   Public Class CAirlineReservation
5      Inherits System.Web.UI.MobileControls.MobilePage
6
7      ' first form
8      Protected WithEvents frmReservation As _
9         System.Web.UI.MobileControls.Form
10
11     ' controls used in form frmReservation
12     Protected WithEvents lblInstruction As _
13        System.Web.UI.MobileControls.Label
14     Protected WithEvents seatList As _
15        System.Web.UI.MobileControls.SelectionList
16     Protected WithEvents classList As _
17        System.Web.UI.MobileControls.SelectionList
18     Protected WithEvents cmdReserve As _
19        System.Web.UI.MobileControls.Command
20     Protected WithEvents lblSeat As _
21        System.Web.UI.MobileControls.Label
```

Fig. 21.21 Code-behind file for mobile Web application that accesses a Web Service.
(Part 1 of 4.) (Image courtesy Openwave System, Inc.)

```
22       Protected WithEvents lblClass As _
23          System.Web.UI.MobileControls.Label
24       Protected WithEvents lblSpacer As _
25          System.Web.UI.MobileControls.Label
26
27       ' second form
28       Protected WithEvents frmConfirmation As _
29          System.Web.UI.MobileControls.Form
30
31       ' control used in form frmConfirmation
32       Protected WithEvents lblConfirmation As _
33          System.Web.UI.MobileControls.Label
34       Protected WithEvents lblConfirmSeat As _
35          System.Web.UI.MobileControls.Label
36       Protected WithEvents lblConfirmClass As _
37          System.Web.UI.MobileControls.Label
38
39       ' Visual Studio .NET generated code
40
41       Private agent As New localhost.Reservation()
42
43       Private Sub cmdReserve_Click(ByVal sender As System.Object, _
44          ByVal e As System.EventArgs) Handles cmdReserve.Click
45
46          ActiveForm = frmConfirmation
47
48       End Sub ' cmdReserve_Click
49
50       Private Sub frmConfirmation_Activate( _
51          ByVal sender As System.Object, ByVal e As System.EventArgs) _
52          Handles frmConfirmation.Activate
53
54          ' if WebMethod returned true, signal success
55          If agent.Reserve(seatList.Selection.Text, _
56             classList.Selection.Text) Then
57
58             lblConfirmation.Text = "Your reservation has been made." & _
59                "Thank You!"
60
61          lblConfirmSeat.Text = "Seat: " & _
62             seatList.Selection.Text
63
64          lblConfirmClass.Text = "Class: " & _
65             classList.Selection.Text
66
67          Else
68             lblConfirmation.Text = "This seat is not available, " & _
69                "please hit back your browser's Back " & _
70                "and try again."
71          End If
72
73       End Sub ' frmConfirmation_Activate
```

Fig. 21.21 Code-behind file for mobile Web application that accesses a Web Service. (Part 2 of 4.) (Image courtesy Openwave System, Inc.)

```
74
75   End Class  ' CAirlineReservation
```

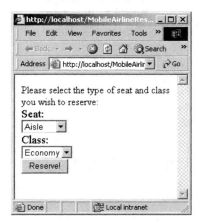

Fig. 21.21 Code-behind file for mobile Web application that accesses a Web Service. (Part 3 of 4.) (Image courtesy Openwave System, Inc.)

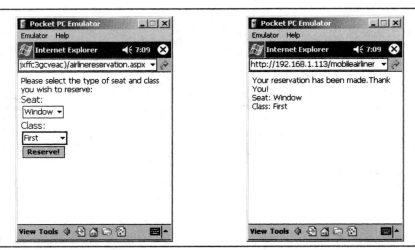

Fig. 21.21 Code-behind file for mobile Web application that accesses a Web Service. (Part 4 of 4.) (Image courtesy Openwave System, Inc.)

Well, that's it for now. We sincerely hope that you have enjoyed learning with *Visual Basic .NET for Experienced Programmers*. As this book went to the presses, we were already at work on *ASP .NET with Visual Basic .NET for Experienced Programmers*, a book appropriate for professional developers writing enterprise applications.

21.8 Summary

The Microsoft® Mobile Internet Toolkit (MIT) allows programmers to create mobile Web applications. The MIT extends the functionality of Visual Studio .NET and is a powerful tool that uses the .NET Framework to create Web content for mobile devices, using languages such as Visual Basic .NET and C#.

The Wireless Application Protocol (WAP) is a set of communications protocols that are designed to enable wireless devices to access the Internet. The Wireless Markup Language (WML) is the markup language used to describe content for WAP devices. WAP supports WML to deliver wireless content. The MIT supports three main clients—HTML devices, WAP devices and iMode devices. HTML devices are those that display HTML markup, such as Internet Explorer or Pocket PC.

Creating a mobile Web application in Visual Studio .NET generates an ASPX page (with the **.aspx** file extension), which contains the markup for the page's user interface. The business logic for the application can be embedded in the ASPX file as a script or in a code-behind file. The business logic is executed on the Web server.

Mobile Web Form controls (or mobile controls) are the objects used to create mobile applications. Some basic mobile controls include labels and buttons. Every mobile control's start tag has its **runat** attribute set to **"server"** to indicate that the control is executed on the server.

The MIT tests for whether multiple controls can fit on the same line by checking the device's screen size. Each device's screen size and other device-specific information, such as support for color graphics or the ability to initiate a phone call, are stored in the **machine.config** file.

A **Stylesheet** control is a collection of **Style** elements. Many MIT controls have a **StyleReference** property, which sets the control's font, color, alignment and so on. **Stylesheet** controls allow the developer to specify the style of the page elements (headers, fonts, colors, etc.) separately from the structure of the document (i.e., mobile tags) and allow developers to target specific devices (called Device-Specific Rendering).

A **DeviceSpecific** element is present when multiple devices are being targeted. A **DeviceSpecific** element contains one or more **Choice** elements. The **Choice** element contains a **Filter** attribute that is evaluated and compared to the **Filter**s specified within the **deviceFilters** element in **Web.config**. Each **filter** element in **Web.config** contains three attributes: **name**, **compare** and **argument**. The **name** value is selected from a predefined list in **Web.config** by the programmer. The **compare** attribute's value must be one of several predefined browser properties specified in **machine.config**. The **argument** attribute is the expected value of the browser property.

21.9 Internet and Web Resources

msdn.microsoft.com/vstudio/nextgen/technology/mobilewebforms.asp
This site presents an online introduction to mobile Web Forms, as well as other useful links.

www.devx.com
This online information source does not yet contain information about the MIT, but it does offer information on wireless technologies and .NET, including discussions, help and code.

www.w3.org/TR/1998/NOTE-compactHTML-19980209
This site provides detailed information on cHTML, including how to use cHTML and what devices cHTML can be used with.

msdn.microsoft.com/library/default.asp?url=/library/en-us/mwsdk/html/mwstartpage.asp
This documentation site provides some background information on the MIT, as well as links to documentation on more specific topics, such as information on the MIT's runtime.

www.asp.net/Default.aspx?tabindex=4&tabid=44
This all-purpose ASP .NET site provides links to several downloads and samples using the MIT.

Newsgroups

microsoft.public.dotnet.framework.aspnet.mobile
Questions and answers on several MIT topics are posted frequently on this Microsoft newsgroup. All levels of programmers can communicate and learn from each other.

Operator Precedence Chart

Operators are shown in decreasing order of precedence from top to bottom with each level of precedence separated by a horizontal line. Visual Basic operators associate from left to right.

Operator	Type
^	exponentiation
+	unary plus
−	unary minus
*	multiplication
/	division
\	integer division
Mod	modulus
+	addition
−	subtraction
&	concatenation
=	relational is equal to
<>	relational is not equal to
<	relational less than
<=	relational less than or equal to
>	relational greater than
>=	relational greater than or equal to
Like	pattern matching
Is	reference comparison
TypeOf	type comparison

Fig. A.1   Operator precedence chart. (Part 1 of 2.)

Operator	Type
Not	logical negation
And	logical AND without short-circuit evaluation
AndAlso	logical AND with short-circuit evaluation
Or	logical inclusive OR without short-circuit evaluation
OrElse	logical inclusive OR with short-circuit evaluation
Xor	logical exclusive OR

Fig. A.1   Operator precedence chart. (Part 2 of 2.)

Visual Studio .NET Debugger

Objectives

- To understand syntax and logic errors.
- To become familiar with the Visual Studio .NET debugging tools.
- To understand the use of breakpoints to suspend program execution.
- To examine data using expressions in the debugging windows.
- To debug procedures and objects.

And often times excusing of a fault
Doth make the fault the worse by the excuse.
William Shakespeare

To err is human, to forgive divine.
Alexander Pope

Outline

B.1 Introduction

Syntax errors (or compilation errors) occur when program statements violate the grammatical rules of a programming language, such as forgetting to end a module with **End Module** (Fig. B.1). Syntax errors are caught by the compiler. In Visual Studio .NET, syntax errors appear in the *Task List* window along with a description, line number and the file name. For additional information on a specific syntax error, select it in the **Task List** and press *F1* to open a help window. Programs that contain syntax errors cannot be executed.

Testing and Debugging Tip B.1

When the compiler reports a syntax error on a particular line, check that line for the syntax error. If the error is not on that line, check the preceding few lines of code for the cause of the syntax error.

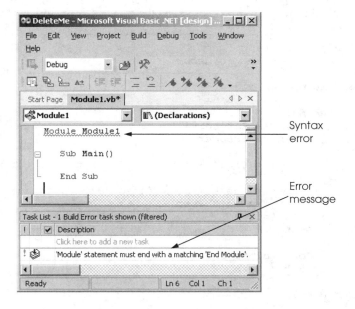

Fig. B.1   Syntax error.

Testing and Debugging Tip B.2

After fixing one error, recompile your program. You may observe that the number of overall errors perceived by the compiler is significantly reduced.

Debugging is the process of finding and correcting *logic errors* in applications. Logic errors are more subtle than syntax errors because the program compiles successfully, but does not run as expected. Logic errors are often difficult to debug because the programmer cannot see the code as it is executing. Some programmers attempt to debug programs using message boxes or **Console.WriteLine** statements. For example, the programmer might print the value of a variable when the variable's value changes to determine if it is being set correctly. This method is cumbersome, because programmers must write a line of code wherever they suspect may be a problem. Once the program has been debugged, the programmer must remove these printing statements.

Debuggers provide a set of tools that allow the programmer to analyze a program while it is running. These tools allow the programmer to suspend program execution, examine and set variables, call procedures without having to modify the program and much more. In this appendix, we introduce the Visual Studio .NET debugger and several of its debugging tools. [*Note*: A program must successfully compile before it can be used in the debugger.]

B.2 Breakpoints

Breakpoints are a simple but powerful debugging tool. A breakpoint is a marker that can be set at any executable line of code. When a program reaches a breakpoint, execution pauses, allowing the programmer to examine the state of the program and ensure that everything is working properly. We use the following program (Fig. B.2) to demonstrate debugging a loop using the features of the Visual Studio .NET debugger. This program is designed to output the value of ten factorial (10!), but contains two logic errors—the first iteration of the loop multiplies **x** by **10** instead of **9**, and the result of the factorial calculation **0**.

```
1    ' Fig. D.2: DebugExample.vb
2    ' Sample program to debug.
3
4    Module modDebug
5
6       Sub Main()
7          Dim x As Integer = 10
8          Dim i As Integer
9
10         Console.Write("The value of " & x & " factorial is: ")
11
12         ' loop to determine x factorial, contains logic error
13         For i = x To 0 Step -1
14            x *= i
15         Next
16
17         Console.WriteLine(x)
18      End Sub ' Main
19
20   End Module ' modDebug
```

Fig. B.2   Debug sample program. (Part 1 of 2.)

```
The value of 10 factorial is: 0
```

Fig. B.2   Debug sample program. (Part 2 of 2.)

To enable the debugger, compile the program using the debug configuration (Fig. B.3). Select **Debug** from the configuration toolbar item if it is not already selected. Alternatively, select **Build > Configuration Manager** and change the **Active Solution Configuration** to **Debug**.

To set breakpoints in Visual Studio, click the gray area to the left of any line of code (Fig. B.4) or right-click a line of code and select **Insert Breakpoint**. A solid red circle appears, indicating that the breakpoint has been set. When the program executes, it suspends when it reaches the line containing the breakpoint.

Selecting **Debug > Start** begins the debugging process. When debugging a console application, the console window appears (Fig. B.5), allowing program interaction (input and output). When the breakpoint (line 14) is reached, program execution is suspended, and the IDE becomes the active window. Programmers may need to switch between the IDE and the console window while debugging programs.

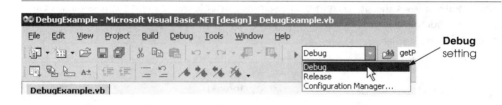

Fig. B.3   Debug configuration setting.

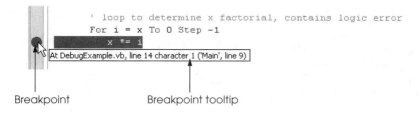

Fig. B.4   Setting a breakpoint.

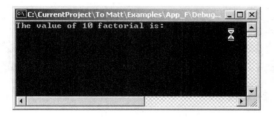

Fig. B.5   Console application suspended for debugging.

Figure B.6 shows the IDE with program execution suspended at a breakpoint. The *yellow arrow* to the left of the statement

```
x *= i
```

indicates that execution is suspended at this line and that this line contains the next statement to execute. Note that the title bar of the IDE displays **[break]**—this indicates that the IDE is in *break mode* (i.e., the debugger is being used). Once the program has reached the breakpoint, you may "hover" with the mouse on a variable (in this case **x** or **i**) in the source code to see the value of that variable.

 Testing and Debugging Tip B.3

*Loops that iterate many times can be executed in full (without stopping every time through the loop) by placing a breakpoint after the loop and selecting **Start** from the **Debug** menu.*

B.3 Examining Data

Visual Studio .NET includes several debugging windows, all accessible from the **Debug > Windows** submenu. Some windows are listed only when the IDE is in break mode (also called *debug mode*). The **Watch** window (Fig. B.7), which is available only in break mode, allows the programmer to examine variable values and expressions. Visual Studio provides a total of four windows that allow programmers to organize and view variables and expressions.

Title bar displays **[break]**

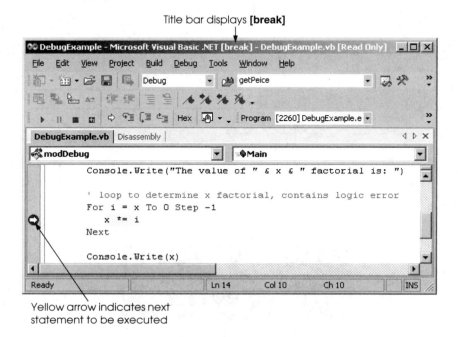

Yellow arrow indicates next
statement to be executed

Fig. B.6   Execution suspended at a breakpoint.

The **Watch** window is initially empty. To examine data, type an expression into the **Name** field. Most valid Visual Basic expressions can be entered in the **Name** field, including expressions that contain procedure calls. Consult the documentation under "debugger, expressions" for a full description of valid expressions.

Once an expression has been entered, its type and value appear in the **Value** and **Type** fields. The first expression in Fig. B.7 is the variable **i**—it is **10** because the **For** loop (line 13) assigns the value of **x** (**10**) to **i**. The **Watch** window also can evaluate more complex arithmetic expressions (e.g, **(i + 3) * 5**). Note that expressions containing the **=** symbol are treated as **Boolean** expressions instead of assignment statements. For example, the expression **i = 3** evaluates to **False**. The value of **i** is not altered.

To debug the program in Fig. B.2, we might enter the expression **i * x** in the **Watch** window. When we reach the breakpoint for the first time, this expression has a value **100**, which indicates a logic error in our program (our calculation contains an extra factor of 10). To fix the error, we could subtract **1** from the initial value of the **For** loop (i.e., change **10** to **9**).

If a **Name** field in the **Watch** window contains a variable name, the variable's value can be modified for debugging purposes. To modify a variable's value, click its value in the **Value** field and enter a new value. Any modified value appears in red.

If an expression is invalid, an error appears in the **Value** field. For example, the fourth expression in Fig. B.7 is an invalid expression because **VariableThatDoesNotExist** is not an identifier used in the program. Visual Studio .NET issues an error message and displays its contents in the **Value** field. To remove an expression, select it and press *Delete*.

Testing and Debugging Tip B.4

*When a procedure is called from a **Watch** window, the program does not stop at breakpoints inside the procedure. Do not call procedures that may have errors from the **Watch** window.*

The **Locals** and **Autos** windows are similar to the **Watch** window, except the programmer does not specify their contents. The **Locals** window displays the name and current value for all the local variables or objects in the current scope. The **Autos** window displays the variables and objects used in the previous statement and the current statement (indicated by the yellow arrow). Variables can be changed in either window by clicking the appropriate **Value** field and entering a new value. When executing an object's procedure, the **Me** window displays data for that object. If the program is inside a procedure that does not belong to an object (such as **Main**), the **Me** window is empty.

Watch 1		
Name	Value	Type
i	10	Integer
(i+3)*5	65	Integer
i = 3	False	Boolean
VariableThatDoesNotExist	Name 'VariableThatDoesNotExist' is not declared.	
Console.WriteLine("Hello")	Expression does not produce a value.	

Expressions

Fig. B.7   Watch window.

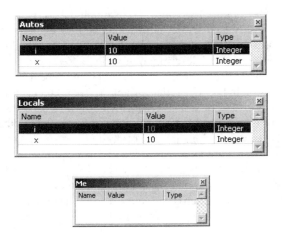

Fig. B.8   Autos and **Locals** windows.

The ***Immediate*** window provides a convenient way to execute statements (Fig. B.9). To execute a statement, type it into the window and press *Enter*. Procedure calls can be executed as well. For example, typing `Console.WriteLine(i)` then pressing *Enter* outputs the value of **i** in the console window. Notice that the = symbol can be used to perform assignments in the **Immediate** window. Notice that the values for **i** and **x** in the **Locals** window contain these updated values.

Testing and Debugging Tip B.5

*Use the **Immediate** window to call a procedure exactly once. Placing a procedure call inside the **Watch** window calls it every time the program breaks.*

B.4 Program Control

The **Debug** toolbar (Fig. B.10) contains buttons for controlling the debugging process. These buttons provide convenient access to actions in the **Debug** menu. To display the **Debug** toolbar, select **View > Toolbars > Debug**.

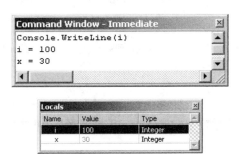

Fig. B.9   Immediate window.

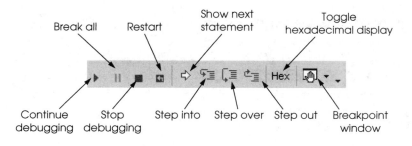

Fig. B.10   **Debug** toolbar icons.

The **_Restart_** button restarts the application, pausing at the beginning of the program to allow the programmer to set breakpoints before the program executes. The **_Continue_** button resumes execution of a suspended program. The **_Stop Debugging_** button ends the debugging session. The **_Break All_** button allows the user to suspend an executing program directly (i.e., without explicitly setting breakpoints). After execution is suspended, the yellow arrow appears indicating the next statement to be executed.

 Testing and Debugging Tip B.6

*When a program is executing, problems such as infinite loops usually can be interrupted by selecting **Debug > Break All** or by clicking the corresponding button on the toolbar.*

Clicking the **_Show Next Statement_** button places the cursor on the same line as the yellow arrow that indicates the next statement to execute. This command is useful when returning to the current execution point after setting breakpoints in a program that contains a large number of lines of code.

The **_Step Over_** button executes the next executable line of code and advances the yellow arrow to the next line. If the next line of code contains a procedure call, the procedure is executed in its entirety as one step. This button allows the user to execute the program one line at a time without seeing the details of every procedure that is called. We discuss the **Step Into** and **Step Out** buttons in the next section.

The **Hex** button toggles the display format of data. If enabled, **Hex** displays data in hexadecimal (base 16) form, rather than decimal (base 10) form. Experienced programmers often prefer to read values in hexadecimal format—especially large numbers. For more information about the hexadecimal and decimal number formats, see Appendix B, Number Systems.

The **Breakpoints** window displays all the breakpoints currently set for the program (Fig. B.11). A checkbox appears next to each breakpoint, indicating whether the breakpoint is *active* (checked) or *disabled* (unchecked). Lines with disabled breakpoints contain an unfilled red circle rather than a solid one (Fig. B.12). The debugger does not pause execution at disabled breakpoints.

The **_Condition_** field displays the condition a that must be satisfied to suspend program execution at that breakpoint. The **_Hit Count_** field displays the number of times the debugger has stopped at each breakpoint. Double-clicking an item in the **Breakpoints** window moves the cursor to the line containing that breakpoint. The down-arrow immediately to the right of the **_Breakpoints_** button provides access to the various debugging windows. [*Note*: Choosing another debugging window from the list changes the icon displayed.]

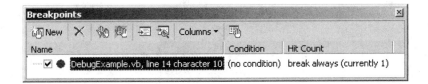

Fig. B.11   Breakpoints window.

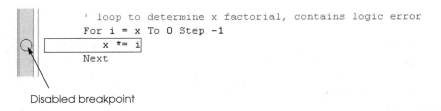

Disabled breakpoint

Fig. B.12   Disabled breakpoint.

Testing and Debugging Tip B.7

Disabled breakpoints allow the programmer to maintain breakpoints in key locations in the program so they can be used again when needed. Disabled breakpoints are always visible.

Breakpoints can be added using the **Breakpoints** window by clicking the ***New*** button, which displays the **New Breakpoint** dialog (Fig. B.13). The **Function**, **File**, **Address** and **Data** tabs allow the programmer to cause execution to suspends at a procedure, a line in a particular file, an instruction in memory or when the value of a variable changes. The **Hit Count...** button (Fig. B.14) can be used to specify when the breakpoint should suspend the program (the default is to always break). A breakpoint can be set to suspend the program when the hit count reaches a specific number, is a multiple of a number or is greater than or equal to a specific number.

The Visual Studio debugger also allows execution to suspend at a breakpoint depending upon the value of an expression. Clicking the **Condition...** button opens the ***Breakpoint Condition*** dialog (Fig. B.15). The **Condition** checkbox indicates whether breakpoint conditions are enabled. The radio buttons determine how the expression in the text box is evaluated. The **is true** radio button pauses execution at the breakpoint whenever the expression is true. The **has changed** radio button causes program execution to suspend when it first encounters the breakpoint and again time the expression differs from its previous value when the breakpoint is encountered.

For example, suppose we set $x * i <> 0$ as the condition for the breakpoint in our loop with the **has changed** option enabled. (We might choose to do this because the program produces an incorrect output of **0**). Program execution suspends when it first reaches the breakpoint and records that the expression has a value of **True**, because $x * i$ is **100** (or **10** if we fixed the earlier logic error). We continue, and the loop decrements **i**. While **i** is between **10** and **1**, the condition's value never changes, and execution is not suspended at that breakpoint. When **i** is **0**, the expression $x * i <> 0$ is **False**, and execution is suspended. This leads to the identification of the second logic error in our program—that the final iteration of the **For** loop multiplies the result by **0**. When finished debugging, click the **Stop Debugging** button on the **Debug** toolbar. The IDE returns to design mode.

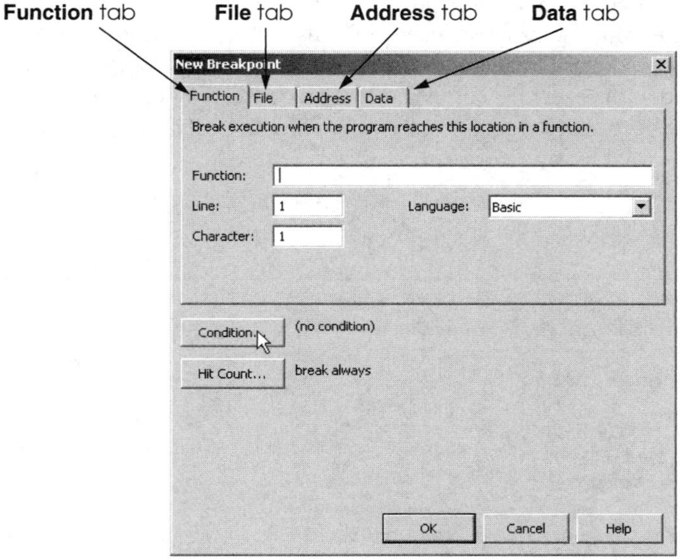

Fig. B.13   **New Breakpoint** dialog.

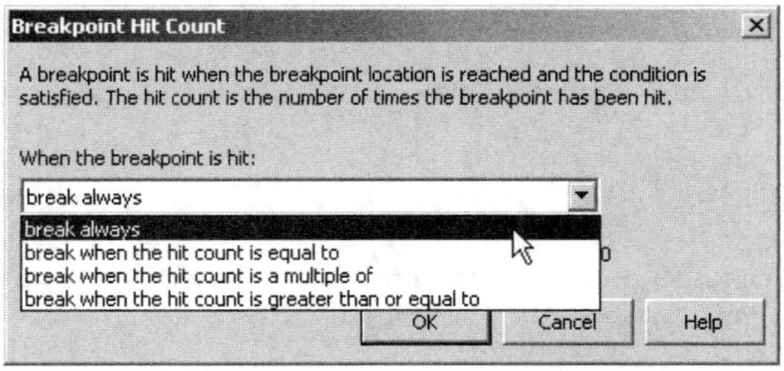

Fig. B.14   **Breakpoint Hit Count** dialog.

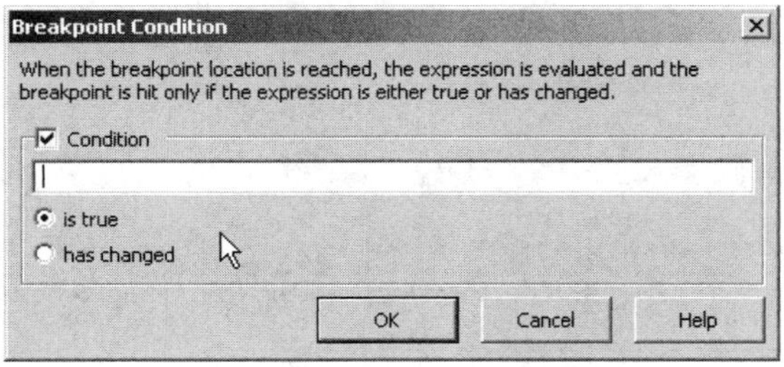

Fig. B.15   **Breakpoint Condition** dialog.

B.5 Additional Procedure Debugging Capabilities

The Visual Studio debugger includes tools for analyzing procedures and procedure calls. We demonstrate some procedure-debugging tools with the following example (Fig. B.16).

The **Call Stack** window contains the program's *procedure call stack*, which allows the programmer to determine the exact sequence of calls that led to the current procedure and to examine calling procedures on the stack. This window helps the programmer see the flow of control that led to the execution of the current procedure. For example, if we place a breakpoint in **MyProcedure**, we get the call stack in Fig. B.17. The program called procedure **Main** first, followed by **MyProcedure**.

```
1    ' Fig. D.16: ProcedureDebugExample.vb
2    ' Demonstrates debugging procedures.
3
4    Module modProcedureDebug
5
6       ' entry point for application
7       Public Sub Main()
8          Dim i As Integer
9
10         ' display MyProcedure return values
11         For i = 0 To 10
12            Console.WriteLine(MyProcedure(i))
13         Next
14      End Sub ' Main
15
16      ' perform calculation
17      Public Function MyProcedure(ByVal x As Integer) As Integer
18         Return (x * x) - (3 * x) + 7
19      End Function ' MyProcedure
20
21      ' method with logic error
22      Public Function BadProcedure(ByVal x As Integer) As Integer
23         Return MyProcedure(x) \ x
24      End Function ' BadProcedure
25
26   End Module ' modProcedureDebug
```

Fig. B.16   Demonstrates procedure debugging.

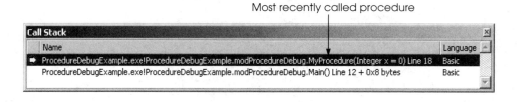

Most recently called procedure

Fig. B.17   Call Stack window.

Double-clicking any line in the **Call Stack** window displays the last executed line in that procedure. Visual Studio .NET highlights the line in green and displays the tooltip shown in Fig. B.18. A green triangle also is displayed to the left of the line to emphasize the line further.

Visual Studio .NET also provides additional program control buttons for debugging-procedures. The **Step Over** button executes one statement in a procedure, then pauses program execution again. As previously mentioned, if a statement contains a procedure call, the called procedure executes in its entirety. The next statement that will be executed is the statement that follows the procedure call. In contrast, the *Step Into* button executes program statements, one per click, including statements in the procedures that are called. **Step Into** transfers control to the procedure, which allows programmers to confirm the procedure's execution, line-by-line. The *Step Out* finishes executing the procedure and returns control to the line that called the procedure.

Testing and Debugging Tip B.8

*Use **Step Out** to finish a procedure that was stepped into accidentally.*

Figure B.19 lists each program-control debug feature, its shortcut key and a description. Experienced programmers often use these shortcut keys in preference to accessing the menu commands.

```
          ' display MyProcedure return values
          For i = 0 To 10
              Console.WriteLine(MyProcedure(i))
This code has called into another function. When that function is finished, this is the next statement that will be executed.
          End Sub ' Main

          ' perform calculation
          Public Function MyProcedure(ByVal x As Integer) As Integer
              Return (x * x) - (3 * x) + 7
          End Function ' MyProcedure
```

Fig. B.18   IDE displaying a procedures calling point.

Control Button	Shortcut Key	Description
Continue	*F5*	Continue running program. Execution continues until either a breakpoint is encountered or the program ends (through normal execution).
Stop Debugging	*Shift + F5*	Stop debugging and return to Visual Studio design mode.
Step Over	*F10*	Step to next command, do not step into procedure calls.
Step Into	*F11*	Execute next statement. If the statement contains a procedure call, control transfers to the procedure for line-by-line debugging. If the statement does not contain a procedure call, **Step Into** behaves like **Step Over**.
Step Out	*Shift + F11*	Finishes executing the current procedure and suspends program execution in the calling procedure.

Fig. B.19   Debug program control features.

The **Immediate** window (Fig. B.20) discussed in Section B.3 is useful for testing arguments passed to a procedure. This helps determine if a procedure is functioning properly without the programmer modifying code.

B.6 Additional Class Debugging Capabilities

Visual Studio includes class debugging features which allow the programmer to determine the current state of objects used in a program. We demonstrate some class debugging features using the code presented in Fig. B.21. We place a breakpoint at the location shown in Fig. B.22. [*Note*: A Visual Basic file may contain multiple classes, as is the case with this example.]

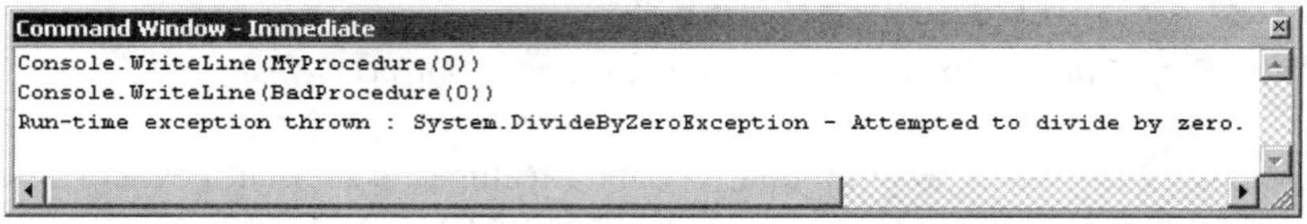

Command Window - Immediate
```
Console.WriteLine(MyProcedure(0))
Console.WriteLine(BadProcedure(0))
Run-time exception thrown : System.DivideByZeroException - Attempted to divide by zero.
```

Fig. B.20   Using the **Immediate** window to debug procedures.

```
1    ' Fig. D.21: DebugClass.vb
2    ' Console application to demonstrate debugging objects.
3
4    Public Class CDebugEntry
5       Private mSomeInteger As Integer = 123
6       Private mIntegerArray As Integer() = {74, 101, 102, 102}
7       Private mDebugClass As CDebugClass
8       Private mRandomObject As Random
9       Private mList As Object() = New Object(2) {}
10
11      Public Sub New()
12         mRandomObject = New Random()
13         mDebugClass = New CDebugClass("Hello World", _
14            New Object())
15
16         mList(0) = mIntegerArray
17         mList(1) = mDebugClass
18         mList(2) = mRandomObject
19      End Sub ' New
20
21      Public Sub DisplayValues()
22         Console.WriteLine(mRandomObject.Next())
23         Console.WriteLine(mDebugClass.SomeString)
24         Console.WriteLine(mIntegerArray(0))
25      End Sub ' DisplayValues
26
27      ' main entry point for application
28      Public Shared Sub Main()
29
```

Fig. B.21   Debugging a class. (Part 1 of 2.)

```
30          Dim entry As CDebugEntry = New CDebugEntry()
31          entry.DisplayValues()
32       End Sub ' Main
33
34    End Class ' DebugEntry
35
36    ' demonstrates class debugging
37    Public Class CDebugClass
38
39       ' declarations
40       Private mSomeString As String
41       Private mPrivateRef As Object
42
43       Public Sub New(ByVal stringData As String, _
44          ByVal objectData As Object)
45
46          mSomeString = stringData
47          mPrivateRef = objectData
48
49       End Sub ' New
50
51       Public Property SomeString() As String
52
53          Get
54             Return SomeString
55          End Get
56
57          Set(ByVal Value As String)
58
59             SomeString = Value
60          End Set
61
62       End Property ' SomeString
63
64    End Class ' CDebugClass
```

Fig. B.21   Debugging a class. (Part 2 of 2.)

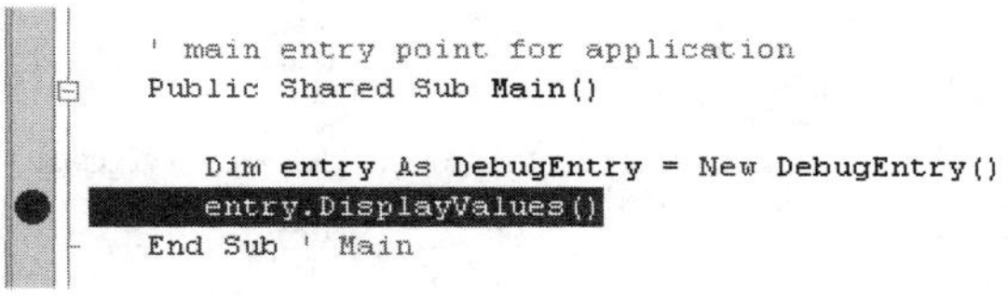

```
' main entry point for application
Public Shared Sub Main()

   Dim entry As DebugEntry = New DebugEntry()
   entry.DisplayValues()
End Sub ' Main
```

Fig. B.22   Breakpoint location for class debugging.

To assist class debugging, Visual Studio .NET allows the programmer to expand and view all data members and properties of a class, including **Private** members. In any of the four windows (i.e., **Watch**, **Locals**, **Autos** and **Me**), a class that has data members is displayed with a plus (**+**) next to it (Fig. B.23). Clicking the plus box displays all of the object's data members and their values. If a member references an object, the object's data members also can be listed by clicking the object's plus box.

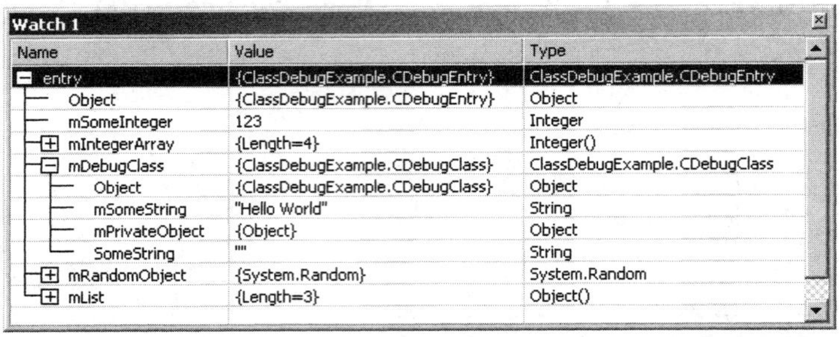

Fig. B.23 Expanded class in **Watch** window.

One of the most valuable features of the debugger is the ability to display all the values in an array. Figure B.24 displays the contents of the **mList** array. At index **0** is **mIntegerArray**, which is expanded to show its contents. Index **1** contains a **Debug-Class** object—expanded to show the object's **Private** data members, as well as a **Public** property. Index **2** contains a **Random** object, defined in the Framework Class Library (FCL).

The Visual Studio debugger contains several other debugging windows, including **Threads**, **Modules**, **Memory**, **Disassembly** and **Registers**. These windows are used by experienced programmers to debug large, complex projects—consult the Visual Studio .NET documentation for more details on these features.

In this appendix, we demonstrated several techniques for debugging programs, procedures and classes. The Visual Studio .NET debugger is a powerful tool that allows programmers to build more robust fault tolerant programs.

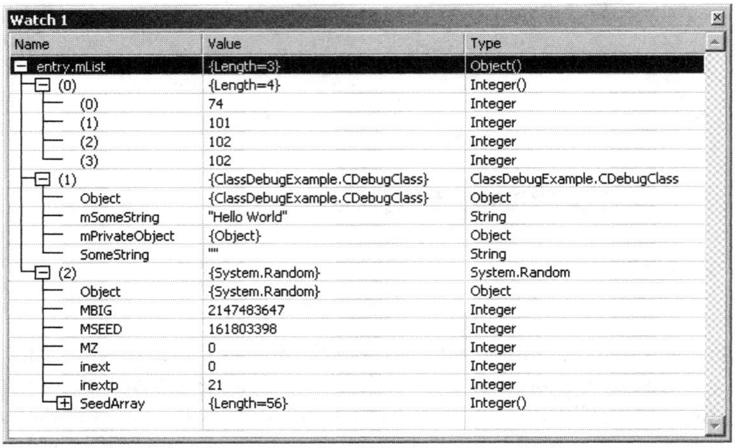

Fig. B.24 Expanded array in **Watch** window.

B.7 Summary

Debugging is the process of finding logic errors in applications. Syntax errors (or compilation errors) occur when program statements violate the grammatical rules of a programming language and are caught by the compiler. Logic errors occur when a program compiles successfully, but does not run as expected. Debuggers allow programmers to examine a program while it is executing.

A breakpoint is a marker set at a line of code. When a program reaches a breakpoint, execution is suspended. The programmer then can examine the state of the program and ensure that the program is working properly. To set breakpoints, click the gray area to the left of any line of code. Alternatively, right-click a line of code and select **Insert Breakpoint**. The **Breakpoints** window displays all the breakpoints currently set for a program. Disabled breakpoints allow the programmer to maintain breakpoints in key locations in the program so that they can be used again when needed.

The **Watch** window allows the programmer to examine the values of variables and expressions. To examine data, type a valid Visual Basic .NET expression, such as a variable name, into the **Name** field. Once the expression has been entered, its type and value appear in the **Type** and **Value** fields. Variables in the **Watch** window can be modified by the user for testing purposes. To modify a variable's value, click the **Value** field and enter a new value.

The **Locals** window displays the name and current value of all the local variables or objects in the current scope. The **Autos** window displays the variables and objects used in the previous statement and the current statement (indicated by the yellow arrow).

The **Immediate** window is useful for testing arguments passed to a method. This helps determine whether a method is functioning properly. To evaluate an expression in the **Immediate** window, simply type the expression into the window and press *Enter*.

The **Call Stack** window contains the program's method call stack, which allows the programmer to determine the exact sequence of calls that led to the current method and to examine calling methods on the stack.

The **Continue** button resumes execution of a suspended program. The **Stop Debugging** button ends the debugging session. The **Break All** button allows the programmer to place an executing program in break mode. The **Show Next Statement** button places the cursor on the same line as the yellow arrow that indicates the next statement to execute. The **Step Over** button executes the next executable line of code, advances the yellow arrow to the executable line that follows and, finally, pauses program execution. If the executed line of code contains a method call, the method is executed in its entirety as one step. The **Step Into** button executes the next statement. If the statement contains a method call, control transfers to the method for line-by-line debugging. If the statement does not contain a method call, **Step Into** behaves like **Step Over**. The **Step Out** button finishes executing the method and returns control to the line that called the method. The **Hex** button toggles the display format of data. If enabled, **Hex** displays data in a hexadecimal (base-16) form, rather than decimal (base-10) form.

Visual Studio .NET includes class debugging features that allow the programmer to determine the current state of any objects used in a program. To assist class debugging, Visual Studio .NET allows the programmer to expand and view all data members, variables and properties of an object, including those declared `Private`.

ASCII Character Set

	0	1	2	3	4	5	6	7	8	9
0	nul	soh	stx	etx	eot	enq	ack	bel	bs	ht
1	nl	vt	ff	cr	so	si	dle	dc1	dc2	dc3
2	dc4	nak	syn	etb	can	em	sub	esc	fs	gs
3	rs	us	sp	!	"	#	$	%	&	`
4	(	)	*	+	,	-	.	/	0	1
5	2	3	4	5	6	7	8	9	:	;
6	<	=	>	?	@	A	B	C	D	E
7	F	G	H	I	J	K	L	M	N	O
8	P	Q	R	S	T	U	V	W	X	Y
9	Z	[	\	]	^	_	'	a	b	c
10	d	e	f	g	h	i	j	k	l	m
11	n	o	p	q	r	s	t	u	v	w
12	x	y	z	{			}	~	del		

Fig. C.1   ASCII character set.

The digits at the left of the table are the left digits of the decimal equivalent (0–127) of the character code, and the digits at the top of the table are the right digits of the character code. For example, the character code for "F" is 70, and the character code for "&" is 38.

Most users of this book are interested in the ASCII character set used to represent English characters on many computers. The ASCII character set is a subset of the Unicode character set used by Visual Basic .NET to represent characters from most of the world's languages. For more information on the Unicode character set, see Appendix D.

Unicode®

Objectives

- To become familiar with Unicode.
- To discuss the mission of the Unicode Consortium.
- To discuss the design basis of Unicode.
- To understand the three Unicode encoding forms: UTF-8, UTF-16 and UTF-32.
- To introduce characters and glyphs.
- To discuss the advantages and disadvantages of using Unicode.
- To provide a brief tour of the Unicode Consortium's Web site.

D.1 Introduction

The use of inconsistent character *encodings* (i.e., numeric values associated with characters) in the developing of global software products causes serious problems, because computers process information as numbers. For instance, the character "a" is converted to a numeric value so that a computer can manipulate that piece of data. Many countries and corporations have developed their own encoding systems that are incompatible with the encoding systems of other countries and corporations. For example, the Microsoft Windows operating system assigns the value 0xC0 to the character "A with a grave accent"; the Apple Macintosh operating system assigns that same value to an upside-down question mark. This results in the misrepresentation and possible corruption of data when data is not processed as intended.

In the absence of a widely-implemented universal character-encoding standard, global software developers had to *localize* their products extensively before distribution. Localization includes the language translation and cultural adaptation of content. The process of localization usually includes significant modifications to the source code (such as the conversion of numeric values and the underlying assumptions made by programmers), which results in increased costs and delays releasing the software. For example, some English-speaking programmers might design global software products assuming that a single character can be represented by one byte. However, when those products are localized for Asian markets, the programmer's assumptions are no longer valid; thus, the majority, if not the entirety, of the code needs to be rewritten. Localization is necessary with each release of a version. By the time a software product is localized for a particular market, a newer version, which needs to be localized as well, may be ready for distribution. As a result, it is cumbersome and costly to produce and distribute global software products in a market where there is no universal character-encoding standard.

In response to this situation, the *Unicode Standard*, an encoding standard that facilitates the production and distribution of software, was created. The Unicode Standard outlines a specification to produce consistent encoding of the world's characters and *symbols*. Software products that handle text encoded in the Unicode Standard need to be localized, but the localization process is simpler and more efficient because the numeric values need not be converted and the assumptions made by programmers about the character encoding are universal. The Unicode Standard is maintained by a nonprofit organization called the

Unicode Consortium, whose members include Apple, IBM, Microsoft, Oracle, Sun Micro-systems, Sybase and many others.

When the Consortium envisioned and developed the Unicode Standard, they wanted an encoding system that was *universal, efficient, uniform* and *unambiguous.* A universal encoding system encompasses all commonly used characters. An efficient encoding system allows text files to be parsed easily. A uniform encoding system assigns fixed values to all characters. An unambiguous encoding system represents a given character in a consistent manner. These four terms are referred to as the Unicode Standard *design basis*.

D.2 Unicode Transformation Formats

Although Unicode incorporates the limited ASCII *character set* (i.e., a collection of char-acters), it encompasses a more comprehensive character set. In ASCII each character is rep-resented by a byte containing 0s and 1s. One byte is capable of storing the binary numbers from 0 to 255. Each character is assigned a number between 0 and 255; thus, ASCII-based systems can support only 256 characters, a tiny fraction of world's characters. Unicode ex-tends the ASCII character set by encoding the vast majority of the world's characters. The Unicode Standard encodes all of those characters in a uniform numerical space from 0 to 10FFFF hexadecimal. An implementation will express these numbers in one of several transformation formats, choosing the one that best fits the particular application at hand.

Three such formats are in use, called *UTF-8, UTF-16* and *UTF-32*, depending on the size of the units—in *bits*—being used. UTF-8, a variable-width encoding form, requires one to four bytes to express each Unicode character. UTF-8 data consists of 8-bit bytes (sequences of one, two, three or four bytes depending on the character being encoded) and is well suited for ASCII-based systems, where there is a predominance of one-byte charac-ters (ASCII represents characters as one byte). Currently, UTF-8 is widely implemented in UNIX systems and in databases.

The variable-width UTF-16 encoding form expresses Unicode characters in units of 16 bits (i.e., as two adjacent bytes, or a short integer in many machines). Most characters of Unicode are expressed in a single 16-bit unit. However, characters with values above FFFF hexadecimal are expressed with an ordered pair of 16-bit units called *surrogates*. Surro-gates are 16-bit integers in the range D800 through DFFF, which are used solely for the pur-pose of "escaping" into higher numbered characters. Approximately one million characters can be expressed in this manner. Although a surrogate pair requires 32 bits to represent characters, it is space-efficient to use these 16-bit units. Surrogates are rare characters in current implementations. Many string-handling implementations are written in terms of UTF-16. [*Note*: Details and sample code for UTF-16 handling are available on the Unicode Consortium Web site at **www.unicode.org**.]

Implementations that require significant use of rare characters or entire scripts encoded above FFFF hexadecimal should use UTF-32, a 32-bit, fixed-width encoding form that usu-ally requires twice as much memory as UTF-16 encoded characters. The major advantage of the fixed-width UTF-32 encoding form is that it expresses all characters uniformly, so it is easy to handle in arrays.

There are few guidelines that state when to use a particular encoding form. The best encoding form to use depends on computer systems and business protocols, not on the data itself. Typically, the UTF-8 encoding form should be used where computer systems and business protocols require data to be handled in 8-bit units, particularly in legacy systems being upgraded, because it often simplifies changes to existing programs. For this reason, UTF-8 has become the encoding form of choice on the Internet. Likewise, UTF-16 is the encoding form of choice on Microsoft Windows applications. UTF-32 is likely to become more widely used in the future as more characters are encoded with values above FFFF hexadecimal. Also, UTF-32 requires less sophisticated handling than UTF-16 in the presence of surrogate pairs. Figure D.1 shows the different ways in which the three encoding forms handle character encoding.

D.3 Characters and Glyphs

The Unicode Standard consists of *characters*, written components (i.e., alphabetic letters, numerals, punctuation marks, accent marks, etc.) that can be represented by numeric values. Examples of characters include: U+0041 LATIN CAPITAL LETTER A. In the first character representation, U+*yyyy* is a *code value*, in which U+ refers to Unicode code values, as opposed to other hexadecimal values. The *yyyy* represents a four-digit hexadecimal number of an encoded character. Code values are bit combinations that represent encoded characters. Characters are represented with *glyphs*, various shapes, fonts and sizes for displaying characters. There are no code values for glyphs in the Unicode Standard. Examples of glyphs are shown in Fig. D.2.

The Unicode Standard encompasses the alphabets, ideographs, syllabaries, punctuation marks, *diacritics*, mathematical operators and so on that compose the written languages and scripts of the world. A diacritic is a special mark added to a character to distinguish it from another letter or to indicate an accent (e.g., in Spanish, the tilde "~" above the character "n"). Currently, Unicode provides code values for 94,140 character representations, with more than 880,000 code values reserved for future expansion.

Character	UTF-8	UTF-16	UTF-32
LATIN CAPITAL LETTER A	0x41	0x0041	0x00000041
GREEK CAPITAL LETTER ALPHA	0xCD 0x91	0x0391	0x00000391
CJK UNIFIED IDEOGRAPH-4E95	0xE4 0xBA 0x95	0x4E95	0x00004E95
OLD ITALIC LETTER A	0xF0 0x80 0x83 0x80	0xDC00 0xDF00	0x00010300

Fig. D.1   Correlation between the three encoding forms.

Fig. D.2   Various glyphs of the character A.

D.4 Advantages/Disadvantages of Unicode

The Unicode Standard has several significant advantages that promote its use. One is the impact it has on the performance of the international economy. Unicode standardizes the characters for the world's writing systems to a uniform model that promotes transferring and sharing data. Programs developed using such a schema maintain their accuracy because each character has a single definition (i.e., *a* is always U+0061, % is always U+0025). This enables corporations to manage the high demands of international markets by processing different writing systems at the same time. Also, all characters can be managed in an identical manner, thus avoiding any confusion caused by different character-code architectures. Moreover, managing data in a consistent manner eliminates data corruption, because data can be sorted, searched and manipulated via a consistent process.

Another advantage of the Unicode Standard is *portability* (i.e., the ability to execute software on disparate computers or with disparate operating systems). Most operating systems, databases, programming languages and Web browsers currently support, or are planning to support, Unicode. Additionally, Unicode includes more characters than any other character set in common use (although it does not yet include all of the world's characters.

A disadvantage of the Unicode Standard is the amount of memory required by UTF-16 and UTF-32. ASCII character sets are 8 bits in length, so they require less storage than the default 16-bit Unicode character set. However, the *double-byte character set (DBCS)* and the *multi-byte character set (MBCS)* that encode Asian characters (ideographs) require two to four bytes, respectively. In such instances, the UTF-16 or the UTF-32 encoding forms may be used with little hindrance on memory and performance.

D.5 Unicode Consortium's Web Site

If you would like to learn more about the Unicode Standard, visit **www.unicode.org**. This site provides a wealth of information about the Unicode Standard. Currently, the home page is organized into various sections: *New to Unicode*, *General Information*, *The Consortium*, *The Unicode Standard*, *Work in Progress* and *For Members*.

The *New to Unicode* section consists of two subsections: **What is Unicode?** and **How to Use this Site**. The first subsection provides a technical introduction to Unicode by describing design principles, character interpretations and assignments, text processing and Unicode conformance. This subsection is recommended reading for anyone new to Unicode. Also, this subsection provides a list of related links that provide the reader with additional information about Unicode. The **How to Use this Site** subsection contains information about using and navigating the site as well hyperlinks to additional resources.

The *General Information* section contains six subsections: **Where is my Character?**, **Display Problems?**, **Useful Resources**, **Enabled Products**, **Mail Lists** and **Conferences**. The main areas covered in this section include a link to the Unicode code charts (a complete listing of code values) assembled by the Unicode Consortium as well as a detailed outline on how to locate an encoded character in the code chart. Also, the section contains advice on how to configure different operating systems and Web browsers so that the Unicode characters can be viewed properly. Moreover, from this section, the user can navigate to other sites that provide information on various topics, such as fonts, linguistics and such other standards as the *Armenian Standards Page* and the *Chinese GB 18030 Encoding Standard*.

The *Consortium* section consists of five subsections: **Who we are**, **Our Members**, **How to Join**, **Press Info** and **Contact Us**. This section provides a list of the current Unicode Consortium members as well as information on how to become a member. Privileges for each member type—*full*, *associate*, *specialist* and *individual*—and the fees assessed to each member are listed here.

The *Unicode Standard* section consists of nine subsections: **Start Here**, **Latest Version**, **Technical Reports**, **Code Charts**, **Unicode Data**, **Updates & Errata**, **Unicode Policies**, **Glossary** and **Technical FAQ**. This section describes the updates applied to the latest version of the Unicode Standard and categorizes all defined encoding. The user can learn how the latest version has been modified to encompass more features and capabilities. For instance, one enhancement of Version 3.1 is that it contains additional encoded characters. Also, if users are unfamiliar with vocabulary terms used by the Unicode Consortium, they can navigate to the **Glossary** subsection.

The *Work in Progress* section consists of three subsections: **Calendar of Meetings**, **Proposed Characters** and **Submitting Proposals**. This section presents the user with a catalog of the recent characters included into the Unicode Standard scheme as well as those characters being considered for inclusion. If users determine that a character has been overlooked, then they can submit a written proposal for the inclusion of that character. The **Submitting Proposals** subsection contains strict guidelines that must be adhered to when submitting written proposals.

The *For Members* section consists of two subsections: **Member Resources** and **Working Documents**. These subsections are password protected; only consortium members can access these links.

D.6 Using Unicode

Visual Studio .NET uses Unicode UTF-16 encoding to represent all characters. Figure D.3 uses Visual Basic to display the text "Welcome to Unicode!" in eight different languages: English, French, German, Japanese, Portuguese, Russian, Spanish and Traditional Chinese. [*Note*: The Unicode Consortium's Web site contains a link to code charts that lists the 16-bit Unicode code values.]

The first welcome message (lines 13–16) contains the hexadecimal codes for the English text. The **Code Charts** page on the Unicode Consortium Web site contains a document that lists the code values for the **Basic Latin** *block* (or category), which includes the English alphabet. The hexadecimal codes in lines 13–14 equate to "Welcome." When using Unicode characters in Visual Basic, the format **&H***yyyy* is used, where *yyyy* represents the hexadecimal Unicode encoding. For example, the letter "W" (in "Welcome") is denoted by **&H57**. [*Note*: The actual code for the letter "W" is **&H0057**, but Visual Studio removes the two zeros.] Line 15 contains the hexadecimal for the *space* character (**&H20**). The hexadecimal value for the word "to" is on line 15 and the word "Unicode" is on line 14. "Unicode" is not encoded because it is a registered trademark and has no equivalent translation in most languages. Line 16 also contains the **&H21** notation for the exclamation mark (**!**).

The remaining welcome messages (lines 18–61) contain the hexadecimal codes for the other seven languages. The code values used for the French, German, Portuguese and Spanish text are located in the **Basic Latin** block, the code values used for the Traditional Chinese text are located in the **CJK Unified Ideographs** block, the code values used for the Russian text are located in the **Cyrillic** block and the code values used for the Japanese text are located in the **Hiragana** block.

```
1   ' Fig. F.3: Unicode.vb
2   ' Using Unicode encoding.
3
4   Public Class FrmUnicode
5       Inherits System.Windows.Forms.Form
6
7       ' Visual Studio .NET generated code
8
9       Private Sub Form1_Load(ByVal sender As System.Object, _
10          ByVal e As System.EventArgs) Handles MyBase.Load
11
12          'English
13          lblEnglish.Text = ChrW(&H57) & ChrW(&H65) & ChrW(&H6C) & _
14              ChrW(&H63) & ChrW(&H6F) & ChrW(&H6D) & ChrW(&H65) & _
15              ChrW(&H20) & ChrW(&H74) & ChrW(&H6F) & ChrW(&H20) & _
16              "Unicode" & ChrW(&H21)
17
18          ' French
19          lblFrench.Text = ChrW(&H42) & ChrW(&H69) & ChrW(&H65) & _
20              ChrW(&H6E) & ChrW(&H76) & ChrW(&H65) & ChrW(&H6E) & _
21              ChrW(&H75) & ChrW(&H65) & ChrW(&H20) & ChrW(&H61) & _
22              ChrW(&H75) & ChrW(&H20) & "Unicode" & ChrW(&H21)
23
24          ' German
25          lblGerman.Text = ChrW(&H57) & ChrW(&H69) & ChrW(&H6C) & _
26              ChrW(&H6B) & ChrW(&H6F) & ChrW(&H6D) & ChrW(&H6D) & _
27              ChrW(&H65) & ChrW(&H6E) & ChrW(&H20) & ChrW(&H7A) & _
28              ChrW(&H75) & ChrW(&H20) & "Unicode" & ChrW(&H21)
29
30          ' Japanese
31          lblJapanese.Text = "Unicode" & ChrW(&H3078) & _
32              ChrW(&H3087) & ChrW(&H3045) & ChrW(&H3053) & _
33              ChrW(&H305D) & ChrW(&H21)
34
35          ' Portuguese
36          lblPortuguese.Text = ChrW(&H53) & ChrW(&HE9) & ChrW(&H6A) & _
37              ChrW(&H61) & ChrW(&H20) & ChrW(&H42) & _
38              ChrW(&H65) & ChrW(&H6D) & ChrW(&H76) & _
39              ChrW(&H69) & ChrW(&H6E) & ChrW(&H64) & _
40              ChrW(&H6F) & ChrW(&H20) & "Unicode" & ChrW(&H21)
41
42          ' Russian
43          lblRussian.Text = ChrW(&H414) & ChrW(&H43E) & ChrW(&H431) & _
44              ChrW(&H440) & ChrW(&H43E) & ChrW(&H20) & _
45              ChrW(&H43F) & ChrW(&H43E) & ChrW(&H436) & _
46              ChrW(&H430) & ChrW(&H43B) & ChrW(&H43E) & _
47              ChrW(&H432) & ChrW(&H430) & ChrW(&H442) & _
48              ChrW(&H44A) & ChrW(&H20) & ChrW(&H432) & _
49              ChrW(&H20) & "Unicode" & ChrW(&H21)
50
```

Fig. D.3   Windows application demonstrating Unicode encoding. (Part 1 of 2.)

```
51          ' Spanish
52          lblSpanish.Text = ChrW(&H42) & ChrW(&H69) & ChrW(&H65) & _
53             ChrW(&H6E) & ChrW(&H76) & ChrW(&H65) & _
54             ChrW(&H6E) & ChrW(&H69) & ChrW(&H64) & _
55             ChrW(&H61) & ChrW(&H20) & ChrW(&H61) & _
56             ChrW(&H20) & "Unicode" & ChrW(&H21)
57
58          ' Traditional Chinese
59          lblChinese.Text = ChrW(&H6B22) & ChrW(&H8FCE) & _
60             ChrW(&H4F7F) & ChrW(&H7528) & ChrW(&H20) & _
61             "Unicode" & ChrW(&H21)
62       End Sub
63
64    End Class
```

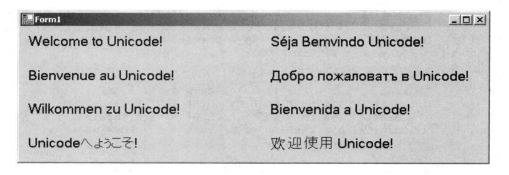

Fig. D.3   Windows application demonstrating Unicode encoding. (Part 2 of 2.)

[*Note*: To render the Asian characters in a Windows application, you would need to install the proper language files on your computer. To do this, open the **Regional Options** dialog from the **Control Panel** (**Start > Settings > Control Panel**). At the bottom of the **General** tab is a list of languages. Check the **Japanese** and the **Traditional Chinese** checkboxes and press **Apply**. Follow the directions of the install wizard to install the languages. For additional assistance, visit **www.unicode.org/help/display_problems.html**.]

D.7 Character Ranges

The Unicode Standard assigns code values, which range from **0000** (**Basic Latin**) to **E007F** (***Tags***), to the written characters of the world. Currently, there are code values for 94,140 characters. To simplify the search for a character and its associated code value, the Unicode Standard generally groups code values by *script* and function (i.e., Latin characters are grouped in a block, mathematical operators are grouped in another block, etc.). As a rule, a script is a single writing system that is used for multiple languages (e.g., the Latin script is used for English, French, Spanish, etc.). The **Code Charts** page on the Unicode Consortium Web site lists all the defined blocks and their respective code values. Figure D.4 lists some blocks (scripts) from the Web site and their range of code values.

Script	Range of Code Values
Arabic	U+0600–U+06FF
Basic Latin	U+0000–U+007F
Bengali (India)	U+0980–U+09FF
Cherokee (Native America)	U+13A0–U+13FF
CJK Unified Ideographs (East Asia)	U+4E00–U+9FAF
Cyrillic (Russia and Eastern Europe)	U+0400–U+04FF
Ethiopic	U+1200–U+137F
Greek	U+0370–U+03FF
Hangul Jamo (Korea)	U+1100–U+11FF
Hebrew	U+0590–U+05FF
Hiragana (Japan)	U+3040–U+309F
Khmer (Cambodia)	U+1780–U+17FF
Lao (Laos)	U+0E80–U+0EFF
Mongolian	U+1800–U+18AF
Myanmar	U+1000–U+109F
Ogham (Ireland)	U+1680–U+169F
Runic (Germany and Scandinavia)	U+16A0–U+16FF
Sinhala (Sri Lanka)	U+0D80–U+0DFF
Telugu (India)	U+0C00–U+0C7F
Thai	U+0E00–U+0E7F

Fig. D.4   Some character ranges.

D.8 Summary

Before Unicode, software developers were plagued by the use of inconsistent character encoding (e.g., using numeric values for characters). Most countries and organizations had their own encoding systems, which were incompatible with each other. Without Unicode, localization of global software requires significant modifications to the source code, which results in increased cost and in delays in releasing the product.

The Unicode Consortium developed the Unicode Standard in response to the serious problems created by multiple character encodings and the use of those encodings. The Unicode Standard facilitates the production and distribution of localized software. It outlines a specification for the consistent encoding of the world's characters and symbols. Software products that handle text encoded in the Unicode Standard need to be localized, but the localization process is simpler and more efficient. The Unicode Standard is designed to be universal, efficient, uniform and unambiguous.

A universal encoding system encompasses all commonly used characters; an efficient encoding system parses text files easily; a uniform encoding system assigns fixed values to all characters; and an unambiguous encoding system represents the same character for any given value. Unicode extends the limited ASCII character set to include all the major characters of the world. Unicode makes use of three Unicode Transformation Formats (UTF)—UTF-8, UTF-16 and UTF-32—each of which may be appropriate for use in different contexts. UTF-8 data consists of 8-bit bytes (sequences of one, two, three or four bytes, depending on the character being encoded) and is well suited for ASCII-based systems when there is a predominance of one-byte characters. (ASCII represents characters with one byte.) UTF-8 is a variable-width encoding form that is more compact for text involving mostly Latin characters and ASCII punctuation. UTF-16, the default encoding form of the Unicode Standard, is a variable-width encoding form that uses 16-bit code units instead of bytes. Most characters are represented by a single unit, but some characters require surrogate pairs. Surrogates are 16-bit integers in the range D800 through DFFF and are used solely for the purpose of "escaping" into higher numbered characters. Without surrogate pairs, the UTF-16 encoding form can encompass only 65,000 characters, but with the surrogate pairs, the number is expanded to include over a million characters. UTF-32 is a 32-bit, fixed-width encoding form whose major advantage is that it expresses all characters uniformly, so that they are easy to handle in arrays and other structures.

A character is any written component that can be represented by a numeric value. Characters are represented with glyphs, shapes, fonts and sizes. Code values are bit combinations that represent encoded characters. The Unicode notation for a code value is U+*yyyy*, in which U+ refers to the Unicode code values, as opposed to other hexadecimal values. The *yyyy* represents a four-digit hexadecimal number.

The Unicode Standard has become the default encoding system for XML and any language derived from XML, such as XHTML. The Visual Studio .NET IDE uses UTF-16 encoding to represent all characters. In using Unicode characters in Visual Basic .NET code, the entity reference **\u***yyyy* is used, where *yyyy* represents the hexadecimal Unicode encoding.

Bibliography

Anderson, R., A. Homer, R. Howard and D. Sussman. *A Preview of Active Server Pages+*. Birmingham, UK: Wrox Press, 2001.

Appleman, D. *Moving to VB .NET: Strategies, Concepts, and Code*. Berkeley, CA: Apress Publishing, 2001.

Archer, T. *Inside C#*. Redmond, WA: Microsoft Press, 2001.

Barwell, F., R. Blair, R. Case, J. Crossland, B. Forgey, W. Hankison, B. S. Hollis, R. Lhotka, T.
McCarthy, J. D. Narkiewicz, J. Pinnock, R. Ramachandran, M. Reynolds, J. Roth, B.
Sempf, B. Sheldon and S. Short. *Professional VB .NET, Second Edition*. Birmingham,
UK: Wrox Press, 2002.

Blaha, M. R., W. J. Premerlani and J. E. Rumbaugh. "Relational Database Design Using an Object-Oriented Methodology." *Communications of the ACM*, Vol. 31, No. 4, April 1988, 414–427.

Carr, D. "Hitting a High Note." *Internet World*. March 2001, 71.

Carr, D. "Slippery SOAP." *Internet World*. March 2001, 72–74.

Carr, D. F. "Dave Winer: The President of Userland and Soap Co-Creator Surveys the Changing
Scene." *Internet World*. March 2001, 53–58.

Chappel, D. "Coming Soon: The Biggest Platform Ever." *Application Development Trends Magazine*, May 2001,15.

Chappel, D. "A Standard for Web Services: SOAP vs. ebXML." *Application Development Trends*,
February 2001, 17.

Codd, E. F. "A Relational Model of Data for Large Shared Data Banks." *Communications of the
ACM*, June 1970.

Codd, E. F. "Further Normalization of the Data Base Relational Model." *Courant Computer Science
Symposia*, Vol. 6, *Data Base Systems*. Upper Saddle River, N.J.: Prentice Hall, 1972.

Codd, E. F. "Fatal Flaws in SQL." *Datamation*, Vol. 34, No. 16, August 15, 1988, 45–48.

Conard, J., P. Dengler, B. Francis, J. Glynn, B. Harvey, B. Hollis, R. Ramachandran, J. Schenken, S.
Short and C. Ullman. *Introducing .NET*. Birmingham, UK: Wrox Press, 2000.

Correia, E. J. "Visual Studio .NET to Speak in Tongues." *Software Development Times*, April 2001, 12.

Cornes, O., C. Goode, J. T. Llibre, C. Ullman, R. Birdwell, J. Kauffman, A. Krishnamoorthy, C. L. Miller, N. Raybould and D. Sussman. *Beginning ASP .NET Using VB .NET.* Birmingham, UK: Wrox Press, 2001.

Date, C. J. *An Introduction to Database Systems, Seventh Edition.* Reading, MA: Addison-Wesley Publishing, 2000.

Davydov, M. "The Road to the Future of Web Services." *Intelligent Enterprise.* May 2001, 50–52.

Deitel, H. M. and Deitel, P. J. *Java How To Program, Fourth Edition.* Upper Saddle River, NJ: Prentice Hall, 2001

Deitel, H. M., Deitel, P. J. and T. R. Nieto. *Visual Basic 6 How To Program.* Upper Saddle River, NJ: Prentice Hall, 1999.

Deitel, H. M., P. J. Deitel, T. R. Nieto, T. M. Lin and P. Sadhu. *XML How To Program.* Upper Saddle River, NJ: Prentice Hall, 2001

Deitel, H. M. *Operating Systems, Second Edition.* Reading, MA: Addison Wesley Publishing, 1990.

Dejong, J. "Raising the Bar." *Software Development Times*, March 2001, 29–30.

Dejong, J. "Microsoft's Clout Drives Web Services." *Software Development Times*, March 2001, 29, 31.

Dejong, J. "One-Stop Shopping: A Favored Method." *Software Development Times*, February 2001, 20.

Erlanger. L. ".NET Services." *Internet World*, March 2001, 47.

Erlanger. L. "Dissecting .NET." *Internet World*, March 2001, 30–36.

Esposito, D. "Data Grid In-Place Editing." *MSDN Magazine*, June 2001, 37–45.

Esposito, D. "Server-Side ASP .NET Data Binding: Part 2: Customizing the Data Grid Control." *MSDN Magazine*, April 2001, 33–45.

Finlay, D. "UDDI Works on Classification, Taxonomy Issues." *Software Development Times*, March 2001, 3.

Finlay, D. "New York Prepares for .NET Conference." *Software Development Times*, June 2001, 23.

Finlay, D. "GoXML Native Database Clusters Data, Reduces Seek Time." *Software Development Times*, March 2001, 5.

Fontana, J. "What You Get in .NET." *Network World*, April 2001, 75.

Galli, P. and R. Holland. ".NET Taking Shape, but Developers Still Wary." *eWeek*, June 2001, pages 9, 13.

Gillen, A. "Sun's Answer to .NET." *EntMag*, March 2001, 38.

Gillen, A. "What a Year It's Been." *EntMag*, December 2000, 54.

Gladwin, L. C. "Microsoft, eBay Strike Web Services Deal." *Computer World*, March 2001, 22.

Grimes, R. "Make COM Programming a Breeze with New Feature in Visual Studio .NET." *MSDN Magazine*, April 2001, 48–62.

Harvey, B., S. Robinson, J. Templeman and K. Watson. *C# Programming With the Public Beta.* Birmingham, UK: Wrox Press, 2000.

Holland, R. "Microsoft Scales Back VB Changes." *eWeek*, April 2001, 16.

Holland, R. "Tools Case Transition to .NET Platform." *eWeek*, March 2001, 21.

Hollis, B. S. and R Lhotka. *VB .NET Programming With the Public Beta*. Birmingham, UK: Wrox Press, 2001.

Hulme, G, V. "XML Specification May Ease PKI Integration." *Information Week*, December 2000, 38.

Hutchinson, J. "Can't Fit Another Byte." *Network Computing*, March 2001, 14.

Jepson, B. "Applying .NET to Web Services." *Web Techniques*, May 2001, 49–54.

Karney. J. ".NET Devices." *Internet World*, March 2001, 49–50.

Kiely, D. "Doing .NET In Internet Time." *Information Week*, December 2000, 137–138, 142–144, 148.

Kirtland, M. "The Programmable Web: Web Services Provides Building Blocks for the Microsoft .NET Framework." *MSDN Magazine*, September 2000 **<msdn.microsoft.com/ msdnmag/issues/0900/WebPlatform/WebPlatform.asp>**.

Levitt, J. "Plug-And-Play Redefined." *Information Week*, April 2001, 63–68.

McCright, J. S. and D. Callaghan. "Lotus Pushes Domino Services." *eWeek*, June 2001, 14.

"Microsoft Chimes in with New C Sharp Programming Language." Xephon Web site. June 30, 2000 **<www.xephon.com/news/00063019.html>**.

Microsoft Developer Network Documentation. Visual Studio .NET CD-ROM, 2001.

Microsoft Developer Network Library. .NET Framework SDK. Microsoft Web site **<msdn.microsoft.com/library/default.asp>**.

Moran, B. "Questions, Answers, and Tips." *SQL Server Magazine*, April 2001, 19–20.

MySQL Manual. MySQL Web site **<www.mysql.com/doc/>**.

Oracle Technology Network Documentation. Oracle Web site. **<otn.oracle.com/docs/con- tent.html>**.

Otey, M. "Me Too .NET." *SQL Server Magazine*, April 2001, 7.

Papa, J. "Revisiting the Ad-Hoc Data Display Web Application." *MSDN Magazine*, June 2001, 27–33.

Pratschner, S. "Simplifying Deployment and Solving DLL Hell with the .NET Framework." *MSDN Library*, September 2000 **<msdn.microsoft.com/library/techart/dply- withnet.htm>**.

Prosise, J. "Wicked Code." *MSDN Magazine*, April 2001, 121–127.

Relational Technology, *INGRES Overview*. Alameda, CA: Relational Technology, 1988.

Ricadela, A. and P. McDougall. "eBay Deal Helps Microsoft Sell .NET Strategy." *Information Week*, March 2001, 33.

Ricadela, A. "IBM Readies XML Middleware." *Information Week*, December 2000, 155.

Richter, J. "An Introduction to Delegates." *MSDN Magazine*, April 2001, 107–111.

Richter, J. "Delegates, Part 2." *MSDN Magazine*, June 2001, 133–139.

Rizzo, T. "Let's Talk Web Services." *Internet World*, April 2001, 4–5.

Rizzo, T. "Moving to Square One." *Internet World*, March 2001, 4–5.

Robinson, S., O. Cornes, J. Glynn, B. Harvey, C. McQueen, J. Moemeka, C. Nagel, M. Skinner and K. Watson. *Professional C#*. Birmingham, UK: Wrox Press, 2001.

Rollman, R. "XML Q & A." *SQL Server Magazine*, April 2001, 57–58.

Rubinstein, D. "Suit Settled, Acrimony Remains." *Software Development Times*, February 2001, pages 1, 8.

Rubinstein, D. "Play It Again, XML." *Software Development Times*, March 2001, 12.

Scott, G. "Adjusting to Adversity." *EntMag*, March 2001, 38.

Scott, G. "Putting on the Breaks." *EntMag*, December 2000,   54.

Sells, C. "Managed Extensions Bring .NET CLR Support to C++." *MSDN Magazine*. July 2001, 115–122.

Seltzer, L. "Standards and .NET." *Internet World*, March 2001, 75–76.

Shohoud, Y. "Tracing, Logging, and Threading Made Easy with .NET." *MSDN Magazine*, July 2001, 60–72.

Sliwa, C. "Microsoft Backs Off Changes to VB .NET." *Computer World*, April 2001, 14.

Songini, Marc. "Despite Tough Times, Novell Users Remain Upbeat." *Computer World*, March 2001, 22.

Spencer, K. "Cleaning House." *SQL Server Magazine*, April 2001, 61–62.

Spencer, K. "Windows Forms in Visual Basic .NET." *MSDN Magazine*, April 2001, 25–45.

Stonebraker, M. "Operating System Support for Database Management." *Communications of the ACM*, Vol. 24, No. 7, July 1981, 412–418.

Surveyor. J. ".NET Framework." *Internet World*, March 2001, 43–44.

Tapang, C. C. "New Definition Languages Expose Your COM Objects to SOAP Clients." *MSDN Magazine*, April 2001, 85–89.

Utley, C. *A Programmer's Introduction to Visual Basic .NET.* Indianapolis, IN: Sams Publishing, 2001.

Visual Studio .NET ADO .NET Overview. Microsoft Developers Network Web site **<msdn.microsoft.com/vstudio/nextgen/technology/adoplusdefault.asp>**.

Ward, K. "Microsoft Attempts to Demystify .NET." *EntMag*, December 2000, 1.

Waymire, R. "Answers from Microsoft." *SQL Server Magazine*, April 2001, 71–72.

Winston, A. "A Distributed Database Primer." *UNIX World*, April 1988, 54–63.

Whitney, R. "XML for Analysis." *SQL Server Magazine*, April 2001, 63–66.

Zeichick, A. "Microsoft Serious About Web Services." *Software Development Times*, March 2001, 3.

Index

The DEITEL™ Suite of Products...

Web Services:
A Technical Introduction

© 2003, 400 pp., paper (0-13-046135-0)

Web Services: A Technical Introduction from the DEITEL™
Developer Series familiarizes programmers, technical
managers and project managers with key Web services
concepts, including what Web services are and why
they are revolutionary. The book covers the business
case for Web services—the underlying technologies,
ways in which Web services can provide competitive
advantages and opportunities for Web services-related
lines of business. Readers learn the latest Web-services
standards, including XML, SOAP, WSDL and UDDI;
learn about Web services implementations in .NET
and Java; benefit from an extensive comparison of
Web services products and vendors; and read about
Web services security options. Although this is not a
programming book, the appendices show .NET and
Java code examples to demonstrate the structure
of Web services applications and documents. In
addition, the book includes numerous case studies
describing ways in which organizations are implementing
Web services to increase efficiency, simplify business
processes, create new revenue streams and interact
better with partners and customers.

Java™ Web Services
for Experienced Programmers

© 2003, 700 pp., paper (0-13-046134-2)

Java™ Web Services for Experienced Programmers from the
DEITEL™ Developer Series provides the experienced
Java programmer with 103 LIVE-CODE™ examples and
covers industry standards including XML, SOAP, WSDL
and UDDI. Learn how to build and integrate Web
services using the Java API for XML RPC, the Java
API for XML Messaging, Apache Axis and the Java
Web Services Developer Pack. Develop and deploy
Web services on several major Web services platforms. Register and discover Web services through
public registries and the Java API for XML Registries.
Build Web Services clients for several platforms,
including J2ME. Significant Web Services case studies also are included.

Visual Basic® .NET
for Experienced Programmers

©2003, paper, approximately 1150 pp., (0-13-046131-8)

Visual Basic .NET for Experienced Programmers from the DEITEL™
Developer Series presents experienced programmers with
a concise introduction to programming fundamentals
before delving into more sophisticated topics. Learn how
to create reusable software components with assemblies,
modules and dynamic link libraries. Learn Visual Basic
.NET through LIVE-CODE™ examples of ASP.NET, multithreading, object-oriented programming, XML processing,
mobile application development and Web services.

Visual C++ .NET
for Experienced Programmers:
A Managed Code Approach

© 2003, 1500 pp., paper (0-13-045821-X)

*Visual C++ .NET for Experienced Programmers: A Managed Code
Approach* from the DEITEL™ Developer Series teaches
programmers with C++ programming experience how to
develop Visual C++ applications for Microsoft's new .NET
Framework. The book begins with a condensed introduction
to Visual C++ programming fundamentals, then covers
more sophisticated .NET application-development topics
in detail. Key topics include: creating reusable software
components with assemblies, modules and dynamic link
libraries; using classes from the Framework Class Library
(FCL); building graphical user interfaces (GUIs) with the
FCL; implementing multithreaded applications; building
networked applications; manipulating databases with
ADO .NET and creating XML Web services. In addition,
the book provides several chapters on unmanaged code
in Visual C++ .NET. These chapters demonstrate how to
use "attributed programming" to simplify common tasks
(such as connecting to a database) and improve code
readability; how to integrate managed- and unmanaged-
code software components; and how to use ATL Server
to create Web-based applications and Web services with
unmanaged code. The book features detailed LIVE-CODE™
examples that highlight crucial .NET-programming concepts
and demonstrate Web services at work. A substantial
introduction to XML also is included.

Java™ How to Program Fourth Edition

BOOK / CD-ROM

©2002, 1546 pp., paper
(0-13-034151-7)

The world's best-selling Java text is now even better! The Fourth Edition of *Java How to Program* includes a new focus on object-oriented design with the UML, design patterns, full-color program listings and figures and the most up-to-date Java coverage available.

Readers will discover key topics in Java programming, such as graphical user interface components, exception handling, multithreading, multimedia, files and streams, networking, data structures and more. In addition, a new chapter on design patterns explains frequently recurring architectural patterns—information that can help save designers considerable time when building large systems.

The highly detailed optional case study focuses on object-oriented design with the UML and presents fully implemented working Java code.

Updated throughout, the text includes new and revised discussions on topics such as Swing, graphics and socket- and packet-based networking. Three introductory chapters heavily emphasize problem solving and programming skills. The chapters on RMI, JDBC™, servlets and JavaBeans have been moved to *Advanced Java 2 Platform How to Program*, where they are now covered in much greater depth. (See *Advanced Java 2 Platform How to Program* below.)

Advanced Java™ 2 Platform How to Program

BOOK / CD-ROM

©2002, 1811 pp., paper
(0-13-089560-1)

Expanding on the world's best-selling Java textbook— *Java How to Program*— *Advanced Java 2 Platform How To Program* presents advanced Java topics for developing sophisticated, user-friendly GUIs; significant, scalable enterprise applications; wireless applications and distributed systems. Primarily based on Java 2 Enterprise Edition (J2EE), this textbook integrates technologies such as XML, JavaBeans, security, Java Database Connectivity (JDBC), JavaServer Pages (JSP), servlets, Remote Method Invocation (RMI), Enterprise JavaBeans™ (EJB) and design patterns into a production-quality system that allows developers to benefit from the leverage and platform independence Java 2 Enterprise Edition provides. The book also features the development of a complete, end-to-end e-business solution using advanced Java technologies. Additional topics include Swing, Java 2D and 3D, XML, design patterns, CORBA, Jini™, JavaSpaces™, Jiro™, Java Management Extensions (JMX) and Peer-to-Peer networking with an introduction to JXTA. This textbook also introduces the Java 2 Micro Edition (J2ME™) for building applications for handheld and wireless devices using MIDP and MIDlets. Wireless technologies covered include WAP, WML and i-mode.

C# How to Program

BOOK / CD-ROM

©2002, 1568 pp., paper
(0-13-062221-4)

An exciting new addition to the How to Program series, *C# How to Program* provides a comprehensive introduction to Microsoft's new object-oriented language. C# builds on the skills already mastered by countless C++ and Java programmers, enabling them to create powerful Web applications and components—ranging from XML-based Web services on Microsoft's .NET platform to middle-tier business objects and system-level applications. *C# How to Program* begins with a strong foundation in the introductory and intermediate programming principles students will need in industry. It then explores such essential topics as object-oriented programming and exception handling. Graphical user interfaces are extensively covered, giving readers the tools to build compelling and fully interactive programs. Internet technologies such as XML, ADO .NET and Web services are also covered as well as topics including regular expressions, multithreading, networking, databases, files and data structures.

Also coming soon in the Deitels' .NET Series:

• *Visual C++ .NET How to Program*

Visual Basic .NET How to Program Second Edition

`BOOK / CD-ROM`

*©2002, 1400 pp., paper
(0-13-029363-6)*

Teach Visual Basic .NET programming from the ground up! This introduction of Microsoft's .NET Framework marks the beginning of major revisions to all of Microsoft's programming languages. This book provides a comprehensive introduction to the next version of Visual Basic—Visual Basic .NET—featuring extensive updates and increased functionality. *Visual Basic .NET How to Program, Second Edition* covers introductory programming techniques as well as more advanced topics, featuring enhanced treatment of developing Web-based applications. Other topics discussed include an extensive treatment of XML and wireless applications, databases, SQL and ADO .NET, Web forms, Web services and ASP .NET.

Also coming soon in the Deitels' .NET Series:

• *Visual C++ .NET How to Program*

C How to Program Third Edition

`BOOK / CD-ROM`

*©2001, 1253 pp., paper
(0-13-089572-5)*

Highly practical in approach, the Third Edition of the world's best-selling C text introduces the fundamentals of structured programming and software engineering and gets up to speed quickly. This comprehensive book not only covers the full C language, but also reviews library functions and introduces object-based and object-oriented programming in C++ and Java. The Third Edition includes a new 346-page introduction to Java 2 and the basics of GUIs, and the 298-page introduction to C++ has been updated to be consistent with the most current ANSI/ISO C++ standards. Plus, icons throughout the book point out valuable programming tips such as Common Programming Errors, Portability Tips and Testing and Debugging Tips.

C++ How to Program Fourth Edition

`BOOK / CD-ROM`

*©2003, 1400 pp., paper
(0-13-038474-7)*

The world's best selling C++ book is now even better! Designed for beginning through intermediate courses, this comprehensive, practical introduction to C++ includes hundreds of hands-on exercises, plus roughly 250 complete programs written and documented for easy learning. It also features exceptional insight into good programming practices, maximizing performance, avoiding errors, debugging and testing. The Fourth Edition features a new code-highlighting style that uses an alternate background color to focus the reader on new code elements in a program. The OOD/UML case study is upgraded to the latest UML standard, and includes significant improvements to the exception handling and operator overloading chapters. It features enhanced treatment of strings and arrays as objects using standard C++ classes, string and vector. It also retains every key concept and technique ANSI C++ developers need to master, including control structures, functions, arrays, pointers and strings, classes and data abstraction, operator overloading, inheritance, virtual functions, polymorphism, I/O, templates, exception handling, file processing, data structures and more. *C++ How to Program Fourth Edition* includes a detailed introduction to Standard Template Library (STL) containers, container adapters, algorithms and iterators.

Getting Started with Microsoft® Visual C++™ 6 with an Introduction to MFC

`BOOK / CD-ROM`

©2000, 163 pp., paper (0-13-016147-0)

Internet & World Wide Web How to Program, Second Edition

`BOOK / CD-ROM`

*©2002, 1428 pp., paper
(0-13-030897-8)*

The revision of this ground-breaking book in the Deitels' *How to Program Series* offers a thorough treatment of

programming concepts that yield visible or audible results in Web pages and Web-based applications. This book discusses effective Web-based design, server- and client-side scripting, multitier Web-based applications development, ActiveX® controls and electronic commerce essentials. This book offers an alternative to traditional programming courses using markup languages (such as XHTML, Dynamic HTML and XML) and scripting languages (such as JavaScript, VBScript, Perl/CGI, Python and PHP) to teach the fundamentals of programming "wrapped in the metaphor of the Web."

Updated material on **www.deitel.com** and **www.prenhall.com/deitel** provides additional resources for instructors who want to cover Microsoft® or non-Microsoft technologies. The Web site includes an extensive treatment of Netscape® 6 and alternate versions of the code from the Dynamic HTML chapters that will work with non-Microsoft environments as well.

Wireless Internet & Mobile Business How to Program

©2002, 1292 pp., paper (0-13-062226-5)

While the rapid expansion of wireless technologies, such as cell phones, pagers and personal digital assistants (PDAs), offers many new opportunities for businesses and programmers, it also presents numerous challenges related to issues such as security and standardization. This book offers a thorough treatment of both the management and technical aspects of this growing area, including coverage of current practices and future trends. The first half explores the business issues surrounding wireless technology and mobile business, including an overview of existing and developing communication technologies and the application of business principles to wireless devices. It also discusses location-based services and location-identifying technologies, a topic that is revisited throughout the book. Wireless payment, security, legal and social issues, international communications and more are also discussed. The book then turns to programming for the wireless Internet, exploring topics such as WAP (including 2.0), WML, WMLScript, XML, XHTML™, wireless Java programming (J2ME)™, Web Clipping and more. Other topics covered include career resources, wireless marketing, accessibility, Palm™, PocketPC, Windows CE,

i-mode, Bluetooth, MIDP, MIDlets, ASP, Microsoft .NET Mobile Framework, BREW™, multimedia, Flash™ and VBScript.

Python How to Program

BOOK / CD-ROM

©2002, 1376 pp., paper (0-13-092361-3)

This exciting new book provides a comprehensive introduction to Python— a powerful object-oriented programming language with clear syntax and the ability to bring together various technologies quickly and easily. This book covers introductory-programming techniques and more advanced topics such as graphical user interfaces, databases, wireless Internet programming, networking, security, process management, multithreading, XHTML, CSS, PSP and multimedia. Readers will learn principles that are applicable to both systems development and Web programming. The book features the consistent and applied pedagogy that the *How to Program Series* is known for, including the Deitels' signature LIVE-CODE™ Approach, with thousands of lines of code in hundreds of working programs; hundreds of valuable programming tips identified with icons throughout the text; an extensive set of exercises, projects and case studies; two-color four-way syntax coloring and much more.

e-Business & e-Commerce for Managers

©2001, 794 pp., cloth (0-13-032364-0)

This comprehensive overview of building and managing e-businesses explores topics such as the decision to bring a business online, choosing a business model, accepting payments, marketing strategies and security, as well as many other important issues (such as career resources). The book features Web resources and online demonstrations that supplement the text and direct readers to additional materials. The book also includes an appendix that develops a complete Web-based shopping-cart application using HTML, JavaScript, VBScript, Active Server Pages, ADO, SQL, HTTP, XML and XSL. Plus, company-specific sections provide "real-world" examples of the concepts presented in the book.

XML How to Program

BOOK / CD-ROM

©2001, 934 pp., paper (0-13-028417-3)

This book is a comprehensive guide to programming in XML. It teaches how to use XML to create customized tags and includes chapters that address standard custom-markup languages for science and technology, multimedia, commerce and many other fields. Concise introductions to Java, JavaServer Pages, VBScript, Active Server Pages and Perl/CGI provide readers with the essentials of these programming languages and server-side development technologies to enable them to work effectively with XML. The book also covers cutting-edge topics such as XSL, DOM™ and SAX, plus a real-world e-commerce case study and a complete chapter on Web accessibility that addresses Voice XML. It includes tips such as Common Programming Errors, Software Engineering Observations, Portability Tips and Debugging Hints. Other topics covered include XHTML, CSS, DTD, schema, parsers, XPath, XLink, namespaces, XBase, XInclude, XPointer, XSLT, XSL Formatting Objects, JavaServer Pages, XForms, topic maps, X3D, MathML, OpenMath, CML, BML, CDF, RDF, SVG, Cocoon, WML, XBRL and BizTalk™ and SOAP™ Web resources.

Perl How to Program

BOOK / CD-ROM

©2001, 1057 pp., paper (0-13-028418-1)

This comprehensive guide to Perl programming emphasizes the use of the Common Gateway Interface (CGI) with Perl to create powerful, dynamic multi-tier Web-based client/server applications. The book begins with a clear and careful introduction to programming concepts at a level suitable for beginners, and proceeds through advanced topics such as references and complex data structures. Key Perl topics such as regular expressions and string manipulation are covered in detail. The authors address important and topical issues such as object-oriented programming, the Perl database interface (DBI), graphics and security. Also included is a treatment of XML, a bonus chapter introducing the Python programming language, supplemental material on career resources and a complete chapter on Web accessibility. The text includes tips such as Common Programming Errors, Software Engineering Observations, Portability Tips and Debugging Hints.

e-Business & e-Commerce How to Program

BOOK / CD-ROM

©2001, 1254 pp., paper (0-13-028419-X)

This innovative book explores programming technologies for developing Web-based e-business and e-commerce solutions, and covers e-business and e-commerce models and business issues. Readers learn a full range of options, from "build-your-own" to turnkey solutions. The book examines scores of the top e-businesses (examples include Amazon, eBay, Priceline, Travelocity, etc.), explaining the technical details of building successful e-business and e-commerce sites and their underlying business premises. Learn how to implement the dominant e-commerce models—shopping carts, auctions, name-your-own-price, comparison shopping and bots/ intelligent agents—by using markup languages (HTML, Dynamic HTML and XML), scripting languages (JavaScript, VBScript and Perl), server-side technologies (Active Server Pages and Perl/CGI) and database (SQL and ADO), security and online payment technologies. Updates are regularly posted to `www.deitel.com` and the book includes a CD-ROM with software tools, source code and live links.

PEARSON PTR interactive
We make it click.

Complete Training Courses

Each complete package includes the corresponding *How to Program Series* book and interactive multimedia CD-ROM Cyber Classroom. *Complete Training Courses* are perfect for anyone interested Web and e-commerce programming. They are affordable resources for college students and professionals learning programming for the first time or reinforcing their knowledge.

Each *Complete Training Course* is compatible with Windows 95, Windows 98, Windows NT and Windows 2000 and includes the following features:

Intuitive Browser-Based Interface

You'll love the *Complete Training Courses'* new browser-based interface, designed to be easy and accessible to anyone who's ever used a Web browser. Every *Complete Training Course* features the full text, illustrations and program listings of its corresponding *How to Program* book—all in full color—with full-text searching and hyperlinking.

Further Enhancements to the Deitels' Signature LIVE-CODE™ Approach

Every code sample from the main text can be found in the interactive, multimedia, CD-ROM-based *Cyber Classrooms* included in the *Complete Training Courses*. Syntax coloring of code is included for the *How to Program* books that are published in full color. Even the recent two-color and one-color books use effective multi-way syntax shading. The *Cyber Classroom* products always are in full color.

Audio Annotations

Hours of detailed, expert audio descriptions of thousands of lines of code help reinforce concepts.

Easily Executable Code

With one click of the mouse, you can execute the code or save it to your hard drive to manipulate using the programming environment of your choice. With selected *Complete Training Courses*, you can also load all of the code into a development environment such as Microsoft® Visual C++™, enabling you to modify and execute the programs with ease.

Abundant Self-Assessment Material

Practice exams test your understanding with hundreds of test questions and answers in addition to those found in the main text. Hundreds of self-review questions, all with answers, are drawn from the text; as are hundreds of programming exercises, half with answers.

www.phptr.com/phptrinteractive

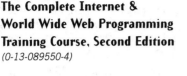

Future Publications

Here are some new titles we are considering for 2002/2003 release:

Computer Science Series: *Operating Systems 3/e, Data Structures in C++, Data Structures in Java, Theory and Principles of Database Systems.*

Database Series: *Oracle, SQL Server, MySQL.*

Internet and Web Programming Series: *Open Source Software Development: Apache, Linux, MySQL and PHP.*

Programming Series: *Flash™.*

.NET Programming Series: *ADO .NET with Visual Basic .NET, ASP .NET with Visual Basic .NET, ADO .NET with C#, ASP .NET with C#.*

Object Technology Series: *OOAD with the UML, Design Patterns, Java™ and XML.*

Advanced Java™ Series: *JDBC, Java 2 Enterprise Edition, Java Media Framework (JMF), Java Security and Java Cryptography (JCE), Java Servlets, Java2D and Java3D, JavaServer Pages™ (JSP), JINI and Java 2 Micro Edition™ (J2ME).*

DEITEL™ BUZZ ONLINE Newsletter

The Deitel and Associates, Inc. free opt-in newsletter includes:

- Updates and commentary on industry trends and developments
- Resources and links to articles from our published books and upcoming publications.
- Information on the Deitel publishing plans, including future publications and product-release schedules
- Support for instructors
- Resources for students
- Information on Deitel Corporate Training

To sign up for the Deitel™ Buzz Online newsletter, visit `www.deitel.com/newsletter/subscribe.html`.

E-Books

We are committed to providing our content in traditional print formats and in emerging electronic formats, such as e-books, to fulfill our customers' needs. Our R&D teams are currently exploring many leading-edge solutions.

Visit `www.deitel.com` and read the DEITEL™ BUZZ ONLINE for periodic updates.

Turn the page to find out more about Deitel & Associates!

TABLE 18-1
The Planets.

Planet	Symbol	Mean distance from sun, earth = 1[a]	Diameter, thousands of km	Mass, earth = 1[b]	Mean density, water = 1[c]	Surface gravity, earth = 1[d]	Escape speed, km/s[e]	Period of rotation on axis	Period of revolution around sun	Eccentricity of orbit[h]	Inclination of orbit to ecliptic[i]	Known satellites
Mercury	☿	0.39	4.9	0.055	5.4	0.38	4.3	59 days	88 days	0.21	7°00'	0
Venus	♀	0.72	12.1	0.82	5.25	0.90	10.4	243 days[f]	225 days	0.01	3°24'	0
Earth	⊕	1.00	12.7	1.00	5.52	1.00	11.2	24 h	365 days	0.02	—	1
Mars	♂	1.52	6.8	0.11	3.93	0.38	5.0	24.5 h	687 days	0.09	1°51'	2
Jupiter	♃	5.20	143	318	1.33	2.6	60	10 h	11.9 yr	0.05	1°18'	14
Saturn	♄	9.54	120	95	0.71	1.2	36	10 h	29.5 yr	0.06	2°29'	17
Uranus	♅	19.2	51	15	1.27	1.1	22	16 h[g]	84 yr	0.05	0°46'	5
Neptune	♆	30.1	49	17	1.70	1.2	24	23 h	165 yr	0.01	1°46'	2
Pluto	♇	39.4	4	0.002	0.4	0.02	1.2	6 days	248 yr	0.25	17°12'	1

[a] The mean earth-sun distance is called the *astronomical unit*, where 1 AU = 1.496×10^8 km.
[b] The earth's mass is 5.98×10^{24} kg.
[c] The density of water is 1 g/cm³ = 10^3 kg/m³.
[d] The acceleration of gravity at the earth's surface is 9.8 m/s².
[e] Speed needed for permanent escape from the planet's gravitational field.
[f] Venus rotates in the opposite direction from the other planets.
[g] The axis of rotation of Uranus is only 8° from the plane of its orbit.
[h] The difference between the minimum and maximum distances from the sun divided by the average distance.
[i] The ecliptic is the plane of the earth's orbit.

THE
PHYSICAL
UNIVERSE

McGRAW-HILL BOOK COMPANY

New York
St. Louis
San Francisco
Auckland
Bogotá
Caracas
Hamburg
Lisbon
London
Madrid
Mexico
Milan
Montreal
New Delhi
Paris
San Juan
São Paulo
Singapore
Sydney
Tokyo
Toronto

THE PHYSICAL UNIVERSE

KONRAD B. KRAUSKOPF

Professor of Geochemistry Emeritus
Stanford University

ARTHUR BEISER

FIFTH EDITION

THE PHYSICAL UNIVERSE

567890 HDHD 99876543210

ISBN 0-07-035484-7

See Acknowledgments on page 749. Copyrights included on this page by reference.

This book was set in Cheltenham Light by Progressive Typographers, Inc.
The editors were Stephen Zlotnick and James R. Belser;
the designer was Jo Jones;
the production supervisor was Joe Campanella.
The photo editor was Rosemarie Rossi.
New drawings were done by J & R Services, Inc.
Halliday Lithograph Corporation was printer and binder.

Library of Congress Cataloging in Publication Data

Krauskopf, Konrad B., date
    The physical universe.

    Includes index.
    1. Science. I. Beiser, Arthur. II. Title.
Q161.2.K7 1986   500.2   85-13216
ISBN 0-07-035484-7

CONTENTS

CONTENTS

CONTENTS

THE TEXT

Our aim in writing *The Physical Universe* is to present, as simply and clearly as possible, the essentials of physics, chemistry, geology, and astronomy.

Because these sciences are so extensive and because we assume a minimum of preparation on the part of the reader, our choice of material and its degree of development has to be limited. We emphasize the basic concepts of each discipline and their role in understanding the natural world, and try to convey something of the historical and philosophical development of the physical sciences as well. We hope the reader will acquire some feeling for both the inductive and deductive approaches of the scientist as a result.

Of the various possible ways to organize a book of this kind, we chose the one that provides the most logical progression of ideas, so that each new topic builds on the ones that came before.

Our first concern in *The Physical Universe* is with motion, how it is described and what factors influence moving bodies. Gravitation, energy, and momentum are carefully examined. Matter in its three phases now draws our attention, and we pursue this theme from the kinetic-molecular model to the laws of thermodynamics. We continue with a grounding in electricity and magnetism that culminates in the electromagnetic theory of light. Then comes a discussion of atoms, atomic structure, the nucleus, and elementary particles. Quantum-mechanical ideas play an important part here. The periodic table takes us to chemistry, which is surveyed through organic chemistry and the chemistry of life.

The transition to the study of the planet on which we live is made with a look at the oceans of air and water that cover it. From there we proceed to the materials of the earth, its ever-evolving crust, and its mysterious interior. After a narrative of the earth's geological history we go on to what we see in the sky and what we know about our immediate neighbors in space. Next the sun, the monarch of the solar system and the provider of nearly all our energy, commands our notice. We then broaden our astronomical sights to include the other stars, both individually and as members of those immense assemblies called galaxies. An inquiry into the evolution of the universe is our last major topic, and we end with the origin of the earth and the likelihood of other inhabited planets in the universe.

We consider it neither possible nor desirable to exclude some quantitative discussions, but these are kept quite simple and supplement rather than dominate the exposition.

STUDENT AIDS

An important feature of *The Physical Universe* is the variety of aids provided to help the reader. These aids make up a built-in study guide that will benefit everyone using the book.

1. *Marginal Notes*. Significant ideas are flagged by brief notes next to their mention in the text. A chapter can be reviewed by just running down its marginal notes.
2. *Important Terms and Formulas*. The meanings of important terms are given at the end of each chapter, which also serves as a chapter summary. A list of formulas needed to solve problems based on the chapter material is given as well.
3. *Multiple-Choice Exercises*. An average chapter has 26 multiple-choice exercises (with answers) that act as a quick check on understanding. Correct answers provide reinforcement and encouragement, and incorrect ones identify areas of weakness.
4. *Questions and Problems*. An average chapter has 40 questions and problems that range from quite easy to moderately challenging. At the back of the book are answers for the odd-numbered questions and complete solutions for the odd-numbered problems. Together with the worked examples in the text, over 400 model answers are provided to typical questions and problems.
5. *Math Refresher*. Although the mathematical level of the book has been kept as low as possible, some algebra is necessary and is reviewed here. Powers-of-ten notation for small and large numbers is carefully explained. This section is self-contained and can provide all the math background needed.
6. *Glossary*. A comprehensive glossary of the basic terms of physics, chemistry, geology, and astronomy concludes the text.

THIS EDITION

In preparing the fifth edition of *The Physical Universe* the entire text was brought up-to-date and revised in the light of classroom experience with the previous edition. We tried to make the book more interesting and the detailed arguments easier to grasp. In particular, the material on physics and chemistry was largely rewritten with the more difficult calculations omitted to make the text more accessible to nontechnical students. The transition from physics to chemistry was made sharper than before in response to requests from users of the fourth edition.

More attention is now paid to the problem of energy supply, both in the near and distant futures, including its environmental aspects. Our aim here and elsewhere is to help prepare the reader for membership in a technological society as well as to be able to follow the progress of science in understanding the universe of which we are part.

Other topics whose treatment is expanded include elementary particles and fundamental interactions, polymers, climatic change, biological extinctions and the disappearance of the dinosaurs, properties of the planets, and the origin and possible fate of the universe. The primacy of observation and experiment in science continues to be emphasized throughout. The new *Introduction* is designed to help orient readers new to science to the scientific approach to the natural world.

To make the reader's task easier, the number of illustrations is increased to nearly 600, about a third of them new, for this edition. Many photographs, including some in full color, supplement the two-color drawings. More exercises, questions, and problems are provided for a total of over 1300. The Instructor's Manual, too, is considerably expanded.

ACKNOWLEDGMENTS

We have had the benefit of comments by Frank Cabrera, Benedict College (South Carolina); Richard A. Cannon, Southeast Missouri State University; Carl O. Clark, South Carolina State College; Duke N. Dayton, Miami-Dade Community College; Lucille B. Garmon, West Georgia College; R. W. Housley, West Georgia College; Donald K. Marchand, Jr., Old Dominion University; Lanny J. Reed, Northeastern Oklahoma State University; and Aaron W. Todd, Middle Tennessee State University. Their generous help was of great value and is much appreciated.

Readers who have suggestions for improving the book are invited to send them to us in care of the publisher.

Konrad B. Krauskopf

Arthur Beiser

INTRODUCTION

All of us belong to two worlds. One is the world of people, the human family. The other is the world of nature, the physical universe of matter and energy and the biological universe of living things.

As members of the world of people, we take an interest in human events of the past and present and find such subjects as politics and economics worth knowing about. As members of the world of nature, we owe ourselves no less an acquaintance with the physical and biological sciences which seek to understand this world.

It is the purpose of this book to survey what the physical sciences of physics, chemistry, geology, and astronomy have to tell us about atoms and molecules, planets and stars, and everything in between. No single volume can cover everything significant in this vast span, but the basic ideas of each discipline can be summarized along with the raw material of observation and reasoning that led to them.

The physical universe, like the world of people, is always changing, so there is plenty of history on a grand scale here. A lot is known about what the universe, and the earth as part of it, were like long ago, and some strong suspicions of what they will be like in the future.

Like any voyage into the unknown, the exploration of nature is an adventure. This book is a record of that adventure, and contains many tales of wonder and discovery. The search for knowledge is far from over, with no end of exciting things still to be found. What some of these things might be and where they are being looked for are part of the story in the chapters to come.

Scientists study nature in different ways. Some are quite direct: a geologist takes a rock sample to his laboratory and, by inspection and analysis, establishes what it is made of, how it was formed, and when. Other methods are indirect: nobody has ever visited the center of the earth or ever will, but by putting together clues from various sources with a lot of thought, it is almost certain that the earth has a core of molten iron.

The words "almost certain" are important. Science is a living body of knowledge, not a set of frozen ideas. Nothing is sacred in science except the constant testing of its findings, which are accepted only if they have been thoroughly checked and if predictions made from them come true. Even then it remains possible for new evidence to modify how earlier results are interpreted.

As an example, it was once believed that heat is an invisible, weightless fluid called "caloric." When a pot of water is placed over a fire, the water becomes hot supposedly because it absorbs caloric from the flames. When the water is taken off the fire, it cools down supposedly because caloric escapes from it. Most scientists of two centuries ago were sure that caloric really existed. But just rubbing two sticks together also produces heat. The more rubbing, the more heat, without limit. This behavior does not make sense in terms of caloric.

Eventually heat was found to be a form of energy, in particular the energy of random motion of the atoms and molecules of which all matter is composed. A pot of water still becomes hot when placed over a fire, but why it does so has nothing to do with an invisible fluid.

Caloric is now part of history. What about atoms and molecules? Is it possible that they, too, will turn out to be imaginary? The difference is that atoms and molecules can actually be detected and their properties studied, which is not the case with caloric. The modern concept of heat thus has a solid foundation. Much remains to be learned about atoms and molecules, but it is clear that they do exist and that their motions give rise to what we call heat.

Scientists are open about the details of their work, so others can follow their thinking and repeat their experiments and observations. Nothing is accepted only on the basis of personal authority or revelation, or because it is part of a religious or political doctrine. "Common sense" is not a valid argument, either: what counts are definite measurements and clear reasoning based on them, not vague notions that vary from person to person.

The power of the scientific approach is shown not only by its success in understanding the natural world but also by the success of the technology based on science. It is hard to think of any aspect of life today untouched in some way by science. The synthetic clothing we wear, the medicines that lengthen our lives, the cars and airplanes we travel in, the telephone, radio, and television by which we communicate — all are ultimately the products of a certain way of thinking. Curiosity and imagination belong to that way of thinking, but the most important part is that nothing is ever taken for granted but is always subject to test and change.

In the past, scientists were burned at the stake for daring to look at nature with their own eyes. Galileo, the first modern scientist, was forced by the Church under threat of torture to deny that the earth moves around the sun. Even today, attempts are being made to compel the teaching of religious beliefs (for instance, the story of the Creation as given in the Bible) under the name of science. Many people find religious beliefs important in their lives, but such beliefs are not part of science because they are matters of faith with principles that are meant to be accepted without question. Skepticism, on the other hand, is at the heart of science. To mix these two ways of looking at the world is good for neither, particularly if compulsion is involved. A free marketplace of ideas is one of the glories of our society, earned with great struggle, and all of us will be the losers if it is allowed to disappear.

1

FORCE AND MOTION

Where shall we begin our study of the physical universe? We want something basic, so what we learn will be useful in as many areas as possible. It should also be fairly simple, so we can follow the discussion even without a background in science. How atoms join together, why the earth is round, what makes the sun shine — these are too complicated for now and belong later in the book. A better plan is to start with the subject of motion: how things move and what makes them go faster or slower.

Everything in the universe is in nonstop movement, from the tiny particles inside atoms to the huge galaxies of stars far away in space. To understand the structure and evolution of the universe we must first classify and interpret the various kinds of motion. In fact, modern science began with Galileo's measurements of moving bodies, which showed how wrong ancient, untested beliefs could be. And an important chapter in the history of ideas was the conflict over how the members of the solar system (sun, moon, and planets) move, whether in orbits around the sun or around the earth.

DESCRIBING MOTION

When something goes from one place to another, we say it *moves*. If it gets there quickly, we say it moves fast; if it takes a long time, we say it moves slowly. The first step in analyzing motion is to be able to say just how fast is fast and how slow is slow.

Speed

How fast is fast

The *speed* of a moving object is the rate at which it covers distance. The higher the speed, the faster it travels and the more distance it covers in a given period of time.

If a car goes through a distance of 40 miles in a time of 1 hour, its speed is 40 miles an hour. Such a speed is also called ''40 miles per hour,'' and is conveniently written 40 miles/hour.

What if the time interval is not exactly 1 hour? For instance, the car might travel 60 miles in 2 hours on another trip. The general formula for speed is distance divided by time:

All motion is relative to a chosen frame of reference. Here the photographer has turned the camera to keep pace with the boys, and relative to them the parked cars are moving. There is no fixed frame of reference in nature, and therefore no such thing as ''absolute motion'': all motion is relative to something.

Speed is rate of change of position

$$\text{Speed} = \frac{\text{distance}}{\text{time}}$$

Hence the car's speed in the second case is

$$\text{Speed} = \frac{\text{distance}}{\text{time}} = \frac{60 \text{ miles}}{2 \text{ hours}} = 30 \text{ miles/hour}$$

The same formula works for times of less than a full hour. The speed of a car that covers 24 miles in half an hour is, since $\frac{1}{2}$ hour $= 0.5$ hour,

$$\text{Speed} = \frac{\text{distance}}{\text{time}} = \frac{24 \text{ miles}}{0.5 \text{ hour}} = 48 \text{ miles/hour}$$

Average speed and instantaneous speed

These speeds are all *average* speeds, because we do not know the details of how the cars moved during their trips. They probably went slower than the average during some periods, faster at others, and even came to a stop now and then at traffic lights. What the speedometer of a car shows is its *instantaneous* speed, that is, how fast it is going at each moment.

For the sake of convenience, quantities such as distance, time, and speed are often abbreviated by letters of the alphabet. By custom

$$d = \text{distance}$$

$$t = \text{time}$$

$$v = \text{speed}$$

In terms of these symbols the formula for speed becomes just

$$v = \frac{d}{t}$$

The formula for speed can be rewritten in two other ways. Suppose we want to know how far a car whose average speed is v goes in a time t. To find out, we must solve $v = d/t$ for the distance d. According to one of the rules of algebra (see the Math Refresher at the back of this book), a quantity that divides one side of an equation can be shifted so it multiplies the other side. Thus

$$v = \frac{d}{t}$$

becomes

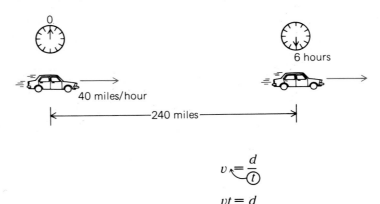

FIG. 1-1

A car whose average speed is 40 miles/hour travels 240 miles in 6 hours.

$$v = \frac{d}{t}$$

$$vt = d$$

which is the same as

Distance covered in a given time

$$d = vt$$

Distance = (speed)(time)

How far does a car travel in 6 hours when its average speed is 40 miles/hour? We put the given quantities into the above formula to find that (Fig. 1-1)

$$d = vt = \left(40\ \frac{\text{miles}}{\text{hour}}\right)(6\ \text{hours}) = 240 \left(\frac{\text{miles}}{\text{hour}}\right)(\text{hours}) = 240\ \text{miles}$$

We note that, since hours/hour = 1, the hours cancel out to give just miles in the answer.

In another situation we might want to know how much time something moving at a certain speed needs to cover a given distance. In other words, we know v and d and want to find the time t. The procedure here is to solve $d = vt$ for the time t. From basic algebra we know that something that multiplies one side of an equation can be shifted so it divides the other side. What we do, then, is shift the v in the formula $d = vt$ to divide the d:

$$d = v\,t$$

$$\frac{d}{v} = t$$

which is the same as

Time needed to cover a given distance

$$t = \frac{d}{v}$$

$$\text{Time} = \frac{\text{distance}}{\text{speed}}$$

How much time is needed for a car whose average speed is 40 miles/hour to travel 100 miles? The answer is

$$t = \frac{d}{v} = \frac{100 \text{ miles}}{40 \text{ miles/hour}} = 2.5 \frac{\text{miles}}{\text{miles/hour}}$$

$$= 2.5 \frac{(\text{miles})(\text{hour})}{\text{miles}} = 2.5 \text{ hours}$$

We notice that

$$\frac{1}{1/(\text{hour})} = \text{hour}$$

Units, such as miles and hours, are always carried along in calculations and treated like ordinary algebraic quantities.

Units

How many of what

When we say that the distance between Chicago and Minneapolis is 405 miles, what we are really doing is comparing this distance with a certain standard length called the mile. Standard quantities such as the mile are known as *units*. The result of every measurement thus has two parts. One is a number (405 for the Chicago–Minneapolis distance) to answer the question "How many?" The other is a unit (the mile in this case) to answer the question "Of what?"

The most widely used units today are those of the International System, abbreviated SI after its French name Système International d'Unités. This set of units is the current version of the metric system, which was introduced in France two centuries ago to replace the hodgepodge of traditional units that were then making commerce and engineering difficult. Examples of SI units are the *meter* (m) for length, the *second* (s) for time, the *kilogram* (kg) for mass, the *joule* (J) for energy, and the *watt* (W) for power.

SI units are used universally by scientists and in most of the world in everyday life as well. Although the British system of units, with its familiar foot and pound, remains in common use in English-speaking countries, it is on the way out and before long will have been replaced by the SI. Since this is a book about science, only SI units will be used here.

The great advantage of SI units is that their subdivisions and multiples are in steps of 10, 100, 1000, and so on, in contrast to the irregularity of British units. In the case of lengths, for instance (Fig. 1-2),

Measurement requires units

SI units

Calculations are easy with SI units

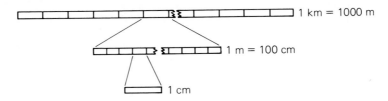

1 km = 1000 m

1 m = 100 cm

1 cm

FIG. 1-2
There are 1000 meters in a kilometer
and 100 centimeters in a meter.

$$1 \text{ meter (m)} = 100 \text{ centimeters (cm)}$$

$$1 \text{ kilometer (km)} = 1000 \text{ meters}$$

whereas

$$1 \text{ foot (ft)} = 12 \text{ inches (in.)}$$

$$1 \text{ mile (mi)} = 5280 \text{ feet}$$

Table 1-1 is a list of conversion factors that make it easy to change a length expressed in one system to its equivalent in the other. (More conversion factors are given inside the back cover of the book.) We note from the table that there are about $2\frac{1}{2}$ centimeters in an inch, so a centimeter is roughly the width of a shirt button; a meter is a few inches longer than 3 feet; and a kilometer is nearly $\frac{2}{3}$ mile.

TABLE 1-1
Conversion Factors for Length.

Multiply	By	To get
Centimeters	$0.394 \frac{\text{in.}}{\text{cm}}$	Inches
Meters	$39.4 \frac{\text{in.}}{\text{m}}$	Inches
Meters	$3.28 \frac{\text{ft}}{\text{m}}$	Feet
Kilometers	$0.621 \frac{\text{mi}}{\text{km}}$	Miles
Inches	$2.54 \frac{\text{cm}}{\text{in.}}$	Centimeters
Feet	$30.5 \frac{\text{cm}}{\text{ft}}$	Centimeters
Feet	$0.305 \frac{\text{m}}{\text{ft}}$	Meters
Miles	$1.61 \frac{\text{km}}{\text{mi}}$	Kilometers

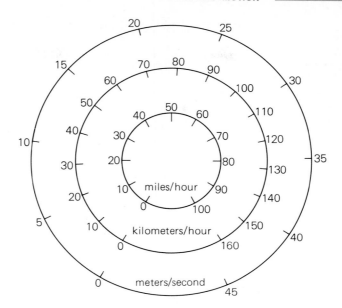

FIG. 1-3
A speedometer calibrated in miles/hour, kilometers/hour, and meters/second, where 100 mi/h = 161 km/h = 44.7 m/s. The speedometer of a car, boat, or airplane indicates its instantaneous speed.

How to convert units

For practice, let us convert the 405-mi distance between Chicago and Minneapolis into km. From Table 1-1, the conversion factor we need is 1.61 km/mi, so

$$d = (405 \text{ mi}) \left(1.61 \frac{\text{km}}{\text{mi}} \right) = 652 \text{ km}$$

Figure 1-3 compares speeds expressed in miles/hour, kilometers/hour, and meters/second.

Acceleration

Vroom!

Acceleration is rate of change of speed

When the speed of something changes, it is said to be *accelerated*. As in Fig. 1-4, the change can be an increase or a decrease in its speed — the moving object can be going faster and faster, or slower and slower. A change in direction, too, is an acceleration, as discussed in Chap. 2. In this chapter we will stick to straight-line motion where accelerations are increases or decreases in speed.

The rate of change of speed is called *acceleration*. That is,

$$a = \frac{v - v_0}{t}$$

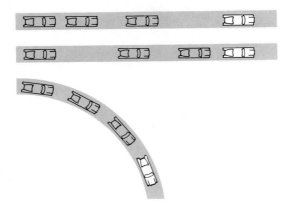

FIG. 1-4
Three cases of accelerated motion, showing successive positions of a body after equal periods of time. At the top the intervals between the positions of the body increase in length because the body is traveling faster and faster. Below it the intervals decrease in length because the body is slowing down. At the bottom the intervals are the same in length because the speed is constant, but the direction of motion is constantly changing.

$$\text{Acceleration} = \frac{\text{change in speed}}{\text{time interval}}$$

where the symbols mean the following:

$a =$ acceleration
$t =$ time interval
$v_0 =$ speed at start of time interval = initial speed
$v =$ speed at end of time interval = final speed

Suppose a car goes from 15 m/s (about 34 mi/h) to 25 m/s (about 56 mi/h) in 20 s when its gas pedal is pressed hard (Fig. 1-5). Here

$$v_0 = 15 \text{ m/s} \qquad v = 25 \text{ m/s} \qquad t = 20 \text{ s}$$

and so the car's acceleration is

$$a = \frac{v - v_0}{t} = \frac{25 \text{ m/s} - 15 \text{ m/s}}{20 \text{ s}}$$

$$= \frac{10 \text{ m/s}}{20 \text{ s}} = 0.5 \frac{\text{m/s}}{\text{s}} = 0.5 \text{ m/s}^2$$

FIG. 1-5
A car whose speed increases from 15 m/s to 25 m/s in 20 s has an acceleration of 0.5 m/s².

It is customary to write (m/s)/s (meters per second per second) as just m/s² (meters per second squared) since

Units of acceleration

$$\frac{m/s}{s} = \frac{m}{(s)(s)} = \frac{m}{s^2}$$

The above result means that the speed of the car increases by 0.5 m/s during each second the acceleration continues.

What is the final speed of something that is accelerated for a certain period of time? To find out, we rewrite the formula for acceleration as follows:

$$a = \frac{v - v_0}{t}$$

$$at = v - v_0$$

Now we add v_0 to both sides of the equation to give

$$at + v_0 = v - v_0 + v_0 = v$$

which is the same as

$$v = v_0 + at$$

Final speed of accelerated object

Final speed = initial speed + (acceleration)(time interval)

This result says that the final speed v is equal to the initial speed v_0 at the start of the acceleration plus the value a of the acceleration multiplied by the time interval t involved (Fig. 1-6).

Let us imagine that we press on the brakes of a car when its speed is 25 m/s. As a result, the car slows down, which means that it is accelerated. Because the acceleration leads to a decrease in speed, it is considered negative. If the car slows down by 5 m/s in each second the brakes are applied, its acceleration is -5 m/s². (A negative acceleration is sometimes called a *deceleration*.) In 3 s the car's speed will have dropped to

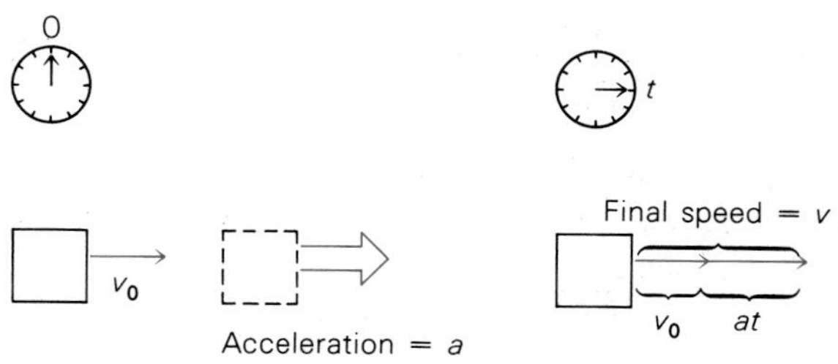

Negative acceleration signifies a decrease in speed

FIG. 1-6

The final speed of an object whose initial speed is v_0 is $v_0 + at$ when it has undergone the acceleration a for the period of time t.

$$v = v_0 + at = 25 \text{ m/s} + (-5 \text{ m/s}^2)(3 \text{ s})$$
$$= 25 \text{ m/s} - (5 \text{ m/s}^2)(3 \text{ s})$$
$$= 25 \text{ m/s} - 15 \text{ m/s} = 10 \text{ m/s}$$

Since the car is losing 5 m/s of speed each second, it will come to a stop in 5 s from the time the brakes are applied. We note that

$$\left(\frac{\text{m}}{\text{s}^2}\right)(\cancel{\text{s}}) = \left[\frac{\text{m}}{(\text{s})(\cancel{\text{s}})}\right](\cancel{\text{s}}) = \frac{\text{m}}{\text{s}}$$

ACCELERATION OF GRAVITY

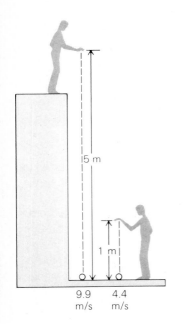

FIG. 1-7
Falling bodies are accelerated downward. A stone dropped from a height of 5 m strikes the ground with a speed more than double that of a stone dropped from a height of 1 m.

Acceleration of gravity is independent of direction of motion

The most familiar acceleration is that of gravity. When something is dropped, it does not fall at a constant speed but goes faster and faster. The higher a stone is when it is dropped, the greater its speed when it reaches the ground (Fig. 1-7). If we jump off a table, we strike the floor with more impact than if we jump off a chair.

Free Fall

What goes up must come down

Under ideal conditions, all falling bodies near the earth's surface have exactly the same acceleration. Large objects and small, heavy ones and light, all have a downward acceleration of 9.8 m/s². This acceleration is usually abbreviated g:

Acceleration of gravity $= g = 9.8$ m/s²

In British units, the value of g is 32 ft/s².

Something that drops from rest (that is, not thrown upward or downward) has a speed of 9.8 m/s at the end of the first second, a speed of 19.6 m/s at the end of the next second, and so on (Fig. 1-8). An imaginary stone dropped from the roof of the Pan Am Building in New York City, which is 253 m above street level, takes 7.2 s to reach the ground. The stone's speed when it reaches the ground is, since its initial speed is $v_0 = 0$,

Final speed = initial speed + (acceleration)(time interval)
$$v = v_0 + at = v_0 + gt$$
$$= 0 + (9.8 \text{ m/s}^2)(7.2 \text{ s}) = 71 \text{ m/s}$$

The downward acceleration g is the same whether an object is just dropped or is thrown upward, downward, or sideways. If a ball is held in the air and

FIG. 1-8
All falling objects have a downward acceleration of 9.8 m/s².

Time

0

1 s

2 s

3 s

4 s

Speed

0

9.8 m/s

19.6 m/s

29.4 m/s

39.2 m/s

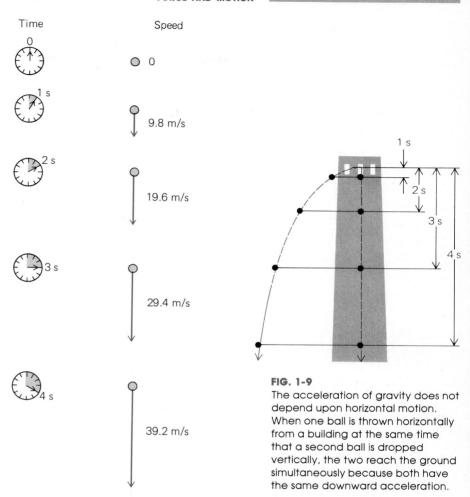

1 s
2 s
3 s
4 s

FIG. 1-9
The acceleration of gravity does not depend upon horizontal motion. When one ball is thrown horizontally from a building at the same time that a second ball is dropped vertically, the two reach the ground simultaneously because both have the same downward acceleration.

FIG. 1-10
When a ball is thrown upward, its downward acceleration reduces its original speed until it comes to a momentary stop. This is the top of its path, and it then begins to fall as if it had been dropped from there. The ball is shown after equal time intervals.

dropped, it goes faster and faster until it hits the ground. If it is thrown horizontally, the ball's motion is a combination of the original horizontal movement plus the downward acceleration of gravity. The result (Fig. 1-9) is a curved path that becomes steeper as the downward speed increases.

When a ball is thrown upward, as in Fig. 1-10, the effect of the downward acceleration of gravity is at first to reduce its upward speed. The upward speed decreases steadily until finally it is zero. This corresponds to the top of the ball's path, when it is momentarily at rest. The ball then begins to fall at ever-increasing speed, exactly as though it had been dropped from the highest point. Interestingly enough, something thrown upward at a certain speed v_0 will return to its starting place with the same final speed v_0, now in the downward direction.

What happens when a ball is thrown downward? Now the ball's original speed is steadily increased by the downward acceleration of gravity. When the ball reaches the ground, its final speed will be the sum of its original speed and the speed due to the acceleration.

Air Resistance

Why raindrops don't kill

Air resistance keeps falling things from developing the full acceleration of gravity. Without this resistance raindrops would reach the ground with bulletlike speeds, and even a light shower would be dangerous.

In air, a stone falls faster than a feather because air resistance affects it less. In a vacuum, however, there is no air, and stone and feather fall with the same acceleration of 9.8 m/s² (Fig. 1-11).

The faster something moves, the more the air in its path resists its motion. At 100 km/h (62 mi/h), the drag force on a car due to air resistance is about 5 times as great as the drag force at 50 km/h (31 mi/h). In the case of a falling object, the air resistance increases with its speed until the object cannot go any faster. It then continues to drop at a constant *terminal speed* that depends on its size and shape and on how heavy it is. A person in free fall has a terminal speed of about 54 m/s

Terminal speed of a falling object

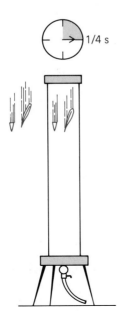
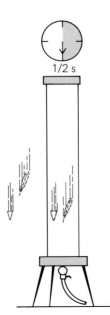

FIG. 1-11

In a vacuum all bodies fall with the same acceleration.

The terminal speed of a sky diver is considerably reduced when his parachute opens, which permits a safe landing.

(120 mi/h), but with an open parachute the terminal speed of only about 6.3 m/s (14 mi/h) permits a safe landing.

Why clouds stay aloft

A cloud consists of tiny water droplets or ice crystals whose terminal speeds are so small, often 1 cm/s or less, that very little updraft is needed to keep them suspended indefinitely. However, when a cloud is rapidly cooled, the water droplets or ice crystals grow in size and weight until their terminal speeds become too great for updrafts to keep them aloft. The result is a fall of raindrops or snowflakes from the cloud.

Galileo

The first modern scientist

Galileo discovered that g is the same for all objects

The fact that, when air resistance is not an important factor, all objects near the earth's surface fall with the same acceleration was first clearly stated by Galileo Galilei (1564 – 1642). For greater accuracy with the primitive instruments of his time, Galileo measured the accelerations of balls rolling down an inclined plane rather than their accelerations in free fall, but his conclusions were perfectly general.

Aristotle's ideas

Galileo's findings directly contradicted the teachings of Aristotle, the famous philosopher of ancient Greece, which had been widely accepted until then. Aristotle's reasoning was based on a picture of the universe in which every kind of material had a ''natural'' place where it belonged and toward which it tried to

The Leaning Tower of Pisa. Although legend has it that Galileo dropped a bullet and a cannonball from this tower to show that all bodies fall with the same acceleration, his conclusions about the behavior of moving bodies actually came from experiments with inclined planes to permit accurate measurements of time and distance.

move. Thus fire rose "naturally" upward toward the sun and stars, whereas stones or pieces of wood were "earthy" and so fell downward toward their home in the earth. A big stone was more earthy than a small one and so ought to fall faster.

The basic ideas of Aristotle's universe — a stationary earth at the center of things, with its human population most important of all — fit well into Christian theology and were made part of Roman Catholic dogma in the writings of St. Thomas Aquinas and his followers. With such powerful backing, it is not surprising that Aristotle's views survived for nearly 2000 years. To challenge them in the early 1600s took a lot of courage.

Yet challenge them Galileo did. His habit of finding out for himself, rather than relying on the notions of Aristotle, caused him to lose his professorship at Pisa. This was only a momentary setback in a remarkable career, however. Galileo continued his work in other Italian cities, where his achievements, such as perfecting the telescope, brought him fame and where his personal charm won him friends among the ruling families of Italy.

Despite fame and friends, Galileo's continued criticisms of accepted ideas brought conflict with Church authorities. Most serious was his support of the idea that the earth and the other planets revolve around the sun. For many years he managed to avoid serious trouble, but finally, as an old man, he was taken before the Inquisition at Rome and forced, under threat of torture, to renounce his beliefs.

The most revolutionary new idea that Galileo introduced, which even the Inquisition could not destroy, was not a specific discovery but the general concept that knowledge about the world could be gained from observation and experiment. Aristotle had tried to explain the world by reasoning alone — reasoning based on what he supposed were self-evident principles, for instance that all materials seek to move toward their "natural" homes. Galileo, on the other hand, found out how falling objects actually behave with the help of a measuring stick and a timer. His experiments led to formulas that described how fast a falling body will move at different times after it is dropped and how far it will go in a given time. These formulas could be checked by further experiments. Galileo's findings turned out to be entirely different from what Aristotle thought ought to be true.

Conclusions linked to observation and experiment rather than to "self-evident" principles or religious beliefs are what distinguish modern science from all other methods of trying to understand the natural world.

Galileo was the first modern scientist because he drew his conclusions about nature from observation and experiment

INERTIA

Imagine a ball lying on a level table. Left alone, it stays where it is. Given a gentle push, the ball rolls a short way and then comes to a stop. The smoother the ball and the tabletop, the farther the ball rolls before stopping. Suppose we have a perfectly round ball and a perfectly smooth and level tabletop, and that no air is present to slow down the ball. If the table is infinitely long and we give the ball a push, will it ever stop rolling?

First Law of Motion

Constant speed is as natural as being at rest

There will never be a perfect ball and a perfect surface for it to roll on, of course. But we can come close. The result is that, as the resistance to its motion becomes less and less, the ball goes farther and farther after the same push. We can reasonably conclude that, under ideal conditions, the ball would keep rolling forever.

This conclusion was first reached by Galileo. Later it was stated by Isaac Newton as a general rule that has become known as Newton's *first law of motion:*

First law of motion

An object will continue in its state of rest or of motion in a straight line at constant speed if no net force acts on it.

An object never begins to move all by itself — a push or a pull is needed to start it off. But once it is moving, the object will continue going at constant speed in a straight line unless a force of some kind acts to bring it to a halt. Friction and air resistance are examples of such forces. Motion at constant speed in a straight line is just as natural as staying at rest.

Inertia

Resistance to change

All matter exhibits inertia

The resistance an object offers to any change in its state of rest or of uniform motion in a straight line is called *inertia*.

When a car begins to move, its riders seem to be pushed backward in their seats (Fig. 1-12). Actually, what is happening is that inertia is trying to keep their bodies in place relative to the ground while the car moves forward. When the car comes to a sudden stop, the riders now seem to be pushed forward. In this case, what is actually happening is that inertia is trying to keep their bodies moving forward.

Inertia is important because it gives us a way to measure the amount of matter in an object. Exactly what do we mean by "amount of matter"? The words seem clear enough, but when we think about it, we realize that in everyday life a number of different ideas are mixed together here. For instance, there is the notion of bulk, the feeling that one of the basic properties of matter is that it occupies space. However, under different circumstances the same sample of matter can have very different volumes — just consider how much steam even a spoonful of water can turn into — so this approach is not satisfactory.

Weight is gravitational pull of the earth

Another idea involved in our mental picture of matter is *weight*. In everyday life we measure the amount of matter in an object by just weighing it. A 2-pound (lb) chicken contains twice as much matter as a 1-lb chicken. The reason we cannot use weight to define quantity of matter is that *weight is the gravitational pull of the earth on an object*. This pull is not the same everywhere on the earth; it is less on mountaintops than at sea level, less near the equator than near the poles because the earth bulges slightly at the equator. These differences are not large, but they are real. A person who weighs 200 lb in Lima, Peru, would weigh nearly 1 lb more in Oslo, Norway. And out in space far from the earth, the same person would weigh nothing at all. It is not the amount of matter in the person that

FIG. 1-12
(a) When a car suddenly starts to move, the inertia of the passengers tends to keep them at rest relative to the earth, and so their heads move backward relative to the car.
(b) When the car comes to a sudden stop, inertia tends to keep the passengers moving, and so their heads move forward relative to the car.

(a) Sudden start

(b) Sudden stop

varies so much from place to place, so weight is not suitable to use in describing matter for the purposes of science.

The property of matter that gives rise to inertia, though, is more promising. Imagine two balls of equal size, one made of lead and the other of wood. Here on earth we would say at once that the lead ball contains more matter because it weighs more. If we were blindfolded and our hands tied, we could still tell the balls apart just by kicking them, because the inertia of the lead ball would resist our kick more than that of the wooden ball (Fig. 1-13).

Now suppose we and the two balls are out in space. Weighing them would be impossible, but inertia would still give the answer because our toe would again hurt more after kicking the lead ball. The resistance the two balls offer to being set in motion is a property more basic than their weights since it does not depend on their position with respect to the earth.

Mass

A measure of inertia

The name *mass* is given to the property of matter that shows itself as the inertia of a body at rest. Mass may properly be thought of as quantity of matter: the more mass something has, the greater its inertia, and the more matter it contains.

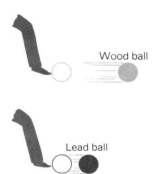

Wood ball

Lead ball

FIG. 1-13
Inertia is an inherent property of matter. The inertia of a lead ball is greater than that of a wood ball of the same size everywhere in the universe. When both are kicked with the same force, the wood ball receives the greater acceleration because its mass is less.

Mass is a measure of inertia

The more mass an object has, the greater its resistance to a change in its state of motion, as this hammer thrower can testify.

The kilogram is the SI unit of mass

In the original metric system the unit of mass was the *gram* (g), defined as the mass of a cubic centimeter of water. (A cubic centimeter is the volume of a box 1 cm on each side.) Because the gram is such a small unit — equivalent to only 0.035 ounce — the *kilogram* (kg), equal to 1000 g, has replaced it. A liter of water, which is a little more than a quart, has a mass of 1 kg (Fig. 1-14).

At the earth's surface, a 1-kg mass weighs about 2.2 lb, so that 5 kg of potatoes weighs (5)(2.2 lb) = 11 lb. Similarly the mass of a person who weighs 160 lb at the earth's surface is 73 kg, since 160/2.2 = 73.

THE ROLE OF FORCE

Force

Pushmipullyu

Let us now return to the last part of Newton's first law of motion, which says that the state of rest or of uniform motion of a body can be changed by the action of a force.

When we think about force, most of us think of a car pulling a trailer, a person pushing a lawnmower or lifting a crate. Also familiar are the force of gravity, which pulls us and things about us down to the ground, the pull of a magnet on a piece of iron, and the force of air pushing against the sails of a boat. In these examples the central idea is one of pushing, pulling, or lifting, a process that either involves muscular effort or produces the same results as such effort. Force is thus a concept based on the direct evidence of our senses.

When a force acts on a body free to move or already moving, the body's state of motion changes — it is *accelerated*. This gives us a way to say more precisely what we mean by force:

Every acceleration is the result of a force

A force is any influence that can change the speed or direction of motion of an object.

When we see something accelerated, we know that a force must be acting upon it.

It is worth emphasizing that just applying a force to an object at rest will not necessarily set it in motion. If we push against a stone wall, the wall is not accelerated as a result. Only if a force is applied to an object that is able to respond will its state of rest or motion change. On the other hand, *every* acceleration can be traced to the action of a force.

An object continues to be accelerated only as long as a net force (that is, a force not balanced out by one or more other forces) acts upon it. An ideal car on a level road would therefore need its engine only to be accelerated to a particular speed, after which it would keep moving at this speed indefinitely with the engine turned off. Actual cars are not so cooperative because of the retarding forces of friction and air resistance, which require counteracting by a force applied by the engine to the wheels.

Second Law of Motion

Force and acceleration

Experiments show that, the greater the net force on an object free to move, the greater the acceleration it produces, in the same proportion. That is, doubling the net force will double the acceleration; tripling the net force will triple the acceleration; and so on (Fig. 1-15).

The greater the mass of the object, on the other hand, the *smaller* the acceleration. For a given net force, doubling the mass cuts the acceleration in half; tripling the mass cuts the acceleration to one-third its original value; and so on.

Newton's *second law of motion* is a statement of these findings. If we let $F =$ force and $m =$ mass, this law states that

$$a = \frac{F}{m}$$

$$\text{Acceleration} = \frac{\text{force}}{\text{mass}}$$

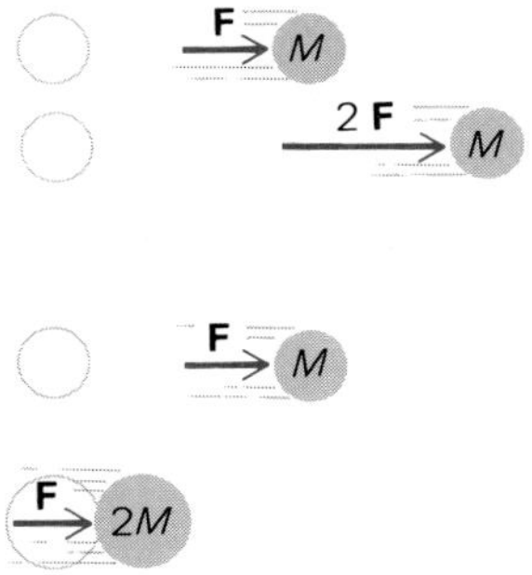

Another way to express the second law of motion is in the form of a definition of force:

$$F = ma$$

$$\text{Force} = (\text{mass})(\text{acceleration})$$

What this formula says is that the net force on an object is equal to the product of its mass and its acceleration.

Although the second law of motion is very simple, it is also very important. When we speak of force from now on, we know exactly what we mean, and we know exactly how an object free to move will behave when a given force is applied to it.

Second law of motion

FIG. 1-15
Newton's second law of motion. When different forces act upon the same mass, the greater force produces the greater acceleration. When the same force acts upon different masses, the greater mass receives the smaller acceleration.

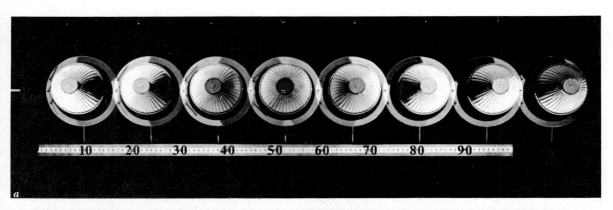

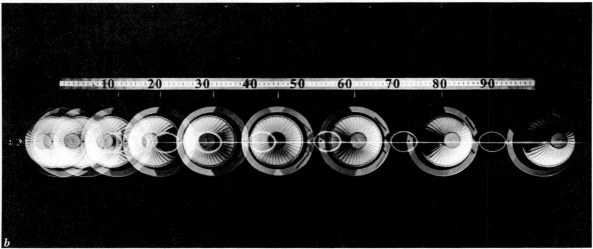

The disks shown moved from left to right on a horizontal sheet of glass while a light was flashed at regular intervals. The scale shown is in centimeters. Each disk consists of a piece of metal containing pieces of Dry Ice (solid carbon dioxide) which gradually vaporize, so that there is a layer of carbon dioxide gas between disk and glass that virtually eliminates friction. In (a) no external force is applied to the disk, and the disk travels equal distances in equal times, which means it has a constant speed. In (b) the disk is pulled to the right by a constant force, and the distance traveled each time interval increases with time: the disk is accelerated. The light flashed every $\frac{10}{24}$ s in each picture.

Direction of acceleration is direction of force

An important aspect of the second law concerns direction. The direction of the acceleration is always the same as the direction of the net force. A car is going faster and faster — therefore the net force on it is in the same direction as that in which the car is headed. The car then slows down — therefore the net force on it is now in the direction *opposite* to that in which it is headed (Fig. 1-16).

FIG. 1-16
The direction of a force is significant. A force applied in the direction in which a body is moving produces a positive acceleration (increase in speed). A force applied opposite to the direction of motion produces a negative acceleration (decrease in speed).

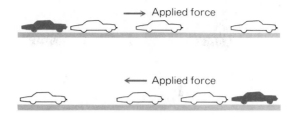

→ Applied force

← Applied force

When the car rounds a curve at constant speed, its direction changes, and it is therefore accelerated (see Fig. 1-4). We shall have more to say in Chap. 2 about force and acceleration with respect to things moving in curved paths. The essential point is that every change in speed or direction of motion is caused by a force acting in the same direction as the change.

The Newton

The SI unit of force

The second law of motion shows us how to define a unit for force. If we express mass m in kilograms and acceleration a in m/s^2, the force F is given in terms of (kg)(m/s^2). This unit is given a special name, the *newton* (N). Thus

The newton is the SI unit of force

$$1 \text{ newton} = 1 \text{ N} = 1 \text{ (kg)(m/s}^2)$$

When a force of 1 N is applied to a 1-kg mass, the mass is given an acceleration of 1 m/s^2 (Fig. 1-17).

We can summarize the second law and its units in this way:

$$F(\text{N}) = [m(\text{kg})][a(\text{m/s}^2)]$$

Force (newtons) = [mass(kilograms)][acceleration(meters/second^2)]

The pound is the British unit of force

In the British system, the unit of force is the *pound* (lb). The pound and the newton are related as follows:

$$1 \text{ N} = 0.225 \text{ lb}$$

$$1 \text{ lb} = 4.45 \text{ N}$$

FIG. 1-17
A force of 1 newton gives a mass of 1 kilogram an acceleration of 1 m/s^2.

$F = 1$ N $m = 1$ kg $a = 1$ m/s^2

FIG. 1-18
A person serving a tennis ball must exert a force of 360 N on it for the ball to have a speed of 30 m/s if the racket is in contact with the ball for 0.005 s.

How to find an applied force

A newton is a little less than $\frac{1}{4}$ lb, and a pound is nearly $4\frac{1}{2}$ newtons.

As an example, let us find the force needed to serve a 60-g tennis ball at 30 m/s. The ball will be in contact with the racket for a time that is typically 5 thousandths of a second, 0.005 s. Since the ball starts from rest, $v_0 = 0$, and the acceleration required is

$$a = \frac{v - v_0}{t} = \frac{30 \text{ m/s} - 0}{0.005 \text{ s}} = 6000 \text{ m/s}^2$$

Because the ball's mass is 60 g = 0.06 kg, the force the racket must exert on it is

$$F = ma = (0.06 \text{ kg})(6000 \text{ m/s}^2) = 360 \text{ N}$$

FIG. 1-19
A force of 2000 N applied to a 1000-kg car produces an acceleration of 2 m/s². If the car's initial speed is 5 m/s and the acceleration lasts for 10 s, the car's final speed is 25 m/s.

$m = 1{,}000$ kg $F = 2{,}000$ N $a = 2$ m/s²

In more familiar units, this force is 81 lb. Of course, it does not seem so great to the person serving because the duration of the impact is so brief (Fig. 1-18).

The relationship between force and acceleration means that the less the acceleration, the less the force. A person dropping to the ground from a height can therefore reduce the force of his impact by coming to a stop gradually instead of suddenly, which he can accomplish by bending his knees as he strikes the ground instead of landing with stiff legs. In this way t is greater, and even though $v - v_0$ and m remain the same, F will be correspondingly smaller.

How to find a final speed

Here is another problem involving force and acceleration. A force of 2000 N is applied to a 1000-kg car that is moving at 5 m/s (Fig. 1-19). What will the car's speed be after 10 s? We begin by finding the car's acceleration, which is

$$a = \frac{F}{m} = \frac{2000 \text{ N}}{1000 \text{ kg}} = 2 \text{ m/s}^2$$

Now we substitute $v_0 = 5$ m/s, $a = 2$ m/s², and $t = 10$ s in the formula $v = v_0 + at$ and find that the final speed will be

$$v = v_0 + at = 5 \text{ m/s} + (2 \text{ m/s}^2)(10 \text{ s})$$
$$= 5 \text{ m/s} + 20 \text{ m/s} = 25 \text{ m/s}$$

Mass and Weight

Weight is a force

The force with which the earth attracts something is called its *weight*. If you weigh 160 lb (711 N), that means the earth is pulling you down with a force of 160 lb. Weight is different from mass, which refers to how much matter something contains. There is a very close relationship between weight and mass, though, and it is important for us to understand it.

Let us look at the situation in the following way. Whenever a net force F is applied to a mass m, Newton's second law of motion tells us that its acceleration a will be in accord with the formula

$$F = ma$$

Force = (mass)(acceleration)

In the case of an object at the earth's surface, the force gravity exerts on it is its weight w. This is the force that causes the object to fall with the constant acceleration $g = 9.8$ m/s² when no other force acts. We may therefore substitute w for F and g for a in the formula $F = ma$ to give

$$w = mg$$

Weight = (mass)(acceleration of gravity)

Since g is a constant, the weight w of an object and its mass m are always proportional to each other: twice the mass means twice the weight, and half the mass means half the weight.

In the metric system, as we know, mass rather than weight is normally used; a customer in a French grocery might ask for a kilogram of bread or 5 kg of potatoes. To find the weight in newtons of something whose mass in kilograms is known, we simply turn to $w = mg$ and set $g = 9.8$ m/s²:

$$w(\text{N}) = [m(\text{kg})](9.8 \text{ m/s}^2)$$

Thus the weight of 5 kg of potatoes is

$$w = (5 \text{ kg})(9.8 \text{ m/s}^2) = 49 \text{ N}$$

This is the force with which the earth attracts a mass of 5 kg.

At the earth's surface, the weight of a 1-kg mass in British units is 2.2 lb. The weight in pounds of 5 kg of potatoes is therefore $(5 \text{ kg})(2.2 \text{ lb/kg}) = 11$ lb.

ACTION AND REACTION

Forces never occur all by themselves. When we think just one force is at work in a situation, a closer look always shows another force present as well. The key idea here is that the forces do not act on the same object.

Third Law of Motion

Forces always come in pairs

We push against a heavy table that stands on a rough floor. At once we become aware of a second force: the table pushes back just as hard as we push against it. The table does not move because our force on it is matched by the opposing force of friction between its legs and the floor, and we do not move because the force of the table on us is matched by a similar force between our shoes and the floor.

Let us imagine ourselves and the table on the frozen surface of a lake, a sheet of ice so smooth and slippery that friction disappears. Again we push on the table, which now is accelerated away from us as a result (Fig. 1-20). But we can stick to

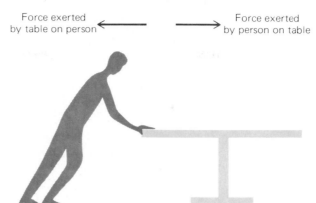

Force exerted
by table on person

Force exerted
by person on table

FIG. 1-20
Action and reaction forces act on
different bodies. Pushing a table on
a frozen lake results in person and
table moving apart in opposite
directions.

the ice no better than the table can, and as we push it away from us, we find
ourselves moving in the opposite direction. There is simply no way that we can
exert a force on the table without its pushing back on us.

Considerations of the above kind led Newton to his *third law of motion:*

Third law of motion

When an object exerts a force on another object, the second object exerts an
equal force in the opposite direction on the first object.

No force ever occurs singly. A chair pushes downward on the floor; the floor
presses upward on the chair (Fig. 1-21). The firing of a rifle exerts a force on the
bullet; at the same time the firing exerts a backward push (recoil) on the rifle. A
pear falls from a tree because of the earth's pull on it; there is an equal upward pull

Reaction force
on rifle

Action force
on bullet

Reaction forces
of floor
on chair

Action forces of
chair on floor

Action force
on pear

Reaction force
on earth

FIG. 1-21
Some examples of action-reaction
pairs of forces.

on the earth by the pear which is not apparent because the earth has so much more mass than the pear, but this upward force is nevertheless present.

Action and Reaction

The ground pushes us when we walk

Action and reaction forces act on different objects

Newton's third law always applies to two different forces on two different objects — the *action* force that one exerts on the second, and the opposite *reaction* force the second exerts on the first.

The third law of motion permits us to walk. When a person walks, what is actually pushing him forward is not his own push on the ground but instead the reaction force of the ground on him (Fig. 1-22). As he moves forward, the earth

Reaction force on person

Action force on earth

FIG. 1-22
When a person pushes backward on the earth with his foot, the earth pushes forward on him. It is the latter reaction force that leads to his forward motion.

When a cannon is fired, the forward force on the cannonball is matched by an equal backward force on the cannon itself. This is an example of Newton's third law of motion.

itself moves backward, though by too small an amount (by virtue of its enormous mass) to be detected.

Sometimes the origin of the reaction force is not obvious. A book lying on a table exerts the downward force of its weight; but how can an apparently rigid object like the table exert an upward force on the book? If the tabletop were made of rubber, the book would obviously depress it, and the upward force would result from the elasticity of the rubber. A similar explanation actually holds for tabletops of wood or metal, which are never perfectly rigid, although the depressions made in them are extremely small ones.

IMPORTANT TERMS

To measure something means to compare it with a standard quantity of the same kind called a **unit.** The **SI** (or **metric**) system of units is used everywhere by scientists and in most of the world in everyday life as well. The SI unit of length is the **meter** (m).

The **speed** of a moving object is the rate at which it covers distance. The **acceleration** of an object is the rate at which its speed changes. Changes in direction are also considered accelerations.

The **acceleration of gravity** is the downward acceleration of a freely falling object near the earth's surface. Its value is $g = 9.8$ m/s^2.

The **inertia** of an object refers to the resistance it offers to any change in its state of rest or motion. The property of matter that shows itself as inertia is called **mass;** it may be thought of as quantity of matter. The unit of mass is the **kilogram** (kg).

A **force** is any influence that can cause an object to be accelerated. The unit of force is the **newton** (N). The **weight** of an object is the gravitational force with which the earth attracts it.

Newton's **first law of motion** states that, if no net force acts on it, every object continues in its state of rest or uniform motion in a straight line. The **second law of motion** states that when a net force F acts on an object of mass m, the object is given an acceleration of F/m in the same direction as that of the force. The **third law of motion** states that when an object exerts a force on another object, the second object exerts an equal but opposite force on the first. Thus for every **action force** there is an equal but opposite **reaction force.**

IMPORTANT FORMULAS

Speed: $v = d/t$

Acceleration: $a = \dfrac{v - v_0}{t}$

Final speed under constant acceleration: $v = v_0 + at$

Weight: $w = mg$

Second law of motion: $F = ma$

MULTIPLE CHOICE

1. In which of the following examples is the motion of the car not accelerated?
   a. A car turns a corner at the constant speed of 20 km/h
   b. A car climbs a steep hill with its speed dropping from 60 km/h at the bottom to 15 km/h at the top
   c. A car climbs a steep hill at the constant speed of 40 km/h
   d. A car climbs a steep hill and goes over the crest and down on the other side, all at the same speed of 40 km/h

2. If two objects which are of the same size and shape but of which one is twice as heavy as the other are dropped simultaneously from a tower,
   a. the heavy object strikes the ground before the light one
   b. they strike the ground at the same time, but the heavy object has the higher speed
   c. they strike the ground at the same time and have the same speed
   d. they strike the ground at the same time, but the heavy object has the lower acceleration because it has more mass

3. The acceleration of a stone thrown upward is
   a. greater than that of a stone thrown downward
   b. the same as that of a stone thrown downward
   c. less than that of a stone thrown downward
   d. zero until it reaches the highest point in its path

4. When an object is accelerated,
   a. its direction never changes
   b. its speed always increases
   c. it always falls toward the earth
   d. a net force always acts on it
5. The mass of an object depends upon
   a. its location relative to the earth's surface
   b. its weight
   c. the acceleration of gravity
   d. how much matter it contains
6. If we know the strength and direction of the net force that acts on an object of known mass, Newton's second law of motion enables us to calculate its
   a. position
   b. speed
   c. acceleration
   d. weight
7. The weight of an object
   a. is the quantity of matter it contains
   b. is the force with which it is attracted to the earth
   c. is basically the same quantity as its mass but is expressed in different units
   d. refers to its inertia
8. The action and reaction forces referred to in the third law of motion
   a. act upon the same object
   b. act upon different bodies
   c. need not be equal in strength but must act in opposite directions
   d. must be equal in strength but need not act in opposite directions
9. A car that is towing a trailer is accelerating on a level road. The force the car exerts on the trailer is
   a. equal to the force the trailer exerts on the car
   b. greater than the force the trailer exerts on the car
   c. equal to the force the trailer exerts on the road
   d. equal to the force the road exerts on the trailer
10. When a boy pulls a cart, the force that causes *him* to move forward is
   a. the force the cart exerts on him
   b. the force he exerts on the cart
   c. the force he exerts on the ground with his feet
   d. the force the ground exerts on his feet
11. Of the following, the shortest is
   a. 1 mm
   b. 0.01 in.
   c. 0.001 m
   d. 0.001 ft
12. Of the following, the longest is
   a. 1000 ft

   b. 500 m
   c. 1 km
   d. 1 mi
13. A bicycle travels 12 km in 40 min. Its average speed is
   a. 0.3 km/h
   b. 8 km/h
   c. 18 km/h
   d. 48 km/h
14. Two cars travel along the same road in the same direction from the same starting place. One car maintains a speed of 50 km/h, and the other car 60 km/h, but the second car starts 1 h later. How many hours will it take for the second car to overtake the first car?
   a. 2
   b. 3
   c. 4
   d. 5
15. In Question 14, how far will the cars have traveled?
   a. 100 km
   b. 200 km
   c. 300 km
   d. 400 km
16. How long does a car whose acceleration is 2 m/s^2 need to go from 10 m/s to 30 m/s?
   a. 10 s
   b. 20 s
   c. 40 s
   d. 400 s
17. A ball is thrown upward at a speed of 12 m/s. It will reach the top of its path in about
   a. 0.6 s
   b. 1.2 s
   c. 1.8 s
   d. 2.4 s
18. The ball of Question 17 will return to the ground from the top of its path in about
   a. 0.6 s
   b. 1.2 s
   c. 1.8 s
   d. 2.4 s
19. When a net force of 1 N acts on a 1-kg body, the body receives
   a. a speed of 1 m/s
   b. an acceleration of 0.1 m/s^2
   c. an acceleration of 1 m/s^2
   d. an acceleration of 9.8 m/s^2
20. When a net force of 1 N acts on a 1-N body, the body receives
   a. a speed of 1 m/s
   b. an acceleration of 0.1 m/s^2

c. an acceleration of 1 m/s²

d. an acceleration of 0.9 m/s²

21. A force gives a 100-kg mass an acceleration of 2 m/s². The same force would give a mass of 1000 kg an acceleration of

    a. 0.2 m/s²

    b. 2 m/s²

    c. 20 m/s²

    d. 200 m/s²

22. A bicycle and its rider together have a mass of 80 kg. If the bicycle's speed is 6 m/s, the force needed to bring it to a stop in 4 s is

    a. 12 N

    b. 53 N

    c. 120 N

    d. 1176 N

23. A net force of 2800 N is applied to a 1400-kg car at rest. The car's speed after 10 s will be

    a. 2 m/s

    b. 5 m/s

    c. 10 m/s

    d. 20 m/s

24. A car whose mass is 1600 kg (including the driver) has a maximum acceleration of 1.2 m/s². If three 80-kg passengers are also in the car, its maximum acceleration will be

    a. 0.5 m/s²

    b. 0.72 m/s²

    c. 1.04 m/s²

    d. 1.2 m/s²

25. The weight of 400 g of onions is

    a. 0.041 N

    b. 0.4 N

    c. 3.9 N

    d. 3920 N

26. A salami weighs 3 lb. Its mass is

    a. 0.31 kg

    b. 1.36 kg

    c. 6.6 kg

    d. 29.4 kg

QUESTIONS

1. Is it necessary that an accelerated object be moving at all times? If not, give some examples of an object at rest that is accelerated.

2. Can a rapidly moving object have the same acceleration as a slowly moving one?

3. Suppose that you are in a barrel going over Niagara Falls and that, during the fall of the barrel, you drop an apple inside the barrel. Would it appear to move toward the top of the barrel or toward its bottom, or would it remain stationary within the barrel?

4. A rifle is aimed directly at a squirrel in a tree. Should the squirrel drop from the tree at the instant the rifle is fired or should it remain where it is? Why?

5. A movie seems to show a ball falling past a meter stick. Is it possible to tell by timing the progress of the ball whether the movie is actually of a ball that has been thrown upward with the film being run backwards in the projector?

6. Every acceleration is the result of a force. Does every applied force produce an acceleration?

7. Is the moon's motion around the earth accelerated? Is a force acting on the moon? If so, what is the direction of the force?

8. When you whirl a stone at the end of a string, the stone seems to be pulling outward against your hand. When you release the string, however, the stone moves along a straight path. Explain each of these effects.

9. Why is it less dangerous to jump from a high wall onto loose earth than onto a concrete pavement?

10. A person in a stationary elevator drops a coin and it reaches the floor of the elevator 0.6 s later. Would the coin reach the floor in less time, the same time, or more time if it were dropped when the elevator was (a) falling at a constant speed? (b) falling at a constant acceleration? (c) rising at a constant speed? (d) rising at a constant acceleration?

11. A book rests on a table. What is the reaction force to the force the book exerts on the table? To the force that gravity exerts on the book?

12. Since the opposite forces of the third law of motion are equal in strength, how can anything ever be accelerated?

13. If you were set down in the center of a frozen lake whose surface was so smooth and slippery that it offered no frictional resistance, how could you get off the lake?

14. Two children wish to break a string. Are they more likely to succeed if each takes one end of the string and they pull against each other, or if they tie one end of the string to a tree and both pull on the free end? Why?

15. An engineer designs a propeller-driven spacecraft. Because there is no air in space, he includes a supply of oxygen as well as a supply of fuel for the motor. What do you think of the idea?

PROBLEMS

1. The distance from Paris to Brussels is 291 km. How many meters is this? How many miles?

2. The tallest tree in the world is a sequoia in California that is 368 ft high. How high is this in meters? In kilometers?

3. The speed of sound in air is about 330 m/s. If a lightning flash occurs 1.5 km from you, how long will it take before you hear the thunder? (The speed of light is nearly a million times greater than that of sound, so the time of travel of the flash can be neglected here.)

4. In 1977 Steve Weldon ate 91.44 m of spaghetti in 28.73 s. At the same speed, how long would it take Mr. Weldon to eat 5 m of spaghetti?

5. If a motorist averages 65 km/h and drives for 9 h per day, how many days will be needed to cover the approximately 3700 km distance by road from Chicago to San Francisco?

6. A car travels at 100 km/h for 2 h, at 60 km/h for the next 2 h, and finally at 80 km/h for 1 h. Find the car's average speed for the entire 5 h.

7. A car moving at 80 km/h is brought to a stop in 3 s. What is its average acceleration (in m/s²) in this period?

8. A DC-8 airplane reaches its takeoff speed of 78 m/s a time of 35 s after starting from rest. What is its average acceleration?

9. A car whose acceleration is constant attains a speed of 80 km/h in 20 s starting from rest. How much additional time is required for it to attain a speed of 130 km/h?

10. The brakes of a car moving at 14 m/s are applied and the car comes to a stop in 4 s. (a) What was the car's acceleration? (b) How long would the car take to come to a stop starting from 20 m/s with the same acceleration? (c) How long would the car take to slow down from 20 m/s to 10 m/s with the same acceleration?

11. A ball is thrown vertically downward with an initial speed of 10 m/s. What is its speed after 1 s? After 3 s?

12. The acceleration of gravity at the surface of Mars is 3.7 m/s². If a ball is thrown vertically downward with an initial speed of 10 m/s on Mars, what will its speed be after 1 s? After 3 s?

13. A ball is thrown vertically upward with an initial speed of 30 m/s. How long will it take the ball to reach the highest point in its path? How long will it take the ball to return to its starting place? What will the ball's speed be there?

14. A ball is thrown vertically upward with an initial speed of 10 m/s. What is its speed after 1 s? After 5 s?

15. A winch can exert a pull of 650 lb. What is the greatest mass in kg it can lift?

16. What is the weight in lb of a 60-kg person?

17. A force of 20 N acts on a body whose weight is 8 N. What is the body's mass? What is its acceleration?

18. A force of 20 N acts on a body whose mass is 4 kg. What is the body's weight? What is its acceleration?

19. A net horizontal force of 4000 N is applied to a 1400-kg car. What will the car's speed be after 10 s if it started from rest?

20. A force of 20 N gives an object an acceleration of 5 m/s². What force would be needed to give the same object an acceleration of 1 m/s²? An acceleration of 10 m/s²?

21. What is the mass of a 700-N man? With how much force is he attracted to the earth? If he falls from a cliff, what will his downward acceleration be?

22. A 100-kg man slides down a rope at constant speed. (a) What is the minimum breaking strength the rope must have? (b) If the rope has precisely this strength, will it support the man if he tries to climb back up?

23. A 1600-kg car goes from 12 m/s to 24 m/s in 15 s. What is the average force acting upon it? What is the origin of this force?

24. The brakes of the above car exert a force of 3000 N. How long will it take for them to slow the car to a stop from an initial speed of 24 m/s?

25. A 60-g tennis ball approaches a racket at 15 m/s, is in contact with the racket for 0.005 s, and then rebounds at 20 m/s. What was the average force the racket exerted on the ball?

26. A 12,000-kg airplane launched by a catapult from an aircraft carrier is accelerated from 0 to 200 km/h in 3 s. (a) How many times the acceleration of gravity is the airplane's acceleration? (b) What is the average force the catapult exerts on the airplane?

27. A woman whose mass is 60 kg is riding in an elevator whose upward acceleration is 2 m/s². What force does she exert on the floor of the elevator?

28. The cable supporting a 2000-kg elevator can safely withstand a tension of 25,000 N. What is the maximum upward acceleration the elevator can have if the tension in the cable is not to exceed this figure?

ANSWERS TO MULTIPLE CHOICE

1. *c*	**8.** *b*	**15.** *c*	**22.** *c*
2. *c*	**9.** *a*	**16.** *a*	**23.** *d*
3. *b*	**10.** *d*	**17.** *b*	**24.** *c*
4. *d*	**11.** *b*	**18.** *b*	**25.** *c*
5. *d*	**12.** *d*	**19.** *c*	**26.** *b*
6. *c*	**13.** *c*	**20.** *b*	
7. *b*	**14.** *d*	**21.** *a*	

2

GRAVITATION

From as far back in history as we can go, people have looked at the sky and wondered at what they saw. The sun and moon, the stars and planets sweep daily from the eastern horizon to the western horizon. Each day, too, the pattern they make in the sky changes slightly, as detailed in Chap. 17. Over the centuries wonder turned to speculation and to measurement, and finally some remarkable regularities were found in the motions of the heavenly bodies. These regularities inspired Newton's discovery that the motions of the planets about the sun, the circling of the moon about the earth, and the behavior of falling objects on the earth all can be traced to a single basic phenomenon of nature, gravitation. On a still larger scale, gravitation helps govern the evolution of the entire universe.

CIRCULAR MOTION

Left to itself, a moving object travels in a straight line at constant speed. A force must be applied to change the object's direction as well as to change its speed. The direction of a planet in orbit about the sun changes all the time, which means a force is always acting on it. Our first step on the road to learning about the nature of this force is a look at the general question of what force is needed to keep an object moving in a circular path.

Vectors

Which way as well as how much

Some quantities have directions as well as magnitudes associated with them, and these directions can be important. Force is an example. Applying a force of 15 N (3.4 lb) upward on this book will lift it from the table; applying a force of 15 N downward on the book will merely press it harder against the table. Motion is another example. If we drive north from Denver, we will end up in Canada; if we drive south, we will end up in Mexico.

A vector quantity has direction and magnitude. A scalar quantity has magnitude only

A *vector quantity* is one that has a direction associated with it. Force is thus a vector quantity, but mass is not. If the mass of a woman is 60 kg when she is standing on her feet, it is also 60 kg when she is sitting, lying down, or standing on her head (Fig. 2-1). A quantity with magnitude but not direction, such as mass, is called *scalar*.

Speed is a scalar quantity, velocity is a vector quantity

The *speed* of a moving object refers only to how fast it is going, regardless of its direction. Speed is a scalar quantity. If we are told that a car has a speed of 100 km/h, we do not know where it is headed, or even if it is moving in a straight

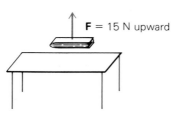

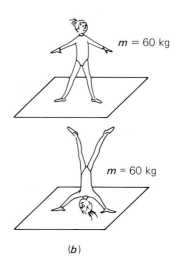

FIG. 2-1
(*a*) A vector quantity is one whose direction is important. Force is an example: an upward force produces a different effect from that of a downward force. (*b*) A scalar quantity has no direction associated with it. Mass is an example.

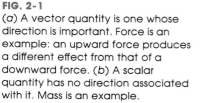

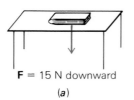

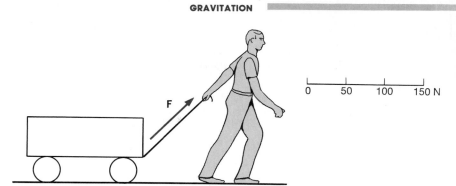

FIG. 2-2
Vector diagram of a person exerting a force of 80 N at an angle of 45° above the horizontal. The scale is 1 cm = 50 N.

line — it might well be going in a circle. The vector quantity that includes both speed and direction is called *velocity*. If we are told that a car has a constant velocity of 100 km/h toward the west, we know all there is to know about its motion and can easily figure out where it will be in an hour, or 2 hours, or at any other time.

A handy way to represent a vector quantity on a drawing is to use a straight line called a *vector* that has an arrowhead at one end to show the direction of the quantity. The length of the line is scaled according to the magnitude of the quantity. Figure 2-2 shows how a force of 80 N at an angle of 45° above the horizontal can be represented by a vector on a scale of 1 cm = 50 N. All vector quantities can be pictured in a similar way.

A vector is a line whose length and direction represent the magnitude and direction of a vector quantity

Vector quantities are usually printed in boldface type (**F** for force, **v** for velocity). Italic type is used for scalar quantities (*m* for mass, *V* for volume). Italic type is also used for the magnitudes of vector quantities: *F* is the magnitude of the force **F**, *v* is the magnitude of the velocity **v**. For instance, the magnitude of a velocity **v** of 100 km/h to the west is its speed $v = 100$ km/h. A vector quantity is usually indicated in handwriting by an arrow over its symbol, so that $\vec{F}$ means the same thing as **F**.

Centripetal Force

The inward pull needed to follow a curved path

Tie a ball to the end of a string and whirl it around your head, as in Fig. 2-3. What you will find is that your hand must pull on the string to keep the ball moving in a circle. If you let go of the string, there is no longer an inward force on the ball, and it flies off to the side.

The force that has to be applied to make something move in a curved path is called *centripetal* ("center-seeking") force:

Centripetal force is needed for motion on a curved path

Centripetal force = inward force on an object moving in a curved path

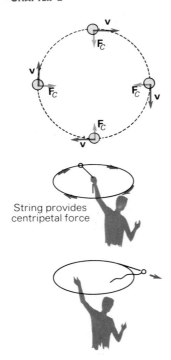

FIG. 2-3
A centripetal force is necessary for circular motion. An inward centripetal force $\mathbf{F}_c$ acts upon every object that moves in a curved path. If the force is removed, the object continues moving in a straight line tangent to its original path.

String provides centripetal force

The centripetal force always points toward the center of curvature of the object's path, which means it is at right angles to the object's direction of motion at each moment. In Fig. 2-3 the ball is moving in a circle, so its velocity vector **v** is always tangent to the circle and the centripetal force vector $\mathbf{F}_c$ is always directed toward the center of the circle.

A detailed calculation shows that the centripetal force $\mathbf{F}_c$ needed for something of mass m and speed v to travel in a circle of radius r has the magnitude

Magnitude of centripetal force; the direction is toward the center of circle

$$\text{Centripetal force} = F_c = \frac{mv^2}{r}$$

To whirl a given object in a circle requires more force if it moves fast or if the circle is small. The more massive the object, the more force is needed as well (Fig. 2-4).

Friction provides centripetal force needed by a car making a turn

From the formula for F_c we can see why cars rounding a curve are so difficult to steer when the curve is sharp (small r) or the speed is high (a large value for v means a very large value for v^2). On a level road, the centripetal force is supplied by friction between the car's tires and the road. If the force needed to make a particular turn at a certain speed is too great for the road surface, the car skids.

Let us consider a 1000-kg car traveling at 5 m/s (11 mi/h) around a turn 30 m (98 ft) in radius, as in Fig. 2-5. The centripetal force needed to make the turn is

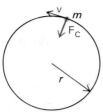

The magnitude of the centripetal force is

$F_c = mv^2/r$

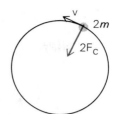

Doubling the mass *m* doubles the needed centripetal force

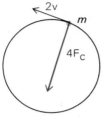

FIG. 2-4
The centripetal force needed to keep an object moving in a circle depends upon the mass and speed of the object and upon the radius of the circle. The direction of the force is always toward the center of the circle.

Doubling the speed *v* quadruples the needed centripetal force because of the *v*² factor

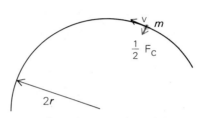

Doubling the radius of the circle halves the needed centripetal force

$$F_c = \frac{mv^2}{r} = \frac{(1000 \text{ kg})(5 \text{ m/s})^2}{30 \text{ m}} = 833 \text{ N}$$

This force, which is about 190 lb, is readily transferred from the road to the car's

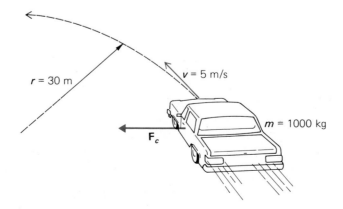

FIG. 2-5
A centripetal force of 833 N is needed by this car to make the turn shown.

The centripetal force needed by a vehicle rounding a turn on a level road is provided by friction between its tires and the road, which may not be sufficient at high speeds. If the turn is banked so that the roadbed tilts inward, additional centripetal force comes from the reaction force of the road on the vehicle (the action force is the vehicle's weight).

Banked turns

tires if the pavement is dry and in good condition. However, if the car's speed were 20 m/s (45 mi/h), the force needed would be 16 times as great, and the car would probably skid outward.

To reduce the chance of skids, particularly when the road is wet and therefore slippery, highway curves are often *banked* so that the roadbed tilts inward. A car going around a banked curve has an inward force acting on it provided by the road itself, apart from friction.

THE SOLAR SYSTEM

The sun, moon, planets, and most stars move from east to west across the sky every day. (The paths are actually close to being circles around Polaris, the North Star, as the photograph on page 582 shows. Hence stars in the northern sky whose circles are above the horizon move from west to east in part of their daily circuits.) These bodies also move relative to one another, though more slowly. There are two ways to explain the general east-to-west motion. The most obvious is that the earth is stationary, with the other bodies revolving around it. The other possibility is that the earth itself turns once a day, so that the heavenly bodies only appear to circle it. How the second alternative came to be recognized as correct and how this finding led to the discovery of the law of gravity are important chapters in the story of civilization.

The Ptolemaic System

The earth as the center of the universe

Although the philosophers of ancient Greece were aware that the apparent daily rotation of the sky could be explained by a rotation of the earth, most of them preferred the commonsense view that the earth is stationary. The scheme most widely accepted was originally the work of Hipparchus. Ptolemy of Alexandria later included Hipparchus's ideas into his *Almagest*, a survey of astronomy that was to remain the standard reference on the subject for over a thousand years. This picture of the universe became known as the *ptolemaic system*.

It was an intricate and ingenious system. Our earth stands at the center, motionless, with everything else in the universe moving about it either in circles or in combinations of circles. To the Greeks, the circle was the only "perfect" curve, hence the only possible path for a celestial object. Enclosing everything is a huge crystal sphere studded with the fixed stars that makes a little more than one

In the ptolemaic system, the earth is stationary at the center of the universe

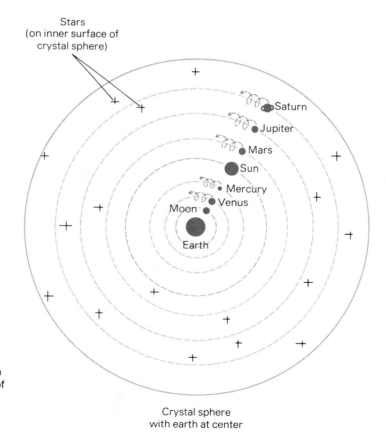

Stars
(on inner surface of
crystal sphere)

Crystal sphere
with earth at center

FIG. 2-6
The ptolemaic system, showing the assumed arrangement of the members of the solar system within the celestial sphere. Each planet is supposed to travel around the earth in a series of loops, while the orbits of the sun and moon are circular. Only the planets known in Ptolemy's time are shown.

revolution each day. Inside the crystal sphere is the sun, which moves around the earth exactly once a day. The difference in speed between sun and stars is just enough so that the sun appears to move eastward past the stars, returning to a given point among them once a year. Near the earth in a small orbit is the moon, revolving more slowly than the sun. The planets Venus and Mercury come between moon and sun, the other planets between sun and stars.

To account for irregularities found in the motions of the planets, Ptolemy imagined that each planet moves in a small circle, called an *epicycle,* about a point that in turn follows a large circle about the earth (Fig. 2-6). By a combination of these circular motions a planet travels in a series of loops. Since we observe these loops edgewise, it appears to us as if the planets move with variable speeds and sometimes reverse their directions of motion in the sky.

From observations made by himself and by others, Ptolemy calculated the relative speed of each celestial object in its assumed orbit. Using these speeds he could then figure out the location in the sky of any object at any time, past or future. These calculated positions checked fairly well, though not perfectly, with positions that had been recorded centuries earlier, and the predictions also agreed fairly well with observations made in later years. So Ptolemy's system fulfilled all the requirements of a scientific theory: it was based on observation, it accounted for the celestial motions known in his time, and it made predictions that could be tested in the future.

The Copernican System

A spinning earth that circles the sun

By the sixteenth century it had become clear that something was wrong with the ptolemaic system. The planets were simply not in the positions in the sky predicted for them. The errors were not large but could be detected easily. There were two ways to remove the discrepancies: either the ptolemaic orbits could be modified further, making the system still more complicated, or the ptolemaic system could be replaced by a completely new picture of the universe.

Nicolaus Copernicus, a versatile and energetic Pole of the early sixteenth century, chose the second approach. He lived in the years following Columbus's voyages, years when intellectual as well as geographical horizons were receding before eager explorers. In Italy it was the time of Leonardo da Vinci and Michelangelo, a time of business expansion and conflicts between rival cities, a time of great fortunes and corrupt governments, a time of brilliant thinkers and inspired artists. To this Italy of the Renaissance Copernicus went as a student, learning medicine, theology, and mathematics in its universities. Back in his native Poland he practiced medicine and became interested in currency reform, but much of his time was devoted to working out an idea that had come to him in Italy — the idea that the sun rather than the earth was at the center of the motions of the planets.

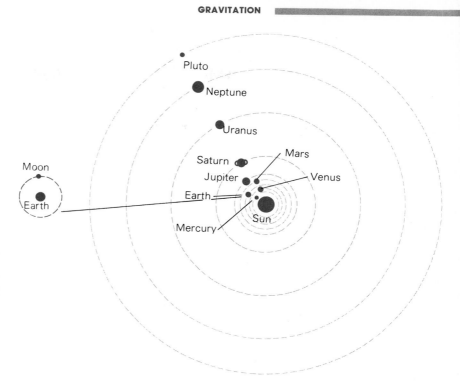

FIG. 2-7

The copernican system, showing the assumed arrangement of the members of the solar system. The planets, including the earth, are supposed to travel around the sun in circular orbits. The earth rotates daily on its axis, the moon revolves around the earth, and the stars are far away. All planets are shown here. The actual orbits are ellipses and are not spaced as shown here, though they do lie in approximately the same plane.

In the copernican system, the earth turns on its axis and revolves with the other planets around the sun

Let us consider the earth, said Copernicus, as one of the planets, a sphere rotating once a day on its axis. Let us also imagine that the planets, including the earth, revolve in circular orbits about the sun (Fig. 2-7), that the moon is relatively near the earth and revolves about it, and that the stars are all far away. In this picture the earth's rotation explains the daily rising and setting of celestial objects. The apparent motion of the sun among the stars is due to the earth's motion in its orbit; as we swing around the sun, it appears to us as if it is the sun that is shifting in position against the background of the fixed stars. The moon's eastward drift is mainly due to its actual orbital motion. Apparently irregular movements of the planets are really just combinations of their actual motions with our own shifts of position as the earth moves.

Here is how Copernicus summed up his picture of the solar system: "Of the moving bodies first comes Saturn, who completes his circuit in thirty years. After him Jupiter, moving in a twelve-year revolution. Then Mars, who revolves biennially. Fourth in order an annual cycle takes place, in which we have said is contained the Earth, with the lunar orbit as an epicycle, that is, with the moon moving in a circle around the earth. In the fifth place Venus is carried around in nine months. Then Mercury holds the sixth place, circulating in the space of eighty days. In the middle of all dwells the Sun. Who indeed in this most beautiful temple would place the torch in any other or better place than one whence it can illuminate the whole at the same time?''

The idea behind Copernicus's scheme was not new, for some of the Greeks, notably Aristarchus, had been aware that celestial motions in the sky could be partly the result of motions of the earth. But Copernicus went further and worked out the planetary orbits and speeds in detail. His calculated positions of the planets were in fair accord with the observed ones, although not really very much more so than Ptolemy's.

Despite a lack of perfect agreement with observation, Copernicus felt that his simple circular orbits gave a truer picture of the universe than the complex orbits within orbits of the ptolemaic system. Such a belief in those days was unpopular, for both Protestant and Catholic churchmen did not want to see the earth taken from its place at the hub of the universe. The publication of Copernicus's manuscript began a long and bitter argument. To us, growing up with the knowledge that the earth moves, it seems odd that this straightforward idea was so long and so violently opposed. But in the sixteenth century good arguments were available to both sides.

Arguments for and against

Consider, said supporters of Ptolemy, how fast the earth's surface must move to complete a full turn every 24 h. Would not everything loose be flung into space by this whirling ball, just as mud is thrown from the rim of a carriage wheel? And would not such dizzy speeds produce a great wind to blow down buildings, trees, plants? The earth does spin rapidly, replied the followers of Copernicus, but the effects are counterbalanced by whatever force it is that holds our feet to the ground. Besides, if the speed of the earth's rotation is a problem, how much more of a problem would be the tremendous speeds of the sun, stars, and planets if they revolve, as Ptolemy thought, once a day around a fixed earth.

Kepler's Laws

How the planets actually move

Fortunately, improvements in astronomical measurements — the first since the time of the Greeks — were not long in coming. Tycho Brahe, an astrologer to the Danish king, built an observatory on the island of Hven near Copenhagen in which the instruments were as rigid and precise as possible. With the help of these instruments, Tycho, blessed with exceptional eyesight and patience, made thousands of measurements, a labor that occupied much of his life. Even without the telescope, which had not yet been invented, Tycho's observatory was able to determine celestial angles to better than $\frac{1}{100}$ of a degree.

At his death in 1601, Tycho left behind his own somewhat peculiar theory of the solar system, a body of superb data extending over many years, and an assistant named Johannes Kepler. Kepler regarded the copernican scheme ''with incredible and ravishing delight'' and fully expected that Tycho's improved figures would prove Copernicus correct once and for all. But this was not the case; after 4

Plan of Tycho Brahe's observatory Uraniburg on the island of Hven between Denmark and Sweden. Here Tycho made the precise astronomical measurements that led to Kepler's discovery of the laws of planetary motion.

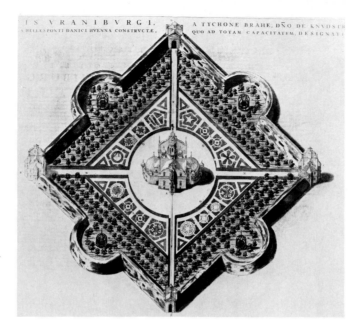

FIG. 2-8

To draw an ellipse, place a loop of string over two tacks a short distance apart. Then move the pencil as shown, keeping the string taut. By varying the length of the string, ellipses of different shapes can be drawn. The points in an ellipse corresponding to the positions of the tacks are called focuses; the orbits of the planets are ellipses with the sun at one focus, which is Kepler's first law.

years of work on the orbit of Mars alone, Kepler could not reconcile the observational data with any of the models of the solar system that had by then been proposed. If the facts do not agree with the theory, then the theory, no matter how attractive, must be discarded. Kepler began a search for a new cosmic design that would be in better accord with Tycho's observations.

After considering every possibility, which meant years of drudgery in making calculations by hand, Kepler found that circular orbits for the planets were out of the question even when modified in various ways. He abandoned circular orbits only reluctantly, for he was something of a mystic and believed, like Copernicus and the Greeks, that circles were the only fitting type of path for celestial bodies. Kepler then examined other geometrical figures, and here he found the key to the puzzle (Fig. 2-8). According to *Kepler's first law*

Kepler's first law of planetary motion

The paths of the planets around the sun are ellipses.

Even this crucial discovery was not enough, as Kepler realized, to establish the courses of the planets through the sky. What was needed next was a way to relate the speeds of the planets to their positions in their elliptical orbits. Kepler could not be sure a general relationship of this kind even existed, and he was overjoyed when he came upon the answer:

FIG. 2-9
Kepler's second law. As a planet goes from a to b in its orbit, its radius vector (an imaginary line joining it with the sun) sweeps out the area A. In the same amount of time the planet can go from c to d, with its radius vector sweeping out the area B, or from e to f, with its radius vector sweeping out the area C. The three areas A, B, and C are equal.

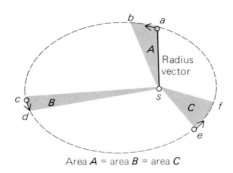

Area **A** = area **B** = area **C**

Kepler's second law

A planet moves so that its radius vector sweeps out equal areas in equal times.

The radius vector of a planet is a line drawn from it to the sun. Thus in Fig. 2-9 each of the shaded areas is covered in the same period of time. This means that each planet travels faster when it is near the sun than when it is far away. The earth, for instance, has a speed of 30 km/s when it is nearest the sun and 29 km/s when it is farthest away, a difference of over 3 percent. This rule of equal areas is known as *Kepler's second law*.

A great achievement, but Kepler was not satisfied. He was obsessed with the idea of order and regularity in the universe, and spent 10 more years making calculations. The result was his *third law* of planetary motion:

Kepler's third law

The ratio between the square of the time needed by a planet to make a revolution around the sun and the cube of its average distance from the sun is the same for all the planets.

In equation form, this law states that

$$\frac{(\text{Period of planet})^2}{(\text{Average orbit radius})^3} = \text{same value for all planets}$$

The period of a planet is the time needed for it to go around the sun; in the case of the earth, the period is 1 year. Figure 2-10 illustrates Kepler's third law. Table 18-1 (see page 619) gives the values of the periods and average orbit radii for the planets.

At last the solar system could be interpreted in terms of simple motions.

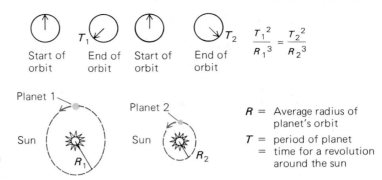

FIG. 2-10
Kepler's third law states that the ratio T^2/R^3 is the same for all the planets.

Planetary positions computed from Kepler's ellipses agreed not only with Tycho's data but with observations made thousands of years earlier. Predictions could be made regarding positions of the planets in the future — accurate predictions this time, no longer approximations. Furthermore, Kepler's laws showed that the speed of a planet in different parts of its orbit was governed by a simple rule and that the speed was related to the size of the orbit.

Why Copernicus Was Right

Simplicity is not enough

It is often said that Kepler proved that Copernicus was "right" and Ptolemy was "wrong." True enough, the copernican system, by having the planets move around the sun rather than around the earth, was simpler than the ptolemaic system. When modified by Kepler, it was also more accurate. However, the ptolemaic system could also be modified to be just as accurate, though in a very much more complicated way. Astronomers of the time squared themselves both with the

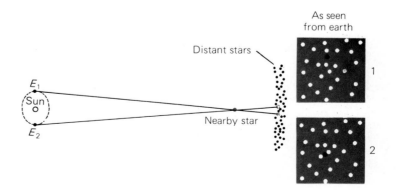

FIG. 2-11
As a consequence of the earth's motion around the sun, nearby stars shift in apparent position relative to distant stars.

Experimental evidence supports the copernican model of the solar system

church and with the practical needs of their profession by using the copernican system for calculations while asserting the ultimate truth of the ptolemaic system.

Though the copernican system is clearly better than the ptolemaic system because more aspects of the natural world fit into it in a straightforward way, only observations that specifically contradict the ptolemaic system can prove it wrong. The copernican system is today considered correct because there is direct experimental evidence of various kinds for the motions of the planets around the sun and of the rotation of the earth. A simple example of such evidence is the change in apparent position of nearby stars relative to distant ones as the earth revolves around the sun (Fig. 2-11). Shifts of this kind are small and hard to detect because all stars are far away, but they unquestionably exist.

UNIVERSAL GRAVITATION

That some force is needed to hold the planets in their orbits had been recognized before Newton, but what kind of force it is had remained open to speculation. It

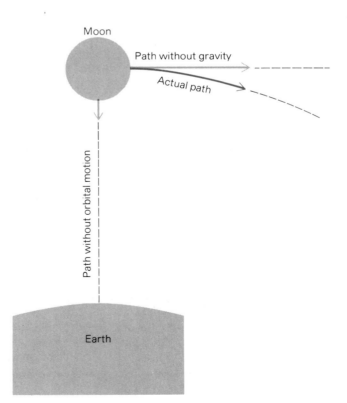

FIG. 2-12
The motion of the moon around the earth represents a balance between the downward pull of gravity and the tendency of the moon to travel in a straight line. Gravity provides the centripetal force required to keep the moon in its orbit.

was Newton's inspired idea that this force might have the same nature as the familiar force of gravity that pulls objects to the earth's surface. Perhaps, thought Newton, the moon revolves around the earth much as a ball on the end of a string revolves around a finger, with gravity taking the place of the pull of the string. In other words, perhaps the moon is a falling object, pulled toward the earth just as we are but moving so fast that the pull is just enough to keep it from flying off away from the earth (Fig. 2-12). The earth and its sister planets might well be held in their orbits by a stronger gravitational pull from the sun.

Isaac Newton

A fortunate genius

The facts of Newton's long life (1642–1727) are simple and undramatic. Born in the year Galileo died, he was the son of an obscure farmer and at first an undistinguished student. In his teens Newton revealed a notable aptitude for science and was sent to Cambridge to complete his studies. In his twenties Newton was appointed professor of mathematics there, and he stayed at Cambridge, living quietly and never marrying, for 30 years. Then, at fifty-four, Newton was appointed an official of the British mint, where he helped reform the currency system and, in his spare time, worked on problems of Biblical dating.

In contrast to this uneventful life are the adventures of his far-ranging mind. In the law of gravitation Newton found the solution to the problem of planetary motion and gave science a powerful tool for understanding natural phenomena. His formulation of the three laws of motion placed the science of mechanics on a solid foundation. By inventing calculus, Newton gave physical science a new and powerful kind of mathematics that is still indispensable. Finally, his work in optics was among the earliest systematic investigations of the properties of light. Newton's great work, the *Principia,* was published in 1687, an event that is a milestone in the history of science.

Of all the tributes that have been paid to Newton's greatness, perhaps the most elegant is that by the mathematician Joseph Louis Lagrange: "Newton was the greatest genius who ever lived, and the most fortunate, for there cannot be more than once a system of the world to establish."

It is worth noting that Newton's discovery of the law of gravitation depended on the copernican picture of the solar system. "Common sense" tells us that the earth is the stationary center of the universe, and terrible penalties were once provided for believing otherwise. Clearly the progress of human knowledge about the world we live in depends upon people who are able to look behind the screen of appearances that make up everyday life and who are willing to think for themselves.

The Law of Gravity

What holds the world together

Newton's problem was to find out what the gravitational force one object exerts upon another depends on. First of all, what is the exact direction of the force? Does the force vary with the distance between the objects, and if so, in what way? Does the force vary with the masses of the objects, and if so, in what way? Are any other factors involved in the gravitational force?

Newton began with Kepler's second law, which states that the radius vector of any planet sweeps out equal areas in equal times (Fig. 2-9). He showed, with the help of his newly invented calculus, that the force responsible for such motion must act directly along the line between sun and planet.

Kepler's third law gave a more specific hint about the nature of the force. This law, shown in Fig. 2-10, together with the fact that the gravitational attractive force on a planet must provide the centripetal force needed to hold it in orbit, enabled Newton to show that the force varies inversely with the square of the distance R between them. That is, the force varies as $1/R^2$. Other things equal, a planet twice as far from the sun as usual would feel only $1/2^2 = 1/4$ as much attractive force. If the planet were half as far from the sun as usual, the force on it would be $1/(\frac{1}{2})^2 = 1/\frac{1}{4} = 4$ times greater. This dependence on distance is illustrated in Fig. 2-13.

The conclusion Newton reached about how gravitational force varies with distance was supported by Kepler's first law: each planet moves in an elliptical orbit. Again making use of calculus, Newton showed that a planet attracted to the sun by a force that varies as $1/R^2$ *must* travel in an ellipse or a circle.

Galileo's work on falling bodies supplied the final clue. All objects in free fall at the earth's surface have the same acceleration g, and

$$\text{Weight of object} = (\text{mass of object})(\text{value of } g)$$

Therefore the weight of an object, which is the force of gravity upon it, is always proportional to its mass m. Newton's third law of motion (action-reaction) requires that, if the earth attracts an object, the object also attracts the earth. If the earth's attraction for a stone depends upon the stone's mass, then the reaction

Gravity decreases as the inverse square of the distance

FIG. 2-13
The gravitational force between two bodies depends upon the square of the distance between them. The gravitational force on a planet would drop to one-fourth its usual amount if the distance of the planet from the sun were to be doubled. If the distance is halved the force would increase to 4 times its usual amount.

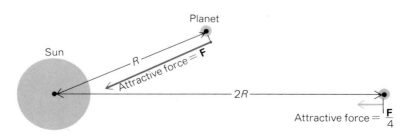

force exerted by the stone on the earth depends upon the earth's mass. Hence the gravitational force between two bodies is proportional to *both* of their masses. We can summarize the above conclusions in a single statement:

Every object in the universe attracts every other object with a force proportional to both of their masses and inversely proportional to the square of the distance between them.

In equation form, *Newton's law of gravitation* states that the force F that acts between two objects whose masses are m_1 and m_2 is

$$F = \frac{G m_1 m_2}{R^2}$$

where R is the distance between them and G is a constant of nature, the same number everywhere in the universe. The value of G is 6.670×10^{-11} N · m²/kg². The point in a body from which R is to be reckoned depends upon the body's shape and the way in which its mass is distributed. The *center of mass* of a uniform sphere is its center (Fig. 2-14).

Variation with Distance

Farther means weaker

The inverse square — $1/R^2$ — variation of gravitational force with distance R means that this force drops rapidly with increasing R. Let us see what this means for a 100-kg astronaut who leaves the earth on a spacecraft.

The law of gravitation

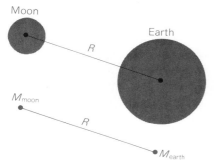

FIG. 2-14
For computing gravitational effects, spherical bodies (such as the earth and moon) may be regarded as though their masses are located at their geometrical centers, provided that they are uniform spheres or consist of concentric uniform spherical shells.

FIG. 2-15
The weight of a person near the earth is the gravitational force the earth exerts upon him. As he goes farther and farther away from the earth's surface, his weight decreases inversely as the square of his distance from the earth's center. The mass of the person here is 100 kg.

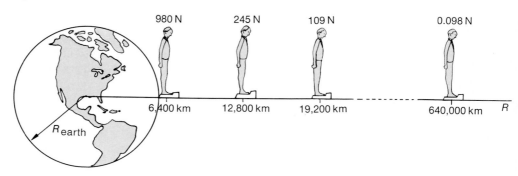

On the earth's surface the astronaut is 6400 km from the earth's center, so $R = 6400$ km and his weight is $mg = 980$ N (220 lb). When he is 12,800 km ($2R$) from the earth's center his weight, which is the gravitational pull of the earth on him, will have fallen to $1/2^2 = 1/4$ of its value on the earth's surface. He now weighs 245 N (Fig. 2-15). At 19,200 km ($3R$) from the earth's center his weight will be only $1/3^2 = 1/9$ of its surface value, or 109 N. When the spacecraft is 640,000 km ($100R$) from the earth's center, the astronaut's weight will have fallen to $1/100^2 = 1/10,000$ of its surface value, or only 0.098 N — the weight of 10 g on the earth's surface.

What Is Gravity?

A fundamental force

Gravity is a *fundamental force* in the sense that it cannot be explained in terms of any other force.

Only four fundamental forces are known: gravitational, electromagnetic, weak, and strong. These forces are responsible for everything that happens in the universe. The weak and strong forces have very short ranges and act within atomic nuclei. The weak force is closely related to the electromagnetic force, and it is probable that the strong force is related to both of them. Electromagnetic forces, which are unlimited in range (like gravity), act between electrically charged particles and govern the structures and behavior of atoms, molecules, solids, and liquids. When one object touches another, an electromagnetic force is what each exerts on the other. Gravitational forces act between all masses and hold together planets, stars, and galaxies of stars.

How can we be sure that the law of gravity, which was obtained from data on the solar system, holds everywhere else in the universe as well?

The evidence for this generalization is indirect but persuasive. First, gravitational forces of some kind certainly act between stars. For instance, there are many double stars in which each member of the pair revolves around the other, which means some force holds them together. Throughout the universe stars occur in giant groups called galaxies, and only gravitation could keep them assembled this way.

But are these the same kinds of gravitation as that which acts in the solar system? Careful analysis of the light and radio waves that reach us from space show that the matter of the rest of the universe is the same as the matter found on the earth. Nowhere do we find reason to suspect that any objects in the universe do not obey Newton's law of gravity, and it would not make sense to propose that such objects exist with no reason whatever to do so. This line of thought may not seem as positive as we might prefer, but taken together with various theoretical arguments, it has convinced nearly all scientists that gravitation is the same phenomenon everywhere.

GRAVITY AND THE EARTH

The law of gravity makes it possible for us to understand a number of aspects of our planet, for instance why it is round and why tides occur in the seas of the world. With the help of this law we can also "weigh" the earth and figure out how to put artificial satellites in orbit.

Why the Earth Is Round

The big squeeze

The earth is round because of gravity

The earth is round because gravity squeezes it into this shape. If any part of it were to stick out very much, the gravitational attraction of the rest of the earth would pull downward on the projection (Fig. 2-16). The material underneath would then flow out sideways until the projection became level or nearly so. The downward forces around the rim of a deep hole would similarly cause the underlying material to flow into it. The same argument applies to the moon, the sun, and the stars.

Such irregularities as mountains and ocean basins are on a very small scale compared with the earth's size. The total range from the Pacific depths to the summit of Everest is less than 20 km; not much compared with the earth's radius of 6400 km.

The earth's rotation causes it to bulge slightly at the equator and be flattened at the poles

While the earth is more nearly round than any other shape, it is not a perfect sphere. This was understood by Isaac Newton three centuries ago. He reasoned that, since the earth is spinning rapidly, inertia would cause the equatorial portion to swing outward, just as a ball on a string does when it is whirled around. As a result the earth bulges slightly at the equator and is slightly flattened at the poles, much like a grapefruit. The total distortion is not great, for the earth is only 43 km wider than it is high (Fig. 2-17).

The earth is about 0.34 percent away from being a perfect sphere. Venus,

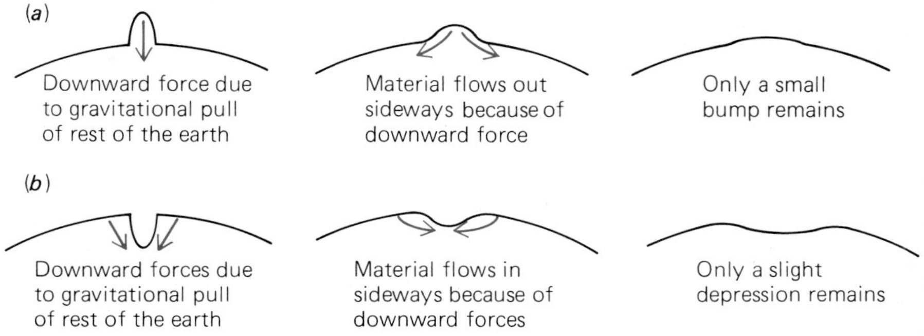

(a) Downward force due to gravitational pull of rest of the earth — Material flows out sideways because of downward force — Only a small bump remains

(b) Downward forces due to gravitational pull of rest of the earth — Material flows in sideways because of downward forces — Only a slight depression remains

FIG. 2-16
Gravity forces the earth to be round. (a) How a large bump would be pulled down. (b) How a large hole would be filled in.

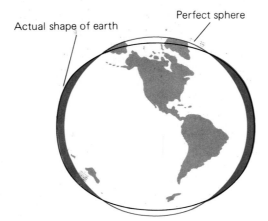

Actual shape of earth   Perfect sphere

FIG. 2-17
The influence of its rotation distorts the earth. The effect is greatly exaggerated in the figure; the equatorial diameter of the earth is actually only 43 km (27 mi) more than its polar diameter.

which rotates very slowly, is hardly distorted at all. Jupiter, Saturn, and Uranus, all of which turn rapidly on their axes, are distorted by 6.2, 9.6, and 6 percent, respectively, and are conspicuously flattened at their poles.

Mass of the Earth

Weighing our planet

On the basis of what we know already, we can find the mass of the earth. It sounds, perhaps, like a formidable job, but it is really a fairly simple calculation, and it is worth following as an example of the indirect way in which scientists go about performing such seemingly impossible feats as "weighing" the earth, the sun, other planets, and even distant stars.

Let us forcus our attention on an apple of mass m on the earth's surface. The downward force of gravity on the apple is its weight of mg:

$$\text{Weight of apple} = F = mg$$

We can also use Newton's law of gravitation to find F, with the result

$$\text{Gravitational force on apple} = F = \frac{GmM}{R^2}$$

Here M is the earth's mass and R is the distance between the apple and the center of the earth, which is the earth's radius of 6400 km $= 6 \times 10^6$ m (Fig. 2-18). The two ways to find F must give the same result, so

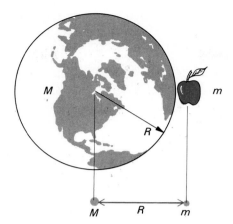

FIG. 2-18
The gravitational force of the earth on an apple at its surface is the same as the force between masses M and m the distance R apart. This force equals the weight of the apple.

Gravitational force on apple = weight of apple

$$\frac{GmM}{R^2} = mg$$

We note that the apple's mass m appears on both sides of this equation, so it cancels out. Solving for the earth's mass M gives

$$M = \frac{gR^2}{G} = \frac{(9.8 \text{ m/s}^2)(6.4 \times 10^6 \text{ m})^2}{6.67 \times 10^{-11} \text{ N} \cdot \text{m}^2/\text{kg}^2} = 6 \times 10^{24} \text{ kg}$$

The number 6×10^{24} is 6 followed by 24 zeros! Enormous as it is, the earth is one of the least massive planets: Saturn has 95 times as much mass, and Jupiter 318 times as much. The sun's mass is more than 300,000 times that of the earth.

The Tides

Up and down twice a day

Those who live near the sea know well the rhythm of the tides, the twice-daily rise and fall of water level. Usually the difference in height between high water and low water is no more than a few meters, but in some regions — the Bay of Fundy in Eastern Canada is one — the tidal range can be over 20 m. What causes the endless advance and return of the sea on such a grand scale?

That there is a relationship of some kind between the moon and the tides was known even in ancient times. It is hard to live on the coast of an ocean and not be aware that the difference between high water and low water is larger at new moon

High and low water at Hall's Harbour, Nova Scotia. Two tidal cycles occur every day. The moon causes the tides by its unequal attraction for parts of the earth at different distances from it.

FIG. 2-19
The origin of the tides. The moon's attraction is greatest at *A*, and so water there is pulled toward the moon. The moon's attraction is least at *B*, hence the solid earth is pulled away from *B* to leave water heaped up there. As the earth rotates, the water bulges stay in place to produce two high and two low tides every day.

(when the moon is entirely dark) and at full moon than it is when only half the moon's disk is visible. Kepler, who succeeded in finding the laws of planetary motion, tried but failed to establish the nature of the connection between the moon and the tides. His efforts were unfairly laughed at by Galileo, who ridiculed Kepler for having "given his ear and assent to the moon's predominancy over the water, and to occult properties and suchlike trifles."

Not until Newton was the cause of the tides finally ascribed to the gravitational attraction of the moon and, to a smaller extent, of the sun as well. The complete theory is somewhat involved, but the following simple explanation accounts for the principal facts.

The moon attracts different parts of the earth with slightly different forces. For matter at *A* in Fig. 2-19 the attraction is strongest, since the distance from the moon is least; at *B*, the point farthest from the moon, the attraction is weakest. Because of these unequal forces, the moon tends to pull matter at *A* away from the rest of the earth, and to pull the entire earth away from matter at *B*. As a result, the earth is somewhat bulged out at *A* and *B*.

Solid rock resists the bulging effect to a large extent, but the fluid ocean responds easily. Water is heaped up on the sides of the earth facing and directly opposite the moon, and is drawn away from other parts of the earth. As the planet rotates, the water bulges are held in place by the moon. The earth, so to speak, moves under the bulges, and a given point on its surface therefore experiences two high tides and two low tides every day.

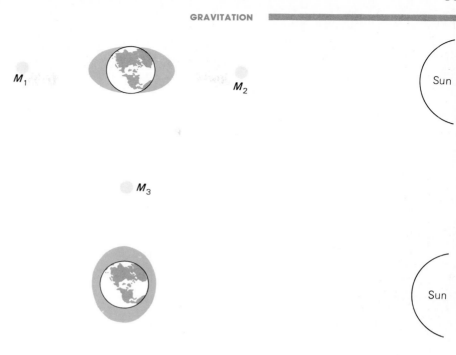

FIG. 2-20
Variation of the tides. Spring tides
are produced when the moon is at
M_1 or M_2, neap tides when the moon
is at M_3 or M_4. The range between
high and low water is greatest for
spring tides.

FIG. 2-21
The tidal bulges are dragged ahead
of the moon by the earth's rotation.
The friction between the bulges and
the earth slows the earth's rotation
on its axis, while the gravitational pull
of the bulges speeds up the moon's
revolution in its orbit. The effect is
greatly exaggerated in the figure.

Why does the moon dominate the tides rather than the sun? After all, the sun
attracts the earth with a gravitational force nearly 180 times as great as that of the
moon. The key to the answer is that what causes the tides is the *difference* between
the gravitational pulls of the moon on the earth's center and on the waters of its
near and far sides. Because the moon is so much closer to the earth than the sun,
this difference is greater for the moon than for the sun.

However, though its tide-raising ability is less than that of the moon, the sun
nevertheless does produce tides of its own. About twice a month, when sun,
moon, and earth are in a straight line, solar tides are added to lunar tides to form
the unusually high (and low) *spring* tides; when the line between moon and earth
is perpendicular to that between sun and earth, the tide-raising forces oppose each
other and tides are the *neap* tides, whose range is small (Fig. 2-20).

The earth does not rotate smoothly beneath the tidal bulges, but tries to carry
them around with it. The moon's attraction prevents them from being dragged very
far, but the line between the bulges is somewhat inclined (about 3°) to the line
between earth and moon (Fig. 2-21). The moon holds the bulges firmly in this
position, and the upraised water drags back on the earth as it rotates. Friction
between water and rotating earth is not very great in the open ocean, but along
irregular coasts it may be considerable. The effect of the friction is, of course, to

slow the earth's rotation. The tidal bulges act like huge but inefficient brake bands clamped on opposite sides of the spinning planet.

In other words, because of tidal friction the day is slowly growing longer. Verification of this effect has come from records of ancient eclipses, among other sources. Using the day's present length, astronomers can calculate precisely when and where eclipses have occurred in the past. These calculations do not agree with the observations recorded by ancient Egyptian and Babylonian astronomers, the discrepancies being greatest for the oldest eclipses. Calculated and observed positions, however, agree well if the slow increase in the day's length is considered. The rate of increase is very small: the time between sunrise and sunrise grows by 0.00002 s per year, 1 s in 50,000 years. Measurements made of daily growth markings on fossil corals extend the data back 380 million years, to a time when the day was only 22 h long.

Artificial Satellites

Why they don't fall down

The first artificial satellite, Sputnik I, was launched by the Soviet Union in 1957. Since then thousands of others have been put into orbits around the earth, most of them by the United States and the Soviet Union. Men and women have been in orbit regularly since 1961, when a Russian cosmonaut circled the globe at a height of about 160 km (100 mi). The first American in orbit was John Glenn the following year. Today the giant 75-ton American space shuttles voyage into orbit and back on a regular schedule.

About 3000 satellites are now in orbits that range from 130 to 36,000 km above the earth. The closer satellites are "eyes in the sky" that survey the earth's surface, both for military purposes and to provide information on weather and earth resources such as mineral deposits, crops, and water. Several satellites at an altitude of 1230 km are used in the Transit navigation system, which enables ships to find their positions with great accuracy day and night.

The most distant satellites circle the equator exactly once a day, so they remain in place indefinitely over a particular location on the earth. A satellite in such a geostationary orbit can "see" about a third of the earth's surface. Nearly 200 of the satellites now in geostationary orbits are used to relay radio and television communications from one place to another, which is cheaper than using cables between them. A typical commercial communications satellite can relay 6000 telephone calls and two television programs at the same time; future ones will have more capacity still.

What keeps all these satellites from falling down? The answer is that a satellite *is* actually falling down, but, like the moon (which is a natural satellite), at exactly such a rate as to circle the earth in a stable orbit. "Stable" is a relative term, to be

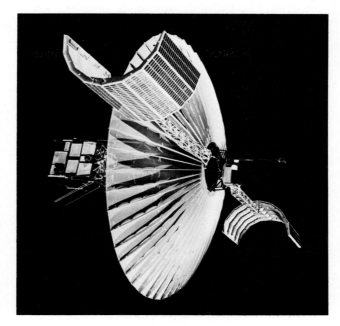

The American satellite Landsat-2 circles the earth at an altitude of 915 km. Landsat-2 carries a television camera and a scanner system powered by solar cells that provides images of the earth's surface using light in four frequency bands. The data radioed back provide information valuable in geology, hydrology, agriculture, and land-use planning.

sure, since friction due to the extremely thin atmosphere present at the altitudes of actual satellites will eventually bring them down. Satellite lifetimes in orbit range from a matter of days to hundreds of years.

How to find the speed needed by a satellite

Let us consider a satellite in a circular orbit. The gravitational force on the satellite is its weight mg, where g is the acceleration of gravity at the satellite's altitude (the value of g decreases with altitude). The centripetal force a satellite of speed v needs to circle the earth at the distance r from the earth's center is mv^2/r. Since the earth's gravity is providing this centripetal force,

$$\text{Centripetal force} = \text{gravitational force}$$

$$\frac{mv^2}{r} = mg$$

$$v^2 = rg$$

$$v = \sqrt{rg} = \text{satellite speed}$$

The mass of the satellite does not matter.

For an orbit just above the earth's surface,

$$r = \text{radius of orbit} = 6.4 \times 10^6 \text{ m}$$

$$g = \text{acceleration of gravity} = 9.8 \text{ m/s}^2$$

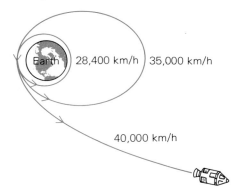

28,400 km/h   35,000 km/h

40,000 km/h

FIG. 2-22
The minimum speed an earth
satellite can have is 28,400 km/h,
while the escape velocity from the
earth is 40,000 km/h.

The satellite speed is therefore

$$v = \sqrt{(6.4 \times 10^6 \text{ m})(9.8 \text{ m/s}^2)} = 7900 \text{ m/s}$$

This speed is about 28,400 km/h (nearly 18,000 mi/h). Anything sent off around the earth at this speed will become a satellite of the earth. (Of course, at such a low altitude air resistance will soon bring it down.) At a lower speed than this an object sent into space would simply fall to the earth, while at a higher speed it would have an elliptical rather than a circular orbit (Fig. 2-22). A satellite initially in an elliptical orbit can be given a circular orbit if it has a small rocket motor to give it a further push at the required distance from the earth.

Escape speed

If its original speed is high enough, at least 40,000 km/h, a spacecraft can escape from the earth entirely. The speed required for something to leave the gravitational influence of an astronomical body permanently is called the *escape speed*. Readers of *Alice in Wonderland* may recall the remark, "Now, here, you see, it takes all the running you can do to stay in the same place. If you want to get somewhere else, you must run at least twice as fast as that!" The ratio between escape speed and minimum orbital speed is actually $\sqrt{2}$, which is 1.41. Escape speeds for the planets are listed in Table 18-1 (see page 619).

Weightlessness

An earth satellite is always falling freely toward the earth. As a result, an astronaut inside feels "weightless," just as a person who jumps off a diving board feels "weightless." But a gravitational force does act on both people — what is missing is the upward reaction force of the ground, a diving board, the floor of a room, the seat of a chair, or whatever each person would otherwise be pressing on. In the case of an astronaut, the floor of the satellite falls just as fast as he does instead of pushing back on him.

THE "SCIENTIFIC METHOD"

After only two chapters, we have already learned a great deal about how the physical universe works. Before going further it is worth looking more closely into how all this knowledge was gathered and why we can have confidence in it. No single procedure was responsible, instead a variety of lines of attack, but underlying all of them was a basic pattern of inquiry, a general scheme for looking at nature, that has become known as the *scientific method*.

Four Steps

But no ultimate truth

It is possible to think of the scientific method in terms of four steps: (1) formulating a problem; (2) observation; (3) interpretation of the observed data; and (4) testing the interpretation by further observations. Observations of the natural world are at the heart of the scientific method, since they serve both as the foundation on which a scientist builds his theories and as the means by which he checks these theories (Fig. 2-23).

FIG. 2-23
The scientific method. No hypothesis is ever final because future data may show that it is incorrect or incomplete. Unless it turns out to be wrong, a hypothesis never leaves the loop of experiment, interpretation, testing. Of course, the more times the hypothesis goes around the loop successfully, the more likely it is to be a valid interpretation of nature. A hypothesis that has survived testing is called a law or theory.

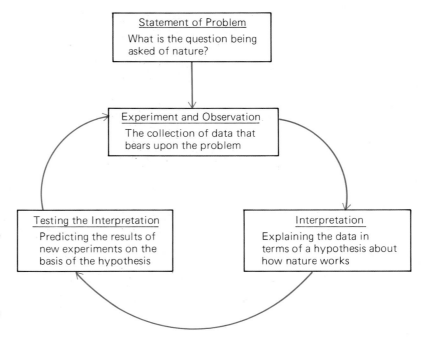

Statement of Problem
What is the question being asked of nature?

Experiment and Observation
The collection of data that bears upon the problem

Testing the Interpretation
Predicting the results of new experiments on the basis of the hypothesis

Interpretation
Explaining the data in terms of a hypothesis about how nature works

1. *Formulating a problem* may mean no more than choosing a certain field to study, but more often a scientist has some specific idea in mind he wishes to investigate further. In many cases there is a good deal of overlap between formulating a problem and interpreting the data. The scientist has a speculation, a hunch, about some aspect of nature, but he or she cannot come to a definite conclusion without further work.

2. *Observation* is carried out painstakingly, to be sure that all relevant data are collected and are accurate. If the amount of data is large, much classification and analysis may be needed before going further.

3. *Interpretation* may lead to a general rule or pattern to which the observations seem to conform. Or it may be a more ambitious attempt to devise a hypothesis that accounts for what has been found in terms of how nature works. Often a *model*— a simplified abstraction of reality — is part of a hypothesis. The ptolemaic and copernican systems are both models of the solar system, for instance. In any case, it must be possible to extend the interpretation from one set of observations to other observations in different circumstances; in other words, to predict the results of other experiments.

4. *Testing the interpretation* involves performing new experiments whose results can be predicted from the hypothesis. If the new observations agree with the predictions, the hypothesis has proved its usefulness. The new observations may well lead to refinements of the original hypothesis, which in turn must be checked by further experiment, and so on indefinitely.

As put forward originally, a scientific interpretation is usually called a *hypothesis*. When it has survived checking and rechecking, the hypothesis becomes a *law* or a *theory*. A law states a regularity or relationship of some kind; Newton's law of gravitation is an example. A law tells us *what*. A theory, on the other hand, tells us *why*. It explains why certain phenomena occur and, if they obey a particular law, how that law originates in terms of broader considerations. Thus Albert Einstein's general theory of relativity (discussed in Chap. 3) interprets gravitation as a distortion in the properties of space and time around a body of matter. From his theory, Einstein made a number of predictions, among them that light should be affected by gravity. The success of these predictions, together with its ability to account for Newton's law, led to the acceptance of the general theory of relativity.

As discussed in the Introduction to this book, it is the essence of science that all its laws and theories are *provisional*. They are accepted only as long as no contradictory evidence comes to light. If such evidence turns up, the law or theory must be modified or discarded. "Ultimate truth" can never be achieved in science because we will never know everything. But an idea that has survived thorough checking and whose predictions have thus far always been successful is likely to have much truth in it, even if it later turns out not to be the whole story. Thus Kepler's discovery that the planetary orbits are ellipses rather than the circles Copernicus suggested does not mean that Copernicus's basic idea that the planets revolve around the sun was wrong, only that it needed improvement.

A breakdown of the scientific method into four steps does not mean that a working scientist always follows these steps in order. Sometimes all four processes go on more or less at the same time. Certainly a scientific beginner cannot expect to make profound discoveries just by going into a laboratory and telling himself or herself to observe, interpret, and check. He would not know, first and most important, what questions to ask of nature. Nor would he know the methods of observation or how to design appropriate experiments. And, finally, he would not have the background or the intuition or the trained imagination to arrive at useful interpretations. The scientific method is not a mechanical process but a human activity that needs creative thinking for all its steps.

An Example of the Scientific Method

How one thing leads to another

A classic example of the scientific method is the history of attempts to explain planetary motions. The original observations are records of the positions of the planets in the sky at various times. The ancient Greeks made several attempts to interpret these data, the most successful being the ptolemaic hypothesis. From this hypothesis future positions of the planets were predicted, and observations were in reasonable agreement with the predictions. As centuries passed and more data were accumulated, the predictions turned out not really so accurate. The original hypothesis had to be modified, but this meant introducing additional complexity.

A rival interpretation then appeared, the copernican hypothesis. Predictions from this hypothesis at first agreed no better with the data, although it had the merit of greater simplicity. Kepler refined Copernicus's idea, basing his detailed laws on the measurements of Tycho Brahe. With these modifications the copernican hypothesis now gave predictions that corresponded well with the data. Because of these results and because of the simplicity of its model, the copernican hypothesis replaced the ptolemaic one.

Behind Kepler's laws and Galileo's analysis of falling bodies Newton found an even broader generalization, the law of gravitation. He and others used that marvel of simplicity and universality to build a comprehensive picture of the astronomical universe. One of the most celebrated of the predictions based on Newton's law led to the discovery of the planet Neptune.

The planet Uranus was found by accident in 1781. Measurements during the next few years enabled astronomers to work out details of the new planet's orbit and to predict its future positions in the sky. To make these predictions, it was necessary to consider not only the sun's attraction but the smaller attractions of the neighboring planets Jupiter and Saturn as well. For 40 years, about half the time required for Uranus to make one complete revolution, calculated positions of the planet seemed to agree well with observed positions.

Then a discrepancy crept in. Little by little the planet moved away from its predicted path among the stars. The calculations were checked and rechecked,

How the planet Neptune was discovered

but no mistake could be found; the attractions of all known bodies had been correctly allowed for. One of two conclusions seemed necessary. Either the law of gravitation, on which the calculations were based, was not accurate, or else some unknown body was attracting Uranus away from its predicted path.

So firmly established was the law of gravitation that two young men, Urbain Leverrier in France and John Couch Adams in England, set themselves the task of calculating by hand the position of an unknown body that might be responsible for the discrepancies in Uranus's position. Adams, completing his computations first, sent them to England's Astronomer Royal. Busy with other matters, the Astronomer Royal put the calculations away to examine later. Meanwhile, Leverrier sent his paper to a young German astronomer, Johann Gottfried Galle, who lost no time in turning his telescope to the part of the sky where the new planet should appear. Very close to the position predicted by Leverrier, Galle found a faint object, which proved to be the eighth member of the sun's family and was called Neptune. A little later the Astronomer Royal showed that Neptune's position had been correctly given in Adams's work also.

It is safe to say that the scientific method has made possible the technological civilization of today. Without it science and engineering would still be in a primitive trial-and-error stage, far away from the present-day state of these disciplines. Observed facts are the foundation of science and the ultimate proof of its results. Usually the facts must be based on observations that can be repeated at will. Always they must be facts that would be clear to anyone with normal senses and sufficient training to understand them. Scientists may disagree about how observations should be interpreted, but about the observations themselves there should be no dispute. This insistence on the primacy of accurate, objective data is what sets the various natural sciences apart from other modes of intellectual endeavor. But it is likewise a limitation that makes it hard to apply the scientific method in fields of thought into which human values enter — because human values are by nature subjective, the products of an individual's emotions, and therefore impossible to deal with in an objective, quantitative fashion.

IMPORTANT TERMS

A **scalar quantity** has magnitude only; mass and speed are examples. A **vector quantity** has both magnitude and direction; force and velocity are examples. An arrowed line that represents the magnitude and direction of a quantity is called a **vector.**

The **centripetal force** on an object moving along a curved path is the inward force needed to cause this motion. In the case of an object moving in a circle, the centripetal force acts toward the center of the circle.

In the **ptolemaic system,** the earth is stationary at the center of the universe. In the **copernican system,** the earth rotates and, with the other planets, revolves around the sun. Observational evidence supports the copernican system.

Newton's **law of gravitation** states that every object in the universe attracts every other object with a force directly proportional to both their masses and inversely proportional to the square of the distance separating them.

The **scientific method** of studying nature can be thought of as consisting of four steps: (1) formulating a problem; (2) observing and experimenting; (3) interpreting the results; (4) testing the interpretation by further observation and experiment. When first proposed, a scientific interpretation is called a **hypothesis.** After thorough checking, it becomes a **law** if it states a regularity or relationship, or a **theory** if it uses general considerations to account for specific phenomena.

IMPORTANT FORMULAS

Centripetal force: $F_c = \dfrac{mv^2}{r}$

Law of gravitation: $F = \dfrac{Gm_1 m_2}{R^2}$

MULTIPLE CHOICE

1. Of the following quantities, the one that is not a vector quantity is
  a. velocity
  b. acceleration
  c. mass
  d. force

2. Which of the following units could be associated with a vector quantity?
  a. kg
  b. h
  c. cm^3
  d. m/s^2

3. In order to cause something to move in a circular path, it is necessary to provide
  a. reaction force
  b. inertial force
  c. centripetal force
  d. gravitational force

4. An object is traveling in a circle with a constant speed. Its acceleration is constant in
  a. magnitude only
  b. direction only
  c. both magnitude and direction
  d. neither magnitude nor direction

5. A body moving in a circle at constant speed is accelerated
  a. in the direction of motion
  b. toward the center of the circle
  c. away from the center of the circle
  d. any of the above, depending upon the circumstances

6. A car rounds a curve on a level road. The centripetal force on the car is provided by
  a. inertia
  b. gravity
  c. friction between the tires and the road
  d. the force applied to the steering wheel

7. The centripetal force that keeps the earth in its orbit around the sun is provided
  a. by inertia
  b. by its rotation on its axis

  c. partly by the gravitational pull of the sun
  d. entirely by the gravitational pull of the sun

8. Kepler modified the copernican system by showing that the planetary orbits are
  a. ellipses
  b. circles
  c. combinations of circles forming looped orbits
  d. the same distance apart from one another

9. According to Kepler's third law, the time needed by a planet to complete an orbit around the sun depends upon the planet's
  a. diameter
  b. distance from the sun
  c. mass
  d. acceleration of gravity

10. The gravitational force with which the earth attracts the moon
  a. is less than the force with which the moon attracts the earth
  b. is the same as the force with which the moon attracts the earth
  c. is more than the force with which the moon attracts the earth
  d. varies with the phase of the moon

11. The shape of the earth is closest to that of
  a. a perfect sphere
  b. an egg
  c. a football
  d. a grapefruit

12. The usual tidal pattern in most parts of the world consists of
  a. a high tide on one day and a low tide on the next
  b. one high tide and one low tide daily
  c. two high tides and two low tides daily
  d. three high tides and three low tides daily

13. Tides are caused
  a. only by the sun
  b. only by the moon
  c. by both the sun and the moon
  d. sometimes by the sun and sometimes by the moon

14. It is not true that, because of the tides,
  a. the earth's rotation is slowing down
  b. the moon's orbital speed is increasing
  c. days are shorter than they used to be
  d. ancient eclipses did not occur when present calculations indicate they should have occurred

15. An astronaut inside an orbiting satellite feels weightless because
  a. he or she is wearing a space suit
  b. the satellite is falling toward the earth just as fast as the

astronaut, so there is no upward reaction force on him or her

c. there is no gravitational pull from the earth so far away

d. the sun's gravitational pull balances out the earth's gravitational pull

16. A scientific law or theory is valid

a. forever

b. for a certain number of years, after which it is retested

c. as long as a committee of scientists say so

d. as long as it is not contradicted by new experimental findings

17. The radius of the circle in which an object is moving at constant speed is doubled. The required centripetal force is

a. one-quarter as great as before

b. half as great as before

c. twice as great as before

d. 4 times as great as before

18. A car rounds a curve at 20 km/h. If it rounds the curve at 40 km/h, its tendency to overturn is

a. halved

b. doubled

c. tripled

d. quadrupled

19. A 1200-kg car whose speed is 6 m/s rounds a turn whose radius is 30 m. The centripetal force on the car is

a. 48 N

b. 147 N

c. 240 N

d. 1440 N

20. A ball of mass 0.2 kg is whirled in a circle at the end of a string 1 m long whose breaking strength is 10 N. Neglecting gravity, the maximum speed of the ball is approximately

a. 2 m/s

b. 7 m/s

c. 10 m/s

d. 50 m/s

21. If the earth were 3 times farther from the sun than it is now, the gravitational force exerted on it by the sun would be

a. 3 times as large as it is now

b. 9 times as large as it is now

c. one-third as large as it is now

d. one-ninth as large as it is now

22. A woman whose mass is 60 kg on the earth's surface is in a spacecraft at an altitude of one earth's radius above the surface. Her mass there is

a. 15 kg

b. 30 kg

c. 60 kg

d. 120 kg

23. A man whose weight is 800 N on the earth's surface is also in the spacecraft of Question 22. His weight there is

a. 200 N

b. 400 N

c. 800 N

d. 1600 N

QUESTIONS

1. Is it correct to say that scalar quantities are abstract, idealized quantities with no precise counterparts in the physical world, whereas vector quantities properly represent reality because they take directions into account?

2. What kind of quantity is the magnitude of a vector quantity?

3. Under what circumstances, if any, can something move in a circular path without a centripetal force acting on it?

4. A car makes a clockwise turn on a level road at too high a speed and overturns. Do its left or right wheels leave the ground first?

5. A person swings an iron ball in a vertical circle at the end of a string. At what point in the circle is the string most likely to break? Why?

6. Ancient astronomers were troubled by variations in the brightnesses of the various planets with time. Does the ptolemaic or the copernican system account better for these variations?

7. According to Kepler's second law, the earth travels fastest when it is closest to the sun. Is this consistent with the law of gravitation? Explain.

8. Compare the weight and mass of an object at the earth's surface with what they would be at an altitude of two earth's radii.

9. Is the sun's gravitational pull on the earth the same at all seasons of the year? Explain.

10. According to the theory of gravitation, the earth must be continually "falling" toward the sun. If this is true, why does the average distance between earth and sun not grow smaller?

11. An artificial satellite is placed in orbit half as far from the earth as the moon is. Would its time of revolution around the earth be longer or shorter than the moon's if its orbit is to be stable?

12. A track team on the moon could set new records for the high jump or pole vault (if they did not need space suits, of course) because of the smaller gravitational force. Could sprinters also improve their times for the 100-m dash?

13. A hole is bored to the center of the earth and a stone is dropped into it. How do the mass and weight of the stone at the earth's center compare with their values at the earth's surface?

14. The earth takes almost exactly 24 h to make a complete rotation about its axis, so one might expect successive high tides to occur 12 h apart. In reality, the interval between high tides is

12 h 25 min. Can you account for the difference?

15. An airplane makes a vertical circle in which it is upside down at the top of the loop. Will the pilot fall out of the seat if there is no belt to hold him or her in place?

PROBLEMS

1. What centripetal force is needed to keep a 1-kg ball moving in a circle of radius 2 m at a speed of 5 m/s?

2. The 200-g head of a golf club moves at 45 m/s in a circular arc of 1 m radius. How much force must the player exert on the handle of the club to prevent it from flying out of his hands? Ignore the mass of the club's shaft.

3. The string of a certain yo-yo is 80 cm long and will break when the tension in it is 10 N. What is the highest speed the 200-g yo-yo can have when it is being whirled in a circle? (Ignore the gravitational pull of the earth on the yo-yo.)

4. A string 1 m long is used to whirl a 500-g stone in a vertical circle at a speed of 5 m/s. Find the tension in the string when the stone is at the top and at the bottom of its path.

5. A road has a hump 12 m in radius. What is the minimum speed at which a car will leave the road at the top of the hump?

6. The maximum force a road can exert on the tires of a certain 1200-kg car is 2500 N. What is the greatest speed with which the car can round a turn of radius 300 m?

7. A 40-kg crate is lying on the flat floor of the rear of a station wagon moving at 15 m/s. A force of 150 N is needed to slide the crate against the friction between the bottom of the crate and the floor. What is the minimum radius of a turn the station wagon can make if the box is not to slip?

8. Find the minimum radius at which an airplane flying at 300 m/s can make a U-turn if the centripetal force on it is not to exceed 4 times the airplane's weight.

9. A 2-kg mass and a 5-kg mass are 1 m apart. Find the gravitational force each one exerts on the other, and find their respective accelerations if they are free to move.

10. A dishonest grocer installs a 100-kg lead block under the pan of his scale. How much gravitational force does the lead exert on 2 kg of cheese placed on the pan if the centers of mass of the lead and cheese are 0.3 m apart? Compare this force with the weight of 1 g of cheese to see if putting the lead under the scale was worth doing.

11. The sun's mass is 2×10^{30} kg, the mass of Jupiter is 1.9×10^{27} kg, and the average radius of its orbit is 7.8×10^{11} m. Find the gravitational force the sun exerts on Jupiter and the orbital speed Jupiter must have in order not to be drawn into the sun nor to fly off into space.

12. With the help of the data in Table 18-1, find the minimum speed artificial satellites must have to pursue stable orbits about Jupiter.

ANSWERS TO MULTIPLE CHOICE

1. c	**7.** d	**13.** c	**19.** d
2. d	**8.** a	**14.** c	**20.** b
3. c	**9.** b	**15.** b	**21.** d
4. a	**10.** b	**16.** d	**22.** c
5. b	**11.** d	**17.** b	**23.** a
6. c	**12.** c	**18.** d	

3

ENERGY

The word energy has become part of everyday life. We say that an active person is energetic. We hear a candy bar described as being full of energy. We complain about the cost of the electric energy that lights our lamps and turns our motors. We worry about some day running out of the energy stored in coal and oil. We argue about whether nuclear energy is a blessing or a curse. What do all of these have in common?

In general, energy refers to an ability to accomplish change. When almost anything happens in the physical world, energy is somehow involved, usually by being transformed from one kind into another. But "change" is not a very precise notion, and we must be sure of exactly what we are talking about in order to go further. Our procedure will be to begin with the simpler idea of *work* and then use it to relate change and energy in the orderly way of science.

WORK

No work done

Work done

FIG. 3-1
The work done by a force on a body is the product of the force and the distance through which the body moves while the force acts upon it. For a force to do work on a body, the body must undergo a displacement while the force acts on it. No work is done by pushing against a rigid wall.

Work is force times distance

No work is done without both a force and a displacement

Changes that take place in the physical world are the result of forces. Forces are needed to pick things up, to move things from one place to another, to squeeze things, to stretch things, and so on. However, not all forces produce changes, and it is the distinction between forces that accomplish change and forces that do not that is central to the idea of work.

The Meaning of Work

A measure of the change a force produces

If we push against a stone wall, nothing happens. We have applied a force, but the wall has not moved and shows no effects of the push. However, if we apply the same force to one of the stones in the wall, the stone flies through the air (Fig. 3-1). In this case something has been accomplished as the result of the push.

The basic difference between the two situations is that, in the first case, our hand did not move while it pushed against the wall. The force was a stationary one. In the second case, when we threw the stone, our hand did move while the force was being applied and before the stone actually left our grasp. It is the motion of the body while the force acts upon it that is responsible for the difference in the two results.

When we examine in detail the results of applying forces to various objects, we find that every force that produces an effect such as an acceleration or a distortion undergoes a change in position as it does so. That is, a moving force does something, a stationary force does not. The physicist makes this observation definite by introducing a quantity called *work:*

The work done by a force acting on an object is equal to the magnitude of the force multiplied by the distance through which the force acts.

If nothing moves, no work is done, no matter how great the force. And even if something moves, work is not done on it unless a force is acting.

What we usually think of as work is in accord with this definition. However, we must be careful not to relate becoming tired with the amount of work done. Pushing against a wall for an afternoon in the hot sun is certainly more tiring than just throwing a stone, but work is done in throwing a stone whereas nothing at all is accomplished by pushing against the wall.

In equation form,

$$W = Fd$$

Work done = (applied force)(distance through which force acts)

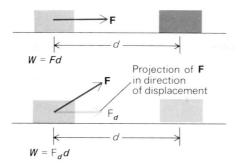

FIG. 3-2
When a force and the distance through which it acts are parallel, the work done is equal to the product of F and d. When they are not in the same direction, the work done is equal to the product of d and the projection of **F** in the direction of **d**.

No work is done when **F** is perpendicular to **d**

The direction of the force **F** is assumed to be the same as the direction of the distance **d**. If it is not, for example in the case of a boy pulling a wagon with a rope not parallel to the ground, we must use for F the projection of the applied force **F** that acts in the direction of motion (Fig. 3-2).

A force that is perpendicular to the motion of an object can do no work upon it. Thus gravity, which results in a downward force on everything near the earth, does no work on objects moving horizontally along the earth's surface. However, if we drop an object, as it falls to the ground work is definitely done upon it.

No work is done when a force is exerted unless there is motion.

The SI unit of work is the *joule* (J), where one joule is the amount of work done by a force of one newton when it acts through a distance of one meter. That is,

$$1 \text{ joule (J)} = 1 \text{ newton-meter (N} \cdot \text{m)}$$

The joule is named after the English scientist James Joule and is pronounced "jool."

If we push a box for 8 m across a floor with a force of 100 N (22.5 lb), the work we perform is

$$W = Fd = (100 \text{ N})(8 \text{ m}) = 800 \text{ J}$$

The mass of the box does not matter; what counts is the force applied and the distance through which the box moves.

Power

The rate of doing work

The time needed to carry out a job is often as important as the amount of work needed. If we have enough time, even the tiny motor of a toy train can lift an elevator as high as we like. However, if we want the elevator to take us up fairly quickly, we must use a motor whose output of work is rapid in terms of the total work needed. Thus the rate at which work is being done is a significant quantity. This rate is called *power:* the more powerful something is, the faster it can do work.

If the amount of work W is done in a period of time t, the power involved is

$$P = \frac{W}{t}$$

$$\text{Power} = \frac{\text{work done}}{\text{time interval}}$$

The SI unit of power is the *watt* (W), where

$$1 \text{ watt (W)} = 1 \text{ joule/second (J/s)}$$

Thus a motor with a power output of 500 W is capable of doing 500 J of work per second. The same motor can do 250 J of work in 0.5 s, 1000 J of work in 2 s, 5000 J of work in 10 s, and so on. The watt is quite a small unit, and often the *kilowatt* (kW) is used instead, where

$$1 \text{ kilowatt (kW)} = 1000 \text{ watts}$$

Horsepower

The horsepower (hp) is the traditional unit of power in engineering. The origin of this unit is interesting. In order to sell the steam engines he had perfected two centuries ago, James Watt had to compare their power outputs with that of a horse. After various tests he found that a typical horse could perform work at a rate of 497 W for as much as 10 hours per day. To avoid any disputes, Watt increased this figure by one-half to establish the unit he called the horsepower. Watt's horsepower therefore represents a rate of doing work of 746 W:

$$1 \text{ horsepower (hp)} = 746 \text{ W} = 0.746 \text{ kW}$$

$$1 \text{ kilowatt (kW)} = 1.34 \text{ hp}$$

The early steam engines ranged from 4 to 100 hp, with the 20-hp model the most popular.

Power output of a person

A person in good physical condition is usually capable of a continuous power output of about 75 W, which is 0.1 hp. An athlete such as a runner or a swimmer during a distance event may have a power output 2 or 3 times greater. What limits the power output of a trained athlete is not muscular development but the supply of oxygen from the lungs through the bloodstream to the muscles, where it is used in the metabolic processes that extract work from nutrients. However, for a period of less than a second, an athlete's power output may exceed 5 kW, which accounts for the feats of weightlifters and jumpers.

ENERGY

We now go from the straightforward idea of work to the complex and many-sided idea of *energy:*

Energy is that property something has that enables it to do work.

Energy is a measure of ability to do work

When we say that something has energy, we mean it is capable, directly or indirectly, of exerting a force on something else and performing work on it. When work is done on something, on the other hand, energy is added to it. Energy is measured in the same unit as work, the joule.

Kinetic Energy

The energy of motion

Kinetic energy is energy of motion

Energy occurs in several forms. One of them is the energy a moving object has because of its motion. Every moving object has the capacity to do work. By striking

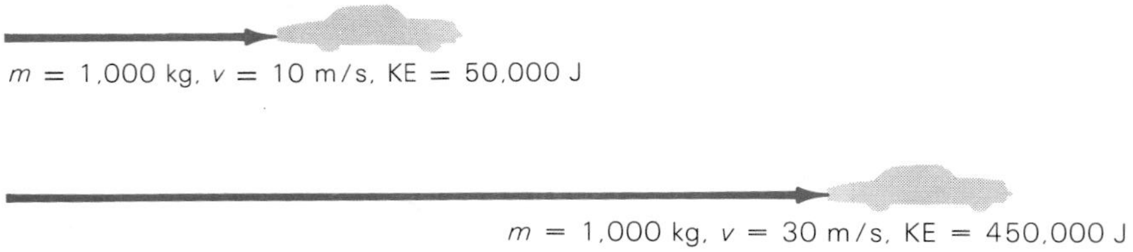

$m = 1{,}000$ kg, $v = 10$ m/s, KE $= 50{,}000$ J

$m = 1{,}000$ kg, $v = 30$ m/s, KE $= 450{,}000$ J

FIG. 3-3
Kinetic energy is proportional to the square of the speed. A car traveling at 30 m/s has 9 times the KE of a car traveling at 10 m/s.

something else, the moving object can exert a force and cause the second object to shift its position, to break apart, or otherwise to show the effects of having work done on it. It is this property that defines energy, so we conclude that all moving things have energy by virtue of their motion. The energy of a moving object is called *kinetic energy* (KE).

The kinetic energy of a moving thing depends upon its mass and its speed. The greater the mass and the greater the speed, the more the KE. A train going at 30 km/h has more energy than a horse galloping at the same speed and more energy than a similar train going at 10 km/h. The exact way KE varies with mass m and speed v is given by the formula

$$\text{Kinetic energy} = \text{KE} = \tfrac{1}{2}mv^2$$

KE depends upon the square of the speed

The v^2 factor means the kinetic energy increases very rapidly with increasing speed. At 30 m/s (67 mi/h) a car has 9 times as much KE as at 10 m/s (22 mi/h) — and requires 9 times as much force to bring to a stop in the same distance (Fig. 3-3). The fact that KE, and hence the ability to do work (in this case, damage), depends upon the square of the speed is what is responsible for the severity of automobile accidents at high speeds. The variation with mass is less marked: a 2000-kg car going at 10 m/s has just twice the KE of a 1000-kg car with the same speed.

The kinetic energy of a 1000-kg car whose speed is 10 m/s is

$$\text{KE} = \tfrac{1}{2}mv^2 = (\tfrac{1}{2})(1000 \text{ kg})(10 \text{ m/s})^2$$
$$= (\tfrac{1}{2})(1000 \text{ kg})(10 \text{ m/s})(10 \text{ m/s}) = 50{,}000 \text{ J}$$

In order to bring the car to this speed from rest, 50,000 J of work had to be done by its engine. To stop the car from this speed, the same amount of work must be done by its brakes.

Potential Energy

The energy of position

When we drop a stone, it falls faster and faster and finally strikes the ground. If we lift the stone afterward, we see that it has done work by making a shallow hole in

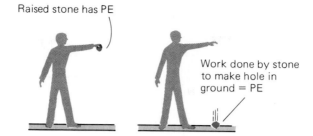

Raised stone has PE

Work done by stone to make hole in ground = PE

FIG. 3-4
A raised stone has potential energy because it can do work on the ground when dropped.

Potential energy is energy of position

the ground (Fig. 3-4). In its original raised position, the stone must have had the capacity to do work even though it was not moving at the time.

The amount of work the stone could do by falling to the ground from its original position is called its *potential energy* (PE). Just as kinetic energy may be thought of as energy of motion, potential energy may be thought of as energy of position.

Examples of potential energy are everywhere. A book on a table has potential energy, since it can fall to the floor. A skier at the top of a slope, water at the top of a waterfall, a car at the top of a hill, anything able to move toward the earth under the influence of gravity has energy because of its position. Nor is the earth's gravity necessary: a stretched spring has potential energy since it can do work when it is

A skier at the top of a slope has potential energy which turns into kinetic energy as he or she descends.

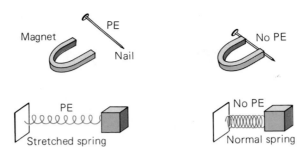

FIG. 3-5
Two examples of potential energy.

let go, and a nail near a magnet has potential energy since it can do work in moving to the magnet (Fig. 3-5).

It is easy to find a formula for the gravitational PE an object has near the earth's surface. The work W needed to raise an object of mass m to a height h above its original position, as in Fig. 3-6, is

$$W = Fd = mgh$$

$$\text{Work} = (\text{force})(\text{distance}) = (\text{weight})(\text{height})$$

since the force needed is the object's weight of mg. Hence the potential energy at the height h is

Gravitational potential energy of mass m at height h

$$\text{Potential energy} = \text{PE} = mgh$$

This result for PE is in accord with our experience. Consider a pile driver, a simple machine that lifts a heavy weight (the "hammer") and allows it to fall on the

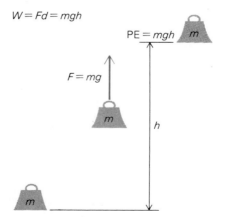

FIG. 3-6
The potential energy of a raised object is equal to the work used to lift it.

In the operation of a pile driver, the potential energy of the raised hammer changes into kinetic energy as it falls and then into work as the pile is pushed down.

head of a pile, which is a wooden or steel post, to drive the pile into the ground. From the formula PE = mgh we would expect the effectiveness of a pile driver to depend on the mass m of its hammer and the height h from which it is dropped, which is exactly what experience shows.

Reference Level

PE is a relative quantity

The gravitational potential energy of an object depends upon the level from which it is reckoned. Often the earth's surface is convenient, but sometimes other references are more appropriate.

Suppose we hold a 10-g (0.01-kg) pencil 10 cm (0.1 m) above a table whose top is 1 m above the floor (Fig. 3-7). The pencil has a potential energy of

$$\text{PE} = mgh = (0.01 \text{ kg})(9.8 \text{ m/s}^2)(0.1 \text{ m}) = 0.0098 \text{ J}$$

relative to the table, and a potential energy of

$$\text{PE} = mgh = (0.01 \text{ kg})(9.8 \text{ m/s}^2)(1.1 \text{ m}) = 0.108 \text{ J}$$

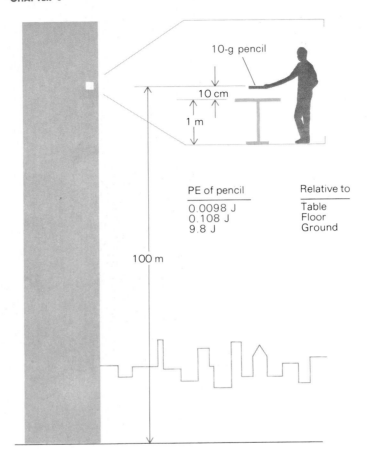

PE of pencil	Relative to
0.0098 J	Table
0.108 J	Floor
9.8 J	Ground

FIG. 3-7
The gravitational potential energy of a body depends upon the choice of reference level. Potential energy is a relative quantity, and only the difference between the potential energies of a body at different points is significant.

relative to the floor. The room in which we are might well be, say, 100 m above the ground, so that the potential energy of the pencil is

$$PE = mgh = (0.01 \text{ kg})(9.8 \text{ m/s}^2)(100 \text{ m}) = 9.8 \text{ J}$$

relative to the ground.

What, then, is the pencil's true potential energy? The answer is that there is no such thing as "true" potential energy. Potential energy is a *relative* quantity that has meaning only in terms of a specific reference location. However, the *difference* between the potential energies of a body at two points in its motion *is* significant, since it is this difference that is changed into work or kinetic energy.

Potential energy is a relative quantity

Energy Transformations

Easy come, easy go

Nearly all familiar mechanical processes involve interchanges of energy among its kinetic and potential forms and work. Thus when the car of Fig. 3-8 is driven to the top of a hill, its engine must do work in order to raise the car. At the top, the car has an amount of potential energy equal to the work done in getting it up there (neglecting friction). If the engine is turned off, the car can still coast down the hill, and its kinetic energy at the bottom of the hill will be the same as its potential energy at the top.

Changes of a similar nature, from kinetic energy to potential and back, are exhibited in the motion of a planet in its orbit around the sun (Fig. 3-9) and in the motion of a pendulum (Fig. 3-10). The orbits of the planets are ellipses with the sun at one focus, and each planet is therefore at a constantly varying distance from the sun. At all times the total of its potential and kinetic energies remains the same.

Most events in the physical world involve energy transformations

FIG. 3-8
In the absence of friction, a car can coast from the top of one hill into a valley and then up to the top of another hill of the same height as the first. In doing this the initial potential energy of the car is converted into kinetic energy as it goes downhill, and this kinetic energy then turns into potential energy as it climbs the next hill. The total amount of energy remains unchanged.

FIG. 3-9
Energy transformations in planetary motion. Near the sun the potential energy of a planet is a minimum and its kinetic energy a maximum, while far from the sun its potential energy is a maximum. The total energy of the planet is the same at all points in its orbit. (Planetary orbits are much more nearly circular than shown here.)

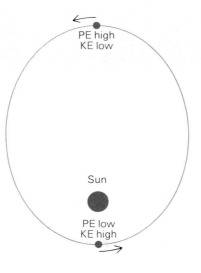

Sun

PE high
KE low

PE low
KE high

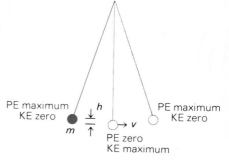

PE maximum
KE zero

PE maximum
KE zero

PE zero
KE maximum

FIG. 3-10
Energy transformations in pendulum motion. The constant total energy of the ball is continuously exchanged between kinetic and potential forms.

At his maximum altitude, a person bouncing on a trampoline has only gravitational potential energy. As he falls, the PE turns into kinetic energy. When he strikes the trampoline, the KE is converted into the elastic potential energy of the stretched springs that hold the trampoline to its supports. The PE of the springs then becomes KE as the person rises into the air to begin another cycle.

When the planet is close to the sun, its potential energy is low and its kinetic energy high. The additional speed due to the increased kinetic energy keeps the planet from being pulled into the sun by the greater gravitational force it experiences at this point in its path. When the planet is far from the sun, its potential energy is high and its kinetic energy correspondingly lower, the reduced speed exactly keeping pace with the reduced gravitational force.

Pendulum

A pendulum, as in Fig. 3-10 consists of a ball suspended by a string. When the ball is pulled to one side with its string taut and then released, it swings back and forth indefinitely. When it is released, the ball has a potential energy relative to the bottom of its path of mgh. At its lowest point all this potential energy has become kinetic energy $\frac{1}{2}mv^2$. After reaching the bottom, the ball continues in its motion until it rises to the same height h on the opposite side from its initial position. Then, momentarily at rest since all its kinetic energy is now potential energy, the ball begins to retrace its path back through the bottom to its initial position.

Energy has many forms

Energy can exist in a variety of modes besides kinetic and potential. The *chemical energy* of gasoline is used to propel our cars and the chemical energy of food enables our bodies to perform work. *Heat energy* from burning coal or oil is used to form the steam that drives the turbines of power stations. *Electric energy* turns motors in home and factory. *Radiant energy* from the sun performs work in lifting water from the earth's surface into clouds, in producing differences in air temperature that cause winds, and in promoting chemical reactions in plants that produce foods.

Just as kinetic energy can be converted into potential energy and potential into kinetic, so other forms of energy can readily be transformed. In the cylinders of a car engine, for example, chemical energy stored in gasoline and air is changed first to heat energy when the mixture is ignited by the spark plugs, then to mechanical energy as the expanding gases push down on the pistons. This mechanical energy is in large part transmitted to the wheels, but some is used to turn the generator and thus produce electric energy for charging the battery, and some is changed to heat by friction in bearings. Energy transformations go on constantly, all about us.

Rest Energy

Matter is a form of energy

In 1905 a young physicist of 26 named Albert Einstein published the results of an analysis of how measurements of time and space are affected by relative motion between an observer and what he is studying. To say that Einstein's *theory of relativity* revolutionized science is no exaggeration.

Mass increases with speed

From the theory of relativity have come a host of remarkable predictions, every one of which has been confirmed by experiment. For instance, Einstein showed that the mass of an object moving with respect to an observer is greater than when it is at rest. The increase in mass is too small to detect at ordinary speeds, but at speeds that approach that of light ($c = 3.0 \times 10^8$ m/s, which is about 186,000 mi/s) it becomes significant, which is the case in the microscopic world of such tiny atomic particles as electrons, protons, and neutrons. At a relative speed equal to that of light, the mass of an object would be infinite, and hence this speed is the absolute limit to how fast anything can travel.

Matter can be converted into energy and energy into matter

The most famous of Einstein's conclusions is that mass and energy are closely related, so closely that matter can be converted into energy and energy into matter. The *rest energy* of a body is the energy equivalent of its mass. If a body has the mass m_0 when it is at rest, its rest energy is

$$E_0 = m_0 c^2$$

Rest energy = (rest mass)(speed of light)^2

A 1.5-kg object, such as this book, has an energy content of

$$E_0 = m_0 c^2 = (1.5 \text{ kg})(3 \times 10^8 \text{ m/s})^2 = 1.35 \times 10^{17} \text{ J}$$

quite apart from any kinetic or potential energy it might have. If liberated, this energy would be more than enough to send a million tons to the moon. By

Rest energy is liberated in many familiar processes

contrast, the PE of this book on top of Mt. Everest, which is 8850 m high, relative to its sea-level PE is less than 10^4 J.

But if even a minute bit of matter represents a vast amount of energy, why are we not aware of it in our everyday lives? As a matter of fact, we *are* aware of the conversion of matter into energy all the time, only we do not normally think about what we experience in these terms. All the energy-producing reactions of chemistry and physics, from the lighting of a match to the nuclear fusion that powers the sun and stars, involve the disappearance of a small amount of matter and its reappearance as energy. Einstein's realization of this fundamental fact led not only to a better understanding of how nature works but also to the nuclear power plants — and nuclear weapons — that are shaping the world of tomorrow.

Albert Einstein

The greatest physicist since Newton

Einstein was born in 1879 in Ulm, Germany. Bitterly unhappy with the rigid discipline of the German schools of the time, at 16 he went to Switzerland to complete his education, and later got a job examining patent applications at the Swiss Patent Office in Berne. Then, in 1905, ideas that had been in his mind for years when he should have been paying attention to other matters blossomed into three short papers that were to change decisively the course, not only of physics, but of modern civilization as well.

Three remarkable papers in 1905 revolutionized physics

The first paper concerned the nature of light, and proposed that light has a dual character with particle as well as wave properties. This work is described in Chap. 8 together with the quantum theory of the atom that flowed from it. The subject of the second paper was brownian motion, the irregular zigzag motion of tiny bits of suspended matter such as pollen grains in water. Einstein arrived at a formula that related brownian motion to the bombardment of the particles by randomly moving molecules of the fluid in which they were suspended. Although the molecular theory of matter had been proposed many years before (see Chap. 4), this was the long-awaited definite link with experiment that convinced the remaining doubters. The third paper introduced the theory of relativity.

Although much of the world of physics was originally either indifferent or skeptical, even the most unexpected of Einstein's conclusions were soon confirmed and the development of what is now called modern physics began in earnest. After university posts in Switzerland and Czechoslovakia, in 1913 he took up an appointment at the Kaiser Wilhelm Institute in Berlin that left him able to do research free of financial worries and routine duties. Einstein's interest was now mainly in gravitation, and he began where Newton had left off more than two hundred years earlier.

General relativity and gravitation

Einstein's *general theory of relativity,* published in 1916, related gravitation to the structure of space and time. What is meant by "the structure of space and time" can be given a quite precise meaning mathematically, but unfortunately no

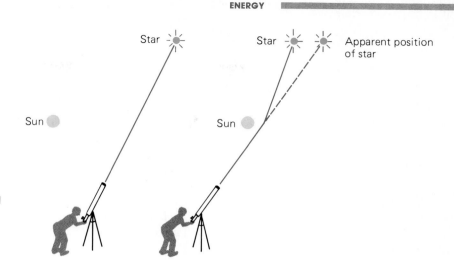

FIG. 3-11
Starlight that passes near the sun is deflected by its strong gravitational pull. The deflection, which is very small, can be measured during a solar eclipse when the sun's disk is covered by the moon.

Light is subject to gravity

such precision is possible using ordinary language. All the same, we can legitimately think of the force of gravity as arising from a warping of space-time around a body of matter so that a nearby mass tends to move toward it, much as a marble rolls toward the bottom of a saucer-shaped hole. It may seem as though one abstract concept is merely replacing another, but in fact the new point of view led Einstein and other scientists to a variety of remarkable discoveries that could not have come from the older way of thinking.

Perhaps the most spectacular of Einstein's results was that light ought to be subject to gravity. The effect is very small, so a large mass, such as that of the sun, is needed to detect its influence on light. If Einstein was right, light rays that pass near the sun should be bent toward it by 0.0005° — the diameter of a dime seen from a mile away. To check this prediction, photographs were taken of stars that appeared in the sky near the sun during an eclipse in 1919, when they could be seen because the sun's disk was covered by the moon (see Chap. 17). These photographs were then compared with photographs of the same region of the sky taken when the sun was far away (Fig. 3-11), and the observed changes in the apparent positions of the stars matched Einstein's calculations. Other predictions based on general relativity have also been verified, and the theory remains today without serious rival.

Einstein immediately became a world celebrity, but his well-earned fame did not provide security when Hitler and the Nazis came to power in Germany in the early 1930s. He left in 1933 and spent the rest of his life at the Institute for Advanced Study in Princeton, New Jersey, thereby escaping the fate of millions of other European Jews at the hands of the Germans. Einstein's last years were spent in a fruitless search for a "unified field theory" that would bring together both gravitation and electromagnetism in a single picture: a problem worthy of his gifts, but one that remains unsolved to this day. He died in 1955.

MOMENTUM

As we know, the mass of an object is a measure of its inertia at rest. The more mass something has, the greater its tendency to remain in place. The corresponding quantity for a moving object is its *linear momentum,* which is a measure of its tendency to continue in motion along a straight path. The more linear momentum something has, the greater the effort needed to deflect it into another path or to bring it to a stop. Another kind of momentum is *angular momentum,* which reflects the tendency of a spinning object to continue to spin. Like energy, the two kinds of momentum are quantities that help us to understand why moving things behave as they do.

Linear Momentum

The inertia of a moving object

The more momentum something has, the harder it is to change its speed or direction

The linear momentum of something of mass m and velocity $\mathbf{v}$ (by velocity, we recall, is meant both speed and direction) is defined as

$$\text{Linear momentum} = (\text{mass})(\text{velocity}) = m\mathbf{v}$$

The greater m and $\mathbf{v}$ are, the harder it is to change the object's speed or direction.

This definition of momentum is in accord with our experience. A baseball hit squarely by a bat (large $\mathbf{v}$) is more difficult to stop than a baseball thrown gently (small $\mathbf{v}$). The heavy iron ball used for the shotput (large m) is more difficult to stop than a baseball (small m) when their speeds are the same (Fig. 3-12).

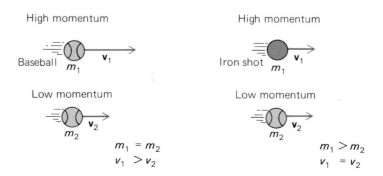

FIG. 3-12
The linear momentum $m\mathbf{v}$ of a moving object is a measure of its tendency to continue in motion at constant velocity. The symbol $>$ means "greater than."

Linear momentum is a vector quantity

An important aspect of momentum is that it is a vector quantity, which means it has a direction associated with it. This direction is the direction of motion. Kinetic energy, which also depends upon mass and speed but according to the different formula $KE = \frac{1}{2}mv^2$, has only magnitude.

Momentum and kinetic energy refer to different properties of a moving object. Its momentum determines its tendency to continue moving with constant speed and direction; its kinetic energy determines the amount of work it can do while being brought to a stop. (The kinetic energy also tells us how much work had to be done to bring the object from rest to the speed it has.) In the early days of physics, even after the time of Newton, the distinction between momentum and kinetic energy was as troublesome to scientists as it often is to students today.

Momentum considerations are most useful in situations that involve, in general terms, explosions and collisions. When outside forces do not act on the objects involved, their combined momentum (taking directions into account) is *conserved:*

Conservation of linear momentum

In the absence of outside forces, the total momentum of a set of objects remains the same no matter how the objects interact with one another.

The total kinetic energies of the objects need not be the same before and after, however. The kinetic energy involved in an explosion is zero to start with, since it all comes from the chemical energy stored in the explosive material, but it is not zero afterward. In a collision, some or even all of the kinetic energy of objects that collide may disappear into heat and sound energy. In both cases the total momentum does not change.

Analyzing a collision

The law of conservation of momentum is often very easy to apply. A simple example is that of a running girl who jumps on a stationary sled, as in Fig. 3-13. Even if there is no friction between the sled and the snow, the combination of girl and sled moves off more slowly than the girl's running speed. This happens because the original amount of momentum, which is that of the girl alone, had to be shared between her and the sled when she jumped on it. With the new total

$$\text{Total momentum} = m_1 \mathbf{v}_1 = (m_1 + m_2)\,\mathbf{v}_2$$

FIG. 3-13

When a running girl jumps on a stationary sled, the combination moves off more slowly than the girl's original speed. The total momentum of girl + sled is the same before and after she jumps on it.

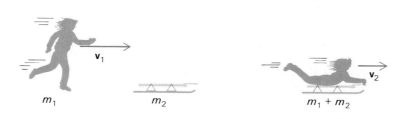

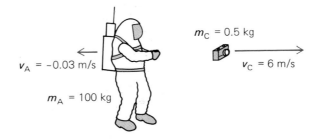

FIG. 3-14
The momentum $m_C v_C$ to the right of the thrown camera is equal in magnitude to the momentum $m_A v_A$ to the left of the astronaut who threw it away.

Analyzing an explosion

mass more than before, the new speed must be less than before in order that the total momentum stay the same.

Let us now see what happens when a single object breaks up into two parts. For a specific case, suppose an astronaut outside a space station throws away his 0.5-kg camera in disgust when it jams (Fig. 3-14). The mass of the astronaut, including his space suit, is 100 kg, and the camera moves off at 6 m/s. What effect does this have on the astronaut?

The total momentum of the astronaut and camera was zero originally. According to the law of conservation of momentum, their total momentum must therefore be zero afterward as well. If we call the astronaut A and the camera C, then

$$\text{Momentum before} = \text{momentum afterward}$$

$$0 = m_A v_A + m_C v_C$$

This means it must be true that

$$m_A v_A = - m_C v_C$$

where the minus sign signifies that $\mathbf{v}_A$ is opposite in direction to $\mathbf{v}_C$. The astronaut is set in motion when he throws the camera away, and he moves away from the camera. Newton's third law of motion (action-reaction) tells us the same thing, but conservation of momentum enables us to find the astronaut's speed at once:

$$v_A = - \frac{m_C v_C}{m_A} = - \frac{(0.5 \text{ kg})(6 \text{ m/s})}{100 \text{ kg}} = -0.03 \text{ m/s}$$

After an hour, which is 3600 s, the camera will have traveled $v_C t = 21{,}600 \text{ m} = 21.6 \text{ km} (13.4 \text{ mi})$ and the astronaut will have traveled $v_A t = 108 \text{ m} (354 \text{ ft})$ in the opposite direction if he was not tethered to the space station.

Rockets

Momentum conservation is the basis of space travel

How a rocket works

The operation of a rocket is based on conservation of linear momentum. When the rocket stands on its launching pad, its momentum is zero. When it is fired, the momentum of the exhaust gases that rush downward is balanced by the momentum in the other direction of the rocket moving upward. The total momentum of the entire system, gases and rocket, remains zero, because momentum is a vector quantity and the upward and downward momenta cancel out (Fig. 3-15). Thus a rocket does not work by "pushing" against its launching pad, the air, or anything else. In fact, rockets function best in space where no atmosphere is present to interfere with their motion.

Energy is also conserved when a rocket is fired off. The kinetic energies of the rocket and of the exhaust gases equal the chemical energy liberated in the rocket engine. Liquid hydrogen and liquid oxygen are used to power many rockets. When a mixture of them is ignited, the result is water vapor, H_2O, and a great deal of energy. The combination of 1 kg of hydrogen and 8 kg of oxygen gives off 245 MJ (million joules). Figure 3-16 shows the basic design of a liquid-fueled rocket.

Multistage rockets

The ultimate speed a single rocket can reach is governed by the amount of fuel it can carry and by the speed of its exhaust gases. Because both these quantities are limited, *multistage rockets* are used in the exploration of space. The first stage is a large rocket which has a smaller one mounted in front of it. When the fuel of the first stage has burnt up, its motor and empty fuel tanks are cast off. Then

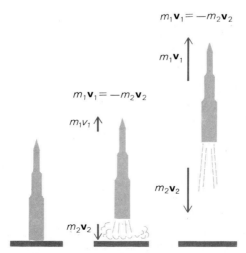

FIG. 3-15
Rocket propulsion is based upon conservation of momentum. In the absence of gravity, the downward momentum of the exhaust gases remains equal in magnitude and opposite in direction to the upward momentum of the rocket itself.

FIG. 3-16
In a liquid-fueled rocket, the reacting substances are mixed and ignited in a combustion chamber. The resulting exhaust gases escape at high speed through a steerable nozzle. The liberated chemical energy of the fuel becomes kinetic energy of the rocket and its exhaust. The momentum of the exhaust is equal and opposite to the momentum of the rocket.

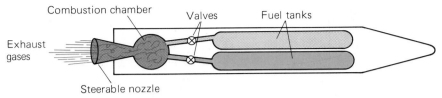

Combustion chamber   Valves   Fuel tanks

Exhaust gases

Steerable nozzle

the second stage is fired. Since the second stage is already moving rapidly and does not have to carry the motor and empty fuel tanks of the first stage, it can reach a much higher final speed than would otherwise be possible.

Depending upon the final speed needed for a given mission, three or even four stages may be required. The Saturn V launch vehicle that carried the Apollo 11 spacecraft to the moon in July 1969 had three stages (Fig. 3-17). Just before takeoff the entire assembly was 111 m long and had a mass of nearly 3,000,000 kg, over 3000 tons.

Apollo 11 lifts off its pad to begin the first manned lunar voyage. The final speeds of the three rocket stages were respectively 2760 m/s, 6935 m/s, and 10,835 m/s. The final speed is equivalent to 24,250 mi/h. Conservation of linear momentum underlies rocket propulsion.

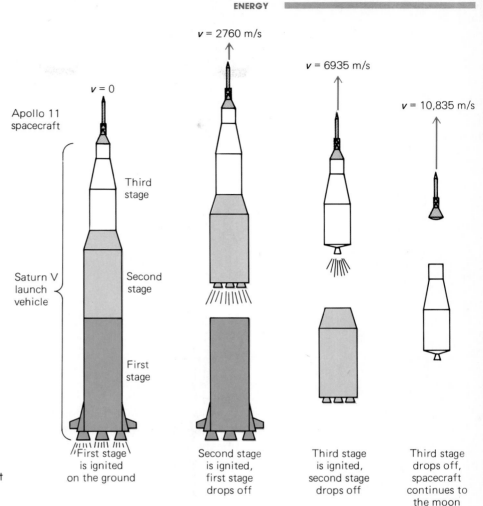

v = 0

v = 2760 m/s

v = 6935 m/s

v = 10,835 m/s

Apollo 11
spacecraft

Third
stage

Saturn V
launch
vehicle

Second
stage

First
stage

First stage
is ignited
on the ground

Second stage
is ignited,
first stage
drops off

Third stage
is ignited,
second stage
drops off

Third stage
drops off,
spacecraft
continues to
the moon

FIG. 3-17
The Saturn V launch vehicle that
propelled the Apollo 11 spacecraft
to the moon for the first manned
landing had three rocket stages.

Angular Momentum

The inertia of rotation

We have all noticed the tendency of rotating objects to continue to spin unless they
are slowed down by an outside agency. A top would spin indefinitely were it not
for friction between its tip and the ground. Another example is the earth, which has
been turning for billions of years and is likely to continue doing so for many more
to come. The earth, too, has a retarding influence on its rotation — the friction of

Axis

Slow spin

Fast spin

FIG. 3-18
Conservation of angular momentum. Angular momentum depends upon both the speed of turning and the distribution of mass. When the skater pulls in her arms and extended leg, she spins faster to compensate for the change.

the tides, as we learned in Chap. 2 — but the slowing down that results is barely detectable.

The rotational quantity that corresponds to linear momentum is called *angular momentum,* and *conservation of angular momentum* is the formal way to describe the tendency of spinning objects to keep spinning.

The precise definition of angular momentum is complicated because it depends not only upon the mass of the object and upon how fast it is turning, but also upon how the mass is arranged in the body. As we might expect, the greater the mass of a body and the more rapidly it rotates, the more angular momentum it has and the more pronounced its tendency to continue to spin. Less obvious is the fact that, the farther away from the axis of rotation the mass is distributed, the more the angular momentum.

An illustration of both the latter peculiarity and the conservation of angular momentum is a skater doing a spin (Fig. 3-18). When the skater starts the spin, she pushes against the ice with one skate to start turning. Initially both arms and one leg are extended, so that her mass is spread as far as possible from the axis of rotation. Then she brings her arms and the outstretched leg in tightly against her body, so that now all her mass is as close as possible to the axis of rotation. As a result she spins faster. To make up for the change in the mass distribution, the speed must change as well to conserve angular momentum.

Like ordinary momentum, angular momentum is a vector quantity with direction as well as magnitude. A spinning body therefore tends to maintain the *direc-*

Conservation of angular momentum

How a skater spins faster

Angular momentum is a vector quantity

FIG. 3-19
The faster a top spins, the more stable it is. When all its angular momentum has been lost through friction, the top falls over.

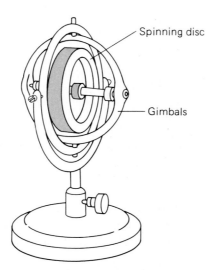

Spinning disc

Gimbals

FIG. 3-20
Conservation of angular momentum underlies the operation of the gyroscope. The spinning disk maintains its orientation in space regardless of how its support is tilted.

tion of its spin axis besides the amount of angular momentum it has. A stationary top falls over at once, but a rapidly spinning top stays upright because its tendency to keep its axis in the same position by virtue of its angular momentum is greater than its tendency to fall over (Fig. 3-19). Footballs and rifle bullets are sent off spinning to prevent them from tumbling during flight, which would increase air resistance and hence shorten their range.

Gyroscope

A *gyroscope* is a disk whose axis is mounted in gimbals, as in Fig. 3-20, so it can move freely. When the disk is spinning, conservation of angular momentum keeps the orientation of the disk's axis fixed in space regardless of how the gyroscope is tilted. Gyroscopes are widely used in airplanes and ships in compasses that are independent of the earth's magnetic field.

CONSERVATION OF ENERGY

A skier slides down a hill and comes to rest at the bottom. What became of the potential energy he or she originally had? The engine of a car is shut off while the

Heat is a form of energy

car itself is allowed to coast along a level road. Eventually the car slows down and comes to a stop. What became of its original kinetic energy?

All of us can give similar examples of the apparent disappearance of kinetic or potential energy. What these examples have in common is that heat is always produced in an amount just equivalent to the "lost" energy. Thus we can conclude not only that heat is a form of energy, but also that energy cannot be either created or destroyed. When energy is transformed from one kind to another, including heat and rest energy, there is always an exact balance between the two. This fundamental observation is called the *law of conservation of energy*.

Temperature

Putting numbers to hot and cold

It is easy to confuse heat and temperature. Certainly the higher its temperature, the more heat something possesses. But we cannot say that one object contains more heat than another only because its temperature is higher. A cup of boiling water is hotter than a pailful of warm water, but the warm water would melt more ice (Fig. 3-21). And the same masses of different substances at the same temperature contain different amounts of heat. A kilogram of boiling water can melt no less than 33 times as much ice as 1 kg of gold at that temperature, for instance.

Temperature, like force, is a physical quantity that has direct meaning for us in terms of our sense impressions. Also like force, a certain amount of discussion is needed before a statement of exactly what temperature signifies can be given. Such a discussion appears in Chap. 4. For the time being, it is sufficient for us simply to regard temperature as that which gives rise to sensations of hot and cold.

Most thermometers are based on thermal expansion

A *thermometer* is a device that measures temperature. Most substances expand when heated and shrink when cooled, and the thermometers we use in everyday life are designed around this property of matter. More precisely, they are based upon the fact that different materials react to a given temperature change to

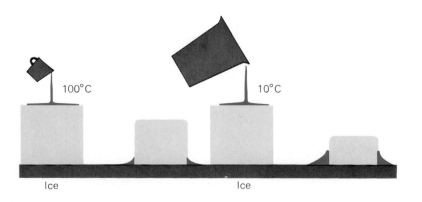

FIG. 3-21
The heat content of a given substance depends upon both its mass and its temperature. A pail of cool water contains more heat than a cup of boiling water.

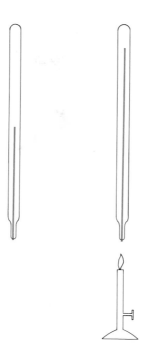

FIG. 3-22
A liquid-in-glass thermometer. Mercury or a colored alcohol solution responds to temperature changes to a greater extent than glass does, and so the length of the liquid column is a measure of the temperature of the thermometer bulb.

different extents. The familiar mercury-in-glass thermometer (Fig. 3-22) works because mercury expands more than glass when heated and contracts more than glass when cooled. Thus the length of the mercury column in the glass tube provides a measure of the temperature around the bulb.

Allowance must be made in the design of a bridge for its expansion and contraction as the temperature changes. The Golden Gate Bridge in San Francisco varies by over a meter in length between summer and winter.

FIG. 3-23
A bimetallic strip thermometer. No matter on which side the heat is applied, the bend is away from the more expansive metal. The higher the temperature, the greater the deflection. At low temperatures the deflection is in the opposite direction. Steel and copper are often used in bimetallic strips; the steel expands less when heated.

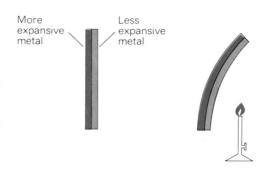

More expansive metal

Less expansive metal

Another common thermometer used for high temperatures, such as in ovens and furnaces, makes use of the different rates of expansion of different kinds of metals. Two straight strips of dissimilar metals are joined together at a particular temperature (Fig. 3-23). At higher temperatures the bimetallic strip bends so that the metal with the greater expansion is on the outside of the curve, and at lower temperatures it bends in the opposite direction. In each case the exact amount of bending depends upon the temperature. Bimetallic strips of this kind are used in the *thermostats* that switch on and off heating systems, refrigerators, and freezers at preset temperatures.

Thermal expansion is not the only property of matter that can be used to make a thermometer. As another example, the color and amount of light emitted by an

The color of a hot object varies with its temperature

The color and brightness of an object heated to incandescence, such as this steel billet, depends upon its temperature. An object that glows white is hotter than one that glows red and radiates more light as well.

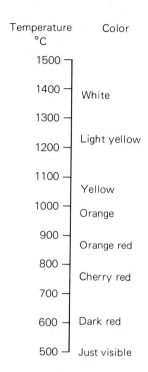

Temperature °C / Color

Temperature °C	Color
1500	
1400	White
1300	
1200	Light yellow
1100	
1000	Yellow / Orange
900	Orange red
800	Cherry red
700	
600	Dark red
500	Just visible

FIG. 3-24
The color of an object hot enough to glow varies with its temperature roughly as shown here.

object vary with its temperature. A poker thrust in a fire first glows dull red, then successively bright red, orange, and yellow. Finally, if the poker achieves a high enough temperature, it becomes "white hot." The precise color of the light given off by a glowing object is thus a measure of its temperature (Fig. 3-24).

Unfortunately two temperature scales are in use in the United States. On the *fahrenheit* scale the freezing point of water is 32° and the boiling point of water is 212°. On the *celsius* scale these points are respectively 0° and 100° (Fig. 3-25). The fahrenheit scale is used only in a few English-speaking countries that cling to it with the same obstinacy that preserves the equally awkward British system of units. The rest of the world, and all scientists, use the more convenient celsius (or centigrade) scale.

Celsius and fahrenheit temperature scales

To go from a fahrenheit temperature T_F to a celsius temperature T_C, and vice versa, we note that 180°F separates the freezing and boiling points of water on the fahrenheit scale. On the celsius scale, however, the difference is 100°C. Therefore fahrenheit degrees are $\frac{100}{180}$ or $\frac{5}{9}$ as large as celsius degrees:

$$5 \text{ celsius degrees} = 9 \text{ fahrenheit degrees}$$

Taking into account that the freezing point of water is 0°C = 32°F, we see that

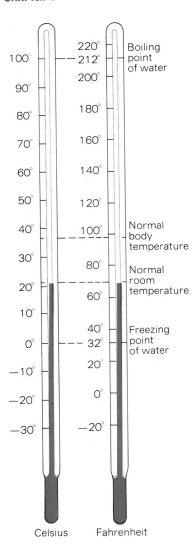

FIG. 3-25
Comparison of celsius and fahrenheit
temperature scales.

$$T_F = \tfrac{9}{5}T_C + 32°$$

$$T_C = \tfrac{5}{9}(T_F - 32°)$$

Thus the celsius equivalent of the normal body temperature of 98.6°F is

$$T_C = \tfrac{5}{9}(98.6° - 32.0°) = \tfrac{5}{9}(66.6°) = 37.0°C$$

Heat Units

The joule, the kilocalorie, and the Btu

Since heat is a form of energy, the joule is the proper SI unit for it. The amount of heat needed to raise or lower the temperature of 1 kg of a substance by 1°C depends upon its nature. In the case of water, 4.19 kJ of heat is required per kilogram per °C. To heat 1 kg of water from, say, room temperature of 20°C to its boiling point of 100°C means raising its temperature by 80°C. The amount of heat that must be added is therefore $(4.19)(80) = 335$ kJ.

Water resists temperature changes more than most other materials

Water must have more heat added to or taken away from it per kilogram for a given temperature change than nearly all other materials. For instance, to change the temperature of 1 kg of ice by 1°C, we must transfer to or from it 2.09 kJ, about half as much as for water. To do the same for 1 kg of iron takes only 0.46 kJ.

Kilocalorie and Btu

Before heat was recognized as a form of energy, different units were used for it. One of them is the *kilocalorie* (kcal), which is the amount of heat needed to change the temperature of 1 kg of water by 1°C. Thus 1 kcal = 4.19 kJ. Another is the *British thermal unit* (Btu), which is the amount of heat needed to change the temperature of 1 lb of water by 1°F. In terms of the kilojoule and the kilocalorie, 1 Btu = 1.05 kJ = 0.252 kcal.

Metabolic Energy

The energy of people and animals

The energy content of the food an animal eats is liberated by the metabolic processes of its body. Table 3-1 lists the energy contents of some common foods.

TABLE 3-1
Energy Contents of Some Common Foods.
(1 kcal = 4.19 kJ)

Food	kcal	Food	kcal
1 raw onion	5	1 broiled hamburger patty	150
1 dill pickle	15		
6 asparagus	20	1 glass milk	165
1 gum drop	35	1 cup bean soup	190
1 poached egg	75	$\frac{1}{2}$ cup tuna salad	220
8 raw oysters	100	1 ice cream soda	325
1 banana	120	$\frac{1}{2}$ broiled chicken	350
1 cupcake	130	1 lamb chop	420

Metabolism and work output

Large and small animals have
different metabolisms

The "calorie" used by dietitians is actually the kilocalorie. This unit is sometimes written Calorie to distinguish it from the calorie of the physicist, which is equal to 0.001 kcal.

The efficiency with which metabolic energy is converted into mechanical work by muscular activity is not very high, only 10 or 20 percent. (An electric motor with the same power output as a person is typically 50 percent efficient, and larger electric motors are more efficient still.) The rest of the energy goes into heat, most of which escapes through the animal's skin. The maximum power output an animal is capable of depends upon its maximum metabolic rate, which in turn depends upon its ability to dissipate the resulting heat, and therefore upon its surface area.

A large animal has more surface area than a small one and so is capable of a higher power output. However, a large animal also has more mass than a small one, and because an animal's mass goes up faster with its size than its skin area does, its metabolic rate per kg decreases. Typical basal metabolic rates, which correspond to an animal resting, are 5.2 W/kg for a pigeon, 1.2 W/kg for a person, and 0.67 W/kg for a cow. African elephants partly overcome the limitation of the small surface/mass ratio of their giant bodies by their enormous ears, which help them get rid of metabolic heat. Birds are small because, with increasing size, a bird's metabolic rate (and hence power output) per kg decreases while the work it

Canada goose coming in for a landing. Birds are limited in size because the larger an animal is, the less is its ability to dissipate waste metabolic energy per unit of body mass.

must perform per kg to fly stays the same. Large birds such as ostriches and emus are not notable for their flying ability.

When an animal is active, its metabolic rate may be much greater than its basal rate. A 70-kg (155-lb) person, to give an example, has a basal metabolic rate of around 80 W. When the person is reading or doing light work while sitting, the rate will go up to perhaps 125 W. Walking means a metabolic rate of 300 W or so, and running hard increases it to as much as 1200 W. If the energy provided by a person's food is more than his or her requirements, the excess goes into additional body tissue: muscle, if enough physical activity is being carried out, otherwise fat. The energy stored as fat can be used by the body if metabolic needs are greater than the food supply at a later time.

Nature of Heat

The downfall of caloric

Although it comes as no surprise to us today to learn that heat is a form of energy, in earlier times this was not so clear. Little more than a century ago most scientists regarded heat as an actual substance called *caloric*. Absorbing caloric caused an object to become warmer; the escape of caloric caused it to become cooler. Because the weight of an object does not change when heated or cooled, caloric was considered to be weightless. It was also supposed to be invisible, odorless, and tasteless, properties that, of course, were why it could not be observed directly.

Actually, the idea of heat as a substance was fairly satisfactory for materials heated over a flame, but it could not account for the unlimited heat that could be generated by friction. One of the first to appreciate this difficulty was an adventurous American, born Benjamin Thompson in 1763, who fled this country during the Revolution and became Count Rumford during a spectacular career in Europe. One of Rumford's many occupations was supervising the making of cannon for a German prince, and he was impressed by the large amounts of heat given off by friction in the boring process. He showed that the heat could be used to boil water and that heat could be produced again and again from the same piece of metal. If heat was a fluid, it was not unreasonable that boring a hole in a piece of metal should allow it to escape. However, even a dull drill which cut no metal produced a great deal of heat. It was hard to imagine a piece of metal as containing an infinite amount of caloric, and Rumford accordingly regarded heat as a form of energy.

James Prescott Joule was an English brewer after whom the SI unit of energy is named in recognition of his classic experiment which settled the nature of heat. Joule's experiment employed a small paddle wheel within a container of water (Fig. 3-26). Work was done in turning the paddle wheel against the resistance of the water, and Joule determined exactly how much heat was supplied to the water by friction during this process. He found that a given amount of mechanical energy invariably produced the same amount of heat. Not only was heat associated with

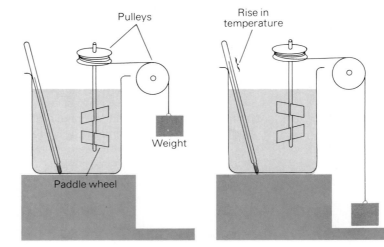

FIG. 3-26
Joule's experimental demonstration that energy is conserved. As the weight falls, it turns the paddle wheel, which heats the water by friction. The potential energy of the weight is converted first into the kinetic energy of the paddle wheel and then into heat.

motion, as Rumford had found, but the *amount of work* performed against friction precisely determined the *amount of heat* produced. This was a clear demonstration that heat is energy and not something else.

Conservation of Energy

A fundamental law of nature

Joule's work led to one of the most basic laws of nature. His experiments showed clearly that, when energy is changed into heat, no energy is lost, nor is any new energy created. One kind of energy is simply converted into another, and every bit of mechanical energy that disappears reappears as heat. In further experiments in which electric, magnetic, radiant, and chemical energies were converted into heat, the amount of heat produced always equaled the vanished energy.

For all known transformations of energy the same rule holds:

Conservation of energy

Energy cannot be created or destroyed, although it can be changed from one form to another (including matter).

This broad generalization is the *law of conservation of energy*. It is probably the principle with the widest application in science, applying equally to distant stars and to biological processes in living cells. We shall learn later of the various ways in which mass is converted into energy and energy into mass in nature.

The conservation principles of energy, linear momentum, and angular momentum are especially interesting because of what they reveal about the underlying symmetrical character of the physical universe. Using advanced mathematics it is possible to show the following:

Conservation principles and symmetry in the universe

1. If the laws of nature are the same at all times, past, present, and future, then energy must be conserved.
2. If the laws of nature are the same everywhere in the universe, then linear momentum must be conserved.
3. If the laws of nature are independent of direction, then angular momentum must be conserved.

Hence these conservation principles, which are observed to be obeyed in all processes, hint at a profound order in the physical universe, despite the random appearance of many aspects of it.

IMPORTANT TERMS

Work is a measure of the change, in a general sense, a force causes when it acts upon something. The work done by a force acting on an object is the product of the magnitude of the force and the distance through which the object moves while the force acts on it. If the direction of the force is not the same as the direction of motion, the projection of the force in the direction of motion must be used. The unit of work is the *joule* (J).

Power is the rate at which work is being done. Its unit is the *watt* (W).

Energy is that property something has that enables it to do work. The unit of energy is the joule. The three broad categories of energy are: *kinetic energy,* which is the energy something has by virtue of its motion; *potential energy,* which is the energy something has by virtue of its position; and *rest energy,* which is the energy something has by virtue of its mass. According to the law of *conservation of energy,* energy cannot be created or destroyed, although it can be changed from one form to another (including mass).

Linear momentum is a measure of the tendency of a moving object to continue in motion along a straight line. *Angular momentum* is a measure of the tendency of a rotating object to continue spinning about a fixed axis. Both are vector quantities and supplement energy in describing situations that involve moving objects. If no outside forces act on a set of objects, then their linear and angular momenta are *conserved,* that is, remain the same regardless of how the objects interact with one another.

Heat is a form of energy, and *temperature* is that property of a body of matter that gives rise to sensations of hot and cold. The natures of heat and temperature are described in Chap. 4.

IMPORTANT FORMULAS

Work: $W = Fd$

Power: $P = \dfrac{W}{t}$

Kinetic energy: $\mathrm{KE} = \frac{1}{2}mv^2$

Gravitational potential energy: $\mathrm{PE} = mgh$

Rest energy: $E_0 = m_0 c^2$

Linear momentum: Linear momentum $= m\mathbf{v}$

Temperature scales: $T_F = \frac{9}{5}T_C + 32°$

$$T_C = \frac{5}{9}(T_F - 32°)$$

MULTIPLE CHOICE

1. An object at rest may have
   a. velocity
   b. momentum
   c. kinetic energy
   d. potential energy

2. A moving object need not have
   a. velocity
   b. momentum
   c. kinetic energy
   d. potential energy
3. An object that has linear momentum must also have
   a. acceleration
   b. angular momentum
   c. kinetic energy
   d. potential energy
4. According to the principle of conservation of energy (with energy interpreted as including rest energy), energy can be
   a. created but not destroyed
   b. destroyed but not created
   c. both created and destroyed
   d. neither created nor destroyed
5. When the speed of a body is doubled,
   a. its kinetic energy is doubled
   b. its potential energy is doubled
   c. its rest energy is doubled
   d. its momentum is doubled
6. Two balls, one of mass 5 kg and the other of mass 10 kg, are dropped simultaneously from a window. When they are 1 m above the ground, the balls have the same
   a. kinetic energy
   b. potential energy
   c. momentum
   d. acceleration
7. A bomb dropped from an airplane explodes in midair.
   a. Its total kinetic energy increases
   b. Its total kinetic energy decreases
   c. Its total momentum increases
   d. Its total momentum decreases
8. What never changes when two or more objects collide is
   a. the momentum of each one
   b. the kinetic energy of each one
   c. the total momentum of all the objects
   d. the total kinetic energy of all the objects
9. It is not true that
   a. light is affected by gravity
   b. the mass of a moving object depends upon its speed
   c. the maximum speed anything can have is the speed of light
   d. momentum is a form of energy
10. Two bars of lead, one twice as heavy as the other, are heated to a temperature of 200°C. The heavy bar
   a. contains half as much heat as the lighter bar
   b. contains the same amount of heat as the lighter bar

   c. contains twice as much heat as the lighter bar
   d. may contain more or less heat than the lighter bar, depending upon the precise shapes of the bars
11. The largest of the following energy units is the
   a. kilocalorie
   b. joule
   c. watthour
   d. newton-meter
12. Which of the following is not a unit of power?
   a. Joule-second
   b. Watt
   c. Newton-meter/second
   d. Horsepower
13. Two thermometers, one calibrated in °F and the other in °C, are used to measure the same temperature. The numerical reading on the fahrenheit thermometer
   a. is less than that on the celsius thermometer
   b. is equal to that on the celsius thermometer
   c. is greater than that on the celsius thermometer
   d. may be any of the above, depending on the temperature
14. The work done in holding a 50-kg object at a height of 2 m above the floor for 10 s is
   a. 0
   b. 250 J
   c. 1000 J
   d. 98,000 J
15. A 40-kg boy runs up a flight of stairs 4 m high in 4 s. His power output is
   a. 160 W
   b. 392 W
   c. 640 W
   d. 1568 W
16. Car A has a mass of 1000 kg and is moving at 60 km/h. Car B has a mass of 2000 kg and is moving at 30 km/h. The kinetic energy of car A is
   a. half that of car B
   b. equal to that of car B
   c. twice that of car B
   d. 4 times that of car B
17. The momentum of car A in Question 16 is
   a. half that of car B
   b. equal to that of car B
   c. twice that of car B
   d. 4 times that of car B
18. A 1-kg ball is thrown in the air. When it is 10 m above the ground, its speed is 3 m/s. At this time most of the ball's total energy is in the form of
   a. kinetic energy

b. potential energy relative to the ground

c. rest energy

d. momentum

19. The smallest part of the total energy of the ball of Question 18 is

    a. kinetic energy

    b. potential energy relative to the ground

    c. rest energy

    d. momentum

20. A 1-kg object has a potential energy of 1 J relative to the ground when it is at a height of

    a. 0.102 m

    b. 1 m

    c. 9.8 m

    d. 98 m

21. A 1-kg object has kinetic energy of 1 J when its speed is

    a. 0.45 m/s

    b. 1 m/s

    c. 1.4 m/s

    d. 4.4 m/s

22. An object has a rest energy of 1 J when its mass is

    a. 1.1×10^{-17} kg

    b. 3.3×10^{-9} kg

    c. 1 kg

    d. 9×10^{16} kg

23. The average momentum of a 70-kg runner who covers 400 m in 50 s is

    a. 8.75 kg · m/s

    b. 57 kg · m/s

    c. 560 kg · m/s

    d. 5488 kg · m/s

24. A 30-kg girl and a 25-kg boy are standing on frictionless roller skates. The girl pushes the boy, who moves off at 1.0 m/s. The girl's speed is

    a. 0.45 m/s

    b. 0.55 m/s

    c. 0.83 m/s

    d. 1.2 m/s

25. Ethyl alcohol boils at 172°F. The celsius equivalent of this temperature is

    a. 64°C

    b. 78°C

    c. 140°C

    d. 278°C

26. A temperature at 20°C is the same as

    a. −20.9°F

    b. −6.4°F

    c. 68°F

    d. 93.6°F

QUESTIONS

1. Is it correct to say that all changes in the physical world involve energy transformations of some sort? Why?

2. Under what circumstances (if any) is no work done on a moving object even though a net force acts upon it?

3. In what part of its orbit is the earth's potential energy greatest with respect to the sun? In what part of its orbit is its kinetic energy greatest? Explain your answers.

4. Does every moving body possess kinetic energy? Does every stationary body possess potential energy?

5. A golf ball and a Ping-Pong ball are dropped in a vacuum chamber. When they have fallen halfway to the bottom, how do their speeds compare? Their kinetic energies? Their potential energies? Their momenta?

6. The potential energy of a golf ball in a hole is negative with respect to the ground. Under what circumstances (if any) is its kinetic energy negative? Its rest energy?

7. Is it possible for an object to have more kinetic energy but less momentum than another object? Less kinetic energy but more momentum?

8. In the formula $E_0 = m_0 c^2$ for rest energy, what does the symbol c represent? What is the difference between m_0 and m?

9. An empty dump truck coasts freely with its engine off along a level road. (a) What happens to the truck's speed if it starts to rain and water collects in it? (b) The rain stops and the accumulated water leaks out. What happens to the truck's speed now?

10. A railway car is at rest on a frictionless track. A man at one end of the car walks to the other end. (a) Does the car move while he is walking? (b) If so, in which direction? (c) What happens when the man comes to a stop?

11. When the kinetic energy of an object is doubled, what happens to its momentum?

12. When the momentum of an object is doubled, what happens to its kinetic energy?

13. Many flywheels have most of their mass concentrated around their rims. What effect does this have?

14. If the polar ice caps melt, the length of the day will increase. Why?

15. Two identical watches, one wound and the other unwound, are dissolved in acid. What do you think becomes of the potential energy of the spring in the wound watch?

16. Why does a nail become hot when it is hammered into a piece of wood?

PROBLEMS

1. A person holds 5 kg of onions 1.5 m above the ground for 2 min. How much work is done?

2. A horizontal force of 80 N is used to move a 20-kg crate across a level floor. How much work is done when the crate is moved 5 m? How much work would have been done if the crate's mass were 30 kg?

3. The average gravitational force the sun exerts on the earth is 4×10^{28} N, and the earth travels 9.4×10^{11} m during each orbit of the sun. How much work does the sun do on the earth per year?

4. A centripetal force of 5 N is used to keep a 200-g ball moving in a circle with uniform speed at the end of a string 80 cm long. How much work is done by the force in each revolution of the ball?

5. Ten thousand joules of work is expended in raising a 90-kg box. How high was it raised? What is its potential energy?

6. A total of 490 J of work is needed to lift a body of unknown mass through a height of 10 m. What is its mass?

7. An 80-kg mountaineer climbs a mountain 3000 m high in 10 h. What is the average power output during the climb?

8. A weightlifter raises a 150-kg barbell from the floor to a height of 2.2 m in 0.8 s. What is the average power output during the lift?

9. A worldwide total of about 2×10^{20} J of energy was obtained from coal, oil, natural gas, falling water, and nuclear power plants in 1970. If the world's population in 1970 was 3.5 billion (3.5×10^9), find the average power consumed per person in watts and in horsepower.

10. A 500-kg pile-driver hammer is dropped from a height of 4 m above the head of a pile. If the pile is driven 10 cm into the ground with each impact of the hammer, what is the average force on the pile when it is struck?

11. Two objects, one with a mass of 1 kg and the other with a weight of 1 N, both have potential energies of 1 J relative to the ground. What are their respective heights above the ground?

12. A 3-kg stone is dropped from a height of 100 m. Find its kinetic and potential energies when it is 50 m from the ground.

13. Is more work needed to increase a car's speed from 0 to 10 km/h or from 40 to 50 km/h?

14. A girl on a swing is 2 m above the ground at her highest point and 1 m above the ground at her lowest point. What is the girl's maximum speed?

15. A 1500-kg car, initially at rest, coasts down a hill 30 m high. Ignoring friction, what is its kinetic energy at the foot of the hill?

16. A force of 500 N is used to lift a 20-kg object to a height of 10 m. There is no friction present. (a) How much work is done by the force? (b) What is the change in the potential energy of the object? (c) What is the change in the kinetic energy of the object?

17. An 80-kg crate is raised 2 m from the ground by a man who uses a rope and a system of pulleys. He exerts a force of 220 N on the rope and pulls a total of 8 m of rope through the pulleys while lifting the crate, which is at rest afterward. How much work does the man do? What is the change in the potential energy of the crate? If the answers to these questions are different, explain why.

18. A person's metabolic processes can usually operate at a power of 6 W/kg of body mass for several hours at a time. If a 60-kg woman carrying a 12-kg pack is walking uphill with an energy-conversion efficiency of 20 percent, at what rate (in m/s) does she move vertically upward?

19. In an effort to lose weight, a person runs 5 km per day at a speed of 4 m/s. While running, the person's body processes consume energy at a rate of 1.4 kW. Fat has an energy content of about 40 kJ/g. How many grams of fat are metabolized during each run?

20. A man drinks a bottle of beer and proposes to work off its 460 kJ by exercising with a 20-kg barbell. If each lift of the barbell from chest height to over his head is through 60 cm and the efficiency of his body is 10 percent under these circumstances, how many times must he lift the barbell?

21. One kilogram of water at 0°C contains 335 kJ of energy more than 1 kg of ice at 0°C. What is the mass equivalent of this amount of energy?

22. Approximately 5.4×10^6 J of chemical energy is released when 1 kg of dynamite explodes. What fraction of the total energy of the dynamite is this?

23. Approximately 4×10^9 kg of matter is converted into energy in the sun per second. Express the power output of the sun in watts.

24. A 70-kg person dives horizontally from a 200-kg boat with a speed of 2 m/s. What is the recoil speed of the boat?

25. A 2000-kg car traveling at 8 m/s strikes a stationary car whose mass is the same. The two cars stick together after the collision. What is their final speed? How much kinetic energy is lost?

26. The 176-g head of a golf club is moving at 45 m/s when it strikes a 46-g golf ball and sends it off at 65 m/s. Find the final speed of the clubhead after the impact, assuming that the mass of the club's shaft can be neglected.

27. A 30-kg girl who is running at 3 m/s jumps on a stationary 10-kg sled on a frozen lake. How fast does the sled with the girl on it then move?

28. The temperature of a room is 70°F. What is this temperature on the celsius scale?

29. The normal temperature of the human body is 37°C. What is this temperature on the fahrenheit scale?

30. How many kJ of heat are needed to raise the temperature of 20 kg of water from the freezing point to the boiling point?

31. How many kJ of heat is needed to raise the temperature of 200 g of water from 20°C to 100°C in preparing a cup of coffee?

32. The diet of a 60-kg person provides 12,000 kJ daily. If this amount of energy were added to 60 kg of water, by how much would its temperature be increased?

33. A 10-kg stone is dropped into a pool of water from a height of 100 m. How much energy in joules does the stone have when it strikes the water? If all this energy goes into heat and if the pool contains 10 m³ of water, by how much is its temperature raised? (The mass of 1 m³ of water is 10^3 kg.)

34. How high is a waterfall if the water at its base is 1°C higher in temperature than the water at the top?

ANSWERS TO MULTIPLE CHOICE

1. *d*	**8.** *c*	**15.** *b*	**22.** *a*
2. *d*	**9.** *d*	**16.** *c*	**23.** *c*
3. *c*	**10.** *c*	**17.** *b*	**24.** *c*
4. *d*	**11.** *a*	**18.** *c*	**25.** *b*
5. *d*	**12.** *a*	**19.** *a*	**26.** *c*
6. *d*	**13.** *d*	**20.** *a*	
7. *a*	**14.** *a*	**21.** *c*	

4

ENERGY IN ACTION

Suppose there were no limit to the power of our microscopes, so that we could examine a drop of water at any magnification we like. What would we find if the drop were enlarged, say, a million times? Would we still see a clear, structureless liquid? Or, if not, what else?

The answer is that, on a very small scale of size, water consists of separate particles. Indeed, *all* matter does, whether solid, liquid, or gas. This much was suspected over 2000 years ago in ancient Greece. Modern science has not only confirmed this suspicion but extended it: the particles are in constant random motion, and it is the kinetic energy of this motion that constitutes heat. In everyday life, matter shows no direct sign of either the particles or their motion. However, there are plenty of indirect signs that support this picture, and we shall consider some of them in this chapter.

Almost all the "raw" energy available to us is liberated in the form of heat. Whether the heat is given off by burning coal or oil or by the fission of uranium in a nuclear reactor, there are quite fundamental limits to how much of it can be changed into another form, such as mechanical or electrical energy. After a discussion of this important topic, the chapter closes with a look at the problem of energy supply, today and in the future. As we shall find, it is a complicated problem with no simple answer.

FLUIDS

Solids, liquids, and gases

As mentioned above, matter consists of particles in random motion. In a solid, the particles vibrate around fixed positions, so the solid has a definite size and shape (Fig. 4-1). In a liquid, the particles stay about as far apart on the average as those in a solid, but are free to move about. Hence a liquid sample has a definite volume but flows to fit its container. In a gas, the particles can move without restriction, and so a gas has neither a definite volume nor shape but fills whatever container it is in.

Liquids and gases are together called fluids because they flow readily. This ability has some interesting consequences. One is *buoyancy*, which permits objects to float in a fluid under certain conditions — a balloon in air, a ship in water. In order to understand how buoyancy occurs, we must first look into the concepts of density and pressure.

Density

A characteristic property of every material

Density is mass per unit volume

The *density* of a material is its mass per unit volume:

$$d = \frac{m}{V}$$

$$\text{Density} = \frac{\text{mass}}{\text{volume}}$$

When we say that lead is a "heavy" metal and aluminum a "light" one, what we actually mean is that lead has a higher density than aluminum: the density of lead is 11,300 kg per cubic meter (kg/m³) whereas that of aluminum is only 2700 kg/m³, a quarter as much.

Units of density

Although the proper SI unit of density is the kg/m³, densities are often given instead in g/cm³ (grams per cubic centimeter). Since there are 1000 g in a kilogram and 100 cm in a meter,

FIG. 4-1
Solids, liquids, and gases. A solid maintains its shape and volume no matter where it is placed; a liquid assumes the shape of its container while maintaining its volume; a gas expands indefinitely unless stopped by the walls of a container.

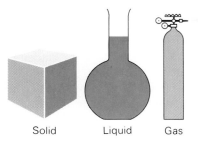

Solid   Liquid   Gas

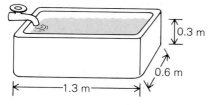

FIG. 4-2
The volume of water in this bathtub is equal to the product (length) (width) (height).

$$1 \text{ g/cm}^3 = 10^3 \text{ kg/m}^3 = 1000 \text{ kg/m}^3$$

$$1 \text{ kg/m}^3 = 10^{-3} \text{ g/cm}^3 = 0.001 \text{ g/cm}^3$$

Thus the density of lead can also be expressed as 11.3 g/cm³. Table 4-1 is a list of the densities of some common substances.

Let us find the mass of the water in a bathtub whose interior is 1.3 m long and 0.6 m wide and is filled to a height of 0.3 m (Fig. 4-2). The water's volume is

$$V = (\text{length})(\text{width})(\text{height}) = (1.3 \text{ m})(0.6 \text{ m})(0.3 \text{ m}) = 0.234 \text{ m}^3$$

According to Table 4-1 the density of water is 1000 kg/m³. From the definition of density as $d = m/V$ we have for the water's mass

TABLE 4-1

Densities of Various Substances at Room Temperature and Atmospheric Pressure.

	Density	
Substance	kg/m³	g/cm³
Air	1.3	1.3×10^{-3}
Alcohol (ethyl)	7.9×10^2	0.79
Aluminum	2.7×10^3	2.7
Balsa wood	1.3×10^2	0.13
Carbon dioxide	2.0	2.0×10^{-3}
Concrete	2.3×10^3	2.3
Gasoline	6.8×10^2	0.68
Gold	1.9×10^4	19
Helium	0.18	1.8×10^{-4}
Hydrogen	0.09	9×10^{-5}
Ice	9.2×10^2	0.92
Iron	7.8×10^3	7.8
Lead	1.1×10^4	11
Mercury	1.4×10^4	14
Oak	7.2×10^2	0.72
Water, pure	1.00×10^3	1.00
Water, sea	1.03×10^3	1.03

$$\text{Mass} = (\text{density})(\text{volume})$$

$$m = dv = \left(1000 \ \frac{\text{kg}}{\text{m}^3}\right)(0.234 \ \text{m}^3) = 234 \ \text{kg}$$

The weight of this amount of water is a little over 500 lb.

Mammals have nearly the same average density as fresh water. Thus the volume of a 70-kg (155-lb) person is, rewriting $d = m/V$ in still another way,

$$\text{Volume} = \frac{\text{mass}}{\text{density}}$$

$$V = \frac{m}{d} = \frac{70 \ \text{kg}}{1000 \ \text{kg/m}^3} = 0.07 \ \text{m}^3$$

which is about $2\frac{1}{2}$ cubic feet.

Specific gravity is density relative to water

The *specific gravity* of something is its density relative to that of water. Since the density of water is almost exactly 1 g/cm³, the specific gravity of a material is just about the same as its density expressed in g/cm³. For example, since the density of aluminum is 2.7 g/cm³, its specific gravity is 2.7. Specific gravity is also called *relative density*.

Pressure

How much of a squeeze

Pressure is perpendicular force per unit area

When a force F acts perpendicular to a surface whose area is A, the *pressure* acting on the surface is the ratio between the force and the area:

$$p = \frac{F}{A}$$

$$\text{Pressure} = \frac{\text{force}}{\text{area}}$$

In the next section we will see why pressure rather than force itself is appropriate when dealing with fluids.

Let us consider a tire pump with a piston whose area is 0.001 m² (Fig. 4-3). If we apply a force of 150 N (34 lb) to the piston, the pressure on the air in the pump is

$$p = \frac{F}{A} = \frac{150 \ \text{N}}{0.001 \ \text{m}^2} = 1.5 \times 10^5 \ \text{N/m}^2$$

The pascal is the SI unit of pressure

The SI unit of pressure is the *pascal* (Pa), where

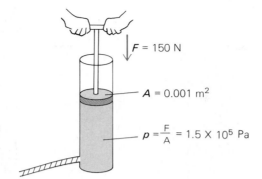

FIG. 4-3
Pressure is force per unit area. A force of 150 N applied to a piston of area 0.001 m² in a tire pump results in a pressure of 1.5×10^5 N/m² = 1.5×10^5 Pa.

$$1 \text{ pascal} = 1 \text{ Pa} = 1 \text{ N/m}^2$$

Hence the above pressure is 1.5×10^5 Pa.

Other pressure units

Because the pascal is rather small, other units are often used as well for pressure, for instance the kilopascal (10^3 Pa) and the megapascal (10^6 Pa). A common unit in practical work is the *bar*, equal to 10^5 Pa, which is almost exactly equal to the pressure of the atmosphere at sea level. A pressure of 1.5×10^5 Pa can therefore also be expressed as 1.5 bars. The *millibar* (mbar), equal to 100 Pa, is familiar from weather maps. The usual British unit of pressure is the lb/in.² (or *psi*, for pounds per square inch), which is equivalent to 6.9 kPa.

Suppose we have a 1000-kg car whose tires are filled with air at a pressure of 2 bars. What is the area of each tire that is in contact with the road? If each tire bears one-quarter of the entire weight *mg* of the car, the force on each tire is

$$F = mg = (250 \text{ kg})(9.8 \text{ m/s}^2) = 2450 \text{ N}$$

Since $p = F/A$ and 1 bar = 10^5 Pa,

$$A = \frac{F}{p} = \frac{2450 \text{ N}}{2 \times 10^5 \text{ Nm}^2} = 0.0123 \text{ m}^2$$

Blood pressure

The *torr*, which represents the pressure of a column of mercury 1 mm high and is equal to 133 Pa, is used in medicine for expressing blood pressures. Arterial blood pressure is usually measured with the help of an inflatable cuff wrapped around a person's upper arm at the level of the heart. The sound of blood flowing in an artery below the cuff is monitored with a stethoscope. The cuff is initially inflated until the flow of blood stops, and the pressure in the cuff is then slowly reduced until a gurgling sound in the stethoscope indicates that the blood has just begun to flow again. The pressure at this point, called *systolic*, represents the maximum pressure the heart produces in the artery. Then the pressure in the cuff is reduced until the gurgling stops, which means that normal blood flow has been

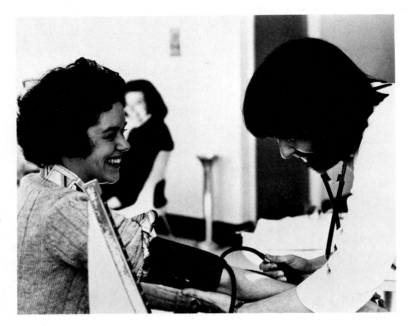

Arterial blood pressures are measured by using an inflatable cuff that is pumped up until the flow of blood stops, as monitored by a stethoscope. Air is then let out of the cuff until the flow just begins again; the pressure at this point is called *systolic* and corresponds to the maximum pressure the heart produces in the artery. Finally, more air is let out until the blood flow becomes normal; the pressure now, called *diastolic*, corresponds to the arterial pressure between strokes of the heart.

restored. The pressure now, called *diastolic*, represents the pressure in the artery between strokes of the heart. A healthy person has systolic and diastolic pressures in the neighborhood of 120 and 80 torr respectively.

Pressure in a Fluid

Why pressure is a useful quantity

In the tire pump of Fig. 4-3, it is impossible for the air just under the piston to be under a pressure of 1.5 bars while the air at the bottom of the cylinder is under a pressure of, say, 0.5 bar. Since the air can flow, it would simply move from the region of high pressure to the region of low pressure until the pressure is the same everywhere. Thus we can say that

When an external pressure acts on a fluid, it is transmitted uniformly throughout the fluid.

Pressure in a fluid increases with depth

The above statement applies only to the pressure imposed from outside the fluid. The fluid at the bottom of a container is always under more pressure than the

A hydraulic ram converts pressure in a liquid into an applied force. The pressure is provided by a pump.

fluid at the top because of the weight of the fluid above it. The increase of pressure with depth is obvious to anyone who dives into a body of water. But such a pressure difference cannot lead to a movement of the fluid because it corresponds exactly to the weight of the overlying fluid.

Another consequence of the ability of a fluid to flow is that

Pressure in a fluid is independent of direction

The pressure at any point within a fluid is the same in all directions.

If the pressure were not the same, again, the fluid would move in such a way as to equalize it. This property of fluids can be demonstrated by the arrangement shown in Fig. 4-4, which consists of a funnel capped by a thin rubber sheet and connected to an instrument for measuring pressure. If the funnel is held with the center of the membrane at a particular level in a liquid or gas, turning the funnel in different directions has no effect on the mercury level.

Pumps

A *pump* is a device that can produce a pressure difference. The way an ordinary piston pump operates is shown in Fig. 4-5. Such a pump can provide high pressure (to inflate a tire or football, for instance) or low pressure (to pump water from a well or the bilge of a boat, for instance). The heart consists of two pumps of this kind, which circulate blood through the lungs and through the body; the

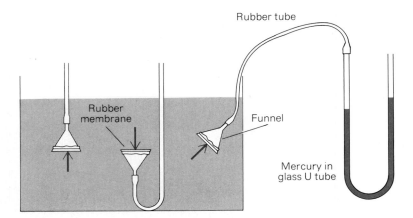

FIG. 4-4
Pressure is the same in all directions at the same level in a fluid.

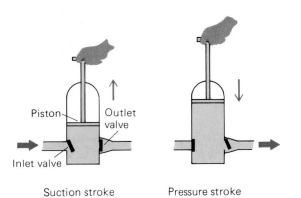

FIG. 4-5
A piston pump. During the suction stroke, the inlet valve opens and the fluid is sucked into the cylinder. When the piston is pushed down, the inlet valve closes and the outlet valve opens, and the fluid is forced out.

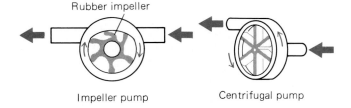

FIG. 4-6
Two kinds of rotary pumps. In an impeller pump, the fluid is compressed when the rubber fins of the impeller are bent over at the flattened top of the chamber. In a centrifugal pump, the rotating blades set the fluid in motion.

contraction and relaxation of the muscular walls of the heart chambers take the place of piston strokes. Two kinds of rotary pumps, which are more suitable for motor drive, are shown in Fig. 4-6.

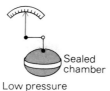

Sealed chamber

Low pressure

High pressure

FIG. 4-7
An aneroid barometer. The flexible ends of a sealed metal cylinder are forced in by a high atmospheric pressure, out by a low atmospheric pressure.

Atmospheric pressure

Since we live at the base of the atmosphere, we are under pressure from the weight of the air above us. This pressure averages 1013 mbars, nearly 15 lb/in.², at sea level. We are not aware of the 15-lb force pushing inward on every square inch of our bodies because our bodies are sufficiently permeable to air so that pressures inside are kept equal to those outside.

Atmospheric pressures are measured with instruments called *barometers*, of which the most common type is the *aneroid*, illustrated in Fig. 4-7.

Buoyancy

Sink or swim

Pressures in liquids rapidly become greater with increasing depth because of the weight of the overlying material. Most submarines cannot descend more than a few hundred meters without the danger of collapsing. At a depth of 10 km in the ocean the pressure is about 1000 times sea-level atmospheric pressure, enough to compress water by 3 percent of its volume. Fish that live at such depths can withstand such enormous pressures for the same reason we can endure the pressures at the bottom of our ocean of air: pressures inside their bodies are kept equal to pressures outside. When brought quickly to the surface, deep-ocean fish may explode because of their high internal pressures.

Buoyancy refers to the upward force exerted by a fluid on an object immersed in it

When something is immersed in water (or any other fluid), it seems to weigh less than it does in air. This effect is called *buoyancy,* and it enables balloons to float in the atmosphere, ships to float in the sea, and the continents to float in the plastic rock that constitutes most of the earth's interior. If the upward buoyant force on a submerged body is greater than its weight, the body floats; if the force is less than its weight, the body sinks.

Imagine a solid body of any kind whose volume is *V* that is immersed in a tank of water. A body of water of the same size and shape in the tank is supported

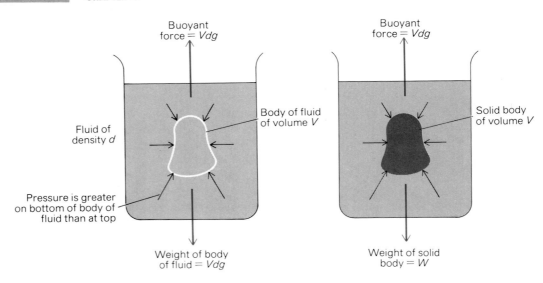

Buoyant force = Vdg

Buoyant force = Vdg

Fluid of density d

Body of fluid of volume V

Solid body of volume V

Pressure is greater on bottom of body of fluid than at top

Weight of body of fluid = Vdg

Weight of solid body = W

FIG. 4-8

Archimedes' principle. The buoyant force on a body in a fluid is equal to the weight of fluid displaced by the body. If the body's weight W is greater than Vdg, the body sinks; otherwise it floats at such a level that the weight of the displaced fluid equals W.

by a buoyant force equal to its weight of Vdg. The buoyant force is the result of all of the forces that the rest of the water in the tank exerts on this particular body of water, and it is always upward because the pressure underneath the volume is greater than the pressure above it; the pressures on the sides cancel one another out. If the body of water is replaced by the solid body, the forces on it are the same (Fig. 4-8), and the buoyant force remains Vdg. In this formula, d is the density of the fluid (which need not be water, of course) and V is the volume of fluid displaced by the submerged body.

Thus we have *Archimedes' principle:*

Archimedes' principle

Buoyant force on a body in a fluid = weight of fluid displaced by the body

Archimedes' principle holds whether the body floats or sinks. If the body's weight is greater than the buoyant force, it sinks. If the weight is less than the buoyant force, it floats, in which case the volume V refers only to the submerged part.

The condition for a body to float in a particular fluid, then, is that its average density be lower than that of the fluid. Why does a steel ship float when the density of steel is nearly 8 times that of water? The answer, of course, is that the ship is a hollow shell, so its average density is less than that of water even when loaded with cargo. If the ship springs a leak and fills with water, its average density goes up, and it sinks. The purpose of a lifejacket is to reduce the average density of a person in the water so that he floats higher and is less likely to get water in his lungs and drown as a result.

At constant pressure, heating a gas reduces its density, which is how a hot-air balloon acquires its buoyancy. These balloons have propane burners in their gondolas to provide the required heat.

An iceberg is a chunk of freshwater ice that has broken off an icecap (such as those that cover Greenland and Antarctica) or a glacier at the edge of the sea. As an illustration of Archimedes' principle, we can find the proportion of an iceberg that is below the water's surface. In order for the iceberg to float in equilibrium, its weight must be exactly balanced by the buoyant force of the sea water. If V_{ice} is the iceberg's volume and V_{sub} is its submerged volume, then

FIG. 4-9
Eighty-nine percent of the volume of an iceberg is submerged because the density of ice is 89 percent of the density of sea water.

Weight of iceberg = weight of displaced water

$$(Vdg)_{ice} = (Vdg)_{water}$$

$$\frac{V_{sub}}{V_{ice}} = \frac{d_{ice}}{d_{water}} = \frac{9.2 \times 10^2 \text{ kg/m}^3}{1.03 \times 10^3 \text{ kg/m}^3} = 0.89$$

Thus 89 percent of the volume of an iceberg is below the surface of the water (Fig. 4-9).

KINETIC THEORY OF MATTER

Matter consists of molecules in motion

The kinetic-molecular theory is an attempt to account for a wide variety of physical and chemical properties of matter in terms of a simple model of its structure. According to this model, all matter is composed of tiny particles called *molecules* that are in constant motion. Later on we shall discuss molecules in some detail, but for the time being we can simply regard them as the basic particles characteristic of a substance.

Brownian Movement

Molecules are never at rest

Today we know a great deal about the actual sizes, speeds, even shapes of the molecules in various kinds of matter.

For example, a molecule of nitrogen, the chief constituent of air, has a diameter of about 0.18 billionth of a meter (1.8×10^{-10} m) and a mass of 4.7×10^{-26} kg. It travels (at 0°C) with an average speed of 500 m/s (about the speed of a rifle bullet), and in each second collides with more than a billion other molecules. Of similar dimensions and moving with similar speeds in each cubic centimeter of air are 2.7×10^{19} other molecules. If all the molecules in such a thimbleful of air were divided equally among all the 4 billion people on the earth, each one would receive nearly 7 billion molecules!

Molecules of a gas or liquid move
irregularly due to collisions among
them

Molecules cannot be seen directly because the resolving power of microscopes is limited by the wave nature of light (Chap. 6). But there are particles small enough to move in response to the blows of swiftly moving molecules yet large enough to be visible in a microscope. Molecular motions are highly erratic, and so these particles are buffeted about in irregular, zigzag paths (Fig. 4-10). The smallest ones move rapidly under molecular bombardment, darting this way and that, now brought to a stop, now starting out in a new direction. Larger particles show only a slight jiggling motion since so many molecules strike them that the forces on all sides very nearly balance out. Called *brownian movement,* this irregular motion

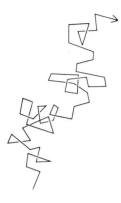

FIG. 4-10
The irregular path of a microscopic particle bombarded by molecules. The line joins the positions of a single particle observed at 10-s intervals. This phenomenon is called brownian movement and is direct evidence of the reality of molecules and their random motions.

is exhibited by particles of various kinds suspended in water and by smoke particles suspended in air. It was discovered in 1827 by the British botanist Robert Brown, who studied the motion of pollen grains in a drop of water. Brownian movement is among the most direct and convincing evidence we have of the reality of molecules and their motions.

The Gas Laws

All gases obey them

In many ways the gaseous state is the one whose behavior is the easiest to describe and account for. As an important example, the pressures, volumes, and temperatures of gas samples are related by simple formulas that have no counterpart in the cases of liquids and solids. The discovery of these formulas led to a search for their explanation in terms of the basic nature of gases, a search that led to the kinetic theory of matter.

Suppose that a sample of some gas is placed in the cylinder of Fig. 4-11 and a pressure of 1 bar is applied. The final volume of the sample is 1 m³. If we double the

FIG. 4-11
Boyle's law: At constant temperature, the volume of a given quantity of any gas is inversely proportional to the pressure applied to it. Here $p_1V_1 = p_2V_2 = p_3V_3$.

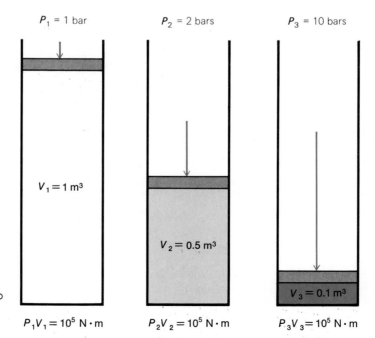

A snowmaking machine in operation. A mixture of compressed air and water is blown through a nozzle, and the expansion of the air cools the mixture sufficiently to freeze the water into the ice crystals of snow.

pressure to 2 bars, the piston will move down until the gas volume is 0.5 m³, half its original amount, provided the gas temperature is kept unchanged. If the pressure is made 10 times greater, the piston will move down farther, until the gas occupies a volume of 0.1 m³, again if the gas temperature is kept unchanged.

The volume of a gas sample is inversely proportional to its pressure

These findings can be summarized by saying that the volume of a given quantity of a gas at constant temperature is inversely proportional to the pressure applied to it. (By "inversely proportional" is meant that as the pressure increases, the volume decreases by the same proportion, and vice versa.) If the volume of the gas is V_1 when the pressure is p_1 and the volume changes to V_2 when the pressure is changed to p_2, the relationship among the various quantities is

Boyle's law

$$\frac{p_1}{p_2} = \frac{V_2}{V_1} \quad \text{(at constant temperature)}$$

This relationship is called *Boyle's law*, in honor of the English physicist who discovered it.

Changes in the volume of a gas sample are also related to temperature changes in a simple way. If a gas is cooled steadily, starting at 0°C, while its pressure is maintained constant, its volume decreases by $\frac{1}{273}$ of its volume at 0°C

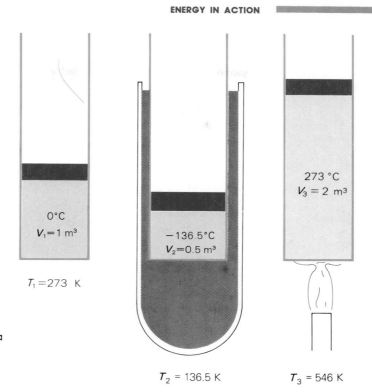

0°C
$V_1 = 1$ m³

$T_1 = 273$ K

−136.5°C
$V_2 = 0.5$ m³

$T_2 = 136.5$ K

273 °C
$V_3 = 2$ m³

$T_3 = 546$ K

FIG. 4-12
Charles's law: At constant pressure, the volume of a given quantity of a gas is directly proportional to its absolute temperature. (To change a celsius temperature to its equivalent absolute temperature, add 273°.) Here $V_1 T_1 = V_2 T_2 = V_3 T_3$.

for every degree the temperature falls. If the gas is heated, its volume increases by the same fraction (Fig. 4-12). If volume rather than pressure is kept fixed, the pressure increases with rising temperature and decreases with falling temperature, again by the fraction $\frac{1}{273}$ of its 0°C value for every degree change.

These figures suggest an obvious question: What would happen to a gas if we could lower its temperature to −273°C? If we should try to maintain constant volume, the pressure at this temperature ought to fall to zero; if the pressure remained constant, the volume ought to fall to zero. It is hardly likely, however, that our experiments would have such results. In the first place, we should find it impossible to reach quite so low a temperature, and in the second place, all known gases liquefy before that temperature is reached. Nevertheless, a temperature of −273°C has a very special significance, a significance that will become clearer shortly. It is called *absolute zero*.

For many scientific purposes it is more convenient to reckon temperatures from absolute zero than from the freezing point of water. Temperatures on such a scale, given as degrees celsius above absolute zero, are called *absolute temperatures*. Thus the freezing point of water is 273° absolute, written 273 K in honor of

Absolute zero is −273°C and is the lowest possible temperature

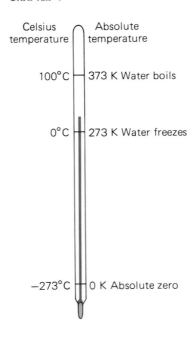

FIG. 4-13
The absolute temperature scale.

the English physicist Lord Kelvin, and the boiling point of water is 373 K. Any celsius temperature T_C can be changed to its equivalent absolute temperature T_K by adding 273 (Fig. 4-13):

$$T_K = T_C + 273$$

Absolute temperature scale

Absolute temperature = celsius temperature + 273

Using the absolute scale, we can express the relationship between gas volumes and temperatures quite simply: the volume of a gas is directly proportional to its absolute temperature (Fig. 4-14). This relation may be expressed in the form

FIG. 4-14
Graphic representation of Charles's law, showing the proportionality between volume and absolute temperature for gases at constant pressure. If the temperature of a gas could be reduced to absolute zero, its volume would fall to zero. Actual gases liquefy at temperatures above absolute zero.

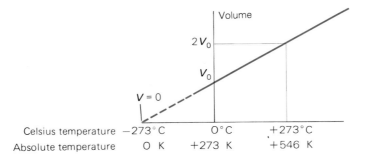

Charles's law

$$\frac{V_1}{V_2} = \frac{T_1}{T_2} \qquad \text{(at constant pressure)}$$

where the V's are volumes and the T's are absolute temperatures. Discovered by two eighteenth-century French physicists, Jacques Alexandre Charles and Joseph Gay-Lussac, this relation is commonly known as *Charles's law*. Like Boyle's law, it is approximately correct for all gases at ordinary pressures, but becomes less accurate at high pressures.

These laws can be combined in the single formula

Ideal gas law

$$\frac{p_1 V_1}{T_1} = \frac{p_2 V_2}{T_2}$$

At constant temperature, $T_1 = T_2$ and we have Boyle's law, while at constant pressure, $p_1 = p_2$ and we have Charles's law. A common way of writing this formula is

$$\frac{pV}{T} = \text{constant}$$

since it reflects the fact that this particular combination of quantities does not change in value even though the individual quantities p, V, and T may vary.

It is very significant that $pV/T =$ constant holds fairly well for *all* gases, and it therefore furnishes a specific goal for theories which attempt to explain the gaseous state of matter. This equation is known as the *ideal gas law*.

Kinetic Theory of Gases

Why gases behave as they do

The three basic assumptions of the kinetic theory for gas molecules, which have been amply verified by experiment, are these:

Assumptions of kinetic theory of gases

1. Gas molecules are small compared with the average distance between them.
2. Gas molecules collide without loss of kinetic energy.
3. Gas molecules exert almost no forces on one another, except when they collide.

A gas, then, is mostly empty space, with its isolated molecules moving helter-skelter like a swarm of angry bees in a closed room. Each molecule collides with others several billion times a second, changing its speed and direction at each collision but unaffected by its neighbors between collisions. If a series of collisions brings it momentarily to a stop, new collisions will set it in motion; if its speed becomes greater than the average, successive collisions will slow it down. There is no order in the motion, no uniformity of speed or direction. All we can say is that the molecules have a certain average speed and that at any instant as many molecules are moving in one direction as in another.

This animated picture readily accounts for the more obvious properties of gases. The ability of a gas to expand and to leak through small openings follows from the rapid motion of its molecules and their lack of attraction for one another. Gases are easily compressed because the molecules are, on the average, widely separated. One gas mixes with another because the spaces between molecules leave ample room for others. Gases are low in density because their volume consists so largely of empty space.

Gas pressure is the effect of bombardment of billions and billions of molecules, the same sort of bombardment that causes the brownian movement; the many tiny, separate blows affect our senses and measuring instruments as a continuous force. When a gas is squeezed into a smaller volume, more molecules strike a square centimeter of surface each second, and the pressure is increased. When the gas is expanded to a larger volume, each square centimeter is struck less often, and the pressure decreases (Fig. 4-15). This is the general relationship summarized in Boyle's law.

The kinetic theory is able to show that the pressure and the volume of a gas at constant temperature should be exactly inversely proportional to each other. Suppose that the molecules of a gas in a cylinder (Fig. 4-16) are thought of as moving in a completely regular manner, some of them vertically between the piston and the base of the cylinder and the remainder horizontally between the cylinder walls. If the piston is raised so that the gas volume is doubled, the vertically moving molecules have twice as far to go between collisions with top and bottom and hence will strike only half as often; the horizontally moving molecules must spread their blows over twice as great an area, and hence the number of impacts

Origin of Boyle's law

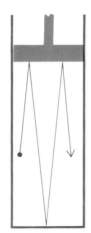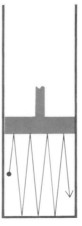

FIG. 4-15
Gas pressure is the result of molecular bombardment. When a gas is compressed into a smaller volume, its molecules strike the walls of the container more often than before, leading to an increase in pressure. For simplicity, only vertical molecular motions are shown.

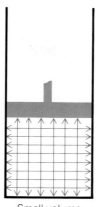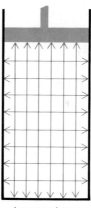

Small volume, high pressure   Large volume, low pressure

FIG. 4-16
Origin of Boyle's law according to the kinetic theory of gases. Expanding a gas sample means that its molecules must travel farther between successive impacts on the container wall and that their blows are spread over a larger area, so the gas pressure drops.

per unit area will be cut in half. Thus the pressure in all parts of the cylinder is exactly halved, as Boyle's law would predict. It is not hard to extend this reasoning to a real gas whose molecules move at random.

Absolute Temperature

The faster the molecules, the higher the temperature

To account for the effects of temperature, the kinetic theory requires a further concept:

Temperature is a measure of average molecular kinetic energy

4. The absolute temperature of a gas is proportional to the average kinetic energy of its molecules.

That temperature should be closely related to molecular speeds, and hence to molecular energies, follows from the fact that the pressure of a confined gas increases as its temperature rises. Increases in pressure must mean that the molecules are striking their confining walls more forcefully and so must be moving faster.

At absolute zero gas molecules would ideally cease to move

Earlier in this chapter we learned that the pressure of a gas approaches zero as its temperature falls toward 0 K, which is −273°C. For the pressure to become zero, molecular bombardment must stop. Thus absolute zero is interpreted in the kinetic theory as the temperature at which gas molecules would lose their kinetic energies completely, as shown in Fig. 4-17. (This is a simplification of the actual situation: in reality, even at 0 K a molecule will have a very small amount of KE.) There can be no lower temperature, simply because there can be no smaller amount of energy than none at all. The regular increase of gas pressure with

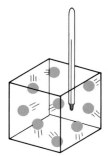

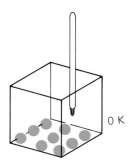

FIG. 4-17
According to the kinetic theory of gases, at absolute zero the molecules of a gas would not move. More advanced theories show that even at 0 K a very slight movement will persist.

0 K

absolute temperature if the volume is constant and the similar increase of volume if the pressure is constant (Charles's law) are understandable from this definition of absolute zero.

Why compressing a gas increases its temperature

If temperature is a measure of average molecular energy, then compressing a gas in a cylinder ought to cause its temperature to rise: as in Fig. 4-18, while the piston is moving down, molecules rebound from it with increased energy just as a baseball rebounds with increased energy from a moving bat. To verify this prediction, it is only necessary to pump up a bicycle tire and notice how hot the pump becomes after the air in it has been compressed a few times. On the other hand, if a gas is expanded by pulling a piston outward, its temperature should fall, since each molecule that strikes the retreating piston gives up some of its kinetic energy.

The cooling effect of gas expansion explains the formation of clouds from rising moist air, as discussed in Chap. 13. Atmospheric pressure decreases with altitude, and the water vapor in the moist air cools as it moves upward until it condenses into the water droplets that constitute clouds.

The picture of a gas as a collection of tiny molecules that fly about in all

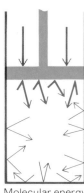

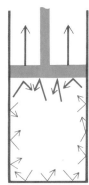

Molecular energy increases

Molecular energy decreases

FIG. 4-18
Compressing a gas causes its temperature to rise because molecules rebound from the piston with more energy. Expanding a gas causes its temperature to drop because molecules rebound from the piston with less energy.

directions brings up the question, What keeps them moving? We might think of molecules as being like billiard balls that move rapidly and collide with one another many times a second. Real billiard balls, after a brief period of such motion, would lose all their kinetic energy and come to rest. All other motions of our experience, except those of the stars and planets, similarly stop sooner or later unless some outside force keeps them going. No outside force acts on molecular motions, yet they continue indefinitely. Why is it that friction of some kind does not affect molecules?

The answer is that friction involves a change of kinetic energy into heat, which is molecular energy. Friction between molecules would mean a change of molecular energy into molecular energy—which is not a change at all. The question of what keeps molecules moving is really meaningless. It seems to make sense only because we are used to thinking of heat and motion as separate concepts. The energy of motion in the molecular world cannot become heat, as it does in the larger world of everyday life, because this energy *is* heat.

Gas molecules keep moving because there is nothing to make them stop

CHANGES OF STATE

Let us now see what the kinetic theory of matter has to say about liquids and solids. In particular, the interpretation of changes of state, between gas and liquid and between liquid and solid, is extremely interesting in molecular terms.

Liquids and Solids

Intermolecular forces hold them together

Gas molecules are far apart, those of liquids and solids are close together

The molecules of a gas are far apart on the average, and as a result gases are easy to compress. A great deal of effort is needed to compress a solid or liquid by even a small amount, however, which suggests that their molecules are quite close together (Fig. 4-19). What keeps them together are electric forces, as discussed in Chap. 9, whose ranges of action are too short to affect the widely spaced gas molecules. When gas molecules do collide, they are moving so fast that the intermolecular forces cannot keep them together and they simply bounce apart.

FIG. 4-19

Molecular models of a solid, a liquid, and a gas. The molecules of a solid are firmly attached to one another; those of a liquid can move about but stay close together; those of a gas have no restrictions on their motion.

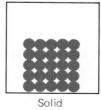
Solid

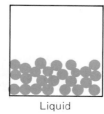
Liquid

Gas

CHAPTER 4

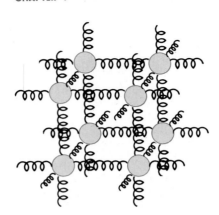

FIG. 4-20
The particles of a solid can be imagined as being held together by tiny springs that permit them to oscillate back and forth. The higher the temperature, the more energetic the oscillations. When a solid is squeezed, the springs are (so to speak) pushed together; when it is stretched, the springs are pulled apart.

Molecules of a liquid move past one another fairly readily

Particles of a solid vibrate about fixed positions

How evaporation occurs

If a gas can be compared with a swarm of angry bees, the molecules of a liquid are more like bees in a hive, crawling over one another constantly. Liquids flow because their molecules slide past one another easily, but they flow less readily than gases because of intermolecular attractions.

The forces between the particles of a solid are stronger than in a liquid, so strong that the particles are no longer free to move about. They are hardly stationary, however. Held in position as if by springs attached to its neighbors, each particle oscillates back and forth rapidly and continuously (Fig. 4-20). A solid is elastic because its particles return to their normal separations after being pulled apart or pushed together when a moderate force is applied. If the force is sufficiently great, the solid may be deformed permanently. In this process, tiny cracks develop throughout the solid, with each fracture healing itself as the particles slide to new positions and find new partners for their attractive forces. Too much force, of course, may break the solid apart.

Boiling

Liquid into gas

Suppose we have two liquids, water and alcohol, in open dishes (Fig. 4-21). Molecules in each dish are moving in all directions, with a variety of speeds. At any instant some molecules are moving fast enough upward to escape into the air in spite of the attractions of their slower neighbors. By this loss of its faster molecules each liquid gradually evaporates. Since the molecules remaining behind are the slower ones, evaporation leaves cool liquids behind. The alcohol evaporates more quickly (or is more *volatile*) and cools itself more noticeably because the attraction of its particles for one another is smaller and a greater number can escape.

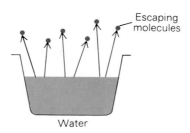

Escaping molecules

Water

FIG. 4-21
Evaporation. Alcohol evaporates more rapidly than water because the attractive forces between its molecules are smaller. In each case, the faster molecules escape; hence the average energy of the remaining molecules is lower and the liquid temperature drops.

Alcohol

Boiling point

Heat of vaporization

When we add heat to a liquid, eventually a temperature is reached at which even molecules of average speed are able to overcome the forces holding them together. Now bubbles of vapor form throughout the liquid, and it begins to boil. This temperature is accordingly called the *boiling point* of the liquid; as we would expect, the boiling point of alcohol is lower than that of water.

Whether evaporation takes place by itself from an open dish or is aided by heating, the formation of vapor from a liquid requires energy. In the first case energy is supplied from the heat energy of the liquid itself (since the liquid grows cooler), in the other case from the external source of heat. For water at its boiling point, 2260 kJ (the *heat of vaporization*) is needed to change each kilogram of liquid into vapor (Fig. 4-22). Here there is no difference in temperature between liquid and vapor, hence no difference in their average molecular kinetic energies.

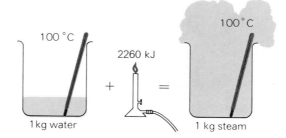

100 °C · 2260 kJ · 100 °C · 1 kg water · 1 kg steam

FIG. 4-22
The heat of vaporization of water is 2260 kJ/kg.

If not into kinetic energy, into what form of molecular energy does the 2260 kJ of heat go?

Intermolecular forces provide the answer. In a liquid these forces are strong, because the molecules are close together. To tear the molecules apart, to separate them by the wide distances that exist in the vapor, requires that these strong forces be overcome. Each molecule must be moved, against the attraction of its neighbors, to a new position in which their attraction for it is very small. Just as a stone thrown upward against the earth's attraction acquires potential energy, so molecules moved apart in this fashion acquire potential energy — potential energy with reference to intermolecular forces. When a vapor condenses to a liquid, the process is reversed: the molecules "fall" toward one another under the influence of their mutual attractions, and their potential energy is taken up as heat by the surroundings.

Melting

Solid into liquid

Crystalline and amorphous solids

Solids fall into two categories. The majority are *crystalline*, with the particles of which they are composed arranged in regular, repeated three-dimensional patterns (Fig. 4-23). Salt, quartz, diamond, and the various metals are familiar examples. Solids whose particles have no regularity of arrangement, for instance glass and many plastics, are *amorphous* ("without form").

Crystalline solids have definite melting points, amorphous solids soften gradually

The temperature changes that accompany the melting of crystalline and amorphous solids are quite different and give an easy experimental method for telling apart the two types of material. A crystalline solid like ice melts sharply, at one definite temperature (0°C for ice), and requires the addition of a certain quantity of energy (335 kJ/kg for ice) at this temperature to change from solid to liquid (Fig. 4-24). An amorphous solid like glass softens gradually on heating, so that no particular temperature can be given as its melting point.

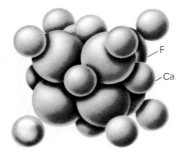

FIG. 4-23
The structure of a fluorite (CaF_2) crystal, showing the regular arrangement of the calcium (Ca) and fluorine (F) atoms.

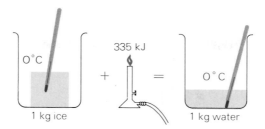

FIG. 4-24
The heat of fusion of ice is 335 kJ/kg.

FIG. 4-25
The orderly arrangement of particles in a crystalline solid is converted to the random arrangement of particles in a liquid when enough energy is supplied to the solid to overcome the bonding forces within it.

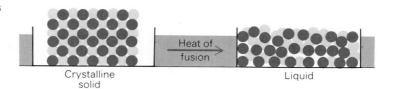

Heat of fusion.

In terms of the kinetic theory, this difference in behavior follows from differences in inner structure. The particles of a crystalline solid are arranged in a definite pattern such that the forces binding each one to its neighbors on all sides are as large as possible. To overcome these forces and give the particles the disorderly arrangement of a liquid requires that they gain potential energy, just as liquid particles must gain potential energy during evaporation (Fig. 4-25). This potential energy is the *heat of fusion* (335 kJ/kg for water) that must be supplied to melt any crystalline solid and is given out again when the liquid crystallizes again.

The particles of an amorphous solid, on the other hand, are organized in no definite pattern but are already in the random, disorderly arrangements characteristic of a liquid. Melting involves a gradual loosening of the ties between adjacent particles, without any sharp increase in potential energy at a certain temperature.

Thus, without any new assumptions, the kinetic theory of matter provides an understanding of changes of state in terms of the motions, potential energies, and arrangements of the basic particles of which every substance is composed.

ENERGY TRANSFORMATION

Transforming heat into other forms of energy is always inefficient

Different kinds of energy, including heat, can be converted from one into another. But heat is unusual in that it cannot be converted *efficiently*. We routinely obtain mechanical energy from the heat given off by burning coal and oil in engines of various types, but a large fraction of the heat is always wasted — about two-thirds in the case of the best modern electric power stations, for example. The problem is an important one because nearly all the primary energy available to modern civilization is liberated from its sources as heat.

The basic inefficiency of all engines whose energy input is heat was discovered in the nineteenth century, at the start of the Industrial Revolution. It is not a question of poor design or construction; the transformation of heat simply will not take place without such losses. Research both by engineers trying to get as much mechanical energy as possible from each ton of coal and by scientists whose interest was in the properties of heat eventually brought to light why such transformations are so wasteful. As we shall see, the ultimate reason is that what we call heat actually consists of the kinetic energy of random molecular motion.

Heat Engines

Turning heat into work

Heat is the easiest and cheapest form of energy to obtain, since all we have to do to liberate it is to burn an appropriate fuel. A device that converts heat into mechanical energy is called a *heat engine*. Examples are the gasoline and diesel engines of cars, the jet engines of aircraft, and the steam turbines of ships and power stations. All these engines operate in the same basic way: a gas is heated and allowed to expand against a piston or the blades of a turbine.

How a heat engine works

Figure 4-26 shows a gas being heated in a cylinder. As the temperature of the gas increases, its pressure increases as well, and the piston is pushed upward. The energy of the upward-moving piston can be used to propel a car or turn a generator or for any other purpose we wish. When the piston reaches the top of the cylinder, however, the conversion of heat into mechanical energy stops. In order to keep

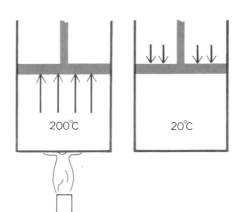

FIG. 4-26
An idealized heat engine. A gas at 200°C gives out more energy in expanding than is required to compress the gas at 20°C, and this excess energy is available for doing work.

the engine working, we must now push the piston back down again in order to begin another energy-producing expansion.

If we push the piston down while the gas in the cylinder is still hot, we will find that we have to do exactly as much work as the energy provided during the expansion. Thus there will be no net work done at all. To make the engine perform a net amount of work in each cycle, we must first cool the gas so that less work is needed to compress it. It is in this cooling process that heat is lost. There is no way to avoid throwing away some of the heat added to the gas in the expansion if the engine is to continue to operate. The wasted heat usually ends up in the atmosphere around the engine.

A heat engine extracts energy from a flow of heat through it

What happens in a complete cycle, then, is that heat flows through the engine from a heat source to the atmosphere, and during the flow we manage to change some of the heat into mechanical energy. Evidently we need *both* a hot reservoir and a cold one in order to produce a flow of heat from which we can extract some of it, as in Fig. 4-27. Figure 4-28 shows the operating cycle of a gasoline engine, in which the hot reservoir is the burning gases of the power stroke and the cold reservoir is the atmosphere.

A refrigerator is a heat engine operated in reverse

A vast amount of heat is contained in the molecular motions of the atmosphere, the oceans, and the earth itself, but only in exceptional circumstances can we use it because we need a colder reservoir nearby to which the heat can flow. What about using a refrigerator as the cold reservoir? A refrigerator is the reverse of a heat engine, as we see in Fig. 4-27. It uses mechanical energy to force heat "uphill" from a cold reservoir (the inside of the refrigerator) to a warm reservoir (the air of the kitchen), which is opposite to its normal direction of flow. Because of the energy needed to drive a refrigerator, using one as the cold reservoir for a heat engine is necessarily a losing proposition.

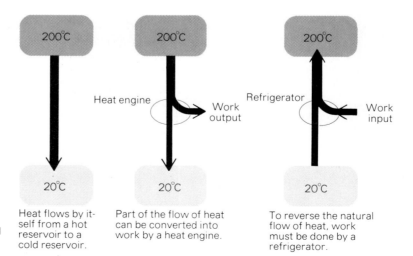

FIG. 4-27
A heat engine is a device that converts part of the heat flowing from a hot reservoir to a cold one into work. A refrigerator is a device that extracts heat from a cold reservoir and delivers it to a hot one by performing work that is converted into heat.

Heat flows by itself from a hot reservoir to a cold reservoir.

Part of the flow of heat can be converted into work by a heat engine.

To reverse the natural flow of heat, work must be done by a refrigerator.

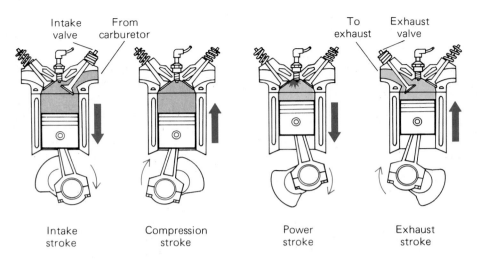

FIG. 4-28
The operating cycle of a four-stroke gasoline engine. In the intake stroke, a mixture of gasoline vapor and air from the carburetor is drawn into the cylinder as the piston moves downward. In the compression stroke, the fuel-air mixture is compressed to perhaps 14 bars. At the end of the compression stroke the spark plug is fired, which ignites the fuel-air mixture. The expanding gases force the piston downward with pressures of 40 to 50 bars in the power stroke. Finally the piston moves upward again to force the spent gases out through the exhaust valve.

Thermodynamics

You can't win

Thermodynamics is the science of heat transformation, and it has two fundamental laws:

Laws of thermodynamics

1. Energy cannot be created or destroyed, but it can be converted from one form to another.
2. It is impossible to take heat from a source and change all of it to mechanical energy; some must be wasted.

The first law of thermodynamics is the same as the law of conservation of energy discussed in Chap. 3. What it means is that we can't get something for nothing. The second law singles out heat from other kinds of energy and recognizes that all conversions of heat into any of the others must be inefficient.

Maximum efficiency of a heat engine depends on the temperatures of its hot and cold reservoirs

Thermodynamics is able to specify the maximum efficiency of a heat engine, ignoring losses to friction and other practical difficulties. The maximum efficiency turns out to depend only on the absolute temperatures T_{hot} and T_{cold} of the hot and cold reservoirs between which the engine operates:

$$\text{Maximum efficiency} = 1 - \frac{T_{cold}}{T_{hot}}$$

The greater the ratio between the two temperatures, the less heat is wasted and the more efficient the engine.

Figure 4-29 shows the basic design of a steam turbine. In a power station, the steam comes from a boiler heated by a coal or oil furnace or by a nuclear reactor,

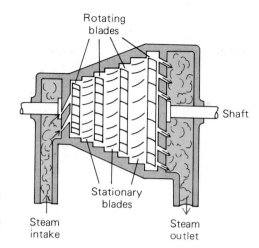

FIG. 4-29
In a steam turbine, steam moves past several sets of rotating blades on the same shaft to obtain as much power as possible. The stationary blades direct the flow of steam in the most effective way.

and the turbine shaft is connected to an electric generator. In a typical power station, steam enters a turbine at about 570°C and leaves at about 95°C into a partial vacuum. The corresponding absolute temperatures are respectively 843 K and 368 K, so the maximum efficiency of such a turbine is

$$\text{Maximum efficiency} = 1 - \frac{T_{\text{cold}}}{T_{\text{hot}}} = 1 - \frac{368 \text{ K}}{843 \text{ K}} = 0.56$$

which is 56 percent. The actual efficiency is likely to be less than 40 percent because of friction and other sources of energy loss.

Why a heat engine must be inefficient

On a molecular level, it is not hard to see why heat resists conversion into other forms of energy. When heat is added to the gas of a heat engine, its molecules increase their average speeds. But the molecules are moving in random directions, whereas the engine can draw upon the increased energies of only those molecules that happen to be moving in the same direction as the piston or turbine blades. If we could line up the molecules and aim them all, like miniature bullets, right at the piston or turbine blades, all the added energy could be turned into mechanical energy. Because this is impossible, only a fraction of any heat given to a gas can be extracted as energy of orderly motion. The nature of heat is responsible for the inefficiency of heat engines, and there is no way around it.

The Fate of the Universe

Order into disorder

Since other kinds of energy can be entirely converted into heat whereas only part of a given amount of heat can be converted the other way, there is an overall tendency toward an increase in the heat energy of the universe at the expense of the other kinds it contains. We see this tendency all around us in everyday life. When coal or oil burns in an engine, much of its chemical energy becomes heat; when any kind of machine is operated, friction turns some of its energy into heat; an electric light bulb emits heat as well as light; and so on. Most of the lost energy is dissipated in the atmosphere, the oceans, and the earth itself where it is largely unavailable for recovery.

Heat death of the universe

In the world of nature a similar steady degradation of energy into unusable heat occurs. In the universe as a whole, the stars (for instance, the sun) constitute the hot reservoir and everything else (for instance, the earth) constitutes the cold reservoir from a thermodynamic point of view. As time goes on, the stars will grow cooler and the rest of the universe will grow warmer, so that less and less energy will be available to power the further evolution of the universe. On a molecular level, order will become disorder. This is the real meaning of the second law of thermodynamics.

ENERGY AND CIVILIZATION

The rise of modern civilization would have been impossible without the discovery of vast resources of energy and the development of ways to transform it into useful forms. All that we do requires energy. The more energy we have at our command, the better we can satisfy our desires for food, clothing, shelter, warmth, light, transport, communication, and manufactured goods.

Unfortunately the most convenient fuels — oil and natural gas — are now expensive and their current abundant supply cannot last much longer. Alternative fuels all have serious handicaps of one kind or another and nuclear fusion, the ultimate energy source, remains a technology of the future. At the same time, world population is increasing and with a need for more and more energy. The choice of an appropriate energy strategy for the next few decades, and perhaps longer, is therefore one of the most ciritical of today's world problems.

The Energy Problem

Limited supply, unlimited demand

The sun is the source of most of the energy available on the earth's surface

Almost all the energy available to us today has a single source — the sun. Light and heat reach us directly from the sun; food and wood owe their energy contents to sunlight falling on plants; water power exists because the sun's heat evaporates water from the oceans to fall later as rain and snow on high ground; wind power comes from motions in the atmosphere due to unequal heating of the earth's surface by the sun. The fossil fuels coal, oil, and natural gas were formed from plants and animals that lived and stored energy derived from sunlight millions of years ago. Only nuclear energy and heat from sources inside the earth cannot be traced to the sun's rays.

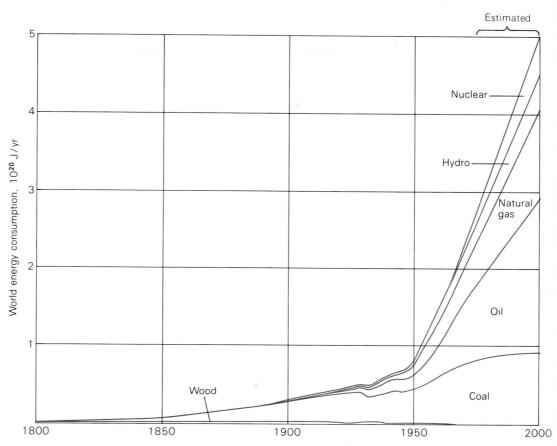

FIG. 4-30
World energy sources and consumption.

Energy use per person has increased throughout history

Our earliest ancestors had only food as their energy source and used energy at an average rate of around 90 W. The mastery of fire and the harnessing of animal power brought this figure up to perhaps 0.5 kW, where it remains for many people even now. With the spread of the steam engine in the last century the Industrial Revolution began in earnest, and energy consumption started a steady rise, largely fueled by coal, in the more advanced countries. After World War II energy demand in these countries soared, to the point where today the average is 11 kW per person in the United States and energy production involves one-third of its industrial plant. Oil and natural gas have overtaken coal as the chief energy source, as Fig. 4-30 shows.

In the advanced countries, the standard of living is already high, and their populations are stable, so their use of energy is not likely to grow very fast. Elsewhere energy consumption is still low, less than 1 kW each for more than half the people of the world. These people seek better lives, which means more energy, and their numbers are increasing rapidly, which means still more energy. Where is it to come from?

Present patterns of energy use leave much scope for conservation. More attention to wasted energy in general and such specific measures as better insulation in buildings and more efficient vehicle engines can make a difference — a saving of perhaps 20 percent is not impossible. But it is nowhere near enough when set against an almost sure tripling and a possible quadrupling of world energy demand in the next 50 years.

Oil and natural gas will be the first fossil fuels to run out

For a number of reasons the trends that have been projected to the year 2000 in Fig. 4-30 cannot be extended further. An obvious one is that the fossil fuels coal, oil, and natural gas, which today furnish by far the greater part of our energy, cannot last forever. Production of natural gas, the least polluting of them, will be the first to decline. Oil will be next, probably by the end of the century. This is a real pity because oil and gas burn efficiently and are easy to produce, process, and transport. In addition, oil and gas are not only fuels but also superb feedstocks for synthetic materials of all kinds. Other raw materials, notably coal, can replace them, but only at much greater expense and greater risk to health and to the environment.

Coal reserves are abundant but pollution is a problem

Even though the coal we consume every year took about two million years to accumulate, enough remains to last at least another two or three hundred years at the present rate of consumption. Coal reserves are equivalent in energy content to 5 times oil reserves. Before 1941, coal was the world's chief fuel, and it is likely to return to first place as oil and gas run out. But coal is far from being a desirable fuel. Not only does its mining usually leave large areas of land unfit for further use, but the air pollution due to burning coal adversely affects the health of millions of people. Acid rain (see Chap. 11) from the same source harms plant and animal life on a large scale. Most estimates put the number of deaths in the United States from cancer and respiratory diseases caused by burning coal at over 10,000 per year. Coal-burning power plants actually expose the people living around them to more radioactivity, from traces of uranium and thorium in their smoke, than do normally operating nuclear plants.

Carbon dioxide and the greenhouse effect

Apart from pollution, another consequence of burning fossil fuels is disturbing. When they are burned, the carbon in coal, oil, and gas becomes carbon dioxide, which is harmless and a normal constituent of air. The trouble is the scale of the burning — billions of tons of carbon dioxide now pour from our chimneys and exhaust pipes each year. The result has been a definite increase in the carbon dioxide content of the atmosphere in the past hundred years. As discussed in Chap. 13, carbon dioxide absorbs heat given off by the earth's surface. This "greenhouse effect" means that, the more carbon dioxide, the warmer the atmosphere becomes, and nobody is sure exactly what the eventual changes in weather and climate patterns will be as a result. Perhaps it is a good thing that the supply of fossil fuels is limited.

Nuclear energy

Nuclear fuel reserves much exceed those of fossil fuels. Mainly this is because "breeder" reactors can be built that convert the normally unusable ^{238}U form of uranium into plutonium, which can serve as a nuclear fuel. (See Chap. 7 for a more complete discussion of nuclear energy.) The United States stockpile of refined ^{238}U about equals in energy content all the country's coal resources. Besides having an abundant fuel supply, properly built and properly operating nuclear plants are in many respects excellent energy sources. Nuclear electricity is less expensive than fossil-fuel electricity everywhere except in regions of the United States near coalfields, and even there the two are competitive if measures are taken to cut pollution from the coal plants. Nuclear energy is already second only to coal in electricity production in the United States, and its use elsewhere in the world is rising steadily.

To be sure, nuclear energy has serious drawbacks. Although the overall public-health record of nuclear installations has been excellent — far better than that of coal-burning plants — even a single major accident could result in enormous harm. A power reactor produces several tons of wastes each year whose radioactivity will remain high for thousands of years, and their safe disposal is still an unsettled issue. And, even though ordinary nuclear fuel cannot be used in weapons, it is not a giant step from a civilian nuclear program to a military one.

The Future

The problem of waste heat

Nuclear fusion is a long-term prospect

In the long run, practical ways to utilize the energy of nuclear fusion (which is how the sun and stars obtain their energy) seem sure to be developed. As described in Chap. 7, a fusion reactor will get its fuel from the sea, will be safe and nonpolluting, and cannot be adapted for military purposes. But nobody can predict when this ultimate source of energy will become an everyday reality.

As energy consumption increases, the disposal of waste heat becomes more difficult

Even given fusion energy, however, the rate of increase of energy consumption that appears in Fig. 4-30 cannot continue indefinitely. The second law of thermodynamics is what stands in the way. As we know, it is impossible to convert heat into mechanical energy efficiently. The best of today's power stations have overall efficiencies of only about 35 percent regardless of whether the heat source is a coal- or oil-burning furnace or a nuclear reactor; a fusion reactor will not be very different. The waste heat must go somewhere, and even now its disposal is difficult in many parts of the world.

Generating plants in the United States already use over 10 percent of the flow of all the rivers and streams of the country for cooling purposes. Serious biological consequences are likely if the scale of heating of inland waters climbs much further. If waste heat is instead discharged into the atmosphere using cooling towers, the weather and climate of the region involved may be changed in a perhaps harmful way. Although the ocean can safely absorb much waste heat, locating power plants on their shores poses the question of carrying the electricity they produce for thousands of miles inland.

The real problem is population growth

In the long term, the need to get rid of waste heat will conflict with the need for more energy that comes from both rising worldwide living standards and rising world population (which is the most ominous threat to civilization for other reasons as well). The second law of thermodynamics is not subject to repeal, and a future energy crisis will represent a social failure, not a technological one.

Nevertheless a large increase in energy production is possible before the waste heat barrier is reached. The big question at the present time is the right course to follow until fusion energy arrives, probably sometime in the next century. More nuclear energy? More burning of fossil fuels? Or alternative energy sources such as winds and tides, direct sunlight, alcohol from crops, or heat from the earth's interior?

Bridging the Gap

What to do until fusion comes

As we have seen, despite certain good aspects, neither fossil nor nuclear energy sources are ideal for bridging the gap until fusion energy arrives an unknown time hence. Let us now look into the chief alternatives to these sources. They fall into two categories, depending on whether they supply energy continuously or only when conditions are favorable.

Energy storage systems

In the second category are solar radiation, winds, and tides. Although their "fuel" is free and cannot run out, they are not reliable and so cannot be used by themselves without a means for storing the energy they produce. One storage scheme is to use the energy to pump water up to a high reservoir. Then, at night or when the wind stops or when the tide is not running, the water can be allowed to fall through turbine generators. Another scheme, practical only on a small scale, is to use storage batteries. Or the energy can be used to produce hydrogen gas from water, with the hydrogen in turn used as a fuel. All these storage methods, however, are quite expensive, and their cost must be added to the already considerable cost of the basic installation. Feeding the output of an intermittent source into the distribution grid of a conventional power system is more likely to be an economic proposition. Unfortunately electric networks do not reach much of the rural populations of Africa, Asia, and Latin America.

Expensive and inefficient now, but a bright future

Solar energy Bright sunlight can deliver over 1 kW of power to each square meter it falls on. At this rate, an area the size of a tennis court receives solar energy equivalent to a gallon of gasoline every 10 min or so. Although the supply of sunshine varies with location (Fig. 4-31), time of day, season, and weather, there is still plenty available, and much study has gone into making use of it.

One approach is to use a series of mirrors arranged to automatically track the sun and concentrate its radiation on a boiler on top of a "tower of power." The resulting steam then drives a turbine and thence an electric generator. Another approach is to use photoelectric cells that convert light energy directly into electric

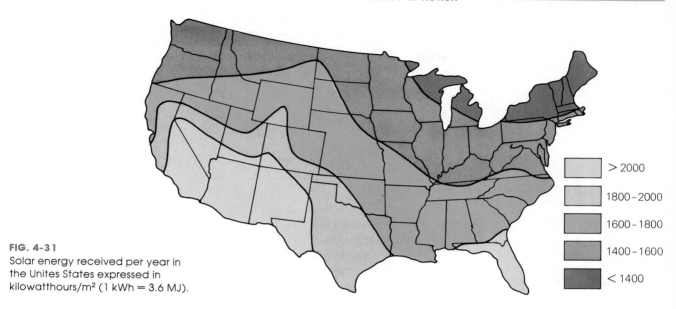

FIG. 4-31
Solar energy received per year in
the Unites States expressed in
kilowatthours/m² (1 kWh = 3.6 MJ).

> 2000

1800 – 2000

1600 – 1800

1400 – 1600

< 1400

Drums of water absorb and store
solar energy for heating this house in
Corrales, New Mexico. At left is a
solar water heater, and the windmill
behind it powers a water pump.
Solar energy involves no hazards and
does not consume irreplaceable
natural resources, but in less favored
climates it can provide only a small
part of the total energy requirements
of a technological society.

Windmills were once widely used for such purposes as grinding grain and pumping water. This photograph shows old windmills near Rotterdam in the Netherlands; the structures were turned to face the wind, and the vanes were covered with cloth to form sails. In a region where steady winds are normal, windmills make sense for generating electric power. Modern windmills use solid propellers rather than sails and rotate much more rapidly than their predecessors.

energy. With no moving parts, and not limited by the second law of thermodynamics because no heat is involved, this would be a perfect method. But (there is always a "but") existing cells are very inefficient, so many of them are needed for a worthwhile output, and very expensive, so the cost of the resulting electricity is well above that of other sources. Fortunately solar-cell technology is steadily improving and may one day reach an economic level.

Practical only in a few places

Wind   For hundreds of years windmills were widely used for such purposes as grinding grain and pumping water. Holland alone once had 9000 of them. Now windmills are coming back into fashion with propeller-type rotors instead of sails and with electricity as their output. A large modern windmill with rotor blades 100 m in diameter might have an output of 3 MW when the wind speed is 12 m/s (about 27 mi/h). Such windmills are cheaper per watt of output than solar cells, though still more expensive than conventional power stations, and make sense only where winds are steady and strong. A number of windmills are operating in the United States, England, Holland, Denmark, and Germany.

Also limited geographically

Tides   The twice-daily rise and fall of the tides is accompanied by corresponding flows of water into and out of bays and river mouths. The energy involved is enormous in regions where the tidal range is great, such as along the English Channel and in the Bay of Fundy between New Brunswick and Nova Scotia in

The ebb and flow of tides in the Rance River estuary in northern France provide energy for generators capable of an output of 240 MW. The lock at right permits ships to enter and leave the river.

Canada. Tides in the Rance River estuary in northern France have driven turbine generators of 240 MW capacity since 1966, but elsewhere the size of the dams needed makes similar projects impractical.

Plenty left to exploit

Hydroelectricity   Now we come to energy sources that can produce electricity on a continuous basis and so substitute for, rather than supplement, nuclear and fossil-fuel power stations. Foremost among them is water power, which today is responsible for 60,000 MW of electricity in the United States alone. Only 3 percent of the approximately 50,000 dams in this country have hydroelectric installations, and if the most suitable of the rest were so equipped, the total power from this source would triple. Untapped water flows exist abroad, too. Still, there is a limit to the possible expansion of hydroelectric power, and it falls short of what will be needed in the future.

Burning wood is not a good idea

Biomass   Green plants use the energy of sunlight to make carbohydrates (such as sugar, starch, cellulose) from water and carbon dioxide. From the time fire came under human control until coal took over a century and a half ago, wood was the world's chief source of energy apart from food. Trees grow almost everywhere and are a renewable resource. But wood smoke is even more polluting than coal smoke, being especially abundant in cancer-producing chemicals. And wood is valuable as a construction material and as a raw material for paper. Managing forests for continuing yield is unfortunately not common; just cutting down all the trees in a forest, the usual practice, leads to such severe ecological damage that an unduly long time is needed for new trees to grow.

Gasohol

Another biomass approach involves converting plant carbohydrates to alcohol for use as vehicle fuel. In Brazil many cars run on pure ethanol (ethyl alcohol)

The kinetic energy of falling water is converted into electric energy as the water turns turbine blades connected to generators in a dam. The ultimate source of the energy is sunlight, which evaporates water that later falls as the rain that drains into the dam's reservoir.

made from sugar cane, and in the United States 4 percent of total gasoline sales are of "gasohol," which contains 10 percent ethanol. Wood is another source of alcohol, in this case methanol (methyl alcohol). Although using alcohol as a fuel does not deplete any natural resources, it is more expensive than gasoline and, on an overall basis that includes the energy used in cultivation and harvesting, may consume more energy to make than it provides. And in the long run, it seems unlikely that much agricultural land can be diverted from food crops: the land needed to operate one car on alcohol can provide food for 8 to 16 people.

Using the earth's heat

Geothermal   Temperature increases with depth in the earth, but only in a few places is it hot enough near the surface for useful energy to be extracted. One such place is the Geysers Geothermal Fields north of San Francisco, where turbines driven by natural steam produce 665 MW of electric power. Other geothermal power plants are located in New Zealand and Italy. Hawaii has enough accessible volcanic heat to furnish double that state's present electricity consumption if put to work, but there seem to be few other regions with such potential. The main use of geothermal zones may turn out to be to supply hot water to heat buildings in northern climates.

A difficult question of engineering

Ocean thermal   A typical temperature for surface water in a tropical ocean is 27°C, whereas at a depth of 1000 m or so it is 5°C or less. As long ago as 1881 it was proposed to operate a heat engine using surface water as the hot reservoir and

Waikei power station in New Zealand uses the heat of the earth's interior as its energy source. Geothermal power is practical in only a few parts of the world.

deep water as the cold reservoir. Although the efficiency of such an engine would be low, only a few percent, the "fuel" in the form of warm surface water is free and unlimited in quantity. But the low efficiency means that an ocean thermal power plant would have to be large in size relative to its capacity. An experimental plant built on the Japanese island of Nauru in 1981 takes in 1400 tons each of hot and cold water per hour to produce 100 kW of electricity. Operating the plant itself uses 90 kW, so the net output is only 10 kW. A full-size 400-MW plant would have to pump 10 million tons of water per hour, the flow of a major river. Despite this, the economics of ocean thermal energy seem promising, but a good many engineering obstacles remain to be overcome.

Disaster is avoidable

Clearly there is no obvious solution possible in the near future to the problem of safe, cheap, and abundant energy. The sensible course is to practice conservation and try to get the best from the various available technologies while pursuing fusion energy as rapidly as possible. As we have seen, each of these technologies has limitations, but may be a reasonable choice in a given situation. If their full potential is realized and population growth slows down, social disaster (starvation, war) and environmental catastrophe (a planet unfit for life) may well be avoided during the wait for fusion.

IMPORTANT TERMS

The **density** of a substance is its mass per unit volume; its **specific gravity** (or **relative density**) is its density relative to that of water.

The **pressure** on a surface is the perpendicular force per unit area that acts on it. The unit of pressure is the **pascal** (Pa), which is equal to the newton/meter². When an external pressure acts on a fluid, it is transmitted uniformly throughout the fluid. The pressure at any point within a fluid is the same in all directions and depends upon the weight of the fluid above the point as well as upon any external pressure.

According to **Archimedes' principle,** the buoyant force on a body in a fluid equals the weight of the fluid displaced by the body.

Boyle's law states that, at constant temperature, the volume of a gas sample is inversely proportional to its pressure. Hence an increase in pressure means a decrease in volume and vice versa at constant temperature.

The **absolute temperature scale** has its zero point at $-273°C$; temperatures in this scale are designated K. **Absolute zero** is $0 K = -273°C$. **Charles's law** states that, at constant pressure, the volume of a gas sample is directly proportional to its absolute temperature. Hence an increase in temperature means an increase in volume and vice versa at constant pressure.

The **ideal gas law,** which states that $pV/T =$ constant for a gas sample regardless of changes in p, V, and T, is a combination of Boyle's and Charles's laws and is obeyed approximately by all gases.

According to the **kinetic theory of matter,** all matter consists of tiny individual **molecules** that are in constant random motion. **Heat** is the kinetic energy of these random molecular motions. The ideal gas law can be explained by the kinetic theory on the basis that the absolute temperature of a gas is proportional to the average kinetic energy of its molecules. At absolute zero, gas molecules would have almost no kinetic energy.

The **heat of vaporization** of a substance is the amount of heat needed to change 1 kg of it at its boiling point from the liquid to the gaseous (or vapor) state. The **heat of fusion** of a substance is the amount of heat needed to change 1 kg of it at its melting point from the solid to the liquid state.

A **heat engine** is a device that converts heat into mechanical energy or work. The **first law of thermodynamics** is the law of conservation of energy. **The second law of thermodynamics** states that some of the heat input to a heat engine must be wasted in order for the engine to operate.

IMPORTANT FORMULAS

Pressure: $p = \dfrac{F}{A}$

Boyle's law: $\dfrac{p_1}{p_2} = \dfrac{V_2}{V_1}$ (at constant temperature)

Absolute temperature scale: $T_K = T_C + 273$

Charles's law: $\dfrac{V_1}{V_2} = \dfrac{T_1}{T_2}$ (at constant pressure; temperatures on absolute scale)

Ideal gas law: $\dfrac{p_1 V_1}{T_1} = \dfrac{p_2 V_2}{T_2}$ (temperatures on absolute scale)

Maximum efficiency of heat engine:

$\text{Eff}_{max} = 1 - \dfrac{T_{cold}}{T_{hot}}$ (temperatures on absolute scale)

MULTIPLE CHOICE

1. The fluid at the bottom of a container is
   a. under less pressure than the fluid at the top
   b. under the same pressure as the fluid at the top
   c. under more pressure than the fluid at the top
   d. any of the above, depending upon the circumstances
2. The pressure of the earth's atmosphere at sea level is due to
   a. the gravitational attraction of the earth for the atmosphere
   b. the heating of the atmosphere by the sun
   c. the fact that most living things constantly breathe air
   d. evaporation of water from the seas and oceans
3. Atmospheric pressure at sea level does not correspond to approximately
   a. 15 lb/in.²
   b. 9.8 Pa
   c. 1013 mbar
   d. 1 bar
4. An object placed in a liquid sinks. The buoyant force on the object
   a. is less than its weight
   b. is zero
   c. is more than its weight
   d. may be any of the above, depending on its shape
5. The density of fresh water is 1.00 g/cm³ and that of sea water is 1.03 g/cm³. A ship will float
   a. higher in fresh water than in sea water
   b. lower in fresh water than in sea water

c. at the same level in fresh water and in sea water

d. any of the above, depending on the shape of its hull

6. The pressure on 100 l of helium is increased from 1 bar to 4 bars. The new volume of the helium is

    a. 25 l

    b. 50 l

    c. 400 l

    d. 1600 l

7. Lead melts at 330°C. On the absolute scale this temperature corresponds to

    a. 57 K

    b. 362 K

    c. 571 K

    d. 603 K

8. At constant pressure, the volume of a gas sample is directly proportional to

    a. the size of its molecules

    b. its fahrenheit temperature

    c. its celsius temperature

    d. its absolute temperature

9. Which of the following statements is not correct?

    a. Matter is composed of tiny particles called molecules

    b. These molecules are in constant motion, even in solids

    c. All molecules have the same size and mass

    d. The differences between the solid, liquid, and gaseous states of matter lie in the relative freedom of motion of their respective molecules

10. Molecular bombardment is not responsible for

    a. the pressure exerted by a gas

    b. Boyle's law

    c. Archimedes' principle

    d. brownian movement

11. On the molecular level, heat is

    a. kinetic energy

    b. potential energy

    c. rest energy

    d. all of the above, in proportions that depend on the circumstances

12. A sample of a gas is compressed to half its original volume while its temperature is held constant. Relative to their original average energy, the new average energy of the molecules is

    a. half as great

    b. the same

    c. twice as great

    d. 4 times as great

13. When a gas is forced into a smaller volume without a change in temperature, its pressure increases because its molecules

    a. strike the container walls more often

    b. strike the container walls at higher speeds

    c. strike the container walls with greater force

    d. have more energy

14. The temperature of a gas sample in a rigid container is raised. The pressure the gas exerts on the container walls increases because

    a. the molecules are in contact with the walls for briefer intervals

    b. the molecular masses increase

    c. the molecules have higher average speeds and so strike the walls more often with greater momentum

    d. the molecules lose more kinetic energy each time they strike the wall

15. According to the kinetic theory of matter, at a given temperature

    a. light gas molecules have the same average energy as heavy gas molecules

    b. all the molecules in a gas have identical speeds

    c. light gas molecules have lower average energies than heavy gas molecules

    d. light gas molecules have higher average energies than heavy gas molecules

16. At which of the following temperatures would the molecules of a gas have twice the average kinetic energy they have at room temperature, 20°C?

    a. 40°C

    b. 80°C

    c. 313°C

    d. 586°C

17. Suppose there were molecules that had no attraction whatever for one another. A collection of such molecules would form a

    a. gas

    b. liquid

    c. amorphous solid

    d. crystalline solid

18. When a vapor condenses into a liquid,

    a. its temperature rises

    b. its temperature falls

    c. it absorbs heat

    d. it gives off heat

19. A heat engine operates by taking in heat at a particular temperature and

    a. converting it all into work

    b. converting some of it into work and exhausting the rest at a lower temperature

    c. converting some of it into work and exhausting the rest at the same temperature

d. converting some of it into work and exhausting the rest at a higher temperature

20. In any process, the maximum amount of heat that can be converted to mechanical energy

    a. depends on the amount of friction present

    b. depends on the intake and exhaust temperatures

    c. depends on whether kinetic or potential energy is involved

    d. is 100 percent

21. In any process, the maximum amount of mechanical energy that can be converted to heat

    a. depends on the amount of friction present

    b. depends on the intake and exhaust temperatures

    c. depends on whether kinetic or potential energy is involved

    d. is 100 percent

22. A refrigerator

    a. produces cold

    b. changes heat to cold

    c. causes heat to disappear

    d. removes heat from a region and carries it elsewhere

23. A heat engine absorbs heat at a temperature of 127°C and exhausts heat at a temperature of 77°C. Its maximum efficiency is

    a. 13 percent

    b. 39 percent

    c. 61 percent

    d. 88 percent

24. The second law of thermodynamics does not lead to the conclusion that

    a. on a molecular level, order will eventually become disorder in the universe

    b. all the matter in the universe will eventually end up at the same temperature

    c. no heat engine can convert heat into work with 100 percent efficiency

    d. the total amount of energy in the universe, including rest energy, is constant

25. The rate at which direct sunlight delivers energy to an area of 1 square meter is roughly

    a. 1 W

    b. 10 W

    c. 1000 W

    d. 1,000,000 W

26. The chief source of energy in the world today is

    a. coal

    b. oil

    c. natural gas

    d. uranium

27. The source of energy whose reserves are greatest is

    a. coal

    b. oil

    c. natural gas

    d. uranium

QUESTIONS

1. When a person drinks a soda through a straw, where does the force come from that causes the soda to move upward?

2. A small amount of water is boiled for a few minutes in a can, which is then sealed while still hot. As the can cools, it collapses. Why?

3. A wooden block is submerged in a tank of water and pressed down against the bottom of the tank so that there is no water underneath it. The block is released. Will it rise to the surface or stay where it is?

4. The height of water at two identical dams is the same, but dam *A* holds back a lake that contains 1 km³ of water whereas dam *B* holds back a lake that contains 2 km³ of water. Compare the forces exerted on the two dams.

5. Why do helium-filled balloons rise to a certain altitude and float there instead of rising indefinitely?

6. An ice cube floats in a glass of water filled to the brim because it has a lower density than water. What will happen when the ice melts?

7. An aluminum canoe is floating in a swimming pool. After a while it begins to leak and sinks to the bottom of the pool. What, if anything, happens to the water level in the pool?

8. Why does bombardment by air molecules not produce brownian motion in large objects such as tables and chairs?

9. How can the conclusion of kinetic theory that molecular motion occurs in solids be reconciled with the observation that solids have definite shapes and volumes?

10. Gas molecules have speeds comparable with those of rifle bullets, yet it is observed that a gas with a strong odor (ammonia, for instance) takes a few minutes to diffuse through a room. Why?

11. At absolute zero, a sample of an ideal gas would have zero volume. Why would this not be true of an actual gas at absolute zero?

12. A sample of hydrogen is expanded to twice its original volume, while its temperature is held constant. What happens to the average speed of the hydrogen molecules?

13. When they are close together, molecules attract one another slightly. As a result of this attraction, are gas pressures higher or lower than expected from the ideal-gas law?

14. How does perspiration give the body a means of cooling itself?

15. How could you tell experimentally whether a fragment of a clear, colorless material is glass or a crystalline solid?

16. A person tries to cool a kitchen in the summer by switching on an electric fan and closing the kitchen door and windows. What will happen?

17. In another attempt to cool the kitchen, the person leaves the refrigerator door open, again with the kitchen door and windows closed. Now what will happen?

18. Why is a piece of ice at $0°C$ more effective in cooling a drink than the same mass of cold water at $0°C$?

19. If an egg is dropped into boiling water over a gas flame, the length of time necessary to cook the egg is not changed by turning the gas higher, although more heat is being supplied to the water. Explain. What becomes of the extra heat?

20. The oceans contain an immense amount of heat energy. Why can a submarine not make use of this energy for propulsion?

21. Is the heat given off by a refrigerator less than, the same as, or more than the heat it absorbs from its contents?

22. What energy sources, if any, cannot be traced to sunlight falling on the earth?

23. What is the nature of the long-term limit to the amount of energy that can be used in the world?

PROBLEMS

1. A piece of balsa wood 10 cm wide, 5 cm thick, and 50 cm long has a mass of 325 g. Find the density of balsa wood.

2. Find the mass of the air in a room 5 m long, 4 m wide, and 3 m high.

3. A 50-g bracelet is suspected of being gold-plated lead instead of pure gold. It is dropped into a full beaker of water and 4.0 cm^3 of water overflows. Is the bracelet pure gold?

4. How many cubic meters of water does a metric ton (1000 kg) of pure water occupy? A metric ton of lead? A metric ton of air?

5. The mercury column in a barometer is about 76 cm high. If water were used instead of mercury, how high would the liquid column be?

6. A 50-kg woman balances on the heel of her right shoe, which is 1 cm in diameter. How much pressure does she exert on the ground? How many atm is this? (The area of a circle of radius r is πr^2.)

7. A cork 1 cm in radius is used to close one end of a tube whose other end is connected to a vacuum pump. The pump removes virtually all the air from the tube. How much force is needed to pull the cork out?

8. The smallest bone in the index finger of a 75-kg circus acrobat's right hand has a cross-sectional area of 0.5 cm^2 and breaks under a pressure of 1.7×10^8 Pa. Is it safe for him to balance his entire weight on this finger?

9. A woman whose mass is 60 kg is standing on a rectangular swimming raft 3 m long and 2 m wide which is floating in fresh water. By how much does the raft rise after she dives off?

10. Find the buoyant force on an 80-kg man in air under the assumption that his density is the same as that of fresh water.

11. Find the minimum area of an ice floe 7 cm thick that can support a 50-kg woman without getting her feet wet. The floe is in a freshwater lake.

12. A 30-kg balloon is filled with 100 cm^3 of hydrogen. How much force is needed to hold it down?

13. A certain quantity of hydrogen occupies a volume of 1000 cm^3 at $0°C$ (273 K) and ordinary atmospheric pressure. If the pressure is tripled but the temperature is held constant, what will the volume of the hydrogen be? If the temperature is increased to $273°C$ but the pressure is held constant, what will the volume of the hydrogen be?

14. A sample of nitrogen occupies 2 m^3 at 300 K and a pressure of 200 kPa. (a) The sample is compressed to a volume of 1 m^3. What is its pressure at the same temperature? (b) What volume does the sample occupy at the same temperature if its pressure is decreased to 150 kPa? (c) What volume does the sample occupy at a temperature of 400 K and a pressure of 200 kPa?

15. To what celsius temperature must a gas sample initially at $20°C$ be heated if its volume is to double while its pressure remains the same?

16. An air tank used for scuba diving has a safety valve set to open at a pressure of 280 bars. The normal pressure of the full tank at $20°C$ is 200 bars. If the tank is heated after being filled to 200 bars, at what temperature will the safety valve open?

17. A tank contains 5 kg of carbon dioxide gas at $20°C$ and a pressure of 1 atm. What happens to the pressure when another 5 kg of carbon dioxide is added to the tank at the same temperature? Explain this result in terms of the kinetic theory of gases.

18. The average speed of a hydrogen molecule at room temperature is about 1.6 km/s. What is the average speed of an oxygen molecule, whose mass is 16 times greater, at the temperature?

19. To what temperature must a gas sample initially at $27°C$ be raised in order for the average energy of its molecules to double?

20. How much heat is required to change 50 g of ice at $0°C$ into water at $20°C$?

21. How much heat is given off when 1 kg of steam at $100°C$ condenses and cools to water at $20°C$?

22. If all the heat given off by a certain quantity of water at $0°C$ when it turns to ice at $0°C$ could be used to lift the ice vertically upward, how high would it be raised?

23. A man is resting in the shade on a hot day in which the air temperature is the same as his body temperature of $37°C$. In this situation the chief way his body dissipates the 120 W his metabolic processes liberate is by the evaporation of sweat. How much sweat per hour is required? The heat of vaporization of water at 37°C is 2430 kJ/kg.

24. An engine that operates between 2000 K and 700 K has an efficiency of 40 percent. What percentage of its maximum possible efficiency is this?

25. An engine is proposed which is to operate between 200°C and 50°C with an efficiency of 35 percent. Will the engine perform as predicted? If not, what would its maximum efficiency be?

26. Three designs for an engine to operate between 450 K and 300 K are proposed. Design A is claimed to require a heat input of 800 J for each 1000 J of work output, design B a heat input of 2500 J, and design C a heat input of 3500 J. Which design would you choose and why?

ANSWERS TO MULTIPLE CHOICE

1. c	**8.** d	**15.** a	**22.** d
2. a	**9.** c	**16.** c	**23.** a
3. b	**10.** c	**17.** a	**24.** d
4. a	**11.** a	**18.** d	**25.** c
5. b	**12.** b	**19.** b	**26.** b
6. a	**13.** a	**20.** b	**27.** d
7. d	**14.** c	**21.** d	

5

ELECTRICITY AND MAGNETISM

We have now learned about force and motion, mass and energy, the law of gravity, and the concept of matter as being made up of tiny, randomly moving molecules. With the help of these ideas we have been able to make sense of a wide variety of observations, from the paths of the planets across the sky to the melting of ice and the boiling of water. Is this enough for us to understand how the entire physical universe works?

A simple demonstration gives the answer. All we need do is run a hard rubber comb through our hair on a dry day: little sparks occur, and the comb afterward is able to pick up small bits of dust and paper. What is revealed in this way is an *electrical* phenomenon, something that neither gravity nor the kinetic theory of matter can account for.

In everyday life electricity is familiar as that which causes our light bulbs to glow, many of our motors to turn, our telephones and radios to bring us sounds, our television screens to bring us sights. But there is more to electricity than its ability to transport energy and information. All matter turns out to be electrical in nature, and electric forces are what bind electrons to nuclei to form atoms and what hold atoms together to form molecules, liquids, and solids. Most of the properties of the ordinary matter around us — with the notable exception of mass — can be traced to electrical forces.

ELECTRIC CHARGE

The first recorded studies of electricity were made in Greece by Thales of Miletus about 2500 years ago. Thales experimented with amber, called *electron* in Greek, and fur. The name *electric charge* is today given to whatever it is that a piece of amber (or hard rubber) possesses as a result of being rubbed with fur. It is this charge that causes sparks to occur and that attracts light objects such as bits of paper.

Positive and Negative Charge

Opposites attract

Charges of the same kind repel

Let us begin by hanging a small pith ball from a thread, as in Fig. 5-1. (Pith is a lightweight substance found in plant stems that is handy for work of this kind.) We

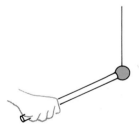

A pith ball held by a string is touched by a hard rubber rod. Nothing happens.

The rubber rod is stroked against a piece of fur

FIG. 5-1
A rubber rod stroked with fur becomes negatively charged. When it is touched against a pith ball, some of the negative charge flows to the ball. The pith ball then flies away because like charges repel each other.

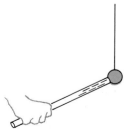

The pith ball is again touched by the rubber rod.

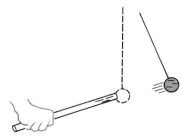

After the touch, the pith ball flies away from the rod.

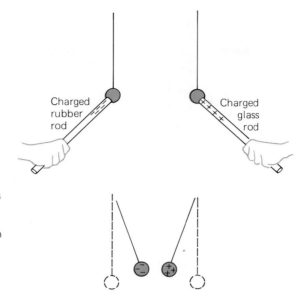

FIG. 5-2
A glass rod stroked with silk becomes positively charged. When one pith ball is touched with a negatively charged rubber rod and another pith ball is touched with a positively charged glass rod, the two balls fly together because unlike charges attract each other.

Unlike charges attract

All charges are either positive or negative

touch the ball with a hard rubber rod, and find that nothing happens. Next we stroke the rod with a piece of fur and again touch the pith ball with it. This time the ball flies away from the rod. Our conclusion is that some of the electric charge on the rod has flowed to the ball, and the fact that the ball then flies away from the rod means that charges of the same kind repel each other.

Is there only one kind of electric charge? To find out, we try other combinations of materials and see what happens when the various charged pith balls are near each other. Figure 5-2 shows the result when one pith ball has been charged by a rubber rod stroked with fur and the other pith ball has been charged by a glass rod stroked with silk: the two balls fly together. This result means that the charges on the rods are somehow different, and that different charges attract each other.

Comprehensive experiments show that *all* electric charges fall into one or the other of the two types described above. Regardless of their actual origin, they always behave as though they originated either on a rubber rod rubbed with fur or on a glass rod rubbed with silk. Benjamin Franklin suggested names for these two basic kinds of electricity. He called the charge produced on the rubber rod *negative charge* and the charge produced on the glass rod *positive charge*. These definitions are still used today.

The above experiments can be summarized very simply:

All charges are either positive or negative. Like charges repel, unlike charges attract.

This man is given an electric charge when he touches the terminal of a static electricity generator. Because all his hairs have the same sign of charge, they repel one another.

We have thus far been paying attention to the positive charge of the glass and the negative charge of the rubber. However, we do not produce positive charge alone by rubbing glass with silk or negative charge alone by stroking rubber with fur. If the fur used with the rubber is brought near a negatively charged pith ball, the ball is attracted. Thus the fur must have a positive charge (Fig. 5-3). Similarly the silk used with the glass turns out to have a negative charge. Whenever electricity is produced by contact between two objects of different material, one of them picks up a positive charge and the other a negative charge. Which is which depends on the particular materials used.

FIG. 5-3
When a rubber rod is stroked against a piece of fur, charges that were originally mixed together evenly become separated so that the rod becomes negatively charged and the fur becomes positively charged.

A neutral object has equal amounts of each kind of charge

It is worth keeping in mind that the rubbing process does not *create* the electric charges that appear as a result. All "uncharged" objects actually contain equal amounts of positive and negative charge. For some combinations of materials, as we have seen, mere rubbing is enough to separate some of the charges from each other. In most cases, however, the charges are firmly held in place and more elaborate treatment is needed to pull them apart. An object whose positive and negative charges exactly balance out is said to be electrically *neutral*.

What Is Charge?

Protons, electrons, and neutrons

In our personal experience, matter and electric charge seem continuous, so that we can imagine dividing either into smaller and smaller bits without limit. But there is another level beyond the direct reach of our senses, though not of our instruments, on which matter is revealed as being composed of just three kinds of *elementary particles*. These particles combine to make up all the different atoms that in turn are assembled into the molecules, solids, and liquids around us: nature is very economical. Two of the particles carry electric charges, so that charge, like mass, comes in small parcels of definite size.

Atoms are composed of protons, electrons, and neutrons

The three elementary particles found in atoms are:

1. The *proton,* which has a mass of 1.673×10^{-27} kg and is positively charged
2. The *electron,* which has a mass of 9.11×10^{-31} kg and is negatively charged
3. The *neutron,* which has a mass of 1.675×10^{-27} kg and is uncharged

The proton and electron have exactly the same amounts of charge, although of opposite sign. Protons and neutrons have almost equal masses, which are nearly 2000 times greater than the electron mass.

Atomic structure

Every atom has a small, central *nucleus* of protons and neutrons with its electrons moving about the nucleus some distance away (Fig. 5-4). Different types of atoms have different combinations of protons and neutrons in their nuclei. For instance, the most common variety of carbon atom has nuclei with six protons and six neutrons each; the most common variety of uranium atom has nuclei with 92 protons and 146 neutrons each. The electrons in an atom are normally equal in number to the protons, so the atom is electrically neutral unless disturbed in some way. The chain of experiments and the reasoning based on them that has led to this picture of the inner structure of matter is outlined in Chap. 7.

The coulomb is the unit of charge

The unit of electric charge is the *coulomb* (C). The proton has a charge of $+1.6 \times 10^{-19}$ C and the electron has a charge of -1.6×10^{-19} C. All charges, both positive and negative, are therefore found only in multiples of 1.6×10^{-19} C. This basic quantity of charge is abbreviated e:

Electric charge comes in multiples of $\pm e$

$$e = 1.6 \times 10^{-19} \text{ C}$$

FIG. 5-4
An atom consists of a central nucleus of protons and neutrons with electrons moving around it some distance away. The protons and electrons have equal but opposite charges and are the same in number, so the atom as a whole is normally electrically neutral. Neutrons are uncharged. Shown is a simplified model of the most common type of carbon atom, which has six protons, six neutrons, and six electrons. Two of the electrons are relatively near the nucleus, the others are farther away.

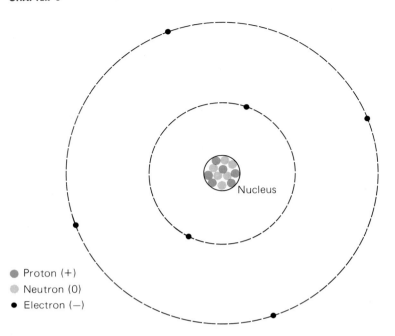

Nucleus

● Proton (+)
● Neutron (0)
● Electron (−)

Electric charge appears continuous outside the laboratory because *e* is such a small quantity. A charge of − 1 C, for example, corresponds to

$$\frac{-1 \text{ C}}{-1.6 \times 10^{-19} \text{ C}} = 6.25 \times 10^{18} \text{ electrons}$$

which is more than six billion billion electrons (Fig. 5-5). Atoms are small, too: coal is almost pure carbon, and six billion billion carbon atoms would make a piece of coal only about the size of a pea.

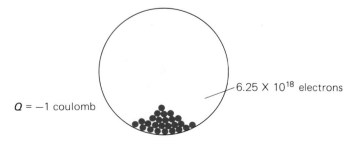

6.25 × 10¹⁸ electrons

Q = −1 coulomb

FIG. 5-5
A charge of − 1 C corresponds to more than 6 billion billion electrons.

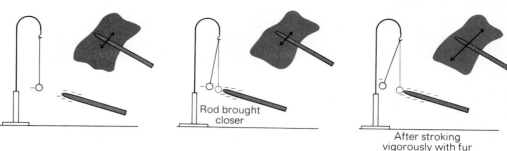

Rod brought
closer

After stroking
vigorously with fur

FIG. 5-6
Forces between charges. When a
rubber rod that has been stroked
with fur is brought near a negatively
charged pith ball, the force on the
ball is greater when the rod is held
close to it and also greater when the
rod has been vigorously stroked.

Coulomb's Law

The law of force for electric charges

The forces between electric charges can be studied in rather simple experiments, such as that shown in Fig. 5-6. What we find is that the force between a charged rod and a charged pith ball depends on two things: how close the rod is to the ball, and how much charge each one has. As we found earlier, when the charges have the same sign — both positive or both negative — the force is repulsive and tends to push them apart. When the charges have opposite signs — one positive and the other negative — the force is attractive and tends to pull them together.

Precise measurements show that the force between charges follows the same inverse-square variation with distance that the gravitational force between two masses does. For instance, when the charges are 2 cm apart, the force between them is $\frac{1}{4}$ as great as the force when they are 1 cm apart; it is 4 times greater when they are $\frac{1}{2}$ cm apart (Fig. 5-7b). If R is the distance between the charges, we can say that the force between them is proportional to $1/R^2$.

The force also depends on the magnitude of each charge: if either charge is doubled, the force doubles too, and if both charges are doubled, the force increases fourfold (Fig. 5-7c). If the charges have the respective magnitudes Q_1 and Q_2, then the force varies as their product $Q_1 Q_2$.

The above results are summarized in *Coulomb's law*

Coulomb's law of electric force

$$F = K \frac{Q_1 Q_2}{R^2}$$

which is named in honor of Charles Coulomb (1736 – 1806), who helped develop it. The quantity K is a constant whose value is almost exactly 9×10^9 N-m²/C². Thus we may rewrite Coulomb's law as

$$F = 9 \times 10^9 \frac{Q_1 Q_2}{R^2}$$

(a)

(b)

FIG. 5-7
(a) Like charges repel, unlike charges attract. (b) The force between two charges varies inversely as the square of their separation; increasing the distance reduces the force. (c) The force is proportional to the product of the charges.

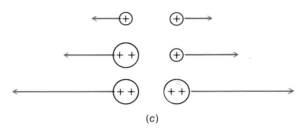

(c)

The coulomb is a very large unit

Just by looking at this formula we can see that the force between two charges of 1 C each that are separated by 1 m is 9×10^9 N. This is an enormous force, equal to about 2 billion lb! We conclude that the coulomb is a very large unit indeed, and that even the most highly charged objects that can be produced cannot contain more than a small fraction of a coulomb of net charge of either sign.

ELECTRICITY AND MATTER

Let us now look into some aspects of the electrical behavior of matter.

Matter in Bulk

Gravity versus electricity

Coulomb's law for the force between charges is one of the fundamental laws of physics, in the same category as Newton's law of gravitation. The latter, as we know, is written in equation form as

$$F = G \frac{m_1 m_2}{R^2}$$

Gravitational forces are always attractive; electric forces can be attractive or repulsive

Coulomb's law and the law of gravitation are remarkably similar, but they have one important difference: gravitational forces are always attractive, tending to draw the objects involved together, but electric forces may be either attractive or repulsive.

This last fact has an important consequence. Because one lump of matter always attracts another lump gravitationally, matter in the universe as a general rule tends to come together into large masses. Even though dispersive influences of various kinds exist, they must fight against this steady attraction. The galaxies, stars, and planets, which condensed from matter that was originally spread out in space, bear witness to this cosmic herd instinct.

To collect a significant electric charge of either sign, however, is far more of a feat. Charges of opposite sign attract each other strongly, so it is hard to separate neutral matter into differently charged portions. And charges of the same sign repel each other, so even if the charge separation is performed a little at a time, putting together a large amount of charge of one sign is difficult.

Gravitational forces dominate on a cosmic scale; electric forces dominate on an atomic scale

To sum up, we can say that a system of electrically neutral particles is most stable (that is, has a minimum potential energy) when the particles make up a single solid body, while a system of electric charges is most stable when charges of opposite sign pair off to cancel each other out. Hence on a cosmic scale gravitational forces are significant and electric ones are not. On an atomic scale, however, the reverse is true. The masses of subatomic particles are too small for them to interact gravitationally to any appreciable extent, whereas their electric charges are enough for electric forces to exert marked effects.

The hydrogen atom

The hydrogen atom serves to illustrate the above statement. Its nucleus is a single proton, and the electron that circles the proton does so at an average distance of 5.3×10^{-11} m (Fig. 5-8). The gravitational force of attraction between the proton and electron is

$$F_{\text{grav}} = G\frac{m_p m_e}{R^2}$$

$$= \frac{(6.7 \times 10^{-11} \text{ N-m}^2/\text{kg}^2)(1.7 \times 10^{-27} \text{ kg})(9.1 \times 10^{-31} \text{ kg})}{(5.3 \times 10^{-11} \text{ m})^2}$$

$$= 3.7 \times 10^{-47} \text{ N}$$

FIG. 5-8
A model of the hydrogen atom. The electric force between the electron and proton is more than 10^{39} times as great as the gravitational force between them.

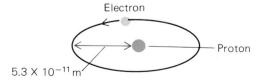

Electron

Proton

5.3×10^{-11} m

The electric force of attraction is

$$F_{\text{elec}} = K \frac{Q_p Q_e}{R^2}$$

$$= \frac{(9 \times 10^9 \text{ N-m}^2/\text{C}^2)(1.6 \times 10^{-19} \text{ C})(1.6 \times 10^{-19} \text{ C})}{(5.3 \times 10^{-11} \text{ m})^2}$$

$$= 8.2 \times 10^{-8} \text{ N}$$

The electric force is more than 10^{39} times greater than the gravitational force! (As we know from the Math Refresher at the back of this book, 10^{39} is 1 followed by 39 zeros.) Clearly, gravitational effects are negligible within atoms as compared with electrical effects.

Conductors and Insulators

How charge flows from one place to another

Electrons can move freely in a metal

A substance through which electric charge can flow readily is called a *conductor.* Metals are the only solid conductors at room temperature, copper being an especially good one. In a metal, each atom gives up one or more electrons to a "gas" of electrons that can move relatively freely inside the metal. The atoms themselves stay in place and are not involved in the movement of charge.

Electrons are firmly bound to the atoms of an insulator

In an *insulator,* charge can flow only with great difficulty. Nonmetallic solids are insulators because all their electrons are tightly bound to particular atoms or groups of atoms. Glass, rubber, and plastics are good insulators.

Superconductivity

No substance is a perfect insulator, but at temperatures near absolute zero certain metals and chemical compounds lose all resistance to the flow of charge through them. This phenomenon, called *superconductivity,* was discovered by Kamerlingh Onnes in Holland in 1911. For example, aluminum is superconducting at temperatures under 1.2 K, which is $-272°$C. If electrons are set in motion in a closed wire loop at room temperature, they will come to a stop in less than a second. In a superconducting wire loop, on the other hand, electrons have continued to circulate for years.

Semiconductors

A few substances, called *semiconductors,* are in between conductors and insulators in ability to allow charge to move through them. Semiconductors are important in technology because they can be made into devices called *transistors,* whose ability to carry charge can be changed at will. Transistors are widely used in modern electronics, notably in radio and television receivers. A computer contains many thousands of transistors that act as miniature switches to perform arithmetic and carry out logical operations. Semiconductor memories are also used in computers, with huge numbers of memory elements built into a "chip" smaller than a fingernail.

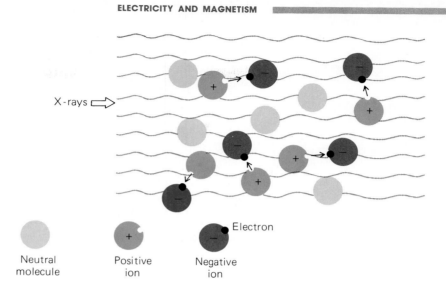

FIG. 5-9
A gas such as air becomes ionized when x-rays disrupt its molecules. A molecule losing an electron becomes a positive ion; a molecule gaining an electron becomes a negative ion. Ultraviolet light, radiation from radioactive substances, sparks, and flames also cause ionization to occur.

An ion is a charged atom or molecule; electric current in a gas or liquid involves the motion of ions

How ionization can occur

Ordinary water is a fair conductor

The conduction of electricity through gases and liquids — in a neon sign, for instance, or in the acid of a storage battery — is a more complicated process. What is involved is the movement of charged atoms and molecules called *ions*. An atom or molecule gains a positive charge (becomes a positive ion) when it loses one or more electrons, and it gains a negative charge (becomes a negative ion) when electrons in excess of its normal number become attached to it.

The process of forming ions, or *ionization*, may take place in a number of ways. A gas like ordinary air, which is normally a poor conductor, becomes ionized when x-rays, ultraviolet light, or radiation from a radioactive material passes through it, when an electric spark is produced, or even when a flame burns in it. Air molecules are sufficiently disturbed by these processes so that electrons are torn loose from some of them; the electrons thus set free may attach themselves to adjacent molecules, so both positive and negative ions are formed (Fig. 5-9). Eventually movements of the gas molecules bring oppositely charged ions together, whereupon the extra electrons on negative ions shift to positive ions to give neutral molecules again. At normal atmospheric pressure and temperature the ions last no more than a few seconds.

In the upper part of the earth's atmosphere, air molecules are so far apart on the average that the neutralization of ions is a slow process. As a result, the ionization produced by x-rays and ultraviolet light from the sun tends to persist, and the ability of the ions to reflect radio waves makes possible long-range radio communication (see Chap. 6).

In contrast with gases, certain liquids may be permanently ionized to a greater or lesser extent (see Chap. 10). The conductivity of pure water itself is extremely small, but even traces of some impurities increase its conductivity enormously.

Since most of the water we use in daily life is somewhat impure, it is usually considered a fair conductor of electricity.

The earth as a whole, at least that part of it beneath the outer dry soil, is also a fairly good conductor. Hence if a charged object is connected with the earth by a piece of metal, the charge is conducted away from the object to the earth. This convenient method of removing the charge from an object is called *grounding* the object. As a safety measure, the metal shells of electrical appliances are grounded through special wires that give electric charges in the shells paths to the earth. The round post in the familiar three-prong electric plug is the ground connection.

Grounding

Force on an Uncharged Object

Why a comb attracts bits of paper

One sign that a body possesses an electric charge is that it causes small, uncharged objects such as dust particles, bits of paper, and suspended pith balls to move toward it. Where does the force come from?

The explanation becomes clear when we reflect that the electrons in a solid have some freedom of movement. In a conductor, this freedom is considerable, but even in an insulator the electrons can shift around a little without leaving their parent atoms or molecules. When a comb is given a negative charge by being run through our hair, electrons in a nearby bit of paper are repelled by the negative charge and move away as far as they can (Fig. 5-10). The side of the paper near the comb is left with a positive charge, and the paper is accordingly attracted to the comb. If the comb is removed without actually touching the paper, the disturbed electrons resume their normal positions. Only a small amount of charge separation actually occurs, and so, with little force available, only very light things can be picked up in this way.

The presence of a charge induces a separation of charge in a nearby object

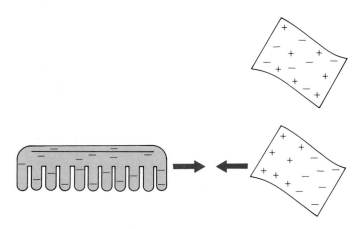

FIG. 5-10
A charged object attracts an uncharged one by first causing a separation of charge in the latter.

ELECTRIC CURRENT

A flow of charge from one place to another constitutes an *electric current*. Currents and not stationary charges are involved in nearly all the practical applications of electricity.

The Ampere

Unit of electric current

A battery is a device that maintains a positive charge on one terminal and a negative charge on the other. This is accomplished by a chemical reaction in the battery, with chemical energy being continuously transformed into electric energy whenever the battery is in use. Connecting a wire between the terminals provides a path for the excess electrons at the negative electrode to move toward the positive electrode. The flow of electrons tends to cancel out the two charges, but chemical processes in the battery build up the charges as fast as they are depleted. Thus the current in the wire consists of a movement of electrons from one end to the other. Note that we do not say, "The electrons carry the current," or "The motion of electrons produces a current"; the moving electrons *are* the current.

> The electric current in a metal consists of moving electrons

In several ways the flow of electricity along a wire resembles the flow of water in a pipe. When we wish to describe the rate at which water moves through a pipe, we give the flow in terms of, say, liters per second. If 5 liters of water pass through a given pipe each second, the flow is 5 l/s.

The description of electric current follows the same pattern. As we know, quantity of electric charge is measured in coulombs, as quantity of water is measured in liters. The natural way to refer to a flow of charge in a wire, then, is in terms of the number of coulombs per second that go past any point in the wire. This unit of electric current is called the *ampere* (A), after the French physicist André Marie Ampère. That is,

FIG. 5-11
The ampere is the unit of electric current. The flow of charge in a circuit is like the flow of water in a pipe except that a return wire is necessary in order to have a complete conducting path.

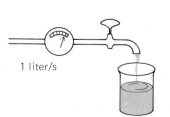

1 liter/s

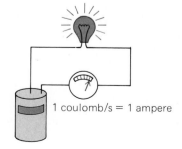

1 coulomb/s = 1 ampere

$$1 \text{ ampere} = 1 \, \frac{\text{coulomb}}{\text{second}}$$

$$1 \text{ A} = 1 \text{ C/s}$$

Batteries are rated in ampere-hours

A battery is rated according to the total amount of charge it can deliver, expressed in ampere-hours (A-h). Thus a battery whose capacity is 60 A-h can supply a current of 60 A for 1 h, a current of 30 A for 2 h, a current of 1 A for 60 h, and so on. The less the current, the longer the battery can supply it.

Potential Difference

The push behind a current

Consider a liter of water at the top of a waterfall. The water has potential energy there, since it can mov downward under the pull of gravity. When the water has fallen all the way down,   PE decreases. The work that can be obtained from the liter of water during its fall is equal to this decrease in PE.

Now consider a coulomb of negative charge on the − terminal of a battery. It is repelled by the − terminal and attracted by the + terminal, and so it has a certain amount of PE. When the coulomb of charge has moved along a wire to the + terminal, its PE is gone. The work the coulomb of charge can perform while flowing from the − to the + terminal of the battery is equal to this decrease in PE.

Potential difference is electric potential energy per coulomb

The decrease in its PE brought about by the motion of 1 C from the − to the + terminal is a quantity called the *potential difference* between the two terminals. It is analogous to difference of height in the case of water (Fig. 5-12). The potential difference between two points is equal to the corresponding energy difference per unit charge. We measure difference of height in meters; we measure difference of potential in *volts* (named for the Italian physicist Alessandro Volta). When 1 coulomb of charge travels through 1 volt of potential difference, this work that it does is equal to 1 joule by definition:

FIG. 5-12
The flow of electric charge in a wire is analogous in many ways to the flow of water in a pipe. Thus at (*b*) having the water fall through a greater height than at (*a*) yields a greater flow of water, which corresponds to using two batteries to obtain a higher potential difference and thereby a greater current.

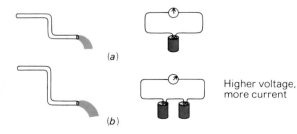

(*a*)

(*b*)

Higher voltage, more current

In a thunderstorm, the electric discharge called lightning occurs when the potential difference between a cloud and the earth exceeds the insulating ability of air.

The volt is the unit of potential difference

$$1 \text{ volt} = 1 \frac{\text{joule}}{\text{coulomb}}$$

$$1 \text{ V} = 1 \text{ J/C}$$

The normal potential difference between the terminals of the storage battery of a car is about 12 V, of a dry cell about 1.5 V. Every coulomb of electricity at the negative terminal of the storage battery, therefore, is capable of doing eight times as much work as a coulomb at the negative electrode of a dry cell — just as a liter of water at the top of a waterfall 12 m high is capable of doing 8 times as much work as a liter at the brink of a 1.5-m fall. If a storage battery and a dry cell are connected in identical circuits, the battery will push 8 times as many electrons around its circuit in a given time as the dry cell, giving a current 8 times as great. We may think of the potential difference between two points as the amount of "push" available to move charge between the points.

Connecting batteries in series increases the voltage

As in Fig. 5-12b, connecting two or more batteries together in series increases the voltage available. The method of connection is − terminal to + terminal, so that each battery in turn supplies its "push" to electrons flowing through them. The voltage of a particular cell is determined by the chemical reactions that take place inside it. In the case of the lead-acid storage battery of a car, each cell has a voltage

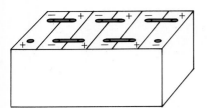

FIG. 5-13
A 12-V storage battery consists of six 2-V cells connected in series.

of 2 V, and six of them are connected together to give the 12 V needed to run the car's electrical equipment (Fig. 5-13). As its name suggests, a storage battery can be *recharged* when the energy it contains is used up. Ordinary batteries, such as those used in flashlights and portable radios, cannot be recharged.

Ohm's Law

Current, voltage, and resistance

If different voltages are applied to the ends of the same piece of wire, we will find that the current in the wire is proportional to the potential difference. Doubling the voltage doubles the current. This generalization is called *Ohm's law* after its discoverer, the German physicist Georg Ohm (1787–1854).

The resistance of a material is a measure of its opposition to the flow of current

The property of a conductor that opposes the flow of current in it is called *resistance*. We can think of resistance as a kind of friction. The more the resistance in a circuit, the less the current for a given applied voltage (Fig. 5-14). If we write I for current, V for voltage, and R for resistance, Ohm's law says that

Ohm's law relates current, potential difference, and resistance in a metal conductor

$$I = \frac{V}{R}$$

$$\text{Current} = \frac{\text{potential difference}}{\text{resistance}}$$

The unit of resistance is the *ohm*, whose abbreviation is Ω, the Greek capital letter "omega." Hence 1 A = 1 V/Ω and

The ohm is the unit of resistance

$$1 \text{ ohm} = 1 \frac{\text{volt}}{\text{ampere}}$$

$$1 \ \Omega = 1 \text{ V/A}$$

FIG. 5-14
At (*a*) a larger pipe yields a greater flow of water, which corresponds to using a large wire that offers less resistance to the flow of charge. At (*b*) a longer pipe yields a smaller flow of water, which corresponds to using a longer wire that offers more resistance to the flow of charge.

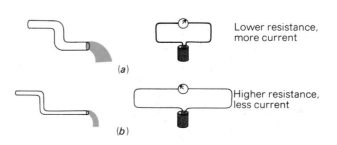

Lower resistance, more current

Higher resistance, less current

(*a*)

(*b*)

FIG. 5-15

(a) Conventional symbols for a battery and a resistance. (b) A current of 3 A flows in a circuit whose resistance is 4 Ω when a potential difference of 12 V is applied. The current consists of a flow of electrons, so its direction is from the − terminal of the battery to the + terminal.

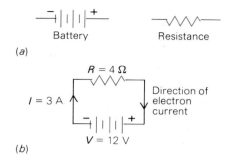

The resistance of a wire or other metallic conductor depends on the material it is made of (an iron wire has 7 times the resistance of a copper wire of the same size); its length (the longer the wire, the more its resistance); its cross-sectional area (the greater this area, the less the resistance); and the temperature (the higher the temperature, the more the resistance).

Let us see how Ohm's law can be applied in a practical situation. How long can a car with a 60 A-h battery have its headlights and taillights, of total resistance 4 Ω, left on before the battery runs down? We assume the engine is not running, so the car's generator is not recharging the battery. To solve the problem, we first calculate the current (Fig. 5-15), which is

$$I = \frac{V}{R} = \frac{12 \text{ V}}{4 \text{ Ω}} = 3 \text{ A}$$

Since the battery's capacity is 60 A-h, the lights can be left on for 20 h before the battery runs down. (Of course, if this is done the battery will then be "dead" and unable to start the engine.)

Ohm's law can also be used to find the resistance of an electrical appliance when its voltage and current ratings are known. An electric toaster draws a current of 4 A when it is plugged into a 120-V supply line. To find its resistance, we rewrite Ohm's law in the form $R = V/I$ and substitute the values given:

$$R = \frac{V}{I} = \frac{120 \text{ V}}{4 \text{ A}} = 30 \text{ Ω}$$

The resistance of the toaster is 30 Ω.

Despite its name, Ohm's law is not a basic physical principle such as the law of conservation of energy. Ohm's law is actually a relationship that is obeyed only by metallic conductors, but not by gaseous or liquid conductors and not by such electronic devices as transistors and vacuum tubes.

Ohm's law holds only for metals

Electrical Safety

Be careful!

Body tissue is a fairly good conductor because it contains ions in solution. Dry skin has more resistance and can protect the rest of the body in case of accidental exposure to a high potential difference, but this protection disappears when the skin is wet. The chief effects of an electric current on tissue are the stimulation of nerves and muscles and the production of heat. Most people can feel a current as small as 0.0005 A, one of 0.005 A is painful, and one of 0.01 A or more leads to muscle contractions which may prevent the person involved from letting go of the source of the current. Breathing becomes impossible when the current is greater than about 0.018 A.

Touching a single "live" conductor has no effect if the body is isolated since a complete conducting path is necessary for a current to occur. However, if a person is at the same time grounded by being in contact with a water pipe, by standing on wet soil, or in some other way, a current will pass through his or her body. The human body's resistance is in the neighborhood of $1000 \ \Omega$, so if a potential difference of 120 V is applied via wet skin, the resulting current will be somewhere near $I = V/R = 120 \ \text{V}/1000 \ \Omega = 0.12$ A. Such a current is exceedingly dangerous because it leads the heart muscles to contract rapidly and irregularly, which is fatal if allowed to continue.

Electrical devices in bathrooms and kitchens are potential sources of danger because the moisture on a wet finger may be enough to provide a conducting path to the interior of the devices. If a person is in a bathtub and thus is grounded through the tub's water to its drainpipe, or the person has one hand on a faucet, even touching a switch with a wet finger is risky.

Electric Power

Current times voltage

Electric energy is so useful both because it is easily carried by wires and because it is readily converted into other kinds of energy. Electric energy in the form of electric current is turned into radiant energy in a light bulb, into chemical energy when a storage battery is charged, into mechanical energy in an electric motor, into heat in an electric oven. In each case the current performs work on the device it passes through, and the device then transforms this work into another kind of energy. A very important quantity in any discussion of electric current, therefore, is the rate at which a current is doing work—in other words, the *power* of the current.

Earlier in this chapter we learned that, when 1 coulomb of charge is pushed through a circuit by a potential difference of 1 volt, the amount of work done is equal to 1 joule. In general, then,

Electric work

$$W = QV$$

$$\text{Electric work} = (\text{charge})(\text{voltage})$$

Since a current I carries the amount of charge $Q = It$ in the time t, the work done during t is

$$W = QV = ItV$$

But power P is by definition W/t, so that $P = W/t = ItV/t = IV$. Thus we have

Electric power

$$P = IV$$

$$\text{Power} = (\text{current})(\text{voltage})$$

Table 5-1 summarizes the various electrical quantities we have been discussing. Now we can see why electrical appliances are rated in watts, which is the unit of power. A 60-W light bulb uses twice the power of a 30-W bulb, and one-tenth the power of a 600-W electric drill. A fuse or circuit breaker opens a power line whenever an unsafe amount of current passes through it. Many of the fuses normally used in homes are rated at 15 A. Since the power-line voltage is 120 V, the greatest power the line can provide without blowing such a fuse is

Watts = (amperes)(volts)

$$P = IV = (15 \text{ A})(120 \text{ V}) = 1800 \text{ W} = 1.8 \text{ kW}$$

Because $P = IV$, it is easy to find how much current is needed by an appliance

TABLE 5-1
Electrical Quantities.

Quantity	Symbol	Unit	Meaning
Charge	Q	Coulomb (C)	A basic property of some elementary particles. The electron has a charge of -1.6×10^{-19} C and the proton has a charge of $+1.6 \times 10^{-19}$ C.
Current	I	Ampere (A) (1 A = 1 C/s)	Rate of flow of charge.
Potential difference (voltage)	V	Volt (V) (1 V = 1 J/C)	Potential energy difference per coulomb of charge between two points; corresponds to pressure in water flow.
Resistance	R	Ohm (Ω) (1 Ω = 1 V/A)	A measure of the opposition to the flow of charge in a particular circuit. For a given voltage, the higher the resistance, the lower the current.
Power	P	Watt (W) (1 W = 1 V-A)	Rate of energy flow.

rated in watts when connected to a power line of given voltage. For instance, a 60-W bulb connected to a 120-V line needs a current of

$$I = \frac{P}{V} = \frac{60 \text{ W}}{120 \text{ V}} = 0.5 \text{ A}$$

The kilowatthour is a unit of energy

Users of electricity pay for the quantity of energy they consume. The usual commerical unit of electric energy is the *kilowatthour* (kWh), which is the energy supplied per hour when the power level is 1 kilowatt. If electricity is sold at $0.12 per kilowatthour, the cost of operating a 1.5-kW electric heater for 7 h would be

$$\text{Cost} = (\text{price per unit of energy})(\text{energy used})$$

$$= (\text{price per unit of energy})(\text{power})(\text{time})$$

$$= (\$0.12)(1.5 \text{ kW})(7 \text{ h}) = \$1.26$$

The electric energy lost in a resistance becomes heat

As in the case of the energy lost due to friction, the energy lost due to the resistance of a conductor reappears as heat. This is the basis of electric heaters and stoves; in a light bulb, the filament is so hot that it glows white. In electric circuits it is obviously important to use wires large enough in diameter, and hence small enough in resistance, to prevent the wires becoming hot enough to melt their insulation and start fires. A thin extension cord suitable for a lamp or radio might well be dangerous used for a heater or power tool.

MAGNETISM

Electricity and magnetism were once considered as completely separate phenomena. One of the great achievements of nineteenth century science was the realization that they are really very closely related, a realization that led to the discovery of the electromagnetic nature of light. And one of the great achievements of nineteenth-century technology was the invention of electric motors and generators, whose operation depends upon the relationship between electricity and magnetism.

Magnets

Poles always come in pairs

North and south magnetic poles

Ordinary magnets are familiar to everybody. The simplest kind consists of a bar of iron that has been magnetized in one way or another, say, by having been stroked by another magnet. A magnetized iron bar is recognized, of course, by its ability to attract and hold other pieces of iron. Another property of a magnet, which is the

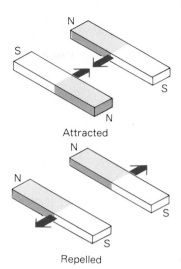

Attracted

Repelled

FIG. 5-16

Like magnetic poles repel each other; unlike magnetic poles attract.

basis of the compass, is its tendency when freely suspended to turn so that one end points north and the other south. The north-pointing end is called the *north pole* of the magnet, the south-pointing end the *south pole*. The greater part of the force exerted by a magnet comes from its ends, as we can see by testing the attraction of various parts of a bar magnet for iron nails.

Like poles repel, unlike poles attract

If two magnets are brought near each other so that the two N poles are opposite, the magnets repel each other. On the other hand, if an N pole is brought near an S pole, the two attract each other (Fig. 5-16). This gives us a simple rule that corresponds to that for electric charges:

Like magnetic poles repel, unlike poles attract.

Magnetic poles always come in pairs

Positive and negative charges in neutral matter can be separated from each other. Can the north and south poles of a magnet be similarly separated? It would seem that all we have to do is to saw the magnet in half. But if we do this, as in Fig. 5-17, we find that the resulting pieces each have an N pole and an S pole. We may cut the resulting magnets in two again, with the same results, and continue as long as we have tools fine enough for the cutting: but each piece, however small, will still have both an N pole and an S pole. There is no such thing as a single free magnetic pole.

Since a magnet can be cut into smaller and smaller pieces indefinitely with each piece a small magnet in itself, we may reasonably conclude that magnetism is a property of the iron atoms themselves. Each atom of iron behaves as if it has an N

FIG. 5-17
Cutting a magnet in half produces two other magnets. There is no such thing as a single free magnetic pole.

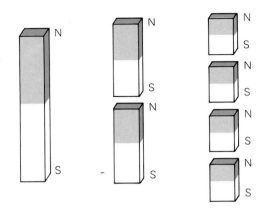

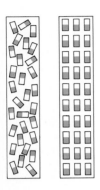

FIG. 5-18
The iron atoms in an unmagnetized iron bar are randomly arranged, whereas in a magnetized bar they are aligned with their north poles pointing in the same direction. The ability of iron atoms to remain aligned in this way is responsible for the magnetic properties of iron.

All substances have magnetic properties

pole and an S pole. In ordinary iron the atoms are arranged haphazardly, and nearby N and S poles cancel out each other's effect. When a bar of iron is magnetized, many or all of the atoms are aligned with the N poles in the same direction, so that the strengths of all the tiny magnets are added together (Fig. 5-18). A "permanent" magnet can be demagnetized by heating it strongly or by hammering it, both processes that agitate the atoms and restore them to their normal random orientations.

Iron is not the only material from which permanent magnets can be made. Nickel, cobalt, and certain combinations of other elements can also be magnetized. Nor is iron the only material affected by magnetism — *all* substances are, though generally only to a very slight extent. Some are attracted to a magnet, but most are repelled. In the cases of mercury and bismuth the repulsion, though weak, is still enough to be observed with simple instruments.

Magnetic Field

How magnetic forces act

We are so familiar with gravitational, electric, and magnetic forces that we take them for granted, but if we think about them, it is clear that something remarkable is going on. Apparently unlike other forces, they occur without actual contact between the objects involved. We cannot move a book from a table by just waving our hand at it, and a golf ball will not fly off until a golf club actually strikes it. An iron nail, however, does not wait until a magnet touches it, but is pulled to the magnet when the two are some distance apart. The region near the magnet is somehow altered by its presence, just as a mass or an electric charge alters the region around itself, in each case in a different way.

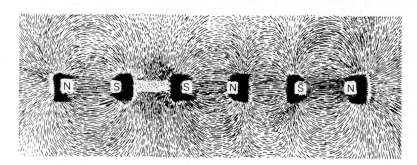

FIG. 5-19
Patterns formed by iron filings sprinkled on card over three bar magnets. The filings align themselves in the direction of the magnetic field. It is convenient to think of the pattern in terms of "lines of force," but such lines do not actually exist since the field is a continuous property of the region of space it occupies.

A force field is a property of space in a certain region that causes a force to be exerted on an appropriate object in that region

The region of altered space around a mass, an electric charge, or a magnet is called a *force field*. The expression "altered space" is hardly precise, and since we normally think of space as emptiness, as the complete absence of anything, it is necessary to make clear what is meant here. A physicist describes a force field in terms of what it does, which is to exert a force on appropriate objects. Although we cannot see a force field, we can readily detect its presence by its effects. In fact, even the forces we think of as being exerted by direct contact turn out to involve the action of force fields. For instance, when a golf club strikes a ball, it is the action of electric forces on the molecular level that leads to the observed transfer of energy and momentum to the ball. There is actually no such thing as "direct contact."

When iron filings are scattered on a card held over a magnet, they form a pattern that suggests the configuration of the magnet's field. In a given place, the filings line up in the direction in which a piece of iron would move if put there, and the filings gather most thickly where the force on the iron would be greatest. Figure 5-19 shows the patterns of iron filings near three bar magnets.

Lines of force

It is traditional, and convenient, to think of a magnetic field in terms of imaginary *lines of force* that correspond to the patterns formed by iron filings. A line of force traces the path that would be taken by a small iron object if placed in the field, with the lines close together where the field is strong and far apart where the field is weak. Although the notion of magnetic lines of force is helpful in illustrating a number of magnetic effects, we must keep in mind that they are imaginary — a force field is a continuous property of the region of space where it is present, not a collection of spaghettilike strings.

Oersted's Experiment

Magnetic fields originate in moving charges

Every electric current has a magnetic field around it

Perhaps unfamiliar to us as sources of magnetic field are electric currents, yet every current is surrounded by such a field. To repeat a famous experiment first

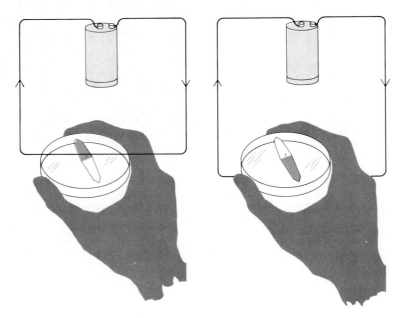

FIG. 5-20
Oersted's experiment showed that a magnetic field surrounds every electric current. The field direction above the wire is opposite to that below the wire.

performed in 1820 by the Danish physicist Hans Christian Oersted, let us connect a horizontal wire to a battery and hold under the wire a small compass needle (Fig. 5-20). The needle at once swings into a position at right angles to the wire. When the compass is placed just above the wire, the needle swings around until it is again perpendicular to the wire but pointing in the opposite direction.

We can use iron filings to determine the magnetic field pattern around a wire carrying a current. When we do this, we find that the lines of force near the wire consist of circles, as in Fig. 5-21. The direction of the lines of force (that is, the direction in which the N pole of the compass points) depends on the direction of flow of electrons through the wire; when one is reversed, the other reverses also.

In general, the direction of the magnetic field around a wire can be found by

FIG. 5-21
Magnetic lines of force around a wire carrying an electric current. The direction of the lines may be found by placing the thumb of the left hand in the direction of electron flow; the curled fingers then point in the direction of the lines of force. In the right-hand diagram the electron current flows up from the paper.

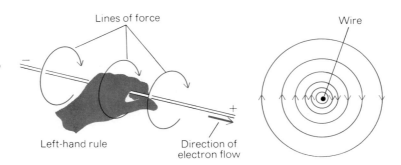

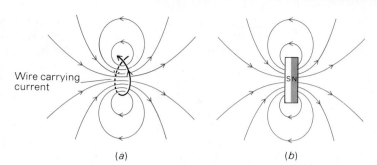

FIG. 5-22
The magnetic field of a loop of electric current is the same as that of a bar magnet.

(a)   *(b)*

Left-hand rule for magnetic field direction

The ultimate source of every magnetic field is a moving charge

encircling the wire with the fingers of the *left hand,* so that the extended thumb points along the wire *in the direction in which the electrons move;* the fingers then point in the direction of the field. (Engineers traditionally think in terms of an imaginary positive current that flows from the + terminal of a battery to its − terminal, the opposite of electron current. In terms of a positive current, the above rule becomes a right-hand rule instead. Either way, the current and the field are perpendicular to each other.)

Oersted's discovery showed for the first time that a connection exists between electricity and magnetism. It was also the first demonstration of the principle on which the electric motor is based. Magnetism and electricity are related, but only through moving charges. An electric charge *at rest* has no magnetic properties. A magnet is not influenced by a stationary electric charge near it, and vice versa.

When a current passes through a wire bent into a circle, the resulting magnetic field, shown in Fig. 5-22, is exactly the same as that produced by a bar magnet. One side of the loop acts as a north pole, the other as a south pole; if suitably suspended, the loop swings to a north-south position. A current loop attracts pieces of iron just as a bar magnet does. Indeed, the magnetic properties of iron and other substances can be traced to tiny currents within their atoms. Thus it is correct to say that

All magnetic fields originate in moving electric charges.

An electric charge at rest is surrounded by an electric field, and when it is moving it is surrounded by a magnetic field as well. Suppose we travel alongside a moving charge, in the same direction and at the same speed. All we detect now is an electric field — the magnetic field has disappeared. But if we move past a stationary charge with our instruments, we find both an electric and a magnetic field! Clearly the *relative motion* between charge and observer is needed to produce a magnetic field: no relative motion, no magnetic field.

Electric and magnetic fields are different aspects of a single electromagnetic field

The proper way to interpret what we perceive as separate electric and magnetic fields is that they are both manifestations of a single electromagnetic field that surrounds every electric charge. The electric field is always there, but the magnetic field only appears when relative motion is present. In the case of a wire that carries an electric current, there is only a magnetic field because the wire itself is electrically neutral. The electric field of the electrons is canceled out by the opposite electric field of the positive ions in the wire, but the ions are stationary and therefore have no magnetic field to cancel the magnetic field of the moving electrons. If we simply move a wire that has no current flowing in it, the electric and magnetic fields of the electrons are canceled by the electric and magnetic fields of the positive ions.

Electromagnets

How to create a strong magnetic field

When several wires that carry currents in the same direction are side by side, their magnetic fields add together to give a stronger total magnetic field. This effect is often used to increase the magnetic field of a current loop. Instead of one loop, many loops of wire are wound into a coil, as in Fig. 5-23, and the resulting magnetic field is as many times stronger than the field of one turn as there are turns in the coil. A coil with 50 turns produces a field 50 times greater than a coil with just one turn.

An electromagnet is a coil of wire with an iron core

The magnetic strength of the coil is enormously increased if a rod of soft iron

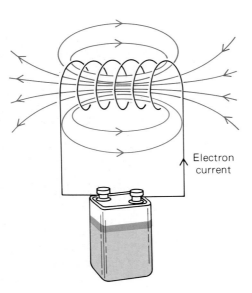

Electron current

FIG. 5-23

The magnetic field of a coil is like that of a single loop but is stronger.

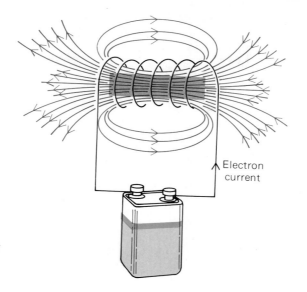

FIG. 5-24
An electromagnet consists of a coil
with an iron core, which considerably
enhances the magnetic field
produced.

Electron
current

Electromagnet loading scrap iron
and steel.

is placed inside it (Fig. 5-24). This combination of coil and iron core is called an
electromagnet. An electromagnet exerts magnetic force only when current flows
through its turns, and so its action can be turned on and off. Also, by using many

turns and enough current, it can be made far more powerful than a permanent magnet of similar size. These two properties make electromagnets among the most widely employed devices in the technical world. They range in size from the tiny coils in telephone receivers to the huge coils that load and unload scrap iron.

USING MAGNETISM

An electric motor uses magnetic fields to turn electric energy into mechanical energy, and a generator uses magnetic fields to turn mechanical energy into electric energy. As we shall find, magnetic fields also play essential roles in television picture tubes, in sound and video recording, and in the transformers used in distributing electric power over large areas.

Magnetic Force on a Current

A sidewise push

Suppose that a horizontal wire connected to a battery is suspended as in Fig. 5-25, so that it is free to move from side to side, and the N pole of a bar magnet is then placed directly beneath it. This arrangement is the reverse of Oersted's experiment: Oersted placed a movable magnet near a wire fixed in position, whereas

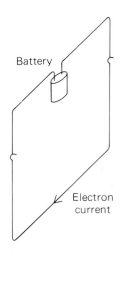
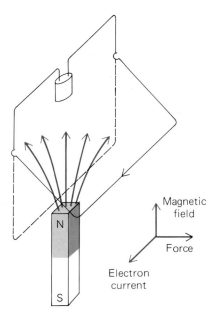

FIG. 5-25
A magnetic field exerts a sidewise push on an electric current. In this arrangement, the wire moves to one side in a direction perpendicular to both the magnetic field and the current.

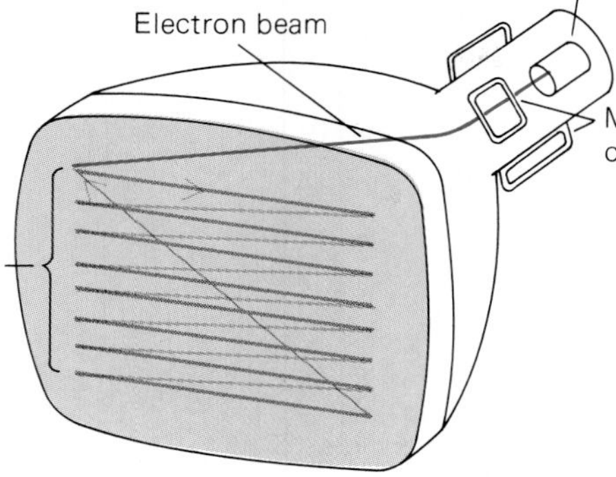

FIG. 5-26
The electron beam of a television picture tube is directed by magnetic fields to cover the screen in a pattern of horizontal lines starting at the upper left. The returns from right to left are much faster than the sweeps from left to right that produce the image. Changes in the beam intensity give the variations in screen brightness that make up the image.

here we have a movable wire near a fixed magnet. We might predict, from Oersted's results and Newton's third law of motion, that in this case the wire will move. It does indeed, swinging out to one side as soon as the circuit is closed. The direction of its motion is perpendicular to the bar magnet's field. Whether it swings to one side or the other depends on the direction of flow of electrons in the wire and on which pole of the magnet is used.

A magnetic field exerts a sidewise push on an electric current

Thus the force a magnetic field exerts on an electric current is not a simple attraction or repulsion but a *sidewise push*. The maximum sidewise push occurs when the current is perpendicular to the magnetic field, as in Fig. 5-25. At other angles the push is less, and it disappears when the current is parallel to the magnetic field.

How the image on a television picture tube is formed

In a television picture tube, a beam of electrons is directed at a fluorescent screen that glows where electrons strike it. A beam of electrons is, of course, an electric current, so magnetic fields produced by coils outside the tube can be used to deflect the beam. By changing the currents in the coils, the magnetic field strengths can be changed, which permits the beam to be aimed anywhere on the screen. As in Fig. 5-26, the beam is moved across the screen in a pattern of horizontal lines starting at the upper left. The returns from right to left take about a tenth as long as the sweeps from left to right that are used to form the picture. During the scans the electron beam intensity is varied to give the variations in brightness that make up the picture.

Electric Motors

Mechanical energy from electric energy

Electric motors are driven by magnetic forces

The sidewise push of a magnetic field on a current-carrying wire can be used to produce continuous motion in an arrangement like that shown in Fig. 5-27. A

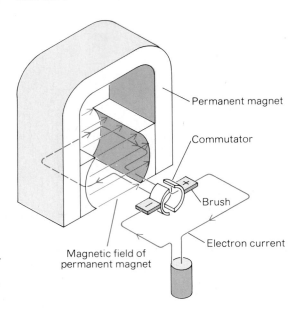

Permanent magnet

Commutator

Brush

Electron current

Magnetic field of
permanent magnet

FIG. 5-27

A simple direct-current electric
motor. The purpose of the commutator is to reverse the current in the
loop periodically so that it always rotates in the same direction.

How an electric motor achieves
continuous rotation

permanent magnet gives rise to a magnetic field inside which a wire loop is free to
rotate. When the plane of the loop is parallel to the magnetic field, there is no force
on the sides of the loop that lie along the magnetic field. The side of the loop at left
in the diagram, however, receives an upward push, and the side at right receives a
downward one. Thus the loop is turned clockwise.

When the plane of the loop is vertical, so that it is perpendicular to the
magnetic field, forces are exerted on all its sides, but these forces are all outward
and so cancel out. To produce a continuous motion, it is necessary to reverse the
direction of the current in the loop when it is vertical. If the loop comes to a stop
when vertical, it will remain there no matter which way its current flows, but in fact
its angular momentum always carries it past this position. When this happens, the
reversed current interacts with the magnetic field to continue to rotate the loop
through 180°. Now the current must have its direction reversed once more,
whereupon it will again swing around through a half-turn. The device used to
automatically change the current direction is called a *commutator;* it is visible on
the shaft of a direct-current motor as a copper sleeve divided into segments.
Normally more than two loops and commutator segments are used in order to
yield the maximum turning force.

Actual electric motors are more complicated than the one shown in Fig. 5-27,
though the basic principle is always the same. Usually electromagnets are employed rather than permanent ones to create the field, and in some motors the coil
is fixed in place and the magnet or magnets rotate within it. Motors built for
alternating rather than direct current do not need commutators because the
current direction changes back and forth many times per second.

Some of the windings of a large electric motor. Magnetic forces underlie the operation of such motors.

Electromagnetic Induction

Electric energy from mechanical energy

The electric energy that our homes and industries use in such quantity comes from generators driven by turbines powered by running water or, more often, by steam. In the latter case the boilers that supply the steam obtain heat from coal, oil, or natural gas, or from nuclear reactors. Ships and isolated farms have smaller generators operated by gasoline or diesel engines. In all cases the energy that is turned into electricity is the kinetic energy of moving machinery.

The principle of the generator was discovered by the nineteenth-century English physicist Michael Faraday. His curiosity aroused by the researches of Ampère and Oersted on the magnetic fields around electric currents, Faraday reasoned that, if a current can produce a magnetic field, then somehow a magnet should be capable of generating an electric current.

A wire placed in a magnetic field and connected to a meter shows no sign of a current. What Faraday found instead is that

A current is produced in a wire when there is relative motion between the wire and a magnetic field.

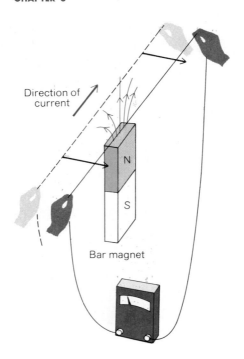

Direction of
current

N

S

Bar magnet

FIG. 5-28
Electromagnetic induction. The
direction of the induced current is
perpendicular both to the magnetic
lines of force and to the direction in
which the wire is moving. No current
is induced when the wire is at rest.

In electromagnetic induction, a
current is induced in a wire moved
across a magnetic field

As long as the wire continues to cut across magnetic lines of force, the current
continues. When the motion stops, the current stops. Because it is produced by
motion through a magnetic field, this sort of current is called an *induced current.*
The entire effect is known as *electromagnetic induction.*

Let us repeat Faraday's experiment. Suppose that the wire of Fig. 5-28 is
moved back and forth across the lines of force of the bar magnet. The meter will
then indicate a current flowing first in one direction, then in the other. Note that the
wire is held approximately at right angles to the lines of force; thus the motion of
electrons along the wire is at right angles to the magnetic field. Which way the
induced current flows through the wire depends on the relative directions of its
motion and of the lines of force. Reverse the direction of motion, or use the
opposite magnetic pole, and the current is reversed. The strength of the current
depends on the strength of the field and on how rapid the motion is.

Origin of electromagnetic induction

Electromagnetic induction is related to the sidewise force a magnetic field
exerts on electrons flowing along a wire. In Faraday's experiment electrons are
again moved through a field, but now by moving the wire as a whole. The electrons
are pushed sidewise as before and, in response to the push, move along the wire as
an electric current.

The generator

In order to obtain a large induced current, a commercial generator employs
several coils rather than a single wire and several electromagnets instead of a bar

magnet. Turned rapidly between the electromagnets by steam engine or water turbine, wires of the coil cut lines of force first in one direction, then in the other. Operation of the generator is illustrated in simplified form in Fig. 5-29, where a coil is shown turning between two magnets. During part of a revolution, each side of the coil cuts the field in one direction, then, during the other part, each cuts the field in the opposite direction. Hence the induced current flows first one way and then the other. Such a back-and-forth current is an *alternating current.*

Alternating and direct currents

The electric currents that come from such sources as batteries and photoelectric cells are always one-way, or *direct,* currents that can be reversed only by changing the connections. In the 60-Hz (1 Hz = 1 hertz = 1 cycle/second) alternating current that we ordinarily use in our homes, electrons change their direction 120 times each second. The usual abbreviation for alternating current is ac and that for direct current is dc.

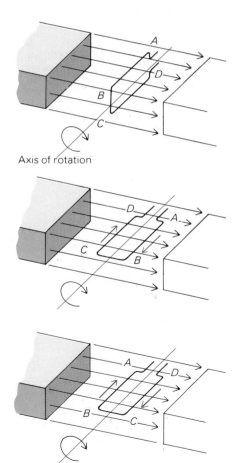

FIG. 5-29

An alternating-current generator. As the loop rotates, current is induced in it first in one direction *(ABCD),* and then in the other *(DCBA).* No current flows at those times when the loop is moving parallel to the magnetic field.

By using commutators similar to those used on direct-current motors, generators can be built that produce direct current. Another way to obtain direct current from an ac generator (or *alternator*) is to use a *rectifier,* which is a device that permits current to pass through it in only one direction. Because alternators are simpler to make and more reliable than dc generators, they are often used together with rectifiers to give the direct current needed to charge the batteries of cars and trucks.

Transformers

Stepping voltage up or down

To generate an induced current requires that magnetic lines of force be made to move across a conductor. As in Fig. 5-28, one way to accomplish this is to move a wire past a magnet. Another way is to hold the wire stationary while the magnet is moved. We come now to a third, less obvious, method, which involves no visible motion at all.

Currents can be induced with no motion of wires

Let us connect coil *A* in Fig. 5-30 to a switch and a battery and connect coil *B* to a meter. When the switch is closed, a current flows through *A*, building up a magnetic field around it. The current and field do not reach their full strengths at once. A fraction of a second is needed for the current to increase from zero to its final value, and the magnetic field increases along with the current. As this happens, the lines of force from coil *A* spread outward across the wires of coil *B*. This

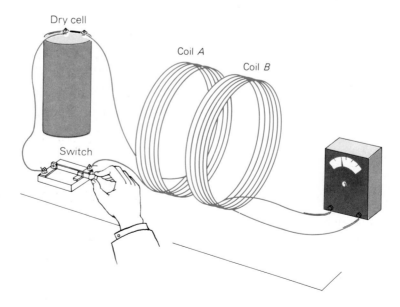

Dry cell

Coil *A*

Coil *B*

Switch

FIG. 5-30
A simple transformer. Momentary currents are detected by the meter when the current in coil *A* is started or stopped.

motion of the lines across coil *B* produces in it a momentary current, recorded by a deflection of the meter needle. Once the current in *A* reaches its normal, steady value, the field becomes stationary and the induced current in *B* stops.

Next let us open the switch. Again in a fraction of a second the current in *A* drops to zero, and its magnetic field collapses. Once more lines of force cut across *B*, and the meter responds with another deflection, this time in the opposite direction since the lines of force are now moving the other way past *B*. Thus starting and stopping the current in *A* has the same effect as moving a magnet in and out of *B*. An induced current is generated whenever the switch is opened or closed.

Suppose that *A* is connected not to a battery but to a 60-Hz alternating current. Now we need no switch; automatically, 120 times each second, the current comes to a complete stop and starts off again in the other direction. Its magnetic field expands and contracts at the same rate, and the lines of force cutting *B* first in one direction, then the other, induce an alternating current similar to that in *A*. An ordinary meter will not respond to these rapid alterations, but an instrument meant for ac will show the induced current.

The transformer

Thus an alternating current in one coil produces an alternating current in a nearby (but unconnected) coil. To generate an induced current most efficiently, the two coils should be close together and wound on a core of soft iron. Such a combination of two coils and an iron core constitutes a *transformer*. The coil into which electricity is fed from an outside source is the primary coil, that in which an induced current is generated is the secondary coil.

The ratio of voltages in a transformer equals the ratio of turns in the coils

Transformers are useful because the voltage of the induced current can be made any desired multiple or fraction of the primary voltage by suitable winding of the coils. If the number of turns of wire in the secondary coil is the same as the number of turns in the primary, the induced voltage will be the same as the primary voltage. If the secondary has twice as many turns, its voltage is twice that of the primary; if it has one-third as many turns its voltage is one-third that of the primary; and so on. By using a suitably designed transformer, we can obtain any desired voltage, high or low, from a given alternating current.

When the secondary coil of a transformer has a higher voltage than the primary coil, its current is lower than that in the primary (and vice versa), so that the power $P = IV$ is the same in both coils.

High-voltage transmission minimizes power loss

For a multitude of purposes, in homes and factories and laboratories, it is useful to change the voltage of alternating currents. But perhaps the most valuable service transformers provide is to make possible the efficient long-distance transmission of power. Currents in long-distance transmission must be as small as possible, since large currents mean energy lost in heating the transmission wires. Hence at the powerhouse electricity from the generator is led into a "step-up" transformer, which increases the voltage and decreases the current, each by several hundred times. On high-voltage lines (sometimes carrying currents at voltages exceeding 1,000,000 V) this current is carried to local substations, where other transformers "step down" its voltage to make it safe for local transmission and use.

Transformers at a power station step up the voltage of the electric power generated there for transmission over long distances. The higher the voltage V, the lower the current I for the same power P, since $P = IV$. The advantage of a low current is that less energy is lost as heat in the transmission lines. Other transformers step down the voltage for the consumer to the usual 220–240 V or 110–120 V.

Tape Recorders

Storing and reproducing sounds

What we have thus far learned about electricity and magnetism allows us to understand how sounds can be changed into electrical signals by a microphone, recorded on a magnetic tape, and then reproduced by a loudspeaker.

The microphone

The first step is to change the pressure variations of a sound wave (described in detail in Chap. 6) into an alternating current. This is done by a *microphone*, of which there are several kinds. One of them is shown in Fig. 5-31. The diaphragm is

FIG. 5-31
A moving-coil microphone. When sound waves reach the diaphragm, it vibrates accordingly. The motion of the coil through the magnetic field of the magnet causes an alternating current to be induced in the coil that corresponds to the original sound. A loudspeaker is similar in construction except that an alternating current in its coil causes the diaphragm to vibrate and thereby produce sound waves.

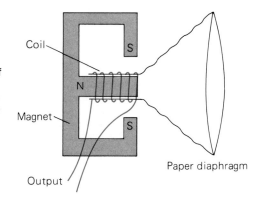

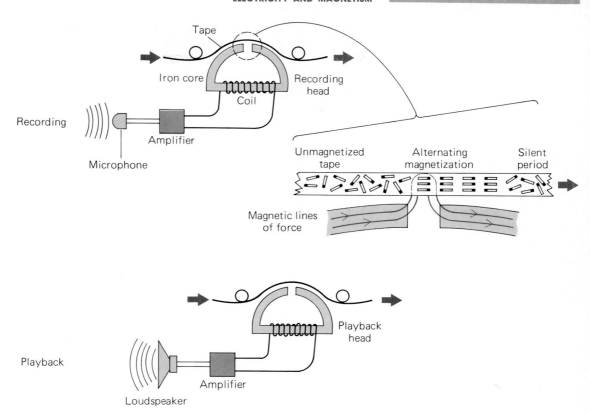

FIG. 5-32
A tape recorder. The polarity and degree of magnetization of the magnetizable coating on the tape correspond to the pressure variations of the original sound wave.

Recording on magnetic tape

a paper cone that vibrates as sound waves strike it. As the diaphragm vibrates, a coil of thin wire at its neck moves back and forth in the field of a permanent magnet, which induces an alternating current in the coil whose variations match those of the sound waves.

The electrical signal from the microphone is then amplified and, in the tape recorder itself, converted into a magnetic pattern on the magnetizable coating of a plastic tape. As in Fig. 5-32, this tape is magnetized by being passed over an electromagnet connected to the amplifier. The air gap in the electromagnet of the recording head permits its magnetic field to reach the tape. The polarity and degree of magnetization of the coating on the tape correspond to the pressure variations of the original sound wave.

Playback

The playing head of the recorder is similar in design to the recording head but makes use of electromagnetic induction. The changing magnetic fields of the moving tape induce an alternating current in the coil of the playing head, which is amplified and fed into a loudspeaker to reconstruct the original sound. A loudspeaker resembles the moving-coil microphone of Fig. 5-31 but is larger in size. An alternating current in its coil causes its conical diaphragm to vibrate and thereby produce a sound wave in the air around it.

A videotape recorder uses recording and playback heads like those in Fig. 5-32, but the electrical signals it records come from a television camera and are played back through a television set.

IMPORTANT TERMS

Electric charge is a fundamental property of certain of the elementary particles of which all matter is composed. The two kinds of charge are called *positive* and *negative.* Charges of the same sign repel, charges of opposite sign attract. The unit of charge is the *coulomb* (C). All charges, of either sign, occur in multiples of $e = 1.6 \times 10^{-19}$ C.

Atoms are composed of *electrons,* whose charge is $-e$; *protons,* whose charge is $+e$; and *neutrons,* which have no charge. Protons and neutrons have almost equal masses, which are nearly 2000 times greater than the electron mass. Every atom has a small, central *nucleus* of protons and neutrons with its electrons moving about the nucleus some distance away. The number of protons and electrons are equal in a normal atom, which is therefore electrically neutral. An atom that has lost one or more electrons is a *positive ion,* and an atom that has picked up one or more electrons in excess of its usual number is a *negative ion.*

A flow of charge from one place to another is an *electric current.* The unit of electric current is the *ampere* (A), which is equal to a flow of 1 coulomb/second.

The *potential difference* between two points is the work needed to take a charge of 1 C from one of the points to the other. The unit of potential difference is the *volt* (V), which is equal to 1 joule/coulomb.

According to *Ohm's law,* the current in a metal conductor is proportional to the potential difference between its ends and inversely proportional to its *resistance.* The unit of resistance is the *ohm* (Ω), which is equal to 1 volt/ampere.

Every electric current (and moving charge) has a *magnetic field* around it that exerts a sidewise force on any other electric current (or moving charge) in its presence. All atoms contain moving electrons, and *permanent magnets* are made from substances, notably iron, whose atomic magnetic fields can be lined up instead of being randomly oriented.

Electromagnetic induction refers to the production of a current in a wire when there is relative motion between the wire and a magnetic field.

The direction of an *alternating current* reverses itself at regu-lar intervals. The *frequency* of such a current is the number of back-and-forth cycles it goes through per second. The unit of frequency is the *hertz* (Hz), where 1 hertz = 1 cycle/second. In a *transformer* an alternating current in one coil of wire induces an alternating current in another nearby coil. Depending on the ratio of turns of the coils, the induced current can have a voltage that is larger, smaller, or the same as that of the primary current.

IMPORTANT FORMULAS

Coulomb's law: $F = K \dfrac{Q_1 Q_2}{R^2}$

Electric current: $I = \dfrac{Q}{t}$

Potential difference: $V = \dfrac{W}{Q}$

Ohm's law: $I = \dfrac{V}{R}$

Electric power: $P = IV$

Transformer: $\dfrac{I_1}{I_2} = \dfrac{V_2}{V_1} = \dfrac{N_2}{N_1}$ (N = number of turns)

MULTIPLE CHOICE

1. Electric charge
   a. can be subdivided indefinitely
   b. occurs only in separate parcels of $\pm 1.6 \times 10^{-19}$ C
   c. occurs only in separate parcels of ± 1 C
   d. occurs only in separate parcels whose value depends on the particle carrying the charge
2. A negative electric charge
   a. interacts only with positive charges
   b. interacts only with negative charges
   c. interacts with both positive and negative charges
   d. may interact with either positive or negative charges, depending on circumstances

3. Which of the following statements is not true?
  a. Protons are positively charged
  b. The proton mass is greater than the electron mass
  c. The proton mass is almost the same as the neutron mass
  d. The proton in an atom circulates around its nucleus

4. Coulomb's law for the force between electric charges belongs in the same general category as
  a. the law of conservation of energy
  b. Newton's second law of motion
  c. Newton's law of gravitation
  d. the second law of thermodynamics

5. The electric force between a proton and an electron
  a. is weaker than the gravitational force between them
  b. is equal in strength to the gravitational force between them
  c. is stronger than the gravitational force between them
  d. any of the above, depending on the distance between the proton and the electron

6. Atoms and molecules are normally
  a. neutral
  b. negatively charged
  c. positively charged
  d. ionized

7. An object has a positive electric charge whenever
  a. it has an excess of electrons
  b. it has a deficiency of electrons
  c. the nuclei of its atoms are positively charged
  d. the electrons of its atoms are positively charged

8. Which of the following statements is correct?
  a. Electrons carry electric current
  b. The motion of electrons produces an electric current
  c. Moving electrons constitute an electric current
  d. Electric currents are carried by conductors and insulators only

9. Match each of the electrical quantities listed below with the appropriate unit from the list on the right:
  a. resistance   volt
  b. current   ampere
  c. potential difference ohm
  d. power   watt

10. The electric energy lost when a current passes through a resistance
  a. becomes magnetic energy
  b. becomes potential energy
  c. becomes heat
  d. disappears completely

11. All magnetic fields originate in
  a. iron atoms
  b. permanent magnets

  c. stationary electric charges
  d. moving electric charges

12. A magnetic field exerts no force on
  a. an electric current
  b. an unmagnetized iron bar
  c. a stationary electric charge
  d. a magnet

13. The magnetic field of a bar magnet resembles most closely the magnetic field of
  a. a straight wire carrying a direct current
  b. a straight wire carrying an alternating current
  c. a wire loop carrying a direct current
  d. a wire loop carrying an alternating current

14. A drawing of the lines of force of a magnetic field provides information on
  a. the direction of the field only
  b. the strength of the field only
  c. both the direction and strength of the field
  d. the source of the field

15. Magnetic lines of force provide a convenient way to visualize a magnetic field. Which of the following statements is not true?
  a. The path followed by an iron particle released near a magnet corresponds to a line of force
  b. The path followed by an electric charge released near a magnet corresponds to a line of force
  c. A compass needle in a magnetic field lines up parallel to the lines of force around it
  d. Lines of force do not actually exist

16. A magnet
  a. attracts all substances
  b. attracts only iron and iron alloys and repels nothing
  c. attracts iron and iron alloys and repels other substances
  d. attracts some substances and repels others

17. An electromagnet
  a. uses an electric current to produce a magnetic field
  b. uses a magnetic field to produce an electric current
  c. is a magnet that has an electric charge
  d. operates only on alternating current

18. The nature of the force that is responsible for the operation of an electric motor is
  a. electric
  b. magnetic
  c. a combination of electric and magnetic
  d. either electric or magnetic depending on the design of the motor

19. A generator is said to "generate electricity." What it actually does is act as a source of
  a. electric charge
  b. electrons

c. magnetism

d. energy

20. The alternating current in the secondary coil of a transformer is induced by

    a. a varying magnetic field

    b. a varying electric field

    c. the iron core of the transformer

    d. a motion of the primary coil

21. A transformer can change

    a. the voltage of an alternating current

    b. the power of an alternating current

    c. alternating current to direct current

    d. direct current to alternating current

22. A positive and a negative charge are initially 4 cm apart. When they are moved closer together so that they are now only 1 cm apart, the force between them is

    a. 4 times smaller than before

    b. 4 times larger than before

    c. 8 times larger than before

    d. 16 times larger than before

23. An electron is placed a certain distance from a positive charge, and the force of attraction between them is measured. Another electron is brought up and placed next to the first electron. The force on the positive charge

    a. does not change

    b. is half as large as before

    c. is twice as large as before

    d. is 4 times as large as before

24. The force between two charges of -3×10^{-9} C that are 5 cm apart is

    a. 1.8×10^{-16} N

    b. 3.6×10^{-15} N

    c. 1.6×10^{-6} N

    d. 3.2×10^{-5} N

25. The potential difference between a certain thundercloud and the ground is 4×10^6 V. A lightning stroke occurs during which 80 C of charge is transferred between the cloud and the ground. The energy dissipated during the lightning stroke is

    a. 5×10^{-6} J

    b. 2×10^5 J

    c. 3.2×10^7 J

    d. 3.2×10^8 J

26. The resistance of a light bulb that draws a current of 2 A when connected to a 12-V battery is

    a. 1.67Ω

    b. 2Ω

    c. 6Ω

    d. 24Ω

27. The current in a 40-W 120-V electric light bulb is

    a. $\frac{1}{3}$ A

    b. 3 A

    c. 80 A

    d. 4800 A

28. A transformer whose primary winding has twice as many turns as its secondary winding is used to convert 240-V ac to 120-V ac. If the current in the secondary circuit is 4 A, the primary current is

    a. 1 A

    b. 2 A

    c. 4 A

    d. 8 A

QUESTIONS

1. What reasons might there be for the universal belief among scientists that there are only two kinds of electric charge?

2. Electricity was once thought to be a weightless fluid, an excess of which was "positive" and a deficiency of which was "negative." What phenomena can this hypothesis still explain? What phenomena can it not explain?

3. List the similarities and differences between electric and gravitational fields.

4. How do we know that the force holding the earth in its orbit about the sun is not an electric force, since both gravitational and electric forces vary inversely with the square of the distance between centers of force?

5. When two objects attract each other electrically, must both of them be charged? When two objects repel each other electrically, must both of them be charged?

6. A person can be electrocuted while taking a bath if he or she touches a poorly insulated light switch. Why is the electric shock received under these conditions so much more dangerous than usual?

7. Name several conductors and insulators of electricity. How well do these substances conduct heat? What general relationship between the ability to conduct heat and the ability to conduct electricity could you infer from this information?

8. Why does the production of electricity by friction always yield equal amounts of positive and negative charge?

9. How is the movement of electricity through air different from its movement through a copper wire?

10. What aspect of superconductivity has prevented its large-scale application thus far?

11. An electrical appliance is sometimes said to "use up" electricity. What does it actually use in its operation?

12. A fuse prevents more than a certain amount of current from flowing in a particular circuit. What might happen if too much current were to flow? What determines how much is too much?

13. Why are two wires used to carry electric current instead of a single one?

14. Why do you think bending a wire does not affect its electrical resistance, even though a bent pipe offers more resistance to the flow of water than a straight one?

15. Why is a piece of iron attracted to either pole of a magnet?

16. What kind of observations would you have to make in order to prepare a map showing the lines of force of the earth's magnetic field?

17. Explain why lines of force can never cross one another.

18. An electron current flows east along a power line. Find the directions of the magnetic field above and below the power line. (Neglect the earth's magnetic field.)

19. A current-carrying wire is in a magnetic field. What angle should the wire make with the direction of the field for the force on it to be zero? What should the angle be for the force to be a maximum?

20. An electric motor requires more current when it is started than when it is running continuously. Why?

21. When a wire loop is rotated in a magnetic field, the direction of the current induced in the loop reverses itself twice per rotation. Why?

22. The shaft of a generator is much easier to turn when the generator is not connected to an outside circuit than when such a connection is made. Why?

23. A long coil is suspended by a thread at its midpoint between the poles of a strong magnet. What (if anything) happens when a direct current is sent through the coil? When an alternating current is sent through the coil?

24. Would you expect to find direct or alternating current in (a) the filament of a light bulb in your home? (b) the filament of a light bulb in a car? (c) the secondary coil of a transformer? (d) the output of a battery charger? (e) an electromagnet?

25. What would happen if the primary winding of a transformer were connected to a battery?

26. Given a coil of wire and a small light bulb, how can you tell whether the current in another coil is direct or alternating without touching the second coil or its connecting wires?

PROBLEMS

1. Two charges of $+10^{-7}$ C are located 10 cm apart. What is the magnitude and direction of the force on each of them? If one of the charges were instead -10^{-7} C, what would be the magnitude and direction of the force on each of them?

2. A charge of $+3 \times 10^{-9}$ C is located 0.5 m from a charge of -5×10^{-9} C. What is the magnitude and direction of the force on each of them?

3. Two small spheres are given identical positive charges. When they are 1 cm apart the repulsive force on each of them is 0.002 N. What would the force be if (a) the distance is increased to 3 cm? (b) one charge is doubled? (c) both charges are tripled? (d) one charge is doubled and the distance is increased to 2 cm?

4. (a) A metal sphere with a charge of $+1 \times 10^{-5}$ C is 10 cm from another metal sphere with a charge of -2×10^{-5} C. Find the magnitude of the attractive force on each sphere. (b) The two spheres are brought in contact and again separated by 10 cm. Find the magnitude of the new force on each sphere.

5. A charge of $+5 \times 10^{-9}$ C is attracted by a charge of -3×10^{-7} C with a force of 0.135 N. How far apart are the charges?

6. Two charges, one of $+3 \times 10^{-5}$ C and the other of $+6 \times 10^{-5}$ C, are 15 cm apart. A test charge of $+5 \times 10^{-5}$ C is placed between the two so that it is 5 cm from the $+3 \times 10^{-5}$ C charge and 10 cm from the $+6 \times 10^{-5}$ C charge. What are the magnitude and direction of the force on the test charge?

7. How much positive charge must be added to the earth and the moon so that the resulting electrical repulsion balances the gravitational attraction between them? Assume equal amounts of charge are added to each body.

8. Two electrons exert forces on each other equal in magnitude to the weight of an electron. How far apart are the electrons?

9. At what distance apart (if any) are the electric and gravitational forces between two electrons equal in magnitude? Between two protons? Between an electron and a proton?

10. How many electrons per second flow past a point in a wire carrying a current of 2 A?

11. About 10^{20} electrons in each cm participate in carrying a 1-A current in a typical wire. Find the average speed of these electrons.

12. What potential difference must be applied across a 1500-Ω resistance in order that the resulting current be 50 mA? (1 mA = 1 milliampere = 0.001 A)

13. How much current passes through a wire of resistance 4 Ω when it is connected across a 12-V battery? How much charge per second does this current represent?

14. Wire A has a potential difference of 50 V across it and carries a current of 2 A. Wire B has a potential difference of 100 V across it and also carries a current of 2 A. Compare the resistances, rates of flow of charge, and rates of flow of energy in the two wires.

15. If a 75-W light bulb is connected to a 120-V power line, how much current flows through it? What is the resistance of the bulb? How much power does the bulb consume?

16. How many coulombs of electric current pass through an electrical appliance in 20 min if the current through the appliance is 0.4 A? If the potential difference across the appliance is 120 V, how much power does it consume? How much energy in joules does it draw from the circuit in 20 min?

17. If your home has a 120-V power line, how much power in watts can you draw from the line before a 30-A fuse will burn out? How many 100-W light bulbs can you put in the circuit before the fuse will burn out?

18. A power rating of 1 horsepower (hp) is equivalent to 746 W. How much current does a $\frac{1}{4}$-hp electric motor require when it is operated at 120 V? Assume 100 percent efficiency.

19. A 1.35-V mercury cell with a capacity of 1.5 A-h is used to power a cardiac pacemaker. If the power required is 0.1 mW (1 mW = 1 milliwatt = 0.001 W), what is the average current? How long will the cell last?

20. How many coulombs of charge can a 12-V battery of 100 A-h capacity supply? How much energy?

21. If electricity costs 6 cents/kWh, how much does it cost to warm a kilogram of water from 10 to 70°C?

22. A hot-water heater employs a 2000-W resistance element. If all the heat from the resistance element is absorbed by the water in the heater, how much water per hour can be warmed from 10 to 70°C?

23. A transformer has a 120-turn primary winding and an 1800-turn secondary winding. A current of 10 A flows in the primary winding when a potential difference of 550 V is placed across it. Find the current in the secondary winding and the potential difference across it.

24. A transformer has a primary coil with 1000 turns and a secondary coil with 200 turns. If the primary voltage is 660, what is the secondary voltage? What primary current is required if 1000 W is to be drawn from the secondary?

25. A transformer rated at a maximum power of 10 kW is used to couple a 5000-V transmission line to a 240-V circuit. What is the ratio of turns in the transformer? What is the maximum current in the 240-V circuit?

26. An electric welding machine employs a current of 400 A. The device uses a transformer whose primary coil has 400 turns and which draws 4 A from a 220-V power line. How many turns are there in the secondary coil of the transformer? What is the potential difference across the secondary coil?

ANSWERS TO MULTIPLE CHOICE

1. *b*	**9.** *a:* ohm	**14.** *c*	**22.** *d*
2. *c*	*b:* ampere	**15.** *b*	**23.** *c*
3. *d*	*c:* volt	**16.** *d*	**24.** *d*
4. *c*	*d:* watt	**17.** *a*	**25.** *d*
5. *c*	**10.** *c*	**18.** *b*	**26.** *c*
6. *a*	**11.** *d*	**19.** *d*	**27.** *a*
7. *b*	**12.** *c*	**20.** *a*	**28.** *b*
8. *c*	**13.** *c*	**21.** *a*	

6

WAVES

Throw a stone into a lake: water waves move outward from the splash. Clap your hands: sound waves carry the noise all around. Switch on a lamp: light waves illuminate the room. Water waves, sound waves, and light waves are very different from one another in important respects, but all have in common the basic properties of wave motion. A wave is a periodic disturbance — a back-and-forth change of some kind (of water height in the case of water waves, of air pressure in the case of sound waves, of electric and magnetic fields in the case of light waves) — that spreads out from a source and carries energy as it goes. Information, too, can be carried by waves, which is how sights and sounds reach us.

WAVE MOTION

In the first part of this chapter we shall examine mechanical waves, that is, waves that move through matter. The disturbances that make up such waves are transmitted from particle to particle in the medium through which they travel. Later we shall consider electromagnetic waves. Such waves consist of coupled electric and magnetic fields that vary periodically like other waves but can move through a perfect vacuum. Light, radio waves, and x-rays are all electromagnetic in nature.

Water Waves

Crests and troughs

If we stand on an ocean beach and watch the waves roll in and break one after the other, we are impressed with their endless progress toward the shore. At first we might guess that water is moving bodily shoreward, carrying along pebbles and shells and bits of driftwood. A few minutes' observation, however, is enough to show us that this cannot be true. Between the breakers water rushes back out to sea, and there is no piling up of water on the beach. The overall motion is really endless back-and-forth movement.

We can see the details of what is happening better by moving out beyond the breakers, say, to the end of a pier. If we fix our attention on a floating cork or piece of seaweed, we find that its actual position changes very little. As the crest of each wave passes, the cork rises and appears to move shoreward. In the trough that follows, it falls and moves an equal distance backward. On the whole its path is approximately a circle, and we can expect the same pattern of circular motion wherever water waves occur.

The illusion of overall movement toward the shore comes about because each molecule of water undergoes its circular motion a moment later than the molecule behind it (Fig. 6-1). At the crest of a wave the molecules move in the

FIG. 6-1
Nature of a water wave in deep water. Each particle performs a periodic motion in a small circle, and because successive particles reach the tops of their circles at slightly later times, their combination appears as a series of crests and troughs moving along the surface of the water. There is no net transfer of water by the wave.

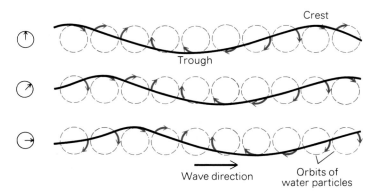

direction of the wave, while in a trough the molecules move in the backward direction.

What does move shoreward is not water but energy. Ocean waves are produced by wind, and it is the energy from the wind out at sea that is carried by means of wave motion to the shore. All mechanical waves behave the same way: they transfer energy from place to place by a series of periodic motions of individual particles, but cause no permanent shift in position of matter.

Wave motion consists of the passage through a medium of a periodic disturbance that transports energy

Transverse and Longitudinal Waves

Up and down; back and forth

In a transverse wave, the particles of the medium move perpendicularly to the wave direction

Surface waves on water are familiar, but they are also complicated. More simple are the waves set up in a stretched rope by a succession of shakes at one end (Fig. 6-2). Clearly the rope as a whole does not change its position, but waves in the rope carry energy from the hand to the point of attachment. If we fix our attention on a part of the rope, we will note that it moves up, then down, then up again as each wave passes, and that this motion is transmitted from one segment to the next down the length of the rope. The motion of particles here is perpendicular to the motion of the wave itself. Such waves are called *transverse waves*.

In a longitudinal wave, the particles of the medium move parallel to the wave direction

Another type of wave can be illustrated by a long horizontal coil spring (Fig. 6-3). If the left-hand end of the spring is moved back and forth, a series of *compressions* and *rarefactions* moves along the spring. The compressions are places where the loops of the spring are pressed together, the rarefactions are places where they are stretched apart. Any one loop simply moves back and forth, transmitting its motion to the next in line, and the regular succession of back-and-forth movements gives rise to the compressions and rarefactions. Waves of this

FIG. 6-2
Transverse waves. The waves travel along the rope in the direction of the black arrow. The individual particles of the rope move back and forth (color arrows) perpendicular to the direction of the waves.

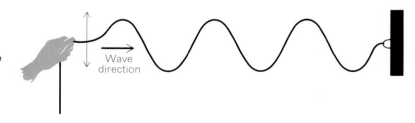

FIG. 6-3
Longitudinal waves. Successive regions of compression and rarefaction move along the spring. The particles of the spring move back and forth parallel to the spring.

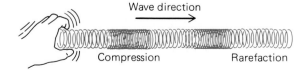

kind, in which the motion of individual units is along the same line that the wave itself travels, are called *longitudinal waves*.

Water waves are evidently a combination of transverse and longitudinal waves.

Only longitudinal waves can travel through a fluid

One reason it is useful to distinguish between the two kinds of waves is that purely transverse waves can occur only in solids, whereas longitudinal waves can travel in any medium, solid or fluid. Why this is true is not hard to see. Transverse motion requires that each particle, as it moves, drag with it adjacent particles to which it is tightly bound. This is impossible in a fluid, where molecules have no rigid attachment to their neighbors. Longitudinal motion, on the other hand, requires simply that each particle exert a push on its neighbors, which can happen as easily in a gas or liquid as in a solid. (Surface waves on water — in fact any waves at the boundary between two fluids — are an exception to the rule, for in part they involve transverse motion.) The fact that longitudinal waves that originate in earthquakes are able to pass through the center of the earth while transverse earthquake waves cannot is one of the reasons the earth is believed to have a liquid core (Chap. 14).

Sound

Pressure waves in a solid, liquid, or gas

Most sounds are produced by a vibrating object, such as the cone of a loudspeaker (Fig. 6-4). When it moves outward, the cone pushes the air molecules in front of it together to form a region of high pressure that spreads outward. The cone then moves backward, which expands the space available to nearby air molecules. These molecules now flow toward the cone, leaving a region of low pressure that

FIG. 6-4
Sound waves produced by a loudspeaker. Alternate regions of compression and rarefaction move outward from the vibrating diaphragm of the loudspeaker.

spreads outward behind the high-pressure region. The repeated vibrations of the loudspeaker cone thus send out a series of compressions and rarefactions that constitute sound waves.

Sound waves are longitudinal

Evidently sound waves are longitudinal, since the molecules in their paths move back and forth in the same direction as that of the waves. This movement is slight, only a tiny fraction of an inch. The movement is superimposed on the normal random movements of the molecules, so that the actual motion of each molecule is a combination of the motion due to thermal energy and the motion impressed on it by the loudspeaker cone. The air (or other material) in the path of a sound wave becomes alternately denser and rarer, and the resulting pressure changes cause our eardrums to vibrate, which produces the sensation of sound.

The great majority of sounds consist of waves of this type, but a few — the crack of a rifle, the first sharp sound of a thunderclap, the noise of an explosion — are essentially single, sudden compressions of the air rather than periodic phenomena.

Sound speeds are highest in solids, lowest in gases

The speed of sound is about 343 m/s (767 mi/h) in sea-level air at ordinary temperatures. Since the particles in liquids and solids are closer together and therefore more immediately responsive to one another's motions than is the case in gases, sound travels faster in liquids and solids. For example, the speed of sound is about 1500 m/s in water and 5000 m/s in iron.

Describing Waves

Wavelength, frequency, amplitude

All waves can be represented by a curve like that in Fig. 6-5. The resemblance to transverse wave motion is easiest to see; in fact the curve is an idealized picture of continuous waves in a rope like that of Fig. 6-2. As the wave moves to the right, each point on the curve can be thought of as moving up or down along a path whose extremes are the heights of the high point and low point of the curve, just as any small segment of the rope would move. The resemblance to longitudinal waves is not so obvious. Here we can say that high points of the curve represent the maximum shifts of particles in one direction, low points their maximum shifts in the other direction.

Wavelength and frequency

A representation like Fig. 6-5 permits us to assign numbers to certain properties of a wave, so that we can compare different waves on the same basis. The

FIG. 6-5
A wave moving in the x direction whose displacements are in the y direction. The wavelength is λ and the amplitude is A.

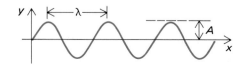

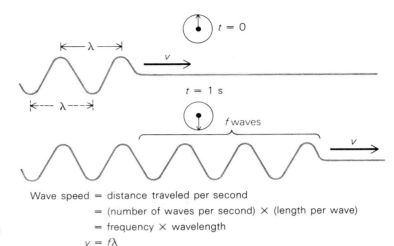

Wave speed = distance traveled per second

= (number of waves per second) × (length per wave)

= frequency × wavelength

$v = f\lambda$

FIG. 6-6
Wave speed equals frequency times wavelength.

distance from crest to crest (or from trough to trough) is called the *wavelength*, usually symbolized by the Greek letter λ (lambda). The *speed* of the waves v is the rate at which each crest moves, and the *frequency f* is the number of crests that pass a given point each second.

The hertz is the unit of frequency

The unit of frequency is the cycle per second (c/s), a unit that is nowadays usually called the *hertz*, abbreviated Hz, after Heinrich Hertz, a pioneer in the study of electromagnetic waves.

The number of waves that pass a point per second multiplied by the length of each wave gives the speed with which the waves travel (Fig. 6-6). If 10 waves, each 2 m long, pass in a second, then each wave must travel 20 m during that second to give a speed of 20 m/s. Thus frequency f times wavelength λ gives speed v:

How wave speed, frequency, and wavelength are related

$$v = \lambda f$$

Wave speed = (wavelength)(frequency)

This formula applies to waves of all kinds. For example, waves on the open sea whose wavelength is 50 m travel at about 8.5 m/s. The frequency of such waves is

$$f = \frac{v}{\lambda} = \frac{8.5 \text{ m/s}}{50 \text{ m}} = 0.17 \text{ Hz}$$

The waves pass a given point 5.9 s apart since 1/0.17 Hz = 5.9 s/wave (Fig. 6-7).

As another example, sound in air travels at 343 m/s and the musical note middle C has a frequency of 261 Hz. The corresponding wavelength is

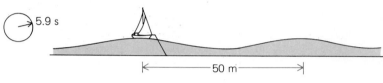

FIG. 6-7
Waves whose speed is 8.5 m/s and whose wavelength is 50 m have a frequency of 0.17 Hz. This means that such waves pass an anchored boat once every 5.9 s.

$$f = \frac{v}{\lambda} = \frac{8.5 \text{ m/s}}{50 \text{ m}} = 0.17 \text{ Hz} = 0.17 \text{ wave/s}$$

$$\text{Time per wave} = \frac{1}{0.17 \text{ wave/s}} = 5.9 \text{ s/wave}$$

$$\lambda = \frac{v}{f} = \frac{343 \text{ m/s}}{261 \text{ Hz}} = 1.3 \text{ m}$$

Wave amplitude is independent of wavelength and frequency

The *amplitude* of a wave refers to the height of the crests above normal (or the depth of the troughs below normal). It is represented by A in Fig. 6-5, and is defined in general as half the length of the path over which each particle moves. It is not surprising that the amount of energy carried by waves depends on their amplitude and their frequency, in other words, on the violence of the waves and the number of waves per second. It turns out that the energy is proportional to the square of each of these quantities.

WAVE BEHAVIOR

A wave behaves in certain respects like a thrown ball: both have certain speeds, both carry energy, both are reflected by a wall in their paths. But in other respects waves are unique. For instance, two balls that meet in midair bounce off each other, but if two waves of the same kind meet, they combine to form a new wave with different properties. We shall look into the behavior of mechanical waves first, since they are easiest to appreciate, and later see how the ideas that result help us to understand the behavior of light waves.

Refraction

A change in direction produced by a change in speed

Water waves that approach a sloping beach, as in Fig. 6-8, illustrate the phenomenon of *refraction*. No matter what direction the wind may be blowing from, the direction of motion of waves near shore is practically at right angles to the shore. Farther out in open water the direction of motion may be oblique (that is, at a slanting angle), but the waves turn as they move in so that their crests become roughly parallel with the shoreline.

Refraction occurs when a wave goes from one region to another in which its speed is different

The explanation is straightforward. As a wave moves obliquely shoreward, its near-shore end encounters shallow water where friction with the bottom slows it down. More and more of the wave is slowed as it continues to move, and the slowing becomes more pronounced as the water gets shallower. As a result the whole wave swings around until it is moving almost directly shoreward. The wave has turned because part of it is forced to move more slowly than the rest. Thus refraction is produced by differences in speed along the wave.

The bending will be at a sharp angle if the waves cross a definite boundary between regions in which they move at different speeds. The photograph on page 197 shows this effect in ripples that move obliquely from deep water to shallow

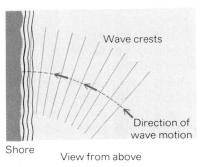

Wave crests

Direction of wave motion

Shore   View from above

View from side

FIG. 6-8
Refraction of water waves. Waves approaching shore obliquely are turned because they move more slowly in shallow water near shore.

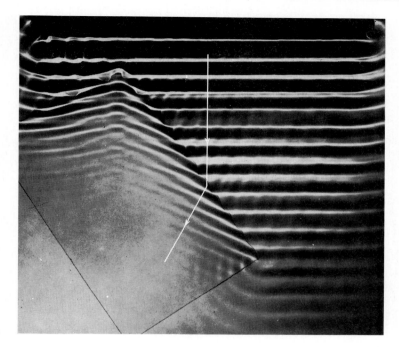

The refraction of water waves in a shallow tank. In the left side of the tank is a glass plate over which the water is shallower than elsewhere. Waves move more slowly in shallow water than in deeper water, and hence refraction occurs at the edge of the plate. The arrows show the direction of movement of the waves.

water in a tank. If the waves approach the boundary at right angles, no refraction occurs because the change in wave speed takes place along each wave at the same time.

Refraction occurs when waves of any kind change speed when they cross a boundary at a slanting angle. The refraction of light waves is responsible for the foreshortened appearance of people standing in shallow water, and their refraction when moving from air into glass and out again accounts for the focusing of light by lenses.

Reflection

Rebounding from an obstacle

Reflection refers to the change in direction of a wave when it strikes an obstacle

Another familiar property of waves is their ability to be *reflected* when they meet an obstacle. When a single wave sent down a stretched rope by a shake of the free end meets the attached end, it re-forms itself and travels back along the rope (Fig. 6-9). Water waves are similarly reflected, as we can see by watching waves strike a breakwater obliquely and re-form themselves into waves that move outward at a similar angle in the other direction (Fig. 6-10).

FIG. 6-9
A wave in a stretched rope is reflected when it reaches a fixed end. The reflected wave is inverted.

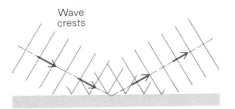

FIG. 6-10
Reflection of water waves. Waves approaching an obstacle obliquely appear to re-form and move away in a different direction.

Strong winds set up standing waves in the Tacoma Narrows Bridge in Washington State soon after its completion in 1940. The bridge collapsed as a result. Today bridges are stiffened to prevent such disasters.

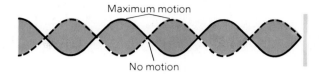

Maximum motion

No motion

FIG. 6-11
Standing waves in a stretched rope.

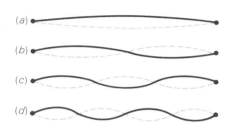

(a)

(b)

(c)

(d)

FIG. 6-12
A few of the possible standing waves in a stretched string, such as a violin string.

Standing waves

If a series of waves is sent along a stretched rope, the reflected waves will meet the forward-moving waves head on. Each segment of the rope must then respond to two different impulses at the same time. The two impulses add together. If the segment is being pushed in the same direction by both wave impulses, it will move in that direction with an amplitude equal to the sum of the two motions. On the other hand, if the two wave impulses are in opposite directions, the segment will have an amplitude equal to the difference of the two.

If the timing is just right, the two motions may cancel out completely for some points of the rope while points between these move with twice the normal amplitude. In this situation the waves appear not to travel at all. Some parts of the rope will simply move up and down, and other parts remain at rest (Fig. 6-11). Waves of this sort are called *standing waves*.

Vibrating strings in musical instruments are the most familiar examples of standing waves (Fig. 6-12). Longitudinal waves traveling in opposite directions over the same path may also set up standing waves, as in the vibrating air columns of whistles, organ pipes, and wind instruments such as flutes and clarinets.

Interference

How waves add together

Interference refers to the adding together of two or more waves of the same kind that pass by the same point at the same time. The formation of standing waves is an example of interference.

A simple demonstration of interference is shown in Fig. 6-13. If waves are started along the stretched strings *AC* and *BC* by shaking them at the ends *A* and

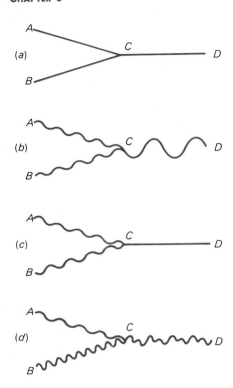

FIG. 6-13
Interference. (*a*) Waves started
along stretched strings *AC* and *BC*
will interfere at *C*. (*b*) Constructive
interference. (*c*) Destructive
interference. (*d*) A mixture of constructive and destructive interference.

In constructive interference, the
original waves are in step and
combine to give a wave of greater
amplitude

In destructive interference, the
original waves are out of step and
combine to give a wave of smaller
amplitude

B, the single string *CD* will be affected by both. Each portion of *CD* must respond
to two different impulses at the same time, and its motion will therefore be
determined by the total of the effects of the two original waves. When *A* and *B* are
shaken in step with each other, the waves add together, so that in *CD* the crests
are twice as high and the troughs twice as deep as in *AC* and *BC*. This situation is
called *constructive* interference.

On the other hand, if *A* and *B* are shaken just out of step with each other, wave
crests in *AC* will arrive at *C* just when troughs get there from *BC*. As a result,
crest matches trough, the wave impulses cancel each other out, and *CD* remains at
rest. This situation is called *destructive* interference. As another possibility, if *A* is
shaken through a smaller range than and half as rapidly as *B*, the two waves add
together to give the complex waveform of Fig. 6-13*d*. The variations are endless,
and the resulting waveforms depend upon the amplitudes, wavelengths, and
timing of the incoming waves.

The interference of water waves is shown by ripples in the photograph on
page 201. Ripples that spread out from the two vibrating rods affect the same
water molecules. In some directions, crests from one source arrive at the same
time as crests from the other source and the ripples are reinforced. Between these
regions of vigorous motion are narrow lanes where the water is quiet, which

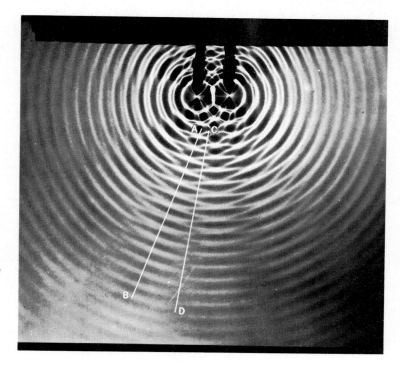

The interference of water waves. Ripples are spreading out across the surface of a shallow tank of water from the two sources at the top. In some directions (for instance *AB*) the ripples reinforce each other and the waves are more prominent. In other directions (for instance *CD*) the ripples are out of step and cancel each other, so that the waves are small or absent.

represent directions in which crests from one source arrive together with troughs from the other so that the wave motions cancel.

Diffraction

Why shadows are never completely dark

In diffraction, waves seem to bend around the edge of an obstacle

An important property of all waves is their ability to bend around the edge of an obstacle in their path. This property is called *diffraction*.

A simple example of diffraction occurs whenever we hear a street noise, such as that of a car horn, around the corner of a building. The noise could not have reached us through the building, and refraction is not involved since the speed of sound does not change between the source of noise and our ears. What has happened is that the sound waves have spread out from the corner of the building into the ''shadow'' as though they originated at the corner (Fig. 6-14). The diffracted waves are not as loud as those that have proceeded directly to a listener, but they have gone around the corner in a way that a stream of particles, for example, cannot.

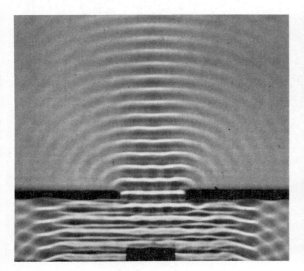

Diffraction of water waves at a gap in an obstacle. The narrower the gap, the more pronounced the diffraction.

FIG. 6-14
Diffraction causes waves to bend around the corner of an obstacle into the "shadow" region. The diffracted waves spread out as though they originated at the corner of the obstacle here, and are weaker than the direct waves. The waves shown here could be of any kind, for instance water waves, sound waves, or light waves.

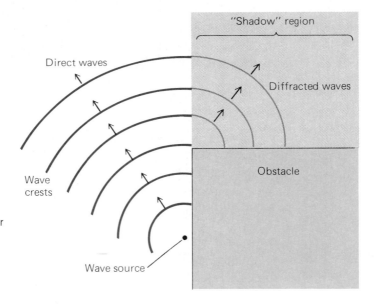

Doppler Effect

Higher pitch when approaching, lower pitch when receding

The doppler effect is the change in frequency of a wave due to motion of source or observer

We all know that sounds produced by vehicles moving toward us seem higher-pitched than usual, whereas sounds produced by vehicles moving away from us seem lower-pitched than usual. Anybody who has listened to the whistle of a train

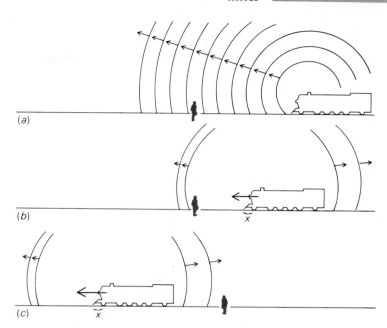

FIG. 6-15
The doppler effect. At (*a*), the train is standing still, and sound waves from the whistle reach the observer at their normal frequency. At (*b*), the train approaches the observer, moving a distance *x* between two successive waves. To the observer, the wavelength seems shorter and the frequency higher. At (*c*), the train moves away from the observer, again moving a distance *x* between successive sound waves. Here the observer finds that the wavelength is longer and the frequency lower.

as it approaches and then leaves a station, or to the siren of a police car as it passes by at high speed, is aware of these changes in frequency, called the *doppler effect*.

The doppler effect arises from the relative motion of the listener and the source of the sound. Either or both may be moving. When the motion lessens their distance apart, as in Fig. 6-15*a*, the apparent wavelength decreases to make the frequency higher. When the motion takes listener and source farther away from each other, as in Fig. 6-15*b*, the apparent wavelength increases to make the frequency lower.

A simple way to visualize the doppler effect is to imagine traveling in a boat on a windy day. If we are headed into the wind, waves strike the boat more often than if it were at rest, and the ride may be very choppy. On the other hand, if we are headed away from the wind, waves catch up with us more slowly than if the boat were at rest, so their apparent frequency is less.

An interesting application of the doppler effect is the measurement of the speed of blood in an artery. When a beam of high-frequency sound waves is directed at an artery, the waves reflected from the moving blood cells show a doppler shift in frequency because the cells then act as moving wave sources. From this shift the speed of the blood can be calculated. It is a few centimeters per second in the main arteries, less in the smaller ones.

Doppler effect in light

The doppler effect occurs in light waves and is one of the methods by which astronomers detect and measure motions of the stars. Stars emit light that contains only certain characteristic wavelengths. When a star moves either toward or away from the earth, these wavelengths appear, respectively, shorter or longer than usual. From the amount of the shift, it is possible to calculate the speed with which the star is approaching or receding. As we shall learn in Chap. 20, this is the method by which the expansion of the universe was discovered.

Musical Sounds

Harmony versus discord

Musical sounds are produced by a variety of vibrating objects — stretched gut or wire in stringed instruments, vocal cords in the larynx, membranes in drums, air columns in wind instruments. We have already considered the behavior of a stretched string. The simplest vibration that can occur is one in which a single standing wave takes up the entire length of the string, as in Fig. 6-12a. The frequency of the note produced may be varied by changing the tension on the string, as a violinist does when he tunes his instrument; the tighter the string, the higher the frequency. For a given tension the frequency may be varied by changing the length of the string, as the violinist does with the pressure of a finger on the string.

Fundamental tone and overtones

Depending on where the string is plucked or bowed, more complex vibrations may be set up: standing waves may form with two, three, or even more maxima (Fig. 6-12b, c, d). Sound waves set up by these shorter standing waves have higher frequencies, and the frequencies are related to the frequency of the longest wave by simple ratios — 2 : 1, 3 : 1, and so on. The tone produced by the string vibrating as a whole is called the *fundamental,* and the higher frequencies produced when it vibrates in segments are called *overtones.*

Sound waves can be generated by a variety of means. Shown here are vibrating strings (guitar and bass), vibrating membranes (cymbal and drum), and vibrating air columns (saxophones and trumpet).

FIG. 6-16

The waveforms of sounds can be analyzed electronically with the help of an oscilloscope, a device that displays electric signals on the screen of a tube like the picture tube of a television set. A microphone is used to convert sound waves into electric waves, and these in turn can be displayed on the oscilloscope screen. "Pure" tones, like those produced by a tuning fork, have simple waveforms, while musical instruments and human vocal cords produce complex waveforms. Ordinary nonmusical noises consist of waves with complex and rapidly changing forms.

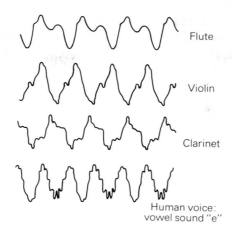

Flute

Violin

Clarinet

Human voice: vowel sound "e"

String instruments

In practice, the strings of a musical instrument are set in motion so that they vibrate not merely to give the fundamental or a single overtone but to produce a combination of the fundamental plus several overtones. The motion of the string, and correspondingly the form of the sound wave, may be very complex (Fig. 6-16). To the ear a fundamental tone by itself seems flat and uninteresting. As overtones are added the tone becomes "richer," with the quality, or timbre, of the tone depending on which particular overtones are emphasized. The emphasis is governed largely by the shape of the instrument, which enables it to *resonate* at particular frequencies. This means that the sounding part of the instrument — the belly of the violin or the soundboard of the piano — has certain natural frequencies of vibration, and that it is more readily set vibrating with these frequencies than with others. The resulting sounds may include a large number of overtones, but the greater emphasis on certain overtones provides the musical quality characteristic of the instrument.

Wind instruments

In wind instruments the sound is produced by a vibrating air column whose length determines the fundamental frequency. The entire air column may be set in motion as a unit, or overtones may be produced by standing waves whose length is a simple fraction of the total length. The performer can control the pitch of a note, in part by controlling the overtones with pressure from his lip and in part by using stops to vary the length of the vibrating column.

The human voice resembles a wind instrument in that the vocal cords produce vibrations in a column of air extending from the throat into the mouth, nose, and sinuses. The shape of this column, which we adjust during speech or singing by manipulating the mouth and tongue, determines the different vowel sounds by emphasizing some overtones and suppressing others. The general shape of the mouth and sinuses is also responsible for the subtle differences in quality which enable us to distinguish one person's voice from another's.

Harmony and discord

Certain mixtures of frequencies are pleasing to the ear. For instance, the combination of a tone and its first overtone, whose frequency is twice as great, appears harmonious to a listener. Such an interval is called an *octave* in music because it includes eight notes. Also agreeable are tones with a frequency ratio of 2 : 3, such as C (264 Hz) and G (396 Hz). This interval is called a *fifth* because it includes five notes, here C, D, E, F, G. Somewhat less agreeable are tones whose frequencies are in the ratio 4 : 5, such as C and E (330 Hz); the interval here spans three notes and is called a *third*. The larger the numbers that express their frequency ratio, the less attractive a combination of tones appears. Thus C and D (ratio 8 : 9) seems discordant, and E and F (ratio 15 : 16) more discordant still.

ELECTROMAGNETIC WAVES

In 1864 the British physicist James Clerk Maxwell made the remarkable suggestion that an accelerated electric charge generates combined electrical and magnetic disturbances able to travel indefinitely through empty space. These disturbances are called *electromagnetic waves*. Such waves are difficult to visualize because they represent fluctuations in fields that are themselves difficult to form mental images of. But they certainly exist — light is an example of an electromagnetic wave.

Faraday and Maxwell

Experimenter and theorist

Faraday was a gifted experimenter

Michael Faraday, the son of a blacksmith, was apprenticed to a bookbinder in his youth, and taught himself chemistry and physics from the books he was learning to bind. At the age of twenty-one he became bottle washer for Sir Humphrey Davy at that chemist's laboratory in the Royal Institution of London. Within 20 years the blacksmith's son succeeded Davy as head of the Institution. During those 20 years Faraday's experiments, particularly in chemistry, had won him the respect of contemporary scientists. To the later years of his life belong the remarkable work in electricity and magnetism whose results include the discovery of electromagnetic induction. Unskilled at mathematics, Faraday is remembered as an experimental genius. Like many of us, he felt the need to work with real, tangible things, such as the coils and magnets of his laboratory. To make sense of the electric and magnetic forces that he could not see or feel, Faraday invented *lines of force* — lines which do not exist, which give at best a crude picture of fields of force, but which students ever since have found useful as they try to understand the subtleties of electricity and magnetism.

Maxwell was a gifted theorist

James Clerk Maxwell was born into an old and distinguished Scottish family in 1831, when Faraday was forty years old. Given the best education that England could provide, Maxwell became a precocious scientist. At fifteen he published his first paper; at twenty-five he was made professor of physics and astronomy at Cambridge University. Maxwell was gifted with extraordinary mathematical ability; for him fields of force could be better expressed by equations than in terms of

Faraday's lines. Starting from the results of Faraday's experiments, Maxwell not only combined electricity and magnetism into a single, all-embracing theory but discovered the nature of light as well.

The work of Faraday and Maxwell is another illustration of the progress of science from experiment to generalization. Sometimes experimental ability and theoretical insight are combined in the same person, but more often we find these talents in different people. As Faraday's work paved the way for Maxwell, so the observations of Tycho Brahe lay behind Kepler's laws of planetary behavior and Galileo's experiments with falling bodies lay behind Newton's laws of motion.

Electromagnetic Waves

Waves without matter

A magnetic field is associated with a changing electric field and vice versa

Maxwell was led to the discovery of electromagnetic (or just em) waves by an argument based on the symmetry of nature. We know that a changing magnetic field gives rise to a current in a nearby wire, from which we conclude that such a field has an electric field associated with it. Maxwell proposed that the opposite effect also exists, so that a changing electric field always has an associated magnetic field. The mathematical statement of this idea is a persuasive one, but it must nevertheless meet the test of experiment. The electric fields produced by electromagnetic induction are easy to measure because metals offer so little resistance to the flow of charges. There is no such thing as a magnetic current, and it is accordingly very difficult to detect the weak magnetic fields Maxwell predicted.

Electromagnetic waves consist of coupled electric and magnetic field fluctuations that travel with the speed of light

However, if Maxwell was right, then em waves must exist in which changing electric and magnetic fields are coupled together by both electromagnetic induction and the converse mechanism that he proposed. The linked fields do not remain stationary in space but spread out, much as ripples spread out when a stone is dropped in a body of water. The energy carried by an em wave is constantly being exchanged between its fluctuating electric and magnetic fields. Calculations show that the wave speed should have the same value as the speed of light, which is 3×10^8 m/s (186,000 mi/s).

How an em wave can be created

To see how an em wave can be created, let us consider what happens when we connect an alternating-current generator to a pair of metal rods, as in Fig. 6-17. For simplicity we will imagine that only a single charge is in each rod at any time. This is not the only way to create em waves, since every accelerated charge emits them, but it is a particularly easy way to visualize how this can occur.

In Fig. 6-17a the charges are moving apart. Some of the electric lines of force between them are shown as color lines; the magnetic lines of force are in the form of circles perpendicular to the page. In b the charges have stopped, so there is no magnetic field being produced at this moment, but the existing magnetic field continues to spread out along with the electric field. Both fields travel with the speed of light. In c the charges are moving toward each other, so the new magnetic field is opposite in direction to the old one although the electric field is in the same direction as before. In d the polarity of the rods has changed and now a negative

FIG. 6-17
A pair of metal rods connected to an electrical oscillator give rise to coupled electric and magnetic fields that constitute electromagnetic waves. The waves spread out from their source with the speed of light.

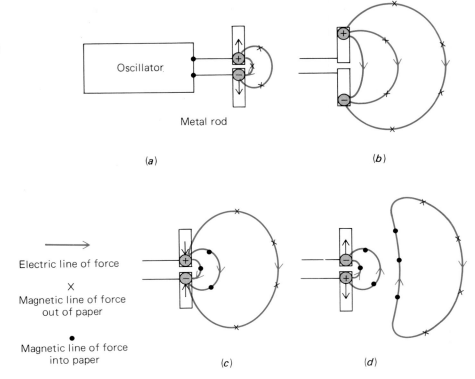

Metal rod

(a)   (b)

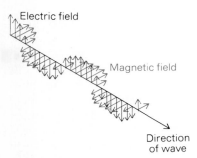

Electric field

Magnetic field

Direction of wave

Electric line of force

X
Magnetic line of force out of paper

•
Magnetic line of force into paper

(c)   (d)

FIG. 6-18
The electric and magnetic fields in an electromagnetic wave vary together. The fields are perpendicular to each other and to the direction of the wave.

The electric and magnetic fields of an em wave form closed loops

charge is in the upper rod and a positive charge is in the lower one. These charges are moving apart. The magnetic field of the moving charges is still in the same direction as in *c* but the electric field is reversed.

The result of the above sequence is that the outermost electric and magnetic lines of force form closed loops which are no longer joined to the oscillating charges. The loops move freely through space and constitute an electromagnetic wave. As the charges continue to oscillate back and forth, additional closed loops of electric and magnetic lines of force are produced that similarly expand outward.

Figure 6-18 shows the relationship between the electric and magnetic fields in an electromagnetic wave. In this drawing the fields are represented by a series of vectors (not lines of force) that indicate the magnitude and direction of the fields in the path of the wave. The fields are perpendicular to each other and to the direction of the wave, and they remain in step as they periodically reverse their directions.

Types of EM Waves

They carry information as well as energy

Radio waves are electromagnetic in character

During Maxwell's lifetime em waves remained an unproven idea. Finally, in 1887, the German physicist Heinrich Hertz showed experimentally that electromagnetic waves indeed exist and behave exactly as Maxwell expected them to.

Hertz was not concerned with the commercial possibilities of em waves, and it remained for others to develop what we now call radio. Radio transmission is accomplished by means of em waves produced by electrons oscillating hundreds of thousands to millions of times per second in the antenna of the sending station. When these waves reach the antenna of a receiving station, the electrons there vibrate in step with the waves. By means of electronic devices of various kinds the receiver can be *tuned* so that it responds to a specific wave frequency only. Since each transmitter operates on a different frequency, a receiver can pick up the signals sent out by whatever station we wish. The original current set up by the radio waves is very feeble, but it can be amplified in the receiver so that its variations are strong enough to produce sounds in a loudspeaker.

The ionosphere makes possible long-range radio communication

High-frequency (short-wavelength) radio waves have the useful property of being reflected from the *ionosphere,* a region of ionized gas high in the atmosphere (Chap. 13). Without the ionosphere, radio communication would be limited to short distances since electromagnetic waves travel in straight lines and would be shielded from more distant receivers by the curvature of the earth. However, since radio waves in a certain frequency range can bounce one or more times between the ionosphere and the earth's surface, transmission is possible for long distances, even to the opposite side of the earth (Fig. 6-19).

FIG. 6-19
The ionosphere is a region in the upper atmosphere whose ionized layers make possible long-range radio communication by their ability to reflect short-wavelength radio waves.

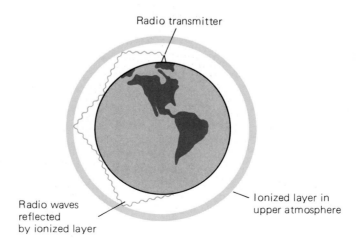

Radio transmitter

Radio waves reflected by ionized layer

Ionized layer in upper atmosphere

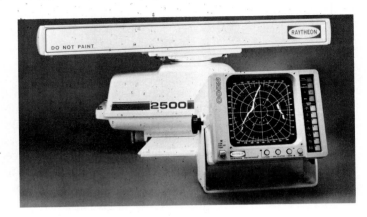

The rotating scanner of a radar set sends out pulses of high-frequency radio waves in a narrow beam and then detects their reflections from objects in their paths. These reflections are then displayed on a screen. Shown here is the image of a harbor entrance; the center of the screen corresponds to the position of the ship carrying the radar.

Radar

In recent years ways have been found to produce em waves of extremely high frequency. The frequencies of ordinary radio waves extend up to about 2 MHz (1 MHz = 1 megahertz = 10^6 Hz) and those of waves used in long-range short-wave communication up to about 30 MHz. Still higher frequencies have found widespread use in television and radar. Such extremely short waves are not reflected by the ionosphere, so direct reception of television is limited by the horizon unless rebroadcast by a satellite station.

Waves whose frequencies are around 10 GHz (1 GHz = 1 gigahertz = 10^9 Hz), corresponding to wavelengths of a few centimeters, can readily be formed into narrow beams. Such beams are reflected by solid objects such as ships and airplanes, which is the basis of *radar*. A rotating antenna is used to send out a

FIG. 6-20

The electromagnetic spectrum. All electromagnetic waves have the same fundamental character and the same speed in vacuum, but many aspects of their behavior depend upon their frequency. The range of frequencies is truly enormous: from 10^4 (10 thousand) Hz to 10^{21} (1000 billion billion) Hz.

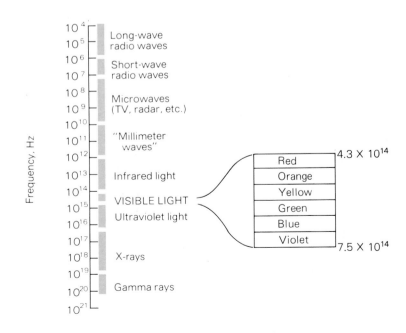

pulsed beam, and the distance of a particular target is found from the time needed for the echo to return to the antenna. The direction of the target is the direction in which the antenna is then pointing.

Light consists of electromagnetic waves of very high frequency

Figure 6-20 shows the range (or *spectrum*) of electromagnetic waves. Light waves cover a very short frequency interval, from about 4.3×10^{14} Hz for red light to about 7.5×10^{14} Hz for violet light. The charges that oscillate in a luminous material so unimaginably fast to produce these waves turn out to be electrons inside atoms. Infrared radiation has lower frequencies than those in visible light, and ultraviolet radiation has higher frequencies. Still higher are the frequencies of x-rays and of the gamma radiation from atomic nuclei. The entire spectrum from radio waves to gamma rays consists of waves having the same basic nature and the same speed.

LIGHT

▬▬▬▬▬▬▬▬▬▬▬▬▬▬▬▬▬

Many aspects of the behavior of light waves can be understood without reference to their electromagnetic character — indeed, it was known that light consists of waves of some kind two centuries before Maxwell's work. As we shall see, it is even possible to adopt a still simpler model in many (but far from all) situations by considering light in terms of "rays" rather than waves.

Light "Rays"

The paths light takes

Early in life we become aware that light travels in straight lines. A simple piece of evidence is the straight beam of a flashlight on a foggy night. Actually, our entire orientation to the world about us, our sense of the location of things in space, depends on *assuming* that light follows straight-line paths. In everyday life we use this property to define straightness, rather than Euclid's "the shortest distance between two points." If we want to know whether a given line is straight or not, we sight along it instead of trying to figure out whether it is the shortest of all possible lines between its end points.

Just as familiar, however, is the fact that light does not always follow straight lines. We see most objects by reflected light, light that has been turned abruptly on striking a surface. The distorted appearance of things seen in a glass of water, through glass objects of irregular shape, or through the heated air rising above a flame, all testify further to the ability of light to be bent from a straight path. In these cases the light is refracted, and we note that this occurs when light moves from one transparent material to a different one.

Although we recognize, with the conscious part of our minds, that light can be reflected and refracted, it is easy to be deceived about the true position of things. When we look in a mirror, for example, we see light that has traveled in a broken path to the mirror and back again, but our eyes seem to tell us that the light has followed a straight path from an image behind the mirror. When we look at someone standing in shallow water, his legs appear shorter than they do in air because light going from water into air is bent. Our eyes have no way to take this into account and so we register the illusion rather than the reality.

Much can be learned about the behavior of light by studying the paths that light follows in various situations. Since light appears to travel in a straight path in a uniform medium, we can represent its motion by straight lines called *rays*. Rays are a convenient abstraction, and we can visualize what we mean by thinking of a narrow pencil of light in a darkened room.

Light "rays" provide a convenient way of thinking for many purposes, although light actually consists of waves

Reflection

Mirror, mirror on the wall

When we look at ourselves in a mirror, light from all parts of the body (this is reflected light, of course, but we may treat it as if it originated in the body) is reflected from the mirror back to our eyes, as in Fig. 6-21. Light from the foot, for example, follows the path $CC'E$. Our eyes, which see the ray $C'E$ and automatically project it in a straight line, register the foot at the proper distance but apparently behind the mirror at C''. A ray from the top of the head is reflected at A', and our eyes see the point A as if it were behind the mirror at A''. Rays from other points of the body are similarly reflected, and in this manner a complete *image* is formed that appears to be behind the mirror.

The fact that the image is a perfect replica of the body (provided the mirror is flat and has no imperfections) means that each ray must be reflected from the mirror at the same angle as the angle of approach. Thus the angle made by CC' with the mirror must equal the angle made by $C'E$. This property of rays is expressed by the statement that

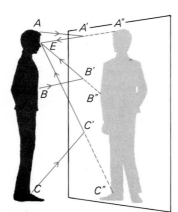

FIG. 6-21
Formation of an image in a plane mirror. The image appears to be behind the mirror because we instinctively respond to light as though it travels in straight lines.

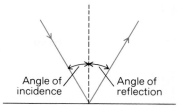

FIG. 6-22
When light is reflected, the angle of incidence equals the angle of reflection.

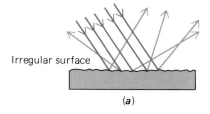

Angle of incidence   Angle of reflection

FIG. 6-23
(a) Light that strikes an irregular surface is scattered randomly and cannot form an image. (b) Light that strikes a smooth, flat surface is reflected at an angle equal to the angle of incidence. Such a surface acts as a mirror.

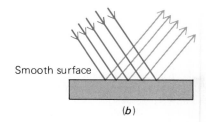

Irregular surface

Smooth surface

(a)

(b)

Law of reflection

The angle of incidence equals the angle of reflection.

In order to make this rule applicable to curved as well as plane surfaces, the angles are usually measured from a perpendicular to the surface (Fig. 6-22) rather than from the surface itself.

Why do we not see images of ourselves in walls and furniture as well as in mirrors? This is simply a question of the relative roughness of surfaces. Rays of light are reflected from walls just as they are from mirrors, but the reflected rays are scattered in all directions by the many surface irregularities (Fig. 6-23). We see the wall by the scattered light reflected from it.

Refraction

Bending light

Now let us consider what happens when light reaches us from something under water. If we look at an angle through a water surface at a stone lying on the bottom of a tank, the stone appears to be higher than it actually is (Fig. 6-24). This is in accord with the familiar observation that a body of water is always deeper than it seems to be. The explanation depends on the refraction of light as it moves from one medium to another, an effect similar to that described earlier in this chapter in connection with water waves. A ray of light from the stone in Fig. 6-24 follows the

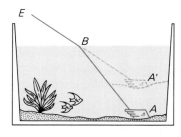

FIG. 6-24
Light is refracted when it travels obliquely from one medium to another. Here the effect of refraction is to make the water appear shallower than it actually is.

FIG. 6-25
Light rays are bent toward the perpendicular when they enter an optically denser medium, away from the perpendicular when they enter an optically less dense medium. A ray moving along the perpendicular is not bent. The paths taken by light rays are always reversible.

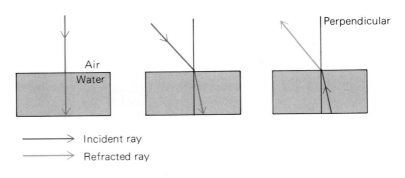

Incident ray
Refracted ray

FIG. 6-26
Refraction occurs whenever light passes from one medium into another in which its speed is different. Here two rays of light, I and II, pass from air, in which their speed is v_a, to glass, in which their speed is v_g. Because v_g is less than v_a, $A'B'$ is longer than AB, and the beam of which I and II are part changes direction when it enters the glass.

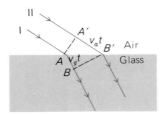

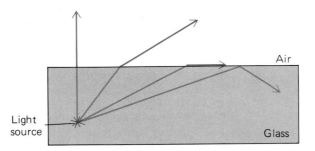

FIG. 6-27
Total internal reflection occurs when the angle through which a light ray going from one medium to a less optically dense medium is refracted by more than 90°.

Which way light bends when it is refracted

broken path *ABE* to our eyes, but our brain registers that the segment *BE* is part of the straight-line path starting at *A'*.

The rays of light from underwater are bent *toward* the water surface as they enter the air. A ray starting in air and going at an angle into water would follow the same path in reverse — as we would find in a dark room by letting a pencil of light fall on the surface of a glass of water mixed with a little milk.

In general, light rays that go obliquely from one medium to another are bent away from a perpendicular to the surface if the second medium is less optically dense than the first. If the second medium is more optically dense, the rays are bent toward the perpendicular (Fig. 6-25). Light going from air into glass, for example, is bent toward the perpendicular; light going from glass into air is bent away from the perpendicular. The reason for the bending, as in the case of water

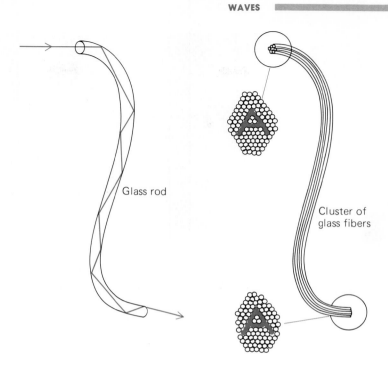

Glass rod

Cluster of
glass fibers

FIG. 6-28
Light can be "piped" from one
place to another by means of internal reflections in a glass rod. Using a
cluster of glass fibers permits an
image to be carried in this way.

Internal reflection

How to pipe light

waves, lies in different speeds of light in different substances (Fig. 6-26). Light that
enters another medium perpendicular to their boundary is evidently not deflected.

As mentioned above, light going from glass to air at a slanting angle is
refracted away from the perpendicular to the glass surface. If the angle of incidence is large enough, the angle of refraction may be so great that the light is bent
back into the glass (Fig. 6-27). This *internal reflection* makes it possible to "pipe"
light by means of successive reflections from the wall of a glass rod, as in Fig. 6-28.

By using a cluster of thin glass fibers instead of a single rod, an image can be
transferred from one end to the other with each fiber carrying a part of the image.
Because a fiber cluster is flexible, it can be used for such purposes as examining a
person's stomach by being passed in through the mouth. Some of the fibers
provide light for illumination, and the rest carry the reflected light back outside for
viewing.

Glass fibers are coming into wide use in telephone systems. The electric
signals that would normally be sent along copper wires are first converted into a
series of pulses according to a standard code and then sent as flashes of light down
a thin (0.005 – 0.1 mm) glass fiber. At the other end the flashes are converted back
into electric signals. Modern electronic methods allow at most 32 telephone
conversations to be carried at the same time by a pair of wires, but several
thousand can be carried by a single fiber with no problems of electrical interfer-

Light can be "piped" from one place to another by means of successive reflections from the wall of a glass rod.

ence. Telephone fiberoptic systems in the United States and elsewhere already link many cities and exchanges within cities.

Color

Each frequency of light produces the sensation of a different color

Each frequency of light produces the visual sensation of a particular color

White light is a mixture of light waves of different frequencies, each of which produces the visual sensation of a particular color. To verify this, we can direct a narrow beam of white light at a glass prism. Because the speed of light in glass varies slightly with frequency, light of each color is refracted to a different extent. This effect is called *dispersion*. The result is that the original beam is separated by the prism into beams of various colors, with red light bent the least and violet light bent the most (Fig. 6-29).

Origin of the rainbow

The dispersion of sunlight by water droplets is responsible for rainbows, which are seen when we face falling rain with the sun behind us. When a ray of sunlight enters a raindrop, as in Fig. 6-30, it is first refracted, then reflected at the back of the drop, and finally refracted again when it goes back out. Dispersion

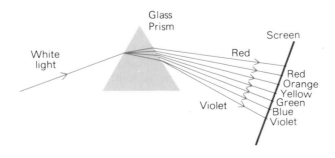

FIG. 6-29
Formation of a spectrum by the dispersion of white light in a glass prism. The different colors blend into one another smoothly.

FIG. 6-30
Rainbows are created by the dispersion of sunlight by raindrops. Red light arrives at the eye of the observer from the upper drop shown here, violet light from the lower drop. Other raindrops yield the other colors and produce a continuous arc in the sky.

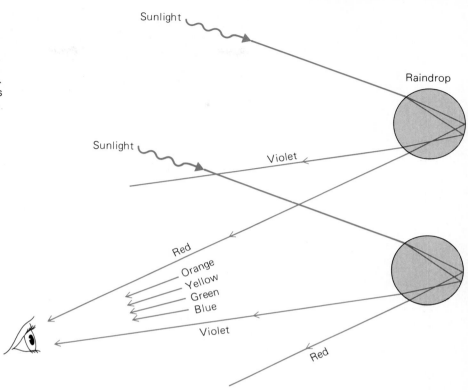

occurs at each refraction. With the sky full of raindrops, the result is a colored arc that has red light on the outside and violet light on the inside. Someone in an airplane can see the entire ring of color, but from the ground only the upper part is visible.

The colors of things we see by reflected light depend on the kind of light that falls on them and on the nature of their surfaces. If a surface reflects all light that falls on it, the color of the surface will be white when white light illuminates it (Fig. 6-31), red when red light illuminates it, and so on. A surface that reflects only, say,

FIG. 6-31
A white surface reflects all light that falls on it. A green surface reflects only green light and absorbs the rest. A black surface absorbs all light that falls on it.

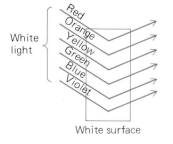
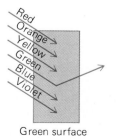
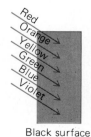

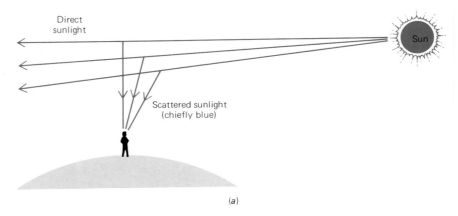

Direct
sunlight

Scattered sunlight
(chiefly blue)

Sun

(a)

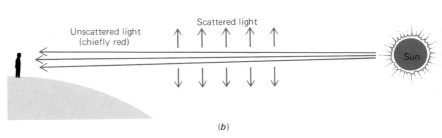

Scattered light

Unscattered light
(chiefly red)

Sun

(b)

FIG. 6-32
(a) The preferential scattering of
blue light in the atmosphere is
responsible for the blue color of the
sky. (b) The remaining direct sunlight
is reddish, which is the reason for the
red color of the sun at sunrise and
sunset.

Why the sky is blue

green light will appear green only when the light illuminating it contains green; otherwise it will appear black. A surface that absorbs all light that falls on it appears black.

The blue color of the sky is due to scattering of the sun's light by molecules and dust particles in the atmosphere. Blue light is scattered more effectively than red. When we look at the sky, what we see is light from the sun that has been scattered out of the direct beam, hence it appears blue (Fig. 6-32). The sun itself is therefore a little more yellowish or reddish than it would appear if there were no atmosphere. At sunrise or sunset, when the sun's light must make a long passage through the atmosphere, much of its blue light is scattered out, and the sun may be a brilliant red as a result. Above the atmosphere the sky is black, and the moon, stars, and planets are visible to astronauts in the daytime.

Interference

Why thin films are brightly colored

All of us have seen the brilliant colors that appear in soap bubbles and thin oil films. This effect can be traced to a combination of reflection and interference. (We

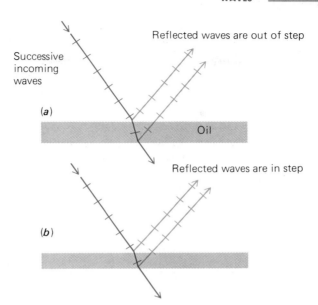

Successive incoming waves

Reflected waves are out of step

(a)

Oil

Reflected waves are in step

(b)

FIG. 6-33
(a) Destructive and (b) constructive interference in a thin film for light of a particular wavelength. When the film has the thickness in (a), it appears dark; when it has the thickness in (b), it appears bright. Light of other wavelengths undergoes destructive and constructive interference at different film thicknesses.

A thin film appears dark where light waves reflected from its upper and lower surfaces are out of step

recall from earlier in this chapter that interference refers to the adding together of two or more waves of the same kind that pass the same place at the same time.)

To understand the origin of the colored areas thin films exhibit, let us consider what happens when light of only one color, and hence only one wavelength, strikes an oil film. As in Fig. 6-33, part of the light passes right through the film, but some is reflected from the upper surface of the film and some from the lower surface. The two reflected waves interfere with each other. At some places in the film its thickness is just right for the reflected waves to be out of step, as in Fig. 6-33a. This is the same effect as the destructive interference shown in Fig. 6-13c. Little or no reflection can take place in this part of the oil film, and nearly all the incoming light simply passes right through it. The oil film accordingly seems black in this region.

Where the film is slightly thicker or thinner than in Fig. 6-33a, the reflected waves may be exactly in step and therefore reinforce each other, as in b. This corresponds to the constructive interference shown in Fig. 6-13b. Here the film is a good reflector and appears bright. Shining light of one color on a thin oil film gives rise in this way to areas of light and dark whose pattern depends on the varying thickness of the film.

Why thin films appear colored in white light

When white light is used, the reflected waves of only one color will be in step at a particular place while waves of other colors will not. The result is a series of brilliant colors. This is the reason for the rainbow effects we see in soap bubbles and in oil films.

Diffraction

The larger the diameter of a telescope, the sharper the image

Diffraction, too, occurs in light waves. As we recall, diffraction refers to the "bending" of waves around the edges of an obstacle in their path. Because of diffraction, a shadow is never completely dark, although the wavelengths of light waves are so short that the effects of diffraction are largely limited to the border of the shadow region.

The larger the lenses or mirrors used in an optical instrument, the sharper the image

Diffraction limits the useful magnification of optical instruments such as those of microscopes and telescopes. The larger the diameter of a lens (or curved mirror which acts like a lens), the less significant is diffraction in its performance. For this reason it is impossible to construct a small telescope capable of high magnification, since the result would be a blurred image instead of a sharp one. The huge Hale telescope at Mt. Palomar in California (page 644) has a concave mirror 5 m in diameter, but even so it can resolve objects only 50 m or more across on the moon's surface.

IMPORTANT TERMS

Waves carry energy from one place to another by a series of periodic motions of the individual particles of the medium in which the waves occur. (Electromagnetic waves are an exception.) There is no net transfer of matter in wave motion.

In a **longitudinal wave** the particles of the medium vibrate back and forth in the direction in which the waves travel. In a **transverse wave** the particles vibrate from side to side perpendicular to the wave direction. Sound waves are longitudinal; waves in a stretched string are transverse; water waves are a combination of both since water molecules move in circular orbits when a wave passes.

The **frequency** of a series of waves is the number of waves that pass a particular point per second. Their **wavelength** is the distance between adjacent crests or troughs. The **amplitude** of a wave is the maximum displacement of a particle of the medium on either side of its normal position when the wave passes.

The change in direction of a train of waves when they enter a region in which their speed changes is called **refraction.** In **reflection,** a train of waves strikes an obstacle and rebounds from it.

Interference refers to the adding together of two or more waves of the same kind that pass by the same point at the same time. In **constructive interference** the new wave has a greater amplitude than any of the original ones; in **destructive interference** the new wave has a smaller amplitude.

The ability of waves to bend around the edge of an obstacle in their path is called **diffraction.**

The **doppler effect** refers to the change in frequency of a wave when there is relative motion between its source and an observer.

Electromagnetic waves are radiated by accelerated electric charges and consist of coupled electric and magnetic field oscillations. Radio waves, light waves, and x-rays are all electromagnetic waves that differ only in their frequency.

White light is a mixture of different frequencies, each of which produces the visual sensation of a particular color. Because the speed of light in a medium is slightly different for different frequencies, white light is **dispersed** into its separate colors when refracted in a glass prism or a water droplet.

IMPORTANT FORMULA

Wave motion: $v = f\lambda$

MULTIPLE CHOICE

1. The distance from crest to crest of any wave is called its
   a. frequency
   b. wavelength
   c. speed
   d. amplitude

2. Of the following properties of a wave, the one that is independent of the others is its
  a. frequency
  b. wavelength
  c. speed
  d. amplitude

3. When waves go from one place to another, they transport
  a. amplitude
  b. frequency
  c. wavelength
  d. energy

4. Sound waves are
  a. longitudinal
  b. transverse
  c. a mixture of longitudinal and transverse
  d. electromagnetic

5. Sound will not travel through
  a. a solid
  b. a liquid
  c. a gas
  d. a vacuum

6. Sound travels fastest in
  a. air
  b. water
  c. iron
  d. a vacuum

7. The amplitude of a sound wave determines its
  a. loudness
  b. pitch
  c. wavelength
  d. overtones

8. An automobile sounding its horn is moving away from an observer. The pitch of the horn's sound relative to its normal pitch is
  a. higher
  b. lower
  c. the same
  d. higher or lower depending upon the exact frequency

9. The higher the frequency of a wave,
  a. the lower its speed
  b. the shorter its wavelength
  c. the smaller its amplitude
  d. the lower its pitch

10. A pure musical note causes a thin wooden panel to vibrate with the same frequency. This is an example of
  a. an overtone
  b. diffraction
  c. resonance
  d. interference

11. Maxwell based his theory of electromagnetic waves on the hypothesis that a changing electric field gives rise to
  a. an electric current
  b. a stream of electrons
  c. a magnetic field
  d. longitudinal waves

12. The direction of the magnetic field in an electromagnetic wave is
  a. parallel to the electric field
  b. perpendicular to the electric field
  c. parallel to the direction of the wave
  d. random

13. In a vacuum, the speed of an electromagnetic wave
  a. depends upon its frequency
  b. depends upon its wavelength
  c. depends upon the strength of its electric and magnetic fields
  d. is a universal constant

14. Which of the following does not consist of electromagnetic waves?
  a. X-rays
  b. Radar waves
  c. Sound waves
  d. Infrared waves

15. The energy of an electromagnetic wave resides in its
  a. frequency
  b. wavelength
  c. speed
  d. electric and magnetic fields

16. Light waves
  a. require air or another gas to travel through
  b. require some kind of matter to travel through
  c. require electric and magnetic fields to travel through
  d. can travel through a perfect vacuum

17. The light emitted by a luminous object comes from
  a. the gas in its atoms
  b. glowing electrons in its atoms
  c. moving electrons in its atoms
  d. combustion on the atomic level

18. A phenomenon that can be explained only if light consists of waves is
  a. reflection
  b. refraction
  c. interference
  d. color

19. The useful magnification of a telescope is limited by
  a. the speed of light
  b. the doppler effect
  c. interference

    d. diffraction

20. Thin films of oil and soapy water owe their brilliant colors to a combination of reflection and

    a. refraction

    b. interference

    c. diffraction

    d. doppler effect

21. The sky is blue because

    a. air molecules are blue

    b. the lens of the eye is blue

    c. the scattering of light is more efficient the shorter its wavelength

    d. the scattering of light is more efficient the longer its wavelength

22. The speed of sound waves having a frequency of 256 Hz compared with the speed of sound waves having frequency of 512 Hz is

    a. half as great

    b. the same

    c. twice as great

    d. 4 times as great

23. The wavelength of sound waves having a frequency of 256 Hz compared with the wavelength of sound waves having a frequency of 512 Hz is

    a. half as great

    b. the same

    c. twice as great

    d. 4 times as great

24. Waves in a lake are observed to be 5 m in length and to pass an anchored boat 1.25 s apart. The speed of the waves is

    a. 0.25 m/s

    b. 4 m/s

    c. 6.25 m/s

    d. impossible to find from the information given

25. A boat at anchor is rocked by waves whose crests are 20 m apart and whose speed is 5 m/s. These waves reach the boat with a frequency of

    a. 0.25 Hz

    b. 4 Hz

    c. 20 Hz

    d. 100 Hz

26. One kHz (kilohertz) is equal to 10^3 Hz. What is the wavelength of the electromagnetic waves sent out by a radio station whose frequency is 660 kHz? The speed of light is 3×10^8 m/s.

    a. 2.2×10^{-3} m

    b. 4.55×10^2 m

    c. 4.55×10^3 m

    d. 1.98×10^{14} m

QUESTIONS

1. Why do you think sound travels fastest in solids and slowest in gases?

2. The speed of sound in a gas depends upon the average speed of the gas molecules. Why is such a relationship reasonable?

3. What types of waves can be refracted? Under what circumstances does refraction occur?

4. What eventually becomes of the energy of sound waves?

5. How can constructive and destructive interference be reconciled with the principle of conservation of energy?

6. The characteristic wavelengths of light emitted by a distant star are observed to be shifted toward the red end of the spectrum. What does this suggest about the motion of the star relative to the earth?

7. If you walk past a bell while it is ringing, you notice no change in pitch, but if you ride past the same bell in a rapidly moving train or car the pitch seems to change markedly. Explain.

8. Why are light waves able to travel through a vacuum whereas sound waves cannot?

9. How could you show that light carries energy?

10. Under what circumstances does an electric charge radiate electromagnetic waves?

11. Light is said to be a transverse wave. What is it that varies at right angles to the direction in which a light wave travels?

12. Light waves carry both energy and momentum. Why doesn't the momentum of the sun diminish with time as its energy content does?

13. Some stars appear red, some yellow, and some blue. Which has the highest temperature? Which the lowest?

14. What color would red cloth appear if it were illuminated by (a) white light? (b) red light? (c) green light?

15. What is the height of the smallest mirror in which you could see yourself at full length? Use a diagram to explain your answer. Does it matter how far away you are?

16. When a beam of white light passes perpendicularly through a flat pane of glass, it is not dispersed into a spectrum. Why not?

17. The period of daylight is increased by a small amount because of the refraction of sunlight by the earth's atmosphere. Show with the help of a diagram how this effect comes about.

18. When a fish looks up through the water surface at an object in the air, will the object appear to be its normal size and distance above the water? Use a diagram to explain your answer, and assume that the fish's eye, like the human eye, is accustomed to interpreting light rays as straight lines.

19. A diamond shows flashes of color when held in white light. Why? If the diamond were exposed to red light, what would happen?

20. Why do large bodies of water appear bluish? How does the sky appear to an astronaut above the earth's atmosphere during the day? During the night?

21. Radio waves are able to diffract readily around buildings, as anybody with a portable radio receiver can verify. However, light waves, which are also electromagnetic waves, undergo no discernible diffraction around buildings. Why not?

22. Can you give two advantages that a telescope lens or mirror of large diameter has over one of small diameter?

PROBLEMS

1. An opera performance is being broadcast by radio. Who will hear a certain sound first, a member of the audience 30 m from the stage or a listener to a radio receiver in a city 5000 km away?

2. The light-year is an astronomical unit of length equal to the distance light travels in a year. What is the length of a light-year in meters?

3. A person is watching as spikes are being driven to hold a steel rail in place. The sound of each sledgehammer blow arrives 0.14 s through the rail and 2 s through the air after the person sees the hammer strike the spike. Find the speed of sound in the rail.

4. The engineer of a train moving at 30 m/s blows its whistle. How much later does someone in the caboose 300 m behind the engine hear the sound?

5. A violin string vibrates 1044 times per second. How many vibrations does it make while its sound travels 10 m?

6. A certain groove in a phonograph record travels past the needle at 40 cm/s and the sound that is produced has a frequency of 3000 Hz. Find the wavelength of the wiggles in the groove.

7. Find the frequency of sound waves in air whose wavelength is 25 cm.

8. Water waves whose crests are 6 m apart reach the shore every 1.2 s. Find the frequency and speed of the waves.

9. The radio frequency used internationally for distress calls from ships is 2182 kHz. What is the corresponding wavelength?

10. Radio amateurs are allowed to communicate on the "10-meter band." What is the frequency of radio waves whose wavelength is 10 m? Of sound waves whose wavelength is 10 m?

ANSWERS TO MULTIPLE CHOICE

1. *b*	**8.** *b*	**15.** *d*	**22.** *b*
2. *d*	**9.** *b*	**16.** *d*	**23.** *c*
3. *d*	**10.** *c*	**17.** *c*	**24.** *b*
4. *a*	**11.** *c*	**18.** *c*	**25.** *a*
5. *d*	**12.** *b*	**19.** *,d*	**26.** *b*
6. *c*	**13.** *d*	**20.** *b*	
7. *a*	**14.** *c*	**21.** *c*	

7

THE NUCLEUS

Atoms are the smallest particles of ordinary matter. Every atom has a central core, or nucleus, of protons and neutrons that provides nearly all its mass. Moving about the nucleus are the much lighter electrons, the same in number as the protons inside so that the atom as a whole is electrically neutral.

The behavior of atomic electrons is responsible for the chief properties (except mass) of atoms, molecules, solids, and liquids. But the atomic nucleus itself is far from insignificant in the grand scheme of things. The continuing evolution of the universe is powered by energy that comes from nuclear reactions and transformations. Like other stars, the sun obtains its energy in this way. On the earth, nuclear reactors are an important source of electric energy. Since wood and the fossil fuels coal, oil, and natural gas, plus falling water and wind, owe their existence to the sun's rays, *all* the energy at our command has a nuclear origin, direct or indirect.

THE NUCLEUS

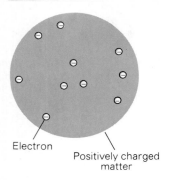

FIG. 7-1
The Thomson model of the atom.
Experiment shows it to be incorrect.

The Rutherford experiment
established the structure of the atom

Until 1911, although it had been established that atoms exist and contain electrons, nothing more was known about them. Since electrons carry negative charges whereas atoms are neutral, everyone agreed that positively charged matter of some kind must be present in atoms. But what kind? And arranged in what way?

One suggestion, made by the British physicist J. J. Thomson in 1898, was that atoms are simply positively charged lumps of matter with electrons embedded in them, like raisins in a fruitcake (Fig. 7-1). Because Thomson had played an important part in discovering the electron, his idea was taken very seriously. But the real atom turned out to be very different.

Rutherford Model of the Atom

An atom is mostly empty space

The most direct way to find out what is inside a fruitcake is to put a finger into it, a method similar to that used by Geiger and Marsden in 1911. At the suggestion of Ernest Rutherford, they used the fast alpha particles emitted by certain radioactive elements as probes. (Alpha particles are discussed later in this chapter. For now, all we need to know about them is that they are almost 8000 times heavier than electrons and each one has a charge of $+2e$.) Geiger and Marsden placed a sample of an alpha-emitting substance behind a lead screen with a small hole in it, as in Fig. 7-2, so that a narrow beam of alpha particles was produced. This beam

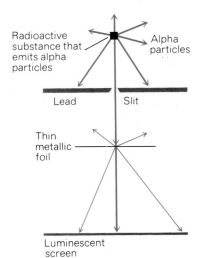

FIG. 7-2
Principle of the Rutherford scattering experiment. The distribution of scattering angles reveals the structure of the atoms in the foil.

was directed at a thin gold foil. A zinc sulfide screen, which gives off a visible flash of light when struck by an alpha particle, was set on the other side of the foil.

It was expected that the alpha particles would go right through the foil with hardly any deflection. This follows from the Thomson model, in which the electric charge inside an atom is assumed to be uniformly spread through its volume. With only weak electric forces exerted on them, alpha particles that pass through a thin foil ought to be deflected only slightly, 1° or less.

What Geiger and Marsden actually found was that, although most of the alpha particles indeed were not deviated by much, a few were scattered through very large angles. Some were even scattered in the backward direction. As Rutherford remarked, "It was as incredible as if you fired a 15-inch shell at a piece of tissue paper and it came back and hit you."

The positive charge and most of the mass of an atom are concentrated in a tiny nucleus at its center

Since alpha particles are relatively heavy and those used in this experiment had high speeds, it was clear that strong forces had to be exerted upon them to cause such marked deflections. The only way to explain the results, Rutherford found, was to picture an atom as being composed of a tiny nucleus, in which its positive charge and nearly all its mass are concentrated, with the electrons some distance away (Fig. 7-3). With an atom largely empty space, it is easy to see why most alpha particles go right through a thin foil. However, when an alpha particle chances to come near a nucleus, the intense electric field there causes it to be

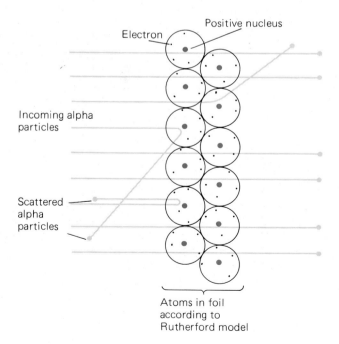

FIG. 7-3
In the Rutherford model of the atom, the positive charge is concentrated in a central nucleus with the electrons some distance away. This model correctly predicts that some alpha particles striking a thin metal foil will be scattered through large angles by the strong electric fields of the nuclei.

scattered through a large angle. The atomic electrons, being so light, do not appreciably affect the alpha particles.

Suppose, as an analogy, that a star approaches the solar system from space at great speed. The chances are good that it will pass through undeflected. Even a collision with a planet would not change its path to any great extent. Only if the star happened to come near the great mass of the sun would its direction change significantly. Similarly, said Rutherford, an alpha particle plows straight through an atom, unaffected by striking an electron now and then. Only a close approach to the heavy central core of an atom can turn it aside.

Ordinary matter, then, is mostly empty space. The solid wood of a table, the steel that supports a bridge, the hard rock underfoot, all are just collections of moving electric charges, comparatively farther away from one another than the sun is from the planets. If all the actual matter, electrons and nuclei, in our bodies could somehow be packed closely together, we would be no larger than specks just visible with a microscope.

An atom is mostly empty space

Nuclear Composition

The nature of an atom depends on the protons in its nucleus

The deflection that an alpha particle undergoes as it comes near an atomic nucleus depends on the amount of positive charge it contains. Rutherford found that all atoms of any particular element have the same nuclear charge and that this charge is different for each element. The nucleus of hydrogen turns out to have a charge of $+e$, where e is the size of the charge of the electron. The nucleus of helium has a charge of $+2e$; that of lithium has a charge of $+3e$; and so on up to the most complex element found on the earth, uranium, whose nucleus has a charge of $+92e$.

As mentioned in Chap. 5, the positive charge in a nucleus comes from particles called *protons* whose charge is $+e$ and whose mass is 1.673×10^{-27} kg, which is 1836 times the electron mass.

Atomic number

The number of protons in the nuclei of the atoms of an element is called the atomic number of the element.

Thus the atomic number of hydrogen is 1, of helium 2, of lithium 3, and of uranium 92. Atomic numbers of the elements are listed in App. II.

The atomic number of an element is its most fundamental property. Atoms with the same atomic number may have somewhat different masses and still be almost identical in other properties. But no change in atomic number is possible without a major change in such properties. The amount of positive charge on the

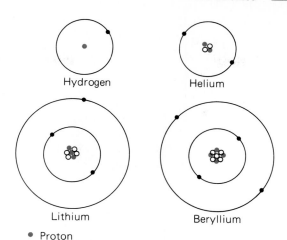

FIG. 7-4
The elements that correspond to the atomic numbers 1, 2, 3, and 4 are respectively hydrogen, helium, lithium, and beryllium. The various particles are actually far too small to be seen even on this scale.

nucleus of an atom serves to determine the basic nature of the atom and to distinguish it from all others.

Atomic nuclei contain both neutrons and protons

The proton is not the only kind of particle found in atomic nuclei. Every nucleus except that of ordinary hydrogen, which consists of a single proton, contains one or more *neutrons* as well (Fig. 7-4). The neutron has no electric charge and its mass of 1.675×10^{-27} kg (1839 times the electron mass) is slightly more than that of the proton. Neutrons and protons make up almost the entire mass of an atom. The electron is so much lighter that even in the largest atoms the total mass of all the electrons is only a small fraction of the mass of a single proton or neutron.

Isotopes

Atoms of the same element may be different

Mass spectrometers measure atomic mass

The mass of an atom can be measured with the help of a *mass spectrometer*. A simple mass spectrometer is shown in Fig. 7-5. Positive ions (atoms missing an electron each) of the element under study are first sent into a device called a velocity selector that permits only ions with a single speed to pass through. The ions then enter a magnetic field which bends their paths into circles. The lighter the ion, the smaller the circle. The mass of an ion can be calculated from its speed and the radius of its circular path. Atomic masses are customarily given in *atomic mass units* (u), where

Atomic mass unit

$$1 \text{ atomic mass unit} = 1 \text{ u} = 1.66 \times 10^{-27} \text{ kg}$$

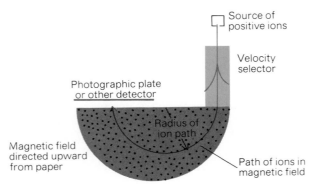

FIG. 7-5
An idealized mass spectrometer. Only ions of a single speed can pass through the velocity selector. In the magnetic field, the ions are bent into circular paths whose radii are proportional to the ion masses; heavy ions are deflected least, light ones most.

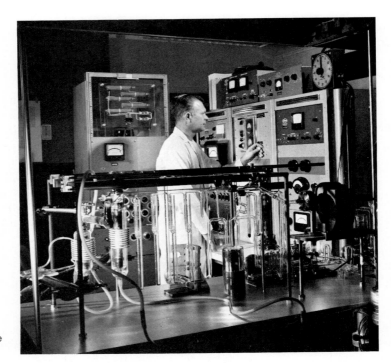

Mass spectrometer used to study the composition of meteorites.

The mass spectrometer reveals that the atoms of a given element do not always have the same mass. In the case of chlorine, for example, about three-quarters of the atoms have a mass of 34.97 u with the rest having a mass of 36.97 u. The result is an average atomic mass of 35.46 for chlorine. The different kinds of chlorine atom are called its *isotopes*.

Isotopes exist because, although all the atoms of an element necessarily have

TABLE 7-1

The Isotopes of Hydrogen, Chlorine, and Zinc.

(The atomic mass of an element is the average of the atomic masses of its isotopes, taking into account their relative abundances. The mass number of a nucleus is the total number of protons and neutrons it contains. Atomic masses are in u.)

| Element | Properties of element | | Properties of isotope | | | | |
	Atomic number	Atomic mass	Protons in nucleus	Neutrons in nucleus	Mass number	Atomic mass	Relative abundance, percent
Hydrogen	1	1.008	1	0	1	1.008	99.985
			1	1	2	2.014	0.015
			1	2	3	3.016	very small
Chlorine	17	35.46	17	18	35	34.97	75.53
			17	20	37	36.97	24.47
Zinc	30	65.37	30	34	64	63.93	48.89
			30	36	66	65.93	27.81
			30	37	67	66.92	4.11
			30	38	68	67.92	18.56
			30	40	70	69.93	0.62

The isotopes of an element differ in the number of neutrons in their nuclei

Deuterium and tritium are hydrogen isotopes

Most of the properties of an element are determined by the electron structures of its atoms

the same number of protons in their nuclei (17 protons for chlorine), the number of neutrons may differ. Thus the lighter isotope of chlorine has nuclei with 18 neutrons and the heavier isotope has nuclei with 20 neutrons (Table 7-1).

Even the element hydrogen has isotopes. Ordinary hydrogen nuclei, of course, consist of a single proton. In addition, an isotope of hydrogen called *deuterium* has nuclei each composed of a proton plus a neutron, and another isotope called *tritium* has nuclei each composed of a proton plus two neutrons (Fig. 7-6). Both these isotopes are found in nature, but only in relatively small amounts. So-called *heavy water* is water in which deuterium atoms instead of hydrogen atoms are present in combination with oxygen.

Most of the physical and chemical properties of an element are determined by the number and arrangement of the electrons in its atoms. Since the isotopes of an element have almost identical electron structures, it is not surprising that the two isotopes of chlorine, for instance, have the same yellow color, the same suffocating odor, the same efficiency as poisons and bleaching agents, and the same ability to combine chemically with metals. Because boiling and freezing points depend somewhat upon atomic mass, these properties differ slightly between the isotopes, as does density. However, such differences are not enough to

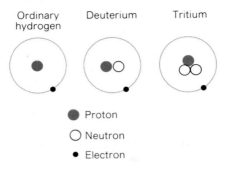

Ordinary hydrogen   Deuterium   Tritium

● Proton
○ Neutron
• Electron

FIG. 7-6
The isotopes of hydrogen.

separate the isotopes of an element in natural processes, which is why their discovery had to wait for the invention of the mass spectrometer.

Describing Atoms and Nuclei

What the symbols mean

Symbols of elements

By convention an atom of an element is represented by an abbreviation of the element's name. For many elements the first letter is used; an atom of oxygen is O, an atom of hydrogen H, an atom of carbon C. When the names of two elements begin with the same letter, two letters are used in the abbreviation for one or both: Cl stands for an atom of chlorine, He for helium, Zn for zinc. For some elements abbreviations of Latin names are used: a copper atom is Cu (cuprum), an iron atom Fe (ferrum), a mercury atom Hg (hydrargyrum). These abbreviations are called *symbols* for the elements. A list of the elements in alphabetical order together with their chemical symbols is given in App. II.

Symbols of nuclei

Because of the existence of isotopes, it is necessary to include more information in the symbols for nuclei. Such symbols follow the pattern

$$\tfrac{A}{Z}X$$

where $X =$ chemical symbol of the element
$Z =$ atomic number of the element
$\quad =$ number of protons in the nucleus
$A =$ mass number of the nucleus
$\quad =$ number of protons and neutrons in the nucleus

Thus the nucleus of the lighter chlorine isotope, which contains 17 protons and 18 neutrons, has the atomic number $Z = 17$ and the mass number $A = 17 + 18 = 35$. Its symbol is accordingly

$$^{35}_{17}Cl$$

Neutrons and protons are jointly called nucleons

The term *nucleon* refers to both protons and neutrons, so that the mass number A is the number of nucleons in a particular nucleus.

RADIOACTIVITY

In 1896 Henri Becquerel accidentally discovered in his Paris laboratory that the element uranium is able to expose covered photographic plates, to ionize gases, and to cause certain substances such as zinc sulfide to glow in the dark. Becquerel concluded that uranium gives off some kind of invisible but penetrating radiation, a property he called *radioactivity*.

Soon afterward, Pierre and Marie Curie, in the course of extracting uranium from the ore pitchblende at the same laboratory, found two other elements that are also radioactive. They named one polonium, after Marie Curie's native Poland. The other, which turned out to be thousands of times more radioactive than uranium, was called radium.

Radioactive tracers

The radioactivity of an element is really due to the radioactivity of one or more of its isotopes. Most elements in nature have no radioactive isotopes, though such isotopes can be prepared artificially and are useful in biological and medical research as "tracers." The procedure is to incorporate a radioisotope in a chemical compound and follow what happens to the compound in a living organism by monitoring the radiation from the isotope. Other elements such as potassium have some stable isotopes and some radioactive ones; a few, such as uranium, have only radioactive isotopes.

Radioactivity is associated with nuclei

Chemical reactions do not change the ability of a radioactive material to emit radiation, nor does heating it in an electric arc or cooling it in liquid air. Radioactivity must therefore be associated with atomic nuclei because these are the only parts of atoms not affected by such treatment.

Radioactive Decay

How unstable nuclei change into stable ones

An alpha particle is a helium nucleus

Early experimenters found that a magnetic field splits the radiation from a radioactive material such as radium into three parts (Fig. 7-7). One part is deflected as though it consists of positively charged particles. Called *alpha particles*, these turned out to be the nuclei of helium atoms. Such nuclei contain two protons and two neutrons, so their symbol is ^4_2He. (These were the probes used in the discovery of the nucleus.)

Beta particles are electrons; gamma rays are high-frequency electromagnetic waves

Another part of the radiation is deflected as though it consists of negatively charged particles. Called *beta particles*, these turned out to be electrons. The rest of the radiation, which is not affected by a magnetic field, consists of *gamma rays*,

FIG. 7-7
The radiations from a radium sample may be analyzed with the help of a magnetic field. Alpha particles are deflected to the left, hence they are positively charged; beta particles are deflected to the right, hence they are negatively charged; and gamma rays are not affected, hence they are uncharged.

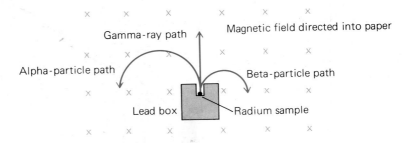

A scintillation counter detects gamma rays and high-speed charged particles by the flashes of light they cause in a luminescent crystal. A sensitive photoelectric cell responds to these flashes, and its electric signals are then fed into a suitable recorder. Here the counter is inside a lead shield to keep out stray radiation.

FIG. 7-8
Alpha particles from radioactive materials are stopped by a piece of cardboard. Beta particles penetrate the cardboard but are stopped by a sheet of aluminum. Even a thick slab of lead may not stop all the gamma rays.

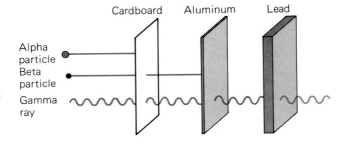

which today are known to be electromagnetic waves whose frequencies are higher than those of x-rays. A gamma ray is emitted by a nucleus that, for one reason or another, has more than its normal amount of energy. The composition of the nucleus does not change in gamma decay, unlike the cases of alpha and beta decay. Gamma rays are the most penetrating of the three kinds of radiation, alpha particles the least (Fig. 7-8).

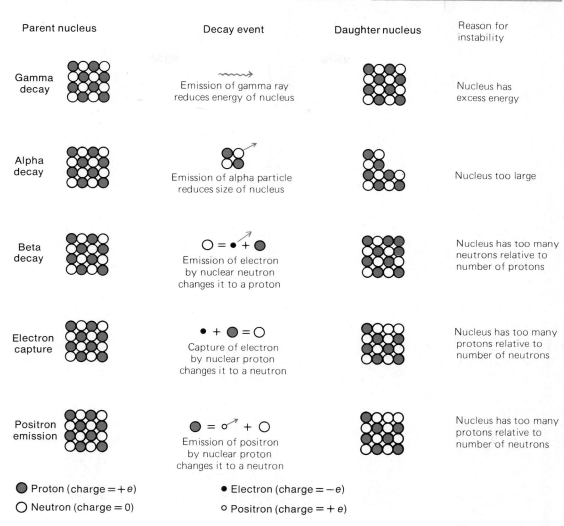

Parent nucleus	Decay event	Daughter nucleus	Reason for instability
Gamma decay	Emission of gamma ray reduces energy of nucleus		Nucleus has excess energy
Alpha decay	Emission of alpha particle reduces size of nucleus		Nucleus too large
Beta decay	Emission of electron by nuclear neutron changes it to a proton		Nucleus has too many neutrons relative to number of protons
Electron capture	Capture of electron by nuclear proton changes it to a neutron		Nucleus has too many protons relative to number of neutrons
Positron emission	Emission of positron by nuclear proton changes it to a neutron		Nucleus has too many protons relative to number of neutrons

● Proton (charge $= +e$)   ● Electron (charge $= -e$)
○ Neutron (charge $= 0$)   ○ Positron (charge $= +e$)

FIG. 7-9
Five kinds of radioactive decay.

Because an alpha particle is a $^4_2$He nucleus, emitting an alpha particle causes a nucleus to have its atomic number reduced by 2 and its mass number reduced by 4 (Fig. 7-9). For example, when the uranium isotope $^{238}_{92}$U undergoes alpha decay, it becomes the thorium isotope $^{234}_{90}$Th:

$$^{238}_{92}\text{U} \longrightarrow \,^{234}_{90}\text{Th} + \,^4_2\text{He}$$

Why alpha decay occurs

Alpha decay occurs in nuclei too large to be stable. The forces that hold protons and neutrons together in a nucleus act only over short distances, and as a result these particles interact strongly only with their nearest neighbors in a nu-

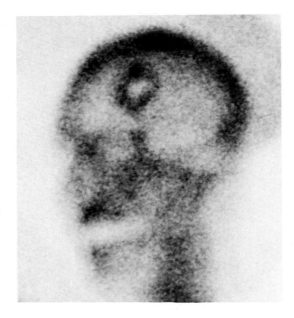

Substances that incorporate a radioactive isotope can be traced in living tissue by the radiation they emit. In this image of the left side of a patient's head a high concentration of the technetium isotope $^{99}_{43}$Tc shows up as a light spot on the temple and indicates a possible malignant tumor there.

Why beta decay occurs

A positron is a positively charged electron

cleus. Because the electrical repulsion of the protons is appreciable throughout the entire nucleus, there is a limit to the ability of neutrons to hold together a large nucleus. This limit is represented by the bismuth isotope $^{209}_{83}$Bi, which is the heaviest stable (that is, nonradioactive) nucleus. All larger nuclei spontaneously transform themselves into smaller ones by alpha decay.

Another factor that can lead to the radioactive decay of a nucleus is a ratio of neutrons to protons that is too large or too small. A small nucleus, such as the helium isotope $^{4}_{2}$He, is stable with equal numbers of neutrons and protons. However, larger nuclei need more neutrons than protons in order to overcome the mutual electrical repulsion of the protons. In beta decay, one of the neutrons in a nucleus with too many of them spontaneously turns into a proton with the emission of an electron, as in Fig. 7-9. A nucleus that emits an electron has its atomic number increased by 1 with no change in its mass number. Thus the rubidium isotope $^{87}_{37}$Rb becomes the strontium isotope $^{87}_{38}$Sr when it undergoes beta decay.

In a nucleus with too few neutrons for stability, one of the protons may become a neutron with the emission of a *positron,* which is an electron that has a positive charge rather than a negative one. Alternatively one of the inner electrons in the atom may be absorbed by one of the protons in its nucleus to form a neutron. Both positron emission and electron capture result in a decrease in atomic number by 1 with no change in mass number.

Sometimes a certain isotope requires a number of radioactive decays before it reaches a stable form. The uranium isotope $^{238}_{92}$U, for instance, undergoes eight alpha decays and six beta decays before it eventually becomes the lead isotope $^{206}_{82}$Pb, which is not radioactive.

Outside a nucleus a neutron decays into a proton and an electron

Free neutrons outside of nuclei are unstable and undergo radioactive decay into a proton and an electron each. Nevertheless it is not correct to think of a neutron as a combination of a proton and an electron: a neutron is a separate particle with unique properties. If we were to try to create a neutron by bringing together a proton and an electron, we would merely get a hydrogen atom as the result, not a neutron. Protons outside a nucleus are apparently stable.

Half-Life

Less and less, but always some left

Nuclei decay at random; the shorter the half-life, the greater the chance a given nucleus will decay in a certain period of time

Radium decay

The *half-life* of a radioisotope is the period of time needed for half of any initial amount of the isotope to decay. As time goes on, the undecayed amount becomes smaller, but it does not become negligible for many half-lives.

Suppose we start with 1 milligram (mg) of the radium isotope $^{226}_{88}Ra$, which alpha decays into the radon isotope $^{222}_{86}Rn$ with a half-life of about 1600 years. After 1600 years, 0.5 mg of radium will remain, with the rest having turned into radon (which, by the way, is a gas; radium is a metal). During the next 1600 years, half the 0.5 mg of radius that is left will itself decay, to leave 0.25 mg of radium (Fig. 7-10). After a further 1600 years, which means a total of 4800 years or three half-lives, 0.125 mg of radium will be left — still a fair amount. Even after 6 half-lives, more than 1 percent of an original sample will remain undecayed.

Half-lives vary widely

Every radioisotope has a characteristic and unchanging half-life. Some half-lives are only a millionth of a second, others are billions of years. Radon, for example, is an alpha emitter like its parent radium, but its half-life is only 3.8 days instead of 1600 years. One of the biggest problems faced by nuclear power plants is the safe disposal of radioactive wastes since some of the isotopes present have long half-lives.

The dating of archeological specimens and rock samples (including those brought back from the moon) by methods based on radioactive decay is described in Chap. 16.

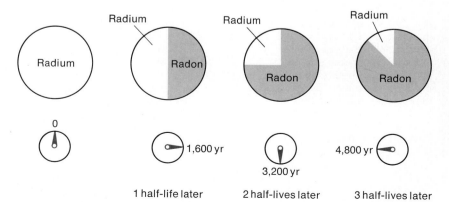

FIG. 7-10
The decay of radium ($^{226}_{88}Ra$) into radon ($^{222}_{86}Rn$). The number of remaining undecayed radium atoms in a sample decreases by one-half in each 1600-year period. This time span is accordingly known as the "half-life" of radium.

CHAPTER 7

Radiation Hazards

Invisible but dangerous

Ionizing radiation is harmful to living things

Like x-rays, the various radiations from radioisotopes are able to ionize matter through which they pass. All ionizing radiation is harmful to living tissue, although if the damage is slight, the tissue often can repair itself with no permanent effect. It is easy to underestimate radiation hazards because there is usually a delay, sometimes of many years, between an exposure and some of its possible consequences, which include cancer, leukemia, and genetic changes that may lead to children handicapped in various ways.

Many useful processes involve ionizing radiation. Some employ such radiation directly, as in the x-rays and gamma rays used in medicine and industry. In other cases the radiation is an unwanted but inescapable by-product, notably in the operation of nuclear reactors and in the disposal of their wastes. It is not always easy to find an appropriate balance between risk and benefit where radiation is concerned. This seems particularly true for medical x-rays, which make up the largest single source of radiation dosage for an average person in the United States (Fig. 7-11).

All x-ray exposures are dangerous; their benefits do not always outweigh the risks

It seems to be an unfortunate fact that many x-ray exposures are made for no strong reason and do more harm than good. In this category are "routine" chest x-rays upon hospital admission, "routine" x-rays as part of regular physical examinations, and "routine" dental x-rays. The once "routine" x-raying of symptomless young women to search for breast cancer is now generally believed to have increased, not decreased, the overall death rate due to cancer. Particularly dangerous is the x-raying of pregnant women, until not long ago another "routine" procedure, which dramatically increases the chance of cancer in their children.

FIG. 7-11
Sources of radiation dosage for an average person in the United States. The total is nearly 2 millisieverts per year, which is about equivalent to two dental x-rays. Actual dosages vary considerably. For example, some people receive more medical x-rays than others; cosmic rays (see Chap. 20) are more intense at high altitudes; concentrations of radioactive minerals exist in some regions; and so on.

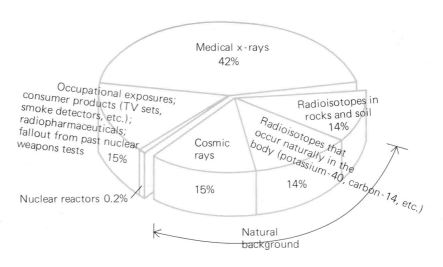

Medical x-rays 42%

Occupational exposures; consumer products (TV sets, smoke detectors, etc.); radiopharmaceuticals; fallout from past nuclear weapons tests 15%

Radioisotopes in rocks and soil 14%

Radioisotopes that occur naturally in the body (potassium-40, carbon-14, etc.)

Cosmic rays 15%

14%

Nuclear reactors 0.2%

Natural background

What is particularly sad about all this is that the carcinogenic properties of x-rays have been known since 1902, only seven years after their discovery. Of course, x-rays have many valuable applications in medicine. The point is that every exposure should have a definite justification that outweighs the risk involved.

The SI unit of radiation dosage is the *sievert,* which is the amount of any radiation that has the same biological effect as that produced by the absorption of 1 J of x- or gamma rays by a kilogram of body tissue. (An older unit, the *rem,* is equal to 0.01 sievert.) Although there is no general agreement, many radiobiologists think that a cancer develops once for every 10 to 70 sieverts of radiation exposure of a population. Such unavoidable natural sources of radiation as cosmic rays (see Chap. 20) and radioactive materials in the earth and in the body itself lead to a dosage rate per person of about 0.8 millisievert/year. Averaged over the United States population, other sources of radiation add 1.06 millisieverts/year, with diagnostic x-rays contributing the largest amount, as shown in Fig. 7-11. Nuclear power stations are responsible for only 0.003 millisievert/year. The total is 1.86 millisieverts/year, about the dose received from two dental x-rays.

BINDING ENERGY

As we all know, the atomic nucleus is the energy source of the reactors that produce more and more of the world's electricity. It is also the energy source of the most destructive weapons ever invented. But there is more to nuclear energy than these applications: nearly all the energy that keeps the sun and stars shining comes from the nucleus as well. Before considering what nuclear energy does, let us look into exactly what it is.

Electron Volt

The energy unit of nuclear physics

The *electron volt,* abbreviated eV, is the energy unit commonly used in nuclear physics. An electron volt is the energy gained by an electron that is accelerated by a potential difference of 1 volt. We recall from Chap. 5 that electric work equals the product of charge and potential difference: $W = QV$. Since the charge on the electron is 1.6×10^{-19} C,

$$W = QV$$
$$1 \text{ eV} = (1.6 \times 10^{-19} \text{ C})(1 \text{ V})$$
$$= 1.6 \times 10^{-19} \text{ J}$$

The electron volt is a very small unit, and frequently its multiples the *MeV* and the *GeV* are used, where

$$1 \text{ MeV} = 1 \text{ million eV} = 10^6 \text{ eV} = 1.6 \times 10^{-13} \text{ J}$$

$$1 \text{ GeV} = 1 \text{ billion eV} = 10^9 \text{ eV} = 1.6 \times 10^{-10} \text{ J}$$

The M and G respectively stand for the prefixes mega ($= 10^6$) and giga ($= 10^9$). The energy equivalent of the atomic mass unit is 931 MeV.

Binding Energy

The missing energy that keeps a nucleus together

Nuclei have less mass than the total mass of their separate neutrons and protons

An ordinary hydrogen atom has a nucleus that consists of a single proton, as its symbol ^1_1H indicates. The isotope of hydrogen called deuterium, ^2_1H, has a neutron as well as a proton in its nucleus. Thus we would expect the mass of the deuterium atom to be equal to the mass of an ordinary ^1_1H hydrogen atom plus the mass of a neutron:

Mass of ^1_1H atom	1.0078 u
$+$ mass of neutron	$+$ 1.0087 u
Expected mass of ^2_1H atom	2.0165 u

However, the measured mass of the ^2_1H atom is only 2.0141 u, which is 0.0024 u *less* than the combined masses of a ^1_1H atom and a neutron (Fig. 7-12).

Nuclei are stable because they lack enough mass to break up into separate neutrons and protons

Deuterium atoms are not the only ones that have less mass than the combined masses of the particles they are composed of — *all* atoms are like that. To explain the "missing" mass, all we need do is recall the formula $E = mc^2$ that relates energy and mass. What must happen when a ^2_1H nucleus is formed is that a certain amount of energy is given off due to the action of the forces that hold the neutron

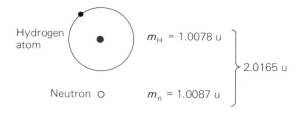

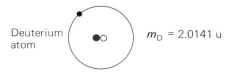

FIG. 7-12
The mass of a deuterium atom (^2_1H) is less than the sum of the masses of a hydrogen atom (^1_1H) and a neutron. The energy equivalent of the missing mass is called the binding energy of the nucleus.

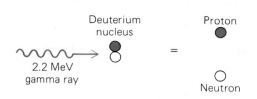

FIG. 7-13
The binding energy of the deuterium nucleus is 2.2 MeV. A gamma ray whose energy is 2.2 MeV or more can split a deuterium nucleus into a proton and a neutron. A gamma ray whose energy is less than 2.2 MeV cannot do this.

and proton together, just as energy is given off when a stone strikes the earth due to the action of gravity. In the case of a nucleus, the energy comes from the mass of the particles that join together, so the resulting nucleus has less mass than the total mass of the particles before they interact.

Since the energy equivalent of 1 u of mass is 931 MeV, the energy that corresponds to the missing deuterium mass of 0.0024 u is

$$\text{Missing energy} = (0.0024 \text{ u})(931 \text{ MeV/u}) = 2.2 \text{ MeV}$$

To test this interpretation of the missing mass, we can perform experiments to see how much energy is needed to break apart a deuterium nucleus into a separate neutron and proton. The required energy turns out to be 2.2 MeV, just as it should (Fig. 7-13). When less energy than 2.2 MeV is given to a $^2_1$H nucleus, the nucleus stays together. When the added energy is more than 2.2 MeV, the extra energy goes into kinetic energy of the neutron and proton as they fly apart.

The binding energy of a nucleus is the energy needed to break it apart

The energy equivalent of the missing mass of a nucleus is called the *binding energy* of the nucleus. The greater its binding energy, the more the energy that must be supplied to break up the nucleus.

Binding energies are very high

Nuclear binding energies are strikingly high. The range for stable nuclei is from 2.2 MeV for $^2_1$H (deuterium) to 1640 MeV for $^{209}_{83}$Bi (an isotope of the metal bismuth). Larger nuclei are all unstable and decay radioactively. To appreciate how high binding energies are, we can compare them with more familiar energies in terms of kilojoules of energy per kilogram of mass. In these units, a typical binding energy is 8×10^{11} kJ/kg — 800 billion kJ/kg. By contrast, to boil water involves a heat of vaporization of a mere 2260 kJ/kg, and even the heat given off by burning gasoline is only 4.7×10^4 kJ/kg, 17 million times smaller.

Binding Energy per Nucleon

The most important graph in science

The *binding energy per nucleon* for a given nucleus is found by dividing its total binding energy by the number of nucleons (protons and neutrons) it contains. Thus the binding energy per nucleon for $^2_1$H is 2.2 MeV/2 = 1.1 MeV/nucleon, and for $^{209}_{83}$Bi it is 1640 MeV/209 = 7.8 MeV/nucleon.

Figure 7-14 shows the binding energy per nucleon plotted against the number

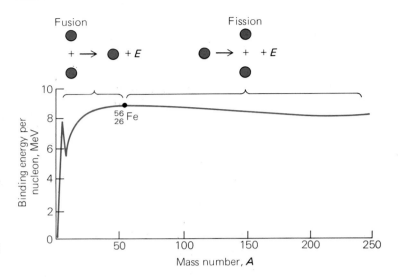

FIG. 7-14
The binding energy per nucleon is a maximum for nuclei of mass number $A = 56$. Such nuclei are the most stable. When two light nuclei join to form a heavier one, a process called *fusion*, the greater binding energy of the product nucleus causes energy to be given off. When a heavy nucleus is split into two lighter ones, a process called *fission*, the greater binding energy of the product nuclei also causes energy to be given off.

Large and small nuclei are less stable than those of intermediate size

Nuclear fission

of nucleons in various atomic nuclei. The greater the binding energy per nucleon, the more stable the nucleus is. The graph has its maximum of 8.8 MeV/nucleon when the number of nucleons is 56. The nucleus that has 56 protons and neutrons is $^{56}_{26}$Fe, an iron isotope. This is the most stable nucleus of them all, since the most energy is needed to pull a nucleon away from it.

Two remarkable conclusions can be drawn from the curve of Fig. 7-14. The first is that, if we somehow split a heavy nucleus into two medium-size ones, each of the new nuclei will have *less* binding energy per nucleon than the original nucleus did. The extra energy will be given off, and it can be a lot. For instance, if the uranium nucleus $^{235}_{92}$U is broken into two smaller nuclei, the binding energy difference per nucleon is about 0.8 MeV. The total energy given off is therefore

$$\left(0.8 \ \frac{\text{MeV}}{\text{nucleon}}\right)(235 \text{ nucleons}) = 188 \text{ MeV}$$

This is a truly enormous amount of energy to be produced in a single atomic event. Ordinary chemical reactions involve rearrangements of the electrons in atoms and liberate only a few eV per reacting atom. Splitting a heavy nucleus, which is called *nuclear fission*, thus involves a hundred million times more energy per atom than, say, the burning of coal or oil.

Nuclear fusion

The other notable conclusion is that joining two light nuclei together to give a single nucleus of medium size also means less binding energy per nucleon in the new nucleus. For instance, if two $^{2}_{1}$H deuterium nuclei combine to form a $^{4}_{2}$He helium nucleus, over 23 MeV is released. Such a process, called *nuclear fusion*, is also a very effective way to obtain energy. In fact, nuclear fusion is the main energy source of the sun and other stars, as described in Chap. 19.

The binding-energy curve is important because it is the key to energy production in the universe

The graph of Fig. 7-14 has a good claim to being the most significant in all of science. The fact that binding energy exists at all means that nuclei more complex than the single proton of hydrogen can be stable. Such stability in turn accounts for the existence of the various elements and so for the existence of the many and diverse forms of matter we see around us. Because the curve peaks in the middle, we have the explanation for the energy that powers, directly or indirectly, the evolution of the entire universe: it comes from the fusion of protons and neutrons to form heavier nuclei. And the harnessing of nuclear fission in reactors and weapons has irreversibly changed modern civilization.

FISSION AND FUSION

The words "nuclear energy" bring to mind two images. One is of a huge building in which a mysterious thing called a nuclear reactor turns an absurdly small amount of uranium into an absurdly large amount of energy. The other image is of a mushroom-shaped cloud rising from the explosion of a nuclear bomb, an explosion that can level the largest city with deaths in the millions.

The first image is a picture of hope, hope for a future of plentiful, cheap, pollution-free energy — a hope only partly fulfilled. The second image is a picture of horror — but such bombs have not been used in war for forty years. So nuclear energy has not turned out as yet to be either the overwhelming blessing or the overwhelming curse it might have been.

As for what lies ahead, it seems possible that fusion energy will someday become a reality, to give all the benefits once envisioned for fission energy without many of its drawbacks. It also seems possible that more countries than the handful that now have nuclear weapons will learn to make them, a peril today's world leaders do not seem to be taking very seriously as they maneuver for short-term political and economic advantage.

Nuclear Fission

Divide and conquer

As we have seen, a great deal of binding energy will be released if we can break a large nucleus into smaller ones. But nuclei are ordinarily not at all easy to split. What we need is a way to disrupt a heavy nucleus without using more energy than we get back from the process.

The answer came in 1939 with the discovery that a nucleus of the uranium isotope $^{235}_{92}$U undergoes fission when struck by a neutron. It is not the impact of the neutron that has this effect. Instead, the $^{235}_{92}$U nucleus absorbs the neutron to become $^{236}_{92}$U, and the new nucleus is so unstable that almost at once it explodes into two fragments (Fig. 7-15). Isotopes of several other elements as well were later found to be fissionable by neutrons in similar processes.

An incident neutron can cause certain heavy nuclei to undergo fission

Most of the energy liberated in fission goes into kinetic energy of the new

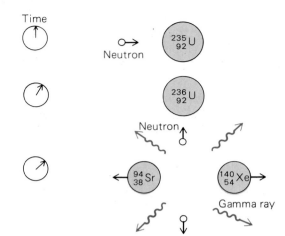

FIG. 7-15
In nuclear fission an absorbed
neutron causes a heavy nucleus to
split into two parts. Several neutrons
and gamma rays are emitted in the
process. The smaller nuclei shown
here are typical of those produced
in the fission of $^{235}_{92}$U.

nuclei. These nuclei are usually radioactive, some with long half-lives. Hence the
products of fission, which are found in reactor fuel rods and in the fallout from a
nuclear weapon burst, are extremely dangerous and remain so for many generations.

Chain reaction

When a nucleus splits during fission, two or three neutrons are set free at the
same time. This suggests a remarkable possibility. Perhaps, under the right conditions, the neutrons emitted by a uranium nucleus as it undergoes fission can cause
other uranium nuclei to split; the neutrons from these other fissions might then go
on to split still more uranium nuclei; and so on, with a series of fission reactions
spreading through a mass of uranium. A *chain reaction* of this kind was first
demonstrated in Chicago in 1942 under the direction of Enrico Fermi, an Italian
physicist who had not long before taken refuge in the United States. Figure 7-16 is a
sketch of the events that occur in a chain reaction.

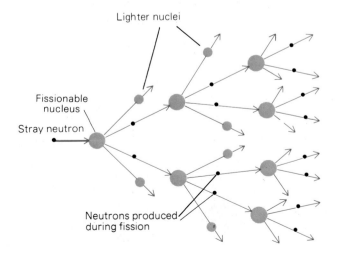

FIG. 7-16
Sketch of a chain reaction. The
reaction is self-sustaining if at least
one neutron from each fission event
on the average induces another
fission event. If more than one
neutron per fission on the average
induces another fission, the reaction
is explosive.

In a nuclear reactor, fission occurs at a controlled rate

The condition for a chain reaction to occur in an assembly of fissionable material is simple: at least one neutron produced by each fission must, on the average, lead to another fission and not either escape or be absorbed without producing fission. If too few neutrons cause fissions, the reaction slows down and stops. If precisely one neutron per fission causes another fission, energy is released at a steady rate. This is the case in a nuclear reactor, which is an arrangement for producing controlled power from nuclear fission.

In an atomic bomb, uncontrolled fission produces an explosion

What happens if more than one neutron from each fission causes other fissions? In such an event the chain reaction rapidly increases in speed and the energy release is so fast that an explosion results. An "atomic" bomb is a device designed to make use of this effect. The destructive power of nuclear weapons does not stop with their detonation but continues long afterward through the radioactive debris that is produced and widely dispersed. Tens of thousands of nuclear weapons of various kinds now exist. The explosion of even a few of them would, by causing dust clouds that block sunlight, probably lead to months of darkness and bitter cold that might well doom those living things that were able to survive the deadly effects of the blasts themselves and the subsequent radioactive fallout.

How a Reactor Works

From uranium to electricity

A nuclear reactor produces heat which can be used for various purposes

For every gram of uranium that undergoes fission in a reactor, 2.6 tons of coal must be burned in an ordinary power plant of the same rating. The energy given off in a nuclear reactor becomes heat in its interior, and this heat is removed by circulating

Research reactor at Brookhaven National Laboratory on Long Island, New York, has a power output of 40 MW and a neutron flux of 1.6×10^{15} neutrons per cm^2 per s.

a liquid or gas coolant. The hot coolant is then used to boil water, and the resulting steam is fed to a turbine that can power an electric generator, a ship, or a submarine.

Only a small proportion of natural uranium is fissionable

In order for a chain reaction to occur at a steady rate, one neutron from each fission must cause another fission to take place. Since each fission in ^{235}U liberates an average of 2.5 neutrons, no more than 1.5 neutrons per fission can be lost on the average. However, natural uranium contains only 0.7 percent of the fissionable isotope ^{235}U. The rest is ^{238}U, an isotope that readily captures the fast neutrons emitted during the fission of ^{235}U but does not undergo fission afterward. The neutrons absorbed by ^{238}U are therefore wasted, and since 99.3 percent of natural uranium is ^{238}U, too many disappear for a chain reaction to occur in a solid lump of natural uranium.

There is an ingenious way around this problem. As it happens, ^{238}U tends to pick up only fast neutrons, not slow ones. In addition, slow neutrons are more apt to induce fission in ^{235}U than fast ones. If the fast neutrons from fission are slowed down, then, many more will produce further fissions despite the small proportion of ^{235}U that is present.

The moderator in a reactor slows down neutrons

To slow down fission neutrons, the uranium fuel in a reactor is mixed with a *moderator,* a substance whose nuclei absorb energy from fast neutrons during collisions. In general, the more nearly equal in mass colliding particles are, the more energy is transferred. A ball bounces off a wall with little loss of energy, but it can lose up to all its energy when it strikes another ball of the same mass. Since hydrogen nuclei are protons with nearly the same mass as neutrons, hydrogen is widely used as a moderator in the form of water, H_2O, each of whose molecules contains two hydrogen atoms along with an oxygen atom.

Enriched uranium contains more of the fissionable isotope ^{235}U than natural uranium

Unfortunately a neutron striking a proton has a certain tendency to stick to it to form a deuterium nucleus, ^2_1H. As a result, a reactor whose moderator is water cannot use ordinary uranium as fuel but must instead use *enriched* uranium whose ^{235}U content has been increased to about 3 percent. Most enriched uranium is produced by the gaseous diffusion process in which uranium hexafluoride (UF_6) gas is exposed to a series of porous barriers. Because of their smaller mass, molecules of $^{235}UF_6$ are slightly more likely to pass through each barrier than molecules of $^{238}UF_6$. In this way any desired amount of enrichment can be achieved. Another method is to use centrifuges for the separation, much as butter is separated from cream in a dairy. Uranium highly enriched in ^{235}U is used in one type of nuclear weapon.

Reactor design

The fuel for a water-moderated reactor consists of uranium oxide (UO_2) pellets sealed in long, thin zirconium alloy tubes. Rods of cadmium or boron, which are good absorbers of slow neutrons, can be slid in and out of the reactor core to control the rate of the chain reaction. In the most common type of reactor, the water that circulates around the fuel in the core is kept at a high pressure, about 155 atmospheres, to prevent boiling. The water, which acts as both moderator and coolant, is passed through a heat exchanger to produce steam that drives a turbine (Fig. 7-17). Such a reactor might contain 90 tons of UO_2 and operate at 3400 MW to yield 1100 MW of electric power. The reactor fuel must be replaced every few years as its ^{235}U content is used up.

The fuel rods of a nuclear reactor consist of pellets of uranium oxide sealed in tubes of zirconium alloy.

FIG. 7-17
Basic design of the most common type of nuclear power plant. Water under pressure is both the moderator and coolant, and transfers heat from the chain reaction in the fuel rods of the core to a steam generator. The resulting steam then passes out of the containment shell, which serves as a barrier to protect the outside world from accidents to the reactor, and is directed to a turbine that drives an electric generator. In a typical plant, the reactor vessel is 13.5 m high and 4.4 m in diameter and weighs 385 tons. It contains about 90 tons of uranium oxide in the form of 50,952 fuel rods each 3.85 m long and 9.5 mm in diameter. Four steam generators are used instead of the single one shown here, and a number of turbine-generators.

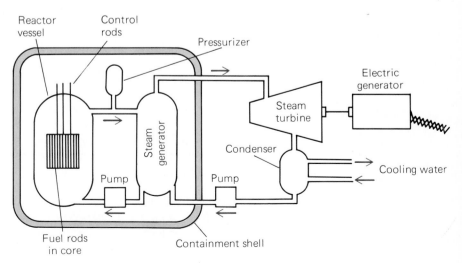

Other kinds of reactor have also been developed. In one, "heavy water," whose molecules contain deuterium ($^2_1$H) atoms rather than ordinary hydrogen ($^1_1$H) atoms, is used as moderator and coolant. The advantage here is that deuterium nuclei are much less likely to capture neutrons than hydrogen nuclei, which permits ordinary uranium to be used as fuel. The disadvantage is that heavy water is expensive.

Another type of reactor uses graphite, a form of pure carbon (the "lead" in a pencil is largely graphite), as the moderator. Although less effective than hydrogen in slowing down neutrons, graphite has little tendency to pick them up and is cheap. Graphite-moderated reactors can be cooled with gases such as helium and carbon dioxide and operate at higher temperatures than water-cooled reactors, which means higher thermal efficiency (Chap. 4).

Gas-cooled reactors

Gas-cooled reactors are safer than water-cooled ones, partly because there is less to go wrong and partly because the huge mass of graphite slows down the rate of temperature rise in case the coolant gas stops circulating. The cooling system in any reactor is a critical element because, even if the chain reaction is stopped by the control rods, the radioactive fission products in the fuel rods continue to decay and give off heat. Without any water around them, the fuel rods in a water-cooled reactor may melt in a few minutes, with disastrous results. In a gas-cooled reactor, many hours would be needed for meltdown if the cooling system fails, which gives time to correct the situation. The United States has one gas-cooled reactor, near Denver, Colorado; over fifty are operating in other countries.

Plutonium

Another fissionable material

How plutonium is produced

Some nonfissionable isotopes can be changed into fissionable ones by absorbing neutrons. A notable example is ^{238}U, which becomes ^{239}U when it captures a fast neutron. This uranium isotope beta-decays soon after its creation into the neptunium isotope $^{239}_{93}$Np. In turn $^{239}_{93}$Np beta-decays into the plutonium isotope $^{239}_{94}$Pu (Fig. 7-18). Like ^{235}U, ^{239}Pu undergoes fission when it absorbs a neutron and can support a chain reaction.

A certain amount of plutonium is produced in the normal operation of a reactor. Because plutonium is chemically different from uranium, it is not hard to separate ^{239}Pu from the uranium that remains in a used fuel rod. The separated ^{239}Pu can then serve as a reactor fuel itself.

Breeder reactors convert nonfissionable ^{238}U into fissionable plutonium

A *breeder reactor* is one especially designed to produce more plutonium than the ^{235}U it consumes. Because the otherwise useless ^{238}U is 140 times more abundant than the fissionable ^{235}U, the widespread use of breeder reactors would mean that known reserves of uranium could fuel reactors for many centuries to come. Because plutonium can also be used in nuclear weapons (unlike the slightly enriched uranium that fuels ordinary reactors), the widespread use of breeder reactors would also complicate the control of nuclear weapons. Several breeder reactors are operating today, all of them outside the United States.

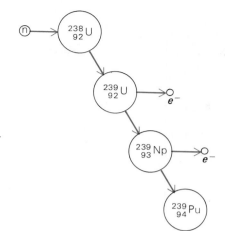

FIG. 7-18
The nonfissionable uranium isotope ^{238}U, which makes up 99.3% of natural uranium, becomes the fissionable plutonium isotope ^{239}Pu by absorbing a neutron and beta-decaying twice. This transformation is the basis of the breeder reactor, which produces many times more nuclear fuel in the form of plutonium than it uses up in the form of ^{235}U.

A Nuclear World?

Not yet

Fission energy was first put to use in 1945 when two atomic bombs, one made from ^{235}U and the other from plutonium, were exploded over Hiroshima and Nagasaki to end the war with Japan. Six years later the first electricity from a nuclear reactor was generated in Idaho. Since then hundreds of reactors have been built around the world.

Nuclear power stations are in wide use

The surge in oil prices that began in 1973, together with the realization of how easily oil imports could be cut off, led many countries to invest heavily in nuclear power stations. Worldwide nuclear energy production has risen by 20 percent per year since 1973, and in 1984 it was over 100,000 MW — the equivalent of 4.5 million barrels of oil per day. By 1990 that figure is expected to double, with some countries, such as France, then obtaining over half their electricity from reactors.

In the United States, in 1983 nuclear energy was responsible for more than one-eighth of the electricity being generated, in second place behind coal. Reactors under construction in that year will increase nuclear electricity to 20 or 25 percent of the total when they are completed (Fig. 7-19). All in all, it would seem that nuclear energy is a great success. Nevertheless, construction has not begun on any new nuclear power stations in this country since 1979, and no new ones are planned. Why?

Three Mile Island

The year 1979 is significant because, in March 1979, failures in its cooling system disabled one of the reactors at Three Mile Island in Pennsylvania. A certain amount of radioactive material escaped from the plant. Although it is impossible for a nuclear reactor to explode in the way an atomic bomb does, poor design, shoddy construction, inadequate maintenance, and errors in operation — all present at Three Mile Island — can lead to breakdowns that put large numbers of

FIG. 7-19
Nuclear power plants in operation or under construction in the United States in 1983. The total is 142. No new plants have been ordered since 1979.

Why nuclear energy is not being expanded in the United States

people at risk. Even though a true catastrophe was narrowly avoided, the Three Mile Island incident made it clear that the dangers associated with nuclear energy are real.

The impact of Three Mile Island on public feeling in the United States about nuclear energy came only in part from the fact of the accident itself. Statements made by company and government officials turned out not to have given the whole truth about what was happening. Another source of unease was the discovery that, throughout the entire nuclear program, the balance between safety and cost had not always favored safety. Far too many accidents were taking place all the time, even though on a smaller scale than at Three Mile Island (and hardly to be compared in their consequences with the damage to the nation's health due to coal-fired power plants). Fairly or unfairly, many people who were basically in favor of nuclear energy developed a lack of trust in both the industry and the government agencies that were supposed to be regulating it.

After 1979, it was inevitable that greater safety would be built into new reactors, adding to their expense. Other costs of construction were going up, too. At the same time, demand for electricity in the United States was not increasing as fast as had been expected; indeed, it even dropped in some years. One reason was a successful effort at conservation. Another was a decline in some of the industries, such as steel, cars, and chemicals, that are heavy users of electricity. The result of all these factors was that new reactors made less economic sense than before, which, together with widespread public displeasure, led to a halt in plans to expand nuclear energy in the United States.

Elsewhere the situation is quite different. In many developing countries without the natural resources of the United States, nuclear reactors seem the best way at present to meet the energy needs of fast-growing populations. In most of the world, coal and oil are expensive, so nuclear energy is favored from a commerical point of view. Public hostility is less abroad, also. The continuing expansion of nuclear energy outside the United States is not limited to generating electricity. In the Soviet Union, for example, reactors are being built to provide heating for the cities of Gorky, Voronezh, and Odessa.

Nuclear waste disposal

Quite apart from the safety of reactors themselves is the issue of what to do with the wastes they produce. Even if old fuel rods are processed to separate out the valuable uranium and plutonium they contain, what is left is still highly radioactive. Although a lot of the activity will be gone in a few months and much of the rest in a few hundred years, some of the radioisotopes have half-lives in the millions of years. At present over 12,000 tons of spent nuclear fuel are being stored in the United States.

The approach being explored most actively is to incorporate nuclear wastes in a borosilicate glass similar to Pyrex. The liquid wastes would be converted to solids and added to the normal ingredients for the glass in a ratio of about 1 : 3. The mixture would then be heated until it melts and cast into blocks for burial deep in the earth. The right location is easy to specify but not easy to find: stable geologically with no earthquakes likely, no nearby population centers, a type of rock that does not disintegrate in the presence of heat and radiation but is easy to drill into, and little or no groundwater that might become contaminated. A key question is just how durable borosilicate glass will turn out to be over the long term. For this reason an alternative process that yields a tough rocklike ceramic is also being considered.

Nuclear Fusion

The energy source of the future?

Enormous as the energy produced by fission is, the fusion of light nuclei to form heavier ones can give out even more per kilogram of starting materials. Nuclear fusion promises to become the ultimate source of energy on the earth: safe, nonpolluting, and with the oceans themselves supplying limitless fuel.

Requirements for a fusion reactor

Three conditions must be met by a successful fusion reactor. The first is a high temperature — 50 million °C or more — so that the nuclei are moving fast enough to come together in collisions despite the repulsion of their positive electric charges. The second condition is a fairly high density of the nuclei to assure that such collisions are frequent. Third, the assembly of reacting nuclei must remain together for a long enough time to give off more energy than the reactor's operation takes. The last two conditions are related, since the more nuclei there are per cm^3, the shorter the minimum confinement time for a net energy output.

A practical fusion reaction

The fusion reaction that is the basis of current research involves the combination of a deuterium nucleus and a tritium nucleus to form a helium nucleus:

$$\;^2_1\text{H} \quad + \quad \;^3_1\text{H} \quad \longrightarrow \quad \;^4_2\text{He} \quad + \quad \;^1_0 n \quad + \; 17.6 \text{ MeV}$$

Deuterium   Tritium   Helium   Neutron   Energy

Most of the energy given off is carried by the neutron that is emitted. To recover this energy, it is proposed to surround the reactor chamber with liquid lithium, which would absorb energy from the neutrons and carry it to a steam generator. (Lithium is the lightest metal, with an atomic number of 3.) The steam would then power a turbine connected to an electric generator, as with fossil-fuel and fission electric plants.

About 1 part in 5000 of the hydrogen in the waters of the world is deuterium, which adds up to a total of over 10^{15} tons — no scarcity there. Sea water contains too little tritium for economic recovery, but, as it happens, neutrons react with lithium nuclei to yield tritium and helium. Thus, once a fusion reactor is given an initial charge of tritium, it will make enough additional tritium for its further operation.

The big problem in making fusion energy practical is to achieve the necessary combination of temperature, density, and confinement time. Such a combination occurs in the explosion of a fission bomb, and including deuterium and tritium in such a bomb leads to a still more destructive weapon, the "hydrogen" bomb.

Two approaches to the controlled release of fusion energy are being explored. In one, strong magnetic fields are used to contain the reacting nuclei.

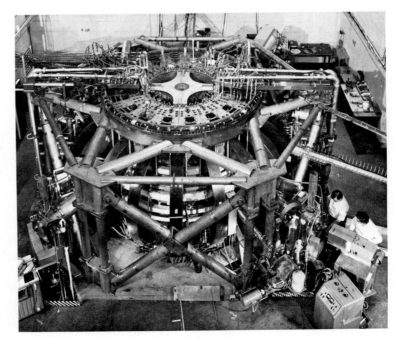

The Princeton Large Torus (PLT) is a device used in research into fusion energy. Based upon a Russian design called a tokamak, it is located at Princeton University. In the PLT, a very hot, ionized gas in a doughnut-shaped chamber 12 ft in diameter is kept away from the chamber walls, where it would be cooled and pick up impurities, by strong magnetic fields. The ionized gas in a tokamak reactor must be heated electrically to about 100 million K and be confined for at least a second in order that enough nuclear fusion reactions occur to yield a worthwhile energy output.

Three decades of research have led to larger and larger magnetic fusion reactors of several designs that seem close to success. Because of the strength needed for the magnetic fields and the volume of several thousand cubic meters they must occupy, electromagnets made with superconducting coils are used. Much less energy is needed to maintain a current in a superconductor than in an ordinary conductor such as copper, but the disadvantage is that superconductivity occurs only at temperatures near absolute zero, $-273°C$, so elaborate refrigeration is needed.

The other approach to practical fusion energy involves using energetic beams to both heat and compress tiny deuterium-tritium pellets to produce what are, in effect, miniature hydrogen-bomb explosions. A series of beams would strike each pellet momentarily from all sides to keep it in place as it is squeezed together. If ten pellets the size of a grain of sand are ignited every second, the energy output would be enough to provide electric power to a city of 175,000 people. Laser beams are being tried for this purpose as well as beams of charged particles such as electrons and protons. It remains to be seen whether magnetic confinement or the pellet method will prove the more practical. It also remains to be seen when a successful fusion reactor will begin to operate.

ELEMENTARY PARTICLES

The building blocks of ordinary matter are atoms, of which over a hundred different kinds are known. Are atoms *elementary particles* in the sense that they cannot

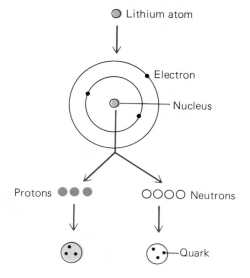

FIG. 7-20
The search for truly elementary particles has led to the discovery of particles within particles. Today all ordinary matter seems to be made up of electrons and quarks. Shown are the various levels of organization of a lithium atom.

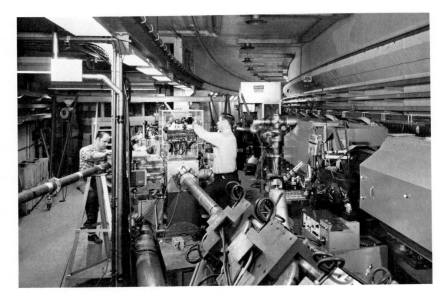

The alternating-gradient synchrotron at Brookhaven National Laboratory accelerates protons to 33 GeV by electromagnetic induction. Protons with energies of 50 MeV from a linear accelerator behind the two men enter the synchrotron through the pipe in the foreground, and then are held in a fixed orbit by the magnets at right while they acquire energy from a changing magnetic field.

The 80-in. hydrogen bubble chamber at Brookhaven. The pressure on the liquid hydrogen at −247°C in the chamber is suddenly reduced to coincide with the arrival of particles from a synchrotron where they have been accelerated to velocities close to that of light. The bubbles that form along the ion trails of charged particles are photographed for subsequent analysis. The main features of the device are: (1) electromagnet to deflect charged particles, which enables their momenta to be determined; (2) beam window of the bubble chamber; (3) vacuum pump; (4) chamber expansion system; (5) liquid hydrogen pipe; (6) camera system; and (7) undercarriage for moving the entire 450-ton assembly.

be broken down further? The answer is no, since every atom consists of a central nucleus surrounded by one or more electrons. Electrons are certainly elementary particles, but nuclei are not: they are made up of protons and neutrons. Because protons and neutrons cannot be split into anything else in experiments, for a long time they were considered to be true elementary particles, like electrons. Today, however, it seems likely that protons and neutrons are actually composed of highly unusual particles called *quarks* (Fig. 7-20). Although quarks have never been isolated in the laboratory, a lot of evidence supports their existence.

A large number of other particles have been discovered in experiments in which atomic nuclei are bombarded by high-energy protons and electrons. These particles are all unstable and seem to play no role in the behavior of ordinary matter. None of them exist for longer than a few millionths of a second, and most have lifetimes of less than a billionth of a second. They decay in various ways, often in a series of steps, and usually end up as protons, neutrons, or electrons; a few become gamma rays. Several of the unstable particles are truly elementary, cousins of the electron. The rest apparently are combinations of quarks, like the proton and neutron.

Antiparticles

The same but different

What an antiparticle is

Nearly all elementary particles have *antiparticles*. The antiparticle of a given particle has the same mass and behaves similarly in most respects, but its electric charge is opposite in sign. Thus the positron e^+ is the antiparticle of the electron e^-, and the negatively charged *antiproton* p^- is the antiparticle of the proton p^+. Certain uncharged elementary particles, such as the neutron, have antiparticles because they have properties other than charge which are different in the particle and its antiparticle.

Matter becomes energy when a particle and its antiparticle annihilate each other

Antiparticles such as positrons and antiprotons are not easy to find for a very basic reason. When a particle and an antiparticle of the same kind happen to come together, they destroy each other in a process called *annihilation*. The lost mass reappears in the form of gamma rays when electrons and positrons are annihilated (Fig. 7-21). Unstable particles of various kinds are also produced when protons and antiprotons (or neutrons and antineutrons) are annihilated. The charges

FIG. 7-21
The mutual annihilation of an electron and a positron results in a pair of gamma rays whose total energy is equal to mc^2, where m is the total mass of the electron and positron.

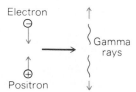

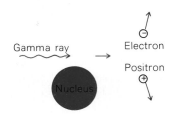

Gamma ray → Electron

Positron

Nucleus

Energy becomes matter when a particle and its antiparticle are created simultaneously

simply vanish, which does not affect the electrical neutrality of the universe since the amounts of + and − charge that disappear are equal.

The reverse of annihilation can also take place, with energy becoming matter and electric charge being created where none existed before. In the remarkable process of *pair production*, a particle and its antiparticle materialize when a high-energy gamma ray passes near an atomic nucleus (Fig. 7-22). According to Einstein's formula $E = mc^2$, the energy equivalent of the electron mass is 0.51 MeV. To produce an electron-positron pair therefore requires a gamma ray whose energy is at least 1.02 MeV. If the gamma ray has more energy than 1.02 MeV, the excess goes into the kinetic energies of the electron and positron. The minimum energy needed for a proton-antiproton or neutron-antineutron pair is nearly 2 GeV. The antiparticles formed in pair production exist for only a short time before they meet up with their particle counterparts in ordinary matter and are annihilated.

There seems to be no reason why atoms could not be composed of antipro-

Bubble-chamber photograph of electron-positron pair formation. The incident beam was composed of antiprotons, one of which interacted with a hydrogen nucleus (which is a proton) in the liquid hydrogen of the bubble chamber to produce an uncharged particle. This particle, which left no track, decayed into an electron and a positron. A magnetic field caused the electron and positron to move in opposite curved paths, which are spirals because the particles lost energy as they moved through the chamber.

Antimatter

tons, antineutrons, and positrons. Such *antimatter* ought to behave exactly like ordinary matter. Of course, if antimatter ever came in contact with ordinary matter, the same amount of both would disappear in a burst of energy. But we can imagine that, when the universe was formed, equal quantities of matter and antimatter came into being that became separate galaxies of stars. If this were true, elsewhere in the universe would be stars, planets, and living things made entirely of antimatter.

The universe is composed entirely or almost entirely of matter

The idea that the universe consists of both matter and antimatter is an attractive one, but unfortunately does not seem to be the case. Although galaxies are far apart on the average, now and then two of them collide. A collision between a matter galaxy and an antimatter galaxy would be a violent explosion giving rise to a flood of gamma rays. No such gamma rays are observed, from which astronomers conclude that there cannot be much, if any, antimatter in the universe. Current theories of elementary particles suggest that matter and antimatter may not be exactly mirror images of each other, with matter being favored for survival when the universe came into being in the "big bang" described in Chap. 20.

Fundamental Interactions

Less is more

Elementary particles interact with each other in only four ways. These fundamental interactions seem able to account for all the physical processes and structures in the universe on all scales of size from atomic nuclei to galaxies of stars (Fig. 7-23). In order of decreasing strength these interactions are:

The four fundamental interactions give rise to all physical processes

1. The *strong interaction,* which holds protons and neutrons together to form atomic nuclei despite the mutual repulsion of the protons. The forces produced by this interaction have short ranges, only about 10^{-15} m, which is why nuclei are limited in size. Because the strong interaction is what its name suggests, nuclear binding energies are high. Electrons are not affected by the strong interaction.

2. The *electromagnetic interaction,* which gives rise to electric and magnetic forces between charged particles. This interaction is responsible for the structures of atoms, molecules, liquids, and solids. The force exerted when a bat hits a ball is electromagnetic. Although the electromagnetic interaction is about 100 times weaker than the strong interaction at short distances, electromagnetic forces are unlimited in range and, unlike strong forces, act on electrons.

3. The *weak interaction,* which affects all particles and, by causing beta decay, helps determine the compositions of atomic nuclei. The range of this interaction is even shorter than that of the strong interaction, and 10 trillion times less powerful.

4. The *gravitational interaction,* which is responsible for the attractive force one

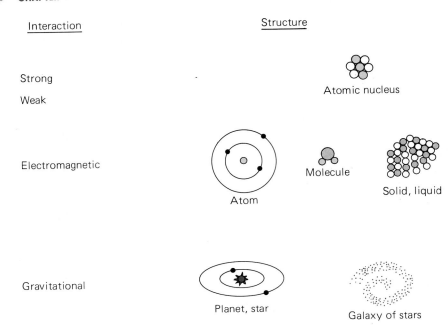

Interaction   Structure

Strong

Weak   Atomic nucleus

Electromagnetic   Molecule   Solid, liquid

                                                  Atom

Gravitational

                                                  Planet, star   Galaxy of stars

FIG. 7-23
The four fundamental interactions determine how matter comes together to form the characteristic structures of the universe.

mass exerts on another. Because the strong and weak forces are severely limited in range and because matter in bulk is electrically neutral, the gravitational interaction dominates on an astronomical scale. Planets, stars, and galaxies owe their existence to the gravitational interaction. This interaction is nevertheless extremely feeble, only 10^{-40} as powerful as the strong interaction.

Before Newton, it was not clear that the gravity that pulls things down to the earth — which we might call terrestrial gravity — is the same as the gravity that holds the planets to their orbits around the sun. One of Newton's great accomplishments was to show that both terrestrial and astronomical gravity have the same nature. Another notable unification was made by Maxwell when he demonstrated that electric and magnetic forces can both be traced to a single interaction between charged particles. What about the four fundamental interactions listed above? Are they all truly fundamental or are any of them, too, related in some way?

Studies made independently by Steven Weinberg and Abdus Salam in the 1960s indicate that the weak and electromagnetic interactions are really different aspects of the same basic phenomenon. Supported by experiment, this conclusion is now generally accepted (Fig. 7-24). A more recent development is a proposed link between the electromagnetic and strong interactions. Although such a grand unified theory is still far from its final form, it seems to be on the right track. One of the merits of the theory is that it can explain why the proton and the electron, which are very different kinds of particle (as discussed in the next section), have electric charges of exactly the same size.

The weak and em interactions are parts of the same basic phenomenon, and the strong interaction may be as well

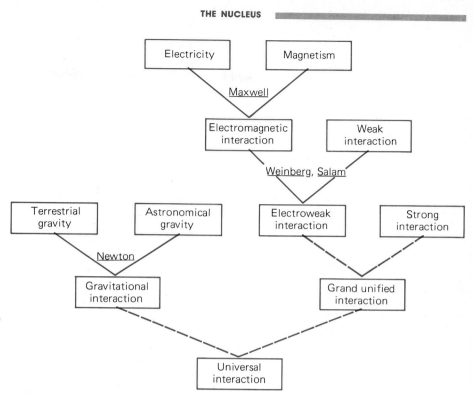

FIG. 7-24
One of the goals of physics is a single theoretical picture that unites all the ways in which particles of matter interact with each other. Much progress has been made, but the task is not finished.

What about gravitation? The final step in understanding how nature works is a single theory that ties together all the particles and interactions that are known. There are hints that this supreme goal is not beyond reach.

Leptons, Hadrons, and Quarks

Ultimate matter

Hadrons are subject to the strong force, leptons are not

All elementary particles, stable and unstable, fall into two broad categories that depend on their response to the strong interaction. *Leptons* are not affected by this interaction and seem to be point particles with no size or internal structures at all; the electron is an example. *Hadrons* are subject to the strong interaction and have definite sizes (they are about 10^{-15} m across) and internal structures; the proton and neutron are examples.

Neutrinos

Two interesting leptons besides the electron are the *neutrino* and the *muon*. The neutrino is a stable particle that has no mass or charge but nevertheless can have both energy and momentum. If this seems impossible, we need only recall that electromagnetic waves, also massless, carry energy and momentum. Electromagnetic waves are associated with the electromagnetic interaction, and neutrinos with the weak interaction. Whenever a nucleus undergoes beta decay, a neutrino as well as an electron (or positron) is emitted.

Because it has neither mass nor charge, a neutrino can pass through vast amounts of matter — over 100 *light-years* of solid iron on the average — before interacting. (A light-year is the distance light travels in a year.) A vast number of neutrinos are produced in the sun in the course of the nuclear reactions that occur within it, and these neutrinos carry into space 6 to 8 percent of all the energy the sun generates. The energy the neutrinos from the sun and other stars carry is apparently lost forever in the sense of being unavailable for conversion into other forms.

Muons

The muon is an unstable, negatively charged particle whose mass is 207 times that of the electron. Two millionths of a second after its creation in the breakup of a heavier unstable particle, a muon decays into an electron and two neutrinos. The secondary particles that reach the earth's surface as the result of the bombardment of the upper atmosphere by cosmic rays from space (see Chap. 20) are nearly all muons; more than one muon per cm² per minute on the average.

Most hadrons are very unstable

Besides the proton and the neutron, the hadron family of particles includes several hundred unstable particles whose masses range from a few hundred to a few thousand electron masses. Their lifetimes are all extremely short, from fifty billionths of a second down to less than a billionth of a billionth of a second. Such a multitude of "elementary" particles where only a few had been expected disturbed most physicists. Unlike leptons, which seem to be point particles of no detectable size, hadrons have definite sizes, and experiments in which fast electrons are scattered by collisions with protons and neutrons show that they have some kind of internal structures. (We recall that the internal structure of the atom was revealed by the similar Rutherford experiment.)

Is it possible that hadrons are composite objects made up of more truly elementary particles? Apparently the answer is yes, but the details of the answer turn out to be just as disturbing as the original problem.

Hadrons seem to be composed of quarks, which have charges smaller than e

The particles that seem to make up hadrons are called *quarks*. Only six kinds of quark are needed to account for all the hundreds of known hadrons. Those hadrons that are lighter than the proton consist of a quark and an antiquark. The proton, neutron, and heavier hadrons consist of three quarks. This is the kind of simplification that was looked for, but quarks turned out to have two unprecedented properties. The first is that, unlike any other particle known, their electric charges must be less than $\pm e$: some quarks have charges of $\pm\frac{1}{3}e$, others have charges of $\pm\frac{2}{3}e$.

Quarks have never been experimentally isolated

The second unusual aspect of quarks is that they do not seem able to exist outside of hadrons. No quark has ever been found by itself, even in experiments that ought to have been able to set them free. Thus there is no direct way to confirm that quarks have fractional charges, or even that they really exist.

Nevertheless there is a great deal of indirect evidence strongly in favor of quarks. For instance, every known hadron matches up with a particular arrangement of quarks, and predictions of hitherto unknown hadrons made on the basis of the quark model have turned out correct. Furthermore, a theory of the strong interaction based on quarks seems very promising. This is the theory mentioned in the previous section that apparently can be linked to the theory of the electromagnetic-weak interaction to make a unified picture that accounts for all aspects of the behavior of matter except — thus far — for gravitation.

Compositions of the proton and neutron

The two quarks that make up the proton and neutron are called u and d. These quarks and their antiquarks $\bar{u}$ and $\bar{d}$ have the following electric charges:

$$u: +\tfrac{2}{3}e \qquad \bar{u}: -\tfrac{2}{3}e$$
$$d: -\tfrac{1}{3}e \qquad \bar{d}: +\tfrac{1}{3}e$$

As shown in Fig. 7-25, a proton consists of one d quark and two u quarks, and a neutron of one u quark and two d quarks. The antiproton and antineutron consist of the corresponding antiquarks. We can see from the figure how the charges of these quarks add up to give the observed charges of the various particles. In the case of the proton, for example

$$(-\tfrac{1}{3} + \tfrac{2}{3} + \tfrac{2}{3})e = +e$$

and in the case of the neutron

$$(+\tfrac{2}{3} - \tfrac{1}{3} - \tfrac{1}{3})e = 0$$

Thus all the properties of ordinary matter can be understood on the basis of just two leptons, the electron and the neutrino, and two quarks, u and d. Considering how diverse these properties are, this is an astonishing achievement. The other leptons and quarks are connected only with unstable particles created in high-energy collisions and seem to play no role in ordinary matter.

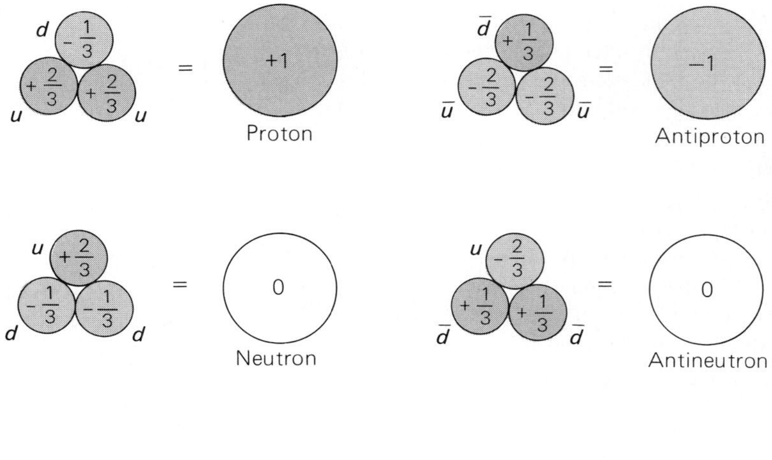

FIG. 7-25
Quark models of the proton, antiproton, neutron, and antineutron. Electric charges are given in units of e.

IMPORTANT TERMS

An **element** is a substance all of whose atoms have the same number of protons in their nuclei. This number is the **atomic number** of the element and is the same as the number of electrons that surround each nucleus of the element's atoms. The **isotopes** of an element have different numbers of neutrons in their nuclei but the same number of protons. A **nucleon** is a neutron or proton.

In **radioactive decay**, certain atomic nuclei spontaneously emit **alpha particles** (helium nuclei), **beta particles** (electrons), or **gamma rays** (high-frequency electromagnetic waves). A **positron** is a positively charged electron emitted in some beta decays.

The **half-life** of a radioisotope is the time needed for half of an original sample to decay.

The **electron volt** (eV) is the energy unit of nuclear physics. It is equal to the energy gained by an electron accelerated by a potential difference of 1 volt, so that $1 \text{ eV} = 1.6 \times 10^{-19}$ J.

The mass of every nucleus is slightly less than the total mass of the same number of free neutrons and protons. The **binding energy** of a nucleus is the energy equivalent of the missing mass and must be supplied to the nucleus to break it up. Nuclei of intermediate size have the highest **binding energies per nucleon.** Hence the **fusion** of light nuclei to form heavier ones and the **fission** of heavy nuclei into lighter ones are both processes that liberate energy.

Fission occurs in certain heavy nuclei (notably the uranium isotope ^{235}U) when they absorb neutrons. Since each fission sets free several neutrons, a rapidly multiplying sequence of fissions called a **chain reaction** can occur if enough of the proper material is brought together. A **nuclear reactor** is a device in which a chain reaction takes place at a controlled rate to produce usable energy in the form of heat.

A large number of **elementary particles** are known, of which the majority decay shortly after their creation. The **antiparticle** of a particle has the same mass and general behavior, but has a charge of opposite sign and differs in certain other respects. A particle and its antiparticle can **annihilate** each other with their masses turning entirely into energy. The opposite process of **pair production,** in which a particle-antiparticle pair materializes from energy, can also occur.

The four **fundamental interactions,** in order of decreasing strength, are the strong, electromagnetic, weak, and gravitational. The electromagnetic and weak interactions, and probably the strong as well, are closely related.

Particles such as the neutron and proton that are subject to the strong interaction are apparently composed of **quarks,** particles with electric charges of $\pm\frac{1}{3}e$ or $\pm\frac{2}{3}e$ that have not been experimentally isolated as yet. Particles such as the electron that are not affected by the strong interaction are point particles without internal structures.

MULTIPLE CHOICE

1. The basic idea of the Rutherford atomic model is that the positive charge in an atom is
   a. spread uniformly throughout its volume
   b. concentrated at its center
   c. readily deflected by an incoming alpha particle
   d. the same for all atoms

2. Nearly all the volume occupied by matter consists of
   a. electrons
   b. protons
   c. neutrons
   d. nothing

3. The atomic number of an element is the number of
   a. protons in its nucleus
   b. neutrons in its nucleus
   c. electrons in its nucleus
   d. protons and neutrons in its nucleus

4. The nuclei of the isotopes of an element all contain the same number of
   a. neutrons
   b. protons
   c. nucleons
   d. electrons

5. An alpha particle consists of
   a. two protons
   b. two protons and two electrons
   c. two protons and two neutrons
   d. four protons

6. A beta particle is
   a. an electron
   b. a photon
   c. a proton
   d. a neutron

7. Radioactive materials do not emit
   a. electrons
   b. protons
   c. alpha particles
   d. gamma rays

8. When a nucleus undergoes radioactive decay, the number of nucleons it contains afterward is

a. always less than the original number
b. always more than the original number
c. never less than the original number
d. never more than the original number

9. As a sample of a radioisotope decays, its half-life
   a. decreases
   b. remains the same
   c. increases
   d. any of the above, depending upon the isotope

10. An atomic nucleus has a mass that is
    a. less than the total mass of its constituent nucleons
    b. the same as the total mass of its constituent nucleons
    c. more than the total mass of its constituent nucleons
    d. any of the above, depending on the nucleus

11. The binding energy per nucleon is
    a. the same for all nuclei
    b. greatest for very small nuclei
    c. greatest for nuclei of intermediate size
    d. greatest for very large nuclei

12. The term *chain reaction* is used to refer to
    a. the linking together of protons and neutrons to form nuclei
    b. the successive fissions of nuclei induced by neutrons from the fissions of other nuclei
    c. the setting off of a hydrogen bomb by an atomic bomb
    d. the burning of uranium in a special furnace called a nuclear reactor

13. Enriched uranium is a better fuel for nuclear reactors than natural uranium because it has a greater proportion of
    a. slow neutrons
    b. deuterium
    c. plutonium
    d. ^{235}U

14. Which of the following does not make use of the energy evolved when two light nuclei fuse together to make a heavier one?
    a. The generation of energy within stars
    b. Proposed thermonuclear power plants
    c. Hydrogen bombs
    d. Nuclear reactors

15. Fusion reactions on the earth are likely to use as fuel
    a. ordinary hydrogen
    b. deuterium
    c. plutonium
    d. uranium

16. Of the following particles, the one that is not an elementary particle is the

a. alpha particle
b. beta particle
c. neutron
d. neutrino

17. An example of a particle-antiparticle pair is the
    a. proton and positron
    b. proton and neutron
    c. neutron and neutrino
    d. electron and positron

18. Atomic nuclei are stable despite the mutual repulsion of the protons they contain because of the action of the
    a. gravitational interaction
    b. electromagnetic interaction
    c. weak interaction
    d. strong interaction

19. The weakest of the four fundamental interactions is the
    a. gravitational interaction
    b. electromagnetic interaction
    c. strong interaction
    d. weak interaction

20. The mass of the neutrino is
    a. equal to that of the neutron
    b. equal to that of the electron
    c. equal to that of a quark
    d. zero

21. A particle that is believed to consist of quarks is the
    a. electron
    b. positron
    c. neutron
    d. neutrino

22. The number of protons in a nucleus of the boron isotope $^{11}_{5}B$ is
    a. 5
    b. 6
    c. 11
    d. 16

23. The number of neutrons in a nucleus of the potassium nucleus $^{40}_{19}K$ is
    a. 19
    b. 21
    c. 40
    d. 59

24. The nucleus of a nitrogen atom contains 7 protons and 8 neutrons. The mass number of the nucleus is
    a. 7
    b. 8
    c. 15

d. 56

25. When the bromine isotope $^{80}_{35}$Br decays into the krypton isotope $^{80}_{36}$Kr, it emits

    a. a gamma ray

    b. an electron

    c. a positron

    d. an alpha particle

26. The product of the alpha decay of the bismuth isotope $^{214}_{83}$Bi is

    a. $^{210}_{79}$Au

    b. $^{210}_{81}$Tl

    c. $^{210}_{83}$Bi

    d. $^{218}_{85}$At

27. After 2 h has elapsed, one-sixteenth of the original quantity of a certain radioactive substance remains undecayed. The half-life of this substance is

    a. 15 min

    b. 30 min

    c. 45 min

    d. 60 min

28. The half-life of tritium is 12.5 years. If we start out with 1 g of tritium, after 25 years there will be

    a. no tritium left

    b. $\frac{1}{4}$ g of tritium left

    c. $\frac{1}{2}$ g of tritium left

    d. a total of 4 g of tritium

QUESTIONS

1. What is the difference between the ways in which the mass and the charge of an atom are distributed?

2. Alpha particle tracks through gases and thin metal foils are nearly always straight lines. To what conclusion regarding atomic structure does this observation lead?

3. The following statements were thought to be correct in the nineteenth century. Which of them are now known to be incorrect? For those that are incorrect, indicate why the statement is wrong and modify it to be in accordance with modern views. (a) Energy can be neither created nor destroyed. (b) The acceleration of an object is proportional to the force applied to it and inversely proportional to its mass. (c) Atoms are indivisible and indestructible. (d) All atoms of a particular element are identical.

4. In what ways are the isotopes of an element similar to one another? In what ways are they different?

5. Find the number of neutrons and protons in each of the following nuclei: $^{6}_{3}$Li; $^{13}_{6}$C; $^{31}_{15}$P; $^{94}_{40}$Zr.

6. Find the number of neutrons and protons in each of the following nuclei: $^{10}_{5}$Be; $^{22}_{10}$Ne; $^{36}_{16}$S; $^{88}_{38}$Sr.

7. What limits the size of a nucleus?

8. What happens to the atomic number and atomic mass of a nucleus when it emits (a) an electron? (b) a positron? (c) a gamma ray?

9. Radium decays spontaneously into radon and helium. Why is radium considered an element rather than a compound of radon and helium?

10. Suppose the strong interaction did not exist, so there were no nuclear binding energies. If the early universe contained protons, neutrons, and electrons, what kind or kinds of matter would eventually fill the universe?

11. What are the differences and similarities between fusion and fission processes?

12. Why are the conditions in the interior of a star favorable for nuclear fusion reactions?

13. What is the function of the moderator in a uranium-fueled nuclear reactor?

14. What is the limitation on the fuel that can be used in a reactor whose moderator is ordinary water? Why is the situation different if the moderator is heavy water?

15. Discuss the similarities and differences between the neutron and the neutrino.

16. Does a gamma ray require more or less energy to materialize into a neutron-antineutron pair than to materialize into a proton-antiproton pair?

17. Leptons and hadrons are the two classes of elementary particle. How do they differ?

18. The gravitational interaction alone governs the motions of the planets around the sun. Why are the other fundamental interactions not significant in planetary motion?

19. No particle of fractional charge has yet been observed. If none is found in the future either, does this necessarily mean that the quark hypothesis is wrong?

20. What enables neutrinos to travel immense distances through matter without interacting?

PROBLEMS

1. Find the energy (in eV) of an electron whose speed is 10^6 m/s.

2. Find the energy (in eV) of a potassium atom of mass 6.5×10^{-26} kg whose speed is 10^6 m/s.

3. Find the speed of an electron whose energy is 26 eV.

4. Find the speed of a neutron whose energy is 50 eV.

5. Using the figures in Table 7-1, verify that the average atomic mass of chlorine is 35.46 u.

6. The carbon nucleus $^{11}_{6}$C decays radioactively by the emission of a positive electron. Find the atomic number, mass number, and chemical name of the resulting nucleus.

7. The thorium nucleus $^{233}_{90}$Th undergoes two successive negative beta decays. Find the atomic number, mass number, and chemical name of the resulting nucleus.

8. A $^{80}_{35}$Br nucleus can decay by emitting an electron or a positron and also by capturing an electron. What is the daughter nucleus in each case?

9. (a) Under what circumstances does a nucleus emit an electron? A positron? (b) The oxygen nuclei $^{14}_{8}$O and $^{19}_{8}$O both undergo beta decay to become stable nuclei. Which would you expect to emit a positron and which an electron?

10. The uranium nucleus $^{238}_{92}$U decays into a lead isotope through the successive emissions of eight alpha particles and six electrons. What is the symbol of the lead isotope?

11. If 1 kg of radium is sealed into a container, how much of it will remain as radium after 1600 years? After 4800 years? If the container is opened after a period of time, what gases would you expect to find inside it?

12. One-sixteenth of a sample of $^{24}_{11}$Na remains undecayed after 60 h. Find the half-life of this radioisotope.

13. The mass of $^{4}_{2}$He is 4.0026 u. Find its binding energy and binding energy per nucleon.

14. The binding energy of $^{20}_{10}$Ne is 160.6 MeV. Find its atomic mass.

15. The neutron decays in free space into a proton and an electron. What must be the minimum binding energy contributed by a neutron to a nucleus in order that the neutron not decay inside the nucleus? How does this figure compare with the observed binding energies per nucleon in stable nuclei?

16. Old stars obtain part of their energy by the fusion of three alpha particles to form a $^{12}_{6}$C nucleus, whose mass is 12.0000 u. How much energy is given off in each such reaction?

17. Would you expect the gravitational attractive force between two protons in a nucleus to counterbalance their electrical repulsion? Calculate the ratio between the electric and gravitational forces acting between two protons. Does this ratio depend upon how far apart the protons are?

ANSWERS TO MULTIPLE CHOICE

1. *b*	**8.** *d*	**15.** *b*	**22.** *b*
2. *d*	**9.** *b*	**16.** *a*	**23.** *b*
3. *a*	**10.** *a*	**17.** *d*	**24.** *c*
4. *b*	**11.** *c*	**18.** *d*	**25.** *b*
5. *c*	**12.** *b*	**19.** *a*	**26.** *b*
6. *a*	**13.** *d*	**20.** *d*	**27.** *b*
7. *b*	**14.** *d*	**21.** *c*	**28.** *b*

8

THE ATOM

Every atom consists of a tiny, positively charged nucleus with negatively charged electrons some distance away. What keeps the electrons out there?

By analogy with the planets of the solar system, we might suppose that atomic electrons avoid being sucked into the nucleus by circling around it at just the right speed. This is not a bad idea, but it raises a serious problem. According to Maxwell's theory, a circling electron should lose energy all the time by emitting electromagnetic waves. Thus the electron's orbit should become smaller and smaller, and soon it should collide with the nucleus. However, atomic electrons do not behave like this. Under ordinary conditions atoms emit no radiation, and, needless to say, they never collapse.

Whenever they have been tested outside the atomic domain, the laws of motion and of electromagnetism have always agreed with experiment—yet atoms are stable. In this chapter we shall see how the strange and radical concepts of the quantum theory of light and the wave theory of moving particles are needed to understand the world of the atom.

QUANTUM THEORY OF LIGHT

To most of us there is nothing mysterious or ambiguous about the concepts of *particle* and *wave*. A stone thrown into a lake and the ripples that spread out from where it lands seem to have in common only the ability to carry energy from one place to another. Classical physics, which describes scientifically the "physical reality" of our sense impressions, treats particles and waves as separate aspects of that reality. The mechanics of particles and the optics of waves are, by tradition, independent subjects, each with its own chain of experiments and hypotheses.

But the physical reality we experience has its roots in events that occur in the small-scale world of atoms and molecules, electrons and nuclei, and in this world there are neither particles nor waves in our sense of these terms. We regard electrons as particles because they have charge and mass and behave according to the laws of particle mechanics in such familiar devices as television picture tubes. However, there is as much evidence in favor of interpreting a moving electron as a type of wave as there is in favor of interpreting it as a type of particle. We regard electromagnetic waves as waves because under suitable circumstances they exhibit such characteristic wave behavior as interference. However, under different circumstances electromagnetic waves behave as though they consist of streams of particles. The wave-particle duality is central to an understanding of modern physics.

Photoelectric Effect

Electrons liberated by light

Light can cause the ejection of electrons from a metal surface

A century ago experiments were performed in which electrons were found to be given off by a metal surface when light was directed on it (Fig. 8-1). For most metals ultraviolet light is needed for this *photoelectric effect* to occur, but active metals, such as potassium and cesium, and certain other substances as well, also respond to visible light. The photoelectric cell that measures light intensity in a camera, the solar cell that produces electric current when sunlight falls on it, and

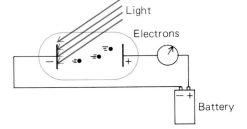

FIG. 8-1

In the photoelectric effect, electrons are emitted from a metal surface when a light beam is directed on it.

All light-sensitive detectors (including the eye) are based upon the absorption by electrons in the target atoms of energy from photons of light. In a camera, the absorbed energy alters silver halide crystals in the film so that chemical treatment can convert them into grains of pure silver.

the television camera tube that converts the image of a scene into an electric signal are all based upon the photoelectric effect.

Since light is electromagnetic in nature and carries energy, there seems nothing unusual about the photoelectric effect — it should be like water waves dislodging pebbles from a beach. But three experimental findings show that no such simple explanation is possible.

Properties of the photoelectric effect

1. The electrons are always emitted at once, even when a faint light is used. However, because the energy in an em wave is spread out across the wave according to theory, a period of time should be needed for an individual electron to accumulate enough energy to leave the metal. Several months ought to be needed for a really weak light beam.

2. A bright light causes more electrons to be emitted than a faint light, but the average kinetic energy of the electrons is the same. The electromagnetic theory of light, on the contrary, predicts that the stronger the light, the greater the KE of the electrons.

3. The higher the frequency of the light, the more KE the electrons have. Blue light yields faster electrons than red light (Fig. 8-2). According to the electromagnetic theory of light, the frequency should not matter.

FIG. 8-2
The higher the frequency of the light, the more KE the photoelectrons have. The brighter the light, the more photoelectrons are emitted. Blue light has a higher frequency than red light.

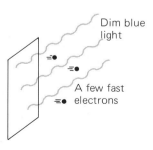

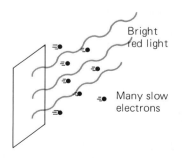

The electromagnetic theory of light cannot explain the photoelectric effect

Until the discovery of the photoelectric effect, the electromagnetic theory of light had been completely successful in accounting for what was known about the behavior of light. But no amount of ingenuity could bring experiment and theory together in this case. The result was the creation of the entirely new *quantum theory of light* in 1905 by Albert Einstein. The same year saw the birth of his equally revolutionary theory of relativity. All of modern physics has its roots in these two theories.

Quantum Theory of Light

Photons are "particles" of light

The energy of light waves travels in bursts called photons

Einstein introduced the idea that light consists of tiny bursts of energy called *photons*. He began with a hypothesis suggested five years earlier by the German physicist Max Planck to account for the spectrum of the light emitted by hot objects. As we recall from Chap. 3, the color of this light varies with the temperature of the object, going from red to yellow to white as it becomes hotter and hotter.

Photon energy is proportional to frequency

Planck found it necessary to assume that hot objects contribute energy in separate units, or *quanta*, to the light they give off. The higher the frequency of the light, the more the energy per quantum. All the quanta associated with a particular frequency f of light have the same energy

$$E = hf$$

Quantum energy = (Planck's constant)(frequency)

In this formula the quantity h, today known as *Planck's constant,* has the value

$$\text{Planck's constant} = h = 6.63 \times 10^{-34} \text{ J} \cdot \text{s}$$

Planck was not happy about this assumption, which made no sense in terms of the physical theories known at that time. He took the position that, although energy apparently had to be given to the light emitted by a glowing object in small bursts, the light nevertheless traveled with its energy spread out in waves exactly as everybody thought.

Einstein, however, felt that, if light is emitted in little packets, it should travel through space and finally be absorbed in the same little packets. His idea fit the experiments on the photoelectric effect perfectly. He supposed that some minimum energy w is required in order to pull an electron away from a metal surface. If the frequency of the light is too low, so that E, the photon energy, is less than w, no electrons can come out. When E is greater than w, a photon of light striking an electron can give the electron enough energy for it to leave the metal with a certain amount of kinetic energy. Einstein's formula for the process is very simple:

Photoelectric equation

$$hf = \text{KE} + w$$

where

$hf =$ energy of a photon of light whose frequency is f
$\text{KE} =$ kinetic energy of the emitted electron
$w =$ energy needed to pull the electron from the metal

Although the photon has no mass and always moves with the speed of light, it has most of the other properties usually associated with the term particle — it is localized in a small region of space, it has energy and momentum, and it interacts with other particles in more or less the same way as a billiard ball interacts with other billiard balls.

What Is Light?

Both wave and particle

The idea that light travels as a series of little packets of energy is directly opposed to the wave theory of light. And the latter, which provides the only way to explain a host of optical effects, notably diffraction and interference, is one of the best established of physical theories. Planck's suggestion that a hot object gives energy to light in separate quanta led to no more than raised eyebrows among physicists in 1900 since it did not apparently conflict with the picture of light itself as a wave. Einstein's suggestion in 1905 that light travels through space in the form of distinct photons, on the other hand, astonished most of his colleagues.

Light as a wave phenomenon

According to the wave theory, light waves spread out from a source in the way

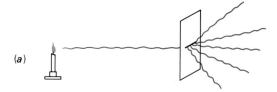

(a)

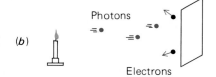

Photons

(b)

Electrons

FIG. 8-3
(a) The wave theory of light accounts for the diffraction of light into the shadow region when it passes through a narrow slit. (b) The quantum theory of light accounts for the photoelectric effect. Neither theory by itself can account for all aspects of the behavior of light. The two theories therefore complement each other.

Light as a quantum phenomenon

ripples spread out on the surface of a lake when a stone falls into it. The energy carried by the light in this picture is spread out through the wave pattern. According to the quantum theory, however, light travels from a source as a series of localized bursts of energy, each so small in size that it can be taken up by a single electron. Curiously, the quantum theory of light, which treats it as a particle phenomenon, incorporates the light frequency f, a wave concept (Fig. 8-3).

Which theory are we to believe? A great many scientific ideas have had to be changed or discarded when they were found to disagree with experiment, but for the first time two entirely different theories are needed to account for a single physical phenomenon.

The wave and quantum theories of light are complementary

In a specific event light exhibits *either* a wave or a particle nature, never both at the same time. This is an important point. The light beam that shows diffraction in passing the edge of an obstacle can also cause photoelectrons to be emitted from a metal surface, but these processes occur independently.

The wave theory of light and the quantum theory of light complement each other.

Electromagnetic waves provide the only possible explanation for some experiments involving light, and photons provide the only possible explanation for all other experiments involving light. Light is a phenomenon that incorporates both wave and particle characters even though there is nothing in everyday life like that to help our imaginations visualize it.

X-Rays

High-energy photons

The photoelectric effect provides convincing evidence that photons of light can transfer energy to electrons. Is the inverse process also possible? That is, can part or all of the kinetic energy of a moving electron be converted into a photon? As it happens, the inverse photoelectric effect not only does occur, but also had been discovered (though not understood) before the work of Planck and Einstein.

The discovery of x-rays

In 1895, in his laboratory at Würzburg, Wilhelm Roentgen accidentally found that a screen coated with a fluorescent salt glowed every time he switched on a nearby cathode-ray tube. (A cathode-ray tube is a tube with the air pumped out in which electrons are accelerated by an electric field.) Roentgen knew that the electrons themselves could not get through the glass walls of his tube, yet it was clear some sort of invisible radiation was falling on the screen. The radiation was very penetrating; thick pieces of wood, glass, and even metal could be placed between tube and screen, and still the screen glowed. Soon Roentgen found that

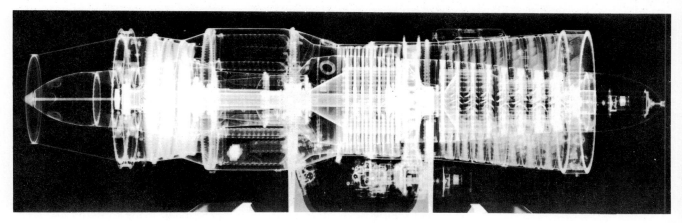

The structure of a jet aircraft engine, laid bare in a single x-ray photo.

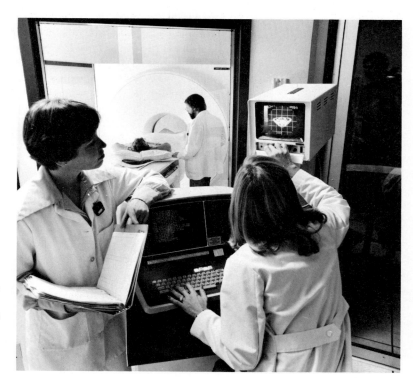

In a "CAT scanner," a series of x-ray exposures of a patient taken from different directions are combined by a computer to give cross-sectional images of the part of the body being examined. In effect, the tissue is sliced up by the computer on the basis of the x-ray exposures, and any desired slice can be displayed. This technique enables an abnormality to be detected and its exact location established, which might be impossible to do from an ordinary x-ray picture.

his mysterious rays would penetrate flesh and produce shadows of the bones inside. He gave them the name x-rays after the algebraic symbol for an unknown quantity.

X-rays are produced whenever fast electrons are stopped suddenly. An x-ray

FIG. 8-4
An x-ray tube. High-frequency electromagnetic waves called x-rays are emitted by a metal target when it is struck by fast electrons. The cathode (negative electrode) is heated by a filament and emits electrons which are accelerated by an electric field between it and the positively charged target.

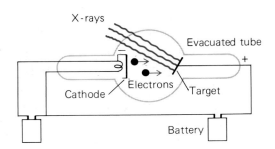

tube is a cathode-ray tube designed for this purpose, with the electrons striking the metal of the positive electrode (Fig. 8-4).

What are x-rays? After many attempts had been made to determine their nature, in 1912 Max von Laue was able to show by means of an interference experiment that they are electromagnetic waves of extremely high frequency. X-ray frequencies are much higher than those of ultraviolet light, but somewhat lower than those of the gamma rays produced by radioactive atomic nuclei.

X-rays are high-frequency electromagnetic waves

The early workers with x-rays noted that increasing the voltage applied to the tube, which means faster electrons, gave rise to x-rays of greater penetrating power. The greater the penetrating ability, the higher the x-ray frequency turned out to be. Hence high-energy electrons meant high-frequency x-rays. The more electrons in the beam, the more x-rays were produced, but their energy depended only on the electron energy.

X-ray production is the inverse of the photoelectric effect

The quantum theory of light is in complete accord with these observations. Instead of photon energy being transformed into electron kinetic energy, electron kinetic energy is transformed into photon energy. The energy of an x-ray photon of frequency f is hf, and therefore the minimum KE of the electron that produced the x-ray should be equal to hf. This prediction agrees with experimental data.

MATTER WAVES

As we have seen, light has both wave and particle aspects. In the topsy-turvy world of the very small, is it possible that what we normally think of as particles — electrons, for instance — have wave properties as well? So extraordinary is this question that it was not asked for two decades after Einstein's work. Soon afterward came the even more extraordinary answer: yes.

de Broglie Wavelength

More momentum means shorter wavelength

The more a particle's momentum, the shorter its de Broglie wavelength

In 1924 the French physicist Louis de Broglie proposed that moving objects act in some respects as though they have wave characters. Reasoning by analogy with

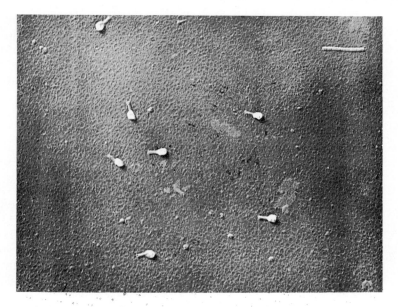

An electron micrograph of bacterio-phages, which are viruses that attack bacteria, magnified 80,000X. Because the wavelengths of the fast electrons in an electron microscope are shorter than those of the light waves in an ordinary microscope, the electron microscope can produce sharp images at higher magnifications. An electron micro-scope uses magnetic fields to focus an electron beam.

the properties of photons, he suggested that a particle of mass m and speed v behaves as though it is a wave whose wavelength is

$$\lambda = \frac{h}{mv}$$

$$\text{de Broglie wavelength} = \frac{\text{Planck's constant}}{\text{momentum}}$$

The more momentum mv a particle has, the shorter its *de Broglie wavelength λ*.

How can de Broglie's hypothesis be tested? Only waves can be diffracted and can reinforce and cancel each other by interference. A few years after de Broglie's work, experiments were performed in the United States and in England in which streams of electrons were shown to exhibit both diffraction and interference. The wavelengths of the electrons could be inferred from the data, and they agreed exactly with the formula $\lambda = h/mv$.

Matter waves are significant only on an atomic scale of size

There is nothing imaginary about these *matter waves*. They are perfectly real, just as light and sound waves are. However, they are not necessarily evident in every situation. A car moving at 80 km/h (50 mi/h) has a de Broglie wavelength of only about 10^{-38} m, which is so extremely small that no wave behavior can be detected. On the other hand, an electron whose speed is 10^7 m/s has a wavelength of 10^{-8} m, which is comparable in size to atomic dimensions. (A speed of 10^7 m/s is not much for an electron; the electrons in a television picture tube move faster.) It is not surprising, then, that the wave nature of moving electrons turns out to be crucial in understanding atomic structure and behavior.

CHAPTER 8

Not only electrons but all other moving particles behave like waves under suitable circumstances. As with electromagnetic waves, the wave and particle aspects of moving bodies can never be observed at the same time. It therefore makes no sense to ask which is the "correct" description. All we can say is that in certain situations a moving body exhibits wave properties and in other situations it exhibits particle properties.

Waves of What?

Waves of probability

In water waves, the quantity that varies periodically is the height of the water surface. In sound waves, it is air pressure. In light waves, electric and magnetic fields vary. What is it that varies in the case of matter waves?

Wave function and probability density

The quantity whose variations make up matter waves is called the *wave function,* symbol ψ (the Greek letter *psi*). The value of ψ^2 at a given place and time for a certain particle determines the probability of finding the particle there at that time. For this reason ψ^2 is called the *probability density* of the particle. A large value of ψ^2 means the strong possibility of the particle's presence, a small value of ψ^2 means its presence is unlikely.

The wave packet associated with a moving body moves with the same speed as the body

The de Broglie waves associated with a moving body are in the form of a group, or packet, of waves, as in Fig. 8-5. This wave packet travels with the same speed v as the body does. Even though we cannot visualize what is meant by ψ and so cannot form a mental image of matter waves, the agreement between theory and experiment means that we must take them seriously.

FIG. 8-5
(*a*) Particle description of a moving object. (*b*) Wave description of a moving object. The packet of matter waves that corresponds to a certain object moves with the same speed *v* as the object does. The waves are waves of probability.

FIG. 8-6
(*a*) A narrow wave packet. The position of the particle can be precisely determined, but the wave-length (and hence the particle's momentum) cannot be established because there are not enough waves to measure λ accurately.
(*b*) A wide wave packet. Now the wavelength can be accurately determined, but not the position of the particle.

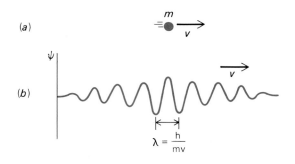

Uncertainty Principle

We cannot know the future because we cannot know the present

To regard a moving object as a wave packet suggests that there are fundamental limits to the accuracy with which we can measure such "particle" properties as position and speed. The particle whose wave packet is shown in Fig. 8-5 may be located anywhere within the packet at a given time. Of course, the probability density ψ^2 is a maximum in the middle of the packet, so it is most likely to be found there. Nevertheless, we may still find the particle anywhere that ψ^2 is not actually 0.

A narrow wave packet permits accurate position determinations

The narrower its wave packet, the more precisely a particle's position can be specified (Fig. 8-6a). However, the wavelength of the waves in a narrow packet is not well defined; there are not enough waves to measure λ accurately. This means that, since $\lambda = h/mv$, the particle's momentum mv (and hence speed v) is not a precise quantity. If we make a series of momentum measurements, we will find a broad range of values.

A wide wave packet permits accurate momentum determinations

On the other hand, a wide wave packet such as that in Fig. 8-6b has a clearly defined wavelength. The momentum that corresponds to this wavelength is therefore a precise quantity, and a series of measurements will give a narrow range of values. But where is the particle located? The width of the packet is now too great for use to be able to say just where it is at a given time.

Thus we have the *uncertainty principle:*

The uncertainty principle

It is impossible to know both the exact position and momentum of an object at the same time.

This principle, which was discovered by Werner Heisenberg, is one of the most significant of physical laws. Some of its implications are discussed in the next section.

Another approach to the uncertainty principle

We can also approach the uncertainty principle from the point of view of the particle nature of waves. Let us suppose we have a microscope powerful enough to see an electron. We cannot use visible light to illuminate the electron because the wavelengths in visible light are billions of times larger than any plausible estimate of an electron's size. A microscope will show details only down to a size near the wavelength of the light employed. But we can imagine using high-frequency gamma rays whose wavelengths are extremely short. Our eyes would not respond to such rays, but instruments exist that do.

So we arrange to get an electron on the stage of our microscope and we illuminate it by turning on the gamma-ray source. There is a momentary flash and then the field of view is blank: the electron has disappeared. Then we recall that gamma rays of high frequency are photons of high energy. At least one of these photons must bounce off an electron for us to see where it is, but when this

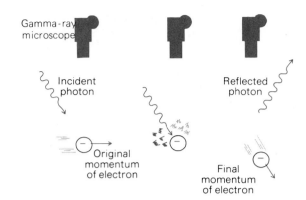

Gamma-ray microscope

Incident photon

Reflected photon

Original momentum of electron

Final momentum of electron

FIG. 8-7
An electron cannot be observed without changing its momentum by an unknown amount. Thus position and momentum cannot both be precisely determined.

An object cannot be observed without disturbing it in some way

happens the electron recoils out of the microscope field of view (Fig. 8-7). We thus have lost the possibility of finding the original state of motion of the electron.

If the electron is to stay in sight, we must use gamma rays of longer wavelength and lower energy. The photons of these gamma rays strike the electron more gently, so we can keep track of its motion. However, the electron itself is now only a hazy blur, because with longer waves our microscope loses its power to show small objects. No matter how we alter the microscope, we cannot improve the situation. So again we have a choice: either precision in measuring position, or precision in measuring motion, but not both. No experiment, either actual or hypothetical, has ever been able to get around the uncertainty principle.

Waves versus Particles

On an atomic level, everything has some properties of both

An electron has mass, and it behaves in many situations as a particle in the sense of being a tiny object that obeys the same laws of motion as the larger objects around us. But in other situations the electron behaves exactly the way a wave does. Similarly, light has both particle and wave properties. In terms of our experience, this seems to make no sense. After all, a wave is a wave, a particle is a particle.

Or, perhaps, is such a conflict meaningless, because we are trying to use models based on everyday life to describe things very different from what we see around us? To put it another way, just because we do not find things that sometimes appear as waves and at other times as particles, this may not mean that such dual characters are not normal in the world of the atom.

The clearest picture we can form of an electron is to regard it as a particle whose associated "waves of probability" govern its position and state of motion. The wave aspect of the electron (and such other small particles as protons and neutrons) means that there is a basic element of unpredictability in its nature. Since

The future cannot be accurately predicted because the present cannot be accurately known we cannot know exactly both where an electron is right now and what its speed is, we cannot say anything definite about where it will be 2 s from now or how fast it will be moving then. We cannot know the future for sure because we cannot know the present for sure. But our ignorance is not total: we can still say that the electron is more likely to be in one place than another and that its speed is more likely to have a certain value than another.

The uncertainty principle is not significant for objects above atomic size

All objects, of whatever size, are governed by the uncertainty principle, which means that their positions and motions likewise can be expressed only as probabilities. There is a chance that this book will someday defy the law of gravity and rise up in the air by itself. But for objects this large — in fact, even for objects the size of molecules — the relevant probabilities are so large as to be practically certainties. The likelihood that this book will continue to obey the law of gravity is so great that we can be quite sure it will stay where it is if left alone. Only in the behavior of electrons and other atomic particles do matter waves play an important part.

THE HYDROGEN ATOM

We now have the key concepts needed to make sense of atomic structure: the Rutherford model of the atom, the quantum theory of light, and the wave theory of moving particles. When linked together, these concepts give rise to a theory of the atom that agrees with experiment. Our starting point will be the hydrogen atom, the simplest of all with a single electron outside a nucleus that consists of just a proton.

Atomic Spectra

Each element has a characteristic line spectrum

The study of the radiation given off by atoms when appropriately stimulated was largely responsible for the growth of modern ideas about atomic structure. Most of this radiation is in the form of visible light. The late nineteenth century saw many studies of *atomic spectra,* the name given to the characteristic series of frequencies emitted by the atoms of particular elements. Since light is an electromagnetic phenomenon that can be produced by moving electrons, the discovery that atoms contain electrons led to the speculation that atomic spectra can somehow be traced to these electrons.

Continuous spectra contain all frequencies; line spectra contain only certain specific ones

In Chap. 6 spectra were mentioned briefly and a distinction made between the rainbow bands produced when light from a hot object passes through a spectrometer (*continuous spectra*) and the sharp, bright lines from the light of an electrically excited gas (*line spectra*); see Fig. 8-8. The continuous colored band from red to violet means that all the frequencies of visible light are present. The discontinuous, bright-line spectrum indicates that only a few frequencies are represented (Fig. 8-9*a*).

Atomic spectra. Shown are portions of the spectra of lithium, neon, helium, sodium, atomic hydrogen, and molecular hydrogen.

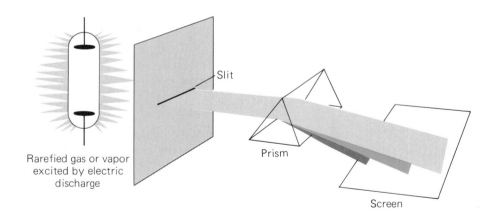

Rarefied gas or vapor excited by electric discharge

Slit

Prism

Screen

FIG. 8-8
An idealized spectrometer. Dispersion in the prism separates light of different frequencies.

FIG. 8-9
(*a*) Emission spectrum of sodium vapor. (*b*) Absorption spectrum of sodium vapor. Each dark line in the absorption spectrum corresponds to a bright line in the emission spectrum.

(*a*)

(*b*)

Absorption spectra

Spectra of a different sort, *absorption spectra,* are produced when light from a glowing source passes through a cool gas before entering the spectrometer. The light source alone would give a continuous spectrum, but the gas absorbs certain frequencies out of the light that passes through it. Hence the continuous spectrum appears to be crossed by dark lines, each line representing one of the frequencies absorbed by the gas.

If the bright-line spectrum of an incandescent gas is compared with the absorption spectrum of the same gas, the dark lines in the latter are found to correspond in frequency to a number of the bright lines in the emission spectrum

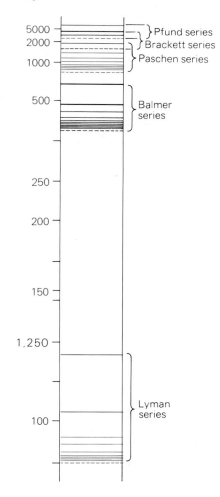

FIG. 8-10
The spectral series of hydrogen. The wavelengths (and hence frequencies) in each series can be related by simple formulas (1 nm = 1 nanometer = 10^{-9} m).

(Fig. 8-9*b*). Thus a cool gas absorbs some of the frequencies of light that it is capable of emitting when excited. The spectrum of sunlight has dark lines in it because the luminous part of the sun, which radiates in a manner much like that of any object heated to 6000 K, is surrounded by an envelope of cooler gas that absorbs light of certain frequencies only.

An element can be identified from its spectrum

Because the line spectrum of each element (either bright-line or dark-line) contains frequencies that are characteristic of that element only, the spectrometer is a valuable tool in chemical analysis. Even the smallest traces of an element can be identified by the lines in a spectrum of an unknown substance.

The number, strength, and position of the lines in the spectrum of an element depend upon temperature, pressure, the presence of electric and magnetic fields, and the motion of the source. It is possible to tell by examining its spectrum not only what elements are present in a light source but much about their physical state. An astronomer, for example, can establish from the spectrum of a star what its atmosphere contains, whether it is approaching or receding from the earth, and what elements in its atmosphere are ionized.

Spectral series

A century ago it was discovered that the frequencies present in the spectrum of an element fall into definite sets called *spectral series* (Fig. 8-10). The frequencies in each series can be described by a simple formula, which suggests that there is some sort of order in the way atomic electrons behave. When the foundations of the modern picture of the atom had been laid, these spectral series provided the final clues for working out the details of atomic structure.

The Bohr Model

Only certain electron energies are possible in an atom

The first successful theory of the hydrogen atom, the simplest of all, was proposed by Niels Bohr, a Dane, in 1913. Bohr applied quantum ideas to atomic structure to obtain a model which, even though it was later replaced by a theory of greater accuracy and usefulness, nevertheless is still the mental picture many scientists have of the atom.

Bohr proposed that an atomic electron can have certain energies only

Bohr applied the basic concept of the quantum theory of light — that energy comes in small packets rather than in a continuous stream — to the problem of atomic structure. He began by proposing that there are certain specific orbits in which an electron inside an atom can circle the nucleus without losing energy. Because these orbits are each a different distance from the nucleus, electrons in them have different amounts of energy. Thus Bohr suggested that electrons within an atom can have only certain particular energy values. An analogy might be with a person on a ladder, who can stand only on its steps and not in between.

Each energy level in an atom is identified by a quantum number

An electron in the innermost orbit has the least energy. The larger the orbit, the more the electron energy. The orbits are identified by a *quantum number, n,* which is $n = 1$ for the innermost orbit, $n = 2$ for the next, and so on. Each orbit corresponds to an *energy level* of the atom.

Origin of spectral lines

The emission and absorption by atoms of light of only certain frequencies,

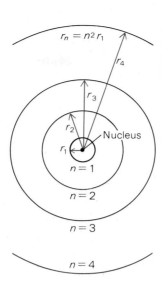

FIG. 8-11
Electron orbits in the Bohr model of the hydrogen atom (not to scale). The radius of each orbit is proportional to n^2, the square of its quantum number. The inner orbit is the electron's normal path and the outer orbits represent states of higher energy. If the electron absorbs enough energy for it to jump to an outer orbit, it may return to its normal one by a suitable jump or combination of jumps; each jump is accompanied by the emission of a photon.

which we observe as spectral lines, fits Bohr's atomic model perfectly. An atomic electron in a particular orbit can absorb only those photons of light whose energy hf will permit it to "jump" to another orbit farther out. When an electron jumps from one orbit to another of less energy, it emits a photon of light. The difference in energy between the two orbits is hf, where f is the frequency of the emitted light.

A ground-state hydrogen atom has its electron in the innermost possible orbit, which corresponds to the lowest energy

Figure 8-11 shows the arrangement of possible orbits for the single electron in a hydrogen atom. Here the circle nearest the nucleus represents the electron orbit under ordinary conditions, when the atom has the lowest possible energy. Such an atom is said to be in its *ground state*. The other circles are possible orbits in which the electron would possess more energy than in its normal orbit, since it would then be farther from the nucleus (much as a stone at the top of a building has more potential energy than on the ground, since it is farther from the earth's center).

Suppose an atom is in its ground state. If the atom is supplied with energy — by strong heating, by an electric discharge, or by radiation — the electron may be induced to jump to a larger orbit (Fig. 8-12). This jump means that the atom has

FIG. 8-12
Excitation by collision. Some of the available energy is absorbed by one of the atoms, which goes into an excited energy state. The atom then emits a photon in returning to its ground (normal) state.

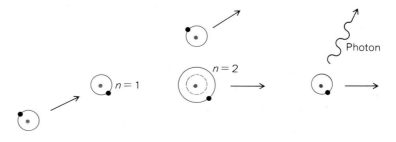

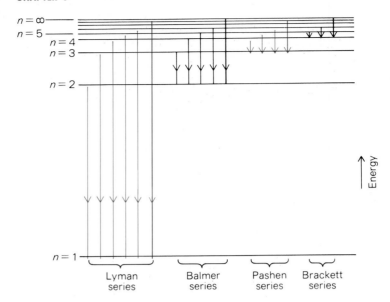

FIG. 8-13
Spectral lines are the result of transitions between energy levels. The spectral series of hydrogen are shown in Fig. 8-10. When $n = \infty$, the electron is free.

Excited states are unstable

absorbed some energy. It keeps the added energy as long as it remains in the *excited state*, that is, as long as its electron stays in the larger orbit. Because excited states are unstable, in a fraction of a second the electron jumps spontaneously back to its original orbit (or to another smaller orbit), emitting a photon of light as it does so.

The energy (and hence the frequency) of the photon emitted from a hydrogen atom is determined, according to Bohr's hypothesis, by the particular jump that its electron makes. If the electron jumps from orbit $n = 4$ to orbit $n = 1$ (Fig. 8-13), the energy of the photon will be greater than if it jumps from 3 to 1 or 2 to 1. Starting from orbit 4, it may return to 1 not by a single leap but by stopping at 2 and 3 on the way; corresponding to these jumps will be photons with energies determined by the energy differences between 4 and 3, 3 and 2, 2 and 1. Each of these jumps gives a photon of a characteristic frequency and will therefore appear in the hydrogen spectrum as a single bright line. The frequencies of the different lines will be related one to another since they correspond to different jumps in the same set of orbits. And the relations among the lines that Bohr predicted by this mechanism precisely matched the observed relations among the lines in the hydrogen spectrum.

Electron Waves and Orbits

Standing waves in the atom

Why is it that an atomic electron can exist in certain orbits only? The answer comes from an analysis of the wave properties of an electron that circles a hydrogen

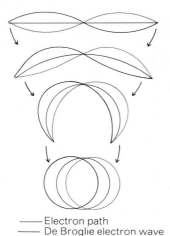

FIG. 8-14
The condition for a stable electron orbit. The orbit of the electron in a hydrogen atom corresponds to a complete electron de Broglie wave joined on itself.

—— Electron path
—— De Broglie electron wave

nucleus. It turns out that the de Broglie wavelength of the electron is exactly equal to the circumference of its normal (that is, innermost) orbit. Thus the normal orbit of the electron in a hydrogen atom corresponds to one complete electron wave joined on itself (Fig. 8-14).

This fact provides us with the clue we need to construct a theory of the atom. If we consider the vibrations of a wire loop (Fig. 8-15), we find that their wavelengths always fit a whole number of times into the loop's circumference, so that each wave joins smoothly with the next. These are the only vibrations possible. Regarding electron waves in an atom as analogous to standing waves in a wire loop leads to an interesting hypothesis:

Condition for orbit

An electron can circle a nucleus only in orbits that contain a whole number of de Broglie wavelengths.

This idea is the decisive one in our understanding of the atom. It combines both the particle and wave characters of the electron into a single statement, since the electron wavelength depends upon the orbital speed needed to balance the

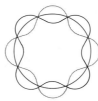

FIG. 8-15
Vibrations of a wire loop. In each case a whole number of wavelengths fit into the circumference of the loop.

Circumference = 2 wavelengths

Circumference = 4 wavelengths

Circumference = 8 wavelengths

electrical attraction of the nucleus. These contradictory characters are fundamental aspects of the atomic world.

It is easy to express the condition that an electron orbit contain a whole number of de Broglie wavelengths. The circumference of a circular orbit of radius r is $2\pi r$. Hence we can write the condition for a possible orbit as

$$n\lambda = 2\pi r_n \qquad n = 1, 2, 3, \ldots$$

$$\binom{\text{Quantum}}{\text{number}}\binom{\text{electron}}{\text{wavelength}} = \binom{\text{circumference}}{\text{of orbit}}$$

Here r_n is the radius of the nth orbit, that is, the orbit that contains n whole wavelengths. The number n is, as before, the quantum number of the orbit.

Orbit radii in the hydrogen atom

A detailed calculation that takes into account the speed the electron must have to circle the nucleus without being drawn into it shows that the electron orbits are specified by the formula

$$\text{Orbit radius} = r_n = n^2 r_1 \qquad n = 1, 2, 3, \ldots$$

The orbit closest to the nucleus in the hydrogen atom has the radius

$$r_1 = 5.3 \times 10^{-11} \text{ m}$$

The n^2 factor means that orbit size increases rapidly with increasing quantum number n. The ratios between successive orbit radii are $1:4:9:16$ and so on.

The Laser

Light waves all in step

Properties of a laser beam

A *laser* is a device that produces an intense beam of single-frequency, "coherent" light from the cooperative radiation of excited atoms. The light waves in a coherent beam are all in step with one another, which greatly increases their effectiveness (Fig. 8-16). Ordinary light is incoherent since the atoms in light sources such as lamps, the sun, and the stars emit light waves randomly. A laser beam hardly spreads out at all; one sent from the earth to a mirror left on the moon by the Apollo 11 expedition remained narrow enough to be detected on its return to the earth, a round-trip distance of over three-quarters of a million km. A light beam produced by any other means would have spread out too much for this to be done. The word laser comes from *l*ight *a*mplification by *s*timulated *e*mission of *r*adiation.

Metastable excited states have longer lifetimes than ordinary ones

The key to the laser is the existence in many atoms of one or more excited energy levels whose lifetimes are as great as 10^{-3} s instead of the usual 10^{-8} s. Such relatively long-lived states are called *metastable*.

A laser contains atoms which have metastable states whose excitation energy

A laser beam is used here to vaporize unwanted material during the manufacture of electronic circuits on semiconductor chips.

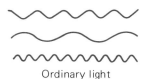

Ordinary light

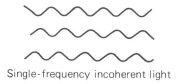

Single-frequency incoherent light

FIG. 8-16
A laser produces a beam of light whose waves all have the same frequency and are in step with one another (coherent). The beam is also very narrow and spreads out very little even over long distances.

Single-frequency coherent light

is E_1 (Fig. 8-17). The first step in its operation is to bring as many as possible of these atoms to this metastable level. Often it is necessary to raise the atoms to a still higher state E_2, from which a number of them fall to the metastable level by emitting a photon of energy $E_2 - E_1$. Several ways exist to do this. One of them, called *optical pumping,* uses an external light source some of whose photons have the right energy. Optical pumping was used in the first lasers, in which xenon-filled flash lamps excited chromium ions in ruby rods to the required level E_2 (Fig. 8-18).

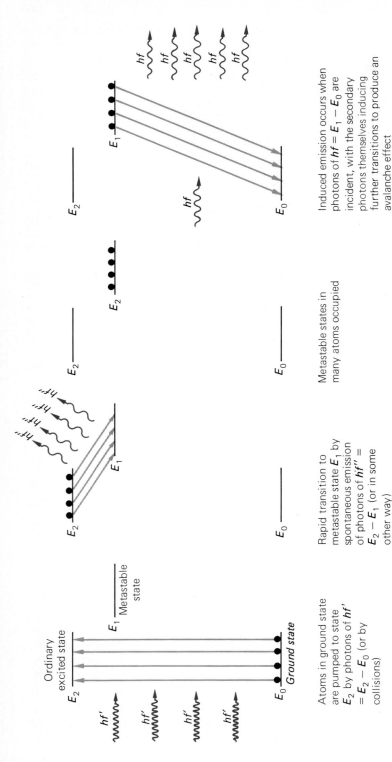

FIG. 8-17

The principle of the laser. A metastable atomic state is one that lasts a much longer time than usual before a photon is emitted that brings the atom to a state of lower energy.

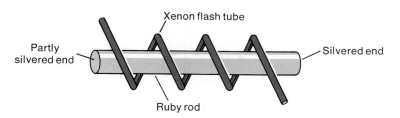

FIG. 8-18
The ruby laser. A ruby is a crystal of aluminum oxide, Al_2O_3, in which some of the aluminum Al^{3+} ions are replaced by chromium Cr^{3+} ions, which are responsible for the red color. A Cr^{3+} ion, which is a Cr atom that has lost three electrons, has a metastable level whose lifetime is about 0.003 s. The xenon flash lamp excites the Cr^{3+} ions to a level of higher energy which falls to the metastable level by losing energy to other ions in the crystal. Photons from the spontaneous decay of some Cr^{3+} ions cause other excited Cr^{3+} ions to radiate. The result is a large pulse of single-frequency, coherent red light from the partly silvered end of the rod.

Why laser light is monochromatic and coherent

Another method is used in the helium-neon laser. Here an electric discharge in the gas mixture produces fast electrons whose impact on the gas atoms brings them to the required energy level. The advantage is that such a laser can operate continuously, whereas a ruby laser produces separate flashes of light.

With a large number of atoms in the metastable state E_1, a few of them are likely to spontaneously emit photons of energy $hf = E_1 - E_0$ before the others, thereby falling to the ground state E_0. A typical laser is a transparent solid (such as a ruby rod) or a gas-filled tube with mirrors at both ends, one of them only partly silvered to allow some of the light inside to get out. The distance between the mirrors is made equal to a whole number of half-wavelengths of light of frequency f, so the trapped light forms an optical standing wave (Fig. 6-11). This standing wave stimulates the other atoms in metastable states to radiate before they would normally do so. The result is an avalanche of photons, all of the same frequency f and all of whose waves are exactly in step, which greatly increases the power they can deliver.

Many kinds of lasers have been built and still others are under development. Some are very small and produce the coded flashes of light that carry telephone signals along glass fiber transmission lines. More powerful lasers are used in surgery where a laser beam has the advantage of sealing small blood vessels it cuts through. Lasers find numerous applications in industry, from cutting fabric for clothing and making holes in nipples for babies' bottles to welding pipelines and heat-treating the surfaces of engine crankshafts and cylinder walls to harden them.

QUANTUM THEORY OF THE ATOM

The theory of the hydrogen atom discussed above, which is basically that developed by Bohr in 1913 (although he did not have de Broglie's idea of electron waves to guide his thinking) is able to account for certain experimental data in a convincing manner. However, it has some severe limitations. For instance, although the Bohr theory correctly predicts the spectral series of hydrogen, it cannot do the same for the spectra of complex atoms having two or more electrons each. Perhaps most important of all, it does not give what a really successful theory of the atom ought to: an understanding of how individual atoms interact with one another to form molecules, solids, and liquids.

These objections to the Bohr theory are not meant to be unfriendly, for it was one of those historic achievements that transform scientific thought, but rather to emphasize that an approach to the atom of greater generality is required. Such an approach was developed in 1925–1926 by Erwin Schrödinger, Werner Heisenberg, and others, under the apt name of *quantum mechanics*. By the early 1930s the application of quantum mechanics to problems involving nuclei, atoms, molecules, and matter in the solid state made it possible to understand a vast body of otherwise puzzling data and — a vital attribute of any theory — led to predictions of remarkable accuracy.

Quantum Mechanics

Physics of the very small

Newtonian mechanics assumes accurate measurements can be made

The real difference between newtonian mechanics and quantum mechanics lies in what they describe. Newtonian mechanics deals with the motion of an object under the influence of applied forces, and it takes for granted that such quantities as the object's position, mass, velocity, and acceleration can be measured. This assumption is, of course, completely valid in our everyday experience. Newtonian mechanics provides the "correct" explanation for the behavior of moving objects in the sense that the values it predicts for observable quantities agree with the measured values of those quantities.

Quantum mechanics deals with probabilities, not certainties

Quantum mechanics, too, consists of relationships between observable quantities, but the uncertainty principle radically alters the meaning of "observable quantity" in the atomic realm. According to the uncertainty principle, the position and momentum of a particle cannot both be accurately known at the same time. In newtonian physics, of course, such quantities are assumed to always have definite, measurable values. What quantum mechanics explores are *probabilities*. Instead of saying, for example, that the electron in a normal hydrogen atom is always exactly 5.3×10^{-11} m from the nucleus, quantum mechanics holds that this is the *most probable* distance. If we could conduct a suitable experiment, many trials would yield different values, but the one most likely to be found would be 5.3×10^{-11} m.

Quantum mechanics does not try to invent a mechanical model based on ideas from everyday life to represent the atom. Instead it deals only with quantities that can actually be measured. We can measure the mass of the electron and its electric charge, we can measure the frequencies of spectral lines emitted by excited atoms, and so on, and the theory must be able to relate them all. But we *cannot* measure the precise diameter of an electron's orbit or watch it jump from one orbit to another, and these notions, therefore, are not part of the theory.

The quantum-mechanical theory of the atom starts with Schrödinger's equation, a formula which unfortunately involves advanced mathematics. The procedure is to substitute into Schrödinger's equation such facts about an atom as the number of protons in its nucleus, the mass and charge of the electron, and so on, and then to solve the resulting equation for the wave function ψ of whichever electrons we are concerned with. From this wave function we can find the probability density of the electron, which is the likelihood that it be found in any given place. The existence of specific atomic energy levels appears as an inevitable part of the theory with no need to imagine actual orbits of fixed radius. The theory covers all atoms, in contrast to the Bohr theory's ability to cover only the hydrogen atom.

Quantum mechanics abandons the traditional approach to physics in which models we can visualize are the starting points of theories. But although quantum mechanics does not give us a look into the inner world of the atom, it does tell us everything we need to know about the measurable properties of atoms. And something more comes from a careful analysis: *newtonian mechanics is just an approximate version of quantum mechanics.* The certainties of Newton are an illusion, and their agreement with experiment is due to the fact that ordinary objects contain so many atoms that deviations from the most probable behavior are unnoticeable. Instead of two sets of physical principles, one for the world of the large and one for the world of the small, there is only a single set, and quantum mechanics represents our best effort to date at formulating it.

Newtonian mechanics is an approximation of quantum mechanics

Quantum Numbers

An atomic electron has four in all

In the Bohr model of the hydrogen atom, the electron moves around the nucleus in a circular orbit. The only quantity that changes as it does so is its position on the circle. The single quantum number n is enough to specify the physical state of such an electron.

Probability clouds of atomic electrons

In the quantum theory of the atom, an electron is not limited to a fixed orbit but is free to move about in three dimensions, as in the real world. We can think of the electron as circulating in a "probability cloud" that forms a certain pattern in space. Where the cloud is most dense (that is, where ψ^2 has a high value), the electron is most likely to be found. Where the cloud is least dense (ψ^2 has a low value), the electron is least likely to be found. Figure 8-19 shows a cross-section of the probability cloud for the normal state of the hydrogen atom.

The energy of an atomic electron depends mainly upon the quantum number n

Three quantum numbers determine the size and shape of the probability cloud of an atomic electron. One of them, the *principal quantum number*, is designated n as in the Bohr theory. This quantum number is the chief factor that governs the electron's energy (the larger n is, the greater the energy) and its average distance from the nucleus (the larger n is, the farther the electron tends to be from the nucleus).

The other two quantum numbers, l and m_l, together govern the electron's angular momentum and the form of its probability cloud. Angular momentum, as we learned in Chap. 3, is the rotational analog of linear momentum. According to quantum mechanics, angular momentum as well as energy is quantized—

The nucleus

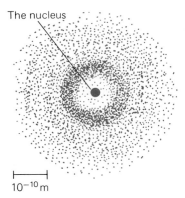

10^{-10} m

FIG. 8-19

Probability cloud for the normal state of the hydrogen atom.

The magnitude of an atomic electron's angular momentum depends upon the quantum number l

The direction of an atomic electron's angular momentum depends upon the quantum number m_l

restricted to certain particular values — in an atom. The possible values of angular momentum for an atomic electron are determined by l, the *orbital quantum number*. An electron whose principal quantum number is n can have an orbital quantum number of 0 or any whole number up to $n-1$. For instance, if $n = 3$, the values l can have are 0, 1, or 2.

The orbital quantum number l determines the *magnitude* of the electron's angular momentum. However, angular momentum, like linear momentum, is a vector quantity, and so to describe it completely requires that its *direction* be specified as well as its magnitude (Fig. 8-20). This is the role of the *magnetic quantum number* m_l. What meaning can a direction in space have for an atom? The answer becomes clear when we reflect that an electron revolving about a nucleus is a current loop and has a magnetic field like that of a tiny bar magnet. In a magnetic field the potential energy of a bar magnet depends both upon how strong it is and upon its orientation with respect to the field. It is the direction of the angular-momentum vector (that is, the direction of the axis about which the electron may be thought to revolve) with respect to a magnetic field that is determined by m_l.

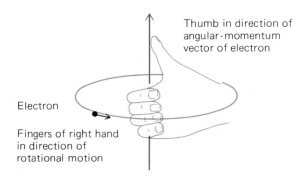

Thumb in direction of angular-momentum vector of electron

Electron

Fingers of right hand in direction of rotational motion

FIG. 8-20

The right-hand rule for direction of angular-momentum vector.

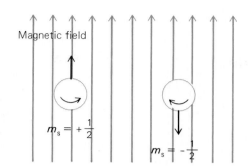

Magnetic field

$m_s = +\frac{1}{2}$

$m_s = -\frac{1}{2}$

FIG. 8-21

The spin magnetic quantum number m_s of an atomic electron has two possible values, $+\frac{1}{2}$ and $-\frac{1}{2}$, depending upon how the electron aligns itself with a magnetic field.

An electron behaves much like a spinning charged sphere

An electron whose orbital quantum number is l can have a magnetic quantum number that is 0 or any whole number between $-l$ and $+l$. For instance, if $l = 2$, the values m_l can have are -2, -1, 0, $+1$, and $+2$.

There is still another quantum number needed to describe completely an atomic electron. This is the electron *spin magnetic quantum number m_s*. Electrons behave as though they were, in themselves, little bar magnets, which we can visualize as arising from electrons spinning on their axes. Since an electron may crudely be thought of as a charged sphere, such spinning means a circular electric current and hence magnetic behavior. A spinning electron can align itself either along a magnetic field, in which case m_s has the value $+\frac{1}{2}$, or opposite to the field, in which case $m_s = -\frac{1}{2}$ (Fig. 8-21). The concept of electron spin is essential for understanding many atomic phenomena.

Exclusion Principle

A different set of quantum numbers for each electron in an atom

In a normal hydrogen atom, the electron is in its quantum state of lowest energy. What about more complex atoms? Are all 92 electrons of a uranium atom in the same quantum state, jammed into a single probability cloud? Many lines of evidence make this idea unlikely.

An example is the great difference in chemical behavior shown by certain elements whose atomic structures differ by just one electron. Thus the elements that have the atomic numbers 9, 10, and 11 are respectively the chemically active gas fluorine, the inert gas neon, and the metal sodium. Since the electron structure of an atom controls how it interacts with other atoms, it makes no sense that the chemical properties of the elements should change so sharply with a small change in atomic number if all the electrons in an atom were in the same quantum state.

In 1925 Wolfgang Pauli solved the problem of the electron arrangement in an atom that has more than one electron. His *exclusion principle* states that

Exclusion principle	Only one electron in an atom can exist in a given quantum state.

Each electron in an atom must have a different set of quantum numbers n, l, m_l, m_s. In the next chapter we will see how the exclusion principle, together with the limits on the possible values of the various quantum numbers, determines the chemical behavior of the elements.

Pauli was led to his principle by a study of atomic spectra. It is possible to determine the various states of an atom from its spectrum, and the quantum numbers of these states can be figured out. In the spectra of every element but hydrogen a number of lines are missing that correspond to electron jumps to and from states having certain combinations of quantum numbers. Pauli showed that every atomic state that does not occur involves two or more electrons with the same quantum numbers. The exclusion principle is a statement of this finding.

IMPORTANT TERMS

The **photoelectric effect** is the emission of electrons from a metal surface when light shines on it. The **quantum theory of light** states that light travels in tiny bursts of energy called **quanta** or **photons.** The photoelectric effect can be explained only by the quantum theory of light, whereas the wave theory of light is needed to account for such other phenomena as interference; the two theories complement each other.

X-rays are high-frequency electromagnetic waves given off when matter is struck by fast electrons.

Moving objects have wave as well as particle properties; the smaller the object, the more conspicuous its wave behavior. The **matter waves** that correspond to a moving object have a **de Broglie** wavelength inversely proportional to its momentum. The quantity that varies in a matter wave is called the **wave function,** and its square is the object's **probability density.** The greater the probability density at a certain time and place, the greater the likelihood of finding the object there at that time. The **uncertainty principle** expresses the limit set by the wave nature of matter on finding both the position and state of motion of a moving object at the same time.

An **emission** (or **bright-line**) spectrum consists of the various frequencies of light given off by an excited substance. An **absorption** (or **dark-line**) spectrum consists of the various frequencies absorbed by a substance when white light is passed through it.

According to the **Bohr model of the atom,** an electron can circle an atomic nucleus only if its orbit is a whole number of de Broglie wavelengths in circumference. The number of wavelengths is the **quantum number** of the orbit. Each orbit corresponds to a specific energy, and spectral lines originate in electron shifts from one orbit, and hence **energy level,** to another.

A **laser** is a device that produces an intense beam of single-frequency light whose waves are all in step with one another, which greatly increases their effectiveness.

Quantum mechanics is based on the wave nature of moving things; newtonian mechanics turns out to be an approximate version of quantum mechanics. Quantum mechanics shows that four quantum numbers in all are needed to specify the physical state of each atomic electron. One of these quantum numbers governs the direction of the **spin** of the electron. According to the **exclusion principle,** no two electrons in an atom can have the same set of quantum numbers.

IMPORTANT FORMULAS

Photon energy: $E = hf$

de Broglie wavelength: $\lambda = \dfrac{h}{mv}$

MULTIPLE CHOICE

1. When light is directed at a metal surface, the emitted electrons
   a. are called photons
   b. have random energies
   c. have energies that depend upon the intensity of the light
   d. have energies that depend upon the frequency of the light
2. The photoelectric effect occurs only when the incident light has more than a certain minimum
   a. frequency
   b. wavelength
   c. speed
   d. charge
3. When the speed of the electrons that strike a metal surface is increased, the result is an increase in
   a. the number of x-rays emitted
   b. the frequency of the x-rays emitted
   c. the speed of the x-rays emitted
   d. the size of the x-rays emitted
4. A phenomenon that cannot be understood with the help of the quantum theory of light is
   a. the photoelectric effect
   b. x-ray production
   c. the spectrum of an element
   d. interference of light
5. According to the theories of modern physics,
   a. only stationary particles exhibit wave behavior
   b. only moving particles exhibit wave behavior
   c. only charged particles exhibit wave behavior
   d. all particles exhibit wave behavior
6. The wave packet corresponding to a moving particle
   a. travels with the same speed as that of the particle
   b. travels with the speed of light
   c. has the same size as that of the particle
   d. consists of x-rays
7. De Broglie waves can be regarded as waves of
   a. pressure
   b. probability
   c. electric charge
   d. momentum
8. According to the uncertainty principle, it is impossible to precisely determine at the same time a particle's
   a. position and charge
   b. position and momentum
   c. momentum and energy
   d. charge and mass
9. If Planck's constant were larger than it is,
   a. moving bodies would have shorter wavelengths
   b. moving bodies would have higher energies
   c. moving bodies would have higher momenta
   d. the uncertainty principle would be significant on a larger scale of size
10. The bright-line spectrum produced by the excited atoms of an element contains frequencies that are
   a. the same for all elements
   b. characteristic of the particular element
   c. evenly distributed throughout the entire visible spectrum
   d. different from the frequencies in its dark-line spectrum
11. A neon sign does not produce
   a. a line spectrum
   b. an emission spectrum
   c. an absorption spectrum
   d. photons
12. The classical model of the hydrogen atom fails because
   a. an accelerated electron radiates electromagnetic waves
   b. a moving electron has more mass than an electron at rest
   c. a moving electron has more charge than an electron at rest
   d. the attractive force of the nucleus is not enough to keep an electron in orbit around it
13. An electron can revolve in an orbit around an atomic nucleus without radiating energy provided that the orbit
   a. is far enough away from the nucleus
   b. is less than a de Broglie wavelength in circumference
   c. is a whole number of de Broglie wavelengths in circumference
   d. is a perfect circle
14. According to the Bohr model of the atom, an electron in a stable orbit
   a. radiates electromagnetic energy continuously
   b. emits only spectral lines
   c. remains there forever
   d. can jump to another orbit if given enough energy
15. In the Bohr model of the atom, the electrons revolve around the nucleus of an atom so as to
   a. emit spectral lines
   b. produce x-rays
   c. form energy levels that depend upon their speeds only
   d. keep from falling into the nucleus
16. A hydrogen atom is said to be in its ground state when the electron
   a. is at rest
   b. is inside the nucleus
   c. is in its lower energy level
   d. has escaped from the atom

17. An atom emits a photon when one of its orbital electrons
    a. jumps from a higher to a lower energy level
    b. jumps from a lower to a higher energy level
    c. is removed by the photoelectric effect
    d. is struck by an x-ray
18. Which of the following types of radiation is not emitted by the electronic structures of atoms?
    a. Ultraviolet light
    b. Visible light
    c. X-rays
    d. Gamma rays
19. The operation of the laser is based upon
    a. the uncertainty principle
    b. the interference of de Broglie waves
    c. stimulated emission of radiation
    d. stimulated absorption of radiation
20. The light waves from a laser
    a. have different wavelengths
    b. have different speeds
    c. are in step with one another
    d. spread out to form a wide beam
21. The quantum-mechanical theory of the atom is
    a. based upon a mechanical model of the atom
    b. a theory that restricts itself to physical quantities that can be measured directly
    c. less accurate than the Bohr theory of the atom
    d. impossible to reconcile with Newton's laws of motion
22. A quantum number is not associated with an atomic electron's
    a. mass
    b. energy
    c. spin
    d. orbital angular momentum
23. The electrons in an atom all have the same
    a. speed
    b. spin
    c. orbit
    d. quantum numbers
24. Light of wavelength 5×10^{-7} m consists of photons whose energy is
    a. 1.1×10^{-48} J
    b. 1.3×10^{-27} J
    c. 4×10^{-19} J
    d. 1.7×10^{-15} J
25. The de Broglie wavelength of a proton is 4×10^{-14} m. The proton's speed is approximately
    a. 10^{-7} m/s

    b. 10^6 m/s
    c. 10^7 m/s
    d. 10^8 m/s

QUESTIONS

1. What are the differences between the photon and the electron?
2. The photon and the neutrino both have neither charge nor mass. What are the differences between them?
3. Compare the evidence for the wave nature of light with the evidence for its particle nature. Why do you think the wave nature of light was established long before its particle nature?
4. Energy is carried in light by means of separate photons, yet even the faintest light we can see does not appear as a series of flashes. Explain.
5. Must a particle have an electric charge in order for matter waves to be associated with its motion?
6. What kind of experiment might you use to distinguish between a gamma ray of wavelength 10^{-11} m and an electron whose de Broglie wavelength is also 10^{-11} m?
7. A photon and a proton have the same wavelength. How does the photon's energy compare with the proton's kinetic energy?
8. The uncertainty principle applies to *all* bodies, yet its consequences are only significant for such extremely small particles as electrons, protons, and neutrons. Explain.
9. What kind of spectrum would you expect to observe if you used a spectroscope to analyze: (a) light from the sun; (b) light from the tungsten filament of a light bulb; (c) light from a sodium-vapor highway lamp; (d) light from an electric light bulb that has passed through cool sodium vapor?
10. Why does the hydrogen spectrum contain many lines, even though the hydrogen atom has only a single electron?
11. Why is the Bohr theory incompatible with the uncertainty principle?
12. On the basis of the Bohr model of the atom, explain why the dark (absorption) lines in the spectrum of hydrogen have the same wavelengths as the bright (emission) lines of the same element.
13. In what way does light from a laser differ from light from other sources?
14. The four quantum numbers needed to describe an atomic electron are n, l, m_l, and m_s. What quantity is governed by each of them?
15. The Bohr theory permits us to visualize the structure of the atom, whereas quantum mechanics is very complex and con-

cerned with such ideas as wave functions and probabilities. What reasons would lead to the replacement of the Bohr theory by quantum mechanics?

16. Under what circumstances do electrons exhibit spin?

17. Under what circumstances can two electrons share the same probability cloud in an atom?

PROBLEMS

1. Calculate the energy of a photon of ultraviolet light whose frequency is 2×10^{16} Hz. Do the same for a photon of radio waves whose frequency is 2×10^5 Hz.

2. Find the energy of the photons in light whose wavelength is 2.5×10^{-7} m.

3. The eye can detect as little as 10^{-18} J of energy in the form of light. How many photons of frequency 5×10^{14} Hz does this amount of energy represent?

4. Yellow light has a frequency of about 5×10^{14} Hz. How many photons are emitted per second by a lamp that radiates yellow light at a power of 100 W?

5. The radiant energy reaching the earth from the sun is about 1400 W/m². If this energy is all green light of wavelength 5.5×10^{-7} m, how many photons strike each square meter per second?

6. How many photons per second are emitted by a 10,000-W radio transmitter whose frequency is 880 kHz?

7. An energy of 4×10^{-19} J is required to remove an electron from the surface of a particular metal. What is the frequency of the light that will just dislodge photoelectrons from the surface? What is the maximum energy of photoelectrons emitted through the action of light of wavelength 2×10^{-7} m?

8. Electrons are accelerated through potential differences of approximately 10,000 V in television picture tubes. Find the maximum frequency of the x-rays that are produced when these electrons strike the screen of the tube.

9. Find the de Broglie wavelength of an electron whose speed is 2×10^7 m/s. How significant are the wave properties of such an electron likely to be?

10. Find the de Broglie wavelength of a 1-mg grain of sand blown by the wind at a speed of 20 m/s. How significant are the wave properties of such a grain of sand likely to be?

11. An electron microscope uses 40-keV (4×10^4 eV) electrons. Find its ultimate resolving power on the assumption that this is equal to the wavelength of the electrons.

12. Find the quantum number of the Bohr orbit in a hydrogen atom that is 1 mm in radius. Why is such an orbit unlikely to actually occur?

13. Find the radius of the $n = 5$ Bohr orbit in a hydrogen atom.

14. The earth has a mass of 6×10^{24} kg, and it circles the sun at 3×10^4 m/s in an orbit 1.5×10^{11} m in radius. How many earth de Broglie wavelengths fit into this orbit?

15. Calculate the speed of the electron in the innermost ($n = 1$) Bohr orbit of a hydrogen atom. [Hint: Begin by setting the centripetal force on the electron equal to the electrical attraction of the proton it circles around.]

16. Of the following transitions in a hydrogen atom (a) which emits the photon of highest frequency, (b) which emits the photon of lowest frequency, and (c) which absorbs the photon of highest frequency? $n = 1$ to $n = 2$, $n = 2$ to $n = 1$, $n = 2$ to $n = 6$, $n = 6$ to $n = 2$.

ANSWERS TO MULTIPLE CHOICE

1. *d*	**8.** *b*	**15.** *d*	**22.** *a*
2. *a*	**9.** *d*	**16.** *c*	**23.** *b*
3. *b*	**10.** *b*	**17.** *a*	**24.** *c*
4. *d*	**11.** *c*	**18.** *d*	**25.** *c*
5. *b*	**12.** *a*	**19.** *c*	
6. *a*	**13.** *c*	**20.** *c*	
7. *b*	**14.** *d*	**21.** *b*	

9

THE PERIODIC LAW

Although the line between physics and chemistry is hazy, with this chaper we are definitely across it. Chemistry began with a search for a way to change ordinary metals into gold. This fruitless task, called *alchemy* by the Arabs, was not abandoned until the seventeenth century. At that time John Mayow and Robert Boyle in England, Jean Rey in France, and Georg Stahl in Germany, among others, started a systematic inquiry into the properties of matter and how they change in chemical reactions.

After a look at exactly what is meant by chemical change, we go on to consider the periodic law, a natural classification of the elements into groups with similar characteristics. As we shall find, the periodic law has its roots in atomic structure. This is not surprising, since the way in which electrons are arranged in an atom is what determines how it interacts with other atoms — in other words, how it behaves chemically.

ELEMENTS AND COMPOUNDS

The properties of matter are altered in a number of processes. When a solid melts into a liquid or a liquid vaporizes into a gas, the cause is a change in the motions and separations of the molecules of the material. In other processes, however, the changes are in the molecules themselves. Examples are the rusting of iron, the burning of wood, and the souring of milk. Such processes are called *chemical reactions*.

Chemical Change

A chemical reaction profoundly alters the substances involved

What happens when zinc reacts with sulfur

Let us examine a specific chemical reaction. Suppose we mix some powdered zinc metal with a somewhat larger volume of powdered sulfur on a ceramic surface and then ignite the mixture with a gas flame. The result is a small explosion with light and heat given off. When the fireworks have died down, we are left with a brittle white substance that resembles neither the original zinc nor the original sulfur (Fig. 9-1). What has happened?

Further experiments would show that neither zinc nor sulfur alone gives such a reaction when heated; that the explosion of the mixture takes place just as well in a vacuum as in air; and that the ceramic surface may be replaced by a metal or asbestos one without affecting the reaction. Evidently the process involves both zinc and sulfur, but nothing else. We conclude that zinc and sulfur have combined chemically to form the new material, which is called *zinc sulfide*.

From Fig. 9-1 we can see that the properties of zinc, sulfur, and zinc sulfide are quite different. Each of them is a pure substance: every particle of sulfur is like every other particle of sulfur, and the same is true for zinc and for zinc sulfide. However, if we simply mix zinc and sulfur together without heating them, the result is a *heterogeneous* substance whose properties vary from one particle to the next.

A heterogeneous substance is composed of particles of different kinds

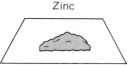

Zinc	Sulfur	Zinc sulfide
Gray metal	Soft yellow solid	Brittle white solid
Melts at 420°C	Melts at 113°C	Does not melt but decomposes into zinc and sulfur at 600°C
Density 7.1 g/cm³	Density 2.0 g/cm³	Density 3.5 g/cm³
Dissolves in dilute acids	Does not dissolve in acids	Does not dissolve in either acids or carbon disulfide
Does not dissolve in carbon disulfide	Dissolves in carbon disulfide	

FIG. 9-1
Zinc and sulfur react chemically to give zinc sulfide, a substance whose properties are different from those of zinc and sulfur.

With a microscope and a needle we can separate particles of zinc from those of sulfur, which cannot be done in the case of zinc sulfide. There has been no change at all in the ingredients of the mixture of zinc and sulfur.

Elements, Compounds, and Mixtures

Three classes of matter

Elements are simple substances that cannot be decomposed or transformed into one another by chemical means

Although the alchemists never reached their goal of turning ordinary metals into gold, their work did have an important result. This was the idea that certain substances, such as zinc, sulfur, and (of course) gold, could neither be decomposed nor be transformed into one another. Slowly the belief grew that only a limited number of such *elements* exist and that all other substances are combinations of them. A new material can be formed from others by chemical change only if its elements are present in the original materials. This observation is what marks the beginning of the science of chemistry.

Elements are the simplest substances present in bulk matter. Over 100 elements are known, of which 10 are gases, 2 are liquids, and the rest are solids at room temperature and atmospheric pressure. Hydrogen, helium, oxygen, chlorine, and neon are familiar gaseous elements, and bromine and mercury are the two liquids. Most of the solid elements are metals.

The symbols of the various elements are listed in a table at the back of this book. They are abbreviations of the elements' names, for instance H for hydrogen, He for helium, and Li for lithium. Sometimes the abbreviations are taken from Latin names, for instance Fe for ferrum (iron), Cu for cuprum (copper), and Au for aurum (gold).

Two or more elements may combine to form a compound with characteristic properties of its own

The matter around us contains elements in a variety of forms. Some materials consist of two or more elements joined together into chemical *compounds,* as in the case of zinc sulfide. Chemical reactions always involve the formation or breaking down of one or more compounds.

Other materials are mixtures of elements or compounds or both. A mixture may be heterogeneous, with its components obvious to the eye and easy to separate. Concrete is an example. When the components are so thoroughly mixed that the result is uniform, we have a homogeneous mixture, or *solution.* Air is a solution of various gases, sea water is a solution of various solids and gases dissolved in water. Figure 9-2 shows how matter is classified into its different forms.

A solution is a uniform mixture of different substances

How can we tell whether two elements have joined to make a compound or are just mixed to make a solution? A number of tests are available. Here are two:

A compound boils and freezes at definite temperatures and is not altered by a change of state

1. See whether the material can be separated into different substances by boiling or freezing. The temperatures at which changes of state occur have specific values for elements and compounds but not for mixtures. Air, for example, is a solution of several gases, mainly nitrogen and oxygen. Nitrogen boils at $-196°C$ and oxygen boils at $-183°C$, 13° higher. If we heat a sample of liquid

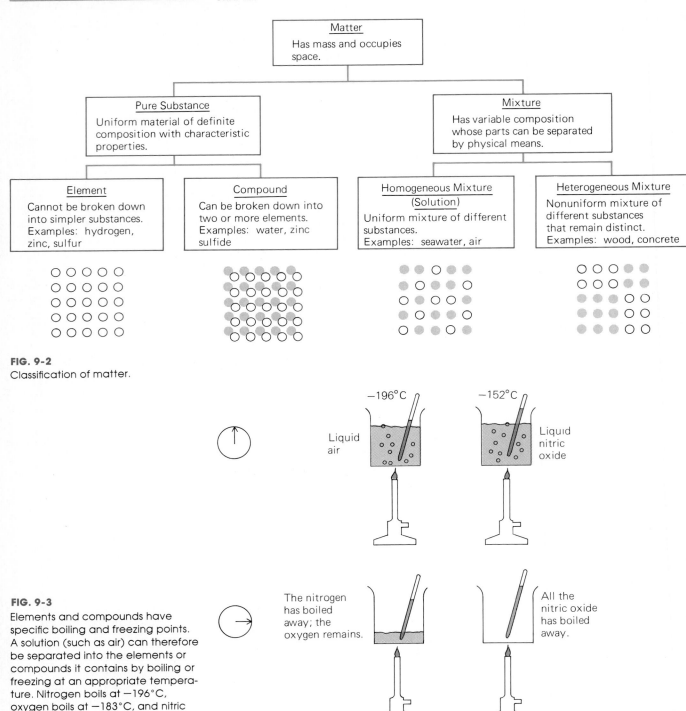

FIG. 9-2
Classification of matter.

FIG. 9-3
Elements and compounds have specific boiling and freezing points. A solution (such as air) can therefore be separated into the elements or compounds it contains by boiling or freezing at an appropriate temperature. Nitrogen boils at −196°C, oxygen boils at −183°C, and nitric oxide boils at −152°C.

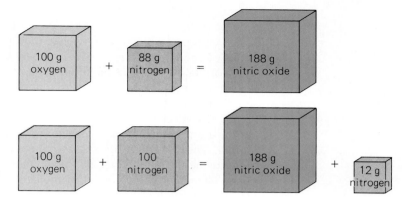

FIG. 9-4

An example of the law of definite proportions. Elements combine in a specific mass ratio when they form a compound.

According to the law of definite proportions, the elements in a compound are present in a specific ratio by mass

air to $-196°C$, nitrogen predominates in the gas that is given off, leaving a liquid behind that is richer in oxygen than the original sample. On the other hand, the compound of nitrogen and oxygen called nitric oxide has a boiling point of $-152°C$. If we heat a sample of liquid nitric oxide to $-152°C$, all of it will boil away at this temperature (Fig. 9-3), with no change in composition.

2. Compare the relative amounts of the elements in different samples of the material. The elements in a given compound are always present in the same proportions, whereas the constituents of a solution may be present in a wide range of proportions. At sea level, the mass ratio of the nitrogen and oxygen in air has an average value of 3.2 : 1, but it is several percent more at high altitudes. However, the mass ratio of these elements in nitric oxide is exactly 0.88 : 1 everywhere. If there is an excess of either nitrogen or oxygen when nitric oxide is being prepared, the additional amount will not combine but will be left over and can easily be separated (Fig. 9-4). The *law of definite proportions* is as basic to chemistry as the law of conservation of momentum is to physics.

The Atomic Theory

The building blocks of matter

Two hundred years ago nobody had any defensible ideas about the structure of matter, of how elements join to make compounds. The theory that answered these questions came from a seemingly unlikely Englishman, an awkward, colorless, poorly educated teacher named John Dalton (1766 – 1844). Dalton was a plodding, literal thinker who had had no formal instruction in physics or chemistry. These liabilities turned out to be assets, because they led him to seek simple explanations for complex phenomena without being hampered by the misconceptions of other people.

The atomic theory of matter emerged from Dalton's attempts at picturing the ultimate particles of which gases were composed. He began with the ancient Greek concept that everything was composed of atoms and developed it into a definite scheme with numerical values that could be checked against experiment. Some of Dalton's notions have had to be modified, and rather than go into the full story of the evolution of the atomic theory we shall simply summarize what is known today about the structure of matter.

In brief, the ultimate particles of any gaseous compound are called *molecules*. Molecules may be further broken down, but when this happens the fragments are no longer representative of the essential characteristics of the compound. The molecules of a gaseous compound consist of the *atoms* of its constituent elements. Although the ultimate particles of any element are atoms, many elemental gases consist of molecules instead of individual atoms. Thus gaseous oxygen contains oxygen molecules, each of which is a pair of oxygen atoms bound together by forces whose nature we shall explore later in this chapter. Other elemental gases, for instance helium and neon, consist of single atoms.

Atoms and most molecules are very small, and even a tiny bit of matter contains huge numbers of them. If each atom in a penny were worth 1 cent, all the money in the world would not be enough to pay for it.

The molecules of a compound have definite, invariable compositions and structures, as Fig. 9-5 shows. Each water molecule contains two hydrogen atoms and one oxygen atom with the hydrogen atoms 105° apart, for example, while each ammonia molecule contains three hydrogen atoms 107.5° apart.

Two or more atoms linked into a molecule are represented by writing their

Molecules are the ultimate particles of a gaseous compound; atoms are the ultimate particles of an element

Molecular formulas

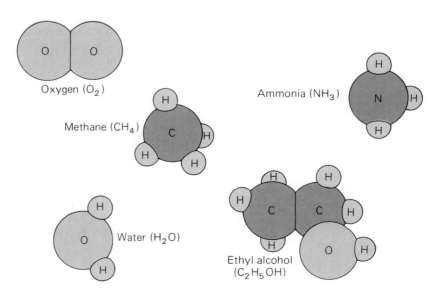

FIG. 9-5
Structures of several common molecules.

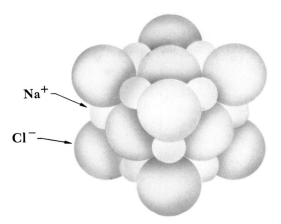

FIG. 9-6
Sodium chloride crystals consist of
Na$^+$ and Cl$^-$ ions rather than of
neutral Na and Cl atoms.

The ultimate particles of liquid and
solid compounds may be atoms,
molecules, or ions

symbols side by side: a carbon monoxide molecule is CO, a zinc sulfide molecule
ZnS, a mercuric oxide molecule HgO. When a molecule contains two or more
atoms of the same kind, a subscript indicates the number present. Thus the familiar
H_2O means that a molecule of water contains two H atoms and one O atom; a
molecule of oxygen, containing two O atoms, is written O_2; a molecule of carbon
tetrachloride (CCl_4) contains one C atom and four Cl atoms; a molecule of nitrogen pentoxide (N_2O_5) contains two N atoms and five O atoms. Each subscript
applies only to the symbol immediately before it. These expressions for molecules
are called *formulas*.

Elements in liquid and solid form are usually assemblies of individual atoms.
Some compounds in these forms are also assemblies of individual molecules, but
more often the situation is not so straightforward, as discussed in Chap. 10. For
example, crystals of table salt, which is a compound of sodium and chlorine,
consist of sodium and chlorine ions rather than of neutral atoms or molecules; the
sodium ions are positively charged and the chlorine ions are negatively charged
(Fig. 9-6). For every sodium ion Na$^+$, there is a chlorine ion Cl$^-$, so the ratio
between them is fixed, and the ions are firmly held together in a definite array.
Sodium chloride is therefore as much a compound as, say, water, even though it is
not composed of separate molecules, and its formula is NaCl.

THE PERIODIC LAW

The periodic law, now over a century old, represents a giant step for chemistry on
its path toward understanding the nature and behavior of the elements. There
cannot be many chemistry laboratories in the world that do not have a copy of the
periodic table hanging on a wall. Before we examine the periodic law itself, we
shall look at some of the background ideas that led to its formulation.

TABLE 9-1
Some Physical Properties of Metals and Nonmetals.

Property	Metals	Nonmetals
Metallic luster	Yes	No
Opaque to light	Yes	Only a few
Can be deformed without breaking	Yes	No
Conducts heat and electricity	Yes	No

Metals and Nonmetals

A fundamental distinction

Most elements are metals

The division between metals and nonmetals is a familiar one. All metals except mercury are solid at room temperature; iron, copper, aluminum, tin, silver, and gold are examples. Nonmetals may be solid (carbon, sulfur), liquid (bromine), or gaseous (chlorine, oxygen, nitrogen) at room temperature. Metals are far more numerous than nonmetals: less than 1 in 5 of the elements is a nonmetal.

Metallic luster

A number of physical properties distinguish metals from nonmetals. An obvious one is *metallic luster*, the characteristic sheen of a clean metal surface. Related to this sheen is the fact that metals are opaque to light even in thin sheets. Solid nonmetals do not show metallic luster and nearly all are transparent in thin sheets.

Metals can be deformed without breaking and conduct heat and electricity readily

Another typical property of metals is their ability to be shaped by being bent or hammered. An ounce of gold can be beaten into 300 ft² of foil, for instance, and a copper rod can be pulled through a die to make a hair-thin wire without breaking. Solid nonmetals, on the other hand, are brittle. Metals are all good conductors of heat and electricity, nonmetals are insulators (Table 9-1). Carbon is intermediate between metals and nonmetals in some respects, since its conductivity is not as poor as those of the other nonmetals and one form of it, graphite (familiar as the "lead" in pencils) is somewhat lustrous; but all forms of carbon are brittle.

Chemical Activity

The more active an element, the more stable its compounds

Metals and nonmetals also differ in their chemical properties, but these differences are less clearcut because the elements in each category vary considerably among themselves. In particular, some metals and nonmetals are very *active*, which

Gold objects such as this Ashanti ring from Africa do not tarnish or corrode because gold is a very inactive metal.

means that they readily combine to form compounds. Inactive elements have little tendency to react chemically.

Active elements liberate more heat when they react than inactive elements do

Sodium is an example of an active metal, gold an example of an inactive one. A few seconds in the open air leaves sodium tarnished, but a gold ring remains bright after a lifetime of exposure to perspiration as well as air. Sodium combines spectacularly with chlorine, evolving much heat and light, but gold does so only sluggishly, with little energy set free. Sodium reacts with dilute acids, even with water; gold is affected only by a mixture of concentrated hydrochloric and nitric acids.

The relative activities of different elements can be established by measuring the heat given off in similar chemical reactions. Suppose we combine a given amount of chlorine with sodium and the same amount with gold. We would find that the formation of sodium chloride gives off over 15 times as much heat as the formation of gold chloride does. The conclusion is that sodium is much more active than gold.

Active elements usually form stable compounds

Or we might start out with similar compounds and ask how easily they can be separated into their component elements or element groups. In the case of gold chloride and sodium chloride, the results are that gold chloride decomposes when it is heated to about 300°C, but sodium chloride must be heated to well over 1000°C for it to break up. Gold chloride is accordingly considered a relatively

TABLE 9-2
Relative Activities of Metals and Nonmetals.

Metals	Nonmetals
Potassium	Fluorine
Sodium	Chlorine
Calcium	Bromine
Magnesium	Oxygen
Aluminum	Iodine
Zinc	Sulfur
Iron	
Lead	
Copper	
Mercury	
Silver	
Gold	

More active / Less active

unstable compound and sodium chloride a relatively stable compound. In general, the more active an element is, the more difficult it is to decompose its compounds: active elements tend to form stable compounds whereas inactive ones tend to form unstable compounds.

There are other means of establishing the relative activity of the elements, but the two mentioned above are probably the most useful. Both metals and nonmetals can be arranged in order of their activities. In the partial listing of Table 9-2 the most active elements are at the top of each series, the least active at the bottom.

Hydrogen is an important element but one that is hard to classify. Its physical properties are certainly not those of a metal, but it combines chemically with nonmetals in a manner typical of a metal. The reason for this behavior will become clear later.

Families of Elements

The members of each family have a lot in common

Some elements resemble one another so much that they seem to be members of the same natural family. Three conspicuous examples of such families are a group of active nonmetals called the *halogens,* a group of active metals called the *alkali metals,* and a group of gases that undergo almost no chemical reactions, the *inert gases.*

The halogens (Table 9-3) are all highly active elements. In fact, fluorine is the most active element of all, and is even able to corrode platinum. The halogens are responsible for some of the vilest odors (*bromos* is Greek for "stink") and most brilliant colors (*chloros* is Greek for "green") to be found in the laboratory. The name halogen means "salt former," a token of the fact that these elements produce white, crystalline solids when they combine with many metals. Fluorine is a pale yellow gas and chlorine a greenish-yellow gas at room temperature; bromine is a reddish-brown liquid; iodine is a steel-gray solid; astatine is a radioactive solid. About one part of chlorine per million parts of water is enough to kill any bacteria present, which is why chlorine is commonly added to water supplies and to swimming pools.

What are the similarities among the halogens? For one thing, their molecules contain two atoms at ordinary temperatures: F_2, Cl_2, Br_2, I_2. Also, the compounds they form with metals have similar formulas. Here are three examples:

NaF	ZnF_2	AlF_3
NaCl	$ZnCl_2$	$AlCl_3$
NaBr	$ZnBr_2$	$AlBr_3$
NaI	ZnI_2	AlI_3

In all compounds with a specific metal, the same number of halogen atoms combine with each metal atom, though this number may vary for different metals.

The halogens

TABLE 9-3
The Halogens.

Element	Symbol	Atomic number
Fluorine	F	9
Chlorine	Cl	17
Bromine	Br	35
Iodine	I	53
Astatine	At	85

TABLE 9-4
The Alkali Metals.

Element	Symbol	Atomic number
Lithium	Li	3
Sodium	Na	11
Potassium	K	19
Rubidium	Rb	37
Cesium	Cs	55
Francium	Fr	87

All the halogens react with hydrogen to form HF, HCl, HBr, and so on. These compounds can be dissolved in water to form acids, of which hydrochloric acid is a familiar example. The halogens dissolve readily in carbon tetrachloride to give solutions colored in the same way as their vapors, but they are only slightly soluble in water.

The *alkali metals* (Table 9-4) are all soft, not very dense, and very active chemically. Like sodium, the other alkali metals tarnish quickly in air, liberate hydrogen from water and dilute acids, and combine with active nonmetals to form very stable compounds. Formulas for their compounds follow similar patterns, for instance

Bromides:	LiBr	NaBr	KBr	RbBr	CsBr
Sulfides:	Li_2S	Na_2S	K_2S	Rb_2S	Cs_2S
Hydroxides:	LiOH	NaOH	KOH	RbOH	CsOH

Among the other properties the alkali metals have in common are rather low melting points for metals: cesium melts in a warm room, and even lithium, which has the hightest melting point of the group, liquefies at only 186°C.

The *inert gases* (Table 9-5), in contrast with the active halogens and alkali metals, are so inactive that they form only a handful of compounds with other elements. In fact, their atoms are so inactive that they do not even join together into molecules like the atoms of other gaseous elements. All the inert gases are found in small amounts in the atmosphere, with argon making up about 1 percent of the air and the others much less. Their scarcity and inactivity prevented their discovery until the very end of the nineteenth century.

Helium, although denser than hydrogen and so less buoyant, cannot burn or explode, and so is ideal for lighter-than-air craft such as balloons and blimps. We have already met radon, a radioactive product of radium decay. The other inert gases glow in various colors when an electric current is passed through them, and are widely used in signs.

The alkali metals

The inert gases

TABLE 9-5
The Inert Gases.

Element	Symbol	Atomic number
Helium	He	2
Neon	Ne	10
Argon	Ar	18
Krypton	Kr	36
Xenon	Xe	54
Radon	Rn	86

The Periodic Table

Organizing the elements

A pattern of recurring similarities among the elements is the basis of the periodic law

A curious feature of the elements listed in Tables 9-3, 9-4, and 9-5 is that each halogen is followed in atomic number by an inert gas and then by an alkali metal. Thus fluorine, neon, and sodium have the atomic numbers 9, 10, and 11 in that order, a sequence that continues through astatine (85), radon (86), and francium (87). When the rest of the elements are examined to see what other regularities are present in their properties, the result is the *periodic law:*

When the elements are listed in order of atomic number, elements with similar chemical and physical properties appear at regular intervals.

Mendeleev

The periodic law was first formulated in detail by the Russian chemist Dmitri Mendeleev about 1869. Born in Siberia, Mendeleev became professor of chemistry at the University of St. Petersburg. He devoted himself to governmental service as well as to scientific work, although his outspoken liberal ideas were frequently embarrassing to the tsarist regime. Mendeleev was a gifted teacher and an able experimenter, but above all a dreamer, a scientific visionary. If some of his speculations seem fantastic, for one vision at least chemistry owes him a great debt, the vision that gave him the key to the classification of the elements. In this vision he was not alone, for a few of his contemporaries reached the same conclusion independently. However, Mendeleev was the first to apply such ideas to all the known elements and to successfully predict the existence and properties of elements then unknown.

Although the modern quantum theory of the atom was many years in the

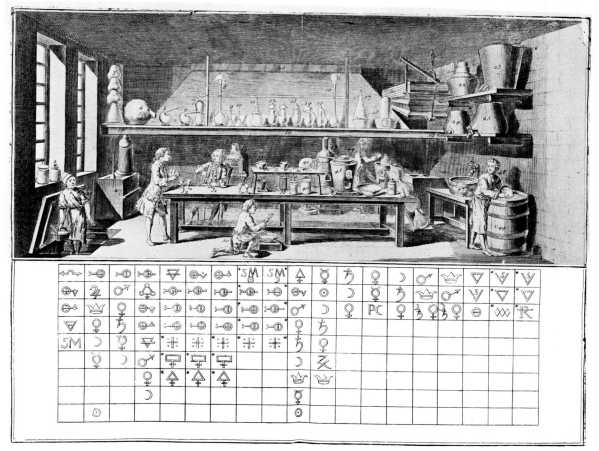

This 1780 table of chemical symbols represents an early attempt at showing relationships among the elements in schematic form. A chemical laboratory of the time is pictured in the engraving.

future, Mendeleev was fully aware of the significance his work would turn out to have. As he remarked, "The periodic law, together with the revelations of spectrum analysis, have contributed to again revive an old but remarkably long-lived hope — that of discovering, if not by experiment, at least by mental effort, the *primary matter*."

A *periodic table* is a listing of the elements according to atomic number in a series of rows such that elements with similar properties form vertical columns. Table 9-6 is a simple form of the periodic table. Let us see how it organizes our knowledge of the elements.

How the periodic table is constructed

The first element in the table is hydrogen, which, as noted earlier, behaves chemically much like an active metal although physically it is a nonmetal. Next comes the inert gas helium, the alkali metal lithium, and the less active metal beryllium. Then follows a series of nonmetals of increasing nonmetallic activity: boron, carbon, nitrogen, oxygen, and finally the halogen fluorine. From lithium to

TABLE 9-6
The Periodic Table of the Elements.

The number above the symbol of each element is its atomic mass, and the number below the symbol is its atomic number. The elements whose atomic masses are given in parentheses do not occur in nature, but have been prepared artificially in nuclear reactions. The atomic mass in such a case is the mass number of the most long-lived radioactive isotope of the element.

Group	I	II	III	IV	V	VI	VII	VIII
Period 1	1.008 H 1							4.00 He 2
2	6.94 Li 3	9.01 Be 4	10.81 B 5	12.01 C 6	14.01 N 7	16.00 O 8	19.00 F 9	20.18 Ne 10
3	22.99 Na 11	24.31 Mg 12	26.98 Al 13	28.09 Si 14	30.97 P 15	32.06 S 16	35.45 Cl 17	39.95 Ar 18
4	39.10 K 19	40.08 Ca 20	44.96 Sc 21					
5	85.47 Rb 37	87.62 Sr 38	88.91 Y 39					
6	132.9 Cs 55	137.3 Ba 56	* 57–71					
7	(223) Fr 87	226.0 Ra 88	† 89–103					

Alkali metals

Halogens Inert gases

Transition elements (Period 4):

47.90 Ti 22	50.94 V 23	52.00 Cr 24	54.94 Mn 25	55.85 Fe 26	58.93 Co 27	58.70 Ni 28	63.55 Cu 29	65.38 Zn 30
69.72 Ga 31	72.59 Ge 32	74.92 As 33	78.96 Se 34	79.90 Br 35	83.8 Kr 36			

Transition elements (Period 5):

91.22 Zr 40	92.91 Nb 41	95.94 Mo 42	(97) Tc 43	101.1 Ru 44	102.9 Rh 45	106.4 Pd 46	107.9 Ag 47	112.4 Cd 48
114.8 In 49	118.7 Sn 50	121.8 Sb 51	127.6 Te 52	126.9 I 53	131.3 Xe 54			

Transition elements (Period 6):

178.5 Hf 72	180.9 Ta 73	183.9 W 74	186.2 Re 75	190.2 Os 76	192.2 Ir 77	195.1 Pt 78	197.0 Au 79	200.6 Hg 80
204.4 Tl 81	207.2 Pb 82	209.0 Bi 83	(209) Po 84	(210) At 85	(222) Rn 86			

Transition elements (Period 7):

(257) Rf 104	(260) Ha 105

*Rare earths

138.91 La 57	140.12 Ce 58	140.91 Pr 59	144.24 Nd 60	(145) Pm 61	150.4 Sm 62	152.0 Eu 63	157.3 Gd 64	158.9 Tb 65	162.5 Dy 66	164.9 Ho 67	167.3 Er 68	168.9 Tm 69	173.0 Yb 70	175.0 Lu 71

†Actinides

(227) Ac 89	232.0 Th 90	231.0 Pa 91	238.0 U 92	(237) Np 93	(244) Pu 94	(243) Am 95	(247) Cm 96	(247) Bk 97	(251) Cf 98	(254) Es 99	(257) Fm 100	(258) Md 101	(255) No 102	(260) Lr 103

Elements created in the laboratory

fluorine is a complete sequence from a highly active metal to a highly active nonmetal. Following fluorine is neon, an inert gas like helium, and after neon is sodium, an alkali metal like lithium.

Clearly it makes sense to break off the rows at helium and neon and start new rows with lithium and sodium under hydrogen. In the seven elements beyond neon, we find again a transition from active metals to active nonmetals.

After calcium, in the fourth row, complications appear. Scandium, the next element, is similar to aluminum in some properties, different in others. Titanium (Ti) is even less like carbon and silicon. Then follow 10 metals (including iron, copper, and zinc) that are quite similar among themselves but differ conspicuously from the nonmetals at the end of the first three rows. Only after the 10 metals do three relatives of these nonmetals appear, arsenic (As), selenium (Se), and bromine. Between the gases helium and neon is a sequence of eight elements; between neon and argon is another sequence of eight; but between argon and krypton the sequence includes 18. Beyond krypton is a second sequence of 18, including again a dozen metals with many properties in common. From xenon to the last inert gas, radon, is a yet more complex sequence of 32 elements.

Groups and Periods

Elements in a group have similar properties; elements in a period have different ones

Elements in a group are similar, those in a period are different

The periodic table shows similar elements in vertical columns called *groups*. The horizontal rows, containing elements with widely different properties, are called *periods* (Fig. 9-7). Across each period is a more or less steady change from an active metal through less active metals and weakly active nonmetals to highly active nonmetals and finally to an inert gas. Within each column there is also a steady change in properties, but much less rapid and less conspicuous than within the periods. Thus increasing atomic number brings increasing activity in the alkali metal family and decreasing activity among the nonmetals of the halogen family. These changes are typical; chemical properties within each group change from top

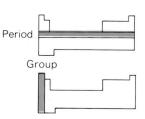

FIG. 9-7
The elements in a group of the periodic table have similar properties, while those in a period have different properties.

FIG. 9-8
How chemical activity varies in the periodic table.

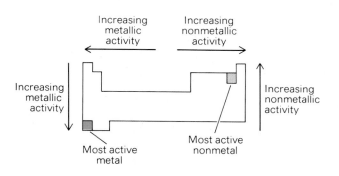

FIG. 9-9
The majority of the elements are metals.

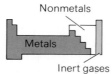

Nonmetals

Metals

Inert gases

FIG. 9-10
The transition elements are metals.

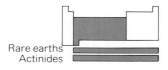

Rare earths
Actinides

to bottom in the direction of increased metallic activity or decreased nonmetallic activity—which amount to the same thing (Fig.9-8).

The periodic table has eight principal groups, which are indicated by Roman numerals in Table 9-6. The inert gases of Group VIII are placed at the right since this puts them with the other nonmetals (Fig. 9-9). Each of the eight-element periods (periods 1 and 2) is broken after the second element in order to keep their members aligned with the most closely related elements of the long periods below.

Transition elements, rare-earth metals, and actinides

The 10 *transition elements* in each long period are metals that resemble one another in chemical behavior but do not much resemble elements in the major groups (Fig. 9-10). Period 6 contains 32 elements altogether, but 15 of these are brought out to a box below the table. These *rare-earth* metals are very much alike, so much so that they are extremely hard to separate and are all lumped together in the spot (marked by as asterisk) below yttrium, Y. A similar group of closely related elements, the *actinides,* appears in the same position in period 7, and these elements are shown with the rare earths below the table itself.

The relationships brought out by the periodic table are a little vague in places, but on the whole the table brings together similar elements with considerable accuracy. Mendeleev's achievement is all the more remarkable when we recall that in 1869, when the periodic law was developed, the notion of atomic number had not been discovered and only 63 elements in all were known. Mendeleev actually used atomic mass, not atomic number, in setting up the periodic table, and he and later chemists found it necessary to deviate from the strict sequence of atomic masses for certain elements. Potassium, for example, has a smaller atomic mass than argon, yet ending the third period with potassium would put this active metal under the inert gases helium and neon, whereas argon would go beneath sodium and lithium. To avoid this discrepancy, the order is reversed to bring argon before potassium, which, of course, fits in with the order of their atomic numbers.

Mendeleev correctly predicted the existence and properties of a number of elements

Because so few elements were known in his time, Mendeleev had to leave gaps in his table in order to have similar elements fall in line. Sure of the correctness of his classification, he proposed that these gaps represented undiscovered elements. From the position of each gap, from the properties of the elements around it, and from the variation of these properties across the periods and down the columns, he went on to predict the properties of the unknown elements. His predictions included not only general chemical activity but precise numerical values for densities, melting points, and so on.

As the unknown elements were discovered one by one and as their properties were found to agree closely with Mendeleev's predictions, the validity and usefulness of the periodic classification became firmly established. Perhaps its greatest triumph came at the end of the last century, when the inert gases were discovered. Here were six new elements whose existence Mendeleev was not aware of, but they fitted perfectly as one more family of similar elements into the periodic table.

ATOMIC STRUCTURE

Now we return to the atomic theory of Chap. 8 to seek the basis of the periodic law. Two basic principles determine the structure of an atom with more than one electron:

The electrons in an atom must be in the lowest energy levels permitted by the exclusion principle

1. The exclusion principle, which states that only one electron can exist in each quantum state of an atom. Thus each electron in a complex atom must have different sets of quantum numbers n, l, m_l, and m_s.
2. An atom, like any other system, is stable when its total energy is a minimum. This means that the various electrons in a normal atom are in the quantum states of lowest energy permitted by the exclusion principle.

Shells and Subshells

They contain atomic electrons with similar energies

The electrons in an atomic shell have the same quantum number n

Let us look into how electron energy varies with quantum state. All the electrons in an atom with the same quantum number n are, on the average, about the same distance from the nucleus. These electrons therefore move around in nearly the same electric field and have similar energies. It is convenient to speak of such electrons as occupying the same atomic *shell*.

The electrons in a subshell have the same quantum number l

The energy of an electron in a particular shell also depends to some extent upon its orbital quantum number l. The higher the value of l, the higher the energy. Electrons that share a certain value of l in a shell are said to occupy the same *subshell*. All the electrons in a subshell have nearly the same energy since electron energy varies only slightly with m_l and m_s, the other two quantum numbers.

A closed shell or subshell contains its full quota of electrons

The exclusion principle limits the number of electrons that can occupy a given shell or subshell. A shell or subshell that contains its full quota of electrons is said to be *closed*. The subshells in a shell of given n can have any value of l from 0 to $n-1$. Thus the $n=1$ shell has only the single subshell $l=0$; the $n=2$ shell has the subshells $l=0$ and $l=1$; the $n=3$ shell has the subshells $l=0$, $l=1$, and $l=2$; and so on.

The greater the value of the orbital quantum number l, the more electrons the corresponding subshell can hold. When $l=0$, the maximum number of electrons turns out to be 2; when $l=1$, it is 6; when $l=2$, it is 10; and so on. Adding up the electrons in its closed subshells gives the maximum number of electrons in a closed shell. Thus a closed $n=1$ shell holds 2 electrons; a closed $n=2$ shell holds $2 + 6 = 8$ electrons; a closed $n = 3$ shell holds $2 + 6 + 10 = 18$ electrons; and so on.

The concept of electron shells and subshells fits perfectly into the pattern of the periodic table, which turns out to mirror the atomic structures of the elements. Let us see how this pattern arises.

Explaining the Periodic Table

How an atom's electron structure determines its chemical behavior

Inert gas atoms have closed shells or subshells

Table 9-7, which is illustrated in Fig. 9-11, shows the occupancy of the various shells in a number of elements. The table is arranged in the same manner as the periodic table to emphasize their relationship. To interpret Table 9-7 we note that the electrons in a closed shell are all tightly bound, since the positive nuclear charge that attracts them is large relative to the negative charge of the inner electrons. An atom that contains only closed shells or subshells has its electric charge uniformly distributed, so it does not attract other electrons and its electrons

TABLE 9-7

Simplified Table of Electron Structures of Some Atoms.
(Subshells are filled when a shell has 2, 8, or 18 electrons.)

Electrons in	H							He
1st shell	1							2
Electrons in	Li	Be	B	C	N	O	F	Ne
1st shell	2	2	2	2	2	2	2	2
2d shell	1	2	3	4	5	6	7	8
Electrons in	Na	Mg	Al	Si	P	S	Cl	Ar
1st shell	2	2	2	2	2	2	2	2
2d shell	8	8	8	8	8	8	8	8
3d shell	1	2	3	4	5	6	7	8
Electrons in	K	Ca	. . . .				Br	Kr
1st shell	2	2					2	2
2d shell	8	8					8	8
3d shell	8	8					18	18
4th shell	1	2					7	8
Electrons in	Rb	Sr	. . . .					Xe
1st shell	2	2					2	2
2d shell	8	8					8	8
3d shell	18	18					18	18
4th shell	8	8					18	18
5th shell	1	2					7	8

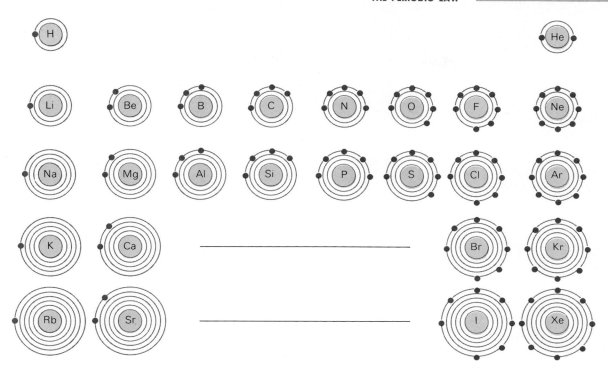

FIG. 9-11
Electron structures of some atoms. In this schematic representation of Table 9-7 the electrons in filled inner shells are not shown.

Why single outer electrons are weakly held

cannot be readily detached. Such atoms we expect to be passive chemically, like the inert gases — and the inert gases all turn out to have closed-subshell electron configurations!

Those atoms with just a single electron in their outermost shell tend to lose this electron because the electric force on it is weak. There are two reasons for this weakness:

1. An outer electron is relatively far from the nucleus.
2. Such an electron is shielded by the electrons closer to the nucleus from nearly all the electric charge of the nucleus.

Alkali metal atoms

Hydrogen and the alkali metals have single outer electrons, according to Fig. 9-11, and so have similar chemical behavior. In the sodium atom, the total nuclear charge of $+11e$ acts on the two innermost electrons, which are held very tightly. These electrons shield part of the nuclear charge from the 8 electrons in the second shell, which are attracted by a net charge of $+9e$. All 10 electrons in the first and second shells act to shield the outmost electron, which therefore "sees" a net nuclear charge of only $+e$ and is held much less securely to the atom than any of the other electrons (Fig. 9-12).

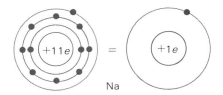

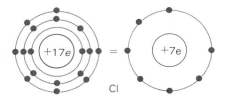

FIG. 9-12
Electron shielding in sodium and chlorine. Each outer electron in a Cl atom is acted upon by an effective nuclear charge seven times greater than that acting upon the outer electron in a Na atom, even though the outer electrons in both cases are in the same shell.

Halogen atoms

Atoms whose outer shells lack a single electron from being closed tend to pick up such an electron through the strong attraction of the poorly shielded nuclear charge. The chemical behavior of the halogens is the result. In the chlorine atom, for instance, there are the same 10 electrons in the inner 2 shells that there are in the sodium atom, but the nuclear charge of chlorine is $+17e$. Hence the net charge "felt" by each of the 7 outer electrons is $+7e$, and the attractive force is accordingly 7 times greater than in the case of the lone outer electron in sodium (Fig. 9-12).

What characterizes an alkali metal atom, then, is a tendency to lose its outer electron. It is not much of a step to a general description of all metal atoms:

Behavior of metal atoms

A metal atom has one or several electrons outside closed shells or subshells and combines chemically by losing these electrons to nonmetal atoms.

In the same way, we can go on to a general description of nonmetal atoms:

Behavior of nonmetal atoms

A nonmetal atom lacks one or several electrons of having closed shells or subshells and combines chemically by picking up electrons from metal atoms or by sharing electrons with other nonmetal atoms.

The inert gases are exceptions, of course, since their structures make it hard for them to gain or lose electrons and so they have almost no ability to react chemically.

The steady change in chemical properties as we go across a period from an

Why chemical properties vary across a period

alkali metal on the left to a halogen on the right is easy to account for. An atom of an element in Group II, for instance magnesium, Mg, has two electrons outside closed inner shells, as we see in Fig. 9-11. These electrons "feel" an effective nuclear charge of $+2e$ and so are more tightly held than the single outer electron in sodium, which "feels" an effective nuclear charge of only $+e$. Not surprisingly, the outer electrons in an Mg atom are harder to pull away than the outer electron in Na, and so Mg is less active as a metal than Na. Aluminum, Al, with three outer electrons, holds them still more securely, which is why Al is less active in turn than Mg.

In a nonmetal atom, the more the gaps in its outer shell, the weaker is the electric field that attracts additional electrons to complete the shell. Sulfur, S, with two electrons missing from its outer shell, is therefore less active a nonmetal than chlorine, which is missing just one electron. Phosphorus, P, with three electrons missing, is still less active. We can now see why, in any period, metallic activity (losing electrons) decreases going to the right whereas nonmetallic activity (gaining electrons) increases (Fig. 9-8).

As Table 9-7 shows, in several places the electron shells and subshells are not always filled in consecutive order. Thus the transition elements in any period have the same outer electron shells and add electrons successively to inner shells, which accounts for their similar properties. Another consequence of the delayed filling of inner shells is the strongly magnetic behavior of iron, nickel, and cobalt.

CHEMICAL BONDS

What is the nature of the forces that bond atoms together to form compounds? This question, of basic importance to the chemist, is no less important to the physicist, whose theory of the atom cannot be correct unless it provides a satisfactory answer. The ability of the quantum theory of the atom to explain chemical bonding is further testimony to the power of this approach.

Types of Bond

Electric forces hold atoms to one another

Let us consider what happens when two atoms are brought closer and closer together. Three extreme situations may occur:

A covalent bond is formed by the sharing of electrons

1. A *covalent bond* is formed. One or more pairs of electrons are shared by the two atoms. These electrons spend more time between the atoms than outside them, which produces an attractive force. An example is H_2, the hydrogen molecule, whose two electrons belong jointly to the two protons (Fig. 9-13).

An ionic bond is formed by the attraction of ions

2. An *ionic bond* is formed. One or more electrons from one atom transfer to another, and the resulting positive and negative ions attract each other. An

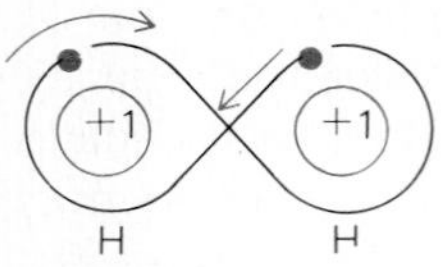

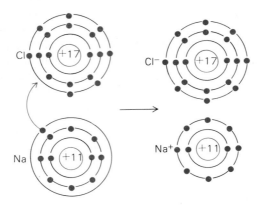

FIG. 9-13 (*above*)
Covalent bonding in hydrogen. The shared electrons spend more time on the average between their parent nuclei and therefore lead to an attractive force.

FIG. 9-14 (*right*)
Ionic bonding. Sodium and chlorine combine chemically by the transfer of electrons from sodium atoms to chlorine atoms. The resulting ions attract electrically.

example is NaCl, where the bond exists between Na^+ and Cl^- ions and not between Na and Cl atoms (Fig. 9-14).

3. No bond is formed. The atoms do not interact to produce an attractive force.

In H_2 the bond is purely covalent and in NaCl it is purely ionic, but in many other molecules an intermediate type of bond occurs in which the atoms share electrons to an unequal extent. An example is the HCl molecule, where the Cl atom attracts the shared electrons more strongly than the H atom.

Ionic bonds usually do not result in the formation of molecules. Strictly speaking, a molecule is an electrically neutral group of atoms that is held together strongly enough to be experimentally observable as a particle. Thus the individual units that constitute gaseous hydrogen each consist of two hydrogen atoms, and we are entitled to regard them as molecules.

On the other hand, the crystals of rock salt (NaCl) are aggregates of sodium and chlorine ions, as we saw in Fig. 9-6. Although arranged in a certain definite structure, the ions do not pair off into individual molecules consisting of one Na^+ ion and one Cl^- ion. Rock salt crystals may in fact be of almost any size. While there are always equal numbers of Na^+ and Cl^- ions in rock salt, so that the formula NaCl correctly represents its composition, these ions form molecules rather than crystals only in the gaseous state. Despite the absence of individual NaCl molecules in solid NaCl, the electric force between adjacent Na^+ and Cl^- ions makes NaCl as characteristic an example of chemical bonding as H_2.

Ionic Bonding

Electron transfer creates ions that attract each other

The simplest example of a chemical reaction involving electron transfer is the combination of a metal and a nonmetal. For a specific case, let us consider the

Formation of sodium chloride, NaCl

burning of sodium in chlorine to give sodium chloride. From Fig. 9-11 it is clear that Na and Cl are perfect mates — one has an electron to lose, the other an electron to gain. In the process of combination, an electron goes from Na to Cl, as shown schematically in Fig. 9-14.

The stability of the resulting closed electron shells in both ions is shown by the large amount of energy in the form of heat and light given off when this reaction takes place. The compound NaCl is quite unreactive because each of its ions has a stable electron structure. To break it apart, which means to return the electron from Cl^- to Na^+, requires the same considerable energy that the combination set free.

As we know, metal atoms tend to lose their outer electrons, like sodium in the above example. Nonmetal atoms, on the other hand, tend to gain electrons so as to fill in gaps in their outer shells. In most reactions of this sort a metal loses all its outer electrons, and a nonmetal fills all the gaps in its structure. When sodium combines with sulfur, for instance, each S atom has two spaces to fill (Fig. 9-11), but each Na atom has only one electron to give. Hence two Na atoms are needed for each S atom, and the resulting compound is Na_2S. When calcium combines with oxygen, each Ca atom contributes two electrons to each O atom, and the formula of the compound is CaO.

Compounds formed by electron transfer are called *ionic compounds*. Some are simple compounds like NaCl, Na_2S, and CaO. Others have more complex formulas, such as Na_2SO_4, KNO_3, and $CaCO_3$. In these compounds electrons from the metal atoms have been transferred to nonmetal atom *groups* (SO_4, NO_3, CO_3) instead of to single nonmetal atoms. Ionic compounds in general contain a metal and one or more nonmetals, and their crystal structures are made up of alternate positive and negative ions. Most of them are crystalline solids with high melting points, as might be expected, since melting involves a separation of the ions. Another important characteristic of ionic compounds, to be discussed later, is their ability in the molten state or in solution to conduct electricity.

Ionic compounds are formed by electron transfer and usually are crystalline in nature

Covalent Bonding

Sharing electron pairs produces an attractive force

A shared pair of electrons constitutes a covalent bond

Ionic bonding cannot account for molecules such as H_2 or Cl_2 that are made up of identical atoms. Instead of having electrons transferred between them, the atoms of these molecules *share* electron pairs. In the course of circulating among the atoms, the electrons spend more time between the atoms than on the outside of the molecule, which leads to a net attractive force that holds the molecule together (Fig. 9-13). This process is called *covalent bonding*.

More than one pair of electrons may be shared

In some molecules more than one pair of electrons is shared. Examples are O_2, which has two shared electron pairs, and N_2, which has three. If we use a pair of dots to stand for a shared pair of electrons, the H_2, O_2, and N_2 molecules can be represented as follows:

$$H \!:\! H \qquad\qquad O \!::\! O \qquad\qquad N \!:::\! N$$

Hydrogen molecule   oxygen molecule   nitrogen molecule

Covalent substances

Substances whose atoms are joined by shared electron pairs are called *covalent substances*. In general, they are nonmetallic elements or compounds of one nonmetal with another, although some compounds that contain metals belong to this class. Because they do not consist of separate ions, covalent substances are poor conductors of electricity.

Polar covalent compounds

In some covalent compounds the bonding electron pairs are closer to one atom than to the other. Two examples are HCl and H_2O:

$$H \quad : \quad Cl \qquad\qquad H \quad :\underset{\cdot\cdot}{O}$$

$$H$$

These substances are called *polar* covalent compounds, because one part of the molecule is relatively negative and another part positive. All gradations can be found between symmetric covalent molecules at one extreme, through polar covalent molecules, to ionic compounds at the other extreme. For example,

Covalent	Cl	:	Cl
Polar covalent	H	:	Cl
Ionic	Na	:	Cl

Organic chemistry is the study of carbon compounds

Most important of the compounds formed by electron sharing are *organic*

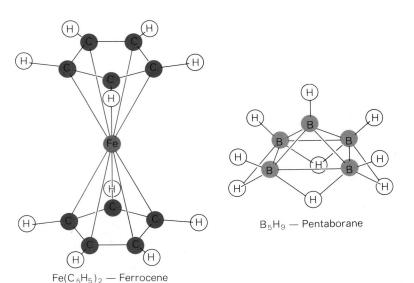

FIG. 9-15
Directed bonds in two complex molecules. Each line represents a covalent bond consisting of a pair of shared electrons.

$Fe(C_5H_5)_2$ — Ferrocene

B_5H_9 — Pentaborane

compounds, which are compounds of the element carbon (Chap. 12). The carbon atom has four outer electrons, which can be shared with other atoms.

The likelihood of finding a particular electron near its parent nucleus depends both upon distance from the nucleus and upon direction. The electron probabilities that can be computed from the quantum theory of the atom are not always symmetric, but instead show "lobes" of high probability in certain directions for electrons in certain quantum states. Covalent bonding occurs when the appropriate probability lobes of adjacent atoms overlap. When an atom combines with two or more other atoms, the latter are therefore generally "attached" at specific places on the atoms corresponding to the lobes of greatest magnitude, instead of being located at random or in some universal arrangement. As a result, molecules with more than two atoms have definite structures in three dimensions. We have already seen this in the cases of some of the simple molecules shown in Fig. 9-5. Two other examples of directed bonds are shown in Fig. 9-15.

Molecular structures

Ionic Compounds

Matching up ions

When a metal and a nonmetal combine to form an ionic compound, the atoms of the metal give up one or more electrons each to atoms of the nonmetal. We can figure out the formula of the compound by knowing how many electrons the metal atoms tend to lose and how many electrons the nonmetal atoms tend to gain.

How to find the formula of an ionic compound

As we have already seen, Na tends to lose one electron to become Na^+ and Cl tends to gain one electron to become Cl^-. Hence the formula of sodium chloride is NaCl. Similarly sulfur tends to gain two electrons to become S^{2-}, so sodium sulfide must have the formula Na_2S in order that two electrons be available for each S atom. Calcium forms Ca^{2+} ions, hence calcium sulfide must have the formula CaS with two electrons shifting from each Ca atom to an S atom.

Table 9-8 shows the ions formed by some common elements when they enter into compounds. A few elements form different ions under different circumstances, for example copper (Cu^+, Cu^{2+}) and iron (Fe^{2+}, Fe^{3+}). In such cases the name of the element in its compound is followed by a Roman numeral to indicate the ionic charge. Thus $FeCl_2$ is called iron(II) chloride because it contains Fe^{2+} ions, and $FeCl_3$ is called iron(III) chloride because it contains Fe^{3+} ions. Special names are sometimes used to distinguish the different ion states. An example is *ferrous* for iron(II) and *ferric* for iron(III). Alternate names for $FeCl_2$ and $FeCl_3$ are accordingly ferrous chloride and ferric chloride.

An element may form ions of different charge

With the help of Table 9-8 we can figure out what would be the result of combining a given metal with a given nonmetal. (How stable the compound would be is another matter, of course.) The positive and negative charges on the ions must always balance out, and a little thought may be needed to find the right combination. Suppose we want the formula of aluminum oxide. We note that aluminum forms Al^{3+} ions and oxygen forms O^{2-} ions. The charges balance out for the formula Al_2O_3 since $2(+3) = +6$ for $2Al^{3+}$ and $3(-2) = -6$ for $3O^{2-}$.

TABLE 9-8
Ions of Some Common Elements.

Element	Ion	Element	Ion
Hydrogen	H^+	Fluorine	F^-
Lithium	Li^+	Chlorine	Cl^-
Sodium	Na^+	Bromine	Br^-
Potassium	K^+	Iodine	I^-
Silver	Ag^+	Oxygen	O^{2-}
Copper	Cu^+, Cu^{2+}	Sulfur	S^{2-}
Mercury	Hg^+, Hg^{2+}	Nitrogen	N^{3-}
Magnesium	Mg^{2+}	Phosphorus	P^{3-}
Calcium	Ca^{2+}		
Barium	Ba^{2+}		
Zinc	Zn^{2+}		
Iron	Fe^{2+}, Fe^{3+}		
Aluminum	Al^{3+}		
Tin	Sn^{2+}, Sn^{4+}		
Lead	Pb^{2+}, Pb^{4+}		

Atom Groups

They stick together during chemical reactions

The sulfate group acts as a unit in reactions

Certain groups of atoms appear as units in many compounds and remain together during chemical reactions. An example is the group SO_4, which consists of a sulfur atom joined to four oxygen atoms. This *sulfate group* is found in a number of compounds:

Sodium sulfate	Na_2SO_4
Potassium sulfate	K_2SO_4
Copper(II) sulfate	$CuSO_4$
Magnesium sulfate	$MgSO_4$

How can we be sure that the sulfate group enters into chemical reactions as a unit? One way is to mix solutions of magnesium sulfate and barium chloride, $BaCl_2$. What happens is that an insoluble precipitate is formed, which analysis shows consists of barium sulfate, $BaSO_4$. The solution left behind contains magnesium chloride, $MgCl_2$; the barium and magnesium atoms have changed partners in the reaction.

When two or more groups of a single kind are present in each molecule of a compound, the formula is written with a pair of parentheses around the group:

TABLE 9-9
Ions of Some Common Atom Groups.

Atom group	Ion
Ammonium	NH_4^+
Nitrate	NO_3^-
Permanganate	MnO_4^-
Chlorate	ClO_3^-
Hydroxide	OH^-
Cyanide	CN^-
Sulfate	SO_4^{2-}
Carbonate	CO_3^{2-}
Chromate	CrO_4^{2-}
Silicate	SiO_3^{2-}
Phosphate	PO_4^{3-}

Calcium nitrate	$Ca(NO_3)_2$
Aluminum sulfate	$Al_2(SO_4)_3$

Naming compounds

Table 9-9 is a list of common atom groups and the charges their ions have. When writing a chemical formula, a metal (if present) always comes first, and oxygen (if present) is usually last. The ending *-ide* indicates a compound with only two elements, and *-ate* indicates a compound with three or more, one of which is oxygen. Examples are NaCl, sodium chloride, and Na_2SO_4, sodium sulfate. Two exceptions are hydroxides (sodium hydroxide has the formula NaOH) and cyanides (sodium cyanide has the formula NaCN). The prefix *bi-* indicates the presence of hydrogen in an atom group. Thus the bicarbonate ion has the formula HCO_3^- and the bisulfide ion has the formula HS^-. There are still other conventions used in naming ions and compounds, but these are the most frequently encountered.

Chemical Equations

The atoms on each side must balance

A chemical equation describes the results of a chemical change

A *chemical equation* is a shorthand way to express the results of a chemical change. In a chemical equation the formulas of the reacting substances appear on the left-hand side and the formulas of the products appear on the right-hand side. When charcoal burns in air, for instance, what is happening is that carbon atoms are reacting with oxygen molecules to form carbon dioxide molecules. The corresponding equation is therefore

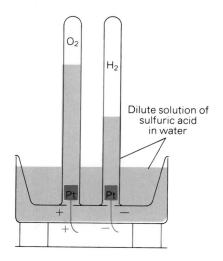

FIG. 9-16

Electrolysis of water. An electric current decomposes water into gaseous hydrogen and oxen. The volume of the hydrogen evolved is twice that of the oxygen, since both are diatomic gases and water contains twice as many hydrogen atoms as oxygen atoms. A trace of sulfuric acid is used to enable the water to conduct electricity.

$$C \ + \ O_2 \ \longrightarrow \ CO_2$$

Carbon $+$ oxygen $\longrightarrow$ carbon dioxide
atom   molecule   molecule

Electrolysis of water

In a chemical reaction the number of atoms of each kind must be the same on both sides of the equation. For example, the decomposition of water that occurs when an electric current is passed through a water sample (Fig. 9-16), a process called *electrolysis,* is written in words as

$$\text{Water} \longrightarrow \text{hydrogen} + \text{oxygen}$$

Using the formulas for these substances, we might write

$$H_2O \longrightarrow H_2 + O_2 \qquad \textit{Unbalanced equation}$$

Here two atoms of oxygen are shown on the right-hand side but only one atom on the left. The equation is therefore *unbalanced.* We cannot help matters by simply writing O instead of O_2 on the right, for gaseous oxygen has the formula O_2. Nor can we write a subscript "2" after the O in H_2O, for H_2O_2 is the formula for hydrogen peroxide, not water. The answer is to show two molecules of H_2O on the left, giving two molecules of hydrogen and one of oxygen:

$$2H_2O \longrightarrow 2H_2 \ + \ O_2$$

2 water $\longrightarrow$ 2 hydrogen $+$ 1 oxygen   *Balanced equation*
molecules   molecules   molecule

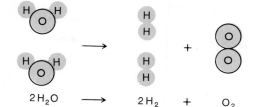

FIG. 9-17
Schematic diagram of the electrolysis of water.

$$2\,H_2O \longrightarrow 2\,H_2 \quad + \quad O_2$$

Now the equation is *balanced* with two O atoms and four H atoms on each side (Fig. 9-17). We note that a number placed in front of a formula multiplies everything in the formula, whereas a subscript applies only to the symbol immediately in front of it.

Burning of propane

A more complicated case is the burning of propane, C_3H_8, a gas widely used in cooking stoves and blowtorches. When it burns, propane combines with oxygen from the air to form carbon dioxide and water vapor. We begin by writing the unbalanced equation of the process:

$$C_3H_8 + O_2 \longrightarrow CO_2 + H_2O \qquad \textit{Unbalanced equation}$$

To balance the three carbon atoms on the left we need three on the right as well:

$$C_3H_8 + O_2 \longrightarrow 3CO_2 + H_2O \qquad \textit{Carbon atoms balanced}$$

The combustion of propane liberates
a great deal of energy.

Eight hydrogen atoms appear on the left, hence we must have eight on the right, which means four H_2O molecules:

$$C_3H_8 + O_2 \longrightarrow 3CO_2 + 4H_2O \qquad \textit{Hydrogen atoms balanced}$$

The three CO_2 molecules have six oxygen atoms and the four H_2O molecules have four, for a total of ten oxygen atoms on the right. Five O_2 molecules on the left will provide the required ten oxygen atoms there:

$$C_3H_8 + 5O_2 \longrightarrow 3CO_2 + 4H_2O \qquad \textit{Balanced equation}$$

This is the balanced equation of the burning of propane. Because a propane stove or torch uses oxygen liberally and produces carbon dioxide, good ventilation is clearly necessary.

It is worth noting that, just because the chemical equation for a certain reaction can be balanced, this is no reason to conclude that the reaction itself can actually take place. And, even if the reaction can take place, the equation does not tell us the particular conditions (of temperature and pressure, for instance) that might be needed.

IMPORTANT TERMS

Elements are the simplest substances present in bulk matter; they cannot be decomposed or transformed into one another by ordinary chemical or physical means. Two or more elements may combine chemically to form a ***compound,*** a new substance whose properties are different from those of the elements it contains. The elements that make up a compound are always combined in the same definite proportions by mass. Other materials are ***mixtures*** of elements or compounds or both whose constituents keep their characteristic properties. A ***solution*** is a uniform (or ***homogeneous***) mixture.

The ultimate particles of any element are called ***atoms.*** The ultimate particles of gaseous compounds consist of atoms of the elements they contain joined together in separate ***molecules.*** Some compounds in the liquid and solid state also consist of molecules, but in many others the atoms are linked in larger arrays. In a given compound, however, the ratios between its various atoms are fixed.

The ***periodic law*** states that if the elements are listed in order of atomic number, elements with similar chemical and physical properties recur at regular intervals. Such similar elements form ***groups,*** such as the halogens, the alkali metals, and the inert gases.

The electrons in an atom that have the same principal quantum number n are said to occupy the same ***shell.*** Electrons in a given shell that have the same orbital quantum number l are said to occupy the same ***subshell.*** Shells and subshells are ***closed*** when they contain the maximum number of electrons permitted by the exclusion principle. Atoms with closed shells and subshells are extremely stable. The concept of shells and subshells is able to account for the periodic law.

In a ***covalent bond*** between atoms, the atoms share one or more electron pairs. In an ***ionic bond,*** electrons are transferred from one atom to another and the resulting ions then attract each other. Many bonds in liquids and solids are intermediate between covalent and ionic.

A ***chemical equation*** expresses the result of a chemical change. When the equation is ***balanced,*** the number of each kind of atom is the same on both sides of the equation.

MULTIPLE CHOICE

1. Which of the following is not a chemical change?
   a. Water is decomposed into hydrogen and oxygen by the

passage of an electric current
  b. Water is frozen into ice
  c. Coal is burned in air
  d. Iron is dissolved in sulfuric acid

2. A substance that cannot be broken down into other substances by chemical means is
  a. an element
  b. a compound
  c. a solution
  d. a molecule

3. Elements can be distinguished unambiguously by their
  a. boiling points
  b. colors
  c. atomic numbers
  d. electrical properties

4. At room temperature and atmospheric pressure, most elements are
  a. gases
  b. liquids
  c. metallic solids
  d. nonmetallic solids

5. The most conspicuous distinction among the elements is their division into
  a. metals and nonmetals
  b. solids, liquids, and gases
  c. atoms and molecules
  d. active and inactive elements

6. Compared with metals, nonmetals in general are
  a. better conductors of heat
  b. better conductors of electricity
  c. more active chemically
  d. less easily deformed (by bending, for instance)

7. Iodine is an example of
  a. an inert gas
  b. an alkali metal
  c. a halogen
  d. a compound

8. Of the following metals, the most active chemically is
  a. gold
  b. aluminum
  c. iron
  d. sodium

9. Of the following metals, the least active chemically is
  a. gold
  b. aluminum
  c. iron
  d. sodium

10. Of the following nonmetals, the most active chemically is
  a. fluorine
  b. chlorine
  c. oxygen
  d. sulfur

11. The place of an element in the periodic table is determined by its
  a. atomic number
  b. atomic mass
  c. density
  d. chemical activity

12. Each vertical row of the periodic table includes elements with chemical characteristics that are, in general,
  a. identical
  b. similar
  c. different
  d. sometimes similar and sometimes different

13. Each horizontal row of the periodic table includes elements with chemical characteristics that are, in general,
  a. identical
  b. similar
  c. different
  d. sometimes similar and sometimes different

14. The periodic table of the elements does not
  a. permit us to make accurate guesses of the properties of undiscovered elements
  b. reveal regularities in the occurrence of elements with similar properties
  c. include the inert gases
  d. tell us the arrangement of the atoms in a molecule

15. An alkali metal atom
  a. has one electron in its outer shell
  b. has two electrons in its outer shell
  c. has a filled outer shell
  d. lacks one electron of having a filled outer shell

16. A halogen atom
  a. has one electron in its outer shell
  b. has two electrons in its outer shell
  c. has a filled outer shell
  d. lacks one electron of having a filled outer shell

17. An inert gas atom
  a. has one electron in its outer shell
  b. has two electrons in its outer shell
  c. has a filled outer shell
  d. lacks one electron of having a filled outer shell

18. The most important factor in determining the chemical behavior of an atom is its
  a. nuclear structure
  b. electron structure
  c. atomic mass
  d. solubility

19. An atom that loses its outer electron or electrons readily is
   a. an active metal
   b. an active nonmetal
   c. an inactive metal
   d. an inactive nonmetal
20. When they combine chemically with metal atoms, non-metal atoms tend to
   a. gain electrons to become negative ions
   b. lose electrons to become positive ions
   c. remain electrically neutral
   d. any of the above, depending upon the circumstances
21. Atoms of two different elements
   a. may form no compounds together
   b. can form only one compound together
   c. can always form more than one compound together
   d. must form ions of the same charge if they are to form a compound together
22. In a covalent molecule,
   a. at least one metal atom is always present
   b. one or more electrons are transferred from one atom to another
   c. adjacent atoms share one or more electrons
   d. adjacent atoms share one or more pairs of electrons
23. Sodium chloride crystals consist of
   a. NaCl molecules
   b. Na and Cl atoms
   c. Na^+ and Cl^- ions
   d. Na^- and Cl^+ ions
24. The number of atoms in a molecule of ammonium sulfide, $(NH_4)_2S$, is
   a. 3
   b. 6
   c. 10
   d. 11
25. The number of oxygen atoms in a molecule of aluminum sulfate, $Al_2(SO_4)_3$, is
   a. 3
   b. 4
   c. 7
   d. 12
26. The nitrate ion has the formula NO_3^-. The formula of mercury(II) nitrate is
   a. $HgNO_3$
   b. Hg_2NO_3
   c. $Hg(NO_3)_2$
   d. $Hg_2(NO_3)_2$
27. Which of the following chemical equations is balanced?
   a. $Fe_2O_3 + CO \rightarrow 2Fe + 2CO_2$
   b. $Na_2S + SO_2 \rightarrow Na_2S_2O_3 + S$

c. $3CuO + 2NH_3 \rightarrow 3Cu + 3H_2O + N_2$
   d. $4Al + 3Fe_3O_4 \rightarrow 4Al_2O_3 + 9Fe$
28. Which of the following chemical equations is unbalanced?
   a. $2Hg + O_2 \rightarrow 2HgO$
   b. $2H_2S + 3O_2 \rightarrow 2H_2O + 2SO_2$
   c. $Na_2O + H_2O \rightarrow 2NaOH$
   d. $SO_2 + H_2O \rightarrow H_2SO_4$

QUESTIONS

1. The conversion of water to ice is considered a physical change whereas the conversion of iron to rust is considered a chemical change. Why?
2. How can you show that water is a compound rather than a homogeneous mixture of hydrogen and oxygen?
3. Which of the following substances are homogeneous and which are heterogeneous? Blood, carbon dioxide gas, solid carbon dioxide, rock, steak, iron, rust, concrete, air, oxygen, salt, milk.
4. Which of the following homogeneous liquids are elements, which are compounds, and which are solutions? Alcohol, mercury, liquid hydrogen, pure water, sea water, rum.
5. Sodium never occurs in nature as the free element, and platinum seldom occurs in combination. How are these observations related to the chemical activities of the two metals?
6. From what physical and chemical characteristics of iron do we conclude that it is a metal? From what physical and chemical characteristics of sulfur do we conclude that it is a nonmetal?
7. The element astatine (At), which appears at the bottom of the halogen column in the periodic table, has been prepared artificially in minute amounts but has not been found in nature. Using the periodic law and your knowledge of the halogens, predict the properties of this element, as follows:
   a. At room temperature, is it solid, liquid, or gaseous?
   b. How many atoms does a molecule of its vapor contain?
   c. Is it very soluble, moderately soluble, or slightly soluble in water?
   d. What is the formula for its compound with hydrogen?
   e. What are the formulas for its compounds with potassium and calcium?
   f. Is its compound with potassium more or less stable than potassium iodide?
8. The following metals are listed in order of decreasing chemical activity: potassium, sodium, calcium, magnesium. How does this order agree with their positions in the periodic table? Where would you place cesium in the above list?
9. Why do fluorine and chlorine exhibit similar chemical behavior?

10. Why do lithium and sodium exhibit similar chemical behavior?

11. Electrons are much more readily liberated from metals than from nonmetals when irradiated with visible or ultraviolet light. Can you explain why this is true? From metals of what group would you expect electrons to be liberated most easily?

12. The rare element selenium has the following arrangement of electrons: 2 in the first shell, 8 in the second, 18 in the third, and 6 in the fourth. Would you expect selenium to be a metal or a nonmetal? To what group in the periodic table would it belong?

13. What is the difference in atomic structure between the two isotopes of chlorine? How would you account for the great chemical similarity of the two isotopes?

14. Would you expect magnesium or calcium to be the more active metal? Explain your answer in terms of atomic structure.

15. Why do chlorine atoms exhibit more pronounced chemical activity than chlorine ions?

16. Why do sodium atoms exhibit more pronounced chemical activity than sodium ions?

17. Illustrate with electronic diagrams (a) the reaction between a lithium atom and a fluorine atom, and (b) the reaction between a magnesium atom and a sulfur atom. Would you expect lithium fluoride and magnesium sulfide to be ionic or covalent compounds?

18. What part of the atom is chiefly involved in each of the following processes?
  a. The burning of charcoal
  b. Radioactive disintegration
  c. The production of x-rays
  d. The ionization of air
  e. The emission of spectral lines
  f. The explosion of a hydrogen bomb
  g. The rusting of iron

19. Why do the inert gas atoms almost never participate in covalent bonds?

20. The atoms in a molecule are said to share electrons, yet some molecules are polar. Explain.

21. Lithium is directly below hydrogen in the periodic table, yet lithium atoms do not join together to form Li_2 molecules the way hydrogen atoms do; instead, lithium is a metal with each atom linked to several others. Why?

22. Which of the following compounds do you expect to be ionic and which covalent? IBr, NO_2, SiF_4, Na_2S, CCl_4, $RbCl$, Ca_3N_2.

23. In each of the following pairs of atoms, which would you expect to be larger, and why? Li and F; Li and Na; F and Cl; Na and Si.

24. The transition elements in any period have the same or nearly the same outer electron shells and add electrons successively to inner shells. How does this bear upon their chemical similarity?

25. The formula for liquid water is H_2O, for solid zinc sulfide ZnS, and for gaseous nitrogen dioxide NO_2. Precisely what information do these formulas convey? What information do they *not* convey?

26. Column II of the periodic table contains the *alkaline earths*. How active chemically would you expect an alkaline earth element to be compared with the alkali metal next to it? Why?

PROBLEMS

1. What is the effective nuclear charge that acts on each electron in the outer shell of the calcium ($Z = 20$) atom? Would you think that such an electron is relatively easy or relatively hard to detach from the atom?

2. What is the effective nuclear charge that acts on each electron in the outer shell of the sulfur ($Z = 16$) atom? Would you think that such an electron is relatively easy or relatively hard to detach from the atom?

3. With the help of Tables 9-8 and 9-9 find the formulas of the following compounds: barium iodide; ammonium chlorate; tin(II) chromate; lithium phosphate.

4. With the help of Tables 9-8 and 9-9 find the formulas of the following compounds: potassium sulfide; sodium nitride; iron(III) hydroxide; calcium carbonate.

5. Name these compounds: BaH_2; $LiPO_4$; PbO; $CuBr_2$; KCN.

6. Name these compounds: $KMnO_4$; $HgBr_2$; Ca_3P_2; $FePO_4$; Na_2CrO_4.

7. Which of the following equations are balanced?
  a. $Zn + H_2SO_4 \rightarrow H_2 + ZnSO_4$
  b. $Al + 3O_2 \rightarrow Al_2O_3$
  c. $H_2CO_3 \rightarrow H_2O + CO_2$
  d. $3CO + Fe_2O_3 \rightarrow 3CO_2 + 2Fe$
  e. $N_2 + H_2 \rightarrow 2NH_3$
  f. $6Na + Fe_2O_3 \rightarrow 2Fe + 3Na_2O$
  g. $MnO + 4HCl \rightarrow MnCl_2 + 2H_2O + Cl_2$

8. Insert the missing numbers in the following equations:
  a. $Ca + [\ ]H_2O \rightarrow Ca(OH)_2 + H_2$
  b. $2Al + [\ ]H_2SO_4 \rightarrow Al_2(SO_4)_3 + 3H_2$
  c. $C_7H_{16} + 11O_2 \rightarrow 7CO_2 + [\ ]H_2O$
  d. $6H_3BO_3 \rightarrow H_4B_6O_{11} + [\ ]H_2O$
  e. $Ca(OH)_2 + 2NH_4Cl \rightarrow CaCl_2 + [\ ]NH_3 + [\ ]H_2O$

Write balanced equations for the following reactions.

9. Sulfur trioxide (SO_3) combines with water to form sulfuric acid (H_2SO_4).

10. Silver oxide decomposes into silver and gaseous oxygen.

11. Sodium reacts with water to give sodium hydroxide and gaseous hydrogen.

12. Potassium chlorate decomposes to give potassium chloride and gaseous oxygen.

13. Aluminum reacts with gaseous chlorine to give aluminum chloride.

14. Aluminum reacts with iron(III) oxide to give iron and aluminum oxide.

15. Aluminum reacts with a solution of hydrochloric acid (HCl) to give gaseous hydrogen and a solution of aluminum chloride.

16. Ethyl alcohol (C_2H_5OH) burns in air (that is, reacts with oxygen) to form carbon dioxide and water.

17. Acetylene gas (C_2H_2) burns in air to form carbon dioxide and water.

18. Sodium hydroxide reacts with copper(II) nitrate to give copper(II) hydroxide and sodium nitrate.

ANSWERS TO MULTIPLE CHOICE

1. *b*	**8.** *d*	**15.** *a*	**22.** *d*
2. *a*	**9.** *a*	**16.** *d*	**23.** *c*
3. *c*	**10.** *a*	**17.** *c*	**24.** *d*
4. *c*	**11.** *a*	**18.** *b*	**25.** *d*
5. *a*	**12.** *b*	**19.** *a*	**26.** *c*
6. *d*	**13.** *c*	**20.** *a*	**27.** *c*
7. *c*	**14.** *d*	**21.** *a*	**28.** *d*

10

CRYSTALS, IONS, AND SOLUTIONS

The modern theory of the atom provides deep insights into many properties of matter we take for granted because they are so familiar. Exactly how are atoms held together in a solid? Why do metals conduct electricity whereas other solids do not? Why do some substances dissolve only in water and others dissolve only in liquids like alcohol or gasoline? We shall look into the answers to these questions and others like them in this chapter.

SOLIDS

Crystalline and amorphous solids

A solid consists of atoms, ions, or molecules packed closely together and held in place by electric forces. These bonding forces can arise in four different ways, and the properties of a given solid depend upon which type of bond is present.

Most solids are *crystalline,* with the particles of which they consist falling into regular, repeated three-dimensional patterns. A crystalline solid melts at a specific temperature when the thermal energy of its particles is enough to break the bonds between them. In some solids, such as glass, pitch, and various plastics, the particles are irregularly arranged with no definite pattern. Such *amorphous* (Greek for "without form") solids are really very stiff liquids that soften gradually when heated because of the random nature of their bonds.

Ionic and Covalent Crystals

Electron transfer and electron sharing in solids

Ionic crystals

Ionic bonds in crystals, as we know, arise when metal atoms, which tend to lose electrons, interact with nonmetal atoms, which tend to pick up electrons. The result is an assembly of positive and negative ions in which the attractive forces between ions of different charge predominate over the repulsive forces between similar ions. Ionic bonds are usually fairly strong and result in hard crystals with high melting points.

Crystal structures can be determined with the help of x-rays

There are 230 different ways in which objects can be regularly arranged in space, so there are 230 different crystal structures possible. X-rays can be used to determine the arrangement of the particles in a given crystal. When a beam of x-rays is directed at a crystal, most of them simply pass right through. A few, however, are scattered at specific angles that vary with the wavelength of the x-rays and with the type of crystal (Fig. 10-1). This phenomenon is an interference

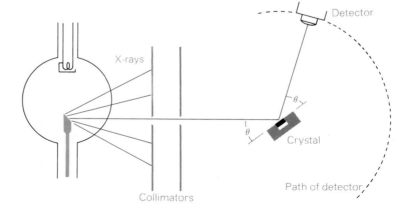

FIG. 10-1
X-ray scattering experiment. At certain angles constructive interference occurs in the x-rays scattered by the various layers of atoms in the crystal.

X-ray-diffraction apparatus being used to study the structures of cell membranes.

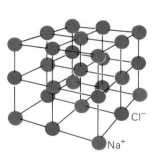

FIG. 10-2
The face-centered-cubic crystal structure of sodium chloride.

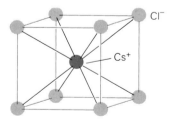

FIG. 10-3
The body-centered-cubic crystal structure of cesium chloride.

Covalent crystals

effect and, from the pattern of the scattered x-rays, the corresponding pattern of ions or atoms in the crystal can be found.

Figure 10-2 shows the arrangement of Na^+ and Cl^- ions in a sodium chloride crystal. The ions of either kind may be regarded as being located at the corners and at the centers of the faces of an assembly of cubes, with the Na^+ and Cl^- assemblies interleaved. Each ion thus has six nearest neighbors of the other kind. Such a crystal structure is called *face-centered cubic.*

A different structure is found in cesium chloride crystals, where each ion is located at the center of a cube at whose corners are ions of the other kind (Fig. 10-3). This structure is called *body-centered cubic,* and each ion has eight nearest neighbors of the other kind. Still other types of structures are found in ionic crystals.

The cohesive forces in covalent crystals arise from the presence of electrons between adjacent atoms. Each atom participating in a covalent bond contributes an electron to the bond, and these electrons are shared by both atoms. Diamond is

Sorting rough diamonds from gravel at a mine in the Namib Desert of Africa. Diamond is one of the crystalline forms of pure carbon; graphite is the other.

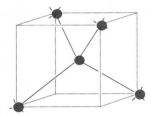

FIG. 10-4
The crystal lattice of diamond. The carbon atoms are held together by covalent bonds.

a crystalline form of carbon in which the atoms are linked by covalent bonds. Figure 10-4 shows the structure of a diamond crystal. Each carbon atom has four nearest neighbors and shares an electron pair with each of them. Since all the electrons in the outer shells of the carbon atoms participate in the bonding, it is not surprising that diamonds are extremely hard and must be heated to over 3500°C before they melt. Purely covalent crystals are few in number. Besides diamond, some examples are silicon, germanium, and silicon carbide ("Carborundum").

As in the case of molecules, it is not always possible to classify a given crystal as being wholly ionic or covalent. Silicon dioxide (quartz) and tungsten carbide, for instance, contain bonds of mixed character.

The Metallic Bond

The electron "gas" that bonds metals makes them good conductors

A "gas" of electrons is present in a metal

The characteristic property of metal atoms is that only a few electrons are present in their outer shells, and these electrons are not very securely attached. When metal atoms come together to form a solid, their outer electrons are given up to a common "gas" of electrons that move relatively freely through the resulting assembly of metal ions. This negatively charged electron gas acts to hold together the positively charged metal ions.

The electron gas gives metals their characteristic behavior

The electron-gas picture of the metallic bond accounts nicely for the properties of metals. The ability of a metal to conduct heat and electricity well follows from the ease with which the free electrons can move about. In other kinds of solids, all the electrons are bound firmly to particular atoms or pairs of atoms. The free electrons respond readily to electromagnetic waves, which is why metals are opaque to light and have shiny surfaces. Since adjacent atoms in a metal are not linked by specific bonds, most alloys — mixtures of different metals — do not obey the law of definite proportions. The copper and tin in bronze, for instance, need not be present in an exact ratio, unlike the sodium and chlorine in sodium chloride.

Molecular Crystals

Van der Waals forces bond molecules together

Many substances have molecules so stable that, when brought together, they have no tendency to join together by transferring or sharing electrons. Most organic compounds are examples of such noninteracting substances. However, even they can exist as liquids and solids through the action of the attractive *van der Waals* intermolecular forces.

Polar-polar attraction

We begin by noting that many molecules, which were called polar molecules in the previous chapter, behave as though they are negatively charged at one end and positively charged at the other. An example is the H_2O molecule, in which the concentration of electrons around the oxygen atom makes that end of the molecule more negative than the end where the hydrogen atoms are (Fig. 10-5). Such molecules tend to line up so that ends of opposite sign are adjacent, as in Fig. 10-6, and in this orientation the molecules strongly attract one another.

The water molecules in a snowflake are held together by van der Waals bonds.

 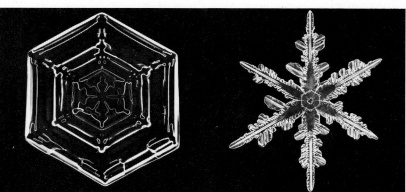

FIG. 10-5
The electron distribution in a water molecule is such that the end where the H atoms are attached behaves as if positively charged and the opposite end behaves as if negatively charged. The water molecule is therefore polar.

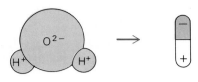

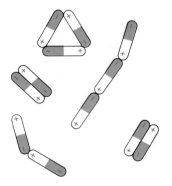

FIG. 10-6
Polar molecules attract each other.

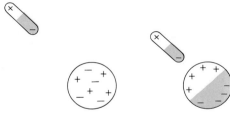

FIG. 10-7
Polar molecules attract normally nonpolar molecules.

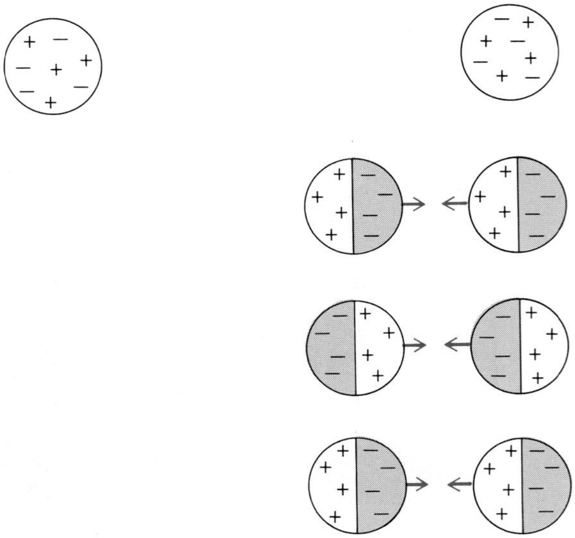

FIG. 10-8
Nonpolar molecules normally have, on the average, uniform distributions of charge, but at any one moment the distributions may be uneven. When two nonpolar molecules are close together, the fluctuations in their charge distributions keep in step, which leads to an attractive force between them.

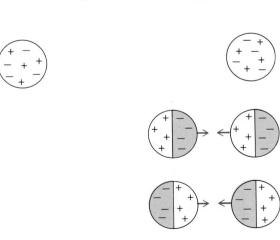

Polar-nonpolar attraction

A polar molecule is also able to attract nonpolar molecules whose charges are normally uniformly distributed. As in Fig. 10-7, the electric field of the polar molecule induces a separation of charge in the other molecule, and the two now attract each other electrically. The thin plastic sheets that cling so readily to whatever they touch do so because of polar molecules on their surfaces.

Nonpolar-nonpolar attraction

More remarkably, two nonpolar molecules can attract each other by the above mechanism. Even though the electrons in a nonpolar molecule are distributed evenly *on the average,* the electrons themselves are in constant motion and *at any moment* one part of the molecule has more than the usual number and the rest of the molecule has fewer. Instead of the fixed charge irregularity of a polar molecule, a nonpolar molecule has a constantly shifting irregularity.

When two nonpolar molecules are close enough, their fluctuating charge distributions tend to shift together with adjacent ends always having opposite sign (Fig. 10-8). The result is an attractive force. Forces based on molecular polarity are

TABLE 10-1
Crystal Types.
(The cohesive energy is equal to the work needed to remove an atom (or molecule) from the crystal and so indicates the strength of the bonds holding it in place.)

Type		Bond	Example	Properties
Ionic	negative ion / positive ion	Electrical attraction	Sodium chloride NaCl $E_{cohesive} = 3.3 \dfrac{eV}{atom}$	Hard; high melting points; may be soluble in polar liquids such as water.
Covalent	shared electrons	Shared electrons	Diamond C $E_{cohesive} = 7.4 \dfrac{eV}{atom}$	Very hard; high melting points; insoluble in nearly all solvents.
Metallic	metal ion / electron gas	Electron gas	Sodium Na $E_{cohesive} = 1.1 \dfrac{eV}{atom}$	Ductile; metallic luster; high electrical and thermal conductivity.
Molecular	instantaneous charge separation in molecule	Van der Waals forces	Methane CH_4 $E_{cohesive} = 0.1 \dfrac{eV}{molecule}$	Soft; low melting and boiling points; soluble in covalent liquids.

named after the Dutch physicist van der Waals, who suggested their existence nearly a century ago to explain observed departures from the ideal-gas law. The explanation of how the forces actually arise is more recent, of course, since it is based on the modern theory of the atom.

Van der Waals forces are present, not only between all molecules, but also between all atoms, including those of the inert gases which do not otherwise interact. Van der Waals bonds are much weaker than ionic and covalent bonds, and as a result molecular crystals, which are composed of whole molecules rather than ions or atoms, generally have low melting and boiling points and little mechanical strength. Ordinary ice and Dry Ice (solid CO_2) are examples of molecular solids.

Table 10-1 summarizes the characteristics of the four kinds of crystalline solids.

Van der Waals forces act between all atoms and molecules but are very weak

SOLUTIONS

A solution is an intimate mixture of two or more different substances. Solutions can be formed of any of the three states of matter. Thus air is a solution of several gases, sea water is a solution of various solids and gases in a liquid, and many alloys are "solid solutions" of two or more metals. Here our concern will be with solutions in liquids.

Solubility

Solvent and solute

In a solution containing two substances, the substance present in larger amount is called the *solvent,* the other the *solute.* When solids or gases dissolve in liquids, the liquid is always considered the solvent. When sugar is stirred into water, the sugar is the solute and the water is the solvent. Water is by far the commonest and most effective of all solvents.

Solutions, like compounds, are homogeneous, but unlike compounds they do not have fixed compositions. To a solution of 10 g of salt in 100 g of water, for example, we can add somewhat more salt or as much more water as we like. The composition of the solution is altered, but it remains homogeneous. Some pairs of liquids form solutions in all proportions. Any amount of alcohol may be mixed with any amount of water to form a homogeneous liquid, for instance.

In general, however, a given liquid will dissolve only a limited amount of another substance. Ordinary salt, NaCl, can be stirred into water at 20°C until the solution contains 36 g of salt for every 100 g of water. More salt will not dissolve, no matter how much we stir (Fig. 10-9). This figure, 36 g per 100 g of water, is called the *solubility* of salt in water at 20°C:

FIG. 10-9
The solubility of ordinary salt, NaCl, is 36 g per 100 g of water at 20°C. (a) 30 g of NaCl in 100 g of water produces an unsaturated solution. (b) 36 g of NaCl is the maximum amount that can dissolve and produces a saturated solution. (c) If 40 g of NaCl is added to 100 g of water, 4 g will remain undissolved.

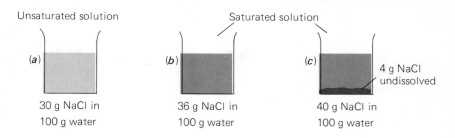

Unsaturated solution   Saturated solution

(a) 30 g NaCl in 100 g water   (b) 36 g NaCl in 100 g water   (c) 40 g NaCl in 100 g water — 4 g NaCl undissolved

Solubility

The solubility of a substance is the maximum amount that can be dissolved in a given quantity of solvent at a given temperature.

Saturated solution

Solubilities of solids increase with temperature

Solubility is usually given in grams of solute per 100 g of water at 20°C. A solution that contains the maximum amount of solute possible is said to be *saturated*.

The solubilities of most solids increase with increasing temperature (Fig. 10-10). It is common experience that hot water is a better solvent than cold water. When a solution of a solid that is saturated at a high temperature is allowed to cool, some of the solid usually crystallizes out. For example, the solubility of potassium nitrate, KNO_3, is 136 g per 100 g at 70°C and 31 g per 100 g at 20°C. If we cool 236 g of a saturated solution of KNO_3 from 70°C to 20°C, 105 g of solid KNO_3 will crystallize out (Fig. 10-11).

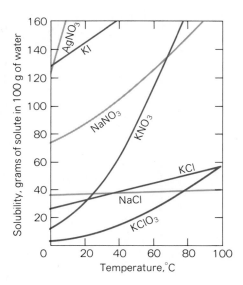

FIG. 10-10
Variation of solubility with temperature for various compounds dissolved in water.

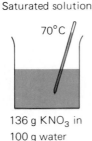 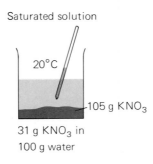

Saturated solution 70°C

136 g KNO_3 in 100 g water

Saturated solution 20°C

105 g KNO_3

31 g KNO_3 in 100 g water

FIG. 10-11
The solubility of potassium nitrate, KNO_3, is 136 g per 100 g of water at 70°C and 31 g at 20°C. Cooling a saturated solution of KNO_3 from 70°C to 20°C causes 105 g of the salt per 100 g of water to crystallize out.

Supersaturated solution

The presence of a solute changes the boiling and freezing points of a solvent

Solubilities of gases decrease with temperature

Sometimes, if the cooling is allowed to take place slowly and without disturbance, a solute may remain in solution even though its solubility is exceeded. The result is a *supersaturated* solution. Supersaturated solutions are often unstable, with the solute crystallizing out suddenly when the solution is jarred or otherwise disturbed.

The boiling point of a solution is usually higher than that of the pure solvent, and its freezing point lower. Thus seawater, which contains about 3.5 percent of various salts (chiefly NaCl), boils at 100.3°C and freezes at −1.2°C. The more concentrated the solution, the greater the changes in boiling and freezing points. Ethylene glycol, $C_2H_4(OH)_2$, is often added to the water in the cooling system of a car to prevent it from freezing in cold weather. A solution of 83 g of ethylene glycol per 100 g of water will not freeze until −25°C (−13°F).

In contrast to the case of solids, the solubilities of gases *decrease* with increasing temperature. We have all noticed that warming a glass of soda water, which is a solution of carbon dioxide in water, causes some of the gas to escape as bubbles. The solubility of a gas in a liquid depends on the pressure as well, increasing with increasing pressure. Soda water is bottled under high pressure, and when a bottle of it is opened, the drop in pressure also causes some of the gas to leave the solution and form bubbles (Fig. 10-12).

    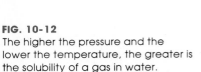

Soda

High pressure

Soda

CO_2 bubbles

Low pressure

Ice cubes

Low temperature

High temperature

FIG. 10-12
The higher the pressure and the lower the temperature, the greater is the solubility of a gas in water.

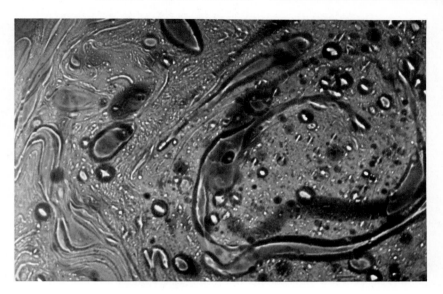

Oil and water do not mix because their molecules are electrically different.

Polar and Nonpolar Liquids

Like dissolves like

We all know that some liquids are better solvents for some substances than for others. Water readily dissolves salt and sugar but not fats or oil. Gasoline, on the other hand, dissolves fats and oils but not salt or sugar.

Water is a polar liquid, gasoline is a nonpolar liquid

The explanation for this behavior depends upon the electrical natures of the solvent and solute. Water is a *polar liquid* since its molecules behave as if negatively charged at one end and positively charged at the other (Fig. 10-5). Gasoline is a *nonpolar liquid* since the charges in its molecules are evenly distributed. Let us see what difference this makes.

Water and other polar liquids consist of groups of molecules rather than single, freely moving molecules. The molecules join together in clumps, positive charges against negative charges, as in Fig. 10-13. Water molecules can join together in a similar way with polar molecules of other substances, such as sugar (Fig. 10-14), so water dissolves these substances with ease.

Molecules of fats and oils are nonpolar or nearly so and do not interact with water molecules. If oil is shaken with water, the strong attraction of water molecules for one another squeezes out the oil molecules from between them, so the liquids separate into layers. Oil or fat molecules mix readily, however, with the similarly nonpolar molecules of gasoline (Fig. 10-15).

"Like dissolves like"

A covalent substance that has distinct molecules, then, dissolves only in liquids whose molecules have similar electrical structures. In general, "like dissolves like."

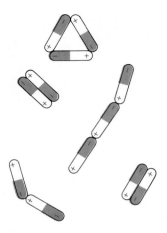

FIG. 10-13
Aggregates of water molecules. Water molecules cluster together because of electric forces that arise from their polar character.

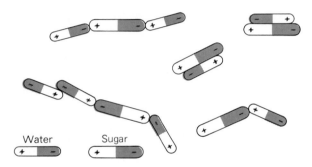

FIG. 10-14
Sugar dissolved in water. Polar compounds readily dissolve in water because their molecules can link up with water molecules.

Water   Sugar

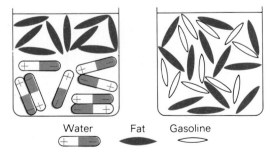

FIG. 10-15
Gasoline dissolves fat; water does not. Nonpolar compounds dissolve only in nonpolar liquids.

Water   Fat   Gasoline

Soaps and detergents are effective cleansing agents because their molecules are polar at one end but nonpolar at the other. With their help dirt particles of all kinds can be loosened and then washed away from a surface on which they are present.

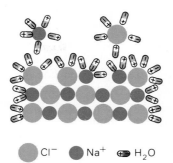

FIG. 10-16
Solution of sodium chloride crystal in water. Water molecules exert electric forces on the Na^+ and Cl^- ions which are strong enough to remove them from the crystal lattice.

Cl^- Na^+ H_2O

Dissociation refers to the separation of a compound into ions when it dissolves

Ionic compounds consist of positive and negative ions and dissolve only in highly polar liquids. Figure 10-16 shows how NaCl dissolves in water. At the surface of a salt crystal water molecules cluster around the ions, positive ends toward negative ions and negative ends toward positive ions. The pull of several water molecules is enough to overcome the electric forces that hold an ion to the crystal, and the ion moves off into the solution with its retinue of water molecules. As each layer of ions is removed, the next is attacked, until either the salt is completely dissolved or the solution becomes saturated. The separation of a compound into ions when it dissolves is called *dissociation*.

The ions released when an ionic compound dissolves are the same as those in its crystal structure. This is true not only for such simple compounds as NaCl, which dissociates into Na^+ and Cl^- ions, but also for compounds that involve atom groups. An example is potassium nitrate, KNO_3, which dissociates into K^+ and NO_3^- ions.

Electrolytes separate into free ions on solution in water

Substances that separate into free ions on solution in water are called *electrolytes*. Electrolytes include all ionic compounds soluble in water and some covalent

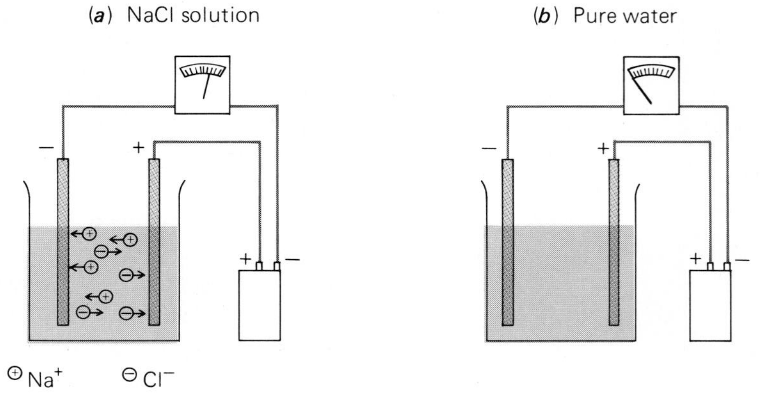

(*a*) NaCl solution   (*b*) Pure water

FIG. 10-17
(*a*) An electrolyte such as NaCl in solution conducts electric current through the motion of its ions.
(*b*) Pure water is a nonelectrolyte, as are solutions of compounds that do not dissociate.

$\oplus Na^+$ $\ominus Cl^-$

compounds containing hydrogen (for example, hydrochloric acid, HCl) that form ions by reaction with water. Other soluble covalent compounds, such as sugar and alcohol, that do not dissociate in solution are *nonelectrolytes*.

A property of electrolytes by which they may be recognized quickly — the property, in fact, that gives them their name — is the ability of their solutions to conduct an electric current. Conduction is possible because the ions are free to move; positive ions migrate through the solution toward the negative electrode, negative ions toward the positive electrode (Fig. 10-17).

Electrolytes in solution conduct electric current by the motion of ions

Ions in Solution

Ions have characteristic properties of their own

One of the early objections to the theory of ionic solutions was that sodium chloride was supposed to break down into separate particles of sodium and chlorine and yet the solution remains colorless. Why, if chlorine is present as free ions, should we not find the greenish-yellow color of chlorine in the solution? The answer is that chloride ion Cl^- has altogether different properties from gaseous chlorine — a different color, a different taste, different chemical reactions. This answer seems straightforward enough, but its full significance is not always easy to appreciate.

Dissociation is a type of chemical change

We must regard a solution of sodium chloride not as a solution of NaCl or of Na and Cl atoms but as a solution of the two ions Na^+ and Cl^-. Each of these substances has its own set of properties, properties that are quite different from those of NaCl crystals or of the active metal Na and the poisonous gas Cl_2. We must think of each ion in an electrolytic solution as a new and separate material.

Ions in solution have their own characteristic properties

By the "properties of an ion" we mean, of course, the properties of solutions in which the ion occurs. A solution of a single kind of ion, all by itself, cannot be prepared; positive ions and negative ions must always be present together, so that the total number of charges of each sign will be the same. But each ion gives its own characteristic properties to all solutions containing it, and these properties can be recognized whenever they are not masked by other ions. For example, a property of the copper ion Cu^{2+} is its blue color, and all solutions of this ion are blue (unless some other ion is present that has a stronger color). A characteristic of the hydrogen ion H^+ is its sour taste, and all solutions containing this ion (namely acids) are sour. The silver ion Ag^+ forms an insoluble white precipitate of AgCl when mixed with solutions of the chloride ion Cl^-. Any solution of an electrolyte that contains silver when mixed with a solution of any chloride will give this precipitate (Fig. 10-18).

A precipitate is an insoluble solid that results from a chemical reaction in solution

To emphasize the differences between the properties of an ion and those of the corresponding neutral substance, Table 10-2 compares the chloride ion, Cl^-, and molecular chlorine, Cl_2. In general, Cl_2 is much more active chemically. This is to be expected, since Cl atoms have only seven outer electrons whereas Cl^- ions have filled outer shells with eight electrons.

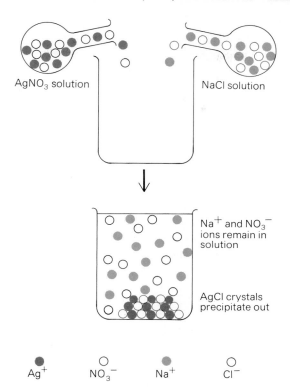

FIG. 10-18

When silver nitrate ($AgNO_3$) and sodium chloride (NaCl) are dissolved in water, a precipitate of the insoluble compound silver chloride is produced. The sodium and nitrate ions remain in solution.

For each ion we may write down a list of properties, which means a list of the properties common to all its solutions. In general, the properties of a solution of an electrolyte are the sum of the properties of the ions that it contains. The properties of sodium chloride are the properties of Na^+ plus those of Cl^-; the properties of copper sulfate are the properties of Cu^{2+} plus those of SO_4^{2-}. Instead of learning

TABLE 10-2

The Properties of Molecular Chlorine, Cl_2, and of the Chloride Ion, Cl^-, in Solution.

Cl_2	Cl^-
Greenish-yellow color	Colorless
Strong, irritating taste and odor	Mild, pleasant taste
Combines with all metals	Does not react with metals
Combines readily with hydrogen	Does not react with hydrogen
Does not react with Ag^+	Forms AgCl with Ag^+
Very soluble in CCl_4	Insoluble in CCl_4

the individual properties of hundreds of different electrolytes, we need only learn the properties of a few ions to be able to predict the behavior of any electrolytic solution that contains them.

Arrhenius

A daring theory in its day

The hypothesis that many substances exist as ions in solution was proposed in 1887 by a young Swedish chemist, Svante Arrhenius. Today the idea of ions in solution follows naturally from the electrical structure of matter. We know that some compounds are formed by the shift of electrons from one kind of atom to another, so that some of the atoms become positive ions and the others negative ions. It is not hard for us to imagine that a polar liquid like water can separate these ions from a crystal. But in 1887 the modern picture of the atom was not even dreamed of. Without this knowledge Arrhenius's fellow chemists had reason to consider his idea that neutral substances can break up into electrically charged fragments in solution as being farfetched.

Until the work of Arrhenius, Faraday's explanation for the ability of certain solutions to conduct electricity was generally accepted. Faraday held that the passage of a current caused the substance in solution to break up into ions. Arrhenius instead felt that ions are set free whenever an electrolyte dissolves, and he gave a number of reasons to support this notion.

Reactions between electrolytes in solution take place extremely fast

One of the points Arrhenius made was that reactions between electrolytes take place almost instantaneously in solution, but are very slow or do not occur at all if the electrolytes are dry. An example is the reaction between the silver nitrate and sodium chloride solutions shown in Fig. 10-18, which is very rapid. The speed with which the insoluble AgCl is formed suggests that its silver and chlorine components are already free in the original solutions and so are ready to combine at once. If dry $AgNO_3$ is mixed with dry NaCl, however, nothing happens, since the components of each salt are held firmly in their respective crystals.

Electrolyte solutions have lower freezing points than comparable solutions of nonelectrolytes

Another piece of evidence cited by Arrhenius was the unexpectedly low freezing points of electrolyte solutions. The amount by which the freezing point of a solution is reduced (or its boiling point increased) depends on the concentration of solute particles present, not upon their nature. Equal numbers of sugar and of alcohol molecules dissolved in the same amount of water lower its freezing point to almost exactly the same extent. But the same number of NaCl units lowers the freezing point nearly twice as much. This suggests that there are no NaCl molecules as such and that solid NaCl breaks up into Na^+ and Cl^- ions when it dissolves. Similarly calcium chloride, $CaCl_2$, lowers the freezing point of water by nearly 3 times as much as sugar or alcohol does, because each $CaCl_2$ unit dissociates in solution into three particles, one Ca^{2+} ion and two Cl^- ions.

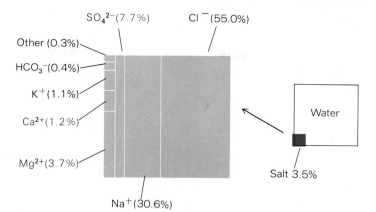

FIG. 10-19
The composition of sea water. In the open ocean the total salt content varies about an average of 3.5% but the relative proportions of the various ions are quite constant. (Percentages given are by mass.)

Water

The most important liquid

Although a minor constituent of the earth as a whole, water covers three-quarters of its surface. All the earth's water was once part of the rock of its interior, and was liberated as a result of geological processes. A large proportion of water vapor is present in the gases that present-day volcanoes emit (Chap. 15). Life probably began in the early oceans, and water is essential to all living things.

The salinity of sea water averages 3.5%; most of the ions are Na^+ and Cl^-

Only 3 percent of the world's water is fresh, and of that a third is trapped as ice in the Arctic and Antarctic. Sea water has a salt content (or *salinity*) that averages 3.5 percent. The composition of sea water is shown in Fig. 10-19. Evidently the ions of ordinary table salt, Na^+ and Cl^-, account for over 85 percent of the total salinity. The salinity of sea water varies around the world, but the proportions of the various ions are virtually the same everywhere because of mixing by currents both on and below the sea surface. Figure 10-20 illustrates the origins of the ions found in sea water.

"Hard" water

Even fresh water is rarely free of ions in solution. "Hard" water contains dissolved minerals that prevent soap from forming suds, react with soap to produce a precipitate, and form insoluble deposits in boilers, water heaters, and teakettles. Calcium and magnesium ions are usually responsible for hard water. Groundwater often picks up these ions through the solvent action of water containing dissolved CO_2 on rocks such as limestone.

To soften water, the Ca^{2+} and Mg^{2+} ions must be removed, which can be done in a variety of ways. In one common method, hard water is passed through a column filled with either a synthetic ion-exchange resin or a natural material called zeolite. Both absorb Ca^{2+} and Mg^{2+} ions into their structures while releasing an equivalent number of Na^+ ions. Since Na^+ ions do not affect soap, nor do sodium

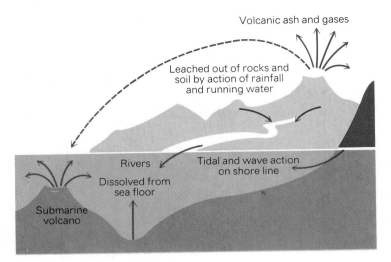

Volcanic ash and gases

Leached out of rocks and
soil by action of rainfall
and running water

Rivers

Tidal and wave action
on shore line

Dissolved from
sea floor

Submarine
volcano

FIG. 10-20
Origins of sea water salts.

compounds precipitate out from hot water, the water is now soft. When the ion-exchange column has reached its capacity of Ca^{2+} and Mg^{2+} ions, it can be flushed with a concentrated solution of NaCl to reverse the process and replace the accumulated Ca^{2+} and Mg^{2+} ions with Na^+ ions.

Water can be polluted — that is, rendered unsuitable for a particular purpose, not necessarily human consumption only — in a variety of ways. A common source of pollution is industry, since such activities as metal refining, food processing, and the manufacture of bulk chemicals and paper require considerable quantities of water: 300 tons of water is needed to produce a ton of steel.

Mercury pollution

Some industrial pollutants are especially dangerous because they are concentrated in the food chain of living things. A notorious example is mercury, which is widely used as an electrode in the production of sodium hydroxide (NaOH) and chlorine gas from solutions of NaCl by electrolysis, as well as in other processes. Mercury-containing wastes have traditionally been discharged into the nearest body of water on the assumption that, since most mercury compounds are insoluble in water, no harm would result. Unfortunately some bacteria are able to convert mercury into the soluble compound dimethyl mercury, $(CH_3)_2Hg$, which is highly toxic. As lower forms of life are eaten by higher ones, the concentration of dimethyl mercury increases. In Japan, thousands of people who regularly ate fish caught in Minamata Bay were afflicted with mercury poisoning due to wastes dumped by a nearby factory. "Minamata disease" is only the most famous of a number of similar occurrences.

The fertilizers and pesticides used in agriculture are another major source of water pollution. Unlike the case of industry, where proper procedures can control the dispersion of harmful wastes, there is no way to keep chemicals deposited on the soil from spreading further. What can happen is illustrated by the potent and

Pollution of the Hudson River in New York. Private greed and public indifference can make our planet uninhabitable.

DDT pollution

long-lasting insecticide DDT. Washed into a body of water, DDT enters the chain of life through the minute organisms called plankton. Starting with a DDT concentration of less than a tenth of a part per million in plankton, the concentration increases rapidly in the fish that eat plankton because it is retained in fat, and can reach 75 parts per million in birds that eat the fish. Because pesticides are of great benefit to agriculture and, in many parts of the world, to disease control, it is not really satisfactory simply to forbid their use. The remedy is clearly to develop pesticides that decompose rapidly, and much has already been done in this direction.

Sewage pollution and biochemical oxygen demand

Sewage is a familiar pollutant. Although water drawn from a contaminated source can be treated to destroy harmful bacteria, notably by adding chlorine, too high a concentration of sewage and other organic wastes (such as those from food-processing plants and paper mills) is nevertheless undesirable. Such wastes are attacked by aerobic bacteria, which use dissolved oxygen to alter the carbon compounds in the wastes to simpler forms, eventually to CO_2 and water.

The oxygen needed to completely oxidize the wastes in a given sample of water is called its *biochemical oxygen demand*, or BOD. BOD is a useful index of pollution because, when it is too great, the oxygen content of the water falls to the point where aquatic life such as fish cannot survive. A high enough BOD can lower the oxygen content so far that aerobic bacteria are unable to degrade the wastes. Anaerobic bacteria, which thrive in the absence of oxygen, then take over to produce such gases as methane (CH_4), which is inflammable, and hydrogen sulfide (H_2S), whose odor is that of rotten eggs.

Thermal pollution

Another way in which the oxygen content of a body of water can be lowered is by heating it, since the solubility of a gas in water decreases with increasing temperature. Because the heat output of an electric power plant is two or more times its electrical output, such a plant has a lot of heat to get rid of, and there are a lot of them. Using water from a nearby river or lake for cooling is the most common method, but it does not benefit the local fish population.

ACIDS AND BASES

We continue our study of ions in solution by considering the three important classes of electrolytes: acids, bases, and salts. All are familiar in everyday life.

Acids

Hydrogen ions give acid solutions their characteristic properties

Properties of acids

Acids are substances that contain hydrogen whose water solutions taste sour and change the color of the dye litmus from blue to red. Strong acids, such as the sulfuric acid used in storage batteries, are poisonous, cause painful burns if allowed to remain on skin, and damage many materials. Weak acids, such as the acetic acid of vinegar and the citric acid of lemons, are far from being harmful and add a pleasant sour taste to foods and drinks.

What is it that underlies the behavior of acids? We have two clues:

1. All acids consist of hydrogen in combination with one or more nonmetals.
2. Solutions of acids conduct electricity and hence must contain ions.

It is therefore tempting to think that acids such as hydrochloric acid, HCl, and sulfuric acid, H_2SO_4, dissociate into hydrogen and nonmetal ions as follows:

$$HCl \longrightarrow H^+ + Cl^-$$

$$H_2SO_4 \longrightarrow 2H^+ + SO_4{}^{2-}$$

From this it is natural to conclude that the characteristic properties of acid solutions are the properties of the free hydrogen ion H^+.

Acids are covalent substances that dissociate only when they react with a polar liquid like water

There are difficulties with this simple picture. For one thing, pure acids in liquid form do not conduct current, as molten NaCl does, so a pure acid cannot be made up of ions. Acids are covalent rather than ionic substances, and they form free ions not by the separation of ions already present but only by reaction with water.

A second difficulty is the nature of the ion H^+, which is just a single proton — the nucleus of a hydrogen atom without its lone electron. All other ions are particles of the same general size as atoms, particles whose structures consist of nuclei and electron clouds. This one ion would be entirely different, a naked positive charge with a volume a million billion times smaller. Such a particle cannot exist by itself in a liquid but must become attached immediately to some other atom or molecule.

To eliminate these difficulties, we could write more correctly

$$HCl + H_2O \longrightarrow H_3O^+ + Cl^-$$

Here the acid is shown reacting with water instead of simply splitting up into ions, and the proton is shown attached to a water molecule as H_3O^+ rather than free in solution. The ion H_3O^+ is called the *hydronium ion;* it is a combination of H^+ with H_2O, a *hydrated* hydrogen ion (Fig. 10-21). The characteristic properties of acids are described more correctly as properties of the hydronium ion than as properties of the simple hydrogen ion.

Nevertheless, it is customary in chemistry to write H^+ for the characteristic ion of acids rather than H_3O^+. This is chiefly for convenience. H_3O^+ is more correct than H^+, but it is still not entirely correct. Often more than one water molecule is attached to a free proton, so to be completely accurate we should have to write sometimes $H_5O_2{}^+$ and $H_7O_3{}^+$ as well as H_3O^+. We should have to use hydrates for other ions also — $Na(H_2O)^+$ instead of Na^+, $Cl(H_2O)^-$ instead of Cl^-, and so on. But in most chemical reactions the water of hydration does not play an important role, and the reactions can be represented well enough by equations from which it is omitted.

For most purposes, then, we can say that

Hydronium

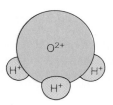

FIG. 10-21
A model of the hydronium ion, H_3O^+.

Definition of acid

An acid is a substance that contains hydrogen whose solution in water increases the number of H^+ ions present.

Although not strictly true, it is still legitimate to think of free hydrogen ions as being present in all acid solutions and giving these solutions their common properties. When we say that acid solutions taste sour, turn litmus pink, and liberate hydrogen gas by reaction with metals, we mean that the hydrogen ion does these things.

Strong and Weak Acids

The more it dissociates, the stronger the acid

A strong acid dissociates completely in solution, a weak acid only slightly

Acids differ greatly in the extent of their dissociation. Some acids, called *strong acids*, dissociate completely. For example, when HCl dissolves in water it breaks down completely into H^+ and Cl^-, with no molecules of undissociated HCl. Other acids, called *weak acids*, dissociate only slightly. The greater dissociation of strong acids means that, in solutions of the same total concentration, a strong acid has a much larger proportion of hydrogen ions than a weak acid: It has a more sour taste, it is a better conductor of electricity, and if the two acids are poured on zinc, the evolution of hydrogen gas is much faster from the reaction with strong acid.

The three most common strong acids are HCl (hydrochloric), H_2SO_4 (sulfuric), and HNO_3 (nitric). The stronger an acid, the weaker is the attachment of hydrogen in its molecules. In a strong acid like HCl the attachment is so weak that all the H^+ and Cl^- ions split apart and go their separate ways in solution. In a weak acid like acetic acid, $HC_2H_3O_2$, on the other hand, the attachment is strong enough so that most of the molecules remain undissociated — in the case of acetic acid, 98 out of 100.

Certain substances that do not contain hydrogen nevertheless yield acid solutions by reacting with water to liberate H^+ from H_2O. An interesting example is the gas CO_2, which when dissolved in water produces H^+ and HCO_3^- (bicarbonate) ions:

$$CO_2 + H_2O \longrightarrow H^+ + HCO_3^-$$

Some bicarbonate ions further dissociate into H^+ and CO_3^{2-} (carbonate) ions:

$$HCO_3^- \longrightarrow H^+ + CO_3^{2-}$$

It is customary to consider a solution of CO_2 in water as containing "carbonic acid," although H_2CO_3 rarely exists as such. "Carbonic acid" is weak because relatively little of the dissolved CO_2 reacts with water to give H^+ ions. Rain and snow are slightly acid because of the dissolved CO_2 they contain.

Bases

Hydroxide ions give bases their characteristic properties

Bases are familiar as substances whose solutions in water have a bitter taste, a slippery or soapy feel, and an ability to turn red litmus to blue. Their formulas, for example, NaOH for sodium hydroxide and $Ba(OH)_2$ for barium hydroxide, show that bases consist of a metal together with one or more hydroxide (OH) groups. On dissolving in water, bases dissociate into ions according to reactions such as

$$NaOH \longrightarrow Na^+ + OH^-$$

$$Ba(OH)_2 \longrightarrow Ba^{2+} + 2OH^-$$

Just as H^+ is the characteristic ion of acid solutions, so OH^- is the character-

Hydrochloric, sulfuric, and nitric acids are strong acids

"Carbonic acid" is formed when CO_2 dissolves in water and is a weak acid

Bases contain the hydroxide (OH) atom group

istic ion in water solutions of bases. The properties of bases are properties of the OH^- ion. We may therefore say that

---

Definition of base

A base is a substance that contains hydroxide groups whose solution in water increases the number of OH^- ions present.

The last part of the definition is needed because not all compounds that contain OH groups release them as OH^- ions in solution. An example is methanol (methyl alcohol), CH_3OH.

A strong base dissociates completely in solution, a weak base only slightly

Like acids, bases may be classed as strong and weak according to their degree of dissociation in solution. Thus potassium hydroxide, KOH, is a strong base because it breaks up completely into K^+ and OH^- ions when it dissolves. The most common strong bases are KOH (ordinary lye or caustic potash), NaOH (soda lye or caustic soda), and calcium hydroxide, $Ca(OH)_2$. Widely used in industry, these bases are all poisonous and just as destructive to flesh and clothing as the strong acids.

Solutions of ammonia, washing soda, and borax are basic although these substances are not bases

Bases differ from acids in that soluble weak bases are rare. However, many substances that do not contain OH in their formulas give basic solutions because they react with water to release OH^- ions from H_2O molecules. An example is the gas ammonia, NH_3, whose reaction with water proceeds as follows:

$$NH_3 + H_2O \longrightarrow NH_4^+ + OH^-$$

The process is analogous to that by which CO_2 reacts with water to give an acid solution. Other familiar compounds that are not bases but that give basic solutions are washing soda (sodium carbonate, Na_2CO_3) and borax (sodium tetraborate, $Na_2B_4O_7$).

A name sometimes used for any substance that dissolves in water to give a basic solution is *alkali*, an old Arabic word that referred originally to a bitter extract obtained from the ashes of a desert plant. Because NaOH and KOH are strong alkalis, sodium and potassium have become known as alkali metals. An alkaline solution is one that contains OH^- ions; the terms alkaline and basic mean the same thing.

The pH Scale

A measure of acidity or basicity

Water dissociates slightly into H^+ and OH^- ions.

Even pure water dissociates to a small extent. The reaction can be written

$$H_2O \longrightarrow H^+ + OH^-$$

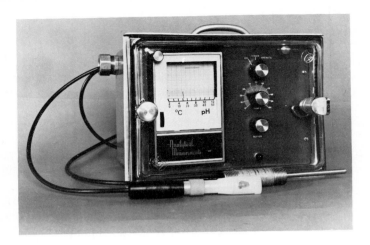

This device records both the temperature and pH of a solution.

The hydroxide ion OH^- attracts protons much more strongly than does the neutral water molecule H_2O, and the reverse reaction

$$H^+ + OH^- \longrightarrow H_2O$$

occurs readily. Thus we can write

$$H_2O \rightleftharpoons H^+ + OH^-$$

where the double arrow means that both reactions take place all the time in water.

The H$^+$ concentration is greater in an acid solution than in pure water and lower in a basic solution

The dissociation of water means that there are always some H^+ and OH^- ions present in pure water, and the tendency for these ions to recombine means that their concentration is small. Only 0.0000002 percent of pure water is dissociated into ions on the average: 2 molecules out of every billion. In an acid solution the concentration of H^+ is greater than in pure water, and that of OH^- is lower. In a basic solution, the concentration of OH^- is greater than in pure water, and that of H^+ is lower.

The *pH scale* is a method for expressing the exact degree of acidity or basicity of a solution in terms of its H^+ ion concentration. This scale is so widely used that an acquaintance with it is worth having, but we need not concern ourselves here with its mathematical basis.

The pH of a neutral solution is 7, that of an acid solution is less than 7, and that of a basic solution is more than 7

A solution that, like pure water, is neither acid nor basic is said to be *neutral* and has, by definition, a pH of 7. Acid solutions have pH values of less than 7; the more strongly acid they are, the lower the pH. Basic solutions have pH values of more than 7; the more strongly basic they are, the higher the pH. A change in pH of 1 means a change in H^+ concentration of a factor of 10. Thus a solution of pH 4 is 10 times more acid than a solution of pH 5 and 100 times more acid than a solution of pH 6. Figure 10-22 illustrates the pH scale, and Fig. 10-23 shows typical pH values of some familiar solutions.

FIG. 10-22
The pH scale. The concentration of hydrogen ion is symbolized by (H^+) and that of the hydroxide ion by (OH^-). An increase of 1 in pH corresponds to a decrease of a factor of 10 in H^+ concentration.

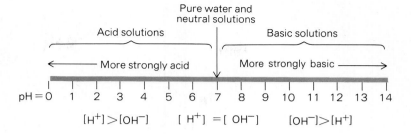

FIG. 10-23
Typical pH values.

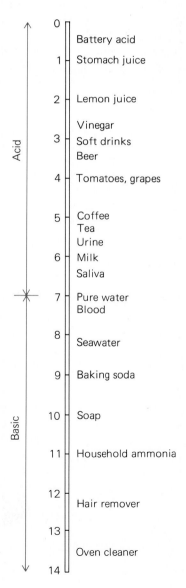

Salts

What happens when an acid reacts with a base

When a sodium hydroxide solution is added slowly to hydrochloric acid, there is no visible sign that a reaction is taking place. Both the original solutions are colorless, and the resulting solution is colorless also. That a reaction does indeed occur can be shown in several ways. An obvious indication is that the mixture becomes warm, which shows that chemical energy is being liberated. If we measure the pH of the mixture, we would find that it gets closer and closer to 7 as the base is added — the concentration of H^+ ions is decreasing.

Acids and bases neutralize each other

Evidently a base destroys, or *neutralizes*, the characteristic acid properties, and the reaction is accordingly called *neutralization*. In the same way the characteristic properties of a base can be neutralized by adding a strong acid.

What is the chemical change in the neutralization of HCl by NaOH? We could write simply

$$HCl + NaOH \longrightarrow H_2O + NaCl$$

However, we can gain more insight into the process by considering the ions involved. HCl, a strong acid, dissociates completely in water to give H^+ and Cl^-; NaOH, a strong base, dissociates into Na^+ and OH^-; the product NaCl, also a soluble electrolyte, remains dissociated in solution. Of the four substances shown, only water is a nonelectrolyte, so it alone should appear intact in the equation. Hence we have

$$H^+ + Cl^- + Na^+ + OH^- \longrightarrow H_2O + Na^+ + Cl^-$$

Since Na^+ and Cl^- appear on both sides, they may be omitted, leaving

$$H^+ + OH^- \longrightarrow H_2O$$

Neutralization involves the formation of H_2O molecules from H^+ and OH^- ions

This is the actual chemical change, stripped of all nonessentials. The neutralization of a strong acid by a strong base in water solution is essentially a reaction between hydrogen ions and hydroxide ions to form water.

Salts

When an NaOH solution is neutralized with HCl, the resulting solution should contain nothing but the ions Na^+ and Cl^+. If the solution is evaporated to dryness, the ions combine to form the white solid NaCl. This substance, ordinary *salt*, gives its name to an important class of compounds, most of which are crystalline solids at ordinary temperatures and most of which consist of a metal combined with one or more nonmetals. Typical salts are KBr, $MgSO_4$, $Al(NO_3)_3$, and $ZnCO_3$.

Crystal structures of salts consist of alternate positive and negative ions, which means that practically all soluble salts dissociate into free ions when dissolved in water. No salt is completely insoluble in water, but some, like AgCl and $CaCO_3$, are so very slightly soluble that they are often considered to be insoluble.

How to prepare a salt

Any salt can be made by mixing the appropriate acid and base and evaporating the solution to dryness. Thus potassium nitrate, KNO_3, is formed when solutions of potassium hydroxide, KOH, and nitric acid, HNO_3, are mixed and evaporated; copper sulfate, $CuSO_4$, is formed when sulfuric acid, H_2SO_4, is poured on insoluble copper hydroxide, $Cu(OH)_2$, and the resulting solution is evaporated. In general, then, neutralization reactions give water and a solution of salt. It is important to remember, however, that the salt itself is not produced directly by the neutralization. Neutralization is essentially a reaction between hydrogen ions and hydroxide ions. As a result of this process ions may be left in solutions that on evaporation will combine to form a salt.

IMPORTANT TERMS

Solids that consist of particles arranged in regular, repeated patterns are called **crystalline.** If the particles are irregularly arranged, the solid is **amorphous.**

The **metallic bond** that holds metal atoms together arises from a "gas" of electrons that can move freely through a solid metal. These electrons are also responsible for the ability of metals to conduct heat and electricity well.

Van der Waals forces arise from the electric attraction between nonuniform charge distributions in atoms and molecules. They enable atoms and molecules to form solids without sharing or transferring electrons.

In a solution, the substance present in larger amount is the **solvent,** the other is the **solute.** When a solid or gas is dissolved in a liquid, the liquid is always considered the solvent. The **solubility** of a substance is the maximum amount that can be dissolved in a given quantity of solvent at a given temperature. A **saturated** solution is one that contains the maximum amount of solute possible.

Polar molecules behave as if negatively charged at one end and positively charged at the other; **nonpolar molecules** are symmetric electrically. **Polar liquids** dissolve only ionic and polar covalent compounds, whereas **nonpolar liquids** dissolve only nonpolar covalent compounds. Water is a highly polar liquid, which is why it is so good a solvent. Ionic compounds **dissociate** into free ions when dissolved in water; ions of a given kind in solution have properties that differ from those of the corresponding neutral substance.

Solutions of **acids** in water contain H^+ ions, solutions of **bases** in water contain OH^- ions. Strong acids and bases dissociate completely in solution, weak ones only partially. The **pH** of a solution is a measure of its degree of acidity or basicity. A **neu-**

tral solution is neither acid nor basic and has a pH of 7. Acid solutions have pH values of less than 7, basic solutions have pH values or more than 7.

Salts are usually crystalline solids whose structures consist of positive metal ions and negative nonmetal ions. A salt can be formed by neutralizing the acid that contains the appropriate nonmetal ion with the base that contains the appropriate metal ion and then evaporating the solution to dryness.

MULTIPLE CHOICE

1. The individual particles in an ionic crystal are
   a. atoms
   b. molecules
   c. ions
   d. electrons
2. The individual particles in a covalent crystal are
   a. atoms
   b. molecules
   c. ions
   d. electrons
3. The individual particles in the van der Waals crystal of a compound are
   a. atoms
   b. molecules
   c. ions
   d. electrons
4. A "gas" of freely moving electrons is present in
   a. ionic crystals
   b. covalent crystals
   c. molecular crystals
   d. metal crystals

5. Van der Waals forces between atoms and between molecules arise from
   a. uniform charge distributions
   b. nonuniform charge distributions
   c. electron transfer
   d. electron sharing

6. The best solid conductors of electricity are held together by
   a. covalent bonds
   b. ionic bonds
   c. metallic bonds
   d. van der Waals bonds

7. The lowest melting points are usually found in solids held together by
   a. covalent bonds
   b. ionic bonds
   c. metallic bonds
   d. van der Waals bonds

8. A saturated solution is a solution that
   a. contains the maximum amount of solute
   b. contains the maximum amount of solvent
   c. is in process of crystallizing
   d. contains polar molecules

9. A gas is dissolved in a liquid. When the temperature of the solution is increased, the solubility of the gas
   a. increases
   b. decreases
   c. remains the same
   d. any of the above, depending upon the nature of the solution

10. A solid is dissolved in a liquid. When the temperature of the solution is increased, the solubility of the solid
   a. increases
   b. decreases
   c. remains the same
   d. any of the above, depending upon the nature of the solution

11. Polar molecules
   a. contain tiny magnetic poles
   b. are completely symmetric in every way
   c. do not dissolve ionic compounds
   d. behave as though positively charged at one end and negatively charged at the other

12. The most strongly polar liquid is
   a. water
   b. alcohol
   c. hydrochloric acid
   d. gasoline

13. Ionic crystals dissolve only in liquids that are
   a. polar
   b. nonpolar
   c. saturated
   d. supersaturated

14. Nonpolar substances usually dissolve most readily in
   a. polar liquids
   b. nonpolar liquids
   c. acids
   d. bases

15. The ions and atoms (or molecules) of an element
   a. have very nearly the same properties except that the ions are electrically charged
   b. may have strikingly different properties
   c. always exhibit different colors
   d. differ in that the ions are always more active chemically than the atoms or molecules

16. Dissociation refers to
   a. the formation of a precipitate
   b. the separation of a mixture of polar and nonpolar liquids (such as oil and water) into separate layers
   c. the separation of a solution containing ions into separate layers of + and − ions
   d. the separation of a substance into free ions

17. Acids invariably contain
   a. hydrogen
   b. oxygen
   c. chlorine
   d. water

18. The reason that pure acids in the liquid state are not dissociated is that their chemical bonds are
   a. ionic
   b. covalent
   c. metallic
   d. van der Waals

19. While it is convenient to regard acid solutions as containing H^+ ions, it is more realistic to describe them as containing
   a. hydronium ions
   b. hydroxide ions
   c. polar molecules
   d. hydrogen atoms

20. A common strong acid is
   a. acetic acid
   b. boric acid
   c. nitric acid
   d. citric acid

21. A base dissolved in water liberates
   a. H^-
   b. OH
   c. OH^+
   d. OH^-

22. A substance whose formula does not contain OH yet which yields a basic solution when dissolved in water is

   a. NH_3
   b. CO_2
   c. HCl
   d. NaCl

23. Water is formed during

   a. dissociation
   b. precipitation
   c. neutralization
   d. crystallization

24. A strong acid or base in solution is completely

   a. dissociated
   b. neutralized
   c. hydrolyzed
   d. precipitated

25. Pure water contains

   a. only H^+ ions
   b. only OH^- ions
   c. both H^+ and OH^- ions
   d. neither H^+ nor OH^- ions

26. A pH of 7 signifies

   a. an acid solution
   b. a basic solution
   c. a neutral solution
   d. a solution of polar molecules

27. A concentrated solution of which of the following has the lowest pH?

   a. Hydrochloric acid
   b. Acetic acid
   c. Sodium hydroxide
   d. Ammonia

28. A concentrated solution of which of the following has the highest pH?

   a. Hydrochloric acid
   b. Acetic acid
   c. Sodium hydroxide
   d. Ammonia

QUESTIONS

1. State the four principal types of bonding in solids and give an example of each. What is the fundamental physical origin of all of them? What kind of particle is present in the crystal structure of each of them?

2. What kind of solid contains a "gas" of freely moving electrons? Does this gas include all the electrons present?

3. Van der Waals forces are strong enough to hold inert gas atoms together to form liquids at low temperatures, yet they do not lead to inert gas molecules at higher temperatures. Why?

4. What ions would you expect to find in the crystal structures of MgO and K_2S?

5. What ions would you expect to find in the crystal structures of CaF_2 and KI?

6. Give two ways to tell whether a sugar solution is saturated or not.

7. Why is the solubility of one gas in another unlimited?

8. Give examples of polar and nonpolar liquids and state several substances soluble in each.

9. How could you distinguish experimentally between an electrolyte and a nonelectrolyte?

10. Contrast the properties and electron structures of Na and Na^+. Which would you expect to be more active chemically?

11. Name one property by which you could distinguish (a) Cl^- from NO_3^-, (b) Ag^+ from Na^+, (c) Cu^{2+} from Ca^{2+}.

12. Why do so many substances dissolve in water? Why do oils and fats not dissolve in water?

13. With the help of Fig. 10-10 predict what will happen when a concentrated solution of sodium nitrate at 50°C is added to a saturated solution of potassium chloride at the same temperature.

14. At 10°C, which is more concentrated, a saturated solution of potassium nitrate or a saturated solution of potassium chloride? At 60°C?

15. Which is more strongly acidic, a solution of pH 3 or one of pH 5? Which is more strongly basic, a solution of pH 8 or one of pH 10?

16. In an acid solution, why is the OH^- concentration lower than it is in pure water?

17. Justify the statement that water is both a weak acid and a weak base.

18. Which of the following are weak acids, and which are weak bases? H_2SO_4, $HC_2H_3O_2$, NH_4OH, H_2CO_3, HCl, NaOH, H_3BO_3.

19. Would you expect HBr to be a weak or strong acid? Why?

20. Nitric acid is a strong acid and benzoic acid is a weak one. Would you expect a solution of sodium nitrate to be acidic, basic, or neutral? Sodium benzoate?

21. How could you tell whether an unknown mixture of salts contains (a) a salt of ammonium ion, (b) a salt of carbonate ion?

22. If the following salts are dissolved in water, which would give acidic solutions, which basic solutions, which neutral solutions? Na_2CO_3, KCl, $KC_2H_3O_2$, $BaCl_2$, $(NH_4)_2SO_4$, $NaNO_3$.

23. From the fact that H_2S is a weak acid, would you predict that a solution of Na_2S would be acidic, basic, or neutral? Explain.

PROBLEMS

1. Give the ionic equation for the neutralization of potassium hydroxide by nitric acid. What actual chemical changes does this equation show?

2. What salt is formed when a solution of sodium hydroxide is neutralized by sulfuric acid? Give the equation of the process.

3. What salt is formed when a solution of calcium hydroxide is neutralized by hydrochloric acid? Give the equation of the process.

4. The Al^{3+} ion tends to form $AlOH^{2+}$ ions in water solution. Would you expect a solution of $AlCl_3$ to be acidic, basic, or neutral? Explain your answer.

5. Boric acid (H_3BO_3) is a weaker acid than carbonic acid. What would happen if solutions of Na_3BO_3 (sodium borate) and HCl were mixed? Would you expect a solution of Na_3BO_3 to be acidic, basic, or neutral?

6. Give the equation of the reaction described below:

Johnny, finding life a bore,
Drank some H_2SO_4.
Johnny's father, an MD,
Gave him $CaCO_3$.
Now he's neutralized, its true,
But he's full of CO_2.

7. How could you prepare the weak acid H_2S from the salt Na_2S (sodium sulfide)?

ANSWERS TO MULTIPLE CHOICE

1. c	**8.** a	**15.** b	**22.** a
2. a	**9.** b	**16.** d	**23.** c
3. b	**10.** a	**17.** a	**24.** a
4. d	**11.** d	**18.** b	**25.** c
5. b	**12.** a	**19.** a	**26.** c
6. c	**13.** a	**20.** c	**27.** a
7. d	**14.** b	**21.** d	**28.** c

11

CHEMICAL REACTIONS

Chemical reactions have significant aspects quite apart from the changes that occur when the reactants combine to form the products. An important one concerns the quantities involved. How much of *A* must be added to how much of *B* to give a certain amount of *C*? Energy considerations are also relevant since some reactions give off energy whereas others must have energy supplied in order to take place. Even those reactions that liberate energy may not occur unless some initial energy is furnished to start the process.

Also, chemical changes take time to be completed: a fraction of a second to many years, depending on a number of factors. Not all reactions even go to completion. Instead, an intermediate equilibrium situation often occurs with the products undergoing reverse reactions to form the starting substances just as fast as the primary reaction proceeds. Topics such as these are considered in this chapter.

COMBUSTION

The first chemical change to be studied intensively was the process of burning or, more formally, combustion. The transformation of wood into smoke and ashes amid dancing flames was the most spectacular chemical change with which our ancestors were familiar. Early explanations were based on demons and spirits, with the fire god having a respected place in many religions. The ancient Greeks made the first attempt at an explanation in nonsupernatural terms, as recorded by Aristotle. Every flammable material was supposed to contain the elements "earth" and "fire," with the fire escaping when the material burned while the earth, as ashes, remained behind. In various forms this idea persisted through the centuries of alchemy down even to the time of the French Revolution.

Phlogiston

Now it's there, now it isn't

Phlogiston is an imaginary substance proposed by early chemists to explain the chemical and physical changes that occur in combustion

The notion of fire as an element was developed by two Germans, Johann Becher (1635–1682) and his student Georg Stahl (1660–1734), into the *phlogiston hypothesis*. The starting point was the same as Aristotle's, but Becher and Stahl showed how it could be extended to reactions other than burning. They used the word *phlogiston* (from the Greek word for flame) for the substance that supposedly escaped during combustion. The story of the overthrow of the phlogiston hypothesis and the growth of the modern picture of chemical change is a notable chapter in the history of ideas.

Today we never hear the word phlogiston, but in its day there was no more respected concept in chemistry. Combustion was explained in the following way. All substances that can be burned contain phlogiston, and the phlogiston escapes as the burning takes place. We observe that air is necessary for combustion, but this is accounted for by assuming that phlogiston can leave a substance only when air is present to absorb it. When heated in air, many metals change slowly to soft powders: zinc and tin give white powders, mercury a reddish powder, iron a black scaly material. These changes, like the changes in ordinary burning, were ascribed to the escape of phlogiston.

A metal was assumed to be a compound of the corresponding powder plus phlogiston, and heating the metal simply caused the compound to decompose. Now, many of the powders can be changed back to metal by heating with charcoal. This observation was interpreted to mean that charcoal must be a form of nearly pure phlogiston that simply reunited with the powder to form the compound (the metal). When hydrogen was discovered in 1766, its ability to burn without leaving any ash suggested that it was another form of pure phlogiston. One could predict, then, that heating an ore or a powder with hydrogen would form a metal, and this prediction was confirmed by experiment.

So far so good, but soon the phlogiston hypothesis ran into serious trouble. When wood burns, its ashes weigh less than the original wood, and the decrease in

Phlogiston could have either positive or negative mass

mass can reasonably be explained as due to the escape of phlogiston. But when a metal is heated until it turns into a powder, the powder weighs *more* than the original metal! The believers in phlogiston were forced to assume that phlogiston sometimes could have negative mass, so that if it left a substance the remaining material could weigh more than before. To us this notion of negative mass is nonsense, but in the eighteenth century it was taken quite seriously.

Lavoisier

A pioneer chemist

The French chemist Antoine Lavoisier carried out a series of experiments in the latter part of the eighteenth century that effectively demolished the phlogiston hypothesis. The son of a wealthy lawyer, Lavoisier had a good education and ample means for carrying on his scientific work. For many years of his busy life he served as a public official and showed himself aware of the acute social problems that France was facing. But neither his scientific reputation nor government service could save him during the Revolution; denounced by Marat, he was sent to the guillotine in 1794.

Lavoisier knew that tin changed to a white powder when it was heated, and that the powder weighed more than the original metal. To study the process in detail, Lavoisier placed a piece of tin on a wooden block floating in water (Fig. 11-1), covered the block with a glass jar, and heated the tin by focusing the sun's rays upon it with a magnifying glass — a common method of heating before gas burners and electric heaters were invented. The tin was partly changed to white

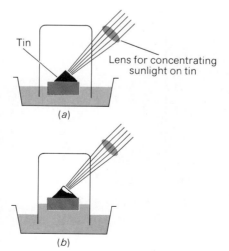

(a)

(b)

FIG. 11-1

Lavoisier's experiment showed that tin, upon heating, combines with a gas from the air. (a) Before heating; (b) after heating. The tin is partly changed to a white powder, and the water level rises until only four-fifths as much air is left as there was at the start. Further heating causes no additional change.

Tin

Lens for concentrating sunlight on tin

powder, and the water level rose in the jar until only four-fifths as much air was left as there had been at the start. Further heating caused nothing more to happen.

In another experiment, Lavoisier heated tin in a sealed flask until as much as possible was turned into powder. The flask was weighed before and after heating, and the two masses were the same. Then the flask was opened, and air rushed in. With the additional air, the mass of the flask was more than it had been at the start, and by the same amount as the increase in mass of the tin.

To Lavoisier these results suggested that the tin had combined with a gas from the air. We need only suppose that one-fifth of air consists of a gas that can combine with tin. Then the powder is a compound of this gas with the metal, and the increase in mass is the mass of the gas. Water rises in the jar of Fig. 11-1 to take the place of the gas that has been removed. When the sealed flask is opened, air rushes in to replace the gas the tin has absorbed. This explanation is simple and direct and involves substances that, unlike phlogiston, have definite masses.

Oxygen

Combustion is rapid oxidation

At about the time these experiments were completed, Lavoisier learned that Joseph Priestley had prepared a new gas with remarkable properties. Priestley was the poverty-striken minister of a small church in England, with only limited time and equipment, yet his scientific talents led him to a number of significant discoveries. The gas he had found caused lighted candles to flare up brightly and glowing charcoal to burst into flames, and a mouse kept in a closed jar of the gas lived longer than one kept in a closed jar of air.

Lavoisier gave the new gas its modern name, *oxygen,* and found it to be involved not only in the changes in metals on heating but in the process of combustion as well. The burning of candles, wood, and coal, according to Lavoisier, involves combining their materials with oxygen. They seem to lose mass because some of the products of the reactions are gases. Actually, as experiment shows, the total mass of the products in each case is more than the original mass of the solid material.

Oxygen under ordinary conditions is a colorless, odorless, tasteless gas. Air owes its ability to support combustion to the free oxygen that it contains. It cannot support combustion as well as pure oxygen because in air the element is so diluted with inactive gases. Air is composed of about one-fifth oxygen and four-fifths nitrogen, with small amounts of other gases.

Oxidation involves the combination of oxygen with another substance; combustion is rapid oxidation that releases energy

When oxygen combines chemically with another substance, the process is called *oxidation,* and the other substance is said to be *oxidized.* Rapid oxidation with a lot of heat and light given off is the process of combustion. In the experiments of Lavoisier, tin and mercury oxidized slowly when heated. A lighted candle oxidized rapidly in air, still more rapidly in pure oxygen. Slow oxidation is involved in many familiar processes, such as the rusting of iron and the hardening of paint. The energy to maintain life comes from the steady oxidation of food in our bodies by oxygen breathed in through the lungs and transported by the bloodstream.

An oxide is a compound of oxygen and another element

A substance formed by the union of another element with oxygen is called an *oxide.* The white powder that Lavoisier obtained by heating tin is tin oxide. Rust is largely iron oxide. In general, oxides of metals are solids. Oxides of other elements may be solid, liquid, or gaseous. The oxide of sulfur is the evil-smelling gas sulfur dioxide, SO_2; carbon forms two gaseous oxides, carbon monoxide (CO) and carbon dioxide (CO_2); the oxide of silicon SiO_2 is found in nature as the solid called quartz, the chief constituent of ordinary sand and abundant in rocks; the oxide of hydrogen is water, H_2O. Oxides of nearly all the elements can be prepared, most of them simply by heating the elements with oxygen. A few oxides (mercury oxide, lead oxide, barium peroxide) are easily decomposed by heating, which provides a convenient laboratory method for preparing oxygen. Other oxides, such as lime (calcium oxide), are not decomposed even at the temperature of an electric arc, 3000°C.

CHEMICAL CALCULATIONS

Lavoisier's discovery of the true nature of combustion was made possible by his use of the balance and by his insistence on the importance of mass in studying chemical reactions. This emphasis on mass marked a profound change in viewpoint and is one of Lavoisier's great contributions to chemistry. From his day to ours the balance has remained the chemist's most valuable tool.

The Mole

The chemist's unit of quantity

Regardless of how small may be the samples of matter involved in a chemical process in industry or the laboratory, so many atoms are present that counting them is out of the question. To measure the mass of a sample, however, is easy. What the chemist therefore needs is a way to relate the number of atoms in a chemical formula or equation to the corresponding masses of the substances.

To make clear the train of thought used to set up such a method, let us consider atoms of carbon and of oxygen. Since the mass of a carbon atom is 12 u and the mass of an oxygen atom is 16 u, the ratio of their masses is exactly 12:16. (We recall from Chap. 7 that u is the abbreviation of the atomic mass unit, which is equal to 1.66×10^{-27} kg.)

Now suppose we have samples of carbon and of oxygen that contain many atoms. However, no matter how many atoms the samples contain, if the ratio between the carbon and oxygen masses is the same 12:16 as the ratio between their atomic masses, the samples contain the same numbers of each kind of atom.

The above reasoning can be extended to the atoms of any element. For convenience a quantity called the *mole* is defined:

Definition of a mole of an element

A mole of any element is that amount of it whose mass in grams is equal to its atomic mass expressed in u.

The abbreviation of the mole is just mol. Thus a mole of carbon is 12 g and a mole of oxygen is 16 g (Fig. 11-2).

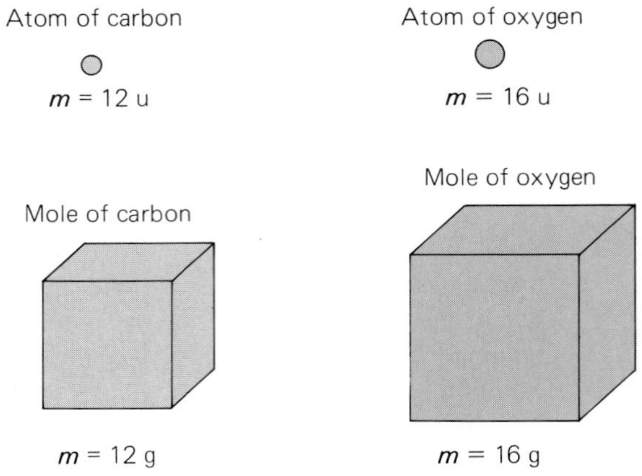

Atom of carbon

$m = 12$ u

Atom of oxygen

$m = 16$ u

Mole of carbon

Mole of oxygen

$m = 12$ g

$m = 16$ g

FIG. 11-2
A mole of any element is equal to its atomic mass expressed in grams.

Avogadro's number is the number of atoms in a mole

Mole of carbon

6.02×10^{23} atoms

Mole of oxygen

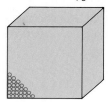

6.02×10^{23} atoms

FIG. 11-3
A mole of any element contains 6.02×10^{23} atoms, which is Avogadro's number.

The way the mole is defined means that *a mole of any element contains the same number of atoms as a mole of any other element.* This number is a constant of nature called *Avogadro's number* (Fig. 11-3):

$$N_0 = 6.02 \times 10^{23} \text{ atoms/mol}$$

Avogadro's number = number of atoms per mole of any element

The number of atoms in a sample of any element is just the number of moles in the sample multiplied by N_0.

We might be curious to know how many atoms are present in 100 g of iron. Since the atomic mass of iron is 55.85 u, the mass of 1 mole of iron is 55.85 g. The number of moles in 100 g of iron is

$$\text{Moles of iron} = \frac{\text{mass of Fe}}{\text{molar mass of Fe}}$$

$$= \frac{100 \text{ g}}{55.85 \text{ g/mol}} = 1.79 \text{ mol}$$

The number of iron atoms is therefore (Fig. 11-4)

$$\text{Atoms of iron} = (\text{moles of iron})(\text{atoms/mol})$$

$$= (1.79 \text{ mol})(6.02 \times 10^{23} \text{ atoms/mol})$$

$$= 1.08 \times 10^{24} \text{ atoms}$$

FIG. 11-4
How the number of atoms in 100 g of iron can be calculated. (*a*) First the number of moles is found. (*b*) Then the total number of atoms is determined.

(*a*) 1 mole of Fe has a mass of 55.85 g   55.85 g

(*b*) 1 mole of any element contains 6.02×10^{23} atoms   6.02 × 10^{23}

Therefore 100 g of Fe   100 g

Therefore 1.79 mol of Fe

contains $\dfrac{100 \text{ g}}{55.85 \text{ g/mol}} = 1.79$ mol   1.00 mol | 0.79 mol

contains $(1.79)(6.02 \times 10^{23})$
$= 1.08 \times 10^{24}$ atoms   1.08 × 10^{24}

Formula Units

A mole of anything contains Avogadro's number of formula units

The concept of the mole is not limited to the elements. For instance, the gas carbon monoxide, CO, is a compound of carbon and oxygen whose molecules contain one atom of each kind. A molecule of CO therefore has a mass of $12\ u + 16\ u = 28\ u$, and a mole of CO has a mass of 28 g. There are N_0 molecules of CO in each mole of it.

Formula unit

Because many compounds, such as sodium chloride, NaCl, do not consist of individual molecules, it is more appropriate to deal with *formula units* rather than molecules in generalizing the definition of the mole. A formula unit of a substance is just the set of atoms given by its formula. In the case of CO, a formula unit is the same combination of one C atom and one O atom each molecule contains. For NaCl, a formula unit consists of one Na atom and one Cl atom. For the more complex compound sodium sulfate, Na_2SO_4, a formula unit consists of two Na atoms, one S atom, and four O atoms.

Formula mass

The formula mass of a substance is the sum of the atomic masses of the elements it contains, each multiplied by the number of times it appears in the formula of the substance.

Evidently the formula mass of carbon monoxide is the same as its molecular mass of 28 u. Here is how the formula masses of sodium chloride and sodium sulfate, which do not exist in molecular form in the solid state, are found:

$$NaCl:\ 1\ Na = 22.99\ u \qquad Na_2SO_4:\ 2Na = 2 \times 22.99 = \ \ 45.98\ u$$
$$1\ Cl = \underline{35.45\ u} \qquad\qquad\quad 1S = 1 \times 32.06 = \ \ 32.06\ u$$
$$Formula\ mass = 58.44\ u \qquad\quad 4O = 4 \times 16.00 = \ \underline{\ \ 64.00\ u}$$
$$Formula\ mass = 142.04\ u$$

Now we can give a general definition of the mole:

General definition of the mole

A mole of any substance is that amount of it whose mass in grams is equal to its formula mass expressed in u.

A mole of NaCl has a mass of 58.44 g, and a mole of Na_2SO_4 has a mass of 142.04 g. The number of formula units in a mole is again Avogadro's number:

$$N_0 = 6.02 \times 10^{23} \text{ formula units/mol}$$

Avogadro's number is also the number of formula units in a mole

Avogadro's number = number of formula units per mole of any substance

The mole is the normal unit of quantity for the chemist

For a grocer, the normal unit of quantity for eggs is the dozen, equal to 12. For a paper manufacturer, the normal unit of quantity for his product is the ream, equal to 500 sheets. For a chemist, the normal unit of quantity of any substance is the mole, equal to N_0 formula units.

Mass Relationships in Reactions

Interpreting chemical equations in terms of moles

Owing to the way the mole is defined, a chemical equation can be interpreted in terms of moles as well as in terms of molecules or formula units. Let us consider the burning of the gas propane, which was discussed at the end of Chap. 9. The process obeys the equation

The burning of propane

$$C_3H_8 + 5O_2 \longrightarrow 3CO_2 + 4H_2O$$

which means that 1 molecule of C_3H_8 combines with 5 molecules of O_2 to yield 3 molecules of CO_2 and 4 molecules of H_2O. The equation equally correctly states that 1 mole of C_3H_8 combines with 5 moles of O_2 to yield 3 moles of CO_2 and 4 moles of H_2O:

$$C_3H_8 + 5O_2 \longrightarrow 3CO_2 + 4H_2O$$

| 1 mole of propane | 5 moles of oxygen | 3 moles of carbon dioxide | 4 moles of water |

A question a chemist ought to be able to answer is this: How many grams of oxygen are needed to burn 100 g of propane? We start by finding the formula masses of oxygen and propane:

$$O_2: 2O = 2 \times 16.00 = 32.00 \text{ u} \qquad C_3H_8: 3C = 3 \times 12.00 = 36.00 \text{ u}$$
$$8H = 8 \times 1.008 = \underline{8.06 \text{ u}}$$
$$44.06 \text{ u}$$

Therefore the molar masses of oxygen and propane are, respectively, 32.00 g and 44.06 g. The number of moles in 100 g of propane is

$$\text{Moles of propane} = \frac{\text{mass of } C_3H_8}{\text{molar mass of } C_3H_8} = \frac{100 \text{ g}}{44.06 \text{ g/mol}} = 2.27 \text{ mol}$$

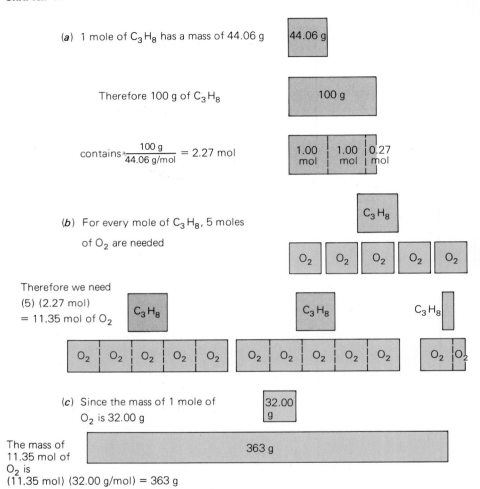

(a) 1 mole of C_3H_8 has a mass of 44.06 g

Therefore 100 g of C_3H_8

contains $\dfrac{100 \text{ g}}{44.06 \text{ g/mol}} = 2.27$ mol

(b) For every mole of C_3H_8, 5 moles of O_2 are needed

Therefore we need
(5) (2.27 mol)
= 11.35 mol of O_2

(c) Since the mass of 1 mole of O_2 is 32.00 g

The mass of 11.35 mol of O_2 is

(11.35 mol) (32.00 g/mol) = 363 g

FIG. 11-5
How the mass of oxygen needed to burn 100 g of propane is calculated. (a) First the number of moles of propane is found. (b) Then the number of moles of oxygen is found. (c) Finally the mass of oxygen is determined. The formula for the process is $C_3H_8 + 5O_2 \rightarrow 3CO_2 + 4H_2O$.

From the equation of the reaction, 5 moles of O_2 are needed for every mole of C_3H_8, so the number of moles of oxygen we need is

$$\text{Moles of oxygen} = \left(\frac{\text{moles of } O_2}{\text{moles of } C_3H_8}\right) (\text{moles of } C_3H_8)$$

$$= (5) (2.27 \text{ mol}) = 11.35 \text{ mol}$$

The mass of oxygen needed is

$$\text{Mass of oxygen} = (\text{moles of } O_2)\ (\text{molar mass of } O_2)$$

$$= (11.35 \text{ mol})\ (32.00 \text{ g/mol}) = 363 \text{ g}$$

A total of 363 g of oxygen is needed for the complete combustion of 100 g of propane (Fig. 11-5). Propane and other hydrocarbon gases, such as butane and methane (natural gas), need surprisingly large amounts of oxygen to burn properly. Good ventilation is obviously important when these gases are used indoors in stoves, heaters, or blowtorches.

Molarity of a solution

The *molarity* of a solution is the number of moles of solute per liter of solution. A solution that contains 2 mol of sulfuric acid per liter is designated $2M$ H_2SO_4. When a certain number of moles of a compound is needed for a particular reaction, it is convenient to be able just to pour out the corresponding volume of a solution of known molarity. Suppose we need 0.082 mol of sulfuric acid and have a bottle of $2M$ H_2SO_4. Since molarity = moles/liter,

$$\text{Volume needed} = \frac{\text{moles needed}}{\text{molarity}} = \frac{0.082 \text{ mol}}{2 \text{ mol/liter}}$$

$$= 0.041 \text{ liter} = 41 \text{ ml}$$

CHEMICAL ENERGY

Ever since our ancestors learned to control fire, people have been putting chemical energy to practical use. Today we transform it not only into heat and light but into mechanical energy and electric energy as well. Locked up in matter, chemical energy long remained a mystery. The modern picture of the atom and of the chemical bond, however, is able to explain the nature of this energy.

Exothermic and Endothermic Reactions

Some reactions liberate energy, others absorb energy

Exothermic reactions liberate energy

Chemical changes that *liberate* heat are called *exothermic reactions*. Familiar examples are the burning of coal, which is largely carbon, and the explosion of a mixture of hydrogen and oxygen. The heat liberated is often given in the equation for the process:

$$C + O_2 \longrightarrow CO_2 + 395 \text{ kJ}$$

$$2H_2 + O_2 \longrightarrow 2H_2O + 490 \text{ kJ}$$

These figures represent the heat produced when the amount of each substance is equal to the number of moles given by its coefficient in the equation. When 1 mol

(12 g) of carbon is burned, 395 kJ is given off; when 2 mol (4.032 g) of hydrogen is burned, 490 kJ is given off. Molar quantities are chosen so that the liberated energies may be compared on the same basis for different reactions.

Endothermic reactions absorb energy

Chemical changes that take place only when heat or some other kind of energy is *absorbed* are called *endothermic reactions*. The decomposition of water into hydrogen and oxygen requires heating to very high temperatures or the supply of electric energy during electrolysis (see Fig. 9-16), so it is endothermic:

$$2H_2O + 490 \text{ kJ} \longrightarrow 2H_2 + O_2$$

The formation of nitric oxide (NO) from the elements N_2 and O_2 is an endothermic reaction that takes place only at high temperatures:

$$N_2 + O_2 + 181 \text{ kJ} \longrightarrow 2NO$$

From the law of conservation of energy we can predict that, if a given reaction is exothermic, the reverse reaction will be endothermic and, further, that the amount of heat liberated by one reaction must be equal to the amount absorbed by the other. This prediction is borne out in the case of water, as we can see above, and is also verified in all other reactions where it can be tested. For example, sodium burning in chlorine liberates 824 kJ for every 2 mol (46 g) of sodium:

$$2Na + Cl_2 \longrightarrow 2NaCl + 824 \text{ kJ}$$

and NaCl is decomposed in an endothermic process requiring the absorption of this same amount of heat:

$$2NaCl + 824 \text{ kJ} \longrightarrow 2Na + Cl_2$$

Dissociation is usually an endothermic process

The energy changes that accompany ionic reactions are represented in the same manner as energy changes for other reactions. The dissociation of most salts is an endothermic process. For example, when KNO_3 is dissolved in water, the container becomes cold, since the dissociation of the salt requires energy:

$$KNO_3 + 36 \text{ kJ} \longrightarrow K^+ + NO_3^-$$

Neutralization is an exothermic process

Neutralization, on the other hand, is an exothermic process. If concentrated solutions of NaOH and HCl are mixed, for instance, the mixture quickly becomes too hot to touch:

$$H^+ + OH^- \longrightarrow H_2O + 57 \text{ kJ}$$

The neutralization of any strong acid by any strong base liberates almost precisely this same amount of heat for each mole (1.008 g) of H^+. This is to be expected, since the actual chemical change in all neutralizations is simply the joining together of hydrogen ions and hydroxide ions.

Chemical Energy and Stability

The less PE the electrons have, the greater the stability

Stability and chemical energy

The heat given out or absorbed in a chemical change is a measure of the stabilities of the substances involved. If much energy is required to decompose a substance, that is, if its decomposition is strongly endothermic, the substance is (with rare exceptions) relatively stable. If its decomposition is exothermic or weakly endothermic, the substance is normally unstable.

From the reactions given before, we can see at a glance that CO_2, H_2O, and NaCl are stable compounds, since the formation of each is strongly exothermic and its decomposition is endothermic. NO, on the other hand, is unstable, since its decomposition liberates heat. The combinations H_2 and O_2, Na and Cl_2, H^+ and OH^- are relatively unstable, since they react with evolution of much energy. On the other hand, N_2 and O_2 form a stable mixture since energy must be supplied for them to react.

Chemical energy is electron potential energy

We can interpret chemical-energy changes in terms of molecular structure on the basis of our earlier discussion of the chemical bond. When sodium reacts with chlorine, for example, an electron from each sodium atom is transferred to the outer shell of a chlorine atom. In its new position the electron has a smaller amount of potential energy with respect to the atomic nuclei. When carbon reacts with oxygen, the atoms are joined by shared electron pairs, and the formation of such covalent bonds also involves a decrease in the potential energy of the electrons. We conclude that *chemical energy is really electron potential energy*.

When electrons move to new locations during an exothermic reaction, some of their potential energy is liberated. This surplus energy may show itself in faster atomic or molecular motions that correspond to a higher temperature, or it may excite outer electrons into higher energy levels from which they return by giving off photons of light. In endothermic reactions, energy must be supplied from outside the atoms involved to enable some of their electrons to form bonds in which their potential energies are greater than before.

Activation Energy

The seed energy needed to start an exothermic reaction

Coal burns in air to give great quantities of heat: how is it possible that coal can be kept indefinitely in contact with air? The decomposition of nitric oxide liberates considerable energy: why does it not break up spontaneously? Indeed, how can this compound exist at all? A mixture of hydrogen and oxygen can explode

FIG. 11-6
Activation energy. The potential energy of the car will be converted into kinetic energy if it moves down into the valley. However, the car requires initial kinetic energy in order to climb the hill between it and the valley, analogous to the activation energy required in many exothermic reactions.

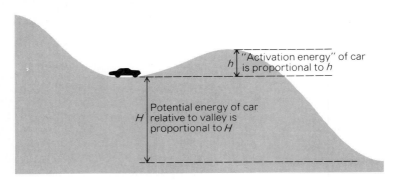

"Activation energy" of car is proportional to h

Potential energy of car relative to valley is proportional to H

Activation energy is the energy needed to start a reaction

An activated molecule has enough energy to participate in a reaction

violently: why should heat or an electric spark be needed to start the explosion? Why, in general, do not all exothermic reactions take place at once of their own accord?

Clearly many exothermic processes occur only if some energy is provided to start them. A mixture of hydrogen and oxygen is like the car of Fig. 11-6, whose potential energy may be converted into kinetic energy if it moves down into the valley. However, this cannot happen unless the car is first given enough energy to climb to the top of the first hill. Similarly the chemical energy of a mixture of hydrogen and oxygen can be freed only if the molecules have enough energy, or are sufficiently *activated,* to make the reaction start. The energy necessary for activation, corresponding to the energy required to move the car up the hill, is called the *activation energy* of the reaction.

The electron picture of chemical combination suggests the reason for activation energy. The reaction of oxygen and hydrogen involves the formation of bonds between O and H atoms, a process that gives out energy. However, before these bonds can be formed, the covalent bonds between the hydrogen atoms in H_2 molecules and the oxygen atoms in O_2 molecules must be broken, and to break these bonds takes energy. After the reaction starts, the energy liberated can supply the needed energy, but in the beginning some outside energy must be supplied besides the thermal energy of the molecules at normal temperatures.

A molecule with sufficient energy above the average to enable it to react is called an *activated molecule.* In some gas reactions an activated molecule may actually have been split into atoms. Other activated molecules may simply have high kinetic energy, or they may have one or two electrons in higher energy levels than usual.

In reactions that take place spontaneously at room temperatures (for example, the reaction between hydrogen and fluorine), enough of the initial molecules have the required kinetic energy of thermal origin for their bonds to "break" during collisions without further activation. In many ionic reactions no bonds need be broken; ions are, so to speak, already activated and react almost instantaneously. But a large number of exothermic reactions require the preliminary activation of some molecules before they can take place in a self-sustaining way.

Once an exothermic reaction is started, it usually supplies its own activation energy. The energy given off when the first molecules react supplies neighboring molecules with the energy to activate them, so the reaction spreads quickly. Thus a mixture of hydrogen and oxygen need only be touched with a flame for the reaction to spread so rapidly that an explosion results. When a bed of coal is set on fire it continues to burn, since the heat liberated in one place is sufficient to ignite the coal around it.

Fuels

Pollution is a burning question

The first requirement of a good fuel is naturally that its combination with oxygen be strongly exothermic. Other desirable features are that it should be cheap, abundant, easy to transport and store, and that the products of combustion should not endanger the environment. Many substances satisfy the first requirement, but none fulfills all the others as well.

Most chemical fuels are carbon or carbon compounds

Carbon and some of its compounds, which occur in nature as wood, coal, petroleum, and natural gas, best fulfill the requirements for fuels. The principal products of their combustion are two gases, CO_2 and water vapor, which escape into the air, and, in the case of wood and coal, ashes. Some of the pros and cons of these fuels were discussed in Chap. 4. Here our interest is in their chemical aspects.

Petroleum is a mixture of hydrocarbon compounds

Liquid fuels Petroleum, formed from the remains of tiny marine organisms buried under sediments millions of years ago, is the source of most liquid fuels. As described in Chap. 12, gasoline, kerosene, diesel fuel, and heating oil are mixtures of various hydrocarbons — compounds of carbon and hydrogen — derived from petroleum. All give off considerable amounts of heat when burned: 44 to 47 kJ per gram. In the engine of a car, the gaseous products of burning gasoline expand rapidly because of the intense heat generated by the reaction. This expansion forces down the pistons of the engine, which in turn causes the crankshaft to turn and provide power to the car's wheels (see Fig. 4-28).

Combustion of gasoline in a car engine

A mixture of gasoline and air is fed into the cylinders of a car's engine, one after another, to be ignited at just the right time by the spark plugs. Each gram of gasoline requires 15 g of air for complete combustion, whose products are CO_2 and H_2O. These gases are odorless and harmless. A "rich" mixture of gasoline and air contains a greater proportion of gasoline than this, and a "lean" mixture contains a smaller proportion.

A typical constituent of gasoline is *octane*, C_8H_{18}, whose complete combustion is given by the equation

$$2C_8H_{18} + 25O_2 \longrightarrow 16CO_2 + 18H_2O \qquad \textit{Complete combustion}$$

Octane   oxygen   carbon   water
dioxide

If the combustion is not complete, which occurs to some extent even under the best circumstances but to a greater extent when the gasoline-air mixture is rich, the result is more likely to be something like this:

$$2C_8H_{18} + 20O_2 \longrightarrow 11CO_2 + 15H_2O + 3CO + C_2H_6 \qquad \textit{Incomplete combustion}$$

Octane   oxygen   carbon   water   carbon   ethane
dioxide   monoxide

Both carbon monoxide and ethane, which is one of various hydrocarbons that may be produced, are harmful substances. The hazard of CO comes from its tendency to combine permanently with the hemoglobin of the blood in place of O_2, thereby depriving the body of some of the oxygen it needs and leading to death if too much CO is inhaled.

We might think that the way to minimize pollution by car exhausts is to use a lean gasoline-air mixture, which increases the chance of complete combustion by providing more than enough O_2. But lean mixtures are hard to ignite. Worse, the leaner the mixture, the hotter it burns, and this promotes the oxidation of the nitrogen present in the air. Nitrogen oxides, such as NO and NO_2, combine with water to form corrosive nitric acid and with unburned hydrocarbons to form a variety of toxic compounds, including potent carcinogens (cancer-producing agents).

Carbon monoxide, unburned hydrocarbons, and nitrogen oxides are not the only menaces to health in car exhausts. In the 1920s it was found that gasoline burns more evenly in an engine when a lead compound called tetraethyllead is added to it. The lead also helps engine performance by lubricating the valves that let fuel into each cylinder and exhaust gases out. Almost all the gasoline used as fuel once contained tetraethyllead, and as a result engine emissions included poisonous lead compounds along with everything else — only a few years ago, over 200 million kg of lead per year was dumped into the atmosphere in the United States alone. Lead that is breathed in tends to stay in the body to produce a variety of ailments, including mental disabilities in children. The problem is especially grave in inner cities, whose heavy traffic conditions make it inevitable that at least some children growing up there will absorb enough lead from the air to affect their intelligence.

There are two ways to reduce the amount of pollutants in car exhausts. One is to build an engine in which just the right mixture of lead-free gasoline and air is completely burned (to minimize CO and unburned hydrocarbons) at just the right temperature (to minimize nitrogen oxides) throughout all the variations in speed and power output involved in driving a car or other vehicle. Such an engine will obviously be very efficient as well. But it is extremely hard to produce an engine with these ideal properties, although much progress has been made, with computer control of engine operation an especially promising development.

Leaded gasoline

Catalytic converters

The other approach is to change the polluting gases into harmless ones by passing the exhaust of a car through a device called a catalytic converter. Reactions that dispose of polluting gases are promoted by the action of such metals as platinum and rhodium (catalysts are discussed later in this chapter), which are the active agents in a catalytic converter. Because lead inactivates the catalysts in a converter, only lead-free fuel can be used. By the mid-1980s, less than half the gasoline sold in the United States contained lead, and even if there is not an outright ban on leaded gasoline, which many people favor, the proportion should drop further as older cars without converters are replaced by new ones.

Natural gas is largely methane

Gas fuels Gas fuels combine with oxygen when burned to give CO_2 and H_2O as liquid fuels do. *Natural gas* consists of lighter hydrocarbons than petroleum, notably *methane,* CH_4. Natural gas is usually transported by pipelines, but sometimes in liquid form in special tankers. Since methane boils at $-161°C$, such tankers must be refrigerated and large compressors are needed at the shipping terminals to turn the gas into a liquid.

Water gas is a mixture of carbon monoxide and hydrogen

Artificial gas fuels can be made from coal or from coke, which is largely carbon. The most common is *water gas,* a mixture of carbon monoxide and hydrogen produced by passing steam over hot coke:

$$H_2O + C \longrightarrow CO + H_2$$

When burned, the H_2 becomes H_2O and the CO becomes CO_2. Because of its carbon monoxide content, water gas is poisonous, unlike natural gas. Hydrogen itself makes an excellent fuel with the extremely high heat of combustion of 143 kJ/g, 3 times that of gasoline. It is too expensive at present for ordinary purposes but is widely used in welding and as a spacecraft fuel.

Coal gasification

Proposals have been made to gasify coal while it is still underground. If the coal is ignited and just the right amount of compressed air is supplied, the combustion will be incomplete and produce carbon monoxide:

$$2C + O_2 \longrightarrow 2CO$$

The carbon monoxide can then be used as a fuel or can be reacted with steam to give hydrogen:

$$CO + H_2O \longrightarrow CO_2 + H_2$$

Coal is abundant

Solid fuels *Coal* was once the chief energy source under human control but, as we saw in Fig. 4-26, it has been overtaken by petroleum. Since coal reserves far exceed those of petroleum and natural gas, it is quite possible that coal will challenge nuclear energy for the position of leadership some day.

The heat of combustion of coal varies, but a typical value is 32 kJ/g. *Coke* is a fuel derived from coal by heating it in the absence of air to drive off volatile constituents, leaving free carbon and ash. Coke is used in place of coal where a hotter and less smoky flame is desired, for instance in steel mills. *Wood* is largely

Coal, shown here piled next to a Consolidated Edison power plant in New York City, is the most abundant fossil fuel and is used to produce about half the electric energy generated in the United States. Opponents of nuclear energy often cite coal as a superior alternative, but coal mining is hazardous and the air pollution that results from burning coal has damaged the health of many people. Acid rain, too, is a result of burning coal. None of today's sources — fossil or nuclear — that is able to provide a substantial fraction of the vast amounts of energy modern civilization requires is free from serious objections of one kind or another.

cellulose, one of the carbohydrates that plants produce by photosynthesis (see Chap. 12). Its heat of combustion is much less than that of coal, ranging from 10 to 19 kJ/g.

If coal were pure carbon, it would be an excellent fuel. Unfortunately coal contains a number of other substances also, one of which — sulfur — is largely responsible for the major ecological problem of acid rain.

Origin of acid rain

Bituminous ("soft") coal, the most common variety, has a sulfur content that averages 3 percent. Anthracite ("hard") coal and much furnace oil derived from petroleum contain somewhat smaller but still significant amounts of sulfur; lignite, another type of coal, contains more. When any of these fuels burns in a furnace, the sulfur is oxidized to sulfur dioxide, SO_2, and some nitrogen from the air is oxidized as well. Car exhausts are also major contributors of nitrogen oxides, as we know. The sulfur and nitrogen oxides combine with atmospheric moisture to give sulfuric and nitric acids. What goes up must come down, and the result is acid rain (and acid snow).

Normal rainwater is slightly acid, with a pH of about 5.6, because of dissolved CO_2. As mentioned in Chap. 10, CO_2 reacts with H_2O to give hydrogen and bicarbonate ions:

$$CO_2 + H_2O \longrightarrow H^+ + HCO_3^-$$

The presence of sulfuric and, to a lesser extent, nitric acid has increased the average acidity of rainwater in much of Canada, the United States, and Europe to pH values of as little as 3.8, which is 60 times more acid than normal rainwater. The record for a single rainfall, set in Scotland in 1970, is a pH of 2.4 — more acid than vinegar.

Effects of acid rain

Acid rain has two main effects on soils. One is to dissolve and carry away valuable plant nutrients. The second is to convert ordinarily harmless aluminum compounds, which are abundant in many soils, to toxic varieties. The results are dying forests on a vast scale and fish disappearing from tens of thousands of lakes and rivers due to aluminum washed into them. Drinking water has already been contaminated in a number of regions by metals released by acidified water, such as cadmium and copper in addition to aluminum. A long-term risk to the world's food supply exists as well since many farm soils are subject to damage by acid rain.

How can so serious a situation have been allowed to arise? Can nothing be done? In fact, several ways exist to reduce the sulfur and nitrogen oxide emissions of power plants, which are the cause of most acid rain, but all cost money.

How to prevent acid rain

The obvious remedy of using low-sulfur coal and oil is seldom possible because such fuels are scarce. However, up to a fifth of the sulfur in bituminous coal can be removed merely by crushing and washing it, and oil refineries can do still better with the petroleum they process if the right measures are taken. Another approach is to "scrub" the exhaust gases from a power-plant smokestack by mixing them with a lime ($CaCO_3$) solution. As much as 95 percent of the sulfur dioxide present can be converted to solid $CaSO_4$ in the reaction

$$2SO_2 + O_2 + 2CaCO_3 \longrightarrow 2CaSO_4 + 2CO_2$$

Unfortunately scrubbers are expensive, and disposing of the resulting sludge is a major undertaking. A third method is to inject limestone (solid $CaCO_3$) into a special combustion chamber along with the coal, which reduces the nitrogen oxides as well as the sulfur dioxide produced. But whatever is done, and especially if nothing is done, an increasing use of coal does not seem to be an ideal solution to the energy problem.

REACTION RATES

Some chemical changes are practically instantaneous. In neutralization, for example, the acid and base react as soon as they are stirred together; silver chloride is precipitated immediately when solutions containing silver ions and chloride ions are mixed; the reaction involved in a dynamite explosion takes a fraction of a second. Other chemical changes, like the rusting of iron, take place slowly. It is possible to measure the speeds of many reactions by determining what fractions of the original substances have disappeared at various times after the reactions start.

The speed of a chemical reaction depends upon four factors

Reaction rates depend first of all on the nature of the reacting substances: iron corrodes faster than copper. For any particular reaction the rate is influenced by four principal factors (Table 11-1). These are temperature, concentrations of the reacting substances, the surface area exposed in the case of reactions that involve solids, and the presence of an appropriate catalyst.

TABLE 11-1
Factors That Affect Reaction Rates.

Factor	Effect
Temperature	The higher the temperature, the faster the reaction
Concentration	The higher the concentration of the reactants, the faster the reaction
Surface area	The greater the surface area of a solid reactant, the faster the reaction
Catalyst	Can increase or decrease the reaction rate

Temperature

Hotter means faster

A 10°C rise in temperature approximately doubles the speed of a chemical reaction

Reaction rates are always increased by a rise in temperature. This is why we put food in the refrigerator to retard its decay and why we use hot water rather than cold for washing. Reaction rates for many common processes near room temperature are approximately doubled for every 10°C increase in temperature.

The kinetic theory of matter suggests one obvious reason for the increase of rate with temperature: Most reactions depend on collisions between particles, and the number of collisions increases with rising temperature because molecular speeds are increased. But a 10°C rise is nowhere near enough to double the number of collisions in a particular sample. To find the real explanation we must go back to the idea of activation energy.

Why reaction rates increase with temperature

If molecules must be activated before they can react, reaction rates should depend not on the total number of collisions per second but on the number of collisions between *activated* molecules. Activated molecules in a fluid (liquid or gas) are produced by ordinary molecular motion as a result of exceptionally energetic collisions. Such molecules remain activated only momentarily before losing energy by further collisions (unless they react in the meantime). In any fluid, then, a certain fraction of the molecules are activated at any time. The fraction may be very small at ordinary temperatures, but it increases rapidly as the temperature rises and molecular motion speeds up. Reaction rates increase with temperature chiefly because the number of activated molecules increases.

A mixture of hydrogen and oxygen, for example, contains at room temperature very few molecules with sufficient energy to react, and the reaction is so exceedingly slow that the gases may remain mixed for years without appreciable change. Even at 400°C the rate is negligibly small, but at 600° enough of the molecules are activated to make the reaction fast, and at 700° so many are activated that the mixture explodes.

This kind of behavior is typical of many reactions between molecules. At low temperatures the chemical change is so slow that for all practical purposes it does not occur; in a range of intermediate temperatures the reaction is moderately rapid; and at high temperatures it becomes practically instantaneous. Reactions between ions, on the other hand, occur immediately even at room temperatures, for the ionic state itself is a form of activation.

Ionic reactions are very fast

Concentration and Surface Area

The greater they are, the faster the reaction

The effect of concentration on reaction speed is illustrated by rates of burning in air and in pure oxygen. The pure gas has almost 5 times as many oxygen molecules per cubic centimeter as air has, and combustion in pure oxygen is correspondingly faster.

Reaction rates are proportional to the concentrations of the reacting substances

As a general rule, the rate of a simple chemical reaction is proportional to the concentration of each reacting substance. This is an experimental result, for which the kinetic theory gives a reasonable explanation. The number of collisions between activated molecules, which determines the reaction speed, depends upon the total number of collisions and this, in turn, depends upon how many molecules each cubic centimeter contains.

The greater the surface area, the faster the reaction

When a reaction takes place between two solids or between a fluid and a solid, its speed depends markedly on the amount of solid surface exposed. A finely powdered solid presents vastly more surface than a few large chunks, and reactions of powders are accordingly much faster. Granulated sugar dissolves more rapidly in water than lump sugar; finely divided zinc is attacked by acid quickly, larger pieces only slowly; ordinary iron rusts slowly, but the oxidation of iron powder is fast enough to produce a flame. The explanation is obvious: the greater the surface, the more quickly atoms and molecules can get together to react. For a similar reason, efficient stirring speeds up reactions between fluids.

Catalysts

Faster or slower by magic (almost)

A catalyst changes the rate of a reaction without itself being altered

The action of catalysts is often hard to account for. These are substances that either speed up or slow down a reaction without themselves being permanently affected.

As an example of catalytic action, let us consider the decomposition of hydrogen peroxide, H_2O_2. At ordinary temperatures solutions of hydrogen peroxide are unstable and slowly turn into water and oxygen:

$$2H_2O_2 \longrightarrow 2H_2O + O_2$$

If a little powdered manganese dioxide is added, the decomposition goes much faster with oxygen bubbling violently from the solution. At the end of the reaction the manganese dioxide remains unchanged. Commercial solutions of hydrogen peroxide usually contain a trace of the compound acetanilid, which acts as a catalyst of the opposite kind to retard their decomposition.

Catalysts accelerate reactions in different ways. In some cases the catalyst forms an unstable intermediate compound with one of the reacting substances, and this compound decomposes later in the reaction. Other catalysts, notably certain metals such as platinum, increase reaction rates by producing activated molecules at their surfaces. For the action of a number of catalysts no adequate explanation is known. A given reaction is usually influenced only by a few catalysts, and these may or may not affect other reactions. Catalysts are essential in many industrial processes, but in searching for new ones a chemist normally relies more on experience and trial-and-error methods than on any overall theory of how catalysts work.

Enzymes are biological catalysts

The many chemical processes that take place in living things, for instance the digestion of food, are controlled by catalysts called *enzymes*. An enzyme is a protein molecule whose physical structure is such that it attracts specific molecules to its surface, promotes their reaction, and then releases the products. Each enzyme catalyzes a particular reaction, and thousands of different ones are present in the human body. The reacting molecules fit into the outside of the enzyme for a process much as a key fits into a lock: if their shapes do not match, nothing will happen.

Chemical Equilibrium

One step forward, one step back

Most chemical reactions are reversible

Most chemical reactions are reversible. That is, the products of a chemical change, under suitable conditions, usually can be made to react "backward" to give the original substances. We have seen many examples in other connections. Hydrogen burns in oxygen to form water, and water decomposes into these elements during electrolysis. Mercury and oxygen combine when heated moderately, and the oxide decomposes when heated more strongly. Carbon dioxide reacts with water to give hydrogen and bicarbonate ions, and these ions recombine all the time to form the original CO_2 and H_2O.

There is no reason, of course, why the forward and backward processes of a chemical change cannot take place at the same time. In a bottle of soda water, some of the CO_2 reacts with the water. But a number of the resulting ions then join together to give CO_2 and H_2O. The recombination rate increases with the ion concentration until, finally, as many ions recombine each second as are being formed. At this point the rates of the forward and backward reactions are the same, and the amounts of the various substances do not change. The situation can be represented by the single equation

$$H_2O + CO_2 \rightleftharpoons H^+ + HCO_3^-$$

in which the double arrow indicates that reactions in both directions occur together.

A chemical equilibrium is a balance between forward and reverse reactions

A situation of this kind is called *chemical equilibrium.* It is a state of balance determined by two opposing processes. The two processes do not reach equilibrium and stop, but instead continue indefinitely because each process constantly undoes what the other accomplishes. As an analogy, we might imagine a person walking up an escalator while the escalator is moving down. If he walks as fast in one direction as the escalator carries him in the other, the two motions will be in equilibrium and he will remain in the same place indefinitely.

Many reactions do not go to completion but reach an intermediate equilibrium state instead

A great many chemical changes reach a state of equilibrium instead of going to completion in one direction or the other. Equilibrium may be established when a reaction is nearly complete, or when it is only just starting, or when both products and reacting substances are present in comparable amounts. The point at which equilibrium occurs depends on the rates of the opposing reactions. The initial reaction always dominates until the concentration of products is sufficient for the reverse reaction to go at the same rate. Thus the extent to which an acid is dissociated depends on how fast its molecules break down into ions compared with how fast the ions recombine. HCl dissociates so rapidly in solution into H^+ and Cl^- that the reverse reaction has no chance to maintain a measurable amount of HCl. On the other hand, acetic acid dissociates slowly, and when only a small concentration of ions has been built up the recombination goes at the same rate as the dissociation.

Altering an Equilibrium

How to get farther up the down escalator

Often a chemist wishing to prepare a compound finds that the reaction that produces it reaches equilibrium before very much of the compound has been formed. Once equilibrium is established, waiting for more of the product to form is useless, for its amount does not change after that. How can equilibrium conditions be altered to increase the yield of the product?

Since equilibrium represents a balance between two rates, a solution to this problem depends on finding a way to change the speed of one reaction or the other. Speeding up or retarding one of the reactions in an equilibrium is not quite so simple as changing the rate of a single reaction, but the same factors that affect reaction rates also influence equilibrium. The chemist has three chief methods available for shifting an equilibrium in one direction or the other. These are:

Methods for adjusting a chemical equilibrium

1. Change the concentration of one or more substances. For example, removing the gaseous product of a reaction will retard the reverse reaction. Thus opening a soda bottle allows CO_2 to escape, which decreases the rate of formation of H^+ and HCO_3^- and so lowers the acidity of the solution.

2. Change the temperature. If one reaction in an equilibrium is exothermic (gives off energy), the other is endothermic (absorbs energy). A rise in temperature, although it increases the rates of both reactions, will therefore favor the endothermic one.

3. Change the pressure. This is especially effective in gas reactions where the number of product molecules differs from the number of initial molecules. Increasing the pressure favors the reaction that gives the fewest molecules. For example, in the case of

$$2SO_2 + O_2 \rightleftharpoons 2SO_3$$

a rise in pressure increases the yield of SO_3 because it occupies only two-thirds the volume of the gases that react to form it.

OXIDATION AND REDUCTION

Until now we have used the term *oxidation* to mean the chemical combination of a substance with oxygen. A related term also in common use is *reduction,* which refers to the removal of oxygen from a compound. Whenever oxygen reacts with another substance (except fluorine), the oxygen atoms pick up electrons donated by the atoms of that substance. When the resulting compound is reduced, its atoms regain the electrons initially lost to the oxygen atoms.

It is convenient to generalize oxidation and reduction to refer to *any* chemical process in which electrons are transferred from one element to another, regardless of whether or not oxygen is involved. Hence

Oxidation and reduction

Oxidation refers to the loss of electrons by the atoms of an element, and reduction refers to the gain of electrons.

The oxidation of one element is always accompanied by the reduction of another; the two processes must take place together. For example, when zinc combines with chlorine, electrons are given up by the zinc atoms to the chlorine atoms. Thus the zinc is oxidized and the chlorine is reduced in the reaction. Reactions that involve electron transfer are called *oxidation-reduction reactions,* and they make up a large and important category.

Oxidation-reduction reactions involve electron transfer

Electrolysis

A chemical reaction caused by electric current

The electrolysis of a compound is an example of an oxidation-reduction process. Let us consider the electrolysis of molten sodium chloride, which consists of the

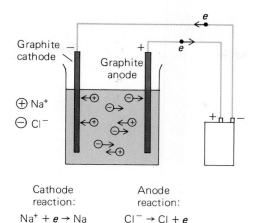

Cathode reaction:

$$Na^+ + e \rightarrow Na$$

Anode reaction:

$$Cl^- \rightarrow Cl + e$$

FIG. 11-7
The electrolysis of molten sodium chloride. The current in the liquid consists of moving Na^+ and Cl^- ions; the current in the wires consists of moving electrons.

In electrolysis, the passage of an electric current through a liquid liberates a free element

ions Na^+ (a sodium atom with its outer electron missing) and Cl^- (a chlorine atom with one excess electron). When electrodes in the liquid are connected to the terminals of a battery, Na^+ ions are attracted to the cathode (negative electrode) and Cl^- ions to the anode (positive electrode), as in Fig. 11-7. At the anode each Cl^- is neutralized by giving up its extra electron and becomes a chlorine atom:

$$Cl^- \longrightarrow Cl + e^-$$

The Cl atoms pair off to form molecules of chlorine gas, Cl_2. At the cathode each Na^+ is neutralized by gaining an electron and becomes a sodium atom:

$$Na^+ + e^- \longrightarrow Na$$

The net result of sending a current through molten salt, then, is to break up the compound NaCl into its constituent elements:

$$2NaCl \longrightarrow 2Na + Cl_2$$

The sodium, a liquid at the temperature of molten salt, collects around the cathode, and chlorine gas bubbles up around the anode. This procedure is commonly used to prepare metallic sodium.

Electroplating involves depositing by electrolysis a thin layer of a metal on an object made of another metal. Sometimes this is done because the plating metal is expensive, for instance gold or silver. In other cases the object is to protect the base metal from corrosion, as in the chromium plating of steel. Nonmetallic items can be plated by first coating them with a conducting material such as graphite.

Figure 11-8 shows an arrangement for silver-plating a spoon. The bath is a solution of silver nitrate, which dissociates into Ag^+ and NO_3^- ions. Silver atoms

Electroplating

Steel plated with tin to prevent corrosion is widely used for food and beverage containers.

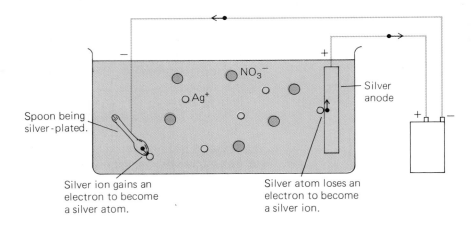

FIG. 11-8
Silver plating. The bath is a solution of silver nitrate, $AgNO_3$. The nitrate ions remain in solution because Ag atoms lose electrons at the anode more readily than NO_3^- ions do.

enter the solution as Ag^+ ions at the anode, and these ions are attracted to the spoon where they pick up electrons to become silver atoms again. Because an Ag atom loses an electron to become Ag^+ more readily than an NO_3^- ion loses its extra electron, the NO_3^- ions stay in solution and do not participate in the plating process.

Displacement Reactions

Active elements displace less active ones from solution

Not all oxidation-reduction reactions require an electric current to take place. For instance, if a piece of copper wire is covered with a solution of silver nitrate and allowed to stand for a few hours, the wire becomes coated with gray crystals and the solution turns pale blue. The crystals are metallic silver, and the telltale blue color shows the presence of copper ions in the solution. The reaction is summarized by the equation

$$Cu + 2Ag^+ + 2NO_3^- \longrightarrow Cu^{2+} + 2Ag + 2NO_3^-$$

Or, since the nitrate ion is not affected, we may write simply

Copper displaces silver from solution

$$Cu + 2Ag^+ \longrightarrow Cu^{2+} + 2Ag$$

This is an oxidation-reduction reaction in which each copper atom has lost two electrons to become a copper ion and each silver ion has gained one electron to become a neutral silver atom. Copper is oxidized; silver is reduced. We may describe this reaction by saying that copper has *displaced* silver from solution.

A similar reaction takes place when a steel knife blade is held in a solution of copper sulfate. After a few moments the blade is coated with a reddish film of copper, and tests would show the presence of iron ions in solution. The equation for the reaction is therefore

Iron displaces copper from solution

$$Fe + Cu^{2+} \longrightarrow Fe^{2+} + Cu$$

Iron atoms reduce copper ions to free copper and are themselves oxidized to positive ions. Or we may say that iron has displaced copper from solution.

Iron atoms give up electrons to copper ions; copper atoms give up electrons to silver ions. Thus the order Fe, Cu, Ag shows the relative tendencies of these metals to give up electrons. By studying other displacement reactions, we find that other metals may be added to this series, each metal being able to give up electrons to the ions of metals that follow it. Table 11-2 is the result. The order

TABLE 11-2
Order of Activity of the Metals.

K	Potassium
Na	Sodium
Ca	Calcium
Mg	Magnesium
Al	Aluminum
Zn	Zinc
Fe	Iron
Pb	Lead
(H)	(Hydrogen)
Cu	Copper
Hg	Mercury
Ag	Silver
Au	Gold

is that of decreasing tendency to lose electrons (decreasing ability to reduce the ions of other metals). Magnesium placed in a solution of copper chloride gives its electrons to the copper ions; lead placed in a silver nitrate solution reduces the silver ions. This is what was described in Chap. 9 as the *order of activity* of the metals. Oxidation-reduction reactions, in fact, furnish a precise measure for the activities of different metals.

Hydrogen fits into the above sequence because dissolving a metal in an acid is really a displacement reaction:

Zinc displaces hydrogen from solution

$$Zn + 2H^+ \longrightarrow Zn^{2+} + H_2$$

Zinc gives up electrons to hydrogen ions, going into solution as zinc ions and setting hydrogen free. To find where hydrogen belongs in the series, we need only see which metals will dissolve in acids and which will not. We find that all the metals from Na to Pb will reduce H^+, but those from Cu to Au are unaffected by ordinary acids. Hence H belongs between Pb and Cu.

Displacement reactions also occur among nonmetals. If chlorine is added to a solution of potassium bromide, for example, the solution turns brownish because bromine is set free:

Chlorine displaces bromine from solution

$$Cl_2 + 2Br^- \longrightarrow Br_2 + 2Cl^-$$

Similarly bromine displaces iodine, and fluorine displaces any one of the other halogens. By means of these reactions, nonmetals also may be arranged in an activity series, as in Table 11-3. The sequence here is in order of decreasing tendency to gain electrons. Note that the activity of nonmetals is measured by their oxidizing ability, that of metals by their reducing ability — which is just another way to say that metals combine chemically by losing electrons to other elements and that nonmetals combine chemically by gaining electrons.

TABLE 11-3
Order of Activity of the Nonmetals.

F	Fluorine
Cl	Chlorine
Br	Bromine
O	Oxygen
I	Iodine
S	Sulfur

Electrochemical Cells

Turning chemical energy into electric energy

Oxidation-reduction reactions underlie the operation of electrochemical cells

An oxidation-reduction reaction can produce an electric current if we arrange matters so that the electrons transferred during the reaction do not move directly between the reactants but instead pass through an external wire. The dry cells of a flashlight, the storage battery in a car, and the fuel cell in a spacecraft are all based upon oxidation-reduction reactions and are known as *electrochemical cells*.

The lead-acid storage battery

In the storage battery of a car, plates of lead and of lead dioxide, PbO_2, are immersed in a solution of sulfuric acid which is dissociated into H^+ and SO_4^{2-} ions. The reactions that take place at each electrode when the battery is providing

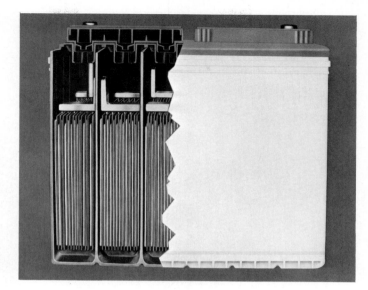

Each cell of a storage battery contains alternate plates of lead and of lead dioxide, PbO_2, in a solution of sulfuric acid. The plates of each kind are connected together and to an outside terminal. The electric current such a battery produces consists of electrons that move from the lead plates through an outside circuit to the lead dioxide plates.

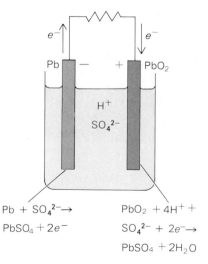

FIG. 11-9
The lead-acid storage battery. The reactions that occur at each electrode when the battery provides current are shown. These reactions are reversed when the battery is being charged.

$$Pb + SO_4^{2-} \rightarrow$$
$$PbSO_4 + 2e^-$$

$$PbO_2 + 4H^+ +$$
$$SO_4^{2-} + 2e^- \rightarrow$$
$$PbSO_4 + 2H_2O$$

current are shown in Fig. 11-9. As the battery is discharged, insoluble lead sulfate, $PbSO_4$, builds up on its plates. When there is no longer enough of the reactants to continue the electrode reactions, the battery is "dead." To recharge the battery, a current is passed through it in the opposite direction. This current causes the two electrode reactions to proceed in reverse, which restores the plates and the acid bath to their original compositions.

Technicians completing assembly of
a hydrogen-oxygen fuel cell used in
a spacecraft to provide electricity
and drinking water.

Fuel cells operate continuously

The state of charge of a storage battery can be found by measuring the
specific gravity of its acid bath. (As we learned in Chap. 4, the specific gravity of
something is its density relative to that of water.) A fully charged battery has a
specific gravity of about 1.26, which means that its density is 1.26 times that of
water. When the battery is fully discharged, its specific gravity drops to about 1.11.
The potential difference across a fully charged storage battery is 2.1 V; a "12-V"
battery contains six cells connected in series.

In a *fuel cell,* the reacting substances are fed in continuously. As a result the
cell can provide current indefinitely without having to be replaced or recharged.
Fuel cells are used in spacecraft since they are very light in proportion to the
electric power they can supply. In the future it is possible that fuel cells will be
perfected to the point where they are economical sources of power for individual
homes and for electric cars.

The combination of 1 lb of hydrogen and 8 lb of oxygen in a hydrogen-oxygen fuel cell produces about 10^8 J of electric energy, which is enough to power a 100-W light bulb for almost 2 weeks. The overall reaction in such a cell is

$$2H_2 + O_2 \longrightarrow 2H_2O + \text{flow of 4 electrons}$$

If a mixture of two volumes of hydrogen gas and one volume of oxygen gas is ignited, the result is a violent explosion with water as the product. In a hydrogen-oxygen fuel cell the same chemical combination occurs, but the liberated energy appears in the form of electric current. The ideal fuel cell would use readily available substances such as natural gas and air. Much progress has been made in recent years in developing such a cell, and large-scale trials are underway.

IMPORTANT TERMS

Combustion is the rapid combination of oxygen with another substance during which heat and light are given off.

The *formula mass* of a substance is the sum of the atomic masses of the elements it contains, each multiplied by the number of times it appears in the formula of the substance. A *mole* of a substance is that amount of it whose mass in grams is equal to its formula mass expressed in atomic mass units (u). A mole of anything contains the same number of formula units as a mole of anything else; this number is called *Avogadro's number.* Because of the way the mole is defined, a chemical equation can be interpreted in terms of moles as well as in terms of formula units such as atoms, molecules, or ions.

Endothermic reactions absorb energy and *exothermic reactions* liberate energy. Many exothermic reactions require initial *activation energy* in order to take place.

A *catalyst* is a substance that can change the rate of a chemical reaction without itself being permanently changed.

In a *chemical equilibrium,* forward and reverse reactions occur at the same rate, so the concentrations of the reactants and products of the reaction remain constant.

Oxidation involves the loss of electrons by the atoms of an element in a chemical reaction, and *reduction* involves the gain of electrons. An example of an oxidation-reduction reaction is *electrolysis,* in which free elements are liberated from a liquid by the passage of an electric current. Batteries and fuel cells produce electric current by means of oxidation-reduction reactions.

MULTIPLE CHOICE

1. When something burns,
   a. it combines with phlogiston
   b. it gives off phlogiston
   c. it combines with oxygen
   d. it gives off oxygen

2. A substance of unknown composition is heated in an open container. As a result,
   a. its mass decreases
   b. its mass remains the same
   c. its mass increases
   d. any of the above, depending on the nature of the substance and the temperature reached

3. The formula mass of gaseous carbon dioxide, CO_2,
   a. is 28 u
   b. is 44 u
   c. is 56 u
   d. depends on the mass of the sample

4. The number of formula units in a mole of a substance
   a. depends on the formula mass of the substance
   b. depends on whether the substance is an element or a compound
   c. depends on whether the substance is in the gaseous, liquid, or solid state
   d. is the same for all substances

5. An oxygen atom has a mass of 16.0 u. The number of moles of molecular oxygen, O_2, in 64 g of oxygen gas is
   a. 2
   b. 4

   c. 32

   d. 64

6. How many moles of H atoms are present in 1 mole of H_2O?

   a. $\frac{2}{3}$

   b. 1

   c. 2

   d. 3

7. The number of moles of carbon present in 3 mol of glucose, $C_6H_{12}O_6$, is

   a. 2

   b. 3

   c. 6

   d. 18

8. The atomic mass of helium is 4.0 u and that of carbon is 12.0 u.

   a. The mass of 1 mole of carbon is $\frac{1}{3}$ the mass of 1 mole of helium

   b. The mass of 1 mole of carbon is 3 times the mass of 1 mole of helium

   c. One mole of carbon contains $\frac{1}{3}$ as many atoms as 1 mole of helium

   d. One mole of carbon contains 3 times as many atoms as 1 mole of helium

9. One mole of which of the following compounds contains the greatest mass of bromine?

   a. HBr

   b. Br_2

   c. $AlBr_3$

   d. $SiBr_4$

10. In round numbers, the atomic mass of nitrogen is 14 u and Avogadro's number is $N_0 = 6 \times 10^{23}$ formula units/mole. One mole of molecular nitrogen, N_2, contains

   a. 6×10^{23} molecules

   b. 12×10^{23} molecules

   c. 84×10^{23} molecules

   d. 168×10^{23} molecules

11. The mass of 1 mole of molecular nitrogen is

   a. 14 g

   b. 28 g

   c. 84×10^{23} g

   d. 168×10^{23} g

12. The mass of 6×10^{23} molecules of N_2 is

   a. 14 g

   b. 28 g

   c. 84×10^{23} g

   d. 168×10^{23} g

13. Six moles of O_2 are consumed in a certain run of the reaction $2H_2S + 3O_2 \rightarrow 2H_2O + 2SO_2$. The number of moles of water produced in the run is

   a. 1

   b. 2

   c. 4

   d. 6

14. Chemical energy is stored within atoms, molecules, and ions as

   a. activation energy

   b. electron kinetic energy

   c. electron potential energy

   d. thermal energy

15. Chemical reactions that evolve energy are said to be

   a. exothermic

   b. endothermic

   c. activated

   d. electrolytic

16. Reactions that evolve energy

   a. never require activation energy

   b. sometimes require activation energy

   c. always require activation energy

   d. always require catalysts

17. The neutralization of a strong acid by a strong base

   a. absorbs energy

   b. liberates energy

   c. involves no energy change

   d. requires a catalyst to occur

18. Acid rain never contains dissolved

   a. carbon dioxide

   b. nitric acid

   c. sulfuric acid

   d. acetic acid

19. Reaction rates increase with temperature primarily because

   a. dissociation into ions is more complete

   b. more collisions occur between the molecules involved

   c. more activated molecules are formed

   d. equilibrium does not occur at high temperatures

20. The speeds of reactions between ions in solution

   a. depend critically upon temperautre

   b. are essentially independent of temperature

   c. depend upon which catalyst is used

   d. are slow in general

21. Most chemical reactions are

   a. reversible

   b. irreversible

   c. exothermic

   d. endothermic

22. At equilibrium,

   a. both forward and reverse reactions have ceased

   b. the forward and reverse reactions are proceeding at the same rate

c. the forward reaction has come to a stop, and the reverse reaction is just about to begin

d. the mass of reactants equals the mass of products

23. When a gas reaction involves a decrease in the total number of molecules, the equilibrium can be shifted in the direction of higher yield by

   a. increasing the pressure
   b. decreasing the pressure
   c. increasing the temperature
   d. decreasing the temperature

24. When an electric current is passed through molten sodium chloride,

   a. sodium metal is deposited at the positive electrode
   b. sodium ions are deposited at the positive electrode
   c. chlorine gas is liberated at the positive electrode
   d. chlorine ions are liberated at the positive electrode

25. The quantity actually stored in a "storage battery" is

   a. electric charge
   b. electric current
   c. voltage
   d. energy

26. A fuel cell does not require

   a. a positive electrode
   b. a negative electrode
   c. oxidation-reduction reactions
   d. recharging

QUESTIONS

1. Which of the following are exothermic reactions and which endothermic?

   a. The explosion of dynamite
   b. The burning of methane
   c. The decomposition of water into its elements
   d. The dissociation of water into ions
   e. The burning of iron in chlorine
   f. The combination of zinc and sulfur to form zinc sulfide

2. From the observation that the slaking of lime [addition of water to CaO to form $Ca(OH)_2$] gives out heat, would you conclude that the following reaction is endothermic or exothermic?

$$Ca(OH)_2 \rightarrow CaO + H_2O$$

3. In what fundamental way is the explosion of an atomic bomb different from the explosion of dynamite?

4. Why does an increase in temperature increase the rate of exothermic as well as endothermic reactions?

5. When carbon in the form of diamond is burned to produce CO_2, 395 kJ/mol of heat is given off, and when carbon in the form of graphite is burned, 394 kJ/mol is given off. What form of carbon is more stable under ordinary conditions? What bearing does this conclusion have on the origin of diamonds?

6. Suggest three ways to increase the rate at which zinc dissolves in sulfuric acid.

7. Give two examples of reactions that are (a) practically instantaneous at room temperatures, (b) fairly slow at room temperatures.

8. Under ordinary circumstances coal burns slowly, but the fine coal dust in mines sometimes burns so rapidly as to cause an explosion. Explain the difference in rates. Would you expect the danger from spontaneous combustion to be greater in a coal pile containing principally large chunks or in one containing finely pulverized coal? Why?

9. Why is a reaction with a high activation energy slow at room temperature?

10. The solubility of a gas in a liquid decreases with increasing temperature. From this observation and what you know of how a change in temperature can affect an equilibrium, would you expect that dissolving a gas in a liquid is an exothermic or an endothermic process?

11. What is the general condition for a reaction to go to completion instead of an equilibrium being established? Give examples of liquid-phase reactions that go to completion.

12. Ammonia gas dissolves in water and reacts according to the equation

$$NH_3 + H_2O \rightleftharpoons NH_4^+ + OH^-$$

How would the amount of ammonium ion in solution be affected by

   a. increasing the pressure of NH_3?
   b. pumping off the gas above the solution?
   c. raising the temperature?
   d. adding a solution of HCl?

13. Hydrogen sulfide gas dissolves in water and ionizes very slightly: $H_2S \rightleftharpoons 2H^+ + S^{2-}$. How would the acidity of the solution (concentration of H^+) be affected by

   a. increasing the pressure of H_2S?
   b. raising the temperature?
   c. adding a solution of KOH?
   d. adding a solution of silver nitrate [silver sulfide (Ag_2S) is insoluble]?

14. Limestone ($CaCO_3$) dissolves in carbonic acid to form calcium bicarbonate. The latter dissociates readily, so that an equilibrium is set up:

$$CaCO_3 + H_2CO_3 \rightleftharpoons Ca^{++} + 2HCO_3^-$$

How would this equilibrium be affected by
  a. raising the temperature?
  b. allowing the solution to evaporate?
  c. increasing the pressure of CO_2, thereby increasing the concentration of H_2CO_3?
Under what natural conditions, then, is limestone most soluble? Under what conditions will it be precipitated from solution?
15. The reaction $2SO_2 + O_2 \rightarrow 2SO_3$ is exothermic. How will a rise in temperature affect the yield of SO_3 in an equilibrium mixture of the three gases? Will an increase in pressure raise or lower this yield? In what possible way can the speed of the reaction be increased at moderate temperatures?
16. The three gases H_2, O_2, and H_2O are in equilibrium at temperatures near 2000°C. Write the equation for the equilibrium. Would the yield of H_2O be increased or decreased by raising the temperature? By raising the pressure?
17. In each of the following displacement reactions, identify the element that is oxidized and the one that is reduced.

$$Zn + Cu^{2+} \rightarrow Zn^{2+} + Cu$$

$$Fe + 2H^+ \rightarrow Fe^{2+} + H_2$$

$$Cl_2 + 2Br^- \rightarrow 2Cl^- + Br_2$$

$$Cl_2 + 2Fe^{2+} \rightarrow 2Cl^- + 2Fe^{3+}$$

18. In each of the following reactions, identify the element that is oxidized and the one that is reduced.

$$Mg + 2H^+ \rightarrow H_2 + Mg^{2+}$$

$$Ca + S \rightarrow CaS$$

$$2Na + 2H_2O \rightarrow 2Na^+ + 2OH^- + H_2$$

$$F_2 + 2Br^- \rightarrow Br_2 + 2F^-$$

$$2Fe^{3+} + 3H_2S \rightarrow 2FeS + S + 6H^+$$

19. Which loses electrons more easily, Na or Fe? Al or Ag? I^- or Cl^-? Which gains electrons more easily, Cl or Br? Hg^{2+} or Mg^{2+}?
20. In what part of the periodic table are the elements that are most easily reduced? In what part are those that are most easily oxidized?
21. How could you demonstrate that magnesium is a better reducing agent (that is, more easily oxidized) than hydrogen?
22. Lithium reacts with water to produce lithium hydroxide. What else is produced? Write the equation of the process. Which element is reduced and which is oxidized?

23. What becomes of the electric energy provided in electrolysis? In what device is this energy transformation reversed?
24. Why must water be added periodically to a lead-acid storage battery when it is in normal operation?
25. A charging current is passed through a fully charged lead-acid storage battery. What happens?
26. In what basic way is a fuel cell different from a dry cell or a storage battery?
27. In the refining of iron, the iron(III) oxide, Fe_2O_3, in iron ore is reduced by carbon (in the form of coke) to yield metallic iron and carbon dioxide. Write the balanced equation of the process.

PROBLEMS

1. Find the mass of 10 mol of uranium, U. How many atoms are present in such a sample?
2. Find the mass of 0.4 mol of magnesium, Mg. How many atoms are present in such a sample?
3. Find the mass of 2 mol of iron(III) oxide, Fe_2O_3.
4. Find the mass of 85 mol of sulfuric acid, H_2SO_4.
5. How many moles are present in 500 kg of glucose, $C_6H_{12}O_6$?
6. How many moles are present in 100 g of lead nitrate, $Pb(NO_3)_2$?
7. How many moles of aluminum are present in 5 mol of $MgAl_2O_4$?
8. How many moles of propane, C_3H_8, can be prepared from 1 mol of carbon? From 1 mol of hydrogen?
9. Ammonia is produced by the reaction $N_2 + 3H_2 \rightarrow 2NH_3$. How many moles of N_2 and how many of H_2 are needed to produce 1 mol of ammonia?
10. When hydrogen is burned in oxygen, water is formed according to the reaction $2H_2 + O_2 \rightarrow 2H_2O$. How many moles of H_2 and how many of O_2 are needed to produce 3 mol of H_2O?
11. How much chlorine is needed to react with 50 g of sodium to form sodium chloride, NaCl? How much sodium chloride is produced?
12. How much sulfur is needed to react with 60 kg of aluminum to form aluminum sulfide, Al_2S_3?
13. How much sulfur is needed to react with 200 g of potassium to form potassium sulfide, K_2S?
14. When potassium chlorate, $KClO_3$, is heated, it decomposes into potassium chloride and oxygen in the reaction $2KClO_3 \rightarrow 2KCl + 3O_2$. How much oxygen is liberated when 50 g of potassium chlorate is heated?
15. How many moles of hydrochloric acid are present in 120 ml of a $2M$ solution?
16. How many ml of $2M$ hydrochloric acid are needed to provide 0.5 mol of this acid?

17. What is the molarity of a solution that contains 100 g of NaCl per liter?

18. How much glucose, $C_6H_{12}O_6$, is needed to prepare 300 ml of a $1.5M$ solution?

19. A cube of zinc 1 cm on each edge takes an hour to dissolve in an acid bath. If the zinc is first cut into eight cubes 0.5 cm on each edge, approximately how much time would be needed?

20. In a hydrogen-oxygen fuel cell, hollow, porous electrodes are used that are made of an inert, conducting material. These electrodes enable the gases to interact with the electrolyte in a gradual way. A typical electrolyte in such a cell is a solution of potassium hydroxide. At one electrode, hydrogen molecules combine with hydroxide ions to form water, and at the other electrode, oxygen molecules combine with water molecules to form hydroxide ions. Which electrode is negative and which is positive when the cell is in operation? What are the reactions that occur at each electrode? Does each reaction occur the same number of times as the other?

ANSWERS TO MULTIPLE CHOICE

1. *c*	**8.** *b*	**15.** *a*	**22.** *b*
2. *d*	**9.** *d*	**16.** *b*	**23.** *a*
3. *b*	**10.** *a*	**17.** *b*	**24.** *c*
4. *d*	**11.** *b*	**18.** *d*	**25.** *d*
5. *a*	**12.** *b*	**19.** *c*	**26.** *d*
6. *c*	**13.** *c*	**20.** *b*	
7. *d*	**14.** *c*	**21.** *a*	

12

ORGANIC CHEMISTRY

In many ways carbon is the most remarkable element. Hundreds of thousands of carbon compounds are known, far more than all other compounds. Further, carbon compounds are the chief constituents of all living things — hence the name *organic chemistry* to describe the chemistry of carbon and the name *inorganic chemistry* to describe the chemistry of all the other elements.

CHAPTER 12

CARBON COMPOUNDS

At one time it was thought that carbon compounds, with the exception of the oxides, the carbonates, and a few others, could be produced only by plants and animals (or indirectly from other compounds produced by them). Carbon was supposed to unite with other elements only under the influence of a mysterious *vital force* possessed by living things. This ancient idea was disproved in 1828 by the German chemist Friedrich Wöhler, who prepared the organic compound urea by heating the inorganic compound ammonium cyanate. Since Wöhler's time a great number of organic compounds have been made in the laboratory from inorganic materials, but the general distinction between the chemistry of carbon compounds and inorganic chemistry nevertheless remains useful.

Carbon Bonds

Carbon atoms can form covalent bonds with each other

What properties of carbon give it such a remarkable ability to form compounds?

Let us see what the periodic table can tell us. Carbon is at the top of Group IV, which means that it is a small atom with four outer electrons. Such an atom cannot readily either lose all these electrons or gain the four more needed to complete its outer shell, and so it almost always combines chemically by sharing four electron pairs. Thus the bonds between carbon atoms and others are covalent. Because of the small size of the carbon atom and the resulting strong attraction of its nucleus for electrons, these bonds are fairly strong.

Carbon atoms form covalent bonds with each other as well as with other atoms

A carbon atom can form firm attachments not only to many different metallic and nonmetallic atoms but to *other carbon atoms* as well. The strength of the bonds between carbon atoms is shown by the hardness of diamond, a crystalline form of carbon in which each atom is linked to four others by electron pairs (Fig. 10-4). It is this capacity of carbon atoms to join together with each other as well as with other atoms in the same molecule that makes possible the immense number and variety of carbon compounds. Atoms of a few elements near carbon in the periodic table, notably boron and silicon, have the same ability, but the range of their compounds is far more limited.

General properties of organic compounds

Because the bonds formed by carbon atoms are covalent, carbon compounds are mostly nonelectrolytes, and their reaction rates are usually slow. The affinity of carbon atoms and hydrogen atoms for oxygen makes many organic compounds subject to slow oxidation in air and to rapid oxidation if heated. Even in the absence of air most organic compounds are stable only at ordinary temperatures, and very few of them resist decomposition at temperatures over a few hundred degrees celsius.

Alkanes

The hydrocarbons in petroleum and natural gas

Hydrocarbons contain only carbon and hydrogen

The simplest organic compounds are the *hydrocarbons* that contain only carbon

TABLE 12-1
The Alkane Series of Hydrocarbons.*

Formula	Name	Freezing point, °C	Boiling point, °C	Commercial name
CH_4	Methane	−184	−161	
C_2H_6	Ethane	−172	−88	
C_3H_8	Propane	−190	−45	Fuel gases
C_4H_{10}	Butane	−135	−1	
C_5H_{12}	Pentane	−132	36	Naphtha
C_6H_{14}	Hexane	−94	69	
C_7H_{16}	Heptane	−90	98	
C_8H_{18}	Octane	−57	125	Gasoline
C_9H_{20}	Nonane	−51	154	
$C_{10}H_{22}$	Decane	−32	174	
$C_{11}H_{24}$	Undecane	−27	197	Kerosene
$C_{16}H_{34}$	Hexadecane	18	287	

$C_{17}H_{36}$ to $C_{22}H_{46}$, constituents of lubricating oil and petroleum jelly
$C_{23}H_{48}$ to $C_{29}H_{60}$, semisolid constituents of paraffin

* The data refer to the normal, or straight-chain, compounds. Isomers of these hydrocarbons (see page 405) have somewhat different properties.

and hydrogen. Even these relatively simple compounds exist in tremendous variety.

Alkane molecules have only single carbon-carbon bonds

A group of hydrocarbons called the *alkanes* include familiar substances such as the gases methane (CH_4), propane (C_3H_8), and butane (C_4H_{10}). Alkane molecules have only single carbon-carbon bonds. The densities, freezing points, and boiling points of the alkanes all increase regularly as the molecular size increases (Table 12-1). Other series of organic compounds show similar regular changes in properties as the number of carbon atoms per molecule increases.

Alkanes are the constituents of petroleum and natural gas

Natural gas and petroleum consist mainly of alkanes. About 80 percent of natural gas is methane, 10 percent ethane, and the rest mostly propane and butane. The heavier alkanes with five or more carbon atoms make up petroleum. Methane is also common outside natural gas as one of the emissions from active volcanoes and as a product of the bacterial decay of plant matter in the absence of oxygen. The "marsh gas" that bubbles up from the black ooze at the bottom of stagnant pools is largely methane, as is the "fire damp" that sometimes causes explosions in coal mines.

The separation of petroleum into the separate alkanes it contains is difficult because their properties are so similar. Suppose we want to separate pentane and hexane. Pentane boils at 36°C and hexane at 69°C, so it would seem that if we heat a mixture of the two, all the pentane would boil away first to leave pure hexane. The trouble is that hexane evaporates readily at 36°C, so the vapor produced by

Catalytic cracking unit at an oil
refinery breaks down complex
hydrocarbons into simpler ones.

boiling the mixture would contain a certain amount of hexane as well as pentane. This procedure would thus give a vapor rich in pentane and a remaining liquid rich in hexane, but would not separate them completely.

The different boiling points of the components of a mixture enable them to be separated by fractional distillation

Usually a complete separation of the alkanes in petroleum is not necessary, however. The basic process in petroleum refining is *fractional distillation,* in which the crude oil is heated and its vapors led off and condensed at progressively higher temperatures. What comes off at the lowest temperature is largely pentane and hexane, with minor amounts of both lighter and heavier hydrocarbons. The resulting colorless, volatile liquid, called naphtha, is used as a solvent and cleaning agent. The next fraction, consisting largely of alkanes from hexane to decane, is gasoline. Still heavier and less volatile fractions make up kerosene and diesel fuel. Higher temperatures give lubricating oil and still higher ones give the semisolid hydrocarbon mixtures called petroleum jelly and paraffin. Grease consists of oil to which a thickening agent has been added to prevent it from running out from between the surfaces being lubricated.

Cracking

Of all these products the most valuable, of course, is gasoline. Unfortunately the constituents of gasoline are present only to a minor extent in most petroleums. Two methods have been developed to increase the yield of gasoline. In one of them the heavier hydrocarbons are *cracked* into smaller molecules by heating them under pressure in the presence of catalysts. A typical cracking reaction is

$$C_{16}H_{34} \longrightarrow C_8H_{18} + C_8H_{16}$$

Here hexadecane, one of the heavier alkanes in kerosene and diesel fuel, is broken down into lighter hydrocarbons that vaporize and burn more readily.

Polymerization

The second procedure is to *polymerize* lighter hydrocarbons, which means to join small molecules into larger ones under the influence of heat, pressure, and appropriate catalysts. An example is

$$C_3H_8 + C_4H_8 \longrightarrow C_7H_{16}$$

in which heptane, a liquid, is formed by the polymerization of two gases.

Alkane molecules have chains of carbon atoms linked together to form symmetrical or nearly symmetrical structures. Such molecules, as we might expect, are nonpolar, with neither end appreciably more positive or negative than the other. Because of this nonpolar character, the alkane hydrocarbons are insoluble in water. Chemically they are fairly unreactive, and neither concentrated acids and bases nor most oxidizing agents affect them at ordinary temperatures. Nor do biological agents such as bacteria attack them to any great extent. The combination of insolubility, relative inertness, and toxicity to living things is what makes the discharge of petroleum and its products into the sea such a serious matter.

Oil spills at sea

Oil spills are common. Some are accidental, the result of shipwreck or a malfunction at an offshore oil well, but a great many are deliberate, the result of tankers flushing out waste oil from their tanks. Although the lighter hydrocarbons soon evaporate, the heavier ones remain floating on the surface or are washed ashore on adjacent coastlines. Depending on the nature of the residues and the region, their effects on marine life may be drastic and immediate — dead plankton, dead fish, dead crustaceans, dead birds — or they may be gradual, taking the form of an altered balance of nature with declining populations. The lumps of tar that are one result of oil spills are already a prominent feature on the surface of much of the world's oceans, and are familiar sights on a great many beaches. To be sure, tankers and oil-well accidents are not the only source of hydrocarbon pollutants: land-based activities involving petroleum products pour a steady stream of them into lakes, rivers, seas, and oceans.

STRUCTURES OF ORGANIC MOLECULES

Structural Formulas

Four covalent bonds per carbon atom

A structural formula shows how the atoms in a molecule are linked together

Instead of using a molecular formula such as CH_4 and C_2H_6, an organic compound is often represented by a *structural formula* that shows the covalent bonds between the atoms in each molecule by dashes. Thus the structural formulas of the alkanes methane, ethane, and propane are

$$
\begin{array}{ccc}
\text{H} & \text{H } \text{ H} & \text{H } \text{ H } \text{ H} \\
| & | \quad | & | \quad | \quad | \\
\text{H—C—H} & \text{H—C—C—H} & \text{H—C—C—C—H} \\
| & | \quad | & | \quad | \quad | \\
\text{H} & \text{H } \text{ H} & \text{H } \text{ H } \text{ H} \\
\text{Methane} & \text{Ethane} & \text{Propane}
\end{array}
$$

FIG. 12-1
Model of the methane molecule, CH_4.

Clearly alkane molecules always have two more H atoms than twice the number of C atoms, so that their compositions follow the general formula C_nH_{n+2}, where $n = 1, 2, 3, \ldots$ Besides the information that the molecular formulas give, the above structural formulas show that, in all three molecules, each hydrogen atom is attached to a carbon atom and that in ethane and propane the carbon atoms are linked together. Figure 12-1 shows a three-dimensional model of the methane molecule.

The number of bonds a given kind of atom forms in an organic compound is the same as the number of electrons it tends to gain or lose. A carbon atom, which has four electrons in its outer shell and lacks four of completing the shell, always participates in four bonds. A hydrogen atom always has a single bond, as does a chlorine atom; an oxygen atom always has two bonds. Here are some examples:

$$
\begin{array}{ccc}
\text{H } \text{ H } \text{ H} & \text{H} & \\
| \quad | \quad | & | & \text{Cl} \\
\text{H—C—C—C—Cl} & \text{H—C—O—H} & | \\
| \quad | \quad | & | & \text{Cl—C=O} \\
\text{H } \text{ H } \text{ H} & \text{H} & \\
\text{Propyl chloride} & \text{Methanol} & \text{Phosgene}
\end{array}
$$

Normal butane

Isobutane

FIG. 12-2
The two isomers of butane, C_4H_{10}.

Isomers have the same molecular
formulas for different structures

Isomers

The same atoms but arranged differently

For methane, ethane, and propane the structural formulas given above are the only possible arrangements of carbon and hydrogen atoms that will satisfy the combination rules. Butane, on the other hand, may have its four C atoms and ten H atoms arranged in two *different* ways:

Normal butane   Isobutane

These formulas show that there are two different compounds with the molecular formula C_4H_{10}. They differ in that one of the carbon atoms in isobutane is linked to three others, while in normal butane the carbon atoms are linked to only one or two others. The physical properties of isobutane are somewhat different from those of normal butane because of this difference in molecular structure; the boiling point of isobutane, for instance, is $-12°C$, whereas that of normal butane, as listed in Table 12-1, is $-1°C$. Another difference is their densities: that of isobutane is 0.622 g/cm³ whereas that of normal butane is 0.604 g/cm³. Figure 12-2 shows three-dimensional models of the two kinds of butane.

Compounds that have the same molecular formulas but different structural formulas are called *isomers*. The number of possible isomers increases rapidly with the number of carbon atoms in the molecule; $C_{13}H_{28}$ has 813 theoretically possible isomers and $C_{20}H_{42}$ has 366,319. Only a few of the possible isomers have actually been prepared.

Determining Structure

Which is which?

Figuring out the possible atomic arrangements that correspond to a given molecular formula is an interesting, though not too difficult, game. The big question is, which structural formula goes with which isomer? This is seldom an easy question to answer and often requires extensive laboratory work.

As an example, let us consider two compounds that have the molecular formula C_2H_6O. One is the familiar liquid ethanol (ethyl alcohol); the other is a gas named dimethyl ether (not the anesthetic called "ether," but a related compound). Two structures for C_2H_6O are possible:

Isomers of C_2H_6O

$$H-\underset{\underset{H}{|}}{\overset{\overset{H}{|}}{C}}-\underset{\underset{H}{|}}{\overset{\overset{H}{|}}{C}}-O-H \qquad H-\underset{\underset{H}{|}}{\overset{\overset{H}{|}}{C}}-O-\underset{\underset{H}{|}}{\overset{\overset{H}{|}}{C}}-H$$

Our problem is to match these structures with the properties of the two substances. Tests such as the following make a choice possible.

1. Sodium reacts with ethanol to liberate hydrogen and form the compound C_2H_5ONa. No further reaction with the other five H's of the ethanol molecule takes place, so one H must be attached in a different manner from the others.
2. Ethanol reacts with HCl to give water and the gas ethyl chloride, C_2H_5Cl. An O and an H have been replaced by a Cl atom, which suggests that the O and H were together in the original molecule.

We need go no further to assign the first of the above structural formulas to ethanol. The second must therefore represent dimethyl ether.

Molecular spectra help in determining molecular structures

Physical as well as chemical methods can be used to investigate molecular structures. An example is molecular spectroscopy. The atoms in a molecule can vibrate back and forth, usually in a variety of ways (Fig. 12-3). If a certain group of atoms in the molecule vibrates with the frequency f, it is able to absorb electromagnetic radiation of this frequency. When it does so, the energy of the vibrations increases by the quantum energy hf. Typical frequencies of molecular vibration are 10^{13} to 10^{14} Hz, which corresponds to the infrared part of the spectrum. If we pass infrared light through the liquid or vapor of a particular compound, then, the frequencies that are absorbed correspond to the vibrational frequencies of its molecules. From these frequencies it is often possible to infer details of the structures of the molecules.

A number of atom groups have characteristic frequencies of vibration that permit them to be identified in any molecule of which they are a part. Thus the —OH group has a vibrational frequency of 1.1×10^{14} Hz and the —NH$_2$ group has a frequency of 1.0×10^{14} Hz; the absorption of infrared light of either of these frequencies by a compound means that the corresponding group is present in its

FIG. 12-3
Three modes of vibration of the H_2O molecule. Each mode has a different characteristic frequency.

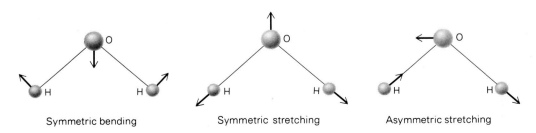

Symmetric bending   Symmetric stretching   Asymmetric stretching

molecules. The nature of carbon-carbon bonds can also be established by this technique: the $-\overset{|}{\underset{|}{C}}-\overset{|}{\underset{|}{C}}-$, $C=C$, and $-C\equiv C-$ groups all have different frequencies of vibration.

Unsaturated Hydrocarbons

Double and triple carbon-carbon bonds

Hydrocarbons are not limited to the alkanes (methane, ethane, and so on) and their isomers. A simple example is *ethene*, also called ethylene, whose formula is C_2H_4. The alkane with two C atoms is ethane, C_2H_6, whose structural formula is

$$H-\overset{\overset{\displaystyle H}{|}}{\underset{\underset{\displaystyle H}{|}}{C}}-\overset{\overset{\displaystyle H}{|}}{\underset{\underset{\displaystyle H}{|}}{C}}-H \qquad \text{Ethane}$$

How can ethene, with two fewer H atoms, still have each C atom share four electron pairs? The answer is that there are *two* covalent bonds between the C atoms in ethene:

$$\overset{\displaystyle H}{\underset{\displaystyle H}{>}}C=C\overset{\displaystyle H}{\underset{\displaystyle H}{<}} \qquad \text{Ethene}$$

Such a link between carbon atoms is called a *double bond.*

Triple bonds, with carbon atoms sharing three electron pairs, are also possible. The simplest case is that of acetylene, C_2H_2, a gas widely used in welding and metal-cutting torches. The structural formula of acetylene is

$$H-C\equiv C-H \qquad \text{Acetylene}$$

Compounds with double and triple bonds are much more reactive than the alkanes, which have only single bonds. Both HCl and Cl_2 combine readily with ethene, for instance:

$$\overset{\displaystyle H}{\underset{\displaystyle H}{>}}C=C\overset{\displaystyle H}{\underset{\displaystyle H}{<}} \;+\; HCl \;\longrightarrow\; H-\overset{\overset{\displaystyle H}{|}}{\underset{\underset{\displaystyle H}{|}}{C}}-\overset{\overset{\displaystyle H}{|}}{\underset{\underset{\displaystyle Cl}{|}}{C}}-H$$

$$\overset{\displaystyle H}{\underset{\displaystyle H}{>}}C=C\overset{\displaystyle H}{\underset{\displaystyle H}{<}} \;+\; Cl_2 \;\longrightarrow\; H-\overset{\overset{\displaystyle H}{|}}{\underset{\underset{\displaystyle Cl}{|}}{C}}-\overset{\overset{\displaystyle H}{|}}{\underset{\underset{\displaystyle Cl}{|}}{C}}-H$$

Unsaturated compounds have double or triple carbon-carbon bonds

The other halogens and many other acids give similar reactions. Since compounds with multiple bonds are able to add other atoms to their molecules, they are called *unsaturated compounds*, in distinction from *saturated compounds* like the alkanes.

Benzene

A stable ring of carbon atoms

What is the nature of the carbon-carbon bonds in the benzene ring?

Benzene, C_6H_6, is a clear liquid that does not mix with water and has a pungent odor. It is an extremely interesting hydrocarbon because its six C atoms are arranged in a flat hexagonal ring (Fig. 12-4). If we think in terms of conventional electron-pair bonds, there are three single and three double bonds between the C atoms in benzene, so that its structure can be drawn in the following way:

Benzene

There are a number of major objections to this simple picture of benzene. One is that double bonds are not particularly stable, so that benzene, like ethylene, should form addition compounds readily. What actually happens, on the contrary, is that benzene forms substitution compounds in which one or more of the H atoms are replaced by other atoms or atom groups, with the ring structure remaining intact. In other words, the benzene ring is stronger than the simple structural formula would indicate.

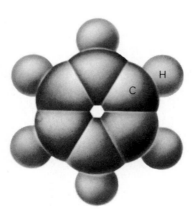

FIG. 12-4
Model of the benzene molecule, C_6H_6.

Another objection arises because C—C bonds are 1.54×10^{-10} m long on the average and C=C bonds are 1.35×10^{-10} m long. The shorter length of the C=C bond is consistent with the participation of four electrons in a double bond, instead of two as in C—C. But benzene molecules are regular hexagons in shape, with all bonds having the same intermediate length of 1.40×10^{-10} m and all bond angles being 120°.

A model of the benzene molecule that is in better accord with its observed properties is provided by a detailed study of how the electron structures of the C atoms join to form the electron structure of the benzene molecule. The conclusion is that there are ordinary single electron-pair bonds between adjacent carbon atoms, and in addition six electrons are shared by the entire ring of six carbon atoms. The latter electrons belong to the molecule as a whole and not to any particular pair of atoms; these electrons are *delocalized*. (We recall that the outer-shell electrons in a metal are similarly delocalized.) The delocalized electrons in benzene can be represented by an inner circle in its structural formula:

The benzene molecule contains six delocalized electrons that contribute to the bonding

Benzene

An *aromatic* compound is defined as one that contains a ring of six carbon atoms like that in benzene. The name arose because many of these compounds are especially fragrant. An example is toluene, which is a common solvent and paint thinner:

Aromatic compounds contain one or more benzene rings in their molecules; aliphatic compounds do not

Toluene

The C and H atoms that are part of a benzene ring are often omitted in representing the structures of aromatic molecules, as shown above. Some aromatic compounds contain two or more benzene rings fused together, as in the case of naphthalene:

Naphthalene

Naphthalene is familiar as the active ingredient in mothballs. Organic compounds whose molecules do not contain ring structures are said to be *aliphatic*.

ORGANIC COMPOUNDS

The remarkable range of organic compounds is hinted at in the hydrocarbons, which contain only carbon and hydrogen. Add just oxygen and the possibilities are multiplied many times over, giving compounds as diverse as they are numerous. Add still other elements and the result is staggering in variety and complexity. But regularities exist which permit the orderly classification of organic compounds and lead to an understanding of how their molecular structures govern their behavior. Given this understanding, the organic chemist can proceed in the reverse direction to create compounds tailored to exhibit specific properties. Evidence of the success of this endeavor is to be found in the synthetic materials, from textile fibers to drugs, so widely used today.

Hydrocarbon Groups

A convenient classification scheme

Hydrocarbon derivatives

To simplify the classification of organic compounds that contain other elements besides carbon and hydrogen, they are often regarded as *derivatives* of hydrocarbons — that is, as compounds obtained by substituting other atoms or atom groups for one or more of the H atoms in hydrocarbon molecules. Ordinarily such compounds are not prepared in this way, but their structural formulas suggest that they might be. For example, ethyl alcohol can be regarded as a derivative of ethane, with an OH group replacing an H atom:

$$
\begin{array}{cc}
\underset{\text{Ethane}}{
\text{H}-\overset{\displaystyle \text{H}}{\underset{\displaystyle \text{H}}{\text{C}}}-\overset{\displaystyle \text{H}}{\underset{\displaystyle \text{H}}{\text{C}}}-\text{H}
} &
\underset{\text{Ethyl alcohol}}{
\text{H}-\overset{\displaystyle \text{H}}{\underset{\displaystyle \text{H}}{\text{C}}}-\overset{\displaystyle \text{H}}{\underset{\displaystyle \text{H}}{\text{C}}}-\text{OH}
}
\end{array}
$$

Similarly acetic acid can be regarded as a derivative of methane, with a COOH group replacing an H atom:

$$
\begin{array}{cc}
\underset{\text{Methane}}{
\text{H}-\overset{\displaystyle \text{H}}{\underset{\displaystyle \text{H}}{\text{C}}}-\text{H}
} &
\underset{\text{Acetic acid}}{
\text{H}-\overset{\displaystyle \text{H}}{\underset{\displaystyle \text{H}}{\text{C}}}-\text{C}\overset{\displaystyle \text{O}}{\underset{\displaystyle \text{OH}}{\Big\langle}}
}
\end{array}
$$

Hydrocarbon groups

The carbon-hydrogen atom groups that appear in hydrocarbon derivatives are named from the hydrocarbons. Groups corresponding to the hydrocarbons methane, ethane, and propane are

$$
\begin{array}{ccc}
& & & H \\
& | & & \\
H-C- & & \\
& | & & \\
& H & & \\
\text{Methyl} & & \\
\text{group} & &
\end{array}
\qquad
\begin{array}{c}
H \quad H \\
| \quad | \\
H-C-C- \\
| \quad | \\
H \quad H \\
\text{Ethyl} \\
\text{group}
\end{array}
\qquad
\begin{array}{c}
H \quad H \quad H \\
| \quad | \quad | \\
H-C-C-C- \\
| \quad | \quad | \\
H \quad H \quad H \\
\text{Propyl} \\
\text{group}
\end{array}
$$

Thus the compound CH_3Cl is methyl chloride, C_3H_7I is propyl iodide, and $CH_3C_2H_5SO_4$ is methyl ethyl sulfate.

Halogen Derivatives

Hydrogen atoms replaced by halogen atoms

One or more of the H atoms in a hydrocarbon molecule may be replaced by halogen atoms to give such compounds as CH_3Br, CH_2I_2, C_2H_5Cl, and C_6H_5Br (Fig. 12-5). The simpler compounds of this sort are gases and volatile liquids, and, as in the alkane series, their boiling points and melting points rise with increasing molecular weight. They can be prepared by the addition of halogens and halogen acids to unsaturated hydrocarbons, as we have seen, but are more conveniently made indirectly from alcohols.

The halogen derivatives are particularly important to the organic chemist because the halogen atoms are easily replaced in turn by various atom groups in building up complex molecules. A few of the simpler of them are useful for other purposes: $CHCl_3$ is the anesthetic chloroform, CCl_4 is carbon tetrachloride and C_2HCl_3 is trichloroethylene, both common cleaning fluids, and CCl_2F_2 (dichlorodifluoromethane) is a gas used in refrigeration under the name Freon 12.

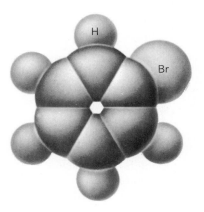

FIG. 12-5
Model of the bromobenzene molecule, C_6H_5Br.

TABLE 12-2
Common Functional Groups.

Name of group	Structural formula	Class of compound		Example	
Hydroxyl	—OH	Alcohol		Ethanol	Used as a solvent and in beverages; prepared by fermenting sugar or starch solution.
Ether	—O—	Ether		Diethyl ether	Once widely used as an anesthetic, its flammability has led to its replacement by safer compounds.
Aldehyde		Aldehyde		Formaldehyde	A gas used to preserve biological specimens and as an embalming fluid when dissolved in water ("formalin").
Ketone		Ketone		Acetone	A common solvent with a toxic vapor.
Carboxyl		Acid		Acetic acid	Responsible for characteristic taste of vinegar; a weak acid like other organic acids.
Ester		Ester		Methyl acetate	Formed by the reaction of methyl alcohol and acetic acid with water as the other product.

Functional Groups

Atom groups with characteristic behaviors

Inorganic compounds that contain a particular atom group, such as NO_3 or SO_4, have much in common, as we know. The chemical behavior of many organic compounds, too, is determined to a large extent by the presence of certain atom groups, called *functional groups*. Table 12-2 shows some of the main functional groups found in organic molecules.

Alcohols contain one or more hydroxyl (OH) groups

Alcohols   The hydroxyl (OH) group they contain makes alcohol molecules somewhat polar, so the simple ones are soluble in water. The polarity is not enough, however, to prevent them from mixing with many less polar compounds, which makes the alcohols useful as solvents. Ethanol (ethyl alcohol) is, of course, the active ingredient in wine, beer, and spirits.

Fermenting sugar yields ethanol and carbon dioxide

Wine is made by fermenting fruit juice, usually grape juice; beer is made by fermenting grain, usually barley, and then adding hops for flavor. Fermentation involves converting sugar to ethanol and carbon dioxide, with enzymes produced by yeast acting as catalysts. For example,

$$C_6H_{12}O_6 \longrightarrow 2C_2H_5OH + 2CO_2$$

Glucose   Ethanol   Carbon
(a sugar)   dioxide

Since yeast cells die when the alcohol concentration reaches about 15 percent, wine and beer cannot be stronger than this. In fact, fermentation generally stops somewhat earlier because the sugar runs out. Distillation can produce stronger liquors. The fermented liquid is heated and the alcohol-rich vapor is then led off and condensed to give brandy (starting from fruit), whiskey (grain), rum (sugar cane), vodka (traditionally potatoes), and so on. Ethanol for industrial purposes is usually made more cheaply by reacting ethene, a by-product of petroleum refining, with water in the presence of an appropriate catalyst:

Ethene   Water   Ethanol

Replacing an H by an OH group in the molecule of a benzene hydrocarbon produces a compound with properties somewhat different from those of ordinary alcohols. The simplest is *phenol* ("carbolic acid"), C_6H_5OH, which was the first antiseptic and today is one of the raw materials for the plastic Bakelite and for the phenolic glues used in plywood:

Phenol

Familiar alcohols with more than one OH group in their molecules are ethylene glycol and glycerol:

$$\underset{\text{OH \quad OH}}{\overset{\text{H \quad H}}{H-C---C-H}}$$ Ethylene glycol $$\underset{\text{OH \quad OH \quad OH}}{\overset{\text{H \quad H \quad H}}{H-C---C---C-H}}$$ Glycerol

Ethylene glycol is used as an antifreeze in car engines. Glycerol, also known as glycerin, is a sweetish, viscous liquid used in many skin lotions and to prevent tobacco from drying out.

Ethers An ether has an oxygen atom bonded between two carbon atoms. Relatively inert chemically, ethers are widely used as solvents in organic processes since there is little or no danger they will interfere with the reactions.

Aldehydes and ketones are soluble in water

Aldehydes and ketones These compounds have similar chemical behavior because both contain the atom group $\diagdown C{=}O$. The double bond between C and O is highly polar and as a result aldehydes and ketones are soluble in water. Ethanol is oxidized in the liver into acetaldehyde,

$$H-\overset{\overset{\textstyle H}{|}}{\underset{\underset{\textstyle H}{|}}{C}}-C\overset{\diagup O}{\diagdown H}$$ Acetaldehyde

which is apparently responsible for many of the ill effects of drinking too much, such as nausea and hangovers. The acetaldehyde is oxidized further in the liver to acetic acid, and the acetic acid to CO_2 and H_2O. The liver oxidizes methanol (methyl alcohol) to the poisonous formaldehyde, which is believed to be the reason why methanol is so toxic. The solvent acetone is the most familiar ketone.

Organic acids are weak

Organic acids Compounds that contain the carboxyl group —COOH are acids because the H atom is loosely held and can detach itself as H^+. Most organic acids are very weak. Familiar examples are the formic acid that causes insect bites to sting, the acetic acid of vinegar, the butyric acid of rancid butter and some cheeses, the citric acid of citrus fruits, the lactic acid of sour milk, and the acetylsalicylic acid of aspirin.

When an opened bottle of wine is stored for some time, the ethanol it contains gradually turns into acetic acid and the eventual result is vinegar. The conversion of ethanol to acetic acid is promoted by enzymes produced by bacteria in the wine:

$$\underset{\underset{\text{H \quad H}}{}}{\overset{\overset{\text{H \quad H}}{}}{H-C-C-OH}} + O_2 \longrightarrow \underset{\underset{\text{H}}{}}{\overset{\overset{\text{H}}{}}{H-C-C}}\overset{\diagup O}{\diagdown OH} + H_2O$$

Ethanol   Oxygen   Acetic acid   Water

Alcohols react with acids to form esters

Esters Alcohols are, so to speak, organic hydroxides, but unlike their inorganic cousins do not dissociate appreciably in water. They react slowly with acids to form compounds called *esters* that are analogous to the salts of inorganic chemistry but are not electrolytes. An example is ethyl acetate, which is made by reacting ethanol with acetic acid:

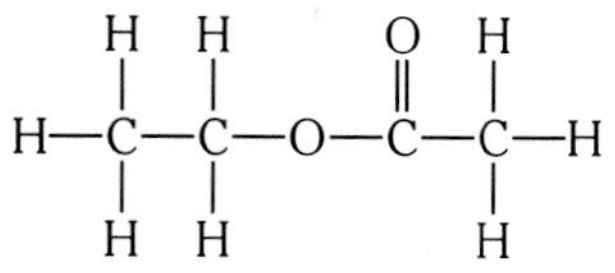

Ethyl acetate

This ester is an important commercial solvent. Several hundred thousand tons of it are used each year in the United States in manufacturing coatings of various kinds, from paint to nail polish.

Many esters have pleasant fruity or flowerlike odors and find extensive use in perfumes and flavors. Propyl acetate is responsible for the fragrance and taste of pears, ethyl butyrate for those of apricots, and butyl butyrate for those of pineapples. The explosive nitroglycerin is an ester formed by the reaction of nitric acid with the alcohol glycerol. Animal and vegetable fats are all esters of glycerol as well.

Polymers

Molecules linked into giant chains

We are already acquainted with the unsaturated hydrocarbon ethene:

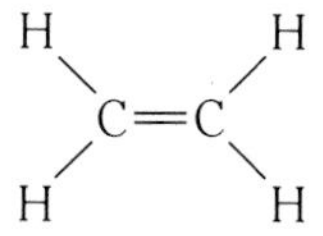

Ethene

Because of the double bond, ethene molecules can, under the proper conditions of heat and pressure, polymerize to form chains thousands of units long whose formula we might write as

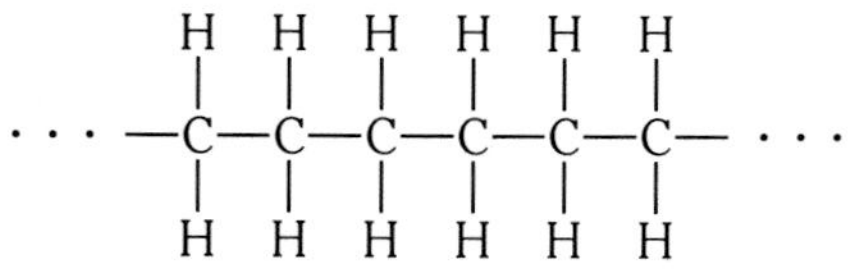

Polythene

A polymer consists of a long chain of monomer molecules

This material is *polythene* (or *polyethylene*), which is widely used as a packaging material because of its inertness and pliability. The ethene is called the *monomer* in the process, and polythene the *polymer*. A train can be thought of as a polymer, with each of its cars as a monomer.

Vinyls

Styrofoam

One of the H atoms in ethene can be replaced by another atom or atom group to form the monomer for a polymer whose properties differ from those of polythene. Because the group

Vinyl group

is called the *vinyl group*, such polymers are classed as vinyls. Some familiar examples are shown in Table 12-3.

The benzene rings attached to alternate C atoms in polystyrene are relatively large and project like knobs from the polymer chain. This prevents adjacent chains

TABLE 12-3
Some Common Vinyl Polymers.

Monomer	Polymer	Uses
Vinyl chloride	Polyvinylchloride	Tubing, insulation, imitation leather, rainwear (PVC, Geon, Koroseal)
Acrylonitrile	Polyacrylonitrile	Textiles, carpets (Acrilon, Orlon)
Propene	Polypropylene	Carpets, ropes, molded objects
Styrene	Polystyrene	Molded objects, insulation, packing material (Styrofoam)

from sliding past one another, and as a result polystyrene is relatively stiff. If a substance that gives off a gas is added to the liquid monomer mixture, gas bubbles will form throughout the liquid as it polymerizes. The result is the familiar light-weight, rigid Styrofoam.

Lucite and Plexiglas

In some monomers, such as methyl methacrylate, two of the H atoms in ethene are replaced by atom groups. Methyl methacrylate polymerizes to form the transparent plastics whose trade names are Lucite and Plexiglas:

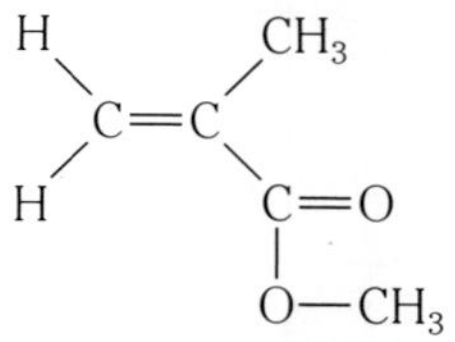

Methyl methacrylate 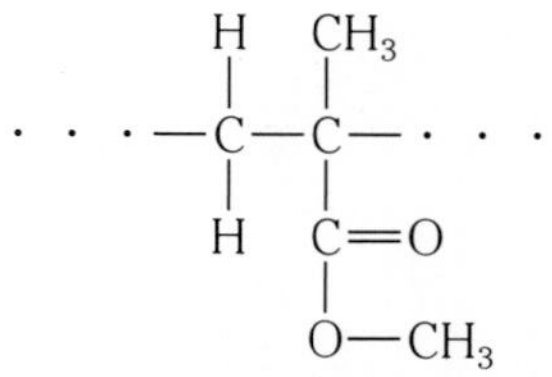   Lucite, Plexiglas

A feature of this material is that it is *thermoplastic*, which means that it softens and can be shaped when heated but becomes rigid again upon cooling.

Teflon

The monomer for Teflon is tetrafluorethene, which is ethene with all the H atoms replaced by fluorine atoms:

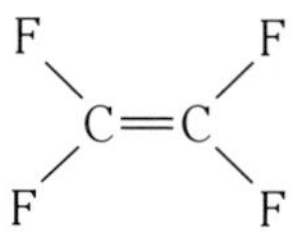

Tetrafluorethene 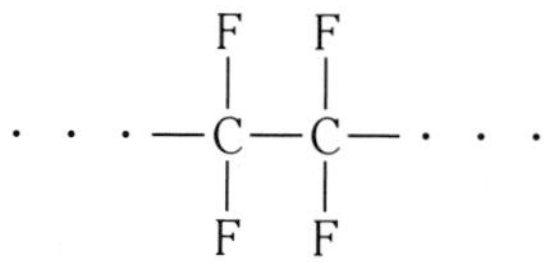   Teflon

The bond between fluorine and carbon is extremely strong, which makes Teflon tough and inert and able to withstand much higher temperatures than other polymers. These properties make Teflon useful industrially for seals and bearings as well as for nonstick coatings for cooking utensils.

Copolymers

Some polymers consist of two different monomers. An example of such a *copolymer* is Dynel, used among other things to make fibers for wigs, whose monomers are vinyl chloride and vinyl acetate. The kitchen wrap Saran is another copolymer.

Elastomers

Certain monomers that contain two double bonds in each molecule form flexible, elastic polymers called *elastomers*. Rubber is a natural elastomer. A widely used synthetic elastomer is neoprene, a polymer of chloroprene:

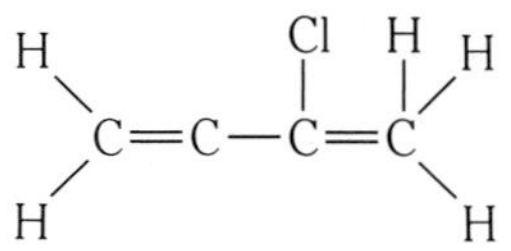

Chloroprene 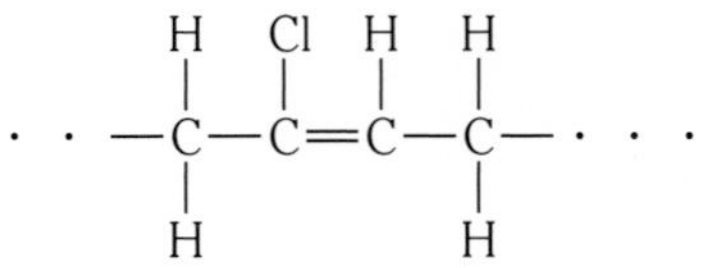   Neoprene

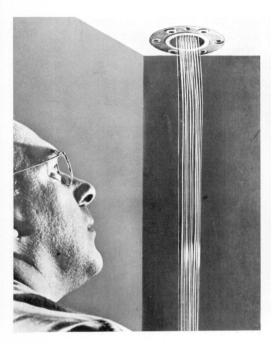

A die called a spinneret is used to form nylon filaments from liquid polyamide.

Mylar film being wound in rolls after manufacture. Mylar is a polyester, like Dacron.

Synthetic fibers

A valuable property of neoprene is that liquid hydrocarbons such as gasoline affect it less than they do natural rubber. Another elastomer, nitrile rubber, is still more resistant to hydrocarbons and is used to line gasoline hoses.

Of the various kinds of synthetic fibers that have been developed, nylon and Dacron are the most familiar. Both are composed of chains of structural elements, just like polymers, but they are produced by chemical reactions rather than by the polymerization of monomer molecules. In the case of nylon, the result is a chain whose elements can be written

$$-N-C-C-C-C-C-C-N-C-C-C-C-C-C-$$

The atom group

$$-N-C-$$

is known as an amide linkage, so nylon is called a polyamide. The N—H and C=O groups in nylon are polar, and their mutual attraction is what holds adjacent chains of molecules firmly together.

Dacron, whose structural elements are different from those of nylon, is a polyester because its elements are linked together by groups of the form

$$\begin{matrix} & O \\ & \| \\ —C& —O— \end{matrix}$$

(see Table 12-2). Polyester resins reinforced with glass fibers are often used in boat hulls, truck bodies, and other large structures.

CHEMISTRY OF LIFE

At one time the physical and biological worlds seemed two separate realms. They interacted with each other to be sure, but nevertheless were thought to be distinct in that some intangible "life force" was thought to be present in living things but absent everywhere else. Nowadays it is clear that there is no life force, and that there is a continuous chain of development from simple chemical compounds through more elaborate ones through viruses (which are neither "alive" nor "dead" by conventional definitions) through primitive one-celled organisms to the complex plants and animals of today. Given the right chemical and physical conditions and plenty of time, there is every reason to believe that life will inevitably come into being from inorganic matter, as it has on our planet. The four chief classes of organic compounds found in living matter are carbohydrates, lipids, proteins, and nucleic acids, which we shall examine in turn.

Carbohydrates

The first link of the food chain

Carbohydrates are made in green plants by photosynthesis

Carbohydrates are compounds of carbon, hydrogen, and oxygen whose molecules contain two atoms of hydrogen for every one of oxygen. They are manufactured in the leaves of green plants from carbon dioxide and water by the process of *photosynthesis*, with energy for the reaction being provided by sunlight. Sugars, starches, and cellulose are all carbohydrates.

Sugars

An important group of sugars consists of isomers that have the same $C_6H_{12}O_6$ composition. These sugars exist both as straight chains of C atoms and as ring structures. The ring forms are more stable and so occur most often, but a sugar molecule of this kind can shift back and forth between the two. Here are the straight-chain and ring forms of glucose, which is the sugar circulated by the blood to provide the body with energy:

Glucose
(straight-chain form)

Glucose
(ring form)

The isomers of glucose, among them fructose (the sweetest-tasting of all), galactose, and mannose, have somewhat different structures and properties.

Simple sugars like those above are called *monosaccharides*. Two monosaccharide rings can link together to form a *disaccharide*. Thus sucrose (ordinary table sugar) consists of one ring of glucose and one of fructose; lactose (milk sugar) consists of one ring of glucose and one of galactose; and maltose (malt sugar) consists of two rings of glucose. The molecular formulas of all three of these disaccharides is $C_{12}H_{22}O_{11}$, but of course their structures are different.

Cellulose and starch are plant carbohydrates

Polysaccharides are complex sugars that consist of chains of more than two simple sugars. They are naturally occurring polymers. In living things the polysaccharides serve both as structural components and as a medium of energy storage. In plants *cellulose*, which consists of a chain of about 1500 glucose rings, is common as the chief constituent of cell walls. Wood is mostly cellulose. Cellulose, in fact, is the most abundant organic compound on earth.

Starch, whose 300 to 1000 glucose units are joined together in a slightly different way from that characteristic of cellulose, is a polysaccharide that plants use to store energy for later use. Starch occurs in grains that have an insoluble outer layer, and so remains in the cell in which it is formed until, when needed as fuel, it is broken down into soluble glucose molecules.

Chitin and glycogen are animal carbohydrates

Two polysaccharides found in animals are *chitin*, which forms the outer shells of insects and crustaceans such as lobsters and crabs, and *glycogen*, which is present in the liver and muscles and is released when energy is required. Glycogen, the animal equivalent of starch, is soluble but its molecules are so large that they cannot pass readily through cell walls. When glucose is needed by an animal, its stored glycogen is split into the much smaller glucose molecules.

The oxidation of glucose provides plants and animals with energy; it is the reverse of photosynthesis

The term *respiration* is used to describe the process by which living things obtain the energy they need by the oxidation of nutrient molecules. Generally the nutrient molecule most directly involved is glucose, and its oxidation is an exothermic reaction that yields carbon dioxide and water as products:

$$C_6H_{12}O_6 + 6O_2 \longrightarrow 6CO_2 + 6H_2O + energy$$

Glucose   Oxygen   Carbon   Water
dioxide

This reaction does not take place all at once, as this equation would indicate, but in a complex series of steps that involve a number of other substances. However, the net effect is the oxidation of glucose. The oxidation of glucose is evidently the reverse of photosynthesis, and is the final process in the transformation of the energy in sunlight into the energy used by living things.

Carbohydrates are converted into simple sugars during digestion

Usually the carbohydrate intake of an animal is in the form of disaccharides and polysaccharides. In digestion, these are *hydrolyzed* with the help of water into monosaccharides. Hydrolysis is promoted by appropriate enzymes, which are the specialized protein molecules that act as catalysts in most biochemical processes. Although many animals are able to hydrolyze starch into glucose, very few can hydrolyze cellulose. Some plant-eating animals, for instance cattle, have microorganisms such as yeasts, protozoa, and bacteria in their digestive tracts whose own enzymes can achieve the hydrolysis of cellulose. The resulting glucose can then be utilized by the animal itself.

After digestion, the glucose passes into the bloodstream for circulation throughout the body. Glucose not immediately needed by the cells is converted into glycogen in the liver and elsewhere. If there is too much glucose present for storage as glycogen, it is synthesized into fats.

Photosynthesis

How the sun powers the living world

As mentioned above, plants combine carbon dioxide from the air with water absorbed through their roots to form carbohydrates in the process of photosynthesis. The overall reaction of photosynthesis is the opposite of the respiration reaction and is highly endothermic, with the necessary energy coming from sunlight.

$$6CO_2 + 6H_2O + energy \longrightarrow C_6H_{12}O_6 + 6O_2$$

Chlorophyll is the catalyst for photosynthesis, the energy for which comes from sunlight

The energy is not absorbed directly by the CO_2 and H_2O but instead by a substance called *chlorophyll*, which is part of the green coloring matter of leaves. Chlorophyll acts as a catalyst that serves to pass solar energy to the reacting molecules in a complicated way.

Perhaps 70 billion tons of carbon dioxide are cycled through plants each year (Fig. 12-6). Photosynthesis is only about 1 percent efficient on the average in utilizing the sunlight that reaches plants. A few plants have much higher efficiencies — as much as 11 percent for sugar cane, which is why the ethanol sometimes used to replace or supplement gasoline is made from this source of sugar.

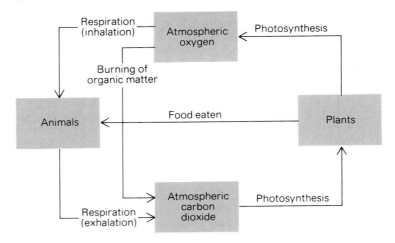

FIG. 12-6
The oxygen–carbon dioxide cycle in the atmosphere.

All atmospheric oxygen comes from photosynthesis

Photosynthesis not only maintains the oxygen content of the atmosphere but was apparently responsible for it in the first place. The early atmosphere of the earth, which is thought to have consisted of gases emitted during volcanic action, contained oxygen only in combination with other elements in compounds such as water (H_2O), carbon dioxide (CO_2), and sulfur dioxide (SO_2). Primitive organisms, which probably obtained their own energy by fermentation, eventually began to produce free oxygen by photosynthesis, and in time the oxygen content of the atmosphere increased to the point where more complex organisms could evolve. In addition to the oxygen now present in the atmosphere, photosynthesis is believed to account for much of the oxygen that is combined with other elements in the oxides, carbonates, and sulfates found in sediments and sedimentary rocks.

Lipids

Where the calories are

Plants and animals synthesize lipids from carbohydrates

Fats and such fatlike substances as oils, waxes, and sterols are collectively known as *lipids*. Like carbohydrates, lipids contain only the elements C, H, and O, which is natural since lipids are synthesized in plants and animals from carbohydrates. The proportions and arrangements of these elements are different in lipids, though.

Saturated fats are solid at room temperature, unsaturated fats are liquid

A fat molecule consists of a glycerol molecule with three *fatty acid* molecules attached to it. The hydrocarbon chains in solid fats have only single bonds between their carbon atoms, so that they are saturated. Liquid fats, such as vegetable oils, are unsaturated, with double bonds linking some carbon atoms. The double bonds introduce bends in such molecules, which prevents them from being closely packed together. As a result the interactions between nearby molecules are weaker than in the case of saturated fat molecules, so unsaturated fats are liquid at room temperature whereas saturated fats are solid. Adding hydrogen atoms to the double-bonded carbon atoms in a liquid fat saturates the chains and gives a solid fat. Margarine is produced by such a *hydrogenation* process, with vegetable oils such as soybean and cottonseed oils being heated with hydrogen in the presence of a catalyst.

Fats provide more energy per gram than carbohydrates

Fats are used for energy storage and other purposes, such as insulation against cold and mechanical protection, in most living things. The digestion of a fat molecule involves the breaking of the ester links between its glycerin and fatty acid parts. The enzyme *lipase* is the catalyst for this reaction. The oxidation of the glycerin and fatty acids then proceeds in a fairly complicated way, and is accompanied by the release of considerably more energy than in the case of an equivalent amount of carbohydrate: 7 kcal/g as against 4 kcal/g. Eating unsaturated rather than saturated fats seems to inhibit the production of cholesterol by the body, which is desirable since cholesterol deposits in the arteries are responsible for atherosclerosis ("hardening of the arteries"), a serious ailment.

Proteins

The building blocks of living matter

Proteins are the chief constituents of living matter and are composed of amino acids

Proteins, which are the principal constituent of living cells, are compounds of carbon, hydrogen, oxygen, nitrogen, and often sulfur and phosphorus; some proteins contain still other elements. The basic chemical units of which the protein molecules are composed are called *amino acids,* of which 20 are primary to life. Typical protein molecules consist of several hundred amino acids joined together in chains, and their structures are accordingly quite complex. The formula of one of the proteins found in milk is $C_{1864}H_{3012}O_{576}N_{468}S_{21}$, which gives an idea of the size of some protein molecules.

Plant and animal tissues contain proteins both in solution, as part of the fluid present in cells and in other fluids such as blood, and in insoluble form, as the skin, muscles, hair, nails, horns, and so forth of animals. Silk is an almost pure protein. The human body contains about 100,000 different proteins, all of which it must make from the amino acids it obtains from the digestion of the food proteins it takes in. One of the great successes of modern biochemistry is the discovery of how living cells build the complex arrangements of amino acids that are found in the proteins they are composed of.

Protein molecules consist of polypeptide chains

A protein molecule may contain hundreds of amino acid units joined together in one or more *polypeptide* chains, so-called because the links between the amino acids consist of *peptide bonds* that are like the amide bonds in nylon. These chains of amino acids are usually coiled or folded in intricate patterns. An important aspect of these patterns is the cross-linking that occurs between different chains and between different parts of the same chain.

FIG. 12-7

The alpha helix form of a protein molecule. Each amino acid unit in the helix is linked by hydrogen bonds (a type of van der Waals bond) to other units above and below it.

Many proteins have a helical form

Other proteins resemble pleated ribbons

The sequence of amino acids in a protein molecule together with the form of the molecule gives it a unique character that is reflected in its biological activity

Many proteins occur in the form of an *alpha helix* whose successive turns are held in position mainly by hydrogen bonds, which are a type of van der Waals bond. An alpha helix may be visualized as a ribbon (representing the polypeptide chain) wrapped in spiral fashion around an imaginary cylinder (Fig. 12-7). Helical protein molecules are usually folded and twisted into compact globules with further bonds to stabilize the assembly.

Heating a protein beyond a certain point breaks the weak hydrogen bonds, although the amino acid units of the helix may still remain together because of the greater strength of the covalent bonds between them. The polypeptide chain then assumes a different structure; the protein has been *denatured,* which is an irreversible process. The coagulation of the white of a boiled egg is an example of denaturation. Proteins can be denatured in a variety of ways other than heating, for instance by exposure to acids and bases.

The polypeptide chains of fibrous proteins such as those found in silk, hair, horn, and cartilage have the form of a pleated ribbon (Fig. 12-8) rather than that of a helix. The pleating occurs because of the angles between the various bonds in each chain. Two or more adjacent chains can bond together side by side with the help of hydrogen bonds.

The sequence of the amino acids in a protein is just as important as which ones they are. There is an astronomical number of possible arrangements of the amino acid units in even a small protein molecule such as insulin, which has 51 units, but only a single arrangement leads to the biological behavior associated with insulin. A close parallel is with the formation of a word from the 26 letters of

FIG. 12-8

The pleated sheet form of a protein molecule. Two or more chains of amino acid units are linked side-to-side along the sheet by hydrogen bonds.

the alphabet: *run* and *urn* contain the same letters but mean different things because the order of the letters is different. The alphabet of the proteins has only 20 letters, corresponding to the various amino acids, but the words may contain hundreds of letters whose relative positions in three dimensions are significant. The extraordinary number of different proteins, each serving a specific biological need in an organism of a specific species, is not surprising in view of this picture of protein structure.

The carbohydrates and lipids do not share the specificity of the proteins. Glucose, for instance, is a carbohydrate found in all plants and animals, but there is no protein similarly widespread. Even individuals of the same species may have proteins that are not quite identical, so that tissues cannot be transplanted because of danger of "rejection" of the graft. The matching of blood types before a transfusion is to ensure that the proteins in the blood of the donor are the same as those in the blood of the recipient.

Amino acids and the diet

The human body can synthesize only some of the amino acids it requires. The others must be present in the diet or the body will not be able to manufacture the various proteins essential to life. A proper diet must therefore include not just an adequate total amount of proteins but also the right ones.

Most proteins of animal origin, such as those in meat, fish, eggs, and milk, contain all the needed amino acids, but plant proteins do not. The important amino acid lysine is missing in corn, wheat, and rice; isoleucine and valine are missing in wheat; threonine is missing in rice; and so on. Although it is certainly possible to live without eating meat or other animal products, a vegetarian diet must not only be sufficiently varied to include all the required amino acids but all of these acids must be provided every day since they are not stored in the body and are needed together for protein manufacture.

Nucleic Acids

The genetic code

Nucleic acid molecules consist of chains of nucleotides

The nucleic acids are very minor constituents of living matter from the point of view of quantity, but, because they control the processes of heredity by which cells and organisms reproduce their proteins and themselves, they are extremely important. If anything may be said to be the key to the distinction between living and nonliving matter, it is the nucleic acids. Nucleic acid molecules consist of long chains of units called *nucleotides*. As in the case of the amino acids in a polypeptide chain, both the kinds of nucleotide present and their arrangement govern the biological behavior of a nucleic acid.

RNA and DNA

Each nucleotide has three parts, a *phosphate group* (PO_4), a *pentose sugar*, and a *nitrogen base*. A pentose sugar is one that contains five carbon atoms. In *ribonucleic acid* (RNA) the sugar is *ribose*, $C_5H_{10}O_5$, and in *deoxyribonucleic acid* (DNA) the sugar is *deoxyribose*, $C_5H_{10}O_4$, which has one O atom less than ribose. The five nitrogen bases usually found in nucleic acid are adenine, guanine, and

Model of a DNA molecule under construction.

DNA has the form of a double helix linked by nitrogen bases; the sequence of these bases is the genetic code

DNA governs protein synthesis in cells and makes possible reproduction and evolution

cytosine, which occur in both RNA and DNA, and thymine and uracil, which occur respectively in DNA and RNA only. Nitrogen bases have characteristic ring structures of nitrogen and carbon atoms.

The structure of a DNA molecule is shown in Fig. 12-9. Pairs of nitrogen bases form the links between a double chain of alternate phosphate and deoxyribose groups. Adenine and thymine are always coupled together, as are cytosine and guanine. The chains are not flat but spiral around each other in a double helix, as in Fig. 12-9*b*. Figure 12-9*c* shows the four "letters" of the genetic code. There may be hundreds of millions of such letters in a DNA molecule, and their precise sequence governs the properties of the cell in which the molecule is located. DNA molecules thus represent the biological blueprints which are translated into the processes of life.

The complexity of living things is mirrored in the complexity of DNA molecules, which are the largest known to science. A DNA molecule is normally folded or coiled into a microscopic package; if it could be stretched out in a straight line, it would be up to a meter or so long.

DNA controls the development and functioning of a cell by determining the character of the proteins it manufactures. This is only one aspect of its role in the life process. Another follows from the ability of DNA molecules to reproduce themselves, so that when a cell divides, all the new cells have the same characteristics (that is, the same *heredity*) as the original cell (Fig. 12-10). Finally, changes in the sequence of bases in a DNA molecule can occur under certain circumstances, for example during exposure to x-rays. These changes will be reflected in

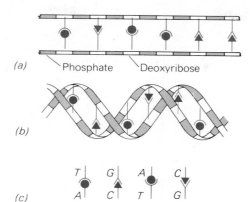

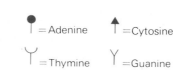

(a)

(b)

(c)

FIG. 12-9

The structure of DNA. (*a*) The nitrogen bases link a double chain of alternate phosphate and deoxyribose groups. Adenine and thymine are always paired and cytosine and guanine are always paired. (*b*) The chains are not flat but form a double helix. (*c*) The four "letters" of the genetic code.

● = Adenine   ↑ = Cytosine

Υ = Thymine   Y = Guanine

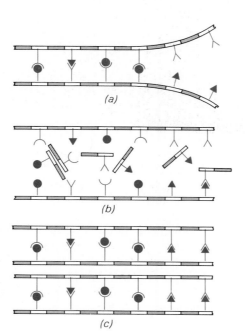

(a)

(b)

(c)

FIG. 12-10

Simplified model of DNA replication. (*a*) When a cell reproduces, each double DNA chain it contains breaks into two single ones, much like a zipper opening. (*b*) The single chains then pick up from the cell material the nucleotides needed to complete their structures. (*c*) The result is two identical DNA chains.

alterations in the properties of the cell containing the molecule, and such a *mutation* may result in the descendants of the original organism being different in some way from their ancestor. Thus three fundamental attributes of life can be traced to DNA: the structure of every organism; its ability to reproduce; and its ability to evolve into different forms in subsequent generations.

The other type of nucleic acid, RNA, differs from DNA in a number of respects. RNA molecules are much smaller than DNA molecules, for example, and usually consist of only single strands of nucleotides. One type of RNA carries instructions for the synthesis of specific proteins from the DNA in a cell's nucleus to the place where the actual synthesis occurs. The instructions are in the form of a code in which each successive group of three nucleotides determines the particular amino acid to be added next to the protein polypeptide chain being formed. For example, the group GCA (guanine-cytosine-adenine) corresponds to the amino acid alanine, and GGA corresponds to glycine. More than one *codon* (three-nucleotide group) corresponds to each amino acid; thus GCA, GCC, GCG, and GCU all refer to alanine.

Molecular biology is still a young and active discipline. The double-helix form of DNA was only discovered in 1953 (by James D. Watson, from the United States and Francis H. C. Crick, from England), and the details of protein synthesis and the operation of the genetic code in general are today being explored at a rapid rate. For all that remains to be understood, it is nevertheless no longer appropriate to speak of the "mystery" of life.

Origin of Life

An inevitable result of natural processes

Whatever the earth's beginnings may have been, it is safe to assume that, at some time in the remote past, the surface was considerably warmer than it is at present. The atmosphere of the young earth almost certainly contained compounds of the elements hydrogen, oxygen, carbon, and nitrogen, of which the most likely were water, methane, ammonia, carbon dioxide, and hydrogen cyanide (HCN). Eventually the outer part of the earth cooled, and torrents of rain began to fall. The rain carried down with it some of the other atmospheric gases, so that the infant oceans had a certain proportion of these gases dissolved in them. Weathering and erosion began at this time also, and the oceans acquired their salt and mineral content early since these processes, along with volcanic activity on the ocean floor, must have been exceptionally rapid at first. Life had its origin in or around these oceans.

Chemical reactions occur most readily in liquids, and furthermore water is the best solvent. Hence the early oceans must have been fertile media for chemical processes of all sorts, with ample energy available in sunlight and lightning discharges. Of the great many compounds that must have been formed, five classes have particular biological significance: the sugars, glycerol, the fatty acids, the amino acids, and the nitrogen bases.

The primary biochemical compounds are likely to have been formed in natural processes that have been duplicated in the laboratory

It is naturally not proper to assume that, because a certain compound contains certain elements, merely bringing together these elements in the ocean will yield the compounds. However, the reaction sequences that are necessary to go from the primitive ingredients of the oceans to the specific compounds listed above seem straightforward and likely to have occurred — or, rather, there is no known reason why they should *not* have occurred. And this is one of the rare hypotheses about the early earth that can be directly verified in the laboratory: when an electric discharge simulating lightning is passed through a mixture of water, methane, and ammonia, it is observed that amino acids and other compounds of biological importance are created (Fig. 12-11). Even fatty acids and the basic structural parts of the chlorophyll molecule have been produced in this way. Later work has shown that atmospheres with other plausible compositions, notably with carbon dioxide predominating, can also yield amino acids.

Confirming the laboratory studies was the discovery of amino acids in meteorites, which are relics of the youth of the solar system. It seems quite likely that there was no shortage of the building blocks of life on the earth's surface long ago.

Given molecules of the five classes of significant organic compounds, further reactions of equal plausibility, though all of them have not yet been verified in the

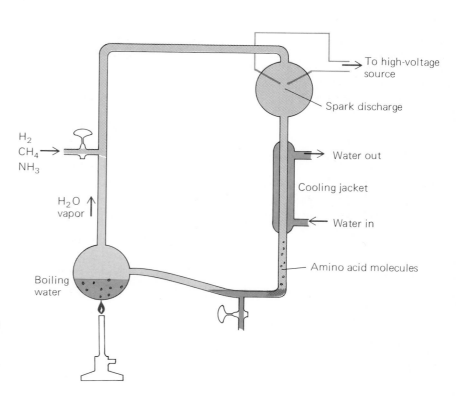

FIG. 12-11
In this experiment, first performed in 1952 by Stanley Miller under the direction of Harold Urey, amino acids were created by passing sparks that simulate lightning through a mixture of water vapor, hydrogen, methane, and ammonia.

laboratory, lead to more complex compounds such as the fats, proteins, and nucleic acids that are directly involved in living matter. And given these latter compounds, most notably the nucleic acids which govern protein synthesis and are able to replicate themselves, the emergence of primitive cells, the basic biological units, becomes inevitable.

The progression from an ocean with dissolved gases, salts, and minerals to living organisms certainly did not occur with the neatness and dispatch with which, say, a baker combines certain ingredients, inserts the mixture in an oven, and removes a cake an hour later. But although pure chance must have dictated which molecules came together and reacted to form a more complex one, just when the reaction occurred, and where it did, the ultimate outcome seems not to have been a matter of chance at all. It is estimated that 1 to $1\frac{1}{2}$ billion years elapsed between the formation of the earth and the formation of the first cells, and the sequence of events proposed by biologists to account for the latter seems reasonable in view of this vast span of time.

IMPORTANT TERMS

Organic chemistry concerns the chemistry of carbon compounds. The number and variety of organic compounds result from the ability of carbon atoms to form covalent bonds with each other as well as with both metallic and nonmetallic atoms. **Double bonds** and **triple bonds** are possible between carbon atoms in addition to single ones. The molecules of a **saturated** organic compound contain only single carbon-carbon bonds; those of an **unsaturated** compound contain one or more double or triple bonds. Unsaturated compounds react more readily than saturated ones.

Structural formulas that show the bonds between atoms in a molecule provide more information on organic compounds than molecular formulas. **Isomers** are compounds with the same molecular formulas but with different structural formulas, corresponding to different arrangements of the same atoms in each molecule.

A **functional group** is a group of atoms whose presence in an organic molecule determines its chemical behavior to a large extent. Thus the hydroxyl (OH) group characterizes the alcohols, the carboxyl (COOH) group characterizes the organic acids, and so on.

A **polymer** is a long chain of simple molecules **(monomers)** linked together. Plastics, synthetic fibers, and synthetic elastomers are polymers.

Carbohydrates are compounds of carbon, hydrogen, and oxygen manufactured in green plants from carbon dioxide and water by **photosynthesis** with sunlight providing the needed energy. Sugars, starches, and cellulose are carbohydrates. **Lipids** are fats and fatlike substances such as oils and waxes synthesized from carbohydrates by plants and animals. **Proteins,** the principal constituents of living matter, consist of long chains of **amino acid** molecules. The sequence of amino acids in a protein molecule together with the form of the molecule determines its biological role. The **nucleic acid** molecules DNA and RNA consist of long chains of **nucleotides,** atom groups whose precise sequence governs the structure and function of cells and organisms. DNA has the form of a double helix and carries the genetic code; one type of RNA has the form of a single helix and acts as a messenger in protein synthesis.

MULTIPLE CHOICE

1. The science of organic chemistry has as its subject
   a. compounds produced by plants and animals
   b. carbon compounds
   c. compounds with complex molecules
   d. the determination of structural formulas

2. Compared with inorganic compounds in general, most organic compounds

a. are more readily soluble in water
b. are more easily decomposed by heat
c. react more slowly
d. form ions more readily in solution

3. The number of covalent bonds each carbon atom has in organic compounds is usually
a. one
b. two
c. four
d. six

4. Carbon atoms do not
a. form covalent bonds by sharing electrons
b. form bonds with other carbon atoms
c. have stability at high temperatures
d. exist only in combination with other elements

5. In general, in the alkane series of hydrocarbons, a high molecular weight implies
a. a low boiling point
b. a high boiling point
c. a low freezing point
d. an artificial origin

6. Methane is not
a. a hydrocarbon
b. an alkane
c. present in natural gas
d. present in gasoline

7. Compounds that have the same molecular formulas but different structural formulas are called
a. hydrocarbons
b. isomers
c. polymers
d. derivatives

8. Unsaturated hydrocarbon molecules are characterized by
a. double or triple bonds between carbon atoms, so that additional atoms can be added readily
b. the ability to absorb water
c. the ability to dissolve in water
d. benzene rings in their structural formulas

9. Hydrocarbons in which only single covalent bonds occur are
a. highly reactive
b. saturated
c. unsaturated
d. isomers

10. Which of the following compounds can exist?
a. C_2H_3
b. C_2H_4
c. C_2H_5
d. C_2H_6

11. The benzene molecule is notable for having
a. a ring of six carbon atoms
b. a ring which can consist of any number of carbon atoms
c. a straight chain of six carbon atoms
d. a helix of carbon atoms

12. All alcohols
a. are safe to drink
b. can be made only by fermentation
c. contain just one OH group
d. contain one or more OH groups

13. The presence of a COOH group is characteristic of an
a. alkane
b. organic acid
c. aldehyde
d. ester

14. The conversion of sugar to ethanol and carbon dioxide with enzymes acting as catalysts is called
a. fermentation
b. polymerization
c. photosynthesis
d. digestion

15. Organic acids are
a. strong and highly corrosive
b. rather weak
c. not found in nature but must be artificially made
d. characterized by simple molecules

16. The process by which small hydrocarbon molecules join together to form heavier ones under the influence of heat and catalysts is called
a. cracking
b. esterification
c. polymerization
d. saturation

17. Living cells consist mainly of
a. carbohydrates
b. lipids
c. proteins
d. nucleic acids

18. Living things differ most from one another in their constituent
a. carbohydrates
b. lipids
c. amino acids
d. proteins

19. The number of amino acids important to life is
a. 2
b. 8
c. 20
d. 69

20. Proteins consist of combinations of
   a. amino acids
   b. nucleic acids
   c. esters of glycerin with organic acids
   d. DNA and RNA molecules
21. Energy is stored in animal cells in the form of
   a. starch
   b. cellulose
   c. chitin
   d. glycogen
22. The oxidation of glucose does not yield
   a. glycogen
   b. water
   c. carbon dioxide
   d. energy
23. Photosynthesis produces
   a. carbohydrates
   b. lipids
   c. proteins
   d. all of the above
24. Most biochemical processes in living matter are catalyzed by
   a. enzymes
   b. glycogen
   c. lipids
   d. DNA
25. Lipids are synthesized in plants and animals from
   a. proteins
   b. carbohydrates
   c. enzymes
   d. nucleic acids
26. Cellulose is not
   a. a carbohydrate
   b. the chief constituent of wood
   c. present in all plants
   d. easily digested by most animals
27. The structure of a DNA molecule resembles
   a. a single helix
   b. a double helix
   c. a pleated ribbon
   d. a straight chain
28. DNA controls the development and functioning of a cell by governing its manufacture of
   a. carbohydrates
   b. lipids
   c. amino acids
   d. proteins

QUESTIONS

1. Why are there more carbon compounds than compounds of any other element?

2. In what ways do organic compounds, as a class, differ from inorganic compounds?

3. What is the principal bonding mechanism in organic molecules?

4. Why are substances whose molecules contain triple carbon-carbon bonds relatively rare?

5. Distinguish between unsaturated and saturated hydrocarbons, giving examples of each.

6. Explain why structural formulas are more important in organic chemistry than in inorganic chemistry.

7. What is wrong with the conventional model of the benzene molecule as having alternate single and double bonds?

8. Why are all aromatic compounds unsaturated?

9. How many covalent bonds are present between the carbon atom and each oxygen atom in carbon dioxide, CO_2?

10. Is it possible for a compound with the formula C_4H_4 to exist? If not, why not?

11. Molecules exist with the formulas C_2H_2, C_2H_4, and C_2H_6. Do you think that C_2H_8 also exists? If not, why not?

12. In which of the following compounds are the carbon-carbon bonds single, in which are they double, and in which are they triple? C_2H_2, C_2H_4, C_4H_8, C_4H_{10}.

13. The aliphatic compound pentene has the molecular formula C_5H_{10}. Are all the bonds in the pentene molecule single ones?

14. The aliphatic compound heptane has the molecular formula C_7H_{16}. Are all the bonds in the heptane molecule single ones?

15. To what class of organic compounds does the compound belong whose structure is shown below?

16. What do you think is the name of the compound whose structural formula is shown below?

17. What do you think is the name of the compound whose structural formula is shown below?

18. Given an example of an ester, an organic acid, an alcohol, a sugar, and a methane derivative.

19. Compare the properties of a simple ester, for instance methyl acetate, with those of a salt, for instance sodium chloride.

20. In each of the following pairs, which substance would you expect to have (a) the higher melting point,(b) the lower density?

C_6H_{14} and $C_{11}H_{24}$
$C_6H_{13}Br$ and $C_{11}H_{23}Br$
$C_5H_{11}COOH$ and $C_{10}H_{21}COOH$

21. Which of the following (a) dissolve in water, (b) are acids, (c) are gaseous at ordinary temperatures, (d) react with Na to liberate hydrogen, (e) react with ethyl alcohol to give esters, (f) react with acetic acid to give esters?

C_2H_5COOH	C_3H_8
C_2H_4	C_2H_5OH
HCl	$C_3H_5(OH)_3$

22. Name one property by which you could distinguish

a. C_2H_4 from CH_4
b. CH_3COOH from CH_3OH
c. C_3H_7OH from $C_5H_{11}OH$
d. C_2H_5OH from H_2O
e. CH_4 from O_2

23. Trace the energy you use in lifting this book back through the various transformations it undergoes to its ultimate source.

24. How does a plant obtain its carbohydrates and fats? An animal?

25. What is believed to be the origin of atmospheric oxygen?

26. Can you think of any function other than energy storage which body fat might have?

27. What are the basic structural units of proteins? How does the human body obtain them?

28. How many different "letters" are found in the genetic code? What is the nature of the "letters"?

PROBLEMS

1. Each molecule of butene, C_4H_8, has a double bond between two of its carbon atoms. Give the structural formula(s) for butene and its isomers, if any.

2. Each molecule of propene, C_3H_6, has a double bond between two of its carbon atoms. Give the structural formula(s) for propene and its isomers, if any.

3. Give structural formulas for the two isomeric propyl alcohols which share the molecular formula C_3H_7OH.

4. Xylene molecules consist of benzene molecules in which two of the hydrogen atoms have been replaced by CH_3 groups. Give structural formulas for the three isomers of xylene.

5. Give structural formulas for the three isomers of pentane, C_5H_{12}.

6. The carbon atoms in normal hexane, C_6H_{14} for a straight chain. All the bonds are single. In cyclohexane the six carbon atoms are arranged in a ring. Give the structural formula of cyclohexane. Are all the bonds single?

7. Bromopropane is propane with one H atom replaced by a Br (bromine) atom. How many isomers does bromopropane have? What are their structural formulas?

8. Use structural formulas to show the reaction between methyl alcohol and acetic acid to produce methyl acetate.

ANSWERS TO MULTIPLE CHOICE

1. *b*	**8.** *a*	**15.** *b*	**22.** *a*
2. *b*	**9.** *b*	**16.** *c*	**23.** *a*
3. *c*	**10.** *b,d*	**17.** *c*	**24.** *a*
4. *d*	**11.** *a*	**18.** *d*	**25.** *b*
5. *b*	**12.** *d*	**19.** *c*	**26.** *d*
6. *d*	**13.** *b*	**20.** *a*	**27.** *b*
7. *b*	**14.** *a*	**21.** *d*	**28.** *d*

13

ATMOSPHERE AND HYDROSPHERE

The earth's atmosphere is an invisible envelope of gas whose presence we hardly notice except when a wind is blowing or when rain or snow is falling. If we think for a moment, though, we recognize that the atmosphere must in some way be responsible for the blue of the sky, the colors of sunrise, sunset, and rainbows, the dramatic spectacle of the aurora, and the reflection of radio waves that permits worldwide radio communication.

Less obvious but more important is the role of the atmosphere in the biological world. Its oxygen, nitrogen, and carbon dioxide are essential for life. It screens out deadly ultraviolet and x-rays from the sun. It transports energy and water over the face of the earth. And by weathering away rocks the atmosphere contributes to the formation of the soil in which plants grow.

All the water of the earth's surface is included in the *hydrosphere*. Water bodies of various kinds, including oceans, lakes, and shallow seas, cover about three-fourths of the total area of our planet. By far the greater part of the hydrosphere, of course, is concentrated in the ocean basins, and the oceans are accordingly a major factor in shaping the environment of life on this planet.

THE ATMOSPHERE

Composition

What we breathe

Atmospheric nitrogen, oxygen, and carbon dioxide are important to living things

The principal gases of the atmosphere and their average abundances are given in Table 13-1. Water vapor is also present but to a variable extent, ranging from nearly none to about 4 percent. In addition, the lower atmosphere contains a great many small particles of different kinds, such as soot, bits of rock and soil, salt grains from the evaporation of seawater droplets, and spores, pollen, and bacteria.

Nitrogen and oxygen are important biologically, and each has a characteristic cycle of interaction with living things. Nitrogen is a key ingredient of the amino acids of which all proteins consist, and certain bacteria are able to convert atmospheric nitrogen into nitrogen compounds which plants can utilize in manufacturing amino acids. The nitrogen cycle is discussed in Chap. 14. Plants also combine carbon dioxide from the air with water absorbed through their roots to form carbohydrates in the process of photosynthesis, with oxygen as a by-product. Animals obtain the carbohydrates and amino acids they need by eating plants (or other animals that eat plants). Plants and animals both derive energy by using atmospheric oxygen to convert carbon in their foods to carbon dioxide. Thus the oxygen–carbon dioxide cycle is an essential aspect of all plant and animal life (Fig. 12-11).

The other major constituent of the atmosphere is argon, which, being chemically inert, escaped detection until the end of the nineteenth century. Argon is more abundant than the other inert gases because the isotope ^{40}K of the common element potassium beta-decays into the argon isotope ^{40}Ar.

TABLE 13-1
The Composition of Dry Air Near Ground Level.

Gas	Percentage by volume
Nitrogen	78.08
Oxygen	20.95
Argon	0.93
Carbon dioxide	0.03
Neon	0.0018
Helium	0.00052
Methane	0.00015
Krypton	0.00011
Hydrogen, carbon monoxide, xenon, ozone, radon	<0.0001

Smog in New York City. Ordinarily air temperature falls steadily with increasing altitude in the lower atmosphere. Sometimes, however, a situation arises in which a layer of air aloft is warmer than the air below it; this constitutes a temperature inversion. Gases emitted by chimneys and vehicle exhausts cannot rise past a temperature inversion because when they reach it their density is greater than the density of the warm air layer. Hence the inversion acts to trap such gases, whose increased concentration is evident as smog.

Regions of the Atmosphere

Four layers

Those of us who have been among mountains know that the higher up we go, the thinner and colder the air becomes. In the lower atmosphere, air temperature falls an average of 6.5°C per km of altitude. At an elevation of only 5 km (about 16,400 ft) the pressure is down to half what it is at sea level (Fig. 13-1) and the temperature is about −20°C. At about 11 km (36,000 ft) the pressure is only one-fourth its sea-level value, which means that 75 percent of the atmosphere lies below, and the temperature has dropped to −55°C—which is cold but not so cold as it sometimes is at ground level during the winter in Siberia and northern Canada—for 14 km more.

Troposphere and stratosphere

A passenger in an airplane would notice a marked change in the atmosphere on passing an elevation of 11 km: above this point there are practically no clouds and no storms, and dust is almost completely absent. Since the character of the atmosphere changes rather abruptly at the 11-km level, this is taken as the boundary between two layers of the atmosphere: the clean, cold upper part, or *stratosphere*, and the denser lower part, or *troposphere*. Such features of the weather as clouds and storms, fog and haze, are confined to the troposphere. The boundary between stratosphere and troposphere is higher near the equator, where it is about 16 km above sea level, and lower near the poles, where it is about 6 km; the 11-km figure is an average. Figure 13-2 shows how the atmosphere is divided into regions.

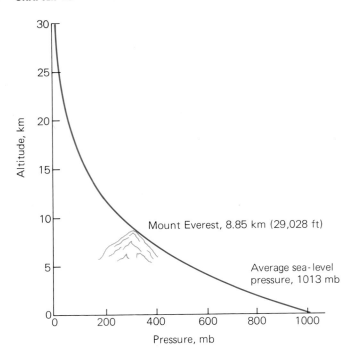

FIG. 13-1
The variation of pressure with altitude in the atmosphere.

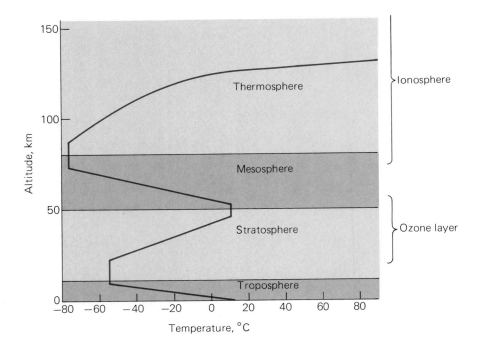

FIG. 13-2
The variation of temperature with altitude in the atmosphere.

Ozone is O_3

The most striking aspect of the stratosphere is the presence of *ozone,* a form of oxygen whose molecules contain three oxygen atoms. The symbol for ozone is accordingly O_3. Ozone is produced in the stratosphere when solar radiation breaks up oxygen molecules, O_2, into separate O atoms. The O atoms then join oxygen molecules to give ozone molecules: $O + O_2 \rightarrow O_3$. As fast as O_3 molecules are formed, others combine with O atoms to give O_2 molecules: $O + O_3 \rightarrow 2O_2$. Hence the situation is one of equilibrium, with ozone being formed and destroyed at the same rates.

Ozone in the stratosphere absorbs harmful solar ultraviolet radiation

Ozone is an excellent absorber of ultraviolet radiation. It is so excellent, in fact, that the relatively small amount of ozone in the stratosphere is able to filter out almost completely the dangerous short-wavelength ultraviolet radiation reaching the earth from the sun. So harmful is this radiation to living things that it is believed life did not leave the sea to become established on land, which took place perhaps 400 million years ago, until the ozone layer had come into being. This layer lies between 15 and 55 km. Its maximum density occurs at 22 km, where less than one molecule in 4 million is O_3 — hardly an impressive concentration for so efficient an absorber. The high temperatures of the upper stratosphere are due to the heating effect of the solar ultraviolet energy absorbed there.

Because the ozone in the stratosphere is so valuable, pollutants that act to decrease the already small ozone concentration are highly undesirable. An example is the Freon gas (CCl_2F_2) once widely used as a spray-can propellant, whose halogen content acts as a catalyst in breaking up O_3 molecules. Very little Freon is needed to produce a large drop in O_3 concentration, which would increase the skin cancer rate in people and reduce crop yields, among other effects. Fortunately the problem was recognized before it was too late, and other gases have replaced Freon in spray cans to a large extent.

Mesosphere

The ozone of the stratosphere causes a rise in temperature to a maximum of $10°C$ or so in the vicinity of 50 km. At this altitude the atmosphere is $\frac{1}{1000}$ of its density at sea level. The temperature then falls once more to another minimum of about $-75°C$ at 80 km. The portion of the atmosphere between 50 and 80 km is known as the *mesosphere.*

Thermosphere

Above 80 km the properties of the atmosphere change radically, for now ions become abundant. The *thermosphere* extends upward to a height of about 600 km, with the temperature increasing to about $2000°C$ where it levels off. (We must keep in mind that the density of the thermosphere is extremely low, so that despite the high temperatures a slowly moving object there would not get hot if shielded from direct sunlight.)

In the year 1901 Marconi was able to send radio signals across the Atlantic Ocean for the first time. Radio waves, like light waves, tend to travel in straight lines, and the curvature of the earth therefore apparently presents an insuperable obstacle to long-distance radio communication. For this reason Marconi's achievement came as a great surprise. In a short time, however, Oliver Heaviside in England and Arthur Kennelly in the United States suggested that the effect could be caused by a reflecting layer high up in the atmosphere. Such a layer, together with the sea, could channel radio waves from one side of the Atlantic to the other

Short-wavelength radio waves from this antenna are reflected by the ionosphere and so can be used for communications over distances of thousands of miles.

Ionosphere layers reflect radio waves and thus make possible long-distance communication

(Fig. 6-20). Electromagnetic theory was able to predict the mechanism of the reflection. If some of the atoms and molecules in the upper atmosphere are ionized by the action of high-energy solar radiation, the resulting layer of charged particles will behave precisely like a mirror to radio waves (though not to the shorter-wavelength light waves).

Direct experimental confirmation of the presence of ionized layers (there are four) high up in the atmosphere followed, and today the region above the mesosphere that contains ions is called the *ionosphere*. It extends from 70 km to several hundred km above the earth's surface. The reason that ions are not distributed throughout the entire atmosphere is straightforward. At very great altitudes there is not enough gas present for the solar ultraviolet and x-rays to interact with, and at low altitudes all the solar radiation energetic enough to cause ionization has already been absorbed.

Atmospheric Moisture

Another vital cycle

Humidity refers to the moisture content of air

The moisture content, or *humidity*, of air refers to the amount of water vapor that it contains. Most of the atmosphere's water vapor comes from evaporation of sea water, but a little comes from evaporation of water in lakes, rivers, moist soil, and vegetation. Since water vapor is continually being added to air by evaporation and periodically removed by condensation as clouds, fog, rain, and snow, the humidity of the atmosphere is extremely variable from day to day and from one region to another (Fig. 13-3). If it were not for the ability of water to evaporate, to be carried by winds, and later to fall to the ground, all the earth's water would be in its oceans and the continents would be lifeless deserts.

Saturated air

Air is said to be *saturated* with water vapor when it holds the maximum amount that will evaporate at a given temperature. Air is unsaturated when its content of water vapor is less than this limiting value, since it is capable of holding more water vapor. We can think of air as a sort of sponge, filled more or less completely with water vapor. Actually, of course, the air has nothing to do with evaporation; if no air existed, vapor would still escape from bodies of water. But, since air is the agent that transports water vapor from one region to another and since air is the medium in which water vapor condenses as clouds, fog, rain, or snow, it is convenient to think of the air as "taking up" and "holding" different amounts of vapor.

FIG. 13-3
The world's water content and its daily cycle. Upward arrows indicate evaporation, downward arrows indicate precipitation. If all the water vapor in the atmosphere were condensed, it would form a layer only about 2.5 cm thick.

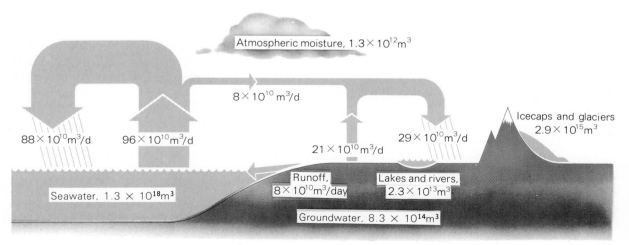

Atmospheric moisture, $1.3 \times 10^{12} m^3$

$8 \times 10^{10} m^3/d$

Icecaps and glaciers $2.9 \times 10^{15} m^3$

$88 \times 10^{10} m^3/d$ $96 \times 10^{10} m^3/d$

$29 \times 10^{10} m^3/d$

$21 \times 10^{10} m^3/d$

Runoff, $8 \times 10^{10} m^3/day$

Lakes and rivers, $2.3 \times 10^{13} m^3$

Seawater, $1.3 \times 10^{18} m^3$

Groundwater, $8.3 \times 10^{14} m^3$

Relative humidity refers to the extent to which air is saturated with water vapor

We usually describe air as humid if it is saturated or nearly saturated, as dry if it is highly unsaturated. Humid weather is oppressive because little moisture can evaporate from the skin into saturated air, and so perspiration does not produce its usual cooling effect. Very dry air is harmful to the skin because its moisture evaporates too rapidly. Meteorologists express the moisture content of air in terms of *relative humidity,* a number indicating the degree to which air is saturated with water vapor. Usually relative humidity is expressed as a percentage: a humidity of 100 percent means that the air is completely saturated with water, 50 percent means that the air contains half of the maximum it could hold, and 0 percent means perfectly dry air.

Relative humidity and temperature

The amount of moisture that air can hold increases with temperature. If air saturated at 20°C is heated to 40°C, it can take up more water vapor and so is no longer saturated (in other words, its relative humidity decreases, although the amount of water vapor does not change). If, on the other hand, air saturated at 20°C is cooled to 0°C, some of its water vapor must condense out as liquid water, since at the lower temperature the air can hold only about one-fourth as much vapor as it contained originally. Further, if air at 40°C containing water vapor corresponding to 100 percent relative humidity at 20°C is cooled to 0°C, it grows steadily more saturated until a temperature of 20°C is reached, after which it remains saturated down to 0°C and some of its vapor condenses out. Thus any sample of ordinary air on heating grows less saturated and on cooling grows more saturated. If the cooling is continued past the saturation point, some liquid water (or ice) must condense out.

Clouds

Some are water droplets, others are ice crystals

Condensed atmospheric moisture is responsible for dew, fog, and clouds

Water condenses when moist air is cooled sufficiently. Dew forms because the ground cools by radiation at night, so that air at the surface has its temperature lowered beyond the saturation point. Fogs result from the cooling of larger masses of air by contact with cold land or water. Clouds occur when air is cooled by expansion when it rises.

Rising air expands and cools, causing its water vapor to condense into clouds

Compressing a gas causes it to heat up, as anyone who has used a tire pump knows. The opposite effect is the cooling of a gas when it expands. When a warm, moist air mass moves upward, it expands because the pressure decreases, and it becomes cooler. A cooling rate of about 1°C for each 100 m of rise is normal. If the temperature drop is enough, the air becomes saturated and some of its water vapor condenses into clouds. The condensation usually occurs around salt and dust particles in the air and results in tiny water droplets or ice crystals, depending on the temperature, that are small enough to remain suspended aloft indefinitely. High clouds consist of ice crystals, low clouds of water droplets.

Fog near Boulder, Colorado.

The three basic types of clouds are *cirrus* (wispy or featherlike), *stratus* (layered), and *cumulus* (puffy or heaped up), shown here from left to right. Cirrus clouds occur at high altitudes, above 7 km, and stratus clouds at low altitudes, below 2 km. Cumulus clouds may extend vertically from below 2 km to above 7 km. A cloud that combines the characteristics of two of these types is designated accordingly, for instance, cirrostratus. A cloud that occurs at a higher altitude than is normal for its type is given the prefix *alto*, as in altostratus. Clouds from which precipitation occurs have the word *nimbus* (Latin for rain) in their names, for instance, nimbostratus.

These are the three processes in the atmosphere that cause clouds to form:

Origins of clouds

1. A warm air mass moving horizontally meets a land barrier such as a mountain and rises (Fig. 13-4). Coastal mountains that lie in the paths of moisture-laden ocean winds may have permanent cloud caps over them.

Air expands and cools as it rises.

Clouds form when moist air cools enough for its moisture to condense.

FIG. 13-4
Why mountains often have cloud caps over them.

2. An air mass is heated by contact with a part of the earth's surface warmer than its surroundings. The air mass then expands and its buoyancy causes it to rise. This process, called convection, is discussed later (see Fig. 13-8).
3. A warm air mass meets a cooler air mass and, being less dense, is forced upward over it. This process is also discussed later (see Fig. 13-16).

Rain and snow fall when clouds are cooled rapidly

Rain falls when a cloud (or part of one) is cooled suddenly, so that condensation is exceptionally rapid. Some of the water droplets in the cloud become larger than others and, because air resistance affects them less, they move within the cloud faster than the smaller droplets. The smaller droplets tend to stick to the larger ones when they come in contact, and the result is larger and larger droplets. Finally these droplets become drops, typically a million times larger than normal cloud droplets, and are too heavy for the updrafts in the cloud to keep aloft. The result is a fall of rain. If the cloud is cold enough, it consists of ice crystals rather than water droplets, and these crystals can grow into snowflakes. Sleet consists of frozen raindrops. Hail occurs when cloud particles alternately freeze and thaw as they grow into rocklike lumps of ice that may be larger than golfballs. Generally hailstones form in thunderclouds, which are tall and have both large water contents and strong updrafts inside them.

Cloud seeding

Clouds are sometimes *seeded* with silver iodide to induce precipitation. The crystal structure of silver iodide resembles that of ice, hence water molecules and droplets in a cloud can readily attach themselves to a silver iodide crystal. Such crystals are thus efficient condensation nuclei and so promote precipitation from a cloud.

WEATHER

The science of meteorology is concerned with what we can think of as a vast air-conditioning system. Our spinning planet is heated strongly at the equator and weakly at the poles, and its moisture is concentrated in the great ocean basins. It is the task of the atmosphere, from our point of view, to redistribute this heat and moisture so that large areas of the land surface will be habitable. Air conditioning by the atmosphere is far from perfect. It fails miserably in deserts, on mountaintops, in the polar regions. On sultry midsummer nights or on bitter January mornings we may question its efficiency even in our favored part of the world. But the atmosphere does succeed in making a surprisingly large part of the globe fit for people to live in.

Weather and climate

The two chief tasks of any air-conditioning system are the regulation of air temperature and humidity. In addition to these, we expect the atmosphere to perform a third function: it must provide us with water in the form of rain or snow. The weather and climate of a given locality describe how effectively these functions are performed. *Weather* refers to the temperature, humidity, pressure, cloudiness, and rainfall at a certain time. *Climate* is a summary of weather conditions over a period of years. Important in a description of climate is the variability of temperature and rainfall with the seasons. For instance, an outstanding feature of the climate of North Dakota is its extreme warmth in summer and extreme cold in winter, whereas the climate of southern California is characterized by comfortable year-round temperatures and by a concentration of rainfall in the winter months. Local barometric pressures and the intensity and direction of wind may be important in descriptions of weather and climate.

Atmospheric Energy

A giant greenhouse in the sky

Insolation is incoming solar radiation

The energy that warms the air, evaporates the water, and drives the winds comes to us from the sun. Solar energy arriving at the upper atmosphere is called *insolation* (for *in*coming *sol*ar radi*ation*) and amounts to 1.4 kW on each square meter of area perpendicular to the sun's rays. In order to understand how energy is provided to the atmosphere by insolation, we must first examine the *greenhouse effect*.

It is an important fact that every object gives off energy in the form of electromagnetic waves, with the intensity and predominant wavelength depending upon the temperature of the object. The hotter the object, the more energy it emits and the shorter the average wavelength. Thus the sun, whose surface temperature is about 5700°C, is extremely bright and its radiation is mainly visible light. The earth, whose surface temperature averages about 15°C, is a feebler source of energy and its radiation is concentrated in the long-wavelength infrared part of the spectrum to which the eye is not sensitive. The interior of a greenhouse is warmer than the outside because sunlight can enter through its windows but the infrared radiation that the warm interior gives off cannot penetrate glass, so the incoming energy is trapped.

The greenhouse effect refers to the heating of the atmosphere by solar energy reradiated from the earth

About 30 percent of the insolation is directly reflected back into space, mainly by clouds (Fig. 13-5). The atmosphere absorbs perhaps 19 percent of the insolation, with ozone, water vapor, and water droplets in clouds taking up most of this amount. Slightly over half of the total insolation therefore reaches the earth's surface, where it is absorbed and converted into heat. A little of this heat is given to

FIG. 13-5

The greenhouse effect. Much of the short-wavelength visible light from the sun that reaches the earth's surface is reradiated as long-wavelength infrared light that is readily absorbed by CO_2 and H_2O in the atmosphere. Some energy also reaches the atmosphere from the earth directly and by means of water evaporated from the sea. Thus the atmosphere is heated mainly from below by the earth rather than from above by the sun. The total energy the earth and its atmosphere radiate into space on the average equals the total energy they receive from the sun.

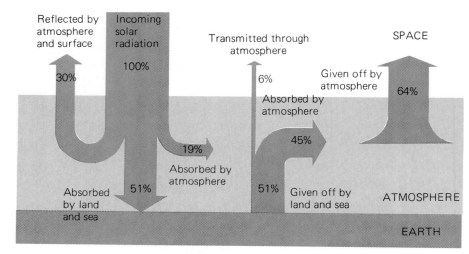

the atmosphere directly by contact with the warm surface, somewhat more by evaporating water from the sea. The warm earth also reradiates energy back into the atmosphere, but the energy now is in the form of long-wavelength infrared radiation. These long waves are readily absorbed by atmospheric carbon dioxide and water vapor whose molecules then transfer energy to the rest of the constituents of the atmosphere. Thus a major source of atmospheric energy is radiation from the earth, not direct sunlight. The atmosphere is, in effect, a giant greenhouse.

The atmosphere prevents temperature extremes

If the earth had no atmosphere, its heated surface would quickly radiate back into space all the energy that reaches it from the sun. Like the moon, the earth would grow intensely hot during the day, unbearably cold during the night. The atmosphere prevents these extremes of temperature. The continual movement of air around the world keeps daytime temperatures at any one place from climbing very high, and the ability of air to absorb the earth's radiation prevents the rapid escape of heat by night.

Why temperatures vary around the earth

How hot the atmosphere becomes over any particular region depends on a number of factors. Air near the equator is on the average much warmer than air near the poles, because the sun's vertical rays are more effective in heating the surface than the slanting rays of polar regions (Fig. 13-6). Air over a mountain may become warm at midday but cools quickly because it is thinner and contains less carbon dioxide and water vapor than air lower down. A region covered with clouds usually has lower air temperatures than a nearby region in sunlight. Because the temperature of water is changed more slowly than that of rocks and soil when it absorbs or gives off radiation, the atmosphere near large bodies of water is usually cooler by day and warmer by night than the atmosphere over regions far from water. Desert regions commonly show abrupt changes in air temperature between

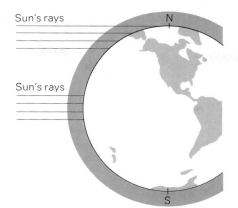

FIG. 13-6
Air near the equator is on the average much warmer than air near the poles because the sun's vertical rays at the equator are more effective in heating the surface than the slanting rays of polar regions.

day and night because so little water vapor is present to absorb infrared radiation. The atmospheric temperatures of some regions are influenced profoundly by winds and by ocean currents.

Because the earth's average temperature does not change by very much with time, there must be a balance on the average between incoming and outgoing energy. That such a balance does indeed occur can be seen with the help of Fig. 13-7, which shows how the rates at which radiant energy enters and leaves the earth vary with latitude.

Winds and ocean currents carry energy from the tropics to the high latitudes

More energy arrives at the tropical regions than is lost there, and the opposite is true at the polar regions. Why then do not the tropics grow warmer and warmer while the poles grow colder and colder? The answer is to be found in the motions

FIG. 13-7
The annual balance between incoming solar radiation and outgoing radiation from the earth. More energy is gained than lost in the tropical regions, and more energy is lost than gained in the polar regions. The latitude scale is spaced so that equal horizontal distances on the graph correspond to equal areas of the earth's surface.

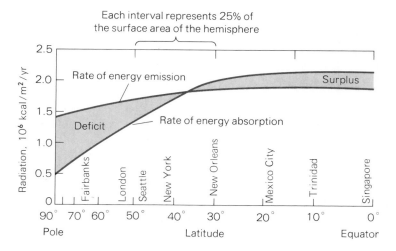

of air and water that shift energy from the regions of surplus to the regions of deficit. About 80 percent of the energy transport around the earth is carried by winds in the atmosphere, and the remainder is carried by ocean currents. We shall examine both of these mechanisms in the remainder of this chapter.

Winds

Currents of air driven by temperature differences

Winds are horizontal movements of air that take place in response to pressure differences in the atmosphere. The greater the difference between the pressures in two regions, the faster the air between them moves. All pressure differences between places on the earth's surface can be traced, directly or indirectly, to temperature differences.

Convection currents are produced by uneven heating of the earth's surface

When a certain region is warmer than its surroundings, the air above it is heated and expands (Fig. 13-8). The hot air rises, leaving behind a low-pressure zone into which cool air from the high-pressure neighborhood flows. The flow toward the heated region at low altitudes is balanced by a flow outward of air that has risen, which cools and sinks to replace the air that has moved inward. Air movements of this kind, produced as the result of unequal heating of the earth's surface, are called *convection currents*.

Sea and land breezes near a coast are caused by convection

On summer days coastal regions often experience onshore winds which at night are replaced by offshore winds. Such sea and land breezes are caused by small-scale convection. Sunlight warms up the land fairly rapidly in the morning, since it is absorbed in a thin surface layer. The water temperature changes very little, partly because the incoming solar energy is shared by a thicker layer of water

FIG. 13-8
Convection currents are produced by unequal heating. The temperature of a land surface rises more rapidly in sunlight than that of a water surface. The resulting convection produces the sea breeze found on sunny days near the shores of a body of water.

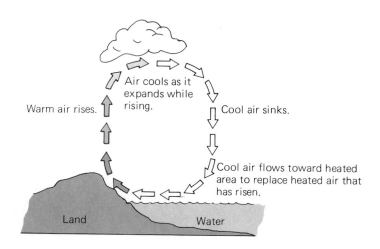

Warm air rises. Air cools as it expands while rising. Cool air sinks. Cool air flows toward heated area to replace heated air that has risen.

Land   Water

FIG. 13-9
Because of the earth's rotation, winds in the northern hemisphere are deflected to the right. As a result, air flows toward a low-pressure region (L) in a counterclockwise spiral as in (a), and air flows away from a high-pressure region (H) in a clockwise spiral as in (b). In the southern hemisphere these deflections are all reversed. An isobar is a line of constant pressure; it corresponds to a contour line of constant altitude on a map.

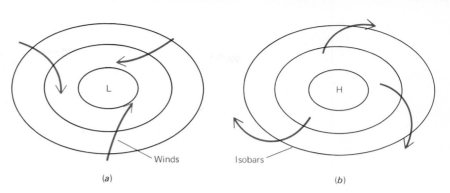

and partly because water requires a relatively large amount of energy per kilogram per degree celsius of temperature rise—more energy than almost any other substance, in fact. The air over the warm land becomes warm in turn and rises by convection, whereupon cooler, denser air from the sea—the sea breeze—sweeps in to replace it. This is the situation shown in Fig. 13-8.

At night the land cools rapidly by radiation while the sea surface remains at about the same temperature as during the day because heat transfer is more efficient in water than in rock and soil. When the land and sea are at the same temperature, the sea breeze stops. If the land cools still further, air warmed by the sea rises and cool air sweeps off the land to replace it—the land breeze.

The rotation of the earth affects the path of an object that moves above its surface as this path is seen by an observer on the surface. In the northern hemisphere a path that would be a straight line across a stationary earth appears instead to be curved to the right; in the southern hemisphere the curvature is to the left. Only motion along the equator is not affected. This phenomenon is called the *coriolis effect*. Because of the coriolis effect, winds are deflected from straight paths into curved ones. Thus the air rushing into a low-pressure region does not move directly inward but instead follows a spiral path which is counterclockwise in the northern hemisphere and clockwise in the southern (Fig. 13-9). Examples of such spiral motion are, in order of decreasing size (but increasing violence), middle-latitude cyclonic weather systems, hurricanes and other tropical cyclones, and tornadoes.

The seasonal winds called *monsoons* are large-scale sea and land breezes modified by the coriolis effect. During the summer, a continent is warmer than the oceans around it. The rising air over the continent creates a low-pressure region that pulls in moisture-laden sea breezes that bring rain. In winter the situation is reversed, with dry air moving out seaward.

These effects are most pronounced in certain parts of Africa and Asia. Figure 13-10 shows how the summer and winter monsoons of India and southeast Asia arise. In summer, the motion of air around the low-pressure center on land is counterclockwise, and it is clockwise around the high-pressure center in the Indian Ocean. The result is a wet southwest monsoon that blows from May to

The coriolis effect refers to the deflection due to the earth's rotation of something moving over the earth's surface

Monsoons

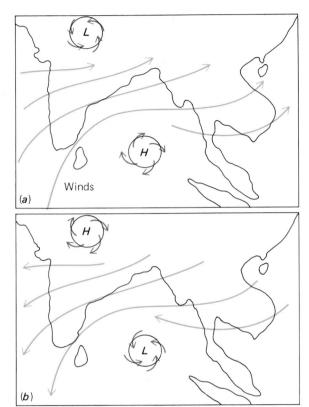

FIG. 13-10
(a) The summer monsoon of India and southeast Asia. Heating of the land produces a low-pressure region centered inland and a high-pressure region centered in the Indian Ocean that cause moisture-laden southwest winds to occur. (b) The winter monsoon. Now the land is cooler than the ocean, so the low- and high-pressure regions are reversed to give dry northeast winds.

September. Every few years this monsoon is weaker than usual, less rain falls, crops suffer, and there may be widespread famine. From October to April dry winds blow from the northeast, as in Fig. 13-10b. A large part of the world's population depends on summer monsoons to provide the rain needed for agriculture.

General Circulation of the Atmosphere

Alternate belts of wind and calm

Air circulation on a stationary earth

The earth is heated most at the equator, least at the poles, so we expect to find convection currents as part of the general atmospheric circulation. Suppose for the moment that our planet did not rotate and that its surface was made up entirely of either land or water. On such an earth air circulation would depend only on the

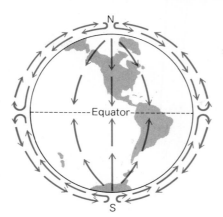

FIG. 13-11

The convectional circulation that would occur if the earth did not rotate and were heated uniformly at the equator. The arrows in the center of the diagram indicate surface winds.

The earth's rotation leads to belts of wind (the westerlies and the trade winds) and belts of calm (the doldrums and the horse latitudes)

difference in temperature between equator and poles. Air would rise along the heated equator, flow at high altitudes toward the poles, and at low altitudes return from the poles toward the equator (Fig. 13-11). We in the northern hemisphere would experience a steady north wind. Around the equator would be a belt of relatively low pressure, near each pole a region of high pressure.

Because the earth does rotate, the above north and south winds are deflected by the coriolis effect into large-scale eddies that lead to a generally eastward drift in the middle latitudes of each hemisphere and a westward drift in the tropics. The principal features of the general circulation of the atmosphere are shown in Fig. 13-12.

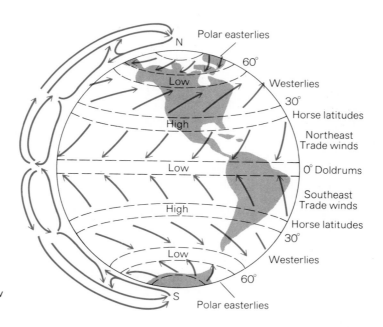

FIG. 13-12

Simplified pattern of horizontal and vertical circulation in the actual atmosphere. Regions of high and low pressure are indicated.

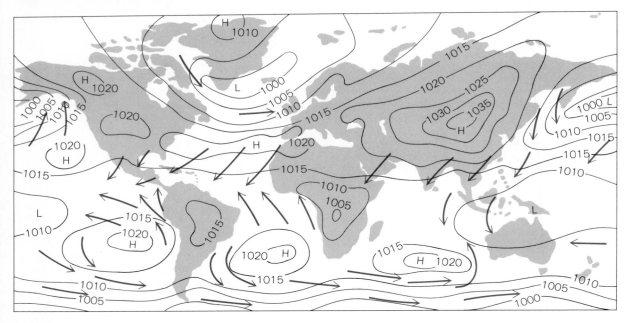

FIG. 13-13
Average January sea-level pressures
(in millibars) and winds. High- and
low-pressure systems are indicated.

The various wind zones were important to shipping in the days of sail, as their names indicate. Thus the steady easterlies on either side of the equator became known as the *trade winds*, while the region of light, erratic wind along the equator itself, where the principal movement of air is upward, constitutes the *doldrums*. The *horse latitudes* that separate the trade winds in both hemispheres from the prevailing westerlies of the middle latitudes are also regions of calm and light winds. Their name is supposed to have come from the practice of throwing overboard horses carried on sailing vessels there that ran short of water while becalmed.

Jet streams

With increasing altitude the belts of westerly winds broaden until almost the enitre flow of air is west to east at the top of the troposphere. The westerly flow aloft is not uniform but contains narrow cores of high-speed winds called *jet streams*. The jet streams form wavelike zigzag patterns around the earth that change continuously and give rise to the variable weather of the middle latitudes by their effect on air masses closer to the surface.

At any given time the circulation near the surface is more complicated than the pattern given in Fig. 13-12. An important factor is the presence of large seasonal low- and high-pressure cells caused by unequal heating due to the irregular distribution of land masses and sea masses (Fig. 13-13). Smaller, short-lived cells also occur which profoundly affect local weather conditions, as described next.

Air Masses, Cyclones, and Anticyclones

Why middle-latitude weather is so variable

Day-to-day weather is more variable in the middle latitudes than anywhere else on earth. If we visit central Mexico or Hawaii, in the belt of the northeast trades, we find that one day follows another with hardly any change in temperature, moisture, or wind direction. On the other hand, in nearly all parts of the continental United States, drastic changes in weather are commonplace. The reason for this variability lies in the movement of warm and cold air masses and of storms derived from them through the belts of the westerlies.

In the northern part of the westerly belt an irregular boundary separates air moving generally northward from the horse latitudes and air moving southward from the polar regions. Great bodies of cold air at times sweep down over North America, and at other times warm air from the tropics extends far northward. The cold air is ultimately warmed and the warm air cooled, but a large volume of air can maintain nearly its original temperature and humidity for days or weeks.

The motion of air masses determines middle-latitude weather

These huge tongues of air, or isolated bodies of air detached from them, are the *air masses* of meteorology. The kind of air in an air mass depends on its source: a mass formed over northern Canada is cold and dry, one from the North

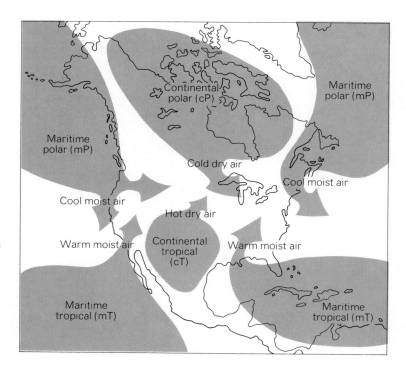

FIG. 13-14

The air masses that affect weather in North America. The importance of the various air masses depends upon the season. In winter, for instance, the continental tropical air mass disappears, whereas the continental polar air mass exerts its greatest influence on the weather then.

Cyclonic weather systems are responsible for the variable weather of the middle latitudes. A typical such cyclone is about 1500 km in diameter and moves eastward at about 40 km/h; its characteristic winds usually do not exceed 65 km/h. The cyclonic weather system here was centered about 2000 km north of Hawaii when it was photographed from a spacecraft.

Atlantic or North Pacific is cold and humid, one from the Gulf of Mexico warm and humid, and so on. Weather prediction in this country depends largely on following the movements of air masses from these various source areas (Fig. 13-14).

Weather systems associated with air masses are usually several hundred to a thousand or more km across and move from west to east. At the center of a *cyclone* the air pressure is low, and as air rushes in toward it the moving air is deflected toward the right in the northern hemisphere and toward the left in the southern

Cyclones are centered on low-pressure regions, anticyclones on high-pressure regions

A hurricane is a large, violent tropical storm typically 160 km in diameter whose winds spiral inward and upward at velocities of 120 km/h or more around an eye of low pressure. Heavy rainfall accompanies the passage of a hurricane except in the eye, which may be 15 to 30 km across. Most hurricanes occur on the western sides of the Pacific, Indian, and North Atlantic oceans during the late summer and early fall, and their most vigorous phases last for a few days to a week or so. Hurricanes usually move at 15 to 50 km/h but may move faster or remain stationary for a day or more. This photograph of Hurricane Katrina was taken on September 3, 1975, by a United States weather satellite when it was off the coast of Baja California.

because of the coriolis effect. As a result cyclonic winds blow in a counterclockwise spiral in the northern hemisphere and in a clockwise spiral in the southern hemisphere (see Fig. 13-9). An *anticyclone* is centered on a high-pressure region from which air moves outward. The coriolis effect therefore causes anticyclonic winds to blow in a clockwise spiral in the northern hemisphere and in a counterclockwise spiral in the southern hemisphere. These spirals are conspicuous in cloud formations photographed from earth satellites.

Cyclonic and anticyclonic weather conditions

A cyclone is a region of low pressure, and air flowing into one rises in an upward spiral. The rising air cools and its moisture content condenses into clouds. As a rule, cyclones bring unstable weather conditions with clouds, rain, strong shifting winds, and abrupt temperature changes. An anticyclone is a region of high pressure, and air flows out of it in a downward spiral. The descent warms the air and its relative humidity accordingly drops, hence condensation does not occur. The weather associated with anticyclones is usually settled and pleasant with clear skies and little wind.

Warm and cold fronts

Middle-latitude cyclones originate at the *polar front,* which is the boundary between the cold polar air mass and the warmed air mass next to it. It is common for a kink to develop in this front with a wedge of warm air protruding into the cold air mass. This produces a low-pressure region which moves eastward as a cyclone. The eastern side of the warm-air wedge is a *warm front* since warm air moves in to replace cold air in its path; the western side is a *cold front* since cold air replaces warm air (Fig. 13-15).

Weather at a front

As warm air rises along an inclined frontal surface it is cooled and part of its moisture condenses out. Clouds and rain are therefore associated with both kinds of fronts (Fig. 13-16). A cold frontal surface is generally steeper, since cold air is actively burrowing under warm air. The temperature difference is greater as well, so rainfall on a cold front is heavier and of shorter duration than on a warm front. A cold front with a large temperature difference is often marked by violent thundersqualls.

A squall line marks the arrival of a cold front.

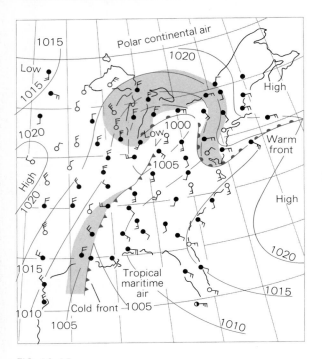

FIG. 13-15
Weather maps show pressure patterns, winds, and precipitation. This is a weather map of the eastern United States one April morning. A cold air mass on the west and north (polar continental air) is separated from a warm air mass (tropical maritime air) by a cold front extending from Louisiana to Michigan and by a warm front from Michigan to Virginia. Where the north end of the warm air mass lies between the two fronts a cyclone has formed, bringing rain (shaded area) to the Great Lakes region. The unit of pressure in this map is the millibar. The small circles indicate clear skies; solid dots indicate cloudy skies. The small lines show wind direction, which is toward the circle or dot, and wind strength; the greater the number of tails, the faster the wind.

FIG. 13-16
Cross-section diagrams of a warm front (a) and a cold front (b).

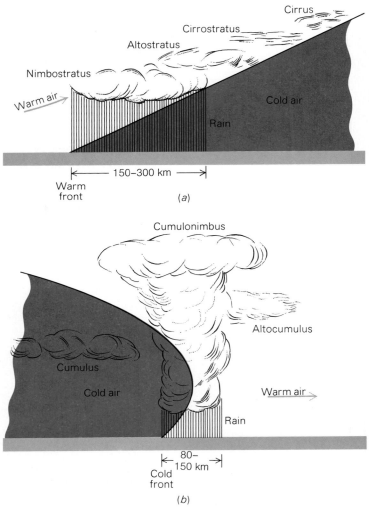

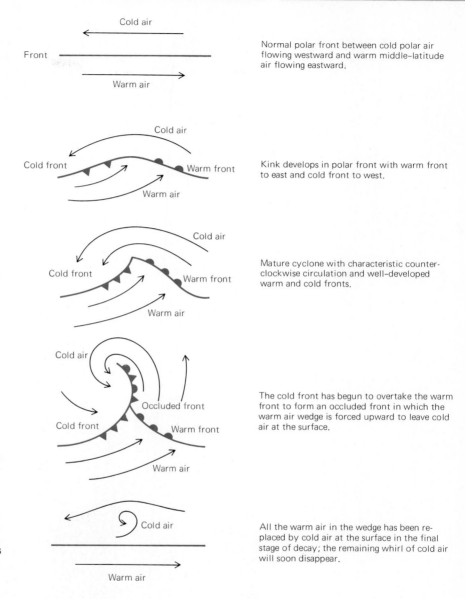

Normal polar front between cold polar air flowing westward and warm middle–latitude air flowing eastward.

Kink develops in polar front with warm front to east and cold front to west.

Mature cyclone with characteristic counter-clockwise circulation and well–developed warm and cold fronts.

The cold front has begun to overtake the warm front to form an occluded front in which the warm air wedge is forced upward to leave cold air at the surface.

All the warm air in the wedge has been replaced by cold air at the surface in the final stage of decay; the remaining whirl of cold air will soon disappear.

FIG. 13-17
Life cycle of a middle-latitude cyclone in the northern hemisphere. Conventional weather-map symbols are used for cold, warm, and occluded fronts.

Occluded front

The cold front associated with a cyclone moves faster than the warm front, and eventually it overtakes the warm front to force the wedge of warm air upward (Fig. 13-17). The formation of such an *occluded front* is the last stage in the evolution of a cyclone, which soon afterward disappears. The total life span of a middle-latitude cyclone may be as little as a few hours or as much as a week, though the usual range is 3 to 5 days.

CLIMATE

The climate of a region refers both to its average weather over a period of years and to the typical amounts by which its weather elements vary during each day and during each year. The most significant weather elements in determining climate are temperature and precipitation. Climates differ considerably around the world, ranging from the tropics where there is no winter to the polar regions where summer is brief.

Tropical Climates

Hot and wet or hot and dry

The equatorial belt of calms, with its rapid evaporation and strong rising air currents, provides an ideal situation for abundant rain. Throughout the year the weather is hot, sultry, with almost daily rains and light, changeable winds. The steaming rain forests of Africa, South America, and the East Indies occur where this belt crosses land.

Weather in the horse latitudes

The horse latitudes, roughly 30° north and south of the equator, are also belts of calm, but their climate is anything but humid. Air in these belts moves chiefly

Year-round high temperatures and abundant rainfall are characteristic of the equatorial regions and encourage plant growth. This forest is in Zaire.

Weather in the trade-wind belts

earthward to become warmer and hence less saturated with water vapor. Thus the climate is perennially dry, with clouds and rain only at long intervals. In a few areas, however, such as the Gulf Coast of the United States, the prevailing aridity is modified by moisture-laden winds of local origin.

Air returning to the warm equatorial belt from the horse latitudes on either side has little reason to lose the small amount of water vapor it possesses, except locally where a mountain range or strong convection currents force it sharply upward. Hence the trade-wind belts are for the most part dry regions. Seasonal movement of the wind belts to the north and south gives rainfall during part of the year to the equatorial margins of the trade-wind belts. The outer portions of these belts, together with the adjacent horse latitudes, are the regions of the world's great deserts — the Sahara, the deserts of South Africa, the arid districts of Mexico and northern Chile, the dry interior of Australia.

Middle-Latitude Climates

Variety is the rule

Weather in the belts of the westerlies

The belts of prevailing westerlies in general have moderate average temperatures, although continental interiors show great seasonal variations. Oceanic islands and the west coasts of continents in these belts have equable temperatures throughout the year. Winds vary greatly in strength and direction, and conditions of moisture and temperature vary with them. In the northern hemisphere the huge land masses of North America and Eurasia introduce further complications.

Climates in the United States

The complexities of the northern belt of westerlies are well illustrated in climates in the United States. Winds from the Pacific Ocean are forced abruptly upward by a succession of mountain ranges along the West Coast, and the western sides of the mountains therefore receive abundant rainfall. Once across the mountain barriers the westerlies have little remaining moisture, so that the region east to the Great Plains is largely dry. If the westerlies maintained their direction as steadily as do the trade winds, arid conditions would continue across the continent to the East Coast. Instead the cyclonic storms characteristic of this belt frequently bring moisture-laden air from the Gulf of Mexico and the Atlantic Ocean into the Mississippi Valley and the Eastern states. Rainfall increases eastward across the country, becoming very large along the Gulf of Mexico.

Temperatures on the West Coast are conditioned by the prevailing wind from the ocean and change relatively little from season to season, but in most other parts of the country the difference between summer and winter is very marked. The fine climates of Florida and southern California owe their mildness to nearby warm oceans and to positions near the junction of the belt of westerlies and the horse latitudes.

In the bleak arctic and antarctic regions, summers are short, winters long and cold. Moderate winds are the rule, although violent gales occur at times. The total amount of snow during the year is small simply because the low temperatures prevent the accumulation of much water vapor in the air.

Climatic Change

An icy past

Climates are subject to long-term change

Weather we expect to vary, both from day to day and from season to season. Nor are we surprised when one year has a colder winter or a drier summer than the one before. Less familiar are changes in climate. Even though climate represents averages in weather conditions over periods of, say, 20 or 30 years, there is plenty of evidence that it, too, is not constant but instead fluctuates markedly over long spans of time. The most dramatic such fluctuations were the *ice ages* of the distant past, of which there have been a great many.

The last ice age

The last ice age reached its peak about 18,000 years ago when huge ice sheets as much as 4 km thick covered much of Europe and North America (see Chap. 16). The vast amount of water locked up as ice lowered sea level nearly 100 m below what it is today. Then the ice began to retreat and climates became progressively less severe; in a period of 12,000 years the average annual temperature of central Europe rose from $-4\,°C$ to $+9\,°C$. By about 4000 B.C. average temperatures were a few degrees higher than those of today. A time of declining temperatures then set in, reaching a minimum in Europe between 900 and 500 B.C.

A gradual warming-up followed that came to a peak between A.D. 800 and 1200. So generally fine were climatic conditions then that the Vikings established flourishing colonies in Iceland and Greenland from which they went on to visit North America. The subsequent deterioration led to cool summers, exceptionally cold winters, and extensive freezing of the Arctic Sea from 1300 to 1700. So extreme was the weather in the first half of the seventeenth century that it has been called the "Little Ice Age." Greenland became a much less attractive place than formerly and the colony there disappeared, the coast of Iceland was surrounded by ice for several months per year (in contrast to a few weeks per year today), and glaciers advanced farther across alpine landscapes than ever before or since in recorded history.

The Little Ice Age

Late in the nineteenth century a trend toward higher temperatures became evident which has led to a marked shrinkage of the world's glaciers. In the first half of the present century especially pronounced temperature increases took place whose most noticeable consequences were milder winters in the higher latitudes. In Spitzbergen, for instance, January temperatures averaged from 1920 to 1940 were nearly $8\,°C$ ($14\,°F$) higher than those averaged from 1900 to 1920, and Greenland became less inhospitable than before.

Recent changes in climate

Alas, these balmy conditions seem to have peaked about 1945, and since then the worldwide average annual temperature has been falling steadily (Fig. 13-18). The total drop in the past 40 years has been less than $0.5\,°C$, which does not seem like very much, but the effects have been dramatic. What has happened has been a shift toward the equator of the various wind and climatic zones. In the northern hemisphere this shift has had a variety of effects. Siberia is growing colder as the polar front moves south. The northern rim of Africa, formerly in the dry zone of the horse latitudes, now receives unaccustomed rain as the cyclonic weather

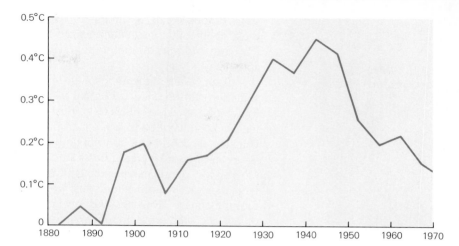

FIG. 13-18
Changes in worldwide average
annual temperatures 1880–1970.
Five-year averages are plotted.

systems of the westerlies sometimes sweep over it. The horse latitudes have moved farther south, depriving vast areas of sub-Sahara Africa, the Middle East, India, and southern Asia of the moist tropical air that formerly brought them abundant rain. Famines have been the result. In North America, the pattern of air flow has changed to bring colder winters and more precipitation to western states while eastern ones have warmer winters.

Origins of Climatic Change

A warm future or a cold one?

Why do climates change? So many different factors influence climate that there is no shortage of possible explanations.

One train of thought blames modern civilization for the temperature behavior shown in Fig. 13-18. The initial temperature rise is attributed to an increase in the carbon dioxide content of the atmosphere. Both the biologic and oceanic cycles are, on the average, balanced in their consumption and production of carbon dioxide. But there are also sources of carbon dioxide that have no absorption processes to counter their effects. The most significant of these sources is our burning of coal and oil to produce heat for dwellings and energy for industry and transportation. At present our chimneys and exhaust pipes pour about 18 billion tons of carbon dioxide each year into the atmosphere.

The carbon dioxide content of the atmosphere is steadily increasing

Since 1860 the carbon dioxide content of the atmosphere has gone up by 13 percent, and today it is increasing at a rate of roughly 0.3 percent a year. This increase represents about half the CO_2 being emitted; the other half is thought to be absorbed by the oceans and by vegetation, mainly forests. Despite the relatively small proportion of CO_2 in the atmosphere — only 335 parts per million — it is a most significant constituent because of its ability to absorb energy reradiated by the earth and thus to contribute to the greenhouse effect that powers the atmosphere.

Dust is also a factor in climatic change

The cooling of the atmosphere since 1945 must have a different explanation since the carbon dioxide content has continued to increase. The culprit here is thought by some scientists to be dust at high altitudes which scatters part of the incoming sunlight back into space. The chief natural source of airborne dust is volcanic eruptions. Our contribution comes from the chimneys of industry, large-scale burning of tropical forests to clear land for agriculture, and soil particles blown away during mechanical cultivation. There is no question that a sufficiently large increase in atmospheric dust would lead to the observed general cooling of the atmosphere. However, just how large an increase is needed and whether it has in fact occurred are not known, nor are the relative importances of the different dust sources.

Variations in solar energy output

Another point of view attributes climatic change to variations in the solar energy arriving at the top of the atmosphere, not to events within the atmosphere. (Of course, the carbon dioxide and dust contents of the atmosphere always play a role in climate: the issue is which influences are primary and which are secondary.) The sun's radiation is not constant but fluctuates through the 11-year sunspot cycle (Chap. 19), and a number of weather phenomena apparently follow a similar cycle. There seem to be longer-term variations in solar output as well; the Little Ice Age may have been caused by one of them.

The Milankovitch theory of climatic change

The most promising explanation of the large-scale ice ages relates them to periodic changes that occur in the tilt of the earth's axis, the shape of its orbit, and the time of year when the earth is closest to the sun (Fig. 13-19). Fifty years ago Milutin Milankovitch, a Yugoslav astronomer, worked out how these changes might affect climate by altering the amount of sunlight (that is, insolation) received

FIG. 13-19
Three variations in the earth's motion that may be responsible for causing ice ages. (a) The time of year when the earth is nearest the sun varies with a period of about 20,000 years. (b) The angle of tilt of the earth's axis of rotation varies with a period of about 40,000 years. (c) The shape of the earth's elliptical orbit varies with a period of about 100,000 years. These variations have relatively little effect on the total sunlight reaching the earth but a considerable effect on the sunlight reaching the polar regions in summer.

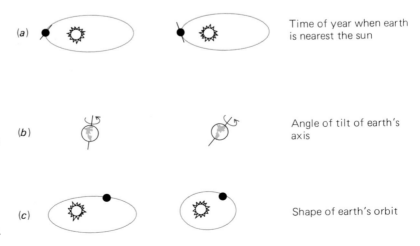

(a)   Time of year when earth
                                                                 is nearest the sun

(b)   Angle of tilt of earth's
                                                                 axis

(c)   Shape of earth's orbit

by the earth. The changes themselves on a global basis are small, 0.3 percent at most, but Milankovitch argued that what really counts is not the total insolation but the insolation in the polar regions in summer, which turns out to vary by up to 20 percent. Too little summer sunshine would not melt all the snow that fell during the winter before, and in time the accumulated snow would turn into great sheets of ice. In the southern hemisphere the ice would melt when it leaves the Antarctic continent and falls into the sea, but in the northern hemisphere the ice would move down across North America and Eurasia to produce an ice age.

Major ice ages have occurred every 100,000 years or so, with smaller cycles of cold and warm at closer intervals. The strongest evidence in favor of Milankovitch's hypothesis is that the periods of advance and retreat of the ice sheets are in accord with the various periods of the earth's orbital variations. Additional support comes from current theoretical models of the earth's climate, which respond to the known insolation changes with a prediction of regular ice ages.

The big question is whether a long-term warming of the atmosphere due to increased carbon dioxide from the burning of fossil fuels will be enough to over-whelm future decreases in insolation. If this is the case, the earth may have seen its last ice age. Or, perhaps, a surge of volcanic activity — or a nuclear war — will produce enough dust to trigger a new ice age. The only certainty is that the atmosphere is in a state of delicate balance, so delicate that human activities may be sufficient to tip the balance one way or the other.

THE OCEANS

Almost 71 percent of the earth's surface is covered by the oceans and the shallower seas that join with them. These waters are home to abundant plant and animal life — indeed, life probably began in the primordial ocean — and in addition influence continental life in a variety of indirect ways. For one thing, the oceans provide the reservoir from which water is evaporated into the atmosphere, later to fall as rain and snow on land. The oceans participate in the oxygen–carbon dioxide cycle both through the life they support and through the vast quantities of these gases dissolved in them. And the oceans help determine climates by their ability to absorb solar energy and transport it around the world. The list of chemical and physical cycles on the earth in which the oceans play significant roles is a long one.

Ocean Basins

Water, water, everywhere

A continental shelf surrounds each continent

Each of the world's oceans lies in a vast basin bounded by continental land masses. Typically an ocean bottom slopes gradually downward from the shore to a depth of 130 m or so before starting to drop more rapidly (Fig. 13-20). The average width of this *continental shelf* is 65 km, but it ranges from less than a kilometer off

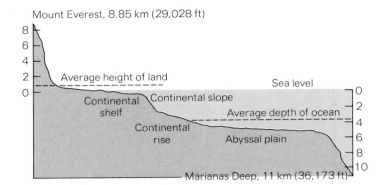

FIG. 13-20
Profile of the earth's surface. The vertical scale is greatly exaggerated. Heights and depths are in km.

The oceans are deep compared with the average height of the continents

such mountainous coasts as the western coast of South America to over 1000 km off the low arctic coasts of the Eurasian land mass. The North, Irish, and Baltic Seas are part of the European continental shelf, while the Grand Banks off Newfoundland are part of the North American shelf. A sharp change in gradient marks the transition from the continental shelf to the steeper *continental slope,* which after a fall of perhaps 2 km joins the *abyssal plain* of the ocean floor via the gentle *continental rise.*

The ocean basins average 3.7 km in depth, while the continents average only about 0.8 km in height above sea level. The deepest known point of the oceans, 11 km below the surface, is found in the Marianas Trench southwest of Guam in the Pacific; by contrast, Mt. Everest is only 80 percent as high above sea level. If the earth were smooth, it would be covered with a layer of water perhaps 2.4 km thick, but it seems likely that the oceans have always been confined to more or less distinct basins and presumably will continue to be.

The ocean floor, like the continents, has mountain ranges and valleys, isolated volcanic peaks and vast plains, many of them rivaling or exceeding in size their counterparts on land. The Hawaiian Islands, for instance, are volcanoes that rise as much as 9000 m above the ocean floor, about half of their altitude being above sea level. Less conspicuous from the surface is the Mid-Atlantic Ridge, an immense submarine mountain range that extends from Iceland past the tip of South America before swinging into the Indian Ocean. Such islands as the Azores, Ascension Island, and Tristan da Cunha are all that protrude from the ocean of this ridge.

The Antarctic ice cap contains most of the world's permanent ice

A considerable amount of water is stored as ice in the form of the glaciers and ice caps which cover one-tenth the land area of the earth. About 90 percent of this ice is located in the Antarctic ice cap, about 9 percent in the Greenland ice cap, and the remaining 1 percent in the various glaciers of the world. If suddenly melted, the ice would raise sea level by perhaps 75 m. (By comparison, if all the water vapor in the atmosphere were condensed, sea level would go up by only about 2.5 cm.) Over a long period of time the rise in sea level would be reduced by about one-third by changes in the levels of the continents and the ocean floors brought about by the changes in the weights they have to bear.

Sea water has always been salty

Most of the earth's surface water probably appeared about 4 billion years ago when the young earth assumed its present internal structure. The water came from the rocks of the interior and took with it the same ions found in sea water today: the oceans have always been salty. Since then, additional salts have continually been added to the oceans in the various ways illustrated in Fig. 10-20. However, seawater salinity has not changed by very much because of the action of various mechanisms that remove salts from the oceans. One of these mechanisms is quite direct, the loss of salts to the atmosphere when wind blows spray off wave tops. The resulting salt particles serve as precipitation nuclei, and a substantial amount falls on land in rain and snow. Another mechanism is the incorporation of various compounds, notably calcium carbonate and silicon dioxide, in the shells of marine organisms, which eventually form part of the sediments that coat the ocean floors.

Ocean Currents

Four great whirlpools

The oceans act as heat reservoirs that moderate the climates of adjacent land areas

The oceans affect climate in two ways. First, they act as reservoirs of heat that moderate the temperature extremes of the seasons. In spring and summer the oceans are cooler than the regions they border, since the insolation they receive is absorbed in a greater volume than in the case of solid, opaque land. The heat stored in the ocean depths means that in fall and winter the oceans are warmer than the regions they border. Heat flows readily between moving air and water. With a sufficient temperature difference, the rate of energy transfer from warm water to cold air (or from warm air to cold water) can exceed the rate at which solar energy arrives at the top of the atmosphere.

Lacking such a nearby heat reservoir, continental interiors experience lower

Waves are produced by winds blowing over the surface of a body of water. The stronger the wind, the longer it blows, and the greater the distance over which the wind has been in contact with the water, the higher the waves that are produced. These factors govern the amount of energy transferred to the water and thus govern the violence of the resulting disturbance.

winter temperatures and higher summer temperatures than those of coastal districts. In Canada, for instance, temperatures in the city of Victoria on the Pacific coast range from an average January minimum of 9°C (36°F) to an average July maximum of 20°C (68°F), whereas in Winnipeg, in the interior, the corresponding figures are −13°C (−8°F) and 27°C (80°F).

Also important in influencing climate are surface drifts in the oceans produced by the friction of wind on water. Such drifts are much slower than movements in the atmosphere, with the fastest normal surface currents having speeds of about 10 km/h.

The wind-driven surface currents parallel to a large extent the major wind systems. The northeast and southeast trade winds drive water before them westward along the equator, forming the *equatorial current*. In the Atlantic Ocean this current runs head on into South America, in the Pacific into the East Indies. At each of these points the current divides into two parts, one flowing south and the other north. Moving away from the equator along the continental margins, these currents then come under the influence of the westerlies, which drive them eastward across the oceans. Thus gigantic whirlpools are set up in both Atlantic and Pacific Oceans on either side of the equator (Fig. 13-21). Many complexities are produced in the four great whirls by islands, continental projections, and undersea mountains and valleys.

The western side of the North Atlantic whirl, a warm current moving partly into the Gulf of Mexico, partly straight north along our southeastern coast, is the famous Gulf Stream. Forced away from the coast in the latitude of New Jersey by the westerlies, this current moves northeastward across the Atlantic, splitting on the European side into one part which moves south to complete the whirl, another

Surface ocean currents are caused by winds

The Gulf Stream

FIG. 13-21
Principal ocean currents of the world. Warm currents are shown by the colored arrows, cool currents by the black ones.

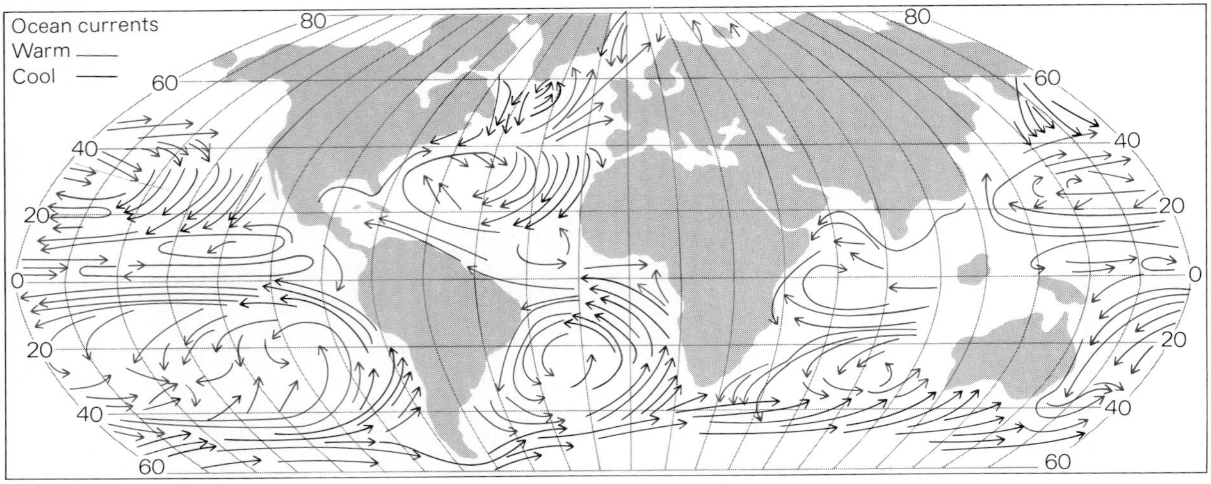

part which continues northeastward past Great Britain and Norway into the Arctic Ocean. To compensate for the addition of water into the polar sea, the cold Labrador Current moves southward along the east coast of North America as far as New York. Down the west coast of North America moves the Japan Current, the southward-flowing eastern part of the North Pacific whirl.

Since ocean currents remain near the temperatures of the latitudes from which they come for a long time, they exert a direct influence on the temperatures of neighboring lands. The influence is greatest, of course, where the prevailing winds blow shoreward from the sea. The warm Gulf Stream has a far greater effect in tempering the climate of northwest Europe than that of eastern United States, since prevailing winds in these latitudes are from the west. Cyclonic storms bring east winds to the Atlantic Seaboard often enough, however, for the Gulf Stream to help raise temperatures in the South Atlantic states, and the Labrador Current is in part responsible for the rigorous climate of New England and eastern Canada.

Thus the oceans, besides acting as water reservoirs for the earth's atmosphere, play a direct part in temperature control — both by preventing abrupt temperature changes in lands along their borders and by aiding the winds, through the motion of ocean currents, in their distribution of heat and cold over the surface of the earth.

IMPORTANT TERMS

The earth's **atmosphere** is its envelope of air. The lowest part of the atmosphere is the **troposphere,** in which such weather phenomena as clouds and storms occur. Next comes the **stratosphere** whose content of **ozone,** a form of oxygen with three atoms per molecule, absorbs most of the dangerous ultraviolet radiation from the sun. Above the stratosphere is the **mesosphere** and still higher the **thermosphere,** which contains layers of ions that make up the **ionosphere.** The ionosphere reflects radio waves and so makes possible long-range radio communication.

Air at a given temperature is said to be **saturated** when it contains the maximum amount that will evaporate at that temperature. The **relative humidity** of a volume of air is the ratio between the water vapor it contains and the amount that would be present at saturation. Low-altitude **clouds** consist of tiny water droplets, high-altitude clouds consist of ice crystals.

The energy that powers weather phenomena is **insolation,** which is **in**coming **sol**ar radi**ation.** Most of the insolation passes through the atmosphere and is absorbed by the earth's surface. The warm earth then reradiates energy back into the atmosphere as infrared radiation that is picked up by the carbon dioxide and water vapor there and then transferred to the other gases present. This indirect heating of the atmosphere from below is called the **greenhouse effect.**

Convection currents are due to the uneven heating of a fluid: the warmer parts of the fluid expand and rise because of their buoyancy while the cooler parts sink. Such currents occur in the atmosphere where air in the equatorial regions is heated strongly, expands and rises, and moves toward the pole in each hemisphere. In the polar regions the air cools and sinks and then flows back on the surface toward the equator. In this way energy is shifted from the tropics to the higher latitudes.

The **coriolis effect** is the deflection of winds to the right in the northern hemisphere, to the left in the southern, as a consequence of the earth's rotation. Because of the coriolis effect, the convection currents in the atmosphere follow curved paths. A **cyclone** is a weather system centered on a low-pressure region. In the northern hemisphere the coriolis effect deflects winds moving inward in a cyclone into a counterclockwise spiral, in the southern hemisphere into a clockwise spiral. An **anticyclone** is a weather system centered on a high-pressure region; winds blowing outward from an anticyclone spiral in the opposite sense about its center to those about a cyclone. A ***front*** is the boundary between a mass of warm air and a mass of cold air; clouds and rain usually occur at a front.

Climate refers to averages in weather conditions over a period of years. The ***ice ages*** were times of severe cold in which ice sheets covered much of Europe and North America.

MULTIPLE CHOICE

1. Arrange the following gases in the order of their abundance in the earth's atmosphere:
   a. oxygen
   b. carbon dioxide
   c. nitrogen
   d. argon

2. Much of Tibet lies in altitudes of over 5.5 km (18,000 ft). At such altitudes the Tibetans are above approximately
   a. 10 percent of the atmosphere
   b. 50 percent of the atmosphere
   c. 90 percent of the atmosphere
   d. 99 percent of the atmosphere

3. The region of the atmosphere closest to the earth's surface is the
   a. thermosphere
   b. ionosphere
   c. troposphere
   d. stratosphere

4. The atmosphere constituent chiefly responsible for absorbing ultraviolet radiation from the sun is
   a. carbon dioxide
   b. water vapor
   c. ozone
   d. helium

5. The formula of ozone is
   a. O
   b. O_2
   c. O_3
   d. O_4

6. The ionosphere
   a. is produced by the action of solar ultraviolet and x-rays
   b. reflects solar ultraviolet and x-rays
   c. consists of ozone ions
   d. occurs at roughly the same altitude as clouds

7. When saturated air is cooled,
   a. it becomes able to take up more water vapor
   b. some of its water content condenses out
   c. the relative humidity goes down
   d. convection currents result

8. If the atmosphere contained fewer salt crystals and dust particles than it now does,
   a. clouds would form less readily
   b. clouds would form more readily
   c. the formation of clouds would be unaffected
   d. snow would never fall

9. Clouds occur when moist air is cooled by
   a. expansion when it rises
   b. expansion when it falls
   c. compression when it rises
   d. compression when it falls

10. The chief source of atmospheric heat is
   a. incoming solar radiation
   b. infrared radiation from the earth itself
   c. ultraviolet radiation absorbed by ozone
   d. ultraviolet radiation absorbed by clouds

11. Air near the equator averages higher temperatures than air near the poles because
   a. polar air is cooled by the ice and snow on the ground
   b. there is more carbon dioxide and water vapor in equatorial air to absorb infrared radiation from the earth
   c. sunlight falls more nearly vertically at the equator than near the poles
   d. the oceans near the equator are warmer than those near the poles

12. Energy is transported from the tropics to the polar regions chiefly by
   a. winds
   b. ocean currents
   c. carbon dioxide
   d. ozone

13. Because of the coriolis effect, a wind in the northern hemisphere is deflected
   a. upward
   b. downward
   c. toward the right
   d. toward the left

14. The flow of air in the upper atmosphere is largely
   a. from east to west
   b. from west to east
   c. from north to south
   d. from south to north

15. The middle latitudes usually experience winds from the
   a. north
   b. south
   c. east
   d. west

16. Weather systems that center about regions of low pressure are called
   a. cyclones
   b. anticyclones
   c. convection currents

d. trade winds
17. The trade-wind belts are regions of generally
    a. little rainfall
    b. much rainfall
    c. low temperatures
    d. westerly winds
18. The winds in a northern hemisphere cyclone spiral
    a. clockwise toward its center
    b. counterclockwise toward its center
    c. clockwise away from its center
    d. counterclockwise away from its center
19. The most pleasant weather is found in
    a. a cold front
    b. a warm front
    c. a cyclone
    d. an anticyclone
20. The greatest seasonal variations in temperature occur in
    a. the west coasts of the continents
    b. the east coasts of the continents
    c. continental interiors
    d. isolated islands
21. Most of the permanent ice of the world is located in
    a. mountain glaciers
    b. Alaska
    c. Greenland
    d. Antarctica
22. Ice ages
    a. cover the entire earth with a sheet of ice
    b. freeze all the oceans
    c. occurred seldom in the past
    d. occurred frequently in the past
23. Compared with the average height of the continents above sea level, the average depth of the ocean basins below sea level is
    a. smaller
    b. greater
    c. about the same
    d. sometimes smaller and sometimes greater, depending upon the tides
24. The deepest known point of the oceans is found in the
    a. Atlantic Ocean
    b. Pacific Ocean
    c. North Sea
    d. Panama Canal
25. The Hawaiian Islands are
    a. part of a sunken continent
    b. floating on the surface of the ocean
    c. located in shallow water
    d. volcanic peaks
26. The most abundant ions in sea water are
    a. Na^+ and Cl^-
    b. H^+ and OH^-
    c. Mg^{2+} and SO_4^{2-}
    d. Fe^{2+} and Cl^-
27. Most surface ocean currents are due to
    a. melting glaciers
    b. rivers
    c. winds
    d. differences in the altitude of the ocean surface
28. The climate of northwest Europe is greatly affected by the
    a. Gulf Stream
    b. abyssal zone
    c. Labrador Current
    d. trade winds

QUESTIONS

1. In what two important processes does the carbon dioxide in the atmosphere have essential roles?
2. What would be the result of the disappearance of ozone from the upper atmosphere?
3. The tropopause, the stratopause, and the mesopause are respectively the upper boundaries of the troposphere, the stratosphere, and the mesosphere. What is characteristic of the air temperature at each of these boundaries?
4. Suppose you are climbing in an airplane that has no altimeter. How could you tell when you are approaching the top of the troposphere?
5. Why do you think temperatures in the troposphere decrease with altitude?
6. What does it mean to say that a certain volume of air has a relative humidity of 50 percent? Of 100 percent?
7. The air in a closed container is saturated with water vapor at 20°C. (a) What is the relative humidity? (b) What happens to the relative humidity if the temperature is reduced to 10°C? (c) If the temperature is increased to 30°C?
8. Why does the air in a heated room tend to be dry?
9. Why does dew form on the ground during clear, calm summer nights?
10. What do high-altitude clouds consist of? Low-altitude clouds?
11. Cumulus clouds form when warm air rises vertically due to convection, and stratus clouds form when a warm air mass moving horizontally encounters a cooler mass and is forced upward on top of it. What kind of clouds would you expect to be characteristic of a warm front?
12. What is the significance of dust and salt particles in the atmosphere for weather phenomena?
13. From time to time a gigantic volcanic explosion sends a large amount of dust into the atmosphere where it may remain for

some years. How many consequences of such an event can you think of?

14. What is the greenhouse effect and how is it related to the absorption of solar energy by the earth's atmosphere?

15. What are the two mechanisms by which energy of solar origin is transported around the earth? Which is the most important?

16. Account for the abrupt changes in temperature between day and night in desert regions.

17. In the northern hemisphere, the longest and shortest days occur respectively in June and December, but the warmest and coldest weather of the year occurs respectively a month or two later. What is the reason for these time lags?

18. What is the direction of the prevailing winds of the middle latitudes in each hemisphere?

19. Where in the atmosphere do the jet streams occur? What is their general direction?

20. A crew is planning to sail from the United States to England and later return home. What routes should they follow across the Atlantic in order to have their course downwind as much of the time as possible?

21. How does the weather associated with a typical cyclone differ from that associated with a typical anticyclone?

22. What is the usual lifetime of a cyclone in the middle latitudes?

23. When you face a wind associated with a cyclone in the northern hemisphere, in what approximate direction will the center of low pressure be? In what direction will the center of low pressure be if you do this in the southern hemisphere?

24. What is the approximate sequence of wind directions when the center of a cyclone passes north of an observer in the northern hemisphere?

25. What is the approximate sequence of wind directions when the center of an anticyclone passes south of an observer in the northern hemisphere?

26. What is the difference between the rainfall that accompanies the passage of a warm front and that which accompanies the passage of a cold front?

27. List the chief reservoirs of the earth's water content in the order of the amount of water each contains.

28. How does the average depth of the ocean basins below sea level compare with the average height of the continents above sea level?

29. The salinity of sea water varies with location, but the relative proportions of the various ions in solution are almost exactly the same everywhere regardless of local circumstances. What is the significance of the latter observation?

30. Do ocean waves actually transport water from one place to another? If not, what if anything do such waves transport?

31. A wind begins to blow over the surface of a calm body of deep water. What factors govern the height of the waves that are produced?

32. The giant whirls of the oceans involve clockwise flows in the northern hemisphere and counterclockwise flows in the southern. Why?

33. (a) If you were planning to drift in a raft across the North Atlantic from the United States to Europe by making use of ocean currents, what would your route be? (b) If you were planning to drift from Europe to the United States, what would your route be?

34. England and Labrador are at about the same latitude on either side of the North Atlantic Ocean, but England is considerably warmer than Labrador on the average. Why?

35. The California Current along the California coast is cooler than the ocean to the west. How does this fact explain the numerous fogs on this coast?

36. The island of Oahu (one of the Hawaiian Islands) is at latitude 21°N and is crossed by a mountain range trending roughly northwest to southeast. Account for the more abundant rainfall on the northeastern side of the range.

37. The northeast and southeast trade winds meet in a belt called the doldrums. What is the characteristic climate of the doldrums and why does it occur?

38. Why are most of the world's deserts found in the horse latitudes, which separate the trade winds from the prevailing westerlies in both hemispheres?

39. If the earth's axis were not tilted, would the differences in climates around the world be greater or smaller than they are today?

40. The Milankovitch theory of ice ages relates them to variations in the tilt of the earth's axis, the shape of its orbit, and the time of year when the earth is closest to the sun. However, these variations affect the total amount of solar energy reaching the earth by no more than 0.3 percent. How did Milankovitch account for this apparent contradiction?

ANSWERS TO MULTIPLE CHOICE

1. *c, a, d, b*	**8.** *a*	**15.** *d*	**22.** *d*
2. *b*	**9.** *a*	**16.** *a*	**23.** *b*
3. *c*	**10.** *b*	**17.** *a*	**24.** *b*
4. *c*	**11.** *c*	**18.** *b*	**25.** *d*
5. *c*	**12.** *a*	**19.** *d*	**26.** *a*
6. *a*	**13.** *c*	**20.** *c*	**27.** *c*
7. *b*	**14.** *b*	**21.** *d*	**28.** *a*

14

EARTH MATERIALS

Soil, vegetation, and rock fragments such as sand and gravel form a thin surface layer on most land areas, but solid rock is always underneath. Rock underlies the sediments on the ocean floors as well. The deepest mines, whose shafts may descend 3 km or so, and the deepest wells, which may penetrate another 5 km, encounter rock similar to that at the surface. Some of the rock now exposed to our view was once buried several km inside the earth, and the material that makes up some volcanic rock probably rose in molten form from still greater depths, perhaps as much as 100 km down. Nevertheless, these samples of rock from well below the surface closely resemble rock formed at higher levels.

Direct observation tells us only that the outer part of the earth is composed almost entirely of rock. This shell of rock, called the *crust* of the earth, is only $\frac{1}{2}$ percent of the earth's 6400-km radius, and we have no firsthand information about the remaining material. Later in this chapter, however, we shall learn how it is possible to probe the interior of our planet by indirect methods, and what the results are.

MINERALS

The study of the earth begins with the solid materials of the crust. Let us see what is known about the rock materials under our feet that we can simply pick up and examine.

Composition of the Crust

Oxygen and silicon are the most abundant elements

The average composition of the crust, not including surface water or the atmosphere, is shown in Fig. 14-1. The figures are percentages of the various elements by mass. Including the oceans and the atmosphere does not change these percentages by very much.

Oxygen is the most abundant element in the earth's crust, most of it combined with silicon

Figure 14-1 illustrates the striking fact that a few elements are abundant in the crust, but most are exceedingly rare. Oxygen alone makes up nearly half the mass of the crust, most of it combined with silicon in silica and the silicates. Silicon and the two metals iron and aluminum account for three-fourths of the rest of the crust's mass. Such familiar metals as copper, tin, lead, and silver are too scarce to be shown. Nitrogen and the halogens are similarly lumped in the 1.4 percent that includes "all others." Carbon and hydrogen, present in all living things, together make up less than 0.2 percent of the total.

The majority of crustal rocks are composed largely of silicon compounds

Next to oxygen, the most common element in the earth's crust is silicon. Silicon never occurs free in nature, and the pure element is not often found even in chemical laboratories, but its compounds make up about 87 percent of the rocks and soil that compose the earth's solid outer portion. In the chemistry of naturally occurring inorganic materials, silicon has the same sort of central role that carbon plays in the chemistry of living things.

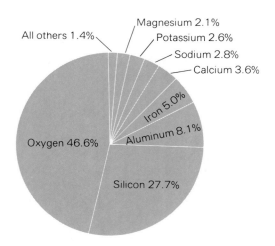

FIG. 14-1
Average chemical composition of the earth's crust. Percentages by mass are given.

Silicates

A variety of crystal structures can occur

Nearly all the earth's silicon is either combined with oxygen in silica (which is silicon dioxide, SiO_2) or combined with oxygen and one or more metals in the various silicates. In number and variety the silicates do not compare with carbon compounds, but their structures are complex enough to make the chemistry of silicon a difficult subject.

As a class, the silicates are crystalline solids that melt at high temperatures to give viscous liquids. Their variations in composition and structure are reflected in a variety of colors, hardnesses, and crystal forms. The softness of talc contrasted with the hardness of zircon and beryl, the transparency of topaz and the deep color of garnet, the platy crystals of mica and the fibrous crystals of asbestos give some idea of the range of silicate properties.

Like most solids, crystalline silicates are assemblies of individual atoms bonded together in a continuous lattice, rather than assemblies of molecules. The basic structural element of all silicates is the SiO_4^{4-} tetrahedron in which each Si^{4+} ion is surrounded by four O^{2-} ions, as in Fig. 14-2. In some silicates the SiO_4^{4-} units occur as single ions linked together by positive metal ions — in a general way like the ionic structure of NaCl, with SiO_4^{4-} ions taking the place of Cl^- ions. In more complex silicates the tetrahedra are linked together in continuous chains (Fig. 14-3) or sheets (Fig. 14-4), with metal ions lying between. Three-dimensional

At ordinary temperatures, the silicates are crystalline solids with widely varying properties

The silicon-oxygen tetrahedron is the basic structural unit of the silicate minerals

FIG. 14-2
The silicon-oxygen tetrahedron is the fundamental unit in all silicate structures. Dashed lines show the tetrahedral form of SiO_4^{4-}, solid lines are bonds between the ions.

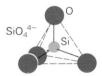

FIG. 14-3
Chain of SiO_4^{4-} tetrahedra. These chains are linked sidewise by metal ions. The solid lines represent bonds between atoms.

FIG. 14-4
Sheet of SiO_4^{4-} tetrahedra. The O^- ions in the top of the sheet form ionic bonds with metal ions.

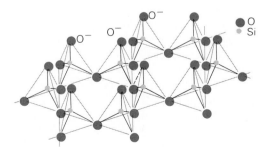

networks of SiO_4^{4-} tetrahedra are also possible in which all the O atoms of each tetrahedron are shared by its neighbors, which is the case in quartz, SiO_2. The number and variety of silicate minerals can be traced to the many different ways in which the basic SiO_4^{4-} tetrahedron can combine with metal ions to form stable crystal structures.

Minerals

What rocks are made of

Rocks are composed of
homogeneous solids called minerals

Most rocks are heterogeneous solids. The different materials, called *minerals,* in a coarse-grained rock like granite are obvious to the eye; for a fine-grained rock the help of a microscope may be needed. As a rule, minerals are crystalline and have fairly definite chemical compositions.

We can predict the kinds of material that can occur as minerals on the basis of the chemistry we learned in earlier chapters. Thus we would anticipate finding the more inactive elements in the free state, active elements in compounds. Soluble compounds should be common minerals only in arid regions; easily oxidized compounds should occur only well beneath the surface. In accord with these expectations, we indeed find free gold, platinum, sulfur, and carbon (both graphite and diamond) as minerals, whereas elements like sodium, chlorine, and calcium always occur in compounds. Sodium chloride, sodium carbonate, and potassium nitrate form deposits in deserts but are seldom found elsewhere. Such reactive compounds as calcium oxide or phosphorus pentoxide never occur in nature.

Only a few minerals are common

Minerals are not usually identified by chemical names for two reasons. First, the same compound may occur in different forms. For instance, both calcite and aragonite are largely calcium carbonate ($CaCO_3$), but they differ in crystal form, hardness, density, and so on. Second, most minerals vary somewhat in composition from sample to sample, unlike compounds whose compositions are invariable. More than 2000 different minerals are known, but the majority are rare. The number of minerals important in ordinary rocks is so small that knowing something about less than a dozen is enough for an introduction to geology.

Common minerals are not only limited in number but are also easily recognizable with some experience, often by appearance alone. To distinguish unusual minerals laboratory tests may be necessary, but for the minerals that compose ordinary rocks such simple physical properties as density, color, hardness, and crystal form make identification straightforward.

Every mineral has a characteristic
crystal form

In describing the important rock-forming minerals, two properties need special attention: *crystal form* and *cleavage.* Most minerals are crystalline solids, which means that their constituent particles are arranged in lattice structures with definite geometric patterns. When a mineral grain develops in a position where its growth is not hindered by neighboring crystals, as in an open cavity, its inner structure expresses itself by the formation of perfect crystals, with smooth faces meeting each other at sharp angles. Each mineral has crystals of a distinctive shape so that well-formed crystals make recognition of a mineral easy. Unfortunately good crystals are rare, since mineral grains usually interfere with one another's growth.

Even when well-developed crystals are not present, however, the characteristic lattice structure of a mineral may reveal itself in the property called *cleavage*. This is the tendency of a substance to split along certain planes, which are determined by the arrangement of particles in its lattice. When a mineral grain is struck with a hammer, its cleavage planes are revealed as the preferred directions of breaking. Even without actual breaking, the existence of cleavage in a mineral is usually shown by flat, parallel faces and minute parallel cracks. The flat surfaces of mica flakes, for instance, and the ability of mica to peel off in thin sheets show that this mineral has almost perfect cleavage. Some minerals (for example, quartz) have practically no cleavage; when struck they shatter, like glass, along random curved surfaces. The ability to recognize different kinds and degrees of cleavage is an important aid in distinguishing minerals.

Cleavage is often helpful in identifying a mineral

Six Common Minerals

All but one contain silicon

Quartz is hard enough to scratch glass

Quartz   Quartz (SiO_2) crystals when well formed are six-sided prisms and pyramids that show no cleavage. They are colorless or milky, often gray, pink, or violet because of impurities, have a glassy luster, and are hard enough to scratch glass and feldspar. They occur in many kinds of rock, appear as veins, and often form aggregates of well-formed crystals on the sides of cavities. Clear quartz (rock crystal) is used in jewelry and in optical instruments; smoky quartz, rose quartz, and amethyst are colored varieties used in jewelry.

Feldspar is the most common type of mineral

Feldspar   This is the name of a group of silicate minerals with very similar properties. The two classes of feldspar are a silicate of K and Al called orthoclase and a series of silicates of Na, Ca, and Al collectively called plagioclase. The crystals are rectangular, with blunt-pointed ends; they show good cleavage in two directions approximately at right angles. Their color is white or light shades of gray and pink, sometimes clear. Feldspar is slightly harder than glass, not so hard as quartz. It is the most abundant single constituent of rocks, making up about 60 percent of the total weight of the earth's crust. Pure feldspar is used in the making of porcelain and as a mild abrasive.

Mica splits readily into flat sheets

Mica   The two chief varieties of this familiar mineral are white mica, a silicate of H, K, and Al, and black mica, a silicate of H, K, Al, Mg, and Fe. Mica is easily recognized by its perfect and conspicuous cleavage in one plane; it is a very soft mineral, only a trifle harder than the fingernail. Large sheets of white mica free from impurities are used as insulators in electrical equipment. Figure 14-4 shows the basic structure of mica.

Water molecules fit readily into the layered structure of clay minerals such as kaolin, shown here. When baked, wet clay loses its water content and attains a hard, almost rocklike character due to the formation of silicates that bind together the clay particles. The transformation of clay from a soft, easily shaped material into a permanent one is the basis of such ceramic products as bricks, pottery, and porcelain.

This sample of orthoclase feldspar has darker inclusions of augite. The feldspars consist of three-dimensional assemblies of silicon-oxygen tetrahedra, and augite consists of single chains of these tetrahedra. Ions of such metals as iron, aluminum, magnesium, calcium, and potassium fit readily into the structures of silicate minerals; orthoclase feldspar contains aluminum and potassium ions, for instance. About 60 percent by weight of the earth's crust consists of feldspar.

Calcite, the chief constituent of limestone and marble, consists of calcium carbonate crystals.

The ferromagnesian minerals are dark green to black in color

Ferromagnesian minerals This name refers to a large group of minerals with diverse properties, all of them silicates of iron and magnesium, nearly all dark green to black in color. Olivine is a common example. Most of these minerals contain other metallic elements besides iron and magnesium, for instance calcium. Black mica really belongs to this group, for its composition includes H, K, and Al in addition to Mg and Fe. No general properties of the group besides color and composition can be set down, since the various minerals differ greatly from one another. For our purposes it will be sufficient to remember that the most abundant dark-colored constituents of common rocks belong to this group.

The clay minerals are very soft and absorb water readily

Clay minerals This is a group of closely related minerals that are the chief constituents of clay. All are silicates of H and Al, some with a little Mg, Fe, and K.

They are aggregates of microscopic crystals, white or light-colored when pure, often discolored with iron compounds. They have a dull luster. They are very soft, forming a smooth powder when rubbed between the fingers, have a low density, and absorb water readily. They are distinguished from chalk by softness and lack of effervescence in acids. Kaolin, one of the clay minerals, is an important ingredient in the manufacture of ceramics, paper, paint, and certain plastics.

Limestone and marble are largely calcite

Calcite   Calcite ($CaCO_3$) crystals are hexagonal, somewhat like those of quartz. Unlike quartz they show perfect cleavage in three directions at angles of about 75°, so that fragments of calcite have a characteristic rhombic shape. They are colorless or light in color, with a glassy luster. They are hard enough to scratch mica or the fingernail, but can be scratched by glass or by a knife blade. Calcite dissolves readily in dilute acid with effervescence. Like quartz, calcite is a common mineral of veins and crystal aggregates in cavities. It is the chief constituent of the common rocks limestone and marble and commercially serves as a source of lime for glass, mortar, and cement.

Of these six kinds of rock-forming minerals, we note that five are compounds of silicon and four are silicates. The light-colored silicates all contain aluminum in addition to silicon and oxygen; two of them (feldspar and mica) contain an alkali metal and two of them (mica and clay) contain hydrogen. The dark-colored silicates contain iron and magnesium.

ROCKS

There seems hardly any limit to the variety of rocks on the earth's surface. We find coarse-grained rocks and fine-grained rocks, light rocks and heavy rocks, soft rocks and hard rocks, rocks of all sizes, shapes, and colors. But close study reveals that there is order in this diversity, and a straightforward scheme for classifying rocks according to their origin has been developed:

The three broad types of rock are igneous, sedimentary, and metamorphic

1. *Igneous rocks* are those that have cooled from a molten state. The formation of some igneous rocks can actually be observed, for instance when molten lava cools on the side of a volcano. For others an igneous origin is inferred from their composition and structure. Two-thirds of crustal rocks are igneous.
2. *Sedimentary rocks* consist of materials derived from other rocks and deposited by water, wind, or glacial ice. Some consist of separate rock fragments cemented together; others contain material precipitated from solution in water. Although sedimentary rocks make up only about 8 percent of the crust, three-quarters of surface rocks are of this kind.
3. *Metamorphic rocks* are rocks that have been changed, or metamorphosed, by heat and pressure deep under the earth's surface. The changes may involve the formation of new minerals or simply the recrystallization of minerals already present.

Igneous Rocks

Once molten, now solid

Igneous rocks have solidified from an originally molten state

Igneous rocks typically have irregular grains that are randomly arranged with intertwinings and embayments. This is to be expected in a mass of crystals that grew together and interfered with one another's development. The principal constituents of these rocks are always minerals that contain silicon: quartz, feldspar, mica, and the ferromagnesians.

Obsidian is a glassy rock of volcanic origin

The siliceous liquids from which igneous rocks form are thick and viscous, much like molten glass. Sometimes, in fact, molten lava has the right composition and cools rapidly enough to form a natural glass—the black, shiny rock called *obsidian*. Usually, however, cooling is slow enough to allow crystalline minerals to form. If cooling is fairly rapid and if the molten material is highly viscous, the resulting rock may consist of tiny crystals or partly of crystals and partly of glass. If cooling is extremely slow, mineral grains have an opportunity to grow large and a coarse-grained rock is formed. The grain size of an igneous rock, therefore, reveals something about its history and gives us one basis for classification.

Mineral composition provides a convenient means of further classification. Nearly all igneous rocks contain feldspar and one or more of the ferromagnesian minerals; many contain quartz as well. A division of igneous rocks based on relative amounts of these three mineral types is shown in Table 14-1. Thus a coarse-grained rock containing quartz, feldspar, and black mica is granite; a fine-grained rock with no quartz and with feldspar in excess of the dark constituents is andesite, and so on. Many more igneous rocks are known, but the six in the table are the most important.

TABLE 14-1
Some Igneous Rocks.
(These have solidified from a molten state.)

Mineral composition	Coarse-grained rocks (intrusive)	Fine-grained rocks (extrusive)
Quartz Feldspar Ferromagnesian minerals	Granite	Rhyolite
No quartz Feldspar predominant Ferromagnesian minerals	Diorite	Andesite
No quartz Feldspar Ferromagnesian minerals predominant	Gabbro	Basalt

Obsidian is a glassy rock of volcanic origin.

Columnar basalt near Haledon, New Jersey. Basalt is a dark, fine-grained rock that emerged molten from the earth's interior and solidified on the surface.

The faces of four American presidents (Washington, Jefferson, Theodore Roosevelt, and Lincoln) carved in the granite of Mt. Rushmore, South Dakota. Granite is a coarse-grained igneous rock, generally light in color, in which quartz and feldspar are abundant.

This classification is convenient for several reasons:

1. Grain size and usually mineral composition can be determined from inspection in the field. Except for a few fine-grained types, a rock can be named without detailed laboratory study.

2. Even if a rock is too fine for its mineral content to be easily determined, its color often shows its place in the table. Granite and rhyolite, which contain only a little ferromagnesian material, are nearly always light-colored; gabbro and basalt, with abundant ferromagnesian minerals, are characteristically dark; diorite and andesite usually have intermediate shades.

Fine-grained igneous rocks have cooled quickly, coarse-grained ones have cooled slowly

3. Grain size usually gives an indication not only of the rate of cooling but also of the environment in which a rock was cooled. Sufficiently rapid cooling to give fine-grained rocks occurs most commonly when molden lava reaches the earth's surface from a volcano and spreads out in a thin flow exposed to the atmosphere. Since fine grain size usually betrays volcanic origin, rhyolite, andesite, and basalt are often called *volcanic* or *extrusive* rocks.

Coarse-grained rocks, on the other hand, have cooled sufficiently slowly for large crystals to have formed, which must have occurred well beneath the earth's surface. Such rocks are now exposed to view only because erosion has carried away the material that once covered them. Since these rocks do not reach the surface as liquids but are intruded into spaces occupied by other rocks, they are often called *intrusive* rocks.

4. The change in mineral composition from top to bottom in Table 14-1 roughly parallels a steady change in chemical composition. Granite and rhyolite are relatively rich in silicon and aluminum; gabbro and basalt contain abundant iron and magnesium.

Sedimentary Rocks

Compacted sediments or precipitates from solution

Most sedimentary rocks are compacted sediments, a few consist of precipitates from solution

Sediments laid down by wind, water, or ice can be consolidated into rock by the weight of overlying deposits and by the gradual cementing of their grains with material deposited from underground water. The resulting rocks usually have distinct, somewhat rounded grains that have not grown together like the crystals of igneous rocks. A few sedimentary rocks, however, consist of intergrowing mineral grains formed by precipitation from solution in water.

Since sediments are normally deposited in layers, the majority of sedimentary rocks have a banded appearance owing to slight differences in color or grain size from one layer to the next. Sedimentary rocks may often be recognized at a glance by the presence of fossils — remains of plants or animals buried with the sediments as they were laid down.

Sedimentary rocks may be divided into two groups according to the nature of the original sediments:

1. *Fragmental* (or *clastic*) *rocks* that consist of the fragments and decomposition products of other rocks
2. *Precipitates* formed from material once dissolved in water and deposited either as a chemical precipitate or as the shells and bone fragments of dead organisms

The more abundant rock varieties in each group are listed in Table 14-2.

Fragmental rocks

The three fragmental rocks are distinguished by their grain size. *Conglomerate* is cemented gravel whose fragments may have any composition and any size

TABLE 14-2
Some Sedimentary Rocks.
(These are compacted sediments or precipitates.)

Group	Type	Constituents
Fragmental rocks	Conglomerate	Rock fragments
	Sandstone	Quartz usually most abundant
	Shale	Clay minerals
Chemical and biochemical precipitates	Chert	Microcrystalline quartz
	Limestone	Calcite

from that of small pebbles to large boulders. Conglomerate grades into *sandstone* as fragment size decreases. Sand grains may consist of many different minerals, but quartz is generally the most abundant. The hardness of sandstone and conglomerate depends largely on how well their grains are cemented together. Some varieties crumble easily; others, especially those with silica as the cementing material, are among the toughest of rocks. *Shale* is consolidated mud or silt, a soft rock usually composed of thin layers. Its chief constituents are one or more of the clay minerals.

Limestone

Limestone is a fine-grained rock that consists chiefly of calcite. It may be formed either as a chemical precipitate or by the consolidation of shell fragments. Like calcite in larger crystals, limestone is only moderately hard and effervesces readily in acid. Small amounts of impurities may give the rock almost any color. *Chalk* is a loosely consolidated variety of limestone, often made up mainly of the shells of tiny, one-celled animals.

Tilted strata of shale near Goshen, New York. Shale is a soft sedimentary rock that has consolidated from mud deposits.

Flint, a type of chert, consists largely of microcrystalline quartz crystals and hence is hard and durable. Many Indian arrowheads were made from flint.

Limestone cliffs near Schenectady, New York. Some limestones originate as precipitates from solution, others have consolidated from shell fragments.

Chert

Most Indian arrowheads are made either of the igneous rock obsidian or the sedimentary rock *chert,* both prized among primitive peoples for their hardness and the sharpness of their edges when broken. The chief mineral constituent of chert is microcrystalline quartz. Two familiar varieties of this rock are *flint* and *jasper.* Fragments of chert show the same sharp edges and smooth, concave surfaces as broken quartz or obsidian, but the surfaces have a characteristic waxy luster. Chert may have almost any color; often a single specimen shows bands and pockets of several different colors. Not nearly as abundant as the other sedimentary rocks just described, chert is nevertheless common in pebble beds and gravel deposits because its hardness and resistance to chemical decay enable it to survive rough treatment from streams, waves, and glaciers.

Metamorphic Rocks

Formed from other rocks by heat and/or pressure

Metamorphic rocks are formed from sedimentary and igneous rocks under the influence of heat and pressure

The enormous pressures and high temperatures below the earth's surface can profoundly change sedimentary and igneous rocks that become deeply buried. Minerals stable at the surface are often unstable under the new conditions and may react to form different substances. Other minerals retain their identities but their crystals increase in size. Hot liquids permeating the rocks may add some new materials and dissolve out others. So many kinds of change are possible that no general rules can be set down for readily distinguishing metamorphic rocks from others.

Many metamorphic rocks are characterized by a property called *foliation*, which means the arrangement of flat or elongated mineral grains in parallel layers. This effect is caused by extreme pressure in one direction, with the mineral grains growing out sideward as the rock is squeezed. Foliated rocks always contain a mineral (like mica) that occurs in thin flakes or a mineral (like some of the ferromagnesian group) that occurs in long needles. Rocks consisting only of minerals like quartz, feldspar, or calcite ordinarily do not show foliation, since these minerals have little tendency to grow larger in one direction than in another, even under pressure. Foliation gives a rock a banded or layered appearance, and, when it is broken, the rock tends to split along the bands. Layering is also characteristic of sedimentary rocks, but in them the layering is caused by slight variations in color or grain size; layering in metamorphic rocks is due to the lining up of mineral grains.

The commoner metamorphic rocks may be classified according to the presence or absence of foliation, as in Table 14-3.

Slate is produced by the low-temperature metamorphism of shale with the unstable clay minerals forming tiny flakes of mica. Although the individual flakes are too small to be seen, mica is responsible for the shiny surfaces produced

Many metamorphic rocks are foliated, which gives them a banded or layered appearance and shiny or spangly surfaces

Slate

TABLE 14-3

Some Metamorphic Rocks.

(These have been altered by heat and/or pressure since originally formed.)

Group	Type	Constituents	Origin
Foliated rocks	Slate	Mica and usually quartz, both in microscopic grains	Shale
	Schist	Mica and/or a ferromagnesian mineral, usually quartz also	Shale or fine-grained igneous rock
Foliated and banded	Gneiss	Quartz, feldspar, mica	Various
Unfoliated rocks	Marble	Chiefly calcite	Limestone
	Quartzite	Chiefly quartz	Sandstone

Gneiss is the most abundant metamorphic rock because it can be formed from a wide variety of sedimentary, igneous, and other metamorphic rocks. This sample was metamorphosed from granite and has the banded appearance characteristic of gneiss.

Schist

Gneiss

Marble and quartzite

whenever slate is split along its foliation. Slate is harder than shale, finely foliated, usually black or dark gray but sometimes lighter colored.

Schist is formed from shale by higher temperatures or from fine-grained igneous rocks. In it the mineral grains responsible for the foliation are large enough to be visible, giving the foliation surfaces a characteristic spangled appearance. Schist does not split so easily along the foliation as slate does, and its surfaces are rougher.

Gneiss is a coarse-grained rock formed under conditions of high temperature and pressure from almost any other rock except pure limestone and pure quartz sandstone. Its composition naturally depends on the nature of the original rock, but quartz, feldspar, and mica are the commonest minerals. In appearance gneiss resembles granite, except for its banding and foliation.

The metamorphism of pure limestone and pure quartz sandstone is a relatively simple process. Since each consists of a single mineral of simple composition, heat and pressure can produce no new substances but instead cause the growth and interlocking of crystals of calcite and quartz. Thus limestone becomes *marble,* a rock composed of calcite in crystals large enough to be easily visible, and sandstone becomes the hard rock *quartzite.* Quartzite sometimes resembles sandstone in appearance, but its grains are so firmly intergrown that it splits across separate grains when it is broken, giving smooth fracture surfaces in contrast with the rough surfaces of sandstone.

The classification of rocks is not as clearcut as, for example, the classification of the elements. In nature there are seldom sharp boundaries between different rock types. A medium-grained igneous rock with no quartz and an abundance of feldspar might be hard to classify as either a diorite or an andesite; some limestones contain so much clay that they may be called either shaly limestones or limy shales; there is no precise point in the metamorphic process when a fine-grained rock ceases to be a shale and becomes a slate. But in spite of these occasional

Quartzite is a hard rock formed by the metamorphism of sandstone; it consists largely of quartz, hence its name.

ambiguities the classification is valuable because it organizes our knowledge about various rocks. When we identify a rock as schist, for instance, we know at once something about its origin and its general properties. The classification summarizes basic information we will need in the study of geological processes.

SOIL

Soil consists largely of rock fragments, clay minerals, and partly decomposed plant matter called humus

Though the bulk of the earth's crust is solid rock, what we see on that part of the surface not covered by water is chiefly soil with only occasional outcrops of bedrock. Soil originates in the weathering of rock, a complex disintegration process whose result is a coat of rock fragments and clay minerals mixed with varying amounts of organic matter.

Any type of rock — igneous, sedimentary, or metamorphic — may form the parent material of a soil. Typically the particles of rock vary in size down to microscopic fineness and are intimately mixed with dark, partly decomposed plant debris called *humus*. The humus content decreases with depth, and it is customary to call the uppermost layer of soil, which is richest in humus, the *topsoil*, and the underlying layer of accumulated rock fragments the *subsoil*.

A great many factors are involved in the production of soil, including microorganisms such as bacteria and fungi which are responsible for the decay of plant and animal residues and are important in maintaining the nitrogen content of soil. A significant fraction of the organic material in soil, in fact, consists of the bodies,

Cross section of a typical soil. The darkening toward the top is due to the presence of humus. Depths are in feet.

living and dead, of these microorganisms. Even so lowly a creature as the worm plays a vital role in mixing together the various soil constituents.

Types of Soil

Some are more fertile than others

A wide variety of soil types have been identified, most of which fall into the four broad classes of podzol, latosol, chernozem, and desert soils (Fig. 14-5).

The four chief classes of soil are podzol, latosol, chernozem, and desert

1. *Podzol soils* are mainly found in cool, moist climates under coniferous or partly coniferous forests, as in most of northern Europe and Canada. They are gray in color because most of the iron and other soluble constituents have been washed away ("leached out"). Such soils are acid, which discourages the work of earthworms and other organisms to such an extent that a sharp line separates a thin upper layer of partly decayed plant matter from a mineral layer underneath that has little organic content. Much of central Europe and the eastern

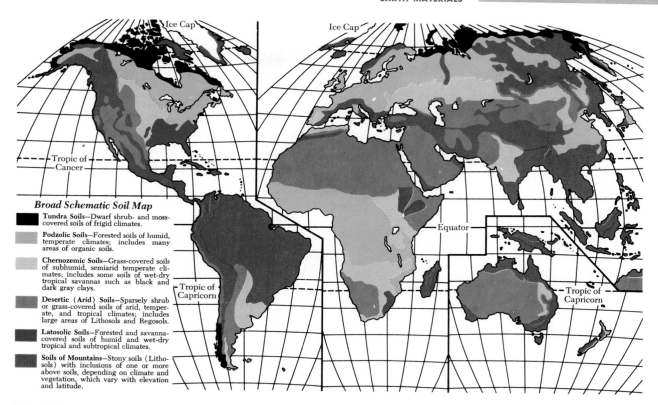

Broad Schematic Soil Map

Tundra Soils—Dwarf shrub- and moss-covered soils of frigid climates.

Podzolic Soils—Forested soils of humid, temperate climates; includes many areas of organic soils.

Chernozemic Soils—Grass-covered soils of subhumid, semiarid temperate climates; includes some soils of wet-dry tropical savannas such as black and dark gray clays.

Desertic (Arid) Soils—Sparsely shrub or grass-covered soils of arid, temperate, and tropical climates; includes large areas of Lithosols and Regosols.

Latosolic Soils—Forested and savanna-covered soils of humid and wet-dry tropical and subtropical climates.

Soils of Mountains—Stony soils (Lithosols) with inclusions of one or more above soils, depending on climate and vegetation, which vary with elevation and latitude.

FIG. 14-5
Principal soils around the world. Localized bodies of soil, for instance, the alluvial soils along such major rivers as the Mississippi, Amazon, Ganges, and Yangtze, are not shown.

United States is covered with gray-brown, red, and yellow podzolic soils which owe their color and agricultural productivity in part to a smaller degree of acidity, which inhibits leaching and is more favorable for the flourishing of soil organisms.

2. *Latosol soils* are typical of rain forests in hot, humid climates, and cover much of Brazil, west and central Africa, and southeast Asia. Latosols are rich in iron and aluminum oxides and are red or yellow in color. They are very porous and have been largely leached of plant nutrients required for cultivation. Driven by poverty and overpopulation, countries such as Brazil are clearing rain forest at a rate of 1 or 2 percent of the world's total per year in an effort to turn it into farmland. The effort is usually in vain because most latosol soils are good only for a few harvests, after which little can grow on them again. A large region of Assam, in India, that is completely barren today was once a thriving rain forest that was destroyed in this way, for instance.

3. *Chernozem* is a Russian word meaning "black earth," and the chernozem soils are indeed black or dark brown in color. They are found in temperate, subhumid climates and were formed under vegetation of prairie grasses rather than forests. Leaching is less effective under such conditions, and mineral constitu-

ents essential for plant growth are largely retained. Southern Russia, a north–south belt in the central United States, and parts of South America, India, Canada, China, and Australia have soils of this kind, which are extremely fertile.

4. *Desert soils* are of various kinds but, being formed in arid regions with little vegetation, are all light in color because organic material is lacking. There is an abundance of soluble minerals, and sometimes a crust of alkaline and salt materials is present on or just under the surface. The richness in soluble minerals partly compensates for the absence of humus, and many desert soils can be cultivated with proper irrigation.

Soil Nitrogen

A vital component

Nitrogen is essential for plant and animal life

The amino acids of which proteins are composed are nitrogen compounds, and since the solid flesh of our bodies is largely protein, nitrogen is one of the most important elements to us. The ultimate source of all our protein is plants, although much of it comes to us secondhand in such animal proteins as those in meat, eggs, and milk. Plants in turn manufacture their proteins from simpler nitrogen compounds which enter their roots from the soil in which they grow.

Green plants cannot directly use the nitrogen of the atmosphere

Green plants are unable to utilize the stable molecules of free nitrogen in the air around them. All their nitrogen, and therefore all the nitrogen that goes into animal bodies as well, comes from nitrogen compounds in the soil. The nitrogen molecules we breathe can do us no good either, for the atoms in these molecules of the free element are held together by bonds which our body processes are unable to break. Like a shipwrecked mariner surrounded by sea water but dying of

Pure ammonia (NH_3) is sometimes applied directly to the soil to supply it with the nitrogen that plants need to manufacture proteins.

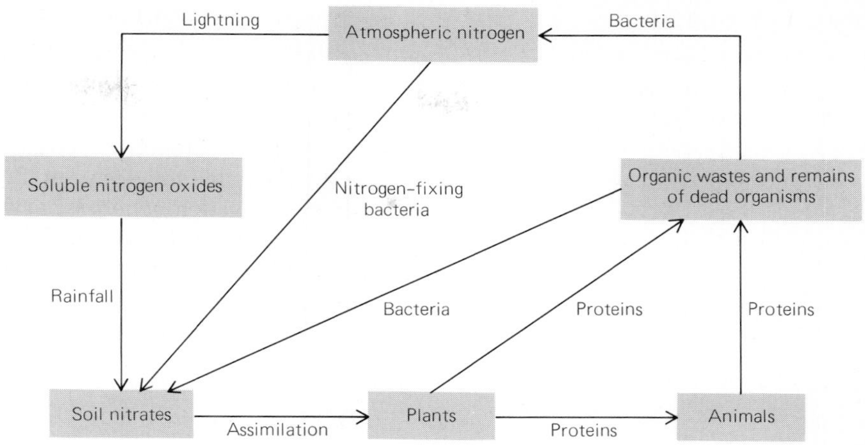

FIG. 14-6
The nitrogen cycle on land.

Atmospheric nitrogen is made
accessible to plants by bacterial
action and by thunderstorms

thirst, humankind is surrounded by an ocean of nitrogen but would perish except for the combined nitrogen which plants can absorb through their roots.

The formation of plant proteins steadily removes nitrogen compounds from the soil. Just as steadily, fixed nitrogen is returned to the soil by the decay of animal excrement and of dead plants and animals, with the nitrogen of proteins being converted by decay into ammonia and ammonium salts which are then oxidized to nitrates by soil bacteria. But the replenishment is never complete: some nitrogen is lost permanently from the soil by solution of nitrates and ammonium salts in streams and rainwash, and by bacteria which decompose nitrates into free nitrogen.

Nature makes good these losses in two ways. Another kind of soil bacteria, the "nitrogen-fixing" bacteria, have the ability to break down the stable nitrogen molecule and to manufacture nitrates from the atoms. Also, electric discharges during thunderstorms cause some atmospheric nitrogen and oxygen to combine into nitrogen oxides, which are carried to the soil in solution in rainwater. So in nature nitrogen goes through a continuous cycle (Fig. 14-6) that keeps the amount of fixed nitrogen in the soil approximately constant.

We have drastically disturbed this natural cycle. Much of the protein that enters our bodies is not returned to the soil but instead is dumped as sewage into the oceans. The use of plant material and manure for fires in primitive areas further contributes to the conversion of combined nitrogen into free nitrogen. To be sure, manure is still used as fertilizer in some regions and legumes (such as beans) on which nitrogen-fixing bacteria grow are widely cultivated, but artificial fertilizers have become essential as sources of nitrogen for a large part of the world's agriculture.

WITHIN THE EARTH

Earthquake waves provide
information on the earth's interior

The earth's solid crust together with the atmosphere and oceans above it are directly accessible to our instruments, and we may legitimately hope one day to understand their structures and behavior in detail. The interior of the earth, however, is beyond our direct reach and, with the exception of shafts that ultimately may be sunk deep enough to barely get through the thinnest part of the crust, is almost certain to remain untouched. What we need is some kind of indirect probe, and it has turned out that the waves sent out by earthquakes are ideal for this purpose. Largely through the analysis of earthquake waves we now know a great deal about the earth's interior, which is hardly less remote than the most distant star, and we are continually learning more.

Earthquakes

When our planet trembles

An earthquake, the most destructive of natural phenomena, consists of rapid vibratory motions of rock near the earth's surface. A single shock usually lasts no more than a few seconds, though severe quakes may last for as much as 3 minutes. Even in such brief times the damage done may be immense. The accelerations associated with the vibrations rather than the actual displacements themselves are responsible for the damage. An acceleration of $1 \text{ m/s}^2 - 0.1g$, a tenth of the acceleration of gravity — is more than many ordinary buildings can withstand, and a major earthquake may produce accelerations several times larger. Widespread fires often follow earthquakes in inhabited regions since broken water mains hinder their control, and landslides are common.

Earthquakes give no obvious warning, though a variety of subtle effects show promise as signs that a quake is about to occur. Usually the first shock is the most severe, with disturbances of lessening intensity following at intervals for days or months afterward. A major earthquake may be felt over many thousands of square kilometers, but its destructiveness is limited to a much smaller area.

Most earthquakes are due to rock
movement along a fracture surface

The great majority of earthquakes are caused by the sudden displacement of crustal blocks along fracture lines. When the stresses developed within the crust in a certain region become too great for the rock to support, a slippage occurs that sends out the waves that are characteristic of an earthquake. The event responsible for an earthquake typically involves an area within the crust some tens of km across located within a few km of the surface, but in a fair number of cases depths of up to several hundred km below the crust have been established.

Seismographs record earthquake
vibrations

Sensitive instruments called *seismographs* can respond to the vibrations of even distant earthquakes. Seismographs of different types record vertical and horizontal movements, as shown in Figs. 14-7 and 14-8. A vertical seismograph and two horizontal ones, one for the north–south direction and the other for the east–west direction, are needed at each observatory. Several hundred seismolog-

FIG. 14-7
The principle of the vertical seismograph. The suspended mass has a very long period of oscillation, hence it remains very nearly stationary in space as the box and scale move up and down when earthquake waves arrive. Only vertical movements of the earth's surface are recorded by this instrument.

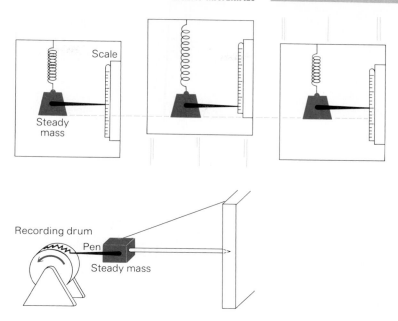

FIG. 14-8
A horizontal pendulum seismograph. This instrument responds to horizontal movements of the earth's surface.

Richter scale of earthquake magnitude

ical stations are in operation around the world, and the data they obtain are routinely compared and correlated. It is possible to establish from such data where a given earthquake has occurred and something about how much energy it has released.

Earthquake magnitudes are often expressed on the *Richter scale*. Each step of 1 on this scale represents a change in vibration amplitude of a factor of 10 and a change in energy release of a factor of about 30. Thus an earthquake of magnitude 5 produces vibrations 10 times larger than a quake of magnitude 4 and releases 30 times more energy. An earthquake of magnitude 0 is barely detectable; if the energy involved could be concentrated, it would be just about enough to blow up a tree stump. An earthquake of magnitude 3 would be felt by people living in the region, and some damage to structures would occur when the magnitude is up to 4 or 5. Significant destruction is likely if the magnitude is 6 or more. The energy given off in a magnitude 8.7 earthquake, the strongest observed thus far, is about double the energy content of the world's yearly production of coal and oil. The Alaska earthquake of 1964 was nearly this severe, the San Francisco earthquake of 1906 somewhat less so.

Of the million or so earthquakes per year strong enough to be experienced as such, only a small proportion liberate enough energy to do serious damage. About 15 really violent earthquakes occur each year on the average. When one of them happens to involve a densely populated urban area, the effects can be appalling: 655,000 people are estimated to have died in the 1976 earthquake in China's Hopeh Province as buildings collapsed around them.

This wing of San Fernando Veteran's Hospital in California collapsed in the earthquake of February 9, 1971. Many patients and hospital workers were trapped in the wreckage and several died. It is not difficult to design structures that can withstand moderate earthquakes.

Severe earthquakes tend to occur in certain regions

Regions in which severe earthquakes are comparatively frequent include the mountain chains that fringe the Pacific and a broad belt that extends from the Mediterranean basin across southern Asia to China. Major earthquakes have occurred sporadically elsewhere, but by far the greatest number have been concentrated in these zones. In or near the earthquake belts lie most of the world's active volcanoes — which, as we shall see in Chap. 15, is no coincidence. Figure 14-9 is a map prepared by the U.S. Coast and Geodetic Survey that shows where earthquakes may be expected in the United States in the next 100 years. Proper design

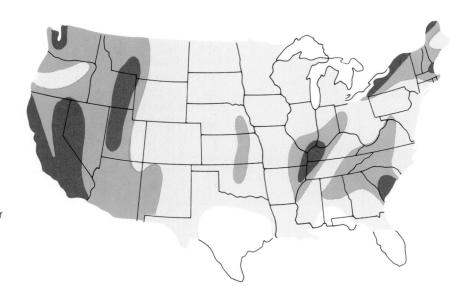

FIG. 14-9
Earthquakes are expected to occur in the regions of the United States shown in color during the next 100 years. The darker the color, the greater the probable damage.

and construction can prevent much of the destruction that accompanies earthquakes, but of course neither the foresight nor the money required is always available.

Earthquake prediction seems to be a goal not beyond reach. Thousands, perhaps millions of lives would be saved if warnings of big quakes could be given in time. Seismologists from the United States, the Soviet Union, and China have already correctly forecast several earthquakes, including the one that devastated Haicheng, a Chinese city whose population of 100,000 was evacuated a few hours before it occurred in 1975.

The buildup of stresses in a region that precedes an earthquake seems to slow down the speed of seismic P waves (see next section) through the region, to increase the electrical resistance of the underlying rocks there, and to affect the local geomagnetic field. Then, shortly before the quake takes place, the seismic wave speed returns to normal. What may be happening is that pressure on the rocks leads to a great many tiny cracks which in turn cause the observed initial effects. Groundwater then seeps into the cracks, which restores the wave speed while also weakening the rocks and thus promoting the disruption that causes the quake. If this picture is correct, then the possibility is opened for earthquake control: by pumping water out of deep holes drilled in appropriate places along an active fault and pumping water into other such holes, minor earthquakes could be induced that would release the accumulated stresses in the fault and prevent a major quake.

Earthquake Waves

They move both through the earth's interior and along its surface

Three kinds of waves are sent out by the vibrations that accompany an earthquake:

1. *Primary (or P) waves* are longitudinal waves that involve back-and-forth vibrations of particles of matter in the same direction as that in which the waves travel. P waves are essentially pressure waves, like sound waves.
2. *Secondary (or S waves)* are transverse waves that involve vibrations of particles of matter perpendicularly to the direction in which the waves travel. The waves produced by shaking a stretched string are similar to S waves. Both P and S waves are body waves that travel through the earth's interior. S waves cannot occur in a liquid, though P waves can.
3. *Surface (or L) waves* involve orbital motions of particles of matter (like water waves) and are limited to the earth's surface.

P and S waves are illustrated in Fig. 14-10, L waves in Fig. 6-1. An easy way to distinguish between P and S waves is to think of P waves as "push-pull" vibrations and S waves as "shakes." Earthquake P waves usually occur 2 or 3 s apart, S waves 10 to 15 s apart, and L waves 10 to 60 s apart.

FIG. 14-10
Two kinds of earthquake waves. The P waves are longitudinal pressure waves, condensations and rarefactions like those in sound. The S waves are transverse waves, like waves in a taut string.

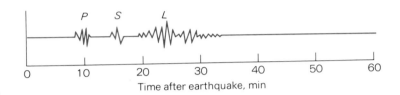

FIG. 14-11
A seismogram of waves from an earthquake that occurred about 5000 km from the recording station.

P waves are the fastest, L waves are the slowest

A simple seismogram is shown in Fig. 14-11. P waves are the fastest, and they accordingly arrive first at a seismograph station when an earthquake occurs somewhere. The S waves, which are slower, arrive next. The surface L waves, which have to travel around the earth instead of through it, appear last. However, their vibrations may be the strongest, particularly when the distance is no more than a few thousand km. The speeds of P and S waves range from $5\frac{1}{2}$ to 14 km/s and from 3 to 7 km/s, respectively. L waves travel along the surface at the more or less uniform speed of 4 km/s.

Core, Mantle, and Crust

The structure of the earth

Earthquake waves are refracted at discontinuities within the earth

Earthquake P and S waves do not travel in straight lines within the earth for two reasons. The first is that the speeds of both kinds of waves increase with depth, so that their paths are somewhat curved owing to refraction. The second reason is more spectacular: there are layers of materials having different properties within the earth. When an earthquake wave traveling in one layer reaches the boundary, or *discontinuity*, that separates it from another layer in which its speed is different, refraction also occurs. Now, however, the refracted wave shows an abrupt change in direction, unlike the more gradual change due to speed variations within each layer (Fig. 14-12).

Shadow zones

Let us suppose a severe earthquake occurs somewhere. We consult the various seismological observatories and find that most of them — never all — have recorded P waves from this event. Curiously, the stations that did not detect any P waves lie along a band from 103° to 143° (11,400 to 15,900 km) distant from the earthquake. We would find, if we consulted the records of other earthquakes, that no matter where they took place, similar *shadow zones* existed. This is the clue

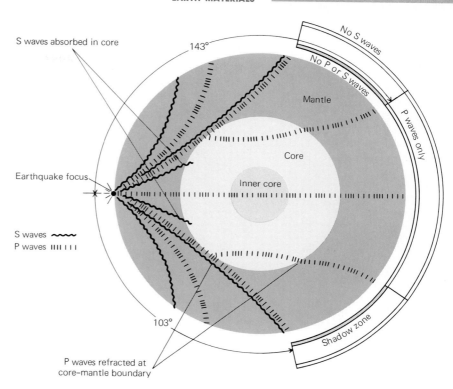

S waves absorbed in core

143°

No S waves

No P or S waves

Mantle

P waves only

Core

Inner core

Earthquake focus

S waves ～～～
P waves ⅢⅠⅠⅠ

103°

Shadow zone

P waves refracted at
core–mantle boundary

FIG. 14-12
How earthquake waves travel
through the earth. The existence of
a shadow zone between 103° and
143° where neither P nor S waves
arrive is evidence for a central core.
The inability of S waves to get
through the core suggests that it is
liquid.

The earth has a liquid core and an
outer solid mantle

Transverse S waves cannot pass
through the outer core, hence it must
be liquid

that confirmed an early suspicion that the earth's interior is made up of concentric layers.

Figure 14-12 shows why this conclusion is necessary. In the picture the earth is divided into a central *core* and a surrounding *mantle*. P waves leaving the earthquake are able to go directly through the mantle only to a limited region slightly larger than a hemisphere. Those P waves that reach the core are bent sharply toward the center of the earth, and, when they emerge, they are 4500 km or more away from those P waves that just barely cleared the core. From an accurate analysis of the available data, it was found that the mantle is 2900 km (1800 mi) thick, which means that the core has a radius of 3470 km (2160 mi), over half the earth's total radius. However, the core constitutes less than 20 percent of the earth's volume.

Supporting the above finding and giving further information about the nature of the core is the behavior of the S waves, which require a solid medium for their passage. These, it is found, cannot get through the core at all. The only explanation is that the core is in liquid form. This would account not only for the absence of S waves in the core but also for the marked changes in the speed of P waves when they enter and leave the core.

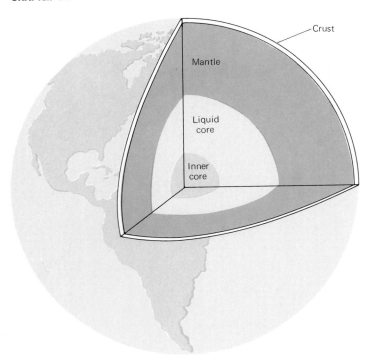

FIG. 14-13
Structure of the earth. The mantle constitutes 80 percent of the earth's volume and about 67 percent of its mass.

The inner core is believed to be solid

The crust is relatively thin

Sensitive seismographs are able to detect faint traces of P waves in the shadow zones, which makes sense if within the liquid core is a smaller solid inner core. This inner core is believed to have a radius of 1390 km (863 mi). Thus the earth's interior has the structure shown in Fig. 14-13.

From observations first made on a 1909 earthquake it became clear that there is a distinct difference between the uppermost layers of the earth and the underlying mantle. The surface of demarcation is known as the *Mohorovicic discontinuity,* after its discoverer, and is considered to be the lower boundary of the crust. Under the oceans the crust is seldom much more than 5 km thick; under the continents it averages about 35 km, and it may reach 70 km under some mountain ranges (Fig. 14-14).

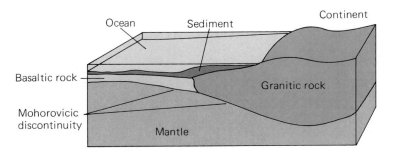

FIG. 14-14
General structure of the earth's crust.

Composition

A mantle of rock, a core of molten iron

The upper mantle may resemble the igneous rocks eclogite and peridotite

In the absence of a hole over 6000 km deep, anything said about the composition of the earth's interior can be no more than an educated guess, but a great deal of evidence supports the guesses that have been made. In the case of the mantle, most studies point to a material similar to such igneous rocks as eclogite and peridotite, which are composed mainly of ferromagnesian minerals. Some of the considerations that have led to this belief are as follows:

1. Only dense rocks such as these transmit seismic waves at the speeds found in the mantle.
2. These rocks are similar in composition to the basalt of the lower crust but are sufficiently different to be able to give rise to the observed Mohorovicic discontinuity in seismic-wave transmission between crust and mantle.
3. Most volcanic magmas come from the upper mantle, and their composition is consistent with an origin in eclogite or peridotite.
4. Diamonds can form only under conditions of high temperature and pressure, such as are found in the mantle but not in the crust, and eclogite and peridotite are common in diamond-bearing rock formations which must have originated in the mantle.

Diamond-bearing rock about to be blasted out in a mine several miles deep near Pretoria in South Africa. Such rock originates in the mantle where temperatures and pressures are high enough for diamonds to be formed.

5. Stony meteorites consist chiefly of the minerals olivine and pyroxene, just as these rocks do, and it is an attractive notion that both the mantle and stony meteorites had the same origin in the early solar system.

Crystal structures change with depth in the mantle

Deep in the mantle pressures of million of pounds per square inch squeeze minerals into crystal structures that are the most compact possible. Olivine, for instance, is known to occur in two forms, the normal one of the crust and another whose particles are packed together in an especially tight arrangement. The more open variety is probably present in the upper mantle, the denser variety lower down. In the innermost part of the mantle, minerals have probably separated into very dense oxides of silicon, iron, and magnesium that occupy even less space.

The density of the earth as a whole is about twice that of surface rocks, hence the core must be very dense and is probably iron

Now we come to the liquid core. An important clue to its nature comes from the average density of the earth. As we found in Chap. 2, the earth's mass is 6.0×10^{24} kg. Since its volume is 1.1×10^{21} m³, the average density of the earth is

$$\text{Density} = \frac{\text{mass}}{\text{volume}} = \frac{6.0 \times 10^{24} \text{ kg}}{1.1 \times 10^{21} \text{ m}^3} = 5.5 \times 10^3 \text{ kg/m}^3$$

This is about twice the average density of the rocks at the earth's surface. The material of the mantle is only moderately denser than surface rocks, so that the core must be very heavy indeed. There are several clues that point to iron as the logical candidate. It has almost the right density, it is in the liquid state at the estimated pressure and temperature of the core, and it is a rather abundant element in the universe generally. Furthermore, iron is a good conductor of electricity, which is necessary in order to explain the earth's magnetism (see below).

Because those meteorites that contain iron also contain some nickel, a good guess is that there is nickel in the core also. Recently it has become clear that the core is actually a little less dense than would be the case if it were composed exclusively of iron or iron and nickel. Therefore a certain proportion of some lighter element, perhaps silicon or sulfur, may be present as well. But there seems little doubt that molten iron is the chief ingredient of the core. As for the solid inner core, the kernel of the earth, many geophysicists believe it to be crystalline iron or iron-nickel.

Temperature

Radioactivity heats the earth

Temperature increases rapidly with depth

Whether or not the fires of Hell lie beneath the surface of the earth, there is no doubt it is hot enough there to satisfy the most critical requirements for this region. Many lines of evidence point to the existence of such high temperatures. The most direct comes from simply taking a thermometer down into the deepest mines and wells: on the average, the temperature goes up by about 1°C for every 35 m of depth. If this rate of increase continued all the way down to the earth's center, the temperature would have to rise to 200,000°C — which is absurd, of course, but nevertheless an indication that considerable temperatures may be expected there.

Heat flow from the earth's interior powers geologic change

One clue to the temperatures inside the earth and their cause is the flow of heat outward. Measurements of this flow have been made in various locations, and it has been found to be almost the same all over the earth. The total amount of heat evolved per year is immense, about 100 times greater than the energy involved in such geological events as volcanoes and earthquakes. There is plenty of heat to spare to account for mountain building and other deformations that occur in the crust. In fact, the geological history of the earth is predominantly a consequence of the steady heat streaming through its outer layers.

Temperatures within the earth are believed to increase fairly rapidly in the mantle from less than 1000°C at its top to perhaps 3000°C at the core boundary. The rise is slower in the core, and the temperature at the center of the earth is estimated to be in the neighborhood of 4200°C, although this figure is far from certain.

Radioactivity is mainly responsible for heating the earth's interior

Part of the earth's heat is a relic of its early history, but most of it comes from radioactive uranium, thorium, and potassium isotopes. The earth is believed to have come into being 4.5 billion years ago as a cold aggregate of smaller bodies of metallic iron and silicate minerals that had been circling the sun. Heat due to radioactivity accumulated in the interior of the infant earth and in time caused partial melting. The influence of gravity then caused the iron to migrate inward to form the core while the lighter silicates rose to form the mantle. Today most of the earth's radioactivity is concentrated in the crust and upper mantle, where the heat it produces escapes through the surface and cannot collect to remelt the rest of the mantle or the inner core.

Geomagnetism

Electric currents in the core seem to be responsible

Although the earliest description of the compass and its use in navigation that we have was published by Alexander Neckham in 1180, knowledge of the compass seems to have been widespread even further back in antiquity. Until 1600, however, it was believed that this phenomenon had its origin in an attractive force exerted by Polaris, the North Star, on magnetized needles. In that year, Sir William Gilbert, physician to Elizabeth I, wrote of experiments he had performed with spherical pieces of lodestone, a naturally magnetized mineral. By comparing the direction of the magnetic force on a test iron needle at various positions near the lodestone sphere with similar measurements made over the earth's surface by explorers, Gilbert concluded that the earth behaves like a giant magnet — *"magnus magnes ipse est globus terrestris."*

The earth's magnetic field closely resembles the field that would be produced

The geomagnetic field is like that of a bar magnet

by a giant bar magnet located a few hundred km from the earth's center and tilted by 11° from the direction of the earth's axis of rotation. No such magnet can possibly exist, since iron loses its magnetic properties above about 1400°C and temperatures exceed this figure in all but the top few dozen km of the earth. Instead, the field is believed to arise from coupled fluid motions and electric currents in the liquid iron of the core. We recall from Fig. 5-22 that a current in the form of a loop is surrounded by a magnetic field of the same form as that of a bar magnet.

The geomagnetic field has undergone many reversals of direction

In many places rock specimens of different ages have opposite magnetic polarities, and it seems the only explanation in most cases is that the earth's field has reversed itself periodically during the period of formation of the various rocks. In the past 76 million years 171 field reversals are believed to have occurred. Such flip-flops seem consistent with the hypothesis that the field is due to electric currents in the core, since changes may well take place in the patterns of flow in the liquid iron there from time to time.

IMPORTANT TERMS

The earth's outer shell of rock is called its **crust.** Oxygen and silicon are the most abundant elements in the crust. Crystalline **silicates** consist of continuous structures of oxygen and silicon ions, often with metal ions as well, rather than separate molecules. **Minerals** are the separate homogeneous substances of which rocks are composed. The most abundant minerals are silicates; also common are carbonates and oxides. Quartz, feldspar, mica, calcite, and the ferromagnesian and clay minerals are six important kinds of minerals.

Igneous rocks (such as granite and basalt) have cooled from a molten state. **Sedimentary rocks** (such as sandstone and limestone) have consolidated from materials derived from the disintegration or solution of other rocks and deposited by water, wind, or glaciers. **Metamorphic rocks** (such as slate and marble) have been altered by heat and pressure beneath the earth's surface. **Soil** consists of rock fragments mixed with varying amounts of organic matter.

Nearly all **earthquakes** are due to the sudden movement of solid rock along faults near the surface. There are three kinds of earthquake waves: **P waves,** which are longitudinal "push-pull" waves; **S waves,** which are transverse "shake" waves; and **L waves,** which are surface waves analogous to water waves. P waves are the fastest, L waves the slowest.

The analysis of earthquake wave records shows that the earth has a **core** 3470 km in radius that probably consists of molten iron with a small solid inner core; a more-or-less solid ferromagnesian silicate **mantle** 2900 km thick; and a thin **crust** whose thickness averages 35 km under the continents and less than 6 km under the oceans. The **geomagnetic field** resembles that which would be produced by a giant bar magnet located near the earth's center. The field is actually due to electric currents in the molten iron core. The direction of the field has reversed itself many times in the past.

MULTIPLE CHOICE

1. The most abundant element in the earth's crust is
   a. oxygen
   b. nitrogen
   c. silicon
   d. carbon
2. Minerals are
   a. silicon compounds
   b. common types of rock
   c. homogeneous solids of which rocks are composed
   d. always compounds
3. Cleavage, the tendency of certain minerals to split along certain planes, is conspicuous in
   a. quartz
   b. mica
   c. chalk
   d. chert

4. The transparent crystalline form of silica is
  a. quartz
  b. mica
  c. feldspar
  d. calcite

5. The most abundant mineral in the earth's crust is
  a. quartz
  b. mica
  c. feldspar
  d. calcite

6. A mineral that is not a silicate is
  a. quartz
  b. mica
  c. feldspar
  d. calcite

7. The ferromagnesian minerals are usually
  a. transparent
  b. white or pink
  c. bluish
  d. dark green or black

8. Rocks that have been formed by cooling from a molten state are called
  a. igneous rocks
  b. sedimentary rocks
  c. metamorphic rocks
  d. precipitated rocks

9. Rocks that have been altered by heat and pressure beneath the earth's surface are called
  a. igneous rocks
  b. sedimentary rocks
  c. metamorphic rocks
  d. precipitated rocks

10. The majority of surface rocks are
  a. sedimentary
  b. metamorphic
  c. intrusive
  d. extrusive

11. A general characteristic of igneous rocks is
  a. random arrangements of grains
  b. grains laid down in layers
  c. coarse grain structure
  d. fine grain structure

12. A general characteristic of rocks of volcanic origin is
  a. glassy appearance
  b. unusually high silica content
  c. coarse grain structure
  d. fine grain structure

13. Of the following rocks, the one that does not originate in sediments laid down by water, wind, or ice is

  a. marble
  b. conglomerate
  c. shale
  d. sandstone

14. The property many metamorphic rocks exhibit of having flat or elongated mineral grains in parallel layers is called
  a. schist
  b. cleavage
  c. sedimentation
  d. foliation

15. Limestone may be metamorphosed into
  a. marble
  b. quartzite
  c. gneiss
  d. schist

16. Mica is not found in
  a. slate
  b. schist
  c. gneiss
  d. marble

17. An unfoliated metamorphic rock is
  a. slate
  b. schist
  c. gneiss
  d. quartzite

18. The black earth found in temperate, subhumid climates is called
  a. podzol
  b. latosol
  c. chernozem
  d. humus

19. Fixed nitrogen is not added to soil by
  a. lightning discharges
  b. bacteria
  c. animal wastes
  d. earthworms

20. Regions in which earthquakes are frequent are also regions in which
  a. the geomagnetic field is strong
  b. hurricanes are common
  c. volcanoes occur
  d. petroleum is found

21. Each step of 1 on the Richter scale of earthquake magnitude corresponds to a change in energy release of a factor of about
  a. 2
  b. 30
  c. 100
  d. 1000

22. Earthquake P waves

    a. are back-and-forth vibrations like sound waves
    b. are transverse vibrations like waves in a taut string
    c. cannot propagate through the earth's core
    d. travel in straight lines through the earth's interior

23. The earth's crust
    a. has an approximately constant thickness of about 100 m
    b. has an approximately constant thickness of about 5 km
    c. has an approximately constant thickness of about 35 km
    d. varies in thickness from about 5 km under the oceans to about 35 km under the continents

24. The radius of the earth's core is roughly
    a. $\frac{1}{10}$ the earth's radius
    b. $\frac{1}{4}$ the earth's radius
    c. $\frac{1}{2}$ the earth's radius
    d. $\frac{3}{4}$ the earth's radius

25. The reasons why the earth's core is believed to be largely molten iron do not include
    a. the magnetic properties of iron
    b. the electrical conductivity of iron
    c. the density of iron
    d. the relative abundance of iron in the universe

26. Most of the heat of the earth's interior is believed to
    a. be left over from its formation
    b. come from radioactive materials
    c. be due to chemical reactions in the core
    d. be provided by solar radiation absorbed by the crust

27. The earth's magnetic field
    a. never changes
    b. has reversed itself many times
    c. is centered exactly at the earth's center
    d. originates in a permanently magnetized iron core

QUESTIONS

1. What is the relationship between rocks and minerals?

2. Which of the following naturally occurring substances are minerals? Diamond, calcite, petroleum, ice, soil, wood, salt, coal.

3. Both cleavange and crystal form characteristic mineral properties. What is the difference between them?

4. Name as many minerals as you can in the following categories:
    a. Minerals that contain carbon
    b. Minerals that contain both aluminum and silicon
    c. Minerals that contain sodium and calcium
    d. Minerals harder than glass
    e. Minerals that can be scratched with a knife
    f. Minerals with cleavage

5. List the three classes of rock in the order of their abundance in the earth's crust.

6. Igneous rocks rich in silicon are often called *silicic,* and rocks in which iron and magnesium are abundant are often called *mafic.* (a) Give examples of silicic and mafic rocks. (b) In general, silicic and mafic rocks are different in color. What is the difference? (c) Which are denser, silicic or mafic rocks?

7. Obsidian is a rock which resembles glass, in particular by sharing the property that its structure is closer to that of a liquid than to that of a crystalline solid. What does this observation suggest about the manner in which obsidian is formed?

8. Granite and rhyolite have similar compositions but granite is coarse-grained whereas rhyolite is fine-grained. What does the difference in grain size indicate about the environments in which each rock formed?

9. Diorite is an intrusive rock and andesite, whose composition is similar, is an extrusive rock. How can they be distinguished from one another?

10. Shale is a sedimentary rock that consolidated from mud deposits. What are the various metamorphic rocks that shale can become under progressively increasing temperature and pressure?

11. What happens to the density of a rock that undergoes metamorphism?

12. Gneiss is formed at greater depths than slate. Which rock would you expect to have the greater density?

13. The mineral grains of many metamorphic rocks are flat or elongated and occur in parallel layers. (a) What is this property called? (b) How does it originate?

14. What are the three most common types of cemented-fragment (or *clastic*) sedimentary rocks? What distinguishes them from one another?

15. What is the nature of chert and why is it so resistant to chemical and mechanical attack?

16. (a) What is the origin of limestone? (b) What rock is formed by the metamorphism of limestone? (c) What is the difference in structure that the metamorphism produces?

17. How could you distinguish (a) granite from gabbro? (b) basalt from limestone? (c) schist from diorite?

18. How could you distinguish (a) chert from obsidian? (b) conglomerate from gneiss? (c) quartz from calcite?

19. Name the following rocks: (a) a fine-grained, unfoliated rock with intergrowing crystals of quartz, feldspar, and black mica; (b) a finely foliated rock with microscopic crystals of quartz and white mica; (c) a fine-grained rock consisting principally of kaolin.

20. Name the following rocks: (a) a rock consisting of intergrown crystals of quartz; (b) the rock resulting from metamorphism of limestone; (c) an intrusive igneous rock with the same composition as andesite.

21. Arrange the following rocks in three general groups as (a) hard, (b) moderately hard, and (c) soft. Indicate which are igneous, which sedimentary, and which metamorphic.

gneiss	obsidian	andesite
limestone	shale	chalk
quartzite	chert	marble

22. Why do plants require nitrogen? Why cannot they use nitrogen from the air? Where do nitrogen compounds in the soil come from?

23. What are the similarities and differences between seismic P and S waves?

24. How is it possible to tell from the seismograph record of the waves from an earthquake how far away the earthquake occurred?

25. The travel times of seismic waves depend only on the distance between earthquke and observing station and do not vary around the earth for the same such distance. What does this indicate about the uniformity of the material in the earth's interior?

26. Why is the mantle thought to be solid?

27. Seismic S waves are never detected beyond about 11,400 km (measured along the earth's surface) from an earthquake. P waves also disappear at this distance but reappear at distances greater than about 15,900 km. How do these observations fit in with the hypothesis that the earth has a liquid core?

28. (a) Why is it considered likely that the earth's outer core is liquid? (b) Why is the liquid thought to be largely iron? (c) Why is nickel believed to be present as well?

29. How does the radius of the earth's core compare with the radius of the earth as a whole?

30. Where is the earth's crust thinnest? Where is it thickest?

31. What evidence is there in favor of the idea that the earth's interior is very hot?

32. What is the principal cause of the high temperatures believed to exist in the earth's interior?

33. Why is it unlikely that the earth's magnetic field originates in a huge bar magnet located in its interior?

34. Why does a compass needle in most places not point due north?

ANSWERS TO MULTIPLE CHOICE

1. *a*	**8.** *a*	**15.** *a*	**22.** *a*
2. *c*	**9.** *c*	**16.** *d*	**23.** *d*
3. *b*	**10.** *a*	**17.** *d*	**24.** *c*
4. *a*	**11.** *a*	**18.** *c*	**25.** *a*
5. *c*	**12.** *d*	**19.** *d*	**26.** *b*
6. *d*	**13.** *a*	**20.** *c*	**27.** *b*
7. *d*	**14.** *d*	**21.** *b*	

15

THE CHANGING CRUST

Now that we know something about the structure of our planet and about the rocks and minerals, atmosphere, and oceans that clothe it, we can turn to the processes whose action has produced the landscapes around us.

Sudden, violent changes and slow, gentle ones have combined through the ages to create the wrinkled face of the earth. Tracing the origins of the earth's surface features, like many of the classic problems of science, is like solving a jigsaw puzzle. Nearly all the pieces are in hand, and the trick is to put them together into a coherent pattern. Today, though some elements are lacking or do not quite fit the rest of the picture, the outlines of that picture exist, and the development of the earth's topography is no longer the mystery it once seemed.

EROSION

It is not obvious that this solid earth under us, made up largely of hard, strong rock, is in a state of constant change. But rocks, hills, and mountains are permanent only by comparison with the brief span of human life, and the long history of the earth goes back not scores of years but billions of years. In this immense stretch of time continents have shifted across the globe, mountain ranges have been thrust upward and then leveled, and broad seas have appeared and disappeared.

Gravity is ultimately responsible for erosion

All the processes by which rocks are worn down and by which the debris is carried away are included in the general term *erosion*. The underlying cause of erosion is gravity. Such agents of erosion as running water and glaciers derive their destructive energy from gravity, and gravity is responsible for the transport of removed material to lower and lower elevations. The leveling of landscape by erosion is often referred to as *gradation*.

Weathering

How exposed rocks decay

Weathering refers to the disintegration of rock surfaces in the open air

We have all seen the rough, pitted surfaces of old stone buildings. This kind of disintegration, brought about by rainwater and the gases in the air, is called *weathering*. Weathering participates in erosion in an important way by preparing rock material for easy removal by the more active erosional agents.

Chemical weathering

Some of the minerals in igneous and metamorphic rocks are especially susceptible to *chemical weathering*, since they were formed under conditions very different from those at the earth's surface. Ferromagnesian minerals are readily attacked by atmospheric oxygen, aided by carbon dioxide dissolved in water (which gives an acid solution) and by organic acids from decaying vegetation. Their iron(II) is oxidized to a hydrate of iron(III) oxide, whose red and brown colors commonly appear as stains on the surface of rocks containing these minerals. Feldspars and other silicates containing aluminum are in large part altered to clay minerals. Among common sedimentary rocks limestone is most readily attacked by chemical weathering because of the solubility of calcite in weak acids. Exposures of this rock can often be identified simply from the pitted surfaces and enlarged cracks that solution produces.

Quartz and white mica are extremely resistant to chemical attack and usually remain as loose grains when the rest of a rock is thoroughly decayed. Rocks consisting wholly of silica, like chert and most quartzites, are practically immune to chemical weathering.

Mechanical weathering

Mechanical weathering is often aided by chemical attack. Not only is the structure of a rock weakened by the decomposition of its minerals, but fragments are actively wedged apart because the chemical changes in a mineral grain usually result in an increased volume. The most effective process of mechanical disintegration that does not require chemical action is the freezing of water in crevices.

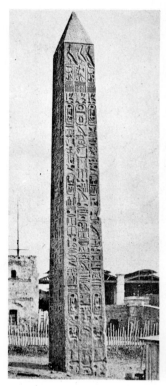

The rate at which weathering occurs depends upon the environment. (Left) The stone obelisk Cleopatra's Needle after standing for 30 centuries in the clean, dry air of Egypt. (Right) Cleopatra's Needle after an exposure of less than a century to the climate and atmospheric contaminants of New York City.

Weathering and soil formation

Just as water freezing in an automobile engine on a cold night may split the block, so water freezing in tiny cracks is an effective wedge for disrupting rocks. Plant roots aid in rock disintegration by growing and enlarging themselves in cracks.

Weathering processes coat the naked rock of the earth's crust with a layer of debris made up largely of clay mixed with rock and mineral fragments. The upper part of the weathered layer, in which rock debris is mixed with decaying vegetable matter, is the soil. From a biological point of view the formation of soil is an important result of weathering.

Stream Erosion

Running water is the chief agent of erosion

By far the most important agent of erosion is the running water of streams. The work of glaciers, wind, and waves is impressive locally but, by comparison with running water, they play only minor roles in the shaping of the earth's landscapes.

Running water is the most important agent of erosion. Shown here is McMullin Creek in Oregon, which feeds into Lake Salmac. Agricultural land is lost by the wearing away of the banks of the creek, and the silt brought to the lake will eventually turn it into a mudflat.

Even in deserts, mountainsides are carved with the unmistakable forms of stream-made valleys.

What streams do

A stream performs two functions in erosion:

1. Active cutting at the sides and bottom of its channel
2. Transportation of debris supplied by weathering and by its own cutting

The effectiveness of a stream in carrying debris depends on its slope and on the volume of water that flows. Its ability to cut a channel depends on these factors and also on the amount and kind of debris with which it is supplied. Sand grains, pebbles, and boulders are the tools that a stream uses to dig into its bed. Scraping them along its bottom and ramming them against its banks, a stream can cut its way through the hardest rocks. The rounded forms of stream channels in hard rock and the smoothly rounded surfaces of the pebbles in stream gravel testify to the power of this process.

Running water is the chief erosional agent even in deserts

Another factor of prime importance in determining how rapidly a stream will erode its valley is the frequency of violent storms in its neighborhood. Often during a few hours of a heavy rain a stream accomplishes more than in months or years of normal flow. One reason that running water is the dominant erosional agent in deserts is that desert storms, when they do occur, are violent enough to send raging torrents down the normally dry valleys.

Streams cut V-shaped channels

If we could watch the development of a river cutting downward through rock of uniform hardness, we would see repeated in slow motion the events that mark the growth of a gully cut in the soft material of a hillside. The gully is deepened, lengthened, and widened by the temporary stream formed during each successive rain. Deepening is accomplished by the downcutting of the stream. Lengthening takes place at the head of the gully, where the stream eats farther and farther into the hill. Widening is a direct result not so much of the stream's activity but of rainwash and slumping of material on the gully's sides. Thus the stream itself cuts like a blunt knife downward and backward into the hill, while secondary processes widen the gash. The combination of deepening and widening gives the gully its characteristic V-shaped cross section; the V is steep when downcutting is rapid compared with the work of rainwash and slumping, broader when downcutting is slow. As a gully grows older the rate of downcutting slackens, and the processes of widening make its cross section a broader and broader V.

Evolution of Eroded Landscapes

Youth, maturity, and old age

In the same manner, at first the river would dig a deep gorge, its cross section steeply V-shaped. A profile drawn to represent the slope of the river would show a steep channel with numerous rapids and waterfalls (Fig. 15-1). Then the part of the gorge near the river's mouth would be deepened to the level of an adjacent valley or perhaps nearly to sea level. Below this the river cannot cut, and downcutting would gradually slacken along its entire course. Its long profile would grow less steep and its cross section more broadly V-shaped.

Later, when the slope of the river flattens, downcutting would practically cease. From this point the river would devote its energy to cutting into the sides of

In a young landscape, streams are starting their work and valleys are few and steep

In a mature landscape, tributary streams are well-developed and the region is cut into ridges and valleys

FIG. 15-1
Successive stages in the development of a river valley. The general appearance of the valley at various times is shown at the right and the corresponding cross sections at the left.

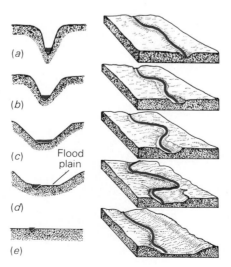

The drainage pattern of the Wadi Hadramawt in Aden is conspicuous from the air. The Gulf of Aden is at the top.

The flood plain of the Christian River in Alaska. The meandering, shifting channel is typical of the old age of a river.

its channel to give its valley a flat floor, or *flood plain*. In dry weather the river would wander over its plain in a meandering channel; in very wet weather it would overflow its channel and spread across the plain. The flood plain would grow wider and wider, the river would become more and more sluggish, the sides of its valley would become lower and lower.

During this development of the major valley, secondary streams would extend their smaller valleys on either side. Soon a characteristic treelike pattern would be fully developed, separated from the patterns of adjacent rivers by sharp divides. As flood plains develop along the main streams, divides would slowly be lowered by attack from the streams on either side. In the final stages of valley growth, when flood plains are wide and rivers broadly meandering, most of the divides would be erased and those remaining would be low and rounded.

Actual landscapes seldom conform exactly to the simple valley shapes and patterns just described. One reason is the presence of rocks of different hardness: hard rocks usually remain as cliffs and high ridges, while the more easily eroded soft rocks wear away. In the Grand Canyon, the typical V shape of a young stream valley is modified by steps because the stream has cut through horizontal layers of hard and soft rocks; the hard layers form the cliffs, the soft layers the more gentle slopes between. In the Appalachian Mountains treelike patterns of secondary streams are not developed, because here alternate hard and soft layers are tilted on end and streams erode the soft layers most (Fig. 15-2). Many of the striking landforms produced by erosion are due simply to differences in resistance from one rock layer to the next.

Whatever the valley shapes produced in various stages of landscape development, whatever different kinds of rock may be present, the ultimate goal of stream erosion is to reduce the land surface to a flat plain almost at sea level. However, this goal is never attained because, as we shall learn, other geologic processes continually counteract the effects of running water. There are very few regions in which geologic processes involving uplift do not occur at the same time as stream erosion. Thus most actual landscapes are the result of a complex of different factors, and reflect a balance among them rather than the action of stream erosion alone.

In an old landscape, flood plains are broad and further erosion is slow

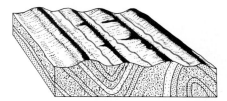

FIG. 15-2
Parallel ridges and valleys produced by stream erosion in tilted layers of hard and soft rocks. Soft layers underlie the valleys, hard layers the ridges. Landscapes and rock structures of this sort are typical of the Appalachian Mountains.

The ultimate result of stream erosion would be a flat plain if no other processes acted

Glaciers

Rivers and seas of ice

A glacier is a moving mass of ice

In a cold climate with abundant snowfall, the snow of winter may not completely melt during the following summer, and so a deposit of snow accumulates from year to year. Partial melting and continual increase in pressure cause the lower part of a snow deposit to change gradually into ice. If the ice is sufficiently thick, its weight forces it slowly downhill. A moving mass of ice formed in this manner is called a *glacier*. About 10 percent of the earth's land area is covered by glacial ice at the present time.

Today's glaciers are of two principal types:

The U-shaped cross section of this valley in Switzerland suggests that it was cut by the ancestor of the shrunken glacier at its head at a time when the climate there was colder than at present.

Glacial erosion produces U-shaped valleys

1. *Valley glaciers* — found, for instance, in the Alps, on the Alaskan coast, in the western United States — are patches and tongues of dirty ice lying in mountain valleys. These glaciers move slowly down their valleys and melt at their lower ends. The combination of downward movement and melting keeps their ends in roughly the same position from year to year. Such valleys have U-shaped cross sections instead of the V shapes produced by stream erosion. Movement in the faster valley glaciers (a meter or more per day) is sufficient to keep their lower ends well below the timber line.

Continental glaciers

2. Glaciers of another type cover most of Greenland and Antarctica. These huge masses of ice thousands of square km in area that engulf hills as well as valleys are called *continental glaciers* or *icecaps*. They, too, move downhill, but the "hill" is the slope of their upper surfaces. An icecap has the shape of a broad dome with its surface sloping outward from a thick central portion of greatest snow accumulation. Its motion is radially outward in all directions from its center. The icebergs of the polar seas are fragments that have broken off the edges of icecaps. Similar sheets of ice extended across Canada and northern Eurasia during the ice ages.

How a glacier moves

Apparently a glacier moves in part by sliding, in part by internal fracture and healing in the crystals of solid ice. Like a stream, a glacier picks up rock fragments which serve as tools in cutting its bed. Fragments at the bottom surface of the glacier, held firmly in the grip of the ice and dragged slowly along its bed, scrape and polish the bedrock and are themselves flattened and scratched. Smoothed

The Greenland icecap covers an area of over 1.3 million km² and is as much as 3.2 km thick in places. The icebergs that menace shipping in the North Atlantic are fragments that have broken off from the edges of this icecap.

and striated rock surfaces and deposits of debris that contain boulders with flattened sides are common near the ends of valley glaciers. Where such evidence of the grinding and polishing of ice erosion is found far from present-day glaciers, we have reason to believe that glaciers were active there in the past.

Glacial erosion is minor on a worldwide basis

Glacial erosion is locally very impressive, particularly in high mountains. The amount of debris and the size of the boulders that a glacier can carry or push ahead of itself is often startling. But overall, the erosion accomplished by glaciers is small. Only rarely have they gouged rock surfaces deeply, and the amount of material they transport long distances is little compared with that carried by streams. Most glaciers of today are only feeble descendants of mighty ancestors, but even these ancestors succeeded only in modifying landscapes already shaped by running water.

Groundwater

Water, water everywhere (almost)

Must of the water that falls as rain does not run off at once in streams but instead soaks into the ground. All water that thus penetrates the surface is called *groundwater*. There is more groundwater than all the fresh water of the world's lakes and rivers, though less than the water locked up in icecaps and glaciers (see Fig. 13-3).

The water table is the upper surface of the saturated zone

The soil, the weathered layer, and any porous rocks below act together as a huge sponge that can absorb great quantities of water. During and immediately after a heavy rain all empty spaces in the sponge may be filled, and the ground is then said to be *saturated* with water. When the rain has stopped, water slowly drains away from hills into the adjacent valleys. A few days after a rain porous

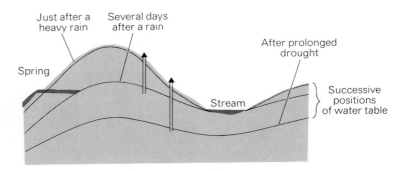

Just after a heavy rain

Several days after a rain

After prolonged drought

Spring

Stream

Successive positions of water table

FIG. 15-3
Cross section through a landscape underlain by porous material. The position of the water table is shown just after a heavy rain, several days later, and after a prolonged drought. The spring and upper well would be dry during the drought.

Springs consist of groundwater that emerges from beneath the surface

Aquifers

How caves are formed

material in the upper part of a hill contains relatively little moisture, while that in the lower part may still be saturated. Another rain would raise the upper level of the saturated zone, prolonged drought would lower it. The fluctuating upper surface of the saturated zone is called the *water table.*

Beneath valleys the water table is usually nearer the surface than under nearby hills (Fig. 15-3). The movement of groundwater in the saturated zone is mainly a slow seeping downward and sideward into streams, lakes, and swamps. The motion is rapid through coarse material like sand or gravel, slow through fine material like clay. It is this flow of groundwater that maintains streams when rain is not falling; a stream goes dry only when the water table drops below the level of its bed. A *spring* is formed where groundwater comes to the surface in a more or less definite channel.

An *aquifer* is a body of porous rock through which groundwater moves. Aquifers underlie more than half the area of the continental United States.

Although groundwater movement is slow, its erosional activity is by no means negligible. It can accomplish little mechanical wear, but its prolonged contact with rocks and soil enables it to dissolve much soluble material. The dissolved substances are in part transported to neighboring streams, in part redeposited at other points in the weathered layer or bedrock. Dissolved material is responsible for the hardness of water from many wells (Chap. 10). In regions underlain by limestone, the most soluble of ordinary rocks, the solvent action of groundwater makes itself conspicuous by the formation of caves. A cave is produced when water moving through tiny cracks in limestone gradually enlarges the cracks by dissolving and removing adjacent rock material.

The activity of groundwater extends downward for some hundreds or thousands of feet, depending on the kinds of rock present. Nearly all rocks within a short distance of the surface have enough pore space or are sufficiently cracked to permit some circulation, although in massive igneous and metamorphic rocks the amount of groundwater may be very small. At lower levels the great pressure leaves cracks too small and too scarce to permit free movement of groundwater. Thus deep mines often have plenty of water in their upper parts but so little at lower levels that dust from drilling and blasting becomes a problem.

Carlsbad Caverns in New Mexico
were produced by the solvent
action of groundwater on limestone
and the subsequent deposition of
the dissolved material.

SEDIMENTATION

The largest sediment deposits occur
near continental margins

Most of the material transported by the agents of erosion is eventually deposited to form *sediments* of various sorts. Only substances in solution can escape such deposition; ions of various salts carried by streams to lakes and oceans may remain dissolved indefinitely. Under some conditions, however, part of the dissolved material may form sediments. Slightly soluble salts like calcium carbonate precipitate readily, and others appear when evaporation concentrates the water of a salt lake or an arm of the sea.

The ultimate destination of erosional debris is the ocean, and the most widespread sediments accumulate in shallow parts of the ocean near continental margins. But much sedimentary material is carried to the sea in stages, deposited first in thick layers elsewhere — in lakes, in desert basins, in stream valleys. Each of the various erosional agents has its own characteristic ways of depositing its load, and these ways leave their stamp on the character of the deposits formed. Since sediments laid down ages ago often retain many of their original characteristics, a knowledge of the processes of deposition enables us to figure out the probable origin of older deposits. In this way we can reconstruct past conditions of erosion and sedimentation and so gain insight into many chapters of earth history.

Deposition of Sediments

What becomes of the debris of erosion

Streams, the chief agents of erosion, deposit some of the abundant debris they carry whenever their speeds drop or their volumes of water decrease. Four sites of deposition are common:

Sites of sediment deposition

1. Debris carried in time of flood is deposited in gravel banks and sandbars on the stream bed when the swiftly flowing waters begin to recede.
2. The flood plain of a meandering river is a site of deposition whenever the river overflows its banks and loses speed as it spreads over the plain. In Egypt, for example, before construction of the Aswan Dam, the fertility of the soil was maintained for centuries by the deposit of black silt left each year when the Nile was in flood.

Alluvial fan

3. A common site of deposition, especially in the western United States, is the point where a stream emerges from a steep mountain valley and slows down as it flows onto a plain. Such a deposit, usually taking the form of a low cone pointing upstream, is called an *alluvial fan.*

Origin of a delta

4. A similar deposit is formed when a stream's flow is stopped abruptly as it flows into a lake or sea. This kind of deposit, built largely under water and with a surface usually flatter than that of an alluvial fan, is called a *delta.*

Glacial moraine

Some of the material scraped from its channel by a glacier is heaped up at its lower end where the ice melts and some is spread as a layer of irregular thickness beneath the ice. The pile of debris around the end and along the sides of the glacier, called a *moraine,* is left as a low ridge of hummocky topography when the glacier melts back. Moraines in mountain valleys and in the North Central states are part of the evidence for a former wide extent of glaciation.

Till is the material deposited directly by a glacier

All the material deposited directly by ice goes by the name of *till,* characteristically an indiscriminate mixture of fine and coarse material. Huge boulders are often embedded in the abundant, fine, claylike material that a glacier produces by its polishing action. Typically, most of the boulders are angular; a few are rounded and show the flat scratched faces produced as they were dragged along the bed of the glacier.

Most important of the agents of deposition, since they handle by far the largest amount of sediment, are the currents of the sea. Currents deposit not only the materials eroded from coastlines by wave action but also the abundant debris brought to the ocean by streams, wind, and glaciers. Visible deposits of waves and currents include beaches and sandbars, but the great bulk of the sediments brought to the ocean are laid down under water.

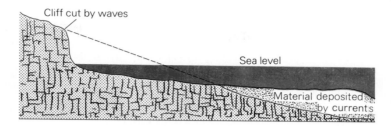

Cliff cut by waves

Sea level

Material deposited by currents

FIG. 15-4
Cross section of a steep, rocky shoreline.

Deposition beneath the sea takes place in several ways. Sand, gravel, and clay are carried outward by rivers and also directly from the shore by *rip currents*, strong but narrow seaward currents found in the midst of breaking waves, and these materials are dropped wherever the current becomes too weak to carry them (Fig. 15-4). Some salts, notably calcium carbonate, are deposited as chemical precipitates when sea water becomes locally oversaturated. In some places living organisms are so abundant that their shells, when the organisms die, become an important part of the material deposited. Coral is a notable example.

Coral

These depositional processes operate chiefly in the shallow parts of the ocean bordering the continents, out to depths of a few hundred meters. In shallow arms of the sea, like Hudson Bay and the Baltic Sea, active deposition may take place over the entire bottom. Little material from the land is directly deposited in the deeper parts of the ocean, but some of the mud and sand deposited on the shallow continental shelves may move to greater depths in the form of *turbidity currents*. These are masses of water and sediment, with the sediment held in suspension by extreme turbulence, which occasionally roll down the relatively steep slope beyond the shelf when triggered by earthquakes or oversteepening.

Turbidity currents shift sediments deposited in shallow water to greater depths offshore

Veins consist of minerals deposited from solution

Deposition by groundwater is almost entirely chemical precipitation from solution. One of the most important geologic activities of groundwater is the depositing of material in the pore spaces of sediments, which helps to convert the sediments into rock. Much dissolved material is deposited along open cracks to form *veins*, common in all kinds of rocks. The commonest vein minerals are quartz and calcite, but some veins contain commercially valuable minerals. More spectacular examples of groundwater deposition are the *stalactites* that hang from the roofs of limestone caverns and the colorful deposits often found around hot springs and geysers.

Lithification

How sedimentary rocks are formed

Lithification is the process by which sediments become rock

Sediments buried beneath later deposits are gradually hardened into rock, a process called *lithification*. Lithification is often a complex process, completed only after slow changes have gone on for thousands or even millions of years. One important change in the sediment is compaction, the squeezing together of its

These sandstone beds in Zion National Park, Utah, were once sand dunes that had been deposited by winds.

Groundwater promotes the hardening of many sediments

Sedimentary rocks provide information on the history of the earth's surface

grains under the pressure of overlying deposits. Some recrystallization may accompany compaction. The calcite crystals of limy sediments, in particular, grow larger and interlock with one another.

Chemical changes brought about by circulating groundwater contribute to the hardening of many sediments. The grains of coarse sediments are cemented by material precipitated from solution in groundwater, and some sediments have much of their original material dissolved away and replaced by other substances. The profound changes groundwater can accomplish are strikingly illustrated by petrified wood, in which the original organic compounds have been removed, molecule by molecule, and replaced by silica. The whole process takes place so gradually that the finest details of the wood structure may be preserved.

The usual cementing materials with which groundwater binds together the grains of sediments are silica, calcium carbonate, and hydrated iron(III) oxide. The iron oxide betrays its presence by the red, yellow, and brown colors of many sandstones and conglomerates. The hardening of sediments by cementation, compaction, and recrystallization produces the ordinary varieties of sedimentary rock. Gravel beds are cemented into tough conglomerates, sand deposits into sandstones. Layers of clay become shale, and precipitates of calcium carbonate become limestone. The origin of chert is more obscure, perhaps because it may come into being in more than one way.

Sedimentary rocks are especially important in geology because they contain material that was deposited at or near the earth's surface. In this material is preserved a record of the changing surface conditions of past time. If we read the record with sufficient insight and imagination, we find before us a panorama of earth history: seas that once spread widely over the land, the advance and retreat of immense glaciers, the shifting sand dunes of ancient deserts, and much more. Revealed are the living creatures that inhabited lands and seas of the past, for many sedimentary rocks contain abundant fossil remains of plants and animals. Igneous and metamorphic rocks tell us by their structures something about conditions in the earth's interior; sedimentary rocks tell us about the varied and interesting history of surface landscapes.

VULCANISM

Erosion and sedimentation are leveling processes through which the higher parts of the earth's surface are worn down and the lower parts are filled with the resulting debris. If their work could be carried to completion, the continents would disappear and the earth would become a smooth sphere covered with sea water. The fact that the continents still exist, not to mention the mountain ranges upon them, is in itself evidence that other agencies exist that can undo the effects of gradation. Such agencies are of two kinds:

1. Processes of *vulcanism,* which involve movements of molten rock
2. Processes of *diastrophism* (or *tectonism*), which involve movements of the solid materials of the crust

Vulcanism and diastrophism often occur together. The flow of molten rock may cause adjacent rock structures to be distorted, and it is common for major crustal shifts to be accompanied by volcanic eruptions and subsurface migrations of molten rock.

Volcanoes

Rivers of lava, clouds of gas and dust

A volcano is an opening through which molten rock and gas emerge from the earth's interior

A volcano is an opening in the earth's crust through which molten rock, usually called *magma* while underground and *lava* aboveground, pours forth. Because the emerging material accumulates near the orifice, most volcanoes in the course of time build up mountains with a characteristic conical shape that steepens toward the top, with a small depression or crater at the summit. Lava escapes almost continuously from a few volcanoes, but the majority are active only at intervals.

What happens in a volcanic eruption

A volcanic eruption is one of the most awesome spectacles in all nature. Earthquakes may provide a warning a few hours or a few days beforehand — minor shocks probably caused by the movement of gases and liquids underground. Volcanic eruptions follow a variety of patterns. Usually an explosion or a series of explosions comes first, sending a great cloud billowing upward from the crater. In

A volcano seen from above. Ash-laden clouds rise from Taal volcano, 40 miles south of Manila, the Philippines, during a recent eruption.

The properties of the magma (underground molten rock) involved determine the nature of a volcanic eruption

the cloud are various gases, dust, fragments of solid material blown from the crater and the upper part of the volcano's orifice, and larger solid fragments representing molten rock blown to bits and hurled upward by the force of the explosions. The exceptionally violent eruption of the volcano Tambora in Indonesia in 1815 is thought to have ejected over 150 cubic km of pumice and ash into the atmosphere. Enough stayed aloft to keep a substantial amount of sunlight from reaching Europe and North America the following year — the "year without a summer."

Gas may continue to emerge in large quantities after the first explosion, and further bursts may recur at intervals. The cloud may persist for days or weeks with its lower part glowing red at night. Activity gradually slackens, and soon a tongue of white-hot (1100°C or so) lava spills over the edge of the crater or pours out of a fissure on the mountain slope. Other flows may follow the first, and explosive activity may continue with diminished intensity. Slowly the volcano quiets down with only a small steam cloud above the crater to suggest its activity.

The chief factors that determine whether an eruption will be a largely quiet lava flow or be explosive are the viscosity of the magma and the amount of gas it contains. (The greater the viscosity of a liquid, the less freely it flows; honey is more viscous than water.) Magma is a complex mixture of the oxides of various metals with silica and usually has an abundance of gas dissolved in it under pressure. Like most molten silicates it is extremely viscous, and with rare exceptions lava creeps downhill slowly, like thick syrup or tar. The viscosity depends upon chemical composition: magmas with high percentages of silica are the most

Kilaueaiki volcano in Hawaii sent fountains of lava and flame as high as 450 m when it erupted in 1959.

viscous. The presence of gas also affects viscosity: magmas with little gas are the most viscous. If the magma feeding a volcano happens to be rich in both gas and silica, the eruption will be explosive. A magma with modest gas and silica contents results in a quiet eruption.

The main volcanic gas is water vapor

The gaseous products of volcanic activity include water vapor, carbon dioxide, nitrogen, hydrogen, and various sulfur compounds. The most prominent constituent is water vapor. Some of it comes from groundwater heated by magma, some comes from the combination of hydrogen in the magma with atmospheric oxygen, and some was formerly incorporated in rocks deep in the crust and carried upward by the magma to be released at the surface. Much of the water vapor condenses when it escapes to give rise to the torrential rains that often accompany eruptions.

Basalt is the most common volcanic rock

Lava solidifies to form one or another of the various volcanic rocks (Fig. 15-5). These are all fine-grained because lava cools too rapidly for large mineral crystals to grow. Basalt is by far the commonest volcanic rock and, when molten, is fluid enough to spread out over a wide area. The more viscous andesite usually

FIG. 15-5
Cross section of a volcano. During explosive eruptions much liquid rock is blown into fragments. Deposits of the finer material may form the rock tuff, and deposits of the coarser material may form a kind of conglomerate called volcanic breccia. In the volcano shown lava flows (solid color) alternate with beds of tuff and volcanic breccia.

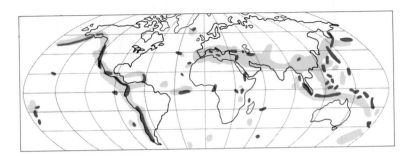

FIG. 15-6
The principal earthquake (light color) and volcanic (dark color) regions of the world

produces steep, conical mountains and, in general, is associated with more rugged landscapes than basalt. Rhyolite, the most siliceous of ordinary lavas, forms small, thick flows and domes. Rhyolitic lava is sometimes so viscous and cools so rapidly that crystallizaton does not take place, leaving the natural glass obsidian. Volcanic rocks of all kinds frequently have rounded holes due to gas bubbles that were trapped during the final stages of solidification. Viscous lavas may harden with so many cavities that the light, porous rock *pumice* results.

Volcanoes occur in belts around the earth

Several hundred active volcanoes are today found around the borders of the Pacific Ocean, on some of the Pacific Islands, in Iceland, in the Mediterranean region, in the West Indies, and in East Africa (Fig. 15-6). In many other parts of the world volcanoes have been active in earlier times. Where volcanoes have become extinct in the recent geologic past, we find evidence of their former splendor in isolated, cone-shaped mountains, in solidified lava flows, and in hot springs, geysers, and steam vents. Some of the great mountains in the western United States are old volcanoes, in a few cases with lava flows so recent that vegetation has not yet gained a foothold on them. In regions where volcanoes have been inactive for a longer period, erosion may have removed all evidence of the original mountains and left only patches of volcanic rocks to indicate former igneous activity.

Intrusive Rocks

They have hardened underground from magma

Intrusive rocks have coarser grains than volcanic rocks

Molten rock that rises through the earth's crust but does not reach the surface solidifies to form intrusive bodies (often called *plutons*) of various kinds. Because these bodies cool slowly, intrusive igneous rocks are coarser-grained than volcanic rocks. We find such rocks exposed at the surface only where erosion has uncovered them after they hardened. The igneous origin of volcanic rocks is clear enough, for we can actually watch lava harden to solid rock. But no one has ever seen an intrusive rock like granite in a liquid state in nature. The belief that granite was once molten follows from indirect evidence such as the following:

Why granite is believed to have hardened from a molten state

1. Granite shows the same relations among its minerals that a volcanic rock shows under the microscope. The separate grains are intergrown, and those with higher melting points show by their better crystal forms that they crystallized a little earlier.

2. In some small intrusive formations every gradation can be found between coarse granite and a rock indistinguishable from the volcanic rock rhyolite, whose igneous origin is clear.

3. Granite is found in masses that cut across layers of sedimentary rock and from which small irregular branches and stringers penetrate into the surrounding rocks. Sometimes blocks of the sedimentary rocks are found completely engulfed by the granite.

4. That granite was at a high enough temperature to be molten is shown by the baking and recystallization of the rocks that it intrudes.

These four types of evidence apply equally well to the other intrusive rocks.

Dikes

A *dike* is a wall-like mass of igneous rock intruded along a fissure that cuts across existing rock layers. The largest dikes are hundreds of meters thick, but more often their thickness is between a few tenths of a meter and a few meters. The distinction between dikes and veins is that a dike is molten rock that has filled a fissure and solidified, whereas a vein consists of material deposited along a fissure from solution in water.

Three dikes of igneous rock intruded in sedimentary beds. The beds on either side of the large dike do not match, which suggests that the dike was intruded along a fault.

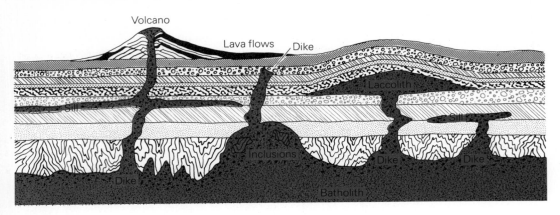

FIG. 15-7
A batholith and associated dikes and sills; a laccolith and a volcano are also shown.

Any kind of igneous rock may occur in a dike. Rapid cooling in small dikes may give rocks similar to those of volcanic origin, and slow cooling in larger dikes often gives coarse-grained rocks. Dikes may cut any other kind of rock. They are frequently associated with volcanoes; apparently some of the magma forces its way into cracks instead of ascending through the central orifice. In regions of intrusive rocks, dikes are often found as offshoots of larger masses, as in Fig. 15-7. Also shown in the figure are *sills* and *laccoliths*, intrusive bodies that lie parallel to the strata they are found in.

Batholiths

Batholiths are very large plutons that extend downwards as much as several km. Visible exposures of batholiths cover hundreds of thousands of square km. The great batholith that forms the central part of the Sierra Nevada in California, for example, is about 800 km long and, in places, over 160 km wide. Granite is the principal rock in batholiths, although many have local patches of diorite and gabbro. Batholiths are always associated with mountain ranges, either mountains of the present or regions whose rock structure shows evidence of mountains in the distant past. The intrusion of a batholith is evidently one of the events that occurs in the process of mountain building.

The Rock Cycle

Rocks are not necessarily forever

As we have seen, rocks can change from one kind to another in a variety of ways. An igneous rock, for instance, can be broken up by erosion into fragments that eventually end up in a deposit of sediments which in time lithifies into sedimentary rock. Heat and pressure can later transform this rock into a metamorphic counterpart, which may later be melted into magma and still later harden into an igneous rock—probably not the same as the one the cycle began with, but perhaps a cousin to it. Other life histories are also possible, as shown in Fig. 15-8.

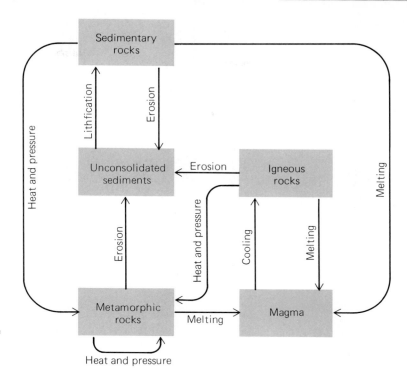

FIG. 15-8
The rock cycle. Depending upon circumstances, different paths are possible, including the conversion of one kind of metamorphic rock into another.

TECTONIC MOVEMENT

Tectonic movement occurs on all scales including continental drift

Terra firma, the solid earth, has come to be a symbol of stability and strength. On foundations of rock, we confidently anchor our buildings, our dams, our bridges. The massive rock of mountain ranges seems strong enough to withstand any conceivable force that might be exerted upon it. Yet even casual observation shows at once how naïve are such notions of the earth's stability. In the strata of high mountains we find shells of marine animals, shells that can be there only if solid rock formed beneath the sea has been lifted high above sea level. Sedimentary rocks, which must have been deposited originally in horizontal layers, are found tilted at steep angles or folded into arches and basins. Other layers have broken along cracks, and the fractured ends have moved apart. Gigantic forces must occur in the crust in order to lift, bend, and break even the strongest rocks.

During the past two decades a major advance has occurred in our understanding of the large-scale forces that are at work shaping and reshaping the earth's crust. The notion that the continents are slowly drifting relative to one another across the globe — a notion over half a century old, but largely scorned until recently — has turned out to be the only way to explain a variety of striking observations. These same observations also provide clues to the physical processes that cause the continents to drift. So far-reaching are the implications of the new picture of continental drift, and so suddenly have they come to light, that it is legitimate to speak of a revolution in geologic thought.

Types of Deformation

Faults and folds, rises and falls, tilts and warps

A fault is a rock fracture along which one side has moved relative to the other

Rock formations of all kinds exhibit fractures, which may be caused by the contraction of molten rock as it cools as well as by mechanical stresses in the crust. A fracture surface along which motion has taken place is called a *fault*. In a rock outcrop a fault appears as a fairly straight line against which sedimentary layers and other structures end abruptly. Near the fault, layers may be bent or crumpled, and along the fault itself streaks of finely powdered material may have developed from friction during movement. Three important kinds of fault are illustrated in Fig. 15-9.

Fault scarps are cliffs formed by faulting

Movement along faults usually takes place as a series of small sudden displacements, with intervals of years or centuries between successive jerks. An immediate effect of displacement along a thrust fault or normal fault is a small cliff. Erosion attacks the cliff at once, and may level it before the next movement. If successive movements follow one another fast enough, erosion may not be able to keep up with diastrophism, with a high cliff only slightly modified by erosion as the result. Cliffs of this sort are called *fault scarps*. Good examples of scarps produced by normal faults are the steep mountain fronts of many of the desert ranges in Utah, Nevada, and eastern California. A more deeply eroded scarp produced by thrust faulting is the eastern front of the Rocky Mountains in Glacier National Park.

Folding takes place by slow, continuous movement, in contrast to the sudden displacements along faults (Fig. 15-10). Sometimes folding produces hills and depressions in the landscape directly, but more commonly erosion keeps pace with it. Indirectly folds affect landforms by exposing tilted beds of varying degrees of resistance to the action of streams, so that characteristic long, parallel ridges and valleys develop, like those of the Appalachian Mountains (see Fig. 15-3). In

FIG. 15-9
(*a*) A normal fault is an inclined surface along which a rock mass has slipped downward; it is the result of tension in the crust. (*b*) A thrust fault is an inclined surface along which a rock mass has moved upward to override the neighboring mass; it is the result of compression in the crust. (*c*) A strike-slip fault is a surface along which one rock mass has moved horizontally with respect to the other; it is the result of oppositely directed forces in the crust that do not act along the same line. Erosion modifies the fault scarps left by normal and thrust faults.

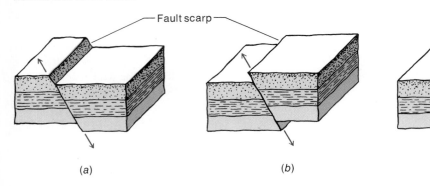

Fault scarp

(*a*) (*b*) (*c*)

Material fractured and pulverized by movement along a fault is especially susceptible to stream erosion. This mosaic of aerial photographs shows a long, straight valley eroded along the San Andreas Fault rift zone from Hughes Lake to Lake Palmdale, California.

STATUTE MILES

0   1   2   3   4

FIG. 15-10
Cross section showing effect of folding in horizontal strata. Folds always shorten the crust and hence are produced by compressional forces. Brittle rocks yield to compression by thrust faults, which are often associated with intense folding. An anticline is an arch or a fold convex upward, and a syncline is a trough or a fold convex downward. In regions of intense folding, anticlines and synclines follow one another in long series.

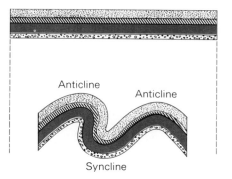

Anticline

Anticline

Syncline

Folded shale beds in Newfoundland.

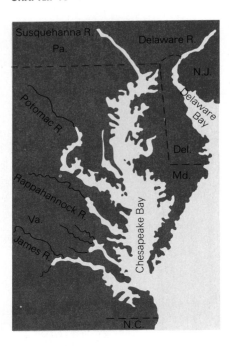

FIG. 15-11
Drowned valleys on the Atlantic
Coast of the United States.

Origin of Chesapeake Bay

these mountains, as in many others, the actual folding is very ancient; the present ridges are due to deep erosion after successive uplifts of the stumps of the old folds.

Large-scale crustal movements may involve whole continents or large parts of them, which may rise or fall, tilt or warp. Such events are not confined to the past but are occurring today as well. Coastal features in many parts of the world provide obvious evidence. For instance, a wave-cut cliff and terrace high above the present shore means that the coast there has been raised in relatively recent times, or stream erosion would have eaten them away.

The sinking of land with respect to sea level is clearly shown by long, narrow bays that fill the mouths of large stream valleys. A body of water like Chesapeake Bay (Fig. 15-11) could not be formed by wave erosion, since wave attack normally straightens a coastline rather than deeply indenting it. Instead, the shape of the bay suggests that it lies in a stream-carved valley whose lower part has been submerged beneath the sea. Elsewhere in the landscapes and sedimentary rocks of the United States a multitude of regional movements are recorded, as seen in Chap. 16.

Mountain Building

The rock record tells a complicated story

Mountains can form in a number of ways. Some are accumulations of lava and fragmental material ejected by a volcano. Some are small blocks of the earth's

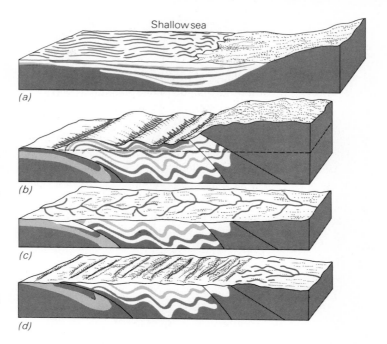

Shallow sea

(a)

(b)

(c)

(d)

FIG. 15-12
Successive stages in the evolution of the Appalachian Mountains. (*a*) Sediments accumulating in the Appalachian basin; (*b*) folding and thrust faulting of rocks in the basin; (*c*) original mountains worn down to a nearly level plain by stream erosion; (*d*) renewed erosion of the folded strata following vertical uplift, producing the parallel ridges and valleys of the present landscape.

Mountain ranges have thicker sedimentary layers than nearby regions

Sideways compression has helped form mountain ranges

crust raised along faults. But the great mountain ranges of the earth, like the Appalachians, the Rockies, the Alps, and the Himalayas, have a much longer and more complex history involving sedimentation, folding, faulting, igneous activity, repeated uplifts, and deep erosion.

The layers of sedimentary rock observed in a mountain range are usually thicker than layers of similar age found under adjacent plains (Fig. 15-12). Most of the layers in both mountains and plains, as shown by their sedimentary structures and their fossils, were formed from deposits that accumulated in shallow seas or on low-lying parts of the land — that is, on surfaces not very far above or below sea level. As deposition continued, the surface must have been slowly sinking at the same time. The greater thickness of the strata in the present mountain area means that this part of the earth's surface was sinking more rapidly than nearby areas.

Besides their thickness, another conspicuous feature of the sedimentary rocks in major mountain ranges is their complex structure. They are crumpled by intense folding and locally broken along huge thrust faults and minor normal faults. Thus in the development of a mountain range the next step must be a period in which the piled-up sediments are subjected to intense compressional forces. (Later in this chapter we will see how these forces arise.) The compression raises part of the folded layers high above the sea, and erosion begins to wear down the exposed beds as folding continues. The appearance of most present-day mountain landscapes is not due directly to the compressional forces that folded and faulted their rocks but instead to long erosion in regions subjected to periodic uplifts.

Continental Drift

An evolving jigsaw puzzle

Matching continental margins

A glance at a map of the world suggests that at some time in the past the continents may have been joined together in one or two giant supercontinents. If the margins of the continents are taken to be on their continental slopes (see Fig. 13-20) at a depth of 3000 ft, instead of their present sea-level boundaries, the fit between North and South America, Africa, Greenland, and western Europe is remarkably exact, as Fig. 15-13 shows. But merely matching up outlines of continents is not by itself sufficient evidence that the continents have migrated around the globe. The first really comprehensive theory of continental drift was proposed early in this century by the German meteorologist Alfred Wegener, who based his argument on biological and geologic evidence.

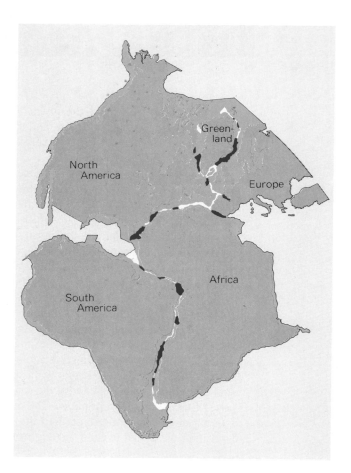

FIG. 15-13
How some of the continents fit together. The boundary of each continent is taken at a depth of 3000 ft (914 m) on its continental slope; the gray regions represent land above sea level at present, and the light-colored regions represent submerged land on the continental shelf and slope. Overlaps are shown in dark color and gaps in white.

Biological evidence for continental drift

Wegener was troubled by the parallel evolution of living things. Going back through the ages, the fossil record shows that, until about 200 million years ago, whenever a new species appeared it did so in many now-distant regions where suitable habitats existed. Evolution, in other words, proceeded at the same rate and in the same way in continents and oceans that today are widely separated. Only in the last 200 million years have plants and animals in the different continents developed in markedly different ways.

At one time the standard explanation for the similarity of patterns of early life around the world was a series of land bridges linking the continents together. But this meant that the oceans were then separated from one another, so a series of channels had to be devised to permit aquatic plants and animals to pass between the oceans. No really believable scheme of bridges and channels could be figured out, and even if one had been, it would still be necessary to account for the disappearance of all traces of them. Wegener was on firm ground when he searched for an alternative to this notion.

Wegener believed all the continents were once part of a single landmass he called Pangaea

What Wegener suggested instead was that originally the continents were all part of a huge landmass he called Pangaea. A few hundred million years ago Pangaea was supposed to have begun to break up and the continents to slowly drift to their present locations. This model found additional support in geologic data regarding prehistoric climates. A little over 200 million years ago South Africa, India, Australia, and part of South America were burdened with great ice sheets, while at the same time a tropical rain forest covered North America, Europe, and China. At various other times, there was sufficient vegetation in Alaska and Antarctica for coal deposits to have resulted, and so currently frigid a place as Baffin Bay was a desert.

Strong evidence supports continental drift

Wegener and his followers examined what was known about the climates of the distant past, and tried to arrange the continents in each geologic period so that the glaciers were near the poles and the hot regions were near the equator. The results, in general, were quite convincing, and in some cases startlingly so. Deposits of glacial debris and fossil remains of certain distinctive plant species follow each other in the same succession in Argentina, Brazil, South Africa, Antarctica, India, and Australia, for example. A recent discovery of this kind was the identification of a skull of the reptile Lystrosaurus in a sandstone layer in the Alexandra mountain range of Antarctica. This creature, which was about 3 feet long, flourished long ago in Africa. It is as unlikely that Lystrosaurus swam the 4300 km between Africa and Antarctica as it is that a land bridge this long connected them, only to vanish completely later on.

Laurasia and Gondwanaland

Supercontinents of the past

Pangaea split into Laurasia and Gondwanaland

Today it seems almost certain that Pangaea did once exist. About 200 million years ago Pangaea began to break apart into two supercontinents, *Laurasia* (which consisted of what is now North America, Greenland, and most of Eurasia) and

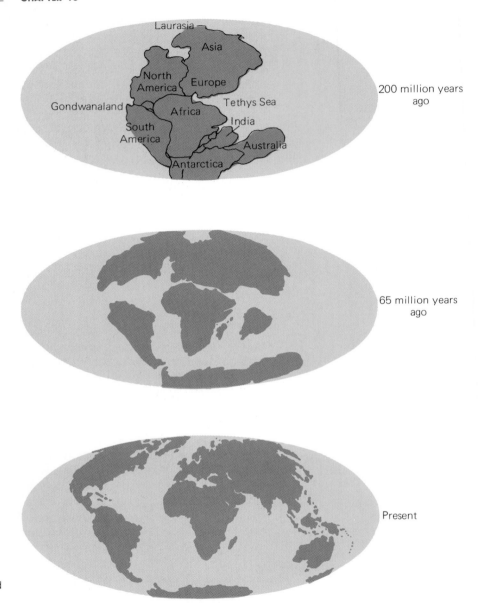

200 million years
ago

65 million years
ago

Present

FIG. 15-14
The landmasses of the earth as they
may have appeared in the past and
as they are today.

Gondwanaland (South America, Africa, Antarctica, India, and Australia). Laurasia
and Gondwanaland were almost equal in size (Fig. 15-14). The separation of
Pangaea into these supercontinents is supported by detailed geologic and biological evidence, for instance certain differences between Laurasian and Gondwanaland fossils of the same age.

The Tethys Sea separated Laurasia and Gondwanaland

Laurasia and Gondwanaland were separated by a body of water called the *Tethys Sea*. Today a little of the Tethys Sea survives as the Mediterranean, Caspian, and Black Seas, but its original extent can be gauged from the sediments that were subsequently uplifted to form the mountain ranges that stretch from Gibraltar eastward to the Pacific. The Pyrenees, Alps, and Caucasus of Europe, the Atlas Mountains of North Africa, and the Himalayas of Asia all were once part of the Tethys Sea.

Origin of today's continents

Not long after Pangaea divided into Laurasia and Gondwanaland, the supercontinents themselves started to break up. The North Atlantic and Indian Oceans were the first to open, followed by the South Atlantic. Perhaps 80 million years ago Greenland began to move away from North America; 45 million years ago Australia split off from Antarctica and India finished its journey north to Asia; and 20 million years ago Arabia separated from Africa.

The ocean floors are too hard and rigid for the continents to move through them

Why was the idea of continental drift rejected by most geologists until only recently? Wegener, who lacked a knowledge of the mechanical properties of the various parts of the earth's crust, thought of the continents as floating freely over the mantle and having no trouble in moving *through* the ocean floors. If this were the case only relatively weak forces would be needed to move the continents over the face of the earth, and Wegener was able to cite several such forces. The evidence available at that time, however, suggested that the crust and upper mantle consisted of rock far too hard and strong to give way before Wegener's proposed forces, making continental drift impossible. Only when more had been learned about the properties of the earth's materials, and when a mechanism entirely different from those of Wegener had been proposed, did the idea of continental drift become accepted.

PLATE TECTONICS

"Continental drift" is not too accurate a description, because the continents themselves turn out to be merely passengers on a number of rigid rock plates that are continually moving across the face of the earth. Before we examine how this motion occurs and what its consequences are, we must first see why it is possible in the first place.

Lithosphere and Asthenosphere

A hard layer over a soft layer

At the heart of all current explanations for major crustal diastrophism is the idea that the mantle of the earth is not a stiff structure, like the crust, but contains a layer near the top that is able to flow.

The lithosphere is a rigid rock shell that consists of the crust and upper mantle; the asthenosphere is a layer of relatively soft rock just beneath it

The crust and the outermost part of the mantle together make up a shell of hard rock 50 to 100 km thick called the *lithosphere*. The lithosphere has no sharp boundary, as the crust does, but gradually turns into the softer *asthenosphere*, a

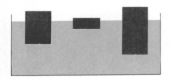

FIG. 15-15
Large blocks of wood float higher and extend farther downward than smaller blocks of wood. This is why the thicker continental crust extends lower into the mantle than the oceanic crust, as shown in Fig. 14-14.

The lithosphere floats on the asthenosphere

region about 100 km thick. (*Lithos* means "rock" in Greek and *astheno* means "weak.") The asthenosphere is soft because its material is close to the melting point under the conditions of temperature and pressure found at such depths. Above the asthenosphere the temperature is too low and below it the pressure is too high for the material to deform easily.

The crust is distinguished from the mantle by a sharp difference in seismic-wave speed, which suggests that the minerals involved are different in composition or in crystal structure or both. The lithosphere is distinguished from the asthenosphere by a difference in their degrees of rigidity. Insofar as brief, suddenly applied forces are concerned, the asthenosphere behaves like a solid and so can transmit the transverse S waves of earthquakes, for example. But when forces act on the asthenosphere over long periods of time, it responds like a thick, viscous fluid.

The notion of a relatively soft asthenosphere makes it possible to understand both why the continents are elevated above the rest of the crust and why the crust is much thicker beneath them than beneath the oceans (see Fig. 14-14). Suppose that we place several blocks of wood of different sizes in a pool of water. The larger blocks float higher than the smaller while simultaneously extending down farther into the water (Fig.15-15). Thus, if the lithosphere with its continents is imagined as floating in equilibrium on a denser asthenosphere capable of plastic deformation, we have the analog of wooden blocks of different sizes floating on water. This implies that exceptionally elevated regions — mountain ranges and plateaus — have corresponding roots extending an exceptional distance downward. Such is actually the case; in fact, its discovery led the British scientist Sir George Biddle Airy a century ago to propose the floating of the entire lithosphere.

The Ocean Floors

The youngest part of the crust

The mountains and valleys, plains and plateaus of the continents have been known for a long time, and few surprises are in store for future explorers. But the continents occupy less than 30 percent of the area of the earth's crust, while the rest lies hidden in perpetual darkness thousands of meters below the seas and oceans. Only in the past few decades have the floors of the oceans been mapped and their physical characters determined. It is largely these findings that have clarified the evolution of the crust.

Echo sounding

Methods used to investigate the ocean floors are not particularly subtle — the real problem has been the vastness of the area to be covered. These days depths are charted by means of echo sounders. An instrument of this kind sends out a pulse of high-frequency sound waves, and the time needed for it to reach the sea floor, be reflected there, and then return to the surface is a measure of how deep the water is (Fig. 15-16). A variant of this method reveals something of the structure of the sea floor itself. What is done is to set off an explosive charge

FIG. 15-16

The principle of echo sounding. (*a*) A pulse of high-frequency sound waves is sent out by a suitable device on a ship. (*b*) The time at which the pulse returns to the ship is a measure of the sea depth.

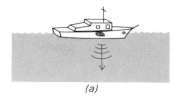 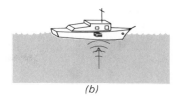

(a)   (b)

in the water and study the returning echoes — one echo will come from the top of the sediment layer, and a later one from the hard rock underneath.

Samples of the sea floor can be obtained by dropping a hollow tube to the bottom on a long cable and then pulling it up filled with a core of the sediments into which it sank. Longer sediment cores can be obtained by drilling. These sediments can be examined later in the laboratory for their composition, their age (by radioactive dating), the fossils they contain, their magnetization, and so forth. Another important technique is to tow a magnetometer behind a survey ship to obtain an idea of the direction and intensity of the magnetization of the rocks of the ocean floor over wide areas.

Four findings about ocean floors have proved of crucial importance:

FIG. 15-17

The worldwide system of oceanic ridges and trenches. The ridges are offset by transverse fracture zones.

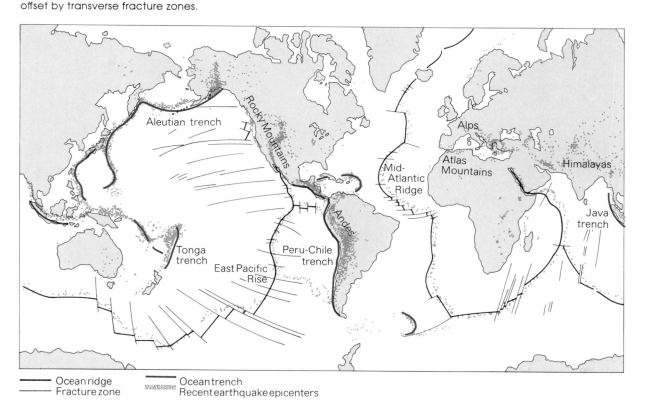

Ocean ridge
Fracture zone
Ocean trench
Recent earthquake epicenters

The ocean floors are relatively young

1. The ocean floors are, geologically speaking, very young. The oldest oceanic crust dates back only about 200 million years, in contrast to continental rocks which date back as much as 3800 million years. Many parts of the ocean floor are much younger still; about one-third of the earth's surface has come into existence in $1\frac{1}{2}$ percent of the earth's history.

Ocean ridges and rises

2. A worldwide system of narrow ridges and somewhat broader *rises* runs across the oceans (Fig. 15-17). An example is the Mid-Atlantic Ridge, which virtually bisects the Atlantic Ocean from north to south. Iceland, the Azores, Ascension Island, and Tristan da Cunha are some of the higher peaks in this ridge. These ridges are offset at intervals by fracture zones that indicate transverse shifts of the ocean floors.

Ocean trenches and island arcs

3. There is also a system of *trenches* several kilometers deep that rims much of the Pacific Ocean. These trenches parallel the belts in which most of today's earthquakes and volcanoes occur. Some of them have *island arcs* on their landward sides that consist largely of volcanic mountains projecting above sea level.

Magnetization of the ocean floors

4. The direction in which ocean-floor rocks are magnetized is the same along strips parallel to the midocean ridges, but the direction is reversed from strip to strip going away from a ridge on either side (Fig. 15-18).

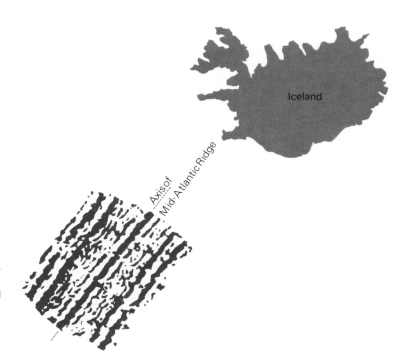

FIG. 15-18
Pattern of magnetization along the Mid-Atlantic Ridge southeast of Iceland. Sea-floor rocks whose directions of magnetization are the same as that of today's geomagnetic field are shown in color; the intervening white spaces represent rocks whose magnetization is in the opposite direction.

Ocean-Floor Spreading

Alternate magnetization is the proof

The first step toward understanding the above observations was taken in the early 1960s by the American geologists Harry H. Hess and Robert S. Dietz, who independently proposed that the ocean floors are widening. (A similar hypothesis was put forward in 1928 by Arthur Holmes in England, but it remained practically unnoticed because supporting data were lacking.)

How the ocean floors spread

The basic idea of ocean-floor spreading is that molten rock is continually rising up along the midocean ridges and flowing outward from them. The parts of the lithosphere on either side of a ridge are moving apart at speeds of 1 to 10 cm/year, with the new material taking their place as it hardens.

Why the ocean floors show strips of normal and reverse magnetizations

The fourth key observation mentioned earlier, which concerns the magnetization of rocks on either side of an ocean ridge, confirms the hypothesis of sea-floor spreading in a convincing way. As Fig. 15-18 shows in the case of a portion of the Mid-Atlantic Ridge southeast of Iceland, successive strips of rock lying parallel to the ridge are magnetized in alternate directions. To interpret this pattern we draw upon the fact that the earth's magnetic field has periodically reversed itself many times in the past. What must have been happening is obvious. As molten rock, unmagnetized in its liquid state, comes to the surface of the crust at a ridge, it hardens and the iron content of its minerals becomes magnetized in the same direction as that of the geomagnetic field at the time. When the direction of the geomagnetic field reverses, the molten rock that cools then becomes magnetized in the opposite direction. Thus strips of alternate magnetization follow one another going away on both sides from a ridge.

The reversals of the earth's magnetic field have been dated by measurements made on magnetized lava flows on land using methods based on radioactivity. This information can be used to find the ages of the magnetized strips that make up the sea floor, and thereby to establish the speeds with which the lithosphere plates have been moving.

Plate Tectonics

How the continents drift

Although the ocean floors are widening at the midocean ridges, the earth as a whole does not expand. The spread of the ocean floors must therefore be accompanied by other large-scale processes in the lithosphere. The study of these processes and their consequences has come to be known as *plate tectonics*.

The lithosphere consists of a number of huge moving plates

The starting point of plate tectonics is the observation that the lithosphere is split not only along the ridges of the ocean floors but also along the trenches and fracture zones of Fig. 15-17. These cracks divide the lithosphere into seven huge *plates* and a number of smaller ones, all of which float on the plastic asthenosphere (Fig. 15-19).

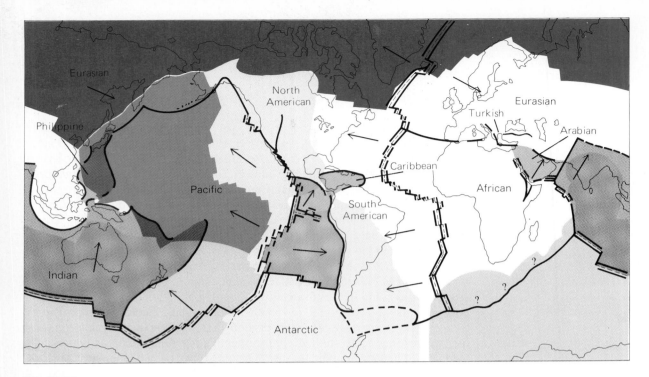

FIG. 15-19

The chief lithosphere plates whose motion results in continental drift. The plates are bounded by ridges, trenches, and faults. The arrows show the direction of motion of the plates except for the African plate, which is thought to be stationary.

FIG. 15-20

Plates can move relative to each other at a boundary between them. (a) The plates move apart, and molten rock from below rises into the gap to form a midocean ridge. New ocean floor is created in this way. (b) The plates move together. If both are continental plates, rock is pushed upward where they come together to form a mountain range such as the Himalayas. (c) If one is an oceanic plate, it is forced under the edge of the other to form a subduction zone. A mountain range is again the result; an example is the Andes. (d) Seen from above, the plates slide past each other. This is what is happening at the San Andreas Fault in California.

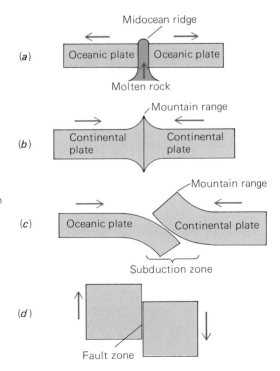

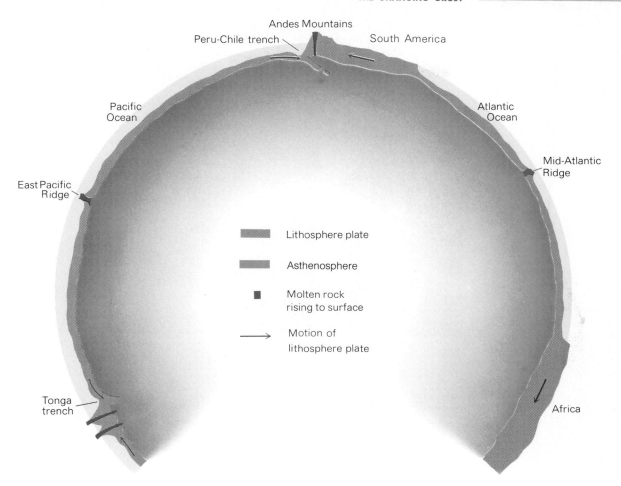

Pacific
Ocean

Andes Mountains

Peru-Chile trench

South America

Atlantic
Ocean

Mid-Atlantic
Ridge

East Pacific
Ridge

Lithosphere plate

Asthenosphere

Molten rock
rising to surface

Motion of
lithosphere plate

Tonga
trench

Africa

FIG. 15-21
The sea floor spreads apart at
midocean ridges where molten rock
rises to the surface of the lithosphere. At a trench, one lithosphere
plate is forced under another into
the asthenoshere, where it melts.
Mountain ranges, volcanoes, and island arcs are found where plates
collide. The vertical scale is greatly
exaggerated.

A plate margin descends into the
asthenosphere at a subduction zone

Origin of the Andes

At one boundary of each plate, molten rock rises to form new ocean floor
(Fig. 15-20). At the opposite boundary, the plate usually slides underneath the
adjacent one and melts when it reaches the asthenosphere. An oceanic trench is
produced at such a *subduction zone*. At the other boundaries the adjacent plates
are simply sliding past each other. In this manner the plates shift around the earth
despite their rigidity and carry the continents with them to produce continental
drift.

An example of a subduction zone occurs where the East Pacific plate (which
is moving eastward) collides with the American plate (which is moving westward)
along the western margin of South America (Fig. 15-21). The result is the formation of a trench along the coasts of Peru and Chile where the East Pacific plate sinks
into the asthenosphere and melts, and also the formation of a mountain range, the
Andes, at the edge of the American plate. From the depths at which earthquake

540

The Andes are a young mountain range thrust upward along the western edge of South America where the eastward-moving East Pacific plate is forced under the westward-moving Atlantic plate.

centers occur at subduction zones, it appears that plate material may not melt completely until it has descended as much as 600 km.

Origin of island arcs

The western Pacific plate, in its westward movement, has produced the island arcs that border the Asiatic side of the Pacific — the Aleutians, Japan, the Philippines, Indonesia, the Marianas. It seems likely that part of the rock in these and similar island arcs elsewhere (the West Indies, for instance) consists of the lighter materials of the lithosphere plates carried downward to melt in the hot asthenosphere. After melting, the buoyancy of these lighter materials would carry them upward again to penetrate cracks in the lithosphere overhead to form volcanoes at the surface and bodies of intrusive rock below the surface. According to one point of view, all the continents had their origins in processes of this kind. As a plate is forced under and melts, the lighter rock rises to create island arcs that eventually grow into continents or become attached to existing continents. Traces of what may have been former island arcs have been detected in the interiors of such present-day continents as North America.

Origin of the Himalayas

The moving apart of lithosphere plates and their collisions are not confined to ocean basins. Thus the Red Sea and the Gulf of California, both extensions of ocean ridges or rises, are currently widening. The massive Himalayas that divide India from the rest of Asia apparently owe their status as the world's highest mountains to the fact that continental blocks are too light relative to the underlying plate material to be forced under when two plates with continental margins come

Mt. Everest, the highest mountain on earth, is part of the Himalaya range in Asia that was thrust upward when the Indian plate collided with the Eurasian plate starting about 45 million years ago.

together. The collision of the Indian plate and the Eurasian plate, which began 45 million years ago, therefore resulted in a gigantic buckling that thrust up the Himalayas (see Fig. 15-20*b*). The geologic evidence for this event is backed up by the fossil record. The oldest mammal fossils in India date back only 45 million years and are similar to those found in Mongolia, the part of Asia with which India collided.

The San Andreas Fault

Earthquakes are common where plates slide past each other, as we would expect. Since most of these regions are in ocean basins, the quakes associated with them usually pass unnoticed except by seismologists. A conspicuous exception is the San Andreas Fault in California (see photograph on page 527), which lies along the boundary between the Pacific and American plates. This is a strike-slip fault, with the Pacific plate moving northward relative to the American plate at an average of about 6 cm (2.4 in.) per year. Movement along the fault does not occur continuously but in sudden jerks which release accumulated strains. The San Francisco earthquake of 1906 was caused by such an abrupt slippage, which amounted to nearly 7 m in places. The strains built up in the fault since then must inevitably lead to further earthquakes in that region.

Mechanism of Spreading

Convection currents may be doing the job

What is the mechanism that drives the lithosphere plates as though on huge conveyor belts from the ridges where they are formed to the trenches where they disappear back into the asthenosphere? Although the motion of the plates, and the drift of the continents that are embedded within them, seems well established, the details of how the motion occurs are still in doubt.

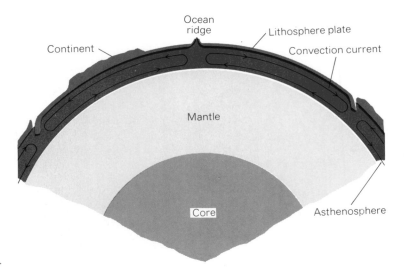

FIG. 15-22

A proposed system of convection currents in the asthenosphere. The vertical scale is greatly exaggerated.

The picture many geologists accept starts from the observations that the asthenosphere is soft enough to permit the lithosphere plates to slide over it and that its temperature increases from top to bottom due to heat generated by radioactive decay in the earth's interior. Not much imagination is needed to go on from these facts to speculate whether convection currents might not occur in the asthenosphere. We have encountered such currents before both in the atmosphere and in the oceans, and they are familiar to anyone who has placed a pan of cold soup on a stove. As the soup is heated, liquid from underneath rises to the surface in some places while surface liquid, which is cooler and therefore denser, sinks downward in other places; the motion in between is horizontal.

Hypothesis of convection spreading

A convective circulation of some kind, on a huge scale and very slow, might well be dragging the lithosphere plates across the face of the earth. Figure 15-22 shows an idealized flow pattern in the asthenosphere that fits the motion of the plates. A virtue of this pattern is that it is in accord with the forcing upward of the lithosphere where the asthenosphere material is rising and with its being sucked downward where the asthenosphere material is sinking. But for all its elegance, there are serious objections to the theory of convection currents. The chief difficulty is that the dense, viscous asthenosphere is supposed to flow in a manner that does not seem to be consistent with what is known about convection from theory and laboratory experiment.

Other hypotheses

Another hypothesis for the origin of the plate movement that avoids such objections has received some support. This is the idea that the elevated ridges push sideways on the adjacent plates simply by virtue of their weight. Forced upward by its buoyancy through the crack in the lithosphere between two plates, molten rock from the asthenosphere piles up and, as in the case of a person whose feet are in two adjacent rowboats, the plates inevitably spread apart. A contributing factor

FIG. 15-23
How the earth may appear in 30 million years from now if present trends continue.

The future

may also be the sinking of the edge of a plate where it melts, which might help pull the rest of the plate across the earth's surface. These lines of thought, too, are open to dispute. Possibly several mechanisms are involved in plate motion.

Regardless of the details of how their motions occur, the continents are definitely drifting across the globe, and new landmasses are coming into being at the various island arcs. A projection of present trends 30 million years into the future yields a picture like that shown in Fig. 15-23. The Atlantic Ocean has grown wider, the Pacific narrower. California has been detached from the rest of North America, and the Arabian peninsula has been forced around to become an integral part of Asia. The West Indies island arc has grown into a land bridge between the Americas, and the western Pacific island arcs have also increased markedly in extent.

And after that? All that can be said is that the face of the earth will probably continue to change in the future, just as it has been changing as far back in the past as we have any evidence.

IMPORTANT TERMS

The processes by which rocks are worn down and the debris carried away are included in the term *erosion.* The chief agent of erosion is running water, although *weathering* (the gradual disintegration of exposed rocks), *glaciers* (rivers and seas of ice formed from accumulated snow), and *groundwater* (subsurface water) also contribute. Most of the material carried by agents of erosion is deposited to form sediments, the bulk of which are laid down on ocean bottoms. *Lithification* refers to the gradual hardening into rock of sediments buried under later deposits.

A *volcano* is an opening in the crust through which molten rock (called *magma* while underground, *lava* above ground) comes out, usually at intervals rather than continuously. Intrusive bodies called *plutons* are formed by the solidification of magma under the surface. *Batholiths* are giant plutons composed mainly of granite that are found in mountain ranges.

Movements of the solid materials of the earth's crust are called *tectonic.* The principal kinds are faulting, folding, regional uplift, subsidence, and tilting. A *fault* is a fracture surface along which motion has taken place. *Mountain building* begins with the deposition of sediments in a sinking area, followed by tectonic movement and erosion.

The crust and the upper part of the mantle make up a shell of hard rock called the **lithosphere.** Below the lithosphere is a layer of plastic rock called the **asthenosphere.** According to the theory of **plate tectonics,** the lithosphere is divided into seven huge **plates** and a number of smaller ones. The plates can move relative to one another in three ways: by moving apart with molten rock rising to form new ocean floor at the gap; one plate can slide under another and melt; and adjacent plates can slide past each other. **Continental drift** occurs because of plate motion. Today's continents were once part of two supercontinents called **Laurasia** (North America, Greenland, Europe, and most of Asia) and **Gondwanaland** (South America, Africa, Antarctica, India, and Australia) which were separated by the **Tethys Sea.**

MULTIPLE CHOICE

1. A rock readily attacked by chemical weathering is
   a. limestone
   b. obsidian
   c. granite
   d. chert
2. The most important agents of erosion are
   a. streams
   b. glaciers
   c. winds
   d. waves
3. Which of the following are not produced by rivers?
   a. Flood plains
   b. Deltas
   c. Alluvial fans
   d. Moraines
4. In their early stages, river valleys exhibit characteristic
   a. U-shaped cross sections
   b. V-shaped cross sections
   c. water tables
   d. moraines
5. A typical speed for a valley glacier is
   a. 1 meter/hour
   b. 1 meter/day
   c. 1 meter/month
   d. 1 meter/year
6. The sediment deposited where a stream flows into a lake or sea forms
   a. a moraine
   b. an alluvial fan
   c. a dike
   d. a delta
7. The largest amounts of sediment are deposited
   a. by glaciers
   b. on river beds
   c. on the ocean floors
   d. by chemical precipitation
8. Most of the groundwater present in soil and underlying porous rocks comes from
   a. streams and rivers
   b. melting glaciers
   c. springs
   d. rain
9. The icicles of stone found hanging from the roofs of caves are called
   a. moraines
   b. stalactites
   c. veins
   d. crustaceans
10. Molten rock underneath the earth's surface is called
    a. magma
    b. lava
    c. obsidian
    d. till
11. The most common volcanic rock is
    a. granite
    b. basalt
    c. limestone
    d. shale
12. The holes found in most volcanic rocks are due to
    a. gases trapped in solidifying lava
    b. erosion
    c. marine organisms
    d. rapid cooling
13. The viscosity of a liquid is a measure of its
    a. temperature
    b. purity
    c. fluidity
    d. silica content
14. Thermal metamorphism is often found
    a. in veins
    b. in tuff
    c. near bodies of intrusive rock
    d. near bodies of sedimentary rock
15. A batholith is
    a. a fissure from which groundwater emerges
    b. a natural rock pillar
    c. a large body of intrusive rock
    d. a volcanic cone
16. A surface in the earth's crust along which movement has taken place is called
    a. a fault

b. a fold

c. an earthquake

d. a moraine

17. The thickness of the lithosphere varies between

  a. 2 and 5 km

  b. 5 and 35 km

  c. 50 and 100 km

  d. 500 and 1000 km

18. The layer of plastic rock beneath the lithosphere is called the

  a. stratosphere

  b. thermosphere

  c. asthenosphere

  d. mantle

19. As compared with the continents, the ocean floors are

  a. much younger

  b. much older

  c. about the same age

  d. in some places older and in others younger

20. According to the hypothesis of sea-floor spreading, molten rock is rising up along the

  a. trenches that rim the Pacific Ocean

  b. midocean floors

  c. location of the Tethys Sea

  d. equator

21. The Andes seem to be the result of

  a. the collision of two giant lithospheric plates

  b. magma welling up from the Peru-Chile trench

  c. the drift of a part of the Himalayas across the Pacific

  d. an enormous earthquake

22. A mountan range that was not once part of the Tethys Sea is the

  a. Alps

  b. Pyrenees

  c. Andes

  d. Himalayas

23. It is currently believed that India

  a. was always part of the Asian landmass

  b. rose from the Tethys Sea

  c. was once separated from Asia and later migrated to its present position

  d. is moving away from the Asian landmass

24. A typical speed for a lithospheric plate is

  a. 3 mm/year

  b. 3 cm/year

  c. 3 m/year

  d. 3 km/year

25. The ancient supercontinents Laurasia and Gondwanaland were separated by

  a. the Atlantic Ocean

  b. the Pacific Ocean

  c. the Tethys Sea

  d. the Caribbean Sea

26. If present trends continue,

  a. California will be detached from the rest of North America

  b. the Atlantic will become narrower

  c. the Pacific will become wider

  d. the West Indies will sink below the ocean surface

QUESTIONS

1. In what way is the weathering of rock important to life on earth?

2. What common rocks are almost immune to chemical weathering?

3. Both marble and slate are metamorphic rocks. Would you expect a marble tombstone or a slate one to be more resistant to weathering?

4. Granite consists of feldspars, quartz, and ferromagnesian minerals. (a) What becomes of these minerals when granite undergoes weathering? (b) What kinds of sedimentary rocks can the weathering products form?

5. What is the source of energy that makes possible the erosion of landscapes?

6. Why are streams the principal agents of erosion on the earth's surface?

7. Is there a limit to the depth to which streams can erode a particular landscape? Is there a limit in the case of glaciers?

8. What agent of erosion produces valleys with a V-shaped cross section? A U-shaped cross section?

9. Under what circumstances does a glacier form?

10. Glaciers grind away rock with far more force than rivers or streams, yet running water has had more influence in shaping landscapes around the world than glaciers have. Why?

11. How is it possible for glaciers to wear down rocks that are harder than glacial ice?

12. What is the eventual site of deposition of most sediments?

13. Why are clay minerals and quartz particles abundant in sediments which have not been chemically deposited?

14. In sand derived from the attack of waves on granite, what mineral or minerals would you expect to be most abundant?

15. What is the probable origin of the following sedimentary rocks?

  a. A thick, evenly bedded limestone

  b. A conglomerate with well-rounded boulders and numerous thin beds of sandy and clayey material

  c. A sandstone consisting of well-sorted, well-rounded grains of quartz

16. Why are hot-spring deposits thicker than the deposits found around ordinary springs?

17. What kinds of rocks are likely to be found in lava flows? What is the most common volcanic rock?

18. What factors determine the viscosity of a magma? What kinds of landscapes are produced by volcanoes whose lavas have relatively high and relatively low viscosities?

19. What is the cause of the holes found in many volcanic rocks?

20. What is the main constituent of volcanic gases?

21. What characteristic topographic features do active volcanoes produce? From what features could you conclude that volcanoes had once been active in a region where actual eruptions have long since ceased?

22. Distinguish between a dike and a vein.

23. (a) Why are metamorphic rocks often found near plutons? (b) Where would you expect to find the wider zone of thermal metamorphism, near a dike or a batholith?

24. Suppose that you find a nearly vertical contact between granite and sedimentary rocks, the sedimentary beds ending abruptly against the granite. How could you tell whether the granite had intruded the sedimentary rocks or had moved up against them after its solidification by tectonic movement along a fault?

25. Distinguish between the foliation of a metamorphic rock and the stratification of a sedimentary rock.

26. An experiment is performed to determine the lowest temperature at which a certain magma can exist within the earth by melting a sample of rock that has hardened from this magma in a furnace. How meaningful are the results of this experiment?

27. The energy source of erosional processes is the sun. Where does the energy involved in tectonic activity come from?

28. List all the evidence you can for each of the following statements:

    a. Granite is an igneous rock.
    b. Mica schist is a rock that has been subjected to nonuniform pressure.
    c. Compressional forces exist in the earth's crust.
    d. Tectonic movement is going on at present.

29. What topographical features are associated with faults?

30. When stream erosion has been active for a long time in a region underlain by folded strata, what determines the position of the ridges and valleys?

31. What geologic process is chiefly responsible for the topography of a mountain range?

32. Why is it believed that the region where the Rocky Mountains now stand was once near or below sea level?

33. What is the difference between the earth's crust and its lithosphere? How is it possible for a plastic asthenosphere to occur between a rigid lithosphere and a rigid mantle? If the asthenosphere is plastic, how can transverse seismic waves travel through it?

34. When continental drift was first proposed half a century ago, it was assumed that the continents move through soft ocean floors. Why is this hypothesis no longer considered valid? How does continental drift actually occur?

35. How do the ages of the ocean floors compare with the ages of continental rocks? What is the reason for the difference, if any?

36. What kind of biological evidence supports the notion that all the continents were once part of a single supercontinent? What kind of climatological evidence supports the concept of continental drift?

37. The east coast of South America is a good fit against the west coast of Africa. What sort of evidence would you look for to confirm that the two continents had once been parts of the same landmass?

38. What mountain ranges of today were once part of the Tethys Sea? What kind of evidence would indicate that the region where these mountains are present was once below sea level?

39. North America, Greenland, and Eurasia fit quite well together in reconstructing Laurasia, but there is no space available for Iceland. Why is the omission of Iceland from Laurasia reasonable?

40. How does the origin of the Himalayas differ from that of the oceanic mountains that constitute the Mid-Atlantic Ridge?

41. The San Andreas Fault in California is a strike-slip fault that lies along the boundary between the Pacific and American plates. What does this indicate about the nature of the boundary?

42. How would you expect the ages of the South Pacific islands far away from the East Pacific Rise to compare with those near this rise?

43. Why is there a mountain range on the western edge of South America but not one on its eastern edge?

44. The distance between the continental shelves of the east coast of Greenland and the west coast of Norway is about 1300 km. If Greenland separated from Norway 65 million years ago and their respective plates have been moving apart ever since at the same rate, find the average speed of each plate.

45. The oldest sediments found on the floor of the South Atlantic Ocean, which are 1300 km west of the axis of the Mid-Atlantic Ridge, were deposited about 70 million years ago. What rate of plate movement does this finding suggest?

ANSWERS TO MULTIPLE CHOICE

1. *a*	**8.** *d*	**15.** *c*	**22.** *c*
2. *a*	**9.** *b*	**16.** *a*	**23.** *c*
3. *d*	**10.** *a*	**17.** *c*	**24.** *b*
4. *b*	**11.** *b*	**18.** *c*	**25.** *c*
5. *b*	**12.** *a*	**19.** *a*	**26.** *a*
6. *d*	**13.** *c*	**20.** *b*	
7. *c*	**14.** *c*	**21.** *a*	

16

EARTH HISTORY

Nothing about the earth is fixed, permanent, unchanging. What is today a great mountain that pierces the sky may in the future be nibbled down into a mere hill, while elsewhere an undersea accumulation of sediments may be thrust upward into a lofty plateau. How do we know that such things can happen? After all, though plenty of geologic activity is taking place around us, for the most part the pace is exceedingly slow. Only after millions of years can the processes now at work yield large-scale changes in the pattern of the continents and in their landscapes. What justifies the belief that the earth's crust never stops evolving is the record of the past, a record that can be read in the rocks of the present.

Two kinds of events in the history of the crust are significant. In one category are physical changes such as the drift of the continents, the upthrust and wearing away of mountains, the spread and retreat of glaciers and ice sheets. In the other are changes in the living things that populate the earth, from primitive one-celled organisms to the complex plants and animals of today. Naturally the rock record is less complete the farther back we go, but it is still possible to trace the physical and biological evolution of the crust for billions of years into the past.

METHODS OF HISTORICAL GEOLOGY

Principle of Uniform Change

"No vestige of a beginning, no prospect of an end"

The modern view of geologic evolution is hardly more than a century old. In earlier times a major obstacle to scientific thinking on the earth's history was the Bible. The Book of Genesis tells the story of the earth's beginning with beauty and simplicity and some precision as to dates. So carefully are things dated in the Bible that a seventeenth-century theologian, Bishop Ussher, was able to compute that the creation of our planet from a formless void took place at 9 o'clock in the morning of October 12, 4004 B.C. However, even the most casual dabbling in geology shows that the events clearly recorded in the present landscape cannot possibly have occurred in only a few thousand years. Despite this, early investigators devoted their best efforts to trying to fit what they found into a literal interpretation of Genesis.

Even when freed from biblical shackles, geologists of the past usually went far astray in their arguments. One reason was their habit of generalizing from limited evidence. Another was their readiness to postulate tremendous events to explain particular findings. For instance, a comprehensive theory was formulated by Abraham Gottlob Werner on the basis of the geologic structures he found near his home in Freiberg, Germany: granite overlain by folded, somewhat metamorphosed rocks, these in turn overlain by flat sedimentary beds. Untraveled and deaf to the reports of others, Werner considered this sequence worldwide. Each of the three types of rock, he presumed, was deposited by a universal ocean, with granite precipitating first and the upper beds last. All rocks, in Werner's system, were sedimentary rocks, and the geologic history of the earth consisted of three sudden precipitations from an ancient ocean that were followed by the disappearance of most of the water.

The French biologist Georges Cuvier greatly influenced geology at the beginning of the nineteenth century. In successive rock layers around Paris, Cuvier found distinct groups of animal fossils, different from one another and from the present animals of that region. He concluded that each group appeared on the earth as the result of a special creation and that each was destroyed by a universal disaster before the next creation. Thus Cuvier regarded the earth's history as a succession of catastrophes that were separated by intervals of stable conditions.

James Hutton, a Scot, based his thinking on a much larger body of observational evidence than Werner or Cuvier did. He found no need to invoke special mechanisms since he could account for what he saw in terms of processes under way in the present-day world: "In the phenomena of the earth," Hutton concluded, "I see no vestige of a beginning, no prospect of an end."

Hutton's ideas were soon taken up by others who modified and extended them. Chief among Hutton's followers was the English geologist Charles Lyell (1797–1875), whose goal was "to explain the former changes of the earth's

Early geologists relied more on imagination than on observation and proposed sudden, catastrophic events to explain geologic change

Hutton saw a cycle of continuous change in the rock record

The principle of uniform change is fundamental to geology

surface by forces now in operation.'' This he was largely able to do, and his thesis became known as the *principle of uniform change*. Of course, the vigor of geologic processes has varied from time to time and from place to place, so that ''uniform'' is perhaps not the best word, but such irregularities are quite different from the catastrophic happenings earlier thinkers were so fond of.

Theory of evolution

An important link in the chain of ideas that was forming was supplied by Charles Darwin in 1859. Darwin's theory of evolution showed that changes in living things as well as in the inorganic world of rocks could be explained in terms of processes operating all around us. The fossil groups found by Cuvier near Paris did not come from special creations but were stages in a continuous line of development. Lyell understood at once the significance of Darwin's work and became one of his most active supporters.

How far back does the principle of uniform change hold? It must break down eventually because the earth in its early stages as a planet was certainly different from today's earth. All geology can say for certain is that the oldest rocks now exposed contain a clear record of processes very similar to those of the present. Beyond that lies the realm of hypothesis, and in Chap. 20 we shall see how theories of the origin of the earth connect up with geologic history.

Rock Formations

History under our feet

The crustal events of the past are recorded in the rocks and landscapes of the present. It is often possible to reconstruct these events in terms of processes still at work which are once again reshaping the face of the earth. Thus from moraines, lakes, and U-shaped valleys we learn of the spread and retreat of ancient glaciers. Wave-cut cliffs and terraces above the sea suggest recent elevation of the land. Hot springs and isolated, cone-shaped mountains signify past volcanic activity.

Earlier episodes are recorded more dimly in the rocks. A geologist finds a bed of salt or gypsum buried beneath other strata, and he or she knows that the region must once have had a desert climate in which a lake or an arm of the sea evaporated. A layer of coal implies an ancient swamp in which partly decayed vegetation accumulated. A limestone bed with numerous fossils suggests a clear, shallow sea in which lived clams, snails, and other hard-shelled organisms. As the long history is carried further and further back, the evidence becomes more shadowy and the geologist's reconstruction of the earth's surface similarly imprecise.

Historical geology is faced with two fundamental problems: to arrange in order the events recorded in the rocks of a single outcrop or small region, and to correlate events in various regions of the world to give a connected history of the earth as a whole. We begin with the first of these problems.

Some of the principles used in reading the history of a small area are not hard to arrive at:

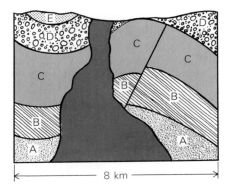

FIG. 16-1
Schematic cross section showing folded sedimentary rocks that were displaced along a fault and then intruded by granite (solid color).

Basic ideas of historical geology

1. In a sequence of sedimentary rocks, the lowest bed is the oldest and the highest bed is the youngest. In Fig. 16-1 bed *A* must have been deposited before the others and bed *E* last. A not very common exception to this rule is a sequence of strata completely overturned by intense folding.
2. Sedimentary beds were originally deposited in approximately horizontal layers.
3. Tectonic movement took place after the deposition of the youngest bed affected. Thus the strata of Fig. 16-1 were not folded until after bed *D* was laid down, and the fault must be younger than bed *C*.
4. An igneous rock is younger than the youngest bed it intrudes. The granite pluton shown in Fig. 16-1 is younger than bed *D*. (The age of an igneous rock refers to the time at which it solidified.)

Obvious as these rules are, to apply them in regions of heavily folded and faulted strata requires much ingenuity. The problem is especially difficult in regions where much of the rock structure is hidden by later sediments or vegetation.

A structure like that shown in Fig. 16-2 requires further attention. Here the lower, tilted beds are cut off by an uneven surface on which rest the upper horizontal beds. An irregular surface of this sort, separating two series of rocks, is called an *unconformity*.

An unconformity is a buried surface of erosion

An unconformity is a buried surface of erosion. It always involves at least four geologic events: the deposition of the oldest strata; tectonic movement that raises

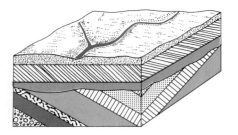

FIG. 16-2
An unconformity is an irregular eroded surface that separates one set of rock strata from an earlier set. Shown is an angular unconformity; the strata above and below an unconformity can also be parallel.

The Grand Canyon in Arizona, 1.6 km deep and 21 km wide, represents about 7 million years of erosion by the Colorado River of uplifted sediments laid down at intervals from 300 million to over 1 billion years ago. This photograph was taken looking west along the rim of the inner gorge from Plateau Point. The inner gorge here is carved through metamorphic rock with sedimentary layers above.

and perhaps tilts the existing strata; erosion of the elevated strata to produce an irregular surface; and finally a new period of deposition that buried the eroded surface. Usually the last of these events involves the lowering of the eroded surface either beneath the sea or to a level where stream deposition can occur.

Why unconformities are important

Unconformities are important in historical geology for several reasons. First of all, they make possible the approximate dating of past tectonic movements. Obviously the movement responsible for an unconformity must have occurred *after* the latest rocks of the older series and *before* the oldest of the upper layers. Second, unconformities tell us something about the distribution of land and sea at different periods of the earth's past, for an unconformity always means that dry land must have existed during the period of erosion that formed it. And unconformities are important in a negative sense, for they indicate gaps in the geologic record, times when no deposits were forming in particular regions. An unconformity tells us that a region was above sea level, but all details of the region's history for that span of time are lost.

The Grand Canyon has several unconformities

As an example of the geologic interpretation of the exposed rocks of a small region, Fig. 16-3 shows a cross section through part of the Grand Canyon together with a brief account of its varied history. Evidently the record has several gaps represented by major unconformities.

Radiometric Dating

A clock based on radioactivity

To trace the sequence of geologic events in various places is not enough: we must also know which events in each place happened at the same time in order to

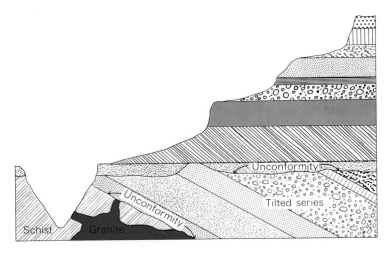

FIG. 16-3
Diagrammatic cross section of the Grand Canyon. In the upper part are the massive, nearly horizontal sedimentary layers responsible for the sculptured cliffs and the brilliant hues so evident to a visitor. Near the top of the steep inner gorge where the river is now cutting, the lowest of these beds rests on an uneven surface which bevels a series of tilted sedimentary strata. The tilted beds in turn are separated by an irregular surface from a still lower series of dark-colored schists and gneisses, complexly folded and intruded by dikes and irregular masses of gray granite.

The oldest rocks in the canyon are evidently the schists and gneisses of the inner gorge. The history of these rocks is obscure, for metamorphism has all but obliterated their original structures. Probably they were once sedimentary layers interbedded with lava flows, lying in an approximately horizontal sequence. In a period of diastrophism they were folded and metamorphosed; then or later they were intruded by granite. These are events that accompany mountain building, so we may picture a range

of mountains here at some distant time in the earth's past.

The uneven surface that planes off schist and granite alike is an unconformity, representing a long period of erosion when the ancient mountains were reduced to a nearly level plain. Sinking of the land or rising of other mountains nearby at length made this plain a basin of deposition, and beds which now form the tilted series were laid down—originally, of course, in a more nearly horizontal position. These beds contain no fossils, so it is difficult to reconstruct accurately the conditions under which they were formed. Because the rocks are mostly fine-grained sandstone and shale, and because each stratum is relatively thin and often shows irregularities, we may picture as a probable site of deposition the flood plain of a large river. After the deposition of these layers they were tilted in another period of diastrophism, and then long erosion reduced the land to the nearly level surface of the second unconformity, on which the horizontal strata rest.

From here on the record becomes clearer. Many of the

horizontal beds contain fossils, and from these and other evidence the conditions of their deposition can be inferred. The thick limestone at the top of the canyon and some of the massive sandstones are typical marine deposits. Some thin shale beds show tracks of amphibians, and so probably represent ancient mudflats along a river or a beach. A sandstone layer shows the rounded grains and other characteristics of windblown sand in an arid climate. Transitions between some layers are gradual, suggesting that deposition was continuous in spite of changing conditions. Other layers are separated by distinct unconformities, showing that at times the land was elevated sufficiently for erosion to take place. The careful study of the different layers provides an accurate reconstruction of changing conditions through a long part of earth history.

The last geologic events recorded at the canyon are elevation of the land high above the sea and erosion by the Colorado River, events which probably took place simultaneously.

understand how the earth's crust evolved. This would not be difficult if rock layers could be followed from one region to another around the globe. In general such a procedure is impossible, however, since a particular layer when followed for a long distance is either cut off by erosion or concealed by later deposits. There are two methods that can be used to figure out the worldwide sequence of the events that have shaped the earth's surface: radioactive dating and fossil identification. As we shall find, each method has different advantages and disadvantages.

Methods based on radioactive decay make it possible to establish the ages of many rocks on an absolute rather than a relative time scale. Because the decay of any particular radioactive isotope proceeds at a constant rate regardless of external conditions, the ratio between the amounts of that isotope and its stable daughter in a rock sample gives an indication of the age of the rock. The greater the proportion of the daughter isotope, the older the rock. Radioactive decay was discussed in Chap. 7.

The procedure may be illustrated with a rock that contains uranium. The chief isotope of this element is ^{238}U, which decays in a series of steps into the stable lead isotope ^{206}Pb. The various alpha particles that are emitted pick up electrons to become helium atoms. Since the rate of decay of ^{238}U itself is extremely slow compared with those of the intermediate radioisotopes, only the ^{206}Pb and helium end products need to be considered.

What we must measure are the amounts of ^{206}Pb and undecayed ^{238}U or the amounts of helium and undecayed ^{238}U. The amount of either ^{206}Pb or helium tells us how much uranium decayed, and this figure added to the uranium still there gives the original amount. Comparing the two reveals the age of the rock, since the half-life of ^{238}U is known (it is 4.5 billion years). Because helium is a gas and some may escape from the rock, the most reliable age determinations are based on the ^{206}Pb content.

Table 16-1 lists the radioisotopes that have been found most useful in dating igneous and metamorphic rocks. For accurate results, the age of the rock should normally be no more than 100 times more or less than the half-life of the isotope; the more nearly comparable the two are, the better.

The presence of long-lived radioisotopes and their decay products permits rock ages to be determined

Dating rocks with uranium

TABLE 16-1

Radioisotopes Found in Common Minerals That Are Often Used for Dating Rocks.

Parent isotope	Stable daughter isotope	Half-life, billion years
Potassium 40	Argon 40	1.3
Rubidium 87	Strontium 87	47
Uranium 235	Lead 207	0.7
Uranium 238	Lead 206	4.5

Some radiometric age measurements

Age measurements with the radioactive clock reveal that relatively large-brained humanlike creatures walked erect in Africa about 2 million years ago; that their ancestors branched away from the apes 7 or 8 million years ago; that primitive mammals existed about 200 million years ago; that sea animals with hard shells first became abundant about 600 million years ago. The most ancient rocks whose ages have been determined are found in Greenland and are believed to be 3.8 billion years old. Both igneous and sedimentary rocks of that age have been found, which suggests that geologic processes cannot have been very different than from what they are today.

Radiocarbon

Dating the recent past

Radiocarbon is found in all living things

The carbon isotope ^{14}C, called *radiocarbon,* is beta radioactive with a half-life of 5700 years. Radiocarbon is produced in small quantities in the earth's atmosphere by the action of cosmic rays (discussed in Chap. 20) on nitrogen atoms, and the carbon dioxide of the atmosphere contains a small proportion of radiocarbon as a result. Green plants take in carbon dioxide in order to live, and so every plant contains radioactive carbon which it absorbed along with its ordinary intake of carbon dioxide. Animals eat plants and in so doing become radioactive themselves. As a result, every living thing on earth is slightly radioactive because of the radiocarbon it takes in. The mixing of radiocarbon is very efficient, and so living

In order to measure its ^{14}C content, the carbon in a sample of organic origin is usually converted into a gas such as carbon dioxide which is then used to fill a special beta-sensitive detector. An early stage in this process is the heating of the sample to remove its volatile constituents, leaving nearly pure carbon which is shown being removed from the tube in which the reduction took place. Next the sample will be further purified in an acid bath.

Time after death of animal or plant	^{14}C content of sample	^{12}C content of sample
0 years	^{14}C ●	^{12}C
5,700 years ($\frac{1}{2}$ of original ^{14}C remains undecayed)	^{14}C ●	^{12}C
11,400 years ($\frac{1}{4}$ of original ^{14}C remains undecayed)	^{14}C •	^{12}C
17,100 years ($\frac{1}{8}$ of original ^{14}C remains undecayed)	^{14}C •	^{12}C

FIG. 16-4
The principle of radiocarbon dating. The radioactive ^{14}C content of a sample of dead animal or plant tissue decreases steadily, while its ^{12}C content remains constant. Hence the ratio of ^{14}C to ^{12}C contents indicates the time that has elapsed since the death of the organism.

The proportion of radiocarbon in living matter decreases after death, which permits the remains to be dated

plants and animals all have the same proportion of radiocarbon to ordinary carbon (^{12}C).

After death, however, the remains of living things no longer absorb radiocarbon, and the radiocarbon they contain keeps decaying away to nitrogen. After 5700 years, then, they have only half as much radiocarbon left — relative to their total carbon content — as they had as living matter, after 11,400 years only one-fourth as much, and so on. Determining the proportion of radiocarbon to ordinary carbon thus makes it possible to evaluate the ages of ancient objects and remains of organic origin (Fig. 16-4). This elegant method permits the dating of archeological specimens such as mummies, wooden implements, cloth, leather, charcoal from campfires, and similar remains of ancient civilizations as much as 40,000 years old.

Fossils

Tracing the history of life

Fossils are the remains or traces of living things of the past

Perhaps the most fascinating technique at the geologist's command for establishing relationships among rocks of different regions and for arranging beds in sequence makes use of *fossils*. Fossils are the remains or traces of organisms preserved in rocks. The most common, of course, are the hard parts of animals, such as shells, bones, and teeth. On rare occasions an entire animal may be preserved: ancient insects have been preserved in amber, and immense woolly mammoths have been found frozen in the arctic.

Plant fossils are relatively scarce, since plants do not contain easily preserved hard parts. The structure of tree trunks is sometimes beautifully shown in petrified

Fossil palate of early humanlike creature found in Olduvai Gorge, Tanzania.

Fossils are most common in marine sediments

Living things have gradually changed from simple forms to complex ones, which accords with the theory of evolution

wood, which is wood whose original organic materials have been replaced by silica deposited from solution in groundwater. The incomplete decay of buried leaves and wood fragments produces black, carbonaceous material which may preserve the original organic structures — coal is a thick deposit of such material. Occasionally fine sediments preserve impressions of delicate structures like leaves, feathers, and skin fragments. Some fossils are merely trails or footprints left in soft mud and covered by later sediments.

Conditions necessary for preservation have been much the same throughout geologic history. Chemical decay, bacteria, and scavengers have quickly disposed of most of the organisms that have lived on the earth, and only special conditions of burial occasionally permit the survival of fossil groups. These conditions most often occur on the floor of shallow seas, where life is abundant and deposition of sediment is sometimes rapid. Our picture of marine life in the past is accordingly far more complete than our picture of the organisms that lived on land, but even the marine record is fragmentary. Marine strata may contain no fossils at all, and the fossils that do occur are frequently broken and poorly preserved.

An important conclusion that comes from a study of the fossil record is that groups of organisms show a progressive change from those buried in ancient rocks to those of the most recent strata. In general, the change is from simple forms to more complex forms, from forms very different from those in the present world to creatures much like those around us today. These observations are part of the foundation for Darwin's theory that life has evolved by a steady development from simple organisms to complex ones.

How fossils are used in geology

Because plants and animals have changed continuously through the ages, rock layers from different periods can be recognized by the kinds of fossils they contain. This fact makes possible the arrangement of beds in a relative time sequence, even when their relationships are not directly apparent, and also provides a means of correlating the strata of different localities. If, for example, fossil snail shells and clamshells are found in a rock layer in New York that are similar to fossil shells from a layer in the Grand Canyon, the two layers are likely to be approximately the same age. Suppose that above the layer in New York is an unconformity and that at the Grand Canyon continuous deposition is recorded into a higher layer with a different group of marine fossils. We can infer that, in this later time, the New York region was a land area undergoing erosion while northern Arizona was still covered by the sea. Thus fossils are an important tool in historical geology for linking together the events of distant regions.

Fossils are useful not only in tracing the development of life and in correlating strata but in helping us to reconstruct the environment in which the organisms lived. Some creatures, like barnacles and scallops, live only in the sea, and it is probable that their close relatives in the past were similarly restricted to salt water.

Samples from a core of sediments extracted from the ocean floor are removed for examination. The record of the past is most complete in marine sediments.

Other animals can exist only in fresh water. On land some organisms prefer desert climates, others cold climates, others warm and humid climates. Evidently many details about the conditions in which a rock was formed are revealed by its fossil organisms.

Geochronology

Precambrian, Paleozoic, Mesozoic, Cenozoic

Fossils make possible a chronological arrangement of geologic events over the entire earth. Enough of these events can be dated accurately by measurements of radioactive decay so that good estimates can be made for the dates of the others.

The most recent 570 million years of the earth's history have been divided by geologists into three major divisions called *eras*. The era in which we are now living, the *Cenozoic* ("recent life") *era*, began about 65 million years ago. Before that came the *Mesozoic* ("intermediate life") *era*, which lasted 160 million years, and the *Paleozoic* ("ancient life") *era*, which lasted about 345 million years. The record of events before the Paleozoic era is so dim that geologists are not agreed about the proper division of this early time into eras. Although the nearly 4 billion years before the Paleozoic makes up seven-eighths of the history of our planet, it is usually considered as a single long division, *Precambrian time.*

The divisions of geologic time shown in Table 16-2 were originally made on the basis of evidence of dramatic changes that seemed to have occurred from time to time in the earth's history — changes in landscapes, in climates, in types of organisms. In particular, the fossil record shows that there were a number of occasions when animal and plant life became sharply reduced in both number and variety, to be followed in each case by the rapid evolution of new forms. The intervals of extinction were used to divide geologic history into periods. During a typical period there is an expansion of living things followed by a time in which biological change is more gradual, then an interval of extinction ends the period. The division into eras was based on exceptionally marked worldwide extinctions and subsequent expansions, and correlations were found between large-scale events in the earth's crust and the biological record. Not all these correlations have turned out to be as clear-cut as they once appeared, but the traditional organization of geologic time is still convenient and is universally used by scientists.

PRECAMBRIAN TIME

The earth came into existence about 4.5 billion years ago. Current ideas on its origin and that of the other planets are discussed in Chap. 20. With the oldest surface rocks, gneisses from western Greenland that date back 3.8 billion years according to radioisotope measurements, the story of the earth leaves the realm of speculation. These rocks and others of comparable age are igneous and are found intruding and interbedded with sedimentary and metamorphic rocks, which sug-

Cenozoic, Mesozoic, and Paleozoic eras

Precambrian time

How geologic time is divided

The earth is about 4.5 billion years old, and the oldest known surface rocks were formed 3.8 billion years ago

TABLE 16-2
Geologic Time.

(The earth came into existence 4500 million years ago, and the oldest known surface rocks were formed 3800 million years ago)

Millions of years before the present	Era	Period	Epoch	Duration in millions of years	The biologic record	
65	Cenozoic	Quaternary	Recent	0.01	Man becomes dominant	
225			Pleistocene	2.5	Rise of man; large mammals abundant	
570		Tertiary	Pliocene	4.5	Flowering plants abundant	Age of Mammals
			Miocene	19	Grasses abundant; rapid spread of grazing mammals	
			Oligocene	12	Apes and elephants appear	
			Eocene	16	Primitive horses, camels, rhinoceroses	
			Paleocene	11	First primates	
	Mesozoic	Cretaceous		71	First flowering plants, dinosaurs die out	Age of Reptiles
		Jurassic		54	First birds; dinosaurs at their peak	
		Triassic		35	Dinosaurs and first mammals appear	
	Paleozoic	Permian		55	Rise of reptiles; large insects abundant	
		Pennsylvanian	Carboniferous	45	Large nonflowering plants in enormous swamps	
		Mississippian		20	Large amphibians; extensive forests; sharks abundant	
		Devonian		50	First forests and amphibians; fish abundant	
4,000		Silurian		35	First land plants and large coral reefs	
		Ordovician		70	First vertebrates (fish) appear	
		Cambrian		70	Marine shelled invertebrates (earliest abundant fossils)	
	Precambrian time	Late Precambrian			Marine invertebrates, mainly without shells	
4,500		Early Precambrian			Marine algae (primitive one-celled plants)	

gests that the cycle of erosion and diastrophism was already well established as far back as the visible record of the earth's history extends.

Precambrian Rocks

Long ago but not far away

PRECAMBRIAN TIME
(4,500–570)

early Precambrian
(4,500–2,500)
marine algae (primitive one-celled plants)

late Precambrian
(2,500–570)
marine invertebrates, mainly without shells

(dates are millions of years ago)

Nothing is known for certain about the locations of the continents in Precambrian time. The splitting of Pangaea into Laurasia and Gondwanaland and their subsequent breakup into today's continents began less than 200 million years ago, a mere 4 percent of the earth's age. If plate movement had been going on further back in the past, the Precambrian continents must have been differently arranged in the midst of a different set of oceans. Whether the initial separation of the earth into crust, mantle, and core resulted in relative amounts of continental and oceanic crust about what they are today or quite different proportions is an unanswered question at this time. Nevertheless by 3 billion years ago recognizable ancestors of the present continents existed.

In any case, the geologic history of a number of regions of the present continents in much of Precambrian time can be traced. For instance, Precambrian rocks are exposed at the surface over a broad area covering most of eastern Canada and adjacent parts of the United States. This immense region of ancient rocks, one of the largest in the world, has stood above sea level for most of the 570

A sample of Precambrian rock that shows ripples and cracks characteristic of fine sediments deposited in shallow water and occasionally dried by exposure to the sun. Similar conditions occur along the shores of present-day lakes and seas.

million years since the beginning of the Paleozoic era. Smaller areas of Precambrian rocks are found in many parts of the country, particularly in the cores of mountain ranges where repeated uplifts and deep erosion have combined to expose them. In the Grand Canyon the Colorado River has cut through more than 1500 m of Paleozoic strata to reveal the older rocks at their base. It is natural to surmise that the Precambrian mountain ranges originated in the collision of lithosphere plates, much like the Andes and other youthful ranges which can be correlated with present-day plate movement. In this view ancient mountain ranges, or what is left of them after erosion did its work, are found wherever plates came together. Such locations are either subduction zones, as in the case of the Andes, or where former oceans shrank and closed, as in the case of the Himalayas where the Tethys Sea was squeezed out of existence by the northward migration of India.

Precambrian geologic processes resemble those of today

Although in places the later Precambrian strata are practically unaltered sedimentary and volcanic rocks, these old rocks more often show considerable metamorphism and often have been greatly deformed. For all the remoteness of the time when they came into being, Precambrian rocks embody events familiar from more recent geologic periods. The sedimentary beds are in part stream deposits, in part marine. In late Precambrian strata we even find rocks of glacial origin — coarse, angular conglomerates containing smoothed and striated boulders, resting on grooved rock surfaces — indicating at least two distinct periods of glaciation in this early stage of earth history. The volcanic rocks include all types, with basalt flows then as now the most common. Intrusive rocks are represented in great abundance and variety. Evidently geologic processes a billion years ago were not very different from those in the modern world.

Early Life

Living things have populated the earth for most of its existence

Evidence of ancient life

Precisely when and where life began on earth nobody knows, because primitive organisms usually leave no hint of their existence behind when they die. A rare piece of direct evidence is the finding of traces of bacterialike structures in 3.4-billion-year-old rocks in South Africa. Indirect evidence is more abundant in the form of beds of marble, whose ultimate source is typically the shells of aquatic creatures, and of layers of graphite (a form of pure carbon), which are most reasonably explained as originating in organic debris since all living things contain considerable carbon. Both marble and graphite are found in rocks up to 3 billion years old.

Oxygen and ozone

During the billion or so years that followed the appearance of life, primitive blue-green algae apparently grew widely in the oceans. These algae presumably could survive solar ultraviolet light that is deadly to most other organisms, and their photosynthetic activity provided the atmosphere with its oxygen content. This oxygen, together with the ozone layer it made possible which screens out solar ultraviolet light, established the final conditions required for the development of advanced forms of life. Evidence of multicellular algae and fungi has been discovered in the Gunflint Formation in Ontario, Canada, that dates from 1.9 billion years ago.

PALEOZOIC ERA

PALEOZOIC ERA

Cambrian (570–500)
marine invertebrates with shells
(earliest abundant fossils)

Ordovician (500–430)
first vertebrates (fish) appear

Silurian (430–395)
first land plants and large coral reefs

Devonian (395–345)
first forests and amphibians; fish
abundant

Mississippian (345–325)
large amphibians;
extensive forests; sharks abundant

Pennsylvanian (325–290)
large nonflowering plants in
enormous swamps

Permian (290–225)
rise of reptiles; large insects abundant

(dates are millions of years ago)

The Paleozoic ("ancient life") era begins in mystery, but its history is remarkably complete. No longer are there the doubts and the vagueness that characterize Precambrian events, for Paleozoic strata are widely exposed, and their wealth of fossils makes possible correlation of rocks and events from one side of the earth to the other.

Paleozoic North America

Shallow seas on the east and west

North America in the early Paleozoic bore little resemblance to the present continent. To the northeast was a highland of Precambrian rocks, perhaps with erosional remnants of late Precambrian mountains still standing. At either side of the continent was a broad sinking trough, covered during most of this time with a shallow sea. Across the middle of the continent stretched a low plain, parts of which were submerged at intervals by spreading of the shallow seas. The Appalachian trough was continuous with a trough in northwestern Europe, which during at least most of the Paleozoic formed part of a single continent with North America.

The chief physical events of the early Paleozoic were advances and retreats of the shallow sea which covered the sides of the continent most of the time and parts of the interior occasionally. At one time nearly 65 percent of the continent was under water (Fig. 16-5). In general this was a time when the earth's crust in North America was stable, its movements consisting simply of minor ups and downs of the continent as a whole. The only important exception was a mountain-building disturbance in New England toward the end of the Ordovician period.

The nature and distribution of fossil animals suggest that the early Paleozoic climates were mild over the entire continent, without the marked divisions into hot and cold regions present today. One exception was an interval of desert conditions recorded by beds of salt and gypsum in the Silurian strata of New York and Michigan.

Rocks of the later periods reveal, in contrast to the wide seas and the minor amount of diastrophic movement in the early Paleozoic, smaller seas and great diastrophic activity. Sedimentation, largely in shallow marine waters, continued through most of this time in parts of the two major troughs at the sides of the continent. Occasionally seas spread over the continental interior, but never widely as in earlier periods.

Fossils of trilobites that lived about
450 million years ago. The larger one
is 3 in. long.

FIG. 16-5
North America during part of the
Ordovician period of the Paleozoic.
Shallow seas are shown in light color
and present-day outcrops of
Ordovician rocks are shown in dark
color.

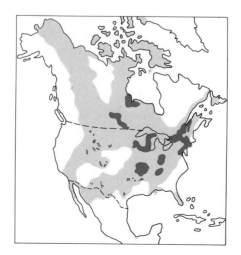

The Carboniferous period

A peculiar type of sedimentation in some regions characterized part of the Mississippian and Pennsylvanian periods: marine deposition alternated with non-marine, so that thin beds of sandstone, shale, and limestone follow one another in a regular sequence repeated time after time. The nonmarine parts of these cycles, especially in the Pennsylvanian, often contain layers of coal, indicating times of widespread, low-lying swamps with abundant vegetation. These are the great coal deposits of the central Mississippi Valley and the Appalachian region. So abundantly was coal formed at this time both in this country and in Europe that the Mississippian and Pennsylvanian are frequently lumped together as the *Carboniferous period.*

Widespread tectonic activity marked the end of the Paleozoic era

Volcanic activity in the Devonian period is shown by lava flows in the extreme eastern part of Canada, and flows of later periods are found in British Columbia and the northwestern part of the United States. Minor mountain-building disturbances occurred in New England during the late Devonian, in the Appalachian region and Oklahoma at the end of the Mississippian, and in western Texas toward the close of the Pennsylvanian. But these and earlier Paleozoic disturbances were dwarfed by the disturbances which ended the Permian period. During this intense tectonic activity, which affected many other parts of the world besides the North American continent, the sediments that had accumulated for more than 300 million years in the Appalachian geosyncline were crumpled, fractured, and uplifted into a mountain chain which must have rivaled any modern range in height and grandeur. It is not hard to connect these dramatic geologic events with the crushing together of the continental masses that formed the supercontinent Pangaea at this time.

Life Moves Ashore

Plants and animals in variety and abundance

Invertebrates have shells but not internal skeletons

The oldest fossils of the Paleozoic era are those of *invertebrates*, creatures without internal skeletons but with external shells of various kinds. All the major groups of the invertebrates are represented, some by organisms that must have had complex internal structures. It seems unlikely that such varied and complex forms could have evolved rapidly, but the fact remains that fossils of these creatures are not found in late Precambrian rocks. Perhaps fairly complex invertebrates were indeed present in the seas of late Precambrian times but they were not yet able to grow hard shells that could be preserved. This idea would allow a long period of evolutionary development during Precambrian times, the only radical advance being the development of shells 600 million or so years ago.

Marine life later in the Paleozoic era shows many changes from that in earlier seas, but was still far different from marine life of the present. Clams and snails increased in numbers and showed considerable evolutionary advances. Corals built widespread reefs in the middle Devonian but thereafter were not conspicuous. Starfish and sea urchins were not common, but some of their distant relatives that today are extinct or rare were more numerous then. Fishes were more abundant than earlier and showed greater variety of form.

In late Paleozoic rocks there is for the first time considerable evidence of land-dwelling organisms. In the coal swamps of Pennsylvanian times grew dense forests of primitive plants — huge fernlike trees, enormous horsetails, primitive conifers. A modern person wandering through such a forest would find no bright-colored flowers, no grasses, few plants at all familiar except possibly some of the ferns and mosses. In and near these primeval forests lived a great variety of animals: scorpions, land snails, primitive insects. The land-living vertebrates of the late Paleozoic are early members of our own family tree. Fossil amphibians, oldest of the land vertebrates, appear first in Devonian rocks. These are relatives of modern frogs and salamanders, sluggish creatures that laid their eggs and spent the early part of their lives in water. Their body structure and dependence on water suggest that they were descended from fishes, but the complete line of development cannot be traced.

Reptiles were the chief land animals in the Permian period

In Pennsylvanian rocks appear fossils of reptiles, animals that looked at first much like their amphibian ancestors but had the great advantage of being able to lay their eggs on dry land. The dry climate at the end of this era wrought havoc upon the amphibians, but the reptiles, no longer dependent on water for hatching their eggs, multiplied rapidly and developed a great variety of species. During the Permian reptiles became the dominant creatures of the land.

Coal and Oil

Both came from once-living matter

Coal beds are the sites of ancient swamps

Coal and oil are plentiful in Paleozoic rocks. Coal was formed from plant matter that accumulated under conditions where complete decay was prevented. A bed of coal nearly always implies an ancient swamp. Coal has been formed in swamps from the Devonian to the present day, but seldom have conditions been so favorable for large-scale accumulation as in the Pennsylvanian period. Apparently there were broad swamps almost at sea level that became periodically submerged so that partly decayed vegetation was covered with thin layers of marine sediments.

The formation of coal begins with the slow bacterial decay of the cellulose content of plants. Taking place largely under water and in the absence of air, this decay results in a gradual removal of oxygen and hydrogen from the cellulose to leave a residue which is largely carbon. Also contributing to coal formation was the action of heat and pressure resulting from burial beneath later sediments.

The origin of petroleum is more obscure, for two reasons: fossils cannot be preserved in a fluid, and oil often migrates long distances from the place where it forms. Because petroleum hydrocarbons can be detected in modern marine sediments, because oils resembling petroleum can be prepared artificially from organic material, and because petroleum is commonly found in rocks formed

High-capacity loading machine in a coal mine in Pennsylvania sweeps coal dislodged from a seam onto a conveyor belt and then into a shuttle car. About half the coal extracted in the United States comes from underground mines, whose average depth is 150 m. The rest is gouged in the open from deposits that lie near the surface after the overlying soil has been stripped away. Most of the underground mines are in the eastern part of the country; most of the surface mines are in the western part. The coal currently consumed in the world each year took about 2 million years to accumulate.

Fossil fern of the Pennsylvanian period found in Illinois.

from sediments deposited in shallow seas, most geologists consider that the origin of petroleum from organic material is established. Probably both plant and animal matter contributed to its formation, the substances involved being largely proteins, fats, and waxes rather than cellulose.

Origin of petroleum and natural gas

Three steps seem to have been involved in producing petroleum. The first consisted of bacterial decay in the absence of oxygen, an ideal site being the floor of a shallow sea. Then, as the organic debris was buried under later sediments, it was further modified by low-temperature chemical reactions. The final step was the "cracking" of complex hydrocarbons to straight-chain alkane hydrocarbons (Chap. 12) under the influence of temperatures of 70 – 130°C deep underground. If the temperatures became higher, the result was natural gas rather than oil.

Where oil is found today

Both gas and oil, like groundwater, can migrate freely through such porous rocks as loosely cemented sandstones and conglomerates. Wherever they may be formed, they often find their way into porous beds, and it is from these beds that they are obtained by drilling. Migration along a porous bed may be induced by a number of factors — gravity, pressure due to the weight of overlying material or to tectonic movement, gas pressure, movement of groundwater. Since both oil and gas are lighter than water, they may be displaced by groundwater and so move upward to the surface to form oil seeps.

In general, oil becomes available in large quantities only when it is trapped underground by impervious material such as shale or salt beds. The most common kind of trap is one formed by an anticline (a fold convex upward), as in Fig. 16-6.

Drilling rig *Unifor I* in the North Sea, where extensive deposits of oil occur between England and Norway. Oil furnishes about half the energy needs of today's industrial societies as well as being a valuable industrial raw material. Demand may exceed supply before the end of this century.

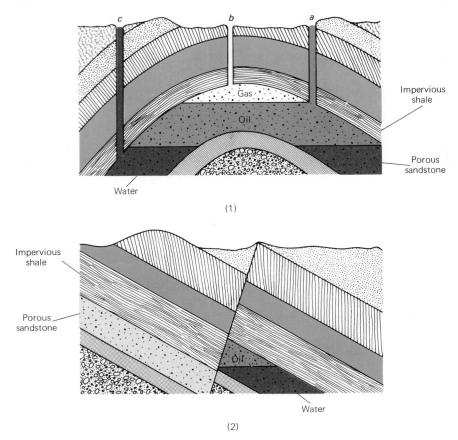

(1)

(2)

FIG. 16-6
Two common types of structural traps in which oil accumulates are (1) a trap formed by an anticline and (2) a trap formed by a fault. In both cases oil in a porous layer is prevented from moving upward by an impervious layer. A well drilled at *a* would strike oil, one drilled at *b* would strike gas, and one at *c* only water. About 80 percent of known oil deposits are found in anticline traps.

MESOZOIC ERA

The earliest Mesozoic ("intermediate life") sediments were laid down about 225 million years ago, a long time by ordinary reckoning. But the earth was already very old. Some 345 million years had elapsed since the beginning of the Paleozoic and $3\frac{1}{2}$ billion years since the oldest known rocks in the Precambrian. All the time that we include in the Mesozoic and Cenozoic eras is only one-sixteenth of the history recorded in rocks of the earth's crust.

Mesozoic North America

A separate continent at last

Laurasia and Gondwanaland broke up in the Mesozoic era

The Mesozoic era saw Pangaea split into Laurasia and Gondwanaland, and this division was followed by their own breakup. Early in the Mesozoic era North

MESOZOIC ERA

Triassic (225–190)
dinosaurs and first mammals appear

Jurassic (190–136)
first birds; dinosaurs at their peak

Cretaceous (136–65)
first flowering plants;
dinosaurs die out

(dates are millions of years ago)

America began to part from Europe, and somewhat later, perhaps 120 million years ago, South America and Africa began to drift apart. By the end of the era Gondwanaland no longer existed: Australia, New Zealand, and India had all left Africa, though Arabia still remained attached. Africa itself was in the process of a shift northeastward, thus closing the western end of the Tethys Sea, while India, well on its way toward Asia, was moving into the eastern end. The Mid-Atlantic Ridge was already a prominent feature of the floor of the infant Atlantic Ocean.

For the North American continent — first as part of Laurasia, then as a separate continent — the history of the era can be reconstructed from the distribution of Mesozoic rocks. At first almost the entire landmass stood above sea level, its surface a broad plain except for the new-formed Appalachians on the east and a few low ranges elsewhere. Streams from the eastern Appalachians carried sediments into narrow valleys along the mountain front. Dry conditions in the Southwest made possible the heaping up of windblown sand. Then, toward the middle of the era, shallow seas along the Pacific Coast became more prominent. From the Arctic Ocean a sea invaded the western part of the continent, at the time of its widest extent spreading out over the plains states and connecting with the Gulf of Mexico (Fig. 16-7). Fluctuations of this sea led to the formation of inland basins where river and lake deposits were formed. Finally, at the end of the era, the entire continent was once more above water.

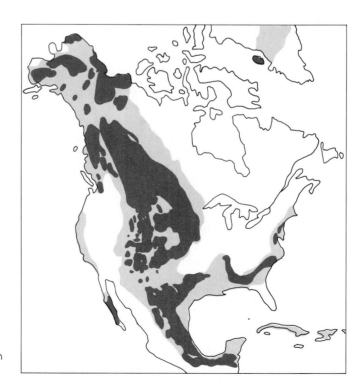

FIG. 16-7
North America during the Cretaceous period of the Mesozoic era. Shallow seas are shown in light color and present-day outcrops are shown in dark color.

The Mesozoic, like the early Paleozoic, was for the most part a time of crustal stability interrupted only by minor uplifts and subsidences. One local disturbance broke into this peaceful picture: toward the end of the Jurassic, subduction along the western edge of the continent led to folding and the intrusion of granite batholiths, forming a mountain range on the site of the present Sierra Nevada of California and lesser ranges to the north and south. Volcanic activity during the early Mesozoic is recorded in basalt flows and intrusive sheets in the red Triassic sediments of the Appalachians. Volcanic materials are also abundant in Triassic beds in British Columbia and in the northwestern states. Eruptions in California and adjacent regions accompanied the mountain building at the end of the Jurassic.

Climates of the Mesozoic were in general mild, although arid conditions prevailed in the southwestern states for at least part of this era.

Like the Paleozoic, the Mesozoic era in North America closed with a time of intense tectonic activity, this time centering in the Rocky Mountain region. Sediments which had accumulated intermittently since earliest Cambrian times were folded, thrust eastward, and uplifted high above sea level. At the same time other parts of the continent were raised vertically; in particular the Old Appalachian range, worn down by the end of the Cretaceous to a nearly level plain, was warped upward and erosion began anew. This period of disturbance, like earlier ones, was accompanied by extremes of climate and by rapid shifts in the position of land and sea.

Mesozoic Life

What happened to the dinosaurs?

On Mesozoic lands developed a group of reptiles that included some of the largest animals the earth has seen — the *dinosaurs*, descendants of the primitive reptiles that had survived from the Paleozoic. Some were carnivores with bodies designed for pursuing and eating other animals. Some were herbivores with jaws and digestive organs adapted for a vegetarian diet. Active species lived in open plains, more sluggish ones in swamps. Some had bony armor for protection; others depended on speed to escape their enemies. Not all the dinosaurs by any means grew to large size, but the biggest ones were enormous beasts over 25 m in length that weighed more than 40 tons.

Meanwhile other land organisms were developing. Flowering plants appeared in mid-Mesozoic and with them a host of modern-looking insects suited for helping in the pollination of flowers. The first true birds, with feathered wings rather than membranes, arose from reptilian ancestors in the Jurassic. Sometime in the Triassic appeared the first *mammals*, tiny creatures probably descended from a group of small Permian reptiles. All during the Mesozoic mammals remained small and inconspicuous, but in several respects they represented an evolutionary advance over reptiles: they were warm-blooded, hence better able to cope with

Skeleton of *Allosaurus fragilis,* a carnivorous dinosaur that lived in North America 130 million years ago.

changes of temperature; they had bigger brains relative to their body size; and they cared for their young after birth, so some of the experience of one generation could be passed on to the next.

The extinction of the dinosaurs

For over 100 million years dinosaurs large and small roamed the earth. Then, 65 million years ago, all of them disappeared. Not a single dinosaur fossil has ever been found in rocks formed after the end of the Mesozoic era. Dinosaurs were not the only victims: as many as 90 percent of the plant and animal species of the world were wiped out at about the same time. This mass extinction is what divides the Mesozoic era from the Cenozoic, and its cause has become the subject of much controversy.

On one side of the argument is the fact that extinctions of organisms are by no means unusual in geologic history. New species have evolved, flourished, and then died out as far back as the fossil record exists. There is no shortage of past events that could have led to these extinctions. The shifting of the continents and surges in volcanic activity associated with such shifts certainly led to repeated changes in climate, in sea level, in the amount of sunlight reaching the surface (which affects the photosynthesis that is at the base of the chain of life), in the carbon dioxide content of the atmosphere, and so forth. In particular, the end of the Mesozoic was a time of worldwide tectonic and volcanic activity, and it would have been surprising if large-scale extinctions had not occurred then. The late Mesozoic extinctions are noteworthy only in their magnitude: at no other time in the earth's history have so many species vanished simultaneously or nearly so.

A layer rich in iridium suggests that a meteorite impact may have caused the dinosaurs and other life forms to disappear

Until recently there seemed no reason to suppose that the fate of the dinosaurs was unusual in any fundamental way. Then came the discovery of exceptionally large traces of the element iridium in a thin clay layer in Gubbio, Italy, that separated marine limestones of the late Mesozoic from younger limestones. Iridium, a metal similar to platinum, is rare in the earth's crust but relatively abundant in the meteorites that bombard the earth from space (Chap. 17). Other late-Mesozoic deposits rich in iridium were soon found elsewhere as well. The obvious inference was that a giant meteorite, perhaps 10 km across, struck the earth 65 million years ago. The impact would have sent up a vast cloud of dust that remained in the stratosphere for some months, blocking sunlight and thereby wiping out much of the life on our planet.

Support for a meteorite impact does not end with the iridium findings. It would be rather peculiar if, in the long history of the earth, exactly one such impact had occurred. In fact, craters that record past impacts of meteorites are not uncommon, a notable one being the famous Great Meteor Crater in Arizona (page 608). Most such craters are fairly small, but three very large ones are known, one in Canada and two in the Soviet Union. They are 70 to 100 km across, consistent with meteorites 10 km or so in diameter. Other meteorites may well have fallen in the ocean, where craters would have filled quickly. So it is possible that every few hundred million years a great meteorite strikes the earth, with the most recent one marking the end of the Mesozoic.

A meteorite impact is not the only possible explanation

The question of whether the dinosaur extinction had a geologic or an astronomical origin does not stop with the above considerations. For one thing, it is not at all certain that all the species that disappeared at the end of the Mesozoic did so at the same time as the dinosaurs. For another, a layer rich in iridium has been found in Montana well above the highest rocks that contain Mesozoic fossils, indeed above rocks that contain fossils from the Cenozoic era that followed, which suggests that the dinosaurs there were gone long before the iridium was deposited. Furthermore, the most intense volcanic activity in the earth's history took place at the end of the Mesozoic, leaving 300,000 square km of India covered with several km of lava. Perhaps the CO_2 that must also have been emitted made the oceans so acid that plankton shells dissolved in it. This would have allowed the normal steady rain of small iridium-containing meteorites to accumulate without being heavily diluted by the shells of dead plankton, as is the case today. Thus the iridium layer need not be the result of a giant meteorite collision at all.

Whatever the reason (or reasons) dinosaurs are no longer with us, it is clear that the history of our planet is far from being a dull subject.

Extinctions and the principle of uniform change

The widespread biological extinctions of the past, in particular the drastic one in which the dinosaurs disappeared, lead to an interesting question. How can the violent events that caused them be reconciled with the principle of uniform change, according to which the earth's geologic history can be explained, in Lyell's words, by "forces now in operation"? Certainly the event that caused not only the dinosaurs but a large proportion of the world's other living things to perish is a catastrophe in the usual definition of the word. But we should note that the ideas proposed to account for this catastrophe are all in accord with the same laws of nature we find in today's universe. Such is not the case with Werner's idea that all rocks were formed in three precipitations from a universal ocean or with Cuvier's idea of the periodic destruction and re-creation of life by divine edict. Their catastrophes make no sense in terms of what we know about physics, chemistry, and biology. On the other hand, volcanoes and giant meteorites certainly exist, and even though they may only affect the earth drastically at intervals of many millions of years, they still fit into the pattern of the principle of uniform change.

CENOZOIC ERA

CENOZOIC ERA

Tertiary {
Paleocene (65–54)
first primates

Eocene (54–38)
primitive horses, camels, rhinoceroses

Oligocene (38–26)
apes and elephants appear

Miocene (26–7)
grasses abundant; rapid spread of grazing mammals

Pliocene (7–2.5)
flowering plants abundant
}

Quaternary {
Pleistocene (2.5–0.01)
rise of man; large mammals abundant

Recent (0.01–0)
man is most complex and successful form of life

(dates are millions of years ago)
}

Tectonic activity in the Cenozoic

In many ways the Cenozoic ("recent life") era, in which we exist today, has been markedly different from preceding eras. During the Cenozoic the continents have stood for the most part well above sea level. No longer do shallow seas spread widely. In North America, marine beds are found only in narrow strips along the Pacific Coast and on the Atlantic Coast from New Jersey south to Yucatan. The thick Tertiary beds east and west of the Rocky Mountains are river, lake, and wind deposits made in continental basins. And climates during much of the Cenozoic have had a diversity like those of the present. The distribution of plants and animals shows that, instead of having widespread moderate climates like those of other eras, Cenozoic continents have had zones of distinct hot, cold, humid, and dry climates.

Geologic Activity

An era of violence

A characteristic of Cenozoic times has been widespread volcanic activity. From the Rockies to the Pacific Coast lava flows and tuff beds testify to former volcanoes, some of which have only recently become extinct. In the mid-Tertiary, immense flows of basalt inundated an area of nearly a half-million square km in Oregon, Idaho, and Washington. Some of these flows today form the somber cliffs of the Columbia River Gorge.

The Cenozoic has also been a time of almost continuous tectonic disturbance, in contrast with the long periods of crustal stability in previous eras. Movements associated with the mountain-building episodes that divide the Cenozoic from the Mesozoic lasted well into the Tertiary. In mid-Tertiary the Alps and Carpathians of Europe and the Himalayas of Asia were folded and uplifted. Toward the end of the Tertiary the Cascade range of Washington and Oregon was formed, and other mountain ranges began to form around the border of the Pacific which have continued active to the present day. Mountain ranges that had been folded earlier — the Appalachians, the Rockies, the Sierra Nevada — were repeatedly uplifted during the Cenozoic, and erosion following these uplifts has created their present topography.

It is not hard to associate the above reshaping of continental landscapes with the spreading of sea floors and the grinding together of lithospheric plates that are still in action today. In the Cenozoic the continents continued their earlier drifts, and in addition Greenland parted from Norway, Australia parted from Antarctica (New Zealand had done so earlier), and the Bay of Biscay opened up. More recently the Arabian peninsula broke off from Africa, the Gulf of California opened to separate Baja California from mainland Mexico, and Iceland rose above the surface of the Atlantic Ocean.

Cenozoic Life

The age of mammals

Animal life in the Cenozoic

Thanks to their greater adaptability, some mammals managed to survive the mass extinction that ended the Mesozoic era. Without the dinosaurs to keep them in check, they multiplied and evolved rapidly. Carnivores like cats and wolves, armored beasts like rhinoceroses, agile creatures like deer and rabbits—ancestors of all these modern forms roamed the early Tertiary landscape. A few mammals, like the whales and porpoises, took to life in the sea; another line, the bats, developed wings. By the middle Tertiary, mammals dominated the earth as reptiles had before them. Side by side with the mammals developed modern birds, modern insects, and the deciduous trees of modern forests. As the end of the Tertiary approached, both the physical and the organic worlds assumed more and more closely their present aspect.

The continents became biologically isolated in the Cenozoic

Until well into the Mesozoic era primitive mammals were apparently able to move more or less freely between many of today's continents despite the fragmentation of Laurasia and Gondwanaland. Land bridges joined North America with both Europe and Asia, for instance, so even though an inland sea from the Tethys Sea to the Arctic Ocean cut Europe off from Asia directly, a roundabout route between them existed. But in the Cenozoic the biological isolation of the continents became increasingly effective—there was not even a land link between North and South America until only a few million years ago—and separate lines of mammalian development appeared. In place of the division of the world's land area into two self-contained biological units in the Mesozoic, when reptiles were the dominant form of animal life, the Cenozoic lands seem to have been effectively split into at least eight biological units.

The Ice Age

One of many

During the Pleistocene epoch great icecaps formed in Canada and Northern Europe and valley glaciers advanced in high mountains elsewhere. This was only the latest in a series of glacial periods that have punctuated earth history (see Chap. 13), but, since these particular glaciers have taken part so directly in shaping present landscapes, the Pleistocene is often referred to simply as the Ice Age.

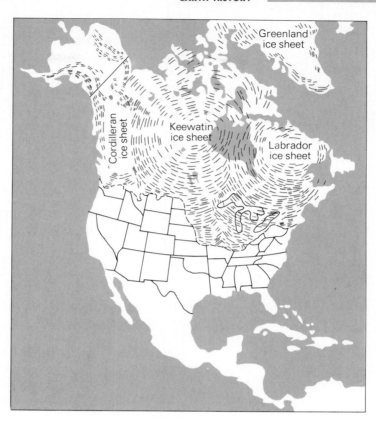

FIG. 16-8
The maximum extent of Pleistocene
glaciers.

The Ice Age in North America

Glacial deposits in North America show that ice spread outward from three centers of accumulation in Canada, the ice front in its farthest advance reaching the Missouri River on the west and the Ohio River to the east (Fig. 16-8). Many different times of ice advance can be distinguished, with long interglacial periods between. During at least one of these interglacial times the ice disappeared completely, and the climate became warmer than it is today.

The changing climates of the Pleistocene proved a severe ordeal for living things. In the present world mammals are still dominant, but in numbers and diversity of species they have declined markedly since the later Tertiary. Against this background of shifting ice fronts and a declining mammalian population was played the drama of early human history. Probably sometime in the late Tertiary the human evolutionary branch split off from that of the apes and monkeys, for humanlike fossils and crude stone implements are sometimes found in Pliocene beds in east Africa.

Early human fossils

By early in the Ice Age human creatures had spread widely over the earth; their remains have been found in Java and China as well as in Africa. The later record is most complete in Europe, where stone implements, burial sites, drawings on caves, and skeletal fragments give a fairly connected history. There does not seem to have been a continuous development but rather a succession of races, each flourishing for a time and then being followed by another. The immediate ancestors of present-day Europeans did not appear until the retreat of the last ice sheet some 20,000 years ago.

Population and the Future

The biggest problem of all

In the past biological changes have been brought about largely by changes in the physical environment, so the biological narrative follows the physical one through the ages. The modern world seems to be witnessing a reversal of this sequence. We are not only able by virtue of our ingenuity to flourish in the environment that nature has provided, but we are able to alter the environment in a number of ways. These alterations, small but numerous, have permitted a vast number of people to live relatively free (by historical standards) of starvation and disease. Today deaths due to ailments brought on by chronic overeating compete in number with those due to famine.

Apparently no irreversible worldwide damage to the interplay between organism and environment has as yet occurred. But continued into the future and swollen many times over in scale by population growth, our present patterns of industry, agriculture, and warfare seem certain to menace this interplay. The indiscriminate use of pesticides and artificial fertilizers has already destroyed the ecological balance in many areas; numerous inland waters have been poisoned by industrial waste; noxious gases fill the air in most densely populated regions; acid rain due to power-plant emissions has damaged forests and lakes on a large scale; deposits of radioactive by-products lie waiting for chance catastrophe to disperse them; and so on. Most ominous of all is that, whatever the character of our terrestrial activity, an increase in this activity is inevitable: from perhaps 500 million in 1650, 1 billion in 1850, 2 billion in the 1920s, and 4.5 billion today, the world's population will climb to at least 6 billion by the year 2000 (and to 60 billion by 2100 if the current rate of increase continues).

The world's population is increasing at an unprecedented rate

How will all these people be fed? Where will the natural resources come from to accommodate their other needs? How will the environment respond to the increased assaults upon it when it is deteriorating even now? And, even if these problems can be solved, what kind of lives will our children and grandchildren have if the earth becomes a human anthill?

Overpopulation is the principal hazard facing the world

Since safe and efficient means of family planning exist, there is no reason why the world's population cannot be stabilized at a reasonable level. What is lacking is a general realization of how grave the situation is becoming in many countries, a realization that, if postponed too long, may have disastrous consequences.

IMPORTANT TERMS

According to the **principle of uniform change,** geologic processes in the past were the same as those in the present. An **unconformity,** which is a buried surface of erosion, indicates that tectonic uplift, erosion, and sedimentation have occurred in that order.

Radioactive isotopes and their decay products in rocks make it possible to date geologic formations. The remains of living things can be dated with the help of **radiocarbon,** the radioactive carbon isotope ^{14}C. **Fossils,** the remains of organisms preserved in rocks, are useful in correlating strata, in tracing the development of living things, and in reconstructing ancient environments.

Geologic time is divided into **Precambrian time** and the **Paleozoic, Mesozoic,** and **Cenozoic eras;** the latter started 570, 225, and 65 million years ago, respectively. Eras are subdivided into **periods** and the periods into **epochs.**

MULTIPLE CHOICE

1. An uneven surface on which a horizontal upper bed rests is called
   a. a stratum
   b. a fault
   c. a dike
   d. an unconformity

2. An unconformity can be interpreted as
   a. the result of volcanic action
   b. an intrusion of igneous rock
   c. a buried surface of erosion
   d. an example of radioactive decay

3. Each of the following elements has at least one radioactive isotope. Which is not useful in geochronology?
   a. Potassium
   b. Rubidium
   c. Uranium
   d. Plutonium

4. Radiocarbon dating is based upon the fact that
   a. ^{14}C is continually being formed in the remains of living things after their death
   b. ^{14}C is not radioactive
   c. the ^{14}C content of the remains of living things depends upon the time in the past when they came into being
   d. the ^{14}C content of the remains of living things depends upon the time in the past when they died

5. Radiocarbon dating is limited to the remains of plants and animals that died no longer ago than about
   a. 100 years
   b. 5700 years
   c. 40,000 years
   d. 1,000,000 years

6. Conditions for the preservation of fossils are best fulfilled
   a. in the desert
   b. on the floors of shallow seas
   c. on ocean floors
   d. on river beds

7. Arrange the following eras of geologic time in their proper sequence:
   a. Paleozoic era
   b. Precambrian time
   c. Cenozoic era
   d. Mesozoic era

8. The earth was formed
   a. in 4004 B.C.
   b. about 2 million years ago
   c. about 4.5 billion years ago
   d. about 10 billion years ago

9. The oldest rocks that have been dated are approximately
   a. 2 million years old
   b. 200 million years old
   c. 4 billion years old
   d. 10 billion years old

10. In rocks of which of the following eras does evidence of life appear?
    a. Precambrian
    b. Paleozoic
    c. Mesozoic
    d. Cenozoic

11. Ancient geologic processes as revealed in Precambrian strata were
    a. primarily volcanic
    b. primarily glacial
    c. primarily erosion and sedimentation
    d. quite similar to those of the present time

12. Large exposures of Precambrian rocks are to be found in
    a. eastern Canada and adjacent parts of the United States
    b. the Rocky Mountains
    c. Texas and New Mexico
    d. the Middle West

13. At one time during the Paleozoic era
    a. all North America was a vast mountain range
    b. two-thirds of North America was covered by water
    c. mammals were abundant in North America
    d. prehistoric man arrived in North America

14. Coal is composed of
   a. petrified wood
   b. buried plant material that has partially decayed
   c. buried animal material that has partially decayed
   d. a variety of igneous rock

15. Most coal deposits were formed in the
   a. Cenozoic
   b. Mesozoic
   c. Paleozoic
   d. Precambrian

16. Amphibians, fishes, and marine invertebrates were the dominant form of life in the
   a. Cenozoic
   b. Mesozoic
   c. Paleozoic
   d. Precambrian

17. The dinosaurs disappeared at the end of
   a. Precambrian time
   b. the Paleozoic era
   c. the Mesozoic era
   d. the Cenozoic era

18. Iridium is an element
   a. relatively abundant on earth but rare in meteorites
   b. relatively rare on earth but abundant in meteorites
   c. relatively abundant both on earth and in meteorites
   d. relatively rare both on earth and in meteorites

19. Mammals were the dominant form of life in the
   a. Cenozoic
   b. Mesozoic
   c. Paleozoic
   d. Precambrian

20. Laurasia and Gondwanaland broke up in the
   a. Cenozoic
   b. Mesozoic
   c. Paleozoic
   d. Precambrian

21. Evidences of past volcanic action include all except
   a. hot springs
   b. isolated conical mountains
   c. moraines
   d. geysers

22. The Cenozoic era represents a period
   a. of almost continuous tectonic activity
   b. of relative stability, with erosion and sedimentation the chief geologic processes
   c. of relatively uniform climate around the world
   d. in which the reptile was the most advanced form of life

23. During the Ice Age
   a. there was a single glacial advance
   b. there were several glacial advances and retreats
   c. the entire earth was covered with an ice sheet
   d. all animal life perished and had to start over again afterward

QUESTIONS

1. In Fig. 16-9, beds *A* to *F* consist of sedimentary rocks formed from marine deposits and rocks *G* and *H* are granite. What sequence of events must have occurred in this region?

2. What is an unconformity?

3. In parts of Colorado and Wyoming, a long period during which marine sediments were deposited in a subsiding basin ended with intense tectonic movement at the close of the Mesozoic era. A mountain range was formed, which in the early part of the Cenozoic era was worn down by erosion to a nearly level plain. On parts of this plain stream and lake sediments were deposited. Describe the rocks and rock structures that you would expect to find in this region.

4. What is the age of the oldest rocks known? How was this age determined?

5. What are the two basic conditions that must be met by a radioisotope in order that it be useful in dating a particular kind of rock?

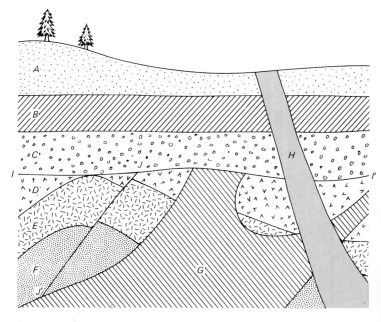

FIG. 16-9

6. What are the chief assumptions involved in the determination of the age of a rock by measurements of its uranium and lead contents?

7. What is the basis of the radiocarbon dating procedure?

8. What steps would you take to find the age of an ancient piece of wood by radiocarbon dating?

9. List as many different kinds of fossils as you can.

10. Why are fossils still useful in dating rock formations despite the development of radioactive methods?

11. Why are fossils never found in igneous rocks and only rarely in metamorphic rocks?

12. Why are most fossils found in beds that were once the floors of shallow seas?

13. The earth's history is sometimes divided into two *eons*, Cryptozoic ("hidden life") and Phanerozoic ("visible life"), with the first corresponding to Precambrian time and the second extending from the beginning of the Paleozoic era to the present day. What do you think is the reason for this division?

14. The early atmosphere of the earth probably consisted of carbon dioxide, water vapor, and nitrogen, with little free oxygen. What is believed to be the source of the oxygen in the present-day atmosphere? What bearing has this question on the relatively rapid development of varied and complex forms of life that marks the start of the Paleozoic era?

15. Precambrian rocks include sedimentary, igneous, and metamorphic varieties. What does this suggest about the geologic activity in Precambrian time?

16. Precambrian rocks are exposed over a large part of eastern Canada. What does this suggest about the geologic history of this region since the end of Precambrian time?

17. What conspicuous difference is there between Precambrian sedimentary rocks and those of later eras?

18. What are the chief kinds of organisms that have left traces in Precambrian sedimentary rocks?

19. Paleozoic sedimentary rocks derived from marine deposits are widely distributed in all of the continents. What does this indicate about the height of the continents relative to sea level in the Paleozoic era?

20. Why is it believed that large parts of the United States were once covered by shallow seas?

21. About 200 million years ago today's continents were all part of the supercontinent Pangaea. During what geologic era did Pangaea break apart into Laurasia and Gondwanaland? During what era did Laurasia break up into North America, Greenland, and Eurasia?

22. Under what circumstances is coal formed?

23. What is believed to be the origin of petroleum? Of natural gas?

24. What major change in land-animal life occurred between the late Mesozoic and early Cenozoic eras?

25. What are some of the events associated with continental drift that could produce a widespread biological extinction?

26. What is the evidence that a meteorite impact caused the great extinction at the end of the Mesozoic in which the dinosaurs disappeared? Are any other explanations possible?

27. During what geologic era did birds develop? From what type of animal did they evolve?

28. What are some of the chief differences between reptiles and mammals?

29. The same reptiles were present on all continents during the Mesozoic era, but the mammals of the Cenozoic era are often different on different continents. Why?

30. In rocks of what era or eras would you expect to find fossils of the following: (a) horses; (b) ferns; (c) clams; (d) insects; (e) apes?

31. What were the Ice Ages? When did they occur?

32. Describe the landscape in the Appalachian Mountain region of eastern Pennsylvania as it appeared (a) in the early Paleozoic, (b) during the Pennsylvanian period, (c) at the beginning of the Mesozoic.

33. At what time in geologic history (a) was most of the Mississippi Valley covered by a shallow sea? (b) were extensive mountains first formed in the Rocky Mountain region? (c) were the North Central states covered by an icecap?

34. Minnesota has a great many shallow lakes. How do you think they originated?

35. The Scandinavian landmass has been rising since the end of the most recent Ice Age; the current rate is about 1 cm/year. Can you think of any reason for this?

ANSWERS TO MULTIPLE CHOICE

1. *d*	**7.** *b, a, d, c*	**13.** *b*	**19.** *a*
2. *c*	**8.** *c*	**14.** *b*	**20.** *b*
3. *d*	**9.** *c*	**15.** *c*	**21.** *c*
4. *d*	**10.** *a, b, c, d*	**16.** *c*	**22.** *a*
5. *c*	**11.** *d*	**17.** *c*	**23.** *b*
6. *b*	**12.** *a*	**18.** *b*	

17

EARTH
AND SKY

Hardly anything in nature can compare with the sky on a clear night in open country or at sea, away from city lights and haze. Before us are millions of stars that seem to form patterns (or do they?), the glowing band that is the Milky Way, the quick tracks of meteors, and dominating all the cold gleam of the moon. If we are lucky, the dancing flames of an aurora will add a touch of sorcery to the scene. It is not surprising that the sky has always been a source of wonder and speculation, nor that astronomy today should fascinate so many people. Before going on to the planets, stars, and galaxies that populate the universe, let us first survey what we see in the sky with the naked eye and how it is affected by the motions of the earth.

CHAPTER 17

THE MOVING EARTH

A Survey of the Sky

Everything circles the North Star

The position in the sky of Polaris (the North Star) changes very little

Among the first things a watcher of the sky becomes aware of is the cyclic nature of what is seen. The sun rises in the east, moves across the sky, and sets in the west, only to repeat this journey the next day. The moon and stars move daily in a similar fashion. But one star in the northern sky hardly seems to move at all. This is the North Star, or *Polaris*, for centuries used as a guide by travelers because of its nearly unchanging position. Stars in its vicinity do not rise or set, but move around it in circles, circles that carry them under Polaris from west to east and over it from east to west. Farther from Polaris the circles get ever larger, until eventually they dip below the northern horizon. Looking to the south, the paths of the stars, like the paths of the sun and moon, are also large circles, all with their centers near Polaris.

Time exposure of stars in the northern sky. The trail of Polaris is the bright one slightly above and to the right of the center of the circles. Thus Polaris is not quite on the line of the earth's axis, a deviation that must be allowed for in surveying and navigation.

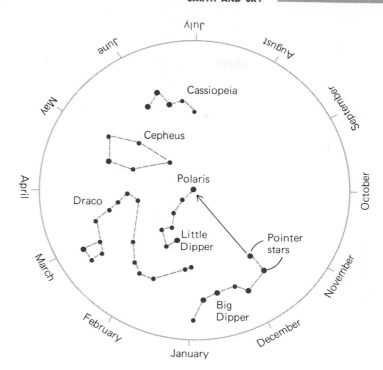

FIG. 17-1

Constellations near Polaris as they appear in the early evening to an observer who faces north with the figure turned so that the current month is at the bottom. Polaris is located on an imaginary line drawn through the two "pointer" stars at the end of the bowl of the Big Dipper. The brighter stars are shown in larger size.

Polaris lies nearly directly over the north pole

A constellation is a pattern of stars as seen from the earth

Sun, moon, and stars rise and set because their circles lie partly below the horizon. Thus the whole sky, to an observer north of the equator, appears to revolve once a day about this otherwise inconspicuous star.

That Polaris occupies such a central position is no more than an accident. The earth rotates once a day on its axis, and Polaris happens to lie almost directly over the north pole. As the earth turns, everything else around it in space seems to be moving. Except for their circular motion around Polaris, the stars appear fixed in their positions with respect to one another. Stars of the Big Dipper move halfway around Polaris between every sunset and sunrise, but the shape of the Dipper itself remains unaltered. (Actually, as discussed in Chap. 19, the stars *do* change their relative positions, but they are so far away that these changes appear very gradual to us.)

Easily recognized groups of stars, like those that form the Big Dipper, are called *constellations* (Fig. 17-1). Near the Big Dipper (Ursa Major, the Great Bear, to astronomers) is the less conspicuous Little Dipper (Ursa Minor, the Little Bear) with Polaris at the end of its handle. On the other side of Polaris from the Big Dipper are Cepheus and the W-shaped Cassiopeia, named for an ancient king and queen of Ethiopia. Next to Cepheus is Draco, which means dragon.

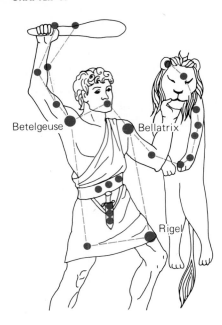

FIG. 17-2
Orion, the mighty hunter. Betelgeuse is a bright red star, and Bellatrix and Rigel are bright blue stars.

Sun and moon move eastward relative to the stars

Elsewhere in the sky are dozens of other constellations that represent animals, heroes, and beautiful women. An especially easy one to recognize on winter evenings is Orion, the mighty hunter of legend. Orion has four stars, three of them quite bright, at the corners of a warped rectangle with a belt of three stars in line across its middle (Fig. 17-2). Except for the Dippers, a lot of imagination is needed to connect a given star pattern with its corresponding figure, but the constellations nevertheless are useful as convenient labels for regions of the sky.

In their daily east-west crossing of the sky, the sun and moon move more slowly than the stars and so appear to drift eastward among the constellations. In other words, *relative* to the stars, the sun and moon move eastward — just as a person on a train traveling southward may walk toward the rear car and so move northward *relative* to the train. The slow eastward motion is most easily observed for the moon. If the moon is seen near a bright star on one evening, by the next evening it will be some distance east of that star, and on later nights it will be farther and farther to the east. In about 4 weeks the moon drifts eastward completely around the sky and returns to its starting point.

The sun's relative motion is less easily followed, because we cannot observe directly what stars it is near. But if we note what constellations appear just after sundown, we can estimate the sun's approximate location among the stars and follow it from day to day. We find that the sun drifts eastward more slowly than the moon, so slowly that the day-to-day change is scarcely noticeable. Because of the sun's motion each constellation appears to rise a few minutes earlier each night,

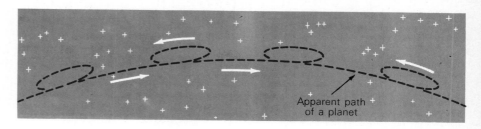

and so, after a few weeks or months, the appearance of the night sky becomes quite different. By the time the sun has migrated eastward completely around the sky, we find that a year has elapsed. The length of the year, in fact, is determined from this apparent motion of the sun among the stars.

The planets also shift their positions relative to the stars

Five other celestial objects visible to the naked eye also shift their positions with respect to the stars. These objects, to all appearances like five bright stars, were called *planets* (Greek for "wanderer") by the ancients and were named for the Roman gods Mercury, Venus, Mars, Jupiter, and Saturn. Like the sun, the planets shift their positions so slowly that their day-to-day motion is hard to detect, but, unlike the sun, they move in complex paths. In general each planet moves eastward among the stars, but its rate of motion is variable and at times it reverses direction to move westward for a brief interval. Thus the path of a planet appears to consist of loops (Fig. 17-3) that recur regularly.

The Earth's Shape and Size

A giant sphere

The ancient Greeks were aware of the earth's spherical shape

A clue to the shape of the earth comes from observations of the sky made at different places. As early as the fifth century B.C., the Greek Parmenides of Elea declared that the earth was a sphere. It is likely that he was led to this conclusion from the tales of travelers, who discovered that, when they went north, a greater number of stars remained above the horizon all night (Fig. 17-4) and that, when they went south, additional stars became visible (for instance Canopus, not visible in Greece). The early travelers also reported that the length of the day changed with what we call latitude, a rather difficult fact to explain in terms of a flat earth.

How the earth's size was first accurately determined

In time, as the notion that the earth was round became accepted in ancient Greece, attempts were made to estimate its size. The best of the early measurements of the earth's circumference was made by Eratosthenes (276–194 B.C.), who spent the latter half of his life in charge of the great museum and library at Alexandria. Eratosthenes knew that, at Syene, which was due south of Alexandria, the sun was directly overhead at noon on the first day of summer. On the first day of summer in 250 B.C. he carefully measured the extent to which the sun's rays slanted away from the vertical at noon in Alexandria, an angle he found to be $\frac{1}{50}$ of a

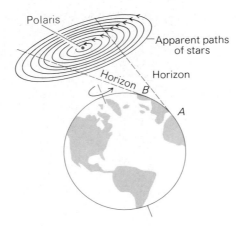

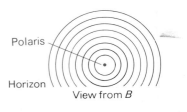

FIG. 17-4
At high latitudes more stars remain above the horizon all night than at low latitudes, evidence of the earth's sphericity.

Today there is no doubt that the earth is round. Astronauts in the Apollo 11 spacecraft saw this view of the earth as they orbited the moon, part of whose surface appears in the foreground.

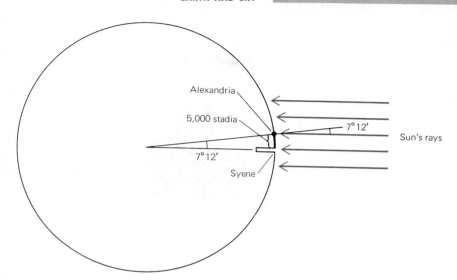

FIG. 17-5
How Eratosthenes determined the circumference of the earth. At noon on the first day of summer, the sun's rays are vertically overhead at Syene but are at an angle of 7°12′ (which is $\frac{1}{50}$ of a complete circle) from the vertical at Alexandria, which is 5000 stadia north of Syene. Hence the earth's circumference is 50 × 5000 = 250,000 stadia.

complete circle, or a little over 7° (Fig. 17-5). Since the distance from Syene to Alexandria was 5000 stadia, the circumference of the earth, corresponding to a full circle of 360°, must be 50 times 5000 or 250,000 stadia.

How long is a stadium? There were several different stadia in use in the ancient world, but it seems likely that Eratosthenes used the stadium of 158 m that was employed by the professional pacers of the time in surveying distances. This means a circumference of 39,500 km, only slightly less than the circumference of more recent determinations. In round numbers, the earth's radius is 6400 km (4000 mi).

Day and Year

The periods of rotation and revolution

The earth rotates on its axis and revolves around the sun. The *day* is the time needed for a complete rotation, and the *year* is the time needed for a complete revolution. An analogy with a clock is inevitable, but a close look reveals that this clock ticks rather less regularly than we might hope. All sorts of tilts and wiggles, accelerations and decelerations disturb the symmetry of the earth's movements. Because these peculiarities, and similar ones in the motions of the moon and of the other members of the solar system, all obey the laws of physics, it is still fair to think of the solar system as a kind of gigantic clock. It is also not surprising that the most precise measurements of time are nowadays based on atomic phenomena, not on astronomical ones.

Why leap years are necessary

Unfortunately the year is not equal to a whole number of days. The length of the year is 365 days 5 h 48 min 46 s. Since the difference between the actual length of the year and 365 days is very nearly 6 h, which is $\frac{1}{4}$ day, adding an extra day to February every 4 years enables the seasons to recur at very nearly the same dates each year. A year with such an extra day is called a *leap year*. By convention, leap years are those which are divisible by 4, for example 1988, 1992, 1996, and so on.

The discrepancy of 11 min 14 s per year that remains adds up to a full day after 128 years. To remove most of this discrepancy, century years not divisible by 400 are not leap years. Thus 1900 was not a leap year, but 2000 will be one. This step makes the calendar accurate to 1 day per 3300 years. A further modification leaves 4000, 8000, 12000, and so on as 365-day years rather than leap years. The resulting calendar is accurate to 1 day per 20,000 years, which seems adequate for the time being.

Precession

The wobble of the earth's axis

The axis about which the earth rotates is tilted by 23.5° with respect to a perpendicular to the plane of its orbit. Such a tilt is not unusual in the solar system. Among the planets, Jupiter's axis is tilted least, only about 3°, whereas that of Uranus is tilted so much that it is only 8° from the plane of its orbit. In effect, Uranus spins sideways.

Precession refers to a regular shift in the direction of the earth's axis

The angle of tilt of the earth's axis is practically constant, but the direction of the axis changes gradually so that it traces out a cone in space, as in Fig. 17-6. This effect is called *precession* and is due to the gravitational pulls of the sun and moon on the earth's equatorial bulge (see Fig. 2-17). The wobble of a spinning top is another example of precession.

The period of the earth's precession is about 26,000 years, which means that the shift of the axis is extremely slow, only about 0.014° per year. Nevertheless precession was known to the ancient Greek astronomers. Today Polaris is almost directly over the north pole, but in 5500 years Alpha Cephei will be the North Star and in 12,000 years it will be Vega. Since Vega is one of the brightest stars in the northern sky, we might speculate what people 12,000 years from now will make of this coincidence if a new Dark Age should have left no remnant of scientific knowledge by then.

The Seasons

They are due to the tilt of the earth's axis

The average distance between the earth and the sun is about 150 million km (93 million mi). Because the earth's orbit is an ellipse rather than a circle, the actual distance varies during the year from about 2.4 million km closer than the average

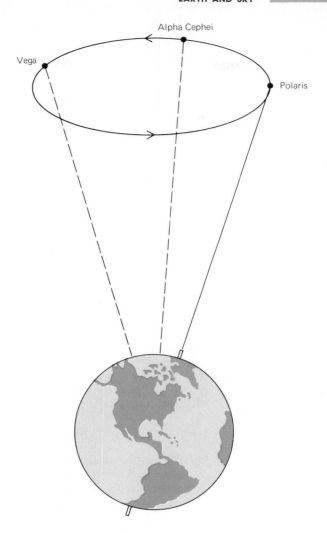

FIG. 17-6
The direction of the earth's axis
gradually changes, so that it
completes a circle every 26,000
years.

Perihelion and aphelion

to the same amount farther away. The earth is nearest the sun early in January, a situation known as *perihelion* (from the Greek *peri* = around or near and *helios* = sun), and is farthest from the sun early in July, a situation known as *aphelion* (*ap* = away from).

We might be tempted to attribute the seasons to the shape of the earth's orbit, especially if we happen to live in the southern hemisphere where January is a summer month and July a winter month. But this cannot be the true explanation, for one thing because the seasons are reversed in the northern hemisphere. Also, the variation in the amount of sunlight reaching the earth between perihelion and aphelion is too small to give rise to the difference between summer and winter that is so pronounced poleward of the tropics. After all, the deviation of the earth's orbit from a perfect circle is only ±1.6 percent.

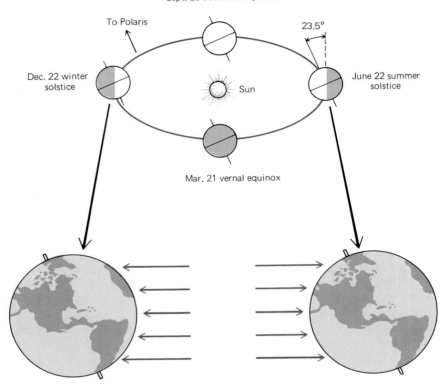

Sept. 23 autumnal equinox

To Polaris

23.5°

Dec. 22 winter solstice

Sun

June 22 summer solstice

Mar. 21 vernal equinox

FIG. 17-7
The seasons are caused by the tilt of the earth's axis together with its annual orbit around the sun. As a result the daylight side of the northern hemisphere is tilted away from the sun in January, which means that sunlight strikes this hemisphere at a glancing angle and delivers less energy to a given area than in June. The seasons are reversed in the southern hemisphere.

The seasons occur because of the tilt of the earth's axis

Solstices and equinoxes

The tilt of the earth's axis, not the shape of its orbit, is what causes the seasons. As a result of this tilt, for half of each year one hemisphere receives more direct sunlight than the other hemisphere, and in the other half of the year it receives less (Fig. 17-7). A beam of light that arrives at a 30° angle to a surface delivers only half as much energy per square meter as does a similar beam that arrives perpendicularly, as we can see in Fig. 17-8.

The noon sun is at its highest in the sky in the northern hemisphere on about June 22 (the time of the *summer solstice*) when the north pole is tilted toward the sun. The period of daylight in the northern hemisphere is longest on this date. The noon sun is at its lowest 6 months later (the time of the winter solstice) when the north pole is tilted away from the sun. The period of daylight is shortest on this date. In the southern hemisphere the situation is, of course, reversed. On March 21 (the time of the *vernal equinox;* vernal = spring) and September 23 (the time of the *autumnal equinox*) the sun is directly overhead at noon at the equator and the periods of daylight and darkness are equal everywhere on the earth.

The dates of the solstices and equinoxes are not always the same from year to year. The vernal equinox, for instance, may occur on either March 20 or 21. This

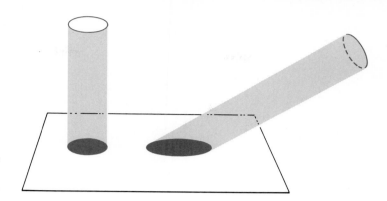

FIG. 17-8
Sunlight that strikes a surface obliquely has its energy spread over a larger area than sunlight that strikes it perpendicularly.

variation is due to the difference between the 365¼-day true year and the 365-day calendar year, which adds up to a full day every 4 years when an extra day is added to February.

The duration of twilight varies

If the earth had no atmosphere, the periods of twilight at sunrise and sunset would only last the few minutes the sun needs to appear or disappear at the horizon. The duration of twilight is extended by the scattering of sunlight by air molecules, moisture droplets, and dust particles in the atmosphere, which provides some illumination for up to an hour or two before the sun actually rises and after it has set. Twilight is brief when the sun crosses the horizon perpendicularly or nearly so, longer when it crosses the horizon at a shallow angle. Hence twilight is shorter in the tropics than in the high latitudes and shorter in summer than in winter.

MAPPING EARTH AND SKY

Latitude and Longitude

North-south and east-west coordinates on the earth's surface

Meridians and the equator are great circles

Locations on the earth's surface are specified in terms of the earth's axis of rotation. We need a few definitions to begin with. A *great circle* is any circle on the earth's surface whose center is the earth's center. The *equator* is a great circle midway between the north and south poles (Fig. 17-9). A *meridian* is a great circle that passes through both poles, and it forms a right angle with the equator. The meridian which passes through Greenwich, England, is called the *prime meridian* (Fig. 17-10).

Longitude measures angular distance east or west of the prime meridian through Greenwich

The *longitude* of a point on the earth's surface is the angular distance between a meridian through this point and the prime meridian. The prime meridian itself is assigned the longitude 0° and longitudes are given in degrees east or west

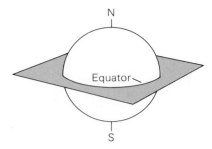

FIG. 17-9
The equator is a great circle around the earth halfway between the poles.

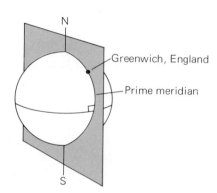

FIG. 17-10
The prime meridian is a great circle perpendicular to the equator that passes through Greenwich, England.

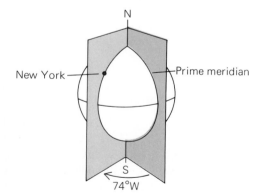

FIG. 17-11
The longitude of a place on the earth's surface is the angle between the meridian it lies on and the prime meridian. The longitude of New York is 74°W because its meridian is 74° west of the prime meridian. The longitude of the prime meridian is 0°.

of the prime meridian (Fig. 17-11). For instance, the longitude of New York is 74°W, which means that its meridian is 74° westward from the prime meridian, and the longitude of Moscow is 38°E, which means that its meridian is 38° eastward from the prime meridian.

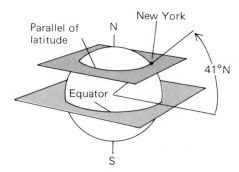

FIG. 17-12

New York lies on a parallel of latitude 41° north of the equator.

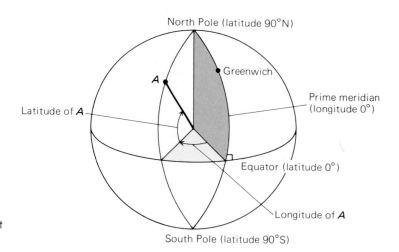

FIG. 17-13

The latitude and longitude of a point A on the earth's surface.

Latitude measures angular distance north or south of the equator

Degrees are subdivided into minutes and seconds

The *latitude* of a point on the earth's surface is the angle between a line drawn from the earth's center to it and another line drawn from the center to a point on the equator on the same meridian (Fig. 17-12). Thus the latitude of the north pole is 90°N, that of the south pole is 90°S, and that of the equator itself is just 0°. The latitude of New York is 41°N, which means it lies on a circle (smaller than a great circle) called a *parallel of latitude* whose angular distance north of the equator is 41°. Figure 17-13 summarizes the definitions of latitude and longitude. Degrees of latitude and longitude are further divided into *minutes* (1° = 60 minutes = 60′) and minutes are further divided into *seconds* (1′ = 60 seconds = 60″).

A *map* is a representation of all or part of the earth's surface on a sheet of paper. Because the earth is round and a sheet of paper is flat, some distortion must occur in preparing a map. Either the shapes of geographic features such as the continents will not be correct, or the scale of areas will vary from place to place, or both. Figure 17-14 shows how the earth appears on a *Mercator projection*, in

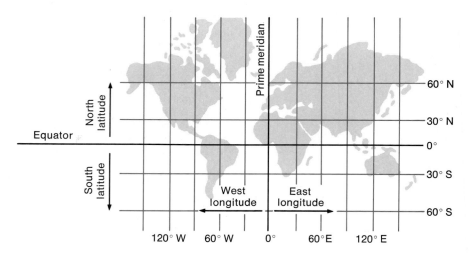

FIG. 17-14
Latitude and longitude on a
Mercator projection of the globe.
In this projection, the spacing of
parallels of latitude increases from
equator to poles in order to avoid
distorting the shapes of geographic
features. As a result, the scale of the
map varies with latitude; Greenland
is actually smaller than South
America, for instance.

which lines of constant latitude and longitude are straight. Shapes are correct on
this projection, but not areas.

Parallels of latitude are almost but not quite equally spaced on the earth's
surface. The deviations from constancy arise because the earth is not a perfect
sphere; a degree of latitude is about 1 percent longer at the poles than at the
equator. The *nautical mile,* equal to 1852 m or 6076 ft, is very nearly the length of
1′ of latitude anywhere on earth. A statute mile, used on land, is 5280 ft in length,
so that a nautical mile equals 1.151 statute miles.

A nautical mile is a minute of latitude

The nautical mile is universally used for air and sea navigation because many
map projections vary the spacing of parallels of latitude in order to preserve the
shapes of geographic features, so there is no single scale of distance on a particular
map. However, distances in nautical miles can always be read off the nearest
latitude scale with adequate accuracy. The *knot* is a unit of speed equal to one
nautical mile per hour.

A knot is a nautical mile per hour

Meridians of longitude are farthest apart at the equator, where 1° of longitude
is equal to a trifle more than 60 nautical miles, and come together at the poles. At
the latitude of New York, 1° of longitude = 46 nautical miles, and at Anchorage,
Alaska, 1° of longitude = 30 nautical miles.

Arctic and Antarctic circles

On December 22, the time of the winter solstice in the northern hemisphere,
the 23.5° tilt of the earth's axis means that no sunlight reaches any point within
23.5° from the north pole; see Fig. 17-7. The *Arctic circle* is the boundary of this
region of darkness (Fig. 17-15). On the same day, which is the time of the summer
solstice in the southern hemisphere, there is unbroken daylight at all points within
23.5° of the south pole, and the *Antarctic circle* is the boundary of this region. On
June 22 the situations in the two hemispheres are reversed.

Tropics of Cancer and Capricorn

The *Tropic of Cancer* is the most northerly latitude in the northern hemisphere at which the sun is ever directly overhead at noon. The *Tropic of Capricorn*

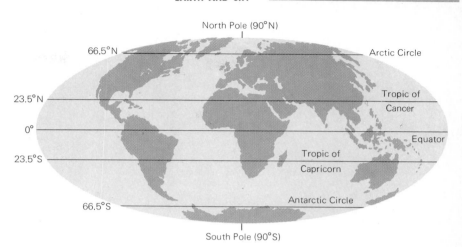

FIG. 17-15
On June 22, when the north pole is tilted closest to the sun, the sun is overhead on the Tropic of Cancer and there is unbroken daylight north of the Arctic circle, unbroken darkness south of the Antarctic circle (see also Fig. 17-7). On December 22, when the south pole is tilted closest to the sun, the sun is overhead on the Tropic of Capricorn and there is unbroken darkness north of the Arctic circle, unbroken daylight south of the Antarctic circle. The projection used here does not vary in scale as much as the Mercator projection, but shapes are distorted.

is the corresponding latitude in the southern hemisphere. On June 22, when the north pole is tilted closest to the sun and which is therefore the day of maximum sunlight in the northern hemisphere, the noon sun is directly overhead 23.5° north of the equator. Hence the latitude of the Tropic of Cancer is 23.5°N. Similarly the latitude of the Tropic of Capricorn is 23.5°S, and the noon sun is directly overhead at this latitude on December 22.

Time Zones

Other places, other times

Solar and sidereal days

A *solar day* is the period of the earth's rotation with respect to the sun. A *sidereal day* is the period with respect to the stars. Because the earth revolves around the sun, the sidereal day is about 4 min shorter than the solar day, which corresponds to 1 day's difference per year. (In other words, if we see the sun at a particular place against the stars at sunset today, a year will have to pass before it is in the same place at sunset the next time.) Ordinary timekeeping is based on the average solar day, which is divided into 24 h with each hour further divided into minutes and seconds.

The world is divided into 24 time zones

From the point of view of a stationary observer on the earth, the sun moves around the earth in a westward direction once every 24 h, which is 15° of longitude/h. This means that noon (or any other time reckoned with respect to the sun) occurs 1 h later at a longitude 15° west of a particular place and 1 h earlier at a longitude 15° east of it. For convenience, the world is divided into 24 *time zones*, each about 15° of longitude wide and each keeping time 1 h ahead of the zone west of it and 1 h behind the zone east of it (Fig. 17-16).

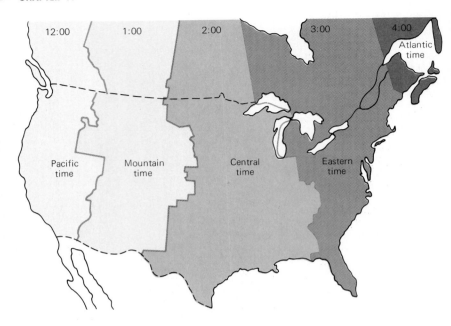

FIG. 17-16
Time zones in the United States.

International date line

The *international date line,* which follows the 180° meridian except for deviations to avoid going through Alaska and island groups in the Pacific, separates one day from the next. A person traveling eastward around the world sets his watch ahead at each successive time zone, and when he crosses the date line he subtracts a day from his calendar in order to compensate. A person traveling westward sets her watch behind at each successive time zone, and when she crosses the date line she adds a day to her calendar.

The Zodiac

The constellations through which the sun passes in a year

Constellations are used to identify regions of the celestial sphere

Let us imagine that the stars are located on the inside of a giant *celestial sphere* centered on the earth, which is in fact the impression the night sky gives. Although the constellations are entirely the product of the human imagination — the stars in a particular constellation have no relationship to one another except the accident of being in the same part of the sky as seen from the earth — they provide a handy way to identify regions of the celestial sphere. Astronomers have divided the celestial sphere into a total of 88 regions, each named after a constellation, much in the manner in which a continent is divided into countries. In both cases history rather than logic is responsible for the actual boundaries, so there is no consistency about the sizes or shapes of either constellations or countries.

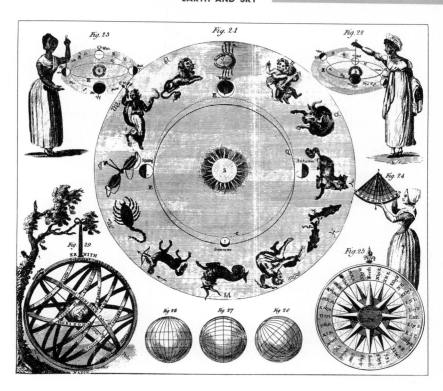

Signs of the zodiac shown in an eighteenth-century engraving.

Because a constellation is a pattern of stars as seen from the earth, the stars themselves may vary considerably in distance from each other and from us. The principal stars of the constellation Taurus, the Bull, for instance, are between 68 and 1000 light-years away from the earth. (The light-year is an astronomical unit of length equal to the distance light travels in a year. A light-year is 9.5×10^{15} m; the star nearest the earth, Proxima Centauri, is 4 light-years away.)

How stars are named

The most conspicuous stars are identified by the genitive form of the Latin name of the constellation in which they are located plus a Greek letter in descending order of brightness. Thus the brightest star in the constellation Lyra, the Harp, is denoted α (alpha) Lyrae, the next brightest is β (beta) Lyrae, and so on. Especially brilliant stars usually have names of their own inherited from the past, so that α Lyrae is also known as Vega. When there are not enough letters in the Greek alphabet, numbers are used. Roman letters are used for stars whose brightness varies, sometimes double letters if there are many in a particular constellation; for example, RR Lyrae. Faint stars, galaxies, nebulas, pulsars, and so forth are identified by their number in one of the various catalogs of such objects that have been compiled. Thus the Crab nebula in the constellation Taurus is also known as both M1 and NGC 1952, where M stands for Messier's catalog and NGC for the New General Catalog.

FIG. 17-17

Because the orbits of the earth, moon, and all the planets except Pluto lie in very nearly the same plane, the sun, the moon, and these planets follow paths in the celestial sphere that lie within a narrow belt called the zodiac. The ecliptic is the path in the celestial sphere followed by the sun in the course of a year. Ancient astronomers divided the zodiac into 12 equal segments and named each according to the constellation it contains. The ecliptic is tilted by 23.5° relative to the celestial equator, which corresponds to the tilt of the earth's axis relative to the axis of its orbit around the sun. At the summer solstice, the sun is at its most northerly point in the celestial sphere; at the winter solstice, the sun is at its most southerly point. At the equinoxes the sun crosses the celestial equator.

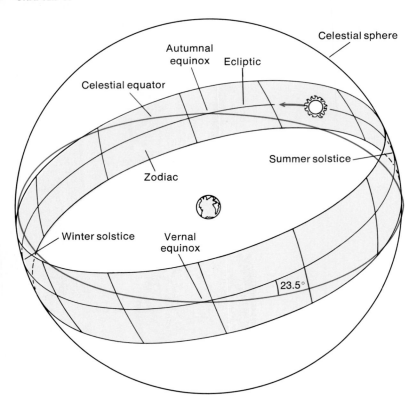

The ecliptic is the path the sun follows in the sky; the 12 constellations through which it passes are the zodiac

As seen from the earth, the sun moves along a great circle across the celestial sphere that is inclined at an angle of 23.5° relative to the celestial equator, which is the projection on the celestial sphere of the earth's equator. The circle along which the sun appears to move is called the *ecliptic*. (The same name is given to the plane of the earth's orbit.) The ecliptic passes through 12 constellations, which make up a belt in the sky called the *zodiac* (Fig. 17-17). Because the orbits of the moon and of all the planets except Pluto lie in planes which are tilted by only a few degrees from the plane of the earth's orbit, to an observer on the earth the moon and planets as well as the sun are restricted to the zodiac in their travels across the celestial sphere.

The different members of the solar system move at different speeds along the ecliptic. Since the earth revolves once a year around the sun, the sun naturally appears to us to traverse the ecliptic in the same period of time. The moon, Mercury, and Venus move faster than the sun as they circle the ecliptic, and the other planets move more slowly.

The constellations generally regarded as part of the zodiac are listed in Table 17-1. They are different in size and prominence, and in fact parts of two other

TABLE 17-1
The Chief Constellations of the Zodiac.

Latin name	English translation
1 Aquarius	The water bearer
2 Capricornus	The sea goat
3 Sagittarius	The archer
4 Scorpius	The scorpion
5 Libra	The balance
6 Virgo	The virgin
7 Leo	The lion
8 Cancer	The crab
9 Gemini	The twins
10 Taurus	The bull
11 Aries	The ram
12 Pisces	The fishes

Astrology holds that the positions of celestial bodies control events on earth; there is no evidence for this belief

constellations — Ophiuchus, the Snake Bearer, and Cetus, the Whale — enter the belt of the Zodiac. The ancient astronomers divided the zodiac into 12 equal segments and named each according to the principal constellation found in it, but these 30°-wide segments correspond only very loosely to the regions of the celestial sphere given the same names by contemporary astronomers.

Astrology

Do the planets and stars control our lives?

To our ancestors of thousands of years ago, things happened in the world because gods caused them to happen. Famine and war, earthquake and eclipse all occurred under divine control. In time the chief gods were identified with the sun, the moon, and the five planets visible to the naked eye, Mercury, Venus, Mars, Jupiter, and Saturn. Early observers of the sky were primarily interested in finding links between celestial events and earthly ones, a study that became known as *astrology.*

Until only a few hundred years ago, astronomy was almost entirely in the service of astrology. The wealth of precise astronomical measurements that ancient civilizations compiled had as their purpose interpreting the ways of the gods. Few people today take seriously the mythology of old, yet although the basis of the connection has disappeared, many still believe that the position in the sky of various celestial bodies at certain times controls the world we live in and our individual destinies as well. It does not seem very gracious for contemporary science to dismiss astrology in view of the great debt astronomy owes its practitioners of long ago. However, it is hard to have confidence in a doctrine that, for all its internal consistency and often delightful notions, nevertheless lacks any basis in scientific theory or observation and has proved no more useful in predicting the future than a crystal ball.

MOTIONS OF THE MOON

The same hemisphere of the moon always faces the earth

Although closer to the earth than any other celestial body, the moon is nevertheless an average of 384,400 km (almost 240,000 mi) away. Its diameter of 3476 km (2160 mi) — a little more than a quarter of the earth's diameter — places it among the largest satellites in the solar system. The moon circles the earth every $27\frac{1}{3}$ days and, like the earth, turns on its axis as it revolves. In the case of the moon the rotation keeps pace exactly with the revolution, so the moon turns completely around only once during each circuit of the earth. This means that the same face of our satellite is always turned toward us and that the other side remains hidden from the earth, though not from spacecraft.

Phases

A 4-week cycle

Phases of the moon

Each month the moon completes its familiar cycle of *phases*. First there is a thin crescent in the western sky at sunset which grows and moves eastward (relative to the stars); then a half-moon, until after 2 weeks the full moon rises in the east at sunset; next the moon wanes, becoming a thin crescent that rises just before the sun; finally it disappears altogether a few days before its next appearance as a crescent.

These different aspects represent the amounts of the moon's illuminated surface visible to us in different parts of its orbit. When the moon is full, it is on the opposite side of the earth from the sun, so the side facing us is fully illuminated. In the "dark of the moon" (or new moon), it is moving approximately between us and the sun, so the side toward the earth is in shadow. Figure 17-18 illustrates the origin of the moon's phases.

Times of moonrise and moonset

From Fig. 17-18 we can figure out the times of moonrise and moonset for each phase, keeping in mind that the earth rotates counterclockwise when viewed from above the north pole. Because a number of factors such as the effect of the observer's latitude will be ignored, actual times of moonrise and moonset may vary by an hour or more from those we shall find.

Crescent moon three days after new moon.

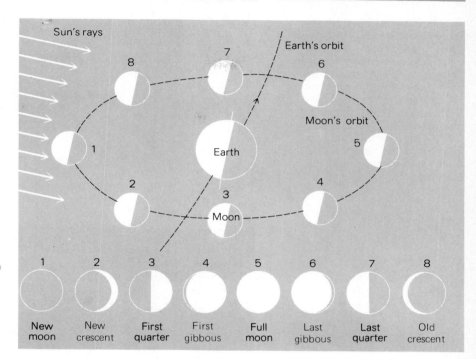

FIG. 17-18
The origin of the moon's phases. As the moon revolves around the earth we see it from different angles; when it is between us and the sun we see only the dark side (new moon), and when it is on the opposite side of us from the sun we see only the illuminated side (full moon). At other times we see parts of both sides.

TABLE 17.2
Approximate Times of Moonrise and Moonset.

Phase	Rise time	Set time
New moon	6 A.M.	6 P.M.
New crescent	9 A.M.	9 P.M.
First quarter	Noon	Midnight
First gibbous	3 P.M.	3 A.M.
Full moon	6 P.M.	6 A.M.
Last gibbous	9 P.M.	9 A.M.
Last quarter	Midnight	Noon
Old crescent	3 A.M.	3 P.M.

Let us start with new moon. Since the new moon is nearly in line with the sun, it rises when the sun does at about 6 A.M. local time, is on the observer's meridian at noon, and sets at about 6 P.M. The full moon is along the same earth-sun line but on the opposite side of the earth, so it rises at 6 P.M. when the sun sets, is on the meridian at midnight, and sets at 6 A.M. A first-quarter moon is halfway between new moon and full moon, hence it rises at noon and sets at midnight. A last-quarter moon is halfway between full moon and new moon, hence it rises at midnight and sets at noon. The rises and sets of crescent and gibbous phases can be estimated in the same way (Table 17-2). For instance, a new crescent moon, which is at position 2 in Fig. 17-18, is intermediate between new moon and first quarter, and therefore rises at about 9 A.M. and sets at about 9 P.M.

Eclipses

Now you see it, now you don't

When the moon is behind the earth (full moon), how can the sun illuminate it at all? Why doesn't the earth's shadow hide it completely? And when the moon passes between sun and earth, why isn't the sun hidden from view?

FIG. 17-19
The orbit of the moon is tilted with respect to that of the earth. For this reason the moon normally passes above or below the direct line from the sun to the earth. Eclipses occur only on the rare occasions when the moon passes exactly between the earth and the sun (a solar eclipse, with the moon blocking out light from the sun) or exactly behind the earth (a lunar eclipse, with the earth blocking out light from the sun).

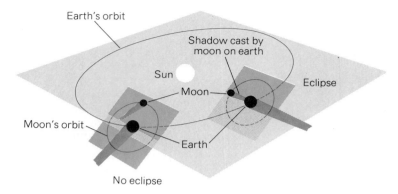

In a solar eclipse, the sun's disk is obscured by the moon. The solar corona, a glowing cloud of gas, is visible during such an eclipse.

Eclipses of the sun and moon

The answers to these questions follow from the fact that the moon's orbit is tilted at an angle of 5.2° to the earth's orbit, so that ordinarily the moon passes either slightly above or slightly below the direct line between sun and earth (Fig. 17-19). On the rare occasions when the moon does pass more or less directly before or behind the earth, an *eclipse* occurs — an eclipse of the moon when the earth's shadow obscures the moon, an eclipse of the sun when the moon's shadow touches the earth.

Total eclipses

Total eclipses of the sun can occur because, though the sun's diameter is about 400 times as great as that of the moon, it is also about 400 times as far away from the earth much of the time during its orbit. At these times the apparent diameters of both the sun and the moon are the same as seen from the earth, and total eclipses are possible.

Partial eclipses

When the moon is farthest from the earth, its apparent diameter is less than that of the sun, and the moon cannot block the entire solar disk even when it lies directly between the sun and the earth. In the latter situation the result is an *annular* eclipse of the sun, with a ring of sunlight appearing around the rim of the moon. Partial eclipses of the sun take place when the moon is not quite aligned with the sun, so that only part of the solar disk is obscured.

During a lunar eclipse the moon is not completely dark because the earth's atmosphere acts as a lens to bend a small amount of sunlight toward it. Blue light from the sun that passes through the atmosphere is scattered more than that of other colors (which is why the sky is blue, as discussed in Chap. 6), and so the light that reaches the eclipsed moon is reddish, the least scattered color. The circular shape of the earth's shadow during a lunar eclipse is evidence for its spherical form, as the ancient Greek astronomers realized.

OTHER PHENOMENA OF THE NIGHT SKY

Besides the stars, planets, and moon that are its permanent inhabitants, the night sky is occasionally host to the transient visitors known as comets and meteors. And in the high latitudes of both hemispheres, the spectacle of the aurora may appear to dazzle and enchant the observer's eye.

Comets

Regular visitors from far away in the solar system

Comets appear as small, hazy patches of light, often accompanied by long, filmy tails — hence their name, which comes from the Greek word for hairy. Most comets are visible only with the help of a telescope, but from time to time one becomes conspicuous enough to be seen with the naked eye. Watched for a few weeks or months, a comet at first grows larger and its tail longer and more brilliant; then it fades gradually, loses its tail, and eventually disappears.

Most comets have long, narrow orbits around the sun

The paths followed by comets may be quite different from the nearly circular planetary orbits. Some comets approach the sun from far out in space beyond the orbit of Pluto, swing around the sun, and then retreat. In such a case the orbit is a long, narrow ellipse, and the comet returns at regular intervals. Although most orbits are so large that their periods range up to millions of years, a few are smaller;

Halley's comet

Halley's comet, for instance, reappears every 76 years. This notable comet has returned 28 times since the first sure record of its observation was made in 239 B.C. It was named after the English astronomer Edmund Halley, a contemporary of

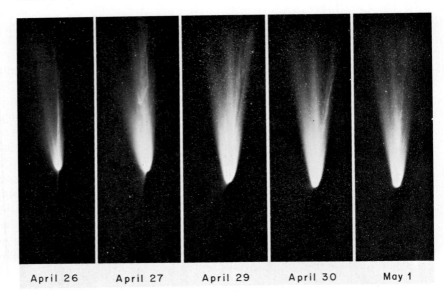

These photographs of the Arend-Roland comet were taken on successive nights from April 26 to May 1, 1957. Comets form tails when near the sun due to solar radiation.

| April 26 | April 27 | April 29 | April 30 | May 1 |

Newton, who in 1705 predicted that a comet last seen in 1682 would reappear in 1758, as it did. Halley's comet came within 93 million km of the earth in November 1985 on its most recent visit, when it was studied at close range by European, Russian, and Japanese spacecraft, and will return next in 2061.

Comets are visible only when they are close to the sun. This is partly because of the reflection of sunlight by cometary material but mostly because the comet's gases are excited by solar ultraviolet radiation and reradiate visible light. Comet tails come into being only in the solar vicinity, and they have the striking characteristic of always pointing away from the sun, even when the parent comet is receding (Fig. 17-20). To some extent this behavior is a result of the pressure of the sun's radiation pushing gases from the head of the comet, and to some extent it is due to streams of protons and electrons constantly emitted by the sun (the "solar wind") that sweep these gases outward.

Comet tails point away from the sun

FIG. 17-20
The tail of a comet always points away from the sun because of pressure from the sun's radiation and from the solar wind of ions. The tail is longest near the sun, and is probably absent far away from the sun.

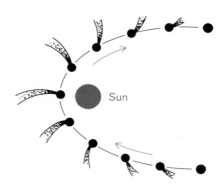

Composition of comets

The current picture of a comet has it as an aggregate chiefly of ice and various frozen gases such as hydrogen cyanide (HCN), with atoms and molecules of other kinds and dust-sized particles of metallic and stony character also present — a "dirty snowball." Comets are thought to be leftover matter from the early history of the solar system that did not become part of larger bodies such as the planets. In the far reaches of the solar system comets are fairly small, only a few km across. Near the sun, though, the frozen gases melt and finally vaporize to form the huge but thin gas clouds that make up comet heads. Comet tails may stretch for tens of millions of km across the sky. Whenever a comet passes near the sun it loses a little of its material to space permanently, and as a result is fainter each time it returns. Once past the sun, a comet begins to contract again into a relatively small body.

Comets and the earth

What would happen if a comet were to strike the earth? In fact, such an event seems to have taken place on June 30, 1908, in the Tunguska River region of Siberia. An object was seen falling from the sky followed by a brilliant flash and a gigantic blast that devastated the forest as far as 40 km away. No large crater was formed and only microscopic iron and silicate particles were found in the soil afterward, which leads to the conclusion that the head of a small comet rather than a solid body was responsible. What happened apparently can be explained on the basis of a swarm of small particles, perhaps mainly ice, whose total mass was several million tons. Most of this material would have vaporized in the atmosphere above the ground, thereby accounting for the large area affected. When the earth passed through the tail of Halley's comet in 1910, on the other hand, there were no observable effects because the density of a comet tail is so low.

Meteors

"Shooting stars" usually smaller than a grain of sand

Meteoroids, meteors, and meteorites

Meteoroids are small fragments of matter, probably the debris of comets, that the earth meets as it travels through space. Most meteoroids are smaller than pebbles with masses of less than a gram. Moving swiftly through the atmosphere, meteoroids are heated rapidly by friction. Usually they burn up completely about 100 km above the earth, appearing as bright streaks in the sky — *meteors,* or "shooting stars." Sometimes, though, they are so large to begin with that a substantial portion may get through the atmosphere to the earth's surface. The largest known fallen meteoroids, called *meteorites,* weigh several tons. The smallest meteoroids are so light that they float through the atmosphere without burning up. Many tons of these fine, dustlike *micrometeorites* reach our planet daily.

Meteor showers

A keen observer on an average clear night can spot 5 to 10 meteors an hour. Most of these meteors are random in occurrence, following no particular pattern either in the time or place in the sky that they appear. At several specific times of year, however, great meteor showers occur, with 50 or more meteors sometimes visible per hour that appear to come from the same region of the sky. The showers come about when the earth moves through a swarm of meteoroids that follow the

Meteor streak in the night sky. Few meteoroids are larger than a grain of sand, and those that enter the earth's atmosphere usually burn up before they can reach the ground. On a clear, dark night, 5 to 10 meteors per hour can be seen.

same orbit about the sun. If the meteoroids are spread out along their common orbit, the number of meteors seen is about the same each year, which is the case with the Perseid showers that occur between August 10 and 14. (The Perseid meteoroids are believed to be the remnants of a comet whose period was 105 years.) If the meteoroids are bunched together, the number of meteors seen varies from year to year. The Leonid showers of mid-November are an example, with intense displays every 33 years. The most recent one was in 1966 when thousands of meteors per hour were seen. Other conspicuous meteor showers are listed in Table 17-3.

Meteoroids are members of the solar system

Meteoroid speeds range up to 72 km/s. This limit is significant, because a higher speed would mean an object arriving from outside the solar system. The

TABLE 17-3
Some Major Meteor Showers.

Shower	Maximum display	Typical hourly rate
Quadrantid	Jan. 3	30
Eta Aquarid	May 4	5
Perseid	Aug. 12	40
Orionid	Oct. 22	13
Taurid	Nov. 1	5
Leonid	Nov. 17	6
Geminid	Dec. 14	55

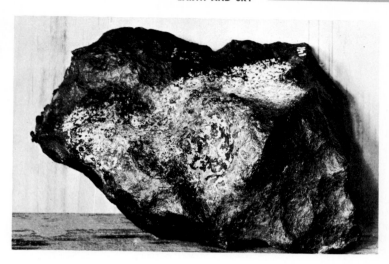

A 5-in. meteorite.

Types of meteorites

Meteor craters

Tektites

conclusion is that all meteoroids, random as well as shower, are members of the solar system that follow regular orbits around the sun until they collide with the earth or another planet.

Most meteorites that have been examined fall into two classes: stony meteorites, which consist of silicate minerals much like those in common rocks, and iron meteorites, which consist largely of iron with a small percentage of nickel. A few meteorites are intermediate in character. All meteorites are sufficiently different from terrestrial rocks to permit their unambiguous identification, although the iron ones, which are in the minority, are more easily recognized.

The earth's neighbors in space — the moon, Mercury, Venus, Mars, and the satellites of Mars — are all deeply pitted with many huge meteor craters. Erosion on the earth has left traces of only 100 or so large craters, but there is no reason to think that a similar rain of giant meteoroids up to 100 or more km across did not fall long ago on our planet as well. By about 3 billion years ago the sizes and rate of arrival of the bombarding objects seem to have fallen to their present levels, which suggests that the planets and their satellites had by then finished sweeping up most of the larger debris left over after the solar system was formed.

Not everything that falls on the earth is a meteoroid from space. In 1982 an unusual greenish-brown rock the size of a golf ball was found in Antarctica whose composition turned out to be identical with those of rocks brought back from the moon by Apollo 15 astronauts in 1971. It seems possible that the impact of a large meteoroid on the moon could have hurled the rock out fast enough to escape the moon's gravitational pull. Other unusual rocks found in Antarctica, India, Egypt, and France show signs of having come from Mars, although positive identification cannot be made because no Martian samples are available (yet?) for comparison.

A lunar origin may also be the case for *tektites*. These are small, glassy objects that have solidified from a molten state whose surface properties point to their

The "Great Meteor Crater" of Arizona is about 1200 m across, 175 m deep, and almost 5 km across the rim, which rises about 30 m above the surrounding plain. It was created during the last interglacial period, or roughly 50,000 years ago.

having passed through the earth's atmosphere. One theory is that tektites were ejected from the moon during particularly violent volcanic eruptions. Another possibility is that they were flung into space from the earth during meteoroid impacts that melted terrestrial rocks into glass, only to fall back again.

The Aurora

Fire in the sky

The aurora (or "northern lights") is one of nature's most awesome spectacles. In a typical auroral display, colored streamers seem to race across the sky, and glowing curtains of light appear which pulsate as they change their shapes into weird forms and images. In the climax of the display the heavens seem on fire, with silent green and red flames dancing everywhere. Then, after a while, the drama fades away, and only a faint reddish arc remains. Auroras are most common in the far north and far south; *aurora borealis* is the name given to this phenomenon in the northern hemisphere, and *aurora australis* in the southern.

Here is how an aurora that occurred in Russia in 1370 was described at the time: "During the autumn there were many signs in the sky. For many nights, people saw pillars in the sky and the sky itself was red, as if covered with blood. So red was the sky that even on the earth covered with snow all seemed red like blood, and this happened many times."

Aurora in northern Sweden. Auroras are caused by streams of fast protons and electrons from the sun that excite gases in the upper atmosphere to emit light.

Auroras are caused by particles from the sun that interact with atmospheric gases

Auroras are caused by streams of protons and electrons emitted by the sun. The particles require about a day to reach the earth, and when they enter the upper atmosphere they interact with the nitrogen and oxygen there so that light is given off. The process is similar to what occurs in a neon-filled glass tube when electricity is passed through it. The gas molecules are excited by the passage near them of charged particles, and this energy is then radiated as light in the characteristic wavelengths of the particular element. The green hues of an auroral display come from oxygen, and the reds originate in both oxygen and nitrogen.

The incoming streams of solar protons and electrons are affected by the earth's magnetic field in a complicated way, and as a result most auroral displays occur in doughnutlike zones about 2000 km in diameter centered about the geomagnetic north and south poles. Sometimes, though, the cloud of particles from the sun is so immense that auroras are visible elsewhere as well.

Airglow

Even when auroras are not obvious as such, there is a faint glow in the night sky due to less concentrated streams of solar particles that interact with the upper atmosphere. The brightness of this *airglow* varies with solar activity, but it is always present to some extent. Auroras and the airglow occur during the day as well as the night, but are too dim to be visible in the daytime.

IMPORTANT TERMS

Polaris, the North Star, lies almost directly above the north pole. A **constellation** is a group of stars that form a pattern in the sky.

The **day** is the time needed by the earth to make a complete rotation on its axis, and the **year** is the time needed to make a complete revolution about the sun. The actual year is a little longer than 365 days, which makes **leap years** of 366 days necessary. The **seasons** occur because the earth's axis is tilted, so that in half of each year one hemisphere receives more direct sunlight than the other one.

The location of a point on the earth's surface is specified by its **latitude** (angular distance north or south of the equator) and **longitude** (angular distance east or west of the prime meridian). The world is divided into 24 **time zones** about 15° of longitude wide. The time in a given zone is 1 h ahead of that in the zone west of it and 1 h behind that in the zone east of it.

The moon shines by virtue of reflected sunlight. The **phases** of the moon occur because the area of its illuminated side visible to us varies with the position of the moon in its orbit. A **lunar eclipse** occurs when the earth's shadow obscures the moon, a **solar eclipse** when the moon obscures the sun.

Comets and **meteoroids** are relatively small objects that pursue regular orbits in the solar system. Comets glow partly by the reflection of sunlight but mainly through the excitation of their gases by solar ultraviolet radiation. **Meteors** are the flashes of light meteoroids produce when they enter the earth's atmosphere. **Auroras** result from the excitation of atmospheric gases by streams of fast ions from the sun.

MULTIPLE CHOICE

1. The object in the sky that apparently moves least in the course of time is
   a. Polaris
   b. Venus
   c. the sun
   d. the moon
2. A planet not visible to the naked eye is
   a. Mars
   b. Venus
   c. Mercury
   d. Pluto
3. Relative to the stars, the sun seems to move
   a. northward
   b. southward

   c. eastward
   d. westward
4. Relative to the stars, the moon seems to move
   a. northward
   b. southward
   c. eastward
   d. westward
5. Leap years are needed because the actual length of the year is
   a. sightly less than 365 days
   b. slightly more than 365 days
   c. sometimes less and sometimes more than 365 days
   d. different at different places on the earth
6. The direction of the earth's axis of rotation
   a. is perpendicular to the plane of its orbit
   b. is parallel to the plane of its orbit
   c. is inclined to the plane of its orbit
   d. is fixed relative to the stars
7. The seasons occur as a result of
   a. variations in the sun's energy output
   b. the ellipticity of the earth's orbit
   c. the tilt of the earth's axis
   d. precession of the earth's axis
8. The time when the noon sun is at its lowest point in the sky in the northern hemisphere is called the
   a. vernal equinox
   b. autumnal equinox
   c. summer solstice
   d. winter solstice
9. At an equinox,
   a. the periods of daylight and darkness are the same everywhere on the earth
   b. the period of daylight is a maximum
   c. the period of darkness is a maximum
   d. eclipses of the moon occur
10. The longitude of Greenwich, England, is
   a. 0°
   b. 90°E
   c. 90°W
   d. 180°
11. A nautical mile is equal to
   a. 1′ of latitude
   b. 1° of latitude
   c. 1′ of longitude
   d. 1° of longitude
12. The sun is never directly overhead at noon on the
   a. Arctic circle

b. Tropic of Cancer
c. Tropic of Capricorn
d. equator

13. At the Arctic circle, the sun remains below the horizon for an unbroken period of
   a. 1 day per year
   b. 1 week per year
   c. 6 months per year
   d. the entire year

14. At the north pole, the sun remains below the horizon for an unbroken period of
   a. 1 day per year
   b. 1 week per year
   c. 6 months per year
   d. the entire year

15. The number of time zones into which the world is divided is
   a. 7
   b. 12
   c. 24
   d. 52

16. Omaha is one time zone west of Boston. When it is 10 A.M. in Boston, in Omaha it is
   a. 9 A.M.
   b. 10 A.M.
   c. 11 A.M.
   d. 10 P.M.

17. The stars in a constellation are
   a. about the same age
   b. about the same distance from the earth
   c. members of the zodiac
   d. unrelated except for proximity in the sky as seen from the earth

18. The circle across the celestial sphere along which the sun moves as seen from the earth is called the
   a. ecliptic
   b. zodiac
   c. international date line
   d. equator

19. The durations of "day" and "night" at a given place on the moon each correspond to about
   a. 1 day on earth
   b. 1 week on earth
   c. 2 weeks on earth
   d. 4 weeks on earth

20. An eclipse of the moon occurs when
   a. the moon passes directly between the earth and the sun
   b. the sun passes directly between the earth and the moon
   c. the earth passes directly between the sun and the moon

   d. the moon's dark side faces the earth

21. Eclipses of the sun occur at
   a. new moon
   b. first or last quarter
   c. full moon
   d. anytime

22. Eclipses of the moon occur at
   a. new moon
   b. first or last quarter
   c. full moon
   d. anytime

23. Comet tails
   a. come into being only near the sun
   b. always point toward the sun
   c. glow by themselves
   d. represent a danger to the earth if they pass nearby

24. Meteors occur in the night sky
   a. only during spring and fall
   b. only during specific shower periods
   c. in approximately the same numbers every night
   d. every night, but with greater frequency during shower periods

25. The majority of meteoroids consist of
   a. silicate minerals
   b. calcite
   c. iron
   d. nickel

26. Auroras are caused by
   a. streams of colored gases from the sun
   b. streams of charged particles from the sun
   c. comets
   d. micrometeorites

27. Auroras occur mainly in the polar regions because of the effect of
   a. the moon
   b. the low temperatures there
   c. the geomagnetic field
   d. the earth's equatorial bulge

QUESTIONS

1. What must be your location if the stars move across the sky in circles centered directly overhead?

2. In terms of what you would actually observe, what does it mean to say that the moon apparently moves eastward among the stars?

3. From observations of the moon, why would you conclude that it is a relatively small body revolving around the earth rather than another planet revolving around the sun?

4. The sun, moon, and planets all follow approximately the same path from east to west across the sky; none of them is ever seen in the far northern or far southern sky. What does this suggest about the arrangement of these members of the solar system in space?

5. As seen from the earth, the sun and moon drift eastward relative to the stars. Through approximately what angle does the sun move eastward each day? The moon?

6. Where on the earth's surface does the sun remain below the horizon for at least 1 full day per year? Where does the sun remain above the horizon for at least 1 full day per year?

7. What is the difference between the Tropic of Cancer and the Tropic of Capricorn?

8. The earth is closest to the sun in January, but January is a winter month in the northern hemisphere. Why?

9. (a) If the earth's axis were tilted by 30° instead of by 23.5°, would the seasons be more or less pronounced than they are now? (b) What would the latitudes of the Arctic circle and the Tropic of Cancer be?

10. In May, does the length of the day (that is, the period between sunrise and sunset) change when one travels north from the Tropic of Cancer? If so, does it become longer or shorter?

11. In May, does the length of the day change when one travels west from the prime meridian? If so, does it become longer or shorter?

12. From what parts of the earth can the entire sky be observed during the course of a year?

13. What is the significance of an equinox? How many times per year does an equinox occur?

14. What is the significance of a solstice? How many times per year does a solstice occur?

15. How does the path of the sun in the sky appear to an observer at the equator at an equinox?

16. What is your location if the sun appears for the first time each year at the vernal equinox, rises above the horizon in a spiral that makes one turn per day until the summer solstice, and then descends in a spiral until it disappears below the horizon at the autumnal equinox?

17. What would be the effect on the seasons of abolishing leap years, so that every year consisted of 365 days?

18. What is the latitude of the north pole? The south pole? The equator?

19. How long is a degree of latitude? Of longitude? Do they have the same values everywhere?

20. Why do you think a nautical mile is used for air and sea navigation in preference to the statute mile or the kilometer?

21. *Greenwich mean time* (GMT) is local time at the prime meridian (0° longitude) when variations in the earth's motions are averaged out. When GMT is 8:00 A.M., what is the local time in New York City, longitude 74°W?

22. What is GMT when it is 6:00 P.M. local time in Tokyo, longitude 140°E?

23. What is your longitude if local noon occurs at 8:00 A.M. GMT?

24. What is the local time in Tokyo, longitude 140°E, when it is local noon in Moscow, longitude 38°E?

25. Los Angeles is three time zones west of New York. When it is 2 P.M. in New York, what time is it in Los Angeles?

26. What is wrong with the statement that the moon is more useful to us than the sun because the moon provides illumination at night when it is needed most?

27. Approximately how much time elapses between new moon and full moon?

28. If the moon were smaller than it is, would total eclipses of the sun still occur? Would total eclipses of the moon still occur?

29. In what phase must the moon be at the time of a solar eclipse? At the time of a lunar eclipse?

30. To what approximate period on the earth do the lengths of "day" and "night" at a given place on the moon each correspond?

31. If the earth had no atmosphere, would comets still be visible from its surface? Would meteors?

32. Why do comets have tails only in the vicinity of the sun? Why do these tails always point away from the sun, even when the comet is receding from it?

33. When a comet is close enough to the sun to be seen from the earth, stars are visible through both the comet's head and tail. What does this imply about the danger to the earth from a collision with a comet?

34. Some meteor showers recur each year at about the same time, for instance the Perseid shower that appears early every August. Does this mean that the orbits of the meteoroids in the Perseid swarm all have periods of exactly 1 year?

35. Over 90 percent of the meteorites found after a known fall are stony, yet most of the meteorites in museums are iron. Why do you think this is so?

36. The moon has virtually no atmosphere. How does the likelihood of being struck by a meteoroid on the moon's surface compare with that on the earth's surface?

37. What would be the effect on the aurora of the disappearance of the earth's magnetic field?

ANSWERS TO MULTIPLE CHOICE

1. *a*	8. *d*	15. *d*	22. *c*
2. *d*	9. *a*	16. *a*	23. *a*
3. *c*	10. *a*	17. *d*	24. *d*
4. *c*	11. *a*	18. *a*	25. *a*
5. *b*	12. *a*	19. *c*	26. *b*
6. *c*	13. *a*	20. *c*	27. *c*
7. *c*	14. *c*	21. *a*	

18

THE SOLAR SYSTEM

To the largest telescope as to the naked eye, a star is no more than a point of light. Most of the planets, on the other hand, are magnified to clear disks by a telescope of even modest power. This does not mean, of course, that the planets are larger than the stars, only that they are much closer to us. The sun, the earth, and the other planets dwell in emptiness and are separated by unimaginable distances from everything else in the universe. Because the sun is its central figure, the family of planets, satellites, and smaller bodies that accompanies it is called the solar system. In this chapter we shall survey briefly what is known about its members.

CHAPTER 18

THE FAMILY OF THE SUN

Until the seventeenth century the solar system was thought to consist of only five planets besides the earth and moon. In 1609, soon after having heard of the invention of the telescope in Holland, Galileo built one of his own and was able to add four new bodies to the system: the brighter of the moons (or *satellites*) that revolve around Jupiter. Since Galileo's time telescopic improvements have made possible the discovery of many more members of the sun's family. The list of planets now include nine; in order from the sun they are Mercury, Venus, Earth, Mars, Jupiter, Saturn, Uranus, Neptune, and Pluto (Fig. 18-1). All except Mercury and Venus have satellites. Thousands of small objects called *asteroids,* all less than 1000 km in diameter, follow separate orbits about the sun in the region between Mars and Jupiter. Comets and meteors, in Galileo's time thought to be atmospheric phenomena, are now recognized as still smaller members of the solar system.

Asteroids are small objects that form a belt between the orbits of Mars and Jupiter

In recent years our knowledge of the solar system has been vastly increased by the voyages of spacecraft, most of them from the United States but with a few notable Russian ones as well. Some spacecraft have landed on Venus and Mars, and astronauts have walked on the surface of the moon. One spacecraft, Pioneer 10, has the distinction of being the first object of human origin to leave the solar system permanently. After leaving Florida in March 1972, Pioneer 10 had a close-up look at Jupiter, its primary mission, in December 1973. Ten years later the

Pioneer 10

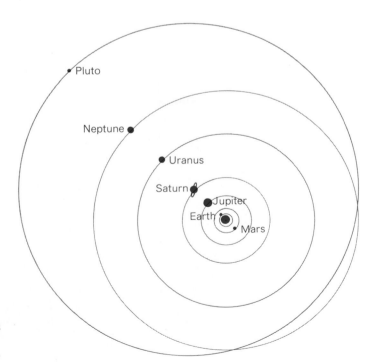

FIG. 18-1

The solar system. The orbits of Mercury and Venus are too small to be shown on this scale. Pluto's orbit is by far the most elliptical. Diameters of sun and planets are exaggerated.

spacecraft crossed the orbit of Neptune; Pluto's orbit was then inside that of Neptune (see Fig. 18-1). Despite a speed of nearly 50,000 km/h, Pioneer 10 will not be near another star for 10,000 years. So remarkable is modern technology that signals from the tiny 8-W transmitter on Pioneer 10 were expected to be picked up on the earth for perhaps 8 years after it left the solar system, nearly 20 years after it left Florida.

The Solar System

The sun has most of the mass, the planets have most of the angular momentum

Not only is the entire solar system isolated in space, but each of its principal members is separated from the others by vast distances. From the earth to our nearest neighbor, the moon, is about 384,000 km; from the earth to the sun is about 150 million km. It took the Apollo 11 spacecraft 3 days to reach the moon, and at the same rate of progress more than 3 years would be needed to reach the sun.

A model of the solar system

If we use a golf ball to represent the sun, a small sand grain 4 m away represents the earth on the same scale. The moon would be a dust speck about 1 cm from the sand grain. The largest planet, Jupiter, would be a small pebble 18 m from the golf ball, and Pluto would be another dust speck 150 m from the golf ball. With three smaller pebbles, three more sand grains, and a few dozen more dust specks, all within the 300-m-wide orbit of Pluto, the model is complete (Fig. 18-2). From the outside, the solar system is not very impressive, with its

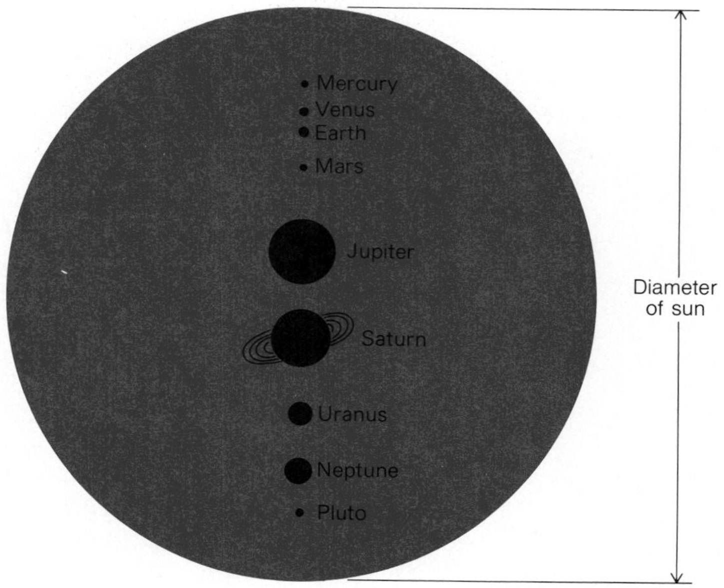

FIG. 18-2
Relative sizes of planets and sun.

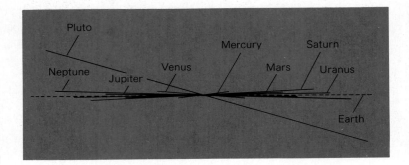

FIG. 18-3
The orbits of the planets seen edgewise. Except for Pluto, they lie nearly in the same plane.

members separated by distances enormous compared with their size.

Planets *revolve* about the sun and *rotate* on their axes. Two further aspects of the solar system are notable:

1. Nearly all the motions — revolutions of planets, asteroids, and satellites, axial rotations of sun and planets — are in the same direction. Only the rotation of Venus and the revolutions of a few minor satellites about their parent planets run contrary to the general motion. (Uranus is an exception of a different kind, since it rotates about an axis only 8° from the plane of its orbit.)
2. All the orbits except those of Pluto and comets lie nearly in the same plane (Fig. 18-3).

Most of the solar system's angular momentum resides in the motions of the planets and satellites

As a consequence of these motions, the solar system has a great deal of angular momentum, nearly all of which belongs to the planets and their satellites even though the sun accounts for the bulk of the entire system's mass. The distribution of angular momentum in the solar system has important implications as regards both the origin of the system and the possibility of planetary systems about other stars, topics we shall consider in Chap. 20.

Planets shine by reflected sunlight

Planets, asteroids, and satellites shine only by reflected sunlight, and observation of any of these objects is limited to the half that is directly exposed to the sun. Planets with orbits larger than the earth's never come between us and the sun, so we can always see nearly the whole of their illuminated sides. Mercury and Venus, however, have orbits smaller than the earth's and therefore exhibit phases like those of the moon to us, though on different time scales.

Properties of the Planets

The inner ones are mostly rocky, the outer ones mostly liquefied gas

The other planets of the solar system have been a source of fascination ever since their special character was discovered through their motions relative to the stars. This fascination has increased with every increase in our knowledge of them. The

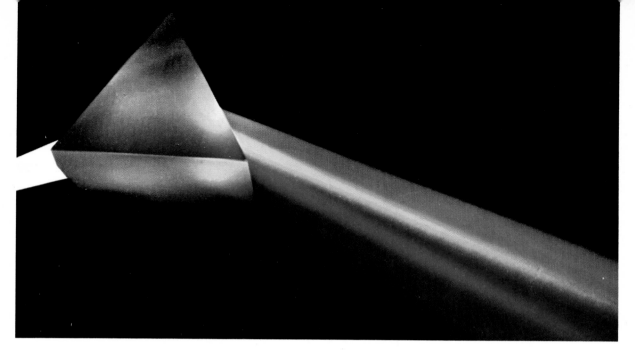

The indexes of refraction of most substances vary with the wavelength of the light sent through them. Here a beam of sunlight is separated into its component wavelengths (each of which causes the sensation of a different color) by a glass prism. (Bausch & Lomb, Inc.)

A colored pattern occurs when an uneven thin film of oil floats on water because light of each wavelength undergoes constructive interference at different oil thickness. (Herman Eisenbeiss)

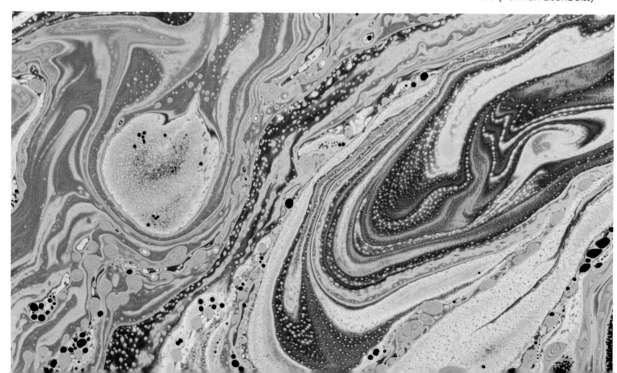

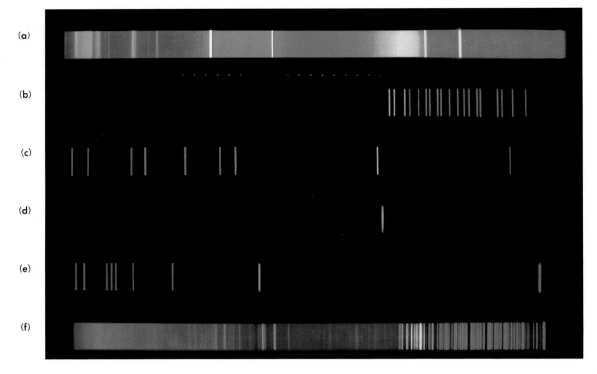

(a)

(b)

(c)

(d)

(e)

(f)

Some emission spectra in the visible region.
These are produced by gases excited electrically (or otherwise) to radiate light whose frequencies are characteristic of the electron structures
of the atoms or molecules present. *(a)* Molecular
hydrogen. *(b)* Atomic hydrogen. *(c)* Sodium
vapor. *(d)* Helium. *(e)* Neon. *(f)* Lithium vapor.
(Bausch & Lomb, Inc.)

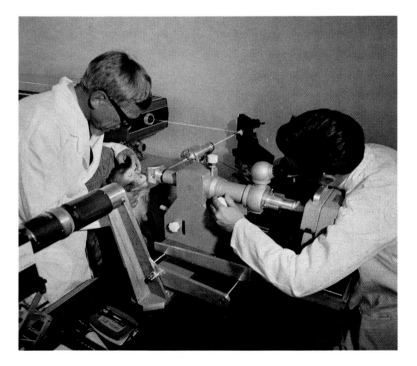

A laser produces an intense beam of monochromatic, coherent light from the cooperative radiation of excited atoms or molecules. The light
waves in a coherent beam are all in step, which
greatly increases their effectiveness. A laser
beam provides an excellent way to "weld" a
detached retina to the tissue behind it. Here researchers at Stanford University are aiming the
blue-green light from an argon laser at a
monkey's eye. (Spectra Physics, Inc.)

Altocumulus lenticularis clouds appear as semi-transparent patches at several levels.

High-altitude cirrus clouds above medium-altitude altocumulus.

Cirrus clouds consist of ice crystals and usually occur at high altitudes (5 to 14 km feet). Shown is cirrus uncinus, commonly called "mares' tails."

Low-altitude stratocumulus clouds formed below 2 km. They are sometimes formed by the horizontal spreading out of cumulus.

Stratus clouds consist of layers of water droplets at low altitudes (here below 1 km) that reveal a horizontal flow of air.

Parallel bands of altocumulus produce a "mackerel sky." (Harper & Row)

Quartz

Amazonite

The Obsidian Cliff in Yellowstone National Park is comprised of black glass of volcanic origin. In the past, Indians in the vicinity used slivers from the cliff for knives and arrowheads. (Golden Press)

Muscovite

Calcite (on amethyst)

Olivine

Kaolin (china clay)

Six common minerals or mineral families are quartz, the feldspars (shown in amazonite), mica (shown is muscovite mica), calcite (on amethyst), the ferromagnesian minerals (shown is olivine), and the clay minerals (shown is kaolin). (Reader's Digest, Inc.)

Andesite porphyry found in Nevada. An igneous rock in which large crystals are embedded in a fine-grained mass is called a porphyry.

An outcrop of conglomerate in New York State that contains many fragments of limestone. The large chunk is about 1 ft in length.

This shale in eastern New York State was mud 350 million years ago in the Devonian period. (Golden Press)

Slate results from the metamorphism of shale under pressure. This scene is in southern New York State.

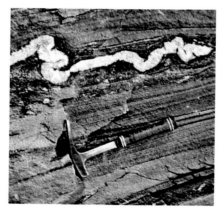

An outcrop of schist which is cut by a vein of quartz in Australia.

The metamorphic rock gneiss shows foliation and bands of different material. (Golden Press)

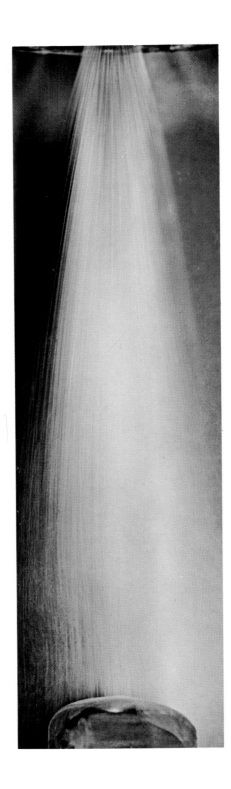

(Above) The zone refining of a silicon rod. The rod is passed through an induction coil which melts a segment of it, and as the rod moves, impurities stay in the molten zone and are thereby carried to the end of the rod. Less than 1 part of impurity in 10^{10} remains. (E. I. du Pont de Nemours & Co.)

(Left) A synthetic ruby rod being "grown" in a furnace. Powdered aluminum oxide (Al_2O_3) with a small amount of chromium oxide (Cr_2O_3) is fed from above through an oxyhydrogen flame and solidifies into a single crystal. The Cr^{3+} ions in the crystal are responsible for the red color. (Union Carbide Corp./Linde Division)

Carlsbad Caverns in New Mexico. Caves such as this occur when groundwater has dissolved limestone and carried it away. The stalactites that hang from the roof consist of material that has precipitated from solution. (Fred E. Mang, Jr./National Park Service)

Sediments laid down as long as 1 billion years ago were uplifted, folded
and metamorphosed, and intruded by granite before being eroded
during the past 7 million years by the Colorado River to form the Grand
Canyon, whose eastern end is shown here. (Nicholas K. Koch)

Snow Creek Glacier in the Stuart Range of the North Cascade Mountains of Washington. (M. Woodbridge Williams/National Park Service)

Mt. St. Helens before, during, and after its eruption on May 18, 1980. The eruption began with an explosion that devastated an area of over 500 km^2 in southwestern Washington and sent a column of ash and smoke to a height of 20 km. About 2.7 km^3 of volcanic rock, 0.5 km^3 of it molten, were expelled. The energy released was about 1.7×10^{18} J, equivalent to 400 million tons of TNT or 27,000 atomic bombs of the size detonated at Hiroshima. Earlier eruptions occurred a number of times in the past 4500 years, most recently between 1831 and 1857. Indians of the region called the mountain Coowit, the Lady of Fire. (Mullineax/Hansen Planetarium; Wilson Scott/Hansen Planetarium; U.S. Geological Service; R.I. Christiansen/U.S. Geological Service)

A multiple-exposure photograph of the solar
eclipse of June 30, 1964. The glowing gaseous
envelope around the sun's disk is the corona.
(M. Tinklenberg)

The moon presents a bleak landscape. The earth
is in the background, 383,000 km away. (NASA)

In 1976 two Viking spacecraft landed on Mars and sent back data and photographs such as this one. Martian rocks are porous and jagged, like basaltic lavas of the earth and moon, and the soil resembles weathered lava. Iron oxides are responsible for the red color. No trace of life was found. (NASA)

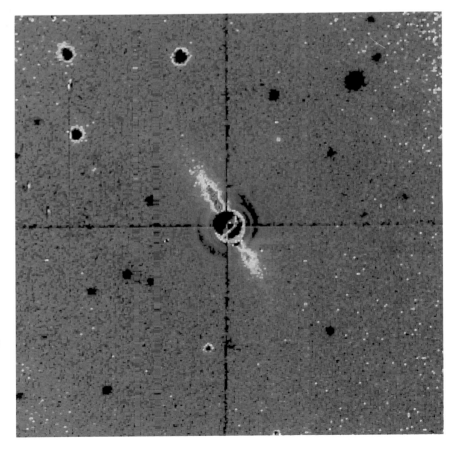

The star Beta Pictoris, 50 light years from the sun, is circled by a disk of gas and particles like that from which the solar system is believed to have evolved. It is possible that several planets have already been formed in the disk. The colors here have been computer-coded to bring out details. (JPL/California Institute of Technology)

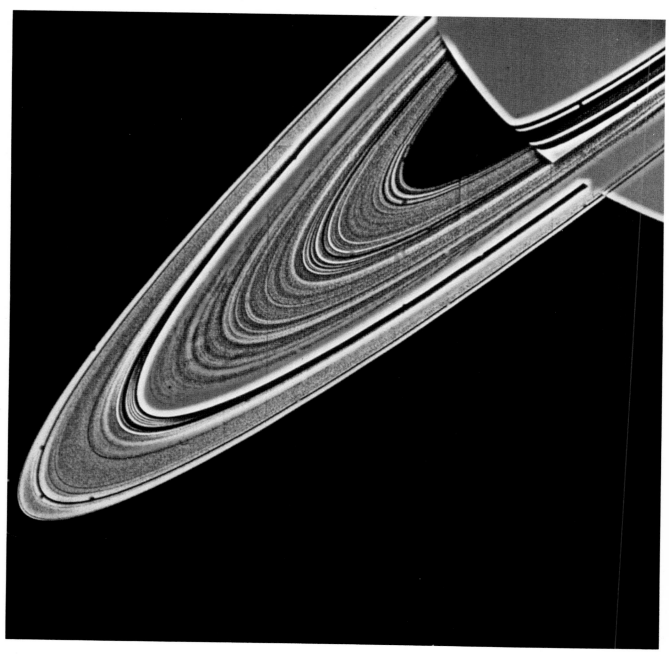

The rings of Saturn as seen by the Voyager 2
spacecraft from a distance of 8 million miles in
August 1981. The complex structure of the rings is
brought out by computer color coding. (NASA)

The Veil Nebula in Cygnus consists of high-speed gas filaments ejected from an exploding star over 50,000 years ago. (Mount Wilson & Palomar Observatories)

The North American Nebula in Cygnus is a gas cloud that is excited to radiate by ultraviolet light from stars embedded in it. The obscured areas that simulate the Atlantic Ocean and Gulf of Mexico are due to absorption of nebular light by dust clouds between the nebula and the earth. (Mount Wilson & Palomar Observatories)

TABLE 18-1
The Planets.

Planet	Symbol	Mean distance from sun, earth = 1 [a]	Diameter, thousands of km	Mass, earth = 1 [b]	Mean density, water = 1 [c]	Surface gravity, earth = 1 [d]	Escape speed, km/s [e]	Period of rotation on axis	Period of revolution around sun	Eccentricity of orbit [h]	Inclination of orbit to ecliptic [i]	Known satellites
Mercury	☿	0.39	4.9	0.055	5.4	0.38	4.3	59 days	88 days	0.21	7°00′	0
Venus	♀	0.72	12.1	0.82	5.25	0.90	10.4	243 days[f]	225 days	0.01	3°24′	0
Earth	⊕	1.00	12.7	1.00	5.52	1.00	11.2	24 h	365 days	0.02	—	1
Mars	♂	1.52	6.8	0.11	3.93	0.38	5.0	24.5 h	687 days	0.09	1°51′	2
Jupiter	♃	5.20	143	318	1.33	2.6	60	10 h	11.9 yr	0.05	1°18′	14
Saturn	♄	9.54	120	95	0.71	1.2	36	10 h	29.5 yr	0.06	2°29′	17
Uranus	⛢	19.2	51	15	1.27	1.1	22	16 h[g]	84 yr	0.05	0°46′	5
Neptune	♆	30.1	49	17	1.70	1.2	24	23 h	165 yr	0.01	1°46′	2
Pluto	♇	39.4	4	0.002	0.4	0.02	1.2	6 days	248 yr	0.25	17°12′	1

[a] The mean earth-sun distance is called the *astronomical unit*, where 1 AU = 1.496×10^8 km.
[b] The earth's mass is 5.98×10^{24} kg.
[c] The density of water is 1 g/cm^3 = 10^3 kg/m^3.
[d] The acceleration of gravity at the earth's surface is 9.8 m/s^2.
[e] Speed needed for permanent escape from the planet's gravitational field.
[f] Venus rotates in the opposite direction from the other planets.
[g] The axis of rotation of Uranus is only 8° from the plane of its orbit.
[h] The difference between the minimum and maximum distances from the sun divided by the average distance.
[i] The ecliptic is the plane of the earth's orbit.

telescopes and spacecraft of today have cleared up many of the mysteries of the planets, but plenty still remain, most notably the question of extraterrestrial life.

The inner planets

The principal data about the planets and their orbits are summarized in Table 18-1. The inner planets of Mercury, Venus, Earth, and Mars are relatively small, have densities comparable with that of the earth, and are composed largely of rocky material. They rotate fairly slowly on their axes. Among them is only one satellite of any size, the moon; the two satellites of Mars are only a few km across.

The outer planets

The outer planets of Jupiter, Saturn, Uranus, and Neptune are large, not very dense compared with the earth (Saturn would float if placed in a large enough bathtub), and are composed largely of gases compressed to liquid form. They rotate fairly rapidly on their axes. These giant planets have among them a total of 38 satellites. The inner planets have low escape speeds, the giant ones have high escape speeds. (Escape speed was discussed in Chap. 2.) Although little is known about Pluto, the outermost planet, because it is so far away, it seems to be only slightly larger than the moon and to be composed of liquid methane. Are there planets beyond Pluto? No one knows, but it does not seem very likely since the sun's gravitational pull is extremely weak that far away.

THE INNER PLANETS

Mercury

It always appears near the sun in the sky

The innermost planet

Mercury was named after the messenger of the gods in classical mythology because its position relative to the stars changes rapidly, and its symbol represents a winged helmet. The innermost planet, Mercury always appears in the sky as a companion to the sun. Although as brilliant an object as Sirius, the brightest star, it is hard to see during the day because it is so near the sun; the best times for observation are near sunrise and sunset. Mercury shows phases like those of the moon because its orbit lies within that of the earth, and its apparent diameter is about three times greater when it is closest to the earth than when it is farthest away.

Because Mercury is so close to the sun, it would not be surprising if it always presented the same face to the sun just as the moon does to the earth. In both cases the effect would be due to tides that act to slow the rotation down until the satellite does not change its orientation relative to the parent body. In fact, until 1965 visual observations of markings on Mercury's surface did seem to indicate that Mercury's day and year were equal. However, in 1965 radar measurements using the doppler effect (Chap. 6) showed that Mercury actually rotates once every 59 of our days, which is two-thirds of its orbital period. Subsequent theoretical studies showed this situation to be as plausible as synchronous rotation for a body whose orbit is as out-of-round as Mercury's. As it happens, the difference between Mercury's day

Mosaic of photographs taken by the Mariner 10 spacecraft show part of Mercury's southern hemisphere as it would appear at an altitude of 50,000 km. The south pole is at the bottom; the large crater near it is 170 km across.

and year is too small to make a great deal of difference in the face we see, which together with the difficulty of making good observations explains the earlier mistaken belief.

Mercury has almost no atmosphere

The long days on Mercury and its closeness to the sun lead to high temperatures on the sunlit side, about 300°C. There is almost no atmosphere to transfer heat from the sunlit side to the dark side or to trap heat radiated by the surface, and as a result the night temperature drops to perhaps −180°C just before sunrise. The only gases found near Mercury are the inert gases helium, argon, neon, and xenon, and only traces of them. Mercury is altogether an inhospitable place.

The surface of Mercury is like that of the moon

In 1974 the Mariner 10 spacecraft passed within a few hundred miles of Mercury and radioed back numerous photographs as well as other data. Mercury turns out to have a crater-pocked surface much like that of the moon. Hills and valleys as well as craters abound in the rugged landscape. However, though plains covered with lava are present on Mercury also, they do not have the vast scale of the lunar maria.

The structure of Mercury

There is no evidence of any general melting in the later stages of Mercury's formation, which presents a problem. Mercury seems to have a crust of silicate rocks whose density is much lower than the density of the planet as a whole, so the interior probably has an iron-rich core like that of the earth. But if there was no melting of the entire planet after it had been formed from the dust and gases of the early solar system, then how did the observed separation of heavy and light materials occur? The simplest explanation is that the iron-rich constituents were picked up first, but such a hypothesis raises other questions in its turn. In any case, it is clear from the heavy cratering still visible on both Mercury and the moon that the youthful earth must also have suffered its share of assault by large meteoroids, with the resulting craters later erased by the melting of the crust and the erosive processes that continue to this day.

Venus

Our sister planet

Venus is the third brightest object in the sky

Venus is the brightest object in the sky apart from the sun and moon. If one knows where to look, it can readily be seen during the day. Because the orbit of Venus, like that of Mercury, lies inside the earth's orbit, it never gets very far away in the sky from the sun, and appears alternately as a "morning star" and an "evening star." Venus may be as much as 47° from the sun, however, unlike 28° in the case of Mercury, and so is visible for longer periods than Mercury. Venus was named after the Roman goddess of love and beauty, and is represented by the traditional female symbol of a mirror.

The phases of Venus

Galileo, the first to study Venus with a telescope, found that it has phases like those of the moon and that its apparent size changes cyclically. He correctly interpreted this evidence as supporting the copernican thesis that Venus revolves

The cloudy atmosphere of Venus as photographed from 720,000 km away by the Mariner 10 spacecraft on its way to Mercury.

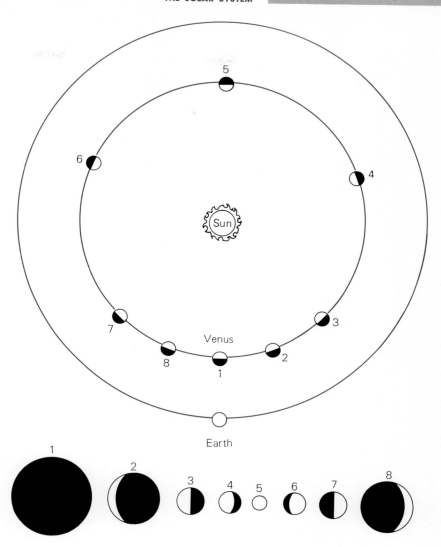

FIG. 18-4

The appearance and apparent size of Venus as seen from the earth depend upon the relative positions of the two planets and the sun. The "new Venus" at 1 is 6 times larger than the "full Venus" at 5. Venus appears brightest between 1 and 2 and between 8 and 1. To an observer on the earth, Venus never appears very far from the sun and either rises just before sunrise or sets just after sunset.

around the sun. Figure 18-4 shows how these effects arise. A year on Venus is only 225 earth days long, so the positions of Venus and the earth relative to each other and to the sun change continually. When Venus is between the sun and the earth, as at 1, it appears dark; if it could be seen, it would have its largest apparent diameter. At 2 and 8 Venus appears as a crescent but, because it is still fairly close to the earth, it is quite bright. At 3 and 7 we see half of Venus illuminated, and at 4 and 6 a gibbous Venus. Although the sun gets in the way of seeing the full Venus at

5, it is so far from the earth that it would not be especially brilliant even if it were visible.

Venus has the distinction of spinning "backward" on its axis. That is, looking downward on its north pole, Venus rotates clockwise, whereas the earth and the other planets rotate counterclockwise. The rotation of Venus is also extremely slow, so that a day on that planet represents 243 of our days. These observations seem odd, but a straightforward explanation has been suggested. As noted already in connection with the moon and with Mercury, a satellite tends to present the same face to its parent body. What may have happened is that, when formed, Venus rotated more or less as the other planets (except Mercury and Uranus) do today, but was eventually slowed down due to tides raised by the sun until its day and year were about the same. Then another gravitational influence came into play, that of the earth whenever the two planets were close together. Although weak compared with that of the sun, the attraction of the earth may have been sufficient to further modify the rotation rate of Venus by the small amount needed for Venus always to present the same face to the earth at closest approach, which is the current situation. Mercury, with only $\frac{1}{18}$ the mass of the earth, cannot have had any appreciable effect on the rotation of Venus.

If it is plausible that the earth can control the rotation of Venus, why doesn't Venus affect the earth's own rotation in a similar way? The answer is that Venus is closer to the sun than the earth and so is influenced by solar gravity to a greater extent. Thus the rotation of Venus may well have been slowed down by the sun to the point where the earth's gravity could take over, while at the same time the earth's spin remained too fast for Venus to do the same to our planet.

In size and mass Venus is more like the earth than any other member of the sun's family. For the most part its surface is relatively smooth, but there are two major highland regions, the larger with about the area of the United States. These "continents" cover only about 5 percent of Venus in contrast to the 30 percent extent of the earth's continents, and no water laps their edges. Some of the mountains of Venus are quite high, one of them topping Everest. Evidence of volcanic activity is abundant, including volcanic peaks, extensive lava flows, and a huge volcanic crater about 100 km across.

The crust of Venus seems to be an unbroken shell of rock instead of the shifting plates whose motion has dominated geologic processes on the earth. Why Venus should be so dead geologically is a mystery. Venus lacks the relatively rapid rotation of the earth, the gravitational tug of a large moon, and water: perhaps one or more of these factors is responsible for the difference in geologic activity between these otherwise similar planets.

Is there life on Venus? Bernard de Fontanelle thought so when he wrote in 1686 that the inhabitants of Venus must "resemble the Moors of Granada; a small, black people, burned by the sun, full of wit and fire, always in love, writing verse, fond of music, arranging festivals, dances, and tournaments every day."

Alas, the truth is less romantic. American spacecraft have passed close to Venus and Russian ones have parachuted instruments to its surface. The information radioed back showed that the atmosphere of Venus is almost all carbon dioxide with only small percentages of water vapor, nitrogen, oxygen, and other gases. The thick clouds that permanently shroud Venus consist mainly of sulfuric acid droplets and are driven by east-to-west winds of 100 m/s (224 mi/h). At the surface, the pressure of the atmosphere is about 100 times the corresponding figure for the earth. On the earth a small percentage of carbon dioxide in the atmosphere absorbs much of the radiation from the ground — the greenhouse effect. Venus, blanketed more effectively by far than the earth, has a surface temperature that averages over 400°C, enough to melt lead. The existence of life on Venus seems impossible.

Venus may have supported life in the past

Although Venus is inhospitable to life now, that may not always have been the case. Quite possibly Venus started out as a twin to our planet with abundant water and moderate temperatures. Life could have evolved there just as it did here. Then, billions of years later, the greenhouse effect on Venus could have somehow begun a runaway course in which evaporated water trapped more and more solar energy. As the atmosphere heated up, the water molecules broke apart under the influence of solar radiation. The hydrogen then could have escaped into space while the oxygen combined with other materials, leaving Venus largely waterless and lifeless. Will the huge increases in the carbon dioxide content of our atmosphere due to burning fossil fuels eventually trigger a similar fate?

Mars

The red planet

Mars is second only to Venus in brightness. Reddish orange in color, it has always been associated with violence and disaster. The Romans named it after their god of war, and the discoverer of its two satellites, the American astronomer Asaph

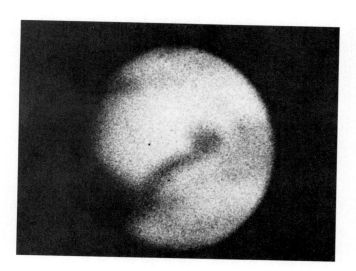

Photograph of Mars in red light.

Hall, continued the tradition by calling them Phobos (fear) and Deimos (terror) after the two sons of the Greek war god Ares. The symbol of Mars is a circle with an arrow, which is also the conventional male symbol.

The satellites of Mars were not discovered until 1877 because they are such tiny objects, far too insignificant to deserve the names they were given. Phobos, the inner one, is only 16 km high and 23 km across; Deimos, the outer one, is even smaller, 9 km high and 11 km across. Irregular shapes like these are possible only for astronomical bodies so small that the rigidity of their material is able to withstand the tendency of gravity to impose a spherical form, as discussed in Chap. 2. Phobos is so close to Mars that its orbital period of 7 h 39 min is shorter than the length of the Martian day, and as a result it rises in the west and sets in the east, speeding across the Martian sky three times each day. The period of Deimos is 30 h 18 min.

In what must be among the most bizarre coincidences in astronomy, the existence of two Martian satellites was conjectured in 1600 by Kepler and elaborated upon by Jonathan Swift in 1726 in *Gulliver's Travels*. Neither of them seems to have had the slightest justification for his belief. In the Voyage to Laputa, Swift has Gulliver learn not only that such satellites existed, but that their periods of revolution were 10 h and $20\frac{1}{2}$ h, not far from their actual periods.

Mars is said to be in *opposition* to the earth when it is on the opposite side of the earth from the sun, with the three bodies in a straight line. Since Mars is then both close to the earth and above the horizon all night, this is the best time to observe our neighbor. Oppositions occur every 780 days, which is 2 years and 50 days, so successive ones take place at different times of year. Because the orbit of Mars is somewhat elongated (the earth is much more nearly circular), the distance to Mars at opposition varies from 56 million km to 101 million km. The most favorable oppositions for viewing Mars are those that take place near the end of August when it is near perihelion, since it is closest to the sun then and hence also closest to the earth.

The diameter of Mars is slightly over half that of the earth and its mass is 11 percent of the earth's mass. As a result the surface gravity on Mars is 38 percent of the earth's; an astronaut weighing 150 lb on the earth would weigh 57 lb on Mars. Although the overall density of Mars is 3.97 g/cm^3 as compared with 5.52 g/cm^3 for the earth, the difference is misleading because materials in the interior of the less massive Mars are not compressed as much as those in the earth''s interior. Reckoned on a comparable basis, the two planets have about the same density, which suggests that Mars probably has about the same composition as the earth.

Mars rotates on its axis in a little over 24 h; its revolution about the sun requires nearly 2 years; and its axis is inclined to the plane of its orbit at nearly the same angle as the earth's. These facts mean that the Martian day and night have about the same lengths as ours and that Martian seasons are 6 months long and at least as pronounced as ours. Mars has long fascinated astronomers and laypeople alike because it is in so many ways similar to the earth, which leads to the question of whether life of some kind is present there.

Is There Life on Mars?

Maybe once, but probably not now

Mars has a thin atmosphere largely of carbon dioxide

If life does exist on Mars, it is adapted to an environment that would soon destroy most earthly organisms. For a start, Martian climates are exceedingly severe by our standards. Over half again farther from the sun than the earth, Mars receives considerably less solar energy per m² than we do. Its atmosphere, largely carbon dioxide, is extremely thin — equivalent to the earth's atmosphere at an altitude of nearly 40 km — so little of the heat from the sun is retained after nightfall. Daytime temperatures in summer at the equator rise to perhaps 20°C, but at night drop to perhaps −70°C. The average surface temperature of the entire planet is about −30°C. The scanty Martian atmosphere is also unable to screen out harmful solar ultraviolet radiation, a function carried out in the earth's atmosphere by the ozone present at high altitudes (see Chap. 13).

Water is scarce on Mars but may have been more abundant in the past

Another difficulty life must face on Mars is the scarcity of water. Some is certainly there, as water vapor in the atmosphere and permanently frozen into ice at the poles, but not a great deal. Some surface features photographed by spacecraft strongly suggest dried-up riverbeds and erosion by running water. The earth's surface water probably was vented from volcanoes early in its history, and there seems no reason why the same process should not have occurred on Mars, whose surface is dotted with extinct volcanoes. The craters we now see in the eroded regions must have been formed by meteoroid impacts after the water disappeared. From the number of these craters it seems clear that there has been no erosion to speak of for at least several hundred million years, perhaps for several billion.

Life of some kind is conceivable on Mars

The fact that most terrestrial life requires liquid water and oxygen plus protection from solar ultraviolet radiation does not necessarily mean that life of some kind could not exist in their absence. Certain bacteria on the earth are known whose life processes require carbon dioxide, not oxygen, so an oxygen-containing atmosphere is not indispensable, at least for primitive forms of life. Conceivably organisms could have evolved which can thrive on water gleaned from traces of it in the minerals of surface rocks. And shells of some sort might protect Martian creatures from ultraviolet radiation. Certainly it is plausible that life could have come into being long ago when conditions on Mars may well have been comparable with those on the earth today. As the original Martian atmosphere and surface water gradually disappeared into space as a result of the low escape speed (some water may have become permanently frozen beneath the surface as well), living things there could have adapted to the progressively harsher environment and have survived in some form to the present.

The absence of any indication of life in photographs taken from thousands of km away from the Martian surface is in itself not significant. At such distances terrestrial life would probably not be apparent to a visitor from elsewhere and a closer look would be likely to suggest that the car is the most conspicuous type of life on earth.

This portion of the Martian land-scape, photographed 2 hours after sunrise on August 3, 1976, by the Viking I Lander, is very similar to desert areas of California and Mexico. The large boulder at left is about 1 by 3 m in size. The object in the middle of the picture is part of the spacecraft.

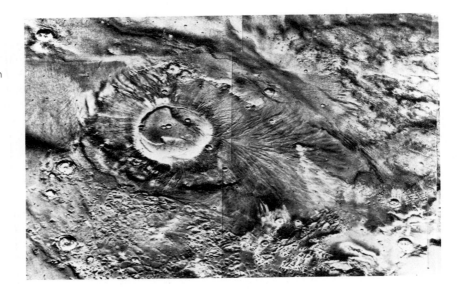

The crater of the Martian volcano Apollinaris Patera is 100 km across. The lava flows that extend about 200 km southeast of the crater apparently originated in a fissure.

The Martian landscape

In 1976 two American Viking spacecraft landed on Mars. Among their various tasks were several sensitive experiments able to detect life in Martian soil. No evidence for present life or chemical traces left by past life was found. But the experiments are hardly conclusive since they were limited to two landing sites, and such essential elements for life as nitrogen and phosphorus were indeed discovered. The best that can be said at present is that conditions suitable for life probably once existed on Mars but probably do not today.

The pictures radioed back by spacecraft that have orbited and landed on Mars show a host of intriguing geologic structures, many apparently of recent origin. The Martian landscape is extremely varied with regions spattered with huge craters, regions broken up into irregular short ridges and depressions, vast lava flows, channels that look as though they were carved by running water, even peculiar areas that seem to suggest glacial activity. Though rainstorms are absent —at least these days—violent winds periodically drive great clouds of dust around the planet that take several months to subside.

Asteroids

Tiny planets between Mars and Jupiter

Ceres is 1000 km across

The asteroids are small, rocky objects nearly all of which circle the sun in a belt between Mars and Jupiter. A few pass inside the earth's orbit in their circuits, and one, Icarus, gets even closer to the sun than Mercury.

The largest asteroid, Ceres, is about 1000 km in diameter and was the first to be discovered, on January 1, 1801, by the Italian astronomer Giuseppi Piazzi. For a long time asteroids were thought to be fragments from the breakup of a planet that was supposed to have once existed between Mars and Jupiter. It now seems more probable that, like the comets and meteoroids, they are bits of matter from the early solar system that never became incorporated into larger bodies.

Over 2000 asteroids have been tracked and named, a small fraction of the total number. Most are small and irregular in shape, no doubt much like the satellites of Mars. When the sunlight reflected by asteroids is analyzed with a spectrometer, the results show that they are probably similar in composition to stony and stony-iron meteorites.

THE OUTER PLANETS

Jupiter

Almost a star

The mammoth planet Jupiter is fittingly named after the most important of the Roman gods. The planet Jupiter is represented by a stylized lightning bolt because lightning was supposed to come from the god Jupiter. The symbolism has turned out to be quite appropriate since electric discharges regularly occur in Jupiter's atmosphere that produce bursts of radio waves detectable on the earth.

Jupiter, like Venus, is shrouded in clouds, but those of Jupiter are more spectacular in appearance. The clouds are responsible for Jupiter's relatively high reflectivity, which together with its size makes it a bright object in the sky despite its distance from the sun. The clouds occur in alternate light and dark bands whose colors — mostly in the yellow-orange-red family — and markings change slightly from time to time. One marking is particularly conspicuous, the Great Red Spot that today is about 25,000 km long and 10,000 km high, larger than the earth. Though its size, shape, and color are known to vary, the Spot itself does not seem to be a transient phenomenon, since it was definitely identified as long ago as 1831 and is probably the same marking described in 1660 by the French astonomer Cassini. Although the nature and origin of the Great Red Spot remain uncertain, a plausible suggestion is that it is a kind of permanent giant hurricane into which energy is constantly fed by the Jovian wind system. The red color may be due to phosphorus from the breakup of the phosphorus compounds believed to contribute to the colors of the bands that circle the planet.

The Great Red Spot

630

Jupiter is the largest planet. The Red Spot at upper left is 3 times larger than the earth and varies in size and appearance.

Jupiter rotates very rapidly

The sc 'ellites of Jupiter

Jupiter, Saturn, Uranus, and Neptune are composed chiefly of hydrogen and helium

Cassini used the spot he found, whatever it was, to determine Jupiter's period of rotation. This is a little less than 10 hours, which means that points on Jupiter's equator travel at the enormous speed of 45,000 km/h; the earth's equatorial speed is only 1670 km/h. Because of its rapid rotation, Jupiter bulges much more at the equator than the earth does.

The four Jovian satellites that Galileo discovered over three centuries ago are readily seen with a pair of binoculars or a small telescope. The largest is as big as Mercury, the smallest is about the size of the moon. One of them, Io, has at least eight active volcanoes. Another, Europa, is covered with ice that has cracks several km deep. Conditions at the bottoms of the cracks could conceivably support simple life forms, such as those that exist under the ice of Antarctica's frozen lakes. The other ten satellites are very small (25 to 250 km across), and one of them escaped detection until 1979. The four outermost satellites revolve ''backward'' around Jupiter, from east to west. Jupiter also has a ring, like those of Saturn but so faint that it can only be detected by spacecraft. It seems to consist of widely spaced rocks the size of boulders.

Jupiter's volume is about 1300 times that of the earth, but its mass is only 318 times as great. The resulting low density — only a third more than that of water — means that Jupiter cannot be composed of rock and iron as is the earth. Like the other giant planets Saturn, Uranus, and Neptune, Jupiter must consist chiefly of hydrogen and helium, the two lightest elements. It is probable that Jupiter has a small rocky inner core surrounded by a large outer core of liquid hydrogen under such enormous pressure that it behaves like a liquid metal. The interior is believed to be very hot, possibly 30,000°C, but not hot enough for nuclear reactions to occur in its hydrogen content that would turn Jupiter into a star. However, if Jupiter's mass were a few dozen times greater, the internal temperatures would be high enough for it to be a miniature star.

The atmosphere of Jupiter

Surrounding the core is a dense layer of liquid hydrogen and helium that gradually turns into a gas. The outer part of Jupiter's atmosphere contains such gases as ammonia, methane, and water vapor as well as hydrogen and helium. Laboratory experiments show that when a mixture of these gases is exposed to energy sources such as are usually present in a planetary atmosphere (for instance, lightning, ultraviolet light, streams of fast ions from the sun), the various organic compounds necessary for life are formed, as described in Chap. 12. Has some form of life evolved in Jupiter's atmosphere? Nobody knows, but simple organisms such as bacteria and yeasts are able to survive when exposed to gas mixtures that simulate the Jovian atmosphere at comparable temperatures and pressures.

Jupiter has a strong magnetic field

United States spacecraft passed close to Jupiter in 1973, 1974, and 1979 after journeys that lasted nearly 2 years and covered over a billion km. Of the wealth of information radioed back, a few items are especially notable. For example, Jupiter has a magnetic field nearly 10 times stronger than the earth's, and this field traps high-energy protons and electrons from the sun in belts that extend many Jovian radii outward. The earth has such belts too, but they are 10,000 times weaker. It is plausible that Jupiter's magnetic field is connected with the metallic nature of part of its volume, with the "metal" being highly compressed liquid hydrogen instead of the molten iron of the earth's core.

Jupiter radiates more energy than it receives from the sun

Another important finding confirmed that Jupiter radiates over twice as much energy as it receives from the sun. By contrast the atmospheres of Venus, Earth, and Mars are in balance, and radiate only as much energy as the sun provides. Apparently Jupiter is still cooling down, so that the extra heat has been left over from the planet's formation.

Saturn

Lord of the rings

In its setting of brilliant rings, Saturn is the most striking and beautiful of the earth's kin. Saturn, the Roman god of sowing seed and the father of Jupiter, was once called Kronos, from which the planet's symbol of a stylized K probably derives. The festivals of worship to Saturn, the saturnalia, were always splendid occasions of joy and revelry; Saturday is also named after him.

Saturn is much like Jupiter in many respects

Saturn resembles Jupiter in many respects, though smaller and less massive. Like Jupiter it consists largely of hydrogen and helium, radiates more heat than it receives from the sun, is flattened at the poles by rapid rotation, has a strong magnetic field and a dense atmosphere, and is surrounded by banded clouds in which gigantic thunderstorms occur. However, Saturn's core seems to have less of the liquid metallic hydrogen of Jupiter's core, with a large rocky kernel at its center.

Farther from the sun than Jupiter, Saturn is considerably colder, only about $-180°C$ at the surface. Nevertheless it gives off over twice as much energy as it receives in sunlight, much more in proportion than Jupiter does. Some of the extra heat traces back to Saturn's formation, but not all of it. A plausible mechanism for

Saturn's rings are not solid but consist of small rock fragments.

the remainder is based upon the fact that helium tends to separate gradually from hydrogen at low temperatures, and, being heavier, sinks downward. The potential energy the helium loses in this way becomes heat. Confirming the idea is the observation that less than 6 percent of helium is in the outer part of Saturn, compared with 10 percent for Jupiter. If the "missing" helium had indeed migrated deeper into Saturn, the planet's energy output would just about be accounted for.

The satellites of Saturn

The 17 known satellites of Saturn range in size from a few tens of km across to the giant Titan, whose 5140-km diameter makes it larger than the moon. Titan is the only satellite in the solar system with an atmosphere, which seems to consist largely of nitrogen. Reddish clouds of organic compounds float in this atmosphere, probably sending showers of methane rain down from time to time to feed the liquid methane oceans that cover much of Titan's surface. Like the other large solid bodies of the solar system unaffected by erosion, Saturn's moons are heavily cratered.

Saturn's rings

A number of rings surround Saturn at its equator, two of them bright and the others faint. The rings are inclined by 27° with respect to the plane of the earth's orbit, so we see them from different angles as Saturn proceeds in its leisurely $29\frac{1}{2}$-year tour around the sun (Fig. 18-5). Twice in each period of revolution the rings are edgewise to the earth, which happened last in 1981 and will happen again in 1996. In this orientation the rings are practically invisible, suggesting that they are very thin. In fact, they are only a km or two thick, in places less than 200 m. Since the outer bright ring is 270,000 km in diameter, a sheet of paper is fat by comparison. In 1988 we will be able to see Saturn's rings in their fullest glory, tipped downward by 27° so that their upper (northern) surfaces face us.

Inside the Roche limit, tidal forces would disrupt a large satellite

The rings are not the solid sheets they appear to be but instead consist of a multitude of small bodies, each of which revolves around Saturn like a miniature satellite. No satellite of substantial size can exist close to its parent planet because of the disruptive effect of tide-producing forces, which are proportionately less the

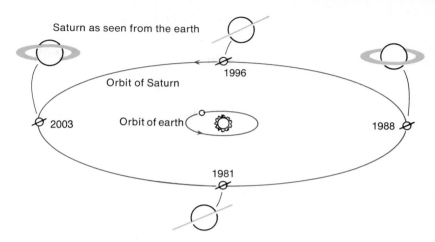

Saturn as seen from the earth

Orbit of Saturn

1996

Orbit of earth

2003

1988

1981

FIG. 18-5
The appearance of Saturn's rings from the earth varies with Saturn's location in its orbit. Saturn's period of revolution is 29.5 years.

The nature of Saturn's rings

more distant the satellite. The *Roche limit* is the minimum radius a satellite orbit can have if the satellite is to remain intact. It is named in honor of E. A. Roche, who investigated the origin of Saturn's rings a century ago. The Roche limit is about 2.4 times a planet's radius, and in fact the outer rim of the outer bright ring is 2.3 radii from the center of Saturn. The innermost of Saturn's large satellite never approaches closer than 2.6 radii, although very small ones are found among the rings. The Roche limit for the earth is a small fraction of the radius of the moon's orbit. Artificial satellites are able to circle the earth inside its Roche limit because they are small.

How do we know for sure that Saturn's rings are not solid? One piece of evidence is that we can see stars through them. Another is that doppler effect measurements show that the inner part of each ring moves faster than the outer part, which is in accord with Kepler's third law that calls for a decrease in orbital speed with an increase in orbital size. (Thus Mercury's orbital speed is 48 km/s, Pluto's is only 5 km/s.) If the rings were solid their outer parts would have the highest speeds, contrary to what is actually found.

Nor can the rings be gaseous — they reflect sunlight and radar signals far too well. The only question left is the size and nature of the particles of which they consist. In 1980 and 1981 two Voyager spacecraft reached Saturn after 4-year journeys. They radioed back vast amounts of data on the planet itself, its satellites, and, of course, its rings. The findings about the rings confirmed what astronomers had suspected earlier: the particles are chunks of rock and ice that range from the size of buildings down to fine dust. In addition, the rings we see from the earth are not uniform but are actually split into thousands of narrow ringlets. Two of the ringlets in one of the outer, faint rings seem to be braided around each other, a peculiarity that may result from the gravitational pulls of two small satellites whose orbits are just inside and just outside the ringlets.

Uranus, Neptune, Pluto

Far out

The three most distant planets, Uranus, Neptune, and Pluto, owe their discovery to the telescope. Uranus was found by accident in 1781 during a systematic survey of the stars by the great English astronomer William Herschel. Herschel, born in Germany in 1738, started out as a musician (he played the oboe and the organ and wrote 24 symphonies), but eventually his hobby of astronomy claimed all his attention. Uranus is just barely visible to the naked eye, and in fact had been identified as a faint star on a number of sky maps prepared during the preceding hundred years.

Herschel at first suspected Uranus to be a comet because, through the telescope, it appeared as a disk rather than as a point of light. Observations made over a period of time showed its position to change relative to the stars, and its orbit, determined from these data, revealed it to be a planet. Six years later Herschel found two satellites circling Uranus; three more were found later. The discoveries of Neptune in 1846 (see Chap. 2) and of Pluto in 1930 were made as the result of predictions based on their gravitational effects on other planets.

Uranus and Neptune are large bodies, each having a diameter about $3\frac{1}{2}$ times that of the earth. In most of their properties these planets resemble Jupiter and Saturn, though they are much colder. Their atmospheres are largely methane, which accounts for their greenish color, with some hydrogen present as well. Because Uranus and Neptune are so far from the sun, their surface temperatures are less than $-200°C$, and any ammonia present would be frozen out of their atmospheres.

Uranus has the distinction of rotating about an axis tilted by 82° from the plane of its orbit, so that we can think of it as spinning on its side. Because of this, summer at a particular place on Uranus is a 42-year period of continuous sunshine, and winter a 42-year period of continuous darkness. To be sure, the sun is so far away that the differences between day and night and between summer and winter cannot be very great.

Uranus has at least nine narrow rings, like those of Jupiter and Saturn, composed of small particles. Does Neptune, too, have rings? Nobody knows as yet.

Pluto may once have been a satellite of Neptune. If this is the case, perhaps the event that left Pluto pursuing its own orbit around the sun also knocked another Neptune satellite, Triton, into its present "backward" orbit. Pluto's orbit is so eccentric that it swings inside Neptune's, and as a result Pluto approaches closer to the sun at times than Neptune ever does (see Fig. 18-1). Pluto is so small, so far away, and so feebly illuminated that reliable information about it is difficult to obtain. It seems to be slightly larger than the moon but only a sixth as massive, and is thought to consist mainly of frozen methane. Pluto has a satellite, Charon (named for the ferryman who takes the dead across the river Styx to Pluto's domain), whose diameter of 2000 km is half that of Pluto and whose composition is probably the same.

The moon rotates on its axis at the same rate that it circles the earth, so it always presents this face to us.

THE MOON

To look at the moon is to wonder. What is it made of? What is its origin? What is the nature of its landscape? What geologic processes occur on its surface and in its interior? Is there life on the moon? What is the ultimate destiny of the earth-moon system? Until July 20, 1969, the study of the moon was more notable for the questions asked than for the answers available. On that day Neil Armstrong set foot on the moon, the first person ever to do so, after a 3-day voyage aboard the spacecraft Apollo 11 with two companions. Four days after that they returned to earth, bringing with them samples of the lunar surface. Since that historic expedition and the others that followed it questions about the moon still outnumber answers, but now the questions are more precise and detailed, reflecting the enormous advance in our knowledge about our companion in space.

The Lunar Surface

Mountains and maria but no water and no atmosphere

The moon has neither an atmosphere nor surface water

The moon was hardly a mystery even before the voyages of Apollo 11 and of the other manned spacecraft that followed it there. Even a small telescope reveals the chief features of the lunar landscape: wide plains, jagged mountain ranges, and innumerable craters of all sizes. Each mountain stands out in vivid clarity, with no clouds or haze to hide the smallest detail. Mountain shadows are black and sharp-edged. When the moon passes before a star, the star remains bright and clear up to the moon's very edge. From these observations we conclude that the moon has little or no atmosphere. Water is likewise absent, as indicated by the complete lack of lakes, oceans, and rivers.

But there is still no substitute for direct observation and laboratory analysis, and each spacecraft that has landed on the moon and returned to earth, whether piloted by human beings or not, has brought back information and samples of the greatest value. The lack of a protective atmosphere and of running water to erode away surface features means that there is much to be learned on the moon about our common environment in space, both past and present. And from the composition and internal structure of the moon hints can be gleaned of its origin and past history, which may well bear upon those of the earth as well. Thus the study of the moon is also a part of the study of the earth, doubly justifying the effort of its exploration.

The maria of the moon consist of lava pulverized by meteorites

With the help of no more than binoculars it is easy to distinguish the two main kinds of lunar landscape, the dark, relatively smooth *maria* and the lighter, ruggedly mountainous highlands. Mare means "sea" in Latin, but the term is still used even though it has been known for a long time that these regions are not covered with water. The largest of the maria is Mare Imbrium, the Sea of Showers, which is over 100 km across. The maria are circular depressions covered with dark, loosely packed material — not solid rock. They are not perfectly smooth, but are marked

Astronaut Charles M. Duke, Jr., collecting lunar samples during Apollo 16 expedition in 1972. The crater at left is 40 m in diameter and 10 m deep. Behind it is the Lunar Roving Vehicle which permitted Duke and his fellow astronaut John W. Young to explore the lunar surface some distance from the landing craft.

by small craters, ridges, and cliffs. The available evidence indicates that maria consist of lava flows similar to basalt that have been broken up by meteorite impacts. It is curious and perhaps significant that nearly all the maria are on the lunar hemisphere that faces the earth.

Lunar craters

The lunar highlands are scarred by innumerable craters ranging up to 236 km in diameter. Most of the craters are circular with raised rims that are steeper on the inside than on the outside, and some have mountain peaks at their centers. Certain craters, such as Tycho and Copernicus, have conspicuous streaks of light-colored matter radiating outward. These *rays* may extend for hundreds or thousands of km, and seem to consist of lunar material sprayed outward. Craters resembling those on the moon are produced on the earth both by volcanic activity and by meteoroid impact. There is no question that some of the lunar craters are of volcanic origin, but meteoroid bombardment is more likely to have been the cause of most of them.

Rilles resemble riverbeds

The *rilles* of the highlands are especially intriguing. These are narrow channels up to 250 km long that look like nothing else than dried-up riverbeds. One of them, called Rima Hadley, is 1.5 km across and 300 to 500 m deep, and meanders down from the edge of a mountain range to the adjoining mare. No convincing hypothesis of the origin of rilles exists as yet, but some suggestions have been advanced. For instance, although water is absent from the moon's surface today, and no trace of hydrated minerals in the lunar samples brought back to the earth has been found, subsurface water may conceivably be present, and could be released by an event such as a meteoroid impact. The water gushing forth could carve out a rille before finally evaporating into space some years, perhaps a century, later. Another theory of rilles, a little less speculative, holds that they were created by the collapse of subsurface lava-filled tubes.

The mountains of the moon

The mountains of the moon are thousands of meters high, which means that the moon's surface is about as irregular as the earth's. In order to support these irregularities, the moon must be quite rigid, which in view of the moon's size suggests that the lunar interior is nowhere near as hot as that of the earth. However, the rigidity argument applies only to the outer few hundred km of the moon's interior. Data from seismographs placed on the lunar surface during Apollo expeditions indicate that, below a depth of 800 km or so, the moon's interior may well be softer. Moonquakes are few and mild compared with earthquakes, which again implies that the lunar interior is relatively cool since it is heat from the earth's interior that powers the tectonic activity of its lithosphere.

Lunar Rocks

All are very old

The oldest lunar rocks solidified 4.6 billion years ago, the youngest 3 billion years ago

The analysis of lunar rock and soil samples has led to a number of tentative conclusions about the past history of our satellite. The story can be taken farther back on the basis of such samples than in the case of the earth because, since the moon lacks an atmosphere, weathering did not occur there. Even particles of pure

This 2-cm rock fragment collected during the Apollo 11 expedition in 1969 resembles a type of terrestrial volcanic rock called breccia.

iron have been found on the moon's surface, whereas only iron compounds occur on the earth's surface. Rocks have been found on the moon which radioactive dating reveals to have crystallized much earlier than the most ancient terrestrial rocks, which are 3.8 billion years old. Some lunar samples apparently solidified 4.6 billion years ago, which is very soon after the solar system came into being.

Because the youngest rocks found on the moon are 3 billion years old, the inference is that, though the lunar surface was once molten and there were widespread volcanic eruptions for some time afterward, all igneous activity must have ceased 3 billion years ago. To be sure, the lunar surface has been disturbed in a variety of small-scale ways since it cooled, but apparently meteorite bombardment was responsible for most of them.

The moon's outer shell was once molten, but apparently not its interior

The density of surface rocks is about the same as the density of the moon as a whole, which implies that the entire moon was never molten. Had it melted all the way through, the heavier materials would have concentrated in a dense core to leave a lighter mantle and crust, as in the case of the earth. Perhaps the outer part of the moon was heated to the melting point by intense meteoroid bombardment. Also possible is that a concentration of radioactive elements there was responsible. The molten layer may have been 150 to 300 km deep.

Origin of the Moon

Still an open question

Theories of the origin of the moon fall into three categories (see Fig. 18-6):

1. The moon was initially part of the earth and split off from it to become an independent body.

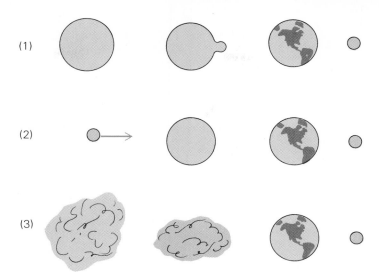

FIG. 18-6
Three theories of the moon's origin. (1) The moon split away from the earth. (2) The moon was captured as it approached the earth from elsewhere. (3) The earth and moon were formed together from a cloud of particles.

2. The moon was formed elsewhere in the solar system and was later captured by the earth's gravitational field.

3. The moon and the earth came into being together as a double-planet system.

Each of these approaches was very fashionable at one time or another, and each has strong arguments both for and against it.

The fragmentation theory

The first hypothesis assumes that the original earth was spinning so fast that it became unstable and broke in two. If we add together the earth's angular momentum of rotation on its axis and the moon's angular momentum of revolution around the earth, the original earth would have rotated every $5\frac{1}{2}$ h or so. This is quite fast, but only half the speed required for such a body to break up. Furthermore, even if it had done so, the mass ratio of the fragments ought to be perhaps $8:1$, not the $81:1$ mass ratio of the earth and moon. And if the moon had originated in this way, it would have escaped from the earth's gravitational field altogether instead of going into orbit around it.

To be sure, some modifications of this idea seem more plausible, in particular the notion that the planet Mars as well as the moon parted from the earth at the same time. Then the angular momentum and mass ratio problems would not occur. But lunar exploration has brought up a new objection: why the composition of the moon is so different from that of the earth.

The capture theory

The second hypothesis must overcome the problem that a body approaching the earth from somewhere far away will, if nothing else happens, simply swing past the earth and move off again. But if the moon lost energy in some way near the earth, it could have been permanently trapped. Apparently only a small energy change would have been enough; three suggestions are friction in an extensive early atmosphere of the earth, friction in a dust cloud filling the early solar system, and the impact of a large meteoroid. The chief difficulty with this hypothesis is perhaps that chance plays more than one role in it. On the other hand, only the earth has a satellite as massive relative to itself as the moon, so the origin of the moon could well be different from the origins of the other planetary satellites. (Pluto's satellite Charon, with half Pluto's mass, is in still another category.)

The double-planet theory

The third hypothesis regards the earth and moon as twin planets that developed in the early solar system instead of a single one. Since the solar system almost certainly originated in the gradual fusing together of small particles of matter in a cloud around the sun (Chap. 20), it seems possible that there could have been two centers of accumulation rather than one. However, nobody has yet proposed a definite mechanism whereby a double planet instead of a single one could have evolved. And if the moon and earth were formed from the same material, why is the moon's density only 60 percent that of the earth? A modification of the common-origin theory accounts for the density difference by proposing that the moon grew from a cloud of matter of different composition near an already-formed earth, but this concept, too, is not free of serious objection.

The origin of the moon is virtually an open question at this time. Only the breaking away of the moon from the earth as a single fragment seems definitely excluded, and neither of the other ideas seems overwhelmingly convincing.

IMPORTANT TERMS

In order from the sun, the planets are **Mercury, Venus, Earth, Mars, Jupiter, Saturn, Uranus, Neptune,** and **Pluto.** All but Mercury and Venus have satellites. In addition, thousands of **asteroids** are in orbits that lie between those of Mars and Jupiter. The planets and their satellites are visible by virtue of the sunlight they reflect.

The **inner planets** (Mercury, Venus, Earth, and Mars) are considerably smaller, less massive, and denser than the **outer planets.** The outer planets apparently consist largely of hydrogen, helium, and hydrogen compounds such as methane, ammonia, and water vapor. Jupiter and Uranus as well as Saturn are circled by **rings** of particles.

The **moon** has neither an atmosphere nor surface water. Although geologically inactive at present, its surface shows signs of having once melted and of having experienced many volcanic eruptions long ago. Meteoroid bombardment has been a more recent factor in shaping its landscapes.

MULTIPLE CHOICE

1. Which of the following statements is correct?
   a. The sun accounts for most of the mass and most of the angular momentum of the solar system
   b. The planets account for most of the mass and most of the angular momentum of the solar system
   c. The sun accounts for most of the mass and the planets account for most of the angular momentum of the solar system
   d. The planets account for most of the mass and the sun accounts for most of the angular momentum of the solar system

2. The planets shine because
   a. they emit light
   b. they reflect sunlight
   c. they reflect moonlight
   d. they reflect starlight

3. The smallest planet is

a. Mercury
b. Venus
c. Mars
d. Jupiter

4. The largest planet is
   a. Mercury
   b. Venus
   c. Jupiter
   d. Saturn

5. The planet nearest the sun is
   a. Mercury
   b. Venus
   c. Saturn
   d. Pluto

6. A planet with virtually no atmosphere is
   a. Mercury
   b. Mars
   c. Jupiter
   d. Saturn

7. The least dense of the following planets is
   a. Mercury
   b. Venus
   c. the earth
   d. Saturn

8. The planet that appears brightest in the sky is
   a. Venus
   b. Mars
   c. Jupiter
   d. Saturn

9. The length of the year is greatest on
   a. Mercury
   b. Jupiter
   c. Uranus
   d. Pluto

10. The largest of Jupiter's satellites is about the size of
    a. a large ship
    b. the moon
    c. Mercury
    d. the earth

11. Two planets that always appear relatively close to the sun in the sky are
    a. Mercury
    b. Venus
    c. Mars
    d. Jupiter

12. A planet on which life of some kind is conceivable is
    a. Mercury
    b. Venus

c. Mars
d. Pluto

13. Most asteroids lie in a belt between
    a. Mercury and the sun
    b. the earth and Mars
    c. the earth and the moon
    d. Mars and Jupiter

14. The planet closest to being a star is
    a. Jupiter
    b. Saturn
    c. Uranus
    d. Pluto

15. The rings of Saturn
    a. are gas clouds
    b. are sheets of liquid
    c. are sheets of solid rock
    d. consist of separate particles

16. The Roche limit refers to
    a. the smallest mass a satellite can have
    b. the largest mass a satellite can have
    c. the smallest orbital radius a satellite can have
    d. the largest orbital radius a satellite can have

17. The spacecraft that traveled to Mars did not find
    a. heavily cratered regions
    b. lava flows
    c. dust storms
    d. liquid water

18. The average density of the moon is
    a. lower than that of the earth
    b. about the same as that of the earth
    c. higher than that of the earth
    d. unknown

19. The maria of the moon are covered with
    a. water
    b. hard, smooth rock
    c. dark, loose soil
    d. frozen carbon dioxide

20. Most of the craters on the moon are probably the result of
    a. volcanic action
    b. meteoroid bombardment
    c. erosion
    d. collisions with asteroids

21. The interior of the moon is probably
    a. liquid
    b. solid
    c. gaseous
    d. hollow

22. The age of the oldest samples of lunar material is
    a. 1 million years

   b. 1 billion years
   c. 3.5 billion years
   d. 4.6 billion years
23. The moon has an abundance of
   a. atmospheric gases
   b. water
   c. ice
   d. craters
24. It is least likely that
   a. the moon broke away from the earth
   b. the moon originated elsewhere in the solar system and was subsequently captured by the earth
   c. the earth and moon originated at the same time as a double-planet system
   d. the moon came into being later than the earth but in its vicinity

QUESTIONS

1. How is it possible to distinguish the planets from the stars by observations with the naked eye? By observations with a telescope?

2. Which of the planets are readily visible to the naked eye?

3. Why do the planets shine?

4. Which planet is the brightest? How does its brightness compare with that of the brightest star? Which planet is the second brightest?

5. Why is Venus a brighter object in the sky than Mars?

6. Which planets would you expect to show phases like those of the moon?

7. Suppose you were on Mars and watched the earth with the help of a telescope. What changes would you see in the earth's appearance as it moves around the sun in its orbit?

8. Why are Mercury and Venus always seen either around sunrise or around sunset?

9. Which is the largest planet? The smallest? Which planet is nearest the sun? Farthest from the sun?

10. On which planet is the length of the year shortest? On which is it longest?

11. On which planets would a person weigh less than on the earth? On which would a person weigh more?

12. Which planet resembles the earth most in size and mass? In surface conditions?

13. About how much time elapses between sunrise and sunset on Mars? On Jupiter?

14. Which planets have crusts of rock?

15. Why is it very unlikely that there is life on Mercury?

16. Why is the average temperature on Mars lower than that on the earth? Why is there a greater variation in Martian temperatures?

17. Mars has surface features that seem to be the result of erosion by running water. Why does the presence of many meteoroid craters in these regions suggest that the running water disappeared long ago?

18. What is the nature of Saturn's rings?

19. Which planets besides Saturn have rings? What is the nature of these rings?

20. Would you expect the rings of Saturn to revolve with the same period, like parts of the same phonograph record?

21. What are thought to be the chief constituents of the giant planets Jupiter, Saturn, Uranus, and Neptune?

22. Jupiter radiates more energy than it receives from the sun. What is the most likely origin for the additional energy?

23. Distinguish between asteroids and meteoroids.

24. Is the moon the largest satellite in the solar system? The smallest?

25. Why is it believed that the moon's interior is different in composition from the earth's interior?

26. The moon's surface is about as irregular as that of the earth. What does this imply about temperatures in the moon's interior?

27. The densities of rocks on the moon's surface are about the same as the density of the moon as a whole. What does this observation suggest about the thermal history of the moon?

28. Why is it believed that large-scale igneous activity ceased on the moon about 3 billion years ago?

29. The moon's maria are dark, relatively smooth regions conspicuous even to the naked eye. What is their nature?

30. If the moon circled Jupiter in an orbit the same size as its present one, would its period of revolution be the same, shorter, or longer? Why?

31. How does the idea of Roche's limit bear on theories of the past history of the moon?

32. List some theories of the moon's origin. Are any of them free from serious objections?

ANSWERS TO MULTIPLE CHOICE

1. c	**7.** d	**13.** d	**19.** c
2. b	**8.** a	**14.** a	**20.** b
3. a	**9.** d	**15.** d	**21.** b
4. c	**10.** c	**16.** c	**22.** d
5. a	**11.** a, b	**17.** d	**23.** d
6. a	**12.** c	**18.** a	**24.** a

19

THE STARS

Modern stellar astronomy began toward the end of the eighteenth century with the work of William Herschel. Herschel sought among the stars something of the regularity of structure and orderliness of motion that Newton and his predecessors had found among the planets. Like a pioneer in any branch of science, Herschel began with observation and spent many years cataloging stars and measuring their apparent motions. From this study he was able to arrive at a structure for the universe that is not far from the one that today's astronomers believe to be correct.

Of the billions of stars in the universe, none appears as more than a point of light to even the most powerful telescope. As recently as the last century most scientists despaired of ever knowing the physical nature of the stars. Thanks to the discovery of spectroscopic analysis, however, we not only have a great deal of detailed information on thousands of stars but are also able to trace the evolution of a star from its birth through maturity to its last agonies and eventual "death."

TOOLS OF ASTRONOMY

Light is the messenger that brings us information about the universe. Because the information arrives in code, so to speak, the astronomer must decipher it before being able to assess its significance. The tools of astronomy consist of devices that collect light and that sort it into its component wavelengths, which are the elements of the code.

The Telescope

All modern ones are reflectors

Advantages of reflecting telescopes

In Herschel's time, as in ours, the telescope was the basic astronomical instrument, and much of his success was due to the improvements he introduced in telescope construction. Herschel was the first to build and use a large reflecting telescope, an instrument in which light is reflected from a concave mirror instead of being refracted through a lens. A large lens tends to sag under its own weight, which produces a distorted image, whereas a mirror of any size can be adequately supported from behind. In addition, there is no problem of the dispersion of light of different wavelengths with a mirror (Chap. 6). All modern astronomical telescopes are reflectors. The largest, located in the Soviet Union, has a mirror 6 m in diameter, but technical problems have prevented it from reaching its full potential. Next in size is a 5-m reflector at Mt. Palomar in California which has been enlarging the horizons of astronomy since 1948.

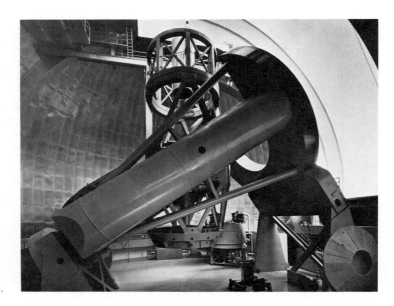

The mounting of the 5-m-diameter reflecting telescope at Mt. Palomar, California, permits it to examine all parts of the sky visible from its location.

The larger the telescope, the fainter the objects it can detect

In stellar astronomy the purpose of a big telescope is not to secure great magnification, for no obtainable magnification can make the stars appear larger than points of light. The virtue of large mirrors and lenses lies in their light-gathering power, which enables more light from a given object to be collected. Thus faint objects that would otherwise be invisible are revealed by a large telescope, and more light from brighter objects is available for study.

Nowadays the light collected by a telescope is directed to a photographic plate or electronic sensor rather than to the astronomer's eye. These devices have the advantage that they respond to the *total amount* of light that falls on them over the period of time they are exposed, whereas the eye responds only to the *brightness* of the light that reaches it. The longer the exposure to faint light, the more distinct the resulting image. A telescope with a camera or sensor attached can be trained on the same area of the sky for hours or, if necessary, for several nights to allow objects too faint for the eye to pick up to be detected. Photographic plates provide permanent records that enable positions and properties of stars as they appear today to be compared with what they were years ago and with what they will be in years to come.

The Spectrometer

Without it, little would be known about the stars

The spectrometer is indispensable to the astronomer

By itself, a telescope is of limited use in studying the stars. What is needed is a combination of a telescope and a spectrometer, the same instrument that contributed so much to our knowledge of atomic structure. A spectrometer breaks light up into its separate wavelengths, as shown in Fig. 8-8. The resulting band of colors, with each wavelength separate from the others, is the spectrum that is recorded on a photographic plate.

The spectrum of a star does not seem impressive. If photographed in natural colors, it generally consists of a rainbow band crossed by a multitude of fine dark lines. Ordinarily color film is not used, so the spectrum shows simply black lines on a light gray background.

At first glance it does not seem that a few black lines on a photographic plate can get us very far in understanding the stars. But each of those lines has its own story to tell about how it was produced, and a specialist can piece together data from different lines into a comprehensive picture of an entire star. Some types of information obtainable from spectra are outlined below.

Spectrum Analysis

Spectra can tell us a surprising amount

Structure   A spectrum of dark lines on a continuous colored background is an *absorption spectrum* that is produced when light from a hot object passes through

A spectrometer mounted on the 1.8-m-diameter reflecting telescope at Lowell Observatory, Arizona. Spectra obtained with such instruments have provided the clues needed to understand the nature and evolution of the universe.

Most stars have hot interiors surrounded by cooler atmospheres

a cooler gas (Chap. 8). Atoms and molecules of the gas absorb light of certain wavelengths — wavelengths that they would emit if they themselves were hot — and so leave narrow gaps in the band of color. Thus a star that has this kind of spectrum (and nearly all of them do) reveals at once something of its structure: it must have a hot, glowing interior surrounded by a relatively cool gaseous atmosphere.

Blue stars are hottest, red stars are coolest

Temperature From the continuous background of a star's spectrum can be found the temperature of its surface, the part of the star from which we receive light. What is necessary is to determine where in the spectrum the star's radiation is brightest. Since the wavelength of maximum intensity decreases as the temperature rises, the point of maximum intensity in the spectrum is a measure of temperature (Fig. 19-1). Thus the hottest stars are blue (maximum intensity at the short-wavelength end of the spectrum), stars of intermediate temperature white, and the coolest visible stars red. This relation holds for materials on the earth as well as for the stars, as we know from experience (Fig. 3-24).

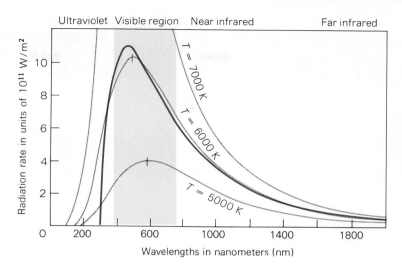

Ultraviolet Visible region Near infrared Far infrared

FIG. 19-1

Relative intensity of the wavelengths of light emitted by bodies with the temperatures indicated. The wavelength whose intensity is greatest is shorter for hot bodies than for cooler ones. The curve in color represents measurements of the sun's photosphere. (1 nm = 10^{-9} m)

The composition of a star can be found from its spectrum

Composition   Since each element has a spectrum consisting of lines with characteristic wavelengths, the elements present in a star's atmosphere can be identified from the dark lines in its spectrum. In principle it is only necessary to determine the wavelength of each line in the spectrum and compare these wavelengths with those produced by various elements in the laboratory.

Condition of matter   In practice the identification of lines in a star's spectrum is not quite so easy. The wavelengths and intensities of the lines characteristic of a given element depend not only on the element but also on such conditions as temperature, pressure, and degree of ionization. These difficulties prove to be blessings in disguise, however, for once the lines are identified they reveal not only which elements are present in a star's atmosphere but something about the physical conditions in which the elements exist.

Chemical compounds also have spectral lines of recognizable wavelengths, so spectra provide a means of determining how much of the matter in a star's atmosphere is in the form of molecules rather than atoms.

The earth's atmosphere absorbs light of certain wavelengths, mainly in the ultraviolet

A serious problem in astronomical spectroscopy is imposed by the absorption of light in the earth's atmosphere. A small amount of ozone in the stratosphere effectively blocks out all ultraviolet radiation except for a small range of wavelengths just below the violet — a fortunate circumstance for living things on earth but a calamity to astronomers, since the lines of several elements occur only in the ultraviolet region. Isolated wavelengths elsewhere in the spectrum are obscured by other atmospheric gases. Spectrometers mounted in sounding rockets, high-altitude balloons, satellites, and in spacecraft are needed to study those parts of solar and stellar spectra that cannot reach the earth's surface.

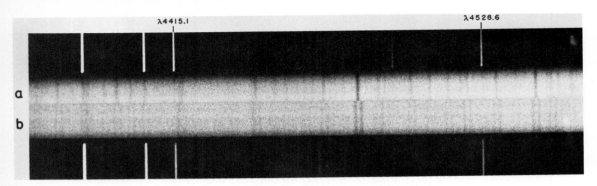

λ4415.1   λ4526.6

a

b

Spectra of the double star Mizar, which consists of two stars that circle their center of mass, taken 2 days apart. In (a) the stars are in line with no motion toward or away from the earth, so their spectral lines are superimposed. In (b) one star is moving toward the earth and the other is moving away from the earth, so the spectral lines of the former are doppler shifted toward the blue end of the spectrum and those of the latter are shifted toward the red end.

Motion of a star toward or away from the earth is shown by doppler shifts in its spectral lines

FIG. 19-2
The doppler effect in stellar spectra. Star A is stationary with respect to the earth. B is receding from the earth; it moves the distance b during the emission of one light wave, whose wavelength is therefore increased by b. C is approaching; it moves the distance c during the emission of one wave, whose wavelength is thus decreased by c. Hence stars receding from the earth have spectral lines shifted toward the red (long-wavelength) end, while stars approaching the earth have spectral lines shifted toward the blue (short-wavelength) end.

Magnetic fields   The presence of a magnetic field causes individual energy levels within atoms to split into several sublevels. When such atoms are excited and radiate, their spectral lines are accordingly split each into a number of lines close to the original ones. This phenomenon is called the *Zeeman effect* after its discoverer, the Dutch physicist Pieter Zeeman. With the help of the Zeeman effect the magnetic nature of sunspots has been established, and a large number of stars and clouds of matter in space have been discovered that appear to be strongly magnetized.

Motion   We all know that sounds produced by vehicles moving toward us seem higher pitched than usual, whereas sounds produced by vehicles receding from us seem lower pitched than usual. Anybody who has listened to the siren of a fire engine as it passes by at high speed is aware of these apparent changes in frequency, called the doppler effect (Chap. 6).

Similarly, a star moving toward the earth has a spectrum whose lines are shifted toward the violet (high-frequency) end, and a star moving away from the earth has a spectrum in which each line is shifted toward the red (low-frequency) end, as in Fig. 19-2. From the amount of the shift we can calculate the speed with which the star is approaching or receding. This special shift records only motion of approach or recession since motion of a star across the line of sight causes no change in its spectrum.

THE SUN

The sun is the glorious body that dominates the solar system, and the origin and destiny of the earth are closely connected with its life cycle. The astronomer has another reason for studying the sun closely, for it is in many ways a typical star, a rather ordinary member of the assembly of perhaps 10^{20} stars that make up the known universe. The properties of the sun that we can observe by virtue of its relative closeness, then, are interesting not only in themselves but also because they provide information about stars in general that would otherwise be out of reach.

Properties of the Sun

The nearest star

Finding the sun's mass

The sun's mass can be found from the characteristics of the earth's orbital motion around it. The calculation is surprisingly easy. For simplicity let us assume that the earth's orbit is a circle with the radius R and that the earth's orbital speed has the constant value v. (Because the orbit is actually an ellipse, both R and v vary somewhat during the course of the year.) From Chap. 2 we know that the centripetal force needed to keep the earth in its orbit is mv^2/R, where m is the earth's mass. This force is provided by the gravitational pull GMm/R^2 the sun exerts on the earth, where M is the sun's mass and G is the gravitational constant. Hence

$$F_{gravitational} = F_{centripetal}$$

$$\frac{GMm}{R^2} = \frac{mv^2}{R}$$

Since m/R appears on both sides of the equation, it drops out, and

$$\frac{GM}{R} = v^2$$

$$M = \frac{v^2R}{G}$$

$$\text{Mass of sun} = \frac{\text{(earth's orbital speed)}^2 \text{ (earth's orbital radius)}}{\text{gravitational constant}}$$

The result is a mass of 1.99×10^{30} kg, more than 300,000 times the earth's mass.

The sun's radius of 6.96×10^8 m can be established by simple geometry from the fact that its angular diameter as seen from the earth is 0.53°. The volume of the sun is such that 1,300,000 earths would fit into it.

The surface temperature of the sun, which is about 6000 K, is determined both from the variation of brightness with wavelength in its spectrum (see Fig. 19-1) and from the amount of energy it emits. At this temperature all matter is gaseous, which means that the surface of the sun is a glowing gas envelope. The thickness of this envelope, which is known as the *photosphere,* is about 300 km. Below it the solar gases contain a small amount of *negative* hydrogen ions (hydrogen atoms with an extra electron) which are so effective in absorbing light of all colors that this region is almost totally opaque. Above the photosphere the gases are thinner and emit little radiation, and are therefore practically transparent. There is no sharp break between the photosphere and the outer atmosphere of the sun on one side and the solar interior on the other but rather gradual transitions between them. The density of the photosphere is only about 1 percent of that of the earth's atmosphere at sea level.

Of the thousands of lines in the sun's spectrum, most can be definitely identified with those of elements known on the earth. About 70 elements have been detected in the sun's atmosphere, and others would probably be found if it were possible to examine the far ultraviolet part of the spectrum. Lines of only a very few extremely stable compounds are recognizable since temperatures in the parts of the solar atmosphere where most of the light is absorbed are high enough to break down nearly all molecules into atoms.

Although conditions on the sun are very different from those on the earth, the basic matter of the two bodies appears to be the same. Even the relative amounts of different elements are similar, except for much more of the light elements hydrogen and helium on the sun. At the relatively low temperatures here on the earth, most elements have combined to form compounds; in the hot sun the elements are present mostly as individual atoms, many of them ionized.

The photosphere is the glowing gas envelope around the sun

The sun consists largely of hydrogen and helium

Solar Energy

It comes from the conversion of hydrogen to helium

Here on the earth, 150 million km from the sun, a surface 1 m^2 in area exposed to the vertical rays of the sun receives energy at a rate of about 1.4 kW. Adding up all the energy received over the earth's surface gives a staggering total, although this is but a tiny fraction of the sun's total radiation. And the sun has been emitting energy at this rate for billions of years. Where does it all come from?

We might be tempted to think of combustion, for fires give off what seem like a lot of heat and light. But a moment's thought shows that the sun is too hot to burn. Burning involves the combination of other elements with oxygen to form compounds, but the terrific temperatures on the sun do not permit compounds to be formed except in its atmosphere. And even if burning were possible, the heat

Solar energy cannot come from chemical processes

obtainable from the best fuels known would be far too little to maintain the sun's temperatures.

Solar energy can only be produced by processes taking place in the sun's interior. Although the interior cannot be observed directly, plausible estimates can be made of conditions there. Pressures are high even at moderate depths because of the weight of overlying material. Temperatures must increase rapidly toward the interior, since a continuous flow of energy is supplied to the photosphere to make good the immense losses by radiation. Calculations based on reasonable assumptions lead to an estimate of 14 million K for the temperature and 1 billion atm for the pressure near the sun's center. The density of the matter there is nearly 10 times that of lead on the earth's surface. Under these conditions atoms of the lighter elements have lost all their electrons, and atoms of the heavier elements retain only their inmost electron shells. Thus matter in the sun's interior consists of atomic debris — free electrons and positive nuclei surrounded by a few electrons or none at all.

Inside the sun are ions and electrons under conditions of high pressure and temperature

These atomic fragments are in extremely rapid motion, traveling far more rapidly than gas molecules at ordinary temperatures. Such speeds mean that two atomic nuclei that collide may get close enough to each other — despite the repulsive electric force due to their positive charges — to react and form a single larger nucleus. When this occurs among the light elements, the new nucleus has a little *less* mass than the combined masses of the reacting nuclei, as we saw in Chap. 7. The missing mass is converted into energy in the process according to Einstein's formula $E = mc^2$. So huge an amount of energy is evolved in nuclear reactions of this kind that there is no doubt they are responsible for solar energy.

Solar energy is derived from the conversion of hydrogen to helium in nuclear fusion reactions

The basic energy-producing reaction in the sun is the conversion of hydrogen into helium. This takes place both directly by collisions of hydrogen nuclei (protons) and indirectly by a series of steps in which carbon nuclei absorb a succession of hydrogen nuclei (Figs. 19-3 and 19-4). Each step can be duplicated in the laboratory and the energy released can be measured. In the sun's interior conditions are ideal for such energy-producing collisions, not as events affecting rare, isolated atoms, like those in our laboratories, but as commonplace events occurring many times a second in every cubic centimeter. For the entire process by either mechanism, the energy available per helium atom corresponds to the 0.0277 u difference in mass between 4 hydrogen nuclei (4×1.0073 u $= 4.0292$ u) and 1 helium nucleus (4.0015 u). Hence every 4 kg of helium that is formed in the sun means the disappearance of about 0.0277 kg of matter, which corresponds to an energy release of

$$E = mc^2 = (0.0277 \text{ kg}) (3 \times 10^8 \text{ m/s})^2 = 2.5 \times 10^{15} \text{ J}$$

About 80 million kg of coal would have to be burned to obtain this amount of energy!

The relative probabilities of the carbon and proton-proton cycles depend upon temperature. In the sun and stars like it, which have interior temperatures up

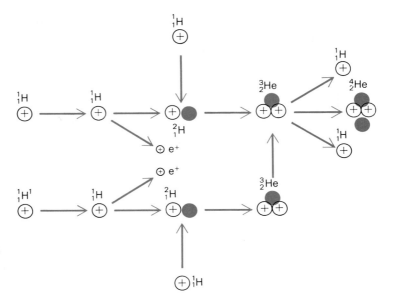

FIG. 19-3
The proton-proton cycle. This is the chief nuclear reaction sequence that takes place in the sun and cooler stars with the evolution of energy at each step. The net result is the combination of four hydrogen nuclei to form a helium nucleus and two positrons.

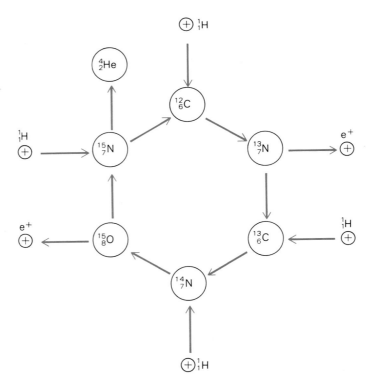

FIG. 19-4
The carbon cycle also involves the combination of four hydrogen nuclei to form a helium nucleus with the evolution of energy. The $^{12}_{6}C$ nucleus is unchanged by the series of reactions. This cycle occurs in stars hotter than the sun.

to about 14 million K, the proton-proton cycle predominates. Most of the energy of hotter stars comes from the carbon cycle, while in cooler stars the proton-proton cycle is by far the chief energy source.

Every second the sun converts over 4 billion kg of matter into energy, and its hydrogen content is such that it should be able to continue releasing energy at this rate for many billions of years more. In fact, the amount of matter lost in all of geologic history is not enough to have changed the sun's radiation appreciably. This confirms other evidence that the earth's surface temperature has remained approximately constant during this period.

The reactions that convert hydrogen to helium are not the only ones that take place in the sun and other stars. With hydrogen and helium as raw materials and high temperatures and pressures to make things happen, most of the other elements are formed as well. A few of the heaviest ones require still more extreme conditions to be produced, conditions that occur during the supernova explosions of heavy stars that are discussed later in this chapter. Such explosions serve as well to scatter the various elements already created in the parent star into space. There these elements, heavy and light, mix with the hydrogen and helium of interstellar space and in turn become incorporated in new stars. The earth's uranium, for instance, seems to have come into being in a supernova explosion 6 billion years ago, over a billion years before the birth of the sun and its planets. The universe was over 6 billion years old at that time.

Sunspots

They appear dark only by comparison with the solar surface around them

Marring the intense luminosity of the sun's surface at times are markings of reduced brightness called *sunspots*. Sunspots change continually in form, each one growing rapidly and then shrinking, with lifetimes of from 2 or 3 days to more than a month. The largest sunspots are many thousands of km across, large enough to engulf several earths.

Sunspots appear dark only because we see them against a brighter background. A spot whose temperature is 5000 K is hot enough to glow brilliantly but is considerably cooler than the rest of the solar surface.

Galileo, one of the first to study sunspots, noted that they moved across the sun's disk. He interpreted this finding, as we do today, as indicating that the sun rotates on its axis. Solar rotation is confirmed by doppler shifts in the spectral lines of radiation from the edges of the sun's disk. The sun rotates faster at its equator, where a complete turn takes 27 days, than near its poles, where a complete turn takes about 31 days.

Sunspots generally appear in groups, each with a single large spot together with a number of smaller ones. Some groups contain as many as 80 separate spots. They tend to occur in two zones on either side of the solar equator and are rarely seen either near the equator or at latitudes on the sun higher than 35°. Sunspots

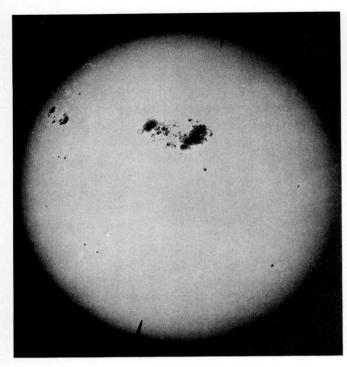

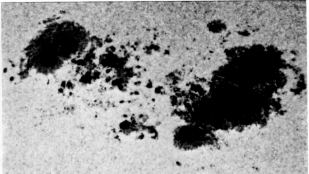

Closeup of the sunspot group.

This unusually large sunspot group
was photographed on April 7, 1947.

The sunspot cycle

Sunspots and the earth

seem to consist of gas that moves upward from the sun's interior, expanding and cooling as it spirals out. Strong magnetic fields are associated with sunspots, and there is little doubt they are closely related to the process of sunspot formation.

The number of spots on the sun changes with time in a regular cycle. Approximately every 11 years the number of spots reaches a maximum and then begins to decrease. Six or seven years later there are virtually no spots at all. Then sunspots begin to reappear and the next maximum occurs.

The sunspot cycle has aroused much interest because a number of effects observable on the earth — such as disturbances in the terrestrial magnetic field (called *magnetic storms*), shortwave radio fadeouts, changes in cosmic-ray intensity, and unusual auroral activity — follow this cycle. It seems likely that the ionosphere changes are due to intense bursts of ultraviolet and x-radiation that are more frequent during sunspot maximum, and that the magnetic, cosmic-ray, and auroral effects are due to vast streams of energetic protons and electrons that shoot out of the sun from the vicinity of sunspot groups.

There is evidence that some aspects of weather and climate are also synchronized with sunspot activity. For instance, very few sunspots appeared between 1645 and 1715, a period during which temperatures were lower than usual — the "Little Ice Age" mentioned in Chap. 13 occurred at about that time. Perhaps the events in the sun that lead to the development of sunspots are correlated with a slightly higher energy output. Not much of a change would be enough to affect terrestrial climates to the extent observed.

Solar Atmosphere

It extends past the earth's orbit

Solar prominences

Above what we can loosely think of as the solar surface is a rapidly thinning atmosphere that contains mainly hydrogen, helium, and calcium. From this atmosphere great, flamelike *prominences* sometimes extend out into space, much like sheets of gas standing on their sides. Prominences occur in a variety of forms; a typical example is about 200,000 km long, 10,000 km wide, and 50,000 km high. Prominences are often associated with sunspots and, like sunspots, seem to have magnetic fields associated with them.

The corona is visible during solar eclipses

During a total eclipse of the sun, when the moon obscures the sun's disk completely, a wide halo of pearly light can be seen around the dark moon. This halo, or *corona*, may extend out as much as a solar diameter and seems to have a great number of fine lines extending outward from the sun immersed in its general luminosity. The corona consists of ionized atoms and electrons in extremely rapid motion.

The solar wind

Although the corona that we see during eclipses is relatively near the sun, it actually extends in very diffuse form much farther out, well beyond the earth's orbit. The outward flow of ions and electrons in this extension of the sun's atmosphere is the *solar wind* that has been detected by spacecraft.

THE STARS IN SPACE

Stellar Distances

The earth's orbit as rangefinder

Aristotle pointed out long ago that, if the earth revolves around the sun, the stars should appear to shift in position, just as trees and buildings shift in position when we ride past them. Since he could detect no such shifts, Aristotle concluded that the earth must be stationary. Another interpretation of the lack of apparent movement among the stars, suggested by some of the Greeks and later by Copernicus, is that the stars are simply too far away for such movement to be detected. When the copernican theory of the solar system had become well established and astronomical instruments had been improved, many observers tried in vain to find the small shifts in position that should result from the earth's motion.

Stars shift in relative position as the earth moves in its orbit

An undoubted shift for one star was finally discovered in 1838 by the German astronomer Friedrich Bessel, and in the following years several others were found. These shifts are so very small that the long failure to detect them is not surprising.

A rangefinder for the nearer stars

Bessel's discovery made possible the direct measurement of distances to the nearer stars. The method is simple, similar to that used in the rangefinder of a camera (Fig. 2-11). The position of a star is determined twice, at times 6 months apart. From the measured change in the angle of the telescope, together with the fact that the telescope was displaced by the 300-million-km diameter of the earth's orbit during the 6 months, the distance to the star can be found by trigonometry.

The *parallax,* or apparent shift in position, is large enough to be measurable for only a few thousand of the nearer stars. Even for these the measurement is difficult; measuring the parallax of the closest star is equivalent to measuring the diameter of a dime seen from a distance of over 6 km. The distance to Proxima Centauri, the star nearest the sun, is about 4×10^{16} m.

A light-year is the distance light travels in a year

As mentioned earlier, a unit commonly used to express stellar distances is the *light-year,* which is the distance light travels in a year and is equal to 9.46×10^{12} km. Thus Proxima Centauri is a little over 4 light-years away — which means that we see the star not as it is today but as it was 4 years ago. Only about 40 stars are within 16 light-years of the solar system. Such distances between stars are typical for much of the visible universe. This means that space is all but completely empty, far more empty even than the solar system with its tiny isolated planets.

Intrinsic and Apparent Brightness

Another way to find stellar distances

Parallax measurements are only possible for distances up to about 300 light-years. However, several indirect methods are available to find the distances of stars farther away than this. A very useful one is based on a comparison of the apparent and intrinsic brightnesses of stars.

The apparent brightness of a star depends upon its intrinsic brightness and upon its distance

The *apparent* brightness of a star is its brightness as we see it from the earth. This quantity expresses the amount of light that reaches us from the star. Its *intrinsic* brightness, on the other hand, is the true brightness of the star, a figure that depends upon the total amount of light it radiates into space. The apparent brightness of a star depends on two things: its intrinsic brightness and its distance from us. A star that is actually very bright may appear faint because it is far away, and a star that is actually faint may have a high apparent brightness because it is close.

If the apparent brightness of a star is measured and if its distance is known, the intrinsic brightness can be calculated by figuring out how bright an object would have to be at the known distance to send us the observed amount of light. Since apparent brightness is easily found for any star, intrinsic brightnesses are known for all stars whose distances can be measured.

Now let us reverse the argument: if both the apparent and the real brightness of a star are known, we can calculate its distance by finding out how far away an object with this intrinsic brightness must be located in order to send us the amount of light we observe. Such a calculation is not hard, and so we can find the distance to any star whose intrinsic brightness can be established.

Intrinsic brightness can be found from spectral data

A suitable method for finding the intrinsic brightness of a star was discovered by the American astronomer W. S. Adams. Studying the spectra of the nearer stars, for which intrinsic brightnesses are known, Adams observed that the relative intensities of certain spectral lines (for stars of a given type) depended on the star's intrinsic brightness. That is, the spectrum of a bright star showed certain relationships among the intensities of its lines, and the spectrum of a faint star showed somewhat different relationships. So definite was the connection between relative intensities of the lines and intrinsic brightnesses of the stars that Adams could establish the brightness of a star simply by examining its spectrum. Assuming that the relationship holds for more distant stars, Adams then was able to use their spectra to find their intrinsic brightnesses and hence their distances.

The spectroscopic method is applicable to any star bright enough to give a good spectrum, except for comparatively uncommon stars of certain spectral types for which Adam's relation does not hold. Through its use stellar distances have been determined up to several thousand light-years.

Variable Stars

Stars whose brightness changes, usually in regular cycles

Many stars, including the sun, vary periodically in brightness

An extension of the above method for finding stellar distances is based upon the properties of a certain type of *variable star*. A variable star is one whose brightness varies continually. Some variables show wholly irregular fluctuations, but the greater number repeat a fairly definite cycle of change.

A typical variable grows brighter for a time, then fainter, then brighter once more, with irregular minor fluctuations during the cycle. Periods separating times of maximum brightness range all the way from a few hours to several years. Maximum brightness for some variables is only slightly greater than minimum brightness, but for others it is several hundred times as great. Since the sun's radiation changes slightly during the sunspot cycle, we may consider it a variable

Superimposed photographs taken at different times of the region of the sky in which the variable star WW Cygni appears. Only the brightness of this star has changed.

star with an extremely small range in brightness (a few percent at most) and a long period (about 11 years).

The light changes in some variable stars are easy to explain. These stars are actually double stars whose orbits we see edgewise, so that one member of each pair periodically gets in the way of the other. In other variables the appearance of numerous spots at regular intervals may be what is dimming their light. Still others seem to be pulsating, expanding and contracting so that their surface areas change periodically. Perhaps the irregular variables are passing through or behind ragged clouds of gas and dust that absorb some of their light.

A special class of variable stars, called *Cepheid variables*, have turned out to be extremely useful to astronomers in determining how far from us certain distant star groups are. The Cepheid variables are very bright yellowish stars five to ten times as heavy as the sun whose periods range from a few days to a few months. They take their name from a typical example discovered in 1784 in the constellation Cepheus.

The value of Cepheid variables in measuring distances was discovered by Henrietta Leavitt in a study of the Cepheids in a single large cluster of stars called the Small Magellanic Cloud, which is visible in the southern hemisphere. The Cepheids of this cluster show a definite relationship between their apparent brightnesses and the periods during which their light fluctuates. A bright Cepheid requires 2 or 3 months to complete its cycle of changes, but a faint Cepheid requires only a few days. The cluster is so far away that all its stars are approximately the same distance from the earth, hence differences in apparent brightness must be due solely to differences in intrinsic brightness. Therefore the observed relationship among the Cepheid variables must be due to some connection between their periods of variation and their actual brightnesses.

Values for the intrinsic brightnesses of stars in the cluster could not be determined directly because of their immense distance. For other Cepheids closer to the earth, however, estimates of intrinsic brightness were possible. By combining figures for these closer Cepheids with data from the cluster, it was possible to establish a definite relationship between brightness and period of variation. If we assume that this relationship holds for Cepheids elsewhere in the universe, then the intrinsic brightness of any Cepheid can be found simply by measuring its period of variation. A comparison of intrinsic brightness with apparent brightness then gives the distance, as we know. This method can be extended to much greater distances than spectroscopic determinations since the period of a Cepheid can be measured regardless of its faintness, but it is limited to a single fairly rare type of star.

Stellar Motions

The stars are not fixed in space

The speeds of stars moving toward or away from the earth can be found from the doppler shifts in their spectral lines. Motion across the line of sight can be followed

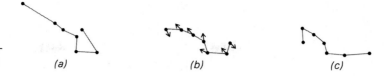

FIG. 19-5

The constellation Big Dipper (*a*) as it was 200,000 years ago, (*b*) as it is today (arrows show directions of motion of the stars), and (*c*) as it will be 200,000 years from now.

by direct observation. The great distances of the stars make their apparent movements exceedingly slow, so slow that it is easy to think of them as "fixed stars." Yet the motion is enough to have caused perceptible changes in the shapes of some constellations during the few thousand years of recorded observations (Fig. 19-5). Most stars are moving with speeds of several km per second relative to the earth.

The sun's motion

Since other stars are moving, we might surmise that the sun is moving also. Such a motion should reveal itself in regularities in the apparent movements of the stars. If the sun is moving toward a certain part of the sky, stars in that direction, on the average, should appear to be approaching us and to be radiating out from a point, just as trees in a forest seem to approach and spread out when we drive toward them. Average stellar motions of this sort are observed in the neighborhood of the constellation Cygnus, and in the opposite part of the sky stars are apparently receding and coming closer together. A study of these motions indicates that the sun and its family of planets are moving toward Cygnus at a speed of 200–300 km/s.

STELLAR PROPERTIES

We now turn to the properties of the stars themselves. Many different types of stars are known, most of which fit into a pattern that can be understood in terms of a regular evolutionary sequence. Some stars, however, are still puzzles to the astronomer.

Mass

A relatively small range

Only the masses of double stars can be determined, but such stars are abundant

The points of light that appear to the eye as single stars are often actually double, two stars close together. The members of such a star pair attract each other gravitationally, and each circles around the other. From the characteristics of the orbits the masses of the stars can be calculated. Although this method is limited to double stars, stars of all kinds are found as members of such pairs.

Stellar masses vary relatively little

What the measurements show is that stellar masses range from $\frac{1}{10}$ to 50 times that of the sun — a smaller span than planetary masses. It is not hard to see why normal stars should be limited in mass. Gravitational forces in a body of matter whose mass is less than about $\frac{1}{10}$ that of the sun cannot produce enough of a

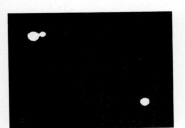  

The double star shown here requires about 50 years for a complete rotation.

contraction to yield the temperatures needed for nuclear reactions to occur. At the other extreme, a star whose mass is too great will become so hot due to accelerated nuclear reactions that its gravity cannot keep it together against the resulting outward pressure.

Temperature

Its color tells us how hot a star is

Most stars are between 3000 and 12,000 K in surface temperature

The temperature of a star is determined from its spectrum by finding the part of its spectrum in which the star's radiation is most intense (Fig. 19-1). This tells us the temperature of the star's surface — the part from which radiation is emitted. The surface temperatures of a few very hot stars range up to 40,000 K but the great majority are between 3000 and 12,000 K. Probably many stars are cooler than 3000 K (which is near the boiling point of iron), but, unless they are relatively close, their radiation is then too feeble for us to detect. Like the sun, stars must have enormously high internal temperatures to maintain their surface radiation. The hottest stars are blue-white, those of intermediate temperature are yellowish, and the coolest are red.

Size

It varies widely

The size of a star can be found from its temperature and its intrinsic brightness

If we know a star's surface temperature and its intrinsic brightness, we can find its size. The temperature tells us how much radiation is emitted from each square meter of the star's surface: the hotter it is, the more intense is the radiation given off. The intrinsic brightness is a measure of the total radiation from the star's entire surface. We need only divide the total radiation by the radiation per square meter to find the number of square meters in the star's surface, and from the area the diameter and volume are simple to calculate.

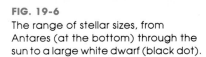

FIG. 19-6
The range of stellar sizes, from
Antares (at the bottom) through the
sun to a large white dwarf (black dot).

Stellar sizes and densities vary widely

There is also a more direct method of measuring stellar diameters based on the interference of light that can be used on the larger stars. Results obtained in this way agree with estimates from temperatures and intrinsic brightness.

The diameters of stars, unlike their masses, have an enormous range (Fig. 19-6). The smallest stars, like the faint companion of the bright star Sirius, are little bigger than the earth. The largest, like the giant red star Antares in the constellation Scorpio, have diameters 500 or more times that of the sun. Antares is so huge that, if the sun were placed at its center, the four inner planets could pursue their normal orbits inside the star with plenty of room to spare.

If the mass and volume of a star are known, finding the average density means simply dividing one by the other. Like the volumes, densities vary greatly from star to star. Giant stars like Antares have densities less than one-thousandth that of ordinary air — densities that correspond to a fairly good vacuum here on earth. At the other extreme are the extraordinary densities of some small stars, for instance the companion of Sirius, densities so great that a cubic centimeter of their substance would weigh a ton on the earth's surface.

Spectra

Stars are classed by their spectra

The analysis of starlight with the spectrometer has provided information on the distances, temperatures, sizes, and motions of the stars. What about the spectra themselves? Are they similar for all stars, are they totally different, or do they exhibit regularities of some kind?

Stellar spectra have two important properties:

1. Almost all stars have absorption (dark-line) spectra, like that of the sun, which implies a hot interior surrounded by a relatively cool atmosphere.
2. The various spectral lines found can be identified with lines found in the spectra of elements known on the earth.

The matter of the visible universe is like that on earth

Thus we know that the matter of the visible universe has the same basic nature as the matter we are familiar with on earth and, further, that most of the large aggregates of matter in the visible universe follow the same general pattern. This uniformity of material and structure is perhaps the most striking discovery of stellar astronomy.

Stellar spectra fall into a natural sequence

Stellar spectra vary considerably in detail. Some have relatively few lines, others have many; some have only sharp lines, other have the diffuse bands characteristic of molecules; some have strong lines of hydrogen, others have strong lines of certain metals. Comparing large numbers of spectra shows that nearly all can be arranged in a single sequence, depending on the intensities of different lines. Lines that are prominent in spectra at one end of this sequence

TABLE 19-1
Spectral Classes of the Stars.

Class	Examples	Color	Surface temperature, K	Spectral characteristics
O	10 Lacertae	Blue	Over 25,000	Lines of ionized helium and other ionized elements, hydrogen lines weak
B	Rigel, Spica	Blue-white	11,000–25,000	Hydrogen and helium prominent
A	Sirius, Vega	White	7,500–11,000	Hydrogen lines very strong
F	Canopus, Procyon	Yellow-white	6,000–7,500	Hydrogen lines weaker, lines of ionized metals becoming prominent
G	The sun, Capella	Yellow	5,000–6,000	Lines of ionized and neutral metals, especially calcium, prominent
K	Arcturus, Aldebaran	Reddish	3,500–5,000	Lines of neutral metals and molecular spectra of simple compounds present
M	Betelgeuse, Antares	Red	2,000–3,500	Molecular spectra of many compounds prominent

grow less intense in successive spectra while other lines become prominent, and then these become faint and still others grow conspicuous.

A convenient classification of stars is based upon the observed sequence of spectral types, even though there is no sharp distinction between adjacent members of the sequence. This classification is given in Table 19-1 together with the surface temperatures that have been found characteristic of each variety of star. As all astronomers know, the sequence of star classes follows the first letters of the words in the request, "Oh be a fine girl, kiss me."

STELLAR EVOLUTION

H-R Diagram

Most stars belong to the main sequence

The H-R diagram is a plot of intrinsic brightness versus temperature for stars

Early in this century two astronomers, Ejnar Hertzsprung in Denmark and Henry Norris Russell in America, independently discovered that the intrinsic brightnesses

Type		Star
O6		λ Cephei
B3		η Aurigae
A0		δ Cygni
F2		β Cassiopeiae
G2		η Pegasi
K5		γ Draconis
M5		α Herculis

Examples of principal types of stellar spectra. Table 19-1 gives their interpretations.

of most stars are related to their spectral types. This relationship is shown in the graph of Fig. 19-7, which is called a *Hertzsprung-Russell* (or *H-R*) *diagram.* Each point on this graph represents a particular star. About 90 percent of all stars belong to the *main sequence,* with most of the others in the *red giant* class at the upper right and in the *white dwarf* class at the lower left. The names *giant* and *dwarf* refer, as we might expect, to very large and very small stars respectively.

Most stars belong to the main sequence; the rest are mainly red giants or white dwarfs

The position of a star on the H-R diagram is correlated with its physical properties. Stars at the upper end of the main sequence are large, hot, massive bodies, with prominent lines of hydrogen and helium in their spectra. Stars at the lower end are small, dense, and reddish, with low enough temperatures so that chemical compounds form a considerable part of their atmosphere. In the middle part of the main sequence are average stars like our sun, with moderate temperatures, densities, and masses, rather small diameters, and spectra in which lines of metallic elements are prominent. The majority of stars show these combinations of principal characteristics.

Red giants

To the giant class belong the huge, diffuse stars like Antares, with low densities and diameters up to several hundred million km. Many of these stars have low surface temperatures, as their reddish color indicates, but their enormous surfaces make them very bright.

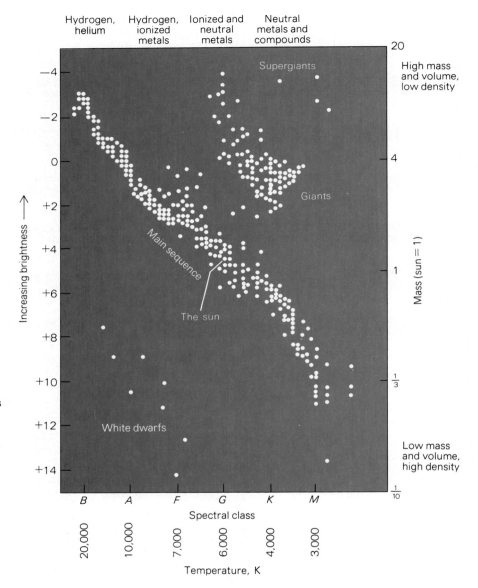

FIG. 19-7
The Hertzsprung-Russell diagram plots stars according to spectral type and intrinsic brightness. The numbers at the left express absolute magnitude (the astronomical measure of intrinsic brightness) with low numbers indicating bright stars and high numbers, faint stars. The letters at the bottom designate spectral classes. Masses at right correspond to main-sequence stars. The most prominent lines in the spectra of the various stars are identified at the top of the figure; see Table 19-1.

White Dwarfs

The size of a planet, the mass of a star

White dwarfs have the size of a planet but the mass of a star and are very hot

The position of the white dwarfs in the H-R diagram reflects their characteristic combination of intensely hot surface and small total radiation. These properties

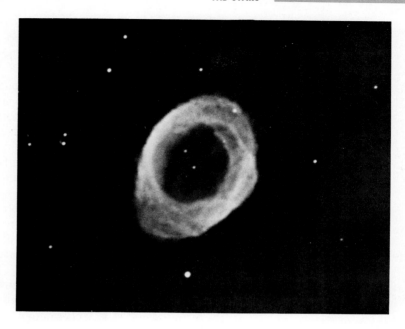

The Ring nebula in the constellation Lyra is a shell of gas moving outward from the star in the center, which is in the process of becoming a white dwarf.

White dwarfs consist of collapsed atoms

suggest that such stars must be small, in fact comparable in size with the earth. However, their masses are all close to that of the sun, so that the density of a white dwarf is about 10^6 g/cm^3! A pinhead of such matter would weigh nearly a pound here on earth, and a cupful would weigh many tons.

Densities like this seem hard to believe but they have been checked by enough methods to leave little doubt of their correctness. The only possible explanation is that atoms in these stars have collapsed. Instead of ordinary atoms with electrons following wide orbits around their nuclei, white dwarfs must have electrons and nuclei packed closely together. Matter in this state does not exist on earth, but its properties can be calculated from theories whose predictions have turned out correct in other situations.

Only a few hundred white dwarfs are known. Their scarcity may be more apparent than real, since they are so faint that only the nearer ones can be seen even in large telescopes. Enough of them have been found in recent years to suggest that the universe probably contains great numbers of these remarkable objects.

Stellar Evolution

Life history of a star

The relationships revealed by the Hertzsprung-Russell diagram cannot have occurred through chance alone. Are the stars in different parts of the diagram perhaps in various stages of development? Does the mass of a star control its temperature and the composition of its atmosphere? The answers to these questions seem to be yes, and the H-R diagram fits in well with modern ideas of the life history of a star.

How stars come into being

Stars are believed to originate in gas clouds in space, which consist largely of hydrogen. Local concentrations occur from time to time, and if the density of one of them is sufficiently great, gravity will both attract more gas and cause the accumulation to contract. The contraction heats the gas, much as the gas in a tire pump is heated by compression, and it begins to glow as a result. Such a very young star appears among the cooler giants in the H-R diagram.

Some thousands or millions of years later, the star's temperature will rise to the point where the nuclear reactions of Fig. 19-3 begin to occur, which convert its hydrogen into helium. The increase in temperature shifts the position of the star on the H-R diagram downward and to the left. From this time on the star's tendency to contract is counterbalanced by the pressure of radiation from its hot interior, and it is a stable member of the main sequence that maintains a constant size as long as its hydrogen supply holds out.

A star does not shine because some mysterious force has caused it to do so — it shines because it has a certain mass and a certain composition.

The greater the mass of a main-sequence star, the higher its temperature

The temperature a star reaches depends upon its mass. Gravitation in a large mass is more powerful than in a small mass and leads to more intense radiation to counterbalance it. Calculations show that the relationship between mass and temperature, for stars with abundant hydrogen, should be exactly that shown by stars in the main sequence of the Hertzsprung-Russell diagram. The large, heavy stars at the upper end of the main sequence have high temperatures and radiate strongly. The small stars at the lower end are relatively cool and only faintly luminous. Stars in the main sequence may be thought of as normal stars in which the hydrogen-helium reaction pours out energy at a rate that depends upon their masses.

A star consumes its hydrogen rapidly if it is large, slowly if it is small. The supply of hydrogen in a fairly small star like our sun might last for 10 billion years; probably the sun is now about halfway through this part of its career.

As a star grows old, it becomes a red giant

When the hydrogen supply at last begins to run low in a star like the sun, the life of the star is by no means over but instead enters its most spectacular phase. Further gravitational contraction makes the interior still hotter, and other nuclear reactions become possible — in particular those in which nuclei larger than helium are built up, for instance the combination of three helium nuclei to form a carbon nucleus. The outer part of the star is heated and expands to as much as 100 times its former diameter. The expansion produces a cooling so that the result is a very large, cool star with a hot core. Such a star is a red giant; the shift from the main sequence to the upper right of the H-R diagram is relatively rapid. Energy is now being poured out at a great rate, so the star's life as a giant is much shorter than its stay in the main sequence.

At the end of its life cycle, the average star becomes a white dwarf

Eventually the new energy-producing reactions run out of fuel too, and again the star shrinks, this time all the way down to the white dwarf state. As a slowly contracting dwarf the star may glow for billions of years more with its energy now coming from the contraction, from nuclear reactions that involve elements heavier than helium, and from proton-proton reactions in a very thin outer atmosphere of hydrogen.

The future of the sun

The distribution of stars on the H-R diagram clearly makes sense on the basis of an evolutionary development. For the sun, the star in which we have the most personal interest, we can expect about 5 billion more years with no marked change from present conditions. Then the sun's temperature will gradually increase, and life on earth will ultimately become impossible — not, as was once thought, because the sun will cool off but rather because it will grow too hot. Eventually the sun will expand into a giant, perhaps as large around as the orbit of Mars, and still later it will collapse into a white dwarf. A dismal end, but one that our most remote descendants are not likely to survive to witness.

Supernovas

Exploding stars

Heavy stars become supernovas after short lifetimes

A heavy star at the upper end of the main sequence has a rather different later history. Such a star does not proceed in the usual way from being a red giant to becoming a white dwarf. Instead, after a relatively short lifetime of some millions of years, the star's great mass causes it to collapse abruptly when its fuel has run out. When the star has become compressed to the point where all its nuclei are in contact, it explodes violently. The explosion flings into space a large part of the star's mass. An event of this kind, called a *supernova*, is billions of times brighter than the original star ever was. A supernova occurs once or twice per century in galaxies of stars like our own.

Neutron stars

What is left after a supernova explosion is a dwarf star of extraordinary density, even in comparison with that of a white dwarf, with a mass not far from that of the sun but a diameter of only about 20 km. The matter of such a star would weigh billions of tons per teaspoonful. If the earth were this dense, it would fit into a large apartment house. Under the pressures that would be present the most stable form of matter is the neutron. Until a decade ago the notion of neutron stars was purely speculative, but the discovery of pulsars has made their existence quite plausible. Figure 19-8 shows how neutron stars and white dwarfs compare in size with the earth and the sun.

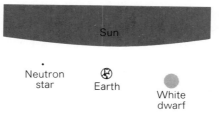

FIG. 19-8

A comparison of a white dwarf and a neutron star with the sun and the earth. Both white dwarfs and neutron stars are thought to have masses similar to that of the sun.

The Crab nebula in Taurus had its origin in a supernova explosion in A.D. 1054. A pulsar at the center of this nebula is what remains of the original star.

Pulsars

Spinning neutron stars

Pulsars emit radio waves as well as light

In 1967 unusual radio signals were detected that came from a source in the constellation Vulpecula. The signals were found to fluctuate with an extremely regular period, exactly 1.33730113 s. Since then several hundred more *pulsars* have been discovered, all with periods of less than 3 s. At first only radio emissions from pulsars could be observed, but in 1969 flashes of visible light were found to be given off by a pulsar in the center of the Crab nebula that are exactly synchronized with the radio signals.

The power output of a pulsar is about 10^{26} W, which is comparable with the total power output of the sun. It is inconceivable that so strong a source of energy can be switched on and off in a fraction of a second, or even that such a source can be the size of the sun. Even if the sun were to suddenly stop radiating, it would take 2.3 s before light stopped reaching us, because all parts of the solar surface that we see are not at the same distance away. Hence we can conclude at once that a pulsar must have roughly the mass of a star, in order to be capable of emitting so much energy, and that it must be very much smaller than a star, in order that its signals fluctuate so rapidly.

Pulsars are spinning neutron stars

From the above and other considerations it seems likely that pulsars are neutron stars that are spinning rapidly. Conceivably a pulsar has a strong magnetic field whose axis is at an angle to the axis of rotation, and this field traps tails of

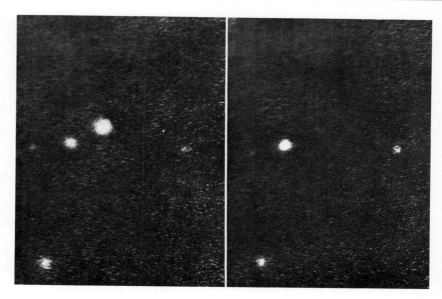

The pulsar at the center of the Crab nebula, which originated in a supernova explosion that occurred in A.D. 1054, flashes 30 times per second. These photographs, taken at maximum and minimum light, were made with the help of a very sensitive television camera.

The Crab nebula pulsar

ionized gases that do the actual radiating. Whatever the actual mechanism, though, a pulsar is apparently like a lighthouse whose flashes are due to a rotating beam of light. The identification of pulsars with neutron stars is supported by evidence that the periods of pulsars are very gradually decreasing, which would be expected as they continue to lose energy.

The fast pulsar in the Crab nebula is of exceptional interest. This nebula is the remnant of a supernova that was seen in A.D. 1054, and it has been expanding rapidly and glowing brightly ever since. Until now it was impossible to understand where all the energy of the nebula is coming from, since the explosion itself occurred so long ago. However, the light and radio flashes from the Crab pulsar are apparently powerful enough to furnish the entire nebula with its energy. This pulsar flashes 30 times per second and is slowing down rapidly — 1 part in 2400 per year. Both these observations are in accord with its formation 900 years ago. A pulsar's lifetime is thought to be about 10 million years before it comes to a stop.

Black Holes

Even light cannot escape from them

Does a neutron star represent the ultimate in compression? Apparently not. A "dead" star — one whose light nuclei have all combined to form heavier ones at the top of the binding energy curve of Fig. 7-14 and so cannot evolve further energy — whose mass exceeds perhaps two solar masses is not stable as a neutron star but will continue to contract gravitationally until it is still smaller, only a few km across. Such an object is called a *black hole* for a most interesting reason.

As we learned in Chap. 3, one of the results of Einstein's general theory of relativity is that light is affected by gravity. Thus starlight passing near the sun is deflected to a small but measurable extent.

Light cannot escape from extremely dense stars, which are accordingly called black holes

The heavier a star and the smaller it is, the stronger the pull of gravity at its surface and the higher the escape speed needed for something to leave the star. In the case of the earth, the escape speed is 11.2 km/s; in the case of the sun, it is 617 km/s. If the ratio M/R between the mass and radius of a star is large enough, the escape speed is more than the speed of light, and nothing, not even light, can ever get out. The star cannot radiate and so is invisible, a black hole in space. For a star with the sun's mass, the critical radius is 3 km, a quarter of a million times smaller than the sun's present radius. Anything passing near a black hole will be sucked into it, never to return to the outside world.

How black holes can be detected

Since it is invisible, how can a black hole be detected? A black hole that is a member of a double-star system (double stars are quite common) will reveal its presence by its gravitational effect on the other star. In addition, the intense gravitational field of the black hole will attract matter from the other star which will be compressed and heated to such high temperatures that x-rays will be emitted profusely. One of a number of invisible objects that astronomers believe to be black holes is known as Cygnus X-1. Its mass is perhaps 8 times that of the sun, and its radius may be only about 10 km.

IMPORTANT TERMS

A star's *spectrum* contains dark lines that correspond to particular frequencies of light absorbed by the ions, atoms, and molecules in its atmosphere. These lines are superimposed on a bright background emitted by the star's surface. The spectrum and the bright background can be analyzed to provide information on the structure, temperature, composition, condition of matter, magnetism, and motion of the star.

The *sun* is a fairly typical star whose temperature is 6000 K at the surface and perhaps 14,000,000 K near the center. *Solar energy* comes from the conversion of hydrogen to helium, which can take place through both the *proton-proton* and *carbon cycles. Sunspots* are regions slightly cooler than the rest of the solar surface and have strong magnetic fields associated with them. Surrounding the sun is a diffuse *corona* of ions and electrons whose outward flow is the *solar wind* that pervades much of the solar system.

The distance to a nearby star can be found from its apparent shift in position, or *parallax,* as the earth moves in its orbit. The distance to a star far away can be found by comparing its *intrinsic* and *apparent brightnesses,* which are its actual brightness and its brightness as seen from the earth. Stellar distances are often expressed in *light-years,* where a light-year is the distance light travels in a year.

Variable stars fluctuate continually in brightness. Notable are the *Cepheid variables,* whose intrinsic brightness and periods of variation are related, which permits their distances to be found. Other variable stars are actually pairs of stars that revolve about their common centers of gravity and periodically block each other's light.

The *Hertzsprung-Russell* diagram is a graph on which the intrinsic brightnesses of stars are plotted versus their spectral types (which are related to their temperatures). Most stars belong to the **main sequence,** which appears as a diagonal band on the diagram, but there are also cool, large, **red giant** stars and hot, small, **white dwarfs** that lie outside the main sequence. The distribution of stars on the diagram corresponds in general to their evolutionary process. Heavy stars have a somewhat different history; at one stage they explode into **supernovas** and later subside into **neutron stars** whose interiors consist entirely of neutrons. A **pulsar** is a spinning neutron star that emits flashes of light and radio waves. A **black hole** is a "dead" star that has contracted so much that its gravitational field is strong enough for the escape speed to be greater than the speed of light. Nothing, not even light, can escape from a black hole.

MULTIPLE CHOICE

1. Large telescopes are valuable in astronomy chiefly because of their
   a. great magnification
   b. ability to gather light
   c. steadiness
   d. wide angle of view

2. The fact that the spectra of most stars consist of dark lines on a bright background means that these stars
   a. have cool interiors surrounded by hot atmospheres
   b. have hot interiors surrounded by cool atmospheres
   c. have hot interiors surrounded by hot atmospheres
   d. have cool interiors surrounded by cool atmospheres

3. The examination of starlight with a spectrometer cannot provide information about an isolated star's
   a. temperature
   b. structure
   c. mass
   d. magnetic field

4. The temperature of the sun's interior is believed to be about
   a. 600 K
   b. 6000 K
   c. 14 million K
   d. 14 billion K

5. Most of the matter in the sun is in the form of
   a. neutral atoms
   b. ions
   c. molecules
   d. liquids

6. The sun obtains its energy from
   a. the combustion of hydrogen and carbon
   b. the fission of uranium
   c. the fusion of hydrogen nuclei to form helium nuclei
   d. the fusion of hydrogen nuclei to form carbon nuclei

7. Sunspots are
   a. dark clouds in the sun's atmosphere
   b. regions somewhat cooler than the rest of the sun's surface
   c. regions somewhat hotter than the rest of the sun's surface
   d. of unknown origin

8. The duration of the sunspot cycle is approximately
   a. 27 days
   b. 6 months
   c. 3 years
   d. 11 years

9. Sunspot activity does not affect
   a. shortwave radio communication
   b. the earth's magnetic field
   c. the aurora
   d. volcanic eruptions

10. The star nearest to the sun is approximately
   a. 1 light-minute away
   b. 4 light-years away
   c. 300 light-years away
   d. 4000 light-years away

11. The intrinsic brightness of a star depends upon
   a. the amount of light reaching us from the star
   b. the amount of light the star radiates into space
   c. the distance beween us and the star
   d. the doppler shift in its spectral lines

12. Cepheid variable stars are valuable to astronomers because
   a. they are very brilliant, easily seen stars
   b. their intrinsic brightnesses and periods of variation are directly related
   c. their periods of variation are short
   d. they all lie in the constellation Cepheus

13. Double stars are valuable to astronomers because they permit the determination of stellar
   a. diameters
   b. distances
   c. masses
   d. temperatures

14. There is a surprisingly small variation among stellar
   a. temperatures
   b. diameters
   c. densities
   d. masses

15. The color of a relatively cool star is
   a. white
   b. yellow
   c. blue
   d. red

16. Stars belonging to the main sequence
   a. have the same mass

    b. have the same temperature

    c. radiate at a steady rate

    d. fluctuate markedly in brightness

17. White dwarf stars are not

    a. comparable in size with the earth

    b. comparable in mass with the sun

    c. extremely hot

    d. extremely bright

18. A white dwarf star

    a. is relatively young

    b. is relatively old

    c. can be of any age

    d. is a member of the main sequence

19. Relatively few stars become

    a. members of the main sequence

    b. red giants

    c. white dwarfs

    d. supernovas

20. A star that explodes as a supernova

    a. has a mass much greater than that of the sun

    b. has a mass much smaller than that of the sun

    c. has a mass about equal to that of the sun

    d. may have any mass

21. Pulsars are unlikely to be

    a. small in size

    b. in rapid rotation

    c. composed largely of neutrons

    d. members of the main sequence

22. A typical pulsar might have a period of

    a. 1 s

    b. 1 min

    c. 1 h

    d. 1 day

23. A "black hole" appears black because

    a. it is too cool to radiate

    b. it is surrounded by an absorbing layer of gas

    c. its gravitational field is too strong to permit light to escape

    d. its magnetic field is too strong to permit light to escape

24. The sun will eventually become a

    a. pulsar

    b. supernova

    c. white dwarf

    d. black hole

QUESTIONS

1. A photograph of a star cluster shows many more stars than can be seen by direct visual observation of the cluster with the same telescope. Why is there a difference?

2. Why do you think it is useful to put an astronomical telescope in a satellite?

3. Arrange the following types of stars in order of decreasing surface temperature: yellow stars, blue stars, white stars, red stars.

4. What part of a star is responsible for the continuous background of its spectrum? What happens to the radiation produced underneath this part of the star? What part is responsible for the dark absorption lines?

5. Suppose that you examine the spectra of two stars receding from the earth and find that the lines in one are displaced farther toward the red end than those in the other. What conclusion can you draw?

6. If the earth were moving toward a star instead of the star toward the earth, would lines in the star's spectrum be shifted? If so, toward which end of the spectrum?

7. What evidence suggests that the sun is almost wholly gaseous?

8. What evidence can you suggest to support the hypothesis that the sun's radiation rate has not changed appreciably in the past 2 billion years or so?

9. Why is it believed that the sun's energy originates in its interior rather than in its surface layers?

10. Why is it impossible for combustion to be the source of the sun's energy?

11. How can the composition of the sun be determined?

12. Helium was discovered in the sun before it was found on the earth (hence its name, which comes from *helios*, the Greek word for "sun"). How can this have come about?

13. What aspect of the formation of helium from hydrogen results in the evolution of energy by the process?

14. Why is the corona of the sun ordinarily not visible? How do we know it exists?

15. Why do sunspots appear dark if their temperatures are over 4500°C?

16. Give two methods for determining how fast the sun rotates on its axis. Is the rotation speed the same for the entire sun?

17. How are stellar masses determined?

18. Which varies more, the masses of the stars or their sizes?

19. Must a star be spherical?

20. What data are needed to determine a star's average density? How would you expect the density to change from the surface layers to the interior?

21. Which stars have the highest densities? The lowest?

22. A red star and a white star of the same apparent brightness are the same distance from the earth. Which is larger? Why?

23. Explain how the distance to a star cluster that contains Cepheid variables is determined.

24. What methods can be used to determine the intrinsic brightness of a star?

25. How is a star's diameter estimated from measurements of temperature and intrinsic brightness?

26. The stars Betelgeuse and Deneb have similar absolute magnitudes but Betelgeuse is red and Deneb is white. Which is larger? Which has the greater density? Which is hotter?

27. How can the motion of a star be detected?

28. The spectrum of a certain star shows a doppler shift that varies periodically from the red to the blue end of the spectrum. What kind of a star is this?

29. Is it possible for an object with the mass and composition of the sun to exist without radiating energy?

30. Why is the sun considered to be a star?

31. Why are most stars part of the main sequence on the H-R diagram?

32. Main-sequence stars are supposed to evolve into red giants, but relatively few stars lie between the main sequence and the group of red giants on the H-R diagram. Why?

33. Why do main-sequence stars have masses that lie between about 0.1 and 100 times the mass of the sun?

34. A giant star is much redder than a main-sequence star of the same intrinsic brightness. How does this observation indicate that the giant star is larger than the main-sequence star?

35. What are the chief characteristics of an average star in the upper left-hand corner of the H-R diagram? In the lower left-hand corner? In the upper right-hand corner? In the middle of the main sequence?

36. The sun is near the middle of the main sequence. Where would a star be located in the main sequence if its mass is 10 times that of the sun? Would it remain in the main sequence for a longer or shorter time than the sun? Would it be hotter or cooler than the sun?

37. Sirius, the brightest star in the sky apart from the sun, is a blue-white star of great intrinsic brightness. What does this suggest about its temperature? About its average density? About the principal lines in its spectrum? About its position in the H-R diagram?

38. As a main-sequence star evolves, what happens to its position on the main sequence?

39. Which of the following types of star is the most common in the sky? Least common? Main-sequence stars, white dwarfs, red giants, supernovas, double stars, Cepheid variables.

40. Why are white dwarfs considered to have such enormous densities?

41. After a very long time, a white dwarf will cool down and become a "black dwarf." What will the corresponding evolutionary path of the star be on the H-R diagram?

42. Into what kind of star will the sun eventually evolve?

43. What is the characteristic behavior of a pulsar? What is believed to be its nature? From what does a pulsar originate?

44. How large are black holes? Can any star evolve into a black hole?

ANSWERS TO MULTIPLE CHOICE

1. *b*	**7.** *b*	**13.** *c*	**19.** *d*
2. *b*	**8.** *a*	**14.** *d*	**20.** *a*
3. *c*	**9.** *d*	**15.** *d*	**21.** *d*
4. *c*	**10.** *b*	**16.** *c*	**22.** *a*
5. *b*	**11.** *b*	**17.** *d*	**23.** *c*
6. *c*	**12.** *b*	**18.** *b*	**24.** *c*

20

THE UNIVERSE

Our sun is a member of an immense swarm of stars, one of many in the universe. These swarms are called *galaxies,* and each is separated from the others by vast reaches of nearly empty space. The stars of the Milky Way are part of our galaxy.

Of the many remarkable properties galaxies have, one stands out: they are moving apart from one another, so that the universe as a whole is expanding at a steady rate. If we project this expansion backward, we find that it began 10 to 15 billion years ago. Can it be that the entire universe was born in a cosmic "big bang" at that time, and has been evolving ever since into the planets, stars, and galaxies of today? As we shall see in this chapter, several lines of evidence support such a picture, which has been filled out in considerable detail. But it is still not clear whether the expansion will continue forever. Quite possibly it will eventually slow down and come to a stop, and the universe will then come back together to start again in a new big bang.

GALAXIES

A galaxy is an island universe of stars. Just as studying the sun tells us a lot about stars in general, so studying our galaxy, the Milky Way, tells us a lot about galaxies in general.

The Milky Way

A spinning disk of stars

The galaxy of which the sun is a member appears in the sky as the Milky Way

The great band of misty light called the Milky Way forms a continuous ring around the heavens. When we look at it with a telescope, the Milky Way is an unforgettable sight. Instead of a dim glow we now see countless individual stars, stars as numerous as sand grains on a beach. In other parts of the sky the telescope also reveals stars too faint for the naked eye, but nowhere else in such numbers. Clearly the stars are not uniformly distributed in space — a basic observation that has profound implications concerning the structure and evolution of the universe.

Our galaxy is in the form of a disk

The appearance of the Milky Way tells us something about the arrangement of stars in our galaxy: most of them are concentrated in a relatively thin disklike region, with the sun located near the central plane of the disk. When we look toward the rim of the disk, we see a great many stars, so many that they seem to form a continuous band of light. When we look above or below the disk, far fewer stars are to be seen. The disk of stars has a thicker central nucleus, so that it is shaped something like a fried egg (Fig. 20-1).

The disk of the galaxy is about 100,000 light-years in diameter and 10,000 light-years thick near the center. It is one of the larger galaxies of the universe. The sun is about two-thirds of the distance from the center, which lies in the direction of the densest part of the Milky Way in the constellation Sagittarius. The 100 billion stars of the galaxy are chiefly located in two spiral arms that extend from the nucleus. Surrounded by so many similar bodies, the sun cannot claim distinction

A mosaic of several photographs of the Milky Way between the constellations Sagittarius and Cassiopeia.

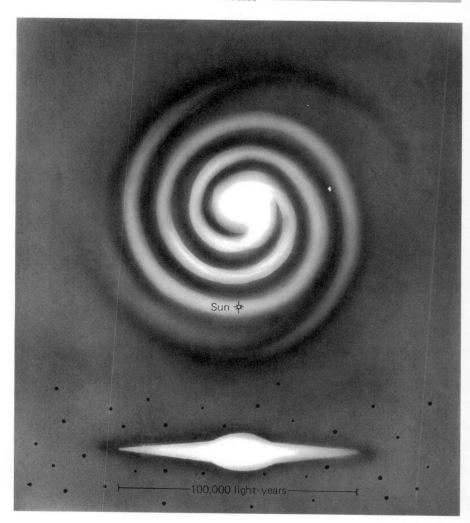

Sun ☆

├──────── 100,000 light-years ────────┤

FIG. 20-1

Approximate structure and size of our galaxy, which is one of the larger ones in the universe. The sun is about 30,000 light-years from the center. Globular clusters are shown as color patches.

Galactic rotation

for its position, size, mass, or temperature. It is probably not even unusual in possessing a family of planets. There may well be millions of planets in our galaxy, many of them no doubt inhabited by some form of advanced life.

The stars of the galaxy are almost all revolving about its center, which is what they must be doing if the galaxy is not to gradually collapse because of the gravitational attraction of its parts. (The planets do not fall into the sun because of their orbital motion, too.) The orbital speed of the sun and the stars in its vicinity around the galactic center is about 280 km/s. At this rate the sun makes a complete circuit once every 200 million years.

In addition to the galactic rotation individual stars move randomly with respect to their neighbors, like molecules in a gas. The sun's speed relative to nearby stars seems to be about 20 km/s. The comparison with molecular motions in a gas is actually quite reasonable, except that the gas must be exceedingly thin to resemble the emptiness of the galaxy. We must imagine a gas more rarefied than the best vacuum we can produce on earth, so rarefied that collisions between its molecules hardly ever take place.

Star Clusters

Two populations of stars

Galactic clusters of stars

Two kinds of star clusters are associated with our galaxy. The *galactic clusters* each consist of up to a thousand stars relatively close to one another that travel together about the center of the galaxy. The Pleiades make up such a cluster; the naked eye can make out six of its stars, and a telescope reveals over a hundred more. The stars in galactic clusters are much the same as the others in the Milky Way, all of which are classed as Population I stars. These stars are of all ages, from those just coming into being to old ones that must have been formed in the early life of the galaxy some 10 billion years ago.

Globular clusters of stars

Clusters of the other type are great assemblies of stars that are distributed in a sort of halo or corona around the central disk of the galaxy. To the naked eye the largest of these *globular clusters* are just visible on a clear night as faint patches of light. Through a telescope they are spectacular aggregates of stars, roughly spheri-

The globular cluster in Hercules contains perhaps a million stars.

(Left) Andromeda galaxy photographed in blue light shows giant
and supergiant stars of Population I
in the spiral arms. (Right) NGC 205,
companion of the Andromeda
galaxy, photographed in yellow light
shows stars of Population II. The
brightest stars are red and 100 times
fainter than the blue giants of
Population I. (The very bright, uniformly distributed stars in both
pictures are foreground stars belonging in our own Milky Way galaxy.)

The stars in globular clusters are very
old

Population I and Population II stars

cal in form, bright and dense near the center and thinning out toward the edges.
About 100 of these objects have been discovered.

In photographs of the great cluster in Hercules, one of the largest, more than
50,000 stars have been counted. These are only the brightest stars, since the
cluster is so far away that faint ones cannot be seen. The total number of stars may
be close to a million. The nearest clusters appear to be about 20,000 light-years
away from us and the farthest more than 100,000 light-years away. Light from the
great Hercules cluster travels 33,000 years before reaching our eyes, so we see it as
it appeared toward the end of the Ice Age. The average distance between stars in a
globular cluster is about 1 light-year, which means they are much more closely
packed than those near the sun.

The stars in globular clusters, which constitute Population II, are all very old,
almost as old as the galaxy. What seems to have happened is that all the matter of
the galaxy was originally a spherical cloud of gas from which stars were forming. In
time the cloud concentrated in a central disk, leaving behind those stars that had
already formed. New stars continued to come into being from the gas clouds of the
disk, which is why the stars there are of all ages.

This picture is supported by the compositions of the stars of the two populations. Population II stars are extremely rich in hydrogen and helium, which is

consistent with their early origin since the materials of the young universe are thought to have been these elements. Population I stars, on the other hand, contain heavier elements in some abundance. Such elements are produced in stars by the nuclear reactions that are responsible for stellar energy, and are ejected into space during the explosions characteristic of the final stages of a star's active life. Population I stars are richer in heavy elements than those of Population II because they were formed from material that already contained such elements, the debris of dying stars from Population II.

Galactic Nebulas

Clouds of gas and dust in the galaxy

Galactic nebulas are irregular masses of diffuse material within our galaxy (nebula is Latin for "cloud"). Some appear as small luminous rings or disks surrounding stars, some take the form of lacy filaments, and many are wholly irregular in outline. The brightest, the great nebula in Orion, is barely visible with the naked eye, but most of them are so faint that long exposure of a photographic plate is necessary to bring out details of structure. Probably these nebulas are masses of rarefied gas and tiny solid particles that shine only because they reflect light from

The Great Nebula in Orion is a gas cloud excited to luminescence by hot stars in its center.

nearby stars or because radiation of various kinds from stars excites their matter to luminescence.

Interstellar space is not completely empty

Clouds of gas and dust similar to galactic nebulas but without any luminosity sometimes reveal their presence as dark patches that obscure the light of stars beyond them. Such dark nebulas may be fairly abundant but are difficult to find because bright stars shine through them except where they are especially dense. In fact, much of our galaxy is filled with rarefied nebular material, with a density somewhere near one atom or molecule per cubic centimeter, and the dark nebulas are only local concentrations of this interstellar matter. Empty space is not nearly so empty as it was once thought to be, but in most places the amount of interstellar material is so small that starlight meets little interference in passing through it.

Radio Astronomy

Molecules in space

A radio telescope is a sensitive radio receiver connected to a directional antenna

A *radio telescope* is basically just an antenna connected to a sensitive radio receiver. Usually a metal dish, like the concave mirror of a reflecting telescope, gathers radio waves over a large area and concentrates them on the antenna itself. With such an arrangement the direction from which a particular radio signal arrives can be established. The largest steerable-dish radio telescope is 100 m in diameter and is located in West Germany. Still larger is a fixed dish 305 m across in Arecibo,

Radio telescope at Greenbank, West Virginia, picks up radio waves from space. Its diameter is 43 m.

Puerto Rico, that consists of wire mesh fitted into a bowl-shaped hollow in the landscape. As the earth turns, a band in the sky can be surveyed; the great sensitivity of the telescope makes up for its limitation to this band. Special types of radio telescopes whose antennas are long wires stretched above the ground for a km or more use interference methods to precisely locate particular sources of radio waves, although their sensitivities are less than those of dish-type telescopes.

Sources of radio waves from space

Radio waves from space seem to originate in three different ways. A common source is the random thermal motion of ions and electrons in a very hot gas, such as the atmosphere of a young star or the remnant thrown out by a supernova explosion. Another kind of source consists of high-speed electrons that move in a magnetic field. The strongest radio sources, called *quasars*, are of this kind and may emit more energy as radio waves than as light waves. Quasars are discussed later in this chapter.

The 21-cm spectral line of hydrogen

Radio waves in space are also produced by hydrogen atoms and by molecules of various kinds. These are spectral lines that happen to lie in the radio-frequency part of the spectrum rather than in the optical part. In particular, the hydrogen line whose wavelength is 21 cm has proved invaluable to astronomers because most interstellar material consists of cool hydrogen. Dark nebulas can be mapped accurately with the help of radio telescopes tuned to receive 21-cm radiation.

Molecules in space can be identified by their radio emissions

A surprisingly large number of chemical compounds have been detected in space by the radio waves their molecules emit when excited by collisions. Most of the molecules are fairly simple, such as carbon monoxide (CO), ammonia (NH_3), and water (H_2O); the hydroxide radical OH is also common. In addition some fairly complex organic molecules have been found, including formaldehyde (H_2CO), acetaldehyde (CH_3CHO), acrylonitrile (CH_2CHCN), and the alcohols methanol (CH_3OH) and ethanol (CH_3CH_2OH), as well as a number of inorganic ones. How these molecules have been formed out in space remains an interesting puzzle.

Spiral Galaxies

Island universes far apart in space

Nebulalike objects outside our galaxy also exist, very often spiral in form. To the naked eye only one of these nebulas is visible in the northern hemisphere, the spiral in Andromeda, and this appears merely as a small, hazy patch of light. But in photographs taken with large telescopes and long exposures the spiral nebulas are impressive objects whose shapes range from fuzzy spheres practically without structure to distinct, flat spirals like Fourth-of-July pinwheels. Members of the most common variety show a definite spiral structure with two curving arms radiating from a brighter nucleus. The telescope shows us spiral nebulas from different angles: some full face, some obliquely, and some edgewise, as in the accompanying illustrations. The general shape of the average nebula is that of a thin circular disk somewhat thicker in the center.

The Great Galaxy in Andromeda, the spiral galaxy nearest the earth, closely resembles our own Milky Way galaxy. The Andromeda galaxy contains about 100 billion stars and its period of rotation is about 200 million years. The two bright objects nearby are dwarf galaxies held as satellites by the gravitational pull of their huge neighbor.

The spiral galaxy in Coma Berenices is edge-on to us, whereas the one in Canes Venatici appears full face. The object near the latter is another galaxy.

Spiral nebulas are distant galaxies of stars

Good spectra of the spiral nebulas are difficult to obtain because of their extreme faintness. The brighter ones have spectra that resemble ordinary star spectra — dark absorption lines of various elements against a continuous background. This suggests that the nebulas are collections of stars, a suggestion borne out by photographs taken with large telescopes which resolve the outer portions of the biggest spirals into separate stars. Possibly the more diffuse spirals and the central parts of others are masses of gas and small particles, but the chief components of the principal nebulas are certainly stars. For this reason spiral nebulas are called *spiral galaxies* today.

The faintness of the stars that can be made out in even the brightest spirals implies that these objects are very far away. Accurate estimates of distances to a few of the nearer ones are made possible by the presence among their stars of Cepheid variables. Measurements of the apparent brightnesses and periods of fluctuation of these variables in the nearest of the large nebulas, the one in Andromeda, give a distance of about $1\frac{1}{2}$ million light-years. Several others are in the range of a few million light-years. Estimates of distances to the farther spirals are not based on so sure a foundation as the periods of Cepheid variables; the faintest spiral that has been found seems to be 10 billion light-years away. Spiral galaxies are exceedingly numerous. Within a distance of a billion light-years from our own galaxy there are at least 100 million others bright enough to be picked up by our telescopes.

William Herschel, the first to study spiral nebulas intensively, suggested that they might be other galaxies of stars which resemble our own, "island universes" in the sea of space. In his time this proposal was hardly more than a guess, but more recently, particularly because of the work of the American astronomer Edwin Hubble, it has been abundantly justified. Even the rotation of some of the spirals about their centers, similar to the rotation of our galaxy, has been detected by the doppler displacement of lines in their spectra. Our galaxy ranks among the larger spirals. Of the 19 known galaxies within a distance of 4 million light-years (the so-called *local group* of galaxies), the largest is the Andromeda nebula and the second in size is ours.

The universe is filled with spiral galaxies isolated from one another

Thus we are able to picture the universe as made up of galaxies of stars, each one isolated in space and separated from its nearest neighbors by distances of a million light-years or more. In all directions, in unbroken succession, these galaxies extend to the farthest parts of the universe that our instruments can reach. Not only is the earth an undistinguished planet circling an undistinguished star, but even the great galaxy that includes the sun is no different from billions of others.

The universe is uniform in material and structure

Through all this vast array of uncounted suns and unimaginable distances runs a uniformity of material and structural pattern. The elements of the earth are the elements of the spiral galaxies, the sun generates energy by a process repeated in billions of other stars, and the form of our galaxy appears again and again in the rest of the universe. Everywhere we find the same ultimate particles of matter, the same kinds of energy, the same patterns of structure. We can study at first hand no more than a tiny fragment of the universe, yet so consistent is the whole that from this fragment we can extend our knowledge wherever our instruments enable us to see.

Cosmic Rays

Atomic nuclei that come from space

Atmospheric ionization increases with altitude

The story of cosmic rays began early in this century, when it was discovered that the ionization in the atmosphere increased with altitude. At that time most scientists thought that the small number of ions always present in the air were due to the alpha, beta, and gamma rays emitted by the naturally radioactive substances, such as radium and uranium, that are found everywhere on the earth in minute quantities. If this were the correct explanation, then when we go high into the atmosphere away from the earth and its content of radioactive materials, the proportion of ions that we find should drop. Instead it increases, as a number of balloon-borne experimenters learned between 1909 and 1914. Finally Victor Hess, an Austrian physicist, suggested an explanation: from somewhere *outside* the earth ionizing radiation is continually bombarding our atmosphere. This radiation was later called *cosmic radiation* because of its extraterrestrial origin.

Primary cosmic rays are high-energy atomic nuclei, mainly protons, that reach the earth's atmosphere from galactic space

Primary cosmic rays, which are the rays as they travel through space before reaching the earth, are atomic nuclei, most of them protons, whose speeds are nearly as great as that of light. A hint of their significance is the fact that about as much energy arrives at the earth in the form of cosmic rays as in the form of starlight — over a billion billion primary cosmic rays arrive at the earth each second and carry with them energy equivalent to the output of a dozen large power plants. The available evidence indicates that nearly all primaries circulate throughout our galaxy, in which they are trapped by magnetic fields, and that they consist of nuclei originally ejected during supernova explosions.

A very few primaries are too energetic to have come from our galaxy and must have originated in another one somehow able to accelerate nuclei to energies of as much as 10^{20} eV, which is 16 J. As far as anyone can tell, these bits of matter from another galaxy, like the cosmic rays from our galaxy, are the same in nature as the matter on earth. This is one of the reasons why it is thought that the universe contains little or no antimatter (see Chap. 7).

Secondary cosmic-ray particles produced in the atmosphere are what reach the earth's surface

When a primary cosmic ray enters the earth's atmosphere, it disrupts atoms in its path to produce a shower of secondary particles. On the average more than one of these secondaries passes through each square centimeter at sea level per minute. Among the secondary particles are neutrons, which interact with nitrogen nuclei to produce the radioactive carbon 14 which is the basis of the radiocarbon dating method discussed in Chap. 16.

THE EXPANDING UNIVERSE

Red Shifts

The galaxies are all moving away from one another

Galactic spectra show red shifts

The spectra of galaxies share a curious feature: the lines in nearly all of them are shifted toward the red end. Furthermore, the amount of the shift increases with the distance of the galaxy from us. This displacement is illustrated in Fig. 20-2, which shows two of the absorption lines of calcium (indicated by arrows) in the spectra of several galaxies. Each galactic spectrum is shown between two comparison spectra, so that the shift of two lines toward the red (right in this picture) for galaxies at different distances is clearly evident.

In Chap. 19 we saw that red shifts in stellar spectra result from motion away from the earth. If we also attribute galactic red shifts to the doppler effect, we must conclude that all the galaxies in the universe (except the 19 in the local group in our own vicinity) are receding from us. From the extent of the red shifts the recession speeds can be computed, and the results are startling: several hundred kilometers per second for the nearer galaxies, nearly 200,000 km/s for the farthest ones. By comparison, the speed of light — the maximum relative speed anything can have — is 300,000 km/s.

The more distant a galaxy, the faster it is receding

If we plot the recession speeds of the galaxies shown in Fig. 20-2 versus their distances from the earth, as in Fig. 20-3, we find that these quantities are proportional. The greater the distance, the faster the galaxies are traveling. The speed increases by about 17 km/s per million light-years of distance. When this graph is extended to cover the still faster and more distant galaxies that have been studied, the experimental points fall on the same line. The proportionality between galactic speed and distance was discovered in 1929 by the astronomer Edwin Hubble and is known as *Hubble's law*.

It might seem at first as though our galaxy had some strange repulsion for all other galaxies, forcing them to move away from us with ever-increasing speed. But it is hardly likely that we occupy so important a place in the universe. A more reasonable conclusion is that all the galaxies are moving away from one another, spreading apart like the fragments of a bursting rocket. An observer on our galaxy *or on any other* would then get this impression that the neighbors are fleeing in all directions.

The entire universe is expanding

The universe, in other words, seems to be expanding, with its component galaxies moving ever farther apart (Fig. 20-4).

The Expanding Universe

Red shifts are not the only evidence

The darkness of the night sky is significant

The discovery that the universe is expanding should not have come as a complete surprise. As long ago as 1826, the German astronomer Heinrich Olbers pointed out

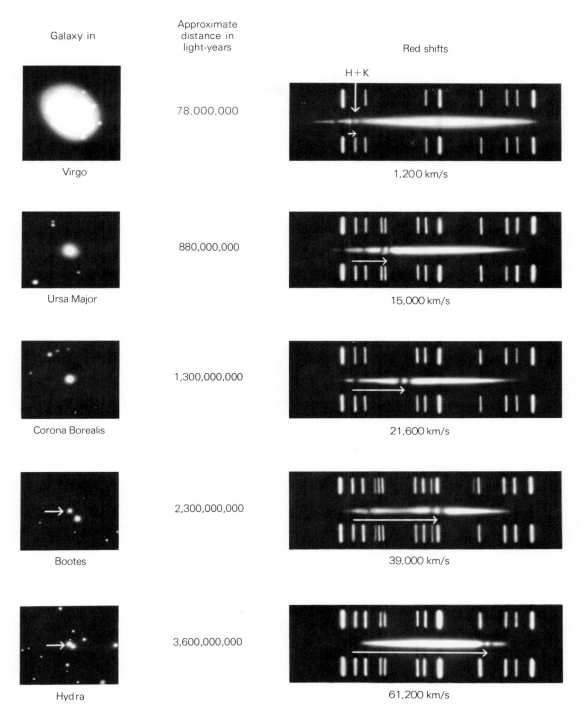

FIG. 20-2

The red shift in the spectral lines of distant galaxies increases with increasing distance. The lines marked H and K occur in the spectrum of calcium. Reference spectra are shown above and below each galactic spectrum.

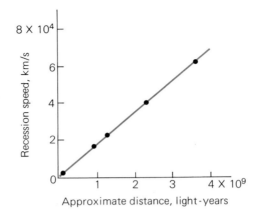

FIG. 20-3
Graph of recession speed versus distance for the galaxies of Fig. 20-2. The speed of recession averages about 17 km/s per million light-years.

FIG. 20-4
Two-dimensional analogy of the expanding universe. As the balloon is inflated, the spots on it become farther apart. A bug on the balloon would find that the farther away a spot is from its location, the faster the spot seems to be moving away; this is true no matter where the bug is.

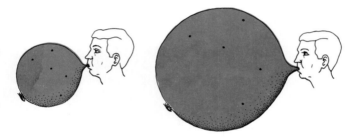

that, if the universe is very large, unchanging, and uniformly populated with stars, then the sky should be a continuous blaze of light both day and night. The reasoning is straightforward. The number of stars at a given distance from the earth increases with distance at the same rate as their apparent brightnesses decrease with distance, so that in such a universe starlight would arrive from all directions with the same intensity. We now know, of course, that it is galaxies of stars and not stars themselves that are uniformly distributed in space, but this does not affect the argument.

The fact that the sky is dark at night yet the universe is filled with bright galaxies must mean one of three things:

1. The universe is very small in size. But reliable distance measurements show that it is, in fact, large enough for Olbers's analysis to be valid.
2. The composition of the universe is not uniform, with no bright galaxies other than the few near us. But galaxies are actually everywhere in the universe, on the average just as bright as our neighbors.

3. The universe is expanding, with distant galaxies receding faster than those close by. This is the only possibility that is not contradicted by the evidence, quite apart from the red-shift data.

General relativity supports the expansion of the universe

A further hint came from Einstein's work on general relativity, which interpreted gravity as a warping of space and time. Among its other successes, this theory predicted correctly that light bends in a gravitational field. Another finding of general relativity was that the universe cannot stand still, so to speak, because all the objects in it attract one another, but must be expanding or contracting. However, when Einstein came to this conclusion in 1917, astronomers were unanimous in thinking that the universe is static and unchanging. Einstein therefore felt his theory must be wrong as it was and arbitrarily altered it to suit this view — the biggest mistake of his scientific career, as he later commented. Today it is clear that Einstein's original ideas were right, and they fit in well with the observed expansion of the universe.

Quasars

Brilliant galaxies perhaps with immense black holes at their hearts

Quasars are strong emitters of radio waves

The most remarkable objects in the sky whose spectra show red shifts are *quasars*. In a telescope, a quasar appears as a point of light, just as a star does. But unlike stars, the first quasars to be discovered, in the early 1960s, were powerful sources of radio waves. Hence their name, a contraction of *quasi-stellar radio sources*. Later on, many quasars were found that did not seem to give off radio waves, but it is now thought that the radio emissions may be directional and are merely not aimed our way in every case. Another possibility is that gas clouds around some quasars absorb the radio waves. Both the light and radio outputs of quasars fluctuate markedly, sometimes over a period of only days or weeks. Hundreds of quasars have been identified and studied, and there seem to be many more.

Quasars are the most distant known objects if their red shifts follow Hubble's law

Quasar red shifts are usually very large, in some cases corresponding to recession speeds of over half the speed of light. This suggests that quasars are far away. But if they are indeed distant objects, then the intensities of the light and radio waves we receive from them mean that they are emitting energy at colossal rates, hundreds or thousands of times more than ordinary galaxies.

To compound the puzzle, quasars vary in brightness too rapidly for them to be large in size. If a quasar were 100,000 light-years across, as our galaxy is, even a simultaneous change in its energy output (if it were possible) over a week's time would appear to us as spaced over 100,000 years. Hence the observed short-period output fluctuations point to a diameter for some quasars not all that much larger than that of the solar system — but their energy output may be thousands of times the output of our entire galaxy.

On the other hand, if quasars are close to us, neither the observed radio and optical brightnesses or their fluctuations would be quite so extraordinary. But then

Quasars radiate many times more energy than do ordinary galaxies like our own Milky Way, yet are far smaller in size. It is possible that quasars have black holes at their centers. The quasar shown here, which is designated 3C273, is 3 billion light-years away, the closest one known. The jet of matter that extends from this quasar is 250,000 light-years long, although the quasar itself is only about 1 light-year across. The image of the quasar appears much larger here than it should because the exposure time of the photograph was increased to show the jet.

A massive black hole may be at the heart of every quasar

we have the problem of explaining the red shifts in quasar spectra, a problem that does not exist if the shifts are traced to the expansion of the universe. And even if we could imagine a way to account for quasar speeds if they are nearby objects, in that case some quasars ought to be moving *toward* us as well as away from us, giving rise to blue shifts. No quasar blue shifts have ever been found, and it is generally agreed today that they are indeed distant objects.

Given that quasars are as far away as their red shifts imply, their energy sources must be small in size yet more powerful than any other energy sources in the universe. What has been suggested is that at the heart of each quasar is a black hole whose mass is hundreds of millions times the mass of the sun. As interstellar gases, or even whole stars, are pulled toward the black hole by its mighty gravitational field, their matter is compressed and heated to temperatures such that abundant radiation is given off. (Once the matter is inside the black hole, of course, it vanishes forever.) Exactly how the observed visible light, ultraviolet light, x-rays, and radio waves emitted by a quasar are produced is still uncertain, but only a supermassive black hole seems able to account for the energy release.

EVOLUTION OF THE UNIVERSE

The big bang

According to the aptly named *big bang theory*, the universe began as an extremely hot and dense lump of matter that exploded violently billions of years ago. As the material spread out and cooled, gravitational attraction caused local concentrations to form that became the galaxies. Given the big bang, no new physical principles seem needed to account for the evolution of the universe as it is today, and the observed expansion of the universe follows naturally.

Age of the Universe

Between 10 and 15 billion years

A rough estimate gives 17 billion years as the maximum

When did the big bang occur? It would seem that we could use the observed figure of approximately 17 km/s per million light-years for the rate of expansion of the universe to calculate backward to a time when the galaxies were together in one place. Let us consider a galaxy 1 million light-years away from us, which is 9.5×10^{21} m. The galaxy's speed is 17 km/s $= 1.7 \times 10^4$ m/s, so it must have started its outward motion at a time

$$T = \frac{\text{distance}}{\text{speed}} = \frac{9.5 \times 10^{21} \text{ m}}{1.7 \times 10^4 \text{ m/s}} = 5.6 \times 10^{17} \text{ s}$$

ago. Since there are 3.2×10^7 s in a year, this would make the age of the universe 1.7×10^{10} years — 17 billion years.

Gravitation has slowed down the expansion

There are two problems with the above calculation. The first is that the figure of 17 km/s per million light-years is not exact because it is hard to establish the distance of remote galaxies independently of their red shifts. Second, the calculation ignores the effect of gravitation on the expanding matter. If the universe were empty, its age would be roughly 17 billion years. Because it contains matter, the rate of expansion must be getting slower and slower, just as a ball thrown up into the air slows down. Since the expansion was faster in the past, the universe is younger than the 17 billion years obtained from Hubble's law.

A precise age is difficult to obtain

How much younger? One way to tell is to determine the present average density of matter in the universe. The greater this density, the more the expansion has been slowing down, and the younger the universe is. Since virtually all the matter in the universe is concentrated in the galaxies, finding the average density of matter boils down to "weighing" them. Most galaxies are found in groups (such as the "local group" of 19 of which our galaxy is a member), and their masses can be found from their gravitational effects on one another. This is the same procedure used to find the masses of the sun, planets, and satellites. An advantage of this method is that it automatically includes invisible matter in the galaxies — dark gas clouds and black holes, for instance. But although weighing galaxies is easy in principle, in practice it is difficult, and there is no general agreement as yet on the precise correction needed to the red-shift figure. An age of somewhere between 10 and 15 billion years is almost certain, around 13 billion years seems a reasonable guess.

Other evidence is consistent with an age of about 13 billion years

Another approach to the age of the universe is to examine the expansion speeds of the most distant galaxies. The light reaching us from a distant galaxy left it long ago; the information we can obtain about a galaxy 5 billion light-years away represents its physical state 5 billion years ago. Hence the galaxies farthest away ought to show recession speeds disproportionately greater than those closer to us, and from the difference the time at which the expansion began can be inferred.

The problem here is that the variation in speed is just on the limit of what is detectable with existing techniques. Again an age of 13 billion years seems consistent with present data.

As a check, we can apply the theory of stellar evolution to the Population II stars of globular clusters, the oldest known stars. They must be at least 10 billion years old, which sets a lower limit to the age of the universe itself. We can also measure the relative abundances of heavy long-lived radioactive isotopes and their decay products. Since these isotopes were formed in supernovas, this gives us a hint of when the first supernovas occurred. Again 10 billion years or so appears as the minimum age of the universe.

The Oscillating Universe

No beginning and no end?

The laws of physics as we know them today can take us from the present universe all the way back to about 10^{-4} s after the big bang, and plausible guesses can get us even closer to that moment of creation. But how did such a concentration of matter and energy arise? What was there before the big bang?

The universe may be undergoing a never-ending series of expansions and contractions

One answer is that perhaps the big bang of 13 billion years ago was only the latest of a succession of big bangs extending infinitely far into the past, a succession that will continue infinitely far into the future.

If the cosmic explosion that led to the present expansion of the universe was not violent enough, the expansion will not continue forever — the universe will be "closed" rather than "open." Eventually gravitation will not only slow down the expansion but will cause it to stop and then be reversed, so that the universe begins to collapse. As the collapse proceeds, galaxies and then individual stars will collide, and finally all of them will come together in a single mass at an extremely high temperature — the *big crunch*. Then another big bang will occur, and another cycle of expansion and contraction will begin (Fig. 20-5).

The big crunch

The cyclic model of the universe is clearly attractive, but is it correct? The key to the answer is the present average density of the universe. If it is less than a

FIG. 20-5

If the universe is "open," its expansion will continue forever. If it is "closed," the universe will eventually stop expanding and then collapse. In that case, a new big bang may conceivably occur which would start a new expansion.

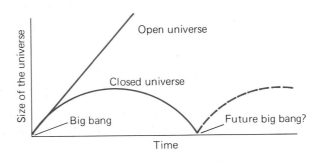

Present data cannot decide
between a closed and an open
universe

certain critical value, the universe is open and will continue to expand forever. If the density is greater than this value, the universe is closed and some day a big crunch will come, probably followed by another big bang. Until recently most of the evidence pointed to a relatively low density and hence to an open universe. However, as measuring techniques improve, more and more matter is being found. Whether there is actually enough to reverse the expansion of the universe remains to be seen.

The Primeval Fireball

A glimmer of it still exists

The early universe

Just after the big bang, the universe was a compact, intensely hot mixture of matter and energy. Particles and antiparticles were constantly annihilating each other to form photons of radiation, and just as often photons were materializing into particle-antiparticle pairs. As the fireball expanded and cooled, the energies of the photons decreased; we recall from Fig. 19-1 that the average wavelength of the radiation from a hot object increases as its temperature drops, which corresponds to a decrease in frequency and hence to a decrease in quantum energy hf. Finally, a few seconds after the big bang, the photons had too little energy to create any more particle-antiparticle pairs. The annihilation of the existing particles and antiparticles continued, however. Current theories of elementary particles suggest that particles outnumbered antiparticles, perhaps a billion and one particles for every billion antiparticles of the same kind. When the annihilation was finished, the surplus of particles — protons, neutrons, and electrons — remained.

When the universe was a minute or so old, nuclear reactions began to form helium nuclei. Calculations show that the ratio of hydrogen nuclei (protons) to helium nuclei ought to have ended up as 3 : 1 by mass, the same ratio found in most of the universe today. (The heavier elements were created later, in the interiors of stars and in supernova bursts.) After several hundred thousand years the universe was down to about 5000 K, cool enough for electrons and nuclei to combine into atoms. Since photons interact strongly with charged particles but only weakly with neutral atoms, at this time matter and radiation were "decoupled" and the universe became transparent. The radiation that was left should then have continued to spread out with the rest of the universe, so that even today remnants of it must be everywhere.

Owing to the expansion of the universe, an observer today would expect to find these remnants to have undergone a red shift to long wavelengths, in the range of radio waves. The radiation would not be easy to find, since it would be very weak, but it ought to have two distinctive characteristics that would permit it to be identified: the radiation should come equally strongly from all directions, and its spectrum should be the same as that which an object at about 3 K would radiate.

Remarkably enough, radiation of exactly this kind has been discovered. In fact, it apparently is one of the sources of the "snow" on television screens. The

Radio waves thought to have originated in the primeval fireball that marked the start of the current expansion of the universe were first detected with a sensitive receiver attached to this 15-m-long antenna at the AT&T Bell Laboratories research facility at Holmdel, New Jersey.

Remnants of the radiation from the early universe constitute a sea of radio waves that pervades the universe

universe is bathed in a sea of radio waves whose ultimate origin seems to have been the primeval fireball. The existence of this radiation is strong support for the big bang picture of the origin of the universe. What is perhaps most exciting about the discovery is that it takes the question of the early history of the universe out of the realm of speculation and into the realm of measurement.

Origin of the Earth

It began with a whisper, not a bang

The first stars

A billion or two years after the big bang the hydrogen and helium of the universe began to accumulate in separate clouds under the influence of gravity. These clouds were the ancestors of today's galaxies. As the young galaxies contracted, local concentrations of gas appeared that became the first stars. Some of the early stars were very massive and went through their life cycles rapidly to end as supernovas. The explosions of these supernovas dumped elements heavier than hydrogen and helium into the remaining galactic gas. As a result the matter from which later stars condensed was a mixture of elements, not just hydrogen and helium. By the time the sun came into being, billions of years after the first generation of stars, the loose material of the galaxy contained between 1 and 2 percent of the heavier elements, often in the form of small solid dust grains.

The sun and planets were formed together

The swirling cloud that became the sun was originally much larger than the present solar system. As it shrank in the process of becoming a star, this *protosun* left behind a spinning disk of gas and dust. Bits of matter in the disk collided and stuck together to form larger and larger grains, perhaps the size of pebbles. Somehow — the details of the process remain unclear — these grains formed larger bodies called *planetesimals* that ultimately joined to become the planets. Near the protosun, which was heated by its gravitational compression, it was too warm for volatile elements to collect in any great amounts on the planetesimals, which is why the inner planets are rocky bodies. Farther out temperatures were lower, and the planetesimals mirrored the composition of the original cloud by being mainly frozen gases.

As the planets were developing with their satellites around them, the protosun was gathering up more and more material. Eventually its internal temperature and pressure became sufficient for fusion reactions to occur in its hydrogen content, and the protosun became a star. Fast ions and electrons then began to stream out of the sun, much like today's solar wind but far more intense, which swept the solar system free of the gas and dust that had not yet been incorporated in the sun, the planets, and the satellites.

The young planets were heated by gravitational compression, which melted the earth

The infant planets were all heated by gravitational compression, which was naturally most effective in giant Jupiter and Saturn. Radioactivity was important as well in heating the inner planets. The earth became hot enough at this time to melt and separate into a dense iron core and a lighter rocky mantle. The remaining planetesimals in the solar system bombarded the planets and satellites heavily, leaving craters on the solid ones that, in the case of the earth, erosion was later to erase.

The future of the solar system

What of the future course of the earth? According to an old Norse legend, the world will come to an end when "an icy winter will seize the earth in its grip, and a great wolf will devour the sun." A rather different fate seems more likely. In 5 billion years or so the sun will swell into a red giant, and its radiation will increase to a hundred times its present rate. The earth will grow warmer and the oceans will begin to boil. Steam will fill the atmosphere and all life will perish. The sun will eventually become as large around as the orbit of Mars, and the earth will in time vaporize with its material dispersed inside the sun. Later a feeble white dwarf will be all that is left.

EXTRATERRESTRIAL LIFE

The recipe for creating life begins with a warm planet whose gravity is able to retain an atmosphere and whose distance from its parent star is such that it receives enough but not too much radiant energy. Then provide an atmosphere of certain quite common gases, allow the planet to cool down a bit so that seas form, and wait perhaps a billion years. This recipe was followed successfully on the earth; let us now see how likely it is to have been followed elsewhere in the universe.

Other Planetary Systems

We are not alone

The modern view of the solar system is that it is a natural accompaniment to the evolution of the sun. Since the sun is by no means an exceptional star in any other respect, it is reasonable to suppose that other stars are also attended by planetary systems.

The above argument is reinforced by the observed rotation rates of stars. These rates are measured with the help of the doppler effect. It is found that stars whose masses are about that of the sun or less rotate slowly, as the sun does; the sun takes 4 weeks for a complete rotation. Heavier stars, on the other hand, spin quite rapidly. What is the reason for this difference?

The sun rotates slowly because the planets have most of the solar system's angular momentum

Stars form from spinning gas clouds, according to current ideas, and so have a great deal of angular momentum. The sun turns so slowly because almost all the angular momentum of the solar system is concentrated in the planets, with the sun having less than 1 percent of the total. If the sun had all the angular momentum of the solar system, it would spin about as fast as heavier stars do. We may therefore conjecture that the stars that rotate slowly do so because they are accompanied by swarms of planets that absorbed most of the available angular momentum.

A great many planetary systems probably exist elsewhere in the universe

Many of the 100 billion stars in the galaxy of stars (the Milky Way) of which the sun is a member are comparable in mass to the sun and share its slow rate of rotation. Some fraction of these stars almost certainly have planetary systems. If the fraction is large, the total number of planets in the galaxy equals or exceeds the number of stars. If the fraction is small — shall we say one in a thousand? — then the number of planets still comes to a billion or so. And there are billions of other galaxies in the known universe. Even a conservative guess at the lower limit to the number of planets in the universe thus yields a billion billion.

Why other planetary systems are hard to find

If planets are such common objects, why are we only certain of the nine in our own solar system? Three interrelated factors stand in the way of identifying planets that belong to other stars. The first is distance: the closest star to us is thousands of times farther away than Pluto, and Pluto is hard enough to detect. The second is that planets shine by reflected light and not by themselves. This makes them very dim compared with their parent stars, far too dim to be seen directly. The third difficulty is size. Planets are necessarily small relative to stars, because if they were of similar size, they would have evolved into stars. In fact, many stars may indeed be overgrown planets, since double stars are common that consist of two stars circling each other in the same way the earth and moon circle each other. (The members of a double star system may well have planets of their own, of course, just as the planets of the solar system have satellites, some of which are pretty big.) The small size of planets helps make them impossible to see at stellar distances and their small mass makes the wobbles they cause in the paths of their parent stars all but imperceptible.

Barnard's star may have two planets

The words "all but imperceptible" are necessary because some wobbles

Photographs of Barnard's Star taken a number of years apart show its change in position relative to other, more distant stars. Periodic irregularities in the path of Barnard's Star may be due to two planets in orbit around it.

seem to have been detected in the positions of several nearby stars. In each case the star itself is less massive than the sun and the planet whose gravitational pull as it swings around in its orbit causes the star to oscillate slightly has an estimated mass equal to or greater than Jupiter's mass. The best-known example is Barnard's Star, a dwarf whose mass is only $\frac{1}{7}$ the mass of the sun and so would exhibit a greater degree of wobble if a planet of a certain mass circled it than would a star more like the sun. Photographs of Barnard's Star taken over a period of 50 years suggest that it has one satellite of nearly Jovian mass and perhaps another, lighter one as well.

From the point of view of life in the universe, it would be nice to have planetary systems confirmed around Barnard's Star and the others, but not crucial. There are so very many stars in the universe that it is hardly conceivable that only our own sun has a planetary system. Whether there are thousands of billions of billions of other planets or merely billions is not really so important. What is important is that a certain proportion of these planets surely meet, in the words of Harlow Shapley, "the happy requirement of suitable distance from the star, near-circular orbit, proper mass, salubrious atmosphere, and reasonable rotation period — all of which are necessary for life as we know it on earth." True, it is unlikely that the hypothesis of life on other worlds will be directly verified in the near future, but no serious arguments that dispute this hypothesis have been advanced. It seems certain that we are not alone in the universe.

CHAPTER 20

Interstellar Travel

Not now, probably not ever

Astronauts have already visited the moon and spacecraft have already traveled to other planets. If the money for such a project were available, there is no reason why people should not be able to set foot on Mars a few years after a decision to do so is made and see for themselves whether life existed in the past. But travel to the planetary systems of other stars is a much more formidable undertaking.

Suppose Barnard's Star turns out to definitely have a planetary system and that we wish to pay a visit to check on the possibility of life there. This star, although one of the nearest to the sun, is still 4×10^{13} km away. The various Apollo spacecraft took 3 days to reach the moon, which is 100 million times closer than Barnard's Star. To reach Barnard's Star at the same rate, a similar spacecraft would therefore need 300 million days, nearly a million years. So existing technology is out of the question.

Nothing can travel faster than the speed of light

What about the future? According to Einstein's special theory of relativity, which has been found to be completely accurate in all its predictions, the ultimate limit to the speed that anything can have is the speed of light. This speed is 300,000 km/s, which is equivalent to 186,000 mi/s. At a speed 1 percent short of this, a spacecraft could reach Barnard's Star in 4.3 years, a reasonable enough period of time. However, the energy required would be fantastic, more than all the energy currently used in the entire world per year for each ton of spacecraft weight — and the spacecraft would have to weigh many tons. How can all this energy be produced? How can it be concentrated at one time and place? How can it be given to the spacecraft? And how could a like amount of energy be provided in the vicinity of Barnard's Star to return the spacecraft to the earth?

These questions are not quibbles, they are fundamental to such an enterprise — and they have no answers that can be envisioned at present. As for visiting the stars that lie millions and billions of times farther away than Barnard's Star, there does not seem to be any hope whatever.

Visits to and from other planetary systems seem impossible

The laws of physics hold everywhere in the universe, which means that the extreme unlikelihood of travel from the earth to another planetary system is also true for travel from such a system to the earth. It is easy to attribute ancient legends and archeological findings that are hard to explain in terms of known events to visitors from another world, but all such attributions have turned out to lack any real evidence to support them. A good story does not constitute proof of anything except the imagination of its author.

Interstellar Communication

Why not?

Existing technology would permit interstellar communication

Although interstellar travel is almost certainly impossible, by contrast interstellar communication by radio seems quite feasible. Existing radio telescopes are probably sensitive enough to respond to a radio signal of plausible strength from a planet of a nearby star. A thousand or so such radio telescopes acting together ought to be able to receive messages sent from any planet in our galaxy, and if operated as transmitters, would be able to send out messages of similar range. A serious attempt at interstellar communication would be expensive — though less in total than the cost of the world's armaments for a single month — and, by virtue of the long distances involved, would mean years at best, more likely centuries for an interchange of information to take place. But what an extraordinary, exhilarating prospect!

The real problem of interstellar communication does not concern technology but instead the average life span of civilizations advanced enough to be capable of such communication. If this life span is short, then there is little chance that more than a very few planets are actually inhabited by intelligent beings at the same time, no matter how many planets have had such beings living on them in the past or will have in the future.

We on earth have had the ability (if not the collective desire) to communicate with other worlds for perhaps 20 years already. How long will this ability persist? With a soaring population and a shrinking stock of natural resources, it is hard to be optimistic. There is no prospect that the needs of future generations can be accommodated nor that the environment can survive their presence unless effective worldwide action is taken soon to limit population, conserve resources, and reduce pollution. If nothing is done, interstellar communication will be the last thing on the minds of the survivors of the catastrophe that may well occur.

Shall we say we have 80 more years before our civilization collapses? This means a total period of 100 years in which intersellar communication would be possible. The universe is about 13 billion years old, and if the average life of other advanced civilizations throughout our galaxy is also 100 years, then there would have to be more than $13,000,000,000/100 = 130,000,000$ habitable planets for more than one of them to contain such a civilization at the same time.

A detailed study has led to the estimate of 600 million habitable planets in our galaxy. On the above basis, this means only four or five civilizations in the galaxy at any time, not many in view of the billions of stars there. Since communication at interstellar distances requires narrow beams of radio waves in order that they not be enfeebled by dispersion, the chance that random scanning of the sky will turn up a signal from another civilization is vastly less than that of finding the proverbial needle in a haystack.

To be sure, it is rather pessimistic to assume that civilizations on other planets have the same self-destructive urges that we on earth do. Given a stable population of moderate size and nonaggressive behavior, a civilization might well last for millions of years. In this case the large number of civilizations current in the galaxy at any one time would certainly make an attempt at communication worthwhile.

The duration of advanced civilizations affects the likelihood that interstellar communication will succeed

It is worth a try

IMPORTANT TERMS

Our **galaxy** is a huge, rotating, disk-shaped group of stars that we see as the **Milky Way** from our location about two-thirds of the way out from the center. Most of the stars of the galaxy are found in two **spiral arms** that extend from the central nucleus. **Globular clusters** of very old stars occur outside the central disk of the galaxy. **Spiral galaxies** are other collections of stars that resemble our galaxy. The universe apparently consists of widely separated galaxies of stars.

A **radio telescope** is a directional antenna connected to a sensitive radio receiver. Radio waves from space are produced by extremely hot gases, by fast electrons that move in magnetic fields, and by atoms and molecules excited to radiate. Especially notable sources are **quasars,** distant objects that emit both light and radio waves strongly and that may be powered by supermassive black holes at their centers.

Cosmic rays are atomic nuclei, mostly protons, that travel through the galaxy at speeds close to that of light. They probably were ejected during supernova explosions and are trapped in the galaxy by magnetic fields.

The spectral lines of distant galaxies show a doppler shift to the red arising from motion away from the earth. Since the speed of recession is observed to be proportional to distance, the **red shift** means that all the galaxies in the universe are moving away from one another. This **expansion of the universe** began about 13 billion years ago.

The **big bang** theory holds that the universe originated in a great explosion about 13 billion years ago. Radiation left over from the big bang and doppler-shifted to radio frequencies has been detected. If the explosion was violent enough, the expansion of the universe will continue forever; if not, the universe will eventually begin to contract and will end up in a **big crunch** after which another cycle of expansion and contraction will occur. It is likely that the solar system and the sun originated together as part of the same evolutionary process, and that planetary systems are quite common elsewhere in the universe.

MULTIPLE CHOICE

1. The stars in space are
   a. uniformly spread out
   b. distributed completely at random
   c. chiefly in the Milky Way
   d. mostly contained within widely separated galaxies
2. The Milky Way is
   a. a galactic cluster of stars
   b. a globular cluster of stars
   c. a galactic nebula
   d. a galaxy of stars
3. Our galaxy is approximately
   a. 4 light-years across
   b. 15,000 light-years across
   c. 100,000 light-years across
   d. 4 million light-years across

4. The number of stars in our galaxy is roughly
   a. 1000
   b. 1 million
   c. 1 billion
   d. 100 billion
5. Each cubic centimeter of space between the stars in our galaxy contains on the average about
   a. 1 atom or molecule
   b. 1 million atoms or molecules
   c. 1 milligram of matter
   d. 1 gram of matter
6. The original form of our galaxy was
   a. spherical
   b. long and thin
   c. like that of a pocket watch
   d. like that of a doughnut
7. Spiral galaxies
   a. are readily visible to the naked eye
   b. may be dark or bright
   c. are usually similar to our galaxy
   d. originate in supernova explosions
8. The stars in a galaxy are
   a. moving outward from its center
   b. moving inward toward its center
   c. revolving around its center
   d. stationary relative to its center
9. The globular clusters of our galaxy
   a. lie in its central disk
   b. consist of several hundred stars each
   c. consist only of very old stars
   d. consist of stars rich in heavy elements
10. A radio telescope is basically
    a. a device for magnifying radio waves
    b. a telescope remotely controlled by radio
    c. a directional antenna connected to a sensitive radio receiver
    d. an optical telescope that uses electronic techniques to produce an image
11. Primary cosmic rays are characteristic phenomena of the
    a. solar system
    b. galaxy
    c. regions between the galaxies
    d. entire universe
12. Primary cosmic rays are composed largely of very fast
    a. protons
    b. neutrons
    c. electrons
    d. gamma rays
13. The red shift in the spectral lines of light reaching us from other galaxies implies that these galaxies

a. are moving closer to one another

b. are moving farther apart from one another

c. are in rapid rotation

d. consist predominantly of red giant stars

14. The idea that the universe is expanding does not receive support from

a. the fact that the sky is dark at night

b. the fact that spiral galaxies rotate

c. Einstein's theory of general relativity

d. red shifts in galactic spectra that increase with increasing distance

15. Current ideas suggest that what is responsible for the observed properties of a quasar is a massive

a. neutron star

b. black hole

c. spiral galaxy

d. star cluster

16. Quasars do not

a. emit radio waves

b. exhibit red shifts in their spectra

c. vary in their output of radiation

d. occur in the solar system

17. The two models of the universe that have most support hold that it is

a. a static assembly of stars and matter that does not change its configuration in time

b. continually expanding

c. alternately expanding and contracting

d. continually contracting

18. Since the big bang the rate of expansion of the universe

a. has been constant

b. has increased

c. has decreased

d. has alternately increased and decreased

19. The age of the universe is probably in the neighborhood of

a. 13 million years

b. $4\frac{1}{2}$ billion years

c. 13 billion years

d. 20 billion years

20. The elements heavier than hydrogen and helium of which the planets are composed probably came from

a. the sun

b. the debris of supernova explosions that occurred before the solar system came into being

c. the big bang

d. the big crunch

21. The planets and their satellites

a. were formed in space and captured by the sun

b. were formed from material ejected by the sun after its formation

c. were formed inside the sun and later ejected

d. came into being at the same time as the sun

22. In the next phase of its evolution, the sun will become a

a. red giant

b. white dwarf

c. neutron star

d. quasar

23. The least likely reason why planetary systems have not been directly observed around stars other than the sun is that

a. planets are small

b. planets shine by reflected light

c. planetary systems are rare

d. other stars are far away

QUESTIONS

1. Are the stars uniformly distributed in space?

2. The earth undergoes four major motions through space. What are they?

3. Why is the sun considered to be part of the central disk of our galaxy?

4. How can the rotation of a spiral galaxy be determined?

5. What sort of evidence would suggest that spiral nebulas are actually galaxies of stars?

6. Both galactic clusters and globular clusters occur in our galaxy. Distinguish between them.

7. What are the properties of globular clusters? Why are they not considered to be a type of galaxy?

8. Distinguish between Population I and Population II stars.

9. A number of elliptically shaped galaxies are known which seem to contain only Population II stars. Would you expect such galaxies to contain abundant gas and dust?

10. Why are spiral nebulas not considered as part of our galaxy?

11. Where is most of the interstellar gas in our galaxy located? What is its chief constituent?

12. Do radio telescopes actually magnify anything? If not, why are larger and larger ones being built?

13. Cosmic-ray intensity varies around the world in a manner that is correlated with the earth's magnetic field. Why is such a correlation plausible? Account for the greater number of cosmic rays that reach the earth near the polar regions than do so near the equator.

14. There is no day-night difference in cosmic-ray intensity. How does this observation bear on the possibility of a solar origin for cosmic rays?

15. What do you think ultimately becomes of the protons and neutrons knocked out of atmospheric atoms by cosmic rays?

16. Cosmic-ray primaries are mostly protons, but few protons are in the cosmic rays that reach the earth's surface. Why?

17. Why are radio-astronomical studies of the distribution of hydrogen in the universe of greater interest than studies of the distribution of other elements?

18. Experiments have been carried out to monitor the 21-cm radio waves emitted by neutral hydrogen in the universe to seek signals produced by intelligent beings on planets outside our solar system. Why do you suppose this particular wavelength was chosen for monitoring?

19. List the three ways in which radio waves from space originate.

20. What kind of evidence supports the belief that molecules of various kinds, including some fairly complex ones, exist in space?

21. According to current ideas, where are elements heavier than hydrogen formed?

22. Why is the universe believed to be expanding?

23. Why must the rate of expansion of the universe be slowing down?

24. How do measurements of the density of matter in space bear on the age of the universe? On the question of whether the universe is cyclic or not?

25. How do measurements of the expansion speeds of galaxies at different distances bear on the age of the universe? On the questions of whether the universe is cyclic or not?

26. What experimental evidence supports the idea that a primeval fireball existed in the early moments of the universe?

27. What is a quasar?

28. The spectra of quasars exhibit red shifts, never blue shifts. Why does this suggest that quasars are not members of our galaxy?

29. Did the sun begin as a small body that grew to its present size, or as a large one that subsequently shrank?

30. The sun and the giant outer planets contain hydrogen and helium in abundance, the inner planets very little. Why?

31. Would you summarize the most likely destiny for the earth as fire or ice?

32. Why is it reasonable to suppose that many other stars have planetary systems circling them?

33. Why is it hard to detect the planetary systems of other stars?

34. Is there an ultimate limit to spacecraft speeds? If so, what is it?

ANSWERS TO MULTIPLE CHOICE

1. *d*	**7.** *c*	**13.** *b*	**19.** *a*
2. *d*	**8.** *c*	**14.** *b*	**20.** *b*
3. *c*	**9.** *c*	**15.** *b*	**21.** *d*
4. *d*	**10.** *c*	**16.** *d*	**22.** *a*
5. *a*	**11.** *b*	**17.** *b, c*	**23.** *c*
6. *a*	**12.** *a*	**18.** *c*	

ANSWERS TO ODD-NUMBERED QUESTIONS AND PROBLEMS

CHAPTER 1   QUESTIONS

1. An accelerated body need not be moving at all times. Examples of a body at rest that is accelerated are a ball at the instant of release when being dropped and a ball at the top of its path after having been thrown vertically upward.

3. The ball will remain stationary with respect to the barrel, since both are falling with the same acceleration.

5. No.

7. The moon's motion around the earth is accelerated because the moon's direction of motion continually changes. Because the moon is accelerated, a force must be acting upon it. This force is directed toward the earth.

9. A person who jumps onto loose earth is slowed down more gradually than if he jumps onto concrete, hence the force acting on him is less.

11. *(a)* The reaction force is the upward force exerted by the table on the book; without this force the book would fall to the floor. *(b)* The reaction force is the gravitational pull the book exerts on the earth.

13. If you throw something away from you, you will begin to move backward since the force it exerts on you is equal and opposite to the force you exert on it in the act of throwing.

15. A propeller works by pushing backward on the air, whose reaction force in turn pushes the propeller itself and the airplane it is attached to forward. No air, no reaction force, so the idea is no good.

CHAPTER 1   PROBLEMS

1. (291 km)(1000 m/km) = 291,000 m; (291 km)(0.621 mi/km) = 181 mi.

3. $t = d/v = $ 1500 m/(330 m/s) = 4.5 s.

5. $t = d/v = $ 3700 km/(65 km/h) = 56.9 h; 56.9 h/(9 h/day) = 6.3 days.

7. $v_0 = $ (80 km/h)(1000 m/km)/3600 s/h) = 22.2 m/s and $v = $ 0. Hence $a = (v - v_0)/t = (0 - 22.2$ m/s)/3 s $= -7.4$ m/s².

9. $a = $ (80 km/h)/20 s = 4 (km/h)/s, hence with $v_0 = $ 80 km/h and $v = $ 130 km/h, $t = (v - v_0)/a = $ 12.5 s.

11. *(a)* $v = v_0 + at = $ 10 m/s + (9.8 m/s²)(1 s) = 19.8 m/s. *(b)* $v = $ 10 m/s + (9.8 m/s²)(3 s) = 39.4 m/s.

13. *(a)* $v_0 = $ 30 m/s and at the highest point $v = $ 0. Since $v = v_0 - gt$, $t = (v_0 - v)/g = $ 3.06 s. *(b)* The time of fall equals the time of rise, so total time is 2 × 3.06 s = 6.12 s. *(c)* 30 m/s.

15. (650 lb)/(2.2 lb/kg) = 295 kg.

17. *(a)* $m = w/g = $ 0.816 kg. *(b)* $a = F/m = $ 24.5 m/s².

19. $a = F/m$, $v = at = Ft/m = $ 28.6 m/s.

21. $m = w/g = $ 71.4 kg; $F = w = $ 700 N; $a = g = $ 9.8 m/s².

23. $a = (v - v_0)/t = $ 0.8 m/s², $F = ma = $ 1280 N. The force is the reaction force of the road on the car's tires.

25. $v_0 = -15$ m/s and $v = $ 20 m/s, so $a = (v - v_0)/t = $ (20 m/s) − (−15 m/s)/0.005 s = (35 m/s)/0.005 s = 7000 m/s² and $F = ma = $ 420 N.

27. The force is her weight of mg plus her mass times her upward acceleration. Hence $F = mg + ma = $ 708 N.

CHAPTER 2   QUESTIONS

1. No. The distinction between vector and scalar quantities is simply that vector quantities have directions associated with them, and both kinds of quantity are found in the physical world.

3. Under no circumstances.

5. At the bottom of the circle, since here the string must support all the ball's weight of mg as well as support the centripetal force mv^2/r. At other positions in the circle, only part of the weight is supported by the string.

7. The earth must travel faster when it is nearest the sun in order to counteract the greater gravitational force of the sun.

9. The sun's gravitational pull on the earth varies during the year since the distance from the earth to the sun varies.

11. The time of revolution will be shorter, since the satellite must revolve faster about the earth than the moon does owing to the greater gravitational pull of the earth at the smaller distance.

13. At the center of the earth, the stone's mass is the same as at the surface but its weight is zero.

15. No, because he and the airplane are ''falling'' at the same rate.

CHAPTER 2   PROBLEMS

1. $F = mv^2/r = 12.5$ N.

3. $v = \sqrt{Fr/m} = 6.3$ m/s.

5. The car will leave the hump when the required centripetal force mv^2/r is more than the car's weight of mg. Hence $mv^2/r = mg$, $v = \sqrt{rg} = 10.8$ m/s.

7. $mv^2/r = F$, $r = mv^2/F = 60$ m.

9. The force on each mass is $GmM/r^2 = 6.67 \times 10^{-10}$ N. The acceleration of the 2-kg mass is $F/m = 3.33 \times 10^{-10}$ m/s^2 and that of the 5-kg mass is 1.33×10^{-10} m/s^2.

11. $F = GmM/r^2 = 4.17 \times 10^{23}$ N; $v = \sqrt{Fr/m} = 1.3 \times 10^4$ m/s.

CHAPTER 3   QUESTIONS

1. Yes, because all changes require the performance of work.

3. When it is farthest from the sun; when it is closest to the sun. The work needed to pull a planet away from the sun to a given distance increases with the distance, so the planet's PE is greatest the farthest it is from the sun. The gravitational force of the sun on a planet is greatest when it is closest to the sun, hence its speed is also greatest there in order that gravitational and centripetal forces be in balance.

5. Their speeds are the same. The golf ball, which has the greater mass, has the greater KE, PE, and momentum.

7. Yes; yes.

9. *(a)* The speed decreases as rainwater collects in the truck, since the total momentum must remain constant. *(b)* The reduced speed is unchanged because the water that leaked out carried with it the momentum it had gained.

11. Since $2 \times (\frac{1}{2}mv^2) = \frac{1}{2}m(\sqrt{2}\,v)^2$, the speed increases by $\sqrt{2}$ and so the momentum increases by $\sqrt{2}$ as well.

13. The angular momentum of such a flywheel is greater than for a simple disk at the same speed of rotation, hence its tendency to keep turning is also greater.

15. The energy goes into heating the acid bath.

CHAPTER 3   PROBLEMS

1. Since the onions do not move, no work is done.

3. No work is done since the force on the earth is perpendicular to its direction of motion.

5. $h = W/mg = 10,000$ J/(90 kg)(9.8 m/s^2) = 11.3; 10,000 J.

7. $P = W/t = mgh/t = 65$W since 10 h = 36,000 s.

9. The energy consumption per person was 2×10^{20} J/3.5 $\times$ $10^9 = 5.7 \times 10^{10}$ J. There are (365 d/yr)(24 h/d)(3600 s/h) = 3.15×10^7 s/yr, hence the power per person is 5.7×10^{10} J/3.15×10^7 s = 1.8×10^3 W. Since 746 W = 1 hp, this is 2.4 hp.

11. *(a)* $h = W/mg = 1$ J/(1 kg $\times$ 9.8 m/s^2) = 0.102 m. *(b)* $h = W/w = 1$ J/1 N = 1 m.

13. Since KE $= \frac{1}{2}mv^2$, much more energy is needed to increase the car's speed from 40 to 50 km/h than from 0 to 10 km/h.

15. KE = PE $= mgh = 4.41 \times 10^5$ J.

17. *(a)* $W = Fd = 1760$ J. *(b)* PE $= mgh = 1568$ J. *(c)* 192 J was dissipated as heat due to friction in the pulleys.

19. $t = d/v = 1250$ s, $W = Pt = 1.75 \times 10^6$ J, hence 1.75×10^6 J/(4 $\times 10^4$ J/g) = 44 g of fat is metabolized.

21. $m = E/c^2 = 3.35 \times 10^5$ J/(3 $\times 10^8$ m/s]^2 = 3.72×10^{-12} kg.

23. $E = mc^2 = 4 \times 10^9$ kg $\times$ (3 $\times 10^8$ m/s)$^2 = 3.6 \times 10^{26}$ J; $P = E/t = 3.6 \times 10^{26}$ W.

25. *(a)* Here $m_2 = 2m_1$, hence $v_2 = m_1 v_1/m_2 = 4$ m/s. *(b)* KE$_1 = \frac{1}{2}m_1 v_1^2 = 64,000$ J, KE$_2 = \frac{1}{2}m_2 v_2^2 = 32,000$ J, so 32,000 J is lost.

27. $v_2 = m_1 v_1/m_2 = 2.25$ m/s.

29. $T_F = \frac{9}{5}(37°) + 32° = 98.6°$F.

31. The temperature difference is 80°C and 4.19 kJ/kg is needed per 1°C change in temperature. Hence $E = (4.19$ kJ/kg$\cdot$°C) (80°C)(0.2 kg) = 67 kJ.

33. The stone's energy is $mgh = 9800$ J = 9.8 kJ. Since 4.19 kJ increases the temperature of 1 kg of water by 1°C and here there is 10^4 kg of water, the temperature rise is (9.8 kJ)/(4.19 kJ/kg$\cdot$°C) (10^4 kg) = 2.3×10^{-4} °C.

CHAPTER 4   QUESTIONS

1. The person reduces the pressure in the straw by sucking on it, and atmospheric pressure then forces the liquid upward.

3. The block will stay where it is since there is no water underneath it to furnish a buoyant force.

5. The density of air decreases with altitude, so the buoyant force on the balloon decreases as it rises. The balloon floats when it reaches an altitude at which its weight is exactly balanced by the buoyant force.

7. The water level falls. The floating canoe displaced a volume of water V whose weight equaled its own weight. The sunken canoe, however, displaces a volume of water equal to the volume of its aluminum shell, which is smaller than V because aluminum is denser than water.

9. The thermal energy of a solid resides in oscillations of its particles about fixed positions.

11. The molecules themselves occupy volume.

13. Lower.

15. By heating it gradually; if it is glass, it will sag slowly, but this will not occur if it is a crystalline solid.

17. The kitchen will warm up because the refrigerator exhausts more heat than it absorbs. Leaving its door open means that it will run continuously and hence add even more heat to the kitchen.

19. The highest temperature that water can have while remaining liquid at atmospheric pressure is its boiling point. Increasing the rate of heat supply thus increases the amount of steam produced without changing the temperature of the boiling water.

21. More.

23. The waste heat produced, which is inevitable according to the second law of thermodynamics.

CHAPTER 4   PROBLEMS

1. $V = (10)(5)(50)$ cm^3 = 2500 cm^3; $d = m/V$ = 0.13 g/cm^3 = 130 kg/m^3.

3. The density of gold is 19 g/cm^3, so 50 g of gold has a volume of $V = m/d$ = 2.63 cm^3. Hence the bracelet is not pure gold.

5. Mercury is 13.6 times denser than water, hence the water column would be 13.6 × 76 cm = 1034 cm = 10.34 m high.

7. $F = pA = p_{atm}\pi r^2$ = 127 N.

9. The volume of water whose mass is 60 kg is 60 kg/(10^3 kg/m^3) = 0.06 m^3. By Archimedes' principle, the raft rises by a height h such that its submerged volume decreases by 0.06 m^3 when the woman dives off. Hence h = 0.06 m^3/(3 m)(2 m) = 0.01 m = 1 cm.

11. $w = w_{ice} + w_{woman} = Ahd_{ice}g + m_{woman}g = Ahd_{water}g$, $A = m_{woman}/h(d_{water} - d_{ice})$ = 8.9 m^2.

13. (a) $V_2 = p_1 V_1/p_2$ = 333 cm^3. (b) T_1 = 273 K, T_2 = 546 K, $V_2 = V_1 T_2/T_1$ = 2000 cm^3.

15. T_1 = 293 K, $T_2 = T_1 V_2/V_1$ = 586 K = 313°C.

17. The pressure doubles because doubling the number of molecules present doubles the number of molecular collisions per second with the walls of the tank.

19. T = 27°C = 300 K. Since the average energy is proportional to the absolute temperature, doubling the energy doubles the temperature to 600 K = 327°C.

21. The heat of vaporization of water is 2260 kJ/kg and (80 kg) (4.19 kJ/kg) is lost by the water in going from 100°C to 20°C, for a total of 2595 kJ.

23. The heat lost per hour is (0.12 kJ/s)(3600 s) = 432 kJ/h. The mass of sweat per hour is (432 kJ/h)/(2430 kJ/kg) = 0.178 kg = 178 g.

25. An engine operating between T_1 = 473 K and T_2 = 323 K has a maximum efficiency of $1 - T_2/T_1$ = 0.317 = 31.7%.

CHAPTER 5   QUESTIONS

1. Experiments show that every charge is either attracted or repelled by a + or a − charge; a charge that is attracted by a + charge is always repelled by a − charge, and vice versa; every charge obeys Coulomb's law when brought near a known charge; and so forth. Since all electrical phenomena can be accounted for on the basis of two kinds of charge only, there is no reason to suppose any other kind of charge exists.

3. Electric fields may be attractive or repulsive, while gravitational fields are always attractive. Electric fields may be created or destroyed, while gravitational fields are present whenever mass is present. Electric fields affect only certain objects, while gravitational fields affect everything with mass.

5. No; yes.

7. Metals are good electrical conductors, nonmetals good electrical insulators. Liquids may be either. Gases are good insulators if un-ionized. Solids that are good electrical conductors are good heat conductors, and vice versa.

9. The movement of electricity in air involves the motion of both positive and negative ions in opposite directions, but in a copper wire only electrons contribute to the current.

11. Energy.

13. With a single wire, charge would be permanently transferred from one end to the other, and soon so large a charge separation would occur that the electric field that produced the current would be canceled out. With two wires, charge can be sent on a round trip, so to speak, and a net flow of energy from one place to another can occur without a net transfer of charge.

15. Either pole of the magnet attracts opposite poles within the iron, leading to a net attractive force since these poles line up facing the external magnet.

17. At a given point a test body free to move travels along a line of force, by definition, and it can travel in only one direction at that point.

19. 0° or 180°; 90°.

21. The magnetic flux through the loop undergoes both an increase and a decrease in each half of a complete rotation.

23. With direct current, the coil rotates in the magnetic field until it is in equilibrium. With alternating current, the coil oscillates back and forth.

25. When the connection is made, a momentary current will occur in the secondary winding as the current in the primary builds up to its final value. Afterward, since the primary current will be constant and hence its magnetic field will not change, there will be no current in the secondary.

CHAPTER 5 PROBLEMS

1. (a) $F = KQ_1Q_2/d^2 = 9 \times 10^{-3}$ N; the force is repulsive. (b) The force would also be 9×10^{-3} N but would be attractive.

3. (a) 0.00022 N. (b) 0.004 N. (c) 0.018 N. (d) 0.001 N.

5. $r = \sqrt{KQ_AQ_B/F} = 0.01$ m = 1 cm.

7. When the forces balance, $Gm_em_m/d^2 = KQ^2/d^2$ and so $Q = \sqrt{Gm_em_m/K} = 5.7 \times 10^{13}$ C.

9. The electric force exceeds the gravitational force for all distances.

11. A current of 1 A means a flow of $1/e$ electrons/s, which is 6.25×10^{18} electrons/s. The average speed of the electrons is therefore $(6.25 \times 10^{18}$ electrons/s)$/(10^{20}$ electrons/cm) = 6.25×10^{-2} cm/s = 6.25×10^{-4} m/s.

13. $I = V/R = 3$ A = 3 C/s.

15. (a) $I = P/V = 0.625$ A.   (b) $R = V/I = 192$ Ω.   (c) $P = 75$ W.

17. $P = IV = 3600$ W; 36 bulbs.

19. (a) $I = P/V = 7.4 \times 10^{-5}$ A. (b) $Q = 1.5$ C/s $\times 3600$ s = 5400 C; $W = QV = 7290$ J; $t = W/P = 7.29 \times 10^3$ J/10^{-4} W = 7.29×10^7 s = 844 days = 2.3 years since 1 day = 86,400 s and 1 year = 365 days.

21. The heat needed is (4.19 kJ/kg·°C)(60°C) = 251 kJ. Since 1 kWh = (1 kW)(3600 s) = 3600 kJ, 251 kJ = 0.0697 kWh. At 6¢/kWh, the cost is 0.4¢.

CHAPTER 6 QUESTIONS

1. Sound travels fastest in solids because their constituent particles are more tightly bound together than those of liquids and gases. Sound travels slowest in gases because their molecules only interact during random collisions.

3. All types of waves can be refracted. Refraction occurs when a wave passes at an oblique angle from one region to another in which its speed is different.

5. The wave energy "missing" at locations of destructive interference supplements the normal wave energy at locations of constructive interference to give a greater amplitude there than if no interference occurred. The total energy remains the same as it would be without interference, but is differently distributed.

7. The pitch change is too small to be detected when the speed of relative motion is a small percentage of the speed of sound.

9. When light is absorbed, the absorbing material is heated.

11. The electric and magnetic fields of an electromagnetic wave are perpendicular to each other and to the direction of propagation.

13. Blue stars have the highest temperature, red stars the lowest.

15. The mirror must be half your own height. It does not matter how far away you are.

19. The flashes of light are the result of dispersion. In red light the flashes would be red only.

21. The wavelengths in visible light are very small relative to the size of a building, whereas those in radio waves are more nearly comparable.

CHAPTER 6 PROBLEMS

1. Sound takes $t = d/v = 30$ m/(340 m/s) = 0.088 s to travel 30 m but radio waves take only 5×10^6 m/$(3 \times 10^8$ m/s) = 0.017 s to travel 5000 km.

3. The distance of the man from the spike is $d = v_st_1 = 680$ m, where $v_s = 340$ m/s is the speed of sound in air. Hence the speed of sound v in the rail is $v = d/t_2 = 680$ m/0.14 s = 4857 m/s.

5. $\lambda = v/f = (340$ m/s)/1044 Hz = 0.326 m. Hence there are $d/\lambda = 10$ m/0.326 m = 31 waves in a wavetrain 10 m long, which means that the string vibrates 31 times while its sound travels 10 m.

7. $f = v/\lambda = (340$ m/s)/0.25 m = 1360 Hz.

9. $\lambda = v/f = 137$ m.

CHAPTER 7 QUESTIONS

1. Nearly all the mass of an atom is located in its small central nucleus. Its positive charge is also in the nucleus. The electrons that carry the atom's negative charge move about the nucleus a relatively large distance away.

3. (a) This statement is no longer exact, since it does not take into account the conversion of mass into energy and energy into mass. A correct statement would be that the total amount of energy plus mass energy in the universe is constant. *(b)* This statement is still correct. *(c)* The statement is no longer exact. Experiments involving the bombardment of atomic nuclei with other particles have shown that atoms may be changed into other atoms or even be completely decomposed into their constituent neutrons, protons, and electrons. A correct statement would be that atoms are indivisible and indestructible by ordinary chemical or physical means. *(d)* This statement is no longer exact, since experiments have shown that isotopes, which are atoms of an element having different atomic masses, exist. A correct statement would be that all atoms of any one element have the same number of protons in their nuclei and the same number of electrons in their electron shells.

5. 3p, 3n; 6p, 7n; 15p, 16n; 40p, 54n.

7. The limited range of the strong interaction.

9. Radium is considered an element because its spontaneous decomposition into radon and helium cannot be affected by ordinary chemical or physical means, nor can radon and helium be combined to form radium.

11. The chief difference is that in fission heavy nuclei split into lighter ones, while in fusion light nuclei join to form heavier ones. The chief similarity is that in both processes mass is converted into energy.

13. Collisions with the nuclei of the moderator slow the fast neutrons produced in fission. This is desirable because ^{235}U undergoes fission more readily when struck by slow neutrons than by fast ones, hence the presence of a moderator promotes a chain reaction when uranium is the fuel.

15. Both are neutral electrically. The neutron is associated with both the strong and weak nuclear interactions, the neutrino with the weak interaction only. The neutron has mass, the neutrino does not. Both have antiparticles. The neutrino is stable, the neutron beta-decays in free space into a proton, an electron, and a neutrino.

17. Leptons are not subject to the strong interaction and are point particles with no detectable size. Hadrons are subject to the strong interaction, have definite sizes, and apparently consist of various combinations of quarks.

19. No; it is possible that there is a reason why quarks cannot exist except in combination with each other as hadrons.

CHAPTER 7   PROBLEMS

1. $KE = \frac{1}{2}mv^2 = (\frac{1}{2})(9.1 \times 10^{-31} \text{ kg})(10^6 \text{ m/s})^2 = 4.55 \times 10^{-19}$ J. Since $1 \text{ eV} = 1.6 \times 10^{-19}$ J, this energy is equal to 2.84 eV.

3. $1 \text{ eV} = 1.6 \times 10^{-19}$ J, so $26 \text{ eV} = 4.16 \times 10^{-18}$ J. Since $KE = \frac{1}{2}mv^2$, $v = \sqrt{2KE/m} = 3.02 \times 10^6$ m/s.

5. $(0.7553)(34.97 \text{ u}) + (0.2447)(36.97 \text{ u}) = 35.46$ u.

7. 92; 233; uranium.

9. *(a)* A nucleus emits an electron when it contains too many neutrons to be stable, and it emits a positron when it contains too many protons. *(b)* $^{14}_{8}$O emits a positron and $^{19}_{8}$O emits an electron.

11. 0.5 kg; 0.125 kg; radon and helium.

13. $2m_H + 2m_n = 4.0330$ u so the mass difference is $0.0304 \text{ u} = 28.3$ MeV. There are four nucleons in $^4_2$He, hence the binding energy per nucleon is 7.1 MeV.

15. $m_p + m_e = 1.0078$ u. The difference between this and m_n is $0.009 \text{ u} = 0.8$ MeV, which is less than the observed binding energies per nucleon in stable nuclei. Hence neutrons do not decay inside nonradioactive nuclei.

17. *(a)* No. *(b)* $(F_{elec}/F_{grav}) = (Ke^2/r^2)/(Gm^2/r^2) = Ke^2/Gm^2 = 1.24 \times 10^{36}$. *(c)* This ratio is independent of how far apart the protons are since both electric and gravitational forces are proportional to $1/r^2$.

CHAPTER 8   QUESTIONS

1. Electrons possess mass, while photons do not. Electrons possess charge, while photons do not. Electrons may be stationary or move with speeds of up to almost the speed of light, while photons always travel with the speed of light. Electrons are constituents of ordinary matter, while photons are not. The energy of a photon depends upon its frequency, while that of an electron depends upon its speed.

3. *(a)* Interference and diffraction phenomena and agreement with the electromagnetic theory of light argue for a wave nature, whereas the photoelectric effect and the nature of line spectra argue for a particle nature. *(b)* Diffraction and interference are much easier to demonstrate than such quantum phenomena as the photoelectric effect.

5. No.

7. The proton's KE may be less than, equal to, or more than the photon energy, depending upon what the wavelength is.

9. *(a)* An absorption line spectrum, since the continuous spectrum emitted by the sun must pass through the cooler solar atmosphere. *(b)* A continuous emission spectrum. *(c)* An emission line spectrum. *(d)* An absorption line spectrum.

11. The Bohr theory assumes that the position and velocity of each electron in an atom may be definitely known at the same time, which is prohibited by the uncertainty principle.

13. The light waves from a laser are coherent; that is, they are exactly in step with one another.

15. The results of quantum mechanics are in better quantitative

agreement with experiment than those of the Bohr theory and can be applied to a greater variety of situations.
17. When their spins are opposite.

CHAPTER 8 PROBLEMS

1. $hf = 1.3 \times 10^{-17}$ J; $hf = 1.3 \times 10^{-28}$ J.
3. 3 photons.
5. The frequency corresponding to a wavelength of 5.5×10^{-7} m is $f = c/\lambda = (3 \times 10^8$ m/s$)/5.5 \times 10^{-7}$ m $= 5.45 \times 10^{14}$ s^{-1}, so $hf = 6.63 \times 10^{-34}$ J-s $\times 5.45 \times 10^{14}$ s$^{-1} = 3.61 \times 10^{-19}$ J. Hence there are $(1400$ J/m^2-s$)/(3.61 \times 10^{-19}$ J/photon$) = 3.88 \times 10^{21}$ photons/m^2-s reaching the earth from the sun.
7. (a) $E = hf$, so $f = E/h = 4 \times 10^{-19}$ J/6.63×10^{-34} J-s $= 6.03 \times 10^{14}$ s$^{-1} = 6.03 \times 10^{14}$ Hz. (b) $f = c/\lambda = (3 \times 10^8$ m/s$)/2 \times 10^{-7}$ m $= 1.5 \times 10^{15}$ Hz. The energy of a photon of light of this frequency is $E = hf = 6.63 \times 10^{-34}$ J-s $\times 1.5 \times 10^{15}$ s$^{-1} = 9.95 \times 10^{-19}$ J, so the maximum energy of the photoelectrons is $(9.95 - 4) \times 10^{-19}$ J $= 5.95 \times 10^{-19}$ J.
9. $\lambda = h/mv = 3.6 \times 10^{-11}$ m. This wavelength is comparable with atomic dimensions, hence the wave character of the electron will affect any interactions it has with atoms in its path.
11. Since 1 eV $= 1.6 \times 10^{-19}$ J, the energy of each electron is 6.4×10^{-15} J and, from KE $= \frac{1}{2}mv^2$, its speed is

$$v = \sqrt{\frac{2 \times 6.4 \times 10^{-15}\ \text{J}}{9.1 \times 10^{-31}\ \text{kg}}} = 1.19 \times 10^8\ \text{m/s}$$

The corresponding de Broglie wavelength is $\lambda = h/mv = 6.63 \times 10^{-34}$ J-s$/(9.1 \times 10^{-31}$ kg $\times 1.19 \times 10^8$ m/s$) = 6.12 \times 10^{-10}$ m.
13. $r_n = n^2 r_1$, hence $r_5 = (5)^2 r_1 = 1.3 \times 10^{-9}$ m.
15. The centripetal force mv^2/r on the electron is provided by the electrical attraction Ke^2/r^2 of the hydrogen nucleus. Hence $mv^2/r = Ke^2/r^2$ and $v = \sqrt{Ke^2/mr}$. In the $n = 1$ orbit, $r = 5.3 \times 10^{-11}$ m, so

$$v = \sqrt{\frac{9 \times 10^9 (1.6 \times 10^{-19})^2}{9.1 \times 10^{-31} \times 5.3 \times 10^{-11}}}\ \text{m/s} = 2.19 \times 10^6\ \text{m/s}$$

CHAPTER 9 QUESTIONS

1. (a) The change from water to ice is a physical change because chemically the substance remains the same; the only differences between ice and water are in their physical properties. (b) The change from iron to rust is a chemical change because the chemical compositions of the two substances are different.
3. Homogeneous: carbon dioxide gas, solid carbon dioxide, iron, rust, air, oxygen, salt.
5. Sodium is a very active metal, and so it combines readily, whereas platinum is highly inactive, and therefore does not tend to combine at all.
7. (a) Solid. (b) 2. (c) Slightly soluble. (d) HAt. (e) KAt, CaAt$_2$. (f) Less stable.
9. Both F and Cl atoms lack one electron of having closed outer shells.
11. Electrons are liberated from metals illuminated by light more easily than from nonmetals because the outer electrons of metal atoms are less tightly bound, which is also the reason they tend to form positive ions. Electrons are most readily liberated from metals in Group I of the periodic table.
13. The two isotopes of chlorine are identical in atomic structure except for a difference in the number of neutrons in their respective nuclei. Since their electron structures are the same, the chemical behavior of the two isotopes is the same.
15. A chlorine ion has a closed outer shell, whereas a chlorine atom lacks an electron of having a closed outer shell.
17. Both are ionic compounds.
19. Inert gas atoms contain only closed outer shells and so cannot accommodate other electrons, as would occur in covalent bonding.
21. A maximum of two electrons can exist in the first shell of an atom, and so only two H atoms can join together at a time. A maximum of eight electrons can exist in the second shell of an atom, so there is no limit to the number of Li atoms that can join together to form an array of atoms; as a result lithium is a metallic solid under ordinary conditions, while hydrogen is a diatomic gas.
23. (a) The Li atom is larger because the effective nuclear charge on its outer electron is less than that on the outer electrons of the F atom. (b) The Na atom is larger because it has an additional electron shell. (c) The Cl atom is larger because it has an additional electron shell. (d) The Na atom is larger for the same reason as in (a) relative to the Si atom.
25. These formulas represent the ratios in which the atoms of the various elements are present in the respective compounds. They do not provide information on the constitutions of the individual molecules or crystals, on the physical properties of the compounds, or on how to prepare the compounds.

CHAPTER 9 PROBLEMS

1. $+2e$; relatively easy.
3. BaI$_2$; NH$_4$ClO$_3$; SnCrO$_4$; LiPO$_4$.

5. Barium hydride; lithium phosphate; lead(II) oxide; copper(II) bromide; potassium cyanide.

7. *a, c, d, f.*

9. $SO_3 + H_2O \rightarrow H_2SO_4$

11. $2Na + 2H_2O \rightarrow 2NaOH + H_2$

13. $2Al + 3Cl_2 \rightarrow 2AlCl_3$

15. $2Al + 6HCl \rightarrow 3H_2 + 2AlCl_3$

17. $2C_2H_2 + 5O_2 \rightarrow 4CO_2 + 2H_2O$

CHAPTER 10 QUESTIONS

1. *(a)* Ionic, NaCl; covalent, diamond; van der Waals, ice; metallic, copper. *(b)* In each case the bonding is due to electric forces. *(c)* Ions; atoms; molecules; ions.

3. These forces are too weak to hold inert gas atoms together to form molecules against the forces exerted during collisions in the gaseous state.

5. Ca^{2+}, F^-; K^+, I^-.

7. The molecules in gases are so far apart that they do not interact with one another in the way a solvent and solute interact in liquid solutions. Hence gas molecules of different kinds can be mixed in any proportions.

9. A solution of an electrolyte conducts electricity, while a solution of a nonelectrolyte does not.

11. *(a)* When Ag^+ is added to a solution containing Cl^-, AgCl is precipitated, but nothing happens if Ag^+ is added to a solution of NO_3^- since $AgNO_3$ is soluble. *(b)* When Cl^- is added to a solution containing Ag^+, AgCl is precipitated, but nothing happens if Cl^- is added to a solution of Na^+ since NaCl is soluble. *(c)* Cu^{2+} is blue in color, while Ca^{2+} is colorless.

13. NaCl will precipitate out since its solubility is less than that of KCl whereas the solubilities of $NaNO_3$ and KNO_3 are greater than that of KCl. (KCl is the less soluble of the two initial compounds.)

15. 3; 10.

17. Water dissociates to a very small extent into H^+ and OH^- ions, hence it is both a weak acid and a weak base.

19. HBr is a strong acid because, like HCl, it is completely dissociated into ions in solution.

21. Dissolve in water and heat. If *(a)*, ammonia will be evolved, and if *(b)*, carbon dioxide will be evolved.

23. Basic, because NaOH is a strong base and so dissociates to a greater extent than the weak acid H_2S.

CHAPTER 10 PROBLEMS

1. The ionic equation is $K^+ + OH^- + H^+ + NO_3^- \rightarrow H_2O + K^+ + NO_3^-$. The actual chemical change is the combination of H^+ and OH^- to form H_2O.

3. *(a)* Calcium chloride, $CaCl_2$. *(b)* $2HCl + Ca(OH)_2 \rightarrow CaCl_2 + 2H_2O$.

5. *(a)* $3Na^+ + BO_3^{3-} + 3H^+ + 3Cl^- \rightarrow H_3BO_3 + 3Na^+ + 3Cl^-$. *(b)* Basic, because H_3BO_3 dissociates less than NaOH.

7. Add a strong acid, for instance HCl: $2Na^+ + S^{--} + 2H^+ + 2Cl^- \rightarrow H_2S + 2Na^+ + 2Cl^-$.

CHAPTER 11 QUESTIONS

1. Exothermic: *a, b, e, f.*

3. In an atomic-bomb explosion, the liberated energy comes from rearrangements of particles within atomic nuclei, whereas in a dynamite explosion the liberated energy comes from rearrangements within the electron clouds of atoms.

5. Graphite is more stable under ordinary conditions because its combustion evolves less energy. Hence diamonds must have been formed under conditions different from those corresponding to room temperature and atmospheric pressure; in fact, they are formed in the earth's interior where the temperature and pressure are both very high.

7. *(a)* The explosion of dynamite; the precipitation of AgCl when solutions containing Ag^+ and Cl^- are mixed. *(b)* The rusting of iron; the formation of ammonia gas from a solution of NH_4OH.

9. At room temperature few of the molecules will have energies as great as the activation energy, and since only these few molecules can react, the process is a slow one.

11. When one of the products of a reaction leaves the system, the reaction must go to completion since the reverse reaction cannot then occur. A reaction in a liquid will go to completion if one of the products is *(a)* a gas which escapes; *(b)* an insoluble precipitate; or *(c)* composed of molecules that do not dissociate when the reaction involves ions.

13. *(a)* Increased, because the greater the gas pressure, the more of it dissolves. *(b)* Decreased, because the solubility of gases decreases with increasing temperature. *(c)* Decreased, because KOH is a strong base. *(d)* Increased, because removing S^{2-} ions by the precipitation of Ag_2S reduces the rate at which H_2S leaves the solution without affecting the rate at which H_2S enters it.

15. Decrease the yield because the reaction is exothermic; increase the yield because in the reaction three molecules combine to form only two; use a catalyst.

17. An element that loses electrons in a reaction is oxidized, and one that gains electrons is reduced. Hence Zn, Fe, Br^-, and Fe^{2+} are oxidized, and Cu^{2+}, H^+, and Cl_2 are reduced.

19. Na; Al; I^-; Cl; Hg^{2+}.

21. To show that magnesium is a better reducing agent than hydrogen, it may be placed in an acid solution. Hydrogen gas is evolved, meaning that the magnesium has reduced hydrogen ions in the solution.

23. During electrolysis, electric energy is converted to chemical energy (that is, electron potential energy). This energy change is reversed in batteries.

25. Electrolysis of water in the electrolyte.

27. $2Fe_2O_3 + 3C \rightarrow 4Fe + 3CO_2$.

CHAPTER 11 PROBLEMS

1. The atomic mass of U is 238 g/mol, so 10 mol has a mass of 2.38 kg. The number of atoms is $(10 \text{ mol})(6.02 \times 10^{23} \text{ atoms/mol}) = 6.02 \times 10^{24}$ atoms since 1 formula unit = 1 atom of U here.

3. $2Fe = 111.70$ u and $3O = 48.00$ u, so the mass of 1 mole of Fe_2O_3 is 159.70 g and the mass of 2 moles is 319.40 g.

5. The formula mass of glucose is 180.16 g/mol and 500 kg = 5×10^5 g, hence the number of moles is 5×10^5 g/(180.16 g/mol) = 2775 mol.

7. Each mole of $MgAl_2O_4$ contains 2 mol of Al, hence 5 mol contains 10 mol of Al.

9. $\frac{1}{2}$ mol of N_2 and $1\frac{1}{2}$ mol of H_2.

11. (a) One mol of Na and 1 mol of Cl combine to form 1 mol of NaCl, so the number of moles is the same for each substance. The number of moles of Na in 50 g is 50 g/(22.99 g/mol) = 2.17 mol. The mass of 2.17 mol of Cl is (2.17 mol)(35.46 g/mol) = 77 g. (b) The mass of 2.17 mol of NaCl is 50 g + 77 g = 127 g.

13. The number of moles in 200 g of K is 200 g/(39.1 g/mol) = 5.12 mol. In K_2S there is 1 mol of S for each 2 mol of K, hence the number of moles of S is half the number of moles of K or 2.56 mol. The corresponding mass of S is (2.56 mol)(32.06 g/mol) = 82 g.

15. Since 120 ml = 0.12 l, the number of moles of HCl is (2 mol/l)(0.12 l) = 0.24 mol.

17. The formula mass of NaCl is 58.45 g/mol, hence 100 g contains 100 g/(58.45 g/mol) = 1.71 mol, and the solution is 1.71 M.

19. A cube has six square faces. The area of a 1-cm square is 1 cm², so the surface area of a 1-cm cube is 6 cm². The area of a 0.5-cm square is (0.5 cm)(0.5 cm) = 0.25 cm², so the surface area of a 0.5-cm is (6)(0.25 cm²) = 1.5 cm². There are eight 0.5-cm cubes in a 1-cm cube, hence the total surface area of the small cubes is (8)(1.5 cm²) = 12 cm². This is twice the area of the large cube, whose mass is the same. Since the speed of a chemical reaction, all else being the same, is proportional to the surface area involved, the eight small cubes should dissolve twice as fast as the one large cube. The time therefore should be 0.5 h.

CHAPTER 12 QUESTIONS

1. There are more carbon compounds than compounds of any other element because of the ability of carbon atoms to form covalent bonds with one another.

3. Covalent bonds that consist of shared electron pairs.

5. In a saturated hydrocarbon, for instance ethane, there is only a single bond between adjacent carbon atoms. In an unsaturated hydrocarbon, for instance ethylene, adjacent carbon atoms are linked by more than one bond. A hydrocarbon derivative is a compound obtained by substituting other atoms or atom groups for some of the hydrogen atoms in hydrocarbon molecules.

7. Double bonds are relatively unstable, yet the benzene ring is a stable structure. Also, the various bonds are all the same length in the benzene ring, and this length is intermediate between that typical of single bonds and that typical of double bonds.

9. Two bonds, so that the structure of CO_2 is O=C=O.

11. C_2H_8 cannot exist because there is no way to have a proper distribution of bonds in such a molecule.

13. One carbon-carbon bond is double.

15. The compound is an aldehyde, namely proprionaldehyde.

17. Trichloroethylene.

19. Esters are nonelectrolytes, while salts in solution are electrolytes. Salts (such as sodium chloride) are crystals in their pure state, while the simpler esters (such as methyl acetate) are liquids or gases.

21. (a) C_2H_5COOH; C_2H_5OH; HCl; $C_3H_5(OH)_3$.
   (b) C_2H_5COOH; HCl.
   (c) C_3H_8; C_2H_4.
   (d) C_2H_5COOH; HCl; C_2H_5OH; $C_3H_5(OH)_3$.
   (e) C_2H_5COOH; HCl.
   (f) C_2H_5OH; $C_3H_5(OH)_3$.

23. The ultimate source is the conversion of hydrogen to helium in thermonuclear reactions in the sun. Solar energy reaches the earth as electromagnetic radiation, which is utilized by plants in photosynthesis to produce carbohydrates. The energy in carbohydrates is liberated in animal respiration.

25. Photosynthesis.

27. Amino acids; some are synthesized by the body, others must be present in food.

CHAPTER 12 PROBLEMS

1. The two isomers are

What might seem to be a third isomer,

is really the first of the above reversed, which is not a true difference.

3.

5.

Normal pentane   Isopentane

Neopentane

7. There are two isomers of bromopropane,

and

CHAPTER 13 QUESTIONS

1. *(a)* In photosynthesis, plants manufacture carbohydrates from atmospheric carbon dioxide and water with oxygen as a by-product. *(b)* By absorbing infrared radiation emitted by the earth, carbon dioxide is an intermediary in the process by which solar energy is transferred to the lower atmosphere and carried around the world by winds.

3. At the tropopause the temperature has decreased to a minimum and is about to increase; at the stratopause it has increased to a maximum and is about to decrease; at the mesopause it has decreased to a minimum and is about to increase.

5. The troposphere is heated largely through the absorption by carbon dioxide and water molecules of infrared radiation emitted by the earth's surface. Because it is heated from below, the temperature of the troposphere decreases with altitude.

7. *(a)* 100 percent. *(b)* The air remains saturated and so the relative humidity remains 100 percent, while the excess water vapor condenses out. *(c)* The relative humidity decreases.

9. On such a night the earth's surface cools by radiation. The air in contact with the surface also cools and may become saturated with water vapor, which then condenses into droplets of liquid water.

11. Stratus clouds are characteristic of a warm front.

13. The dust will increase the amount of scattering of sunlight and so produce exceptionally colorful sunrises and sunsets. Worldwide rainfall will increase. There will be more clouds than usual, and the clouds and dust will reflect more sunlight back into space and so lead to a general cooling of the atmosphere.

15. Winds and ocean currents carry energy around the earth in the forms of warm air and warm water, respectively. Winds are more effective in energy transport than ocean currents.

17. A large amount of heat must be absorbed or lost by a region of the earth's surface before it reaches its final temperature when the rate of arrival of solar energy changes. Since the difference between the rates of energy absorption and energy loss is always small compared with the heat content of the earth's surface, the temperature of the surface cannot change rapidly enough to keep pace with changes in the rate at which solar energy arrives; hence the time lags in seasonal weather conditions.

19. The jet streams occur near the top of the troposphere and flow from west to east.

21. Anticyclonic weather is generally steady with relatively constant temperature, clear skies, and light winds. Cyclonic weather is unsettled with rapid changes in temperature that accompany the passages of cold and warm fronts, cloudy skies, rain, and fairly strong, shifting winds.

23. Cyclonic winds in the northern hemisphere are counterclockwise; hence when you face the wind, the center of low pressure will be on your right. Cyclonic winds in the southern hemisphere are clockwise; hence when you face the wind, the center of low pressure will be on your left.

25. Northwest → west → southwest.

27. Seas and oceans; icecaps and glaciers; groundwater; lakes and rivers; atmospheric moisture.

29. Because their waters must be thoroughly mixed in the course of time to obtain a uniform composition of ions, the seas and oceans of the world cannot be static bodies but must exhibit large-scale currents, both vertical and horizontal.

31. *(a)* The greater the wind velocity, the higher the waves. *(b)*

The longer the period of time during which the wind blows, the higher the waves. (c) The greater the distance (fetch) over which the wind blows across the water, the higher the waves. Each of the above factors cease to have a strong effect on wave height after a certain point; for example, after a day or two the waves will have reached very nearly the maximum height possible for the wind velocity and fetch of a given situation.

33. (a) At first northward with the Gulf Stream, then northeastward with the North Atlantic Drift. (b) At first southward with the Canary Current, then westward and finally northwestward with the North Equatorial Current and the Gulf Stream.

35. When warm moist air from the west blows over the colder California Current, its temperature drops and moisture from the now supersaturated air condenses into tiny droplets to form a fog.

37. The doldrums are at the equator, so it is quite warm there with considerable evaporation of water and thus high humidity. The air flow is largely upward, so surface winds are light and erratic. The rising currents of moist air lead to considerable rainfall.

39. The differences would be smaller.

CHAPTER 14 QUESTIONS

1. A rock is an aggregate of grains of one or more minerals.

3. *Crystal form* refers to the shape of a crystal, which is determined by the pattern in which its constituent particles are linked together. *Cleavage* refers to the tendency, if any, of a crystal to break apart in a regular way, which is determined by the presence of weak bonds in certain directions in its structure.

5. Igneous, metamorphic, and sedimentary.

7. To have the amorphous structure of a liquid, obsidian must have solidified so rapidly that crystals had no chance to develop. This can only have occurred by the cooling of a lava flow at the earth's surface.

9. Diorite is coarse-grained and andesite is fine-grained.

11. The density increases because the pressures under which metamorphism occurs lead to more compact rearrangements of the atoms in the various minerals.

13. (a) Foliation. (b) Foliation results from the growth of platy or needlelike crystals along planes of movement in a rock produced by directed pressure (stress).

15. Chert consists largely of microscopic quartz crystals and hence is hard and durable.

17. (a) Granite, which contains only a small proportion of ferromagnesian material, is light in color, while gabbro, with much ferromagnesian material, is dark. (b) Limestone effervesces readily in acid, unlike basalt. (c) Schist is foliated, while diorite is not.

19. Rhyolite; slate; shale.

21. (a) Hard: quartzite (metamorphic)
chert (sedimentary)

    (b) Moderately hard: limestone (sedimentary)
gneiss (metamorphic)
andesite (igneouus)
marble (metamorphic)

    (c) Soft: chalk (sedimentary)
shale (sedimentary)

23. P and S waves both can travel through a solid medium, but only P waves can travel through a liquid. P waves are longitudinal and, like sound waves, consist of pressure fluctuations; S waves are transverse and are analogous to waves in a stretched string. P waves are faster than S waves in the same medium.

25. Because travel times depend only on distance but not on location, any variations in the material of the interior can only occur along a radius and not transversely. Thus the division of the interior into an inner core, an outer core, and a mantle, which form concentric shells, is consistent with the above observation; but a difference between the material in, say, the northern and southern hemispheres is ruled out.

27. The presence of a liquid core affects both S and P waves: the S waves cannot travel through it at all, and the P waves travel with a different speed than in the mantle. The latter fact means that P waves entering the core change their directions due to refraction, as shown in Fig. 14-12. As a result, a shadow zone occurs in a band around the earth in which P waves are not found, and there is a still larger region in which S waves are absent since they are absorbed in the core.

29. The core's radius is approximately half the radius of the earth.

31. (a) Measurements made in mines and wells indicate that temperature increases with depth. (b) Molten rock from the interior emerges from volcanoes. (c) The outer core is liquid, which means that it must be at a high temperature.

33. Ferromagnetic materials lose their magnetic properties at high temperatures, and sufficiently high temperatures exist throughout all of the earth's interior except near the surface of the crust to cause such a loss. Also, both the direction and strength of the field are observed to vary, and in fact the field has reversed its direction many times in the past, which cannot be reconciled with the notion of a permanent magnet in the interior.

CHAPTER 15 QUESTIONS

1. The rock debris produced by weathering is the principal constituent of soil.

3. Marble exposed to the atmosphere weathers fairly readily because its calcite content is soluble in rainwater that contains dissolved carbon dioxide. Slate consists largely of clay minerals that have metamorphosed to white mica, which is nearly as resistant to weathering as quartz.

5. The ultimate source of the energy that goes into erosion is the sun. Solar energy evaporates surface water, some of which subsequently falls as rain and snow on high ground. The potential energy of the latter water turns into kinetic energy as it flows downhill, and some of the kinetic energy becomes work done in eroding landscapes along its path.

7. The maximum depth to which streams can erode a landscape is sea level, since streams flow downhill into the seas and oceans. Glacial erosion is not limited in this way, and glaciers can wear away landscapes to depths well below sea level.

9. A glacier forms when the average annual snowfall in a region exceeds the annual loss by evaporation and melting.

11. Stones and boulders are embedded in glaciers, some of which are hard enough to erode the bedrock.

13. Quartz is resistant to chemical attack and so survives weathering and erosion. Feldspar, the most common mineral, is converted into clay minerals by the carbonic acid of surface waters.

15. *(a)* Precipitate from groundwater. *(b)* Stream deposits. *(c)* Sand dunes.

17. *(a)* Basalt, rhyolite, andesite, obsidian. *(b)* Basalt.

19. Such holes were produced by bubbles of gas trapped in lava as it solidified.

21. Volcanic mountains are conical, steepening toward the top, with craters at the summit. The presence of isolated, conical mountains, lava flows, hot springs, geysers, and steam vents, as well as of volcanic rocks, indicates a region where volcanoes had once been active.

23. *(a)* The intruded magma that solidifies to form a pluton is very hot, and thus nearby rocks often undergo thermal metamorphism. *(b)* Near a batholith, because of the greater heat that had to be dissipated in its cooling.

25. Metamorphic rocks are foliated because, under heat and pressure, their mineral grains grow in long needles or thin flakes as the rocks are squeezed. The stratification of sedimentary rock, however, arises because the various layers were formed at different times, perhaps from somewhat different materials. In sedimentary rocks the layering is caused by slight variations in color or grain size; in metamorphic rocks the foliation is caused by the alignment of mineral grains.

27. The earth's interior.

29. Both normal and thrust faults produce cliffs called *fault scarps*. A strike-slip fault is often marked by a *rift*, which is a trench or valley caused by erosion of the disintegrated rock produced during the faulting.

31. Erosion.

33. *(a)* The crust is distinguished from the mantle beneath it by a sharp difference in seismic-wave velocity, which suggests a difference in the composition of the minerals involved or in their crystal structures or in both. The lithosphere is distinguished from the asthenosphere beneath it by a difference in their behavior under stress: the lithosphere is rigid whereas the asthenosphere is capable of plastic flow.

(b) The asthenosphere is plastic because its material is close to its melting point under the conditions of temperature and pressure found in that region of the mantle. Above the asthenosphere the temperature is too low and below it the pressure is too high for the material of the mantle to be plastic.

(c) When a large stress is applied over a long period of time, the asthenosphere gradually flows in response to it. When brief, relatively small forces are applied, as is the case with seismic waves, the asthenosphere is rigid enough to transmit them as a solid does.

35. The ocean floors are relatively recent in origin; the oldest sediments date back only about 135 million years. Continental rocks, in contrast, date back as much as 3800 million years. The reason is that, owing to their low density and consequent buoyancy, the continental blocks are not forced down into the mantle in subduction zones but remain as permanent features of the lithosphere plates they are part of. The ocean floors, on the other hand, are continually being destroyed in such zones as new ocean floors are deposited at midocean ridges.

37. If South America and Africa were once joined together, there should be similar geologic formations and fossils of the same kinds at corresponding locations along their respective east and west coasts. This is indeed found for material deposited up to aout 100 million years ago, which is when these continents must have begun to separate.

39. Iceland is less than 70 million years old, much younger than North America, Greenland, and Eurasia, and was formed after the breakup of Laurasia from magma rising through the rift in the Mid-Atlantic Ridge.

41. There is relative motion between the two plates along their boundary; the Pacific plate is moving northwestward relative to the American plate.

43. The boundary of the western Atlantic lithospheric plate is along the western edge of South America, and the Andes are the result of the collision between this plate, which is drifting westward, and the eastern Pacific plate, which is drifting eastward. The eastern edge is not near a plate boundary.

45. 1.9 cm/year.

CHAPTER 16   QUESTIONS

1. *(a)* Deposition of beds *E* and *F* when the region was below sea level. *(b)* Diastrophic movement that produced the fault *JJ'* and the folds in beds *E* and *F*. *(c)* Deposition of bed *D*. *(d)* Intrusion of the granite pluton *G*. *(e)* Erosion that produced the irregular surface *II'*, which is an unconformity. The region must have been elevated above sea level for this erosion to have occurred. *(f)* The region subsided below sea level and beds *A, B,* and *C* were deposited. *(g)* Intrusion of the granite pluton *H*. *(h)* Raising of the region above sea level again and the renewed erosion of the surface.

3. The original sedimentary material will have been converted into such metamorphic rocks as slate, schist, and marble, which will be exposed by the subsequent erosion. The outcrops of metamorphic rocks will be intruded by igneous rocks — granite batholiths and dikes of various kinds. Unconformities will occur where subsequent stream and lake sediments are deposited. Thin sandstone beds, interstratified with shale and conglomerate and exhibiting cross-bedding, will predominate in the overlying sedimentary rocks.

5. The isotope must be found in at least one of the minerals in the rock, and it must have a half-life that is roughly comparable with the age of the rock.

7. The ratio between the radiocarbon and ordinary carbon contents of all living things is the same. When a plant or animal dies, its radiocarbon content decreases at a fixed rate. Hence the ratio between the radiocarbon and ordinary carbon contents of an ancient specimen of organic origin will reveal its age.

9. *(a)* Actual plant or animal tissues, usually of a hard nature such as teeth, bones, hair, and shells. Entire insects have been found preserved in amber. *(b)* Plant tissues that have become coal through partial decay but which retain their original forms. *(c)* Tissues that have been replaced by material (such as silica) deposited from groundwater; petrified wood is an example. Sometimes a porous tissue such as bone will have its pore spaces filled with a deposited mineral. *(d)* Impressions that remain in a rock of plant or animal structures that have themselves disappeared. *(e)* Footprints, wormholes, or other cavities produced by animals in soft ground that have later filled with a different material and so can be distinguished today.

11. Igneous rocks have hardened from a molten state, and no fossil could survive such temperatures. Metamorphic rocks have been altered under conditions of heat and pressure severe enough to distort or destroy most fossils.

13. Abundant fossils exist in rocks belonging to the Phanerozoic eon, which permits tracing the evolution of living things during this span of time. Few fossils exist from the Cryptozoic eon,

making it difficult to determine the forms of life that were present then and how they developed.

15. Precambrian geologic activity must have been similar to that of today.

17. Precambrian sedimentary rocks contain few fossils, whereas later sedimentary rocks usually contain abundant fossils.

19. Much of the area of the continents must have been near or below sea level during at least part of the Paleozoic since shallow seas must have been widespread on their surfaces then.

21. Mesozoic era; Cenozoic era.

23. Petroleum is thought to have originated in the remains of marine animals and plants which became buried under sedimentary deposits. After bacterial decay in the absence of oxygen, low-temperature chemical reactions produced further modifications. Then complex hydrocarbons were "cracked" under the influence of temperatures of $70-130°C$ to the straight-chain alkane hydrocarbons found in petroleum. When the temperatures were higher, the result was the smaller alkanes that make up natural gas.

25. The shifting of the continents and increases in volcanic activity associated with such shifts led to changes in climate partly because the continents moved to different locations on the globe and partly because volcanic dust at times reduced the amount of sunlight reaching the earth's surface. Another effect of widespread vulcanism is an increase in the carbon dioxide content of the atmosphere, which may increase the acidity of the oceans. Sea level, too, must have changed as a result. The changes in climate, in CO_2 concentration, and in the intensity of sunlight at the surface may well have stressed many living things beyond their ability to survive.

27. Mesozoic era; reptiles.

29. During the Mesozoic era today's continents were joined together so the animal populations (which were largely reptiles) could move freely among them. During the Cenozoic era the continents were split apart, and the evolution of some of the mammals that replaced the reptiles proceeded differently on the various landmasses.

31. The Ice Ages involved the formation of ice sheets that covered large areas of the earth's surface. In the most recent of the Ice Ages there were four major episodes during which ice advanced across the continents, separated by interglacial periods during which the ice retreated poleward. The glacial advances took place during the past 2 million years, that is, the Pleistocene epoch of the Quaternary period of the Cenozoic era. In the latest of the glacial episodes, ice covered much of Canada and northeastern United States and began to recede only about 20,000 years ago.

33. *(a)* Ordovician period of the Paleozoic. *(b)* Early in the

Tertiary period of the Cenozoic. *(c)* The Pleistocene epoch. **35.** When the thick sheet of ice that covered this region melted, the continental block became lighter and its buoyancy provided an upward force that has been raising it toward a level of equilibrium.

CHAPTER 17 QUESTIONS

1. At the north or south pole.
3. The moon's apparent diameter remains constant, and its eastward motion through the sky is uniform.
5. *(a)* Since the earth takes a year to revolve counterclockwise (as seen from above the north pole) around the sun, the sun appears to somebody on the earth to drift eastward relative to the stars through 360° in 365 days. The daily drift is therefore 360°/365 days, which is a little less than 1° per day. *(b)* The moon circles the earth in 27.3 days relative to the stars, hence it travels through 360° in 27.3 days or 13° per day.
7. The Tropic of Cancer is the most northerly latitude in the northern hemisphere at which the sun is ever directly overhead at noon. The Tropic of Capricorn is the corresponding latitude in the southern hemisphere.
9. *(a)* More pronounced. *(b)* 60° and 30°.
11. There is no change with longitude.
13. The times at which the noon sun is directly overhead at the equator are called equinoxes. There are two equinoxes per year, the vernal equinox (about March 21) and the autumnal equinox (about September 23).
15. The sun appears to move in a vertical semicircle from the eastern horizon at dawn through a point directly overhead at noon to the western horizon at sunset.
17. The seasons would occur earlier in each successive year.
19. The length of a degree of latitude varies slightly because the earth is not a perfect sphere, but it is always close to 60 nautical miles. The length of a degree of longitude varies from 0 at the poles to a little over 60 nautical miles at the equator.
21. Since a longitude difference of 15° leads to a time difference of 1 h, 1° of longitude difference is equivalent to a 4-min time difference. The longitude of New York City is 74°W; hence the time difference with respect to GMT is 74 × 4 min = 296 min = 4 h 56 min. Since New York is west of the prime meridian, it is earlier in New York than in Greenwich and the time difference must be subtracted from GMT. Hence local time in New York at 8:00 A.M. GMT is 3:04 A.M.
23. 60°E.
25. 11 A.M.
27. Two weeks.

29. New moon; full moon.
31. Yes; no.
33. The density of a comet is extremely low when it is in the vicinity of the earth, and in a collision most or all of the comet material would simply be absorbed in the upper atmosphere.
35. Stony meteorites resemble ordinary rocks whereas iron ones are conspicuously different; also, stony meteorites are more readily eroded than iron ones.
37. If the earth's magnetic field disappeared, auroras would be less frequent than at present since charged particles passing near the earth would no longer be "captured" by the magnetic field. Also, there would be no tendency for auroras to occur in definite zones centered about the geomagnetic poles.

CHAPTER 18 QUESTIONS

1. *(a)* When viewed over a period of time, a planet will be seen to change its position in the sky relative to the stars. *(b)* Seen through a sufficiently powerful telescope, the planets appear as disks whereas the stars, which are much farther away, appear as points of light.
3. The planets shine because of the sunlight they reflect.
5. Venus is closer to the sun than Mars and hence receives more sunlight to reflect. It is larger than Mars, so the reflecting surface is greater in area. Venus is surrounded by clouds whereas Mars has none, and these clouds constitute a better reflector of sunlight than the Martian surface; the white polar caps on Mars are too small to make much difference in this respect. As a result of all these factors, Venus is not only brighter than Mars but is also at times the brightest object in the sky after the sun and moon.
7. The seasons would be visible, due to the widespread ice and snow of winter and the green of summer vegetation. The seasonal changes in the weather systems of the middle latitudes would be obvious from the cloud patterns.
9. Jupiter; Mercury; Mercury; Pluto.
11. Less: Mercury, Venus, Mars, Pluto. More: Jupiter, Saturn, Uranus, Neptune.
13. Mars, 12.3 h; Jupiter, 4.9 h.
15. The sunlit side of Mercury is too hot and its dark side is too cold for life to exist. Also, Mercury has only a trace of an atmosphere, and it contains only inert gases.
17. Because running water would fill craters with sediments and level their raised rims, the presence of many meteoroid craters means that there has been no running water for a long time on the surface of Mars.
19. *(a)* Jupiter and Uranus. *(b)* Fairly small particles, as in the case of Saturn's rings.

21. Hydrogen and helium.

23. Asteroids follow orbits between those of Mars and Jupiter whereas meteoroid orbits are very much larger in size. In general, asteroids are larger than meteoroids—many asteroids are tens or hundreds of km across, whereas few meteoroids are as much as a meter across.

25. The average density of the moon is 3.3 g/cm³ whereas that of the earth is 5.5 g/cm³. Part of the reason is the smaller total mass of the moon, which reduces the pressures in its interior. However, this factor is not enough to account for the large difference in densities. Hence the moon must have a different composition from that of the earth, perhaps by virtue of a smaller proportion of iron.

27. Because the moon apparently has a more or less uniform density, it probably never was entirely molten as the earth was. If the moon had melted all the way through, its heavier constituents would have become concentrated by gravity in a core with the lighter constituents forming a mantle around it, as in the case of the earth.

29. The maria are approximately circular depressions covered with pulverized rocks. They are apparently lava flows that were broken up by meteorite impacts.

31. No satellite can have been closer to the earth than the distance given by Roche's limit or it would have disintegrated. This sets a lower limit to the size of the moon's orbit in the past.

CHAPTER 19 QUESTIONS

1. More stars appear in the photograph because the exposure time can be long, permitting even faint stars to produce images.

3. Blue, white, yellow, red.

5. The star whose spectral lines are displaced farther to the red is moving away from the earth faster than the other star.

7. The 6000 K temperature of the sun's visible surface suggests that the sun is almost wholly gaseous.

9. The solar spectrum is an absorption one, indicating that the surface layers are cooler than those below. An even stronger argument is that only in the sun's interior could conditions of pressure and temperature occur suitable for energy production by nuclear fusion reactions.

11. The presence of the spectral lines of a particular element in the solar spectrum means that this element must be present in the sun.

13. A helium nucleus has less mass than the total mass of the four hydrogen nuclei (protons) that combine to form it, and the "missing" mass appears as energy.

15. Sunspots appear dark only by comparison with the rest of the photosphere, whose temperature is higher.

17. A direct measurement of a star's mass is only possible when it is a member of a system of two stars that revolve around their common center of mass. The mass of a single main-sequence star can be indirectly inferred from its absolute magnitude by using the mass-luminosity relationship.

19. Stars must be spheres or nearly so because if parts of their surfaces were at different distances from their centers, the resulting pressure differences, due to gravity, would cause the material of the stars to flow until they had spherical or spheroidal (if in rotation) shapes.

21. Black holes, neutron stars, and white dwarfs have the highest densities, and giant stars the lowest.

23. One would begin by measuring the apparent brightnesses and periods of the Cepheid variables. From the known relationship between the period of a Cepheid and its intrinsic brightness, the latter can be computed, and a comparison of the intrinsic and apparent brightnesses then yields the distance of the star and, hence, of the cluster.

25. The surface temperature of a star determines the radiation it emits per unit area, while its intrinsic brightness is a measure of its total radiation; knowing both quantities permits computing the star's surface area and hence its diameter.

27. A star moving toward or away from the earth will show a doppler shift in its spectrum toward the blue or the red end, respectively. A star moving across our line of sight will change its position relative to other stars, as revealed by photographs taken at different times.

29. Such an object must contract owing to gravity, which causes both a rise in temperature and an increase in density. As a result the hydrogen present begins to react to form helium with the release of considerable energy. Thus any object with the mass and composition of the sun must radiate energy like the sun.

31. A star on the main sequence is in an equilibrium condition with its tendency to expand owing to high temperature exactly balanced by its tendency to contract gravitationally. The condition lasts until the star's hydrogen content decreases beyond a certain proportion, which requires a relatively long time compared with its earlier and later phases. Therefore most stars are members of the main sequence simply because this is the longest stage in a star's evolution.

33. A star whose mass is less than about $\frac{1}{10}$ the sun's mass is not able by gravitational contraction to reach a high enough temperature for nuclear reactions in its interior to occur. A star whose mass is more than about 100 times the sun's mass would become so hot as a result of accelerated nuclear reactions that the outward pressure would exceed the inward force of its gravitation, and it would not be stable.

35. *(a)* It is large, heavy, hot, and bright, with prominent hydrogen and helium lines in its spectrum. *(b)* It is small, exceedingly dense, very hot, and dim. *(c)* It is huge, diffuse, cool, and bright. *(d)* It is moderately small with moderate temperature, density, and mass, with a spectrum in which lines of metallic elements are prominent.

37. *(a)* It is very hot. *(b)* Its average density is low. *(c)* Lines of hydrogen and helium are prominent in its spectrum. *(d)* Upper end of main sequence.

39. Main-sequence stars; supernovas.

41. Diagonally downward (since the star's luminosity will decrease) and to the right (since its temperature will decrease).

43. *(a)* A pulsar emits bursts of radio waves at regular intervals. *(b)* Pulsars are believed to be very small, dense stars that consist almost entirely of neutrons. *(c)* Pulsars are believed to originate in supernova explosions.

CHAPTER 20 QUESTIONS

1. No. Stars are concentrated in galaxies that are relatively far apart from one another.

3. The Milky Way is composed of stars in the spiral arms of our galaxy and so defines its central disk. Since the earth is close to the plane of the Milky Way, the sun must be part of the central disk of the galaxy.

5. Their spectra resemble ordinary star spectra, and large telescopes have been able to resolve the outer portions of the largest ones into separate stars.

7. A typical globular cluster is an assembly of hundreds of thousands of Population II stars that are relatively close together. They are found in all galaxies; in spiral galaxies, they are mostly located in the corona outside the central disk and move at high speeds about the galactic center. Since globular clusters are much smaller than galaxies and are always found as members of them, they cannot be considered as being themselves galaxies.

9. Since elliptical galaxies contain only Population II stars, which are very old, they cannot contain much gas and dust since young stars would then be present that formed from this gas and dust.

11. Most of the interstellar gas is located in the spiral arms of the galaxy, and its chief constituent is hydrogen.

13. *(a)* Primary cosmic rays are atomic nuclei and so are electrically charged particles, and moving charged particles experience forces in a magnetic field. *(b)* A charged particle approaching the equatorial regions moves perpendicularly through the lines of the geomagnetic field, which means that the maximum deflecting force is exerted on them. A charged particle approaching near the poles, on the other hand, is not deflected or is little deflected, since it moves parallel or nearly parallel to the lines of the geomagnetic field there.

15. The protons pick up electrons and become hydrogen atoms, while most of the neutrons are absorbed by carbon nuclei to form radiocarbon. Some neutrons escape from the earth entirely, and decay into protons and electrons in space.

17. Hydrogen is by far the most abundant element in the universe.

19. Random thermal motion of ions and electrons in a very hot gas; fast electrons moving in a magnetic field; spectral lines of atoms and molecules.

21. Up to iron, they are formed in the interiors of stars; heavier than iron, in supernova explosions.

23. The gravitational attraction of the matter of the universe retards its expansion.

25. The light reaching us from a distant galaxy reflects the state of the universe long ago. From the different recession velocities of galaxies at different distances away, the rate of change of the expansion velocity of the universe can be established, which permits calculating the time that the expansion started. If the universe is now older than about 13 billion years, its rate of expansion is not slowing down enough for it ever to stop, so the universe cannot in that case be cyclic.

27. A quasar appears in a telescope as a point of light, as a star does, but is a far more powerful source of radio waves than any known star. Quasar spectra show large red shifts, which suggests that they are far away and emit energy at prodigious rates. The outputs of quasars sometimes change in periods of a few weeks, so they must be small, which makes their energy rates even harder to account for.

29. The young sun was much larger than it is today, perhaps as far across as the entire present solar system.

31. Fire, in the sense that the earth will probably vaporize when the sun swells into a red giant.

33. Other stars are all very far away; planets are small in size; planets are dim objects because they shine by reflected light.

THE ELEMENTS

Atomic number	Element	Symbol	Atomic mass*	Atomic number	Element	Symbol	Atomic mass*
1	Hydrogen	H	1.008	28	Nickel	Ni	58.70
2	Helium	He	4.003	29	Copper	Cu	63.54
3	Lithium	Li	6.941	30	Zinc	Zn	65.38
4	Beryllium	Be	9.012	31	Gallium	Ga	69.72
5	Boron	B	10.81	32	Germanium	Ge	72.59
6	Carbon	C	12.01	33	Arsenic	As	74.92
7	Nitrogen	N	14.01	34	Selenium	Se	78.96
8	Oxygen	O	16.00	35	Bromine	Br	79.90
9	Fluorine	F	19.00	36	Krypton	Kr	83.80
10	Neon	Ne	20.18	37	Rubidium	Rb	85.47
11	Sodium	Na	22.99	38	Strontium	Sr	87.62
12	Magnesium	Mg	24.31	39	Yttrium	Y	88.91
13	Aluminum	Al	26.98	40	Zirconium	Zr	91.22
14	Silicon	Si	28.09	41	Niobium	Nb	92.91
15	Phosphorus	P	30.97	42	Molybdenum	Mo	95.94
16	Sulfur	S	32.06	43	Technetium	Tc	(97)
17	Chlorine	Cl	35.45	44	Ruthenium	Ru	101.1
18	Argon	Ar	39.95	45	Rhodium	Rh	102.9
19	Potassium	K	39.10	46	Palladium	Pd	106.4
20	Calcium	Ca	40.08	47	Silver	Ag	107.9
21	Scandium	Sc	44.96	48	Cadmium	Cd	112.4
22	Titanium	Ti	47.90	49	Indium	In	114.8
23	Vanadium	V	50.94	50	Tin	Sn	118.7
24	Chromium	Cr	52.00	51	Antimony	Sb	121.8
25	Manganese	Mn	54.94	52	Tellurium	Te	127.6
26	Iron	Fe	55.85	53	Iodine	I	126.9
27	Cobalt	Co	58.93	54	Xenon	Xe	131.3

(Continued)

Atomic number	Element	Symbol	Atomic mass*	Atomic number	Element	Symbol	Atomic mass*
55	Cesium	Cs	132.9	81	Thallium	Tl	204.4
56	Barium	Ba	137.3	82	Lead	Pb	207.2
57	Lanthanum	La	138.9	83	Bismuth	Bi	209.0
58	Cerium	Ce	140.1	84	Polonium	Po	(209)
59	Praseodymium	Pr	140.9	85	Astatine	At	(210)
60	Neodymium	Nd	144.2	86	Radon	Rn	(222)
61	Promethium	Pm	(145)	87	Francium	Fr	(223)
62	Samarium	Sm	150.4	88	Radium	Ra	226.0
63	Europium	Eu	152.0	89	Actinium	Ac	(227)
64	Gadolinium	Gd	157.3	90	Thorium	Th	232.0
65	Terbium	Tb	158.9	91	Protactinium	Pa	231.0
66	Dysprosium	Dy	162.5	92	Uranium	U	238.0
67	Holmium	Ho	164.9	93	Neptunium	Np	(237)
68	Erbium	Er	167.3	94	Plutonium	Pu	(244)
69	Thulium	Tm	168.9	95	Americium	Am	(243)
70	Ytterbium	Yb	173.0	96	Curium	Cm	(247)
71	Lutetium	Lu	175.0	97	Berkelium	Bk	(247)
72	Hafnium	Hf	178.5	98	Californium	Cf	(251)
73	Tantalum	Ta	180.9	99	Einsteinium	Es	(254)
74	Tungsten	W	183.9	100	Fermium	Fm	(257)
75	Rhenium	Re	186.2	101	Mendelevium	Md	(258)
76	Osmium	Os	190.2	102	Nobelium	No	(255)
77	Iridium	Ir	192.2	103	Lawrencium	Lr	(260)
78	Platinum	Pt	195.1	104	Rutherfordium	Rf	(257)
79	Gold	Au	197.0	105	Hahnium	Ha	(260)
80	Mercury	Hg	200.6				

* Masses in parentheses are those of the most stable isotopes of the elements.

MATH REFRESHER

Some familiarity with basic mathematics is necessary to appreciate much of physical science. This review is included primarily to assist those readers whose mathematical skills have become rusty, but it is sufficiently self-contained to introduce such useful ideas as powers-of-ten notation to those who have not been exposed to them elsewhere.

Algebra

Algebra is the arithmetic of symbols that represent numbers. Instead of being restricted to relationships among specific numbers, algebra can express more general relationships among quantities whose numerical values need not be known.

To give an example, in the theory of relativity it is shown that the "rest energy" of any object — that is, the energy it possesses by virtue of its mass alone — is

$$E = mc^2$$

What this formula does is give a way to calculate the rest energy E in terms of mass m and speed of light c. The formula is not restricted to a particular object, but can be applied to any object whose mass is known. What is being expressed is the way in which rest energy E varies with mass m *in general*.

If we are told merely that the rest energy E of some object is 5 joules, we do not know upon what factors E depends or precisely how the value of E varies with those factors. (The joule is a unit of energy widely used in physics; it is equal to 1 kg-m^2/s^2.) The quantities E and m are *variables*, since they have no fixed values. On the other hand, c^2 is a *constant*, since it is the square of the speed of light c and the value of c—almost 300,000,000 m/s, or about 186,000 mi/s—is the same everywhere in the universe. Thus the formula $E = mc^2$ tells us, in a simple and straightforward way, that the rest energy of something varies only with its mass and also how to find the numerical value of E if we are given the mass m of a particular object.

The convenience of algebra in science is increased by the use of standard symbols for constants of nature: c always represents the speed of light, π always represents the ratio between the circumference and diameter of a circle, e always represents the electric charge of the electron, and so on.

Before going further, it is worth reviewing how the arithmetical operations of addition, subtraction, multiplication, and division are expressed in algebra. Addition and subtraction are straightforward:

$$x + y = a$$

means that we obtain the sum a by adding the two quantities x and y together, while

$$x - y = b$$

means that we obtain the difference b when quantity y is subtracted from quantity x.

In algebraic multiplication, no special sign is ordinarily used, and the symbols of the quantities to be multiplied are merely written together. Thus these three expressions have the same meaning:

$$xy = c \qquad (x)(y) = c \qquad x \times y = c$$

When the quantity x is to be divided by y to yield the quotient e, we write

$$\frac{x}{y} = e$$

which can also be expressed as

$$x/y = e$$

whose meaning is the same.

If several operations are to be performed in a certain order, parentheses ( ), brackets [ ], and braces { } are used to indicate this order. For instance, $a(x + y)$ means that we are first to add x and y together and then to multiply their sum $(x + y)$ by a. In essence $a(x + y)$ is an abbreviation for the same quantity written out in full:

$$a(x + y) = ax + ay$$

Let us find the value of

$$v = 5\left[\frac{(x - y)}{z}\right] + w$$

when $x = 15$, $y = 3$, $z = 4$, and $w = 10$. We proceed as follows:

1. Subtract y from x to give

$$x - y = 15 - 3 = 12$$

2. Divide $(x - y)$ by z to give

$$\frac{(x - y)}{z} = \frac{12}{4} = 3$$

3. Multiply $[(x - y)/z]$ by 5 to give

$$5\left[\frac{(x - y)}{z}\right] = 5 \times 3 = 15$$

4. Add w to $5[(x - y)/z]$ to give

$$v = 5\left[\frac{(x - y)}{z}\right] + w = 15 + 10 = 25$$

Positive and Negative Quantities

The rules for multiplying and dividing positive and negative quantities are simple. If the quantities are both positive or both negative, the result is positive; if one is positive and the other negative, the result is negative. In symbolic form,

$$(+ a)(+ b) = (- a)(- b) = + ab$$

$$\frac{+ a}{+ b} = \frac{- a}{- b} = \frac{a}{b}$$

$$(- a)(+ b) = (+ a)(- b) = - ab$$

$$\frac{- a}{+ b} = \frac{+ a}{- b} = - \frac{a}{b}$$

Here are some examples:

$$(-3)(-5) = 15 \qquad \frac{-16}{-4} = 4$$

$$2(-4) = -8 \qquad \frac{10}{-5} = -2$$

$$(-12)6 = -72 \qquad \frac{-24}{4} = -6$$

To find the value of

$$w = \frac{xy}{x+y}$$

when $x = 5$ and $y = -6$, we begin by finding xy and $x + y$. These are:

$$xy = (5)(-6) = -30$$
$$x + y = 5 + (-6) = 5 - 6 = -1$$

Hence

$$w = \frac{xy}{x+y} = \frac{-30}{-1} = 30$$

An example of the use of positive and negative quantities occurs in physics, where there are two kinds of electric charge, one of which is designated positive and the other negative. The force F that a charge Q_1 exerts on another charge Q_2 a distance r away is given by Coulomb's law as

$$F = K\frac{Q_1 Q_2}{r^2}$$

where K is a universal constant. By convention, a positive value of F means a repulsion between the charges — the force tends to push Q_1 and Q_2 apart. A negative value of F means an attraction between the charges — the force tends to pull Q_1 and Q_2 together. Evidently a positive (= repulsive) force acts when *either* both charges are $+$ *or* both are $-$: "like charges repel." When one charge is $+$ and the other one $-$, the force is negative (= attractive): "opposite charges attract." Both the above observations about the types of force that occur together with the way in which the strength of F varies with the magnitudes of Q_1 and Q_2 and with their separation r are included in the simple formula $F = KQ_1 Q_2/r^2$.

Exercises

A. Evaluate the following. The answers are given at the end of the Math Refresher.

1. $\dfrac{3(x+y)}{2}$ when $x=5$ and $y=-2$

2. $\dfrac{1}{x-y}-\dfrac{1}{x+y}$ when $x=3$ and $y=2$

3. $\dfrac{4xy}{y+3x}+5$ when $x=1$ and $y=-2$

4. $\dfrac{x+y}{2z}+\dfrac{z}{x-y}$ when $x=-2$, $y=2$, and $z=4$

5. $\dfrac{x+z}{y}+\dfrac{xy}{2}$ when $x=2$, $y=8$, and $z=10$

6. $\dfrac{3(x+7)}{y+2}$ when $x=3$ and $y=-6$

7. $\dfrac{5(3-x)}{2(x+y)}$ when $x=-5$ and $y=7$

Equations

An equation is a statement of equality: whatever is on the left-hand side of an equation is equal to whatever is on the right-hand side. An example of an arithmetical equation is

$$3 \times 9 + 8 = 35$$

since it contains only numbers, and an example of an algebraic equation is

$$5x - 10 = 20$$

since it contains a symbol as well as numbers.

The symbols in an algebraic equations usually must have only certain values if the equality is to hold. To *solve* an equation is to find the possible values of these symbols. The solution of the equation $5x - 10 = 20$ is $x = 6$ since only when $x = 6$ is this equation a true statement:

$$5x - 10 = 20$$
$$5 \times 6 - 10 = 20$$
$$30 - 10 = 20$$
$$20 = 20$$

The methods that can be used to solve an equation are based on this principle:

Any operation carried out on one side of an equation must be carried out on the other side as well.

Thus an equation remains valid when the same quantity is added to or subtracted from both sides or is used to multiply or divide both sides.

Two helpful rules follow from the above principle. The first is:

Any term on one side of an equation may be shifted to the other side by changing its sign.

To check this rule, let us consider the equation

$$a + b = c$$

If we subtract b from each side of the equation, we obtain

$$a + b - b = c - b$$
$$a = c - b$$

Thus b has disappeared from the left-hand side and $-b$ is now on the right-hand side. Similarly, if

$$a - d = e$$

then it is true that

$$a = e + d$$

The second rule is:

A quantity that multiplies one side of an equation may be shifted so as to divide the other side, and vice versa.

To check this rule, let us consider the equation

$$ab = c$$

If we divide both sides of the equation by b, we obtain

$$\frac{ab}{b} = \frac{c}{b}$$

$$a = \frac{c}{b}$$

Thus b, which was a multiplier on the left-hand side, is now a divisor on the right-hand side. Similarly, if

$$\frac{a}{d} = e$$

then it is true that

$$a = ed$$

Let us use the above rules to solve $5x - 10 = 20$ for the value of x. What we want is to have just x on the left-hand side of the equation. The first step is to shift the -10 to the right-hand side, where it becomes $+10$:

$$5x - 10 = 20$$

$$5x = 20 + 10 = 30$$

Now we transpose the 5 so that it divides the right-hand side:

$$5x = 30$$

$$x = \frac{30}{5} = 6$$

The solution is $x = 6$.

When each side of an equation consists of a fraction, all we need do is *cross multiply* to remove the fractions:

$$\frac{a}{b} = \frac{c}{d} \qquad \frac{a}{b} \times \frac{c}{d} \qquad ad = bc$$

For practice, let us solve the equation

$$\frac{5}{a + 2} = \frac{3}{a - 2}$$

for the value of a. We proceed as follows:

Cross multiply to give	$5(a-2)=3(a+2)$
Multiply out both sides to give	$5a-10=3a+6$
Shift the -10 and the $3a$ to give	$5a-3a=6+10$
Carry out the indicated addition and subtraction to give	$2a=16$
Divide both sides by 2 to give	$a=8$

Exercises

B. Solve each of the following equations for the value of x:

1. $3x+7=13$

2. $5x-8=17$

3. $2(x+5)=6$

4. $7x-10=0.5$

5. $\dfrac{x+7}{6}=x+2$

6. $\dfrac{4x-35}{3}=9(1-x)$

7. $\dfrac{3x-42}{9}=2(7-x)$

8. $\dfrac{1}{x+1}=\dfrac{1}{2x-1}$

9. $\dfrac{3}{x-1}=\dfrac{5}{x+1}$

10. $\dfrac{1}{3x+4}=\dfrac{2}{x+8}$

Exponents

There is a convenient shorthand way to express a quantity that is to be multiplied by itself one or more times. In this scheme a superscript number called an *exponent* is used to indicate how many times the multiplication is to be carried out, as follows:

$$a=a^1$$
$$a\times a=a^2$$
$$a\times a\times a=a^3$$
$$a\times a\times a\times a=a^4$$

and so on. The quantity a^2 is read "a squared" because it is equal to the area of a square whose sides are a long, and a^3 is read as "a cubed" because it is equal to the volume of a cube whose edges are a long. Past an exponent of 3 we read a^n as "a to the nth power," so that a^5 is "a to the fifth power."

Suppose we have a quantity raised to some power, say a^n, that is to be multiplied by the same quantity raised to another power, say a^m. In this event the result is that quantity raised to a power equal to the sum of the original exponents:

$$a^n \times a^m = a^n a^m = a^{n+m}$$

To convince ourselves that this is true, we can work out $a^3 \times a^4$:

$$(a \times a \times a)(a \times a \times a \times a) = a \times a \times a \times a \times a \times a \times a$$
$$a^3 a^4 = a^7$$

Because the process of multiplication is basically one of repeated addition,

$$(a^n)^m = a^{nm}$$

where $(a^n)^m$ means that a^n is to be multiplied by itself the number of times indicated by the exponent m. Thus

$$(a^2)^4 = a^{2 \times 4} = a^8$$

because

$$(a^2)^4 = a^2 \times a^2 \times a^2 \times a^2 = a^{2+2+2+2} = a^8$$

Reciprocal quantities are expressed according to the above scheme but with negative exponents:

$$\frac{1}{a} = a^{-1} \qquad \frac{1}{a^2} = a^{-2} \qquad \frac{1}{a^3} = a^{-3} \qquad \frac{1}{a^4} = a^{-4}$$

Roots

When the *square root* of a quantity is multiplied by itself, the product is equal to the quantity. The usual symbol for the square root of a quantity a is $\sqrt{a}$. Thus

$$\sqrt{a} \times \sqrt{a} = a$$

Here are some examples of square roots:

$$\sqrt{1} = 1 \qquad \text{because} \qquad 1 \times 1 = 1$$
$$\sqrt{4} = 2 \qquad \text{because} \qquad 2 \times 2 = 4$$
$$\sqrt{9} = 3 \qquad \text{because} \qquad 3 \times 3 = 9$$
$$\sqrt{100} = 10 \qquad \text{because} \qquad 10 \times 10 = 100$$
$$\sqrt{30.25} = 5.5 \qquad \text{because} \qquad 5.5 \times 5.5 = 30.25$$
$$\sqrt{16B^2} = 4B \qquad \text{because} \qquad 4B \times 4B = 16B^2$$

In the case of a number smaller than 1, the square root is larger than the number itself:

$$\sqrt{0.01} = 0.1 \quad \text{because} \quad 0.1 \times 0.1 = 0.01$$

$$\sqrt{0.25} = 0.5 \quad \text{because} \quad 0.5 \times 0.5 = 0.25$$

Similarly, multiplying the *cube root* $\sqrt[3]{a}$ of a quantity a by itself twice yields the quantity:

$$\sqrt[3]{a} \times \sqrt[3]{a} \times \sqrt[3]{a} = a$$

An expression of the form $\sqrt[n]{a}$ is read as "the nth root of a"; for instance, $\sqrt[4]{16}$ is "the fourth root of 16" and is equal to 2 since $2 \times 2 \times 2 \times 2 = 16$.

Although procedures exist for finding square and cube roots arithmetically, in practice electronic calculators or printed tables are normally used nowadays.

Here is an example of how a square root arises naturally in physics. Let us solve for r the equation

$$F = K \frac{Q_1 Q_2}{r^2}$$

that expresses Coulomb's law of electric force. What we do is this:

Multiply both sides by r^2 to give $\qquad Fr^2 = KQ_1Q_2$

Divide both sides by F to give $\qquad r^2 = \dfrac{KQ_1Q_2}{F}$

Take square root of both sides to give $\qquad r = \sqrt{\dfrac{KQ_1Q_2}{F}}$

In algebra, a fractional exponent is used to indicate a root of a quantity. In terms of exponents we would write the square root of a as

$$\sqrt{a} = a^{1/2}$$

because

$$a^{1/2} \times a^{1/2} = (a^{1/2})^2 = a^{2 \times 1/2} = a^1 = a$$

In a similar way the "cube root" of a, which is $\sqrt[3]{a}$, is indicated by the exponent $\frac{1}{3}$ since

$$a^{1/3} \times a^{1/3} \times a^{1/3} = (a^{1/3})^3 = a^1 = a$$

In general, the nth root of any quantity is indicated by the exponent $1/n$:

$$\sqrt[n]{a} = a^{1/n}$$

A few examples will indicate how fractional exponents fit into the general pattern of exponential notation:

$$(a^6)^{1/2} = a^{(1/2) \times 6} = a^3$$

$$(a^{1/2})^6 = a^{6 \times 1/2} = a^3$$

$$(a^3)^{-1/3} = a^{(-1/3) \times 3} = a^{-1}$$

$$a^6 a^{1/2} = a^{6 + 1/2} = a^{6 \ 1/2}$$

Powers of 10

There is a convenient and widely used method for expressing very large and very small numbers that makes use of powers of 10. Any number in decimal form can be written as a number between 1 and 10 multiplied by some power of 10, a positive power for numbers larger than 10 and a negative power for numbers smaller than 1. Positive powers of ten follow this pattern:

$10^0 = 1$ $\qquad$ = 1 with decimal point moved 0 places

$10^1 = 10$ $\qquad$ = 1 with decimal point moved 1 place to the right

$10^2 = 100$ $\qquad$ = 1 with decimal point moved 2 places to the right

$10^3 = 1000$ $\qquad$ = 1 with decimal point moved 3 places to the right

$10^4 = 10,000$ $\quad$ = 1 with decimal point moved 4 places to the right

$10^5 = 100,000$ = 1 with decimal point moved 5 places to the right

$10^6 = 1,000,000$ = 1 with decimal point moved 6 places to the right

and so on. The exponent of 10 in each case indicates the number of places through which the decimal point is moved to the right from 1.00000 . . . ; or, equivalently, the exponent gives the number of zeroes that follow the 1.

Negative powers of 10 follow a similar pattern:

$10^0 =$ $\qquad$ 1 = 1 with decimal point moved 0 places

$10^{-1} =$ $\qquad$ 0.1 = 1 with decimal point moved 1 place to the left

$10^{-2} =$ $\qquad$ 0.01 = 1 with decimal point moved 2 places to the left

$10^{-3} =$ $\qquad$ 0.001 = 1 with decimal point moved 3 places to the left

$10^{-4} =$ $\quad$ $0.000,1$ = 1 with decimal point moved 4 places to the left

$10^{-5} =$ $\quad$ $0.000,01$ = 1 with decimal point moved 5 places to the left

$10^{-6} = 0.000,001$ = 1 with decimal point moved 6 places to the left and so on. Here the exponent of 10 in each case indicates the number of places through which the decimal point is moved to the left from 1; the number of zeroes between the decimal point and the 1 is one less than the exponent, that is, $n - 1$.

Here are some examples of powers-of-10 notation:

$$8000 = 8 \times 1000 = 8 \times 10^3$$

$$347 = 3.47 \times 100 = 3.47 \times 10^2$$

$$8,700,000 = 8.7 \times 1,000,000 = 8.7 \times 10^6$$

$$0.22 = 2.2 \times 0.1 = 2.2 \times 10^{-1}$$

$$0.000,035 = 3.5 \times 0.000,01 = 3.5 \times 10^{-5}$$

An advantage of powers-of-10 notation is that it makes calculations involving large and small numbers easier to carry out. The rules for manipulating exponents that were reviewed in the previous section hold for exponents of 10, and so we have here

Multiplication: $\qquad 10^n \times 10^m = 10^{n+m}$

Division: $\qquad \dfrac{10^n}{10^m} = 10^{n-m}$

Raising to power: $\qquad (10^n)^m = 10^{nm}$

Taking a root: $\qquad (10^n)^{1/m} = 10^{n/m}$

An example will show how a calculation involving powers of 10 is worked out:

$$\frac{460 \times 0.000,03 \times 100,000}{9000 \times 0.006,2} = \frac{(4.6 \times 10^2) \times (3 \times 10^{-5}) \times (10^5)}{(9 \times 10^3) \times (6.2 \times 10^{-3})}$$

$$= \frac{4.6 \times 3}{9 \times 6.2} \times \frac{10^2 \times 10^{-5} \times 10^5}{10^3 \times 10^{-3}}$$

$$= 0.25 \times \frac{10^{2-5+5}}{10^{3-3}} = 0.25 \times \frac{10^2}{10^0}$$

$$= 25$$

Another virtue of this notation is that it permits us to express the accuracy with which a quantity is known in a clear way. The speed of light in free space c is often given as simply 3×10^8 m/s. If c were written out as 300,000,000 m/s we might be tempted to think it is precisely equal to this number, right down to the last zero. Actually, the most accurate figure for the speed of light is given by experiment as 299,792,800 m/s, with the last three digits uncertain: they are somewhere between

750 and 850. For our purposes we do not need this much detail, and by writing just $c = 3 \times 10^8$ we automatically indicate both how large the number is (the 10^8 tells how many decimal places are present) and how precise the quoted figure is (the single digit 3 means that c is closer to 3×10^8 than it is to either 2×10^8 or 4×10^8 m/s). If we wanted more precision, we could write $c = 2.998 \times 10^8$ m/s, and again how large c is and how precise the quoted figure is are both obvious at a glance. To be sure, sometimes one or more zeroes in a number are meaningful in their own right, and not solely decimal-point indicators. In the case of the speed of light, we can legitimately state that, to three-digit accuracy

$$c = 3.00 \times 10^8 \text{ m/s}$$

since c is closer to this figure than to 2.99×10^8 or 3.01×10^8 m/s. In the sample calculation of the preceding paragraph, the quantity $(4.6 \times 3)/(9 \times 6.2)$ actually equals 0.2473118 . . . , but it is rounded off to 0.25 because the result of a calculation may have no more significant digits than those in the least precise of the numbers that went into it.

Exercises

C. Express the following numbers in powers-of-10 notation:

1. $720 =$	2. $890,000 =$
3. $0.02 =$	4. $0.000,062 =$
5. $3.6 =$	6. $0.4 =$
7. $49,527 =$	8. $0.002,943 =$
9. $0.0014 =$	10. $49,000,000,000 =$
11. $0.000,000,011 =$	12. $1.4763 =$

D. Express the following numbers in decimal notation:

1. $3 \times 10^{-4} =$	2. $7.5 \times 10^3 =$
3. $8.126 \times 10^{-5} =$	4. $1.01 \times 10^8 =$
5. $5 \times 10^2 =$	6. $3.2 \times 10^{-2} =$
7. $4.32145 \times 10^3 =$	8. $6 \times 10^6 =$
9. $5.7 \times 10^0 =$	10. $6.9 \times 10^{-5} =$

E. Evaluate the following in powers-of-10 notation:

1. $\dfrac{30 \times 80,000,000,000}{0.0004} =$ 2. $\dfrac{30,000 \times 0.000,000,6}{1000 \times 0.02} =$

3. $\dfrac{0.0001}{60,000 \times 200} =$ 4. $5000 \times 0.005 =$

5. $\dfrac{5000}{0.005} =$

6. $\dfrac{200 \times 0.000,04}{400,000} =$

7. $\dfrac{0.002 \times 0.000,000,05}{0.000,004} =$

8. $\dfrac{500,000 \times 18,000}{9,000,000} =$

Answers

A.
1. 4.5
2. 0.8
3. -3
4. -1
5. -6.5
6. -7.5
7. 10

B.
1. 2
2. 5
3. -2
4. 1.5
5. -1
6. 2
7. 8
8. 2
9. 4
10. 0

C.
1. 7.2×10^2
2. 8.9×10^5
3. 2×10^{-2}
4. 6.2×10^{-5}
5. 3.6×10^0
6. 4×10^{-1}
7. 4.9527×10^4
8. 2.943×10^{-3}
9. 1.4×10^{-3}
10. 4.9×10^{10}
11. 1.1×10^{-8}
12. 1.4763×10^0

D.
1. 0.0003
2. 7500
3. 0.000,081,26
4. 101,000,000
5. 500
6. 0.032
7. 4321.45
8. 6,000,000
9. 5.7
10. 0.000,069

E.
1. 6×10^{15}
2. 9×10^{-4}
3. 8.3×10^{-11}
4. 2.5×10^1
5. 10^6
6. 2×10^{-8}
7. 2.5×10^{-5}
8. 10^3

Absolute zero is the lowest temperature possible, corresponding to no random molecular movement. This temperature is $-273°C$. The *absolute temperature scale* gives temperatures in °C above absolute zero, denoted K. Thus the freezing point of water is 273 K.

The **acceleration** of an object is the rate of change of its velocity. An object is accelerated when its speed changes, when its direction of motion changes, or when both change.

The **acceleration of gravity** is the acceleration of an object in free fall near the earth's surface. Its value is 9.8 m/s^2.

An **acid** is a substance whose molecules contain hydrogen and whose water solution contains hydrogen ions.

The **activation energy** of a reaction is the energy that must be supplied initially for the reaction to start.

An **alcohol** is a hydrocarbon derivative in which one or more hydrogen atoms have been replaced by OH groups.

The **alkali metals** are a family of soft, light, extremely active metals with similar chemical properties. The alkali metals are lithium, sodium, potassium, rubidium, cesium, and francium in order of atomic number.

An **alluvial fan** is a deposit of sediments where a stream emerges from a steep mountain valley and flows onto a plain.

An **alpha particle** is the nucleus of a helium atom. It consists of two protons and two neutrons and is emitted in certain radioactive decays.

An **amorphous solid** is one whose constituent particles show no regularity of arrangement.

The **ampere** (A) is the unit of electric current. It is equal to a flow of one coulomb of charge per second.

The **amplitude** of a wave is the maximum value of whatever quantity is periodically varying.

The **angular momentum** of a rotating body is a measure of its tendency to continue to spin. Angular momentum is a vector quantity. The angular momentum of an isolated body or system of bodies is *conserved* (remains unchanged).

The **antiparticle** of a particle has the same mass and general behavior, but has a charge of opposite sign and differs in certain other respects. A particle and its antiparticle can *annihilate* each other with their masses turning entirely into energy. The opposite process of *pair production* in which a particle-antiparticle pair materializes from energy can also occur.

Archimedes' principle states that the buoyant force on an object immersed in a fluid is equal to the weight of the fluid displaced by the object.

An **asteroid** is one of many relatively small bodies that revolve around the sun in orbits that lie between those of Mars and Jupiter.

The **asthenosphere** is a layer of rock capable of plastic deformation that is just below the lithosphere in the earth's mantle.

The earth's **atmosphere** is its gaseous envelope. The four regions of the atmosphere are, from the earth's surface upward, the *troposphere*, the *stratosphere*, the *mesosphere*, and the *thermosphere*.

Atmospheric pressure is the force with which the atmosphere presses down upon each unit area at the earth's surface. Its value is normally about 1.013×10^5 Pa.

An **atom** is the ultimate particle of any element. It consists of a *nucleus,* composed of neutrons and protons, and a number of *electrons* that move about the nucleus relatively far away.

The **atomic mass** of an element is the average mass of its atoms expressed in atomic mass units (u).

The **atomic number** of an element is the number of electrons in each of its atoms or, equivalently, the number of protons in its nucleus. An element is a substance all of whose atoms have the same atomic number.

An **aurora** is a display of changing colored patterns of light that appear in the sky, particularly at high latitudes. The aurora arises from the excitation of atmospheric gases at high altitudes by streams of fast ions of solar origin.

Avogadro's number is the number of atoms in a mole of any element; it is also the number of formula units in a mole of any compound.

A **base** is a substance whose molecules contain OH groups and whose water solutions contain OH^- ions.

A **batholith** is a very large body of intrusive rock, mainly granite, that extends downward as much as 10 km.

A **benzene ring** consists of six carbon atoms linked together in a flat hexagon.

The **big bang theory** holds that the universe originated in the explosion of a hot, dense aggregate of matter about 13 billion years ago. If the explosion was violent enough, the expansion of the universe will continue forever; if not, the universe will eventually begin to contract and will end up in a *big crunch* after which another cycle of expansion and contraction will occur.

A **black hole** is an old star that has contracted to so small a size that its gravitational field prevents the escape of anything, including light.

In the **Bohr model of the atom,** electrons are supposed to move around nuclei in circular orbits of definite size. When an electron jumps from one orbit to another, a photon of light is either emitted or absorbed whose energy corresponds to the difference in the electron's energy in the two orbits.

Boyle's law states that the volume of a gas is inversely proportional to its pressure when the temperature is held constant.

A **carbohydrate** is a compound of carbon, hydrogen, and oxygen whose molecules contain two atoms of hydrogen for each one of oxygen. Carbohydrates are manufactured in green plants from water and carbon dioxide in the process of photosynthesis. Sugars, starches, chitin, and cellulose are carbohydrates.

The **carbon cycle** is one of two series of energy-producing nuclear reactions that take place in the sun and other stars and involve the conversion of hydrogen to helium. In the carbon cycle, carbon nuclei absorb a succession of protons which ultimately results in the formation of helium nuclei and the reemergence of carbon nuclei.

A **catalyst** is a substance that can alter the rate of a chemical reaction without itself being permanently changed by the reaction.

Cathode rays are streams of electrons produced in an evacuated tube when opposite charges are placed on electrodes at each end.

The **Cenozoic era** refers to the past 65 million years of the earth's history; the term means "recent life."

The **centripetal force** on a body moving in a circle is the inward force that must be exerted to produce this motion. It always acts toward the center of the circle in which the body is moving.

737

A **Cepheid variable** is a variable star of a particular type whose intrinsic brightness and period of variation are related.

A **chain reaction** is a succession of nuclear fissions in which neutrons produced by each fission induce further fissions in other atoms.

Charles's law states that the volume of a gas is proportional to its absolute temperature when the pressure is held constant.

Chlorophyll is the catalyst that makes possible the reaction of water and carbon dioxide in green plants to produce carbohydrates. The reaction is called *photosynthesis*.

The **clay minerals** are a group of light, soft silicates of hydrogen and aluminum, sometimes with a little magnesium, iron, or potassium, which occur as aggregates of microscopic crystals.

Cleavage is the tendency of a substance to split along certain planes determined by the arrangement of particles in its crystal lattice.

Climate refers to average in weather conditions over a period of years.

A **cloud** is composed of water droplets or ice crystals small enough to remain suspended aloft indefinitely.

Coal is a fuel, largely carbon, that was formed chiefly from plant material that accumulated under conditions preventing complete decay.

Combustion is the rapid combination of oxygen with another substance accompanied by the evolution of heat and light.

Comets are aggregates of matter that follow regular orbits in the solar system and appear as small, hazy patches of light accompanied by long, filmy tails when near the sun.

A **compound** is a homogeneous combination of elements in definite proportions. The properties of a compound are different from those of its constituent elements.

A **conductor** is a substance through which electric current can flow readily.

A **constellation** is a group of stars whose arrangement in the sky suggests a particular pattern.

According to the theory of **continental drift,** today's continents were once part of two primeval supercontinents called Laurasia (North America, Greenland, Europe, and most of Asia) and Gondwanaland (South America, Africa, Antarctica, India, and Australia), which were separated by the Tethys Sea. The continents are still in motion.

Convection currents result from the uneven heating of a fluid. The warmer parts of the fluid expand and rise because of their buoyancy, while the cooler parts sink.

In the **copernican system** the sun and stars are fixed, the earth and the other planets revolve around the sun, the moon revolves around the earth, and the earth rotates on an axis passing through Polaris.

The earth's **core** is a spherical region around the center of the earth whose radius is about 3500 km (2100 mi). It probably consists mainly of molten iron.

The **Coriolis effect** is the deflection of winds to the right in the northern hemisphere, to the left in the southern as a consequence of the earth's rotation.

The sun's **corona** is a vast cloud of extremely hot, rarefied gas that surrounds the sun. It is visible during solar eclipses.

Cosmic rays are atomic nuclei, mostly protons, that travel through the galaxy at speeds close to that of light. They probably were ejected during supernova explosions and are trapped in the galaxy by magnetic fields.

Coulomb's law states that the force between two electric charges is directly proportional to both charges and inversely proportional to the distance between them. The force is repulsive when the charges have the same sign, attractive when they have different signs.

In a **covalent bond** between atoms, the atoms share one or more electron pairs. The atoms in a molecule are held together by covalent bonds. A *covalent crystal* consists of atoms that share electron pairs with their neighbors.

Cracking a hydrocarbon is the process of heating it under pressure in the presence of a catalyst in order to break its molecules down into simpler hydrocarbons.

The **crust** of the earth is its outer shell of rock which averages 35 km in thickness under the continents and about 5 km under the oceans.

A **crystalline solid** is one whose atoms or molecules are arranged in a definite pattern.

An electric **current** is a flow of charge from one place to another. A direct current is one that always flows in one direction; an alternating current periodically reverses its direction of flow.

Cyclones are weather systems centered about regions of low pressure. In the northern hemisphere cyclones are characterized by counterclockwise winds, in the southern hemisphere by clockwise winds. *Anticyclones* are weather systems centered about regions of high pressure; the characteristic winds of anticyclones are opposite in direction to those of cyclones.

The matter waves that correspond to a moving object have a **de Broglie** wavelength inversely proportional to its momentum.

The law of **definite proportions** states that the elements that make up a chemical compound are always combined in the same definite proportions by mass.

A **delta** is a deposit of sediments where a stream flows into a lake or the sea.

The **density** of a substance is its mass per unit volume.

Diffraction refers to the ability of waves to bend around the edge of an obstacle in their path.

A **dike** is a wall-like mass of igneous rock that cuts across existing rock layers.

The **dinosaurs** were reptiles of various kinds, many huge in size, which flourished in the Mesozoic era.

A **displacement reaction** is an oxidation-reduction reaction in which one metal (or nonmetal) displaces another metal (or nonmetal) from solution.

DNA: See **nucleic acid.**

The **doppler effect** is the change in perceived frequency of a wave due to relative motion between its source and an observer. Light and sound waves exhibit the doppler effect.

A **double star** is actually a pair of stars both revolving about their mutual center of mass.

An **earthquake** consists of rapid vibratory motions of rock near the earth's surface usually caused by the sudden movement of rock along a fault. Earthquake P (for primary) waves are longitudinal oscillations in the solid earth like those in sound waves; earthquake S (for secondary) waves are transverse oscillations in the earth like those in a stretched string; earthquake L (for long) waves are oscillations of the earth's surface like those in water waves.

A lunar **eclipse** occurs when the earth's shadow obscures the moon. A *solar eclipse* occurs when the moon obscures the sun.

Electric charge is a fundamental property of certain of the elementary particles of which all matter is composed. There are two kinds of charge, *positive* and *negative;* charges of like sign repel, unlike charges attract. The unit of charge is the *coulomb* (C). The principle of *conservation of charge* states that the net electric charge in an isolated system remains constant.

In an **electrochemical cell,** electric current is produced by an oxidation-reduction reaction whose two half-reactions take place at different locations.

Electrolysis refers to the liberation of free elements from a liquid when an electric current passes through it.

An **electrolyte** is a substance that separates into free ions on solution in water.

An **electromagnet** is a current-carrying coil of wire with an iron core to increase its magnetic field.

Electromagnetic induction refers to the production of a current in a wire moving through a magnetic field or in a wire loop in the presence of a changing magnetic field.

Electromagnetic waves are coupled periodic electric and magnetic disturbances that spread out from accelerated electric charges. Among the various kinds of electromagnetic waves, distinguished only by their frequencies, are gamma rays, x-rays, ultraviolet radiation, visible light, infrared radiation, millimeter waves, microwaves, and radio waves. Electromagnetic waves all travel in vacuum with the *speed of light.*

An **electron** is a tiny, negatively charged particle found in matter whose charge is -1.6×10^{-19} C and whose mass is 9.1×10^{-31} kg.

The **electron volt** is a unit of energy equal to 1.6×10^{-19} J, which is the amount of energy acquired by an electron accelerated by a potential difference of 1 volt. An *MeV* is 10^6 eV and a *GeV* is 10^9 eV.

An **element** is a substance all of whose atoms have the same number of protons in their nuclei. Elements can neither be decomposed nor transformed into one another by ordinary chemical or physical means. There is a limited number of elements and all other substances are combinations of them in various proportions.

An **elementary particle** is one of the various indivisible particles found in nature of which all matter is composed. Elementary particles that have neither discernible size nor internal structures and are not affected by the strong nuclear force are called *leptons;* the electron is an example. Elementary particles that are associated with the strong nuclear force are called *hadrons* and have both definite sizes and internal structures of some kind; the proton and neutron are examples. Hadrons are believed to be composed of *quarks,* which have fractional electric charges and have never been isolated experimentally.

An **endothermic reaction** is one that must be supplied with energy in order to occur.

Energy is the property something has that enables it to do work. The unit of energy is the *joule* (J). The basic forms of energy are kinetic energy, potential energy, and mass energy. The *law of conservation of energy* states that energy can be neither created nor destroyed, although it may go from one form to another.

A chemical **equation** expresses the result of a chemical change. When the equation is *balanced,* the number of each kind of atom is the same on both sides of the equation.

A chemical **equilibrium** occurs when a chemical reaction and its reverse reaction both take place at the same rate.

At the vernal and autumnal **equinoxes** the sun is directly overhead at noon at the equator. The periods of daylight and darkness on these days are the same everywhere on the earth.

Erosion refers to all processes by which rock is disintegrated and worn away and its debris removed.

The **escape speed** is the minimum speed an object needs to

permanently escape from the gravitational pull of a particular astronomical body.

An **ester** is an organic compound formed when an alcohol reacts with an acid.

The Pauli **exclusion principle** states that no more than one electron in an atom can have a particular set of quantum numbers.

An **exothermic reaction** is one that liberates energy.

The **expanding universe** refers to the fact that all of the galaxies visible to us seem to be rapidly moving apart from one another. The evidence for the recession is the observed *red shift* in galactic spectra, which is a shift of their spectral lines toward the red end of the spectrum that is interpreted as a doppler effect.

A **fault** is a rock fracture along which movement has occurred.

Feldspar is the name of a group of light-colored silicate minerals with similar properties.

The **ferromagnesian minerals** are a group of diverse minerals that are silicates of iron and magnesium and green to black in color.

A **field of force** is a region of altered space (for example, around a mass, an electric charge, a magnet) that exerts a force on appropriate objects in that region.

A **flood plain** is the wide, flat floor of a river valley produced by the sidewise cutting of the stream when its slope has become too gradual for further downcutting.

Foliation refers to the alignment of flat or elongated mineral grains characteristic of many metamorphic rocks.

A **force** is any influence that can cause an object to be accelerated. The unit of force is the *newton* (N).

The **formula mass** of a compound is the sum of the atomic masses of its constituent elements, each multiplied by the number of times it appears in the formula of the compound.

Fossils are the remains or traces of organisms preserved in rocks.

Fractional distillation is a process for separating or partially separating a mixture of chemical compounds in the order of their boiling points.

The **frequency** of a wave is the number of waves that pass a given point per second. The unit of frequency is the *hertz* (Hz). The frequency of a sound wave is its *pitch*.

A **frontal surface** is the surface separating a warm and a cold air mass; a *front* is where this surface touches the ground. A *cold front* generally involves a cold air mass moving approximately eastward. A *warm front* generally involves a warm air mass moving approximately eastward.

A **functional group** is a group of atoms in an organic molecule whose presence determines its chemical behavior to a large extent. An example is the OH group that characterizes the alcohols.

The four **fundamental interactions,** in order of decreasing strength, are the strong, electromagnetic, weak, and gravitational. They give rise to all the physical processes in the universe. The electromagnetic and weak interactions, and probably the strong as well, are closely related.

Galactic nebulas are irregular masses of diffuse material within our galaxy.

Our **galaxy** is a huge, rotating, disk-shaped group of stars that we see as the Milky Way from our location about two-thirds of the way out from the center. *Spiral galaxies* are other collections of stars that resemble our galaxy. The universe apparently consists of widely separated galaxies of stars.

Gamma rays are very high frequency electromagnetic waves.

The **geomagnetic poles** are the points on the earth's surface through which the magnetic axis of the earth passes.

A **glacier** is a large mass of ice formed from compacted snow that gradually moves downhill.

Globular clusters are roughly spherical assemblies of stars outside the plane of our galaxy but associated with it.

Gondwanaland was the primeval supercontinent which later split up to form what are today South America, Africa, Antarctica, India, and Australia.

Newton's **law of gravitation** states that every particle in the universe attracts every other particle with a force that is directly proportional to both of their masses and inversely proportional to the square of the distance between them.

The **greenhouse effect** refers to the process by which a greenhouse is heated: sunlight can enter through its windows, but the infrared radiation the warm interior gives off cannot penetrate glass, so the incoming energy is trapped. The earth's atmosphere is heated in a similar way, with its carbon dioxide and water vapor content absorbing infrared radiation from the warm earth.

A body is **grounded** when its excess charge is permitted to flow to the earth.

Groundwater is rainwater that has soaked into the ground. The *water table* is the upper surface of that part of the ground whose pore spaces are saturated with water. A *spring* is a channel through which groundwater comes to the surface.

The **half-life** of a radioisotope is the period of time required for one-half of an original sample to decay.

The **halogens** are a family of highly active nonmetals with similar chemical properties. The halogens are fluorine, chlorine, bromine, iodine, and astatine in order of atomic number.

Heat is energy of random molecular motion. The heat that a body possesses depends upon its temperature, its mass, and the kind of material of which it is composed. The unit of heat is the joule (J).

The **heat of fusion** of a substance is the amount of heat required to change 1 kg of the substance from solid to liquid at its freezing point. It is also the heat that 1 kg of the substance liberates when it changes from liquid to solid at its freezing point.

The **heat of vaporization** of a substance is the amount of heat required to change 1 kg of the substance from liquid to vapor at its boiling point. It is also the heat that 1 kg of the substance liberates when it changes from vapor to liquid at its boiling point.

The **Hertzsprung-Russell diagram** is a graph on which are plotted the intrinsic brightness and spectral type of the various stars. Most stars belong to the *main sequence,* which follows a diagonal line on the diagram, but there are also small, hot *white dwarf* stars and large, cool *red giant* stars occupying other positions not on the main sequence.

Humidity refers to the moisture content of air. *Relative humidity* is the ratio between the amount of moisture in a volume of air and the maximum amount of moisture that volume of air can hold when completely saturated. It is usually expressed as a percentage.

A **hydrocarbon** is an organic compound containing only carbon and hydrogen. An *unsaturated hydrocarbon* is one whose molecules contain more than one bond (that is, shared electron pair) between adjacent carbon atoms. In a *saturated hydrocarbon* there is only one bond between adjacent carbon atoms.

A **hydrocarbon derivative** is a compound obtained by substituting other atoms or atom groups for some of the hydrogen atoms in hydrocarbon molecules.

The **hydronium ion** consists of a water molecule with a hydrogen ion attached. Its symbol is H_3O^+. (Sometimes more than one water molecule may be attached to a single hydrogen ion; the notion of the hydronium ion is for convenience only.)

A **hypothesis** is an interpretation of scientific results as first proposed. After thorough checking, it becomes a *law* if it states a regularity or relationship, or a *theory* if it uses general considerations to account for specific phenomena. (These terms are often used in senses slightly different from the ones indicated, but the definitions stated here correspond to their usual meanings.)

The **ice ages** were times of severe cold in which ice sheets covered much of Europe and North America.

An **ideal gas** is one that obeys the formula $pV/T =$ constant, which is a combination of Boyle's and Charles's laws. The behavior of actual gases corresponds approximately to that of an ideal gas.

Igneous rocks are rocks that have been formed from a molten state by cooling.

The **inert gases** are a family of almost totally inactive elements consisting of helium, neon, argon, krypton, xenon, and radon in order of atomic number.

Inertia is the apparent resistance a material body offers to any change in its state of motion.

Insolation is an acronym for *in*coming *sol*ar radi*ation*. Insolation is the energy that powers weather phenomena.

An **insulator** is a substance through which charges can move only with difficulty.

Interference occurs when two or more waves of the same kind pass the same point in space at the same time. If the waves are "in step" with each other, their amplitudes add together to produce a strong wave; this situation is called *constructive interference*. If the waves are "out of step" with each other, their amplitudes tend to cancel out and the resulting wave is weaker; this situation is called *destructive interference*.

Intrusive rocks are igneous rocks that flowed into regions below the surface already occupied by other rocks and gradually hardened there.

Invertebrates are animals without internal skeletons.

An **ion** is an atom or molecule that has an electric charge because it has gained or lost one or more electrons. The process of forming ions is called *ionization*.

In an **ionic bond,** electrons are transferred from one atom to another and the resulting ions then attract each other. An *ionic crystal* consists of individual ions in an array in which attractive and repulsive forces balance out.

The **ionosphere** is a region in the upper atmosphere that contains layers of ions. The ionosphere reflects radio waves and so makes possible long-range radio communication.

Isomers are compounds whose molecules contain the same atoms but in different arrangements.

The **isotopes** of an element have atoms with the same atomic number but different atomic masses; their nuclei contain the same number of protons but different numbers of neutrons.

The **jet stream** consists of swift currents of air near the base of the stratosphere that move from west to east.

Kepler's laws of planetary motion state that (1) the paths of the planets around the sun are ellipses, (2) the planets move so that their radius vectors sweep out equal areas in equal times, and (3) the ratio between the square of the time required by a planet to make a complete revolution around the sun and the cube of its average distance from the sun is a constant for all the planets.

Kinetic energy is the energy a body has by virtue of its motion. The kinetic energy of a moving body is equal to $\frac{1}{2}mv^2$, one-half the product of its mass and the square of its speed.

According to the **kinetic theory of matter,** all matter consists of tiny individual molecules that are in constant random motion. Heat is the kinetic energy of these random molecular motions.

A **laser** is a device that produces an intense beam of monochromatic, coherent light from the cooperative radiation of excited atoms. (The waves in a coherent beam are all in step with one another.)

Laurasia was the primeval supercontinent which later split up into what are today the continents North America, Greenland, Europe, and most of Asia.

Lava is molten rock on the earth's surface.

The **left-hand rule** states that when a current-carrying wire is grasped so that the thumb of the left hand points in the direction in which the electrons move, the fingers of that hand point in the direction of the magnetic field around the wire.

A **light-year** is the distance light travels in 1 year; it is about 9.46×10^{12} km

Lines of force are imaginary lines used to describe a field of force. Their direction is that of the force which the field would exert on a test particle, and their density is proportional to the strength of the field (that is, they are closest together where the field is strongest, farthest apart where the field is weakest).

Fats, oils, waxes, and sterols are **lipids,** which are synthesized in plants and animals from carbohydrates.

The **lithosphere** is the earth's outer shell of rigid rock. It consists of the crust and the outermost part of the mantle.

Magma is molten rock below the earth's surface.

A **magnet** is a body that can attract iron objects. When freely suspended, the *north pole* of a magnet points north while its *south pole* points south. Like poles repel each other; unlike poles attract.

Magnetic forces are exerted by moving charges (such as electric currents) on one another. The magnetic force between two charges is a modification of the electric force between them due to their motion; it is a relativistic effect.

The earth's **mantle** is the solid part of the earth between the core and the crust; it is about 2900 km (1800 mi) thick.

The **maria** of the moon are dark, smooth regions on its surface once thought to be seas. They are covered with lava pulverized by meteorite bombardment.

The **mass** of a body is the property of matter that manifests itself as inertia. It may be thought of as the quantity of matter in the body. The unit of mass is the *kilogram* (kg).

A **matter wave** is associated with rapidly moving bodies, whose behavior in certain respects resembles wave behavior. The matter waves associated with a moving body are in the form of a group, or packet, of waves which travel with the same speed as the body.

The **Mesozoic era** is the period in the earth's history from 225 million years ago to 65 million years ago; the term means "intermediate life."

The **metallic bond** that holds metal atoms together arises from a "gas" of electrons that can move freely through a solid metal. These electrons are also responsible for the ability of metals to conduct heat and electricity well.

Metals possess a characteristic sheen (metallic luster) and are good conductors of heat and electricity. They combine with nonmetals more readily than with one another. A metal atom has one or several electrons outside closed shells or subshells and combines chemically by losing these electrons to nonmetal atoms.

Metamorphic rocks are rocks that have been altered by heat and pressure deep under the earth's surface.

Meteoroids are pieces of matter moving through space; *meteors* are the flashes of light they produce when entering the earth's atmosphere; and *meteorites* are the remains of meteoroids that reach the ground.

Mica is a soft mineral with conspicuous cleavage in one plane.

Minerals are the separate homogeneous substances of which rocks are composed. The most abundant minerals are silicates; also common are carbonates and oxides.

A **mole** of a substance is that amount of it whose mass in grams is equal to its formula mass expressed in atomic mass units. A mole of anything contains the same number of formula units as a mole of anything else; this number is called *Avogadro's number.* Because of the way the mole is defined, a chemical equation can be interpreted in terms of moles as well as in terms of formula units such as atoms, molecules, or ions.

A **molecule** is an electrically neutral combination of two or more atoms held together strongly enough to be experimentally observable as a particle.

The linear **momentum** of a body is the product of its mass and its velocity. Momentum is a vector quantity, possessing both a magnitude and a direction; the direction is that of the body's motion. The law of *conservation of momentum* states that, when several objects interact with one another (for instance, in an explosion or a collision), if outside forces do not act upon them, the total momentum of all the objects before they interact is exactly the same as their total momentum afterward. (See also **angular momentum.**)

A **moraine** is the pile of debris around the end of a glacier left as a low, hummocky ridge when the glacier melts back. The deposited material is called *till.*

Newton's **first law of motion** states that every body continues in its state of rest or of uniform motion in a straight line if no force acts upon it. The *second law of motion* states that when a net force F acts on an object of mass m, the object is given an acceleration of F/m in the same direction as that of the force. The *third law of motion* states that when an object exerts a force on another object, the second object exerts an equal but opposite force on the first. Thus for every *action force* there is an equal but opposite *reaction force;* the two forces act on different objects.

The **neutralization** of a strong acid by a strong base in water solution is a reaction between hydrogen and hydroxide ions to form water.

The **neutron** is an electrically neutral elementary particle

whose mass is slightly more than that of the proton. Atomic nuclei consist of neutrons and protons.

A **neutron star** is an extremely small star, smaller than a white dwarf, which is composed almost entirely of neutrons.

Nonmetals have an extreme range of physical properties; in the solid state they are usually lusterless and brittle and are poor conductors of heat and electricity. Some nonmetals form no compounds whatever; the others combine more readily with active metals than with one another. A nonmetal atom lacks one or several electrons of having closed shells or subshells and combines chemically by picking up electrons from metal atoms or by sharing electrons with other nonmetal atoms.

Nuclear fission occurs when a heavy nucleus splits into two or more lighter nuclei. Considerable energy is evolved each time fission occurs.

Nuclear fusion occurs when two light nuclei unite to form a heavier one. Considerable energy is evolved in such processes.

A **nuclear reactor** is a device in which fissions occur at a controlled rate.

Nucleic acid molecules consist of long chains of *nucleotides* whose precise sequence governs the structure and functioning of cells and organisms. *DNA* has the form of a double helix and carries the genetic code. One form of the simpler *RNA* acts as a messenger in protein synthesis.

The **nucleus** of an atom is its small, heavy core, containing all the atom's positive charge and most of its mass. The constituents of a nucleus are neutrons and protons.

Ohm's law states that the current in a metallic conductor is equal to the potential difference between the ends of the conductor divided by its resistance; symbolically, $I = V/R$.

Organic chemistry refers to the chemistry of carbon compounds; *inorganic chemistry* refers to the chemistry of the other elements.

Oxidation is the chemical combination of a substance with oxygen. More generally, an element is *oxidized* when its atoms lose electrons and *reduced* when its atoms gain electrons.

Ozone is a form of oxygen whose molecules consist of three oxygen atoms each. Ozone is present in the upper atmosphere where it absorbs solar ultraviolet radiation.

Pair production is the materialization of a particle-antiparticle pair (for instance, an electron and a positron) when a sufficiently energetic gamma ray passes near an atomic nucleus.

The **Paleozoic era** is the period in the earth's history from 570 million years ago to 225 million years ago; the term means "ancient life."

The **parallax** of a star is the apparent shift in its position relative to more distant stars as the earth revolves in its orbit.

Mendeleev's **periodic law** in modern form states that if the elements are listed in the order of their atomic numbers, elements with similar properties recur at regular intervals. A tabular arrangement of the elements showing this recurrence of properties is called a *periodic table.*

Petroleum is a naturally occurring liquid mixture of hydrocarbons believed to have originated from the protein, fat, and wax content of plant and animal matter buried long ago.

The **pH** of a solution is an expression of its exact degree of acidity or basicity in terms of its hydrogen-ion concentration. A pH of 7 signifies a neutral solution, a smaller pH than 7 signifies an acid solution, and a higher pH than 7 signifies a basic solution.

The **phases of the moon** occur because the amount of the illuminated side of the moon visible to us varies with the position of the moon in its orbit.

The **photoelectric effect** is the emission of electrons from a metal surface when light is shone upon it.

Electromagnetic waves transport energy in tiny bursts called **photons** that resemble particles in many respects. The energy of a photon is related to the frequency f of the corresponding wave by $E = hf$, where h is *Planck's constant.*

Photosynthesis is the reaction between water and carbon dioxide to produce carbohydrates that occurs in green plants with the help of sunlight and the catalyst chlorophyll.

A **planet** is a satellite of the sun that appears in the sky as a bright object whose position changes relative to the stars.

According to the theory of **plate tectonics,** the lithosphere of the earth is divided into seven huge *plates* and a number of smaller ones. Continental drift occurs because the plates can move relative to one another.

A **pluton** is a body of intrusive rock formed by the solidification of magma under the surface.

In a **polar covalent compound** one part of each molecule is relatively negative and another part relatively positive.

A **polar molecule** is one that behaves as if it were negatively charged at one end and positively charged at the other. A *polar liquid* is a liquid whose molecules are polar whereas a *nonpolar liquid* has molecules whose charge is symmetrically arranged.

A **polymer** is a long chain of simple molecules, called *monomers,* that have joined together, usually under the influence of heat and catalysts.

A **positron** is a positively charged electron.

The **potential difference** between two points is the work needed to take a charge of 1 C from one of the points to the other. The unit of potential difference is the *volt* (V), equal to 1 J/C.

Potential energy is the energy an object has by virtue of its position. The gravitational potential energy of an object of mass m that is a height h above some reference level is $PE = mgh$, where g is the acceleration of gravity. Since mg is the object's weight w, an alternative formula is $PE = wh$.

Power is the rate at which work is being done. The unit of power is the *watt* (W), equal to 1 J/s.

Precambrian time is the name given to the period in the earth's history previous to the Paleozoic era, which began 570 million years ago.

A **precipitate** is an insoluble solid that forms as a result of a chemical reaction in solution.

The **pressure** on a surface is the perpendicular force per unit area that acts on it. The unit of pressure is the *pascal* (Pa), equal to 1 N/m². Another common pressure unit is the *bar,* equal to 10^5 Pa, which is very close to atmospheric pressure.

Proteins are the chief constituents of living matter and consist of long chains of amino acid molecules. The sequence of amino acids in a protein molecule together with the form of the molecule determines its biological role.

The **proton** is a positively charged elementary particle found in all atomic nuclei. Its charge is $+1.6 \times 10^{-19}$ C and its mass is 1.67×10^{-27} kg.

The **proton-proton cycle** is one of two series of energy-producing nuclear reactions that take place in the sun and other stars and involve the conversion of hydrogen to helium. In the proton-proton cycle, a series of collisions of protons results in the formation of helium nuclei.

The **ptolemaic system** is an incorrect hypothesis of the astronomical universe in which the earth is at the center with all of the other celestial bodies revolving around it in more or less complex orbits.

A **pulsar** is a star that emits extremely regular flashes of light and radio waves. Pulsars are believed to be neutron stars that are spinning rapidly.

Quantum mechanics is a theory of atomic phenomena based on the wave nature of moving things. Newtonian mechanics is an approximate version of quantum mechanics valid only on a relatively large scale of size.

Four **quantum numbers** are needed to specify completely the physical state of an atomic electron. These are the *total quantum number, n,* which governs the energy of the electron; the *orbital quantum number, l,* which determines the magnitude of the electron's angular momentum; the *magnetic quantum number, m_l,* which determines the direction of the electron's angular momentum; and the *spin magnetic quantum number, m_s,* which determines the orientation of the electron's spin.

Quartz consists of crystals of silicon dioxide, SiO_2.

A **quasar** is a distant celestial object that emits both light and radio waves strongly and that may be powered by a supermassive black hole at its center.

A **radio telescope** is a directional antenna connected to a sensitive radio receiver. Radio waves from space are produced by extremely hot gases, by fast electrons that move in magnetic fields, and by atoms and molecules excited to radiate.

In **radioactive decay,** certain atomic nuclei spontaneously emit *alpha particles* (helium nuclei), *beta particles* (electrons or positrons), or *gamma rays* (high-frequency electromagnetic waves).

Radiocarbon dating is a procedure for establishing the approximate age of once-living matter on the basis of the relative amount of radioactive carbon it contains.

Reflection occurs when a wave bounces off a surface. Light is reflected by a mirror, sound by a wall.

Refraction occurs when a wave changes direction on passing from one medium to another in which its speed is different.

Einstein's **general theory of relativity** deals with problems that arise when one frame of reference is accelerated with respect to another; gravitation is in this category. The *special theory of relativity* deals with problems that arise when one frame of reference moves at constant velocity with respect to another. Special relativity accounts for the relationship between electricity and magnetism, as an example.

The **relativity of mass** refers to the greater mass of an object when measured by an observer in relative motion as compared with the mass measured by an observer at rest relative to the object.

Electrical **resistance** is a measure of the difficulty electric current has in passing through a certain body of matter. The unit of resistance is the *ohm* (Ω, the Greek capital letter *omega*), equal to 1 V/A.

The **rest energy** of an object is the energy it possesses by virtue of its mass alone. An object's rest energy is given by the product of its mass measured when it is at rest and the square of the speed of light, namely m_0c^2.

RNA: See **nucleic acid.**

A **salt** is one of a class of ionic compounds most of which are crystalline solids at ordinary temperatures and most of which consist of a metal combined with one or more nonmetals. Any salt can be formed by mixing the appropriate acid and base and evaporating the solution to dryness.

A **satellite** is, in general, an astronomical body revolving about some other body. Usually the term refers to the satellites of the planets; thus the moon is a satellite of the earth.

A **saturated solution** is one that contains the maximum amount of solute that can be absorbed at a given temperature.

A **scalar quantity** has magnitude only. Mass and speed are examples.

The **scientific method** of studying nature can be thought of as consisting of four steps: (1) formulating a problem; (2) observation and experiment; (3) interpretation of the results; (4) testing the interpretation by further observation and experiment.

Sedimentary rocks consist of materials derived from other rocks that have been decomposed by water, wind, or glacial ice. They may be fragments cemented together or material precipitated from water solution.

A **seismograph** is a sensitive instrument designed to detect earthquake waves.

An electron **shell** in an atom consists of all the electrons having the same principal quantum number n. When a particular shell contains all the electrons possible it is called a *closed shell*. An electron *subshell* in an atom consists of all the electrons having both the same principal quantum number n and the same orbital quantum number l. When a particular subshell contains all the electrons possible it is called a *closed subshell*. Closed shells and subshells are exceptionally stable.

A **sill** is a sheetlike mass of igneous rock lying parallel to preexisting rock layers.

Soil is a mixture of rock fragments, clay minerals, and organic matter. The organic matter consists largely of partially decomposed plant debris called humus.

A **solar prominence** is a large sheet of luminous gas projecting from the solar surface.

The summer **solstice** occurs when the north pole is tilted toward the sun; the period of daylight in the northern hemisphere is longest on this day. The *winter solstice* occurs when the north pole is tilted away from the sun; the period of daylight in the northern hemisphere is shortest on this day.

A **solution** is a homogenous mixture of elements or compounds without any fixed proportions. The substance present in larger amount is the *solvent,* the other is the *solute*. When a solid or gas is dissolved in a liquid, the liquid is always considered the solvent. The *solubility* of a substance is the maximum amount that can be dissolved in a given quantity of solvent at a given temperature.

The **specific gravity** of a substance is its density relative to that of water.

A **spectrometer** is a device for analyzing a beam of light into its component frequencies.

A **spectrum** is the band of different colors produced when a light beam passes through a glass prism or is diffracted by a device called a *grating*. An *emission spectrum* is one produced by a light source alone. It may be a *continuous spectrum* with all colors present, or a *bright-line spectrum,* in which only a few specific frequencies characteristic of the source appear. An *absorption spectrum* is one produced when light from an incandescent source passes through a cool gas. It is also called a *dark-line spectrum* because it appears as a continuous band of colors crossed by dark lines corresponding to characteristic frequencies absorbed by the gas.

The **speed** of a moving object is the rate at which it covers distance. The unit of speed is the m/s. The *terminal speed* of a falling body is the speed at which its weight is balanced by the force of air resistance, so it cannot fall any faster. This limit arises because air resistance increases with speed.

A **star** is a large, self-luminous body of gas held together gravitationally and obtaining its energy from nuclear fusion reactions in its interior.

Stellar brightness. The *apparent* brightness of a star is its brightness as seen from the earth; the *intrinsic* brightness of a star is a measure of the total amount of light it radiates into space.

The **stratosphere** is the relatively constant-temperature part of the atmosphere from the top of the troposphere to an altitude of about 50 km.

The **structural formula** of a compound is a diagram that shows the bonds between the atoms in its molecules.

A **sunspot** is a dark marking on the solar surface. Sunspots range up to some thousands of km across, last from several days to over a month, and have temperatures as much as 1000°C cooler than the rest of the solar surface. The *sunspot cycle* is a regular variation in the number and size of sunspots whose period is about 11 years.

A **supernova** is a heavy star that explodes with spectacular brightness so that it may be visible even in daylight and emits vast amounts of material into space.

A **supersaturated solution** is one in which more solute is dissolved than normally possible at that temperature; it is unstable and the excess solute readily crystallizes out.

The **Système International** (SI) is the current version of the metric system of units. SI units are universally used in science and in most of the world for engineering and in everyday life as well.

The **temperature** of a body is a measure of the average energy of random motion of its constituent particles. When two bodies are in contact, heat flows from the body at the higher temperature to the one at the lower temperature.

The first law of **thermodynamics** is the law of conservation of energy; the *second law* of *thermodynamics* states that, in every energy transformation, some of the original energy is always changed into heat energy not available for further transformations.

A **thermometer** is a device for measuring temperature. In the *fahrenheit* temperature scale, the freezing point of water is defined as 32°F and the boiling point of water as 212°F; in the *celsius* temperature scale, the freezing point of water is defined as 0°C and the boiling point of water as 100°C.

The **tides** are twice-daily rises and falls of the ocean surface. They are due to the different attractive forces exerted by the moon on different parts of the earth. *Spring tides* have a large range between high and low water. They occur when the sun and moon are in line with the earth and thus add together their tide-producing actions. *Neap tides* have small ranges and occur when the sun and moon are 90° apart relative to the earth and thus their tide-producing actions tend to cancel each other out.

Till is the unsorted material deposited by a glacier and left behind when the glacier recedes.

A **transformer** is a device that transfers electric energy in the form of alternating current from one coil to another by means of electromagnetic induction.

The **troposphere** is the lower part of the atmosphere, from sea level to an altitude of about 11 km, in which most weather phenomena take place.

The **uncertainty principle** states that it is impossible to determine simultaneously accurate values for the position and momentum of a particle. Hence, in dealing with electrons within atoms, all we can consider are probabilities rather than specific positions and states of motion.

An **unconformity** is an uneven surface separating two series of rock beds. It is a buried surface of erosion that involves at least four geologic events: formation of the older rocks; diastrophic uplift of these rocks; erosion; and the deposit of sediments on the eroded landscape.

According to the **principle of uniform change,** the geologic processes that shaped the earth's surface in the past are the same as those active today.

Van der Waals forces arise from the electrical attraction between nonuniform charge distributions in atoms and molecules. They enable atoms and molecules to form solids without sharing or transferring electrons.

A **variable star** is one whose brightness changes regularly.

A **vector** is an arrowed line whose length is proportional to the magnitude of some quantity and whose direction is that of the quantity. A *vector quantity* is a quantity that has both magnitude and direction.

Veins consist of minerals deposited from solutions along cracks in rocks.

The **velocity** of a body refers to both its speed and the direction of its motion. A car has a speed of 30 m/s; its velocity is 30 m/s to the northwest.

Viscosity is the resistance of fluids to flowing motion; liquids are more viscous than gases.

A **volcano** is an opening in the earth's crust through which molten rock (called *magma* while underground, *lava* above ground) comes out, usually at intervals rather than continuously.

The variable quantity that characterizes the matter waves of a moving particle is called its **wave function,** symbol ψ. The probability of finding the particle at a certain place at a certain time is proportional to the value of ψ^2, called *probability density*.

The **wavelength** of a wave is the distance between adjacent crests, in the case of transverse waves, or between adjacent compressions, in the case of longitudinal waves.

Waves carry energy from one place to another by a series of periodic motions of the individual particles of the medium in which the waves occur. (Electromagnetic waves are an exception.) There is no net transfer of matter in wave motion. In a *longitudinal wave* the particles of the medium vibrate back and forth in the direction in which the waves travel. In a *transverse wave* the particles vibrate from side to side perpendicular to the wave direction. Sound waves are longitudinal; waves in a stretched string are transverse; water waves are a combination of both since water molecules move in circular orbits when a wave passes.

Weather refers to the state of the atmosphere in a particular place at a particular time, whereas *climate* refers to the weather trends in a region through the years.

Weathering is the surface disintegration of rock by chemical decay and mechanical processes such as the freezing of water in crevices.

The **weight** of an object is the force with which gravity pulls it toward the earth. The weight of an object of mass m is mg, where g is the acceleration of gravity.

Work is a measure of the change, in a general sense, a force causes when it acts upon something. The work done by a force acting on an object is the product of the magnitude of the force and the distance through which the object moves while the force acts on it. If the direction of the force is not the same as the direction of motion, the projection of the force in the direction of motion must be used. The unit of work is the *joule* (J).

X-rays are high-frequency electromagnetic waves given off when matter is struck by fast electrons.

The **zodiac** is the belt of 12 constellations through which the sun moves on its annual journey through the sky as seen from the earth.

ACKNOWLEDGMENTS

The authors and publisher are deeply indebted to the following for their help in obtaining the illustrations listed by page numbers.

Abbott, Berenice: 197, 201
American Iron & Steel Institute: 92, 388
American Museum of Natural History: 554, 560
Analytical Measurements Inc.: 356
Arizona Office of Tourism: 608
Associated Press: 426
Atomic Industrial Forum: 247
Ballooning, Journal of the Balloon Federation of America: 113
Bausch & Lomb, Inc.: 280
Bell Telephone Laboratories: 287, 684
Bendix Corp.: 216
Bettmann Archive: 198, 301, 597
Brookhaven National Laboratory: 230, 245, 254, 256
CBF Systems Inc.: 366
Bruce Coleman photos: 236
John Deere Company: 109
Diamond Information Center: 497
E. I. du Pont de Nemours & Co.: 418
Eastman Kodak Co.: 269, 273
Exxon Corp.: 567
Freeport Minerals Co.: 476
French Embassy Press & Information Division: 139
Gama Liaison Agency: 541
The General Battery Corporation: 391
General Electric Corp.: 177, 335
Geological Survey of Canada: 527
Hale Observatories: 600, 602, 625, 630, 632, 635, 644, 648, 654, 665, 668, 676, 678, 679, 680, 683, 690
Hawaii Visitors Bureau: 521
International Science and Technology Magazine: 337
Kinne, Russell: 510

Lowell Observatory: 646
Metropolitan Museum of Art: 507
Mount Wilson & Palomar Observatories: 604
Museum of Science, Boston: 150
NASA: 55, 84, 454, 455, 586, 621, 622, 628, 636, 638
National Coal Association: 566
NCAR: 443
NOAA: 527
Nusbaum, Korrine: 108
Photo Researchers, Inc.: 3, 14, 24, 36, 57, 71, 78, 89, 94, 137, 161, 204, 329, 351, 380, 437, 458, 484, 485, 515, 540, 552, 556
Pileco Company: 73
Power Authority of the State of New York: 140, 182
Princeton University: 252
Publiofoto Milan: 571
Raytheon Co.: 210
Rijkomuseum voor Volkenkunole: 307
Shell Oil Co.: 402
Smithsonian Institution: 563
Douglas Kirkland/Sygma Photos: 67
Technology for Communications International: 440
United Press International: 12, 492, 520
U. S. Coast Guard: 465, 513
U. S. Dept. of Agriculture: 486, 508
U. S. Geological Survey: 523
Vail: 116
Waywick Corp.: 327
Woodfin Camp and Associates: 273
Woods Hole Oceanographic Institution: 557
Wyckoff, Jerome: 479, 481, 482, 512, 518
Yerkes Observatory: 41, 657, 669

INDEX

753

758

Conversion Factors

1 meter (m) = 100 cm = 39.4 in. = 3.28 ft

1 centimeter (cm) = 10 millimeters (mm) = 0.394 in.

1 kilometer (km) = 1,000 m = 0.621 mi

1 foot (ft) = 12 in. = 0.305 m

1 inch (in.) = 0.0833 ft = 2.54 cm

1 mile (mi) = 5,280 ft = 1.61 km

1 liter = 1,000 cm^3 = 10^{-3} m^3 = 1.056 quart

1 day = 86,400 s = 2.74 × 10^{-3} year

1 year = 3.16 × 10^7 s = 365 days

1 m/s = 3.28 ft/s = 2.24 mi/h = 3.60 km/h

1 ft/s = 0.305 m/s = 0.682 mi/h = 1.10 km/h

1 mi/h = 1.47 ft/s = 0.447 m/s = 1.61 km/h

1 kilogram (kg) = 1,000 grams (g)

(Note: kg corresponds to 2.21 lb in the sense that the weight of 1 kg is 2.21 lb.)

1 slug = 14.6 kg

(Note: 1 slug corresponds to 32.2 lb in the sense that the weight of 1 slug is 32.2 lb.)

1 atomic mass unit (u) = 1.66 × 10^{-27} kg
$\qquad$ = 1.49 × 10^{-10} J
$\qquad$ = 931 MeV

1 newton (N) = 0.225 lb

1 pound (lb) = 4.45 N

1 joule (J) = 2.39 × 10^{-4} kcal
$\qquad$ = 6.24 × 10^{18} eV = 2.78 × 10^{-7} kWh

1 kilocalorie (kcal) = 4,185 J = 3,089 ft·lb

1 electron volt (eV) = 10^{-6} MeV = 10^{-9} GeV
$\qquad$ = 1.60 × 10^{-19} J
$\qquad$ = 1.18 × 10^{-19} ft·lb = 3.83 × 10^{-23} kcal

1 watt (W) = 1 J/s = 1.34 × 10^{-3} hp

1 kilowatt (kW) = 1,000 W = 1.34 hp

1 horsepower (hp) = 746 W

1 atmosphere of pressure (atm) = 1.013 × 10^5 N/m^2
$\qquad$ = 14.7 lb/$in.^2$

1 bar = 10^5 N/m^2 = 14.5 lb/$in.^2$

$°C = \dfrac{5}{9}(°F - 32°)$

$°F = \dfrac{9}{5}°C + 32°$

$K = °C + 273$

Powers of Ten

10^{-10} = 0.000,000,000,1		10^0 = 1	
10^{-9} = 0.000,000,001		10^1 = 10	
10^{-8} = 0.000,000,01		10^2 = 100	
10^{-7} = 0.000,000,1		10^3 = 1000	
10^{-6} = 0.000,001		10^4 = 10,000	
10^{-5} = 0.000,01		10^5 = 100,000	
10^{-4} = 0.000,1		10^6 = 1,000,000	
10^{-3} = 0.001		10^7 = 10,000,000	
10^{-2} = 0.01		10^8 = 100,000,000	
10^{-1} = 0.1		10^9 = 1,000,000,000	
10^0 = 1		10^{10} = 10,000,000,000	

Physical and Chemical Constants

Speed of light in vacuum	c	3.00 × 10^8 m/s
Charge on electron	e	1.60 × 10^{-19} C
Gravitational constant	G	6.67 × 10^{-11} N·m/kg^2
Acceleration of gravity at earth's surface	g	9.81 m/s^2
Planck's constant	h	6.63 × 10^{-34} J·s
Coulomb constant	k	8.99 × 10^9 N·m/C^2
Electron rest mass	m_e	9.11 × 10^{-31} kg
Neutron rest mass	m_n	1.675 × 10^{-27} kg
Proton rest mass	m_p	1.673 × 10^{-27} kg
Avogadro's number	N_o	6.02 × 10^{23} formula units/mole